GUIDE TO FUNDING FOR
INTERNATIONAL
& FOREIGN
PROGRAMS

FOUNDATION CENTER
Knowledge to build on.

ELEVENTH EDITION

GUIDE TO FUNDING FOR
INTERNATIONAL
& FOREIGN
PROGRAMS

Linda Calderon
Manager, New Forms of Philanthropy

CONTRIBUTING STAFF

Vice President for Data Acquisition and Architecture_____ Jeffrey A. Falkenstein

Director, Foundation Information Management _____ David G. Jacobs

Director, Grants Information Management _____ Jeannine Corey

Contributing Managers _____ Andrew Grabois
                                                            Jonathan Miller

Coordinator, Large Foundations _____ Cindy B. Martinez

Coordinator, Foundation Directory _____ Regina Faighes

Coordinator, Foundation Directory Part 2_____ William Giles

Publishing Database Administrator _____ Kathye Giesler

System Administrator_____ Emmy So

Production Manager _____ Christine Innamorato

Director, New York Library _____ Jimmy Tom

Reference/Outreach Librarian_____ Inès Sucre

The editor gratefully acknowledges the many other Foundation Center staff who contributed support, encouragement, and information that was indispensable to the preparation of this volume. Special mention should also be made of the staff members of the New York, Washington, DC, Cleveland, San Francisco, and Atlanta libraries who assisted in tracking changes in foundation information. We would like to express our appreciation as well to the many foundations that cooperated fully in updating information prior to the compilation of the *Guide To Funding For International & Foreign Programs*.

CONTENTS

INTRODUCTION

This volume is intended as a starting point for grantseekers looking for foundation, corporate, and other charitable support in international and foreign programs. It contains a total of 2,232 entries including 1,313 grantmaking foundations, 110 direct corporate giving programs and 809 public charities (including 18 community foundations) that have shown a substantial interest in international and foreign programs, either as part of their stated fields of interest or through the actual grants of $10,000 or more reported to the Foundation Center in the latest year of record. Grants in international and foreign programs are listed for 357 of the foundations listed in this volume. These 11,453 grants represent over $4.1 billion in support for a variety of programs, including public policy groups, legal agencies, educational institutions, and international exchange organizations, among others.

Each entry in the Guide was carefully evaluated by Foundation Center staff to ensure that the grantmaker possesses a sufficient interest in international and foreign programs, either stated or demonstrated. Often, a grantmaker claims interest not only in programs related to international and foreign programs but in dozens of widely diverse fields. To determine if inclusion in this Guide is warranted in such cases, consideration is given to the grantmaker's purpose statement, giving limitations, and, if they exist, subject-related grants. Grantseekers should be aware that inclusion does not imply that these grantmakers will consider all programs in international and foreign programs.

Keep in mind that some grantmakers support particular programs because of their interest in a specific community or organization. Others may do so because the program relates to a highly specific subject interest of the grantmaker, such as amnesty programs, international relief, or economic development. Still others are interested in building the capacity of nonprofit institutions by providing specific types of support such as operating costs or challenge grants. Grantseekers are therefore urged to read each foundation and corporate giving program description carefully to determine the nature of the grantmaker's interests and to note any restrictions on giving that would prevent the grantmaker from considering their proposal.

PRECISE INDEXING

Since 1989 the Foundation Center has used a Grants Classification System (GCS) based on the National Taxonomy of Exempt Entities (NTEE), a comprehensive organizational coding scheme developed by the National Center for Charitable Statistics (NCCS) that was adopted by the IRS in 1995. The GCS builds on the NTEE and is used by the Center to provide subject, types of support, and other grants information both online through two DIALOG files (www.dialog.com), a product of The Thomson Corporation, and Foundation Directory Online (fconline.foundationcenter.org).

This eleventh edition of the Guide to Funding for International & Foreign Programs represents a continuing project to utilize comprehensive and precise GCS terminology across all Foundation Center publications and files. This process enables the Center to maintain a unified system of classification. The results from the implementation of unified indexing terms include:

1. A section in grantmaker descriptive entries identifying any international giving interests of an organization. Because of the conversion to the GCS terminology, the number of index terms describing the countries, continents, and regions in which grantmakers have giving interests has expanded from a few dozen to over 200, providing a much greater level of specificity.

2. The full scope of the terminology used to describe a grantmaker's areas of interests has also expanded following the conversion to unified GCS subject terms. The "Fields of Interest" section of each grantmaker descriptive entry includes all indexed subject terms for the organization, rather than listing only its primary areas of giving. The "Purpose and Activities" section contains a more general statement of foundation funding priorities.

WHAT IS A FOUNDATION?

The Foundation Center defines a foundation as a nongovernmental, nonprofit organization with its own funds (usually derived from a single source, either an individual, family, or corporation) and programs managed by its own trustees and directors, which was established to maintain or aid educational, social, charitable, or other activities serving the common welfare, primarily by making grants to other nonprofit organizations.

The Foundation Center classifies nonprofit organizations under the following types:

An **independent foundation** is a grantmaking organization usually classified by the IRS as a private foundation. Independent foundations may also be known as family foundations, general purpose foundations, special purpose foundations, or private non-operating foundations. The Foundation Center defines independent foundations and company-sponsored foundations separately; however, federal law normally classifies both as private, non-operating foundations subject to the same rules and requirements.

Operating foundations are 501(c)(3) organizations classified by the IRS as private foundations whose primary purpose is to operate research, social welfare, or other programs determined by its governing body or establishment charter. Some grants may be made, but the sum is generally small relative to the funds used for the foundation's own programs.

A **Company-sponsored foundation** is a private foundation whose grant funds are derived primarily from the contributions of a for-profit business organization. The company-sponsored foundation might maintain close ties with the donor company, but it is an independent organization with its own endowment and is subject to the same rules and regulations as other private foundations.

Corporate giving programs are grantmaking programs established and administered within a for-profit business organization. Corporate giving programs do not have a separate endowment and their annual grant totals are generally more directly related to current profits. They are not subject to the same reporting requirements as private foundations. Some companies make charitable contributions through both a corporate giving program and a company-sponsored foundation.

Public Charities, in general, are organizations tax-exempt under code section 501(c) and classified by the IRS as a public charity and not a private foundation. Public charities generally derive their funding or support primarily from the general public in carrying out their social, educational, religious, or other charitable activities serving the common welfare. Some public charities engage in grantmaking activities, although most engage in direct service or other tax-exempt activities. Public charities are eligible for maximum income tax-deductible contributions from the public and are not subject to the same rules and restrictions as private foundations. Some are also referred to as "public foundations" or "publicly supported organizations" and might use the term "foundation" in their names.

Community Foundations are 501(c)(3) organizations that make grants for charitable purposes in a specific community or region. Funds are usually derived from many donors and held in an endowment independently administered; income earned by the endowment is then used to make grants. Although a few community foundations might be classified by the IRS as private foundations, most are classified as public charities eligible for maximum income tax-deductible contributions from the general public.

Grantseekers should be aware that an increasing number of for-profit business have also adopted "foundation" as part of their name to promote their activities. While there are no legal restrictions on the use of the word "foundation," it is important for grantseekers to understand that many of these groups do not make grants and are not governed by the same rules and regulations as private foundations or nonprofit groups.

GRANTSEEKING FROM FOUNDATIONS

Foundations receive many thousands of worthy requests each year. Most of these requests are declined because there are not enough funds to go around or because the application clearly falls outside the foundation's fields of interest. Some of the applications denied are poorly prepared and do not reflect a careful analysis of the applicant organization's needs, its credibility, or its capacity to carry out the proposed project. Sometimes the qualifications of the organization's staff are not well established; the budget or the means of evaluating the project may not be presented convincingly; or the organization may not have asked itself whether it is especially suited to make a contribution to the solution of the problem, whether it can provide the service proposed, or whether others are not already effectively engaged in the same activity.

The first step in researching foundation funding support is to analyze your own program and organization to determine the need you plan to address, the audience you will serve, and the amount and type of support you need. Become familiar with the basic facts about foundations in general and how they operate. Consider other sources of funding, such as individual contributors, government grants, earned income possibilities, and so on. Although foundations are an important source of support for nonprofit organizations, their giving represents a relatively small percentage of the total philanthropic dollars contributed annually, and an even smaller percentage of the total when government grants and earned income are included. If you are new to grantseeking, we strongly urge you to visit one of the Foundation Center's many Cooperating Collections. They provide free access to a core collection of Foundation Center publications, as well as other materials on funding sources, program planning, and fundraising.

Once you have determined the amount and type of foundation support you need and the reasons why you are seeking support, this Guide can help you develop an initial list of foundations that might be interested in funding your project. In determining whether or not it is appropriate to approach a particular foundation with a grant request, keep in mind the following questions:

1. Does the foundation's interest in international and foreign programs include the specific type of service or program you are proposing?

2. Does it seem likely that the foundation will make a grant in your geographic area?

3. Does the amount of money you are requesting fit within the foundation's grant range?

4. Does the foundation have any policy prohibiting grants for the type of support you are requesting?

5. Does the foundation prefer to make grants that cover the full cost of a project or do they favor projects where other foundations or funding sources share the cost?

6. What types of organizations does the foundation tend to support?

7. Does the foundation have specific application deadlines and procedures or does it review proposals continuously?

Some of these questions can be answered from the information provided in this *Guide*, but grantseekers will almost always want to consult a few additional resources before submitting a request for funding. If the foundation issues an annual report, application guidelines, or other printed materials describing its program, it is advisable to obtain copies and study them carefully before preparing your proposal. The foundation's annual information return (Form 990 or 990-PF) includes a list of all grants paid by the foundation in addition to basic data about its finances, officers, and giving policies.

The foundations listed in this *Guide* by no means represent all of the possible foundation funding sources for programs related to international and foreign programs. There are a number of foundations, including over 800 community foundations across the country, that support a wide variety of programs within a specific community or region. Grantseekers should learn as much as possible about the foundations in their own area, particularly when they are seeking relatively small grants for projects with purely local impact. Be sure to check any local or state directories for additional funding resources. Copies of these directories are almost always available for use at your local Foundation Center cooperating library.

The Foundation Center publishes several national directories on an annual basis. *The Foundation Directory* describes the top 10,000 foundations by total giving. *The Foundation Directory Part 2* provides information on the second tier of foundations, the next 10,000 foundations by total giving. The *Directory* and *Directory Part 2* entries include a list of selected grants whenever available, providing concrete examples of a foundation's giving. The directories are arranged by state and include a geographic index to help you identify foundations located or interested in your specific community.

For those who want more detailed information on how to identify appropriate foundation funding sources, the Center also publishes *Foundation Fundamentals*. This guide takes you step-by-step through the research strategies developed and taught by the Foundation Center, describing in the process how to gather the facts you need to best approach foundations for funding. All Foundation Center publications can be examined free of charge at Foundation Center libraries.

GRANTSEEKING FROM CORPORATIONS

The research process for corporate funding is similar to other institutional grantseeking: identifying companies that might be interested in an organization's mission and program, learning as much as possible about those companies, determining the best method of approach, and articulating program objectives so as to be in line with the company's giving rationale. It differs from researching other institutional funders, however, in that it is often more difficult to uncover the needed information. There is great diversity in method and style of giving among corporations, and companies are often looking for a quid pro quo for their giving. Because many corporations see their giving not in terms of altruism but as a responsibility or simply good business, corporate philanthropy is often considered something of an oxymoron. Soliciting support from corporations, therefore, often requires a shift in perspective, from appealing to a company's benevolence to promoting its self-interest.

Identifying corporations to approach is accomplished in several ways. Directories such as the *National Directory of Corporate Giving* describe companies with known corporate giving programs. These guides can help you identify a corporation's subject interests, geographical giving patterns, and/or the benefits it hopes to derive from its giving. General business directories aid in the search, as do the books and guides listed in the bibliography. Staff members, your organization's board, and volunteers often know or work for companies that ultimately may be able to provide funds.

After a list of likely prospects is compiled, you should continue your efforts to locate additional information about the company, its primary and secondary business activities, its officers, giving history, and any details helpful in understanding its giving rationale. Understanding why a company gives is essential, as it may point to a match of the grantseeker's programmatic goals and the corporation's giving goals. Although determining the reasons a company makes contributions can be difficult, it can be accomplished through careful research, including studying annual reports and the materials issued by other organizations the company has supported, as well as by speaking directly with company officials whenever possible.

This kind of research usually uncovers the best method for approaching a company with a request for support. Companies with formal giving programs may have guidelines and application procedures and require a written proposal, while companies with informal giving programs may be better approached through personal contacts made by board members or volunteers. Once the approach is determined, however, a written or oral presentation that articulates how your organization's programs fit into the company's giving rationale should be prepared.

Ultimately, the more you know about a company, the better your chance of obtaining support. A company should not be approached without some knowledge of its business activities or past giving history, as that may jeopardize your chances of receiving funding. This does not mean that corporations without a record of grantmaking should be ignored. Creative fundraisers have found ways of encouraging companies of all sizes, from small businesses to large corporations, to assist in their activities. Success in acquiring such support, however, is usually the result of good research and good contacts. The job of the corporate fundraiser is to be imaginative and thorough, calling on all the knowledge, people, and ideas available. It means learning where to ask, how to ask, and what to ask.

SOURCES OF INFORMATION

Foundation Center publications examine giving interests in two broad ways: what the grantmaker states as its purpose and what can be observed from a listing of its actual grants. In preparing the *Guide to Funding for International & Foreign Programs* we drew on four important tools to identify grantmakers with a specific interest in programs in international and foreign programs in addition to those that make contributions for related projects as part of a broader giving program:

1. *The Foundation Directory* provides descriptions of the nation's largest foundations (the top 10,000 foundations by total giving). The statements of purpose for each foundation listed in the *Directory* are drawn from the descriptions provided by foundations in their annual reports, informational brochures or other publications, responses to our annual questionnaire mailings, and a broad analysis of the foundation's grantmaking program over the last three years. Although some of these statements provide very specific information about the foundation's giving interests, many were developed to last for substantial periods of time and, thus, left purposely broad to allow for future shifts in emphasis. To illustrate a foundation's giving pattern, lists of up to ten selected grants are included, whenever available.

2. *The Foundation Directory Part 2* provides information on the second tier of U.S. grantmaking foundations, (the next 10,000 foundations by total giving). Like the *Directory*, the *Directory Part 2* provides lists of up to ten selected grants whenever available.

3. The *National Directory of Corporate Giving* is the source of information on corporate grantmakers. The seventeenth edition of the *Directory*, published in 2011, profiles over 4,100 companies making contributions to nonprofit organizations. It includes entries describing nearly 1,700 direct corporate giving programs and over 3,300 corporate foundations. The most comprehensive directory on corporate giving available, it lists only corporations that provided information to the Center or for which public documents on giving were available.

4. *Foundation Directory Online* provides information on over 100,000 U.S. grantmakers and their funding activities, including descriptions of more than 2.4 million recent grants. Updated weekly, it's the most comprehensive resource available to grantseekers. *Foundation Directory Online* includes complete profiles on the top 20,000 U.S. foundations including trustees, officers, and donors; profiles of almost 13,000 grantmaking public charities, and over 1,900 corporate giving programs. Information drawn from FDO is continually monitored by the Foundation Center by using more than 35 information sources to verify details, including electronic grant submissions by over 600 grantmakers, ensuring the most recent, comprehensive information available.

These sources provide all the information on foundations, corporate giving programs, public charities, and grants included in this *Guide*.

HOW TO USE THE GUIDE TO FUNDING FOR INTERNATIONAL & FOREIGN PROGRAMS

When using the *Guide* to identify potential funding sources, grantseekers are urged to read each grantmaker description carefully to determine the nature of the grantmaker's interests and to note any restrictions on giving that would prevent the foundation from considering their proposal. Many grantmakers limit their giving to a particular subject field or geographic area; others are unable to provide certain types of support, such as funds for buildings and equipment or for general operating budgets. Even when a grantmaker has not provided an explicit limitations statement, restrictions on giving may exist. This is often the case with entries updated from public records. Further research into the giving patterns of these grantmakers is necessary before applying for funds.

ARRANGEMENT

The *Guide* is arranged alphabetically by state and, within states, by grantmaker name. Each descriptive entry is assigned a sequence number; references in the indexes are to these entry numbers.

WHAT'S IN AN ENTRY?

There are 36 basic data elements that could be included in a descriptive entry. The content of entries varies widely due to differences in the size, nature, and type of grantmaker and its programs and the availability of information from grantmakers. Specific data elements that could be included are:

1. The full legal **name of the grantmaker**.

2. The **former name** of the grantmaker.

3. The **street address, city,** and **zip code** of the grantmaker's principal office.

4. The **telephone number** of the grantmaker.

5. The name and title of the **contact person** at the grantmaker.

6. Any **additional address** (such as a separate application address) supplied by the grantmaker. Additional telephone or FAX numbers as well as E-mail and/or URL address also may be listed here.

7. **Establishment data**, including the legal form (usually a trust or corporation) and the year and state in which the grantmaker was established.

8. The **donor(s)** or principal contributor(s) to the grantmaker, including individuals, families, and corporations. If a donor is deceased, the symbol ‡ follows the name.

9. **Grantmaker type:** community foundation, company-sponsored foundation, independent foundation, operating foundation, corporate giving program, or public charity.

10. The **year-end date** of the grantmaker's accounting period for which financial data is supplied.

11. **Revenue:** The total amount of contributions and support received by the public charity, including investment income, program service revenue, net profits from sale of assets, etc.

12. **Assets:** the total value of the grantmaker's investments at the end of the accounting period. In a few instances, grantmakers that act as "pass- throughs" for annual corporate or individual gifts report zero assets.

13. **Asset type:** generally, assets are reported at market value (M) or ledger value (L).

14. **Gifts received:** the total amount of new capital received by the grantmaker in the year of record.

15. **Expenditures:** total disbursements of the grantmaker, including overhead expenses (salaries; investment, legal, and other professional fees; interest; rent; etc.) and federal excise taxes, as well as the total amount paid for grants, scholarships, and matching gifts.

16. The total amount of **qualifying distributions** made by the grantmaker in the year of record. This figure includes all grants paid, qualifying administrative expenses, loans and program-related investments, set-asides, and amounts paid to acquire assets used directly in carrying out charitable purposes.

17. **Program services expenses:** The total amount of program services expenses made by the public charity in the year of record. This figure includes all expenses directly involved in carrying out charitable activities, including total grants paid.

18. The dollar value and number of **grants paid** within the U.S. and **grants paid outside the U.S.** during the year, with the largest grant paid **(high)** and smallest grant paid **(low)**. When supplied by the grantmaker, the average range of grant payments is also indicated. Grant figures generally do not include commitments for future payment or amounts spent for grants to individuals, employee matching gifts, loans, or grantmaker-administered programs.

19. The total dollar value of **set-asides** made by the grantmaker during the year. Although set-asides count as qualifying distributions toward the grantmaker's annual payout requirement, they are distinct from any amounts listed as grants paid.

20. The total amount and number of **grants made directly to or on behalf of individuals** within the U.S. and **individuals outside the U.S.**, including scholarships, fellowships, awards, and medical payments. When supplied by the grantmaker, high, low, and average range are also indicated.

21. The dollar amount and number of **employee matching gifts** awarded, generally by company- sponsored foundations or corporate giving programs.

22. The total dollars expended for **programs administered by the grantmaker** and the number of grantmakeradministered programs. These programs can include useums or other institutions supported exclusively by the grantmaker, research programs administered by the grantmaker, etc.

23. The dollar amount and number of **loans** made to nonprofit organizations by the grantmaker. These can include program-related investments, emergency loans to help nonprofits that are waiting for grants or other income payments, etc. When supplied by the grantmaker, high, low, and average range are also indicated.

24. The number of **loans to individuals** and the total amount loaned. When supplied by the grantmaker, high, low, and average range are also indicated.

25. The monetary value and number of **in-kind gifts**.

26. The **purpose and activities**, in general terms, of the grantmaker. This statement reflects funding interests as expressed by the grantmaker or, if no grantmaker statement is available, an analysis of the actual grants awarded by the grantmaker during the most recent two-year period for which public records exist. Many grantmakers leave statements of purpose intentionally broad, indicating only the major program areas within which they fund. More specific areas of interest can often be found in the "Fields of Interest" section of the entry.

27. The **fields of interest** reflected in the grantmaker's giving program. The terminology used in this section conforms to the Foundation Center's Grants Classification System (GCS).

28. The **international giving interests** of the grantmaker.

29. The **types of support** (such as endowment funds, support for building/renovation, equipment, fellowships, etc.) offered by the grantmaker. Definitions of the terms used to describe the forms of support available are provided at the beginning of the Type of Support Index at the back of this volume.

30. Any stated **limitations** on the grantmaker's giving program, including geographic preferences, restrictions by subject focus or type of recipient, or specific types of support the grantmaker cannot provide. It is noted here if a grantmaker does not accept unsolicited applications.

31. **Publications** or other printed materials distributed by the grantmaker that describe its activities and giving program. These can include annual or multi-year reports, newsletters, corporate giving reports, informational brochures, grant lists, etc.

32. **Application information**, including the preferred form of application, the number of copies of proposals requested, application deadlines, frequency and dates of board meetings, and the general amount of time the grantmaker requires to notify applicants of the board's decision. Some grantmakers have indicated that their funds are currently committed to ongoing projects.

33. The names and titles of **officers, principal administrators, trustees, or directors,** and members of other governing bodies. An asterisk (*) following the individual's name indicates an officer who is also a trustee or director.

34. The number of professional and support **staff** employed by the grantmaker, and an indication of part-time or full-time status of these employees, as reported by the grantmaker.

35. **EIN:** the Employer Identification Number assigned to a foundation or public charity by the Internal Revenue Service for tax purposes. This number can be useful when accessing copies of the grantmaker's annual information return, Form 990-PF for foundations and Form 990 for public charities.

36. **Recent grants for international and foreign programs** awarded in 2008–2011. Entries include the name and location of the recipient, the grant amount and year awarded, and, where available, a brief description of the purpose of the grant.

INDEX

Six indexes to the descriptive entries are provided at the back of the book to assist grantseekers and other users of this *Guide*:

1. The **Index to Donors, Officers, Trustees** is an alphabetical list of individual and corporate donors, officers, and members of governing boards whose names appear in the descriptive entries. Many grantseekers find this index helpful in determining whether current or prospective members of their own governing boards, alumni of their schools, or current contributors are affiliated with other grantmakers.

2. The **Geographic Index** references grantmaker entries by the state and city in which the grantmaker maintains its principal offices. The index includes "see also" references at the end of each state section to indicate grantmakers that have made substantial grants in that state but are located elsewhere. Grantmakers that award grants on a national, regional, or international basis are indicated in bold type. The remaining grantmakers generally limit their giving to the state or city in which they are located.

3. The **Type of Support Index** provides access to grantmaker entries by the specific types of support the grantmaker awards. A glossary of the forms of support listed appears at the beginning of the index. Under each type of support term, entry numbers are listed by the state location and abbreviated name of the grantmaker. Grantmakers that award grants on a national, regional, or international basis are indicated in bold type. When using this index, grantseekers should focus on grantmakers located in their own state that offer the specific type of support needed, or on grantmakers listed in bold type if their program has national impact.

4. The **Subject Index** provides access to the giving interests of grantmakers based on the "Fields of Interest" sections of their entries. The terminology in the index conforms to the Foundation Center's Grants Classification System (GCS). A list of subject headings for international and foreign programs is provided at the beginning of the index. Under each subject term, entry numbers are listed by the state location and abbreviated name of the grantmaker. As in the Type of Support Index, grantmakers that award grants on a national, regional, or international basis are indicated in bold type. Again, grantseekers should focus on grantmakers located in their own state or on grantmakers listed in bold type if their program is national in scope.

5. The **Index to Grants by Subject** provides access to the individual grants included in this *Guide*. For each subject term, grants are listed first by grantmaker entry number, then by grant number within the grantmaker entry.

6. The **Grantmaker Name Index** is an alphabetical list of all grantmakers appearing in this *Guide*. Former names of foundations appear with "see" references to the appropriate entry numbers.

GLOSSARY

The following list includes important terms used by grantmakers and grantseekers. A number of sources have been consulted in compiling this glossary, including *The Handbook on Private Foundations*, 3rd Edition, by David F. Freeman, John A. Edie, Jane C. Nober, and the Council on Foundations (Washington, DC, 2005); *The Law of Tax-Exempt Organizations*, 9th Edition, by Bruce R. Hopkins (Hoboken, NJ: John Wiley & Sons, 2007); and the *AFP Fund-Raising Dictionary*, (2003).

Annual Report: A *voluntary* report issued by a foundation or corporation that provides financial data and descriptions of grantmaking activities. Annual reports vary in format from simple typewritten documents listing the year's grants to detailed publications that provide substantial information about the grantmaking program.

Assets: The amount of capital or principal—money, stocks, bonds, real estate, or other resources—controlled by the foundation or corporate giving program. Generally, assets are invested and the income is used to make grants.

Beneficiary: In philanthropic terms, the donee or grantee receiving funds from a foundation or corporate giving program is the beneficiary, although society benefits as well. Foundations whose legal terms of establishment restrict their giving to one or more named beneficiaries are not included in this publication.

Bricks and Mortar: An informal term for grants for buildings or construction projects.

Capital Support: Funds provided for endowment purposes, buildings, construction, or equipment, and including, for example, grants for "bricks and mortar."

Challenge Grant: A grant awarded that will be paid only if the donee organization is able to raise additional funds from another source(s). Challenge grants are often used to stimulate giving from other donors. (*See also* **Matching Grant**)

Community Foundation: A 501(c)(3) organization that makes grants for charitable purposes in a specific community or region. Funds are usually derived from many donors and held in an endowment independently administered; income earned by the endowment is then used to make grants. Although a few community foundations may be classified by the IRS as private foundations, most are classified as public charities eligible for maximum income tax-deductible contributions from the general public. (*See also* **501(c)(3)**; **Public Charity**)

Community Fund: An organized community program which makes annual appeals to the general public for funds that are usually not retained in an endowment but are used for the ongoing operational support of local social and health service agencies. (*See also* **Federated Giving Program**)

Company-Sponsored Foundation (also referred to as Corporate Foundation): A private foundation whose grant funds are derived primarily from the contributions of a profit-making business organization. The company-sponsored foundation may maintain close ties with the donor company, but it is an independent organization with its own endowment and is subject to the same rules and regulations as other private foundations. (*See also* **Private Foundation**)

Cooperative Venture: A joint effort between or among two or more grantmakers (including foundations, corporations, and government agencies). Partners may share in funding responsibilities or contribute information and technical resources.

Corporate Giving Program: A grantmaking program established and administered within a profit-making company. Corporate giving programs do not have a separate endowment and their annual grant totals are generally more directly related to current profits. They are not subject to the same reporting requirements as private foundations. Some companies make charitable contributions through both a corporate giving program and a company-sponsored foundation.

Distribution Committee: The board responsible for making grant decisions. For community foundations, it is intended to be broadly representative of the community served by the foundation.

Donee: The recipient of a grant. (Also known as the grantee or the beneficiary.)

Donor: The individual or organization that makes a grant or contribution. (Also known as the grantor.)

Employee Matching Gift: A contribution to a charitable organization by a company employee that is matched by a similar contribution from the employer. Many corporations have employee matching gift programs in higher education that stimulate their employees to give to the college or university of their choice.

Endowment: Funds intended to be kept permanently and invested to provide income for continued support of an organization.

Expenditure Responsibility: In general, when a private foundation makes a grant to an organization that is not classified by the IRS as a "public charity," the foundation is required by law to provide some assurance that the funds will be used for the intended charitable purposes. Special reports on such grants must be filed with the IRS. Most grantee organizations are public charities and many foundations do not make "expenditure responsibility" grants.

Family Foundation: An independent private foundation whose funds are derived from members of a single family. Family members often serve as officers or board members of the foundation and have a significant role in grantmaking decisions. (*See also* **Operating Foundation; Private Foundation; Public Charity**)

Federated Giving Program: A joint fundraising effort usually administered by a nonprofit "umbrella" organization which in turn distributes contributed funds to several nonprofit agencies. United Way and community chests or funds, the United Jewish Appeal and other religious appeals, the United Negro College Fund, and joint arts councils are examples of federated giving programs. (*See also* **Community Fund**)

501(c)(3): The section of the Internal Revenue code that defines nonprofit, charitable (as broadly defined), tax-exempt organizations; 501(c)(3) organizations are further defined as public charities, private operating foundations, and private non-operating foundations. (*See also* **Operating Foundation; Private Foundation; Public Charity**)

Form 990: The annual information return that all tax-exempt organizations, other than private foundations, must submit to the IRS each year and which is also filed with the appropriate state officials. The form requires information on the organization's assets, program services expenses, revenue, contributions and grants, paid staff and salaries, and program funding areas.

Form 990-PF: The annual information return that all private foundations must submit to the IRS each year and which is also filed with appropriate state officials. The form requires information on the foundation's assets, income, operating expenses, contributions and grants, paid staff and salaries, program funding areas, grantmaking guidelines and restrictions, and grant application procedures.

General Purpose Foundation: An independent private foundation that awards grants in many different fields of interest. (*See also* **Special Purpose Foundation**)

General Purpose Grant: A grant made to further the general purpose or work of an organization, rather than for a specific purpose or project. (*See also* **Operating Support Grant**)

Grantee Financial Report: A report detailing how grant funds were used by an organization. Many corporations require this kind of report from grantees. A financial report generally includes a listing of all expenditures from grant funds as well as an overall organizational financial report covering revenue and expenses, assets and liabilities.

Grassroots Fundraising: Efforts to raise money from individuals or groups from the local *community* on a broad basis. Usually an organization's own constituents—people who live in the neighborhood served or clients of the agency's services—are the sources of these funds. Grassroots fundraising activities include membership drives, raffles, auctions, benefits, and a range of other activities.

Independent Foundation: A grantmaking organization usually classified by the IRS as a private foundation. Independent foundations may also be known as family foundations, general purpose foundations, special purpose foundations, or private non-operating foundations. The Foundation Center defines independent foundations and company-sponsored foundations separately; however, federal law normally classifies both as private, non-operating foundations subject to the same rules and requirements. (*See also* **Private Foundation**)

In-Kind Contributions: Contributions of equipment, supplies, or other property as distinguished from monetary grants. Some organizations may also donate space or staff time as an in-kind contribution.

Matching Grant: A grant that is made to match funds provided by another donor. (See also **Challenge Grant; Employee Matching Gift**)

Operating Foundation: A 501(c)(3) organization classified by the IRS as a private foundation whose primary purpose is to conduct research, social welfare, or other programs determined by its governing body or establishment charter. Some grants may be made, but the sum is generally small relative to the funds used for the foundation's own programs. (*See also* **501(c)(3)**)

Operating Support Grant: A grant to cover the regular personnel, administrative, and other expenses of an existing program or project. (*See also* **General Purpose Grant**)

Payout Requirement: The minimum amount that private foundations are required to expend for charitable purposes (includes grants and, within certain limits, the administrative cost of making grants). In general, a private foundation must meet or exceed an annual payout requirement of five percent of the average market value of the foundation's assets.

Private Foundation: A nongovernmental, nonprofit organization with funds (usually from a single source, such as an individual, family, or corporation) and program managed by its own trustees or directors that was established to maintain or aid social, educational, religious, or other charitable activities serving the common welfare, primarily through the making of grants. "Private foundation" also means an organization that is tax-exempt under code section 501(c)(3) and is classified by the IRS as a private foundation as defined in the code. The code definition usually, but not always, identifies a foundation with the characteristics first described. (See also **501(c)(3); Public Charity**)

Program Amount: Funds that are expended to support a particular program administered internally by the foundation or corporate giving program.

Program Officer: A staff member of a foundation who reviews grant proposals and processes applications for the board of trustees. Only a small percentage of foundations have program officers.

Program-Related Investment (PRI): A loan or other investment (as distinguished from a grant) made by a foundation or corporate giving program to another organization for a project related to the grantmaker's stated charitable purpose and interests. Program-related investments are often made from a revolving fund; the foundation generally expects to receive its money back with interest or some other form of return at less than current market rates, and it then becomes available for further program-related investments.

Proposal: A written application, often with supporting documents, submitted to a foundation or corporate giving program in requesting a grant. Preferred procedures and formats vary. Consult published guidelines.

Public Charity: In general, an organization that is tax-exempt under code section 501(c) and is classified by the IRS as a public charity and not a private foundation. Public charities generally derive their funding or support primarily from the general public in carrying out their social, educational, religious, or other charitable activities serving the common welfare. Some public charities engage in grantmaking activities, although most engage in direct service or other tax-exempt activities. Public charities are eligible for maximum income tax-deductible contributions from the public and are not subject to the same rules and restrictions as private foundations. Some are also referred to as "public foundations" or "publicly supported organizations" and may use the term "foundation" in their names. (See also **501(c)(3); Private Foundation**)

Qualifying Distributions: Expenditures of private foundations used to satisfy the annual payout requirement. These can include grants, reasonable administrative expenses, set-asides, loans and program-related investments, and amounts paid to acquire assets used directly in carrying out exempt purposes.

Query Letter: A brief letter outlining an organization's activities and its request for funding sent to a foundation or corporation to determine whether it would be appropriate for that organization to submit a full grant proposal. Many grantmakers prefer to be contacted in this way before receiving a full proposal.

RFP: Request For Proposal. When the government issues a new contract or grant program, it sends out RFPs to agencies that might be qualified to participate. The RFP lists project specifications and application procedures. A few foundations occasionally use RFPs in specific fields, but most prefer to consider proposals that are initiated by applicants.

Seed Money: A grant or contribution used to start a new project or organization. Seed grants may cover salaries and other operating expenses of a new project.

Set-Asides: Funds set aside by a foundation for a specific purpose or project that are counted as qualifying distributions toward the foundation's annual payout requirement. Amounts for the project must be paid within five years of the first set-aside.

Special Purpose Foundation: A private foundation that focuses its grantmaking activities in one or a few special areas of interest. For example, a foundation may only award grants in the area of cancer research or child development. (See also **General Purpose Foundation**)

Technical Assistance: Operational or management assistance given to nonprofit organizations. It can include fundraising assistance, budgeting and financial planning, program planning, legal advice, marketing, and other aids to management. Assistance may be offered directly by a foundation or corporate staff member, or be offered in the form of a grant to pay for the services of an outside consultant. (See also **In-Kind Contributions**)

Trustee: A member of a governing board. A foundation's board of trustees meets to review grant proposals and make decisions. Often also referred to as a "director" or "board member."

ABBREVIATIONS

The following lists contain standard abbreviations frequently used by the Foundation Center's editorial staff. These abbreviations are used most frequently in the addresses of grantmakers and the titles of corporate and grantmaker officers.

STREET ABBREVIATIONS

1st	First*	N.E.	Northeast
2nd	Second*	N.W.	Northwest
3rd	Third*	No.	Number
Apt.	Apartment	Pkwy.	Parkway
Ave.	Avenue	Pl.	Place
Bldg.	Building	Plz.	Plaza
Blvd.	Boulevard	R.R.	Rural Route
Cir.	Circle	Rd.	Road
Ct.	Court	Rm.	Room
Ctr.	Center	Rte.	Route
Dept.	Department	S.	South
Dr.	Drive	S.E.	Southeast
E.	East	S.W.	Southwest
Expwy.	Expressway	Sq.	Square
Fl.	Floor	St.	Saint
Ft.	Fort	St.	Street
Hwy.	Highway	Sta.	Station
Ln.	Lane	Ste.	Suite
M.C.	Mail Code	Terr.	Terrace
M.S.	Mail Stop	Tpke.	Turnpike
Mt.	Mount	Univ.	University
N.	North	W.	West

*Numerics used always

TWO LETTER STATE AND TERRITORY ABBREVIATIONS

AK	Alaska	NC	North Carolina
AL	Alabama	ND	North Dakota
AR	Arkansas	NE	Nebraska
AZ	Arizona	NH	New Hampshire
CA	California	NJ	New Jersey
CO	Colorado	NM	New Mexico
CT	Connecticut	NV	Nevada
DC	District of Columbia	NY	New York
DE	Delaware	OH	Ohio
FL	Florida	OK	Oklahoma
GA	Georgia	OR	Oregon
HI	Hawaii	PA	Pennsylvania
IA	Iowa	PR	Puerto Rico
ID	Idaho	RI	Rhode Island
IL	Illinois	SC	South Carolina
IN	Indiana	SD	South Dakota
KS	Kansas	TN	Tennessee
KY	Kentucky	TX	Texas
LA	Louisiana	UT	Utah
MA	Massachusetts	VA	Virginia
MD	Maryland	VI	Virgin Islands
ME	Maine	VT	Vermont
MI	Michigan	WA	Washington
MN	Minnesota	WI	Wisconsin
MO	Missouri	WV	West Virginia
MS	Mississippi	WY	Wyoming
MT	Montana		

ABBREVIATIONS USED FOR OFFICER TITLES

Acctg.	Accounting	Govt.	Government
ADM.	Admiral	Hon.	Judge
Admin.	Administration	Inf.	Information
Admin.	Administrative	Int.	Internal
Admin.	Administrator	Intl.	International
Adv.	Advertising	Jr.	Junior
Amb.	Ambassador	Lt.	Lieutenant
Assn.	Association	Ltd.	Limited
Assoc(s).	Associate(s)	Maj.	Major
Asst.	Assistant	Mfg.	Manufacturing
Bro.	Brother	Mgmt.	Management
C.A.O.	Chief Accounting Officer	Mgr.	Manager
C.A.O.	Chief Administration Officer	Mktg.	Marketing
		Msgr.	Monsignor
C.E.O.	Chief Executive Officer	Mt.	Mount
C.F.O.	Chief Financial Officer	Natl.	National
C.I.O.	Chief Information Officer	Off.	Officer
		Opers.	Operations
C.I.O.	Chief Investment Officer	Org.	Organization
		Plan.	Planning
C.O.O.	Chief Operating Officer	Pres.	President
Capt.	Captain	Prog(s).	Program(s)
Chair.	Chairperson	RADM.	Rear Admiral
Col.	Colonel	Rels.	Relations
Comm.	Committee	Rep.	Representative
Comms.	Communications	Rev.	Reverend
Commo.	Commodore	Rt. Rev.	Right Reverend
Compt.	Comptroller	Secy.	Secretary
Cont.	Controller	Secy.-Treas.	Secretary-Treasurer
Contrib(s).	Contribution(s)	Sen.	Senator
Coord.	Coordinator	Soc.	Society
Corp.	Corporate, Corporation	Sr.	Senior
Co(s).	Company(s)	Sr.	Sister
Dep.	Deputy	Supt.	Superintendent
Devel.	Development	Supvr.	Supervisor
Dir.	Director	Svc(s).	Service(s)
Distrib(s).	Distribution(s)	Tech.	Technology
Div.	Division	Tr.	Trustee
Exec.	Executive	Treas.	Treasurer
Ext.	External	Univ.	University
Fdn.	Foundation	V.P.	Vice President
Fr.	Father	VADM.	Vice Admiral
Genl.	General	Vice-Chair.	Vice Chairperson
Gov.	Governor		

ADDITIONAL ABBREVIATIONS

E-mail	Electronic mail
FAX	Facsimile
LOI	Letter of Inquiry
RFP	Request for Proposals
SASE	Self-Addressed Stamped Envelope
TDD, TTY	Telecommunication Device for the Deaf
Tel.	Telephone
URL	Uniform Resource Locator (web site)

Jan.	January
Feb.	February
Mar.	March
Apr.	April
Aug.	August
Sept.	September
Oct.	October
Nov.	November
Dec.	December

BIBLIOGRAPHY OF FUNDING FOR INTERNATIONAL AND FOREIGN PROGRAMS

Compiled by Inès Sucre

This selected listing is compiled from the Foundation Center's bibliographic database. Many of the items are available for free reference use in the Center's New York City, Washington, DC, Cleveland, San Francisco, and Atlanta libraries and in many of its cooperating libraries. For further references on such topics as fundraising and proposal development, see the *Catalog of Nonprofit Literature*, which can be accessed online at cnl.foundationcenter.org.

Anheier, Helmut K., Adele Simmons and David Winder (eds.) *Innovation in Strategic Philanthropy: Local and Global Perspectives*. New York, NY: Springer Publishing Company Inc., 2007. xv, 236 p. ISBN 0-387-34252-4
> In Part I, various specialists provide status reports on the third sector in Brazil, Central and Eastern Europe, Mexico, Pakistan, Philippines, South Africa, and Thailand. In Part II, authors provide a global perspective: "Distinct View–Intervening in the Practices of the Public and Private Sector" by Melanie Beth Oliviero and Adele Simmons; "The Global and Local Dimension" by Dan Nielsen; "Philanthropy and Networks in Global Civil Society" by Giuseppe Caruso; "The Role of Philanthropy Within the United Nations System: The Case of the United Nations Foundation" by Stefan Toepler and Natascha Mard; "Philanthropic Foundations' Assistance in Post-Conflict Situations: A Case Study of Post-Communist Southeast Europe" by Natalia Leshchenko; "The Infrastructure of Global Philanthropy: Wings and Wings-CF" by Diana Leat.

Anheier, Helmut K. and Siobhan Daly (eds.) *The Politics of Foundations: A Comparative Analysis*. New York, NY: Routledge, 2007. xvi, 349 p. ISBN 0-415-70167-8
> Contents include analyses for Austria, Belgium, Czech Republic, Denmark, Estonia, France, Germany, Greece, Hungary, Ireland, Italy, Netherlands, Norway, Poland, Spain, Sweden, Switzerland, and the United Kingdom. Indexed.

Ausenda, Fabio (ed.) *Green Volunteers: The World Guide to Voluntary Work in Nature Conservation*. 8th ed. Milano, Italy: Green Volunteers. 2011. 255 p. ISBN-13: 978-88-89060-19-3
> This guide provides detailed information on over 200 short- and long-term organizations and projects around the world that provide conservation volunteering opportunities. Includes sample standard application form. Indexed by location, cost, and species.

Baehr, Erika. *European Philanthropic Support to Address HIV/AIDS in 2010*. Brussels, Belgium: European HIV/AIDS Funders Group, 2011. 48 p.
> Based on survey data from 31 foundations in Europe, the report examines HIV/AIDS funding in 2010 and includes a forecast for 2011. Contains an analysis by geographic distribution, intended use of funding, and target population. Appendices contain a list of corporations that support HIV/AIDS workplace and other programs and web sites of funders mentioned in the report.

Burdenski, Robert A. *More Innovations in Annual Giving: Ten Global Departures That Worked*. Washington, DC: Council for Advancement and Support of Education, 2009. xviii, 107 p. ISBN 0-89964-420-1
> Provides ten case studies of annual giving programs from around the world. The examples highlight strategies related to the Internet, reunion giving, staff appeals, parent programs, data mining, phonathons, leadership gifts, direct mail, and other fundraising topics.

Charities Aid Foundation. *The World Giving Index 2011: A Global View of Giving Trends*. Kent, Great Britain: Charities Aid Foundation. 2011. 67 p.
> This report is based upon survey data carried out in 153 countries. Individuals were asked about three specific charitable acts: donating money, volunteering, and helping strangers. Among the findings: Asia has seen the biggest growth in giving, while the U.S. is currently the world's most giving nation. It also found that despite global economic turmoil, the world is giving more. Includes numerous tables and charts.

Comparative Charts of Foundation Laws. 2009 ed. Brussels, Belgium: European Foundation Centre. 2009. 44 p.
> The comparative charts in this publication provide an overview of the laws governing foundations in member states of the European Union. Issues addressed include the purpose that a foundation may legally pursue, the need for state approval or registration, the minimum capital required, governing structures of different types of foundations, reporting and accountability requirements, remuneration of board members, and many others.

Cracknell, Jon, Heather Godwin, and Harriet Williams. *Where the Green Grants Went: Patterns of UK Funding for Environmental and Conservation Work*. 4th ed. Environmental Funders Network, 2009. 44 p.
> Provides results of an annual analysis grants for environmental programs from trusts and foundations based in the United Kingdom. Includes a geographic comparison of environmental giving in the UK and abroad.

Cravens, Jayne. *Basic Tips for Fund-Raising for Small NGOs/Civil Society in Developing Countries*. 2009. 27 p.
> Provides practical fundraising advice for community-based organizations or civil society organizations in developing countries. Topics covered include establishing credibility, promoting accountability, finding donors, and other subjects.

Directory of Grant Making Trusts. 22nd ed. London, England: Directory of Social Change, 2012. 1072 p.
ISBN-13: 978-1-906294-56-4
> A directory covering the largest 2,500 British grantmaking trusts. Entries include the title of the trust; year established; registration number; contact information; trustees; restrictions; beneficial area; finances; type of grant; type of beneficiary; submission of applications; publications; and notes.

Disaster Grantmaking: A Practical Guide for Foundations and Corporations. 2nd ed. Washington, DC: Council on Foundations, 2007. 40 p.
> Jointly published with the European Foundation Centre, this pamphlet presents the results of a year-long study, outlining the best principles and approaches to funding for disaster relief.

Edie, John A., Jane C. Nober, and Jacob T. Clauson. *Beyond Our Borders: A Guide to Making Grants Outside the United States*. 4th ed. Washington, DC: Council on Foundations. 2011. 113 p.
> This revised edition explains the technical and legal requirements private and community foundations, corporate grantmakers, and public charities must follow for making grants outside the U.S. It includes details of restrictions on cross-border giving found in the USA Patriot Act and in the Foreign Corrupt Practices Act. Appendixes include sample materials, foreign equivalency determination forms, discussion of treaties with Canada, Mexico and Israel, a listing of international organizations designated by executive order, Internal Revenue Service rulings governing friends organizations, suggested grant agreements for public charity grantors, guidance on expenditure responsibility, and more detailed discussions of technical points.

Edwards, Michael (ed.) *The Oxford Handbook of Civil Society*. New York, NY: Oxford University Press. 2011. xiii, 515 p.
ISBN-13: 978-0-195398-57-1
> This collection of essays on civil society in both the developed and developing worlds examines its forms, achievements, and norms and provides a variety of geographical perspectives. The last section analyzes philanthropic support of civil society. Contains bibliographical references and index.

Espinoza, Robert. *A Global Gaze: Lesbian, Gay, Bisexual, Transgender and Intersex Grantmaking in the Global South and East*. New York, NY: Funders for Lesbian and Gay Issues, 2007. 36 p.
> Grants data from 40 funders and survey responses from 278 nongovernmental organizations were examined to help grantmakers identify funding disparities and to develop benchmarks for trends analysis. The report also includes a synopsis of a recent funder gathering, a list of grantmakers, selected profiles of grantmakers, and a brief glossary.

The Europa International Foundation Directory: 2012. 21st ed. London, England: Routledge, 2012. 692 p.
ISBN- 978-1-85743-647-1
> This edition includes information on 2,550 organizations in approximately 100 countries. Arranged alphabetically by country, each entry notes the foundation's name in its native language followed by an English translation, year founded, and founding person or organization; activities, publications, and finances if available (assets and grantmaking expenditures in native country's currency); board of trustees; officers; address with e-mail; and telephone and fax numbers. Contains background essays, a selected bibliography, and indexes.

European Foundations in Times of Crisis. London, UK: Alliance Publishing Trust, 2009. 32 p.
> The Alliance Magazine special supplement contains several features, including highlights from the "Responsible Leadership in Times of Change" symposium in Luxembourg (October 9, 2009), case studies of European foundations responding to the economic crisis, and a number of interviews.

Exploring Transparency and Accountability Regulation of Public-Benefit Foundations in Europe. Brussels, Belgium: European Foundation Centre. 2011. 47 p.
> In this study, the European Foundation Centre and Donors and Foundations Networks in Europe compare and map regulatory frameworks and self-regulatory tools that shape the transparency and accountability of European foundations. It also examines the effectiveness of these mechanisms, discusses the rationale for regulation, and offers recommendations.

Funder Collaborations Addressing HIV/AIDS: Examples From Around the World. New York, NY: Funders Concerned About AIDS, 2008. 28 p.
> 19 case studies illustrate varied effective grantmaker partnerships in fighting the global spread of HIV and AIDS. Names and contact information are provided for each profiled initiative.

Funding Human Rights: An Invitation. New York, NY: International Human Rights Funders Group. 2008. 32 p.
> This booklet for grantmakers explores what human rights can contribute to funders' grantmaking goals. Features stories and examples of how human rights funding has impacted numerous fields and communities, and discusses varied strategies through which human rights objectives can be achieved. Includes a resource list.

Funding Impact: Partnerships, Networks, and Collaborations: A Learning Opportunity. New York, NY: Africa Grantmakers' Affinity Group, 2008. 28 p.
> A conference report from the Africa Grantmakers' Affinity Group's February 2008 meeting on evaluating impact in African development. Includes notes on each session, and a list of participants.

Giving Korea. 2009 ed. Seoul, Korea: Center on Philanthropy at the Beautiful Foundation, 2010. 120 p.
> The annual volume alternates between research results on individual and corporate giving in South Korea. The 2009 edition focuses on corporate giving and corporate social responsibility.

Hammack, David C. and Steven Heydemann (eds.)
Globalization, Philanthropy, and Civil Society: Projecting Institutional Logics Abroad. Bloomington, IN: Indiana University Press, 2009. xiii, 304 p. (Philanthropic and Nonprofit Studies).
ISBN-13: 978-0-253-35303-0
> Experts contribute case studies that examine the spread of nonprofit organizational models, structures, and systems across national boundaries. Contents include: "Philanthropic Projections: Sending Institutional Logics Abroad" by Steven Heydemann and David C. Hammack; "Nongovernmental Organizations and the Making of the International Community" by Akira Iriye; "Philanthropy and the 'Perfect Democracy' of Rotary International" by Brendan Goff; "Social Entrepreneurship: Success Stories and Logic Construction" by Michael Lounsbury and David Strang; "Moral Globalization and Discursive Struggle: Reconciliation, Transition Justice, and Cosmopolitan Discourse" by Jonathan Vanantwerpen; "Philanthropic Foundations in Russia: Western Projection and Local Legitimacy" by John W. Slocum; "Promoting Civil Society or Diffusing NGOs? U.S. Donors in the Former Soviet Union" by Sada Aksartova; "Dialectics of Patronage: Logics of Accountability at the African AIDS-NGO Interface" by Ann Swidler; The Political Logic of Institutional Adaptation: NGO's Strategies Abroad" by Elizabeth Bloodgood; and "Exporting Institutional Logics into the Amazon? American and German Efforts to Protect the Ecosystem and Traditional Peoples of the American Basin" by Sandra Moog. With bibliographical references and index.

Harvard Humanitarian Initiative. *Disaster Relief 2.0: The Future of Information Sharing in Humanitarian Emergencies*. Washington, DC and Berkshire, UK: UN Foundation & Vodafone Foundation Technology Partnership, 2011. 72 p.
> Outlines the challenges of and recommendations for creating an effective interface between humanitarian groups and volunteer and technical communities, aggregating, visualizing, and analyzing data on and from affected communities to support relief efforts.

Hero, Peter deCourcy and Peter Walkenhorst (eds.)
Local Mission-Global Vision: Community Foundations in the 21st Century. New York, NY: Foundation Center, 2008. x, 351 p.
ISBN-13: 978-1-59542-204-0
> The compilation examines current and emerging roles of community foundations from the international perspective. Community foundation practitioners and academic experts contribute chapters that discuss the development of financial resources and social capital; civic leadership by community foundations; and the impact of global trends on community foundations. With bibliographical references and index.

The Index of Global Philanthropy and Remittances 2011. Washington, DC: Hudson Institute, 2011. 35 p.
> The report documents and measures giving overseas by the United States and other developed nations. Various sections present statistics and analyses on giving by governments, foundations, corporations, public charities, universities, religious organizations, volunteers, and remittances.

International Exchange Locator: A Resource Directory for Educational and Cultural Exchange. Washington, DC: Alliance for International Educational and Cultural Exchange. 2011. xii, 292 p.
> This publication lists organizations involved in international exchanges, industry-specific exchanges, research/support organizations, foreign affairs agencies and exchange programs, other federal government exchanges, and key congressional committees and members of congress. Entries contain name and address of the organization, statement of purpose, types of exchange programs, availability of financial assistance, geographic focus, and selected publications. Indexed.

Johnson, Paula D. *Global Institutional Philanthropy: A Preliminary Status Report*. Sao Paulo, Brazil: WINGS. 2010. 53 p.
> This publication reports on findings from a global survey of members of the Worldwide Initiatives for Grantmaker Support (WINGS). It offers an overview of philanthropic models, trends, and regulations in Sub-Saharan Africa, the Arab Region, Asia-Pacific, Europe, Latin America and the Caribbean, and North America. Published in cooperation with the Philanthropic Initiative.

Kiger, Joseph C. *Philanthropists and Foundation Globalization*. New Brunswick, NJ: Transaction Publishers, 2008. xv, 173 p.
ISBN-13: 978-1-4128-0673-2
> The volume presents a biographical-historical account of international giving by twenty-four well-known philanthropists including Andrew Carnegie, George Soros, and Bill Gates. A chapter of the book discusses foundation investigations and studies since 1912, citing examples where foundations were criticized for funding programs abroad. A section also chronicles foundation activities in Europe during the late twentieth century.

Lawrence, Steven, and Reina Mukai. *International Grantmaking Update: A Snapshot of U.S. Foundation Trends*. New York, NY: Foundation Center. 2010. 7 p.
> This report provides a brief update on key trends and the current outlook for international giving. Prepared by the Foundation Center in cooperation with the Council on Foundations, the study includes estimates of overall giving by private and community foundations through 2009; and an analysis of patterns of giving in 2008 and changes in funding priorities between 2006 and 2008. Includes charts and bibliographical references.

MacDonald, Norine and Luc Tayart de Borms (eds.) *Global Philanthropy*. London, UK: MF Publishing. 2010. xii, 401 p.
ISBN-13: 978-0-9564422-0-8
> Leaders and experts from across the globe share stories, perspectives, and insight regarding philanthropy. Chapters cover a number of countries, regions, and topics, including New Zealand, Australia, Japan, Asia and the Pacific, China, India, Pakistan, United Arab Emirates, Arab region, Muslim philanthropy, Turkey, Russia, Europe, South Africa, Africa, Brazil, United States, and Canada.

MacDonald, Norine and Luc Tayart de Borms (eds.) *Philanthropy in Europe: A Rich Past, a Promising Future*. London, UK: Alliance Publishing Trust, 2008. 304 p. ISBN-13: 978-0-9558804-0-7
> Explores the history and unique characteristics of philanthropy in Europe through 13 funder profiles and six essays.

Mersiyanova, I. V. and L. I. Yakobson. *Philanthropy in Russia: Public Attitudes and Participation*. Moscow: State University, Higher School of Economics. 2010. 94 p. ISBN-13: 978-5-7598074-2-1
> This monograph presents survey findings and opinion poll data that describe the participation of Russian citizens in charitable activity, as well as the public perception of the relationship between the State and charity providers. Chapters also discuss volunteerism, donation practices, and the relationship between those giving and receiving aid. Contains bibliographical references.

Mexico Community Foundations: A Comprehensive Profile. Teamworks, 2009. xvi, 92 p.

Provides an environmental scan of community foundations in Mexico, based on survey data, submitted financial data, and interviews with foundation representatives. The report describes organizational characteristics, such as board composition and staffing profile, as well as the developmental needs of the foundations. Includes recommendations for strengthening the community foundation sector in Mexico.

Moyo, Bhekinkosi (ed.) (Dis) *Enabling the Public Sphere: Civil Society Regulation in Africa.* [Midrand, South Africa]: Southern Africa Trust. 2010. xv, 425 p. ISBN-13: 978-1-9202600-9-5

This book covers the regulatory environment under which civil society, in particular nongovernmental organizations, operates in Africa. Articles discuss civil society-state relations, NGO laws and policies, national constitutions and processes, and the general political economy of civil society. Volume 1 includes Zimbabwe, South Africa, Namibia, Lesotho, Swaziland, Malawi, Zambia, Ethiopia, Uganda, Kenya, Tanzania, Angola, Mozambique, Democratic Republic of the Congo, Cameroon, Gabon, Madagascar, and Mauritius. Contains bibliographical references and index.

Norton, Michael. *Worldwide Fundraiser's Handbook: A Resource Guide for NGOs and Community Organizations.* 3rd ed. London, UK: Directory of Social Change, 2009. xii, 324 p. ISBN-13: 978-1-906294-33-5

The fundraising guide provides advice and tips for nongovernmental organizations in developing countries. The handbook explores a number of topics, including basic principles, strategy, funding sources, earned income, communications, and other areas. Indexed.

Parker, Susan. *Lessons from a Ten-Year Funder Collaborative: A Case Study of the Partnership for Higher Education in Africa.* Clear Thinking Communications. 2010. 50 p. ISBN 978-0-9827746-1-8

Examines the funder collaborative's evolution, successes, and challenges, including differences in foundation cultures and lack of data. Offers advice on leadership, goals and expectations, planning, structure, pooled funding, evaluation, and exit plans.

Pharoah, Cathy. *Family Foundation Philanthropy 2009: UK, Germany, Italy, US.* London, UK: Alliance Publishing Trust. 2009. 60 p. ISBN-13: 978-0-9558804-4-5

This research on family foundations in the United Kingdom, United States, Germany, and Italy primarily examines the largest 100 foundations based on data from 2006 and 2007.

Pharoah, Cathy, Charles Keidan, and Jillian Gordon. *Family Foundation Giving Trends 2011.* London, UK: Alliance Publishing Trust. 2011. 70 p. ISBN-13: 978-1-9073761-4-6

Fourth in a series, this report tracks annual trends in the giving of the largest 100 family foundations in the United Kingdom and compares them with U.S.-based foundations. The data are from 2009/2010; the report includes eight case studies of family foundations and their founders. Contains bibliographical references.

Prewitt, Kenneth, Mattei Dogan, Steven Heydemann, and Stephan Toepler (eds.) *The Legitimacy of Philanthropic Foundations: United States and European perspectives.* New York, NY: Russell Sage Foundation, 2006. x, 294 p. ISBN 0-87154-696-5

These scholarly essays, originally presented at a conference in 2004, represent analyses by Helmut K. Anheier, Siobhan Daly, Peter Frumkin, Giuliana Gemelli, Kirsten A. Grønbjerg, David C. Hammack, Diana Leat, Rupert Graf Strachwitz, Steen Thomsen, and Julian Wolpert, in addition to the editors. With bibliographical references and index.

Principles of Accountability for International Philanthropy: An Aspirational Tool for International Donors. Washington, DC: Council on Foundations, 2007. 27 p.

Presents principles and good accountability practices for international philanthropic activities. Includes a resource list.

Ramutsindela, Maano, Marja Spierenburg, and Harry Wels. *Sponsoring Nature: Environmental Philanthropy for Conservation.* New York, NY: Earthscan. 2011. xi, 207 p. ISBN-13: 978-1-84407904-9

This publication offers a comprehensive discussion of global environmental philanthropy, with a focus on the motivations of donors supporting environmental causes. It also looks at how this type of philanthropy might shed light on the charitable impulse in general, and investigates the implications of the current economic crisis on future directions. Chapter seven is devoted to environmental conservation in Africa. Contains bibliographical references and index.

Reid, Elizabeth J., and Janelle A. Kerlin. *The International Charitable Nonprofit Subsector in the United States: International Understanding, International Development and Assistance, and International Affairs.* Washington, DC: Urban Institute. Center on Nonprofits and Philanthropy, 2006. iii, 84 p.

This is the first systematic study of the impact of international nonprofit organizations, based on analysis of their Form 990s. Includes numerous statistical tables and demographic characteristics, such as revenue and size, location, expenditures, and growth.

Rozas, Daniel. *Implementing Client Protection in Microfinance: The State of the Practice, 2011.* Smart Campaign. 2011. 48 p.

In 2008, the microfinance community introduced Client Protection Principles (CPPs) and launched the Smart Campaign to implement them. This report documents the progress of the Campaign, which has reached 2,300 endorsers, including 700 microfinance institutions (MFIs), and, based on third-party assessments, rates MFIs on preventing over-indebtedness, transparency, responsible pricing, fair and respectful treatment of clients, privacy of client data, and mechanisms for complaint resolution.

Salamon, Lester M. *Rethinking Corporate Social Engagement: Lessons from Latin America.* Sterling, VA: Kumarian Press. 2010. xii, 159 p. ISBN-13: 978-1-5654931-3-1

This study looks at the current state of corporate social responsibility (CSR) in Latin America. Through interviews, case studies, and field reports, the author examines the proliferation of corporate social engagement, partnerships between corporations and local grass-roots projects/programs, CSR variations among countries and businesses, and lessons that CSR in Latin America can hold for other regions of the world. The book's origins stem from research initiated by the Inter-American Foundation (Arlington, VA) to determine the status of its efforts to encourage corporate engagement with nonprofit organizations in Latin America. Contains bibliographical references and index.

Shah, Seema, Lawrence T. McGill, and Karen Weisblatt. *Untapped Potential: European Foundation Funding for Women and Girls.* New York, NY: Foundation Center. 2011. 39 p.

This study of the philanthropic activities of European foundations focuses on support for women and girls. Altogether, 145 foundations from 19 countries participated in the study. Sections discuss funding priorities, foundation engagement and approaches to funding, and how foundations fund females in different subject areas. Appendices cover foundation interest in issues affecting women and girls, a chart of grants by subject area, and grantmaker profiles. The study commissioned by Mama Cash and produced in association with Weisblatt & Associates and the European Foundation Centre. Contains bibliographical references.

Simon, Sue. *Expanding Global Philanthropy to Support The Human Rights of Lesbian, Gay, Bisexual and Transgender People: Summary Report from a Convening at the Rockefeller Conference Center, Bellagio, Italy; September 15–19, 2008.* Kalamazoo, MI: Arcus Operating Foundation. 2009. 28 p.

A conference report from the Arcus Operating Foundation's meeting to address the ways in which philanthropy can aid in expanding human rights for lesbian, gay, bisexual, and transgender individuals in the Global South and Global East. The report offers conference proceedings, a list of participants, and a list of relevant research reports available online.

Spero, Joan E. *The Global Role of U.S. Foundations.* New York, NY: Foundation Center. 2010. x, 44 p.

Provides a short history of international philanthropy and examines global philanthropy in the post-Cold War era. The final section explores several key issues, such as measuring impact, global governance, accountability at home and abroad, and future global challenges. Includes related statistics, charts, and bibliographical references.

Tadashi, Yamamoto, Iriye Akira, and Iokibe Makoto (eds.) *Philanthropy and Reconciliation: Rebuilding Postwar U.S.-Japan Relations.* New York, NY: Japan Center for International Exchange, 2006. 406 p. ISBN 4-88907-076-1

Various specialists provide essays on the efforts of foundations and individuals to encourage international exchanges and promote civil society in the era after World War II. Chapters include: "The Role of Philanthropy in Postwar U.S.-Japan Relations, 1945-1975: An Overview" by Yamamoto Tadashi; "The Role of Philanthropy and Civil Society in U.S. Foreign Relations" by Iriye Akira; "U.S.-Japan Intellectual Exchange: The Relationship between Government and Private Foundations" by Iokibe Makoto; "The Evolving Role of American Foundations in Japan: An Institutional Perspective" by Kimberly Gould Ashizawa; "American Philanthropy in Postwar Japan: An Analysis of Grants to Japanese Institutions and Individuals" by Wada Jun; "Understanding the 'Other': Foundation Support for Japanese Studies in the United States" by Kimberly Gould Ashizawa; "The Development of Grassroots International Exchange in Japan and the Impact of American Philanthropy" by Menju Toshihiro; and "Japanese Philanthropy: Its Origins and Impact on U.S.-Japan Relations" by Katsumata Hideko. With bibliographical references.

Taylor, Rupert (ed.) *Third Sector Research.* New York, NY: Springer Publishing Company Inc.. 2010. xiv, 342 p. ISBN-13: 978-1-4419-5707-8

This anthology of essays by various scholars appears at a time when research efforts, formal academic programs, and peer-reviewed journals have all increased substantially. With a focus on the contemporary issues that are being studied internationally, the topics range from new trends in philanthropy and voluntarism, the situation in developing countries, corporate responsibility, global civil society, as well as the history and development of the field. Indexed.

Thompson, Verne (ed.) *Encyclopedia of Associations: International Organizations.* 50th ed. Detroit, MI: Gale/Cengage Learning, 2011. 3 vols. ISBN 0-4144-5895-9

Guide to over 31,000 international nonprofit membership organizations, including multinational and binational groups and national organizations based outside the U.S., as well as U.S.-based multinational associations. Parts 1 and 2 include descriptive listings, arranged under 15 general subject categories and include location, size, objectives, and information on publications, conventions/meetings, annual budget, commercial exhibits, language and affiliations. Part 3 contains a comprehensive alphabetical name and keyword index, geographic, and executive indexes.

Water Access, Sanitation, and Hygiene (WASH): *U.S. Advocacy Landscape.* FSG Social Impact Advisors. 2011. 18 p.

Reviews challenges for WASH advocacy and practice. Outlines a framework of interdependent goals, including boosting the sustainability and effectiveness of interventions and securing more funding from non-government donors, and ways to strengthen the field.

Wiepking, Pamala (ed.) *The State of Giving Research in Europe: Household Donations to Charitable Organizations in Twelve European Countries.* Pallas Publications. 2009. 76 p. ISBN: 978-90-8555-009-9

Examines philanthropic research in twelve European countries: Austria, Belgium, Czech Republic, France, Germany, Hungary, Ireland, Italy, the Netherlands, Spain, Sweden, and the United Kingdom. Contains bibliographical references.

RESOURCES OF THE FOUNDATION CENTER

Established in 1956, the Foundation Center is the leading source of information about philanthropy worldwide. Through data, analysis, and training, it connects people who want to change the world to the resources they need to succeed. The Center maintains the most comprehensive database on U.S. and, increasingly, global grantmakers and their grants — a robust, accessible knowledge bank for the sector. It also operates research, education, and training programs designed to advance knowledge of philanthropy at every level. Thousands of people visit the Center's web site each day and are served in its five regional library/learning centers and its network of more than 450 funding information centers located in public libraries, community foundations, and educational institutions nationwide and around the world.

ONLINE DATABASES

FOUNDATION DIRECTORY ONLINE SUBSCRIPTION PLANS

To meet the needs of grantseekers at every level, *Foundation Directory Online* (FDO) offers five plans—each with monthly, annual, and two-year subscription options. With every plan, subscribers can choose from indexed search terms or keyword-search; search for grantmakers geographically by county, metropolitan area, congressional district, and ZIP code, as well as by state and city.

Professional

FDO *Professional* is acclaimed as the best grantseeking tool on the market. Only *Professional* provides immediate access to nine comprehensive databases, updated weekly: grantmakers, companies, grants, and IRS 990s . . . all with indexed search terms and fully keyword-searchable, plus news, jobs, RFPs, PubHub reports, and nonprofit literature. *Professional* features interactive maps and charts displaying a foundation's giving patterns, and unique funder portfolios with abstracts from *Philanthropy News Digest*, the grantmaker's latest RFPs, job postings, and key staff affiliations.
$179.95: ONE MONTH
$1,295: ONE YEAR

Platinum

The *Platinum* plan includes profiles of all U.S. foundations, corporate funders, and grantmaking public charities in addition to their recently-awarded grants and an index of trustee, officer, and donor names.
$149.95: ONE MONTH
$995: ONE YEAR

Premium

The *Premium* plan features profiles of the nation's top 20,000 funders and an expanded database of recently-awarded grants . . . fully-searchable. With indexed trustee, officer, and donor names, it's a popular starting point for mid-size nonprofits.
$59.95: ONE MONTH
$595: ONE YEAR

Plus

Search two databases: the nation's 10,000 largest foundations and recently-awarded grants. *Plus* includes an index of trustee, officer, and donor names. A terrific value.
$29.95: ONE MONTH
$295: ONE YEAR

Basic

Gain access to profiles of the nation's 10,000 largest foundations. FDO *Basic* includes an index of trustee, officer, and donor names. A great tool for beginning grantseekers.
$19.95: ONE MONTH
$195: ONE YEAR

TO SUBSCRIBE, VISIT foundationcenter.org/fdo

Corporate Giving Online

For nonprofits seeking grants or in-kind donations of equipment, products, professional services, and volunteers from U.S. company-sponsored foundations and giving programs, *Corporate Giving Online* includes three databases, updated weekly: companies, grantmakers, and grants.
$59.95: ONE MONTH
$595: ONE YEAR

TO SUBSCRIBE, VISIT cgonline.foundationcenter.org

Foundation Grants to Individuals Online

Need a scholarship, fellowship or award? Visit the new *Foundation Grants to Individuals Online* built specifically for students, artists, researchers, and individuals like you!
$19.95: ONE MONTH
$36.95: THREE MONTHS
$59.95: SIX MONTHS
$99.95: ONE YEAR

TO SUBSCRIBE, VISIT gtionline.foundationcenter.org

Map of Cross-Border Giving

Who is making a difference outside of the U.S.?
The *Map of Cross-Border Giving* is an online, interactive mapping tool that lets you see over 45,000 grants totaling more than $13 billion— invaluable for quickly finding U.S. foundations and corporations that support non-U.S. organizations.
$59.95: ONE MONTH
$595: ONE YEAR

TO SUBSCRIBE, VISIT crossborder.foundationcenter.org

TRASI (Tools and Resources for Assessing Social Impact)

Browse or search the TRASI database for proven approaches to social impact assessment, guidelines for creating and conducting an assessment, and ready-to-use tools for measuring social change. TRASI also features a community page where individuals can connect with peers and experts.

FREE

PLEASE VISIT trasi.foundationcenter.org

Philanthropy In/Sight®

A grantmaker's essential planning tool.

Philanthropy In/Sight® is an interactive mapping platform designed for grantmakers, policymakers, researchers, academics—virtually anyone interested in the impact of philanthropy around the world today.

$195: ONE MONTH
$1,495: ONE YEAR

TO SUBSCRIBE, VISIT philanthropyinsight.org

Nonprofit Collaboration Database

This database provides hundreds of real-life examples of how nonprofits are working together.

PLEASE VISIT foundationcenter.org/gainknowledge/collaboration

GRANTMAKER DIRECTORIES

THE FOUNDATION DIRECTORY, 2012 Edition

Key facts include fields of interest, contact information, financials, names of decision makers, and over 55,000 sample grants. Convenient indexes are provided for all *Foundation Directories*.

MARCH 2012 / ISBN 978-1-59542-402-0 / $215 / PUBLISHED ANNUALLY

THE FOUNDATION DIRECTORY PART 2, 2012 Edition

Thorough coverage for the next 10,000 largest foundations, with nearly 40,000 sample grants.

MARCH 2012 / ISBN 978-1-59542-403-7 / $185 / PUBLISHED ANNUALLY

THE FOUNDATION DIRECTORY SUPPLEMENT, 2012 Edition

This single volume provides updates for thousands of foundations in *The Foundation Directory* and the *Directory Part 2*. Changes in foundation status, contact information, and giving interests are highlighted in new entries.

SEPTEMBER 2012 / ISBN 978-1-59542-407-5 / $125 / PUBLISHED ANNUALLY

GUIDE TO FUNDING FOR INTERNATIONAL & FOREIGN PROGRAMS, 11th Edition

Profiles of more than 2,200 grantmakers that provide international relief, disaster assistance, human rights, civil liberties, community development, and education.

MAY 2012 / ISBN 978-1-59542-408-2 / $125

THE CELEBRITY FOUNDATION DIRECTORY
3rd Digital Edition

This downloadable directory (PDF) includes detailed descriptions of more than 1,600 foundations started by VIPs in the fields of business, entertainment, politics, and sports.

SEPTEMBER 2011 / ISBN 978-1-59542-375-7 / $59.95

NATIONAL DIRECTORY OF CORPORATE GIVING, 17th Edition

The *National Directory of Corporate Giving* offers comprehensive profiles of nearly 4,400 companies, nearly 1,700 corporate giving programs, and over 11,400 sample grants.

AUGUST 2011 / ISBN 978-1-59542-368-9 / $195 / PUBLISHED ANNUALLY

FOUNDATION GRANTS TO INDIVIDUALS, 20th Edition

The only publication devoted entirely to foundation grant opportunities for qualified individual applicants, this directory features over 9,500 entries with current information: foundation name, address, contact, program description, grant amount, application guidelines, and more.

JULY 2011 / ISBN 978-1-59542-374-0 / $75 / PUBLISHED ANNUALLY

THE PRI DIRECTORY, 3RD EDITION
Charitable Loans and Other Program-Related Investments by Foundations

This *Directory* lists leading funders, recipients, project descriptions, and includes tips on how to secure and manage PRIs. Foundation listings include funder name and state; recipient name, city, and state (or country); and a description of the project funded.

PUBLISHED IN PARTERNSHIP WITH PRI MAKERS NETWORK.

JULY 2010 / ISBN 978-1-59542-214-9 / $95

GRANT GUIDES

Designed for fundraisers who work within specific areas, 25 digital edition *Grant Guides* list actual foundation grants of $10,000 or more. *Guides* include a keyword search tool and indexes to pinpoint grants of interest to you. As a special bonus, each grantmaker entry contains a link to its Foundation Finder profile for even more details, all in a convenient PDF format.

2011 EDITIONS / $39.95 EACH

TO ORDER, VISIT foundationcenter.org/marketplace/grantguides

FUNDRAISING GUIDES

AFTER THE GRANT
The Nonprofit's Guide to Good Stewardship

An invaluable and practical resource for anyone seeking funding from foundations, this *Guide* will help you manage your grant to ensure you get the next one.

MARCH 2010 / ISBN 978-1-59542-301-6 / $39.95

FOUNDATION FUNDAMENTALS, 8th Edition
Expert advice on fundraising research and proposal development.

A go-to resource in academic programs on the nonprofit sector. *Foundation Fundamentals* describes foundation funding provides advice on research strategies, including how to best use *Foundation Directory Online*.

MARCH 2008 / ISBN 978-1-59542-156-2 / $39.95

THE FOUNDATION CENTER'S GUIDE TO PROPOSAL WRITING, 6th Edition

Author Jane Geever provides detailed instructions on preparing successful grant proposals, incorporating the results of interviews with 40 U.S. grantmakers.

JUNE 2012 / ISBN 978-1-59542-404-4 / $39.95

GUÍA PARA ESCRIBIR PROPUESTAS

The Spanish-language translation of *The Foundation Center's Guide to Proposal Writing*, 5th edition.

MARCH 2008 / ISBN 978-1-595423-158-6 / $39.95

THE GRANTSEEKER'S GUIDE TO WINNING PROPOSALS

A collection of 35 actual proposals submitted to international, regional, corporate, and local foundations. Each includes remarks by the program officer who approved the grant.

AUGUST 2008 / ISBN 978-1-59542-195-1 / $39.95

SECURING YOUR ORGANIZATION'S FUTURE
A Complete Guide to Fundraising Strategies, Revised Edition
Author Michael Seltzer explains how to strengthen your nonprofit's capacity to raise funds and achieve long-term financial stability.
FEBRUARY 2001 / ISBN 0-87954-900-9 / $39.95

NONPROFIT MANAGEMENT GUIDES

AMERICA'S NONPROFIT SECTOR
A Primer
The third edition of this publication, by Lester Salamon, is ideal for people who want a thorough, accessible introduction to the nonprofit sector—as well as the nation's social welfare system.
MARCH 2012 / ISBN 978-1-59542-360-3 / $24.95

THE 21ST CENTURY NONPROFIT
Managing in the Age of Governance
This book details the significant improvements in nonprofit management practice that have taken place in recent years.
SEPTEMBER 2009 / ISBN 978-1-59542-249-1 / $39.95

FOUNDATIONS AND PUBLIC POLICY
This book presents a valuable framework for foundations as they plan or implement their engagement with public policy.
Published in partnership with The Center on Philanthropy & Public Policy.
MARCH 2009 / ISBN 978-1-59542-218-7 / $34.95

LOCAL MISSION-GLOBAL VISION
Community Foundations in the 21st Century
This book examines the new role of community foundations, exploring the potential impact of transnational evolution on organized philanthropy.
Published in partnership with Transatlantic Community Foundations Network.
AUGUST 2008 / ISBN 978-1-59542-204-0 / $34.95

WISE DECISION-MAKING IN UNCERTAIN TIMES
Using Nonprofit Resources Effectively
This book highlights the critical challenges of fiscal sustainability for nonprofits, and encourages organizations to take a more expansive approach to funding outreach.
AUGUST 2006 / ISBN 1 59542-099-1 / $34.95

EFFECTIVE ECONOMIC DECISION-MAKING BY NONPROFIT ORGANIZATIONS
Editor Dennis R. Young offers practical guidelines to help nonprofit managers advance their mission while balancing the interests of trustees, funders, government, and staff.
DECEMBER 2003 / ISBN 1-931923-69-8 / $34.95

THE BOARD MEMBER'S BOOK
Making a Difference in Voluntary Organizations, 3rd Edition
Written by former Independent Sector President Brian O'Connell, this is the perfect guide to the issues, challenges, and possibilities facing a nonprofit organization and its board.
MAY 2003 / ISBN 1-931923-17-5 / $29.95

PHILANTHROPY'S CHALLENGE
Building Nonprofit Capacity Through Venture Grantmaking
Author Paul Firstenberg explores the roles of grantmaker and grantee within various models of venture grantmaking. He outlines the characteristics that qualify an organization for a venture grant, and outlines the steps a grantmaker can take to build the grantees' organizational capacity.
FEBRUARY 2003 / SOFTBOUND: ISBN 1-931923-15-9 / $29.95
HARDBOUND: ISBN 1-931923-53-1 / $39.95

INVESTING IN CAPACITY BUILDING
A Guide to High-Impact Approaches
Author Barbara Blumenthal helps grantmakers and consultants design better methods to help nonprofits, while showing nonprofit managers how to get more effective support.
NOVEMBER 2003 / ISBN 1-931923-65-5 / $34.95

RESEARCH REPORTS

THE GLOBAL ROLE OF U.S. FOUNDATIONS
This study looks at private foundations as growing political actors with great potential as global players pursuing foreign policies and focuses in particular on how foundations have addressed five major global challenges: health disparities, poverty, climate change, democracy and civil society, and peace and security—and raises important questions regarding the assessment of foundation impact, the role of foundations in global governance, and institutional accountability.
MAY 2010 / ISBN 978-1-59542-312-2 / $19.95

SOCIAL JUSTICE GRANTMAKING II
This research report includes an analysis of social justice giving by private and public foundations, and examines the evolving nature of social justice funding through interviews with leading grantmakers.
AUGUST 2009 / ISBN 978-1-59542-213-2 / $40

Accelerating Change for Women and Girls:
THE ROLE OF WOMEN'S FUNDS
Philanthropy by and for women has increased since the 1970s, calling attention to critical women's issues like human trafficking and domestic violence. Published in partnership with the Women's Funding Network, this report examines patterns of giving by women's funds and their role in spearheading social change.
JUNE 2009 / ISBN 978-1-59542-262-0 / $19.95

FOUNDATIONS TODAY SERIES 2011
The *Foundations Today Series* provides the latest information on foundation growth and trends in foundation giving.
THREE BOOK SET / $95

Foundation Giving Trends: Update on Funding Priorities—Examines recent grantmaking patterns of more than 1,000 large U.S. foundations and compares current giving priorities with trends since 1980.
JULY 2011 / ISBN 978-1-59542-364-1 / $45

Foundation Growth and Giving Estimates: Current Outlook—Includes the new top 100 foundations list and the outlook for 2010.
APRIL 2012 / ISBN 978-1-59542-406-8 / $20

Foundation Yearbook: Facts and Figures on Private and Community Foundations—The growth in number, giving amounts, and assets of all active U.S. foundations from 1975 through 2009.
DECEMBER 2011 / ISBN 978-1-59542-366-5 / $45

INTERNATIONAL GRANTMAKING IV
This report examines grantmakers' international giving strategies and practices, assesses the outlook for future funding and documents trends based on grants awarded by over 1,000 of the largest U.S. foundations.
DECEMBER 2008 / ISBN 978-1-59542-211-8 / $40

ARTS FUNDING IV
An Update on Foundation Trends
This report provides a framework for understanding trends in foundation funding for arts and culture through 2001, based on a sample of over 800 foundations.
JUNE 2003 / ISBN 1-931923-48-5 / $19.95

ASSOCIATES PROGRAM

For just $995 a year or $695 for six months, the Associates Program experts will answer all of your questions about foundation giving, corporate philanthropy, and individual donors.

You will receive online access to several lists that are updated monthly, including new grantmakers and grantmaker application deadlines. In addition, you will receive most results within the next business day.

JOIN NOW AT foundationcenter.org/marketplace/associates

ADDITIONAL ONLINE RESOURCES

foundationcenter.org

◆ *Philanthropy News Digest* is a daily digest of philanthropy-related articles. Read interviews with leaders, look for RFPs, learn from the experts, and share ideas with others in the field.

◆ PubHub provides links to reports and white papers covering the full scope of philanthropic activity in the United States.

◆ FC Stats provides thousands of tables of national, state, and metropolitan area data on U.S. foundations and their grants, including assets and giving, grant distribution patterns, and top recipients.

◆ Access research studies to track trends in foundation growth and giving in grantmaker policies and practices.

◆ To stay current on the latest research trends visit foundationcenter.org/gainknowledge.

grantspace.org

GrantSpace, the Foundation Center's learning community for the social sector, features resources organized under the 13 most common subject areas of funding research — including health, education, and the arts.

◆ Dig into the GrantSpace knowledge base for answers to more than 150 questions asked about grantseeking and nonprofits.

◆ Stay up-to-date on classes and events happening in person and online with the GrantSpace training calendar.

◆ Add your voice and help build a community-driven knowledge base: share your expertise, rate content, ask questions, and add comments.

glasspockets.org

◆ Learn about the online transparency and accountability practices of the largest foundations, and see who has "glass pockets."

◆ Transparency Talk, the Glasspockets blog and podcast series, highlights strategies, findings, and best practices related to foundation transparency.

www.GrantCraft.org

GrantCraft, a former project of the Ford Foundation, operates under the leadership of the Foundation Center in New York and the European Foundation Centre in Brussels. GrantCraft's signature approach has been to tap the "practical wisdom" of a diverse group of experienced grantmakers to improve the practice of philanthropy.

◆ Find real-life examples and tested solutions for overcoming hurdles faced by funders.

◆ Learn about grantmaking tools and techniques through guides, case studies, videos, surveys, workshops, and translations.

FOUNDATION CENTER

Cooperating Collections
Free Funding Information Centers

For free fundraising information and other funding-related technical assistance, visit our Cooperating Collections. Located across the U.S. and in many locations around the world, in libraries, nonprofit resource centers, or other agencies, Cooperating Collections provide visitors with free access to core Foundation Center electronic and print resources and fundraising research guidance, along with access to the Internet and our searchable databases. Many offer workshops and programs for local nonprofits. For the most current contact information, visit foundationcenter.org/collections or call (800) 424-9836. Individual Collection hours vary, so please confirm specifics before paying a visit. No appointment is necessary, and no fee is charged for use of Foundation Center resources.

National

ALABAMA

Birmingham: Birmingham Public Library, Government Documents Dept., 2100 Park Place (205) 226-3620

Hoover: Hoover Public Library, 200 Municipal Dr. (205) 444-7800

Huntsville: Huntsville-Madison County Public Library, Information and Periodicals Dept., 915 Monroe St. (256) 532-5940

Mobile: Mobile Public Library, 5555 Grelot Rd. (251) 340-8555

Montgomery: Auburn University at Montgomery, 74-40 East Dr. (334) 244-3200

Montgomery: Montgomery City-County Public Library, Juliette Hampton Morgan Memorial Library, 245 High St. (334) 240-4300

Tuscaloosa: Tuscaloosa Public Library, 1801 Jack Warner Pkwy. (205) 345-5820

ALASKA

Anchorage: University of Alaska - Anchorage, Consortium Library, 3211 Providence Dr. (907) 786-1848

Juneau: Juneau Public Library, 292 Marine Way (907) 586-5267

ARIZONA

Flagstaff: Flagstaff City-Coconino County Public Library, 300 W. Aspen Ave. (928) 779-7670

Phoenix: Phoenix Public Library, Information Services Dept., 1221 N. Central Ave. (602) 262-4636

Prescott: Prescott Public Library, 215 E. Goodwin St. (928) 777-1500

Tucson: Pima County Public Library, 101 N. Stone Ave. (520) 594-5500

Yuma: Yuma County Library District, Main Branch, 2951 S. 21st Dr. (928) 782-1871

ARKANSAS

Fayetteville: Fayetteville Public Library, 401 W. Mountain St. (479) 856-7000

Fort Smith: University of Arkansas—Fort Smith, Boreham Library, 5210 Grand Ave. (479) 788-7204

Hot Springs: Garland Public Library, 1427 Malvern Ave. (501) 623-4161

Little Rock: Central Arkansas Library System, 100 Rock St. (501) 918-3000

Little Rock: Charles A. Frueauff Foundation, 200 S. Commerce, Ste. 100 (501) 324-2233

Mountain Home: Arkansas State University, Norma Wood Library, 1600 S. College St. (870) 508-6112

CALIFORNIA

Aptos: Community Foundation of Santa Cruz County, 7807 Soquel Dr. (831) 662-2000

Bakersfield: Kern County Library, Beale Memorial Library, 701 Truxtun Ave. (661) 868-0701

Bayside: Rooney Resource Center, Humboldt Area Foundation, 373 Indianola Rd. (707) 442-2993

Berkeley: Berkeley Public Library, 2090 Kittredge St. (510) 981-6100

Camarillo: Ventura County Community Foundation, Center for Nonprofit Leadership, 1317 Del Norte Rd., Ste. 150 (805) 988-0196

Fairfield: Solano Community Foundation, 470 Chadbourne Rd., Ste. D (2nd Fl.) (707) 399-3846

Fresno: Fresno County Library, 2420 Mariposa St. (559) 600-7323

Livermore: Las Positas College Library, 3000 Campus Hill Dr., Bldg. 2000 (925) 424-1151

Long Beach: Long Beach Nonprofit Partnership, 4900 E. Conant St. (562) 290-0018

Los Angeles: Southern California Library for Social Studies and Research, 6120 S. Vermont Ave. (323) 759-6063

Modesto: Stanislaus County Library, 1500 I St. (209) 558-7800

Oakland: Oakland Public Library, 125 14th St. (510) 238-6611

Pasadena: Flintridge Center, Philanthropy Resource Library, 236 W. Mountain St., Ste. 118 (626) 449-0839

Quincy: Plumas County Library, 445 Jackson St (530) 283-6310

Redding: Shasta College Library, Shasta-Tehama-Trinity Joint Community College District, 11555 Old Oregon Trail (530) 242-7551

Richmond: Richmond Public Library, 325 Civic Center Plaza (510) 620-6561

Riverside: Volunteer Center of Riverside County, Resource Center for Nonprofit Management, 2060 University Ave., Ste. 201 (951) 686-4402

Roseville: Roseville Public Library, 225 Taylor St. (916) 774-5221

Sacramento: Nonprofit Resource Center, 1331 Garden Highway (916) 285-1840

Salinas: Salinas Public Library, John Steinbeck Library, 350 Lincoln Ave. (831) 758-7311

San Diego: Nonprofit Management Solutions, 8265 Vickers St., Ste. C (858) 292-5702

San Diego: San Diego Foundation, 2508 Historic Decatur, Ste. 200 (619) 235-2300

San Mateo: San Mateo Public Library, 55 W. 3rd Ave. (650) 522-7802

San Pedro: Los Angeles Public Library, San Pedro Regional Branch, 931 S. Gaffey St. (310) 548-7779

San Rafael: Center for Volunteer and Nonprofit Leadership of Marin, 555 Northgate Dr. (415) 479-5710

Santa Ana: OneOC, 1901 E. 4th St., Ste. 100 (714) 953-5757

Santa Barbara: Santa Barbara Public Library, 40 E. Anapamu St. (805) 962-7653

Santa Monica: Santa Monica Public Library, 601 Santa Monica Blvd. (310) 458-8600

Santa Rosa: Sonoma County Library, 211 E St. (707) 545-0831

Seaside: Seaside Branch Library, 550 Harcourt Ave. (831) 899-2055

Sonora: Sierra Nonprofit Services, 591 S. Washington St. (209) 533-1093

Stockton: University of the Pacific, Global Center for Social Entrepreneurship, Callison Hall, 3601 Pacific Avenue (209) 946-7654

Victorville: High Desert Resource Network, Asuza Pacific University High Desert Center, 15283 Pahute Ave. (760) 949-2930

Walnut Creek: Walnut Creek Library, 1644 N. Broadway (925) 977-3340

COLORADO

Aspen: Pitkin County Library, 120 N. Mill St. (970) 429-1900

Basalt: Basalt Regional Library District, 14 Midland Ave. (970) 927-4311

Colorado Springs: El Pomar Nonprofit Resource Center, Penrose Library, 20 N. Cascade Ave. (719) 531-6333

Denver: Denver Public Library, 10 W. 14th Ave. Pkwy. (720) 865-1111

Durango: Durango Public Library, 1900 East 3rd Ave. (970) 375-3380

Grand Junction: Mesa County Libraries, 530 Grand Ave. (970) 243-4443

Greeley: High Plains Library District, Farr Branch Library, 1939 61st Ave. (970) 506-8550

Lakewood: Rocky Mountain Center for Health Promotion and Education, Prevention Information Center Library, 7525 West 10th Ave. (303) 239-8633

Pueblo: Pueblo City-County Library District, Doris D. Kester Southern Colorado Community Foundation, Nonprofit Resource Center, 100 E. Abriendo Ave. (719) 562-5626

Steamboat Springs: Yampa Valley Community Foundation, 465 Anglers Dr., Ste. 2-G (970) 879-8632

CONNECTICUT

Greenwich: Greenwich Library, 101 W. Putnam Ave. (203) 622-7900

Hartford: Hartford Public Library, 500 Main St. (860) 695-6295

Middletown: Russell Library, 123 Broad St. (860) 347-2520

New Haven: New Haven Free Public Library, 133 Elm St. (203) 946-7431

New London: Public Library of New London, 63 Huntington St. (840) 447-1411

Ridgefield: Ridgefield Library, 472 Main St. (203) 438-2282

Vernon: Rockville Public Library, 52 Union St. (860) 875-5892

Westport: Westport Public Library, Arnold Bernhard Plaza, 20 Jesup Rd. (203) 291-4800

DELAWARE

Dover: Dover Public Library, 45 S. State St. (302) 736-7030

Newark: University of Delaware, Hugh M. Morris Library, 181 S. College Ave. (302) 831-2432

Wilmington: University of Delaware, Center for Community Research and Service, 100 W. 10th St., Ste. 812 (302) 573-4475

DISTRICT OF COLUMBIA

Washington: University of the District of Columbia, Learning Resources Division, 4200 Connecticut Ave., N.W., Bldg. 41 - 5th Fl. (202) 274-5104

FLORIDA

Bartow: Bartow Public Library, 2150 S. Broadway Ave. (863) 534-0131

Boca Raton: Junior League of Boca Raton, Vegso Community Resource Center, 261 NW 13th St. (561) 620-2553

Clermont: Community Foundation of South Lake County, George Hovis and Don Wickham Community and Nonprofit Resource Center, 2150 Oakley Seaver Dr. (352) 394-3818

Daytona Beach: Volusia County Library Center, Daytona Beach Regional Library, City Island, 105 E. Magnolia Ave. (386) 257-6036

Fort Lauderdale: Nova Southeastern University, Alvin Sherman Library, Research, and Information Technology Center, 3100 Ray Ferrero Jr. Blvd. (954) 262-4613

Fort Myers: Southwest Florida Community Foundation, 8771 College Pkwy., Bldg. 2, Ste. 201 (239) 274-5900

Fort Pierce: Indian River Community College, Miley Library, Learning Resources Center, 3209 Virginia Ave. (866) 866-4722

Gainesville: Alachua County Library District, 401 E. University Ave. (352) 334-3900

Jacksonville: Jacksonville Public Libraries, 303 N. Laura St. (904) 630-2665

Miami: Miami-Dade College, North Campus Library, 11380 NW 27th Ave. (305) 237-1142

Miami: Miami-Dade Public Library, Humanities/Social Science Department, 101 W. Flagler St. (305) 375-5575

Orlando: Orange County Library System, Orlando Public Library, 101 E. Central Blvd. (407) 835-7323

Sarasota: Selby Public Library, 1331 1st St. (941) 861-1100

St. Petersburg: St. Petersburg College, Allstate Center, 3200 34th St. S. (727) 341-4112

Stuart: Martin County Library System, Blake Library, 2351 SE Monterey Rd. (772) 288-5702

Tampa: Hillsborough County Public Library Cooperative, John F. Germany Public Library, 900 N. Ashley Dr. (813) 273-3652

West Palm Beach: Community Foundation for Palm Beach and Martin Counties, 700 S. Dixie Highway, Ste. 200 (561) 659-6800

Winter Park: Rollins College, Philanthropy and Nonprofit Leadership Center Library, 200 E. New England Ave., Ste. 250 (407) 975-6414

GEORGIA

Atlanta: Atlanta-Fulton Public Library System, Ivan Allen Jr. Reference Dept., One Margaret Mitchell Square (404) 730-1900

Brunswick: United Way of Coastal Georgia, Coastal Georgia Nonprofit Center, 3400 Parkwood Dr., Ste. A - 2nd Fl. (912) 265-1850

Columbus: Chattahoochee Valley Regional Library System, Columbus Public Library, 3000 Macon Rd. (706) 243-2669

Gainesville: Hall County Library System, 127 Main St. NW (770) 532-3311

Macon: Methodist Home, Rumford Center, 304 Pierce Ave., 1st Fl. (478) 751-2800

Milledgeville: Digital Bridges, Knight Community Innovation Center, 127 W. Hancock St. (478) 387-0254

Thomasville: Thomas County Public Library, 201 N. Madison St. (229) 225-5252

Vienna: Southwest Georgia United, 1150 Industrial Dr. (229) 268-7592

HAWAII

Kapolei: Hawaii Maoli, Prince Kuhio Community Center, Kipuka Computer Resource Center, 91-1270 Kinoiki St. (808) 394-0050

IDAHO

Boise: Boise Public Library, 715 S. Capitol Blvd. (208) 384-4024

Coeur d'Alene: United Way of Kootenai County, 501 E. Lakeside Ave., Ste. 3 (208) 667-8112

Pocatello: Marshall Public Library, 113 S. Garfield (208) 232-1263

ILLINOIS

Carbondale: Carbondale Public Library, 405 W. Main St. (618) 457-0354

Chicago: Donors Forum, 208 S. LaSalle, Ste. 1535 (312) 578-0175

Evanston: Evanston Public Library, 1703 Orrington Ave. (847) 448-8630

Glen Ellyn: College of DuPage, Philanthropy Center, Student Resource Center, 425 Fawell Blvd. (630) 942-3364

Grayslake: College of Lake County, John C. Murphy Memorial Library, Lake County Philanthropy Center, 19351 W. Washington St. (847) 543-2071

Joliet: Joliet Junior College Library, 1215 Houbolt Rd., J-Bldg., 3rd Fl. (815) 729-9020

Quincy: John Wood Community College, West Central Illinois Philanthropy Center, 1301 S. 48th St. (217) 224-6500

Rock Island: Rock Island Public Library, 401 19th St. (309) 732-7323

Schaumburg: Schaumburg Township District Library, Northwest Suburban Philanthropy Center, 130 S. Roselle Rd. (847) 985-4000

Springfield: University of Illinois at Springfield, Central Illinois Nonprofit Resources Center, Brookens Library, One University Plaza, MS BRK 140 (217) 206-6633

INDIANA

Anderson: Anderson Public Library, 111 E. 12th St. (765) 641-2456

Bloomington: Monroe County Public Library, 303 E. Kirkwood Ave. (812) 349-3050

Columbus: Bartholomew County Public Library, Cleo Rogers Memorial Library, 536 Fifth St. (812) 379-1255

Evansville: Evansville Vanderburgh Public Library, 200 SE Martin Luther King Jr. Blvd. (812) 428-8218

Fort Wayne: Allen County Public Library, Paul Clarke Nonprofit Resource Center, 900 Library Plaza (260) 421-1200

Gary: Indiana University Northwest, 3400 Broadway (219) 980-6580

Indianapolis: First Samuel (W)Holistic Resource Center, 1402 N. Belleview Place (317) 636-7653

Indianapolis: Indianapolis-Marion County Public Library, 40 E. St. Clair St. (317) 275-4100

Muncie: Muncie Public Library, 2005 S. High St. (765) 747-8204

Shelbyville: Shelbyville-Shelby County Public Library, 57 W. Broadway St. (317) 398-7121

South Bend: St. Joseph County Public Library, 304 S. Main St. (574) 282-4630

Terre Haute: Vigo County Public Library, One Library Square (812) 232-1113

Valparaiso: Valparaiso University, Christopher Center for Library and Information Resources, 1410 Chapel Dr. (219) 464-5500

Vincennes: Knox County Public Library, 502 N. 7th St. (812) 886-4380

IOWA

Ames: Iowa State University, 204 Parks Library (515) 294-3642

Cedar Rapids: Cedar Rapids Public Library, 2600 Edgewood Rd. SW (319) 398-5123

Council Bluffs: Council Bluffs Public Library, 400 Willow Ave. (712) 323-7553

Des Moines: Des Moines Public Library, 1000 Grand Ave. (515) 283-4152

Dubuque: Community Foundation of Greater Dubuque, 700 Locust St., Ste. 195 (563) 588-2700

Fairfield: Fairfield Public Library, 104 W. Adams (641) 472-6551

Sioux City: Sioux City Public Library, 529 Pierce St. (712) 255-2933

KANSAS

Ellis: Ellis Public Library, 907 Washington St. (785) 726-3464

Junction City: Dorothy Bramlage Public Library, 230 W. 7th St. (785) 238-4311

Lawrence: Lawrence Public Library, Business Center, 707 Vermont St. (785) 843-3833

Ness City: Ness City Public Library, 113 S. Iowa Ave. (785) 798-3415

Phillipsburg: Phillips County Community Foundation, Entrepreneurial Center (E-Center), 205 F. St. (785) 540-4110

Salina: Salina Public Library, 301 W. Elm (785) 825-4624

Topeka: Topeka and Shawnee County Public Library, Adult Services, 1515 SW 10th Ave. (785) 580-4400

Wichita: Wichita Public Library, 223 S. Main St. (316) 261-8500

KENTUCKY

Bowling Green: Western Kentucky University, Helm-Cravens Library, 110 Helm Library (270) 745-6163

Covington: Kenton County Public Library, 502 Scott Blvd. (859) 962-4060

Highland Heights: Northern Kentucky University, W. Frank Steely Library, Nunn Drive (859) 572-5456

Lexington: Lexington Public Library, 140 E. Main St. (859) 231-5520

Louisville: Bellarmine University, W.L. Lyons Brown Library, 2001 Newburg Rd. (502) 452-8317

Louisville: Louisville Free Public Library, 301 York St. (502) 574-1617

LOUISIANA

Alexandria: Community Development Works, 1101 4th St., Ste. 101B (318) 443-7880

Baton Rouge: East Baton Rouge Parish Library, River Center Branch, 120 St. Louis St. (225) 389-4967

DeRidder: Beauregard Parish Library, 205 S. Washington Ave. (337) 463-6217

Lafayette: Community Foundation of Acadiana, Louisiana Association of Nonprofit Organizations (LANO), 1035 Camellia Blvd., Ste. 100 (337) 769-4840

New Orleans: Louisiana Association of Nonprofit Organizations (LANO), 935 Gravier Pl., Ste. 850 (504) 309-2081

New Orleans: New Orleans Public Library, Business and Science Division, 219 Loyola Ave. (504) 596-2580

Shreveport: Louisiana Association of Nonprofit Organizations (LANO), 2601 Line Ave. Ste. D (318) 865-5510

Shreveport: Shreve Memorial Library, 424 Texas St. (318) 226-5894

MAINE

Portland: Maine Philanthropy Center, USM Glickman Family Library, 314 Forest Ave., Room 321 (207) 780-5039

Presque Isle: Mark and Emily Turner Memorial Library, 39 Second St. (207) 764-2571

MARYLAND

Annapolis: Anne Arundel County Public Library, Annapolis Area Branch, 1410 West St. (410) 222-1750

Baltimore: Enoch Pratt Free Library, Social Science and History Dept., 400 Cathedral St. (410) 396-5320

Columbia: Howard County Library, Central Library, 10375 Little Patuxent Pkwy. (410) 313-7860

Frederick: Frederick County Public Libraries, C. Burr Artz Central Library, 110 E. Patrick St. (301) 600-1383

Hagerstown: Washington County Free Library, 59 W. Washington St. (301) 791-5149

Hyattsville: Prince George's County Memorial Library, Hyattsville Branch Library, 6530 Adelphi Rd. (301) 985-4690

Lexington Park: St. Mary's County Library, Lexington Park Library, 21677 FDR Blvd. (301) 863-8188

Prince Frederick: Calvert Library, 850 Costley Way (410) 535-0291

Rockville: Rockville Library, 21 Maryland Ave. (240) 777-0140

Salisbury: Community Foundation of the Eastern Shore, 1324 Belmont Ave. (410) 742-9911

Waldorf: Charles County Public Library, P.D. Brown Memorial Branch, 50 Village St. (301) 645-2864

Wye Mills: Chesapeake College Library, 1000 College Dr. (410) 827-5860

MASSACHUSETTS

Boston: Boston Public Library, Social Sciences Reference Dept., 700 Boylston St. (617) 536-5400

Leominster: Leominster Public Library, 30 West St. (978) 534-7522

Natick: Morse Institute Library, 14 E. Central St. (508) 647-6520

Oak Bluffs: Oak Bluffs Public Library, 56R School St. (508) 693-9433

Pittsfield: Berkshire Athenaeum, One Wendell Ave. (413) 499-9480

Springfield: Springfield City Library, 220 State St. (413) 263-6828

West Barnstable: Cape Cod Community College, Wilkens Library, 2240 Iyannough Rd. (508) 362-2131 x4480

Worcester: Worcester Public Library, 3 Salem Square (508) 799-1655

MICHIGAN

Alpena: Alpena County Library, 211 N. 1st St. (989) 356-6188

Ann Arbor: University of Michigan, Harlan Hatcher Graduate Library, 209 Hatcher Graduate Library (734) 615-8610

Battle Creek: Willard Public Library, 7 W. Van Buren St. (269) 968-8166

Detroit: Purdy/Kresge Library, Wayne State University, 134 Purdy/Kresge Library (313) 577-6424

East Lansing: Michigan State University, Funding Center, 100 Library (517) 432-6123

Farmington Hills: Farmington Community Library, 32737 W. 12 Mile Rd. (248) 553-0300

Flint: Flint Public Library, 1026 E. Kearsley St. (810) 232-7111

Fremont: Fremont Area District Library, 104 E. Main St. (231) 924-3480

Grand Rapids: Grand Rapids Public Library, Reference Dept., 111 Library St. NE (616) 988-5400

Houghton: Portage Lake District Library, 58 Huron St. (906) 482-4570

Kalamazoo: Kalamazoo Public Library, ONEplace, 315 S. Rose St. (269) 553-7844

Ludington: Mason County District Library, Ludington Library, 217 E. Ludington Ave. (231) 843-8465

Marquette: Peter White Public Library, 217 N. Front St. (906) 226-4311

Petoskey: Petoskey District Library, 500 E. Mitchell St. (231) 758-3100

Roscommon: Kirtland Community College Library, 10775 N. St. Hellen Rd. (989) 275-5000

Saginaw: Public Libraries of Saginaw, Hoyt Public Library, 505 Janes Ave. (989) 755-0904

Sault Ste. Marie: Lake Superior State University, Kenneth J. Shouldice Library, 906 Ryan St. (906) 635-2815

Traverse City: Traverse Area District Library, 610 Woodmere Ave. (231) 932-8500

Washington: Romeo District Library, Graubner Library, 65821 Van Dyke (586) 752-0603

MINNESOTA

Brainerd: Brainerd Public Library, 416 S. 5th St. (218) 829-5574

Duluth: Duluth Public Library, 520 W. Superior St. (218) 730-4200

Minneapolis: Hennepin County Library, Central Library, 300 Nicollet Mall (612) 630-6000

North Mankato: Taylor Library, 1001 Belgrade Avenue (507) 345-5120

Rochester: Rochester Public Library, 101 2nd St. SE (507) 328-2300

St. Cloud: Central Minnesota Community Foundation, 101 S. 7th Ave., Ste. 100 (320) 253-4380

St. Paul: St. Paul Public Library, 90 W. 4th St. (651) 266-7000

MISSISSIPPI

Jackson: Jackson/Hinds Library System, 300 N. State St. (601) 968-5803

Long Beach: University of Southern Mississippi, Gulf Coast Library, 730 E. Beach Blvd. (228) 214-3450

MISSOURI

Joplin: Missouri Southern State University, Resource Development Center, 3950 E. Newman Rd., L-329 (417) 659-5472

Kansas City: Kansas City Public Library, 14 W. 10th St. (816) 701-3400

Kirkwood: Kirkwood Public Library, 140 E. Jefferson Ave. (314) 821-5770

Moberly: Randolph County Caring Community Partnership, 423 E. Logan (660) 263-7173

O'Fallon: St. Charles City-County Library District, Middendorf-Kredell Branch, 2750 Hwy. K (636) 978-7997

Springfield: Springfield-Greene County Library, 4653 S. Campbell (417) 882-0714

St. Louis: St. Louis Public Library, Schlafly Branch, 225 N. Euclid Ave. (314) 539-0357

MONTANA

Baker: Fallon County Library, 6 W. Fallon Ave. (406) 778-7160

Billings: Montana State University—Billings, Library-Special Collections, 1500 University Dr. (406) 657-2262

Bozeman: Bozeman Public Library, 626 E. Main St. (406) 582-2402

Kalispell: Flathead County Library, 247 1st Ave. E. (406) 758-5819

Missoula: University of Montana, Mansfield Library, 32 Campus Dr. #9936 (406) 243-6800

NEBRASKA

Cambridge: Butler Memorial Library, 621 Penn St. (308) 697-3836

Hastings: Hastings Public Library, 517 W. 4th St. (402) 461-2346

Lincoln: University of Nebraska-Lincoln, Love Library, 13th and R Sts. (402) 472-2526

Omaha: Omaha Public Library, W. Dale Clark (Main) Library, 215 S. 15th St. (402) 444-4800

NEVADA

Carson City: Business Resource Innovation Center (BRIC), 108 E. Proctor St. (775) 283-7123

Carson City: Nevada State Library and Archives, 100 N. Stewart St. (775) 684-3314

Elko: Great Basin College Library, 1500 College Pkwy. (775) 753-2222

Incline Village: Tahoe CAN, The Smallwood Collaboration Resource Center, 948 Incline Way (775) 298-0119

Las Vegas: Clark County Library, 1401 E. Flamingo Rd. (702) 507-3421

NEW HAMPSHIRE

Concord: Concord Public Library, 45 Green St. (603) 225-8670

Plymouth: Plymouth State University, Herbert H. Lamson Library, 17 High St. (603) 535-2258

NEW JERSEY

Elizabeth: Free Public Library of Elizabeth, 11 S. Broad St. (908) 354-6060

Galloway: United Way of Atlantic County, 4 E. Jimmie Leeds Rd., Ste. 10 (609) 404-4483

New Brunswick: Rutgers, The State University of New Jersey, School of Social Work, Center for Nonprofit Management and Governance, 390 George St., Ste. 511 (732) 932-8758

Piscataway: Piscataway Public Library, John F. Kennedy Branch, 500 Hoes Lane (732) 463-1633

Randolph: County College of Morris, Learning Resource Center, 214 Center Grove Rd. (973) 328-5296

Trenton: New Jersey State Library, 185 W. State St. (609) 278-2640

Vineland: Cumberland County College, Center for Leadership, Community and Neighborhood Development, 3322 College Dr. (856) 691-8600

NEW MEXICO

Albuquerque: Albuquerque/Bernalillo County Library System, 501 Copper Ave. NW (505) 768-5141

Eagle Nest: Eagle Nest Library, 74 N. Tomboy Dr. (575) 377-0657

Las Cruces: Thomas Branigan Memorial Library, 200 E. Picacho Ave. (575) 528-4000

Santa Fe: New Mexico State Library, 1209 Camino Carlos Rey (505) 476-9702

NEW YORK

Albany: New York State Library, Cultural Education Center, 222 Madison Ave., Empire State Plaza (518) 474-5355

Auburn: Central New York Grants Information Center, 2 State St. (315) 252-7291

Auburn: Seymour Public Library District, 176-178 Genesee St. (315) 252-2571

Binghamton: Broome County Public Library, 185 Court St. (607) 778-6400

Bronx: New York Public Library, Bronx Library Center, 310 E. Kingsbridge Rd. (718) 579-4244

Brooklyn: Brooklyn Public Library, Society, Sciences, and Technology Division, 10 Grand Army Plaza (718) 230-2145

Buffalo: Buffalo and Erie County Public Library, Business, Science, and Technology Dept., One Lafayette Square (716) 858-8900

Corning: Southeast Steuben County Library, 300 Nasser Civic Center Plaza (607) 936-3713

Geneva: Geneva Public Library, 244 Main St. (315) 789-5303

Huntington: Huntington Public Library, 338 Main St. (631) 427-5165

Jamaica: Queens Borough Public Library, Social Sciences Division, 89-11 Merrick Blvd. (718) 990-0700

Jamestown: James Prendergast Library, 509 Cherry St. (716) 484-7135

Kingston: Kingston Library, 55 Franklin St. (845) 331-0507

Levittown: Levittown Public Library, One Bluegrass Lane (516) 731-5728

Mahopac: Mahopac Public Library, 668 Rte. 6 (845) 628-2009

Margaretville: Blue Deer Center, 1155 County Rte. 6 (845) 586-3225

New York: The Riverside Church, Cloister Library, 490 Riverside Dr. (212) 870-6728

Newburgh: Newburgh Free Library, 124 Grand St. (845) 563-3601

Poughkeepsie: Adriance Memorial Library, 93 Market St. (845) 485-3445

Riverhead: Riverhead Free Library, 330 Court St. (631) 727-3228

Rochester: Central Library of Rochester and Monroe County, 115 South Ave. (585) 428-8127

Saratoga Springs: Saratoga Springs Public Library, 49 Henry St. (518) 584-7860

Southampton: Rogers Memorial Library, 91 Coopers Farm Rd. (631) 283-0774

Staten Island: New York Public Library, St. George Library Center, 5 Central Ave. (718) 442-8560

Staten Island: Wagner College, Horrmann Library, One Campus Rd. (718) 390-3401

Stephentown: Stephentown Memorial Library, 472 State Rte. 43 (518) 733-5750

Suffern: Suffern Free Library, 210 Lafayette Ave. (845) 357-1237

Syracuse: Onondaga County Public Library, 447 S. Salina St. (315) 435-1900

White Plains: White Plains Public Library, 100 Martine Ave. (914) 422-1480

Yonkers: Yonkers Public Library, Riverfront Library, One Larkin Center (914) 337-1500

NORTH CAROLINA

Asheville: Pack Memorial Library, Community Foundation of Western North Carolina, 67 Haywood St. (828) 250-4711

Brevard: Transylvania County Library, 212 S. Gaston St. (828) 884-3151

Chapel Hill: Chapel Hill Public Library, 100 Library Dr. (919) 968-2780

Charlotte: Charlotte Mecklenburg Library, 310 N. Tryon St. (704) 416-0101

Durham: Durham County Public Library, 300 N. Roxboro St. (919) 560-0100

Flat Rock: Blue Ridge Community College, Small Business Center, 180 W. Campus Dr. (828) 694-1779

Greensboro: Greensboro Public Library, Glenwood Branch Nonprofit Resource Center, 1901 W. Florida St. (336) 297-5000

High Point: High Point Public Library, Business Research Services, 901 N. Main St. (336) 883-3670

Jacksonville: Onslow County Public Library, 58 Doris Ave. E. (910) 455-7350

Raleigh: Nonprofit Resource Center, Olivia Raney Local History and Research Library, 4016 Carya Dr. (919) 250-1229

Spruce Pine: Avery-Mitchell-Yancey (AMY) Regional Library, Spruce Pine Public Library, 142 Walnut Ave. (828) 765-4673

Wilmington: New Hanover County Public Library, 201 Chestnut St. (910) 798-6301

Winston-Salem: Forsyth County Public Library, 660 W. 5th St. (336) 703-3020

NORTH DAKOTA

Bismarck: Bismarck Public Library, 515 N. 5th St. (701) 222-6410

Fargo: Fargo Public Library, 102 N. 3rd St. (701) 241-1472

Minot: Minot Public Library, 516 2nd Ave. SW (701) 852-1045

OHIO

Akron: Akron-Summit County Public Library, 60 S. High St. (330) 643-9000

Akron: BVU: The Center for Nonprofit Excellence, 703 S. Main St., Ste. 200 (330) 762-9670

Ashtabula: Ashtabula County District Library, 335 W. 44th St. (440) 997-9341

Canton: Stark County District Library, 715 Market Ave. N. (330) 452-0665

Cincinnati: Public Library of Cincinnati and Hamilton County, 800 Vine St. (513) 369-6900

Cleveland: Cleveland Public Library, 325 Superior Ave., NE (216) 623-2800

Cleveland Heights: Cleveland Heights-University Heights Public Library, Lee Road Library Branch, 2345 Lee Rd. (216) 932-3600

Columbus: Columbus Metropolitan Library, Business and Technology Dept., 96 S. Grant Ave. (614) 645-2275

Dayton: Dayton Metro Library, 215 E. 3rd St. (937) 463-2665

Elyria: Elyria Public Library, West River Branch, 1194 W. River Road N. (440) 324-9827

Elyria: Lorain County Community College, Barbara and Mike Bass Library, 1005 N. Abbe Rd. (440) 366-4106

Independence: Cuyahoga County Public Library, Independence Branch, 6361 Selig Dr. (216) 447-0160

Lima: Lima Public Library, 650 W. Market St. (419) 228-5113

Mansfield: Mansfield/Richland County Public Library, 43 W. 3rd St. (419) 521-3110

Marietta: Marietta College, Legacy Library, 220 5th St. (740) 376-4741

Newark: Licking County Library, 101 W. Main St. (740) 349-5500

Painesville: Morley Library, 184 Phelps St. (440) 352-3383

Piqua: Edison Community College Library, 1973 Edison Dr. (937) 778-7950

Port Clinton: Ida Rupp Public Library, 310 Madison St. (419) 732-3212

Portsmouth: Portsmouth Public Library, 1220 Gallia St. (740) 354-5688

Rio Grande: University of Rio Grande, Jeanette Albiez Davis Library, 218 N. College Ave. (740) 245-7005

Sandusky: The Volunteer Center of Erie County, 300 Central Ave. (419) 627-0074

Toledo: Toledo-Lucas County Public Library, Business Technology Dept., 325 N. Michigan St. (419) 259-5209

Twinsburg: Twinsburg Public Library, 10050 Ravenna Rd. (330) 425-4268

Urbana: Urbana University, Swedenborg Memorial Library, 579 College Way (937) 484-1335

Warren: Kent State University, Trumbull Campus Library, 4314 Mahoning Ave. NW (330) 847-0571

Westlake: Westlake Porter Public Library, 27333 Center Ridge Rd. (440) 871-2600

Wooster: Wayne County Public Library, 220 W. Liberty St. (330) 262-0916

Xenia: Greene County Public Library, Xenia Community Library, 76 E. Market St. (937) 352-4000

Youngstown: Public Library of Youngstown and Mahoning County, 305 Wick Ave. (330) 744-8636

Zanesville: Muskingum County Community Foundation, 534 Putnam Ave. (740) 453-5192

OKLAHOMA

Durant: Southeastern Center For Funding Research, Southeastern Oklahoma State University, Henry G. Bennett Memorial Library, 1405 N. 4th, PMB 4105 (580) 745-2702

Enid: Public Library of Enid and Garfield County, 120 W. Maine (580) 234-6313

Muskogee: Nonprofit Resource Center, 207 N. 2nd St. (918) 683-4600

Norman: Pioneer Library System, Norman Public Library, 225 N. Webster (405) 701-2600

Oklahoma City: Oklahoma City University, Dulaney Browne Library, 2501 N. Blackwelder (405) 208-5065

Tulsa: Tulsa City-County Library, 400 Civic Center (918) 596-7977

OREGON

Eugene: Eugene Public Library, 100 W. 10th Ave. (541) 682-5450

Eugene: University of Oregon, Knight Library, 1501 Kincaid (541) 346-3053

Klamath Falls: Oregon Institute of Technology Library, 3201 Campus Dr. (541) 885-1000

Medford: Jackson County Library Services, 205 S. Central Ave. (541) 774-8679

North Bend: North Bend Public Library, 1800 Sherman Ave. (541) 756-0400

Portland: Multnomah County Library, Government Documents, 801 SW 10th Ave. (503) 988-5123

Roseburg: Umpqua Community College Library, 1140 Umpqua College Rd., P.O. Box 967 (541) 440-4640

PENNSYLVANIA

Aliquippa: Beaver County Library System, 109 Pleasant Dr., Ste. 101 (724) 728-3737

Allentown: Allentown Public Library, 1210 Hamilton St. (610) 820-2400

Bethlehem: Northampton Community College, Paul and Harriett Mack Library, 3835 Green Pond Rd. (610) 861-5360

Blue Bell: Montgomery County Community College, The Brendlinger Library, 340 DeKalb Pike (215) 641-6596

Bristol: Margaret R. Grundy Memorial Library, 680 Radcliffe St. (215) 788-7891

East Stroudsburg: East Stroudsburg University of Pennsylvania, Kemp Library, 200 Prospect Ave. (570) 422-3594

Erie: Erie County Public Library, 160 E. Front St. (814) 451-6927

Franklin: Franklin Public Library, 421 12th St. (814) 432-5062

Harrisburg: Dauphin County Library System, East Shore Area Library, 4501 Ethel St. (717) 652-9380

Hazleton: Hazleton Area Public Library, 55 N. Church St. (570) 454-2961

Lancaster: Lancaster Public Library, 125 N. Duke St. (717) 394-2651

Philadelphia: Free Library of Philadelphia, Regional Foundation Center, 1901 Vine St., 2nd Fl. (215) 686-5423

Philadelphia: The Johnson-UGO Foundation Library, United Methodist Neighborhood Services, 804 North Broad St. (215) 236-1003

Phoenixville: Phoenixville Public Library, 183 2nd Ave. (610) 933-3013

Pittsburgh: Carnegie Library of Pittsburgh, 4400 Forbes Ave. (412) 622-3158

Pittston: Nonprofit and Community Assistance Center, 1151 Oak St. (570) 655-5581

Reading: Reading Public Library, 100 S. 5th St. (610) 655-6355

Scranton: Albright Memorial Library, 500 Vine St. (570) 348-3000

Sharon: Community Library of the Shenango Valley, 11 N. Sharpsville Ave. (724) 981-4360

Washington: Citizens Library, 55 S. College St. (724) 222-2400

Williamsport: James V. Brown Library, 19 E. 4th St. (570) 326-0536

York: Martin Library, 159 E. Market St. (717) 846-5300

PUERTO RICO

San Juan: Universidad Del Sagrado Corazón, Biblioteca Madre Maria Teresa Guevara, PO Box 12383 (787) 728-1515

RHODE ISLAND

Providence: Providence Public Library, 150 Empire St. (401) 455-8088

SOUTH CAROLINA

Anderson: Anderson County Library, 300 N. McDuffie St. (864) 260-4500

Charleston: Charleston County Library, 68 Calhoun St. (843) 805-6930

Columbia: South Carolina State Library, 1500 Senate St. (803) 734-8026

Florence: Florence County Library System, Doctors Bruce and Lee Foundation Library, 509 S. Dargan St. (843) 662-8424

Greenville: Greenville County Library System, 25 Heritage Green Place (864) 242-5000

Spartanburg: Spartanburg County Public Libraries, 151 S. Church St. (864) 596-3500

SOUTH DAKOTA

Madison: Dakota State University, Karl E. Mundt Library, 820 N. Washington Ave. (605) 256-5100

Pierre: South Dakota State Library, 800 Governors Dr. (605) 773-3131

Rapid City: Rapid City Public Library, 610 Quincy St. (605) 394-4171

TENNESSEE

Chattanooga: United Way of Greater Chattanooga, 630 Market St. (423) 752-0300

Johnson City: Johnson City Public Library, 100 W. Millard St. (423) 434-4450

Knoxville: Knox County Public Library, 500 W. Church Ave. (865) 215-8751

Memphis: Alliance for Nonprofit Excellence, 5100 Poplar Ave., Ste. 502 (901) 684-6605

Memphis: Memphis Public Library and Information Center, 3030 Poplar Ave. (901) 415-2734

Nashville: Nashville Public Library, 615 Church St. (615) 862-5800

TEXAS

Amarillo: Amarillo Area Foundation, 801 S. Filmore, Ste. 700 (806) 376-4521

Arlington: Arlington Public Library, George W. Hawkes Central Library, 101 E. Abram St. (817) 459-6900

Austin: Regional Foundation Library, Community Engagement Center, 1009 East 11th St. (512) 475-7373

Beaumont: Southeast Texas Nonprofit Development Center, 700 North St., Suite D (409) 832-6565

Dallas: Dallas Public Library, Urban Information, 1515 Young St. (214) 670-1400

Edinburg: Southwest Border Nonprofit Resource Center, The University of Texas-Pan American, 1201 West University Drive, ITT 1.404H (956) 292-7566

El Paso: University of Texas at El Paso, Community Non-Profit Grant Library, 500 W. University, Benedict Hall Room 103 (915) 747-5672

Fort Worth: Funding Information Center of Fort Worth, 2701 W. Berry St., Ste. 128 (817) 334-0228

Houston: Houston Public Library, Bibliographic Information Center, 500 McKinney St. (832) 393-1313

Houston: United Way of Greater Houston, 50 Waugh Dr. (713) 685-2300

Kingsville: Texas A&M University - Kingsville, James C. Jernigan Library, 700 University Blvd., MSC 197 (361) 593-3416

Laredo: Texas A&M International University, Bi-National Center, 5201 University Blvd., LBV #201 (956) 326-2834

Longview: Longview Public Library, 222 W. Cotton St. (903) 237-1350

Lubbock: Lubbock Area Foundation, 2509 80th St. (806) 762-8061

North Richland Hills: North Richland Hills Public Library, 9015 Grand Ave. (817) 427-6800

San Angelo: Tom Green County Public Library, 33 W. Beauregard Ave. (325) 655-7321

San Antonio: Center for Nonprofit Support, 110 Broadway, Ste. 230 (210) 227-4333

Tyler: United Way of Tyler/Smith County, 4000 Southpark Dr. (903) 581-6376

Victoria: Victoria College/University of Houston, Victoria Library, 2602 N. Ben Jordan (361) 570-4166

Waco: Waco-McLennan County Library, West Waco Library & Genealogy Center, 5301 Bosque Blvd., Ste. 275 (254) 745-6018

Wichita Falls: Nonprofit Management Center of Wichita Falls, 2301 Kell Blvd., Ste. 218 (940) 322-4961

UTAH

Cedar City: Southern Utah University, Gerald R. Sherratt Library, 351 W. University Blvd. (435) 586-7700

Ogden: United Way of Northern Utah, Zada Haws Community Grant Center, 2955 Harrison Blvd., Ste. 201 (801) 399-5584

Salt Lake City: Salt Lake City Public Library, 210 E. 400 S. (801) 524-8200

Salt Lake City: Utah Nonprofits Association, 231 E. 400 S., Ste. 345 (801) 596-1800

VERMONT

Middlebury: Ilsley Public Library, 75 Main St. (802) 388-4095

Montpelier: Vermont Dept. of Libraries, Reference and Law Information Services, 109 State St. (802) 828-3261

VIRGINIA

Abingdon: Washington County Public Library, 205 Oak Hill St. (276) 676-6222

Alexandria: Alexandria Library, Kate Waller Barrett Branch, 717 Queen St. (703) 838-4555

Arlington: Arlington County Public Library, 1015 N. Quincy St. (703) 228-5990

Ashburn: George Washington University, The Virginia Science and Technology Campus Library, 44983 Knoll Square, Ste. 179 (703) 726-8230

Bealeton: Fauquier County Public Library, Bealeton Library, 10877 Willow Dr. N. (540) 422-8500

Charlottesville: Center for Nonprofit Excellence, 1701-A Allied St. (434) 244-3330

Culpeper: Culpeper County Library, 271 Southgate Shopping Ctr. (540) 825-8691

Fairfax: Fairfax County Public Library, 12000 Government Center Pkwy., Ste. 329 (703) 324-3100

Farmville: Longwood University, The Janet D. Greenwood Library, Redford and Race Sts. (434) 395-2433

Fredericksburg: Central Rappahannock Regional Library, 1201 Caroline St. (540) 372-1144

Hampton: Hampton Public Library, 4207 Victoria Blvd. (757) 727-1314

Hopewell: Appomattox Regional Library System, 209 E. Cawson St. (804) 458-0110

Norfolk: VOLUNTEER Hampton Roads, 400 W. Olney Rd., Ste. B (757) 624-2400

Richmond: Richmond Public Library, 101 E. Franklin St. (804) 646-7223

Roanoke: Roanoke City Public Library System, 706 S. Jefferson St. (540) 853-2477

Virginia Beach: Virginia Beach Public Library, 4100 Virginia Beach Blvd. (757) 385-0120

WASHINGTON

Bellingham: Bellingham Public Library, 210 Central Ave. (360) 778-7323

Bremerton: United Way of Kitsap County, 647 4th St. (360) 377-8505

Port Townsend: Port Townsend Public Library, 1220 Lawrence St. (360) 385-3181

Redmond: King County Library System, Redmond Regional Library, Nonprofit and Philanthropy Resource Center, 15990 NE 85th (425) 885-1861

Seattle: Seattle Public Library, 1000 4th Ave. (206) 386-4636

Spokane: Spokane Public Library, 906 W. Main Ave. (509) 444-5300

Tacoma: University of Washington Tacoma Library, 1902 Commerce St. (253) 692-4440

WEST VIRGINIA

Bluefield: Craft Memorial Library, 600 Commerce St. (304) 325-3943

Charleston: Kanawha County Public Library, 123 Capitol St. (304) 343-4646

Huntington: Cabell County Public Library, 455 9th St. (304) 528-5700

Marlinton: Pocahontas County Free Libraries, McClintic Library, 500 Eighth St. (304) 799-6000

Parkersburg: West Virginia University at Parkersburg, 300 Campus Dr. (304) 424-8260

Shepherdstown: Shepherd University, Ruth A. Scarborough Library, 301 N. King St. (304) 876-5420

Weirton: Mary H. Weir Public Library, 3442 Main St. (304) 797-8510

Wheeling: Wheeling Jesuit University, Bishop Hodges Library, 316 Washington Ave. (304) 243-2226

WISCONSIN

Eau Claire: L.E. Phillips Memorial Public Library, 400 Eau Claire St. (715) 839-1648

La Crosse: La Crosse Public Library, 800 Main St. (608) 789-7100

Madison: University of Wisconsin—Madison, Memorial Library, Grants Information Center, 728 State St., Room 262 (608) 262-3242

Milwaukee: Marquette University Raynor Memorial Library, 1355 W. Wisconsin Ave. (414) 288-1515

Stevens Point: University of Wisconsin—Stevens Point, 900 Reserve St. (715) 346-2540

Superior: University of Wisconsin - Superior, Jim Dan Hill Library, 907 N. 19th St. (715) 394-8343

WYOMING

Casper: Natrona County Public Library, 307 E. 2nd St. (307) 237-4935

Cheyenne: Laramie County Community College, Ludden Library, 1400 E. College Dr. (307) 778-1205

Cody: Park County Public Library, 1500 Heart Mountain St. (307) 527-1880

Gillette: Campbell County Public Library, 2101 S. 4-J Rd. (307) 687-0115

Jackson: Teton County Library, 125 Virginian Lane (307) 733-2164

Sheridan: Sheridan County Fulmer Public Library, 335 W. Alger St. (307) 674-8585

International

AUSTRALIA

Brisbane, QLD: Queensland University of Technology, Gardens Point Library, 2 George St., Level 7, V Block (+61) 7-3138-2083

BRAZIL

Belo Horizonte, Minas Gerais: Instituto Hartmann Regueira, Rua Nicaragua, 36 - Sion (+55) 31-3228-1750

CANADA

Ontario: University of Toronto, Robarts Library, 130 St. George St. (416) 978-6215

COLOMBIA

Barranquilla, Atlántico: Fundación Gestión y Desarrollo Global, FUNDAGESGLOBAL, Carrera 43B No. 85 - 76 (001) 57-53041711

GHANA

Accra: Solid Rock Association, P.O. Box 571, Art Center (233) 24-3322-558

LAO P.D.R.

Vientiane: Village Focus International (VFI), LINK Resource Centre, PhonsavanTai Village, Unit 14, No 207, Sisattanak District (+856) 21-312519

MEXICO

D.F.: Centro Mexicano para la Filantropía A.C. (Cemefi), (Mexican Center for Philanthropy), Cerrada de Salvador Alvarado #7, Col. Escandón, C.P. 11800 +52 (55) 5276-8530

Guanajuato: Biblioteca Publica de San Miguel de Allende, A.C., Insurgentes 25, San Miguel de Allende (+52) 415-152-0293

Hermosillo, Sonora: Fundacion Eduardo Bours Castelo, A.C., 'Blvd. Navarrete No. 82, Int. 14 Col. Valle Escondido (+52) 662-213-33-13

Querétaro, Qro: Centro De Recursos Internacionales Para Organizaciones Civiles, Madero 46, Oficina 7, Centro Histórico (+52) 442-212-6849

NIGERIA

Wuse II, Abuja: Ty Danjuma Foundation, 47, Lobito Cresent/Plot 2015, Dar-Salam Crescent, Cadastral Zone, A07 District (+234) 807-394-4120

P.R.CHINA

Beijing: China Foundation Center, Rm. 216, Bldg. A, Tianhai Business Plaza, 107 Dongsi North Ave., Dongcheng District (+86)10-65691231

SINGAPORE

Asia Center for Social Entrepreneurship and Philanthropy, NUS Business School, Biz II Bldg., 05-01, 10 Kent Ridge Crescent (+65) 6516-5277

SOUTH AFRICA

Cape Town: South African Institute for Advancement (Inyathelo), 2nd Fl., Fairweather House, 176 Sir Lowry Rd., Woodstock (+27) 021-465 6981/2

SOUTH KOREA

Seoul: The Beautiful Foundation, 16-3 Gahoe-dong, Jongno-Gu (+82) 2-766-1004

THAILAND

Chiang Mai: Payap University - Funding Resource Center, Sirindhorn Learning Resource Center (Central Library), Super-highway Chiang Mai - Lumpang Rd., Amphur Muang (+66) 53-851-478 x7450

FOUNDATION CENTER
Knowledge to build on.

About the Foundation Center Established in 1956, the Foundation Center is the leading source of information about philanthropy worldwide. Through data, analysis, and training, it connects people who want to change the world to the resources they need to succeed. The Center maintains the most comprehensive database on U.S. and, increasingly, global grantmakers and their grants—a robust, accessible knowledge bank for the sector. It also operates research, education, and training programs designed to advance knowledge of philanthropy at every level. Thousands of people visit the Center's web site each day and are served in its five regional library/learning centers and its network of more than 450 funding information centers located in public libraries, community foundations, and educational institutions nationwide and around the world. For more information, please visit foundationcenter.org or call (212) 620-4230.

Interested in Becoming a Cooperating Collection? Cooperating Collections provide under-resourced and underserved populations across the U.S. with crucial information and education. To expand the network in regions where nonprofit communities are most in need of Foundation Center resources, we welcome proposals from qualified institutions—public, academic, or special libraries; community foundations; nonprofit resource centers; and other technical assistance providers—that can partner with us to help grantseekers succeed. If you are interested in establishing a Collection in your area or would like to learn more about the program, please visit foundationcenter.org/collections or contact: Coordinator of Cooperating Collections, Foundation Center, 79 Fifth Avenue, New York, NY 10003 (e-mail: ccmail@foundationcenter.org).

DESCRIPTIVE DIRECTORY

ALABAMA

1

The Ard Family Foundation

c/o Garry Ard
120 Office Park Dr., Ste. 200
Birmingham, AL 35223-3407
Contact: Garry Ard

Established in 2002 in AL.
Donors: George Garrabant Ard; James Ard; Dan Matheson; Richard Simmons III.
Grantmaker type: Operating foundation.
Financial data (yr. ended 12/31/10): Assets, $1,993,225 (M); gifts received, $765,823; expenditures, $1,163,375; qualifying distributions, $1,156,872; giving activities include $1,156,872 for 60 grants (high: $150,000; low: $100).
Purpose and activities: Giving primarily for human services, and to Christian churches and organizations.
Fields of interest: Human services; Children/youth, services; Foundations (private grantmaking); Christian agencies & churches; Substance abusers; Homeless.
International interests: Africa; Romania.
Type of support: Capital campaigns; Emergency funds; Matching/challenge support.
Limitations: Applications not accepted. Giving primarily in AL. No support for political organizations or for family planning organizations. No grants to individuals.
Application information: Contributes only to pre-selected organizations.
Board meeting date(s): Dec. 31
Officers: George Garrabant Ard, Pres.; Katherine L. Ard, V.P. and Secy.
EIN: 431990285

2

S.E. Belcher, Jr. Private Foundation No. 2

c/o Canterbury Trust
800 Shades Creek Pkwy., Ste. 325
Birmingham, AL 35209-4534 (800) 626-8446
Application address: c/o Robert Ingram, Jr., 204 Marina Dr., Ste. 100, Tuscaloosa, AL 35406; tel.: (205) 349-1322

Donor: S.E. Belcher, Jr.†
Grantmaker type: Independent foundation.
Financial data (yr. ended 12/31/09): Assets, $41,204,521 (M); expenditures, $8,517,515; qualifying distributions, $8,171,390; giving activities include $8,171,390 for 10 grants.
Fields of interest: Christian agencies & churches; Education.
Limitations: Giving primarily in AL, FL and MS.
Governors: Ashley Belcher Ferry; Sam P. Faucett; Robert L. Ingram, Jr.
Trustee: Canterbury Trust.
EIN: 631259859
Recent grants for international programs:
2-1 Campus Crusade for Christ International, Orlando, FL, $1,500,000. 2009.
2-2 English Language Institute in China, Fort Collins, CO, $36,390. 2009.

3

Corman Foundation, Inc.

P.O. Box 1268
Atmore, AL 36504-1268 (251) 446-1610
Contact: Linda G. Parsons
Additional e-mail: lparsons@trinsic.com

Established in 1993 in AL.
Donors: James F. Corman; Jane D. Corman.
Grantmaker type: Independent foundation.
Financial data (yr. ended 12/31/08): Assets, $3,545,866 (M); expenditures, $565,156; qualifying distributions, $502,404; giving activities include $430,736 for 17 grants (high: $192,250; low: $100).
Purpose and activities: Giving limited to major Evangelical Christian ministries involved in evangelism, discipleship, leadership training, development, and church planting.
Fields of interest: Christian agencies & churches.
International interests: Western Africa; Soviet Union (Former); Latin America; India; Eastern & Central Europe.
Type of support: Technical assistance; Matching/challenge support; Internship funds; General/operating support; Consulting services; Conferences/seminars; Continuing support; Program development.
Limitations: Giving in the U.S., with emphasis on Fort Lauderdale and Orlando, FL. No support for colleges, schools, local organizations, or directly to foreign charities. No grants to individuals, or for domestic church construction.
Application information: Application form not required.
Initial approach: Letter
Deadline(s): None
Board meeting date(s): Every other Thurs.
Officer and Directors:* James F. Corman,* Pres.; Jane D. Corman; Charles R. Dettling.
Number of staff: 1 full-time professional; 2 part-time professional.
EIN: 631084918

4

Ekta Foundation

115 Mountain Brook Blvd.
Madison, AL 35758-7915
URL: http://www.ektafoundationusa.org/main/

Established in 2007 in AL.
Donor: Ashok K. Mahbubani.
Grantmaker type: Independent foundation.
Financial data (yr. ended 11/30/10): Assets, $496,684 (M); gifts received, $250,000; expenditures, $483,065; qualifying distributions, $474,500; giving activities include $474,500 for grants.
Fields of interest: International development; Human services.
Limitations: Applications not accepted. Giving primarily in AR. No grants to individuals.
Application information: Contributes only to pre-selected organizations.
Directors: Scott E. Ludwig; Amrita Mahbubani; Ashok K. Mahbubani.
EIN: 261644753

5

The Kairos Foundation Trust

61 White Ave.
Fairhope, AL 36532-1317 (251) 929-1266
Contact: Thomas L. Yearwood, Tr.

Established in 2004 in AL.
Donors: Thomas L. Yearwood; Lisa W. Yearwood.
Grantmaker type: Independent foundation.
Financial data (yr. ended 12/31/10): Assets, $555,788 (M); gifts received, $398,625; expenditures, $237,178; qualifying distributions, $231,300; giving activities include $231,300 for 23 grants (high: $81,500; low: $200).
Fields of interest: International development; United Ways and Federated Giving Programs; Christian agencies & churches.
Type of support: General/operating support.
Limitations: Applications accepted. Giving primarily in AL and GA, with some giving in Rotherham, South Yorkshire, England. No grants to individuals.
Application information:
Initial approach: Letter
Deadline(s): None
Trustees: Lisa W. Yearwood; Thomas L. Yearwood.
EIN: 206214789

6

The Nabers Charitable Foundation

1901 6th Ave. N., Ste. 2400
Birmingham, AL 35203-4604

Established in 1998 in AL.
Donor: Drayton Nabers, Jr.
Grantmaker type: Independent foundation.
Financial data (yr. ended 12/31/09): Assets, $9,893,420 (M); gifts received, $720,000; expenditures, $236,740; qualifying distributions, $192,739; giving activities include $182,251 for 16 grants (high: $91,000; low: $60).
Purpose and activities: Giving primarily to Christian churches and agencies, and for education.
Fields of interest: Christian agencies & churches; International development; Arts; Education; Human services; Children/youth, services; Protestant agencies & churches.
Limitations: Applications not accepted. Giving primarily in AL, with emphasis on Birmingham. No grants to individuals.
Application information: Contributes only to pre-selected organizations.
Officers: Drayton Nabers, Jr., Pres.; Fairfax Smathers Nabers, Secy.; Mary Nabers Doyle, Treas.
EIN: 631189714

7

Protective Life Insurance Company Contributions Program

2801 Hwy. 280 S.
Birmingham, AL 35223-2488
URL: http://www.protective.com/default.asp?id=4

Grantmaker type: Corporate giving program.
Purpose and activities: As a complement to its foundation, Protective Life Insurance also makes charitable contributions to nonprofit organizations directly. Support is given primarily in areas of company operations in Alabama, California, Georgia, Illinois, Kansas, Minnesota, Missouri, Nebraska, North Carolina, Ohio, Tennessee, and Virginia, and in Canada.

Fields of interest: Human services; Arts; Education; Community/economic development.
International interests: Canada.
Type of support: Employee volunteer services; Sponsorships.
Limitations: Giving primarily in areas of company operations in AL, CA, GA, IL, KS, MN, MO, NC, NE, OH, TN, and VA, and in Canada.

ALASKA

8

The Alaska Community Foundation

400 L St., Ste. 100
Anchorage, AK 99501-1900 (907) 334-6700
Contact: Candace Winkler, C.E.O.
FAX: (907) 334-5780; E-mail: info@alaskacf.org;
Additional e-mail: cwinkler@alaskacf.org;
URL: http://www.alaskacf.org
Facebook: http://www.facebook.com/pages/
The-Alaska-Community-Foundation/97080836858
Twitter: http://twitter.com/AKCommunity

Incorporated in 1995.
Grantmaker type: Community foundation.
Financial data (yr. ended 12/31/10): Assets, $46,833,383 (M); gifts received, $12,095,911; expenditures, $12,213,199; giving activities include $4,155,530 for 67+ grants (high: $475,536), $178,217 for grants to organizations outside the U.S., and $56,600 for grants to individuals.
Purpose and activities: The foundation is a nonprofit public charity promoting personal philanthropy and providing financial management, strategic development and donor development services to communities, organizations and donors across AK.
Type of support: General/operating support; Equipment; Matching/challenge support; Program development; Scholarship funds.
Limitations: Applications accepted. Giving generally limited to AK. No support for religious organizations for religious purposes. No grants for fundraising activities, sponsorships, membership solicitations, debt reduction, or funding after the fact.
Publications: Annual report; Grants list; Informational brochure; Newsletter.
Application information: Visit foundation web site for application forms and guidelines per grant type. Application form required.
    Initial approach: Telephone
    Copies of proposal: 1
    Deadline(s): Varies
    Board meeting date(s): Quarterly
Officers and Directors:* Susan Behlke Foley,* Chair.; Blythe Campbell,* Vice-Chair.; Angela Cox,* Vice-Chair.; Candace Winkler,* C.E.O. and Pres.; Kris Norosz,* Secy.; Kate Gerlek, C.F.O.; Bernie Washington,* Treas.; Carla Beam; Dr. Leo Bustad; Hon. Morgan Christen; Kathryn Dodge; Jason Evans; Rick Nerland; Alex Slivka; Reed Stoops; Don Zoerb.
Number of staff: 4 full-time professional; 1 part-time professional.
EIN: 920155067
Recent grants for international programs:
8-1 Institute of the North, Anchorage, AK, $13,107. For general support. 2010.

8-2 Malawi Childrens Village Foundation, Anchorage, AK, $22,415. For orphanage operating support. 2010.
8-3 Malawi Childrens Village Foundation, Anchorage, AK, $20,944. 2010.
8-4 Malawi Childrens Village Foundation, Anchorage, AK, $20,849. For salaries. 2010.
8-5 Malawi Childrens Village Foundation, Anchorage, AK, $13,250. To support orphanage. 2010.
8-6 Malawi Childrens Village Foundation, Anchorage, AK, $12,199. For salaries and tuition. 2010.
8-7 Malawi Childrens Village Foundation, Anchorage, AK, $11,699. For operating support. 2010.
8-8 Malawi Childrens Village Foundation, Anchorage, AK, $11,489. For salaries and tuition. 2010.
8-9 Malawi Childrens Village Foundation, Anchorage, AK, $11,197. For salaries. 2010.
8-10 Malawi Childrens Village Foundation, Anchorage, AK, $10,750. For salaries and tuition. 2010.
8-11 Malawi Childrens Village Foundation, Anchorage, AK, $10,699. For salaries and tuition. 2010.
8-12 Solace International, Anchorage, AK, $10,000. For Kenya and Liberia Project. 2010.
8-13 Solace International, Young Generation Center Orphanage, Anchorage, AK, $10,000. For general operating support for the Young Generation Center in Kisumu, Kenya. 2010.

9

Benieo & Frances C. Gaguine Foundation

10117 Silver St.
Juneau, AK 99801-8745
Contact: John Gaguine, Pres.

Grantmaker type: Independent foundation.
Financial data (yr. ended 12/31/10): Assets, $13,070,484 (M); expenditures, $576,634; qualifying distributions, $550,550; giving activities include $550,550 for 4 grants (high: $250,000; low: $550).
Fields of interest: International relief; Human services.
Application information: Application form not required.
    Initial approach: Letter
    Deadline(s): None
Officers and Directors:* John Gaguine,* Pres. and Treas.; Patricia Dobbins,* V.P. and Secy.; Mary Alice McKeen.
EIN: 111792380
Recent grants for international programs:
9-1 International Rescue Committee, New York, NY, $250,000. 2010.
9-2 United States Fund for UNICEF, New York, NY, $100,000. 2010.

10

Gottstein Family Foundation

c/o B. J. Gottstein
935 W. 3rd Ave.
Anchorage, AK 99501-2003

Established in AK.
Donor: Barnard J. Gottstein.
Grantmaker type: Independent foundation.

Financial data (yr. ended 12/31/10): Assets, $4,121,901 (M); gifts received, $262,500; expenditures, $450,459; qualifying distributions, $414,460; giving activities include $411,375 for 49 grants (high: $231,500; low: $100).
Purpose and activities: Giving primarily for Jewish organizations; funding also for the arts and human services.
Fields of interest: Museums; Arts; Higher education; Medical research; Human services; United Ways and Federated Giving Programs; Jewish federated giving programs; Jewish agencies & synagogues.
Limitations: Applications not accepted. Giving primarily in AK, with emphasis on Anchorage; giving also in NY. No grants to individuals.
Application information: Contributes only to pre-selected organizations.
Officers: Barnard J. Gottstein, Pres.; Robert W. Gottstein, V.P.; James B. Gottstein, Secy.; David R. Gottstein, Treas.
Directors: Rachel L. Gottstein; Sandra L. Gottstein; Eytan Jacobsen.
EIN: 943152524
Recent grants for international programs:
10-1 American Friends of Magen David Adom, Encino, CA, $20,000. 2009.
10-2 New Israel Fund, Washington, DC, $10,000. 2009.
10-3 North American Conference on Ethiopian Jewry, New York, NY, $30,000. 2009.
10-4 Washington Institute for Near East Policy, Washington, DC, $10,000. 2009.

11

Steve Nash Foundation

9400 Sugar Cir.
Anchorage, AK 99507-6033
Contact: Jenny L. Miller, Exec. Dir.
E-mail: foundation@stevenash.org; E-mail for Jenny Miller: jenny@stevenach.org; URL: http://www.stevenash.org

Established in 2001 in TX.
Donor: Stephen Nash.
Grantmaker type: Independent foundation.
Financial data (yr. ended 12/31/10): Assets, $514,754 (M); gifts received, $461,594; expenditures, $486,849; qualifying distributions, $244,622; giving activities include $213,625 for 3 grants (high: $189,000; low: $200).
Purpose and activities: The foundation is dedicated to assisting underserved children in their health, personal development, education and enjoyment of life. The foundation awards grants to youth-focused organizations that foster children's development by addressing underlying conditions of poverty, medical need, and restricted access to those resources that contribute to their well-being. The foundation looks for organizations that work directly with children, or those that work to benefit children through social change and policy reform.
Fields of interest: Health care; Youth development; Children; Economically disadvantaged.
International interests: Canada.
Type of support: General/operating support.
Limitations: Applications accepted. Giving limited to British Columbia. No support for governmental agencies, or for religious programs or programs based within a religious institution, schools, colleges or university administrations or for sports teams or sporting events. No grants to individuals, or for salaries, general operating expenses or travel.

Application information: Unsolicited full proposals will not be accepted. Letters will not be accepted via fax or FedEx.

Initial approach: See application guidelines on foundation web site, then send letter of interest

Board meeting date(s): Mar. and Sept.

Final notification: None

Officers and Directors: Stephen Nash,* Pres.; Joann Nash,* Secy.-Treas.; Jenny Miller, Exec. Dir.

EIN: 311753206

Recent grants for international programs:

11-1 Hospital Nacional Itaugua, Itaugua, Paraguay, $83,861. For Welch Allyn clinic equipment. 2009.

12

Sealaska Heritage Institute

(formerly Sealaska Heritage Foundation)

1 Sealaska Plz., Ste. 301

Juneau, AK 99801-1245 (907) 463-4844

Contact: Deena LaRue, Mgr., Grants

FAX: (907) 586-9293;

E-mail: scholarship@sealaska.com; URL: http://www.sealaskaheritage.org

Established in 1980 in AK.

Donor: Sealaska Corp.

Grantmaker type: Public charity.

Financial data (yr. ended 12/31/10): Revenue, $2,849,322; assets, $2,800,259 (M); gifts received, $2,561,314; expenditures, $2,703,211; giving activities include $298,375 for grants to individuals.

Purpose and activities: The foundation seeks to harness all available resources to preserve, promote, and maintain the cultures and heritage of the Tlingit, Haida, and Tsimshian people for the benefit of present and future generations and the public; to encourage and support cultural heritage cooperation among all tribes and organizations; to encourage and foster the education of Native Americans so that the public may benefit from their talents; and to cooperate with other heritage programs.

Fields of interest: Arts education; Arts; Business school/education; Engineering school/education; Environment, management/technical assistance; Environment, natural resources; International affairs, goodwill promotion; Civil rights, race/intergroup relations; Native Americans/American Indians.

Type of support: Grants to individuals; Scholarships—to individuals.

Limitations: Applications accepted. Giving limited to southeast AK.

Publications: Application guidelines; Informational brochure; Newsletter.

Application information: Applicants must be Alaska natives who are defined as "Native" under the Alaska Claims Settlement Act 43 U.S.C. 1602(b) and enrolled to Sealaska Corporation or native lineal descendants of Alaska Natives enrolled to Sealaska Corporation, whether or not the applicant owns Sealaska Corporate stock. Application form required.

Initial approach: Download application form

Deadline(s): Mar. 1

Final notification: May 1

Officers and Directors:* Marlene Johnson,* Chair.; Robert Martin,* Vice-Chair.; Dr. Rosita Worl,* Pres.;

Joe Nelson,* Secy.; Nancy Barnes; Jeane Breinig; Clarence Jackson; Ethel Lund; Mike Miller.

EIN: 920081844

AMERICAN SAMOA

13

Amerika Samoa Humanities Council

P.O. Box 5800

Pago Pago, AS 96799-5800

Contact: Niualama E. Taifane, Exec. Dir.

Established in AS.

Grantmaker type: Public charity.

Financial data (yr. ended 10/31/10): Revenue, $531,108; assets, $100,627 (M); gifts received, $405,348; expenditures, $465,403.

Purpose and activities: The council seeks to promote the humanities and Samoan culture in the territory of American Samoa.

Fields of interest: Humanities.

International interests: Samoa.

Type of support: Program development.

Limitations: Giving primarily in American Samoa.

Officers: Fonoti Savali Vaeao, Chair.; Ufagafa Ray Tulafono, Vice-Chair.; Minareta Thompson, Secy.; Tauiliili Lauifi Tauilii, Treas.; Niualama E. Taifane, Exec. Dir.

EIN: 660519082

ARIZONA

14

Craig and Barbara Barrett Foundation

4617 E. Ocotillo Rd.

Paradise Valley, AZ 85253-4032

Established in 2004 in AZ.

Donors: Barbara Barrett; Craig Barrett.

Grantmaker type: Independent foundation.

Financial data (yr. ended 12/31/10): Assets, $1,422,038 (M); gifts received, $1,567,460; expenditures, $1,870,370; qualifying distributions, $1,850,432; giving activities include $1,850,432 for 78 grants (high: $750,000; low: $75).

Purpose and activities: Giving primarily for higher education; funding also for animal and wildlife protection, environmental conservation, and social services.

Fields of interest: Higher education; Engineering school/education; Education; Environment, natural resources; Animals/wildlife; Human services; Children/youth, services; International affairs; Engineering/technology.

Limitations: Applications not accepted. Giving primarily in AZ.

Application information: Contributes only to pre-selected organizations.

Officers: Craig Barrett, Pres.; Barbara Barrett, V.P.

EIN: 201539507

15

Vaughn L. & Eleanore M. Beals Charitable Foundation

P.O. Box 3260

Carefree, AZ 85377-3260

Established in 1989 in WI.

Donors: Eleanore M. Beals; Vaughn L. Beals.

Grantmaker type: Independent foundation.

Financial data (yr. ended 12/31/10): Assets, $4,529,985 (M); expenditures, $220,288; qualifying distributions, $192,600; giving activities include $192,600 for grants.

Purpose and activities: Giving primarily for education, health care, and community services.

Fields of interest: Higher education; Museums; Arts; Education; Hospitals (general); Health organizations, association; Human services.

International interests: Canada.

Limitations: Giving primarily in AZ, MA and OH. No grants to individuals.

Trustees: Eleanore M. Beals; Vaughn L. Beals, Jr.

EIN: 391653407

16

Children's Emergency Medical Fund, Inc.

20439 N. Fletcher Wy.

Peoria, AZ 85382-1421 (602) 241-2873

E-mail: info@cemfund.org; Mailing address: P.O. Box 83775, Phoenix, AZ 85071-3774; URL: http://www.cemfund.org

Established in 2000 in AZ.

Grantmaker type: Public charity.

Financial data (yr. ended 09/30/10): Revenue, $3,105,337; assets, $74,775 (M); gifts received, $3,105,337; expenditures, $3,109,285; giving activities include $2,193,183 for grants, $301,725 for 1 grant to an organization outside the U.S., and $553,825 for grants to individuals.

Purpose and activities: The organization aims to meet the desperate emergency medical, nutritional, and portable water needs of hurting and suffering children in the Philippines and Arizona, by providing critically needed medical supplies, nutritional food, and grants; the organization also educates and trains families on health, nutrition, sanitation, pre- and post-natal care, and family planning.

Fields of interest: Human services, emergency aid; Health care; Children.

International interests: Philippines.

Type of support: In-kind gifts.

Limitations: Giving limited to AZ, Haiti, and the Philippines.

Publications: Annual report.

Officers: Lee Taylor, Pres.; Daryl Brumbaugh, V.P.; Lordwin Clarisa, Secy.-Treas.

EIN: 861004356

17

Community Foundation for Southern Arizona

2250 E. Broadway Blvd.

Tucson, AZ 85719-6014 (520) 770-0800

Contact: J. Clint Mabie, C.E.O.

FAX: (520) 770-1500;

E-mail: philanthropy@cfsoaz.org; Additional e-mail: cmabie@cfsoaz.org; URL: http://www.cfsoaz.org

Community Matters: http://www.cfsoaz.blogspot.com/

Facebook: http://www.facebook.com/
communityfoundationfor.southernarizona
Twitter: http://twitter.com/SoAZCommunityFd

Established in 1980 in AZ.
Grantmaker type: Community foundation.
Financial data (yr. ended 06/30/10): Assets,
$92,268,416 (M); gifts received, $16,781,967;
expenditures, $12,668,761; giving activities
include $7,811,576 for grants.
Purpose and activities: The mission of the
foundation is to work with charitably minded
individuals and organizations to strengthen
southern AZ communities, now and for generations
to come. The foundation also administers a variety
of donor-initiated funds and conducts competitive
scholarship and grant rounds.
Fields of interest: Community/economic
development; Recreation; Human services; Arts;
Education; Environment; Health care; AIDS;
Children/youth, services.
International interests: Mexico.
Type of support: Program development; Scholarship
funds; Research; Scholarships—to individuals;
Matching/challenge support.
Limitations: Applications accepted. Giving limited to
southern AZ, with particular emphasis on Pima and
Santa Cruz counties. No support for sectarian
organizations or individual schools (except for
special literacy grants). No grants to individuals
(except for scholarships), or for operating expenses,
endowment building, capital campaigns, debt
retirement, research or fundraising events.
Publications: Application guidelines; Annual report;
Financial statement; Informational brochure.
Application information: Visit foundation web site
for guidelines per grant type. Application form
required.
  Deadline(s): Varies
  Board meeting date(s): Bimonthly
  Final notification: 60 days
Officers and Trustees:* Nancy Davis,* Chair.; Roger
Vogel,* 1st Vice-Chair.; Mary B. Bernal,* 2nd
Vice-Chair.; J. Clinton Mabie, C.E.O. and Pres.; Evan
Mendelson, V.P., Donor Rels. and Prog. Svcs.; Bill
Holmes,* Secy.; Richard Mundinger,* Treas.; Ron
Barber; Kerstin Block; Carrie Brennan; Tony
Dabdoub; Megan Davis; Darryl Dobras; Robert
Friesen; James J. Glasser; Paul Lindsey; Don Luria;
Scott Neeley; Bradley Jon Nystedt; Jim Rowley;
Roman Sandoval; R. Michael Sullivan; Beth Walkup;
Craig Wisnom.
Number of staff: 5 full-time professional; 10 full-time
support; 2 part-time support.
EIN: 942681765
Recent grants for international programs:
17-1 Business Foundation of Sonora, Nogales,
  Mexico, $14,550. For Desarrollo Integral
  Juvenile program. 2010.
17-2 Doctors Without Borders USA, New York, NY,
  $10,000. For Haiti relief efforts. 2010.
17-3 Give2Asia, San Francisco, CA, $11,000. For
  $5,000 to National Chiao Tung University for
  Management Science Department Scholarship
  Fund, $5,000 to Ichen Jingo Chen and
  Kuang-Shen Chen Memorial Scholarship for
  Deaf-Agape Social Welfare Association, and
  $1,000 to Agape Social Welfare Association
  general support. 2010.
17-4 World Care, Tucson, AZ, $10,000. For Haiti
  relief efforts. 2010.

18
John & Anne Duffy Foundation, Inc.
c/o John P. Duffy
2420 E. Camino La Zorrela
Tucson, AZ 85718-3021
E-mail: jpmacduff@earthlink.net

Established in 1986 in NJ.
Donor: John P. Duffy.
Grantmaker type: Independent foundation.
Financial data (yr. ended 11/30/10): Assets,
$3,453,785 (M); expenditures, $161,305;
qualifying distributions, $129,000; giving activities
include $129,000 for grants.
Fields of interest: Arts; Education; Environment;
Cancer research; Human services; Children/youth,
services.
International interests: Africa.
Type of support: Seed money; Management
development/capacity building; Land acquisition;
General/operating support; Annual campaigns;
Emergency funds; Curriculum development;
Fellowships; Internship funds; Scholarship funds;
Exchange programs.
Limitations: Applications not accepted. Giving
primarily in AZ, CT, NJ, NY and RI. No grants to
individuals.
Application information: Contributes only to
pre-selected organizations.
  Board meeting date(s): Dec. 15
Officers: John P. Duffy, Pres. and Treas.; Anne Duffy,
Secy.
Directors: Hilary Duffy; Kevin Duffy; Peter R. Kellogg.
EIN: 222598324

19
Esperanca, Inc.
1911 W. Earll Dr.
Phoenix, AZ 85015-6095 (602) 252-7772
Contact: Raul Espericueta M.S.W., Pres. and C.E.O.
FAX: (602) 340-9197; E-mail: info@esperanca.org;
Toll-free tel.: (888) 701-5150; URL: http://
www.esperanca.org

Established in 1970 in Phoenix, AZ.
Grantmaker type: Public charity.
Financial data (yr. ended 09/30/10): Revenue,
$2,677,996; assets, $3,048,440 (M); gifts
received, $2,642,577; expenditures, $2,905,787;
giving activities include $637,951 for grants to
organizations outside the U.S.
Purpose and activities: The organization aims to
provide medical services and public health programs
in the poorest areas of the world throughout North
America, South America, and Africa.
Fields of interest: Health organizations, public
education; Health care, volunteer services.
International interests: South America; Africa.
Limitations: Giving on a national and international
basis, with emphasis on Africa, North America, and
South America.
Publications: Annual report; Newsletter.
Application information:
  Board meeting date(s): Monthly from September
    through May
Officers and Directors:* Bill Wichterman,* Chair.;
Brian Roberts, Chair.-Elect; Raul Espericueta,*
M.S.W., Pres. and C.E.O.; Jerry Morgan,* Secy.;
Charlie Broucek,* Treas.; Gregg Abbott; Rick Baker;
Kathryn Bradley; and 13 additional directors.
Number of staff: 4 full-time professional; 2 part-time
professional.
EIN: 237087997

20
Food for the Hungry, Inc.
1224 E. Washington St.
Phoenix, AZ 85034-1102 (480) 998-3100
Toll-free tel.: (800) 248-6437; URL: http://
www.fh.org
Facebook: http://www.facebook.com/
foodforthehungry
Food for the Hungry: Relief: http://
fhrelief.wordpress.com/2010/10/29/
fh-responds-to-the-mentawai-indonesia-tsunami/
Twitter: http://twitter.com/food4thehungry
YouTube: http://www.youtube.com/user/
foodforthehungry

Established in 1971.
Grantmaker type: Public charity.
Financial data (yr. ended 09/30/10): Revenue,
$87,417,777; assets, $14,447,348 (M); gifts
received, $86,955,052; expenditures,
$89,848,679; giving activities include
$38,036,336 for grants, and $33,343,309 for
grants to organizations outside the U.S.
Purpose and activities: The organization provides
disaster and emergency relief, and implements
sustainable development programs to transform
communities physically and spiritually.
Fields of interest: International relief; Agriculture/
food; Safety/disasters.
Type of support: In-kind gifts.
Limitations: Giving on a national and international
basis.
Officers and Board Members: Ben Homan,* Pres.;
David Evans,* V.P., Govt. and Gifts-in-Kind
Resources; Matt Panos,* V.P., Ministry
Partnerships and Resources; Gary St. John,* V.P.,
Ministry Support Svcs.; Scott Krippayne; Gregg
Vestri.
EIN: 952680390

21
Freeport-McMoRan Copper & Gold
Foundation
(formerly Phelps Dodge Foundation)
333 N. Central Ave.
Phoenix, AZ 85004-2189 (602) 366-8116
Contact: Nicolle Turner
FAX: (602) 366-7305; E-mail: Foundation@fmi.com;
Additional tel.: (800) 528-1182, ext. 8116, fax:
(602) 366-7323, e-mail:
communityaffairs@fmi.com; URL: http://
www.fcx.com/envir/grants.htm
Contact for Scholarship Program: Valerie Beach,
e-mail: valerie_beach@fmi.com

Incorporated in 1953 in NY.
Donor: Phelps Dodge Corp.
Grantmaker type: Company-sponsored foundation.
Financial data (yr. ended 12/31/10): Assets,
$5,123,790 (M); expenditures, $11,905,580;
qualifying distributions, $11,890,945; giving
activities include $10,453,264 for 147+ grants
(high: $1,000,000), and $1,437,681 for employee
matching gifts.
Purpose and activities: The foundation supports
organizations involved with arts and culture,
education, the environment, wildlife preservation,
crime and violence prevention, employment, safety,
human services, community development, science,
economics, public policy, minorities, women, and
economically disadvantaged people.

Fields of interest: Human services; Arts, cultural/ethnic awareness; Visual arts; Museums; Performing arts; Arts; Elementary/secondary education; Vocational education; Higher education; Business school/education; Teacher school/education; Education, reading; Education; Environment, natural resources; Botanical gardens; Environmental education; Environment; Animals/wildlife, preservation/protection; Zoos/zoological societies; Hospitals (general); Crime/violence prevention; Crime/violence prevention, abuse prevention; Employment, training; Employment; Safety/disasters, public education; Disasters, preparedness/services; Safety/disasters; Children/youth, services; Family services; Family services, parent education; Family services, domestic violence; Economic development; Business/industry; Community/economic development; United Ways and Federated Giving Programs; Science, formal/general education; Physical/earth sciences; Mathematics; Geology; Engineering/technology; Science; Economics; Public policy, research; Minorities; Women; Economically disadvantaged.
Type of support: General/operating support; Continuing support; Management development/capacity building; Annual campaigns; Curriculum development; Internship funds; Scholarship funds; Research; Employee volunteer services; Employee matching gifts; Employee-related scholarships; Scholarships—to individuals; Matching/challenge support.
Limitations: Applications accepted. Giving primarily in areas of company operations, with emphasis on AZ and NM. No support for discriminatory organizations, fraternal, veterans', or labor organizations, churches or religious organizations not of direct benefit to the entire community, political or lobbying organizations, pass-through foundations, or auxiliary organizations. No grants to individuals (except for scholarships), or for travel, conference fees, medical procedures, advertising, religious activities, or debt reduction or operational deficits.
Publications: Application guidelines; Corporate report; Informational brochure (including application guidelines); Program policy statement.
Application information: Proposals for STEM Innovation Grants should be no longer than 6 pages. Proposals for Mini Grants for Education should be no longer than 4 pages. Organizations receiving STEM Innovation Grants are required to submit a final report. An application form is required for scholarships. Application form required.
Initial approach: Download application form and mail or e-mail to foundation; download application form and mail to participating schools for scholarships
Copies of proposal: 1
Deadline(s): Aug. 30; Mar. 1 for STEM Innovation Grants; Oct. 30 for Mini Grants for Education; Mar. 4 for scholarships
Board meeting date(s): May
Final notification: Dec. 15; May 15 for STEM Innovation Grants; Jan. 15 for Mini Grants for Education
Officers and Directors:* Tracy L. Bame,* Pres.; Kathleen L. Quirk,* Exec. V.P. and Treas.; Catherine R. Hardwick, Secy.; Richard C. Adkerson; Michael J. Arnold; L. Richards McMillan II.
Number of staff: 2 part-time professional; 1 part-time support.
EIN: 136077350
Recent grants for international programs:

21-1 Center for a New American Security, Washington, DC, $15,000. 2010.
21-2 Clinton Bush Haiti Fund, Washington, DC, $250,000. 2010.
21-3 Clinton Bush Haiti Fund, Washington, DC, $250,000. 2010.
21-4 Dikembe Mutombo Foundation, Atlanta, GA, $35,000. For soccer program. 2010.
21-5 Dikembe Mutombo Foundation, Atlanta, GA, $23,500. For hospital equipment. 2010.
21-6 Dikembe Mutombo Foundation, Atlanta, GA, $21,927. For hospital. 2010.
21-7 Ducks Unlimited, Memphis, TN, $50,000. 2010.
21-8 Food for the Hungry, Phoenix, AZ, $10,000. For Phoenix Fire Training at Melobolah. 2010.
21-9 Initiative for Global Development, Seattle, WA, $25,000. 2010.
21-10 Institute of International Education, New York, NY, $16,570. For children of employees. 2010.
21-11 Johns Hopkins University, Baltimore, MD, $50,000. For School of Advanced International Studies (SAIS) student fellowships. 2010.
21-12 Johns Hopkins University, Baltimore, MD, $15,000. For School of Advanced International Studies (SAIS) Africa Studies Program. 2010.
21-13 Stop Hunger Now, Raleigh, NC, $10,000. 2010.
21-14 United States Indonesia Society, Washington, DC, $100,000. For School of Advanced International Studies (SAIS) Fellowship Program. 2010.
21-15 University College London, Institute of Archaeo-Metallurgical Studies, London, England, $25,000. 2010.

22
Jewish Federation of Southern Arizona
3822 E. River Rd., Ste. 100
Tucson, AZ 85718-6685 (520) 577-9393
Contact: Gail Barnhill
FAX: (520) 577-0734; E-mail: gbarnhill@jfsa.org; URL: http://jewishtucson.org/
Facebook: http://www.facebook.com/pages/Jewish-Tucson/116106780151
Twitter: http://twitter.com/jewishtucson

Established in 1947 in AZ.
Grantmaker type: Public charity.
Financial data (yr. ended 12/31/10): Revenue, $5,565,717; assets, $16,089,870 (M); gifts received, $4,080,963; expenditures, $5,029,894; giving activities include $2,442,170 for grants, and $17,950 for grants to individuals.
Purpose and activities: The organization works to bring the Jewish community of southern Arizona together to help those in need and strengthen community bonds.
Fields of interest: Jewish agencies & synagogues; Community/economic development; Human services.
International interests: Israel.
Type of support: Grants to individuals; Seed money.
Limitations: Giving primarily in AZ and Israel.
Officers and Directors:* Steve Lightman,* Co-Chair.; Jennifer Miller Grant,* Co-Chair.; Don Baker, Vice-Chair.; Donna Beyer,* Vice-Chair.; Jeff Katz,* Vice-Chair.; Karen Katz,* Vice-Chair.; Robert Glaser,* Secy.; Kathryn Unger,* Treas.; Stuart Mellan,* Pres. and C.E.O.; Jeff Artzi; Janet Ash; Paul Ash; Randie Collier; Ralph Duchin; Rodney Glassman; and 48 additional directors.

Number of staff: 13 full-time professional; 7 part-time professional; 7 full-time support; 1 part-time support.
EIN: 860096795

23
Kearny Alliance, Inc.
14901 N. Scottsdale Rd., Ste. 201A
Scottsdale, AZ 85254-2718

Established in 2001 in DE and AZ.
Donor: The Kearny Foundation.
Grantmaker type: Independent foundation.
Financial data (yr. ended 12/31/10): Assets, $12,407 (M); expenditures, $148,944; qualifying distributions, $138,244; giving activities include $138,244 for grants.
Purpose and activities: Giving for innovative business education and training, applied research, and other initiatives to promote increased participation in fair and reciprocal international trade.
Fields of interest: International economic development; International development; Higher education, university.
International interests: Asia.
Limitations: Applications not accepted. Giving primarily in AZ; some funding also in Washington, DC. No grants to individuals.
Application information: Contributes only to pre-selected organizations.
Officer and Director:* Dr. John E. Walsh, Jr.,* Pres.
EIN: 861041247

24
Lincoln Institute of Land Policy
(formerly Lincoln Foundation, Inc.)
11010 N. Tatum Blvd., No. D-101
Phoenix, AZ 85028-6071 (602) 393-4300
Contact: Kathryn Lincoln
FAX: (602) 393-4319;
E-mail: katelincoln@lincolninst.edu; URL: http://www.lincolninst.edu
Blog: http://www.lincolninst.edu/news/atlincolnhouse.asp

Established in 1946 in AZ and MA; Founded as Lincoln Foundation; merged into the Lincoln Institute of Land Policy and adopted current name in 2006.
Grantmaker type: Operating foundation.
Financial data (yr. ended 06/30/09): Assets, $340,333,873 (M); expenditures, $20,128,956; qualifying distributions, $16,887,356; giving activities include $127,167 for 6 grants (high: $50,000; low: $10,000), $162,950 for 14 grants to individuals (high: $19,700; low: $10,000), and $10,528,681 for 4 foundation-administered programs.
Purpose and activities: The Institute improves the dialogue about urban development, the built environment, and tax policy in the United States and abroad. Through research, training, conferences, demonstration projects, publications, and multi-media, the organization provides non-partisan analysis and evaluation for today's regulatory, planning, and policy decisions.
Fields of interest: Public affairs, public education; Public affairs, research; Public affairs, information services.
International interests: China; Europe; Latin America.

Type of support: Research; Publication; Fellowships.
Limitations: Applications not accepted. Giving on a national and international basis.
Publications: Informational brochure; Newsletter.
Application information: Unsolicited requests for funds not accepted.
Officers and Directors:* Kathryn Lincoln,* Chair. and C.I.O.; Gregory K. Ingram, C.E.O. and Pres.; Levering F.T. White,* V.P., Admin; Dennis W. Robinson,* V.P., Finance and Opers., and Treas.; Dione Etter, Secy.; Roy W. Bahl; Henry Coleman; Gary Cornia; and 15 additional directors.
EIN: 866021106

25
The Lodestar Charitable Foundation
(formerly The Lodestar Foundation)
4455 E. Camelback Rd., Ste. 215A
Phoenix, AZ 85018-2897 (602) 840-4800
Contact: Bonnie N. Fujii, Grants Mgr.
FAX: (602) 840-1543;
E-mail: bfujii@lodestarfoundation.org; URL: http://www.lodestarfoundation.org

Established in 1999 in AZ; supporting organization of the Arizona Community Foundation.
Grantmaker type: Public charity.
Financial data (yr. ended 03/31/10): Assets, $703,081 (M); gifts received, $900,000; expenditures, $1,147,289; program services expenses, $1,113,567; giving activities include $791,303 for grants.
Purpose and activities: The foundation encourages and supports philanthropy utilizing two strategies: philanthropy capacity-building in general community philanthropic, volunteer, and public service organizations; and supporting collaborations among nonprofits to eliminate duplication and encourage efficiency.
Fields of interest: Public affairs, reform.
International interests: Africa; Asia; Eastern & Central Europe.
Type of support: General/operating support; Management development/capacity building; Capital campaigns; Endowments; Program development; Technical assistance; Consulting services; Program evaluation; Program-related investments/loans.
Limitations: Applications accepted. Giving primarily in AZ.
Publications: Application guidelines; Grants list; Program policy statement.
Application information: Application form not required.
Initial approach: E-mail or letter preferred
Copies of proposal: 1
Deadline(s): July 16 for Collaboration Prize
Officers: Lois Savage, Pres.; Caroline Young, V.P., Progs.
Directors: G. Peter Bidstrup; Daryl Burton; M. Joyce Geyser; Lisa Hirsch Handley; Jerry Hirsch; Kyle Hirsch; Neal Kurn; William J. Macomber; F. Francis Najafi; John C. Ogden; C.J. Theobald.
Number of staff: 1 part-time professional.
EIN: 860965287

26
PetSmart Charities, Inc.
19601 N. 27th Ave.
Phoenix, AZ 85027-4008
Contact: Monica Neal, Dir., Charitable Giving and Progs.
FAX: (623) 580-6561;
E-mail: info@petsmartcharities.org; Toll-free tel.: (800) 423-7387; URL: http://www.petsmartcharities.org

Established in 1994.
Donor: PetSmart, Inc.
Grantmaker type: Public charity.
Financial data (yr. ended 01/31/11): Revenue, $39,182,367; assets, $42,979,560 (M); gifts received, $38,309,502; expenditures, $31,525,330; giving activities include $19,431,714 for grants.
Purpose and activities: The organization gives grants to help homeless pets and end euthanasia as a means to controlling the pet population.
Fields of interest: Animal welfare.
International interests: Canada.
Type of support: Equipment; Emergency funds; Program development; Conferences/seminars; Seed money.
Limitations: Applications accepted. Giving on a national basis, as well as in Canada and U.S. territories. No support for wildlife or endangered species programs. No grants to individuals, or for building projects, endowments, or operating expenses.
Publications: Application guidelines; Annual report; Financial statement; Informational brochure; Newsletter.
Application information: See web site for additional application information. Application form required.
Copies of proposal: 1
Deadline(s): Varies
Board meeting date(s): Feb., June and Oct.
Final notification: About 30 to 60 days after deadline; Day of receipt for emergency relief grants
Officers and Directors:* Philip L. Francis,* Chair.; Sophie Engelhard Craighead,* Pres.; Dale Brunk,* Secy.; Bob Moran,* Treas.; Barbara Fitzgerald; Donna Fleischer; Ken Hall; Chuck Latham; Francesca Spinelli.
Number of staff: 16 full-time professional; 7 full-time support.
EIN: 931140967

27
Rosztoczy Foundation
c/o Wendy Cooper
11111 W. McDowell Rd.
Avondale, AZ 85392-5000
E-mail: ferenc@rosztoczyfoundation.org;
URL: http://www.rosztoczyfoundation.com

Established in 2005 in AZ.
Donors: Ferenc E. Rosztoczy; Thomas F. Rosztoczy.
Grantmaker type: Independent foundation.
Financial data (yr. ended 01/31/11): Assets, $427,036 (M); gifts received, $315,500; expenditures, $358,228; qualifying distributions, $354,000; giving activities include $354,000 for 40 grants to individuals (high: $30,000; low: $7,000).
Purpose and activities: Giving for students and scientists from Hungary to come to the United States for a period of one year to study at a university or research institute.
Fields of interest: Education; Religion.
International interests: Hungary.
Type of support: Scholarship funds; Scholarships—to individuals.
Application information: See web site for complete application policies and guidelines and for downloadable application form. Application form required.
Initial approach: See grantmaker web site
Deadline(s): None
Trustees: Diane E. Rosztoczy; Ferenc E. Rosztoczy; Robert A. Rosztoczy; Thomas F. Rosztoczy.
EIN: 721583507

28
Solheim Foundation
P.O. Box 84558
Phoenix, AZ 85071-4558

Established in 1985 in AZ.
Donors: Karsten Solheim†; Louise C. Solheim; Karsten Manufacturing Co.
Grantmaker type: Independent foundation.
Financial data (yr. ended 06/30/10): Assets, $5,477,485 (M); gifts received, $800,000; expenditures, $1,363,680; qualifying distributions, $1,361,080; giving activities include $1,361,000 for 28 grants (high: $150,000; low: $10,000).
Purpose and activities: Giving primarily for Christian education, missions, and other related activities.
Fields of interest: International relief; Human services; Christian agencies & churches.
Limitations: Applications not accepted. Giving primarily in AZ, CA, CO, MD and TX. No grants to individuals.
Application information: Contributes only to pre-selected organizations.
Trustees: Allan Solheim; Allan Solheim, Jr.; Andrew Solheim; David Solheim; Joy Solheim; Karsten Louis Solheim; Louise Solheim.
EIN: 742378207

29
U-Haul International, Inc. Corporate Giving Program
c/o Public Rels., Attn.: Sponsorship
2727 N. Central Ave.
Phoenix, AZ 85004-1158
FAX: (602) 263-6772;
E-mail: publicrelations@uhaul.com; URL: http://www.uhaul.com/About/Philanthropy.aspx

Grantmaker type: Corporate giving program.
Purpose and activities: U-Haul makes charitable contributions to nonprofit organizations involved with food, shelter, and clothing and provides self-storage services to people affected by natural disasters. Support is given on a national basis in areas of company operations, with some emphasis on Phoenix, Arizona, and in Canada.
Fields of interest: Disasters, preparedness/services; Food services; Housing/shelter; Human services, emergency aid.
International interests: Canada.
Type of support: Sponsorships; Grants to individuals; Donated products.
Limitations: Applications accepted. Giving on a national basis in areas of company operations, with some emphasis on Phoenix, AZ, and in Canada. No grants for beauty pageants or individual

competitions, race teams or car clubs, school activities or sports teams.
Application information: Application form not required.
  Initial approach: Mail, fax, or e-mail proposal to headquarters; e-mail or telephone for self-storage facilities
  Copies of proposal: 1
  Deadline(s): 3 weeks prior to need

30
World Care
3538 E. Ellington Pl.
Tucson, AZ 85713-4214 (520) 514-1588
FAX: (520) 514-1589; URL: http://www.worldcare.org

Established in 1996 in AZ.
Grantmaker type: Public charity.
Financial data (yr. ended 12/31/10): Revenue, $4,834,052; assets, $908,664 (M); gifts received, $4,596,940; expenditures, $5,357,356; giving activities include $2,869,568 for grants, $1,813,338 for grants to organizations outside the U.S., and $162,948 for grants to individuals.
Purpose and activities: The organization seeks to improve world health, education, and the state of the environment.
Fields of interest: International development; International affairs; Education; Health care; Environment.
Officers and Directors:* Lee Coble,* Pres.; Lisa Hopper, C.E.O.; Frances Goodenough,* Secy.; Maureen Earhardt,* Treas.; Jodi Bain; Lindsey Biaggi; Janet Blakely; Maggie Guzman; Hassan Hijazi; John Pfersdorf; Edina Strum; Adriel Tavel; Janet Wood.
EIN: 860830973

ARKANSAS

31
Irvin C. & Evea J. Bainum Foundation, Inc.
P.O. Box 500
Glenwood, AR 71943-0500
Application address: c/o David Cypes, 6500 Rock Spring Dr., Ste. 200, Bethesda MD, 20008, tel.: (301) 571-1900

Established in 1999 in MD.
Donors: Evea Bainum; Mark Bainum; Tim Bainum.
Grantmaker type: Independent foundation.
Financial data (yr. ended 12/31/10): Assets, $3,424,946 (M); gifts received, $17,540; expenditures, $168,877; qualifying distributions, $166,596; giving activities include $164,346 for 7 grants (high: $70,982; low: $1,750).
Fields of interest: International affairs, volunteer services; Higher education; Health care; Protestant agencies & churches.
Limitations: Applications accepted. Giving primarily in CA and TN. No grants to individuals.
Application information: Application form required.
  Initial approach: Letter
  Deadline(s): None

Officers: Evea Bainum, Pres.; Tim Bainum, Secy.-Treas.
EIN: 522135981

32
Fred Darragh Foundation
P.O. Box 250746
Little Rock, AR 72225-0746
Contact: Ernie Dumas, Pres.; Freddie Nixon, V.P.
E-mail: edumas@aristotle.net

Established in 1968 in AR.
Donor: Fred K. Darragh, Jr.‡.
Grantmaker type: Independent foundation.
Financial data (yr. ended 12/31/10): Assets, $3,857,797 (M); gifts received, $100; expenditures, $302,781; qualifying distributions, $270,390; giving activities include $270,390 for 18 grants (high: $50,000; low: $500).
Fields of interest: Higher education; Environment; International peace/security; Civil liberties, advocacy; Civil/human rights; Minorities; Children; Single parents; LGBTQ; Economically disadvantaged.
Type of support: General/operating support; Endowments; Program development; Conferences/seminars; Film/video/radio; Scholarship funds; Research.
Limitations: Applications accepted. Giving limited to AR. No support for non-ecumenical religious organizations or for political organizations. No grants to individuals.
Publications: Financial statement.
Application information: Application form not required.
  Initial approach: Letter
  Copies of proposal: 5
  Deadline(s): None
  Board meeting date(s): Varies
  Final notification: 1 month
Officers and Directors:* Ernie Dumas,* Pres.; Freddie Nixon,* V.P.; Charles B. Cliett, Jr.,* Secy.; Max Brantley; Kathy Wells.
Number of staff: None.
EIN: 710406242

33
Heifer International Foundation
1015 Louisiana St.
P.O. Box 727
Little Rock, AR 72203-0727 (501) 907-4900
FAX: (501) 907-4902;
E-mail: foundation@heifer.org; Toll-free tel.: (888) 422-1161; URL: http://www.heiferfoundation.org

Established in 1992; supporting organization of Heifer International.
Grantmaker type: Public charity.
Financial data (yr. ended 12/31/10): Revenue, $9,864,854; assets, $71,012,945 (M); gifts received, $5,924,573; expenditures, $2,808,663; giving activities include $387,792 for grants.
Fields of interest: International development; International agricultural development.
Limitations: Applications not accepted.
Publications: Annual report; Newsletter.
Officers and Trustees:* Ardyth Neill,* Acting Pres. and C.E.O.; Greg Spradlin, V.P., Comms.; Vicki Bailyn; Carol N. Brown; Miller Davis; James Howell;

Bayard U. Livingston; Ron McLean; Steve Mondora; C. Douglas Smith.
EIN: 710699939

34
Little Door International
12100 Cave Creek Rd.
Paron, AR 72122-8048 (501) 594-5771
Contact: Tom K. Arnold, Chair.

Established in 2006 in AR.
Donors: Ray Roles; Tom K. Arnold; Curtis Thomas; Charlene Yarbrough; Chenal West Development, Inc.; Foothills Fellowship Bible Church.
Grantmaker type: Independent foundation.
Financial data (yr. ended 12/31/10): Assets, $61,244 (M); gifts received, $145,674; expenditures, $168,381; qualifying distributions, $164,921; giving activities include $159,919 for 1 grant.
Fields of interest: International development; Education; Christian agencies & churches.
Limitations: Giving primarily in Myanmar.
Application information: Application form required.
Officers: Tom K. Arnold, Chair. and Pres.; Curtis Thomas, V.P.; Nancy Arnold, Secy.-Treas.
EIN: 205550137

35
Winthrop Rockefeller Trust
2230 Cottondale Ln., Ste. 6
Little Rock, AR 72202-2048 (501) 661-9294
Contact: Marion Burton, Tr.

Established in 1973 in AR.
Donor: Winthrop Rockefeller‡.
Grantmaker type: Independent foundation.
Financial data (yr. ended 06/30/10): Assets, $109,487,444 (M); gifts received, $47,180; expenditures, $6,874,015; qualifying distributions, $5,650,988; giving activities include $5,445,180 for 12 grants (high: $4,266,868; low: $1).
Purpose and activities: Support primarily for an agricultural development institute and a historic preservation foundation.
Fields of interest: Higher education, university; Historic preservation/historical societies; Agriculture.
Type of support: General/operating support.
Limitations: Applications accepted. Giving limited to AR. No grants to individuals.
Application information: Application form not required.
  Deadline(s): None
Officer: Donna Huckabee, C.E.O.
Trustees: Bruce Bartley; Marion Burton; Donal C. O'Brien, Jr.; Robert Schults; John W. Ward.
EIN: 716082655
Recent grants for international programs:
35-1 University of Arkansas, Fayetteville, AR, $4,266,868. For operations of Winthrop Rockefeller Institute in Morrilton. 2010.
35-2 University of Arkansas, Fayetteville, AR, $648,269. For other operations of Winthrop Rockefeller Institute in Morrilton. 2010.
35-3 University of Arkansas, Fayetteville, AR, $28,000. For five-year facility upgrade for Winthrop Rockefeller Institute in Morrilton. 2010.
35-4 University of Arkansas, Fayetteville, AR, $15,000. For capital support for Winthrop Rockefeller Institute in Morrilton. 2010.

36
Tech Serve International, Inc.
P.O. Box 598
Greenbrier, AR   72058-0598   (501) 679-2120
Contact: Wes L. Syverson, Pres.
FAX: (501) 679-2017; E-mail: tsi@tech-serve.org;
URL: http://www.techserve.org

Established in 1990.
Grantmaker type: Public charity.
Financial data (yr. ended 12/31/10): Revenue,
$330,426; assets, $720,018 (M); gifts received,
$140,796; expenditures, $403,829; giving
activities include $6,800 for grants to individuals.
Purpose and activities: The organization provides
technical assistance and equipment to missions
and missionaries, and gives volunteers an
opportunity to be personally involved in mission
endeavors in various areas of service.
Fields of interest: International affairs, volunteer
services; Christian agencies & churches.
Type of support: Building/renovation; Technical
assistance; Consulting services.
Limitations: Giving on a worldwide basis. No grants
to individuals.
Officers: Wes L. Syverson,* Chair.; Wes L.
Syverson, Jr., Pres.; Clarence Shrader, Secy.; H. Leo
Gillman, Treas.
Directors: David Adolfson; Ken Brunk.
EIN: 330386510

37
Walton Family Foundation, Inc.
P.O. Box 2030
Bentonville, AR   72712-2030   (479) 464-1570
Contact: Buddy D. Philpot, Exec. Dir.
FAX: (479) 464-1580; E-mail: info@wffmail.com;
URL: http://www.waltonfamilyfoundation.org
Facebook: http://www.waltonfamilyfoundation.org/
about/follow-us-on-facebook
Application address for environment projects: The
Walton Family Foundation, Attn.: Letter of Inquiry,
919 18th St., N.W., Ste. 650, Washington, DC
20006

Established in 1987 in AR.
Donors: Sam M. Walton†; Helen R. Walton†; John
T. Walton†; Walton Enterprises, LLC.
Grantmaker type: Independent foundation.
Financial data (yr. ended 12/31/10): Assets,
$1,282,168,113 (M); gifts received,
$406,362,732; expenditures, $1,491,544,999;
qualifying distributions, $1,509,382,927; giving
activities include $1,342,345,745 for 967 grants
(high: $800,000,000; low: $100), $137,290,308
for in-kind gifts, and $19,451,098 for loans/
program-related investments.
Purpose and activities: Giving is focused in four
areas: 1) Systemic reform of primary education
(K-12); 2) The environment as it relates to marine
and freshwater conservation; 3) The delta region of
Arkansas and Mississippi; and 4) Northwest
Arkansas.
Fields of interest: Elementary/secondary school
reform; Elementary/secondary education; Child
development, education; Environment, natural
resources.
Type of support: General/operating support;
Continuing support; Management development/
capacity building; Equipment; Program
development; Curriculum development; Technical
assistance; Program evaluation; Program-related

investments/loans; Employee-related scholarships;
Matching/challenge support.
Limitations: Applications accepted. Giving through
two of four funding areas is limited to northwest AR
and the Mississippi River's delta region of AR and
MS. Educational funding is limited to target school
districts. No support for non-established medical
research programs. No grants to individuals, or for
endowments for operations, church-related
construction projects, travel expenses for groups to
compete or perform, or business-related activities
such as start-up costs, or expenses related to
groups or individuals participating in non-curricular
programs.
Publications: Annual report; Grants list.
Application information: Proposals by invitation
only. See web site for more information.
   Initial approach: Letter of inquiry
Officer and Directors:* Buddy D. Philpot,* Exec.
Dir.; Carrie W. Penner; Alice A. Walton; Alice L.
Walton; Benjamin S. Walton; Jim C. Walton; Lukas
T. Walton; S. Robson Walton; Samuel R. Walton;
Steuart L. Walton; Thomas L. Walton.
Number of staff: 6 full-time professional.
EIN: 133441466
Recent grants for international programs:
37-1 Comunidad y Biodiversidad, Guaymas, Mexico,
$651,150. 2009.
37-2 Conservation International, Arlington, VA,
$20,989,768. 2009.
37-3 Consultative Group on Biological Diversity, San
Francisco, CA, $80,000. 2009.
37-4 Ecology Project International, Missoula, MT,
$504,250. 2009.
37-5 Floresta USA, San Diego, CA, $10,000. 2009.
37-6 Fundacion Cayetano Heredia, Lima, Peru,
$117,875. 2009.
37-7 Global Explorers, Fort Collins, CO, $50,000.
2009.
37-8 Holy Land Christians Society, Falls Church, VA,
$25,000. 2009.
37-9 International Community Foundation, National
City, CA, $27,115. 2009.
37-10 Marine Stewardship Council, London,
England, $1,700,000. 2009.
37-11 Mexican Nature Conservation Fund, Mexico
City, Mexico, $304,096. 2009.
37-12 Noroeste Sustentable, La Paz, Mexico,
$572,459. 2009.
37-13 Ocean Conservancy, Washington, DC,
$2,352,919. 2009.
37-14 Playing for Change Foundation, Los Angeles,
CA, $20,000. 2009.
37-15 RARE, Arlington, VA, $186,773. 2009.
37-16 Sociedad de Historia Natural Niparaja, La
Paz, Mexico, $462,389. 2009.
37-17 Walton Family Charitable Support Foundation,
Bentonville, AR, $100,848,750. To provide
endowment funds for the Walton International
Scholarship Program. 2009.
37-18 Wild Salmon Center, Portland, OR,
$450,000. 2009.
37-19 World Wildlife Fund, Washington, DC,
$624,944. 2009.

CALIFORNIA

38
ACTION Council of Monterey Council
369 Main St., Ste. 201
Salinas, CA   93901-2770   (831) 783-1276
Contact: Ricki Mazzullo, Exec. Dir.
E-mail: richard@actioncouncil.org; URL: http://
www.actioncouncil.org

Established in 1994.
Grantmaker type: Public charity.
Financial data (yr. ended 06/30/10): Revenue,
$2,412,714; assets, $1,984,674 (M); gifts
received, $1,075,178; expenditures, $1,997,005;
program services expenses, $1,953,086; giving
activities include $123,264 for 4 grants (high:
$50,000; low: $10,000), $5,836 for grants to
organizations outside the U.S., $19,519 for 157
in-kind gifts, and $1,804,467 for
foundation-administered programs.
Purpose and activities: The organization is
committed to economic and social justice by
providing fiscal sponsorship, incubating new
programs for sustainability, providing research,
assessing and evaluating services, developing
resources, and facilitating partnerships among
public and private agencies.
Fields of interest: Community/economic
development; Youth development; Family services;
Children/youth, services; Environment;
International development; Housing/shelter;
Nutrition; Arts; Human services; Children/youth;
Minorities; Women.
Limitations: Applications accepted. Giving primarily
in Monterey County, CA.
Application information:
   Initial approach: Download fiscal sponsorship
   request
Officer: Ricki Mazzullo, Exec. Dir.
EIN: 770357101

39
**Adobe Systems Incorporated Corporate
   Giving Program**
c/o Community Rels.
345 Park Ave.
San Jose, CA   95110-2704   (408) 536-5163
FAX: (408) 537-4779; Contact for North America
Software Donation Prog.: tel.: (703) 836-2121, FAX:
(866) 531-6028, E-mail:
adobeprogram@giftsinkind.org; Application address
for International Software Donation Prog.: Gifts in
Kind Intl., 333 N. Fairfax St., Alexandria, VA 22314,
tel.: (703) 836-2121, FAX: (703) 549-1481, E-mail:
adobeprogram@giftsinkind.org; URL: http://
www.adobe.com/aboutadobe/philanthropy/
main.html

Grantmaker type: Corporate giving program.
Financial data (yr. ended 12/31/08): Total giving,
$39,907,774, including $4,366,056 for grants,
$1,624,410 for employee matching gifts, and
$33,917,308 for in-kind gifts.
Purpose and activities: Adobe makes charitable
contributions to nonprofit organizations involved
with arts and culture, education, the environment,
hunger, housing, community development, youth,
senior citizens, disabled people, economically

disadvantaged people, and homeless people. Special emphasis is directed toward programs designed to improve the quality of life for underserved populations in the community. Support is given primarily in southern Alameda County, San Francisco, southern San Mateo County, and Santa Clara County, CA, King County and Seattle, Washington, and Ottawa, Canada, and on a national and international basis for software donations. Grants and scholarships are made through the Adobe Foundation Fund at the Community Foundation Silicon Valley.

Fields of interest: Community/economic development; Human services, emergency aid; Neighborhood centers; Zoos/zoological societies; Environment, natural resources; Education; Libraries/library science; Arts; Arts, services; Humanities; Performing arts, theater; Performing arts; Museums; Arts, folk arts; Arts, cultural/ethnic awareness; Arts education; Visual arts; Elementary/secondary education; Environment, beautification programs; Environment; Food services; Housing/shelter; Aging; Youth; Disabilities, people with; Economically disadvantaged; Homeless.

International interests: Taiwan; Canada; France; Ireland; Italy; United Kingdom; Germany; Sweden; India; China; Japan; Hong Kong; Australia.

Type of support: General/operating support; Continuing support; Program development; Scholarship funds; Technical assistance; Employee volunteer services; Use of facilities; Employee matching gifts; Scholarships—to individuals; Donated products.

Limitations: Applications accepted. Giving primarily in southern Alameda County, San Francisco, southern San Mateo County, and Santa Clara County, CA, Newton, MA, King County and Seattle, WA, and Ottawa, Canada; giving on a national basis and in Australia, Canada, China, France, Germany, Hong Kong, India, Ireland, Italy, Japan, Sweden, Taiwan, and the United Kingdom for software donations. No support for private foundations, political organizations, religious organizations not of direct benefit to the entire community, organizations with unlawful employment practices or discriminatory organizations, lobbying organizations, research or advocacy organizations, think-tanks not providing direct services to the end-beneficiary, information services organizations, or fraternal organizations, scholarship organizations, organizations whose clients are other nonprofit organizations, or medical service organizations not providing services to disabled people; no North America Software Donations—Nonprofit or International Software Donations for organizations with an annual operating budget of over $10 million; no International Software Donations for fundraising organizations located in China, Hong Kong, or Taiwan. No grants to individuals (except for scholarships), or for endowments; no software donations for raffles, door prizes, auctions, or other fundraising activities or individual awards.

Publications: Application guidelines; Corporate giving report.

Application information: Adobe Action Grants are one-time general operating and program development grants. Grants range from $5,000 to $20,000. Adobe Community Investment Grants are multi-year cash, software, volunteer, and facility use grants. Support is limited to 1 contribution per organization during any given year for Adobe Action Grants. The company utilizes an invitation only Request For Proposal (RFP) process for Adobe

Community Investment Grants; unsolicited requests are not accepted. Support is limited to 3 years in length for Adobe Community Investment Grants. Unsolicited requests for employee volunteer services from organizations located in San Francisco, CA, are not accepted. Software donations are limited to 4 individually titled software products or 1 bundled software package per organization during any given year. The Community Relations Department handles giving. A contributions committee reviews all requests for employee volunteer services. Application form required.

Initial approach: Complete online application form for Adobe Action Grants; download application form and mail or fax to headquarters for employee volunteer services; complete online application form at giftsinkind.org for North America Software Donation Program—Education

Copies of proposal: 1

Deadline(s): Mar. 31, June 30, Sept. 30, and Dec. 31 for Adobe Action Grants; 8 weeks prior to need for employee volunteer services

Committee meeting date(s): Quarterly for employee volunteer services

Final notification: Feb. 28, May 31, Aug. 31, and Nov. 30 for Adobe Action Grants; 1 month for software donations

Number of staff: 4 full-time professional.

40
Advent Software, Inc. Corporate Giving Program
600 Townsend St.
San Francisco, CA 94103 (415) 543-7696
URL: http://www.advent.com/about/community-involvement

Grantmaker type: Corporate giving program.
Purpose and activities: Advent Software makes charitable contributions to nonprofit organizations to nonprofit organizations involved with education and low-performing K-12 schools. Support is given primarily in areas of company operations in California, Massachusetts, and New York, and in China, Denmark, India, the Netherlands, Norway, Singapore, Sweden, Switzerland, and the United Kingdom.
Fields of interest: Elementary/secondary education.
International interests: China; Denmark; India; Netherlands; Norway; Singapore; Sweden; Switzerland; United Kingdom.
Type of support: General/operating support; Employee volunteer services.
Limitations: Giving primarily in areas of company operations in CA, MA, and NY, and in China, Denmark, India, the Netherlands, Norway, Singapore, Sweden, Switzerland, and the United Kingdom.

41
Afghanistan Relief
P.O. Box 866
Cypress, CA 90630-0866
FAX: (714) 661-5932; Toll-free tel.: (877) 276-2440;
URL: http://www.afghanrelief.org

Grantmaker type: Public charity.

Financial data (yr. ended 12/31/10): Revenue, $64,941; assets, $156,671 (M); gifts received, $64,941; expenditures, $84,064.
Purpose and activities: The organization provides relief aid to the needy throughout Afghanistan.
Fields of interest: International relief.
International interests: Afghanistan.
Limitations: Giving limited to Afghanistan.
Officers and Directors:* Abul F. Khalili,* Chair.; Abdul Satar,* Vice-Chair.; Mumtaz Soleman, Treas.; Nahid Etemadi; Mostafa Khairzada; Ehsan Khawajazada; Parween Omidi; Mary Adams Urashima.
EIN: 954822766

42
African American Self-Help Foundation
182 Farmers Ln., Ste. 201
Santa Rosa, CA 95405-4761 (707) 528-3499
Contact: Jeff Baugham, Director
E-mail: info@aashf.org; URL: http://www.aashf.org
Application address for Emergency Assistance Fund: AASHF c/o Samaritan Outreach P.O. Box 3842, Dayton OH 45401

Established in 1981.
Grantmaker type: Public charity.
Financial data (yr. ended 04/30/11): Revenue, $4,366,767; assets, $313,529 (M); gifts received, $4,341,099; expenditures, $4,352,868; giving activities include $46,922 for grants, and $4,151,975 for grants to organizations outside the U.S.
Purpose and activities: The foundation seeks to provide relief and self-help to African children and families as well as single, working African American mothers in the U.S.
Fields of interest: Human services; African Americans/Blacks.
International interests: Sudan; Africa; Kenya; Uganda; Zambia.
Type of support: In-kind gifts.
Limitations: Giving on a national and international basis, with emphasis on Africa.
Publications: Annual report.
Officers and Directors:* Monte E. Wilson,* Chair.; Joseph Spiccia,* Vice-Chair.; Jeff Baugham,* Secy.-Treas.; Warren Hayes; Doug Weber.
EIN: 521224507

43
African Orphans Foundation
34 Paseo Mirasol
Tiburon, CA 94920-2021
URL: http://www.africanorphansfoundation.org/
Facebook: http://www.facebook.com/pages/African-Orphans-Foundation/106077864361

Established in 2003 in CA.
Donor: Donald E. Dana.
Grantmaker type: Public charity.
Purpose and activities: The foundation works to provide food, clothing, shelter, and education to female children orphaned by AIDS, famine, war, and other misfortunes of life in Africa.
Fields of interest: Youth, services; Children/youth.
International interests: Africa.
Limitations: Applications not accepted. Giving limited to Africa.
Application information: Unsolicited requests for funds not considered or acknowledged.

Officers: Donald E. Dana, Pres.; Danielle M. Dana, Secy.; Natalie A. Dana, Treas.
Trustees: Brad Goodhart; Paddy Moore-Goodhart.
EIN: 201576039

44
Agilent Technologies Foundation
5301 Stevens Creek Blvd., MS 1B-07
Santa Clara, CA 95051-7201
Contact: Kimberly Henderson, Grants Admin.
E-mail: foundation@agilent.com; URL: http://
www.agilent.com/contributions/foundation.html

Established in 2001 in CA.
Donor: Agilent Technologies, Inc.
Grantmaker type: Company-sponsored foundation.
Financial data (yr. ended 10/31/10): Assets, $7,453,939 (M); expenditures, $4,373,138; qualifying distributions, $4,307,031; giving activities include $2,737,976 for 88 grants (high: $152,000; low: $2,000), and $999,268 for employee matching gifts.
Purpose and activities: The foundation focuses on advancing pre-university science education around the world by creating and supporting strategic initiatives linked to change and improvement in student learning and engagement. It also funds university research at the frontiers of measurement in electronics and biosciences.
Fields of interest: Chemistry; Elementary/ secondary education; Higher education; Employment, services; Disasters, preparedness/ services; Science, formal/general education; Engineering/technology; Biology/life sciences; Science; Minorities; Women.
International interests: Asia; Europe.
Type of support: Building/renovation; General/ operating support; Program development; Conferences/seminars; Seed money; Curriculum development; Research; Employee volunteer services; Sponsorships; Program evaluation; Employee matching gifts.
Limitations: Giving primarily in areas of company operations, with emphasis on CA, CO, DE, Asia, and Europe. No support for home schools, sectarian or denominational organizations, discriminatory organizations, or health or human services organizations. No grants to individuals, or for luncheons, dinners, or auctions, annual campaigns, endowments or capital campaigns, political activities, television or radio productions, or personal websites.
Publications: Application guidelines; Corporate giving report; Financial statement.
Application information: Application form required.
Initial approach: E-mail foundation
Deadline(s): Quarterly
Board meeting date(s): Apr.
Officers: William P. Sullivan, Chair. and Pres.; Marie Oh Huber, V.P. and Secy.; Hilliard C. Terry III, V.P. and Treas.; Cynthia D. Johnson, V.P.; Laurie Nichol, Exec. Dir.
Number of staff: 2 full-time professional; 1 full-time support.
EIN: 770532250

45
The Agouron Institute
1055 E. Colorado Blvd., Ste. 250
Pasadena, CA 91106-2359 (626) 744-5100
E-mail: info@agi.org; URL: http://www.agi.org/
Knowledge Center: http://www.agi.org/
publications.html

Established in 1978.
Grantmaker type: Independent foundation.
Financial data (yr. ended 06/30/10): Assets, $42,063,490 (M); expenditures, $4,788,605; qualifying distributions, $4,215,711; giving activities include $3,266,991 for 29 grants (high: $809,373; low: $3,500).
Purpose and activities: Giving primarily for scientific research and education.
Fields of interest: Biology/life sciences; Science, research; Education; Higher education.
International interests: United Kingdom; Sweden.
Limitations: Applications not accepted. Giving in the U.S. is primarily in CA, international giving includes Stockholm, Sweden, and Cambridge, United Kingdom.
Application information: Contributes only to pre-selected organizations.
Officers and Directors: * Melvin Simon,* Ph.D., Chair.; John Abelson,* Ph.D., Pres. and Exec. Dir.; Willis Wood,* Ph.D., V.P.; Gary Friedman,* Exec. V.P. and Secy.; Gustaf Arrhenius, Ph.D.; Dr. Theodore Friedmann, M.D.; Gordon Gill, M.D.; John Grotzinger, Ph.D.; David Hirsch, Ph.D.; Peter Johnson; Deborah Spector, Ph.D.; Edward Stolper, Ph.D.
EIN: 953248387
Recent grants for international programs:
45-1 Gordon Research Conferences, West Kingston, RI, $20,000. For scientific research and education. 2009.
45-2 Universidad de Concepcion, Concepcion, Chile, $809,420. For scientific research and education. 2009.
45-3 University of Queensland, Brisbane, Australia, $10,000. For scientific research and education. 2009.
45-4 University of Southern Denmark, Odense, Denmark, $398,245. For scientific research and education. 2009.

46
AIDS Healthcare Foundation
(also known as AHF)
6255 Sunset Blvd., Fl. 21
Los Angeles, CA 90028-7422 (323) 860-5200
FAX: (323) 962-8513;
E-mail: webmaster@aidshealth.org; URL: http://
www.aidshealth.org

Established in 1987 as the AIDS Hospice Foundation; current name adopted in 1990.
Grantmaker type: Public charity.
Financial data (yr. ended 12/31/10): Revenue, $97,221,629; assets, $89,116,415 (M); gifts received, $19,022,411; expenditures, $77,128,239; giving activities include $561,629 for grants.
Purpose and activities: The foundation provides medical care for those affected by HIV or living with AIDS. In addition, the foundation participates in scientific research and patient advocacy for those in need.
Fields of interest: Health care; AIDS; AIDS, people with.

International interests: Central America; Asia; Africa.
Type of support: Research; Grants to individuals.
Limitations: Giving primarily in the U.S., Africa, Asia, and Central America.
Publications: Annual report.
Officers and Directors: * Judith Briggs Marsh,* Co-Chair.; Kathy Mendez,* Esq., Co-Chair; Diana Hoorzuk,* Vice-Chair.; Michael Weinstein,* C.E.O.; Peter Reis,* V.P.; Laurent Fischer,* M.D., Secy.; Laura Nelson, C.F.O.; Agapito Diaz,* Treas.; Gregg Alton; Cynthia Davis; Sam Mall; Scott Galvin; Lawrence Peters; and 12 additional directors.
EIN: 954112121

47
Airline Ambassadors International, Inc.
418 California Ave.
P.O. Box 459
Moss Beach, CA 94038-0459 (650) 728-7844
Contact: Nancy Rivard, Pres.
FAX: (650) 728-7855;
E-mail: contact@airlineamb.org; Toll-free tel.: (866) 153-2486; URL: http://www.airlineamb.org
YouTube: http://www.youtube.com/user/ airlineamb

Established in 1996 in TX.
Donors: American Airlines, Inc.; Bill and Melinda Gates Foundation; Buckner Orphan Care International; Care Bags Foundation; Cape Classics; Cathay Pacific Airlines; Catholic Relief Services; CROCS; Dallas Mavericks; Dallas Stars, LP.
Grantmaker type: Public charity.
Financial data (yr. ended 12/31/08): Revenue, $4,980,823; assets $1,157,855 (M); gifts received, $4,884,893; expenditures, $3,943,680; program services expenses, $3,657,820; giving activities include $979 for grants, and $70,804 for foundation-administered programs.
Purpose and activities: The organization provides humanitarian aid to children and families in need, as well as international relief and development, to underprivileged communities throughout the world through utilizing the resources of airline personnel and other individuals.
Fields of interest: International relief; Community/ economic development; Human services; Human services, emergency aid.
Type of support: Grants to individuals.
Limitations: Giving on a worldwide basis.
Publications: Annual report.
Officer and Directors: * Nancy Rivard,* Pres.; Frank Campagna; Steven Crane; Stephen Forneris; Maya Grant; Peter Greenberg; Leilei LeLaulu; H.E. Francis Lorenzo; Nana Patricia McPeak; David Rivard; Daniel Sheth.
EIN: 752679444

48
Akian Foundation
26235 Technology Dr.
Valencia, CA 91355

Established in 2009 in CA.
Grantmaker type: Independent foundation.
Financial data (yr. ended 11/30/10): Assets, $5,083,808 (M); expenditures, $255,903; qualifying distributions, $243,677; giving activities include $225,722 for grants.
Fields of interest: Higher education.

International interests: Armenia.
Limitations: Applications not accepted. Giving primarily in CA.
Application information: Unsolicited requests for funds not accepted.
Officers: Haig P. Akian, Pres.; Lori J. Stephan, V.P. and Secy.; Lena G. Akian, V.P. and C.F.O.
Directors: Sonia Akian; Zaven P. Akien.
EIN: 263913336

49
The Al-Ameen Foundation
1301 Ocean Ave.
Santa Monica, CA 90401-1019

Established in 1998 in CA.
Donors: Ahmad Adaya; Adaya Family Trust.
Grantmaker type: Independent foundation.
Financial data (yr. ended 12/31/10): Assets, $5,831,524 (M); expenditures, $621,814; qualifying distributions, $601,645; giving activities include $601,645 for grants.
Fields of interest: Education; Hospitals (general); Health care; Human services; Family services, domestic violence; Islam.
International interests: Pakistan.
Limitations: Applications not accepted. Giving primarily in CA, and in Karachi, Pakistan.
Application information: Contributes only to pre-selected organizations.
Officers: Ahmad Adaya, Pres.; Tehmina Adaya, Secy.; Gazala Shauk, C.F.O.
Directors: Amina Adaya; Salim Adaya; Nargis Dada; Nasreen Haroon; Ruksana Mohammed.
EIN: 954698812

50
Alalusi Foundation
1975 National Ave.
Hayward, CA 94545-1709 (510) 887-2281
E-mail: info@alalusifoundation.org; URL: http://www.alalusifoundation.org/

Established in 2001 in CA.
Donor: Hesham Al Alusi.
Grantmaker type: Independent foundation.
Financial data (yr. ended 03/31/11): Assets, $0 (M); gifts received, $648,391; expenditures, $638,595; qualifying distributions, $638,595; giving activities include $577,639 for 14 grants (high: $185,000; low: $25).
Purpose and activities: Giving primarily for Muslim and Islamic relief and affairs, as well as for humanitarian assistance in other regions.
Fields of interest: International relief; International human rights; Islam; Religion.
International interests: China.
Type of support: Grants to individuals; General/operating support.
Limitations: Applications accepted. Giving on an international basis with emphasis on China; some giving also in CA.
Application information:
 Initial approach: Letter
 Deadline(s): None
Director: Hesham Al Alusi.
EIN: 912158518

51
Amar Foundation
c/o McCabe & Totah, LLP
1760 The Almeda, Ste. 300
San Jose, CA 95126-1728
Vinod and Neeru Khosla's Giving Pledge: http://givingpledge.org/#vinod_khosla

Established in 1987 in CA.
Donors: Neeru Khosla; Vinod Khosla.
Grantmaker type: Independent foundation.
Financial data (yr. ended 12/31/09): Assets, $42,649,795 (M); gifts received, $4,376,592; expenditures, $4,624,393; qualifying distributions, $4,945,308; giving activities include $4,516,667 for 5 grants (high: $3,325,000; low: $50,000), and $428,631 for 1 loan/program-related investment.
Purpose and activities: Giving primarily for education, and to U.S.-based organizations concerning India that support social, economic, and educational programs.
Fields of interest: Education; Human services; International affairs.
International interests: India.
Limitations: Applications not accepted. Giving primarily in CA. No grants to individuals.
Application information: Contributes only to pre-selected organizations.
Officers and Director:* Neeru Khosla,* Pres.; Vinod Khosla,* Secy.
EIN: 943055731

52
America Gives Back
(formerly Charity Projects Entertainment Fund)
9720 Wilshire Blvd., 4th Fl.
Beverly Hills, CA 90212-2000
E-mail: info@americagivesback.org; URL: http://www.americagivesback.org
Facebook: http://www.facebook.com/comicrelief

Established in 2006.
Grantmaker type: Public charity.
Financial data (yr. ended 12/31/10): Revenue, $1,117,739; assets, $2,694,973 (M); gifts received, $1,090,385; expenditures, $1,276,820; program services expenses, $1,249,024; giving activities include $1,183,000 for grants to organizations outside the U.S.
Purpose and activities: The fund helps combat extreme poverty in the United States and throughout the world, particularly in Africa.
Fields of interest: Youth development, centers/clubs; Education; Health care; AIDS; Crime/violence prevention, child abuse; Food services; Human services; Children, day care; International relief; Economically disadvantaged.
International interests: Africa.
Limitations: Giving on a national and international basis, with emphasis on Africa.
Board Members: Kevin Cahill,* Pres.; Richard Curtis; Richard Hofstetter; Richard L. Scott.
EIN: 010885377

53
American Friends of Neve Shalom/Wahat Al-Salam, Inc.
12925 Riverside Dr., 3rd Fl.
Sherman Oaks, CA 91423-2231
(818) 325-8884
Contact: Perrine Vaillant, Exec. Dir.

FAX: (818) 465-9498;
E-mail: afnswas@oasisofpeace.org; E-mail for Perrine Vaillant: perrine@oasisofpeace.org; URL: http://www.oasisofpeace.org

Established in 1986 in CA.
Grantmaker type: Public charity.
Financial data (yr. ended 08/31/10): Revenue, $673,665; assets, $1,219,592 (M); gifts received, $691,736; expenditures, $825,463; program services expenses, $636,711; giving activities include $469,665 for grants to organizations outside the U.S.
Purpose and activities: The organization is dedicated to dialogue, cooperation, and a genuine and durable peace between Arabs and Jews, Palestinians, and Israelis by encouraging, supporting, and publicizing the projects of Neve Shalom/Wahat al-Salam, the "Oasis of Peace".
Fields of interest: Education, single organization support; International affairs, single organization support; International peace/security; International conflict resolution; International affairs.
International interests: Israel.
Limitations: Giving on an international basis, primarily in Israel.
Publications: Annual report.
Officers: Rev. Gordon Webster, Pres.; Jeanine Shama, V.P.; Judith Tuller, Secy.; David Matz, Treas.; Perrine Vaillant, Exec. Dir.
Directors: Judy Dubin; Adeeb Fadil; Gordon Fellman; Richard Goodwin; Roberta Gordon; and 6 additional directors.
Number of staff: 3
EIN: 133441742

54
Amgen Foundation, Inc.
1 Amgen Center Dr., M.S. 28-1-B
Thousand Oaks, CA 91320-1799
(805) 447-4056
Contact: Eduardo Cetlin, Sr. Mgr., Corp. Contribs
FAX: (805) 376-1258;
E-mail: amgenfoundation@amgen.com; Additional e-mail for Eduardo Cetlin: ccetlin@amgen.com; URL: http://www.amgen.com/citizenship/foundation.html
Grants List: http://wwwext.amgen.com/citizenship/foundation_donation_list.html
Twitter: http://twitter.com/AmgenFoundation

Established in 1991 in CA.
Donor: Amgen Inc.
Grantmaker type: Company-sponsored foundation.
Financial data (yr. ended 12/31/09): Assets, $101,711,817 (M); gifts received, $31,107,500; expenditures, $18,210,650; qualifying distributions, $18,239,641; giving activities include $13,825,998 for 173 grants (high: $1,303,179; low: $480), and $2,995,625 for employee matching gifts.
Purpose and activities: The foundation supports programs designed to advance science education; improve quality of care and access for patients; and create sound communities where Amgen staff members live and work.
Fields of interest: Health care, equal rights; Arts; Higher education; Teacher school/education; Education; Health care, reform; Health care, information services; Health care, patient services; Health care; Human services; Community/economic development; United Ways and Federated Giving

Programs; Science, formal/general education; Mathematics; Engineering/technology; Science.

Type of support: Grants to individuals; General/operating support; Continuing support; Capital campaigns; Equipment; Endowments; Program development; Research; Employee volunteer services; Program evaluation; Employee matching gifts; Matching/challenge support.

Limitations: Applications accepted. Giving on a national and international basis in areas of company operations, with emphasis on Los Angeles, San Francisco, and Ventura, CA, CO, KY, Greater Boston, Middlesex, and Suffolk counties, MA, Juncos, PR, RI, King and South Snohomish counties, WA, and Europe; giving also to regional and national organizations. No support for religious organizations not of direct benefit to the entire community, political organizations, labor unions or fraternal, service, or veterans' organizations, international organizations, private foundations, or discriminatory organizations. No grants to individuals (except for AASTE), or for fundraising or sports-related events, corporate sponsorships, or lobbying activities.

Publications: Application guidelines; Annual report; Grants list; Program policy statement.

Application information: A full proposal may be requested at a later date. Support is limited to 1 contribution per organization during any given year. Application form required.

  Initial approach: Complete online letter of inquiry; complete online application for AASTE
  Deadline(s): None; Varies for AASTE
  Board meeting date(s): Quarterly
  Final notification: June for AASTE

Officer and Directors:* David J. Scott, Chair.; Jean J. Lim, Pres.; Phyllis J. Piano,* V.P.; Andrea A. Robinson, Secy.; Peter O'Hara, Treas.; Stephen Canepa, C.F.O.; Fabrizio Bonanni; Michael A. Kelly; Brian M. McNamee; Joseph P. Miletich; Helen I. Torley.

EIN: 770252898

Recent grants for international programs:

54-1 Amelie Civic Association, Czech Republic, $37,682. For Guide to Living with Cancer for Patients, and Prevention Information. Grant made in collaboration with the United Way Worldwide. 2010.

54-2 Cambridge University, Cambridge, England, $1,287,721. For Amgen Scholars Program, which provides undergraduate students with the opportunity to engage in hands-on summer research experience. 2010.

54-3 Cambridge University, Cambridge, England, $1,000,000. For Amgen Scholars Program, which provides undergraduate students with the opportunity to engage in hands-on summer research experience. 2010.

54-4 Direct Relief International, Santa Barbara, CA, $400,000. For disaster relief efforts for Haiti Earthquake. 2010.

54-5 Direct Relief International, Santa Barbara, CA, $100,000. For disaster relief efforts for Haiti Earthquake. 2010.

54-6 Euroscience, Athens, Greece, $46,613. For Knowledge Outside the City. Grant made in collaboration with the United Way Worldwide. 2010.

54-7 Hungarian Research Students Association, Budapest, Hungary, $10,000. For High School Research Support Project. Grant made in collaboration with the United Way Worldwide. 2010.

54-8 Hungarian Research Teachers Association, Budapest, Hungary, $10,000. For Open Science

Inquiry Based Science in Classroom Practice. Grant made in collaboration with the United Way Worldwide. 2010.

54-9 International Medical Corps, Santa Monica, CA, $50,000. For Pakistan flood relief efforts. 2010.

54-10 Karolinska Institute, Stockholm, Sweden, $770,133. For Amgen Scholars Program, which provides undergraduate students with the opportunity to engage in hands-on summer research experience. 2010.

54-11 Lambrakis Foundation, Athens, Greece, $85,969. For The Science Education Network. Grant made in collaboration with the United Way Worldwide. 2010.

54-12 Liga Portuguesa Contra o Cancro, Lisbon, Portugal, $26,452. For Living Longer and Better Program. Grant made in collaboration with the United Way Worldwide. 2010.

54-13 Ludwig-Maximilians University, Munich, Germany, $1,000,000. For Amgen Scholars Program, which provides undergraduate students with the opportunity to engage in hands-on summer research experience. 2010.

54-14 National Association of Hungarian Biology Teachers Collaboration, Budapest, Hungary, $93,000. For Attracting New Science Teachers: Analysis and Strategic Blueprint for the Future. Grant made in collaboration with the United Way Worldwide. 2010.

54-15 UNICEF, New York, NY, $50,000. For Pakistan flood relief efforts. 2010.

54-16 United States Fund for UNICEF, New York, NY, $500,000. For disaster relief efforts for Haiti Earthquake. 2010.

54-17 Universite Pierre et Marie Curie, Paris, France, $89,163. For E-Patient University to leverage the patient experience through online curriculum to train patient educators. Grant made in collaboration with the United Way Worldwide. 2010.

54-18 University of Zurich, Life Science Learning Center, Zurich, Switzerland, $103,724. For School Ambassador Program to create opportunities that allow for exposure to research at higher education level for both teachers and students. Grant made in collaboration with the United Way Worldwide. 2010.

55
The Vijay Amritraj Foundation

16501 Sherman Way, Ste. 130
Van Nuys, CA 91406-7013   (818) 988-9977
FAX: (818) 988-5812;
E-mail: info@vijayamritrajfoundation.org;
URL: http://www.vijayamritrajfoundation.org

Established in 2006 in CA.

Grantmaker type: Public charity.

Financial data (yr. ended 12/31/10): Revenue, $198,015; assets, $103,081 (M); gifts received, $320,099; expenditures, $185,630; program services expenses, $174,140; giving activities include $1,900 for grants, $107,025 for grants to organizations outside the U.S., and $65,215 for foundation-administered programs.

Purpose and activities: The foundation seeks to bring hope, help, and healing to the defenseless and innocent victims of disease, tragedy, and circumstance in India.

Fields of interest: International relief.

International interests: India.

Limitations: Applications accepted. Giving limited to India. No support for religious activities or programs serving specific religious groups or denominations. No grants to individuals, or for capital development, research, project replication, or endowment (unless these activities grow out of work already being funded by the foundation). No loans to individuals. Generally, no grants for film or video projects, books, scholarships, or fellowships.

Application information:

  Initial approach: Letter of inquiry submitted preferably via e-mail

Officers: Vijay Amritraj, Pres.; Gautam M. Shah, Secy.; Randhir S. Tuli, Treas.; Michael Donohue, Exec. Dir.

EIN: 205017416

56
ANGELCARE

(also known as Children's ANGELCARE Aid International)
P.O. Box 600370
San Diego, CA   92160-0370
Contact: T.J. Grosser, Pres. and C.E.O.
FAX: (619) 795-6238; E-mail: info@angelcare.org;
Toll-free tel.: (888) 264-5227; URL: http://www.angelcare.org/

Established in 1977 in DC as Children's Aid International; in 1997 became ANGELCARE.

Grantmaker type: Public charity.

Financial data (yr. ended 08/31/08): Revenue, $1,299,459; assets, $250,179 (M); gifts received, $1,299,459; expenditures, $1,897,771; program services expenses, $39,943; giving activities include $6,756 for grants.

Purpose and activities: The organization offers an opportunity for a partnership of caring people who become members of the board of angels to answer the prayers of the world's poor children for food, medicine, clothing, schooling and disaster relief.

Fields of interest: Safety/disasters; Education, early childhood education; Elementary school/education; Education; Health care; Food services; Nutrition; Agriculture/food; Children, services; Community/economic development.

International interests: Africa; Canada; Central America; Eastern & Central Europe; Latin America; Mexico; Southeast Asia.

Type of support: General/operating support; Continuing support; Equipment; Emergency funds; Program development; Program evaluation; In-kind gifts.

Limitations: Applications not accepted. Giving on a national and international basis, primarily in Africa, Southeast Asia, Central America, Eastern Europe, and North America. No grants to individuals.

Publications: Annual report; Financial statement; Informational brochure; Newsletter.

Application information: Contributes only to pre-selected organizations.

  Board meeting date(s): 4th Mon. of each month via teleconference, quarterly on-site meetings

Officers and Directors:* Daniel K. Park,* Chair.; T.J. Grosser,* Ed.D., D.D., Pres.; Janet Grosser,* Secy.; Wayne Peimann, Treas.; Debbie Lou Smith.

Number of staff: 7 full-time professional; 1 full-time support.

EIN: 330776776

57
Appleton Foundation
P.O. Box 1460
Santa Cruz, CA 95061-1460 (831) 469-3941
Contact: Don Lane, Mgr.
E-mail: appleton@calcentral.com

Established in 1998 in CA.
Donors: Alexander Gaguine; Jane Yett; John Hellwig; John Gaguine; Benito Gaguine.
Grantmaker type: Independent foundation.
Financial data (yr. ended 12/31/10): Assets, $11,203,729 (M); expenditures, $1,357,384; qualifying distributions, $1,208,276; giving activities include $1,206,071 for 43 grants (high: $332,885; low: $4,500).
Fields of interest: Education; Environment; Health care; Human services; International affairs; Community/economic development.
Type of support: General/operating support.
Limitations: Applications not accepted. Giving primarily in Latin America and Santa Cruz County, CA. No grants to individuals.
Application information: Contributes only to pre-selected organizations. Unsolicited requests for funds not accepted.
Officers: Alexander Gaguine, Pres.; Phil McManus, Secy.; Bill Leland, Treas.; Don Lane, Mgr.; David Foster; Jane Weed Pomerantaz.
EIN: 911792407

58
The Applied Materials Foundation
3050 Bowers Ave., MS 0106
P.O. Box 58039
Santa Clara, CA 95054-3201
E-mail: applied_materials_foundation@amat.com; E-mail contact for organizations located outside of the US: community_affairs@amat.com; URL: http://www.appliedmaterials.com/about/cr

Established in 1994.
Donor: Applied Materials, Inc.
Grantmaker type: Company-sponsored foundation.
Financial data (yr. ended 10/31/09): Assets, $16,743,711 (M); gifts received, $5,631,263; expenditures, $7,036,755; qualifying distributions, $6,984,327; giving activities include $6,984,327 for grants.
Purpose and activities: The foundation supports food banks and organizations involved with arts and culture, education, the environment, housing, disaster relief, human services, international relief, civic affairs, and economically disadvantaged people.
Fields of interest: Adult/continuing education; Environmental education; Youth development, adult & child programs; Youth, services; Housing/shelter; Museums (science/technology); Arts; Elementary/secondary education; Higher education; Education; Environment; Food banks; Disasters, preparedness/services; Homeless, human services; Human services; International relief; Public affairs; Economically disadvantaged.
Type of support: Continuing support; Program development; Scholarship funds; Employee volunteer services; Sponsorships; Employee matching gifts; Matching/challenge support.
Limitations: Applications accepted. Giving primarily in areas of company operations, with emphasis on San Jose, CA; giving also to organizations outside of the United States. No support for missing children organizations, fraternities, religious or political

organizations, commencements, PTAs, or alumni groups. No grants to individuals, or for general operating support, capital campaigns, research, sporting events for schools or civic teams, health-related programs or sponsorships, or fundraisers.
Publications: Application guidelines; Corporate giving report.
Application information:
  Initial approach: Complete online application; e-mail letter of inquiry for Women in Science & Technology Scholarship Program; e-mail community affairs for organizations located outside of the United States
  Deadline(s): Jan. 15 and June 15; None for Women in Science & Technology Scholarship Program
  Board meeting date(s): Semi-annually
  Final notification: Mar. 15 and Aug. 15
Officers: Michael R. Splinter, Pres.; Charmaine F. Mesina, Secy.; Robert M. Friess, C.F.O.; Mark L. Walker, Exec. Dir.; George Davis; James C. Morgan.
EIN: 770386898
Recent grants for international programs:
58-1 Akshaya Patra Foundation USA, Stoneham, MA, $38,000. 2009.
58-2 American India Foundation, Santa Clara, CA, $61,079. 2009.
58-3 American Israel Environmental Council, New York, NY, $72,850. 2009.
58-4 Friends of Ofanim, Wynnewood, PA, $84,000. 2009.
58-5 Global Impact, Alexandria, VA, $1,309,863. 2009.
58-6 GlobalGiving Foundation, Washington, DC, $20,355. 2009.

59
Applied Materials, Inc. Corporate Giving Program
3050 Bowers Ave.
P.O. Box 58039
Santa Clara, CA 95054-3299 (408) 727-5555
E-mail: community_affairs@appliedmaterials.com; URL: http://www.appliedmaterials.com/about/cr
The Applied Materials Corporate Responsibility Blog: http://blog.appliedmaterials.com/corporate-responsibility

Grantmaker type: Corporate giving program.
Purpose and activities: As a complement to its foundation, Applied Materials also makes charitable contributions to K-12 educational institutions and nonprofit organizations directly. Support is limited to areas of company operations in California, Massachusetts, Montana, Texas, and Utah, with emphasis on Silicon Valley, California, and in Canada, China, France, Germany, India, Israel, Japan, Malaysia, the Philippines, Singapore, South Korea, Switzerland, and Taiwan.
Fields of interest: Elementary/secondary education; Arts; Environment, energy; Environmental education; Human services; Community/economic development.
International interests: Canada; China; France; Germany; India; Israel; Japan; Malaysia; Philippines; Singapore; South Korea; Switzerland; Taiwan.
Type of support: Continuing support; Program development; Faculty/staff development; Curriculum development.
Limitations: Applications accepted. Giving limited to areas of company operations in CA, MA, MT, TX, and

UT, with emphasis on Silicon Valley, CA, and in Canada, China, France, Germany, India, Israel, Japan, Malaysia, the Philippines, Singapore, South Korea, Switzerland, and Taiwan. No support for fraternities, religious, or political organizations, or missing children organizations. No grants to individuals, or for general operating support, research, commencements, PTAs, alumni groups, health-related programs or sponsorships, fundraisers such as walk-a-thons, runs, team in training, sporting events for school or civic teams, capital campaigns, bricks/mortar, equipment, home building, or physical structures.
Application information: Application form required.
  Initial approach: Complete online application form; e-mail letter of inquiry for organizations located outside of the U.S.
  Deadline(s): Jan. 15 and June 15
  Committee meeting date(s): Semi-annually

60
Arlene Foundation
100 Wilshire Blvd., Ste. 1760
Santa Monica, CA 90401-1142

Established in 2005 in CA.
Donors: Steven D. Levine; Loren L. Levine.
Grantmaker type: Independent foundation.
Financial data (yr. ended 12/31/10): Assets, $155,816 (M); gifts received, $304,790; expenditures, $256,836; qualifying distributions, $251,950; giving activities include $251,950 for grants.
Fields of interest: Human services; International relief; Civil/human rights.
Limitations: Applications not accepted. Giving primarily in CA and NY. No grants to individuals.
Application information: Contributes only to pre-selected organizations.
Trustees: Loren L. Levine; Steven D. Levine.
EIN: 320158768

61
Armenian Gospel Mission
2650 E. Foothill Blvd., Ste. 205
Pasadena, CA 91107-3439 (626) 744-3221
FAX: (626) 744-3224;
E-mail: office@armeniangospelmission.org; Mailing address: P.O. Box 5727, Pasadena, CA 91117-0727; URL: http://www.armeniangospelmission.org

Established in 1970 in CA.
Grantmaker type: Public charity.
Financial data (yr. ended 12/31/10): Revenue, $1,812,927; assets, $2,235,515 (M); gifts received, $1,441,655; expenditures, $1,785,670; giving activities include $2,000 for grants, $552,272 for 1 grant to an organization outside the U.S., and $26,400 for grants to individuals outside the U.S.
Purpose and activities: The mission is a Christian humanitarian relief and development organization that ministers to the needs of the most vulnerable and socially-deprived children, elderly, and families in Armenia who lack support structures to sustain their basic human and spiritual needs.
Fields of interest: Human services; Family services; Children/youth, services; Christian agencies & churches; Children/youth; Economically disadvantaged.

International interests: Armenia.
Type of support: Emergency funds; In-kind gifts.
Limitations: Giving limited to Armenia.
Officers and Directors:* Ariel Babikian; Silva Balouzian; Anita Goodall; John Jemelian; Stan Lazarian; Steve Lazarian; Armineh Mooshagian; Raymond Savoian; Leonard Sunukjian; George Terzian.
EIN: 237089113

62
Arntz Family Foundation
(formerly Eugene S. Arntz Foundation)
P.O. Box 66488
Scotts Valley, CA 95067-6488
Contact: Nancy Rosa
E-mail: nancy@arntzfamilyfoundation.org;
URL: http://www.arntzfamilyfoundation.org

Established in 1994 in CA.
Donors: Eugene S. Arntz‡; K. Allan Arntz; Thomas E. Arntz; Donald M. Arntz; Arntz Builders Inc.
Grantmaker type: Independent foundation.
Financial data (yr. ended 09/30/10): Assets, $12,717,443 (M); gifts received, $21,000; expenditures, $579,877; qualifying distributions, $531,857; giving activities include $420,180 for grants.
Purpose and activities: The purpose of the foundation is to support environmental organizations, with an emphasis on those organizations that work toward systematic change and sustainability, particularly where the areas of environment and economic development come together.
Fields of interest: Environment.
International interests: Central America; Mexico.
Type of support: General/operating support; Program development.
Limitations: Applications not accepted. Giving primarily in CA. No grants to individuals.
Publications: Grants list.
Application information: Contributes only to pre-selected organizations. Unsolicited requests for funds not accepted. Proposal submissions are by invitation only.
   Board meeting date(s): Feb. and July
Trustees: Donald M. Arntz; K. Allan Arntz; Katherine J. Jones; Thomas E. Arntz.
Number of staff: 1 part-time professional.
EIN: 686109096

63
Artists for a New South Africa
(also known as ANSA)
2999 Overland Ave., Ste. 102
Los Angeles, CA 90064-4256 (310) 204-1748
Contact: Sharon Gelman, Pres. and Exec. Dir.
FAX: (310) 204-4277; E-mail: info@ansafrica.org;
URL: http://www.ansafrica.org
Facebook: http://www.facebook.com/pages/Artists-for-a-New-South-Africa/102019626580?ref=ts
Twitter: http://twitter.com/ansafrica
YouTube: http://www.youtube.com/ArtistsNewSAfrica

Established in 1989.
Grantmaker type: Public charity.
Financial data (yr. ended 12/31/10): Revenue, $290,640; assets, $580,573 (M); gifts received,

$283,654; expenditures, $588,714; giving activities include $266,424 for grants to organizations outside the U.S.
Purpose and activities: The organization is dedicated to combating the African AIDS pandemic and advancing democracy and equality in South Africa.
Fields of interest: AIDS.
International interests: South Africa.
Limitations: Applications not accepted. Giving limited to South Africa.
Application information: Unsolicited requests for funds not considered or acknowledged.
Officer and Directors:* Sharon Gelman,* Pres. and Exec. Dir.; Gillian Anderson; Latanya Richardson Jackson; Michael Jensen; Kitsaun King; Ron Kunene; Artis Lane; Sarah Pillsbury; Deborah Santana; Marlene Saritzky; Gary Schwartz; Bradley Silver; Jurnee Smollett; Roderick Spencer; Blair Underwood; Yvonne E. White; Alfre Woodard.
EIN: 954544830

64
The Asia Foundation
465 California St., 9th Fl.
San Francisco, CA 94104-1822 (415) 982-4640
Contact: Gordon R. Hein, V.P., Progs.
FAX: (415) 392-8863; E-mail: info@asiafound.org;
Additional address (DC office): 1779 Massachusetts Ave., N.W., Ste. 815, Washington, DC 20036-2109, tel.: (202) 588-9420, fax: (202) 588-9409, email: info@asiafound-dc.org; additional mailing address (CA office): P.O. Box 193223, San Francisco, CA 94119-3223; URL: http://www.asiafoundation.org
RSS Feed: http://feeds.feedburner.com/TheAsiaFoundationNews
Twitter: http://twitter.com/Asia_Foundation

Established in 1954 in CA.
Donors: David R. Andrews; Michael H. Armacost; Jennifer Armstrong; Purnima Bajpai; William L. Ball III; Doris Bebb; Doug Bereuter; Louise Bereuter; Jeffrey T. Bergner; Susan P. Besemer.
Grantmaker type: Public charity.
Financial data (yr. ended 09/30/10): Revenue, $154,023,805; assets, $68,567,032 (M); gifts received, $153,318,660; expenditures, $151,924,948; giving activities include $745,477 for grants, $24,165,977 for grants to organizations outside the U.S., and $330,101 for grants to individuals outside the U.S.
Purpose and activities: The foundation is a nonprofit, non-governmental organization committed to the development of a peaceful, prosperous, just, and open Asia-Pacific region; the foundation supports programs in Asia that help improve governance, law, civil society, women's empowerment, economic reform and development, and international relations.
Fields of interest: International affairs.
International interests: Asia.
Type of support: General/operating support; Continuing support; Income development; Equipment; Program development; Conferences/seminars; Publication; Curriculum development; Fellowships; Internship funds; Scholarship funds; Research; Technical assistance; Program evaluation; Exchange programs; In-kind gifts.
Limitations: Applications accepted. Giving primarily in Asia and the Pacific, especially to Afghanistan, Bangladesh, Cambodia, China, East Timor, India, Indonesia, Malaysia, Mongolia, Nepal, Pakistan,

Philippines, Sri Lanka, Thailand, and Vietnam. No grants to individuals (except for Junior Associates in Asian Affairs Program) or U.S.-based organizations.
Publications: Annual report; Financial statement; Grants list; Occasional report.
Application information: After receiving the letter of inquiry, foundation staff may reply, informing the grant seeker as to whether or not the project fits within the foundation's interests. If it does, foundation staff may ask the grant seeker to submit a formal proposal and/or raise questions for clarification of project. Application form not required.
   Initial approach: Letter of inquiry
   Copies of proposal: 1
   Board meeting date(s): Quarterly
Officers and Trustees:* Michael H. Armacost,* Chair.; Harry Harding,* Vice-Chair.; Missie Rennie,* Vice-Chair.; David D. Arnold, Pres. and C.E.O.; Barnett F. Baron, Exec. V.P.; Allen C. Choate, V.P., Partners in Asia Devel.; Richard H. Fuller, V.P., Field Opers.; Gordon R. Hein, V.P., Progs.; Nancy Yuan, V.P.; Philip W. Yun, V.P., Resource Devel.; Susan J. Pharr,* Secy.; John Croizat, C.F.O.; Paul S. Slawson,* Treas.; Terrence B. Adamson; David R. Andrews; William L. Ball III; Mary Brown Bullock, Ph.D.; Alexander D. Calhoun; William H.C. Chang; Gina Lin Chu; and 19 additional trustees.
Number of staff: 120 full-time professional; 3 part-time professional; 280 full-time support; 4 part-time support.
EIN: 941191246

65
Atkinson Foundation
1720 S. Amphlett Blvd., Ste. 100
San Mateo, CA 94402-2710
Contact: Elizabeth H. Curtis, V.P., Admin.
E-mail: atkinfdn@aol.com; Tel./fax: (650) 357-1101; URL: http://www.atkinsonfdn.org

Incorporated in 1939 in CA.
Donors: George H. Atkinson‡; Mildred M. Atkinson‡.
Grantmaker type: Independent foundation.
Financial data (yr. ended 12/31/10): Assets, $15,743,580 (M); expenditures, $991,100; qualifying distributions, $853,304; giving activities include $745,403 for 90 grants (high: $40,000; low: $972).
Purpose and activities: Primary areas of interest include the disadvantaged and the homeless, child welfare, family planning, and the handicapped. Broad purposes are to help people reach their highest potential and to reach self-sufficiency. Giving for social services, including youth and the aged, education, family planning programs, and international development programs.
Fields of interest: Child development, education; Secondary school/education; Vocational education; Higher education; Adult education—literacy, basic skills & GED; Reproductive health, family planning; Substance abuse, services; Mental health/crisis services; AIDS; Alcoholism; Crime/violence prevention, youth; Food services; Human services; Children/youth, services; Child development, services; Family services; Aging, centers/services; Minorities/immigrants, centers/services; Homeless, human services; International economic development; Infants/toddlers; Children/youth; Youth; Adults; Aging; Disabilities, people with; Physically disabled; Mentally disabled; Minorities; Asians/Pacific Islanders; Hispanics/Latinos; Women; Offenders/ex-offenders; Substance

abusers; Single parents; Crime/abuse victims; LGBTQ; Immigrants/refugees; Economically disadvantaged; Homeless; Migrant workers.
International interests: Central America; Mexico.
Type of support: Management development/capacity building; General/operating support; Continuing support; Income development; Program development; Seed money; Scholarship funds; Technical assistance.
Limitations: Applications accepted. Giving limited for the benefit of San Mateo County, CA, for social welfare, secondary schools, colleges, and church activities. Some international grantmaking (through U.S.-based nonprofit organizations) to benefit Mexico and Central America for technical assistance, population issues, economic development, and water and food resources. No support for sports groups, or national or statewide umbrella organizations. No grants to individuals directly (including scholarships), or for research or doctoral study, annual campaigns, travel to conferences or events, media presentations, or fundraising events; no loans.
Publications: Annual report (including application guidelines); Grants list.
Application information: Applications should include a grant proposal cover sheet, which is available online or from the foundation. Application form required.
  Initial approach: Telephone
  Copies of proposal: 1
  Deadline(s): Feb. 1, May 1, Aug. 1, and Nov. 1
  Board meeting date(s): Mar., June, Sept., and Dec.
  Final notification: 2 months, maximum
Officers and Directors:* Linda L. Lanier,* Pres.; James R. Avedisian,* V.P., Fin. and Treas.; Elizabeth H. Curtis,* V.P., Admin.; Ray N. Atkinson,* V.P.; James C. Ingwersen,* Secy.; Olivia O. Aranda; Jean S. Atkinson; William W. Crandall, Jr.; Dirk Damonte; John E. Herrell; Shirley Moore.
Number of staff: 1 full-time professional.
EIN: 946075613

66
Auroville International USA
P.O. Box 1534
Lodi, CA 95241-1534 (916) 416-0041
E-mail: info@aviusa.org; URL: http://www.aviusa.org

Established in 1974.
Grantmaker type: Public charity.
Financial data (yr. ended 06/30/10): Revenue, $74,930; assets, $132,747 (M); gifts received, $63,582; expenditures, $141,265; program services expenses, $12,309; giving activities include $128,956 for grants.
Fields of interest: Human services.
International interests: India.
Limitations: Giving primarily in India.
Officers: Bryan Walton, Pres.; David Walker, Secy.; Mary Alexander, Treas.
Board Members: Roesemary Carpendale; John-Robert Cornell; Bill Leon; Nilauro Markus.
EIN: 237360183

67
Australians in Film
2800 28th St., Ste. 320
Santa Monica, CA 90405-6201 (310) 452-5939
FAX: (323) 446-8724;
E-mail: administrator@australiansinfilm.org;
URL: http://www.australiansinfilm.org
Facebook: http://www.facebook.com/australiansinfilm
Twitter: http://twitter.com/#!/australiansfilm

Established in 2001 as the Los Angeles Australian Film and Television Association (LAAFTA); current name adopted in 2004.
Grantmaker type: Public charity.
Financial data (yr. ended 12/31/09): Revenue, $79,363; assets, $43,461 (M); gifts received, $110,022; expenditures, $54,624.
Purpose and activities: The organization seeks to celebrate and promote the work of Australian film and television makers; create a Los Angeles-based networking forum for professionals working in the film, television, and allied industries who are Australian or who have a close association with Australia; increase the visibility of the Los Angeles-based Australian film and television community; and provide a vehicle for raising the profile of Australian film and television productions.
Fields of interest: Performing arts.
International interests: Australia.
Type of support: Scholarships—to individuals.
Limitations: Giving on a national basis.
Publications: Application guidelines.
Application information:
  Initial approach: Submit application
  Deadline(s): Dec. 22 for Heath Ledger Scholarship Fund
Officers and Directors: Susie Dobson,* Pres.; Paula Palzes,* V.P.; Jenny Cooney Carrillo; Michelle Day; Rob Marsala; David Pratt; Andrew Warne; Megan Worthy.
EIN: 954862600

68
Autodesk, Inc. Corporate Giving Program
c/o Community Rels. Dept.
111 McInnis Pkwy.
San Rafael, CA 94903-2773 (415) 507-6603
Contact: Julie Wilder, Mgr., Worldwide Community Rels.
E-mail: julie.wilder@autodesk.com; Application address for product donations: Gifts In Kind Intl., 1330 Bradock Pl. Alexandria, VA 22314;
URL: http://usa.autodesk.com/adsk/servlet/index?siteID=123112&id=1064603

Grantmaker type: Corporate giving program.
Financial data (yr. ended 01/31/11): Total giving, $2,422,000, including $700,000 for grants, $222,000 for employee matching gifts, and $1,500,000 for in-kind gifts.
Purpose and activities: Autodesk makes charitable contributions to nonprofit organizations involved with arts and culture, education, the environment, health and human services, and community development. Support is given on a national and international basis.
Fields of interest: Science; Human services; Health care; Environment; Engineering/technology; Education; Community/economic development; Arts; Youth; Young adults, male; Young adults, female; Young adults; Women; Terminal illness, people with; Substance abusers; Single parents;

Physically disabled; Native Americans/American Indians; Minorities; Military/veterans; Migrant workers; Mentally disabled; Men; LGBTQ; Infants/toddlers, male; Infants/toddlers, female; Infants/toddlers; Indigenous peoples; Immigrants/refugees; Homeless; Hispanics/Latinos; Girls; Economically disadvantaged; Disabilities, people with; Deaf/hearing impaired; Crime/abuse victims; Children/youth; Children; Boys; Blind/visually impaired; Asians/Pacific Islanders; AIDS, people with; Aging; African Americans/Blacks; Adults, women; Adults, men; Adults.
International interests: Asia; Canada; Central America; Europe; South America.
Type of support: Annual campaigns; Building/renovation; Capital campaigns; Continuing support; Curriculum development; Donated products; Emergency funds; Employee matching gifts; Employee volunteer services; Equipment; General/operating support; In-kind gifts; Matching/challenge support; Program development; Scholarship funds; Sponsorships; Use of facilities.
Limitations: Applications accepted. Giving on a national and international basis primarily in areas of company operations, including in Canada, Asia, and Europe; also giving in Latin America via employee matching. No support for athletic teams, religious organizations, political organizations, or discriminatory organizations. No grants for sporting events or advertising.
Publications: Application guidelines; Corporate report.
Application information: An online application form through giftsinkind.org is required for product donations. The Community Relations Department handles giving. The company has a staff that only handles contributions. A contributions committee reviews all requests. Application form required.
  Initial approach: Complete online application
  Copies of proposal: 1
  Deadline(s): None
  Committee meeting date(s): Monthly
  Final notification: 8 to 10 weeks
Number of staff: 1 full-time professional.

69
AWESNA, Inc.
(formerly Adventist Mission Society of America)
1712 Orchard Ave.
Glendale, CA 91206-4123

Established in 1990.
Grantmaker type: Public charity.
Financial data (yr. ended 12/31/10): Revenue, $53,775; assets, $311,914 (M); expenditures, $52,545.
Purpose and activities: The society promotes and advances Seventh-day Adventist Church mission work.
Fields of interest: Christian agencies & churches.
International interests: Philippines.
Type of support: Continuing support; Building/renovation.
Limitations: Giving on an international basis, primarily in the Philippines.
Officers: Alfonso Miguel, Jr., Pres.; Francisco Diongzon, V.P.; Wilma A. Dauglash, Secy.; Filomeno Alcaide, Treas.
EIN: 330397600

70
Bangladesh Relief Fund
519 Stassi Ln.
Santa Monica, CA 90402-1337 (513) 561-0996
FAX: (513) 561-1301;
E-mail: info@bangladeshrelief.org; URL: http://
www.bangladeshrelief.org

Established in 2004 in OH.
Grantmaker type: Public charity.
Financial data (yr. ended 12/31/09): Revenue,
$4,804; assets, $218,195 (M); gifts received,
$13,681; expenditures, $34,566; program services
expenses, $34,595; giving activities include
$34,595 for grants.
Purpose and activities: The organization works to
raise and distribute funds for poverty alleviation in
Bangladesh.
Fields of interest: International relief.
International interests: Bangladesh.
Type of support: In-kind gifts.
Limitations: Giving primarily in Bangladesh.
Officer: Muhit Rahman, Pres.
Director: Sarah Bachman.
EIN: 201527760

71
Battle Family Foundation
c/o A. George Battle
35 Vicente Rd.
Berkeley, CA 94705-1603
E-mail: sb@skipbattle.com

Established in 1999 in CA.
Donor: A. George Battle.
Grantmaker type: Independent foundation.
Financial data (yr. ended 12/31/10): Assets,
$4,987,218 (M); expenditures, $242,195;
qualifying distributions, $185,004; giving activities
include $185,004 for grants.
Purpose and activities: Giving primarily for higher
education.
Fields of interest: Arts; Higher education.
International interests: Africa.
Limitations: Applications not accepted. Giving
primarily in NH. No grants to individuals.
Application information: Contributes only to
pre-selected organizations.
Officers: A. George Battle, Pres.; Emily T. Battle, V.P.
and Treas.; Daniel K. Battle, Secy.
EIN: 943350554

72
The Benaka Foundation
36 Paseo de Castana
Rancho Palos Verdes, CA 90275-6385

Established in 1999 in CA.
Grantmaker type: Independent foundation.
Financial data (yr. ended 12/31/10): Assets,
$1,018,685 (M); expenditures, $262,543;
qualifying distributions, $262,533; giving activities
include $262,533 for 7 grants (high: $250,000;
low: $28).
Fields of interest: Education; Human services.
International interests: India.
Limitations: Applications not accepted. No grants to
individuals.
Application information: Contributes only to
pre-selected organizations.

Officer: Sundaresh Ramayya, C.E.O. and Pres.
EIN: 954748730

73
Maribeth Benham Family Foundation
20611 Ritanna Ct.
Saratoga, CA 95070-3021

Established in 1998 in CA.
Donor: Maribeth Benham.
Grantmaker type: Independent foundation.
Financial data (yr. ended 12/31/10): Assets,
$390,758 (M); expenditures, $335,370; qualifying
distributions, $332,500; giving activities include
$332,500 for grants.
Purpose and activities: Giving primarily to human
services and Roman Catholic organizations.
Fields of interest: Housing/shelter, homeless;
Human services; Children/youth, services; Family
services; Residential/custodial care; International
relief; Catholic agencies & churches; Economically
disadvantaged.
Limitations: Applications not accepted. Giving
primarily in CA. No grants to individuals.
Application information: Contributes only to
pre-selected organizations.
Officers: Maribeth Benham, Pres.; William Benham,
Secy. and C.F.O.
EIN: 770486557

74
The Benificus Foundation
(formerly Vallejo Ventures Private Foundation)
555 Bryant St., No. 722
Palo Alto, CA 94301
Ann and John Doerr's Giving Pledge: http://
givingpledge.org/#enter

Established in 1997 in CA.
Donors: Ann Howland Doerr; L. John Doerr.
Grantmaker type: Independent foundation.
Financial data (yr. ended 09/30/09): Assets,
$77,988,010 (M); expenditures, $20,259,324;
qualifying distributions, $20,257,208; giving
activities include $20,149,271 for 10 grants (high:
$10,524,861; low: $10,000).
Purpose and activities: Giving primarily for
education; funding also for medical research.
Fields of interest: Environment; Higher education;
Education; Medical research, institute; Foundations
(private grantmaking).
Type of support: Program-related investments/
loans.
Limitations: Applications not accepted. Giving
primarily in CA. No grants to individuals.
Application information: Contributes only to
pre-selected organizations.
Officers: Barbara S. Hager, C.E.O. and C.F.O.; L.
John Doerr III, Pres.; Ann Howland Doerr, V.P. and
Secy.
EIN: 770444504
Recent grants for international programs:
74-1 Alliance for Climate Protection, Washington,
DC, $10,524,861. 2009.
74-2 Conservation International, Arlington, VA,
$1,000,000. 2009.
74-3 Grameen Foundation USA, Washington, DC,
$1,000,000. 2009.
74-4 Kickstart International, San Francisco, CA,
$100,000. 2009.

75
The Benjamin Fund, Inc.
17 Peralta Ave.
San Francisco, CA 94110-4828

Established in 2003 in CA.
Donors: Alvin Benjamin; Rose Benjamin†.
Grantmaker type: Independent foundation.
Financial data (yr. ended 12/31/10): Assets,
$12,735,427 (M); gifts received, $10,863,060;
expenditures, $1,082,197; qualifying distributions,
$1,032,514; giving activities include $1,004,929
for 65 grants (high: $730,000; low: $100).
Fields of interest: Minorities/immigrants, centers/
services; International human rights.
Limitations: Applications not accepted. Giving
primarily in CA, DC, and NY. No grants to individuals.
Application information: Contributes only to
pre-selected organizations.
Officers: Medea Susan Benjamin, Pres.; Kirsten
Irgens-Moller, Secy.; Kevin Danaher, Treas.
EIN: 841618483

76
Bercaw Family Foundation
3530 W. Garry Ave.
Santa Ana, CA 92704-6423

Established in 2002 in CA.
Donors: Thomas Bercaw; Lisa Bercaw; The Todos
Santos Charitable Trust.
Grantmaker type: Independent foundation.
Financial data (yr. ended 12/31/10): Assets,
$872,575 (M); gifts received, $150,000;
expenditures, $175,862; qualifying distributions,
$170,000; giving activities include $170,000 for
grants.
Purpose and activities: Giving primarily to
Protestant churches, family services, and to a
cancer organization.
Fields of interest: Cancer; Family services;
Protestant agencies & churches.
International interests: Bahamas.
Limitations: Applications not accepted. Giving
primarily in CA and Nassau, Bahamas.
Application information: Unsolicited requests for
funds not accepted.
Officer: Thomas Bercaw, Pres.
EIN: 061649745

77
Bergman Family Foundation
c/o James R. Bergman
1217 Emerald Bay
Laguna Beach, CA 92651-1261
E-mail: jbergman@pacebell.net

Established in 1997 in CA.
Donor: James R. Bergman.
Grantmaker type: Independent foundation.
Financial data (yr. ended 12/31/10): Assets,
$1,552,856 (M); expenditures, $138,649;
qualifying distributions, $127,163; giving activities
include $127,163 for 24 grants (high: $28,663;
low: $500).
Fields of interest: Theological school/education;
International development; International economic
development; Protestant agencies & churches.
Type of support: General/operating support.
Limitations: Applications not accepted. Giving
primarily in CA. No grants to individuals.

Application information: Unsolicited requests for funds not accepted.
Officers: James R. Bergman, Pres. and C.F.O.; Judy G. Bergman, Secy.
EIN: 330743999

78
Erik E. and Edith H. Bergstrom Foundation, A Charitable Trust
P.O. Box 520
Palo Alto, CA 94302-0520

Newly formed in 2002 in CA; previously Erik E. and Edith H. Bergstrom Foundation, Inc.
Donors: Edith H. Bergstrom; Erik E. Bergstrom.
Grantmaker type: Independent foundation.
Financial data (yr. ended 09/30/10): Assets, $69,925,637 (M); expenditures, $3,623,015; qualifying distributions, $2,798,285; giving activities include $2,798,285 for grants.
Purpose and activities: Giving primarily for international affairs.
Fields of interest: Reproductive health, family planning; Health care; International affairs.
Limitations: Applications not accepted. Giving primarily in the U.S., Mexico and Central America. No grants to individuals.
Application information: Contributes only to pre-selected organizations.
Directors: Edith H. Bergstrom; Erik E. Bergstrom.
EIN: 912155835

79
The Philip and Muriel Berman Foundation
P.O. Box 48558
Los Angeles, CA 90048-0558
Contact: Jan Heffner, Admin.
FAX: (610) 437-1435; *E-mail:* pmbfound@ptd.net

Established in 1960 in PA.
Donors: Philip I. Berman†; Muriel M. Berman†.
Grantmaker type: Independent foundation.
Financial data (yr. ended 05/31/10): Assets, $37,115,121 (M); expenditures, $762,366; qualifying distributions, $575,398; giving activities include $447,857 for 32 grants (high: $125,000; low: $250).
Purpose and activities: Giving primarily for arts and culture, education, health and Jewish causes with special focus on eastern PA and Israel.
Fields of interest: Health care; Arts, cultural/ethnic awareness; Education; Jewish agencies & synagogues.
International interests: Israel.
Type of support: Technical assistance; Seed money; Research; Program development; Endowments.
Limitations: Applications not accepted. Giving limited to CA, eastern PA and Israel. No grants to individuals.
Application information: Contributes only to pre-selected organizations.
   Board meeting date(s): Biannually
Officers and Directors:* Nancy Berman Bloch,* Pres. and Exec. Dir.; Jack Kushner,* Secy.; Alan Bloch,* Treas.
Number of staff: 1 full-time professional; 1 part-time professional.
EIN: 236270983

80
Better U
11812 San Vicente Blvd., 4th Fl.
Los Angeles, CA 90049-5022
E-mail: comments@betterufoundation.org;
URL: http://betterufoundation.org/

Established in 2005 in CA.
Donors: James Carrey; Carrey Family Trust.
Grantmaker type: Independent foundation.
Financial data (yr. ended 12/31/10): Assets, $537,650 (M); gifts received, $319,846; expenditures, $1,097,577; qualifying distributions, $545,482; giving activities include $545,482 for grants.
Purpose and activities: Giving to provide global assistance that transforms the daily lives of people through imaginative and self-improving methods.
Fields of interest: International human rights; Independent living, disability; Education, reading; Higher education; Physically disabled.
Limitations: Applications not accepted. Giving primarily in CA; some giving also in Washington, DC. No grants to individuals.
Application information: Contributes only to pre-selected organizations.
Officers: James Carrey, C.E.O. and Pres.; John Rigney, Secy.-Treas. and C.F.O.
EIN: 203752045

81
Bickerstaff Family Foundation
c/o Gursey Schneider
1888 Century Park, E.
Century City, CA 90067-1702
Contact: Amy White
E-mail: bickfamilyfound@aol.com; Application address: P.O. Box 41100, Long Beach, CA 90853; Tel./Fax: (562) 433-5661

Established in 2000 in CA.
Donors: Deborah J. Bickerstaff; Glen E. Bickerstaff.
Grantmaker type: Independent foundation.
Financial data (yr. ended 12/31/10): Assets, $4,590,169 (M); expenditures, $1,708,667; qualifying distributions, $1,707,800; giving activities include $1,707,800 for grants.
Purpose and activities: Giving primarily for health associations and health care, including a hospital which provides medical treatment for pediatric HIV; funding also for other HIV programs, children, youth and social services, including scholarships for HIV infected teens to go to colleges or vocational schools.
Fields of interest: Higher education; Health care; Health organizations, association; Cancer; Crime/violence prevention, abuse prevention; Housing/shelter, homeless; Human services; Children/youth, services; Family services; Youth; Young adults; Terminal illness, people with; Crime/abuse victims; Children/youth; AIDS, people with; Adults, women; Women.
International interests: Malawi; South Africa.
Type of support: Curriculum development; Endowments; Grants to individuals; Research; Scholarships—to individuals.
Limitations: Applications accepted. Giving primarily in CA; giving limited to residents of Los Angeles and Orange counties in CA for scholarships.
Application information: Application form not required.
   Initial approach: Letter
   Copies of proposal: 1

Officers: Deborah J. Bickerstaff, Pres.; Glen E. Bickerstaff, Secy.
EIN: 954819633

82
Amy Biehl Foundation
P.O. Box 66
San Marcos, CA 92079-0066 (949) 650-5356
E-mail: info@amybiehl.co.za; Additional address (Cape Town office): 1 Plein St., 7th FL., Cape Town, 8001 South Africa; URL: http://www.amybiehl.org

Established in 1994 in CA.
Grantmaker type: Public charity.
Financial data (yr. ended 12/31/10): Revenue, $43,320; assets, $42,462 (M); gifts received, $43,063; expenditures, $41,441; giving activities include $9,500 for 1 grant to an organization outside the U.S.
Purpose and activities: The foundation supports human rights programs that promote small businesses for women, non-violence training, and a girls' soccer club.
Fields of interest: Athletics/sports, soccer; Civil/human rights, women; Community development, small businesses; Women.
International interests: South Africa.
Limitations: Giving limited to South Africa.
Publications: Newsletter.
Officers and Directors:* Linda R. Biehl,* Chair. and C.E.O.; Larry Kendall,* Secy.-Treas.; Kimberly Biehl; Molly Corbin; Carole Hoeneke; Judy Kendall; Scott Meinert.
EIN: 330641697

83
The Aaron and Marie Blackman Foundation, Inc.
423 Broadway, Rm. 706
Millbrae, CA 94030-1905 (650) 589-5111
Contact: Milton Jacobs, Pres.

Established in 1989 in CA.
Donor: Marie Blackman.
Grantmaker type: Independent foundation.
Financial data (yr. ended 12/31/10): Assets, $7,902,291 (M); gifts received, $1,000; expenditures, $154,871; qualifying distributions, $199,185.
Purpose and activities: Giving primarily to Jewish organizations, temples, and schools.
Fields of interest: Education; Human services; Aging, centers/services; Jewish agencies & synagogues.
International interests: Israel.
Application information: Application form not required.
   Initial approach: Letter or telephone
   Deadline(s): None
Officers and Directors:* Milton Jacobs,* Pres.; Elizabeth Landers,* Secy.; Matook Nissim; Peter Samuels; Ron Solomon; Stuart Weinstein.
EIN: 943105905

84
Saul Brandman Foundation
9595 Wilshire Blvd., No. 200
Beverly Hills, CA 90212-2502

Established in 1993 in CA.

Donor: Saul Brandman.
Grantmaker type: Independent foundation.
Financial data (yr. ended 12/31/09): Assets, $3,278,738 (M); gifts received, $11,526,739; expenditures, $11,783,741; qualifying distributions, $11,769,395; giving activities include $11,559,828 for 95 grants (high: $1,510,125; low: $100), and $10,000 for 1 grant to an individual.
Purpose and activities: Giving primarily for education and human services.
Fields of interest: Higher education; Education; Medical research, institute; Human services; Jewish federated giving programs; Children.
Limitations: Applications not accepted. Giving primarily in CA.
Application information: Unsolicited requests for funds not accepted.
Director: Joyce Christian O'Donnell.
EIN: 954456430
Recent grants for international programs:
84-1 American Friends of the Hebrew University, Los Angeles, CA, $1,510,125. 2009.
84-2 HELPS International, Addison, TX, $10,000. 2009.
84-3 Israel Guide Dog Center for the Blind, Warrington, PA, $25,000. 2009.

85

Brilliant Earth, Inc. Corporate Giving Program
12 Geary St., Ste. 605
San Francisco, CA 94108-5716 (415) 354-4623
URL: http://www.brilliantearth.com/giving-back/

Grantmaker type: Corporate giving program.
Purpose and activities: Brilliant Earth makes charitable donations to nonprofit organizations involved with helping communities in gemstone regions recover from abuses in the past and develop the skills needed to manage their natural resources effectively.
Fields of interest: Business/industry; Children's rights; Environment; International human rights; Children.
Type of support: General/operating support.
Limitations: Giving primarily in gemstone producing regions in Africa.

86

The Brin Wojcicki Foundation
(formerly The Brin Foundation)
1080 Marsh Rd., Ste. 100
Menlo Park, CA 94025-1025

Established in 2004 in CA.
Donor: Sergey Brin.
Grantmaker type: Independent foundation.
Financial data (yr. ended 12/31/09): Assets, $126,781,720 (M); expenditures, $7,852,712; qualifying distributions, $7,770,978; giving activities include $7,750,513 for 23 grants (high: $3,500,000; low: $5,000).
Purpose and activities: Giving primarily for private grantmaking foundation, as well as for human services; funding also for a Parkinson's disease organization.
Fields of interest: Parkinson's disease; Human services; Foundations (private grantmaking).
Limitations: Applications not accepted. Giving primarily in CA; some funding also in NY and VA. No grants to individuals.

Application information: Contributes only to pre-selected organizations.
Officers: Sergey Brin, Pres.; Michael Brin, Secy.
Director: Anne Wojcicki.
EIN: 201922947
Recent grants for international programs:
86-1 Ashoka: Innovators for the Public, Arlington, VA, $1,000,000. For general support. 2009.
86-2 Flip Flop Foundation, New York, NY, $30,513. For general support. 2009.
86-3 Friends of the Institut des Hautes Etudes Scientifiques, New York, NY, $200,000. For general support. 2009.
86-4 Ina Esaine Foundation, Burlingame, CA, $15,000. For general support. 2009.
86-5 Lurdes Mutola Foundation, Friends of, Palo Alto, CA, $20,000. For general support. 2009.

87

Harold and Colene Brown Family Foundation
1640 S. Sepulveda Blvd., Rm. 515
Los Angeles, CA 90025

Established in 1997 in CA.
Donors: Colene Brown; Harold Brown.
Grantmaker type: Independent foundation.
Financial data (yr. ended 12/31/10): Assets, $7,290,541 (M); gifts received, $265,651; expenditures, $397,467; qualifying distributions, $348,230; giving activities include $348,230 for grants.
Fields of interest: Higher education; Education; International affairs, research.
Type of support: General/operating support.
Limitations: Applications not accepted. Giving primarily in CA, Washington, DC, and NY. No grants to individuals.
Application information: Contributes only to pre-selected organizations.
Trustees: Colene Brown; Harold Brown; Ellen Brown Merewether; Deborah Brown Ploumis.
EIN: 336203761

88

Burnam Charitable Foundation
2951 28th St., No. 2070
Santa Monica, CA 90405

Grantmaker type: Independent foundation.
Financial data (yr. ended 03/31/11): Assets, $1,064,200 (M); expenditures, $149,843; qualifying distributions, $138,646; giving activities include $138,646 for grants.
Fields of interest: Health organizations; Arts; Education; Jewish agencies & synagogues.
International interests: Israel.
Limitations: Applications not accepted. Giving primarily in CA and NY. No grants to individuals.
Application information: Contributes only to pre-selected organizations.
Officer: Beth Burnam, C.E.O.
EIN: 954680145

89

Cadence Design Systems, Inc. Corporate Giving Program
c/o Community Involvement
2655 Seely Ave.
San Jose, CA 95134-1931 (408) 943-1234
Contact: Kathy Wheeler, Mgr., Community Rels.
E-mail: kwheeler@cadence.com; URL: http://www.cadence.com/community/

Grantmaker type: Corporate giving program.
Purpose and activities: Cadence makes charitable contributions to nonprofit organizations involved with education, the military, homeless women, children, and youth, and technology. Support is given primarily in areas of company operations in Arizona, Florida, Maryland, Massachusetts, Minnesota, New Jersey, New York, North Carolina, Oregon, Pennsylvania, Texas, Utah, and Washington, with emphasis on California, and in India, Japan, and the United Kingdom.
Fields of interest: Children/youth, services; Engineering/technology; Homeless, human services; Women, centers/services; Vocational education; Elementary/secondary education; Museums (science/technology); General charitable giving; Military/veterans.
International interests: United Kingdom; Japan; India.
Type of support: General/operating support; Employee volunteer services; Sponsorships; Employee matching gifts; Donated equipment; In-kind gifts.
Limitations: Giving primarily in areas of company operations in AZ, FL, MA, MD, MN, NC, NJ, NY, OR, PA, TX, UT, and WA, with emphasis on CA, and in India, Japan, and the United Kingdom.
Application information: Unsolicited requests for general operating support and sponsorships are not accepted.
 Initial approach: Letter of inquiry for equipment donations

90

Caipirinha Foundation
c/o The Presidio
39 Mesa St., Ste. 300
San Francisco, CA 94129-1019

Established in 2006 in DE.
Donors: George Gund III; Iara Lee; Riverbank Technologies, Inc.
Grantmaker type: Operating foundation.
Financial data (yr. ended 12/31/10): Assets, $98,188 (M); expenditures, $262,222; qualifying distributions, $238,541; giving activities include $225,550 for 40 grants (high: $10,000; low: $500).
Purpose and activities: Support for human rights, international law, United States foreign policy, independent media, and arts and culture.
Fields of interest: Arts; Media, film/video; Human services; International relief; International democracy & civil society development; International affairs, national security; International affairs, foreign policy; International human rights; Law/international law.
Limitations: Applications not accepted. Giving primarily in CA, Washington, DC, and NY.
Application information: Unsolicited requests for funds not accepted.
Officers and Director:* Iara Lee,* Pres.; Thomas Suniville, Secy.-Treas.
EIN: 203587464

91
The Capital Group Companies Charitable Foundation

333 S. Hope St.
Los Angeles, CA 90071-1406
URL: http://www.capgroup.com/about_us/charitable_programs.html

Established in 1997 in CA.
Donors: Capital Management Services, Inc.; Capital Bank & Trust Co.; The Capital Group Cos., Inc.; Capital Research & Management Co.; Capital International, Inc.
Grantmaker type: Company-sponsored foundation.
Financial data (yr. ended 06/30/10): Assets, $218,995,945 (M); gifts received, $9,303,042; expenditures, $15,998,460; qualifying distributions, $15,779,392; giving activities include $15,738,993 for 4,909 grants (high: $253,800; low: $40).
Purpose and activities: The foundation supports organizations involved with arts and culture, education, and human services.
Fields of interest: Museums; Performing arts, music; Arts; Higher education; Education; Children, services; Family services; Human services.
Type of support: Employee matching gifts; General/operating support.
Limitations: Applications not accepted. Giving on a national and international basis, with emphasis on CA, NY, Indonesia, Mexico, Pakistan, and Russia. No support for religious, political, or fraternal organizations or professional organizations. No grants to individuals.
Application information: Contributes only to pre-selected organizations.
Officers and Directors:* James M. Brown,* Chair.; Naomi H. Kobayashi, Secy.; Edith H.L. Van Huss, C.F.O.; James B. Lovelace; Theodore R. Samuels.
EIN: 954658856
Recent grants for international programs:
91-1 AFS-USA, New York, NY, $10,000. 2010.
91-2 AFS-USA, New York, NY, $10,000. 2010.
91-3 American School in London Foundation, Princeton, NJ, $29,400. 2010.
91-4 American School in London Foundation, Princeton, NJ, $11,400. 2010.
91-5 American Service to India Medical and Educational Foundations, Prerana, Costa Mesa, CA, $25,000. 2010.
91-6 Biosphere Foundation, Big Pine, CA, $34,000. 2010.
91-7 Biosphere Foundation, Big Pine, CA, $10,000. 2010.
91-8 Brazil Foundation, New York, NY, $37,000. 2010.
91-9 Caring for Cambodia, Austin, TX, $24,000. 2010.
91-10 Citizens Foundation USA, Schaumburg, IL, $30,000. 2010.
91-11 Developing Radio Partners, Washington, DC, $12,500. 2010.
91-12 Direct Relief International, Santa Barbara, CA, $15,000. 2010.
91-13 Doctors Without Borders USA, New York, NY, $11,700. 2010.
91-14 Embrace Global, San Francisco, CA, $50,000. 2010.
91-15 Embrace Global, San Francisco, CA, $10,500. 2010.
91-16 FLAX, Los Angeles, CA, $47,700. 2010.
91-17 Folk Arts Rajasthan, New York, NY, $20,000. 2010.

91-18 Folk Arts Rajasthan, New York, NY, $20,000. 2010.
91-19 Friends Without A Border, New York, NY, $10,800. 2010.
91-20 Grameen Foundation USA, Washington, DC, $50,000. 2010.
91-21 Half the Sky Foundation, Berkeley, CA, $25,000. 2010.
91-22 Himalayan Youth Foundation, Winter Park, FL, $15,000. 2010.
91-23 HOPE Worldwide, Wayne, PA, $25,000. 2010.
91-24 Human Development and Children Foundation, Atlanta, GA, $16,000. 2010.
91-25 International Justice Mission, Arlington, VA, $13,800. 2010.
91-26 Israel Cancer Research Fund, Beverly Hills, CA, $12,500. 2010.
91-27 Landesa, Seattle, WA, $20,000. 2010.
91-28 Landesa, Seattle, WA, $15,000. 2010.
91-29 Nepalese Youth Opportunity Foundation, Sausalito, CA, $20,000. 2010.
91-30 Operation Smile International, Norfolk, VA, $25,000. 2010.
91-31 Oxfam America, Boston, MA, $100,000. 2010.
91-32 Oxfam America, Boston, MA, $14,100. 2010.
91-33 Oxfam America, Boston, MA, $10,000. 2010.
91-34 Pacific Council on International Policy, Los Angeles, CA, $37,500. 2010.
91-35 Philip Hayden Foundation, Temecula, CA, $25,000. 2010.
91-36 Pratham USA, Pratham Mumbai Education, Houston, TX, $37,000. 2010.
91-37 Rainforest Action Network, San Francisco, CA, $15,000. 2010.
91-38 Salzburg Global Seminar, Washington, DC, $145,000. 2010.
91-39 Salzburg Global Seminar, Washington, DC, $65,000. 2010.
91-40 Salzburg Global Seminar, Washington, DC, $20,000. 2010.
91-41 Salzburg Global Seminar, Washington, DC, $14,901. 2010.
91-42 Sihanouk Hospital Corporation, Fort Worth, TX, $18,000. 2010.
91-43 Smile Train, New York, NY, $10,000. 2010.
91-44 Starfish Greathearts Foundation USA, Westport, CT, $37,000. 2010.
91-45 Survivor Corps, Washington, DC, $75,000. 2010.
91-46 Synapse Fund, Washington, DC, $11,400. 2010.
91-47 William Holden Wildlife Foundation, Beverly Hills, CA, $10,000. 2010.
91-48 World Fund, New York, NY, $18,000. 2010.

92
Caufield Family Foundation

4 Embarcadero Ctr., Ste. 3620
San Francisco, CA 94111-4155

Established in 1993 in CA.
Donor: Frank J. Caufield.
Grantmaker type: Independent foundation.
Financial data (yr. ended 06/30/11): Assets, $3,191,252 (M); gifts received, $751; expenditures, $536,620; qualifying distributions, $485,063; giving activities include $485,063 for grants.
Purpose and activities: Giving primarily for child abuse prevention, education, and the arts.

Fields of interest: Media, film/video; Museums; Arts; Education; Environment; Health organizations; Crime/violence prevention, child abuse; Human services; Children/youth, services; International affairs; Civil/human rights, immigrants; United Ways and Federated Giving Programs.
Limitations: Applications not accepted. Giving primarily in San Francisco, CA. No grants to individuals.
Application information: Contributes only to pre-selected organizations.
Officers: Frank J. Caufield, Pres.; Frank R. Caufield, V.P.; Kirsten N. Caufield, V.P.; Eva Jefferies, Secy.-Treas.
EIN: 943187012

93
Ping and Amy Chao Family Foundation

800 High St., Ste. 408
Palo Alto, CA 94301-2450 (650) 924-1104
FAX: (650) 323-2179;
E-mail: info@chaofoundation.org; URL: http://www.chaofoundation.org

Established in 2006 in CA.
Donor: Chao Family Trust.
Grantmaker type: Independent foundation.
Financial data (yr. ended 11/30/10): Assets, $10,718,402 (M); gifts received, $2,704,000; expenditures, $957,951; qualifying distributions, $940,534; giving activities include $744,950 for 21 grants (high: $200,000; low: $400), and $71,980 for 1 foundation-administered program.
Purpose and activities: Giving primarily to fund and nurture initiatives improving the health and well-being of children and youth in economically disadvantaged regions throughout the world, as well as to promote the spirit of philanthropy and developing awareness of non-profit practices and opportunities for service for the younger generation of China and the greater Chinese Diaspora. Because of these focuses, the foundation seeks to fund grants that either are run by a member of the Asian American community, or that focus on work in Asia or the Asian American community.
Fields of interest: Education; Human services; International affairs, goodwill promotion; Christian agencies & churches.
Limitations: Giving primarily in CA; some giving also NY. No grants to individuals.
Application information:
Initial approach: Use online application on foundation web site
Officers and Trustees:* Ping Chao,* Chair.; Amy Chao,* V.P.; Nancy Nguyen, Exec. Dir.; Shiu-Kai Chao.
EIN: 206750125

94
Chevron Global Fund

(formerly ChevronTexaco Global Fund)
c/o Chevron Corp., Public and Govt. Affairs
6001 Bollinger Canyon Rd.
San Ramon, CA 94583-2324 (925) 842-1000

Established in 1999 in NY.
Donor: Texaco Inc.
Grantmaker type: Company-sponsored foundation.
Financial data (yr. ended 12/31/10): Assets, $2,006,910 (M); expenditures, $3,021,453;

qualifying distributions, $2,954,517; giving activities include $2,954,517 for grants.
Purpose and activities: The foundation supports organizations involved with education, disaster relief, and international development.
Fields of interest: Disasters, preparedness/services; International development; Education.
International interests: Global programs.
Type of support: Building/renovation; Program development; Research.
Limitations: Applications not accepted. Giving to international organizations located in Silver Spring, MD and Portland, OR. No grants to individuals.
Application information: Contributes only to pre-selected organizations.
Officers and Directors:* Matthew Lonner,* Pres.; Ramiro Estrada,* Secy.; Rhonda Zygocki.
EIN: 311634478

95
Children's Hunger Fund
P.O. Box 7085
Mission Hills, CA 91346-7085   (818) 899-5122
FAX: (818) 899-9552;
E-mail: info@childrenshungerfund.org; Toll-free tel.: (800) 708-7589; URL: http://www.childrenshungerfund.org
Facebook: http://www.facebook.com/ChildrensHungerFund
Twitter: http://twitter.com/@isupportCHF
YouTube: http://www.youtube.com/user/chfcomm

Established in 1991.
Grantmaker type: Public charity.
Financial data (yr. ended 12/31/10): Revenue, $66,623,399; assets, $5,972,899 (M); gifts received, $66,590,703; expenditures, $66,409,963; giving activities include $1,986,820 for grants, $40,803,861 for grants to organizations outside the U.S., and $17,755,251 for grants to individuals.
Purpose and activities: The fund seeks to break this cycle of hunger and suffering, at least for some, so that hope can be restored, life can be lived, and dreams can be fulfilled.
Fields of interest: Agriculture/food; Children.
Type of support: Grants to individuals.
Limitations: Giving on a national and international basis.
Publications: Annual report; Financial statement.
Officers and Directors:* Ted Cox,* Chair.; Dick Griffith, Vice-Chair.; David K. Phillips,* Pres.; Tim Kirk, V.P., Opers.; Bryan McKinney, V.P., Ministry Devel.; Jane Harvey,* Secy.; Mark Chao,* Treas.; Barbara Cameron; Sue Hagen; Eric Heard; Greg Mitchell.
EIN: 954335462

96
Chintu Gudiya Foundation
453 Lincoln Ave.
Alameda, CA 94501-3235

Established in 1999 in CA.
Donors: Donald Ajit Lobo; Mari Tilos.
Grantmaker type: Independent foundation.
Financial data (yr. ended 06/30/10): Assets, $10,235,888 (M); expenditures, $624,272; qualifying distributions, $540,750; giving activities include $540,750 for grants.

Purpose and activities: Giving primarily for education and human services.
Fields of interest: International relief; Education; Human services; Children/youth, services; International development.
Limitations: Applications not accepted. Giving primarily in CA; some funding also in Washington, DC, and TX. No grants to individuals.
Application information: Contributes only to pre-selected organizations.
Officers and Directors:* Donald Ajit Lobo,* Pres.; Mari Grace Tilos,* Secy.-Treas.
EIN: 943315265

97
The Christensen Fund
260 Townsend St., Ste. 600
San Francisco, CA 94107   (415) 644-1600
Contact: Lourdes Inga, Grants Admin.
FAX: (415) 644-1601;
E-mail: info@christensenfund.org; URL: http://www.christensenfund.org
Facebook: http://www.facebook.com/pages/The-Christensen-Fund/170421729636697
Grants Database: http://www.christensenfund.org/funding/grants-search/
Twitter: http://twitter.com/christensenfund
YouTube: https://www.youtube.com/user/ChristensenFund?feature=mhee

Incorporated in 1957 in CA.
Donors: Allen D. Christensen†; Carmen M. Christensen†.
Grantmaker type: Independent foundation.
Financial data (yr. ended 12/31/09): Assets, $75,384,083 (M); gifts received, $2,900,000; expenditures, $20,192,093; qualifying distributions, $19,326,568; giving activities include $14,205,187 for 226 grants (high: $750,000; low: $1,000; average: $5,000–$100,000), and $236,000 for 4 foundation-administered programs.
Purpose and activities: The fund believes in the power of biological and cultural diversity to sustain and enrich a world faced with great change and uncertainty. Focus is on "bio-cultural" - the rich but neglected adaptive interweave of people and place, culture and ecology. The fund's mission is to buttress the efforts of people and institutions who believe in a biodiverse world infused with artistic expression and work to secure ways of life and landscapes that are beautiful, bountiful and resilient. The fund pursues this mission through place-based work in the region chosen for their potential to withstand and recover from the global erosion of diversity. Focus is on backing the efforts of locally-recognized community custodians of this heritage, and their alliances with scholars, artists, advocates and others. International efforts are also funded to help build global understanding of these issues. The fund works primarily through capacity and network building, knowledge generation, collaboration and mission-related investments.
Fields of interest: Arts, cultural/ethnic awareness; Visual arts; Museums; Environment, research; Environment, natural resources; Environment; Biology/life sciences; Indigenous peoples; Native Americans/American Indians.
International interests: Papua New Guinea; Kyrgyzstan; Australia; Vanuatu; Tajikistan; Mexico.
Type of support: Continuing support; Equipment; Program development; Conferences/seminars; Seed money; Fellowships; Research; Program evaluation; Matching/challenge support.

Limitations: Applications accepted. Giving primarily in the Southwest (Four Corners region), northern Mexico (including the Colorado Plateau and Delta, the Pueblo and Hispanic communities of the Rio Arriba/Rio Grande, the Sonoran Desert on both sides of the Mexican-U.S. border and east of the Colorado River, and the Sierra Tarahumara Montane West), Central Asia (the mountains and associated valleys of northeastern Turkey, the Kyrgyz Republic, and Tajikistan), the Rift Valley (especially southwest Ethiopia and adjacent areas of northern Kenya) Northern Australia (especially Arhem Land, Far Northern Queensland, and the Kimberley and Torres Strait Islands), and Melanesia, (Papua New Giunea and Vanuatu). No grants to individuals, or for capital funds, or building or renovation funding; no loans.
Publications: Financial statement; Grants list; Program policy statement (including application guidelines).
Application information: Please refer to the fund's web site for guidelines and program areas. For events such as conferences and workshops, apply at least six months in advance of their starting date to enable timely review and grant processing. Application form required.
  Initial approach: Pre-proposal as outlined on fund's web site
  Copies of proposal: 1
  Deadline(s): Submit pre-proposal between July 15 and Sept. 15 (for next calendar year)
  Board meeting date(s): Quarterly
  Final notification: 8 weeks
Officers and Directors:* C. Diane Christensen,* Chair. and Pres.; Thomas K. Seligman, V.P.; Tara Diann Stein,* Secy.; Kenneth Kirshenbaum,* Treas.; Kenneth Wilson, Ph.D., Exec. Dir.; E. Walter Coward, Jr., Ph.D.; Rodolfo Dirzo; Winona LaDuke; Peter Liu; John G. Robinson; Atossa Soltani; Richard Williams; Michael Nicoll Yahgulanaas.
Number of staff: 4 full-time professional; 5 full-time support; 1 part-time support.
EIN: 946055879
Recent grants for international programs:
97-1 Aboriginal Centre for the Performing Arts, South Brisbane, Australia, $50,000. For collaborative cultural exchange program between two innovative Indigenous performing arts organizations based in Australia (ACPA) and Brazil (Silo Cultural) to enrich personal, artistic and cultural practices of participating students and wider Indigenous arts communities in both countries. 2010.
97-2 Act Now, Port Moresby, Papua New Guinea, $25,000. To assist in creation of online community campaign for effective action on transparency, wise use of resources, and protection of biocultural diversity in Papua New Guinea. 2010.
97-3 Action for Environmental Public Advocacy, Addis Ababa, Ethiopia, $70,000. To underwrite partnership between AEPA, local governments and communities in Hadiya and Yayo in the Southern Region and in Oromiya, Ethiopia, to introduce eco-tourism and establish tourist lodges as livelihood options, based on cultural and natural resources. 2010.
97-4 Agency for Technical Cooperation and Development, Paris, France, $100,000. To strengthen the capacity of Central Asian creative practitioners as catalysts of social development in Tajikistan and Kyrgyzstan through educational, artistic and social programs as well as through artists' creative engagement with the local rural communities. 2010.

97-5 Agency for Technical Cooperation and Development, Paris, France, $100,000. To work with Kyrgyz pastoral communities in the Murghab plateau of Badakhshan Province in Tajikistan to develop environmentally-sustainable approaches for pastures and sustainable energy. 2010.

97-6 AID/WATCH, Woollahra, Australia, $100,000. For advocacy and outreach campaign carried out in collaboration with the Melanesian Indigenous Land Defense Alliance to investigate and expose where Australian aid practice in Melanesia undermines customary land tenure and practices to the benefit of commercial interests. 2010.

97-7 Alotau Environment, Alotau, Papua New Guinea, $21,500. To underwrite program of community awareness training on range of related biocultural issues in Milne Bay Province, Papua New Guinea. 2010.

97-8 Amesha Spenta, Khorog, Tajikistan, $16,900. To underwrite production of documentary film that portrays living pre-Islamic traditions, including the ancient seasonal calendar, celebrations and festivals as practiced today in the local Pamir communities in Tajik and Afghan Badakhshan. 2010.

97-9 Association for Nature and Sustainable Development, Cusco, Peru, $65,000. For institutional support and funds to host South-to-South exchanges on local knowledge and best practice for designing, planning, implementing and managing Agrobiodiversity Conservation Areas with groups from Central Asia and Ethiopia who are developing similar programs for their traditional crop varieties. 2010.

97-10 Australian Conservation Foundation, Carlton, Australia, $50,000. For return of Wuthathi Traditional Owners to their traditional lands in the Shelburne Bay region on eastern Cape York Peninsula, Queensland, and to assist them in the care, management and preservation of their culturally and ecologically significant lands. 2010.

97-11 Bangor University, Bangor, Wales, $101,000. To underwrite the cost of a PhD for Ethiopian student at the University of Bangor School of Environment, Natural Resources and Geography to support the building of national environmental leadership. 2010.

97-12 Barnard College, New York, NY, $185,000. To underwrite third and fourth phases of eco-anthropological research regarding local perceptions of socio-ecological change in New Ireland, Papua New Guinea, due to various drivers, including the growth of the oil palm plantation sector, carried out in collaboration with Ailan Awenes and the National Fisheries College. 2010.

97-13 Bio-Muras, Bishkek, Kyrgyzstan, $30,000. For efforts to re-establish reciprocal relations between culture, livelihoods and ecology through organization of annual Blooming Apricot festival, convening of workshop and Apricot fair in Samarkandek village and other local communities in Batken province of Kyrgyzstan. 2010.

97-14 Bioversity International, Rome, Italy, $430,000. To foster alliance between indigenous peoples, local communities, international research and advocacy organizations to co-create research and advocacy agendas to enhance agrobiodiversity, strengthen and maintain diverse local food systems within Indigenous Peoples and food sovereignty framework. 2010.

97-15 Bioversity International, Rome, Italy, $25,000. For roundtable discussions related to agrobiodiversity at La Settimana della Biodiversita, week-long celebration of Biodiversity in Rome as part of the International Year of Biodiversity. 2010.

97-16 Bismarck Ramu Group, Madang, Papua New Guinea, $200,000. For continued support for indigenous landholder capacity-building on environmental issues, land rights, and legal literacy in Madang, Papua New Guinea. 2010.

97-17 Bismarck Ramu Group, Madang, Papua New Guinea, $50,000. For continued support for indigenous landholder capacity-building on environmental issues, land rights, and legal literacy in Madang, Papua New Guinea. 2010.

97-18 Botanical Research Institute of Texas, Fort Worth, TX, $40,000. For final phase of botanical fieldwork in New Guinea, to update important reference materials on forest trees and poorly known plant groups, and to build a publicly accessible digital database on the distribution of plant diversity on the island. 2010.

97-19 Buku-Larrnggay Mulka Art Centre, Yirrkala, Australia, $90,000. For Yolngu Cultural Directors in carrying out the mission of the Mulka Project to sustain and protect Yolngu cultural knowledge in Northeast Arnhem Land under the leadership of Yolngu Elders. 2010.

97-20 Center of Museum Initiatives, Bishkek, Kyrgyzstan, $25,000. For capacity building of museum in Naryn Province and to support its innovative program utilizing space and expertise of local and national museums for promotion of biocultural thinking, place-based education and appreciation of the concepts of resilience and co-evolution. 2010.

97-21 Central Asia-Arts Management, Bishkek, Kyrgyzstan, $170,000. To promote Central Asian art of musical improvisation through cultural restoration of archival records of Kyrgyz traditional instrumental tunes - K'uus, production of anthology of these tunes and to underwrite ethnojazz program of the annual Bishkek jazz festival. 2010.

97-22 Central Asian Network for Arts and Culture, Bishkek, Kyrgyzstan, $50,000. For transboundary eco-cultural caravan/annual spring festival Aiguli-Guli-Surh, which celebrates endemic flowers as shared natural and cultural treasures and involves borderland communities of Batken-Isfana (Kyrgyzstan) and Isfara-Khudjand (Tajikistan). 2010.

97-23 Centre Francais des Etudes Ethiopiennes, Addis Ababa, Ethiopia, $25,000. To underwrite cost of filming last part of the late Maale King's funerary rite, and succession and installation of the new King as part of Christensen support for cultural expression and heritage transmission of southwest Ethiopian community. 2010.

97-24 Cobanaras Federacion Estatel de Sociedades de Solidandad Social, Ciudad Obregon, Mexico, $100,000. To continue production and transmission of Mayo language radio program Pajara Pinta around women's rights, health and the environment, and to build indigenous women's capacity to manage revolving loan funds that support sustainable rural micro-enterprises and livelihoods. 2010.

97-25 Common River, Mill Valley, CA, $50,000. To foster sense of pride in Sidama food, folklore and architectural traditions in the community of Aleta Wondo, in Southern Ethiopia, and to build a synergy between these traditions and emerging ideas to validate this tradition and to enhance a culturally based progress. 2010.

97-26 Confederation Europeenne des Proprietaires Forestiers, Luxembourg City, Luxembourg, $35,000. For travel and meetings to increase dialogue and cooperation between a coalition of forest rights holders groups to advocate globally the importance of locally controlled forestry, especially within the context of Reduced Emissions from Deforestation and Degradation (REDD). 2010.

97-27 Consejo EcoRegional Sierra Tarahumara, Chihuahua, Mexico, $100,000. To develop community strategies around adaptation to climate change effects through biodiversity monitoring and community consultation in Tarahumara's Urique-Batopilas Biological Corridor. 2010.

97-28 Consultative Group on Biological Diversity, San Francisco, CA, $55,000. For general support and support toward salaries for Gulf of California Funders Group for this association of North American funders of environmental concerns that supports learning and collaboration between foundations toward biodiversity conservation internationally. 2010.

97-29 Cross Cultural Journeys Foundation, Sausalito, CA, $20,000. For participation of international group of indigenous elders in Beyond Sustainability meeting in Hawaii, in order for them to share their insights with global leaders from mainstream sectors about how to bring about systemic change in the way humankind deals with the planet. 2010.

97-30 Culture and Art Society of Ethiopia, Addis Ababa, Ethiopia, $27,490. To underwrite publishing of book of Kambata tales and stories and three illustrated booklets and their dissemination across the southwest and the rest of Ethiopia to support local cultural expression and to encourage heritage transmission. 2010.

97-31 De Pamiri Handicrafts, Khorog, Tajikistan, $110,000. For continued support to the artisans of Badakhshan, by promoting livelihoods connected with local landscapes rich in cultural expression through training, design, materials and market development to revive the crafts traditions of the Pamirs in ways that are ecologically and economically sustainable. 2010.

97-32 Dir Biyabir, Mountain View, CA, $25,000. For renewal grant to underwrite partnership between Ethiopian Diaspora and rural community through environmental stewardship program among young men and women in Northern Shewa to regenerate degraded landscapes by growing indigenous trees and water source management. 2010.

97-33 Duke University, Durham, NC, $100,000. To strengthen Comcaac fisheries' governance for sustainability and resilience and build knowledge of how Comcaac culture and ecological characteristics of their fisheries plays a role in sustaining the fishing system in the Infiernillo Channel and in the Gulf of California. 2010.

97-34 Embassy of the Federal Democratic Republic of Ethiopia, London, England, $35,500. To underwrite public gathering to showcase Ethiopian culture, tradition and popular products to encourage development of balanced knowledge about the country, the people and its richness in cultural and biological diversity. 2010.

97-35 Erromango Cultural Association, Port Vila, Vanuatu, $18,500. For supplemental support to underwrite documentation and promotion of unique language, culture and customs of Erromango Island in Vanuatu through production of early reader books in vernacular language and about Erromangan customs and culture, and through other activities aimed at revival of the traditional system of governance. 2010.

97-36 Ethiopian Arts Forum, San Jose, CA, $53,290. To underwrite staging of exhibition of paintings and sculptures of Diaspora artist in Ethiopia's capital and Rift Valley towns to create dialogue between artists in the Diaspora, the general public and artists in the homeland. 2010.

97-37 Fahamu Limited, Oxford, England, $100,000. To enhance participation of network of West African women's rural organizations in the continent-wide We are the Solution Campaign for African agro-ecological solutions to the food crisis. 2010.

97-38 Fondi Zaboni Tojiki, Dushanbe, Tajikistan, $35,000. For activities of special working groups composed of academics, teachers, elders, stewards and youth on comprehensive research and re-enactment of forgotten ancient Tajik folk festivals, connected to celebration of nature seasons, agricultural cycles and stages of human life. 2010.

97-39 Fundacion Tarahumara Jose A. Llaguno, Monterrey, Mexico, $200,000. To continue comprehensive higher education program to enable Warijio, Pina, Pima, and Raramuri students to access the Autonomous University of Chihuahua and other state institutions to train a generation of Indigenous professionals; co-funding with Mexican private and public agencies. 2010.

97-40 Gaia Foundation, London, England, $50,000. For core support for general programs of organization committed to furthering biocultural diversity. 2010.

97-41 Gaia Foundation, London, England, $40,000. For supporting production of audio-visual and written materials, based on years of experience in protecting and sustaining sacred sites in Africa, South America and Asia, to stimulate discussion of long-term strategies on sacred sites protection at the International Society of Ethnobiology Congress. 2010.

97-42 Ganji Tabiat, Kulyab, Tajikistan, $30,000. For development of mechanisms and opportunities for domestication of wild zeera (Bunium persicum) and other culturally significant plants as means to improve livelihoods in rural mountainous communities in the Kulyab zone of Tajikistan and to lessen anthropogenic pressure on the landscape. 2010.

97-43 Global Diversity Fund, Brooklyn, NY, $40,000. For ongoing exchange of experience and practice in community-based approaches to biocultural heritage with partners from Christensen priority regions including at the International Society for Ethnobiology and International Funders for Indigenous Peoples meetings in Tofino. 2010.

97-44 Global Fund for Women, San Francisco, CA, $20,000. For general support to provide vital flexible financial support to community-based women's organizations responding to the needs of flood-affected communities in Pakistan. 2010.

97-45 GOLA Culture, Arts and Ecology Association, Istanbul, Turkey, $100,000. For continuing support for the Green Yayla Culture, Arts and Ecology Festivals of local music, dance, drama, history, folklore and ecological education coupled with livelihood development including through crafts and ecotourism in the mountain pastures of the Turkish Black Sea. 2010.

97-46 Grantmakers Without Borders, San Francisco, CA, $20,000. For renewal grant to provide general support to underwrite efforts to increase funding for international social change. 2010.

97-47 Greenstone Group, Warriewood, Australia, $55,000. To develop, in partnership with Rio Tinto Aboriginal Fund, Indigenous Guide for Philanthropists and Social Investors to encourage more effective Indigenous philanthropy and to improve relationships between grantmakers and Indigenous grant recipients. 2010.

97-48 Hawassa University, Awassa, Ethiopia, $150,000. To underwrite consensus building process among scientists, government and farmers in order to ensure sustained capacity to conserve agrobiodiversity and biocultural systems through the establishment of Agrobiodiversity Parks in the Gamo Highlands and Konso Special Woreda. 2010.

97-49 Hokotehi Moriori Trust, Rekohu, New Zealand, $21,000. For meeting of representatives from indigenous communities at International Society for Ethnobiology Congress to provide group forum for learning about and presenting sacred peace keeping traditions and their importance for sustaining biocultural diversity and resilience. 2010.

97-50 Indigenous Environmental Network, Bemidji, MN, $65,550. To bring indigenous traditional knowledge-based perspective and indigenous human-rights approach to the international climate negotiations by bringing indigenous experts in person and through the use of participatory media in international meetings on climate change. 2010.

97-51 Initiative for Living Community Action, Addis Ababa, Ethiopia, $200,000. To underwrite support to southwest Ethiopian schools providing laptops to help young students engage with their communities and environment to meet the challenges of climate change in the face of its increasing negative impact and communities' continued search for solutions. 2010.

97-52 Inochi, Berkeley, CA, $194,000. To develop and support local capacity to use digital technology in sustaining and enhancing transmission of oral traditions in Christensen regions, including meaningful engagement by Living Cultural Storybases project with the Conservation with the Earth(CWE) collaborative. 2010.

97-53 InsightShare, Oxford, England, $240,000. To develop capacity of indigenous communities and organizations in Northwest Mexico and Ethiopia to use Participatory Video and become active participants in a growing global community of local indigenous media hubs exploring climate change and biocultural diversity on their own terms. 2010.

97-54 Institute of International Education, New York, NY, $485,000. For continuing support for a Global Travel Fund to enable travel opportunities and exchanges that build on priorities in the regions or link them to international events,

including meetings of the International Society of Ethnobiology and the Conference on Biological Diversity. 2010.

97-55 Institute of International Education, New York, NY, $420,000. For continuing support for Global Travel Fund to enable opportunities of exchanges that build on priorities in the regions or link them to key biocultural diversity international events. 2010.

97-56 International Funders for Indigenous Peoples, Akwesasne, NY, $75,000. For core support and matching grant for important funders' association closely linked to the mission of The Christensen Fund. 2010.

97-57 International Humanities Center, Pacific Palisades, CA, $25,000. To underwrite production of special issue on contemporary Central Asia of the arts and ideas journal Gallerie to foster broad awareness and understanding of the region and explore the role of artistic creativity and culture in regional development. 2010.

97-58 International Society of Ethnobiology, Athens, GA, $70,000. To underwrite institutional development, including re-envisioning exercise with its members to frame new strategies, streamlining operations, enhancing membership benefits, expanding and diversifying membership, and supporting Indigenous and local participation in the biennial congresses. 2010.

97-59 James Cook University, Townsville, Australia, $50,000. For preparation for and participation of Indigenous Australian students from participating Indigenous communities to undertake the Master's of Development Practice (MDP) program at James Cook University and to meet the costs of their field work. 2010.

97-60 Kalpavriksh, Pune, India, $30,000. For consultation and side events of Indigenous and Community Conserved Areas (ICCAs) Consortium, at Tenth Conference of Parties of the UN Convention on Biological Diversity in October, at Nagoya, Japan to share experiences and push for legal recognition of ICCAs. 2010.

97-61 Kapululangu Aboriginal Women's Association, Halls Creek, Australia, $50,000. For Kapululangu Circles of Cultural Learning Pathways initiative for the intergenerational transfer of cultural knowledge at Balgo in the southern Kimberley region in Western Australia by funding the Aboriginal Women's Law Camp and the Dreaming Track Trip. 2010.

97-62 Kenya Community Development Foundation, Nairobi, Kenya, $96,700. For capacity building for Ethiopian and Kenyan Christensen partners working with stewards in Kenya and Ethiopia to deliver their services in ways that understand the ground, respect locally existing knowledge and enhance opportunities for diversified livelihoods. 2010.

97-63 Kivulini Trust, Nairobi, Kenya, $63,400. To facilitate use by Gabbras of Kenya of traditional pilgrimage routes to their ancestral sacred sites located in southern Ethiopia by building dialogue and negotiating passage with the Ethiopian Boran and to build capacity of Kivulini Trust. 2010.

97-64 Kyrgyz El, Bishkek, Kyrgyzstan, $35,000. To enable return of original meaning and cultural significance of Kyrgyz kalpak, traditional male headwear, through revival and adaptation of ancient methods of production and by strengthening connections between older custodians of traditions and youth. 2010.

97-65 Lambi Fund of Haiti, Washington, DC, $20,000. For general support for secondary relief and rehabilitation efforts to Haiti earthquake victims. 2010.

97-66 Land Is Life, Somerville, MA, $200,000. To build capacity of indigenous communities to protect their rights in climate change-related mitigation and adaptation initiatives, while informing international audiences about the critical role indigenous peoples play in developing appropriate and effective responses to the challenges of climate change. 2010.

97-67 Maji Culture and Natural Resource Protection and Development Association, Maji, Ethiopia, $30,000. To underwrite capacity building for community association in hills and coffee forests of Maji in southwestern Ethiopia to strengthen Dizzi identity, livelihoods and landscape relationships through representation in festivals, attention to traditional agriculture and maintaining the sacred forest of Wurug. 2010.

97-68 Melanesian Organizational Development Limited, Lae, Papua New Guinea, $52,800. For facilitation of healthy organizational development processes among people's organizations in Papua New Guinea and Bougainville, particularly groups working on issues related to protection of biocultural diversity. 2010.

97-69 Mizan-Tepi University, Mizan Teferi, Ethiopia, $30,000. To underwrite showcasing of music, dance, food and creative artifacts of Indigenous communities living around Tepi and Mizan Teferi as a medium to initiate dialogue, validate traditional knowledge and lifeways, and bridge the gap between the university and the communities. 2010.

97-70 Mountain Societies Development Support Programme, Osh, Kyrgyzstan, $25,000. For children in pastoralist communities of Karakulja district (Southern Kyrgyzstan) with culturally appropriate quality learning opportunities and enhance their biocultural learning through establishment of mobile kindergartens and mobile libraries. 2010.

97-71 Mountain Societies Development Support Programme, Dushanbe, Tajikistan, $25,000. To convene grantees and stewards of agrobiodiversity from Tajikistan and Kyrgyzstan with the Global Partnership for Indigenous Agrobiodiversity and Food Sovereignty, to facilitate collective learning and advance common objectives and concerns for agrobiodiversity and resilience of local food systems. 2010.

97-72 Mukogodo Pastoralist Integrated Development Organization, Nairobi, Kenya, $20,000. To underwrite participatory mapping of Il Ngwesi conservancy to help better understand, represent and communicate biocultural knowledge of the Il Ngwesi Community of Kenya and to maintain socio-cultural connections and meanings to the landscape. 2010.

97-73 Nancy Sullivan and Associates, Madang, Papua New Guinea, $30,000. For research and biocultural documentation of a series of caves at the headwaters of the Arafundi and Karawari Rivers in East Sepik Province, Papua New Guinea, to protect the area from urgent threats including industrial logging and mining. 2010.

97-74 Native Seeds/Southwestern Endangered Aridland Resource Clearing House, Tucson, AZ, $150,000. For continued support to foster and promote agrobiodiversity and health leading to food and livelihood security within Tarahumara communities in regions of the Sierra Madre. 2010.

97-75 Northern Gulf Resource Management Group, Georgetown, Australia, $50,000. For indigenous traditional cultural knowledge mapping and recording by Traditional Owners of their traditional country in the Northern Gulf of Carpentaria region of Australia. 2010.

97-76 Norwegian Peoples Aid, Oslo, Norway, $40,000. To bridge knowledge gap that exists between communities in south Ethiopia, agencies that facilitate tourism, institutions that view tourism as vehicle for poverty reduction and the private sector whose funds are sought to complement the development of the industry. 2010.

97-77 Oxfam Australia, Carlton, Australia, $50,000. For participation of Indigenous women from north Australia at a summit in Canberra as part of the Straight Talk national program which seeks to build lasting relationships between Australian Indigenous women and women in parliament. 2010.

97-78 Oxford University, Oxford, England, $46,500. To underwrite translation of historical manuscripts written about southwest Ethiopia that focus on received knowledge with regards to governance systems, territorial structure and conquest, from French into the English Language, to encourage heritage transmission and to complement social memory. 2010.

97-79 Oxford University, Oxford, England, $28,000. To establish sustainable heritage program amongst Mursi of Lower Omo to safeguard heritage, to enhance local livelihoods, and to build knowledge about past and present rangeland cultures in southwest Ethiopia. 2010.

97-80 Papua New Guinea Institute of Biological Research, Goroka, Papua New Guinea, $200,000. For continued core support to PNG Institute of Biological Research for its biocultural research and training efforts, aiming to contribute to the emergence of a culturally appropriate national indigenous conservation strategy. 2010.

97-81 PO Science and Education, Dushanbe, Tajikistan, $110,000. To contribute to preservation and restoration of folklore and music archives in private Tajik collections both through digitization and then by sharing the material with communities from which they were collected in order to support intergenerational cultural transfer. 2010.

97-82 Prescott College, Prescott, AZ, $70,000. To create education and participatory research opportunities with Seri youth building capacity for effective resource management of their territory including new Ramsar site in the Infiernillo Canal, and ecosystems ranging from Desemboque de las Seris to Bahia de Kino. 2010.

97-83 Pronatura Noroeste-Mar de Cortes, Ensenada, Mexico, $75,000. To foster radio programming and communication processes to heighten recognition of biocultural values of the Mayo, Yaqui and Guarijio groups and to build indigenous capacity for decision-making around sustainable land use in Southern Sonoran region. 2010.

97-84 Rainforest Action Network, San Francisco, CA, $100,000. For continued support to RAN's Rainforest Agribusiness Campaign in New Guinea through strengthening relationships with local allies; bringing international attention to the issues surrounding commodity plantation expansion; and influencing corporate and public sector operations that impact forests and communities. 2010.

97-85 Regional Environmental Centre for Central Asia, Kyrgyz Branch, Bishkek, Kyrgyzstan, $50,000. To mobilize and channel creative forces of artistic intelligentsia toward the formation of modern environmental consciousness rooted in traditional worldviews of Kyrgyz people and toward improvement of culturally appropriate landscape management in Jalalabad (South) and Chui (North) regions of Kyrgyzstan. 2010.

97-86 Research and Conservation Foundation of Papua New Guinea, Port Moresby, Papua New Guinea, $200,000. To support Conservation Education Program for training in indigenous biocultural knowledge and conservation for practicing and trainee teachers and students in Eastern Highlands, Morobe, and Madang, and for Conservation Education Resource Centres in provinces. 2010.

97-87 Resilience Alliance, Wolfville, Canada, $40,000. To enable development of updated version of Resilience Workbook designed to enable practical application of resilience theory based on the lessons learned from testing the pilot version of the Workbook. 2010.

97-88 Rural Development Fund, Bishkek, Kyrgyzstan, $300,000. For development of local co-management models for forest resources in Batken and Chui regions of Kyrgyzstan based on integration of traditional knowledge and sound science recommendations, active partnership of local communities, local governments and state agencies. 2010.

97-89 Rushnoe, Rasht, Tajikistan, $35,000. For local garden museum of living traditional horticulture as educational, cultural and agrobiodiversity space created and maintained by stewards of biocultural diversity in the community of Jaffr, in the Rasht valley of Tajikistan. 2010.

97-90 Saint Ignatius Church, San Francisco, CA, $15,000. For Native American component exhibition and symposium in San Francisco centered on visual dialogue between representatives of Native American artists and artists from Nauiyu Nambiyu Aboriginal community of Daly River, Northern Territory, Australia. 2010.

97-91 Save Papua New Guinea, Lae, Papua New Guinea, $50,000. To underwrite production and launching of educational video series promoting the traditional food cultures and culinary arts of indigenous Papua New Guinean societies. 2010.

97-92 Slow Food International, Cuneo, Italy, $140,000. For core support to increase engagement of major global social movement around good, clean and fair food with indigenous communities, who are custodians of agricultural biodiversity, through workshops, an Indigenous Coordinator, and improved communications and networking. 2010.

97-93 SnowChange Project, Finland, $20,000. To enable representatives of nomadic communities to share their experience in maintaining traditional modes of transmission of pastoral knowledge through Nomadic Education initiative, while providing opportunity for developing a strategy and a plan for future collaborative work. 2010.

97-94 Social and Environmental Entrepreneurs, Calabasas, CA, $50,000. To advance recognition of indigenous rights and strengthen autonomous indigenous organization in communities in the Sierra Madre Occidental who are struggling with the respective environmental, cultural and economic impacts of mining and tourism development. 2010.

97-95 Social Justice Forum, Addis Ababa, Ethiopia, $25,000. For renewal grant to underwrite dissemination of ideas of justice and law among civil servants, communities and other stake holders and to provide free legal service to benefit vulnerable groups in the southern Regional State of Ethiopia. 2010.

97-96 Stanford University, Stanford, CA, $20,000. For supplemental support for conservation science fellowship for Senior Research Scientist to implement ornithological and bio-cultural diversity field research, education and local partnerships in Kars and Idgir, Turkey. 2010.

97-97 Taalim-Forum, Bishkek, Kyrgyzstan, $185,000. To facilitate biocultural learning in Kyrgyzstan through advancing place-based education, support of community initiatives related to biocultural diversity, backing the Ak-Talaa village resource center in Naryn province and continuation of the training program in participatory video. 2010.

97-98 Taalim-Forum, Bishkek, Kyrgyzstan, $12,000. To facilitate biocultural learning in Kyrgyzstan through advancing place-based education, support of community initiatives related to biocultural diversity, backing the Ak-Talaa village resource center in Naryn province and continuation of the training program in participatory video. 2010.

97-99 Tahoe-Baikal Institute, South Lake Tahoe, CA, $10,000. For exchange between Washoe and Buryat peoples to further enhance and sustain their relationship by sharing mutual efforts to protect sacred sites and to revitalize their native languages, traditional cultures and youth engagement. 2010.

97-100 Tajik Dance Initiative, Dushanbe, Tajikistan, $45,000. For revitalization of authentic Tajik dance culture through networking of stewards of dance traditions from all regions of Tajikistan, workshops/masterclasses by the stewards for professional and nascent choreographers, and documenting the current state of performing arts in visual media. 2010.

97-101 Tampara Duanta Melanesia, Buka, Papua New Guinea, $125,000. To strengthen biocultural revitalization efforts, including the Kaur Festival, with a continued focus on Central Bougainville (Wakunai and Kieta Districts). 2010.

97-102 Tides Center, San Francisco, CA, $40,000. For development of articles, by indigenous writers and others, contrasting traditional land-management practices and adaptation approaches to climate change with the solutions emerging under the REDD program proposed under the UN Climate Change Convention, and exploring the experience of indigenous communities with REDD program. 2010.

97-103 Tulele Peisa, Buka, Papua New Guinea, $30,000. For ecologically and culturally sustainable relocation and resettlement of the Carteret/Tulun Islands community (facing threats from climate change) to Tinputz, Bougainville. 2010.

97-104 Union of Creative Forces, Bishkek, Kyrgyzstan, $15,000. For rebuilding capacity and restoring instruments and equipment of Manas Presidential Chamber Orchestra, vandalized and destroyed during mass riot in Bishkek, Kyrgyzstan. 2010.

97-105 United Nations Development Fund for Women, New Delhi, India, $30,000. For globally important applied research around indigenous women's knowledge and practice within selected shifting cultivation systems of Himalayan South Asia in the face of growing commercialization, land and forest privatization, climate change and changes in gender relations. 2010.

97-106 United Nations University, Tokyo, Japan, $47,000. For various activities around Indigenous peoples, biocultural diversity, and traditional knowledge maintenance, with a focus on traditional marine resource management in Melanesia. 2010.

97-107 Universita di Roma, Rome, Italy, $50,000. For fellowship program to build capacity of Ethiopian youth from indigenous communities to be leaders in development in their communities through internship in international development organization and study in a world class university. 2010.

97-108 University of California, Santa Cruz, CA, $45,000. For supplemental support for building capacity of two young scholars currently with the University California, Santa Cruz, to give intellectual leadership in landscape stewardship and to raise knowledge about biodiversity in Ethiopia's southwest. 2010.

97-109 University of Central Asia, Bishkek, Kyrgyzstan, $50,000. For publication of original academic research on musical arts of Pamir, Tajikistan and herder's manual, designed for pastoralist communities, Pasture Committees and governmental authorities as a practical tool for improvement of pasture and livestock management in Kyrgyzstan. 2010.

97-110 University of Kent, Kent, England, $138,200. To fund a PhD project in the School of Anthropology and Conservation at University of Kent, for the study of the role, current status, ethnobotany and social value of the spiritual ecology within sacred sites in southwestern Ethiopia. 2010.

97-111 University of Kent, Kent, England, $138,100. To underwrite the training of a young Environmental Leader from southwest Ethiopia at Kent Law School, at the University of Kent, to pursue a PhD and to conduct research. 2010.

97-112 Vanuatu National Cultural Council, Port Vila, Vanuatu, $55,000. For supplemental support to underwrite planning process for international convening regarding possible development of new indicators of wealth and well-being for Melanesia. 2010.

97-113 Water Users Association, Porshnev, Tajikistan, $30,000. For efforts of the water user association Ob Umed to enhance resilience and climate change adaptation of the nine communities of Porshnev in Tajik Badakhshan through rehabilitation and strengthening of traditional water management institutions. 2010.

97-114 World Wildlife Fund, Washington, DC, $25,000. For continued funding to empower Raramuri in Chihuahua to participate in planning and decision-making for sustainable livelihoods and in protecting biodiversity and to facilitate regional planning and activities around biocultural diversity with NGOs working in Sierra Tarahumara region. 2010.

97-115 Wungal Environment Foundation, Mooroobool, Australia, $375,000. To enable Wungal Environment Foundation to establish its administrative infrastructure, solicit funds from the donor community and begin operations to instigate projects to empower Indigenous Australians to care for their country and sustainably use their natural resources. 2010.

97-116 Yarrabah Police Citizens Youth Club, Yarrabah, Australia, $45,237. For production and distribution of lasting, accurate portrayal of the origins, oral history and settlement of the Yarrabah Aboriginal Community, Far North Queensland in DVD format. 2010.

98
Christian Children's Health and Hope Mission

(also known as United Cambodian Charity)
2000 S. Melrose Dr., Rm. 134
Vista, CA 92081-8772

Established in 1998 in CA.
Grantmaker type: Public charity.
Financial data (yr. ended 12/31/10): Revenue, $998,693; assets, $26,724 (M); gifts received, $998,693; expenditures, $1,014,630; giving activities include $894,378 for grants, and $85,575 for grants to organizations outside the U.S.
Purpose and activities: The organization works to provide clean water, food, healthcare, education, and safety to suffering children in Cambodia.
Fields of interest: Education; Agriculture/food; Nutrition; Health care; Aging.
International interests: Cambodia.
Limitations: Giving primarily to Cambodia.
Officers: Stan Schmunk, Chair.; Michael Sholer, Pres.; Joyce Schmunk, Secy.-Treas.
EIN: 330801951

99
Chino Cienega Foundation

901 N. Palm Canyon Dr., Ste. 200
Palm Springs, CA 92262-4451
E-mail: info@chinofound.org; URL: http://www.chinofound.org/

Established in 1985 in CA; funded in 2003.
Donor: Frank Culver Nichols Revocable Trust.
Grantmaker type: Independent foundation.
Financial data (yr. ended 12/31/10): Assets, $6,912,470 (M); expenditures, $332,570; qualifying distributions, $312,308; giving activities include $297,300 for 12 grants (high: $50,000; low: $300).

Purpose and activities: Giving to engage in and support educational and charitable activities that foster crosscultural and international understanding and cooperation, that encourage the viability of local communities and that promote sustainable natural ecosystems.
Fields of interest: Higher education, university; International affairs, goodwill promotion; International development; International economic development.
International interests: Cambodia; Cuba; Laos; Vietnam.
Type of support: Mission-related investments/loans.
Limitations: Applications not accepted. Giving primarily in NC and NY. No grants to individuals.

Application information: Contributes only to pre-selected organizations.
Officers: Steven C. Nichols, Pres.; Sarah J. Benson, Secy.-Treas.
Director: Robert Wolcott.
EIN: 412075864

100
Cisco Systems Foundation
170 W. Tasman Dr.
San Jose, CA   95134-1706   (408) 527-3040
Contact: Peter Tavernise, Exec. Dir.
E-mail: ciscofoundation@cisco.com; URL: http://www.cisco.com/go/foundation
Grants List: http://www.cisco.com/web/about/ac48/svig_recipients_fy2011.html

Established in 1997 in CA.
Donors: Cisco Systems, Inc.; Scientific-Atlanta Fdn. Inc.
Grantmaker type: Company-sponsored foundation.
Financial data (yr. ended 07/31/10): Assets, $124,500,407 (M); gifts received, $19,704,829; expenditures, $10,795,948; qualifying distributions, $10,298,583; giving activities include $6,155,986 for 92 grants (high: $541,166; low: $10,000), and $3,885,496 for employee matching gifts.
Purpose and activities: The foundation supports programs designed to improve access to basic human needs, education, and economic opportunity. Special emphasis is directed toward programs designed to address underserved communities; and provide solutions that utilizes the power of the internet and communications technology.
Fields of interest: Crime/violence prevention; Public health, obesity; Elementary/secondary education; Vocational education; Health sciences school/education; Adult/continuing education; Education, reading; Education; Public health, clean water supply; Health care; Employment, training; Employment, retraining; Food services; Housing/shelter, development; Housing/shelter; Disasters, preparedness/services; Children, services; Human services, financial counseling; Human services; Economic development; Social entrepreneurship; Community development, small businesses; Microfinance/microlending; Mathematics; Engineering/technology; Science; Children/youth; Minorities; Women; Girls; Economically disadvantaged; Homeless.
Type of support: General/operating support; Continuing support; Program development; Curriculum development; Employee volunteer services; Employee matching gifts.
Limitations: Applications accepted. Giving primarily in areas of company operations, with emphasis on San Jose, CA. No support for discriminatory organizations, religious, political, or sectarian organizations no of direct benefit to the entire community, public schools or school systems, charter schools, school foundations, booster clubs, colleges or universities, pass-through organizations, or grantmaking foundations. No grants to individuals, or for research, start-up needs, scholarships, stipends, or loans, athletic events, competitions, or tournaments, conferences or seminars, festival or similar one day events, field trips, fundraising events or sponsorships, capital campaigns, or challenge or matching grants; generally, no equipment funding.

Publications: Application guidelines; Grants list; IRS Form 990 or 990-PF printed copy available upon request.
Application information: A full proposal may be requested at a later date for Global Impact Grants. Organizations receiving Community Impact Cash Grants -Silicon Valley are asked to provide periodic progress reports. Application form required.
  Initial approach: Complete online eligibility quiz and application form
  Deadline(s): None for Global Impact Grants; Jan. 30 to Feb. 17 for Community Impact Cash Grants -Silicon Valley
  Board meeting date(s): Fall and Spring
  Final notification: June for Community Impact Cash Grants -Silicon Valley
Officer and Trustees:* John P. Morgridge,* Chair.; John T. Chambers, Pres.; Larry R. Carter,* Secy.-Treas.; Peter Tavernise, Exec. Dir.; Carlos Dominguez; Patrick Finn; Karen McFadzen; Michael Quinn; Michael Vessey; Tae Yoo.
Number of staff: 1 part-time support.
EIN: 770443347
Recent grants for international programs:
100-1 American Red Cross National Headquarters, Washington, DC, $250,000. Toward immediate response efforts to earthquake in Haiti. 2010.
100-2 Blue Planet Run Foundation, Redwood City, CA, $75,000. For expanding the first global water network to increase group collaboration, capacity to implement sustainable water projects at lower costs, and impact data to attract more funders and improve the worldwide delivery of safe drinking water. 2010.
100-3 BluWorld, Montour Falls, NY, $200,000. For empowering users by providing them with a means to connect and communicate (via email accounts), as well as access to information and resources (portal) to develop knowledge and skills they need to participate in social and economic growth and development. 2010.
100-4 Build Change, Mill Valley, CA, $150,000. For expanding technical assistance in China to reach thousands of homeowners. 2010.
100-5 Gemin-i.Org, London, England, $200,000. To develop skills across the curriculum among pupils from primary schools globally, through online, collaborative learning. 2010.
100-6 Give2Asia, San Francisco, CA, $166,985. For strengthening the delivery capacity of China Foundation for Poverty Alleviation's micro-finance project management and IT systems. 2010.
100-7 Give2Asia, San Francisco, CA, $107,000. For building healthy, resilient futures for youth in earthquake-affected communities in Dujiangyan region, Sichuan Province through targeted psychosocial programs and capacity building for the institutions and organizations that support them. 2010.
100-8 Give2Asia, San Francisco, CA, $107,000. For providing psychological aid and training to teachers in seriously earthquake impacted areas to help the children and communities of these areas healthily recover. 2010.
100-9 Give2Asia, San Francisco, CA, $21,400. For supporting 50 rural high school students with financial need with 3-year scholarships. 2010.
100-10 Grameen Foundation USA, Washington, DC, $495,942. For dramatically increasing the scale, efficiency, and poverty alleviation impact of microfinance. 2010.
100-11 Lu'ma Native Housing Society, Vancouver, Canada, $25,000. For empowering the homeless to help themselves. 2010.

100-12 Unitus, Inc., Seattle, WA, $73,098. To provide training, and pilot online global community with e-enabled training materials, best practices, and collaboration technology to accelerate Unitus microfinance partners capabilities so they can scale operations. 2010.
100-13 Water.org, Kansas City, MO, $74,250. Toward the development and release of the Online Giving Network thereby deferring infrastructure costs whose savings can be redirected to other program work. 2010.

101
The Clara Fund
101 1st St., No. 235
Los Altos, CA   94022-2778

Established in 2003 in CA.
Donor: Lorene Arey.
Grantmaker type: Independent foundation.
Financial data (yr. ended 12/31/10): Assets, $5,044,234 (M); gifts received, $3,267; expenditures, $831,136; qualifying distributions, $619,667; giving activities include $619,667 for grants.
Fields of interest: International development; Philanthropy/voluntarism; Education; Women, centers/services; Children/youth; Women; Economically disadvantaged.
Limitations: Applications not accepted. Giving primarily in CA. No grants to individuals.
Application information: Unsolicited requests for funds not accepted.
Officers: Lorene Arey, Pres.; Paris Arey, V.P.; Holly Marr, Secy.
Directors: Haley Perkins; Hansen Perkins.
EIN: 582672863

102
The Clarity Project Contributions Program
2784 Homestead Rd.
Santa Clara, CA   95051-5353   (408) 921-1990
E-mail: info@clarityproject.com; URL: http://www.the-clarity-project.com
B Corporation Profile: http://www.bcorporation.net/theclarityproject

Grantmaker type: Corporate giving program.
Purpose and activities: The Clarity Project is a certified B Corporation that donates a percentage of net profits to charitable organizations. Support is given primarily in Sierra Leone.
Fields of interest: Elementary/secondary education; Education, reading; Employment, training; International development; Rural development.
International interests: Sierra Leone.
Type of support: General/operating support; Program development.
Limitations: Giving primarily in Sierra Leone.

103
Coalition to Abolish Slavery & Trafficking
5042 Wilshire Blvd., Ste. 586
Los Angeles, CA   90036-4305   (213) 365-1906
FAX: (213) 365-5257; E-mail: info@castla.org;
URL: http://www.castla.org
Facebook: http://www.facebook.com/pages/CAST-Los-Angeles/114867600162
Twitter: http://twitter.com/antitrafficking

Established in 1998.
Grantmaker type: Public charity.
Financial data (yr. ended 06/30/10): Revenue, $1,474,913; assets, $536,761 (M); gifts received, $1,468,096; expenditures, $1,617,064; giving activities include $25,000 for grants to organizations outside the U.S.
Purpose and activities: The coalition provides services to survivors of trafficking through crisis intervention, case management, and social services coordination.
Fields of interest: Education, ESL programs; Education; Health care; Mental health/crisis services; Legal services; Women, centers/services; International human rights.
Publications: Newsletter.
Officers and Directors:* Sr. Catherine Marie Kreta,* C.S.J., Pres.; Kevin R. Davis,* V.P.; Sal Varela, Secy.; Rachel J. Lee,* Treas.; Kay Buck,* Exec. Dir.; Kenneth Bloch; Cathy King; Chancee Martorell; Kathryn McMahon; Liliana T. Perez; Molly Rhodes.
EIN: 100008533

104
Columbia Foundation
77 Van Ness Ave., Ste. 200
San Francisco, CA 94102-6042 (415) 861-5657
Contact: Susan Reed Clark, Exec. Dir.
E-mail: info@columbia.org; Letter of inquiry e-mail: loi@columbia.org; e-mail for confirmation of LOI receipt (if a confirm has not been received within a week following appropriate deadline) Alex Hoskyns-Abrahall: alex@columbia.org; URL: http://www.columbia.org

Incorporated in 1940 in CA.
Donors: Madeleine H. Russell‡; Christine H. Russell; SIT Investment Assocs., Inc.
Grantmaker type: Independent foundation.
Financial data (yr. ended 05/31/11): Assets, $81,532,388 (M); gifts received, $13,837; expenditures, $3,248,246; qualifying distributions, $2,264,708; giving activities include $2,264,708 for grants.
Purpose and activities: While the foundation's broad philanthropic purpose has given it flexibility to respond to changing social conditions, it has nevertheless maintained its long-standing interest in world peace, human rights, the environment, cross-cultural and international understanding, the quality of urban life, and the arts. Within each of these areas the board of directors sets new priorities as conditions change.
Fields of interest: Arts; Environment, natural resources; Environment; Animals/wildlife, preservation/protection; Agriculture/food; Civil/human rights, advocacy; Civil liberties, advocacy; Civil liberties, right to die; Urban/community development; Social sciences.
International interests: England.
Type of support: Program-related investments/loans; General/operating support; Continuing support; Management development/capacity building; Building/renovation; Program development; Film/video/radio; Publication; Seed money; Curriculum development; Research.
Limitations: Applications accepted. Giving primarily in the San Francisco Bay Area, CA. Some foundation-initiated giving in the United Kingdom and other countries for the arts. No support for private foundations, institutions supported by federated campaigns or heavily subsidized by government funds, or projects in medicine or

religion. No grants to individuals, (except for filmmakers with a fiscal sponsorship for their projects), or for scholarships, fellowships, ongoing programs, or operating budgets of established agencies.
Publications: Annual report (including application guidelines); Grants list; Program policy statement (including application guidelines).
Application information: Application cover sheet available on foundation web site. Grants to programs based in the United Kingdom or other countries are initiated by the foundation; unsolicited proposals are not considered. Please note that U.K. organizations need not complete a "foreign public charity equivalency" process when applying to the foundation. However, applications are only considered from organizations in the U.K. that are charities registered with The Charity Commission. The foundation does not accept applications from for-profit organizations or individuals. Complete application guidelines available on foundation web site. Application form required.
 Initial approach: Letter of inquiry sent as an attachment with application cover sheet via e-mail
 Copies of proposal: 1
 Deadline(s): Arts and Culture: Mar. 1; Human Rights: Aug. 1; Food and Farming: Dec. 1. Deadlines for media projects should coincide with the relevant program area the project is based upon
 Board meeting date(s): 4 times per year
Officers and Directors:* Alice C. Russell-Shapiro,* Pres.; Christine H. Russell,* Secy.; Charles P. Russell,* Treas.; Susan Reed Clark, Exec. Dir.
Number of staff: 2 full-time professional; 1 full-time support.
EIN: 941196186

105
Compton Foundation, Inc.
101 Montgomery St., Ste. 850
San Francisco, CA 94104 (415) 391-9001
Contact: Allen Friedman, Exec. Dir.
FAX: (415) 391-9005; URL: http://www.comptonfoundation.org
Blog: http://www.comptonfoundation.org/news/updates/
Compton Foundation's Philanthropy Promise: http://www.ncrp.org/philanthropys-promise/who
Grants Database: http://www.comptonfoundation.org/grants-awarded/schedule-of-grants/

Incorporated in 1972 in NY as successor to the Compton Trust; reincorporated in 1992 in CA.
Donor: Members of the Compton family.
Grantmaker type: Independent foundation.
Financial data (yr. ended 12/31/09): Assets, $64,316,869 (M); gifts received, $250,000; expenditures, $5,906,364; qualifying distributions, $5,259,569; giving activities include $4,407,309 for 288 grants (high: $118,150; low: $100).
Purpose and activities: In a world that is increasingly interrelated, the Compton Foundation seeks to foster human and ecological security by addressing contemporary threats to these inalienable rights. The foundation supports responsible stewardship that respects the rights of future generations to a balanced and healthy ecology, both personal and global, allowing for the full richness of human experience. The foundation

envisions a world in which humans live in harmony with each other, and in sustainable balance with the earth. To realize this vision, the foundation focuses most of its grantmaking in the areas of Peace & Security, Environment & Sustainability, and Population & Reproductive Health, with a special emphasis on projects that explore the interconnections between these categories. The foundation seeks to foster positive and sustainable models of change in each of its three program areas. It believes that research and activism should inform each other, and that both perspectives are necessary for productive public debate and effective policy change. The foundation actively encourages creative collaboration between agencies, institutions and/or foundations, and projects that advance human knowledge by connecting theory with practice.
Fields of interest: Population studies; Environment.
International interests: Central America; Mexico; Sub-Saharan Africa.
Type of support: Mission-related investments/loans; General/operating support; Continuing support; Land acquisition; Program development; Fellowships; Research; Consulting services; Matching/challenge support.
Limitations: Applications not accepted. Giving on an international basis to U.S.-based organizations for projects in Mexico, Central America, and Sub-Saharan Africa and on a national basis for programs in peace and population and the environment. Other funding limited to areas where board members reside: primarily San Francisco, Marin, and Santa Clara counties, CA. No grants to individuals, or for capital or building funds, no loans.
Application information: As a result of the foundation beginning a planning process, there will not be an open grants cycle in 2011. Grants will be made by invitation only during that time.
 Board meeting date(s): June and Dec.
Officers and Directors:* Rebecca DiDomenico,* Pres.; Vanessa Compton,* V.P.; W. Danforth Compton,* Secy.; Marty Krasney,* Treas.; Ellen Friedman, Exec. Dir.; Marshal J. Compton; Betty L. Farrell; J. Martin Goebel; Stephen Perry; Steven M. Riskin; Terry Tempest Williams.
Number of staff: 4 full-time professional; 2 part-time support.
EIN: 943142932
Recent grants for international programs:
105-1 Aftermath Project, Los Angeles, CA, $39,500. For pilot curriculum development project with Facing History and Ourselves for youth education initiative related to War Is Only Half the Story, book featuring photographs and essays related to war and international conflict. The book is distributed for free to every US senator, university and high school journalism and media programs, academics in peacebuilding and post-conflict studies, human rights organizations and museum curators. 2010.
105-2 Arts Education International, San Francisco, CA, $13,000. For programs in Makeni, Sierra Leone that will provide vocational training and emotional rehabilitation through the arts for orphaned and abandoned children at Young Shall Grow Orphanage. Children will learn skills in batik fabric-dyeing, t-shirt and sign printing, dance, drama and studio recording in an immersive two-week arts camp taught by local artisans. Following the camp, students will continue study in twice-weekly group lessons, with opportunities for further training in apprenticeship settings. This program will provide children with career

opportunities and a connection to their community. 2010.

105-3 Barefoot Artists, Philadelphia, PA, $28,000. For Phase 2 of Rwanda Twa Village Transformation Project. Goals are to: 1) Strengthen Twa Art House with deep rooting through individual and collective storytelling in words, images, music and dance so that they connect with one another and reclaim their ancestry; 2) Empower Twa Art House by making possible new ways of earning a livelihood including land cultivation, sewing training, the development of a professional performing troupe, and assistance in marketing their pottery and other products; 3) Renovate the roof of the main building of the Rubavu 2 Primary School to secure weatherproof indoor spaces for project activities, especially during the rainy seasons; 4) Raise the visibility of the Twa Art House through a documentary video film that will be promoted widely both in Rwanda and the United States. 2010.

105-4 Bulletin of the Atomic Scientists, Chicago, IL, $30,000. To deliver expert analysis of global environmental with focus on continuing editorial coverage of climate change and environmental issues. 2010.

105-5 Cape Farewell, London, England, $30,000. For expedition to Franz Joseph Land, which will take artists and scientists on a voyage to the north seas of Russia. Grant will support the North American places (ideally two North American artists) on this voyage and associated media projects, which will enable the North American public to engage directly with the work. Franz Joseph Land is an archipelago located in the far north of Russia. 2010.

105-6 Catholics for a Free Choice, Washington, DC, $25,000. To promote reproductive health and justice in Central America. 2010.

105-7 Center for International Policy, Washington, DC, $25,142. For project, Innovation or Militarization: Colombia, which will analyze U.S.-supported post-conflict, state-building and counterinsurgency programs in Colombia. 2010.

105-8 CERES, Boston, MA, $30,000. To leverage investor action to address water risk by 1) educating investors; 2) leading direct company engagement; 3) catalyzing corporate transparency; 4) driving sustainable investment in water-intensive sectors; and 5) launching a comprehensive media campaign. 2010.

105-9 Citizens for Global Solutions Education Fund, Washington, DC, $50,000. To support U.S. Engagement in U.N. Peacekeeping Operations by organizing Partnership for Effective Peacekeeping, high-level conference and preparatory meetings to formulate blueprint for the Obama administration in the areas of funding, equipment and training, standing civilian and police capabilities, and committing active U.S military personnel. 2010.

105-10 Clark University, Department of International Development, Community and Environment (IDCE), Worcester, MA, $24,000. For fellowships for Masters level graduate students in environment and sustainable development. Fellowships will be used to leverage other fellowship funds to enable three mid-career professionals to enroll in one of IDCE's three MA Programs that address issues of the environment and sustainability: the programs in International Development and Social Change (ID), Environmental Science and Policy (ES&P), and Geographical Information Science for Development and Environment (GISDE). 2010.

105-11 Connexus Communications, Arcata, CA, $20,500. For After the War is Over, two one-hour radio programs. The first program will focus on war-affected communities in Northern Uganda using photography, story-telling, chanting, dancing, songs, theatre and writing to access suppressed emotions and heal from the ravages of decades-long civil war. The second will profile the work of several Ashoka Peace Fellows for their contributions to the peacebuilding field. 2010.

105-12 Consultative Group on Biological Diversity, San Francisco, CA, $10,000. For Biennium support. 2010.

105-13 Crisis Action, New York, NY, $50,000. To employ New York-based staff member to lead work on Democratic Republic of Congo (DRC) in protecting civilians from conflict in that country. Additionally New York office will consolidate its presence at the United Nations, creating additional elements of synergy among NGOs, to enable them to respond to emergency situations better. 2010.

105-14 Dalhousie University, Halifax, Canada, $50,000. For work of Child Soldiers Initiative to develop standards of proficiency for pre-deployment training and to facilitate training on child soldiering for South African and Botswana police. Training will be conducted with local partners, Institute of Security Studies, Save the Children Sweden and the Network of Young People Affected by War. 2010.

105-15 Eastern Mennonite University, Harrisonburg, VA, $42,850. To identify and develop range of consultative mechanisms for U.S. government to interface with civil society organizations in elements of planning and policymaking related to peace operations and peacebuilding. Grant will facilitate civil-military roundtables, publish reports and policy briefs. 2010.

105-16 Ecotrust, Portland, OR, $30,000. For project, The Social Cost of Carbon (SCC), defined as the estimated cost to society for each additional ton of carbon dioxide released into the atmosphere. 2010.

105-17 EngenderHealth, New York, NY, $45,000. For Program H for Young Men in Latin America. Program H (for hombres and homens, the words for men in Spanish and Portuguese) Initiative consists of group educational activities to engage young men and adult men in gender equality, community campaigns, staff training and an impact evaluation model. 2010.

105-18 Environmental Law Institute, Washington, DC, $25,000. For Peacebuilding through Natural Resource Management. 2010.

105-19 Extreme Ice Survey, Boulder, CO, $25,000. For Art Meets Science for Public Awareness to expand effectiveness and scope of outreach program by focusing on high-impact, mission-oriented speaking engagements devoted to improving public awareness of the anthropogenic impacts on Earth, especially climate change. Speaking engagements tel captivating visual stories that inspire positive social action. 2010.

105-20 Fambul Tok International, Freetown, Sierra Leone, $50,000. For Fambul Tok: Lessons from Sierra Leone, outreach campaign, which uses the Fambul Tok movie as its cornerstone in leading community-based dialogues across the U.S. and in Sierra Leone. There are three parts: 1) securing community screenings of the film; 2) publishing a photo-intensive companion book to the organizers of the screenings. 2010.

105-21 Friends Committee on National Legislation Education Fund, Washington, DC, $42,000. For Rebalancing the U.S. Foreign Policy Toolbox, initiative which leverages a moment of policy change opportunity to strengthen U.S. civilian capacities for peacebuilding and violence prevention. Program will lead coordinated advocacy to inform key policy processes underway in the Executive Branch and Congress that will shape the future of U.S. civilian peacebuilding capacities. Project also includes coordinating and strengthening a new advocacy coalition and expanding a strategic circle of congressional support.. 2010.

105-22 Friends of the Earth, Washington, DC, $25,000. For California Greenhouse Gas Transportation Solutions, initiative to shape strong alternative fuel and vehicle regulatory requirements, promote and support updated greenhouse gas vehicle standards, and lend legal and policy expertise to efforts to strengthen such policies. 2010.

105-23 Gender Action, Washington, DC, $40,000. To build capacity in Kenya related to International Financial Institution (IFI) investments related to population, women's rights and gender equality. 2010.

105-24 Gender Equity: Citizenship and Work and Family, Washington, DC, $31,000. For advocacy to increase family planning funding. 2010.

105-25 Global Action Network Net, iScale, Seattle, WA, $25,000. For Peace and Security Development Global Action Network Initiative. 2010.

105-26 Global Justice Center, New York, NY, $45,000. To ensure sustainable peace and security in Sierra Leone through legislative reform that upholds international human rights standards. 2010.

105-27 Guttmacher Institute, New York, NY, $20,000. For Past Due: EC and USAID. 2010.

105-28 Henry L. Stimson Center, Washington, DC, $40,000. For Future of Peace Operations Program (FOPO) which works with allies in the United States and the international community to transform the rhetoric of civilian protection into a working reality. 2010.

105-29 Henry L. Stimson Center, Washington, DC, $40,000. For Rebalancing the Tools of Statecraft, project to analyze and understand budgets and policy options involving Department of Defense (DOD) and the civilian side of the equation. 2010.

105-30 International Center for Transitional Justice, New York, NY, $20,000. For Policy: Transitional Justice and Peace. 2010.

105-31 International Rescue Committee, New York, NY, $30,000. For adolescent reproductive health programs in Liberia. 2010.

105-32 Island Press, Center for Resource Economics, Washington, DC, $10,000. For stakeholder research effort that will lead to a comprehensive plan of action on water resulting in a better framework for understanding the issues surrounding water, which can help inform the work of policymakers, practitioners, funders, and academics seeking to resolve problems impacting this finite and exhaustible resource. 2010.

105-33 Leadership Institute for Ecology and the Economy, Santa Rosa, CA, $64,138. For Compton International Fellowship Program. 2010.

105-34 New York University, Center on International Cooperation (CIC), New York, NY, $30,000. For Peace Operations Outreach Project, component of CIC's Peacekeeping and Security Sector Reform Program. Project will use the substantive content of its flagship publication, The Annual Review of Global Peace Operations, as the basis for two workshops in the global south. Project will convene workshops in the capitals of India and Ethiopia that will provide a platform for the voices of government and nongovernmental organizations in the global south to bear on both the critical function that peace operations have come to play and areas where they can be improved upon. 2010.

105-35 Oxfam America, Boston, MA, $40,000. To develop policies and procedures on how to provide humanitarian, recovery and development assistance in persistently contested areas that do not leave these areas even less safe. 2010.

105-36 Physicians for Social Responsibility, Washington, DC, $30,000. For work to reduce and reverse global climate change, as well as goals of closing coal plants and implementing state policy, PSR will identify, recruit and train physicians and health professionals in how to use new tools and new information to make the public health case for health-protective policies on climate. 2010.

105-37 Ploughshares Fund, San Francisco, CA, $10,000. For Peace and Security Funders Group. 2010.

105-38 Population Action International, Washington, DC, $40,000. For U.S. Policy Impact Project. 2010.

105-39 Population Reference Bureau, Washington, DC, $118,000. For Compton International Population Fellowship Program Support Services. 2010.

105-40 PROOF: Media for Social Justice, Larchmont, NY, $20,000. For Rescuers Project, which will collect, preserve, and present rescue stories from Cambodia and Bosnia-Herzegovina. PROOF will work with local NGOs in each country to identify and collect rescuer testimonies, create a learning exhibit for each country-setting with a curriculum, as well as work with local youth groups to develop theater pieces that reflect young people's understanding of the Rescuer concept. PROOF will work with each NGO to evaluate and measure the outputs and impact of the project. 2010.

105-41 Refugees International, Washington, DC, $50,000. For Peacekeeping Program activities related to improving civilian protection capacity of multilateral peacekeeping operations. Program activities will include: (1) urging the U.S. and United Nations to work together to define and write doctrine on how peacekeepers can and should provide protection to civilians; (2) working with Congress to authorize and appropriate funds for the U.S. military to provide support for international peacekeeping troops, and to create a U.S. program that will provide refurbished aircraft to international peacekeeping missions; and (3) convincing the U.S. Executive Branch to increase training and equipment it provides for the African Union's Standby Force, and to ensure that U.S. military training of international peacekeeping forces meets or exceeds

international and federal standards for the protection of women.. 2010.

105-42 Sierra Club Foundation, San Francisco, CA, $25,000. For Global Population and Environment Program. 2010.

105-43 Trash Island Project, San Francisco, CA, $35,000. For Midway Journey with Chris Jordan, project to photograph expeditions to Midway Atoll which will document an environmental disaster showing the massive plastic pollution of the Pacific Ocean. All of the multimedia materials resulting from these expeditions will be geared towards fostering a shift in public consciousness from a human-centered perspective to a holistic view that underscores the interconnectedness of life. Tangible results will be: a series of exhibitions, a book, a Google Earth tour, a documentary film, a free image library and educational materials, and web and social media campaigns.. 2010.

105-44 Trinity University, San Antonio, TX, $10,000. To publish Moral Ground: Ethical Action for a Planet in Peril, anthology that brings together the testimony of the world's moral and religious leaders, scientists, activists, poets and authors, all calling on us to honor our moral responsibility to the Earth. 2010.

105-45 Tufts University, Feinstein International Center (FIC), Medford, MA, $35,000. For Phase II of People First, popular education tool outlining how local and national authorities, traditional leaders, parents, and victims' representatives can jointly promote accountability and reparation from the perspective of the war-affected communities, including Uganda. 2010.

105-46 University of Florida, Department Wildlife Ecology and Conservation, Gainesville, FL, $40,000. For Compton International Fellowships in Environment and Sustainability. 2010.

105-47 Worldwatch Institute, Washington, DC, $30,000. For Relinking Population and Climate. 2010.

105-48 Yale University, School of Forestry and Environmental Studies, New Haven, CT, $36,000. For Compton International Fellows. 2010.

106
The Conservation Land Trust
1062 Fort Cronkhite
Sausalito, CA 94965-2609
E-mail: info@theconservationlandtrust.org;
URL: http://www.theconservationlandtrust.org

Established in 1999 in CA.
Donors: Douglas R. Tompkins; Kristine M. Tompkins; Addison M. Fischer; Charities Aid Foundation.
Grantmaker type: Operating foundation.
Financial data (yr. ended 03/31/10): Assets, $111,830,879 (M); gifts received, $88,168; expenditures, $3,756,176; qualifying distributions, $5,337,989; giving activities include $3,209,176 for 2+ grants (high: $2,805,044), $290,761 for foundation-administered programs and $1,838,048 for 2 loans/program-related investments.
Purpose and activities: Giving to the conservation of biodiversity and strategically important biota. Important but secondary considerations are good public access, public educational and interpretive programs, appropriate and ecologically sustainable economic activities, and tourist possibilities.

Fields of interest: Environment, natural resources; Environment, water resources; Environment, forests.
International interests: Argentina; Chile.
Type of support: Program-related investments/ loans.
Limitations: Applications not accepted. Giving primarily in Argentina and Chile; funding also in Sausalito, CA for a Chile-based cause. No grants to individuals.
Application information: Contributes only to pre-selected organizations.
Officers and Directors:* Douglas R. Tompkins,* Pres.; Quincey T. Imhoff,* V.P.; Debra B. Ryker,* Secy.-Treas.; Peter Buckley; Thomas Butler; Kristine M. Tompkins; George Wuerthner.
EIN: 680245471

107
Consortium for Global Development
P.O. Box 51050
Palo Alto, CA 94303-0683

Established in 1992; supporting organization of the International Development Exchange, Just Art: Youth Action for Global Justice, Inc., and Volunteers in Asia, Inc.
Grantmaker type: Public charity.
Financial data (yr. ended 12/31/09): Revenue, $18; assets, $10,979 (M).
Fields of interest: International affairs.
Type of support: General/operating support.
Limitations: Applications not accepted.
Application information: Contributes only to pre-selected organizations; unsolicited requests for funds not considered or acknowledged.
Officers and Directors:* Peter Miller,* Chair. and Pres.; Terry Kelly,* Secy. and C.F.O.; Lalit Balchandani; Ron Herring.
EIN: 943152543

108
Crankstart Foundation
c/o Frank, Rimerman & Co., LLP
1801 Page Mill Rd.
Palo Alto, CA 94304-1216 (650) 845-8100

Established in 2000 in CA.
Donors: Michael Moritz; Harriet Heyman.
Grantmaker type: Independent foundation.
Financial data (yr. ended 12/31/10): Assets, $342,540,850 (M); gifts received, $241,592,734; expenditures, $7,648,289; qualifying distributions, $465,000; giving activities include $465,000 for grants.
Fields of interest: Performing arts, orchestras; Community/economic development.
Type of support: General/operating support.
Limitations: Applications accepted. Giving primarily in CA. No grants to individuals.
Application information: Application form not required.
Initial approach: Proposal
Deadline(s): None
Officer: Michael Moritz, Pres. and C.F.O.
EIN: 943377099
Recent grants for international programs:
108-1 American Friends of Christ Church, Willsboro, NY, $15,849,442. To support the restoration of buildings and support education. 2008.

109
Cuore Foundation
859 Corporate Way
Fremont, CA 94539-6115

Established in 2007 in CA.
Grantmaker type: Independent foundation.
Financial data (yr. ended 03/31/11): Assets, $1,028,104 (M); gifts received, $1,186,118; expenditures, $202,112; qualifying distributions, $200,212; giving activities include $200,212 for 8 grants (high: $153,412; low: $1,000).
Fields of interest: International affairs.
Limitations: Applications not accepted. Giving primarily in Brazil.
Application information: Unsolicited requests for funds not accepted.
Officer: Daniel Dalarossa, Pres.; Elza Harumi Dalarossa, Secy.
EIN: 205106120

110
CW Film Foundation, Inc.
145 9th St., Ste. 105
San Francisco, CA 94103-2637   (415) 934-9500
Contact: Santhosh Daniel, Dir., Progs.
FAX: (415) 934-9501;
E-mail: gfi-info@globalfilm.org; URL: http://www.globalfilm.org

Grantmaker type: Independent foundation.
Financial data (yr. ended 06/30/10): Assets, $816,530 (M); gifts received, $1,343,003; expenditures, $817,618; qualifying distributions, $140,000; giving activities include $140,000 for grants.
Purpose and activities: The initiative promotes cross-cultural understanding through the medium of cinema by supporting the production of authentic and accessible stories created in the developing world, and their distribution through the schools and leading cultural institutions of the U.S.
Fields of interest: International affairs; Education; Media, film/video.
Type of support: Film/video/radio; Grants to individuals.
Limitations: Applications accepted. Giving limited to Africa, Asia, the Caribbean, Central and Eastern Europe, Latin America, the Middle East, and Oceana. No support for projects from Australia, Cuba, the European Union, Iran, Japan, New Zealand, Singapore, South Korea, and Taiwan. No grants for documentaries or short films.
Publications: Application guidelines.
Application information: Application form required.
  Initial approach: Submit application
  Copies of proposal: 2
  Deadline(s): July 15 for Feature-Film Production Grants
Officer: Susan Weeks Coulter, Chair.
Board Members: Pedro Almodovar; Lucy Barreto; Jean-Pierre Bekolo; Noah Cowan; Sandra den Hamer; Christopher Doyle; Adoor Gopalakrishnan; Rashid Masharawi; Mira Nair; Carlos Reygadas; Pierre Rissient; Lita Stantic; Bela Tarr; Djamshed Usmonov; Lars von Trier; Apichatpong Weerasethakul.
EIN: 010738276

111
The Ruth and Leo David Foundation
2222 E. 17th St.
Santa Ana, CA 92705-8608

Established in 2004 in CA.
Donors: Leo David; JPIII Inc.
Grantmaker type: Independent foundation.
Financial data (yr. ended 12/31/10): Assets, $195,765 (M); gifts received, $9,000; expenditures, $345,000; qualifying distributions, $345,000; giving activities include $345,000 for grants.
Fields of interest: Jewish agencies & synagogues.
International interests: Israel.
Limitations: Applications not accepted. Giving primarily in CA. No grants to individuals.
Application information: Contributes only to pre-selected organizations.
Directors: Leo David; Ruth David; Boros David.
EIN: 201199793

112
The Leonard & Sophie Davis Fund
c/o Alan Davis
P.O. Box 590780
San Francisco, CA 94159-0780

Established in 2001 in CA.
Donors: Alan Stephen Davis; Alan Stephen Davis Charitable Lead Annuity Trust.
Grantmaker type: Independent foundation.
Financial data (yr. ended 11/30/10): Assets, $76,575,643 (M); gifts received, $6,255,338; expenditures, $4,749,997; qualifying distributions, $4,401,573; giving activities include $4,210,000 for 45 grants (high: $1,250,000; low: $3,000).
Fields of interest: Medical research, institute; Higher education; Museums (art); Performing arts; Arts; Education; Human services; Jewish federated giving programs; Jewish agencies & synagogues.
International interests: Israel.
Limitations: Applications not accepted. Giving primarily in NY. No grants to individuals.
Application information: Contributes only to pre-selected organizations.
Officers: Alan Stephen Davis, C.E.O.; Mary Lou Davis, C.F.O.
EIN: 943402266

113
Delzell Foundation, Inc.
1482 E. Valley Rd., No. 481
Santa Barbara, CA 93108-1200

Established in 1996 in CA.
Donor: Robert M. Delzell.
Grantmaker type: Independent foundation.
Financial data (yr. ended 12/31/10): Assets, $213,684 (M); gifts received, $50,000; expenditures, $351,903; qualifying distributions, $278,065; giving activities include $278,065 for grants.
Purpose and activities: To improve the medical and cultural welfare in St. Petersburg, Russia.
Fields of interest: Arts; Performing arts, theater; Performing arts, opera; Libraries (medical); Health care.
International interests: Russia.

Limitations: Applications not accepted. Giving primarily in St. Petersburg, Russia. No grants to individuals.
Application information: Contributes only to pre-selected organizations.
Officer: Robert M. Delzell, Chair.
Directors: Eugene Polzik; Tatiana Polzik; Ekaterina Sirakanian.
EIN: 330725441

114
The Valentino Achak Deng Foundation
849 Valencia St.
San Francisco, CA 94110-1736
URL: http://www.valentinoachakdeng.org

Established in 2007.
Grantmaker type: Public charity.
Financial data (yr. ended 12/31/10): Revenue, $631,561; assets, $1,192,872 (M); gifts received, $595,886; expenditures, $420,283.
Purpose and activities: The foundation works to build a peaceful and prosperous future for those who are affected by war in Sudan through helping members of the southern Sudanese diaspora in the U.S. to enhance their educational, social, and economic opportunities; rebuilding southern Sudanese communities through the implementation of community-driven development projects that increase access to educational opportunities for children, women, and men; and improving U.S. policy toward Sudan by educating the public and policy makers on the situation in Sudan.
Fields of interest: International affairs; International migration/refugee issues; Immigrants/refugees.
International interests: Sudan.
Limitations: Giving primarily to San Francisco, CA and Alexandria, VA.
Officers: Valentino Achak Deng, Pres.; Dave Eggers, V.P.; Barbara Bersche, Secy.; Phil Mays, Treas.
EIN: 205961736

115
Dharma Merchant Services Corporate Giving Program
353 Kearny St., Ste. 32
San Francisco, CA 94108-3236   (415) 632-1920
FAX: (415) 632-1921; URL: http://www.dharmamerchantservices.com/GivingBack.html

Grantmaker type: Corporate giving program.
Purpose and activities: Dharma Merchant Services is a certified B Corporation that donates a percentage of profits to nonprofit organizations.
Fields of interest: Animals/wildlife, preservation/protection; Arts; Education; Environment; Animal welfare; Health care; Human services; International development; Public affairs; Religion.
Type of support: Cause-related marketing.

116

Do Unto Others Americas Emergency Relief, Development and Humanitarian Outreach Charities
(also known as DUO)
1100 Larkspur Landing Cir., Ste. 340
Larkspur, CA 94939-1880
Toll-free tel.: (800) 934-9755; URL: http://www.duo.org

Established in 1991 in CA.
Grantmaker type: Public charity.
Financial data (yr. ended 04/30/11): Revenue, $2,101,049; assets, $1,994,313 (M); gifts received, $2,101,049; expenditures, $2,101,049; giving activities include $1,872,331 for grants.
Purpose and activities: The organization is a nonprofit federation that supports charities working in every area of the world to ease the suffering of people who have been affected by war, natural disaster, famine, and epidemic.
Fields of interest: International relief; International affairs.
Limitations: Applications not accepted.
Publications: Annual report; Financial statement.
Application information: Contributes only to pre-selected organizations.
Officers: Karen Dempsey, Pres.; Timothy Romps, V.P.; Kate Kappel Haba, Treas.
Board Members: Patricia Daniels; James McNeil.
EIN: 943148590

117

The Dragon Fund
c/o The 1990 Institute
P.O. Box 1681
Burlingame, CA 94011-1681 (650) 558-9939
FAX: (650) 558-9499;
E-mail: jcrehan@1990institute.org; URL: http://1990institute.org/en/projects

Donor-advised fund of the 1990 Institute.
Grantmaker type: Public charity.
Purpose and activities: The fund makes grants to organizations working toward economic development for women and girls in rural China.
Fields of interest: International economic development; Women; Girls.
International interests: China.
Limitations: Giving primarily in China.

118

The Draper Foundation
c/o Draper Fisher Jurvetson
2882 Sand Hill Rd., Ste. 150
Menlo Park, CA 94025-7057 (650) 233-9000
Contact: Tim C. Draper, Pres.

Established in 1996 in CA.
Donors: William Draper; Phyllis Draper; Tim C. Draper; Melissa Draper; Polly Draper.
Grantmaker type: Independent foundation.
Financial data (yr. ended 12/31/10): Assets, $34,516,061 (M); gifts received, $5,644,417; expenditures, $4,034,598; qualifying distributions, $3,961,183; giving activities include $3,961,183 for grants.
Purpose and activities: Giving primarily for the arts, education, medical research, and children and social services.

Fields of interest: Arts; Higher education; Education; Health organizations, association; Medical research, institute; Human services; Children, services; International affairs; United Ways and Federated Giving Programs.
Limitations: Applications accepted. Giving primarily in CA.
Application information:
  Initial approach: Proposal
  Deadline(s): None
Officers: Tim C. Draper, Pres.; Rebecca Draper, Secy.; William Draper, C.F.O.
EIN: 943256415

119

The Draper Richards Kaplan Foundation
(formerly The Draper Richards Foundation)
50 California St., Ste. 2925
San Francisco, CA 94111-4779 (415) 616-4050
Contact: Jennifer Shilling Stein, Exec. Dir.; Anne Marie Burgoyne, Dir.; Christy Chin, Dir.; Breanna DiGiammarino, Assoc.
FAX: (415) 616-4060;
E-mail: info@draperrichards.org; Application e-mail: proposals@draperrichards.org; URL: http://www.draperrichards.org/

Established in 2001 in CA.
Donors: William H. Draper III; Robin R. Donohoe; Robert S. Kaplan.
Grantmaker type: Operating foundation.
Financial data (yr. ended 12/31/09): Assets, $14,751,338 (M); gifts received, $1,328,477; expenditures, $2,020,823; qualifying distributions, $1,957,900; giving activities include $1,200,000 for 15 grants, and $1,957,900 for foundation-administered programs.
Purpose and activities: The foundation awards grants to entrepreneurial leaders at new nonprofits that seek to solve existing social problems in innovative ways at a large scale. The applicant must also be the organization's founder. Grants include seed funding of $100,000 annually for three years, advisory support in the form of a board seat, and access to a network of social entrepreneurs in the Draper Richards Kaplan Foundation portfolio. The foundation only awards six fellowships per year (less than 2 percent of grantees). The foundation selects proposals from a variety of public service areas, including but not limited to, education, youth and families, the environment, health, and community and economic development. The foundation does not fund organizations later in their lifecycle. The foundation does not fund organizations that are unable to scale their impact.
Fields of interest: Education; Environment; Health care; Crime/law enforcement; Employment; Housing/shelter; Youth development, adult & child programs; Youth development; Human services; International affairs, equal rights; International economic development; Civil/human rights; Economic development; Nonprofit management; Community/economic development; Philanthropy/voluntarism; Philanthropy/voluntarism; Public affairs.
Type of support: General/operating support; Management development/capacity building; Program development; Seed money; Fellowships; Technical assistance.
Limitations: Applications accepted. Giving to new high impact nonprofit organizations with headquarters in the U.S., and operations that are domestic or international. No support for faith-based

models, single community-based models, lobbying or advocacy. No grants for research or scholarships.
Publications: Application guidelines.
Application information: Please see foundation web site for submission guidelines. Application form not required.
  Initial approach: Brief proposal, no more than 3 pages
  Copies of proposal: 1
  Deadline(s): None
  Final notification: Acknowledgement of receipt within 14 business days
Officers: Jennifer Shilling Stein, Pres. and Exec. Dir.; Cynthia Lam, Secy.-Treas.
Directors: Anne Marie Burgoyne; Christy Remy Chin; Robin R. Donohoe; William H. Draper III; Robert S. Kaplan.
Number of staff: 4 full-time professional; 1 full-time support; 1 part-time support.
EIN: 912172351
Recent grants for international programs:
119-1 Agora Partnerships, Washington, DC, $50,000. For fellowship. 2010.
119-2 Global Citizen Year, San Francisco, CA, $100,000. For fellowship. 2010.
119-3 Global Health Corps, New York, NY, $100,000. For fellowship. 2010.
119-4 Kiva Microfunds, San Francisco, CA, $50,000. For fellowship. 2010.
119-5 KOMAZA USA, San Francisco, CA, $50,000. For fellowship. 2010.
119-6 Mapendo International, Cambridge, MA, $50,000. For fellowship. 2010.
119-7 Naya Jeevan, Artesia, CA, $100,000. For fellowship. 2010.
119-8 Wild4Life, San Francisco, CA, $100,000. For fellowship. 2010.

120

Dzambuling Imports LLC Contributions Program
807 Richmond St.
El Cerrito, CA 94530-2924 (510) 524-9926
E-mail: info@lhasabeerusa.com; URL: http://lhasabeerusa.com
B Corporation Profile: http://www.bcorporation.net/dzambulingimports

Grantmaker type: Corporate giving program.
Purpose and activities: Dzambuling Imports is a certified B Corporation that donates a percentage of profits to charitable organizations. Support is limited to Tibet.
Fields of interest: Disasters, preparedness/services; Arts, cultural/ethnic awareness; Historic preservation/historical societies; Education; Environment; Health care; Employment, training; Human services; Economic development; Religion, equal rights; Buddhism.
International interests: Asia.
Type of support: General/operating support; Continuing support; Program development.
Limitations: Giving limited to Tibet.

121

East Meets West Foundation
1611 Telegraph Ave., Ste. 1420
Oakland, CA 94612-2129 (510) 763-7045
FAX: (510) 763-6545;
E-mail: info@eastmeetswest.org; Toll-free tel.: (800) 561-3378; mailing address: P.O. Box 29292,

Oakland, CA 94604-9292; URL: http://www.eastmeetswest.org

Established in 1988 in CA.
Grantmaker type: Public charity.
Financial data (yr. ended 12/31/10): Revenue, $29,839,742; assets, $27,225,174 (M); gifts received, $29,827,164; expenditures, $13,371,513; giving activities include $98,160 for 6 grants to organizations outside the U.S.
Purpose and activities: The foundation seeks to transform the health, education, and communities of disadvantaged people in southeast Asia by building partnerships, developing opportunities, and creating sustainable solutions.
Fields of interest: Dental care; Education; International relief; Economically disadvantaged.
International interests: Southeast Asia; Vietnam.
Limitations: Giving limited to Oakland, CA and to Vietnam.
Officers and Directors:* Peter A. Singer,* M.D., Chair.; Stephen Gunther,* M.D., Vice-Chair. and Secy.; Craig Fox, C.O.O.; Eric Hemel, Treas.; John Anner, Exec. Dir.; Jerome Falk; Gil Kemp; Barbara Kemp; Alexander Nguyen; Lena Tran.
EIN: 330316095

122
Egg Foundation
1 Letterman Dr., Bldg. D, Ste. DM700
San Francisco, CA 94129-1494

Established in 2006 in CA.
Donors: Cecily Cameron; Derek Schrier.
Grantmaker type: Independent foundation.
Financial data (yr. ended 12/31/10): Assets, $18,079,731 (M); expenditures, $967,960; qualifying distributions, $967,690; giving activities include $759,964 for 21 grants (high: $125,745; low: $1,770).
Fields of interest: Leadership development; International democracy & civil society development; International relief.
International interests: Africa.
Limitations: Applications not accepted. Giving primarily in CA. No grants to individuals.
Application information: Contributes only to pre-selected organizations.
Directors: Cecily Cameron; Derek Schrier.
EIN: 208090285

123
Ben B. and Joyce E. Eisenberg Foundation
c/o Richard A. Bender
12400 Wilshire Blvd., Ste. 1250
Los Angeles, CA 90025-1042

Established in 1986 in CA.
Grantmaker type: Independent foundation.
Financial data (yr. ended 05/31/10): Assets, $56,903,761 (M); expenditures, $3,563,132; qualifying distributions, $2,493,310; giving activities include $2,493,310 for 41 grants (high: $1,038,600; low: $250).
Fields of interest: Higher education; Hospitals (general); Health care; Health organizations, association; Medical research, institute; Cancer research; Government/public administration; Jewish agencies & synagogues.
International interests: Israel.

Type of support: Continuing support; Annual campaigns; Research.
Limitations: Applications not accepted. Giving primarily in the Los Angeles, CA, area.
Application information: Contributes only to pre-selected organizations.
Officers and Directors:* Joyce Eisenberg-Keefer,* Pres.; Richard A. Bender, Secy.-Treas.; Joyce Green; Edna Weiss.
Number of staff: 3 full-time support.
EIN: 990246427

124
Energy Foundation
301 Battery St., 5th Fl.
San Francisco, CA 94111-3237 (415) 561-6700
Contact: Eric Heitz, Pres.
FAX: (415) 561-6709; E-mail: energyfund@ef.org;
URL: http://www.ef.org
Grants feed for Buildings Program: http://hgrants.ef.org/?sector%5B%5D=c7c8bccb771f6f33bf6672a2b6b4f65a&begin=2009-01-01&end=&filter=&on=all&sort=begin&order=asc
Grants Feed for Climate Program: http://hgrants.ef.org/?sector%5B%5D=60277a3cd47173fb17f8e8656e7537c1&begin=2009-01-01&end=&filter=&on=all&sort=begin&order=asc
Grants feed for Power Program: http://hgrants.ef.org/?sector%5B%5D=5c997f164b1871440c09e3c762eccfd9&begin=2009-01-01&end=&filter=&on=all&sort=begin&order=asc
Grants Feed for Transportation Program: http://hgrants.ef.org/?sector%5B%5D=eaebe624178d2e9c1227068bd998ff44&begin=2009-01-01&end=&filter=&on=all&sort=begin&order=asc

Established in 1991 in CA; became a public charity in 2008.
Donors: The Blue Moon Fund; The William and Flora Hewlett Foundation; John D. and Catherine T. MacArthur Foundation; The McKnight Foundation; Mertz Gilmore Foundation; The David and Lucile Packard Foundation; The Pew Charitable Trusts; The Rockefeller Foundation.
Grantmaker type: Public charity.
Financial data (yr. ended 12/31/09): Assets, $68,673,826 (M); gifts received, $90,717,384; expenditures, $114,313,929; giving activities include $91,293,849 for grants.
Purpose and activities: The foundation works to assist in a transition to a sustainable energy future by promoting energy efficiency and renewable energy.
Fields of interest: Environment, energy.
International interests: China.
Type of support: Program development.
Limitations: Applications accepted. Giving limited to the U.S. and China. No support for sectarian or religious purposes or political organizations. No grants to individuals, or for endowment funds; debt reduction; planning, renovation, maintenance, retrofit, or purchase of buildings; equipment purchases; land acquisition; general support grants; annual fundraising campaigns; research and development of technology; demonstration projects; or capital construction.
Publications: Annual report (including application guidelines); Financial statement.

Application information: Only those organizations who submit letters of intent of interest to the foundation will be asked to submit full proposals. Application form required.
Initial approach: Letter of inquiry
Copies of proposal: 1
Deadline(s): At least 12 weeks in advance of next board meeting (for inclusion in a specific docket)
Board meeting date(s): 3rd week of Mar., 3rd week of June, and 1st week of Nov.
Final notification: Approximately four to six weeks
Officers and Directors:* Susan F. Tierney, Chair.; Eric Heitz,* Pres.; Jiang Lin, Senior V.P., and Dir., CSEP; Robert O'Connor, Senior V.P. and C.O.O.; Charlotte Pera, Senior V.P., U.S. Opers.; David Wooley, V.P. and Power Utilities Program Dir.; Rosina Bierbaum; Robert Crane; Larry Goulder; Denis Hayes; Knee Poh Lam; Alan Lloyd; Rose McKinney-James; Victor Rabinowitch; William Ruckelshaus; Phil Sharp; Michael Wang; Hongjun Zhang.
Number of staff: 26
EIN: 943126848

125
Esperanto League for North America, Inc.
(also known as Esperanto-USA)
1335 Stanford Ave., Ste. 300
Emeryville, CA 94608-2537
URL: http://esperanto-usa.org

Grantmaker type: Public charity.
Financial data (yr. ended 12/31/10): Revenue, $106,131; assets, $470,448 (M); gifts received, $60,663; expenditures, $108,437; giving activities include $285 for grants to organizations outside the U.S., and $7,534 for grants to individuals.
Purpose and activities: The league supports Esperanto speakers in the U.S. who have a common interest in using and promoting Esperanto as an answer to the world language problem.
Fields of interest: International exchange; International affairs; Language/linguistics.
Publications: Occasional report.
Officers and Board Members:* Phil Dorcas,* Pres.; Tim Westover,* V.P.; Julie Spickler,* Secy.; Anna Bennett,* Treas.; Jenja Amis; Mar Cardenas; D. Gary Grady; Anjo Harlow; Ros Haruo; Tor Kinlok; Orlando Raola; Julie Winberg; Christopher Zervic.
EIN: 942240404

126
Falling Leaves Foundation, Inc.
16902 Bolsa Chica Rd., Ste. 203
Huntington Beach, CA 92649-5306

Established in 2006 in CA and DE.
Donor: Adeline Yen Mah.
Grantmaker type: Independent foundation.
Financial data (yr. ended 12/31/10): Assets, $4,461,324 (M); gifts received, $295,000; expenditures, $406,085; qualifying distributions, $175,838; giving activities include $164,550 for 8 grants (high: $150,000; low: $50).
Fields of interest: International human rights; Museums (art); Foundations (community).
Limitations: Applications not accepted. No grants to individuals.
Application information: Contributes only to pre-selected organizations.

Officers: Adeline Yen Mah, Pres.; Robert Mah, V.P.; Earl Mar, Secy.; Larry Mar, Treas.
EIN: 204861119

127
Fanuk Human Resourcees Foundation
1844 Glendon Ave., Ste. 101
Los Angeles, CA 90025-4775

Grantmaker type: Independent foundation.
Financial data (yr. ended 12/31/09): Assets, $4,386,517 (M); expenditures, $542,921; qualifying distributions, $542,921; giving activities include $486,028 for 4 grants (high: $256,027; low: $13,250), and $256,027 for foundation-administered programs.
Fields of interest: International relief.
Limitations: Applications not accepted. Giving primarily in Indonesia; some giving also in CA, GA, and NY.
Application information: Contributes only to pre-selected organizations.
Officers: Stephen M. Olson, Pres.; Bruce Payne, Secy.; Endang Purwati, Treas.
EIN: 912156712

128
Farahnik Family Foundation Charitable Trust
10250 Constellation Blvd., Ste. 2820
Los Angeles, CA 90067-6244

Established in 1993 in CA.
Donor: Leon Farahnik.
Grantmaker type: Operating foundation.
Financial data (yr. ended 03/31/10): Assets, $0 (M); gifts received, $143,000; expenditures, $161,170; qualifying distributions, $161,170; giving activities include $160,077 for 24 grants (high: $41,544; low: $100).
Fields of interest: Higher education, university; Education; Human services; Jewish federated giving programs; Jewish agencies & synagogues.
International interests: Israel.
Type of support: General/operating support; Scholarship funds.
Limitations: Applications not accepted. Giving primarily in CA; some giving in Israel. No grants to individuals.
Application information: Contributes only to pre-selected organizations.
Trustee: Leon Farahnik.
EIN: 956959966

129
Joseph F. Farivar Educational Foundation
c/o Micheal J. Grobstein
15233 Ventura Blvd., 9th Fl.
Sherman Oaks, CA 91403-2289

Established in 1998 in CA.
Donor: Joseph F. Farivar.
Grantmaker type: Independent foundation.
Financial data (yr. ended 12/31/10): Assets, $1,034,949 (M); gifts received, $700,000; expenditures, $206,066; qualifying distributions, $206,056; giving activities include $202,256 for 11 grants (high: $120,278; low: $18).
Purpose and activities: Giving primarily to Jewish educational institutions.

Fields of interest: Religion, interfaith issues; Education; Hospitals (general); Jewish agencies & synagogues.
International interests: Iran.
Limitations: Applications not accepted. Giving primarily in CA, with some giving in Ontario, Canada and Buenos Aires, Argentina. No grants to individuals.
Application information: Contributes only to pre-selected organizations.
Officers and Directors:* Joseph F. Farivar,* Pres.; Fred Farivar,* Secy.
EIN: 954718204

130
Fatima Welfare Foundation
8 Corporate Park, Ste. 100
Irvine, CA 92606
Application address: c/o Tariq Chaudhary, 84 Fairlake, Irvine, CA 92614

Established in 1994 in CA.
Donors: Interchange Standards Corp.; Tariq Mahmood Chaudhary; Zapways Corporations.
Grantmaker type: Operating foundation.
Financial data (yr. ended 11/30/09): Assets, $1,401,475 (M); gifts received, $247,654; expenditures, $145,872; qualifying distributions, $140,887; giving activities include $140,887 for 6 grants (high: $117,630; low: $250).
Fields of interest: Education; Islam.
International interests: Pakistan.
Limitations: Applications accepted. Giving primarily in CA.
Application information:
    Initial approach: Letter
    Deadline(s): None
Officers: Tariq Mahmood Chaudhary, Pres.; Uzma Chaudhary, V.P.
EIN: 330643401

131
Firedoll Foundation
1460 Maria Ln., Ste. 420
Walnut Creek, CA 94596-5355
Contact: Neil Sims, Prog. Off.
E-mail: info@firedoll.org; URL: http://www.firedoll.org

Established in 1998 in CA.
Donor: Straus Family Trust.
Grantmaker type: Independent foundation.
Financial data (yr. ended 05/31/10): Assets, $9,234,976 (M); gifts received, $1,715,687; expenditures, $1,618,532; qualifying distributions, $1,594,533; giving activities include $1,442,355 for 96 grants (high: $40,000; low: $2,500).
Purpose and activities: The foundation offers grants to nonprofits in the areas of environmental conservation, immigrant/human rights, community development, Mid-East peace, and offers support for Bay Area non-profits servicing victims of traumatic brain injury.
Fields of interest: Environment, natural resources; Environment, water resources; Environment, forests; Animals/wildlife, fisheries; Housing/shelter, homeless; International peace/security; Civil/human rights, immigrants; Community development, small businesses.
International interests: Middle East.

Type of support: General/operating support; Continuing support; Capital campaigns; Building/renovation; Equipment; Land acquisition; Emergency funds; Program development; Seed money; Technical assistance; Program evaluation; Program-related investments/loans; Matching/challenge support.
Limitations: Applications accepted. Giving primarily in the San Francisco Bay Area, CA, with emphasis on Alameda and Contra Costa counties; some giving to national organizations promoting environmental conservation. No grants to individuals or for the arts.
Publications: Application guidelines; Grants list; Program policy statement.
Application information: Consult application guidelines on web site before sending proposals. Proposals not following guidelines will be returned. Application form required.
    Initial approach: E-mail or written letter of inquiry or proposal after consulting web site
    Copies of proposal: 1
    Deadline(s): Between Oct. 1 and Dec. 31 for Environmental Conservation, Immigration/Human Rights and Community Development. No deadline for other areas
    Final notification: 6-10 weeks
Officers: Sandor Straus, Pres. and Treas.; Faye Straus, V.P. and Secy.
Number of staff: 1 full-time professional; 1 part-time professional.
EIN: 943301999

132
Firelight Foundation
740 Front St., Ste. 380
Santa Cruz, CA 95060-4559 (831) 429-8750
FAX: (831) 429-2036;
E-mail: info@firelightfoundation.org; URL: http://www.firelightfoundation.org
Blog: http://blog.firelightfoundation.org/
E-Newsletter: http://www.firelightfoundation.org/subscribe-here.php
Facebook: http://www.facebook.com/pages/Firelight-Foundation/186636331584?ref=nf
Grants Database: http://grants.firelightfoundation.org/
LinkedIn: http://www.linkedin.com/companies/478035
RSS Feed: http://feeds.feedburner.com/firelightfoundation/KvAb.rss
Twitter: http://twitter.com/peter_laugharn

Established in 1999 in CA.
Donors: David M. Katz; Kerry A. Olson.
Grantmaker type: Independent foundation.
Financial data (yr. ended 06/30/10): Assets, $6,635,679 (M); gifts received, $192,900; expenditures, $2,919,347; qualifying distributions, $2,873,914; giving activities include $1,137,500 for 94 grants (high: $107,000; low: $1,000).
Purpose and activities: The mission of the Firelight Foundation is to support and advocate for the needs and rights of children who are orphaned or affected by HIV/AIDS in Sub-Saharan Africa. Firelight strives to increase the resources available to grassroots organizations that are strengthening the capacity of families and communities to care for children made vulnerable by HIV/AIDS.
Fields of interest: AIDS; Children/youth, services; Women, centers/services.
International interests: Lesotho; Malawi; Rwanda; South Africa; Sub-Saharan Africa; Tanzania, Zanzibar and Pemba; Zambia; Zimbabwe.

Type of support: General/operating support; Continuing support; Management development/ capacity building; Building/renovation; Program development; Technical assistance.

Limitations: Giving primarily in Sub-Saharan Africa; few grants to U.S.-based organizations. No grants to individuals, or for academic or medical research, endowments, or fundraisers.

Publications: Application guidelines; Annual report; Grants list; Informational brochure; Informational brochure (including application guidelines); Newsletter; Occasional report.

Application information: The foundation is not accepting letters of inquiry or proposals at this time. See foundation web site for updates and information, or check the foundation's Newsflash newsletter: http://www.firelightfoundation.org/newsflash.php.

  Board meeting date(s): Spring (Apr.) and fall (Sept.)

Officers and Directors:* Kerry A. Olson,* Ph.D., Pres.; David M. Katz,* V.P.; Debra Evans,* Secy.; Jonathan C. Lewis, Treas.; Peter Laugharn, Exec. Dir.; Barbara Fagan-Smith; Geoff Foster; Diana Aubourg Millner.

Number of staff: 6 full-time professional; 2 part-time support.

EIN: 770529657

Recent grants for international programs:

132-1 Action pour le Developpement du Peuple, Gisenyi, Rwanda, $15,000. 2011.

132-2 Action pour le Developpement du Peuple, Gisenyi, Rwanda, $15,000. 2011.

132-3 AIDS Care Counselling Campaign Project, Nsanje, Malawi, $13,000. 2011.

132-4 AIDS Outreach Programme - Nyakato, Nyakato, Tanzania, Zanzibar and Pemba, $20,000. 2011.

132-5 Association Benimpuhwe, Center Familial Mu Rugo, Kigali, Rwanda, $15,000. 2011.

132-6 Association Ihorere Munyarwanda, Kigali, Rwanda, $15,000. 2011.

132-7 Association Tuvuge Twiyubaka, Gikongoro, Rwanda, $15,000. 2011.

132-8 Association Tuvuge Twiyubaka, Gikongoro, Rwanda, $12,000. 2011.

132-9 Association Ubumwe Saint Kisito, Ruhengeri, Rwanda, $10,300. 2011.

132-10 Basilwizi Trust, Bulawayo, Zimbabwe, $12,000. 2011.

132-11 Center for Youth Development and Adult Education, Uvinza, Tanzania, Zanzibar and Pemba, $12,000. 2011.

132-12 Centre for Environment Technology and Rural Development, Kasese, Uganda, $15,000. 2011.

132-13 Centre Presbyterien d'Amour des Jeunes, Kigali, Rwanda, $10,000. 2011.

132-14 Chikwawa Diocese Health Commission, Chikwawa, Malawi, $13,000. 2011.

132-15 Child Care and Adoption Society, Chilenje Transient Home, Lusaka, Zambia, $15,000. 2011.

132-16 Childrens Rights Center, Durban, South Africa, $14,000. 2011.

132-17 Childrens Rights Center, Durban, South Africa, $10,000. 2011.

132-18 Chilimba Women and Orphans Care Group, Zomba, Malawi, $13,000. 2011.

132-19 Chintelelwe Health Education and Livelihood Programme, Ndola, Zambia, $13,000. 2011.

132-20 Communaute des Potiers du Rwanda, Kigali, Rwanda, $13,000. 2011.

132-21 Community Based Care Foundation, Kasama, Zambia, $15,000. 2011.

132-22 Community Health Environmental Care Trust, Lilongwe, Malawi, $12,000. 2011.

132-23 Dlalanathi, Pietermaritzburg, South Africa, $15,000. 2011.

132-24 Educational, Self-Sustainability and Improvement of Economy Development Group, Nairobi, Kenya, $15,000. 2011.

132-25 Esandleni Sothando, Plumtree, Zimbabwe, $15,000. 2011.

132-26 Farm Orphan Support Trust of Zimbabwe, Harare, Zimbabwe, $15,000. 2011.

132-27 Foundation for Community Support Services, Karonga, Malawi, $15,000. 2011.

132-28 Foundation for Community Support Services, Karonga, Malawi, $13,000. 2011.

132-29 Fountain of Hope, Lusaka, Zambia, $10,000. 2011.

132-30 Gwai Grandmothers Group, Mberengwa, Zimbabwe, $12,200. 2011.

132-31 Imvani Womens Support Group, Mchinji, Malawi, $13,000. 2011.

132-32 Ingalo Zomusa Orphan Care, Gwanda, Zimbabwe, $14,000. 2011.

132-33 Jerusalem Children and Community Development Organization, Addis Ababa, Ethiopia, $75,000. 2011.

132-34 Kyetume Community Based Health Care Programme, Mukono, Uganda, $15,000. 2011.

132-35 Les Enfants de Dieu, Kigali, Rwanda, $10,000. 2011.

132-36 Lupwa Lwabumi Trust, Kapiri Mposhi, Zambia, $10,000. 2011.

132-37 Matero Care Center, Lusaka, Zambia, $15,000. 2011.

132-38 Maunganidze Kindhearted Childrens Organisation, Chitungwiza, Zimbabwe, $12,000. 2011.

132-39 Monze Mission Hospital/Buntolo Drop-In Center, Mazabuka, Zambia, $13,000. 2011.

132-40 Motivation Community Development, Welkom, South Africa, $15,000. 2011.

132-41 Mphatso Development Foundation, Nyimba, Zambia, $13,000. 2011.

132-42 Mulumbo Early Childhood Care and Development Foundation, Lusaka, Zambia, $15,000. 2011.

132-43 Mulumbo Early Childhood Care and Development Foundation, Lusaka, Zambia, $13,000. 2011.

132-44 Mwanje Orphan Care and Home Based Care, Chiradzulu, Malawi, $13,000. 2011.

132-45 Namwera AIDS Coordinating Committee, Namwera, Malawi, $13,000. 2011.

132-46 Nehemiah AIDS Relief Project, Bulawayo, Zimbabwe, $12,000. 2011.

132-47 Nkhotakota AIDS Support Organization, Nkhotakota, Malawi, $15,000. 2011.

132-48 Nkhotakota AIDS Support Organization, Nkhotakota, Malawi, $13,000. 2011.

132-49 Nkhotakota AIDS Support Organization, Nkhotakota, Malawi, $10,000. 2011.

132-50 Peace in God Organisation, Blantyre, Malawi, $13,000. 2011.

132-51 Rwanda Womens Network, Kigali, Rwanda, $75,000. 2011.

132-52 Simukai Street Youth Programme, Mutare, Zimbabwe, $15,000. 2011.

132-53 Teens Against AIDS, Dar es Salaam, Tanzania, Zanzibar and Pemba, $15,000. 2011.

132-54 Teresa Group-Child and Family Aid, Toronto, Canada, $15,000. 2011.

132-55 Touch Roots Africa, Metsong Africa, Maseru, Lesotho, $125,000. 2011.

132-56 Trust and Care, Kigali, Rwanda, $15,000. 2011.

132-57 Tsosane Support Group, Maseru, Lesotho, $20,000. 2011.

132-58 Tusa Munyandi Association, Livingstone, Zambia, $13,000. 2011.

132-59 Ulupwa Project, Ndola, Zambia, $15,000. 2011.

132-60 Ulupwa Project, Ndola, Zambia, $13,000. 2011.

132-61 WEM Integrated Health Services, Thika, Kenya, $75,000. 2011.

132-62 WEM Integrated Health Services, Thika, Kenya, $15,000. 2011.

132-63 Women Emancipation and Development Agency, Kayanga, Tanzania, Zanzibar and Pemba, $15,000. 2011.

132-64 Youth Activists Organization, Lusaka, Zambia, $12,000. 2011.

132-65 YWCA of Zambia, Western Region, Mongu, Zambia, $10,000. 2011.

133
Fishman Family Foundation, Inc.
730 E. Cypress Ave.
Monrovia, CA 91016-4253 (626) 930-0101
Contact: Betty Fishman, Pres.
URL: http://www.fishman.org

Established in 1997 in CA.
Donors: Daniel Fishman; Erica Fishman; Yehuda Fishman.
Grantmaker type: Independent foundation.
Financial data (yr. ended 12/31/10): Assets, $460,711 (M); gifts received, $200,750; expenditures, $130,027; qualifying distributions, $125,434; giving activities include $125,434 for 75 grants (high: $12,500; low: $50).
Fields of interest: Medical research; Science, research; Education.
International interests: Israel.
Limitations: Applications accepted. Giving primarily in CA. No grants to individuals.
Application information: Application form not required.
  Initial approach: Proposal
  Copies of proposal: 1
  Deadline(s): Mar. 31 for spring review; Sept. 30 for fall review
  Board meeting date(s): Apr. and Oct.
Officers and Directors:* Betty Fishman,* Pres.; Daniel Fishman,* Secy.; Kirk Brattkus; Erica Fishman; J. Bert Fishman; Jane Fishman; Yehuda Fishman; Sandra Lavine.
EIN: 954644459

134
The Fistula Foundation
1900 The Alameda, Ste. 500
San Jose, CA 95126-1427 (408) 249-9596
FAX: (408) 244-7328;
E-mail: info@fistulafoundation.org; Toll-free tel.: (866) 756-3700; URL: http://www.fistulafoundation.org
Facebook: http://www.facebook.com/pages/Fistula-Foundation/108147992546867?sk=info
Grants List: http://www.fistulafoundation.org/whatwedo/2010grantees.html

Established in 2000 in CA.
Grantmaker type: Public charity.
Financial data (yr. ended 12/31/10): Revenue, $2,995,340; assets, $5,204,702 (M); gifts received, $2,960,175; expenditures, $2,983,760; giving activities include $192,500 for grants, and $2,063,713 for 3 grants to organizations outside the U.S.
Purpose and activities: The foundation is dedicated to treating and preventing the childbirth injury obstetric fistula, the devastating injury caused by obstructed labor, through support of the Hamlin Fistula Hospitals in Ethiopia.
Fields of interest: Obstetrics/gynecology research.
International interests: Ethiopia.
Type of support: In-kind gifts; Research.
Limitations: Applications not accepted. Giving on an international basis, primarily in Ethiopia.
Publications: Annual report; Financial statement; Informational brochure; Newsletter.
Application information: Contributes only to pre-selected organizations.
Board meeting date(s): May and Oct.
Officers and Directors: Kassahun Kebede,* Chair.; Cleopatra Kiros,* Secy.-Treas.; Kate Grant, Exec. Dir.; Abaynesh Asrat; France Anne Donnay, M.D., M.Ph.; Linda Levee Samuels; C. Stephen Saunders, Esq.; Gerald Shefren, M.D.; Mary Tadesse; Robert Tessler, Esq.; Whitney Tilson; Linda Tripp; Larry William, M.D.
Number of staff: 1 full-time professional; 2 part-time professional.
EIN: 770547201

135
Flora Family Foundation

2121 Sand Hill Rd., Ste. 123
Menlo Park, CA 94025-6909 · (650) 233-1335
Contact: B. Stephen Toben, Pres.
FAX: (650) 233-1340; E-mail: info@florafamily.org;
URL: http://www.florafamily.org
Grants List: http://www.florafamily.org/grantees.html

Established in 1998 in CA.
Donors: William Hewlett‡; Flora Lamson Hewlett‡.
Grantmaker type: Independent foundation.
Financial data (yr. ended 12/31/10): Assets, $105,771,163 (M); expenditures, $5,500,070; qualifying distributions, $5,214,853; giving activities include $4,418,589 for grants, and $178,010 for 71 employee matching gifts.
Purpose and activities: Giving to support programs in education, arts and culture, international development, the advancement of women, health, the environment, human services, economic development, humanitarian assistance, cultural preservation, and international security.
Fields of interest: Economic development; International economic development; International development; Museums; Higher education; Environment; Health care; Health organizations, association; Health organizations; Disasters, preparedness/services; Human services; Children, services; Women, centers/services; United Ways and Federated Giving Programs; Philanthropy/voluntarism; Women.
Type of support: Mission-related investments/loans; General/operating support; Continuing support; Income development; Management development/capacity building; Annual campaigns; Capital campaigns; Building/renovation; Equipment; Land acquisition; Endowments; Debt

reduction; Emergency funds; Program development; Conferences/seminars; Professorships; Publication; Seed money; Curriculum development; Fellowships; Internship funds; Scholarship funds; Research; Consulting services; Program evaluation; Employee matching gifts; Exchange programs; Matching/challenge support.
Limitations: Applications not accepted. No grants to individuals.
Publications: Grants list.
Application information: Contributes only to pre-selected organizations.
Board meeting date(s): Feb., June, and Oct.
Officers and Directors: Susan S. Briggs,* Chair.; B. Stephen Toben,* Pres.; Patricia Gump, Corp. Secy.; Annette Rado, C.F.O.; Eleanor Gimon; Emma Gimon; Billy Hewlett; Esther Hewlett; Sarah Jaffe; Carrie Zeisler.
Number of staff: 1 full-time professional; 1 part-time professional; 1 part-time support.
EIN: 770500183
Recent grants for international programs:
135-1 African Leadership Foundation, New York, NY, $60,000. For general support. 2008.
135-2 Amistad International, Palo Alto, CA, $18,000. For construction of two classrooms in Buddhas School in India. 2008.
135-3 Ashoka: Innovators for the Public, Arlington, VA, $20,000. For Changemaker Program. 2008.
135-4 Bangladesh Centre for Advanced Studies, Dhaka, Bangladesh, $300,000. For general support. Grant made through the Tides Foundation. 2008.
135-5 Catholic Relief Services, Baltimore, MD, $40,000. For Gaza Strip violence. 2008.
135-6 Catholic Relief Services, Baltimore, MD, $10,000. For general support. 2008.
135-7 Columbia University, New York, NY, $20,000. For South Asian Institute. 2008.
135-8 Debo, Inc., Tarzana, CA, $50,000. For general support. 2008.
135-9 Development Society, Bangladesh, $60,000. For general support. Grant made through the Tides Foundation. 2008.
135-10 Dian Fossey Gorilla Fund International, Atlanta, GA, $10,000. For general support. 2008.
135-11 Energy Foundation, San Francisco, CA, $100,000. For climate control. 2008.
135-12 Environment and Population Research Centre, Dhaka, Bangladesh, $60,000. For general support. Grant made through the Tides Foundation. 2008.
135-13 Film Education, London, England, $20,000. For distribution of the film, A Crude Awakening. 2008.
135-14 Focus the Nation, Portland, OR, $20,000. For Focus the Nation. 2008.
135-15 Folk Arts Center of New England, Melrose, MA, $12,000. For the Afghan Songbook publication. 2008.
135-16 Global Fund for Children, Washington, DC, $90,000. For general support. 2008.
135-17 HealthStore Foundation, Minneapolis, MN, $80,000. For general support. 2008.
135-18 Hesperian Foundation, Berkeley, CA, $50,000. For general support. 2008.
135-19 Internews Network, Arcata, CA, $15,000. For Earth Journalism Network. 2008.
135-20 Living Water International, Houston, TX, $20,000. For Central America program. 2008.
135-21 Meedan, Inc., San Francisco, CA, $20,000. For general support. 2008.

135-22 Mercy Corps, Portland, OR, $10,000. For earthquake in China. 2008.
135-23 Nari Uddug Kendra, Dhaka, Bangladesh, $300,000. For general support. Grant made through the Tides Foundation. 2008.
135-24 National Association of Secondary School Head Teachers of Uganda, Kampala, Uganda, $45,000. For general support. 2008.
135-25 Near East Foundation, New York, NY, $100,000. For general support. 2008.
135-26 Near East Foundation, New York, NY, $90,000. For Iraqui refugees. 2008.
135-27 NGO Forum for Drinking Water Supply and Sanitation, Dhaka, Bangladesh, $200,000. For projects in the Chittagong Hill Tracts. Grant made through the Tides Foundation. 2008.
135-28 Pacific Institute for Studies in Development, Environment and Security, Oakland, CA, $10,000. For general support. 2008.
135-29 Pathfinder International, Watertown, MA, $80,000. For New Dehli projects. 2008.
135-30 Planet Care/Global Health Access Program, San Francisco, CA, $40,000. For cyclone relief. 2008.
135-31 Rainforest Action Network, San Francisco, CA, $60,000. For Global Finance campaign. 2008.
135-32 Reseau Action Climat France, Montreuil, France, $19,000. For general support. 2008.
135-33 Root Capital, Cambridge, MA, $125,000. For general support. 2008.
135-34 Royal United Services Institute for Defence Studies, London, England, $20,000. For Iran in the Middle East conference. Grant made through Tides Foundation. 2008.
135-35 Rural Energy and Development Initiative, Bangladesh, $75,000. For general support. Grant made through the Tides Foundation. 2008.
135-36 Save the Children Federation, Westport, CT, $40,000. For cyclone relief in Myanmar. 2008.
135-37 Snowflake School for Children with Autism, London, England, $10,000. For general support. Grant made through Tides Foundation. 2008.
135-38 Stanford University, Stanford, CA, $200,000. For Center for International Security and Cooperation (CISAC). 2008.
135-39 Stanford University, Stanford, CA, $11,000. For Hamburg archives of interviews on genocide. 2008.
135-40 Tibet Fund, New York, NY, $50,000. For organic farming program. 2008.
135-41 VillageReach, Seattle, WA, $40,000. For vaccinations in Mozambique. 2008.
135-42 Voices on the Border, Washington, DC, $10,000. For El Salvador projects. 2008.
135-43 Wildlife Conservation Society, Bronx, NY, $40,000. For Asiatic cheetah. 2008.
135-44 World Learning, Brattleboro, VT, $10,000. For Turkish Experiment in International Living. 2008.

136
Kay Richard and Elizabeth Bates Flynt Foundation

13350 Country Way
Los Altos Hills, CA 94022-2437

Donor: Christine F. Hemrick.
Grantmaker type: Independent foundation.
Financial data (yr. ended 12/31/10): Assets, $2,137,666 (M); expenditures, $203,248; qualifying distributions, $249,373; giving activities

include $195,500 for 6 grants (high: $150,000; low: $500).
Fields of interest: Animals/wildlife, preservation/protection.
International interests: Africa.
Limitations: Applications not accepted. Giving primarily in CA and Washington, DC. No grants to individuals.
Application information: Contributes only to pre-selected organizations.
Officer: Peggy Flynt Reavis, Secy. and C.F.O.
Trustee: Christine F. Hemrick.
EIN: 770498527

137
ForceBrain.com Contributions Program
1920 Leslie St.
San Mateo, CA 94403-1325 (650) 513-1668
URL: http://www.ForceBrain.com

Grantmaker type: Corporate giving program.
Purpose and activities: ForceBrain.com is a certified B Corporation that donates a percentage of profits to charitable organizations. Support is given primarily in areas of company operations in Georgia, Illinois, Massachusetts, Minnesota, Nevada, New York, Pennsylvania, Texas, and Washington, with emphasis on California, and in Argentina, Canada, England, India, Ireland, Mexico, and the Philippines.
International interests: Argentina; Canada; England; India; Ireland; Mexico; Philippines.
Type of support: General/operating support; In-kind gifts.
Limitations: Giving primarily in areas of company operations in GA, IL, MA, MN, NV, NY, PA, TX, and WA, with emphasis on CA, and in Argentina, Canada, England, India, Ireland, Mexico, and the Philippines.

138
Foundation for Deep Ecology
1062 Fort Cronkhite
Sausalito, CA 94965-2609 (415) 229-9339
Contact: Lizzie Udwin, Prog. Admin.
FAX: (415) 229-9340;
E-mail: info@deepecology.org; URL: http://www.deepecology.org

Established in 1989 in CA.
Donors: Douglas R. Tompkins; Clark Family Foundation.
Grantmaker type: Independent foundation.
Financial data (yr. ended 06/30/10): Assets, $43,216,776 (M); gifts received, $5,000; expenditures, $2,342,708; qualifying distributions, $1,167,854; giving activities include $1,167,854 for grants.
Purpose and activities: Focus on fundamental ecological issues: 1) protection of forests, aquatic ecosystems and other habitats, including wildlands philanthropy (buying land to save it), wilderness recovery (supporting the design and implementation of large-scale wilderness recovery networks), funding for activists fighting for full protection of species and ecosystems and funding for efforts to eliminate resource extraction on public lands; 2) support for alternative models of agriculture that support biodiversity, local self-reliance and healthy agrarian communities, support for efforts in the fight against industrial agriculture, and support for efforts to link conservationists with farmers and activists in order to integrate habitat preservation and

restoration with diverse farming practices; 3) campaigns for effective analysis, organizing and action in response to the rapid acceleration in macroeconomic trends toward global economic integration and free trade that has shifted real political power away from citizen democracies to global corporate bureaucracies, and the further centralization of global corporate power caused by new technological innovation. Supported projects include educational programs exposing the full consequences of the global economy and new free trade agreements, technological critiques and campaigns, and groups fighting large road-building, infrastructure, and dam projects.
Fields of interest: Environment, natural resources; Environment, land resources; Environment; Animals/wildlife, preservation/protection; Agriculture; International affairs.
International interests: South America; Argentina; Chile.
Type of support: General/operating support; Continuing support; Land acquisition; Program development; Conferences/seminars; Publication; Seed money; Grants to individuals.
Limitations: Applications not accepted. Giving primarily in CA and South America, with emphasis on Chile and Argentina. No support for curriculum development or K-12 educational projects, or for businesses or debt. No grants for television, video, photography (visual arts) or film productions, research, or individual academic pursuits (including graduate work or scholarships).
Publications: Multi-year report.
Application information: Contributes only to pre-selected organizations. Unsolicited requests for funds will not be accepted.
Board meeting date(s): Annually
Officers and Directors:* Douglas R. Tompkins,* Pres.; Quincey Imhoff,* V.P.; Kristine McDivitt Tompkins,* V.P.; Debra B. Ryker,* Secy.-Treas.; Marita Albert, Cont.
Number of staff: 3 full-time professional; 2 part-time professional; 3 full-time support.
EIN: 943100115

139
Foundation for Excellence, Inc.
1850 Warburton Ave., Ste. 201
Santa Clara, CA 95050-4169 (408) 985-2001
FAX: (408) 985-1877; E-mail: vishnu@ffe.org;
URL: http://www.ffe.org

Established in 1997.
Grantmaker type: Public charity.
Financial data (yr. ended 06/30/10): Revenue, $741,105; assets, $175,101 (M); gifts received, $738,035; expenditures, $753,484; giving activities include $606,765 for grants to organizations outside the U.S.
Purpose and activities: The organization works to bring about a transformation in the lives of academically brilliant and economically underprivileged students in India, though administering a scholarship program that allows awardees to continue and complete their higher education.
Fields of interest: Higher education; Scholarships/financial aid; Education.
International interests: India.
Type of support: Scholarships—to individuals.
Limitations: Giving limited to India.
Publications: Application guidelines.

Application information: The foundation does not provide application forms directly to applicants; rather, scholarship application forms are only available through facilitators throughout India.
Initial approach: Contact foundation for list of facilitators who administer scholarship applications
Officers and Trustees:* Venktesh Shukla,* Pres.; Vishnu Sharma,* Exec. Dir.; Kailash Joshi; Kanwal S. Rekhi; Bilin Shah.
EIN: 770474749

140
Foundation for Global Community
251 High St., Ste. B
Palo Alto, CA 94301-1097
E-mail: trustees@globalcommunity.org; URL: http://www.globalcommunity.org

Grantmaker type: Public charity.
Financial data (yr. ended 06/30/10): Revenue, $36,178; assets, $1,607,431 (M); gifts received, $6,770; expenditures, $2,754,686; giving activities include $2,373,104 for grants, and $10,000 for grants to organizations outside the U.S.
Purpose and activities: The foundation seeks to help people focus on the belief that the destiny of humankind rests on the willingness of people to put aside self-interest and cooperate as races, nations, and religions for the well-being of the planet.
Fields of interest: International exchange; International affairs, goodwill promotion; Environment.
Limitations: Applications accepted. Giving on a national and international basis.
Application information:
Initial approach: Letter via e-mail
Officer: Bill Wall, C.F.O.
Trustees: Jim Burch; Bill DeVincenzi; Virginia Fitton; Richard Rathbun; Libby Traubman.
EIN: 941675981

141
Foundation for the People of Burma
225 Bush St., Ste. 590
San Francisco, CA 94104-4294
FAX: (415) 477-2787;
E-mail: info@foundationburma.org; URL: http://www.foundationburma.org

Established in 1999 in CA as the Burma People's Relief Group; established as a public charity in 2000.
Grantmaker type: Public charity.
Financial data (yr. ended 12/31/10): Revenue, $2,010,146; assets, $2,244,861 (M); gifts received, $2,008,629; expenditures, $1,825,886; giving activities include $1,177,777 for grants to organizations outside the U.S., and $18,857 for grants to individuals.
Purpose and activities: The foundation works to provide humanitarian aid to Burmese people of all ethnic backgrounds and religious beliefs, and responds to the basic health, education, and leadership development needs of communities.
Fields of interest: Education; Public health; Human services; International economic development; International affairs; Immigrants/refugees.
International interests: Thailand; Philippines; Burma (Myanmar); India.

Type of support: Program development; Grants to individuals.
Limitations: Giving limited to Burma, India, Philippines, and Thailand.
Publications: Newsletter.
Officers and Directors:* Hal Nathan,* Ph.D., Pres.; Alan Senauke,* V.P.; Gail Seneca,* Treas.; Jane Dudley; Rina Hirai; Maung Tin-Wa; Jack Kornfield, Ph.D.; Eileen Moncoeur.
EIN: 943375666

142
Sidney E. Frank Foundation
50 California St., Ste. 3165
San Francisco, CA 94111-4725
Contact: Rae Richman, Philanthropic Advisor
FAX: (415) 543-0753; E-mail for Rae Richman: rrichman@rockpa.org

Established in 2004 in NY.
Donor: Sidney E. Frank†.
Grantmaker type: Independent foundation.
Financial data (yr. ended 12/31/09): Assets, $270,023,903 (M); gifts received, $29,724,321; expenditures, $14,084,579; qualifying distributions, $12,627,981; giving activities include $11,402,655 for 136 grants (high: $1,000,000; low: $500; average: $10,000–$300,000).
Fields of interest: Cancer; Arts, multipurpose centers/programs; Elementary/secondary education; Education; Environment, beautification programs; Environment; Medical research.
Limitations: Applications not accepted. Giving primarily in the San Francisco Bay Area and San Diego, CA, HI, and New York City. No grants to individuals.
Application information: Contributes only to pre-selected organizations.
Trustees: Peter Halstead; Cathy Halstead.
Number of staff: 1 full-time professional.
EIN: 206383779
Recent grants for international programs:
142-1 Acumen Fund, New York, NY, $250,000. ForEnergy Portfolio. 2009.
142-2 American Associates of the Royal National Theater, New York, NY, $79,200. For screenings of All's Well That Ends Well through National Theatre Live and digitization of video performance archive. 2009.
142-3 American Associates, Ben-Gurion University of the Negev, Corte Madera, CA, $25,000. For scholarships for disadvantaged undergraduate students. 2009.
142-4 American Friends of the Hebrew University, New York, NY, $25,000. For scholarships for disadvantaged undergraduate students. 2009.
142-5 American Friends of the Open University of Israel, New York, NY, $25,000. For scholarships for disadvantaged undergraduate students. 2009.
142-6 American Friends of the Tel Aviv University, New York, NY, $25,000. For scholarships for disadvantaged undergraduate students. 2009.
142-7 Bletchley Park Trust, Bletchley, England, $248,190. To restore several huts for use as exhibit space for Enigma Museum. 2009.
142-8 Earthjustice, Oakland, CA, $200,000. For projects aimed at reducing black carbon and international shipping emissions. 2009.
142-9 Give2Asia, San Francisco, CA, $100,000. For support of Joint U.S.-China Collaboration on Clean Energy (JUCCCE). 2009.

142-10 Holon Institute of Technology, Holon, Israel, $125,000. For scholarships for low-income and disadvantaged youth. 2009.
142-11 Interplast, Mountain View, CA, $10,000. For general support. 2009.
142-12 Natural Resources Defense Council, San Francisco, CA, $300,000. For work related to greening of China, protecting and revitalizing oceans and other projects. 2009.
142-13 Nature Conservancy, Arlington, VA, $200,000. For Forest Carbon and Climate Adaptation Programs. 2009.
142-14 North American Friends of AMCHA/Israel, New York, NY, $100,000. For general operating support. 2009.
142-15 Prince's Foundation for Children and the Arts, London, England, $50,000. For START, program which provides funding and support to cultural venues (e.g. theatres, museums, galleries and orchestras) to enable them to build partnerships with selected primary and secondary schools in their local areas. 2009.
142-16 R. J. Mitchell Memorial Museum, Solent Sky, Southampton, England, $20,000. To host and update R. J. Mitchell website. 2009.
142-17 Royal Shakespeare Company, Stratford-upon-Avon, England, $100,000. For digital transfer of video productions archive and secure installation of digital archive in multiple locations. 2009.
142-18 Schechter Institutes, Philadelphia, PA, $30,000. For Sarah Becker Frank project to expand Women and Gender Studies. 2009.
142-19 Shakespeare's Globe, London, England, $75,000. For tour in the U.S. of Love's Labour's Lost and for digital transfer of video performance archive. 2009.
142-20 Village Enterprise Fund, San Carlos, CA, $10,000. For general support. 2009.

143
The Fremont Group Foundation
P.O. Box 193809
San Francisco, CA 94119-3809
Contact: Nancy Hair
FAX: (415) 284-8128;
E-mail: nhair@fremontgroup.com; URL: http://www.fremontgroup.com/values/commitment.html

Established in 1996 in CA.
Donor: Fremont Sequoia Holding, L.P.
Grantmaker type: Company-sponsored foundation.
Financial data (yr. ended 12/31/10): Assets, $8,668,928 (M); expenditures, $443,949; qualifying distributions, $358,464; giving activities include $358,464 for grants.
Purpose and activities: The foundation supports food banks and organizations involved with education, the environment, animal welfare, child welfare, human services, and international affairs and matches contributions made by its employees.
Fields of interest: Elementary/secondary education; Education, early childhood education; Higher education; Education; Environment, natural resources; Environment; Animal welfare; Crime/violence prevention, child abuse; Food banks; Boy scouts; Human services; International affairs.
Type of support: General/operating support; Annual campaigns; Program development; Scholarship funds; Employee volunteer services; Employee matching gifts.
Limitations: Applications not accepted. Giving primarily in CA. No support for political or religious

organizations or organizations involved with reproductive issues. No grants to individuals.
Application information: Contributes only to pre-selected organizations.
Board meeting date(s): Twice per year
Officers and Directors:* Alan M. Dachs,* Pres.; Richard S. Kopf,* V.P. and Secy.; Deborah L. Duncan,* V.P. and Treas.
Number of staff: 1 part-time support.
EIN: 333255428

144
Friends of Sheba Medical Center, Inc.
2566 Overland Ave., No. 670
Los Angeles, CA 90064-3376 (310) 838-0700
FAX: (310) 838-0707; E-mail: info@shebamed.org; URL: http://www.shebamed.org

Established in 1970 in CA.
Grantmaker type: Public charity.
Financial data (yr. ended 12/31/10): Revenue, $1,859,386; assets, $891,454 (M); gifts received, $1,894,595; expenditures, $1,483,515; giving activities include $520,030 for grants to organizations outside the U.S.
Purpose and activities: The organization supports Sheba Medical Center in Israel.
Fields of interest: Health care, single organization support; Health care; Hospitals (general).
International interests: Israel.
Limitations: Applications not accepted. Giving limited to Israel.
Application information: Contributes only to a pre-selected organization.
Officers and Directors:* Ruth Steinberger,* Chair.; Gal Ben-Naim,* Pres.; Carol Green,* Secy.; Aron Shapiro, Treas.; Jack Saltzberg,* Exec. Dir.; Marianne Berman; Martin Berman; Ben Boston; R. Ricardo Brechner, M.D., Ph.D.; Hon. Barry Brucker; Sue Brucker; Ruth Cooper; Harry L. Green, M.D.; Aviva Harari; Stephanie Hibler; and 28 additional directors.
EIN: 237076117

145
The Alfred & Hanna Fromm Fund
80 E. Sir Francis Drake Blvd., No. 4D
Larkspur, CA 94939-1748

Established in 1965 in CA.
Donors: Alfred Fromm†; Hanna Fromm; Alfred and Hanna Fromm Charitable Lead Annuity Trust.
Grantmaker type: Independent foundation.
Financial data (yr. ended 09/30/10): Assets, $20,621,620 (M); gifts received, $2,352,225; expenditures, $1,275,760; qualifying distributions, $1,079,223; giving activities include $1,000,000 for 4 grants (high: $800,000; low: $30,000).
Purpose and activities: Giving primarily to Jewish federated giving funds and to a university's education program for retired persons.
Fields of interest: Higher education; Adult/continuing education; Human services; Jewish federated giving programs; Jewish agencies & synagogues.
International interests: Israel.
Limitations: Applications not accepted. Giving primarily in San Francisco and Larkspur, CA. No grants to individuals.
Application information: Contributes only to pre-selected organizations.

Officers and Directors: * Rabbi Brian L. Lurie, Pres.; Caroline Lurie, V.P.; David George Fromm, Secy.; Peter K. Maier,* Treas.; Barbara Fromm.
Agent: Susan Lechter.
Number of staff: 2 full-time professional; 1 full-time support.
EIN: 946100399

146
The Fuller Foundation
135 N. Los Robles, Ste. 660
Pasadena, CA 91101-4503
Contact: Samuel L. Delcamp, Exec. Dir.
FAX: (626) 792-3232;
E-mail: info@thefullerfoundation.org; Toll-free tel.: (888) 792-3232; URL: http://www.thefullerfoundation.org/

Established in 1987.
Grantmaker type: Public charity.
Financial data (yr. ended 12/31/09): Revenue, $4,406,350; assets, $446,828,711 (M); gifts received, $2,366,273; expenditures, $17,858,383; giving activities include $14,207,544 for grants, and $80,600 for grants to organizations outside the U.S.
Purpose and activities: The foundation primarily gives to Christian agencies, including theological education; support is also given for international development and human services, with an emphasis on children and youth.
Fields of interest: Secondary school/education; Theological school/education; Youth development, religion; Youth development; Human services; Children/youth, services; International development; International economic development; Christian agencies & churches; Protestant agencies & churches.
Limitations: Applications not accepted. Giving on a national basis, with some emphasis on CA.
Application information: Unsolicited requests for funds not considered or acknowledged.
Officers and Directors: * Dennis K. Metzler,* Chair.; Daniel Villanueva,* Vice-Chair.; Peggy C. Still,* Secy.; Katherine L. Saigeon,* Treas.; Samuel L. Delcamp, Exec. Dir.; Scott Bedford; David L. Bere; Gaylen J. Byker; Merlin W. Call; Robert J. Ceremsak; Todd B. Derrick; Larry R. Langdon; Richard J. Mouw; Roy L. Rogers.
EIN: 954124436

147
The Jamie Lynn Fullmer Memorial Fund
(formerly J. L. Fullmer Charitable Fund)
2552 Walnut Ave., No. 230
Tustin, CA 92780-6935

Established in 2001 in CA.
Donor: James L. Fullmer.
Grantmaker type: Independent foundation.
Financial data (yr. ended 11/30/10): Assets, $311,989 (M); expenditures, $144,045; qualifying distributions, $144,045; giving activities include $144,000 for 13+ grants (high: $15,000).
Fields of interest: International development; Higher education; Family services.
Limitations: Applications not accepted. No grants to individuals.
Application information: Contributes only to pre-selected organizations.

Officer: James L. Fullmer, Pres.
EIN: 470847296

148
Fund for Nonviolence
303 Potero, No. 54
Santa Cruz, CA 95060-2760 (831) 460-9321
Contact: Betsy Fairbanks, C.E.O. and Pres.
FAX: (831) 460-9137;
E-mail: mail@fundfornonviolence.org; Toll-free tel.: (866) 454-8006; URL: http://www.fundfornonviolence.org
Grants List: http://www.fundfornonviolence.org/grants/grants.html

Established in 1997 in CA.
Grantmaker type: Independent foundation.
Financial data (yr. ended 12/31/10): Assets, $4,722,402 (M); expenditures, $1,475,306; qualifying distributions, $1,046,215; giving activities include $1,046,215 for grants.
Purpose and activities: The fund cultivates and supports efforts to bring about social change that moves humanity towards a more just and compassionate coexistence. Primary interest is placed on proposals from organizations that: 1) pursue structural changes to root causes of race, class, and gender injustice; 2) value the active involvement of members of the communities most impacted by the violence and social injustice being addressed; 3) understand and articulate the impact of their work on women and promote the leadership of women within the organization; 4) work through networks, coalitions and alliances; 5) reflect the spirit of nonviolence in their organizational relations, structure, and process; and 6) demonstrate the capacity to reflect on their experience and adapt to lessons and insights.
Fields of interest: International human rights; Civil/human rights, advocacy; Civil liberties, advocacy; Civil liberties, death penalty issues.
International interests: Latin America.
Type of support: General/operating support; Continuing support; Management development/capacity building; Program development; Conferences/seminars; Seed money; Technical assistance; Program evaluation; Program-related investments/loans.
Limitations: Applications accepted. Giving on a national and international basis; giving through Prison Program primarily in CA. No support for direct services not in the context of social change. No grants for one time events or experiences without meaningful follow up; or for individually designed academic research or media projects.
Publications: Application guidelines; Grants list; Informational brochure (including application guidelines).
Application information: Applications for the Latin America program will not be accepted. Please contact fund for description of programs, letter of inquiry questions, and upcoming grant cycle. Specific questions need to be addressed in letter of inquiry (questions available on Web site). Application form required.
Initial approach: Letter of inquiry (not to exceed 2 pages)
Copies of proposal: 2
Deadline(s): Check foundation Web site for deadlines
Board meeting date(s): Quarterly
Final notification: Varies

Officers and Directors: * Betsy Fairbanks,* C.E.O. and Pres.; Carolina Martinez,* Secy.; Lynda Marin,* Treas.; Raquel Mariscal, Esq.
Number of staff: 2 part-time professional; 1 part-time support.
EIN: 770457185
Recent grants for international programs:
148-1 Accion Ecologica, Quito, Ecuador, $20,000. 2009.
148-2 Asociacion Filomena Tomaira Pacsi, Lima, Peru, $20,000. 2009.
148-3 Asociacion Nacional de Mujeres Rurales e Indigenas, Santiago, Chile, $20,000. 2009.
148-4 Asociacion para la Promocion Social Alternativa, Bogota, Colombia, $30,000. 2009.
148-5 Coalition for Justice in the Maquiladoras, Missouri City, TX, $20,000. 2009.
148-6 Coordinadora Latinoamericana de Organizaciones del Campo, Brazilia, Brazil, $20,000. 2009.
148-7 Corporacion Juridica Libertad, Medellin, Colombia, $30,000. 2009.
148-8 Global Greengrants Fund, Boulder, CO, $20,000. 2009.
148-9 Grupo de Formacion e Intervencion para el Desarrollo Sostenible, Cajamarca, Peru, $22,500. 2009.
148-10 Human Rights Watch, Los Angeles, CA, $50,000. 2009.
148-11 Instituto Politicas Alternativas para o Cone Sul, Rio de Janeiro, Brazil, $25,000. 2009.
148-12 Iraq Veterans Against the War, New York, NY, $50,000. 2009.
148-13 Jubilee South, Buenos Aires, Argentina, $10,000. 2009.
148-14 Marcha Mundial das Mulheres, Sao Paulo, Brazil, $30,000. 2009.
148-15 Observatorio Latinoamericano de Conflictos Ambientales, Santiago, Chile, $12,000. 2009.
148-16 Organizacion Femenina Popular, Barrancabermeja, Colombia, $20,000. 2009.
148-17 Organizacion Nacional Indigena de Colombia, Bogota, Colombia, $20,000. 2009.
148-18 Peace Brigades International, London, England, $20,000. For Mexico Project. 2009.
148-19 Urgent Action Fund for Womens Human Rights, Boulder, CO, $20,000. 2009.
148-20 Win Without War, Washington, DC, $50,000. 2009.

149
Fund for Santa Barbara, Inc.
26 W. Anapamu St.
Santa Barbara, CA 93101-2514
(805) 962-9164
Contact: Geoff Green, Exec. Dir.
FAX: (805) 965-0217;
E-mail: email@fundforsantabarbara.org; Additional address: 120 E. Jones St., Ste. 127, Santa Maria, CA 93454-5101; URL: http://www.fundforsantabarbara.org/
Fund for Santa Barbara's Philanthropy Promise: http://www.ncrp.org/philanthropys-promise/who

Established in 1980 in CA.
Grantmaker type: Public charity.
Financial data (yr. ended 12/31/10): Revenue, $739,993; assets, $2,338,554 (M); gifts received, $784,684; expenditures, $835,713; giving activities include $385,013 for grants.
Purpose and activities: The fund supports projects that advocate, educate, and organize, in order to

examine and address the root causes of social, economic, and environmental problems.

Fields of interest: Arts, cultural/ethnic awareness; Environment; Health care; International peace/ security; International human rights; Civil/human rights; Public affairs.

Type of support: General/operating support; Emergency funds; Seed money; Technical assistance.

Limitations: Applications accepted. Giving limited to Santa Barbara County, CA. No support for individual candidates in electoral campaigns, or direct service organizations. No grants to individuals, or for capital ventures, building improvement, or equipment (except for basic office equipment).

Publications: Application guidelines; Grants list; Informational brochure; Newsletter; Program policy statement.

Application information: Santa Barbara Foundation Roundtable's Common Grant Application Form accepted. Application form required.

  Initial approach: Contact organization for application packet
  Copies of proposal: 20
  Deadline(s): 2nd Fri. in Mar. and Sept.
  Board meeting date(s): Monthly
  Final notification: Ten weeks

Officers and Directors:* Rand Clark,* Co-Pres.; Cristina Gonzalez,* Co-Pres.; Kyle Richards,* V.P.; Jo Ann Bell,* Secy.; Kate Silsbury,* Treas.; Geoff Green,* Exec. Dir.; Ignacio Alarcon; Olga Aguliera; Angela Antenore; Jane Brody; Angela Caballero de Cordero; Don Daves-Rougeaux; Elsa Granados; Mark Hamilton; Carol Keator; and 6 additional directors.

Number of staff: 2 full-time professional; 2 part-time professional; 1 part-time support.

EIN: 770070742

150

The Gap Foundation

2 Folsom St.
15th Fl.
San Francisco, CA   94105-1205   (415) 427-6473
E-mail: dotti_hatcher@gap.com; URL: http:// www.gapinc.com/content/gapinc/html/csr.html

Established in 1977 in CA.

Donor: The Gap, Inc.

Grantmaker type: Company-sponsored foundation.

Financial data (yr. ended 01/31/11): Assets, $15,745,562 (M); gifts received, $3,749,473; expenditures, $3,685,657; qualifying distributions, $3,684,151; giving activities include $3,684,151 for 49 grants (high: $788,500; low: $7,500).

Purpose and activities: The foundation supports programs designed to reach underserved youth in the developed world and women in the developing world.

Fields of interest: Secondary school/education; International affairs; Boys & girls clubs; Youth development; Human services; Youth; Women; Economically disadvantaged.

International interests: Canada; India; United Kingdom.

Type of support: General/operating support; Management development/capacity building; Program development; Scholarship funds; Employee volunteer services; Sponsorships; Employee matching gifts; Donated equipment; Donated products; In-kind gifts.

Limitations: Applications not accepted. Giving primarily in areas of company operations, with emphasis on San Francisco, CA, Chicago, IL, New York, NY, Canada, India, and the United Kingdom. No support for religious, political, or discriminatory organizations. No grants to individuals, or for scholarships, conferences, travel, films, videos, or fundraisers (except for gift card donations).

Application information: The foundation does not accept unsolicited proposals for grants or event sponsorships.

Officers and Trustees: Bobbi Silten, Pres.; Forrest Bryant, Treas.; Doris F. Fisher; Marka Hansen; Dan Henkle; Art Peck; Stan Raggio; Steve Stickel; Tom Wyatt.

EIN: 942474426

151

The Genocide Education Project

51 Commonwealth Ave.
San Francisco, CA   94118-2601
E-mail: info@genocideeducation.org; URL: http:// www.genocideeducation.org/

Established in 2005.

Grantmaker type: Public charity.

Financial data (yr. ended 08/31/10): Revenue, $22,312; assets, $28,240 (M); gifts received, $21,653; expenditures, $62,592.

Purpose and activities: The project seeks to help prevent genocide by assisting educators, students, and educational organizations.

Fields of interest: International human rights.

Officers and Directors: Raffi Momjian,* Pres. and C.E.O.; Roxanne Makasdjian,* Secy.; Khajag Sarkissian,* Treas.; Dr. Stephan Astourian; Dr. Dikran Kaligian.

EIN: 593791802

152

The Gere Foundation

c/o International Business Mgmt.
9696 Culver Blvd., No. 203
Culver City, CA   90232-2754
URL: http://www.gerefoundation.org/

Established in 1991 in CA.

Donors: Richard Gere; The Conde Nast Publications, Inc.; Warner Brothers; Visages RPS, Inc.; Lakeshore International Corporation.

Grantmaker type: Independent foundation.

Financial data (yr. ended 12/31/10): Assets, $4,482,118 (M); gifts received, $168,292; expenditures, $420,909; qualifying distributions, $413,730; giving activities include $413,730 for grants.

Purpose and activities: The foundation awards grants to humanitarian organizations supporting victims of war and natural disasters, providing HIV/ AIDS care and research, and addressing human rights violations occurring around the world. Its primary mission is to assist the cultural survival of the Tibetan people through health, technological and educational projects.

Fields of interest: Arts, cultural/ethnic awareness; Education; Health care; AIDS; International development; International human rights.

International interests: Asia.

Limitations: Applications not accepted. Giving on a national basis. No grants to individuals, or for capital campaigns, for-profit organizations, or feature film projects.

Publications: Grants list.

Application information: Unsolicited requests for funds not accepted.

Officers: Richard Gere, Pres.; Edgar Gross, Secy.-Treas.

EIN: 954305828

153

J. Paul Getty Trust

1200 Getty Ctr. Dr., Ste. 800
Los Angeles, CA   90049-1679   (310) 440-7320
Contact: The Getty Foundation
FAX: (310) 440-7703;
E-mail: GettyFoundation@getty.edu; URL: http:// www.getty.edu
E-Newsletter: http://www.getty.edu/subscribe/ index.html
Grants List: http://www.getty.edu/foundation/ grants/
Twitter: http://twitter.com/gettytrust

Operating trust established in 1953 in CA as J. Paul Getty Museum; Grant Program established in 1984.

Donor: J. Paul Getty‡.

Grantmaker type: Operating foundation.

Financial data (yr. ended 06/30/10): Assets, $9,584,879,219 (M); gifts received, $5,172,069; expenditures, $276,129,799; qualifying distributions, $210,398,710; giving activities include $11,218,468 for 145 grants (high: $1,000,000), $1,529,190 for 148 grants to individuals (high: $75,000; low: $500), $463,000 for 33 employee matching gifts, and $209,431,727 for 4 foundation-administered programs.

Purpose and activities: The Getty Foundation fulfills the philanthropic mission of the Getty Trust by supporting individuals and institutions committed to advancing the understanding and preservation of the visual arts locally and throughout the world. Through strategic grants and programs, the foundation strengthens art history as a global discipline, promotes the interdisciplinary practice of conservation, increases access to museum and archival collections, and develops current and future leaders in the visual arts. The foundation carries out its work in collaboration with the Getty Museum, Research Institute, and Conservation Institute, to ensure that the Getty programs achieve maximum impact.

Fields of interest: Arts education; Art history; Arts; Arts, cultural/ethnic awareness; Museums; Visual arts; Visual arts, art conservation; Minorities.

Type of support: Program development; Publication; Fellowships; Internship funds; Research; Employee matching gifts; Grants to individuals; Matching/ challenge support.

Limitations: Applications accepted. Giving on a national and international basis, with emphasis on Los Angeles and Southern CA. No grants for operating or endowment purposes, start-up, construction or maintenance of buildings, or acquisition of works of art.

Publications: Application guidelines; Annual report; Grants list.

Application information: The foundation maintains its commitment to increasing the understanding and preservation of the visual arts, both in Los Angeles and throughout the world. The foundation's four strategic priorities are: 1) access to museum and archival collections; 2) art history as a global discipline; 3) advancing conservation practice; and 4) leadership and professional development. Within these focus areas, current initiatives range from support for exhibitions about the development of avant-garde art in Southern California to the conservation of mosaics in the Mediterranean. The Getty Foundation also maintains support for long-standing leadership and professional development programs including internships and the Getty Leadership Institute. For additional information, guidelines and updates, or to review current initiatives and programs in detail, please visit the foundation's web site. Application form not required.

Initial approach: See web site for online applications

Officers and Trustees: * Mark S. Siegel,* Chair.; Neil Rudenstine,* Vice-Chair.; James Cuno,* C.E.O. and Pres.; Patricia Woodworth, V.P., C.O.O. and C.F.O.; Stephen W. Clark, V.P., Secy. and Genl. Counsel; James M. Williams, V.P., Treas. and C.I.O.; Ron Hartwig, V.P., Comms.; William Humphries, Cont.; Frances Daly Ferguson; Maria D. Hummer-Tuttle; Joanne Corday Kozberg; Paul LeClerc; David Lee; Luis G. Nogales; Stewart A. Resnick; William E.B. Siart; Ronald P. Spogli; Peter J. Taylor; Jay S. Wintrob.

Number of staff: 1406

EIN: 951790021

Recent grants for international programs:

153-1 Association for Preservation Technology International, Springfield, IL, $75,000. For participants from Latin America to attend the 2011 conference in Victoria, Canada. 2011.

153-2 British Museum, London, England, $885,244. For a three-year East Africa Museum Training Program. (545,000). 2011.

153-3 Cambridge University, Hamilton Kerr Institute, Cambridge, England, $224,153. For training and treatment related to five panel paintings in the Royal Collection as part of the Panel Paintings Initiative. (138,000). 2011.

153-4 College Art Association, New York, NY, $100,000. For participants from developing countries to attend the 2012 Annual Conference in Los Angeles. 2011.

153-5 Foundation of the American Institute for Conservation of Historic and Artistic Works, Washington, DC, $73,600. For participants from Latin America and the Caribbean to attend the 2012 annual meeting in Albuquerque, New Mexico. 2011.

153-6 Fundacao de Apoio a Universidade de Sao Paulo, Sao Paulo, Brazil, $248,000. For faculty and student exchanges and the research seminars New Art Histories: Relating Ideas, Objects and Institutions in Latin America. 2011.

153-7 Fundacion ArtNexus, Bogota, Colombia, $127,500. For the research seminars Intellectual Networks: Art and Politics in Latin America. 2011.

153-8 International Association of Art Critics, Paris, France, $34,000. For participants from developing countries to attend the 2011 Congress in Asuncion, Paraguay. 2011.

153-9 International Centre for the Study of the Preservation and Restoration of Cultural Property, Rome, Italy, $159,672. For participants in the Tyre, Lebanon Mosaikon course to implement pilot projects, as part of the Mosaikon initiative. 2011.

153-10 International Council of Museums, Paris, France, $91,686. For participants from developing countries and Central and Eastern Europe to attend the Sixteenth Triennial Meeting of the Conservation Committee in Lisbon, Portugal. 2011.

153-11 International Council of Museums, Paris, France, $30,000. For museum professionals from Southern Africa to attend the fourth International Conference on the Inclusive Museum in Johannesburg, South Africa. 2011.

153-12 International Council of Museums, CIMAM, Paris, France, $56,696. For participants from developing countries to attend the 2011 Annual Conference of the International Committee for Museums and Collections of Modern Art (CIMAM) in Ljubljana, Zagreb, and Sarajevo. (38,600 EUR). 2011.

153-13 International Council of Museums, ICOM-CIDOC, Paris, France, $73,750. For participants from developing countries to attend the 2011 Annual Conference of the International Committee for Documentation (ICOM-CIDOC) in Sibiu, Romania. 2011.

153-14 International Council of Museums, International Committee on Management (INTERCOM), Paris, France, $25,000. For participants from developing countries to attend the 2011 Annual Conference of the International Committee on Management (ICOM-INTERCOM) in Copenhagen, Denmark. 2011.

153-15 International Council on Monuments and Sites, Paris, France, $75,000. For participants from developing countries and Central and Eastern Europe to attend the 17th General Assembly and Scientific Symposium. 2011.

153-16 International Institute for Conservation of Historic and Artistic Works, London, England, $154,851. For the IIC website and for participants from developing countries to attend the 24th International Congress in Vienna, Austria. (94,600). 2011.

153-17 International National Trusts Organisation, London, England, $75,000. For participants from developing countries and Central and Eastern Europe to attend the 14th International Conference of National Trusts in Victoria, Canada. 2011.

153-18 Kings College London, London, England, $98,905. To organize two workshops on mosaic conservation in Libya for site managers, archaeologists and technicians. 2011.

153-19 Kulturveranstaltungen des Bundes in Berlin GmbH, Martin Gropius Bau, Berlin, Germany, $240,000. For the exhibition +Pacific Standard Time: Crosscurrents in L.A. Painting and Sculpture 1950-1970+ and related programming at the Martin-Gropius-Bau, Berlin. 2011.

153-20 Louisiana Museum of Modern Art, Humlebaek, Denmark, $60,000. For the production of illustrated scholarly catalogue to accompany the American and European tour of artist Ed Kienholz's +Five Car Stud+ (1969-1972), as part of the special initiative +Pacific Standard Time: Art in L.A. 1945-1980.+. 2011.

153-21 Max Planck Society for the Advancement of Science, Kunsthistorisches Institut in Florenz, Munich, Germany, $236,000. For the third phase of the research seminars Art, Space, and Mobility in the Early Ages of Globalization organized by the Kunsthistorisches Institut in Florence, Italy. 2011.

153-22 Museo Nacional del Prado, Museo del Prado, Madrid, Spain, $389,043. For training and treatment related to a series of six panel paintings by Peter Paul Rubens as part of the Panel Paintings Initiative. (270,000 Euros). 2011.

153-23 Museum of Latin American Art, Long Beach, CA, $25,000. For the publication MEX/LA: The Legacy of Mexican Modernism(s) in Los Angeles 1930-1985, as part of the special initiative Pacific Standard Time: Art in L.A. 1945-1980. 2011.

153-24 Netherlands Organisation for Scientific Research, The Hague, Netherlands, $95,304. For interactive image web application related to the Ghent Altarpiece. (66,000 Euros). 2011.

153-25 Netherlands Organisation for Scientific Research, The Hague, Netherlands, $77,802. For experts meeting on panel paintings conservation and a film on the Ghent Altarpiece, as part of the Panel Paintings Initiative. 2011.

153-26 Pontifical Catholic University of Peru, Lima, Peru, $75,000. For participants from developing countries to attend the 11th International Conference on the Study and the Conservation of Earthen Architectural Heritage (TERRA 2012). 2011.

153-27 Royal Museums of Fine Arts of Belgium, Brussels, Belgium, $404,320. For training and treatment related to nine Old Master paintings in the collection as part of the Panel Paintings Initiative. (280,000 Euros). 2011.

153-28 School of African Heritage, Porto-Novo, Benin, $80,000. For the completion of a two-year university diploma course in Preventative Conservation. 2011.

153-29 Seton Hall University, South Orange, NJ, $23,000. For the planning of a symposium, China and the West: Visual and Artistic Encounters, Qing Dynasty. 2011.

153-30 Sterling and Francine Clark Art Institute, Williamstown, MA, $20,000. For Unfolding Narratives: Art Histories in East-Central Europe after 1989. 2011.

153-31 University of California, Los Angeles, CA, $85,800. For participants from Africa to attend the Arts Council of the African Studies Association's Fifteenth Triennial Symposium on African Art at the University of California, Los Angeles. 2011.

153-32 University of Cyprus, Nicosia, Cyprus, $230,194. For activities related to the 11th Triennial Conference of the International Committee for the Conservation of Mosaics in Morocco and support for the Mosaikon Regional Coordinator. 2011.

154
The Rosalinde and Arthur Gilbert Foundation

2730 Wilshire Blvd., Ste. 301
Santa Monica, CA   90403-4749
Contact: Robbie Diamond
URL: http://www.thegilbertfoundation.org
E-Newsletter: http://visitor.constantcontact.com/manage/optin/ea?
v=001NKYjl8JNhwpsy202CsrHcw%3D%3D
Grants List: http://web.me.com/seanxyz/gilbert/recent.html

Established in 2002 in CA; funded in 2003 through a merger with another foundation with the same name.

Donor: A & R Gilbert 1982 Trust.

Grantmaker type: Independent foundation.

Financial data (yr. ended 12/31/09): Assets, $198,707,085 (M); gifts received, $500,000; expenditures, $12,113,806; qualifying distributions, $7,763,879; giving activities include $6,729,436 for grants.

Purpose and activities: Support primarily for access to college, healthcare, Israel, arts education, Jewish organizations and universities in California.

Fields of interest: Education; Human services; Higher education; Jewish agencies & synagogues.

International interests: Israel.

Limitations: Applications accepted. Giving primarily in Los Angeles, CA and Israel. No grants for individuals, capital campaigns or legislation.

Application information: Full proposals accepted by invitation only following a letter of inquiry. After receiving a letter of inquiry, the foundation will send a notice of acknowledgement. If the foundation decides not to proceed, applicants will be notified with an explanation. If the foundation determines from an applicant's letter of inquiry that a request is consistent with the foundation's priorities and interests, the applicant will be asked to submit a full proposal. Only when an organization is invited to submit a proposal, will a full application e-mailed.

Initial approach: Letters of inquiry (1-2 pages). Use the form on the contact page of the foundation's web site

Deadline(s): None for letters of inquiry; If you submit a letter of inquiry and it is declined you must wait 12 months from the date of declination to submit another request

Final notification: Receipt of proposal is acknowledged immediately; Decisions are communicated in a timely manner

Officers: Richard Ziman, C.E.O.; Martin Blank, Jr., Secy.

EIN: 562305694

Recent grants for international programs:

154-1 American Friends of Koret Israel Economic Development Fund, San Francisco, CA, $25,000. For SAWA, microfinance program in Israel, modeled on Grameen Bank and focusing on loans to Bedouin communities in southern Israel. 2009.

154-2 American Friends of the Association for the Advancement of Community Centers in Israel, New York, NY, $62,500. For programs for discharged soldiers. 2009.

154-3 American Friends of the Association for the Advancement of Community Centers in Israel, New York, NY, $50,000. For Budding Scientists program. 2009.

154-4 American Friends of the Association for the Advancement of Community Centers in Israel, New York, NY, $50,000. For programs for discharged soldiers. 2009.

154-5 American Friends of the Association for the Advancement of Community Centers in Israel, New York, NY, $40,000. For Budding Scientists Program. 2009.

154-6 American Friends of the Hebrew University, Los Angeles, CA, $55,000. For Saltiel Center for Pre-Academic Studies. 2009.

154-7 American Friends of the Hebrew University, Los Angeles, CA, $55,000. For Saltiel Center for Pre-Academic Studies. 2009.

154-8 American Friends of the Hebrew University, Los Angeles, CA, $39,200. For Project Nurture, initiative to retain students vulnerable to dropping out of university by creating pilot program to enhance retention and career development for first-year and second-year Israeli-Arab law school students. 2009.

154-9 American Friends of the Hebrew University, Los Angeles, CA, $30,000. For Tennis and Table Tennis programs. 2009.

154-10 American Friends of the Hebrew University, Los Angeles, CA, $14,500. For general support. 2009.

154-11 American Friends of the Hebrew University, Los Angeles, CA, $10,000. For Leadership Education Forum. 2009.

154-12 American Friends of the Israel Philharmonic Orchestra, New York, NY, $25,000. For general support. 2009.

154-13 American Friends of the Reut Institute, Beverly Hills, CA, $15,000. For general support. 2009.

154-14 American Israel Education Foundation, Washington, DC, $100,000. For American Israel Public Affairs Committe (AIPAC). 2009.

154-15 American Jewish Joint Distribution Committee, New York, NY, $50,000. For Project Tsofia. 2009.

154-16 American Jewish Joint Distribution Committee, New York, NY, $25,000. For Or 'Aquiva Parent and Child Center. 2009.

154-17 American Society for Technion-Israel Institute of Technology, Los Angeles, CA, $40,000. For Sci-Tech, scientific summer camp for talented students at Technion Israel Institute of Technology. 2009.

154-18 American Society for Technion-Israel Institute of Technology, Los Angeles, CA, $39,000. For general support. 2009.

154-19 American Society for Technion-Israel Institute of Technology, New York, NY, $17,500. For Pre-University Program, where selected students learn basic education such as math, science and English. 2009.

154-20 American Supporters of YEDID, Teaneck, NJ, $50,000. For programs to end homelessness in Israel and the West Bank. 2009.

154-21 American Supporters of YEDID, Teaneck, NJ, $50,000. For programs to end homelessness in Israel and the West Bank. 2009.

154-22 Central Europe Center for Research and Documentation, Atlanta, GA, $25,000. For educational outreach programs. 2009.

154-23 Economic Empowerment for Women, Haifa, Israel, $30,000. For program, A Business of One's Own. 2009.

154-24 Economic Empowerment for Women, Haifa, Israel, $30,000. For program, A Business of One's Own. 2009.

154-25 Friends of Ethiopian Jews, Boston, MA, $30,000. For programs in the Gedara Community. 2009.

154-26 Friends of Ethiopian Jews, Boston, MA, $30,000. For programs in the Geran Community. 2009.

154-27 Friends of Yemin Orde, Rockville, MD, $20,000. For Excellence in Education Initiative. 2009.

154-28 Hadassah College Jerusalem, Jerusalem, Israel, $72,000. For Gateway to Hope and Promising Prospect. 2009.

154-29 Hadassah College Jerusalem, Jerusalem, Israel, $52,500. For Promising Project. 2009.

154-30 Hadassah College Jerusalem, Jerusalem, Israel, $52,500. For Promising Project. 2009.

154-31 Israel Free Loan Association, Jerusalem, Israel, $37,500. For Haredi Employment Training and Placement program. 2009.

154-32 Israel Free Loan Association, Jerusalem, Israel, $37,500. For Haredi Employment Training and Placement program. 2009.

154-33 Israel Tennis Association, Tel Aviv, Israel, $37,500. For Girls' Tennis programs. 2009.

154-34 Israel Tennis Association, Tel Aviv, Israel, $37,500. For Girls' Tennis programs. 2009.

154-35 Kol Ha-Isha, The Jerusalem Womens Center, Jerusalem, Israel, $30,000. For economic empowerment programs. 2009.

154-36 Maccabi Union USA, Beverly Hills, CA, $15,000. For general support. 2009.

154-37 MATI-Jerusalem Business Development Center, Jerusalem, Israel, $40,000. To export Pilot Program. 2009.

154-38 MATI-Jerusalem Business Development Center, Jerusalem, Israel, $37,500. For program, From Unemployed to Entrepreneur. 2009.

154-39 MATI-Jerusalem Business Development Center, Jerusalem, Israel, $37,500. For program, From Unemployed to Entrepreneur. 2009.

154-40 MATI-Jerusalem Business Development Center, Jerusalem, Israel, $37,500. For program, From Unemployed to Entrepreneur. 2009.

154-41 Milken Institute, Santa Monica, CA, $25,000. For Milken Institute Israel Center (MIIC). 2009.

154-42 Negev Institute for Strategies of Peace and Development, Beer Sheva, Israel, $45,000. For economic empowerment and enhancement of employment opportunities for Negev Arab Bedouin women and men. 2009.

154-43 Negev Institute for Strategies of Peace and Development, Beer Sheva, Israel, $45,000. For economic empowerment and enhancement of employment opportunities for Negev Arab Bedouin women and men. 2009.

154-44 Negev Institute for Strategies of Peace and Development, Beer Sheva, Israel, $36,000. For economic empowerment and enhancement of employment opportunities for Negev Arab Bedouin women and men. 2009.

154-45 Negev Institute for Strategies of Peace and Development, Beer Sheva, Israel, $36,000. For economic empowerment and enhancement of employment opportunities for Negev Arab Bedouin women and men. 2009.

154-46 PEF Israel Endowment Funds, New York, NY, $50,000. For programs in Rishon Lezion. 2009.

154-47 Rashi Foundation, Tafnit Turn Around, Ben-Shemen, Israel, $44,000. For Last Hurdle Program with the aim of closing the educational gap between underachievers and their classmates, and on reducing the disparity between low-performing schools in weak communities and schools in the center of the country. 2009.

154-48 UCLA Foundation, Los Angeles, CA, $225,000. For Israel Studies Program. 2009.

154-49 Womens Courtyard, Jaffa, Israel, $42,500. For general support. 2009.

154-50 Womens Courtyard, Jaffa, Israel, $42,500. For general support. 2009.

154-51 Zionism 2000, Beit Yehoshea, Israel, $15,000. For Youth in Yerucham. 2009.

154-52 Zionism 2000, Beit Yehoshea, Israel, $15,000. For Youth in Yerucham. 2009.

154-53 Zionism 2000, Beit Yehoshea, Israel, $12,000. For Youth in Yerucham. 2009.

154-54 Zionism 2000, Beit Yehoshea, Israel, $12,000. For Youth in Yerucham. 2009.

155
Give2Asia

465 California St., Ste. 806
San Francisco, CA 94104-1832 (415) 743-3336
Contact: Ray Klinke, C.F.O.; Birger Stamperdahl, Dir., Mktg.
FAX: (415) 391-4075; E-mail: info@give2asia.org;
Mailing address: P.O. Box 193223, San Francisco, CA 94119-3223; URL: http://www.give2asia.org/
Ammado Profile: http://www.ammado.com/nonprofit/give2asia
Facebook: http://www.facebook.com/pages/San-Francisco-CA/Give2Asia/26233666109?ref=ts
LinkedIn: http://www.linkedin.com/companies/give2asia
Twitter: http://twitter.com/give2asia

Established in 2000 in CA by the Asia Foundation.
Grantmaker type: Public charity.
Financial data (yr. ended 09/30/10): Revenue, $21,317,531; assets, $10,699,592 (M); gifts received, $20,834,423; expenditures, $24,256,192; giving activities include $731,830 for grants, and $21,357,886 for grants to organizations outside the U.S.
Purpose and activities: The organization seeks to provide individuals, families, corporations, and foundations with the tools for fulfilling their charitable goals in Asia.
Fields of interest: International affairs; Asians/Pacific Islanders.
International interests: Asia.
Type of support: Scholarship funds; Research; Program development; Management development/capacity building; General/operating support; Employee matching gifts; Emergency funds; Consulting services.
Limitations: Applications not accepted. Giving limited for the benefit of Asia.
Publications: Annual report; Informational brochure; Newsletter.
Application information: The organization makes grants to area organizations in response a list of greatest needs it identifies every year; unsolicited requests for funds not otherwise considered or acknowledged.
  Board meeting date(s): Jan., May, and Oct.
Officers and Trustees: Bill S. Kim,* Chair.; Michael Howe, Pres. and C.E.O.; Ray Klinke, C.F.O.; Naren Agrawal, Ph.D.; Doug Bereuter; Alexander D. Calhoun; Gina Lin Chu; Weili Dai; Frank L. Ellsworth; William P. Fuller; Edwin Go; Eugene Hong; Bill Kim; Kai-Fu Lee; Joe Lumarda; Teresa Orr; Susan J. Pharr; and 7 additional trustees.
Number of staff: 10 full-time professional.
EIN: 943373670

156
Global Catalyst Foundation

255 Shoreline Dr., Ste. 520
Redwood City, CA 94065-1432 (650) 486-2430
FAX: (650) 593-0419;
E-mail: info@global-catalyst.org; URL: http://www.global-catalyst.org

Established in 2000 in CA.
Donors: Kamran Elahian; Global Catalyst Partners; Art Schneiderman.
Grantmaker type: Independent foundation.
Financial data (yr. ended 12/31/10): Assets, $71,291 (M); gifts received, $196,310; expenditures, $183,110; qualifying distributions,

$183,110; giving activities include $182,961 for 5 grants (high: $50,000; low: $950).
Purpose and activities: The foundation's mission is to improve people's lives through the effective application of information technologies. It initiates and supports innovative projects worldwide to improve education, alleviate poverty, promote social tolerance and celebrate diversity.
Fields of interest: Education; Economic development; Computer science; Immigrants/refugees.
International interests: United Kingdom.
Type of support: Equipment; Program development; Technical assistance.
Limitations: Applications not accepted. Giving primarily for U.S.-based NGO's delivering services to developing countries. No grants to individuals, or for capital campaigns.
Application information: Contributes only to pre-selected organizations.
Officer and Directors: Kamran Elahian,* Chair.; Arthur Schneiderman, Secy.; Zohre Elahian, Treas.; Koji Osawa; Vijay Parikh.
EIN: 770555801

157
Global Exchange

2017 Mission St., 2nd Fl.
San Francisco, CA 94110-1296 (415) 255-7296
Contact: Kirsten Irgens-Moller, Exec. Dir.
FAX: (415) 255-7498;
E-mail: web@globalexchange.or; URL: http://www.globalexchange.org

Established in 1988.
Grantmaker type: Public charity.
Financial data (yr. ended 12/31/10): Revenue, $4,684,434; assets, $1,181,989 (M); gifts received, $2,209,603; expenditures, $5,068,919.
Purpose and activities: The organization is dedicated to promoting political, social, and environmental justice globally.
Fields of interest: International human rights.
Type of support: General/operating support; Program development.
Limitations: Applications not accepted. Giving on a national and international basis.
Publications: Newsletter.
Application information:
  Board meeting date(s): Mar. and Oct.
Officers: Walter Turner, Pres.; Wanda Whitaker, V.P.; John Harrington, Treas.; Kevin Danaher, Secy.; Kirsten Irgens-Moller, Exec. Dir.
Directors: Medea Susan Benjamin; Delvis Fernandez; Michele Frank, M.D.; Isao Fujimoto; Tony Newman; Thuyen Wguyen; Bob Wing.
Number of staff: 23 full-time professional; 5 part-time professional; 5 full-time support; 11 part-time support.
EIN: 943066686

158
The Global Fund for Women

222 Sutter St., No. 500
San Francisco, CA 94108-4445
Contact: Rachel Humphrey, Dir., Philanthropic Partnerships
FAX: (415) 248-4801;
E-mail: gfw@globalfundforwomen.org; URL: http://www.globalfundforwomen.org
Twitter: http://twitter.com/GlobalFundWomen

Established in 1987 in CA.
Grantmaker type: Public charity.
Financial data (yr. ended 06/30/10): Revenue, $12,137,100; assets, $20,581,667 (M); gifts received, $11,894,909; expenditures, $14,833,203; giving activities include $8,512,111 for grants, and for 504 grants to organizations outside the U.S.
Purpose and activities: The fund provides flexible general support to seed, strengthen, and link women's rights groups outside the United States.
Fields of interest: Education, equal rights; Youth development, equal rights; Women, centers/services; International affairs, equal rights; International human rights; Civil/human rights, women; Civil/human rights, LGBTQ; Civil liberties, reproductive rights; Community development, women's clubs; Women's studies; Public affairs, equal rights; Religion, equal rights; Immigrants/refugees; Girls; Disabilities, people with; Women; LGBTQ.
Type of support: General/operating support; Continuing support; Income development; Management development/capacity building; Building/renovation; Equipment; Emergency funds; Program development; Conferences/seminars; Film/video/radio; Publication; Seed money; Curriculum development; Research; Technical assistance; In-kind gifts.
Limitations: Applications accepted. Giving to Africa, Europe and the Former Soviet States, Middle East and North Africa, the Americas, Asia and Oceania. No support for organizations based and working primarily in the U.S., groups whose main purpose is to generate income for its members or the community, or organizations without women in important management functions. No grants to individuals, or for government entities, political parties or election campaigns, or scholarships.
Publications: Application guidelines; Annual report; Financial statement; Grants list; Informational brochure; Newsletter; Occasional report.
Application information: Application form not required.
  Initial approach: Proposal
  Copies of proposal: 1
  Deadline(s): None
  Board meeting date(s): Biannually
  Final notification: Three times annually
Officers and Directors: Lelia Hessini,* Chair.; Pilar Gonzales, Interim V.P., Devel.; Deborah Holmes, V.P., Comms.; Shalini Nataraj, V.P., Progs.; Dina Dublon,* Secy.; Stans Kleijnen,* Treas.; Dale Needles, C.F.O.; Charlotte Bunch; Myrna Cunningham; Abigail Disney; Lydia Alpizar Duran; Linder Gruber; Boriana Jonsson; Gay McDougall; Zenebeworke Tadesse; Sakena Yacoobi; and 6 additional directors.
Number of staff: 24 full-time professional; 3 part-time professional; 20 full-time support; 3 part-time support.
EIN: 770155782

159
Global Green USA

2218 Main St., 2nd Fl.
Santa Monica, CA 90405-2273 (310) 581-2700
FAX: (310) 581-2702;
E-mail: ggusa@globalgreen.org; URL: http://www.globalgreen.org
Facebook: http://www.facebook.com/globalgreenfans

Flickr: http://www.flickr.com/photos/
globalgreenusa
Twitter: http://twitter.com/#!/globalgreenusa
YouTube: http://www.youtube.com/user/
GlobalGreen2008

Established in 1993 in CA.
Grantmaker type: Public charity.
Financial data (yr. ended 12/31/09): Revenue, $3,872,324; assets, $5,293,431 (M); gifts received, $3,468,908; expenditures, $3,912,504; giving activities include $34,250 for grants, $150,000 for grants to organizations outside the U.S., and $25,000 for grants to individuals.
Purpose and activities: The organization works toward the stemming of global climate change by creating green buildings and cities, eliminating weapons of mass destruction that threaten lives and the environment, and providing clean, safe drinking water for those who lack access to clean water.
Fields of interest: International affairs, arms control; Environment, water resources; Environment, public education; Environment, pollution control; Environment, climate change/global warming; Environment.
Limitations: Giving on a national and international basis.
Publications: Informational brochure; Newsletter; Occasional report.
Officers and Directors:* Scott Seydel,* Chair.; Matt Petersen, Pres. and C.E.O.; Robert S. Bucklin,* Treas.; Andrew Beebe; Jason Berman, Ph.D.; Sebastian Copeland; Leonardo DiCaprio; Amb. Wyche Fowler; Hon. Lee Hamilton; Jordan Harris; Bruce Katz; Pat Mitchell; Jerry Moss; Edward Norton; Steven Schneider, Ph.D.; Lisa Shields; Zem Spire-Joaquin; Jeremy Wiesen.
EIN: 770387124

160
The Goldrich Family Foundation
5150 Overland Ave.
Culver City, CA 90230-4914
Contact: Jona Goldrich, Pres.

Established in 1987 in CA.
Donors: Jona Goldrich; Ana Hirth; Emanuel Hirth; Goldrich & Kest Industries; Goldrich Trust; Hirth Family Foundation; Z Valet Inc.; Phoenix Life Insurance Co.
Grantmaker type: Independent foundation.
Financial data (yr. ended 11/30/09): Assets, $70,699,422 (M); gifts received, $5,000,000; expenditures, $3,552,332; qualifying distributions, $3,134,936; giving activities include $3,103,769 for 82 grants (high: $2,047,595; low: $100).
Purpose and activities: Support for Jewish education and for other Jewish organizations.
Fields of interest: Education; Community/economic development; Jewish federated giving programs; Jewish agencies & synagogues.
International interests: Israel.
Limitations: Applications not accepted. Giving primarily in Los Angeles, CA, and New York, NY; some funding also in CO. No grants to individuals.
Application information: Contributes only to pre-selected organizations.
Officers: Jona Goldrich, Pres.; Andrea Goldrich Cayton, Secy.; Melinda Goldrich, Treas.; David Rochkind, C.F.O.
Directors: Barry Cayton; Doretta Goldrich.
EIN: 954155986

161
Goldsmith Family Foundation
c/o Bram Goldsmith
400 N. Roxbury Dr.
Beverly Hills, CA 90210-5002

Established in 1980 in CA.
Donors: Mrs. Bram Goldsmith; Bram Goldsmith; Karen Goldsmith; Russell Goldsmith; Elm 2006 Charitable Trust; Spruce 2007 Charitable Trust.
Grantmaker type: Independent foundation.
Financial data (yr. ended 09/30/10): Assets, $13,483,064 (M); gifts received, $403,493; expenditures, $436,295; qualifying distributions, $432,350; giving activities include $428,286 for grants.
Fields of interest: Performing arts; Arts; Education; Hospitals (general); Medical research, institute; Human services; Jewish federated giving programs; Jewish agencies & synagogues.
International interests: Israel.
Type of support: Continuing support; Annual campaigns; Capital campaigns; Building/renovation; Endowments; Professorships; Research; Matching/challenge support.
Limitations: Applications not accepted. Giving primarily in southern CA. No grants to individuals.
Application information: Contributes only to pre-selected organizations.
  Board meeting date(s): As needed
Officers: Bram Goldsmith, Pres.; Elaine Goldsmith, V.P. and Treas.
Directors: Bruce L. Goldsmith; Russell Goldsmith.
Number of staff: 1 part-time support.
EIN: 953545880

162
The Gondobay Manga Foundation
c/o Steven G. Churchwell
1101 South Flower St., Ste. 4
Burbank, CA 91502-2022 (818) 333-1905
FAX: (818) 333-1935; URL: http://
www.gondobaymangafoundation.org/
Facebook: http://www.facebook.com/pages/
The-Gondobay-Manga-Foundation/
272576724729?ref=ts

Grantmaker type: Public charity.
Financial data (yr. ended 05/31/10): Revenue, $98,130; assets, $5,683 (M); gifts received, $98,130; expenditures, $86,091.
Purpose and activities: The foundation works to foster cooperative planning to achieve positive, timely improvement in the lives of the people of Sierra Leone.
Fields of interest: Human services.
International interests: Sierra Leone.
Limitations: Giving limited to Sierra Leone.
Officer and Directors: Isaiah Washington,* Chair.; L.D. Britt, M.D., M.P.H.; Brian M. Fischer; Barbara Gothard, Ph.D.; Andre Panossian, M.D.; Steven Ross; Esther H. Vassar; Breton F. Washington; Jenisa Washington.
EIN: 205434913

163
Google.org
1600 Amphitheatre Pkwy.
Mountain View, CA 94043-1351
URL: http://www.google.org
Google Earth Outreach Tweets: http://twitter.com/
statuses/user_timeline/41865658.rss
Google for Non-Profits: https://groups.google.com/
group/googlefornonprofits?hl=en
Google Grants Blog: http://
googlegrants.blogspot.com/
Google Grants Discussion Groups: http://
www.google.com/support/forum/p/grants?hl=en
Twitter: http://twitter.com/earthoutreach

Grantmaker type: Corporate giving program.
Financial data (yr. ended 12/31/10): Total giving, $183,100,000, including $183,100,000 for grants.
Purpose and activities: As a complement to its foundation, Google makes charitable contributions to nonprofit organizations directly. Support is given on a national and international basis in areas of company operations.
Fields of interest: Arts; Youth development; Environment; Public health; Education; Science.
International interests: Australia; Brazil; Canada; Denmark; France; Germany; India; Ireland; Italy; Japan; Netherlands; Spain; Sweden; Switzerland; United Kingdom.
Type of support: Employee matching gifts; Employee volunteer services; Technical assistance; Donated products; In-kind gifts.
Limitations: Applications accepted. Giving on a national and international basis in areas of company operations. No support for organizations participating in the Google AdSense program, religious or political organizations, or lobbying organizations.
Publications: Application guidelines.
Application information: All qualifying NTEN organizations will be considered for Google Grants on an expedited basis. A contributions committee reviews all requests. Application form required.
  Initial approach: Complete online application form for Google Grants program
  Copies of proposal: 1
  Deadline(s): None
  Final notification: 4 months for Google Grants

164
Grameen de la Frontera Norte
1330 Orange Ave., Ste. 309
Coronado, CA 92118-2949 (858) 646-7799
Contact: Marshall Saunders, Pres.
Telephone for Marshall Saunders: (619) 435-7980

Grantmaker type: Public charity.
Financial data (yr. ended 12/31/10): Revenue, $20,820; assets, $4,999 (M); gifts received, $20,820; expenditures, $29,632; giving activities include $28,190 for grants, and for 1 grant to an organization outside the U.S.
Purpose and activities: The organization supports efforts to reduce poverty and promote economic self-sufficiency among the world's poor.
Fields of interest: International economic development; International relief.
Limitations: Applications not accepted. Giving limited to Mexico.
Publications: Annual report.

Officers and Directors: * Marshall Saunders,* Pres.; Edward Law,* Secy.-Treas.; Ray Delagrave; Timi C. Gleason.
EIN: 330843234

165
Greenlight Apparel Corporate Giving Program
48521 Warm Springs Blvd.
Fremont, CA   94539-7792   (510) 474-3965
E-mail: info@greenlightapparel.com; URL: http://www.greenlightapparel.com
B Corporation Profile: http://www.bcorporation.net/greenlightapparel

Grantmaker type: Corporate giving program.
Purpose and activities: Greenlight Apparel is a certified B Corporation that donates a percentage of profits to charitable organizations.
Fields of interest: Anti-slavery/human trafficking; Children's rights.
Type of support: General/operating support.

166
Grousbeck Family Foundation
c/o Stanford University
655 Knight Way
Graduate School of Business, Rm. L-336
Stanford, CA   94305-5015   (650) 723-0709
Contact: H. Irving Grousbeck, Pres.

Established in 1990 in CA.
Donors: H. Irving Grousbeck; E. Grousbeck‡.
Grantmaker type: Independent foundation.
Financial data (yr. ended 11/30/10): Assets, $179,112,949 (M); gifts received, $338; expenditures, $16,537,878; qualifying distributions, $14,877,736; giving activities include $14,817,860 for 142 grants (high: $2,000,000; low: $250; average: $20,000–$200,000).
Purpose and activities: Grants primarily for higher education, hospitals, eye research and for the environment.
Fields of interest: Higher education; Eye diseases; Eye research.
Limitations: Applications accepted. Giving primarily in CA and MA, with some giving in IA and NY. No grants to individuals.
Application information: Application form not required.
Deadline(s): None
Officers: H. Irving Grousbeck, Pres.; Susanne B. Grousbeck, V.P.; Wycliffe K. Grousbeck, Secy.-Treas.; Anne H.G. Matta, C.F.O.
EIN: 770267061
Recent grants for international programs:
166-1 African Leadership Foundation, New York, NY, $50,000. For general support. 2009.
166-2 Amistad International, Palo Alto, CA, $20,000. For general support. 2009.
166-3 Center for Global Development, Washington, DC, $550,000. For general support. 2009.
166-4 Doctors Without Borders USA, New York, NY, $500,000. For general support. 2009.
166-5 Earth Island Institute, SLFP, Berkeley, CA, $50,000. For general support. 2009.
166-6 EcoLogic Development Fund, Cambridge, MA, $150,000. For general support. 2009.
166-7 Generation Rwanda, New York, NY, $30,000. For general support. 2009.

166-8 Global Fund for Women, San Francisco, CA, $50,000. For general support. 2009.
166-9 Hesperian Foundation, Berkeley, CA, $250,000. For general support. 2009.
166-10 Hosana Global Ministries, Carrollton, TX, $85,000. For general support. 2009.
166-11 Interplast, Mountain View, CA, $75,000. For general support. 2009.
166-12 Maranyundo Initiative, South Boston, MA, $10,000. For general support. 2009.
166-13 Nuru International, Palo Alto, CA, $60,000. For general support. 2009.
166-14 Nuru International, Palo Alto, CA, $40,000. For general support. 2009.
166-15 Oxfam America, Boston, MA, $500,000. For general support. 2009.
166-16 Partners in Health, Boston, MA, $25,000. For general support. 2009.
166-17 Project Healthy Children, Newton, MA, $80,000. For general support. 2009.

167
The Grove Foundation
P.O. Box 1667
Los Altos, CA   94023-1667

Established in 1986 in CA.
Donors: Andrew S. Grove; Eva K. Grove.
Grantmaker type: Independent foundation.
Financial data (yr. ended 09/30/10): Assets, $120,871,122 (M); gifts received, $54,786,356; expenditures, $13,326,960; qualifying distributions, $12,376,909; giving activities include $9,869,401 for 194 grants (high: $600,000; low: $500).
Purpose and activities: Giving primarily for family planning and other social services, vocational or professional education, Jewish welfare, international refugee assistance, and the performing arts.
Fields of interest: Food banks; Health care; Performing arts; Higher education; Reproductive health, family planning; Homeless, human services; International relief; Civil/human rights, advocacy; Civil liberties, reproductive rights; Aging; Women; Immigrants/refugees; Economically disadvantaged; Homeless.
Limitations: Applications not accepted. Giving primarily in CA. No grants to individuals, or for construction.
Application information: Unsolicited requests not considered; funds are fully committed.
Officers and Directors: * Andrew S. Grove,* Chair.; Karen Grove,* Vice-Chair.; Leslie Dorsin, C.F.O.; Eva K. Grove; Robbie Grove Livingstone.
EIN: 770108124
Recent grants for international programs:
167-1 American Jewish Joint Distribution Committee, New York, NY, $30,000. For project support. 2010.
167-2 American Jewish World Service, New York, NY, $10,000. For project support. 2010.
167-3 American Supporters of YEDID, Teaneck, NJ, $20,000. For general support. 2010.
167-4 CARE, San Francisco, CA, $12,500. For project support. 2010.
167-5 International Rescue Committee, New York, NY, $100,000. For general support. 2010.

168
The Naren & Vinita Gupta Foundation
1252 Canada Rd.
Woodside, CA   94062-3511

Established in 1994 in CA.
Donors: Naren Gupta; Vinita Gupta.
Grantmaker type: Independent foundation.
Financial data (yr. ended 12/31/10): Assets, $1,001,011 (M); gifts received, $958,000; expenditures, $200,556; qualifying distributions, $200,336; giving activities include $198,806 for 16 grants (high: $126,000; low: $200).
Purpose and activities: Giving primarily to foundations serving causes concerning India, as well as to specific organizations which help South Asian women who are facing domestic violence; funding also for education and social services.
Fields of interest: Education; Human services; Women, centers/services.
International interests: Asia; India.
Limitations: Applications not accepted. Giving primarily in CA, with emphasis on San Francisco, and New York, NY. No grants to individuals.
Application information: Contributes only to pre-selected organizations.
Trustees: Naren Gupta; Vinita Gupta.
EIN: 770388598

169
The Armen and Gloria Hampar Family Foundation
10247 Valley Spring Ln.
Toluca Lake, CA   91602-2931

Established in 1998 in CA.
Donor: Armen Hampar.
Grantmaker type: Independent foundation.
Financial data (yr. ended 12/31/10): Assets, $3,098,436 (M); gifts received, $112,989; expenditures, $185,037; qualifying distributions, $174,105; giving activities include $174,105 for grants.
Purpose and activities: Giving primarily to Armenian organizations and churches.
Fields of interest: Education; Human services; Christian agencies & churches.
International interests: Armenia.
Limitations: Applications not accepted. Giving primarily in CA. No grants to individuals.
Application information: Contributes only to pre-selected organizations.
Officers: Armen Hampar, Pres.; Audrey L. Matoesian, Secy.; Steven Hampar, C.F.O.
EIN: 954714147

170
The Handlery Foundation
180 Geary St., Ste. 700
San Francisco, CA   94108-5604
Contact: Margaret Handlery, Chair.

Established in 1998 in CA.
Donors: Ardyce A. Handlery; Paul R. Handlery.
Grantmaker type: Independent foundation.
Financial data (yr. ended 12/31/10): Assets, $4,993,175 (M); expenditures, $214,875; qualifying distributions, $205,505; giving activities include $189,070 for 41 grants (high: $13,221; low: $100).

Purpose and activities: Giving primarily for higher education, with a particular focus on hotel and hospitality management, and human services.
Fields of interest: Museums (art); Higher education, university; Hospitals (general); Health organizations, association; Cancer, leukemia; Safety/disasters; Human services; American Red Cross; International relief, 2004 tsunami; Protestant agencies & churches; Jewish agencies & synagogues.
Type of support: General/operating support; Program development; Research.
Limitations: Applications accepted. Giving for human services primarily in the San Francisco Bay Area, CA.
Application information: Application form not required.
  Deadline(s): None
Officers: Margaret Handlery, Chair.; Michael K. Handlery, Secy.-Treas.
Trustee: A. John Pekrul.
EIN: 943302912

171
Harkham Foundation
857 S. San Pedro St., Ste. 300
Los Angeles, CA 90014-2435

Established in 1980 in CA.
Donors: Efrem Harkham; Uri Harkham; Harkham Industries; JM Shoe Group Inc.
Grantmaker type: Independent foundation.
Financial data (yr. ended 03/31/10): Assets, $380,560 (M); gifts received, $194,850; expenditures, $315,826; qualifying distributions, $312,816; giving activities include $312,561 for 33 + grants.
Purpose and activities: Giving for Jewish education and organizations.
Fields of interest: Elementary/secondary education; Higher education; Jewish federated giving programs; Jewish agencies & synagogues.
International interests: Israel.
Type of support: General/operating support.
Limitations: Applications not accepted. Giving primarily in CA and Israel. No grants to individuals.
Application information: Contributes only to pre-selected organizations.
Officers: Uri Harkham, Pres.; Naji Harkham, Secy.; Dan Harkham, Treas.
EIN: 953532383

172
The William and Flora Hewlett Foundation
2121 Sand Hill Rd.
Menlo Park, CA 94025-6909 (650) 234-4500
Contact: Eric Brown, Dir., Comms.
FAX: (650) 234-4501; E-mail for Eric Brown: ebrown@hewlett.org; URL: http://www.hewlett.org
E-Newsletter: http://www.hewlett.org/newsroom/subscribe
Facebook: http://www.facebook.com/pages/William-and-Flora-Hewlett-Foundation/132972610943?ref=mf
Grantee Perception Report: http://www.hewlett.org/what-we-re-learning/our-approach-to-philanthropy/grantee-perception-report/2009-grantee-perception-report
Grants Database: http://www.hewlett.org/grants/search?order=field_date_of_award_value&sort=desc

Library Database: http://www.hewlett.org/library/search
Library Feed: http://www.hewlett.org/rss/library
News Feed: http://www.hewlett.org/rss/newsroom
RSS Grants Feed: http://grantsfeed.hewlett.org/
Twitter: http://www.twitter.com/hewlett_found
YouTube: http://www.youtube.com/hewlettfoundation

Incorporated in 1966 in CA.
Donors: Flora Lamson Hewlett‡; William R. Hewlett‡.
Grantmaker type: Independent foundation.
Financial data (yr. ended 12/31/10): Assets, $7,377,414,000 (M); expenditures, $402,861,000; qualifying distributions, $358,100,000; giving activities include $358,100,000 for grants, and $8,819,000 for foundation-administered programs.
Purpose and activities: The foundation makes grants to help solve social and environmental problems at home and around the world. It concentrates its resources on activities in education, the environment, global development, performing arts, philanthropy, and population, and makes grants to support disadvantaged communities in the San Francisco Bay Area. A full list of all the Hewlett Foundation's grants can be found on its website.
Fields of interest: Performing arts; Performing arts, dance; Performing arts, theater; Performing arts, music; Arts; Elementary/secondary education; Higher education; Higher education, college (community/junior); Environment, natural resources; Environment; Reproductive health, family planning; International economic development; Urban/community development; Community/economic development; Philanthropy/voluntarism; Population studies; International studies; Public policy, research; Minorities.
International interests: China; Latin America; Sub-Saharan Africa.
Type of support: General/operating support; Continuing support; Program development; Employee matching gifts; Matching/challenge support.
Limitations: Applications accepted. Giving limited to the San Francisco Bay Area and Central Valley, CA, for family and community development programs; performing arts primarily limited to the Bay Area. No funds for individuals and generally the foundation does not fund scholarships, endowments, capital campaigns, building construction, for-profit organizations, or unincorporated associations or groups. In addition, the foundation's funds can be used only for purposes that are consistent with its status as a charitable organization.
Publications: Application guidelines; Annual report; Grants list; Informational brochure; Newsletter; Program policy statement.
Application information: The Hewlett Foundation prefers to receive letters of inquiry via its online submission form on its website. The foundation is not currently accepting letters of inquiry for the following programs: Performing Arts, Philanthropy, or Special Projects. The foundation accepts unsolicited letters of inquiry for various areas of work within its Education, Environment, and Global Development and Population programs. Please visit the foundation's Grantseekers page at http://www.hewlett.org/grants/grantseekers to learn more. Application form not required.
  Initial approach: Letter of inquiry
  Copies of proposal: 1

Deadline(s): None
Board meeting date(s): Feb., June, and Oct.
Final notification: 2 to 3 months
Officers and Directors:* Walter B. Hewlett,* Chair.; Harvey V. Fineberg, M.D., Vice-Chair.; Paul Brest,* Pres.; Laurance Hoagland, Jr., V.P. and C.I.O.; Susan Bell, V.P.; Elizabeth Peters, Corp. Secy. and Genl. Counsel; Susan Ketcham, C.F.O. and Treas.; Byron Auguste; Eleanor H. Gimon; Marianne Gimon; Patricia House; Koh Boon Hwee; Mary H. Jaffe; Richard C. Levin; Stephen C. Neal; Rakesh Ranjani; Jean Gleason Stromberg.
Number of staff: 68 full-time professional; 6 part-time professional; 27 full-time support; 2 part-time support.
EIN: 941655673
Recent grants for international programs:
172-1 Africa Agriculture Development Company, London, England, $400,000. For Beira Agricultural Growth Corridor initiative. 2010.
172-2 African Center for Economic Transformation, Washington, DC, $1,310,000. For establishing a unit to advise on extractive resource issues. 2010.
172-3 African Center for Economic Transformation, Washington, DC, $190,000. For establishing a unit to advise on extractive resource issues. 2010.
172-4 African Population and Health Research Center, Nairobi, Kenya, $35,000. For videoconferencing project. 2010.
172-5 Alliance Publishing Trust, London, England, $10,000. For support of free access of Alliance magazine content. 2010.
172-6 American University in Cairo, Cairo, Egypt, $150,000. For Reproductive Health and Policy Formulation workshops. 2010.
172-7 Arius Association, Baden, Switzerland, $75,000. For scoping project to determine level of international support for multi-nationalized fuel disposal facilities. 2010.
172-8 Arms Control Association, Washington, DC, $200,000. For general operating support. 2010.
172-9 Arms Control Association, Washington, DC, $110,000. For a project to reduce the role of tactical nuclear weapons in European security. 2010.
172-10 ARTICLE 19, London, England, $550,000. For promoting right to information in Mexico and globally through advocacy and legal assistance. 2010.
172-11 Aspen Institute, Washington, DC, $1,350,000. For establishment of the TransFarm Africa policy network on agriculture, trade, and food security. 2010.
172-12 Aspen Institute, Washington, DC, $400,000. For the Global Leaders Council for Reproductive Health. 2010.
172-13 Aspen Institute, Washington, DC, $25,000. For a project to examine the effectiveness of U.S. foreign assistance in insecure countries. 2010.
172-14 Association pour le Developpement de la Langue Saafi, Thies, Senegal, $850,000. For mother tongue reading and math instruction in Senegal with transitional support. 2010.
172-15 Athabasca University, Athabasca, Canada, $121,000. For interaction and networking within the international OER community. 2010.
172-16 Bayan Association for Indigenous Socio-Economic Development, Tegucigalpa, Honduras, $96,000. For emergency funding for Sistema de Aprendizaje Tutorial, a rural education program in Honduras. 2010.

172-17 Bread for the World Institute, Washington, DC, $1,550,000. For the Modernizing Foreign Assistance Network. 2010.

172-18 Bread for the World Institute, Washington, DC, $25,000. For IT systems planning. 2010.

172-19 British American Security Information Council, Washington, DC, $130,000. For a project to reduce the role of tactical nuclear weapons in European security. 2010.

172-20 Brookings Institution, Washington, DC, $1,200,000. For general support of the Global Economy and Development Program. 2010.

172-21 Calvert Social Investment Foundation, Bethesda, MD, $2,700,000. For general operating support. 2010.

172-22 Calvert Social Investment Foundation, Bethesda, MD, $400,000. For metrics and monitoring framework for Viazi Halisi project. 2010.

172-23 Carter Center, Atlanta, GA, $115,000. For finalizing and disseminating access to information legislation implementation assessment tool. 2010.

172-24 Center for American Progress, Washington, DC, $300,000. For effort to reform U.S. foreign aid to ensure the foreign policy goal of sustainable security. 2010.

172-25 Center for Global Development, Washington, DC, $2,400,000. For general operating support. 2010.

172-26 Center for Strategic and International Studies, Washington, DC, $80,000. For a project to explore the United States' approach to technical cooperation agreements. 2010.

172-27 Centre for Policy Research, New Delhi, India, $564,000. For strengthening the transparency and accountability of public expenditures on education in India. 2010.

172-28 Centro de Investigacion para el Desarrollo, Mexico City, Mexico, $500,000. For general operating support. 2010.

172-29 Centro de Investigacion y Docencia Economicas, Mexico City, Mexico, $400,000. For a research, analysis, and dissemination project on transparency and accountability in Mexico. 2010.

172-30 Centro de Investigacion y Docencia Economicas, Mexico City, Mexico, $70,000. For fostering use of collective actions in Mexico through public interest litigation. 2010.

172-31 Centro de Transporte Sustentable de Mexico, Mexico City, Mexico, $1,200,000. For promoting public transportation in Mexico's largest cities. 2010.

172-32 Centro Mexicano de Derecho Ambiental, Mexico City, Mexico, $500,000. For Air and Energy Program. 2010.

172-33 China Arms Control and Disarmament Association, Beijing, China, $40,000. For a conference to explore the implications of reprocessing in Asia. 2010.

172-34 Clear Fund, GiveWell, Brooklyn, NY, $60,000. For general operating support. 2010.

172-35 College of William and Mary, Williamsburg, VA, $1,000,000. For a project to simplify and help access to more complete and comparable data on aid flows. 2010.

172-36 College of William and Mary, Williamsburg, VA, $69,200. For strategic communications planning. 2010.

172-37 Commonwealth of Learning, Vancouver, Canada, $300,000. For Virtual University of the Small States of the Commonwealth. 2010.

172-38 Cornell University, Ithaca, NY, $400,000. For demographic training, research and policy dissemination in sub-Saharan Africa. 2010.

172-39 CUTS Geneva Resource Centre, Geneva, Switzerland, $600,000. For implementation of Fostering Equitable Agricultural Development project in E. Africa. 2010.

172-40 Deutsche Stiftung Weltbevoelkerung, Hannover, Germany, $30,000. For strategic planning. 2010.

172-41 DKT International, Washington, DC, $1,300,000. For general operating support. 2010.

172-42 Educational Initiatives, Ahmadabad, India, $101,500. For workshops to help governments use assessment results to improve practice and policy in education. 2010.

172-43 Ekonomi ve Dis Politika Arastirmalar Merkezi, Istanbul, Turkey, $100,000. For a project to explore Turkey's interests and preferences regarding nuclear policy. 2010.

172-44 El Colegio de Mexico, Mexico City, Mexico, $400,000. For PRECESAM program. 2010.

172-45 El Poder del Consumidor, Mexico City, Mexico, $150,000. For a project to promote the benefits of clean transportation systems in Mexico's largest cities. 2010.

172-46 Energy Foundation, San Francisco, CA, $7,000,000. For China Sustainable Cities Initiative. 2010.

172-47 Energy Foundation, San Francisco, CA, $5,000,000. For general operating support. 2010.

172-48 EngenderHealth, New York, NY, $1,250,000. For general operating support. 2010.

172-49 European Climate Foundation, The Hague, Netherlands, $30,500. For organizational assessment to strengthen ECF's charitable work on GHG reductions in Europe. 2010.

172-50 FinalsClub.Org, Cambridge, MA, $152,000. For expansion of the FinalsClub OER platform. 2010.

172-51 Foundation Center, New York, NY, $250,000. For a project to develop a common data standard with the International Aid Transparency Initiative. 2010.

172-52 Fundar Center for Research and Analysis, Mexico City, Mexico, $700,000. For Fundar's access to information and public budget accountability projects in Mexico. 2010.

172-53 German Marshall Fund of the United States, Washington, DC, $1,300,000. For promoting trade, aid, and development policy reform in United States and European Union. 2010.

172-54 Global AIDS Alliance, Washington, DC, $40,000. For strategic planning. 2010.

172-55 Global Citizen Year, San Francisco, CA, $200,000. For program to allow low-income Bay Area youth to participate in experiential learning abroad. 2010.

172-56 Global Fund for Women, San Francisco, CA, $10,000. For executive search. 2010.

172-57 Global Integrity, Washington, DC, $450,000. For examining municipal-state relations affecting budget transparency and FOIA in Mexico. 2010.

172-58 Global Integrity, Washington, DC, $285,000. For tool improving efficiency of field-based data collection teams. 2010.

172-59 Global Integrity, Washington, DC, $22,000. For staff development. 2010.

172-60 Guttmacher Institute, New York, NY, $200,000. For documenting the cost of unsafe abortion in Rwanda. 2010.

172-61 Harvard University, Cambridge, MA, $265,000. For implementing and evaluating the impact of a peer-to-peer teaching model in Kenya. 2010.

172-62 Health Effects Institute, Boston, MA, $500,000. For the Science to Inform Transportation and Air Quality Decision Initiative. 2010.

172-63 Ibis Reproductive Health, Cambridge, MA, $375,000. For general operating support. 2010.

172-64 INDEPTH Network, Accra, Ghana, $35,000. For videoconferencing project. 2010.

172-65 Iniciativa Ciudadana y Desarrollo Social, Mexico City, Mexico, $100,000. For strengthening citizens' social policy observatory. 2010.

172-66 Innovation Center for Energy and Transportation, South Pasadena, CA, $300,000. For general operating support. 2010.

172-67 Innovation Center for Energy and Transportation, South Pasadena, CA, $30,000. For organization planning. 2010.

172-68 Innovations for Poverty Action, New Haven, CT, $250,000. For evaluating a remedial education program in Ghana. 2010.

172-69 Institute for State Effectiveness, Washington, DC, $100,000. For the Kabul Conference. 2010.

172-70 Institute for Transportation and Development Policy, New York, NY, $1,000,000. For general operating support. 2010.

172-71 Instituto de Energia e Meio Ambiente, Sao Paulo, Brazil, $3,000,000. For promoting clean air and sustainable transportation policies in Brazil. 2010.

172-72 Instituto de Energia e Meio Ambiente, Sao Paulo, Brazil, $50,000. For strategic planning to improve work on sustainable and clean transportation. 2010.

172-73 Instituto Mexicano para la Competitividad, Mexico City, Mexico, $1,800,000. For IMCO's research and analysis on economic competitiveness in Mexico. 2010.

172-74 InterAction: American Council for Voluntary International Action, Washington, DC, $275,000. For a project to reform U.S. foreign assistance. 2010.

172-75 International Association for K-12 Online Learning, Vienna, VA, $315,000. For a coalition around uses of federal education stimulus funding for OER (Open Educational Resources) adoption. 2010.

172-76 International Crisis Group, Washington, DC, $300,000. For general operating support. 2010.

172-77 International Initiative for Impact Evaluation, Washington, DC, $2,000,000. For general operating support. 2010.

172-78 International Sustainable Systems Research Center, La Habra, CA, $68,000. For the International Air Quality Management Improvement Project. 2010.

172-79 International Union for the Scientific Study of Population, Paris, France, $400,000. For a project to develop policy-relevant population sciences. 2010.

172-80 Keio University, Keio Research Institute, Tokyo, Japan, $200,000. To deepen the value of and promote the vision of OER within Japan. 2010.

172-81 Mango Tree Educational Enterprises, Kampala, Uganda, $63,500. For supporting students to transition from Lango reading fluency to English reading fluency. 2010.

172-82 Massachusetts Institute of Technology, Cambridge, MA, $24,712. For a study on voting behavior to help design more effective voter education campaigns in India. 2010.

172-83 Massachusetts Institute of Technology, Cambridge, MA, $15,000. For strengthening financial management systems. 2010.

172-84 Meridian Institute, Dillon, CO, $400,000. For Phase I implementation of the Foundation Working Group on Food and Agriculture Policy initiative. 2010.

172-85 Mexico Evalua - Centro de Analisis de Politicas Publicas, Mexico City, Mexico, $200,000. For public expenditure program. 2010.

172-86 Michigan State University, East Lansing, MI, $400,000. For general support of the Partnership to Cut Hunger and Poverty in Africa program. 2010.

172-87 Mongolian American Scientific Research Center, Ulaanbaatar, Mongolia, $75,000. For a workshop to explore a Mongolian-led multinational nuclear arrangement for Northeast Asia. 2010.

172-88 National Campaign on Dalit Human Rights, New Delhi, India, $25,000. For a project to track education budget expenditures for Dalits in Bihar and Rajasthan, India. 2010.

172-89 National Security Initiative, Washington, DC, $300,000. For general operating support. 2010.

172-90 Natural Resources Defense Council, San Francisco, CA, $100,000. For scoping project to determine feasibility of International Nuclear Fuel Agency. 2010.

172-91 NEPAD Business Foundation, Johannesburg, South Africa, $3,000,000. For Removing the Barriers program. 2010.

172-92 Nonproliferation for Global Security Foundation, Buenos Aires, Argentina, $180,000. For a Brazilian-Argentine commission to assess possible shifts in nuclear policies. 2010.

172-93 Oeuvre Malienne dAide a lEnfance du Sahel, Bamako, Mali, $307,000. For the preparatory phase of a civil society initiative to assess student learning in Mali. 2010.

172-94 Ontario College of Art and Design, Toronto, Canada, $500,000. For OER community in meeting diverse learner needs. 2010.

172-95 Open University, Milton Keynes, England, $275,000. For creation of African Teacher Education OER network. 2010.

172-96 Organisation for Economic Co-operation and Development, Paris, France, $1,020,000. For PISA Lite project. 2010.

172-97 Organisation for Economic Co-operation and Development, Paris, France, $100,000. For Teaching and Learning International Survey video study planning phase. 2010.

172-98 Oxfam America, Boston, MA, $1,200,000. For the Aid Effectiveness Team. 2010.

172-99 Oxfam America, Boston, MA, $500,000. For civil society to participate in developing a transparent system for managing Ghana's oil wealth. 2010.

172-100 Oxfam Novib, The Hague, Netherlands, $1,400,000. For project promoting universal access to female condoms. 2010.

172-101 Pacific Council on International Policy, Los Angeles, CA, $100,000. For general operating support. 2010.

172-102 Partners in Population and Development, Kampala, Uganda, $2,100,000. For building the capacity of African policymakers for reproductive health issues. 2010.

172-103 PATH, Seattle, WA, $1,250,000. For PATHs Reproductive Health Global Program. 2010.

172-104 Pathfinder International, Watertown, MA, $1,750,000. For general operating support. 2010.

172-105 Planned Parenthood Federation, International, Washington, DC, $6,565,000. For general operating support. 2010.

172-106 Planned Parenthood Federation, International, Washington, DC, $75,000. For the Safe Abortion Action Fund. 2010.

172-107 Planned Parenthood Federation, International, Washington, DC, $17,000. For organization planning. 2010.

172-108 Planned Parenthood Federation, International, Western Hemisphere Region, New York, NY, $500,000. For emergency relief in Haiti. 2010.

172-109 Ploughshares Fund, San Francisco, CA, $350,000. For general operating support. 2010.

172-110 Population Action International, Washington, DC, $50,000. For organization planning. 2010.

172-111 Population Council, New York, NY, $3,000,000. For the Reproductive Health and Poverty, Gender and Youth programs. 2010.

172-112 Population Reference Bureau, Washington, DC, $400,000. For communication and dissemination of population-poverty research. 2010.

172-113 Pratham USA, Houston, TX, $6,500,000. For Read India Phase II, a nationwide program to improve learning achievement in the primary grades. 2010.

172-114 Pratham USA, Houston, TX, $3,000,000. For the Annual Status of Education Report (ASER) and the related activities of the ASER Centre. 2010.

172-115 Raising Voices, Kampala, Uganda, $663,000. For implementing a Good Schools Toolkit to improve the classroom environment in Ugandan schools. 2010.

172-116 Reproductive Health Matters, London, England, $500,000. For the charitable purposes of the Reproductive Health Matters Journal. 2010.

172-117 Results for Development Institute, Washington, DC, $4,000,000. For Transparency and Accountability Program. 2010.

172-118 Royal United Services Institute for Defence Studies, London, England, $120,000. To work to support evidence-based debate about role of nuclear weapons in European security. 2010.

172-119 San Francisco Film Society, San Francisco, CA, $25,000. For disseminating award-winning documentary Presumed Guilty to targeted audiences in Mexico. 2010.

172-120 Save the Children Federation, Westport, CT, $250,000. For research and advocacy to promote improvements to U.S. development assistance. 2010.

172-121 Security Council Report, New York, NY, $40,000. For fundraising planning. 2010.

172-122 Shirkat Gah Womens Resource Centre, Karachi, Pakistan, $100,000. For emergency access to reproductive and primary health care services in Pakistan. 2010.

172-123 Social and Development Network Kenya, SODNET, Nairobi, Kenya, $150,000. For the INFONET Program. 2010.

172-124 Sonora Ciudadana, Hermosillo, Mexico, $290,000. For the charitable project to empower users of public health systems in Mexico. 2010.

172-125 South African Institute for Distance Education, Braamfontein, South Africa, $275,000. For creation of African Teacher Education OER network. 2010.

172-126 Stanford University, Stanford, CA, $237,000. For evaluation of Nali Kali, a primary school activity-based learning program in Karnataka, India. 2010.

172-127 Stanford University, Stanford, CA, $200,000. For the Toward a World Free of Nuclear Weapons project. 2010.

172-128 Stanford University, Stanford, CA, $180,000. For the Managing Global Insecurity project. 2010.

172-129 Stanford University, Stanford, CA, $140,000. For the CISAC (Center for International Security and Cooperation) project on US-Russian ballistic missile defense. 2010.

172-130 Tel Aviv University, Institute for National Security Studies, A Think Tank, Tel Aviv, Israel, $150,000. For a project to develop regional expertise on nuclear security and arms control in the Middle East. 2010.

172-131 Tides Canada Foundation, Vancouver, Canada, $400,000. For efforts to reduce fossil fuel development. 2010.

172-132 Tides Center, San Francisco, CA, $20,000. For the Africa Grantmakers Affinity Group. 2010.

172-133 Tides Foundation, San Francisco, CA, $2,000,000. For reducing the environmental impacts of oil and gas development in Northern Canada. 2010.

172-134 Tostan, Washington, DC, $3,814,000. To empower communities to play a central role in improving children's learning achievement. 2010.

172-135 Transparencia Mexicana, Mexico City, Mexico, $350,000. For general operating support. 2010.

172-136 United States Department of State, Washington, DC, $125,000. For a Franklin Fellow to serve as a science advisor to the Special Advisor for Nonproliferation. 2010.

172-137 University of California, Davis, CA, $450,000. For documenting and analyzing changes in Mexico's rural poverty during the global economic crisis. 2010.

172-138 University of Cape Town, Cape Town, South Africa, $1,000,000. For establishing unit to promote impact evaluations of poverty reduction programs. 2010.

172-139 University of Cape Town, Cape Town, South Africa, $500,000. For the Centre of Actuarial Research's (CARe) population science training program. 2010.

172-140 University of Ghana, Legon, Ghana, $550,000. For Regional Institute for Population Studies program. 2010.

172-141 University of Ghana, Legon, Ghana, $40,000. For videoconferencing project. 2010.

172-142 University of San Diego, San Diego, CA, $200,000. For analyzing and promoting efforts to strengthen judicial institutions in Mexico. 2010.

172-143 Vietnam Foundation, U.S. Office, Washington, DC, $30,000. For modulating and posting Vietnamese college textbooks and learning modules on VOER website. 2010.

172-144 W N E T Channel 13, WNET.ORG, New York, NY, $50,000. For the International Summit on the Future of the Teaching Profession. 2010.

172-145 Wikimedia Foundation, San Francisco, CA, $800,000. For general operating support. 2010.

172-146 Women Deliver, New York, NY, $40,000. For Women Deliver Conference. 2010.

172-147 Women Thrive Worldwide, Washington, DC, $600,000. For project promoting U.S. development assistance. 2010.

172-148 Woodrow Wilson International Center for Scholars, Washington, DC, $175,000. For educating policymakers and staff about trade and development. 2010.

172-149 Woodrow Wilson International Center for Scholars, Washington, DC, $44,275. For fundraising planning. 2010.

172-150 World Affairs Council of Northern California, San Francisco, CA, $20,000. For the Global Philanthropy Forum. 2010.

172-151 World Neighbors, Oklahoma City, OK, $150,000. For general operating support. 2010.

172-152 World Population Foundation, Utrecht, Netherlands, $600,000. For general operating support. 2010.

172-153 World Population Foundation, Utrecht, Netherlands, $30,000. For strategic communications planning. 2010.

172-154 World Wide Web Foundation, Cambridge, MA, $100,000. For developing a flexible data collection tool for users in developing countries. 2010.

173
The Hexberg Family Foundation
921 Emerald Bay
Laguna Beach, CA 92651-1260

Established in 2001 in CA.
Donors: Eric Hexberg†, Jane Hexberg†; The Hexberg Charitable Trust.
Grantmaker type: Independent foundation.
Financial data (yr. ended 12/31/10): Assets, $9,792,835 (M); gifts received, $1,347,935; expenditures, $326,923; qualifying distributions, $278,000; giving activities include $278,000 for 56 grants (high: $50,000; low: $500).
Fields of interest: Health care; International relief; Higher education; Human services.
Limitations: Applications not accepted. Giving primarily in CA and IL. No grants to individuals.
Application information: Contributes only to pre-selected organizations.
Trustees: Deborah L. Hexberg; Gregory Hexberg; Jill Hexberg.
EIN: 912172555

174
Hidaya Foundation
1765 Scott Blvd., Ste. 115
Santa Clara, CA 95056-5481   (408) 244-3282
E-mail: mail@hidaya.org; Toll-free tel.: (866) 244-3292; Toll-free fax: (866) 344-3292;
URL: http://www.hidaya.org

Established in 1999.
Grantmaker type: Public charity.
Financial data (yr. ended 12/31/10): Revenue, $6,325,270; assets, $3,724,146 (M); gifts received, $6,469,161; expenditures, $5,216,317; giving activities include $28,000 for grants, $4,255,918 for grants to organizations outside the U.S., and $92,750 for grants to individuals outside the U.S.

Purpose and activities: The foundation seeks to implement educational, social welfare, and charitable programs in economically depressed areas of south Asia, west Africa and North America, with a focus on projects which promote self-employment.
Fields of interest: Employment; International relief.
Type of support: In-kind gifts.
Limitations: Giving on a national and international basis, with emphasis on Bangladesh, Canada, India, Indonesia, Pakistan, Sri Lanka, and West Africa.
Publications: Financial statement.
Officers and Directors:* Waseem Baloch,* Chair. and Pres.; Mazhar Uddin,* V.P.; Tufail Memon, Secy.; Mohamed S. Shamsuddin,* Treas.; Adeel Ahmed; Irfan Baloch.
EIN: 770502583

175
Hidden Leaf Foundation
(formerly David A. Brown Foundation)
c/o David A. Brown
1200 Concord Ave., Ste. 200
Concord, CA 94520-4900

Established in 1988 in CA.
Grantmaker type: Independent foundation.
Financial data (yr. ended 12/31/09): Assets, $493,975 (M); gifts received, $400,000; expenditures, $421,510; qualifying distributions, $405,000; giving activities include $405,000 for grants.
Purpose and activities: The foundation supports organizations that use contemplative practices to further their social or environmental goals.
Fields of interest: Environment; Employment; equal rights; Human services, mind/body enrichment; International affairs, goodwill promotion; Civil/human rights, advocacy; Community/economic development; Leadership development; Spirituality.
Limitations: Applications not accepted. Giving primarily in CA, CO, Washington, DC, FL, MA, NC, and New York, NY. No grants to individuals.
Application information: Contributes only to pre-selected organizations.
Officers: David A. Brown, Pres.; Tara Brown, V.P.; Karen Brown, Secy.-Treas.
Director: Kristen Brown.
EIN: 680154341

176
The Higgins-Trapnell Family Foundation
1777 Fletcher Way
Santa Ynez, CA 93460-9484

Established in 2000 in CA.
Donors: Priscilla Higgins; Roger Higgins.
Grantmaker type: Independent foundation.
Financial data (yr. ended 12/31/10): Assets, $1,464,190 (M); expenditures, $191,073; qualifying distributions, $130,650; giving activities include $130,650 for 24 grants (high: $17,500; low: $250).
Fields of interest: Environment, natural resources; International development; International relief.
Limitations: Applications not accepted. Giving primarily in CA and Washington, DC. No grants to individuals.
Application information: Contributes only to pre-selected organizations.

Officers and Directors:* Priscilla Higgins,* Pres.; Mark Higgins,* V.P.; Neal Higgins,* V.P.; Roger Higgins,* C.F.O.
EIN: 770537256

177
The Edward E. Hills Fund
119 Sheridan Way
Woodside, CA 94062-2345

Incorporated in 1953 in CA.
Donor: Edward E. Hills†.
Grantmaker type: Operating foundation.
Financial data (yr. ended 12/31/10): Assets, $11,766,526 (M); expenditures, $911,745; qualifying distributions, $710,785; giving activities include $649,641 for 30 grants (high: $127,000; low: $1,000).
Purpose and activities: Giving primarily for education, including a veterinary school, as well as for the arts, and to an institute for international studies.
Fields of interest: International affairs, research; Human services; Education; Arts; Environment, natural resources.
Limitations: Applications not accepted. Giving primarily in CA. No grants to individuals.
Application information: Contributes only to pre-selected organizations.
Officers and Directors:* Ingrid von Mangoldt Hills,* Pres.; Joseph M. Breall, Secy.; William S. Breall,* M.D., Treas.; Keith Kelson; Ken Monnono.
EIN: 946062537

178
Conrad N. Hilton Foundation
10100 Santa Monica Blvd., Ste. 1000
Los Angeles, CA 90067   (310) 556-4694
Contact: Jordan Faires, Sr. Grants Manager; Rose M. Arnold, Grants Mgr.
FAX: (310) 556-2301;
E-mail: cnhf@hiltonfoundation.org; Additional address (Reno office): 100 W. Liberty St., Ste. 840, Reno NV, 89501, tel.: (775) 323-4221, fax: (775) 323-4150; URL: http://www.hiltonfoundation.org
Barron Hilton's Giving Pledge: http://givingpledge.org/#enter
Conrad N. Hilton Foundation's Philanthropy Promise: http://www.ncrp.org/philanthropys-promise/who
E-Newsletter: http://www.hiltonfoundation.org/prize/signup
Impact & Learning: http://www.hiltonfoundation.org/index.php?option=com_ninjarsssyndicator&feed_id=1&format=raw
Knowledge Center: http://www.hiltonfoundation.org/impact-learning

Conrad N. Hilton, founder of Hilton Hotels, established the Conrad N. Hilton Foundation as a philanthropic trust in 1944. In 1950, the foundation was legally established as a nonprofit corporation, separate from Hilton Hotels.
Donors: Conrad N. Hilton†; Barron Hilton.
Grantmaker type: Independent foundation.
Financial data (yr. ended 12/31/10): Assets, $2,140,385,894 (M); gifts received, $3,821,456; expenditures, $122,211,531; qualifying distributions, $112,165,054; giving activities include $99,070,768 for 433 grants (high:

$11,500,000; low: $500), $249,427 for foundation-administered programs and $1,000,000 for 1 loan/program-related investment.

Purpose and activities: The Conrad N. Hilton Foundation supports efforts to improve the lives of disadvantaged and vulnerable people throughout the world by focusing on five strategic initiatives and five major program areas. Potential applicants should see Current Programs for more information.

Fields of interest: Public utilities, sewage; Public utilities, water; Public health, sanitation; Public health, hygiene; Public health, clean water supply; Education; Environment, water resources; Mental health/crisis services; Health organizations, association; Medical research; Agriculture/food; Housing/shelter; Safety/disasters; Youth development; Human services; Religion; Infants/toddlers; Children/youth; Children; Youth; Disabilities, people with; Blind/visually impaired; Substance abusers; Economically disadvantaged; Homeless.

International interests: Africa; Asia; Global programs; Mexico.

Type of support: General/operating support; Continuing support; Management development/capacity building; Capital campaigns; Building/renovation; Equipment; Endowments; Emergency funds; Program development; Publication; Curriculum development; Fellowships; Scholarship funds; Research; Technical assistance; Program evaluation; Program-related investments/loans; Employee matching gifts; Matching/challenge support.

Limitations: Applications not accepted. Giving on a balanced national and international basis. No support for political organizations. No grants to individuals, or for fundraising events.

Publications: Annual report; Financial statement; Occasional report.

Application information: The foundation accepts applications primarily from its specified beneficiaries; unsolicited proposals generally not considered. If application is invited, information will be requested.

   Board meeting date(s): Quarterly

Board of Directors: Barron Hilton,* Chair.; Steven M. Hilton,* C.E.O. and Pres.; William H. Foege, M.D., M.P.H.; James R. Galbraith; Conrad N. Hilton III; Eric M. Hilton; William B. Hilton, Jr.; Hawley Hilton McAuliffe; Sr. Joyce Meyer; John L. Notter; William G. Ouchi.

Officers: Edmund J. Cain, V.P., Grant Progs.; Randy Kim, V.P. and C.I.O.; Judy M. Miller, V.P. and Dir., Humanitarian Prize; Patrick J. Modugno, V.P., Admin. and C.F.O.; Marcia Trujillo-Penman, Corp. Secy.; Timothy J. Ortez, Treas.

Number of staff: 23 full-time professional; 1 part-time professional; 5 full-time support.

EIN: 943100217

Recent grants for international programs:

178-1 Aravind Eye Care System, Madurai, India, $1,500,000. For Conrad N. Hilton Humanitarian Prize Recipient selected by Jury. 2010.

178-2 BRAC USA, New York, NY, $100,000. For emergency disaster relief to flood victims in Pakistan with a focus on WASH (water, sanitation, and hygiene) activities. 2010.

178-3 Carter Center, Atlanta, GA, $2,000,000. For Guinea Worm Eradication Programs in Ghana and Mali, with any residual funding going to stop transmission in Sudan. 2010.

178-4 Catholic Relief Services, Baltimore, MD, $148,000. For implementation of water and sanitation activities specifically targeting 50,000 people displaced by the earthquake who are now living in temporary camps in and around Port-au-Prince. 2010.

178-5 CDC Foundation, Atlanta, GA, $750,000. To develop, implement and evaluate, in partnership with Institute of Road Traffic Education, pilot safety program designed to address occupational road safety in India. 2010.

178-6 CDC Foundation, Atlanta, GA, $15,000. For Louise Martin Fund for work in Kenya. 2010.

178-7 Friends of Ciudad Oculta, San Diego, CA, $10,000. For expansion of Little Dreams Day Care Center in Argentina. 2010.

178-8 Global Fund for Children, Washington, DC, $275,000. To help facilitate post-earthquake recovery efforts in Haiti for vulnerable children, including orphans and children affected by AIDS. 2010.

178-9 Global Water Challenge, Washington, DC, $34,000. For World Water Day held in Washington, DC and across the US on March 22 to let the world know what Americans are doing to increase support for WASH internationally, and to inform how Americans can make sustainable access to water, sanitation and hygiene a reality for millions of people around the world. 2010.

178-10 Grant Foundation, Pittsburgh, PA, $25,000. For Hospital Albert Schweitzer for emergency relief for victims of the Haiti earthquake. 2010.

178-11 Haitian Health Foundation, Norwich, CT, $25,000. For child feeding and rural health programs. 2010.

178-12 Headington Institute, Pasadena, CA, $15,000. For their work in Haiti. 2010.

178-13 Hugh OBrian World Youth Network, Beverly Hills, CA, $25,000. For general operating support. 2010.

178-14 International Medical Corps, Santa Monica, CA, $100,000. For emergency medical relief and health related services to flood affected people in Pakistan. 2010.

178-15 International Medical Corps, Santa Monica, CA, $25,000. For post-earthquake emergency relief in Haiti including general operating support, logistics coordination and provision of assistance for orphans. 2010.

178-16 International Presentation Association, New York, NY, $10,000. For scholarships for sisters from the developing world to attend short-term programs at the United Nations. 2010.

178-17 Kilimanjaro Centre for Community Ophthalmology, Moshi, Tanzania, Zanzibar and Pemba, $337,400. To conduct research and implementation activities aimed at improving the delivery and outcomes of trichiasis surgery. 2010.

178-18 Los Medicos Voladores, Auburn, CA, $10,000. For general operating support. 2010.

178-19 Los Medicos Voladores, Auburn, CA, $10,000. For operating support for work of Reno Chapter. 2010.

178-20 Marywood University, Scranton, PA, $2,000,000. To extend Sisters Leadership Development Initiative to increase technical, management, and leadership skills for Sisters ministering in Africa. 2010.

178-21 Medical Emergency Relief International USA, Washington, DC, $150,000. For Emergency relief to support malaria treatment and prevention activities in flood-affected areas of Pakistan. 2010.

178-22 Miles Jesu, Chicago, IL, $10,000. For Udaya Nakshatra, home for destitute boys in Sirsi, India. 2010.

178-23 Millennium Water Alliance, Houston, TX, $822,000. For Millennium Water Program; to support continued implementation of water, sanitation and hygiene programming in Ethiopia; and, coordination and review of the Millennium Water Program. 2010.

178-24 Mission Doctors Association, Los Angeles, CA, $25,000. For construction of new building at St. Martin de Porres Hospital in Cameroon. 2010.

178-25 Nuclear Age Peace Foundation, Santa Barbara, CA, $10,000. For general operating support. 2010.

178-26 Our Task, Arlington, VA, $25,000. For general operating support. 2010.

178-27 Oxfam America, Boston, MA, $250,000. For WASH (water, sanitation, and hygiene) and agriculture livelihood activities in flood-affected Pakistan. 2010.

178-28 Oxfam America, Boston, MA, $150,000. For emergency WASH (water, sanitation, and hygiene) activities in flood-affected areas of Pakistan. 2010.

178-29 Partners in Health, Boston, MA, $300,000. For post-earthquake recovery efforts in Haiti for vulnerable children in collaboration with SOS Children's Villages. 2010.

178-30 Partners in Health, Boston, MA, $250,000. To support the immediate needs of the earthquake-affected people of Haiti; funds may also be used for emergency supplies, as well as to respond to logistical and operational needs as they arise during the disaster and its aftermath. 2010.

178-31 Partners in Health, Boston, MA, $10,000. For relief and recovery efforts in Haiti. 2010.

178-32 Project Concern International, San Diego, CA, $50,000. For C-FISH (Captive Fisheries for Income and Strengthened Households) program activities in Malawi. 2010.

178-33 Save the Children Federation, Westport, CT, $10,000. For general operating support. 2010.

178-34 Skirball Cultural Center, Los Angeles, CA, $25,000. For Half the Sky: Turning Oppression into Opportunity for Women Worldwide. 2010.

178-35 SurfAid International USA, Carlsbad, CA, $20,000. For relief and recovery work in Mentawai Islands, Indonesia following the October tsunami. 2010.

178-36 TOUCH Foundation, New York, NY, $10,000. For general operating support of healthcare capacity work in Africa. 2010.

178-37 University of California, Santa Barbara, CA, $10,000. For Orfalea Center for Global and International Studies. 2010.

178-38 University of Washington Foundation, Seattle, WA, $15,000. For the Thomas Francis Jr. Global Health Fund. 2010.

178-39 WIKS-USA, New Haven, CT, $10,000. For Nambale Magnet School, residential school for AIDS orphans in western Kenya. 2010.

178-40 William J. Clinton Foundation, New York, NY, $77,000. For transport of 33,000 square foot tent to Haiti, where it will be used for office and administrative space for the city government of Port-au-Prince. 2010.

179
The Hirshberg Foundation for Pancreatic Cancer Research

(formerly The Ronald S. Hirshberg Memorial Foundation)
2990 S. Sepulveda Blvd., Ste. 300C
Los Angeles, CA 90064-3996 (310) 473-5121
Contact: Lisa Manheim, Dir.; Agi Hirshberg, C.E.O.
FAX: (310) 473-5107;
E-mail: AHirshberg@pancreatic.org; Additional
e-mail: lmanheim@pancreatic.org; URL: http://
www.pancreatic.org

Established in 1997 in CA.
Donors: Agnes Berliner Hirshberg; Paul A. Hughes
Foundation; Linda Tallen & David Kane Foundation.
Grantmaker type: Operating foundation.
Financial data (yr. ended 12/31/09): Assets,
$1,232,225 (M); gifts received, $556,926;
expenditures, $1,197,362; qualifying distributions,
$398,043; giving activities include $398,043 for
grants.
Purpose and activities: Giving to a medical center
laboratory for research directed at mechanisms,
treatments, and potential cures for pancreatic
cancer, as well as providing support to charities for
the support of families with pancreatic cancer.
Grants to individuals are made through Cancer Care,
Inc. The foundation only supports pancreatic cancer
research and related topics.
Fields of interest: Hospitals (general); Cancer
research; Adults, men; Adults, women.
International interests: Japan; Germany.
Type of support: General/operating support;
Conferences/seminars; Seed money; Research.
Limitations: Applications accepted. Giving primarily
in the U.S. No grants to individuals directly.
Publications: Financial statement; Grants list;
Informational brochure; Newsletter; Occasional
report (including application guidelines).
Application information: Application guidelines
available on foundation web site. Application form
required.
  Initial approach: E-mail
  Copies of proposal: 1
  Deadline(s): Aug. 15
  Board meeting date(s): Jan. and June
  Final notification: 8 weeks
Officer and Directors:* Agi Hirshberg,* C.E.O.; Lisa
Manheim.
Trustees: Mike Berliner; Jon Hirshberg; Lisa
Hirshberg; Stephen Prince; Michael Scott.
Advisory Board: Vay Liang W. Go, M.D., Chair.;
Laszlo G. Boros, M.D.; Murray Korc, M.D.; Laurence
J. Miller, M.D.; Stephen Pandol, M.D.; Howard A.
Reber, M.D.; Diane M. Simeone, M.D.
Number of staff: 3 full-time professional.
EIN: 954640311

180
Hispanics in Philanthropy

55 Second St., Ste. 1500
San Francisco, CA 94105-3499 (415) 837-0427
Contact: Diana Campoamor, Pres.
FAX: (415) 837-1074; E-mail: Diana@hiponline.org;
URL: http://www.hiponline.org
Hispanics in Philanthropy's Philanthropy
Promise: http://www.ncrp.org/
philanthropys-promise/who

Established in 1983 in CA.
Grantmaker type: Public charity.

Financial data (yr. ended 12/31/10): Revenue,
$2,648,627; assets, $8,466,145 (M); gifts
received, $2,392,296; expenditures, $3,461,333;
giving activities include $1,586,825 for grants, and
$92,358 for grants to organizations outside the U.S.
Purpose and activities: The organization's mission
is to strengthen Latino communities by increasing
resources for the Latino and Latin American civil
sector and by increasing Latino participation and
leadership throughout the field of philanthropy.
Fields of interest: Hispanics/Latinos.
International interests: Latin America.
Type of support: Publication; Research.
Limitations: Giving in the U.S. and Latin America.
Publications: Financial statement.
Officers and Directors:* Janice Petrovich,* Chair.;
Diana Campoamor,* Pres.; Ana Gloria
Rivas-Vazquez, V.P.; Christa Roth, V.P., Progs. and
Finance; Nelson Colon,* Secy.; Phillippe Wallace,*
Treas.; Elisa Arevalo; Aixa Beauchamp; Cristina
Eguizabal; Herman Gallegos; John Govea; Sandra
Licon; Julio Marcial; Kica Matos; Benita Melton;
Arelis M. Rodriguez; G. Albert Ruesga; Tara
Sandercock; Paul Spivey; Marta Tellado; Vivian
Vasallo; Luz Vega-Marquis; Alejandro Villanueva.
EIN: 943040607

181
The Hitz Foundation

(formerly The XYZZY Foundation)
c/o Frank, Rimerman Co., LLP
1801 Page Mill Rd.
Palo Alto, CA 94304-1211

Established in 2000 in CA.
Donor: David Hitz.
Grantmaker type: Independent foundation.
Financial data (yr. ended 12/31/10): Assets,
$27,732,208 (M); gifts received, $5,784,565;
expenditures, $845,142; qualifying distributions,
$542,640; giving activities include $542,640 for
grants.
Fields of interest: Higher education; Media/
communications; Arts; Education; Environment,
energy; Environment; Human services; International
affairs; Civil liberties, advocacy.
Limitations: Applications not accepted. Giving
primarily in CA, NV and Washington D.C., some
giving also in NY. No grants to individuals.
Application information: Contributes only to
pre-selected organizations.
Officers: David Hitz, C.E.O. and Pres.; Kevin P.
McAuliffe, Secy.; Yen Hitz, Treas.
EIN: 943379521

182
The Hoppe Foundation

P.O. Box 398
Fallbrook, CA 92088-0398

Grantmaker type: Independent foundation.
Financial data (yr. ended 06/30/11): Assets,
$10,990,846 (M); expenditures, $553,238;
qualifying distributions, $402,000; giving activities
include $402,000 for grants.
Fields of interest: International affairs; Media,
radio; Education; Youth, services; Christian
agencies & churches.
Limitations: Applications not accepted. No grants to
individuals.

Application information: Contributes only to
pre-selected organizations.
Officers: William James Hoppe, C.E.O.; Lea Ann
Hoppe, Secy.
EIN: 912144087

183
The Humanitarian Media Foundation

9663 Santa Monica Blvd., Ste. 792
Beverly Hills, CA 90210-4303
Contact: M. Morgan

Established in 2008.
Grantmaker type: Public charity.
Purpose and activities: The foundation works to
employ multiple forms of media (film, television,
journalism, photojournalism art, photography, and
music) to explore aspects of domestic and
international humanitarian crises, issues, and
histories; raise awareness for humanitarian
matters; and facilitate change in areas where it is
most needed.
Fields of interest: International human rights;
Media/communications; Media, film/video; Media,
print publishing; Visual arts; Visual arts,
photography; Performing arts, music; Civil/human
rights; Community/economic development.
Type of support: Grants to individuals.
Publications: Application guidelines.
Application information: All applications must be
accompanied by a $15 entry fee. Application form
required.
  Initial approach: Submit work with application
  form
  Deadline(s): Jan. 1 for International Film/Media
  Festival and Conference Art/Photography
  Exhibition
Officer: K.J. Wetherholt, Chair.

184
Humanity United

1991 Broadway St., No. 320
Redwood City, CA 94063-1959 (650) 587-2000
FAX: (650) 587-2039; URL: http://
www.humanityunited.org/
Blog: http://www.humanityunited.org/meet/media
Facebook: http://www.facebook.com/
humanityunited
Pierre and Pam Omidyar's Giving Pledge: http://
givingpledge.org/#enter
RSS Feed: http://www.humanityunited.org/blog/
rss
Twitter: http://twitter.com/HUtweets

Established in 2008 in CA.
Grantmaker type: Public charity.
Financial data (yr. ended 12/31/09): Revenue,
$240,004,272; assets, $5,640,942 (M); gifts
received, $24,000,000; expenditures,
$23,030,679; program services expenses,
$20,276,305; giving activities include
$13,672,996 for 74 grants (high: $2,250,000; low:
$8,000), $2,577,305 for 11 grants to organizations
outside the U.S., and $4,026,004 for
foundation-administered programs.
Purpose and activities: The organization promotes
social welfare by seeking and supporting local and
global solutions to eliminate modern-day slavery and
mass atrocities and to alleviate human suffering on
a broad scale.

Fields of interest: International affairs; International migration/refugee issues; Anti-slavery/human trafficking; International conflict resolution; International relief; Crime/violence prevention, abuse prevention; Human services.
Limitations: Applications not accepted. Giving primarily on a national basis, and to Europe and the Sub-Saharan Africa.
Application information: Contributes only to pre-selected organizations.
Officers and Trustees:* Pam Omidyar,* Chair.; Randy Newcomb,* Pres. and C.E.O.; Daniel Boggan, Jr.; Shannon Sedgwick Davis; Susan McCue.
EIN: 262583379

185
The Huneeus Foundation
1010 Lombard St.
San Francisco, CA   94109-1515   (415) 931-5146

Established in 1999 in DE.
Donor: Augustin C. Huneeus.
Grantmaker type: Operating foundation.
Financial data (yr. ended 12/31/09): Assets, $255,160 (M); expenditures, $200,396; qualifying distributions, $190,000; giving activities include $190,000 for 3 grants (high: $125,000; low: $25,000).
Fields of interest: Catholic agencies & churches; International affairs.
International interests: India.
Application information: Application form required.
  Initial approach: Proposal
  Deadline(s): None
Officers: Augustin C. Huneeus, Pres.; Valeria Huneeus, Secy.-Treas.
EIN: 510395298

186
India Literacy Project-USA
P.O. Box 361143
Milpitas, CA   95035-9998
E-mail: ilp@ilpnet.org; *URL:* http://www.ilpnet.org

Established in 1990 in IL.
Grantmaker type: Public charity.
Financial data (yr. ended 12/31/10): Revenue, $413,389; assets, $586,208 (M); gifts received, $231,394; expenditures, $294,552; giving activities include $284,545 for grants to organizations outside the U.S.
Purpose and activities: The organization works to eradicate illiteracy within India.
Fields of interest: Education; Education, reading.
International interests: India.
Publications: Annual report.
Officer: Sandeep Shroff, Treas.
EIN: 363779020

187
Ingram Micro Inc. Corporate Giving Program
P.O. Box 25125
Santa Ana, CA   92799-5125
Contact: Nicole Trombly, Specialist, Comm. Rels.
FAX: (714) 382-4978;
E-mail: communityrelations@ingrammicro.com;
E-mail: tamara.sharp@ingrammicro.com;

URL: http://www.ingrammicro.com/imdocs/display/main/1,,591,00.html
Twitter: http://twitter.com/IngramMicroInc

Grantmaker type: Corporate giving program.
Purpose and activities: Ingram Micro makes charitable contributions to nonprofit organizations involved with arts and culture, education, technology, and health and human services. Support is given primarily in Orange County, California, Carol Stream, Illinois, Buffalo, New York, Harrisburg, Pennsylvania, Memphis and Millington, Tennessee, and Carrollton, Texas.
Fields of interest: Engineering/technology; Education.
International interests: Asia; Canada; Europe; Latin America; Mexico; Oceania.
Type of support: Annual campaigns; Donated products; Employee matching gifts; Employee volunteer services; In-kind gifts; Matching/challenge support; Program development.
Limitations: Applications accepted. Giving primarily in Orange County, CA, Carol Stream, IL, Buffalo, NY, Harrisburg, PA, Memphis and Millington, TN, and Carrollton, TX; limited giving in Asia, Canada, Latin America, Mexico, Oceania, and western Europe. No support for sectarian, denominational, or religious organizations, political candidates, sports or sports-related organizations, organizations not of direct benefit to the entire community, or discriminatory organizations. No grants to individuals, or for fundraising.
Publications: Application guidelines.
Application information: Faxed requests are not accepted. Unsolicited requests for contributions of over $5,000 are not accepted. The Community Relations Department handles giving. The company has a staff that only handles contributions. A contributions committee reviews all requests. Application form not required.
  Initial approach: E-mail proposal to headquarters
  Copies of proposal: 1
  Deadline(s): None
  Committee meeting date(s): Bi-weekly
  Final notification: 30 days
Administrators: Nicole Trombly, Specialist, Comm. Rels.

188
Institute for OneWorld Health
50 California St., Ste. 500
San Francisco, CA   94111-4608   (415) 421-4700
FAX: (415) 421-4747;
E-mail: info@oneworldhealth.org; *URL:* http://www.oneworldhealth.org

Established in 2001; institute operates in conjunction with the University of California - San Francisco Medical Center, Kala-Azar Medical Research Centre, International Centre for Diarrhea Disease Research, and Massachusetts General Hospital.
Grantmaker type: Public charity.
Financial data (yr. ended 12/31/10): Revenue, $26,399,862; assets, $26,215,343 (M); gifts received, $26,173,980; expenditures, $17,804,343; giving activities include $120,000 for grants, and $5,321,466 for grants to organizations outside the U.S.
Purpose and activities: The institute serves as a positive agent for change by saving lives, improving health, and fulfilling the promise of medicine for those most in need by: identifying potential new

medicines for disease disproportionately affecting developing countries; assessing the safety and effectiveness of investigational medicines; honoring international ethical standards for research; establishing collaborations with partners to manufacture and distribute new medicines; and ensuring that medicines will be affordable and available for distribution.
Fields of interest: Medical research, information services; Tropical diseases research; Parasitic diseases research; Medical research; Economically disadvantaged.
International interests: Developing countries.
Limitations: Applications not accepted.
Application information: Contributes only to pre-selected organizations.
Officer and Directors:* Victoria G. Hale,* Ph.D., Chair. and C.E.O.; Leslie Z. Benet, Ph.D.; William A. Haseltine, Ph.D.; Frederick W. Kyle; Bernardita Mendez, Ph.D.; Herbert D. Montgomery; Keith Olson; Regina Rabinovich, M.D., M.P.H.
EIN: 943384500

189
International Community Foundation
2505 N. Ave.
National City, CA   91950-6019   (619) 336-2250
Contact: Denisse Newell, Dir., Devel. and Mktg.
FAX: (619) 336-2249; *E-mail:* lisa@icfdn.org;
URL: http://www.icfdn.org

Established in 1990 in CA.
Grantmaker type: Public charity.
Financial data (yr. ended 06/30/10): Revenue, $6,600,431; assets, $11,579,251 (M); gifts received, $6,318,747; expenditures, $9,927,046; program services expenses, $9,326,938; giving activities include $4,017,034 for 23 grants (high: $2,996,531; low: $10,000), $4,817,664 for 91 grants to organizations outside the U.S., and $492,240 for foundation-administered programs.
Purpose and activities: The foundation seeks to increase charitable giving and volunteerism across U.S. borders to benefit overseas communities and nonprofit organizations.
Fields of interest: Arts; Education; Environment; Health care; Human services; Economic development; Community/economic development.
International interests: South America; Mexico; Latin America; Asia.
Type of support: General/operating support; Continuing support.
Limitations: Applications not accepted. Giving on an international basis, primarily in Latin America and the Pacific Rim region of Asia. No grants to individuals.
Publications: Annual report; Newsletter.
Application information: The foundation only sends out requests for proposals to organizations of interest; unsolicited requests for funds not considered or acknowledged.
  Board meeting date(s): 1st Wed. of Jan., Mar., June, Sept., and Nov.
Officers and Governors:* Irma Gigli,* M.D., Chair.; Samuel Simon Dychter,* Vice-Chair.; Richard Kiy, Pres. and C.E.O.; Yuri A. Calderon,* Secy.; Atul Patel,* Treas.; Mary Correia-Moreno; Cheryl Hammond; Anthony "Tony" Kinninger; Gabriela Manriquez; John McNeece; Alejandra Mier y Teran; Edward J.G. Mracek; Dr. Deborah L. Riner; Richard "Rick" L. Romney; Mary L. Walshok, Ph.D.
Number of staff: 5
EIN: 330457858

190
International Humanities Center
(also known as IHCenter)
860 Via de la Paz, Ste. B-1
Pacific Palisades, CA 90272-3640
(310) 526-9665
Contact: Steve Sugarman, Exec. Dir.
FAX: (206) 333-1797; E-mail: info@ihcenter.org

Established in 1998.
Grantmaker type: Public charity.
Purpose and activities: The center's mission is to work with other independent nonprofit organizations and sponsored projects that are devoted to a vision of ecological and humanitarian stewardship that benefits all of creation; and to reverse the current situation of pollution, disease, and disconnection by focusing efforts on creating a civilization that is centered on love, peace, and natural harmony.
Fields of interest: Community/economic development; International affairs; Human services.
Publications: Application guidelines; Financial statement; Program policy statement.
Application information: Application form required.
   Initial approach: Download fiscal sponsorship application form and return completed form via regular mail or fax
   Board meeting date(s): Varies
   Final notification: Three to five weeks
Officer and Directors:* Steven Sugarman,* M.A., Exec. Dir.; Catherine Carroll; Timothy Hall; Katherine O'Flaherty; David Michael Tanner.
Number of staff: 3 full-time professional; 1 part-time professional; 1 full-time support; 1 part-time support.
EIN: 330767921

191
International Medical Corps
1919 Santa Monica Blvd., Ste. 400
Santa Monica, CA 90404-1950   (310) 826-7800
FAX: (310) 442-6622;
E-mail: imc@imcworldwide.org; Additional address: 1313 L St., N.W., Unit 220, Washington, DC 20006, tel.: (202) 828-5155, FAX: (202) 828-5156; URL: http://www.imcworldwide.org

Established in 1984.
Grantmaker type: Public charity.
Financial data (yr. ended 06/30/10): Revenue, $131,132,443; assets, $30,944,789 (M); gifts received, $130,703,278; expenditures, $122,080,674; giving activities include $6,000 for grants, and $1,642,641 for grants to organizations outside the U.S.
Purpose and activities: The organization is dedicated to relieving suffering, saving lives, and fostering self-reliance through health care training and relief and development programs.
Fields of interest: Human services; Health care; International relief.
Limitations: Giving on a national and international basis.
Publications: Annual report.
Officer: Nancy A. Aossey, Pres. and C.E.O.
EIN: 953949646

192
International Project Advisory Board
2003 Santa Cruz Ave.
Menlo Park, CA 94025-6237   (650) 854-2770
Contact: Max Rondoni, Secy.

Grantmaker type: Public charity.
Purpose and activities: The organization supports Evangelistic bible colleges, schools, and related ministries working in the former CIS (Russia).
Fields of interest: Religion.
International interests: Ukraine.
Limitations: Giving limited to the Ukraine.
Officers and Directors:* Rev. Donald B. Sheley,* Chair.; Max Rondoni,* Secy.; M. Lyman Bates, Jr.,* Treas.; William Clauson, M.D., Ph.D.; Richard Dorst; Joseph C. Hickingbotham III; Marlowe Rondoni.
EIN: 943169854

193
The Intuit Foundation
P.O. Box 7850, MS MTV-07-02
Mountain View, CA 94043
E-mail: communityimpact@intuit.com; URL: http://www.intuit.com/about_intuit/philanthropy/how.jsp#Foundation

Established in 2002 in CA.
Donor: Intuit Inc.
Grantmaker type: Company-sponsored foundation.
Financial data (yr. ended 03/31/11): Assets, $484,523 (M); gifts received, $1,036,000; expenditures, $971,097; qualifying distributions, $836,380; giving activities include $836,380 for grants.
Purpose and activities: The foundation supports organizations involved with education, health, children and youth, human services, community development, and economically disadvantaged people. Special emphasis is directed toward programs designed to foster economic empowerment.
Fields of interest: Human services, financial counseling; Community development, small businesses; Economic development; Education; Health care; Children/youth, services; Human services; Community/economic development; Economically disadvantaged.
International interests: Canada.
Type of support: Program development; Employee volunteer services; Employee matching gifts.
Limitations: Applications not accepted. Giving primarily in Tucson, AZ, Mountain View, San Diego, and Sebastopol, CA, Denver, CO, Stamford, CT, Boston, MA, Reno, NV, Plano, TX, Fredericksburg, VA, and Edmonton, Canada. No support for religious organizations, political or labor organizations, private foundations, or discriminatory organizations. No grants to individuals, or for fundraising events or sponsorships, advertising, souvenir journals, or dinner programs, or conferences, exhibits, or academic research.
Application information: Contributes only to pre-selected organizations.
Officers and Director: Sherry Whiteley, C.E.O. and Pres.; Ken Wach, V.P.; Tyler Cozzens, Secy.; David Merenbach, Treas.; Terilyn Monroe, Exec. Dir.; Scott D. Cook.
EIN: 470860921

194
Invisible Children, Inc.
1620 5th Ave., Ste. 400
San Diego, CA 92101-2738   (619) 562-2799
FAX: (619) 660-0576;
E-mail: info@invisiblechildren.com; Additional fax: (619) 660-0689; URL: http://www.invisiblechildren.com
Facebook: http://www.facebook.com/invisiblechildren
MySpace: http://www.myspace.com/invisiblechildren
Twitter: http://twitter.com/invisible
YouTube: http://www.youtube.com/invisiblechildreninc

Established in 2004.
Grantmaker type: Public charity.
Financial data (yr. ended 06/30/11): Revenue, $13,765,180; assets, $6,931,285 (M); gifts received, $10,334,060; expenditures, $8,894,632; giving activities include $2,810,681 for 1 grant to an organization outside the U.S.
Purpose and activities: The organization works to transform apathy into activism by documenting the lives of those living in regions of conflict and injustice, with the hopes of educating and inspiring individuals in the Western world to use their voices for change.
Fields of interest: Education; Media/communications; Media, film/video; International peace/security; International conflict resolution; Children.
International interests: Uganda.
Type of support: Film/video/radio; Scholarships—to individuals.
Limitations: Giving limited to Uganda.
Publications: Annual report; Financial statement.
Officers and Board Members:* Scott Wolfe,* Chair.; Jason Russell,* Pres.; Bobby Bailey,* Secy.; Ben Keesey,* Exec. Dir. and C.F.O.; John Bradel; Glenn Guthridge; Rich McCullen; Shawn Parr; Laren Poole; Keven Relyea; Sheryl Russell.
EIN: 542164338

195
The Ishiyama Foundation
465 California St., Ste. 800
San Francisco, CA 94104-1847
Contact: Margaret Raffin, Secy.

Established in 1968 in CA.
Donor: George S. Ishiyama.
Grantmaker type: Independent foundation.
Financial data (yr. ended 12/31/10): Assets, $84,868,616 (M); expenditures, $4,125,873; qualifying distributions, $3,362,900; giving activities include $3,362,900 for grants.
Purpose and activities: Giving primarily for the environment, as well as for education, health care, social services and the arts.
Fields of interest: Arts; Higher education; Education; Environment; Health organizations; Human services; Foundations (private grantmaking).
International interests: South Africa.
Limitations: Applications accepted. Giving primarily in CA; some funding also in South Africa. No support for study programs. No grants to individuals.
Application information: Application form not required.
   Deadline(s): None
Officers: Margaret Raffin, Pres.; Patsy Ishiyama, V.P.; Nelson Ishiyama, Secy.

Directors: Alan Arai; Sheryl Lynn Suzuki.
EIN: 941659373

196
Israel Venture Network
540 Cowper St., Ste. 200
Palo Alto, CA   94301-1806   (650) 325-4200
FAX: (650) 649-1974;
E-mail: info@israelventurenetwork.org; Additional
address: P.O. Box 5064, Kadima, Israel 60920, tel.:
972-9-891-2117, E-mail: info@ivn.org.il;
URL: http://www.israelventurenetwork.org

Grantmaker type: Public charity.
Financial data (yr. ended 12/31/09): Revenue,
$694,221; assets, $254,512 (M); gifts received,
$694,059; expenditures, $954,085; giving
activities include $776,114 for grants to
organizations outside the U.S.
Purpose and activities: The organization is a
venture philanthropy network of high-tech executives
from Israel and the U.S. that aims to increase
Israel's national competitiveness by advancing its
educational systems and promoting social
programs.
Fields of interest: Education; Social
entrepreneurship; Venture philanthropy.
International interests: Israel.
Type of support: Fellowships.
Limitations: Giving limited to Israel.
Publications: Annual report.
Officers and Directors: * Eric Benhamov,* Chair.;
Benny Levin,* Vice-Chair.; Alona Barkat; Nir Barkat;
Bernie Belkin; Ofer Ben Shachar; and 12 additional
directors.
EIN: 141891915

197
Jacobs Engineering Foundation
P.O. Box 7084
Pasadena, CA   91109-7084   (626) 578-3500
Contact: John W. Prosser, Jr., Treas.

Established in 1978 in CA.
Donor: Jacobs Engineering Group Inc.
Grantmaker type: Company-sponsored foundation.
Financial data (yr. ended 12/31/10): Assets,
$2,756,202 (M); gifts received, $725,389;
expenditures, $875,574; qualifying distributions,
$875,414; giving activities include $875,414 for
grants.
Purpose and activities: The foundation supports
organizations involved with choral music, education,
environmental policy, Alzheimer's disease, human
services, international affairs, community
development, science, and civic affairs.
Fields of interest: Performing arts, music (choral);
Secondary school/education; Education;
Environment, public policy; Alzheimer's disease; Boy
scouts; American Red Cross; Salvation Army; Youth,
services; Aging, centers/services; Human services;
International affairs; Business/industry;
Community/economic development; United Ways
and Federated Giving Programs; Science; Public
affairs.
Type of support: General/operating support; Annual
campaigns; Scholarship funds; Sponsorships;
Matching/challenge support.
Limitations: Applications accepted. Giving primarily
in CA, Washington, DC, IL, MO, SC, TX, and VA.

Application information: Application form not
required.
Initial approach: Proposal
Deadline(s): None
Officers and Directors: * Noel G. Watson,* Chair.;
Craig L. Martin,* Pres.; Michael S. Udovic, Secy.;
John W. Prosser, Jr.,* Treas.; Nazim G. Thawerbhoy,
Cont.
EIN: 953195445

198
Jagadeesh Family Foundation
14232 Shady Oak Ct.
Saratoga, CA   95070-5568

Established in 1999 in CA.
Donors: Anu Jagadeesh; B.V. Jagadeesh.
Grantmaker type: Independent foundation.
Financial data (yr. ended 12/31/10): Assets,
$3,293 (M); gifts received, $70,000; expenditures,
$127,586; qualifying distributions, $127,385;
giving activities include $127,385 for grants.
Purpose and activities: Giving primarily for
international development in India; and for higher
education.
Fields of interest: Higher education; International
development; International conflict resolution.
International interests: India.
Type of support: General/operating support;
Research.
Limitations: Applications not accepted. Giving
primarily in CA. No grants to individuals.
Application information: Unsolicited requests for
funds not accepted.
Officers and Director: * B.V. Jagadeesh,* C.E.O.
and C.F.O.; Anu Jagadeesh, Secy.
EIN: 770511893

199
The Jao Foundation
8907 Warner Ave., Ste. 108
Huntington Beach, CA   92647-5079

Established in CA.
Donors: Frank Jao; Catherine Jao.
Grantmaker type: Independent foundation.
Financial data (yr. ended 12/31/10): Assets,
$410,753 (M); gifts received, $350,301;
expenditures, $159,475; qualifying distributions,
$158,145; giving activities include $158,145 for 3
grants (high: $100,000; low: $7,789).
Fields of interest: International affairs, research;
Higher education.
Limitations: Applications not accepted. Giving
primarily in CA. No grants to individuals.
Application information: Unsolicited requests for
funds not accepted.
Officers: Catherine Jao, Pres.; Felicia Jao, Secy.;
Alicia Jao, Treas.
EIN: 200114436

200
The Alan K. and Cledith M. Jennings
Foundation
P.O. Box 111
Penn Valley, CA   95946-0111

Established in 2000 in CA.
Donors: A.K. Jennings; Cledith Jennings.
Grantmaker type: Independent foundation.

Financial data (yr. ended 12/31/10): Assets,
$8,529,198 (M); expenditures, $386,597;
qualifying distributions, $386,597; giving activities
include $147,900 for 25 grants (high: $10,000;
low: $50).
Fields of interest: Legal services; Reproductive
health, family planning; Education; Health
organizations, association; Human services;
International relief; International human rights;
United Ways and Federated Giving Programs.
Limitations: Applications not accepted. Giving
primarily in CA. No grants to individuals.
Application information: Unsolicited requests for
funds not accepted.
Officers: A.K. Jennings, Pres.; C.M. Jennings, V.P.;
T.L. Jennings, V.P.
EIN: 943363468

201
Jerome Foundation
541 E. Chapman Ave., Ste. B
Orange, CA   92866-1648   (714) 538-2393
Contact: Sherrie Spray

Incorporated in 1956 in CA.
Donors: James M. Andreoli; Frank Jerome;
members of the Jerome family; Baker Commodities,
Inc.
Grantmaker type: Independent foundation.
Financial data (yr. ended 12/31/10): Assets,
$10,150,814 (M); gifts received, $50,000;
expenditures, $489,874; qualifying distributions,
$463,456; giving activities include $463,456 for
grants.
Purpose and activities: Giving primarily to an
affiliated foundation; giving also for hospitals, youth,
and education.
Fields of interest: Children/youth, services;
Education; Hospitals (general); Medical research,
institute; Human services; YM/YWCAs & YM/
YWHAs; Foundations (private grantmaking).
International interests: Philippines.
Limitations: Giving primarily in southern CA; some
giving in Rizal, Philippines. No grants to individuals.
Publications: Annual report.
Application information: Application form not
required.
Deadline(s): None
Officers: James M. Andreoli, Pres.; Mitchell Ebright,
Secy.-Treas.
Directors: Andrew Andreoli; Anthony Andreoli;
James A. Andreoli; Richard Jerome; Maxine Taylor.
EIN: 956039063

202
Jewish Community Federation of San
Francisco, the Peninsula, Marin and
Sonoma Counties
121 Steuart St.
San Francisco, CA   94105-1236   (415) 777-0411
Contact: Phyllis Cook, Exec. Dir.
E-mail: info@sfjcf.org; URL: http://www.sfjcf.org
Facebook: http://www.facebook.com/jewishfed
Jewish Community Federation: http://
sfjcf.wordpress.com/
Jewish Community Federation: http://
feeds.feedburner.com/sfjcf
Twitter: http://twitter.com/JewishBayArea

Established in 1910 in CA.
Grantmaker type: Public charity.

Financial data (yr. ended 06/30/10): Revenue, $67,819,979; assets, $591,227,651 (M); gifts received, $59,112,305; expenditures, $89,785,231; giving activities include $61,595,926 for grants, $500,000 for grants to organizations outside the U.S., and $23,258 for grants to individuals.

Purpose and activities: The federation works to protect and enhance Jewish life in the San Francisco community through fundraising, strategic planning, and providing funding for programs that care for those in need, strengthen and secure the safety of the Jewish people, and foster Jewish renaissance at home, in Israel, and in other Jewish communities.

Fields of interest: Museums (ethnic/folk arts); Education; Jewish federated giving programs; Jewish agencies & synagogues; Aging.

International interests: Israel.

Application information: Application form required.

  Deadline(s): Varies

Officers and Directors:* James M. Koshland,* Pres.; David Agger, V.P.; Susan Diamond, V.P.; Nancy Grand, V.P.; Daniel Grossman, V.P.; H. Michael Feldman, V.P.; Jennifer Gorovitz, C.E.O.; Deena Soulon,* C.O.O. and C.F.O.; Barbara Farber,* Secy.; Michael A. Jacobs,* Treas.; Phyllis Cook, Exec. Dir.; Ruvim Baude; Valli Benesch Tandler; and 36 additional directors.

EIN: 941156533

203
Jewish Community Foundation of Los Angeles

6505 Wilshire Blvd., Ste. 1200
Los Angeles, CA   90048-4960   (323) 761-8700
Contact: Naomi Strongin, Grants Coord.
FAX: (323) 761-8666;
E-mail: info@jewishfoundationla.org; Toll-free tel.: (877) 363-6966; tel. for Naomi Strongin, (323) 761-8705; URL: http://www.jewishfoundationla.org
YouTube: http://www.youtube.com/user/JCFLATV

Established in 1954 in CA.
Grantmaker type: Public charity.
Financial data (yr. ended 12/31/10): Revenue, $31,614,000; assets, $730,935,000 (M); expenditures, $76,581,000; giving activities include $65,252,000 for grants.

Purpose and activities: The foundation serves as a long-term, stable funding resource to help the Jewish and general community of Los Angeles grow and thrive, meet emergencies, and foster innovative responses to new challenges.

Fields of interest: Arts; Education; Environment; Health care; Community/economic development; Jewish agencies & synagogues.

International interests: Israel.

Type of support: Building/renovation; Conferences/seminars; Seed money.

Limitations: Applications accepted. Giving primarily in Los Angeles County, CA. No grants to individuals.

Publications: Application guidelines; Annual report; Grants list; Newsletter; Program policy statement.

Application information: Application form required.

  Deadline(s): Oct. 29 for concept papers for Cutting Edge Grants Initiative; varies for all others

Officers and Trustees:* Lorin M. Fife,* Chair.; Marvin I. Schotland, Pres. and C.E.O.; Daniel M. Rothblatt, Sr. V.P., Philanthropic Services; Michael J. Januzik, Sr. V.P., Finance & Admin.; Elliot B. Kristal, V.P., Charitable Gift Planning; Baruch S.

Littman, V.P., Devel.; Amelia Xann, V.P., Family Foundation Center & Grants Program; Kenneth A. August,* V.P.; Leah M. Bishop, V.P.; Max Factor III, V.P.; Bertrand I. Ginsberg, V.P.; Harold J. Masor, V.P.; Alan Stern, V.P.; Selwyn Gerber,* Secy.; Lawrence Rauch, Treas.; Martin S. Appel; Anthony Chanin; Allan B. Cutrow; and 26 additional trustees.
Number of staff: 26
EIN: 956111928

204
Jewish Family and Children's Services of San Francisco, the Peninsula, Marin and Sonoma Counties

(formerly JFCS)
2150 Post St.
San Francisco, CA   94115-3508   (415) 449-1226
Contact: Anita Friedman Ph.D., Exec. Dir.
FAX: (415) 922-5938; E-mail: erics@jfcs.org; TDD: (415) 567-1044; URL: http://www.jfcs.org

Founded in 1850.
Grantmaker type: Public charity.
Financial data (yr. ended 06/30/10): Revenue, $39,174,514; assets, $66,647,223 (M); gifts received, $21,612,493; expenditures, $29,921,036; giving activities include $210,445 for grants, $32,400 for grants to organizations outside the U.S., and $1,620,847 for grants to individuals.

Purpose and activities: The organization exists to provide professional and volunteer services for the purposes of developing, restoring, and maintaining the competency of families and individuals of all ages.

Fields of interest: Humanities; Vocational education; Higher education; Education; International affairs.

Type of support: Scholarships—to individuals; Grants to individuals.

Limitations: Applications accepted. Giving primarily to the San Francisco Bay Area, CA.

Publications: Application guidelines; Annual report; Informational brochure.

Application information: See web site for additional application information and forms. Application form required.

  Initial approach: Telephone foundation or contact school counselor for application form and guidelines

Officers and Directors:* Dr. Raquel Newman,* Pres.; Nancy Goldberg,* V.P.; Michael J. Kaplan,* V.P.; Susan Kolb,* V.P.; Galina Miloslavsky,* Secy.; Mark S. Menell,* Treas.; Anita Friedman, Ph.D., Exec. Dir.; Joseph Alouf; Ian H. Altman; Suzy Colvin; Paul Crane Dorfman; Don Friend; Lynn Ganz; Paul Gelburd; Carl Grunfeld, M.D., Ph.D.; and 16 additional directors.
EIN: 941156528

205
Jewish World Watch

5551 Balboa Blvd
Encino, CA   91316-1506   (818) 501-1836
E-mail: info@jewishworldwatch.org; URL: http://www.jewishworldwatch.org
Facebook: http://www.facebook.com/JewishWorldWatch
Flickr: http://www.flickr.com/photos/36054082@N08/
Twitter: http://twitter.com/#!/jworldwatch

YouTube: http://www.youtube.com/user/JWW17514

Established in 2004.
Grantmaker type: Public charity.
Financial data (yr. ended 12/31/10): Revenue, $1,230,775; assets, $2,101,044 (M); gifts received, $1,227,685; expenditures, $1,605,051; giving activities include $189,947 for grants, and $340,649 for grants to organizations outside the U.S.

Purpose and activities: The organization works to mobilize synagogues, their schools, their members, and the community to combat genocide and other violations of human rights around the world through education, advocacy, and refugee relief.

Fields of interest: International relief; International affairs; International migration/refugee issues; International human rights; Jewish agencies & synagogues.

Limitations: Giving on a worldwide basis.

Officers and Directors:* Janice Kamenir-Reznik,* J.D., Pres. and C.E.O.; Abby J. Leibman, J.D., Secy. and C.F.O.; Tzivia Schwartz-Getzug, Exec. Dir.; Rabbi Eli Herscher; Rabbi Stephen B. Jacobs; Rabbi Harold M. Schulweis; Sheila Gordon Wasserman; Rabbi David Wolpe.
EIN: 203406211

206
Kadima Foundation

38 Miller Ave., Ste. 220
Mill Valley, CA   94941-1939   (415) 435-6995
Contact: Chara Schreyer, Pres.

Established in 1997 in CA.
Donors: MCR Foundation; The Max Webb Lead Unitrust.
Grantmaker type: Independent foundation.
Financial data (yr. ended 12/31/10): Assets, $1,486,727 (M); gifts received, $322,674; expenditures, $497,698; qualifying distributions, $453,000; giving activities include $453,000 for grants.

Purpose and activities: The mission of the foundation focuses primarily on creating opportunities for promising young adults to access education and training that will help them realize their potential. In addition, the foundation also supports institutions and programs dedicated to the cure, prevention, and management of insulin-dependent diabetes whose goals are to cure diabetes, to delay and/or prevent complications, and to improve the quality of life through disease management to ultimately prevent the disease. Also giving for the understanding and encouragement of contemporary art, as well as the encouragement and support of emerging young artists, and causes that promote the people of Israel, with a special interest in women's rights.

Fields of interest: Arts; Museums; Elementary/secondary education; Higher education; Diabetes research; Youth development, services; International affairs, fund raising/fund distribution; Jewish federated giving programs; Jewish agencies & synagogues.

Limitations: Applications accepted. Giving primarily in CA.

Application information: Application form not required.

  Deadline(s): None

Officers: Chara Schreyer, Pres.; Justine Schreyer, Secy.-Treas.

Director: Mira Kon.
EIN: 943254834

207
The Henry J. Kaiser Family Foundation
2400 Sand Hill Rd.
Menlo Park, CA 94025-6941 (650) 854-9400
Contact: Renee Wells, Contracts Mgr.
FAX: (650) 854-4800; E-mail: rwells@kff.org;
Washington, DC Office Address: 1330 G St., N.W.,
Washington, DC 20005, tel.: (202) 347-5270; fax:
(202) 347-5274; URL: http://www.kff.org
E-Newsletter: http://profile.kff.org/
Knowledge Center: http://www.kff.org/content/
reports.cfm
RSS Feed: http://www.kff.org/Content/rss.cfm
Twitter: http://twitter.com/KaiserFamFound
YouTube: http://www.youtube.com/
kaiserfoundation

Trust established in 1948 in CA; changed status to
operating foundation in 1999.
Donors: Bess F. Kaiser†; Henry J. Kaiser†; Henry J.
Kaiser, Jr.†; and others.
Grantmaker type: Operating foundation.
Financial data (yr. ended 12/31/10): Assets,
$576,659,804 (M); gifts received, $2,064,326;
expenditures, $57,639,460; qualifying
distributions, $40,710,960; giving activities include
$483,915 for 50+ grants (high: $35,000),
$115,911 for employee matching gifts, and
$7,584,432 for foundation-administered programs.
Purpose and activities: The foundation is a
nonprofit, private operating foundation that
develops and runs its own research and
communications programs and does not accept
unsolicited funding requests.
Fields of interest: Health care, public policy;
Reproductive health; AIDS; Minorities; Women;
Economically disadvantaged.
International interests: South Africa.
Limitations: Applications not accepted. Giving in
South Africa for the international grants program;
other grants nationwide.
Application information: The foundation does not
accept unsolicited funding requests.
Officers and Trustees:* Richard T. Scholsberg,*
Chair.; Drew E. Altman,* Ph.D., C.E.O. and Pres.;
Diane Rowland, Sc.D., Exec. V.P. and Exec. Dir.,
Kaiser Commission on Medicaid and the Uninsured;
Bruce W. Madding, Sr. V.P., C.F.O., and C.I.O.; Matt
James, Sr. V.P., Media and Public Education and
Exec. Dir., kaisernetwork.org; Michael R. Sinclair,
Ph.D., Sr. V.P., Health and Development in South
Africa; David Orcutt, V.P. and Cont.; Mollyann
Brodie, Ph.D., V.P. and Dir., Public Opinion and
Survey Research; Gary Claxton, V.P. and Dir., Health
Care Marketplace Project; Esther Dicks, V.P., and
Dir., Human Resources; Tina Hoff, V.P. and Dir.,
Entertainment Media Partnerships; Jackie Judd, V.P.
and Sr. Advisor, Comms.; Jennifer Kates, V.P. and
Dir., HIV Policy; Barbara Lyons, Ph.D., V.P. and
Deputy Dir., Kaiser Commission on Medicaid and
the Uninsured; Tricia Neuman,* Sc.D., V.P. and Dir.,
Medicare Policy Project; Vicky Rideout, V.P. and Dir.,
Program for the Study of Media and Health; Alina
Salganicoff, Ph.D., V.P. and Dir., Women's Health
Policy and kaiser.edu; Rakesh Singh, V.P., Comms.;
Susan V. Berresford; Tom Campbell; Jennifer
Drobac; Jacob Lew; Cokie Roberts; Gerald Rosberg;
Allan Rosenfield, M.D.; David Satcher, M.D.; Donna
E. Shalala, Ph.D.; Diana Chapman Walsh; Kathy
Wehle; W. Richard West.

Number of staff: 82 full-time professional; 36
full-time support.
EIN: 946064808

208
**Kaiser Permanente Northern California
Regional Community Grants Program**
c/o Community Benefit Progs.
1800 Harrison St., 25th Fl.
Oakland, CA 94612-3434 (510) 625-6101
FAX: (510) 625-6398;
E-mail: NCAL-CB-Programs@kp.org; URL: http://
info.kp.org/communitybenefit/html/
our_communities/northern-california/
our_communities_1_a.html

Grantmaker type: Corporate giving program.
Purpose and activities: Kaiser Permanente
Northern California Regional Community Grants
Program supports organizations that provide critical
health and human services to vulnerable
populations, including the safety net of community
clinics, public hospitals and health care systems.
Support is limited to areas of company operations
in northern California.
Fields of interest: International relief; Disasters,
preparedness/services; Health care, public policy;
Health care, equal rights; Public health; Health care;
Economically disadvantaged.
Type of support: General/operating support.
Limitations: Applications accepted. Giving limited to
CA. No support for organizations lacking 501(c)(3)
status, religious organizations for religious
purposes, or for partisan, political, fraternal,
athletic, international, or social organizations. No
grants to individuals, or for endowments,
memorials, field trips, or tours.
Publications: Application guidelines; Corporate
giving report.
Application information: The LOI should be
submitted with a cover letter on agency letterhead
signed by the organization's chief executive(s), and
should include requested amount. Subject line of
e-mail should include following: "LOI - Name of
requesting organization". Application form required.
Initial approach: Complete letter of inquiry
template and e-mail to headquarters
Deadline(s): None
Final notification: 4 to 6 weeks

209
The J. F. Kapnek Charitable Trust
(formerly Kapnek Charitable Trust)
936 Dewing Ave., Ste. E3
Lafayette, CA 94549-4277 (925) 962-7150
FAX: (925) 962-7151;
E-mail: dan@jfkapnektrust.org; URL: http://
www.jfkapnektrust.org

Established in 1973 in PA.
Donors: Fivelight Foundation; Elizabeth Glaser
Pediatric A.I.D.S. Foundation; U.N.I.C.E.F.
Grantmaker type: Public charity.
Financial data (yr. ended 06/30/10): Revenue,
$1,857,618; assets, $763,299 (M); gifts received,
$404,527; expenditures, $1,778,243; giving
activities include $1,425,478 for grants to
organizations outside the U.S.
Purpose and activities: The trust provides support
for medical research, education, nursing training for
the prevention of mother to child transmission of

HIV, and seeks to develop a national preschool
program to support orphans and vulnerable children.
Fields of interest: AIDS research; AIDS; Medical
school/education; Medical research, institute.
International interests: Zimbabwe.
Type of support: Research.
Limitations: Applications not accepted. Giving
primarily in Zimbabwe. No grants for capacity
building or training.
Publications: Annual report; Newsletter.
Application information: Contributes only to
pre-selected organizations.
Board meeting date(s): Apr.
Officer and Trustees:* Daniel Robbins,* M.D.,
Chair.; Mary Bassett, M.D.; Robert Kapnok; Barbara
Kramer, J.D.; Arnold Perkins; Lester Steppacher,
M.D.; Cynthia Stokes-Brown, Ph.D.; Candice Toute.
Number of staff: 36 full-time professional; 4
part-time professional.
EIN: 237165692

210
Karisma Foundation
c/o Karen Bedrosian Coyne
2934 1/2 Beverly Glen Cir., Ste. 419
Los Angeles, CA 90077-1724

Established in 2005 in CA.
Donors: John C. Bedrosian; Judith D. Bedrosian.
Grantmaker type: Independent foundation.
Financial data (yr. ended 06/30/10): Assets,
$8,462,975 (M); expenditures, $661,265;
qualifying distributions, $500,000; giving activities
include $500,000 for 12 grants (high: $50,000;
low: $25,000).
Purpose and activities: Giving for organizations
serving people in Armenia; funding for organizations
serving children in the Los Angeles area.
Fields of interest: Children/youth, services;
Children/youth.
International interests: Armenia.
Type of support: General/operating support;
Equipment; Continuing support.
Limitations: Applications not accepted. Giving on a
national and international basis, primarily in Los
Angeles, CA and Armenia. No support for religious
organizations.
Application information: Unsolicited requests for
funds not accepted.
Board meeting date(s): Spring and Fall
Officers and Directors:* John C. Bedrosian,* Pres.;
Judith D. Bedrosian,* Secy.; Karen Bedrosian
Coyne, C.F.O.
Number of staff: 1 part-time professional.
EIN: 201982120

211
The Kavli Foundation
1801 Solar Drive, Ste. 250
Oxnard, CA 93030-8297 (805) 683-6000
Contact: Dr. Robert W. Conn, Pres.
FAX: (805) 988-4800; URL: http://
www.kavlifoundation.org/
E-Newsletter: http://visitor.constantcontact.com/
manage/optin/ea?
v=001nQUq2GTjwCh2XVyu9nQt_g%3D%3D
RSS Feed: http://www.kavlifoundation.org/rss.xml
Twitter: http://twitter.com/KavliFoundation
YouTube: http://www.youtube.com/
KavliFoundation

Established in 2000 in CA.
Donor: Fred Kavli.
Grantmaker type: Independent foundation.
Financial data (yr. ended 12/31/10): Assets, $155,824,484 (M); expenditures, $15,187,299; qualifying distributions, $10,831,242; giving activities include $5,770,691 for 14+ grants (high: $1,250,000).
Purpose and activities: The foundation is dedicated to the goals of advancing science for the benefit of humanity and promoting increased public understanding of and support for scientists and their work. The foundation has selected three areas in which to focus its activities: astrophysics, neuroscience, and nanoscience. An international program of research institutes, prizes, symposia, and endowed professorships is being established to further these goals.
Fields of interest: Education; Science.
Type of support: Professorships; Research.
Limitations: Applications not accepted. Giving primarily on a national basis; some giving internationally. No grants to individuals.
Publications: Informational brochure.
Application information: Participation in the foundation's programs of fellowships, professorships, symposia and prizes is by invitation only; the foundation does not respond to unsolicited proposals.
Officers and Directors:* Fred Kavli,* Chair.; Rockell N. Hankin,* Vice-Chair.; Dr. Robert W. Conn,* Pres.; Mi Young Chun, V.P., Science Progs.; Charles M. Vest; Thomas E. Everhart; Douglas K. Freeman; Henry T. Yang.
Number of staff: 2 full-time professional; 1 part-time professional; 3 full-time support.
EIN: 770560142
Recent grants for international programs:
211-1 Beijing University, Beijing, China, $575,000. For scientific support. 2009.
211-2 Cambridge University, Kavli Institute of Cosmology, Cambridge, England, $1,250,000. For scientific support. 2009.
211-3 Chinese Academy of Sciences, Beijing, China, $575,000. For scientific support. 2009.
211-4 Delft University of Technology, Kavli Institute for Nanoscience, Delft, Netherlands, $1,750,000. For scientific support. 2009.
211-5 Norwegian University of Science and Technology, Kavli Institute for Systems Neuroscience, Trondheim, Norway, $1,250,000. For scientific support. 2009.
211-6 Royal Society, Kavli International Center, London, England, $714,750. For scientific support. 2009.

212
B. K. Kee Foundation
102 Fey Dr.
Burlingame, CA 94010-6027 (650) 491-3434
Contact: Stanley Sze, Pres.
FAX: (650) 490-3153;
E-mail: thekeefoundation@gmail.com

Established in 2005 in CA.
Donor: Dr. Lay K. Kay.
Grantmaker type: Independent foundation.
Financial data (yr. ended 12/31/10): Assets, $16,098,144 (M); expenditures, $831,413; qualifying distributions, $544,817; giving activities include $544,817 for grants.
Purpose and activities: To provide humanitarian aid to the people of Myanmar.

Fields of interest: Health care; Human services; Education.
International interests: Burma (Myanmar).
Type of support: Management development/capacity building; Emergency funds; Seed money; Scholarship funds.
Limitations: Applications not accepted. Giving primarily in CA and Myanmar.
Application information: Unsolicited requests for funds not accepted.
Officers and Directors:* Stanley Sze,* Pres.; Dr. Lay K. Kay,* C.F.O. and Secy.-Treas.
EIN: 562545977

213
David and Anita Keller Foundation
90 Broadacres Rd.
Atherton, CA 94027-6408 (650) 854-7238
Contact: David Keller, Pres.

Established in 2002 in CA.
Donors: Anita Keller; David Keller.
Grantmaker type: Independent foundation.
Financial data (yr. ended 12/31/10): Assets, $2,205,621 (M); gifts received, $37,254; expenditures, $222,045; qualifying distributions, $180,200; giving activities include $180,200 for 12 grants (high: $100,000; low: $2,000).
Fields of interest: Civil/human rights, women; International human rights; Museums (art); Animals/wildlife, preservation/protection; Higher education; Human services; Children/youth, services.
Application information: Application form not required.
    Initial approach: Proposal
    Deadline(s): None
Officers and Directors:* David Keller,* Pres.; Anita Keller,* Secy.-Treas. and C.F.O.; Kimberly Keller; Michael Keller.
EIN: 270006184

214
Kerby Family Foundation
P.O. Box 2971
Grass Valley, CA 95945-2971

Established in 2000 in CA.
Donors: Camille L. Kerby; Lynn A. Kerby.
Grantmaker type: Independent foundation.
Financial data (yr. ended 12/31/10): Assets, $17,182 (M); expenditures, $2,420,277; qualifying distributions, $2,406,000; giving activities include $2,406,000 for 15 grants (high: $2,280,000; low: $2,000).
Fields of interest: Residential/custodial care, hospices; Performing arts, music; Education; Health care, volunteer services; Health care; Cancer research; Human services; Children/youth, services; International affairs, volunteer services; International relief; Orthodox agencies & churches.
Limitations: Applications not accepted. Giving primarily in CA and NY. No grants to individuals.
Application information: Contributes only to pre-selected organizations.
Trustees: Camille L. Kerby; Lynn A. Kerby.
EIN: 680458359

215
Kiva Microfunds
3180 18th St., Ste. 201
San Francisco, CA 94110-2042
E-mail: contactus@kiva.org; URL: http://www.kiva.org

Established in 2005 in CA.
Grantmaker type: Public charity.
Financial data (yr. ended 12/31/10): Revenue, $11,515,298; assets, $11,565,224 (M); gifts received, $11,322,524; expenditures, $6,225,091.
Purpose and activities: The organization manages and develops international microlending by helping to bring together borrowers and lenders and facilitate the advancement and repayment of funds between each party.
Fields of interest: International development.
Type of support: Fellowships; Program-related investments/loans.
Limitations: Applications accepted. Giving on an international basis.
Application information:
    Deadline(s): Rolling basis for Kiva Fellows Program
Officers: Premal Shah, Pres.; Matt Flannery, C.E.O.; Olana Hirsch Khan, C.O.O.
Directors: Leslie Crutchfield; Geoff Davis; Alex Edelstein; Reid Hoffman; Jenny Shilling Stein; Tabreez Berjee.
EIN: 710992446

216
Koret Foundation
33 New Montgomery St., Ste. 1090
San Francisco, CA 94105-4526
Contact: Susan Wolfe, Dir., Grantmaking Progs. and Comms.
FAX: (415) 882-7775;
E-mail: info@koretfoundation.org; URL: http://www.koretfoundation.org
E-Newsletter: http://www.koretfoundation.org/news/index.html
Facebook: http://www.facebook.com/pages/Koret-Foundation/139817769439751
Grants List: http://www.koretfoundation.org/awards/index.html
Knowledge Center: http://www.koretfoundation.org/publications/index.html

Grantmaking commenced in 1979.
Donors: Joseph Koret‡; Stephanie Koret‡.
Grantmaker type: Independent foundation.
Financial data (yr. ended 12/31/10): Assets, $444,724,401 (M); gifts received, $646,419; expenditures, $41,584,726; qualifying distributions, $25,324,201; giving activities include $22,128,614 for 448 grants (high: $2,250,000; low: $500; average: $10,000–$600,000).
Purpose and activities: Koret seeks to address societal challenges and to strengthen Bay Area life. The foundation seeks to invest in strategic, local solutions to help to inspire a multiplier effect-encouraging collaborative funding and developing model initiatives. Koret promotes educational opportunity, the community of Israel, and free market expansion. Areas of focus include arts/culture and civic institutions, K-12 education reform, Israel advocacy (including education and economic development), as well as Jewish community organizations.

Fields of interest: Elementary/secondary school reform; Arts; Higher education; Community/economic development; Jewish federated giving programs; Jewish agencies & synagogues.
International interests: Israel.
Type of support: General/operating support; Continuing support; Management development/capacity building; Annual campaigns; Program development; Conferences/seminars; Fellowships; Scholarship funds; Research; Technical assistance; Program evaluation; Matching/challenge support.
Limitations: Applications accepted. Giving limited to the Bay Area counties of San Francisco, Alameda, Contra Costa, Marin, Santa Clara, and San Mateo, CA; giving also in Israel and on a national basis for Jewish funding requests. No support for private foundations, or veterans', fraternal, military, religious, or sectarian organizations whose principal activity is for the benefit of their own membership. No grants to individuals, or for endowment funds or deficit financing.
Publications: Application guidelines; Biennial report; Financial statement; Grants list; Informational brochure; Newsletter; Occasional report.
Application information: Full proposals are accepted by invitation only. Application form not required.
  Initial approach: Review application guidelines, then send letter of inquiry
  Copies of proposal: 1
  Deadline(s): Ongoing basis
  Board meeting date(s): 4 times per year
  Final notification: 4 to 6 months
Officers and Directors:* Susan Koret,* Chair.; Jeffrey A. Farber, C.E.O.; Tad Taube,* Pres.; Claudia J. Hardin, C.F.O. and C.A.O.; Richard C. Atkinson; Michael J. Boskin, Ph.D.; William K. Coblentz; Anita Friedman; Robert Friend; Richard L. Greene; Abraham D. Sofaer.
Number of staff: 10 full-time professional; 5 full-time support; 1 part-time support.
EIN: 941624987
Recent grants for international programs:
216-1 American Friends of Koret Israel Economic Development Fund, San Francisco, CA, $500,000. For General Operating Support. 2009.
216-2 American Friends of Koret Israel Economic Development Fund, San Francisco, CA, $20,000. For General Operating Support. 2009.
216-3 American Friends of NATAL, New York, NY, $20,000. For General Operating Support. 2009.
216-4 American Friends of Sarah Herzog Hospital, New York, NY, $25,000. For General Operating Support. 2009.
216-5 American Friends of the Hebrew University, New York, NY, $50,000. For General Operating Support to Koret School of Veterinarian Medicine in Honor of the Tails of Love Benefit Gala. 2009.
216-6 American Friends of the Israel Philharmonic Orchestra, New York, NY, $20,000. For General Operating Support. 2009.
216-7 American Israel Education Foundation, Washington, DC, $25,000. For General Operating Support. 2009.
216-8 American Jewish Joint Distribution Committee, New York, NY, $50,000. For Emergency Relief in Georgia. 2009.
216-9 American Society of the University of Haifa, New York, NY, $10,000. For Hippos Excavation Project. 2009.

216-10 Birthright Israel Foundation, New York, NY, $50,000. For Educational Trips from Poland. 2009.
216-11 BlueStar, San Francisco, CA, $55,000. For Write On for Israel. 2009.
216-12 Business Executives for National Security, Washington, DC, $60,000. For General Operating Support and Bay Area Business Force. 2009.
216-13 Business Executives for National Security, Washington, DC, $20,000. For American Heroes Project. 2009.
216-14 Cantors Assembly Foundation, Baltimore, MD, $25,000. For Anniversary Mission to Poland and Israel. 2009.
216-15 Cantors Assembly Foundation, Baltimore, MD, $25,000. For Anniversary Mission to Poland and Israel. 2009.
216-16 Central Fund of Israel, New York, NY, $25,000. For Israel's Media Watch. 2009.
216-17 Central Fund of Israel, New York, NY, $20,000. For Western Galilee College. 2009.
216-18 Claremont McKenna College, Claremont, CA, $10,000. For The Center for Human Rights Leadership. 2009.
216-19 Committee for Accuracy in Middle East Reporting in America, Boston, MA, $10,000. For Eyes on Israel Educational Program. 2009.
216-20 David Horowitz Freedom Center, Sherman Oaks, CA, $25,000. For The Defense of Israel Project. 2009.
216-21 El Camino Youth Symphony Association, Palo Alto, CA, $10,000. For Poland and Germany Summer Tour. 2009.
216-22 Friends of Ofanim, Wynnewood, PA, $10,000. For General Operating Support. 2009.
216-23 International Survey of Jewish Monuments, Syracuse, NY, $10,000. For Synagogue Restoration in Kerala, India. 2009.
216-24 Israel Project, Washington, DC, $25,000. For General Operating Support. 2009.
216-25 Israel21c, Sherman Oaks, CA, $15,000. For General Operating Support. 2009.
216-26 Jewish Community Federation of San Francisco, the Peninsula, Marin and Sonoma Counties, San Francisco, CA, $140,000. For Impact Projects in Poland. 2009.
216-27 Jewish Community Federation of San Francisco, the Peninsula, Marin and Sonoma Counties, San Francisco, CA, $20,000. For Israel in the Gardens. 2009.
216-28 Jewish National Fund, New York, NY, $100,000. For Sderot Indoor Recreation Center. 2009.
216-29 Jews Indigenous to the Middle East and North Africa, San Francisco, CA, $30,000. For General Operating Support. 2009.
216-30 Museum of Jewish Heritage, New York, NY, $10,000. For Taube Fellow at Auschwitz Jewish Center in Poland. 2009.
216-31 NCSJ: Advocates on Behalf of Jews in Russia, Ukraine, the Baltic States and Eurasia, Washington, DC, $35,000. For Student Leadership Program's An Educational Experience in Moscow. 2009.
216-32 North American Council of the Museum of the History of Polish Jews, New York, NY, $500,000. For Capital Support. 2009.
216-33 PEF Israel Endowment Funds, New York, NY, $20,000. For Shurat HaDin Israel Law Center. 2009.
216-34 Shalem Foundation, New York, NY, $100,000. For General Operating Support. 2009.

216-35 Stanford University, Stanford, CA, $150,000. For Koret Fellowship in Korean Studies Program. 2009.
216-36 Stanford University, Stanford, CA, $20,000. To work on International Nuclear Disarmament. 2009.
216-37 Stanford University, Stanford, CA, $20,000. To work on International Nuclear Disarmament. 2009.

217
The Trustees of Ivan V. Koulaieff Educational Fund
c/o Rothstein, Kass & Co., LLP
101 Montgomery St., 22nd Fl.
San Francisco, CA 94104-4104

Incorporated in 1930 in CA.
Donor: Ivan V. Koulaieff.
Grantmaker type: Independent foundation.
Financial data (yr. ended 12/31/10): Assets, $7,787,405 (M); expenditures, $557,844; qualifying distributions, $474,920; giving activities include $474,920 for grants.
Purpose and activities: The fund awards aid to Russian immigrants throughout the world through grants, scholarships, and loans; support also for Russian publications and Russian Orthodox education and churches in the U.S.
Fields of interest: Orthodox agencies & churches; Immigrants/refugees.
International interests: Russia.
Type of support: Publication; Program-related investments/loans; Grants to individuals; Scholarships—to individuals.
Limitations: Applications not accepted. Giving on a national and international basis.
Application information: Unsolicited requests for funds not accepted.
Officers and Trustees:* Olga P. Hughes, Pres.; Peter A. Yakoubovsky-Lerke, V.P.; Nikolai A. Kaliakin,* Secy.; Alex D. Psiol, Treas.; Nicolai A. Hidchenko; Michel Mirkovitch; Anatol Shmelev.
Candidate: Natalia Tkachov.
EIN: 946088762

218
The Kulkarni Foundation
1149 Valley Quail Cir.
San Jose, CA 95120-4128

Established in 1999 in CA.
Donors: Ashok Kulkarni; Ranjana Kulkarni; Vishwas Godbole; Arati Godbole.
Grantmaker type: Independent foundation.
Financial data (yr. ended 12/31/10): Assets, $97,490 (M); gifts received, $130,000; expenditures, $225,745; qualifying distributions, $221,008; giving activities include $221,008 for 2 grants (high: $220,000; low: $1,008).
Fields of interest: Elementary school/education.
International interests: India.
Limitations: Applications not accepted. Giving primarily in India.
Application information: Unsolicited requests for funds not accepted.
Officers: Ashok Kulkarni, Pres.; Ranjana Kulkarni, C.F.O.; Vedant Kulkarni, Secy.
EIN: 770527357

219
The Jean & E. Floyd Kvamme Foundation
P.O. Box 2494
Saratoga, CA 95070-0494
Contact: Jean Kvamme, Tr.

Established in 1993 in CA.
Donors: E. Floyd Kvamme; Jean Kvamme.
Grantmaker type: Independent foundation.
Financial data (yr. ended 06/30/11): Assets, $14,831,639 (M); gifts received, $281,265; expenditures, $1,176,450; qualifying distributions, $1,059,700; giving activities include $1,059,700 for grants.
Purpose and activities: Giving primarily to Christian religious organizations, medical grants for Alzheimer's, leukemia, arthritis, and spondylitis research and to the community of northern California for education and the arts.
Fields of interest: Arts; Engineering school/education; Education; Health organizations, association; Medical research, institute; United Ways and Federated Giving Programs; Christian agencies & churches.
International interests: Ecuador.
Type of support: General/operating support; Continuing support; Building/renovation; Equipment; Research; Matching/challenge support.
Limitations: Applications not accepted. Giving primarily in northern CA. No grants to individuals.
Application information: Unsolicited requests for funds not accepted.
Trustees: Damon Kvamme; E. Floyd Kvamme; Jean Kvamme; Todd Kvamme.
Number of staff: 3 part time support.
EIN: 770359484

220
Lee and Luis Lainer Family Foundation
16216 Kittridge St.
Van Nuys, CA 91406-5846

Established in 2008 in CA.
Donor: Simha Lainer‡.
Grantmaker type: Independent foundation.
Financial data (yr. ended 12/31/10): Assets, $9,723,490 (M); expenditures, $468,962; qualifying distributions, $457,300; giving activities include $457,300 for grants.
Fields of interest: Jewish agencies & synagogues; International peace/security; Jewish federated giving programs; Human services.
Limitations: Applications not accepted. Giving primarily in CA, Washington, DC, and New York, NY. No grants to individuals.
Application information: Contributes only to pre-selected organizations.
Trustees: Anne E. Lainer; Jesse S. Lainer; Lee Lainer; Luis Lainer; Zachary Lainer.
EIN: 260494276

221
Leadership Thru Books
1849 Firestone Blvd.
La Mirada, CA 90638
E-mail: leadershipthrubooks@yahoo.com

Established in 1996 in CA.
Grantmaker type: Public charity.
Financial data (yr. ended 03/31/10): Revenue, $58,463; assets, $29,830 (M); gifts received, $60,969; expenditures, $81,967; giving activities include $72,806 for grants to organizations outside the U.S.
Purpose and activities: The foundation supports a library for the community of Patulul, Guatemala.
Fields of interest: Libraries/library science.
International interests: Guatemala.
Limitations: Applications not accepted. Giving primarily in Patulul, Guatemala. No grants to individuals.
Application information: Contributes only to pre-selected organizations.
Officers and Directors:* Gregorio Ruiz, Chair.; Dora Orellana, C.E.O.; Ana Karenina, Treas.; Francis Leon,* C.F.O.
EIN: 954593229

222
The L. S. B. Leakey Foundation
(formerly L. S. B. Leakey Foundation for Research Related to Human Origins, Behavior and Survival)
1003B O'Reilly Ave.
San Francisco, CA 94129-1359 (415) 561-4646
Contact: Sharal Camisa, Assoc. Exec. Dir.
FAX: (415) 561-4647;
E-mail: sharal@leakeyfoundation.org; URL: http://www.leakeyfoundation.org

Founded in 1968.
Grantmaker type: Public charity.
Financial data (yr. ended 08/31/10): Revenue, $1,788,117; assets, $15,577,099 (M); gifts received, $1,292,818; expenditures, $1,446,915; giving activities include $297,241 for grants to organizations outside the U.S., and $439,231 for grants to individuals.
Purpose and activities: The foundation seeks to promote education and research human origins, evolution, behavior and survival.
Fields of interest: History/archaeology; Geology; Anthropology/sociology.
International interests: Europe; Africa; Asia.
Type of support: Fellowships; Research.
Limitations: Applications accepted. Giving on a national and international basis. No grants for salary or fringe benefits of applicant, tuition, non-project personnel, equipment, travel to meetings, or general operating expenses.
Publications: Application guidelines; Financial statement; Grants list; Informational brochure; Newsletter.
Application information: Application form required.
Initial approach: Download application
Copies of proposal: 13
Deadline(s): Jan. 5 and July 15 for General Research Grants; Feb. 15 for Franklin Mosher Baldwin Memorial Fellowships
Board meeting date(s): Apr., Oct., and Dec.
Final notification: Mid-May for spring session and fellowships; mid-Jan. for fall session
Officers and Trustees:* Gordon P. Getty,* Chair.; William M. Wirthlin II,* Pres.; Don Dana,* V.P.; C. Paul Johnson,* V.P.; Alice M. Corning,* Secy.; William P. Richards, Jr.,* Treas.; Hernan Buchi; Nina Carroll; Joan C. Donner; Carolyn Farris; and 13 additional trustees.
Number of staff: 3 full-time professional; 3 part-time professional.
EIN: 952536475

223
Lebanese Ladies Cultural Society
315 Arden Ave., Ste. 18
Glendale, CA 91203-1155 (818) 547-5701

Established in 1988.
Grantmaker type: Public charity.
Financial data (yr. ended 12/31/10): Revenue, $319,980; assets, $2,754,914 (M); gifts received, $186,918; expenditures, $512,579; giving activities include $485,275 for grants.
Purpose and activities: The society provides scholarship funds to assist needy students in Lebanon.
Fields of interest: Education.
International interests: Lebanon.
Type of support: Scholarship funds.
Limitations: Giving limited to Lebanon.
Officers: Falak Beyhum, Pres.; Joanna Nachef, V.P.; Rajia Husami, Treas.
EIN: 954141592

224
The Iara Lee & George Gund III Foundation
The Presidio
39 Mesa St., Ste. 300
San Francisco, CA 94129-1018
Contact: Thomas Suniville, V.P.

Established in 2004 in CA, funded in 2005.
Donors: George Gund III; Iara Lee.
Grantmaker type: Independent foundation.
Financial data (yr. ended 12/31/10): Assets, $48,330 (M); gifts received, $107,740; expenditures, $253,265; qualifying distributions, $246,053; giving activities include $245,750 for 9 grants (high: $60,000; low: $250).
Fields of interest: Animal welfare; International affairs; Environment.
International interests: Africa.
Limitations: Applications not accepted. Giving primarily in CA, Washington, DC, and NY.
Application information: Contributes only to pre-selected organizations.
Officers and Directors:* Iara Lee,* Pres.; George Gund III,* Sr. V.P.; Thomas Suniville,* V.P. and C.F.O.; George Gund IV.
EIN: 912146075

225
Leibowitz Photography, Inc. Contributions Program
5482 Wilshire Blvd., Ste. 1510
Los Angeles, CA 90036-4218 (323) 933-1013
E-mail: mark@leibowitzpictures.com; URL: http://www.leibowitzpictures.com
B Corporation Profile: http://www.bcorporation.net/leibowitzphotography

Grantmaker type: Corporate giving program.
Purpose and activities: Leibowitz Photography is a certified B Corporation that donates a percentage of net profits to charitable organizations.
Fields of interest: Human services; Environment; International development; International human rights.
Type of support: General/operating support; Continuing support.

226

The Leichtag Family Foundation
c/o Sheldon Scharlin, C.P.A.
5800 Armada Dr., Ste. 100
Carlsbad, CA   92008-4611
URL: http://www.jcfsandiego.org/Default.aspx?tabid=614
Grants List: http://www.jcfsandiego.org/Default.aspx?tabid=1097

Established in 1991 in CA.
Donors: Max Leichtag; Andre Leichtag; Leichtag Family Trust; Lee and Toni Leichtag Family Trust.
Grantmaker type: Independent foundation.
Financial data (yr. ended 12/31/10): Assets, $130,528,726 (M); gifts received, $101,505,050; expenditures, $12,405,701; qualifying distributions, $12,176,518; giving activities include $11,514,010 for 99 grants (high: $2,000,000; low: $250).
Purpose and activities: Giving primarily for federated giving programs and human services.
Fields of interest: Hospitals (general); Human services; United Ways and Federated Giving Programs; Jewish federated giving programs; Religion.
Type of support: Equipment; Building/renovation; Capital campaigns; Annual campaigns.
Limitations: Applications not accepted. Giving primarily in CA. No grants to individuals.
Application information: Contributes only to pre-selected organizations.
   Board meeting date(s): May and Nov.
Officers: Bernard Reiter, Chair.; Murray Galinson, Vice-Chair.; James S. Farley, C.E.O. and Pres.; Rabbi Lenore Bohm,* V.P.; Robert Brunst, M.D., C.F.O.; Sheldon Scharlin,* Chair., Audit Comm.
Number of staff: None.
EIN: 330466189
Recent grants for international programs:
226-1 America-Israel Cultural Foundation, New York, NY, $25,000. 2010.
226-2 American Friends of Magen David Adom, New York, NY, $46,000. 2010.
226-3 American Friends of Shalom Hartman Institute, New York, NY, $25,000. 2010.
226-4 American Jewish Joint Distribution Committee, New York, NY, $650,000. 2010.
226-5 Daniel Pearl Foundation, Encino, CA, $10,000. 2010.
226-6 Foundation for Women, San Diego, CA, $695,000. 2010.
226-7 Friends of Ikamva Labantu, New Rochelle, NY, $18,000. 2010.
226-8 Hand in Hand, American Friends of the Center for Jewish-Arab Education in Israel, Portland, OR, $25,000. 2010.
226-9 Israel Guide Dog Center for the Blind, Warrington, PA, $25,000. 2010.
226-10 Jewish National Fund, New York, NY, $36,000. 2010.
226-11 PEF Israel Endowment Funds, New York, NY, $25,000. 2010.
226-12 Shalem Foundation, New York, NY, $50,000. 2010.

227

The Robert Lemelson and Susan Morse Lemelson Family Foundation
17411 Revello Dr.
Pacific Palisades, CA   90272-4160

Established in 1999 in CA.
Donors: Robert Lemelson, Ph.D.; Susan Morse Lemelson.
Grantmaker type: Independent foundation.
Financial data (yr. ended 11/30/10): Assets, $582,933 (M); expenditures, $223,389; qualifying distributions, $212,050; giving activities include $212,050 for 9 grants (high: $81,000; low: $100).
Fields of interest: International affairs; Education; African Americans/Blacks; Men.
Limitations: Applications not accepted. Giving primarily in CA, Washington, DC and Singapore. No grants to individuals.
Application information: Contributes only to pre-selected organizations.
Officers: Robert Lemelson, Ph.D., Pres.; Susan Morse Lemelson, Secy.-Treas. and C.F.O.
EIN: 954774899

228

The Carol Anne Levy Foundation
10960 Wilshire Blvd., Ste. 1100
Los Angeles, CA   90024-3714
URL: http://www.pilotlightfund.org/

Established in 1996 in MI.
Donors: Carol Anne Levy; R.H. Bluestein and Company.
Grantmaker type: Independent foundation.
Financial data (yr. ended 12/31/10): Assets, $975,603 (M); gifts received, $39,369; expenditures, $294,017; qualifying distributions, $278,558; giving activities include $278,558 for grants.
Purpose and activities: Giving primarily for international development.
Fields of interest: AIDS; AIDS research; International development; International human rights; Civil/human rights, advocacy; Economically disadvantaged.
Limitations: Applications not accepted. Giving primarily in New York, NY and Los Angeles, CA. No grants to individuals.
Application information: Contributes only to pre-selected organizations.
Officers and Directors:* Carol Anne Levy, Pres.; John D. Johnstone,* Secy.; Ellen Levy,* Treas.
EIN: 383331960

229

Hyman Jebb Levy Foundation
6634 Valjean Ave.
Van Nuys, CA   91406-5816
Contact: Hyman Levy, Pres.

Established in 1974 in CA.
Donors: Hyman Levy; Raymond Mallel; Aaron Cohen.
Grantmaker type: Independent foundation.
Financial data (yr. ended 12/31/10): Assets, $5,192,898 (M); gifts received, $1,024,581; expenditures, $356,026; qualifying distributions, $329,335; giving activities include $329,300 for 21 grants (high: $200,000; low: $1,000).
Purpose and activities: Grants primarily for Jewish education and temple support, including support for institutions in Israel.
Fields of interest: Elementary/secondary education; Education; Human services; Jewish federated giving programs; Jewish agencies & synagogues.
International interests: Israel.
Limitations: Applications accepted. Giving primarily in CA and NY. No support for private foundations. No grants to individuals.
Application information: Application form not required.
   Initial approach: Letter
   Deadline(s): None
Officers: Hyman Levy, Pres.; Donna Levy, Secy.
EIN: 237422872

230

Lidow Foundation
233 Kansas St.
El Segundo, CA   90245-4316

Donors: Alexander Lidow; Eric Lidow; Derek Lidow.
Grantmaker type: Independent foundation.
Financial data (yr. ended 12/31/10): Assets, $617,628 (M); gifts received, $24,200; expenditures, $443,974; qualifying distributions, $443,224; giving activities include $441,000 for 8 grants (high: $200,000; low: $1,500).
Fields of interest: Secondary school/education; International studies; United Ways and Federated Giving Programs; Hospitals (specialty).
Type of support: General/operating support.
Limitations: Applications not accepted. Giving primarily in southern CA and Washington, DC. No grants to individuals.
Application information: Contributes only to pre-selected organizations.
Officers: Eric Lidow, C.E.O. and C.F.O.; Elizabeth Lidow, V.P.; Verna Kuykendall, Secy.-Treas.
Directors: Alan Lidow; Alexander Lidow; Derek Lidow.
EIN: 952406726

231

Lift the Children
(formerly The LIFT Foundation)
c/o Katherine M. Smith
4700 Roseville Rd.
North Highlands, CA   95660-5143
E-mail: info@liftfoundation.org; *URL:* http://www.liftchildren.org

Established in 1998 in CA.
Donors: Katherine M. Miller; Richard C. Miller; Scott Hanson; Valerie Hanson; Ceres Foundation; McFarlane Martin Foundation; Romania America Sustain PT RSP.
Grantmaker type: Public charity.
Financial data (yr. ended 12/31/10): Revenue, $144,047; assets, $657,959 (M); gifts received, $130,871; expenditures, $225,551; giving activities include $68,762 for grants to organizations outside the U.S.
Purpose and activities: Giving primarily in Romania for child welfare programs, projects that prevent the abuse, abandonment, and neglect of children, and efforts to educate and integrate children into society through social assistance and counseling.
Fields of interest: Education; Crime/violence prevention, child abuse; Youth development; Children/youth, services; International human rights.
International interests: Romania.
Type of support: Program development.
Limitations: Applications not accepted. Giving on an international basis, primarily to benefit Romania. No

support for state-run institutions or religious purposes. No grants to individuals, or for projects for street children, or building and infrastructure projects.

Publications: Annual report; Grants list; Informational brochure; Newsletter.
Application information: Contributes only to pre-selected organizations.
   Board meeting date(s): Quarterly
Officers and Board Members:* Katherine M. Miller, Pres.; Paul S. Aronowitz,* Secy.; Katherine M. Smith, Exec. Dir.; Donald J. Clutter, M.D., F.A.C.S.; John Crisan; Maureen Gill, R.N.; Ed Goldman; Scott Hanson; Kipp Johnson; George Muntean; Karen O'Brien; Ken Plumlee.
Number of staff: 1 full-time professional.
EIN: 680404790

232
Lindholm Foundation
25 Vista Montemar
Laguna Niguel, CA 92677-7954

Established in 2003 in CA.
Donor: Wayne Lindholm.
Grantmaker type: Independent foundation.
Financial data (yr. ended 12/31/10): Assets, $2,876,904 (M); gifts received, $550,000; expenditures, $367,742; qualifying distributions, $135,435; giving activities include $132,370 for 8 grants (high: $100,000; low: $1,000).
Fields of interest: Health care; International development; Education; Protestant agencies & churches.
Limitations: Applications not accepted. No grants to individuals.
Application information: Unsolicited requests for funds not accepted.
Officers: Wayne Lindholm, Pres.; Linda Lindholm, Secy.
EIN: 200411464

233
Linked Foundation
c/o 3
3749 Santa Claus Ln., Ste. B
Carpinteria, CA 93013-1104
URL: http://www.linkedfoundation.org
Blog: http://www.linkedfoundation.org/blog

Established in 2006 in CA.
Donors: Dorothy F. Largay; Wayne E. Rosing; Tabasgo Foundation.
Grantmaker type: Independent foundation.
Financial data (yr. ended 12/31/10): Assets, $7,809,076 (M); gifts received, $850,000; expenditures, $869,638; qualifying distributions, $520,721; giving activities include $520,721 for grants.
Purpose and activities: The foundation supports alleviation of poverty by promoting solutions that improve the health and economic self-reliance of women, internationally.
Fields of interest: International economic development; Human services; Civil/human rights, women; Economic development; Women.
Limitations: Applications not accepted. Giving primarily in CA. No grants to individuals.
Application information: Contributes only to pre-selected organizations.

Officers: Dorothy F. Largay, Pres.; Wayne E. Rossing, Secy.
EIN: 203880761

234
The Lunchbox Fund
9229 Sunset Blvd., Ste. 414
Los Angeles, CA 90069-3404
E-mail: info@thelunchboxfund.org; URL: http://www.thelunchboxfund.org
Facebook: http://www.facebook.com/thelunchboxfund?v=wall
Twitter: http://twitter.com/#!/thelunchboxfund
YouTube: http://www.youtube.com/user/TheLunchboxFund

Established in 2004.
Grantmaker type: Public charity.
Financial data (yr. ended 12/31/10): Revenue, $157,281; assets, $191,056 (M); gifts received, $157,281; expenditures, $33,383.
Purpose and activities: The fund aims to provide disadvantaged and impoverished pre- and secondary school children in South Africa with the food they need to help them achieve their goals in life.
Fields of interest: Higher education; Education; Food services; Nutrition; Economically disadvantaged.
International interests: South Africa.
Limitations: Giving primarily in South Africa.
Directors: Balthazar Getty; John Krysko; Topaz Page-Green; Joaquin Phoenix.
EIN: 201232903

235
Lutz Foundation
1251 Grizzly Peak Blvd.
Berkeley, CA 94708-2127
Contact: Elizabeth G. Lutz, Tr.

Established in 1986 in CA.
Donor: Gregory P. Lutz.
Grantmaker type: Independent foundation.
Financial data (yr. ended 12/31/10): Assets, $862,817 (M); expenditures, $268,441; qualifying distributions, $260,004; giving activities include $259,000 for 18 grants (high: $30,000; low: $1,000).
Purpose and activities: Giving for local performing arts, human rights, and civil liberties.
Fields of interest: Civil/human rights; Performing arts; International human rights.
Type of support: Continuing support; General/operating support; Endowments; Emergency funds; Program development.
Limitations: Applications not accepted. Giving primarily in the San Francisco Bay Area, CA. No grants to individuals.
Application information: The foundation prefers to initiate contact with potential donees; unsolicited requests for funds not considered or acknowledged.
Trustees: Elizabeth G. Lutz; Gregory P. Lutz.
EIN: 943033875

236
Chuan Lyu Foundation
(formerly The Lee Foundation)
P.O. Box 1294
Menlo Park, CA 94026-1294

Established in 1986 in CA.
Donor: Dr. Hwalin Lee.
Grantmaker type: Independent foundation.
Financial data (yr. ended 11/30/10): Assets, $10,619,724 (M); expenditures, $942,389; qualifying distributions, $745,725; giving activities include $745,725 for 12+ grants (high: $487,710).
Purpose and activities: Giving primarily for the study of topics related to Taiwan.
Fields of interest: Arts, cultural/ethnic awareness; Education.
International interests: Taiwan.
Limitations: Applications not accepted. Giving for Taiwan-related projects. No grants to individuals.
Application information: Contributes only to pre-selected organizations.
Officer and Trustee:* Dr. Hwalin Lee,* Mgr.
EIN: 586203563

237
Magbit Foundation
433 N. Camden Dr., 4th Fl., No. 215
Beverly Hills, CA 90210-4409
URL: http://www.magbit.org

Established in 1990.
Grantmaker type: Public charity.
Financial data (yr. ended 12/31/10): Revenue, $682,195; assets, $845,501 (M); gifts received, $678,631; expenditures, $610,325; giving activities include $216,900 for grants, $2,500 for grants to organizations outside the U.S., and $2,000 for grants to individuals.
Fields of interest: Jewish agencies & synagogues.
International interests: Israel.
Officers: Avi Cohen, Pres.; Shushana Djavaheri, V.P.; Babak Naffas, Secy.; Carolyn Afari, Treas.
EIN: 954307648

238
The Marisla Foundation
668 N. Coast Hwy., PMB 1400
Laguna Beach, CA 92651-1513   (949) 494-0365
Contact: Glenda Menges, Admin.
E-mail: glenda@marisla.org; URL: http://www.fsrequests.com/marisla

Established in 1986 in CA.
Grantmaker type: Independent foundation.
Financial data (yr. ended 12/31/09): Assets, $61,912,925 (M); gifts received, $20,000,000; expenditures, $35,694,619; qualifying distributions, $35,679,777; giving activities include $34,792,400 for 224 grants (high: $5,000,000; low: $500).
Purpose and activities: Giving primarily through two programs: an Environmental Program, and a Human Services Program.
Fields of interest: Environment, toxics; Women, centers/services; Marine science; Women.
International interests: Chile; Mexico.
Type of support: General/operating support; Program development.
Limitations: Applications accepted. Giving primarily on the West Coast of the U.S. (including Baja, CA), and in HI, Chile, and the Western Pacific for the environment; funding for women limited to Los Angeles and Orange County, CA. No support for political campaigns. No grants to individuals, or for scholarships, fellowships, or film or video projects.
Publications: Application guidelines.

Application information: Applications accepted via foundation web site. All applicants must complete the online application form which can be found on the foundation's web site. The foundation does not accept applications by mail, fax or e-mail. Application form required.

Initial approach: Proposal
Copies of proposal: 1
Deadline(s): Jan. 15, Apr. 15, Jul. 15, and Oct. 15
Board meeting date(s): Quarterly
Final notification: Immediate confirmation of receipt; 2-3 months for a decision

Officers and Directors: Anne G. Earhart, Pres.; Glenda Menges,* Secy. and Prog. Dir., Admin.; Oliver N. Crary, Treas.; Herbert M. Bedolfe,* Exec. Dir.; Sara M. Lowell.

Number of staff: 2 full-time professional.

EIN: 330200133

Recent grants for international programs:

238-1 1% for the Planet, Waitsfield, VT, $50,000. For General Support for Activities that Stimulate Corporate Giving to the Environment. 2009.

238-2 Alaska Wilderness League, Washington, DC, $35,000. For Arctic Solutions. 2009.

238-3 Antarctic and Southern Ocean Coalition, Washington, DC, $50,000. For Southern Ocean Initiative. 2009.

238-4 Asociacion Interamericana para la Defensa del Ambiente, Oakland, CA, $45,000. For Protection of Biodiversity and Marine Resources in Mexico and Costa Rica. 2009.

238-5 Basel Action Network, Seattle, WA, $25,000. For Global Environment Health and Justice Campaign. 2009.

238-6 Biosphere Foundation, Big Pine, CA, $20,000. For Menjangan Island Reef. 2009.

238-7 Catholic Relief Services, Baltimore, MD, $50,000. For Sumatra Earthquake Relief. 2009.

238-8 Center for Climate Strategies, Washington, DC, $250,000. For General Support. 2009.

238-9 Center for International Environmental Law, Washington, DC, $150,000. For International Persistent Organic Pollutants Elimination Network. 2009.

238-10 CERES, Boston, MA, $200,000. For Investor Strategy on Climate Change. 2009.

238-11 Cetacean Society International, Georgetown, CT, $100,000. For Grant Program in Latin America and the Caribbean. 2009.

238-12 Climate Group, New York, NY, $250,000. For climate change work. 2009.

238-13 Consultative Group on Biological Diversity, San Francisco, CA, $30,000. For General Support of Foundation Consortium. 2009.

238-14 Coral Reef Alliance, San Francisco, CA, $45,000. For Coral Reef Sustainable Destinations. 2009.

238-15 Doctors Without Borders USA, New York, NY, $50,000. For Bangladesh Cyclone Relief. 2009.

238-16 Earth Island Institute, Berkeley, CA, $100,000. For Energy Action Coalition/Power Shift Campaign. 2009.

238-17 Earth Island Institute, Berkeley, CA, $50,000. For Dolphin-Safe Tuna. 2009.

238-18 Earth Island Institute, Berkeley, CA, $20,000. For C-Saw/BC to BC Cruise Industry Reform Campaign. 2009.

238-19 EcoHealth Alliance, New York, NY, $50,000. For Sea Turtles and Marine Mammals Stranding Training and Monitoring in Baja California. 2009.

238-20 Ecology Center, Berkeley, CA, $175,000. For Global Alliance for Incinerator Alternatives and Environmental Health and Justice. 2009.

238-21 Environmental Flying Services, Tucson, AZ, $15,000. For National and Global Environmental Health Initiatives. 2009.

238-22 Environmental Health Fund, Jamaica Plain, MA, $175,000. For National and Global Environmental Health Initiatives. 2009.

238-23 Environmental Investigation Agency, Washington, DC, $125,000. For Campaign to Reduce Commercial Trade of Cetacean Products in Japan. 2009.

238-24 Environmental Law Alliance Worldwide, Eugene, OR, $40,000. For Protecting Communities from Toxic Chemicals. 2009.

238-25 Great Ape World Heritage Species Project, Cambridge, MA, $50,000. For Conservation of Tropical Forest Landscapes. 2009.

238-26 High Road for Human Rights Education Project, Salt Lake City, UT, $50,000. For General Support. 2009.

238-27 Humane Society of the United States, Washington, DC, $25,000. For Campaign to End Canada's Commercial Seal Hunt. 2009.

238-28 InMER Expeditions, Monterey, CA, $30,000. For Ocean Air Project. 2009.

238-29 Institute for Americas Future, Washington, DC, $75,000. For Energy and Climate Messaging Project. 2009.

238-30 International Community Foundation, National City, CA, $1,000,000. For Marisla Fund. 2009.

238-31 International Community Foundation, National City, CA, $500,000. For Marisla Fund. 2009.

238-32 International Community Foundation, National City, CA, $85,000. For Sea of Cortez Fund, Gulf of California Sustainable Tourism, World Heritage Alliance and Hurricane Jimena Relief. 2009.

238-33 International Fund for Animal Welfare, Yarmouth Port, MA, $150,000. For Global Campaign to End Commercial Whaling. 2009.

238-34 Internews Network, Arcata, CA, $50,000. For Earth Journalism Network. 2009.

238-35 Kentucky Environmental Foundation, Berea, KY, $160,000. For Coming Clean Collaborative. 2009.

238-36 MacGillivray Freeman Films Educational Foundation, Laguna Beach, CA, $1,000,000. For To the Arctic. 2009.

238-37 Mangrove Action Project, Port Angeles, WA, $30,000. For Mangrove Conservation. 2009.

238-38 Meridian Institute, Dillon, CO, $100,000. For Joint Ocean Commission Initiative. 2009.

238-39 Nature Conservancy, Arlington, VA, $1,050,000. For Pacific, Hawaii, Mexico, California, and Alaska Projects. 2009.

238-40 New York Botanical Garden, Bronx, NY, $50,000. For Ethnobotany and Conservation in Micronesia. 2009.

238-41 Ocean Foundation, Washington, DC, $30,000. For the Ocean Project/General Support. 2009.

238-42 Ocean Foundation, Washington, DC, $25,000. For Ocean Revolution/Sea Turtles. 2009.

238-43 Oceana, Washington, DC, $1,200,000. For General Support of International Marine Conservation. 2009.

238-44 Oceana, Washington, DC, $50,000. For Development Efforts. 2009.

238-45 Oceana, Washington, DC, $40,000. For End of the Line Film Promotion. 2009.

238-46 Oceana, Washington, DC, $35,000. For Development Efforts. 2009.

238-47 Oikonos, Benicia, CA, $35,000. For Seabird and Plastics Project. 2009.

238-48 Paso Pacifico, Ventura, CA, $40,000. For Nicaragua Sea Turtle Protection and Conservation. 2009.

238-49 Pesticide Action Network, North America Regional Center, San Francisco, CA, $75,000. For Eliminating Pesticides and Promoting Sustainable Alternatives Globally. 2009.

238-50 Pesticide Action Network, North America Regional Center, San Francisco, CA, $25,000. For International Campaign for Justice in Bhopal. 2009.

238-51 Physicians for Social Responsibility, Washington, DC, $40,000. For Environmental and Reproductive Health. 2009.

238-52 Pro Peninsula, San Diego, CA, $80,000. For Laguna San Ignacio Science Program. 2009.

238-53 Resources Legacy Fund, Sacramento, CA, $5,000,000. For Land Conservation in Northwest Mexico. 2009.

238-54 Rockefeller Family Fund, New York, NY, $200,000. For Climate Accountability Project. 2009.

238-55 Save the Waves Coalition, Davenport, CA, $30,000. For Chile Coastkeeper. 2009.

238-56 Sea Turtle Conservancy, Gainesville, FL, $25,000. For Sea Turtle Research, Protection and Conservation in Costa Rica. 2009.

238-57 Seacology, Berkeley, CA, $30,000. For Marine Projects in the Western Pacific. 2009.

238-58 Silicon Valley Toxics Coalition, San Jose, CA, $40,000. For Global E-Waste. 2009.

238-59 Smithsonian Institution, Washington, DC, $40,000. For Central Amazonia Project. 2009.

238-60 Smithsonian Institution, Washington, DC, $35,000. For Conservation and Study of the Whale Shark in Central America. 2009.

238-61 Transfair USA, Oakland, CA, $45,000. For empowering farming communities and working women by taking fair trade to scale. 2009.

238-62 Trust for Conservation Innovation, San Francisco, CA, $75,000. For Roots of Change. 2009.

238-63 University of California, Santa Barbara, CA, $200,000. For Coral Reef Research in the Palmyra Atoll. 2009.

238-64 Waterkeeper Alliance, New York, NY, $80,000. For Grassroots Movement and Clean Water Campaign. 2009.

238-65 World Resources Institute, Washington, DC, $60,000. For Reefs At Risk Report. 2009.

238-66 Yellowstone to Yukon Conservation Initiative, Bozeman, MT, $25,000. For the Center for Large Landscape Conservation. 2009.

239
Marra Foundation

c/o Leventhal Kline Mgmt., Inc.
127 University Ave.
Berkeley, CA 94710-1616 (510) 841-4016
Contact: Benita Kline, Mgr.
E-mail: Benita@lkmi.com.; Additional e-mail: benita@marrafoundation.org; URL: http://www.marrafoundation.org

Established in 1999 in CA.
Donors: Milan Momirov; Letitia Momirov.
Grantmaker type: Independent foundation.
Financial data (yr. ended 12/31/10): Assets, $284,542 (M); expenditures, $180,649; qualifying distributions, $176,802; giving activities include

$174,950 for 11 grants (high: $25,500; low: $1,500).

Purpose and activities: Giving primarily for projects that benefit the health and wholeness of all participants by addressing issues of water use, work and economic opportunity, women's welfare, and spiritual well being.

Fields of interest: Arts; Environment; Human services; Economic development; Religion.

International interests: Africa; Central America; India.

Type of support: General/operating support; Continuing support; Program development; Seed money; Matching/challenge support.

Limitations: Applications not accepted. Giving primarily in the San Francisco Bay Area, CA. No grants to individuals.

Application information: Contributes only to pre-selected organizations.

Officers: Letitia Momirov, Pres.; Milan Momirov, V.P. and Treas.

EIN: 943347337

240
Mashhoon Family Foundation
4525 District Blvd.
Vernon, CA 90058-2711 (323) 584-9500
Contact: Mahasti Mashhoon, Dir.

Established in 2007 in CA.

Grantmaker type: Independent foundation.

Financial data (yr. ended 12/31/10): Assets, $153 (M); gifts received, $713,000; expenditures, $767,635; qualifying distributions, $767,550; giving activities include $767,550 for 11 grants (high: $300,000; low: $300).

Fields of interest: Health organizations; Hospitals (specialty); Medical research; International development.

Type of support: General/operating support.

Limitations: Applications accepted. Giving primarily in Los Angeles, CA, Washington, DC, New York, NY, Memphis, TN, and Arlington, VA.

Application information:

Initial approach: Letter in narrative form
Deadline(s): None

Directors: Hamid Mashhoon; Mahasti Mashhoon.

EIN: 260663435

241
MAZON: A Jewish Response to Hunger
10495 Santa Monica Blvd., Ste. 100
Los Angeles, CA 90025-5031 (310) 442-0020
FAX: (310) 442-0030;
E-mail: mazonmail@mazon.org; URL: http://www.mazon.org
Facebook: http://www.facebook.com/mazonusa
Flickr: http://www.flickr.com/photos/mazonusa
RSS Feed: http://mazon.org/feed/
Twitter: http://twitter.com/stophunger
YouTube: http://www.youtube.com/user/mazonusa

Established in 1985 in MA.

Grantmaker type: Public charity.

Financial data (yr. ended 06/30/10): Revenue, $6,516,310; assets, $2,331,320 (M); gifts received, $6,501,386; expenditures, $6,294,236; giving activities include $3,994,846 for grants, and $135,214 for grants to organizations outside the U.S.

Purpose and activities: This national nonprofit agency allocates donations from the Jewish community to provide food, help, and hope to hungry people of all faiths and backgrounds.

Fields of interest: Human services, emergency aid; Food services; Food banks; International agricultural development.

Type of support: General/operating support; Continuing support; Seed money; Matching/challenge support.

Limitations: Applications not accepted. Giving primarily in the U.S., with some giving in Israel and in developing countries. No support for professional associations, government initiatives, or projects focusing on the prevention of homelessness. No grants to individuals, or for capital grants for building projects.

Publications: Annual report; Financial statement; Grants list; Informational brochure; Newsletter.

Application information: The organization is not currently accepting applications from organizations who are not previous grantees; see web site for current status of grantmaking programs.

Board meeting date(s): Jan., Apr., and Oct.

Officers and Directors:* Joel E. Jacob,* Chair.; David Pinzur,* Vice-Chair.; Evelyn Laser Shlensky,* Vice-Chair.; H. Eric Schockman, Pres.; Leslie Friedman, V.P.; Ruth Segal Laibson,* Secy.; Neil E. Salowitz,* Treas.; Erwin Chemerinsky; Shirley Davidoff; Leonard Fein; Lois Frank; Dan Glickman; Jeff Hollander; Rabbi Elliott Kleinman; Eve Biskind Klothen; and 12 additional directors.

Number of staff: 7 full-time professional; 6 full-time support; 1 part-time support.

EIN: 222624532

242
The McConnell Foundation
800 Shasta View Dr.
Redding, CA 96003-8208 (530) 226-6200
Contact: Lee W. Salter, C.E.O. and Pres.
FAX: (530) 226-6230;
E-mail: info@mcconnellfoundation.org; URL: http://www.mcconnellfoundation.org
E-Newsletter: http://www.mcconnellfoundation.org/contact/

Established in 1964 in CA.

Donors: Carl R. McConnell†; Leah F. McConnell†; National Park Service.

Grantmaker type: Independent foundation.

Financial data (yr. ended 12/31/09): Assets, $360,903,129 (M); expenditures, $17,203,164; qualifying distributions, $14,908,973; giving activities include $7,834,503 for 39 grants (high: $875,000; low: $385), $457,098 for grants to individuals, $138,691 for 83 employee matching gifts, and $3,975,182 for 4 foundation-administered programs.

Purpose and activities: Primary interests include the children, youth and education, sustainable livable communities, international grantmaking, environment, environmental education, recreation; projects that demonstrate broad based community support, and the promotion of voluntarism and philanthropy.

Fields of interest: Museums; Performing arts; Arts; Secondary school/education; Environment; Health care; Recreation; Aging, centers/services; Community/economic development; Voluntarism promotion.

International interests: Laos; Nepal.

Type of support: Building/renovation; Capital campaigns; Employee matching gifts; Endowments; Equipment; General/operating support; In-kind gifts; Matching/challenge support; Scholarship funds; Technical assistance.

Limitations: Giving limited to Shasta, Trinity, Modoc, Tehama and Siskiyou counties, CA; and Nepal and Laos. No support for sectarian religious purposes or for businesses or non 501(c) (3) organizations. No grants for annual fund drives or budget deficits.

Publications: Annual report; Newsletter.

Application information: Check foundation web site for current active programs.

Board meeting date(s): Feb., Mar., June, Sept., and Dec.

Officers and Directors:* Robert P. Blankenship,* Chair.; Lee W. Salter,* C.E.O. and Pres.; John A. Mancasola,* Exec. V.P. and Secy.; Shannon E. Phillips, V.P., Opers.; Doreeta J. Domke,* Treas.; William B. Nystrom, Dir. Emeritus; Richard J. Stimpel.

Number of staff: 9 full-time professional; 27 full-time support.

EIN: 946102700

Recent grants for international programs:

242-1 Asia Foundation, San Francisco, CA, $306,000. For community mediation. 2009.

242-2 Asia Foundation, San Francisco, CA, $282,090. For community mediation program improvement and expansion. 2009.

242-3 Asia Foundation, San Francisco, CA, $250,000. For access to Justice for Poor and Rural Citizens of Laos. 2009.

242-4 Asia Foundation, San Francisco, CA, $75,000. For Community Mediation: Building the Foundation for Program Sustainability. 2009.

242-5 Asia Foundation, Mahila Shakti Bikash Kendra, Nepal, San Francisco, CA, $278,000. For Women's Leadership Development Program. 2009.

242-6 Federation of Community Forestry Users, Kathmandu, Nepal, $306,000. For Nature Resources Conflict Management. 2009.

243
Medical Missions Adventures
11540 Bonham Ave.
Lake View Terrace, CA 91342-6608

Grantmaker type: Public charity.

Financial data (yr. ended 12/31/10): Revenue, $176,080; assets, $54,683 (M); gifts received, $164,612; expenditures, $161,227; program services expenses, $161,227; giving activities include $132,532 for grants.

Purpose and activities: The organization provides medical supplies to the poor in developing countries.

Fields of interest: International relief; Health care.

International interests: Developing countries.

Type of support: In-kind gifts.

Limitations: Applications not accepted. Giving primarily on an international basis.

Application information: Unsolicited requests for funds not accepted.

Officers and Board Members:* Louie Rosado,* Pres.; Ron Radachy,* V.P.; Barbara Rosado,* Secy.; Randall Blayney,* Treas.; Juan Caldentey; Mike Davis; Gail Davis; Jake DeLeon; Mark De Leon; Charles Funaro; Todd Kunkler; Dennis Ware.

EIN: 043661520

244
MicroCredit Enterprises
5758 Geary Blvd., Ste. 261
San Francisco, CA 94121-2112 (415) 230-4330
URL: http://www.mcenterprises.org
Facebook: http://www.facebook.com/MCEorg
Twitter: http://twitter.com/mceorg

Established in 2005.
Grantmaker type: Public charity.
Financial data (yr. ended 12/31/10): Revenue, $2,371,034; assets, $17,058,342 (M); gifts received, $1,036,929; expenditures, $1,983,224.
Purpose and activities: The organization leverages private capital and guarantees as security for loans to finance the micro-businesses of impoverished families throughout the developing world.
Fields of interest: Venture philanthropy; International development; Economic development.
International interests: Developing countries.
Type of support: Program-related investments/loans.
Officers: Jonathan C. Lewis, C.E.O.; Michael H. Katcher, C.O.O. and C.F.O.; Kyle R. Sayer, Exec. V.P., Portfolio Mgmt.; Dawnie M. Andrak, Sr. V.P., Devel.; Gary M. Ford, Genl. Counsel.
EIN: 203154063

245
Middle East Children's Alliance
1101 Eighth St., Ste. 100
Berkeley, CA 94710-2525 (510) 548-0542
Contact: Barbara Lubin, Exec. Dir.
FAX: (510) 548-0543;
E-mail: meca@mecaforpeace.org; URL: http://www.mecaforpeace.org

Established in 1994 in CA.
Grantmaker type: Public charity.
Financial data (yr. ended 06/30/10): Revenue, $1,073,968; assets, $710,882 (M); gifts received, $1,056,573; expenditures, $1,231,183; program services expenses, $903,450; giving activities include $90,286 for 7 grants (high: $42,000; low: $2,500), and $506,126 for grants to organizations outside the U.S.
Purpose and activities: The alliance works on behalf of children through: direct aid including food, medicine, medical supplies, clothes, books, toys, and school supplies; financial support and professional assistance to community organizations in the East Jerusalem, West Bank and Gaza that help meet children's needs; educational and cultural programs in the U.S. to increase understanding about the lives of children in the Middle East; and scholarships for Palestinian refugees in Gaza, the West Bank, East Jerusalem and the U.S.
Fields of interest: Human services; International affairs; International conflict resolution; Scholarships/financial aid.
Type of support: Scholarships—to individuals; In-kind gifts.
Limitations: Applications accepted. Giving in the U.S., East Jerusalem, West Bank, Gaza Strip, Israel, and Palestine.
Publications: Application guidelines.
Application information: Application form required.
  Initial approach: Download application form
  Deadline(s): July 15 for Elly Jaensch Memorial Scholarship
Officer: Barbara Lubin, Exec. Dir.

Directors: Sherry Gendelman; Barbara Lubin; Osha Neumann; Eugene Newport; Michel Shehadeh.
EIN: 943074600

246
Middle East Fellowship
(formerly Holy Land Trust)
P.O. Box 1252
Brea, CA 92822-1252 (562) 653-4252
E-mail: info@middleeastfellowship.org; URL: http://www.middleeastfellowship.org
Facebook: http://www.facebook.com/middleeastfellowship

Established in 1982 in CA.
Grantmaker type: Public charity.
Financial data (yr. ended 12/31/10): Revenue, $259,740; assets, $25,339 (M); gifts received, $72,249; expenditures, $361,098; giving activities include $250,092 for 268 grants to organizations outside the U.S.
Purpose and activities: The organization seeks to encourage, strengthen and improve the lives of Christians and Christian communities everywhere, with particular attention to those communities in the Middle East.
Fields of interest: Christian agencies & churches; Children/youth.
International interests: Syria; Middle East.
Type of support: Fellowships.
Limitations: Applications accepted. Giving primarily in the Middle East.
Publications: Application guidelines.
Application information: Applicants must pay fellowship costs in full; limited financial aid is available under the Lucius Battle Peace Fellows Program. Application form required.
  Initial approach: Submit application
  Deadline(s): Apr. 28 and May 30 for Palestine Summer Encounters
Officers: Robin Wainwright, Pres.; Phil Elkins, Secy.
Directors: Yves Accad; Murbark Awad; Gary Burge, Ph.D.; Fred Bush, Ph.D.; Farouk Eldeiry; Brice Harris, Ph.D.; Carolyn Harris; Darrel Myers; Dale Ryan; Rev. Nuhad Tomeh; Don Wagner; Nancy Wainwright.
EIN: 953910004

247
Milarepa Foundation, Inc.
1880 Century Park E., Ste. 1600
Los Angeles, CA 90067-1661 (310) 553-1707
URL: http://www.milarepa.org/

Established in 1994 in CA.
Grantmaker type: Public charity.
Financial data (yr. ended 12/31/10): Revenue, $650; assets, $78,065 (M); gifts received, $591; expenditures, $39,829; giving activities include $34,000 for grants.
Purpose and activities: The foundation is committed to funding political organizations involved in the Free Tibet movement worldwide; the foundation also seeks to promote public awareness of Tibet, non-violence, and humanitarian issues.
Fields of interest: International peace/security; International human rights.
Type of support: General/operating support; Continuing support; Building/renovation; Emergency funds; Program development; Publication; Seed money; Research; Technical assistance; Matching/challenge support.

Limitations: Applications not accepted. Giving on a national and international basis. No grants for media projects.
Publications: Annual report; Informational brochure.
Application information: Contributes only to pre-selected organizations; unsolicited requests for funds not considered or acknowledged.
Officers: Adam Yauch, Pres.; Michael Diamond, V.P.; Adam Horovitz, Secy.
Number of staff: 5 full-time professional.
EIN: 133767290

248
Milkcare Foundation
P.O. Box 3575
Santa Clara, CA 95055-3575

Established in 2001.
Donors: Hoang Nguyen; Alastor Capital Mgmt.; Samartan Foundation; Christina Ngo; Jean-Marc Verdiell; Quang Nguyen; Thanh-Thuy T. Doan.
Grantmaker type: Operating foundation.
Financial data (yr. ended 12/31/10): Assets, $0 (M); gifts received, $111,627; expenditures, $132,466; qualifying distributions, $132,466; giving activities include $129,171 for 30 grants (high: $56,708; low: $100).
Purpose and activities: Giving primarily to support schools and orphanages in Vietnam.
Fields of interest: Children/youth, services; Residential/custodial care.
International interests: Vietnam.
Limitations: Applications not accepted. Giving limited to Vietnam. No grants to individuals.
Application information: Contributes only to pre-selected organizations.
Director: Hoang Nguyen.
EIN: 770561742

249
The Millard Foundation
1521 Las Trampas Rd.
Alamo, CA 94507-1821

Established in 1982 in CA.
Donors: William H. Millard; ComputerLand Corp.
Grantmaker type: Independent foundation.
Financial data (yr. ended 12/31/10): Assets, $325,039 (M); expenditures, $138,988; qualifying distributions, $136,500; giving activities include $136,500 for 9 grants (high: $129,000; low: $500).
Fields of interest: Arts.
International interests: Canada; Japan.
Limitations: Applications not accepted. Giving primarily in Orlando, FL. No grants to individuals.
Application information: Unsolicited requests for funds not accepted.
Officers and Director:* William H. Millard, Pres.; Patricia H. Millard,* Secy.
EIN: 942894847

250
The Yao Ming Foundation
c/o The Giving Back Fund
6033 W. Century Blvd., Ste. 240
Los Angeles, CA 90045-6427 (310) 649-5222
FAX: (310) 649-5070;
E-mail: yaomingfoundation@givingback.org;
URL: http://www.theyaomingfoundation.org/

Established in 2008 in CA; donor-advised fund of The Giving Back Fund.

Grantmaker type: Public charity.

Purpose and activities: The foundation works to support rebuilding efforts in China, with an emphasis on rebuilding earthquake-resistant high-quality schools; the foundation also supports youth programs in China and the U.S.

Fields of interest: Youth development; Education.

International interests: China.

Limitations: Applications not accepted. Giving primarily in China.

Application information: Unsolicited requests for funding not considered or acknowledged.

Directors: Julie Brothers; Charlie Wan.

251
Gordon and Betty Moore Foundation

1661 Page Mill Rd.
Palo Alto, CA 94304-1209 (650) 213-3000
Contact: Genny Biggs, Comm. Manager
FAX: (650) 213-3003; E-mail for Genny Biggs: genny.biggs@moore.org. Additional e-mail: grantprocessing@moore.org; URL: http://www.moore.org/
Grantee Perception Report: http://www.moore.org/grantee-perception-2008.aspx
Grants Database: http://www.moore.org/grants-awarded.aspx

Established in 2000 in CA.

Donors: Gordon E. Moore; Betty I. Moore.

Grantmaker type: Independent foundation.

Financial data (yr. ended 12/31/10): Assets, $5,585,288,763 (M); expenditures, $288,641,024; qualifying distributions, $274,867,200; giving activities include $247,769,481 for grants.

Purpose and activities: As responsible stewards of the resources entrusted to them, the foundation forms and invests in partnerships to achieve significant, lasting and measurable results in environmental conservation, science and the San Francisco Bay Area. The majority of funding is directed to organizations whose work supports the foundation's initiatives in its three major program areas.

Fields of interest: Environment; Science.

Type of support: Conferences/seminars; Land acquisition; Program development; Research; Program-related investments/loans.

Limitations: Applications not accepted. Giving on a worldwide basis (North Pacific Rim and Andes-Amazon), with some focus on the San Francisco Bay Area, CA, for selected projects. No grants to individuals, or for arts, building/renovation, endowments, capital campaigns, labor issues, or for sports programs.

Publications: Financial statement; Grants list.

Application information: The foundation does not accept unsolicited proposals.

Officers and Trustees:* Gordon E. Moore,* Chair.; Steven J. McCormick,* Pres.; William G. Green, Corp. Secy. Genl. Counsel; Denise Strack, C.I.O.; Chris McCrum, Chief Admin. Officer; Kenneth G. Moore,* Dir., Eval. and Inf. Tech.; Bruce Alberts, Ph.D.; Rosina Bierbaum, Ph.D.; James C. Gaither; Paul Gray, Ph.D.; Kathleen Justice-Moore; Kristen L. Moore; Steven E. Moore; Edward E. Penhoet, Ph.D.; Kenneth F. Siebel.

Number of staff: 72 full-time professional; 4 part-time professional.

EIN: 943397785

Recent grants for international programs:

251-1 Alianca da Terra, Goiania, Brazil, $606,625. For Sustainable Lands in Production Incenting Conservation on Priv Lands in Brazil. 2009.

251-2 Amazon Alliance for Indigenous and Traditional Peoples of the Amazon Basin, Washington, DC, $30,000. For Indigenous Peoples' Global Summit on Climate Change. 2009.

251-3 Amazon Conservation Team, Arlington, VA, $30,000. For Publishing UNFCC (United Nations Framework Convention on Climate Change) REDD (Reducing Emissions from Deforestation and Forest Degradation) Negotiation Articles on Mongaba.Com in Portuguese and Spanish. 2009.

251-4 Amazon Institute of People and the Environment, Belem, Brazil, $582,134. For consolidation of state forests and to monitor protected areas in the Brazilian Amazon. 2009.

251-5 American Bird Conservancy, The Plains, VA, $513,500. For Sustaining Biodiversity in Key Protected Areas in the Andes. 2009.

251-6 Brazilian Biodiversity Fund, Rio de Janeiro, Brazil, $127,365. For project titled: Biodiversity Conservation Investment Database. 2009.

251-7 Brazilian Biodiversity Fund, Rio de Janeiro, Brazil, $90,000. For Conservation Finance Alliance. 2009.

251-8 Brazilian Biodiversity Fund, Rio de Janeiro, Brazil, $20,000. For 11th Annual RedLAC General Assembly. 2009.

251-9 Canadian Parks and Wilderness Society, British Columbia Chapter, Vancouver, Canada, $95,564. For Provincial Government Engagement in Marine Spatial Planning. 2009.

251-10 CARE USA, Atlanta, GA, $60,000. For Social and Environmental Standards Development for REDD (Reducing Emissions from Deforestation and Forest Degradation). 2009.

251-11 Center for International Environmental Law, Washington, DC, $20,000. For Consultation Process at the Inter-American Development Bank. 2009.

251-12 Centro de Conservacion Investigacion y Manejo de Areas Naturales, Lima, Peru, $250,000. For Consolidation of Cordillera Azul National Park, Peru. 2009.

251-13 Conservation International, Arlington, VA, $11,121,568. For Efforts to Integrate the Sustainable Mission and Vision. 2009.

251-14 Conservation International, Arlington, VA, $1,577,000. For Guiana Shield Action Plan. 2009.

251-15 Conservation International, Arlington, VA, $1,078,092. For Global Conservation Fund, Centers for Biodiversity Conservation, and Scientific Field Stations. 2009.

251-16 Conservation International, Arlington, VA, $685,635. For Marine Management Area Science Program. 2009.

251-17 Conservation International, Arlington, VA, $352,000. For Atlantic Forest Hotspot. 2009.

251-18 Conservation International, Arlington, VA, $35,000. For General Operations. 2009.

251-19 Conservation International, Arlington, VA, $25,000. For General Operations. 2009.

251-20 Conservation International, Arlington, VA, $20,000. For General Operations. 2009.

251-21 Conservation International, Arlington, VA, $10,000. For General Operations. 2009.

251-22 Conservation Strategy Fund, Arcata, CA, $417,133. For Frontier Conservation Planning. 2009.

251-23 Consultative Group on Biological Diversity, San Francisco, CA, $50,000. For General Operations. 2009.

251-24 Consultative Group on Biological Diversity, San Francisco, CA, $20,000. For Website and Information Technology Improvement. 2009.

251-25 David Suzuki Foundation, Vancouver, Canada, $104,014. For Sustaining an Area-Based Management Constituency for Pincima Initiative. 2009.

251-26 Driftwood Foundation, Smithers, Canada, $373,690. For project titled: Skeena Headwaters Habitat Protection. 2009.

251-27 Ecotrust Canada, Vancouver, Canada, $215,757. For Skeena Commercial Fishery Transition. 2009.

251-28 Environmental Defense, New York, NY, $50,000. For Cattle and Soy Producer Meeting hosted By Alianca Da Terra in Brazil. 2009.

251-29 Forest Trends Association, Washington, DC, $200,000. For project titled, Strengthening National and Project-Level Capacity for REDD (Reduced Emissions from Deforestation and Forest Degradation) in Ghana. 2009.

251-30 Fundacao de Desenvolvimento da Pesquisa, Belo Horizonte, Brazil, $912,967. For Setting the Technical and Social Conditions for Carbon Programs in the Map Region. 2009.

251-31 Fundacao Djalma Batista, Manaus, Brazil, $1,497,827. For Building a Large-Scale Biodiversity Conservation Network in the State of Amazonas. 2009.

251-32 Fundacao Instituto de Biodiversidade e Manejo de Ecossistemas da Amazonia Ocidental, Rio Branco, Brazil, $41,806. For Federal University of Acre Institutional Strengthening. 2009.

251-33 Fundacao Vitoria Amazonica, Manaus, Brazil, $494,743. For Rio Negro Basin Conservation Geopolitics II. 2009.

251-34 Fundacion Amigos de la Naturaleza, Santa Cruz, Bolivia, $400,000. For Reducing Emissions from Deforestation and Forest Degradation (REDD) in the Bolivian Amazon. 2009.

251-35 Gitgaat Development Corporation, Hartley Bay, Canada, $108,713. For Science and Legal Analyses to Support First Nations Marine Spatial Planning. 2009.

251-36 Global Canopy Foundation, Oxford, England, $88,012. For REDD (Reducing Emissions from Deforestation and Forest Degradation) and Forest Financing Resources. 2009.

251-37 Gordon Research Conferences, West Kingston, RI, $15,000. For Gordon Research Conference on Marine Microbes: From Genes to Global Cycles. 2009.

251-38 Green Belt Movement International-North America, Washington, DC, $300,000. For REDD (Reducing Emissions from Deforestation and Degradation) Capacity Building and Consultation in Kenya and Neighboring Countries. 2009.

251-39 Instituto del Bien Comun, Lima, Peru, $452,022. For Indigenous People, Resource Management and Conservation. 2009.

251-40 Instituto Floresta Tropical, Belem, Brazil, $385,029. For Sustainable Forest Management in Brazil. 2009.

251-41 Instituto Socioambiental, Sao Paulo, Brazil, $1,241,460. For Amazonia Socioambiental: Consolidation of Protected Areas in the Brazilian Amazon. 2009.

251-42 International Forum on Globalization, San Francisco, CA, $139,961. For Building Civil Society Consensus on Mechanisms for

Participation By Forest Communities in REDD (Reducing Emissions from Deforestation and Forest Degradation). 2009.

251-43 International Institute for Environment and Development, London, England, $99,214. For REDD (Reducing Emissions from Deforestation and Forest Degradation) Resource Support. 2009.

251-44 J. Craig Venter Institute, Rockville, MD, $794,635. For A Metagenomic Study of Unique Antarctic Environments. 2009.

251-45 La Fundacion para la Sobrevivencia del Pueblo Cofan, Quito, Ecuador, $212,532. For Consolidation of the Cofan Conservation Program. 2009.

251-46 Living Oceans Society, Sointula, Canada, $822,312. For Coastal Alliance for Aquaculture Reform in British Columbia. 2009.

251-47 Ministere de lEnvironnement de la Protection de la Nature et du Developpement Durable, Libreville, Gabon, $326,360. For Forest Carbon Mapping in Gabon. 2009.

251-48 Nature and Culture International, Del Mar, CA, $10,000. For Consolidation of the Operation of Biological Station La Sata and Support for Impact Livestock Mitigation Plan. 2009.

251-49 Northern Illinois University, DeKalb, IL, $800,000. For Remotely Operated Instrumentation System for Subglacial Environments. 2009.

251-50 Northwest Institute for Bioregional Research, Smithers, Canada, $174,182. For Skeena Water Quality Protection. 2009.

251-51 Organization for Tropical Studies, Durham, NC, $109,638. For Educating US Policymakers on International Forest Carbon. 2009.

251-52 Our Savior Lutheran Church, Lafayette, CA, $13,200. For Hope for the Heart of Africa, Guatemala, Music Ministry, and OSLC Foundation. 2009.

251-53 Pacific Salmon Foundation, Vancouver, Canada, $470,081. For Skeena Watershed Participant Process. 2009.

251-54 Pacific Salmon Foundation, Vancouver, Canada, $408,957. For Skeena Watershed Monitoring Baseline Research. 2009.

251-55 Pacific Salmon Foundation, Vancouver, Canada, $50,448. For Terrestrial Salmon Aquaculture Pilot Project Planning. 2009.

251-56 Patrimonio Natural - Fondo para la Biodiversidad y Areas Protegidas, Bogota, Colombia, $809,000. For Securing Protected Areas in Colombia. 2009.

251-57 Pembina Foundation for Environmental Research and Education, Drayton Valley, Canada, $236,479. For Skeena Energy Development. 2009.

251-58 Plymouth Marine Laboratory, Plymouth, England, $50,469. For Ocean Acidification/Marine Microbes Workshop. 2009.

251-59 Secretaria de Estado do Meio Ambiente e Desenvolvimento Sustentavel, Manaus, Brazil, $975,498. For Building a Large-Scale Biodiversity Conservation Network in the State of Amazonas. 2009.

251-60 Sociedad Peruana de Derecho Ambiental, Lima, Peru, $316,187. For Consolidating Private Conservation Strategies in Peru. 2009.

251-61 Tech Museum of Innovation, San Jose, CA, $15,000. For Tech Awards Program. 2009.

251-62 Tides Canada Foundation, Vancouver, Canada, $902,172. For Skeena Integrated Management Reform. 2009.

251-63 Tides Canada Foundation, Vancouver, Canada, $523,037. For Developing an Innovative Oceans Partnership to Support the PNCIMA (Pacific North Coast Integrated Management Area) I Initiative. 2009.

251-64 Tides Canada Foundation, Vancouver, Canada, $395,910. For British Columbia Wild Salmon Conservation - Small Grants Fund. 2009.

251-65 Tides Canada Foundation, Vancouver, Canada, $222,315. For Aquaculture Innovation. 2009.

251-66 Tides Canada Foundation, Vancouver, Canada, $195,053. For Informing Area Based Management Through Collaborative Scientific Analyses. 2009.

251-67 Tides Canada Foundation, Vancouver, Canada, $162,785. For Sustainability Plan. 2009.

251-68 Tides Center, San Francisco, CA, $271,166. For Taku Habitat Protection, Rivers Without Borders Project. 2009.

251-69 Turning Point Initiative Society, Vancouver, Canada, $676,035. For First Nations Area-Based Management. 2009.

251-70 Turning Point Initiative Society, Vancouver, Canada, $247,727. For project titled, First Nations Marine Spatial Planning Leadership. 2009.

251-71 United Nations Educational, Scientific and Cultural Organization, Paris, France, $111,620. For Incorporating Best Practice Guidelines Into Area-Based Management Efforts in British Columbia and Massachusetts. 2009.

251-72 Universidad de Concepcion, Departamento de Oceanografia, Concepcion, Chile, $30,000. For Course Ecology and Diversity of Marine Microorganisms Course. 2009.

251-73 University of Colorado, Boulder, CO, $221,043. For Implementing REDD (Reducing Emissions from Deforestation and Degradation) Between California and Brazilian and Indonesian States. 2009.

251-74 University of Leeds, Leeds, England, $794,956. For Quantifying The Role of Tropical Forests in the Global Carbon Balance and Future Climate Change. 2009.

251-75 University of Michigan, Ann Arbor, MI, $15,000. For Climate Adaptation Fellows. 2009.

251-76 University of the Andes, Bogota, Colombia, $178,000. For Conservation Management and Policy Masters Program. 2009.

251-77 Vancouver Aquarium Marine Science Center, Vancouver, Canada, $496,360. For Pacific Ocean Shelf Tracking Project. 2009.

251-78 Watershed Watch Salmon Society, Port Coquitlam, Canada, $150,000. For Implementation of Wild Salmon Policy. 2009.

251-79 West Coast Vancouver Island Aquatic Management Board, Port Alberni, Canada, $284,830. For Securing Area-Based Management in West Coast Vancouver Island Coastal-Marine Ecosystem. 2009.

251-80 Wild Salmon Center, Portland, OR, $1,533,939. For Kamchatka Wild Salmon Conservation. 2009.

251-81 Wildlife Conservation Society, Bronx, NY, $1,350,000. For Amazon Conservation Landscapes. 2009.

251-82 Wildlife Conservation Society, Bronx, NY, $360,777. For Conserving Wildlife Migration By Creation and Consolidation of Southern Sudan's Protected Area System. 2009.

251-83 Wildlife Conservation Society, Bronx, NY, $249,767. For Coral Reef Ecosystem Protection. 2009.

251-84 Wildlife Conservation Society, Bronx, NY, $20,000. For International Conference on Wildlife Management. 2009.

251-85 Woods Hole Research Center, Falmouth, MA, $100,000. For Development of A Global Framework to support the Climate and Land Use Alliance. 2009.

251-86 World Wildlife Fund, Washington, DC, $1,843,000. For Amazon Protected Area Project (ARPA) II. 2009.

251-87 World Wildlife Fund, Washington, DC, $1,500,000. For Phase III of Amazon Headwaters Initiative. 2009.

251-88 World Wildlife Fund, Washington, DC, $1,179,616. For Kamchatka Salmon Fisheries Reform. 2009.

251-89 World Wildlife Fund, Washington, DC, $154,336. For Defining Science-Driven Habitat and Spatial Criteria for Protected Areas in the Amazon. 2009.

251-90 World Wildlife Fund, Washington, DC, $25,000. For Connecting Amazon Protected Areas and Indigenous Lands to REDD (Reducing Emissions from Deforestation and Forest Degradation) Frameworks. 2009.

251-91 World Wildlife Fund Canada, Vancouver, Canada, $499,484. For Facilitating Federal Government Commitment to Area-Based Management. 2009.

252
Lucille and Ronald Neeley Foundation

P.O. Box 371347
San Diego, CA   92137-1347

Established in 1989 in CA.
Donors: Lucille A. Neeley; Ronald Neeley.
Grantmaker type: Independent foundation.
Financial data (yr. ended 12/31/10): Assets, $5,281,839 (M); expenditures, $328,480; qualifying distributions, $299,715; giving activities include $299,545 for 8 grants (high: $156,545; low: $500).
Fields of interest: Cancer; Museums (art); Arts; International relief; Foundations (community).
Limitations: Applications not accepted. Giving primarily in San Diego, CA; some funding in New York, NY. No grants to individuals.
Application information: Contributes only to pre-selected organizations.
Officers: Lucille Neeley, Chair. and Pres.; Ronald Neeley, V.P. and C.F.O.; Alison Neeley, Secy.
EIN: 330386127

253
Craig H. Neilsen Foundation

16633 Ventura Blvd., No. 1050
Encino, CA   91436-1864
E-mail: contact@chnfoundation.org; URL: http://www.chnfoundation.org

Established in 2002 in ID and NV.
Donors: Craig H. Neilsen†; Gordon Kanofsky; Marcia Kanofsky; John Boushy; Lisa Boushy; Bally Gaming; Wells Fargo Bank Nevada, N.A.
Grantmaker type: Independent foundation.
Financial data (yr. ended 12/31/09): Assets, $400,184,900 (M); gifts received, $10,500,000;

expenditures, $7,887,614; qualifying distributions, $7,586,287; giving activities include $6,736,286 for 137 grants (high: $125,000; low: $2,182).

Purpose and activities: The primary mission of the foundation is to find a cure for spinal cord injury (SCI). In an effort to reach this goal, the foundation supports: 1) Cutting edge research that seeks to understand the biological basis for recovery of function after SCI, and to translate these findings to a clinical setting; 2) Clinical research that will develop new treatments for people living with SCI, and; 3) Innovative rehabilitation programs for people living with spinal cord injuries throughout the U.S.

Fields of interest: Medical research, institute; Disabilities, people with.

International interests: Canada.

Type of support: Research.

Limitations: Applications accepted. Giving in the U.S. and Canada. No support for religious or political organizations. No grants to individuals.

Publications: Grants list.

Application information: Application information (search by foundation name) available at Proposal Central web site: https://proposalcentral.altum.com/.

Initial approach: Letter of Intent (online only)
Final notification: 3 months

Officer and Directors:* Beth Goldsmith, Exec. Dir.; Robert D. Brown, M.D., M.P.H.; Gordon R. Kanofsky; Lorne D. Mendell, Ph.D.; Ray H. Neilsen; Michael K. Young.

Number of staff: 1 full-time professional.

EIN: 061695275

Recent grants for international programs:

253-1 University of British Columbia, Vancouver, Canada, $125,000. For spinal cord injury research. 2009.

253-2 University of British Columbia, Vancouver, Canada, $85,440. For spinal cord injury research. 2009.

253-3 University of British Columbia, Vancouver, Canada, $28,000. For programs/services for persons living with a spinal cord injury. 2009.

253-4 University of Toronto, Toronto, Canada, $110,203. For spinal cord injury research. 2009.

254

Network in Solidarity with the People of Guatemala

(also known as NISGUA)
436 14th St., Ste. 409
Oakland, CA 94612-2728 (510) 238-8400
E-mail: info@nisgua.org; URL: http://www.nisgua.org/home.asp

Established in 1981.

Grantmaker type: Public charity.

Financial data (yr. ended 12/31/10): Revenue, $315,711; assets, $107,058 (M); gifts received, $251,442; expenditures, $320,003; giving activities include $3,200 for grants, and $31,694 for grants to organizations outside the U.S.

Purpose and activities: The organization works for real democracy in Guatemala and the U.S. and strengthens the global movement for justice by building mutually beneficial grassroots ties between the people of the U.S. and Guatemala.

Fields of interest: International affairs; International human rights; International affairs, alliance/advocacy; Human services.

International interests: Guatemala.

Limitations: Giving limited to Guatemala.

Publications: Occasional report.

Officers and Directors:* Melinda Van Slyke,* Pres.; Sue Ellen Kingsley,* Secy.; Todd Kolze,* Treas.; Josue Revolorio Illescas; Amanda Kistler; Jerry Kohler; Matthew Lowen.

EIN: 521650978

255

New Field Foundation

1016 Lincoln Blvd., Mailbox 14, 3rd Fl.
San Francisco, CA 94129-0903 (415) 561-3417
FAX: (415) 561-3419;
E-mail: info@newfieldfound.org; URL: http://www.newfieldfound.org

Established in 2003 in CA; supporting organization of the Tides Foundation.

Grantmaker type: Public charity.

Financial data (yr. ended 12/31/09): Revenue, $2,918,179; assets, $14,306,388 (M); gifts received, $3,000,018; expenditures, $3,124,676; giving activities include $2,950,000 for grants.

Purpose and activities: The foundation works to contribute to the creation of a peaceful and equitable world by supporting women and their families to overcome poverty, violence, and injustice in their communities.

Fields of interest: International affairs; Crime/law enforcement; Human services; Foundations (public); Women; Economically disadvantaged.

International interests: Niger; Mali; Burkina Faso; Sierra Leone; Liberia; Guinea; Senegal; Africa.

Limitations: Applications accepted. Giving limited to the U.S. and Africa. No support for natural disaster relief; lobbying activities, including activities to influence legislators or voters on specific, pending legislation; participation or intervention in an election campaign that expresses a view in support or opposition to a candidate for public office; or religious activities. No grants to individuals.

Application information: Preliminary inquiry form is available for download from the foundation's web site.

Initial approach: Preliminary inquiry form

Officers and Directors:* Barbara Sargent,* Pres.; Janis Burger,* Secy.; Ellen Friedman,* Treas.; Sarah Hobson, Exec. Dir.; D. Thomson Sargent; Barbara Taylor.

EIN: 270029270

256

The New Jerusalem Foundation

28123 Ridgefern Ct.
Rancho Palos Verdes, CA 90275-3265

Established in 2007 in CA.

Donors: Zhi-Qiang Jacob Zhou; Nan Zou.

Grantmaker type: Independent foundation.

Financial data (yr. ended 12/31/10): Assets, $7,960,619 (M); expenditures, $474,419; qualifying distributions, $326,000; giving activities include $326,000 for grants.

Purpose and activities: Giving for Christian missionary work in China.

Fields of interest: Christian agencies & churches.

International interests: China.

Limitations: Applications not accepted. Giving primarily in CA.

Application information: Contributes only to pre-selected organizations.

Trustees: Andrew Wang; Zhi-Qiang Jacob Zhou; Nan Zou.

EIN: 207370119

257

Nonprofit Enterprise and Self-Sustainability Team, Inc.

(also known as NESST)
4401 Tahama Ln.
Turlock, CA 95382-8639
FAX: (815) 846-1775; E-mail: nesst@nesst.org; URL: http://www.nesst.org

Established in 1997 in CA.

Grantmaker type: Public charity.

Financial data (yr. ended 12/31/10): Revenue, $3,195,359; assets, $2,560,051 (M); gifts received, $2,930,244; expenditures, $2,609,700; giving activities include $778,216 for grants to organizations outside the U.S.

Purpose and activities: The organization is dedicated to finding lasting solutions to critical social problems in emerging markets through the development of social enterprises.

Fields of interest: Community/economic development; Social entrepreneurship; Venture philanthropy.

International interests: Latin America; Eastern & Central Europe.

Type of support: Consulting services; General/operating support; Income development; Management development/capacity building; Seed money; Technical assistance.

Limitations: Applications not accepted. Giving limited to Argentina, Brazil, Chile, Croatia, Czech Republic, Ecuador, Hungary, Peru, Romania, and Slovakia. No support for religious or political purposes.

Publications: Annual report; Financial statement; Grants list; Informational brochure; Newsletter.

Application information: Unsolicited requests for funds not accepted.

Officers and Directors:* Felipe Medina,* Chair.; Lee Davis,* Co-C.E.O.; Nicole Etchart,* Co-C.E.O.; Katherine Downs,* Secy.; Julian Garel-Jones,* Treas.; Ernest Boles; Joseph Schull; Richard Surrey; Frank van Beuningen; Tulio P. Vera.

Number of staff: 20 full-time professional; 2 part-time professional.

EIN: 522018791

258

Nora Lam Chinese Ministries International

5442 Thornwood Dr.
San Jose, CA 95123-1200 (408) 629-5000

Established in 1974 in CA.

Grantmaker type: Public charity.

Financial data (yr. ended 03/31/10): Revenue, $3,232,405; assets, $362,896 (M); gifts received, $3,234,761; expenditures, $3,195,623; program services expenses, $1,672,945; giving activities include $60,000 for grants, and $710,205 for grants to organizations outside the U.S.

Fields of interest: International relief.

International interests: China.

Type of support: In-kind gifts.

Limitations: Applications not accepted. Giving on an international basis, with emphasis on China.

Application information: Contributes only to pre-selected organizations.

Officers: Joseph Lam, Pres.-C.E.O.; Susan Lam, Secy.; Bruce Barnes, Treas.
EIN: 237418355

259
Novellus Systems, Inc. Corporate Giving Program
4000 N. 1st St.
San Jose, CA 95134-1568 (408) 943-9700
URL: http://ir.novellus.com/releasedetail.cfm?ReleaseID=556446

Grantmaker type: Corporate giving program.
Purpose and activities: Novellus Systems, Inc. makes charitable contributions to nonprofit organizations on a case by case basis.
Fields of interest: International relief; Disasters, floods; Disasters, preparedness/services.
Type of support: General/operating support.

260
Nuclear Age Peace Foundation
1622 Anacapa St.
Santa Barbara, CA 93101-1910
(805) 965-3443
FAX: (805) 568-0466; Mailing address: 1187 Coast Village Rd., Ste. 1, PMB 121, Santa Barbara, CA 93108-2794; URL: http://www.wagingpeace.org
Facebook: http://www.facebook.com/wagingpeace
RSS Feed: http://www.wagingpeace.org/rss/index.php
Twitter: http://twitter.com/napf
YouTube: http://www.youtube.com/user/NuclearAgePeace

Established in 1982 in CA.
Grantmaker type: Public charity.
Financial data (yr. ended 12/31/10): Revenue, $478,673; assets, $4,694,694 (M); gifts received, $266,539; expenditures, $918,772; giving activities include $62,387 for 2 grants to organizations outside the U.S., and $26,435 for grants to individuals.
Purpose and activities: The foundation initiates and supports worldwide efforts to abolish nuclear weapons, strengthen international law and institutions, and inspire and empower a new generation of peace leaders.
Fields of interest: International conflict resolution; International affairs, arms control; Dispute resolution; International peace/security.
Limitations: Giving on a national and international basis.
Publications: Informational brochure; Newsletter.
Officers and Directors:* Richard Falk,* J.S.D., Chair.; Mark Hamilton,* Vice-Chair.; David Krieger,* J.D., Ph.D., Pres.; Frank K. Kelly,* Sr. V.P.; Peter R. MacDougall,* Ed.D., V.P.; Robert B. Laney,* J.D., Secy.; Steve Parry,* Treas.; Laurie Ashton, J.D.; Mary Becker, J.D.; Jill Dexter; Diandra M. Douglas; Anna Grotenhuis, J.D.; Peter O. Haslund, Ph.D.; Sue Hawes, J.D.; George Haynes, Ph.D.; John Randolph Parten, J.D.; Chris Pizzinat; Selma Rubin; Lessie Nixon Schontzler, J.D.; Imagene Spence.
EIN: 953825265

261
NVIDIA Foundation
2701 San Tomas Expwy.
Santa Clara, CA 95050-2519 (408) 486-2000
Contact: Tonie Hansen, Dir., NVIDIA Foundation
E-mail: corporategrants@siliconvalleycf.org; E-mail for Tonie Hansen: thansen@nvidia.com;
URL: http://www.nvidia.com/object/gcr-community.html

Grantmaker type: Corporate giving program.
Purpose and activities: NVIDIA makes charitable contributions to nonprofit organizations involved with education, the environment, health care, medical research, youth development, and human services. Support is given primarily in areas of company operations in Alabama, California, Colorado, Florida, Massachusetts, Missouri, North Carolina, Oregon, Texas, Utah, Virginia, and Washington, and in China, Finland, France, Germany, Hong Kong, Japan, Russia, Singapore, Switzerland, Taiwan, and the United Kingdom.
Fields of interest: Disasters, preparedness/services; General charitable giving.
International interests: China; Finland; France; Germany; Hong Kong; Japan; Russia; Singapore; Switzerland; Taiwan; United Kingdom.
Type of support: Continuing support; General/operating support; Employee volunteer services; Employee matching gifts.
Limitations: Giving primarily in areas of company operations in AL, CA, CO, FL, MA, MO, NC, OR, TX, UT, VA, and WA, and in China, Finland, France, Germany, Hong Kong, Japan, Russia, Singapore, Switzerland, Taiwan, and the United Kingdom.
Application information: Applications must have an employee sponsor and be submitted by the employee. Support is limited to 1 contribution per organization during any given year. Application form required.
  Initial approach: Download application form and e-mail with proposal to Silicon Valley Foundation
  Deadline(s): Apr. 22
  Final notification: July

262
The Oak Tree Philanthropic Foundation
330 Oxford St., Ste. 212
Chula Vista, CA 91911-3119

Established in 1992 in CA.
Grantmaker type: Independent foundation.
Financial data (yr. ended 12/31/10): Assets, $7,899,172 (M); expenditures, $545,660; qualifying distributions, $404,100; giving activities include $364,500 for 36 grants (high: $110,000; low: $1,000).
Purpose and activities: Giving primarily for children and social services, including hurricane and international relief, as well as for education, including support of U.S.-based Lithuanian education.
Fields of interest: International relief; Higher education; Education; Hospitals (general); Safety/disasters; Human services; Children/youth, services; Catholic agencies & churches.
Limitations: Applications not accepted. Giving primarily in CA, IL, and NY. No grants to individuals.
Application information: Contributes only to pre-selected organizations.
Officers and Directors:* Dr. Dana Maciunas-Mockus,* C.E.O. and Pres.; Dr. Robert

Maciunas, V.P.; Dr. Vytautas Mockus, Secy.-Treas.; Ann L. Failinger.
EIN: 363779795

263
Omega Global Caring Ministries
6745 Riverside Blvd.
Sacramento, CA 95831-1939
URL: http://www.omegacaringministries.com/

Established in 2005 in CA.
Grantmaker type: Public charity.
Financial data (yr. ended 12/31/10): Revenue, $12,770; assets, $695 (M); gifts received, $12,770; expenditures, $12,770.
Purpose and activities: The ministries support missionary work in Fiji.
Fields of interest: Christian agencies & churches.
International interests: Fiji.
Type of support: Emergency funds.
Limitations: Giving primarily to Fiji.
Officers and Directors:* Sailosi V. Tawake,* Pres.; Joe Bulivou, Secy.; Bill Yacarogovinka,* Treas.; Poasa Vesikula.
EIN: 680607708

264
Omidyar Network Fund, Inc.
1991 Broadway St., Ste. 200
Redwood City, CA 94063-1958
E-mail: info@omidyar.net; URL: http://www.omidyar.com/
Facebook: http://www.facebook.com/OmidyarNetwork
Pierre and Pam Omidyar's Giving Pledge: http://givingpledge.org/#enter
RSS Feed: http://www.omidyar.com/about_us/news/feed
Twitter: http://twitter.com/OmidyarNetwork

Established in 2004 in CA from the transfer of funds from the Omidyar Foundation.
Donors: Pierre Omidyar; Omidyar Network, LLC.
Grantmaker type: Independent foundation.
Financial data (yr. ended 12/31/09): Assets, $249,429,410 (M); expenditures, $20,857,993; qualifying distributions, $24,478,114; giving activities include $20,352,759 for 23 grants (high: $4,000,000; low: $25,000), $160,758 for 83 employee matching gifts, and $3,964,597 for 4 loans/program-related investments.
Purpose and activities: The fund makes both investments and grants, identifying likeminded organizations to support, help scale, and collaborate with to help realize their full potential. The fund's efforts are organized around two investment initiatives: 1) Access to Capital - The fund works to create economic opportunity for people in emerging markets. The focus of this initiative is on microfinance, small/medium enterprises, emerging market ventures, and property rights; 2) Media, Markets and Transparency- The fund emphasizes technology that promotes transparency, accountability, and trust across media, markets, and government. The focus of this initiative is on social media, marketplaces, government transparency, and trust/reputation and identity.
Fields of interest: Community development, small businesses; International economic development; Economic development; Social entrepreneurship;

Engineering/technology; Computer science; Public affairs, information services; Public affairs; Economically disadvantaged.

Type of support: General/operating support; Program-related investments/loans; Employee matching gifts.

Limitations: Applications not accepted. Giving primarily on a national and international basis. No grants to individuals.

Application information: Contributes only to pre-selected organizations.

Officers: Pierre Omidyar, Chair.; Matthew Bannick, Pres.; Will Fitzpatrick, Secy.

Trustees: Matt Halprin; Michael Mohr; Pam Omidyar; Iqbal Paroo.

Number of staff: 30

EIN: 201173866

Recent grants for international programs:

264-1 BRAC, Dhaka, Bangladesh, $1,039,417. For microfinance operations in Sierra Leone with objective increasing economic opportunities and job creation for low-income persons in Sierra Leone and revitalizing distressed communities by providing technical assistance and financial products and services to small scale enterprises. 2009.

264-2 BRAC, Dhaka, Bangladesh, $1,039,417. For microfinance operations in Liberia with objective increasing economic opportunities and job creation for low-income persons in Liberia and revitalizing distressed communities by providing technical assistance and financial products and services to small scale enterprises. 2009.

264-3 BRAC, Dhaka, Bangladesh, $682,277. For projects delivering health care and agriculture development services to Liberia. 2009.

264-4 BRAC, Dhaka, Bangladesh, $347,323. For project delivering health care and agriculture development services to Sierra Leone. 2009.

264-5 Endeavor Global, New York, NY, $2,424,325. For general operating support. 2009.

264-6 Endeavor Global, New York, NY, $75,000. For recruiting purposes to fill positions in marketing, economic research and fund raising. 2009.

264-7 Global Integrity, Washington, DC, $300,000. For operating support. 2009.

264-8 Global Integrity, Washington, DC, $25,000. For leadership recruiting efforts. 2009.

264-9 GlobalGiving Foundation, Washington, DC, $2,000,000. For general operating support. 2009.

264-10 International Bank for Reconstruction and Development, Washington, DC, $300,000. For Consultative Group to Assist The Poor Activities Trust Fund. 2009.

264-11 International Finance Corporation, Washington, DC, $198,000. For project to establish foundation for microfinance credit bureaus in India. 2009.

264-12 Landesa, Seattle, WA, $2,500,000. For general operating support. 2009.

264-13 Microfinance Information Exchange, Washington, DC, $200,000. For general operating support. 2009.

264-14 Silicon Valley Microfinance Network, San Francisco, CA, $25,000. For general operating support. 2009.

264-15 Unitus, Inc., Seattle, WA, $115,000. For consulting study to review governance function. 2009.

265
Open Doors International, Inc.
2953 S. Pullman St.
Santa Ana, CA 92705-5840
E-mail for United States Office: opendoorsusa.org;
URL: http://www.od.org

Established in 1993 in CA.

Grantmaker type: Operating foundation.

Financial data (yr. ended 12/31/10): Assets, $19,604,536 (M); gifts received, $24,407,581; expenditures, $23,250,008; qualifying distributions, $23,000,849; giving activities include $19,376,374 for 12 grants (high: $5,464,274; low: $15,537), and $20,267,322 for 4 foundation-administered programs.

Purpose and activities: The purpose of the foundation is to "strengthen and equip the Body of Christ living under or facing restriction and persecution because of their faith in Jesus Christ, and to encourage their involvement in world evangelism" by providing bibles and literature, media, leadership training, socio-economic development, as well as mobilizing the free world to identify with threatened and persecuted Christians and be actively involved in assisting them.

Fields of interest: Christian agencies & churches.

International interests: Africa; Asia; Latin America; Middle East; Southeast Asia.

Limitations: Applications not accepted. Giving on an international basis. No grants to individuals.

Application information: Contributes only to pre-selected organizations.

Officers and Directors:* Brian McFarlane,* Chair.; Jeff Taylor, C.E.O.; Kelley Valdez, C.F.O.; Evert Schut, C.O.O.; Robert Dalton; Maarton Dees; Robert Martin; Gunnhild Oftedal; Gabrielle Searle; Roger Spoelman; David Stone; Deryck Stone.

Number of staff: 21 full-time professional; 6 full-time support.

EIN: 330523832

Recent grants for international programs:

265-1 Open Doors Asia, Quezon City, Philippines, $3,481,361. 2009.

265-2 Open Doors Central Asia, Ermelo, Netherlands, $522,613. 2009.

265-3 Open Doors Egypt, Ermelo, Netherlands, $1,136,619. 2009.

265-4 Open Doors Gulf, Santa Ana, CA, $1,744,976. 2009.

265-5 Open Doors Holland, Ermelo, Netherlands, $5,187,286. 2009.

265-6 Open Doors India, Noida, India, $662,431. 2009.

265-7 Open Doors Latin America, Santa Ana, CA, $761,789. 2009.

265-8 Open Doors Middle East, Ermelo, Netherlands, $143,532. 2009.

265-9 Open Doors Southeast Asia, Quezon City, Philippines, $1,665,386. 2009.

265-10 Open Doors Sub-Saharan Africa, Johannesburg, South Africa, $2,622,993. 2009.

265-11 Open Doors Sweden, Orebro, Sweden, $180,050. 2009.

266
Operation USA
(formerly Operation California, Inc.)
3617 Hayden Ave., Ste. A
Culver City, CA 90232-2448 (310) 838-3455
Contact: Richard Walden, Pres. and C.E.O.

FAX: (310) 838-3477; E-mail: info@opusa.org; Toll-free tel.: (800) 678-7255; URL: http://www.opusa.org
Facebook: http://www.facebook.com/operationusa?ref=ts
Twitter: http://twitter.com/#!/OperationUSA/

Established in 1979 in CA.

Grantmaker type: Public charity.

Financial data (yr. ended 06/30/10): Revenue, $22,680,870; assets, $8,434,653 (M); gifts received, $22,672,339; expenditures, $20,317,746; giving activities include $2,838,830 for grants, and $15,506,640 for grants to organizations outside the U.S.

Purpose and activities: The organization collects and distributes donated supplies for the relief of refugees and the victims of natural disasters around the world, and also has a role in promoting the transfer of advanced technology from many fields to detect and destroy anti-personnel mines.

Fields of interest: Disasters, Hurricane Katrina; Disasters, floods; Safety/disasters, fund raising/fund distribution; Disasters, preparedness/services; Disasters, domestic resettlement; International relief, 2004 tsunami; International relief.

Limitations: Applications not accepted. Giving primarily in LA.

Publications: Annual report; Financial statement; Newsletter.

Application information: Unsolicited requests for funds not considered or acknowledged.

Officers and Board Members:* Jonathan Estrin,* Chair.; Gary Larsen,* Vice-Chair.; Richard Walden,* Pres. and C.E.O.; Dave Brubaker; Jeff Franklin; Drew Hagen; Louis J. Ignarro, Ph.D.; Bob L. Johnson; Michael Mahdesian; Tom Moore, Jr.; Paul O'Rourke, M.D.; Jack Shakely; and 5 additional board members.

Number of staff: 9 full-time professional; 1 part-time professional.

EIN: 953504080

267
The Orangutan Conservancy
(formerly BOS-USA, Inc.)
5001 Wilshire Blvd., No. 112
P.O. Box 513
Los Angeles, CA 90036-6104
Contact: Christine Mallar, V.P., Prog. Dir.
E-mail: micasowards@wildblue.net; Application address: P.O. Box 968, Clark, CO 80428-0968; tel./fax: (970) 879-9113; URL: http://www.orangutan.com

Established in 1998.

Grantmaker type: Public charity.

Financial data (yr. ended 12/31/10): Revenue, $123,931; assets, $69,518 (M); gifts received, $123,663; expenditures, $129,051; giving activities include $68,044 for grants.

Purpose and activities: The organization fosters conservation of orangutans and the rainforest.

Fields of interest: Environment, forests; Environment, water resources; Animals/wildlife, preservation/protection.

International interests: Indonesia; Malaysia.

Type of support: General/operating support; Continuing support; Emergency funds; Conferences/seminars; Research.

Limitations: Giving on an international basis, primarily in Indonesia and Malaysia. No support for religious or political organizations.
Publications: Annual report; Financial statement; Informational brochure; Newsletter.
Application information:
 Board meeting date(s): Nov.
Officers and Directors:* Norm Rosen,* Chair.; Doug Cress, V.P., Devel.; Christine Mallar, V.P., Prog. Dir.; Vanessa Rogier, V.P., Special Events; Sarita Siegel, V.P., Media Devel.; Stacey Sowards, Ph.D., V.P., Educ.; Margaret Clune Giblin,* Secy.; Ms. Michael Sowards,* Treas.; Christine Mallar; Roger E. Nelson; Anne Russon; Rob Shumaker; Wayne Sowards.
EIN: 841461579

268
Ormsby Hill Trust
c/o James Hardyman
4802 Glenhollow Cir.
Oceanside, CA 92057-7935

Established in 1962 in CA.
Grantmaker type: Independent foundation.
Financial data (yr. ended 06/30/11): Assets, $2,362,793 (M); expenditures, $238,360; qualifying distributions, $203,000; giving activities include $203,000 for grants.
Fields of interest: Recreation, camps; Education; Children/youth, services.
International interests: Mexico.
Limitations: Applications not accepted. Giving on a national and international basis. No grants to individuals.
Application information: Contributes only to pre-selected organizations.
Officers and Trustees:* Maitland Hardyman,* Pres.; James Hardyman,* Secy.-Treas.; Norman Frank.
EIN: 951866004

269
Otto Family Foundation
16935 W. Bernardo Dr., Ste. 120
San Diego, CA 92127
E-mail: neiott@aol.com

Established in 2000 in CA.
Donors: Neil Otto; Margaret Otto.
Grantmaker type: Independent foundation.
Financial data (yr. ended 06/30/10): Assets, $3,886,831 (M); expenditures, $222,849; qualifying distributions, $192,842; giving activities include $181,048 for 3 grants (high: $171,238; low: $4,810).
Purpose and activities: Giving to protect the lives of children in our communities and around the world.
Fields of interest: Minorities/immigrants, centers/services; International migration/refugee issues; Vocational education; Children, services; Human services; International development; International economic development; International relief; International human rights.
International interests: Africa; Asia; Burma (Myanmar); Ethiopia; Kenya; Mexico; Somalia, Somaliland and Puntland; Thailand.
Limitations: Applications not accepted. Giving primarily in San Diego, CA. No grants to individuals.
Application information: Unsolicited requests for funds not accepted.

Officer: Neil Otto, Pres.
Directors: Daniel Otto; Madeline Otto; Margaret Otto; Michel Otto.
Number of staff: None.
EIN: 330916411

270
Pacific Environment and Resources Center
251 Kearny St., 2nd Fl.
San Francisco, CA 94108-4530 (415) 399-8850
Contact: David Gordon, Exec. Dir.
FAX: (415) 399-8860;
E-mail: info@pacificenvironment.org; URL: http://www.pacificenvironment.org

Established in 1987.
Grantmaker type: Public charity.
Financial data (yr. ended 03/31/10): Revenue, $2,678,572; assets, $3,184,715 (M); gifts received, $2,635,351; expenditures, $2,894,499; giving activities include $807,500 for grants to organizations outside the U.S.
Purpose and activities: The organization protects the living environment of the Pacific Rim by strengthening democracy, supporting grassroots activism, empowering communities, and redefining international policies.
Fields of interest: International affairs.
International interests: China; Japan; Russia.
Type of support: Program development; Management development/capacity building; General/operating support; Continuing support.
Limitations: Giving primarily in China, Japan, and Russia.
Publications: Annual report.
Application information:
 Initial approach: Proposal
 Copies of proposal: 1
 Board meeting date(s): Quarterly
 Final notification: Within one month of receipt of proposal
Officers and Directors:* Debbie Chapman,* Chair.; Stephen Fowler,* Secy.-Treas.; David Gordon, Exec. Dir.; Phillip S. Berry; Helena Brykarz; Barbara J. Chisholm; Craig Cramer; Keith Gayler; Karen Hoy; Loretta Lynch; Walter Parker; Sunil Parthasarathy; Josh Perfetto; Suzanne Sheuerman; Lisa Tracy; Jane Zhang.
Number of staff: 17 full-time professional; 2 full-time support.
EIN: 942628924

271
The David and Lucile Packard Foundation
300 2nd St.
Los Altos, CA 94022-3632 (650) 948-7658
Contact: Communications Dept.
E-mail: communications@packard.org; URL: http://www.packard.org
E-Newsletter: http://www.packard.org/about-the-foundation/news/subscribe-to-mailing-list/
Grantee Perception Report: http://www.packard.org/about-the-foundation/how-we-operate-2/grantee-experience/about-grantee-perception-report-content/
Grants Database: http://www.packard.org/grants/grants-database/

Incorporated in 1964 in CA.

Donors: David Packard†; Lucile Packard†.
Grantmaker type: Independent foundation.
Financial data (yr. ended 12/31/10): Assets, $6,100,637,478 (M); gifts received, $400,000; expenditures, $312,688,044; qualifying distributions, $324,626,302; giving activities include $260,622,415 for 1,052 grants (high: $46,757,793; low: $1,314), $1,823,191 for employee matching gifts, $6,194,698 for foundation-administered programs and $22,944,351 for 9 loans/program-related investments (high: $5,000,000; low: $500,000).
Purpose and activities: The David and Lucile Packard Foundation is a family foundation. The foundation works on the issues its founders cared about most: improving the lives of children, enabling the creative pursuit of science, advancing reproductive health, and conserving and restoring the earth's natural systems. The foundation invests in effective organizations and leaders, collaborates with them to identify strategic solutions, and supports them over time to reach their common goals.
Fields of interest: Engineering; Agriculture/food; Animals/wildlife, fisheries; Arts; Arts, cultural/ethnic awareness; Child development, services; Civil liberties, reproductive rights; Education; Education, early childhood education; Environment; Environment, beautification programs; Environment, energy; Environment, natural resources; Environment, public education; Family services; Food services; Foundations (private operating); Health care, insurance; Housing/shelter; Marine science; Museums; Performing arts; Philanthropy/voluntarism; Philanthropy/voluntarism, management/technical assistance; Population studies; Reproductive health; Reproductive health, family planning; Science; Youth development.
International interests: Global programs; Oceania; South Asia; Sub-Saharan Africa.
Type of support: General/operating support; Continuing support; Management development/capacity building; Land acquisition; Program development; Fellowships; Research; Consulting services; Program evaluation; Program-related investments/loans; Employee matching gifts; Matching/challenge support.
Limitations: Applications accepted. Giving for national and international grants, with special focus on the Northern CA counties of San Mateo, Santa Clara, Santa Cruz, Monterey, and San Benito; giving also on Pueblo, CO. No support for religious or political organizations. No grants to individuals.
Publications: Application guidelines; Annual report; Financial statement; Grants list; Newsletter; Occasional report; Program policy statement; Program policy statement (including application guidelines).
Application information: Review program guidelines online; foundation does not accept proposals for all of their areas of interest. Application form not required.
 Initial approach: Proposal or 2- to 3-page letter of inquiry
 Copies of proposal: 1
 Deadline(s): None
 Board meeting date(s): Mar., June, Sept., and Dec.
 Final notification: Varies
Officers and Trustees:* Susan Packard Orr,* Chair.; Nancy Packard Burnett,* Vice-Chair.; Julie E. Packard,* Vice-Chair.; Carol S. Larson,* C.E.O. and Pres.; Chris DeCardy, V.P. and Dir., Progs.; Craig Neyman, V.P. and C.F.O.; John H. Moehling, C.I.O.; Mary Anne Rodgers, Secy. and Genl. Counsel;

Edward W. Barnholt; Jason K. Burnett; Sierra Clark; Linda Griego; Donald Kennedy; David Orr; William K. Reilly; Louise Stephens; Colburn S. Wilbur; Ward W. Woods.

Number of staff: 56 full-time professional; 4 part-time professional; 34 full-time support; 6 part-time support.

EIN: 942278431

Recent grants for international programs:

271-1 Action Health, Lagos, Nigeria, $350,000. For expanded access to secondary education and sexual and reproductive health information and services for married adolescents in Northern Nigeria. 2010.

271-2 Alianza para la Sustentabilidad del Noroeste Costero, Hermosillo, Mexico, $60,000. For documenting the impact of the National Trust Fund for Tourism Development (FONATUR) on tourism development, and encouraging FONATUR and the Ministry of Tourism (SECTUR) to include sustainable tourism criteria in planning processes. 2010.

271-3 Amhara Development Association, Bahir Dar, Ethiopia, $800,000. To improve reproductive health of young girls in the Amhara region of Ethiopia by helping them stay in school and mainstreaming sexual reproductive health services into the school system. 2010.

271-4 Aspen Institute, Washington, DC, $750,000. For the Global Leaders Council for Reproductive Health. 2010.

271-5 Association for Reproductive and Family Health, Ibadan, Nigeria, $125,000. To implement a plan for sustaining maternal health service provision and utilization in northern Nigeria. 2010.

271-6 Association for Stimulating Know How, Gurgaon, India, $25,000. For the Evaluation Conclave to be used for scholarships to attend the event for those who would otherwise not be able to afford the registration fees. 2010.

271-7 Basic Education Association in Ethiopia, Addis Ababa, Ethiopia, $300,000. To integrate reproductive health education and services into adult literacy and alternative basic education programs in Amhara and Oromia regions of Ethiopia. 2010.

271-8 Better Sugar Cane Initiative, London, England, $90,000. For continued development and implementation of global sustainability standard for sugarcane feedstock. 2010.

271-9 Better Sugar Cane Initiative, London, England, $40,000. For strategic communications planning. 2010.

271-10 BirdLife International, Cambridge, England, $250,000. To promote adoption and evaluation of seabird bycatch mitigation measures in tuna longline fisheries in the Pacific. 2010.

271-11 BirdLife International, Cambridge, England, $250,000. To protect critically endangered Spoon-billed Sandpiper on breeding grounds in northeast Russia. 2010.

271-12 California Environmental Associates, San Francisco, CA, $131,248. To design and lead expert-driven assessment and plan to reform commercial fisheries worldwide. 2010.

271-13 California State University San Bernardino, Foundation for the, San Bernardino, CA, $25,000. For the California and the World Ocean 10 Conference in San Francisco, CA. 2010.

271-14 Canadian Parks and Wilderness Society, British Columbia Chapter, Vancouver, Canada, $600,000. To continue Sustainable Seafood Canada's SeaChoice program. 2010.

271-15 Canadian Parks and Wilderness Society, British Columbia Chapter, Vancouver, Canada, $32,622. To develop a strategic plan for the SeaChoice network. 2010.

271-16 CARE USA, Atlanta, GA, $250,000. For Haiti Emergency Response Fund. 2010.

271-17 Center for Cultural and Technical Interchange Between East and West, East-West Center, Honolulu, HI, $20,872. For China-U.S. Philanthropy Partnership (CUSPP). 2010.

271-18 Center for Responsible Travel, Washington, DC, $24,100. To promote sustainable tourism development in Mexico. 2010.

271-19 Centre for African Family Studies, Nairobi, Kenya, $40,575. For business planning and executive transition. 2010.

271-20 Centre for Development and Population Activities, Washington, DC, $500,000. To improve access and quality of family planning services in selected areas of Northern Nigeria by working with local partners to improve capacity and develop sustainability strategies. 2010.

271-21 Centre for Development and Population Activities, Washington, DC, $200,000. To train women leaders from developing countries to mobilize attention and resources for family planning and reproductive health. 2010.

271-22 Centre for Development and Population Activities, New Delhi, India, $1,000,000. To improve reproductive health outcomes for couples in Bihar by enhancing leadership competencies of elected women leaders in communities and leveraging positions of established women leaders active in NGOs and state government. 2010.

271-23 Centre for Environmental Law and Community Rights, Port Moresby, Papua New Guinea, $35,000. For board development. 2010.

271-24 Centre for the Study of Adolescence, Nairobi, Kenya, $250,000. To promote contraceptive uptake among youth, ages 15-24, in Western Kenya through use of innovative information and communication technologies and interactive media. 2010.

271-25 Centro de Colaboracion Civica, Socios-Mexico, Mexico City, Mexico, $84,000. For collaboration and consensus-building around sustainable fishing and sustainable development in Northwest Mexico. 2010.

271-26 Centro Mexicano de Derecho Ambiental, Mexico City, Mexico, $100,000. To ensure that environmental laws and regulations in Gulf of California region are followed by providing legal advice to local groups. 2010.

271-27 Centro para el Desarrollo Social y la Sustentabilidad Nuiwari, Tepic, Mexico, $35,000. For community participation in development of Marismas Nacionales and San Pedro Mezquital River basin. 2010.

271-28 Circus in Ethiopia for Youth and Social Development, Addis Ababa, Ethiopia, $51,000. To enhance capacity of Circus in Ethiopia for Youth and Social Development to promote family planning and reproductive health issues through circus art. 2010.

271-29 ClimateWorks Foundation, San Francisco, CA, $46,757,793. For efforts to reduce global greenhouse gas emissions and avert catastrophic climate change. 2010.

271-30 Communications Consortium Media Center, Washington, DC, $200,000. For a final grant to the Global Population, Health and Development 2015 Program. 2010.

271-31 Comunidad y Biodiversidad, Guaymas, Mexico, $250,000. To strengthen community-based marine conservation in northwest Mexico using new fisheries management tools and policies. 2010.

271-32 Concept Foundation, Bangkok, Thailand, $300,000. For general support. 2010.

271-33 Conselva Conservacion y Uso Sustentable de la Selva Tropical Seca, Mazatlan, Mexico, $115,000. To lead the scientific evaluation of a large-scale tourism development project being proposed in Marismas Nacionales, and to help coordinate a coalition that will propose alternative development vision for the area. 2010.

271-34 Conservation Society of Pohnpei, Kolonia, Federated States of Micronesia, $25,153. For fund development and staff development. 2010.

271-35 Consultative Group on Biological Diversity, San Francisco, CA, $100,000. For general support and membership dues. 2010.

271-36 Consultative Group on Biological Diversity, San Francisco, CA, $40,000. For the Gulf of California Coordinator. 2010.

271-37 Dalberg Consulting U.S., LLC, San Francisco, CA, $250,000. To lead a joint scoping effort with grantees on opportunities for fisheries or aquaculture conservation in China. 2010.

271-38 Defensa Ambiental del Noroeste, Ensenada, Mexico, $144,000. For litigation against ill-advised coastal development projects and to provide legal support and training to environmental organizations and communities in Northwest Mexico. 2010.

271-39 Deutsche Stiftung Weltbevoelkerung, Hannover, Germany, $500,000. To strengthen the youth-to-youth program and positive impact on the sexual and reproductive health needs and rights of young Ethiopians. 2010.

271-40 Deutsche Stiftung Weltbevoelkerung, Hannover, Germany, $300,000. For general support. 2010.

271-41 DKT International, Washington, DC, $1,000,000. For the Janani program in India. 2010.

271-42 Ecole Polytechnique Federale de Lausanne, Lausanne, Switzerland, $400,000. To continue the development and implementation of global sustainability standards for biofuels. 2010.

271-43 Embrace Global, San Francisco, CA, $315,000. For start-up costs for testing, production and initial distribution of low-cost infant warmer to families and medical providers in developing nations. 2010.

271-44 Environmental Defense, New York, NY, $225,000. For policy-focused efforts to transform the marine ornamental trade and, in turn, help protect coral reef habitats. 2010.

271-45 Ethiopian Public Health Association, Addis Ababa, Ethiopia, $800,000. To enhance provision of family planning and reproductive health services at the community level in Ethiopia. 2010.

271-46 Family Planning Association of India, Mumbai, India, $250,000. To mobilize commitment to family planning and advocate for inclusion of safer and more effective contraceptive methods through a network of NGOs called Advocating Reproductive Choices. 2010.

271-47 Felidae Conservation Fund, Sausalito, CA, $35,000. For establishing environmental education initiative over one year. 2010.

271-48 Fondo para la Comunicacion y Educacion Ambiental, Mexico City, Mexico, $49,600. To increase the level of awareness and understanding of the value of coastal environmental services in Northwest Mexico among key federal and state legislators. 2010.

271-49 Forest Trends Association, Washington, DC, $25,000. For a meeting aimed at developing frameworks for the payment of marine ecosystem services, with emphasis on coastal mangroves of Northwest Mexico. 2010.

271-50 Forum for African Women Educationalists, Nairobi, Kenya, $750,000. To address the sexual and reproductive health issues which negatively affect girls participation and retention in school in four African countries: Ethiopia, Kenya, Rwanda, and Uganda. 2010.

271-51 Foundations of Success, Bethesda, MD, $100,000. For the second phase of the 1999-2010 evaluation of the Gulf of California subprogram. 2010.

271-52 Friends of the Earth, Washington, DC, $250,000. To advance the sustainability of biofuels and reduce incentives for non-sustainable biofuels. 2010.

271-53 Friends of the Earth Europe, Brussels, Belgium, $87,000. To work to raise public awareness of the environmental and climate impacts of increased biofuels production. 2010.

271-54 Futures Group, Washington, DC, $250,000. To develop analytical framework and interactive computer model that demonstrates the linkages between women's empowerment, family planning and achieving development goals (Population Program Area). 2010.

271-55 Global Fund for Women, San Francisco, CA, $50,000. For executive transition. 2010.

271-56 Global Greengrants Fund, Boulder, CO, $125,000. To fund small grants to grassroots environmental organizations in the Western Pacific. 2010.

271-57 Global Greengrants Fund, Boulder, CO, $75,000. To enable Fondo Accion Solidaria to provide strategic small grants to grassroots organizations working on conservation and sustainable development initiatives in Mexico. 2010.

271-58 Global Greengrants Fund, Boulder, CO, $30,000. To develop a strategic plan for Global Greengrants Fund. 2010.

271-59 Global Training Research and Evaluation Services, LLC, San Clemente, CA, $165,000. To review the Sub-Saharan Africa portfolio and develop a system for monitoring and communicating progress toward strategic objectives (Population Program Area). 2010.

271-60 Guraghe People Self Help Development Organization, Addis Ababa, Ethiopia, $500,000. To improve the reproductive health status of young people through economic and social empowerment. 2010.

271-61 Gynuity Health Projects, New York, NY, $300,000. To demonstrate how misoprostol for post-abortion care can be incorporated into selected countries service delivery programs. 2010.

271-62 Hatohobei Organization for People and Environment, Koror, Palau, $50,000. For management of the Helen Reef Atoll marine protected area in Palau. 2010.

271-63 Hatohobei Organization for People and Environment, Koror, Palau, $32,572. For needs assessment, planning, and board training. 2010.

271-64 Health and Nutrition Development Society, Karachi, Pakistan, $750,000. To improve family planning and reproductive health in marginalized communities of Sindh, Pakistan through viable and demonstrated initiatives. 2010.

271-65 Health and Nutrition Development Society, Karachi, Pakistan, $300,000. For emergency relief to those affected by the flooding in Pakistan. 2010.

271-66 IEMANYA Oceanica, Woodland Hills, CA, $50,000. To engage artisanal shark fishers in sustainable fishing practices. 2010.

271-67 Indonesian Coral Reef Foundation, Jakarta, Indonesia, $250,000. To develop, promote and implement best practices in community-based ecotourism and ornamental fisheries management in Indonesia. 2010.

271-68 Indonesian Coral Reef Foundation, Jakarta, Indonesia, $35,000. For organizational assessment and staff training. 2010.

271-69 Institute for Agriculture and Trade Policy, Minneapolis, MN, $250,000. To work to advance critical policies, innovations and relationships needed to build sustainable biofuels sector that helps meet climate, agricultural and environmental goals. 2010.

271-70 Institute of International Education, New York, NY, $4,600,000. For the Technical Assistance Program in South Asia and Sub-Saharan Africa and for Population and Reproductive Health Program Analysts (Population Program Area). 2010.

271-71 Intercultural Center for the Study of Deserts and Oceans, Tucson, AZ, $200,000. For effective management and conservation of key coastal and marine habitats and species of the northern Gulf of California. 2010.

271-72 International Biochar Initiative, Westerville, OH, $250,000. To continue promoting a viable role for biochar in national and international climate mitigation and energy policy schemes. 2010.

271-73 International Biochar Initiative, Westerville, OH, $35,000. For board development. 2010.

271-74 International Community Foundation, National City, CA, $50,000. For the RED Sustainable Tourism project in Northwest Mexico. 2010.

271-75 International Council on Clean Transportation, Washington, DC, $50,000. To foster the exchange of information and to establish long term collaborations among low carbon fuels regulators in the United States and Europe. 2010.

271-76 International Council on Management of Population Programmes, Ampang, Malaysia, $100,000. To explore potential of developing a regional advocacy mechanism to engage parliamentarians and civil society leaders to increase commitment to family planning and reproductive health in South Asia. 2010.

271-77 International Projects Assistance Services, Chapel Hill, NC, $350,000. For technical support to the government of Bihar to implement, monitor, and build evidence of a sustainable public-private partnership to increase access to safe abortion services. 2010.

271-78 International Projects Assistance Services, Chapel Hill, NC, $150,000. To evaluate and disseminate a collaborative project to increase access to comprehensive abortion care in India, focused to two districts. 2010.

271-79 International Projects Assistance Services, Chapel Hill, NC, $50,000. To increase grassroots knowledge on abortion in select rural communities in Kenya. 2010.

271-80 International Womens Health Coalition, New York, NY, $300,000. To promote increased financial and political commitment to reproductive health and rights especially in Sub-Saharan Africa and South Asia. 2010.

271-81 International Womens Tribune Centre, New York, NY, $50,000. To develop a three-year strategy and to plan executive transition. 2010.

271-82 Internews Network, Arcata, CA, $200,000. For environmental media capacity-building in Indonesia. 2010.

271-83 ISEAL Alliance, London, England, $146,644. To help the coordination and integration of biofuels standards systems. 2010.

271-84 Island Conservation, Ensenada, Mexico, $250,000. For restoration on islands of Northwest Mexico through the eradication of invasive species, monitoring of ecosystem recovery, applied scientific research and environmental education. 2010.

271-85 Island Conservation, Ensenada, Mexico, $150,000. To complete and begin to implement a careful plan to eradicate invasive mouse and to help restore San Benito Oeste Island in Baja, Mexico. 2010.

271-86 Johns Hopkins University, Baltimore, MD, $150,000. For technical support to the government of Bihar, India to develop a strategy and implementation plan for strengthening postpartum family planning programs in the public and private sectors. 2010.

271-87 LaFrance Associates, San Francisco, CA, $195,000. To develop and distribute monitoring, evaluation and learning framework for Global and U.S. subprograms (Population Program Area). 2010.

271-88 Lahore University of Management Sciences, Lahore, Pakistan, $500,000. To launch a national women's leadership network to advocate for family planning and reproductive health to mobilize policy changes in the corporate social responsibility agenda. 2010.

271-89 Leadership for Environment and Development-Pakistan, Islamabad, Pakistan, $400,000. To create cross-sectoral network of influential women leaders in Pakistan who are connected to community networks for advancing reproductive health agenda in networks and for influencing policies and resource allocation at government level. 2010.

271-90 Live and Learn Environmental Education, Melbourne, Australia, $250,000. To strengthen marine conservation leadership in the Solomon Islands, Papua New Guinea and Indonesia. 2010.

271-91 Living Oceans Society, Sointula, Canada, $100,000. To strengthen social media strategies and build a senior management team to lead the implementation of the new strategic plan. 2010.

271-92 Manomet Center for Conservation Sciences, Manomet, MA, $250,000. To improve shorebird habitat management on Chiloe Island, Chile. 2010.

271-93 Marine Stewardship Council, London, England, $125,000. To evaluate the environmental impacts that have resulted from the Marine Stewardship Council's fishery certification program during the first ten years of operations. 2010.

271-94 Mexican Nature Conservation Fund, Mexico City, Mexico, $115,000. For the Gulf of California

Conservation Fund and for the production of outreach materials for existing MPAs in Baja California. 2010.

271-95 Micronesia Conservation Trust, Kolonia, Federated States of Micronesia, $32,781. For board development and strategic planning. 2010.

271-96 Mustashaar, Social Development Advisors, Islamabad, Pakistan, $50,000. To increase grantee effectiveness and program impact through technical assistance and capacity building in monitoring, learning, and evaluation in Pakistan. 2010.

271-97 National Marine Educators Association, Gulfport, MS, $50,000. For the 2010 conference of the International Pacific Marine Educators Network. 2010.

271-98 National Rural Support Programme, Islamabad, Pakistan, $300,000. For emergency relief to those affected by the flooding in Pakistan. 2010.

271-99 National Rural Support Programme, Islamabad, Pakistan, $48,023. For technology systems development. 2010.

271-100 Nature Conservancy, Narragansett, RI, $234,600. To continue to develop and refine the Gulf of Mexico Ecosystem Decision Support effort to provide salient and credible information to bear on the many decisions that will be made in response to the oil spill in the Gulf of Mexico. 2010.

271-101 NatureServe, Arlington, VA, $35,000. To analyze and improve NatureServe's network. 2010.

271-102 New England Aquarium, Boston, MA, $500,000. To eradicate invasive species from two important seabird islands in the Phoenix Islands Protected Area, Kirabati, an island nation located in the central tropical Pacific Ocean. 2010.

271-103 Niparaja, La Paz, Mexico, $200,000. For Niparajas Marine Conservation Program in the southern Gulf of California region. 2010.

271-104 Niparaja, La Paz, Mexico, $26,286. For strategic planning. 2010.

271-105 Noroeste Sustentable, La Paz, Mexico, $150,000. To advance sustainable development in the Upper Gulf and Bahia de La Paz. 2010.

271-106 Ocean Foundation, Washington, DC, $150,000. For capacity building, small-scale sustainable fisheries management, and sea turtle conservation in the Gulf of California. 2010.

271-107 Ocean Foundation, Washington, DC, $30,000. For Ocean Revolutions native oyster and scallop aquaculture project in Sonora, Mexico. 2010.

271-108 Oceana, Washington, DC, $450,000. To continue work on U.S. Arctic Large Marine Ecosystems conservation. 2010.

271-109 Opportunities Industrialization Centers International, Philadelphia, PA, $400,000. For adolescent reproductive health education and skill training for youth in Ethiopia. 2010.

271-110 Pacific Seabird Group, Little River, CA, $50,000. For travel stipends to individuals attending the World Seabird Conference in Victoria, Canada. 2010.

271-111 Palau Conservation Society, Koror, Palau, $200,000. For scientific research that will help resource planners and habitat managers make better informed decisions about Palaus sustainable development. 2010.

271-112 Palau Conservation Society, Koror, Palau, $28,000. For board development. 2010.

271-113 Papua New Guinea Centre for Locally Managed Areas, Boroko, Papua New Guinea, $115,000. To improve management and expand implementation of locally managed marine areas in Papua New Guinea. 2010.

271-114 Parliamentary Centre of Canada, Ottawa, Canada, $50,000. For the participation of African delegates at the G-8/20 Global Parliamentarians Summit. 2010.

271-115 Partners for Development, Silver Spring, MD, $150,000. For the second phase of a program to integrate family planning services into micro-credit networks in northern Nigeria. 2010.

271-116 Pathfinder International, Watertown, MA, $30,500. For strategic communications planning. 2010.

271-117 Planned Parenthood Association of Thailand, Bangkok, Thailand, $600,000. For renewed support for the Asia Pacific Alliance secretariat and advocacy to increase financial and political commitment to international reproductive health and family planning. 2010.

271-118 Planned Parenthood Federation of America, New York, NY, $700,000. To consolidate and sustain critical reproductive health care in Northern Nigeria by developing sustainability initiatives, expand funding base, and forging partnerships with governments and communities. 2010.

271-119 Planned Parenthood Federation of America, New York, NY, $250,000. For the Reproductive Health and Rights Alliance in Kenya and for the Planned Parenthood Federation of America Africa Regional Office. 2010.

271-120 Planned Parenthood Federation, International, Washington, DC, $1,500,000. To mobilize support for sexual and reproductive health (SRH) by increasing awareness about the link between poor SRH outcomes and poverty and about the impact of abortion stigma on reproductive health. 2010.

271-121 Planned Parenthood Federation, International, Western Hemisphere Region, New York, NY, $500,000. For renovation and rebuilding of PROFAMIL facilities in Haiti. 2010.

271-122 Population Action International, Washington, DC, $42,000. For fund development. 2010.

271-123 Population Council, New York, NY, $145,000. To advance research on youth demography and support policy makers to develop evidence-informed policies on midlevel provision of safe abortion and post-abortion care services in South Asia. 2010.

271-124 Population Reference Bureau, Washington, DC, $1,000,000. For general support. 2010.

271-125 Population Services International, Washington, DC, $500,000. To expand access to modern contraceptives to reduce unwanted pregnancies and improve maternal health in Bihar, India. 2010.

271-126 Prescott College, Prescott, AZ, $70,000. For the Research and Conservation Program of the Kino Bay Center for Cultural and Ecological Studies, Prescott College's field station on the shores of the Gulf of California, one of the most remote and unexplored seas remaining in the world today. 2010.

271-127 Pronatura Noroeste-Mar de Cortes, Ensenada, Mexico, $225,000. For regional and site-based conservation of fisheries resources in the Gulf of California. 2010.

271-128 Public Health Institute, Santa Cruz, CA, $250,000. For management and technical support to AdvocacyNigeria's efforts to expand the provision of reproductive health services in northern Nigeria. 2010.

271-129 Reach Global, Berkeley, CA, $600,000. To strengthen and expand the Reach India social franchise to provide health, livelihood, and household finance training for girls and women in rural India. 2010.

271-130 Reproductive Health Training Center of the Republic of Moldova, Chisinau, Moldova, $150,000. To strengthen the African and Asian regional networks of the International Consortium for Medical Abortion. 2010.

271-131 Resource Media, San Francisco, CA, $50,000. For strategic communications support for the Intergovernmental Panel on Climate Change. 2010.

271-132 Resources Legacy Fund, Sacramento, CA, $2,000,000. For the third year of grantmaking activities under the Northwest Mexico Land Conservation subprogram. 2010.

271-133 Rockefeller Philanthropy Advisors, New York, NY, $20,000. For the Global Impact Investing Network (GIIN) Investors Council and development of the Impact Reporting and Investment Standards (IRIS). 2010.

271-134 Rozan, Islamabad, Pakistan, $34,000. For human resources management systems. 2010.

271-135 SeaWeb, Silver Spring, MD, $600,000. For a marine-focused communications program in the Western Pacific. 2010.

271-136 Service for Information Technology in International Agriculture, Menlo Park, CA, $250,000. For high-level computer and network technical support to population experts in four focus countries. 2010.

271-137 Shirkat Gah Womens Resource Centre, Lahore, Pakistan, $50,800. For team development. 2010.

271-138 Sierra Club Foundation, San Francisco, CA, $100,000. For final grant for the Global Population and Environment Program. 2010.

271-139 Society of Obstetricians and Gynecologists of Pakistan, Karachi, Pakistan, $100,000. For emergency relief to those affected by the flooding in Pakistan. 2010.

271-140 Sonoran Institute, Tucson, AZ, $127,000. For restoration and conservation of the Colorado River Delta region. 2010.

271-141 Spitfire Strategies, Washington, DC, $49,125. To develop strategies aimed at halting the development of destructive mass coastal tourism projects in Mexico. 2010.

271-142 Stanford University, Stanford, CA, $150,000. To continue and expand upon research studying the Chinese aquaculture industry and use of feed resources. 2010.

271-143 Stichting BirdLife Europe, Brussels, Belgium, $174,854. For stakeholder engagement during the implementation phase of the European Union Renewable Energy Directive. 2010.

271-144 Terra Peninsular, Coronado, CA, $100,000. For the development of a management plan for the new San Quintin federal protected area in Baja California. 2010.

271-145 United Nations Foundation, Washington, DC, $400,000. To raise awareness and mobilize resources for programs that promote reproductive health, self-esteem and economic empowerment of girls. 2010.

271-146 United Nations University, Bonn, Germany, $94,000. To improve the role of social science in the global environmental change community. 2010.

271-147 University of Arizona, Tucson, AZ, $900,000. For Pesca Artesanal del Norte del Golfo de California: Ambiente y Sociedad (PANGAS) Project. PANGAS is collaboration between three academic institutions and two research and conservation NGO's for ecosystem-based research and management of coastal fisheries. 2010.

271-148 University of California, Berkeley, CA, $150,000. For the next phase of educational intervention aimed at delaying marriage and first birth in Northern Nigeria. 2010.

271-149 University of California, Los Angeles, CA, $290,000. For continuation of the Immigrant Remittance Corridors Project over two years. 2010.

271-150 University of California at San Diego, La Jolla, CA, $75,000. To study spatial and temporal connections between human use activities and marine ecosystems within priority areas in the Gulf of California. 2010.

271-151 University of Hawaii, Hilo, HI, $200,000. To develop sustainable mariculture enterprises as a form of income generation for conservation communities in Micronesia. Mariculture is specialized branch of aquaculture involving the cultivation of marine organisms for food and other products in the open ocean, an enclosed section of the ocean, or in tanks, ponds or raceways which are filled with seawater. 2010.

271-152 University of the South Pacific, Suva, Fiji, $34,380. To develop a strategic plan for the Institute of Applied Sciences. 2010.

271-153 Utrecht University, Utrecht, Netherlands, $79,300. To develop integrated modeling framework assessing global biomass supply and impact on direct and indirect land-use change. 2010.

271-154 Voces por la Naturaleza, Guaymas, Mexico, $140,000. For a campaign to strengthen leadership in coastal communities to improve coastal and fisheries management. 2010.

271-155 W N E T Channel 13, WNET.ORG, New York, NY, $100,000. To produce one of a five-part documentary series titled Afghanistan: The End Game that focuses on the lives of women in situations of conflict and leadership to bring about change. 2010.

271-156 Wild Salmon Center, Portland, OR, $225,000. To continue to catalyze market incentives that can activate improvements in Asian and Russian Far East wild salmon fisheries. 2010.

271-157 WildAid, San Francisco, CA, $250,000. For a campaign against shark finning. 2010.

271-158 Wildcoast, Inc., Imperial Beach, CA, $200,000. For Defiende el Mar, a campaign to preserve coastal and marine ecosystems and endangered wildlife in Baja California. 2010.

271-159 Wildlife Conservation Society, Bronx, NY, $600,000. For strengthening marine protected area management in Fiji and Indonesia. 2010.

271-160 Winrock International, Arlington, VA, $75,000. For travel scholarships for the 5th Biennial Partnership for Clean Indoor Air Forum in Lima, Peru. 2010.

271-161 WomanCare Global, Chapel Hill, NC, $250,000. To strengthen management systems

and improve the delivery of reproductive health products to women in low resource settings. 2010.

271-162 Women Deliver, New York, NY, $100,000. For planning and implementation of the Women Deliver Conference, which will bring together thousands of global leaders focused on improving the health of girls and women. 2010.

271-163 Womens Funding Network, San Francisco, CA, $250,000. To develop a fundraising campaign for reproductive health and rights. 2010.

271-164 Womens Health and Action Research Centre, Benin City, Nigeria, $125,000. For strengthening the provision of medical abortion services in five states in northern Nigeria. 2010.

271-165 World Health Organization, Geneva, Switzerland, $500,000. To disseminate updated evidence on the global prevalence of unsafe abortion and updated guidance on comprehensive abortion care. 2010.

271-166 World Health Organization, Geneva, Switzerland, $250,000. For the development of regional agenda for accelerating universal access to sexual and reproductive health in the African region. 2010.

271-167 World Population Foundation, Utrecht, Netherlands, $42,993. For strategic and operational planning. 2010.

271-168 World Wide Fund for Nature-Australia, Ultimo, Australia, $450,000. For continued support to promote independent certification of fisheries and provide incentives for better fishery management in Australia, New Zealand and South Pacific. 2010.

271-169 World Wide Fund for Nature-Singapore, Singapore, Singapore, $200,000. For management of community-based marine managed areas in Fiji. 2010.

271-170 World Wildlife Fund, Washington, DC, $1,900,000. To promote market-based improvements of fisheries worldwide by harnessing and leveraging purchasing power at various points in the seafood value chain. 2010.

271-171 World Wildlife Fund, Washington, DC, $400,000. To eliminate harmful subsidies for fisheries and to secure adoption of rights-based management by Regional Fisheries Management Organizations. 2010.

271-172 World Wildlife Fund, Washington, DC, $380,000. To complete the development of global aquaculture standards and support small scale capacity building. 2010.

271-173 World Wildlife Fund, Washington, DC, $20,000. For the fifth annual Kathryn S. Fuller Symposium. 2010.

271-174 YWCA, World Office, Geneva, Switzerland, $50,000. For developing a monitoring and evaluation plan. 2010.

272
The Packard Humanities Institute
300 2nd St.
Los Altos, CA 94022-3694

Established in 1987 in CA.
Donor: The David and Lucile Packard Foundation.
Grantmaker type: Operating foundation.
Financial data (yr. ended 12/31/10): Assets, $732,975,558 (M); expenditures, $21,091,543; qualifying distributions, $22,986,056; giving activities include $10,800,378 for 29 grants (high:

$3,000,000; low: $2,100), and $6,355,170 for 4 foundation-administered programs.
Purpose and activities: Giving primarily for education and the arts.
Fields of interest: Arts; Education; Human services.
Limitations: Applications not accepted. Giving primarily in CA. No grants to individuals.
Application information: Contributes only to pre-selected organizations.
Officers and Directors:* David W. Packard,* Chair. and Pres.; Susan Packard Orr,* V.P.; Barbara P. Wright, Secy.; Alberta Astras, C.F.O. and Treas.; G. Gervaise Davis III; Robert J. Glaser, M.D.; Walter B. Hewlett; Richard Hodges; William A. Johnson; Pamela M. Packard; Christopher J. Wolff.
EIN: 943038401
Recent grants for international programs:

272-1 American School of Classical Studies at Athens, Princeton, NJ, $367,700. For excavations in the ancient Agora (marketplace) of Athens. 2009.

272-2 Bach-Archiv, Leipzig, Germany, $236,600. For historical research, conservation and publication of music by Bach. 2009.

272-3 British School at Athens, Athens, Greece, $100,000. For excavations at ancient Greek site of Lefkandi. 2009.

272-4 British School at Rome, Rome, Italy, $3,000,000. For conservation of ancient Roman town of Herculaneum. 2009.

272-5 British School at Rome, Rome, Italy, $250,000. For Web-Based report on archaelogical excavations in Italy. 2009.

272-6 Butrint Foundation, London, England, $750,000. For archaeological excavation and study in Albania. 2009.

272-7 Butrint Foundation, London, England, $500,000. For excavation of ancient city of Butrint in Albania. 2009.

272-8 CORA, Prague, Czech Republic, $23,400. For expenses of Plasy Organ restoration in the Czech Republic. 2009.

272-9 Humboldt-Universitat zu Berlin, Berlin, Germany, $100,000. For analysis and restoration of archaeological artifacts from Sudan. 2009.

272-10 Michigan State University, East Lansing, MI, $24,442. For archaeological research at Butrint in Albania. 2009.

272-11 Mihai Eminescu Trust, London, England, $720,000. For conservation of historic village architecture and traditions in Romania. 2009.

272-12 Ohio State University, Columbus, OH, $127,776. For excavations at ancient Greek site of Isthmia. 2009.

272-13 Saxon Academy of Sciences, Leipzig, Germany, $125,000. For research and publication concerning music by Bach. 2009.

272-14 University of California, Santa Barbara, CA, $250,000. For archaeological research in Fourth Nile Cataract Region of Sudan. 2009.

272-15 University of Texas, Austin, TX, $1,500,000. For archaeological research at Metaponto, Italy and at Chersonesus, Ukraine. 2009.

272-16 University of Western Australia, Perth, Australia, $250,000. For Aerial survey of archaeological sites in Jordan. 2009.

273
PADI Foundation
(also known as Professional Association of Diving Instructors Foundation)
9150 Wilshire Blvd., Ste. 300
Beverly Hills, CA 90212-3414   (310) 281-3200
Contact: Charles P. Rettig, Pres.
E-mail: grants@padifoundation.org; URL: http://www.padifoundation.org
Grants List: http://www.padifoundation.org/Recipients/Recipient10.htm

Established as a company-sponsored operating foundation in 1991 in CA.
Donors: Department of Justice, State of California; Capital Investments & Ventures Corp.
Grantmaker type: Operating foundation.
Financial data (yr. ended 05/31/10): Assets, $2,919,913 (M); gifts received, $341,308; expenditures, $248,166; qualifying distributions, $222,637; giving activities include $197,108 for 40 grants to individuals (high: $13,678; low: $1,517).
Purpose and activities: The foundation supports organizations involved with underwater science, the underwater environment, education, and sports diving and awards grants to individuals undertaking projects in underwater science.
Fields of interest: Marine science; Education; Environment, water pollution; Environment, natural resources; Environment, water resources; Environment; Athletics/sports, water sports.
International interests: Asia; Australia; Brazil; Europe; South Africa.
Type of support: Research; Grants to individuals.
Limitations: Applications accepted. Giving on a national and international basis. No grants for diving equipment, standard photographic equipment, personal computers, overhead costs, or indirect expenses.
Publications: Application guidelines; Financial statement; Grants list.
Application information: The foundation utilizes the Common Grant Application, a web-based management program to receive and administer grant proposals. Application form not required.
  Initial approach: Complete online application
  Copies of proposal: 1
  Deadline(s): Nov. 1 to Jan. 31
  Board meeting date(s): Apr.
  Final notification: May 3
Officer and Directors:* Charles P. Rettig,* Pres.; Paul K. Dayton, Ph.D.; John Englander; Daniel M. Hanes, Ph.D.; Andrew Saxon, M.D.
EIN: 954326850

274
The Palm Foundation
(formerly Palm, Inc. Corporate Giving Program)
950 West Maude Ave.
Sunnyvale, CA 94085-2801
Contact: Gisela B. Bushey, Fdn. Mgr.
FAX: (408) 224-7563;
E-mail: gisela.bushey@palm.com; URL: http://www.hpwebos.com/us/company/palm-foundation-template.html

Established in 2005.
Grantmaker type: Corporate giving program.
Purpose and activities: The Palm Foundation makes charitable contributions to nonprofit organizations involved with child and youth development and education. Special emphasis is directed towards programs that demonstrate the innovative use of Palm mobile computing devices. Support is given primarily in areas of company operations in California and Massachusetts, and in Brazil, France, Ireland, Singapore, and the United Kingdom.
Fields of interest: Elementary/secondary education; Child development, education; Education, special; Youth development; Children/youth, services; Children, foster care.
International interests: United Kingdom; Brazil; France; Ireland; Singapore.
Type of support: General/operating support; Employee volunteer services; Employee matching gifts; Donated products.
Limitations: Giving primarily in areas of company operations in CA and MA, and in Brazil, France, Ireland, Singapore, and the United Kingdom.
Application information: The foundation is not accepting new proposals until further notice.

275
The Panda Charitable Foundation
1683 Walnut Grove Ave.
Rosemead, CA 91770-3711   (626) 372-8450
Contact: Winnie Chan

Changed status to a company-sponsored operating foundation in 1999.
Donors: Panda Management Co., Inc.; Panda Restaurant Group, Inc.
Grantmaker type: Operating foundation.
Financial data (yr. ended 12/31/10): Assets, $2,330,261 (M); gifts received, $1,771,760; expenditures, $1,374,257; qualifying distributions, $1,265,399; giving activities include $1,265,399 for 27 grants (high: $266,184; low: $100).
Purpose and activities: The foundation supports organizations involved with Asian culture, education, health, cancer, pediatrics, and children services.
Fields of interest: Pediatrics; Arts, cultural/ethnic awareness; Higher education; Education; Hospitals (general); Health care; Cancer; Children, services.
International interests: China.
Type of support: General/operating support.
Limitations: Applications accepted. Giving primarily in CA, some giving also in China.
Application information: Application form not required.
  Initial approach: Letter of inquiry
  Deadline(s): None
Trustee: Andrew Cherng.
EIN: 954142346

276
Partnerships for Change
Presidio of San Francisco
P.O. Box 471647
San Francisco, CA 94147-1647   (415) 922-1851
FAX: (415) 440-2940; URL: http://www.partnershipsforchange.org

Established in 1990 in CA.
Grantmaker type: Public charity.
Financial data (yr. ended 06/30/10): Revenue, $26,750; assets, $1,120 (M); gifts received, $26,750; expenditures, $25,630.
Purpose and activities: The organization is dedicated to positive transformation at the community level, and works with communities around the world to empower individuals to achieve their full potential as well as build and strengthen community alliances.
Fields of interest: International development; Community/economic development.
Limitations: Giving primarily in India.
Officers and Directors:* Jacqueline Miller,* Pres.; Linda Alber, Secy.; Dr. Mary Weiss,* Treas.; Heidi Alber; Joel Cohn; Diane Federico; Andrew Michael, Esq.
EIN: 880303288

277
Ravi & Naina Patel Foundation
(formerly Shree Krishna Karuna Foundation)
6501 Truxtun Ave.
Bakersfield, CA 93309-0633   (661) 322-2206
Contact: Pradip Shah

Established in 1998 in CA.
Donor: Ravi Patel, M.D., Inc.
Grantmaker type: Independent foundation.
Financial data (yr. ended 12/31/10): Assets, $10,714,683 (M); gifts received, $2,014,065; expenditures, $413,801; qualifying distributions, $367,920; giving activities include $367,920 for grants.
Purpose and activities: Giving to raise cancer awareness, including early detection, and to fund cancer research, in India.
Fields of interest: Cancer; Cancer research; Economically disadvantaged.
International interests: India.
Limitations: Giving primarily in CA, IA and in India. No grants to individuals.
Application information:
  Initial approach: Letter
  Deadline(s): None
Officers: Ravi Patel, M.D., Pres.; Naina Patel, V.P.
EIN: 770490360

278
The Stephen Philibosian Foundation
46-930 W. El Dorado Dr.
Indian Wells, CA 92210-8649

Established in 1969 in PA.
Donor: Armenian Missionary Association of America.
Grantmaker type: Independent foundation.
Financial data (yr. ended 12/31/10): Assets, $8,144,029 (M); expenditures, $676,925; qualifying distributions, $618,755; giving activities include $618,755 for grants.
Purpose and activities: Giving primarily for Armenian-American churches and organizations, as well as for other Christian organizations, education, arts and culture, and health and human services.
Fields of interest: Human services; Arts; Health care; Education; Children/youth, services; Christian agencies & churches.
International interests: Middle East.
Type of support: Continuing support; Annual campaigns; Endowments; Scholarship funds.
Limitations: Applications not accepted. Giving primarily in CA. No grants to individuals, or for operating budgets, seed money, emergency funds, deficit financing, building funds, matching gifts, research, special projects, publications, or conferences; no loans.
Application information: Contributes only to pre-selected organizations.
  Board meeting date(s): Spring and fall

Trustees: Mrs. Richard Danelian; Mrs. Stephanie Landes; Mr. Albert Momjian; Mr. George Phillips; Mrs. Joyce Stein.
EIN: 237029751

279
Philippine Development Foundation

(formerly Ayala Foundation USA, also known as PhilDev USA)
1065 E. Hillsdale Blvd., Ste. 105
Foster City, CA 94404-1688   (650) 288-3937
E-mail: info@af-usa.org; URL: http://www.af-usa.org
Twitter: http://twitter.com/ayalafoundation

Established in 2000.
Grantmaker type: Public charity.
Financial data (yr. ended 12/31/10): Revenue, $1,776,260; assets, $943,685 (M); gifts received, $1,751,463; expenditures, $1,590,261; giving activities include $1,237,582 for grants to organizations outside the U.S.
Purpose and activities: The foundation seeks to empower a global Filipino community that is passionately committed to sustainable and equitable development in the Philippines, enhancing the lives of its people.
Fields of interest: Community/economic development; Asians/Pacific Islanders.
International interests: Philippines.
Limitations: Applications accepted. Giving on a national and international basis, with emphasis on the Philippines.
Publications: Application guidelines; Annual report; Newsletter.
Application information: Application form required.
   Initial approach: Download application
   Deadline(s): None
Officers: Diosdado "Dado" Banatao, Chair.; Fernando Zobel de Ayala, Vice-Chair.; Victoria P. Garchitorena, Pres.; Michael John Balaoing, Esq., Secy.; Denny S. Roja, Esq., Treas.
Trustees: Sally Anda-Munoz; Maria Banatao; Sherri Burke; Gloria Caoile; Eddie Flores; Lynn M. Hess; Loida Niolas Lewis; Joe M. Lumarda; Greg B. Macabenta; Sheila Lirio Marcelo; Ofelia Maristela, M.D.; Alexander G. Yap, M.D.
EIN: 943369973

280
Ploughshares Fund

1808 Wedermeyer St., Ste. 200
San Francisco, CA 94129   (415) 668-2244
E-mail: ploughshares@ploughshares.org; Additional address (DC office): 1430 K St., N.W., Ste. 550, Washington, DC 20005-2504, tel.: (202) 783-4401, fax: (202) 783-4407; URL: http://www.ploughshares.org
RSS Feed: http://www.ploughshares.org/news-analysis/feed

Established in 1981 in CA.
Grantmaker type: Public charity.
Financial data (yr. ended 06/30/10): Revenue, $6,029,323; assets, $35,675,909 (M); gifts received, $3,993,562; expenditures, $9,583,437; program services expenses, $8,163,038; giving activities include $5,634,622 for 61 grants (high: $650,000; low: $7,500), $507,282 for 5 grants to organizations outside the U.S., $345,896 for 6 grants to individuals, $17,250 for 6 grants to individuals outside the U.S., and $1,657,988 for foundation-administered programs.
Purpose and activities: The fund is dedicated to stopping the spread of weapons of mass destruction, controlling the sale of conventional weapons, addressing the environmental legacy of nuclear weapons production, promoting new approaches to conflict prevention, and building global and regional security.
Fields of interest: International peace/security; International affairs, arms control; International conflict resolution.
International interests: Africa; Asia; Europe; Japan; Middle East; North Korea; Russia; Southeast Asia.
Type of support: General/operating support; Continuing support; Emergency funds; Program development; Conferences/seminars; Seed money; Technical assistance; Grants to individuals.
Limitations: Applications accepted. Giving on a national and international basis. No grants for research, film, video, or book production, or writing academic dissertations.
Publications: Annual report (including application guidelines); Grants list; Informational brochure (including application guidelines); Newsletter.
Application information: Application e-mails should be sent to proposals@ploughshares.org. Application form not required.
   Initial approach: Letter or e-mail
   Copies of proposal: 1
   Deadline(s): Feb. 27
   Board meeting date(s): Three times per year
Officers and Directors:* Roger Hale,* Chair.; Joseph Cirincione,* Pres.; Brooks Walker III,* Secy.; Edie Allen; Reza Aslan; Terry Gamble Boyer; Doug Carlston; Michael Douglas; Gloria Duffy; Mary Lloyd Estrin; Angela Foster; Chuck Hagel; David Holloway; John Hoyt; Robert A. Rubinstein; Cynthia Ryan; Gail Seneca; Robert E. Sims; Philip Yun.
Number of staff: 5 full-time professional; 1 part-time professional; 2 full-time support.
EIN: 942764520

281
The Preuss Family Foundation, Inc.

2223 Avenida De La Playa, Ste. 220
La Jolla, CA 92037-3218

Established in 1985 in CA and DE.
Donors: Peter G. Preuss; Peggy Preuss.
Grantmaker type: Independent foundation.
Financial data (yr. ended 12/31/10): Assets, $478,265 (M); expenditures, $365,544; qualifying distributions, $355,853; giving activities include $354,088 for 13 grants (high: $40,000; low: $5,000).
Purpose and activities: Giving for the opera and to support scientific research, especially related to brain tumors.
Fields of interest: Foundations (private grantmaking); Performing arts, opera; Education; Diabetes; Cancer research; Brain research; YM/YWCAs & YM/YWHAs; Mathematics.
International interests: Germany.
Type of support: General/operating support; Scholarship funds; Research.
Limitations: Applications not accepted. Giving primarily in La Jolla, CA. No grants to individuals.
Application information: Contributes only to pre-selected organizations.
Officers: Peter G. Preuss, Pres.; Peter J. Preuss, V.P.; Peggy Preuss, Secy.
EIN: 330229180

282
Project Concern International

5151 Murphy Canyon Rd., Ste. 320
San Diego, CA 92123-4339   (858) 279-9690
FAX: (858) 694-0294; Toll-free tel.: (877) 724-4673;
URL: http://www.projectconcern.org
Facebook: http://www.facebook.com/pages/Project-Concern-International/38603229664
Twitter: http://twitter.com/#!/pciglobal

Established in 1961.
Grantmaker type: Public charity.
Financial data (yr. ended 09/30/10): Revenue, $29,420,533; assets, $12,194,844 (M); gifts received, $29,348,785; expenditures, $29,446,319; giving activities include $196,631 for grants, and $4,920,121 for grants to organizations outside the U.S.
Purpose and activities: The organization works to prevent disease, improve community, and promote sustainable development around the world.
Fields of interest: Community/economic development; Public health; International development.
Limitations: Giving nationally, and to Bolivia, Botswana, El Salvador, Ethiopia, Guatemala, Honduras, India, Indonesia, Malawi, Mexico, Nicaragua, South Africa, and Zambia.
Officer and Directors:* Amb. Kevin E. Moley,* Chair.; John D. Collins, Esq.; Ruth M. Covell, M.D.; Karen Zable Cox; Amb. Jeffrey Davidow; Judith A. Ettinger; Sandra Hadley; Norman F. Hapke, Jr.; Kurt Honold; Donald M. Ings; Catherine J. Mackey, Ph.D.; Philip R. Matthews, Esq.; Karen Mercaldo; Royce Pepin, G.C.S.J., Ph.C.; Cheryl Pia; and 11 additional directors.
EIN: 952248462

283
PTSRK Foundation

18 Crow Canyon Ct., Ste. 250
San Ramon, CA 94583-1669

Established in 2005 in CA.
Donors: Ross Koningstein; Patrisia Spezzaferro.
Grantmaker type: Independent foundation.
Financial data (yr. ended 12/31/10): Assets, $3,749,572 (M); gifts received, $12,929; expenditures, $186,421; qualifying distributions, $172,000; giving activities include $172,000 for grants (high: $30,000; low: $1,000).
Fields of interest: International human rights; Human services; Higher education, university.
Limitations: Applications not accepted. Giving primarily in CA. No grants to individuals.
Application information: Contributes only to pre-selected organizations.
Officers: Ross Koningstein, C.E.O.; Patrisia Spezzaferro, Secy. and C.F.O.
EIN: 203960774

284
Quiksilver Foundation

15202 Graham St.
Huntington Beach, CA 92649-1109
(714) 889-7132
Contact: Ryan Ashton, Dir.
E-mail: ryan.ashton@quiksilver.com; Additional contact: Kathie Armstrong, Dir., kathie.armstrong@quicksilver.com; E-mail for U.S., Canada, and Latin America inquiries:

foundation@quicksilver.com; E-mail for South Pacific and Australia inquiries: quicksilver.foundation@quicksilver.com.au; URL: http://www.quiksilverfoundation.org/ RSS Feed: http://www.quiksilverfoundation.org/ feed/

Established in 2004 in CA.
Donor: Quiksilver, Inc.
Grantmaker type: Company-sponsored foundation.
Financial data (yr. ended 10/31/10): Assets, $224,449 (M); gifts received, $577,989; expenditures, $491,498; qualifying distributions, $431,874; giving activities include $431,874 for grants.
Purpose and activities: The foundation supports programs that benefit and enhance the quality of life for communities of boardriders across the world. Special emphasis is directed towards community-based organizations involved with education, oceans, the environment, health, science, children, and youth.
Fields of interest: Environmental education; Education; Environment, water resources; Environment; Health care; Community/economic development; Science; Children; Youth.
International interests: Asia; Australia; Europe.
Type of support: Research; General/operating support; Continuing support; Program development; Scholarship funds; Donated products; In-kind gifts.
Limitations: Applications accepted. Giving primarily in areas of company operations, with emphasis on CA, Asia, Australia, and Europe. No grants to individuals or for fundraising activities.
Publications: Application guidelines; Annual report; Grants list; Informational brochure; Newsletter.
Application information: Organizations receiving support are asked to submit periodic reports. Application form required.
> *Initial approach:* Download application and e-mail to foundation
> *Deadline(s):* None
> *Final notification:* Following review
Directors: * Fernando Aguerre; Kathie Armstrong; Ryan Ashton; Maritxu Darrigrand; Scott Fullerton; Richard A. Gadbois III; Julia Ladgrove; Sean Pence; Jeff Wilson.
Number of staff: 1 full-time professional; 1 part-time professional.
EIN: 200986472

285
Raising Malawi
c/o Philippe Van Den Bossche
1108 S. Robertson Blvd.
Los Angeles, CA 90035-1404
Contact: Philippe van den Bossche, Exec. Dir.
E-mail: philippe@raisingmalawi.org; URL: http://www.raisingmalawi.org
Facebook: http://www.facebook.com/raisingmalawi?v=wall
Organization blog: http://www.raisingmalawi.org/blog/rss
Twitter: http://twitter.com/RaisingMalawi
YouTube: http://www.youtube.com/raisingmalawi

Established in 2006.
Grantmaker type: Public charity.
Financial data (yr. ended 12/31/09): Revenue, $3,337,342; assets, $5,389,964 (M); gifts received, $3,231,423; expenditures, $4,411,164; giving activities include $3,560,676 for grants to organizations outside the U.S.

Purpose and activities: The organization provides direct physical assistance to Malawi's orphans, including food, clothing, shelter, formal education, and targeted medical care, with the goal of ending their extreme poverty in a sustainable manner over time.
Fields of interest: International affairs.
International interests: Malawi.
Limitations: Giving limited to Malawi.
Officers: Michael Berg, Chair.; Rachel Almog, Vice-Chair.; John Larkin, Secy.; Philippe van den Bossche, Exec. Dir.
EIN: 743248665

286
Rancho Santa Fe Foundation
(formerly Rancho Santa Fe Community Foundation)
P.O. Box 811
Rancho Santa Fe, CA 92067-0811
(858) 756-6557
Contact: Christina Wilson, Exec. Dir.
FAX: (858) 756-6561;
E-mail: info@rsffoundation.org; URL: http://www.rsffoundation.org

Established in 1981 in CA.
Grantmaker type: Community foundation.
Financial data (yr. ended 12/31/10): Assets, $28,953,418 (M); gifts received, $4,103,827; expenditures, $3,458,718; giving activities include $3,000,397 for grants.
Purpose and activities: The foundation promotes philanthropy by: 1) assisting donors to build assets for their chosen charitable purposes; 2) enhancing the awareness of ways to give purposefully; 3) exploring and evaluating local and regional charitable needs; and 4) building endowments for charitable organizations.
Fields of interest: Community/economic development.
Type of support: Management development/capacity building; Grants to individuals; General/operating support; Continuing support; Building/renovation; Equipment; Land acquisition; Emergency funds; Program development; Publication; Seed money; Curriculum development; Scholarship funds; Technical assistance.
Limitations: Giving primarily in San Diego County, CA. No support for religious organizations (from discretionary funds). No grants for capital campaigns, annual campaigns, or endowments (from discretionary funds).
Publications: Annual report; Financial statement; Informational brochure; Newsletter.
Application information: Grants through Donor-Advised funds only; unsolicited requests for funds not accepted. However, if your organization wishes to be included in the foundation's Resource Library, please contact the foundation in writing and include the most recent copy of an annual report to the community and any marketing materials that would be helpful to a potential donor.
> *Board meeting date(s):* Bimonthly
Officers and Directors: * Charles J. Yash,* Chair.; Robert H. Goldsmith,* Vice-Chair.; Gigi Fenley,* Secy.; Scott B. Robinson,* Treas.; Christina P. Wilson, Exec. Dir.; James A. Boyce; Richard E. Carlson; Craig Dado; David Down; Gigi Fenley; Doug Forsyth; Franci Free; Mary T. Hart; William J. Herrick; Neil C. Hokanson; Candace A. Humber; Ron Kimura; Dr. Michael Lobatz; John Major; Connie L. Matsui; Ronald D. McMahon; E. Tyler Miller III; Mark Pulido; Scott B. Robinson; R. Roger Rowe; William J. Ruh;

Edward J. Sanderson, Jr.; Richard Sapp; Robert Vanosky; Philip White; Kate Williams; Richard Woltman.
Number of staff: 1 full-time professional; 3 part-time professional.
EIN: 953709639
Recent grants for international programs:
286-1 Asian Access Life Ministries, San Dimas, CA, $60,000. For general support. 2008.
286-2 Catholic Near East Welfare Association, New York, NY, $50,000. For endowment funds. 2008.
286-3 Christian International Scholarship Foundation, Lake Forest, IL, $10,000. For general support. 2008.
286-4 Food for the Hungry, Phoenix, AZ, $33,000. For general support. 2008.
286-5 Fresh Start Surgical Gifts, Carlsbad, CA, $30,000. For Surgery Weekend. 2008.
286-6 Mingei International Museum, San Diego, CA, $43,000. For 30th Anniversary Gala. 2008.
286-7 Opportunity International, Oak Brook, IL, $77,500. For general support. 2008.
286-8 Pontifical North American College, Washington, DC, $75,000. For program development. 2008.
286-9 Serving Hands International, San Diego, CA, $100,000. For general support. 2008.
286-10 Thornston Educational Fund, Glendora, CA, $20,000. For Chinese Migrant School. 2008.
286-11 World Vision, Federal Way, WA, $12,500. For general support. 2008.

287
The Prem Rawat Foundation
P.O. Box 241498
Los Angeles, CA 90024-9298 (310) 392-5700
FAX: (310) 388-3231; URL: http://www.tprf.org/

Established in 2001 in CA.
Grantmaker type: Public charity.
Financial data (yr. ended 12/31/09): Revenue, $2,220,681; assets, $1,055,905 (M); gifts received, $1,729,022; expenditures, $2,519,332; giving activities include $120,000 for grants, and $692,800 for grants to organizations outside the U.S.
Purpose and activities: The foundation works to fulfill a dual purpose: to bring Prem Rawat's message of peace to people around the world and to provide essential humanitarian aid to those who need it most.
Fields of interest: International relief.
Limitations: Giving on a national and international basis.
Officers and Directors: * Linda Pascotto,* Pres.; Premlata Rawat Hudson,* V.P.; Edward Hanzelik,* Secy.; Kenneth deLaski, Treas.; Stephen Sordoni.
EIN: 912166236

288
Ray of Light Foundation
c/o NKSF
10960 Wilshire Blvd., 5th Fl.
Los Angeles, CA 90024-3702 (310) 277-4657
Application address: c/o Richard Feldstein, 10100 Santa Monica Blvd., No. 1300, Los Angeles, CA 90067, tel.: (310) 277-4657

Established in 1998 in CA.
Donor: Madonna Ciccone.
Grantmaker type: Independent foundation.

Financial data (yr. ended 12/31/10): Assets, $9,858,233 (M); gifts received, $5,000,000; expenditures, $1,234,971; qualifying distributions, $1,134,033; giving activities include $1,134,033 for grants.
Fields of interest: International relief; Children, services; American Red Cross; Human services.
International interests: Malawi.
Limitations: Applications accepted. Giving primarily in CA, with emphasis on Los Angeles; some funding also in NY.
Trustee: Melanie Ciccone.
EIN: 954716881

289
The Myra Reinhard Family Foundation
c/o Myra Reinhard
15729 Los Gatos Blvd., Ste. 201
Los Gatos, CA 95032-2539
E-mail: MRFfoundation@verizon.net

Established in 1999 in CA.
Donor: Myra Reinhard.
Grantmaker type: Independent foundation.
Financial data (yr. ended 12/31/10): Assets, $1,061,502 (M); gifts received, $1,000,000; expenditures, $919,408; qualifying distributions, $888,061; giving activities include $878,500 for 38 grants (high: $120,000; low: $1,000).
Fields of interest: Media, film/video; Arts; Education; Hospitals (general); Health organizations, association; Medical research; Children/youth, services; Family services; Jewish agencies & synagogues.
International interests: Israel.
Type of support: Curriculum development; Continuing support; Program development.
Limitations: Applications not accepted. Giving primarily in CA and Washington, DC. No grants for building funds.
Application information: Unsolicited requests for funds not accepted.
Board meeting date(s): Mar.
Officers and Directors:* Myra Reinhard,* Pres.; Ian Reinhard,* V.P.; Ruth Fletcher,* Secy.; Neil Reinhard,* C.F.O. and Treas.; Erica Krauss.
Number of staff: 1 part-time professional.
EIN: 770514955

290
Rescue Task Force
(formerly Gary D. Becks International Ministries)
864 N. 2nd St., No. 340
El Cajon, CA 92021-5806 (619) 328-6511
FAX: (619) 334-0946;
E-mail: info@rescuetaskforce.org; URL: http://www.rescuetaskforce.org

Established in 1988.
Grantmaker type: Public charity.
Financial data (yr. ended 12/31/08): Revenue, $758,265; assets, $118,524 (M); gifts received, $757,501; expenditures, $784,799; giving activities include $408,648 for grants.
Purpose and activities: The organization provides volunteer medical teams, medical supplies and clinics, humanitarian aid, and livestock to remote, isolated regions of the globe.
Fields of interest: Human services; Children; Adults; Disabilities, people with; Indigenous peoples;

Military/veterans; Crime/abuse victims; Economically disadvantaged.
International interests: Asia; Central America.
Type of support: In-kind gifts.
Limitations: Applications not accepted. Giving on a national and international basis.
Publications: Informational brochure; Newsletter; Occasional report.
Application information: Unsolicited requests for funds not accepted.
Board meeting date(s): Quarterly
Officers and Directors:* John E. Linehan,* Chair.; Andrea Stone, C.E.O.; Gary D. Becks, Pres.; Mary Carlson; Lawrence Cutting; Lynn LaSauer; W. Foster Rich, Ph.D.; Robert L. Schroeder; Jimmy Valentine.
Number of staff: 3 full-time professional; 1 part-time support.
EIN: 330320141

291
Resnick Foundation
(formerly Resnick Family Foundation)
11444 W. Olympic Blvd., 10th Fl.
Los Angeles, CA 90064-1557
Contact: Jessica Aronoff, Dir., Char. Giving
E-mail: info@rollgiving.com

Established in 1997 in CA.
Donors: Lynda R. Resnick; Stewart A. Resnick; Resnick Family Foundation, Inc.
Grantmaker type: Independent foundation.
Financial data (yr. ended 09/30/10): Assets, $517,686 (M); gifts received, $6,593;882; expenditures, $7,424,294; qualifying distributions, $7,424,284; giving activities include $7,407,947 for grants.
Purpose and activities: Giving primarily for museums, education, especially medical schools, 9/11 disaster support, and conservation.
Fields of interest: Museums; Education; Environment, natural resources; Disasters, 9/11/01; Human services; Jewish agencies & synagogues; Young adults; Mentally disabled; Infants/toddlers; Economically disadvantaged; Children/youth; Children.
International interests: Fiji.
Type of support: General/operating support; Program development.
Limitations: Giving primarily in the Central Valley, CA. No grants to individuals.
Application information: Application form not required.
Initial approach: Letter
Copies of proposal: 1
Officers and Directors:* Lynda R. Resnick,* Co-Pres.; Stewart A. Resnick,* Co-Pres.; Craig B. Cooper, Secy.; Jordan P. Weiss.
Number of staff: 2 full-time professional; 1 part-time support.
EIN: 954658095

292
The Reve Foundation
550 Hamilton Ave., Ste. 300
Palo Alto, CA 94301-2031

Established in 1998 in CA.
Donor: Tae Yoo.
Grantmaker type: Independent foundation.
Financial data (yr. ended 12/31/10): Assets, $1,107,949 (M); expenditures, $266,339;

qualifying distributions, $245,000; giving activities include $245,000 for 1 grant.
Purpose and activities: Giving primarily for museums and children's hospitals.
Fields of interest: Hospitals (specialty); Museums; Education; Children; Economically disadvantaged.
International interests: India.
Type of support: Building/renovation.
Limitations: Applications not accepted. Giving primarily in CA, Washington, DC and MA. No grants to individuals.
Application information: Contributes only to pre-selected organizations.
Officers: Paul H. Roskoph, Pres.; Robert K. Roskoph, Secy.; Tae Yoo, Mgr.
EIN: 770483982

293
Rex Foundation
P.O. Box 29608
San Francisco, CA 94129-0608 (415) 561-3134
Contact: Sandy Sohcot, Exec. Dir.
FAX: (415) 561-3136;
E-mail: info@rexfoundation.org; URL: http://www.rexfoundation.org
Blog: http://www.rexfoundation.org/blog/
Facebook: http://www.facebook.com/rexfoundation
LinkedIn: http://www.linkedin.com/groups?gid=66423
Multimedia: http://www.myspace.com/rexfoundationmusicevents
RSS Feed: http://rexfoundation.org/?feed=rss2
Twitter: http://twitter.com/Rex_Foundation

Established in 1983 in CA.
Grantmaker type: Public charity.
Financial data (yr. ended 12/31/10): Revenue, $191,507; assets, $239,037 (M); gifts received, $190,845; expenditures, $178,310; giving activities include $20,900 for grants, and $10,000 for grants to individuals.
Purpose and activities: The foundation helps to secure a healthy environment, promote individuality in the arts, provide support to critical and necessary social services, protect the rights of indigenous people, build a stronger community, and educate children and adults.
Fields of interest: Arts; Education; Human services; Community/economic development; Indigenous peoples.
Type of support: General/operating support; Continuing support; Seed money.
Limitations: Applications not accepted. Giving on a national basis.
Publications: Annual report; Grants list; Newsletter.
Application information: Unsolicited requests for funds not accepted.
Officer and Directors:* Sandy Sohcot,* Exec. Dir.; Dennis Alpert; Diane Blagman; Matt Butler; Barry Caplan; Stefanie Coyote; Tim Duncan; Andy Gadiel; Carolyn Garcia; Trixie Garcia; Freddy Hahne; Mickey Hart; Rosalie Howarth; Roger McNamee; Nick Morgan; and 8 additional directors.
Number of staff: 1 full-time professional; 1 part-time professional.
EIN: 680033257

294
Robert Gore Rifkind Foundation
4335 Marina City Dr., No. 734 ETS
Marina del Rey, CA   90292-5826
(310) 823-9608
Contact: Robert Gore Rifkind, Dir.

Established in 1979 in CA.
Donor: Robert Gore Rifkind.
Grantmaker type: Operating foundation.
Financial data (yr. ended 03/31/10): Assets, $7,974,741 (M); expenditures, $537,715; qualifying distributions, $413,271; giving activities include $350,947 for 48 grants (high: $50,000; low: $500).
Purpose and activities: Giving primarily for the arts, especially art museums; in addition, grant awards enable scholars to come to Los Angeles to study at the Rifkind Center for German Expressionist Studies.
Fields of interest: Animals/wildlife; Medical research; Arts; Performing arts, orchestras; Arts education; Museums; Libraries/library science; Jewish agencies & synagogues.
International interests: Israel.
Type of support: General/operating support; Continuing support; Research.
Limitations: Applications accepted. Giving primarily in southern CA.
Application information: Application form required.
  Initial approach: Letter
  Deadline(s): None
Directors: Jonathan Davidson; Max Rifkind-Barron; Robert Gore Rifkind.
EIN: 953397350

295
Rivendell Stewards' Trust
P.O. Box 6009
Santa Barbara, CA   93160-6009
Contact: Amity Wicks, Admin.
FAX: (805) 823-4594; *E-mail:* info@rstrust.org; *URL:* http://www.rstrust.org

Established in 1985 in CA.
Donors: K.N. Hansen, Sr.; K.N. Hansen, Jr.; G.W. Hansen; Vince Nelson.
Grantmaker type: Independent foundation.
Financial data (yr. ended 12/31/10): Assets, $30,930,005 (M); gifts received, $28,335,396; expenditures, $533,226; qualifying distributions, $420,900; giving activities include $420,900 for grants.
Purpose and activities: Giving for Christian institutions and missionary efforts in the two-thirds world.
Fields of interest: Theological school/education; Religion.
International interests: Developing countries.
Type of support: General/operating support; Management development/capacity building; Program development; Seed money; Curriculum development; Scholarship funds; Matching/challenge support.
Limitations: Giving limited to developing countries. No support for Western ministries. No grants to individuals (except for program for retired missionaries).
Publications: Application guidelines.
Application information: At this time, the foundation is only accepting proposals and synopses from those ministries it currently supports. See

foundation web site for full submission guidelines. Application form not required.
  Initial approach: Synopsis (1-2 pages, and only from ministries the foundation currently supports)
  Copies of proposal: 1
  Deadline(s): July 1 for synopsis. Full proposals (if invited to submit) are due Sept. 1 for the following calendar year
  Board meeting date(s): Early Nov.
  Final notification: Dec. 15
Officers: Walter Hansen, Pres.; Vince Nelson, Treas.; Darlene Hansen, Secy.
Trustee: Jean Johnson.
Number of staff: 1 part-time support.
EIN: 776016389

296
The RM Liu Foundation
500 W. 190th St., 6th Fl.
Gardena, CA   90248-4265

Established in 2007 in CA.
Donors: Justin Liu; Emily Liu; Tireco, Inc.
Grantmaker type: Company-sponsored foundation.
Financial data (yr. ended 12/31/10): Assets, $2,092,061 (M); gifts received, $1,582,802; expenditures, $1,528,020; qualifying distributions, $1,514,131; giving activities include $1,514,131 for grants.
Fields of interest: Higher education; International affairs.
Limitations: Applications not accepted. Giving primarily in CA. No grants to individuals.
Application information: Contributes only to pre-selected organizations.
Officers: Justin R. Liu, Pres.; Robert W. Liu, V.P.; Emily F. Liu, Secy.; Mimi W. Liu, C.F.O.
EIN: 208643551

297
The Rock Foundation
(also known as The DJ Rock Foundation)
9100 Wilshire Blvd., Ste. 1000W
Beverly Hills, CA   90212-3463   (310) 841-0800
Contact: Katie Kornfield, Exec. Dir.
FAX: (310) 841-0808;
E-mail: therockfoundation@primeprinc.com;
URL: http://www.djrockfoundation.org

Established in 2006; granted 501(c)(3) status in 2007.
Grantmaker type: Public charity.
Financial data (yr. ended 12/31/09): Revenue, $245,038; assets, $78,125 (M); gifts received, $245,038; expenditures, $196,622; program services expenses, $144,068.
Purpose and activities: The foundation seeks to provide a platform of hope and possibility for children worldwide by providing programs designed to enrich and empower the lives and self-esteem of under-served, at-risk youth and children hospitalized for medical disabilities, disorders and illnesses; the foundation also strives to improve the health and self-esteem of children through physical fitness programs, educating children about nutrition and health.
Fields of interest: Public health, physical fitness; Children.
International interests: Zimbabwe; South Africa; Lesotho; Cambodia; Guatemala.

Type of support: Continuing support; Equipment; General/operating support; In-kind gifts; Program development.
Limitations: Applications not accepted. Giving on a national and international basis. No support for religious or political purposes. No grants to individuals, or for film projects.
Application information: Contributes only to pre-selected organizations; unsolicited requests for funds not considered or acknowledged.
Officers and Directors:* Dwayne Johnson,* Chair.; Katie Kornfield, Exec. Dir.; Harold A. Brown; Dany Garcia; Emery B. Sheer, C.P.A.., C.V.A.; Darren Statt.
EIN: 208797894

298
Rock, Paper, Scissors Foundation, Inc.
13769 Wildflower Ln.
Los Altos Hills, CA   94022-6205

Established in 2005 in CA.
Donors: Keith H. Randall; Kay Marie Boissicat.
Grantmaker type: Independent foundation.
Financial data (yr. ended 12/31/10): Assets, $10,111,837 (M); gifts received, $1,252,870; expenditures, $511,837; qualifying distributions, $506,243; giving activities include $502,350 for 14 grants (high: $100,000; low: $500).
Purpose and activities: Giving primarily for international development, health care, and human services.
Fields of interest: Elementary/secondary education; Human services; Health care; International development.
Limitations: Applications not accepted. Giving primarily in CA, Washington, DC, GA, IL, and NY. No grants to individuals.
Application information: Contributes only to pre-selected organizations.
Officers and Director:* Keith H. Randall,* Pres. and Treas.; Kay Marie Boissicat, Secy.
EIN: 202427803

299
Roth Family Foundation
3700 Wilshire Blvd., Ste. 1050A
Los Angeles, CA   90010-3090   (213) 383-9207
Contact: Rachel Roth, Exec. Dir.
FAX: (213) 383-9222; *E-mail:* rachel@roth-la.org;
URL: http://www.rothfamilyfoundation.org

Established in 1966 in CA.
Donors: Louis Roth and Co.; Louis Roth†; Fannie Roth†; Harry Roth†.
Grantmaker type: Independent foundation.
Financial data (yr. ended 12/31/10): Assets, $10,901,621 (M); expenditures, $480,090; qualifying distributions, $457,758; giving activities include $380,755 for grants.
Purpose and activities: The Foundation seeks to improve lives through a variety of focus areas, primarily in the Los Angeles area. Specifically, it provides general operating support and new and/or on-going program/project support to organizations that fall into the following focus areas: 1) Arts and Culture; 2) Youth; 3) Environment; 4) Economic Development; 5) International Development; 6) Reproductive Health and Rights/Sex Education.
Fields of interest: Media/communications; Performing arts, education; Economic development;

Environment; Environment, beautification programs; Environment, formal/general education; International development; Media, radio; Performing arts, music; Reproductive health; Youth development; Children/youth; Economically disadvantaged; Girls; Women; Youth.
International interests: Africa.
Type of support: General/operating support; Program development; Matching/challenge support.
Limitations: Giving primarily in Los Angeles County, CA. No support for fraternal organizations, or for religious or political organizations. No grants to individuals; generally no grants to fund dinners, special events or fundraising events.
Publications: Application guidelines; Annual report; Grants list.
Application information: The foundation does not accept unsolicited proposals. However, the foundation will accept a letter of inquiry. See foundation web site for complete guidelines.
   Initial approach: Letter of inquiry (no longer than 3 pages)
   Board meeting date(s): Semiannually
Officers and Directors:* Rachel Roth,* C.E.O. and Exec. Dir.; Michael P. Roth,* Pres.; Gil Garcetti,* V.P.; Sukey Garcetti,* Secy.-Treas.; Dana Boldt; Eric Garcetti; Sarah Roth; Andrea Roth-Fedida.
Number of staff: 1 full-time professional.
EIN: 880352682

300
S.G. Foundation
P.O. Box 444
Buellton, CA   93427-0444   (805) 688-0088
Contact: Pamela Grattan, Admin.; Dee Reed, Progs. Analyst
FAX: (805) 686-1250; E-mail: sgfound@utech.net; E-mail address for Dee Reed, Progs. Analyst, for questions regarding proposals: dpreed@verizon.net; URL: http://www.sgfoundation.org

Established in 1984 in CA.
Grantmaker type: Independent foundation.
Financial data (yr. ended 12/31/10): Assets, $11,819,647 (M); expenditures, $742,253; qualifying distributions, $607,255; giving activities include $607,255 for grants (high: $55,000; low: $500).
Purpose and activities: The foundation's purpose is to encourage and enable individuals and communities to partner together to help people help themselves. The foundation supports projects that are self-help in nature, affirm individual dignity, and create incentives for people to participate in their own self-development. The foundation accepts proposals for program expenses for national and international human service relief and development projects. Projects must demonstrate a specific and focused community-based strategy for economic development in the areas of hunger relief, jobs, and small business start-up. The foundation also accepts proposals for senior care, and educational/leadership development programs for youth, child abuse and neglect prevention, and strengthening family values.
Fields of interest: Health care; Family services; Christian agencies & churches; Community/economic development.
International interests: Central America; Haiti; Mexico.
Type of support: General/operating support; Continuing support; Equipment; Program

development; Seed money; Matching/challenge support.
Limitations: Giving primarily in central CA, as well as Central America, Mexico, and Haiti. No support for athletics, politics, the arts, music, or museums. No grants for building projects, capital improvement, endowments, research, books, films, or media.
Application information: See web site for application guidelines. Application form not required.
   Initial approach: Proposal in accordance with guidelines posted on foundation web site
   Copies of proposal: 1
   Deadline(s): None
   Board meeting date(s): Monthly
   Final notification: 60-90 days
Officers and Trustees:* Lynn R. Gildred,* Pres.; William Sauer,* V.P.; Duane Serritslev, Secy.; Stuart Gildred, Jr.,* Treas.
Directors: John Crowell; John Donati; Joseph Lambert.
Number of staff: 2 part-time professional.
EIN: 330048410

301
Sabadia Family Foundation
23231 La Palma Ave.
Yorba Linda, CA   92887-4768
E-mail: info@sabadiafoundation.org; URL: http://www.sabadiafoundation.org/

Established in 1999 in CA.
Donor: Rahim Sabadia.
Grantmaker type: Independent foundation.
Financial data (yr. ended 12/31/10): Assets, $24,629 (M); gifts received, $325,000; expenditures, $309,564; qualifying distributions, $307,644; giving activities include $307,644 for 9 grants (high: $242,060; low: $500).
Purpose and activities: Support primarily for Islamic and Muslim organizations and programs.
Fields of interest: Human services; International relief; Islam; Religion.
Limitations: Applications not accepted. Giving primarily in CA. No support for private foundations. No grants to individuals.
Application information: Contributes only to pre-selected organizations.
Officers: Rahim Sabadia, Pres.; Nafees Batool, Secy.
EIN: 330884886

302
Saban Family Foundation
10100 Santa Monica Blvd., Ste. 2600
Los Angeles, CA   90067-4003   (310) 557-5100
Contact: Alex De Campo

Established in 1999 in CA.
Donors: Haim Saban; Cheryl Saban.
Grantmaker type: Independent foundation.
Financial data (yr. ended 12/31/10): Assets, $5,374,073 (M); expenditures, $13,712,847; qualifying distributions, $13,700,192; giving activities include $13,198,052 for 71 grants (high: $4,141,507; low: $264).
Purpose and activities: Support for children's health research and social welfare in Los Angeles, CA, and in Israel.
Fields of interest: Hospitals (specialty); Medical research, institute; Nutrition; Children, services;

International affairs; Jewish agencies & synagogues.
International interests: Israel.
Type of support: General/operating support; Continuing support; Annual campaigns; Building/renovation; Program development; Conferences/seminars; Seed money; Curriculum development; Scholarship funds; Research; Matching/challenge support.
Limitations: Applications accepted. Giving primarily in CA and Israel, some giving in AR and Washington, DC. No grants to individuals.
Publications: Application guidelines.
Application information: Application form required.
   Initial approach: Letter on organization letterhead
   Copies of proposal: 1
   Deadline(s): None
   Final notification: Within 6 months
Officers and Directors:* Cheryl Saban,* Co-Pres.; Adam Chesnoff,* V.P.; Niveen Tadros, Secy.; Haim Saban, Treas.; Judy Friedman; Fred Gluckman; Laura Hartigan.
Number of staff: 1 full-time professional; 1 full-time support.
EIN: 954769273
Recent grants for international programs:
302-1 American Israel Education Foundation, Washington, DC, $1,000,000. For educating opinion leaders about United States/Israel relationship. 2009.
302-2 Endeavor Global, New York, NY, $100,000. To transform economies of emerging markets by identifying and supporting high-impact entrepreneurs. 2009.
302-3 Friends of Israel Scouts, New York, NY, $30,000. To develop and maintain the connection between Tzofim (Israel Scouts) movement in Israel, and to strengthen relationships between Israel and North American Jewry. 2009.
302-4 Friends of the Israel Defense Forces, National/NY Tri-State Region, New York, NY, $3,572,000. To help support social, educational and recreational programs and facilities for Israel soldiers including services to widows and children of fallen soldiers. 2009.
302-5 Israeli Leadership Club, Beverly Hills, CA, $85,000. To fortify and enhance productive and continuous relationship between Israeli-Americans and the State of Israel through community empowerment, activism, and philanthropy. 2009.
302-6 Jewish National Fund, New York, NY, $25,000. To promote and further cultural, physical, social, medical, agricultural and general welfare of the people of Israel. 2009.
302-7 Malaria No More, New York, NY, $500,000. For mosquito nets for everyone at risk for malaria in Africa. 2009.
302-8 Mercy Corps, Portland, OR, $10,000. To alleviate suffering, poverty and oppression by helping people build secure, productive and just communities. 2009.
302-9 Oceana, Washington, DC, $10,000. For ocean conservation. 2009.

303
The Sai Ram Foundation
1118 E. Colorado St.
Glendale, CA   91205-1309
Contact: Harshadray Patel, Pres.

Established in 2001 in CA.

Donors: Rajan Geeta Ghayal; Urvashi Parikh; Arun Patel; Harshadray Patel; Nilesh Patel; Shirish Patel.
Grantmaker type: Independent foundation.
Financial data (yr. ended 12/31/10): Assets, $1 (M); gifts received, $332,491; expenditures, $271,615; qualifying distributions, $262,734; giving activities include $262,734 for grants.
Fields of interest: Hospitals (general); Foundations (public).
International interests: India.
Limitations: Applications accepted. Giving primarily in India. No grants to individuals.
Application information:
Initial approach: Letter
Deadline(s): None
Officers: Harshadray Patel, Pres.; Nilesh Patel, Secy.; Ramila Patel, Treas.
EIN: 954825779

304
The Saje Foundation
17291 Irvine Blvd., No. 351
Tustin, CA 92780-2931 (714) 734-7808
FAX: (714) 734-7834;
E-mail: info@sajefoundation.org; URL: http://www.sajefoundation.org

Established in 1998 in IL.
Donors: Elaine McKay; Robert L. McKay.
Grantmaker type: Independent foundation.
Financial data (yr. ended 12/31/10): Assets, $25,873 (M); gifts received, $1,423,659; expenditures, $1,439,996; qualifying distributions, $1,295,000; giving activities include $1,295,000 for 20 grants (high: $350,000; low: $2,500).
Purpose and activities: The mission of the foundation is to support Christian organizations in the United States and in the developing world. Focus areas include: 1) HIV/Aids in Africa; 2) Christian Community Development; 3) Spread of Evangelism; 4) Emergency crisis relief and 5) Christian Micro-Enterprise Development.
Fields of interest: AIDS; Education; Youth development; Human services; International economic development; International relief; International affairs; Christian agencies & churches.
International interests: Developing countries.
Limitations: Applications not accepted. Giving primarily in CA and IL. No grants to individuals.
Application information: Contributes only to pre-selected organizations.
Officers and Trustees:* John McKay,* Pres.; Elaine McKay,* Secy.; Robert L. McKay, Jr.,* Treas.; Christine McKay.
EIN: 364309903

305
salesforce.com Foundation
1 Market St., Ste. 300
San Francisco, CA 94105-1315 (415) 901-7000
Contact: Suzanne DiBianca, Exec. Dir.
FAX: (415) 901-8501;
E-mail: foundation@salesforce.com; URL: http://www.salesforcefoundation.org
Facebook: http://www.facebook.com/Salesforce.comFoundation
Twitter: http://twitter.com/SFDCFoundation
YouTube: http://www.youtube.com/salesforcefoundation

Established in 2000.

Donor: salesforce.com, inc.
Grantmaker type: Public charity.
Financial data (yr. ended 09/30/10): Revenue, $2,481,172; assets, $18,535,133 (M); gifts received, $502,327; expenditures, $4,427,356; giving activities include $2,357,251 for grants, $551,738 for grants to organizations outside the U.S., and $54,916 for grants to individuals.
Purpose and activities: The foundation exposes and educates underserved youth to technology, and builds a salesforce.com corporate culture of employee volunteerism in the community.
Fields of interest: Children/youth, services; Engineering/technology; Economically disadvantaged.
International interests: Asia; Europe; Japan; Middle East.
Type of support: Equipment; Program development; Technical assistance; Employee matching gifts.
Limitations: Applications accepted. Giving on a national and international basis.
Publications: Application guidelines.
Application information: Application form required.
Initial approach: Complete online application form
Deadline(s): Feb. 27 for Turn It Up Grants
Final notification: Mar. 31 for Turn It Up Grants
Officers and Directors:* Marc R. Benioff,* Chair. and C.E.O.; Suzanne DiBianca, Exec. Dir.; Rebecca Enonchong; Alan Hassenfeld; F. Warren Hellman; Dave Moellenhoff; Laura Scher; Robert Thurman.
Number of staff: 7 full-time professional; 1 part-time support.
EIN: 943347800

306
The San Carlos Foundation
1065 Creston Rd.
Berkeley, CA 94708-1545 (510) 525-3787
Contact: Davida Coady, Pres.
FAX: (510) 525-3278; E-mail: dcoady@igc.org;
URL: http://sancarlosfoundation.org

Grantmaker type: Public charity.
Financial data (yr. ended 04/30/11): Revenue, $274,309; assets, $209,888 (M); gifts received, $274,103; expenditures, $418,105; giving activities include $417,565 for grants.
Purpose and activities: The organization provides health and educational assistance to refugees and other people living in extreme poverty in the Third World, particularly in Central America.
Fields of interest: Education; Health care; Immigrants/refugees; Economically disadvantaged.
International interests: Developing countries; Central America.
Limitations: Applications not accepted. Giving in the Third World, particularly in Central America.
Application information: Unsolicited requests for funds not accepted or acknowledged.
Officers and Directors:* Davida Coady,* Pres.; Martin Sheen,* V.P.; Barbara Erickson,* Secy.; Michael Blake,* Treas.; Pauline Butcher; Todd Jailer; Bill Joyce; Owen Murphy; Arthur Naiman; Leonard Post; John Roark, M.D.; Fred Ross; Vivian Zelaya.
EIN: 680040121

307
The San Diego Foundation
(formerly San Diego Community Foundation)
2508 Historic Decatur Rd., Ste. 200
San Diego, CA 92106-6138 (619) 235-2300
Contact: Robert A. Kelly, C.E.O.
FAX: (619) 239-1710;
E-mail: info@sdfoundation.org; URL: http://www.sdfoundation.org
Knowledge Center: http://www.sdfoundation.org/communityimpact/index.html
Twitter: http://twitter.com/sd_fdn

Established in 1975 in CA.
Grantmaker type: Community foundation.
Financial data (yr. ended 06/30/11): Assets, $560,136,000 (M); gifts received, $60,380,000; expenditures, $48,339,000; giving activities include $38,004,000 for grants.
Purpose and activities: The foundation seeks to improve the quality of life within all local communities by promoting and increasing responsible and effective philanthropy, with giving to nonprofit organizations in the areas of asset building, civil society, education, environment/animal welfare, scholarship, human/social services, health, arts and culture.
Fields of interest: Adult education—literacy, basic skills & GED; Arts; Child development, services; Education; Education, reading; Elementary school/education; Environment; Environment, land resources; Environment, pollution control; Environment, public policy; Environment, research; Environment, water resources; Higher education; Human services; Medical research, institute; Science; Science, research; Secondary school/education; Vocational education; Aging; Disabilities, people with; Economically disadvantaged; Homeless; Minorities; Women.
International interests: Mexico.
Type of support: Scholarships—to individuals; Research; Program evaluation; Program development; Matching/challenge support; Land acquisition; General/operating support; Equipment; Employee matching gifts.
Limitations: Applications accepted. Giving primarily in the greater San Diego, CA, region. No support for religious organizations. No grants to individuals (except for scholarships), or for annual or capital fund campaigns, endowment funds, conferences, travel, or to underwrite fundraising events and performances.
Publications: Annual report; Financial statement; Grants list; Informational brochure; Newsletter.
Application information: Visit foundation web site for grant application and guidelines. Application form required.
Initial approach: Submit online application and proposal
Deadline(s): Varies
Board meeting date(s): Bimonthly beginning July through May
Final notification: 3 to 5 months
Officers and Board Members:* Jennifer Adams-Brooks,* Chair.; Robert C. Dynes,* Ph.D., Vice-Chair., Center for Civic Engagement; Garry Ridge,* Vice-Chair., Charitable Giving and External Rels.; Steve Smith,* Vice-Chair. and Secy.; John D. Wylie,* Vice-Chair., Finance; Robert A. Kelly, C.E.O. and Pres.; Dan Beintema, V.P., Opers. and Community Partnerships; Anna-Marie Rooney, V.P., Mktg. and External Affairs; Adrienne Vargas, V.P., Charitable Giving and Donor Experience and Engagement; Hal Orr, C.F.O. and C.I.O.; Doug

Hegebarth,* Treas.; Mike Pattison, Cont. and Assoc. V.P., Finance and Admin.; Yamila M. Ayad; Darcy C. Bingham; James Cahill; John Cambon, Ph.D.; Constance M. Carroll, Ph.D.; Ted Chan, M.D.; Kay Chandler; Richard A. Collato; Roger Cornell, M.D.; Sandra Daley, M.D.; William K. Geppert; Benjamin Haddad; Thomas Hall; Jerry E. Hoffmeister; Connie L. Matsui; Paul I. Meyer; Scott H. Peters; Hollyce J. Phillips; Derek J. Quackenbush; Barbara A. Sawrey, Ph.D.; Nancy Spector; Carisa M. Wisniewski; James "Jim" Ziegler.

Number of staff: 26 full-time professional; 8 part-time professional; 11 full-time support; 1 part-time support.

EIN: 952942582

Recent grants for international programs:

307-1 Africa Inland Mission International, Pearl River, NY, $12,000. For missionary support. 2011.

307-2 African Conservation Fund, Tucson, AZ, $10,000. For the conservation research of the African Conservation Center. 2011.

307-3 American Friends of the Louvre, New York, NY, $16,000. For Liaisons au Louvre II. 2011.

307-4 American Red Cross National Headquarters, Washington, DC, $10,000. For Japan relief. 2011.

307-5 Armenian Gospel Mission, Pasadena, CA, $50,000. For the church/community center project in Maralik, Armenia. 2011.

307-6 Casa de los Pobres USA, San Diego, CA, $12,000. 2011.

307-7 De Colores Foundation, Chula Vista, CA, $16,171. For program support for disabled individuals. 2011.

307-8 Doctors Without Borders USA, New York, NY, $10,000. For Pakistan flood relief efforts. 2011.

307-9 Doctors Without Borders USA, New York, NY, $10,000. For relief efforts for the Japan earthquake and tsunami. 2011.

307-10 Edify, San Diego, CA, $25,000. For Financing Sustainable Christian Schools. 2011.

307-11 Fresh Start Surgical Gifts, Carlsbad, CA, $25,000. For the Butterfly Ball. 2011.

307-12 Fresh Start Surgical Gifts, Carlsbad, CA, $25,000. Toward a Fresh Start Surgical Weekend. 2011.

307-13 Friends of the Earth, Washington, DC, $25,000. For Climate Crisis Coalition in its efforts to promote awareness and understanding of a price and dividend mechanism to control greenhouse gas emissions in the U.S., through Earth Equity News, videos and a national meeting on carbon pricing. 2011.

307-14 Helen Keller National Center, San Diego, CA, $198,880. For training program for Support Service Providers (SSP) to serve individuals who are deaf-blind. 2011.

307-15 International Foundation for the Community, Tijuana, Mexico, $20,000. To partner with Caritas Mexicali Food Bank in Mexicali, Baja California, to provide distributions of food and household items to approximately 1,400 survivors of the April 4, 2010 Baja California earthquake. 2011.

307-16 International Foundation for the Community, Tijuana, Mexico, $13,420. To partner with Lions Club of Mexicali in Mexicali, Baja California, to provide distributions of food and household items to approximately 420 survivor households of the April 4, 2010 Baja California earthquake. 2011.

307-17 Kyoto Symposium Organization, La Jolla, CA, $11,500. For unrestricted support. 2011.

307-18 Lazarian World Homes, Oceanside, CA, $75,000. To continue work in Haiti, Brazil, US Indian Reservations, and in Mexico. 2011.

307-19 Medical Benevolence Foundation, Houston, TX, $10,000. For general support. 2011.

307-20 Mingei International Museum, San Diego, CA, $50,000. For general support. 2011.

307-21 Mingei International Museum, San Diego, CA, $45,000. For museum exhibitions, Mingei Fusion. 2011.

307-22 Pontifical North American College, Washington, DC, $10,000. For general support. 2011.

307-23 Power of Love Foundation, San Diego, CA, $10,000. For microcredit project in Zambia in partnership with Nkwazi Rotary Club in Lusaka. 2011.

307-24 Power of Love Foundation, San Diego, CA, $10,000. For the Zambia - Kusinta Rotary Microcredit Project, a microcredit program in Lusaka, Zambia in partnership with the Kusinta Rotary Club. 2011.

307-25 Project Concern International, San Diego, CA, $12,500. For unrestricted annual gift. 2011.

307-26 Rotary Club of San Diego, San Diego, CA, $20,850. For the Cure Malawi Rotary Project. 2011.

307-27 Rotary Foundation of Rotary International, Evanston, IL, $10,500. For India-Bhatkal microcredit matching gift project from the La Jolla Sunrise Rotary Club, Rotary Club of San Diego, El Cajon Rotary Club, Rancho Bernardo Noon Rotary club, and San Diego Breakfast Rotary club. 2011.

307-28 Sydney Opera House, Sydney, Australia, $10,000. For the Chairman's Leadership Circle. 2011.

308
San Diego Padres Baseball Club L.P. Corporate Giving Program

c/o Community Rels., Charitable Donation
P.O. Box 122000
San Diego, CA   92112-2000   (619) 795-5275
URL: http://sandiego.padres.mlb.com/sd/community/donations.jsp

Grantmaker type: Corporate giving program.

Purpose and activities: The San Diego Padres make charitable contributions to nonprofit organizations on a case by case basis. Support is given primarily in the greater San Diego, California, area.

Fields of interest: Education; Hospitals (general); Public health, physical fitness; Cancer; Athletics/sports, baseball; Boys & girls clubs; General charitable giving; Youth.

International interests: Mexico.

Type of support: Income development; Donated products; In-kind gifts.

Limitations: Applications accepted. Giving primarily in area of company operations in the greater San Diego, CA, area, including Imperial and San Diego counties and Baja California, Mexico.

Publications: Application guidelines.

Application information: Proposals should be submitted using organization letterhead. The Community Relations Department handles giving.

Initial approach: Proposal to headquarters for memorabilia donations; complete online application form for Charity Ticket Program

Copies of proposal: 1

Deadline(s): 4 to 6 weeks prior to need for memorabilia donations; none for Charity Ticket Program

309
The San Francisco Foundation

225 Bush St., Ste. 500
San Francisco, CA   94104-4224   (415) 733-8500
Contact: Sandra R. Hernandez M.D., C.E.O.
FAX: (415) 477-2783; E-mail: info@sff.org; Intent to Apply e-mail: apps@sff.org; URL: http://www.sff.org
E-Newsletter: http://www.sff.org/about/publications/ENews
Facebook: http://www.facebook.com/TheSanFranciscoFoundation
The San Francisco Foundation's Philanthropy Promise: http://www.ncrp.org/philanthropys-promise/who

Established in 1948 in CA by resolution and declaration of trust.

Grantmaker type: Community foundation.

Financial data (yr. ended 06/30/11): Assets, $1,101,069,000 (M); gifts received, $56,712,000; expenditures, $95,338,000; giving activities include $82,473,000 for grants.

Purpose and activities: The foundation mobilizes resources and acts as a catalyst for change to build strong communities, foster civic leadership, and promote philanthropy. Grants principally in six categories: the arts and culture, community health, education, environment, neighborhood and community development, and social justice.

Fields of interest: Arts, cultural/ethnic awareness; Media/communications; Performing arts; Performing arts, dance; Humanities; Arts, artist's services; Arts; Education, early childhood education; Child development, education; Elementary school/education; Higher education; Adult education—literacy, basic skills & GED; Education, reading; Education; Environment, natural resources; Environment; Reproductive health, family planning; Health care; Substance abuse, services; Mental health/crisis services; Health organizations, association; Cancer; AIDS; Alcoholism; Crime/violence prevention, youth; Legal services; Employment; Housing/shelter, development; Youth development, services; Children/youth, services; Child development, services; Family services; Aging, centers/services; Homeless, human services; Human services; International human rights; Civil/human rights; Urban/community development; Community/economic development; Voluntarism promotion; Public policy, research; Government/public administration; Leadership development; Public affairs; Aging; Disabilities, people with; Minorities; Immigrants/refugees; Economically disadvantaged; Homeless.

Type of support: General/operating support; Program development; Fellowships; Technical assistance; Program-related investments/loans; Employee matching gifts; Scholarships—to individuals.

Limitations: Applications accepted. Giving limited to the San Francisco Bay Area, CA, counties of Alameda, Contra Costa, Marin, San Francisco, and San Mateo. No support for religious purposes, or medical, academic, or scientific research. No grants to individuals (except scholarships and fellowships designated by a donor) or for conferences or one-time events.

Publications: Annual report; Financial statement; Grants list; Newsletter; Program policy statement.
Application information: Visit foundation web site for Grantee Center online application, application guidelines and specific deadlines. Application form required.
  Initial approach: Complete online grant application
  Deadline(s): Nov.
  Board meeting date(s): Monthly except Jan., Apr., and Aug.; applications are reviewed two times each year
  Final notification: Approx. 16 weeks after deadline
Officers and Trustees:* David Friedman,* Chair.; Stephanie DiMarco,* Vice-Chair.; Sandra R. Hernandez,* M.D., C.E.O. and Secy.; Dee Dee Brantley, V.P., Human Resources and C.O.O.; James W. Head, V.P., Progs.; Sara Ying Rounsaville,* V.P., Public Affairs and Comms.; Monica Pressley, C.F.O.; Susan Frohlich, Cont.; Andy Ballard; Charlene Harvey; James C. Hormel; Tatwina Lee; Marcela C. Medina; Hugo Morales; John Murray; Kurt C. Organista, Ph.D.; Peggy Saika.
Number of staff: 35 full-time professional; 2 part-time professional; 13 full-time support; 3 part-time support.
EIN: 010679337
Recent grants for international programs:
309-1 Accordia Global Health Foundation, Washington, DC, $50,000. For general support. 2010.
309-2 Acumen Fund, New York, NY, $50,000. For general support. 2010.
309-3 Acumen Fund, New York, NY, $50,000. For general support. 2010.
309-4 Afghan Coalition, Fremont, CA, $30,000. For the Afghan Health Partnership Program (AHPP), promoting access to direct health-related services for underserved Afghan women, youth and their families. 2010.
309-5 Alliance to Stop Slavery and End Trafficking, Los Angeles, CA, $10,000. For general support. 2010.
309-6 American Associates, Ben-Gurion University of the Negev, Corte Madera, CA, $500,000. To fund two career development chairs at BGU, specifically for young, untenured faculty. 2010.
309-7 American Friends of Meali, Cambridge, MA, $10,000. For general support. 2010.
309-8 American India Foundation, Santa Clara, CA, $10,000. For Annual Bow Ties and Bangles Gala. 2010.
309-9 American Red Cross, Central Iowa Chapter, Des Moines, IA, $12,340. For Haiti Relief and Development. 2010.
309-10 AmeriCares, Stamford, CT, $25,000. For general support. 2010.
309-11 AmeriCares, Stamford, CT, $20,000. For general support. 2010.
309-12 Artists for a New South Africa, Los Angeles, CA, $20,000. For the challenge grant. 2010.
309-13 Boys Hope Girls Hope, Bridgeton, MO, $10,000. For Esperanza Juvenil, Guatemalan arm of Boys Hope Girls Hope. 2010.
309-14 BRAC USA, New York, NY, $11,000. For operating support for BRAC Uganda and BRAC USA. 2010.
309-15 Cambodian Childrens Fund, Santa Monica, CA, $10,000. For general support. 2010.
309-16 CARE, San Francisco, CA, $40,000. For general support. 2010.
309-17 Carr Educational Foundation, San Rafael, CA, $100,000. To build new dorm at Daraja Academy. 2010.

309-18 Carr Educational Foundation, San Rafael, CA, $20,000. For Daraja Academy. 2010.
309-19 Carr Educational Foundation, San Rafael, CA, $20,000. For scholarships at Daraja Academy. 2010.
309-20 Carr Educational Foundation, San Rafael, CA, $20,000. To find a sustainable source of water for Daraja Academy. 2010.
309-21 Carr Educational Foundation, San Rafael, CA, $19,200. For scholarships for four girls for one year in student sponsorship program at Daraja Academy. 2010.
309-22 Carr Educational Foundation, San Rafael, CA, $15,000. For Daraja Academy Scholarship Fund. 2010.
309-23 Carr Educational Foundation, San Rafael, CA, $10,000. For maintenance needs at Daraja Academy. 2010.
309-24 Catholic Relief Services, Baltimore, MD, $20,000. For general support. 2010.
309-25 Center for Art in Translation, San Francisco, CA, $150,000. For general support. 2010.
309-26 Chhandam Chitresh Das Dance Company, San Francisco, CA, $10,000. For Traditions Engaged 2010 International Indian Festival of classical Indian dance and music in contemporary contexts at Yerba Buena Center for the Arts. 2010.
309-27 ChildFund, Richmond, VA, $20,000. For general support. 2010.
309-28 Citizen Effect, Washington, DC, $10,000. For general support. 2010.
309-29 Columbia University, New York, NY, $10,800. For Institute for Medieval Japanese Studies. 2010.
309-30 Conservation International, Arlington, VA, $10,000. For general support. 2010.
309-31 Conservation Strategy Fund, Arcata, CA, $15,000. For general support. 2010.
309-32 Dance/USA, Washington, DC, $15,000. For participation of Bay Area dance artists, managers and presenters in the Internationale Tanzmesse in Dusseldorf. 2010.
309-33 Direct Relief International, Santa Barbara, CA, $20,000. For general support. 2010.
309-34 Doctors Outreach Clinics, San Francisco, CA, $10,000. For disaster relief in Haiti. 2010.
309-35 Doctors Without Borders USA, New York, NY, $40,000. For general support. 2010.
309-36 Doctors Without Borders USA, New York, NY, $25,000. For Haiti Earthquake Emergency Fund. 2010.
309-37 Doctors Without Borders USA, New York, NY, $25,000. For relief efforts in Haiti. 2010.
309-38 Doctors Without Borders USA, New York, NY, $16,873. For relief efforts in Haiti. 2010.
309-39 Doctors Without Borders USA, New York, NY, $15,000. For general support. 2010.
309-40 Doctors Without Borders USA, New York, NY, $13,750. For relief work in Haiti. 2010.
309-41 Doctors Without Borders USA, New York, NY, $11,230. For relief efforts in Haiti. 2010.
309-42 Doctors Without Borders USA, New York, NY, $10,000. For Haiti Earthquake Relief. 2010.
309-43 Doctors Without Borders USA, New York, NY, $10,000. For Haiti Relief. 2010.
309-44 Doctors Without Borders USA, New York, NY, $10,000. For relief efforts in Haiti. 2010.
309-45 Doctors Without Borders USA, New York, NY, $10,000. For relief efforts in Haiti. 2010.
309-46 Door Dog Music Productions, San Francisco, CA, $12,000. For core operating support. 2010.
309-47 East Meets West Foundation, Oakland, CA, $20,000. For Vietnam water projects. 2010.

309-48 Friends of the Earth, San Francisco, CA, $20,000. To protect human health and environment from a significant expansion of short sea shipping. 2010.
309-49 Futures Without Violence, San Francisco, CA, $12,500. For general support. 2010.
309-50 Futures Without Violence, San Francisco, CA, $10,000. For general support. 2010.
309-51 Global AIDS Interfaith Alliance, Larkspur, CA, $25,000. For general support. 2010.
309-52 Global AIDS Interfaith Alliance, Larkspur, CA, $15,000. For general support. 2010.
309-53 Global Community Monitor, El Cerrito, CA, $20,000. To prevent public health threats from industrial air pollution in urban redevelopment projects in San Francisco Bay Area and to develop model urban redevelopment policies to guide future planning. 2010.
309-54 Global Fund for Women, San Francisco, CA, $50,000. For general support. 2010.
309-55 Global Fund for Women, San Francisco, CA, $40,000. For Reclaiming Peace and Genuine Security - a Special Initiative. 2010.
309-56 Global Fund for Women, San Francisco, CA, $25,000. For general support. 2010.
309-57 Global Hunger Project, New York, NY, $20,000. For general support. 2010.
309-58 Grameen Foundation USA, Washington, DC, $835,000. 2010.
309-59 Hands Across the World, Sherborn, MA, $10,000. For general support. 2010.
309-60 Harambee Arts, San Rafael, CA, $10,000. For Harambee Arts. 2010.
309-61 Harvard University, Cambridge, MA, $200,000. For Katherine and T.R. Burke Fund for Global Health. 2010.
309-62 Human Rights Watch, San Francisco, CA, $10,000. For general support. 2010.
309-63 Initiative for Medicines, Access and Knowledge, Lewes, DE, $150,000. For general support. 2010.
309-64 Inter American Press Association, Miami, FL, $40,000. For the Chapultepec Project. 2010.
309-65 International Center for Research on Women, Washington, DC, $10,000. For unrestricted funds. 2010.
309-66 International Rescue Committee, Washington, DC, $20,000. For Haiti Earthquake Relief. 2010.
309-67 International Rescue Committee, New York, NY, $10,000. For Humanitarian Matching Grant. 2010.
309-68 J.F. Kapnek Charitable Trust, Lafayette, CA, $15,000. For general support. 2010.
309-69 Kickstart International, San Francisco, CA, $10,000. For general support. 2010.
309-70 Kids with Cameras, Salt Lake City, UT, $10,000. For Hope House. 2010.
309-71 Monterey Institute of International Studies, Monterey, CA, $25,000. For general support. 2010.
309-72 New China Education Foundation, San Francisco, CA, $31,930. For general support. 2010.
309-73 New China Education Foundation, San Francisco, CA, $14,420. For general support. 2010.
309-74 New Israel Fund, San Francisco, CA, $10,000. For general support. 2010.
309-75 Nonprofit Enterprise and Self-sustainability Team, San Francisco, CA, $10,000. For Levantando Chile Fund. 2010.
309-76 Nurturing Minds, Valley Forge, PA, $10,000. For general support. 2010.

309-77 Oxfam America, Boston, MA, $100,000. For a matching gift for Haiti relief. 2010.

309-78 Oxfam America, Boston, MA, $16,873. For relief efforts in Haiti. 2010.

309-79 Oxfam America, Boston, MA, $12,500. For Haiti Relief. 2010.

309-80 Oxfam America, Boston, MA, $11,230. For relief efforts in Haiti. 2010.

309-81 Oxfam America, Boston, MA, $10,000. For Haiti Earthquake Relief. 2010.

309-82 Oxfam America, Boston, MA, $10,000. For Haiti Earthquake Relief. 2010.

309-83 Oxfam America, Boston, MA, $10,000. For Haiti Earthquake Response Fund. 2010.

309-84 Oxfam America, Boston, MA, $10,000. For Haiti Relief. 2010.

309-85 Oxfam America, Boston, MA, $10,000. For Haiti relief effort. 2010.

309-86 Oxfam America, Boston, MA, $10,000. For relief efforts in Haiti. 2010.

309-87 Oxfam America, Boston, MA, $10,000. For relief efforts in Haiti. 2010.

309-88 Oxfam America, Boston, MA, $10,000. For relief efforts in Haiti. 2010.

309-89 Pacific Environment, San Francisco, CA, $20,000. To produce, distribute, and promote Bay Area Smart Energy 2020 report. 2010.

309-90 Partners in Health, Boston, MA, $28,750. For relief work in Haiti. 2010.

309-91 Partners in Health, Boston, MA, $25,000. For corporate-level support for Haiti Earthquake Relief campaign to match employee and Board donations. 2010.

309-92 Partners in Health, Boston, MA, $25,000. For relief efforts in Haiti. 2010.

309-93 Partners in Health, Boston, MA, $25,000. For relief efforts in Haiti. 2010.

309-94 Partners in Health, Boston, MA, $21,230. For relief efforts in Haiti. 2010.

309-95 Partners in Health, Boston, MA, $20,000. For Haiti earthquake relief. 2010.

309-96 Partners in Health, Boston, MA, $16,873. For relief efforts in Haiti. 2010.

309-97 Partners in Health, Boston, MA, $12,500. For corporate-level support for Haiti Earthquake Relief fund. 2010.

309-98 Partners in Health, Boston, MA, $10,000. For earthquake relief in Haiti. 2010.

309-99 Partners in Health, Boston, MA, $10,000. For Haiti Earthquake Relief. 2010.

309-100 Partners in Health, Boston, MA, $10,000. For Haiti Earthquake Relief Fund Stand with Haiti. 2010.

309-101 Partners in Health, Boston, MA, $10,000. For Haiti Relief. 2010.

309-102 Partners in Health, Boston, MA, $10,000. For Haitian relief efforts. 2010.

309-103 Ploughshares Fund, San Francisco, CA, $10,000. For general support. 2010.

309-104 Ploughshares Fund, San Francisco, CA, $10,000. For Mother's Day effort. 2010.

309-105 Population Action International, Washington, DC, $10,000. For general support. 2010.

309-106 Rainforest Action Network, San Francisco, CA, $25,000. For general support. 2010.

309-107 Right to Play USA, New York, NY, $100,000. For general support. 2010.

309-108 Right to Play USA, New York, NY, $25,000. For general support. 2010.

309-109 Room to Read, San Francisco, CA, $15,000. For Girl's Education Program. 2010.

309-110 Room to Read, San Francisco, CA, $10,000. For general support. 2010.

309-111 Save the Children Federation, Westport, CT, $30,000. For Guatemala Water Project. 2010.

309-112 Save the Children Federation, Westport, CT, $20,000. For Haiti Earthquake Children in Emergency Fund. 2010.

309-113 Save the Children Federation, Westport, CT, $16,873. For relief efforts in Haiti. 2010.

309-114 Seacology, Berkeley, CA, $12,500. For annual support. 2010.

309-115 Sionfonds for Haiti, Canyon, CA, $10,000. For general support of the orphanage and earthquake relief for the children. 2010.

309-116 Truman National Security Project Educational Institute, Washington, DC, $15,000. For general support. 2010.

309-117 UNICEF, New York, NY, $20,000. For Vitamin A Supplementation Program. 2010.

309-118 UNICEF, New York, NY, $15,000. For Vitamin A Supplementation Program. 2010.

309-119 United States Fund for UNICEF, Los Angeles, CA, $16,000. For general support. 2010.

309-120 United States Fund for UNICEF, Los Angeles, CA, $10,000. For Haiti Relief. 2010.

309-121 University of California San Francisco Foundation, San Francisco, CA, $200,000. For Global Health Sciences Faculty Scholars Program. 2010.

309-122 World Wildlife Fund, Washington, DC, $10,000. To further work to save Amur tigers. 2010.

309-123 Worldwide Fistula Fund, Saint Louis, MO, $15,000. For general support. 2010.

310

Sathya Sai Society of America
P.O. Box 660908
Arcadia, CA   91066-0908
Contact: Robert A. Bozzani, Treas.

Donor: Robert Baskin.
Grantmaker type: Public charity.
Financial data (yr. ended 12/31/10): Revenue, $3,781,118; assets, $214,585 (M); gifts received, $3,759,767; expenditures, $3,954,666; giving activities include $2,500 for grants, and $3,951,612 for grants to organizations outside the U.S.
Purpose and activities: Giving to organizations that provide medical assistance to Sathya Sai in India.
Fields of interest: International relief, 2004 tsunami; Medical research.
International interests: India.
Type of support: General/operating support.
Limitations: Giving limited to India. No grants to individuals.
Application information: Application form not required.
Deadline(s): None
Officers and Director:* Dr. Narendra Reddy, Pres.; Michael Goldstein,* V.P.; Robert Baskin, Secy.; Robert A. Bozzani, Treas.
EIN: 237024944

311

Saturno Foundation
c/o Wells Fargo Bank, N.A.
P.O. Box 63954, MAC A0330-011
San Francisco, CA   94163-0001
Contact: Eugene Ranghiasci

Application address: c/o Wells Fargo Bank, N.A., 420 Montgomery St., MAC No. 0101-056, San Francisco, CA 94104-1298

Established in 1957 in CA.
Donors: Joseph Saturno†; Victor Saturno.
Grantmaker type: Independent foundation.
Financial data (yr. ended 10/31/10): Assets, $10,769,486 (M); expenditures, $573,834; qualifying distributions, $471,419; giving activities include $440,000 for grants.
Purpose and activities: Grants to U.S.-based human service organizations for the benefit of Italy. Emphasis is on organizations which care for impoverished orphan children.
Fields of interest: American Red Cross; Children/youth, services.
International interests: Italy.
Limitations: Giving to national organizations for the benefit of Italy, primarily in Washington, DC, and New York, NY. No grants to individuals, or for general support, building or endowment funds, research, scholarships, fellowships, or matching gifts; no loans.
Application information:
Initial approach: Letter
Deadline(s): None
Trustee: Wells Fargo Bank, N.A.
EIN: 946073765

312

The Schmidt Family Foundation
555 Bryant St., No. 370
Palo Alto, CA   94301-1704
Contact: Sarah Bell, Prog. Mgr., 11th Hour Project
FAX: (650) 321-2103; E-mail: staff@theschmidt.org;
URL: http://www.theschmidtfamilyfoundation.org

Established in 2006 in CA.
Donors: Eric Schmidt; Wendy Schmidt.
Grantmaker type: Independent foundation.
Financial data (yr. ended 12/31/09): Assets, $168,961,799 (M); gifts received, $4,401,216; expenditures, $16,336,830; qualifying distributions, $18,232,738; giving activities include $13,913,163 for 35 grants (high: $4,800,000; low: $2,000), $2,248,243 for 3 foundation-administered programs and $2,659,451 for 3 loans/program-related investments.
Purpose and activities: The foundation supports efforts, using best expert information, to help transform the world's environmental and energy practices in the 21st century. The foundation's mission, at its broadest, is to advance the creation of an increasingly intelligent relationship between human activity and the use of the world's natural resources. The foundation works strategically, and often in collaboration, to create successful models of their vision. This includes the restoration and protection of vulnerable historic places while improving their environmental profile, using new technologies, and the growing knowledge about the impact of the built environment on the Earth's climate system. The foundation supports efforts around the world to improve health, education, transportation and communications through investing in a pattern of economic development that includes green, sustainable environmental practices and design. In addition, the foundation supports public education around issues of energy and the environment and promote public understanding of the science of climate change.
Fields of interest: Environment.

Limitations: Applications accepted. Giving primarily in CA.
Publications: Annual report; Financial statement; Grants list; IRS Form 990 or 990-PF printed copy available upon request.
Application information: Application guidelines and form available on foundation web site. Application form required.
Initial approach: Online letter of inquiry
Deadline(s): None
Officers and Directors:* Wendy Schmidt,* Pres.; Eric Schmidt,* V.P.; Sophie Schmidt,* V.P.; Joe Rose, Treas.; Jeanne W. Huey, C.F.O.
EIN: 204170342
Recent grants for international programs:
312-1 Alliance for Climate Protection, Washington, DC, $1,000,000. For education and communication on climate change. 2009.
312-2 Asia Society, New York, NY, $45,000. To produce visually striking glacier photography that illustrates immediacy of global warning and to quantify glacial recession. 2009.
312-3 Clean Economy Network Education Fund, Washington, DC, $30,000. To develop infrastructure and other startup support related to launch of clean technology/green business advocacy organization. 2009.
312-4 Climate Central, Princeton, NJ, $100,000. For general operating support to launch new group of scientists and communicators to develop honest, nonpartisan and up-to-date information to help people make sound decisions about climate and energy. 2009.
312-5 Columbia University, Center for Children's Environmental Health, New York, NY, $50,000. For longitudinal study of health risks to mothers and children from environmental pollutants generated by coal-fired power plants in China. 2009.
312-6 Energy Foundation, San Francisco, CA, $500,000. To advance clean energy technologies as means of reducing global warming and pollution in the U.S. and China. 2009.
312-7 Generation Rwanda, New York, NY, $100,000. To provide core scholarships for university students. 2009.
312-8 George Washington University, Washington, DC, $25,000. Toward Planet Forward project's PBS programming, as well as web outreach. 2009.
312-9 Golden Gate National Parks Conservancy, Institute at the Golden Gate, San Francisco, CA, $10,000. To sponsor Turning of the Tide Conference, bringing together leading voices of the environmental movement to envision a sustainable future for our world. 2009.
312-10 Natural Resources Defense Council, New York, NY, $1,000,000. Toward communications about international and domestic environmental priorities. 2009.
312-11 Permaculture Research Institute USA, Pahoa, HI, $10,000. To support campaign to bring permaculutre practices around the world to a larger audience. 2009.
312-12 Rwanda Community Works, Rwanda Works, New York, NY, $500,000. To construct new health centers in Gashora Sector in Rwanda's Bugesera District. 2009.
312-13 Sailors for the Sea, Boston, MA, $75,000. For outreach work on ocean conservation and related climate change impact. 2009.

312-14 Schmidt Research Vessel Institute, Palo Alto, CA, $4,009,163. For general support. 2009.
312-15 Tides Foundation, San Francisco, CA, $100,000. To act as fiscal sponsor for Tar Sands Project to support efforts to reduce supply of high-carbon tar sands fuels in Canada and minimize environmental degradation associated with tar sands mining. 2009.
312-16 Tides Foundation, San Francisco, CA, $25,000. To act as fiscal sponsor for Instituto Terra's Atlantic Rainforest Recovery Program in Brazil's Rio Doce Basin. 2009.
312-17 Union of Concerned Scientists, Cambridge, MA, $25,000. Toward publication of Consumer's Guide to Effective Climate Choices. 2009.

313
Sea Change Foundation
301 Battery St., Fl. 5
San Francisco, CA 94111 (415) 830-9330
URL: http://www.seachange.org
James and Marilyn Simons' Giving Pledge: http://givingpledge.org/#jim+and+marilyn+_simons

Established in 2006 in CA.
Donors: Nathaniel Simons Trust; Nathaniel Simons; Laura Simons.
Grantmaker type: Independent foundation.
Financial data (yr. ended 07/31/10): Assets, $124,496,992 (M); gifts received, $63,900,000; expenditures, $56,971,508; qualifying distributions, $56,971,508; giving activities include $54,266,549 for 66 grants (high: $3,000,000; low: $50,000).
Purpose and activities: Giving to address the serious threats posed by global warming.
Fields of interest: Environment, research; Education.
Limitations: Applications not accepted. Giving primarily in CA; Washington, DC., and NY, with some giving in AK and FL.
Application information: Contributes only to pre-selected organizations.
Officers: Nathaniel Simons, Pres.; Shawn Reifsteck, C.O.O.; Laura Baxter-Simons, Secy.; Stephen Colwell, Exec. Dir.
EIN: 204952986
Recent grants for international programs:
313-1 CERES, Boston, MA, $350,000. To educate business about climate and clean energy. 2010.
313-2 CERES, Boston, MA, $110,000. To reduce reliance on high carbon energy. 2010.
313-3 European Climate Foundation, The Hague, Netherlands, $3,000,000. To promote clean energy and energy efficiency. 2010.
313-4 Global Campaign for Climate Action, Montreal, Canada, $1,750,000. To promote awareness of climate change and reduce reliance on high carbon energy. 2010.
313-5 Global Campaign for Climate Action, Montreal, Canada, $500,000. To promote awareness of climate change and reduce reliance on high carbon energy. 2010.
313-6 U.S. Climate Action Network, Washington, DC, $500,000. To promote awareness of climate change and reduce reliance on high carbon energy. 2010.
313-7 U.S. Climate Action Network, Washington, DC, $250,000. To promote awareness of climate change and reduce reliance on high carbon energy. 2010.

313-8 Union of Concerned Scientists, Cambridge, MA, $168,000. To educate public about climate and clean energy policy. 2010.
313-9 Union of Concerned Scientists, Cambridge, MA, $122,200. To educate public about climate and clean energy policy. 2010.
313-10 World Resources Institute, Washington, DC, $825,000. For research and analysis of climate change. 2010.
313-11 World Wildlife Fund, Washington, DC, $1,500,000. To promote awareness of climate change and reduce reliance on high carbon energy. 2010.

314
Seacology
1623 Solano Ave.
Berkeley, CA 94707-2406 (510) 559-3505
Contact: Susan Racanelli, Devel. Dir.
FAX: (510) 559-3506;
E-mail: islands@seacology.org; URL: http://www.seacology.org

Established in 1992 in UT; relocated to CA in 1999.
Grantmaker type: Public charity.
Financial data (yr. ended 12/31/10): Revenue, $1,278,498; assets, $3,005,510 (M); gifts received, $1,262,354; expenditures, $1,456,992; giving activities include $15,498 for grants, $493,953 for grants to organizations outside the U.S., and $21,997 for grants to individuals.
Purpose and activities: The organization aims to preserve the highly endangered biodiversity of islands throughout the world.
Fields of interest: Environment, beautification programs; Environment, natural resources; Environment, water resources; Environment, land resources; Environment, forests; Indigenous peoples.
International interests: Tanzania, Zanzibar and Pemba, Sri Lanka, Seychelles; Maldives; Madagascar; India; Papua New Guinea; Indonesia; Malaysia; Philippines; Vietnam; China; Southeast Asia; Marshall Islands; Palau; Federated States of Micronesia; Vanuatu; Solomon Islands; Fiji; Samoa; Oceania.
Type of support: Building/renovation; Equipment; Grants to individuals; Income development; Scholarships—to individuals; Seed money; Technical assistance.
Limitations: Applications not accepted. Giving on a national and international basis.
Publications: Annual report; Newsletter.
Application information: Unsolicited requests for funds not accepted.
Board meeting date(s): Jan., June, and Oct.
Officers and Directors:* Paul Alan Cox,* Chair.; Ken Murdock,* Pres.; Shari Sant Plummer,* V.P.; Sandie Tillotson,* V.P.; Paul Felton,* Treas.; Donald M. Arntz; Larry Barels; Michael Burbank; Kimo Campbell; Scott S. Halsted; Douglas Herst; Masayuki Kishinoyo; Cathy Klema; Matsumo Kuhara Patrick; Peter Pistor; Gordon Radley; James Sandler; Michael Staffieri; Cindy Troop; Eric van Boer; Jake Walker; Marsha Gares Williams.
Number of staff: 6 full-time professional; 2 part-time support.
EIN: 870495235

315
Sempra Energy Corporate Giving Program
c/o Corp. Community Rels. Dept.
101 Ash St.
San Diego, CA 92101-3017 (877) 736-7729
Contact: Molly Cartmill, Dir., Corp. Community Rels.
E-mail: gifts@sempra.com; Additional tel.: (877)
SEMPRA9; FAX: (619) 696-1868; E-mail:
sempracommunity@sempra.com; URL: http://
sempra.com/corporateresponsibility/

Grantmaker type: Corporate giving program.
Purpose and activities: As a complement to its
foundation, Sempra Energy makes charitable
contributions to nonprofit organizations involved
with arts and culture, education, the environment,
health and human services, community
development, and civic affairs. Support is given on
a national and international basis.
Fields of interest: Arts; Education; Environment;
Health care; Human services; Economic
development; Business/industry; Community/
economic development; Public affairs.
International interests: Canada; Mexico; South
America.
Type of support: Annual campaigns; Program
development; Conferences/seminars;
Cause-related marketing; Employee volunteer
services; Public relations services; Sponsorships;
Employee matching gifts; Employee-related
scholarships.
Limitations: Applications accepted. Giving in areas
of company operations, on a national and
international basis, with emphasis on central and
southern CA, including Inland Empire, Los Angeles,
San Diego, and Orange County, and in Canada,
Mexico, and South America. No support for private
foundations, pass-through organizations,
discriminatory organizations, sectarian or
denominational organizations not of direct benefit to
the entire community, sports teams or groups not
available to the general public, political parties or
candidates or partisan political organizations, or
non-educational government organizations. No
grants to individuals (except for employee-related
scholarships), or for general operating support,
travel, debt reduction, liquidation, continuing
support, advertising, or sports programs or events
not available to the general public; no gas or electric
service discounts.
Publications: Application guidelines; Informational
brochure (including application guidelines); Program
policy statement.
Application information: The Corporate Community
Relations Department handles giving. The company
has a staff that only handles contributions. A
contributions committee reviews all requests.
Application form not required.
  Initial approach: Proposal to headquarters
  Copies of proposal: 1
  Deadline(s): None
  Final notification: 8 to 10 weeks
Administrators: Molly Cartmill, Dir., Corp.
Community Rels.; David Jay, Mgr.; Cathy Lavin, Mgr.
Number of staff: 2 full-time professional; 3 full-time
support.

316
Seva Foundation
1786 5th St.
Berkeley, CA 94710-1716 (510) 845-7382
Contact: Mark Lancaster, Exec. Dir.

FAX: (510) 845-7410; E-mail: admin@seva.org;
URL: http://www.seva.org/
Twitter: http://twitter.com/Seva_Foundation
YouTube: http://youtube.com/user/
SevaFoundation

Founded in 1978.
Grantmaker type: Public charity.
Financial data (yr. ended 06/30/11): Revenue,
$3,027,352; assets, $3,515,121 (M); gifts
received, $2,833,357; expenditures, $2,896,013;
giving activities include $30,000 for grants, and
$249,488 for grants to organizations outside the
U.S.
Purpose and activities: The foundation works to
prevent and relieve suffering, and to generate hope
through compassionate action, by serving
partnerships and projects around the world that
promote health, nutrition, education, economic
sustainability, environmental protection, cultural
survival, human dignity, and social and economic
justice.
Fields of interest: Education; Health care; Eye
diseases; Diabetes; Nutrition; International relief;
Civil/human rights, advocacy; Economic
development; Blind/visually impaired; Native
Americans/American Indians.
Limitations: Applications not accepted. Giving
primarily on an international basis; giving also in
support of Native American projects across the U.S.
Publications: Annual report; Financial statement.
Application information: Contributes only to
pre-selected organizations.
Officers and Directors:* Gary Hahn,* Chair.; Steve
Miller,* M.D., Chair.-Elect and Treas.; Jahanara
Romney,* Secy.; Mark Lancaster,* Exec. Dir.;
Michael E. Bird, M.P.H.; Jonathan Brilliant; Wavy
Gravy; David Green, M.P.H.; T. Stephen Jones, M.D.;
Lisa M. Laird, C.S.A.; Michael Lemle; Leslie Louie,
M.P.H., Ph.D.; Michael Maurer; Pamela Siliato;
Martin Spencer, M.D., FRCSC; Dr. M. Srinivasan,
MBBS, DO, MS; Ken Wilson, Ph.D.; Dr. Mariano Yee,
M.D.
EIN: 382231279

317
Seventh Generation Fund
(also known as Seventh Generation Fund for Indian
Development, Inc.)
P.O. Box 4569
Arcata, CA 95518-4569 (707) 825-7640
Contact: Tia Oros Peters, Exec. Dir.
FAX: (707) 825-7639; E-mail: of7gen@pacbell.net;
Mailing Address : 425 I Street, Arcata, CA
95521E-Mail for Tia Oros Peters : tia@7genfund.org;
URL: http://www.7genfund.org

Established in 1984 in CA.
Donors: America's Charities; Chumash Casino and
Resort; Community Resource Alliance; Corporation
of the Fine Arts Museums; Flowering Tree
Permaculture; Fund for Santa Barbara, Inc.; Grant
Distributing; Grousbeck Family Foundation;
Hampshire Group Limited; Humboldt Area
Foundation.
Grantmaker type: Public charity.
Financial data (yr. ended 06/30/10): Revenue,
$1,377,286; assets, $866,015 (M); gifts received,
$1,340,484; expenditures, $1,473,819; program
services expenses, $1,146,079; giving activities
include $285,526 for 6 grants (high: $32,430; low:
$6,500), and $7,627 for grants to organizations
outside the U.S.

Purpose and activities: The fund is a national Native
American advocacy and intermediary grantmaking
organization dedicated to maintaining and
promoting the uniqueness of Native peoples and the
distinctiveness of their nations.
Fields of interest: Environment, natural resources;
Environment; Religion; Native Americans/American
Indians.
International interests: Canada; Central America;
South America.
Type of support: General/operating support;
Continuing support; Annual campaigns; Building/
renovation; Equipment; Emergency funds; Program
development; Conferences/seminars; Publication;
Seed money; Technical assistance.
Limitations: Applications accepted. Giving limited to
U.S., Canada, and Central and South America.
Publications: Annual report (including application
guidelines); Occasional report.
Application information: See web site for
application guidelines and cover sheet. Application
form not required.
  Initial approach: Letter or telephone
  Copies of proposal: 1
  Deadline(s): None
  Board meeting date(s): Varies
Officers and Directors:* Rosalie Little Thunder,*
Chair.; Tonya Gonnella Frichner, Vice-Chair.;
Christopher Peters, Pres. and C.E.O.; Susana
Geliga, Secy.; Arthur Manuel, Treas.; Tia Oros
Peters,* Exec. Dir.; Tupac Enrique-Acosta; Oren
Lyons; Luis Macas, M.D.; Henrietta Mann, M.D.; Ray
Williams.
Number of staff: 2 full-time professional; 2 part-time
professional; 1 full-time support; 2 part-time
support.
EIN: 680027247

318
David and Fela Shapell Family Foundation
(formerly David and Fela Shapell Foundation)
9401 Wilshire Blvd., Ste. 1200
Beverly Hills, CA 90212-2926

Established in 1967.
Donors: David Shapell; Fela Shapell; David Shapell
2009 Charitable Lead Trust; Fela Shapell 2009
Charitable Lead Trust.
Grantmaker type: Independent foundation.
Financial data (yr. ended 12/31/10): Assets,
$4,482,940 (M); gifts received, $3,791,460;
expenditures, $4,859,856; qualifying distributions,
$4,738,503; giving activities include $4,698,980
for grants.
Purpose and activities: Giving primarily for higher
education and Jewish temple support.
Fields of interest: Higher education; Hospitals
(general); Health organizations, association; Jewish
agencies & synagogues.
International interests: Israel.
Limitations: Applications not accepted. Giving
primarily in CA; some giving also in NY. No grants to
individuals.
Application information: Contributes only to
pre-selected organizations.
Officers: Rochelle Shapell, C.E.O.; David Shapell,
V.P.; Benjamin Shapell, Secy.; Irvin N. Shapell,
C.F.O.
EIN: 956187271

319
Benjamin and Susan Shapell Foundation, Inc.

9401 Wilshire Blvd., Ste. 1200
Beverly Hills, CA 90212-2926

Established in 1997 in CA.
Donor: The David and Fela Shapell Lead Unitrust.
Grantmaker type: Independent foundation.
Financial data (yr. ended 12/31/10): Assets, $1,857,209 (M); gifts received, $45,000; expenditures, $168,109; qualifying distributions, $166,725; giving activities include $166,725 for grants.
Purpose and activities: Giving primarily for Jewish organizations.
Fields of interest: Libraries (public); Jewish agencies & synagogues.
International interests: Israel.
Limitations: Applications not accepted. Giving primarily in NY; some giving also in Israel. No grants to individuals.
Application information: Contributes only to pre-selected organizations.
Officers: Benjamin Shapell, Pres.; Susan Shapell, Secy.-Treas.
EIN: 954653430

320
The Thomas and Stacey Siebel Foundation

P.O. Box 240
Palo Alto, CA 94302-0240 (650) 752-1000
Contact: Thomas M. Siebel, Pres.

Established in 1996 in CA.
Donors: Stacey Siebel; Thomas M. Siebel.
Grantmaker type: Independent foundation.
Financial data (yr. ended 12/31/09): Assets, $212,482,497 (M); expenditures, $22,109,288; qualifying distributions, $20,231,708; giving activities include $19,182,274 for 62 grants (high: $2,080,000; low: $160).
Purpose and activities: Giving primarily to the Salvation Arm as well as for land conservation and children's scholarships and services.
Fields of interest: Higher education, university; Education, single organization support; Elementary/secondary education; Environment, land resources; Salvation Army; Children, services; Homeless, human services.
Limitations: Applications not accepted. Giving primarily in CA, with some giving in MA, MD and NY.
Application information: Contributes only to pre-selected organizations.
Officers: Thomas M. Siebel, Pres.; Stacey Siebel, Secy.; Nitsa Zuppas, Exec. Dir.
EIN: 943256331
Recent grants for international programs:
320-1 Childrens Shelter of Hope Foundation, Wauconda, IL, $20,000. To provide food, shelter and medical supplies to needy children in Puerto Vallarta, Mexico area. 2009.
320-2 Eagles on Assignment, Children of the Dump, Enumclaw, WA, $20,000. For general support. 2009.
320-3 Princeton University, Princeton, NJ, $1,000,000. For Siebel Energy Grand Challenge project within Princeton Grand Challenges Initiative. Energy Challenge confronts climate change, management of fossil-fuel carbon, expansion of non-fossil energy sources and other environmental impacts of the energy system. 2009.

320-4 Tsinghua University, Beijing, China, $2,000,000. To establish Siebel Scholars Program. 2009.

321
The Sikand Foundation, Inc.

15230 Burbank Blvd.
Van Nuys, CA 91411-3534

Established in 1986 in CA.
Donor: Gunjit S. Sikand.
Grantmaker type: Operating foundation.
Financial data (yr. ended 11/30/10): Assets, $5,045,825 (M); gifts received, $625,000; expenditures, $407,356; qualifying distributions, $136,675; giving activities include $136,675 for 84 grants (high: $15,000; low: $50).
Purpose and activities: Giving primarily for education and health.
Fields of interest: Education; Medical school/education; Health organizations; United Ways and Federated Giving Programs.
International interests: India.
Type of support: General/operating support.
Limitations: Applications not accepted. Giving primarily in CA. No grants to individuals.
Application information: Contributes only to pre-selected organizations.
Officers: Gunjit S. Sikand, Pres.; Annette C. Sikand, Secy.
EIN: 954109267

322
The Stephen M. Silberstein Foundation

c/o Stephen M. Silberstein
29 Eucalyptus Rd.
Belvedere, CA 94920-2435 (415) 435-1692

Established in 1997 in CA.
Donor: Stephen M. Silberstein.
Grantmaker type: Independent foundation.
Financial data (yr. ended 12/31/09): Assets, $81,422,060 (M); gifts received, $148,671; expenditures, $4,401,777; qualifying distributions, $4,327,175; giving activities include $4,327,175 for 51 grants (high: $500,000; low: $1,000).
Fields of interest: Education; Civil/human rights; Public affairs, equal rights.
Type of support: General/operating support.
Limitations: Applications not accepted. Giving primarily in CA, some funding also in Washington, DC and NY. No grants to individuals.
Application information: Contributes only to pre-selected organizations.
Officers: Stephen M. Silberstein, Pres. and Treas.; Paul Silberstein, Secy.
EIN: 911852739
Recent grants for international programs:
322-1 Amazon Watch, San Francisco, CA, $10,000. To protect rainforest and advance rights of indigenous people of Amazon Basin. 2009.
322-2 Amnesty International USA, New York, NY, $300,000. To defend and preserve individual rights and liberties. 2009.
322-3 Asia Society, New York, NY, $10,000. To bring awareness to recession of Himalayan glaciers. 2009.
322-4 Human Rights Watch, New York, NY, $500,000. To defend and preserve individual rights and liberties. 2009.

322-5 J Street Education Fund, Washington, DC, $15,000. To raise awareness for a two-state solution to the Israeli-Palestinian conflict. 2009.
322-6 Worldwatch Institute, Washington, DC, $10,000. To build an ecologically sustainable society. 2009.

323
Silicon Valley Community Foundation

2440 West El Camino Real, Ste. 300
Mountain View, CA 94040-1498
(650) 450-5400
Contact: Vera Bennett, C.F.O.
FAX: (650) 450-5401;
E-mail: info@siliconvalleycf.org; Additional E-mail: vlbennett@siliconvalleycf.org; Grant inquiry E-mail: grants@siliconvalleycf.org; Grant application E-mail: grantproposals@siliconvalleycf.org; URL: http://www.siliconvalleycf.org/
E-Newsletter: http://www.siliconvalleycf.org/news-resources/enewsletters.html
Facebook: http://www.facebook.com/pages/Silicon-Valley-Community-Foundation/89110242053
LinkedIn: http://www.linkedin.com/companies/silicon valley community foundation
Silicon Valley Community Foundation's Philanthropy Promise: http://www.ncrp.org/philanthropys-promise/who
Twitter: http://twitter.com/siliconvalleycf
Vimeo: http://vimeo.oom/0174001
YouTube: http://www.youtube.com/TheSVCF

Established in 2007 in CA.
Grantmaker type: Community foundation.
Financial data (yr. ended 12/31/09): Assets, $1,749,109,000 (M); gifts received, $237,591,000; expenditures, $181,515,000; giving activities include $153,533,000 for grants, and $722,000 for 304 grants to individuals.
Purpose and activities: The mission of the foundation is to strengthen the common good, improve quality of life and address the most challenging problems of the community. The foundation's endowment grantmaking strategies are focused on five key areas: Economic Security, Education, Immigrant Integration, Regional Planning, and Community Opportunity Fund.
Fields of interest: Education; Human services; Economic development; Community/economic development; Public affairs; Youth; Immigrants/refugees; Homeless; Economically disadvantaged; Children/youth; Adults.
Type of support: Mission-related investments/loans; General/operating support; Continuing support; Management development/capacity building; Program development; Conferences/seminars; Seed money; Scholarship funds; Scholarships—to individuals.
Limitations: Applications accepted. Giving of endowment grants are restricted to programs, services, and efforts that benefit the San Mateo and Santa Clara counties in CA. No support for religious purposes or private non-operating foundations.
Publications: Application guidelines; Annual report; Financial statement; Grants list; Informational brochure; Newsletter; Occasional report.
Application information: Visit foundation web site for request for proposal forms (which includes application), guidelines, and deadlines per grant type. Application form required.
Initial approach: Attend an information session, request for proposal

Deadline(s): Varies, see web site for requests for proposals specific deadline dates

Board meeting date(s): Mar., June, Oct., and Dec.

Final notification: Within 6 to 12 weeks

Officers and Directors: * John M. Sobrato,* Chair.; Thomas J. Friel,* Vice-Chair.; Emmett D. Carson, Ph.D., C.E.O. and Pres.; Leigh Stilwell, Sr. V.P., Donor Experience and Engagement; John Stuckey, Sr. V.P., Finance; Don Aguilar, V.P., Human Resources; Bert Feuss, V.P., Investments; Oris Miller, V.P., Information Svcs.; Rebecca Salner, V.P., Mktg. and Comms.; Michelle Sklar, V.P., Devel. and Business Svcs.; Erica Wood, V.P., Community Leadership and Grantmaking; Mari Ellen Reynolds Loijens, Chief of Philanthropic Devel. and Information; Vera Bennett, C.F.A.O.; Sarah Valencia, Cont.; Jane Battey; Gloria Brown; Caretha Coleman; Gregory M. Gallo; Narendra Gupta; Nancy H. Handel; Susan M. Hyatt; Samuel Johnson, Jr.; William S. Johnson; Robert A. Keller; Anne F. Macdonald; Ivonne Montes de Oca; C.S. Park; Eduardo Rallo; Sanjay Vaswani; Richard Wilkolaski; Erika Williams; Gordon Yamate.

Number of staff: 81 full-time professional; 5 part-time professional; 7 full-time support.

EIN: 205205488

Recent grants for international programs:

323-1 Aalto University School of Science of Technology, Espoo, Finland, $84,000. For research proposal entitled: Understanding and Reporting on IPTV Behavior. 2010.

323-2 ACCION New York, New York, NY, $100,000. For Fundacion Paraguaya. 2010.

323-3 Acumen Fund, New York, NY, $34,000. For general support. 2010.

323-4 Acumen Fund, New York, NY, $10,000. For general support. 2010.

323-5 African Leadership Foundation, New York, NY, $100,000. For general support. 2010.

323-6 American Assistance for Cambodia, Tokyo, Japan, $25,000. For various programs previously discussed for two schools in Cambodia: Sophia Noelle Carson School and Clay Alexander Carson School, No. 454 and No. 455. 2010.

323-7 American Associates, Ben-Gurion University of the Negev, Corte Madera, CA, $700,000. To create a $1 Million Endowment Fund. 2010.

323-8 American Himalayan Foundation, San Francisco, CA, $47,250. For various projects. 2010.

323-9 American Himalayan Foundation, San Francisco, CA, $10,000. For general support. 2010.

323-10 American India Foundation, New York, NY, $30,000. For Digital Equalizer Program. 2010.

323-11 American India Foundation, New York, NY, $25,000. For general support. 2010.

323-12 American Ireland Fund, Los Altos, CA, $19,416. For Camara Education, specifically in support of the Africa Headquarters. 2010.

323-13 American Israel Education Foundation, Washington, DC, $500,000. For educational trips to Israel. 2010.

323-14 American Jewish World Service, New York, NY, $200,000. For Haiti Earthquake Relief Fund. 2010.

323-15 American Jewish World Service, New York, NY, $100,000. For general support. 2010.

323-16 American Jewish World Service, New York, NY, $10,000. For Haiti Earthquake Relief. 2010.

323-17 American Jewish World Service, New York, NY, $10,000. For Haiti Earthquake Relief Fund. 2010.

323-18 American Red Cross, San Jose, CA, $30,000. For employee matching donations to Red Cross for Haiti. 2010.

323-19 American Red Cross, Greater Chicago Chapter, Chicago, IL, $100,000. For Haiti Relief and Development. 2010.

323-20 American Red Cross, Greater Chicago Chapter, Chicago, IL, $25,000. For disaster relief for Yushu China Earthquake. 2010.

323-21 American Red Cross, Greater Chicago Chapter, Chicago, IL, $25,000. For infrastructure support for Haiti Earthquake Relief. 2010.

323-22 American Red Cross, Greater Chicago Chapter, Chicago, IL, $25,000. To support Haiti Earthquake Relief Efforts. 2010.

323-23 American Red Cross, Greater Chicago Chapter, Chicago, IL, $25,000. For disaster relief for the Pakistan Flooding. 2010.

323-24 American Red Cross, Greater Chicago Chapter, Chicago, IL, $10,495. For Haiti Relief Infrastructure support as matching gift. 2010.

323-25 American Red Cross, Greater Chicago Chapter, Chicago, IL, $10,000. For relief efforts in Haiti to help victims of the recent earthquake. 2010.

323-26 American Red Cross, Greater Chicago Chapter, Chicago, IL, $10,000. For general support of International Response Fund in honor of Haiti earthquake victims. 2010.

323-27 American Red Cross, Greater Chicago Chapter, Chicago, IL, $10,000. For Haiti Relief. 2010.

323-28 American Red Cross, Greater Chicago Chapter, Chicago, IL, $10,000. For Haiti relief for International Response Fund. 2010.

323-29 American Red Cross, Greater Chicago Chapter, Chicago, IL, $10,000. For relief and recovery in Haiti. 2010.

323-30 American Red Cross, Greater Chicago Chapter, Chicago, IL, $10,000. For relief of January 2010 earthquake damage in Haiti. 2010.

323-31 American Red Cross, Greater Chicago Chapter, Chicago, IL, $10,000. For general support of the International Response Fund in honor of Pakistan flood victims. 2010.

323-32 American Red Cross, Santa Clara Valley Chapter, San Jose, CA, $35,000. For relief and recovery efforts in Haiti. 2010.

323-33 American Red Cross, Bay Area Chapter, Bay Area Chapter, San Francisco, CA, $10,000. To provide aid to Haiti. 2010.

323-34 American Society for Technion-Israel Institute of Technology, San Francisco, CA, $10,000. For research in Wind Turbine. 2010.

323-35 APLBA, Sao Paulo, Brazil, $150,785. For INPE to work with PSI to further co-develop and test PSI's Forestry Skin in the Amazon, SE Asia and in Africa for broad public benefit. 2010.

323-36 Architecture for Humanity, San Francisco, CA, $50,000. For Haiti rebuilding project. 2010.

323-37 Ashoka: Innovators for the Public, Arlington, VA, $1,500,000. For core support and Collaborative Action and Tropical Forests Initiative. 2010.

323-38 Ashoka: Innovators for the Public, Arlington, VA, $26,000. For general support and Imam Blbars' Arab World Program. 2010.

323-39 Ashoka: Innovators for the Public, Arlington, VA, $25,000. For general operating support. 2010.

323-40 Asia Foundation, San Francisco, CA, $10,000. For general support. 2010.

323-41 Asia Society Northern California, San Francisco, CA, $25,000. For general support. 2010.

323-42 Asia Society Northern California, San Francisco, CA, $25,000. For general support. 2010.

323-43 Association for Computing Machinery, New York, NY, $12,000. For ACM SIGCOMM 2010, held in New Delhi, India. 2010.

323-44 Association for Indias Development, College Park, MD, $24,959. For JSS Phulwari Program - Bay Area Chapter. 2010.

323-45 Australian Indigenous Education Foundation, Edgecliff, Australia, $25,000. For a technology platform for AIEF scholarship students. 2010.

323-46 AVINA Americas, Washington, DC, $90,000. For Global Social Competitiveness Index. 2010.

323-47 Bay Area Environmental Research Institute, Sonoma, CA, $233,884. For Planetary Skin Institute. 2010.

323-48 Bay Area Environmental Research Institute, Sonoma, CA, $100,649. For the Planetary Skin Institute. 2010.

323-49 Better World Fund, Washington, DC, $1,500,000. For The Elders, group of world leaders and activists who have united to collectively contribute their wisdom and leadership to tackling some of the world's toughest issues, including the crisis in Darfur. 2010.

323-50 Better World Fund, Washington, DC, $212,520. For The Elders. 2010.

323-51 Black Dog Institute, Randwick, Australia, $15,000. For development of teaching and learning resource. 2010.

323-52 Blue Metropolis Foundation, Montreal, Canada, $25,000. For educational programs. 2010.

323-53 Blue Planet Run Foundation, Redwood City, CA, $40,000. For Where There's A Well, There's A Way: Phase 2. 2010.

323-54 BRAC USA, New York, NY, $200,000. For Pakistan Disaster Relief. 2010.

323-55 BRAC USA, New York, NY, $10,000. For general support. 2010.

323-56 Brookings Institution, Washington, DC, $25,000. For the Foreign Policy Leadership Council. 2010.

323-57 Business Executives for National Security, Washington, DC, $15,000. For general support. 2010.

323-58 Business Executives for National Security, Washington, DC, $10,000. For general support. 2010.

323-59 California Academy of Sciences, San Francisco, CA, $40,000. For Madagascar Fund, support for one Malagasy student for doctoral training at University of Antananarivo, Madagascar. 2010.

323-60 California State University at Fresno Foundation, Fresno, CA, $24,000. For Professorship of International Business. 2010.

323-61 Cambodian Childrens Fund, Santa Monica, CA, $20,000. For general support. 2010.

323-62 Camfed USA Foundation, San Francisco, CA, $150,000. For general support. 2010.

323-63 CARE USA, Atlanta, GA, $38,500. For general support, and is available as part of the board matching grant program. 2010.

323-64 Carolina for Kibera, Chapel Hill, NC, $10,000. For general support. 2010.

323-65 Carter Center, Atlanta, GA, $75,000. For general support. 2010.

323-66 Catalyst Foundation, Redwood City, CA, $30,000. For general support. 2010.

323-67 Catholic Relief Services, Baltimore, MD, $85,000. To support Haiti Earthquake Relief Efforts. 2010.

323-68 Catholic Relief Services, Baltimore, MD, $25,000. For Haiti Earthquake Relief - support for continuing efforts to provide life-preserving services such as water, food, sanitation to Haitian residents in Port-au-Prince and environs. 2010.

323-69 Catholic Relief Services, Baltimore, MD, $10,000. For relief efforts in Haiti. 2010.

323-70 Catholic Relief Services, Baltimore, MD, $10,000. For support for Catholic Relief Services' programs to rebuild Haiti's schools and hospitals after the earthquake. 2010.

323-71 Center for Justice and Accountability, San Francisco, CA, $20,000. For social support and legal services for U.S.-based Cambodian diaspora survivors of the Khmer Rouge regime. 2010.

323-72 Center for Strategic and International Studies, Washington, DC, $250,000. For general support. 2010.

323-73 Centers for Social Responsibility, Montpelier, VT, $40,000. For Rwanda Knits-Ingenzi Knit Union Sustainability Project. 2010.

323-74 Central Asia Institute, Bozeman, MT, $10,000. For advancement of educational development. 2010.

323-75 Charitable Care Foundation, Gilroy, CA, $18,500. For work of Nividya Trust's education programs and schools. 2010.

323-76 China Youth Development Foundation, Beijing, China, $20,000. For the Center for Project Hope Teacher Training Program. 2010.

323-77 Chinese University of Hong Kong Foundation, Boston, MA, $80,000. For research proposal entitled: Two Problems in Network Coding. 2010.

323-78 Chinese University of Hong Kong Foundation, Boston, MA, $77,000. For research entitled: Physical Defect Test for NTF with Minimized Test Efforts. 2010.

323-79 Climate Group, New York, NY, $350,000. For Planetary Skin Institute. 2010.

323-80 Committee of 100, New York, NY, $50,000. For general support. 2010.

323-81 Committee of 100, New York, NY, $25,000. For Chinese in America Exhibit for USA Pavilion at 2010 World Expo in Shanghai. 2010.

323-82 Community Foundation of Ottawa, Ottawa, Canada, $1,142,400. For work of Seven Churches and Charitable Works, nonprofit organization based in Quebec. 2010.

323-83 Conservation International, Arlington, VA, $250,000. For general operating support. 2010.

323-84 Conservation International, Arlington, VA, $95,000. For Greater Mekong Program. 2010.

323-85 Conservation International, Arlington, VA, $50,000. For conservation work related to climate change. 2010.

323-86 Conservation Through Poverty Alleviation International, Lincoln, MA, $10,000. For upkeep and maintenance of silk worm/moth harvesting project in Maroansetra, Madagascar; to help establish new silk moth growing projects in nearby areas such as Ambodivoangy, Madagascar; and to help develop silk moth products that can be sold in Madagascar and internationally. 2010.

323-87 Craighead Institute, Bozeman, MT, $20,000. For Traditional Community Center construction projects in Aceh Region. 2010.

323-88 Craighead Institute, Bozeman, MT, $20,000. For Aceh Leuser Community Centers. 2010.

323-89 CREATE-NET, Trento, Italy, $80,000. For research proposal entitled: Dynamic Mesh Protection/Restoration (Protectoration) in Impairment and 3R Regenerator Aware GMPLS-Based WDM Optical Networks. 2010.

323-90 Creating Hope International, Dearborn, MI, $50,000. To support Afghan Institute of Learning. 2010.

323-91 Creating Hope International, Dearborn, MI, $10,000. For Afghan Institute of Learning. 2010.

323-92 Cross International Catholic Outreach, Boca Raton, FL, $10,000. For Haiti Disaster Fund. 2010.

323-93 Cross International Catholic Outreach, Boca Raton, FL, $10,000. For additional Haiti Relief. 2010.

323-94 D-REV: Design for the Other 90%, Palo Alto, CA, $100,000. For general support. 2010.

323-95 D-REV: Design for the Other 90%, Palo Alto, CA, $50,000. For general support. 2010.

323-96 D-REV: Design for the Other 90%, Palo Alto, CA, $50,000. To set up challenge grant as determined by the CEO. 2010.

323-97 D-REV: Design for the Other 90%, Palo Alto, CA, $10,000. For Founders contribution. 2010.

323-98 Dian Fossey Gorilla Fund International, Atlanta, GA, $140,000. For preservation and protection of world's remaining population of mountain gorillas in Rwanda and the Democratic Republic of Congo. 2010.

323-99 Direct Relief International, Santa Barbara, CA, $10,000. For Haiti earthquake victims and relief efforts in Haiti. 2010.

323-100 Doctors Without Borders USA, New York, NY, $300,000. For relief efforts in Haiti as result of earthquake in January 2010. 2010.

323-101 Doctors Without Borders USA, New York, NY, $85,000. To support Haiti Earthquake Relief Efforts. 2010.

323-102 Doctors Without Borders USA, New York, NY, $50,000. For efforts to provide medical assistance to those in need around the world. 2010.

323-103 Doctors Without Borders USA, New York, NY, $50,000. For efforts to provide medical assistance to those in need around the world. 2010.

323-104 Doctors Without Borders USA, New York, NY, $25,000. For general support. 2010.

323-105 Doctors Without Borders USA, New York, NY, $25,000. For Haiti Earthquake Relief. 2010.

323-106 Doctors Without Borders USA, New York, NY, $25,000. For general support. 2010.

323-107 Doctors Without Borders USA, New York, NY, $11,971. 2010.

323-108 Doctors Without Borders USA, New York, NY, $10,000. For general support. 2010.

323-109 Doctors Without Borders USA, New York, NY, $10,000. For Pakistan Flooding Employee Match. 2010.

323-110 Down Syndrome NSW, Harris Park, Australia, $20,000. For the Technology Access Project. 2010.

323-111 Dream A Dream, Bangalore, India, $20,000. For life skill building in India. 2010.

323-112 Dream School Foundation, Bangalore, India, $21,267. For the Holistic School Development Program Phase II. 2010.

323-113 Dublin Simon Community, Dublin, Ireland, $10,000. For Literacy Programs and GED Certification. 2010.

323-114 Earth Island Institute, Berkeley, CA, $150,000. For Sacred Land Film Project. 2010.

323-115 Earth Island Institute, Berkeley, CA, $10,000. For matching grant and general support. 2010.

323-116 Edify, San Diego, CA, $30,000. For matching grant fund for Starfish School. 2010.

323-117 Empower Dalit Women of Nepal, North Waltham, MA, $10,000. For general support. 2010.

323-118 Encounter, New York, NY, $25,000. For general support. 2010.

323-119 Engineers Without Borders San Francisco Professionals, San Francisco, CA, $50,000. For High Impact Grant Program. 2010.

323-120 Eyebeam, New York, NY, $10,000. For Eve Sibley's sustainable gardening project in India. 2010.

323-121 FACE AIDS, Palo Alto, CA, $50,000. To support Global Health Corps. 2010.

323-122 FACE AIDS, Palo Alto, CA, $40,000. For FACE AIDS youth leadership development activities in the U.S. 2010.

323-123 FACE AIDS, Palo Alto, CA, $15,000. For general support. 2010.

323-124 FACE AIDS, Palo Alto, CA, $10,000. For general support. 2010.

323-125 Feed the Hungry San Miguel, Laredo, TX, $35,000. For operating costs for kitchen, that feeds over 350 poor school children in Las Clavellinas, a town outside San Miguel de Allende, Mexico and pay for funds to continue gardening program. 2010.

323-126 Fonkoze USA, Washington, DC, $35,000. For Haiti Earthquake Relief - support for microfinance activities will boost grassroots economic activity and help improve the livelihoods and long-term financial well-being of Haitians living in rural areas. 2010.

323-127 Forest Trends Association, Washington, DC, $300,000. For REDD tracking. 2010.

323-128 Foundation for Worldwide Mercy and Sharing, Aspen, CO, $20,000. For organization's work associated with John Branchizio School project in Haiti. 2010.

323-129 Fraunhofer-Gesellschaft, Berlin, Germany, $50,000. For research at Fraunhofer FOKUS. 2010.

323-130 Free the Children USA, Hartford, CT, $750,000. For core support. 2010.

323-131 Free the Children USA, Hartford, CT, $150,000. For core support. 2010.

323-132 Free the Children USA, Hartford, CT, $17,500. To fund building of library for San Miguel community in Ecuador. 2010.

323-133 Free the Children USA, Hartford, CT, $10,000. For Take Action Academy. 2010.

323-134 Freiburger Munsterbauverein e.V., Freiburg, Germany, $20,000. For the Freiburg Cathedral (Muenster) Restoration. 2010.

323-135 Friends of Burma, Fort Wayne, IN, $10,000. For EXODUS in India, for support of education and career counseling. 2010.

323-136 Friends of Via, Pittsburgh, PA, $12,000. For community development. 2010.

323-137 Friends Without A Border, New York, NY, $14,411. For Clean Water and Literacy Project. 2010.

323-138 Friends-International, Phnom Penh, Cambodia, $1,033,560. For core support. 2010.

323-139 Friends-International, Phnom Penh, Cambodia, $150,000. For core support. 2010.

323-140 Fundacion Escuela Nueva, Bogota, Colombia, $250,000. For core support. 2010.

323-141 Fundacion Escuela Nueva, Bogota, Colombia, $150,000. For core support. 2010.

323-142 Galapagos Conservancy, Fairfax, VA, $25,000. For general support. 2010.

323-143 Geohazards International, Palo Alto, CA, $10,000. For general support. 2010.

323-144 Give Foundation, Ladera Ranch, CA, $26,935. For Dream A Dream (India) for the Dream Sports Program (Football and Rugby). 2010.

323-145 Give2Asia, San Francisco, CA, $50,000. For Pakistan Flood Relief Fund. 2010.

323-146 Give2Asia, San Francisco, CA, $45,000. For Educational Ecosystem Katong School in Singapore to National Council of Social Services, E-Learning, Yvonee Swim School, and Oh Kah Tuan Dolph NRIC. 2010.

323-147 Give2Asia, San Francisco, CA, $27,000. For Agastya Foundation in Bangalore, India for Synopsys Mobile Science Lab program. 2010.

323-148 Give2Asia, San Francisco, CA, $27,000. For Parikrma Humanity Foundation for Year 2 (of 3-year) plan for Synopsys Universe2You Science Program. 2010.

323-149 Give2Asia, San Francisco, CA, $21,400. For general support. 2010.

323-150 Give2Asia, San Francisco, CA, $15,377. For Community Chest for Give A Hand support of $14,000.00 for donation in Singapore local currency and $1,377 for fees. 2010.

323-151 Give2Asia, San Francisco, CA, $11,000. For the Chi Heng Foundation Fund in Hong Kong - Walk for Chalk. 2010.

323-152 Global Citizen Year, San Francisco, CA, $100,000. For general support. 2010.

323-153 Global Citizen Year, San Francisco, CA, $23,668. For the GCY/YEF Access Fund. 2010.

323-154 Global Citizen Year, San Francisco, CA, $10,000. For general support. 2010.

323-155 Global Footprint Network, Oakland, CA, $250,000. For core support. 2010.

323-156 Global Footprint Network, Oakland, CA, $150,000. For core support. 2010.

323-157 Global Fund for Children, Washington, DC, $40,000. For general support. 2010.

323-158 Global Fund for Children, Washington, DC, $30,000. For endowment and annual support. 2010.

323-159 Global Fund for Children, Washington, DC, $20,000. For general support. 2010.

323-160 Global Fund for Children, Washington, DC, $19,250. 2010.

323-161 Global Fund for Children, Washington, DC, $10,000. For general support. 2010.

323-162 Global Fund for Women, San Francisco, CA, $25,000. For general support. 2010.

323-163 Global Greengrants Fund, Boulder, CO, $20,000. To fund work with the Council on Foundation's International Philanthropy for the Clinton Global Philanthropy Initiative Project. 2010.

323-164 Global Heritage Fund, Palo Alto, CA, $100,000. For the Global Heritage Fund Challenge. 2010.

323-165 Global Heritage Fund, Palo Alto, CA, $77,000. For general support. 2010.

323-166 Global Heritage Fund, Palo Alto, CA, $50,000. For Indus Heritage Centre Planning and Design Project. 2010.

323-167 Global Heritage Fund, Palo Alto, CA, $33,000. For general support for Global Heritage Network. 2010.

323-168 Global Heritage Fund, Palo Alto, CA, $25,000. For Global Heritage Fund goals. 2010.

323-169 Global Heritage Fund, Palo Alto, CA, $20,000. For Global Heritage Network Engineering. 2010.

323-170 Global Heritage Fund, Palo Alto, CA, $10,000. For general support. 2010.

323-171 GlobalGiving Foundation, Washington, DC, $14,000. For Books for At-Risk Children with Raising A Reader. 2010.

323-172 GlobalGiving Foundation, Washington, DC, $10,000. For Books for At-Risk Children with Raising A Reader. 2010.

323-173 Gram Vikas, Berhampur, India, $500,000. For core support. 2010.

323-174 Gram Vikas, Berhampur, India, $150,000. For core support. 2010.

323-175 Grant Foundation, Pittsburgh, PA, $50,000. For response efforts for victims of earthquake. 2010.

323-176 Grassroots Alliance for Community Education USA, Half Moon Bay, CA, $50,000. For general support. 2010.

323-177 Guanacaste Dry Forest Conservation Fund, Philadelphia, PA, $50,000. For general support. 2010.

323-178 H. John Heinz III Center for Science, Economics and the Environment, Washington, DC, $150,000. For Terrestrial Carbon Group/ Heonz Center for the Environment, for Planetary Skin Institute. 2010.

323-179 H. John Heinz III Center for Science, Economics and the Environment, Washington, DC, $150,000. For furtherance of global public good and exempt purposes of PSI and Heinz Center to promote collaborative research, capacity strengthening and dissemination in areas of global and localized modeling of terrestrial carbon management and integrated land use. 2010.

323-180 Haiti Outreach - Pwoje Espwa, Rochester, NY, $10,000. For general support. 2010.

323-181 Hands Together, Springfield, MA, $10,000. For greatest need. 2010.

323-182 Harvard University, Cambridge, MA, $450,000. For international expansion for the Center for the Developing Child at Harvard University. 2010.

323-183 Harvest Heralds, Beaverton, OR, $25,000. For continuing program funding. 2010.

323-184 Heifer Project International, Little Rock, AR, $40,000. For general support. 2010.

323-185 Help Them Grow, Sunnyvale, CA, $30,389. For Sikshana. 2010.

323-186 Helping Children Worldwide, Herndon, VA, $20,000. For Child Rescue Center in Bo, Sierra Leone. 2010.

323-187 Hillel of Silicon Valley, San Jose, CA, $10,000. For the Israel Fellowship Program. 2010.

323-188 Himanchal Educational Foundation, Kearney, NE, $19,600. For Nepal Wireless program utilizing Juniper Networks products. 2010.

323-189 Hogar Amanacer, San Nicolas, Argentina, $25,000. For (Hogar Amanacer) Orphanage in San Nicolas, Argentina. 2010.

323-190 Hope Springs Institute, Peebles, OH, $20,000. To support work of Makkala Jagriti in India. 2010.

323-191 Hope With Sudan, San Jose, CA, $22,000. For general support. 2010.

323-192 Human Rights Watch, New York, NY, $50,000. For Middle East/North Africa group. 2010.

323-193 India Literacy Project, Milpitas, CA, $15,743. For Community Empowerment through Education. 2010.

323-194 Innovations for Poverty Action, New Haven, CT, $25,000. For Impact of Impact research. 2010.

323-195 Institute for Development Studies and Practices, Quetta, Pakistan, $10,000. For general operating support. 2010.

323-196 Institute for OneWorld Health, San Francisco, CA, $25,000. For general support. 2010.

323-197 Institute for OneWorld Health, San Francisco, CA, $25,000. For general support. 2010.

323-198 International Association for Human Values, Bowie, MD, $25,160. For YES! Program at Yerba Buena High School. 2010.

323-199 International Forum on Globalization, San Francisco, CA, $10,000. For general support. 2010.

323-200 International Humanities Center, Pacific Palisades, CA, $15,000. For the Palast Investigative Fund in their Amazon to Arctic media project. 2010.

323-201 International Rescue Committee, New York, NY, $50,000. To expand IRC's Immigration Program to include additional support for clients applying for citizenship through classes, tutoring, and technology. 2010.

323-202 International Rescue Committee, New York, NY, $15,000. For general support. 2010.

323-203 International Youth Foundation, Baltimore, MD, $40,000. For general support. 2010.

323-204 Internews Network, Arcata, CA, $200,000. For restricted grant to support InterNews work in Haiti, in response to January 2010 earthquake. 2010.

323-205 Internews Network, Arcata, CA, $100,000. For general support. 2010.

323-206 Internews Network, Arcata, CA, $20,000. For general support. 2010.

323-207 Interplast, Mountain View, CA, $50,000. For general support. 2010.

323-208 Interplast, Mountain View, CA, $25,000. For general support. 2010.

323-209 Interplast, Mountain View, CA, $15,000. 2010.

323-210 Interplast, Mountain View, CA, $10,000. For general support. 2010.

323-211 Invisible Children, San Diego, CA, $50,000. For general support. 2010.

323-212 Invisible Children, San Diego, CA, $20,000. For general support. 2010.

323-213 Israel Venture Network, Palo Alto, CA, $100,000. For general support. 2010.

323-214 Jesuit Refugee Service, Washington, DC, $10,000. For Haiti Relief. 2010.

323-215 Jews Indigenous to the Middle East and North Africa, San Francisco, CA, $15,000. For general support. 2010.

323-216 Kashf Foundation, Lahore, Pakistan, $150,000. For core support. 2010.

323-217 Kashf Foundation, Lahore, Pakistan, $100,000. For core support. 2010.

323-218 Kashf Foundation, Lahore, Pakistan, $10,000. For general operating support. 2010.

323-219 Keio University, Tokyo, Japan, $98,000. For research proposal entitled: Explanation of

BGP Update Background Noise and Spikes in the Internet. 2010.

323-220 Kickstart International, San Francisco, CA, $100,000. For general support. 2010.

323-221 KOMAZA USA, San Francisco, CA, $100,000. For general support. 2010.

323-222 KTH Royal Institute of Technology, Stockholm, Sweden, $97,448. For research proposal entitled: Network Search for Network Management. 2010.

323-223 Lambi Fund of Haiti, Washington, DC, $25,000. To support Lambi's earthquake recovery and community development strategy already underway to help rural communities throughout Haiti cope with mass exodus of people from Port-au-Prince to the rural areas, to use funding to support sustainable agriculture projects to meet the demand for food and to increase opportunities livelihoods through pig and goat breeding, grain mills and sugar cane mills. 2010.

323-224 Le Fonds d'Excellence Massey-Vanier, Cowansville, Canada, $30,000. For Scholarship Fund. 2010.

323-225 Lehigh University, Bethlehem, PA, $50,000. For Global Initiative Fund. 2010.

323-226 Leo Baeck Education Center Foundation, Houston, TX, $400,000. For construction of new floor to the existing elementary school building, made in support of the current matching opportunity. 2010.

323-227 Lewa Wildlife Conservancy USA, Woodbridge, VA, $60,000. For education and conservancy. 2010.

323-228 London Grid for Learning Trust, New Malden, England, $20,000. For suite of online academic programs in London schools. 2010.

323-229 Lost Frontiers Foundation, Fairfax, CA, $25,000. To assist in the assessment of water needs in the village of Maruvango, Tanzania and to begin the building of needed water catchers. 2010.

323-230 Makerere University, Kampala, Uganda, $50,000. For research proposal entitled: Large-scale WiMAX Mesh Networks. 2010.

323-231 Mama Cares Foundation, Carlsbad, CA, $80,031. For matching funds. 2010.

323-232 Marine Stewardship Council, London, England, $1,800,000. For core support. 2010.

323-233 Marine Stewardship Council, London, England, $150,000. For core support. 2010.

323-234 Maryknoll Sisters of Saint Dominic, Maryknoll, NY, $10,000. For work in Burma/Myanmar. 2010.

323-235 McGill University, Friends of, New Rochelle, NY, $50,000. For Innovative Research Awards at McGill Cancer Center. 2010.

323-236 Mercy Corps, Portland, OR, $10,000. For Haiti Earthquake Relief Efforts. 2010.

323-237 Mercy Ships, Garden Valley, TX, $10,000. For general support. 2010.

323-238 Mission Aviation Fellowship, Nampa, ID, $200,000. For Asas De Socorro Kodiak. 2010.

323-239 Mission Aviation Fellowship, Nampa, ID, $10,000. For Haiti Earthquake Relief. 2010.

323-240 Missions Ministries, Littleton, CO, $28,600. For van, college students' and high school or middle school students' school expenses, and for library setup and building expenses. 2010.

323-241 Music of Bhutan Research Center, Santa Cruz, CA, $30,000. For general support of archival traditional music projects in the country of Bhutan. 2010.

323-242 Music of Bhutan Research Center, Santa Cruz, CA, $10,000. For general support of the archival traditional music projects in the country of Bhutan. 2010.

323-243 National Geographic Society, Washington, DC, $10,000. For LEX/NG Fund - Galapagos Conservation. 2010.

323-244 National Peace Corps Association, Washington, DC, $50,000. For The Promise of the Peace Corps Campaign. 2010.

323-245 National Peace Corps Association, Washington, DC, $12,500. For 50th Anniversary Campaign and for general support. 2010.

323-246 Natural Resources Defense Council, New York, NY, $25,000. For AB 32 or China project. 2010.

323-247 Nature Conservancy, Arlington, VA, $1,000,000. For Forever Costa Rica. 2010.

323-248 Nature Conservancy, Arlington, VA, $50,000. For Montana chapter's Annual Fund. 2010.

323-249 Nature Conservancy, Arlington, VA, $50,000. For Plant a Billion Trees campaign in Brazil. 2010.

323-250 Nature Conservancy, Arlington, VA, $45,000. For general support. 2010.

323-251 Nature Conservancy, Arlington, VA, $35,000. For general support. 2010.

323-252 Nuru International, Palo Alto, CA, $150,000. For general support. 2010.

323-253 Nuru International, Palo Alto, CA, $100,000. For general support. 2010.

323-254 Ocean Conservancy, Washington, DC, $110,000. For general support and Arctic Initiative. 2010.

323-255 One Acre Fund, Falcon Heights, MN, $765,000. For core support. 2010.

323-256 One Acre Fund, Falcon Heights, MN, $100,000. For general support. 2010.

323-257 One World Childrens Fund, San Francisco, CA, $20,000. For general support. 2010.

323-258 One World Childrens Fund, San Francisco, CA, $10,000. For general support. 2010.

323-259 Opportunity International, Oak Brook, IL, $50,000. For general support. 2010.

323-260 Opportunity International, Oak Brook, IL, $50,000. For general support. 2010.

323-261 Opportunity International, Oak Brook, IL, $15,000. For the Africa Campaign. 2010.

323-262 Opportunity International, Oak Brook, IL, $10,000. For general support. 2010.

323-263 Ottawa Community Immigrant Services Organization, Ottawa, Canada, $20,000. For immigrant and refugee children and Youth Support Project. 2010.

323-264 Our Lady Queen of Peace Church, Arlington, VA, $30,441. For the second phase of construction project to re-build eight primary school classrooms of St. Joseph Elementary School in Medor, Haiti. 2010.

323-265 Oxfam America, Boston, MA, $85,000. To support Haiti Earthquake Relief Efforts. 2010.

323-266 Oxfam America, Boston, MA, $30,000. For earthquake relief and recovery work in Haiti. 2010.

323-267 Oxfam America, Boston, MA, $25,000. For general support. 2010.

323-268 Oxfam America, Boston, MA, $10,000. For relief efforts in Haiti. 2010.

323-269 Oxford University, Oxford, England, $39,825. For project entitled: Machian Quantum Gravity. 2010.

323-270 Pachamama Alliance, San Francisco, CA, $40,000. For general support. 2010.

323-271 Pan African Childrens Fund, Save Africa's Children, Los Angeles, CA, $20,000. For general support. 2010.

323-272 Pan American Development Foundation, Washington, DC, $11,770. For Synopsys Chile Disaster Relief - employee match to Un Techo Para Chile for housing program. 2010.

323-273 Partners in Health, Boston, MA, $200,000. For emergency relief after earthquake in Haiti. 2010.

323-274 Partners in Health, Boston, MA, $190,000. For the Haiti earthquake relief. 2010.

323-275 Partners in Health, Boston, MA, $85,000. To support Haiti Earthquake Relief Efforts. 2010.

323-276 Partners in Health, Boston, MA, $50,000. For general support. 2010.

323-277 Partners in Health, Boston, MA, $50,000. For Haiti Earthquake Relief. 2010.

323-278 Partners in Health, Boston, MA, $25,000. For Haiti Earthquake Relief. 2010.

323-279 Partners in Health, Boston, MA, $25,000. For general support. 2010.

323-280 Partners in Health, Boston, MA, $25,000. For relief work in Haiti. 2010.

323-281 Partners in Health, Boston, MA, $20,000. For the Stand with Haiti Fund. 2010.

323-282 Partners in Health, Boston, MA, $10,000. For Haiti Earthquake Relief Efforts. 2010.

323-283 Partners in Health, Boston, MA, $10,000. To support Haitians post-earthquake. 2010.

323-284 Partners in Health, Boston, MA, $10,000. For treating patients in Haiti. 2010.

323-285 Partners International, Spokane, WA, $10,000. For general fund. 2010.

323-286 Partners International, Spokane, WA, $10,000. For general fund. 2010.

323-287 Peace Education Fund, Berkeley, CA, $10,000. For general support to promote education on peace issues and foreign policy legislation. 2010.

323-288 PEF Israel Endowment Funds, New York, NY, $300,000. For organization TMURA: The Israel Public Service Venture Fund. 2010.

323-289 PEF Israel Endowment Funds, New York, NY, $20,000. To PUSH Foundation for volunteer and remedial teaching projects Israel. 2010.

323-290 Pembina Foundation for Environmental Research and Education, Drayton Valley, Canada, $50,000. For work on climate change. 2010.

323-291 Pew Charitable Trusts, Philadelphia, PA, $100,000. For Oceans North Initiative. 2010.

323-292 Philanthropic Ventures Foundation, Oakland, CA, $25,000. For the ICE 911 designated fund. 2010.

323-293 Politecnico di Turino, Turin, Italy, $81,511. For research proposal entitled: Fast and memory-efficient regular expression matching. 2010.

323-294 Presbyterian Church USA, Pittsburgh, PA, $35,000. For Extra Commitment Opportunity (ECO) for Tajikistan Relief, for funding of medical and educational projects. 2010.

323-295 Pro Mujer, New York, NY, $50,000. For women's education and microlending. 2010.

323-296 Protection and Education re: Animals, Culture and Environment, Vail, CO, $32,500. For Animal Program, to support full-time veterinarian in Mexico. 2010.

323-297 Protection and Education re: Animals, Culture and Environment, Vail, CO, $32,500. For general support. 2010.

323-298 Protection and Education re: Animals, Culture and Environment, Vail, CO, $20,000. To sponsor spay/neuter clinics and sponsor one full-time English teacher for a whole year. 2010.

323-299 Protection and Education re: Animals, Culture and Environment, Vail, CO, $10,000. For Microfinance project. 2010.

323-300 Protection and Education re: Animals, Culture and Environment, Vail, CO, $10,000. For student scholarships. 2010.

323-301 Rain for the Sahel and Sahara, Newmarket, NH, $70,000. For general support. 2010.

323-302 Rain for the Sahel and Sahara, Newmarket, NH, $21,000. For general support. 2010.

323-303 RARE, Arlington, VA, $25,000. For general support. 2010.

323-304 Relief International, Los Angeles, CA, $50,000. For general operating support. 2010.

323-305 Right to Play USA, New York, NY, $100,000. For general operating support. 2010.

323-306 Right to Play USA, New York, NY, $10,000. For May Playday. 2010.

323-307 Room to Read, San Francisco, CA, $1,250,000. For growth plan of Room to Read. 2010.

323-308 Room to Read, San Francisco, CA, $50,000. For financial aid for girls' scholarships in Southeast Asia. 2010.

323-309 Room to Read, San Francisco, CA, $25,479. For libraries in India and publishing of local language books. 2010.

323-310 Room to Read, San Francisco, CA, $19,000. To fund construction of stand-alone library building in Cambodia or Laos. 2010.

323-311 Room to Read, San Francisco, CA, $15,000. For libraries in Cambodia. 2010.

323-312 Root Capital, Cambridge, MA, $50,000. For general support. 2010.

323-313 Root Capital, Cambridge, MA, $50,000. For the Talent Initiative. 2010.

323-314 Saint Elizabeth Catholic School, Ottawa, Canada, $18,500. For SMART Board Technology. 2010.

323-315 Saint Michael Catholic Elementary School, Ottawa, Canada, $18,500. For SMART Board technology for classrooms. 2010.

323-316 Saint Pauls United Church, Waterloo, Canada, $16,000. For general support. 2010.

323-317 Saint Thomas Church, Leipzig, Germany, $10,000. For Cantata Music Series. 2010.

323-318 Salvation Army of Long Beach, Long Beach, CA, $10,000. For the disadvantaged locally and abroad. 2010.

323-319 Samasource, San Francisco, CA, $100,000. For general support. 2010.

323-320 Samasource, San Francisco, CA, $25,000. For general support. 2010.

323-321 Santa Clara University, Santa Clara, CA, $14,000. For the German Language Abroad Program. 2010.

323-322 Save the Children Federation, Westport, CT, $85,000. To support Haiti Earthquake Relief Efforts. 2010.

323-323 Save the Children Federation, Westport, CT, $50,000. For Pakistan Flood Relief Fund. 2010.

323-324 Save the Children Federation, Westport, CT, $35,000. For earthquake relief and recovery efforts in Haiti. 2010.

323-325 Save the Children Federation, Westport, CT, $25,000. For Haiti Earthquake Relief. 2010.

323-326 Save the Children Federation, Westport, CT, $20,000. For general support. 2010.

323-327 Save the Children Federation, Westport, CT, $15,000. For general support and domestic programs. 2010.

323-328 Save the Children Federation, Westport, CT, $12,226. 2010.

323-329 Save the Children Federation, Westport, CT, $10,000. For Haiti Quake Relief. 2010.

323-330 Science World, Vancouver, Canada, $20,000. For Super Science Club. 2010.

323-331 Seed International, Merrifield, VA, $20,000. For The Morning Star of Cambodia for new project to build Christian community to help poor people in Cambodia. 2010.

323-332 Seva Foundation, Berkeley, CA, $15,000. For The Sight Program. 2010.

323-333 Shin Shin Education Foundation, San Francisco, CA, $10,000. For ECTT programs. 2010.

323-334 Shirley Ann Sullivan Educational Foundation, Lindsborg, KS, $19,567. For SASEF Reading Corner in Porte Alegre City, Brazil. 2010.

323-335 Singapore American School Foundation, Princeton, NJ, $10,000. For Singapore American School to fund Wish Kids for the Philippines. 2010.

323-336 Smile Train, New York, NY, $25,000. For general support. 2010.

323-337 Smile Train, New York, NY, $25,000. For general support. 2010.

323-338 Smith Family, Camperdown, Australia, $20,000. For Technology Pack Program in Australia. 2010.

323-339 Somaly Mam Foundation, Wheat Ridge, CO, $10,000. For general support. 2010.

323-340 Stanford University, Stanford, CA, $50,000. For Stanford's Center for International Conflict and Negotiation (SCICN). 2010.

323-341 Stanford University, Stanford, CA, $25,000. For Stanford Fund, Bing School Endowment, Critical Issues in International Women's Health for undergraduate research and service learning projects, and Stanford Poverty Internship to support undergraduate scholarship. 2010.

323-342 Stanford University, Stanford, CA, $25,000. To support the work of Center for International Security and Cooperation. 2010.

323-343 Students in Free Enterprise, Springfield, MO, $11,730. For SIFE China to support Community Development Project, specifically eight different University student projects that will create economic opportunity for the community. 2010.

323-344 SurfAid International USA, Carlsbad, CA, $50,000. For restricted grant to support the relief efforts in Mentawai. 2010.

323-345 Swami Vivekananda Youth Movement of North America, Fullerton, CA, $25,000. For general support for the education and youth literacy services provided by the PremaVidya program. 2010.

323-346 Swinburne University of Technology, Hawthorn, Australia, $89,708. For research proposal entitled: Extending Open Source Packet Filtering to Support Distributed Statistical Traffic Classification. 2010.

323-347 TeachAIDS, Palo Alto, CA, $26,107. For funding to develop culturally-appropriate and medically-accurate HIV/AIDS prevention materials to be utilized in every primary, secondary and tertiary institutions across Botswana. 2010.

323-348 Telapak Indonesia, Bogor, Indonesia, $15,000. For general operating support. 2010.

323-349 Thames Community Foundation, Teddington, England, $35,000. 2010.

323-350 Ties to the World, Lafayette, CA, $50,000. For general support. 2010.

323-351 Tongji University, College of Electronics and Info Engineering, Shanghai, China, $55,000. For research proposal entitled: Service Access on Highway VANETs. 2010.

323-352 Tony Blair Faith Foundation-US, Washington, DC, $10,000. For general support. 2010.

323-353 Tostan, Washington, DC, $765,000. For core support. 2010.

323-354 Transfair USA, Oakland, CA, $100,000. For general support. 2010.

323-355 Transfair USA, Oakland, CA, $10,000. For production of Micro-Documentaries. 2010.

323-356 TurtleWill, Inc., Carefree, AZ, $70,000. For general support. 2010.

323-357 TurtleWill, Inc., Carefree, AZ, $21,000. For general support. 2010.

323-358 United States Association for United Nations High Commissioner for Refugees, Washington, DC, $400,000. For Pakistan Disaster Relief. 2010.

323-359 United States Fund for UNICEF, New York, NY, $50,000. To be used for relief efforts in Pakistan. 2010.

323-360 United States Fund for UNICEF, New York, NY, $25,000. For Haiti Earthquake Relief. 2010.

323-361 United States Fund for UNICEF, New York, NY, $25,000. For Haiti Earthquake Relief. 2010.

323-362 United States Fund for UNICEF, New York, NY, $10,000. For Haiti Earthquake Relief. 2010.

323-363 United States Fund for UNICEF, New York, NY, $10,000. For general support. 2010.

323-364 United States Fund for UNICEF, New York, NY, $10,000. For Pakistani flood victims. 2010.

323-365 United Way Worldwide, Alexandria, VA, $125,611. For matching gift. 2010.

323-366 United Way Worldwide, Alexandria, VA, $46,764. For matching gift. 2010.

323-367 University College London, London, England, $23,263. For the FQXi grant project: Abstract Quantum Probability. 2010.

323-368 University of Edinburgh, Edinburgh, Scotland, $99,953. For research proposal entitled: Robust Acoustic Segmentation for Conversational Speech Recognition. 2010.

323-369 University of Glasgow, Glasgow, Scotland, $144,465. For research proposal entitled: Architecture and Protocols for Massively Scalable IP Media Streaming. 2010.

323-370 University of Minnesota, Minneapolis, MN, $300,000. For Planetary Skin Institute. 2010.

323-371 University of Pennsylvania, Philadelphia, PA, $10,000. For Penn Museum, support for two Mark Goodman Preservation Fellows at Gordion, Turkey. 2010.

323-372 University of Prince Edward Island, Charlottetown, Canada, $10,000. For the continuation of the Pegasus Fund Neutering Program at the Atlantic Veterinary College. 2010.

323-373 University of Science and Technology of China, Hefei, China, $50,000. For research proposal entitled: Mobile Cloud Computing. 2010.

323-374 University of Science and Technology of China, Hefei, China, $30,000. For research proposal entitled: Malware Detection for Smartphones. 2010.

323-375 University of Science and Technology of China, Hefei, China, $30,000. For research proposal entitled: Malware Detection for Smartphones. 2010.

323-376 Verite, Inc., Amherst, MA, $250,000. For core support. 2010.

323-377 Verite, Inc., Amherst, MA, $150,000. For core support. 2010.

323-378 Village Enterprise Fund, San Carlos, CA, $40,000. For general support. 2010.

323-379 Village Enterprise Fund, San Carlos, CA, $40,000. For general support. 2010.

323-380 Village Enterprise Fund, San Carlos, CA, $15,000. To begin site assessment, business mentor selection and training. 2010.

323-381 Virunga Fund, Brooklyn, NY, $50,000. For general support. 2010.

323-382 VisionSpring, New York, NY, $83,333. For general support of SEGUE. 2010.

323-383 Vittana Foundation, Seattle, WA, $25,000. For general support. 2010.

323-384 Vittana Foundation, Vittana, Seattle, WA, $100,000. For general support. 2010.

323-385 Wild Cat Education and Conservation Fund, Occidental, CA, $20,000. For general support. 2010.

323-386 Wildlife Conservation Network, Los Altos, CA, $18,000. For the Small Cat Conservation Alliance, for Cheetah Conservation Botswana, and for Snow Leopard Conservancy. 2010.

323-387 William J. Clinton Foundation, Little Rock, AR, $20,000. For general support of the Clinton Global Initiative. 2010.

323-388 William J. Clinton Foundation, Little Rock, AR, $19,000. For the Clinton Global Initiative Program. 2010.

323-389 William J. Clinton Foundation, Little Rock, AR, $19,000. To fund programs in the development of international philanthropy, through the Clinton Global Initiative. 2010.

323-390 Witness, Inc., Brooklyn, NY, $250,000. For core support. 2010.

323-391 Witness, Inc., Brooklyn, NY, $20,000. For general support. 2010.

323-392 World Land Trust-US, Washington, DC, $20,000. For Ride for the Trees campaign to preserve forests of Paraguay. 2010.

323-393 World Learning, Brattleboro, VT, $10,000. For Outbound Ambassadors program. 2010.

323-394 World Neighbors, Oklahoma City, OK, $50,000. For matching gift campaign. 2010.

323-395 World Savvy, San Francisco, CA, $15,000. For the Global Youth Media and Arts program. 2010.

323-396 World Savvy, San Francisco, CA, $12,500. For Global Youth Media and Arts program. 2010.

323-397 World Spine Care, Santa Ana, CA, $25,000. For general operating support. 2010.

323-398 World Vision, Federal Way, WA, $25,000. For Haiti Earthquake Relief. 2010.

323-399 World Vision, Federal Way, WA, $25,000. For general support. 2010.

323-400 World Wildlife Fund, Washington, DC, $10,000. For general support. 2010.

323-401 Youth Action International, New York, NY, $25,000. For general support. 2010.

323-402 Zhejiang University, Hangzhou, China, $85,000. For research proposal entitled: Moving Object Detention Based Adaptive 3D Filtering and Video Coding Optimization. 2010.

324
Simms Family Foundation
10153 1/2 Riverside Dr., Ste. 670
Toluca Lake, CA 91602-2561
Contact: Margaret S. Simms, Pres.

Established in 1998 in CA.
Donors: Thomas M. Simms; Margaret S. Simms.
Grantmaker type: Independent foundation.
Financial data (yr. ended 12/31/10): Assets, $3,789,061 (M); expenditures, $257,430; qualifying distributions, $257,430; giving activities include $236,800 for 17 grants (high: $100,000; low: $1,000).
Fields of interest: Hospitals (specialty); Education; Health care; Family services; International relief; International relief, 2004 tsunami; Christian agencies & churches.
Type of support: General/operating support.
Limitations: Applications accepted. Giving primarily in CA.
Application information: Application form required.
Deadline(s): None
Officers and Directors: * Margaret S. Simms,* Pres.; Christopher S. Simms,* V.P.; Thomas M. Simms,* Secy. and C.F.O.
EIN: 954692270

325
The Skoll Foundation
250 University Ave., Ste. 200
Palo Alto, CA 94301-1738   (650) 331-1031
FAX: (650) 331-1033;
E-mail: grants@skollfoundation.org; URL: http://www.skollfoundation.org/
Foundation News: http://feeds.feedburner.com/SkollFoundationNews
Jeff Skoll's Giving Pledge: http://www.givingpledge.org/#enter
Twitter: http://www.twitter.com/skollfoundation
YouTube: http://www.youtube.com/user/skollfoundation

Established in 2002 in CA. In 2004, the foundation incorporated the Skoll Community Fund, a supporting organization associated with the Silicon Valley Community Foundation of San Jose, CA, into its operations.
Donor: Jeffrey S. Skoll.
Grantmaker type: Independent foundation.
Financial data (yr. ended 12/31/09): Assets, $463,297,672 (M); gifts received, $79,483,580; expenditures, $52,503,726; qualifying distributions, $50,372,174; giving activities include $33,383,519 for 81 grants (high: $10,000,000; low: $3,374), $5,011,545 for foundation-administered programs and $5,330,522 for 7 loans/program-related investments (high: $2,200,000; low: $3,378).
Purpose and activities: The Skoll Foundation drives large-scale change by investing in, connecting, and celebrating social entrepreneurs and other innovators dedicated to solving the world's most pressing problems.
Fields of interest: Social entrepreneurship.
Type of support: Mission-related investments/loans; General/operating support; Program-related investments/loans.
Limitations: Applications accepted. No support for organizations new or early-stage business plans or ideas, schools and school districts, or programs promoting religious doctrine. No grants to individuals, or for scholarships, endowments, deficit reduction or land acquisition.
Publications: Application guidelines; Annual report; Financial statement; Newsletter.
Application information: New SASE award winners celebrated once each year in Mar. at the annual Skoll World Forum on Social Entrepreneurship. Application form required.
Initial approach: Online eligibility quiz and application
Deadline(s): Online applications are accepted between Jan. 4 and the deadline of Mar. 1, 2012
Board meeting date(s): Annually
Final notification: Application status: July. Award decisions: Nov.
Officers and Directors: * Jeffrey S. Skoll,* Chair.; Sally Osberg, C.E.O. and Pres.; Sandy Herz, Interim V.P., Program & Impact and Dir., Strategic Alliances; Ben Binswanger, C.A.O.; Richard Fahey, C.O.O.; Renee Kaplan, Chief Marketing Off.; Larry Brilliant; James G.B. DeMartini III; Debra L. Dunn; Kirk O. Hanson; Peter Hero; Roger L. Martin.
Number of staff: 33
EIN: 113659133
Recent grants for international programs:

325-1 Amazon Institute of People and the Environment, Belem, Brazil, $765,000. For core support. 2010.

325-2 Ashoka: Innovators for the Public, Arlington, VA, $1,500,000. For core support and Collaborative Action and Tropical Forests Initiative. 2010.

325-3 Ashoka: Innovators for the Public, Arlington, VA, $25,000. For general operating support. 2010.

325-4 AVINA Americas, Washington, DC, $90,000. For Global Social Competitiveness Index (GSCI). 2010.

325-5 Better World Fund, Washington, DC, $1,500,000. For The Elders. 2010.

325-6 Better World Fund, Washington, DC, $212,520. For The Elders. 2010.

325-7 Centre for Addiction and Mental Health, Toronto, Canada, $25,000. For Jennifer Frances Martin Fund. 2010.

325-8 Creating Hope International, Dearborn, MI, $10,000. For Afghan Institute of Learning. 2010.

325-9 Endeavor Global, New York, NY, $15,000. For Endeavor Gala. 2010.

325-10 Forest Trends Association, Washington, DC, $765,000. For core support. 2010.

325-11 Forest Trends Association, Washington, DC, $300,000. For REDD tracking. 2010.

325-12 Free the Children USA, Hartford, CT, $750,000. For core support. 2010.

325-13 Free the Children USA, Hartford, CT, $150,000. For core support. 2010.

325-14 Free the Children USA, Hartford, CT, $50,000. For general operating support. 2010.

325-15 Friends of Via, Pittsburgh, PA, $12,000. For community development. 2010.

325-16 Friends-International, Phnom Penh, Cambodia, $1,033,560. For core support. 2010.

325-17 Friends-International, Phnom Penh, Cambodia, $150,000. For core support. 2010.

325-18 Fundacion Escuela Nueva, Bogota, Colombia, $250,000. For core support. 2010.

325-19 Fundacion Escuela Nueva, Bogota, Colombia, $150,000. For core support. 2010.

325-20 Global Footprint Network, Oakland, CA, $250,000. For core support. 2010.

325-21 Global Footprint Network, Oakland, CA, $150,000. For core support. 2010.

325-22 Gram Vikas, Berhampur, India, $500,000. For core support. 2010.

325-23 Gram Vikas, Berhampur, India, $150,000. For core support. 2010.

325-24 Institute for Development Studies and Practices, Quetta, Pakistan, $10,000. For general operating support. 2010.

325-25 Institute for Development Studies and Practices, Quetta, Pakistan, $10,000. For general operating support. 2010.

325-26 Kashf Foundation, Lahore, Pakistan, $150,000. For core support. 2010.

325-27 Kashf Foundation, Lahore, Pakistan, $100,000. For core support. 2010.

325-28 Kashf Foundation, Lahore, Pakistan, $10,000. For general operating support. 2010.

325-29 Marine Stewardship Council, London, England, $1,800,000. For core support. 2010.

325-30 Marine Stewardship Council, London, England, $150,000. For core support. 2010.

325-31 One Acre Fund, Falcon Heights, MN, $765,000. For core support. 2010.

325-32 Partners for Sustainable Development, Ramallah, West Bank/Gaza (Palestinian Territories), $200,000. For NETKETABi Project. 2010.

325-33 Partners for Sustainable Development, Ramallah, West Bank/Gaza (Palestinian Territories), $30,000. For Youth Capacity Building Project. 2010.

325-34 Partners in Health, Boston, MA, $200,000. For core support. 2010.

325-35 Partners in Health, Boston, MA, $50,000. For general operating support. 2010.

325-36 Relief International, Los Angeles, CA, $50,000. For general operating support. 2010.

325-37 Root Capital, Cambridge, MA, $50,000. For Talent Initiative. 2010.

325-38 Salman and Samina Global Wellness Initiative, Tappan, NY, $50,000. For Pakistan Hai Hamara Project. 2010.

325-39 Seva Foundation, Berkeley, CA, $15,000. For Sight Program. 2010.

325-40 Telapak Indonesia, Bogor, Indonesia, $765,000. For core support. 2010.

325-41 Telapak Indonesia, Bogor, Indonesia, $15,000. For general operating support. 2010.

325-42 Tostan, Washington, DC, $765,000. For core support. 2010.

325-43 Verite, Inc., Amherst, MA, $250,000. For core support. 2010.

325-44 Verite, Inc., Amherst, MA, $150,000. For core support. 2010.

325-45 William J. Clinton Foundation, Little Rock, AR, $19,000. For Clinton Global Initiative support. 2010.

325-46 Witness, Inc., Brooklyn, NY, $250,000. For core support. 2010.

325-47 World Affairs Council of Northern California, San Francisco, CA, $34,210. For Global Philanthropy Forum (GPF). 2010.

325-48 World Spine Care, Santa Ana, CA, $25,000. For general operating support. 2010.

326
Margaret K. Sloss Foundation

818 Cherry St.
Santa Rosa, CA   95404-4207
Contact: Louis Sloss, Jr., Tr.

Established about 1958.
Donor: Members of the Sloss family.
Grantmaker type: Independent foundation.

Financial data (yr. ended 12/31/10): Assets, $18,869 (M); gifts received, $128,196; expenditures, $129,434; qualifying distributions, $128,086; giving activities include $128,086 for grants.

Fields of interest: Arts; Higher education; Environment; Reproductive health, family planning; Health organizations, association; Human services; International relief; International peace/security; Civil/human rights; Community/economic development; Jewish agencies & synagogues; Economically disadvantaged.

Limitations: Applications not accepted. Giving on a national basis. No grants to individuals.

Application information: Unsolicited applications not accepted.

  Board meeting date(s): Annually

Trustees: Anthony Sloss; Karen Sloss; Louis Sloss, Jr.

Number of staff: None.

EIN: 946065985

327
May and Stanley Smith Charitable Trust

2320 Marinship Way, Ste. 150
Sausalito, CA   94965-2830   (415) 332-0166
Contact: Ruth Collins, Admin.
E-mail: grantsmanager@adminitrustllc.com;
URL: http://www.adminitrustllc.com/
may-and-stanley-smith-charitable-trust/

Established in 1989.
Donor: May Smith†.
Grantmaker type: Independent foundation.

Financial data (yr. ended 12/31/10): Assets, $397,009,481 (M); expenditures, $12,462,353; qualifying distributions, $10,370,643; giving activities include $9,994,171 for grants.

Purpose and activities: Provide grants to organizations that serve the needs of children, the elderly, the disabled, and the disadvantaged.

Fields of interest: Art & music therapy; Arts education; Education; Human services; Aging; Blind/visually impaired; Children/youth; Deaf/hearing impaired; Disabilities, people with; Economically disadvantaged; Immigrants/refugees; Mentally disabled; Minorities; Physically disabled.

International interests: Australia; Bahamas; Canada; Hong Kong; United Kingdom.

Type of support: General/operating support; Continuing support; Management development/capacity building; Equipment; Program development; Scholarship funds.

Limitations: Applications accepted. Giving on a national basis, with international particularly focused on Australia, Bahamas, Canada, United Kingdom and Hong Kong. No support for hospitals or hospital foundations, or for government programs or organizations receiving significant government funding. No grants to individuals or for endowment funds, capital funding or for general support to organizations that enjoy broad popular support.

Application information: Full proposals are by invitation only. The foundation provides a step-by-step guide to the grant application process on their web site. It is highly recommended that grantseekers review these steps in the order presented before beginning the application process.

  Initial approach: Submit online Letter of Intent
  Deadline(s): None
  Board meeting date(s): Quarterly
  Final notification: One month for letters of intent. Three to six months for full proposals

Trustees: Ruth M. Collins; David C. Cuneo; Daniel F. Piombo, Jr.

EIN: 946622075

328
The Crawford Smith Foundation

2827 Caminito Merion
La Jolla, CA   92037-5817

Established in 2001 in CA.
Grantmaker type: Independent foundation.

Financial data (yr. ended 12/31/09): Assets, $562,173 (M); expenditures, $228,251; qualifying distributions, $227,471; giving activities include $149,962 for 33 grants (high: $29,000; low: $50).

Fields of interest: Performing arts, orchestras; Performing arts, theater; Education; Human services.

International interests: Tanzania, Zanzibar and Pemba.

Type of support: General/operating support; Scholarship funds.

Limitations: Applications not accepted. Giving primarily in CA.

Application information: Unsolicited requests for funds not accepted.

Officers: Judith C. Smith, Pres.; Stephen W. Smith, C.F.O.; Peter C. Smith, Secy.

Directors: Constance S. Lundy; Stephen W. Smith, Jr.

EIN: 330964075

329
William D. Smythe Family Foundation

142 S. Santa Cruz Ave.
Los Gatos, CA   95030-6712   (408) 399-5551
Contact: Michael D. Smythe, V.P.

Established in 2000 in CA.
Donors: William D. Smythe; Michael D. Smythe; Linda Smythe; Karen Smythe Cocumelli; William D. Smythe, Jr.; Catherine Smythe Grasso; James J. Smythe; Sally Smythe Godwin; Stephen Godwin.

Grantmaker type: Independent foundation.

Financial data (yr. ended 12/31/10): Assets, $1,159,779 (M); expenditures, $227,458; qualifying distributions, $153,500; giving activities include $153,500 for 9 grants (high: $50,000; low: $2,500).

Fields of interest: Boy scouts; Education; Health organizations; Boys & girls clubs; Children/youth, services; Human services; International affairs, foreign policy.

Limitations: Applications accepted. Giving primarily in San Jose, CA.

Application information: Application form required.

  Initial approach: Letter
  Deadline(s): Dec. 31

Officers: William D. Smythe, Jr., C.F.O.; Karen Smythe Cocumelli, Secy.

Directors: Sally Smythe Godwin; Catherine Smythe Grasso; James J. Smythe.

EIN: 770535273

330
Social and Environmental Entrepreneurs
22231 Mulholland Hwy., Ste. 209
Calabasas, CA 91302-5151 (310) 737-9148
FAX: (310) 737-9151;
E-mail: seefinance2@earthlink.net; URL: http://www.saveourplanet.org

Established in 1994.
Grantmaker type: Public charity.
Financial data (yr. ended 12/31/09): Revenue, $3,279,853; assets, $2,469,590 (M); gifts received, $3,310,488; expenditures, $2,734,717; giving activities include for 7 grants to organizations outside the U.S.
Purpose and activities: The organization's mission is to empower, encourage, and catalyze individuals to facilitate progressive change in areas of social justice and ecological restoration.
Fields of interest: Environment.
International interests: Asia; Latin America; South America.
Type of support: General/operating support; Program development; Use of facilities.
Limitations: Applications accepted. Giving primarily in CA. No support for private shareholders, attempts to influence legislation, or campaign activities. No grants to individuals.
Publications: Application guidelines; Occasional report.
Application information: Application form required.
 Initial approach: Download fiscal sponsorship application form and mail or deliver
 Copies of proposal: 1
 Deadline(s): None
 Final notification: Three to four weeks
Officers and Directors:* Andrew Beath,* Chair.; Atossa Soltani,* V.P.; Sarah Vaill,* Secy.; John F. Feldsted,* Treas.; Max Gail, Jr.; Doe Mayer.
Number of staff: 2 full-time professional.
EIN: 954116679

331
Spansion Inc. Corporate Giving Program
915 DeGuigne Dr.
Sunnyvale, CA 94085-3836 (408) 962-2500
FAX: (408) 962-2502; URL: http://www.spansion.com/About/SocialResponsiblity/Pages/CorporateSocialResponsibility.aspx

Grantmaker type: Corporate giving program.
Purpose and activities: Spansion makes charitable contributions to nonprofit organizations involved with education, basic needs, and community development. Support is given primarily in areas of company operations in California, and in China, Japan, Malaysia, Singapore, South Korea, Taiwan, and Thailand.
Fields of interest: Science, formal/general education; Elementary/secondary education; Education; Health care; Food services; Housing/shelter; Community/economic development; Mathematics; Leadership development.
International interests: Malaysia; China; Japan; Singapore; South Korea; Taiwan; Thailand.
Type of support: General/operating support; Program development; Employee volunteer services; Sponsorships; Donated equipment; In-kind gifts.
Limitations: Giving primarily in areas of company operations in CA, and in China, Japan, Malaysia, Singapore, South Korea, Taiwan, and Thailand.

332
The W. L. S. Spencer Foundation
1660 Bush St., Ste. 300
San Francisco, CA 94109-5308 (415) 561-6540
Contact: Mary L. Gregory, Admin.
FAX: (415) 561-6477; E-mail: mgregory@pfs-llc.net; URL: http://www.pfs-llc.net/spencer/spencer.html

Established in 1994 in DE.
Grantmaker type: Independent foundation.
Financial data (yr. ended 12/31/09): Assets, $10,148,599 (M); gifts received, $609,357; expenditures, $1,450,721; qualifying distributions, $1,409,879; giving activities include $1,329,201 for 40 grants (high: $401,868; low: $500).
Purpose and activities: The mission of the foundation is to fund activities anywhere in the world which foster new ideas in education and encourage creativity. The foundation prefers specific initiatives that conform with this mission. The foundation enjoys the leverage that arises from seed grants, challenge grants, and matching grants.
Fields of interest: Arts; Education.
International interests: Asia.
Type of support: Program development; Seed money; Matching/challenge support.
Limitations: Applications accepted. Giving on a worldwide basis through intermediaries based in the United States. No grants to individuals or for events, no grants for endowments or ongoing operational expenses.
Publications: Application guidelines; Annual report (including application guidelines); Grants list; Program policy statement.
Application information: The foundation will ONLY consider grant requests for compelling needs within previously funded organizations. Unsolicited full proposals are accepted by invitation only. Application form not required.
 Initial approach: Letter
 Copies of proposal: 2
 Deadline(s): None
 Board meeting date(s): Varies
 Final notification: Up to 1 month from receipt of application
EIN: 133799186

333
Sri Sathya Sai World Foundation
1220 Oaklawn Rd.
Arcadia, CA 91006-2130
URL: http://www.sathyasai.org/organize/06mar12foundation.pdf

Established in 2006 in CA.
Donors: Narendranath Reddy; Vijay C. Desai.
Grantmaker type: Public charity.
Financial data (yr. ended 12/31/10): Revenue, $3,321,180; assets, $794,812 (M); gifts received, $3,318,979; expenditures, $2,760,417; giving activities include $2,675,482 for grants to organizations outside the U.S.
Purpose and activities: The foundation's mission is to ensure the authenticity of all programs engaged in by International Sri Sathya Sai organizations, and to incorporate the teachings of Sri Sathya Sai Baba for the good will and spiritual being of mankind.
Fields of interest: Education; Youth development; International relief.
International interests: India.
Limitations: Giving primarily in India.

Officers: Michael Goldstein, Chair.; Narendranath A. Reddy, Secy.
EIN: 204536634

334
John Stott Ministries
1050 Chestnut St., Ste. 203
Menlo Park, CA 94025-4516 (650) 617-0390
FAX: (650) 617-0389;
E-mail: info.jsm@johnstott.org; URL: http://www.johnstott.org/

Established around 1974.
Grantmaker type: Public charity.
Financial data (yr. ended 06/30/10): Revenue, $1,851,113; assets, $3,326,863 (M); gifts received, $1,761,283; expenditures, $2,244,248; giving activities include $152,300 for grants to organizations outside the U.S., and $474,305 for grants to individuals.
Purpose and activities: The organization works to support evangelical graduate students in the developing world who plan to disciple and train leaders and pastors around the world and in local contexts, by providing Ph.D. scholarships and facilitating programs to help pastors preach and lead efficiently.
Fields of interest: Theological school/education.
International interests: Developing countries.
Type of support: Scholarships—to individuals.
Limitations: Applications not accepted. Giving primarily in developing countries.
Publications: Annual report.
Application information: Unsolicited requests for funds not accepted.
Officers and Directors:* Greg Scharf,* Chair.; Tim Stafford,* Vice-Chair.; Ken Perez,* Pres.; Jack Swanson,* Secy.-Treas.; Guy Anthony; Chip Combs; Lynn Cohick; Fred Gale; Gene Green; Greg Haroutunian; Crissy Haslam; Joel Manby; Jeff McColloch; John Rain; David Spence; and 6 additional directors.
EIN: 237417198

335
Levi Strauss Foundation
1155 Battery St.
Levi Plaza
San Francisco, CA 94111-1203 (415) 501-3577
Contact: Daniel Jae-Won Lee, Exec. Dir.
FAX: (415) 501-6575;
E-mail: LeviStraussFoundation@levi.com; E-mail for Daniel Jae-Won Lee: dlee4@levi.com; URL: http://www.levistrauss.com/about/foundations/levi-strauss-foundation
Levi Strauss Foundation's Philanthropy Promise: http://www.ncrp.org/philanthropys-promise/who
LS&CO. Unzipped: http://levistrauss.com/category/blog-tags/social-responsibility

Incorporated in 1952 in CA.
Donors: Levi Strauss & Co.; Peter E. Haas, Jr.; F. Warren Hellman.
Grantmaker type: Company-sponsored foundation.
Financial data (yr. ended 11/30/10): Assets, $67,918,540 (M); gifts received, $1,715,000; expenditures, $5,163,447; qualifying distributions, $5,139,314; giving activities include $4,989,926 for 129 grants (high: $625,000; low: $126).

Purpose and activities: The foundation supports organizations involved with education, health, HIV/AIDS prevention, HIV/AIDS research, legal aid, employment, disaster relief, human services, community development, civic affairs, and women. Special emphasis is directed toward programs designed to advance human rights and well-being of underserved people.

Fields of interest: Community development, small businesses; Education; Reproductive health; Public health; Public health, hygiene; Health care; AIDS; AIDS research; Legal services; Employment, equal rights; Employment; Disasters, preparedness/services; American Red Cross; Human services, financial counseling; Human services; Civil/human rights, equal rights; Civil/human rights, advocacy; Business/industry; Community/economic development; Public policy, research; Financial services; Public affairs; Women; Economically disadvantaged.

International interests: Africa; Asia; Canada; China; Europe; Haiti; Latin America.

Type of support: General/operating support; Continuing support; Management development/capacity building; Capital campaigns; Equipment; Program development; Publication; Scholarship funds; Research; Technical assistance; Employee volunteer services; Sponsorships; Employee matching gifts.

Limitations: Applications not accepted. Giving on a national and international basis in areas of company operations, with emphasis on CA, NY, Africa, Asia, Canada, China, Europe, Latin America, and Mexico. No support for political, sectarian, religious, or discriminatory organizations, or sports teams. No grants to individuals, or for capital, endowment, or building funds, athletic competition, or advertising.

Application information: Contributes only to pre-selected organizations.

Officers and Directors:* Robert D. Haas,* Pres.; Hilary K. Krane, V.P.; Daniel Jae-Won Lee, Secy. and Exec. Dir.; Roger Fleischmann, Treas.; R. John Anderson; Sandrine Besnard-Corblet; Dorota Gotkowska; Peter E. Haas, Jr.; Jennifer Haas-Dehejia; Jeff Harlowe; Michael Kobori; Amy Leonard; Daniel Lurie; Babur Rifiq.

Number of staff: 14

EIN: 946064702

Recent grants for international programs:

335-1 Action for Health Initiatives, Quezon City, Philippines, $45,500. For renewal support for HIV/AIDS policy reform and media training for people living with HIV/AIDS in the Philippines. 2010.

335-2 AIDS Care China - Guangxi, Nanning, China, $100,000. For critical HIV/AIDS services for migrant workers in Guangdong Province and to build capacity among people living with HIV/AIDS in China to advocate for policy and social change. 2010.

335-3 AIDS Legal Network, Cape Town, South Africa, $150,000. For advocacy to create responsive communities, increase legal literacy, and enable supportive social and legal environments for HIV/AIDS work in South Africa. 2010.

335-4 AIDS Project Los Angeles, Los Angeles, CA, $100,000. To strengthen global advocacy to address HIV/AIDS stigma and discrimination among men having sex with men (MSM) and transgender people. 2010.

335-5 Alternative Financing Network, Brussels, Belgium, $80,000. To build the capacity of low-income communities in Belgium to build and protect assets through financial education and group matched savings programs. 2010.

335-6 Andrey Rylkov Foundation for the Protection of Health and Social Justice, Moscow, Russia, $30,000. For media advocacy for improved access to health and human rights protection for people affected by HIV/AIDS in Russia. 2010.

335-7 Apparel Lesotho Alliance to Fight AIDS, Maseru, Lesotho, $75,000. For peer-led interventions to address HIV/AIDS among garment workers and supervisors in Lesotho through implementation of a curriculum focusing on gender equality, gender-based violence, stigma and discrimination, and life skills. 2010.

335-8 Asia Catalyst, New York, NY, $75,000. For renewal support for development and testing of a model human rights training curriculum for HIV/AIDS-affected communities. 2010.

335-9 Asia Pacific Network of People Living with HIV/AIDS, Bangkok, Thailand, $100,000. For general support for a regional network advocating for the human rights and participation of people living with HIV/AIDS in Asia and the Pacific. 2010.

335-10 Asia Pacific Network of People Living with HIV/AIDS, Bangkok, Thailand, $100,000. For the Coalition of Asia Pacific Regional Networks on HIV/AIDS (7 Sisters) to address stigma and discrimination and advance policy and social change. 2010.

335-11 Asociacion Dominicana para el Desarrollo de la Mujer, Santo Domingo, Dominican Republic, $100,000. For technical assistance to displaced workers in the Esperanza region of the Dominican Republic to find employment, learn new technical skills or start a small business. 2010.

335-12 Association for Women's Rights in Development, Toronto, Canada, $40,000. For general support - human rights leadership grant. 2010.

335-13 Autonomia Foundation, Budapest, Hungary, $95,000. For asset building opportunities among low-income Roma families in Hungary through financial education, matched savings, and affordable credit for home improvements. 2010.

335-14 Better Cotton Initiative, Nyon, Switzerland, $100,000. For social and environmentally sustainable cultivation practices and asset building opportunities among cotton farmers in India. 2010.

335-15 Business for Social Responsibility, San Francisco, CA, $50,000. For renewal support for peer-education programs on general and reproductive health and facilitating access to health services for female and male garment workers in Pakistan. 2010.

335-16 Business for Social Responsibility, San Francisco, CA, $25,000. For renewal support for Moving the Needle: Taking Workers' Rights to Scale, a partnership to expand factory-based rights and responsibilities trainings within the apparel industry. 2010.

335-17 Canadian HIV/AIDS Legal Network, Toronto, Canada, $30,000. For a communications toolkit for the Donor Collaboration to Advance the Human Rights of Sex Work project. 2010.

335-18 Canadian Working Group on HIV and Rehabilitation, Toronto, Canada, $75,000. To build the capacity of people living with HIV/AIDS in Canada to address stigma and discrimination in employment in the context of the United Nations Convention on the Rights of Persons with Disabilities. 2010.

335-19 CARE USA, Atlanta, GA, $170,000. For renewal support to expand and enhance the Sewing for a Brighter Future program for women garment workers in Cambodia. 2010.

335-20 Catholic Relief Services, Baltimore, MD, $75,000. For the expansion of three worker rights centers providing legal aid, remediation and trainings on rights and responsibilities in Northeastern Mexico. 2010.

335-21 Center for Promotion of Quality of Life, Ho Chi Minh City, Vietnam, $50,000. For expanded support for in-factory trainings to strengthen communication mechanisms; build capacity on labor rights and responsibilities; promote health, asset building and life skills development among apparel workers in Vietnam. 2010.

335-22 Colectivo Sol, Mexico City, Mexico, $80,000. To address HIV/AIDS stigma and discrimination in health care, law enforcement and legal settings in Mexico City, Puebla, and Aguascalientes, Mexico. 2010.

335-23 European Microfinance Network, Paris, France, $100,000. For dissemination, replication and scaling of asset building innovation by influencing microfinance organizations and policy makers across Europe. 2010.

335-24 Fair Finance, London, England, $80,000. For a pilot program to promote savings among low-income clients of Fair Finance in the United Kingdom. 2010.

335-25 Forum de ONGs AIDS do Estado de Sao Paulo, Sao Paulo, Brazil, $40,000. For changes in laws, policies, and practices promoting human rights in the context of HIV/AIDS throughout the state of Sao Paulo, Brazil. 2010.

335-26 Foundation for AIDS Research, New York, NY, $100,000. For renewal support for the Men Having Sex With Men (MSM) HIV/AIDS Prevention and Advocacy Initiative in Asia and the Pacific. 2010.

335-27 Fundacion Huesped, Buenos Aires, Argentina, $75,000. For human rights advocacy and legal aid to reduce HIV/AIDS stigma and discrimination in Argentina. 2010.

335-28 Fundusz Grantowy dla Plocka, Plock, Poland, $50,000. For general support to the Grant Fund for Plock, a public-private partnership improving the capacity of local organizations to address critical community development needs in Plock, Poland. 2010.

335-29 Give to Colombia, Coral Gables, FL, $100,000. To expand a financial literacy, matched savings and micro-enterprise development program for workers in the apparel industry in Medellin, Colombia. 2010.

335-30 Global Fund for Women, San Francisco, CA, $25,000. For disaster relief and rebuilding efforts by women's organizations in the wake of the Haiti earthquake. 2010.

335-31 Grupo de Incentivo a Vida, Sao Paulo, Brazil, $40,000. For advocacy and legal aid to ensure access to treatment and advance the human rights of people living with HIV/AIDS in Brazil. 2010.

335-32 Grupo Pela Vidda, Sao Paulo, Brazil, $40,000. For legal advocacy work protecting the human rights of marginalized communities affected by HIV/AIDS in Brazil. 2010.

335-33 HealthRight International, New York, NY, $25,000. To sponsor the 20th anniversary Health and Human Rights Awards Dinner. 2010.

335-34 Human Rights Watch, New York, NY, $100,000. For general support for the Health and Human Rights Division. 2010.

335-35 Intercambios, Buenos Aires, Argentina, $75,000. For harm reduction policies to prevent the spread of HIV/AIDS in Argentina. 2010.

335-36 International Association for Community Development, Falkland, Scotland, $55,000. To help the expansion of the Indigo Asset Building Innovation Network in Europe. 2010.

335-37 International Association for Community Development, Falkland, Scotland, $25,000. To help the expansion of the Indigo Asset Building Innovation Program in Europe. 2010.

335-38 International Bridges to Justice, Geneva, Switzerland, $15,000. To safeguard legal rights for people living with or vulnerable to HIV/AIDS through sponsorship of the 2011 JusticeMakers Competition. 2010.

335-39 International Gay and Lesbian Human Rights Commission, New York, NY, $50,000. For human rights leadership grant supporting IGLHRC's 20th anniversary event and advocacy on the Yogyakarta Principles on sexual orientation and gender identity. 2010.

335-40 International HIV/AIDS Alliance, Brighton, England, $120,000. For renewal support to build a supportive legal, policy and social environment for effective harm reduction programs to prevent HIV infection among intravenous drug users in western China. 2010.

335-41 International Labour Organization, Geneva, Switzerland, $100,000. For the Better Work program to implement life skills and asset building training pilots for apparel workers in Haiti and Lesotho. 2010.

335-42 International Labour Organization, Geneva, Switzerland, $75,000. For renewal support to build the capacity of the Vietnam General Confederation of Labor (VGCL) to strengthen the ILO Better Work program and improve industrial relations in Vietnam. 2010.

335-43 KIZ, Offenbach am Main, Germany, $75,000. To promote asset building in low-income communities in Germany through a saving and loan program for micro-entrepreneurs. 2010.

335-44 Lawyers Collective, New Delhi, India, $80,000. For the human rights advocacy work of the United Nations Special Rapporteur on the Right to Health. 2010.

335-45 Lawyers Collective, New Delhi, India, $16,000. For two satellite meetings on HIV/AIDS-related policy issues about commercial sex work and access to medicines at the XVIII International AIDS Conference. 2010.

335-46 Lembaga Bantuan Hukum Masyarakat, Jakarta, Indonesia, $25,000. For general support for a community legal aid institute serving marginalized and detained populations at greater risk of HIV infection in Indonesia. 2010.

335-47 Mercado Global, New Haven, CT, $32,500. For development of a film spotlighting the asset building work of Mercado Global. 2010.

335-48 Microfinance Centre, Warsaw, Poland, $85,000. To promote asset building among low-income communities in Poland by testing and strengthening incentives to save and invest. 2010.

335-49 National Association of People Living with HIV/AIDS, Newtown, Australia, $50,000. To improve access to social justice, laws and policies, and the human rights of people living with HIV/AIDS in Australia by understanding and combating HIV/AIDS-related stigma. 2010.

335-50 Oxfam America, Boston, MA, $50,000. For disaster relief efforts in Chile. 2010.

335-51 Oxfam America, Boston, MA, $50,000. For emergency relief efforts in response to the January 2010 earthquake in Haiti. 2010.

335-52 Oxfam America, Boston, MA, $10,000. For relief efforts for Hurricane Karl in Mexico. 2010.

335-53 Partners in Health, Boston, MA, $25,000. For health emergency relief efforts in response to the January 2010 earthquake in Haiti. 2010.

335-54 Popular Education Research Group, Toronto, Canada, $75,000. To promote fair labor practices and respect for labor rights through NGO capacity building and strategic collaboration in Mexico and Central America. 2010.

335-55 Runnymede Trust, London, England, $100,000. For creation of advocacy network on ethnicity, migration and asset building in Europe. 2010.

335-56 Social and Enterprise Development Innovations, North York, Canada, $20,000. For the inaugural gathering of the Global Asset Action Network (GAAN). 2010.

335-57 Sociedad Mexicana pro Derechos de la Mujer, Mexico City, Mexico, $100,000. For renewal support for a program providing technical and capacity building assistance to organizations supporting the labor rights of women in Mexico. 2010.

335-58 Thai AIDS Treatment Action Group, Bangkok, Thailand, $100,000. For general support for a health and rights advocacy organization in Thailand working with populations highly vulnerable to HIV/AIDS. 2010.

335-59 Tides Center, San Francisco, CA, $100,000. For renewal support for advocacy to ensure comprehensive and equitable access to HIV/AIDS treatment and services in China and Southeast Asia. 2010.

335-60 Tides Center New York, New York, NY, $80,000. To build the advocacy capacity of people living with HIV/AIDS and other vulnerable groups to ensure access to essential treatment in Russia. 2010.

335-61 United Nations High Commissioner for Refugees, Geneva, Switzerland, $50,000. To support emergency relief efforts in the north where flooding has been most severe. 2010.

335-62 Washington University, Center for Social Development, Saint Louis, MO, $100,000. For inaugural regional conference in 2012 to advance the field of asset building in Asia. 2010.

335-63 Washington University, Center for Social Development, Saint Louis, MO, $100,000. For renewal support for The Global Assets Project. 2010.

336
Strome Family Foundation
100 Wilshire Blvd., Ste. 1750
Santa Monica, CA 90401-1161
Contact: Peter N.C. Davies

Established in 1993 in CA.
Donors: Jeffrey Lambert; Mark E. Strome.
Grantmaker type: Independent foundation.
Financial data (yr. ended 06/30/08): Assets, $3,762,408 (M); expenditures, $458,299; qualifying distributions, $387,654; giving activities include $320,050 for 22 grants (high: $200,000; low: $100).

Purpose and activities: Giving primarily for education and human services.
Fields of interest: Elementary/secondary education; Secondary school/education; Human services; Family services; Science.
International interests: Asia; Africa.
Type of support: Research; Program development; General/operating support; Annual campaigns.
Limitations: Applications not accepted. Giving primarily in CA. No grants to individuals.
Application information: Contributes only to pre-selected organizations.
Officers and Director:* Mark E. Strome,* Pres.; Tammy Strome, Secy.; Peter N.C. Davies, Treas.
EIN: 954460987

337
Symantec Corporation Contributions Program
c/o Symantec Community Rels.
350 Ellis St.
Mountain View, CA 94043 (650) 527-2900
E-mail: community_relations@symantec.com;
URL: http://www.symantec.com/about/profile/responsibility/community/index.jsp

Grantmaker type: Corporate giving program.
Financial data (yr. ended 03/31/09): Total giving, $19,507,396, including $3,147,560 for grants, $659,836 for employee matching gifts, and $15,700,000 for in-kind gifts.
Purpose and activities: As a complement to its foundation, Symantec also makes charitable contributions to nonprofit organizations directly. Special emphasis is directed toward programs designed to incorporate technology in teaching; engage minorities and women in the technological sciences; and better the lives of young people. Grants range from $1,000 to $100,000. Software donations to organizations located in the U.S. and Canada are administered by techsoup.org.
Fields of interest: Education; Engineering/technology; Human services; Youth development; Hispanics/Latinos; Girls; Economically disadvantaged; Children; Minorities; Women.
International interests: Asia; Canada; Europe; Mexico; Oceania; South America.
Type of support: Donated products; Employee matching gifts; Employee volunteer services; General/operating support; Program development; Sponsorships.
Limitations: Giving on a national and international basis within 50 miles of areas of company operations; giving also to national organizations, national organizations located in countries of company operations, and international organizations. No support for religious organizations not of direct benefit to the entire community, veterans' organizations, or fraternal organizations, political candidates, organizations deemed detrimental to Symantec's business goals or that can be classified as "anti-business", private foundations, or K-12 schools; no software donations for organizations with an annual operating budget of greater than $10 million, political organizations, or discriminatory organizations. No grants to individuals, or for political causes, courtesy advertising, capital campaigns, or conferences or symposia; no software donations for fundraisers, raffles, or auctions or personal use.
Publications: Application guidelines.
Application information: Organizations receiving support may be asked to provide a final report. An

interview may be requested. Software and software subscription renewal donations are limited to two contributions each per organization during any given year. The Corporate Responsibility Department handles giving. The company has a staff that only handles contributions. A contributions committee reviews all requests.

Initial approach: Complete online Letter of Intent
Deadline(s): None
Final notification: 3 months if approved for grants
Number of staff: 1 full-time professional.

338

The Tabasgo Foundation
3463 State St., Ste. 255
Santa Barbara, CA 93105-2603

Established in 2005 in CA.
Donors: Wayne E. Rosing; Dorothy F. Largay.
Grantmaker type: Independent foundation.
Financial data (yr. ended 12/31/09): Assets, $29,391,050 (M); gifts received, $4,910; expenditures, $12,104,681; qualifying distributions, $11,958,720; giving activities include $11,958,720 for 8 grants (high: $10,980,000; low: $20).
Fields of interest: Astronomy; Higher education.
Limitations: Applications not accepted. Giving primarily in CA.
Application information: Contributes only to pre-selected organizations.
Officers: Wayne Rosing, Pres.; Dorothy F. Largay, Secy.
EIN: 651251997
Recent grants for international programs:
338-1 Las Cumbres Observatory, Goleta, CA, $10,980,000. For studies in astronomy. 2009.

339

Taiwan Buddhist Tzu Chi Foundation, U.S.A.
(also known as Tzu Chi Foundation)
1100 S. Valley Center Ave.
San Dimas, CA 91773-3728   (909) 447-7799
Contact: William Keh, C.E.O.
FAX: (909) 447-7948; E-mail: info@us.tzuchi.org; URL: http://www.us.tzuchi.org

Established in 1984 in CA.
Grantmaker type: Public charity.
Financial data (yr. ended 12/31/09): Revenue, $31,986; gifts received, $27,135; expenditures, $29,011,000; giving activities include $6,624,000 for grants.
Purpose and activities: The foundation provides shelter, financial assistance, education, health care, and social services to needy people around the world.
Fields of interest: Health care; Disasters, Hurricane Katrina; Human services; International peace/security.
Type of support: Scholarships—to individuals; In-kind gifts; Emergency funds.
Limitations: Applications not accepted. Giving on a worldwide basis.
Publications: Informational brochure; Newsletter.
Application information: Unsolicited requests for funds not accepted.
Officers: Master Shih Cheng Yen,* Chair.; William Keh,* C.E.O.; Debra Boudreaux,* Exec. V.P.; Han Huang, Exec. V.P.; Paulina Luan, Exec. V.P.; Jackson

Chen, V.P.; Calvin Hsi, V.P.; Mei Kuo, V.P.; Shiu Yun Tsai, V.P.
Number of staff: 61 full-time professional; 11 part-time professional.
EIN: 942952782

340

Henri & Tomoye Takahashi Charitable Foundation
c/o Martha Suzuki
1661 Pine St., No. 1113
San Francisco, CA 94109-0413

Established in 1985 in CA.
Donors: Tomoye Takahashi; Masako M. Suzuki; Masako Takahashi.
Grantmaker type: Independent foundation.
Financial data (yr. ended 12/31/10): Assets, $4,273,854 (M); gifts received, $2,000; expenditures, $246,696; qualifying distributions, $225,000; giving activities include $225,000 for 10 grants (high: $75,000; low: $5,000).
Purpose and activities: Supports Americans of Japanese ancestry through cultural programs.
Fields of interest: Arts, cultural/ethnic awareness; Media, television; Media, radio; Arts.
International interests: Japan.
Limitations: Applications not accepted. Giving primarily in northern CA. No grants to individuals.
Application information: Contributes only to pre-selected organizations.
Board meeting date(s): Nov. 4
Officers and Directors:* Tomoye Takahashi,* Pres.; Masako M. Suzuki,* Secy.
Number of staff: None.
EIN: 942977890

341

Tarsadia Foundation
(formerly Singgod Foundation)
620 Newport Center Dr., 14th Fl.
Newport Beach, CA 92660-6420

Established in 1999 in CA.
Donors: B.U. Patel; Tushar Patel; T-Twelve Legacy Trust; Krishan Tarsadia Trust.
Grantmaker type: Independent foundation.
Financial data (yr. ended 12/31/10): Assets, $29,645,483 (M); gifts received, $10,650,000; expenditures, $1,246,660; qualifying distributions, $1,237,119; giving activities include $1,029,775 for 63 grants (high: $98,500; low: $150).
Fields of interest: Education; Higher education; Human services.
International interests: India.
Limitations: Applications not accepted. Giving primarily in CA and India. No grants to individuals.
Application information: Contributes only to pre-selected organizations.
Officers: B.U. Patel, C.E.O.; Tushar Patel, Secy.
Director: Shirish Dayal.
EIN: 330879062

342

Tawa Charitable Foundation
6281 Regio Ave.
Buena Park, CA 90620-7323

Established in 2007 in CA.
Donor: Ho-Yuan Chen.

Grantmaker type: Operating foundation.
Financial data (yr. ended 12/31/09): Assets, $1,626,207 (M); gifts received, $500,000; expenditures, $214,349; qualifying distributions, $149,700; giving activities include $149,700 for grants.
Fields of interest: Education; Disasters, preparedness/services; American Red Cross.
International interests: China.
Type of support: General/operating support; Scholarships—to individuals.
Limitations: Giving primarily in CA.
Officers and Directors:* Ho-Yuan Chen,* Pres.; Chang-Hua Chen,* Secy.; Chen Hong Lee, Treas.; Robert Chang; Tzu Tse Kao; Chi Kuang Lee.
EIN: 711035371

343

The Teichman Family Charitable Foundation
6100 Bandini Blvd.
Los Angeles, CA 90040-3112

Established in 1982 in CA.
Donors: Marcia Teichman; Ruth Teichman; Sidney Teichman; Sol Teichman; Teichman Enterprises, Inc.; Bernard Teichman; Alan Teichman; Samuel Teichman.
Grantmaker type: Independent foundation.
Financial data (yr. ended 03/31/11): Assets, $2,729,055 (M); gifts received, $81,000; expenditures, $186,841; qualifying distributions, $168,200; giving activities include $168,200 for grants.
Purpose and activities: Giving primarily for education and for Jewish organizations.
Fields of interest: Museums (specialized); Education; Human services; Jewish agencies & synagogues.
International interests: Israel.
Type of support: General/operating support; Continuing support; Annual campaigns; Building/renovation; Emergency funds; Conferences/seminars; Publication; Curriculum development; Scholarship funds; Research.
Limitations: Applications not accepted. Giving primarily in NY. No grants to individuals.
Publications: Annual report.
Application information: Contributes only to pre-selected organizations.
Officers: Sol Teichman, Pres.; Ruth Teichman, V.P.; Sidney Teichman, Secy.-Treas.
Number of staff: None.
EIN: 953710911

344

Tibetan Nyingma Relief Foundation
2210 Harold Way
Berkeley, CA 94704-1425   (510) 848-4238
FAX: (510) 548-2230;
E-mail: tap@tibetanaidproject.org; Toll-free tel.: (800) 338-4238; URL: http://www.tibetanaidproject.org

Established in 1975 in CA.
Grantmaker type: Public charity.
Financial data (yr. ended 12/31/10): Revenue, $431,859; assets, $95,125 (M); gifts received, $364,002; expenditures, $534,755; giving activities include $7,850 for grants to organizations outside the U.S.

Purpose and activities: The foundation is dedicated to supporting Tibetans dispersed throughout Asia and in Tibet. It provides financial support for monastic centers, lamas, monks, nuns, and lay people.

Fields of interest: International relief; Buddhism.

Limitations: Giving primarily on an international basis, with emphasis on Asia.

Officers and Board Members: Tarthang Tulku,* Pres.; Wangmo Dixey, V.P.; Tsering Gellek, Treas.; Pema Gellek; Jack Petranker; Rosalyn White.

EIN: 237433901

345
Tides Center

The Presidio
P.O. Box 29907
San Francisco, CA   94129-0907   (415) 561-6300
Contact: Jane Levikow, Dir., External Relations
FAX: (415) 561-6301; E-mail: info@tides.org;
Additional contact inf. to become a project: tel.:
(415) 561-7830, E-mail: newprojects@tides.org;
URL: http://www.tidescenter.org

Established in 1996.

Grantmaker type: Public charity.

Financial data (yr. ended 12/31/10): Revenue, $94,248,024; assets, $77,295,676 (M); gifts received, $84,029,370; expenditures, $95,220,606; giving activities include $17,218,024 for grants, $5,273 for grants to organizations outside the U.S., and $103,011 for grants to individuals.

Purpose and activities: The center actively promotes change towards a healthy society, one which is founded on principles of social justice, broadly-shared economic opportunity, a robust democratic process, and sustainable environmental practices.

Fields of interest: Human services; Environment, administration/regulation; Environment; International affairs; Economic development; Community/economic development; Philanthropy/voluntarism.

Type of support: Continuing support; Program development; Program evaluation; In-kind gifts.

Publications: Application guidelines; Annual report; Informational brochure.

Application information:

Initial approach: Submit nomination form for Union Square Awards

Deadline(s): None for Union Square Awards

Officers and Directors:* Stephanie J. Clohesy,* Chair.; Larry Litvak,* Vice-Chair.; Melissa Bradley,* C.E.O.; Ellen Friedman,* Exec. V.P.; Martha Jimenez,* Secy.; John R. O'Neil,* Treas.; Nao Emmett Aluli; Dan Carol; Maya Wiley.

Number of staff: 52 full-time professional.

EIN: 943213100

346
Tides Foundation

P.O. Box 29198
San Francisco, CA   94129-0198   (415) 561-6400
Contact: Christine Coleman, Dir., Comms.
FAX: (415) 561-6401; E-mail: info@tides.org;
Additional address: 55 Exchange Pl., Ste. 402, New York, NY 10005-3304, tel.: (212) 509-1049, fax: (212) 509-1059, additional e-mail: nyinfo@tides.org; Address for Honor the Earth Native Communities Program: 2104 Stevens Ave.

S., Minneapolis, MN 55404-2533, tel.: (612) 879-7529; URL: http://www.tidesfoundation.org
Facebook: http://www.facebook.com/TidesCommunity
Flickr: http://www.flickr.com/photos/tidescommunity/
RSS Feed: http://blog.tides.org/feed/
Tides Foundation's Philanthropy Promise: http://www.ncrp.org/philanthropys-promise/who
Twitter: http://twitter.com/TidesCommunity
What's Possible: The Tides Blog: http://blog.tides.org/
Pizzigati Prize e-mail: pizzigatiprize@tides.org; Jane Bagley Lehman e-mail: jblawards@tides.org

Established in 1976 in CA.

Grantmaker type: Public charity.

Financial data (yr. ended 12/31/10): Revenue, $132,896,487; assets, $169,615,992 (M); gifts received, $126,111,188; expenditures, $157,152,701; giving activities include $115,780,587 for grants, $28,727,745 for 1,632 grants to organizations outside the U.S., and $125,350 for grants to individuals.

Purpose and activities: The foundation gives primarily in the areas of the environment and natural resources, international affairs, economic public policy and enterprise development, social justice, and community affairs.

Fields of interest: Population studies; Civil liberties, reproductive rights; Media/communications; Environment, natural resources; Environment; Reproductive health; AIDS; Disasters, 9/11/01; Youth development, services; International affairs; Community development, citizen coalitions; Community development, civic centers; Economic development; Community/economic development; Economics; Public policy, research; Minorities; Native Americans/American Indians; Women; LGBTQ; Economically disadvantaged.

Type of support: General/operating support; Continuing support; Annual campaigns; Land acquisition; Program development; Publication; Seed money; Research; Technical assistance; Matching/challenge support.

Limitations: Applications accepted. Giving primarily on a national basis, with some international giving. No support for universities or organizations with budgets exceeding $2 million. No grants to individuals (except for honoraria), or for capital campaigns, endowments, or media projects.

Publications: Annual report; Informational brochure (including application guidelines).

Application information: Applications are normally only accepted in response to specific RFPs. The foundation is longer accepting applications for funding for the Moloka'i Environmental Protection Fund; see website for further information. The foundation accepts the New York/ New Jersey Area Common Application Form and the New York/ New Jersey Common Report Form.

Deadline(s): Mar., June, Sept., and Dec. for California Wildlands Grassroots Fund; May 14 for Fund for Drug Policy Reform; May 15 for Syringe Access Fund; Aug. 16 for Death Penalty Mobilization Fund; Dec.15 for Pizzigati Prize; varies for all others

Officers and Directors:* Joel Solomon,* Chair.; Drummond Pike,* C.E.O.; Ellen Friedman, Exec. V.P.; Brian Byrnes, Sr. V.P. and Managing Dir.; Melissa Lynn Bradley,* Secy.; Lauren Webster,* C.F.O. and Treas.; Joanie Bronfman; Anne Mosle; John A. Powell; Charles C. Savitt.

Number of staff: 40 full-time professional; 1 part-time professional; 12 full-time support.

EIN: 510198509

347
Tosa Foundation

(formerly Morgridge Family Foundation)
c/o Tashia F. Morgridge
3130 Alpine Road, PMB 705, Ste. 288
Portola Valley, CA   94028-8005
Contact: Tashia F. Morgridge, Pres.
Tashia and John Morgridge's Giving Pledge: http://givingpledge.org/#enter

Established in 1992 in CA.

Donors: Tashia F. Morgridge; John P. Morgridge.

Grantmaker type: Independent foundation.

Financial data (yr. ended 12/31/09): Assets, $495,404,135 (M); expenditures, $46,372,874; qualifying distributions, $46,234,856; giving activities include $46,051,120 for 297 grants (high: $12,949,200; low: $15).

Purpose and activities: Giving support to education, the environment, medical research, the arts, and human services.

Fields of interest: Arts; Higher education; Education; Environment; Animal welfare; Youth development, services; Human services; International development; International affairs.

Limitations: Applications not accepted. Giving primarily in CA and MA. No grants to individuals.

Application information: Contributes only to pre-selected organizations.

Officers and Directors:* Tashia F. Morgridge,* Pres.; Kate M. Greswold,* Secy.; John P. Morgridge,* C.F.O.; John D. Morgridge.

EIN: 943165171

Recent grants for international programs:

347-1 African Leadership Foundation, New York, NY, $250,000. For general support. 2009.

347-2 Akshaya Patra Foundation, Bangalore, India, $225,635. For general support. 2009.

347-3 Business Executives for National Security, Washington, DC, $25,000. For general support. 2009.

347-4 Business Executives for National Security, Washington, DC, $22,000. For general support. 2009.

347-5 CARE USA, Atlanta, GA, $500,000. For general support. 2009.

347-6 CARE USA, Atlanta, GA, $500,000. For general support. 2009.

347-7 CARE USA, Atlanta, GA, $13,737. For general support. 2009.

347-8 Global Heritage Fund, Palo Alto, CA, $25,000. For general support. 2009.

347-9 Interplast, Mountain View, CA, $65,000. For general support. 2009.

347-10 Ottawa Food Bank, Gloucester, Canada, $24,918. For general support. 2009.

347-11 Room to Read, San Francisco, CA, $10,000. For general support. 2009.

347-12 Village Enterprise Fund, San Carlos, CA, $10,000. For general support. 2009.

348
The Tres Chicas Foundation

P.O. Box 5145
Santa Barbara, CA   93150-5145

Established in 2000 in CA and classified as a private operating foundation.
Donor: Alison Zuber.
Grantmaker type: Independent foundation.
Financial data (yr. ended 12/31/10): Assets, $5,468,840 (M); gifts received, $300,000; expenditures, $260,175; qualifying distributions, $260,175; giving activities include $240,000 for 19 grants (high: $100,000; low: $5,000).
Fields of interest: Higher education; Health care; Human services; International relief.
Limitations: Applications not accepted. Giving primarily in CA. No grants to individuals.
Application information: Unsolicited requests for funds not accepted.
Officers: Alison Zuber, Chair.; Amisha Zuber, Pres.
EIN: 770544704

349
Turkish Educational Foundation
1113 Sladky Ave.
Mountain View, CA 94040-3628

Grantmaker type: Public charity.
Financial data (yr. ended 05/31/09): Revenue, $96,941; assets, $309,010 (M); gifts received, $111,280; expenditures, $64,590; giving activities include $61,580 for grants.
Purpose and activities: The foundation is dedicated to educating needy children in Turkey.
Fields of interest: Education.
International interests: Turkey.
Limitations: Giving primarily in Turkey.
Officers: Duygu Demirlioglu, Pres.; Erdem Esengil, V.P.; Muge Bakircioglu, Treas.
EIN: 237050060

350
U.S.-Mexico Border Philanthropy Partnership
(also known as Alianza Fronteriza de Filantropia Mexico EEUU)
2508 Historic Decatur Rd., Ste. 130
San Diego, CA 92106-6138 (619) 814-1387
Contact: Andy Carey, Exec. Dir.
FAX: (619) 814-1389;
E-mail: andy@borderpartnership.org; URL: http://www.borderpartnership.org
Facebook: http://www.facebook.com/group.php?gid=172102528248
Podcasts: http://www.borderpartnership.org/membership/publications.html

Established in 2002.
Grantmaker type: Public charity.
Financial data (yr. ended 12/31/10): Revenue, $537,834; assets, $246,549 (M); gifts received, $527,350; expenditures, $513,077; giving activities include $15,000 for grants, $6,884 for grants to organizations outside the U.S., and $20,000 for grants to individuals outside the U.S.
Purpose and activities: The organization works to strengthen and grow community philanthropy along the U.S.-Mexico border region, and to improve the quality of life for residents along the border.
Fields of interest: Human services; International affairs; Community/economic development; Hispanics/Latinos.
Limitations: Giving limited to AZ, CA, NM, TX, and Mexico.
Publications: Occasional report.

Officers and Directors:* Richard Kiy,* Co-Chair.; Karen Yarza,* Co-Chair.; Andy Carey,* Exec. Dir.; Alfredo Alvarez-Cardenas; Dr. Robert F. Ashcraft; Tony Banegas; Lic. Antonia Beguerisse de Beltran Tone; Jorge Contreras; Ana Maria de la Garza; Ruben Gonzalez; Jaime Gonzalez-Rodriguez; Russell Jones; Cheryl Alethia Phelps; Francisco Solis.
EIN: 262946180

351
Unique Zan Foundation
P.O. Box 1257
Menlo Park, CA 94026-1257 (650) 321-5021
Contact: Diane Tober, Exec. Dir.
FAX: (650) 321-5042;
E-mail: info@uniquezanfoundation.org; URL: http://www.uniquezanfoundation.org

Established in 2007 in CA.
Donor: Bita Daryabari.
Grantmaker type: Independent foundation.
Financial data (yr. ended 12/31/10): Assets, $3,217,487 (M); expenditures, $478,655; qualifying distributions, $450,835; giving activities include $203,740 for 4 grants (high: $100,000; low: $10,000).
Purpose and activities: Giving to promote health, literacy, and peace for women in and from the Middle East.
Fields of interest: Community/economic development; Education; Health care; Human services; International affairs; Civil/human rights; Women.
International interests: Middle East.
Limitations: Applications accepted. Giving primarily in CA.
Application information: Complete application details and funding opportunities available on foundation web site.
Initial approach: Letter
Officers and Directors:* Bita Daryabari,* Pres.; Diane M. Tober, Exec. Dir., Secy., and C.F.O.
EIN: 208385631

352
The United Armenian Fund
1101 N. Pacific Ave., No. 204
Glendale, CA 91202-3250 (818) 241-8900
FAX: (818) 241-6900; E-mail: sassoun@pacbell.net

Established in 1989 in CA.
Grantmaker type: Public charity.
Financial data (yr. ended 09/30/10): Revenue, $33,071,557; assets, $616,447 (M); gifts received, $33,068,581; expenditures, $33,095,157; giving activities include $31,022,520 for grants to organizations outside the U.S.
Purpose and activities: The fund seeks to bring short- and long-term humanitarian aid to indigent persons residing in Armenia.
Fields of interest: Community/economic development; Economically disadvantaged.
International interests: Armenia.
Type of support: In-kind gifts.
Limitations: Applications not accepted. Giving limited to Armenia.
Application information: Unsolicited requests for funds not accepted.
Board meeting date(s): Various

Officers and Directors:* Alex Yemenidjian,* Chair.; Harut Sassounian,* Pres. and C.E.O.; Sonia Peltekian,* Secy.; Savey Tufenkian,* Treas.; Arch. Hovnan Derderian; Arch. Moushegh Mardirossian; Louise Simone; Andrew Torigian.
Number of staff: 2 full-time professional; 1 part-time support.
EIN: 954247860

353
United Jewish Federation of San Diego County
4950 Murphy Canyon Rd.
San Diego, CA 92123-4900 (858) 571-3444
E-mail: fedujf@ujfsd.org; URL: http://www.jewishinsandiego.org

Established in 1937 in CA.
Grantmaker type: Public charity.
Financial data (yr. ended 06/30/10): Revenue, $8,586,935; assets, $12,737,011 (M); gifts received, $8,192,138; expenditures, $8,208,292; giving activities include $5,577,206 for grants, and $10,000 for grants to organizations outside the U.S.
Purpose and activities: The organization is dedicated to building a vibrant and inclusive local Jewish community, and to enhancing the well being of Jews in San Diego, Israel, and throughout the world.
Fields of interest: Religion, alliance/advocacy; Religious federated giving programs; International affairs, alliance/advocacy.
Limitations: Giving on a national and international basis.
Officers and Directors:* Steven Solomon,* Pres.; Steven J, Morris, C.E.O.; Ken Bender,* V.P.; Gene Berkenstadt,* V.P.; Howard Berkson,* V.P.; Claire Ellman,* V.P.; Tammy Moch,* V.P.; Kenneth Polin,* V.P.; Jane Scher,* V.P.; Brian Tauber,* V.P.; Andrea Oster,* Secy.; Marty Klitzner,* Treas.; Dr. Howard Bear; Juli Bear; Lori Bolotin; and 38 additional directors.
EIN: 951319015

354
The Uplands Family Foundation
(formerly Rosengarten Horowitz Fund)
134 The Uplands
Berkeley, CA 94705-2817

Established in 1996 in CA.
Donors: Jeffrey Horowitz; Lynn Horowitz.
Grantmaker type: Independent foundation.
Financial data (yr. ended 12/31/10): Assets, $7,588,404 (M); expenditures, $519,271; qualifying distributions, $408,192; giving activities include $350,000 for 59 grants (high: $92,000; low: $100).
Fields of interest: International affairs; Education; Environment; Animals/wildlife; Human services.
Limitations: Applications not accepted. Giving primarily in CA, Washington, DC, and MA. No grants to individuals.
Application information: Contributes only to pre-selected organizations.
Officers and Directors:* Lynn Horowitz,* Pres.; Jeffrey Horowitz,* Secy.
EIN: 943257271

355
Van Konynenburg Foundation
13681 W. Sunset Blvd.
Pacific Palisades, CA 90272-4019

Established in CA.
Donors: Claire Van Konynenburg; D. Michael Van Konynenburg.
Grantmaker type: Independent foundation.
Financial data (yr. ended 12/31/10): Assets, $3,261,322 (M); gifts received, $348,328; expenditures, $1,014,383; qualifying distributions, $1,009,814; giving activities include $1,009,814 for 19 grants (high: $365,000; low: $500).
Fields of interest: Medical research; Hospitals (specialty); Education; Human services; International affairs, goodwill promotion; Christian agencies & churches; Children.
Type of support: General/operating support.
Limitations: Applications not accepted. Giving primarily in CA and WA. No grants to individuals.
Application information: Contributes only to pre-selected organizations.
Trustees: Claire Van Konynenburg; D. Michael Van Konynenburg.
EIN: 954505575

356
Venture Beyond
23426 Via Codurniz
Coto de Caza, CA 92679 (949) 400-1778

Supporting organization of Purpose Driven Ministries.
Grantmaker type: Public charity.
Fields of interest: International affairs.
Officers: Forrest D. Reinhardt, Pres.; Doug Slagbaugh, Secy.; Lance Witt, Treas.
EIN: 200841989

357
Village Enterprise Fund
751 Laurel St., Ste. 222
San Carlos, CA 94070-3113 (650) 802-8891
Contact: Dianne Calvi, C.E.O.
FAX: (650) 802-8890;
E-mail: info@villageenterprise.org; URL: http://www.villageef.org

Established in 1987 in CA.
Grantmaker type: Public charity.
Financial data (yr. ended 06/30/10): Revenue, $1,320,915; assets, $471,722 (M); gifts received, $1,316,359; expenditures, $1,221,716; program services expenses, $740,466; giving activities include $249,200 for grants to organizations outside the U.S.
Purpose and activities: The organization funds micro businesses in developing countries.
Fields of interest: International economic development; International development; Community/economic development; Venture philanthropy.
International interests: Developing countries.
Limitations: Giving primarily in Africa.
Publications: Annual report.
Officers and Directors:* Dianne Calvi,* C.E.O.; Emeka Ajoku; Jay Friedrichs; Tim Geisse; Deborah A. Hall; Larry Langdon; Safa Rashtchy; Tim Tight; Christopher Wuthmann.
EIN: 222852248

358
Theodore A. Von der Ahe, Jr. Trust
177 Sierra View Rd.
Pasadena, CA 91105-1447

Established in 1978 in CA.
Grantmaker type: Independent foundation.
Financial data (yr. ended 01/31/11): Assets, $2,926,870 (M); expenditures, $174,423; qualifying distributions, $139,778; giving activities include $139,000 for 53 grants (high: $8,000; low: $1,000).
Purpose and activities: Grants primarily for religious giving, with emphasis on Catholic welfare; support also for international affairs programs and social services.
Fields of interest: Religion; Human services; International development; International human rights; International affairs; Civil rights, race/intergroup relations; Civil/human rights; Foundations (public); Christian agencies & churches; Catholic agencies & churches.
Limitations: Applications not accepted. Giving primarily in CA, Washington, DC, and NY. No grants to individuals.
Application information: Unsolicited requests for funds not accepted.
Trustee: Ted Von der Ahe, Jr.
Number of staff: 1 part-time support.
EIN: 953371127

359
Wade Family Charitable Foundation
1716 Catalina Ave.
Seal Beach, CA 90740-5711 (562) 431-9593
Contact: Chris Wade, Pres.
E-mail: chris.wade@wfcf.org

Established in 2008 in CA.
Donors: Charles Wade; Diana Wade; Chris Wade.
Grantmaker type: Independent foundation.
Financial data (yr. ended 12/31/10): Assets, $4,013,550 (M); expenditures, $428,616; qualifying distributions, $415,681; giving activities include $310,395 for 10 grants (high: $75,780; low: $3,000).
Fields of interest: Education; Christian agencies & churches.
International interests: Philippines; Tanzania, Zanzibar and Pemba.
Limitations: Applications accepted. Giving primarily in CA, Philippines and Tanzania.
Application information: Application form required.
   Initial approach: E-mail
   Deadline(s): None
Officers: Chris Wade, Pres. and C.E.O.; Diana Wade, C.F.O.
Director: Angela Wade.
EIN: 263664913

360
Wadhwani Foundation
(formerly Tekchand Foundation)
2475 Hanover St.
Palo Alto, CA 94304-1114
E-mail: info@wadhwani-foundation.org; Application address: c/o Divya Singh Gurbuxani, 2 Bina Apartments, Ground Fl., Guru Gangeshwar Marg, 6th Rd., Khar (W), Mumbai 400052, India, tel.: 91 22 26006158, fax: 91 22 26460129, e-mail: divya@wadhwani-foundation.org

Established in 1997 in CA.
Donors: Kathleen E. Wadhwani; Romesh T. Wadhwani.
Grantmaker type: Independent foundation.
Financial data (yr. ended 03/31/10): Assets, $6,367,854 (M); expenditures, $1,854,959; qualifying distributions, $1,627,183; giving activities include $588,907 for 12 grants (high: $260,000; low: $1,000).
Purpose and activities: Giving primarily for international affairs, particularly concerning India; funding also for the arts, education, and social services.
Fields of interest: Disasters, floods; Arts education; Performing arts, music; Arts; Secondary school/education; Safety/disasters; Human services; International affairs; Philanthropy/voluntarism.
International interests: India.
Limitations: Giving primarily in CA and India. No grants to individuals.
Application information: Applicants must be a legally registered (under 80G and FCRA) NGO in India. Application information available on foundation web site.
Officers: Dr. Romesh T. Wadhwani, Chair. and Pres.; Kathleen E. Wadhwani, Secy. and C.F.O.; Laura Parkin, Exec. Dir.
EIN: 770450893

361
Wang Foundation
P.O. Box 234
Pebble Beach, CA 93953-0234 (831) 624-1694
Contact: Dr. Peter C.C. Wang, Chair. and Pres.
E-mail: petercwang@aol.com; URL: http://www.wangfoundation.net

Established in 2004 in CA.
Grantmaker type: Public charity.
Financial data (yr. ended 12/31/10): Revenue, $502; assets, $4,454 (M); gifts received, $500; expenditures, $10,280; giving activities include $4,000 for grants, and for 1 grant to an organization outside the U.S.
Purpose and activities: The foundation works to advance international exchange and service learning as key elements in poverty alleviation.
Fields of interest: International exchange, students; International exchange; International development; International economic development; Poverty studies; Economically disadvantaged.
Limitations: Giving primarily in China and the U.S.
Officers: Dr. Peter C.C. Wang, Pres. and C.E.O.; Grace L. Wang, V.P. and C.F.O.
Director: Hu Dongcheng.
EIN: 753158135

362
The Joe Weider Foundation
21100 Erwin St.
Woodland Hills, CA 91367-3712

Established in 1993 in CA.
Donor: Weider Health & Fitness.
Grantmaker type: Independent foundation.
Financial data (yr. ended 11/30/10): Assets, $336,107 (M); gifts received, $400,000; expenditures, $628,582; qualifying distributions, $619,570; giving activities include $610,560 for 17 grants (high: $400,000; low: $560).

Purpose and activities: Giving primarily for education and to Jewish organizations.
Fields of interest: Education; Human services; Jewish agencies & synagogues.
International interests: Canada.
Limitations: Applications not accepted. Giving primarily in CA and NY; some giving also in Montreal, Canada. No grants to individuals.
Application information: Contributes only to pre-selected organizations.
Officers: Joe Weider, C.E.O.; Sidney Machtinger, Secy.; Eric Weider, C.F.O.
EIN: 954349698

363
Western Christian Foundation
130 W. Woodward Ave.
Escondido, CA 92025-2614

Established in 2005 in CA.
Donors: Winter Family Revocable Trust; National Assurance Group.
Grantmaker type: Independent foundation.
Financial data (yr. ended 08/31/08): Assets, $10,796,259 (M); gifts received, $14,053; expenditures, $454,918; qualifying distributions, $428,105; giving activities include $425,250 for 8 grants (high: $388,500; low: $250).
Fields of interest: Human services; Foundations (community); Christian agencies & churches.
International interests: Rwanda.
Limitations: Applications not accepted. Giving primarily in CA. No grants to individuals.
Application information: Contributes only to pre-selected organizations.
Officers and Directors:* Jim Oestreich,* Pres.; Paul Winter,* Secy.; Charlie D. Eaton,* Treas.
EIN: 134287538

364
The Whalen Family Foundation
5866 Ostrander Rd.
Oakland, CA 94618-2040 (410) 537-5452

Established in 1999 in CA.
Donors: C. Fesler; Daniel C. Whalen; Katharine C. Whalen.
Grantmaker type: Independent foundation.
Financial data (yr. ended 12/31/10): Assets, $17,765 (M); gifts received, $571,167; expenditures, $555,059; qualifying distributions, $555,047; giving activities include $458,940 for 11 grants (high: $337,452; low: $1,000).
Fields of interest: Youth, services; Youth.
International interests: Bosnia-Herzegovina.
Limitations: Applications not accepted. Giving primarily in Sarajevo, Bosnia-Herzegovina. No grants to individuals.
Application information: Contributes only to pre-selected organizations.
Officers: Daniel A. Whalen, Pres.; Katharine C. Whalen, V.P. and Secy.-Treas.
EIN: 943348069

365
The Howard & Betty White Foundation
131 Durazno
Portola Valley, CA 94028-7408

Established in 1990 in CA.

Donors: Betty D. White; Betty D. White Living Trust.
Grantmaker type: Independent foundation.
Financial data (yr. ended 06/30/11): Assets, $15,902,740 (M); expenditures, $1,086,300; qualifying distributions, $441,000; giving activities include $441,000 for grants.
Purpose and activities: Giving for religious organizations.
Fields of interest: International development; Cancer; Athletics/sports, amateur leagues; Human services; Youth, services; Christian agencies & churches; Religion.
Limitations: Applications not accepted. Giving primarily in CA. No grants to individuals.
Application information: Unsolicited requests for funds not accepted.
Officers: Eddie Dove, Pres.; Carolee White, Secy.; Mary M. McDowell, Treas.
EIN: 770250057

366
Wildlife Concern International
c/o Janice Gleason Skow
P.O. Box 7310, Mission 4SW
Carmel by the Sea, CA 93921-7310

Grantmaker type: Public charity.
Financial data (yr. ended 12/31/10): Revenue, $182,365; assets, $19,189 (M); gifts received, $182,341; expenditures, $175,397; giving activities include $160,854 for grants, and for 4 grants to organizations outside the U.S.
Purpose and activities: The organization provides funds for education and wildlife support in African countries.
Fields of interest: Animals/wildlife; Animals/wildlife, preservation/protection.
International interests: Africa.
Limitations: Giving limited to Africa.
Officer: Janice Gleason Skow, Pres.
Directors: Marcus Borner; Richard Skow.
EIN: 593141703

367
Wilson Thornhill Foundation
c/o Dreyer, Edmonds & Robbins
355 S. Grand Ave., No. 1710
Los Angeles, CA 90071-1532

Established in 1992 in CA.
Donor: Gary L. Wilson.
Grantmaker type: Independent foundation.
Financial data (yr. ended 12/31/10): Assets, $12,764,429 (M); expenditures, $733,524; qualifying distributions, $646,016; giving activities include $645,490 for 27 grants (high: $300,000; low: $1,000).
Purpose and activities: Giving primarily to an international affairs organization dedicated to the Millennium Development Goals; funding also for higher and other education, and for social services.
Fields of interest: International affairs, U.N.; Arts; Higher education; Education; Human services; Children/youth, services.
Limitations: Applications not accepted. Giving in the U.S., with emphasis on NY, as well as CA and NC. No grants to individuals.
Application information: Contributes only to pre-selected organizations.
Trustees: Gary L. Wilson; Derek Wilson.
EIN: 954400754

368
The Winnick Family Foundation
(formerly The Gary and Karen Winnick Foundation)
9355 Wilshire Blvd., 4th Floor
Beverly Hills, CA 90210-5421
Contact: Rosalie Zalis, Exec. Dir.

Established in 1983 in MD.
Donors: Gary Winnick; Karen Winnick; Pacific Capital Group; GKW Unified Holdings, LLC.
Grantmaker type: Independent foundation.
Financial data (yr. ended 12/31/10): Assets, $17,911 (M); gifts received, $1,060,000; expenditures, $728,508; qualifying distributions, $609,688; giving activities include $609,688 for grants.
Purpose and activities: Giving primarily for education, health organizations and Jewish organizations.
Fields of interest: Arts; Higher education; Education; Animals/wildlife; Health organizations, association; Jewish federated giving programs.
International interests: Israel.
Limitations: Applications accepted. Giving primarily in CA and NY. No support for political organizations. No grants to individuals.
Publications: Application guidelines.
Application information: Application form required.
  Initial approach: 3-page proposal
  Copies of proposal: 1
  Deadline(s): None
  Board meeting date(s): Rolling review
  Final notification: Up to 3 months
Officers and Directors:* Gary Winnick,* Chair.; Karen Winnick,* Pres.; Alex Winnick,* V.P.; Rosalie Zalis, Secy. and Exec. Dir.; Gregg W. Ritchie, C.F.O.; Kurt Tomita, C.F.O.; Gerry Ginsberg, Genl. Counsel; Lodwrick Cook; Adam Winnick.
Number of staff: 1 part-time professional; 1 part-time support.
EIN: 953855792

369
Wokai
653 11th St.
Oakland, CA 94607-3650
URL: http://wokai.org
Organization blog: http://wokai.org/blog

Grantmaker type: Public charity.
Financial data (yr. ended 12/31/10): Revenue, $352,476; assets, $157,008 (M); gifts received, $352,669; expenditures, $279,940; giving activities include $204,756 for grants to organizations outside the U.S.
Purpose and activities: The organization works to connect donors with rural entrepreneurs in China to help them lift themselves from poverty.
Fields of interest: Community/economic development; Community development, small businesses; Economic development; Human services.
International interests: China.
Type of support: Program-related investments/loans.
Limitations: Giving limited to China.
Officer: Casey Wilson, C.E.O.
Directors: Maya Chorengel; Michael Hsieh; Mark Hsu; Courtney McColgan.
EIN: 113814740

370
I. S. Wong Foundation

P.O. Box 80121
San Marino, CA 91118-8121

Established in 1989 in CA.
Donors: Ellen H. Sam; Wah-Pui Sam; Dr. Hing-Lan Ho.
Grantmaker type: Independent foundation.
Financial data (yr. ended 12/31/10): Assets, $13,661,859 (M); expenditures, $687,630; qualifying distributions, $643,961; giving activities include $639,000 for 24 grants (high: $100,000; low: $1,000).
Fields of interest: Disasters, preparedness/services; Human services; International affairs; Christian agencies & churches.
Limitations: Applications not accepted. Giving in the U.S., with some emphasis on CA and Washington, DC; some funding also in Singapore. No grants to individuals.
Application information: Contributes only to pre-selected organizations.
Officers: Wah-Pui Sam, Pres.; Ellen H. Sam, Secy.
EIN: 954194427

371
Working Assets Funding Service, Inc. Corporate Giving Program

c/o Mgr., Donations
101 Market St., Ste. 700
San Francisco, CA 94105-1533 (415) 788-0777
E-mail: info@credoaction.com; *URL:* http://www.workingassets.com

Grantmaker type: Corporate giving program.
Financial data (yr. ended 12/31/08): Total giving, $3,345,331, including $3,345,331 for grants.
Purpose and activities: Working Assets makes charitable contributions to nonprofit organizations involved with education and freedom of expression, the environment, peace and international freedom, economic and social justice, and civil rights. Support is given to national and international organizations.
Fields of interest: Civil liberties, first amendment; Civil rights, voter education; Civil/human rights; Civil/human rights, equal rights; Education; Environment; International affairs, arms control; International human rights.
Type of support: General/operating support.
Limitations: Giving to national and international organizations. No support for disease-specific organizations, religious organizations, or organizations established less than one year ago.
Publications: Grants list.
Application information: Contributes only to organizations nominated by the company's customers. An independent foundation reviews all nominations. Application form not required.
  Initial approach: Nomination to headquarters
  Copies of proposal: 1
  Deadline(s): June 30

372
World Affairs Council of Northern California

312 Sutter St., Ste. 200
San Francisco, CA 94108-4311 (415) 293-4600
Contact: Jane Wales, Pres. and C.E.O.

FAX: (415) 982-5028; *URL:* http://www.itsyourworld.org
Facebook: http://www.facebook.com/WorldAffairsCouncil
Flickr: http://www.flickr.com/photos/worldaffairscouncil
Organization blog: http://itsyourworldblog.wordpress.com/
Twitter: http://twitter.com/World_Affairs
Vimeo: http://vimeo.com/channels/worldaffairs
YouTube: http://www.youtube.com/worldaffairscouncil

Founded in 1947 in CA.
Grantmaker type: Public charity.
Financial data (yr. ended 12/31/10): Revenue, $7,285,925; assets, $11,592,444 (M); gifts received, $5,995,898; expenditures, $4,035,806.
Purpose and activities: The organization promotes public understanding of international affairs by offering public forums.
Fields of interest: Education, services; International affairs.
Type of support: Scholarships—to individuals.
Limitations: Applications accepted. Giving primarily to northern CA.
Publications: Application guidelines; Informational brochure; Newsletter (including application guidelines).
Application information: See web site for additional application information. Application form required.
  Initial approach: Telephone
  Copies of proposal: 1
  Deadline(s): Mar. 1 for Asilomar scholarships; Dec. 13 for Study Abroad Scholarships
  Final notification: Varies
Officers and Trustees:* Peter J. Robertson,* Chair.; Martha M. Hertelendy,* Vice-Chair.; Maria Starr,* Vice-Chair.; Jane Wales,* Pres. and C.E.O.; Kerry King, C.O.O.; Sara Abbasi,* Secy.; William Fuller,* Treas.; Charlyn Belluzzo; Douglas Boreuter; W. Richard Bingham; Maureen Blanc; John L. Boland; J. Dennis Bonney; Jennifer Burstedt; Richard M. Chong; and 46 additional trustees.
Number of staff: 20 full-time professional; 3 full-time support.
EIN: 943053917

373
World Children's Fund

5442 Thornwood Dr., Ste. 250
San Jose, CA 95123-1200 (408) 363-8100
Contact: Ruth Kendrick
FAX: (408) 629-4846; *E-mail:* info@wcf-intl.org; *URL:* http://www.worldchildrensfund.org

Established in 1984 in CA.
Donors: Universal Aide Society; World Childrens Fund-Europe (CH); World Harvest Church; Window to Asia.
Grantmaker type: Independent foundation.
Financial data (yr. ended 03/31/10): Assets, $610,665 (M); gifts received, $4,327,812; expenditures, $4,660,370; qualifying distributions, $1,786,434; giving activities include $1,786,434 for grants.
Purpose and activities: Giving for aid to needy, suffering children in crisis situations worldwide.
Fields of interest: Children/youth, services; International relief.
Type of support: In-kind gifts.
Limitations: Applications accepted. Giving on an international basis. No grants to individuals.

Publications: Annual report; Financial statement.
Application information:
  Initial approach: Proposal
  Deadline(s): None
Officers and Directors:* Joseph Lam,* C.E.O. and Pres.; Ruth Kendrick,* V.P.; Paul Chiar, Secy.; Stanley Chen,* Treas.; Douglas Kendrick, C.F.O.; Anne Chiang, Cont.; Bruce Barnes.
EIN: 770210616

374
World Emergency Relief

27715 Jefferson Ave., Ste. 205
Temecula, CA 92590-6618 (951) 225-6700
Contact: Rev. Joel MacCollam, Pres. and C.E.O.
FAX: (951) 225-6799; *E-mail:* info@wer-us.org;
Mailing address: P.O. Box 1760, Temecula, CA 92593-1760; Toll-free tel.: (888) 484-4543;
URL: http://www.worldemergency.org/
Twitter: http://twitter.com/WER_US

Established in 1985 in CA.
Grantmaker type: Public charity.
Financial data (yr. ended 12/31/09): Revenue, $21,342,178; assets, $1,034,626 (M); gifts received, $21,342,996; expenditures, $21,474,520; program services expenses, $20,103,219; giving activities include $15,309,562 for grants to organizations outside the U.S., $63,013 for grants to individuals outside the U.S., and $3,833,343 for 230 in-kind gifts.
Purpose and activities: The organization is dedicated to spreading the gospel throughout the world by evangelism, feeding the hungry, providing medical assistance, establishing churches, fostering economic development, and providing disaster relief.
Fields of interest: Health organizations; Disasters, preparedness/services; International relief; International migration/refugee issues; Native Americans/American Indians.
International interests: Caribbean; Eastern & Central Europe; Africa; Developing countries; Central America; Asia.
Type of support: General/operating support; Building/renovation; Equipment; Emergency funds; Seed money; Program evaluation; In-kind gifts; Matching/challenge support.
Limitations: Applications not accepted. Giving limited to Native American tribes in AZ and CA, and to developing countries.
Publications: Annual report; Financial statement; Informational brochure; Newsletter; Occasional report.
Application information: Unsolicited requests for funds not considered or acknowledged.
  Board meeting date(s): Four to six times annually
Officers and Directors:* Gary Becks,* Chair.; W. Foster Rich,* Vice-Chair.; Kristy Scott,* C.E.O.; Peggy Reiber,* V.P., Devel.; Kristy Scott, V.P., Prog. Logistics; Andrea Stone, V.P., Progs.; Lawrence E. Cutting,* Secy.; Michael Batarseh,* C.F.O.; Mary Carlson; Lawrence E. Cutting; Gayle Lynn Falkenthal, A.P.R.; Erica Holloway; Bob Kilpatrick; Lynn LaSuer; Robert L. Schroeder; Jimmy Valentine.
Number of staff: 6 full-time professional; 4 full-time support; 2 part-time support.
EIN: 954014743

375
World Vision International
800 W. Chestnut Ave.
Monrovia, CA   91016-3198   (626) 303-8811
E-mail: worvis@wvi.org; URL: http://www.wvi.org

Established in 1950.
Grantmaker type: Public charity.
Purpose and activities: The organization works for the well-being of all people, especially children, by providing emergency relief, education, health care, economic development and promotion of justice.
Fields of interest: Economic development; Health care; Education; International relief; Children.
Type of support: In-kind gifts.
Limitations: Giving on a national and international basis.
Officers and Directors:* Denis St. Amour,* Chair.; Rev. A. Seth Ayettey,* Vice-Chair.; Dr. Saisuree Chutikul,* Secy.; James F. Bere, Jr.,* Treas.; Max W. Buskens; David Chitundu; Berhanu Habte; Rev. Dr. Stephen A. Hayner; and 12 additional directors.
EIN: 953202116

376
X Prize Foundation, Inc.
5510 Lincoln Blvd., Ste. 100
Playa Vista, CA   90094-2015   (310) 741-4880
FAX: (310) 741-4974; E-mail: info@xprize.org;
URL: http://www.xprize.org
Facebook: http://www.facebook.com/xprize
RSS Feed: http://feeds.feedburner.com/
XPrizeFoundationBlogsRssFeed?format=xml
Twitter: http://twitter.com/xprize
YouTube: http://youtube.com/user/xprize

Established in 1995.
Grantmaker type: Public charity.
Financial data (yr. ended 12/31/10): Revenue, $18,422,678; assets, $18,840,487 (M); gifts received, $17,962,401; expenditures, $16,886,527.
Purpose and activities: The foundation's mission is to bring about radical breakthroughs for the benefit of humanity through incentivized competition that motivates individuals, companies, and organizations across all disciplines to develop innovative ideas and technologies that help solve the grand challenges that restrict humanity's progress.
Fields of interest: Medical research; International affairs; Environment; Engineering; Engineering/technology; Education; Economic development; Biomedicine research; Biomedicine; Space/aviation; Science.
Limitations: Applications not accepted. Giving on a national and international basis.
Application information: Prizes are only given out in response to specific competitions and awards programs; unsolicited requests for funding not considered or acknowledged.
Officers and Trustees:* Peter H. Diamandis,* M.D., Chair. and C.E.O.; Robert K. Weiss,* Vice-Chair. and Pres.; Keith Kegley, V.P., Alliances; Gregg E. Maryniak,* Secy. and Exec. Dir.; J. Barry Thompson,* Treas.; Bretton S. F. Alexander, Exec. Dir., Space Prizes; Bard J. Geesaman, Exec. Dir., Life Sciences; Eric C. Anderson; Amir Ansari; Anousheh Ansari; Jack Bader; Gil Elbaz; Arianna Huffington; Ratan Tata; and 14 additional trustees.
EIN: 521876879

377
Xilinx, Inc. Contributions Program
c/o Community Rels.
2100 Logic Dr.
San Jose, CA   95124-3400   (408) 559-7778
FAX: (408) 559-7114; URL: http://www.xilinx.com/about/community-relations/index.htm

Grantmaker type: Corporate giving program.
Purpose and activities: Xilinx makes charitable contributions to nonprofit organizations involved with arts and culture, education, health care, and community and social services. Support is given primarily in areas of company operations in California, Colorado, New Mexico, and Oregon, and in China, India, Ireland, Japan, and Singapore.
Fields of interest: Science, formal/general education; Engineering/technology; Mathematics; Human services; Health care; Elementary/secondary education; Education, special; Arts.
International interests: China; India; Ireland; Japan; Singapore.
Type of support: General/operating support; Program development; Employee volunteer services; In-kind gifts.
Limitations: Giving primarily in areas of company operations in CA, CO, NM, and OR, and in China, India, Ireland, Japan, and Singapore. No support for religious organizations not of direct benefit to the entire community, political organizations, fraternal organizations, or discriminatory organizations. No grants for athletic programs, athletic scholarships, tournaments, youth and adult sports leagues, or recreational activities.

378
Yen Chuang Foundation
(formerly Yen Chuang Charitable Corporation)
1247 Elko Dr.
Sunnyvale, CA   94089-2211   (408) 474-1769
Contact: Yung Tsai Yen, Pres.

Established in 1984 in CA.
Donors: Yung-Tsai Yen; Ho-Tzu Yen.
Grantmaker type: Independent foundation.
Financial data (yr. ended 11/30/10): Assets, $3,937,298 (M); gifts received, $197,623; expenditures, $228,365; qualifying distributions, $213,345; giving activities include $211,031 for 25 grants (high: $30,000; low: $90).
Purpose and activities: Giving primarily for cultural, scientific and educational endeavors.
Fields of interest: Leadership development; Crime/violence prevention; Media, radio; Arts; Education, public education; Higher education; Health care, public policy; Health care, formal/general education; Reproductive health; Reproductive health, family planning; Reproductive health, sexuality education; Public health, STDs; Health care; Crime/violence prevention, domestic violence; Family services, parent education; International human rights; Children; Asians/Pacific Islanders.
Type of support: General/operating support; Student loans—to individuals.
Limitations: Applications accepted. Giving primarily in San Francisco, CA, CO, Washington, DC, and Chicago, IL and NY.
Application information: Application form not required.
   Deadline(s): None
Officers: Yung Tsai Yen, Pres.; Ho-Tzu Yen, Secy.; Sophia Yen, Treas.
EIN: 770071175

379
The Ying Family Charitable Foundation
c/o I/O Controls Corp.
1357 W. Foothill Blvd.
Azusa, CA   91702-2853

Established in 2001 in CA.
Donors: Jeffrey Ying; Renee H. Ying.
Grantmaker type: Independent foundation.
Financial data (yr. ended 06/30/10): Assets, $1,577,171 (M); gifts received, $300,000; expenditures, $167,878; qualifying distributions, $151,134; giving activities include $133,796 for 5 grants (high: $100,000; low: $1,796).
Fields of interest: United Ways and Federated Giving Programs; Elementary/secondary education; International relief.
Limitations: Applications not accepted. No grants to individuals.
Application information: Contributes only to pre-selected organizations.
Officers: Jeffrey Ying, Pres.; Renee H. Ying, V.P. and Secy.
EIN: 912172516

COLORADO

380
AfricAid, Inc.
P.O. Box 13725
Denver, CO   80201-5741   (303) 351-4928
Contact: Elizabeth Abshire, Exec. Dir.
E-mail: africaid@gmail.com; Elizabeth Abshire Email: elizabeth@africaid.com; URL: http://www.africaid.com

Established in 2001 in CO.
Grantmaker type: Public charity.
Financial data (yr. ended 12/31/10): Revenue, $252,229; assets, $184,854 (M); gifts received, $239,799; expenditures, $171,924; giving activities include $47,917 for grants to organizations outside the U.S.
Purpose and activities: The organization supports girls' education in Africa in order to provide young women with the opportunity to transform their own lives and the futures of their communities.
Fields of interest: Education; Women; Indigenous peoples; AIDS, people with; Children/youth; Girls.
International interests: Africa; Tanzania, Zanzibar and Pemba.
Type of support: Building/renovation; Equipment; Program development; Curriculum development; Program evaluation; Scholarships—to individuals.
Limitations: Applications not accepted. Giving limited to Africa, primarily in Tanzania.
Publications: Informational brochure; Newsletter.
Application information: Unsolicited requests for funds not considered or acknowledged.
Officer and Directors:* Elizabeth Abshire, Exec. Dir.; Rocco Dodson; Emily Droll; Felicity Hannay; Dr. Carrie Besnette Hauser; Gretchen Healey; Betsy Hoke; Bazi Kanani; Amy Livingston; Dr. Doug Millham; and 7 additional directors.
EIN: 841549841

381
The Arsenault Family Foundation, Inc.
1450 Infinite Dr., Ste. E2
Louisville, CO 80027-9440

Established in 2000 in CO.
Donor: Marcel J.C. Arsenault.
Grantmaker type: Independent foundation.
Financial data (yr. ended 12/31/10): Assets,
$11,377,884 (M); gifts received, $62,500;
expenditures, $633,571; qualifying distributions,
$613,676; giving activities include $590,700 for 12
grants (high: $112,700; low: $5,000).
Fields of interest: Higher education; Human
services; International peace/security.
Limitations: Applications not accepted. Giving
primarily in NY; funding also in CO, Washington, DC,
and Portland, OR. No grants to individuals.
Application information: Contributes only to
pre-selected organizations.
Officers: Marcel J.C. Arsenault, Pres.; Sharon K.
Eshima, V.P. and Secy.; Cynda Collins Arsenault,
V.P.; John F.C. Arsenault, Treas.
EIN: 841569419

382
Asia Transpacific Foundation
2995 Center Green Ct.
Boulder, CO 80301-5421 (303) 443-6789
URL: http://www.asiatranspacific.com/ATJ/
philanthropy/projects.aspx

Established in 1998.
Grantmaker type: Public charity.
Financial data (yr. ended 12/31/10): Revenue,
$24,661; assets, $103,141 (M); gifts received,
$24,616; expenditures, $47,024; program services
expenses, $35,000; giving activities include
$35,000 for grants.
Purpose and activities: The foundation provides
medical aid and services to refugees in
impoverished areas of Asia.
Fields of interest: Human services, emergency aid;
International affairs; Immigrants/refugees.
International interests: Asia.
Limitations: Giving on an international basis,
primarily in Asia.
Officer: Marilyn Staff, Exec. Dir.
Board Members: Rick Blauvelt; Melody Massey;
James Terman; Robin van Norman.
EIN: 841451040

383
Avenir Foundation, Inc.
215 Union Blvd. Ste. 300
Lakewood, CO 80228-1841 (303) 232-2262

Established in 1993 in CO.
Donors: Alice Dodge Wallace; William Dodge
Wallace; Margaret Boynton Wallace; Berkshire
Hathaway Inc.; Varki Investments, Inc.; Beaumont
Investments, Ltd.
Grantmaker type: Independent foundation.
Financial data (yr. ended 06/30/09): Assets,
$2,290,207 (M); gifts received, $3,357,905;
expenditures, $3,434,974; qualifying distributions,
$3,360,633; giving activities include $3,360,633
for 17 grants (high: $1,000,000; low: $10,000).
Purpose and activities: Giving primarily for
education, and the arts, particularly museums;
funding also for a public research center for music

theory in Vienna, Austria, which focuses on the
methods of Arnold Schonberg.
Fields of interest: Museums (specialized); Arts;
Higher education; Education; Neuroscience
research.
International interests: Austria.
Limitations: Applications not accepted. Giving
primarily in CO, NY, as well as in Vienna, Austria. No
grants to individuals.
Application information: Contributes only to
pre-selected organizations.
Officers and Directors:* Alice Dodge Wallace,*
Pres.; William Dodge Wallace,* V.P.; Margaret
Boynton Wallace,* Secy.; Norman L. Wilson, Treas.
EIN: 841245939

384
Bohemian Foundation
(formerly The Stryker-Short Foundation)
262 E. Mountain Ave.
Fort Collins, CO 80524 (970) 221-2636
Contact: Tana Atwood, Grants Admin.
E-mail: info@bohemianfoundation.org; URL: http://
www.bohemianfoundation.org

Established in MI in 1995.
Donors: Patricia A. Short; Pat Stryker.
Grantmaker type: Independent foundation.
Financial data (yr. ended 12/31/10): Assets,
$45,508,423 (M); gifts received, $1,574;
expenditures, $14,139,840; qualifying
distributions, $14,050,640; giving activities include
$13,530,436 for 223 grants (high: $2,500,000;
low: $500; average: $5,000–$100,000).
Purpose and activities: The mission of the
foundation is to involve fellow citizens in the care
and improvement of the community.
Fields of interest: Children/youth, services.
Type of support: General/operating support;
Continuing support; Capital campaigns; Building/
renovation; Equipment; Program development;
Publication; Seed money; Research; Technical
assistance; Consulting services; Program
evaluation; Matching/challenge support.
Limitations: Applications accepted. Giving limited to
the Fort Collins, CO, area. No support for specific
religious programs, tuition-based private schools,
private foundations, individual team requests or
discriminatory programs. No grants to individuals, or
for scholarships, debt reduction, multi-year
requests, multi-program requests, fundraising
events, or for program-related investments.
Publications: Application guidelines.
Application information: Please visit the foundation
Web site for more information as well as grant
guidelines and application form. Application form
required.
  Initial approach: Website
  Copies of proposal: 1
  Deadline(s): Feb. and Sept.; specific dates
    available on foundation web site
  Final notification: May for Feb. deadline; Dec. for
    Sept. deadline; specific dates available on
    foundation web site
Officers and Director:* Pat Stryker, Pres.; Joe
Zimlich,* Secy.-Treas.
Number of staff: 2 full-time professional; 1 part-time
professional; 2 full-time support.
EIN: 841605993
Recent grants for international programs:
384-1 Acumen Fund, New York, NY, $200,000. For
  Energy Fund/Education Fund. 2010.

384-2 Central Asia Institute, Bozeman, MT,
  $168,081. For general operating support. 2010.
384-3 Colorado State University Foundation, Fort
  Collins, CO, $100,000. For College of Business
  GSSE Program. 2010.
384-4 Colorado State University Foundation, Fort
  Collins, CO, $100,000. For Global Social and
  Sustainable Enterprise (GSSE) General
  Operating. 2010.
384-5 Colorado State University Foundation, Fort
  Collins, CO, $100,000. For International
  Development Design Summit. 2010.
384-6 Colorado State University Foundation, Fort
  Collins, CO, $35,000. For International
  Development Design Summit. 2010.
384-7 Come Lets Dance, Steamboat Springs, CO,
  $15,000. For Global Institute. 2010.
384-8 Doctors Without Borders USA, New York, NY,
  $200,000. For Haiti Earthquake Relief Efforts.
  2010.
384-9 Edgemar Center for the Arts, Santa Monica,
  CA, $250,000. For Climate Refugees
  Documentary. 2010.
384-10 Global Explorers, Fort Collins, CO, $18,000.
  For Leadership Immersion for Poudre School
  District's Most Promising Yet Underserved
  Youth. 2010.
384-11 International Rescue Committee, New York,
  NY, $200,000. For Haiti Earthquake Relief
  Efforts. 2010.
384-12 Lambi Fund of Haiti, Washington, DC,
  $200,000. For Haiti Earthquake Relief Efforts.
  2010.
384-13 Oxfam America, Boston, MA, $200,000. For
  Haiti Earthquake Relief Efforts. 2010.
384-14 Partners in Health, Boston, MA, $200,000.
  For Haiti Earthquake Relief Efforts. 2010.
384-15 Root Capital, Cambridge, MA, $100,000.
  For Permanent Lending Capital. 2010.
384-16 Sustainable Schools International, Fort
  Collins, CO, $18,000. For Awareness to Action
  Service Learning Program. 2010.
384-17 Waterkeeper Alliance, New York, NY,
  $50,000. For general operating support. 2010.

385
Colorado Friends of the Lost Boys of Sudan
454 Owl Dr.
Louisville, CO 80027-2256 (303) 666-0139
Contact: Jean Wood, Pres.
FAX: (303) 449-8554;
E-mail: jeanawood@comcast.net; URL: http://
www.cflbs.com

Grantmaker type: Public charity.
Financial data (yr. ended 12/31/08): Revenue,
$83,442; assets, $7,348 (M); gifts received,
$77,220; expenditures, $94,446; program services
expenses, $89,633; giving activities include
$89,633 for grants to individuals.
Purpose and activities: The organization is
committed to assisting in the education, job training
and general welfare of Sudanese refugees known as
the Lost Boys and Girls of Sudan who have been
displaced by civil war in Sudan and currently living in
Colorado.
Fields of interest: Employment, training; Education;
International migration/refugee issues;
Immigrants/refugees.
International interests: Sudan.
Type of support: Grants to individuals.
Limitations: Giving limited to residents of CO.
Publications: Newsletter.

Officers: Jean Wood, Pres.; Bill L. Wedum, Secy.; Walt DeWolf, Treas.
Board Members: Deanna Chilton; Terry McClain; Chuck Miller; David Vorlage.
EIN: 320094224

386
Colorado Haiti Project, Inc.
841 Front St., Ste. 100
Louisville, CO 80027-1849 (303) 938-5021
Contact: Melissa Mahaney, Exec. Dir.
E-mail: melissa.mahaney@coloradohaitiproject.org;
URL: http://www.coloradohaitiproject.org

Established in 1989 in CO.
Grantmaker type: Public charity.
Financial data (yr. ended 12/31/10): Revenue, $705,518; assets, $448,139 (M); gifts received, $705,518; expenditures, $537,262; giving activities include $410,078 for grants to organizations outside the U.S.
Purpose and activities: The organization provides Colorado citizens and youth the opportunity to extend aid to the poorest of the poor in rural Haiti.
Fields of interest: International relief; International economic development.
International interests: Haiti.
Limitations: Applications not accepted. Giving limited to Haiti.
Application information: Contributes only to pre-selected organizations.
Officers and Directors:* Don Snyder,* Pres.; Jack Morris,* Ph.D., V.P.; Marti O'Dell,* R.N., Secy.; Michael Coffey,* Ph.D., Treas.; Melissa Mahaney, Exec. Dir.; Warren Berggren, M.D.; Eben Carsey, M.D.; Fr. Kesner Gracia; James Smith, M.D.; Marcia E. Walsh.
EIN: 841330243

387
Econscious Market Corporate Giving Program
603 Alpine Dr.
Boulder, CO 80304-3211 (303) 444-4144
URL: http://www.econsciousmarket.com/default/about

Grantmaker type: Corporate giving program.
Purpose and activities: Econscious Market donates a percentage of each online transaction to nonprofit organizations.
Fields of interest: Children/youth, services; International economic development; Environmental education; Food services; Animal welfare; Environment; International human rights.
Type of support: Cause-related marketing; General/operating support.

388
Ecumenical Project for International Cooperation, Inc.
(also known as EPIC)
322 Lab Rd.
P.O. Box 433
Allenspark, CO 80510-0433 (303) 747-2059
Contact: Paul T. McKay, Exec. Dir.

Established in 1977 in NY.
Grantmaker type: Public charity.

Financial data (yr. ended 12/31/10): Revenue, $117,705; assets, $290,619 (M); gifts received, $110,217; expenditures, $135,735; giving activities include $86,765 for grants.
Purpose and activities: The project seeks to promote peace, human rights, sustainable development, and preservation of the environment through research, education and action and by encouraging cooperation among organizations involved in these areas.
Fields of interest: Health care; Agriculture; Education; Environment, natural resources; International development; International peace/security; International human rights; International affairs.
Type of support: Research; Technical assistance.
Limitations: Applications not accepted. Giving on a national and international basis.
Publications: Annual report; Program policy statement.
Application information: Contributes only to pre-selected organizations.
Board meeting date(s): 2nd or 3rd weekend of Feb.
Officers and Directors:* Christie R. McKay,* Chair.; Barbara Johnson,* Secy.; Richard Williams,* Treas.; Paul T. McKay, Exec. Dir.; Tony Brun; Dana DeLoca; John Fitch; Mary E. McKay; Loren Raymond.
Number of staff: 2 full-time professional.
EIN: 132931242

389
First Data Foundation
6200 S. Quebec St., Ste. 330
Greenwood Village, CO 80111-4729
(303) 967-7700
Contact: Glora Schoch, Prog. Dir.
FAX: (954) 509-2842;
E-mail: gloria.schoch@firstdata.com; Additional contact: Ellen Sandberg, Pres., tel.: (303) 967-8287, E-mail: ellen.sansberg@firstdata.com; URL: http://www.firstdata.com/en_us/about-first-data/corporate-responsibility/foundation

Established in 2006 in CO.
Donor: First Data Corp.
Grantmaker type: Company-sponsored foundation.
Financial data (yr. ended 12/31/10): Assets, $21,612 (M); gifts received, $1,792,009; expenditures, $1,791,807; qualifying distributions, $1,791,524; giving activities include $1,791,524 for grants.
Purpose and activities: The foundation supports food banks and organizations involved with education, health, housing, disaster relief, human services, economically disadvantaged people and other areas.
Fields of interest: Human services, financial counseling; Education; Health care; Food banks; Housing/shelter; Disasters, preparedness/services; American Red Cross; Children/youth, services; Homeless, human services; Human services; United Ways and Federated Giving Programs; General charitable giving; Economically disadvantaged.
International interests: Argentina; Australia; Germany; Greece; United Kingdom.
Type of support: General/operating support; Program development; Employee volunteer services; Employee matching gifts.
Limitations: Applications not accepted. Giving primarily in Denver, CO, Omaha, NE, and Long Island, NY, giving also in Australia, Argentina,

Germany, Greece, and the United Kingdom. No support for religious or political organizations. No grants for films.
Publications: Corporate report; Grants list.
Application information: Contributes only to pre-selected organizations.
Board meeting date(s): Jan., Apr., July, and Oct.
Officers and Directors:* Grace Tent,* Chair.; Ellen Sanderg, Pres.; Joe Samuel, Secy.; Barry Cooper, Treas.; Grant Lines; Nancy Disman; Donna Mullilgan; Lisa Olson; Kim Patmore; Richard Shillito.
Number of staff: 2 full-time professional.
EIN: 205626313

390
Harmes C. Fishback Foundation Trust
8 Village Rd.
Englewood, CO 80113-4908
Contact: Katharine H. Stapleton, Tr.
E-mail: kties@aol.com

Trust established in 1972 in CO.
Donor: Harmes C. Fishback†.
Grantmaker type: Independent foundation.
Financial data (yr. ended 12/31/10): Assets, $8,863,214 (M); expenditures, $403,930; qualifying distributions, $373,505; giving activities include $342,500 for 79 grants (high: $16,000; low: $100).
Purpose and activities: Giving primarily for education, health and human services, and the arts.
Fields of interest: Museums; Medical research, institute; Hospitals (general); Historical activities; Higher education; Health organizations, association; Children/youth, services; Arts; Young adults; Physically disabled; Adults.
International interests: France.
Type of support: Continuing support; General/operating support; Scholarship funds.
Limitations: Applications accepted. Giving primarily in the metropolitan Denver, CO, area. No support for health organizations or hospitals, with few exceptions. No grants to individuals.
Application information: Application form not required.
Initial approach: Letter
Copies of proposal: 1
Deadline(s): None
Trustees: Benjamin F. Stepleton III; Craig R. Stapleton; Katharine H. Stapleton.
Number of staff: None.
EIN: 846094542

391
Free A Child
1576 Hawthorn
Boulder, CO 80304-2217 (720) 890-1457
E-mail: info@freeachild.org; URL: http://www.freeachild.org

Established in 1998 in CO.
Grantmaker type: Public charity.
Financial data (yr. ended 12/31/08): Revenue, $13,156; assets, $4,822 (M); gifts received, $13,156; expenditures, $13,245; program services expenses, $12,741; giving activities include $12,741 for 3 grants (high: $5,383; low: $1,360).
Purpose and activities: The organization is dedicated to preventing the exploitation and trafficking of individuals into the U.S. and global sex trade by delivering micro-economic aid and

prevention education to girls and young women in Nepal who are in danger of being sold into brothels in India, and by empowering homeless youth in the Denver area who are at-risk to exploitation and trafficking.
Fields of interest: International human rights; Crime/violence prevention; Crime/violence prevention, youth; Crime/violence prevention, sexual abuse; Children/youth, services; Girls; Women.
International interests: Nepal.
Limitations: Giving limited to the metropolitan Denver, CO area and Nepal.
Officer and Directors:* Kenlyn Kolleen,* Pres.; Rebecca Callahan; Elizabeth Dining; Kendall Rames; Helaine Unger.
EIN: 841450336

392
General Service Foundation
557 N. Mill St., Ste. 201
Aspen, CO   81611-1513   (970) 920-6834
FAX: (970) 920-4578;
E-mail: info@generalservice.org; E-mail for Letters of Inquiry (if applicant cannot apply online): grantmanager@generalservice.org; Additional tel. (for William M. Repplinger, Cont.): (970) 920-6834, ext. 5; URL: http://www.generalservice.org

Incorporated in 1946 in IL.
Donors: Clifton R. Musser†; Margaret K. Musser†.
Grantmaker type: Independent foundation.
Financial data (yr. ended 12/31/10): Assets, $60,848,547 (M); expenditures, $4,162,537; qualifying distributions, $3,382,852; giving activities include $2,550,930 for 94 grants (high: $120,000; low: $2,000), and $22,443 for foundation-administered programs.
Purpose and activities: The foundation believes it can make its best contribution at this point in time by addressing some of the world's basic long-term problems in three areas: Human Rights and Economic Justice, Reproductive Justice and the Colorado Program.
Fields of interest: Environment, natural resources; Reproductive health; Reproductive health, family planning; Youth, pregnancy prevention; International peace/security; International human rights; Civil liberties, reproductive rights.
International interests: Caribbean; Central America; Mexico.
Type of support: Mission-related investments/ loans; General/operating support; Emergency funds; Program development; Conferences/ seminars; Seed money; Technical assistance.
Limitations: Applications accepted. Giving limited to the U.S., Mexico, Central America, and the Caribbean.
Publications: Application guidelines; Financial statement; Grants list; Informational brochure (including application guidelines).
Application information: Applicants are strongly encouraged to submit letters of inquiry via e-mail or using the online submission form on the foundation web site. Applicants who are unable to apply online may submit their letters of inquiry via e-mail or U.S. mail, but this only if applying online is not an option. The foundation encourages applicants to who apply via U.S. mail to use non-chlorine bleached recycled paper, and not to use plastic binders. Application form required.
   Initial approach: Online letter of inquiry (4 pages)
   Copies of proposal: 1

Deadline(s): Feb. 1 and Sept. 1 for letter of inquiry; Mar. 1 and Oct. 1 for invited proposals
Board meeting date(s): Apr. and Nov.
Final notification: 6 months
Officers and Directors:* Robin Snidow,* Chair.; Zoe Estrin,* Vice-Chair.; Marcie J. Musser,* Secy.; Will Halby,* Treas.; William M. Repplinger, CPA, C.F.O.; Lani A. Shaw, Exec. Dir.; Mary Lloyd Estrin; Robert L. Estrin; Zoe L. Foxley; Peter C. Halby; Cleo Hill; Marcie J. Musser; Robert W. Musser; Crystal Plati; Arturo Sandoval; Bill Vandenberg.
Number of staff: 4 full-time professional; 1 full-time support.
EIN: 366018535

393
The Global Volunteer Network Foundation
P.O. Box 294
Littleton, CO   80160-0294
E-mail: info@gvnfoundation.org; Toll-free tel.: (800) 963-1198; URL: http://www.gvnfoundation.org

Established in 2005 in CO.
Grantmaker type: Public charity.
Financial data (yr. ended 12/31/10): Revenue, $384,730; assets, $99,867 (M); gifts received, $482,475; expenditures, $360,711; giving activities include $174,643 for grants to organizations outside the U.S.
Purpose and activities: The foundation works to support the charitable and educational work of local community organizations in various countries through the distribution of financial, in-kind, and material donations.
Fields of interest: Environment; International development; Community/economic development.
Type of support: General/operating support; Emergency funds; Building/renovation; Annual campaigns; In-kind gifts.
Limitations: Applications not accepted. Giving primarily to Ecuador, Ethiopia, Kenya, Nepal, Peru, Philippines, Romania, South Africa, Tanzania, Uganda and Vietnam.
Publications: Annual report; Grants list; Newsletter.
Application information: Contributes only to pre-selected organizations.
Officers and Directors:* Colin Salisbury,* Chair. and C.E.O.; Barbara Courtney,* Secy.; Leslie Plomondon,* Treas.; Courtney Montague, Exec. Dir.; Chris Bryan; Mike Cornish; Emma Cahilog Rahman.
EIN: 203087760

394
Grassroots Asia
P.O. Box 6750
Snowmass Village, CO   81615-6750
(970) 923-1700
FAX: (970) 923-0655;
E-mail: info@grassrootsasia.org; URL: http:// www.grassrootsasia.org

Established in CO.
Grantmaker type: Public charity.
Financial data (yr. ended 12/31/09): Revenue, $45,049; assets, $122,559 (M); gifts received, $39,538; expenditures, $62,217.
Purpose and activities: The organization identifies and empowers grassroots projects in Asia which offer emergency relief, access to basic care, and education for children and the under-privileged by providing fundraising and marketing support in the

U.S. for efforts that are self-sustaining, aid the most vulnerable, and offer creative solutions to those in need.
Fields of interest: Philanthropy/voluntarism; Children/youth, services; Family services; Human services; Human services, emergency aid; Economically disadvantaged.
International interests: Asia.
Type of support: Grants to individuals.
Limitations: Giving limited to Asia, primarily in India.
Publications: Newsletter.
Officers: Debra Pennington, Pres.; Ann Cassidy Brink, V.P.; Steve Alldredge, Secy.
EIN: 020700384

395
H.E.L.P. International
1041 S. Country Rd. 3
Johnstown, CO   80534-4097   (303) 678-7788
E-mail: info@helpint.org; Toll-free tel.: (800) 955-9444; additional address: 629 14th St., S.W., Loveland, CO 80537-6329, tel.: (970) 224-2233; URL: http://www.helpint.org

Established in 2000 in CO.
Grantmaker type: Public charity.
Financial data (yr. ended 12/31/10): Revenue, $6,730,146; assets, $72,574 (M); gifts received, $6,525,750; expenditures, $6,706,209; giving activities include $1,066,052 for grants, and $5,132,921 for grants to organizations outside the U.S.
Purpose and activities: The organization works to provide medical services to the needy by linking arms with other ministries having shared beliefs and values, to help develop medical clinics and centers in areas of the world where people have been underserved by medical services by providing supplies, doctors, and other qualified medical personnel; and volunteer for organizations working with underserved communities.
Fields of interest: International relief; Health care; Health care, clinics/centers.
Type of support: In-kind gifts.
Limitations: Giving on a national and international basis.
Publications: Newsletter.
Officers and Directors:* Jean Kaye Wilson,* Pres.; Don Wilson,* Treas.; Pastor Brett Costigan; Katherine Elmore; Ben Fetzer; Dr. George Kandel; Shauna King; Randy Mirowski.
EIN: 841531749

396
Hunter-White Foundation
1520 S. University Blvd.
Denver, CO   80210-2813

Established in 1998 in CO.
Donor: Catherine P. Cole.
Grantmaker type: Independent foundation.
Financial data (yr. ended 12/31/10): Assets, $3,011,971 (M); gifts received, $41,000; expenditures, $220,645; qualifying distributions, $203,749; giving activities include $200,000 for 10 grants (high: $40,000; low: $5,000).
Purpose and activities: Giving primarily for human services, employment programs, and the environment.

Fields of interest: Disasters, Hurricane Katrina; Environment, natural resources; Employment; Human services; International peace/security.
Limitations: Applications not accepted. Giving primarily in CO, MA and NY. No support for religious and political programs. No grants to individuals.
Application information: Unsolicited requests for funds not accepted.
Directors: Amy C. Berkley; Linda C. Call; Catherine P. Cole; Lisa A. Cole.
EIN: 841443958

397
Japan America Society of Colorado
1625 Broadway, Ste. 680
Denver, CO 80202-4725 (303) 592-5364
Contact: Dilek Eccles, Exec. Dir.
FAX: (303) 592-5367; E-mail: info@jascolorado.org;
URL: http://www.jascolorado.org

Established in 1989 in CO.
Grantmaker type: Public charity.
Financial data (yr. ended 12/31/09): Revenue, $93,045; assets, $111,431 (M); gifts received, $50,086; expenditures, $75,028; giving activities include $7,730 for grants.
Purpose and activities: The society promotes mutual understanding and commerce between the people of Japan and Colorado at a grassroots level, by serving as an important resource in Colorado for all things relating to Japan; and by providing opportunities for cultural, historical, language, arts, educational, and personal exchange to further contacts and knowledge.
Fields of interest: International affairs, goodwill promotion; International affairs; International exchange.
International interests: Japan.
Limitations: Giving limited to CO, primarily in Denver. No grants to individuals.
Publications: Newsletter.
Officers and Board Members:* Shinobu Yoshitomi, Pres.; Richard K Clark, V.P.; John Bywaters, Secy. and Treas.; Dilek Eccles, Exec. Dir.; Hiraga Eric; Ajisaka Kathy; Bywaters John; Driver Michael; and 19 additional Board Members.
EIN: 841125146

398
The JFM Foundation
P.O. Box 17965
Denver, CO 80217-0965 (303) 864-2316
Contact: Joanie Wimberg Pacheco, Fdn. Admin.
FAX: (303) 894-9088;
E-mail: info@jfmfoundation.org; URL: http://www.jfmfoundation.org

Established in 1980 in CO.
Donor: Frederick R. Mayer†.
Grantmaker type: Independent foundation.
Financial data (yr. ended 11/30/09): Assets, $4,219,854 (M); gifts received, $853,334; expenditures, $7,426,006; qualifying distributions, $7,252,756; giving activities include $7,194,993 for 35 grants (high: $2,500,000; low: $1,000).
Purpose and activities: Support for innovative and cooperative projects in the areas of art, education, child development, women's issues and economic development that achieve long lasting and tangible impact.

Fields of interest: Arts; Education; Children/youth, services; Community/economic development; Women.
International interests: Mexico.
Type of support: Program development; Seed money; Matching/challenge support.
Limitations: Applications not accepted. Giving limited to CO for community projects and social issues; cultural programs having national or international significance are considered. No support for medical or health-related fields or religious organizations for religious purposes. No grants to individuals, or for endowments, deficit financing, fundraising, testimonials, or basic research.
Publications: Annual report.
Application information: Unsolicited requests for funds are not accepted.
Board meeting date(s): Varies
Officers and Trustees:* Jan Perry Mayer,* Pres.; Frederick M. Mayer,* V.P. and Secy.; Anthony R. Mayer,* V.P. and Treas.; Barbara Ann Atkeson; Ann Daley; Gloria J. Higgins; Harold R. Logan, Jr.
Number of staff: 1 part-time professional.
EIN: 840833163
Recent grants for international programs:
398-1 Cordillera Presidents Foundation, Denver, CO, $12,500. For general operating support. 2009.

399
The Kenney Brothers Foundation
(formerly Jay P.K. Kenney Private Foundation)
910 Gaylord St.
Denver, CO 80206-3754

Established in 1993 in CO.
Donor: Jay P.K. Kenney.
Grantmaker type: Independent foundation.
Financial data (yr. ended 12/31/10): Assets, $1,674,206 (M); gifts received, $10,000; expenditures, $329,787; qualifying distributions, $324,250; giving activities include $324,250 for 60 grants (high: $15,000; low: $250).
Fields of interest: AIDS; Arts; Elementary/secondary education; Environment; Animals/wildlife, preservation/protection; Legal services; Recreation.
International interests: China.
Limitations: Applications not accepted. Giving primarily in CO. No grants to individuals.
Application information: Contributes only to pre-selected organizations.
Officers: Jay P.K. Kenney, Pres.; Thomas J. Barrett, Jr., Secy.
Trustees: Clayton Kendall Kenney; Duncan Stross Kenney.
EIN: 841249377

400
Living Stones Foundation
(formerly Praise The Lord Foundation)
1544 Oxbow Dr., Ste. 200
Montrose, CO 81401 (970) 497-5001
FAX: (970) 497-5670;
E-mail: info@lsfoundation.org; URL: http://www.lsfoundation.org/

Established in 1986 in CA.
Donors: Kenneth A. Eldred; Roberta E. Eldred.
Grantmaker type: Independent foundation.

Financial data (yr. ended 11/30/09): Assets, $7,077,294 (M); expenditures, $340,024; qualifying distributions, $245,785; giving activities include $208,917 for 13 grants (high: $60,800; low: $450).
Purpose and activities: Giving primarily for projects relating to: Community Transformation, Family Values, Business as Mission and Evangelism.
Fields of interest: Christian agencies & churches; Minorities; Women.
International interests: Central America; Europe; India; Middle East; Oceania; South America.
Type of support: Seed money; Research; Matching/challenge support.
Limitations: Applications not accepted. Giving on a national and international basis. No grants to individuals.
Application information: Due to its commitments and limitations, the foundation will not add any new grantees.
Board meeting date(s): Varies
Officers and Trustees:* Kenneth A. Eldred,* Chair.; Roberta E. Eldred, Pres.; Paul H. J. Kim,* V.P.; Kary N. Eldred,* Secy.; Justin A. Eldred,* Treas.; Monica Eldred; Rachel Eldred; and 5 additional trustees.
Number of staff: 2 part-time professional; 1 part-time support.
EIN: 770140039

401
Lutheran Social Service of Colorado
363 S. Harlan St., Ste. 200
Denver, CO 80226-3552 (303) 922-3433
Contact: James Barclay, Pres. and C.E.O.; Dianne Reyer, Dir., Prog. Support
FAX: (303) 922-7335; E-mail: info@lfsco.org;
Toll-free tel.: (800) 579-9496; URL: http://www.lfsco.org

Established in 1948 in CO.
Grantmaker type: Public charity.
Financial data (yr. ended 06/30/11): Revenue, $12,241,439; assets, $2,727,989 (M); gifts received, $2,101,064; expenditures, $11,569,785; giving activities include $3,766,580 for grants to individuals.
Purpose and activities: The organization gives aid to vulnerable members of society through services that heal, strengthen, and provide hope, in an inclusive and non-discriminatory manner.
Fields of interest: Housing/shelter; Human services; Single parents; Infants/toddlers; Children/youth; Aging; African Americans/Blacks; Crime/abuse victims; Immigrants/refugees; Economically disadvantaged.
Publications: Annual report; Financial statement; Informational brochure; Newsletter.
Application information:
Board meeting date(s): Feb., June, Sept., and Dec.
Officers and Directors:* Jim Swaeby,* Chair.; Greg Johnson,* Vice-Chair., Finance; Jerry Paul,* Vice-Chair., Board Devel.; Matt Rauh,* Vice-Chair., Resource Devel.; James Barclay, Pres. and C.E.O.; John Samuelson,* Secy.; Jennifer Bick; Betty Boyd; Phyllis Eifler; and 7 additional directors.
Number of staff: 97
EIN: 840775550

COLORADO—Rio—406

402
Mercy and Sharing
(formerly Foundation for Worldwide Mercy & Sharing)
201 N. Mill St., Ste. 201
Aspen, CO 81611-1503 (970) 925-1492
FAX: (970) 925-1181;
E-mail: contactus1@haitichildren.com; Toll-free tel.:
(877) 424-8454; URL: http://
www.haitichildren.com
Facebook: http://www.facebook.com/pages/
The-Mercy-and-Sharing-Foundation/52849460750
Twitter: http://twitter.com/MercyandSharing

Established in 1995 in CO.
Donors: Joseph Krabacher; Susan Krabacher; Dave Anderson; Robert Brining; Linda Brining; Anthony Caine; Terri Caine; Doris Carver; Buck Deane; Natasha Dean; Christopher Hewett; Frances Johnson; Edwin Joseph; Jeffrey Leck; Carolyn McRae; Ginger Reddington; Rotary Foundation of Washington; Fund for the Poor, Inc.; Bridgeway Charitable Foundation; Crystal Foundation; John A. Griffin Foundation, Inc.; Heart to Heart for Kids, Inc.; The Anschutz Foundation; Blake Okland; Eydie Okland; Cactus Jacks Restaurants; Campbell Soup Company; Cargo Express International; Christopher L. Tolk Rev. Trust; Claire Stilwell; Comme Il Faut; Dallas Haiti Project; Diagnostic Instruments Inc.; Dolphin Outdoor Power Equipment; Feed My Starving Children; Frank Woods; Tamara Woods; Fund for the Poor Inc.; Iselin Foundation; Kellogg's Corporation; Ken Delaski; LDS Humanitarian Services; Lester & Frances Johnson Foundation; Marcos Rodriguez; Sony Rodriguez; Medical Bridges; Michael Lypka; Samaritans International Inc.; Snowmass Chapel; Stop Hunger Now Organization; Sysco Corporation; The Capital Trust Co. of Delaware; The Helen Hayes Foundation; The Louis L. Borick Foundation; The Pacific Charitable Trust; Tom Turnbull; Ros Turnbull.
Grantmaker type: Public charity.
Financial data (yr. ended 03/31/10): Revenue, $3,360,070; assets, $2,451,239; gifts received, $3,308,662; expenditures, $2,340,332; program services expenses, $2,003,029; giving activities include $3,000 for grants, and $2,000,029 for foundation-administered programs.
Purpose and activities: Giving primarily for health and medical care for children in Haiti.
Fields of interest: Education; Health care; Children, services.
International interests: Haiti.
Type of support: General/operating support; Building/renovation; Program development.
Limitations: Giving primarily in CO, FL, IL and NY, with program giving in Haiti. No grants to individuals.
Publications: Financial statement; Newsletter.
Application information: Application form not required.
   Deadline(s): None
   Board meeting date(s): Monthly
Officers and Board Members:* Susan Krabacher,* Pres.; B. Joseph Krabacher,* Secy.-Treas.; Colin Brown; John Cripe; Marie Ginther; Ray Ginther; Jennefer Hirshberg; Jeffrey Leck; Connie O'Murray; Richard K. Taylor; Laura Wright.
EIN: 841323007

403
Oreg Foundation
(formerly Weaver Family Foundation)
P.O. Box 20587
Boulder, CO 80308-0587 (720) 565-4064
Contact: Julie Shaffer, Secy.

Established in 1999 in CO as the Weaver Family Foundation; assets split in 2008 to create two separate foundations. Name changed in 2008.
Donors: Lindsey A. Weaver, Jr.; Francine Lavin Weaver.
Grantmaker type: Independent foundation.
Financial data (yr. ended 12/31/10): Assets, $9,227,262 (M); expenditures, $285,340; qualifying distributions, $259,084; giving activities include $131,598 for 57 grants (high: $18,000; low: $180).
Purpose and activities: The foundation funds Colorado based, non-sectarian charitable programs that focus on education, community service, and the preservation of our natural environment. The foundation also supports programs that enhance Jewish life and spiritual renewal in the United States, Israel, and other countries around the world.
Fields of interest: Education; Environment; Housing/shelter, development; Human services; Jewish agencies & synagogues.
International interests: Israel.
Type of support: General/operating support; Continuing support; Program development; Conferences/seminars; Curriculum development; Fellowships; Consulting services; Program-related investments/loans; Matching/challenge support.
Limitations: Applications accepted. Giving primarily in Boulder, CO, and Israel. No grants to individuals.
Application information: Colorado Common Grant Application form required. Application form required.
   Initial approach: Proposal
   Deadline(s): None
Officer: Julie Shaffer, Secy.
Director: Lindsay A. Weaver, Jr.
Number of staff: 1 full-time professional.
EIN: 841513850

404
ProLogis Foundation
4545 Airport Way
Denver, CO 80239-5716 (303) 567-5000
Contact: Edward S. Nekritz, Sr. V.P. and Secy.-Treas.
URL: http://www.prologis.com/en/aboutus/CommunityInvolvement.aspx

Established in 2001 in CO.
Donors: Catellus Land & Development Corporation and Subsidiaries; Development Services Trust; ProLogis.
Grantmaker type: Company-sponsored foundation.
Financial data (yr. ended 12/31/10): Assets, $11,900,707 (M); gifts received, $2,000,262; expenditures, $596,518; qualifying distributions, $594,012; giving activities include $594,012 for 41 grants (high: $140,000; low: $50).
Purpose and activities: The foundation supports museums and organizations involved with education, health, spine injuries, human services, and international relief.
Fields of interest: Museums; Elementary school/education; Higher education; Scholarships/financial aid; Education; Hospitals (general); Health care, patient services; Spine disorders; Boys & girls clubs; Youth development, adult & child programs; Boy scouts; Youth development, business;

Children/youth, services; Human services; International relief.
Type of support: General/operating support; Program development; Scholarship funds; Employee matching gifts.
Limitations: Applications accepted. Giving primarily in areas of company operations, with emphasis in CO; giving also to national organizations.
Application information: Application form not required.
   Initial approach: Proposal
   Deadline(s): None
Officers and Directors:* Walter C. Rakowich,* Pres.; Edward S. Nekritz,* Sr. V.P. and Secy.-Treas.; Lori Palazzolo, V.P.
EIN: 364439409

405
Queen of Apostles Mission Association
c/o St. Elizabeth of Hungary Church
1060 St. Francis Way
Denver, CO 80204-2025 (720) 234-7223
Contact: A. Matt Werner, Pres.
E-mail: qama@aol.com; URL: http://www.qama.org

Established in 1993 in CO.
Grantmaker type: Public charity.
Financial data (yr. ended 03/31/11): Revenue, $51,891; assets, $2,905 (M); expenditures, $51,124; giving activities include $26,350 for grants.
Purpose and activities: The association provides funds for to Catholic Church for rebuilding in Russia and other countries of the former Soviet Union.
Fields of interest: Catholic agencies & churches.
International interests: Soviet Union (Former).
Type of support: General/operating support; Continuing support; Building/renovation; Publication.
Limitations: Giving limited to benefit Russia, Ukraine, Belarus, and other former Soviet Union countries.
Publications: Corporate giving report; Informational brochure (including application guidelines); Newsletter.
Application information:
   Board meeting date(s): First week in Jan.
Officers and Directors: A. Matt Werner,* Pres.; Kitty Kolody,* Secy.; Sylvia Groeger,* Treas.; Jane Brennan; Rachel Bresnahan; Joe McAleer.
Number of staff: 1 part-time professional; 1 part-time support.
EIN: 841212760

406
Rio Tinto Borax Corporate Giving Program
c/o Rio Tinto Minerals
8000 E. Maplewood Ave.
Greenwood Village, CO 80111-4714
URL: http://www.borax.com/practices5.html

Grantmaker type: Corporate giving program.
Purpose and activities: Rio Tinto Borax makes charitable contributions to nonprofit organizations on a case by case basis. Support is given primarily in areas of company operations in California, Colorado, and Illinois, and in Argentina, Belgium, Brazil, China, England, France, Germany, Italy, the Netherlands, Singapore, Spain, and Taiwan.
Fields of interest: General charitable giving; United Ways and Federated Giving Programs.

International interests: Argentina; Belgium; Brazil; China; England; France; Germany; Italy; Netherlands; Singapore; Spain; Taiwan.
Type of support: General/operating support.
Limitations: Giving primarily in areas of company operations in CA, CO, and IL, and in Argentina, Belgium, Brazil, China, England, France, Germany, Italy, the Netherlands, Singapore, Spain, and Taiwan.

407
The Salvador Foundation
5061 N. 30th St., Ste. 103
Colorado Springs, CO   80919-3248
(719) 598-6006
FAX: (719) 598-6556;
E-mail: info@salvadorfoundation.org; E-mail address for applications: grants@salvadorfoundation.org;
URL: http://www.salvadorfoundation.org/

Established in 2005 in CO.
Donor: Salvador Imaging, Inc.
Grantmaker type: Company-sponsored foundation.
Financial data (yr. ended 12/31/10): Assets, $20,260,659 (M); gifts received, $520; expenditures, $848,172; qualifying distributions, $712,588; giving activities include $671,200 for 10 grants (high: $350,000; low: $11,000).
Purpose and activities: The foundation supports programs designed empower individuals, organizations, and communities through Christianity. Special emphasis is directed toward helping people who are truly in need.
Fields of interest: Human services; Education; Environment, water resources; Health care; Agriculture; Economic development; Microfinance/microlending; Christian agencies & churches; Economically disadvantaged.
International interests: Latin America.
Type of support: General/operating support.
Limitations: Applications accepted. Giving primarily in Miami, FL, and in Latin America. No support for organizations that advocate abortion or the taking of human life. No grants to individuals, or for sports activities (unless participants are mentally or physically handicapped), general operating support of K-12 schools or colleges, or mission trips.
Publications: Application guidelines; Newsletter.
Application information:
   Initial approach: Download application form and e-mail to foundation
   Deadline(s): None
Officers: H. William Mahaffey, Chair.; David W. Gardner, Pres.; Mary Gardner, Secy.-Treas.
Director: Nick Gonzales.
EIN: 202760889

408
Society of Economic Geologists Foundation, Inc.
7811 Shaffer Pkwy.
Littleton, CO   80127-3732   (720) 981-7882
FAX: (720) 981-7874; E-mail: seg@segweb.org;
URL: http://www.segweb.org/foundation/mission.aspx

Established in 1966.
Grantmaker type: Operating foundation.
Financial data (yr. ended 12/31/10): Assets, $4,575,540 (M); gifts received, $397,219; expenditures, $586,320; qualifying distributions,

$1,024,428; giving activities include $449,446 for 12 grants.
Purpose and activities: Giving to fund education, research, publications, student support, public outreach and other geoscientific programs endorsed by the Society of Economic Geologists, Inc. (SEG), or other programs considered for funding by the trustees of the corporation. Support is limited to programs, projects, and research in economic geology as they relate to metallic mineral deposits.
Fields of interest: Geology.
International interests: Global programs.
Type of support: Publication; Seed money; Grants to individuals.
Limitations: Applications not accepted.
Publications: Informational brochure; Newsletter.
Application information: Unsolicited requests for funds not accepted.
Officers and Trustees:* Donald Birak,* Pres.; Peter K.M. Megaw,* V.P.; David W. Broughton,* Secy.; Brian G. Hoal, Exec. Dir.; A. Geoff Loudon; Barton J. Suchomel.
Number of staff: 1 part-time support.
EIN: 516020487

409
Someone Cares Charitable Trust
P.O. Box 2062
Wheat Ridge, CO   80034-2062
Contact: Philip Yancey, Pres.

Established in 1986 in IL.
Grantmaker type: Independent foundation.
Financial data (yr. ended 05/31/11): Assets, $820,340 (M); gifts received, $318,904; expenditures, $286,576; qualifying distributions, $268,450; giving activities include $268,450 for grants.
Purpose and activities: Giving primarily for education, health centers, human services, and community service organizations.
Fields of interest: Health care; Education; Human services; International development; International relief; Christian agencies & churches; Immigrants/refugees; Economically disadvantaged.
Type of support: General/operating support; Building/renovation.
Limitations: Applications not accepted. Giving on a national and international basis.
Application information: Unsolicited requests for funds not accepted.
   Board meeting date(s): Varies
Officers: Philip Yancey, Pres.; Janet Yancey, V.P.; Diane Davis, Secy.; Bruce Otto, Treas.
EIN: 363415880

410
Steffens Foundation
P.O. Box 271170
Louisville, CO   80027-5021

Established in 2005 in CO.
Donor: Mary S. Schweitzer.
Grantmaker type: Independent foundation.
Financial data (yr. ended 12/31/10): Assets, $5,649,413 (M); gifts received, $183,830; expenditures, $283,819; qualifying distributions, $253,500; giving activities include $253,500 for 44 grants (high: $50,000; low: $250).
Fields of interest: Higher education; International economic development; Catholic agencies &

churches; Education; Women, centers/services; Human services; Science; Immigrants/refugees.
Limitations: Applications not accepted. Giving primarily in IL, KS, MD, and WA. No grants to individuals.
Application information: Contributes only to pre-selected organizations.
Officers: Mary S. Schweitzer, Pres.; Stephanie L. Schweitzer, V.P.; Edmund A. Schweitzer, Secy.; Paul A. Schweitzer, Treas.
EIN: 202420941

411
Urgent Action Fund for Women's Human Rights
3100 Arapahoe Ave., Ste. 201
Boulder, CO   80303-1050   (303) 442-2388
FAX: (303) 442-2370;
E-mail: urgentact@urgentactionfund.org; Application address for Africa: Urgent Action Fund - Africa, P.O. Box 53841-00200, Nairobi, Kenya, Tel: 254 20 2731095, FAX: 254 20 2731094, E-mail: proposals@urgentactionfund-africa.or.ke;
URL: http://www.urgentactionfund.org

Established in 1997.
Grantmaker type: Public charity.
Financial data (yr. ended 12/31/10): Revenue, $1,504,529; assets, $1,268,417 (M); gifts received, $1,505,581; expenditures, $1,559,917; giving activities include $422,500 for grants, and $299,035 for grants to organizations outside the U.S.
Purpose and activities: The fund provides funding for strategic interventions that take advantage of unanticipated opportunities to advance women's human rights or to safeguard rights that have already been won. Fund grants support short-term measures that comprise vital elements of long-term strategies for advancing women's human rights.
Fields of interest: International human rights; Women.
Type of support: Emergency funds.
Limitations: Applications accepted. Giving on a worldwide basis. No grants for development projects, natural disaster relief, humanitarian aid, travel to conferences or general support.
Publications: Annual report.
Application information: The fund only provides support to organizations in which women are the primary decision-makers. Application form required.
   Initial approach: Download application
   Copies of proposal: 1
   Deadline(s): Rolling
   Board meeting date(s): Biannually; generally, Mar. and Oct.
   Final notification: Response within 72 hours; funds can usually be delivered within a week following approval
Officers and Directors:* Eleanor Douglas,* Co-Chair.; Sunila Abeysekera, Co-Chair.; Rachel Wareham,* Secy.; Jelena Djordjevic,* Treas.; Terry Greenblatt, Exec. Dir.; Marta Drury; Amalia Fischer; Anissa Helie.
Number of staff: 7 full-time professional.
EIN: 030419743

412
Albert & Bessie Warner Fund
P.O. Box 2784
Telluride, CO   81435-2784

Trust established in 1955 in NY.

Grantmaker type: Independent foundation.

Financial data (yr. ended 12/31/10): Assets, $3,212,407 (M); expenditures, $255,166; qualifying distributions, $154,490; giving activities include $154,490 for grants.

Fields of interest: Hospitals (general); Environment; Health care; Legal services; Crime/law enforcement; Employment, labor unions/organizations; Children/youth, services; International peace/security; International affairs, arms control; International human rights; Civil rights, race/intergroup relations; Civil/human rights; United Ways and Federated Giving Programs; Native Americans/American Indians; Immigrants/refugees.

Type of support: General/operating support; Land acquisition; Program development; Seed money; Technical assistance.

Application information: Application form not required.

  Initial approach: Letter

  Deadline(s): None

  Board meeting date(s): Feb., May, Aug., and Nov.

Trustees: Bernice Freidus; John Steel; Kitty Steel; Lewis M. Steel.

Number of staff: 1 part-time support.

EIN: 136095213

413
Western Union Foundation
12500 E. Belford Ave., Ste. M1-I
Englewood, CO 80112-5939   (720) 332-6606
Contact: Luella Chavez D'Angelo, Pres.
FAX: (720) 332-4772;
E-mail: foundation@westernunion.com; Tel. and E-mail for Luella Chavez D'Angelo: (720) 332-4763, luella.dangelo@westernunion.com; Scholarship application address: Institute of International Education, 475 17th St., Ste. 800, Denver, CO 80202, tel.: (303) 837-0788, fax: (303) 837-1409, e-mail: wufamily@iie.org; URL: http://foundation.westernunion.com/
Grants List: http://foundation.westernunion.com/giving_map.html

Established as a company-sponsored operating foundation in 2000 in CO.

Donors: First Data Corp.; Western Union Co.

Grantmaker type: Operating foundation.

Financial data (yr. ended 12/31/10): Assets, $3,147,671 (M); gifts received, $11,279,541; expenditures, $9,379,899; qualifying distributions, $9,374,984; giving activities include $7,227,541 for 235 grants (high: $459,575; low: $72), and $530,365 for employee matching gifts.

Purpose and activities: The foundation supports programs designed to provide individuals with better access to educational opportunities, economic development, and provide basic human services to communities in developing countries. Special emphasis is directed toward programs designed to promote job training, life skills and small business development, financial literacy, community integration, and assistance to migrants and immigrants.

Fields of interest: Community development, small businesses; Education, ESL programs; Education; Employment, training; Disasters, preparedness/services; Human services, financial counseling; Human services; International affairs, U.N.; Economic development; Business/industry; Social entrepreneurship; Community/economic development; Engineering/technology; Public affairs; Children; Adults; Minorities; Immigrants/refugees; Economically disadvantaged; Migrant workers.

International interests: Brazil; China; Global programs; India; Mexico; Philippines.

Type of support: Continuing support; Building/renovation; Equipment; Program development; Scholarship funds; Employee volunteer services; Employee matching gifts; Scholarships—to individuals; Matching/challenge support.

Limitations: Giving on a national and international basis, with emphasis on Phoenix, AZ, Los Angeles and San Francisco, CA, Denver, CO, Washington, DC, Miami, FL, Chicago, IL, New York, NY, Argentina, Australia, Austria, Brazil, Canada, China, Costa Rica, Haiti, India, Indonesia, Kenya, Lithuania, Mexico, Morocco, Pakistan, Philippines, Romania, Russia, South Africa, Uganda, United Arab Emirates, and Yemen. No support for pass-through organizations, health organizations, arts, media, or humanities organizations, or religious or political organizations. No grants for general operating support, endowments, special events, capital campaigns, post-secondary scholarship programs, early childhood education, debt reduction, disease research, environmental causes, sports, or athletics.

Publications: Application guidelines; Annual report; Financial statement; Grants list; Newsletter.

Application information: Unsolicited requests for general grants are not accepted at this time. The foundation is working with its current NGO partners and will solicit proposals from NGOs that align with its giving platform. Application form required.

  Initial approach: Complete online application for Family Scholarship Program

  Copies of proposal: 1

  Deadline(s): Sept. 15 for Family Scholarship Program

  Board meeting date(s): Quarterly

  Final notification: Dec. 31 for Family Scholarship Program

Officers and Directors:* David Schlapbach, Chair.; Luella Chavez D'Angelo,* Pres.; Scott Coad, Treas.; Odilon Almeida; Jean Claude Farah; Davida Fedeli; Paul Foster; Christopher Kawula; Jo-Anne Scharmann; Diane Scott; Drina Yue.

Number of staff: 3 full-time professional; 2 full-time support.

EIN: 311738614

Recent grants for international programs:

413-1 Akhuwat, Lahore, Pakistan, $40,000. For restricted support. 2010.

413-2 Akshaya Patra Foundation USA, Stoneham, MA, $10,000. For unrestricted support. 2010.

413-3 Al Yateem Development Foundation, Sanaa, Yemen, $20,000. For restricted support. 2010.

413-4 Apafe Muso Danbe, Bamako, Mali, $13,702. For restricted support. 2010.

413-5 Ashoka: Innovators for the Public, Arlington, VA, $25,000. For unrestricted support. 2010.

413-6 Asociacion Alimentando Esperanzas, Santa Ana, Costa Rica, $10,000. For unrestricted support. 2010.

413-7 Asociacion de Amigos del Museo de Arte Popular, Mexico City, Mexico, $300,000. For restricted support. 2010.

413-8 Asociacion de Cooperacion Bolivia-Espana, Madrid, Spain, $68,955. For restricted support. 2010.

413-9 Belize Red Cross, Belize City, Belize, $22,722. For restricted support. 2010.

413-10 Bharti Foundation, Gurgaon, India, $10,000. For unrestricted support. 2010.

413-11 Bridges of Hope Project, New York, NY, $10,000. For unrestricted support. 2010.

413-12 Candelasolidarity, Zurich, Switzerland, $40,000. For restricted support. 2010.

413-13 CARE Bosnia and Herzegovina, Sarajevo, Bosnia-Herzegovina, $20,000. For restricted support. 2010.

413-14 CARE USA, Atlanta, GA, $18,000. For restricted support. 2010.

413-15 Caritas Osterreich, Vienna, Austria, $83,536. For restricted support. 2010.

413-16 Center for International Migration and Integration, Jerusalem, Israel, $10,000. For unrestricted support. 2010.

413-17 Centro de Apoio ao Migrante, Servio Pastoral dos Migrantes, Sao Paulo, Brazil, $10,000. For unrestricted support. 2010.

413-18 Charitable Society for Social Welfare, Sanaa, Yemen, $200,000. For restricted support. 2010.

413-19 Clinton Global Initiative, New York, NY, $20,000. For unrestricted support. 2010.

413-20 Clinton Global Initiative, New York, NY, $20,000. For unrestricted support. 2010.

413-21 Costa Rican Investment Promotion Agency, Escazu, Costa Rica, $10,000. For unrestricted support. 2010.

413-22 Developing Minds Foundation, Miami Beach, FL, $10,000. For unrestricted support. 2010.

413-23 Ecumenical Institute for Labor Education and Research, Quezon City, Philippines, $10,000. For unrestricted support. 2010.

413-24 Ethioplan Orthodox Church, Child and Family Affairs Organization (EOC-CFAO), Addis Ababa, Ethiopia, $10,000. For unrestricted support. 2010.

413-25 Eurasia Foundation, Washington, DC, $20,000. For unrestricted support. 2010.

413-26 Foundation for Development Cooperation, Brisbane, Australia, $15,000. For unrestricted support. 2010.

413-27 Foundation for Development Cooperation, Brisbane, Australia, $10,000. For unrestricted support. 2010.

413-28 Fundacion Lucha Contra la Desercion Estudiantil, San Jose, Costa Rica, $10,000. For unrestricted support. 2010.

413-29 Fundacion Manos Abiertas, Buenos Aires, Argentina, $10,000. For unrestricted support. 2010.

413-30 Fundacion ProEmpleo Productivo, Mexico City, Mexico, $10,000. For unrestricted support. 2010.

413-31 Fundacion TV Azteca, Mexico City, Mexico, $300,000. For restricted support. 2010.

413-32 Gokongwei Brothers Foundation Learning and Development Center, Pasig City, Philippines, $69,166. For restricted support. 2010.

413-33 Grameen Foundation USA, Washington, DC, $50,000. For unrestricted support. 2010.

413-34 Groupement Feminin Rayuwa Mata de Koubia, Niamey, Niger, $22,026. For restricted support. 2010.

413-35 Habitat for Humanity Canada, Waterloo, Canada, $45,000. For unrestricted support. 2010.

413-36 Habitat for Humanity Philippines, Makati, Philippines, $38,470. For restricted support. 2010.

413-37 Institute of International Education, Denver, CO, $30,000. For unrestricted support. 2010.

413-38 Interkulturelles Zentrum, Vienna, Austria, $60,000. For unrestricted support. 2010.

413-39 International Organization for Migration-Ukraine, Kiev, Ukraine, $15,000. For unrestricted support. 2010.

413-40 International Rescue Committee, New York, NY, $100,000. For unrestricted support. 2010.

413-41 International Rescue Committee, New York, NY, $50,000. For unrestricted support. 2010.

413-42 International Rescue Committee, New York, NY, $10,000. For unrestricted support. 2010.

413-43 Iraqi Youth League, Baghdad, Iraq, $200,000. For restricted support. 2010.

413-44 Kamwokya Christian Caring Community, Kampala, Uganda, $35,068. For restricted support. 2010.

413-45 Kottayam Social Service Society, Kottayam, India, $50,000. For unrestricted support. 2010.

413-46 Leadership for Environment and Development International, London, England, $36,800. For restricted support for Congo program. 2010.

413-47 Mercy Corps, Portland, OR, $313,188. For restricted support. 2010.

413-48 Mercy Corps, Portland, OR, $162,900. For unrestricted support. 2010.

413-49 Mercy Corps, Portland, OR, $112,000. For unrestricted support. 2010.

413-50 Mercy Corps, Portland, OR, $50,000. For unrestricted support. 2010.

413-51 Mercy Corps, Portland, OR, $10,000. For restricted support. 2010.

413-52 Namlo International, Denver, CO, $20,000. For restricted support. 2010.

413-53 Opportunity International, Oak Brook, IL, $50,000. For unrestricted support. 2010.

413-54 Paragon Charitable Trust, Mumbai, India, $20,000. For restricted support. 2010.

413-55 Pro Mujer, New York, NY, $20,000. For unrestricted support. 2010.

413-56 Save the Children Federation, Westport, CT, $89,908. For restricted support. 2010.

413-57 Save the Children Federation, Westport, CT, $50,000. For unrestricted support. 2010.

413-58 Save the Children Federation, Westport, CT, $15,600. For restricted support. 2010.

413-59 Sheikh Khalifa Bin Zayed Bangladesh Islamia Private School, Abu Dhabi, United Arab Emirates, $10,000. For unrestricted support. 2010.

413-60 Skills for Change, Toronto, Canada, $10,000. For unrestricted support. 2010.

413-61 SNV Netherlands Development Organization, The Hague, Netherlands, $10,000. For unrestricted support for Honduras program. 2010.

413-62 Soldier's Families Welfare Society, Az-Zarqa, Jordan, $20,000. For restricted support. 2010.

413-63 Teach for All, New York, NY, $50,000. For unrestricted support. 2010.

413-64 Toplum Gonulluleri Vakfi, Istanbul, Turkey, $50,548. For restricted support. 2010.

413-65 United Nations Development Programme, New York, NY, $150,000. For unrestricted support. 2010.

413-66 United Nations Development Programme, New York, NY, $100,000. For unrestricted support. 2010.

413-67 United Nations Foundation, Washington, DC, $100,000. For unrestricted support. 2010.

413-68 United Nations Foundation, Washington, DC, $50,000. For unrestricted support. 2010.

413-69 United States Association for United Nations High Commissioner for Refugees, Washington, DC, $50,000. For unrestricted support. 2010.

413-70 Vietnam Association of Manpower Supply, Hanoi, Vietnam, $30,000. For restricted support. 2010.

413-71 Womens World Banking, New York, NY, $10,000. For unrestricted support. 2010.

413-72 World Vision International, Monrovia, CA, $60,000. For restricted support. 2010.

413-73 World Vision International, Monrovia, CA, $50,000. For unrestricted support. 2010.

413-74 World Vision International, Monrovia, CA, $17,293. For unrestricted support. 2010.

413-75 Young Afghan Professionals for Reconstruction and Development, Westminster, CO, $10,000. For unrestricted support. 2010.

413-76 Zambia National Education Coalition, Lusaka, Zambia, $32,796. For restricted support. 2010.

414
Whetstone Mountain Foundation

c/o Michael G. Johnson
P.O. Box 2506
Crested Butte, CO   81224-2506

Established in 2001 in TX.
Donors: John J. Johnson; Michael G. Johnson.
Grantmaker type: Independent foundation.
Financial data (yr. ended 12/31/10): Assets, $575,907 (M); gifts received, $20,000; expenditures, $162,879; qualifying distributions, $161,600; giving activities include $161,600 for 5 grants (high: $80,000; low: $2,000).
Fields of interest: Recreation, adaptive sports; Health care; International development.
Limitations: Applications not accepted. No grants to individuals.
Application information: Unsolicited requests for funds not accepted.
Officers: Nancy T. Johnson, Pres.; John J. Johnson, V.P.; Michael G. Johnson, Secy.; Steven M. Johnson, Treas.
EIN: 760691948

415
World Orphans

(formerly Wiseman-Roosen-Winslow Foundation)
P.O. Box 1840
Castle Rock, CO   80104-1501   (719) 487-1700
Contact: Robert C. Roosen, Chair.; Paul Myhill, Pres.
FAX: (719) 487-1800;
E-mail: info@worldorphans.org; Toll-free tel.: (888) 677-4267; URL: http://www.worldorphans.org
Facebook: http://www.facebook.com/worldorphans
Flickr: http://www.flickr.com/photos/worldorphans/
Paul Myhill's Blog: http://abandoned-orphaned.typepad.com/
Twitter: http://twitter.com/worldorphans

Established in 1993 in CA and IL.
Grantmaker type: Public charity.
Financial data (yr. ended 12/31/10): Revenue, $2,460,442; assets, $1,193,263 (M); gifts received, $2,460,097; expenditures, $2,453,326; giving activities include $531,359 for grants to organizations outside the U.S.

Purpose and activities: The organization works to rescue orphaned and abandoned children in underdeveloped countries by funding the construction of orphan homes required for local Christian churches to meet the spiritual, physical, nutritional, social, educational, economic and skills training needs of these children.
Fields of interest: Christian agencies & churches; Children, services.
International interests: Developing countries.
Type of support: Building/renovation.
Limitations: Applications accepted. Giving in developing countries.
Publications: Annual report; Newsletter.
Application information: Application form required.
Initial approach: E-mail
Copies of proposal: 1
Board meeting date(s): 2 times per year minimum
Final notification: 30 to 60 days
Officers and Directors:* Paul Myhill,* Chair.; Brian Becker,* Secy.; Mark Haverkate, Treas.; Ty Albright; Pete Allen; Douglas Strecker.
Number of staff: 1 full-time professional; 3 full-time support; 1 part-time support.
EIN: 330571309

416
YPI Charitable Trust

c/o J. Harvey
P.O. Box 2132
Crested Butte, CO   81224-2132

Established in 1991.
Donors: John T. Dorrance III; Charles A. Dorrance.
Grantmaker type: Independent foundation.
Financial data (yr. ended 05/31/11): Assets, $1,106,540 (M); expenditures, $1,177,808; qualifying distributions, $1,176,750; giving activities include $1,176,750 for grants.
Fields of interest: Arts; Education; Environment; natural resources; Human services; Foundations (private grantmaking).
International interests: Bahamas; England; Ireland.
Limitations: Applications not accepted. Giving primarily in FL, NY, TN, and WY; some giving in the Bahamas, England, and Ireland. No grants to individuals.
Application information: Contributes only to pre-selected organizations.
Trustees: Charles A. Dorrance; Gunda S. Dorrance; John T. Dorrance III; John T. Dorrance IV.
EIN: 237675355
Recent grants for international programs:

416-1 American Associates of the Old Vic Theater, New York, NY, $100,000. 2009.

416-2 Cape Eleuthera Foundation, Lawrenceville, NJ, $60,000. 2009.

416-3 Charities Aid Foundation America, Alexandria, VA, $26,548. For American Donor Fund. 2009.

416-4 Countryside Alliance, London, England, $36,458. 2009.

416-5 Dublin City University, Dublin, Ireland, $25,000. 2009.

416-6 Lyford Cay Foundation, Nassau, Bahamas, $74,000. 2009.

416-7 Lyford Cay School Development Fund, Nassau, Bahamas, $50,000. 2009.

416-8 Naked Heart Foundation, White Plains, NY, $100,000. 2009.

416-9 University of Dublin, Trinity College, Dublin, Ireland, $26,686. 2009.

416-10 Versailles Foundation, New York, NY, $90,000. 2009.

CONNECTICUT

417
Aid to Artisans, Inc.
1030 New Britain Ave., Ste. 102
West Hartford, CT 06110-2215 (860) 756-5550
FAX: (860) 756-5558;
E-mail: info@aidtoartisans.org; Application email:
small_grants@aidtoartisans.org; URL: http://
www.aidtoartisans.org

Established in 1975.
Grantmaker type: Public charity.
Financial data (yr. ended 09/30/10): Revenue,
$5,326,140; assets, $1,225,280 (M); gifts
received, $2,987,211; expenditures, $5,259,278;
program services expenses, $4,264,825; giving
activities include $10,000 for grants to
organizations outside the U.S.
Purpose and activities: The organization offers
practical assistance to artisan groups worldwide,
working in partnerships to foster artistic traditions,
cultural vitality, and community well-being.
Fields of interest: Business/industry; Arts, folk arts;
Arts.
International interests: Developing countries.
Type of support: Continuing support; Equipment;
Program development; Technical assistance;
Matching/challenge support.
Limitations: Applications accepted. Giving in
developing communities around the world. No
support for groups in the building trades. No grants
to individuals, or for travel, salaries, start-up
expenses, or for the production of industrial articles.
Publications: Application guidelines; Annual report;
Financial statement; Informational brochure;
Newsletter.
Application information: Only grant requests
accompanied by a letter of recommendation from
organizations already known to the foundation (or
part of the foundation's network) will be considered.
Application form not required.
  Initial approach: Submit proposal and budget (in
    U.S. dollars) via email
  Copies of proposal: 1
  Deadline(s): July 1 for Small Grants
  Board meeting date(s): Fall and spring
Officers and Directors:* Eric O'Leary, Chair.;
Thomas Blinkhorn,* Vice-Chair.; Alfredo Espinosa,
Pres.; Edmund See,* Secy.; Charles Mann,* Treas.;
Melinda Brayton,* Genl. Mgr.; Alexandra Ballard;
Charles Clifford; Andrew Corrie; Susan Ginsberg;
Mac McCoy.
Number of staff: 22 full-time professional; 1
part-time professional.
EIN: 042577837

418
The Allison Foundation, Inc.
(formerly The Allison Family Foundation, Inc.)
P.O. Box 122
Greens Farms, CT 06838-0122

Established in 1998 in NY.
Donor: Herbert M. Allison, Jr.
Grantmaker type: Independent foundation.
Financial data (yr. ended 05/31/11): Assets,
$8,239,469 (M); gifts received, $5,625;
expenditures, $272,631; qualifying distributions,
$253,125; giving activities include $250,000 for 1
grant.
Fields of interest: International affairs; Performing
arts, dance; Business school/education; Human
services.
Type of support: General/operating support.
Limitations: Applications not accepted. Giving
primarily in New York, NY; some funding also in
Stanford, CA. No grants to individuals.
Application information: Contributes only to
pre-selected organizations.
Officers: Simin N. Allison, Pres.; John R. Allison, V.P.
and Secy.; Andrew G. Allison, V.P. and Treas.
EIN: 134011223

419
American Friends of the Verbier Festival & Academy
c/o FCSN
88 Field Point Rd.
Greenwich, CT 06830-6468 (203) 661-1000

Grantmaker type: Public charity.
Financial data (yr. ended 12/31/10): Revenue,
$47,560; assets, $59,392 (M); gifts received,
$47,556; expenditures, $26,718; program services
expenses, $59,392; giving activities include
$24,300 for 1 grant, and $35,092 for
foundation-administered programs.
Purpose and activities: The organization provides
support to the Foundation du Festival Verbier.
Fields of interest: Arts education; Arts; Education.
International interests: Switzerland.
Limitations: Applications not accepted. Giving
limited to Switzerland. No grants to individuals.
Application information: Contributes only to a
pre-selected organization.
Officers and Directors:* Peter W. Williams, Pres.;
Leland C. Selby,* Secy.; Neville Sargeant,* Treas.;
Maria H. Bergendahl; Martin Engstroem; Avraham
Shoshani.
EIN: 133882864

420
American Friends of the Victoria and Albert Museum, Inc.
(formerly American and International Friends of the
Victoria and Albert Museum)
61 Londonderry Dr.
Greenwich, CT 06830-3508
Contact: Savita Monie, V.P.
E-mail: diana.seaton@afvam.org; URL: http://
www.afvam.org

Established in 1984 in DE.
Grantmaker type: Public charity.
Financial data (yr. ended 12/31/09): Revenue,
$2,631,315; assets, $2,936,565 (M); gifts
received, $2,630,027; expenditures, $1,375,320;
program services expenses, $1,307,702; giving
activities include $1,291,963 for grants to
organizations outside the U.S.
Purpose and activities: The organization aims to
enhance the status and further the objectives of
organizations that further the appreciation of art.
Fields of interest: Arts; Museums (art).
International interests: England.
Limitations: Giving limited to London, England.
Officers and Trustees:* Diana Quasha, Chair. and
Pres.; Jeremy Weinberg,* Treas.; Richard

Greenfield; Audrey Gruss; Leslie Schreyer; Dr.
Susan Weber.
EIN: 133212077

421
AmeriCares
88 Hamilton Ave.
Stamford, CT 06902-3111 (203) 658-9500
E-mail: giving@americares.org; Toll-free tel.: (800)
486-4357; URL: http://www.americares.org
Facebook: http://www.facebook.com/americares
RSS Feed: http://www.americares.org/system/
rss/channel.jsp?
subsiteID=33969&feed=feed-638182
Twitter: http://twitter.com/AmeriCares
YouTube: http://www.youtube.com/user/
AmeriCares

Established in 1982 in CT.
Grantmaker type: Public charity.
Financial data (yr. ended 06/30/10): Revenue,
$795,078,846; assets, $159,618,587 (M); gifts
received, $794,563,561; expenditures,
$854,604,824; giving activities include
$24,318,222 for grants, $568,307,550 for grants
to organizations outside the U.S., and
$217,223,280 for grants to individuals.
Purpose and activities: The organization provides
disaster relief and humanitarian aid in response to
emergency medical needs in support of long-term
health care programs for all people around the
world.
Fields of interest: Health care; Safety/disasters;
Human services; International relief.
Type of support: Grants to individuals; Emergency
funds; In-kind gifts.
Limitations: Applications not accepted. Giving on a
national and international basis.
Publications: Annual report; Financial statement.
Application information: Contributes only to
pre-selected organizations.
Officers and Directors:* Alma Jane "Leila"
Macauley,* Co-Founder and Vice-Chair.; Curtis R.
Welling,* Pres. and C.E.O.; Carol Bauer; John L.
Kelly; Jerry Leamon; C. Dean Maglaris; Joseph W.
Merrill; Joseph J. Rucci, Jr.; Beverly Schuch; Fred
Weisman; James C. Wheat III; Stephen Winter, M.D.
EIN: 061008595

422
Avatar Meher Baba Foundation, Inc.
c/o Emory D. Ayers
P.O. Box 398
Mystic, CT 06355-0398

Established in 1998 in CT.
Donors: Emory D. Ayers; Susan A. Ayers; Elinor
Griest; David Alcorn; Winnie Alcorn; Richard Medina;
Lynda Medina; Jonathan Meyer; Deborah Meyer;
Dinah Smith.
Grantmaker type: Independent foundation.
Financial data (yr. ended 12/31/10): Assets,
$1,366,070 (M); gifts received, $151,547;
expenditures, $245,413; qualifying distributions,
$241,329; giving activities include $206,870 for 4
grants (high: $144,550; low: $1,000), and $19,800
for 11 grants to individuals.
Purpose and activities: Giving for spiritual
development in accordance with the teaching of
Avatar Meher Baba.
Fields of interest: Religion.

International interests: India.
Limitations: Applications not accepted. Giving primarily in India.
Application information: Unsolicited requests for funds not accepted.
Officers: Emory D. Ayers, Pres.; Susan A. Ayers, Secy.-Treas.
Directors: Ananda Jones; Jonathan Meyer.
EIN: 061516691

423
Belgian American Educational Foundation, Inc.
195 Church St.
New Haven, CT   06510-2009
Contact: Emile L. Boulpaep M.D., Chair. and Pres.
E-mail: emile.boulpaep@yale.edu; Tel./Fax: (203) 777-5765; URL: http://www.baef.be

Incorporated in 1920 in DE.
Donor: The Commission for Relief in Belgium.
Grantmaker type: Public charity.
Financial data (yr. ended 08/31/10): Revenue, $5,170,739; assets, $65,047,216 (M); gifts received, $1,347,376; expenditures, $2,639,154; giving activities include $13,584 for grants to organizations outside the U.S., and $2,149,375 for grants to individuals.
Purpose and activities: The foundation provides grants to promote closer relations between Belgium and the United States through graduate exchange fellowships in diverse fields and to assist higher education, scientific research, and the exchange of intellectual ideas.
Fields of interest: Media, film/video; Visual arts; Visual arts, architecture; Performing arts; Performing arts, music; History/archaeology; Arts; Child development, education; Higher education; Business school/education; Law school/education; Medical school/education; Engineering school/education; Environment, natural resources; Environment; Health care; Health organizations; Human services; Child development, services; International affairs, foreign policy; Business/industry; Mathematics; Physics; Engineering/technology; Computer science; Engineering; Biology/life sciences; Science; Economics; International studies.
International interests: Belgium.
Type of support: Fellowships; Research; Grants to individuals; Scholarships—to individuals; Exchange programs.
Limitations: Applications accepted. Giving limited to students from Belgium and the U.S. No grants for general support, endowment funds, matching gifts, or fellowships (except for Belgian and American graduate students).
Publications: Application guidelines; Financial statement; Newsletter.
Application information: Application form required.
  Initial approach: Letter or submit online application
  Copies of proposal: 1
  Deadline(s): Oct. 31 for Graduate Fellowships for Study or Research in Belgium
  Board meeting date(s): Jan., Apr., June, and Oct.
  Final notification: On or about Jan. 31 for Graduate Fellowships for Study or Research in Belgium
Officers and Directors:* Emile L. Boulpaep,* M.D., Chair. and Pres.; L. Gilles Sion,* Secy.; Sherman Gray,* Treas.; Maryan Ainsworth; Marcel Crochet;

Jacques de Groote; Diego du Monceau; Susan Friberg; John H.F. Haskell, Jr.; Andre Jacques; Daniel Janssen; Edward H.A. Tuck; Luc Wauters; Jacques Willems.
Number of staff: 1 full-time support.
EIN: 131606002

424
China Care Foundation, Inc.
P.O. Box 607
Westport, CT   06881-0607   (203) 227-3655
E-mail: info@chinacare.org; URL: http://www.chinacare.org
Facebook: http://www.facebook.com/group.php?gid=2258395310&v=wall
Facebook: http://www.facebook.com/pages/China-Care-Foundation/101931353207?sk=info
Twitter: http://twitter.com/#!/ChinaCare
YouTube: http://www.youtube.com/user/ChinaCareFoundation

Grantmaker type: Public charity.
Financial data (yr. ended 12/31/10): Revenue, $1,958,970; assets, $1,203,158 (M); gifts received, $2,229,138; expenditures, $2,431,092; giving activities include $1,712,314 for grants, and $100,500 for grants to organizations outside the U.S.
Purpose and activities: The foundation works to give special-needs Chinese orphans the opportunity for a better life and empower youth through direct humanitarian service. It provides specialized care for infants who are orphaned, life saving medical treatments and surgeries, foster care in loving families as well as encourage and promote adoptions of special needs children.
Fields of interest: Health care; Children, adoption; Human services.
International interests: China.
Limitations: Giving in the U.S. and China.
Officer and Directors:* Matt Dalio,* Pres.; Marilyn Caufield; Ray Dalio; Ted Johnson; Lorraine Kennedy; Ray Rivers; Richard Whitcomb; Gu Zeqing; Yunfang Zhang.
EIN: 311732062

425
Creative Connections, Inc.
Mathews Park
303 West Ave.
Norwalk, CT   06850-4002   (203) 803-4376
FAX: (203) 803-4386;
E-mail: worldlink@creativeconnections.org;
URL: http://www.creativeconnections.org/

Established in 1992 in CT.
Donors: Alan R. Steckler; Lois R. Steckler Charitable Lead Trust.
Grantmaker type: Public charity.
Financial data (yr. ended 06/30/10): Revenue, $274,868; assets, $128,763 (M); gifts received, $175,079; expenditures, $303,149.
Purpose and activities: The organization works to educate young people by encouraging their awareness, understanding, and appreciation of other cultures, as well as their own.
Fields of interest: Education; International exchange, arts.
Officers and Directors:* David Hurwitt,* Chair.; Alan R. Steckler,* Exec. Dir.; Cherie Lyeth Burton; Chris

Filmer; Judy Kirst-Kolkman; Sharon Lauer; Nancy Romberg; Susie Salomon; Deborah S. Steckler.
EIN: 133697184

426
The Crew Family Foundation, Inc.
100 E. Main St.
Plainville, CT   06062-1954   (860) 793-6955

Established in 1986 in CT.
Donors: Ted J. Crew; Peggy Lynn Crew.
Grantmaker type: Independent foundation.
Financial data (yr. ended 10/31/10): Assets, $1,423,932 (M); gifts received, $175,000; expenditures, $304,012; qualifying distributions, $303,500; giving activities include $303,500 for 27 grants (high: $50,000; low: $100).
Fields of interest: International relief; Human services; Christian agencies & churches.
Type of support: General/operating support.
Application information: Application form not required.
  Initial approach: Proposal
  Deadline(s): None
Officers and Directors:* Ted J. Crew,* Pres.; Peggy Lynn Crew,* Secy.; Kimberly Crew; Pamela Crew-Baker.
EIN: 061191170

427
Richard Davoud Donchian Foundation, Inc.
(formerly Richard D. Donchian Charitable Foundation, Inc.)
c/o Foundation Svcs. LLC
88 Field Point Rd.
Greenwich, CT   06836-2508
E-mail: rdd@fsllc.net; URL: http://www.rddonchian.org

Established in 1991 in CT; reincorporated in 1998.
Donor: Richard D. Donchian†.
Grantmaker type: Independent foundation.
Financial data (yr. ended 12/31/10): Assets, $9,143,843 (M); expenditures, $613,173; qualifying distributions, $526,414; giving activities include $428,500 for 51 grants (high: $50,000; low: $500).
Purpose and activities: The foundation focuses its grantmaking in four key areas: 1) Literacy & Education; 2) Humanitarian Efforts; 3) Health; and 4) Ethics and Personal Development.
Fields of interest: Health care; Adult/continuing education; Education; Employment, ethics; Employment; Housing/shelter, homeless; Housing/shelter; Disasters, search/rescue; Youth development; Human services; Homeless, human services; International economic development; Business/industry; Leadership development.
Limitations: Applications accepted. Giving primarily in the northeastern U.S. No grants to individuals, or for endowments.
Application information: Online application form required. Application form required.
  Initial approach: See Web site for guidelines
  Deadline(s): None
  Board meeting date(s): Quarterly
Officers and Directors:* Geoffrey M. Parkinson,* Pres.; Leland C. Selby,* Secy.-Treas.; Geoffrey M. Parkinson, Jr.; Clark M. Whittemore, Jr.
EIN: 061514402

428
GE Foundation
(formerly GE Fund)
3135 Easton Tpke.
Fairfield, CT 06828-0001 (203) 373-3216
Contact: Robert L. Corcoran, Chair. and Pres.
FAX: (203) 373-3029;
E-mail: gefoundation@ge.com; E-mail for Corporate Citizenship Team: citizenship@ge.com; URL: http://www.gefoundation.com
Blog: http://www.gereports.com/tag/ge-foundation/
Citizenship Newsletter: http://www.ge.com/citizenship/news_features/newsletters.jsp
Grants List: http://www.ge.com/files_foundation/pdf/ge_foundation_2008_contributions_above_10k.pdf

Trust established in 1952 in NY.
Donor: General Electric Co.
Grantmaker type: Company-sponsored foundation.
Financial data (yr. ended 12/31/10): Assets, $17,199,287 (M); gifts received, $130,627,400; expenditures, $114,372,133; qualifying distributions, $114,305,622; giving activities include $74,462,439 for 210 grants (high: $8,888,880; low: $4,660), $37,759,301 for 18,976 employee matching gifts and $16,000,000 for set-asides.
Purpose and activities: The foundation supports programs designed to promote U.S. and international education; global health; the environment; disaster relief; human rights; public policy; and community success around the globe.
Fields of interest: International economics/trade policy; Legal services, public interest law; Legal services; Environment, water resources; Environment, climate change/global warming; Education, reform; Elementary/secondary education; Middle schools/education; Higher education; Business school/education; Scholarships/financial aid; Education; Environment; Health care, clinics/centers; Health care, infants; Health care; AIDS; Diabetes; Tropical diseases; Crime/law enforcement; Disasters, preparedness/services; Youth development, business; Human services; International affairs, U.N.; International affairs; Civil/human rights; Community/economic development; United Ways and Federated Giving Programs; Mathematics; Engineering/technology; Science; Public policy, research; Girls; Economically disadvantaged.
International interests: Africa; China; Ghana; Uganda.
Type of support: Continuing support; Management development/capacity building; Program development; Faculty/staff development; Publication; Curriculum development; Scholarship funds; Research; Employee matching gifts; Employee-related scholarships.
Limitations: Applications not accepted. Giving on a national and international basis, with emphasis on Stamford, CT, Atlanta, GA, Jefferson County and Louisville, KY, New Orleans, LA, Baltimore, MD, New York and Schenectady, NY, Cincinnati, OH, Erie, PA, Greenville, SC, Houston, TX, VA, Milwaukee, WI, Africa, China, Ghana, Latin America, Southeast Asia, and Uganda. No support for religious or political organizations. No grants to individuals (except for employee-related scholarships), or for capital campaigns, endowments, or other special purpose campaigns; no loans; no equipment donations.
Publications: Grants list.

Application information: Contributes only to pre-selected organizations.
Board meeting date(s): Quarterly
Officers and Directors: Robert L. Corcoran,* Chair. and Pres.; Paul Bueker, Secy. and Cont.; Michael J. Cosgrove, Treas.; E. W. Fraser, Genl. Counsel; Alfredo Arguello; Nani Beccalli; Pamela Daley; Brackett Denniston; Nancy Dorn; John F. Lynch; John G. Rice; Keith S. Sherin; Dmitri Stockton.
Number of staff: 6 full-time professional; 1 part-time professional; 4 full-time support.
EIN: 222621967
Recent grants for international programs:
428-1 AmeriCares, Stamford, CT, $530,000. 2010.
428-2 Americas Society, New York, NY, $100,000. 2010.
428-3 Arab Science and Technology Foundation, Sharjah, United Arab Emirates, $100,000. 2010.
428-4 Assist International, Scotts Valley, CA, $1,000,000. 2010.
428-5 Assist International, Scotts Valley, CA, $1,000,000. 2010.
428-6 Assist International, Scotts Valley, CA, $250,000. 2010.
428-7 Bocskai Istvan Gimnazium, Hungary, $27,335. 2010.
428-8 Brazil Foundation, New York, NY, $90,000. 2010.
428-9 CARE USA, Atlanta, GA, $70,000. 2010.
428-10 Center for a New American Security, Washington, DC, $50,000. 2010.
428-11 Center for Strategic and International Studies, Washington, DC, $85,000. 2010.
428-12 Doctors for Developing Countries, Frankfurt am Main, Germany, $50,000. 2010.
428-13 ENTHUSE Charitable Trust, London, England, $325,980. 2010.
428-14 Executive Council on Diplomacy, Washington, DC, $20,000. 2010.
428-15 Foundation for the Global Compact, New York, NY, $275,000. 2010.
428-16 Foundation for the Global Compact, New York, NY, $100,000. 2010.
428-17 Friends of the World Food Program, Washington, DC, $1,000,000. 2010.
428-18 Give to Colombia, Coral Gables, FL, $30,000. 2010.
428-19 Global Reporting Initiative, Amsterdam, Netherlands, $85,000. 2010.
428-20 Harmony Foundation of Canada, Canada, $100,000. 2010.
428-21 HelpArgentina, New York, NY, $45,000. 2010.
428-22 Hogar de Cristo USA, Miami, FL, $180,000. 2010.
428-23 INMED Partnerships for Children, Ashburn, VA, $150,000. 2010.
428-24 Institute for Human Rights and Business, London, England, $90,000. 2010.
428-25 Institute of International Education, New York, NY, $1,090,250. 2010.
428-26 Institute of International Education, New York, NY, $615,300. 2010.
428-27 Institute of International Education, New York, NY, $567,300. 2010.
428-28 Institute of International Education, New York, NY, $311,750. 2010.
428-29 Institute of International Education, New York, NY, $306,250. 2010.
428-30 Institute of International Education, New York, NY, $209,750. 2010.
428-31 Institute of International Education, New York, NY, $100,000. 2010.

428-32 Instituto Mexicano para la Excelencia Educativa, Mexico City, Mexico, $100,000. 2010.
428-33 International Business Leaders Forum North America, San Francisco, CA, $74,704. 2010.
428-34 International Center, Washington, DC, $100,000. 2010.
428-35 International Judicial Academy, Washington, DC, $30,000. 2010.
428-36 International Mediation Institute, The Hague, Netherlands, $50,000. 2010.
428-37 International Rescue Committee, New York, NY, $333,333. 2010.
428-38 International Rescue Committee, New York, NY, $100,000. 2010.
428-39 Jozsef Attila Gimnazium, Mako, Hungary, $29,400. 2010.
428-40 National Institute of Occupational Health and Poison Control, China CDC, Beijing, China, $60,000. 2010.
428-41 Peter G. Peterson Institute for International Economics, Washington, DC, $80,000. 2010.
428-42 Pratham USA, Houston, TX, $220,000. 2010.
428-43 Prince's Trust, London, England, $18,000. 2010.
428-44 Red Cross Society of China, Beijing, China, $150,000. 2010.
428-45 Save the Children Federation, Westport, CT, $99,638. 2010.
428-46 Save the Children Federation, Westport, CT, $75,000. 2010.
428-47 Transparency International, Washington, DC, $75,000. 2010.
428-48 United States Fund for UNICEF, New York, NY, $500,000. 2010.
428-49 United States Fund for UNICEF, New York, NY, $12,198. 2010.
428-50 United States Fund for UNICEF, New York, NY, $11,651. 2010.
428-51 United States Indonesia Society, Washington, DC, $80,000. 2010.
428-52 United Way of Peel Region, Mississauga, Canada, $349,121. 2010.
428-53 United Way Worldwide, Alexandria, VA, $8,888,880. 2010.
428-54 University of Monterrey, Monterrey, Mexico, $96,000. 2010.
428-55 University of Monterrey, Monterrey, Mexico, $83,080. 2010.
428-56 University of Monterrey, Monterrey, Mexico, $83,080. 2010.
428-57 University of Monterrey, Monterrey, Mexico, $76,606. 2010.
428-58 VIDYA, Pune, India, $50,000. 2010.
428-59 World Justice Project, Washington, DC, $100,000. 2010.
428-60 World Justice Project, Washington, DC, $25,000. 2010.
428-61 World Resources Institute, Washington, DC, $96,000. 2010.

429
Sanford J. Grossman Charitable Trust
c/o QFS, Inc.
10 Glenville St.
Greenwich, CT 06831-3680

Established in 2002 in CT.
Donor: Sanford J. Grossman.
Grantmaker type: Independent foundation.
Financial data (yr. ended 12/31/10): Assets, $3,316,852 (M); expenditures, $229,100;

qualifying distributions, $213,969; giving activities include $212,056 for 12 grants (high: $100,000; low: $120).

Purpose and activities: Giving primarily for education, the arts, and health associations.

Fields of interest: Arts; Higher education; Health organizations, association; Medical research, institute; Human services; International terrorism.

Limitations: Applications not accepted. Giving primarily in CA, Washington, DC, IL, and New York, NY. No grants to individuals.

Application information: Contributes only to pre-selected organizations.

Officers: Mitchell Maresco, V.P.; David Zimmerman, Secy.

Trustee: Sanford J. Grossman.

EIN: 336316059

430
The Hampshire Foundation
151 New Park Ave., Ste. 7
Hartford, CT   06106   (860) 236-5751
Contact: Sabina E. Shelby, Tr.
FAX: (860) 586-7035;
E-mail: info@hampshirefoundation.org; URL: http://www.hampshirefoundation.org

Established in 2000 in CT.

Donor: The Hadley Trust.

Grantmaker type: Independent foundation.

Financial data (yr. ended 12/31/09): Assets, $18,060,673 (M); gifts received, $1,000; expenditures, $710,907; qualifying distributions, $657,420; giving activities include $374,000 for 6 grants (high: $150,000; low: $1,000).

Purpose and activities: The purpose of the foundation is to achieve sustainable growth for rural Peruvians.

Fields of interest: Education; Human services; International economic development.

International interests: Peru.

Limitations: Applications not accepted. Giving primarily in Peru. No grants to individuals.

Application information: Primary funding is through Peru Opportunity Fund. See web site for additional information.

Trustees: Nicholas N. Cournoyer; Sabina G. Cournoyer; Sabina E. Shelby.

EIN: 061584535

431
International Institute of Connecticut, Inc.
670 Clinton Ave.
Bridgeport, CT   06605-1704   (203) 336-0141
Contact: Angela Rossi Zurowski, Exec. Dir.
FAX: (203) 339-4400; E-mail: admin@iiconn.org;
URL: http://www.iiconn.org

Established in 1918 in CT.

Grantmaker type: Public charity.

Financial data (yr. ended 12/31/10): Revenue, $1,023,353; assets, $282,881 (M); gifts received, $532,495; expenditures, $1,097,917; giving activities include $103,211 for grants to individuals.

Purpose and activities: The organization provides immigration and citizenship counseling, refugee resettlement services, interpreter and translation services, immigration court representation, English as a Second Language education, and community education and training, to help facilitate the immigration of refugees who settle in Connecticut.

Fields of interest: International migration/refugee issues; Education, ESL programs; Immigrants/refugees.

Type of support: Emergency funds; Grants to individuals.

Limitations: Applications accepted. Giving limited to CT.

Publications: Annual report; Newsletter.

Application information: Application form not required.

Initial approach: Email or telephone

Officers and Directors:* Robert Maresca,* Pres.; Franck Adjisegbe,* V.P.; Richard Ryscavage, S.J.,* Secy.; Jorge Atencio,* Treas.; Angela Rossi Zurowski,* Exec. Dir.; Viviana Atienzar; Carol Dreznick; Sharon Kish; Jane Norgren; Peter Penczer, Esq.; and 8 additional directors.

EIN: 060669118

432
Lingnan Foundation
(formerly Trustees of Lingnan University)
P.O. Box 208223
New Haven, CT   06520-8223   (203) 432-1063
Contact: Leslie Stone, Exec. Dir.
FAX: (203) 432-7246; E-mail: lingnan@yale.edu; Application e-mail: lingnan@yale.edu; URL: http://www.lingnanfoundation.org

Established in 1893 in NY.

Donors: Anna Luk Liu; Huey Wong; Pausang Wong; Sinclair Louie; May Louie; Jennie Lee Mui Yi-Ching; I.U. Lai.

Grantmaker type: Independent foundation.

Financial data (yr. ended 06/30/11): Assets, $21,345,722 (M); gifts received, $21,186; expenditures, $1,083,867; qualifying distributions, $783,391; giving activities include $783,391 for grants.

Purpose and activities: To contribute to the advancement of higher education in South China, and through that process, to promote understanding between Chinese and Americans. The foundation supports scholarly exchange, educational innovation, and service to society.

Fields of interest: Higher education; Social sciences; International studies.

International interests: China; Hong Kong.

Type of support: General/operating support; Continuing support; Management development/capacity building; Building/renovation; Program development; Conferences/seminars; Professorships; Publication; Seed money; Curriculum development; Fellowships; Internship funds; Scholarship funds; Research; Exchange programs.

Limitations: Applications accepted. Giving primarily in Hong Kong and in the People's Republic of China. No grants to individuals, or for annual campaigns or emergency, capital or endowment funds; no loans.

Publications: Application guidelines; Biennial report; Program policy statement.

Application information: See foundation web site for application guidelines and procedures. Application form not required.

Initial approach: Proposal or letter
Copies of proposal: 1
Deadline(s): Inquire with foundation
Board meeting date(s): May and Nov.
Final notification: 1 month after meetings

Officers and Trustees:* Edward Chow,* Chair.; Jane S. Permaul,* Pres.; Bobby Fong,* Secy.; Alex Banker,* Treas.; Leslie B. Stone, Exec. Dir.; Frederic

C. Chang, M.D., Tr. Emeritus; Elizabeth D. Knup, Tr. Emeritus; Douglas P. Murray, Tr. Emeritus; Shenyu Belsky; Chi-Chao Chan; Kenyon Chan; Larry Hudspeth; Edward Rhoads; Roy C. Sheldon; Chui L. Tsang; Michael Woo.

Number of staff: 2 part-time professional.

EIN: 136400470

433
The Macauley Foundation, Inc.
131 Hazel Plain Rd.
Woodbury, CT   06798-1919
E-mail: info@themacauleyfoundation.org;
URL: http://www.themacauleyfoundation.com

Established in 1995 in CT.

Donor: Robert C. Macauley.

Grantmaker type: Independent foundation.

Financial data (yr. ended 06/30/11): Assets, $1,692,878 (M); gifts received, $25,000; expenditures, $496,287; qualifying distributions, $327,600; giving activities include $327,600 for grants.

Purpose and activities: Funding for various human service agencies.

Fields of interest: Cancer research; Human services; Children, services; International relief; Foundations (public).

Limitations: Applications accepted. Giving primarily in CT, FL, and NY; some funding also in AZ. No grants to individuals.

Publications: Financial statement.

Application information: Once received, applications in Spanish will need to be translated, therefore, response time may be longer. At this time, the foundation is not considering funding for homeless and feeding programs which are located outside of its local area. Application form required.

Initial approach: Letter for application
Copies of proposal: 3
Deadline(s): None
Board meeting date(s): Nov. and June
Final notification: Up to 6 months

Officers and Directors:* Robert C. Macauley,* Pres.; Alma Jane Macauley,* Exec. V.P.; Anne Marie Weirether, Secy.; Melinda Rice Macauley; Robert C. Macauley, Jr., M.D.

Number of staff: 1 part-time professional.

EIN: 061439255

434
Mahadeva Family Foundation
15 E. Putnam Ave., No. 407
Greenwich, CT   06830-5424

Established in 2004 in NJ.

Donor: Wijeyaraj A. Mahadeva.

Grantmaker type: Independent foundation.

Financial data (yr. ended 12/31/10): Assets, $5,727,443 (M); expenditures, $289,035; qualifying distributions, $281,100; giving activities include $281,100 for 10 grants (high: $168,100; low: $500).

Fields of interest: International human rights; United Ways and Federated Giving Programs; Arts, cultural/ethnic awareness; Education; Minorities/immigrants, centers/services.

Limitations: Applications not accepted. Giving primarily in MA and NY. No grants to individuals.

Application information: Contributes only to pre-selected organizations.

Director: Wijeyaraj A. Mahadeva.
EIN: 137437490

435
Newman's Own Foundation

790 Farmington Ave., No. 4B
Farmington, CT 06032-2300
E-mail: info@newmansownfoundation.org;
URL: http://www.newmansownfoundation.org/
Campus Community Service Challenge on
YouTube: http://www.youtube.com/watch?
v=rPeFysaqoJU&feature=player_embedded
Campus Community Service Challenge
Website: http://newmansownfoundation.org/
challenge/

Established in 2004 in DE and CT.
Donors: Paul L. Newman†; Newman's Own.
Grantmaker type: Company-sponsored foundation.
Financial data (yr. ended 12/31/09): Assets,
$188,203,761 (M); gifts received, $20,611,227;
expenditures, $30,885,039; qualifying
distributions, $29,847,937; giving activities include
$27,889,000 for 660 grants (high: $1,325,000;
low: $1,000).
Purpose and activities: The foundation supports
camps and organizations involved with arts and
culture, education, the environment, health, hunger,
disaster relief, human services, international
affairs, community economic development,
philanthropy, and economically disadvantaged
people.
Fields of interest: Media/communications;
Museums; Performing arts, theater; Arts; Higher
education; Education; Environment; Hospitals
(general); Health care; Food services; Food banks;
Disasters, preparedness/services; Recreation,
camps; Children/youth, services; Human services;
International affairs; Community/economic
development; Philanthropy/voluntarism;
Economically disadvantaged.
Type of support: General/operating support;
Management development/capacity building;
Program development; Scholarship funds;
Research; Sponsorships; Matching/challenge
support.
Limitations: Applications not accepted. Giving on a
national and international basis, with emphasis on
CA, CT, DC, FL, IL, MA, NY, OH, and WA, and in
Australia, Canada, and South Africa. No support for
organizations that promote a business purpose,
lobbying or political organizations, litigations of any
type, private foundations, or other entities which
require expenditure responsibility. No grants to
individuals, or for religious activities or beliefs,
annual campaigns, endowments, donor-advised
funds, special events, or building campaigns.
Application information: Contributes only to
pre-selected organizations.
Officers and Directors:* Robert Patricelli,*
Co-Chair.; Henry Schacht,* Co-Chair.; Robert
Forrester,* C.E.O. and Pres.; Brian Murphy,* V.P.
and Treas.; Clea Newman Soderlund,* V.P.; Jamie
Gerard,* Esq., Secy.; Robert M. Haggett, C.O.O. and
C.F.O.
EIN: 061606588
Recent grants for international programs:
435-1 1% for the Planet, Waitsfield, VT, $35,000.
For general operating support. 2009.
435-2 Africa Bridge, Marylhurst, OR, $20,000. For
Primary Education/Project Access. 2009.
435-3 Africa Bridge, Marylhurst, OR, $12,500. For
Masoko Ward Project. 2009.

435-4 African Medical and Research Foundation,
New York, NY, $20,000. For Leprosy and
Reconstructive Surgery. 2009.
435-5 Boys Town Jerusalem Foundation of America,
Roseland, NJ, $10,000. For scholarships. 2009.
435-6 buildOn, Stamford, CT, $15,000. For School
in Mali. 2009.
435-7 Carter Center, Atlanta, GA, $10,000. For
Human Rights Defenders Initiative. 2009.
435-8 Children of Armenia Fund, New York, NY,
$45,000. For Lernagog Project. 2009.
435-9 Coffee Kids, Santa Fe, NM, $20,000. For
Chiapas Mexico Project. 2009.
435-10 Concern Worldwide U.S., Chicago, IL,
$25,000. For Humanitarian Funding for Pakistan.
2009.
435-11 Doctors Without Borders USA, New York,
NY, $50,000. For general support. 2009.
435-12 Dynamo Foundation, Milan, Italy, $50,000.
For Dynamo - Middle East Project. 2009.
435-13 Education and Hope, Norwalk, CT, $10,000.
For Guatemala Program. 2009.
435-14 Fauna and Flora International, Washington,
DC, $100,000. For challenge grant. 2009.
435-15 Fauna and Flora International, Washington,
DC, $100,000. For challenge grant. 2009.
435-16 FIRST LEGO League, Manchester, NH,
$10,000. For US and Israel Programs. 2009.
435-17 Global AIDS Interfaith Alliance, Larkspur,
CA, $10,000. For GAIA Villages Program. 2009.
435-18 Global Hunger Project, New York, NY,
$10,000. For Epicenter Project in Ghana. 2009.
435-19 Hands Along the Nile Development
Services, Arlington, VA, $10,000. For
American-Egyptian Dialogue Program. 2009.
435-20 Hope for Haiti, Naples, FL, $30,000. For
Clinic of Hope Project. 2009.
435-21 Institute for International Sport, Kingston,
RI, $10,000. For World Youth Peace Summit.
2009.
435-22 International Rescue Committee, New York,
NY, $150,000. For From Surviving to Thriving.
2009.
435-23 International Rescue Committee, New York,
NY, $51,500. For general support. 2009.
435-24 International Rescue Committee, New York,
NY, $50,000. For Freedom Award. 2009.
435-25 Interplast, Mountain View, CA, $10,000. For
general program support. 2009.
435-26 Island Conservation, Santa Cruz, CA,
$35,000. For Caribbean Program. 2009.
435-27 K C E T Community Television of Southern
California, Los Angeles, CA, $200,000. For BBC
World News. 2009.
435-28 MADRE, New York, NY, $25,000. For
general support. 2009.
435-29 Mercy Center Foundation USA, Silver Spring,
MD, $17,000. For Lare Staff Housing Project.
2009.
435-30 Project HOPE - The People-to-People Health
Foundation, Millwood, VA, $80,000. For Iraqi
Project. 2009.
435-31 Rain for the Sahel and Sahara, Newmarket,
NH, $10,000. For Literacy for Girls and Women.
2009.
435-32 Rainforest Foundation International, New
York, NY, $25,000. For program support. 2009.
435-33 RARE, Arlington, VA, $25,000. For Borneo
Orangutan Campaign. 2009.
435-34 Right to Play USA, New York, NY, $50,000.
For Lebanese Project. 2009.
435-35 Safe Water Network, Westport, CT,
$625,000. For strategic initiatives and programs
at Safe Water Network, which provides

sustainable water and sanitation solutions such
as safe water kiosks and rainwater harvesting
systems for households and communities in
Ghana, India, and Kenya. 2009.
435-36 Safe Water Network, Westport, CT,
$625,000. For strategic initiatives and programs
at Safe Water Network, which provides
sustainable water and sanitation solutions such
as safe water kiosks and rainwater harvesting
systems for households and communities in
Ghana, India, and Kenya. 2009.
435-37 Save the Children Federation, Westport, CT,
$20,000. For Saving Newborns. 2009.
435-38 Seacology, Berkeley, CA, $50,000. For
general program support. 2009.
435-39 Survivor Corps, Washington, DC, $10,000.
For Global Sports Initiative. 2009.
435-40 Sustainable Harvest International, Surry,
ME, $27,500. For Field Trainers Sponsorship.
2009.
435-41 Tanzania Wildlife Fund, New York, NY,
$45,000. For Eastern Arc Program. 2009.
435-42 Tanzania Wildlife Fund, New York, NY,
$15,000. For Eastern Arc Project. 2009.
435-43 Union of Concerned Scientists, Cambridge,
MA, $25,000. For Food and Environment
Program. 2009.
435-44 United Nations Association of the United
States of America, New York, NY, $150,000. For
Leo Nevas Human Rights Program. 2009.
435-45 United Nations Association of the United
States of America, New York, NY, $150,000. For
Leo Nevas Human Rights Program. 2009.
435-46 United Nations Association of the United
States of America, New York, NY, $50,000. For
Global Leadership Awards Gala. 2009.
435-47 United Nations Association of the United
States of America, New York, NY, $10,000. For
general support. 2009.

436
The Oristano Foundation

1764 Litchfield Tpke., Ste. 203
Woodbridge, CT 06525-2353

Established in 1984 in DE and CT.
Donor: Victor Oristano.
Grantmaker type: Independent foundation.
Financial data (yr. ended 12/31/10): Assets,
$3,572,648 (M); expenditures, $230,726;
qualifying distributions, $165,780; giving activities
include $165,780 for grants.
Purpose and activities: Giving primarily to
educational institutions; support also for community
and family service organizations.
Fields of interest: Family services; Child
development, education; Vocational education;
Education; Reproductive health, family planning;
Housing/shelter, development; Human services;
Children/youth, services; Child development,
services; Minorities/immigrants, centers/services;
International affairs, arms control; Civil rights, race/
intergroup relations; Disabilities, people with;
Minorities; Economically disadvantaged.
Type of support: General/operating support;
Continuing support; Annual campaigns; Capital
campaigns; Building/renovation; Seed money.
Limitations: Applications not accepted. No grants to
individuals.
Application information: Unsolicited requests for
funds not accepted.
Board meeting date(s): 3 times annually

Directors: Mark Oristano; Matthew Oristano; Michael Oristano; Victor Oristano.
Number of staff: 1 part-time support.
EIN: 222471915

437
Rett Syndrome Research Trust, Inc.

67 Under Cliff Rd.
Trumbull, CT   06611-2550   (203) 445-0041
E-mail: monica@rsrt.org; *URL:* http://www.rsrt.org
Facebook: http://www.facebook.com/group.php?gid=162270035694
Trust Blog: http://rettsyndrome.wordpress.com/
Twitter: http://twitter.com/RSRT

Established in 2007 in CT.
Grantmaker type: Public charity.
Financial data (yr. ended 12/31/10): Revenue, $2,169,196; assets, $2,066,355 (M); gifts received, $2,160,051; expenditures, $1,596,570; giving activities include $1,335,210 for grants, and $13,535 for 1 grant to an organization outside the U.S.
Purpose and activities: The trust is focused on the development of treatments and cures for Rett Syndrome and related MECP2 disorders.
Fields of interest: Medical research; Genetic diseases and disorders research; Genetic diseases and disorders.
International interests: England.
Type of support: Research.
Limitations: Giving primarily to Dallas and Houston, TX and Seattle, WA, and to England.
Publications: Financial statement; Newsletter; IRS Form 990 or 990-PF printed copy available upon request.
Officer and Trustees:* Monica Coenraadds,* Exec. Dir.; Adrian P. Bird, Ph.D.; Heidi Epstein; Ingrid Love Harding; Lawrence Mattis.
EIN: 260687439

438
Faye and Michael Richardson Charitable Trust

33 Joshuatown Rd.
Lyme, CT   06371-3119   (860) 434-3349
Contact: Faye Richardson, Tr.

Established in 1994 in CT.
Donor: Michael Richardson.
Grantmaker type: Independent foundation.
Financial data (yr. ended 06/30/11): Assets, $2,729,990 (M); gifts received, $500,000; expenditures, $186,107; qualifying distributions, $181,804; giving activities include $181,804 for grants.
Fields of interest: Environment; Christian agencies & churches.
International interests: Burma (Myanmar); Guatemala.
Limitations: Giving primarily in CT and NY. No grants to individuals.
Application information: Application form required.
  Initial approach: Proposal
  Deadline(s): None
Trustees: Faye Richardson; J. Michael Richardson; Peter Richardson; Thomas Richardson.
EIN: 137044993

439
Smith Richardson Foundation, Inc.

60 Jesup Rd.
Westport, CT   06880-4311   (203) 222-6222
Contact: Marin J. Strmecki, Sr. V.P. and Dir., Progs.
FAX: (203) 222-6282; *URL:* http://www.srf.org
Grants Database: http://www.srf.org/grants/grantsdb.php

Incorporated in 1935 in NC.
Donors: H.S. Richardson, Sr.†; Grace Jones Richardson†.
Grantmaker type: Independent foundation.
Financial data (yr. ended 12/31/09): Assets, $441,100,393 (M); gifts received, $1,841,000; expenditures, $27,377,198; qualifying distributions, $25,683,114; giving activities include $21,741,648 for 315 grants (high: $700,000; low: $400).
Purpose and activities: The mission of the foundation is to contribute to important public debates and to help address serious public policy challenges facing the United States. The foundation seeks to help ensure the vitality of social, economic, and governmental institutions. It also seeks to assist with the development of effective policies to compete internationally and advance U.S. interests and values abroad. This mission is embodied in their domestic and international grant programs.
Fields of interest: Education; International affairs, foreign policy; International affairs; Social sciences; Economics; Political science; International studies; Public policy, research; Government/public administration.
International interests: Asia; Europe; Middle East; Soviet Union (Former).
Type of support: Fellowships; Conferences/seminars; Publication; Research.
Limitations: Applications accepted. Giving limited to U.S.-based organizations only. No support for programs in the arts and humanities, direct service programs, or historic restoration projects. No grants to individuals, or for deficit financing, building or construction projects, or research in the physical sciences; no loans.
Publications: Annual report (including application guidelines).
Application information: Most projects funded are initiated by the foundation. The staff does not meet with applicants. Application form not required.
  Initial approach: Concept paper (no longer than 5 pages)
  Copies of proposal: 1
  Deadline(s): None
  Final notification: 45 to 60 days
Officers and Trustees:* Peter L. Richardson,* Chair., Pres. and Gov.; Stuart S. Richardson, Vice-Chair.; Marin J. Strmecki, Sr. V.P. and Dir., Progs.; Ross F. Hemphill, V.P. and C.F.O.; Arvid R. Nelson,* Secy. and Gov.; Michael Blair; W. Winburne King III; Adele Richardson Ray; Lunsford Richardson, Jr.; Stuart S. Richardson; E. William Stetson III.
Board of Governors: Hon. Zbigniew Brzezinski; Christopher DeMuth; Martin Feldstein; Stephen Goldsmith; Fred C. Ikle; Dr. Roderick MacFarquhar; Genl. Edward C. Meyer; Dr. June E. O'Neill; Jane B. Preyer; Peter L. Richardson; Dr. Lawrence Sherman; Dr. Ashley Tellis; R. James Woolsey; Edward F. Zigler.
Number of staff: 6 full-time professional; 7 full-time support.
EIN: 560611550
Recent grants for international programs:

439-1 America Abroad Media, Washington, DC, $600,000. For Engaging the Muslim World through Media to lead effort to enhance political and ideological engagement with audiences in the Muslim world through a private-sector media initiative, developing public affairs programming jointly with television stations in Afghanistan, Pakistan, Indonesia, and Turkey and with Arab satellite stations such as Al Arabiya and Al Jazeera. 2009.

439-2 America Abroad Media, Washington, DC, $325,000. For Journalism Fellowship Program to lead effort to help the public in Muslim-majority countries better understand the United States. The program will bring journalists from the Middle East and Asia to Washington for a series of meetings with members of the U.S. policy community. The fellows will produce articles or video pieces for readers or audiences in their home countries. 2009.

439-3 American Enterprise Institute for Public Policy Research, Washington, DC, $20,000. For Bridging the Gap: An Economic and Security Strategy for U.S.-China Relations to research and write a monograph that sets forth two competing analytical perspectives on U.S. policy toward China - one grounded in a military-strategic perspective and the other in economic perspective - in order to identify the strengths and weaknesses of each approach. 2009.

439-4 Atlantic Council of the United States, Washington, DC, $150,000. To research and write a book, Impact of the Global Economic Crisis on China's Economic Evolution, that will examine the impact of the global financial crisis on the economic foundation of China's rise as a global power. The study will collect and analyze statistical and policy data and conduct field work in China in order to assess the efficacy of China's policies to cope with the fallout from the financial crisis. 2009.

439-5 Brookings Institution, Washington, DC, $100,000. For Pakistan's Uncertain Futures to lead effort to explore the political future of Pakistan, research from a group of American, Pakistani, European, and Indian analysts to develop alternative futures analysis of Pakistan and then synthesize those diverse assessments into analysis to appear in a series of papers. 2009.

439-6 Brookings Institution, Washington, DC, $100,000. For Winning our Longest War: Our Prospects in Afghanistan, to research and write a book that will assess the progress of U.S. military and political efforts in Afghanistan. They will discuss the history and culture of Afghanistan, track the U.S. political-military strategy to stabilize the country, develop metrics to gauge progress, and craft recommendations on key issues such as the building of Afghan security forces, the establishment of the rule of law, and economic development. 2009.

439-7 Carnegie Endowment for International Peace, Washington, DC, $150,000. For Net Assessment of Japan-China Defense Forces to research and write a monograph that will assess the impact of China's military buildup for the balance of power in East Asia. They will conduct a net assessment of political-military competition between China and Japan based on analysis of open data and supplemented by interviews with officials and analysts in China, Japan, and the United States. 2009.

439-8 Carnegie Endowment for International Peace, Washington, DC, $150,000. To research and write a book, Mapping the Saudi Clerical Establishment, exploring the role of the clerical establishment in Saudi Arabia's society and politics. The study will analyze existing Saudi and western research on the Saudi clerical establishment and carry out field work in Saudi Arabia involving interviews with a wide array of Saudi clerics. 2009.

439-9 Carnegie Endowment for International Peace, Washington, DC, $50,000. To research and write a book, Hegemon: U.S. Foreign Policy from 1900 into the Early 21st Century, which will examine how tensions between America's principles and its ambition for influence have shaped its foreign policy decisions and actions. The study will identify and explain how policy makers have misinterpreted history and analyze how these have shaped U.S. foreign policies, particularly regarding political and military interventions abroad. 2009.

439-10 Center for Democracy and Human Rights in Saudi Arabia, Washington, DC, $15,000. 2009.

439-11 Center for Media and Security, Millwood, NY, $200,000. To organize a series of meetings that bring defense officials together with reporters from print and electronic media to discuss key national security and defense policy issues. 2009.

439-12 Center for Strategic and Budgetary Assessments, Washington, DC, $600,000. For Strategy for the Long Haul to lead effort to inform the policy debate over how to revise the U.S. defense program to address the principal security challenges facing the United States more effectively. The study will engage in policy outreach and public education regarding the findings and recommendations of the center's study. 2009.

439-13 Center for Strategic and International Studies, Washington, DC, $149,816. For U.S.-China Dialogue on Instability in North Korea and Potential Responses to convene meetings with the Chinese Institute for Contemporary International Relations that bring U.S. and Chinese policy thinkers together to discuss prospects for discontinuous political change in North Korea and potential responses to it. The project's findings will appear in a report. 2009.

439-14 Center for Strategic and International Studies, Washington, DC, $143,517. For Supporting European Energy Security to examine approaches that the United States and key European Union countries could employ to counter Russia's use of energy policies to further its geopolitical influence in Europe. The study will develop strategies to reduce vulnerability to politically motivated energy disruptions and to build a coalition of European political and security leaders to work toward a common energy security strategy. The project's findings will appear in a series of papers and a monograph. 2009.

439-15 Center for Strategic and International Studies, Washington, DC, $114,675. For Georgian Lessons for the NATO Alliance to research and write a monograph that will analyze Russia's strategies and tactics toward its Central and East European neighbors, examine European reactions to Russia's policies, and develop policy recommendations to develop a common U.S.-European approach to Russian policy. 2009.

439-16 Center for Strategic and International Studies, Washington, DC, $100,000. For Anchor and Drift: The Future of U.S.-Israeli Strategic Ties; to lead effort to assess the future of the U.S. relationship with Israel. They will conduct a survey of open source material in English and Hebrew on the strategic and political components of the partnership; conduct interviews with a wide range of current and former government officials, academics, businessmen, and journalists in the United States and Israel; and form core groups of American and Israeli experts to assess the dynamics affecting the future of U.S.-Israeli relations. The project's findings will appear in a monograph. 2009.

439-17 Center for the National Interest, Washington, DC, $125,000. For Maritime Security East of Suez: Sustaining the U.S. Role as the Key Policeman to examine strategies to protect sea lanes in and around the Persian Gulf in light of the fiscal constraints the United States will face in the coming years. The study will conduct interviews with military and civilian experts in the United States, Japan, China, India, and the Persian Gulf nations to identify and analyze their outlooks concerning how to preserve commercial and energy access to the gulf. The project's findings will appear in a monograph and a series of journal articles. 2009.

439-18 Center for the National Interest, Washington, DC, $50,000. To research and write a book, China on the Edge: China's Border Provinces and Chinese Security Policy, that will analyze China's political strategy for its relations with and influence on the countries on its borders. 2009.

439-19 Center for the Study of the Presidency and Congress, Washington, DC, $200,000. For NATO in Afghanistan: Saving the Alliance's Future to lead effort to catalyze improvements in NATO's strategies and policies in Afghanistan. The study will lead a net assessment of the terrorist threat emanating from Afghanistan and Pakistan and develop a set of strategies and implementation plans to improve NATO's performance in Afghanistan. The project's findings will appear in policy briefings and a monograph. 2009.

439-20 CNA Corporation, Alexandria, VA, $100,097. To research and write a book, History of the War in Al Anbar, exploring the history of the U.S. military's efforts to combat insurgents in Iraq's Al Anbar province. The study will examine the political, military, and intelligence actions that were taken in order to quell the Sunni Arab insurgency and to enlist tribal groups in efforts to defeat al Qaeda in Iraq. 2009.

439-21 Columbia University, New York, NY, $125,000. For U.S. Policy toward Georgia After the War to research and write a monograph assessing U.S. policies toward Georgia in the run up to its war with Russia and consider how the United States should define and pursue its interests in the Caucasus region in the future. 2009.

439-22 Council for a Community of Democracies, Washington, DC, $100,000. For Training Diplomats to Support Democracy Development to research and write a handbook to improve the ability of diplomats to develop and implement policies to support indigenous democratic political movements and transitions. They will update existing edition of the handbook with new material drawn from case studies of Poland,

Egypt, Cuba, Nepal, Haiti, Vietnam, Cambodia, Zimbabwe, and Burma. 2009.

439-23 Council on Foreign Relations, New York, NY, $85,675. To research and write a book, The Future of Saudi Arabia, exploring the evolution of Saudi Arabia. The study will interview members of the Saudi elite as well as citizens from diverse sectors of Saudi society to identify and analyze internal Saudi debates on the economy, women's rights, education, and Saudi relations with neighboring nations. 2009.

439-24 Council on Foreign Relations, New York, NY, $75,000. To research and write a book, Partners in Peril: Understanding the U.S.-Pakistan Relationship, that will examine why the United States and Pakistan have consistently failed to develop a constructive and stable bilateral partnership even though they have professed to share important geopolitical interests. The study will analyze existing literature and conduct interviews with officials and experts in Afghanistan, India, Saudi Arabia, the United Arab Emirates, and China. 2009.

439-25 Council on Foreign Relations, New York, NY, $40,000. To research and write a book, Invisible Armies: A History of Guerrilla Warfare and Terrorism, that will identify patterns in how guerrilla wars have unfolded, the conditions under which guerrilla forces have tended to succeed, and the most effective counterinsurgency strategies and practices over time. 2009.

439-26 Foreign Policy Research Institute, Philadelphia, PA, $125,000. To research and write a book, Managing the Second Nuclear Age, analyzing how key features of the second nuclear age will challenge traditional approaches to deterrence and affect geostrategic competition among states. 2009.

439-27 Foreign Policy Research Institute, Philadelphia, PA, $109,800. For Border Nation: A Regional Security Strategy for Northern Mexico and the U.S. Southwest to research and write a monograph that will analyze security, economic, and political trends in the border regions of the United States and Mexico. The study will assess the degree of cooperation among local levels of government in both countries and develop recommendations for strategies and capabilities needed to reduce violence and criminality in the area. 2009.

439-28 Freedom House, Washington, DC, $166,465. For The American Committee for Peace in the Caucasus to lead effort to explore the geopolitical implications of instability in the Caucasus region. They will collect information about developments in the North Caucasus and analyze their effects on regional stability and Russia's political trajectory. This project's findings will appear on a website and in a series of briefings. 2009.

439-29 Freedom House, Washington, DC, $15,000. 2009.

439-30 Georgetown University, Washington, DC, $200,000. To research and write a book, Global Authoritarianism and the Challenge of International Order, that will explore whether informal coalition of authoritarian states is taking shape to challenge the current international order. They will commission research papers and organize workshops that will examine empirical evidence of policy coordination among key authoritarian states. 2009.

439-31 Georgetown University, Washington, DC, $50,000. To research and write a book, Staying Power and the Future of the American Era, that will examine the degree to which America's power is eroding across a range of key variables, including economic performance, demography, military capacity, and societal and political cohesion. 2009.

439-32 Hamilton Foundation, Los Angeles, CA, $150,000. For SME-Focused Development Project to explore whether financing mechanisms to support start ups of small- and medium-sized enterprises could help accelerate economic development in less-developed countries. They will prepare a blueprint for actions based on lessons learned from past or existing programs and through discussions with political, business, and educational leaders in Indonesia, the United Arab Emirates, and Morocco. The project's findings will appear in a monograph and a series of articles. 2009.

439-33 Harvard University, Cambridge, MA, $119,439. For Changing Chinese Attitudes toward Inequality and Distributive Injustice: A 5-Year Follow-up Survey to assemble a team of Chinese social science researchers to design and carry out opinion and attitude survey in eight urban and rural areas in China regarding the issues of social equality and justice. The project's findings will appear in a book and a series of articles. 2009.

439-34 Henry L. Stimson Center, Washington, DC, $116,730. To research and write a book, Building and Reforming Armies in the Middle East and South Asia: Western Military Assistance in Comparative Perspective. The study will conduct archival research and conduct interviews to study the history of Western and Soviet attempts to build or train modern militaries in the Middle East and South Asia. 2009.

439-35 Hobart and William Smith Colleges, Geneva, NY, $60,000. To research and write a book, Banking with Allah: Sharia-Compliant Banking and the Quest to Make Pakistan More Islamic, that will explore efforts to make the Pakistani financial sector comply with Islamic law. The study will analyze primary documents and interview leading figures in the Pakistani government and financial sector in order to develop a better understanding of their motivations and thinking regarding Islamic banking. 2009.

439-36 Hudson Institute, Washington, DC, $39,820. For Organizing a Strategic Ideas Campaign to convene a working group, undertake interviews, and explore historical parallels in order to develop concrete recommendations for how the U.S. government should organize itself to implement a soft power strategic ideas campaign. The project's findings will appear in a report. 2009.

439-37 Institute for Foreign Policy Analysis, Cambridge, MA, $178,164. For New Strategic Dynamics in the Arctic Region: Implications for National Security and International Collaboration to research and write a monograph that will explore the potential for strategic competition in the Arctic. They will assess security challenges likely to arise in the Arctic, examine the implications of these challenges for U.S. military force structure, and identify opportunities for constructive private sector and multilateral involvement in the region. 2009.

439-38 Institute for State Effectiveness, Washington, DC, $600,000. For The State Effectiveness Program to lead effort to advance approaches to help developing countries build effective state institutions. The study will prepare handbooks on the creation of institutions that carry out key government functions, document successful cases of state and institution building, and work with political and civil society leaders in select countries to develop state-building plans. The project's findings will appear in a series of reports, handbooks, and articles. 2009.

439-39 Instituto Libertad y Democracia, Lima, Peru, $25,000. For Bringing the Market Economy and the Rule of Law to the Peruvian Amazon to explore new ways to use economic empowerment to defuse internal conflicts in developing countries stemming from the marginalization of indigenous or native groups. The study will convene a conference that will bring together leaders of indigenous peoples from the Peruvian Amazon with those of similar communities from the United States and Canada to explore how programs to formalize property could contribute to economic development. The project's findings will appear in a report and a series of papers. 2009.

439-40 International Center for Religion and Diplomacy, Washington, DC, $200,000. For Best Practices in Islamic Education Research and Madrasa Curriculum Development to lead effort to catalyze and facilitate reform within Pakistan's system of religious educational institutions. They will work with a team of Pakistani social and political leaders to produce a reformed madrasa curriculum. They will organize a series of meetings in the United States to provide opportunities for Pakistani participants to exchange ideas with their American counterparts about designing and implementing pedagogy based on critical thinking and values such as religious tolerance and respect for human rights. The project's findings will be presented in a report and disseminated through a series of workshops in Pakistan. 2009.

439-41 International Studies Association, Tucson, AZ, $40,000. 2009.

439-42 Jamestown Foundation, Washington, DC, $75,000. To research and write a book, The Reform and Modernization of Russia's Conventional Armed Forces: Problems, Challenges, and Policy Implications, examining the nature, progress, and implications of Russia's military reform and modernization programs. The study will identify the drivers and the design of reforms across key military sectors; examine and evaluate doctrine, training, and equipment modernization initiatives; and analyze the political-military objectives behind the reform process. 2009.

439-43 Johns Hopkins University, Baltimore, MD, $170,220. For A Regional Strategy for Afghanistan and Steps Necessary for its Implementation to lead effort to develop a regional development strategy for stabilizing Afghanistan to complement the new U.S. military strategy. The project organizers will engage U.S. and regional policy makers to develop actionable agenda for using trade and transit as engine for economic growth in Afghanistan and the wider region. The project's findings will be presented in a report. At the School of Advanced International Studies. 2009.

439-44 Johns Hopkins University, Baltimore, MD, $96,000. To research and write a book, Chechnya's Secret Wartime Diplomacy: Efforts to Win Western Support for Independence, on the war in Chechnya based on the confidential communications between Akhmadov and the former Chechen president, Aslan Maskhadov. They will publish transcripts of these audio letters, accompanied by editorial material to provide historical context. At the School of Advanced International Studies. 2009.

439-45 National Bureau of Economic Research, Cambridge, MA, $200,000. The Design and Implementation of U.S. Climate Policy to explore issues related to the design, implementation, and administration of climate change policies. They will commission research on topics such as the impact of climate policy on employment and innovation, how carbon markets can be administered and regulated, and how climate mitigation efforts might interact with international trade rules. The project's findings will appear in a series of papers. 2009.

439-46 National Endowment for Democracy, Washington, DC, $50,000. For Assessing Democracy Assistance to lead effort to evaluate the the strengths and weaknesses of international democracy assistance in Afghanistan, Ukraine, and Russia. They will commission a survey, analyze available program evaluations, and map the assistance programs that have been undertaken. The project's findings will appear in a report. 2009.

439-47 National Institute for Public Policy, Fairfax, VA, $49,553. For Comprehensive Test Ban Treaty to convene a task force of experts to examine its security implications. The project's findings will appear in a report. 2009.

439-48 Naval War College Foundation, Newport, RI, $42,357. For Teaching about Irregular Warfare and Armed Groups to convene a symposium to disseminate new curricula and reading mateials for instructors teaching about irregular warfare. 2009.

439-49 New America Foundation, Washington, DC, $300,000. For Understanding Extremism in Pakistan and Afghanistan and its Strategic Implications to lead effort to improve the policy community's knowledge of insurgent groups in western Pakistan and the wider social and political dynamics underlying the conflict in the region. They will develop a network of local journalists and analysts who will produce a bottom-up picture of the human terrain of the war and analyze key cross-cutting questions. The project's findings will appear in a series of interim reports, a capstone report, and edited volume of policy essay. 2009.

439-50 New America Foundation, Washington, DC, $50,000. To research and write a book, Private Military Companies and Foreign Policy, that examines the drivers behind the rise of the private military industry and analyze the costs and benefits of using non-governmental personnel to train foreign militaries and conduct operations that potentially involve the use of force. 2009.

439-51 Nonproliferation Policy Education Center, Washington, DC, $400,000. For The Next Arms Race to commission research and organize workshops to explore the potential scenarios stemming from a significant reduction in nuclear arsenals of the major nuclear powers and accelerating proliferation of nuclear weapons and weapons-grade materials around the world. The project's findings will be published in a single-author volume, edited volume, and a series of shorter articles. 2009.

439-52 Peter G. Peterson Institute for International Economics, Washington, DC, $300,000. For America and the World after the Global Financial Crisis to lead effort to develop policy prescriptions to preserve U.S. leadership in the global financial and trading system. They seek support to examine how the major powers are restructuring themselves economically in response to the current crisis and how this will affect their power and influence in the world. The project's findings will appear in a series of co-authored monographs and articles. 2009.

439-53 Princeton University, Princeton, NJ, $125,000. To research and write a book, A Political History of Saudi Arabia, examining the internal politics and drivers of potential change in Saudi Arabia. The study will analyze primary and secondary literature and conduct interviews with the members of the royal family, the clerical establishment, and technocrats. The study will then use this material in order to present analytical history of Saudi politics based on the dynamic interrelationships among those three social and political groups. 2009.

439-54 Rights Action, Washington, DC, $15,000. 2009.

439-55 Small Wars Foundation, Bethesda, MD, $150,500. For Small Wars Journal, a web-based publication designed to increase the policy community's understanding of irregular warfare. 2009.

439-56 Technology Policy Institute, Washington, DC, $50,000. For Maintaining U.S. Leadership in Information and Communications Technology: Antitrust and the Dynamics of Competition in New Economy Industries to examine how the United States can best maintain its leadership in information and communications technologies. They will commission papers on the regulation of the technology industry, with a particular emphasis on the role of antitrust laws in promoting and hindering innovation. The project's findings will appear in a series papers and a report making policy recommendations. 2009.

439-57 Transnational Crisis Project, Washington, DC, $250,000. For Frontier Digital Gazette to lead effort to improve the ability of civilian and military operators in the field to understand the social and political contexts of the localities in which they are working. They will launch a pilot project in Pakistan's Malakand Division to test the possibility of creating online collaborative platform in which international and Pakistani stakeholders can accumulate detailed local social knowledge. 2009.

439-58 Truman National Security Project Educational Institute, Washington, DC, $100,000. For The Promise of Distributed Energy for Developing and Post-Conflict Countries to lead effort to catalyze new thinking in the policy community on employing distributed renewable energy systems to support economic growth in developing and post-conflict countries. They will examine how distributed renewable energy systems could be financed and deployed in the developing world and think through how such systems could be fielded to support economic growth and stabilization of Afghanistan. The

project's findings will be published in two monographs. 2009.

439-59 U.S. Cyber Consequences Unit, Norwich, VT, $75,000. To research and write a book, Cyber-Attacks: A Handbook for Understanding the Economic and Strategic Risks, that will develop a risk management paradigm that will allow policy makers to quantify the costs and challenges of defending against cyber threats. 2009.

439-60 University of Maryland-College Park, College Park, MD, $150,000. For The History of International Financial Crises: A Living Data Base to examine the history of financial crises around the world to inform contemporary debates over how best to avoid and recover from future crises. They will create on-line, database on the history of financial crises, commission research to address key issues surrounding them, and develop a set of standards that could be used to identify and date them. The project's findings will appear in a series of papers. 2009.

439-61 University of Maryland-College Park, College Park, MD, $81,400. To research and write a book, The Historical Obstacle to Global Zero in Nuclear Weapons, that will analyze whether worldwide nuclear disarmament would make the world more or less stable and secure. The study will conduct historical research into the debates and calculations concerning nuclear abolition among political leaders and the top scientists on the eve of the atomic age. The study will use this historical record to reflect on the dynamics of a world in which competitive states have access to nuclear technologies amid uncertainties about the intentions and capabilities of rivals. 2009.

439-62 University of Pennsylvania, Philadelphia, PA, $60,000. To research and write a book, Religious Dynamics and International Conflict, that will use case studies to assess whether religiously motivated combatants behave differently from their secular counterparts in armed conflicts. 2009.

439-63 Vanderbilt University, Nashville, TN, $60,000. To research and write a book, Political Influence of Foreign Graduates of U.S. Military Staff and War Colleges, that will examine the political implications of sponsoring foreign military officials at U.S. military staff and war colleges. The study will analyze data and conduct interviews to assess whether education of officers at these institutions correlates with the development of democratic political institutions in authoritarian countries. 2009.

439-64 Washington Institute for Near East Policy, Washington, DC, $75,000. For The Regent of God: A Political Biography of Iran's Supreme Leader to research and write a biography of Ayatollah Ali Khamenei, the most important religious and political figure in Iran. The study will examine Khamenei's rise to political prominence, religious and political worldviews, political strategies for managing contending factions over the course of almost two decades, and influence over key structures of power. 2009.

439-65 Wisconsin Project on Nuclear Arms Control, Washington, DC, $440,000. For Iran Watch to lead effort to research and analyze Iran's ongoing efforts to develop weapons of mass destruction and ballistic missile delivery capabilities. The project's findings will appear on the Iran Watch website and a series of articles and electronic bulletins. 2009.

439-66 Woodrow Wilson International Center for Scholars, Washington, DC, $150,000. For Developing a Comprehensive Binational Strategy to Address Mexican Drug Trafficking Organizations to lead effort to develop a U.S.-Mexico strategy to reduce the power of drug trafficking organizations. They will address issues such as increased law enforcement and intelligence cooperation, the disruption of southbound supply chains of money and assault weapons, the strengthening of law enforcement and judicial institutions in Mexico, the reduction of demand for narcotics, and building hemispheric cooperation against organized crime. The project's findings will appear in a report and a handbook for policy officials. 2009.

439-67 World Organization for Resource Development and Education, Washington, DC, $50,000. For Understanding the Socio-Political Groups of Pakistan to invite a group of Pakistani social, political, and religious leaders to the United States to provide opportunities for the U.S. policy community to gain a more sophisticated knowledge of the political and religious terrain of Pakistan. 2009.

439-68 Wright State University, Dayton, OH, $60,000. To research and write a book, Wiring the World: Information Technology, Strategy and U.S. Foreign Policy Across the Twentieth Century, that will explore how U.S. policy makers and communications industry leaders view the role of information technology in advancing U.S. economic and national security objectives. 2009.

439-69 Yale University, New Haven, CT, $149,861. To research and write a book, Can We Make Better Use of Medical Evidence? Political Incentives and the Prospects for Sustainable Reform, that will explore whether research on the effectiveness of medical treatments can play a larger role in improving the quality and efficiency of the U.S. health care system. They will examine how other countries have used medical evidence to inform treatment decisions, assess how medical evidence is currently used in the health care system, and interview key private-and public-sector actors in the health care field. 2009.

440

Save The Children Federation, Inc.
54 Wilton Rd.
Westport, CT 06880-3108 (203) 221-4030
E-mail: twebster@savethechildren.org; Toll-free tel.: (800) 728-3843; Additional address: 2000 M St., N.W., Ste. 500, Washington, DC 20036-3316, tel.: (202) 293-4170; URL: http://www.savethechildren.org
RSS Feed: http://www.savethechildren.org/rss/stc_topstories.xml

Established in 1932.
Grantmaker type: Public charity.
Financial data (yr. ended 12/31/10): Revenue, $541,850,058; assets, $315,121,126 (M); gifts received, $529,965,504; expenditures, $516,090,817; giving activities include $27,647,294 for grants, and $134,635,343 for grants to organizations outside the U.S.
Purpose and activities: The federation attempts to create real and lasting change for children in need in the United States and around the world by creating opportunities for the world's children to live safe, healthy, and fulfilling lives.

Fields of interest: Children/youth, services; International development; Children.
Type of support: Grants to individuals; In-kind gifts.
Limitations: Giving on a national and international basis.
Publications: Annual report; Financial statement.
Trustees: Susan Blumenthal, M.D.; Roxanne Mankin Cason; Andrea Collins; Robert Daly; Martha De Laurentis; Gretchen Dykstra; William Harrison Frist, M.D.; Tina Georgeou; Thomas R. Gerety; Charlotte M. Guyman; Bill Haber; Catherine Herman; Eric H. Holder, Jr.; Lawrence C. Horowitz, M.D.; Brad Irwin; and 17 additional trustees.
EIN: 060726487

441
The Shenandoah Foundation
c/o Walter, Berlingo & Co.
P.O. Box 4080
Darien, CT   06820-1480

Established in 1992 in CT.
Donor: Winifred Read Wilson.
Grantmaker type: Independent foundation.
Financial data (yr. ended 11/30/10): Assets, $4,301,937 (M); expenditures, $274,202; qualifying distributions, $247,000; giving activities include $247,000 for 12 grants (high: $55,000; low: $5,000).
Purpose and activities: Giving primarily for family planning and population studies.
Fields of interest: Reproductive health, family planning; International affairs; Population studies.
Limitations: Applications not accepted. Giving primarily in Washington, DC. No grants to individuals.
Application information: Contributes only to pre-selected organizations.
Trustees: Robert S. Anderson; Susan Brown; Douglas Wilson.
EIN: 223259552

442
The Tierney Family Foundation, Inc.
17 Butlers Island Rd.
Darien, CT   06820-6203

Established around 1990.
Donor: Paul E. Tierney, Jr.
Grantmaker type: Independent foundation.
Financial data (yr. ended 12/31/10): Assets, $7,343,355 (M); expenditures, $412,147; qualifying distributions, $407,171; giving activities include $402,195 for 55+ grants (high: $124,590).
Purpose and activities: Giving primarily for higher education and social issues.
Fields of interest: Higher education; Children/youth, services; International economic development; International human rights.
Limitations: Applications not accepted. Giving primarily in MA and NY.
Application information: Unsolicited requests for funds not accepted.
Officers: Susan E. Tierney, Pres.; Michael P. Tierney, V.P.; Patricia E. Tierney, V.P.; Paul E. Tierney, Jr., Secy.
EIN: 133541596

443
The Tudor Foundation, Inc.
1275 King St.
Greenwich, CT   06831-2936

Established in 1997 in CT.
Donors: Tudor Arbitrage Partners; Tudor Group Holdings, LLC; Tudor Proprietary Trading, LLC; Tudor Investment Corp.
Grantmaker type: Independent foundation.
Financial data (yr. ended 12/31/10): Assets, $1,646,038 (M); gifts received, $6,750,000; expenditures, $5,109,955; qualifying distributions, $5,037,946; giving activities include $5,037,946 for grants.
Purpose and activities: Giving primarily for education and human services, with emphasis on children and youth services.
Fields of interest: Education; Human services; Children/youth, services.
International interests: England; Australia.
Limitations: Applications not accepted. Giving primarily in CT, MA, NY and England; some funding also in Australia. No grants to individuals.
Application information: Contributes only to pre-selected organizations.
Officers and Directors:* Andrew S. Paul,* Pres. and Secy.-Treas.; Paul T. Jones II; John G. Macfarlane III.
EIN: 061502288
Recent grants for international programs:
443-1 Anika Foundation, Birchgrove, Australia, $30,000. 2010.
443-2 Autism Spectrum Australia, Frenchs Forest, Australia, $60,000. 2010.
443-3 Cerebral Palsy Foundation, Terrey Hills, Australia, $30,000. 2010.
443-4 Children Action, Geneva, Switzerland, $125,000. 2010.
443-5 Children of Mother Earth, Gorakhpur, India, $10,000. 2010.
443-6 Children's Trust, Tadworth, England, $81,165. 2010.
443-7 Council for Music in Hospitals, Walton-on-Thames, England, $40,688. 2010.
443-8 Country Holidays for Inner-City Kids, Tavistock, England, $40,665. 2010.
443-9 Disability Challengers, Guildford, England, $58,774. 2010.
443-10 East Surrey Domestic Abuse Services, Redhill, England, $32,556. 2010.
443-11 Fairbridge, London, England, $40,667. 2010.
443-12 Friends Without A Border, New York, NY, $25,000. 2010.
443-13 Medical Engineering Resource Unit, Epsom, England, $56,791. 2010.
443-14 National Society for the Prevention of Cruelty to Children, London, England, $56,798. 2010.
443-15 New Hope Foundation Limited, Hong Kong office, Beijing, China, $105,000. 2010.
443-16 Queen Elizabeths Foundation for Disabled People, Leatherhead, England, $56,822. 2010.
443-17 Rainbow Trust Childrens Charity, Leatherhead, England, $73,017. 2010.
443-18 Right to Play USA, New York, NY, $10,000. 2010.
443-19 Royal Hospital for Neuro Disability, London, England, $58,421. 2010.
443-20 SeeAbility, Epsom, England, $56,819. 2010.
443-21 SHINE, Ewell Village, England, $100,528. 2010.
443-22 Shooting Star CHASE, Guildford, England, $55,731. 2010.

443-23 Temple Garden Foundation Limited, Siem Reap Office, Cambodia, London, England, $15,000. 2010.

444
United Technologies Corporation Contributions Program
1 Financial Plz.
Hartford, CT   06103-2608   (860) 728-7000
Contact: Andrea Doane, Dir., Corp. Citizenship and Community Investment
URL: http://www.utc.com/utc/ Corporate_Responsibility/Community.html

Grantmaker type: Corporate giving program.
Financial data (yr. ended 12/31/09): Total giving, $19,000,000, including $19,000,000 for grants.
Purpose and activities: UTC makes charitable contributions to programs designed to build sustainable cities; support vibrant communities; advance STEM education; and invest in emerging markets. Support is given on a national and international basis in areas of company operations.
Fields of interest: Secondary school/education; Athletics/sports, Special Olympics; Museums; Housing/shelter, development; Arts; Education; Environment, natural resources; Environment; Health care; Human services; Community/economic development; United Ways and Federated Giving Programs; Mathematics; Engineering/technology; Science; Minorities; Women.
International interests: China; India.
Type of support: Donated products; In-kind gifts; General/operating support; Continuing support; Capital campaigns; Program development; Conferences/seminars; Curriculum development; Technical assistance; Employee volunteer services; Sponsorships; Employee matching gifts.
Limitations: Applications accepted. Giving on a national and international basis in areas of company operations, with emphasis on Hartford, CT, New York, NY, China, and India. No support for religious organizations, municipalities, booster clubs, sororities or fraternities, political groups, or organizations engaged in or advocating illegal action. No grants to individuals, or for religious activities, or publications or merchandise.
Publications: Application guidelines.
Application information: UTC administers grants for its corporate headquarters and its business units including Carrier, Hamilton Sundstrand, Otis, Pratt & Whitney, Sikorsky, United Technologies Research Center, UTC Fire & Security, and UT Power. Nonprofit organizations may apply to only one UTC business during any given year. The Community Affairs Department handles giving. The company has a staff that only handles contributions. Application form required.
Initial approach: Complete online eligibility quiz and application form
Copies of proposal: 1
Deadline(s): None for corporate headquarters grants; Mar. 1 to June 1 for business unit grants
Final notification: Up to 3 months
Number of staff: 3 full-time professional; 1 part-time professional; 1 full-time support.

445
Lawson Valentine Foundation
1000 Farmington Ave.
West Hartford, CT 06107-2138
Contact: Valentine Doyle, Prog. Off.
E-mail: valentinedoyle@sbcglobal.net

Established in 1989 in CT.
Donor: Alice P. Doyle†.
Grantmaker type: Independent foundation.
Financial data (yr. ended 12/31/09): Assets, $12,498,963 (M); expenditures, $800,416; qualifying distributions, $688,236; giving activities include $543,685 for 51 grants (high: $50,000; low: $1,000).
Purpose and activities: Primary areas of interest include human rights, environmental and economic justice, and food systems, including sustainable agriculture.
Fields of interest: Environment, legal rights; Agriculture, sustainable programs; Agriculture/food; International human rights; Civil/human rights, advocacy.
Type of support: General/operating support; Continuing support; Program development; Seed money; Technical assistance.
Limitations: Applications accepted. Giving primarily in CT, NJ and NY; some giving in CA. No support for religious activities, schools, or land trusts. No grants to individuals.
Publications: Annual report (including application guidelines).
Application information: Certified mail and express mail applications not accepted; AGM Common Proposal Form accepted. Application form not required.
  Initial approach: Letter
  Deadline(s): None
  Board meeting date(s): Spring and fall
  Final notification: Following board meetings
Trustees: Allen Doyle; Valentine Doyle; Mark Lindeman; Lucy Miller; Paul E. Vawter; William D. Zabel.
Number of staff: 2 part-time professional.
EIN: 136920044

446
The Vranos Family Foundation
c/o Ellington Mgmt. Group
53 Forest Ave., 2nd Fl.
Old Greenwich, CT 06870-1526

Established in 1997 in DE.
Donor: Michael Vranos.
Grantmaker type: Independent foundation.
Financial data (yr. ended 12/31/10): Assets, $1,349,019 (M); gifts received, $2,699,288; expenditures, $2,513,778; qualifying distributions, $2,508,154; giving activities include $2,494,106 for 107 grants (high: $100,000; low: $35).
Purpose and activities: Giving primarily for health care, education, human services, children's services, and international relief.
Fields of interest: Education; Health care; Cancer research; Human services; Children, services; International development; International relief.
Limitations: Applications not accepted. Giving primarily in CT and NY. No grants to individuals.
Application information: Contributes only to pre-selected organizations.
Trustees: James Ledley; Michael Vranos.
EIN: 133948273

DELAWARE

447
Adobe Foundation
c/o Foundation Source
501 Silverside Rd., Ste. 123
Wilmington, DE 19809-1377

Donor: Adobe Systems Incorporated.
Grantmaker type: Independent foundation.
Financial data (yr. ended 11/30/10): Assets, $29,430,384 (M); gifts received, $10,000,000; expenditures, $9,679,764; qualifying distributions, $9,639,868; giving activities include $7,314,879 for 179 grants (high: $300,000; low: $750), and $1,922,584 for 1 foundation-administered program.
Fields of interest: Children/youth, services; International affairs; Human services; Education.
Limitations: Applications not accepted. Giving primarily in CA and NY.
Application information: Contributes only to pre-selected organizations.
Officers and Directors:* Shantanu Narayen,* Pres.; Ann Lewnes, Secy.; Mark Garrett, Treas.; Johnny Loiacono; Michelle Mann; Donna Morris.
EIN: 260233808
Recent grants for international programs:
447-1 Akshaya Patra Foundation USA, Stoneham, MA, $10,000. For Bangalore Project. 2010.
447-2 American India Foundation, New York, NY, $93,583. For Year 5 of the Adobe Youth Voices Program. 2010.
447-3 American India Foundation, New York, NY, $74,626. To Implement AYV India in Bangalore. 2010.
447-4 American Red Cross of the National Capital Area, Fairfax, VA, $25,000. For International Response Fund Efforts in Chile. 2010.
447-5 Designers Accord, Oakland, CA, $30,000. For General Operating Support. 2010.
447-6 Free the Children USA, Hartford, CT, $49,475. To Implement Adobe Youth Voices within the Free the Children Network in Toronto and Florida. 2010.
447-7 Free the Children USA, Hartford, CT, $49,475. To implement Adobe Youth Voices within the Free the Children Network in Toronto and New York. 2010.
447-8 Free the Children USA, Hartford, CT, $29,458. To Implement Adobe Youth Voices within the Free the Children Network. 2010.
447-9 Friends of the World Food Program, Washington, DC, $50,000. For Haiti Disaster Relief Fund. 2010.
447-10 Friends of the World Food Program, Washington, DC, $25,000. For Disaster Relief Grant to the World Food Program for Pakistan flooding. 2010.
447-11 Give2Asia, San Francisco, CA, $466,000. For Adobe Foundation Donor Advised Fund. 2010.
447-12 Global Fund for Children, Washington, DC, $92,219. For Adobe Youth Voices Program. 2010.
447-13 Global Lives Project, Mountain View, CA, $30,000. For general operating support. 2010.
447-14 Global Youth Action Network, Brooklyn, NY, $186,560. To Implement Adobe Youth Voices through the Taking IT Global Network Project. 2010.

447-15 Human Rights Watch, New York, NY, $200,000. For Human Rights Watch International Film Festival and its signature program Youth Producing Change. 2010.
447-16 iEARN, International Education and Resource Network, New York, NY, $149,293. For Year 5 of the Adobe Youth Voices Program. 2010.
447-17 iEARN, International Education and Resource Network, New York, NY, $141,000. For Summer Teacher Internship through Industry Initiatives for Science and Math Education Program. 2010.
447-18 iEARN, International Education and Resource Network, New York, NY, $15,740. For International Conference and Youth Summit Program. 2010.
447-19 King Baudouin Foundation United States, New York, NY, $110,000. For Adobe Youth Voices Fund. 2010.
447-20 King Baudouin Foundation United States, New York, NY, $33,000. To replenish AYV donor advised fund at KBFUS for a grant to Eastside Educational Trust. 2010.
447-21 Learning Matters, New York, NY, $21,250. For Beyond Green Program. 2010.
447-22 NetHope, Fairfax, VA, $50,000. For general and unrestricted support. 2010.
447-23 Parikrma USA, New York, NY, $95,000. To support learning at Jayanagar (Bangalore). 2010.
447-24 Stanford University, Stanford, CA, $15,000. For Rural Education Action Project Computer Assisted Learning Program. 2010.
447-25 Tides Foundation, San Francisco, CA, $52,500. For Tides Canada Division. 2010.
447-26 Tides Foundation, San Francisco, CA, $32,000. For Tides Canada Division Arts and Creativity Program. 2010.
447-27 Tides Foundation, San Francisco, CA, $16,000. For Tides Foundation to be directed to Tides Canada Exchange Fund (No. 1481) for your cross-border. 2010.

448
American College International Foundation
1105 N. Market St., Ste. 200
Wilmington, DE 19801-1276

Established in 2001 in DE.
Grantmaker type: Public charity.
Financial data (yr. ended 12/31/09): Revenue, $19,250; assets, $3,460 (M); gifts received, $19,250; expenditures, $26,450; giving activities include $0 for grants.
Purpose and activities: The foundation works to establish educational partnerships and initiatives to promote world peace.
Fields of interest: Education.
International interests: Ireland.
Limitations: Giving limited to Ireland.
Officers and Directors:* Patrick J. Rooney,* Pres.; John P. Garniewski,* Secy.-Treas.; Donald E. Ross.
EIN: 510413197

449
American Fund for Charities
c/o Chapel & York
1000 N.W. St., Ste. 1200
Wilmington, DE 19801-1058 (302) 295-4959
Contact: David Wickert, Chair.

URL: http://www.americanfund.info/charities.html

Grantmaker type: Public charity.
Financial data (yr. ended 12/31/09): Revenue, $2,183,596; assets, $160,493 (M); gifts received, $2,171,834; expenditures, $2,945,095; giving activities include $2,874,716 for grants to organizations outside the U.S.
Purpose and activities: The fund supports various charities throughout the world in areas of arts, health, education, the environment, and other worthwhile causes.
Fields of interest: Environment; Health care; Education; Arts.
International interests: South Africa; United Kingdom.
Limitations: Giving on an international basis, primarily in the United Kingdom and South Africa.
Officers: David Wickert, Chair.; Gayle Levin, Pres.; Nancy Bikson, Secy-Treas.
EIN: 522109597

450
American Trust for Oxford University and East M.
c/o Wilmington Trust Co.
1100 N. Market St.
Wilmington, DE 19890-0001

Established in 1928 in NY.
Grantmaker type: Public charity.
Financial data (yr. ended 12/31/10): Revenue, $2,493,826; assets, $3,349,449 (M); gifts received, $1,795,886; expenditures, $1,924,955; giving activities include $1,883,459 for 1 grant to an organization outside the U.S.
Purpose and activities: The trust supports Oxford University.
Fields of interest: Education, single organization support; Higher education, university.
International interests: England.
Limitations: Applications not accepted. Giving limited to Oxford, England.
Application information: Contributes only to a pre-selected organization.
Trustee: Wilmington Trust Co.
EIN: 136024454

451
The Bertuzzi Family Foundation
c/o Foundation Source
501 Silverside Rd., Ste. 123
Wilmington, DE 19809-1377

Established in 2005 in DE.
Donor: John D. Bertuzzi.
Grantmaker type: Independent foundation.
Financial data (yr. ended 12/31/10): Assets, $943,087 (M); expenditures, $222,017; qualifying distributions, $212,000; giving activities include $212,000 for grants.
Fields of interest: International development; Media, film/video; Libraries (public); Higher education; Museums (art).
Limitations: Applications not accepted. No grants to individuals.
Application information: Contributes only to pre-selected organizations.

Officers and Directors:* John D. Bertuzzi,* Pres. and Secy.; Gail Bertuzzi,* V.P.; James Bertuzzi, V.P.; John A. Bertuzzi, V.P.
EIN: 203864006

452
Stephen and Mary Birch Foundation, Inc.
103 Foulk Rd., Ste. 200
Wilmington, DE 19803-3742   (888) 372-6303
Contact: Rose B. Patek, Secy.-Treas.

Incorporated in 1938 in DE.
Donor: Stephen Birch†.
Grantmaker type: Independent foundation.
Financial data (yr. ended 12/31/09): Assets, $211,137,953 (M); expenditures, $14,598,346; qualifying distributions, $12,254,906; giving activities include $11,492,888 for 168 grants (high: $5,371,570; low: $750; average: $1,000–$500,000).
Purpose and activities: The foundation provides funding in support of other nonprofit institutions, communities, and organizations that are or that have been instrumental in strengthening and heightening both culturally and educationally, the impact of research, medical, health, educational, sports, social service, and artistic programs in communities across the nation, from coast to coast.
Fields of interest: Arts education; Museums (sports/hobby); Arts; Education; Health care; Human services; Youth, services; International relief; Government/public administration; Christian agencies & churches.
Limitations: Applications accepted. Giving on a national basis. No support for political organizations.
Application information: Application form not required.
   Initial approach: Letter only
   Copies of proposal: 1
   Deadline(s): None
   Board meeting date(s): Quarterly
Officers: Rose B. Patek, Pres. and Treas.; Debra D. Durkin, V.P. and Secy.; Christopher Patek, V.P.
EIN: 221713022
Recent grants for international programs:
452-1 Diocese of Mandeville, Mandeville, Jamaica, $10,000. For Pastoral Centre. 2009.

453
Russell Colgate Fund, Inc.
c/o The Corporation Trust Co.
1209 Orange St.
Wilmington, DE 19801-1120

Established in 1943 in NJ and DE.
Grantmaker type: Independent foundation.
Financial data (yr. ended 12/31/09): Assets, $5,383,613 (M); expenditures, $270,947; qualifying distributions, $251,478; giving activities include $251,478 for 53 grants (high: $35,550; low: $500).
Fields of interest: YM/YWCAs & YM/YWHAs; Arts; Higher education; Hospitals (general); Health organizations, association; Human services; International affairs; United Ways and Federated Giving Programs.
International interests: France.
Type of support: General/operating support; Annual campaigns; Endowments.

Limitations: Applications not accepted. Giving primarily in Greenwich, CT, Boston, MA, and New York, NY. No grants to individuals.
Application information: Contributes only to pre-selected organizations.
Officers: Russell C. Wilkinson, Pres.; John C. Colgate, Jr., V.P.; Mary C. Kirk, Secy.
EIN: 221713065

454
Dominique Cornwell and Peter Mann Family Foundation
c/o JPMorgan Services
P.O. Box 6089
Newark, DE 19714-6089

Donor: Victoria Mann.
Grantmaker type: Independent foundation.
Financial data (yr. ended 09/30/10): Assets, $2,272,245 (M); gifts received, $1,500,000; expenditures, $471,519; qualifying distributions, $428,209; giving activities include $428,209 for grants.
Fields of interest: Multiple sclerosis research; Cancer research.
International interests: France.
Limitations: Applications not accepted. Giving primarily in NY and IL.
Application information: Unsolicited requests for funds not accepted.
Trustees: Dominique Cornwell; Peter Mann; Helen Lovely Francis.
EIN: 266848909

455
The Happy Davis Foundation, Inc.
c/o Foundation Source
501 Silverside Rd., Ste. 123
Wilmington, DE 19809-1377

Established in 2005 in DE.
Donor: Ray C. Davis.
Grantmaker type: Independent foundation.
Financial data (yr. ended 12/31/09): Assets, $3,311,948 (M); gifts received, $4,000,000; expenditures, $3,143,589; qualifying distributions, $3,143,084; giving activities include $3,084,415 for 27 grants (high: $1,500,000; low: $1,000).
Fields of interest: Health care; Cancer; Youth development; Children, services.
Limitations: Applications not accepted. Giving primarily in TX. No grants to individuals.
Application information: Contributes only to pre-selected organizations.
Officers and Directors:* Ray C. Davis,* Pres. and Secy.; Kris D. Leitzman,* V.P.
EIN: 203246052
Recent grants for international programs:
455-1 International Justice Mission, Arlington, VA, $350,000. For general support and unrestricted support. 2009.
455-2 YWAM Mercy Ships, Lindale, TX, $1,500,000. For general support. 2009.

456
Glencoe Foundation, Inc.
Greenville Ctr., Bldg. C, Ste. 300
3801 Kennett Pike, Ste. C-300
Greenville, DE 19807-2377
Contact: Ellice McDonald, Jr., Pres.

Established in 1975 in DE.
Donors: Ellice McDonald, Jr.; Rosa H. McDonald.
Grantmaker type: Independent foundation.
Financial data (yr. ended 12/31/10): Assets, $5,640,123 (M); gifts received, $134,191; expenditures, $499,024; qualifying distributions, $490,997; giving activities include $490,997 for 1 grant.
Purpose and activities: Gives exclusively to Scottish and American charitable organizations, such as museums, hospitals, educational institutions, and other publicly-oriented organizations that promote and preserve Scottish-American traditions and culture located in the Highlands and the islands of Scotland.
International interests: Scotland.
Type of support: General/operating support; Continuing support; Building/renovation; Equipment; Emergency funds.
Limitations: Applications not accepted. Giving limited to the Highlands and islands of Scotland. No grants to individuals, or for scholarships, fellowships, or matching gifts; no loans.
Application information: Unsolicited requests for funds not accepted.
   Board meeting date(s): Annually and as required
Officers and Directors:* Ellice McDonald, Jr.,* Pres.; Gregory A. Inskip, V.P.; Rosa H. McDonald,* V.P.; John C. Milner, Secy.-Treas.
EIN: 510164761

457
Renate, Hans & Maria Hofmann Trust
(formerly Hofmann Article 5 Charitable Trust)
c/o JPMorgan Chase Bank, N.A., Svcs. Dept.
P.O. Box 6089
Newark, DE   19714-6089

Established in 1996 in NY.
Donor: Renate Hofmann†.
Grantmaker type: Independent foundation.
Financial data (yr. ended 06/30/09): Assets, $42,324,984 (M); gifts received, $85,893; expenditures, $1,853,834; qualifying distributions, $1,639,769; giving activities include $1,055,000 for 8 grants (high: $725,000; low: $5,000).
Purpose and activities: Giving primarily to a Roman Catholic diocese in Germany; funding also for the arts.
Fields of interest: Arts; Catholic agencies & churches.
International interests: Germany.
Limitations: Applications not accepted. Giving primarily in Germany; some giving also in New York, NY. No grants to individuals.
Application information: Contributes only to pre-selected organizations.
Trustees: Patricia A. Gallagher, Esq.; Robert S. Warshaw, Esq.; JPMorgan Chase Bank, N.A.
EIN: 137102172

458
ING DIRECT Corporate Giving Program
1 S. Orange St.
Wilmington, DE   19801-5006   (302) 467-6076
URL: http://home.ingdirect.com/about/about.asp?s=CommunityAffairs

Grantmaker type: Corporate giving program.
Purpose and activities: ING DIRECT makes charitable contributions to nonprofit organizations involved with helping individuals achieve financial stability and become productive, self-sufficient citizens. Support is given primarily in areas of company operations in California, Delaware, Hawaii, Illinois, Minnesota, New York, and Pennsylvania, and in Australia, Austria, Canada, France, Germany, Italy, Spain, and the United Kingdom.
Fields of interest: Community/economic development; Youth development; Human services, financial counseling.
International interests: United Kingdom; Spain; Italy; Germany; France; Canada; Austria; Australia.
Type of support: General/operating support; Employee volunteer services; Loaned talent; Sponsorships.
Limitations: Applications accepted. Giving primarily in areas of company operations in CA, DE, HI, IL, MN, NY, and PA, and in Australia, Austria, Canada, France, Germany, Italy, Spain, and the United Kingdom.
Publications: Application guidelines.
Application information: The Community Affairs Department handles giving. A contributions committee reviews all requests. Application form required.
   Initial approach: Complete online application form
   Deadline(s): Jan. 1 to Sept. 30
   Final notification: 60 days

459
The Jackman Family Foundation
c/o Foundation Source
501 Silverside Rd., Ste. 123
Wilmington, DE   19809-1377

Established in 2006 in DE.
Donors: Hugh Jackman; Deborra-Lee Furness.
Grantmaker type: Independent foundation.
Financial data (yr. ended 12/31/10): Assets, $1,912,409 (M); expenditures, $206,123; qualifying distributions, $193,623; giving activities include $181,324 for 49 grants (high: $20,000; low: $250).
Fields of interest: Education, special; International development; Arts education; Performing arts, theater; Performing arts, education; Philosophy/ethics; Education; Environment, water pollution; Medical care, rehabilitation; Cancer; American Red Cross; Children/youth, services; Human services, mind/body enrichment; International relief.
International interests: Global programs; Zimbabwe.
Type of support: General/operating support; Income development; Program development; Curriculum development.
Limitations: Applications not accepted. No grants to individuals.
Application information: Unsolicited requests for funds not accepted.
Officers and Directors:* Hugh Jackman,* Pres. and Secy.; Deborra-Lee Furness,* V.P.
EIN: 204702478

460
Robert & Ardis James Foundation
c/o Foundation Source
501 Silverside Rd., Ste. 123
Wilmington, DE   19809-1377

Established in 1986 in NY.
Donor: Robert James.
Grantmaker type: Independent foundation.
Financial data (yr. ended 12/31/09): Assets, $65,789,468 (M); expenditures, $4,698,223; qualifying distributions, $3,233,090; giving activities include $3,104,466 for 88 grants (high: $1,300,000; low: $35).
Purpose and activities: Giving primarily for higher education, international affairs, and to Presbyterian churches.
Fields of interest: Higher education; International affairs, arms control; International affairs, foreign policy; International human rights; Public policy, research; Protestant agencies & churches.
Limitations: Applications not accepted. Giving primarily in NE and NY; some funding also in Washington, DC. No grants to individuals.
Application information: Unsolicited requests for funds not accepted.
Trustees: Ardis James; Ralph M. James; Robert James; Catherine James Paglia.
Number of staff: 1 part-time support.
EIN: 136880057
Recent grants for international programs:
460-1 Executives Without Borders USA, New York, NY, $15,000. For general and unrestricted support. 2009.
460-2 Human Rights in China, New York, NY, $10,000. For general and unrestricted support. 2009.
460-3 Human Rights Watch, New York, NY, $76,000. For general and unrestricted support. 2009.
460-4 International Council for the Life Sciences, Washington, DC, $25,000. For general and unrestricted support. 2009.
460-5 International Institute for Strategic Studies, Washington, DC, $50,000. For general and unrestricted support. 2009.
460-6 International Institute for Strategic Studies, Washington, DC, $50,000. To update and republish of Iran Dossier. 2009.
460-7 Partners in Health, Boston, MA, $200,000. For capital campaign. 2009.
460-8 PEF Israel Endowment Funds, New York, NY, $20,000. For Sikkuy Program. 2009.
460-9 World Security Institute, Washington, DC, $25,000. For general and unrestricted support. 2009.

461
Jewish Federation of Delaware, Inc.
100 W. 10th St., Ste. 301
Wilmington, DE   19801-1642   (302) 427-2100
Contact: Ruth Rosenberg, Asst. Exec. Dir.
E-mail: ruth.rosenberg@shalomdel.org; URL: http://www.shalomdelaware.org

Established in DE.
Grantmaker type: Public charity.
Financial data (yr. ended 06/30/10): Revenue, $3,649,970; assets, $31,890,348 (M); gifts received, $2,122,591; expenditures, $4,236,327; giving activities include $1,575,719 for grants.
Purpose and activities: The federation seeks to bring Jewish people together into a community coalition, grounded in Jewish teaching and heritage, to strengthen Israel, the global Jewish family and local organizations in order to further the survival of the Jewish people.
Fields of interest: Community/economic development; American Red Cross; Jewish agencies & synagogues.
International interests: Israel.

Type of support: Management development/capacity building; Annual campaigns; Capital campaigns; Building/renovation; Program development; Conferences/seminars; Consulting services; Use of facilities; Scholarships—to individuals; Matching/challenge support.

Limitations: Applications not accepted. Giving primarily in DE and southern PA.

Publications: Annual report.

Application information: Unsolicited requests for funds not considered or acknowledged.

Board meeting date(s): 3rd Thurs. of every month

Officers and Directors: Suzanne B. Grant,* Pres.; Samuel H. Asher, Exec. V.P.; Glenn M. Engelmann,* Esq., 1st V.P.; Robin Kauffman Saran,* V.P.; Connie J. Sugarman,* V.P.; Wendy J. Berger,* Secy.; William W. Wagner,* Treas.; Barry Bakst; Jack Blumenfeld, Esq.; John Elzufon; Douglas Herrmann, Esq.; Dr. Neil Hockstein; Dr. Robin Karol-Eng; Barry S. Kayne, D.D.S.; Laura Kramer; and 6 additional directors.

Number of staff: 6 full-time professional; 1 part-time professional; 2 full-time support; 1 part-time support.

EIN: 510064315

462
JNT Foundation

c/o JPMorgan Chase Bank, N.A.
P.O. Box 6089
Newark, DE   19714-6089

Established in 1999 in IA.

Grantmaker type: Independent foundation.

Financial data (yr. ended 08/31/10): Assets, $5,369,738 (M); expenditures, $525,152; qualifying distributions, $485,000; giving activities include $485,000 for grants.

Fields of interest: Higher education; Health care; Human services; Family services, domestic violence; International affairs.

Limitations: Applications not accepted. Giving primarily in IA. No grants to individuals.

Application information: Contributes only to pre-selected organizations.

EIN: 421493980

463
Jolie-Pitt Foundation

c/o Foundation Source
501 Silverside Rd., Ste. 123
Wilmington, DE   19809-1377

Established in 2006.

Donors: Brad Pitt; Angelina Jolie; Robert Offer; Potter Inc.; Weintraub Family Trust.

Grantmaker type: Independent foundation.

Financial data (yr. ended 12/31/09): Assets, $6,765,836 (M); gifts received, $341,012; expenditures, $5,927,628; qualifying distributions, $5,945,495; giving activities include $4,867,204 for 22 grants (high: $2,000,000; low: $2,000), $3,437 for 52 loans to individuals, and $866,606 for 1 foundation-administered program.

Fields of interest: International affairs, volunteer services; International human rights; International relief.

Limitations: Applications not accepted. Giving primarily in Washington, DC, New York, NY, New Orleans, LA and Boston, MA. No grants to individuals.

Application information: Unsolicited requests for funds not accepted.

Officers and Directors: Brad Pitt,* Co-Pres. and Secy.; Angelina Jolie,* Co-Pres.

EIN: 205176706

Recent grants for international programs:

463-1 Brookings Institution, Washington, DC, $100,000. For U.S. Policy toward international justice and the international criminal court. 2009.

463-2 Charities Aid Foundation America, Alexandria, VA, $10,870. For SOS Children's Village Association of Jordan. 2009.

463-3 Concern Worldwide U.S., New York, NY, $125,000. For Rebuilding Lives in Haiti Project, to rebuild three schools in Saut D'eau and repair six schools in La Gonave. 2009.

463-4 Council on Foreign Relations, New York, NY, $50,000. For special report on international law. 2009.

463-5 Global Health Committee, Boston, MA, $225,000. For Maddox Chivan Children's Center for AIDS infected children in Cambodia. 2009.

463-6 Maasai Foundation of East Africa, Santa Barbara, CA, $26,000. To support fundraising efforts. 2009.

463-7 Three Generations, New York, NY, $60,000. For Lubanga Chronicles/Katanga Trial Project. 2009.

463-8 United States Association for United Nations High Commissioner for Refugees, Washington, DC, $1,000,000. For Pakistan Emergency Fund. 2009.

463-9 United States Association for United Nations High Commissioner for Refugees, Washington, DC, $75,000. To Afghan Bureau for Reconstruction, NGO Implementing Partner of Sub Office Kabul in Central Region. 2009.

463-10 United States Association for United Nations High Commissioner for Refugees, Washington, DC, $75,000. To National Consultancy and Relief Association, NGO Implementing Partner of Sub Office Jalalabad in Eastern Region. 2009.

463-11 United States Association for United Nations High Commissioner for Refugees, Washington, DC, $10,000. For computer at the Kakuma School for Girls. 2009.

463-12 Valentino Achak Deng Foundation, San Francisco, CA, $50,000. For general and unrestricted support. 2009.

463-13 Wyclef Jean Foundation, New York, NY, $125,000. To rebuild, repair, and upgrade Haitian schools for underprivileged communities in Port-Au-Prince, Gonaives, Jakmel, and Cabaret. 2009.

464
The Kendeda Fund

c/o Foundation Source
501 Silverside Rd., Ste. 123
Wilmington, DE   19809-1377   (800) 839-1754

Donor: The March 23, 2006 Trust.

Grantmaker type: Independent foundation.

Financial data (yr. ended 12/31/10): Assets, $6,207,321 (M); gifts received, $20,063,500; expenditures, $29,688,319; qualifying distributions, $29,113,392; giving activities include $28,741,506 for 115 grants (high: $3,000,000; low: $3,000; average: $15,000–$150,000).

Fields of interest: Animals/wildlife; Higher education; Environment, climate change/global warming; Environment; Housing/shelter, development.

Limitations: Applications not accepted. Giving primarily in CA, Washington, DC, MA, MT, NY and VA.

Application information: Unsolicited requests for funds not accepted.

Trustee: Atlantic Trust Co., N.A.

EIN: 206881642

Recent grants for international programs:

464-1 Biomimicry Institute, Missoula, MT, $600,000. For general and unrestricted support. 2009.

464-2 Center for Climate Strategies, Washington, DC, $250,000. For general and unrestricted support. 2009.

464-3 Consultative Group on Biological Diversity, San Francisco, CA, $35,000. For health and environmental network program. 2009.

464-4 Earth Island Institute, Berkeley, CA, $700,000. For Energy Action Coalition's Power Shift Project. 2009.

464-5 EcoLogic Development Fund, Cambridge, MA, $500,000. For general and unrestricted support. 2009.

464-6 Ecology Center, Berkeley, CA, $100,000. For Global Alliance for Incinerator Alternatives project (GAIA). 2009.

464-7 Fund for Global Human Rights, Washington, DC, $150,000. For environmental justice program. 2009.

464-8 Global Greengrants Fund, Boulder, CO, $200,000. For general and unrestricted support. 2009.

464-9 Harvard University, Cambridge, MA, $250,000. For Center for Health and the Global Environment's Scientist-Evangelical initiative. 2009.

464-10 International Rivers Network, Berkeley, CA, $450,000. For general and unrestricted support. 2009.

464-11 Natural Capital Institute, Sausalito, CA, $50,000. For Wiser Earth program. 2009.

464-12 Oregon Jewish Community Foundation, Portland, OR, $164,372. For Amigos Hospitalito Atitlan project (friends of the little hospital in Atitlan). 2009.

464-13 Pueblo a Pueblo, Washington, DC, $117,970. For Hospitalito Santiago Atitlan construction project. 2009.

464-14 Rockefeller Family Fund, New York, NY, $700,000. For Re-Amp global warming strategic actions fund. 2009.

464-15 Rockefeller Family Fund, New York, NY, $50,000. For Re-Amp Steering Committee. 2009.

464-16 Root Capital, Cambridge, MA, $1,400,000. For general and unrestricted support. 2009.

464-17 Root Capital, Cambridge, MA, $350,000. 2009.

464-18 Safe Passage, Yarmouth, ME, $15,000. For charitable event. 2009.

464-19 Sustainable Markets Foundation, New York, NY, $175,000. For Project 350. 2009.

464-20 World Security Institute, Washington, DC, $52,400. For Heat of the Moment: The Faces of Climate Change Project. 2009.

464-21 Yale University, Corporate and Foundation Relations, New Haven, CT, $100,000. For the Yale Center for Green Chemistry and Engineering: Leading the Way to a Sustainable World project. 2009.

465
Paul and Patricia Kuehner Family Foundation

c/o Foundation Source
501 Silverside Rd., Ste. 123
Wilmington, DE 19809-1377

Established in 2007 in DE.
Donors: Patricia Kuehner; Paul J. Kuehner.
Grantmaker type: Independent foundation.
Financial data (yr. ended 12/31/10): Assets, $437,674 (M); expenditures, $569,002; qualifying distributions, $568,871; giving activities include $481,000 for 19 grants (high: $60,000; low: $1,000), and $3,198 for foundation-administered programs.
Fields of interest: Human services; International relief.
Limitations: Applications not accepted. Giving in the U.S., with emphasis on CT. No grants to individuals.
Application information: Contributes only to pre-selected organizations.
Officers and Directors:* Paul J. Kuehner,* Pres. and Secy.; Patricia Kuehner,* V.P.
EIN: 260849308

466
Mackenzie Family Foundation

c/o Foundation Source
501 Silverside Rd., Ste. 123
Wilmington, DE 19809-1377

Established in 2006 in CA.
Donors: Douglas Mackenzie; Shawn Mackenzie.
Grantmaker type: Independent foundation.
Financial data (yr. ended 12/31/10): Assets, $22,810,775 (M); gifts received, $1,797,528; expenditures, $3,022,049; qualifying distributions, $2,450,000; giving activities include $2,450,000 for grants.
Fields of interest: Higher education; Human services.
Limitations: Applications not accepted. No grants to individuals.
Application information: Contributes only to pre-selected organizations.
Officers and Directors:* Douglas Mackenzie,* Pres.; Shawn Mackenzie,* Secy.
EIN: 205700615
Recent grants for international programs:
466-1 Opportunity International, Oak Brook, IL, $500,000. For Africa campaign. 2008.

467
Raskob Foundation for Catholic Activities, Inc.

P.O. Box 4019
Wilmington, DE 19807-0019 (302) 655-4440
Contact: Paul A. Zambernardi, Exec. V.P.
FAX: (302) 655-3223; E-mail: info@rfca.org;
URL: http://www.rfca.org

Incorporated in 1945 in DE.
Donors: John J. Raskob†; Helena Raskob†.
Grantmaker type: Independent foundation.
Financial data (yr. ended 12/31/10): Assets, $143,802,443 (M); expenditures, $7,323,986; qualifying distributions, $6,221,006; giving activities include $4,482,749 for 339 grants (high: $95,800; low: $250).

Purpose and activities: To support Roman Catholic church organizations and activities worldwide by providing funds to official Catholic organizations for education, training, social services, health, emergency relief, as well as a wide variety of charitable needs.
Fields of interest: Education; Environment, water resources; Health care; Agriculture, sustainable programs; Human services; Children/youth, services; International relief; Catholic federated giving programs; Catholic agencies & churches; Religion; Infants/toddlers, female; Aging; Infants/toddlers; Children/youth; Children; Youth; Adults; Young adults; Disabilities, people with; Physically disabled; Blind/visually impaired; Deaf/hearing impaired; Mentally disabled; Minorities; Asians/Pacific Islanders; African Americans/Blacks; Hispanics/Latinos; Native Americans/American Indians; Indigenous peoples; Women; Girls; Adults, women; Young adults, female; Men; Infants/toddlers, male; Boys; Adults, men; Young adults, male; Military/veterans; Offenders/ex-offenders; Substance abusers; AIDS, people with; Single parents; Crime/abuse victims; Terminal illness, people with; LGBTQ; Immigrants/refugees; Economically disadvantaged; Homeless; Migrant workers.
International interests: Global programs.
Type of support: General/operating support; Management development/capacity building; Building/renovation; Equipment; Land acquisition; Emergency funds; Program development; Conferences/seminars; Film/video/radio; Publication; Seed money; Curriculum development; Technical assistance; Consulting services; Program evaluation; Program-related investments/loans; Matching/challenge support.
Limitations: Applications accepted. Giving to domestic and international programs affiliated with the Roman Catholic church. No grants to individuals, or for continuing support, annual campaigns, deficit financing (except missions), endowment funds, tuition, scholarships, fellowships, individual research, capital campaigns, building projects prior to the start or after the completion of construction, continuing subsidies, or requests that are after-the-fact by the time of the spring and fall trustee meetings.
Publications: Application guidelines; Grants list; IRS Form 990 or 990-PF printed copy available upon request.
Application information: The foundation does not accept applications via e-mail. Application form required.
Initial approach: Applications can be completed and submitted online or request application package via mail or fax on organization letterhead, or request downloadable application from foundation web site
Copies of proposal: 1
Deadline(s): Applications accepted for spring meeting from Dec. 8 to Feb. 8, for fall meeting from June 8 to Aug. 8
Board meeting date(s): May and mid-Nov.
Final notification: 4 months
Officers and Trustees:* Patrick W. McGrory III,* Chair.; Edward H. Robinson,* Pres.; Paul A. Zambernardi, Exec. V.P.; Noelle M. Fracyon,* 1st V.P.; Carolina R. Heinle, 2nd V.P.; L. Charles Rotunno, Jr., V.P., Grants Mgmt.; Timothy T. Raskob,* Secy.; Russell Raskob,* Treas.; Theodore H. Bremekamp III; Erin E. Henderson; Christopher R. Raskob; Richard G. Raskob; T. Mark Raskob; Maria R. Robinson; Katherine R. Van Loan.

Number of staff: 3 full-time professional; 5 full-time support; 1 part-time support.
EIN: 510070060
Recent grants for international programs:
467-1 African Benedictine Sisters of Saint Getrud Convent Imiliwaha, Njombe, Tanzania, Zanzibar and Pemba, $15,000. Toward the construction and furnishing of a primary school for orphans whose parents have died of AIDS and for street children whose extended families cannot support them. 2009.
467-2 Apostolic Vicariate of Isiolo, Isiolo, Kenya, $10,000. Toward the costs of food, facilitators' fees, stationery and transportation to organize workshops to promote inter-faith dialogue and enhance relationships among Catholics, Christians and Muslims. 2009.
467-3 Archbishop Joseph Cabana Ssunga Health Centre, Masaka, Uganda, $10,000. Toward the cost of repairing/renovating the male and female wards, the out-patient building and the staff quarters in order to better serve the community. 2009.
467-4 Archdiocese of Ernakulam-Angamaly, Kochi, India, $14,936. To establish, publicize and operate rural market centers to promote self-help group products and increase income of women entrepreneurs. 2009.
467-5 Archdiocese of Tegucigalpa, Tegucigalpa, Honduras, $20,000. Toward text books, materials/supplies, travel, room and board for 20 local participants to attend a week-long seminar of Hope for A Healthier Humanity and the Pan American Catholic Health Care Network to develop and implement programs to support those afflicted with HIV/AIDS as well as provide counseling, education and encouragement to those at-risk. 2009.
467-6 Archdiocese of Verapoly, Kochi, India, $13,000. To organize, train and support unemployed women in backwater island villages through the establishment/financing of a micro-credit business in duck farming. 2009.
467-7 Bannabikira Sisters, Daughters of Mary, Kampala, Uganda, $15,958. Toward the costs (salaries, administrative expenses, and training materials) of a Vocational and Apprenticeship Skills Development Project for orphans and vulnerable children, helping them to be self-reliant and less vulnerable to cross-generational sexual relationships, HIV infection, early marriage, and pregnancy. 2009.
467-8 Benebikira Sisters, Rwanda, $28,000. Toward the salary and expenses of a Development Director to establish a legal entity in the U.S. to enable U.S. citizens to make contributions to the Sisters and to coordinate all fundraising efforts for the Sisters, over 3 years. 2009.
467-9 Benebikira Sisters, Rwanda, $25,000. To construct additional building in order to add grades 4-6 at Our Lady of the Angels School in the Remera neighborhood of Kigali. 2009.
467-10 Benedictine Sisters of Saint Agnes, Peramiho, Tanzania, Zanzibar and Pemba, $15,000. Toward building materials to construct a water tank to provide clean, safe water to St. Joseph Vocational Training Center and the surrounding villages. 2009.
467-11 Caltec Academy, Makerere, Kampala, Uganda, $11,920. Toward materials and labor to construct a water harvesting and storage system to improve the water supply at this Senior Secondary School. 2009.

467-12 Caritas Developpement Niger, Niamey, Niger, $25,000. Toward a program to teach young farmers the use of organic grass mulch as a means of dramatically increasing crop productivity, specifically to construct a training center, drill a well with water pump, generator and related materials, purchase grass seed and adobe brick press and fence. 2009.

467-13 Carmelites of Mary Immaculate, India, $15,000. To construct a shelter/home to accommodate street children, ages 5-17. 2009.

467-14 Casa Corazon de la Misericordia, San Pedro Sula, Honduras, $14,000. For salary of tutor and/or non-tuition educational expenses (books/supplies, uniforms, snacks, bus fare/gasoline) for school-age residents at 24-hour Complete Care Program at Casa Corazon de la Misericordia. 2009.

467-15 Catholic Charities Health and Human Services, Cleveland, OH, $20,000. Toward equipment, supplies and labor to drill wells to provide clean water for drinking, cooking and bathing for the villagers in Duluit Bol in Southern Sudan which currently has only one water pump to serve a population of 41,000 people. 2009.

467-16 Catholic Medical Mission Board, New York, NY, $20,000. Toward program costs (salaries/benefits, clinical and community training, travel, medicines, monitoring and evaluation) to strengthen primary-level, maternal, antenatal and post-natal healthcare for children 5-and-under by partnering with selected clinics in the Diocese of Les Gonaives, Haiti. 2009.

467-17 Catholic Near East Welfare Association, New York, NY, $25,000. For medical services in the Gaza Strip and reconstruction assistance to the Mother and Child Health Care Clinic in Shija'ia, Gaza Strip, Palestine. 2009.

467-18 Catholic Relief Services, Cotonou, Benin, $21,224. To improve the quality of life and preserve the dignity of orphans and vulnerable children in dioceses of Benin by improving existing partner and community structures to provide care and counseling services; to ensure access of orphans/OVCs to formal and nonformal education, improve the income capacity of at least OVC households, and increase government and civil society involvement in the Issue of OVCs. 2009.

467-19 Catholic Relief Services, Baltimore, MD, $30,000. To implement a Homesteads to Markets project to train Afghan refugee women in vocational and life skills in urban Quetta, Pakistan to produce/market high quality products to generate family income. 2009.

467-20 Catholic Relief Services, Baltimore, MD, $25,000. For relief and cholera-fighting efforts for persons from Zimbabwe and along the Zimbabwe/South Africa border. 2009.

467-21 Church of Saint Francis of Assisi, Vilnius, Lithuania, $10,000. Toward the purchase of a minibus (or similar vehicle) for the Bernardinai Youth Center to conduct evangelization programs in rural areas. 2009.

467-22 Congregation of the Rosarians, Bangalore, India, $21,500. To underwrite construction/installation of sump tanks to harvest rain water for drinking, irrigation and farming (crops and fishery) to increase self-sufficiency of the Monastery. 2009.

467-23 Congregation of the Sisters of the Blessed Virgin, Kisii, Kenya, $15,178. Toward construction of a two-room daycare center for orphans and vulnerable children, ages 0-6 years. 2009.

467-24 Daughters of Charity of Saint Vincent de Paul, Province of Argentina, Buenos Aires, Argentina, $13,000. Toward costs of labor/material to construct additional classrooms at Miraculous Medal School to accommodate additional students and provide space for rescue intervention programs for children in marginalized and dysfunctional situations. 2009.

467-25 Daughters of Charity of Saint Vincent de Paul, Province of Burundi, Kicukiro, Rwanda, $26,000. Toward cost of construction/labor of Early Education School in Ruzo Parish, Burundi. 2009.

467-26 Daughters of Charity of Saint Vincent de Paul, Province of South India, Bangalore, India, $15,000. Toward costs of labor/materials to construct additional floor on top of the existing building at De Paul Bhavan Home for children with mental and physical disabilities. 2009.

467-27 Daughters of Charity of Saint Vincent de Paul, Province of the Middle East, Egypt, Beirut, Lebanon, $15,000. Toward the purchase of a locally-manufactured bus to provide safe transportation on a regular basis for young girls to attend St. Joseph School. 2009.

467-28 Diocese of Abomey, Abomey, Benin, $18,182. Toward computers, printers, converters, photocopiers, phones, credit charge and installation costs to effectively communicate between diocesan offices and parishes. 2009.

467-29 Diocese of Bungoma, Kenya, $13,251. Toward cost of financing capital for farming incentives and training for families to become self-reliant through the efforts of Agricultural Sustainability and Food Production Program. 2009.

467-30 Diocese of Calicut, Calicut, India, $15,000. For cows and goats for households of unwed and abandoned women in Pozhuthana to start income-generating projects to achieve self-sufficiency. 2009.

467-31 Diocese of Chimbote, Chimbote, Peru, $13,000. Toward expenses of workshops/educational materials to train pastoral agents in 3 parishes on the care of creation and preservation of nature and the cost of materials/campaigns to educate the public on protecting the environment. 2009.

467-32 Diocese of Chulucanas, Chulucanas, Peru, $10,500. Toward the costs (room and board) of conducting formation workshops at Villa La Buena Nueva Formation House in the mountain parish of Santo Domingo to prepare young men, ages 18-22, for service as diocesan priests and lay ministers. 2009.

467-33 Diocese of Guntur Society, India, $18,000. Toward construction of houses with toilets for flood-affected families. 2009.

467-34 Diocese of Iringa, Iringa, Tanzania, Zanzibar and Pemba, $15,000. For continued funding of Diocesan programs, specifically toward building materials to construct a 3-classroom building to offer orphan girls vocational training in cooking and nutrition. 2009.

467-35 Diocese of Irinjalakuda, Irinjalakuda, India, $13,500. Toward establishing income-generating domestic dairy unit for women, specifically to construct cattle sheds, purchase cows and increase organic backyard farming. 2009.

467-36 Diocese of Kanjirapally, Kanjirapally, India, $15,400. Toward the purchase of ambulance to provide emergency medical care and transportation to medical facilities for patients at various Diocesan facilities namely, Good Samaritan Home, a mental institution for women and Bethlehem Ashram, a home for unwed mothers and children. 2009.

467-37 Diocese of Kumbakonam, Kumbakonam, India, $11,000. To underwrite start-up costs of a Decentralized Collective Womens Initiative and create a revolving loan fund to empower rural women to optimize income from agricultural produce. 2009.

467-38 Diocese of Madurai, Madurai, India, $10,000. To underwrite the construction of new toilet blocks, with bathrooms/washrooms per block, at Nobili Pastoral Center, the institution that coordinates the 12 Archdiocesan Commissions. 2009.

467-39 Diocese of Marthandam, Marthandam, India, $16,300. Toward the costs of establishing income-generating rabbit program for poor, rural families: food, facility rental, personnel, coordinator's salary, administrative expenses and purchase/insurance/transportation of rabbits. 2009.

467-40 Diocese of Melipilla, Melipilla, Chile, $11,000. For the Hope and Solidarity Foundation, specifically leadership training seminars/workshops for female seasonal agricultural workers. 2009.

467-41 Discalced Carmelites, India, $14,000. To conduct health awareness camps in schools and organize/implement healthcare activities in rural villages. 2009.

467-42 Education for Life Program, Nairobi, Kenya, $69,266. To address the problems of the continued spread of HIV/AIDS, especially as it affects the youth, through replication and extension of existing prevention programs; to improve and multiply facilitation of such programs through facilitator training, refresher and monitoring programs; for advocacy to address the stigmatization and exploitation of PLWA's, HIV/AIDS orphans and vulnerable children; and to provide special programs for the children and their caregivers. 2009.

467-43 Familia Padre Fabretto, Managua, Nicaragua, $15,000. Toward program expenses, evaluation/monitoring, training, salaries and administrative expenses to expand the Fabretto education and nutrition programs to boys and girls, ages 0-5, by offering early childhood and pre-education programs in the communities of Somoto and Cusmapa in northern Nicaragua. 2009.

467-44 Fonkoze USA, Washington, DC, $25,000. Toward on-site salaries/benefits, loan capital, furniture, staff training, printed materials and/or in-country Fonkoze administrative expenses to launch the Ti Kredi (little credit) Program at one of the branches of Haiti's Alternative Bank for the Organized Poor to provide poor women in Haiti with small loans needed to start/expand micro-businesses. 2009.

467-45 Franciscan Sisters of Our Lady of Bon Secours, India, $13,000. Toward labor/materials to construct additional toilet facilities at St. Francis Xavier Middle School. 2009.

467-46 Franciscan Sisters of the Immaculate Heart of Mary, Dar es Salaam, Tanzania, Zanzibar and Pemba, $35,000. To complete construction of the hospital at Ubungo-Msewe. 2009.

467-47 Franciscan Sisters of the Sacred Heart, Philippines, $14,000. To underwrite the installation of a new well at Mary Immaculate Children's Center: a temporary shelter for 26 orphaned, abandoned, neglected and street children, ages 4-12. 2009.

467-48 Fundacion Nosotros, Acassuso, Argentina, $30,000. For a building to house a Center of Inclusive Education to train professionals in dealing with the mentally-disabled, open a special primary school and raise awareness and inclusion through community outreach. 2009.

467-49 Handmaids of the Holy Child Jesus, Nigeria, $13,000. Toward materials and labor to drill a borehole, lay pipeline and purchase a 100-gallon tank to provide clean drinking water for Handmaids of the Holy Child Jesus Nursery Primary School and surrounding community. 2009.

467-50 Hands Together of the Palm Beaches, North Palm Beach, FL, $10,000. Toward costs of assisting Haitian immigrants to transition to living in the United States, specifically for software, computer maintenance, gas/time stipends and food allowance for counseling and literacy/computer classes and health awareness programs for adults and enrichment classes and a summer academic institute for middle school students. 2009.

467-51 Instituto Fe y Vida, Stockton, CA, $30,000. To subsidize the purchase of La Biblia Catolica para Jovenes to make Bibles more accessible to economically-disadvantaged young evangelizers participating in a Biblical initiative to bring the Word of God to Spanish-speaking young people in the Americas. 2009.

467-52 Instituto Superior de Ciencias Religiosas de San Bernardo, San Bernardo, Chile, $10,000. Toward teachers' fees to continue the Parish Catechist Degree program to promote Christian education. 2009.

467-53 Kenya Episcopal Conference, Nairobi, Kenya, $25,000. For the Pontifical Missionary Societies of the Conference: toward training materials, facilitation, transportation, medical services, consultation fee, and food to organize and implement a formation, rehabilitation and counseling program to improve the living standards of children throughout the dioceses in Kenya. 2009.

467-54 Lay Centre at Foyer Unitas, Rome, Italy, $10,000. Toward renovation/furnishing/technological costs of relocation to the Passionist Monastery of John and Paul, to increase student rooms, provide lecture/dining facilities, industrial kitchen and additional office space to expand into international, inter-faith residence for young adult Catholics, Orthodox Christians, Muslims and Jews studying at Rome's pontifical universities. 2009.

467-55 Matero Boys Secondary School, Lusaka, Zambia, $30,000. Toward materials to build a fence around the school property for security purposes. 2009.

467-56 Misioneras de Cristo Resucitado, Vina Del Mar, Chile, $10,000. Toward capital renovations to a residence/formation house for the community. 2009.

467-57 Missionary Oblates of Mary Immaculate, Lusaka, Zambia, $25,000. For building materials toward Phase 1 construction of a Chapel for the Oblate Community at Radio Liseli in Mongu, Zambia. 2009.

467-58 Missionary Oblates of Mary Immaculate, Justice, Peace, & Integrity of Creation Office, Washington, DC, $40,000. For expenses to

continue the joint dialogue and exploration of relationships between Catholic and Islamic traditions as Part 2 (Religious Fidelity in Islam and Christianity) of a two-part series of colloquia co-sponsored by Catholic University (Washington, DC), Mofid University (Qom, Iran) and Tehran Institute of Philosophy and the publication and distribution of jointly-created documents. 2009.

467-59 Missionary Oblates of Mary Immaculate, Justice, Peace, and Integrity of Creation Office, Washington, DC, $27,500. To underwrite the cost of Education Specialist, diagnosis and therapy, training of parents/support teams, education materials (books, CD's, DVD's) and transportation to implement the Giving Hope to Special Kids Project - educational and spiritual outreach to the hidden children of San Eugenio Mission: physically- and mentally-handicapped youth in track houses, closed-gate and squatter communities on the outskirts of Tijuana, Mexico. 2009.

467-60 Missionary Oblates of Mary Immaculate, Justice, Peace/Integrity of Creation Office, Washington, DC, $10,000. To underwrite participants' travel, room and board, speakers' fees, marketing and staff costs of a 2-day Lay-Oblate Evangelization Communications Conference to explore the challenges facing Oblate-Catholic communications in the 21st century. 2009.

467-61 Musha Parish, Kigali, Rwanda, $11,000. Toward the purchase of water tanks, pipelines, materials and labor to construct a water system to provide clean drinking water to the rectory and the parish community. 2009.

467-62 Mwange Parish, Ruhengeri, Rwanda, $12,000. Toward construction of ecological public latrines, septic ditches and a rainwater harvesting system at the parish. 2009.

467-63 New Mariahout Parish, Yellapur, India, $16,000. For mulch cows as income-generating projects for the members of Mahila Mandal women's groups in the villages of Hasanparthy, Jayagiri, Palavelpula, Seethampeta and Yellapur. 2009.

467-64 Nyadri Urban Secondary School, Arua, Uganda, $15,000. Toward construction of a dormitory to house female students. 2009.

467-65 Oblate Sisters of Saint Francis de Sales, Riobamba, Ecuador, $20,000. Toward the cost of rebuilding the soup kitchen at tuition-free Isidro Narvaez Catholic School in Alausi that was damaged by an earthquake. 2009.

467-66 Our Lady of Fatima Church, India, $10,800. For income-generating dairy project, specifically to underwrite the purchase of milk buffalo for poor women in rural villages. 2009.

467-67 Our Lady of Lourdes Church, India, $16,154. For tools (carts, tables, irons/ironing boards, shelves) for washerman families in Marripadu to take in laundry to sustain their livelihood. 2009.

467-68 Our Lady of the Philippines Trappist Abbey, Jordan, Philippines, $25,000. Toward construction of a health care center to serve the poor of Guimaras. 2009.

467-69 Parroquia Nuestra Senora de Guadalupe, La Libertad, Guatemala, $15,000. To subsidize training and technical support provided by Concern America, Santa Ana, CA to conduct Integrated Community Health Program in Melchor and La Libertad parishes and expand community-based health projects throughout the parishes of Peten, specifically for foreign/local

personnel, health promoter training courses, education materials, transportation, site visits and administrative expenses. 2009.

467-70 PICO National Network, Oakland, CA, $25,000. For funding of PICO Central America staffing, travel and leadership training costs to expand the PICO organizing experience into Guatemala and additional dioceses in Central America, and establish a Central America Institute for Community Organizations. 2009.

467-71 Presentation Sisters of the Blessed Virgin Mary, Saint Kilda, Australia, $26,000. To underwrite the purchase of a Toyota Hilux 4-wheel drive truck, single cabin with canopy (or similar vehicle) for the Sisters to carry out their teaching, nursing and pastoral ministries in remote bush outstations of Papua New Guinea.. 2009.

467-72 Rutabo Preparatory Seminary, Kamachumu, Tanzania, Zanzibar and Pemba, $12,000. Toward cost of constructing additional water tank to collect and store 60,000 liters of rain water. 2009.

467-73 Sacred Heart School, Nalgonda, India, $13,500. Toward the purchase of a 42-passenger Tourister bus (or similar vehicle) to combat child labor by providing transportation for underprivileged children from rural villages to school. 2009.

467-74 Saint Andrews Catholic Parish, Kondoa, Tanzania, Zanzibar and Pemba, $15,000. Toward the cost of drilling one borewell to provide safe drinking water and sanitary facilities for the parish community. 2009.

467-75 Saint Balikuddembe Senior Secondary School, Buwama, Uganda, $12,942. Toward materials and labor to construct underground water storage tank, drainage system and pumps to distribute clean rain water to the school buildings for use by students and staff members. 2009.

467-76 Saint Cecilia Villa Girls Primary School, Masaka, Uganda, $13,000. Toward construction of a reservoir to provide clean water and sanitary facilities for the school. 2009.

467-77 Saint John the Baptist Parish, Hola, Kenya, $30,000. Toward the purchase of medicine, lab equipment, fuel for ambulance and boat for mobile clinics, and salaries of a clinical officer and nurse to provide health services and reduce the rate of malnutrition within the parish community which includes hard to reach areas along the Tana River District. 2009.

467-78 Saint Josephs Church, Chittoor, India, $13,500. Toward stipends of a project coordinator and teachers, books, food and lodging to offer tribal children a Residential Bridge Course to prepare them for mainstreaming into regular schools in effort to eradicate child labor. 2009.

467-79 Saint Martins Boys High School, Meru, Kenya, $10,000. Toward expenses of replacing materials and supplies (beds, blankets, bed sheets, uniforms, books) lost in a dormitory fire at St. Martin's High School, in order for students in Form IV to prepare for final examinations and/or costs of housing replacement for the students. 2009.

467-80 Saint Marys Church, India, $11,100. For drinking water for the parish complex (church, rectory, St. Mary's Primary and High Schools and St. Anthony's Orphanage) in Guntur District and classroom/library furniture, computers and laboratory equipment for St. Mary's High School in Pedaparimi. 2009.

467-81 Saint Renatus Malankara Catholic Church, Nooranadu, India, $10,800. To construct cow sheds and purchase mulch cows to establish income-generating project for unemployed women in Nooranadu Village. 2009.

467-82 Saint Theresas Riiji Health Center, Meru, Kenya, $14,700. Toward the purchase of building materials and labor to construct a water tank and lay pipeline to provide adequate water supply to the health center. 2009.

467-83 Salesian Missionaries of Mary Immaculate, India, $15,000. Toward construction of additional classrooms at Fatima Girls Higher Secondary School in Jayankondam. 2009.

467-84 Salesians of Don Bosco, India, $10,000. To underwrite the cost of labor/materials to construct toilets for students attending Don Bosco Academy. 2009.

467-85 San Vicente de Paulo Hogar de Ancianos, Buenos Aires, Argentina, $15,000. To repair, renovate and refurbish sections of the Pavilion, gardens and walkways at the Home providing refuge and services for the infirmed elderly. 2009.

467-86 Sisters of Charity of Leavenworth, Leavenworth, KS, $10,000. Toward the costs of formation and training workshops for the development of leadership among young lay women who volunteer for service in their local community in the Diocese of Chulucanas, Peru. 2009.

467-87 Sisters of Mary Immaculate, Kenya, $10,000. Toward the purchase of rabbits, chickens, and dairy goats to provide income and improve the nutritional status of orphans, in addition to textbooks, uniforms, and food items. 2009.

467-88 Sisters of Saint Joseph of Tarbes, India, $22,500. For funding of a community-based Rehabilitation Program for mentally- and physically-disabled residents of Cheshire Home, specifically to provide medical services, offer vocational courses, organize and hold community meetings in neighboring villages to promote/develop environment whereby the handicapped can be integrated into society. 2009.

467-89 Sisters of Saint Therese of the Child Jesus, Cameroon, $14,125. Toward general operating expenses. 2009.

467-90 Sisters of the Adoration of the Blessed Sacrament, Ernakulam, India, $12,917. To underwrite cost of labor/materials to construct rooftop tanks to harvest rain water for tribal families in Velliyamattam with disabled members resulting from alcoholism, tribal practices and/or inter-familial marriages. 2009.

467-91 Solidarity Bridge, Evanston, IL, $10,000. To continue the Pacemaker Implant Program in Cochabamba and Santa Cruz - bringing donated pacemakers to Bolivian poor infected with the parasitic disease, Chagas; and toward the cost of the Heart Surgery Program in Santa Cruz - providing open heart surgery to young adults needing valve replacement. 2009.

467-92 Taweta Parish, Mlimba, Tanzania, Zanzibar and Pemba, $10,365. Toward the purchase and installation of a water pump and motor to provide clean water to the parish dispensary. 2009.

467-93 Ukrainian Greek-Catholic Church, Lviv, Ukraine, $20,000. Toward salaries/benefits of a director, financial consultant and administrative assistant and/or annual operating expenses of

the Development Office of the Patriarchal Curia. 2009.

467-94 Unidad Academica Campesina-Carmen Pampa, Coroico, Bolivia, $50,000. Toward the costs of labor/materials to construct and furnish additional student dormitory as part of a capital campaign to provide new housing for students/faculty to alleviate overcrowding. 2009.

467-95 University of Notre Dame, Notre Dame, IN, $11,000. Toward salary, travel, lodging and per diem costs of a language interpreter essential in the production of Romero: Seeker of Justice - Martyr for Truth, a 90-minute bilingual documentary examining the life and death of Archbishop Oscar Romero of El Salvador, a project of Latin American/North American Church and the Kellogg Institute for International Studies. 2009.

467-96 University of San Diego, San Diego, CA, $10,000. For speakers' travel/accommodations and transportation for students from Catholic high schools in Mexico and inner-city San Diego neighborhoods to Worldlink's annual Youth Town Meeting, a program of the Joan B. Kroc Institute for Peace and Justice at the University. 2009.

467-97 Ursuline Sisters of Mount Saint Joseph, Maple Mount, KY, $12,000. Toward labor/materials to renovate first and second floors of Dianna Ortiz Ursuline Center for Women in order to expand programs, work/office space and living quarters to accommodate volunteers working with low-income women in the Poblacion Vicente Perez Rosales, one of the poorest areas of Chillan, Chile. 2009.

467-98 Vincentian Congregation, Kochi, India, $14,833. To improve the quality of life of the rural people of Ayyampuzha Grama Panchayath, specifically for weekly visits by medical personnel and administrative/program costs of counseling programs and literacy workshops, training programs and awareness camps on HIV/AIDS, drug abuse and parenting. 2009.

467-99 Volunteer Missionary Movement, Greendale, WI, $22,000. To construct a water catchment system for the community of Las Mezas in El Salvador in conjunction with Fundacion Hermano Mercedes Ruiz (FUNDAHMER), specifically the purchase/transport of materials, cost of labor and living expenses of the volunteer engineer designing and constructing the catchment system and training the local community in its maintenance. 2009.

468
The Sager Family Traveling Foundation and Road Show, Inc.

c/o Foundation Source
501 Silverside Rd., Ste. 123
Wilmington, DE 19809-1377
E-mail: contact@teamsager.org; URL: http://www.teamsager.org
E-Newsletter: http://www.teamsager.org/contact-us.php
Facebook: http://www.facebook.com/pages/The-Sager-Family-Traveling-Foundation-and-Roadshow/300545282648?ref=ts
Twitter: http://twitter.com/sagerfoundation

Established in 2000 in MA.
Donors: Robert C. Sager; Elaine H. Sager; Tess Sager; Shane E. Sager.
Grantmaker type: Independent foundation.

Financial data (yr. ended 07/31/09): Assets, $1,185,929 (M); gifts received, $1,000,000; expenditures, $774,114; qualifying distributions, $1,205,624; giving activities include $249,920 for grants, $717,806 for foundation-administered programs and $103,600 for 1 loan/program-related investment.
Purpose and activities: The foundation's goal is to educate children, teachers, community activists and doctors in underprivileged regions of the world to become better leaders.
Fields of interest: Higher education; Education; Environment; Human services; International affairs.
International interests: England; Nepal; South Africa; Sub-Saharan Africa.
Limitations: Applications not accepted. Giving on a national and international basis, particularly MA, PA, Dover, England, Nepal, Rwanda, and South Africa. No grants to individuals.
Application information: Contributes only to pre-selected organizations.
Officers and Directors:* Robert C. Sager,* Pres.; Elaine H. Sager,* V.P.; Brian D. Ferullo, Secy.-Treas.; Ken Tsunoda, Exec. Dir.
EIN: 043528688

469
Sall Family Foundation, Inc.

c/o JP Morgan Services, Inc.
P.O. Box 6089
Newark, DE 19714-6089
Contact: John Phillip Sall, Chair.

Established in 1993 in NC.
Donors: John Phillip Sall; Virginia B. Sall.
Grantmaker type: Independent foundation.
Financial data (yr. ended 12/31/10): Assets, $4,906,259 (M); gifts received, $6,500,000; expenditures, $6,439,521; qualifying distributions, $6,434,411; giving activities include $6,434,411 for 4 grants (high: $3,600,329; low: $125,082).
Purpose and activities: Giving primarily for health, education, environmental protection, and community development.
Fields of interest: Education; Environment, natural resources; Health care; Community/economic development.
Limitations: Applications accepted. Giving limited to Washington DC, NC and VA. No grants to individuals.
Application information:
  Initial approach: Letter
  Deadline(s): Sept. 30
Officers: John Phillip Sall, Chair. and Pres.; Virginia B. Sall, Secy.-Treas.
Board Members: John McMillan; William B. Messer; Elizabeth A. Sall; Leslie C. Sall.
Agent: JPMorgan Chase Bank, N.A.
EIN: 582016050
Recent grants for international programs:
469-1 CARE USA, Atlanta, GA, $3,600,329. For general support. 2010.
469-2 Nature Conservancy, Arlington, VA, $1,480,000. For general support. 2010.
469-3 World Wildlife Fund, Washington, DC, $1,229,000. For general support. 2010.

470
Myles D. and J. Faye Sampson Family Foundation

501 Silverside Rd., Ste. 123
Wilmington, DE 19809-1377

Established in 1993 in PA.
Donors: Myles D. Sampson; J. Faye Sampson; Twila Sampson Foundation; Rimdo Properties Inc.; Toro Development Company.
Grantmaker type: Independent foundation.
Financial data (yr. ended 12/31/10): Assets, $22,450,634 (M); gifts received, $17,760; expenditures, $869,836; qualifying distributions, $292,495; giving activities include $292,495 for grants.
Purpose and activities: Giving for senior citizen care, youth services, higher education, and public welfare services.
Fields of interest: Arts; Higher education; Hospitals (general); Health organizations, association; Youth development, scouting agencies (general); Human services; YM/YWCAs & YM/YWHAs; International development; United Ways and Federated Giving Programs; Protestant agencies & churches.
Limitations: Applications not accepted. Giving primarily in southwestern, PA. No grants to individuals.
Application information: Contributes only to pre-selected organizations.
Officer and Trustees: Katharine Sampson Boscia,* Secy; Kristy Sampson Rodriguez; J. Faye Sampson; Myles D. Sampson.
EIN: 256407379

471
Micol Schejola Foundation

c/o Foundation Source
501 Silverside Rd., Ste. 123
Wilmington, DE 19809-1377

Established in 2000 in NY.
Donor: Linda Schejola.
Grantmaker type: Independent foundation.
Financial data (yr. ended 12/31/10): Assets, $9,726,840 (M); gifts received, $1,008,222; expenditures, $692,263; qualifying distributions, $664,057; giving activities include $627,138 for 21 grants (high: $200,000; low: $500).
Fields of interest: Museums (art); Hospitals (general); Health care; Boys & girls clubs; International relief.
Limitations: Applications not accepted. Giving primarily in GA and NY. No grants to individuals.
Application information: Contributes only to pre-selected organizations.
Trustees: Jeff Akin; Linda Schejola; Lisa Schejola.
EIN: 137257959

472
The Thomas H. and Mary Williams Shoemaker Fund

c/o Advisory Trust Co. of Delaware
1100 N. Market St.
Wilmington, DE 19890-0900
Application address: c/o TH & MW Shoemaker Distributing Trustees, P.O. Box 390, Gwynedd, PA, 19736

Established in 1953 in PA.
Donors: Mary Williams Shoemaker†; Thomas H. Shoemaker†; Thomas H. and Mary Williams Shoemaker Trust.
Grantmaker type: Independent foundation.
Financial data (yr. ended 09/30/10): Assets, $7,545,026 (M); expenditures, $385,397; qualifying distributions, $341,056; giving activities

include $315,500 for 13 grants (high: $200,000; low: $2,500).
Purpose and activities: Emphasis on religious, charitable, and educational institutions of the Religious Society of Friends.
Fields of interest: Education; Environment; Human services; International peace/security; Religious federated giving programs; Protestant agencies & churches.
Type of support: General/operating support; Continuing support; Capital campaigns; Building/renovation; Endowments; Program development; Publication; Seed money; Curriculum development; Scholarship funds.
Limitations: Applications accepted. Giving primarily in PA. No grants to individuals, or for matching gifts; no loans.
Publications: Application guidelines; Informational brochure (including application guidelines).
Application information: Application form not required.
> *Initial approach:* Brief proposal and cover letter
> *Copies of proposal:* 6
> *Deadline(s):* Apr. 15, May 15, Oct. 15 and Nov. 15
> *Board meeting date(s):* May and Nov.
> *Final notification:* 3 weeks after meetings

Officers and Trustees:* Edward W. Marshall III,* Chair.; Martha B. Bryans,* Secy.; Samuel D. Caldwell; Mary Ellen McNish; Parker Snowe; Advisory Trust Co. of Delaware.
Number of staff: 1 full-time support.
EIN: 236209783

473
The Michael and Karen Stone Family Foundation, Inc.

501 Silverside Rd., Ste. 123
Wilmington, DE 19809-1377

Established in 2002 in DE.
Donors: Michael R. Stone; Karen Stone.
Grantmaker type: Independent foundation.
Financial data (yr. ended 12/31/10): Assets, $6,018,634 (M); gifts received, $508,625; expenditures, $295,206; qualifying distributions, $265,660; giving activities include $265,660 for grants.
Fields of interest: Higher education; Education; Children, services.
International interests: Kenya.
Limitations: Applications not accepted. No grants to individuals.
Application information: Unsolicited requests for funds not accepted.
Officer and Director:* Michael R. Stone,* Pres. and Secy.
EIN: 050544633

474
The Three Sisters Foundation

(formerly The Deutsch Foundation)
c/o Foundation Source
501 Silverside Rd., Ste. 123
Wilmington, DE 19809-1377
Contact: Alexis Deutsch-Adler, Secy.

Incorporated in 1947 in CA.
Donors: The Deutsch Co.; Carl Deutsch; Eleanor Deutsch; Lester Deutsch; Dworman Foundation,

Inc.; Alexis Deutsch-Adler; Gina Deutsch-Zakarin; Victoria D. Sutherland.
Grantmaker type: Company-sponsored foundation.
Financial data (yr. ended 12/31/10): Assets, $4,814,321 (M); expenditures, $203,088; qualifying distributions, $183,500; giving activities include $183,500 for grants.
Purpose and activities: The foundation supports organizations involved with elementary education, health, human services, and international relief.
Fields of interest: Elementary school/education; Health care; Children/youth, services; Children, services; Aging, centers/services; Human services; International relief; Jewish federated giving programs.
Type of support: General/operating support.
Limitations: Applications not accepted. Giving primarily in CA. No grants to individuals.
Application information: Contributes only to pre-selected organizations.
Officers and Directors:* Gina Deutsche-Zakarin,* Pres.; Alexis Deutsch-Adler,* Secy.; Lester Deutsch; Leslie Lichtenstein; Victoria D. Sutherland.
EIN: 956027369

475
Trust in Diversity

c/o Thomas E. Peckham
1100 N. Market St.
Wilmington, DE 19890-0900

Established in 1994 in MA.
Donors: John R. Bemis; Charlotte H. Bemis; The Charlotte H. Bemis Trust.
Grantmaker type: Operating foundation.
Financial data (yr. ended 07/31/09): Assets, $8,361,207 (M); gifts received, $3,476,996; expenditures, $483,816; qualifying distributions, $399,055; giving activities include $370,000 for 4 grants (high: $250,000; low: $10,000).
Fields of interest: Cancer research; International conflict resolution; United Ways and Federated Giving Programs.
Type of support: General/operating support.
Limitations: Applications not accepted. Giving primarily in MA. No grants to individuals.
Application information: Contributes only to pre-selected organizations.
Trustees: Eleanor Bemis; Gordon H. Bemis; Marjorie Bemis; Alice Bemis Bueti; Thomas E. Peckham.
EIN: 046747335

476
The Adam J. Weissman Foundation

(formerly The Joby Foundation, Inc.)
c/o Foundation Source
501 Silverside Rd., Ste. 123
Wilmington, DE 19809-1377

Established in 2005 in DE.
Donors: Adam J. Weissman; Google Inc.
Grantmaker type: Independent foundation.
Financial data (yr. ended 12/31/10): Assets, $7,316,748 (M); expenditures, $384,540; qualifying distributions, $379,321; giving activities include $342,250 for 11 grants (high: $15,000; low: $500).
Fields of interest: Human services; International relief; Catholic agencies & churches.

Limitations: Applications not accepted. Giving primarily in AR, CA, NY and WA. No grants to individuals.
Application information: Contributes only to pre-selected organizations.
Officers and Director:* Adam J. Weissman,* Pres. and Secy.; Tabitha Jordan, V.P.
EIN: 202624778

477
Thomas Lyle Williams Care-Salvation Army
(formerly Thomas Lyle Williams Trust)
c/o JPMorgan Chase Bank, N.A.
P.O. Box 6089
Newark, DE 19714-6089

Established in 1968 in IL; supporting organization of Care Inc., and The Salvation Army.
Grantmaker type: Public charity.
Financial data (yr. ended 12/31/10): Revenue, $9,167,147; assets, $128,114,045 (M); expenditures, $8,602,773; giving activities include $7,755,036 for grants.
Fields of interest: Salvation Army; International relief.
Limitations: Applications not accepted. Giving limited to Atlanta, GA and Alexandria, VA. No grants to individuals.
Application information: Contributes only to pre-selected organizations.
Trustees: Diane W. Parker; Thomas L. Williams III; JPMorgan Chase Bank, N.A.
EIN: 366673112

478
The Winky Foundation
c/o Wilmington Trust Co.
1100 N. Market St.
Wilmington, DE 19890-0900

Established in 1998 in DE.
Donor: Gerrish H. Milliken III.
Grantmaker type: Independent foundation.
Financial data (yr. ended 12/31/10): Assets, $4,843,956 (M); gifts received, $310,000; expenditures, $317,354; qualifying distributions, $312,000; giving activities include $312,000 for 202 grants (high: $9,000; low: $500).
Purpose and activities: Giving primarily for conservation organizations, as well as for education, health, and human services.
Fields of interest: Education; Environment, natural resources; Health organizations; Human services; International peace/security; Civil/human rights; Social sciences, public policy.
Limitations: Applications not accepted. Giving primarily in CA, NY, and Washington, DC. No grants to individuals.
Application information: Contributes only to pre-selected organizations.
Trustee: Wilmington Trust Co.
Advisors: Gerrish H. Milliken III; Stephen G. Milliken.
EIN: 516508170

DISTRICT OF COLUMBIA

479
Accordia Global Health Foundation
(formerly Academic Alliance Foundation for AIDS Care and Prevention in Africa)
1101 14th St., N.W., Ste. 801
Washington, DC 20005-5601 (202) 534-1200
FAX: (202) 534-1220;
E-mail: into@academicalliancefoundation.org;
URL: http://www.accordiafoundation.org
RSS Feed: http://www.accordiafoundation.org/latest-news/rss.xml

Established in 2001.
Grantmaker type: Public charity.
Financial data (yr. ended 12/31/10): Revenue, $8,357,936; assets, $12,167,269 (M); gifts received, $8,103,338; expenditures, $8,781,666; program services expenses, $7,602,813; giving activities include $3,899,101 for grants to organizations outside the U.S., and $3,703,712 for foundation-administered programs.
Purpose and activities: The alliance encourages the development of innovative, sustainable projects and programs that respond to the critical global health epidemic, especially the HIV/AIDS crisis engulfing Sub-Saharan Africa.
Fields of interest: AIDS research; AIDS.
International interests: Sub-Saharan Africa.
Type of support: Grants to individuals.
Limitations: Applications not accepted. Giving on a national and international basis, with emphasis on Sub-Saharan Africa.
Publications: Newsletter.
Application information: Unsolicited requests for funds not accepted.
Officers and Directors:* Henry A. McKinnell, Jr.,* Ph.D., Chair; Merle A. Sande,* M.D., Pres.; Nelson Sewankamba,* M.D., V.P.; Paula Luff,* Secy.; Robert Mallett,* Treas.; Susan Desmond-Hellmann, M.D., M.P.H.; Warner C. Greene, M.D., Ph.D.; King K. Holmes, M.D., Ph.D.; and 5 additional directors.
EIN: 043774897

480
ACDI VOCA
50 F St., N.W., Ste. 1075
Washington, DC 20001-1532 (202) 469-6000
FAX: (202) 469-6257; URL: http://www.acdivoca.org
Facebook: http://www.facebook.com/pages/ACDIVOCA/56475092041?v=wall&viewas=5308513
LinkedIn: http://www.linkedin.com/companies/acdivoca
RSS Feed: http://www.acdivoca.org/852571DC00681414/pagesbycategory.rss?openview&category=About%20Us-Newsroom-News
Twitter: http://twitter.com/acdivoca
YouTube: http://www.youtube.com/acdivocaDC

Established in 1997 from the merger of Agricultural Cooperative Development International and Volunteers in Overseas Cooperative Assistance.
Grantmaker type: Public charity.

Financial data (yr. ended 12/31/10): Revenue, $138,356,769; assets, $65,571,698 (M); gifts received, $138,243,359; expenditures, $137,587,412; giving activities include $10,411,832 for grants, and $39,725,877 for grants to organizations outside the U.S.
Purpose and activities: The organization promotes broad-based economic growth and the development of civil society in emerging democracies and developing countries.
Fields of interest: Community/economic development; Business/industry.
International interests: Developing countries.
Type of support: Technical assistance; In-kind gifts.
Limitations: Giving on a national and international basis.
Publications: Financial statement.
Officers and Directors:* Mortimer Neufville,* Chair.; Hon. Timothy J. Penny,* Vice-Chair.; Carl H. Leonard,* Pres. and C.E.O.; Marsha Moulton,* Sr. V.P., Human Resources and Admin.; Bill Polidoro,* C.O.O.; Matt Renaud, C.F.O.; Deborah Atwood; Dr. U.S. Awasthi; Charles F. Conner; Patricia Wilkinson Garamendi; Douglas Graham; William Harris; James K. Hoyt; R. Bruce Johnson; Richard Owen; Don Theuninck; Tom Verdoorn.
EIN: 520811461

481
African Wildlife Foundation
1400 16th St. N.W., Ste. 120
Washington, DC 20036-2217 (202) 939-3333
Contact: Kurt Redenbo, Dir., Fdn. Rels.
FAX: (202) 939-3332;
E-mail: africanwildlife@awf.org; URL: http://www.awf.org
YouTube: http://youtube.com/user/AfricanWildlife

Established in 1961.
Grantmaker type: Public charity.
Financial data (yr. ended 06/30/10): Revenue, $21,270,063; assets, $34,951,122 (M); gifts received, $20,418,220; expenditures, $21,097,992; giving activities include $279,274 for grants, and $1,469,014 for grants to organizations outside the U.S.
Purpose and activities: The foundation works together with the people of Africa to ensure that the wildlife and wildlands of Africa will endure forever.
Fields of interest: Community/economic development; Environment; Animals/wildlife.
International interests: Africa.
Type of support: Management development/capacity building.
Limitations: Giving primarily in Africa.
Publications: Annual report; Informational brochure; Newsletter.
Officers and Directors:* Dennis Keller,* Chair.; Matthew T. Weir,* Vice-Chair.; Helen W. Gichohi, Ph.D., Pres.; Patrick J. Bergin, Ph.D., C.E.O.; Joanna R. Elliott, V.P., Programming; Gregg Mitchell, V.P., Mktg. and Philanthropy; Thomas W. Nichols, C.F.O.; Edward M. Armfield, Jr.; Robin Berkeley; Wendy McCrary Breck; and 27 additional trustees.
EIN: 520781390

482
Aga Khan Foundation U.S.A.
1825 K St. N.W., Ste. 901
Washington, DC 20006-1202
URL: http://www.akdn.org/AKF

Established in 1981 in DC.
Grantmaker type: Public charity.
Financial data (yr. ended 12/31/10): Revenue, $27,795,480; assets, $173,641,359 (M); gifts received, $28,083,631; expenditures, $36,464,845; program services expenses, $30,312,868; giving activities include $299,202 for 3 grants (high: $129,790; low: $72,575), $29,873,220 for 19 grants to organizations outside the U.S., and $140,446 for 12 grants to individuals.
Purpose and activities: The foundation's mission is to develop and promote creative solutions to problems that impede social development, primarily in Asia and East Africa.
Fields of interest: International affairs.
International interests: Uganda; United Kingdom; Tanzania, Zanzibar and Pemba; Tajikistan; Syria; Switzerland; Portugal; Pakistan; Mozambique; Kyrgyzstan; Kenya; India; Bangladesh; Afghanistan; Canada; Africa; Asia.
Limitations: Applications accepted. Giving on a national and international basis, with emphasis on Afghanistan, Bangladesh, Canada, Egypt, France, Great Britain, India, Kenya, Madagascar, Mozambique, Pakistan, Portugal, Syria, Tajikistan, Tanzania, and Uganda. No grants for construction.
Publications: Application guidelines; Annual report.
Application information:
    Initial approach: Submit proposal
    Deadline(s): Mar. 31
    Final notification: Late June or early July
Officers and Directors:* Shah Karim Al-Husseini Aga Khan,* Chair.; Dr. Mirza Jahani, C.E.O.; Mohamed Ashraf Ramji,* Secy.-Treas.; Maitre Andre Ardoin; Guillame de Spoelberch; Prince Amyn Aga Khan.
EIN: 521231983

483
Agora Partnerships

920 U St., NW
Washington, DC 20001-4048 (202) 580-8776
URL: http://www.agorapartnerships.org
B Corporation Profile: http://www.bcorporation.net/agorapartnerships
Blog: http://agorapartnerships.org/about-us/blog

Grantmaker type: Corporate giving program.
Purpose and activities: Agora Partnerships is a certified B Corporation that donates a percentage of profits to charitable organizations. Support is given primarily in Central America, with emphasis on Nicaragua.
Fields of interest: Community development, small businesses; Economically disadvantaged.
International interests: Central America.
Type of support: Income development.
Limitations: Giving primarily in Central America, with emphasis on Nicaragua.

484
Alliance for Global Justice

1247 E St. S.E.
Washington, DC 20003-2221 (202) 544-9355
E-mail: afgj@afgj.org; URL: http://www.clrlabor.org/afgj/index.html

Established in 1998 in DC.
Grantmaker type: Public charity.

Financial data (yr. ended 03/31/11): Revenue, $1,410,526; assets, $784,621 (M); gifts received, $1,399,432; expenditures, $1,081,636.
Purpose and activities: The alliance works to achieve social change and economic justice by helping to build a stronger and more unified grassroots movement, through recognizing that the concentration of wealth and power is the root cause of oppression, and working together across ideologies issues, and communities.
Fields of interest: Community/economic development; International affairs; Civil/human rights.
Application information:
    Initial approach: Telephone or e-mail
Officers: Katherine Hoyt, Pres.; Charles Kaufman, Secy.; Robert Moses, Treas.
Directors: Tom Baker; Charles Delaney; Tim Jeffries; Barbara Larcom; Donna Leist; Arnold Matlin, M.D.; Shelly Scribner; Robert Siegel; Jean Midge Quandt.
EIN: 522094677

485
Amazon Conservation Association

1731 Connecticut Ave., N.W., 3rd Fl.
Washington, DC 20009-1137 (202) 234-2356
FAX: (202) 234-2358;
E-mail: info@amazonconservation.org; Additional tel.: (202) 234-2357; URL: http://www.amazonconservation.org
YouTube: http://www.youtube.com/user/AmazonConservation

Grantmaker type: Public charity.
Financial data (yr. ended 12/31/10): Revenue, $4,268,353; assets, $3,908,209 (M); gifts received, $4,168,834; expenditures, $4,045,678; giving activities include $400,000 for grants, and $2,832,149 for grants to organizations outside the U.S.
Purpose and activities: The association works to conserve the biological diversity of the Amazon Basin through a network of state, community and private lands managed for conservation.
Fields of interest: Animals/wildlife, preservation/protection; Environment; Environment, plant conservation; Environment, natural resources.
International interests: Peru; Brazil; Bolivia.
Type of support: Research; Scholarships—to individuals.
Limitations: Applications accepted. Giving limited to Bolivia, Brazil, and Peru.
Publications: Application guidelines; Newsletter.
Application information: Application form required.
    Initial approach: Concept letter (one page) for Matching Grants for Long-Term Research Projects
    Deadline(s): June 7 for Fondo para Investigacion de Campo para Tesis de Bachiller, Licenciatura o Maestria (Feb. 1 and Oct. 1 for Wayqecha Cloud Forest Research Center); Oct. 1 for Graduate Research Grants (Feb. 1 and Oct. 1 for Wayqecha Cloud Forest Research Center); Mar. 15 for Seed Grants and Matching Grants for Long-Term Research Projects
Officers and Directors:* Adrian Forsyth,* Pres.; Enrique Ortiz,* V.P.; John Tobin de la Puente,* Secy.-Treas.; Cesar Moran-Cahusac, Exec. Dir.; Dorothy Batten; Sarah duPont; Elizabeth Losos; Jessica Nagle; and 2 additional directors.
EIN: 522211305

486
American Association of Spinal Cord Injury Nurses

(also known as AASCIN)
801 18th St., N.W.
Washington, DC 20006-3517 (202) 872-1300
Contact: Sara Lerman M.P.H., Prog. Mgr.
E-mail: slerman@unitedspinal.org; URL: http://www.aascin.org

Established in 1983 in DE.
Grantmaker type: Public charity.
Financial data (yr. ended 06/30/09): Revenue, $200,142; assets, $189,826 (M); gifts received, $188,859; expenditures, $112,011.
Purpose and activities: The organization is dedicated to promoting quality care for individuals with Spinal Cord Impairment (SCI). This is achieved by advancing nursing practice through education, research, advocacy, health care policy, and collaboration with consumers and health care delivery systems.
Fields of interest: Spine disorders.
International interests: Canada.
Limitations: Applications not accepted. Giving on a national basis.
Publications: Informational brochure.
Application information: Unsolicited requests for funds not accepted.
    Board meeting date(s): Mar. and Sept.; June and Dec. teleconference
Officers and Directors:* Terrie Price,* Pres.; William Bockenek, V.P.; Mary Ann Reilly,* Secy.; Eliane Rogers, Treas.
EIN: 133206492

487
American Councils for International Education

1776 Massachusetts Ave., N.W., Ste. 700
Washington, DC 20036-1911 (202) 833-7522
Contact: William J. Brown, V.P., Devel.
FAX: (202) 833-7523;
E-mail: general@americancouncils.org; E-mail for William J. Brown: wbrown@americancouncils.org; URL: http://www.americancouncils.org
Facebook: http://en-gb.facebook.com/pages/American-Councils-for-International-Education/32669288562
YouTube: http://www.youtube.com/user/AmericanCouncils

Established in 1974.
Grantmaker type: Public charity.
Financial data (yr. ended 06/30/10): Revenue, $53,773,572; assets, $20,344,997 (M); gifts received, $48,072,263; expenditures, $53,966,291; giving activities include $439,308 for grants to organizations outside the U.S.
Purpose and activities: The organization works to advance education, research, and mutual understanding across the United States, Canada and the nations of southeastern Europe, Eurasia, South Asia, the Middle East, and China.
Fields of interest: Education; International exchange; Adults; Minorities; Young adults, female; Young adults, male.
International interests: Asia; Canada; Eastern & Central Europe; Russia; Soviet Union (Former).
Type of support: Fellowships; Research; Scholarships—to individuals.

Limitations: Applications accepted. Giving on a national and international basis, primarily in China, southeastern Europe, Eurasia, the Middle East, and Russia.
Publications: Annual report.
Application information: Application form required.
  Deadline(s): Varies
  Board meeting date(s): July and Dec.
Officers and Trustees: Richard D. Brecht,* Ph.D., Chair.; Dan E. Davidson,* Ph.D., Pres.; William J. Brown, V.P., Devel.; Lisa Choate, V.P.; Dr. David Patton, V.P.; John Henderson, C.F.O.; Hon. James F. Collins; Harriet Mayor Fulbright; Billie Davis Gaines, Ph.D.; David J. Gotaas; Lawrence T. Kurlander; Amb. Richard Morningstar; Robert Rose; Roald Sagdeev, Ph.D.; Jane W. Shuffelton.
Number of staff: 375
EIN: 521067256

488
American Enterprise Institute for Public Policy Research

1150 Seventeenth St., N.W.
Washington, DC 20036-4670 (202) 862-5800
FAX: (202) 862-7177; E-mail: webmaster@aei.org;
URL: http://www.aei.org
Institute Blog: http://blog.american.com/

Established in 1943.
Grantmaker type: Public charity.
Financial data (yr. ended 06/30/10): Revenue, $13,185,521; assets, $138,205,460 (M); gifts received, $12,427,227; expenditures, $13,967,167; program services expenses, $9,978,954.
Purpose and activities: The institute is dedicated to research and education on issues of government, politics, economics, and social welfare.
Fields of interest: Political science; Government/public administration; Economics; Civil/human rights; International affairs.
Limitations: Giving primarily to Washington, DC.
Publications: Annual report.
Officers and Trustees: Kevin B. Rollins,* Chair.; Arthur C. Brooks,* Pres.; Tully M. Friedman,* Treas.; Gordon M. Binder; Hon. Richard B. Cheney; Harlan Crow; Daniel A. D'aniello; John V. Faraci; Christopher B. Galvin; Raymond V. Gilmartin; Harvey Golub; Robert F. Greenhill; Roger Hertog; Bruce Kovner; Marc S. Lipschultz; and 10 additional trustees.
EIN: 530218495

489
American Friends of the Alexander von Humboldt Foundation

1012 14th St. N.W., Ste. 1015
Washington, DC 20005-3415 (202) 783-1907
FAX: (202) 783-1908; URL: http://www.americanfriends-of-avh.org

Established in 1999.
Grantmaker type: Public charity.
Financial data (yr. ended 12/31/09): Revenue, $686,971; assets, $1,036,870 (M); gifts received, $765,994; expenditures, $701,861.
Purpose and activities: The foundation promotes international scholarship and cross-cultural understanding by supporting the mission of the Alexander von Humboldt Foundation to foster German scholarship and research, and to benefit

scholarly research and educational programs in areas of interest to the foundation.
Fields of interest: International exchange; International exchange, arts; Education.
Type of support: Fellowships; Research; Scholarships—to individuals.
Limitations: Giving on a national basis.
Publications: Application guidelines; Newsletter.
Officers and Board Members: Robert P. Grathwol,* Pres.; Ulrike Albrecht,* Ph.D., V.P.; Donita M. Moorhus,* Secy.-Treas.; A. Stephen Dahms, Ph.D.; Daniel Fallon, Ph.D.; Thomas Hesse, Ph.D.; Eric Koenig.
EIN: 522217136

490
American Hellenic Institute Foundation, Inc.

1220 16th St. N.W.
Washington, DC 20036-3202 (202) 785-8430
Contact: Nick Larigakis, Exec. Dir.
FAX: (202) 785-5178; E-mail: info@ahiworld.org;
URL: http://www.ahiworld.com

Established in 1993 in DC as a private foundation; status changed to a public charity in 2003.
Grantmaker type: Public charity.
Financial data (yr. ended 12/31/09): Revenue, $763,254; assets, $3,120,737 (M); gifts received, $156,630; expenditures, $751,202.
Purpose and activities: The foundation seeks to develop policies and practical programs that will advance the interests of the Hellenic community and United States relations with Greece and Cyprus.
Fields of interest: International affairs; History/archaeology; Education.
International interests: Cyprus; Greece.
Publications: Annual report; Newsletter.
Officers and Directors: Aleco Haralambides,* Pres.; James H. Lagos, V.P.; Nick Karambelas, Secy.; Nick Larigakis, Exec. Dir.; Kostas Alexakis; Nicholas Chimicles, Esq.; James Marketos, Esq.; Gene Rossides, Esq.
EIN: 521061633

491
American Israel Education Foundation, Inc.

251 H. St., N.W.
Washington, DC 20001-2028
Contact: Richard Fishman, Exec. Dir.

Grantmaker type: Public charity.
Financial data (yr. ended 09/30/10): Revenue, $26,267,231; assets, $42,823,365 (M); gifts received, $26,122,122; expenditures, $24,369,000; program services expenses, $18,013,991; giving activities include $13,503,472 for grants.
Purpose and activities: The organization aims to provide education and information about the relationship between the U.S. and Israel.
Fields of interest: International affairs; Higher education.
International interests: Israel.
Type of support: Program development; Conferences/seminars.
Limitations: Giving limited to Washington, DC.
Officer and Directors: Howard E. Friedman,* Pres.; Robert Cohen,* Secy.; Donna Sternberg,* Treas.; Richard Fishman, Exec. Dir.; Melvin Dow; Russel

Holdstein; Claire Mazer; and 24 additional directors; Barry Silverman.
EIN: 521623781

492
American Near East Refugee Aid, Inc.

1522 K St., N.W., Ste. 600
Washington, DC 20005-1202 (202) 842-2766
URL: http://www.anera.org
ANERA: http://www.anera.org/anera-main.xml
Facebook: http://www.facebook.com/group.php?gid=12914486063
Twitter: http://twitter.com/ANERAorg
YouTube: http://www.youtube.com/user/ANERAorg

Established in 1968.
Grantmaker type: Public charity.
Financial data (yr. ended 05/31/10): Revenue, $50,585,386; assets, $11,878,733 (M); gifts received, $50,176,360; expenditures, $50,929,521; giving activities include $44,478,521 for grants to organizations outside the U.S.
Purpose and activities: The organization provides development, health, education, and employment programs to Palestinian communities and impoverished families throughout the Middle East.
Fields of interest: Human services, emergency aid; Community/economic development; Human services; Economically disadvantaged; Children/youth.
International interests: East Jerusalem; Jordan; Lebanon; Middle East; West Bank/Gaza (Palestinian Territories).
Type of support: Emergency funds; In-kind gifts; Loans—to individuals.
Limitations: Giving limited to Gaza, Jordan, Lebanon, East Jerusalem, and the West Bank.
Publications: Annual report; Informational brochure; Newsletter.
Officers and Directors: Curtis W. Brand,* Chair.; Edward Gnehm,* Vice-Chair.; William D. Corcoran,* Pres. and C.E.O.; Philip E. Davies,* V.P.; Mike de Graffenreid,* Secy.-Treas.; Gaby Ajram; Tim A. Attalla; Thomas D. Cabot; Diana D. Dajani; Ronald A. Dudum; James Gallagher; Curtis C. Giesen; James Hagerty; Richard C. Hall; Mona Aboelnaga Kanaan; and 18 additional directors.
EIN: 520882226

493
Americans for Informed Democracy Corporation, Inc.

218 D St., S.E.
Washington, DC 20003-1900 (410) 962-8770
FAX: (410) 962-8771; URL: http://www.aidemocracy.org/
Organization blog: http://aidemocracy.wordpress.com

Grantmaker type: Public charity.
Financial data (yr. ended 06/30/09): Revenue, $576,859; assets, $205,481 (M); gifts received, $548,396; expenditures, $636,884; program services expenses, $569,308; giving activities include $14,840 for grants, and $554,468 for foundation-administered programs.
Purpose and activities: The organization works to bring world issues to university campuses by coordinating town hall meetings on the U.S. role in

the world, hosting leadership retreats, and publishing opinion pieces and reports on issues of global importance.

Fields of interest: Media, print publishing; Media, film/video; Higher education, college; Education; International affairs; Civil/human rights.

Type of support: Program development; Film/video/radio.

Limitations: Applications accepted. Giving on a national basis.

Publications: Application guidelines.

Application information:
  Initial approach: Submit one- to two-page proposal online
  Deadline(s): Jan. 18 for Rights Camera Action Grants

Officers and Board Members:* Seth Green,* Chair.; Lynne Steuerle Schofield,* M.S., M.Phil., Vice-Chair.; Marceline White, Pres.; Sarah Bush,* Secy.; Patricia Langan,* Treas.; Mariam Asmar; Veronica Canton; Robert T. Coonrod; David Devlin-Foltz; Eric Gardner, M.P.P.; Tim Ruckh; Zeeshan Suhali.

EIN: 300216496

494
Americans for Peace Now, Inc.

1101 14th St. N.W., 6th Fl.
Washington, DC 20005-5601 (202) 728-1893
Contact: Debra DeLee, Pres. and C.E.O.
FAX: (202) 728-1895;
E-mail: apndc@peacenow.org; URL: http://www.peacenow.org

Established in 1978.

Grantmaker type: Public charity.

Financial data (yr. ended 12/31/10): Revenue, $1,905,807; assets, $780,948 (M); gifts received, $1,904,394; expenditures, $1,869,122; giving activities include $350,000 for grants to organizations outside the U.S.

Purpose and activities: The organization's mission is to help Israel and the Shalom Achshav movement to achieve a comprehensive political settlement of the Arab-Israeli conflict consistent with Israel's long-term security needs and its Jewish and democratic values.

Fields of interest: International conflict resolution.

International interests: Middle East; Israel.

Limitations: Giving primarily in the Middle East and Israel.

Officers and Directors:* Franklin M. Fisher,* Chair.; Martin Bresler,* Vice-Chair.; Debra DeLee,* Pres. and C.E.O.; Jo-Ann Mort,* Secy.; Elaine Hoffman,* Treas.; Elaine Attias; Jeremy Ben-Ami; David E. Birenbaum; Ernest Bogen; Luis Lainer; and 38 additional directors.

EIN: 133509867

495
Anti-Slavery International, Inc.

1320 19th St., N.W., Ste. 600
Washington, DC 20036-1633 (202) 775-7480
E-mail: info@freetheslaves.net; URL: http://www.freetheslaves.net
Facebook: http://www.facebook.com/group.php?gid=6186394386
MySpace: http://www.myspace.com/freetheslavesofficial

Grantmaker type: Public charity.

Financial data (yr. ended 12/31/10): Revenue, $2,969,934; assets, $1,445,754 (M); gifts received, $2,939,709; expenditures, $3,175,781; giving activities include $969,579 for grants to organizations outside the U.S., $20,000 for grants to individuals, and $7,500 for grants to individuals outside the U.S.

Purpose and activities: The organization works to liberate slaves around the world, help them rebuild their lives and research real-world solutions to eradicate slavery forever.

Fields of interest: Anti-slavery/human trafficking; International human rights; Civil/human rights, research; Civil/human rights.

Type of support: Research.

Officers: Kevin Bales, Pres.; Jolene Smith, Exec. Dir.

Directors: Robert Boneberg; David Brewer; Jean-Robert Cadet; Franka Jordan; Siddharth Kara; Stephen Maher; Kathy Sreedhar; John Zarafonetis.

EIN: 562189635

496
The Arca Foundation

1308 19th St. N.W.
Washington, DC 20036-1602
Contact: Anna Lefer Kuhn, Exec. Dir.
FAX: (202) 785-1446;
E-mail: proposals@arcafoundation.org; URL: http://www.arcafoundation.org
Grants List: http://www.arcafoundation.org/current_grantees.htm
The Arca Foundation's Philanthropy Promise: http://www.ncrp.org/philanthropys-promise/who

Incorporated in 1952 in NY.

Donor: Nancy R. Reynolds†.

Grantmaker type: Independent foundation.

Financial data (yr. ended 12/31/10): Assets, $51,130,475 (M); gifts received, $4,100; expenditures, $2,872,909; qualifying distributions, $2,622,299; giving activities include $1,931,990 for 58 grants (high: $300,000; low: $450).

Purpose and activities: The foundation is dedicated to advancing social equity and justice. It believes that a vibrant democracy requires an organized and informed citizenry that has access to information and free expression. In pursuit of these principles, the foundation supports innovative and strategic efforts that work to advance equity, accountability, social justice, and participatory democracy in the U.S. and abroad. While its areas of focus evolve over time, it achieves its fundamental purpose by supporting efforts that affect public policy.

Fields of interest: Public affairs; Civil/human rights; Civil/human rights, advocacy; International affairs, national security; International affairs, foreign policy; International human rights; Public policy, research.

Type of support: General/operating support; Continuing support; Management development/capacity building; Program development; Conferences/seminars; Film/video/radio; Publication; Seed money; Research; Program evaluation; Matching/challenge support.

Limitations: Applications accepted. Giving on a national basis. No support for direct social services, government programs, or groups outside the U.S. No grants to individuals, or for annual campaigns, emergency funds, capital or endowment funds, scholarly research, deficit financing, scholarships, or fellowships; no loans.

Publications: Application guidelines; Financial statement; Grants list.

Application information: Applications guidelines and form available on foundation web site. Preliminary letters of inquiry are not considered; proposals received outside the biennial deadlines will not be considered. Application form required.
  Initial approach: Proposal (8 pages maximum), via online application process on foundation web site only
  Copies of proposal: 1
  Deadline(s): Feb. 1 and Sept. 1
  Board meeting date(s): June and Dec.
  Final notification: June and Dec.

Officers and Directors:* Nancy R. Bagley,* Pres.; Nicole Bagley,* V.P.; Mary E. King,* Secy.; Anna Lefer Kuhn, Exec. Dir.; The Rev. Joseph Eldrige; Michael Lux; Janet Shenk; Margery A. Tabankin.

Number of staff: 2 full-time professional.

EIN: 132751798

497
The Aspen Institute

1 Dupont Cir., N.W., Ste. 700
Washington, DC 20036-1133 (202) 736-5800
Contact: Winnifred Levy, Comms. Mgr.
FAX: (202) 467-0790;
E-mail: info@aspeninstitute.org; Additional address (Aspen office): 1000 N. Third St., Aspen, CO 81611-1330, tel.: (970) 925-7010, fax: (970) 925-4188; URL: http://www.aspeninstitute.org
Additional URL: http://www.nonprofitresearch.org
Facebook: http://www.facebook.com/AspenInstitute
YouTube: http://www.youtube.com/user/AspenInstitute

Established in 1950 in DC.

Donors: Daniel Abraham; Fred Abrams; Penny Abrams; Ruth C. Anderson; John Adams; Lizbeth Adams; Michael B. Adams; Mrs. Michael B. Adams; Scarlett N. Adams; Joe Agley.

Grantmaker type: Public charity.

Financial data (yr. ended 12/31/10): Revenue, $69,095,692; assets, $170,674,815 (M); gifts received, $49,399,174; expenditures, $66,067,040; giving activities include $2,100,816 for grants, $445,365 for 10 grants to organizations outside the U.S., and $420,355 for grants to individuals.

Purpose and activities: The institute increases the legitimacy and visibility of nonprofit scholarship; encourages new investments in sector research; supports the exploration of tough, neglected questions; and enlarges the number of creative scholars and practitioners pursuing nonprofit studies.

Fields of interest: Philanthropy/voluntarism; Education; Environment; Health care; Economic development; Business/industry; International studies; Government/public administration.

Type of support: Conferences/seminars; Fellowships; Research; Scholarships—to individuals.

Limitations: Giving on a national basis.

Publications: Application guidelines; Annual report; Newsletter.

Application information:
  Deadline(s): Feb. 12 for Bezos Scholar Program; none for Aspen Institute-Rodel Fellowships in Public Leadership; varies for all others
  Board meeting date(s): Dec.

Officers and Trustees:* Robert K. Steel,* Chair.; Henry E. Catto, Vice-Chair.; Walter Isaacson, Pres. and C.E.O.; Elliot Gerson, Exec. V.P., Policy and

Public Progs.; Amy L. Margerum, Exec. V.P., Opers., and Corp. Secy.; Peter A. Reiling, Exec. V.P., Leadership and Seminar Progs.; Susan Sherwin, Exec. V.P., Devel.; Kitty Boone, V.P.; Jamie Miller, V.P.; Jane Wales, V.P., Philanthropy and Society; Madeleine K. Albright; Paul F. Anderson; Mercedes Bass; Berl Bernhard; Melva Bucksbaum; and 74 additional trustees.
Number of staff: 182 full-time professional; 15 part-time professional.
EIN: 840399006

498
Atlas Service Corps

1133 19th St., N.W., 9th Fl.
Washington, DC 20036-3612 (202) 669-4497
Contact: Scott Beale, Exec. Dir.
E-mail: info@atlascorps.org; URL: http://www.atlascorps.org
Change.org URL: http://www.change.org/atlascorps
Facebook: http://www.facebook.com/atlascorps
LinkedIn: http://www.linkedin.com/groupInvitation?
gid=47982&sharedKey=752BAB125FEB
Ned.org URL: http://www.ned.com/home/

Established in 2006 in DC.
Grantmaker type: Public charity.
Financial data (yr. ended 12/31/10): Revenue, $817,409; assets, $369,590 (M); gifts received, $239,112; expenditures, $719,052.
Purpose and activities: The organization works to integrate a global citizen sector in order to create a global partnership for development through facilitating international fellowships for rising citizen sector leaders who contribute to service both in the U.S. and their home country.
Fields of interest: International exchange; International development; International affairs; Community/economic development; Leadership development.
Type of support: Program development; Fellowships; Grants to individuals.
Limitations: Applications accepted. Giving primarily in the U.S., Colombia, Ecuador, and India.
Publications: Application guidelines; Annual report; Newsletter.
Application information: Two or three reference letters and a resume must accompany applications. Application form required.
  Initial approach: Complete online eligibility survey to download application
  Deadline(s): Jan. 1 for Host Partnership Opportunity; Apr. 31 for Fellows Program
Officers and Directors:* Gared Price Jones,* Chair.; Courtney Kramer,* Secy.; Lincoln D. Willis,* Treas.; Scott Beale,* Exec. Dir.; Julia Cohen; Manmeet Mehta; Camila Payan; Pratichi Shah; Jamie Zembruski.
EIN: 760834735

499
Banyan Tree Foundation

1775 Pennsylvania Ave., Ste. 1200
Washington, DC 20006-4671
Contact: Carolyn Stremlau, Exec. Dir.

Established in 1986 in CA.
Donors: Peter Ackerman; Joanne Leedom Ackerman.

Grantmaker type: Independent foundation.
Financial data (yr. ended 12/31/10): Assets, $55,767 (M); gifts received, $5,080,000; expenditures, $5,071,562; qualifying distributions, $5,069,307; giving activities include $4,374,001 for 46 grants (high: $629,533; low: $12,000).
Purpose and activities: Giving primarily to international education in selected countries; support also for education programs in Washington, DC.
Fields of interest: Education; Economically disadvantaged; Children/youth; Children.
International interests: Africa; Southeast Asia.
Type of support: General/operating support; Continuing support; Program development; Matching/challenge support.
Limitations: Applications not accepted. Giving on an international basis to select countries in Africa and Southeast Asia and on a limited basis in Washington, DC. No support for organizations with religious affiliations and/or medical or environmental focus or for individual schools; no grants outside listed geographic focus. No grants to individuals.
Application information: Unsolicited requests for funds not accepted.
Officers: Joanne Leedom-Ackerman, Pres.; Peter Ackerman, Secy.-Treas.; Carolyn Stremlau, Exec. Dir.
Number of staff: 3 full-time professional.
EIN: 954088915
Recent grants for international programs:

499-1 A Self-Help Assistance Program, Peachtree City, GA, $33,649. To improve student performance in mathematics in primary and secondary schools. 2009.

499-2 ActionAid, London, England, $119,150. To improve education quality and conditions for expanding education access. 2009.

499-3 ActionAid Sierra Leone, Freetown, Sierra Leone, $135,400. To improve quality and consolidate government support for community schools, and to demonstrate a district-wide approach for wider replication. 2009.

499-4 Afar Pastoralist Development Association, Addis Ababa, Ethiopia, $68,500. To provide literacy and primary education to pastoralist adults and children in the Afar region. 2009.

499-5 Africa Educational Trust, London, England, $116,993. To provide access to relevant, appropriate non-formal education for pastoralist youth who have missed out on school. 2009.

499-6 Backward Society Education, Tulsipur, Nepal, $144,500. To eliminate child labor system in districts by forming Child Friendly Villages and ensuring that all children attend school. 2009.

499-7 Camfed International, Cambridge, England, $100,000. To ensure that girls complete secondary school and become productive members and leaders of their communities. 2009.

499-8 Centre for Rural Studies and Development, Anantapur, India, $71,550. To achieve universal enrollment, regular school attendance, and prescribed learning achievements in 76 villages in rural Anantapur district. 2009.

499-9 Childrens Book Project, Dar es Salaam, Tanzania, Zanzibar and Pemba, $83,200. To improve reading and writing skills in primary schools. 2009.

499-10 Defence for Children International - Sierra Leone, Freetown, Sierra Leone, $44,200. To create a violence-free school environment. 2009.

499-11 Dupoto-E-Maa, Kajiado, Kenya, $98,950. To improve access, retention, and performance of pastoralist children in remote areas of Kajiado District. 2009.

499-12 Education Action International, London, England, $123,677. To increase pupil retention through a family learning program in primary schools (via support to Sierra Leone program) and to strengthen EAI's capacity for program growth in education (via support to the HQ). 2009.

499-13 Education Action International, London, England, $119,800. To increase pupil retention through a family learning program in primary schools (via support to Sierra Leone program) and to strengthen EAI's capacity for program growth in education (via support to the HQ). 2009.

499-14 Emmanuel Development Association, Addis Ababa, Ethiopia, $60,000. To improve quality of learning in nonformal schools supported by EDA. 2009.

499-15 Family Literacy Project, Hillcrest, South Africa, $32,600. To improve both adult literacy and development of literacy skills of young children. 2009.

499-16 FARM-Africa, London, England, $85,409. To improve delivery, quality, and relevance of primary education in northern Tanzania. 2009.

499-17 Human Rights Watch, New York, NY, $62,500. To monitor and advocate for children's rights worldwide. 2009.

499-18 International Institute of Rural Reconstruction, Addis Ababa, Ethiopia, $185,100. To strengthen pastoralist capacity for quality basic education. 2009.

499-19 International Institute of Rural Reconstruction, Addis Ababa, Ethiopia, $143,000. To strengthen pastoralist capacity for quality basic education. 2009.

499-20 International Institute of Rural Reconstruction, Addis Ababa, Ethiopia, $14,800. To strengthen pastoralist capacity for quality basic education. 2009.

499-21 International Institute of Rural Reconstruction, Addis Ababa, Ethiopia, $11,700. To strengthen pastoralist capacity for quality basic education. 2009.

499-22 International Institute of Rural Reconstruction, Nairobi, Kenya, $146,600. To strengthen pastoralist capacity for quality basic education. 2009.

499-23 International Institute of Rural Reconstruction, Nairobi, Kenya, $97,200. To strengthen pastoralist capacity for quality basic education. 2009.

499-24 Janarth, Aurangabad, India, $151,750. To provide education for children whose parents migrate annually to cut sugar cane. 2009.

499-25 Kinnapa Development Programme, Mwanza, Tanzania, Zanzibar and Pemba, $89,800. To provide scholarships to children from pastoralist area to allow them to attend secondary schools with boarding facilities. 2009.

499-26 Movement for Alternatives and Youth Awareness, Bangalore, India, $142,000. To improve education quality by institutionalizing participation of communities in schools and improving teaching and learning in the classroom. 2009.

499-27 National Youth Awareness Forum, Freetown, Sierra Leone, $47,580. To provide children access to school and to sustain community nonformal primary schools. 2009.

499-28 Nepalese Youth Opportunity Foundation, Sausalito, CA, $102,950. To free young girls from indentured labor and to enroll and retain them in school. 2009.

499-29 Nepalese Youth Opportunity Foundation, Sausalito, CA, $79,420. To free young girls from indentured labor and to enroll and retain them in school. 2009.

499-30 Ntataise Trust, Viljoenskroon, South Africa, $73,900. To implement Enrichment Program developed for Free State pre-schools in other provinces of South Africa with members of Ntataise network. 2009.

499-31 Partners in Adult Education Coordinating Office, Freetown, Sierra Leone, $61,000. To strengthen and consolidate community primary schools (non-formal primary schools) in Porto Loko, Moyamba and Kenema Districts and continue lobbying campaign to achieve sustained government support. 2009.

499-32 PEN International, London, England, $58,000. For institutional support. 2009.

499-33 Rift Valley Children and Women Development, Addis Ababa, Ethiopia, $77,300. To provide access to basic education to marginalized children in Arsi Negelle area of Oromia region. 2009.

499-34 Tostan, Washington, DC, $75,450. To foster literacy learning and community development in Senegal's most disadvantaged communities. 2009.

500

Diane & Norman Bernstein Foundation, Inc.

1156 15th St. N.W., Ste. 601
Washington, DC 20005-4802 (202) 223-2002
E-mail: annalee@bernsteinfoundation.org

Established in 1965 in DC.
Donors: Diane Bernstein; Norman Bernstein.
Grantmaker type: Independent foundation.
Financial data (yr. ended 12/31/10): Assets, $14,297,473 (M); gifts received, $1,000,000; expenditures, $1,025,642; qualifying distributions, $533,750; giving activities include $533,750 for grants.
Purpose and activities: Primary areas of interest include the arts, health, social services, Jewish welfare, and Israel. Support for those institutions and organizations, identified by the foundation's donors and their family members, which perpetuate and nurture the educational, religious, humanitarian, health, cultural and social aspects of society, including support for the Jewish community.
Fields of interest: Performing arts; Performing arts, music; Arts; Elementary/secondary education; Health care; Health organizations, association; AIDS; AIDS research; Human services; Child development, services; Jewish federated giving programs; Biology/life sciences; Religion; Youth; Women; Economically disadvantaged; Children/youth; Children.
International interests: Israel.
Type of support: General/operating support; Continuing support; Annual campaigns; Capital campaigns; Program development.
Limitations: Applications not accepted. Giving primarily in Washington, DC; support for the Jewish community on a local, national, and international basis. No grants to individuals.
Publications: Annual report.

Application information: Contributes only to pre-selected organizations.
   Board meeting date(s): Oct. and Aug.
Officers and Directors:* Norman Bernstein,* Chair.; Diane Bernstein,* Pres.; Elizabeth B. Norton,* Secy.; Joshua Benjamin Bernstein,* Treas.; Celia Ellen Bernstein; Lisa Bernstein; Susan Amy Bernstein; Marianne Bernstein Kalb; Robert Kalb; Robert Norton; Nancy Bernstein Schoen; Robert Schoen.
Number of staff: 1 full-time professional.
EIN: 526047356

501

Better World Fund

1800 Massachusetts Ave., N.W.
Washington, DC 20036-1806 (202) 462-4900
Contact: Timothy E. Wirth, Pres.
FAX: (202) 462-2686; *URL:* http://www.betterworldfund.org
Ted Turner's Giving Pledge: http://givingpledge.org/#enter

Established in 1998 in DC.
Grantmaker type: Public charity.
Financial data (yr. ended 12/31/10): Revenue, $10,450,964; assets, $22,912,269 (M); gifts received, $10,435,520; expenditures, $12,493,706; giving activities include $2,413,478 for grants, and $58,000 for 4 grants to organizations outside the U.S.
Purpose and activities: The fund supports select programs that increase awareness of and appreciation for the United Nation's contributions to the world and highlight its vital role as the vehicle for global cooperation; the fund also promotes outreach, education, and grassroots activities to engage youth, academia, non-governmental organizations, the business community, and policy makers in the work of the United Nations.
Fields of interest: International peace/security; International affairs, U.N.; International affairs.
Limitations: Giving on a national and international basis.
Officers and Directors:* R.E. "Ted" Turner III,* Chair.; Timothy E. Wirth,* Pres.; Kathryn A. Bushkin,* Exec. V.P.; Rutherford Seydel,* Secy.; David Carter,* C.F.O. and Treas.; Deborah Derrick, Exec. Dir.; Kofi Annan; H.M. Queen Raina Al-Abdullah; Gro Harlem Brundtland; Fernando Henrique Cardoso; Graca Machel; Yuan Ming; N.R. Narayana Murthy; Hisashi Owada; Emma Rothschild; Nafis Sadik; Andrew J. Young; Muhammad Yunus.
EIN: 582366765

502

The Butler Family Fund

1634 I St. NW, Ste. 1000
Washington, DC 20006-4015 (202) 463-8288
Contact: Martha A. Toll, Exec. Dir.; Anne H. Morin, Prog. Assoc.
FAX: (202) 783-8499;
E-mail: info@butlerfamilyfund.org; *URL:* http://www.butlerfamilyfund.org

Established in 1992 in DC.
Donor: J.E. and Z.B. Butler Foundation.
Grantmaker type: Independent foundation.
Financial data (yr. ended 12/31/10): Assets, $9,753,604 (M); gifts received, $704,480; expenditures, $914,093; qualifying distributions, $645,000; giving activities include $645,000 for grants.
Purpose and activities: Support for homeless families and criminal justice reform (death penalty and juvenile justice).
Fields of interest: Environment, climate change/global warming; Crime/law enforcement, reform; Housing/shelter; Civil liberties, death penalty issues; Homeless.
International interests: United Kingdom.
Type of support: General/operating support; Program development; Seed money.
Limitations: Applications not accepted. Giving primarily in Los Angeles, San Diego and the San Francisco Bay Area, CA, Washington, DC, Chicago, IL, NY, Philadelphia, PA, WI, and London, England. No grants to individuals.
Publications: Grants list; Multi-year report; Program policy statement.
Application information: Unsolicited proposals or letters of inquiry are not accepted. No grants for more than 3 consecutive years.
   Board meeting date(s): Biannually
Officers and Directors:* Eve B. Wildrick,* Pres.; Jody Snider,* V.P. and Treas.; Dina Hirsch,* Secy.; Martha A. Toll, Exec. Dir.; Phineas Hirsch; Steven R. Hirsch; Jasmine Horan; Lucia Horan; Peggy A. Horan.
Number of staff: 1 part-time professional; 1 part-time support.
EIN: 521786778

503

The Case Foundation

(formerly The Stephen Case Foundation)
1717 Rhode Island Ave. N.W., 7th Fl.
Washington, DC 20036-3023 (202) 467-5788
Contact: Brian Sasscer, Sr. V.P., Strategic Opers.
FAX: (202) 775-8513;
E-mail: contactus@casefoundation.org; *URL:* http://www.casefoundation.org
Case Foundation Blog: http://www.casefoundation.org/blog
Case Foundation Video Library: http://www.casefoundation.org/videos
Case Soup: http://www.casefoundation.org/videos/case-soup
Facebook: http://www.facebook.com/casefoundation
Jean and Steve Case's Giving Pledge: http://givingpledge.org/#enter
LinkedIn: http://www.linkedin.com/company/the-case-foundation
RSS Feed: http://feed.casefoundation.org/casefoundation
Twitter: http://www.twitter.com/CaseFoundation
YouTube: http://www.youtube.com/casefoundation

Established in 1997 in VA.
Donors: Stephen M. Case; Jean N. Case.
Grantmaker type: Independent foundation.
Financial data (yr. ended 12/31/10): Assets, $2,911,007 (M); gifts received, $15,000; expenditures, $3,858,032; qualifying distributions, $3,819,058; giving activities include $1,224,912 for 39+ grants (high: $200,000), and $13,002 for in-kind gifts.
Purpose and activities: Giving to achieve sustainable solutions to complex social problems by investing in collaboration, leadership, and entrepreneurship. Supports individuals and organizations that have the strategy, leadership,

and commitment to make positive, widespread social change. The foundation seeks to meet the needs of families and children in poverty; create thriving and sustainable economic development for communities; bridge cultural and religious divides; expand civic engagement and volunteerism; and accelerate innovative approaches to health care.

Fields of interest: Education; Health care; Youth development, services; Community/economic development; Engineering/technology.

International interests: Global programs.

Type of support: Program-related investments/loans.

Limitations: Giving in the U.S. and abroad. No grants to individuals.

Application information: Contributes only to pre-selected organizations except for the Make it Your Own grants program. Please see foundation web site for additional information.

Officers and Directors: Stephen M. Case,* Chair.; Jean N. Case,* C.E.O.; Erich Brokas, Sr. V.P., Innovation and Investment; Brad Burns, Sr. V.P., Comms.; Brian Sasscer, Sr., V.P., Strategic Operations; Michael Smith, Sr.V.P., Social Innovation; Gail Franck, V.P., Finance; Kari Dunn Saratovsky, V.P., Social Innovation.

Number of staff: 2 full-time professional; 1 part-time professional; 3 full-time support; 1 part-time support.

EIN: 541848791

Recent grants for international programs:

503-1 Aspen Institute, Washington, DC, $25,000. For international development. 2009.

503-2 Change.org, San Francisco, CA, $15,000. For youth development. 2009.

503-3 Education Development Center, Newton, MA, $20,000. For international development. 2009.

503-4 Malaria No More, New York, NY, $50,000. For international development. 2009.

503-5 Millennium Promise Alliance, New York, NY, $300,000. For international development. 2009.

503-6 One Foundation, London, England, $40,000. For general support. 2009.

503-7 PlayPumps International, Washington, DC, $373,243. To bring play opportunities and improved access to safe water to communities and schools in Africa. 2009.

503-8 United Nations Foundation, Washington, DC, $50,000. For international development. 2009.

503-9 Water for People, Denver, CO, $200,000. For general support. 2009.

503-10 World Affairs Council of Northern California, San Francisco, CA, $25,000. For general support. 2009.

504

Center for Global Development

1800 Massachusetts Ave., N.W., 3rd Fl.
Washington, DC 20036-1806 (202) 416-4000
FAX: (202) 416-4050; URL: http://www.cgdev.org/
Facebook: http://www.facebook.com/CGDev
Global Prosperity Wonkcast: http://blogs.cgdev.org/global_prosperity_wonkcast/
RSS Feed: http://www.cgdev.org/section/about_enews/sitefeeds/
Twitter: http://twitter.com/cgdev
YouTube: http://www.youtube.com/globaldevelopment

Established in 2001 in DC.
Grantmaker type: Public charity.
Financial data (yr. ended 12/31/10): Revenue, $8,256,365; assets, $32,002,508 (M); gifts

received, $6,822,069; expenditures, $10,482,039; giving activities include $69,799 for grants, and $137,715 for grants to organizations outside the U.S.

Purpose and activities: The organization is dedicated to reducing global property and inequality, and to making globalization work for the poor.

Fields of interest: International economic development; International peace/security; Community/economic development; Human services; International affairs; Economically disadvantaged.

Limitations: Giving limited to Washington, DC.
Publications: Annual report.

Officers and Directors: Edward Scott,* Chair.; Nancy Birdsall,* Pres.; Timothy D. Adams; Bernard Aronson; C. Fred Bergsten; Mark Malloch Brown; Jessica P. Einhorn; David Gergen; Thomas R. Gibian; C. Boyden Gray; Bruns Grayson; James Harmon; Jose Angel Gurria Trevino; Enrique V. Iglesias; Kassahun Kebede; and 12 additional directors.
EIN: 522351337

505

Center for Interfaith Action on Global Poverty

c/o Washington Natl. Cathedral
Massachusetts and Wisconsin Aves.
Washington, DC 20016 (202) 537-6561

Grantmaker type: Public charity.
Financial data (yr. ended 12/31/10): Revenue, $1,297,240; assets, $658,506 (M); gifts received, $1,285,286; expenditures, $1,985,182; giving activities include $285,365 for grants, and $151,776 for grants to organizations outside the U.S.

Purpose and activities: The organization works to improve the capacity and effectiveness of the faith community in its collective effort to reduce global poverty and disease.

Fields of interest: Health organizations; AIDS; Human services; International development; International economic development; International affairs; Religion; Economically disadvantaged.

Type of support: Grants to individuals.
Publications: Application guidelines.
Application information:
    Deadline(s): Oct. 15 for SEVEN-CIFA Essay Competition

Officers and Directors: Timothy Shriver,* Pres.; Edward Scott,* C.E.O.; Jean Duff,* Exec. Dir.; Nancy Birdsall; Dale Hanson Bourke; Rich Cizik; Rajmund Dabrowski; David Dahlin; John J. Degioia; Mark Dybul; Dr. Hany el Banna; William H. Frist; Ken Hackett; Rev. Samuel T. Lloyd; Ruth W. Messinger; and 5 additional directors.
EIN: 943446667

506

Center for International Private Enterprise, Inc.

1155 15th St. N.W., Ste. 700
Washington, DC 20005-2706 (202) 721-9200
FAX: (202) 721-9250; E-mail: cipe@cipe.org;
URL: http://www.cipe.org
Facebook: http://www.facebook.com/pages/Center-for-International-Private-Enterprise/100141625685
Twitter: http://twitter.com/CIPEglobal

Established in 1983.
Grantmaker type: Public charity.
Financial data (yr. ended 09/30/10): Revenue, $20,116,005; assets, $1,647,697 (M); gifts received, $20,107,490; expenditures, $20,118,622; giving activities include $3,938,485 for grants to organizations outside the U.S.

Purpose and activities: The center provides management assistance, practical experience, and financial support to local organizations around the world to strengthen their capacity to implement democratic and economic reforms.

Fields of interest: International economic development; International democracy & civil society development; International affairs.

Limitations: Applications accepted. Giving on an international basis. No support for commercial operations, trade or investment promotions, revolving credit funds, the establishment of new organizations, or partisan political activity.

Publications: Application guidelines; Annual report.
Application information: Application form required.
    Initial approach: Proposal
    Copies of proposal: 3
    Final notification: Up to six months after receipt of proposal

Officers and Directors: Gregori Lebedev,* Chair.; Thomas J. Donohue,* Pres.; Myron A. Brilliant,* V.P.; John D. Sullivan,* Secy.-Treas. and Exec. Dir.; Grant D. Aldonas; Stanton D. Anderson; Amb. Barbara Barrett; Karan Bhatia; Harry Clark; Peter M. Cleveland; Lynda Y. de la Vina, Ph.D.; Joseph Ha, Ph.D.; Michael J. Hershman; Amb. Richard N. Holwill; Karen Kerrigan; and 8 additional directors.
EIN: 521398742

507

Center for the Study of Islam and Democracy, Inc.

1625 Massachusetts Ave., N.W., Ste. 601
Washington, DC 20036-2244 (202) 265-1200
FAX: (202) 265-1222;
E-mail: feedback@islam-democracy.org;
URL: http://www.csidonline.org

Established in 1999 in DC.
Grantmaker type: Public charity.
Financial data (yr. ended 12/31/09): Revenue, $346,407; assets, $23,063 (M); gifts received, $300,677; expenditures, $407,607.

Purpose and activities: The center is dedicated to studying Islamic and democratic political thought and merging them into a modern Islamic democratic discourse.

Fields of interest: International democracy & civil society development; Islam.

Limitations: Giving on a national and international basis.

Publications: Newsletter; Occasional report.
Officers and Directors: Asma Afsaruddin,* Chair.; Anthony Sullivan,* Vice-Chair.; Radwan Masmoudi,* Pres.; Akbar S. Ahmed; Omar Kader; Ali Nawaz Memon; Abdulaziz Sachedina; Robert Schadler; S. Abdallah Schleiffer; Tamara Sonn.
EIN: 522167254

508
Centre for Development and Population Activities
(also known as CEDPA)
1133 21st St., N.W., Ste. 800
Washington, DC 20036-3371 (202) 667-1142
Contact: Ashley Bennett, Assoc., Comms. and Devel.
FAX: (202) 332-4496; *E-mail:* abennett@cedpa.org;
URL: http://www.cedpa.org
MySpace: http://www.myspace.com/cedpa

Established in 1975.
Grantmaker type: Public charity.
Financial data (yr. ended 12/31/10): Revenue, $9,780,967; assets, $4,695,731 (M); gifts received, $9,482,831; expenditures, $10,998,559; giving activities include $100,000 for grants, and $992,468 for grants to organizations outside the U.S.
Purpose and activities: The centre works to equip and mobilize women to achieve equality by seeking to increase educational opportunities for girls and youth, ensuring access to lifesaving reproductive health and HIV/AIDS information and services, and strengthening governance and women's leadership in developing countries.
Fields of interest: Education; Reproductive health; AIDS; Civil/human rights, women; Civil liberties, reproductive rights; Girls; Women.
International interests: Nigeria; South Africa; Nepal; India; Developing countries.
Type of support: Management development/capacity building; Annual campaigns; Program development; Matching/challenge support.
Limitations: Applications not accepted. Giving on an international basis.
Publications: Annual report; Newsletter.
Application information: Unsolicited requests for funds not encouraged or acknowledged.
Board meeting date(s): Nov. 9-10 and May 4-5
Officers and Board Members:* Ann Van Dusen,* Chair.; Carol A. Peasley, Pres. and C.E.O.; Doris Mason Martin,* Secy.; Cheri Alexander; Hon. Phoebe M. Asiyo; Susan Maria Benton; Barie Carmichael; Kaval Gulhati; and 8 additional board members.
EIN: 521021663

509
The CityBridge Foundation, Inc.
(formerly The Advisory Board Foundation, Inc.)
600 New Hampshire Ave. N.W., Ste. 800
Washington, DC 20037-2403 (202) 266-7990
E-mail: info@citybridgefoundation.org; *URL:* http://www.citybridgefoundation.org

Established in 1993 in DC.
Donors: David G. Bradley; Katherine B. Bradley; Atlantic Media; Capital Source Finance LLC; Acumen Solutions; Glover Park Group LLC.
Grantmaker type: Independent foundation.
Financial data (yr. ended 12/31/10): Assets, $6,609,517 (M); gifts received, $240,000; expenditures, $4,459,263; qualifying distributions, $3,350,484; giving activities include $3,196,099 for 66 grants (high: $333,000; low: $50), and $3,157,616 for 3 foundation-administered programs.
Purpose and activities: Giving primarily for youth, voluntarism promotion, and international development and relief.

Fields of interest: Education; Health care; Children/youth, services; Employment; International development; International relief; Public health; Voluntarism promotion; Youth development; Adults; Asians/Pacific Islanders; Children; Children/youth; Crime/abuse victims; Economically disadvantaged; Infants/toddlers; Young adults; Youth.
International interests: Philippines; South Africa.
Type of support: Program development; Research; Program evaluation.
Limitations: Applications not accepted. Giving in the U.S. (primarily in the greater metropolitan Washington, DC, area) and internationally, with emphasis on South Africa and the Philippines. No grants to individuals.
Application information: Contributes only to pre-selected organizations.
Officers and Directors:* Katherine Brittain Bradley,* Pres.; David G. Bradley,* V.P. and Secy.-Treas.; Mieka Wick, Exec. Dir.; Spencer Bradley.
Number of staff: 6 full-time professional.
EIN: 521870074

510
George E. Coleman, Jr. Foundation
c/o Webster
1747 Pennsylvania Ave.
Washington, DC 20006-4604
Application address: c/o Daniel Oliver, 3105 Woodley Rd. N.W., Washington, DC 20008, tel.: (202) 986-2888

Established in DC.
Grantmaker type: Independent foundation.
Financial data (yr. ended 12/31/10): Assets, $7,021,106 (M); expenditures, $365,024; qualifying distributions, $304,500; giving activities include $304,500 for grants.
Fields of interest: Arts; Higher education; International affairs; Public policy, research.
Limitations: Applications accepted. Giving primarily in Washington, DC. No grants to individuals.
Application information:
Initial approach: Letter
Deadline(s): None
Trustees: Andrew Oliver, Jr.; Daniel Oliver; Louise Oliver.
EIN: 527044220

511
Connect U.S. Fund
1730 Pennsylvania Ave., N.W., Fl. 7
Washington, DC 20006-4706
Contact: Karl Horberg, Program Associate
E-mail: info@connectusfund.org; *URL:* http://www.connectusfund.org

Established in 2004; component fund of the Tides Center.
Grantmaker type: Public charity.
Purpose and activities: The fund seeks to advance a vision for responsible U.S. global engagement in an increasingly interdependent world by uniting individuals, initiatives, and organizations that share the goal of promoting responsible U.S. engagement and using a collaboration as a strategy to accomplish policy objectives; global issues include human rights, economic development, global health, nuclear weapons proliferation,

environmental protection, and democracy and good governance.
Fields of interest: International peace/security; International affairs, arms control; International economics/trade policy; Environment, climate change/global warming; Environment, energy; International affairs, public policy; International human rights; International exchange; International affairs.
Publications: Application guidelines; Grants list.
Application information: The fund is no longer accepting letters of inquiry for their 2009-2010 Global Security and Cooperation Initiative. See website for further information.
Initial approach: Contact Program Associate
Deadline(s): Rolling
Final notification: Rolling
Officers: Nancy Soderberg, Pres.; Alexandra Toma, Exec. Dir.

512
Consortium for Elections and Political Process Strengthening
1225 Eye St. N.W., Ste. 700
Washington, DC 20005-5962
Wiki: http://en.wikipedia.org/wiki/Consortium_for_Elections_and_Political_Process_Strengthening

Grantmaker type: Public charity.
Financial data (yr. ended 09/30/10): Revenue, $124,498,513; assets, $759,628 (M); gifts received, $124,498,513; expenditures, $124,498,513; giving activities include $124,385,296 for grants.
Purpose and activities: The consortium encourages sustainable democratic political development around the world.
Fields of interest: International democracy & civil society development; Public affairs.
Limitations: Applications not accepted.
Application information: Contributes only to pre-selected organizations.
Directors: Lauren M. Cramer; Sandra Govatski; William R. Sweeney, Jr.; Kenneth D. Wollack.
EIN: 521943638

513
Council of American Overseas Research Centers
(formerly Council of American Research Centers)
P.O. Box 37012
NHB Rm. CE-123, MRC 178
Washington, DC 20013-7012 (202) 633-1599
Contact: Lisa Rogers, Grants Admin.
FAX: (202) 786-2430;
E-mail: fellowships@caorc.org; Additional e-mail: caorc@caorc.org; *URL:* http://www.caorc.org

Founded in 1981; status changed to a public charity.
Grantmaker type: Public charity.
Financial data (yr. ended 09/30/10): Revenue, $11,740,720; assets, $3,054,071 (M); gifts received, $11,715,315; expenditures, $11,686,474; giving activities include $7,838,802 for grants, $1,202,475 for 9 grants to organizations outside the U.S., and $6,000 for grant to an individual outside the U.S.
Purpose and activities: The council supports a world-wide network of institutes of advanced study which foster international scholarly exchange

primarily through fellowship programs allowing American scholars to pursue independent research important to the increase of knowledge and the understanding of foreign cultures.

Fields of interest: Humanities; International affairs.

Type of support: Scholarships—to individuals; Fellowships; Matching/challenge support.

Limitations: Applications accepted. Giving on a national and international basis.

Publications: Application guidelines; Newsletter.

Application information: Contact individual participating institutes for application guidelines and deadlines for Andrew W. Mellon East-Central European Research Fellowships and Getty Research Exchange Fellowship Program for the Mediterranean Basin and Middle East. Application form required.

   Initial approach: Download application form
   Deadline(s): Jan. 12 for Multi-County Research Fellowship Program; Jan. 25 for Critical Language Scholarships for Intensive Summer Institutes

Officers and Board Members: Dr. Jeanne Marecek, Chair.; Prof. John Spencer,* Vice-Chair.; Dr. Erica Ehrenberg,* Secy.; Dr. Leonardo Villalon,* Treas.; Mary Ellen Lane, Ph.D., Exec. Dir.; Thomas Barfield; Dr. Mbye Cham; Dr. Kevin Clinton; Dr. Lois Pattison de Menil; Shelley Feldman; Dr. William Fitzhugh; Nan Frederick; McGuire Gibson; Charles Hallisey; Dr. Benson Harer; Dr. Timothy Harrison; Dr. Ellen Herscher; Philip Lutgendorf; Dr. Philip Mattar; Kevin Reinhart; Dr. Irene Bald Romano; Brian Rose; Catherine deG. Vanderpool, Ph.D.; I. William Zartman.

EIN: 521395971

514
Counterterrorism & Security Education & Research Foundation

4200 Wisconsin Ave., N.W., Ste. 128
Washington, DC   20016-2143

Grantmaker type: Public charity.

Financial data (yr. ended 12/31/09): Revenue, $2,735,447; assets, $280,200 (M); gifts received, $2,735,350; expenditures, $3,003,771; giving activities include $2,997,699 for grants.

Purpose and activities: The foundation seeks to provide grants for research on issues of terrorism and counterterrorism.

Fields of interest: International terrorism; International affairs.

Type of support: Research.

Officers: Steven Fustero, Pres.; Phil Friedman, Secy.; Richard Horowitz, Treas.

EIN: 522099490

515
Una Chapman Cox Foundation

1200 18th St., N.W., Ste. 902
Washington, DC   20036-2558   (202) 331-3918
FAX: (202) 833-4555;
E-mail: programs@uccoxfoundation.org;
URL: http://www.uccoxfoundation.org

Established in 1980 in TX; supporting organization of the United States Foreign Service.

Donor: Una Chapman Cox‡.

Grantmaker type: Public charity.

Financial data (yr. ended 11/30/10): Revenue, $1,691,967; assets, $36,567,451 (M); expenditures, $1,159,408; program services

expenses, $572,464; giving activities include $394,155 for 5 grants (high: $155,000; low: $17,500), and $10,200 for 1 grant to an individual.

Fields of interest: International affairs, foreign policy.

Limitations: Applications not accepted. Giving limited to Washington, DC and Arlington, VA.

Application information: Contributes only to pre-selected organizations.

Officers and Trustees: Margo Branscomb,* Chair.; Dian Owen VandeMark, Pres.; Harvie Branscomb, Jr.,* Secy.; Shannon M. Wilde,* Treas.; Clyde Taylor, Exec. Dir.; Elizabeth Jones.

Number of staff: 1 part-time professional; 1 part-time support.

EIN: 311680916

516
Arthur S. DeMoss Foundation

1747 Pennsylvania Ave. N.W., Ste. 1000
Washington, DC   20006-3944
Contact: Nancy S. DeMoss, Chair.

Incorporated in PA in 1955 as the National Liberty Foundation of Valley Forge, Inc.

Donor: Arthur S. DeMoss‡.

Grantmaker type: Independent foundation.

Financial data (yr. ended 12/31/09): Assets, $238,121,792 (M); expenditures, $42,359,394; qualifying distributions, $41,122,078; giving activities include $35,271,848 for 50 grants (high: $12,424,363; low: $4,000), and $751,237 for 2 foundation-administered programs.

Purpose and activities: Support primarily for operating programs initiated and managed by the foundation itself that are evangelistic and disciplined in nature in the U.S. and other countries, primarily the Third World. To a limited extent, a few grants are made to organizations both in the U.S. and overseas that have these same goals.

Fields of interest: Christian agencies & churches.

International interests: Kenya; Tanzania, Zanzibar and Pemba; Uganda.

Type of support: Program development.

Limitations: Applications not accepted. Giving on an international basis. No support for local churches, denominational agencies and/or schools or colleges. No grants to individuals, or for scholarships or endowments; no loans.

Publications: Informational brochure.

Application information: Unsolicited requests for funds not accepted.

   Board meeting date(s): Quarterly

Officers and Directors: Nancy S. DeMoss,* Chair., C.E.O., and Treas.; Robert G. DeMoss,* Pres.; Charlotte DeMoss,* Secy.; Larry R. Nelson, C.F.O.; Elizabeth J. DeMoss.

Number of staff: 9 full-time professional; 8 full-time support.

EIN: 236404136

Recent grants for international programs:

516-1 Agape France, Ozoir La Ferriere, France, $68,000. 2009.

516-2 Bikur Cholim Hospital, Jerusalem, Israel, $63,000. 2009.

516-3 Campus Crusade for Christ International, Orlando, FL, $26,000. For work in Aisa. 2009.

516-4 Campus Crusade for Christ International, Orlando, FL, $10,000. For work in Korea. 2009.

516-5 Evangelism Explosion International, Fort Lauderdale, FL, $3,045,000. 2009.

516-6 Greater Europe Mission, Monument, CO, $89,000. 2009.

516-7 Mission to the World, Lawrenceville, GA, $71,375. 2009.

516-8 Samaritans Purse, Boone, NC, $2,390,000. 2009.

516-9 SIM International, Fort Mill, SC, $100,000. For El Afarero Student Center in Sucre, Bolivia. 2009.

516-10 SIM International, Fort Mill, SC, $11,500. 2009.

517
Development Gateway Foundation, Inc.

1889 F St., N.W., 2nd Fl.
Washington, DC   20006-4401   (202) 572-9200
FAX: (202) 572-9290;
E-mail: info@dgfoundation.org; URL: http://www.dgfoundation.org/

Grantmaker type: Public charity.

Financial data (yr. ended 06/30/10): Revenue, $6,887,406; assets, $5,144,353 (M); gifts received, $3,790,783; expenditures, $6,596,481.

Purpose and activities: The organization improves people's lives in developing countries by building partnerships and information systems that provide access to knowledge for development.

Fields of interest: Telecommunications; International development; Economically disadvantaged.

International interests: Developing countries.

Limitations: Applications accepted. Giving on an international basis, primarily in developing countries.

Publications: Annual report; Newsletter.

Application information: Entries for the Photo Contest must be accompanied by a written statement explaining how that image is representative of development. Application form required.

   Deadline(s): Sept. 19 for Photo Contest
   Final notification: Oct. 31 for Photo Contest

Officers and Directors: Mary O'Kane,* Chair.; Mark Fleeton, C.E.O.; Gianluigi Benedetti; Julian Casasbuenas; Rudolf Haggenmueller, Ph.D.; Walter Hofer; Michael J. Hoffmann, Ph.D.; Olav Kjorven; Shri Dhanendra Kumar; Motoo Kusakabe, Ph.D.; Miguel Marques; John H. McArthur, Ph.D.; Romain Murenzi, Ph.D.; Margaret Nzuki; and 7 additional directors.

EIN: 522318905

518
William Orr Dingwall Foundation, Inc.

2201 N St. N.W., Ste. 117
Washington, DC   20037-1113
E-mail: apply@dingwallfoundation.org; URL: http://www.dingwallfoundation.org/

Established in 1994 in MO.

Donors: Marion Orr Dingwall Trust; Dingwall Family, LP.

Grantmaker type: Independent foundation.

Financial data (yr. ended 12/31/10): Assets, $6,211,003 (M); expenditures, $412,469; qualifying distributions, $381,230; giving activities include $381,230 for grants to individuals.

Purpose and activities: Scholarship awards to individuals of Asian ancestry to pursue undergraduate or graduate studies in any subject offered by well-established universities throughout the world and to individuals of any national origin to pursue graduate studies devoted to the neural bases of language.

Fields of interest: Language/linguistics; Higher education; Graduate/professional education.

International interests: South Korea; Asia.

Type of support: Scholarships—to individuals.

Limitations: Applications accepted. Giving primarily in VA.

Application information: See foundation web site for complete application information and materials. Application form required.

Deadline(s): Varies

Final notification: Varies

Officer and Directors: John D. Ward,* Pres.; Christopher Grant,* Secy.-Treas.; William Hodos, Ph.D.; Chin-Wu Kim, Ph.D.; Young-Key-Renaud Kim, Ph.D.

Number of staff: 1 full-time professional.

EIN: 521877552

519
El-Hibri Charitable Foundation

1420 16th St. N.W.
Ibrahim El-Hibri Bldg.
Washington, DC 20036-2202 (202) 387-9500
FAX: (202) 387-9050;
E-mail: info@elhibrifoundation.org; Application address: c/o Zen Hunter-Ishikawa, 12001 Glen Rd., Potomac, MD 20854, tel.: (301) 983-1133;
URL: http://elhibrifoundation.org
Grants List: http://www.elhibrifoundation.org/granthistory.html

Established in 2001 in DC.

Donors: Fuad El-Hibri; Ibrahim Y. El-Hibri‡.

Grantmaker type: Independent foundation.

Financial data (yr. ended 12/31/10): Assets, $43,262,737 (M); gifts received, $833,715; expenditures, $2,213,049; qualifying distributions, $2,221,895; giving activities include $1,420,833 for 5 grants (high: $1,183,333; low: $25,000), and $16,317 for foundation-administered programs.

Purpose and activities: The foundation seeks to build a better world by encouraging interfaith dialogue. The foundation seeks to: 1) Improve the human condition through application of the universally shared values of Islam: peace, charity and civic responsibility; 2) Foster interfaith dialogue; and; 3) Find common ground and solutions for global challenges affecting humankind.

Fields of interest: International human rights; International relief; Education; International democracy & civil society development; International peace/security; International conflict resolution; Islam; Religion, interfaith issues.

International interests: Lebanon; Middle East.

Type of support: Seed money; General/operating support; Management development/capacity building; Capital campaigns.

Limitations: Applications accepted. Giving primarily in the Washington, DC area, and Lebanon.

Publications: Application guidelines.

Application information: Full proposals are by invitation only, upon review of letter of intent. Application form not required.

Initial approach: Letter of intent (1-2 pages)

Deadline(s): Letters of intent are accepted from July 1 to Sept. 30

Officers and Directors: Fuad El-Hibri, Chair.; Robert L. Buchanan, Jr.,* Pres.; Marcia Thayer Nass, V.P., Strategic Planning, Secy. and Genl. Counsel; Greg Siegrist, V.P., Fin. and Admin. and Treas.; Zen Hunter-Ishikawa, V.P., Opers.; Karim

El-Hibri,* Sr. Prog. Assoc.; Lynn Kunkle; Abdul Aziz Said; Abdo Sabban; Allen Shofe.

EIN: 522306995

520
Endowment of the U.S. Institute of Peace

2301 Constitution Ave., N.W.
Washington, DC 20037-2900 (202) 457-1700
Contact: Richard H. Solomon, Pres.
FAX: (202) 429-6063;
E-mail: grant_program@usip.org; URL: http://www.usip.org
RSS Feed: http://www.usip.org/rss-feeds

Established in 1986 in DC.

Grantmaker type: Public charity.

Financial data (yr. ended 09/30/10): Revenue, $24,447,975; assets, $24,492,827 (M); gifts received, $23,841,834; expenditures, $30,284,229; giving activities include $1,909,174 for grants; $3,825,364 for 34 grants to organizations outside the U.S., and $864,100 for grants to individuals.

Purpose and activities: The institute aims to strengthen the nation's capacity to promote the peaceful resolution of international conflict. It meets this congressional mandate through an array of programs, including grants, fellowships, conferences, workshops, library services, publications, and other educational activities.

Fields of interest: International affairs, public education; International peace/security; International conflict resolution.

Type of support: Curriculum development; Fellowships; Scholarship funds; Research.

Limitations: Giving on a national and international basis. No support for for-profit organizations. No grants for indirect costs, institutional support, or development.

Publications: Application guidelines; Annual report, Newsletter; Occasional report.

Application information: See web site for application forms and additional guidelines. Application form required.

Initial approach: Letter, telephone, or e-mail

Copies of proposal: 10

Deadline(s): Apr. 1 for Priority Grants Program; Oct. 3 for Annual Grants Program; Sept. 8 for Jennings Randolph Senior Fellowship Program

Officers and Directors: J. Robinson West,* Chair.; George E. Moose,* Vice-Chair.; Richard H. Solomon,* Pres.; Patricia P. Thomson,* Exec. V.P.; Anne H. Cahn; Chester A. Crocker; Kerry Kennedy; Ikram U. Khan; Stephen D. Krasner; Jeremy A. Rabkin; Judy van Rest; Nancy Zirkin.

EIN: 521503251

521
Eritrean Development Foundation, Inc.

(formerly Eritrean Relief Committee, Inc.)
1012 14th St. N.W., Ste. 1030
Washington, DC 20005-3415 (202) 783-3273
FAX: (202) 783-3274; E-mail: edf@edfonline.org;
URL: http://www.edfonline.org

Established in 1999 in DC.

Grantmaker type: Public charity.

Financial data (yr. ended 12/31/09): Revenue, $13,828; assets, $289,163 (M); gifts received, $7,129; expenditures, $55,810.

Purpose and activities: The foundation works in partnership with grassroots nongovernmental organizations, community groups and other local institutions engaged in education, healthcare and agriculture development in Eritrea, Africa. It also provides financial support and material aid for emergency relief, community development and capacity building in the region.

Fields of interest: International affairs.

International interests: Africa; Eritrea.

Type of support: Continuing support; Emergency funds; Publication; In-kind gifts.

Limitations: Applications not accepted. Giving primarily in Eritrea, Africa.

Publications: Annual report; Financial statement; Grants list; Informational brochure.

Application information: Unsolicited requests for funds not accepted.

Board meeting date(s): Quarterly

Officers and Directors: Yacob Fisseha,* M.D., Chair.; Solomon Teklu,* Vice-Chair.; Martin Ganzglass,* Secy.; Mesfin Zaid,* Treas.; Prof. Astier M. Almedom; Yobi Amdemariam; Almaz A. Armstead; Dr. "Fee" Fickak Habtes; Gebre Hiwet-Tesfagiorgis; Jack Ladenson, Ph.D.; Kip Mackey.

Number of staff: 1 full-time professional; 1 part-time professional.

EIN: 132888880

522
The Eurasia Foundation

1350 Connecticut Ave., N.W., Ste. 1000
Washington, DC 20036-1730 (202) 234-7370
FAX: (202) 234-7377; E-mail: eurasia@eurasia.org;
URL: http://www.eurasia.org
Twitter: http://twitter.com/efnetwork

Established in 1993 in DC.

Grantmaker type: Public charity.

Financial data (yr. ended 09/30/10): Revenue, $11,929,234; assets, $20,170,907 (M); gifts received, $11,857,212; expenditures, $11,048,450; giving activities include $5,203,038 for grants to organizations outside the U.S.

Purpose and activities: The foundation supports economic reform and democratic institution building in the New Independent States of the former Soviet Union. It promotes innovation in programming, unique evaluation mechanisms, new collaborative efforts and imaginative co-funding ideas by supporting projects in the following areas: Private Enterprise Development: accelerated development and growth of private enterprise; Public Administration and Policy: more effective, responsive and accountable local government; and Civil Society: increased citizen participation in the political and economic decision-making process.

Fields of interest: Media/communications; Business school/education; International affairs, management/technical assistance; International affairs, government agencies; International economic development; Law/international law; Government/public administration.

International interests: Armenia; Azerbaijan; Belarus; Georgia (Republic of); Kazakhstan; Kyrgyzstan; Moldova; Russia; Soviet Union (Former); Tajikistan; Turkmenistan; Ukraine; Uzbekistan.

Type of support: Equipment; Program development; Conferences/seminars; Publication; Curriculum development; Consulting services; Matching/challenge support.

Limitations: Applications accepted. Giving limited to the New Independent States of the former Soviet Union. Generally no support for health care, humanitarian aid, scientific or technical research, or the environment (unless related to economic development and improving management of non-governmental organizations). No grants to individuals, or for scholarships supporting long-term study abroad.
Publications: Application guidelines; Annual report; Grants list; Informational brochure; Newsletter.
Application information: Application form not required.

> *Initial approach:* 2-3 page letter of inquiry for grants; Submit nomination form for Bill Maynes Fund for Future Leaders of Eurasia
> *Copies of proposal:* 1
> *Deadline(s):* Mar. 15 for Bill Maynes Fund for Future Leaders of Eurasia

Officers and Trustees:* Jan Kalicki,* Chair.; Daniel Witt,* Vice-Chair.; William Horton Beebe-Center, Pres.; Randy Bregman; Esther Dyson; Terrence J. English; William Frenzel; Andrew Guff; George Helland; George M. Ingram; Sandra Willett Jackson; Margery Kraus; Eugene Lawson; Thomas Pickering; Margaret Richardson; William B. Taylor, Jr.; Maurice Tempelsman.
Number of staff: 100 full-time professional.
EIN: 521780162

523
FINCA International, Inc.
1101 14th St., N.W., 11th Fl.
Washington, DC   20005-5637   (202) 682-1510
FAX: (202) 682-1535; E-mail: info@finca.org;
URL: http://www.finca.org
Facebook: http://www.facebook.com/
VillageBanking
MySpace: http://www.myspace.com/
villagebanking
Twitter: http://twitter.com/#!/finca
YouTube: http://www.youtube.com/user/
Villagebanking2009

Established in 1985.
Donors: Alpern Family Foundation; John T. Archer; Dennis M. Berryman; Brewester Foundation; Suzette J. Clayton; Ostara Foundation; Margaret Little; Million Dollar Round Table Foundation; The Osprey Foundation; Pam Phelan.
Grantmaker type: Public charity.
Financial data (yr. ended 12/31/10): Revenue, $36,842,120; assets, $130,949,321 (M); gifts received, $19,228,973; expenditures, $38,828,685.
Purpose and activities: The organization's mission is to provide financial services to the world's lowest-income entrepreneurs so they can create jobs, build assets, and improve their standard of living.
Fields of interest: International economic development; Financial services.
Type of support: Loans—to individuals.
Limitations: Giving on an international basis.
Publications: Annual report; Financial statement.
Officers and Directors:* Robert W. Hatch,* Chair.; Rupert Scofield,* Pres. and C.E.O.; Dr. John Hatch,* Secy.; Richard Williamson,* Treas.; Rupert Scofield, Exec. Dir.; H.M. Queen Raina Al-Abdullah; Carlos Camacho; John Elkins; JoAnn Field; Michael Green; Shawn Hassel; Soledad DeLeon Hurst; Harold D.

Jastram, Esq.; Paul LeFort; Agrina Mussa; James Semakkadde; Rita Spillman; David E. Weisman.
EIN: 133240109

524
Foundation for Middle East Peace
1761 N St. N.W.
Washington, DC   20036-2801   (202) 835-3650
Contact: Grant Applications
FAX: (202) 835-3651; E-mail: info@fmep.org;
URL: http://www.fmep.org

Incorporated in 1979 in DC.
Donors: Merle Thorpe, Jr.†; Stephen Hartwell; Nelson B. Delavan Foundation; W.H. Rosenwald Family Fund.
Grantmaker type: Independent foundation.
Financial data (yr. ended 09/30/10): Assets, $9,942,256 (M); gifts received, $267,372; expenditures, $909,414; qualifying distributions, $895,407; giving activities include $315,030 for 26 grants (high: $40,000; low: $530).
Purpose and activities: To promote an understanding of the Israeli-Palestinian conflict, including the identification of U.S. interests, and to contribute to a just and peaceful resolution of the conflict with security for both peoples. Support directed to elements within the Arab and Jewish communities working for a peaceful resolution of the conflict.
Fields of interest: International peace/security.
International interests: Israel; Middle East.
Type of support: General/operating support; Conferences/seminars; Publication; Research; Matching/challenge support.
Limitations: Giving primarily in Washington, DC, Israel, and Palestine.
Publications: Application guidelines; Informational brochure; Newsletter; Program policy statement.
Application information: Application form not required.

> *Initial approach:* Cover letter and proposal
> *Deadline(s):* None
> *Board meeting date(s):* As required
> *Final notification:* 30 days

Officers and Trustees:* Calvin Hayes Cobb, Jr.,* Esq., Chair.; Amb. Philip C. Wilcox, Jr.,* Pres.; Richard S.T. Marsh, Esq., Secy.; Stephen Hartwell, Treas.; A. Lucius Battle; Landrum R. Bolling; James J. Cromwell, Esq.; Peter Gubser; Hon. Richard Murphy; Jean Newsom; Gail Pressberg; Dr. William B. Quandt; Nicholas A. Veliotes.
Number of staff: 2 full-time professional; 1 full-time support.
EIN: 526055574

525
Franciscan Foundation for the Holy Land
P.O. Box 29086
Washington, DC   20017-9086
Contact: Rev. Peter F. Vasko O.F.M., Pres.
E-mail: info@ffhl.org; Toll-free tel.: (866) 905-3787;
Toll-free fax: (866) 905-3788; URL: http://
www.ffhl.org

Established in 1994 in DC.
Grantmaker type: Public charity.
Financial data (yr. ended 12/31/10): Revenue, $1,900,925; assets, $3,293,263 (M); gifts received, $1,751,966; expenditures, $1,990,578; giving activities include $10,000 for grants, and

$1,390,850 for grants to organizations outside the U.S.
Purpose and activities: The foundation was created to inform and educate the general public about the plight of Christians in the Middle East. By increasing awareness of the complex human rights issues involving Christians in this part of the world, the foundation seeks to establish equality of opportunity for this unrepresented minority group and safeguard their right to remain in their homeland.
Fields of interest: Christian agencies & churches.
International interests: East Jerusalem; Israel; Middle East; West Bank/Gaza (Palestinian Territories).
Type of support: Emergency funds; Scholarships—to individuals.
Limitations: Applications not accepted. Giving on an international basis, primarily in Israel and the Middle East.
Publications: Newsletter.
Application information: Unsolicited requests for funds not accepted.

> *Board meeting date(s):* Spring and fall

Officers and Trustees:* Rev. Pierbattista Pizzaballa,* O.F.M., Chair.; Rev. Peter F. Vasko,* O.F.M., Pres.; Denise M. Scalzo,* V.P.; Frank L. Nageotte,* Secy.; Br. Callistus Welch,* O.F.M., Treas.; Raymond Arroyo; Jorge J. Bosch; Karen M. Carroll; Christopher T. Maloney, M.D.; and 10 additional trustees.
Number of staff: 2 part-time professional.
EIN: 330628775

526
The Free Africa Foundation, Inc.
910 17th St., N.W., Ste. 419
Washington, DC   20006-2605   (202) 296-7081
Contact: George B.N. Ayittey Ph.D., Pres.
FAX: (202) 296-5909; E-mail: info@freeafrica.org;
Additional e-mail address: africa@erols.com;
URL: http://www.freeafrica.org

Established in DC.
Grantmaker type: Public charity.
Financial data (yr. ended 12/31/10): Revenue, $75,450; assets, $24,100 (M); gifts received, $68,550; expenditures, $75,660.
Purpose and activities: The foundation seeks to free Africans from intellectual bondage, empower them to take charge of their own destiny, and devise African-based solutions to Africa's problems.
Fields of interest: International development; International affairs.
International interests: Africa.
Limitations: Applications not accepted. Giving primarily in Africa.
Application information: Unsolicited requests for funds not considered or acknowledged.
Officer: George B. Ayittey, Pres.; Kate Anderson, Secy.
Board Members: John Fund; Audna Nicholson.
EIN: 521849803

527
Freedom House, Inc.
1301 Connecticut Ave. N.W., 6th Fl.
Washington, DC   20036-1802   (202) 296-5101
FAX: (202) 293-2840;
E-mail: info@freedomhouse.org; URL: http://
www.freedomhouse.org

Established in 1941 in NY.
Grantmaker type: Public charity.
Financial data (yr. ended 06/30/10): Revenue, $33,511,970; assets, $9,284,227 (M); gifts received, $33,501,344; expenditures, $32,976,608; giving activities include $14,115,236 for grants, and $1,584,845 for grants to organizations outside the U.S.
Purpose and activities: The organization supports the expansion of freedom in the world.
Fields of interest: International human rights; International democracy & civil society development; Civil/human rights, advocacy; Civil/human rights.
Officers and Trustees:* Peter Ackerman,* Chair.; Stuart Eizenstat,* Vice-Chair.; Mark Palmer,* Vice-Chair.; Ned W. Bandler,* Secy.; Walter J. Schloss,* Treas.; Jacqueline Adams; Kenneth L. Adelman; Bernard Aronson; Antonia Cortese; Alan P. Dye; and 26 additional trustees.
EIN: 131656647

528
The Alfred Friendly Foundation
1100 Connecticut Ave. N.W., Ste. 440
Washington, DC 20036-4119
E-mail: info@pressfellowships.org; URL: http://www.pressfellowships.org

Established in 1983 in DC.
Donor: Alfred Friendly‡.
Grantmaker type: Operating foundation.
Financial data (yr. ended 12/31/09): Assets, $1,869,304 (M); gifts received, $300,980; expenditures, $537,814; qualifying distributions, $521,181; giving activities include $228,115 for grants to individuals.
Purpose and activities: Funding only for the Alfred Friendly Press Fellowships, which is a fellowship program providing foreign print journalists working experience in the U.S.; main purposes of the program are to enable the Fellow to gain an understanding of the significance of the free press in American society and to foster continuing working ties between free institutions and journalists in the U.S. and other countries, particularly developing countries. Applicants must be English-speaking, mid-career journalists employed at independent, non-U.S. publications in the developing world.
Fields of interest: Media, print publishing.
International interests: Developing countries.
Type of support: Fellowships; Grants to individuals.
Limitations: Applications not accepted. Giving limited to journalists from developing countries, who are recipients of Alfred Friendly Fellowships.
Publications: Financial statement.
Application information: Unsolicited requests for funds not accepted.
Board meeting date(s): Oct.
Officers and Directors:* Jonathan Friendly,* Pres.; Lucinda F. Murphy,* 1st V.P.; John G. Murphy, Jr.,* 2nd V.P.; Nicholas Friendly, Treas.; Susan Albrecht, Exec. Dir.; Byron Calame; Victoria Friendly; Nabeeha Kazi; Randall Smith; Patrick Stueve.
Number of staff: None.
EIN: 521307387

529
Friends of the World Food Program, Inc.
1819 L St. N.W., Ste. 900
Washington, DC 20036-3801 (202) 530-1694
FAX: (202) 530-1698; E-mail: info@friendsofwfp.org;
URL: http://www.friendsofwfp.org
Facebook: http://www.facebook.com/WFPUSA?ref=ts&msource=%7BFacebook%7D
RSS Feed: http://usa.wfp.org/rss
Twitter: http://twitter.com/#!/WFPUSA
YouTube: http://www.youtube.com/user/WORLDFOODPROGRAM

Grantmaker type: Public charity.
Financial data (yr. ended 12/31/10): Revenue, $39,485,580; assets, $14,470,231 (M); gifts received, $39,508,348; expenditures, $37,321,207; giving activities include $68,000 for grants, and $33,075,956 for grants to organizations outside the U.S.
Purpose and activities: The organization is dedicated to building support for the World Food Program (WFP) and other hunger relief efforts.
Fields of interest: International agricultural development; Agriculture/food; Food services.
Limitations: Applications not accepted.
Application information: Contributes only to pre-selected organizations.
Officers and Directors:* Marshall Matz,* Chair.; Randy Russell,* Vice-Chair.; Karen Sendelback,* Pres. and C.E.O.; Barbara S. Belmont,* C.A.E., Secy.-Treas.; John Block; Rudy Boschwitz; Frank Mitchell Corso, Jr.; Robert Dole; Jim Edgar; and 7 additional directors.
EIN: 133843435

530
The Fund for American Studies
1706 New Hampshire Ave., N.W.
Washington, DC 20009-2502 (202) 986-0384
Contact: Roger Ream, Pres.
FAX: (202) 986-0390; E-mail: info@tfas.org; Toll-free tel.: (800) 741-6964; URL: http://www.tfas.org
Facebook: http://www.facebook.com/TFASfan?ref=ts
Flickr: http://www.flickr.com/photos/tfas1967/
LinkedIn: http://www.linkedin.com/groupInvitation?gid=25022&sharedKey=72F6FF77559E
Twitter: http://twitter.com/tfas_tweet

Established in 1967 in DC.
Grantmaker type: Public charity.
Financial data (yr. ended 12/31/10): Revenue, $9,082,503; assets, $23,507,228 (M); gifts received, $3,124,565; expenditures, $9,735,469; giving activities include $1,783 for grants, $783,939 for grants to organizations outside the U.S., and $1,090,521 for grants to individuals.
Purpose and activities: The fund conducts educational programs to introduce college students to the political, economic, and moral principles of a free society.
Fields of interest: Economics; Political science; American studies.
International interests: Czech Republic; Greece; Hong Kong.
Type of support: Scholarships—to individuals.
Limitations: Giving primarily in the U.S., Czech Republic, Greece, and Hong Kong.
Publications: Annual report; Financial statement; Informational brochure; Newsletter.

Application information: See Web site for additional information. Application form not required.
Initial approach: Telephone or e-mail
Copies of proposal: 6
Deadline(s): Mar. 1 for Mollenhoff Award; Mar. 15 for Economic Journalism Award
Board meeting date(s): Jan., Feb., Oct., and Nov.
Officers and Trustees:* Randal C. Teague,* Chair. and C.E.O.; Michael W. Thompson,* Vice-Chair.; Roger R. Ream,* Pres.; Daniel H. Branch,* Secy.; John W. Farley,* Treas.; Fred Barnes; Charles R. Black, Jr.; James B. Culbertson; Louis DeJoy; Dr. Paula J. Dobriansky; Frank J. Donatelli; Juanita Duggan; William J. Hybl; Frank Lauinger; Mark A. Stansberry; Leon J. Weil; Catherine Windels.
Number of staff: 13 full-time professional; 3 full-time support; 1 part-time support.
EIN: 136223604

531
Fund For Global Human Rights, Inc.
1666 Connecticut Ave., N.W., Ste. 410
Washington, DC 20009-1039 (202) 347-7488
Contact: Regan E. Ralph, Exec. Dir.; Kathryn Sommers, Dir., Opers.
FAX: (202) 347-7487;
E-mail: info@globalhumanrights.org; URL: http://www.globalhumanrights.org

Established in 2002 in DC.
Grantmaker type: Public charity.
Financial data (yr. ended 06/30/10): Revenue, $5,863,956; assets, $4,596,736 (M); gifts received, $5,817,577; expenditures, $5,434,705; giving activities include $15,000 for grants, and $4,120,136 for 639 grants to organizations outside the U.S.
Purpose and activities: The fund's purpose is to support local, national, and regional human rights groups and networks abroad in becoming stronger, more effective, and better funded.
Fields of interest: International human rights; Youth; Women; Physically disabled; Minorities; Migrant workers; Men; LGBTQ; Indigenous peoples; Immigrants/refugees; Girls; Children/youth; Adults.
International interests: Algeria; Burundi; Democratic Republic of the Congo; Guatemala; Guinea; India; Liberia; Mexico; Morocco and the Western Sahara; Pakistan; Philippines; Sierra Leone; Thailand; Tunisia; Uganda.
Type of support: Technical assistance; Seed money; Program development; General/operating support.
Limitations: Applications accepted. Giving limited to Algeria, Burundi, Democratic Republic of the Congo, Guatemala, Guinea, India, Liberia, Mexico, Morocco, Pakistan, the Philippines, Sierra Leone, Thailand, Tunisia, and Uganda. No support for activities directly or indirectly intended to support candidates for political office, businesses, government agencies, or micro-credit programs. No grants to individuals, or for fundraising events, scholarships, stand-alone conferences, university-based research, or the construction of roads, bridges, buildings, wells, or medical facilities.
Publications: Application guidelines; Grants list; Informational brochure; Newsletter.
Application information: The organization offers various requests for proposals to eligible organizations working in the fund's service areas; contact organization for current requests and eligibility guidelines. Application form required.
Initial approach: Download application
Copies of proposal: 1

Deadline(s): Varies
Board meeting date(s): Spring and fall
Officers and Board Members:* Hina Jilani,* Chair.; Regan E. Ralph, Exec. Dir.; Mariclaire Acosta; Kemal Ahmed; Philip Alston; Hossam Bahgat; George Biddle; Holly Cartner; Helen Mack; Josh Mailman; Chidi Anselm Odinkalu; Mary Robinson; Cynthia Ryan; Darian Weltman Swig.
Number of staff: 10 full-time professional.
EIN: 753029336

532

The German Marshall Fund of the United States

1744 R St., N.W.
Washington, DC 20009-2410 (202) 745-3950
FAX: (202) 265-1662; E-mail: info@gmfus.org;
URL: http://www.gmfus.org
Twitter: http://twitter.com/gmfus
Internship/Fellowships Contact: Tisha Spriggs Pugh, Sr. H.R. Coord.

Incorporated in 1972 in DC; founded through a gift from Germany as a permanent memorial to Marshall Plan assistance; status changed to a public charity.
Donor: Federal Republic of Germany.
Grantmaker type: Public charity.
Financial data (yr. ended 05/31/10): Revenue, $23,501,298; assets, $206,851,537 (M); gifts received, $13,215,344; expenditures, $38,141,656; giving activities include $753,850 for grants, and $7,861,443 for grants to organizations outside the U.S.
Purpose and activities: The fund is an American public policy and grantmaking institution dedicated to promoting greater cooperation and understanding between the United States and Europe by supporting individuals and institutions working on transatlantic issues, by convening leaders to discuss the most pressing transatlantic themes, and by examining ways in which transatlantic cooperation can address a variety of global policy challenges.
Fields of interest: Media, print publishing; Environment; International affairs, foreign policy.
International interests: Eastern & Central Europe; Europe.
Type of support: Conferences/seminars; Publication; Fellowships; Research.
Limitations: Applications accepted. Giving limited to the U.S. and Europe. No support for the arts and humanities, medicine and health, arms control, or diplomatic studies. No grants for building or operating budgets, annual campaigns, emergency funds, deficit financing, medical or scientific research, or graduate or undergraduate studies.
Publications: Annual report.
Application information: Application form only required for fellowship programs. See web site for current requests for proposals. Application form required.
Initial approach: Proposal
Copies of proposal: 1
Deadline(s): Varies
Board meeting date(s): Feb., May, and Oct.
Officers and Trustees:* Guido Goldman,* Co-Chair.; Marc Leland,* Co-Chair.; Craig Kennedy,* Pres.; Calvin M. Dooley; Jeffrey A. Goldstein; Marc Grossman; David Ignatius; Nike Irvin; Scott Klug; Roman Martinez IV; Richard Powers; J. Thomas Presby; John A. Ross; Barbara Shailor; Amity Shlaes; Jenonne Walker; Leah Zell Wanger; J. Robinson West; Suzanne H. Woolsey.

Number of staff: 30 full-time professional; 1 part-time professional; 4 full-time support; 11 part-time support.
EIN: 520954751

533

Global Fund for Children

1101 14th St., N.W., Ste. 420
Washington, DC 20005-5616 (202) 331-9003
FAX: (202) 331-9004;
E-mail: info@globalfundforchildren.org; URL: http://www.globalfundforchildren.org/

Established in 1994.
Grantmaker type: Public charity.
Financial data (yr. ended 06/30/10): Revenue, $6,244,044; assets, $7,342,199 (M); gifts received, $6,169,471; expenditures, $6,934,511; giving activities include $64,000 for grants, and $3,349,698 for grants to organizations outside the U.S.
Purpose and activities: The fund advances the education and dignity of young people around the world by targeting and strengthening small grassroots organizations that improve education for children who would otherwise be left behind.
Fields of interest: Education; International development; Children/youth; Economically disadvantaged.
International interests: Global programs.
Limitations: Applications accepted. Giving primarily on an international basis; minor funding also in the U.S.
Publications: Annual report; Financial statement; Newsletter.
Application information: Organizations with successful letters of inquiry will be asked to submit a full proposal, generally ranging from five to ten pages in length. Grants typically range from $5,000 to $20,000 per year, with a typical funding relationship of three to six years. Application form required.
Initial approach: Letter of inquiry
Deadline(s): Rolling basis
Final notification: June and Dec.
Officers and Directors:* Juliette Gimon,* Chair.; Robert Scully,* Vice-Chair.; Maya Ajmera,* Pres.; Isabel Carter Stewart,* Secy.; Robert D. Stillman,* Treas.; Peter Briger; Sanjiv Khattri; Mark McGoldrick; Sarah Perot; Sandra Pinnavaia; Patricia Rosenfield; Roy Salameh; Raj Singh.
EIN: 561834887

534

Global Health Council

1111 19th St. N.W., Ste. 1120
Washington, DC 20036-3636 (202) 833-5900
E-mail: ghc@globalhealth.org; Additional address: 1111 19th St. N.W., Ste. 1120, Washington, DC 20036-3636, tel.: (202) 833-5900, fax: (202) 833-0075; URL: http://www.globalhealth.org

Established in 1974 in DE.
Grantmaker type: Public charity.
Financial data (yr. ended 09/30/10): Revenue, $3,481,570; assets, $5,482,409 (M); gifts received, $798,358; expenditures, $7,105,083; giving activities include $1,000,000 for 3 grants to organizations outside the U.S.
Purpose and activities: The council works to ensure that all who strive for improvement and equity in

global health have the information and resources they need to succeed.
Fields of interest: International affairs; Health care.
Type of support: Grants to individuals.
Limitations: Applications accepted. Giving on a national and international basis.
Application information: Application form required.
Initial approach: Complete online nomination form
Deadline(s): Jan. 15 for Jonathan Mann Award; Feb. 1 for Excellence in Media Award for Global Health; Feb. 15 for Best Practices Award; Oct. 31 for Gates Award for Global Health
Officers and Directors:* Joel Lamstein,* Chair.; Reeta Roy, M.A., Vice-Chair.; Jeffrey L. Sturchio,* Pres. and C.E.O.; Kathryn Guare, V.P., Membership Resources; Maurice Middleberg, V.P., Public Policy; Alvaro Bermejo,* M.D., M.Ph., Secy.; Elizabeth Furst Frank,* M.B.A., Treas.; Valerie Nkamgang Bemo, M.D., M.P.H.; George F. Brown, M.D., M.P.H.; Rev. Dr. Joan Brown Campbell; Christopher J. Elias, M.D., M.Ph.; William Foege, M.D., M.P.H.; Julio Frenk; Michele Galen, MS, JD; Gretchen Howard; Jim Kolbe; Patricia McGrath.
EIN: 521048393

535

Global Rights

1200 18th St. N.W., Ste. 602
Washington, DC 20036-2526 (202) 822-4600
FAX: (202) 822-4606; URL: http://www.globalrights.org

Grantmaker type: Public charity.
Financial data (yr. ended 09/30/10): Revenue, $6,073,215; assets, $4,099,592 (M); gifts received, $6,199,402; expenditures, $5,453,128; giving activities include $313,580 for grants to organizations outside the U.S.
Purpose and activities: The organization is a human rights advocacy group that partners with local activists internationally to challenge injustice and amplify new voices within the global discourse.
Fields of interest: International human rights; Civil/human rights; International affairs.
Limitations: Giving on a worldwide basis.
Publications: Newsletter.
Officers and Directors:* James F. Fitzpatrick,* Chair.; J. Stuart Lemle,* Vice-Chair.; Susan Schneider,* Secy.; Antoine W. van Agtmael,* Treas.; Salih Brooks,* Exec. Dir.; Tim Brodhead; David Carliner; Russell H. Carpenter, Jr.; Vivian Derryck; Bradley P. Holmes; Niloo Razi Howe; Robert Kapp; Eric Koenig; William Lake; Bill Lann Lee; and 12 additional directors.
EIN: 521295669

536

Gorongosa Restoration Project, Inc.

(formerly Gregory C. Carr Foundation)
1250 24th St. N.W., Rm. 300
Washington, DC 20037-1186 (202) 466-0577
Contact: Gregory Carr, Pres. and Treas.
E-mail: MLgray@prodigy.net

Established in 1999 in MA.
Donors: Gregory C. Carr; Jan Sousa; Academy for Education Development; United States Agency for International Development; IPAD; Fundacao Ciocle AE Tecnologia.
Grantmaker type: Independent foundation.

Financial data (yr. ended 12/31/09): Assets, $2,959,071 (M); gifts received, $6,334,637; expenditures, $11,952,719; qualifying distributions, $10,983,294; giving activities include $488,405 for 15 grants (high: $100,000; low: $100), $2,000 for 2 grants to individuals (high: $1,000; low: $1,000), and $8,482,720 for 1 foundation-administered program.
Purpose and activities: Giving primarily to further public education in the area of human rights, African development, and health care in rural areas.
Fields of interest: Performing arts, theater; Museums; Higher education; Human services; International human rights.
Limitations: Giving primarily in MA; some funding also in Boise, ID.
Application information: Application form not required.
> *Initial approach:* Letter
> *Copies of proposal:* 8
> *Deadline(s):* None

Officers and Directors:* Gregory C. Carr, Pres. and Treas.; Katherine Raphaelson,* Secy.; Judy Oglethorpe.
EIN: 043452643

537
The Gottesman Fund
1818 N St. N.W., Ste. 400
Washington, DC 20036-2477
Contact: Diane Bennett Eidman, Dir.; Elaine Randall, Asst. Secy.
E-mail: deidman@firstmanhattan.com; New York City Address: 437 Madison Ave., 28th Fl., New York, NY 10022

Established in 1965 in DC.
Donor: Members of the Gottesman family.
Grantmaker type: Independent foundation.
Financial data (yr. ended 08/31/10): Assets, $258,945,062 (M); gifts received, $3,526,521; expenditures, $14,600,349; qualifying distributions, $14,338,766; giving activities include $13,921,375 for 106 grants (high: $2,857,500; low: $300).
Purpose and activities: The Gottesman Fund is dedicated to the enhancement and perpetuation of Jewish life in the United States and Israel through the support of programs that increase the appreciation of and commitment to Jewish ideals among youth and adults. The fund also sees its responsibility in serving the communities in which its board members reside, helping a variety of cultural, medical and educational institutions.
Fields of interest: Museums (ethnic/folk arts); Arts; Higher education; Hospitals (general); Human services; Jewish federated giving programs; Jewish agencies & synagogues.
Type of support: General/operating support; Capital campaigns; Building/renovation; Emergency funds; Program development; Scholarship funds.
Limitations: Applications not accepted. Giving primarily in NY. No grants to individuals.
Application information: Contributes only to pre-selected organizations.
> *Board meeting date(s):* Sept. 18

Officers: David S. Gottesman, Pres.; Alice R. Gottesman, V.P.; Ruth L. Gottesman, V.P.; William L. Gottesman, V.P.; Diane Bennett Eidman, Secy.; Robert W. Gottesman, Treas.
Number of staff: 1 full-time professional; 2 part-time professional.
EIN: 526061469

Recent grants for international programs:
537-1 American Friends of NATAL, New York, NY, $15,000. For general support. 2010.
537-2 American Jewish Joint Distribution Committee, New York, NY, $10,000. For general support. 2010.
537-3 American Jewish World Service, New York, NY, $110,000. For general support. 2010.
537-4 American Pardes Foundation, New York, NY, $25,000. For general support. 2010.
537-5 Birthright Israel Foundation, New York, NY, $29,745. For general support. 2010.
537-6 Committee to Protect Journalists, New York, NY, $10,000. For general support. 2010.
537-7 Israel Center of Vermont, Burlington, VT, $40,000. For general support. 2010.
537-8 Israel on Campus Coalition, Washington, DC, $51,500. For general support. 2010.
537-9 PEF Israel Endowment Funds, New York, NY, $2,857,500. For general support. 2010.
537-10 Save the Children Federation, Westport, CT, $10,000. For general support. 2010.

538
The Isadore and Bertha Gudelsky Family Foundation, Inc.
c/o Margolius Firm LLC
4201 Connecticut Ave. N.W., Ste. 600
Washington, DC 20008-1128
Contact: Philip Margolius, Secy.-Treas.
FAX: (202) 332-1800;
E-mail: jennifer@themargoliusfirm.com

Incorporated in 1955 in MD.
Donor: Members of the Gudelsky family.
Grantmaker type: Independent foundation.
Financial data (yr. ended 04/30/11): Assets, $12,911,220 (M); expenditures, $642,676; qualifying distributions, $573,488; giving activities include $554,951 for 24 grants (high: $125,000; low: $5,000).
Purpose and activities: Giving primarily to Jewish organizations, education, and for the arts.
Fields of interest: Performing arts centers; Arts; Education; Human services; Jewish federated giving programs; Jewish agencies & synagogues.
International interests: Israel.
Type of support: Endowments; General/operating support; Continuing support; Capital campaigns; Building/renovation; Emergency funds; Program development; Conferences/seminars; Professorships; Fellowships; Scholarship funds.
Limitations: Applications not accepted. Giving primarily in the metropolitan Washington, DC, and surrounding areas, including MD; funding also in New York, NY. No grants to individuals.
Application information: Unsolicited requests for funds not accepted.
> *Board meeting date(s):* May or June

Officers: Arlene G. Kaufman, Pres.; Shelley G. Mulitz, V.P.; Philip Margolius, Secy.-Treas.
Board Members: Paul S. Berger; Michael Friedman; Laura Bryna Gudelsky Mulitz.
Number of staff: 1 part-time professional.
EIN: 526036621

539
The Henry Foundation, Inc.
1990 M St. N.W., Ste. 250
Washington, DC 20036-3430 (202) 887-8992
Contact: C. Wolcott Henry III, Pres.

Established in 1986 in FL.
Grantmaker type: Independent foundation.
Financial data (yr. ended 12/31/09): Assets, $10,310,999 (M); expenditures, $591,489; qualifying distributions, $517,649; giving activities include $433,600 for 87 grants (high: $50,000; low: $200).
Purpose and activities: Giving primarily for education, coral reef conservation and for animal welfare.
Fields of interest: Secondary school/education; Higher education; Environment, water resources; Animals/wildlife, preservation/protection; Mental health/crisis services.
International interests: Caribbean.
Type of support: Program development; Conferences/seminars; Publication; Seed money; Matching/challenge support.
Limitations: Applications accepted. Giving primarily in FL and Washington, DC. No grants to individuals, or for capital campaigns or endowments.
Publications: Application guidelines; Grants list.
Application information: Applications are accepted only for the Coral Reef Conservation Program. No other applications will be considered.
> *Initial approach:* Letter of inquiry (for Coral Reef Program only)
> *Copies of proposal:* 1
> *Deadline(s):* July 31
> *Board meeting date(s):* Dec.
> *Final notification:* 4-6 months

Officers and Directors:* C. Wolcott Henry III,* Pres.; Nancy H. McKelvy,* Secy.; H. Alexander Henry,*** Treas.
Number of staff: 1 part-time professional.
EIN: 592827461

540
The Heritage Foundation
214 Massachusetts Ave., N.E.
Washington, DC 20002-4961 (202) 546-4400
Contact: Edwin J. Feulner, Pres.
FAX: (202) 546-8328; *E-mail:* info@heritage.org;
URL: http://www.heritage.org
Blog: http://blog.heritage.org
RSS Feed: http://rss.heritage.org/xml/researchpapers/allResearchPapers.xml
Twitter: http://twitter.com/Heritage
Ustream Channel: http://www.ustream.tv/channel/heritage-foundation-live
YouTube: http://www.youtube.com/HeritageFoundation
Application contact for fellowships: Jonathan Butcher, Domestic Policy, tel.: (202) 608-6073, E-mail: familydatabase@heritage.org

Established in 1973.
Grantmaker type: Public charity.
Financial data (yr. ended 12/31/10): Revenue, $78,253,864; assets, $196,167,571 (M); gifts received, $73,957,186; expenditures, $80,378,250; giving activities include $474,170 for grants.
Purpose and activities: The foundation formulates and promotes conservative public policies based on the principles of free enterprise, limited government, individual freedom, traditional American values, and a strong national defense.
Fields of interest: Economics; International studies.
Type of support: Fellowships; Research.
Limitations: Giving on a national basis.

Publications: Annual report; Financial statement; Newsletter.

Officers and Trustees:* Thomas A. Saunders III,* Chair.; Richard M. Scaife,* Vice-Chair.; Edwin J. Feulner,* Pres.; Phillip N. Truluck,* Exec. V.P.; John Von Kannon, V.P. and Treas.; J. Frederic Rench,* Secy.; Douglas F. Allison; Larry P. Arnn, Ph.D.; Hon. Belden H. Bell; Amb. Holland H. Coors; and 15 additional trustees.

Number of staff: 190

EIN: 237327730

541

The Eric D. & Steven D. Hovde Foundation

c/o Hovde Financial, Inc.
1826 Jefferson Pl. N.W.
Washington, DC 20036-2550   (202) 261-0857
Contact: Jeffrey Boyd, Exec. Dir.
E-mail: jboyd@hovdefoundation.org; URL: http://www.hovdefoundation.org

Established in 1998 in IL.

Donors: Eric D. Hovde; Steven D. Hovde; Curt Sidden; Jennifer Sidden; Hovde Financial, Inc.; Banco Popular North America; Hovde Capital I, LLC; The Lili Claire Foundation, Inc.; Ellis Management Svcs., Inc.

Grantmaker type: Independent foundation.

Financial data (yr. ended 12/31/10): Assets, $12,169,161 (M); gifts received, $662,737; expenditures, $1,762,873; qualifying distributions, $2,046,025; giving activities include $1,398,974 for 30 grants (high: $315,470; low: $100), and $395,455 for foundation-administered programs.

Fields of interest: Human services; Medical research, institute; Multiple sclerosis research; International development; Christian agencies & churches.

Limitations: Applications not accepted. Giving in the U.S., with emphasis on Washington, DC, and NY. No grants to individuals.

Application information: Contributes only to pre-selected organizations.

Officers: Jeffrey Cashdin, C.F.O.; Jeffrey Boyd, Exec. Dir.

Trustees: Eric D. Hovde; Steven D. Hovde; Richard J. Perry, Jr.

EIN: 522107093

542

Institute of Current World Affairs, Inc.

(also known as The Crane-Rogers Foundation)
4545 42nd St. N.W., Ste. 311
Washington, DC 20016-4623   (202) 364-4068
Contact: Steven Butler, Exec. Dir.
FAX: (202) 364-0498; E-mail: icwa@icwa.org;
URL: http://www.icwa.org
Application e-mail: apply@icwa.org

Incorporated in 1925 in NY as a private operating foundation.

Donors: Charles R. Crane; Robert McColl; Suzanne McColl; The Beinecke Foundation; Friendship Fund, Inc.

Grantmaker type: Operating foundation.

Financial data (yr. ended 12/31/09): Assets, $4,922,274 (M); gifts received, $575,625; expenditures, $685,722; qualifying distributions, $541,247; giving activities include $192,318 for 8 grants to individuals (high: $33,238; low: $9,185).

Purpose and activities: Support for a limited number of long-term fellowships to persons 35 years or younger of exceptional ability to enable them to work in and write about foreign areas of significance to the U.S.

Fields of interest: International affairs.

Type of support: Fellowships.

Limitations: Applications accepted. Giving limited to fellowships conducted outside the U.S. No support for formal education. No grants for research projects.

Publications: Application guidelines; Informational brochure.

Application information: Complete application information available on Institute web site. Application form not required.
  Initial approach: Letter of interest and resume (by email preferred)
  Copies of proposal: 1
  Deadline(s): See Institute web site for deadlines for letter of interest and resume. If appropriate, candidates will be invited to submit a more detailed written application
  Board meeting date(s): June and Dec.

Officers and Trustees:* Gary Hartshorn,* Chair.; Pramila Jayapal,* Vice-Chair.; Boris Weintraub,* Secy.; Edmund Sutton,* Treas.; Steven Butler,* Exec. Dir.; Bryn Barnard; Carole Beaulieu; Mary Lynne Bird; Virginia Foote; Peter Geithner; Robert Levinson; Cheng Li; David Robinson; John Spencer; Susan Stemer.

Number of staff: 1 full-time professional; 2 full-time support.

EIN: 131621044

543

Institute of Turkish Studies

c/o Georgetown Univ., Intercultural Ctr.
P.O. Box 571033
Washington, DC 20057-1033   (202) 687-0295
Contact: David C. Cuthell, Exec. Dir.
FAX: (202) 687-3780;
E-mail: institute_turkishstudies@yahoo.com;
URL: http://www.turkishstudies.org
Application address: 1524 18th St., N.W., No. 1, Washington, DC 20036-1333, tel.: (202) 328-6208

Established in 1982.

Grantmaker type: Independent foundation.

Financial data (yr. ended 09/30/10): Assets, $645,396 (M); gifts received, $589,808; expenditures, $339,511; qualifying distributions, $201,428; giving activities include $148,908 for 8 grants (high: $10,000; low: $771), and $52,520 for 17 grants to individuals (high: $7,200; low: $1,000).

Purpose and activities: Grant awards to the academic community of U.S. specialists in the field of Turkish studies; support includes awards to individual scholars and to institutions for the humanities and social sciences.

Fields of interest: Higher education.

International interests: Turkey.

Type of support: General/operating support; Program development; Conferences/seminars; Publication; Seed money; Curriculum development; Fellowships; Scholarship funds; Research; Grants to individuals; Scholarships—to individuals; Matching/challenge support.

Limitations: Giving on a national basis.

Publications: Application guidelines; Grants list; Informational brochure; Multi-year report.

Application information: Application forms available on web site. Application form required.
  Initial approach: Proposal
  Copies of proposal: 4
  Deadline(s): Mar. 12
  Board meeting date(s): 1st week in May
  Final notification: May

Officers and Board of Governors:* Donald Quataert,* Chair.; Madeline Zilfi,* Treas.; David C. Cuthell, Exec. Dir.; Richard Barkley; Walter Denny; Ahmet Ertegun; Halil Inalcik; Heath W. Lowry; Mike Mustafoglu; Kenan Sahin.

Number of staff: 2 full-time professional.

EIN: 521294029

544

International Campaign for Tibet

1825 Jefferson Pl., N.W.
Washington, DC 20036-2504   (202) 785-1515
FAX: (202) 785-4343; E-mail: info@savetibet.org;
URL: http://www.savetibet.org
Campaign Blog: http://weblog.savetibet.org/
Facebook: http://www.facebook.com/pages/International-Campaign-for-Tibet/16266289036
RSS Feed: http://www.savetibet.org/rss.xml
Twitter: http://twitter.com/savetibetorg
YouTube: http://www.youtube.com/intercampaigntibet

Established in 1988 in DC.

Grantmaker type: Public charity.

Financial data (yr. ended 12/31/10): Revenue, $4,145,807; assets, $4,678,355 (M); gifts received, $4,027,883; giving activities include $27,220 for grants, $83,814 for 3 grants to organizations outside the U.S., $101,818 for grants to individuals, and $30,680 for grants to individuals outside the U.S.

Purpose and activities: The campaign works to promote human rights and democratic freedoms for the people of Tibet.

Fields of interest: International democracy & civil society development; International human rights; International affairs.

International interests: China.

Type of support: Grants to individuals.

Limitations: Applications accepted. Giving on a national and international basis, primarily to Tibet.

Publications: Annual report; Financial statement.

Application information:
  Initial approach: Submit application
  Deadline(s): Sept. 30 for Rowell Fund for Tibet

Officers and Directors:* Richard Gere,* Chair.; Gare Smith,* Vice-Chair.; John Ackerly; Ellen Bork; Lodi Gyari; Jim Kane; Marco Antonio Karam; Melissa Mathison; Joel McCleary; Keith Pitts; Steve Schroeder; Grace Spring.

EIN: 521570071

545

The International Center for Journalists, Inc.

1616 H St., N.W., 3rd Fl.
Washington, DC 20006-4903   (202) 737-3700
Contact: Nancy P. Frye, V.P., Finance and Admin.
FAX: (202) 737-0530; E-mail: editor@icfj.org;
Additional URL (for Knight Fellowships): http://www.knight.ifcj.org; URL: http://www.icfj.org
Additional URL: http://www.ijnet.org
Facebook: http://www.facebook.com/icfj.org?ref=s

LinkedIn: http://www.linkedin.com/groups?
home=&gid=1802658&trk=anet_ug_hm&goback=.
ana_1802658_1242743670734_3_1
Twitter: http://twitter.com/icfj
YouTube: http://www.youtube.com/icfjournalists

Established in 1984 in DC.
Grantmaker type: Public charity.
Financial data (yr. ended 12/31/10): Revenue,
$12,156,079; assets, $21,958,767 (M); gifts
received, $11,684,621; expenditures,
$8,120,617; giving activities include $1,412,342
for grants to organizations outside the U.S., and
$424,785 for grants to individuals.
Purpose and activities: The center is committed to
working with colleagues around the globe to: share
journalistic, managerial, and technical expertise;
provide the latest information on media
developments, journalism ethics, and professional
practices; offer support services relevant to
changing needs; and encourage vital and
independent media that are professionally,
ethically, and financially grounded.
Fields of interest: Media/communications; Media,
print publishing.
Type of support: Fellowships.
Limitations: Applications accepted. Giving on a
national and international basis.
Publications: Application guidelines; Newsletter.
Application information: Application form required.
  Initial approach: Complete online application
  Deadline(s): Mar. 9 for World Affairs Journalism
    Fellowships; Mar. 11 for Arthur F. Burns
    Fellowship Program; Apr. 16 for McGee
    Journalism Fellowship; June 1 for International
    Journalism Exchange; June 10 for World Affairs
    Journalism Fellowships; Aug. 29 for Knight
    International Journalism Fellowship; Sept. 1 for
    Faith in the Media Grants
  Board meeting date(s): May and Nov.
Officers and Directors:* James F. Hoge, Jr.,* Chair.;
Pamela Howard,* Vice-Chair.; Joyce Barnathan,
Pres.; Patrick Butler, V.P., Progs.; Nancy P. Frye,
V.P., Finance and Admin.; Vjollca Shtylla, V.P.,
Devel.; John Maxwell Hamilton,* Treas.; Louis D.
Boccardi; Mary Boies; Marcus Brauchli; Tom Curley;
Michael Elliott; Anne Finucane; Michael Golden;
George B. Irish; and 11 additional directors.
Number of staff: 29 full-time professional; 6
part-time professional.
EIN: 112724905

546
International Crisis Group
1629 K St., N.W., Ste. 450
Washington, DC 20006-1677 (202) 785-1601
FAX: (202) 785-1630; URL: http://
www.crisisgroup.org
Facebook: http://www.facebook.com/crisisgroup?
ref=mf
Twitter: http://twitter.com/#!/CrisisGroup

Established in 1995.
Grantmaker type: Public charity.
Financial data (yr. ended 06/30/10): Revenue,
$24,659,144; assets, $48,013,761 (M); gifts
received, $23,816,897; expenditures,
$16,975,452.
Purpose and activities: The group is an international
non-governmental organization that is recognized as
the world's leading independent, nonpartisan
source of analysis and advice to governments and
intergovernmental bodies.

Fields of interest: International affairs, information
services; International peace/security; International
conflict resolution; International human rights;
International affairs.
Type of support: Program development; Grants to
individuals.
Limitations: Giving on an international basis.
Publications: Annual report.
Officers and Board Members:* Lord Christopher
Patten of Barnes,* Co-Chair.; Amb. Thomas R.
Pickering,* Co-Chair.; Emma Bonino,* Vice-Chair.;
Gareth Evans,* Pres. and C.E.O.; Morton
Abramowitz; Adnan Abu-Odeh; Kenneth L. Adelman;
Turki al-Faisal; Kofi Annan; Louise Arbour; Richard
Armitage; Paddy Ashdown; Shlomo Ben-Ami;
Lakhdar Brahimi; and 39 additional board members.
EIN: 525170039

547
International Food Policy Research
Institute
(also known as IFPRI)
2033 K St., N.W.
Washington, DC 20006-1002 (202) 862-5600
FAX: (202) 467-4439; E-mail: ifpri@cgiar.org;
URL: http://www.ifpri.org
Facebook: http://www.facebook.com/pages/
International-Food-Policy-Research-Institute-IFPRI/
15653394685
RSS Feed: http://www.ifpri.org/rss
SlideShare URL: http://www.slideshare.net/ifpri
Twitter: http://twitter.com/ifpri
YouTube: http://www.youtube.com/ifpri

Established in 1975 in DC.
Grantmaker type: Public charity.
Financial data (yr. ended 12/31/10): Revenue,
$70,681,528; assets, $91,423,720 (M); gifts
received, $70,460,016; expenditures,
$66,179,714; giving activities include $800,389
for grants, and $470,477 for grants to organizations
outside the U.S.
Purpose and activities: The institute seeks
sustainable solutions for ending hunger and poverty
throughout the world.
Fields of interest: International affairs; Agriculture/
food; Nutrition.
Limitations: Giving on a national and international
basis.
Publications: Annual report; Informational brochure;
Occasional report.
Trustees: Fawzi Al-Sultan; Csaba Csaki; Shenggen
Fan; Ross G. Garnaut; Barbara Harriss-White;
Masayoshi Honma; Mohamad Ikhsan; Kabba
Thomas Joiner; Jean Kinsey; Zhu Ling; Cecilia Lopez
Montano; Amrita Patel; Liliana Rojas-Suarez; Gunnar
M. Sorbo; Michele Veeman; Samuel Wangwe.
EIN: 521041632

548
International Foundation for Electoral
Systems
(also known as IFES, Inc.)
1850 K St., N.W., 5th Fl.
Washington, DC 20006-2213 (202) 350-6700
FAX: (202) 350-6701;
E-mail: applied.research@ifes.org; URL: http://
www.ifes.org

Established in 1987.
Grantmaker type: Public charity.

Financial data (yr. ended 09/30/10): Revenue,
$94,754,333; assets, $21,580,909 (M); gifts
received, $94,808,790; expenditures,
$92,489,758; giving activities include
$19,193,428 for grants to organizations outside the
U.S.
Purpose and activities: The organization is
committed to providing professional support to
electoral democracy through field work, applied
research, and advocacy, in order to promote citizen
participation, transparency, and accountability in
political and civic life.
Fields of interest: Civil rights, voter education;
International development; International affairs,
equal rights; International affairs.
Limitations: Applications accepted. Giving on a
national and international basis.
Publications: Occasional report.
Application information: Application form required.
  Initial approach: Download application
  Copies of proposal: 3
  Deadline(s): Apr. 3 for fellowships
Officers and Directors:* Peter G. Kelly,* Chair.;
Wiliam J. Hybl,* Vice-Chair.; William "Bill" Sweeney,
Pres. and C.E.O.; Hon. Leon J. Weil, Secy.; Lesley
Israel, Treas.; Hon. Howard Henry Baker, Jr.; Hon.
Mary Banotti; Judy A. Black; Ken Blackwell; Hank
Brown; Sean Cleary; Hon. Paula J. Dobriansky;
Frederick P. Furth, Esq.; Jeffrey L. Glassman; Stuart
Holliday; Steny Hoyer; and 11 additional directors.
EIN: 521527835

549
International Republican Institute
1225 Eye St., N.W., Ste. 700
Washington, DC 20005-5962 (202) 408-9450
FAX: (202) 408-9462; E-mail: info@iri.org;
URL: http://www.iri.org

Established in 1983 in DC.
Donors: American Gaming Association; Akin, Gump,
Strauss, Hauer & Feld, LLP; Alliance of Automobile
Manufacturers; Alliance for Democracy in Iran;
Americans for Freedom and Prosperity; American
International Group, Inc.; The Annenberg
Foundation; Archipelago Exchange, LLC; Bank of
America Specialists, Inc.; Bernard S. and Sarah M.
Gerwirz Foundation, Inc.
Grantmaker type: Public charity.
Financial data (yr. ended 09/30/10): Revenue,
$85,286,280; assets, $11,219,683 (M); gifts
received, $85,458,313; expenditures,
$85,345,131; giving activities include $250,000
for grants, and $1,323,780 for grants to
organizations outside the U.S.
Purpose and activities: The institute works to
advance freedom and democracy worldwide by
developing political parties, civic institutions, open
elections, good governance, and the rule of law.
Fields of interest: International peace/security;
International human rights; International affairs.
Limitations: Giving to the U.S. and Afghanistan,
Albania, Angola, Armenia, Azerbaijan, Bangladesh,
Belarus, Bolivia, Bosnia and Herzegovina, Bulgaria,
Burma, Cambodia, China, Colombia, Croatia, Cuba,
Czech Republic, East Timor, Egypt, Estonia, Georgia,
Guatemala, Haiti, Hungary, Indonesia, Iran, Iraq,
Jordan, Kazakhstan, Kenya, Kuwait, Kyrgyz
Republic, Latvia, Lebanon, Liberia, Lithuania,
Macedonia, Malaysia, Mali, Mexico, Moldova,
Mongolia, Montenegro, Morocco, Nicaragua,
Nigeria, Oman, Pakistan, Peru, Poland, Romania,
Russia, Serbia, Slovakia, Slovenia, Somaliland,

South Africa, Sri Lanka, Sudan, Syria, Turkey, Uganda, Ukraine, Venezuela, West Bank and Gaza, and Zimbabwe.
Publications: Annual report; Informational brochure; Newsletter.
Officers and Directors:* Sen. John McCain,* Chair.; Peter T. Madigan,* Vice-Chair.; Lorne W. Craner, Pres.; Harold W. Collamer, C.O.O.; Judy van Rest, Exec. V.P.; Georges A. Fauriol, Sr. V.P.; Elizabeth Dugan, V.P., Progs.; J. William Middendorf II,* Secy.-Treas.; Sonya Vekstein, C.F.O.; Amb. L. Paul Bremer III; Gahl Hodges Burt; Rep. David Dreier; Lawrence S. Eagleburger; Frank J. Fahrenkopf, Jr.; Alison B. Fortier; James A. Garner; Janet G. Mullins Grissom; Sen. Chuck Hagel; and 15 additional directors.
EIN: 521340267

550
International Utility Efficiency Partnerships, Inc.

2000 L St., N.W., Ste. 805
Washington, DC   20036-4913   (202) 293-7992
FAX: (202) 478-2525; E-mail: contact@iuep.org;
URL: http://www.iuep.org

Established in 1997.
Grantmaker type: Public charity.
Financial data (yr. ended 07/31/10): Revenue, $396,440; assets, $6,010 (M); expenditures, $275,930.
Purpose and activities: The organization seeks to reduce emissions by identifying, coordinating, and providing funding for the development of international environmentally-friendly energy development projects.
Fields of interest: International exchange; Environment, fund raising/fund distribution; Environment, air pollution; Environment, energy.
Type of support: Program development.
Limitations: Applications accepted. Giving on a national and international basis.
Publications: Application guidelines.
Application information: See web site for current RFP focus and guidelines.
Officer: Ronald C. Shiflett, Jr., Exec. Dir.
Directors: John Daniel; John Easton, Jr.; John Novak.
EIN: 521985160

551
International Women's Media Foundation

1625 K St., N.W., Ste. 1275
Washington, DC   20006-1680   (202) 496-1992
Contact: Jane Ransom, Exec. Dir.
FAX: (202) 496-1977; E-mail: info@iwmf.org;
URL: http://www.iwmf.org
Facebook: http://www.facebook.com/IWMFpage
Flickr: http://www.flickr.com/photos/iwmfphotos
Twitter: http://twitter.com/#!/iwmf
YouTube: http://www.youtube.com/user/Thelwmf

Founded in 1990 in DE.
Grantmaker type: Public charity.
Financial data (yr. ended 06/30/10): Revenue, $1,081,678; assets, $2,572,056 (M); gifts received, $1,059,223; expenditures, $2,068,388.
Purpose and activities: The foundation strengthens the role of women in the news media worldwide and helps protect freedom of the press.

Fields of interest: Media/communications; Media, print publishing; Women.
International interests: Africa; Latin America.
Type of support: Grants to individuals; Fellowships.
Limitations: Applications accepted. Giving on a national and international basis.
Publications: Application guidelines; Annual report; Informational brochure; Newsletter; Occasional report.
Application information: Application form required.
  Deadline(s): Mar. 1 for Courage Awards; Apr. 1 for Elizabeth Neuffer Fellowship; Apr. 16 for Leadership Institute for Women Journalists; Nov. 30 for Women Entrepreneurs in the Global Digital News Frontier Grants
  Final notification: May
Officers and Directors:* Campbell Brown, Co-Chair.; Barbara Cochran,* Co-Chair.; Theodore J. Boutrous, Jr.,* Vice-Chair.; Carolan K. Stiles,* Secy.; Jennifer Moyer,* Treas.; Jane Ransom, Exec. Dir.; Christiane Amanpour; Akwe Amosu; Merrill Brown; Eleanor Clift; Ann Curry; Raghida Dergham; Ferial Haffajee; Katty Kay; Cindi Leive; and 9 additional directors.
Number of staff: 12
EIN: 521648942

552
The Jerusalem Fund for Education and Community Development

(formerly The Jerusalem Fund)
2425 Virginia Ave., N.W.
Washington, DC   20037-2637   (202) 338-1958
Contact: Samar Assad, Exec. Dir.
FAX: (202) 333-7742;
E-mail: info@palestinecenter.org; URL: http://www.palestinecenter.org

Established in 1977 in DC.
Donor: Jerusalem Fund.
Grantmaker type: Public charity.
Financial data (yr. ended 12/31/10): Revenue, $735,257; assets, $5,018,616 (M); gifts received, $464,064; expenditures, $741,912; giving activities include $6,000 for grants, and $54,550 for grants to organizations outside the U.S.
Purpose and activities: Support primarily for emergency aid to Palestinians in East Jerusalem, the West Bank and Gaza Strip and young people's education and welfare in Palestinian communities in Israel; scholarships, fellowships, and travel and research grants for individuals who reside in those communities.
Fields of interest: Education; Health care; Family services.
International interests: East Jerusalem; Middle East; West Bank/Gaza (Palestinian Territories).
Type of support: Emergency funds; Program development; Conferences/seminars; Fellowships; Research; Scholarships—to individuals; Student loans—to individuals.
Limitations: Giving primarily in Palestinian communities in Israel.
Publications: Annual report; Financial statement; Grants list; Newsletter.
Application information:
  Initial approach: Letter
  Deadline(s): Aug. 31 and Dec. 15 for individual applicants; none for organizations
Officers and Directors:* Subhi D. Ali,* M.D., F.A.C.S., Chair.; Omar J. Fayez,* Esq., Secy.; Eid B. Musatafa,* M.D., F.A.C.S., Treas.; Samar Assad, Exec. Dir.; George Hishmeh; Mohayya H. Khilfeh;

M.D., M.P.H.; Nabil E. Khoury, M.D.; Sari A. Nabulso, M.D., M.B.A.; William Youmans.
Number of staff: 5
EIN: 521238142

553
Joint Aid Management

900 19th St., N.W., Ste. 400
Washington, DC   20006-2110   (202) 380-3566
FAX: (202) 380-3627; URL: https://www.jamint.com/index.php?option=com_content&task=view&id=633&Itemid=589

Grantmaker type: Public charity.
Financial data (yr. ended 12/31/10): Revenue, $29,128,806; assets, $4,648,111 (M); gifts received, $29,123,383; expenditures, $29,396,011; giving activities include $26,126,199 for grants to organizations outside the U.S.
Purpose and activities: The organization supports the South Africa-based Joint Aid Management, which works to help Africa help itself by contributing toward the alleviation of poverty through sustainable development programs.
Fields of interest: Human services, emergency aid; International economic development; International agricultural development; Nutrition.
International interests: Sub-Saharan Africa; Africa.
Limitations: Applications not accepted. Giving primarily to sub-Saharan Africa.
Application information: Contributes only to a pre-selected organization.
Officer: Isak Pretorius, Pres.
Trustees: Thomas Demery; James Carson Pack; Peter Desmond Pretorius; Albert Simon; Ellen Sue Simon.
EIN: 382726350

554
Jordan River Foundation

c/o Earl F. Glock
1100 Connecticut Ave., N.W.
Washington, DC   20036-4101
E-mail: info@jrf.org.jo; URL: http://www.jordanriver.jo
Facebook: http://www.facebook.com/group.php?gid=10194312059
Twitter: http://twitter.com/JordanRiverFDN
YouTube: http://www.youtube.com/user/JRFAmman

Established in 1995 in VA.
Grantmaker type: Public charity.
Financial data (yr. ended 12/31/10): Revenue, $300,868; assets, $79,600 (M); gifts received, $297,705; expenditures, $399,644; giving activities include $386,000 for 1 grant to an organization outside the U.S.
Purpose and activities: The foundation's mission is to promote the development of a dynamic Jordanian society by initiating and supporting sustainable social, economic and cultural programs that empower communities and individuals based on their needs and priorities.
Fields of interest: International economic development; International development.
International interests: Jordan.
Limitations: Giving primarily to Amman, Jordan.
Publications: Annual report.

Officers and Directors:* Pat Mitchell,* Pres.; Earl F. Glock,* Secy.-Treas.; Nancy Aossey; Alexander Cappello; Phil Condit; Beth Dozoretz; Sharon Patrick; Julia Tolkan.
EIN: 522218780

555
Danny Kaye and Sylvia Fine Kaye Foundation
c/o The Weidenfeld Law Firm
888 17th St. N.W., Rm. 1250
Washington, DC 20006-3328

Established in 1995 in CO.
Donors: Danny Kaye†; Sylvia Fine Kaye†.
Grantmaker type: Independent foundation.
Financial data (yr. ended 12/31/10): Assets, $13,101,197 (M); expenditures, $1,565,129; qualifying distributions, $1,379,150; giving activities include $1,363,150 for 17 grants (high: $750,000; low: $1,500).
Purpose and activities: Giving primarily for the arts, health, human services, and international affairs.
Fields of interest: Media, film/video; Performing arts; Arts; Biomedicine research; Medical research; Human services; International affairs, goodwill promotion; International relief; Civil liberties, reproductive rights; Social sciences.
Type of support: Program development; General/operating support.
Limitations: Applications not accepted. Giving in the U.S., with emphasis on CA, Aspen, CO, New York, NY, and VA. No grants to individuals.
Application information: Contributes only to pre-selected organizations.
Directors: Richard Fallin; Dena Kaye; Edward L. Weidenfeld.
EIN: 841283914

556
The Joseph P. Kennedy, Jr. Foundation
1133 19th St. N.W., 12th Fl.
Washington, DC 20036-3604 (202) 393-1250
Contact: Steve Eidelman, Mgr.
FAX: (202) 824-0351; E-mail: info@jpkf.org; URL: http://www.jpkf.org

Incorporated in 1946 in DC.
Donors: Joseph P. Kennedy†; Mrs. Joseph P. Kennedy†.
Grantmaker type: Independent foundation.
Financial data (yr. ended 12/31/10): Assets, $15,067,209 (M); expenditures, $618,017; qualifying distributions, $448,549; giving activities include $448,549 for grants.
Purpose and activities: The foundation's main objectives are the prevention of mental retardation by identifying its causes and improving means by which society deals with its mentally retarded citizens. Emphasis on the use of funds in areas where a multiplier effect is possible. Fellowships limited to four one-year Washington, DC-based Kennedy Foundation Public Policy Leadership Fellows.
Fields of interest: Learning disorders research; Developmentally disabled, centers & services; Disabilities, people with.
International interests: Central America; Nicaragua.
Type of support: Program development; Seed money; Fellowships; Technical assistance; Consulting services.

Limitations: Giving on a national basis. No grants to individuals (except for fellowships), or for building or endowment funds, equipment, or operating budgets of schools or service organizations.
Application information: The foundation does not accept grant applications or inquiries.
Board meeting date(s): Usually spring
Officers and Trustees:* Amb. Jean Kennedy Smith, Vice-Chair.; Steve Eidelman, Mgr.; Caroline Kennedy; Christopher Kennedy; Edward M. Kennedy, Jr.; Rory E. Kennedy; Sydney McKelvy; Mark Shriver; Stephen E. Smith, Jr.
Number of staff: 1 full-time professional; 1 part-time professional; 1 full-time support; 1 part-time support.
EIN: 136083407

557
Kimsey Foundation
c/o Lydia Miles, V.P., Progs.
1700 Pennsylvania Ave. N.W., Ste. 900
Washington, DC 20006-4722
FAX: (202) 638-7272; E-mail: kimseyfdn@aol.com; URL: http://www.kimseyfoundation.org

Established in 1997 in VA.
Donor: James V. Kimsey.
Grantmaker type: Independent foundation.
Financial data (yr. ended 12/31/10): Assets, $16,954,599 (M); gifts received, $159,301; expenditures, $1,220,644; qualifying distributions, $1,053,571; giving activities include $462,800 for 35 grants (high: $100,000; low: $500).
Purpose and activities: The foundation focuses on educational and cultural initiatives; supporting thriving communities that offer hope and opportunity to youth. The foundation gives preference to organizations using a proactive collaborative approach. The foundation participates in funding partnerships. It also serves the international community through policy research and humanitarian outreach. The foundation has narrowed its focus to include a few specific projects that leverage systemic change in public education and community development. The majority of new grants will be related to existing partnerships and initiatives.
Fields of interest: Arts; Education; Children/youth, services; International affairs, public policy; International human rights; Community/economic development; Public affairs, political organizations; Immigrants/refugees.
Type of support: General/operating support; Program development; Technical assistance; Matching/challenge support.
Limitations: Applications not accepted. Giving primarily in Washington, DC. No grants to individuals, or for building or renovations, endowments, capital campaigns, conferences, or for competition expenses.
Application information: The foundation does not accept unsolicited proposals. A few focused projects are chosen each year based on research in the field.
Officers: James V. Kimsey, Chair.; Michael P. Kimsey, Exec. Dir.
Directors: Mark J. Kimsey; Raymond C. Kimsey.
Number of staff: 2 full-time professional; 1 part-time professional.
EIN: 522007895

558
The Lambi Fund of Haiti
P.O. Box 18955
Washington, DC 20036-8955 (202) 833-3713
URL: http://www.lambifund.org

Established in 1994.
Grantmaker type: Public charity.
Financial data (yr. ended 12/31/08): Revenue, $991,912; assets, $878,286 (M); gifts received, $981,510; expenditures, $705,045; program services expenses, $580,984.
Purpose and activities: The fund works to assist the popular, democratic movement in Haiti, and to strengthen civil society in Haiti as a necessary foundation for democracy and government.
Fields of interest: International affairs; Community/economic development; Economic development.
Limitations: Giving primarily to Haiti.
Officers and Directors:* Marie Marthe St. Cyr,* Chair.; Max Blanchet,* M.S., Vice-Chair.; Wendy Emrich,* Secy.; Gyliane Morgan,* Treas.; Nadege T. Clitandre; Julie Meyer; Marie M.B. Racine, Ph.D.; Benjamin Saint-Dic; Jay Schoenberger; Anouk Shambrook; Fr. William Smarth.

559
MAG America, Inc.
(also known as MAG)
1750 K St., N.W., Ste. 350
Washington, DC 20006-2327 (202) 293-1908
E-mail: info@magamerica.org; URL: http://www.maginternational.org/usa/

Established in 1989 in the UK, incorporated in the U.S. in 2000.
Grantmaker type: Public charity.
Financial data (yr. ended 12/31/10): Revenue, $17,242,358; assets, $3,090,824 (M); gifts received, $17,231,490; expenditures, $17,089,036; giving activities include $16,420,543 for grants to organizations outside the U.S.
Purpose and activities: By supporting a combination of weapons clearance, education, and awareness programs, the organization seeks to remove the threat that remains from conflict and enable people to build their livelihoods in safety.
Fields of interest: International conflict resolution; International affairs, arms control; International human rights; International affairs.
International interests: South Asia; Middle East; Africa.
Limitations: Giving primarily in Angola, Cambodia, Congo, Iraq, Laos, Lebanon, Sudan, and Vietnam.
Officer and Board Members:* Amb. Barbara Bodine,* Pres.; Donald F. "Pat" Patierno; Virgil Wiebe.
Number of staff: 2 full-time professional.
EIN: 522302253

560
Merriman Foundation
1747 Pennsylvania Ave.
Washington, DC 20006-4604

Established in MO.
Donors: Trading Partners I; Trading Partners II; Joe Jack Merriman†.
Grantmaker type: Independent foundation.

Financial data (yr. ended 12/31/10): Assets, $7,419,972 (M); gifts received, $44; expenditures, $581,204; qualifying distributions, $565,236; giving activities include $565,236 for grants.
Fields of interest: Boy scouts; Arts; Education; Medical research, institute; Boys & girls clubs; Human services; United Ways and Federated Giving Programs; Religion.
International interests: Bahamas.
Limitations: Applications not accepted. No grants to individuals.
Application information: Unsolicited requests for funds not accepted.
Officers: Michael A. Merriman, Pres. and Treas.; Elaine A. Merriman, V.P.; Marybeth M. Sotos, Secy.
EIN: 237113720

561

Migration Policy Institute

1400 16th St., N.W.
Washington, DC 20036-2217 (202) 266-1940
FAX: (202) 266-1900;
E-mail: info@migrationpolicy.org; URL: http://www.migrationpolicy.org
Grants List: http://www.migrationinformation.org/integrationawards/winners.cfm

Established in 2000 in DC.
Grantmaker type: Public charity.
Financial data (yr. ended 06/30/10): Revenue, $3,539,796; assets, $7,846,598 (M); gifts received, $3,529,718; expenditures, $4,660,619; giving activities include $200,000 for grants.
Purpose and activities: The institute is dedicated to the analysis of the movement of people worldwide, and provides analysis, development, and evaluation of migration and refugee policies at the local, national, and international levels.
Fields of interest: International affairs; International migration/refugee issues.
Limitations: Applications accepted. Giving on a national basis.
Publications: Annual report; Grants list; Occasional report.
Application information: Application form required.
  Initial approach: Submit application
  Deadline(s): Dec. 15 for E Pluribus Unum Prizes
Officers and Trustees:* Most Rev. Nicholas DiMarzio,* Chair.; Demetrios G. Papademetriou,* Pres.; Warren R. Leiden; Antonio L. Maciel; Kathleen Newland; Amb. Andres Rozental; Rita Sussmuth.
EIN: 522279789

562

Moriah Fund

1 Farragut Sq. S.
1634 I St. N.W., Ste. 1000
Washington, DC 20006-4015 (202) 783-8488
Contact: Mary Ann Stein, Pres.
FAX: (202) 783-8499; E-mail: info@moriahfund.org;
Israel office e-mail: MoriahF@actcom.net.il;
Requests in Israel: Don Futterman, 18 Weizman St., Kfar Saba, Israel 44247; URL: http://www.moriahfund.org/index.htm
Grants List: http://www.moriahfund.org/grants/index.htm

Established in 1985 in IN.
Donors: Clarence W. Efroymson†; Robert A. Efroymson†; Ben-Ephraim Gershon Fund; Gustave Aaron Efroymson Fund.

Grantmaker type: Independent foundation.
Financial data (yr. ended 12/31/09): Assets, $115,323,005 (M); expenditures, $8,632,712; qualifying distributions, $8,608,170; giving activities include $7,317,500 for 162 grants (high: $1,500,000; low: $500; average: $25,000–$100,000), and $100,000 for 1 loan/program-related investment.
Purpose and activities: Promote human rights and democracy, help disadvantaged people gain self-sufficiency and control over their lives, and promote women's rights and reproductive health. The fund supports programs that strengthen local involvement, leadership and institutional development. The fund focuses on areas where private funding can make a difference, that is, areas that receive inadequate government funds, or that leverage public and private support through advocacy and the modeling of innovative programs.
Fields of interest: Reproductive health; Reproductive health, family planning; Family services, single parents; International human rights; Civil/human rights; Community/economic development; Leadership development.
International interests: Guatemala; Israel; Latin America.
Type of support: General/operating support; Continuing support; Income development; Management development/capacity building; Endowments; Emergency funds; Program development; Conferences/seminars; Seed money; Technical assistance; Program evaluation; Program-related investments/loans; In-kind gifts; Matching/challenge support.
Limitations: Applications not accepted. Giving nationally and internationally in the United States and Israel. Giving for the Economic Justice Program focuses on Washington, DC, MD and VA. No support for lobbying or political campaigns, private foundations, or arts organizations. No grants to individuals, or for medical research.
Publications: Grants list; Program policy statement.
Application information: The Moriah Fund will no longer accept or review unsolicited proposals. This new policy, a result of the current economic situation and decline in Moriah's assets, is intended to save organizations the work of preparing proposals that cannot be funded. As Moriah determines new strategies, policies and plans, the foundation will keep you updated on the website. In the meantime, grantmaking will continue on an invitation-only basis.
  Board meeting date(s): May and Nov.
Officers and Program Board:* Mary Ann Stein,* Pres.; Barbara Schrirfer, C.F.O.; Craig Cramer; Debra Delee; Jane Fox Johnson; Kim Jones; Judith Lichtman; Norman Rosenberg; Gideon Stein; Noah Stein; Dorothy Swamy.
Number of staff: 8 full-time professional; 1 part-time professional; 3 full-time support.
EIN: 311129589

Recent grants for international programs:
562-1 ActionAid USA, Washington, DC, $20,000. For ActionAid Haiti's Grain Processing Plant Project, which will provide food for the growing population in the Grand-Anse region, and increase the income of participating farmers by 40 percent. 2010.
562-2 American Jewish World Service, New York, NY, $10,000. For Pakistan Flood Relief project, which is providing desperately needed services to people affected by flooding. 2010.
562-3 Americans for Peace Now, Washington, DC, $25,000. For general support of this

organization, which seeks to support Israel's grassroots peace movement, Shalom Achshav (Peace Now), and bolster support for peace among Israelis, the Palestinians and Arab states in order to enhance Israel's security and bring stability to the Middle East. 2010.
562-4 Asylum Access, San Francisco, CA, $35,000. For general support of this organization, which advocates for the rights of refugees - particularly female refugees - through direct legal services and through policy advocacy at the national and international levels. 2010.
562-5 Better World Fund, Washington, DC, $25,000. For project, RH Reality Check, which seeks (a) to foster evidence-based coverage in the online, broadcast, and print media of sexual and reproductive rights, health and justice issues; (b) provide rapid response to distortions of these issues; and (c) offer a platform through which members of the reproductive and sexual health communities can share ideas. 2010.
562-6 Catholics for a Free Choice, Washington, DC, $20,000. For the Instancia por la Salud y el Desarrollo de las Mujeres (Alliance for Women's Health and Development), which educates policymakers, health officials, advocates and the public about policies to improve women's health in Guatemala. 2010.
562-7 Center for Health and Gender Equity, Washington, DC, $60,000. For general support of this organization, which seeks to ensure that U.S. policy and funding levels promote and advance women's sexual and reproductive health and rights. 2010.
562-8 Center for International Environmental Law, Washington, DC, $45,000. For Empowering Indigenous Communities Affected by Mining in Guatemala project, which provides legal counsel and services and international campaign support to indigenous communities affected by the Marlin goldmine, as well as to those challenging other proposed mines in the Guatemala Highlands. 2010.
562-9 Doctors Without Borders USA, New York, NY, $35,000. For Emergency Relief Fund, which allows MSF to flexibly respond to critical humanitarian needs, including those that may not be receiving public or media attention. 2010.
562-10 Doctors Without Borders USA, New York, NY, $25,000. For Emergency Relief Fund, which allows MSF to flexibly respond to critical humanitarian needs, including those that may not be receiving public or media attention. 2010.
562-11 Fondo Centroamericano de Mujeres, Managua, Nicaragua, $30,000. For general support of this organization, which provides direct grants to women's organizations in Central America that are committed to advancing women's human rights. 2010.
562-12 Freedom Now, Washington, DC, $20,000. For general support of this organization, which promotes respect for human rights worldwide by working to free prisoners of conscience through targeted legal, political and public relations advocacy efforts. 2010.
562-13 Fund for Global Human Rights, Washington, DC, $450,000. For general support of this organization, which provides funding to local human rights organizations around the world. 2010.
562-14 Fund for Global Human Rights, Washington, DC, $365,500. For fundraising and communication project, which seeks to increase

donor base and improve communication strategy. 2010.

562-15 Fund for Global Human Rights, Washington, DC, $85,000. For project to advance resource rights in Guatemala, that is, for efforts to ensure that mining and other development strategies respect the human rights of individuals and communities in rural Guatemala. 2010.

562-16 Fund for Global Human Rights, Washington, DC, $50,000. For general support of Centro Mujeres (CM), community health and rights organization dedicated to fostering empowerment and well-being of women, adolescents and migrant workers; providing community health education and leadership training; and advocating for changes in policies and programs that promote respect for reproductive and sexual rights in Baja California Sur, Mexico. 2010.

562-17 Fund for Global Human Rights, Washington, DC, $30,000. For Minga Peru, which produces educational radio programs and trains a network of community promoters to provide culturally appropriate health and income generation education in indigenous communities in the Peruvian Amazon. 2010.

562-18 Human Rights First, New York, NY, $25,000. For general support of this organization, which seeks to promote effective and principled U.S. human rights policies at home and abroad, to expand the rule of law, and ensure the dignity to which every individual is entitled. 2010.

562-19 Human Rights Watch, New York, NY, $30,000. For Women's Rights Division, which seeks to assist women in the fight for their rights and end widespread impunity for violence and discrimination against them. 2010.

562-20 Institute for Policy Studies, Washington, DC, $125,000. For Promoting Resource Rights in the Global Economy Project, which seeks to advance resource rights within the global economic system, bringing together advocates, activists and funders across silos and disciplines to identify and promote successful strategies to enforce these human rights within global economic institutions. 2010.

562-21 International Center for Research on Women, Washington, DC, $25,000. For general support of this organization, which seeks to empower women, advance gender equality and fight poverty in the developing world. 2010.

562-22 International Labor Rights Forum, Washington, DC, $20,000. For general support of this organization, which is dedicated to achieving just and humane treatment for workers worldwide. 2010.

562-23 International Rescue Committee, New York, NY, $40,000. For the IRC's Women's Refugee Commission, and specifically, for its Detention and Asylum Program, which promotes reforms in U.S. law, policy and practice to ensure human rights protections for women, children, and families who are fleeing persecution and seeking asylum. 2010.

562-24 International Rescue Committee, New York, NY, $33,000. For Pakistan Flood Relief, to provide hygiene, water supplies, and other relief to people affected by the recent floods in Pakistan. 2010.

562-25 International Rivers Network, Berkeley, CA, $25,000. For Mesoamerica Program, which works with communities in Central America and Mexico that are affected by dams, helping them to oppose socially and environmentally destructive mega-projects and to propose alternative development plans. 2010.

562-26 Latin America Working Group Education Fund, Washington, DC, $35,000. For general support of this organization, which seeks to promote human rights in U.S. foreign policy toward Latin America. 2010.

562-27 Law Students for Reproductive Justice, Oakland, CA, $30,000. For general support of this organization, which seeks to develop legal expertise and leadership for the future of reproductive freedom in the US and around the world. 2010.

562-28 Network in Solidarity with the People of Guatemala, Oakland, CA, $50,000. For general support of this organization, which supports human rights and social and economic justice in Guatemala and promotes a U.S. policy that supports these goals. 2010.

562-29 New Israel Fund, Washington, DC, $380,000. For general support of this organization, which seeks to promote democratic change and advance social justice and equality for all Israelis. 2010.

562-30 New Israel Fund, Washington, DC, $300,000. For The Israel Center for Educational Innovation (ICEI) for its Netanya and Petach Tikvah Initiatives, to raise literacy achievement levels of students in elementary schools with high concentrations of Ethiopian pupils, to strengthen school management and leadership, and to increase parental involvement in the life of the school and their children's learning. 2010.

562-31 New Israel Fund, Washington, DC, $195,000. For NIF's Core Grants Program, which provides institution-building grants to social change organizations working to strengthen democracy and promote social and economic justice in Israel. NIF proposes the use of Moriah funds to fulfill its commitments to the following organizations: (a) Adalah ($40,000), (b) The Arab Center for Law and Policy ($10,000), (c) Association for Civil Rights in Israel ($125,000), (d) Machsom Watch ($20,000). 2010.

562-32 New Israel Fund, Washington, DC, $160,000. For Shatil, which works to empower and marginalized communities to realize their rights and play active role in determining policies that affect their lives; Shatil provides technical support to hundreds of NGOs and operates independent projects to build capacity in specific sectors of civil society. 2010.

562-33 New Israel Fund, Washington, DC, $150,000. For NIF's Palestinian Society Program which provides grants to organizations working to promote equality and justice for the Palestinian minority in Israel. 2010.

562-34 New Israel Fund, Washington, DC, $115,000. For Shatil's Assistance to Ethiopian Immigrants Project, which trains Ethiopian Israelis to assume leadership positions in and take responsibility for their communities. 2010.

562-35 New Israel Fund, Washington, DC, $110,000. For FIDEL: The Association for Education and Social Integration for Ethiopian Jews in Israel, which works to strengthen and expand mediation, empowerment, and advocacy services for the Ethiopian community. 2010.

562-36 New Israel Fund, Washington, DC, $100,000. For The Israel Center for Educational Innovation (ICEI), which is now operating in 13 schools in three cities, to raise literacy achievement levels of students in elementary schools with high concentrations of Ethiopian pupils, to strengthen school management and leadership, and to increase parental involvement in the life of the school and their children's learning. 2010.

562-37 New Israel Fund, Washington, DC, $80,000. For the Israel Association for Ethiopian Jews (IAEJ), which advocates for community empowerment initiatives for improved education and employment policies for Ethiopian Israelis. 2010.

562-38 New Israel Fund, Washington, DC, $75,000. For Proactive Media Campaign to Promote a Positive Image of NIF and Values, a positive media campaign designed to respond to the troubling atmosphere of repression that has been mounting in Israel in recent months. The campaign will seek to promote NIF's core values and regain legitimacy for NIF as a positive force for change. 2010.

562-39 New Israel Fund, Washington, DC, $60,000. For Shatil's Palestinian Initiative, which augments NIF's grantmaking to Israel's Palestinian communities through consulting, training and proactive support for vital voices in the Palestinian community. Shatil's advocacy efforts bring the needs of the Palestinian community directly to the top echelons of the government, demanding the democratic rights Israel's Palestinian citizens are guaranteed by law. 2010.

562-40 New Israel Fund, Washington, DC, $45,000. For South Wing to Zion (SWZ), which is the leading advocate for the continued immigration to Israel of the Remnant of Israel (the Falash Mura), and which helps Ethiopian Immigrants in their initial integration into Israeli society. 2010.

562-41 New Israel Fund, Washington, DC, $40,000. For Bimkom - Planners for Planning Rights, organization of urban and municipal planners that supports the planning rights of disadvantaged communities. 2010.

562-42 New Israel Fund, Washington, DC, $40,000. For Mossawa Center: The Advocacy Center for Arabs in Israel, and specifically for this organization's Socio-Economic Justice and Economic Development Program. 2010.

562-43 New Israel Fund, Washington, DC, $40,000. For NISPED: Hirakuna the Forum for Social Solidarity and Community Voluntarism for Young Leadership, a coalition of eight Arab and Jewish-Arab NGOs to advance public support within the government and Palestinian leadership in Israel for leadership development and volunteer programs for young adults aged 18-22 in Arab communities in Israel. 2010.

562-44 New Israel Fund, Washington, DC, $40,000. For Shatil's Social and Economic Initiative (SEJI), which aims to enable marginalized populations to avoid and escape poverty and reduce the gap between rich and poor in Israel by promoting policy changes, encouraging participatory democracy and advancing alternative forms of economic development. 2010.

562-45 New Israel Fund, Washington, DC, $40,000. For Tebeka: The Center for Legal Aid and Advocacy for Ethiopian-Israelis, which works to protect the legal rights of Ethiopian Israelis and to nurture a cadre of young Ethiopian Israeli leaders in the field of law. 2010.

562-46 New Israel Fund, Washington, DC, $35,000. For Breaking the Silence (BTS) for its project, Soldiers Speak Out, which collects, verifies, edits and publishes soldiers testimonies about their service in the Occupied Territories, to break the silence and educate Israelis about the nature of the occupation. 2010.

562-47 New Israel Fund, Washington, DC, $30,000. For Agenda -The Israel Center for Strategic Communications, which seeks to influence the way social change issues are presented in the media, to improve the media capacity of social change organizations, and to serve as information dissemination hub for monitoring, research and analysis of social change topics. 2010.

562-48 New Israel Fund, Washington, DC, $30,000. For Sawt el-Amel - The Laborer's Voice, and specifically for its Grassroots Organizing Forum (GOF), including its Alternative Wisconsin Center, Women's Platform and Young Workers Platform. 2010.

562-49 New Israel Fund, Washington, DC, $30,000. For Women Against Violence (WAV), which concentrates on policy change for the advancement of Palestinian women citizens of Israel. 2010.

562-50 New Israel Fund, Washington, DC, $30,000. For Yesh Din (There is Law), which seeks to create long-term structural improvement in the human rights situation in the Occupied Palestinian Territories through documentation of abuses, legal action and raising public awareness. 2010.

562-51 New Israel Fund, Washington, DC, $25,000. For Alnuhud (reaching up/renewal): the Association to Promote Education for Bedouin Women in the Negev for its efforts to promote higher education for Bedouin girls and women. 2010.

562-52 New Israel Fund, Washington, DC, $25,000. For Ir Amim, for its efforts to shape policy to meet the needs of both peoples sharing Jerusalem and to minimize the damage caused by unilateral actions such as the construction of the separation barrier, and the expansion of settlements in East Jerusalem and in the Old City's historic basin. 2010.

562-53 New Israel Fund, Washington, DC, $25,000. For National Budget Reform Project (NBRP), which seeks to address the lack of accountability and transparency in social, economic and financial matters, especially in relation to the approval process for the annual State budget. 2010.

562-54 New Israel Fund, Washington, DC, $25,000. For Sidreh to promote the development and advancement of Bedouin women in the Negev through education and business projects. 2010.

562-55 New Israel Fund, Washington, DC, $20,000. For Al Manarah (The Lighthouse) for its advocacy work for rights and accessibility to services for blind and other disabled people in Israel's Palestinian community. 2010.

562-56 New Israel Fund, Washington, DC, $20,000. For Ma'an for its Forum of Negev Bedouin Women's Organizations. 2010.

562-57 New Israel Fund, Washington, DC, $20,000. For Olim Together-Leadership and Employment Excellence, for its program to find and place Ethiopian-Israeli graduates and students in employment suitable to their education and abilities. 2010.

562-58 New Israel Fund, Washington, DC, $20,000. For Sikkuy: The Association for the Advancement of Civic Equality, for its Intervention and Monitoring of the Government of Israel's five-year Economic Development Plan for the Arab community in Israel. 2010.

562-59 New Israel Fund, Washington, DC, $20,000. For Step Forward, for its Bedouin Women Community Based Economic Leadership Project. 2010.

562-60 New Israel Fund, Washington, DC, $20,000. For the Hotline for Migrant Workers for the project: Safeguarding Rights for Asylum Seekers. 2010.

562-61 New Israel Fund, Washington, DC, $10,000. For Ir Amim to counter a libel suit by the Elad organization, related to Ir Amim report about Elad's activities in East Jerusalem. 2010.

562-62 New Israel Fund, Washington, DC, $10,000. For Merchavim, for its program Teaching Across School Streams, designed to promote national integration of Arab Israeli teachers in the Jewish school system in Israel; and for Let's Talk language and shared citizenship education programs in Israel's Jewish school system. 2010.

562-63 New Israel Fund, Washington, DC, $10,000. For the Israel AIDS Task Force for its project: HIV/AIDS Prevention and Treatment-Spotlight on the Ethiopian Community. 2010.

562-64 North American Conference on Ethiopian Jewry, New York, NY, $35,000. For school program for Ethiopian Jewish children in the NACOEJ Community Primary School in Gondar, Ethiopia, including the lunch program, and for extension of the feeding program for children ages 0-3 to children ages 4-6. 2010.

562-65 Palestinian Human Rights Monitoring Group, Los Angeles, CA, $25,000. For general support of this organization, which works to end violations of human rights committed against Palestinians in the West Bank, Gaza Strip and East Jerusalem, whether committed by Palestinian or Israeli agencies or individuals. 2010.

562-66 Refugees International, Washington, DC, $30,000. For general support of this organization, which generates life saving humanitarian assistance and protection for displaced people around the world, and which works to end the conditions that create displacement. 2010.

562-67 San Miguel - CASA, Austin, TX, $50,000. For general support of this organization, which raises funds for the Centro para los Adolescentes de San Miguel de Allende (CASA); CASA trains peer promoters and develops young leaders, operates Mexico's first nationally accredited midwifery college, and provides reproductive health services and education in the state of Guanajuato, Mexico. 2010.

562-68 Universities Allied for Essential Medicines, Berkeley, CA, $25,000. For general support of this organization, which seeks to promote access to medicines for people in developing countries by changing norms and practices on university patenting and licensing; encourage development of treatments for neglected diseases that disproportionately affect the poorest patients in the world; and empower students to respond to the access and innovation crisis. 2010.

562-69 University of California Hastings College of Law, San Francisco, CA, $30,000. For Center for Gender and Refugee Studies, which works to advance women's human rights by protecting women and girls seeking asylum in the U.S. while simultaneously addressing the systemic gender-based human rights abuses that force them to flee their home countries. 2010.

562-70 Urgent Action Fund for Womens Human Rights, Boulder, CO, $20,000. For general support of this organization, which promotes the human rights of women and girls through rapid response grantmaking; research and publications about women in conflict areas; and collaborative programs to promote women's participation in conflict prevention and resolution, peace building, and post-conflict reconstruction. 2010.

562-71 Washington Office on Latin America, Washington, DC, $30,000. For general support of this organization, which promotes human rights, democracy, and social justice by working with partners in Latin America and the Caribbean to shape policies in the US and abroad. 2010.

562-72 Womens Link Worldwide, Northfield, VT, $30,000. For general support of this organization, which is dedicated to advancing women's rights, with a special focus on sexual and reproductive rights, gender violence, and gender discrimination, through the development and strategic implementation of human rights law worldwide. 2010.

562-73 World Organization for Human Rights USA, Washington, DC, $40,000. For general support of this organization, which uses litigation to advance compliance with international human rights norms in the U.S. and to protect refugees from gender-based violence. 2010.

563
Mosaic Foundation USA

730 11th St., N.W., Ste. 302
Washington, DC 20001-4580   (202) 388-0000
FAX: (202) 388-0061;
E-mail: grants@mosaicfound.org; URL: http://www.mosaicfound.org

Established in 1997.

Grantmaker type: Public charity.

Financial data (yr. ended 09/30/08): Revenue, $1,659,712; assets, $2,737,765 (M); gifts received, $1,563,187; expenditures, $1,769,193; program services expenses, $1,315,030; giving activities include $633,500 for grants, and $681,530 for foundation-administered programs.

Purpose and activities: The organization aims to make a positive difference in the lives of women and children, while promoting awareness, understanding, and appreciation between the peoples of the Arab world and the United States through its charitable, humanitarian, and cultural involvement in both regions.

Fields of interest: International relief; International exchange, arts; International exchange; Children; Women.

Application information:
  Initial approach: Download letter of intent form
  Deadline(s): Apr. 17, Aug. 1, and Nov. 13 for letter of intent, and May 17, Sept. 1, and Dec. 13 for proposals for Trustees Grants
  Final notification: Jan. 30, June 30, and Oct. 17 for Trustees Grants

Officers and Trustees:* Nermin Fahmy,* Chair. and Pres.; Nevine Hassouna,* V.P., Progs. and Public Outreach; Ilse Kherbi,* V.P., Planning and Financial Affairs; Rafif Al-Sayed Moustapha,* Secy.; Kathleen El Maaroufi,* Treas.; Cherifa Bennammour Al-Balooshi; Sheikha Rima Al-Sabah; Amina Farah

Olhaye; Nichole Shedid; Princess Sarah Zeid; and 7 additional trustees.
Number of staff: 5 full-time professional; 1 part-time professional; 1 full-time support.
EIN: 432109703

564
American Society of the Most Venerable Order of Hospital of St. John of Jerusalem
1875 K St., N.W., Ste. 603
Washington, DC 20006-1251 (202) 510-9691
Contact: Barbara Hayward, Exec Dir.
FAX: (202) 822-0040;
E-mail: prioryusa@saintjohn.org; NY tel.: (212) 753-5544; URL: http://www.saintjohn.org

Established in 1962; supporting organization of the Order of St. John in London and the St. John Eye Hospital in Jerusalem.
Grantmaker type: Public charity.
Financial data (yr. ended 12/31/10): Revenue, $1,560,006; assets, $1,815,311 (M); gifts received, $1,425,260; expenditures, $1,681,733; giving activities include $9,040 for grants, and $983,069 for grants to organizations outside the U.S.
Purpose and activities: The society seeks to encourage, promote, and support, financially and otherwise, all works of humanity and charity for the relief of persons in sickness, distress, suffering and danger, without distinction as to race, class or creed; the principle beneficiaries of the society's support are the Order of St. John in London and the St. John Eye Hospital in Jerusalem.
Fields of interest: Hospitals (general); Eye diseases; Catholic agencies & churches.
International interests: England; Middle East.
Type of support: In-kind gifts.
Limitations: Applications not accepted. Giving on a national and international basis.
Application information: Contributes only to pre-selected organizations.
Officers: Suzanne P. Bishorric, Chancellor; Allen Curtis Greer II, Esq., Vice-Chancellor; Guy Stair Sainty, Esq., Vice-Chancellor; Barbara Hayward, Secy. and Exec. Dir.; A. Marshall Acuff, Jr., Treas.
EIN: 136161455

565
Stewart R. Mott Foundation
(formerly Stewart R. Mott Charitable Trust)
122 Maryland Ave. N.E.
Washington, DC 20002-5610
Contact: Conrad Martin, Exec. Dir.
FAX: (202) 543-3156; E-mail: info@srmtrust.org;
URL: http://www.srmtrust.org

Trust established in 1968 in NY; reorganized in 1989 in NY.
Donors: Stewart R. Mott†; Ruth R. Mott†.
Grantmaker type: Independent foundation.
Financial data (yr. ended 12/31/09): Assets, $0 (M); expenditures, $2,154,431; qualifying distributions, $2,086,484; giving activities include $1,649,000 for 41 grants (high: $1,000,000; low: $100).
Purpose and activities: The foundation funds organizations with small general operating grants. Areas of interest are those shared by Stewart Mott and the trustees. These include: peace, arms

control and foreign policy; population issues and reproductive rights; government reform and public policy; and civil rights and civil liberties.
Fields of interest: Reproductive health, family planning; International peace/security; International affairs, arms control; International affairs, foreign policy; International human rights; Civil/human rights; Government/public administration; Public affairs.
Type of support: General/operating support.
Limitations: Applications accepted. Giving primarily in the U.S. with emphasis on Washington, DC and internationally. Generally, no support for local, regional, grassroots efforts, or ethnic-specific organizations. No grants to individuals, or for emergency support, conferences, media/arts projects or exchange programs.
Publications: Application guidelines.
Application information: The trust accepts the Common Grant Application of the National Network of Grantmakers. See foundation web site for application guidelines and procedures.
  Initial approach: Proposal
  Deadline(s): None
  Board meeting date(s): 4 to 6 meetings per year
Officer: Conrad Martin, Exec. Dir.
Trustees: Stewart R. Mott; Kappy J. Wells.
Number of staff: 2 full-time professional; 1 part-time professional.
EIN: 237002554

566
The Mountain Institute, Inc.
3000 Connecticut Ave., N.W., Ste. 138
Washington, DC 20008-2549 (202) 234-4050
Contact: Robert M. Davis, Pres. and C.E.O.
E-mail: summit@mountain.org; URL: http://www.mountain.org/

Established in 1971.
Grantmaker type: Public charity.
Financial data (yr. ended 09/30/10): Revenue, $3,121,670; assets, $3,059,078 (M); gifts received, $2,728,831; expenditures, $4,152,925; giving activities include $1,280,224 for grants to organizations outside the U.S.
Purpose and activities: The institute's general focus is program delivery with partners in mountain regions around the world. Its organizational mission is to develop mountain livelihoods, conserve mountain environments and support mountain cultures.
Fields of interest: Environment; Environment, beautification programs; Environment, forests; Environmental education; International development.
Limitations: Applications not accepted. Giving on a national and international basis. No grants to individuals.
Application information: Unsolicited requests for funds not considered or acknowledged.
Officers and Board Members:* Joseph D. Teplitz,* Chair.; Elsie Walker,* Vice-Chair.; Robert M. Davis,* Pres. and C.E.O.; Jim Underwood,* Secy.; Eliot Kalter,* Treas.; Ted Armbrecht; Jack Bluestein; Walt Coward; Pauline Danino; Lee Elman; Jane Farmer; Indira Mansingh; Gail Percy; Robert Reynolds; Robert Rhoades; David Sloan; Harvey Sloane.
Number of staff: 50
EIN: 550541323

567
NAFSA: Association of International Educators
1307 New York Ave., N.W., 8th Fl.
Washington, DC 20005-4701 (202) 737-3699
Contact: Marlene M. Johnson, C.E.O. and Exec. Dir.
FAX: (202) 737-3657; E-mail: inbox@nafsa.org;
URL: http://www.nafsa.org

Established in 1948 in DC.
Grantmaker type: Public charity.
Financial data (yr. ended 12/31/09): Revenue, $13,395,168; assets, $10,628,828 (M); gifts received, $4,367,973; expenditures, $13,743,697; program services expenses, $9,745,132; giving activities include $28,000 for grants to organizations outside the U.S.
Purpose and activities: The association promotes the exchange of students and scholars to and from the U.S. NAFSA also offers conferences, publications, and training for international educators.
Fields of interest: Higher education; Education; International exchange.
Type of support: Program development; Seed money.
Limitations: Applications accepted. Giving on a national basis. No grants to individuals.
Publications: Application guidelines; Annual report; Multi-year report.
Application information: Application form required.
  Initial approach: Download application form
  Copies of proposal: 8
  Deadline(s): Aug. 11 for APPP; Sept. 22 for ETS Excellence Awards
  Board meeting date(s): Varies
Officers and Directors:* Marlene M. Johnson, C.E.O. and Exec. Dir.; Meredith M. McQuaid,* J.D., Pres. and Chair.; Sherif Barsoum,* V.P., Public Policy and Practice; Susan Thompson,* V.P., Member Rels.; Deborah L. Pierce, Ph.D., V.P., Ed. and Professional Devel.; William P. Newman, Jr., C.F.O.; Charles A. S. Bankart, Ph.D., Secy.; Lars Heikensten, Ph.D., Treas.; Fanta Aw, Ph.D.; and 9 additional directors.
EIN: 131878953

568
National Council for International Visitors
1420 K St. N.W., Ste. 800
Washington, DC 20005-2500 (202) 842-1414
FAX: (202) 289-4625; E-mail: info@nciv.org;
URL: http://www.nciv.org/

Established in 1961.
Grantmaker type: Public charity.
Financial data (yr. ended 09/30/10): Revenue, $5,700,628; assets, $881,240 (M); gifts received, $5,651,827; expenditures, $5,630,908; giving activities include $4,141,783 for grants.
Purpose and activities: The council promotes excellence in citizen diplomacy, and serves as a professional association for the international exchange community.
Fields of interest: International affairs; International exchange.
Limitations: Applications not accepted. Giving on a national basis. No support for non-members.
Publications: Annual report; Informational brochure.
Application information: Contributes only to pre-selected organizations.
  Board meeting date(s): Feb., July, and Nov.

Officers and Board Members:* Lawrence J. Chastang,* Chair.; Al Durtka,* 1st Vice-Chair.; Carol Engebretson Byrne,* 2nd Vice-Chair.; Sherry L. Mueller, Pres.; Carina Black,* Ph.D., Secy.; Laura Dupuy,* Treas.; Chris Ajemian; Quincy Carter; Tarik S. Daoud; Karen de Bartolome; Nancy Gilboy; Eurica Huggins-Axum; Jerrold Keilson; Kyle Moyer; Peter C. Simpson; Samuel "Sandy" B. Sterrett, Jr.
EIN: 520848094

569
National Democratic Institute for International Affairs

2030 M St., N.W., 5th Fl.
Washington, DC 20036-3341 (202) 728-5500
FAX: (202) 728-5520; URL: http://www.ndi.org

Grantmaker type: Public charity.
Financial data (yr. ended 09/30/10): Revenue, $130,207,368; assets, $20,800,462 (M); gifts received, $130,328,641; expenditures, $130,086,031; giving activities include $4,070,904 for grants, and $9,428,240 for grants to organizations outside the U.S.
Purpose and activities: The institute works to strengthen and expand democracy worldwide.
Fields of interest: International democracy & civil society development.
Officers and Directors:* Madeleine K. Albright,* Chair.; Rachelle Horowitz,* Vice-Chair.; Marc B. Nathanson,* Vice-Chair.; Kenneth D. Wollack,* Pres.; Kenneth F. Melley,* Secy.; Eugene Eideneberg,* Treas.; Bernard W. Aronson; J. Brian Atwood; Hon. Harriet C. Babbitt; Elizabeth Frawley Bagley; and 30 additional directors.
EIN: 521338892

570
National Endowment for Democracy

1025 F St., N.W., Ste. 800
Washington, DC 20004-1432 (202) 378-9700
Contact: Carl Gershman, Pres.
FAX: (202) 378-9407; E-mail: info@ned.org; E-mail for fellowship inf.: fellowships@ned.org;
URL: http://www.ned.org
Facebook: http://www.facebook.com/National.Endowment.for.Democracy
Twitter: http://twitter.com/nedemocracy

Established in 1983 in DC.
Grantmaker type: Public charity.
Financial data (yr. ended 09/30/10): Revenue, $136,692,723; assets, $108,149,741 (M); gifts received, $136,450,471; expenditures, $136,760,415; program services expenses, $114,489,282; giving activities include $64,432,522 for grants, and $50,056,760 for grants to organizations outside the U.S.
Purpose and activities: The endowment seeks to strengthen democratic institutions (including political parties and business, labor, civic, education, media, human rights, and other groups that are working for democratic goals) around the world through nongovernmental efforts.
Fields of interest: International democracy & civil society development; International affairs, goodwill promotion.
Type of support: Program development; Fellowships.
Limitations: Applications accepted. Giving on an international basis, with emphasis on Africa, Asia,

Central and Eastern Europe, Latin America, the Middle East, and the former Soviet Union. No grants to individuals.
Publications: Application guidelines; Annual report; Informational brochure.
Application information: Application form not required.
Initial approach: Proposal
Deadline(s): Jan. 20 for proposals
Board meeting date(s): Jan. 13, Mar. 30, June 15, and Sept. 7
Officers and Directors:* Hon. Richard A. Gephardt,* Chair.; Dr. Judy Shelton,* Vice-Chair.; Carl Gershman,* Pres.; Dr. Robert Miller,* Secy.; Robert H. Tuttle,* Treas.; John Bohn; Norm Coleman; Rita DiMartino; Hon. Kenneth M. Duberstein; Patricia S. Friend; Dr. Francis Fukuyama; Dr. William A. Galston; and 14 additional directors.
EIN: 521344831

571
National Peace Corps Association

1900 L St., N.W., Ste. 205
Washington, DC 20036-5028 (202) 293-7728
FAX: (202) 293-7554; E-mail: npca@rpcv.org;
URL: http://www.rpcv.org

Established in 1983 in NC.
Grantmaker type: Public charity.
Financial data (yr. ended 12/31/10): Revenue, $1,447,984; assets, $704,620 (M); gifts received, $928,375; expenditures, $1,573,185; giving activities include $2,000 for grants to organizations outside the U.S., and $1,360 for grants to individuals.
Purpose and activities: The mission of the association is to lead the Peace Corps community and others to foster peace by working together in service, education, and advocacy.
Fields of interest: International peace/security.
Type of support: Grants to individuals.
Publications: Application guidelines.
Application information: Application form required.
Initial approach: Submit application
Deadline(s): June 3 for Global Community Project Competition
Final notification: July 15 for Global Community Project Competition
Officers and Directors:* Jan Guifarro,* Chair.; Chris Glaudel,* Vice-Chair.; Sharon Stash,* Secy.; Bruce Anderson,* Treas.; Frances Holliday Alford; Betty Currie; Don Dakin; Robert A. Findlay; and 11 additional directors.
EIN: 581431113

572
National Press Foundation, Inc.

1211 Connecticut Ave., N.W., Ste. 310
Washington, DC 20036-2709 (202) 663-7280
Contact: Nolan Walters, Dir., Progs.
E-mail: npf@nationalpress.org; E-mail for Nolan Walters: nolan@nationalpress.org; URL: http://www.nationalpress.org/index.htm
Facebook: http://www.facebook.com/NationalPressFoundation
Flickr: http://www.flickr.com/photos/nationalpress
Foundation blog: http://nationalpress.org/blogs/
Twitter: http://twitter.com/#!/natpress
YouTube: http://www.youtube.com/NTLPressFoundation

Established in 1975 in DC.
Grantmaker type: Public charity.
Financial data (yr. ended 12/31/10): Revenue, $1,208,145; assets, $3,095,361 (M); gifts received, $1,255,830; expenditures, $1,189,617.
Purpose and activities: The foundation is dedicated to the professional development of working print and broadcast journalists; pursues an agenda of topical forums, seminars, and fellowships for journalists; and confers national awards that recognize high standards of excellence.
Fields of interest: Media/communications; Media, print publishing.
Type of support: Fellowships; Grants to individuals.
Limitations: Applications accepted. Giving limited to Washington, DC, and Canada.
Publications: Application guidelines; Annual report; Financial statement; Informational brochure; Occasional report.
Application information:
Initial approach: Submit application
Deadline(s): June 30 for Evert Clark/Seth Payne Award for Young Science Writers; Oct. 17 for The "Feddie" Award for Reporting on Federal Rules and Local Impact; varies for all others
Officers and Directors:* Gerald Seib,* Chair.; John Walcott,* Vice-Chair.; Bob Meyers,* Pres.; Kathy Gest,* Secy.; Johanna Schneider,* Treas.; Jeffrey Birnbaum; Jim Brady; Peter Cherukuri; George Condon; Karen Doyne; Kevin M. Goldberg; Imani Greene; Melinda Henneberger; Sandy Johnson; Susan Swain; and 8 additional directors.
Number of staff: 5
EIN: 521069481

573
New Mighty Foundation

c/o Stephen K. Vetter
1666 K St., N.W., Ste. 400
Washington, DC 20006-1219 (202) 457-7200
Contact: George Harris

Established in 2007 in DC.
Donors: New Mighty US Trust; Goldman Sachs.
Grantmaker type: Operating foundation.
Financial data (yr. ended 12/31/10): Assets, $30,123,601 (M); expenditures, $29,199,919; qualifying distributions, $29,177,945; giving activities include $29,177,945 for 57 grants (high: $1,423,000; low: $51,290).
Fields of interest: Education.
Limitations: Giving primarily in China.
Application information:
Initial approach: Letter of pre-grant inquiry
Deadline(s): None
Officer: Wen-Hsiung Hung, Chair.
Directors: Sandy R.Y. Wang; Susan R.H. Wang; Wilfred Wang; William H. Wong.
EIN: 204282979
Recent grants for international programs:
573-1 Anhui Provincial Department of Education, Hefei, China, $1,423,000. For school contribution. 2010.
573-2 Anhui Provincial Department of Education, Hefei, China, $826,000. For school contribution. 2010.
573-3 Anhui Provincial Department of Education, Hefei, China, $465,000. For school contribution. 2010.
573-4 Anhui Provincial Department of Education, Hefei, China, $228,000. For school contribution. 2010.

573-5 Chongqing Education Commission, Chongqing, China, $356,000. For school contribution. 2010.

573-6 Chongqing Education Commission, Chongqing, China, $294,000. For school contribution. 2010.

573-7 Department of Education Jiangsu Province, Nanjing City, China, $162,000. For school contribution. 2010.

573-8 Department of Education of Guizhou Province, Guiyang City, China, $438,000. For school contribution. 2010.

573-9 Education Bureau of Qinghai Province, Xining, China, $779,500. For school contribution. 2010.

573-10 Education Bureau of Qinghai Province, Xining, China, $463,000. For school contribution. 2010.

573-11 Education Department of Henan Province, Zhengzhou, China, $722,000. For school contribution. 2010.

573-12 Education Department of Henan Province, Zhengzhou, China, $533,000. For school contribution. 2010.

573-13 Education Department of Henan Province, Zhengzhou, China, $296,000. For school contribution. 2010.

573-14 Education Department of Inner Mongolia Autonomous Region, Hohhot, China, $198,500. For school contribution. 2010.

573-15 Education Department of Inner Mongolia Autonomous Region, Hohhot, China, $176,500. For school contribution. 2010.

573-16 Education Department of Liaoning Province, Shenyang, China, $467,000. For school contribution. 2010.

573-17 Education Department of Liaoning Province, Shenyang, China, $368,500. For school contribution. 2010.

573-18 Education Department of Ningxia Hui Autonomous Region, Yinchuan, China, $593,000. For school contribution. 2010.

573-19 Education Department of Ningxia Hui Autonomous Region, Yinchuan, China, $238,000. For school contribution. 2010.

573-20 Education Department of Zhejiang Province, Hangzhou City, China, $99,500. For school contribution. 2010.

573-21 Hebei Education Department, Shijanzhuang City, China, $925,000. 2010.

573-22 Hebei Education Department, Shijanzhuang City, China, $760,000. For school contribution. 2010.

573-23 Hebei Education Department, Shijanzhuang City, China, $681,000. For school contribution. 2010.

573-24 Hebei Education Department, Shijanzhuang City, China, $336,500. For school contribution. 2010.

573-25 Heilongjiang Provincial Education Department, Harbin, China, $793,000. For school contribution. 2010.

573-26 Heilongjiang Provincial Education Department, Harbin, China, $690,000. For school contribution. 2010.

573-27 Heilongjiang Provincial Education Department, Harbin, China, $51,290. For school contribution. 2010.

573-28 Hubei Education Foundation, Wuhan, China, $962,000. For school contribution. 2010.

573-29 Hubei Education Foundation, Wuhan, China, $904,500. For school contribution. 2010.

573-30 Hubei Education Foundation, Wuhan, China, $183,500. For school contribution. 2010.

573-31 Hunan Provincial Education Department, Changsha, China, $1,288,000. For school contribution. 2010.

573-32 Hunan Provincial Education Department, Changsha, China, $686,500. For school contribution. 2010.

573-33 Hunan Provincial Education Department, Changsha, China, $379,500. For school contribution. 2010.

573-34 Jiangxi Provincial Department of Education, Nanchang, China, $760,000. For school contribution. 2010.

573-35 Jiangxi Provincial Department of Education, Nanchang, China, $573,000. For school contribution. 2010.

573-36 Jiangxi Provincial Department of Education, Nanchang, China, $305,000. For school contribution. 2010.

573-37 Jilin Provincial Education Department, Changchun, China, $474,000. For school contribution. 2010.

573-38 Jilin Provincial Education Department, Changchun, China, $52,500. For school contribution. 2010.

573-39 Provincial Education Department of Gansu, Lanshou City, China, $778,000. For school contribution. 2010.

573-40 Provincial Education Department of Gansu, Lanshou City, China, $554,500. For school contribution. 2010.

573-41 Provincial Education Department of Gansu, Lanshou City, China, $287,500. For school contribution. 2010.

573-42 Shaanxisheng Jiaoyuting Mingdexiaoxue Xiangmuzhuanhu, Xian, China, $442,500. For school contribution. 2010.

573-43 Shaanxisheng Jiaoyuting Mingdexiaoxue Xiangmuzhuanhu, Xian, China, $431,500. For school contribution. 2010.

573-44 Shaanxisheng Jiaoyuting Mingdexiaoxue Xiangmuzhuanhu, Xian, China, $297,500. For school contribution. 2010.

573-45 Shandong Provincial Education Department, Jinan, China, $857,500. For school contribution. 2010.

573-46 Shandong Provincial Education Department, Jinan, China, $460,500. For school contribution. 2010.

573-47 Shandong Provincial Education Department, Jinan, China, $231,500. For school contribution. 2010.

573-48 Shanxi Province Department of Education, Taiyuan, China, $740,000. For school contribution. 2010.

573-49 Shanxi Province Department of Education, Taiyuan, China, $231,500. For school contribution. 2010.

573-50 Sichuan Province Education Foundation, Chengdu City, China, $698,000. For school contribution. 2010.

573-51 Tianjin Municipal Education Commission, China, $312,500. For school contribution. 2010.

574
Nuclear Threat Initiative, Inc.
(also known as NTI)
1747 Pennsylvania Ave. N.W., 7th Fl.
Washington, DC 20006-4602 (202) 296-4810
FAX: (202) 296-4811; E-mail: contact@nti.org;
URL: http://www.nti.org/
Ted Turner's Giving Pledge: http://givingpledge.org/#enter

Established in 2001 in DC.
Donors: Better World Fund; Susan Thompson Buffett†; Buffett Foundation; Carnegie Corporation of New York; J.B. Fuqua; Bill & Melinda Gates Foundation; Google Foundation; Fred Isemon; MacArthur Foundation; Russell Family Foundation; R.E. "Ted" Turner III; R.E. Turner Charitable Remainder Unitrust No. 3; The World Bank; Martin Zonnenberg.
Grantmaker type: Public charity.
Financial data (yr. ended 06/30/10): Revenue, $22,568,951; assets, $89,205,571 (M); gifts received, $22,459,607; expenditures, $14,233,542; giving activities include $1,605,817 for grants, and $1,987,906 for 17 grants to organizations outside the U.S.
Purpose and activities: The organization works to strengthen global security by reducing the risk of use and preventing the spread of nuclear, biological, and chemical weapons; and to work to build the trust, transparency, and security that are preconditions to the ultimate fulfillment of the goals and ambitions of the Non-Proliferation Treaty.
Fields of interest: International peace/security; International affairs, arms control.
Limitations: Applications not accepted. Giving on a worldwide basis.
Publications: Annual report.
Application information: Contributes only to pre-selected organizations.
    Board meeting date(s): Up to four times per year
Officers and Directors:* Sam Nunn,* Co-Chair. and C.E.O., R.E. "Ted" Turner III,* Co-Chair.; Joan Rohlfing,* Pres. and C.O.O.; Brooke D. Anderson, V.P., Comms.; Kraig M. Butrum, V.P., Devel.; Laura S.H. Holgate, V.P., Russia/NIS Prog.; Terence Taylor, V.P., Global Health and Security; Charlotte S. Atkinson, Treas.; Dr. Alexei Arbatov; HRH Prince El Hassan bin Talal; Charles B. Curtis; Pete V. Domenici; Susan Eisenhower; Amb. Rolf Ekeus; Genl. Eugene E. Habiger; Igor S. Ivanov; Hon. Pierre Lellouche; Sen. Richard G. Lugar; Jessica Tuchman Mathews, Ph.D.; Ronald L. Olson; Hon. Hisashi Owada, Dr. William J. Perry, Nafis Sadik, M.D.; Amartya Sen; Rt. Hon. Shirley Williams; Fujia Yang.
Advisors: Warren E. Buffett; Dr. David A. Hamburg; Dr. Siegfried S. Hecker; Frederick Iseman; George F. Russell, Jr.
Number of staff: 20 full-time professional; 1 part-time professional; 11 full-time support.
EIN: 522289435

575
The Ocean Foundation
1990 M St. N.W., Ste. 250
Washington, DC 20036-3430 (202) 887-8992
FAX: (202) 887-8987; E-mail: info@oceanfdn.org;
URL: http://www.oceanfdn.org

Established in 2001 in CA.
Grantmaker type: Public charity.
Financial data (yr. ended 06/30/10): Revenue, $5,843,518; assets, $4,112,786 (M); gifts received, $5,673,864; expenditures, $4,548,768; giving activities include $667,133 for grants, $838,543 for grants to organizations outside the U.S., and $20,471 for grants to individuals.
Purpose and activities: The organization aims to support, strengthen, and promote those organizations dedicated to reversing the trend of destruction of ocean environments around the world.

Fields of interest: Environment, water resources; Environment, water pollution.
International interests: Middle East; Latin America; Caribbean; Asia; Africa.
Type of support: Technical assistance; Seed money; Scholarships—to individuals; Scholarship funds; Research; Publication; Program evaluation; Program development; Matching/challenge support; Management development/capacity building; Internship funds; General/operating support; Film/video/radio; Fellowships; Equipment; Employee-related scholarships; Emergency funds; Curriculum development; Consulting services; Conferences/seminars; Building/renovation; Grants to individuals.
Limitations: Applications not accepted. Giving primarily on an international basis with emphasis on coastal communities/states and island communities/states. No support for religious or political organizations. No grants for endowments, capital campaigns, land acquisition, basic science research, or more than 20 percent overhead, administrative, or infrastructure costs.
Publications: Annual report; Informational brochure; Newsletter; Occasional report.
Application information: Unsolicited requests for funds not considered or acknowledged.
 Board meeting date(s): Jan., Apr., July, and Oct.
Officers and Directors:* J. Thomas McMurray,* Ph.D., Chair.; Mark J. Spalding,* Pres.; C. Bowdoin Train,* Treas.; Angel Braestrup; Wolcott Henry; Lisa Hook.
Number of staff: 3 full-time professional; 1 part-time support.
EIN: 710863908

576
The Omega Foundation
c/o James Feldman
3750 Oliver St. N.W.
Washington, DC 20015-2532

Established in 2002 in DC.
Donor: Myer Feldman.
Grantmaker type: Independent foundation.
Financial data (yr. ended 12/31/10): Assets, $1,920,114 (M); expenditures, $142,311; qualifying distributions, $137,500; giving activities include $137,500 for grants.
Fields of interest: Elementary/secondary education; Higher education; International relief.
Type of support: General/operating support.
Limitations: Applications not accepted. Giving primarily in Washington, DC, and St. Louis, MO. No grants to individuals.
Application information: Contributes only to pre-selected organizations.
Directors: James Feldman; Natalie Wexler.
EIN: 542075805

577
The One Campaign
(formerly DATA Foundation, also known as Debt AIDS Trade Africa Foundation)
1400 Eye St. N.W., Ste. 600
Washington, DC 20005-6517 (202) 495-2700
URL: http://www.one.org/us/
Facebook: http://www.facebook.com/ONE?v=wall
MySpace: http://www.myspace.com/theonecampaign
Organization blog: http://www.one.org/blog/

Twitter: http://twitter.com/onecampaign
YouTube: http://www.youtube.com/user/TheONECampaign

Established in 2002 in DC.
Grantmaker type: Public charity.
Financial data (yr. ended 12/31/09): Revenue, $35,212,269; assets, $38,442,945 (M); gifts received, $34,963,239; expenditures, $20,109,396; program services expenses, $17,038,148; giving activities include $26,595 for 2 grants (high: $16,595; low: $10,000), $107,493 for 2 grants to organizations outside the U.S., and $16,904,090 for foundation-administered programs.
Purpose and activities: The organization aims to fight extreme poverty and preventable disease around the world, particularly in Africa, through public education and grassroots mobilization in support of the Millennium Development Goals, and through educating global leaders to adopt smart policies and invest in tested, proven solutions.
Fields of interest: Human services, emergency aid; Human services.
International interests: Africa.
Limitations: Giving on a national and international basis, primarily to Africa.
Publications: Annual report.
Officers and Directors:* Tom Freston, Chair.; Joshua Bolten,* Interim C.E.O.; Jamie Drummond, Exec. Dir.; Howard G. Buffett; Susan A. Buffett; Joe Cerrell; John Doerr; Helene D. Gayle; Morton H. Halperin; Paul David "Bono" Hewson; Dr. Mo Ibrahim; Dr. Ngozi Okonjo-Iweala; Jeff Raikes; Kevin Sheekey; Bobby Shriver.
EIN: 010593565

578
Open Society Policy Center
1730 Pennsylvania Ave., N.W., 7th Fl.
Washington, DC 20006-4706 (202) 721-5600
URL: http://www.opensocietypolicycenter.org

Established in 2001 in DC, in response to the September 2001 attacks on the World Trade Center.
Grantmaker type: Public charity.
Financial data (yr. ended 12/31/09): Revenue, $1,501,033; assets, $337,647 (M); gifts received, $1,500,000; expenditures, $2,700,821; giving activities include $1,385,674 for grants.
Purpose and activities: The center engages in policy advocacy on U.S. and international issues, including domestic civil liberties, multilateralism, economic development, civil rights, human rights, women's rights, and criminal justice reform.
Fields of interest: International development; International affairs, information services; International affairs, public education; International affairs, foreign policy; International human rights; International affairs; Civil/human rights; Economic development; Women.
Limitations: Giving primarily in Washington, DC.
Officers and Directors:* Aryeh Neier,* Chair.; Gara LaMarche,* Secy.; Lynthia Gibson Price, Treas.; Morton H. Halperin,* Pres. and Exec. Dir.; Ann Beeson; Stephen Rickard.
EIN: 522028955

579
The Palmer Foundation
734 15th St. N.W., Ste. 600
Washington, DC 20005-1029 (202) 595-1020
FAX: (202) 833-5540;
E-mail: admin@thepalmerfoundation.org; E-mail address for Betsy Erickson: betsy@thepalmerfoundation.org; URL: http://www.thepalmerfoundation.org

Established in 1990 in IL.
Donors: Rogers Palmer†; Mary Palmer†; Mary P. Enroth.
Grantmaker type: Independent foundation.
Financial data (yr. ended 12/31/10): Assets, $13,379,273 (M); gifts received, $100,000; expenditures, $621,904; qualifying distributions, $457,200; giving activities include $457,200 for grants.
Purpose and activities: Giving primarily for youth, the environment and public health.
Fields of interest: Human services; Environment; Public health; Children/youth; Youth.
International interests: Guatemala; Mexico.
Type of support: Program development; Matching/challenge support.
Limitations: Applications not accepted. Giving limited to the Midwest states of: IL and WI, and the Mid Atlantic states of: MD, NC, VA, and in Washington, DC, unless one of the foundation's directors has a personal interest elsewhere. No support for lobbying, sectarian religious purposes, individual medical purposes, or for scientific research. No grants to individuals, or for multi-year grants, endowment drives, operational support, annual campaigns, or salaries.
Publications: Annual report; Grants list; Program policy statement.
Application information: Unsolicited requests for funds not accepted.
 Board meeting date(s): Apr. and Oct.
Officers and Directors:* Mary P. Enroth,* Pres.; Karen E. Lischick,* V.P.; Jay L. Owen,* Secy.-Treas.; Charly Enroth; Susan Le Mieux Enroth; Matt Lischick.
Number of staff: 1 part-time support.
EIN: 363700897

580
Pan American Development Foundation
1889 F St., N.W., 2nd Fl.
Washington, DC 20006-4401 (202) 458-3969
FAX: (202) 458-6316; E-mail: padf-dc@padf.org;
URL: http://www.padf.org/

Established in 1962.
Grantmaker type: Public charity.
Financial data (yr. ended 09/30/10): Revenue, $55,670,340; assets, $15,302,872 (M); gifts received, $10,625,222; expenditures, $55,324,421; giving activities include $30,145,566 for grants to organizations outside the U.S.
Purpose and activities: The mission of the foundation is to increase opportunity for the disadvantaged in Latin America and the Caribbean through innovative partnerships with private, public, and nonprofit organizations, in support of the priorities of the Organization of American States (OAS).
Fields of interest: International human rights; International relief; International development.

International interests: Caribbean; Central America; Latin America; Mexico; South America.
Type of support: In-kind gifts.
Limitations: Applications not accepted. Giving primarily in Latin America and the Caribbean.
Publications: Annual report; Informational brochure.
Application information:
  Board meeting date(s): Apr. and Sept.
Officers and Trustees:* Jose Miguel Insulza,* Chair.; Albert R. Ramdin,* Vice-Chair.; Amb. Alexander F. Watson,* Pres.; Carlos Marino Garcia,* 1st V.P.; Philippe R. Armand,* 2nd V.P.; Kathleen C. Barclay,* Secy.; William D. Gambrel,* Treas.; John Sanbrailo, Exec. Dir.; and 19 additional trustees.
Number of staff: None.
EIN: 526054268

581
Pan American Health and Education Foundation
525 23rd St., N.W.
Washington, DC 20037-2895 (202) 974-3416
FAX: (202) 974-3636; URL: http://www.pahef.org/

Established in 1968 in DC.
Grantmaker type: Public charity.
Financial data (yr. ended 12/31/10): Revenue, $4,744,031; assets, $31,442,745 (M); gifts received, $1,154,762; expenditures, $4,260,585; giving activities include $780,006 for grants to organizations outside the U.S.
Purpose and activities: The foundation works in conjunction with the Pan American Health Organization to combat disease, lengthen life, improve health care services, foster health research, and enhance the capacities of health care workers primarily in the Americas through grantmaking and direct program implementation.
Fields of interest: International development; Medical research; Health care.
International interests: Caribbean; Central America; Latin America; South America.
Type of support: Scholarships—to individuals.
Limitations: Giving primarily for the benefit of the Americas.
Publications: Application guidelines.
Application information: The foundation is not currently accepting proposals for funding that falls outside its Awards for Excellence in Inter-American Public Health Program; see web site for current status of grantmaking.
  Initial approach: Submit nomination form for Awards for Excellence in Inter-American Public Health Program
  Deadline(s): June 15 and June 30 for Awards for Excellence in Inter-American Public Health Program
  Board meeting date(s): Nov.
Officers: Benjamin Caballero, M.D., Ph.D., Chair.; Patricia P. Barry, M.D., M.P.H., Vice-Chair.; Fernando Mendoza, M.D., M.P.H., Secy.; Arnold Simonse, D.S.W., Treas.; Edward L. Kadunc, M.P.H., Exec. Dir.
EIN: 237072046

582
The Phelps Stokes Fund
1400 I St. N.W., Ste. 750
Washington, DC 20005-6521 (202) 371-9544
Contact: Badi Foster Ph.D., Pres.

FAX: (202) 371-9522;
E-mail: info@phelpsstokes.org; URL: http://www.phelpsstokes.org/

Established in 1911 in NY.
Grantmaker type: Public charity.
Financial data (yr. ended 09/30/10): Revenue, $4,591,321; assets, $2,431,744 (M); gifts received, $4,444,015; expenditures, $4,732,636; giving activities include $2,109,436 for grants to individuals.
Purpose and activities: The fund promotes education and social development for the underprivileged and needy in the Americas and Africa. Education of African Americans, Native Americans, and Africans, and an international visitor program are the principle activities of the fund.
Fields of interest: Education, research; Education, reform; Education, services; International exchange; Civil rights, race/intergroup relations; African Americans/Blacks; Native Americans/American Indians; Women; Economically disadvantaged.
International interests: South America; Central America; Africa; Liberia.
Type of support: Program development; Research; Exchange programs.
Limitations: Applications not accepted. Giving limited to the Americas and Africa; primarily Liberia.
Publications: Newsletter.
Application information: Unsolicited requests for funds not accepted.
  Board meeting date(s): Apr. and Nov.
Officers and Trustees:* Jonathan Cahn,* Esq., Chair.; Richard Fletcher,* Vice-Chair.; Badi Foster,* Ph.D., Pres.; Dr. Gail Christopher,* Treas.; Dr. Euric Bobb; Lou Capozzi; Amb. Raul Gangotena; Sarah Hatch; Gerald LeMelle; William Smith; and 6 additional trustees.
Number of staff: 14 full-time professional.
EIN: 131624208

583
Physicians for Social Responsibility
1875 Connecticut Ave. N.W., Ste. 1012
Washington, DC 20009-5747 (202) 667-4260
Contact: Catherine Thomasson, Exec. Dir.
FAX: (202) 667-4201; E-mail: psrnatl@psr.org;
URL: http://www.psr.org

Established in 1961 in MA.
Grantmaker type: Public charity.
Financial data (yr. ended 12/31/10): Revenue, $2,550,446; assets, $908,740 (M); gifts received, $2,456,853; expenditures, $2,959,147; giving activities include $96,972 for grants.
Purpose and activities: The organization seeks to be the medical and public health voice working to prevent the use or spread of nuclear weapons, and to slow, stop, and reverse global warming and toxic degradation of the environment.
Fields of interest: Environment, climate change/global warming; International affairs, arms control.
Limitations: Applications not accepted. Giving on a national basis.
Publications: Financial statement; Newsletter; Occasional report.
Application information: Contributes only to pre-selected organizations.
Officers and Directors:* Catherine Thonasson, M.D., Exec. Dir.; Sid Alexander, M.D.; Kennette Benedict, Ph.D.; Steven G. Gilbert, Ph.D., D.A.B.T.; Robert Gould,, M.D.; Richard Grady, M.D.; Ira Helfand, M.D.; Edward Ifft, Ph.D.; Andy Kanter, M.D.,

M.P.H.; Andy Kanter, M.D., M.P.H.; and 13 additional directors.
Number of staff: 11 full-time professional; 1 part-time professional; 1 full-time support.
EIN: 237059731

584
PlayPumps International, Inc.
1718 M St., N.W.
PMB 249
Washington, DC 20036-4504

Grantmaker type: Public charity.
Financial data (yr. ended 02/28/09): Revenue, $2,376,663; assets, $1,530,489 (M); gifts received, $1,828,666; expenditures, $2,836,640; giving activities include $24,000 for grants, and $1,666,420 for grants to organizations outside the U.S.
Purpose and activities: As the U.S. affiliate of PlayPumps International, the organization works to provide rural African communities with clean drinking water.
Fields of interest: Health care; Environment, water pollution.
International interests: Africa.
Limitations: Applications not accepted. Giving limited to Africa.
Application information: Contributes only to a pre-selected organization.
Officers: Jean Case,* Chair.; Dale Jones, Pres. and C.E.O.; John Richardson, Secy., C.F.O., and Treas.
Directors: Thomas D. Eckert; Doug Holladay.
EIN: 043839391

585
Population Action International
1300 19th St., N.W., Ste. 200
Washington, DC 20036-1624 (202) 557-3400
FAX: (202) 728-4177; E-mail: pai@popact.org;
URL: http://www.populationaction.org
Facebook: http://www.facebook.com/pages/Population-Action-International/17303018426
LinkedIn: http://www.linkedin.com/groups?gid=1000347
Twitter: http://twitter.com/popact
YouTube: http://www.youtube.com/paiwdc

Established in 1965 to DC.
Grantmaker type: Public charity.
Financial data (yr. ended 12/31/10): Revenue, $3,978,598; assets, $5,922,352 (M); gifts received, $3,930,055; expenditures, $5,025,649; giving activities include $44,500 for grants, and $427,682 for grants to organizations outside the U.S.
Purpose and activities: The organization works to improve individual well-being and preserve global resources by mobilizing political and financial support for population, family planning, and reproductive health policies and programs.
Fields of interest: International affairs; Reproductive health; Reproductive health, family planning.
Limitations: Giving on a national and international basis.
Publications: Annual report.
Officers and Directors:* Jacqueline C. Morby,* Chair.; Moises Naim,* Ph.D., Vice-Chair.; Suzanne Ehlers, Pres. and C.E.O.; Michele Duryea, V.P., Devel.; Karen Hardee, V.P., Research; Michael

Khoo, V.P., Comms.; Rachael Murray Rakestraw, V.P., Finance and Admin.; Hon. Harriet C. Babbitt,* Secy.; Dr. Pouru Bhiwandi,* Treas.; Pamela Bevier, Ph.D., M.P.H.; Hon. Lee H. Hamilton; Hon. Amory Houghton, Jr.; Lt. Genl. Claudia Kennedy; Dr. Thomas E. Lovejoy; Dr. Elizabeth Lule; Maj. Genl. William L. Nash; Dr. Nafis Sadik; James Gustave Speth, Esq.; and 4 additional directors.
EIN: 520812075

586
The Rita Poretsky Foundation, Inc.
c/o Margaret Siegel
P.O. Box 11519
Washington, DC   20008-0719

Established in 1992 in MD.
Donor: Rita Poretsky‡.
Grantmaker type: Independent foundation.
Financial data (yr. ended 12/31/10): Assets, $326,330 (M); expenditures, $554,162; qualifying distributions, $535,710; giving activities include $525,000 for 41 grants (high: $75,000; low: $2,000).
Purpose and activities: Giving primarily for the arts, Jewish organizations, and for Israel.
Fields of interest: Arts; Women, centers/services; Jewish agencies & synagogues; Immigrants/ refugees; Children/youth.
International interests: Israel.
Type of support: General/operating support; Continuing support; Annual campaigns; Program development; Publication; Scholarship funds.
Limitations: Applications not accepted. Giving primarily in the Washington, DC, area; giving also in Israel. No grants to individuals.
Publications: Grants list.
Application information: Contributes only to pre-selected organizations.
    Board meeting date(s): Annually
Officer and Trustees:* Esther Ticktin,* Treas.; Margaret Siegel; Max Ticktin.
Number of staff: None.
EIN: 521688160

587
PVA Spinal Cord Research Foundation
(also known as SCRF)
801 18th St., N.W.
Washington, DC   20006-3517   (202) 416-7652
Contact: Barbara Zupnik, Grants Portfolio Mgr.
FAX: (202) 416-7641; E-mail: foundations@pva.org; Toll-free tel.: (800) 424-8200, ext. 652; TTY: (202) 416-7622; URL: http://www.pva.org/site/ PageServer?pagename=research_resfdn

Established in 1976.
Donor: Paralyzed Veterans of America.
Grantmaker type: Public charity.
Financial data (yr. ended 09/30/10): Revenue, $1,113,532; assets, $1,619,395 (M); gifts received, $1,110,346; expenditures, $1,173,421; giving activities include $1,020,852 for grants, and $149,139 for grants to organizations outside the U.S.
Purpose and activities: The foundation works to discover better treatments and cures for spinal cord injury and/or disease, promote innovative research, support and encourage new investigators to specialize in the area of spinal cord injury and/or disease, and support efforts to improve the quality

of life of individuals with spinal cord injury and/or disease.
Fields of interest: Spine disorders research; Spine disorders; Medical research, institute.
International interests: Canada.
Type of support: Conferences/seminars; Fellowships; Research.
Limitations: Applications accepted. Giving primarily in the U.S. and Canada.
Publications: Application guidelines; Annual report; Grants list.
Application information: Application form required.
    Initial approach: Online application
    Deadline(s): Sept. 2
    Board meeting date(s): Nov.
Officers and Trustees:* Randy Pleva,* Chair.; Thomas E. Stripling,* Secy; John Ring,* Treas.; Peter W. Axelson, M.S., M.E.; Terry L. Blackwell, Ed.D.; Rory A. Cooper, Ph.D.; Donald J. Eastmead, M.D.; Ivenhoe T. Richey II; Ross F. "Rick" Rogers III, M.Ed.
Number of staff: 2 full-time professional.
EIN: 521064398

588
San Giacomo Charitable Foundation
2801 New Mexico Ave. N.W., Ste. 209
Washington, DC   20007-3907   (202) 338-5728
Contact: Luigi R. Einaudi, Tr.

Established in DC.
Grantmaker type: Independent foundation.
Financial data (yr. ended 12/31/10): Assets, $9,065,569 (M); expenditures, $582,503; qualifying distributions, $525,000; giving activities include $525,000 for grants.
Purpose and activities: The foundation's goals are to foster international, cultural and educational exchange; to support institutional development and research, primarily in the economic and social sciences; and to support medical research, particularly towards cures for various forms of cancer.
Fields of interest: Medical research, institute; Cancer research; International exchange, arts; International exchange; Social sciences; Economics.
International interests: Italy.
Limitations: Applications accepted. Giving limited to Italy. No grants to individuals.
Application information: Application form not required.
    Initial approach: 2-3 page proposal
    Deadline(s): None
Trustees: Luigi R. Einaudi; Roberta Einaudi.
EIN: 521963583

589
Save Darfur Coalition
1025 Connecticut Ave., N.W., Ste. 310
Washington, DC   20036-5405
FAX: (202) 467-0001; E-mail: info@savedarfur.org; Toll-free tel.: (800) 917-2034; URL: http:// www.savedarfur.org
Blog: http://blogfordarfur.org/

Grantmaker type: Public charity.
Financial data (yr. ended 09/30/10): Revenue, $3,307,088; assets, $1,536,091 (M); gifts received, $3,256,358; expenditures, $4,359,027; giving activities include $59,386 for grants, and

$649,812 for grants to organizations outside the U.S.
Purpose and activities: The coalition works to raise public awareness and mobilize a massive response to the atrocities in Sudan's western region of Darfur.
Fields of interest: Civil/human rights; International conflict resolution; International migration/refugee issues; International human rights; Immigrants/ refugees.
International interests: Sudan.
Limitations: Giving on a national and international basis.
Publications: Annual report.
Officers: Dr. Antonios Kireopoulos, Chair.; Sam Bell, Vice-Chair.; Jerry Fowler, Pres.; Omer Ismail, Secy.; Mike Edington, Treas.
Directors: Dr. Mahmoud Braima; Zeinab Eyega; Rev. David Emmanuel Goatley, Ph.D.; Rabbi Steve Gutow; Ruth Messinger; John Prendergast; Jill Savitt; Rev. Gloria White-Hammond, M.D.
EIN: 300335420

590
Sister Cities International, Inc.
(formerly Town Affiliation Association of the U.S., Inc., Sister Cities International)
915 15th St., NW, 4th Fl.
Washington, DC   20005-1735   (202) 347-8630
FAX: (202) 393-6524; E-mail: info@sister-cities.org; URL: http://www.sister-cities.org

Established in 1967 in DC.
Grantmaker type: Public charity.
Financial data (yr. ended 12/31/09): Revenue, $1,797,446; assets, $1,739,776 (M); gifts received, $1,493,783; expenditures, $2,043,227; program services expenses, $1,759,486; giving activities include $63,444 for grants, and $85,198 for grants to organizations outside the U.S.
Purpose and activities: The organization promotes local community development and volunteer action to provide opportunities for citizens of different countries to share culture, develop trade relationships, and provide an atmosphere for learning and problem solving between countries.
Fields of interest: International development; Community/economic development.
Limitations: Giving on a national and international basis.
Application information: Application form required.
Officers and Directors:* Brad Cole, Chair.; Thomas Lisk, Vice-Chair.; Carol Robertson Lopez, Secy.; Bill Boerum, Treas.; Lalit Acharya; Leroy Allala; Carolyn Bishop; Carla Walker; Paula West; and 16 additional directors; Mark Walton.
EIN: 520859021

591
Sons of Italy Foundation
219 E St., N.E.
Washington, DC   20002-4922   (202) 547-2900
Contact: Margaret Cirona O'Rourke, Admin. Asst., Scholarships
FAX: (202) 546-8168;
E-mail: scholarships@osia.org; Toll-free tel.: (800) 522-6742; e-mail for Margaret Cirona O'Rourke: morourke@osia.org; URL: http://www.osia.org/sif/ index.php
Facebook: http://www.facebook.com/Sons.of.Italy

Established in 1959 in PA.

Grantmaker type: Public charity.
Financial data (yr. ended 09/30/10): Revenue, $1,857,834; assets, $1,716,596 (M); gifts received, $1,967,743; expenditures, $1,413,830; program services expenses, $576,843; giving activities include $47,640 for 4 grants (high: $27,000), $85,843 for 16 grants to individuals, and $443,360 for foundation-administered programs.
Purpose and activities: The foundation helps educate and improve the lives of Americans, especially those of Italian descent.
Fields of interest: Arts, cultural/ethnic awareness; Student services/organizations; Medical research, institute; Crime/law enforcement; Disasters, preparedness/services; Children, foster care; Human services; International affairs; Community/economic development.
Type of support: Continuing support; Annual campaigns; Emergency funds; Program development; Internship funds; Scholarship funds; Research; Scholarships—to individuals.
Limitations: Applications accepted. Giving on a national basis. No support for government agencies, for-profit organizations, foreign countries, or religious groups and denominations. No grants to individuals (except through annual scholarship program), or for endowments, advertising, membership campaigns, propaganda, lobbying to influence legislation, political or election campaigns, or activities designed to financially benefit the applicant or employees of the applicant.
Publications: Application guidelines; Biennial report; Newsletter.
Application information: The foundation has currently suspended its grants program; contact foundation for current status. Application form required.
Initial approach: Letter, telephone, or e-mail
Copies of proposal: 7
Deadline(s): Feb. 28
Board meeting date(s): May and Nov.
Final notification: May 1
Officers and Trustees:* Joseph J. DiTrapani,* Chair.; Vincent Sarno,* Pres.; Anthony J. Baratta,* V.P.; Nancy di Fiore Quinn,* Treas.; Philip R. Piccigallo, Ph.D., Exec. Dir.; Alfred A. Affinito; Louis C. Ambrosio; Angelo R. Bianchi; Joseph Cicippio; Edward Innella; Carlo Matteucci; Robert A. Messa; Michael G. Polo; Philip R. Privitera; Joseph A. Russo; Joseph Sciame; Joanne L. Strollo.
Number of staff: 2 full-time professional; 5 full-time support.
EIN: 236276526

592
The Summit Foundation
(also known as The Summit Charitable Foundation, Inc.)
2100 Pennsylvania Ave., N.W., Ste. 525
Washington, DC 20037-3223
Contact: Carlos Saavedra, Exec. Dir.
FAX: (202) 912-2901; URL: http://www.summitfdn.org/foundation/index.html
Roger and Victoria Sant's Giving Pledge: http://givingpledge.org/#enter

Established in 1991 in DE.
Donors: Roger Sant; Victoria P. Sant; AES Corp.; Aspen Charitable Remainder Unitrust No. 3.
Grantmaker type: Independent foundation.
Financial data (yr. ended 12/31/09): Assets, $68,269,520 (M); expenditures, $6,691,440; qualifying distributions, $6,541,219; giving

activities include $5,375,715 for 64 grants (high: $662,585; low: $150).
Purpose and activities: Funding currently for three program areas: Conservation of the Mesoamerican Reef, Leadership for Adolescent Reproductive Health, and Sustainable Cities. The foundation seeks to promote the health and well being of the planet - its people and its natural environment - by achieving a sustainable population, empowering young people, and protecting the earth's biodiversity.
Fields of interest: Youth, pregnancy prevention; Health care; Environment, natural resources; Environment; Reproductive health; Reproductive health, family planning; Reproductive health, sexuality education; Youth development; International human rights.
International interests: Belize; Guatemala; Honduras; Mexico.
Type of support: General/operating support; Continuing support; Program development; Seed money; Technical assistance; Program evaluation; Matching/challenge support.
Limitations: Applications not accepted. Giving through Biodiversity Program focuses on international Mesoamerican Reef countries only; Population Advocacy and Sustainable Cities Programs focus on the United States; and Youth Leadership Program focuses on Mesoamerican Reef countries only. No grants to individuals, or for freestanding conferences, film and video projects or basic research.
Publications: Grants list.
Application information: Unsolicited requests for funds not considered.
Board meeting date(s): 2 times a year
Officers and Trustees:* Roger Sant,* Chair.; Victoria P. Sant,* Pres.; Shari Sant Plummer,* Secy.; Alexis Sant,* Treas.; Carlos Saavedra, Exec. Dir. and Sr. Prog. Off., Conservation of the Mesoamerican Reef Program; Kathryn S. Fuller; Dan Plummer; Ali Sant; Chrissie Sant; Kristin Sant; Michael Sant; Shira Saperstein.
Number of staff: 4 full-time professional.
EIN: 521743817

593
Teamster Disaster Relief Fund
25 Louisiana Ave. N.W.
Washington, DC 20001-2198 (202) 624-6800
Contact: James P. Hoffa, Pres.

Established in DC.
Grantmaker type: Public charity.
Financial data (yr. ended 12/31/10): Revenue, $78,856; assets, $367,527 (M); gifts received, $78,856; expenditures, $83,500; giving activities include $83,500 for grants.
Purpose and activities: The fund provides monetary and non-monetary relief to individuals in the U.S. and Canada who are victims of disasters such as hurricanes and earthquakes.
Fields of interest: Disasters, preparedness/services; Safety/disasters; Economically disadvantaged.
International interests: Canada.
Type of support: In-kind gifts; Grants to individuals.
Limitations: Applications not accepted. Giving limited to the U.S. and Canada.
Application information: Requests for aid must come from the local union office and not by individual members; unsolicited requests for funds not otherwise considered or acknowledged.

Officers and Directors:* James P. Hoffa,* Pres.; Dotty Malinsky,* V.P.; Cheryl Johnson,* Secy.; C. Thomas Keegel,* Treas.; John Steger.
EIN: 521790540

594
Trust for Civil Society in Central and Eastern Europe
c/o German Marshall Fund
1744 R St., N.W.
Washington, DC 20009-2410
E-mail: trust@ceetrust.org; URL: http://www.ceetrust.org
Grants Database: http://www.ceetrust.org/grants-database.html

Supporting organization of the German Marshall Fund of the United States.
Grantmaker type: Public charity.
Financial data (yr. ended 12/31/10): Revenue, $653,133; assets, $16,606,174 (M); gifts received, $530,000; expenditures, $6,754,697; giving activities include $6,010,378 for grants to organizations outside the U.S.
Purpose and activities: The organization aims to promote the development of civil societies in Bulgaria, the Czech Republic, Hungary, Poland, Romania, Slovakia and Slovenia by supporting civil society organizations to gain greater effectiveness and stability.
International interests: Slovakia; Slovenia; Romania; Poland; Hungary; Czech Republic; Bulgaria.
Limitations: Applications accepted. Giving primarily to Bulgaria, Hungary, and Romania, with some giving to the Czech Republic, Poland, Slovakia, and Slovenia. No support for political organizations, trade unions, or business organizations and businesses.
Publications: Application guidelines; Annual report; Financial statement.
Application information: Application form required.
Initial approach: Submit letter of intent
Deadline(s): Oct. 26
Final notification: Nov. 25
Officers and Directors:* Helke MacKerron,* Chair.; Haki Abazi,* Secy.-Treas.; Rayna Gavrilova, Exec. Dir.; Lisa Jordan; Annette Laborey; Jiri Pehe; Maureen Smyth.
EIN: 522250772

595
U.S. for Belize Foundation for Research & Environmental Education, Inc.
2101 Connecticut Ave., NW
Washington, DC 20008-1728

Grantmaker type: Public charity.
Financial data (yr. ended 12/31/10): Revenue, $167,998; assets, $103,759 (M); gifts received, $51,667; expenditures, $162,634.
Fields of interest: Environment, research; Environment.
International interests: Belize.
Type of support: Research.
Officers: Jacob A. Marlin, Pres.; Steven Brewer, Secy.; Kelly K. Marlin, Treas.
Board Members: Mark Ginsberg; John Zabaneh.
EIN: 593340282

596
Union Plus Education Foundation
1125 15th St. N.W., Ste. 300
Washington, DC 20005-2707
Contact: Shana E. Higgins, Prog. Asst.
FAX: (202) 293-5311;
E-mail: shiggins@unionprivilege.org; Application
address: c/o Union Privilege, P.O. Box 34800,
Washington, D.C. 20043-4800; URL: http://
www.unionplus.org/benefits/education/
scholarships

Established in 1993 in DC.
Donor: Household Bank.
Grantmaker type: Independent foundation.
Financial data (yr. ended 12/31/09): Assets,
$174,932 (M); gifts received, $150,000;
expenditures, $266,226; qualifying distributions,
$259,061; giving activities include $25,000 for 1
grant, and $234,061 for 144 grants to individuals
(high: $4,000; low: $500).
Purpose and activities: Provides scholarships to
members of unions participating in any Union Plus
program, their spouses, and their dependent
children (foster children, step-children, and any
other child for whom the individual member provides
greater than 50 percent of their support).
Participating members from Canada and U.S.
territories of Guam, Puerto Rico, and the Virgin
Islands are also eligible. The individual must be
accepted into an accredited college or university,
community college or recognized technical or trade
school at the time the award is issued.
Fields of interest: Military/veterans' organizations;
Scholarships/financial aid; Human services; Young
adults, male; Young adults, female; Young adults;
Women; Single parents; Physically disabled; Native
Americans/American Indians; Minorities; Men;
LGBTQ; Hispanics/Latinos; Girls; Economically
disadvantaged; Disabilities, people with; Deaf/
hearing impaired; Children; Boys; Blind/visually
impaired; Asians/Pacific Islanders; African
Americans/Blacks; Adults, women; Adults, men;
Adults.
International interests: Canada.
Type of support: Scholarship funds; Scholarships—
to individuals.
Limitations: Applications accepted. Giving in the
U.S., Guam, Puerto Rico, the Virgin Islands, and
Canada.
Publications: Informational brochure; Newsletter.
Application information: The program is open to
students attending or planning to attend a college
or university, a community college, or a technical
college or trade school. The amount of the award
ranges from $500-$4,000. Application information
available on foundation web site. Graduate students
are now eligible. Application form required.
   Deadline(s): Jan. 31
   Board meeting date(s): Apr.
   Final notification: 4 months
Trustees: Randall Renjilian; Leslie A. Tolf.
Number of staff: None.
EIN: 383647522

597
United Nations Foundation
1800 Massachusetts Ave. N.W., Ste. 400
Washington, DC 20036-1218 (202) 887-9040
FAX: (202) 887-9021; URL: http://
www.unfoundation.org
Facebook: http://www.facebook.com/
unitednationsfoundation
Ted Turner's Giving Pledge: http://givingpledge.org/
#enter
Twitter: http://twitter.com/unfoundation
Vimeo: http://vimeo.com/unfoundation
YouTube: http://www.youtube.com/unfoundation

Established in 1997 in NY.
Donor: R.E. "Ted" Turner III.
Grantmaker type: Public charity.
Financial data (yr. ended 12/31/10): Revenue,
$137,514,520; assets, $180,980,264 (M); gifts
received, $124,098,656; expenditures,
$107,661,444; giving activities include
$14,434,718 for grants, and $58,079,846 for
grants to organizations outside the U.S.
Purpose and activities: The foundation promotes a
more peaceful, prosperous, and just world through
the support of the United Nations.
Fields of interest: Reproductive health; Civil
liberties, reproductive rights; Population studies;
Environment; International development;
International affairs, U.N.; International human
rights; Civil/human rights.
Type of support: Program development; Program
evaluation.
Limitations: Applications not accepted. Giving on an
international basis. No grants to individuals.
Application information: Unsolicited requests for
funds not considered or acknowledged.
Officers and Directors:* R.E. "Ted" Turner III,*
Chair.; Timothy E. Wirth,* Pres.; Kathryn A.
Bushkin,* Exec. V.P.; Melinda Kimble,* Sr. V.P.,
Programs; Jean-Claude Faby,* V.P.; Michael
Machick,* V.P.; Amy Weiss,* V.P., Public Affairs;
David H. Carter,* C.F.O.; Tamara Kreinin, Exec. Dir.,
Women and Population Prog.; H.M. Queen Raina
Al-Abdullah; Kofi Annan; Gro Harlem Brundtland;
Liang Dan; Igor Ivanov; Graca Machel; Yuan Ming;
N.R. Naranya Murthy; Amb. Hisashi Owada; Emma
Rothschild; Nafis Sadik, M.D.; Andrew J. Young;
Muhammad Yunus.
Number of staff: 12 full-time professional; 1
part-time professional; 8 full-time support.
EIN: 582368165

598
United Palestinian Appeal, Inc.
1330 New Hampshire Ave., N.W., Ste. 104
Washington, DC 20036-6300 (202) 659-5007
FAX: (202) 296-0224;
E-mail: contact@helpupa.com; URL: http://
helpupa.com
Facebook: http://www.facebook.com/group.php?
gid=2679855588
YouTube: http://www.youtube.com/user/helpUPA

Established in 1978.
Grantmaker type: Public charity.
Financial data (yr. ended 12/31/10): Revenue,
$5,604,620; assets, $3,128,002 (M); gifts
received, $5,579,677; expenditures, $5,692,622;
giving activities include $10,500 for grants, and
$5,122,867 for grants to organizations outside the
U.S.

Purpose and activities: The organization provides
aid to Palestinians in need, especially children, in
East Jerusalem, the West Bank, the Gaza Strip, and
Palestinian refugee camps in Lebanon.
Fields of interest: Community/economic
development.
International interests: East Jerusalem; Lebanon;
West Bank/Gaza (Palestinian Territories).
Type of support: Scholarships—to individuals.
Limitations: Giving limited to East Jerusalem, the
Gaza Strip, Lebanon, and the West Bank.
Publications: Application guidelines; Annual report;
Financial statement.
Application information:
   Initial approach: Submit application for University
      Scholarship Program
   Deadline(s): Apr. 30 for University Scholarship
      Program
   Final notification: June for University Scholarship
      Program
Officer: Ghassan Tarazi, Exec. Dir.
Directors: Afaf Nasr; Isam Salah; George Salem; Dr.
Mohammad Tarbush.
EIN: 112494808

599
United States Association for UNHCR
1775 K St. N.W., Ste. 290
Washington, DC 20006-1517 (202) 296-1115
FAX: (202) 296-1081; E-mail: info@usforunhcr.org;
Toll-free tel.: (800) 770-1100; URL: http://
www.usaforunhcr.org
Facebook: http://www.facebook.com/
UNREFUGEES
Facebook Causes URL: http://www.causes.com/
causes/1860
Twitter: http://twitter.com/UNRefugeeAgency
YouTube: http://www.youtube.com/user/
usaforunhcr

Established in 1950 in DC.
Grantmaker type: Public charity.
Financial data (yr. ended 12/31/10): Revenue,
$8,587,031; assets, $1,683,858 (M); gifts
received, $8,586,068; expenditures, $9,025,687;
giving activities include $6,175,120 for grants to
organizations outside the U.S.
Purpose and activities: The organization builds
support in the United States for the humanitarian
work of the United Nations High Commission for
Refugees (UNHCR) by informing Americans about
the plight of refugees and advocate for their
protection, shelter, emergency food, water, medical
care and other life-saving assistance worldwide.
Fields of interest: International affairs, U.N.;
International affairs, alliance/advocacy; Human
services; Safety/disasters, association; Health
care; Immigrants/refugees.
Type of support: Emergency funds.
Limitations: Applications not accepted. Giving
primarily to Europe.
Publications: Annual report; Financial statement;
Newsletter.
Application information: Contributes only to
pre-selected organizations.
Officers and Directors:* Loretta Feehan,* Chair.;
Marc Breslaw, Exec. Dir.; Marcia W. Dam; Christina
R. Davis; Wendy B. Doyle; Patrick M. Hanlon;
Stephanie Hunt; Richard Marks; Pam Omidyar; Keith
Patten; Ellen Rose; Anna Eliasson Schamis; David
Tafuri.
Number of staff: 6 full-time professional.
EIN: 521662800

600
United States Committee for UNDP
(also known as UNDP-USA)
P.O. Box 65345
Washington, DC 20035-5345 (202) 558-7104
FAX: (202) 558-7105; E-mail: info@undp.org;
URL: http://www.undp.org/
RSS Feed: https://www.z2systems.com/np/feed?
orgId=undp

Established in 1995 in DE.
Grantmaker type: Public charity.
Purpose and activities: The organization supports the work of the United Nations Development Program to improve the quality of life for millions of people around the world by promoting democratic governance, poverty reduction, crisis prevention, and recovery, energy and environmental issues, and reducing the impact of the HIV/AIDS pandemic.
Fields of interest: Environment, formal/general education; AIDS; Human services, mind/body enrichment; Human services, emergency aid; Human services; International relief; International affairs; Economically disadvantaged; Adults; Young adults; Minorities; Indigenous peoples; Women; AIDS, people with.
Type of support: Scholarships—to individuals; Program-related investments/loans; Management development/capacity building; In-kind gifts; Emergency funds; General/operating support; Continuing support; Program development; Technical assistance.
Limitations: Applications not accepted. Giving on an international basis, to UNDP only.
Publications: Annual report; Newsletter.
Application information: Contributes only to pre-selected organizations.
Officers and Directors:* Kenneth D. Wollack,* Chair.; Priscilla Rabb Ayres; Lisa Barry; Isabel "Didi" Cutler; Jim Dyer; Nancy Ely-Raphael; Ann Hunter-Welborn; Lionel Johnson; Sonal Shah; John Calvin Williams.
Number of staff: 2 full-time professional.
EIN: 521990876

601
United States-Israel Science and Technology Foundation, Inc.
1300 Pennsylvania Ave., N.W., Ste. 700
Washington, DC 20004-3024 (202) 419-0430
Contact: Ann Liebschultz, Exec. Dir.
FAX: (202) 419-0435; URL: http://www.usistf.org

Established in 1995 in D.C.
Grantmaker type: Public charity.
Financial data (yr. ended 09/30/10): Revenue, $9,513; assets, $2,778,240 (M); expenditures, $674,463.
Purpose and activities: The foundation aims to foster growth of science and technology in the U.S. and Israel.
Fields of interest: Science.
International interests: Israel.
Limitations: Applications accepted. Giving to the U.S. and Israel.
Publications: Application guidelines; Informational brochure; Newsletter.
Application information: See Web site for current RFP.
Officers: Eli Opper, Ph.D., Chair.; Ann Liebschutz, Exec. Dir.

Directors: Arnold Brenner; Uzia Galil; Valerie Herold; Kenneth W. Rind, Ph.D.; Dennis Fred Simon, Ph.D.; Zehev Tadmor.
EIN: 521965628

602
The United States-Mexico Foundation for Science
Keck Bldg. 443
500 5th St. N.W.
Washington, DC 20001-2736 (202) 334-2522
FAX: (202) 334-3094;
E-mail: general@fumec.org.mx; URL: http://www.fumec.org.mx

Grantmaker type: Public charity.
Financial data (yr. ended 12/31/09): Revenue, $10,051,393; assets, $30,830,123 (M); gifts received, $7,080,862; expenditures, $7,315,843; giving activities include $3,721,277 for grants to organizations outside the U.S.
Purpose and activities: The foundation's mission is to foster innovative cooperation in science and technology that contributes to solving issues of interest to both the U.S. and Mexico. The foundation has the following objectives: to identify and develop opportunities for bi-national cooperation in science and technology; to promote the development of stakeholder and information networks; to identify and support management of bi-national financial resources, in order to sustain programs that can lead to medium range solutions; to study, facilitate and promote science and technology policy-making that enhances and strengthens bi-national cooperation between the U.S. and Mexico; and to base programs and actions firmly in communities and local institutions to ensure continuity and permanence.
Fields of interest: Engineering/technology; Science; International exchange.
International interests: Mexico.
Limitations: Giving limited to the U.S. and Mexico.
Officers and Governors:* Leopoldo Rodriguez Sanchez,* Chair.; Diana Natalicio,* Vice-Chair.; Karl A. Ruggeberg,* Treas.; Antonio Zarate Negorn; Bernard Robertson; Alvaro Alberto Aldama Rodriguez; Cipriano Santos; Blanca Trevino; and 7 additional governors.
EIN: 980143306

603
Vishnevskaya-Rostropovich Foundation
1776 K St., N.W., Ste. 800
Washington, DC 20006-2333 (202) 296-5730
FAX: (202) 452-7989; E-mail: info@rostropovich.org;
URL: http://www.rostropovich.org

Established in 1991.
Donors: Mstislav Rostropovich‡; Galina Vishnevskaya.
Grantmaker type: Public charity.
Financial data (yr. ended 11/30/10): Revenue, $3,068,207; assets, $3,662,804 (M); gifts received, $3,067,109; expenditures, $3,093,259; giving activities include $1,000 for grants.
Purpose and activities: The foundation's mission is to improve the health care of children in Russia and the former Soviet Union by conducting sustainable public health programs for children that focus on vaccine-preventable diseases and HIV/AIDS.
Fields of interest: Public health; Children.

International interests: Russia; Soviet Union (Former).
Type of support: In-kind gifts.
Limitations: Giving limited to Armenia, Azerbaijan, Georgia, Kyrgyzstan, and Russia.
Officer and Directors:* Leonard L. Silverstein,* Chair. and Treas.; Elena Rostropovich, Pres.; William P. Amoss, Exec. Dir.; James H. Billington; Monique Duroc-Danner; Harold M. Koenig, M.D.; Dominique Limet; Richard Miles; Thomas R. Pickering; Stanley Plotkin, M.D.; Yasuhiko Sata; Jerome Seydoux; Paul R. Smith; John F. Stapleton, M.D.; Charles H. Taylor; Galina Vishnevskaya; Russ Zajtchuk, M.D.
EIN: 521752473

604
Voices on the Border
3321 12th St. N.E.
Washington, DC 20017-4008 (202) 529-2912
FAX: (202) 526-4611; E-mail: voices@votb.org;
URL: http://www.votb.org

Grantmaker type: Public charity.
Financial data (yr. ended 12/31/10): Revenue, $188,507; assets, $29,279 (M); gifts received, $108,768; expenditures, $180,898; giving activities include $81,317 for grants.
Purpose and activities: The organization provides financial, logistical, and technical assistance to community-based non-governmental organizations in El Salvador that work to unite residents to improve living conditions and human capacity.
Fields of interest: International development; International relief.
International interests: El Salvador.
Limitations: Giving limited to El Salvador.
Officers: Betsy Shepard Cruz, Pres.; Annette Marshall, Secy.; Mark Reedy, Treas.; Tanya Snyder, Exec. Dir.
Board Members: Rebecca Cramer; Amy Hernandez; James Munro; Michael Terry; Janice Valder.
EIN: 521758738

605
Wallace Genetic Foundation, Inc.
4910 Massachusetts Ave., NW, Ste. 221
Washington, DC 20016-4368 (202) 966-2932
Contact: Patricia Lee, Co-Exec. Dir.; Carolyn Sand, Co-Exec. Dir.
FAX: (202) 966-3370;
E-mail: info@wallacegenetic.org; Additional e-mail: president@wallacegenetic.org; URL: http://www.wallacegenetic.org

Incorporated in 1959 in NY.
Donors: Henry A. Wallace‡; Jean Douglas.
Grantmaker type: Independent foundation.
Financial data (yr. ended 12/31/10): Assets, $167,962,024 (M); gifts received, $63,345,000; expenditures, $6,971,102; qualifying distributions, $6,620,384; giving activities include $6,221,000 for 92 grants (high: $2,000,000; low: $5,000).
Purpose and activities: Areas of interest are sustainable agriculture, protection of farmland near cities, plant genetic research, biodiversity protection, and environmental education.
Fields of interest: Public health, clean water supply; Public policy, research; Environmental education; Environment, natural resources; Agriculture.

International interests: Latin America; Soviet Union (Former).

Type of support: General/operating support; Continuing support; Land acquisition; Program development; Seed money; Research; Matching/challenge support.

Limitations: Applications accepted. Giving on a national basis. No grants to individuals, or for scholarships, endowments, multi-year commitments, or university overhead expenses; no loans.

Publications: Grants list.

Application information: Faxed or e-mailed proposals will not be accepted. Application form not required.

   Initial approach: 1- or 2-page letter and proposal
   Copies of proposal: 1
   Deadline(s): None
   Board meeting date(s): Six times a year
   Final notification: None

Officers and Directors:* Jean W. Douglas,* Pres.; Ann D. Cornell,* V.P. and Secy.; Joan D. Murray,* V.P. and Treas.; David W. Douglas,* V.P., Research; Patricia Lee, Co-Exec. Dir.; Carolyn Sand, Co-Exec. Dir.

Number of staff: 2 part-time professional.

EIN: 136162575

Recent grants for international programs:

605-1 ActionAid USA, Washington, DC, $75,000. For research and advocacy efforts on the impacts of biofuels on hunger and development in the US, Guatemala and Brazil. 2010.

605-2 Amazon Conservation Team, Arlington, VA, $75,000. For supporting Agroforestry and Biodiversity Conservation at the Inga Yachaicuri School. 2010.

605-3 American Bird Conservancy, The Plains, VA, $60,000. For the Birds, Pesticides and Toxics Program. 2010.

605-4 Canadian Rotarian Water Foundation, Toronto, Canada, $24,000. For the work of Steve Werner. 2010.

605-5 CARE USA, Atlanta, GA, $75,000. For the WASH Advocacy Initiative. 2010.

605-6 Center for Strategic and International Studies, Washington, DC, $50,000. For their WASH University Initiative. 2010.

605-7 Commonweal, Bolinas, CA, $25,000. For the work of the Friends of the Ganges. 2010.

605-8 Doctors Without Borders USA, New York, NY, $50,000. For general support. 2010.

605-9 Earth Policy Institute, Washington, DC, $50,000. For general support. 2010.

605-10 EcoLogic Development Fund, Cambridge, MA, $10,000. For the project, Community Water as a Catalyst for Biodiversity Conservation in Pico Bonito National Park, Honduras. 2010.

605-11 Global Community Monitor, El Cerrito, CA, $25,000. For general support. 2010.

605-12 Global Water Challenge, Washington, DC, $75,000. For WASH Advocacy Initiative. 2010.

605-13 Global Water Challenge, Washington, DC, $50,000. For general support. 2010.

605-14 Institute for Multi-Track Diplomacy, Arlington, VA, $25,000. For general support. 2010.

605-15 International Fund for Animal Welfare, Yarmouth Port, MA, $75,000. For Animal Action Week. 2010.

605-16 International Housing Coalition, Washington, DC, $25,000. For the assessment of the Senator Paul Simon Water for the Poor Act. 2010.

605-17 Millennium Water Alliance, Houston, TX, $25,000. For their advocacy work. 2010.

605-18 Natural Resources Defense Council, New York, NY, $50,000. For Global Safe Water Initiative. 2010.

605-19 Physicians for Social Responsibility, Washington, DC, $35,000. For the Confronting Toxics program. 2010.

605-20 Solar Electric Light Fund, Washington, DC, $50,000. For general support. 2010.

605-21 Tropics Foundation, Athens, GA, $50,000. For CATIE's joint graduate program in sustainable tourism, the Orton Library, the 6th Wallace Scientific Conference, and the coffee genetic improvement program. 2010.

605-22 Union of Concerned Scientists, Cambridge, MA, $75,000. For climate change program. 2010.

605-23 Water Advocates, Washington, DC, $250,000. For general support. 2010.

605-24 Water Engineers for the Americas, Santa Fe, NM, $25,000. For general support. 2010.

605-25 Water for People, Denver, CO, $75,000. For the WASH Advocacy Initiative. 2010.

605-26 Water.org, Kansas City, MO, $75,000. For the WASH Advocacy Initiative. 2010.

605-27 Wateraid America, New York, NY, $25,000. For the Water, Sanitation, and Hygiene (WASH) Working Group housed at InterAction. 2010.

605-28 Waterlines, Santa Fe, NM, $25,000. For general support. 2010.

605-29 Worldwatch Institute, Washington, DC, $25,000. For general support. 2010.

606

Woodrow Wilson International Center for Scholars

1 Woodrow Wilson Plz.
1300 Pennsylvania Ave., N.W.
Washington, DC 20004-3027 (202) 691-4000
Contact: Lee H. Hamilton, Pres.
FAX: (202) 691-4001;
E-mail: wwics@wilsoncenter.org; URL: http://www.wilsoncenter.org

Established by an act of Congress in 1968 in DC.

Grantmaker type: Public charity.

Financial data (yr. ended 09/30/10): Revenue, $16,452,666; assets, $106,395,510 (M); gifts received, $14,576,999; expenditures, $20,218,504; giving activities include $832,854 for 2 grants to organizations outside the U.S., and $413,628 for grants to individuals.

Purpose and activities: The mission of the center is to commemorate the ideals and concerns of Woodrow Wilson by providing a link between the world of ideas and the world of policy, and fostering research, study, discussion, and collaboration among a full spectrum of individuals concerned with policy and scholarship in national and world affairs.

Fields of interest: Historical activities; Environment, energy; Environment; Dispute resolution; International economic development; International affairs; Economics; Urban studies; American studies; Public policy, research; Public affairs, government agencies; Government/public administration; Public affairs.

International interests: Africa; Asia; Canada; China; Eastern & Central Europe; Latin America; Middle East; Mexico; Russia.

Type of support: Fellowships; Internship funds; Research; Scholarships—to individuals.

Limitations: Applications accepted. Giving on a national and international basis.

Publications: Application guidelines; Annual report; Informational brochure; Newsletter.

Application information: See web site for current fellowship opportunities, application guidelines, and deadlines. Application form required.

   Initial approach: Download application form and mail completed form to the center
   Copies of proposal: 10
   Deadline(s): Oct. 1
   Board meeting date(s): Feb., June, and Oct.
   Final notification: Mar.

Officers and Trustees:* Joseph B. Gildenhorn,* Chair.; Sander R. Gerber,* Vice-Chair.; Lee H. Hamilton,* Pres.; John T. Dysland,* C.F.O.; James H. Billington; Hillary R. Clinton; Wayne Clough; Charles Cobb; Robin Cook; Arne Duncan; David Ferriero; Charles L. Glazer; Carlos Gutierrez; Susan Hutchison; Barry S. Jackson; James Leach; Ignacio E. Sanchez; Kathleen Sebelius.

Number of staff: 83 full-time professional; 5 part-time professional; 52 full-time support; 2 part-time support.

EIN: 521067541

607

Women for Women International

4455 Connecticut Ave., N.W., Ste. 200
Washington, DC 20008-2300 (202) 737-7705
FAX: (202) 737-7709;
E-mail: general@womenforwomen.org; URL: http://www.womenforwomen.org
Blog: http://wfwnotesfromthefield.wordpress.com/
Facebook: http://www.facebook.com/womenforwomen
Flickr: http://www.flickr.com/photos/womenforwomen/
LinkedIn: http://www.linkedin.com/company/women-for-women-international
Twitter: http://twitter.com/#!/womenforwomen
YouTube: http://www.youtube.com/user/WomenforWomenIntl

Grantmaker type: Public charity.

Financial data (yr. ended 12/31/10): Revenue, $31,197,464; assets, $20,320,020 (M); gifts received, $31,345,352; expenditures, $27,417,656; giving activities include $4,772,919 for grants to organizations outside the U.S.

Purpose and activities: The organization helps women in war-torn regions rebuild their lives by giving them financial and emotional support, job skills training, rights education, access to capital, and assistance for small business development.

Fields of interest: Civil/human rights, women; International development; Employment; Women.

International interests: Kosovo; Afghanistan; Bosnia-Herzegovina; Colombia; Congo; Iraq; Nigeria; Rwanda; Serbia; Sudan.

Type of support: Grants to individuals; Loans—to individuals.

Limitations: Applications not accepted. Giving on an international basis in Afghanistan, Bosnia-Herzegovina, Colombia, the Democratic Republic of Congo, Iraq, Kosovo, Nigeria, Rwanda, and Sudan.

Publications: Annual report.

Application information: Unsolicited requests for funds not accepted.

Officers and Directors:* Mary Menell Zients,* Chair.; Zainab Salbi,* C.E.O.; Amjad Atallah; Andrea Bernstein; Jewelle Bickford; Katherine Borsecnik;

Jan Brandt; Gay Browne; Christine Fisher; Eva Haller; Dr. Kedi Letlaka-Rennert; Sharon Marcil; Nancy Rubin; Cythnia Ryan; Lekha Singh; Anne B. Zill.
EIN: 521838756

608
Women Thrive Worldwide
(formerly Women's Edge Coalition, Inc.)
1825 Connecticut Ave., N.W., Ste. 600
Washington, DC   20009-5743   (202) 884-8396
FAX: (202) 884-8366;
E-mail: thrive@womenthrive.org; URL: http://www.womenthrive.org
Facebook: http://www.facebook.com/womenthrive
Twitter: http://twitter.com/WomenThrive
YouTube: http://www.youtube.com/user/WomenThriveWorldwide

Established in 1998 in DC.
Grantmaker type: Public charity.
Financial data (yr. ended 12/31/10): Revenue, $2,068,175; assets, $1,690,850 (M); gifts received, $2,058,108; expenditures, $2,222,812; giving activities include $20,000 for grants, $36,631 for grants to organizations outside the U.S., and $7 for grants to individuals.
Purpose and activities: The organization advocates for international economic policies and human rights that support women worldwide in their actions to end poverty in their lives, communities and nations.
Fields of interest: International economic development; International development; International human rights; Women.
Limitations: Giving on a worldwide basis.
Publications: Financial statement; Newsletter.
Officers and Directors:* Shamaya Gilo,* Chair.; Susan Cornell Wilkes,* Vice-Chair.; Ritu Sharma Fox,* Pres.; Bill Reese,* Secy.; Mike Caggiano,* Treas.; Mona Dave; Carol Head; Suzanne Lerner; Joe Keefe; Sarah Newhall; Farhiya Noor; Cathy Novelli; Elise Fiber Smith.
EIN: 522100597

609
The Zients Family Foundation, Inc.
4500 Garfield St., NW
Washington, DC   20007-1131

Established in 2003 in DC.
Donor: Jeffery Zients.
Grantmaker type: Independent foundation.
Financial data (yr. ended 12/31/10): Assets, $4,620,794 (M); gifts received, $375,000; expenditures, $988,207; qualifying distributions, $872,925; giving activities include $864,125 for 54 grants (high: $231,500; low: $330).
Purpose and activities: Giving primarily for education, health organizations, children, youth and social services, and to an organization supporting women of conflict.
Fields of interest: International conflict resolution; Education; Health organizations; Human services; Children/youth, services; Women, centers/services.
Type of support: Annual campaigns; Program development.
Limitations: Applications not accepted. Giving primarily in Washington, DC.
Application information: Unsolicited requests for funds not accepted.

Trustees: Jennifer Nance; Mary Zients; Steven Farina.
EIN: 546520936

610
The Jennie Zoline Foundation
2099 Pennsylvania Ave. N.W., Ste. 900
Washington, DC   20006-6804

Established in 1987 in DC.
Donor: Frank H. Pearl.
Grantmaker type: Independent foundation.
Financial data (yr. ended 09/30/10): Assets, $15,578 (M); gifts received, $220,000; expenditures, $208,121; qualifying distributions, $207,500; giving activities include $207,500 for 7 grants (high: $100,000; low: $5,000).
Fields of interest: Performing arts; International economic development; Higher education; Human services.
Limitations: Applications not accepted. Giving primarily in Washington, DC.
Application information: Contributes only to pre-selected organizations.
Officers and Directors:* Frank H. Pearl,* Pres.; Geryl T. Pearl,* V.P.
EIN: 133445391

611
Zonta Club of Washington, D.C. Foundation
5002 Hurst Terr.
Washington, DC   20016-3413
E-mail: wdcfoundation@zontawashingtondc.org;
URL: http://www.zontawashingtondc.org/foundation.html

Established in 2003 in DC.
Grantmaker type: Public charity.
Financial data (yr. ended 05/31/11): Revenue, $46,133; assets, $42,555 (M); gifts received, $36,242; expenditures, $48,222; giving activities include $47,500 for grants.
Purpose and activities: Grants awarded to both local and international service projects; scholarships awarded to women attending universities in Washington, DC.
Fields of interest: International relief; Human services; Women.
Type of support: Scholarships—to individuals.
Application information: Scholarship applications accepted through the students' institution; the foundation does not accept direct applications from students.
Officers and Directors:* Sandra Shaw,* Pres.; Carol Beaver,* V.P.; Janet Southby,* Secy.; Judy Fitzpatrick,* Treas.; Marie Bundy; Liz Folsom.
EIN: 521226538

612
Anthony R. Abraham Foundation, Inc.
1320 S. Dixie Hwy., Ste. 241
Coral Gables, FL   33146-2937   (305) 665-2222
Contact: Anthony R. Abraham, Chair.

Established in 1978 in FL.
Donor: Anthony R. Abraham.
Grantmaker type: Independent foundation.
Financial data (yr. ended 12/31/10): Assets, $34,587,573 (M); expenditures, $1,479,208; qualifying distributions, $1,479,208; giving activities include $1,322,151 for 87 grants (high: $215,000; low: $150).
Purpose and activities: Giving primarily for health, children, youth and social services, education, and Christian churches and organizations.
Fields of interest: International relief; Education; Health organizations, association; Medical research, institute; Human services; Children/youth, services; Foundations (private grantmaking); Christian agencies & churches.
Limitations: Giving primarily in Miami, FL. No grants to individuals.
Application information: Application form not required.
  Initial approach: Letter
  Copies of proposal: 1
  Deadline(s): None
  Board meeting date(s): Various
Officers and Directors:* Anthony R. Abraham,* Chair.; Thomas G. Abraham,* Secy.-Treas.; George Abraham; Nicholas Daniels; Richard Shadyac; Anthony Shaker; Joseph Shaker.
EIN: 591837290

613
The Abramson Family Foundation
376 Regatta Dr.
Jupiter, FL   33477-4076   (215) 542-1222
Contact: Judith Abramson Felgoise, Tr.

Established in 1996 in FL.
Donor: Judith Abramson Felgoise.
Grantmaker type: Independent foundation.
Financial data (yr. ended 06/30/10): Assets, $60,330,389 (M); gifts received, $8,674,226; expenditures, $9,866,016; qualifying distributions, $9,561,904; giving activities include $9,224,671 for 64 grants (high: $3,091,781; low: $100).
Purpose and activities: Giving primarily to Jewish organizations, educational institutions, and health associations.
Fields of interest: Arts; Higher education; Education; Hospitals (general); Human services; Jewish federated giving programs; Jewish agencies & synagogues.
International interests: Israel.
Type of support: Scholarships—to individuals.
Limitations: Applications accepted. Giving primarily in PA.
Application information: Contact foundation for scholarship application guidelines. Application form required.
  Initial approach: Proposal
  Deadline(s): None

FLORIDA

Trustees: Leonard Abramson; Madlyn Abramson; Judith Abramson Felgoise; Jerome S. Goodman; Marcy Abramson Shoemaker; Nancy Abramson Wolfson; Joseph M. Yohlin.
EIN: 311482888
Recent grants for international programs:
613-1 American Friends of Lubavitch, Washington, DC, $10,000. For general support. 2010.
613-2 American Friends of the Israel Museum, New York, NY, $100,000. For general support. 2010.
613-3 Birthright Israel Foundation, NEXT, New York, NY, $1,000,000. For general support and for NEXT, the young Jewish adult organization, mostly Birthright Israel alumni. 2010.
613-4 Israel Sports Center for the Disabled, Friends of, Laguna Hills, CA, $36,000. For general support. 2010.
613-5 Seeds of Peace, New York, NY, $10,000. For general support. 2010.

614
Alfalit International, Inc.
3026 N.W. 79th Ave.
Miami, FL 33122-1010 (305) 597-9077
FAX: (305) 597-9078; E-mail: alfalit@alfalit.org;
URL: http://www.alfalit.org
Twitter: http://twitter.com/#!/alfalit

Established in 1961.
Grantmaker type: Public charity.
Financial data (yr. ended 12/31/09): Revenue, $2,320,021; assets, $780,027 (M); gifts received, $1,886,955; expenditures, $2,474,603; giving activities include $109,517 for grants to organizations outside the U.S.
Purpose and activities: The organization promotes pre-school, literacy, elementary education, health, nutrition, and Christianity in Latin America, Portugal, and Spanish and Portuguese-speaking African countries.
Fields of interest: Education, early childhood education; Elementary school/education; Adult education—literacy, basic skills & GED; Health care; Nutrition; Christian agencies & churches.
International interests: Portugal; Spain; Africa; Latin America; South America.
Type of support: In-kind gifts.
Limitations: Applications not accepted. Giving on an international basis, with emphasis on Latin America, Portugal, and Spanish and Portuguese-speaking African countries.
Application information: Unsolicited requests for funds not accepted.
Officers and Directors:* Roberto Perez, Pres.; Joseph Milton, V.P.; William C. Murff, Secy.; Eugenio M. Fernandez, Treas.; Aida Iglesias.
EIN: 591595459

615
American Nicaraguan Foundation, Inc.
1000 N.W. 57th Court St., Ste. 770
Miami, FL 33126 (305) 374-3391
FAX: (305) 374-5993;
E-mail: info@aidnicaragua.org; URL: http://www.aidnicaragua.org
Blog: http://aidnicaragua.blogspot.com/
Facebook: http://www.facebook.com/anfni?ref=search&sid=1606879.3925604929..1
Flickr: http://www.flickr.com/photos/aidnicaragua
Twitter: http://twitter.com/anf

Grantmaker type: Public charity.
Financial data (yr. ended 12/31/10): Revenue, $172,977,949; assets, $34,916,764 (M); gifts received, $169,452,068; expenditures, $167,214,538; giving activities include $162,180,413 for grants to organizations outside the U.S.
Purpose and activities: The foundation seeks to aid the poor in Nicaragua by forging strategic alliances to procure and distribute commodity donations and funds to community-based organizations that have been selected based on their effectiveness, transparency, and spirit of service.
Fields of interest: Community/economic development; Community development, neighborhood associations; Community development, neighborhood development; Disasters, floods; Disasters, preparedness/services; Education; Education, services; Food services; Food services, commodity distribution; Health care; Health care, support services; Homeless, human services; Hospitals (general); Housing/shelter; Housing/shelter, development; Housing/shelter, homeless; Human services; International affairs; International development; International relief; Medical care, community health systems; Medical care, outpatient care; Nursing home/convalescent facility; Nutrition; Public health school/education; Rural development; Safety, education; Secondary school/education; Tropical diseases; Urban/community development; Women, centers/services; Youth development.
International interests: Nicaragua.
Type of support: In-kind gifts.
Limitations: Giving primarily in Nicaragua.
Publications: Annual report; Financial statement.
Officers: F. Alfredo Pellas, Jr., Pres.; Ricardo Roman, V.P.; Armando J. Rodriguez, C.E.O. and Exec. Dir.; Ruben Diaz, Esq., Secy.
Board Members: Carlos Abaunza-Hunter; Carla Barrow; Paco Bendana-McEwan; Helen Aguirre Ferre; and 24 additional board members.
EIN: 650326517

616
Ted Arison Family Foundation USA, Inc.
(formerly Arison Foundation, Inc.)
c/o Safo, LLC
20900 N. E. 30th Ave., Ste. 1015
Aventura, FL 33180-2166 (305) 891-0017
E-mail: hanna@SAFOUSA.com; URL: http://www.arison.co.il/group/en/

Incorporated in 1981 in FL.
Donors: Carnival Cruise Lines, Inc.; Festivale Maritime, Inc.; Intercon Overseas, Inc.; Ted Arison Charitable Trust.
Grantmaker type: Independent foundation.
Financial data (yr. ended 12/31/09): Assets, $446,513,460 (M); expenditures, $17,237,954; qualifying distributions, $17,445,091; giving activities include $11,744,573 for 57 grants (high: $3,866,856; low: $2,500)..
Purpose and activities: Emphasis on arts and cultural programs; support also for Jewish welfare funds.
Fields of interest: Children/youth, services; Health care; Education; Arts; Human services; Jewish federated giving programs; Disabilities, people with.
Limitations: Applications accepted. Giving primarily in NY and Israel.
Publications: Grants list.
Application information:

Initial approach: Letter
Deadline(s): None
Officers and Trustees:* Shari Arison Glazer,* Chair.; Jason Arison,* C.E.O.; Arnaldo Perez, V.P.; Cassie Arison; David Arison; Marilyn Arison.
EIN: 592128429
Recent grants for international programs:
616-1 Al-Manarah Association for the Advancement of the Arab Blind in Israel, Nazareth, Israel, $32,800. For activities to promote social awareness for the blind. 2009.
616-2 Alexander Muss Institute for Israel Education, Rockville Centre, NY, $100,000. For general support. 2009.
616-3 America-Israel Cultural Foundation, New York, NY, $250,000. For general support. 2009.
616-4 American Associates, Ben-Gurion University of the Negev, New York, NY, $113,939. For Youth Mathematics Forum. 2009.
616-5 American Friends of Ilan, New York, NY, $23,100. For therapeutic treatments at Day Care Center in Israel. 2009.
616-6 American Friends of Ilan, New York, NY, $10,000. To support integration of disabled children in the community in Israel. 2009.
616-7 American Friends of Migdal Ohr, New York, NY, $18,000. To provide support to children in Israel. 2009.
616-8 American Friends of the Tel Aviv Museum, New York, NY, $1,000,000. For support for Museum in Tel Aviv. 2009.
616-9 American Friends of the Tel Aviv University, New York, NY, $80,000. For mentoring programs for girls in distress. 2009.
616-10 American Society for Yad Vashem, New York, NY, $100,000. For training program for teachers. 2009.
616-11 Amutat Al - Promoting Unique Programs in the Community in the Negev, Beer Sheva, Israel, $16,344. For therapeutic horse riding lessons for disabled youth. 2009.
616-12 Anonymous for Animal Rights, Tel Aviv, Israel, $24,300. For national education projects for youth. 2009.
616-13 Athena Fund, Tel Aviv, Israel, $180,000. For teacher kits. 2009.
616-14 Beit Noam, Tel Aviv, Israel, $20,500. For therapeutic groups for adolescents. 2009.
616-15 ERAN - Israeli Association for Emotional First Aid by Phone, Netanya, Israel, $13,000. For emergency support to keep Emotional First Aid Hotline of Israeli Coalition for Trauma in operation. 2009.
616-16 Essence of Life-International, Miami, FL, $3,866,856. For operating support. 2009.
616-17 Etgarim Association, Tel Aviv, Israel, $13,333. To support integrating disabled youth into the military. 2009.
616-18 Givat Haviva Educational Foundation, New York, NY, $27,150. For Face to Face - Dialogue meetings for Jewish and Arab youth. 2009.
616-19 Hadassah, The Womens Zionist Organization of America, New York, NY, $46,620. To support Hadassah Medical Center. 2009.
616-20 Hakfar Hayarok, Ramat HaSharon, Israel, $40,100. To purchase basic furniture for boarding school. 2009.
616-21 Heznek La-Atid, Tel Aviv, Israel, $35,000. For Heznek Program in Meir Shfaya boarding school. 2009.
616-22 Interdisciplinary Center Herzliya, Herzliya, Israel, $290,000. To train students to compete and participate in the global economy. 2009.

616-23 Interdisciplinary Center Herzliya, Herzliya, Israel, $250,000. For research and promotion of Communication Awareness Concept, study of the importance of an individual's inner balance as a driving force that allows him or her to develop and achieve self-realization. 2009.

616-24 Israeli Center for Human Dignity, Tel Aviv, Israel, $30,000. For teachers' seminar, Regaining Teachers' Authority. 2009.

616-25 Jaffa Institute, Jaffa, Israel, $12,285. For scholarships. 2009.

616-26 Krembo Wings, Tel Aviv, Israel, $40,530. To provide transportation for Maayan Baruch facility. 2009.

616-27 Lautman Foundation, Israel, $20,194. For Tzamarot Interservice Principal Training. 2009.

616-28 Lifeline for the Old, Jerusalem, Israel, $25,369. To purchase equipment for day care center for the elderly. 2009.

616-29 Magen David Adom, Jerusalem, Israel, $40,000. To print manuals for Youth Volunteer Project. 2009.

616-30 MATAN - Your Way to Give, Tel Aviv, Israel, $100,000. For special support. 2009.

616-31 NATAL - Israel Trauma Center for Victims of Terrorism, Tel Aviv, Israel, $25,900. For emergency aid supporting therapy for individuals as a result of the fighting in Gaza. 2009.

616-32 North American Conference on Ethiopian Jewry-Israel, Jerusalem, Israel, $30,000. For intensive after-school education program for Ethiopian children in Rishon Le Tzion. 2009.

616-33 PEF Israel Endowment Funds, New York, NY, $1,116,194. 2009.

616-34 Prisoner Rehabilitation Authority, Jerusalem, Israel, $23,040. To support preparatory school for rehabilitation of former female convicts. 2009.

616-35 Rashi Foundation, Ben-Shemen, Israel, $121,099. For scholarships for single mothers. 2009.

616-36 Ruach Tova, Tel Aviv, Israel, $665,000. For operating support. 2009.

616-37 School of Arts Foundation, Tel Aviv, Israel, $77,500. For renovations to school's Conservatory. 2009.

616-38 SELAH - Israel Crisis Management Center, Tel Aviv, Israel, $29,549. For operating support to provide services to groups from elementary schools in Hatikva Neighborhood. 2009.

616-39 Shoval Kibbutz, Shoval, Israel, $12,007. For surgical equipment for Community Dental Clinic. 2009.

616-40 Special Olympics Israel, Netanya, Israel, $50,000. For general support. 2009.

616-41 Technoda-Mada'at Non-Profit Organization, Givat Olga - Hadera, Israel, $37,500. For Young Inventor Program. 2009.

616-42 Tel Aviv Foundation, Tel Aviv, Israel, $600,000. For construction of Conservatory. 2009.

616-43 United Kibbutz Movement, Israel, $25,300. For Parents Involved Program. 2009.

616-44 Weizmann Institute of Science, Rehovot, Israel, $27,270. For One Camp Class in Active Science Group. 2009.

616-45 Yokneam Community Center, Yokneam, Israel, $19,625. For Bait Ham after-school program for at-risk children. 2009.

616-46 ZAKA Search and Rescue, Jerusalem, Israel, $42,800. To send rescue to team to Mumbai, India to assist with the work after terror attack. 2009.

617
The Around Foundation
c/o James Gleick
808 Windsor Ln.
Key West, FL 33040-6441

Established in 1997 in NY.
Donor: James Gleick.
Grantmaker type: Independent foundation.
Financial data (yr. ended 04/30/10): Assets, $4,247,487 (M); expenditures, $247,665; qualifying distributions, $200,050; giving activities include $200,050 for 30 grants (high: $25,000; low: $250).
Fields of interest: Media, radio; Arts; Education; Human services; International human rights.
Limitations: Applications not accepted. Giving primarily in NY. No grants to individuals.
Application information: Contributes only to pre-selected organizations.
Trustees: Cynthia Crossen; James Gleick.
EIN: 113377271

618
Association of American Schools in South America, Inc.
1911 N.W. 150th Ave., Ste. 101
Pembroke Pines, FL 33028-2871
(954) 436-4034
FAX: (954) 436-4092; E-mail: enicolau@aassa.com; URL: http://www.aassa.com

Established in 1977 in FL.
Grantmaker type: Public charity.
Financial data (yr. ended 06/30/11): Revenue, $1,221,365; assets, $1,011,615 (M); gifts received, $530,545; expenditures, $1,004,193.
Purpose and activities: The association works to provide and promote programs and services to member schools to enhance the quality of American international education, particularly in South America.
Fields of interest: Elementary/secondary education; International affairs, formal/general education; International affairs; Education.
Officers and Trustees:* Philip Joslin,* Pres.; Susan Barba,* V.P.; Steven Herrera,* Secy.; Bill Pearson,* Treas.; Paul Poore, Exec. Dir.; David Cardenas; David Wells.
EIN: 581333760

619
Assurant Corporate Giving Program
c/o Charitable Giving Prog. Office
11222 Quail Roost Dr.
Miami, FL 33157-6596
Contact: Debbie Burbridge
E-mail: debbie.burbridge@assurant.com; URL: http://www.assurantsolutions.com/inCommunity.html
Additional URL: http://www.assurant.com/inc/assurant/community/solutions.html

Grantmaker type: Corporate giving program.
Financial data (yr. ended 12/31/10): Total giving, $1,584,369, including $832,098 for grants, and $752,271 for employee matching gifts.
Purpose and activities: As a complement to its foundation, Assurant also makes charitable contributions to nonprofit organizations directly. Special emphasis is directed towards programs

designed to address arts and culture, education, health care, and human services. Support is given primarily in areas of company operations, with emphasis on southern Florida, Atlanta, Georgia, and Lawton, Oklahoma, and in Argentina, Brazil, Canada, Chile, China, Germany, Ireland, Italy, Mexico, Puerto Rico, Spain, and the United Kingdom.
Fields of interest: Housing/shelter; Food services; Arts; Education; Health care; Disasters, preparedness/services; United Ways and Federated Giving Programs; Children/youth.
International interests: Argentina; Brazil; Canada; Chile; China; Germany; Ireland; Italy; Mexico; Spain; United Kingdom.
Type of support: General/operating support; Continuing support; Program development; Scholarship funds; Employee volunteer services; Sponsorships; Employee matching gifts.
Limitations: Applications accepted. Giving primarily in areas of company operations, with emphasis on southern FL, Atlanta, GA, and Lawton OK, and in Argentina, Brazil, Canada, Chile, China, Germany, Ireland, Italy, Mexico, Puerto Rico, Spain, and the United Kingdom. No support for government agencies, social, or political organizations, religious organizations not of direct benefit to the entire community, trade, industry, or professional associations, or fraternal, labor, or veterans' organizations. No grants to individuals, or for sports events or sponsorships or fundraising, advertising or tickets, travel, or discretionary social functions.
Publications: Application guidelines; Corporate giving report; Informational brochure; Program policy statement (including application guidelines).
Application information: Proposals should be submitted using organization letterhead. Multi-year funding is not automatic. The Corporate Communications Department handles giving. The company has a staff that only handles contributions. Application form not required.
  Initial approach: Proposal to headquarters
  Copies of proposal: 1
  Deadline(s): None
  Committee meeting date(s): Quarterly
  Final notification: 6 to 8 weeks
Number of staff: 1 full time professional.

620
Atlantic Center for the Arts, Inc.
1414 Art Center Ave.
New Smyrna Beach, FL 32168-5560
(386) 427-6975
Contact: Ann Brady, Exec. Dir.
FAX: (386) 427-5669;
E-mail: program@atlanticcenterforthearts.org;
URL: http://www.atlanticcenterforthearts.org

Founded in 1977.
Grantmaker type: Public charity.
Financial data (yr. ended 12/31/10): Revenue, $698,585; assets, $8,805,340 (M); gifts received, $405,501; expenditures, $1,417,423.
Purpose and activities: The center provides and promotes art and humanities in all their forms, including the visual and performing arts and cultural education through instruction.
Fields of interest: Arts; Literature; Performing arts; Visual arts.
Type of support: Capital campaigns; Endowments; Use of facilities; Employee matching gifts; Scholarships—to individuals; In-kind gifts.
Limitations: Applications accepted. Giving limited to FL.

Publications: Application guidelines; Annual report; Informational brochure; Newsletter.
Application information: Application form required.
Initial approach: Download application form
Deadline(s): Jan. 16, Feb. 6, Mar. 6, May 23, and Oct. 17 for Residencies
Board meeting date(s): 4th Wed. of Jan., Mar., May, July, Sept., and Nov.
Officers and Trustees: Margery Pabst,* Chair.; Ann Brady, Exec. Dir.; Bradley D. Blum; Lynn Conte; Charlotte Everbach; Jose B. Fernandez, Ph.D.; Marcia Frey; Edward N. Harris; Steven "Woody" Igou; Beverly P. Lassiter; A.C. Leerdam; Van Massey; Andrew McCorkle; Hiram Powell, Ph.D.; and William Preston; and 9 additional trustees.
Number of staff: 10 full-time professional; 3 full-time support; 1 part-time support.
EIN: 591998321

621

Danker Basham Foundation, Inc.
3717 W. North B St.
Tampa, FL   33609-1335

Established in 1994 in FL.
Donor: Robert D. Basham.
Grantmaker type: Independent foundation.
Financial data (yr. ended 12/31/10): Assets, $10,113,998 (M); expenditures, $411,590; qualifying distributions, $356,914; giving activities include $356,914 for 16 grants.
Purpose and activities: Giving primarily for Christian ministries, and children, youth, and human services.
Fields of interest: United Ways and Federated Giving Programs; Boys & girls clubs; Education; Youth development, centers/clubs; Human services; Children/youth, services; International relief, 2004 tsunami; Christian agencies & churches.
Limitations: Applications not accepted. Giving primarily in FL. No grants to individuals.
Application information: Contributes only to pre-selected organizations.
Officer: Robert D. Basham, Pres.
Director: Richard Danker.
EIN: 593284079

622

The Blank Family Foundation, Inc.
(formerly The New Blank Family Foundation, Inc.)
3455 N.W. 54th St.
Miami, FL   33142-3309
Contact: Robin Reiter
URL: http://www.blankfamily.org

Established in 2002 in FL.
Donor: Rose Blank Kramer Revocable Living Trust.
Grantmaker type: Independent foundation.
Financial data (yr. ended 12/31/10): Assets, $22,229,059 (M); expenditures, $1,206,806; qualifying distributions, $1,116,250; giving activities include $1,116,250 for 32 grants (high: $725,000; low: $250).
Purpose and activities: Giving primarily for Jewish causes, including federated giving programs; support also for human services, and the environment.
Fields of interest: Environment; Health organizations; Human services; Jewish federated giving programs; Jewish agencies & synagogues.
International interests: Israel.
Type of support: General/operating support.

Limitations: Applications not accepted. Giving primarily in FL, some funding nationally. No support for political or social organizations. No grants to individuals.
Application information: Contributes only to pre-selected organizations. Unsolicited requests for funds not accepted.
Board meeting date(s): Quarterly
Officers and Directors:* Jerome Blank,* Chair.; Andrew S. Blank,* Pres.; Kathleen Blank,* Secy.; Robert Frehling; Kathy Martin.
Number of staff: 1 part-time professional.
EIN: 920185953

623

The Cafesjian Family Foundation, Inc.
2400 9th St. N., Ste. 401
Naples, FL   34103
E-mail: info@cafesjianfoundation.org; *URL:* http://www.cafesjianfoundation.org

Established in 1996 in FL.
Donor: Gerard L. Cafesjian.
Grantmaker type: Independent foundation.
Financial data (yr. ended 12/31/09): Assets, $63,936,106 (M); gifts received, $2,674,392; expenditures, $948,192; qualifying distributions, $178,000; giving activities include $178,000 for 5 grants (high: $150,000; low: $1,000).
Purpose and activities: Giving primarily for economic development in the Republic of Armenia and for U.S.-Armenia friendship. Current interests are to: 1) promote Armenia's energy independence; 2) invest to support other economic development initiatives in Armenia; 3) promote Armenia's independent media sector, 4) giving for The Cafesjian Museum Foundation to create an international-caliber Center for the Arts in Armenia; 5) to bring new sources of debt and equity, capital, and direct foreign investment to Armenia; and 6) to build a stronger U.S.-Armenia relationship.
Fields of interest: Arts; Education; Health care; Housing/shelter; Human services; Children, services; International affairs; Community/economic development; Social sciences; Public affairs; Orthodox agencies & churches.
International interests: Armenia.
Type of support: General/operating support; Annual campaigns; Capital campaigns; Endowments; Technical assistance; Program-related investments/loans; Matching/challenge support.
Limitations: Applications not accepted. Giving primarily in the Republics of Armenia and Nagorno Karabakh; national funding in Washington, DC, and New York, NY; some funding also in MN. No grants to individuals.
Application information: Contributes only to pre-selected organizations.
Officers and Directors:* Gerard L. Cafesjian,* Pres.; Cleo T. Cafesjian,* V.P.; John Waters,* Secy.-Treas.
EIN: 593417473

624

Michael G. Cantonis Foundation, Inc.
P.O. Box 338
Tarpon Springs, FL   34688-0338

Established in 1982.

Donors: Michael G. Cantonis; Anastasia H. Cantonis; George H. Cantonis; Acme Sponge and Chamois Co.
Grantmaker type: Independent foundation.
Financial data (yr. ended 12/31/10): Assets, $2,439,173 (M); expenditures, $153,998; qualifying distributions, $138,535; giving activities include $138,535 for 19 grants (high: $41,000; low: $200).
Purpose and activities: Giving primarily for the Greek Orthodox Church, medicine and nursing, and medical-related fields on the island of Symi, Greece. Scholarships will be granted to students who have made the commitment to become a priest in the Greek Orthodox Church. The directors will also grant scholarship loans to students selected by a special committee who will study medicine or nursing and will serve in the medical-related field on the island of Symi, Greece.
Fields of interest: Education; Orthodox agencies & churches.
International interests: Greece.
Type of support: General/operating support.
Limitations: Giving primarily in FL; some giving also in NY and in Greece. No grants to individuals.
Application information:
Initial approach: Letter
Deadline(s): None
Officers and Directors:* George M. Cantonis,* Pres.; Cynthia Heller,* V.P. and Secy.; James M. Cantons,* V.P. and Treas.; Anastasia H. Cantonis,* V.P.
EIN: 592214565

625

Caribbean Conservation Corporation
4424 N.W. 13th St., Ste. B-11
Gainesville, FL   32609-1879   (352) 373-6441
Contact: David Godfrey, Exec. Dir.
FAX: (352) 375-2449; *E-mail:* ccc@cccturtle.org; *Toll-free tel.:* (800) 678-7853; *URL:* http://www.cccturtle.org

Established in 1959.
Grantmaker type: Public charity.
Financial data (yr. ended 12/31/09): Revenue, $1,692,218; assets, $3,593,065 (M); gifts received, $1,395,772; expenditures, $1,776,627; giving activities include $327,836 for grants, and $4,250 for grants to organizations outside the U.S.
Purpose and activities: The organization aims to ensure the survival of sea turtles within the wider Caribbean basin and Atlantic through research, education, training, advocacy and the protection of the natural habits upon which they depend.
Fields of interest: Animals/wildlife, preservation/protection.
International interests: Caribbean.
Type of support: Research.
Limitations: Applications accepted. Giving limited to FL and the Caribbean.
Publications: Application guidelines.
Application information: Application form required.
Deadline(s): Nov. 16
Final notification: Mar.
Officers and Board Members:* Landon T. Clay,* Chair.; Peggy M. Cavanaugh,* Pres.; F. Peter Rose,* Secy.; Anthony Knorr,* Ph.D., Treas.; David Godfrey, Exec. Dir.; Mario A. Boza; Archie F. Carr III, Ph.D.; and 18 additional board members.
EIN: 596151069

626
The Chatlos Foundation, Inc.
P.O. Box 915048
Longwood, FL 32791-5048 (407) 862-5077
Contact: William J. Chatlos, C.E.O. and Pres.
E-mail: info@chatlos.org; URL: http://www.chatlos.org

Incorporated in 1953 in NY.
Donors: Bristol Door and Lumber Co., Inc.; William F. Chatlos†.
Grantmaker type: Independent foundation.
Financial data (yr. ended 12/31/10): Assets, $67,887,339 (M); expenditures, $4,221,739; qualifying distributions, $3,144,512; giving activities include $2,369,323 for 308 grants (average: $1,000–$50,000).
Purpose and activities: Grants for higher education and religious causes; giving also for hospitals, health agencies, social services, and child welfare.
Fields of interest: Higher education; Nursing school/education; Theological school/education; Education; Hospitals (general); Health care; Health organizations, association; Human services; Children/youth, services.
Type of support: General/operating support; Equipment; Debt reduction; Program development; Publication; Curriculum development; Scholarship funds; Technical assistance; Matching/challenge support.
Limitations: Applications accepted. Giving on a national basis. No support for individual church congregations, primary or secondary schools or for the arts, or for organizations in existence for less than two years. No grants to individuals, or for seed money, deficit financing, endowment funds, medical research, conferences, bricks and mortar, or multi-year grants; no loans.
Publications: Application guidelines; Informational brochure (including application guidelines).
Application information: See foundation web site for proposal instructions. Application form may be requested in writing or printed from the foundation web site. Only 1 grant to an organization within a 12-month period. Application form required.
  Initial approach: Proposal (no more than 5 pages)
  Copies of proposal: 1
  Deadline(s): None
  Board meeting date(s): Quarterly
  Final notification: Immediately
Officers and Trustees:* Kathryn A. Randle,* Chair.; William J. Chatlos,* C.E.O. and Pres.; Michele C. Roach, Sr. V.P.; William J. Chatlos III, V.P.; Cindee L. Random, Treas.; Janet Chatlos; Cherlyn Dannhaeuser; Kimberly C. Grimm; Charles O. Morgan; Brianne Ortt.
Number of staff: 4 full-time professional; 1 part-time professional.
EIN: 136161425
Recent grants for international programs:
626-1 American Leprosy Missions, Greenville, SC, $10,000. For the Buruli ulcer projects, which will provide life-changing treatment for children and adults. 2010.
626-2 Cedarville University, Cedarville, OH, $10,000. For faculty and staff leaders of short-term student missions teams participating in the Mission Involvement Services program. 2010.
626-3 Christian Broadcasting Network, Virginia Beach, VA, $20,000. To produce and broadcast live Farsi programs from the Mohabat studios in Chatsworth, CA for broadcast in Iran. 2010.

626-4 Christian Research Institute, Charlotte, NC, $15,000. To partially fund staffing, software and hardware for the development of video capabilities for new television program. 2010.
626-5 Elam Ministries, Alpharetta, GA, $15,000. For the Leadership Development training program for the Iranian Church. 2010.
626-6 Evangelical Christian Humanitarian Outreach for Cuba, Miami, FL, $10,000. To supply independent Christian seminaries in Cuba with laptop computers for training and outreach programs. 2010.
626-7 Evangelism Explosion International, Fort Lauderdale, FL, $15,000. To print student books for training Christian children how to share the gospel. 2010.
626-8 Faith Comes By Hearing International Foundation, Albuquerque, NM, $10,000. To implement new Audio Bible School listening program at the request of the Bible Society of Peru and the governments of Arequipa, Huancayo and Lima. 2010.
626-9 Focus on the Family, Colorado Springs, CO, $10,000. For the Focus Leadership Institute designed to educate, mentor and develop young, college-age leaders. 2010.
626-10 Friends of Israel Gospel Ministry, Bellmawr, NJ, $10,000. To expand the worldwide outreach of the ministry. 2010.
626-11 Gordon-Conwell Theological Seminary, South Hamilton, MA, $20,000. For scholarship funds to foreign nationals agreeing to return to their home countries to minister. 2010.
626-12 Jews for Jesus, San Francisco, CA, $10,000. For funding to purchase and renovate a building in the land of Israel, to be used as a secure base of operations. 2010.
626-13 Larry McFadden Ministries, Orlando, FL, $10,000. For Pastors' training conferences in Ghana, West Africa and South India. 2010.
626-14 Leading the Way International, Atlanta, GA, $10,000. For 24/7 satellite channel THE KINGDOM SAT which airs biblically sound programming throughout the Middle East, North Africa and Europe. 2010.
626-15 Luis Palau Association, Beaverton, OR, $10,000. For training and mentoring for Next Generation Alliance evangelists from 5 continents. 2010.
626-16 New Tribes Mission, Sanford, FL, $10,000. For the missionary training, education and livelihood skill development of members of the Tagbanwa Tribal Church in Palawan Island, Philippines. 2010.
626-17 ORBIS International, New York, NY, $10,000. For the blindness prevention and treatment programs in developing countries. 2010.
626-18 Peter Deyneka Russian Ministries, Wheaton, IL, $15,000. To continue to evangelize, train, equip and mobilize the Next Generation in the former Soviet Union and Central Asia. 2010.
626-19 Pioneers, Inc., Orlando, FL, $15,000. For the CPM Muslim World expansion and training initiative. 2010.
626-20 SAT-7 North American, Easton, MD, $10,000. For SAT-7 PARS Seminary of the Air (SOTA) curriculum production. 2010.
626-21 SIM USA, Charlotte, NC, $10,000. For library material and facilities' needs for the Theological Institutions of the Evangelical Church of West Africa. 2010.

626-22 Trans World Radio, Cary, NC, $10,000. For airtime costs of the Strategic Programming to China project. 2010.
626-23 Tyndale Theological Seminary, Amsterdam, Netherlands, $25,000. For scholarships for needy students from Eastern Europe, Africa, and Asia. 2010.
626-24 World Team, Warrington, PA, $10,000. For the Mission: Mobilization program designed to impact long-term church planting by increasing the number of missionaries to meet growing demands for ministry. 2010.
626-25 Wycliffe Bible Translators, Orlando, FL, $20,000. To continue the Asia Area Consultant Development Project. 2010.

627
Cigar Family Charitable Foundation, Inc.
P.O. Box 2030
Tampa, FL 33601-2030 (813) 248-2124
E-mail: cfcf@cigarfamily.com; URL: http://www.cigarfamilycharitablefoundation.com

Grantmaker type: Public charity.
Financial data (yr. ended 12/31/10): Revenue, $837,713; assets, $640,046 (M); gifts received, $825,430; expenditures, $999,305; giving activities include $958,463 for grants.
Fields of interest: Health care; Education; International development.
International interests: Dominican Republic.
Limitations: Giving primarily in the Dominican Republic.
Officers: Carlos Fuente, Jr., Pres.; Carlos Fuente, Sr., V.P.; Robert Newman, V.P.; Eric Newman, Secy.-Treas.; Camille Wingfield, Exec. Dir.
EIN: 593735324

628
James H. Clark Charitable Foundation
505 South Flagler Dr., Ste. 900
West Palm Beach, FL 33401-5948

Established in 1999 in NV.
Donors: James H. Clark; Monaco Partners, LP; James K. Clark.
Grantmaker type: Independent foundation.
Financial data (yr. ended 03/31/11): Assets, $39,025,288 (M); expenditures, $3,149,134; qualifying distributions, $2,690,728; giving activities include $2,690,728 for grants.
Fields of interest: Performing arts, music; Environment, water resources; Animals/wildlife; Youth, services.
Limitations: Applications not accepted. Giving primarily in CT, CO, Washington, DC, and NY. No grants to individuals.
Application information: Contributes only to pre-selected organizations.
Officer and Director:* Harvey L. Armstrong,* Secy.
EIN: 943346273
Recent grants for international programs:
628-1 Wildlife Australia Fund, New York, NY, $646,375. For general support. 2009.

629
Wallace H. Coulter Foundation
790 N.W. 107th Ave., Ste. 215
Miami, FL 33172-3158 (305) 559-2991
Contact: Wayne A. Barlin, V.P. and Genl. Counsel

FAX: (305) 559-5490; URL: http://www.whcf.org Grants List: http://www.whcf.org/ coulter-translational-research-award-recipients

Established in 2000 in DE and FL.
Donors: Wallace H. Coulter Charitable Remainder Unitrust; Wallace H. Coulter Trust.
Grantmaker type: Independent foundation.
Financial data (yr. ended 09/30/10): Assets, $318,009,823 (M); expenditures, $30,181,761; qualifying distributions, $27,629,110; giving activities include $23,374,318 for 66 grants (high: $1,000,000; low: $25,000; average: $120,000–$1,000,000), and $110,000 for 23 employee matching gifts.
Purpose and activities: The foundation is dedicated to improving human health care by supporting translational research in biomedical engineering-research directed at the transfer of promising technologies within the university research laboratory that are progressing towards commercial development and clinical practice.
Fields of interest: Health care; Biomedicine; Medical research, institute; United Ways and Federated Giving Programs; Science.
Type of support: Research.
Limitations: Applications accepted. Giving primarily in FL, GA, MO and NY. No support for religious organizations. No grants to individuals.
Application information: See foundation web site for more application information. Application forms are available on the foundation web site. Application form required.
Initial approach: Preliminary application
Officers: Sue Van, C.E.O. and Pres.; Susan Racher, V.P. and C.F.O.; Wayne A. Barlin, V.P. and Genl. Counsel; Elias Caro, V.P., Tech. Devel.; Greg Thornton, Cont.
EIN: 311546126
Recent grants for international programs:
629-1 American Association for Clinical Chemistry, Washington, DC, $250,000. For the Wallace H. Coulter lectureship award for contributions to education, practice, and/or research in laboratory medicine; remainder will be used for education and training in laboratory medicine in developing countries. 2009.
629-2 American Nicaraguan Foundation, Miami, FL, $250,000. For improving education in Nicaragua. 2009.
629-3 American Nicaraguan Foundation, Miami, FL, $10,000. For contribution through employee donation program. 2009.
629-4 American Society of Hematology, Washington, DC, $400,000. For Wallace H. Coulter Lifetime Achievement Award in Hematology for contributions to education, practice, and/or research in discipline of clinical hematology; remainder will be used for education and training in hematology in developing countries. 2009.
629-5 Engineering World Health, Durham, NC, $200,000. For operating support to send engineers to less developed countries to repair equipment and train personnel. 2009.
629-6 Georgia Tech Foundation, Atlanta, GA, $500,000. For ongoing collaborative effort between Georgia Tech and Peking University in China. 2009.
629-7 Leiden University Medical Center, Leiden, Netherlands, $555,378. For collaborative research developing standards in T-cell immune monitoring, assuring results of tests are reproducible and do not vary from lab to lab. 2009.
629-8 Peking University Education Foundation USA, Millbrae, CA, $1,000,000. For a matching grant to stimulate alumni giving in this country and benefit the school in China. 2009.

630
The Arthur Vining Davis Foundations
225 Water St., Ste. 1510
Jacksonville, FL 32202-5185 (904) 359-0670
Contact: Dr. Jonathan T. Howe, Exec. Dir.
FAX: (904) 359-0675; E-mail: office@avdf.org;
URL: http://www.avdf.org/

The Foundations are comprised of three separate foundations established in 1952 and 1965 in PA; and in 1965 in FL. In early 2001, Foundation No. 1 merged with Foundation No. 2.
Donor: Arthur Vining Davis†.
Grantmaker type: Independent foundation.
Financial data (yr. ended 12/31/10): Assets, $222,871,018 (M); expenditures, $10,938,072; qualifying distributions, $10,283,116; giving activities include $8,814,716 for 40 grants.
Purpose and activities: Support largely for private higher education; secondary education, to strengthen teachers and their teaching in high schools, health care with emphasis on caring attitudes, public television, and graduate theological education.
Fields of interest: Media, film/video; Secondary school/education; Higher education; Medical school/education; Theological school/education.
Type of support: Employee matching gifts; General/operating support; Continuing support; Capital campaigns; Building/renovation; Equipment; Endowments; Program development; Professorships; Publication; Curriculum development; Fellowships; Internship funds; Scholarship funds; Research; Technical assistance; Consulting services; Program evaluation; Matching/challenge support.
Limitations: Applications accepted. Giving limited to the U.S., including possessions and territories. No support for community chests, publicly governed colleges and universities, and institutions primarily supported by government funds (except in secondary education and health care programs), voter education, voter registration drives, or projects incurring obligations extending over many years. No grants to individuals; no loans.
Publications: Grants list; Informational brochure.
Application information: Proposals are not accepted via fax or e-mail. Applicants for higher education and religion program grants should complete the Institutional Information form on foundation web site. Application form not required.
Initial approach: Letter
Copies of proposal: 1
Deadline(s): None
Board meeting date(s): Spring, fall, and winter
Final notification: 10 to 15 months for approvals
Officers and Trustees:* J.H. Dow Davis,* Chair.; W.R. Wright, Emeritus; Holbrook R. Davis; Joel P. Davis; Maynard K. Davis; Serena Davis Hall; Mrs. John L. Kee, Jr.; John L. Kee III; Haley Davis Melanson; BNY Mellon; SunTrust Bank.
Number of staff: 5 full-time professional; 1 full-time support.
Recent grants for international programs:

630-1 Pitzer College, Claremont, CA, $250,000. For endowment for leadership position in the Center for Study of Global Communities. 2010.
630-2 Vanderbilt University, Divinity School, Nashville, TN, $200,000. For the Global Education program. 2010.
630-3 W G B H Educational Foundation, Boston, MA, $200,000. For completion funding for The Panama Canal. 2010.
630-4 Wellesley College, Wellesley, MA, $250,000. For endowment for the Madeleine Albright Institute for Global Affairs. 2010.

631
De La Pena Foundation
1000 S.W. 184th Terr.
Pembroke Pines, FL 33029-6044

Established in 2001 in FL.
Donors: Mario De La Pena; Miriam De La Pena.
Grantmaker type: Independent foundation.
Financial data (yr. ended 12/31/10): Assets, $2,445,604 (M); expenditures, $182,156; qualifying distributions, $161,000; giving activities include $157,500 for 9 grants (high: $116,000; low: $1,500).
Fields of interest: Public affairs; International affairs.
International interests: Cuba.
Limitations: Applications not accepted. No grants to individuals.
Application information: Contributes only to pre-selected organizations.
Officer and Directors:* Mario De La Pena,* Chair.; Michael De La Pena; Miriam De La Pena.
EIN: 651057681

632
The Ferdinand and Anna Duda Foundation, Inc.
P.O. Box 620257
Oviedo, FL 32762-0257

Established in 1991 in FL as partial successor to the Duda Foundation.
Donors: Ferdinand S. Duda; A. Duda & Sons, Inc.
Grantmaker type: Independent foundation.
Financial data (yr. ended 12/31/10): Assets, $2,968,829 (M); expenditures, $195,863; qualifying distributions, $170,131; giving activities include $162,500 for 12 grants (high: $30,000; low: $1,000).
Fields of interest: Secondary school/education; Higher education; Graduate/professional education; Protestant agencies & churches.
International interests: Slovakia.
Type of support: Research.
Limitations: Applications not accepted. Giving primarily in CO, FL, MO, and WI; some giving in Slovakia. No grants to individuals.
Application information: Contributes only to pre-selected organizations.
Officers: Ferdinand S. Duda, Pres.; Eleanor Hrncir, V.P.; Susan V. Hanas, Secy.; Elaine D. Lavender, Treas.
Trustee: Joseph A. Duda.
EIN: 593041353

633
EIS Foundation, Inc.
550 S.E. Mizner Blvd., Ste. 503
Boca Raton, FL   33432-6094
Contact: Maurice L. Schwarz, Pres.

Incorporated in 1951 in CT.
Donors: Joseph W. Gilfix†; C.C. Weiss†; Maurice L. Schwarz; and members of the Weiss and Schwarz families.
Grantmaker type: Independent foundation.
Financial data (yr. ended 12/31/10): Assets, $1,329,862 (M); gifts received, $3,813; expenditures, $163,950; qualifying distributions, $159,250; giving activities include $159,250 for 61 grants (high: $15,000; low: $25).
Purpose and activities: Grants largely for Jewish welfare funds, hospitals, higher education, care of the aged and physically handicapped, temple support, and the State of Israel.
Fields of interest: Higher education; Hospitals (general); Human services; Children/youth, services; Aging, centers/services; Jewish federated giving programs; Jewish agencies & synagogues; Disabilities, people with; Aging.
International interests: Israel.
Type of support: General/operating support; Continuing support; Capital campaigns; Emergency funds; Scholarship funds.
Limitations: Applications accepted. Giving primarily in CT, FL, and NY. No grants to individuals.
Application information: Application form not required.
   Initial approach: Letter
   Copies of proposal: 1
   Deadline(s): None
   Board meeting date(s): Annually
Officers and Directors: * Maurice L. Schwarz,* Pres.; Michael Schwarz, V.P. and Secy.; Nedra J. Mirkin.
Number of staff: None.
EIN: 066021896

634
The Engelberg Foundation
1050 N. Lake Way
Palm Beach, FL   33480-3252
Contact: Alfred B. Engelberg, Tr.
E-mail: aengelberg@nglbrg.com

Established in 1990 in CT.
Donor: Alfred Engelberg.
Grantmaker type: Independent foundation.
Financial data (yr. ended 01/31/10): Assets, $18,966,619 (M); gifts received, $1,871,632; expenditures, $3,472,805; qualifying distributions, $3,360,800; giving activities include $3,359,300 for 54 grants (high: $2,075,000; low: $250).
Purpose and activities: Primary areas of interest include primary healthcare coverage and serving the disadvantaged; some support also for issues concerning intellectual property law, Jewish organizations, and arts education.
Fields of interest: Arts, formal/general education; Arts education; Health care; Human services; Children/youth, services; Child development, services; Jewish agencies & synagogues; Children/youth; Economically disadvantaged.
International interests: Israel.
Type of support: General/operating support; Continuing support; Annual campaigns; Capital campaigns; Building/renovation; Emergency funds; Program development; Conferences/seminars;

Professorships; Seed money; Curriculum development; Fellowships; Program evaluation; Program-related investments/loans.
Limitations: Applications not accepted. Giving primarily in FL and NY. No grants to individuals.
Application information:
   Board meeting date(s): None
Trustee: Alfred Engelberg.
Number of staff: None.
EIN: 061309603

635
Food for the Poor, Inc.
6401 Lyons Rd., Dept. 9662
Coconut Creek, FL   33073-3602   (954) 427-2222
FAX: (954) 570-7654; URL: http://
www.foodforthepoor.org
Blog: http://
www.officialfoodforthepoor.blogspot.com/
Facebook: http://www.facebook.com/
FoodForThePoor
Twitter: http://twitter.com/foodforthepoor
YouTube: http://www.youtube.com/user/
FoodForThePoorInc

Established in 1982.
Grantmaker type: Public charity.
Financial data (yr. ended 12/31/10): Revenue, $1,047,115,087; assets, $39,602,242 (M); gifts received, $1,046,978,905; expenditures, $1,050,829,851; giving activities include $398,440 for grants, $985,756,253 for grants to organizations outside the U.S., and $43 for grants to individuals.
Purpose and activities: The organization seeks to improve the health, economic, social, and spiritual conditions of men, women, and children.
Fields of interest: Economically disadvantaged.
International interests: Caribbean; Latin America.
Type of support: Grants to individuals.
Limitations: Giving primarily in Latin America and the Caribbean.
Publications: Annual report.
Officers and Directors: * P. Todd Kennedy,* Chair.; Bill Benson,* Vice-Chair.; Robin G. Mahfood,* Pres. and C.E.O.; David T. Price, Secy.-Treas.; Angel A. Aloma, Exec. Dir.; Grace Bonina; Most Rev. Pierre-Andre Dumas; Rev. Leopold Frade, D.D.; Rhonda Maingot; His Eminence Oscar Andres Cardinal Rodriguez Maradiaga, S.D.B.; Lynne G. Nasrallah, Ed.D.; Alvaro J. Pereira; Rev. Gregory Ramkissoon.
EIN: 592174510

636
Freewill Charitable Trust
657 N.W. Hooten Hollow Rd.
Greenville, FL   32331-4800

Established in 2005 in FL.
Donor: E. Peter H. Wilkens.
Grantmaker type: Independent foundation.
Financial data (yr. ended 12/31/10): Assets, $1,877,706 (M); expenditures, $173,531; qualifying distributions, $173,231; giving activities include $173,231 for 11 grants (high: $61,090; low: $4,141).
Purpose and activities: Giving primarily for the support of Christian evangelism, training, and aid.
Fields of interest: Christian agencies & churches.

International interests: Philippines; South Africa; Nigeria; Vietnam; Paraguay; Poland; China; Sudan; Benin; Senegal; Bangladesh; India.
Type of support: Building/renovation; Conferences/ seminars; Continuing support; Curriculum development; Emergency funds; Equipment; General/operating support; Income development; Land acquisition; Matching/challenge support; Program evaluation; Publication; Research; Scholarship funds.
Limitations: Applications not accepted. Giving primarily in CA and VA. No grants to individuals.
Application information: Contributes only to pre-selected organizations.
Trustees: Laura Holland; E. Peter H. Wilkens; Dena Woodburn.
EIN: 202911795

637
Victor & Sandra Fuller Family Foundation, Inc.
2 Alhambra Plz., Ste. 1280
Coral Gables, FL   33134-5237

Established in 2006 in FL.
Donors: Sandra Fuller; Stephen M. Fuller; Victor Fuller.
Grantmaker type: Independent foundation.
Financial data (yr. ended 12/31/10): Assets, $2,284,051 (M); gifts received, $134,604; expenditures, $195,366; qualifying distributions, $175,000; giving activities include $175,000 for 2 grants (high: $125,000; low: $50,000).
Fields of interest: Military/veterans' organizations; International affairs, research; Education; Christian agencies & churches; Arts; Speech/hearing centers; Athletics/sports, baseball.
Limitations: Applications not accepted. Giving primarily in FL, MA, SC, and TX. No grants to individuals.
Application information: Unsolicited requests for funds not accepted.
Officers: Victor Fuller, Pres.; Sandra Fuller, V.P. and Treas.; Michael Katz, Secy.
EIN: 203736887

638
Gainesville Community Foundation, Inc.
5214 S.W. 91 Dr., Ste. A
Gainesville, FL   32608   (352) 367-0060
FAX: (352) 378-1718; E-mail: office@gnvcf.org;
URL: http://www.gnvcf.org

Established in 1998 in FL.
Grantmaker type: Community foundation.
Financial data (yr. ended 12/31/10): Assets, $9,623,270 (M); gifts received, $1,506,772; expenditures, $1,205,693; giving activities include $973,495 for 50 grants (high: $249,000), $4,279 for grants to organizations outside the U.S., and $5,000 for grants to individuals.
Purpose and activities: The foundation seeks to promote and sustain philanthropy among the citizens of Gainesville and the surrounding areas.
Fields of interest: Arts; Higher education; Libraries/ library science; Education; Environment; Animal welfare; Hospitals (general); Health care; Substance abuse, prevention; Medical research; Housing/ shelter; Athletics/sports, water sports; Recreation; Family services; Human services; Philanthropy/ voluntarism; Religion; Girls; Women; Children/

youth; Aging; Economically disadvantaged; Homeless.

International interests: Costa Rica.
Type of support: General/operating support; Program development; Scholarship funds.
Limitations: Giving limited to Gainesville and the surrounding areas in north central FL.
Publications: Application guidelines; Annual report; Financial statement.
Application information:
   Board meeting date(s): 3rd Thurs of Jan., Mar. May, Sept. and Nov.
Officers and Directors:* Perry McGriff,* Chair.; Eric Godet,* Vice-Chair.; Barzella Papa, C.E.O. and Pres.; Chris McLaughlin,* Secy.; Mitch Gleaser,* Treas.; Mark Avera; Luis Diaz; Phil Emmer; Dink Henderson; Clark Hodge; Linda Kallman; Tony Kendzior; Wes Marston; Susan Parrish; Susannah Peddie; Nancy Perry; Howard W. Patrick; Mike Ryals; Melanie Shore; Portia Taylor; Ester Tibbs; Michael Tillman; Marilyn Tubb; Terry Van Nortwick; Stuart Wegener; Richard White.
Number of staff: 1 full-time professional; 1 full-time support.
EIN: 593532330

639
Give to Colombia, Inc.
6705 Red Rd., Ste. 502
Coral Gables, FL 33143-3644   (305) 669-4630
URL: http://www.givetocolombia.org/
Facebook: http://www.facebook.com/pages/
GIVE-TO-COLOMBIA/148265430742?ref=ts
Twitter: http://twitter.com/GIVETOCOLOMBIA

Established in 2003 in FL.
Grantmaker type: Public charity.
Financial data (yr. ended 12/31/10): Revenue, $2,333,002; assets, $852,760 (M); gifts received, $2,547,170; expenditures, $2,120,087; giving activities include $848,941 for grants, and $900,112 for grants to organizations outside the U.S.
Purpose and activities: The organization creates, promotes, and facilitates partnerships between international donors and Colombian non-profit organizations; the foundation also as a fiscal sponsors to private international donors to channel their contributions to high-impact social organizations throughout the country.
Fields of interest: International economic development; International development; International affairs.
International interests: Colombia.
Limitations: Giving primarily to Colombia.
Publications: Annual report; Newsletter; IRS Form 990 or 990-PF printed copy available upon request.
Directors: Orlando Ayala; Gabriela Febres Cordero; Robert Eichfeld; Rodrigo Arboleda Halaby; Maria Camila Leiva; Felipe Medina; Geoffrey Randall.
EIN: 260073580

640
Global Servants, Inc.
P.O. Box 740737
Orange City, FL 32774-0737   (386) 775-9968
Toll-free tel.: (888) 823-8772; URL: http://www.globalservants.org

Established in 1985.
Grantmaker type: Public charity.

Financial data (yr. ended 03/31/10): Revenue, $1,079,191; assets, $2,706,847 (M); gifts received, $656,938; expenditures, $1,356,314; giving activities include $295,038 for grants to organizations outside the U.S., and $3,360 for grants to individuals.
Fields of interest: International affairs; Religion.
Type of support: Grants to individuals.
Limitations: Giving on a national and international basis.
Officers and Directors:* Jim Moye,* Chair.; Mark Rutland,* Pres.; Rev. Lawrence Lockett,* Secy.; Doug Beacham,* Treas.; Rev. John Anderson; John Bohlayer; Rev. Ronny Brannen; Tom Brown; Don Martin.
EIN: 581291607

641
Mark J. Gordon Foundation
(formerly Gail and Mark Gordon Foundation)
2875 N.E. 191st St., Ste. 400
Aventura, FL 33180-2831

Established in 1999 in DE and FL.
Donor: Mark J. Gordon.
Grantmaker type: Independent foundation.
Financial data (yr. ended 12/31/10): Assets, $2,204,576 (M); expenditures, $671,281; qualifying distributions, $430,600; giving activities include $430,600 for 20 grants (high: $225,000; low: $100).
Purpose and activities: Giving primarily for children, youth and social services, as well as for health organizations.
Fields of interest: Health care; Human services; Children/youth, services; Leadership development.
International interests: Kenya.
Limitations: Applications not accepted. Giving primarily in FL. No grants to individuals.
Application information: Contributes only to pre-selected organizations.
Officer: Mark J. Gordon, Pres.
Directors: Dorothy Dedario; Nancy Platt.
EIN: 650995291

642
Nehemias Gorin Foundation
7028 Leopardi Ct.
Naples, FL 34114-2650
Contact: Stephen Goldenberg, Tr.

Established in 1964 in MA.
Donors: Nehemias Gorin†; William Gorin†; Ida G. Leckart†.
Grantmaker type: Independent foundation.
Financial data (yr. ended 11/30/10): Assets, $1,314,822 (M); expenditures, $1,301,931; qualifying distributions, $1,255,163; giving activities include $1,240,000 for 94 grants (high: $110,000; low: $2,500).
Purpose and activities: Giving primarily for the arts, particularly symphony orchestras, as well as for higher education, hospitals and health associations, Jewish agencies and temples, and social services.
Fields of interest: Performing arts, orchestras; Arts; Higher education; Education; Hospitals (general); Health organizations, association; Cancer research; Human services; Jewish federated giving programs; Jewish agencies & synagogues.
International interests: Israel.

Limitations: Giving primarily in MA. No grants to individuals.
Application information: Application form not required.
   Initial approach: Letter. Phone calls will not be accepted
   Copies of proposal: 1
   Deadline(s): None
   Board meeting date(s): Varies
Trustees: Stephen Goldenberg; Howard Gorin; Ralph Gorin.
EIN: 046119939

643
Green Family Foundation, Inc.
2601 S. Bayshore Dr., 9th Fl.
Coconut Grove, FL 33133-5417   (305) 858-4225
E-mail: info@greenff.org; URL: http://www.greenff.org
Facebook: http://www.facebook.com/greenff
YouTube: http://www.youtube.com/greenfamilymiami

Established in 1991 in FL.
Donor: Steven J. Green.
Grantmaker type: Independent foundation.
Financial data (yr. ended 12/31/10): Assets, $16,661,263 (M); expenditures, $2,396,842; qualifying distributions, $1,816,454; giving activities include $1,816,454 for 33+ grants (high: $1,500,001).
Purpose and activities: The foundation provides seed grants to support holistic programs that empower entire communities. The end goal is to enable underserved communities to achieve sustainability and self-reliance by alleviating the cycle of poverty and disease. The foundation lends resources to programs that focus on, 1) global health and development, 2) community empowerment, 3) youth arts, and 4) education.
Fields of interest: Arts; Education; Human services; Children/youth, services; International development; Foundations (private grantmaking); Immigrants/refugees; Economically disadvantaged.
Limitations: Applications not accepted. Giving primarily in FL. No grants to individuals, or for emergency funding to cover ongoing program or operational deficits.
Publications: Grants list.
Application information: Contributes only to pre-selected organizations. See foundation Web site for current RFP information.
Officers: Kimberly Green, Pres.; Kevin Coster, V.P.
EIN: 650284913

644
Green Park Foundation
9611 N. US Hwy. 1, Ste. 340
Sebastian, FL 32958-6363
E-mail: greenparkfdn@aol.com

Established in 1999 in DC.
Donors: Melissa Baron Murdoch; Stephen Murdoch.
Grantmaker type: Independent foundation.
Financial data (yr. ended 12/31/10): Assets, $3,789,186 (M); expenditures, $312,221; qualifying distributions, $306,834; giving activities include $306,834 for grants.
Fields of interest: Libraries (public); Education, reading; Education; Environment, natural resources;

Public health; Human services; International relief; Women.
Limitations: Applications not accepted. Giving primarily in CA and Washington, DC. No grants to individuals.
Application information: Contributes only to pre-selected organizations.
Directors: Nancy C. Baron; Melissa Baron Murdoch; Stephen I. Murdoch.
EIN: 522178078

645
The Greenburg-May Foundation, Inc.
P.O. Box 54-5816
Miami, FL 33154-5816
Contact: Isabel May, Pres.
Application address: 9999 Collins Ave., Apt. 15A, Bal Harbour, FL 33154

Incorporated in 1947 in DE.
Donors: Harry Greenburg†; Samuel D. May†.
Grantmaker type: Independent foundation.
Financial data (yr. ended 12/31/10): Assets, $12,093,059 (M); expenditures, $761,901; qualifying distributions, $599,470; giving activities include $599,470 for 97 grants (high: $162,250; low: $100).
Purpose and activities: Grants almost entirely for medical research, primarily cancer, heart, diabetes, Parkinson's, and neurological research; support also for the aged, hospitals, Jewish welfare funds, and temples.
Fields of interest: Hospitals (general); Cancer; Heart & circulatory diseases; Neuroscience; Medical research, institute; Cancer research; Human services; Aging, centers/services; Jewish federated giving programs; Jewish agencies & synagogues; Children; Blind/visually impaired; Aging.
International interests: Israel.
Type of support: General/operating support; Continuing support; Annual campaigns; Endowments; Emergency funds; Program development; Internship funds; Scholarship funds; Research; Consulting services.
Limitations: Applications accepted. Giving primarily in southern FL and Long Island, NY. No grants to individuals, or for conferences; generally no grants for scholarships or fellowships; no loans.
Application information: Application form required.
Initial approach: Letter
Copies of proposal: 1
Deadline(s): None
Board meeting date(s): Jan., Apr., July, and Oct.
Final notification: 1 to 2 months
Officers and Directors:* Isabel May,* Pres.; Peter May,* V.P. and Treas.; Jonathan May, V.P.; Linda Sklar,* V.P.
Number of staff: 2 part-time support.
EIN: 136162935

646
Hertog Foundation, Inc.
c/o Rampell and Rampell, P.A.
223 Sunset Ave., Ste. 200
Palm Beach, FL 33480-3855

Donors: Roger Hertog; Susan Hertog.
Grantmaker type: Independent foundation.
Financial data (yr. ended 02/28/11): Assets, $36,414,759 (M); gifts received, $5,018,942; expenditures, $16,858,590; qualifying

distributions, $16,538,786; giving activities include $15,575,830 for 114 grants (high: $2,682,550; low: $175).
Fields of interest: Medical research, institute; Higher education; Jewish agencies & synagogues; Jewish federated giving programs; Historic preservation/historical societies; Libraries (public); Public affairs.
Limitations: Applications not accepted. Giving primarily in Washington, DC and New York, NY.
Application information: Contributes only to pre-selected organizations.
Officers and Directors:* Roger Hertog,* Pres. and Treas.; Susan Hertog,* Secy.
EIN: 262002295
Recent grants for international programs:
646-1 America-Israel Friendship League, New York, NY, $24,550. 2011.
646-2 Birthright Israel North America, New York, NY, $1,000,000. 2011.
646-3 David Project, New York Office, Boston, MA, $50,000. 2011.
646-4 ELEM Youth in Distress, New York, NY, $23,150. 2011.
646-5 Foundation for the Defense of Democracies, Washington, DC, $50,000. 2011.
646-6 Friends of Ir David, Brooklyn, NY, $1,000,000. 2011.
646-7 Friends of Israel Initiative, Miami, FL, $25,000. 2011.
646-8 Friends of the Israel Center for Social and Economic Progress, Great Neck, NY, $40,000. 2011.
646-9 Institute for the Study of War, Washington, DC, $50,000. 2011.
646-10 Institute for Zionist Strategies, Jerusalem, Israel, $60,000. 2011.
646-11 Institute of World Politics, Washington, DC, $10,000. 2011.
646-12 Israel Project, Washington, DC, $100,000. 2011.
646-13 Middle East Forum, Philadelphia, PA, $25,000. 2011.
646-14 Ohr Torah Stone Colleges and Graduate Programs, New York, NY, $550,000. 2011.
646-15 Schechter Institutes, Philadelphia, PA, $25,000. 2011.
646-16 Trialogue Educational Trust, Institute for Strategic Dialogue, London, England, $50,000. 2011.
646-17 U.S. Friends of the Van Leer Jerusalem Institute, Washington, DC, $25,000. 2011.
646-18 Vets for Freedom, Washington, DC, $10,000. 2011.
646-19 Washington Institute for Near East Policy, Washington, DC, $204,500. 2011.

647
The Himmel Anton Foundation, Inc.
c/o Himmel Mgmt. Co.
4500 PGA Blvd.
Palm Beach Gardens, FL 33418-3994

Established in 2007 in FL.
Donor: Jeffrey S. Himmel.
Grantmaker type: Public charity.
Financial data (yr. ended 12/31/10): Revenue, $3,499; assets, $1,484 (M); gifts received, $3,499; expenditures, $8,211; giving activities include $1,600 for grants.
Fields of interest: International development.
International interests: Nicaragua.

Limitations: Applications not accepted. Giving primarily in FL. No grants to individuals.
Application information: Contributes only to pre-selected organizations.
Officer: Jeffrey S. Himmel, Pres.
EIN: 320208732

648
Holland & Knight Charitable Foundation, Inc.
P.O. Box 2877
Tampa, FL 33601-2877 (813) 227-8500
FAX: (813) 229-0134;
E-mail: foundation@hklaw.com; Toll-free tel.: (866) 452-2737; URL: http://foundation.hklaw.com
Application address for African American Heritage: Holland & Knight LLP, Attn. Lura Battle, 1201 W. Peachtree St., N.E., 1 Atlantic Center, Ste., 2000, Atlanta, GA 30309-3453; E-mail and URL for Holocaust Project: holocaust@hklaw.com, www.holocaust.hklaw.com; E-mail for Young Native Writers' Contest: indian@hklaw.com

Established in 1996 in FL.
Grantmaker type: Public charity.
Financial data (yr. ended 12/31/10): Revenue, $653,110; assets, $1,068,493 (M); gifts received, $651,841; expenditures, $776,203; giving activities include $549,693 for grants, and $41,872 for grants to individuals.
Purpose and activities: The foundation provides support to organizations working in the fields of arts and sciences, child services, education, health and disability issues, homelessness assistance, indigent legal services, and international relief and civic causes.
Fields of interest: Science; Arts; Education; Legal services; Housing/shelter; Children, services; Family resources and services, disability; Homeless, human services; International relief; African Americans/Blacks; Native Americans/American Indians.
Type of support: Grants to individuals.
Limitations: Applications accepted. Giving on a national and international basis.
Publications: Application guidelines.
Application information: Application form required.
Deadline(s): Apr. 15 for Young Native Writers Essay Contest; Dec. 3 for Living the Dream Essay and Scholarship Program
Officers and Directors:* Marie Lefere,* Chair.; Brian Starer,* Vice-Chair.; Andrew H. Weinstein,* Pres.; Richard P. Sills,* V.P.; Chris Kolos, Secy.; Charles L. Stutts,* Treas.; Angela M. Ruth,* Exec. Dir.; Susan E. Edlein; John F. Germany; George B. Howell III; John Arthur Jones; Darrell Kelley; D. Burke Kibler III; Shari A. Levitan; Michael R. Marget; Bobbie Pease; Edward Ryan; William S. Sessions.
EIN: 311472972

649
Hope for Haiti, Inc.
1021 5th Ave. N.
Naples, FL 34102-5603 (239) 434-7183
FAX: (239) 434-2839;
E-mail: info@hopeforhaiti.com; URL: http://www.hopeforhaiti.com/

Established in 1997.
Grantmaker type: Public charity.

Financial data (yr. ended 06/30/10): Revenue, $58,768,474; assets, $6,741,486 (M); gifts received, $58,328,182; expenditures, $53,734,364; giving activities include $51,704,967 for grants to organizations outside the U.S.

Purpose and activities: The organization works to improve the quality of life for the people of Haiti, particularly children, through education, nutrition, and healthcare.

Fields of interest: Human services; Community/economic development; Agriculture/food; Health care; Education.

International interests: Haiti.

Type of support: In-kind gifts.

Limitations: Giving limited to Haiti.

Publications: Annual report; Newsletter.

Officers and Board Members:* JoAnne Kuehner,* Pres.; Lacey King,* Secy.; Francis J. Proto,* Treas.; Bill Earls; Collette Hall; Howard M. Hujsa; Todd Kendall; Christina Kolbjornsen; James B. Lancaster, Jr.; Vladimir J. Mathieu, M.D.; Gilbert Saint-Jean, M.D., Ph.D.

EIN: 593564329

650

Hsu Family Foundation, Inc.

4100 E. Lake Estates Dr.
Davie, FL 33328-3074
Contact: Jane H. Hsiao, Pres.

Established in 2006 in FL.

Donor: Jane H. Hsiao.

Grantmaker type: Independent foundation.

Financial data (yr. ended 03/31/10): Assets, $20,030,719 (M); expenditures, $5,449,341; qualifying distributions, $5,410,724; giving activities include $5,410,724 for 8 grants (high: $4,523,724; low: $10,000).

Fields of interest: International affairs, goodwill promotion; Health care.

Limitations: Giving primarily in FL and NJ; some giving in Taiwan.

Application information:
Initial approach: Letter
Deadline(s): None

Officers and Directors:* Jane H. Hsiao,* Pres. and Treas.; Kristy Hsiao,* Secy.; Bernard Hsiao; Michael Hsiao.

EIN: 711017117

651

Israel Cancer Association USA

525 S. Flagler Dr., Ste. 202
West Palm Beach, FL 33401-5932
(561) 832-9277
Contact: Jill Cooper, Exec. Dir.
FAX: (561) 832-9337; E-mail: icausa@icausa.org;
URL: http://www.icausa.org

Established in 1967.

Grantmaker type: Public charity.

Financial data (yr. ended 06/30/10): Revenue, $713,184; assets, $990,091 (M); gifts received, $598,400; expenditures, $592,615; program services expenses $505,149; giving activities include $263,532 for grants to organizations outside the U.S.

Purpose and activities: The association raises money to distribute to Israel Cancer Association in Israel.

Fields of interest: Cancer research; Cancer.

International interests: Israel.

Type of support: Research.

Limitations: Giving on an international basis, primarily in Israel.

Publications: Newsletter.

Officers and Directors:* Eliezer Robinson, Chair.; Leon Recanati,* Vice Chair.; Peter D. Brown,* Pres.; Lexye Aversa, Exec. V.P.; Deena Freeman, Exec. V.P.; Wilma Mooney, Exec. V.P.; Harvey L. Poppel, Exec. V.P.; Jeremy Schneider, Exec. V.P.; Celia R. Jacobs, Secy.; Dianne Meckler, Treas.; Jill Cooper, Exec. Dir.; Adam Brown; Beatrice Brown; David Genser; and 21 additional directors.

EIN: 136218184

652

Jabil Circuit, Inc. Contributions Program

10560 Dr. Martin Luther King Jr. St. N.
St. Petersburg, FL 33716-3718 (727) 577-9749
URL: http://www.jabil.com/SER_statement.html

Grantmaker type: Corporate giving program.

Purpose and activities: Jabil Circuit makes charitable contributions to nonprofit organizations involved with education, the environment, natural disasters, and on a case by case basis. Support is given primarily in areas of company operations in Arizona, California, Colorado, Florida, Kentucky, Michigan, New York, Tennessee, and Texas, and in Austria, Belgium, Brazil, China, England, France, Germany, Hungary, India, Italy, Japan, Malaysia, Mexico, the Netherlands, Poland, Russia, Scotland, Singapore, Taiwan, Ukraine, and Vietnam.

Fields of interest: Disasters, preparedness/services; Environment; Education; General charitable giving.

International interests: Austria; Belgium; Brazil; China; England; France; Germany; Hungary; India; Italy; Japan; Malaysia; Mexico; Netherlands; Poland; Russia; Scotland; Singapore; Taiwan; Ukraine; Vietnam.

Type of support: Scholarships—to individuals; In-kind gifts; Employee volunteer services; Program development; General/operating support.

Limitations: Giving primarily in areas of company operations in AZ, CA, CO, FL, KY, MI, NY, TN, and TX, and in Austria, Belgium, Brazil, China, England, France, Germany, Hungary, India, Italy, Japan, Malaysia, Mexico, the Netherlands, Poland, Russia, Scotland, Singapore, Taiwan, Ukraine, and Vietnam.

653

Jewish Federation of Broward County, Inc.

5890 S. Pine Island Rd.
Davie, FL 33328-5933 (954) 252-6900
Contact: Eric B. Stillman, Pres. and C.E.O.
FAX: (954) 252-6892;
E-mail: info@jewishbroward.org; URL: http://www.jewishbroward.org

Established in FL.

Grantmaker type: Public charity.

Financial data (yr. ended 06/30/10): Revenue, $950,130; assets, $85,640,385 (M); gifts received, $5,405,716; expenditures, $10,025,721; giving activities include $7,223,767 for grants.

Purpose and activities: The organization exists to safeguard and address the educational and social service needs of the local community, perpetuate Jewish heritage and ensure the continuity and survival of the Jewish family in Israel and around the world.

Fields of interest: Religion; Jewish agencies & synagogues; Community/economic development; International affairs, alliance/advocacy; Human services.

Type of support: Continuing support; General/operating support.

Limitations: Applications not accepted. Giving on a national and international basis.

Publications: Annual report.

Application information: Contributes only to pre-selected organizations.

Officers and Directors:* Stephen Jackman,* Chair.; Gordon Deckelbaum,* Vice-Chair.; Adrienne Frank,* Vice-Chair.; David Garfinkle,* Vice-Chair.; Carolyn Shapir,* Vice-Chair.; Sharon Schwartz,* Secy.; Mark Schmidt,* Treas.; Bryan Drowos; Bernie Friedman; Ben J. Genet; Debra Gober; Laura Goldblum; and 26 additional directors.

EIN: 590967823

654

Jewish Federation of South Palm Beach County, Inc.

9901 Donna Klein Blvd.
Boca Raton, FL 33428-1756 (561) 852-3100
FAX: (561) 852-3150; URL: http://www.jewishboca.org

Established in 1976 in FL.

Grantmaker type: Public charity.

Financial data (yr. ended 08/31/10): Revenue, $17,241,068; assets, $81,414,446 (M); gifts received, $15,852,717; expenditures, $16,588,675; giving activities include $8,861,882 for grants.

Purpose and activities: The federation works to further the welfare of the Jewish community in South Palm Beach County and elsewhere.

Fields of interest: Human services; Community/economic development; Jewish agencies & synagogues.

International interests: Israel.

Publications: Annual report.

Officers and Directors:* Etta Gross Zimmerman,* Chair.; Steven D. Bedowitz,* Vice-Chair.; Alan Cornell,* Vice-Chair.; Warren Greenspoon,* Vice-Chair.; Thomas R. Kaplan,* Vice-Chair.; Ellen R. Sarnoff,* Vice-Chair.; Ted Struhl,* Vice-Chair.; William S. Bernstein, Pres. and C.E.O.; Albert Gortz,* Secy.; Ira M. Gerstein,* Treas.; Jerome Altheimer; James Baer; and 68 additional directors.

EIN: 591945109

655

The Lillian Jean Kaplan Foundation, Inc.

330 S.W. 2nd St., Ste. 213
Fort Lauderdale, FL 33312-1712
(786) 385-6525
Contact: Luis Aguiar

Established in FL.

Donors: Thomas Kaplan; Guma Aguiar; Dafna Recanati Kaplan; Consolidated Commodities Ltd.

Grantmaker type: Independent foundation.

Financial data (yr. ended 12/31/10): Assets, $23,135,509 (M); expenditures, $872,343; qualifying distributions, $628,822; giving activities

include $536,150 for 12 grants (high: $110,000; low: $10,000).

Purpose and activities: Giving primarily to support and recognize outstanding achievement in clinical research and excellence in kidney and pancreas-related programs, and to improving the overall quality of life; funding also for Jewish organizations, the film and media arts, and to an organization for the preservation of wild cats.

Fields of interest: Media, film/video; Animals/wildlife; Kidney research; Jewish agencies & synagogues.

Limitations: Applications accepted. Giving primarily in CA, FL and NY.

Application information:
Initial approach: Letter
Directors: Ellen Aguiar; Luis Aguiar; Justin Corey Drew.
EIN: 300127083

Recent grants for international programs:
655-1 American Friends of Bet El, Forest Hills, NY, $500,000. For development in Beit El. 2009.

655-2 American Friends of the Hebrew University, New York, NY, $262,500. For higher education and interdisciplinary research. 2009.

655-3 American Friends of the Old City Cheder in Jerusalem, Allentown, PA, $74,500. To develop Old City of Jerusalem. 2009.

655-4 American Friends of Yeshivas Bircas Hatorah, East Windsor, NJ, $74,500. For Jewish education programs. 2009.

655-5 Central Fund of Israel, New York, NY, $331,000. For emergency assistance to Jewish communities in Israel. 2009.

655-6 Federation of Jewish Communities of the CIS and Baltic States, New York, NY, $103,000. For professional assistance, educational support and funding to member communities. 2009.

655-7 International March of the Living, New York, NY, $500,000. To bring together Jews from different countries and cultures, secular and religious and every religious denomination, to share common a Jewish experience. 2009.

655-8 Jerusalem Foundation, New York, NY, $12,500. For educational programming. 2009.

655-9 Machne Israel, Brooklyn, NY, $1,540,000. To offer direct help to Jews in Israel and the former Soviet Union. 2009.

655-10 Nefesh BNefesh - Jewish Souls United, New York, NY, $1,000,000. To revitalize Aliyah (the immigration of Jews to Israel) and increase the number of future Olim (those who make Aliyah). 2009.

655-11 Orthodox Union - Union of Orthodox Jewish Congregations of America, New York, NY, $14,000. To serve North American Jewish community through education, outreach and social services. 2009.

655-12 Outreach Judaism, Monsey, NY, $150,000. For international Jewish education programs. 2009.

655-13 PEF Israel Endowment Funds, New York, NY, $175,000. For direct distribution to selected and approved charitable organizations in Israel. 2009.

655-14 United Jewish Community of Broward County, Davie, FL, $25,000. To save and improve Jewish lives in Broward County, in Israel and around the world. 2009.

656
The Eleanor M. and Herbert D. Katz Family Foundation, Inc.
c/o Thomas O. Katz, Secy.-Treas.
21218 St. Andrews Blvd., No. 404
Boca Raton, FL   33433-2449

Established in 1983 in FL.
Donors: Eleanor M. Katz; Herbert D. Katz.
Grantmaker type: Independent foundation.
Financial data (yr. ended 12/31/10): Assets, $13,532,368 (M); expenditures, $1,277,537; qualifying distributions, $1,168,716; giving activities include $1,168,716 for grants.
Purpose and activities: Primary areas of interest include higher education, and Jewish organizations.
Fields of interest: Higher education; Education; Health organizations, association; Human services; Jewish federated giving programs; Leadership development; Jewish agencies & synagogues.
International interests: Israel.
Type of support: Continuing support; Annual campaigns; Capital campaigns; Program development.
Limitations: Applications not accepted. Giving on a national and international basis. No grants to individuals.
Application information: Contributes only to pre-selected organizations.
Board meeting date(s): Quarterly
Officers and Directors:* Eleanor M. Katz,* Pres.; Thomas O. Katz,* V.P. and Secy.-Treas.; Laura Katz Cutler; Daniel Katz, Sally Katz, Walter Katz.
Number of staff: 1 part-time support.
EIN: 592320940

657
Henry & Elaine Kaufman Foundation, Inc.
c/o Edward I. Speer, CPA
4400 N. Federal Hwy., Ste. 210
Boca Raton, FL   33431-5195
Application address: c/o Henry Kaufman, Pres., and Elaine Kaufman, V.P., 590 Madison Ave., New York, NY 10022

Established in 1969.
Donors: Elaine Kaufman; Henry Kaufman; Henry Kaufman Charitable Lead Trust.
Grantmaker type: Independent foundation.
Financial data (yr. ended 12/31/09): Assets, $16,304,468 (M); expenditures, $7,236,387; qualifying distributions, $7,133,203; giving activities include $7,132,453 for 118 grants (high: $6,042,598; low: $100).
Purpose and activities: Support primarily for Jewish organizations, museums and other cultural institutions, and education; funding also for human services and hospitals.
Fields of interest: Museums; Arts; Higher education; Business school/education; Education; Animal welfare; Hospitals (general); Human services; Jewish federated giving programs; Jewish agencies & synagogues.
Type of support: General/operating support; Annual campaigns.
Limitations: Applications accepted. Giving primarily in the metropolitan New York, NY, area, including portions of NJ; some funding also in Atlanta, GA.
Application information:
Initial approach: Letter
Deadline(s): None

Officers and Directors:* Henry Kaufman,* Pres. and Treas.; Elaine Kaufman,* V.P.; Daniel S. Kaufman,* Secy.; Craig S. Kaufman; Glenn D. Kaufman.
EIN: 237045903

Recent grants for international programs:
657-1 Council on Foreign Relations, New York, NY, $35,000. For general operating support. 2009.

657-2 Institute for Middle East Peace and Development USA, Teaneck, NJ, $50,000. For general operating support. 2009.

657-3 Institute of International Education, New York, NY, $6,042,598. For general operating support. 2009.

657-4 Institute of International Education, New York, NY, $23,250. For general operating support. 2009.

657-5 Institute of International Education, New York, NY, $15,000. For general operating support. 2009.

657-6 Jerusalem Fellowships, New York, NY, $25,000. For general operating support. 2009.

658
Kerzner Marine Foundation, Inc.
1000 S. Pine Island Rd., Ste. 800
Plantation, FL   33324-3909
Contact: Debra Erickson, Exec. Dir.
E-mail: info@kerznermarinefoundation.org; E-mail for Debra Erickson: debra.erickson@kerzner.com; URL: http://www.kerznermarinefoundation.org

Established in 2005 in FL.
Donor: Kerzner International Bahamas.
Grantmaker type: Company-sponsored foundation.
Financial data (yr. ended 12/31/10): Assets, $156,607 (M); gifts received, $469,760; expenditures, $432,430; qualifying distributions, $387,000; giving activities include $387,000 for grants.
Purpose and activities: The foundation supports programs designed to preserve and enhance global marine ecosystems through scientific research, education, and community outreach. Special emphasis is directed toward marine protected areas, coral reef conservation, cetacean conservation, and research in the Caribbean, Middle East, and Southeast Asia.
Fields of interest: Environment, research; Environment, natural resources; Environment, water resources; Animals/wildlife, research; Animals/wildlife, endangered species; Animals/wildlife.
International interests: Asia; Caribbean; Middle East.
Type of support: Building/renovation; Continuing support; Management development/capacity building; Program development; Research.
Limitations: Applications accepted. Giving primarily in CA, FL, NY and in the Caribbean, Middle East, and Southeast Asia. No support for political activism. No grants for litigation, or for fundraising, scholarships, endowments or overhead costs for universities.
Publications: Informational brochure.
Application information: Proposals should include a cover page; 2 page abstract; a program or research description of up to 20 pages; an intuitional capacity description of up to 3 pages; a project team description with resumes; and past performance references.
Initial approach: Proposal
Copies of proposal: 5
Deadline(s): Apr. 15 and Sept. 15
Officers and Directors:* George Markantonis,* Pres. and Managing Dir.; Paul K. Dayton,* V.P.; Tim

Wise,* Treas.; Debra Erickson, Exec. Dir.; Steve Kaiser.
EIN: 342045752

659
The Samuel Aba and Sisel Klurman Foundation, Inc.
(formerly The Klurman Foundation, Inc.)
c/o Sisel Klurman
4000 Hollywood Blvd., Ste. 530N
Hollywood, FL   33021-6744

Established in 1984 in FL.
Donors: Samuel A. Klurman†; Sisel Klurman; Matan Ben-Aviv; Ganot Corp.
Grantmaker type: Independent foundation.
Financial data (yr. ended 12/31/10): Assets, $11,792,750 (M); gifts received, $10,000; expenditures, $523,368; qualifying distributions, $469,248; giving activities include $468,134 for 82 grants (high: $50,000; low: $2).
Fields of interest: Education; Health organizations, association; Human services; Jewish federated giving programs; Jewish agencies & synagogues.
International interests: Israel.
Type of support: General/operating support.
Limitations: Applications not accepted. Giving primarily in FL and NY. No grants to individuals.
Application information: Contributes only to pre-selected organizations.
Officers and Directors:* Zipora Ben-Aviv,* Pres.; Matan Ben-Aviv,* V.P.; Harvey L. Lichtman,* Secy.-Treas.
EIN: 592532272

660
Koch Foundation, Inc.
4421 N.W. 39th Ave., Bldg. 1, Ste. 1
Gainesville, FL   32606-7223
Contact: Carolyn A. Young, Exec. Dir.
E-mail: staff@thekochfoundation.org; URL: http://www.thekochfoundation.org

Incorporated in 1979 in FL.
Donors: Carl E. Koch†; Paula Koch†.
Grantmaker type: Independent foundation.
Financial data (yr. ended 03/31/11): Assets, $117,137,342 (M); expenditures, $11,106,170; qualifying distributions, $10,460,166; giving activities include $10,091,774 for 676 grants (high: $300,000; low: $2,500).
Purpose and activities: Grants only for Roman Catholic organizations that propagate the faith. Grants are made for direct evangelization programs, preparation of evangelists, Roman Catholic schools in resource-poor areas, and where the schools are the principal means of evangelization, and a Roman Catholic presence in the media.
Fields of interest: Catholic agencies & churches.
Type of support: Equipment; Program development; Conferences/seminars; Publication; Seed money; Curriculum development; Matching/challenge support.
Limitations: Applications accepted. Giving on a national and international basis. No grants to individuals, or for endowment funds, deficit financing, emergency funds, operating expenses, or for scholarships or fellowships; no loans.
Publications: Application guidelines; Annual report.
Application information: All applicants outside the U.S. must list a diocese or religious congregation in the U.S. to act as Fiscal Agent through which funds may be distributed. The fiscal agent must be an organization listed in the Official Catholic Directory (OCD). The foundation currently has a moratorium on funds for building. Application form required.
Initial approach: Letter of request for an application that briefly describes the project; submit between Jan. 1 and May 1. All requests must be made in English. Fax, telephone, or e-mail requests will not be accepted
Copies of proposal: 1
Deadline(s): 90 days after receipt of application
Board meeting date(s): Feb.
Final notification: 1 month after Feb. board meeting
Officers and Directors:* Rachel A. Bomberger,* Pres.; Inge L. Vraney,* V.P.; William A. Bomberger,* Secy.; Carolyn L. Bomberger,* Treas.; Carolyn A. Young, Exec. Dir.; Dorothy C. Bomberger; Matthew A. Bomberger; Michelle H. Bomberger; Charlotte L. Spacinsky; Lawrence E. Vraney, Jr.; Maura J. Vraney.
Number of staff: 2 full-time professional; 2 full-time support.
EIN: 591885997
Recent grants for international programs:
660-1 All Hallows College, Dublin, Ireland, $10,000. For spiritual training of adults. 2010.
660-2 All Saints of Ukrainian People Parish, Temopil, Ukraine, $15,000. For construction of parish church. 2010.
660-3 Andean Pastoral Institute, Cuzco, Peru, $10,000. For training of laity and religious on evangelization in Peru. 2010.
660-4 Angelic Sisters of Saint Paul, Maumere, Indonesia, $20,000. For renovation of formation house. 2010.
660-5 Apostolic Vicariate of Soddo, Wolayta Soddo, Ethiopia, $15,000. For expansion and reconstruction of four parish chapels. 2010.
660-6 Archdiocese of Ernakulam-Angamaly, Kochi, India, $15,000. For construction of cloistered monastery for women religious. 2010.
660-7 Archdiocese of Tabora, Tabora, Tanzania, Zanzibar and Pemba, $15,000. For construction of convent for women religious to minister as teachers in a secondary school. 2010.
660-8 Archeparchy of Beirut, Beirut, Lebanon, $10,000. For retreats for students. 2010.
660-9 Asmara Catholic Theological Institute, Asmara, Eritrea, $15,000. For renovation of theological institute. 2010.
660-10 Barnabite Fathers, Marikina City, Philippines, $15,000. For training and formation of religious men. 2010.
660-11 Benedictine Nuns of Perpetual Adoration, Warsaw, Poland, $30,000. For renovation of convent roof. 2010.
660-12 Benedictine Sisters of Saint Agnes, Peramiho, Tanzania, Zanzibar and Pemba, $20,000. For training and formation of religious women and to purchase bicycles for evangelization outreach. 2010.
660-13 Blessed Mariam Thresia Church, Delhi, India, $15,000. For construction of parish church. 2010.
660-14 Brothers of Saint Charles Lwanga, Uganda, $10,000. For construction of classrooms for primary school. 2010.
660-15 Brothers of the Holy Cross, Notre Dame, IN, $20,000. For construction of formation house for religious men in Ghana. 2010.
660-16 Carmelite Missions, Darien, IL, $10,000. For library development project in Philippines. 2010.
660-17 Carmelite Missions, Darien, IL, $10,000. For construction of temporary residence for religious women. 2010.
660-18 Carmelite Missions, Darien, IL, $10,000. For expansion of school and to provide furnishings and teaching materials. 2010.
660-19 Carmelite Missions, Darien, IL, $10,000. For expansion of school and to purchase furnishings for two classrooms. 2010.
660-20 Carmelite Missions, Darien, IL, $10,000. For ongoing training and formation of six religious women. 2010.
660-21 Carmelite Missions, Darien, IL, $10,000. For renovation of hostel for women in Guyana. 2010.
660-22 Carmelite Missions, Darien, IL, $10,000. For training and formation of religious women in Zimbabwe. 2010.
660-23 Carmelite Missions, Darien, IL, $10,000. For training and formation of seminarians in Kenya. 2010.
660-24 Carmelite Sisters of Our Lady, Quezon City, Philippines, $10,000. For formation of women religious in Indonesia and the Philippines. 2010.
660-25 Carmelites of Mary Immaculate, India, $10,000. For publishing and distribution of religious materials for evangelization. 2010.
660-26 Carmelites of Mary Immaculate, Machakos, Kenya, $10,000. For construction of retreat center. 2010.
660-27 Catholic Diocese of Jhabua, Meghnagar, India, $10,000. For expansion of parish mission school. 2010.
660-28 Catholic Education Committee, Indonesia, $10,000. For education and spiritual formation of youth, parents, and school faculty. 2010.
660-29 Catholic Media Center, Kiev, Ukraine, $15,000. For printing of religious newspaper for children. 2010.
660-30 Catholic Medical Mission Board, New York, NY, $40,000. For medical volunteer program. 2010.
660-31 Catholic Ministry to Deaf People, Quezon City, Philippines, $10,000. For salaries, continuing education and teaching materials for catechists ministering to the deaf. 2010.
660-32 Catholic World Mission, Hamden, CT, $20,000. For training and formation of six lay evangelists in Mexico. 2010.
660-33 Centro de Valores Humanos Emaus, Matamoros, Mexico, $20,000. For completion of a conference room for retreat center. 2010.
660-34 Centro Francisco de Reflexion, Guatemala City, Guatemala, $15,000. For training of religious and laity as missionaries. 2010.
660-35 Chaithanya Pastoral Center, Kottayam, India, $10,000. For diocesan faith formation program. 2010.
660-36 Christ the King Catholic Parish, Kamieskroon, South Africa, $15,000. For renovation of building into catechetical/pastoral training center. 2010.
660-37 Christ the Redeemer Parish, Bolivia, $10,864. For purchase of furniture for parish house. 2010.
660-38 Comunidad Jesed, Monterrey, Mexico, $10,000. For house for formation household. 2010.
660-39 Cong Doan Con En, Cho Moi, Vietnam, $15,000. For construction of parish library, purchase of religious books and materials, and training of catechists. 2010.

660-40 Congregation of Holy Cross, Bridgeport, CT, $15,000. For education and formation of seminarians in Peru. 2010.

660-41 Congregation of Holy Cross, Bridgeport, CT, $15,000. To continue to support reconstruction of parish pastoral center in Peru. 2010.

660-42 Congregation of the Holy Cross, District of East Africa, Kampala, Uganda, $15,000. For family ministry programs. 2010.

660-43 Congregation of the Mission, Enugu, Nigeria, $15,000. For completion of seminary building. 2010.

660-44 Congregation of the Mission of Saint Vincent de Paul, Dublin, Ireland, $15,000. For mission teams in Ireland and Great Britain. 2010.

660-45 Congregation of the Mission of Saint Vincent de Paul, Da Lat, Vietnam, $10,000. For construction of chapel and mission center. 2010.

660-46 Congregation of the Mother of Carmel, Jayamatha Province, Pala, India, $20,000. For construction of primary school. 2010.

660-47 Congregation of the Sisters of Mercy, Mazabuka, Zambia, $15,000. For evangelization programs. 2010.

660-48 Coprodeli USA, Chicago, IL, $15,000. For construction of chapel in Peru. 2010.

660-49 Crosier Community of Phoenix, Phoenix, AZ, $15,000. For seminarians in different stages of multiyear program in Indonesia. 2010.

660-50 Daughters of Charity of Saint Vincent de Paul, Cochabamba, Bolivia, $12,000. For Bibles, religion texts, audiovisual materials, salary of school teacher, and to provide retreat expenses. 2010.

660-51 Daughters of Charity of Saint Vincent de Paul, Province of South India, Bangalore, India, $15,000. For construction of parish Pastoral Ministry Center. 2010.

660-52 Daughters of Divine Love Congregation, Nigeria, $15,000. For completion of convent in Kenya. 2010.

660-53 Daughters of Divine Love Congregation, Nigeria, $12,000. For evangelization ministry in Cuba. 2010.

660-54 Daughters of Mary, Tabora, Tanzania, Zanzibar and Pemba, $15,000. For construction of kindergarten and sisters' residence. 2010.

660-55 Daughters of Mary, Uganda, $10,000. For completion of convent. 2010.

660-56 Daughters of Mary Help of Christians, Bangalore, India, $15,000. For training and formation of novices. 2010.

660-57 Daughters of Mary Immaculate, San Antonio, TX, $15,000. For equipment and furnishings for school in Ecuador. 2010.

660-58 Daughters of Mary Immaculate, San Antonio, TX, $15,000. For construction of novitiate/hostel for young women in India. 2010.

660-59 Daughters of Mercy of the Third Order Regular of Saint Francis, Rome, Italy, $15,000. For renovations to motherhouse. 2010.

660-60 Daughters of Saint Francis de Sales, Katani, Nairobi, Kenya, $10,000. For construction of restrooms for nursery school. 2010.

660-61 Daughters of Saint Therese/Banyatereza Sisters, Uganda, $10,000. For renovation of the roof of motherhouse. 2010.

660-62 Deen Bandhu Samaj, India, $10,000. For construction of residence for religious women. 2010.

660-63 Diocese of Barentu, Barentu, Eritrea, $15,000. For diocesan catechetical formation program. 2010.

660-64 Diocese of Berhampur, Berhampur, India, $20,000. For training and formation of lay leaders. 2010.

660-65 Diocese of Chulucanas, Chulucanas, Peru, $10,000. For purchase of furniture for dormitory rooms for seminarians. 2010.

660-66 Diocese of Djibouti, Djibouti, Djibouti, $10,000. For living expenses of four Catholic school directors. 2010.

660-67 Diocese of Huancavelica, Huancavelica, Peru, $10,000. For education and training of religion teachers. 2010.

660-68 Diocese of Jasikan, Jasikan, Ghana, $10,000. For completion of outstation chapel. 2010.

660-69 Diocese of Kabankalan, Philippines, $10,000. For training and formation of catechists. 2010.

660-70 Diocese of Kasana-Luweero, Mary Mother of the Divine Shepherd Parish, Mulajje, Luweero, Uganda, $10,000. For purchase of church pews. 2010.

660-71 Diocese of Keren, Keren, Eritrea, $10,000. For diocesan catechetical formation program. 2010.

660-72 Diocese of Kiyinda-Mityana, Mityana, Uganda, $15,000. For purchase of four motorcycles for diocesan pastoral ministry. 2010.

660-73 Diocese of Kiyinda-Mityana, Kyankwanzi Chaplaincy and Institutions, Mityana, Uganda, $10,000. For completion of church. 2010.

660-74 Diocese of Kiyinda-Mityana, Our Lady of Presentation Parish, Ndibata, Mityana, Uganda, $15,000. For completion and expansion of secondary school. 2010.

660-75 Diocese of Kokstad, Kokstad, South Africa, $20,000. For training and formation of laity. 2010.

660-76 Diocese of Kokstad, Kokstad, South Africa, $15,000. For construction of outstation church. 2010.

660-77 Diocese of Kottayam, India, $10,000. For formation of religious and lay leaders and evangelization programs. 2010.

660-78 Diocese of Machakos, Machakos, Kenya, $15,000. For construction of outstation church. 2010.

660-79 Diocese of Nha Trang, Khanh Hoa, Vietnam, $10,000. For formation program for college seminarians. 2010.

660-80 Diocese of Port-de-Paix, Port-au-Prince, Haiti, $10,000. For renovation of parish hall. 2010.

660-81 Diocese of Purwokerto, Purwokerto, Indonesia, $10,000. For education and training of catechists. 2010.

660-82 Diocese of San Pablo, San Pablo, Philippines, $10,000. For ongoing training and formation of catechists. 2010.

660-83 Discalced Carmelite Friars, Manjummel Province, India, $10,000. For completion of formation house. 2010.

660-84 Discalced Carmelite Order, Krakow Province, Krakow, Poland, $10,000. For replacement of windows in monastery. 2010.

660-85 Divine Word Missionaries, Techny, IL, $20,000. For scholarship assistance for clergy, women religious and seminarians from Vietnam. 2010.

660-86 Divine Word Missionaries, India, $10,000. For construction of primary school. 2010.

660-87 Dominican Order of the Catholic Church, Mexico City, Mexico, $20,000. For training and formation of seminarians. 2010.

660-88 Dominican Sisters Congregation of Blessed Imelda, Trnava, Slovakia, $20,000. For living expenses of religious women in Slovakia and the Ukraine. 2010.

660-89 Episcopia Romano-Catolica Chisinau, Chisinau, Moldova, $20,000. For renovation of village church. 2010.

660-90 Eucharistic Heart of Jesus Sisters, Lagos, Nigeria, $12,000. For education of two religious women. 2010.

660-91 Evangelizing Sisters of Mary, Nairobi, Kenya, $10,000. For evangelization program for women. 2010.

660-92 Evangelizing Sisters of Mary, Nairobi, Kenya, $10,000. For construction of convent. 2010.

660-93 Fathers of the Holy Cross, South India Province, India, $10,000. For construction of priests' residence. 2010.

660-94 Franciscan Clarist Congregation, Nirmalrani Province, India, $15,000. For completion of formation house. 2010.

660-95 Franciscan Federation of Morocco, Morocco and the Western Sahara, $15,000. For operation of mission center, and living expenses and formation of resident friars. 2010.

660-96 Franciscan Foundation for Russia and Kazakhstan, Almaty, Kazakhstan, $10,000. For renovation of church basement into religious education center. 2010.

660-97 Franciscan Friars Minor, Seraphic Province of Saint Francis, Assisi, Italy, $20,000. For living expenses and formation of seminarians. 2010.

660-98 Franciscan Friars Minor, Seraphic Province of Saint Francis, Assisi, Italy, $20,000. For ongoing formation and living expenses of professed friars and novices. 2010.

660-99 Franciscan Friars Minor, Venetian Province of Saint Anthony of Padua, Venice, Italy, $15,000. For healing and renewal of priests and religious. 2010.

660-100 Franciscan Friars Minor, Venetian Province of Saint Anthony of Padua, Venice, Italy, $15,000. For training and formation of priests and laity for interfaith religious dialogue. 2010.

660-101 Franciscan General Curia, Cairo, Egypt, $15,000. For education and formation of seminarians. 2010.

660-102 Franciscan Missionary Sisters for Africa, Nakuru, Kenya, $10,000. For parish-based empowerment program for care and support of children infected with HIV/AIDS. 2010.

660-103 Franciscan Sisters of Little Falls, Little Falls, MN, $12,000. For living expenses of women religious ministering in Mexico. 2010.

660-104 Franciscan Sisters of Saint Joseph Asumbi, Kisii, Kenya, $10,000. For renovation and furnishing of convent. 2010.

660-105 Franciscan Sisters of the Poor, New York, NY, $15,000. For construction of school in Louanga, Senegal. 2010.

660-106 Franciscan Vice Province of Saint Benedict, Santarem, Brazil, $15,000. For education and formation of seminarians. 2010.

660-107 Fraternidad Marianna de la Reconciliation, Lima, Peru, $15,000. For training and formation of religious women. 2010.

660-108 Fraternidad Misionera Verbum Dei, Madrid, Spain, $20,000. For salary of woman religious working in evangelization outreach. 2010.

660-109 Grail Sisters, Mwanga, Tanzania, Zanzibar and Pemba, $10,000. For construction of multipurpose building. 2010.

660-110 Handmaids of the Holy Child Jesus, Kenya, $10,000. For expansion of classrooms for vocational training center. 2010.

660-111 Handmaids of the Holy Child Jesus, Central Eastern Province in Onitsha, Nigeria, $20,000. For completion of convent. 2010.

660-112 Hearts Home USA, Brooklyn, NY, $10,000. For development of recruitment and formation program for lay missionaries. 2010.

660-113 Hiep Hoa Parish, Hiep Hoa, Vietnam, $10,000. For construction of parish school. 2010.

660-114 Holy Cross Congregation, Notre Dame, IN, $30,000. For renovation of novitiate in Uganda and equipment and repairs of formation house in Mexico. 2010.

660-115 Holy Family Parish, Tanzania, Zanzibar and Pemba, $15,000. For construction of two classrooms for catechetical instruction. 2010.

660-116 Holy Ghost Fathers, Foundation of Kenya, Nairobi, Kenya, $15,000. For formation of 40 lay leaders. 2010.

660-117 Holy Saviors Major Seminary, Keren, Eritrea, $20,000. For education and formation of seminarians. 2010.

660-118 Holy Spirit, Velke Slemence, Slovakia, $15,000. For renovation of parish church. 2010.

660-119 Holy Spirit Religious Missionary Congregation Foundation of Sierra Leone, Freetown, Sierra Leone, $15,000. For completion of parish church. 2010.

660-120 Immaculate Conception of the Blessed Virgin Mary Parish, Miroslawiec, Poland, $15,000. For renovation of parochial house and two churches. 2010.

660-121 Immaculate Heart Sisters of Africa, Musoma, Tanzania, Zanzibar and Pemba, $15,000. For renovation of convent. 2010.

660-122 Institute Servants of the Lord and the Virgin of Matara, Rome, Italy, $20,000. For living and travel expenses for women religious in Siberia, to purchase evangelization materials, and to repair convent. 2010.

660-123 Instituto de Formacion Filosofica Intercongregacional de Mexico, Mexico, $10,000. For basic academic skills to religious men. 2010.

660-124 Instituto de Pastoral Regional, Belem, Brazil, $15,000. For training and formation of lay catechists and BCC leaders. 2010.

660-125 International Theological Institute for Studies on Marriage and the Family, Trumau, Austria, $15,000. For education and living expenses of students. 2010.

660-126 Kanyakine Parish, Meru, Kenya, $10,000. For training and formation of laity. 2010.

660-127 King Christ Church, Da Lat, Vietnam, $20,000. For construction of parish church. 2010.

660-128 Kinh Ba Parish, Vietnam, $20,000. For construction of mission church. 2010.

660-129 Lebanese Maronite Missionaries, Jounieh, Lebanon, $10,000. For purchase of media equipment for laity formation training program. 2010.

660-130 Legionaries of Christ, Cornwall, Canada, $20,000. For education and formation of Latin American seminarians. 2010.

660-131 Likulezi Catechetical Training Centre, Namadzi, Malawi, $15,000. For education and training of catechists. 2010.

660-132 Little Brothers of the Good Shepherd, Hamilton, Canada, $10,000. For vocation literature advertising project. 2010.

660-133 Little Servants of Mary Immaculate, Saint Charles Lwanga Province, Lusaka, Zambia, $10,000. For renovation of convent. 2010.

660-134 Liturgical Catechetical Institute, Goroka, Papua New Guinea, $15,000. For purchase of color printer and electric cutting machine for liturgical and catechetical material production. 2010.

660-135 Living Stones Catholic Community, Kaunas, Lithuania, $15,000. For evangelization and faith formation programs. 2010.

660-136 Living Waters International, Antigo, WI, $20,000. For construction of formation house for religious men in Tanzania. 2010.

660-137 Living Waters International, Antigo, WI, $15,000. For construction of catechetical and women's empowerment center in Tanzania. 2010.

660-138 Living Waters International, Antigo, WI, $10,000. For furnishings for school in Tanzania. 2010.

660-139 Living Waters International, Antigo, WI, $10,000. For completion of sub-parish presbytery in Tanzania. 2010.

660-140 Living Waters International, Antigo, WI, $10,000. For completion of outstation chapel in Tanzania. 2010.

660-141 Living Waters International, Antigo, WI, $10,000. For completion of outstation chapel in Tanzania. 2010.

660-142 Living Waters International, Antigo, WI, $10,000. For construction of dormitory for girls in secondary school in Uganda. 2010.

660-143 Living Waters International, Antigo, WI, $10,000. For construction of mission chapel in Mozambique. 2010.

660-144 Living Waters International, Antigo, WI, $10,000. For construction of mission chapel in Tanzania. 2010.

660-145 Living Waters International, Antigo, WI, $10,000. For construction of sub-station church in Tanzania. 2010.

660-146 Living Waters International, Antigo, WI, $10,000. For construction of outstation church in Tanzania. 2010.

660-147 Lovers of the Holy Cross, Vietnam, $15,000. For formation and daily living expenses of women religious. 2010.

660-148 Magadi Catholic Parish, Magadi, Kenya, $10,000. For construction of two classrooms. 2010.

660-149 Marianists, Province of the United States, Saint Louis, MO, $20,000. For formation materials for pastoral agents and Bibles and missals for the poor in Mexico. 2010.

660-150 Marianists, Province of the United States, Saint Louis, MO, $15,000. For construction of parish church in India. 2010.

660-151 Marist Brothers of the Schools, Bayonne, NJ, $10,000. For campus ministry program for a mission in Mexico. 2010.

660-152 Mary Mother of God Mission Society, Saint Paul, MN, $15,000. For expansion of evangelization outreach program to university students. 2010.

660-153 Maryknoll Mission Association of the Faithful, Maryknoll, NY, $15,000. For salary and living expenses of education program coordinator ministering in Kenya. 2010.

660-154 Missionaries of Compassion, Hyderabad, India, $15,000. For construction of parish church. 2010.

660-155 Missionaries of Little Flower Congregation, Changanachery, India, $15,000. For expansion of school building. 2010.

660-156 Missionaries of Saint Francis de Sales, India, $15,000. For construction of parish church. 2010.

660-157 Missionaries of the Sacred Heart, Dublin, Ireland, $15,000. For renovation of Mission House to make it handicapped accessible. 2010.

660-158 Missionary Oblates of Mary Immaculate, Maseru, Lesotho, $20,000. For farming project for men's congregation. 2010.

660-159 Missionary Oblates of Mary Immaculate, Lusaka, Zambia, $20,000. For construction of chapel in Zambia. 2010.

660-160 Missionary Sisters of the Holy Family, Poland, $15,000. For training and formation of religious women in Belarus. 2010.

660-161 Missionary Sisters of the Holy Family, Poland, $15,000. For training and formation of religious women in Kenya. 2010.

660-162 Molopo District Catholic Church, Mmabatho, South Africa, $15,000. For renovation and expansion of parish church. 2010.

660-163 Monasterio Santa Teresa de Jesus, Santo Domingo, Dominican Republic, $15,000. For tuition support for young girls in Catholic school. 2010.

660-164 Monastero di Santa Chiara, Naples, Italy, $15,000. For daily living expenses of women religious and to purchase host-making machine. 2010.

660-165 Monastery of Poor Clares, Myanga, Bungoma, Kenya, $15,000. For formation and training of women religious. 2010.

660-166 Munkeby Mariakloster, Levanger, Norway, $30,000. For construction of monastery in Norway. 2010.

660-167 Oblates of Mary Immaculate, Brazil Province, Sao Paulo, Brazil, $20,000. For construction of multipurpose building. 2010.

660-168 Opifices Christi Missionary Priests, Philippines, $15,000. For completion of dining and conference hall. 2010.

660-169 Our Lady of Fatima Church, Haiti, $15,000. For generator for parish. 2010.

660-170 Our Lady of Fatima Parish, Urambo, Tabora, Tanzania, Zanzibar and Pemba, $10,000. For construction of student hostels. 2010.

660-171 Our Lady of Lourdes Grotto, Egyam, Takoradi, Ghana, $15,000. For construction of mechanized borehole for potable water. 2010.

660-172 Our Lady of Visitation Church, Timau Parish, Timau, Kenya, $10,000. For construction of outstation chapel. 2010.

660-173 Our Lady Queen of Angels Bukalagi Parish, Mityana, Uganda, $10,000. For construction of girls' school dormitory. 2010.

660-174 Our Lady Source of Joy Kasambya Parish, Mubende, Uganda, $15,000. For completion of six outstation churches. 2010.

660-175 Parroquia Nuestra Senora del Carmen, Ecuador, $15,000. For printing of family catechism books. 2010.

660-176 Perpetual Adoration of the Blessed Sacrament Sisters, Rancagua, Chile, $20,000. For construction of multipurpose building. 2010.

660-177 Peter Cao Parish, Peter Cao, Vietnam, $10,000. For construction of kindergarten. 2010.

660-178 Polish Piarist Province, Krakow, Poland, $10,000. For completion of parish house in Belarus. 2010.

660-179 Poor Clare Missionary Sisters, Rome, Italy, $20,000. For construction of phase II of pastoral center in Mexico. 2010.

660-180 Poor Clare Nuns, Abidjan, Ivory Coast, $10,000. For living expenses of contemplative religious women. 2010.

660-181 Poor Clare Sisters, Kigali, Rwanda, $15,000. For living expenses of women religious. 2010.

660-182 Poor Clare Sisters, Kigali, Rwanda, $10,000. For living expenses of women religious. 2010.

660-183 Poor Clare Sisters of Cortona, Cortona, Italy, $10,000. For daily living expenses of women religious. 2010.

660-184 Poor Clares Monastery of Our Lady of Africa, Lubango, Angola, $10,000. For daily expenses of women religious. 2010.

660-185 Poor Clares Monastery of the Holy Family, San Ysidro, CA, $15,000. For living expenses of religious women in Mexico. 2010.

660-186 Poor Clares, Saint Clare Monastery, Ijebu Ode, Nigeria, $15,000. For formation and living expenses of religious women. 2010.

660-187 Prelatura de Sicuani, Sicuani, Peru, $10,500. For religious formation workshops for teachers. 2010.

660-188 Prelatura de Yauyos, Lima, Peru, $15,000. To continue to support education and formation of seminarians. 2010.

660-189 Prelatura de Yauyos, Lima, Peru, $10,000. To continue to support training of catechists for evangelization outreach. 2010.

660-190 Province of Our Mother of Good Counsel, Olympia Fields, IL, $15,000. For formation and living expenses of seminarians in Peru. 2010.

660-191 Rakama FM Radio, Vohipeno, Madagascar, $20,000. For additional airtime for Catholic radio station. 2010.

660-192 Redemptoris Mater Diocesan Seminary, Austria, $15,000. For training and formation of seminarians. 2010.

660-193 Redemptorists-Denver Province, Denver, CO, $15,000. For education and formation of seminarians in Brazil. 2010.

660-194 Redemptorists-Denver Province, Denver, CO, $15,000. For living expenses, training and formation of seminarians in Nigeria. 2010.

660-195 Sacred Apostles Peter and Paul Ukrainian Church, Ukraine, $15,000. For renovations of parish church. 2010.

660-196 Sacred Heart Brothers, Angelo Province, India, $20,000. For construction of refectory, kitchen and storeroom. 2010.

660-197 Sacred Heart of Jesus Parish, Babahoyo, Ecuador, $15,000. For renovation of parish buildings into classrooms for religious education. 2010.

660-198 Saint Alfred Parish, Jema, Elubo, Ghana, $15,000. For water construction project. 2010.

660-199 Saint Andrew the Apostle Catholic Chaplaincy, Kaliro, Uganda, $10,000. For completion of multipurpose hall. 2010.

660-200 Saint Ann Sisters of Providence, India, $10,000. For construction of convent. 2010.

660-201 Saint Anthony of Padua Monastery, Mexico, $15,000. For education and formation of religious women. 2010.

660-202 Saint Anthony of Padua Parish, Kwesimintsim, Takoradi, Ghana, $10,000. For construction of parish school and nursery. 2010.

660-203 Saint Anthonys Catholic Church, Ghana, $20,000. For construction of substation church. 2010.

660-204 Saint Anthonys Catholic Church, Ghana, $19,000. For construction of mechanized borehole for potable water for parish. 2010.

660-205 Saint Anthonys Catholic Church, Ghana, $15,000. For completion of presbytery. 2010.

660-206 Saint Anthonys Catholic Church, Ghana, $10,000. For renovation of parish school. 2010.

660-207 Saint Augustines School Chaplaincy, Bogoso, Ghana, $10,000. For construction of high school chapel. 2010.

660-208 Saint Benedict Parish, Mabugai, Lushoto, Tanzania, Zanzibar and Pemba, $25,000. For expansion of Catholic school. 2010.

660-209 Saint Brother Albert Catholic Parish, Poland, $20,000. For renovation of parish building for religious education. 2010.

660-210 Saint Francis of Assisi Parish, Dakao, Ho Chi Minh City, Vietnam, $20,000. For expansion of parish church. 2010.

660-211 Saint James Catholic Church, Ilesa, Nigeria, $10,000. For construction of priest's residence. 2010.

660-212 Saint James the Apostle Parish, Yanaoca, Sicuani, Peru, $10,000. For construction of parish catechetical center. 2010.

660-213 Saint John the Evangelist Parish, Ghana, $15,600. For potable water for parish outstation community. 2010.

660-214 Saint John the Evangelist Parish, Ghana, $10,000. For pews for parish church. 2010.

660-215 Saint Johns Parish, Euthini, Malawi, $10,000. For construction of two classroom blocks and teachers' residence. 2010.

660-216 Saint Joseph Major Seminary, Kenya, $11,539. For installation of plastic tanks to harvest rainwater for seminary. 2010.

660-217 Saint Joseph the Worker Catholic Parish, Kenya, $15,000. For construction of parish primary school. 2010.

660-218 Saint Josephs Mission, Mataleng, Barkly West, South Africa, $15,000. For renovation of multipurpose building. 2010.

660-219 Saint Josephs Monastery, Benedictine Monks, Mineiros, Brazil, $15,000. For education and formation of young monks. 2010.

660-220 Saint Josephs Parish, Ghana, $10,000. For completion of outstation chapel. 2010.

660-221 Saint Josephs Parish, Haiti, $20,000. For construction of parish church. 2010.

660-222 Saint Josephs Parish, Gvardeysk, Russia, $17,000. For apartment for worship, gatherings and living quarters for priest. 2010.

660-223 Saint Josephs Parish, Uganda, $10,000. For evangelization programs for women in Jinja. 2010.

660-224 Saint Josephs Parish, Asem Asa, Ghana, $15,000. For renovation of parish church. 2010.

660-225 Saint Josephs Parish, La Croix, Haiti, $10,000. For purchase of pews for parish church. 2010.

660-226 Saint Josephs Pontifical Seminary, India, $15,000. For maintenance and operational expenses of seminary. 2010.

660-227 Saint Margarets Kasaba Parish, Mansa, Zambia, $10,000. For roofing of five outstation churches. 2010.

660-228 Saint Mary Queen of the Apostles Parish, Chomachankola, Nzega, Tanzania, Zanzibar and Pemba, $15,000. For completion of presbytery. 2010.

660-229 Saint Marys Girls High School, Isiolo, Kenya, $10,000. For purchase of books and furniture for secondary school library. 2010.

660-230 Saint Marys Parish, Ghana, $15,000. For construction of pastoral/social center. 2010.

660-231 Saint Matthews Catholic Church, Moree, Ghana, $15,000. For construction of parish rectory. 2010.

660-232 Saint Michaels Catholic Parish, Asankrang Bremang, Asankrangwa, Ghana, $15,000. To install mechanized borehole for potable water for parish. 2010.

660-233 Saint Paul of Chartres Sisters, Ho Chi Minh City, Vietnam, $15,000. For renovation of chapel. 2010.

660-234 Saint Paul the Apostle Catholic Church, Mukono, Uganda, $10,000. For pews for parish church. 2010.

660-235 Saint Peters Catholic Church, Gouyave, Grenada, $20,000. For restoration of presbytery. 2010.

660-236 Saint Therese Parish, Gaspard, Haiti, $15,000. For completion of parish hall/school. 2010.

660-237 Saint Thomas Apostolic Seminary, Vadavathoor, India, $15,000. For training and formation of seminarians. 2010.

660-238 Saint Vlasa Church, Andrushivka, Ukraine, $15,000. For completion of parish church. 2010.

660-239 Salesians of Don Bosco, India, $15,000. For construction of small chapel. 2010.

660-240 Salesians of Don Bosco, ZMB Vice Province, Lusaka, Zambia, $10,000. For renovation and expansion of primary school. 2010.

660-241 Santa Chiara Poor Clare Monastery, Kokstad, South Africa, $15,000. For daily living expenses of women religious. 2010.

660-242 School for Adult Catechesis, Kaunas, Lithuania, $15,000. For religious education for adults. 2010.

660-243 Servants of Mary Mother of Sorrows, Alexis Province, India, $15,000. For construction of multipurpose rooms in primary school. 2010.

660-244 Servants of the Immaculate Heart of Mary Brothers, Iringa, Tanzania, Zanzibar and Pemba, $10,000. For construction of chapel. 2010.

660-245 Service Foundation Rural Missionary, Santiago, Chile, $15,000. For formation of lay missioners for promotion of pastoral letter to rural world. 2010.

660-246 Siervas del Plan de Dios, Lima, Peru, $10,000. For training of pastoral agents. 2010.

660-247 Sisters of Charity of Nazareth, Nazareth, KY, $10,000. For training and formation of religious women in India. 2010.

660-248 Sisters of Charity of Seton Hill, Korean Province, Gwangju, South Korea, $15,000. For training and formation of religious women. 2010.

660-249 Sisters of Mercy of Saint Charles Borromeo, Lusaka, Zambia, $10,000. For construction of convent. 2010.

660-250 Sisters of Our Lady of Nazareth, Suva, Fiji, $30,000. For preparation for congregation's General Chapter conference. 2010.

660-251 Sisters of Our Lady Queen of Africa, Sumbawanga, Tanzania, Zanzibar and Pemba, $14,000. For drilling of borehole for potable water for orphanage. 2010.

660-252 Sisters of Our Lady Queen of Africa, Sumbawanga, Tanzania, Zanzibar and Pemba,

$10,000. For construction of nursery school. 2010.

660-253 Sisters of Saint Ann, Brazil, $15,000. For training and formation of women religious. 2010.

660-254 Sisters of Saint Ann, Cameroon, $20,000. For training and formation of women religious. 2010.

660-255 Sisters of Saint Ann, Peru, $11,000. For daily living expenses of women religious. 2010.

660-256 Sisters of Saint Ann, Tanzania, Zanzibar and Pemba, $15,000. For installation of windmill for electricity at girls' school. 2010.

660-257 Sisters of Saint Felix of Cantalice, Warsaw, Poland, $20,000. For renovation of utility rooms of convent for pastoral activities. 2010.

660-258 Sisters of Saint Felix of Cantalice, Warsaw, Poland, $10,000. For evangelization program for youth and adults. 2010.

660-259 Sisters of Saint Louis, Ibadan, Nigeria, $15,000. For renovation of formation house for religious women. 2010.

660-260 Sisters of Saint Michael the Archangel, Nigeria, $25,000. For completion of convent. 2010.

660-261 Sisters of the Cross and Passion, Manchester, England, $15,000. For course in adult faith formation. 2010.

660-262 Sisters of the Divine Savior, Milwaukee, WI, $15,000. For expansion of primary school in Democratic Republic of Congo. 2010.

660-263 Sisters of the Good Shepherd, Province of New York, Astoria, NY, $20,000. For construction of infirmary for women religious in Ecuador. 2010.

660-264 Sisters of the Holy Faith, Dublin, Ireland, $10,000. For evangelization through Prayer and Music Ministry. 2010.

660-265 Sisters of the Mother of God of Loreto, Warsaw, Poland, $20,000. For renovation of home for elderly. 2010.

660-266 Sisters of the Order of Augustinian Recollects, Ahuacatlan de Jesus, San Luis Potosi, Mexico, $15,000. For construction of infirmary for elderly and retired women religious. 2010.

660-267 Sociedade Civil Sao Rafael, Belem, Brazil, $15,000. For renovation of seminary. 2010.

660-268 Society for the Propagation of the Faith, New York, NY, $300,000. For education and formation of major seminarians in Africa. 2010.

660-269 Society of African Missions, Cork, Ireland, $15,000. For construction of parish church. 2010.

660-270 Society of Jesus, China Province, Macau, China, $20,000. For formation of lay missionaries. 2010.

660-271 Society of Jesus, Czech Province, Prague, Czech Republic, $15,000. For operating costs of elementary school. 2010.

660-272 Society of Jesus, South Poland Province, Krakow, Poland, $15,000. For renovation and refurnishing of seminary. 2010.

660-273 Society of Jesus, South Poland Province, Krakow, Poland, $15,000. For renovation and refurnishing of dormitories and to provide scholarship assistance for students. 2010.

660-274 Society of Jesus, South Poland Province, Krakow, Poland, $10,000. For retreat and Ignatian Youth Days celebration. 2010.

660-275 Society of Mary, Wellington, New Zealand, $20,000. For youth website and salaries for youth ministers. 2010.

660-276 Society of Mary, Wellington, New Zealand, $15,000. For leadership and evangelization program. 2010.

660-277 Society of Nirmala Dasi Sisters, Thrissur, India, $15,000. For construction of home for elderly and infirm women. 2010.

660-278 Soeurs de Misericorde, Montreal, Canada, $10,000. For religious formation of children. 2010.

660-279 Teresian Carmelite Congregation, Amala Province in Tamil Nadu, India, $10,000. For construction of convent. 2010.

660-280 Ternopil-Zboriv Eparchy, Ternopil, Ukraine, $10,000. To continue to support education of priest. 2010.

660-281 Tho Loc Parish, Tho Loc, Vietnam, $10,000. For construction of kindergarten. 2010.

660-282 Uganda Martyrs Parish, Misigi, Mityana, Uganda, $10,000. For completion of presbytery. 2010.

660-283 University of Saint Mary of the Lake-Mundelein Seminary, Mundelein, IL, $15,000. For education and formation of international seminarians. 2010.

660-284 Ursuline Sisters of Saint Jerome in Somasca, Dumaguete City, Philippines, $10,000. For catechetical formation of women religious, faculty and staff of diocesan parish school. 2010.

660-285 Vicariato Apostolico de Galapagos, Puerto Baquerizo Moreno, Ecuador, $15,000. For training and formation of seminarians. 2010.

660-286 Volunteer Missionary Movement, Greendale, WI, $15,000. For training of lay missionaries in Central America. 2010.

661

KTW Foundation Ltd., Inc.

c/o Franz & Beame, P.A.
2425 Hollywood Blvd.
Hollywood, FL 33020-6605

Established in 1980; supporting organization of Beth Israel V'Damesk Elizer Inc., B'nai Brith, Israel.
Grantmaker type: Public charity.
Financial data (yr. ended 10/31/10): Revenue, $236,232; assets, $15,451,565 (M); expenditures, $650,150; giving activities include $650,000 for grants to organizations outside the U.S.
Fields of interest: Jewish agencies & synagogues.
International interests: Israel.
Limitations: Applications not accepted. Giving primarily in Israel.
Application information: Contributes only to a pre-selected organization.
Officers: Emanuel Edelstein,* Pres.; Sol Kest,* V.P.
EIN: 591950712

662

Matthew 28:18-20 Charitable Trust

12635 S.W. 112th St. Rd.
Dunnellon, FL 34432-5419 (352) 694-3175
Contact: Stephen F. Saint, Pres.

Established around 1992 in FL.
Donors: Stephen F. Saint; Abraham C. Van Der Puy; Marjorie Van Der Puy.
Grantmaker type: Operating foundation.

Financial data (yr. ended 12/31/10): Assets, $2,640,524 (M); gifts received, $418,640; expenditures, $229,387; qualifying distributions, $216,041; giving activities include $201,972 for 7 grants (high: $168,000; low: $820).
Purpose and activities: Giving generally for religious missionary activities.
Fields of interest: Religion; General charitable giving.
International interests: Ecuador.
Limitations: Giving primarily in CO, FL and MO.
Application information: Application form not required.
    Deadline(s): None
Officer and Trustees:* Stephen F. Saint,* Pres.; Jesse Saint.
EIN: 593091298

663

Katherine John Murphy Foundation

c/o SunTrust Bank
P.O. Box 1908
Orlando, FL 32802-1908
Contact: Allan Mast, 1st V.P., SunTrust Bank
E-mail: info@murphyfoundation.org; URL: http://www.murphyfoundation.org/

Trust established in 1954 in GA.
Donor: Katherine Murphy Riley†.
Grantmaker type: Independent foundation.
Financial data (yr. ended 12/31/10): Assets, $15,937,531 (M); expenditures, $973,221; qualifying distributions, $831,500; giving activities include $831,500 for grants.
Fields of interest: Arts; Higher education; Environment; Health care; Children/youth, services.
International interests: Latin America.
Limitations: Applications not accepted. Giving primarily in Atlanta, GA. No grants to individuals, or for research, or matching gifts; no loans.
Application information: The foundation has suspended grantmaking for the foreseeable future. Please check foundation web site for updates.
    Board meeting date(s): Annually, and as necessary
Officer and Trustees:* Martin Gatins,* Chair.; Dameron Black III; Phillip Gatins.
Number of staff: None.
EIN: 586026045

664

Drs. Kiran & Pallavi Patel Family Foundation, Inc.

5600 Mariner St., Ste. 227
Tampa, FL 33609-3471
Contact: Kiran C. Patel M.D., Secy.-Treas.

Established in 2006 in FL.
Donors: Kiran C. Patel, M.D.; Pallavi C. Patel, M.D.; Ace Endowment Fund; Bay Area Primary Care.
Grantmaker type: Independent foundation.
Financial data (yr. ended 06/30/10): Assets, $3,236,878 (M); gifts received, $505,644; expenditures, $489,640; qualifying distributions, $471,110; giving activities include $440,963 for 11 grants (high: $177,500; low: $180).
Fields of interest: Performing arts centers; Education; Hospitals (general); Health care; Human services; International development; International relief; International human rights.
International interests: India.

Type of support: General/operating support; Program development; Scholarships—to individuals.
Limitations: Giving primarily in FL, Bangladesh, India, and the Congo.
Application information:
Initial approach: Letter
Deadline(s): None
Officers: Pallavi C. Patel, M.D., Pres.; Shilen Patel, V.P.; Kiran C. Patel, M.D., Secy.-Treas.
Trustees: Sonali Judd; Sheetal Patel.
EIN: 203916634

665

Drs. Kiran & Pallavi Patel Foundation for Global Understanding, Inc.

5600 Mariner St., Ste. 200
Tampa, FL 33609-3417 (813) 471-4380
Contact: Bharati Shah, Exec. Dir.
URL: http://www.global-understanding.org

Established in 2003.
Grantmaker type: Public charity.
Financial data (yr. ended 06/30/10): Revenue, $221,047; assets, $318,074 (M); gifts received, $220,547; expenditures, $159,492; program services expenses, $126,026; giving activities include $125,495 for 2 grants (high: $100,000; low: $10,000).
Purpose and activities: The foundation is dedicated to creating educational, health and cultural programs that build healthy communities and empower individuals to be their best.
Fields of interest: Higher education; Vocational education; Arts; Education; Health care; International affairs; Community/economic development.
International interests: India; Africa.
Type of support: Scholarships—to individuals.
Officers and Directors:* Frank Sanchez,* Chair.; Clark Jordan Holmes,* Secy.; Dr. Martin Silbiger,* Treas.; Bharati Shah, Exec. Dir.; Chip Diehl; Jeff Knott; Gene Marshall; Dr. Kiran C. Patel; Dr. Pallavi Patel; Kathy Rydell; Dr. Juel Shannon Smith.
EIN: 200020142

666

The Patricia Price Peterson Foundation

c/o AUREOS
P.O. Box 25331
Miami, FL 33102-5331
Contact: Erik Peterson, Pres.
E-mail: epeterson@aureos.co.cr

Established about 1964.
Donor: Rudolph A. Peterson†.
Grantmaker type: Independent foundation.
Financial data (yr. ended 12/31/10): Assets, $10,459,028 (M); expenditures, $551,128; qualifying distributions, $549,149; giving activities include $546,269 for 9 grants (high: $245,000; low: $1,500).
Purpose and activities: Giving primarily for education and for environmental programs, including agricultural university scholarships, an orphanage, environmental education, community development, and nature reserve-conservation.
Fields of interest: Agriculture; Teacher school/education; Education; Environment, natural resources; Physically disabled.
International interests: Central America.

Type of support: General/operating support; Management development/capacity building; Equipment; Land acquisition; Emergency funds; Program development; Professorships; Seed money; Scholarship funds.
Limitations: Giving limited to Central America and Panama.
Application information: Application form not required.
Initial approach: E-mail
Copies of proposal: 1
Deadline(s): None
Board meeting date(s): Mid-year
Officer: Erik Peterson, Pres.
Directors: Merrill K. Bennett; Stephen W. Bennett; R. Price Peterson; Peter Stirling.
EIN: 946109098

667

Posnack Foundation of Hollywood

(formerly Posnack Family Foundation of Hollywood)
c/o Bank of America, N.A.
P.O. Box 40200, MC FL9-100-10-19
Jacksonville, FL 32203-0200
Application address: c/o Bank of America, N.A., 401 E. Las Olas Blvd., Fort Lauderdale, FL 33301-2230

Established in 1984 in FL.
Grantmaker type: Independent foundation.
Financial data (yr. ended 01/31/11): Assets, $2,022,388 (M); expenditures, $436,051; qualifying distributions, $410,890; giving activities include $410,890 for grants.
Purpose and activities: Support for Jewish organizations, including welfare funds and educational institutions.
Fields of interest: Education; Higher education; Elementary/secondary education; Human services; Jewish federated giving programs; Jewish agencies & synagogues.
International interests: Israel.
Limitations: Applications accepted. Giving primarily in FL and NY. No grants to individuals.
Application information: Application form not required.
Deadline(s): None
Trustee: Bank of America, N.A.
EIN: 592484512

668

J. Crayton Pruitt Foundation, Inc.

c/o Peter R. Wallace
1 Beach Dr. S.E., Ste. 320E
St. Petersburg, FL 33701-3953
E-mail: prw@swblaw.com

Established in 1989 in FL; funded in 1990.
Donors: J. Crayton Pruitt; Secret Promise, Ltd.; J. Crayton Pruitt Charitable Lead Trust I; J. Crayton Pruitt Charitable Lead Trust II; J. Crayton Pruitt Charitable Lead Trust III.
Grantmaker type: Independent foundation.
Financial data (yr. ended 12/31/10): Assets, $4,434,357 (M); gifts received, $1,378,137; expenditures, $1,410,570; qualifying distributions, $1,384,136; giving activities include $1,384,136 for grants.
Fields of interest: Higher education.
International interests: Chile.
Type of support: Professorships; Curriculum development; Research.

Limitations: Applications not accepted. Giving primarily in FL. No grants to individuals.
Application information: Unsolicited requests for funds not accepted.
Board meeting date(s): Dec.
Directors: Natalie Pruitt Judge; Frances M. Pruitt; J. Crayton Pruitt; Helen G. Pruitt Wallace.
EIN: 592876499

669

Robert Russell Memorial Foundation

c/o Norman H. Lipoff, Esq.
1221 Brickell Ave., 17th Fl.
Miami, FL 33131-2804 (305) 579-0503
Contact: Norman H. Lipoff, Chair.
FAX: (305) 961-5503; E-mail: Lipoffn@Gtlaw.com

Established in 1984 in FL.
Donor: Robert Russell†.
Grantmaker type: Independent foundation.
Financial data (yr. ended 08/31/10): Assets, $15,053,112 (M); expenditures, $624,861; qualifying distributions, $558,683; giving activities include $451,000 for 57 grants (high: $36,000; low: $1,000).
Purpose and activities: Support primarily for Jewish and Israeli programs and agencies, including education, social or research programs, capital projects, religious tolerance, Middle East studies, Jewish leadership development, and interfaith activity.
Fields of interest: Jewish federated giving programs.
International interests: Israel.
Type of support: General/operating support; Continuing support; Annual campaigns; Capital campaigns; Building/renovation; Program development; Fellowships; Scholarship funds; Matching/challenge support.
Limitations: Applications accepted. Giving primarily in the Miami-Dade County, FL, area; limited giving also in Israel. No grants to individuals.
Publications: Application guidelines.
Application information: Application form required.
Initial approach: Letter
Copies of proposal: 5
Deadline(s): Mar. 31
Board meeting date(s): May
Final notification: Following board meeting
Officer and Trustees:* Norman H. Lipoff,* Chair.; Joel Goldman; Bill Lehman; Jacob Solomon; Harry Weitzer; Northern Trust Bank, N.A.
EIN: 592486579

670

The Milton and Marilyn Safenowitz Family Foundation, Inc.

7124 Queenferry Cir.
Boca Raton, FL 33496-5950

Established in 2001 in FL.
Donor: Marilyn Safenowitz.
Grantmaker type: Independent foundation.
Financial data (yr. ended 12/31/10): Assets, $4,333,214 (M); expenditures, $166,949; qualifying distributions, $162,100; giving activities include $162,100 for 6 grants (high: $100,000; low: $5,000).
Fields of interest: ALS; Health care; Jewish federated giving programs.
International interests: Israel.

Limitations: Applications not accepted. Giving primarily in FL and NY. No grants to individuals.
Application information: Contributes only to pre-selected organizations.
Officers: Marilyn Safenowitz, Pres.; Susan Levine, V.P.; Ellen Silverman, V.P.; Howard Safenowitz, Secy.-Treas.
EIN: 651118908

671
Salvadoran American Humanitarian Foundation, Inc.
2050 Coral Way, Ste. 5600
Miami, FL   33145-2636   (305) 860-0300
FAX: (305) 860-1415; E-mail: contact@sahf.org;
Toll-free tel.: (800) 992-8858; URL: http://www.sahf.org

Established in 1983 in FL.
Grantmaker type: Public charity.
Financial data (yr. ended 12/31/10): Revenue, $40,311,593; assets, $2,079,195 (M); gifts received, $40,043,163; expenditures, $40,414,611; giving activities include $39,862,840 for grants to organizations outside the U.S.
Purpose and activities: The organization works to enhance the well-being of the underserved people of El Salvador through human development programs, implemented in partnership with local organizations.
Fields of interest: Safety/disasters; International affairs; Children/youth.
International interests: El Salvador.
Limitations: Giving limited to El Salvador.
Publications: Annual report; Newsletter; IRS Form 990 or 990-PF printed copy available upon request.
Officers and Directors:* Jos Eduardo Siman,* Pres.; Ernesto Poma,* V.P.; Maga Lie-Nielsen,* Secy.; William Freund,* Treas.; Guillermo Argumedo; Leon R. Avila; Carmen Elena Palomo de Mohlman; Jacobo Gadala-Maria; Raul Henriquez; Fernando Melo; Ricardo Menendez; Roxana Aguirreurreta O'Neill; Mauricio Samayoa; Roberto Schaps; Daniel Schwartz; and 4 additional directors.
EIN: 592339140

672
Aaron & Martha Schecter Private Foundation
3900 Hollywood Blvd., PH-N
Hollywood, FL   33021

Established in 1981 in FL.
Donors: Aaron Schecter; Martha Schecter†; Laurie Schecter; Julie Schecter.
Grantmaker type: Independent foundation.
Financial data (yr. ended 09/30/11): Assets, $14,470,942 (M); gifts received, $3,645,760; expenditures, $1,022,847; qualifying distributions, $862,000; giving activities include $862,000 for grants.
Purpose and activities: Giving primarily for international affairs, public policy groups promoting peace and social responsibility, and civil rights organizations.
Fields of interest: Arts; Scholarships/financial aid; International peace/security; International affairs; Civil/human rights; Philanthropy/voluntarism; Public policy, research.

Limitations: Applications not accepted. Giving in the U.S., with emphasis on CA and NY. No grants to individuals.
Application information: Contributes only to pre-selected organizations.
Trustees: Aaron Schecter; Julie Schecter; Laurie Schecter.
EIN: 592185762

673
Scholarship Fund for Ethiopian Jews
19202 Black Mangrove Ct.
Boca Raton, FL   33498-4835
URL: http://www.sfej.org

Established in FL.
Grantmaker type: Public charity.
Financial data (yr. ended 06/30/10): Revenue, $39,139; assets, $66,569 (M); gifts received, $38,981; expenditures, $18,446; giving activities include $15,000 for grants.
Purpose and activities: The fund is dedicated to developing a pool of talented, well-educated, and highly-motivated Ethiopian Israelis, committed to serving their own community and the society at large.
Fields of interest: Education; Jewish agencies & synagogues.
International interests: Israel.
Type of support: Scholarship funds.
Limitations: Giving primarily to Israel.
Officers and Directors:* Asher Naim,* Chair.; Rabbi Richard Yellin,* Pres.; Jerome Krassenstein,* C.P.A., V.P.; Roger Gorman,* M.D., Secy.; J.D. Krassenstein,* Treas.; Harry Adwar; Stanton Cherry; Marlene Herzog; Rabbi Peter Kasdan; Victor Levadi, Ph.D.; Edwin Sherman.
EIN: 650938714

674
The Second Chance Foundation
194 Ridge Dr.
Naples, FL   34108-3415

Established in 1986 in FL.
Donors: Lloyd S. Taylor†; Lorraine Huloschman.
Grantmaker type: Independent foundation.
Financial data (yr. ended 12/31/10): Assets, $7,171,056 (M); gifts received, $1,500; expenditures, $419,973; qualifying distributions, $284,203; giving activities include $284,203 for grants.
Fields of interest: Museums (history); Humanities; Secondary school/education; Higher education; Education; Cystic fibrosis; Cancer; Cancer, leukemia; International development.
Type of support: Program-related investments/loans.
Limitations: Applications not accepted. Giving primarily in Naples, FL. No grants to individuals.
Application information: Unsolicited requests for funds not accepted.
Trustee: Bruce Conley.
EIN: 592708392

675
Festus and Helen Stacy Foundation, Inc.
5200 N. Federal Hwy.
P.M.B. 1065
Fort Lauderdale, FL   33308-3848
(954) 776-3386
Contact: Sharon Bizzell, Grants Mgr.
FAX: (954) 776-6469; E-mail: grants@fsfnd.org;
Sharon Bizzell e-mail: sbizzell@fsfnd.org;
URL: http://www.fsfnd.org

Established in 1980 in FL.
Donors: Festus Stacy†; Helen Stacy Charitable Trust.
Grantmaker type: Independent foundation.
Financial data (yr. ended 10/31/10): Assets, $46,471,528 (M); gifts received, $585,034; expenditures, $2,299,269; qualifying distributions, $622,690; giving activities include $622,690 for grants.
Purpose and activities: Support of charitable works that are consistent with making a genuine Christian impact benefiting mankind.
Fields of interest: Children/youth, services; Human services; International development; Foundations (community); Christian agencies & churches.
International interests: Africa; Asia; Europe.
Type of support: Seed money; In-kind gifts; Matching/challenge support.
Limitations: Giving primarily in Broward County, FL; some giving on a national and international basis. No support for No support to secular organizations or for for-profit organizations, as well as to churches other than those that the trustees are personally involved with, or those who are proposing unified multi-church outreaches. No grants to individuals, or for endowments, scholarship funds, long term Christian education, emergency funds, general operating budgets and/or capital expenditures to churches.
Publications: Application guidelines.
Application information: Application guidelines and form available on foundation web site. Application form required.
Initial approach: Telephone or e-mail requesting application form or download form from web site
Copies of proposal: 3
Deadline(s): None
Board meeting date(s): Feb. and June
Final notification: 60 days
Officers and Directors:* Douglas A. Stepelton,* Pres.; Brett S. Stepelton,* V.P.; Sean D. Stepelton,* V.P.; Virlee Stacy Stepelton,* Secy.-Treas.
EIN: 311706311

676
Taylor Family Foundation, Inc.
1111 9th Ave. W., Ste. E
Bradenton, FL   34205-7745

Established in 1996 in WI and FL.
Grantmaker type: Independent foundation.
Financial data (yr. ended 12/31/10): Assets, $13,210,765 (M); expenditures, $771,567; qualifying distributions, $314,945; giving activities include $314,945 for grants.
Purpose and activities: Giving primarily for children, youth and social services, medical research, and Christian organizations.
Fields of interest: Animal welfare; Medical research, institute; Human services; Children/youth, services;

Christian agencies & churches; Economically disadvantaged.
International interests: United Kingdom; Chile; Scotland.
Limitations: Applications not accepted. Giving primarily in FL; some giving also in Chile, Aberdeen, Scotland and United Kingdom. No grants to individuals.
Application information: Contributes only to pre-selected organizations.
Officers and Directors: * Ritchey Nelson Taylor,* Pres. and Treas.; Katherine Kittsmiller, V.P. and Secy.; Elaine Ackel, Exec. Dir.; Darlene Westermeyer.
EIN: 396058301

677
Transitions Foundation of Guatemala, Inc.
A-146 P.O. Box 669004
Miami Springs, FL   33266-9004
E-mail: transitionsguatemala@yahoo.com; Tel. (Guatemala): 011-502-7832-4261; URL: http://www.transitionsfoundation.org/
Blog: http://www.transitionsfoundation.org/index.php/en/news?format=feed&type=rss
Facebook: http://www.facebook.com/pages/Transitions-Foundation/93384265759
Twitter: http://twitter.com/#!/TransitionsGuat
YouTube: http://www.youtube.com/transitionsguate

Established in 2000 in RI.
Grantmaker type: Public charity.
Financial data (yr. ended 12/31/08): Revenue, $373,254; assets, $239,000 (M); gifts received, $355,436; expenditures, $397,171; program services expenses, $329,863; giving activities include $26,388 for 51 grants to organizations outside the U.S., and $303,475 for foundation-administered programs.
Purpose and activities: The foundation works to mobilize disabled Guatemalans through health, rehabilitation, education, spiritual development, leadership skills, and social integration.
Fields of interest: Physical therapy; Medical care, rehabilitation; Health care; Human services; Disabilities, people with.
International interests: Guatemala.
Limitations: Applications not accepted. Giving limited to Guatemala.
Application information: Unsolicited requests for funds not considered or acknowledged.
Officers: Robert L. Benham, Pres.; Maureen Welsh, Secy.; Constance Hargis, Treas.; John Bell, Exec. Dir.
Directors: William Bell; Ronald Bevacqua; Alexander Galvez; John Hartman; Jennifer Hewitt; Rick Mazur; Rebecca Moscoso; Mike Neher; Jennifer Rundell.
EIN: 223749558

678
Uncle Larry's Fund
c/o Winterer
P.O. Box 1009
Boca Grande, FL   33921-1009

Established in 2000.
Donors: William G. Winterer; Victoria T. Winterer; Theresa S. Thompson.
Grantmaker type: Independent foundation.

Financial data (yr. ended 12/31/10): Assets, $2,672,087 (M); gifts received, $500,000; expenditures, $153,662; qualifying distributions, $144,595; giving activities include $144,100 for 27 grants (high: $25,000; low: $100).
Purpose and activities: The fund's primary focus is education. But it also supports opportunities that provide for creativity, growth towards self-sufficiency, and leadership. The fund will consider environmental, cultural and spiritual projects that contribute to a community's well-being, as well as projects that develop personal responsibility, initiative, moral standards and leadership.
Fields of interest: Christian agencies & churches; Education; Human services.
International interests: South America; Central America.
Type of support: General/operating support; Management development/capacity building; Annual campaigns; Capital campaigns; Building/renovation; Equipment; Land acquisition; Endowments; Curriculum development; Internship funds; Scholarship funds; Consulting services; Exchange programs; Matching/challenge support.
Limitations: Applications not accepted. Giving on a national basis, with preference given to organizations in communities with a personal connection to the trustees.
Application information: Unsolicited requests for funds not accepted.
Board meeting date(s): June, Nov. and as needed
Trustees: Theresa S. Thompson; Victoria T. Winterer; William G. Winterer.
Number of staff: 2 part-time professional.
EIN: 316653673

679
Wahlert Foundation
P.O. Box 61477
Fort Myers, FL   33906-1477
Contact: Amy Principi, Pres.; R.H. Wahlert, V.P. and Treas.
E-mail: info@wahlertfoundation.org; Summer address: P.O. Box 736, Dubuque, IA 52004-0736.
E-mail: Bob16307@aol.com; URL: http://www.wahlertfoundation.org

Incorporated in 1948 in IA.
Donors: H.W. Wahlert†; and officers of the foundation.
Grantmaker type: Independent foundation.
Financial data (yr. ended 08/31/09): Assets, $5,021,963 (M); gifts received, $5,055; expenditures, $450,653; qualifying distributions, $401,210; giving activities include $401,210 for 49 grants (high: $125,000; low: $1,000).
Purpose and activities: Support primarily for higher, secondary, and medical education; grants also for health services and hospitals, including medical and cancer research, social service agencies, including drug abuse prevention programs and services for families, the homeless and the handicapped, child welfare programs for minorities, cultural activities, including the arts and museums, and Catholic welfare organizations and schools.
Fields of interest: Secondary school/education; Higher education; Health care; Human services; Aging, centers/services; Catholic agencies & churches; Terminal illness, people with; Native Americans/American Indians; Children; Aging; Hispanics/Latinos; Women; Economically disadvantaged; Homeless; Migrant workers.

International interests: Honduras.
Type of support: General/operating support; Annual campaigns; Capital campaigns; Building/renovation; Equipment; Emergency funds; Program development; Scholarship funds.
Limitations: Applications accepted. Giving primarily in the metropolitan Dubuque, IA, area. No grants to individuals, or for publications, conferences, or matching gifts; no loans.
Application information: Application form not required.
Initial approach: 1-page letter
Copies of proposal: 1
Deadline(s): Aug. 25
Board meeting date(s): 2nd Sat. of Sept.
Final notification: 1 month after board meeting
Officers and Trustees: * Amy Wahlert Principi,* Pres.; Robert H. Wahlert,* V.P. and Treas.; David Wahlert,* V.P.; Brian Kane,* Secy.; Kathy Wahlert Chameli; Marni Wahlert Peck; Alan Wahlert; Donna Wahlert; James Wahlert; Mark Wahlert; Nancy Wahlert; R.C. Wahlert II; Susan Wahlert.
Number of staff: 1 part-time professional.
EIN: 426051124

680
Watoto Child Care Ministry, Inc.
258 Crystal Grove Blvd.
Lutz, FL   33548-1320   (813) 948-4343
FAX: (813) 948-4346; E-mail: usa@watoto.com;
URL: http://www.watoto.com/home
Facebook: http://www.facebook.com/group.php?gid=2256403083
Flickr: http://www.flickr.com/photos/38341888@N03/
MySpace: http://www.myspace.com/watotochildrenuganda/
Twitter: http://twitter.com/watoto
YouTube: http://www.youtube.com/watotonews

Established in 1997 in FL.
Grantmaker type: Public charity.
Financial data (yr. ended 12/31/10): Revenue, $6,166,420; assets, $1,531,678 (M); gifts received, $5,715,621; expenditures, $6,409,334; giving activities include $3,298,258 for 1 grant to an organization outside the U.S.
Purpose and activities: The organization supports Watoto, an organization based in Uganda that supports orphaned children and vulnerable women, and works to raise the next generation of African leaders by pursuing excellence in academic and practical skills, integrity in conduct, and moral values.
Fields of interest: Youth development; Children/youth, services; Family services; Christian agencies & churches.
International interests: Uganda.
Limitations: Giving limited to Uganda.
Officers and Directors: * Gary Skinner,* Chair.; Don Champion, Co-Exec. Dir; Eugene Stutzman,* Co-Exec. Dir.; Gary Beesley; John Rayner; Randy Sohnchen; Ben Wendland; Scott Young.
EIN: 593445250

681
Working Partners Foundation
400 Royal Palm Way, Ste. 304C
Palm Beach, FL   33480-4117
E-mail: info@wpfintl.org; URL: http://www.wpfint.org

Established in 2005 in CO.
Donor: The New Millennium Trust.
Grantmaker type: Independent foundation.
Financial data (yr. ended 12/31/10): Assets,
$1,531,290 (M); gifts received, $1,797,445;
expenditures, $1,535,914; qualifying distributions,
$1,325,770; giving activities include $1,325,770
for grants.
Purpose and activities: The goal of the foundation
is to improve basic health and living conditions for
people in need through health care, micro-economic
financing, sanitation and water, education, food,
prevention and a magnitude of other community
development assistance programs around the
globe.
Fields of interest: International agricultural
development; International economic development;
International relief.
International interests: Africa; Global programs.
Limitations: Applications not accepted. Giving
primarily to U.S-based organizations with
international focus.
Application information: Contributes only to
pre-selected organizations.
Director: Robert G. Simses.
EIN: 201783302

GEORGIA

682
**American Friends of the Israel Democracy
Institute, Inc.**
1266 W. Paces Ferry Rd., Ste. 615
Atlanta, GA 30327-2306   (404) 240-7700
URL: http://www.idi.org.il/sites/english/afidi/
pages/afidilobby.aspx

Grantmaker type: Public charity.
Financial data (yr. ended 12/31/09): Revenue,
$8,077,920; assets, $144,924 (M); gifts received,
$8,077,920; expenditures, $8,179,582; giving
activities include $7,731,000 for 1 grant to an
organization outside the U.S.
Purpose and activities: The organization works to
fund the activities of the Israeli Democracy Institute,
and support its mission of working toward the
development of a modern, democratic, and
pluralistic Jewish state.
Fields of interest: International affairs; Jewish
agencies & synagogues.
Type of support: Grants to individuals.
Limitations: Giving limited to New York, NY and
Jerusalem, Israel.
Directors: Elliott Broidy; Susan Crown; David Fox;
Tony Gelbart; Mike Leven; Fred Marcus; Roberto
Sonabend.
EIN: 133348313

683
Amigos for Christ
1845 S. Lee Ct., Ste. A
Buford, GA 30518-8811   (770) 614-9250
Contact: John Bland, Exec. Dir.; Kristin Monacella
FAX: (770) 614-9850;
E-mail: johnb@amigosforchrist.org; URL: http://
www.amigosforchrist.org

Established in 1997 in GA.
Grantmaker type: Public charity.
Financial data (yr. ended 12/31/10): Revenue,
$2,013,799; assets, $358,507 (M); gifts received,
$1,668,526; expenditures, $2,150,553; giving
activities include $1,543,074 for grants to
organizations outside the U.S.
Purpose and activities: The organization works to
strengthen families without resources in Nicaragua
by providing community housing, medical and
educational services, clean water, and small
business, cooperative, and agricultural programs.
Fields of interest: Agriculture/food; Education;
Health care; Housing/shelter; Human services,
victim aid; Human services; Community/economic
development; Economically disadvantaged.
International interests: Nicaragua.
Type of support: General/operating support; In-kind
gifts.
Limitations: Applications not accepted. Giving
limited to Nicaragua. No support for political
organizations.
Publications: Annual report; Financial statement;
Informational brochure; Newsletter.
Application information: Contributes only to a
pre-selected organization.
Board meeting date(s): 1st Mon. of each month
Officers and Board Members:* Robert Evola,*
Pres.; Rick Floress,* V.P.; Gloria Whidby,* Secy.;
Mary Mastrogiovanni,* Treas.; John Bland,* Exec.
Dir.; Richard Nutt, M.D.; Jack Schiveree.
Number of staff: 2 full-time professional; 1 part-time
professional.
EIN: 582484257

684
Daniel P. Amos Family Foundation
(formerly Daniel P. and Shannon L. Amos
Foundation, Inc.)
c/o Selection Comm.
P.O. Box 5346
Columbus, GA 31906-0346
E-mail: CCBradshaw@AmosFamilyFoundation.org;
URL: http://amosfamilyfoundation.org/index.htm

Established in 1992 in GA.
Donors: Daniel P. Amos; Paul Amos Trust; Jean
Amos Trust; Paul S. and Jean R. Amos Trust.
Grantmaker type: Independent foundation.
Financial data (yr. ended 12/31/09): Assets,
$107,490,590 (M); gifts received, $7,740,894;
expenditures, $5,821,517; qualifying distributions,
$5,645,792; giving activities include $5,645,792
for 44 grants (high: $2,150,000; low: $1,000).
Purpose and activities: Giving primarily for human
services, health associations, Christian and
Protestant organizations, as well as to an
interdenominational theological seminary.
Fields of interest: Arts; Higher education;
Theological school/education; Health
organizations, association; Human services;
Children/youth, services; Christian agencies &
churches; Protestant agencies & churches.
Type of support: Building/renovation.
Limitations: Applications accepted. Giving primarily
in Columbus, GA. No grants to individuals.
Application information: Application forms available
on foundation web site. Application form required.
Initial approach: Complete appropriate
application form

Officers and Trustees:* Lauren A. Amos,*
Vice-Chair.; Daniel P. Amos, Pres.; David B. Plyler,
Secy.
EIN: 582005391
Recent grants for international programs:
684-1 Asian Access Life Ministries, San Dimas, CA,
$500,000. For Japan Ministries. 2009.
684-2 Central Conference Pension Initiative,
Glenview, IL, $1,000,000. 2009.
684-3 Samaritans Purse, Boone, NC, $250,000.
For medical diagnosed TB. 2009.
684-4 University of North Carolina, Chapel Hill, NC,
$50,000. For International Friends. 2009.

685
Amos-Cheves Foundation, Inc.
(formerly His Trust Foundation, Inc.)
P.O. Box 1199
Columbus, GA 31902-1199

Established in 2002 in GA.
Donors: Olivia D. Amos; Bettye A. Cheves; Cecil
Chevez; Elizabeth Cheves Meeks.
Grantmaker type: Independent foundation.
Financial data (yr. ended 12/31/10): Assets,
$20,571,773 (M); gifts received, $1,517,080;
expenditures, $927,435; qualifying distributions,
$885,180; giving activities include $885,180 for
grants.
Purpose and activities: Giving primarily for
Christian-based education, youth programs, and
human services.
Fields of interest: Higher education; Youth
development; Human services; YM/YWCAs & YM/
YWHAs; Children/youth, services; International
relief; Christian agencies & churches; Economically
disadvantaged.
Type of support: Building/renovation; Equipment;
Program development; Scholarship funds; Grants to
individuals; Scholarships—to individuals.
Limitations: Applications not accepted. Giving
primarily in GA; some giving also in AL, SC, and TN.
Application information: Unsolicited requests for
funds not accepted.
Officers: Cecil M. Cheves,* Chair.; Bettye A.
Cheves,* Pres. and Secy.-Treas.
Board Members: Blanchard C. Olivia; William R.
Blanchard; Avery C. Wolf; Luther H. Wolf III; Elizabeth
C. Meeks.
EIN: 582634947

686
The Atlanta Resource Foundation, Inc.
2001 Martin Luther King Jr. Dr., S.W., Ste. 540
Atlanta, GA 30310-5807   (404) 842-7878
E-mail: bell@connections.org; Mailing address: P.O.
Box 20057, Atlanta, GA 30325-0057; URL: http://
www.connections.org

Established in 1990.
Grantmaker type: Public charity.
Financial data (yr. ended 06/30/11): Revenue,
$157,650; assets, $288,009 (M); gifts received,
$153,440; expenditures, $268,704.
Purpose and activities: The foundation enhances
the welfare of Atlanta, Georgia and leadership
development among people in the Caribbean and
Latin America.
Fields of interest: Community/economic
development.
International interests: Caribbean; Latin America.

Limitations: Applications not accepted. Giving primarily in Atlanta, GA.
Publications: Annual report; Newsletter.
Application information: Unsolicited requests for funds not accepted.
  Board meeting date(s): May and Nov.
Officer: W. Allen Bell, Exec. Dir.
Directors: Keith Eigel; Rawson Haverty, Jr.; George H. Johnson; Dale E. Jones; William A. Mitchell, Jr.; Thomas R. Roddy; Christy Simmons; McKittrick Simmons.
Number of staff: 1 full-time professional; 1 part-time support.
EIN: 581895227

687
The Bancker-Williams Foundation, Inc.
c/o Thomas Oastler
130 Riverwood Pl.
Atlanta, GA 30327-4280

Established in 1989 in GA.
Grantmaker type: Independent foundation.
Financial data (yr. ended 06/30/11): Assets, $2,787,018 (M); expenditures, $182,699; qualifying distributions, $138,000; giving activities include $138,000 for grants.
Fields of interest: Environment, natural resources; Environment; Animals/wildlife, preservation/protection; Women, centers/services; Women.
International interests: Latin America; Africa.
Type of support: Continuing support; Program development; Seed money; Scholarship funds.
Limitations: Applications not accepted. Giving primarily in GA and TN. No grants to individuals.
Application information: Contributes only to pre-selected organizations.
Officers and Trustees:* Elaine O. Blackmon,* Chair.; Beverly Kelly,* Secy.-Treas.; Belitje B. Bull; Elizabeth O. Jackson; Katharine B. Johnson; Dorothy B. Robertson; Charlotte H. Versfeld.
EIN: 581868577

688
Belize Children's Fund, Inc.
22 Sweetgum Crossing
Savannah, GA 31411-2711

Established in 2007 in GA.
Donors: Frank H. McNeal; Christ Church.
Grantmaker type: Public charity.
Financial data (yr. ended 12/31/08): Revenue, $43,525; assets, $43,774 (M); gifts received, $41,636; expenditures, $28,509; giving activities include $4,000 for grants, and $24,183 for grants to organizations outside the U.S.
Purpose and activities: Scholarship awards to underprivileged children in Belize.
Fields of interest: Higher education.
International interests: Belize.
Type of support: Scholarship funds.
Limitations: Applications not accepted. Giving primarily in Belize.
Application information: Unsolicited requests for funds not accepted.
Officers: Frank H. McNeal, Pres.; Mary McNeal, Secy.-Treas.
Trustees: Thomas Knight; Margaret Walworth.
EIN: 260612403

689
Cambodia Corps, Inc.
915 Goebel Ave.
Savannah, GA 31404-2422
E-mail: tommy@cambodiacorps.org; *URL:* http://www.cambodiacorps.org/

Grantmaker type: Public charity.
Financial data (yr. ended 12/31/09): Revenue, $36,807; assets, $3,089 (M); gifts received, $36,804; expenditures, $38,723; giving activities include $6,471 for grants.
Purpose and activities: The organization works to improve the effectiveness of non-governmental organizations in Mondulkiri and Ratanakiri provinces, Cambodia, by providing them with university-educated employees who are ethnic minority Montagnards indigenous to those provinces.
Fields of interest: Community/economic development.
International interests: Cambodia.
Type of support: Scholarships—to individuals.
Limitations: Giving limited to Cambodia.
Officers and Directors:* Thomas M. Daniels III,* Pres. and Treas.; Gary M. Gregg,* V.P.; Dorothy A. Daniels,* Secy.; Jack W. Jarnigan; Richard R. Steinmetz.
EIN: 562199508

690
The Carter Center, Inc.
1 Copenhill
453 Freedom Pkwy.
Atlanta, GA 30307-1400 (404) 420-5100
Contact: Thom Bornemann, Dir., Mental Health Program
FAX: (404) 420-5158;
E-mail: carterweb@emory.edu; *URL:* http://www.cartercenter.org

Established in 1982 in GA.
Grantmaker type: Public charity.
Financial data (yr. ended 08/31/10): Revenue, $81,394,211; assets, $431,995,460 (M); gifts received, $62,811,963; expenditures, $75,268,975; giving activities include $3,137,399 for grants, $8,315,163 for grants to organizations outside the U.S., and $81,802 for grants to individuals.
Purpose and activities: The center seeks to wage peace, fight disease, and build hope.
Fields of interest: Media, print publishing; Health care; International affairs.
Type of support: Fellowships.
Limitations: Applications accepted. Giving on a national and international basis.
Publications: Annual report; Informational brochure (including application guidelines).
Application information: Prospective fellowship applicants must submit an application packet that includes a personal and professional profile, resume, letters of recommendation and support, samples of professional work, and essay of objectives for fellowship and project description. Profile may be submitted electronically to ccmhp@emory.edu or printed and included in the application packet. Applications are only accepted for fellowships; the center does not provide assistance outside of its fellowship program and unsolicited requests for funds will not be considered or acknowledged. Application form not required.
  Copies of proposal: 1

Deadline(s): Apr. 19 for Fellowships for Mental Health Journalism
Board meeting date(s): Mar., July, and Nov.
Final notification: July 9
Officer and Trustees:* Kent C. "Oz" Nelson,* Chair.; Terrence B. Adamson; Arthur M. Blank; Richard C. Blum; James E. Carter; Jason Carter; Rosalynn Carter; Bradley N. Currey, Jr.; Hon. Gordon D. Giffin; Charlayne Hunter-Gault; Ben F. Johnson III; Frank C. Jones; Hon. James T. Laney; Sherry Lansing; and 6 additional trustees.
EIN: 581454716

691
Chesed, Inc.
c/o Marcus Family Office, LLC
1266 W. Paces Ferry Rd., Ste. 615
Atlanta, GA 30327-2306

Established in 1993 in GA.
Donor: Frederick R. Marcus.
Grantmaker type: Independent foundation.
Financial data (yr. ended 12/31/10): Assets, $6,364,635 (M); expenditures, $650,846; qualifying distributions, $580,806; giving activities include $580,806 for grants.
Purpose and activities: Giving primarily for Jewish education and organizations.
Fields of interest: Secondary school/education; Higher education; Jewish agencies & synagogues.
International interests: Canada.
Limitations: Applications not accepted. Giving primarily in the U.S., with some emphasis on GA. No grants to individuals.
Application information: Contributes only to pre-selected organizations.
Officers and Directors: Frederick R. Marcus, Pres.; Sara Ognibene Loft, Secy.; Douglas Dinapoli, Treas.; Nancy Dubois Marcus; Frederick Slagle.
EIN: 580231691

692
Coca-Cola Enterprises Inc. Corporate Giving Program
2500 Windy Ridge Pkwy.
Atlanta, GA 30339-5677 (678) 260-3000
URL: http://www.cokecce.com/pages/_content.asp?page_id=72

Grantmaker type: Corporate giving program.
Purpose and activities: Coca-Cola Enterprises makes charitable contributions to nonprofit organizations involved with water conservation, recycling, healthy active living, youth development, and diversity. Support is given primarily in areas of company operations in Belgium, Great Britain, France, Luxembourg, Monaco, and the Netherlands.
Fields of interest: Nutrition; Environment, recycling; Environment, water resources; Public health, physical fitness; Youth development; Civil/human rights, equal rights; General charitable giving.
International interests: Belgium; England; France; Luxembourg; Monaco; Netherlands; Scotland; Wales.
Type of support: General/operating support; Program development; Employee volunteer services; In-kind gifts.
Limitations: Giving primarily in areas of company operations in Belgium, Great Britain, France, Luxembourg, Monaco, and the Netherlands.

693
The Coca-Cola Foundation, Inc.
1 Coca-Cola Plaza, NW
Atlanta, GA   30313-2420   (404) 676-2568
Contact: Helen Smith Price, Exec. Dir.
FAX: (404) 676-8804;
E-mail: cocacolacommunityrequest@na.ko.com;
Additional tel.: (404) 676-3525; URL: http://
www.thecoca-colacompany.com/citizenship/
foundation_coke.html

Incorporated in 1984 in GA.
Donor: The Coca-Cola Co.
Grantmaker type: Company-sponsored foundation.
Financial data (yr. ended 12/31/09): Assets,
$119,126,648 (M); gifts received, $105,701,398;
expenditures, $41,240,634; qualifying
distributions, $40,968,382; giving activities include
$40,968,382 for grants.
Purpose and activities: The foundation supports
programs designed to promote water stewardship;
healthy and active lifestyles; community recycling,
and education.
Fields of interest: Public health, clean water supply;
Higher education; Scholarships/financial aid;
Education, services; Education, drop-out prevention;
Education; Environment, water pollution;
Environment, recycling; Environment, water
resources; Public health, physical fitness; AIDS;
Nutrition.
International interests: Africa; Europe; Latin
America.
Type of support: General/operating support;
Continuing support; Emergency funds; Program
development; Fellowships; Scholarship funds;
Sponsorships; Employee matching gifts.
Limitations: Applications accepted. Giving on a
national and international basis in areas of company
operations, with emphasis on Washington, DC, GA,
NY, VA, WA, Africa, Colombia, Europe, Japan, Latin
America, Philippines, and Swaziland. No support for
discriminatory organizations, political, legislative, or
lobbying organizations, fraternal organizations,
athletic teams, or U.S. based local schools,
including charter schools, pre-schools, elementary
schools, middle schools, or high schools. No grants
to individuals (except for the Coca-Cola First
Generation Scholarship), or for movie, film, or
television documentaries, website development,
concerts or other entertainment events, beauty
contests, fashion shows, or hair shows, local
sports, travel or organized field trips, family
reunions, marketing sponsorships, cause
marketing, or advertising projects, land, building, or
equipment, or construction or renovation projects.
Publications: Application guidelines; Grants list;
Program policy statement.
Application information: Application form required.
   Initial approach: Complete online application
      form; contact participating universities for
      Coca-Cola First Generation Scholarship
   Copies of proposal: 1
   Deadline(s): None
   Board meeting date(s): Quarterly
   Final notification: 2 months
Officers and Directors:* Ingrid Saunders Jones,*
Chair.; Melody C. Justice,* Secy.; Gary P. Fayard,*
Treas.; Lawton Hawkins, Genl. Counsel; William
Hawkins,* Genl. Tax Counsel; Helen Smith Price,*
Exec. Dir.; Ahmet C. Bozer; Alexander B. Cummings;
John H. Downs, Jr.; Jose Octavio Reyes; Clyde C.
Tuggle.

Number of staff: 6 full-time professional; 5 full-time
support.
EIN: 581574705
Recent grants for international programs:
693-1 American University of Beirut, New York, NY,
$500,000. 2009.
693-2 Atma Jaya Yayasan, Jakarta, Indonesia,
$43,039. 2009.
693-3 AVINA Americas, Washington, DC, $452,691.
2009.
693-4 Beijing Environmental Protection Foundation,
Beijing, China, $25,000. 2009.
693-5 British Nutrition Foundation, London,
England, $890,000. 2009.
693-6 Cambodian Women for Peace and
Development Association, Phnom Penh,
Cambodia, $20,000. 2009.
693-7 CARE USA, Atlanta, GA, $20,000. 2009.
693-8 Casa de la Paz, Santiago, Chile, $93,750.
2009.
693-9 China Youth Concern Committee for the
Advancement of Health and Physical Culture
Development, Beijing, China, $279,000. 2009.
693-10 China Youth Development Foundation,
Beijing, China, $3,000,000. 2009.
693-11 China Youth Development Foundation,
Beijing, China, $153,000. 2009.
693-12 Chinese Foundation for Prevention of STD
and AIDS, Beijing, China, $154,000. 2009.
693-13 Coca-Cola Africa Foundation, Manzini,
Swaziland, $9,975,000. 2009.
693-14 Coca-Cola Africa Foundation, Manzini,
Swaziland, $1,170,000. 2009.
693-15 Coca-Cola Australia Foundation, Sydney,
Australia, $86,000. 2009.
693-16 Coca-Cola Australia Foundation, Sydney,
Australia, $71,000. 2009.
693-17 Coca-Cola Australia Foundation, Sydney,
Australia, $29,000. 2009.
693-18 Coca-Cola Australia Foundation, Sydney,
Australia, $23,000. 2009.
693-19 Coca-Cola Brazil Institute, Rio de Janeiro,
Brazil, $783,564. 2009.
693-20 Coca-Cola Brazil Institute, Rio de Janeiro,
Brazil, $516,736. 2009.
693-21 Coca-Cola Brazil Institute, Rio de Janeiro,
Brazil, $325,009. 2009.
693-22 Coca-Cola Environmental Educational
Foundation, Tokyo, Japan, $1,720,000. 2009.
693-23 Coca-Cola Korea Youth Foundation, Seoul,
South Korea, $80,000. 2009.
693-24 Colombian Foundation for Education and
Opportunity, Bogota, Colombia, $2,000,000.
2009.
693-25 Elie Wiesel Foundation for Humanity, New
York, NY, $100,000. 2009.
693-26 European Water Partnership, Brussels,
Belgium, $253,252. 2009.
693-27 Family Health Research and Development
Center, Hanoi, Vietnam, $50,000. 2009.
693-28 Forum for Organised Resource Conservation
and Enhancement, New Delhi, India, $50,000.
2009.
693-29 Fundacion Cimientos, Buenos Aires,
Argentina, $214,000. 2009.
693-30 Fundacion Desde el Surco, Quito, Ecuador,
$40,000. 2009.
693-31 Fundacion Edad&Vida, Barcelona, Spain,
$148,972. 2009.
693-32 Fundacion Galapagos Ecuador, Quito,
Ecuador, $20,000. 2009.
693-33 Fundacion Vida Silvestre Argentina, Buenos
Aires, Argentina, $168,750. 2009.

693-34 Gawad Kalinga, Manila, Philippines,
$100,000. 2009.
693-35 Haribon Foundation for the Conservation of
Natural Resources, Quezon City, Philippines,
$44,000. 2009.
693-36 Hellenic Ornithological Society, Athens,
Greece, $84,417. 2009.
693-37 Hydro and Agro Informatics Institute,
Bangkok, Thailand, $92,000. 2009.
693-38 International Center for Agricultural
Research in the Dry Areas, Aleppo, Syria,
$200,000. 2009.
693-39 International Center for Agricultural
Research in the Dry Areas, Aleppo, Syria,
$200,000. 2009.
693-40 Keep Australia Beautiful, Harris Park,
Australia, $167,024. 2009.
693-41 Khao Kwan Foundation, Suphanburi,
Thailand, $112,900. 2009.
693-42 Korea Green Foundation, Seoul, South
Korea, $80,000. 2009.
693-43 Lahore Businessmen Association for
Rehabilitation of the Disabled, Lahore, Pakistan,
$200,000. 2009.
693-44 Malayan Nature Society, Kuala Lumpur,
Malaysia, $90,883. 2009.
693-45 Millennium Water Alliance, Houston, TX,
$200,000. 2009.
693-46 Nature Conservancy, Arlington, VA,
$100,000. 2009.
693-47 New Names International Foundation,
Moscow, Russia, $50,000. 2009.
693-48 Ocean Conservancy, Washington, DC,
$300,000. 2009.
693-49 Philippine Business for Social Progress,
Manila, Philippines, $172,000. 2009.
693-50 Pos Keadilan Peduli Umat, Jakarta,
Indonesia, $76,000. 2009.
693-51 Pronatura Mexico, Colonia Sanclemente,
Mexico, $375,000. 2009.
693-52 Solid Waste Management Association of the
Philippines, Makati City, Philippines, $40,000.
2009.
693-53 Special Olympics Nippon, Kumamoto,
Japan, $33,000. 2009.
693-54 Special Olympics Ukraine, Kiev, Ukraine,
$10,000. 2009.
693-55 State Hermitage Museum, Saint Petersburg,
Russia, $150,000. 2009.
693-56 State University - Higher School of
Economics, Institute for International Business,
Moscow, Russia, $70,000. 2009.
693-57 Universitat Pompeu Fabra, Barcelona,
Spain, $665,000. For the Center for Research in
Environmental Epidemiology. 2009.
693-58 University of Edinburgh USA Development
Trust, New York, NY, $250,000. 2009.
693-59 Way Home, Odessa, Ukraine, $62,000.
2009.
693-60 World Wildlife Fund, Washington, DC,
$112,500. 2009.
693-61 World Wildlife Fund, Washington, DC,
$30,000. 2009.
693-62 World Wildlife Fund, Madrid, Spain,
$104,280. 2009.
693-63 World Wildlife Fund Canada, Toronto,
Canada, $120,000. 2009.
693-64 World Wildlife Fund Russia, Moscow,
Russia, $100,000. 2009.
693-65 World Wildlife Fund Russia, Moscow,
Russia, $89,950. 2009.

694

Delta Air Lines, Inc. Corporate Giving Program

c/o Community Relations
1050 Delta Blvd.
Atlanta, GA 30354-1989
Contact: Scarlet Pressley-Brown, Dir., External Affairs & Community Rels.
URL: http://www.delta.com/about_delta/global_good/
Facebook: http://www.facebook.com/pages/Deltas-Force-for-Global-Good/35548488237
RSS Feed: http://news.delta.com/index.php?s=43&pagetemplate=rss&category=4

Grantmaker type: Corporate giving program.
Purpose and activities: As a complement to its foundation, Delta also makes charitable contributions to nonprofit organizations directly. Support is given on a national and international basis.
Fields of interest: Diabetes; Museums; Performing arts; Performing arts, orchestras; Historic preservation/historical societies; Arts; Education, fund raising/fund distribution; Higher education; Environment, natural resources; Hospitals (general); Health care, patient services; Health care; Cancer; Breast cancer; Housing/shelter, development; Athletics/sports, baseball; Salvation Army; Children/youth, services; Human services; Civil/human rights, equal rights; Economically disadvantaged.
International interests: India; Japan.
Type of support: General/operating support; Continuing support; Building/renovation; Scholarship funds; Research; Employee volunteer services; Sponsorships; Donated equipment; Donated products; In-kind gifts.
Limitations: Applications accepted. Giving primarily on a national and international basis in areas of company operations, with emphasis on Washington, DC, Atlanta, GA, Minneapolis, MN, VA, India, and Japan; giving also to national organizations. No support for partisan political organizations, sectarian, religious, or denominational organizations, tax-supported city, county, or state organizations, or local sports organizations. No grants to individuals, or for local events in areas without Delta facilities, academic or medical research, or fundraisers.
Publications: Application guidelines.
Application information: Application form required.
  Initial approach: Complete online proposal for sponsorships
  Deadline(s): 90 days prior to need for sponsorships
  Final notification: 4 weeks for sponsorships
Number of staff: 1 full-time support.

695

Global Aviation Holdings Inc. Corporate Giving Program

(formerly Global Aero Logistics Corporate Giving Program, Inc.)
101 World Dr.
Peachtree City, GA 30269-6965
Contact: Steven E. Forsyth, Dir., Corp. Comms.
FAX: (770) 632-8055; E-mail: sforsyth@glah.com

Grantmaker type: Corporate giving program.
Financial data (yr. ended 12/31/10): Total giving, $208,400, including $77,800 for 28 grants (high:

$10,400; low: $400), $30,600 for 200 employee matching gifts, and $100,000 for 1 in-kind gift.
Purpose and activities: Global Aviation Holdings makes charitable contributions to nonprofit organizations involved with human services, international affairs, and military interests. Support is given on a national basis in areas of company operations, with emphasis on Fayette County, Georgia.
Fields of interest: Human services; Military/veterans' organizations.
International interests: Afghanistan.
Type of support: Annual campaigns; Continuing support; Emergency funds; Employee volunteer services; General/operating support.
Limitations: Applications not accepted. Giving on a national basis in areas of company operations, with emphasis on Fayette County, GA. No support for political organizations.
Application information: The Corporate Communications Department handles giving.
Number of staff: 1 full-time professional.

696

Gray Matters Charitable Foundation, Inc.

(formerly The Rockdale Foundation, Inc.)
2200 Century Pkwy., Ste. 100
Atlanta, GA 30345-3103

Established in 1995 in GA.
Donors: Robert A. Patillo; Katy Patillo; Robert Pattillo Properties, Inc.
Grantmaker type: Company-sponsored foundation.
Financial data (yr. ended 12/31/10): Assets, $2,548,989 (M); expenditures, $690,720; qualifying distributions, $649,075; giving activities include $584,683 for 79 grants (high: $108,055; low: $25).
Purpose and activities: The foundation supports organizations involved with education, international economic development, community development, and civic affairs.
Fields of interest: Microfinance/microlending; Education, reform; Higher education; Business school/education; Teacher school/education; Education; International economic development; Community/economic development; Financial services; Public affairs.
International interests: Dominican Republic; Ghana; India.
Type of support: General/operating support; Program development; Conferences/seminars; Research; Sponsorships; Employee matching gifts; Matching/challenge support.
Limitations: Applications not accepted. Giving primarily in the metropolitan Atlanta, GA area; giving also on an international basis in Dominican Republic, Ghana, and India. No grants to individuals.
Application information: Contributes only to pre-selected organizations.
Officers and Directors:* Robert A. Pattillo,* Pres.; Terry L. Galloway, Secy.; Eugenia Topple Cayce, Treas.; Ricardo Carvalho.
Number of staff: 2 full-time professional; 2 full-time support.
EIN: 582147850

697

The Halle Foundation

P.O. Box 724075
Atlanta, GA 31139-1075   (770) 437-1000
Contact: Marnite B. Calder, Exec. Dir.
FAX: (770) 433-1211;
E-mail: mbcalder@thehallefoundation.org;
URL: http://www.thehallefoundation.org/

Established in 1986 in GA; supporting organization of American Council on Germany, American Institute for Contemporary German Studies, Atlantik Brucke - Youth for Understanding USA Inc., Emory University, Georgia Institute of Technology, Georgia Rotary Student Program, German-American Chamber of Commerce South, German School of Atlanta, International University - Bremen, Oglethorpe University, The Robert W. Woodruff Arts Center, and The Southern Center for International Studies.
Grantmaker type: Public charity.
Financial data (yr. ended 12/31/10): Revenue, $1,111,837; assets, $12,343,967 (M); expenditures, $359,359; giving activities include $120,000 for grants.
Purpose and activities: The foundation promotes understanding, knowledge and friendship between people of Germany, as seen in its European context, and those of the U.S. It supports initiatives in the fields of culture, science, technology, commerce, language, scholarship and international relations.
Fields of interest: International affairs.
International interests: Germany.
Limitations: Applications accepted. Giving on an international and national basis, with some emphasis on Atlanta, GA. No support for religious or political organizations, churches, or sports booster clubs. No grants to individuals, or for legislative lobbying, operating budget relief, or debt relief.
Publications: Application guidelines; Grants list.
Application information: Application form not required.
  Initial approach: Letter
  Copies of proposal: 1
  Deadline(s): Jan. 15, Apr. 1, and Sept. 15
  Board meeting date(s): Feb., May, and Oct.
  Final notification: 30 days following board meeting
Officers and Trustees:* Dr. Eike Jordan,* Chair.; Marnite B. Calder, Exec. Dir.; Charles Battle; Dr. Rosemary Magee; Neil Williams.
Number of staff: 1 full-time professional.
EIN: 586201529

698

His Hands Foundation, Inc.

c/o Steven M. Craig
437 Latimer St.
Woodstock, GA 30188

Donors: Steve Craig; Susan Craig; Juan Butler.
Grantmaker type: Independent foundation.
Financial data (yr. ended 09/30/09): Assets, $13,829 (M); gifts received, $56,000; expenditures, $252,097; qualifying distributions, $175,900; giving activities include $175,900 for 2 grants (high: $130,900; low: $45,000).
Fields of interest: Christian agencies & churches.
International interests: Uganda.
Limitations: Applications not accepted. Giving primarily in Uganda.
Application information: Unsolicited requests for funds not accepted.

Officers: Steven M. Craig, Pres.; Susan L. Craig, V.P.; Juan Butler, Treas.; Doug Bentle, Mgr.
EIN: 202028309

699
Home Depot Foundation, Inc.
2455 Paces Ferry Rd. N.W.
Atlanta, GA 30339-1834   (770) 384-3889
Contact: Kelly Caffarelli, Pres.
FAX: (770) 384-3908;
E-mail: hd_foundation@homedepot.com; Toll-free tel.: (866) 593-7019; toll-free fax: (866) 593-7027;
URL: http://www.homedepotfoundation.org
Building Healthy Communities: http://www.homedepotfoundation.org/blog/
Home Depot Foundation: http://twitter.com/HomeDepotFdn

Established in 2002.
Grantmaker type: Public charity.
Financial data (yr. ended 12/31/08): Revenue, $28,125,003; assets, $1 (M); gifts received, $27,999,533; expenditures, $52,936,428; giving activities include $50,244,613 for grants, and $168,300 for grants to organizations outside the U.S.
Purpose and activities: The foundation aims to build affordable, efficient, and healthy homes while promoting sustainability by supporting nonprofit organizations with funding and volunteers.
Fields of interest: Environment, energy; Environment, beautification programs; Environment; Housing/shelter; Community/economic development.
International interests: Canada.
Limitations: Applications accepted. Giving on a national basis and to Canada. No support for political or religious campaigns. No grants to individuals, or for capital campaigns, conferences, sports competitions, endowments, or equipment.
Publications: Annual report.
Application information: If letter of inquiry is approved, applicant will be instructed to submit a full application; foundation staff will provide information regarding how to access an online full application. Application form required.
   Initial approach: Complete online letter of inquiry; in order to access the letter of inquiry, an applicant must pass an online eligibility test
   Deadline(s): Jan. 15 and July 1 (letter of inquiry) and Mar. 15 and Sept. 15 (full project descriptions) for Housing Impact Grants; Dec. 14 for Awards of Excellence for Community Trees; Mar. 31 for Affordable Housing Built Responsibly
Officers and Directors:* Craig Menear,* Chair.; Kelly Caffarelli,* Pres.; Dominic Piccininni,* Secy.; Giles Bowman; Lyne Castonguay; Ron Jarvis; Jim Kane; Darryl Tieken.
EIN: 550800151

700
Livingston Foundation, Inc.
171 17th St. N.W., Ste. 2100
Atlanta, GA 30363-1031   (404) 873-8500
Contact: Milton W. Brannon, Pres.

Incorporated in 1964 in GA.
Donors: Roy N. Livingston†; Leslie Livingston Kellar†; Bess B. Livingston†.
Grantmaker type: Independent foundation.

Financial data (yr. ended 09/30/10): Assets, $7,604,982 (M); expenditures, $434,459; qualifying distributions, $317,600; giving activities include $317,600 for 16+ grants (high: $67,500; low: $4,500).
Purpose and activities: Giving primarily for education, the fine arts, and health care.
Fields of interest: Education; Visual arts; Museums; Performing arts; Historic preservation/historical societies; Arts; Hospitals (general); Medical research, institute; Community/economic development; International studies.
Type of support: General/operating support; Continuing support; Annual campaigns; Capital campaigns; Building/renovation; Endowments; Seed money; Curriculum development; Matching/challenge support.
Limitations: Applications not accepted. Giving primarily in the metropolitan Atlanta, GA, area. No support for religious or political organizations. No grants to individuals, or for scholarships or fellowships; no loans.
Application information: Unsolicited requests for funds not accepted.
   Board meeting date(s): Quarterly
Officers and Trustees:* Jonathan Golden,* Chair.; Milton W. Brannon,* Pres. and Treas.; C.E. Gregory III,* Secy.; Greer Brannon; Michael Golden; Charles Gregory; Bill Jacobs.
Number of staff: 1 part-time support.
EIN: 586044858

701
The Marcus Foundation, Inc.
1266 W. Paces Ferry Rd., No. 615
Atlanta, GA 30327-2306   (404) 240-7700
Contact: Frederick Slagle, Exec. Dir.
Bernie and Billi Marcus's Giving Pledge: http://givingpledge.org/#enter

Established in 1989 in GA.
Donor: Bernard Marcus.
Grantmaker type: Independent foundation.
Financial data (yr. ended 12/31/10): Assets, $136,565,122 (M); expenditures, $45,013,372; qualifying distributions, $43,825,253; giving activities include $40,430,393 for 193 grants (high: $4,000,000; low: $250).
Purpose and activities: Support primarily for human services, mental health, Jewish federated giving programs, education, and public affairs.
Fields of interest: Education; Health care; Mental health, treatment; Jewish agencies & synagogues.
Type of support: Program-related investments/loans.
Limitations: Applications not accepted. Giving primarily in Atlanta, GA. No grants to individuals.
Application information: Contributes only to pre-selected organizations.
Officers and Directors:* Bernard Marcus,* Chair.; Michael Leven,* Vice-Chair.; Doug Hertz, Pres.; Frederick Slagle, Secy.-Treas. and Exec. Dir.; Douglas D. Napoli, C.F.O.; Lisa Brill; Dennis Cooper; James Grien; Jeffrey Koplan; Ken Langone; Frederick R. Marcus; Michael Morris; Larry Smith.
EIN: 581815651
Recent grants for international programs:
701-1 American Friends of Brothers Aid, Boisbriand, Canada, $2,000,000. For general support. 2009.
701-2 American Friends of the Israel Democracy Institute, Atlanta, GA, $2,140,000. For operating support. 2009.

701-3 American Friends of the Israel Democracy Institute, Atlanta, GA, $101,000. For operating support. 2009.
701-4 American Friends of the Israel Free Loan Association, Washington, DC, $250,000. For micro-lending in Northern Israel. 2009.
701-5 American Israel Education Foundation, Washington, DC, $500,000. For Global Leadership Institute for Public Affairs. 2009.
701-6 American Israel Education Foundation, Washington, DC, $100,000. For annual campaign. 2009.
701-7 Birthright Israel Foundation, New York, NY, $1,000,000. For Israel Program for Young Adults, Cohort II. 2009.
701-8 Business Executives for National Security, Southeast Regional Office, Atlanta, GA, $50,000. For general operating support. 2009.
701-9 Emory University, Middle Eastern Research Program, Atlanta, GA, $150,000. For Pre-Collegiate Israel Curriculum Development Program. 2009.
701-10 Foundation for the Defense of Democracies, Washington, DC, $1,000,000. For operating support and program support. 2009.
701-11 Foundation for the Defense of Democracies, Washington, DC, $700,000. For program support. 2009.
701-12 Foundation for the Defense of Democracies, Washington, DC, $300,000. For program support. 2009.
701-13 Foundation for the Defense of Democracies, Washington, DC, $20,000. For general operating support. 2009.
701-14 Friends of Yemin Orde, Rockville, MD, $2,858,646. For challenge grant for 5 Villages national initiative. 2009.
701-15 Friends of Yemin Orde, Rockville, MD, $250,000. For Rejuvenation: Neve Amiel Youth Village. 2009.
701-16 Georgia International Law Enforcement Exchange, Atlanta, GA, $100,000. For exchange program. 2009.
701-17 Israel Encounter, Dunwoody, GA, $118,204. For Israel Encounter III. 2009.
701-18 Israel Encounter, Dunwoody, GA, $46,025. For Israel Encounter II. 2009.
701-19 Israel Encounter, Dunwoody, GA, $28,331. For Israel Encounter I. 2009.
701-20 Israel Project, Washington, DC, $250,000. For general operating support. 2009.
701-21 Middle East Media Research Institute, Washington, DC, $100,000. For general operating support. 2009.
701-22 Nefesh BNefesh - Jewish Souls United, New York, NY, $1,000,000. For outreach. 2009.

702
M. A. Masroor Foundation, Inc.
P.O. Box 8375
Savannah, GA 31412-8375   (912) 233-5492
Contact: M.A. Masroor

Established in 1988.
Donor: M.A. Masroor.
Grantmaker type: Independent foundation.
Financial data (yr. ended 03/31/11): Assets, $12,432 (M); gifts received, $124,069; expenditures, $202,674; qualifying distributions, $201,000; giving activities include $201,000 for grants.
Purpose and activities: Grants must be used exclusively for religious, educational, charitable or

scientific purposes as set forth by Zakah of the Muslim religion.
Fields of interest: Medical school/education; Health care; International relief; Islam.
International interests: Pakistan.
Limitations: Applications accepted. Giving primarily in Savannah, GA; giving also in NY.
Application information: Application form not required.
  Initial approach: Letter
  Deadline(s): None
Directors: Edgar L.T. Gay; M.A. Masroor; W.N. Searcy.
EIN: 581786413

703
Murray & Sydell Rosenberg Foundation
(formerly Murray M. Rosenberg Foundation)
3330 Cumberland Blvd., Ste. 900
Atlanta, GA 30339

Established in 1991 in GA.
Donor: Greystone Funding Corp.
Grantmaker type: Company-sponsored foundation.
Financial data (yr. ended 06/30/11): Assets, $83,556 (M); gifts received, $980,969; expenditures, $945,369; qualifying distributions, $910,798; giving activities include $910,798 for grants.
Purpose and activities: The foundation supports programs designed to help impoverished Jewish families.
Fields of interest: Education; Jewish agencies & synagogues; Economically disadvantaged.
International interests: Soviet Union (Former); Israel; Argentina.
Type of support: Grants to individuals.
Limitations: Applications accepted. Giving primarily in NY, NJ, and Israel.
Application information: Application form required.
  Initial approach: Contact foundation for application form
  Copies of proposal: 1
Directors: Lisa Lifshitz; Cheryl Rosenberg; Stephen Rosenberg.
Number of staff: 3 full-time professional.
EIN: 581947342

704
Scientific-Atlanta Foundation, Inc.
5030 Sugarloaf Pkwy.
P.O. Box 465447
Lawrenceville, GA 30042-5447 (770) 236-7961
Contact: Renee Byrd-Lewis, Secy.
E-mail: safoundation@sciatl.com

Established in 1998 in GA.
Donor: Scientific-Atlanta, Inc.
Grantmaker type: Company-sponsored foundation.
Financial data (yr. ended 07/31/09): Assets, $19,101,877 (M); gifts received, $1,068,030; expenditures, $1,136,701; qualifying distributions, $1,039,056; giving activities include $1,039,056 for 56 grants (high: $150,000; low: $750).
Purpose and activities: The foundation supports organizations involved with arts and culture, health, human services, economic development, and civic affairs. Special emphasis is directed toward programs designed to promote education in the areas of science, math, and technology.

Fields of interest: Computer science; Arts, cultural/ethnic awareness; Arts; Education; Health care; Human services; Economic development; Science, formal/general education; Mathematics; Public affairs.
International interests: Canada; Mexico.
Type of support: General/operating support; Continuing support; Annual campaigns; Capital campaigns; Building/renovation; Program development; Curriculum development; Scholarship funds; Technical assistance; Employee matching gifts; Employee-related scholarships; In-kind gifts; Matching/challenge support.
Limitations: Applications accepted. Giving primarily in Cupertino, CA, Orlando, FL, Atlanta, GA, and Chicago, IL; some giving also in Toronto and Vancouver, Canada, and Juarez, Mexico. No support for religious organizations, athletic organizations, or discriminatory organizations. No grants to individuals (except for employee-related scholarships), or for political causes, theological functions or church-sponsored programs, conferences, seminars, trips, or tours, or fundraising activities related to individual sponsorship.
Publications: Application guidelines; Program policy statement.
Application information: Application form not required.
  Initial approach: Proposal
  Board meeting date(s): Annually
Officers and Trustees:* J. Lawrence Bradner,* Pres.; Bryan D. Benfield, V.P. and Treas., Beverly A. Wright, V.P. and Treas.; Steven D. Boyd,* V.P., Finance; William F. McCargo, V.P.; Renee Byrd-Lewis, Secy.; Peggy Ballard; Hector Baro; Dwight B. Duke; Michael P. Harney; Beth A. Pollard; Michael C. Veysey.
EIN: 582452986

705
South Arts
(formerly Southern Arts Federation)
1800 Peachtree St. N.W., Ste. 808
Atlanta, GA 30309-7603 (404) 874-7244
Contact: Gerri Combs, Exec. Dir.
FAX: (404) 873-2148; *E-mail:* saf@southarts.org;
TTD: (404) 876-6240; URL: http://www.southarts.org
YouTube: http://www.youtube.com/southarts

Established in 1975 in NC.
Grantmaker type: Public charity.
Financial data (yr. ended 06/30/11): Revenue, $2,955,050; assets, $1,437,195 (M); gifts received, $2,425,555; expenditures, $2,829,534; giving activities include $995,911 for grants.
Purpose and activities: The federation promotes and supports arts regionally, nationally, and internationally; enhances the artistic excellence and professionalism of Southern arts organizations and artists; and serves the diverse population of the South.
Fields of interest: Arts, artist's services; Arts, public education; Visual arts; Performing arts; Literature.
International interests: Canada; Mexico; Netherlands.
Type of support: Management development/capacity building; Program development; Technical assistance; Consulting services; Matching/challenge support.

Limitations: Applications accepted. Giving limited to AL, FL, GA, KY, LA, MS, NC, SC, and TN. No grants to individuals.
Publications: Application guidelines; Annual report; Financial statement; Grants list; Informational brochure; Informational brochure (including application guidelines); Newsletter; Occasional report.
Application information: Application form required.
  Copies of proposal: 2
  Deadline(s): Feb. 2 for International Puppetry Arts Tour Grants; Mar. 2 for NEA/SAF Regional Touring Program; sixty days prior to the start date for Technical Assistance Grants and Southern Fast Track Touring Program
  Board meeting date(s): Fall and spring
Officers and Directors:* Todd Parker Lowe,* Chair.; Dr. Margaret S. Mertz,* Vice-Chair., Strategic Planning; Sandy Shaughnessy,* Vice-Chair., Progs. and Svcs.; Jan Selman, Vice-Chair., Ext. Rels.; Scott Shanklin-Peterson,* Secy.; Richard Ranta,* Ph.D., Treas.; Gerri Combs, Exec. Dir.; Betsy Baker; Pam Breaux; Jim Clinton; Stephanie Conner; Jeffrey Dunn; Derek Gordon; Dr. Remedios Gomez-Arnau; Al Head; and 9 additional directors.
Number of staff: 11 full-time professional; 1 full-time support.
EIN: 561129587

706
Southwire Company Contributions Program
1 Southwire Dr.
Carrollton, GA 30119-4400
URL: http://www.southwire.com/ourcompany/Community.htm
RSS Feed: http://www.southwire.com/rss.jsp?channelId=36391dc51235df00VgnVCM1000004c026564RCRD&channelName=Community

Grantmaker type: Corporate giving program.
Purpose and activities: Southwire makes charitable contributions to nonprofit organizations involved with education, the environment, youth development, human services, and community development. Support is given primarily in areas of company operations, with emphasis on Alabama, Arizona, California, Florida, Georgia, Illinois, Indiana, Kentucky, Mississippi, Pennsylvania, Texas, and Utah, and in Canada and Mexico.
Fields of interest: Education; Environment; Youth development; Human services; Community/economic development.
International interests: Mexico; Canada.
Type of support: General/operating support; Employee volunteer services.
Limitations: Giving primarily in areas of company operations in AL, AZ, CA, FL, GA, IL, IN, KY, MS, PA, TX, and UT, and in Canada and Mexico.

707
St. Marys United Methodist Church Foundation, Inc.
P.O. Box 160
St. Marys, GA 31558-6858 (912) 510-9350
FAX: (912) 510-9346; *E-mail:* smumcf@tds.net;
URL: http://www.smumcfoundation.org
Grants List: http://www.smumcfoundation.org/grant-program/grant-recipients
RSS Feed: http://smumcf.wordpress.com/feed/

Established in 2001; supporting organization of St. Marys United Methodist Church.

Grantmaker type: Public charity.

Financial data (yr. ended 12/31/10): Assets, $36,178,468 (M); expenditures, $1,711,198; giving activities include $1,157,329 for grants.

Purpose and activities: The foundation's mission is to be a lasting, effective, and compassionate charitable resource for agencies in southeast Georgia, the nation, and the world that respond to people in need, for institutions related to United Methodism, and for organizations that promote evangelical Christianity.

Fields of interest: Theological school/education; Health care; Mental health/crisis services; AIDS; Children/youth, services; Family services; Aging, centers/services; Religion, public education; Christian agencies & churches; Adults; Disabilities, people with; Children.

International interests: Africa; Kenya; Mozambique; Rwanda; Southern Africa; Tanzania, Zanzibar and Pemba; Uganda; Zambia.

Limitations: Applications accepted. Giving primarily to agencies of the South Georgia Annual Conference of the United Methodist Church and programs in southeast GA (Camden, Glynn, Brantley and Charlton counties). No support for organizations lacking 501(c)(3) status, business ventures, arts and culture, environmental projects, animals, social clubs, sports, recreation, leisure, historic preservation projects, or individual church projects where a collaborative effort with other churches may be more beneficial and effective. No grants to individuals, or for debt reduction, individual scholarships, endowments, brick and mortar projects for individual churches, meetings, conferences, or production of films, videos, or other recordings; no loans.

Publications: Application guidelines; Annual report; Grants list.

Application information: Proposals chosen for further consideration will be asked to submit a completed application, which will be provided by the foundation. Applications will only be provided when a proposal has been selected for further review. Response time to an application is approximately one week. Application form required.

   Initial approach: Proposal (no more than two pages) on organization's letterhead
   Copies of proposal: 1
   Deadline(s): June 1 and Dec. 1 for proposals
   Final notification: One week

Officers and Directors:* Ginna Stein,* Chair.; Jeff Barker, Pres.; Kathleen Duddleston,* V.P.; Sheila Ulmer,* Secy.; Robert Bennett,* Treas.; Richard Anderson; Buddy McGhin; Tricia Smith.

EIN: 582591172

708
Turner Foundation, Inc.

c/o Raymond Goodreau
133 Luckie St. N.W., 2nd Fl.
Atlanta, GA 30303-2038 (404) 681-9900
Contact: Michael Finley, Pres.
FAX: (404) 681-0172; URL: http://www.turnerfoundation.org
Ted Turner's Giving Pledge: http://givingpledge.org/#enter

Established in 1990 in GA.

Donor: R.E. "Ted" Turner III.

Grantmaker type: Independent foundation.

Financial data (yr. ended 12/31/10): Assets, $5,833,975 (M); gifts received, $12,134,371; expenditures, $12,981,599; qualifying distributions, $12,893,635; giving activities include $11,011,517 for 417 grants (high: $300,000; low: $75).

Purpose and activities: The foundation is committed to preventing damage to the natural systems - water, air, and land - on which all life depends.

Fields of interest: Environment, natural resources; Environment, water resources; Environment, energy; Animals/wildlife, preservation/protection; Animals/wildlife; Population studies.

Type of support: General/operating support; Continuing support; Program development; Research; Technical assistance; Matching/challenge support.

Limitations: Applications not accepted. Giving primarily on a regional and national basis; priority consideration to programs in FL, GA, MT, NM, and SC. No grants to individuals, or for buildings, land acquisition, endowments, start-up funds, films, books, magazines, and other specific media projects.

Application information: The foundation has implemented an invitation-only grantmaking process. Letters of inquiry and unsolicited proposals are not accepted.

   Board meeting date(s): April, Aug., and Dec.

Officers and Trustees:* R.E. "Ted" Turner III,* Chair.; Michael Finley,* Pres. and Treas.; J. Rutherford Seydel II, Secy.; Jennie Turner Garlington; Laura Turner Seydel; Beau Turner; Rhett Lee Turner; Teddy Turner.

Number of staff: 7 full-time professional.

EIN: 581924590

Recent grants for international programs:

708-1 Alaska Wilderness League, Washington, DC, $40,000. 2009.

708-2 American Bird Conservancy, The Plains, VA, $25,000. 2009.

708-3 Better World Fund, Washington, DC, $250,000. 2009.

708-4 Better World Fund, Washington, DC, $238,232. 2009.

708-5 Business Executives for National Security, Washington, DC, $10,000. 2009.

708-6 Center for Climate Strategies, Washington, DC, $60,000. 2009.

708-7 Dian Fossey Gorilla Fund International, Atlanta, GA, $10,000. 2009.

708-8 Olusegun Obasanjo Presidential Library Foundation in the U. S, Washington, DC, $25,000. 2009.

708-9 Rome Chamber Music Festival, New York, NY, $10,000. 2009.

708-10 Sky Island Alliance, Tucson, AZ, $40,000. 2009.

708-11 V-Day, New York, NY, $25,000. 2009.

708-12 Waterkeeper Alliance, New York, NY, $60,000. 2009.

708-13 Wild Salmon Center, Portland, OR, $100,000. 2009.

709
The UPS Foundation

55 Glenlake Pkwy., N.E.
Atlanta, GA 30328-3474 (404) 828-6374
Contact: Ken Sternad, Pres.
FAX: (404) 828-7435; URL: http://community.ups.com/UPS+Foundation

Incorporated in 1951 in DE.

Donor: United Parcel Service of America, Inc.

Grantmaker type: Company-sponsored foundation.

Financial data (yr. ended 12/31/10): Assets, $1,739,183 (M); gifts received, $39,685,916; expenditures, $42,173,667; qualifying distributions, $39,513,804; giving activities include $39,497,732 for 1,952 grants (high: $7,148,082; low: $100).

Purpose and activities: The foundation supports programs designed to promote economic and global literacy; environmental sustainability; nonprofit effectiveness; diversity; and community safety.

Fields of interest: Boys & girls clubs; Business school/education; Education, reading; Education; Environment, climate change/global warming; Environment, natural resources; Environment, energy; Environment, forests; Environment; Public health, clean water supply; Food services; Disasters, preparedness/services; Safety, automotive safety; Children/youth, services; Human services, financial counseling; Human services; Civil/human rights, equal rights; Civil/human rights; Social entrepreneurship; Microfinance/microlending; Nonprofit management; Community/economic development; Voluntarism promotion; Leadership development; Economically disadvantaged.

International interests: Brazil; Canada; China; Malaysia; Mexico; South Africa.

Type of support: Continuing support; Management development/capacity building; Program development; Scholarship funds; Research; Technical assistance; Employee volunteer services; Employee matching gifts; In-kind gifts.

Limitations: Applications not accepted. Giving on a national basis and in Brazil, Canada, China, Malaysia, Mexico, and South Africa; giving also to statewide, regional, national, and international organizations. No support for religious organizations not of direct benefit to the entire community. No grants to individuals; generally, no grants for capital campaigns, endowments, or general operating support.

Publications: Annual report; Informational brochure.

Application information: Contributes only to pre-selected organizations.

   Board meeting date(s): Oct. and Nov.

Officers and Trustees:* Allen E. Hill,* Chair.; Edward Martinez, Pres.; Ken Sternad, Pres.; David P. Abney,* Secy.; Kurt P. Kuehn,* Treas.; D. Scott Davis; Teri P. McClure; Christine M. Owens.

Number of staff: 7 full-time professional; 4 full-time support.

EIN: 136099176

Recent grants for international programs:

709-1 AAKAR, New Delhi, India, $19,890. 2009.

709-2 Africare, Washington, DC, $125,000. 2009.

709-3 Africare, Washington, DC, $125,000. 2009.

709-4 Agency for International Development, Washington, DC, $31,051. For the Chennai Community Health Education Society, India (AIDS relief and education for children). 2009.

709-5 Aids-Hilfe Koln e.V., Cologne, Germany, $65,000. 2009.

709-6 ASPRODIS, Elda, Spain, $19,000. 2009.

709-7 Association Pierre Favre, Saint Jean d'Illac, France, $44,630. 2009.

709-8 Association pour le Droit a L'Initiative Economique, Strasbourg, France, $26,628. 2009.

709-9 Associazione di Volontariato di Protezione Civile, Italy, $28,270. 2009.

709-10 Associazione Italiana Dislessia, Bologna, Italy, $20,000. 2009.

709-11 Associazione Italiana Sclerosi Multipla, Italy, $49,000. 2009.

709-12 Australian Red Cross, Carlton, Australia, $10,000. 2009.

709-13 Autism Society Philippines, Quezon City, Philippines, $40,000. 2009.

709-14 Bandra Holy Family Hospital Society, Mumbai, India, $32,559. 2009.

709-15 Cancer Patients Aid Association, New Delhi, India, $32,571. 2009.

709-16 CARE Internacional Brasil, Sao Paulo, Brazil, $60,000. 2009.

709-17 CARE USA, Atlanta, GA, $50,000. 2009.

709-18 Centro Rieducazione Equestre L'Arca Del Seprio Onlus, Vedano Olona, Italy, $45,000. 2009.

709-19 China Population Welfare Foundation, Beijing, China, $50,000. 2009.

709-20 Chofu Gakuen, Japan, $34,150. 2009.

709-21 Christel House de Mexico, Mexico City, Mexico, $15,000. 2009.

709-22 City of Refuge Orphanage, Abuja, Nigeria, $50,000. 2009.

709-23 Clean Up Australia, Australia, $10,000. 2009.

709-24 Corpo Volontari Protezione Civile - Peschiera Borromeo, Peschiera Borromeo, Italy, $20,000. 2009.

709-25 Dartford, Gravesham & Swanley MIND, Dartford, England, $15,450. 2009.

709-26 Dc Amicitia, Gargantilla del Lozoya, Spain, $20,040. 2009.

709-27 Dum tri prani, o.s., Prague, Czech Republic, $15,600. 2009.

709-28 East Anglian Air Ambulance, Norwich, England, $32,799. 2009.

709-29 Entrajuda, Lisbon, Portugal, $20,633. 2009.

709-30 Erika Muller Stiftung, Bremen, Germany, $36,500. 2009.

709-31 Fitted for Work, Melbourne, Australia, $27,000. 2009.

709-32 Forderverein der Gemeinschaftsgrundschule Grefrath e.V., Grefrath, Germany, $20,245. 2009.

709-33 Foreign Press Association, New York, NY, $10,000. 2009.

709-34 Full Gospel Assemblies Foundation, Agapa Home, Chiang Mai, Thailand, $30,000. 2009.

709-35 Fundacion para el Desarrollo Solidario, Lima, Peru, $25,000. 2009.

709-36 Fundacja DZieciom Zdazyc z Pomoca, Warsaw, Poland, $22,000. 2009.

709-37 Fundacja Forum Obywatelskiego Rozwoju, Warsaw, Poland, $49,500. 2009.

709-38 Good360, Alexandria, VA, $150,000. 2009.

709-39 Gram Vikas, Berhampur, India, $27,669. 2009.

709-40 Great Orchestra of Christmas Charity Foundation, Warsaw, Poland, $49,000. 2009.

709-41 Guangzhou Youth Development Foundation, Guangzhou, China, $61,873. 2009.

709-42 Guangzhou Youth Development Foundation, Guangzhou, China, $29,258. 2009.

709-43 Guangzhou Youth Development Foundation, Guangzhou, China, $20,480. 2009.

709-44 Guangzhou Youth Development Foundation, Guangzhou, China, $10,387. 2009.

709-45 Guias de Mexico, A.C., Cuauhtemoc, Mexico, $15,000. 2009.

709-46 Guias de Mexico, A.C., Cuauhtemoc, Mexico, $12,700. 2009.

709-47 Guias de Mexico, A.C., Cuauhtemoc, Mexico, $10,000. 2009.

709-48 Habitat for Humanity Canada, Waterloo, Canada, $10,000. 2009.

709-49 HandsOn Shanghai, HandsOn China, China, $50,000. 2009.

709-50 Heathrow Special Needs Farm, Longford, England, $14,822. 2009.

709-51 Hellenic Ornithological Society, Athens, Greece, $20,000. 2009.

709-52 Hong Kong Association of the Deaf, Hong Kong, China, $16,655. 2009.

709-53 Hong Kong Council of Social Service, Hong Kong, China, $50,000. 2009.

709-54 Hospital Municipal de Zamora, Zamora, Mexico, $15,000. 2009.

709-55 Hwasung Baby Home, Seoul, South Korea, $16,900. 2009.

709-56 Impact Foundation, Warsaw, Poland, $10,000. For a program about the Vistula River. 2009.

709-57 International Association for Volunteer Effort, Washington, DC, $50,000. 2009.

709-58 International Franchise Association Educational Foundation, Washington, DC, $10,000. 2009.

709-59 International Medical Equipment Collaborative of America, North Andover, MA, $25,000. 2009.

709-60 Irish Heart Foundation, Dublin, Ireland, $24,691. 2009.

709-61 Keech Hospice Care, Luton, England, $17,584. 2009.

709-62 LAlbero della Vita, Milan, Italy, $49,000. 2009.

709-63 LARAMARA-Associacao Brasileira de Assistencia ao Deficiente Visual, Sao Paulo, Brazil, $40,525. 2009.

709-64 Lastenklinikoiden Kummit ry, Helsinki, Finland, $14,000. 2009.

709-65 Lebenshilfe fur Menschen mit Geistiger Behinderung Viernheim, Viernheim, Germany, $60,000. 2009.

709-66 Leibnizschule In Frankfurt-Hochst, e.V., Verein zur Forderung der, Frankfurt, Germany, $78,000. 2009.

709-67 Lions Home for the Elders, Singapore, Singapore, $38,000. 2009.

709-68 London Wildlife Trust, London, England, $46,600. 2009.

709-69 MedShare International, Decatur, GA, $20,000. 2009.

709-70 Men on the Side of the Road, Woodstock, South Africa, $15,571. 2009.

709-71 National Bureau of Asian Research, Seattle, WA, $50,000. 2009.

709-72 National Nikkei Museum and Heritage Centre, Burnaby, Canada, $15,000. 2009.

709-73 National Peace Corps Association, Washington, DC, $50,000. 2009.

709-74 Naturschutzbund Deutschland, Bonn, Germany, $33,152. 2009.

709-75 Natuurpunt, Mechelen, Belgium, $48,667. 2009.

709-76 Nav Maharashtra Community Foundation, Pune, India, $30,174. 2009.

709-77 Never-ending International workCamps Exchange, Tokyo, Japan, $41,910. 2009.

709-78 New Life Psychiatric Rehabilitation Association, Hong Kong, China, $15,560. 2009.

709-79 New Zealand Landcare Trust, Hamilton, New Zealand, $20,000. 2009.

709-80 Norges Rode Kors, Oslo, Norway, $14,000. 2009.

709-81 Ny Gemenskap, Stockholm, Sweden, $13,000. 2009.

709-82 Oasis d'amour, Decines-Charpieu, France, $57,000. 2009.

709-83 Operation Blessing China, Beijing, China, $59,697. 2009.

709-84 Operation Blessing International Relief and Development Corporation, Virginia Beach, VA, $15,000. For Mexico AC. 2009.

709-85 Operation Smile International, Norfolk, VA, $50,000. For Hangzhou Operation Smile Charity Hospital. 2009.

709-86 Opportunity International, Oak Brook, IL, $80,000. 2009.

709-87 Papel de Gente, Sao Paulo, Brazil, $46,345. 2009.

709-88 Paranaque Don Galo Volunteer Firefighters, Manila, Philippines, $35,000. 2009.

709-89 Parkdale Project Read, Toronto, Canada, $50,000. 2009.

709-90 Partnership Council, Nottingham, England, $16,415. 2009.

709-91 Peace Corps of the United States, Washington, DC, $250,000. 2009.

709-92 Persatuan Rumah Kebajikan Rita, Klang, Malaysia, $26,700. 2009.

709-93 Philippine Association for the Gifted, Pasig City, Philippines, $40,000. 2009.

709-94 Polish Ukrainian Cooperation Foundation, Kiev, Ukraine, $166,096. 2009.

709-95 PRAYAS: Initiatives in Health, Energy, Learning and Parenthood, Pune, India, $26,266. 2009.

709-96 Progetto Arca, Milan, Italy, $18,730. 2009.

709-97 Rainbow Trust Childrens Charity, Leatherhead, England, $16,000. 2009.

709-98 Rajapruek Institute Foundation, Bangkok, Thailand, $60,000. 2009.

709-99 Red Cross of France, Paris, France, $43,824. 2009.

709-100 Reef Check Foundation, Pacific Palisades, CA, $10,000. 2009.

709-101 Rowny Start, Poznan, Poland, $13,500. 2009.

709-102 Rumah Charis, Kuala Lumpur, Malaysia, $10,736. 2009.

709-103 Saathi, Lalitpur, Nepal, $32,491. 2009.

709-104 Saigon Childrens Charity, Ho Chi Minh City, Vietnam, $11,190. 2009.

709-105 Saint Patricks Family Centre, Moncton, Canada, $30,000. 2009.

709-106 School of Human Genetics and Population Health, Kolkata, India, $29,412. 2009.

709-107 Servicio, Educacion y Desarrollo a la Comunidad IAP, Mexico City, Mexico, $15,000. 2009.

709-108 Slezska Humanita, o.s., Karvina, Czech Republic, $39,424. 2009.

709-109 Societe de l'autisme des Laurentides, Saint Jerome, Canada, $70,000. 2009.

709-110 SOS Childrens Villages Romania, Bucharest, Romania, $30,000. 2009.

709-111 Staffordshire Wildlife Trust, Stafford, England, $30,000. 2009.

709-112 Stowarzyszenie Przyjaciol Integracji, Warsaw, Poland, $10,000. 2009.

709-113 Stretch-A-Family, Marrickville, Australia, $10,620. 2009.

709-114 Sutton Nature Conservation Volunteers, Sutton, England, $15,000. 2009.

709-115 Thai Environmental Corporation Foundation, Bangkok, Thailand, $10,000. 2009.

709-116 Thai Fund Foundation, Bangkok, Thailand, $47,750. 2009.

709-117 Thusanang Study Project, Jane Furse, South Africa, $11,109. 2009.

709-118 Thusanang Study Project, Thusanang Sewing School, Jane Furse, South Africa, $11,109. 2009.

709-119 Towarzystwo Opieki nad Ociemnialymi, Izabelin, Poland, $28,000. 2009.

709-120 Treetops Hospice, Derby, England, $57,040. 2009.

709-121 United Nations Association of the United States of America, New York, NY, $100,000. 2009.

709-122 United States Fund for UNICEF, New York, NY, $350,000. 2009.

709-123 United Way of Taiwan, Taipei, Taiwan, $48,192. 2009.

709-124 United Way Worldwide, Alexandria, VA, $7,917,527. 2009.

709-125 Uplift International, Seattle, WA, $48,036. 2009.

709-126 Vecsesi Serult Gyermekekert Kozhasznu Alapitvany, Vecses, Hungary, $13,000. 2009.

709-127 Verein zur Forderung und Betreuung spastisch gelahmter und anderen Korperbehinderter, Frankfurt, Germany, $28,000. 2009.

709-128 Vision Mexico, Arlington, VA, $100,000. 2009.

709-129 Vision Mundial Mexico, Bay of All Saints, Mexico, $15,000. 2009.

709-130 Volunteer Canada, Ottawa, Canada, $85,000. 2009.

709-131 Welcome Hall Mission, Montreal, Canada, $55,000. 2009.

709-132 Women for Women International, Washington, DC, $40,000. 2009.

709-133 Women for Women International, Washington, DC, $10,000. 2009.

709-134 World Association of Girl Guides and Girl Scouts, London, England, $195,588. 2009.

709-135 World Association of Girl Guides and Girl Scouts, London, England, $195,588. 2009.

709-136 World Resources Institute, Washington, DC, $200,000. 2009.

709-137 Yayasan Sunbeams Home, Kuala Lumpur, Malaysia, $17,000. 2009.

709-138 YMCA of Greater Moncton, Moncton, Canada, $25,000. 2009.

709-139 Young Nak Aeneass Home, Seoul, South Korea, $30,600. 2009.

710
The Edna Wardlaw Charitable Trust
c/o GenSpring Family Offices
4401 Northside Pkwy., Ste. 120
Atlanta, GA   30327-5220
Contact: Gregorie Guthrie, Secy.

Established in 1992 in GA.
Donor: Edna Wardlaw.
Grantmaker type: Independent foundation.
Financial data (yr. ended 12/31/10): Assets, $17,079,219 (M); expenditures, $873,009; qualifying distributions, $745,594; giving activities include $725,500 for 75 grants (high: $42,500; low: $2,000).
Purpose and activities: Giving primarily for children's services and environmental conservation.
Fields of interest: Environment, natural resources; Reproductive health, family planning; Children/youth, services; Homeless, human services; International affairs, goodwill promotion;

International peace/security; International human rights.
Limitations: Applications accepted. Giving on a national basis.
Application information: Application form not required.
   Initial approach: Letter
   Copies of proposal: 1
   Deadline(s): June 15
Distribution Committee: Edna Raine Coker; Elizabeth H. Coker; Charlotte S. Hoffman; Trudie Olavarrieta-Coker; Julia Milner Wardlaw; William C. Wardlaw III.
Trustee: SunTrust Bank.
EIN: 586278167

HAWAII

711
Crown Prince Akihito Scholarship Foundation
P.O. Box 1412
Honolulu, HI   96806-1412   (808) 524-4450
FAX: (808) 524-4451;
E-mail: ehawkins@jashawaii.org; URL: http://www.jashawaii.org/cpas.asp

Established in 1959 in HI.
Grantmaker type: Public charity.
Financial data (yr. ended 12/31/09): Revenue, $202,994; assets, $2,706,236 (M); gifts received, $377,176; expenditures, $1,063,131; program services expenses, $547,731; giving activities include $48,400 for 4 grants to organizations outside the U.S., and $175,960 for 5 grants to individuals.
Purpose and activities: The foundation seeks to promote understanding between the U.S. and Japan by offering scholarships for study in Hawaii and Japan.
Fields of interest: International exchange; Higher education, university; Education.
Type of support: Scholarships—to individuals.
Limitations: Applications accepted. Giving limited to HI and Japan.
Publications: Application guidelines.
Application information: Application form required.
   Initial approach: Download application
   Deadline(s): Nov. 8 for American students
Trustees:* Robin Campaniano; Walter Dods; Dennis Esaki; Howard H. Hamamoto; Howard Karr; Larry Kumabe; Dr. David McClain; Marjorie Midkiff; Katsugo Miho; Dr. Glenn Miyataki; and 13 additional trustees.
EIN: 990261751

712
Alexander & Baldwin Foundation
P.O. Box 3440
Honolulu, HI   96801-3440   (808) 525-6642
Contact: Meredith J. Ching, Pres.
FAX: (808) 525-6677; E-mail: lhowe@abinc.com;
Application address for organizations located outside HI and the Pacific: Mathew Cox, Chair. Mainland Contrib. Comm., c/o Matson Navigation Co., Inc., 555 12th St., Oakland, CA 94607;

Additional contact for organizations located outside of HI and the Pacific: Paul Merwin, tel.: (707) 421-8121, Fax: (707) 421-1835, E-mail: plmifm@aol.com; URL: http://www.alexanderbaldwinfoundation.org
Grants List: http://www.alexanderbaldwinfoundation.org/grants.htm

Established in 1991 in HI.
Donors: Alexander & Baldwin, Inc.; A&B Properties, Inc.; East Maui Irrigation Co., Ltd.; Hawaiian Commercial and Sugar Co.; Kahului Trucking and Storage; Kauai Coffee Co.; Kauai Commercial Co., Inc.; Matson Navigation Co., Inc.
Grantmaker type: Company-sponsored foundation.
Financial data (yr. ended 12/31/10): Assets, $581,986 (M); gifts received, $852,500; expenditures, $1,632,565; qualifying distributions, $1,632,565; giving activities include $1,618,235 for 782+ grants (high: $100,000).
Purpose and activities: The foundation supports organizations involved with arts and culture, education, the environment, health, human services, and community development.
Fields of interest: Environment, natural resources; Museums (marine/maritime); Arts; Education, reading; Education; Environment; Health care; Children/youth, services; Human services; Community/economic development; United Ways and Federated Giving Programs.
International interests: Oceania.
Type of support: General/operating support; Continuing support; Annual campaigns; Capital campaigns; Building/renovation; Equipment; Program development; Seed money; Employee volunteer services; Employee matching gifts; Employee-related scholarships.
Limitations: Applications accepted. Giving primarily in areas of company operations, with emphasis on AZ, CA, HI, IL, and in the Pacific. No support for religious organizations or veterans', fraternal, or labor organizations. No grants to individuals, or for travel or endowments, secondary giving, religious activities not of direct benefit to the entire community, advertising, sponsorship of events, or general operating support for United Way agencies; no product or service donations.
Publications: Application guidelines; Annual report; Grants list; Program policy statement.
Application information: Support is limited to 1 contribution per organization during any given year. Proposals for requests of less than $2,000 should be no longer than 3 pages. Proposals for requests greater than $2,000 should also include an executive summary if proposal exceeds 3 pages. Executive summaries should be no longer than 250 words. Application form required.
   Initial approach: Download application form and mail proposal and application form to foundation for organizations located in HI and the Pacific; mail to application address for organizations located outside HI and the Pacific
   Copies of proposal: 1
   Deadline(s): Feb. 1, Apr. 1, June 1, Aug. 1, Oct. 1, and Dec. 1 for organizations located in HI and the Pacific; first of the month for organizations located outside HI and the Pacific
   Board meeting date(s): Jan., Mar., May, July, Sept., and Nov. for organizations located in HI and the Pacific; monthly for organizations located outside HI and the Pacific
   Final notification: Within 2 weeks of committee meetings

Officers and Directors:* Meredith J. Ching,* Pres.; Christopher J. Benjamin,* V.P. and Treas.; Linda M. Howe, V.P.; Paul K. Ito, V.P.; Alyson J. Nakamura, Secy.; Vic S. Angoco, Jr.; Grant Y.M. Chun; Norbert M. Buelsing; Stanley M. Kuriyama.
Number of staff: 2 part-time professional; 1 part-time support.
EIN: 990291942

713
The Julia Burke Foundation
73-1397 Hamiha St.
Kailua Kona, HI 96740-9213   (808) 960-1705
Contact: Joy Johnson, Exec. Dir.
FAX: (866) 437-8579;
E-mail: Projects@JuliaBurkeFoundation.com; E-mail address for Joy Johnson, Exec. Dir.: Joy_Johnson@burkefoundation.org; URL: http://www.juliaburkefoundation.com/

Established in 1998 in CA.
Donors: Gerald P. Burke; Marilyn Burke; Janice Hamill; Stephen Hamill.
Grantmaker type: Independent foundation.
Financial data (yr. ended 11/30/09): Assets, $5,712,848 (M); gifts received, $564,372; expenditures, $1,394,448; qualifying distributions, $1,335,033; giving activities include $1,026,549 for 24 grants (high: $300,000; low: $2,000).
Fields of interest: Family services, parent education; Medical school/education; Scholarships/financial aid; Education; International peace/security; International affairs.
Limitations: Applications accepted. Giving worldwide, with an emphasis on CA. No grants to individuals.
Publications: Newsletter.
Application information: See grantmaker web site for specific policies and guidelines. Application form required.
  Initial approach: E-mail
  Deadline(s): None
Officers: Marilyn C. Burke, Pres. and Secy.; Gerald P. Burke, V.P. and Treas.; Joy Johnson, Exec. Dir.
Members: Donald M. Burke; Robert M. Burke; Timothy J. Campion; Jonathan E. Cowperthwait; Stephen A. Hamill; Robbie Murphy; Eric S. Zampol.
Number of staff: 1 full-time professional.
EIN: 943314266

714
Center for Cultural and Technical Interchange Between East and West, Inc.
(also known as East-West Center)
1601 East-West Rd.
Honolulu, HI 96848-1601   (808) 944-7111
FAX: (808) 944-7376; URL: http://www.eastwestcenter.org
Facebook: http://www.facebook.com/EastWestCenter.org
Flickr: http://www.flickr.com/photos/eastwestcenter/collections/
LinkedIn: http://www.linkedin.com/groups?home=&gid=130651&trk=anet_ug_hm
RSS Feed: http://www.eastwestcenter.org/about-ewc/rss-feeds/
YouTube: http://www.youtube.com/eastwestcenter

Established in 1960 in HI.
Grantmaker type: Public charity.

Financial data (yr. ended 09/30/10): Revenue, $32,786,830; assets, $33,851,252 (M); gifts received, $23,352,675; expenditures, $33,328,705; giving activities include $167,101 for grants to organizations outside the U.S., and $5,414,744 for grants to individuals.
Purpose and activities: The center contributes to a peaceful, prosperous, and just Asia Pacific community by serving as a vigorous hub for cooperative research, education, and dialogue on critical issues of common concern to the Asia Pacific region and the United States.
Fields of interest: Media, print publishing; Graduate/professional education; International affairs; Higher education.
International interests: Oceania; Asia.
Type of support: Fellowships; Use of facilities; Scholarships—to individuals; In-kind gifts.
Limitations: Applications accepted. Giving on a national and international basis, with emphasis on Asia and the Pacific Rim.
Publications: Annual report.
Application information: Application form required.
  Deadline(s): Feb. 15 for Asia Pacific Leadership Program Scholarship Funds; May 21 for Hong Kong Journalism Fellowships; June 8 for East-West Center Student Affiliate Program; Nov. for Asian Development Bank-Government of Japan Scholarship; Dec. for Obuchi Student Scholarships
Officers and Governors:* Puongpun Sananikone,* Chair.; Roland Lagareta,* Vice-Chair.; Charles E. Morrison, Pres.; Ricky Kubota, Treas.; Tarun Das; Eddie Flores, Jr.; Lori A. Forman; Daniel Fung, S.B.S.; Miriam Hellreich; Theodore B. Lee; Theodore Em-Po Liu; Jean E. Rolles; Il SaKong; Hon. Patricia F. Saiki; S. Linn Williams; Tadashi Yamamoto; Michael K. Young; Hon. Tun Daim Zainuddin.
EIN: 990161603

715
Community Conservation Network
923 Nuuanu Ave.
Honolulu, HI 96817-5115   (808) 528-3700
FAX: (808) 528-3701;
E-mail: info@conservationpractice.org; Mailing address: P.O. Box 4674, Honolulu, HI 96812-4674

Established in 1998 in HI.
Grantmaker type: Public charity.
Financial data (yr. ended 12/31/09): Revenue, $83,738; assets, $36,101 (M); gifts received, $83,738; expenditures, $265,375; giving activities include $131,054 for grants.
Purpose and activities: The network assists local communities and their partners to sustain vital ecosystems and resources by fostering relationships and building capacity that results in improved long-term conservation, management effectiveness, and human security.
Fields of interest: International affairs; Environment, land resources; Environment; Animals/wildlife.
Limitations: Giving primarily to HI.
Publications: Annual report; Newsletter.
Officers and Board Members:* Dr. Alan White,* Pres.; Mark Ridgley, V.P.; Dawn Southard, Exec. Dir.; Scott R. Atkinson; Dr. Kitty Courtney; John Parks.
EIN: 990346183

716
East-West Center Foundation
1601 East-West Rd.
Honolulu, HI 96848-1601   (808) 944-7111
Contact: Gerald J. Keir, Co-Chair.
FAX: (808) 944-7376; URL: http://www.eastwestcenter.org/support-the-ewc/

Established in 1982 in HI; supporting organization of Center for Cultural & Technical Interchange Between East & West, Inc.
Grantmaker type: Public charity.
Financial data (yr. ended 09/30/10): Revenue, $2,493,263; assets, $5,318,339 (M); gifts received, $2,371,918; expenditures, $723,157; giving activities include $346,818 for grants.
Purpose and activities: The foundation aims to broaden the financial support to the center for cultural and technical interchange between East and West, Inc., a public educational nonprofit corporation.
Fields of interest: International affairs, goodwill promotion.
Type of support: Research.
Limitations: Giving limited to Honolulu, HI.
Officers and Directors:* Neal K. Kanda,* Co-Chair.; Don K. Kim,* Co-Chair.; Cynthia J.C. Ai; Jean M. Ariyoshi; Joan M. Bickson; Paul M.F. Cheng; Robin Campaniano; Bruce A. Coppa; Karl Essig; Dr. John N. Hawkins; and 14 additional directors.
EIN: 990218752

717
The Hau'Oli Mau Loa Foundation
701 Bishop St.
Honolulu, HI 96813-4814   (808) 545-4212
FAX: (808) 440-0061;
E-mail: info@hauolimauloa.org; URL: http://www.hauolimauloa.org

Established in 1990 in NY.
Donors: Helga Glaesel-Hollenback†; Edwin Hollenback; Edwin Hollenback 1998 Trust; Helga Glaesel-Hollenback 1990 Trust.
Grantmaker type: Operating foundation.
Financial data (yr. ended 12/31/09): Assets, $127,419,131 (M); expenditures, $13,290,169; qualifying distributions, $5,964,018; giving activities include $3,722,330 for 35 grants (high: $500,000; low: $2,500).
Purpose and activities: Giving primarily to help the less fortunate, especially children, and to enhance stewardship, preservation, and protection of the environment.
Fields of interest: Performing arts, theater; Environment; Food services; Human services; Children/youth, services.
Type of support: General/operating support.
Limitations: Applications not accepted. Giving primarily in HI. No grants to individuals.
Application information: Contributes only to pre-selected organizations.
Officers and Directors:* Hans Bertram-Nothnagel,* Pres.; Wayne M. Pitluck,* V.P.; Liora Brener, Secy.-Treas.; Janis A. Reischmann, Exec. Dir.
EIN: 133588071
Recent grants for international programs:
717-1 Doctors Without Borders USA, New York, NY, $100,000. For humanitarian relief, emergency relief fund. 2009.
717-2 Save the Children Federation, Westport, CT, $250,000. For alliance cooperation in

emergencies and for continued support for Hahima Institute. 2009.

718

The Honda Foundation

2969 Kalakaua Ave., Ste. 1204
Honolulu, HI 96815-4651
Contact: Paul S. Honda, Pres.

Established in 1989 in HI.
Donor: Paul S. Honda.
Grantmaker type: Independent foundation.
Financial data (yr. ended 12/31/10): Assets, $3,526,058 (M); expenditures, $154,786; qualifying distributions, $140,170; giving activities include $140,170 for grants.
Purpose and activities: Giving primarily for education.
Fields of interest: Arts; Higher education; Education; Health organizations, association; International affairs, goodwill promotion; International affairs.
Type of support: General/operating support; Endowments; Scholarship funds.
Limitations: Applications accepted. Giving primarily in HI. No grants to individuals.
Application information:
　Initial approach: Letter
　Deadline(s): None
Officers: Paul S. Honda, Pres.; Mitsuko Honda, V.P.
Directors: Erika Honda; James A. Honda.
EIN: 990272268

719

The Kosasa Foundation

766 Pohukaina St.
Honolulu, HI 96813-5307
Contact: Paul J. Kosasa, Pres.

Established in 1994 in HI.
Donors: Gloria J. Gainsley; Stephen E. Gainsley; Lisa C. Kosasa; Minnie Kosasa; Sidney S. Kosasa; Paul J. Kosasa; Susan M. Kosasa; Thomas S. Kosasa; Wilfred Nishi; Atlanta/Sosnoff Capital Corp.; Central Pacific Bank; Island Insurance Foundation.
Grantmaker type: Independent foundation.
Financial data (yr. ended 07/31/10): Assets, $14,151,197 (M); gifts received, $2,222,000; expenditures, $576,287; qualifying distributions, $491,000; giving activities include $491,000 for grants.
Purpose and activities: Giving primarily for the arts, education, and children, youth, and social services.
Fields of interest: Arts; Education; Health care; Human services; Children/youth, services.
Limitations: Giving primarily in Honolulu, HI.
Application information: Application form not required.
　Initial approach: Letter
　Deadline(s): None
Officers and Directors:* Paul J. Kosasa,* Pres. and Treas.; Minnie Kosasa,* V.P.; Gloria Gainsley,* V.P.; Susan M. Kosasa,* Secy.; Sidney S. Kosasa, Chair. Emeritus; Thomas S. Kosasa.
EIN: 990313279
Recent grants for international programs:
719-1 Book Bank USA, San Rafael, CA, $10,000. To ship equipment to schools and health centers. 2008.

719-2 Crown Prince Akihito Scholarship Foundation, Honolulu, HI, $25,000. For Scholars. 2008.
719-3 Hawaii International Film Festival, Honolulu, HI, $10,000. For Guest Filmmaker Program. 2008.

720

Pacific and Asian Affairs Council

(also known as PAAC)
1601 East-West Rd., 4th Fl.
Honolulu, HI 96848-1601　(808) 944-7780
FAX: (808) 944-7785;
E-mail: admin@paachawaii.org; URL: http://www.paachawaii.org
Facebook: http://www.facebook.com/group.php?gid=18553101777
Flickr: http://www.flickr.com/photos/paachawaii
Twitter: http://twitter.com/#!/paachawaii
YouTube: http://www.youtube.com/user/paachawaii?feature=mhum

Established in 1954 in HI.
Grantmaker type: Public charity.
Financial data (yr. ended 06/30/10): Revenue, $609,204; assets, $580,821 (M); gifts received, $553,963; expenditures, $509,246; program services expenses, $450,780; giving activities include $18,900 for 12 grants to individuals, and $431,880 for foundation-administered programs.
Purpose and activities: The council serves as the World Affairs Council for the state of Hawaii, and promotes a greater awareness and understanding of foreign affairs issues with special attention to Hawaii's role in the Asia-Pacific region.
Fields of interest: Scholarships/financial aid; International affairs; Asians/Pacific Islanders.
Type of support: Scholarships—to individuals.
Limitations: Giving limited to HI.
Publications: Application guidelines.
Application information:
　Deadline(s): Apr. 18 for Eddie Tangen Award and Paul S. Honda Scholarships
Officers and Governors:* Warren K.K. Luke,* Chair.; Ruth Limtiaco,* Pres.; Mitchell Imanaka,* V.P.; Roland Lagareta,* V.P.; Jean E. Rolles,* V.P.; Dr. Carlos E. Juarez,* Secy.; Arthur Tokin,* Treas.; Lisa Maruyama, Exec. Dir.; David Bramlett; Betty Brow; Robin Campaniano; Tom Chapman; Ralph Cossa; Judith Dawson; Fumiko Halloran; and 17 additional governors.
EIN: 990073501

721

The People's Fund

(also known as Hawaii People's Fund)
949 Kapiolani Blvd., Ste. 100
Honolulu, HI 96814-2128　(808) 593-9969
Contact: Nancy Aleck, Exec. Dir.
E-mail: peoples@lava.net; Tel./FAX: (808) 845-4800; URL: http://www.hawaiipeoplesfund.org
The People's Fund Philanthropy Promise: http://www.ncrp.org/philanthropys-promise/who

Established in 1972 in HI.
Grantmaker type: Public charity.
Financial data (yr. ended 06/30/11): Revenue, $187,361; assets, $349,910 (M); gifts received, $171,255; expenditures, $182,614; giving activities include $63,225 for grants.
Purpose and activities: The fund provides financial support and technical assistance of up to $3,000 to

progressive grassroots social change organizations, especially those considered too small, too new, or too radical by traditional funders. The fund invites applications from organizations and individuals working against discrimination based on race, sex, age, religion, economic status, sexual orientation, ethnic background, illness/disease, or physical or mental disabilities; struggling for the rights of workers; promoting self-determination in low-income and disenfranchised communities; creating alternative arts and media; and promoting peace and responsible U.S. foreign policy. Emergency grants of up to $1,000 are available for response to issues that arise unexpectedly (does not affect eligibility for a grant during regularly scheduled funding cycle).
Fields of interest: Environment; Employment, equal rights; Aging, centers/services; International peace/security; Civil/human rights, LGBTQ; Civil rights, race/intergroup relations; Civil/human rights; Aging.
Type of support: Matching/challenge support; Management development/capacity building; Internship funds; Film/video/radio; General/operating support; Equipment; Emergency funds; Program development; Conferences/seminars; Publication; Seed money; Curriculum development; Research; Technical assistance; Program evaluation.
Limitations: Applications accepted. Giving limited to HI and the Pacific Basin. No support for groups with annual budgets exceeding $150,000 or organizations that have received a grant from the fund in the previous 12 months.
Publications: Application guidelines; Biennial report; Financial statement; Grants list; Informational brochure; Newsletter; Occasional report.
Application information: Faxed and e-mailed applications are accepted for emergency grants. Application forms are available on the fund's Web site. Application form required.
　Initial approach: Letter, telephone, or e-mail
　Copies of proposal: 15
　Deadline(s): Apr. 1 and Oct. 1; None for emergency grants
　Board meeting date(s): Monthly
　Final notification: May and Nov.
Officers and Directors:* Stanford Masui,* Pres.; Judy Kiehm Kern,* V.P.; Sabina Fajardo Swift,* Secy.; Guy Kaulukukui,* Treas.; Nancy Aleck, Exec. Dir.; Chris Conybeare; Charmaine Crockett; Shirley Garcia; Noelani Goodyear-Ka'opua; Kim Coco Iwamoto; Irene Tayay.
Number of staff: 1 full-time professional.
EIN: 237250803

722

Sangham Foundation

P.O. Box 449
Kula, HI 96790-0449
Contact: Christiane Santoro, Treas.
URL: http://www.sanghamfoundation.org/
Grants List: http://www.sanghamfoundation.org/grant-portfolio.php

Established in 2003 in HI.
Donors: The Hecht Family, LLC; Margaret Hecht; 2008 Hecht Trust.
Grantmaker type: Independent foundation.
Financial data (yr. ended 12/31/10): Assets, $6,033,683 (M); expenditures, $402,768; qualifying distributions, $391,899; giving activities

include $368,500 for 30 grants (high: $52,000; low: $1,000).

Purpose and activities: Giving for non-profit organizations committed to protecting water resources, improving water quality, and improving the lives of children.

Fields of interest: Environment, forests; Environment, water resources; Family services; Food services; Youth; Young adults; Children; Children/youth; Girls; Infants/toddlers; Infants/toddlers, female; Infants/toddlers, male; Young adults, female; Young adults, male.

International interests: Africa; India.

Type of support: General/operating support; Continuing support; Income development; Management development/capacity building; Capital campaigns; Program development; Publication; Consulting services; Matching/challenge support.

Limitations: Applications not accepted. Giving primarily in ID and OR.

Publications: Grants list.

Application information: Unsolicited requests for funds not accepted.

Officers and Directors:* Sean Hecht,* Pres.; Dayvin Turchiano,* V.P.; Nicoya Hecht,* Secy.; Christiane Santoro,* Treas.; Amara Hecht; James Christopher Hecht; James Grey Hecht; Jennifer Hecht; Margaret Hecht; Marya Hecht.

Number of staff: 1 part-time professional; 1 full-time support; 1 part-time support.

EIN: 731681596

723
M. M. Scott Scholarship Fund - Gertrude S. Straub Trust Estate

c/o Bank of Hawaii
P.O. Box 3170, Dept. 715
Honolulu, HI 96802-3170
Scholarship address: c/o Hawaii Community Fdn., Scholarships, 1164 Bishop St., Ste. 800, Honolulu, HI 96813, tel.: (808) 566-5570 or toll free (888) 731-3863, e-mail: scholarships@hcf-hawaii.org, URL: http://www.hawaiicommunityfoundation.org

Established in 1966.

Donor: Gertrude S. Straub‡.

Grantmaker type: Independent foundation.

Financial data (yr. ended 03/31/11): Assets, $7,214,190 (M); expenditures, $347,429; qualifying distributions, $244,750; giving activities include $244,750 for grants to individuals.

Purpose and activities: Scholarship grants to HI public high school graduates to attend mainland colleges and major in a subject relating to the better understanding of peace and the promotion of international peace.

Fields of interest: International peace/security; International affairs; International studies.

Type of support: Scholarships—to individuals.

Limitations: Giving primarily to residents of HI.

Publications: Informational brochure (including application guidelines).

Application information: See web site for complete application policies and forms. Applicants must be graduates of public high schools in HI. Application form required.

　Initial approach: Complete online application form
　Copies of proposal: 1
　Deadline(s): Mar. 1
　Board meeting date(s): Apr.
　Final notification: Apr.

Trustee: Bank of Hawaii.

EIN: 996003243

724
The Shaw "U.S." Foundation

c/o Deloitte & Touche, LLP
1132 Bishop St., Ste. 1200
Honolulu, HI 96813-2870

Established in 1995 in DE and HI.

Donor: Sir Run Run Shaw.

Grantmaker type: Independent foundation.

Financial data (yr. ended 12/31/10): Assets, $20,717,903 (M); gifts received, $3,000,000; expenditures, $6,240,113; qualifying distributions, $6,225,815; giving activities include $6,219,575 for 6 grants (high: $3,000,000; low: $643,915).

Purpose and activities: Giving primarily for higher education in China and Hong Kong.

Fields of interest: Engineering school/education; Higher education.

Limitations: Applications not accepted. Giving primarily in Hong Kong and China. No grants to individuals.

Application information: Contributes only to pre-selected organizations.

Officers and Directors:* Mona Fong,* Pres.; Choy Meage,* V.P.; Roger Epstein, Secy.; Jerry Rajakulendran, Treas.; Kit Yee Jenny Li; Venus Choy.

EIN: 990291105

Recent grants for international programs:

724-1 Anhui University of Architecture, Hefei, China, $643,915. For operating support. 2010.

724-2 East China Jiaotong University, Nanchang, China, $643,915. For operating support. 2010.

724-3 Jinan University, Guangzhou, China, $643,915. For operating support. 2010.

724-4 Shaw Prize Foundation, Kowloon, China, $3,000,000. For the Shaw Prize Award. 2010.

724-5 Suzhou University of Science and Technology, Suzhou, China, $643,915. For operating support. 2010.

724-6 Tianjin University of Science and Technology, Tianjin, China, $643,915. For operating support. 2010.

725
Shiraki Memorial Foundation

2020 Vancouver Dr.
Honolulu, HI 96822-2452
Contact: Stanley Togikawa, Secy.
E-mail: stan.togikawa@hawaiiantel.net

Established in 1997 in HI.

Donor: Hilda Kikuno Shiraki Trust.

Grantmaker type: Independent foundation.

Financial data (yr. ended 12/31/10): Assets, $3,619,004 (M); gifts received, $9,520; expenditures, $353,967; qualifying distributions, $223,147; giving activities include $223,147 for 5 grants.

Purpose and activities: Giving primarily for scholarships benefiting students at Southern Baptist seminaries and organizations. Scholarships are limited to Hawaii residents who are attending Southern Baptist seminaries or schools, and who are also Southern Baptist church members.

Fields of interest: Theological school/education; Protestant agencies & churches.

International interests: Southeast Asia.

Type of support: Scholarship funds.

Limitations: Applications accepted. Giving limited to residents of HI. No grants to individuals directly.

Application information: Applications by students for financial aid should be submitted to the seminary they are attending. Application form required.

　Initial approach: Proposal
　Deadline(s): None

Officers: Mary Kong, Pres.; Clyde Kakiuchi, V.P.; Stanley Togikawa, Secy.

Number of staff: None.

EIN: 943274547

726
J. Watumull Fund

(formerly J. Watumull Estate, Inc.)
c/o Watumull Bros., Ltd.
P.O. Box 88296
Honolulu, HI 96830-8296　(808) 971-8800
Contact: Gulab Watumull, Pres.
Application address: Watumull Bldg., 307 Lewers St., 6th Fl., Honolulu, HI 96815; fax: (808) 971-8824

Established in 1980 in HI.

Donors: Jhamandos Watumull‡; Watumull Bros., Ltd.

Grantmaker type: Independent foundation.

Financial data (yr. ended 12/31/10): Assets, $9,859,541 (M); expenditures, $513,791; qualifying distributions, $432,525; giving activities include $432,525 for grants.

Purpose and activities: Support for community development, education, including higher education, social services, and culture; foundation is interested in programs in HI and India.

Fields of interest: Museums; Arts; Higher education; Hospitals (general); Human services; Family services.

International interests: India.

Type of support: General/operating support; Capital campaigns; Building/renovation; Endowments; Program development; Fellowships; Scholarship funds; Scholarships—to individuals.

Limitations: Applications accepted. Giving primarily in HI, and nationally to organizations interested in India.

Application information: Application form not required.

　Initial approach: Letter
　Copies of proposal: 1
　Deadline(s): None
　Board meeting date(s): Apr., June, and Nov.

Officers and Directors:* Gulab Watumull,* Pres.; Jaidev Watumull,* V.P. and Treas.; Khubchand Watumull,* V.P.; Vik Watumull, V.P.; Jyoti Watumull,* Secy.

EIN: 510205431

727
W. T. Yoshimoto Foundation

P.O. Box 17160
Honolulu, HI 96817-0160
Contact: Randy Harris, Pres.

Established in 1978.

Donor: Watson T. Yoshimoto‡.

Grantmaker type: Independent foundation.

Financial data (yr. ended 12/31/10): Assets, $4,699,593 (M); gifts received, $18,881; expenditures, $290,673; qualifying distributions,

$288,502; giving activities include $210,338 for 8 grants (high: $200,000; low: $200).
Purpose and activities: Giving for education and scientific study related to wildlife conservation.
Fields of interest: Higher education; Animals/wildlife, preservation/protection.
International interests: Japan.
Type of support: Program development; General/operating support; Fellowships.
Limitations: Applications not accepted. Giving primarily in HI. No grants to individuals.
Application information: Contributes only to pre-selected organizations.
Officers: Randy A. Harris, Pres.; Wendell W.S. Kam, V.P.; Jeanine V. Davidson, Secy.-Treas.
Number of staff: None.
EIN: 990190570

IDAHO

728
Boise Legacy Constructors Foundation, Inc.

(formerly Washington Group Foundation)
102 S. 17th St., Ste. 200
Boise, ID · 83702-5172
Contact: Marlene M. Puckett, Secy. and Exec. Dir.
FAX: (208) 424-7627;
E-mail: blcfoundation@qwestoffice.net; URL: http://boiselegacyconstructorsfoundation.com/

Established in 1947 in ID as a company-sponsored operating foundation.
Donors: Morrison Knudsen Corp.; Washington Group International, Inc.; WGI Holdings England.
Grantmaker type: Operating foundation.
Financial data (yr. ended 12/31/09): Assets, $6,504,599 (M); gifts received, $59,529; expenditures, $372,844; qualifying distributions, $367,200; giving activities include $117,697 for 176 grants (high: $15,000; low: $13), and $160,000 for 194 grants to individuals (high: $9,500).
Purpose and activities: The foundation supports programs designed to promote health and human services; civic and community; education; and culture and arts; and awards grants to needy individuals to assist with basic necessities.
Fields of interest: Salvation Army; Visual arts; Performing arts; Arts; Education; Environment; Health care; Human services; Community/economic development; Mathematics; Engineering/technology; Science; Public affairs; Youth; Aging; Economically disadvantaged.
Type of support: Sponsorships; Emergency funds; Equipment; Program development; Grants to individuals.
Limitations: Applications not accepted. Giving limited to Boise, ID. No support for political, labor, or fraternal organizations, merchant associations, civic clubs, memberships primarily to lobby, discriminatory organizations, or churches or religious organizations. No grants for trust funds, sporting events, seminars, contests, sponsorships, travel, student trips or tours, books, films, television or video production, research or feasibility studies, or tickets for raffles or other prize-oriented activities.

Application information: Individuals must be referred by a social service agency.
Officers and Directors:* Frank Finlayson,* Pres.; Marlene M. Puckett,* Secy. and Exec. Dir.; Scott Wilson,* Treas.; James McCallum; Matthew Reece; Tony Sander; Dawn Yantek.
Number of staff: 1 full-time professional.
EIN: 826005410
Recent grants for international programs:
728-1 Engineers Without Borders Canada, Toronto, Canada, $16,600. For general fund. 2008.

729
The Good Works Institute, Inc.

P.O. Box 1811
Sun Valley, ID   83353-1811   (208) 726-4421
Contact: Ann M. Down, Pres.
FAX: (208) 622-8003; E-mail address for Ann Down: anndown@yahoo.com

Established in 1999 in ID.
Donor: Ann M. Down.
Grantmaker type: Independent foundation.
Financial data (yr. ended 09/30/09): Assets, $355,599 (M); gifts received, $199,440; expenditures, $442,609; qualifying distributions, $441,712; giving activities include $437,700 for 26 grants (high: $100,000; low: $4,200).
Purpose and activities: Giving in support of the health and welfare of children and the preservation and protection of the environment.
Fields of interest: Environment, land resources; Human services; Education; Health care; Children/youth, services.
Application information: Contact foundation for complete application requirements. Application form not required.
  Initial approach: Letter, e-mail, or fax
  Deadline(s): None
Officers: Ann M. Down, Pres.; Douglas I. Aanestad, Secy.; Sandra Clapp, Treas.
EIN: 820518035
Recent grants for international programs:
729-1 Amistad International, Palo Alto, CA, $12,000. For general support. 2009.
729-2 Friends of SODA, Hailey, ID, $15,000. For general support. 2009.
729-3 Green Empowerment, Portland, OR, $21,000. For general support. 2009.
729-4 Hope Haven, Hope Haven Guatemala, Rock Valley, IA, $18,000. For general support. 2009.
729-5 Little Sisters Fund, Ketchum, ID, $20,000. For general support. 2009.
729-6 Machik, Washington, DC, $100,000. For general support. 2009.
729-7 One HEART, Salt Lake City, UT, $30,000. For general support. 2009.
729-8 Pachamama Alliance, San Francisco, CA, $20,000. For general support. 2009.
729-9 Tributary Fund, Bozeman, MT, $15,000. For general support. 2009.

730
Micron Technology Foundation, Inc.

8000 S. Federal Way, MS 1-407
P.O. Box 6
Boise, ID   83707-0006
Contact: Dee K. Mooney, Exec. Dir.

E-mail: mtf@micron.com; Contact for applications: Kami Faylor, Community Relations Mgr.;
URL: http://www.micron.com/foundation
The Micron Bulletin: http://bulletin.micron.com/
Twitter: http://twitter.com/Micron_Giving

Established in 1999 in ID.
Donors: Micron Technology, Inc.; Micron Semiconductor Products, Inc.; Blue Cross of Idaho Health Service, Inc.
Grantmaker type: Company-sponsored foundation.
Financial data (yr. ended 12/31/10): Assets, $91,696,689; expenditures, $14,321,125; qualifying distributions, $13,752,835; giving activities include $12,902,656 for 256 grants (high: $10,811,345; low: $70), and $91,525 for 29 grants to individuals (high: $6,250; low: $2,500).
Purpose and activities: The foundation supports organizations involved with K-12 and higher education. Special emphasis is directed toward programs designed to promote education in the areas of engineering, science, chemistry, mathematics, and computer science.
Fields of interest: Teacher school/education; Education, research; Elementary/secondary education; Secondary school/education; Higher education; Engineering school/education; Science, formal/general education; Chemistry; Mathematics; Engineering/technology; Computer science.
International interests: Italy; Singapore.
Type of support: Continuing support; Program development; Professorships; Curriculum development; Fellowships; Scholarship funds; Research; Employee volunteer services; Sponsorships; Employee matching gifts; Scholarships—to individuals.
Limitations: Applications accepted. Giving limited to areas of company operations in Boise, ID, Manassas, VA, Avezzano, Italy, and Singapore. No support for religious, fraternal, veterans', or political organizations, discriminatory organizations, or pass-through organizations or private foundations. No grants to individuals (except for scholarships), or for general operating support, luncheons, dinners, auctions, or events, travel or related expenses, courtesy advertisements, endowments, annual campaigns, or lobbying activities.
Publications: Application guidelines.
Application information: University participation in the University Partnerships program is by invitation only. Applications for Chip Camp requires a teacher recommendation. Application form required.
  Initial approach: Download application form and mail proposal and application form to foundation for Community and K-12 Grants; visit website for Chip Camp
  Deadline(s): None; Apr. 15 for Chip Camp
  Final notification: Monthly
Officers and Directors:* Mark D. Duncan,* Chair.; Kipp A. Bedard,* Pres.; Roderick W. Lewis,* Secy.; Tom L. Laws, Treas.; Dee K. Mooney, Exec. Dir.; Jay L. Hawkins.
Number of staff: 8 full-time professional; 2 part-time professional.
EIN: 820516178
Recent grants for international programs:
730-1 Associazione Culturale Harmonia Novissima, Avezzano, Italy, $15,516. 2009.
730-2 Fondazione dell'Universita degli Studi dell'Aquila, Antrodoco, Italy, $15,000. 2009.
730-3 Fondazione Marco Biagi, Modena, Italy, $28,814. 2009.
730-4 Gran Sasso National Laboratory, Assergi, Italy, $17,764. 2009.

730-5 Intercultura, Colle Val d'Elsa, Italy, $16,647. 2009.

730-6 Osaka University, Osaka Daigaku Seikatso Kyoudou Kumiai, Osaka, Japan, $21,962. 2009.

730-7 Taiwan Buddhist Tzu Chi Foundation USA, San Dimas, CA, $33,000. 2009.

730-8 University of Bristol, Bristol, England, $50,000. 2009.

730-9 University of Hyogo, Hyogo, Japan, $11,229. 2009.

730-10 University of Perugia, Dipartimento di Ingegneria Elettronica e dell'Informazione, Perugia, Italy, $27,504. 2009.

731

Micron Technology, Inc. Corporate Giving Program

8000 S. Federal Way
P.O. Box 6
Boise, ID   83716-9632
URL: http://www.micron.com/about/communities/

Grantmaker type: Corporate giving program.
Purpose and activities: As a complement to its foundation, Micron Technology also makes charitable contributions to nonprofit organizations directly. Support is given primarily in areas of company operations in California, Colorado, Idaho, Minnesota, Texas, Utah, and Virginia, and in China, India, Israel, Italy, Japan, Malaysia, the Philippines, Puerto Rico, Singapore, South Korea, Switzerland, Taiwan, and the United Kingdom.
Fields of interest: Engineering/technology; Education; Disasters, preparedness/services; Science.
International interests: China; India; Israel; Italy; Japan; Malaysia; Philippines; Singapore; South Korea; Switzerland; Taiwan; United Kingdom.
Type of support: General/operating support; Employee volunteer services.
Limitations: Giving primarily in areas of company operations in CA, CO, ID, MN, TX, UT, and VA, and in China, India, Israel, Italy, Japan, Malaysia, the Philippines, Puerto Rico, Singapore, South Korea, Switzerland, Taiwan, and the United Kingdom.
Number of staff: 3 full-time professional; 1 full-time support.

732

The Rebholtz Family Foundation, Inc.

1555 Shoreline Dr., 3rd Fl.
Boise, ID   83702-9106

Established in 1996 in ID.
Donors: Dorothy Rebholtz; Agri Beef Co.
Grantmaker type: Independent foundation.
Financial data (yr. ended 09/30/10): Assets, $2,411,113 (M); gifts received, $1,002,300; expenditures, $691,959; qualifying distributions, $669,415; giving activities include $668,500 for 8 grants (high: $400,000; low: $3,500).
Fields of interest: Human services; Foundations (private grantmaking).
Type of support: General/operating support; Grants to individuals.
Limitations: Applications not accepted. Giving primarily in ID and MN.
Application information: Unsolicited requests for funds not accepted.

Officers: Dorothy Rebholtz, Pres.; Teresa A. Cleary, Secy.; Thomas M. Rebholtz, Treas.
EIN: 820496018
Recent grants for international programs:
732-1 Catholic Relief Services, Baltimore, MD, $400,000. For disaster relief. 2010.

733

The Arthur B. Schultz Foundation

P.O. Box 5339
Ketchum, ID   83340-5339   (208) 340-3397
Contact: Erik B. Schultz, Exec. Dir.; Rachael Richards, Prog. Off.; Linn Kincannon, Strategic Rels.
E-mail: info@absfoundation.org; E-mail for Erik B. Schultz: ebs@absfoundation.org. Tel. for Rachael Richards: (208) 841-7351; URL: http://www.absfoundation.org
Facebook: http://www.facebook.com/pages/The-Arthur-B-Schultz-Foundation/103668762718
Grants List: http://www.absfoundation.org/index.php?id=3

Established in 1985 in CA.
Donor: Arthur B. Schultz.
Grantmaker type: Independent foundation.
Financial data (yr. ended 11/30/10): Assets, $6,732,222 (M); gifts received, $465,270; expenditures, $755,630; qualifying distributions, $728,767; giving activities include $341,966 for 16 grants (high: $88,154; low: $200), and $40,000 for loans/program-related investments.
Purpose and activities: The foundation is dedicated to improving the quality of life on earth through supporting small business entrepreneurs, women's empowerment, and disabled mobility solutions.
Fields of interest: Economic development; International relief; Physical therapy; Disabilities, people with; Economically disadvantaged; Physically disabled; Women; Young adults.
International interests: Afghanistan; Cambodia; Central America; East Jerusalem; Israel; Kenya; Vietnam; West Bank/Gaza (Palestinian Territories).
Type of support: General/operating support; Continuing support; Income development; Management development/capacity building; Building/renovation; Equipment; Program development; Program-related investments/loans; Exchange programs; Matching/challenge support.
Limitations: Applications accepted. Giving primarily in the developing world for social microenterprise and disabled mobility solutions. For global understanding, focus is on Israel-Palestine and West-Middle East relations. No support for strictly religious organizations. No grants to individuals.
Publications: Application guidelines; Financial statement; Grants list; Program policy statement; Program policy statement (including application guidelines).
Application information: Electronic submission only. Application guidelines are available on foundation web site; unsolicited inquiries are accepted but unsolicited proposals are not accepted. Other publications available online include grant guidelines, program descriptions and selected grant descriptions. The foundation requires letters of inquiry received by e-mail, with attachments in MS Office (Word, Excel, etc.), and/or Adobe PDF format. Eligible organizations will be invited to submit a full proposal. Application form not required.
   Initial approach: See foundation web site for letter of inquiry guidelines. Electronic submissions only.

Copies of proposal: 1
Deadline(s): Varies
Board meeting date(s): Irregular basis
Final notification: Immediately following board meetings
Officer and Director:* Erik B. Schultz, Exec. Dir.
Number of staff: 1 full-time professional; 2 part-time professional.
EIN: 953980014

734

Harold E. & Phyllis S. Thomas Foundation

12549 W. Bowmont Ct.
Boise, ID   83713-0023
Contact: Judy Rasmussen, Dir.

Established in 1995 in ID.
Donors: Harold Thomas; Phyllis Thomas; Patrick W. Feenstra.
Grantmaker type: Independent foundation.
Financial data (yr. ended 12/31/10): Assets, $0 (M); expenditures, $1,372,638; qualifying distributions, $604,597; giving activities include $604,597 for 26+ grants (high: $50,000).
Purpose and activities: Grants are awarded for Christian evangelical work with particular consideration for missions and organizations engaged in missionary teachings and work. Some giving also for other religious philanthropic organizations.
Fields of interest: Christian agencies & churches
Limitations: Applications not accepted. Giving in the U.S., with emphasis on ID and WA.
Application information: Contributes only to pre-selected organizations. Unsolicited requests for funds not accepted.
Directors: Patrick W. Feenstra; Judy Rasmussen.
Trustees: Dave Hills; James Mitchell; Robert Renfro; Harold E. Thomas; Phyllis S. Thomas; Rick Thomas.
EIN: 820477243
Recent grants for international programs:
734-1 Baptist Mid-Mission, Cleveland, OH, $15,000. 2009.
734-2 Expansion International, Meridian, ID, $20,000. 2009.
734-3 Frontiers, Phoenix, AZ, $15,000. For religious activities. 2009.
734-4 Global Events Group, Dacula, GA, $12,000. For religious activity. 2009.
734-5 Harvest Foundation, Phoenix, AZ, $25,000. For religious activity. 2009.
734-6 Partners International, Spokane, WA, $50,000. For religious activities. 2009.
734-7 Praise International, Meridian, ID, $18,000. For religious activities. 2009.
734-8 TeachBeyond, Bloomingdale, IL, $40,000. For religious activity. 2009.
734-9 TellAsia Ministries, Arvada, CO, $20,000. 2009.
734-10 VisionSynergy, Edmonds, WA, $30,000. For religious activity. 2009.

ILLINOIS

735
Abbott Fund

(formerly Abbott Laboratories Fund)
100 Abbott Park Rd., D379/AP6D
Abbott Park, IL 60064-3500 (847) 937-7075
URL: http://www.abbottfund.org

Incorporated in 1951 in IL.
Donor: Abbott Laboratories.
Grantmaker type: Company-sponsored foundation.
Financial data (yr. ended 12/31/10): Assets,
$205,032,015 (M); gifts received, $80,809,490;
expenditures, $37,934,992; qualifying
distributions, $37,855,725; giving activities include
$21,624,676 for 185 grants (high: $2,770,000;
low: $1,000), $4,587,062 for 2,678 employee
matching gifts, and $9,427,892 for
foundation-administered programs.
Purpose and activities: The fund supports
organizations involved with arts and culture,
education, water conservation, health, HIV/AIDS,
diabetes, tropical diseases, hunger, nutrition,
disaster relief, human services, community
development, science, children, minorities, women,
and economically disadvantaged people. Special
emphasis is directed toward programs designed to
promote science and medical innovation; expand
access to healthcare; and strengthen communities
around the globe.
Fields of interest: Museums; Museums (science/
technology); Arts; Elementary/secondary education;
Higher education; Libraries (public); Education;
Environment, water resources; Medical care,
community health systems; Hospitals (general);
Health care, clinics/centers; Health care, infants;
Health care, rural areas; Reproductive health,
OBGYN/Birthing centers; Public health, physical
fitness; Health care; AIDS; Diabetes; Tropical
diseases; Food services; Food banks; Nutrition;
Disasters, preparedness/services; American Red
Cross; Family services; Homeless, human services;
Human services; Community/economic
development; United Ways and Federated Giving
Programs; Mathematics; Engineering/technology;
Science; Children; Minorities; Women; Economically
disadvantaged.
Type of support: General/operating support;
Continuing support; Management development/
capacity building; Building/renovation; Program
development; Conferences/seminars; Faculty/staff
development; Curriculum development; Scholarship
funds; Research; Sponsorships; Employee matching
gifts.
Limitations: Giving on a national and international
basis in areas of company operations, with
emphasis on AR, CA, CT, Washington, DC, IL, IN,
MA, NH, NY, OH, OR, PR, TX, VA, Afghanistan, Africa,
Haiti, India, Kenya, and Tanzania; giving also to
national and international organizations. No support
for social organizations, political parties or
candidates, sectarian religious organizations, or
trade or business associations. No grants to
individuals, or for scholarships, advertising journals
or booklets, capital campaigns, congresses,
symposiums, or meetings, medical research that
supports Abbott products, political activities,
fundraising events, ticket purchases, sporting
events, travel, trips, tours, or cultural exchange
programs; no employee volunteer services.

Publications: Application guidelines.
Application information: The foundation is currently
not accepting unsolicited applications. Visit website
to view future opportunities for funding.
   Board meeting date(s): Ongoing
Officers and Directors:* John B. Thomas,* Pres.;
Katherine Pickus, V.P.; Cindy Schwab, V.P.; Stephen
R. Fussel; Miles D. White.
Number of staff: 1 full-time professional; 1 part-time
professional; 1 full-time support; 1 part-time
support.
EIN: 366069793
Recent grants for international programs:
735-1 Africa Infectious Disease Village Clinics,
Chicago, IL, $75,000. 2009.
735-2 Africaid Trust, WhizzKids United, Durban,
South Africa, $15,000. 2009.
735-3 African Mothers Health Initiative, Austin, TX,
$25,000. 2009.
735-4 AmeriCares, Stamford, CT, $209,802. 2009.
735-5 Anna Abdallah Secondary School, Masasi,
Tanzania, Zanzibar and Pemba, $200,000.
2009.
735-6 Arzu, Inc., Chicago, IL, $100,000. 2009.
735-7 Baylor College of Medicine International
Pediatric AIDS Initiative, Houston, TX,
$4,901,286. 2009.
735-8 CARE, Chicago Regional Office, Chicago, IL,
$105,000. 2009.
735-9 Catholic Medical Mission Board, New York,
NY, $425,000. 2009.
735-10 Cita International, SEED International,
Golden, CO, $10,000. 2009.
735-11 Corporate Council on Africa, Washington,
DC, $25,000. 2009.
735-12 DAP Foundation, Inglewood, CA, $170,000.
2009.
735-13 Direct Relief International, Santa Barbara,
CA, $487,007. 2009.
735-14 FACE AIDS, Palo Alto, CA, $20,000. 2009.
735-15 Family Health International, Washington
Office, Arlington, VA, $1,500,000. 2009.
735-16 Faraja Trust Fund, Morogoro, Tanzania,
Zanzibar and Pemba, $86,000. 2009.
735-17 Floating Doctors, Topanga, CA, $30,000.
2009.
735-18 Fritz Institute, San Francisco, CA, $30,000.
2009.
735-19 GBCHealth, New York, NY, $15,000. 2009.
735-20 Global AIDS Interfaith Alliance, Larkspur,
CA, $20,000. 2009.
735-21 Global Medical Relief Program, Evanston, IL,
$30,000. 2009.
735-22 Initiative Privee et Communautaire de lutte
contre le VIH/SIDA au Burkina Faso,
Ouagadougou, Burkina Faso, $55,556. 2009.
735-23 Intensive Care Foundation, Melbourne,
Australia, $33,000. 2009.
735-24 Interchurch Medical Assistance, New
Windsor, MD, $150,000. 2009.
735-25 International Conservation Caucus
Foundation, Washington, DC, $50,000. 2009.
735-26 Lesideng Soup Kitchen, Libertyville, IL,
$22,000. 2009.
735-27 Mamta-Health Institute for Mother and
Child, New Delhi, India, $125,790. 2009.
735-28 Muhimbili National Hospital, Dar es Salaam,
Tanzania, Zanzibar and Pemba, $420,000.
2009.
735-29 Oasis for Orphans, Wadsworth, IL, $20,000.
2009.
735-30 Operation Smile International, Norfolk, VA,
$240,950. 2009.

735-31 PRAYAS: Initiatives in Health, Energy,
Learning and Parenthood, Pune, India,
$151,381. 2009.
735-32 Project HOPE - The People-to-People Health
Foundation, Millwood, VA, $825,000. 2009.
735-33 PWDS, Marthandam, India, $340,062.
2009.
735-34 Sarhad Rural Support Programme,
Peshawar, Pakistan, $20,000. 2009.
735-35 Siempre Unidos, Mill Valley, CA, $92,000.
2009.
735-36 TOUCH Foundation, New York, NY,
$920,489. 2009.
735-37 Vasavya Mahila Mandali, Vijayawada, India,
$263,333. 2009.

736
Stuart & Benjamin Abelson Foundation

131 S. Dearborn St., Ste. 2400
Chicago, IL 60603-5577

Established in 2005 in IL.
Grantmaker type: Independent foundation.
Financial data (yr. ended 12/31/10): Assets,
$3,596,163 (M); expenditures, $177,644;
qualifying distributions, $150,000; giving activities
include $150,000 for 10 grants (high: $50,000;
low: $5,000).
Fields of interest: Environment; Human services;
International affairs; Foundations (community).
Limitations: Applications not accepted. No grants to
individuals.
Application information: Unsolicited requests for
funds not accepted.
Trustees: Benjamin Abelson; H. Debra Levin.
EIN: 201704170

737
Alphawood Foundation

(formerly WPWR-TV Channel 50 Foundation)
2451 N. Lincoln Ave., Ste. 205
Chicago, IL 60614-2422 (773) 477-8984
Contact: Agnes Meneses, Prog. Off. and Grants Mgr.
FAX: (773) 477-9019;
E-mail: info@alphawoodfoundation.org

Established in 1991 in IL.
Donors: Fred Eychaner; Newsweb Corp.
Grantmaker type: Independent foundation.
Financial data (yr. ended 02/28/11): Assets,
$159,633,170 (M); expenditures, $15,350,823;
qualifying distributions, $14,793,807; giving
activities include $14,644,810 for 243 grants (high:
$4,000,000; low: $916).
Purpose and activities: The foundation provides
general operating support to nonprofit organizations
whose primary mission involves the arts, arts
education for children, institutional advocacy for
social change, domestic violence intervention/
prevention, and architecture and historical
preservation. Arts education funding is specifically
for children only.
Fields of interest: Family services, domestic
violence; Arts education; Visual arts; Performing
arts, dance; Performing arts, theater; Performing
arts, music; Performing arts (multimedia);
Literature; Historic preservation/historical
societies; Arts.
Type of support: General/operating support.
Limitations: Giving primarily in the metropolitan
Chicago, IL, area and northwestern IN. No support

for religious or fraternal purposes, political campaigns or for public schools. No grants to individuals, or for scholarships, underwriting or tables for events, capital campaigns, or special projects.

Publications: Program policy statement (including application guidelines).

Application information: New proposals from organizations not currently being funded are by invitation only. Prospective new applications for funding must demonstrate a very strong match between their work and the foundation's priorities and guidelines; in order to be invited to apply contact foundation for more information.

  Board meeting date(s): Varies

Officers and Directors:* Fred Eychaner,* Pres. and Treas.; Don Hilliker,* Secy.; Laura Samson, Exec. Dir.; Barbara Richardson.

Number of staff: 2 full-time professional.

EIN: 363805338

Recent grants for international programs:

737-1 Boston University, Boston, MA, $48,568. For Holmul archeology project in Guatemala. 2010.

737-2 Dance Center of Columbia College, Chicago, IL, $137,000. For performances of Cloud Gate Dance Theatre of Taiwan. 2010.

737-3 Give2Asia, San Francisco, CA, $362,000. For advised grant for Asian Harm Reduction Network. 2010.

737-4 Global Network of People Living with HIV-AIDS North America, Silver Spring, MD, $150,000. For general operating support. 2010.

737-5 Trent University, Department of Anthropology, Peterborough, Canada, $193,090. For North Vaca Plateau archeological project in Belize. 2010.

737-6 University of Central Florida Research Foundation, Orlando, FL, $29,893. For Caracol Archaeological Project coordinated through Winter Springs, FL campus. 2010.

737-7 University of Cincinnati Foundation, Cincinnati, OH, $93,094. For water management and agroforestry work in Tikal, Guatemala. 2010.

737-8 University of Louisiana at Lafayette Foundation, Lafayette, LA, $67,600. For Nuevo Cerros archeology project in Guatemala. 2010.

737-9 University of New Mexico Foundation, Albuquerque, NM, $53,571. For Uxbenka archeological project in Belize. 2010.

737-10 Vanderbilt University, Nashville, TN, $78,980. For Cancuen Regional Archeological Project in Guatemala. 2010.

738
American Institute of Indian Studies
1130 E. 59th St.
Chicago, IL 60637-1539 (773) 702-8638
E-mail: aiis@uchicago.edu; *URL:* http://www.indiastudies.org

Established in 1961.
Grantmaker type: Public charity.
Financial data (yr. ended 06/30/10): Revenue, $4,330,349; assets, $7,598,031 (M); gifts received, $4,068,882; expenditures, $3,972,875; giving activities include $257,264 for grants to organizations outside the U.S., and $174,684 for grants to individuals.
Purpose and activities: The institute promotes scholarly studies on India in the U.S. through fellowship support, training, and the maintenance of research facilities.
Fields of interest: Education.

International interests: India.
Type of support: Fellowships; Research; Grants to individuals.
Limitations: Applications accepted. Giving on a national basis.
Publications: Application guidelines; Informational brochure; Newsletter.
Application information: Application fee of $25 must be submitted. Application form required.
  Initial approach: Download application form
  Copies of proposal: 1
  Deadline(s): July 1
  Board meeting date(s): Mar.
  Final notification: Oct.
Officers and Executive Committee:* Frederick M. Asher,* Chair.; Philip Lutendorf,* Pres.; Priti Ramamurthy,* V.P.; John Cort,* Secy.; John Echeveri-Gent,* Treas.; Vinayak Chaturvedi; Sanjay Joshi; Margery Sabin.
Number of staff: 1 full-time professional.
EIN: 236297039

739
Aon Foundation
(formerly Combined International Foundation)
200 East. Randolph, 8th Fl.
Chicago, IL 60601-6419 (312) 381-2422
Contact: Carolyn Barry Frost, Pres. and Treas.
URL: http://www.aon.com/usa/about-aon/community-involvement.jsp

Established in 1984 in IL.
Donor: Aon Corp.
Grantmaker type: Company-sponsored foundation.
Financial data (yr. ended 12/31/10): Assets, $113,806 (M); gifts received, $10,033,943; expenditures, $10,473,390; qualifying distributions, $10,473,390; giving activities include $10,472,240 for 3,084 grants (high: $750,000; low: $25).
Purpose and activities: The foundation supports organizations involved with arts and culture, civic and community affairs, environmental issues, and human services, with a focus on the development of at-risk youth. Special emphasis is directed toward programs designed to promote access to and excellence in education; advance school readiness, academic achievement for school-aged children, and college preparedness and admission for underserved populations; and programs that prepare future workforce and help develop leadership skills.
Fields of interest: Developmentally disabled, centers & services; YM/YWCAs & YM/YWHAs; Athletics/sports, Special Olympics; Youth development, business; Housing/shelter, development; Arts; Elementary/secondary education; Higher education; Business school/education; Education; Environment; Employment; Boys & girls clubs; Youth development; Human services; Community/economic development; Leadership development; Public affairs; Youth; Minorities; Economically disadvantaged.
Type of support: General/operating support; Building/renovation; Endowments; Program development; Scholarship funds; Employee matching gifts.
Limitations: Applications not accepted. Giving on a national basis in areas of company operations, with emphasis on Chicago, IL. No grants for general operating support for secondary or vocational schools.

Application information: Contributes only to pre-selected organizations. The foundation utilizes an invitation only process for giving.
  Board meeting date(s): 3 times per year
Officers and Directors: Carolyn Barry Frost, Pres. and Treas.; Jennifer Kraft, Secy.; Gregory J. Besio; Gregory C. Chase; Christa Davies.
Number of staff: 4
EIN: 363337340
Recent grants for international programs:

739-1 American Ireland Fund, Boston, MA, $10,000. 2009.

739-2 American Israel Education Foundation, Washington, DC, $15,000. To Maintain and Further the Understanding of the Issues Affecting Relations Between the United States and Israel through Information and Education Provided to Public and Private Parties Interested in Such Relations. 2009.

739-3 Business in the Community, London, England, $37,500. For Undertaking Vital Research Into How Greenhouse Gases Could Affect the Marine Life of the Arctic Ocean, Including Some Species That Can Be Described as the Core of Life Our Planet. 2009.

739-4 Chicago Council on Global Affairs, Chicago, IL, $50,000. To Promote Public Understanding of the Foreign Policy of the United States and World Affairs. 2009.

739-5 Chicago Council on Global Affairs, Chicago, IL, $25,000. To Promote Public Understanding of the Foreign Policy of the United States and World Affairs. 2009.

739-6 Foreign Policy Association, New York, NY, $15,000. 2009.

739-7 INSEAD Management Education Foundation, New York, NY, $371,263. For MBA Program. 2009.

739-8 INSEAD Management Education Foundation, New York, NY, $354,580. For MBA Program. 2009.

739-9 INSEAD Management Education Foundation, New York, NY, $331,820. For MBA Program. 2009.

739-10 INSEAD Management Education Foundation, New York, NY, $318,606. For MBA Program. 2009.

739-11 Singer Museum, Laren, Netherlands, $10,000. 2009.

739-12 United World Colleges, Mostar, Bosnia-Herzegovina, $142,000. 2009.

740
Archer Daniels Midland Company Contributions Program
4666 Faries Pkwy.
Decatur, IL 62526-5678 (217) 424-5200
E-mail: responsibility@adm.com; *URL:* http://origin.adm.com/en-US/responsibility/2010CR/Pages/default.aspx

Grantmaker type: Corporate giving program.
Purpose and activities: Archer Daniels Midland makes charitable contributions to nonprofit organizations involved with agricultural development and education. Special emphasis is directed towards educational programs for children and young adults. Support is given on a national and international basis in areas of company operations, with some emphasis on central Illinois.
Fields of interest: Education; Environment; Employment; Agriculture/food, formal/general education; Agriculture, sustainable programs; Food

services; Disasters, preparedness/services; International development; United Ways and Federated Giving Programs; Children; Young adults.
Type of support: General/operating support; Program development; Employee volunteer services; Employee matching gifts.
Limitations: Giving on a national and international basis in areas of company operations, with some emphasis on central IL.

741
The Baxter International Foundation
(formerly The Baxter Allegiance Foundation)
1 Baxter Pkwy.
Deerfield, IL 60015-4625 (847) 948-4605
Contact: Donna Namath, Secy. and Exec. Dir.
FAX: (847) 948-4559; E-mail: fdninfo@baxter.com;
Additional tel.: (847) 948-2000; URL: http://www.baxter.com/about_baxter/sustainability/international_foundation/index.html
Recent Grants: http://www.baxter.com/about_baxter/sustainability/international_foundation/recent_foundation_grants.html

Established in 1982 in IL.
Donors: Baxter International Inc.; American Hospital Supply Corp.; Allegiance Corp.
Grantmaker type: Company-sponsored foundation.
Financial data (yr. ended 12/31/10): Assets, $35,860,913 (M); expenditures, $4,327,792; qualifying distributions, $4,213,482; giving activities include $3,176,477 for 134 grants (high: $164,440; low: $300), and $836,862 for employee matching gifts.
Purpose and activities: The foundation supports programs designed to improve access, quality, and cost-effectiveness of direct healthcare. Special emphasis is directed toward programs designed to expand access to direct healthcare services to disadvantaged or underserved populations in communities where a significant number of Baxter employees live and work.
Fields of interest: Health care, insurance; Dental care; Health care, cost containment; Health care; Substance abuse, services; Mental health/crisis services; Crime/violence prevention, domestic violence; Crime/violence prevention, child abuse; Crime/violence prevention, sexual abuse; Disabilities, people with; Economically disadvantaged.
International interests: Asia; Canada; Europe; Latin America; Mexico.
Type of support: Continuing support; Program development; Employee volunteer services; Employee matching gifts; Employee-related scholarships.
Limitations: Applications accepted. Giving on a national and international basis in areas of company operations, including CA, Cook, Lake, and McHenry County, IL, IN, Asia, Australia, Canada, Europe, Latin America, and Mexico. No support for disease or condition-specific organizations, hospitals, lobby or political organizations, or organizations with a limited constituency, such as fraternal, veterans', or religious organizations. No grant to individuals (except for employee-related scholarships) or for capital or endowment campaigns, non-healthcare activities at educational institutions, general operating support, magazines, professional journals, documentaries, film, video, radio, or website productions, medical missions, advertising, tickets to dinners, benefits, social or fund-raising

events, sponsorships or promotional materials, or research.
Publications: Application guidelines; Grants list.
Application information: Multi-year funding is not automatic. A majority of grants are awarded based on recommendations from Baxter employees. Organizations receiving support are asked to provide a final report. Application form not required.
   Initial approach: Proposal
   Copies of proposal: 1
   Deadline(s): Feb. 13, June 22, and Oct. 11
   Board meeting date(s): Quarterly
   Final notification: Following board meetings
Officers and Directors: Robert J. Hombach, Pres.; Donna Namath, Secy. and Exec. Dir.; Charles W. Thurman, Treas.; Katherine Azuara; Alice J. Campbell; Robert M. Davis; Shaun Newlon; Peter Nicklin; John S. Park.
Number of staff: 1 full-time professional; 1 full-time support.
EIN: 363159396

742
The Bobolink Foundation
(formerly Henry M. & Wendy J. Paulson, Jr. Foundation)
c/o Robbins and Assocs. LLC
333 W. Wacker Dr., Ste. 830
Chicago, IL 60606-1225

Established in 1985 in IL.
Donors: Henry M. Paulson, Jr.; Goldman Sachs & Co.
Grantmaker type: Independent foundation.
Financial data (yr. ended 03/31/10): Assets, $89,926,814 (M); expenditures, $8,309,861; qualifying distributions, $8,146,757; giving activities include $8,117,500 for 46 grants (high: $5,000,000; low: $2,500).
Purpose and activities: Support primarily for Christian Science churches, environmental conservation and wildlife preservation, and higher education.
Fields of interest: Higher education; Business school/education; Environment, natural resources; Animals/wildlife, preservation/protection; Children, services; Protestant agencies & churches.
Limitations: Applications not accepted. Giving primarily in New York, NY, Washington, DC, Arlington, VA, and Boston, MA. No grants to individuals; no loans.
Application information: Contributes only to pre-selected organizations.
Trustees: Amanda Clark Paulson; Henry Merritt Paulson III; Wendy J. Paulson.
EIN: 942988627
Recent grants for international programs:
742-1 African Wildlife Foundation, Washington, DC, $10,000. For unrestricted support. 2009.
742-2 American Bird Conservancy, The Plains, VA, $100,000. For unrestricted support. 2009.
742-3 American Friends of Birdlife International, Washington, DC, $100,000. For unrestricted support. 2009.
742-4 International Crane Foundation, Baraboo, WI, $10,000. For unrestricted support. 2009.
742-5 Nature Conservancy, Arlington, VA, $1,400,000. For unrestricted support. 2009.
742-6 NatureServe, Arlington, VA, $10,000. For unrestricted support. 2009.
742-7 RARE, Arlington, VA, $5,000,000. For unrestricted support. 2009.

742-8 World Land Trust-US, Washington, DC, $100,000. For Antisana. 2009.
742-9 World Wildlife Fund, Washington, DC, $100,000. For unrestricted support. 2009.

743
The Boeing Company Contributions Program
100 N. Riverside
Chicago, IL 60606-1596
URL: http://www.boeing.com/companyoffices/aboutus/community/

Grantmaker type: Corporate giving program.
Purpose and activities: As a complement to its foundation, Boeing also makes charitable contributions to nonprofit organizations directly. Support is given on a national and international basis.
Fields of interest: Arts; Elementary/secondary education; Higher education; Education; Environment; Health care; Substance abuse, services; Family services, domestic violence; Human services; Public affairs; Aging.
International interests: Canada; Australia.
Type of support: Continuing support; Capital campaigns; Building/renovation; Equipment; Emergency funds; Program development; Conferences/seminars; Professorships; Seed money; Fellowships; Scholarship funds; Research; Technical assistance; Consulting services; Employee volunteer services; Loaned talent; Public relations services; Use of facilities; Sponsorships; Employee matching gifts; Donated equipment; In-kind gifts; Matching/challenge support.
Limitations: Giving on a national and international basis in areas of company operations, including AL, AZ, CA, CO, FL, GA, HI, IL, KS, MD, MO, NV, NM, OH, OK, OR, PA, SC, TX, UT, DC, WA, and in Australia, Canada, including Richmond, British Columbia and Winnipeg, Manitoba, and in Africa, and Europe including France, Germany, Great Britain, Spain, Italy, Russia and Commonwealth of Independent States, and Central, Eastern and Northern Europe, and The Middle East and Persian Gulf, including Saudi Arabia, Israel, Turkey, and Latin America including Brazil, and Mexico. No support for political candidates, committees, or organizations, religious organizations, hospital or medical research organizations, or athletic organizations. No grants to individuals, or for travel, agency-sponsored walks, runs, or golf tournaments, auction booklet printing, tickets, or one-time events.
Application information: Contact headquarters for nearest company facility. Printing services are provided on an every-other year basis for educational and awareness materials. The Community and Educational Relations Department handles giving. Application form required.
   Initial approach: Contact nearest company facility for application form
   Copies of proposal: 1
   Deadline(s): None; 6 to 8 weeks prior to need for printing services
   Final notification: 1 to 2 months

744
Howard G. Buffett Foundation
145 N. Merchant St.
Decatur, IL 62523-1442 (217) 423-9286
URL: http://www.thehowardgbuffettfoundation.org/
Multimedia: http://
www.thehowardgbuffettfoundation.org/media/
video

Established in 1999 in IL and NE.
Donors: Warren E. Buffett; Susan T. Buffett†.
Grantmaker type: Independent foundation.
Financial data (yr. ended 12/31/10): Assets, $226,205,520 (M); gifts received, $56,167,099; expenditures, $82,119,685; qualifying distributions, $91,732,545; giving activities include $75,833,873 for 104 grants (high: $10,034,250; low: $624), and $12,731,460 for 2 foundation-administered programs.
Purpose and activities: The primary mission of the foundation is to improve the standard of living and quality of life for the world's most impoverished and marginalized populations. It's focus is on international programs that operate in challenging environments, including areas with reasonable risk, where there is great need for our support. The highest priorities are agricultural resource development for smallholder and subsistence farmers and clean water delivery to vulnerable communities in Africa and Central America. The foundation's second-tier funding includes nutrition-based programs, projects for refugees and internally displaced people, support for journalism-based projects primarily directed at student learning and improved governance, limited work in specific areas of conservation and programs in the local communities in which the foundation has a presence.
Fields of interest: Public health, clean water supply; Education; Environment; Animals/wildlife; Agriculture; Human services.
Limitations: Applications not accepted. Giving primarily in GA, IL and MD, and in England and Italy. No grants to individuals.
Application information: Contributes only to pre-selected organizations.
Officers and Directors: * Howard G. Buffett,* Pres.; Devon G. Buffett,* Exec. V.P. and Secy.; Trisha A. Cook, Treas.; Howard W. Buffett, Exec. Dir.; Susan S. Bell; Nicolette DeBruyn; Erin M. Morgan; Michael D. Walter; Chelsea M. Zillmer.
EIN: 470824756
Recent grants for international programs:
744-1 African Agricultural Technology Foundation, Nairobi, Kenya, $1,000,000. For Development of Water. 2010.
744-2 African American Empowerment Network, Omaha, NE, $20,000. For General Support, Africa. 2010.
744-3 Barefoot Foundation, Santa Monica, CA, $80,000. For operational support. 2010.
744-4 CARE USA, OSA, Atlanta, GA, $4,426,576. For Global Water Initiative in Ethiopia, Kenya, Tanzania. 2010.
744-5 Catholic Relief Services, Baltimore, MD, $10,034,250. For Borderlands Coffee Project-Colombia. 2010.
744-6 Catholic Relief Services, Baltimore, MD, $5,000,000. For Agriculture for Basic Needs (A4N), Central America. 2010.
744-7 Catholic Relief Services, Baltimore, MD, $4,467,979. For Global Water Initiative in Central America. 2010.

744-8 Catholic Relief Services, Baltimore, MD, $2,554,619. For Agriculture for Basic Needs (A4N), Me. 2010.
744-9 Catholic Relief Services, Baltimore, MD, $1,002,394. For Jornaleros SAFE - Mexico. 2010.
744-10 Catholic Relief Services, Baltimore, MD, $607,911. For Breaking the Cycle of Malnutrition. 2010.
744-11 Catholic Relief Services, Baltimore, MD, $574,325. For No-Till Agriculture in Maniema Province, Democratic Republic of Congo. 2010.
744-12 Catholic Relief Services, Baltimore, MD, $374,995. For Camp for Progress (C4P), El Salvador, Nicaraugua. 2010.
744-13 Catholic Relief Services, Baltimore, MD, $293,000. For Central America Maize-Bean Systems/Changing E. 2010.
744-14 Catholic Relief Services, Baltimore, MD, $150,000. For General Support. 2010.
744-15 Cheetah Conservation Fund USA, Alexandria, VA, $100,000. For Extension Officer in Namibia. 2010.
744-16 Cheetah Conservation Fund USA, Alexandria, VA, $66,666. For Extension Officer. 2010.
744-17 Donald Danforth Plant Science Center, Saint Louis, MO, $4,241,365. For Bio-Fortified Sorghum for Africa. 2010.
744-18 Donald Danforth Plant Science Center, Saint Louis, MO, $866,036. For Virus Resistance Cassava for Africa. 2010.
744-19 Donald Danforth Plant Science Center, Saint Louis, MO, $65,050. For field test site for evaluation of improved crops in Africa. 2010.
744-20 Educational Concerns for Hunger Organization, North Fort Myers, FL, $355,910. For Increasing Soil Ecology and Crop Yield. 2010.
744-21 Endangered Wildlife Trust, Johannesburg, South Africa, $122,729. For Metapopulation Strategy for Cheetahs. 2010.
744-22 Foods Resource Bank, Western Springs, IL, $25,000. For operational support. 2010.
744-23 Friends of the Laguna Hom, Dolni Brezany, Czech Republic, $123,317. For Handicap Van for Special Needs Children School. 2010.
744-24 Future Farmers of America Foundation, National, Indianapolis, IN, $100,780. For Global Outreach, Africa. 2010.
744-25 Global Fund for Children, Washington, DC, $477,590. For Child Return Reintegration Program-Guatemala. 2010.
744-26 Global Fund for Children, Washington, DC, $20,000. For General Support. 2010.
744-27 Indiana Institute for Global Health, Indianapolis, IN, $163,440. For AMPATH/World Food Programme, Kenya. 2010.
744-28 International Institute for Environment and Development, London, England, $4,297,442. For GWIwest Africa Cluster. 2010.
744-29 International Justice Mission, Arlington, VA, $69,262. To Investigate trafficking IDP Camps, Kenya. 2010.
744-30 International Maize and Wheat Improvement Center, Mexico City, Mexico, $104,000. For production of basic seed maize in Africa. 2010.
744-31 International Womens Media Foundation, Washington, DC, $220,000. For International Conference of Women Media Leaders. 2010.
744-32 Kids in Need of Defense, Washington, DC, $524,631. For Child Return Reintegration Program-Guatemala. 2010.
744-33 National Democratic Institute for International Affairs, Washington, DC,

$525,000. For Support for the Presidential Debate. 2010.
744-34 National Democratic Institute for International Affairs, Washington, DC, $73,836. For the Presidential Debate. 2010.
744-35 National Geographic Society, Washington, DC, $550,000. For Discretionary Cheetah Funding, Africa. 2010.
744-36 Nature Conservation Trust, South Africa, $900,000. For Development of Plant Science Infrastructure. 2010.
744-37 Nature Conservation Trust, South Africa, $850,000. For Purchase of Equipment for Agricultural Research Project. 2010.
744-38 Nature Conservation Trust, South Africa, $650,000. For Development of Plant Science Infrastructure. 2010.
744-39 Nature Conservation Trust, South Africa, $500,000. For Development of Plant Science Infrastructure. 2010.
744-40 Nature Conservation Trust, South Africa, $420,000. For Development of Plant Science Infrastructure. 2010.
744-41 Nature Conservation Trust, South Africa, $350,000. For Operations/South Africa. 2010.
744-42 Nature Conservation Trust, South Africa, $320,000. For Purchase of Equipment for Agricultural Research Project. 2010.
744-43 Nature Conservation Trust, South Africa, $300,000. For Operations/South Africa. 2010.
744-44 Nature Conservation Trust, South Africa, $200,000. For Purchase of Equipment for Agricultural Research Project. 2010.
744-45 Nature Conservation Trust, South Africa, $80,000. For Development of Plant Science Infrastructure. 2010.
744-46 Nature Conservation Trust, South Africa, $50,000. For Operations/South Africa. 2010.
744-47 Natures Best Photography Fund, Reston, VA, $58,000. For Public Power of Nature Project, Africa. 2010.
744-48 New Venture Fund, Washington, DC, $1,632,000. For Partnership for Seed Development, Africa. 2010.
744-49 New Venture Fund, Washington, DC, $200,000. For Greenhouse Project-Democratic Republic of Congo. 2010.
744-50 Norman Borlaug Foundation, College Station, TX, $167,703. For Farm Management Plan for Ukulima Farm-Africa. 2010.
744-51 ONE Campaign, Washington, DC, $1,500,000. For Agriculture Project-Africa. 2010.
744-52 ONE Campaign, Washington, DC, $150,000. For Endowment for the ONE Africa Award. 2010.
744-53 Pennsylvania State University, State College, PA, $249,685. For development. 2010.
744-54 Survivor Corps, Washington, DC, $39,471. For Recovery and Reconcil San Rafael. 2010.
744-55 TechnoServe, Washington, DC, $200,000. For Helping Smallholder Farmers to Thrive. 2010.
744-56 University of Tennessee, Knoxville, TN, $42,927. For Africa: A Literature Review Orphan. 2010.
744-57 Virunga Fund, Brooklyn, NY, $80,250. For Gorilla Sanctuary-Democratic Republic of Congo. 2010.
744-58 Wildlife Conservation Network, Los Altos, CA, $100,245. For Western Kalahari Cheetah Project. 2010.
744-59 Wildlife Conservation Society, Bronx, NY, $500,000. For COMACO: Community Markets for Conservation, Zambia. 2010.

744-60 Wildlife Conservation Society, Bronx, NY, $72,033. For Community Assessment, Mbomo and Odzala-Kokoua. 2010.

744-61 Wildlife Conservation Society, Bronx, NY, $36,200. For Purchase of Survey Equipment, Tanzania. 2010.

744-62 Wildlife Conservation Society, Bronx, NY, $11,279. For Ethiopian National Conservation Action Plan. 2010.

744-63 World Food Programme, Rome, Italy, $3,997,208. For Purchase for Progress (P4P), El Salvador, Guatemala. 2010.

744-64 World Food Programme, Rome, Italy, $3,600,000. For Fortified Beverage Partnership-Celom. 2010.

744-65 World Food Programme, Rome, Italy, $1,200,000. For School Meals Program, Sierra Leone. 2010.

744-66 World Food Programme, Rome, Italy, $277,953. For Purchase for Progress (P4P), El Salvador, Guatemala. 2010.

744-67 World Food Programme, Rome, Italy, $250,000. For Infra Development for Grain Products. 2010.

744-68 World Food Programme, Rome, Italy, $149,800. For Purchase for Progress (P4P) Feasibility Assessment, Somalia. 2010.

744-69 World Food Programme, Rome, Italy, $20,000. For Fil lthe Cup Campaign-Italy. 2010.

745
Build Cambodia, Inc.
1555 N. Astor St., Apt. 45W
Chicago, IL 60610-5787   (312) 423-6689
FAX: (773) 304-2888;
E-mail: info@buildcambodia.org; Additional tel.: (773) 306-8159; URL: http://www.buildcambodia.org

Established in 2006 in IL.
Donor: Ed Bachrach.
Grantmaker type: Public charity.
Financial data (yr. ended 12/31/10): Revenue, $119,785; assets, $42,953 (M); gifts received, $119,780; expenditures, $92,379; program services expenses, $84,820; giving activities include $58,325 for 3 grants (high: $40,910; low: $5,500), and $26,495 for foundation-administered programs.
Purpose and activities: The organization is dedicated to helping Cambodians build their lives and society and ensuring that a steady flow of attention and resources for worthwhile efforts in Cambodia.
Fields of interest: International affairs; International democracy & civil society development.
International interests: Cambodia.
Limitations: Giving primarily to Concord, MA.
Board Members: Susan Axelrod; Ed Bachrach; Laurie Bachrach; Lori Jackson; Kathryn Lucatelli; David Prichard; Sophally Showalter; Kheang Un.
EIN: 204864316

746
Gerald and Janet Carrus Foundation
c/o Bank of America, N.A.
231 S. LaSalle St.
Chicago, IL 60697-0001   (312) 828-1029
Contact: Kristin Carlson Vogen

Established in 1997.

Donors: Janet Carrus; Gerald Carrus†.
Grantmaker type: Independent foundation.
Financial data (yr. ended 12/31/10): Assets, $11,428,053 (M); expenditures, $492,965; qualifying distributions, $381,615; giving activities include $381,615 for grants.
Fields of interest: Health organizations; Arts; Human services; Children, services; International relief.
Limitations: Giving primarily in NY. No grants to individuals.
Application information: Application form not required.
　Initial approach: Letter of inquiry
　Deadline(s): None
　Final notification: Positive responses only
Officers and Directors:* Janet Carrus,* Pres.; Irving Sitnick,* V.P. and Secy.; Cathey Romano, Exec. Dir.; Robin Miller; Michelle Peperone; Renee Peperone.
EIN: 133929249

747
Casten Family Foundation, Inc.
8 E. 3rd St.
Hinsdale, IL 60521-4401   (630) 321-1095
Contact: Judith A. Casten, Pres.

Established in 2000 in NY.
Donor: Michael Weiser.
Grantmaker type: Independent foundation.
Financial data (yr. ended 12/31/10): Assets, $3,194,874 (M); gifts received, $1,500; expenditures, $389,535; qualifying distributions, $357,407; giving activities include $357,407 for grants.
Fields of interest: United Ways and Federated Giving Programs; International affairs, formal/general education; Education; Arts; Museums (children's); Human services.
Application information: Application form required.
　Initial approach: Proposal
　Deadline(s): None
Officers: Judith A. Casten, Pres.; Thomas R. Casten, V.P.
EIN: 134074089

748
Caterpillar Foundation
100 N.E. Adams St.
Peoria, IL 61629-1480   (309) 675-5941
Contact: Jennifer Zammuto, V.P.
E-mail: Foundation@cat.com; Additional tel.: (309) 675-4464; URL: http://www.cat.com/foundation

Established in 1952 in IL.
Donor: Caterpillar Inc.
Grantmaker type: Company-sponsored foundation.
Financial data (yr. ended 12/31/10): Assets, $32,137,196 (M); gifts received, $35,986,700; expenditures, $35,995,143; qualifying distributions, $35,992,935; giving activities include $35,807,264 for 1,138 grants (high: $4,000,000; low: $50).
Purpose and activities: The foundation supports programs designed to advance knowledge and education; protect the environment and conservation of resources; and promote access to basic human needs.
Fields of interest: Microfinance/microlending; Breast cancer; Hospitals (general); Zoos/zoological societies; Environment, land resources;

Environment, forests; Media/communications; Media, television; Museums; Arts; Higher education; Education; Environment, natural resources; Environment, water resources; Environment; Health care; Youth development, business; Human services; Community/economic development; United Ways and Federated Giving Programs; Mathematics; Engineering/technology; Public policy, research; Public affairs; Economically disadvantaged.
Type of support: General/operating support; Annual campaigns; Capital campaigns; Building/renovation; Equipment; Program development; Curriculum development; Scholarship funds; Employee volunteer services; Sponsorships; Employee matching gifts; Matching/challenge support.
Limitations: Applications accepted. Giving primarily in areas of company operations on a national basis, with some emphasis on IL. No support for fraternal organizations or exclusive membership societies, hospitals, political action committees or candidates, private foundations, or religious organizations not of direct benefit to the entire community. No grants to individuals, or for graduate student scholarships or fellowships, capital campaigns, building construction, debt reduction, development or production of books, videos, films, or television programs, research papers or articles in professional journals, endowments, general operating or agency programs funded by the United Way, political causes, research, sponsorships, tickets, or advertising for fund-raising, or travel; no product or service donations; no loans.
Publications: Application guidelines; Corporate giving report (including application guidelines); Program policy statement.
Application information: Application form required.
　Initial approach: Complete online application
　Copies of proposal: 1
　Deadline(s): None
　Board meeting date(s): Dec. 1
　Final notification: 2 months
Officers and Directors:* Douglas R. Oberhelman,* Pres.; E. J. Rapp,* Exec. V.P.; W. N. Ball, V.P.; J. A. Baumgartner,* V.P.; M. H. Collier, V.P.; K. S. Hauer, V.P.; Jennifer L. Zammuto, V.P.; C. D. Patterson III, Secy.; Robin D. Beran, Treas.
EIN: 376022314
Recent grants for international programs:
748-1 Africa University, Mutare, Zimbabwe, $20,000. 2009.
748-2 Build Change, Mill Valley, CA, $100,000. 2009.
748-3 Bulembu International, Vancouver, Canada, $230,000. 2009.
748-4 Cambridge in America, New York, NY, $25,000. 2009.
748-5 Center for Global Development, Washington, DC, $25,000. 2009.
748-6 CHF International, Silver Spring, MD, $252,000. 2009.
748-7 CHF International, Silver Spring, MD, $226,000. 2009.
748-8 Council on Foreign Relations, New York, NY, $15,000. 2009.
748-9 Engineers Without Borders USA, Boulder, CO, $37,500. 2009.
748-10 Friends of the World Food Program, Washington, DC, $100,000. 2009.
748-11 Give2Asia, San Francisco, CA, $100,000. 2009.
748-12 Give2Asia, San Francisco, CA, $65,000. 2009.

748-13 Give2Asia, San Francisco, CA, $50,835. 2009.

748-14 Give2Asia, San Francisco, CA, $50,000. 2009.

748-15 Give2Asia, San Francisco, CA, $50,000. 2009.

748-16 Give2Asia, San Francisco, CA, $50,000. 2009.

748-17 Give2Asia, San Francisco, CA, $50,000. 2009.

748-18 Give2Asia, San Francisco, CA, $50,000. 2009.

748-19 Give2Asia, San Francisco, CA, $50,000. 2009.

748-20 Give2Asia, San Francisco, CA, $50,000. 2009.

748-21 Give2Asia, San Francisco, CA, $50,000. 2009.

748-22 Give2Asia, San Francisco, CA, $50,000. 2009.

748-23 Give2Asia, San Francisco, CA, $50,000. 2009.

748-24 Give2Asia, San Francisco, CA, $49,963. 2009.

748-25 Give2Asia, San Francisco, CA, $49,175. 2009.

748-26 Give2Asia, San Francisco, CA, $48,940. 2009.

748-27 Give2Asia, San Francisco, CA, $47,808. 2009.

748-28 Give2Asia, San Francisco, CA, $46,623. 2009.

748-29 Give2Asia, San Francisco, CA, $40,000. 2009.

748-30 Give2Asia, San Francisco, CA, $22,500. 2009.

748-31 Hope for Tomorrow Foundation, Williamsville, NY, $10,000. 2009.

748-32 International Youth Foundation, Baltimore, MD, $256,079. 2009.

748-33 King Baudouin Foundation United States, New York, NY, $45,000. 2009.

748-34 King Baudouin Foundation United States, New York, NY, $45,000. 2009.

748-35 King Baudouin Foundation United States, New York, NY, $45,000. 2009.

748-36 King Baudouin Foundation United States, New York, NY, $40,500. 2009.

748-37 King Baudouin Foundation United States, New York, NY, $40,000. 2009.

748-38 King Baudouin Foundation United States, New York, NY, $40,000. 2009.

748-39 King Baudouin Foundation United States, New York, NY, $40,000. 2009.

748-40 King Baudouin Foundation United States, New York, NY, $38,000. 2009.

748-41 King Baudouin Foundation United States, New York, NY, $30,000. 2009.

748-42 King Baudouin Foundation United States, New York, NY, $25,000. 2009.

748-43 King Baudouin Foundation United States, New York, NY, $14,000. 2009.

748-44 Mano a Mano Medical Resources, Mendota Heights, MN, $225,000. 2009.

748-45 Northern Alberta Institute of Technology, Edmonton, Canada, $200,000. 2009.

748-46 Northern Alberta Institute of Technology, Edmonton, Canada, $200,000. 2009.

748-47 Opportunity International, Oak Brook, IL, $1,000,000. 2009.

748-48 Pan American Development Foundation, Washington, DC, $35,000. 2009.

748-49 Pan American Development Foundation, Washington, DC, $15,000. 2009.

748-50 Queens University of Belfast, Friends of the, Washington, DC, $25,008. 2009.

748-51 Resource Foundation, New York, NY, $50,000. 2009.

748-52 Resource Foundation, New York, NY, $50,000. 2009.

748-53 Resource Foundation, New York, NY, $50,000. 2009.

748-54 Resource Foundation, New York, NY, $49,878. 2009.

748-55 Resource Foundation, New York, NY, $45,000. 2009.

748-56 Resource Foundation, New York, NY, $43,500. 2009.

748-57 Resource Foundation, New York, NY, $40,000. 2009.

748-58 Room to Read, San Francisco, CA, $250,000. 2009.

748-59 Sir Sandford Fleming College, Peterborough, Canada, $15,000. 2009.

748-60 Tropical Forest Foundation, Alexandria, VA, $85,000. 2009.

748-61 United States Indonesia Society, Washington, DC, $100,000. 2009.

748-62 United States Indonesia Society, Washington, DC, $100,000. 2009.

748-63 University of Alberta Foundation USA, Chicago, IL, $150,000. 2009.

748-64 VNB Nationale Bedevaarten, Hertogenbosch, Netherlands, $15,000. 2009.

748-65 World Affairs Council of Peoria, Peoria, IL, $10,000. 2009.

748-66 World Resources Institute, Washington, DC, $1,500,000. 2009.

749
CF Industries, Inc. Corporate Giving Program
c/o Community Rels.
4 Pkwy. N., Ste. 400
Deerfield, IL 60015-2590
URL: http://www.cfindustries.com/community_relations.html

Grantmaker type: Corporate giving program.
Purpose and activities: CF Industries makes charitable contributions to nonprofit organizations involved with K-12 education, the environment, youth development, and human services. Support is given primarily in areas of company operations in Florida, Iowa, Illinois, Mississippi, and Oklahoma, and in Canada.
Fields of interest: Elementary/secondary education; Environment; Youth development; Human services; General charitable giving.
International interests: Canada.
Type of support: General/operating support; Program development; Grants to individuals.
Limitations: Giving primarily in areas of company operations in FL, IA, IL, MS, and OK, and in Canada.
Application information:
  Initial approach: Contact nearest plant distribution facility for Classroom Minigrant Program

750
Nicholas and Eleanor Chabraja Foundation
2 Westminster Pl., Ste. 201
Lake Forest, IL 60045-1804

Established in 2004 in VA.

Donors: Nicholas Chabraja; Eleanor Chabraja.
Grantmaker type: Independent foundation.
Financial data (yr. ended 12/31/10): Assets, $6,362,192 (M); gifts received, $484,843; expenditures, $295,034; qualifying distributions, $256,693; giving activities include $245,000 for 8 grants (high: $65,000; low: $10,000).
Fields of interest: Christian agencies & churches; Museums (art); Performing arts, theater; Historic preservation/historical societies; Theological school/education; Food services; International affairs, public policy.
Limitations: Applications not accepted. Giving primarily in IL, NY and VA. No grants to individuals.
Application information: Unsolicited requests for funds not accepted.
Officers: Nicholas Chabraja, Pres. and Treas.; Eleanor Chabraja, V.P. and Secy.
EIN: 202020571

751
Circle of Love Foundation
4804 Innsbruck Dr.
Rockford, IL 61114-7312 (815) 282-9243
E-mail: information@circleoflovefoundation.net;
URL: http://www.circleoflovefoundation.net

Established in 1995.
Grantmaker type: Public charity.
Financial data (yr. ended 12/31/10): Revenue, $380,650; assets, $42,451 (M); gifts received, $364,400; expenditures, $378,810; program services expenses, $369,198; giving activities include $91,565 for grants to organizations outside the U.S.
Purpose and activities: The foundation supports faith-based current ministry partners and provides medical, physical, and spiritual comfort to underdeveloped countries.
Fields of interest: Health care; Human services.
International interests: Guatemala; Southern Africa; Sri Lanka; Sudan; Thailand.
Type of support: Continuing support; Emergency funds; Grants to individuals; In-kind gifts.
Limitations: Applications not accepted. Giving on an international basis.
Publications: Annual report; Financial statement; Informational brochure; Newsletter.
Application information: Contributes only to pre-selected organizations.
  Board meeting date(s): Monthly
Officers and Directors: David Laib,* Chair.; Helen Laib,* Pres.; Janet Lei,* Secy.; Thomas Munson, Treas.; Dena Koehler; Atef Tawfik; Rev. Sharon Theroux; Mary Linda Wing; Martha Zuniga.
EIN: 364064032

752
Communitas Charitable Trust
c/o Harold M. Baron
5555 N. Sheridan Rd., Ste. 1011
Chicago, IL 60640-1624

Established in 1991 in IL.
Donors: Harold M. Baron; Paula L. Baron.
Grantmaker type: Independent foundation.
Financial data (yr. ended 12/31/10): Assets, $1,987,273 (M); expenditures, $242,883; qualifying distributions, $242,166; giving activities include $222,935 for 16 grants (high: $87,035; low: $1,500).

Fields of interest: Jewish agencies & synagogues; Arts; Education; Human services; International peace/security; International affairs; Public affairs.
Type of support: General/operating support.
Limitations: Applications not accepted. Giving primarily in IL. No grants to individuals.
Application information: Unsolicited requests for funds not accepted.
Trustees: Harold M. Baron; Paula L. Baron.
EIN: 366947593

753
The Conduit Foundation
c/o Strategic Philanthropy
1700 W. Irving Park Rd., No. 203
Chicago, IL 60613-2599 (773) 360-5998
URL: http://www.theconduitfoundation.org

Established in 2002.
Donor: Oak Tree Trust.
Grantmaker type: Independent foundation.
Financial data (yr. ended 12/31/10): Assets, $25,139,037 (M); expenditures, $6,114,168; qualifying distributions, $5,944,000; giving activities include $5,944,000 for 8 grants (high: $3,500,000; low: $2,000).
Purpose and activities: Giving primarily for Jewish education.
Fields of interest: Elementary/secondary education.
Limitations: Applications not accepted. Giving primarily in Westchester, NY. No grants to individuals.
Application information: Contributes only to pre-selected organizations.
Officers: William M. Doyle, Jr., Pres. and Secy.; Dennis J. Kelly, Treas.; Betsy Brill, Exec. Dir.
EIN: 043684566
Recent grants for international programs:
753-1 Israel Renaissance Fund, Brooklyn, NY, $50,000. 2010.
753-2 Shalem Foundation, New York, NY, $3,500,000. 2010.

754
Cooper Family Foundation
(formerly Richard W. Cooper Foundation)
611 Enterprise Dr.
Oak Brook, IL 60523-8811

Established in 1969 in IL.
Donors: Richard H. Cooper; Cooperfund, Inc.
Grantmaker type: Independent foundation.
Financial data (yr. ended 12/31/10): Assets, $9,580,582 (M); expenditures, $172,768; qualifying distributions, $165,700; giving activities include $165,700 for 9 grants (high: $126,000; low: $100).
Fields of interest: Health organizations, association; Lupus research; Human services; International affairs, foreign policy.
Type of support: General/operating support.
Limitations: Applications not accepted. Giving primarily in IL, with emphasis on Chicago. No grants to individuals.
Application information: Unsolicited requests for funds not accepted.
EIN: 237024516

755
Crane Foundation, Inc.
1908 Kingsbrook Ct., Ste. B
Wheaton, IL 60187-3199

Established in 1951 in MO.
Donor: Crane Co.
Grantmaker type: Company-sponsored foundation.
Financial data (yr. ended 12/31/10): Assets, $5,736,776 (M); expenditures, $238,343; qualifying distributions, $167,954; giving activities include $167,954 for grants.
Purpose and activities: The foundation supports organizations involved with performing arts, K-12 and higher education, health, recreation, human services, philanthropy and voluntarism, and minorities.
Fields of interest: Recreation; Performing arts; Elementary/secondary education; Higher education; Health care; Children/youth, services; Child development, services; Family services; Human services; Philanthropy/voluntarism; Minorities.
International interests: Canada.
Type of support: General/operating support; Continuing support; Annual campaigns; Scholarship funds; Employee matching gifts.
Limitations: Applications not accepted.
Application information: Unsolicited requests for funds not accepted.
Officers and Directors:* Robert S. Evans,* Chair.; Eric C. Fast,* Pres.; Augustus I. DuPont,* V.P., Secy., and Genl. Counsel; T.J. MacCarrick,* V.P.; Elise M. Kopczick, V.P.; T.M. Noonan, V.P.; A.L. Krawitt,* Treas.
EIN: 436051752

756
Arie and Ida Crown Memorial
222 N. LaSalle St., Ste. 2000
Chicago, IL 60601-1109 (312) 750-6671
Contact: Caren Yanis, Exec. Dir.
FAX: (312) 984-1499;
E-mail: aicm@crown-chicago.com; URL: http://www.crownmemorial.org/

Incorporated in 1947 in IL.
Donor: members of the Crown family.
Grantmaker type: Independent foundation.
Financial data (yr. ended 12/31/10): Assets, $470,489,043 (M); gifts received, $7,653,682; expenditures, $26,155,965; qualifying distributions, $23,579,806; giving activities include $22,895,293 for 580 grants (high: $1,000,000; low: $3).
Purpose and activities: Giving primarily for arts and culture, civic affairs, education, the environment, health, human services, and Jewish causes.
Fields of interest: Environment; Arts; Education; Health care; Human services; Public affairs; Jewish agencies & synagogues.
International interests: Israel.
Type of support: General/operating support; Continuing support; Annual campaigns; Capital campaigns; Building/renovation; Equipment; Endowments; Program development; Professorships; Fellowships; Scholarship funds; Employee matching gifts; Matching/challenge support.
Limitations: Applications accepted. Giving primarily in metropolitan Chicago, IL, with some giving in NY. No support for government-sponsored programs, or to organizations with budgets under $200,000. No

grants to individuals, or for film, video, exhibitions, conference, associations or coalitions.
Publications: Application guidelines.
Application information: Application guidelines available on foundation web site. Application form not required.
  Initial approach: E-mail letter of intent (2 pages maximum)
  Copies of proposal: 1
  Deadline(s): See web site deadlines for specific program areas
  Board meeting date(s): Spring and fall
Officers and Directors:* Susan Crown, Pres.; A. Steven Crown,* V.P.; James S. Crown,* V.P.; Rebecca Crown,* V.P.; William Crown,* V.P.; Charles Goodman, V.P.; Barbara Goodman Manilow,* V.P.; Sara Crown Star,* V.P.; Arnold Weber,* V.P.; Lester Crown, Treas.; Caren Yanis, Exec. Dir.
Number of staff: 6 full-time professional.
EIN: 366076088
Recent grants for international programs:
756-1 Acumen Fund, New York, NY, $10,000. 2009.
756-2 American Committee for the Weizmann Institute of Science, New York, NY, $25,000. 2009.
756-3 American Foreign Policy Council, Washington, DC, $25,000. 2009.
756-4 American Friends of the Israel Democracy Institute, Atlanta, GA, $30,000. 2009.
756-5 American Friends of the Israel Museum, New York, NY, $100,000. 2009.
756-6 American Friends of the Israel Museum, New York, NY, $15,000. 2009.
756-7 American Friends of the Tel Aviv University, New York, NY, $15,000. 2009.
756-8 American Israel Education Foundation, Washington, DC, $100,000. 2009.
756-9 American Jewish World Service, New York, NY, $25,000. 2009.
756-10 Bar-Ilan University in Israel, New York, NY, $200,000. 2009.
756-11 Birthright Israel Foundation, New York, NY, $100,000. 2009.
756-12 Bridges of Understanding Foundation, Washington, DC, $25,000. 2009.
756-13 Chicago Council on Global Affairs, Chicago, IL, $100,000. 2009.
756-14 Chicago Council on Global Affairs, Chicago, IL, $100,000. 2009.
756-15 Conservation International, Arlington, VA, $400,000. 2009.
756-16 Council on Foreign Relations, New York, NY, $15,000. 2009.
756-17 Elie Wiesel Foundation for Humanity, New York, NY, $250,000. 2009.
756-18 Global Fund for Children, Washington, DC, $100,000. 2009.
756-19 Hebrew University of Jerusalem, Jerusalem, Israel, $35,000. 2009.
756-20 Hebrew University of Jerusalem, Jerusalem, Israel, $10,000. 2009.
756-21 Human Rights Watch, New York, NY, $25,000. 2009.
756-22 International Rescue Committee, New York, NY, $10,000. 2009.
756-23 Israel Childrens Centers, Deerfield Beach, FL, $10,000. 2009.
756-24 Jewish Institute for National Security Affairs, Washington, DC, $20,000. 2009.
756-25 National Strategy Forum, Chicago, IL, $25,000. 2009.

756-26 Tom Lantos Foundation for Human Rights and Justice, Concord, NH, $10,000. 2009.

756-27 United Nations Foundation, Washington, DC, $10,000. 2009.

756-28 WHITIA, Chicago, IL, $25,000. 2009.

756-29 World Wildlife Fund, Washington, DC, $40,000. 2009.

757
John Deere Foundation
1 John Deere Pl.
Moline, IL 61265-8010
Contact: John W. Bustle, V.P.
FAX: (309) 748-7953;
E-mail: bustlejohnw@johndeere.com; URL: http://www.deere.com/en_US/globalcitizenship/socialinvestment/index.html

Incorporated in 1948 in IL.
Donor: Deere & Co.
Grantmaker type: Company-sponsored foundation.
Financial data (yr. ended 10/31/10): Assets, $120,494,329 (M); gifts received, $60,000,000; expenditures, $8,020,752; qualifying distributions, $7,934,020; giving activities include $7,934,020 for 584 grants (high: $1,000,000; low: $50), and $166,654 for 1 foundation-administered program.
Purpose and activities: The foundation supports programs designed to promote education; community betterment through community development, human services, and arts and culture; and solutions for world hunger through agricultural development that results in sustainable food supplies and economic growth in underdeveloped countries.
Fields of interest: Disasters, preparedness/services; Arts; Higher education; Agriculture, sustainable programs; Food services; Food banks; Agriculture/food; Youth development, business; American Red Cross; Human services; Community development, business promotion; Community development, small businesses; Community/economic development; Mathematics; Engineering/technology; Science; Minorities; Economically disadvantaged.
International interests: Africa; Global programs; India.
Type of support: General/operating support; Continuing support; Annual campaigns; Building/renovation; Emergency funds; Program development; Scholarship funds; Research; Employee matching gifts.
Limitations: Applications accepted. Giving primarily in areas of company operations in Atlanta and Augusta, GA, Des Moines, Dubuque, Iowa Quad cities, Ottumwa, and Waterloo, IA, Quad City Region, IL, Coffeyville and Greater Kansas City, KS, Thibodaux, LA, Cary and Fuquay-Varina, NC, Fargo, ND, Greeneville, TN, and Horicon and Madison, WI; giving also to Africa and global programs. No support for religious organizations, athletic organizations, political organizations, foundations, tax-supported organizations, or fraternal organizations or sororities. No grants to individuals, or for sports programs, political campaigns, advertising, or marketing; no loans; no in-kind equipment donations.
Publications: Application guidelines; Corporate report.
Application information: Application form required.
Initial approach: Complete online eligibility quiz and application
Deadline(s): None

Board meeting date(s): Quarterly
Final notification: 30 days following board meetings
Officers and Directors:* Samuel R. Allen, Chair.; Mara L. Sovey, Pres.; John W. Bustle, V.P.; Gregory R. Noe, Secy.; Dennis R. Schwartz, Treas.; Frances B. Emerson; David C. Everitt; James M. Field; James R. Jenkins; Marie Z. Ziegler.
Number of staff: 2.5 full-time professional.
EIN: 366051024

758
N. Demos Foundation, Inc.
c/o The Northern Trust Co.
50 S. LaSalle St.
Chicago, IL 60675-0001   (312) 444-7922
Contact: Carrie M. Stanton, Secy.

Incorporated in 1964 in NY.
Donor: Nicholas Demos‡.
Grantmaker type: Independent foundation.
Financial data (yr. ended 06/30/11): Assets, $3,544,485 (M); expenditures, $206,836; qualifying distributions, $160,850; giving activities include $160,850 for grants.
Purpose and activities: Grants for educational projects, social work activities, and health care assistance in Greece.
Fields of interest: Education; Children/youth, services.
International interests: Greece.
Type of support: General/operating support; Scholarship funds.
Limitations: Applications accepted. Giving limited to Greece. No grants to individuals.
Publications: Application guidelines.
Application information: Application form required.
Initial approach: Letter
Copies of proposal: 1
Deadline(s): Sept. 1
Board meeting date(s): Fall
Final notification: Dec. 31
Officers: Robert F. Reusche, Chair.; Charles Gray, Pres.; Carrie M. Stanton, Secy.; R. Hugh Magill, Treas.
Directors: Mrs. Desi Bakalis; Elizabeth Gebhard; Metropolitan Iakovos; Hon. Paul C. Lillios.
EIN: 366165689

759
Peter Deyneka Russian Ministries, Inc.
P.O. Box 496
Wheaton, IL 60187-0496   (630) 462-1739
FAX: (630) 690-2976;
E-mail: info@russian-ministries.org; Toll-free tel.: (888) 462-1739; international address (Canada office): P.O. Box 511, Niagara Falls, ON L2E 6V2, tel.: (905) 354-3540, email: pdrm@bellnet.ca; international address (UK office): 28 Maple Ct., The Gables, Clarendon Park, Oxshott, Surrey, KT22 OSD, England, tel.: (011-44) 0137284418, email: sdhsib@aol.com; URL: http://www.russian-ministries.org
Facebook: http://www.facebook.com/pages/Peter-Deyneka-Russian-Ministries/203550186579
YouTube: http://www.youtube.com/user/RussianMinistries

Established in 1991 in IL.
Grantmaker type: Public charity.

Financial data (yr. ended 09/30/10): Revenue, $1,714,649; assets, $1,609,511 (M); gifts received, $1,672,951; expenditures, $2,077,621; program services expenses, $1,471,322; giving activities include $22,600 for grants, and $1,024,415 for grants to organizations outside the U.S.
Purpose and activities: The organization works to promote indigenous evangelism, church-planning, church growth, and humanitarian aid in the former Soviet Union by developing creative and strategic partnerships between nationals and Western Christians.
Fields of interest: Christian agencies & churches; Human services.
International interests: Ukraine; Russia; Moldova; Belarus.
Limitations: Giving on a national basis, and to Belarus, Moldova, Russia, and Ukraine.
Officers and Directors:* Jason Dorsey, Chair.; Anita Deyneka,* Pres.; Wayne Shephard, Secy.; Barry Gardner,* Treas.; Ron Braund; Richard Scheuerman*; Alex Kaye.
EIN: 351835273

760
Divac Children's Foundation
(formerly Group Seven Children's Foundation Corporation, also known as Humanitarian Organization Divac Corporation)
18704 S. 114th Ave.
Mokena, IL 60448-8209   (310) 593-0920
Contact: Ralph Flores, Jr., Dir.
FAX: (310) 943-3100; E-mail: info@divac.org; Toll-free tel.: (8888) 348-2212; URL: http://www.divac.com/

Established in 1992.
Grantmaker type: Public charity.
Financial data (yr. ended 12/31/09): Revenue, $277,849; assets, $256 (M); gifts received, $277,849; expenditures, $374,330; giving activities include $277,010 for grants.
Purpose and activities: The foundation provides care for children who suffer from the isolation, poverty, and displacement inherent to the break-up of a country.
Fields of interest: International affairs; Children, services.
Type of support: Grants to individuals.
Directors: Alex Dimitrijevic; Vlade Divac.
EIN: 320014351

761
The Richard H. Driehaus Foundation
333 N. Michigan Ave., Ste. 510
Chicago, IL 60601   (312) 641-5772
FAX: (312) 641-5736; Contact for arts and culture groups with budgets under $500,000: Richard Cahan, Prog. Off., e-mail: RichardCahan@aol.com, tel.: (847) 722-9244; Contact for small theater and dance companies with budgets under $150,000, Peter Handler, Prog. Dir., e-mail: peterhandler@driehausfoundation.org; E-mail for general inquiries, Kim Romero, Admin.: kimromero@driehausfoundation.org; URL: http://www.driehausfoundation.org
RSS Feed: http://www.driehausfoundation.org/rss.xml
YouTube: http://www.youtube.com/user/DriehausFoundation

Established in 1983 in IL.
Donors: Richard H. Driehaus; John D. and Catherine T. MacArthur Foundation; Reva and David Logan Foundation; Leveraging Investment in Creativity.
Grantmaker type: Independent foundation.
Financial data (yr. ended 12/31/10): Assets, $68,525,174 (M); gifts received, $577,622; expenditures, $5,748,974; qualifying distributions, $5,251,586; giving activities include $4,498,343 for 442 grants (high: $100,000; low: $45).
Purpose and activities: The foundation benefits individuals and communities primarily by preserving and enhancing built and natural environments through historic preservation, recognition of quality community and landscape design, and conserving open space. The foundation also supports the performing and visual arts and helps organizations that provide opportunities for economically disadvantaged individuals.
Fields of interest: Visual arts, design; Historic preservation/historical societies; Arts; Housing/shelter, development; Human services; Economic development.
International interests: Scotland.
Type of support: Grants to individuals; General/operating support; Capital campaigns; Emergency funds; Program development; Publication; Seed money; Matching/challenge support.
Limitations: Applications accepted. Giving primarily in the metropolitan Chicago, IL, area which includes Cook, DuPage, Lake, McHenry, Kane and Will counties. Generally, no support for arts education or arts outreach, community theater or community dance, public, private or parochial education, or health care.
Publications: Application guidelines; Biennial report; Multi-year report.
Application information: Application guidelines and form are available on foundation web site. Faxed proposals are not accepted. Application form required.
> *Initial approach:* Letter of inquiry or telephone for Built Environment, Economic Opportunity for the Working Poor, Government Accountability/Investigative Reporting, Small Museums and Cultural Centers funding areas; Arts and culture groups with budgets under $500,000, and small theater and dance companies with budgets under $150,000 may apply online through foundation web site
> *Copies of proposal:* 2
> *Deadline(s):* See foundation web site for current deadlines in each funding area
> *Final notification:* 4 - 5 months
Officers and Directors: * Richard H. Driehaus,* Pres.; Elizabeth Driehaus,* Secy.; Dorothy Mellin,* Treas.; Sonia Fischer, Exec. Dir.
Number of staff: 2 full-time professional; 1 full-time support.
EIN: 363261347

762
Dunard Fund USA, Ltd.
555 Skokie Blvd., Ste. 555
Northbrook, IL   60062-2845

Established around 1993 in IL.
Donors: Consolidated Electrical Distributors, Inc.; LCR-M Corp.; Carol C. Hogel.
Grantmaker type: Company-sponsored foundation.
Financial data (yr. ended 12/31/09): Assets, $25,097,750 (M); gifts received, $4,425,000; expenditures, $4,765,006; qualifying distributions,

$4,494,903; giving activities include $4,432,888 for 22 grants (high: $2,123,200; low: $4,050).
Purpose and activities: The foundation supports organizations involved with arts and culture and education.
Fields of interest: Performing arts, music; Museums; Performing arts, orchestras; Performing arts, opera; Performing arts, education; Arts; Higher education.
Type of support: General/operating support; Continuing support; Annual campaigns; Endowments; Program development; Scholarship funds.
Limitations: Applications not accepted. Giving primarily in CA, New York, NY, and Philadelphia, PA. No grants to individuals.
Application information: Contributes only to organizations referred by known and highly respected figures.
> *Board meeting date(s):* Weekly
Officers and Directors: * Carol C. Hogel,* Pres. and Treas.; David T. Bradford, Secy.; Catherine C. Hogel; Elisabeth Hogel.
EIN: 980087034
Recent grants for international programs:
762-1 American Friends of the Monteverdi Choir and Orchestra, Washington, DC, $50,000. For general support. 2009.
762-2 Americans for Oxford, New York, NY, $500,000. For endowment. 2009.

763
Eades Foundation
1701 Broadmoor Dr., Ste. 200
Champaign, IL   61821-5933

Established in 1969 in IL; classified as a private operating foundation in 1981; changed to an independent foundation in 1996.
Grantmaker type: Independent foundation.
Financial data (yr. ended 12/31/10): Assets, $2,867,426 (M); expenditures, $128,849; qualifying distributions, $125,000; giving activities include $125,000 for 7 grants (high: $50,000; low: $5,000).
Purpose and activities: Giving for charitable purposes of interest to the trustees.
Fields of interest: Science, research.
International interests: Taiwan; Pakistan.
Type of support: Scholarship funds.
Limitations: Applications not accepted. Giving primarily in IL and IN. No grants to individuals.
Application information: Contributes only to pre-selected organizations.
> *Board meeting date(s):* Varies
Officer: David Grill.
Trustees: David C. Eades; Elizabeth E. Frank; Katherine A. Grill; Amelia Koplow; Rebecca Willrich.
Number of staff: None.
EIN: 237045810

764
The Edgerly Foundation
(formerly Foundation for Partnerships Trust)
P.O. Box 803878
Chicago, IL   60680-3878

Established in 1992 in MA.
Donors: William S. Edgerly; Lois Stiles Edgerly.
Grantmaker type: Independent foundation.

Financial data (yr. ended 12/31/10): Assets, $2,797,625 (M); expenditures, $732,955; qualifying distributions, $705,872; giving activities include $705,300 for 73 grants (high: $200,000; low: $100).
Purpose and activities: Giving primarily for education and community development.
Fields of interest: Elementary/secondary education; Higher education; Education; Legal services; Employment, labor unions/organizations; International affairs, foreign policy; Community/economic development; United Ways and Federated Giving Programs; Protestant agencies & churches.
Limitations: Applications not accepted. Giving primarily in MA. No grants to individuals.
Application information: Contributes only to pre-selected organizations.
Trustees: Lois Stiles Edgerly; William S. Edgerly; Edward P. Lawrence; The Northern Trust Co.
EIN: 043165980

765
Foods Resource Bank
4479 Central Ave.
Western Springs, IL   60558-1714
(312) 612-1939
FAX: (312) 612-1966;
E-mail: admin@foodsresourcebank.org; Toll-free tel.: (888) 276-4372; URL: http://www.foodsresourcebank.org
Facebook: http://www.facebook.com/pages/Foods-Resource-Bank/319234830448
Flickr: http://www.flickr.com/photos/foodsresourcebank/collections/
iTunes: http://itunes.apple.com/us/podcast/foodsresourcebank/id413056922
Podbead.com: http://www.foodsresourcebank.podbean.com/
Twitter: http://twitter.com/FRBFarmers
YouTube: http://www.youtube.com/user/FoodsResourceBank

Established in 1986 in VA.
Grantmaker type: Public charity.
Financial data (yr. ended 03/31/11): Revenue, $3,766,775; assets, $3,543,247 (M); gifts received, $3,757,005; expenditures, $3,845,327; program services expenses, $3,508,209; giving activities include $2,989,453 for 14 grants (high: $555,739; low: $26,814), and $518,756 for foundation-administered programs.
Purpose and activities: The organization is committed to providing food security in the developing world through sustainable small-scale agricultural production, thereby allowing hungry people to know the dignity of feeding themselves.
Fields of interest: Agriculture, sustainable programs; Nutrition; Christian agencies & churches; Economically disadvantaged.
International interests: Developing countries.
Limitations: Applications not accepted. Giving on an international basis, primarily in developing countries.
Application information: Contributes only to pre-selected organizations.
Officers and Board Members: * Bill Adams,* Chair.; Arlyn Schipper, Vice-Chair.; Brian Backe, Treas.; Randy Ackley; Donna Derr; Ken Flemmer; David Husby; June H. Kim; Howard Royer; Sherwin Rulloda; Susan Sanders; Darrin Yoder; and 10 additional board members.
EIN: 541940516

766
Gochnauer Family Foundation
335 Woodley Rd.
Winnetka, IL 60093-3740

Established in 1998 in CA.
Donor: Richard W. Gochnauer.
Grantmaker type: Independent foundation.
Financial data (yr. ended 12/31/10): Assets, $3,855,234 (M); gifts received, $688,289; expenditures, $172,381; qualifying distributions, $151,100; giving activities include $151,100 for 29 grants (high: $25,000; low: $100).
Purpose and activities: Giving to provide financial help for families and children, by supporting organizations and programs that promote spiritual, medical, cultural, and educational growth or provide essential services.
Fields of interest: International development; Arts; Human services; Children/youth, services; United Ways and Federated Giving Programs; Christian agencies & churches.
Type of support: General/operating support; Capital campaigns.
Limitations: Applications accepted. Giving primarily in southern CA, the greater Chicago, IL, area, and in MT. No grants to individuals.
Application information: Larger requests, in amounts of $5,000 or more, must include additional information. Contact foundation for complete application details.
 Initial approach: Letter
 Copies of proposal: 2
 Deadline(s): None
 Board meeting date(s): Quarterly
Officers and Trustees: Beth A. Gochnauer, Chair. and Secy.; Richard W. Gochnauer, Pres. and Treas.; Grant D. Gochnauer,* V.P.; Meg Gochnauer,* V.P.
EIN: 330833479

767
Lillian and Larry Goodman Foundations
c/o Lawrence Goodman
4711 W. Golf Rd., Ste. 1000
Skokie, IL 60076-1235 (847) 674-1400
FAX: (847) 674-8157; URL: http://www.llgoodmanfdn.org/

Established in 1994 in IL.
Donors: Lawrence Goodman; Cebrin Goodman†; Goodman Real Estate Partnership; Lawrence Goodman Revocable Trust.
Grantmaker type: Independent foundation.
Financial data (yr. ended 12/31/10): Assets, $18,259,353 (M); gifts received, $903,720; expenditures, $1,413,201; qualifying distributions, $980,073; giving activities include $856,306 for 4 + grants (high: $325,000).
Purpose and activities: Giving primarily for Jewish causes and to drug prevention programs.
Fields of interest: Substance abuse, prevention; Jewish federated giving programs; Jewish agencies & synagogues.
International interests: Israel.
Limitations: Giving primarily in Chicago, IL; some funding also in West Palm Beach, FL. Funding also in the area of Be'er Sheva, Israel and the surrounding Negev. No support for political campaigns, or to organizations that aspire to build or renovate places of business, or purchase or refurbish capital as needed. No grants to individuals, or for conferences, festivals, exhibitions, or debt reduction.

Application information: Unsolicited grant proposals are not accepted.
 Initial approach: Complete grant inquiry form on foundation web site
Officers: Lawrence Goodman, Pres.; Lawrence Etchell, Secy.-Treas.; Susan Karlinsky, Exec. Dir.
EIN: 363956748

768
Hebrew Immigrant Aid Society of Chicago
216 W. Jackson, Ste. 700
Chicago, IL 60606-6921

Established in 1939 in IL.
Grantmaker type: Public charity.
Financial data (yr. ended 06/30/10): Revenue, $459,375; assets, $4,083,842 (M); gifts received, $402,715; expenditures, $790,725; program services expenses, $790,725; giving activities include $741,725 for 1 grant, and $49,000 for 11 grants to individuals.
Purpose and activities: The society seeks to guide Jewish immigrants and others through the immigration process to the ultimate goal of U.S. citizenship; to aid them in bringing their families to the U.S. as new immigrants and to reunite them with family or friends already here; to foster American ideals among the newcomers and to instill in them, through knowledge of American history and institutions, a sense of patriotism and love for their adopted country; to make better known to the people of the U.S. the need to foster immigration; and to promote this by means of meetings, lectures, and publications.
Fields of interest: International migration/refugee issues; Immigrants/refugees.
Type of support: Scholarships—to individuals.
Limitations: Giving primarily to Chicago, IL.
Officers and Directors: Jeffrey Kriezelman,* Pres.; Vadim Muchnik,* Exec. V.P.; Stephen D. Berman,* V.P.; Igor Boguslavsky,* V.P.; Stanley Horn,* V.P.; Irena Persky, V.P.; Eleanor Wolfe,* Secy.; Ellen Gutiontov,* Treas.; Arthur Babakoff; Melanie H. Berkowitz; Justin Burton; Samuel Cohen; Randy Felsenthal; Leonid Gelfgat; Otto Grenton; and 15 additional directors.
EIN: 362167094

769
The Heritage Foundation of First Security Federal Savings Bank, Inc.
2329 W. Chicago Ave.
Chicago, IL 60622-4723 (773) 486-6645
Contact: Julian E. Kulas, Pres.

Established in 1997 in IL.
Donors: First Security Federal Savings Bank; Maria Olijnyk.
Grantmaker type: Company-sponsored foundation.
Financial data (yr. ended 12/31/10): Assets, $12,715,137 (M); gifts received, $381,009; expenditures, $577,602; qualifying distributions, $475,500; giving activities include $475,500 for 75 grants (high: $68,000; low: $250).
Purpose and activities: The foundation supports programs designed to preserve Ukrainian culture and heritage; and promote democracy and a free market economy.
Fields of interest: International affairs, foreign policy; Arts, alliance/advocacy; Arts, cultural/ethnic awareness; Museums; Arts; Higher education;

Education; Public affairs, alliance/advocacy; Catholic agencies & churches.
International interests: Ukraine.
Type of support: General/operating support; Program development; Conferences/seminars; Publication.
Limitations: Applications accepted. Giving primarily in IL. No grants to individuals.
Application information: Application form not required.
 Initial approach: Proposal
 Deadline(s): None
Officers and Trustees: Julian E. Kulas, Pres.; Paul Nadzikewycz, V.P.; Terry Gawryk, Secy.; Taras Drozd; Dmytro Shtohryn; Chrysta Wereszczak.
Number of staff: 1 part-time support.
EIN: 364135415

770
IDP Foundation, Inc.
321 N. Clark St., Ste. 2350
Chicago, IL 60654-4784
E-mail for letters of inquiry: grantinquiry@idpfoundation.org; URL: http://www.idpfoundation.org
Blog: http://www.idpfoundation.org/blog/
E-Newsletter: http://idpfoundation.us1.list-manage.com/subscribe?u=b4f2abb075ed4830f7d64a21a&id=874bee3ac5
Facebook: http://www.facebook.com/IDPFoundation
LinkedIn: http://www.linkedin.com/in/idpfoundation
RSS Feed: http://www.idpfoundation.org/feed/
Twitter: http://twitter.com/IDPFoundation

Established in 2007 in IL.
Grantmaker type: Independent foundation.
Financial data (yr. ended 12/31/10): Assets, $76,322 (M); expenditures, $262,775; qualifying distributions, $261,925; giving activities include $261,925 for 12 grants (high: $220,000; low: $50).
Purpose and activities: To develop and support innovative programs devoted to improving the quality of life for people and organizations in need particularly as it relates to poverty alleviation.
Fields of interest: Performing arts; Education; Health care; Medical research.
International interests: Africa.
Limitations: Applications accepted. Giving primarily in Chicago, IL; some focus also on Ghana. No support for lobbying, or for religious missionary or indoctrination activities. No grants to individuals, or for endowments, capital construction, or deficit financing.
Application information: Unsolicited full proposals not accepted. For more information see http://www.idpfoundation.org/grant-seekers.
 Initial approach: Letter of inquiry via mail or e-mail
EIN: 261614687

771
IFSA Foundation, Inc.
1715 Pavilion Way, No. 501
Park Ridge, IL 60068-6500
Contact: Tom Roberts, Pres.
E-mail: troberts@theifsafoundation.org

Established in 2004 in IN.
Donor: Institute for Study Abroad.

Grantmaker type: Independent foundation.
Financial data (yr. ended 05/31/11): Assets, $670,193 (M); gifts received, $631,500; expenditures, $870,841; qualifying distributions, $623,840; giving activities include $600,000 for 1 grant.
Purpose and activities: Giving to assist accredited colleges, universities, or organizations with the mission to further international education through direct and indirect support to study abroad by undergraduate students.
Fields of interest: International exchange, students; Higher education.
Type of support: Program development; Film/video/radio; Fellowships; Internship funds; Scholarship funds; Research; Exchange programs; Matching/challenge support.
Limitations: Applications not accepted. Giving primarily in the U.S.
Publications: Grants list.
Application information: Unsolicited requests for funds not accepted or acknowledged.
 Board meeting date(s): Quarterly
Officers: Tom Roberts, Pres.; David Gray, Secy.; M. Jean White, Treas.
EIN: 201238211

772
Illinois Arts Council Foundation
100 W. Randolph, Ste. 10-500
Chicago, IL 60601-3230 (312) 814-6750
Contact: Terry A. Scrogum, Exec. Dir.
FAX: (312) 814-1471; E-mail: iac.info@illinois.gov; Toll-free tel.: (800) 237-6994; E-mail for Terry A. Scrogum: terry.scrogum@illinois.gov, tel.: (312) 814-6758; URL: http://www.arts.illinois.gov/grants-programs/overview

Established in 1967 in IL.
Grantmaker type: Public charity.
Financial data (yr. ended 06/30/10): Revenue, $3,285; assets, $81,039 (M); gifts received, $2,150; expenditures, $843.
Purpose and activities: The foundation serves the Illinois Arts Council constituency by augmenting limited state funds for the purpose of outreach and communication initiatives within the arts community and the general public.
Fields of interest: Boys clubs.
International interests: Europe; Africa; South America; Asia; Australia.
Limitations: Applications accepted. Giving limited to IL.
Publications: Application guidelines; Annual report.
Application information: Application form required.
 Initial approach: Download application
 Deadline(s): Varies
Officer and Directors:* Shirley R. Madigan,* Chair.; Rhoda A. Pierce,* Vice-Chair.; Andy Van Meter,* Secy.; Terry A. Scrogum, Exec. Dir.; Virginia G. Bobins; Hon. Charles E. Box; William E. Brattain, Ph.D.; Patrice Bugelas-Brandt; Christina Kemper Gidwitz; Jodie Shagrin Kavensky; and 5 additional directors.
EIN: 362680757

773
India Development Service
1307 Dunrobin Rd.
Naperville, IL 60302-1355 (708) 524-2041
E-mail: idsusa@gmail.com; Mailing address: P.O. Box 980, Chicago, IL 60690-0980; URL: http://www.idsusa.org

Grantmaker type: Public charity.
Financial data (yr. ended 12/31/10): Revenue, $114,844; assets, $528,464 (M); gifts received, $104,044; expenditures, $92,500; program services expenses, $87,234; giving activities include $58,225 for grants to organizations outside the U.S.
Purpose and activities: The organization supports economic and social development in India.
Fields of interest: International development.
International interests: India.
Limitations: Giving primarily in India.
Officer and Directors:* Kaushik Pancholi,* Treas.; Shiban Ganju; Jerry Gosenpud, Ph.D.; Nilesh Kothari; Varsha Pancholi; Sameer Prasad; Suman Sachdeva; Dershi Saxena; Naimish Shah; Sonesh Shah; Nayeem Sharif; Roop Shivpuri; Anita Sinha; Elizabeth Vogt.
EIN: 237355796

774
International Fellowship of Christians and Jews, Inc.
30 N. LaSalle St., Ste. 2600
Chicago, IL 60602-3356
Contact: Rabbi Yechiel Eckstein, Pres.
E-mail: info@ifcj.org; Toll-free tel.: (800) 486-8844; URL: http://www.ifcj.org
Facebook: http://www.facebook.com/FellowshipFan
Flickr: http://www.flickr.com/people/the-fellowship
RSS Feed: http://feeds.feedburner.com/ifcj/thebridge
Twitter: http://twitter.com/#!/TheFellowship
YouTube: http://www.youtube.com/user/IFCJ25

Established in 1983 in IL.
Grantmaker type: Public charity.
Financial data (yr. ended 12/31/10): Revenue, $97,019,588; assets, $17,610,801 (M); gifts received, $96,424,433; expenditures, $96,626,001; program services expenses, $77,521,072; giving activities include $18,675,000 for 8 grants (high: $13,500,000; low: $5,000), $37,636,624 for grants to organizations outside the U.S., and $21,209,448 for foundation-administered programs.
Purpose and activities: The fellowship seeks to foster better relations and understanding between Christians and Jews, encourage greater cooperation between both communities on issues of shared biblical concern, and help build support for Israel and Jews in crisis or need.
Fields of interest: Religion, interfaith issues.
International interests: Israel.
Limitations: Applications not accepted. Giving to the U.S. and Israel.
Publications: Annual report; Financial statement.
Application information: Unsolicited requests for funds not accepted.
Officers and Directors:* John P. French,* Chair.; Rabbi Yechiel Eckstein,* Pres.; Barbara Manuel,* Secy.; Edward Lasky,* Treas.; David Clark; J.R.

Dupell; John French; Steven Hefter; Andrew Lappin; Melvin Myland; Suzanne Peyser; Joseph Wein.
Number of staff: 12 full-time professional; 45 full-time support.
EIN: 363256096

775
Jocarno Fund
333 North Michigan, Ste. 510
Chicago, IL 60601-3934
Contact: John Schlossman, Pres.

Established in 1959 in IL.
Donors: Shirley Schlossman; John Schlossman.
Grantmaker type: Independent foundation.
Financial data (yr. ended 12/31/10): Assets, $1,872,137 (M); expenditures, $253,631; qualifying distributions, $233,680; giving activities include $226,500 for 116 grants (high: $10,000; low: $250).
Purpose and activities: Giving primarily for the arts, education, and health and human services.
Fields of interest: Arts; Higher education; Environment, natural resources; Health care; Youth development; Human services; International peace/security; Civil/human rights; Foundations (community); United Ways and Federated Giving Programs; Religion.
Type of support: General/operating support; Continuing support; Annual campaigns; Land acquisition; Emergency funds.
Limitations: Applications accepted. Giving primarily in Chicago, IL. No grants to individuals.
Application information: Application form required.
 Initial approach: Letter
 Copies of proposal: 1
 Deadline(s): None
Officer: John Schlossman, Pres.
Director: Donald Lubin.
Number of staff: 9
EIN: 366062019

776
Joy Foundation
1540 N. Lake Shore Dr., No. 14N
Chicago, IL 60610-6684

Established in 2000 in IL.
Donors: Rochelle Zell†; Leah Zell Wanger.
Grantmaker type: Independent foundation.
Financial data (yr. ended 12/31/10): Assets, $5,509,351 (M); gifts received, $81,760; expenditures, $461,737; qualifying distributions, $408,900; giving activities include $408,900 for grants.
Purpose and activities: Giving primarily for higher education and international affairs.
Fields of interest: International affairs; Cancer; Higher education; Education; Human services.
Limitations: Applications not accepted. Giving primarily in Chicago, IL, and Cambridge, MA. No grants to individuals.
Application information: Contributes only to pre-selected organizations.
Officers: Leah Zell Wanger, Pres. and Treas.; Ralph Wanger, V.P.
Director: Jenny Wanger.
EIN: 364410533

777

King Family Foundation
(formerly Flagg Creek Foundation)
c/o Emily H. King
15W090 Sedgley Rd.
Burr Ridge, IL 60527-5281

Established in 1995 in IL.
Donor: Robert E. King.
Grantmaker type: Independent foundation.
Financial data (yr. ended 09/30/10): Assets, $3,928,148 (M); expenditures, $1,396,458; qualifying distributions, $1,216,704; giving activities include $1,211,104 for 52 grants (high: $433,334; low: $50).
Purpose and activities: Giving primarily for the arts, education, and health. The grantmaker also gives toward African Wildlife Foundation scholarships.
Fields of interest: Performing arts; Arts; Education; Health care; Human services; Native Americans/American Indians; Indigenous peoples; Children; African Americans/Blacks; Hispanics/Latinos; Economically disadvantaged.
International interests: Africa.
Type of support: General/operating support; Continuing support; Management development/capacity building; Annual campaigns; Capital campaigns; Building/renovation; Endowments; Emergency funds; Program development; Curriculum development; Internship funds; Scholarship funds; Technical assistance; Program evaluation; Matching/challenge support.
Limitations: Applications not accepted. Giving primarily in IL. No grants to individuals.
Application information: Contributes only to pre-selected organizations.
Officers: Emily H. King, Pres.; Robert E. King, Jr., V.P.
Directors: Elizabeth K. Alden; Robert E. King; Heather K. Pines.
Number of staff: None.
EIN: 363991717

778

The Kraft Foods Foundation
3 Lakes Dr., NF-132
Northfield, IL 60093-2753

Established in 2005 in IL.
Donor: Kraft Foods Global, Inc.
Grantmaker type: Company-sponsored foundation.
Financial data (yr. ended 12/31/09): Assets, $28,304,349 (M); gifts received, $18,300,000; expenditures, $8,181,396; qualifying distributions, $8,180,776; giving activities include $8,180,776 for grants.
Fields of interest: Food services; International development.
Limitations: Giving on an international basis, primarily in Australia, Belgium, Brazil, China, England, Hungary, Lithuania, Mexico, Poland, Romania, Sweden, and Venezuela.
Officers and Directors:* Cynthia P. Yeatman,* Pres.; Nancy Daigle, V.P. and Secy.; Carol J. Ward, V.P. and Secy.; Marc S. Firestone,* V.P.; Nicole R. Robinson, V.P.; Joseph Klauke, Counsel; James Portnoy, Counsel.
EIN: 203881590

779

Krehbiel Family Foundation
c/o Robert J. Reichner & Assoc., Inc.
807 Chestnut Ave.
Wilmette, IL 60091-1743

Established in 2003 in IL as s successor to the original Krehbiel Family Foundation.
Grantmaker type: Independent foundation.
Financial data (yr. ended 10/31/10): Assets, $7,103,278 (M); expenditures, $334,096; qualifying distributions, $300,935; giving activities include $295,000 for 7 grants (high: $85,000; low: $15,000).
Fields of interest: International affairs; Hospitals (specialty); Museums (art); Higher education; Environment; Children/youth, services; Children.
Limitations: Applications not accepted. Giving primarily in IL, NH and NY.
Application information: Unsolicited requests for funds not accepted.
Officers and Directors:* Margaret V. Krehbiel-Ellsworth,* Pres. and Secy.; William V. Krehbiel,* Treas.; Frederick A. Krehbiel; Frederick L. Krehbiel; Jay F. Krehbiel; John H. Krehbiel, Jr.; John H. Krehbiel III.
EIN: 841621866

780

Landau Family Foundation
P.O. Box 577880
Chicago, IL 60657-7880

Established in 1955 in IL.
Donor: Howard M. Landau†.
Grantmaker type: Independent foundation.
Financial data (yr. ended 11/30/10): Assets, $7,564,595 (M); expenditures, $536,180; qualifying distributions, $463,000; giving activities include $463,000 for grants.
Purpose and activities: Support primarily for social and economic justice.
Fields of interest: Legal services, public interest law; Human services; Civil/human rights; Jewish federated giving programs; Public affairs; Jewish agencies & synagogues; Immigrants/refugees; Economically disadvantaged.
International interests: Middle East; Israel.
Type of support: General/operating support; Continuing support; Emergency funds; Program development; Seed money; Program-related investments/loans.
Limitations: Applications accepted. Giving primarily in Chicago, IL. No grants to individuals.
Application information: Application form not required.
   Deadline(s): None
Officers and Directors:* Kay Berkson,* Pres.; Kenneth J. Landau,* Secy.; Sidney Hollander, Treas.; Daniel Berkson.
EIN: 366089098

781

Legion of Young Polish Women
3340 N. Page Ave.
Chicago, IL 60634-2915
Contact: Dr. Geraldine Balut Coleman, Treas.
E-mail: gbalutc@sbcglobal.net; URL: http://www.lmp-chicago.org/

Established in 1939 in IL.

Grantmaker type: Public charity.
Financial data (yr. ended 09/30/10): Revenue, $49,985; assets, $39,979 (M); gifts received, $8,824; expenditures, $53,758; giving activities include $33,600 for grants.
Purpose and activities: The organization seeks to help Poland and Poles scattered throughout the world; raise funds for the relief of needy individuals of Polish heritage, institutions in Poland and wherever Polish communities exist; support local, national and international fund drives to promote charitable and Polish cultural endeavors; ensure that Polish culture, heritage and traditions remain an integral part of our ethnically diverse country; support young people, recognizing that they will carry on Polish cultural legacy in the generations to come; and to donate to numerous institutions, including the Polish Youth Association, Polish language schools, the Polish Museum of America, scholarship funding for the Knights of Dabrowski and other charitable institutions.
Fields of interest: Human services; Health care.
International interests: Poland.
Officers: Teresa Sinkowski, Pres.; Teresa Skawski, 1st V.P.; Jane Kobos, 2nd V.P.; Jenny Crissey, Secy.; Dr. Geraldine Balut Coleman, Treas.
Directors: Connie Malinowski; Kathy Wojdyla.
EIN: 362552579

782

The Libra Foundation
1700 W. Irving Park Rd., Rm. 203
Chicago, IL 60613-2599 (773) 325-1235
E-mail: info@thelibrafoundation.org; URL: http://www.thelibrafoundation.org

Established in 2002 in IL.
Donors: Rhoda Pritzker†; Pritzker Foundation; Nicholas J. Pritzker.
Grantmaker type: Independent foundation.
Financial data (yr. ended 12/31/10). Assets, $68,316,711 (M); gifts received, $3,626,927; expenditures, $3,605,272; qualifying distributions, $2,678,500; giving activities include $2,678,500 for grants.
Purpose and activities: The foundation seeks to support programs that contribute to improving the quality of life and promoting human rights and social justice for the disenfranchised or marginalized populations, as well as those initiatives that protect and sustain the ecosystems that surround us. Emphasis is on organizations in the Chicago, IL and San Francisco, CA areas whose work is national in scope. The foundation funds social and economic justice organizations that integrate human rights into their work in and across the following priority areas: women's rights, with an emphasis on reproductive rights and the elevation of women's rights as human rights; environmental sustainability, with an emphasis on promoting social justice within climate change mitigation and adaptation strategies; peace and justice, with an emphasis on fair application of the law, government accountability and human rights field-building.
Fields of interest: Environment; Human services; Civil/human rights; Community/economic development; Economically disadvantaged.
Limitations: Giving primarily in San Francisco, CA and Chicago, IL. No support for international organizations not registered in the U.S., or for organizations that are heavily supported by the government (except for specific advocacy or public policy projects of interest). No grants to individuals,

or for fundraising events, capital fund drives or campaigns, debt reduction, international work that focuses on a single country or on a small set of countries, or for religious activities.

Publications: Application guidelines; Grants list.

Application information: In general, the foundation does not accept unsolicited proposals. Brief letters of inquiry are accepted however, on a rolling basis. Refer to foundation web site for complete application information and guidelines. Application form required.

Initial approach: Letter of Inquiry only
Deadline(s): None

Officers and Directors:* Nicholas J. Pritzker,* C.E.O.; Susan S. Pritzker,* Pres. and Treas.; Regan Pritzker,* V.P. and Secy.; Thomas Dykstra, V.P.; Jacob Pritzker; Joseph Pritzker; Isaac Pritzker.

Number of staff: 1 full-time professional; 1 part-time professional; 1 part-time support.

EIN: 300031117

Recent grants for international programs:

782-1 1Sky Education Fund, Takoma Park, MD, $50,000. For the Climate Precinct Captains (CPCs) initiative to catalyze individual action around climate change solutions and expand volunteer leadership at the grassroots level nationwide pushing for bold federal climate policy in the U.S. 2010.

782-2 American Civil Liberties Union Foundation, New York, NY, $60,000. For the ACLU's Human Rights Program in its work on the Campaign for Human Rights at Home which uses human rights to advance the social justice agenda of the ACLU, with particular attention to issues of torture, women's rights, children's rights and racial justice. 2010.

782-3 Amnesty International USA, New York, NY, $35,000. For Amnesty International USA's work with the reconstituted Interagency Working Group to ratify human rights treaties, push for the integration of economic, social, and cultural rights, and implement all human rights principles in U.S. domestic policy. 2010.

782-4 Center for Constitutional Rights, New York, NY, $20,000. For CCR's Global Detentions and Rendition Project to advance a human rights model and focus on four main areas: 1) the Guantanamo Global Justice Initiative; 2) holding U.S. officials accountable for serious human rights violations, including torture; 3) challenging racial profiling and the detention of immigrants; and 4) holding corporations accountable for complicity in abusive programs that were part of the so-called war on terror. 2010.

782-5 CERES, Boston, MA, $25,000. For continued engagement with the Securities and Exchange Commission (SEC) on climate and Environmental, Social and Governance risk disclosure in corporate SEC filings. 2010.

782-6 EarthRights International, Washington, DC, $50,000. For EarthRights International's Legal Program which seeks to bring the power of the law to bear directly on earth rights abusers to secure justice and develop laws for human rights and environmental accountability with regards to multinational corporations that operate with impunity in remote areas of the world. 2010.

782-7 Environmental Law and Policy Center of the Midwest, Chicago, IL, $50,000. For the Environmental Law and Policy Center's Global Warming Solutions Project in Illinois to: (a) advance renewable energy development; (b) promote strong energy efficiency programs; (c) clean up or shut down old, dirty coal plants; and

(d) advance the Midwest high-speed rail network and other transportation reforms. 2010.

782-8 Fund for Global Human Rights, Washington, DC, $35,000. For grant-making programs in six regions around the world and facilitating meaningful technical assistance to grantees seeking to augment their skills and capacity. 2010.

782-9 Gender Action, Washington, DC, $30,000. For general operating support to ensure that International Financial Institution investments support poor women's and men's access to health, water, housing, education, livelihoods, freedom from violence and other basic human rights in developing countries. 2010.

782-10 Genocide Intervention Network, Washington, DC, $20,000. For the Genocide Prevention Campaign, a multi-year grassroots mobilization campaign to implement the recommendations made by the Genocide Prevention Task Force (co-chaired by former Secretaries Madeleine Albright and William Cohen) in its report, Preventing Genocide: A Blueprint for U.S. Policymakers. 2010.

782-11 Global Fund for Children, Washington, DC, $40,000. For the Global Fund for Children's Safety portfolio to invest in programs that protect and promote the rights of children and youth by keeping them safe from danger and the risk of exploitation and by developing safe spaces in which children can grow to their full potential and thrive. 2010.

782-12 Global Fund for Women, San Francisco, CA, $50,000. For investments in emerging women-led social change initiatives; strengthen the capacity of women's rights groups; and build collective power to achieve lasting change by linking women's rights' organizations and movements. 2010.

782-13 Global Greengrants Fund, Boulder, CO, $50,000. For general operating support and support for Global Greengrants Fund's recently launched Climate Fund. 2010.

782-14 Global Justice Center, New York, NY, $25,000. For efforts to expose and change US law and policies which define gender equality rights too narrowly, including the exclusion of abortion laws from equality scrutiny. 2010.

782-15 Heartland Alliance for Human Needs and Human Rights, Chicago, IL, $50,000. For the From Poverty to Opportunity Campaign: Realizing Human Rights in Illinois, which is focused on cutting extreme poverty in half by 2015. 2010.

782-16 Human Rights First, New York, NY, $25,000. To work to consolidate and advance the recent progress toward ending the policies and practices of torture and cruel or degrading treatment; advance policies to dismantle mechanisms that facilitate torture, including unlawful detention; and promote accountability for human rights violations that result from such policies and practices. 2010.

782-17 Indian Law Resource Center, Helena, MT, $50,000. For legal assistance, litigation and outreach to protect the human and the environmental rights of Indian and Alaska Native nations and indigenous communities throughout North, Central, and South America. 2010.

782-18 International Coalition of Sites of Conscience, New York, NY, $20,000. For the Guantanamo Public Memory Project to raise awareness of how Guantanamo has been used and reused over the last century, and foster action on its future. 2010.

782-19 International Development Exchange, San Francisco, CA, $20,000. To support IDEX's current grantmaking portfolio, exploration of programs in new countries and the development of organizational blue print for growth. 2010.

782-20 International Projects Assistance Services, Chapel Hill, NC, $20,000. For advocacy efforts to build public and political support for decriminalizing abortion and ensuring better access to safe care. 2010.

782-21 National Economic and Social Rights Initiative, New York, NY, $45,000. For programs which: 1) Build the capacity of grassroots organizations to use human rights analysis and strategies; 2) Introduce human rights analysis to influence policy debates toward greater protection of economic and social rights; 3) Increase recognition of economic and social rights in various sectors; 4) Build and support new alliances across issues, communities and/ or borders; and 5) Engage international human rights monitors and United Nations organs as appropriate. 2010.

782-22 Physicians for Human Rights, Cambridge, MA, $20,000. For efforts to apply a wide range of medical and scientific skills to investigate and document human rights violations around the world and mobilize the voices, passion and expertise of physicians and other health professionals to advocate to protect and save lives and prevent further abuses. 2010.

782-23 Planned Parenthood Federation, International, New York, NY, $50,000. For advocacy work at various levels in support of sexual rights and reproductive rights in Latin America and the Caribbean. 2010.

782-24 Population Council, New York, NY, $40,000. For the Rethinking Sexuality Education Project which is aimed at shifting public discourse and providing the tools for implementing a next generation of sex and HIV education. 2010.

782-25 United States International Council on Disabilities, Washington, DC, $20,000. For efforts to strengthen ties between disability and human rights groups and advance the movement for US ratification of the Convention on the Rights of Persons with Disabilities. 2010.

782-26 Witness, Inc., Brooklyn, NY, $50,000. For continuation of the U.S. campaign to end elder abuse; selection of new partners for the North America video advocacy program; work with the U.S. Human Rights Network on the Testify Project; expansion of the training program to activists through a new online training Toolkit; and promotion of best practices and the development of standards and norms in online and mobile video for human rights. 2010.

782-27 Womens Learning Partnership for Rights, Development and Peace, Bethesda, MD, $25,000. For training, capacity building, advocacy and curriculum development that advances women's rights worldwide. 2010.

782-28 Womens Link Worldwide, Madrid, Spain, $35,000. For efforts to advance and implement gender equality, with a special focus on sexual and reproductive rights. 2010.

782-29 World Resources Institute, Washington, DC, $20,000. For The Access Initiative's continued work to test and refine the Rapid Institutional Analysis for Adaptation tool that will aid civil society in responding to climate change through formal and informal mechanisms. 2010.

783
Elick and Charlotte Lindon Foundation
c/o Charlotte Lindon
2500 Indigo Ln., Ste. 337
Glenview, IL 60025-8306

Established in 1978 in IL.
Donors: Charlotte Lindon; Elick Lindon†.
Grantmaker type: Independent foundation.
Financial data (yr. ended 12/31/10): Assets, $4,255,500 (M); gifts received, $200,000; expenditures, $312,244; qualifying distributions, $284,807; giving activities include $284,807 for 63 grants (high: $50,000; low: $18).
Purpose and activities: Giving to Jewish organizations, human services, and medical and health purposes.
Fields of interest: Foundations (community); Arts; Housing/shelter; Human services; Jewish agencies & synagogues; Disabilities, people with; Economically disadvantaged.
International interests: Israel.
Type of support: General/operating support; Continuing support; Annual campaigns; Capital campaigns; Emergency funds; Program development; Seed money.
Limitations: Applications not accepted. Giving primarily in IL. No support for political organizations. No grants to individuals.
Application information: Unsolicited requests for funds not accepted.
  Board meeting date(s): Varies
Director: Charlotte Lindon.
EIN: 363071211

784
Lithuanian Foundation
14911 127th St.
Lemont, IL 60439-6466 (630) 257-1616
FAX: (630) 257-1647; E-mail: admin@lithfund.org; URL: http://www.lietuviufondas.org/

Established in 1962 in IL.
Grantmaker type: Public charity.
Financial data (yr. ended 12/31/10): Revenue, $1,209,716; assets, $14,390,673 (M); gifts received, $382,952; expenditures, $643,453; program services expenses, $453,613; giving activities include $352,072 for 12 grants (high: $78,250; low: $7,500), $26,928 for 36 grants to individuals, $32,500 for 36 grants to individuals outside the U.S., and $42,113 for foundation-administered programs.
Purpose and activities: The organization supports Lithuanian language, culture, and traditions in the United States, Lithuania, and Lithuanian communities worldwide.
Fields of interest: Arts, cultural/ethnic awareness; Education.
International interests: Lithuania.
Type of support: Scholarship funds; Scholarships—to individuals.
Limitations: Applications accepted. Giving on an international basis, primarily in Lithuania.
Publications: Application guidelines; Newsletter.
Application information: Applications must be written in Lithuanian. Application form required.
  Initial approach: Download application form
  Deadline(s): Apr. 20 for Grants; Oct. 10 for Scholarships
  Final notification: Aug.
Officers and Directors:* Rimantas Griskelis,* Chair.; Marius Kasniunas,* Pres. and C.E.O.; Rimas

Domanskis,* Secy.; Saulius Cyvas; Violeta Gedgaudas; Sarunas Griganavicius; Juozas Kapacinskas; Rita Kisielius; Daina Kojelis; Almis Kuolas; Dale Lukas; Laurynas Misevicius; Vytautas Narutis; Algirdas Saulis; Arvydas Tamulis; and 4 additional directors.
EIN: 366118312

785
Logos Charitable Fund, Inc.
200 W. Monroe, Ste. 1440
Chicago, IL 60606-5399

Established in 1994 in IL & DE.
Grantmaker type: Independent foundation.
Financial data (yr. ended 11/30/10): Assets, $2,317,614 (M); gifts received, $380,325; expenditures, $146,897; qualifying distributions, $146,250; giving activities include $146,250 for 23 grants (high: $50,000; low: $250).
Purpose and activities: Giving primarily to Catholic agencies and churches, and for human services.
Fields of interest: Higher education, university; Scholarships/financial aid; Salvation Army; International development; Christian agencies & churches; Catholic agencies & churches.
Type of support: Continuing support; Annual campaigns; Program development; Curriculum development; Scholarship funds.
Limitations: Applications not accepted. Giving primarily in IL. No grants to individuals.
Application information: Contributes only to pre-selected organizations.
Officers and Directors:* Noel G. Moore,* Pres.; Jeff McKinley,* Secy.; Michele Moore.
EIN: 363994192

786
Lohengrin Foundation, Inc.
c/o Peter & Lucy Ascoli
5744 S. Kimbark Ave.
Chicago, IL 60637-1615

Established in 1963.
Donors: Peter M. Ascoli; Lucy B. Ascoli.
Grantmaker type: Independent foundation.
Financial data (yr. ended 12/31/10): Assets, $299,170 (M); gifts received, $148,194; expenditures, $227,428; qualifying distributions, $224,632; giving activities include $224,517 for 30 grants (high: $50,000; low: $350).
Fields of interest: Performing arts; Humanities; Arts; Secondary school/education; Higher education; International relief; Community/economic development; Jewish agencies & synagogues.
Type of support: General/operating support.
Limitations: Applications not accepted. Giving primarily in Chicago, IL. No grants to individuals.
Application information: Unsolicited requests for funds not accepted.
Officers: Peter M. Ascoli, Pres. and Treas.; Elizabeth Tsapira, V.P.; Lucy B. Ascoli, Secy.
EIN: 136141339

787
Ann and Robert H. Lurie Foundation
(formerly Ann and Robert H. Lurie Family Foundation)
440 W. Ontario St.
Chicago, IL 60610-4014 (312) 466-3982

Established in 1986 in IL.
Donors: Ann Lurie; Robert Lurie†; Robert H. & Ann Lurie Trust.
Grantmaker type: Independent foundation.
Financial data (yr. ended 12/31/10): Assets, $6,199,676 (M); gifts received, $10,930,000; expenditures, $28,753,972; qualifying distributions, $28,745,000; giving activities include $28,745,000 for 23 grants (high: $20,000,000; low: $2,500; average: $50,000–$1,000,000).
Purpose and activities: Giving primarily for education, human services, and health.
Fields of interest: Higher education; Environment, research; Environment, natural resources; Health care; Health organizations, association; Children/youth, services.
Type of support: Endowments.
Limitations: Applications not accepted. Giving primarily in Chicago, IL. No grants to individuals.
Application information: Contributes only to pre-selected organizations.
Officers and Directors:* Ann Lurie,* Pres. and Treas.; Sheli Z. Rosenberg,* V.P. and Secy.; Andrew Lurie,* V.P.; Benjamin Lurie,* V.P.; Elizabeth Lurie, V.P.; Mark Slezak,* V.P.
EIN: 363486274
Recent grants for international programs:
787-1 Africa Infectious Disease Village Clinics, Chicago, IL, $5,677,593. For unrestricted support. 2009.
787-2 Ancient Egypt Research Associates, Cambridge, MA, $450,000. For unrestricted support. 2009.
787-3 Human Rights Watch, New York, NY, $175,000. For unrestricted support. 2009.
787-4 Pangaea Global AIDS Foundation, San Francisco, CA, $457,366. For unrestricted support. 2009.
787-5 Trust for African Rock Art, Nairobi, Kenya, $125,000. For unrestricted support. 2009.

788
The John D. and Catherine T. MacArthur Foundation
140 S. Dearborn St., Ste. 1200
Chicago, IL 60603-5285 (312) 726-8000
Contact: Richard J. Kaplan, Assoc. V.P., Institutional Research and Grants Mgmt.
FAX: (312) 920-6258;
E-mail: 4answers@macfound.org; TDD: (312) 920-6285; URL: http://www.macfound.org
Asia Security Initiative: http://asiasecurity.macfound.org/blog
E-Newsletter: http://www.macfound.org/site/c.lkLXJ8MQKrH/b.4357343/k.7FF4/Subscribe_to_eNews__Custom/apps/ka/ct/contactcustom.asp
Grants Database: http://www.macfound.org/site/c.lkLXJ8MQKrH/b.4979973/k.8E29/Recent_Grants.htm
Knowledge Center: http://www.macfound.org/site/c.lkLXJ8MQKrH/b.2722017/k.62D0/What_We_Have_Learned.htm
RSS Feed: http://feeds.feedburner.com/macfound
Spotlight on Digital Media and Learning: http://spotlight.macfound.org/blog
Twitter: http://www.twitter.com/macfound
YouTube: http://www.youtube.com/macfound

Incorporated in 1970 in IL.
Donors: John D. MacArthur†; Catherine T. MacArthur†.

Grantmaker type: Independent foundation.

Financial data (yr. ended 12/31/10): Assets, $5,737,270,000 (M); expenditures, $280,999,078; qualifying distributions, $243,776,078; giving activities include $243,776,078 for grants.

Purpose and activities: The foundation supports creative people and effective institutions committed to building a more just, verdant, and peaceful world. In addition to selecting the MacArthur Fellows, the foundation works to defend human rights, advance global conservation and security, make cities better places, and understand how technology is affecting children and society.

Fields of interest: Media/communications; Media, film/video; Education, public education; Higher education; Environment, natural resources; Reproductive health; Mental health/crisis services, public policy; Crime/violence prevention, youth; International peace/security; International human rights; Community development, neighborhood development; Public policy, research.

International interests: India; Mexico; Nigeria; Russia.

Type of support: General/operating support; Program development; Fellowships; Research; Program-related investments/loans; Employee matching gifts; Matching/challenge support.

Limitations: Applications accepted. Giving on a national and international basis. No support for religious programs, political activities or campaigns. No grants for fundraising appeals, institutional benefits, honorary functions or similar projects, tuition expenses, scholarships, or fellowships (other than those sponsored by the foundation).

Publications: Annual report; Newsletter.

Application information: Please do not send the letter of inquiry by fax. Send it by mail to the office of Grants Management or by e-mail. Direct applications for MacArthur Fellows programs not accepted. Grants increasingly initiated by the board. Application form not required.

   Initial approach: Letter of inquiry (2 to 3 pages) and one-page summary
   Copies of proposal: 1
   Deadline(s): None
   Board meeting date(s): Mar., June, Sept., and Dec.
   Final notification: 8 to 10 weeks

Officers and Directors: * Robert E. Denham,* Chair.; Robert L. Gallucci, Pres.; Marc P. Yanchura, V.P., and C.F.O.; Susan E. Manske, V.P. and C.I.O.; Joshua J. Mintz, V.P. and Genl. Counsel; Barry Lowenkron, V.P., International Progs.; Elspeth A. Revere, V.P., Media, Culture and Special Initiatives; Andrew Solomon, V.P., Public Affairs; Julia M. Stasch, V.P., U.S. Progs.; Elizabeth Kane, Secy.; Lloyd Axworthy; John Seely Brown; Jack Fuller; Jamie S. Gorelick; Mary Graham; Donald R. Hopkins, M.D.; Daniel Huttenlocher; Joi Ito; Will Miller; Mario J. Molina; Marjorie M. Scardino; Claude M. Steele.

Number of staff: 92 full-time professional; 85 full-time support.

EIN: 237093598

Recent grants for international programs:

788-1 Academic Educational Forum on International Relations, Moscow, Russia, $175,000. For development of a new generation of international relations expertise in Russia and the CIS. 2010.

788-2 Action Health, Lagos, Nigeria, $250,000. To promote pre-service Family Life and HIV Education quality assurance and youth-friendly reproductive health services in Nigeria (over 18 months). 2010.

788-3 Action Research and Training for Health Society, Udaipur, India, $375,000. To improve the quality of maternal-newborn health services, and pilot intervention to improve young women's access to reproductive health services in Rajasthan (over three years). 2010.

788-4 Action Research and Training for Health Society, Udaipur, India, $350,000. For the purchase of office space, partial construction costs for a field campus, and contribute to the endowment. 2010.

788-5 Adolescent Health and Information Project, Kano, Nigeria, $430,000. To implement the Family Life and HIV/AIDS Education Curriculum in Kano State (over three years). 2010.

788-6 Afluentes, Mexico City, Mexico, $92,000. To research sexuality education needs of young seasonal migrant workers. 2010.

788-7 African Centre for Democracy and Human Rights Studies, Serrekunda, Gambia, $300,000. For networking and advocacy by African NGOs with the African Commission on Human and Peoples' Rights (over three years). 2010.

788-8 African Court on Human and Peoples Rights, Arusha, Tanzania, Zanzibar and Pemba, $200,000. To procure books, journals and other resources for its library (over two years). 2010.

788-9 African Diaspora Policy Centre, Amsterdam, Netherlands, $185,000. To build capacity for African officials responsible for working with the diaspora to promote better treatment of migrants and economic development. 2010.

788-10 Ahmadu Bello University, Zaria, Nigeria, $950,000. To strengthen program in development communication (over three years). 2010.

788-11 Ahmadu Bello University, Zaria, Nigeria, $29,159. To plan for a Master's in Veterinary Epidemiology program. 2010.

788-12 Ahmadu Bello University Teaching Hospital, Zaria, Nigeria, $300,000. For the Community Prevention of Postpartum Hemorrhage Initiative. 2010.

788-13 All-Russian Public Movement for Human Rights, Moscow, Russia, $150,000. For research on human rights abuses in child care facilities and the federal penitentiary system (over two years). 2010.

788-14 America Abroad Media, Washington, DC, $200,000. To support America Abroad, international affairs radio series (over two years). 2010.

788-15 American Bar Association Fund for Justice and Education, Washington, DC, $600,000. To improve access to justice for victims of sexual and gender-based violence in the eastern Democratic Republic of Congo (over two years). 2010.

788-16 American Museum of Natural History, New York, NY, $315,000. To consolidate and sustain community based conservation in the western Solomon Islands (over three years). 2010.

788-17 Amnesty International UK, London, England, $265,000. For a project entitled, Protection and Promotion of Human Rights in the Russian Federation (over two years). 2010.

788-18 Arms Control Association, Washington, DC, $500,000. To establish operating reserve, a strategic plan for donor outreach, and a communications plan (over two years). 2010.

788-19 Ashish Gram Rachna Trust, Maharashtra, India, $330,000. To increase access to maternal and reproductive health information and services

among married adolescents in Maharashtra (over three years). 2010.

788-20 ASITY: Ligue Malgache pour la Protection des Oiseaux, Antananarivo, Madagascar, $250,000. To improve conservation, sustain natural resource use, and increase resilience to climate change in Mangoky-Ihotry Wetland Complex (over three years). 2010.

788-21 Aspen Institute, Washington, DC, $300,000. To promote effective implementation of the World Health Organization's Global Code of Practice on the International Recruitment of Health Personnel (over two years). 2010.

788-22 Bangladesh Institute of Peace and Security Studies, Dhaka, Bangladesh, $350,000. To research the security implications of climate change in South Asia (over two years). 2010.

788-23 Bayero University, Kano, Nigeria, $43,000. To plan and prepare activities for the establishment of a University Center for Dryland Agriculture. 2010.

788-24 BirdLife International, Cambridge, England, $250,000. For the organizational and technical development of Societe Audubon Haiti (over three years). 2010.

788-25 BirdLife International, Cambridge, England, $235,000. To develop a public/private alliance among Caribbean and international agencies and organizations to conserve Caribbean mangrove forests (over three years). 2010.

788-26 BirdLife International, Cambridge, England, $150,000. To design, test, and monitor the effectiveness of site based ecosystem based approaches to climate change adaptation in Cambodia (over two years). 2010.

788-27 BirdLife International, Cambridge, England, $70,000. To raise awareness among key decisionmakers about the impact of climate change on biodiversity at the Tenth Conference of Parties to the Convention on Biological Diversity. 2010.

788-28 Bishop Museum, Honolulu, HI, $500,000. To develop information infrastructure and modeling tools that advance biodiversity conservation in Melanesia in the face of climate change (over three years). 2010.

788-29 Blue Ventures Conservation, London, England, $670,000. To build the foundation of a national locally-managed marine area network to safeguard Madagascar's coastal fisheries and biodiversity (over three years). 2010.

788-30 Blue Ventures Conservation, London, England, $300,000. To develop integrated population, health, and environment project in Madagascar (over 42 months). 2010.

788-31 Blue Ventures Conservation, London, England, $275,000. To link the conservation of Madagascar's mangrove habitats to international carbon markets (over three years). 2010.

788-32 Blue Ventures Conservation, London, England, $40,800. To improve girls' education in Velondriake Locally Managed Marine Area in southwest Madagascar (over two years). 2010.

788-33 Brookings Institution, Washington, DC, $450,000. For the Geopolitics and Scarcity: Energy and Resource Competition Among the Major and Rising Powers project (over two years). 2010.

788-34 Brookings Institution, Washington, DC, $200,000. For research and a task force to advance agenda for secondary education in developing countries, with a focus on girls (over 18 months). 2010.

788-35 Brown University, Providence, RI, $500,000. To study the relationship between compulsory savings and homeownership in Mexico (over three years). 2010.

788-36 Bulletin of the Atomic Scientists, Chicago, IL, $250,000. For information to policymakers and the public on nuclear weapons, nuclear energy, climate change and bioterrorism and to foster informed dialogue on solutions to such global risks. 2010.

788-37 CARE USA, Atlanta, GA, $625,000. To research climate change and its impact on migration (over two years). 2010.

788-38 Caribbean Natural Resources Institute, Laventille, Trinidad & Tobago, $475,000. To strengthen civil society organizations as effective advocates for biodiversity conservation and sustainable development (over three years). 2010.

788-39 Carnegie Endowment for International Peace, Washington, DC, $650,000. For general operations (over one year). 2010.

788-40 Carnegie Endowment for International Peace, Washington, DC, $350,000. To expand the Democracy and Rule of Law Program (over three years). 2010.

788-41 Carnegie Endowment for International Peace, Washington, DC, $300,000. For the policy journal, Pro et Contra (over three years). 2010.

788-42 Center for Citizens Participation with the African Union, Nairobi, Kenya, $300,000. To promote the participation and engagement of African citizens and civil society organizations with the African Union and its institutions (over two years). 2010.

788-43 Center for Health and Gender Equity, Washington, DC, $300,000. For maternal health advocacy (over three years). 2010.

788-44 Center for Reproductive Rights, New York, NY, $600,000. For the international legal program (over three years). 2010.

788-45 Center for Strategic and International Studies, Washington, DC, $800,000. For the Sustainable Nuclear Futures project (over three years). 2010.

788-46 Center for Strategic and International Studies, Washington, DC, $200,000. To involve immigrant leaders in policy dialogue on migration and development in the U.S. and Mexico (over two years). 2010.

788-47 Center of Applied Research and Programs, Moscow, Russia, $150,000. For Russia's participation in the European Social Survey. 2010.

788-48 Center of Social Policy and Gender Studies, Saratov, Russia, $300,000. For a comparative analysis of social policy processes in the post-socialist space (over three years). 2010.

788-49 Centre for Constitutionalism and Demilitarisation, Lagos, Nigeria, $200,000. To research, document, and publish annual report on the state of human rights in Nigeria (over two years). 2010.

788-50 Centre for Independent Social Research, Saint Petersburg, Russia, $175,000. For a research project on the societal role of universities in provincial Russia (over three years). 2010.

788-51 Centre for Socio-Legal Studies, Abuja, Nigeria, $100,000. To consolidate justice sector reform. 2010.

788-52 Centro Agronomico Tropical de Investigacion y Ensenanza, Turrialba, Costa Rica, $600,000.

To create a Master's in Development Practice degree program (over three years). 2010.

788-53 Centro de Investigaciones en Salud de Comitan, Comitan de Dominguez, Mexico, $210,000. To disseminate intervention models for the prevention of maternal mortality (over three years). 2010.

788-54 Chicago Fair Trade, Chicago, IL, $70,000. For Fair Play, a project to increase public and institutional support for the principles of fair trade (over two years). 2010.

788-55 Citizens to Stop Nuclear Terrorism, Dallas, TX, $25,000. For a project titled, Business Initiative on Nuclear Terrorism, to educate U.S. business leaders on the threat from nuclear terrorism and the need for policies and actions to prevent it. 2010.

788-56 CIVIC-Campaign for Innocent Victims in Conflict, Washington, DC, $300,000. For general operations (over three years). 2010.

788-57 Columbia University, Earth Institute, New York, NY, $500,000. For the Master of Public Administration in Development Practice Secretariat (over 21 months). 2010.

788-58 Community Action for Popular Participation, Abuja, Nigeria, $250,000. For community-driven peace building in Plateau State, Nigeria (over two years). 2010.

788-59 Community Health and Research Initiative, Kano, Nigeria, $300,000. For advocacy and budget tracking for improved maternal health services, with a view to reducing maternal mortality and morbidity in Kano, Bauchi and Sokoto states (over three years). 2010.

788-60 Conservation International, Arlington, VA, $250,000. To foster the sustainable development and financing of Fiji's Locally Managed Marine Areas network through targeted research, monitoring, and outreach (over three years). 2010.

788-61 Conservation International, Arlington, VA, $200,000. To design, test, and monitor the effectiveness of site based ecosystem based approaches to climate change adaptation in Cambodia (over two years). 2010.

788-62 Consortium of Womens Nongovernmental Organizations, Moscow, Russia, $300,000. To work with regional and municipal public authorities and the mass media to combat gender discrimination through the implementation of existing laws in the Russian Federation (over three years). 2010.

788-63 Cornell University, Cornell Laboratory of Ornithology, Ithaca, NY, $300,000. For training and monitoring for conservation and management of natural resources in Cuban protected areas (over three years). 2010.

788-64 Council on Foreign Relations, New York, NY, $400,000. For policy research on security challenges on China's periphery (over two years). 2010.

788-65 Counterpart International, Arlington, VA, $340,000. To improve agriculture and fishery practices in the buffer zone of Monte Cristi National Park, Dominican Republic (over three years). 2010.

788-66 Development and Environmental Law Center Madagascar-Mizana Maitso, Fianarantsoa, Madagascar, $200,000. To build capacity to apply public interest law to environmental law and to improve community governance and management of natural resources in Madagascar (over two years). 2010.

788-67 Dose na Tsenzuru, Moscow, Russia, $90,000. For a human rights journal and its quarterly publication covering human rights violations in the criminal justice and penitentiary system. 2010.

788-68 Due Process of Law Foundation, Washington, DC, $80,000. For the protection of indigenous rights in the implementation of the new criminal justice system in Mexico. 2010.

788-69 Durrell Wildlife Conservation Trust, Trinity, Jersey, $240,000. To manage sustainable resources through integration of community-based monitoring within protected area management in Madagascar (over three years). 2010.

788-70 Elige: Youth Network for Sexual and Reproductive Rights, Mexico City, Mexico, $150,000. To advance federal policies supportive of youth sexual and reproductive health and rights in Mexico (over three years). 2010.

788-71 Endowment of the United States Institute of Peace, Washington, DC, $100,000. To develop a student educational toolkit for the Global Peacebuilding Center. 2010.

788-72 EngenderHealth, New York, NY, $125,000. To advance the global knowledge base of maternal health. 2010.

788-73 Environmental Defender's Office, Sydney, Australia, $210,000. To use the law to promote environmental protection and conservation in Melanesia (over three years). 2010.

788-74 Environmental Defense, New York, NY, $220,000. To improve cooperation between the United States and Cuba on natural resource management and environmental protection (over two years). 2010.

788-75 Environmental Law Alliance Worldwide, Eugene, OR, $300,000. To strengthen public interest law to sustain conservation in the Caribbean (over three years). 2010.

788-76 Environmental Law Institute, Washington, DC, $180,000. To build the capacity of judges to protect biodiversity in Jamaica, Haiti, and the Dominican Republic (over three years). 2010.

788-77 European University of Saint Petersburg, Institute for Professional Training, Saint Petersburg, Russia, $400,000. To conduct research on the functioning of the court system in Russia (over two years). 2010.

788-78 Fairchild Tropical Botanic Garden, Coral Gables, FL, $250,000. To apply conservation science to protect the Greater Cockpit Country ecosystem in Western Jamaica (over three years). 2010.

788-79 Family Care International, New York, NY, $350,000. To strengthen accountability mechanisms for maternal health programs in Latin America (over three years). 2010.

788-80 FANAMBY, Antananarivo, Madagascar, $200,000. To enhance participation of local communities in the design and management of Loky Manambato protected area in Madagascar. 2010.

788-81 Federal Rural University of Rio de Janeiro, Rio de Janeiro, Brazil, $800,000. To develop and offer a Master's in Development Practice degree program (over three years). 2010.

788-82 Field Museum of Natural History, Chicago, IL, $350,000. To involve local communities in conserving critical habitats that lack official protection and to build Malagasy capacity for conservation biology (over three years). 2010.

788-83 Foundation of the Peoples of the South Pacific International Regional Secretariat, Suva, Fiji, $300,000. To consolidate and expand the Locally Managed Marine Area Network in Vanuatu and the Solomon Islands (over three years). 2010.

788-84 George Washington University, Elliott School of International Affairs, Washington, DC, $200,000. For the Project on Forward Engagement (over two years). 2010.

788-85 George Washington University, Office of Sponsored Research, Washington, DC, $630,000. To monitor implementation of the Voluntary Code of Conduct for the Ethical International Recruitment of Foreign-Educated Nurses to the United States, and to explore the extension of ethical recruitment codes to allied health professionals, physicians, and teachers (over two years). 2010.

788-86 Georgetown University, Institute for the Study of International Migration, Washington, DC, $360,000. To create a module of questions on migration and remittances for inclusion in household surveys in developing countries (over two years). 2010.

788-87 Girls Power Initiative, Calabar, Nigeria, $250,000. To scale up implementation of the national sexuality education curriculum and training of health providers on youth friendly services in Cross River State (over three years). 2010.

788-88 Global Rights, Washington, DC, $500,000. For general operations (over two years). 2010.

788-89 Global Witness, London, England, $205,000. For the project, Breaking the Links Between Natural Resource Exploitation, Conflict, and Corruption in the Democratic Republic of Congo (over two years). 2010.

788-90 Groupe detude et de Recherche sur les Primates de Madagascar, Antananarivo, Madagascar, $140,000. To demonstrate contribution of lemur conservation to human well-being for communities living next to Makira protected area (over three years). 2010.

788-91 Grupo de Informacion en Reproduccion Elegida, Mexico City, Mexico, $270,000. For national, state-level and international advocacy (over three years). 2010.

788-92 Grupo Jaragua, Santo Domingo, Dominican Republic, $350,000. To conserve the Jaragua-Bahoruco-Enriquillo Biosphere Reserve in the Dominican Republic (over three years). 2010.

788-93 Gynuity Health Projects, New York, NY, $100,000. To raise awareness about the use of misoprostol for post abortion care (over 18 months). 2010.

788-94 Health Partners International, Lewes, England, $120,000. For research on emergency transport schemes in Nigeria (over two years). 2010.

788-95 Henry L. Stimson Center, Washington, DC, $650,000. For a research project titled, South Asia's Nuclear Future (over three years). 2010.

788-96 Henry L. Stimson Center, Washington, DC, $400,000. To broaden and deepen understanding of the risks posed by the construction of hydropower dams on the Mekong River's mainstream. 2010.

788-97 Henry L. Stimson Center, Washington, DC, $300,000. For general operations. 2010.

788-98 Human Rights Resource Center, Saint Petersburg, Russia, $375,000. For legal support to Russian NGOs and promote the professional growth of these organizations (over three years). 2010.

788-99 Independent Television Service, San Francisco, CA, $1,500,000. For the Global Perspectives Project, a program to bring documentary content from international producers to U.S. audiences, and from U.S. producers to international audiences (over three years). 2010.

788-100 Indonesia Locally Managed Marine Areas Foundation, Biak City, Indonesia, $150,000. To strengthen a network of Locally Managed Marine Areas in Papua Province, Indonesia (over three years). 2010.

788-101 Institute for Study and Dissemination on Migration, Mexico City, Mexico, $225,000. To study and assess recruitment mechanisms and access to social protection benefits for temporary migrant workers in the U.S., Canada, Mexico and Central America (over 21 months). 2010.

788-102 Institute of International Education, New York, NY, $50,000. To develop implementation plan for Asia Security Initiative Emerging Leaders program. 2010.

788-103 Institute of Sociology of the Russian Academy of Sciences, Moscow, Russia, $600,000. For the Center for Sociological Education's training program in the social sciences and humanities for young Russian regional university faculty and researchers (over three years). 2010.

788-104 Instituto para la Seguridad y la Democracia, Mexico City, Mexico, $500,000. For public security policy reform in Mexico (over three years). 2010.

788-105 Inter-American Institute for Global Change Research, Sao Jose dos Campos, Brazil, $500,000. To develop a standard methodology to estimate climate change risk for biodiversity at local scales in the Tropical Andes (over three years). 2010.

788-106 International Centre for Integrated Mountain Development, Kathmandu, Nepal, $400,000. To understand the impact of climate change on biodiversity and related ecosystem services in the Eastern Himalayas and advance collaboration on regional adaptation strategies (over two years). 2010.

788-107 International Institute for Strategic Studies, London, England, $535,000. For a policy research project titled, Fostering Cooperation with China on Nuclear and Radiological Security (over two years). 2010.

788-108 International Projects Assistance Services, Chapel Hill, NC, $300,000. For advancing access to safe legal abortion in three Mexican states (over three years). 2010.

788-109 International Womens Health Coalition, New York, NY, $1,000,000. For general operations (over three years). 2010.

788-110 Internews Network, Washington, DC, $175,000. For Haitian media. 2010.

788-111 Inveneo, San Francisco, CA, $725,000. For portable solar devices to improve maternal health outcomes (over 18 months). 2010.

788-112 Johns Hopkins University, Paul H. Nitze School of Advanced International Studies/ U.S.-Korea Institute, Baltimore, MD, $50,000. For a policy research project to improve understanding of the constraints on spent fuel storage in South Korea. 2010.

788-113 Kazan Human Rights Center, Kazan, Russia, $250,000. To combat police abuse in Russia (over three years). 2010.

788-114 Kudirat Initiative for Democracy, Lagos, Nigeria, $100,000. For special program support. 2010.

788-115 Legal Resources Consortium, Lagos, Nigeria, $60,000. To plan a meeting to launch African Working Group on Human Rights Council advocacy. 2010.

788-116 Link Media, San Francisco, CA, $1,500,000. To produce and distribute Link TV's global news programs (over three years). 2010.

788-117 Madagascar Foundation for Protected Areas and Biodiversity, Antananarivo, Madagascar, $150,000. To strengthen fundraising capacity and to diversify sources of funding (over two years). 2010.

788-118 Malagasy Environment Foundation in Environment Tany Meva, Antananarivo, Madagascar, $320,000. To reduce the vulnerability of communities living in and around Mikea forest through improved management of natural resources (over three years). 2010.

788-119 Management Systems International, Washington, DC, $200,000. To scale up NGO and public sector innovations on reducing maternal mortality and morbidity and to advance young people's sexual and reproductive health in India. 2010.

788-120 Marie Stopes Mexico, San Cristobal de las Casas, Mexico, $210,000. For outreach to indigenous and rural adolescents on reproductive and sexual health information and services (over three years). 2010.

788-121 Massachusetts Institute of Technology, Office of Sponsored Programs, Cambridge, MA, $980,000. For action-research program on improving maternal health in Nigeria (over three years). 2010.

788-122 Middlebury College, Monterey Institute of International Studies, Middlebury, VT, $475,000. For the James Martin Center for Nonproliferation Studies program of education and training in the areas of nuclear nonproliferation and terrorism (over two years). 2010.

788-123 Mud Horse Pictures, Brooklyn, NY, $50,000. For support of High Tech, Low Life , a documentary film exploring citizen reporting in China. 2010.

788-124 National Alliance of Latin American and Caribbean Communities, Chicago, IL, $400,000. To involve immigrant leaders in policy dialogue on migration and development in the U.S .and Mexico (over two years). 2010.

788-125 National Committee on American Foreign Policy, New York, NY, $330,000. For Track II Dialogues on Asia-Pacific Security (over two years). 2010.

788-126 National Democratic Institute for International Affairs, Washington, DC, $50,000. To promote closer EU-U.S. cooperation on democracy assistance. 2010.

788-127 National Security Archive Fund, Washington, DC, $900,000. For the International Human Rights Evidence Program (over three years). 2010.

788-128 National Universities Commission, Abuja, Nigeria, $350,000. To enhance capacity to meet the challenges of monitoring and coordinating the university system and to bring to scale some of the positive developments in the Nigerian university system (over two years). 2010.

788-129 Nature Conservancy, Arlington, VA, $350,000. For integrated conservation of coastal and terrestrial ecosystems in the Solomon Islands (over three years). 2010.

788-130 Nature Conservancy, Arlington, VA, $200,000. To establish a sustainable conservation funding mechanism for protected areas in the Caribbean region (over two years). 2010.

788-131 Nature Conservancy, Arlington, VA, $150,000. To become a more strategically-focused global conservation organization. 2010.

788-132 Nature Conservancy, Arlington, VA, $75,000. To developing a tri-national, Haiti-Dominican Republic-Cuba marine action plan for the Caribbean Biological Corridor. 2010.

788-133 Network of African National Human Rights Institutions, Nairobi, Kenya, $37,000. For a workshop on best practices for National Human Rights Institutions. 2010.

788-134 Network of University Legal Aid Institutions, NULAI-Nigeria, Abuja, Nigeria, $380,000. For implementation of law clinics and the Clinical Legal Education program in Nigerian law schools to complement official legal aid services (over three years). 2010.

788-135 New York Botanical Garden, Bronx, NY, $250,000. To identify the most vulnerable plant species in Cuba (over three years). 2010.

788-136 Nigeria Coalition on the International Criminal Court, Abuja, Nigeria, $250,000. To promote the International Criminal Court in Nigeria and Africa (over two years). 2010.

788-137 Nizhny Novgorod Regional Committee Against Torture, Nizhny Novgorod, Russia, $375,000. To combat police abuse in Russia (over three years). 2010.

788-138 Nonproliferation Policy Education Center, Washington, DC, $400,000. For a policy research project titled, Nuclear Power Development We Can Live With: What International Security Requires (over two years). 2010.

788-139 Northwestern University, Northwestern University School of Law, Center for International Human Rights, Evanston, IL, $20,000. For the Atrocity Crimes Litigation Year in Review Conference. 2010.

788-140 Nuclear Threat Initiative, Washington, DC, $1,000,000. For general operations (over two years). 2010.

788-141 Nuevos Codices Compatia, San Cristobal De Las Casas, Mexico, $75,000. To promote the reproductive and sexual health of indigenous youth in four municipalities in Chiapas (over 18 months). 2010.

788-142 Organisation for Economic Co-operation and Development, Paris, France, $70,000. For the Connected Minds report, international comparative analysis of student experience with digital media. 2010.

788-143 Organization for Social Development, Addis Ababa, Ethiopia, $30,000. To promote corporate social responsibility good practices related to reproductive health in Ethiopia. 2010.

788-144 Oxfam America, Boston, MA, $500,000. To empower indigenous peoples and organizations in the Andean-Amazon in efforts to reduce vulnerability to climate extremes and protect their environments and livelihoods (over three years). 2010.

788-145 Oxford University, Refugee Studies Centre, Oxford, England, $480,000. To research the emergence of the concept of environmental migrant, and how vulnerable populations in developing countries cope with the threat of climate change-induced displacement (over two years). 2010.

788-146 Panos Institute, Jamaica Office, Kingston, Jamaica, $365,000. For the participation of environmentally vulnerable communities in Haiti's national earthquake recovery debate (over two years). 2010.

788-147 Papua New Guinea Centre for Locally Managed Areas, Boroko, Papua New Guinea, $150,000. To strengthen a network of Locally Managed Marine Areas in Papua New Guinea (over three years). 2010.

788-148 Partners in Expanding Health Quality and Access, Ann Arbor, MI, $250,000. To scale up promising maternal and adolescent reproductive health programs (over three years). 2010.

788-149 Partners in Health, Boston, MA, $1,000,000. For construction of the new Mirebalais hospital in Haiti. 2010.

788-150 Partnership for Justice, Ikeja, Nigeria, $200,000. To monitor the Nigerian government's implementation of the Human Rights National Action Plan (over two years). 2010.

788-151 Peregrine Fund, Boise, ID, $160,000. To create a wetland and forest protected area in western Madagascar that is sustainably managed by local communities to maintain their livelihoods and conserve biodiversity (over three years). 2010.

788-152 PIR - Center for Policy Studies in Russia, Moscow, Russia, $600,000. For policy research and advanced training in the field of nuclear security (over two years). 2010.

788-153 Planned Parenthood Federation of Nigeria, Abuja, Nigeria, $1,200,000. For action-research program on improving maternal health in Nigeria (over three years). 2010.

788-154 Planned Parenthood Federation, International, London, England, $400,000. For the accreditation process for member associations (over three years). 2010.

788-155 Planned Parenthood Federation, International, New York, NY, $500,000. To increase access to sexual and reproductive health care among the Haitian population displaced by the 2010 earthquake. 2010.

788-156 Policy and Legal Advocacy Center, Abuja, Nigeria, $400,000. To improve the administration and credibility of elections in Nigeria. 2010.

788-157 Population Foundation of India, New Delhi, India, $300,000. To scale up NGO and public sector innovations on reducing maternal mortality and morbidity and to advance young people's sexual and reproductive health in India (over two years). 2010.

788-158 Princeton University, Woodrow Wilson School of Public and International Affairs, Princeton, NJ, $225,000. For joint U.S.-China research on the security challenges posted by dual-use biotechnology (over two years). 2010.

788-159 Proteus Fund, Amherst, MA, $150,000. For the International Human Rights Funders Group (over three years). 2010.

788-160 Red por los Derechos de la Infancia, Mexico City, Mexico, $500,000. To improve the judicial system's defense of vulnerable groups and individuals in Mexico (over 42 months). 2010.

788-161 Redress Trust Limited, London, England, $500,000. For security upgrades, communications system improvements, and contributions to operating reserve (over two years). 2010.

788-162 Reef Check Foundation, Pacific Palisades, CA, $150,000. For post-earthquake strategies for marine resource management in Haiti (over three years). 2010.

788-163 Reproductive Health Matters, London, England, $250,000. For general operations. 2010.

788-164 Research Foundation of State University of New York, Rockefeller College of Public Affairs and Policy, University at Albany-State University of New York, Albany, NY, $450,000. To research the interaction between immigration policy debates in the U.S. and Mexico and on cooperative migration management practices (over three years). 2010.

788-165 Ritinjali, New Delhi, India, $300,000. To deliver sexuality education program in public schools in three districts of Rajasthan (over three years). 2010.

788-166 Rostros y Voces, Mexico City, Mexico, $250,000. To integrate development concerns into the migration policy community in Mexico, strengthen civil society input into global migration discussions, and protect the rights of migrants on Mexico's southern border. 2010.

788-167 Royal Society for the Protection of Nature, Thimphu, Bhutan, $350,000. To contribute to endowment, construct a library and conference center for public use, and to create operating reserve. 2010.

788-168 Sciences Po, Paris, France, $800,000. To create a Master's in Development Practice degree program (over three years). 2010.

788-169 Sea to Shore Alliance, Saint Petersburg, FL, $150,000. For coastal wildlife conservation in Cuba (over three years). 2010.

788-170 Search for Common Ground, Washington, DC, $400,000. For TV, radio, and internet programming to promote reconciliation in transitional societies (over two years). 2010.

788-171 SeaWeb, Silver Spring, MD, $300,000. For communications training to enhance ocean conservation in Fiji and Papua Province, Indonesia through the Locally Managed Marine Area Network (over three years). 2010.

788-172 Secretaria de Relaciones Exteriores, Mexico City, Mexico, $136,000. For the fourth Global Forum on Migration and Development. 2010.

788-173 Security Council Report, New York, NY, $350,000. To produce detailed reports and publications. 2010.

788-174 Self Employed Women's Association, Ahmadabad, India, $200,000. To develop and demonstrate a young people's sexual and reproductive health program in the Ahmedabad district of Gujarat (over three years). 2010.

788-175 Shan Shui Conservation Center, Beijing, China, $400,000. For locally led ecosystem conservation in southwest and western China (over three years). 2010.

788-176 Sin Fronteras, Mexico City, Mexico, $350,000. To strengthen institutional capacity with the aim of continuing and expanding work to promote and defend the human rights of migrants, asylum seekers, and refugees in Mexico. 2010.

788-177 Social and Economic Rights Action Center, Lagos, Nigeria, $350,000. For the construction and procurement of materials for a resource and conference center in Lagos, Nigeria (over two years). 2010.

788-178 Social Science Research Council, Brooklyn, NY, $172,000. For Track II dialogue with North Korea. 2010.

788-179 Sociedad Mexicana pro Derechos de la Mujer, Mexico City, Mexico, $750,000. For office space and to contribute to endowment (over two years). 2010.

788-180 Sociedad Mexicana pro Derechos de la Mujer, Mexico City, Mexico, $700,000. To strengthen local capacity and organizing to decrease maternal mortality in rural indigenous areas of Mexico (over three years). 2010.

788-181 Society for Conservation Biology, Washington, DC, $300,000. To expand Conservation Magazine's distribution and reporting on key environment issues through the development of Conservation Conversations (over three years). 2010.

788-182 Stichting Global Voices, Amsterdam, Netherlands, $75,000. For the Citizen Media Summit. 2010.

788-183 Stichting Govcom.org, Amsterdam, Netherlands, $75,000. For network analysis to map the field of digital media and learning (over 15 months). 2010.

788-184 Tides Center, San Francisco, CA, $150,000. For a NGO-Summit on Nuclear Security, to be held in Washington D.C.. 2010.

788-185 Tides Center, Connect U.S. Fund, Washington, DC, $50,000. To strengthen collaboration among NGOs on nuclear nonproliferation and disarmament. 2010.

788-186 Transition Monitoring Group, Abuja, Nigeria, $400,000. To improve civic education for the 2011 general elections. 2010.

788-187 United Nations, Department of Economic and Social Affairs, New York, NY, $237,000. For the fourth and fifth meetings of the Global Forum on Migration and Development (over 18 months). 2010.

788-188 United Nations Association of the United States of America, New York, NY, $150,000. For the international Global Classrooms program (over three years). 2010.

788-189 United Nations Environment Programme World Conservation Monitoring Centre, Cambridge, England, $500,000. To expand the Integrated Biodiversity Assessment Tool into a family of decision support systems targeting three key sectors: research and conservation planning, business, and development finance (over two years). 2010.

788-190 United Nations Institute for Training and Research, Geneva, Switzerland, $500,000. To expand the use of geospatial technologies to advance human rights (over two years). 2010.

788-191 United Nations Population Fund, New York, NY, $500,000. To identify near-term reconstructive needs in Haiti and to support funding for longer term reconstructive efforts. 2010.

788-192 United Nations Population Fund, New York, NY, $350,000. To increase access to reproductive health services among the Pakistani population affected by the 2010 floods. 2010.

788-193 University of Ibadan, Ibadan, Nigeria, $980,000. To establish a graduate training and research program in Petroleum and Energy Economics and Law (over three years). 2010.

788-194 University of Ibadan, Ibadan, Nigeria, $950,000. To build training and research

capacity in the fields of population and public health (over four years). 2010.

788-195 University of Ibadan, Ibadan, Nigeria, $950,000. To improve child and adolescent mental health service delivery through a new Master's degree program (over four years). 2010.

788-196 University of Maryland Foundation, Adelphi, MD, $350,000. For the Advanced Methods of Cooperative Security Program at the Center for International Security Studies. 2010.

788-197 University of Port Harcourt, Port Harcourt, Nigeria, $990,000. To establish a new program in petroleum geosciences at the Institute of Petroleum Studies (over three years). 2010.

788-198 University of Queensland, School of Engineering, Brisbane, Australia, $275,000. To implement community management systems to protect the coral reefs and marine ecosystems of Marovo Lagoon in the Solomon Islands (over three years). 2010.

788-199 University of Sydney, Centre for International Security Studies, Sydney, Australia, $400,000. To research relationships between food security and conflict in the Asia-Pacific (over two years). 2010.

788-200 University of the Andes, Bogota, Colombia, $800,000. To create a Master's in Development Practice degree program to be housed in the School of Management (over three years). 2010.

788-201 University of the South Pacific, Institute of Applied Sciences South Pacific Regional Herbarium, Suva, Fiji, $600,000. To develop and implement successful community-based marine management in Melanesia by acting as the focal point for the Locally-Managed Marine Area Network (over three years). 2010.

788-202 University of the West Indies, Department of Life Sciences, Mona, Jamaica, $340,000. For natural resource conservation in the Cockpit Country and Black River Lower Morass, Jamaica (over three years). 2010.

788-203 University of Toronto, Munk Centre for International Studies, Toronto, Canada, $350,000. For the Citizen Lab (over two years). 2010.

788-204 University of Winnipeg, Winnipeg, Canada, $800,000. To develop and offer a Master's in Development Practice degree program (over three years). 2010.

788-205 W N E T Channel 13, New York, NY, $100,000. For support of Cuba: The Accidental Eden , a documentary film about Cuba's threatened natural environment for PBS NATURE. 2010.

788-206 WANGONeT, Lagos, Nigeria, $230,000. For credible elections in Nigeria. 2010.

788-207 Washington Office on Latin America, Washington, DC, $52,000. To promote bilateral U.S.-Mexico dialogue on the connection between migration and development. 2010.

788-208 Wildlife Conservation Society, Bronx, NY, $600,000. For community-based natural resource management and sustainable livelihood initiatives in Madagascar's MaMaBay ecosystems (over three years). 2010.

788-209 Wildlife Conservation Society, Bronx, NY, $250,000. For ecosystem-based management approach to Fiji's Vatu-i-Ra Seascape (over two years). 2010.

788-210 Wildlife Conservation Society, Bronx, NY, $150,000. To build consensus on key recommendations for addressing climate change

adaptation for conservation in the Albertine Rift region. 2010.

788-211 Wildlife Conservation Society, Bronx, NY, $150,000. To conserve wetlands and strengthening biodiversity conservation capacity in Cuba (over three years). 2010.

788-212 Wildlife Conservation Society, Bronx, NY, $17,000. To test the ability of new remote sensing tools to map and monitor disturbances caused by illegal logging within protected areas in Northeast Madagascar. 2010.

788-213 Windsor Research Centre, Trelawny, Jamaica, $250,000. For improving environmental impact assessment processes in Jamaica (over three years). 2010.

788-214 Women of the Don, Novocherkassk, Russia, $300,000. To promote reform of the regional police force (over three years). 2010.

788-215 Womens Rights Advancement and Protection Alternative, Abuja, Nigeria, $350,000. For a project on Islamic Family Law (over three years). 2010.

788-216 Woodrow Wilson International Center for Scholars, Washington, DC, $300,000. To promote bilateral dialogue among government representatives, policy experts and migrant leaders on U.S.-Mexico migration issues (over two years). 2010.

788-217 Woodrow Wilson International Center for Scholars, Washington, DC, $65,000. To develop a Public Diplomacy Initiative. 2010.

788-218 Woodstock Theological Center, Washington, DC, $30,000. For a public forum, God and the Bomb: Deterrence, Disarmament and Human Security, to improve understanding of contemporary nuclear weapons policy choices and the Catholic Church's approach to them. 2010.

788-219 World Affairs Council of Northern California, San Francisco, CA, $90,000. For the Global Philanthropy Forum (over three years). 2010.

788-220 World Policy Institute, New York, NY, $150,000. For the United Nations' Special Advisor on the Prevention of Genocide with tools to limit the catastrophic effects of violent speech in pre-genocidal situations (over 18 months). 2010.

788-221 World Security Institute, Washington, DC, $100,000. To support Johnson's Russia List , a daily electronic digest of news and analysis on political, economic, and security developments in Russia (over two years). 2010.

788-222 World Wide Fund for Nature-Madagascar, Madagascar and West Indian Ocean Programme Office, Antananarivo, Madagascar, $210,000. To develop and implement climate change adaptation strategies in two vulnerable hotspots in the mangrove ecosystems of Tsiribihina and Manambolo along the west coast of Madagascar (over two years). 2010.

788-223 World Wide Fund for Nature-Madagascar, Madagascar and West Indian Ocean Programme Office, Antananarivo, Madagascar, $81,600. To improve school infrastructure and secondary school education for girls in coastal villages of Southwest Madagascar (over two years). 2010.

788-224 World Wildlife Fund, Washington, DC, $400,000. To implement stronger environmental practices in Chinese investment and business operations overseas and in China, while simultaneously promoting sustainable development (over two years). 2010.

788-225 World Wildlife Fund, Washington, DC, $200,000. For a collaborative program that designs, tests, and monitors the effectiveness of site-based ecosystem based approaches to climate change adaptation in Cambodia (over two years). 2010.

788-226 World Wildlife Fund, Washington, DC, $200,000. To build capacity in the Wider Caribbean to climate change threats on coastal biodiversity and marine turtle habitat (over three years). 2010.

788-227 World Wildlife Fund, Washington, DC, $100,000. To improve the lives of communities within the Sakteng Wildlife Sanctuary. 2010.

788-228 Yayasan Pengembangan Hak Asasi Manusia Untuk ASEAN, Depok, Indonesia, $300,000. For research and education on human rights in Southeast Asia (over three years). 2010.

788-229 Youth, Adolescent, Reflection and Action Centre, Jos, Nigeria, $125,000. To expand young people's access to quality Family Life and HIV/AIDS Education in Plateau State. 2010.

789
Marquis George MacDonald Foundation, Inc.

c/o Northern Trust Bank of Florida, N.A.
P.O. Box 803878
Chicago, IL 60680-3878

Incorporated in 1951 in NY.
Donor: Marquis George MacDonald‡.
Grantmaker type: Independent foundation.
Financial data (yr. ended 12/31/10): Assets, $7,860,926 (M); expenditures, $440,077; qualifying distributions, $395,460.
Fields of interest: Christian agencies & churches; Media/communications; Visual arts; Museums; Performing arts; Performing arts, dance; Performing arts, theater; Performing arts, music; Arts; Secondary school/education; Higher education; Environment, natural resources; Environment; Animal welfare; Hospitals (general); Health care; Health organizations, association; Cancer; AIDS; Alcoholism; Cancer research; AIDS research; Food services; Human services; Aging, centers/services; Women, centers/services; International affairs, arms control; Community/economic development; Religion; Aging; Disabilities, people with; Women.
Type of support: Continuing support; Program development; Scholarship funds.
Limitations: Applications not accepted. Giving primarily in FL, NY and PA. No grants to individuals, or for matching gifts; no loans.
Application information: Contributes only to pre-selected organizations.
Officers and Directors:* John Lee McDonald, Pres.; Catherine MacDonald, V.P.; Helen MacDonald, V.P.; Joseph MacDonald, V.P.; Kevin McDonald, V.P.; Lauren McDonald,* Secy.; Kristen McDonald; Lee McDonald; Charles Shea III.
Number of staff: 1 part-time professional.
EIN: 131957181

790
Madigan Family Foundation

c/o Madden, Jiganti, Moore & Sinars
190 S. LaSalle St., Ste. 1700
Chicago, IL 60603-3496

Established in 1997 in IL.
Donor: John W. Madigan.
Grantmaker type: Independent foundation.
Financial data (yr. ended 03/31/11): Assets, $1,844,981 (M); expenditures, $792,829; qualifying distributions, $781,770; giving activities include $781,770 for grants.
Purpose and activities: Giving primarily for the arts, education, health organizations, and children, youth, and social services.
Fields of interest: Museums (art); Museums (children's); Museums (specialized); Performing arts; Arts; Higher education, university; Education; Health organizations, association; Human services; Children/youth, services; International affairs, foreign policy; United Ways and Federated Giving Programs; Christian agencies & churches; Catholic agencies & churches.
Limitations: Applications not accepted. Giving primarily in IL. No grants to individuals.
Application information: Contributes only to pre-selected organizations.
Officers and Directors:* Holly W. Madigan,* Pres.; John W. Madigan,* Secy.-Treas.; John J. Jiganti.
EIN: 364155300

791
Magnus Charitable Trust

600 W. Rand Rd., Ste. A-104
Arlington Heights, IL 60004-2355
(847) 255-1100
FAX: (847) 632-0616;
E-mail: info@magnuscharitable.org; URL: http://www.magnuscharitable.org

Established in 1995 in IL.
Donors: Alexander B. Magnus, Jr.‡; The Magnus Asset Management Trust.
Grantmaker type: Independent foundation.
Financial data (yr. ended 12/31/10): Assets, $9,973,061 (M); gifts received, $500; expenditures, $1,497,631; qualifying distributions, $326,065; giving activities include $326,065 for grants.
Purpose and activities: The mission of the Trust is to make a positive impact on the world by helping to educate those that are greatly in need. Since its inception, the trust has partnered with many organizations to help eliminate hunger and obstacles to obtaining education. Giving primarily for education scholarships to needy individuals; some funding for higher education, health and human services.
Fields of interest: Higher education; Health organizations, association; International human rights; Education; Human services.
Limitations: Applications accepted. Giving primarily in IL, with some emphasis on Chicago.
Application information: Application and guidelines are available on Trust web site. Application form required.
 Deadline(s): Apr. 18
Trustees: Maria Magnus; Krzysztof Szewczul.
EIN: 364049284

792
Robert R. McCormick Foundation

(formerly McCormick Tribune Foundation)
205 N. Michigan Ave., Ste. 4300
Chicago, IL 60601-5983 (312) 445-5000
Contact: Donald A. Cooke, Sr. V.P., Philanthropy

FAX: (312) 445-5001;
E-mail: info@mccormickfoundation.org; Additional address (Cantigny Park office): 1S151 Winfield Rd., Wheaton, IL 60189-3353; URL: http://www.mccormickfoundation.org
Facebook: http://www.facebook.com/McCormickFoundation
Twitter: http://twitter.com/McCormick_Fdn
YouTube: http://www.youtube.com/user/McCormickFoundation

Trust established in 1955 in IL; became a foundation in 1990; converted to a public charity in 2002.
Donors: Robert R. McCormick‡; The National Football League; Uni-Mart.
Grantmaker type: Public charity.
Financial data (yr. ended 12/31/10): Revenue, $32,784,582; assets, $1,176,585,115 (M); gifts received, $13,534,410; expenditures, $67,272,202; giving activities include $56,875,049 for grants, and $6,000 for 1 grant to an organization outside the U.S.
Purpose and activities: The foundation aims to improve social and economic environments, encourage a free and responsible discussion of issues affecting the nation, enhance the effectiveness of American education, and stimulate responsible citizenship within the Chicago metropolitan region.
Fields of interest: Media, print publishing; Education, early childhood education; Child development, education; Vocational education; Employment; Housing/shelter, development; Youth development, citizenship; Human services; Children/youth, services; Child development, services; Homeless, human services; Civil liberties, first amendment; Community/economic development; Voluntarism promotion; Government/public administration; Public affairs, citizen participation; Minorities; Economically disadvantaged; Homeless.
International interests: Latin America.
Type of support: General/operating support; Continuing support; Building/renovation; Program development; Conferences/seminars; Seed money; Curriculum development; Research; Technical assistance; Program evaluation; Program-related investments/loans; Employee matching gifts; Matching/challenge support.
Limitations: Giving primarily in the Chicagoland, IL region. No grants to individuals, or for scholarships or endowment funds.
Publications: Application guidelines; Annual report; Annual report (including application guidelines); Informational brochure (including application guidelines).
Application information: See web site for specific application information for each program, including contact information and application deadlines.
 Initial approach: Submit letter of inquiry online
 Copies of proposal: 1
 Deadline(s): Varies
 Board meeting date(s): Feb., May, Sept., and Dec.
Officers: Dennis J. FitzSimons,* Chair.; David D. Hiller, Pres. and C.E.O.; Donald A. Cooke,* Sr. V.P., Philanthropy; Louis J. Marsico, Jr.,* Sr. V.P., Opers.; Melinda Rosenbraugh, Treas.
Directors: James C. Dowdle; John W. Madigan; Ruthellyn Musil; Scott C. Smith; Don Wycliff.
Number of staff: 16 full-time professional; 6 full-time support.
EIN: 363689171

793

The McShane Foundation
9550 W. Higgins Rd., Ste. 200
Rosemont, IL   60018-4906   (847) 292-4300
Contact: James A. McShane, Pres. and Secy.

Established in 1988 in IL.
Donors: McShane Builders, Inc.; James A. McShane.
Grantmaker type: Company-sponsored foundation.
Financial data (yr. ended 12/31/10): Assets, $812,296 (M); expenditures, $165,230; qualifying distributions, $158,200; giving activities include $158,200 for grants.
Purpose and activities: The foundation supports organizations involved with education, youth development, human services, international relief, and Christianity.
Fields of interest: Human services; Christian agencies & churches; International relief; Youth development; Education.
Type of support: General/operating support.
Limitations: Applications accepted. Giving primarily in IL.
Application information: Application form required.
   Initial approach: Letter
   Deadline(s): None
Officer and Directors:* James A. McShane,* Pres. and Secy.; Pat Glascow; Mary G. McShane.
EIN: 363627198

794

Mead Johnson Nutrition Company Contributions Program
2701 Patriot Blvd.
Glenview, IL   60026-8039   (847) 832-2420
URL: http://www.meadjohnson.com/CorporateCitizenship/Pages/Nurturing-Communities.aspx

Grantmaker type: Corporate giving program.
Purpose and activities: Mead Johnson Nutrition Company makes charitable contributions to nonprofit organizations involved with nutritional care for vulnerable children and nutrition information for their caregivers. Support is given primarily in areas of company operations worldwide.
Fields of interest: Child development, services; Children, services; Reproductive health, prenatal care; Nutrition; Children.
International interests: Asia; Europe; Latin America.
Type of support: General/operating support; Curriculum development; Employee volunteer services; Donated products; In-kind gifts.
Limitations: Giving on an international basis in areas of company operations.

795

Henry and Louise Mermelstein Charitable Foundation
6500 North Hamlin
Lincolnwood, IL   60712-3904

Established in 1986 in IL.
Donors: Henry Mermelstein; Louise Mermelstein; Doreen Mermelstein; Marvin Mermelstein.
Grantmaker type: Independent foundation.
Financial data (yr. ended 06/30/11): Assets, $1,177,037 (M); gifts received, $266,006; expenditures, $228,098; qualifying distributions,

$225,842; giving activities include $225,842 for 99 grants (high: $42,000; low: $18).
Purpose and activities: Support for Jewish organizations, including yeshivas and congregations.
Fields of interest: Education; Jewish agencies & synagogues.
International interests: Canada; Israel.
Limitations: Applications not accepted. Giving primarily in the U.S., with some emphasis on Chicago, IL, NJ and NY. No grants to individuals.
Application information: Contributes only to pre-selected organizations.
Officer: Henry Mermelstein, Pres.
Directors: Joseph Mermelstein; Louise Mermelstein; Marvin Mermelstein.
EIN: 363481731

796

Messengers of Mercy
25 W. 560 Geneva Rd.
Carol Stream, IL   60188-2231   (630) 580-5074
FAX: (630) 580-5075; *URL:* http://www.messengersofmercy.org

Established in 1996.
Grantmaker type: Public charity.
Financial data (yr. ended 12/31/10): Revenue, $1,841,126; assets, $217,843 (M); gifts received, $1,840,535; expenditures, $1,747,621; giving activities include $1,626,400 for grants to organizations outside the U.S.
Purpose and activities: The organization provides humanitarian relief by providing medical equipment, medical supplies, new or used clothing, shoes, books, and educational supplies.
Fields of interest: Human services; International relief.
International interests: Bulgaria; Guatemala; Argentina; Nepal; Chile; Honduras; Nicaragua; Peru; New Zealand; Burma (Myanmar); Ethiopia; Pakistan; Bangladesh; Cambodia; Jamaica; Egypt; Mexico; Eritrea; Turkmenistan; Afghanistan; Thailand; Turkey; Tajikistan; Brazil; Paraguay; Mongolia; Indonesia; Gambia, The; India; Uganda; Kenya; Nigeria; Kazakhstan; Kyrgyzstan; China; Uzbekistan; Tanzania, Zanzibar and Pemba; Albania; North Korea.
Type of support: In-kind gifts.
Limitations: Giving limited to Afghanistan, Albania, Argentina, Bangladesh, Brazil, Bulgaria, Cambodia, Chile, China, Egypt, Eritrea, Ethiopia, Gambia, Guatemala, Honduras, India, Indonesia, Jamaica, Kazakhstan, Kenya, Kyrgyzstan, Mexico, Mongolia, Myanmar, Nepal, New Zealand, Nicaragua, Nigeria, North Korea, Pakistan, Paraguay, Peru, Tajikistan, Tanzania, Thailand, Turkey, Turkmenistan, Uganda, Uzbekistan, and West Samoa.
Publications: Newsletter.
Officers and Directors:* David K. Lee,* Chair.; Matthew Lee, Secy.; Yong S. Park, Treas.; Dr. Soon Ja Choi, Exec. Dir.; John Hyunsoo Kim; Dr. Byung In Lee; Dr. Yong E. Lee; Dr. Sung Chul Moon; and 8 additional directors.
EIN: 364203666

797

Mission Honduras International
P.O. Box 56007
Chicago, IL   60656-0007   (773) 809-4008
Contact: Robert O'Dwyer, Pres.

E-mail: info@missionhonduras.com; *URL:* http://www.missionhonduras.com
Facebook: http://www.facebook.com/pages/Liberia-Mission-Inc/192377907488?ref=ts

Established in 1970 in IL.
Grantmaker type: Public charity.
Financial data (yr. ended 12/31/10): Revenue, $436,045; assets, $197,675 (M); gifts received, $421,961; expenditures, $716,171; program services expenses, $565,425; giving activities include $303,319 for 1 grant, $189,174 for 1 grant to an organization outside the U.S., and $72,932 for foundation-administered programs.
Purpose and activities: The organization seeks to provide missionary support to poor orphans in Honduras, the Dominican Republic, and Liberia.
Fields of interest: Christian agencies & churches; Education.
International interests: Liberia; Honduras; Dominican Republic.
Limitations: Applications not accepted. Giving primarily in the Dominican Republic, Honduras, and Liberia.
Application information: Contributes only to pre-selected organizations.
Officers and Directors:* Robert O'Dwyer,* Pres.; John Dewan,* Treas.; Jerome Cabeen; Clarissa Chavarria-Lara; Sue Dewan; Dave Dionisi; Fr. Don Halpin, O.F.M. Conv.; Jennie Martin; Kathy O'Dwyer.
EIN: 237116589

798

Motorola Solutions Foundation
(formerly Motorola Foundation)
c/o Motorola Solutions, Inc.
1303 East Algonquin Rd.
Schaumburg, IL   60196-4041   (847) 538-7639
Contact: Matt Blakely, Dir.
FAX: (847) 538-1456;
E-mail: foundation@motorolasolutions.com;
URL: http://www.motorolasolutions.com/giving
Facebook: http://www.facebook.com/MSIFoundation
Innovation Generation Grant Recipients: http://responsibility.motorolasolutions.com/index.php/communityinvestment/education/igg/ig2011/
Twitter: http://twitter.com/#!/msifoundation

Established in 1953 in IL.
Donor: Motorola, Inc.
Grantmaker type: Company-sponsored foundation.
Financial data (yr. ended 12/31/10): Assets, $101,344,313 (M); expenditures, $18,223,029; qualifying distributions, $18,140,012; giving activities include $17,890,729 for 428 grants (high: $500,700; low: $55).
Purpose and activities: The foundation supports programs designed to promote education, disaster relief, public safety, and Motorola employee involvement. Special emphasis is directed toward science, technology, engineering, and math programming.
Fields of interest: Elementary/secondary education; Education; Disasters, preparedness/services; Disasters, fire prevention/control; Safety/disasters; American Red Cross; Human services; United Ways and Federated Giving Programs; Science, formal/general education; Mathematics; Engineering/technology; Science; Youth; Minorities; Girls.

Type of support: General/operating support; Equipment; Program development; Curriculum development; Employee volunteer services.
Limitations: Applications accepted. Giving primarily on a national and international basis in areas of company operations, with emphasis on CA, Washington, DC, FL, GA, IL, MA, MD, NJ, NY, TX, Argentina, Belgium, Brazil, China, England, France, Mexico, Poland, and Singapore. No support for political or lobbying organizations, political candidates, or private foundations described under the U.S. IRS Code Section 509(a). No grants to individuals, or for endowments, sports sponsorships, or capital campaigns; no Motorola Solutions product or equipment donations.
Publications: Application guidelines; Grants list; Program policy statement.
Application information: Application form required.
   Initial approach: Complete online eligibility quiz and application
   Deadline(s): None; Mar. 23 for Innovation Generation Grants
   Board meeting date(s): Monthly and as required
Director: Matt Blakely, Dir.
Number of staff: 1 part-time professional; 2 part-time support.
EIN: 366109323
Recent grants for international programs:
798-1 ABTI-American University of Nigeria, African Center, Yola, Nigeria, $50,000. 2009.
798-2 American Society for Technion-Israel Institute of Technology, New York, NY, $40,000. For Israel Technion Society. 2009.
798-3 BAPS Care International, Piscataway, NJ, $20,378. 2009.
798-4 BAPS Care International, Piscataway, NJ, $12,854. 2009.
798-5 BDA Fund, New York, NY, $15,000. 2009.
798-6 Boldrini Childrens Cancer Center, Sao Paulo, Brazil, $100,000. 2009.
798-7 Canadian Fallen Firefighters Foundation, Ottawa, Canada, $10,000. 2009.
798-8 CARE USA, Atlanta, GA, $200,000. 2009.
798-9 CARE USA, Atlanta, GA, $100,000. 2009.
798-10 CARE USA, Atlanta, GA, $50,000. 2009.
798-11 Casa dos Menores de Campinas, Campinas, Brazil, $15,000. 2009.
798-12 CDI International, New York, NY, $100,000. 2009.
798-13 CDI International, New York, NY, $75,000. 2009.
798-14 China Youth Development Foundation, Beijing, China, $300,000. 2009.
798-15 Clinton Global Initiative, New York, NY, $19,000. 2009.
798-16 Comite de Soutien a La Scotarisation des Filles Rurales, Rabat, Morocco and the Western Sahara, $70,000. 2009.
798-17 Daphne Jackson Trust, Guildford, England, $35,000. 2009.
798-18 Dikembe Mutombo Foundation, Atlanta, GA, $100,000. 2009.
798-19 e-learning Foundation, Chertsey, England, $60,000. 2009.
798-20 Ecole Superieure de Electricite, Gif-sur-Yvette, France, $100,000. 2009.
798-21 Educational Cooperation Society, Lagos, Nigeria, $50,000. 2009.
798-22 Fidel - Association for Education and Social Integration of Ethiopian Jews in Israel, Yehud, Israel, $38,000. 2009.
798-23 Fundacion Michou y Mau, I.A.P., Mexico City, Mexico, $75,000. 2009.

798-24 Give to Colombia, Coral Gables, FL, $52,000. 2009.
798-25 Halev Center, Tel Aviv, Israel, $40,000. 2009.
798-26 Hands On Technology, Leipzig, Germany, $50,000. 2009.
798-27 Instituto de Ensenanza Superior Simon Bolivar, Anexo de Villa El Libertador, Cordoba, Argentina, $61,700. 2009.
798-28 Instituto Superior Tecnico, Lisbon, Portugal, $100,000. 2009.
798-29 International Center for Missing and Exploited Children, Alexandria, VA, $100,000. 2009.
798-30 International Scientific Exchange Foundation of China, Beijing, China, $50,000. 2009.
798-31 Junior Achievement China, Beijing, China, $50,000. 2009.
798-32 Junior Achievement of Argentina, Buenos Aires, Argentina, $13,500. 2009.
798-33 Kids Help Phone, Toronto, Canada, $100,000. 2009.
798-34 Kidscape, London, England, $20,000. 2009.
798-35 King Baudouin Foundation United States, New York, NY, $10,000. 2009.
798-36 Korea Firemens Mutual Aid Association, Seoul, South Korea, $50,000. 2009.
798-37 Minority Supplier Development China, Beijing, China, $25,000. 2009.
798-38 Nanyang Polytechnic, Singapore, $19,300. 2009.
798-39 Nanyang Technological University, Singapore, $50,000. 2009.
798-40 Nanyang Technological University, Singapore, $18,000. 2009.
798-41 National University of Singapore, Singapore, $15,000. 2009.
798-42 Netanya Academic College, Netanya, Israel, $59,825. 2009.
798-43 Parikrma USA, New York, NY, $250,000. 2009.
798-44 Parikrma USA, New York, NY, $100,000. 2009.
798-45 Quantum Leaps, Washington, DC, $25,000. 2009.
798-46 Royal Institution of Great Britain, London, England, $100,000. 2009.
798-47 Saint Petersburg Electrotechnical University, Saint Petersburg, Russia, $30,000. 2009.
798-48 Saint Petersburg State Technical University, Saint Petersburg, Russia, $35,000. 2009.
798-49 Saint Petersburg State University of Aerospace Instrumentation, Saint Petersburg, Russia, $20,000. 2009.
798-50 Shanghai Expo 2010, Pasadena, CA, $250,000. 2009.
798-51 Shanghai Science and Education Development Foundation, Shanghai, China, $100,000. 2009.
798-52 Slovenska Komore Mladych, Bratislava, Slovakia, $20,000. 2009.
798-53 Sociedade Pro Menor Barao Geraldo, Campinas, Brazil, $12,500. 2009.
798-54 Sociedade Sal Da Terra, Sao Paulo, Brazil, $30,000. 2009.
798-55 Stichting International Institute for Communication and Development, The Hague, Netherlands, $98,500. 2009.
798-56 Techsploration, Halifax, Canada, $33,000. 2009.

798-57 Tel Aviv University, Tel Aviv, Israel, $45,000. For Students Aid Unit. 2009.
798-58 Umicore Solar Team, Leuven, Belgium, $100,000. 2009.
798-59 United States Association for United Nations High Commissioner for Refugees, Washington, DC, $100,000. 2009.
798-60 United States Association for United Nations High Commissioner for Refugees, Washington, DC, $25,000. 2009.
798-61 United States Association for United Nations High Commissioner for Refugees, Washington, DC, $25,000. 2009.
798-62 United States Fund for UNICEF, New York, NY, $50,000. 2009.
798-63 United States-Mexico Foundation for Science, Mexico City, Mexico, $90,000. 2009.
798-64 Universidad Simon Bolivar, Caracas, Venezuela, $59,057. 2009.
798-65 University College Dublin, Dublin, Ireland, $100,000. 2009.
798-66 University of Southampton, Southampton, England, $20,000. 2009.
798-67 Wicklow Montessori School, Wicklow Town, Ireland, $21,000. 2009.
798-68 World Vision, Federal Way, WA, $12,906. 2009.
798-69 Wyclef Jean Foundation, New York, NY, $100,000. 2009.

799
New Horizon Foundation
1625 Hinman Ave., No. 202
Evanston, IL 60201-4522
Contact: Ethelyn C. Bond, Secy.-Treas.
E-mail: nhf@revelle.net

Established in 1985 in IL.
Donors: Roger R. Revelle†; Ellen C. Revelle; William R. Revelle; Eleanor M. Revelle; Piero F. Paci†; Mary Paci; Carolyn R. Revelle; Gary C. Hufbauer.
Grantmaker type: Independent foundation.
Financial data (yr. ended 08/31/10): Assets, $1,293,431 (M); expenditures, $400,571; qualifying distributions, $369,900; giving activities include $369,900 for grants.
Purpose and activities: The foundation is interested in developing and funding direct and indirect programs in which it can encourage interest and foster education in the arts and sciences. It also funds projects concerned with issues in human rights, social welfare and global security.
Fields of interest: Arts; Higher education; Human services; International peace/security; International human rights; Public policy, research.
Type of support: General/operating support; Continuing support; Annual campaigns; Capital campaigns; Endowments; Scholarship funds; Research.
Limitations: Applications not accepted. Giving on a national basis. No grants to individuals.
Publications: Annual report.
Application information: Contributes only to pre-selected organizations.
Officers and Directors:* William R. Revelle,* Pres.; Mary Paci,* V.P.; Carolyn Revelle,* V.P.; Ethelyn C. Bond, Secy.-Treas.; Eleanor M. Revelle.
Number of staff: 1 part-time professional.
EIN: 363406294

800

New Visions Foundation
485 E. Half Day Rd., Ste. 200
Buffalo Grove, IL 60089-8806
Contact: Elizabeth Versten
Online application process URL: http://tinyurl.com/
NewVisions

Established in 1999 in IL.
Donors: Ronald J. Miller; Harvey L. Miller.
Grantmaker type: Independent foundation.
Financial data (yr. ended 12/31/10): Assets,
$1,645,768 (M); gifts received, $365,322;
expenditures, $351,189; qualifying distributions,
$299,500; giving activities include $299,500 for
grants.
Purpose and activities: The New Visions Foundation
(NVF) is dedicated to building a more just, peaceful,
compassionate and ecologically balanced culture.
The foundation strives to promote a holistic
worldview as an antidote to the fragmentation that
dominates modern society. NVF's grantmaking is
based on a belief that the problems of contemporary
society can best be solved with "new
visions"-significant innovations and alternatives to
the materialist and violent culture of the modern
world. Therefore, the foundation is committed to
supporting organizations that educate people and
communities about innovative cultural possibilities
or actively engage people and communities in the
task of creating a nonviolent and life-affirming
society.
Fields of interest: International peace/security;
Arts; Education; Environment; Human services;
Human services, mind/body enrichment; Civil/
human rights; Social entrepreneurship; Spirituality.
Limitations: Giving on a national and international
basis, with some emphasis on VT. No support for
non public charities. No grants to individuals.
Application information: Full proposals will be
accepted by invitation only. Application form not
required.
 Initial approach: Letter of inquiry (not exceeding 2
 pages) via online process
 Deadline(s): Sept. for invited proposals only
 Board meeting date(s): Oct.
 Final notification: Approximately two months after
 deadline
Officers and Directors:* Ronald J. Miller,* Pres.;
Jennie Kristel,* Secy.; Eric F. Achepohl,* Treas.
EIN: 364291720

801

**The David C. and Wendy L. Novak
 Foundation, Inc.**
3023 N. Clark St., No. 303
Chicago, IL 60657-5200

Established in 1999 in KY.
Donors: David C. Novak; Wendy L. Novak.
Grantmaker type: Independent foundation.
Financial data (yr. ended 12/31/10): Assets,
$18,948,972 (M); gifts received, $8,000,000;
expenditures, $1,962,502; qualifying distributions,
$1,888,945; giving activities include $1,888,945
for 31 grants (high: $583,945; low: $500).
Purpose and activities: Giving primarily for Christian
agencies and human services.
Fields of interest: Food services; Human services;
United Ways and Federated Giving Programs;
Christian agencies & churches.

Limitations: Applications not accepted. Giving in the
U.S., with some emphasis on Louisville, KY, and
Washington, D.C. No grants to individuals.
Application information: Contributes only to
pre-selected organizations.
Officers and Directors:* David C. Novak,* Pres.;
Wendy L. Novak,* V.P. and Secy.-Treas.; Ashley
Novak Butler; Susan B. Novak.
EIN: 611359337
Recent grants for international programs:
801-1 Friends of the World Food Program,
 Washington, DC, $583,945. For general support.
 2010.
801-2 Friends of the World Food Program,
 Washington, DC, $100,000. For general support.
 2010.

802

Opportunity International, Inc.
2122 York Rd., Ste. 150
Oak Brook, IL 60523-1996 (630) 242-4100
FAX: (630) 645-1458;
E-mail: getinfo@opportunity.org; Toll-free tel.: (800)
793-9455; URL: http://www.opportunity.org
Facebook: http://www.facebook.com/
OpportunityIntl
Organization Blog: http://www.opportunity.org/
blog/
Twitter: http://twitter.com/OpportunityIntl
YouTube: http://www.youtube.com/
opportunitydotorg

Established in 1971.
Grantmaker type: Public charity.
Financial data (yr. ended 12/31/10): Revenue,
$79,330,922; assets, $87,879,375 (M); gifts
received, $16,394,946; expenditures,
$110,852,770; giving activities include
$14,259,211 for grants to organizations outside the
U.S.
Purpose and activities: The organization's mission
is to provide opportunities for people in chronic
poverty to transform their lives by offering emerging
entrepreneurs access to small loans and training
that will enable them to start or expand their own
businesses.
Fields of interest: Economically disadvantaged.
International interests: Africa; Asia; Eastern &
Central Europe; Latin America.
Type of support: Program-related investments/
loans; Loans—to individuals.
Limitations: Giving primarily in Africa, Asia, Eastern
Europe, and Latin America.
Officers and Directors:* Peter Thorrington,* Chair.;
Betty Jane "BJ" Hess,* Vice-Chair.; Bill
Morgenstern, C.E.O.; Richard C. John, Sr. V.P.,
Finance and Admin., and C.F.O.; Mark Lutz, Sr. V.P.,
Mktg.; Dennis Ripley, Sr. V.P., Intl. Business Devel.;
Connie Stryjak, Sr. V.P., Human Resources; Betty S.
Perdue,* Secy.; Mark Vaselkiv,* Treas.; Bradley J.
Bell; Steve D. Cosler; Rodney Dammeyler; Dawn
Parsons Feller; James W. Hamilton; Julie
Hindmarsh; and 15 additional directors.
EIN: 540907624

803

**The Sheila A. Penrose & R. Ernest
 Mahaffey Charitable Foundation**
c/o Northern Trust Co.
P.O. Box 803878
Chicago, IL 60680-3878

Established in 1998 in IL.
Donors: Sheila A. Penrose; R. Ernest Mahaffey.
Grantmaker type: Independent foundation.
Financial data (yr. ended 12/31/10): Assets,
$2,813,346 (M); expenditures, $240,910;
qualifying distributions, $215,791; giving activities
include $187,403 for 28 grants (high: $45,000;
low: $500).
Fields of interest: International affairs; United Ways
and Federated Giving Programs; Higher education;
Education; Health care; Human services.
Limitations: Applications not accepted. Giving
primarily in IL. No grants to individuals.
Application information: Contributes only to
pre-selected organizations.
Officers: R. Ernest Mahaffey, Pres.; Sheila A.
Penrose, V.P.
Director: Barbara Gaines.
EIN: 364220588

804

**Margot & Thomas Pritzker Family
 Foundation**
c/o Thomas J. Pritzker
71 S. Wacker Dr., Ste. 4600
Chicago, IL 60606-4637

Established in IL.
Grantmaker type: Independent foundation.
Financial data (yr. ended 10/31/10): Assets,
$44,296,766 (M); expenditures, $2,805,189;
qualifying distributions, $2,378,887; giving
activities include $2,367,200 for 18 grants (high:
$1,037,500; low: $100).
Fields of interest: Museums (art); Arts; Higher
education, university; International affairs;
Philanthropy/voluntarism.
Type of support: General/operating support.
Limitations: Applications not accepted. Giving in the
U.S., with emphasis on CA, Chicago, IL, and New
York, NY. No grants to individuals.
Application information: Contributes only to
pre-selected organizations.
 Board meeting date(s): Nov., and as necessary
Officers and Directors:* Thomas J. Pritzker,* Pres.;
Ronald Wray, V.P. and Secy.-Treas.; Margot
Pritzker,* V.P.; Marshall Eisenberg.
EIN: 363852559

805

Benjamin J. Rosenthal Foundation
P.O. Box 166037
Chicago, IL 60616-6037

Incorporated in 1922 in IL.
Donor: Benjamin J. Rosenthal†.
Grantmaker type: Independent foundation.
Financial data (yr. ended 12/31/10): Assets,
$3,483,658 (M); expenditures, $352,137;
qualifying distributions, $294,646; giving activities
include $214,500 for 73 grants (high: $17,000;
low: $1,000).
Purpose and activities: Support primarily for youth,
child welfare, human services, arts and culture, and
protection of animals.
Fields of interest: International affairs; Arts;
Scholarships/financial aid; Education; Environment,
natural resources; Animal welfare; Human services;
Children/youth, services; Social sciences, public
policy.

Limitations: Applications not accepted. Giving primarily in Chicago, IL. No grants to individuals.
Application information: Unsolicited requests for funds not accepted.
Officers: Elaine Broadhead, Pres.; Walter Roth, Secy.; Rodger Mandel, Treas.; Erica Wise, Exec. Dir.
Trustees: Mellisa Foulke; Joseph Glossberg.
EIN: 362523643

806
Rossman Family Foundation
333 W. Wacker Dr., Ste. 1700
Chicago, IL   60606-1247

Established in 2005 in IL.
Donor: Howard Rossman.
Grantmaker type: Independent foundation.
Financial data (yr. ended 12/31/10): Assets, $10,692,376 (M); gifts received, $1,000,000; expenditures, $435,841; qualifying distributions, $383,900; giving activities include $383,900 for grants.
Fields of interest: Charter schools; International development; Higher education, university; Public policy, research; Leadership development.
Limitations: Applications not accepted. Giving primarily in Washington, DC, and the greater metropolitan Chicago, IL, area. No grants to individuals.
Application information: Contributes only to pre-selected organizations.
Officers: Howard Rossman, Pres. and Treas.; Erin Rossman, V.P.; Jeremy Rossman, V.P.; Beverly Rossman, Secy.
EIN: 203928172

807
The Rotary Foundation of Rotary
International
1 Rotary Ctr.
1560 Sherman Ave.
Evanston, IL   60201-3698   (847) 866-3000
Contact: Edwin H. Futa, Genl. Secy.
FAX: (847) 328-8554; URL: http://www.rotary.org/
en/aboutus/therotaryfoundation/Pages/
ridefault.aspx
Facebook: http://www.facebook.com/rotary
Flickr: http://www.flickr.com/groups/
familyofrotary/
LinkedIn: http://www.linkedin.com/groups?
gid=858557
Twitter: http://twitter.com/rotary
YouTube: http://www.youtube.com/user/
RotaryInternational

Established in 1917 in OR.
Grantmaker type: Public charity.
Financial data (yr. ended 06/30/10): Revenue, $275,377,951; assets, $731,289,105 (M); gifts received, $268,412,480; expenditures, $228,468,710; program services expenses, $204,899,325; giving activities include $40,323,605 for 385 grants (high: $31,566,026; low: $5,000), $122,700,366 for 2,111 grants to organizations outside the U.S., $2,712,028 for 289 grants to individuals, $21,306,621 for 289 grants to individuals outside the U.S., and $17,919,801 for foundation-administered programs.
Purpose and activities: The foundation supports the efforts of Rotary International to achieve world understanding and peace through international

humanitarian, educational, and cultural exchange programs; sends graduate, undergraduate, and vocational students to study abroad; and supports international health organizations in their effort to combat polio by sending funds for vaccines and technical support and promoting support for the community.
Fields of interest: Diseases (rare); International exchange, students.
Type of support: Annual campaigns; Equipment; Emergency funds; Program development; Scholarship funds; Scholarships—to individuals; Matching/challenge support.
Limitations: Applications accepted. Giving on a national and international basis.
Publications: Annual report.
Application information: Contact local chapter for application forms and guidelines. Application form required.
 Initial approach: Letter
 Deadline(s): Varies
Officers and Trustees: Glenn E. Estess, Sr.,* Chair.; Carl-Wilhem Stenhammar, Chair.-Elect; John F. Germ,* Vice-Chair.; Doh Bae; William B. Boyd; Ron D. Burton; Gustavo Gross; Lynn A. Hammond; Ashok M. Mahajan; David D. Morgan; Samuel A. Okudzeto; Louis Piconi; Jose Antonio Salazar-Cruz; Sakuji Tanaka; Wilfrid J. Wilkinson.
Number of staff: 450
EIN: 363245072

808
Rothman Family Foundation
311 S. Wacker Dr., Ste. 4190
Chicago, IL   60606-6621   (312) 663-4700
Contact: Patricia C. Rothman, V.P.

Established in 1986 in IL.
Donor: Members of the Rothman family.
Grantmaker type: Independent foundation.
Financial data (yr. ended 12/31/10): Assets, $4,229,861 (M); gifts received, $283,500; expenditures, $497,116; qualifying distributions, $403,000; giving activities include $403,000 for grants.
Fields of interest: Children/youth, services; Arts; Education; Reproductive health, family planning; Health organizations, association; Legal services; International relief; International human rights; Civil/human rights, advocacy; Jewish agencies & synagogues.
Limitations: Applications accepted. Giving primarily in IL. No grants to individuals.
Application information:
 Initial approach: Letter or proposal
 Deadline(s): None
 Final notification: 90 days
Officers: Florence C. Rothman, Pres.; Patricia C. Rothman, V.P. and Secy.; Gregory C. Rothman, V.P.; Hermine C. Rothman, V.P.; Michael C. Rothman, V.P.; Noel N. Rothman, V.P.
EIN: 363490566

809
Robert E. & Judith O. Rubin Foundation
c/o The Northern Trust Co.
P.O. Box 803878
Chicago, IL   60680-3878

Established in 1980 in NY.
Donor: Robert E. Rubin.

Grantmaker type: Independent foundation.
Financial data (yr. ended 08/31/10): Assets, $496 (M); gifts received, $1,384,250; expenditures, $1,384,300; qualifying distributions, $1,380,300; giving activities include $1,380,250 for 16 grants (high: $640,000; low: $750).
Purpose and activities: Giving primarily for the arts and international affairs.
Fields of interest: International affairs, foreign policy; Social sciences, public policy; Performing arts, theater; Arts; Higher education; Human services.
Limitations: Applications not accepted. Giving primarily in New York, NY; some funding also in Washington, DC. No grants to individuals.
Application information: Contributes only to pre-selected organizations.
Trustees: Judith O. Rubin; Robert E. Rubin; Roy E. Zuckerberg.
EIN: 133050749

810
Rumsfeld Foundation
333 W. Wacker Dr., Ste. 830
Chicago, IL   60606-1225

Established in 2007 in DC.
Donors: Donald H. Rumsfeld; Joyce P. Rumsfeld; Ralph Eberhart; Joyce and Donald Rumsfeld Foundation.
Grantmaker type: Independent foundation.
Financial data (yr. ended 12/31/10): Assets, $9,359,892 (M); gifts received, $23,425; expenditures, $775,492; qualifying distributions, $715,020; giving activities include $715,020 for grants.
Fields of interest: Higher education; Human services; International affairs, research; Military/veterans' organizations.
Limitations: Applications not accepted. Giving in the U.S., with emphasis on Washington, DC.
Application information: Unsolicited requests for funds not accepted.
Officers: Donald H. Rumsfeld, Pres. and Secy.; Joyce P. Rumsfeld, V.P. and Treas.
Director: Lawrence Di Rita.
EIN: 260580915

811
Sarkisian Foundation
55 E. Erie St., Ste. 2701
Chicago, IL   60611-2254   (312) 943-0646
Contact: Ralph Sarkisian, Pres.

Established in IL.
Donor: Ralph Sarkisian.
Grantmaker type: Independent foundation.
Financial data (yr. ended 12/31/10): Assets, $952,578 (M); gifts received, $200,255; expenditures, $217,777; qualifying distributions, $215,251; giving activities include $215,251 for 27 grants (high: $16,000; low: $1,000).
Fields of interest: International development; Food services; Children/youth, services; Christian agencies & churches.
International interests: Armenia.
Limitations: Applications accepted. Giving primarily in IL.
Application information: Application form required.
 Initial approach: Letter
 Deadline(s): None

Officers: Ralph Sarkisian, Pres.; Mike Noble, V.P.; John J. Hayes, Secy.
EIN: 203983247

812

The John D. and Minnie R. Schneider Charitable Trust

(formerly John D. Schneider Charitable Trust)
c/o Richard T. Zwirner
130 E. Randolph St., Ste. 3800
Chicago, IL   60601-6317

Established in 1985 in IL.
Donor: Hollister, Inc.
Grantmaker type: Independent foundation.
Financial data (yr. ended 12/31/10): Assets, $5,387,113 (M); gifts received, $28,739; expenditures, $231,956; qualifying distributions, $220,000; giving activities include $220,000 for 3 grants (high: $200,000; low: $10,000).
Fields of interest: Spine disorders; Higher education; Disasters, Hurricane Katrina; International relief, 2004 tsunami; Disabilities, people with.
Limitations: Applications not accepted. Giving primarily in IL and Washington, DC. No grants to individuals.
Application information: Contributes only to pre-selected organizations.
Officer and Trustees: Richard T. Zwirner,* Pres.; Loretta L. Stempinski.
EIN: 363388493

813

Scholar Leaders International

(formerly Christian International Scholarship Foundation)
27850 Irma Lee Cir.
Lake Forest, IL   60045-1554   (847) 295-9308
Contact: Larry Smith, Pres.
FAX: (847) 234-1047;
E-mail: info@scholarleaders.org; URL: http://www.scholarleaders.org/
Facebook: http://www.facebook.com/pages/ScholarLeaders-International/162258963820022
Google Plus URL: https://plus.google.com/109089617998906301719/posts
LinkedIn: http://www.linkedin.com/pub/scholarleaders-international/35/736/360
Twitter: https://twitter.com/scholarleaders

Established in 1983 in IL.
Grantmaker type: Public charity.
Financial data (yr. ended 08/31/10): Revenue, $744,471; assets, $886,165 (M); gifts received, $732,791; expenditures, $835,853; program services expenses, $545,354; giving activities include $2,500 for grants, $73,273 for 1 grant to an organization outside the U.S., $282,308 for 31 grants to individuals, $136,150 for 31 grants to individuals outside the U.S., and $51,123 for foundation-administered programs.
Purpose and activities: The foundation works to support Christian theological leaders from around the world.
Fields of interest: Scholarships/financial aid; Theological school/education.
International interests: Africa; Asia; Eastern & Central Europe; Latin America.
Type of support: Scholarships—to individuals.

Limitations: Applications accepted. Giving primarily on an international basis, with emphasis on Africa, Asia, Eastern Europe, and Latin America.
Publications: Application guidelines.
Application information: Application form required.
  Initial approach: Submit one-page letter of interest
  Deadline(s): Jan. 1
Officers and Directors: Tite Tienou,* Chair.; Larry Smith, Pres.; Rob Bloss, V.P.; Evan Hunter, V.P.; Barbara Ames; Gary Ames; Bruce Baker; Mark Conroe; Tom Cooper; Kerry Dearborn; Tim Dearborn; Debbie Evans; Paul Evans; Clair Fung; David Fung; Steve Hayner; and 20 additional directors.
EIN: 942923639

814

Dr. Scholl Foundation

1033 Skokie Blvd., Ste. 230
Northbrook, IL   60062-4109   (847) 559-7430
Contact: Pamela Scholl, Chair. and Pres.
URL: http://www.drschollfoundation.com

Incorporated in 1947 in IL.
Donor: William M. Scholl, M.D.†.
Grantmaker type: Independent foundation.
Financial data (yr. ended 12/31/10): Assets, $157,382,670 (M); expenditures, $9,306,553; qualifying distributions, $7,791,844; giving activities include $6,471,660 for 364 grants (high: $400,000; low: $1,000).
Purpose and activities: Support for private education at all levels, including elementary, secondary, and postsecondary schools, colleges and universities, and medical and nursing institutions; general charitable programs, including grants to hospitals, and programs for children, the developmentally disabled, and senior citizens; and civic, cultural, social welfare, economic, and religious activities.
Fields of interest: General charitable giving.
Type of support: Continuing support; Equipment; Program development; Fellowships; Internship funds; Scholarship funds; Research.
Limitations: Applications accepted. Giving primarily in the U.S., with some emphasis on the Chicago, IL area. No support for public education, political organizations, or political action committees. No grants to individuals, or for deficit financing, or unrestricted purposes, or to endowments, or capital campaigns, event sponsorship, liquidation of debt; no loans.
Publications: Application guidelines; Informational brochure.
Application information: Applications sent by fax or e-mail not accepted; only one request per organization, per year is permitted. Application form required.
  Initial approach: Letter on organization letterhead
  Copies of proposal: 1
  Deadline(s): Mar. 1
  Board meeting date(s): Feb., May, Aug., and Nov.
  Final notification: Nov.
Officers and Directors: Pamela Scholl,* Chair. and Pres.; Jeanne M. Scholl,* V.P. and Secy.; Anne Mosely, V.P.; John A. Nitschke, Treas.; Mary Ann Hynes; Stephen Meer; Richard B. Patterson; Daniel Scholl; Susan Scholl.
Number of staff: 3 full-time professional; 3 full-time support.
EIN: 366068724
Recent grants for international programs:

814-1 America Abroad Media, Washington, DC, $10,000. For Journalism Fellowship Initiative. 2009.

814-2 American Committee for the Weizmann Institute of Science, Chicago, IL, $500,000. For water and climate research. 2009.

814-3 American Friends of Ilan, New York, NY, $10,000. For Sports Wheelchair Campaign. 2009.

814-4 American Society for Yad Vashem, New York, NY, $20,000. For scholarships. 2009.

814-5 British Red Cross Society, Winchester, England, $10,000. Toward purchase of a new ambulance. 2009.

814-6 Center for Strategic and International Studies, Washington, DC, $90,000. For William M. Scholl Chair in International Business. 2009.

814-7 Center for the Study of the Presidency and Congress, Washington, DC, $100,000. For Strengthening America's Future Initiative (SAFI), Foundation for International Understanding (FIU), Character-Based Leadership, Syria's relationship with the U.S. and other programs. 2009.

814-8 Chicago Council on Global Affairs, Chicago, IL, $40,000. For Focus on China series and lecture on U.S.-China relations. 2009.

814-9 Empowering Lives International, Upland, CA, $10,000. For Hope and Health program in Western Kenya. 2009.

814-10 Global Arthroscopy Foundation, Northbrook, IL, $25,000. For operating support and to purchase surgical equipment. 2009.

814-11 Hospice Care, Douglas, Isle of Man, $105,000. To purchase and install combined heat and power generator. 2009.

814-12 International Center for Religion and Diplomacy, Washington, DC, $25,000. For university training in Pakistan for Madrasa faculty. 2009.

814-13 International Rescue Committee, New York, NY, $25,000. For programs for children affected by violent conflict and disaster. 2009.

814-14 Jackson Hole Center for Global Affairs, Jackson, WY, $10,000. For series of public presentations and events. 2009.

814-15 Layalina Productions, Washington, DC, $30,000. For Layalina Review on Public Diplomacy and Arab Media. 2009.

814-16 Manx Housing Trust, Douglas, Isle of Man, $20,000. To repair dampness problems in Douglas Properties flats. 2009.

814-17 Manx Wildlife Trust, Peel, Isle of Man, $10,000. For new Marine Officer project. 2009.

814-18 Mercy Ships Foundation, Lindale, TX, $10,000. For orthopedic projects in Benin. 2009.

814-19 National Society for the Prevention of Cruelty to Children, London, England, $40,000. For Young Witness Support Service program. 2009.

814-20 National Strategy Forum, Chicago, IL, $25,000. To publish National Strategy Forum Review. 2009.

814-21 Neil D. Levin Graduate Institute Foundation, New York, NY, $20,000. For Globalization 101.org project. 2009.

814-22 Opportunity International, Oak Brook, IL, $20,000. For Leadership, Empowerment, Access and Development (LEAD) Campaign, which promotes development and sustenance of transformational leaders and women in leadership at all levels of the organization-from clients to loan officers to decision makers. Each of the people served becomes an advisor, mentor, advocate and servant leader for their communities, providing resources and opportunities for impoverished women and their families. 2009.

814-23 Partners in Christ International, Tempe, AZ, $25,000. To conduct four medical clinics in Mexico. 2009.

814-24 Riding for the Disabled Association, Leominster, England, $10,000. For programs at Holme Lacey Riding Center. 2009.

814-25 Roy Castle Lung Cancer Foundation, Liverpool, England, $32,000. To provide Anti-Tobacco Youth Campaign (ATYC) Action Weekends for young people. 2009.

814-26 UNICEF of the Greater Chicago Area, Chicago, IL, $35,000. For Accelerated Child Survival Initiative. 2009.

814-27 Whizz-Kidz, London, England, $30,000. To provide customized mobility equipment to disabled children. 2009.

815
Shamrock Foundation
747 Sheridan Rd.
Wilmette, IL   60091-1959

Established in 2004 in IL.
Donors: Edwardson Family Foundation; Catharine O. Edwardson.
Grantmaker type: Independent foundation.
Financial data (yr. ended 12/31/10): Assets, $3,700,134 (M); gifts received, $150,000; expenditures, $192,495; qualifying distributions, $178,362; giving activities include $175,000 for 10 grants (high: $110,000; low: $3,300).
Fields of interest: International economic development; Christian agencies & churches.
Limitations: Applications not accepted. Giving primarily in DC, IL and TX. No grants to individuals.
Application information: Contributes only to pre-selected organizations.
Officer: Catharine O. Edwardson, Pres.
Trustees: Anne L. Edwardson; Laura K. Edwardson; Shelly M. Edwardson.
EIN: 061720127

816
Earl & Brenda Shapiro Foundation
111 E. Wacker Dr., Ste. 2607
Chicago, IL   60601-4211   (312) 552-7660
Contact: Benjamin Shapiro, V.P. and Treas.

Established in 2003 in IL.
Donors: Earl W. Shapiro; Soretta Shapiro; Soretta and Henry Shapiro Family Foundation.
Grantmaker type: Independent foundation.
Financial data (yr. ended 12/31/10): Assets, $29,867,571 (M); expenditures, $1,777,324; qualifying distributions, $1,663,302; giving activities include $1,635,667 for 48 grants (high: $200,000; low: $2,500).
Fields of interest: Jewish federated giving programs; Environment, natural resources; Higher education; Arts.
Type of support: General/operating support.
Limitations: Giving primarily in Chicago, IL and New York, NY. No grants to individuals.
Application information: Application form not required.
Initial approach: Letter
Deadline(s): None

Officers and Directors:* Brenda M. Shapiro,* Pres.; Matthew I. Shapiro,* V.P. and Secy.; Alexandra E. F. Shapiro, V.P. and Treas.; Benjamin M. Shapiro,* V.P. and Treas.
EIN: 450524597
Recent grants for international programs:
816-1 American Israel Education Foundation, Washington, DC, $135,000. For general support. 2009.
816-2 American Israel Education Foundation, Washington, DC, $75,000. For general support. 2009.
816-3 Jewish National Fund, New York, NY, $10,000. For general support. 2009.

817
The Shifting Foundation
70 W. Madison St., Ste. 4500
Chicago, IL   60602-4227

Established in 1982 in IL.
Donors: Julie Breskin; David Breskin.
Grantmaker type: Independent foundation.
Financial data (yr. ended 12/31/10): Assets, $12,213,410 (M); gifts received, $810,000; expenditures, $1,192,500; qualifying distributions, $600,000; giving activities include $600,000 for grants.
Purpose and activities: Giving primarily for human services and international affairs.
Fields of interest: Arts; Education; Environment; Human services; International relief; International affairs.
Type of support: General/operating support; Continuing support; Capital campaigns; Program development.
Limitations: Applications not accepted. Giving primarily in CA, MA and NY. No grants to individuals.
Application information: Contributes only to pre-selected organizations.
Officers and Directors:* David Breskin,* Pres.; Julie Breskin,* V.P.; William Biederman, Secy.; Samuel M. Seaman, Treas.
EIN: 366108560

818
Sigma Chi Foundation
1714 Hinman Ave.
P.O. Box 469
Evanston, IL   60201-4517   (847) 869-3655
Contact: Frank Raymond, Pres.
FAX: (847) 869-4906;
E-mail: foundation@sigmachi.org; *URL:* http://www.sigmachi.org/foundation
Application e-mail: scholarship@sigmachi.org

Established in 1939 in CO.
Grantmaker type: Public charity.
Financial data (yr. ended 06/30/10): Revenue, $5,342,748; assets, $16,831,094 (M); gifts received, $4,631,201; expenditures, $5,097,048; program services expenses, $3,009,648; giving activities include $2,045,283 for 9 grants (high: $566,000; low: $33,359), $8,500 for 2 grants to organizations outside the U.S., $436,784 for 825 grants to individuals, and $519,081 for foundation-administered programs.
Purpose and activities: The foundation grants scholarships to worthy individuals, conducts leadership training meetings and workshops, and

maintains a museum of historical objects and matters.
Fields of interest: Students, sororities/fraternities; Scholarships/financial aid; Education.
Type of support: Scholarships—to individuals.
Limitations: Applications accepted. Giving on a national basis.
Publications: Application guidelines; Annual report; Grants list; Newsletter.
Application information:
Initial approach: Download application form
Deadline(s): June 15
Board meeting date(s): Biannually
Final notification: Aug. 15
Officers and Directors:* Charles L. "Chuck" Watson,* Chair.; Timothy A. Michael,* Vice-Chair.; Greg Harbaugh,* Pres. and C.E.O.; Wade Overstreet,* V.P., Devel.; John A. Clerico, Treas.; Michael Pemberton, Cont.; Lee A. Beauchamp; John G. Berylson; Edward W. Blessing; Matthew R. Bradshaw; Thomas E. "Tommy" Bronson; Richard J. "Ric" Campo; Constantine Curris, Ph.D.; Stephen W. Goodroe; Robert E. "Bob" Joseph; D. Kerry McCluggage; and 6 additional directors.
EIN: 362208386

819
Arnold J. Simonsen Foundation
P.O. Box 5139
Buffalo Grove, IL   60089-5139

Established in 1998 in IL.
Donor: Arnold J. Simonsen.
Grantmaker type: Independent foundation.
Financial data (yr. ended 06/30/11): Assets, $606,962 (M); gifts received, $5,000; expenditures, $226,070; qualifying distributions, $170,000; giving activities include $170,000 for 7 grants (high: $120,000; low: $5,000).
Fields of interest: Environment; Health organizations, Children/youth, services; International development; Christian agencies & churches.
International interests: Russia.
Limitations: Applications not accepted. Giving primarily in IL and FL. No grants to individuals.
Application information: Contributes only to pre-selected organizations.
Trustee: Arnold J. Simonsen.
EIN: 367213624

820
The Spencer Foundation
625 N. Michigan Ave., Ste. 1600
Chicago, IL   60611-3109   (312) 337-7000
Contact: Michael S. McPherson, Pres.
FAX: (312) 337-0282; *E-mail:* pres@spencer.org;
URL: http://www.spencer.org
Grants List: http://www.spencer.org/content.cfm/foundation-reports

Incorporated in 1962 in IL.
Donor: Lyle M. Spencer†.
Grantmaker type: Independent foundation.
Financial data (yr. ended 03/31/11): Assets, $431,614,578 (M); expenditures, $20,072,325; qualifying distributions, $19,022,026; giving activities include $13,197,191 for 189 grants (high: $798,038; low: $2,500), $261,915 for employee matching gifts, and $251,239 for foundation-administered programs.

Purpose and activities: The foundation is committed to supporting high-quality investigation of education through its research programs and to strengthening and renewing the educational research community through its fellowship and by strengthening the connections among education research, policy and practice through its communication and networking.

Fields of interest: Education, research.

Type of support: Fellowships; Research; Employee matching gifts.

Limitations: Applications accepted. Giving on a national and international basis. No grants to individuals, or for capital funds, general purposes, operating or continuing support, sabbatical supplements, work in instructional or curriculum development, any kind of training or service program, scholarships, travel fellowships, endowment funds, or pre-doctoral research; no loans.

Publications: Annual report; Financial statement; Grants list; Informational brochure; Newsletter.

Application information: Application information for specific foundation programs available on foundation website. Submit full proposal only upon request. Information on program and application forms required for NAEd/Spencer Postdoctoral Fellowships or NAEd/Spencer Dissertation Fellowships should be requested from the National Academy of Education, 500 5th St. N.W., Washington, DC 20001. Application form not required.

Initial approach: See foundation web site for program-specific guidelines

Deadline(s): See program-specific deadlines on foundation website

Board meeting date(s): Jan., June, and Oct.

Final notification: Program-specific dates available on foundation website

Officers and Directors:* Derek C. Bok,* Chair.; Deborah Lowenberg Ball,* Vice-Chair.; Michael S. McPherson,* Pres.; Diana Hess, Sr. V.P.; Mary J. Cahillane, V.P., Finance and Investments and Treas.; Elizabeth Carrick, V.P., Admin.; Judy Klippenstein, Secy.; Maria H. Carlos, Cont.; Pamela Grossman; Christopher Jencks; Carol R. Johnson; Lyle Logan; Richard Murnane; Stephen Raudenbush; Cybele Raver; Richard J. Shavelson; T. Dennis Sullivan.

Number of staff: 11 full-time professional; 10 full-time support; 2 part-time support.

EIN: 366078558

Recent grants for international programs:

820-1 Cambridge University, Girton College, Cambridge, England, $37,675. For university and life experience website. 2010.

820-2 Carleton University, Department of Psychology, Ottawa, Canada, $40,000. For Looking Beyond Trucks vs. Dolls - Teachers' Attitudes and Responses to Young Children's Gender Stereotypical and Atypical Social Behaviors at School. 2010.

820-3 Cornell University, Department of Education, Ithaca, NY, $25,000. For From Global Projects to Classroom Practice - The Localization of Democratic Citizenship Education in Post-Communist Albania. 2010.

820-4 Emory University, Atlanta, GA, $40,000. For Engaging Transnational Citizens - A Comparative Study of Civic Teaching and Learning for Civic Action. 2010.

820-5 Harvard University, Cambridge, MA, $25,000. For 500 Maori Doctorates in 15 Years - Exploring the Process of Change in Higher Education and Community Development. 2010.

820-6 Harvard University, Graduate School of Education, Cambridge, MA, $209,175. For Phase II of International, Comparative Program of Research on Test-Based Educational Accountability Systems. 2010.

820-7 Kent State University, School of Foundations, Leadership, and Administration, Kent, OH, $39,700. For The Silent Revolution of the Activity Based Learning Movement in Tamil Nadu, India. 2010.

820-8 Teachers College Columbia University, New York, NY, $40,000. For What Does it Take to Improve Schools - An Exploration of Approaches to Accountability and School Capacity in Singapore, the Netherlands, and New York City. 2010.

820-9 Tel Aviv University, School of Education, Tel Aviv, Israel, $39,425. For Promoting Conceptual Understanding Through Activities Involving Student-Generated Representations. 2010.

820-10 University of California, Berkeley, CA, $25,000. For Randomized Evaluations of New Forms of Education Targeting Marginalized Children and Youth in Africa. 2010.

820-11 University of Wisconsin System, Madison, WI, $25,000. For Educational Opportunity and Parental Wealth in the U.S. and Germany. 2010.

821

State Farm Companies Foundation

1 State Farm Plz.
Bloomington, IL 61710-0001   (309) 766-2161
Contact: Karen Mayfield, Asst. Secy., Fdn Board of Mgrs.
FAX: (309) 766-2314; E-mail: home.sf-foundation.494b00@statefarm.com; Additional E-mail: home.sf-foundation.494b00@statefarm.com;
URL: http://www.statefarm.com/aboutus/community/grants/foundation/foundation.asp

Incorporated in 1963 in IL.

Donor: State Farm Mutual Automobile Insurance Co.

Grantmaker type: Company-sponsored foundation.

Financial data (yr. ended 12/31/10): Assets, $9,191,871 (M); gifts received, $12,516,375; expenditures, $16,571,812; qualifying distributions, $16,364,685; giving activities include $13,091,995 for 692+ grants (high: $3,000,000), $90,000 for 9 grants to individuals (high: $10,000; low: $10,000), and $3,182,690 for employee matching gifts.

Purpose and activities: The foundation supports key initiatives and scholarships, as well as associate-directed programs, including grants supporting volunteerism and matching gifts to two- and four-year colleges and universities.

Fields of interest: Voluntarism promotion; Education; Higher education.

International interests: Canada.

Type of support: Scholarship funds; Employee matching gifts; Employee volunteer services; Employee-related scholarships; General/operating support.

Limitations: Applications accepted. Giving on a national basis and in Canada. No support for Houses of Worship or organizations established for religious, political, or special interest purposes; veterans, fraternal, or social organizations under Section 501(c)(4); professional organizations under Section 501(c)(6); organizations that discriminate against any person or group on the basis of age, political affiliation, race or national origin, ethnicity, gender, disability, sexual orientation, or religious beliefs; or nonprofit, tax-exempt organizations under Section 501(c)(3) of the U.S. Internal Revenue Code that are not private foundations because they are described in Code Section 509(a)(3) or 509(a)(4). No grants to individuals.

Application information: Application form required.

Initial approach: Letter

Copies of proposal: 1

Deadline(s): None

Final notification: 60 days

Officers and Directors:* Edward B. Rust, Jr.,* Chair. and Pres.; Mary Crego, V.P. and Secy.; Don Heltner, V.P., Fixed Income; David Beigie, V.P., Progs.; Duane Farrington, V.P.; Michael L. Tipsord, V.P.; Paul J. Smith, Treas.; Brian V. Boyden; Kellie Clapper; Dale Egeberg; W.H. Knight, Jr.; Lori Manning; Karen Mayfield; Susan M. Phillips.

EIN: 366110423

Recent grants for international programs:

821-1 United Way of York Region, Markham, Canada, $34,053. 2010.

822

Irvin Stern Foundation

4 E. Ohio St., Studio 6
Chicago, IL 60611-4750
Contact: Christine Flood, Grants Admin.
E-mail: christine@irvinstern.org; URL: http://www.irvinstern.org

Established in 1957 in IL.

Donor: Irvin Stern†.

Grantmaker type: Independent foundation.

Financial data (yr. ended 09/30/10): Assets, $11,336,303 (M); expenditures, $1,159,518; qualifying distributions, $955,623; giving activities include $921,200 for 71 grants (high: $120,000; low: $1,000).

Purpose and activities: Grants for human services, particularly aid to the underserved, the poor and disadvantaged, via innovative social service programs, physical and mental health outreach, literacy and vocational training; civic affairs aimed at improving the quality of life in urban communities through grass roots and neighborhood organizations; and for the enhancement of the Jewish community through education and spirituality.

Fields of interest: Education; Mental health/crisis services; Food services; Human services; Homeless, human services; Community/economic development; Jewish federated giving programs; Public affairs.

International interests: Israel.

Type of support: General/operating support; Continuing support; Equipment; Emergency funds; Program development; Seed money.

Limitations: Applications accepted. Giving primarily in Chicago, IL. Some giving in New York by invitation only. No grants to individuals, or for endowment funds, deficit financing, building funds, capital campaigns, construction projects, medical research, or advertising or program books.

Publications: Application guidelines.

Application information: Letter of inquiry form and application guidelines available on foundation web site. All requests for funding from outside the City of Chicago are by invitation only. Application form required.

Initial approach: Brief letter of inquiry available on foundation web site
Copies of proposal: 1
Deadline(s): Submit proposal preferably by Mar. 1 or Sept. 1
Board meeting date(s): Apr./May and Oct./Nov.
Final notification: Up to 90 days
Trustees: Heidi Boncher; Kirsten Boncher; Jeffrey R. Epstein; Nicholas Epstein; Samantha Epstein; Stuart A. Epstein; Arthur Winter; Dorothy Winter.
Number of staff: 1 part-time professional.
EIN: 366047947

823
Stuart Family Foundation

(formerly The Barbara and Robert Stuart Foundation)
150 Field Dr., Ste. 100
Lake Forest, IL 60045-2597
Contact: Truman O. Anderson, Exec. Dir.

Established in 1985 in IL.
Donor: Robert D. Stuart, Jr.
Grantmaker type: Independent foundation.
Financial data (yr. ended 12/31/10): Assets, $7,488,539 (M); expenditures, $2,782,083; qualifying distributions, $2,765,145; giving activities include $2,387,973 for 110 grants (high: $175,000; low: $300).
Fields of interest: Media/communications; Arts; Education; International affairs, goodwill promotion; Civil rights, race/intergroup relations.
Type of support: General/operating support; Continuing support; Annual campaigns; Capital campaigns.
Limitations: Applications not accepted. Giving primarily in Chicago, IL. No grants to individuals.
Application information: Contributes only to pre-selected organizations.
Board meeting date(s): Nov.
Officers and Directors:* Robert D. Stuart, Jr.,* Pres.; Alexander D. Stuart,* V.P.; Marian S. Pillsbury,* V.P.; Teresa Acuna,* Treas.; Catherine A. Bertini; Blair Pillsbury Enders; James M. Stuart; Maren M. Stuart; Robert D. Stuart III.
Number of staff: 1 full-time professional; 3 part-time professional.
EIN: 363422731

824
Terra Foundation for American Art

980 N. Michigan Ave., Ste. 1315
Chicago, IL 60611-4501 (312) 664-3939
Contact: Amy Zinck, V.P.
FAX: (312) 664-2052;
E-mail: grants@terraamericanart.org; Additional e-mail: contact@terraamericanart.org and tsr@terraamericanart.org; URL: http://www.terraamericanart.org
Grants Database: http://www.terraamericanart.org/grants/awarded/?key=32&category=Exhibition&location=International&year=2010

Classified as a private operating foundation in 1981 in IL.
Donors: Daniel J. Terra†; Lawter Intl.; James D. Terra.
Grantmaker type: Operating foundation.
Financial data (yr. ended 06/30/11): Assets, $444,761,954 (M); expenditures, $11,301,550; qualifying distributions, $9,645,371; giving

activities include $4,920,136 for 44 grants (high: $350,000; low: $1,758), and $53,112 for 13 grants to individuals (high: $5,200; low: $700).
Purpose and activities: The foundation is dedicated to fostering exploration, understanding, and enjoyment of the visual arts of the United States for national and international audiences. Recognizing the importance of experiencing original works of art, the foundation provides opportunities for interaction and study, beginning with the presentation and growth of its own art collection in Chicago. To further cross-cultural dialogue on American art, the foundation supports and collaborates on innovative exhibitions, research, and educational programs. The foundation's grant areas are Exhibition, Academic and Public Programs, Chicago K-12 Education, and Publication. Publication grants will provide support for publication projects on historical American art (circa 1500 to 1980) that make a significant contribution to scholarship and have an international dimension. "International dimensions" vary by project, but include translations of important texts on American art; publications that are written by non-U.S. scholars or that have a significant number of non-U.S. contributors; and publications with a focused thesis exploring American art in an international context. The grants are designed to advance and internationalize scholarship on American art and provide individuals outside the United States with greater access to resources in the field.
Fields of interest: Visual arts; Arts, multipurpose centers/programs; Arts education; Museums (art).
International interests: Asia; Europe; South America.
Type of support: Program development; Fellowships.
Limitations: Applications accepted. Giving in the U.S., with emphasis on Chicago, IL, and internationally. No support for artwork conservation. No grants to individuals.
Publications: Application guidelines; Annual report; Grants list.
Application information: Application guidelines available on foundation web site. Formal proposals accepted by invitation only, after review of letter of inquiry. Application form not required.
Initial approach: Letter of inquiry (1 copy only, 3 pages maximum, written in English and e-mailed to Grants Mgr.)
Copies of proposal: 5
Deadline(s): See foundation web site for current deadlines
Board meeting date(s): Quarterly
Final notification: Within 3 weeks
Officers and Trustees:* Gerhard Casper, Chair.; Elizabeth Glassman, C.E.O. and Pres.; Donald Ratner, Exec. V.P. and C.F.O.; Amy Zinck, V.P.; Max N. Berry; Charles C. Eldredge; Ruth Fine; Mimi Gardner Gates; David G. Kabiller; Peter Krikovich; Peter Lunder; Clare Munana; William A. Osborn; John Rogers, Jr.; Gloria Scoby; Michael Syhapiro; Marilynn Thoma; David B. Weinberg.
Number of staff: 14 full-time professional.
EIN: 362999442
Recent grants for international programs:
824-1 Art Gallery of Ontario, Toronto, Canada, $20,000. For At Work, group of concurrent exhibitions focusing on the issue of labor in the production of art, specifically that of Eva Hesse, Agnes Martin, and Betty Goodwin. 2010.
824-2 Art Institute of Chicago, Chicago, IL, $20,000. For internationally collaborative pre-exhibition convening for the Roy Lichtenstein

retrospective organized by the Institute and the Tate Modern London, which is scheduled to open in Chicago, followed by the National Gallery of Art in D.C. and the Tate Modern London. 2010.
824-3 Association des Amis de Pontigny-Cerisy, Cerisy, France, $35,000. For international conference, The Sign of Stieglitz, which will examine Stieglitz and his influence on the New York avant-garde between 1890 and 1930. 2010.
824-4 Courtauld Institute of Art, London, England, $179,280. For short-term visiting professorships and postdoctoral teaching fellowship in American art. 2010.
824-5 Dulwich Picture Gallery, London, England, $25,000. For exhibition, The Wyeth Family: Three Generations of American Art. 2010.
824-6 Freer Gallery of Art and Arthur M. Sackler Gallery, Washington, DC, $22,360. For the initial meeting of International Scholarly Advisory Board and online seminars. 2010.
824-7 Musee des Impressionnismes Giverny, Giverny, France, $14,500. For loan of three works from the Terra Foundation for American Art collection to exhibition Impressionism on the Seine. 2010.
824-8 Museo Carlo Bilotti, Rome, Italy, $140,000. For catalogue and exhibition, Philip Guston, Roma, which examines the relationships between his work, his return to figuration and Italian culture, landscape and artistic patrimony. 2010.
824-9 Museo de Arte de Lima, Lima, Peru, $250,000. For exhibition, Gordon Matta-Clark: Undoing Spaces, at MALI and Paco Imperial in Rio de Janciro, Brazil. 2010.
824-10 National Gallery Trust, London, England, $165,250. For catalogue, Study Day and exhibition, George Bellows and His Contemporaries. 2010.
824-11 New Museum of Contemporary Art, New York, NY, $63,500. For the catalogue and exhibition, Brion Gysin: Dream Machine at the New Museum, Zurich Kunsthalle in Zurich, Switzerland and Musee d'art Moderne de la Ville de Paris. 2010.
824-12 Peggy Guggenheim Collection, Venice, Italy, $100,000. For catalogue and exhibition of Adolph Gottlieb, American abstract expressionist painter, sculptor and graphic artist. 2010.
824-13 Pierpont Morgan Library, New York, NY, $225,000. For catalogue and exhibition, Roy Lichtenstein: The Black-and-White Drawings, 1961-1968 at the Morgan Library and the Albertina in Vienna, Austria. 2010.
824-14 Tate, London, England, $165,000. For London presentation of exhibition, Eadweard Muybridge, an English photographer. 2010.
824-15 Universite de Caen Basse-Normandie, Caen, France, $27,500. For international symposium, Collaboration and the Artist's Book: A Transatlantic Perspective, which focuses on the evolution of artists' books from the beginning of the twentieth century to 1980 in Europe and the United States. 2010.
824-16 University of Nottingham, School of American and Canadian Studies, Nottingham, England, $12,650. For Art Across Frontiers: Cross-Cultural Encounters in America, international symposium which will explore the impact of trans-nationalism on the visual arts in the United States through cultures in migration. It will look at trans-cultural exchange between Euro-American, Native-American,

African-American, and Latino-American interactions within the U.S., as well as cross-border relations between the art of the United States and the visual cultures of the Americas from the colonial period to the present. 2010.

825
The Tinberg Foundation
159 Sheridan Rd.
Winnetka, IL 60093-1554 (847) 441-9152
Contact: Richard W. Tinberg, Pres.; Elaine M. Tinberg, V.P.

Established in 1990 in IL.
Donors: Elaine M. Tinberg; Richard W. Tinberg.
Grantmaker type: Independent foundation.
Financial data (yr. ended 12/31/10): Assets, $2,321,954 (M); expenditures, $131,698; qualifying distributions, $127,100; giving activities include $127,100 for 34 grants (high: $35,000; low: $50).
Fields of interest: Cancer research; Neuroscience research; Cancer; Higher education, university; Education, public education; Human services; Children, services; International development.
Limitations: Applications accepted. Giving primarily in Chicago, IL.
Application information: Application form required.
  Initial approach: Letter
  Deadline(s): None
Officers: Richard W. Tinberg, Pres.; Elaine M. Tinberg, V.P.
Directors: Christine Tinberg; Richard J. Tinberg.
EIN: 363742179

826
Two Blades Foundation
1630 Chicago Ave., Ste. 1907
Evanston, IL 60201-6024 (847) 425-1277
E-mail: info@2blades.org; URL: http://www.2blades.org/

Grantmaker type: Public charity.
Financial data (yr. ended 12/31/09): Revenue, $958,543; assets, $521,820 (M); gifts received, $956,660; expenditures, $846,596; giving activities include $270,600 for grants, and for 3 grants to organizations outside the U.S.
Purpose and activities: The foundation works to identify and support the best available technologies and strategies for developing durable resistance to important crop diseases.
Fields of interest: Agriculture; Science, research; Botany.
International interests: Germany; Australia.
Type of support: Research.
Limitations: Giving primarily to St. Paul, MN, and Australia and Germany.
Officers and Directors:* Dr. Roger Freedman,* Chair.; Dr. Eric Ward,* Pres.; Dr. Diana Horvath, C.O.O.; Susan Nycum; Dr. Michael Pauly.
EIN: 562455310

827
United Holy Land Fund
6000 W. 79th St.
Burbank, IL 60459-3110 (708) 430-9731

Grantmaker type: Public charity.

Financial data (yr. ended 12/31/10): Revenue, $577,697; assets, $1,704,788 (M); gifts received, $604,041; expenditures, $551,793; giving activities include $7,000 for grants, and $373,736 for grants to organizations outside the U.S.
Fields of interest: International relief; Human services.
International interests: East Jerusalem; West Bank/Gaza (Palestinian Territories).
Type of support: Scholarship funds.
Limitations: Giving primarily in Palestine.
Officers: Jamil El Samna, Pres.; Isam Moalla, V.P.; Hatem Abdallah, Secy.; Ali Naji, Treas.
Directors: Awni Abuhadba; Mohammed Aburmishan; Maryam Alrazzaq; Katie Bayoud; Imad Daboob; Ryad Elagha; Nazmi Elrabie; and 10 additional directors.
EIN: 436100111

828
Van Dyke Family Charitable Foundation
11900 W. Roosevelt Rd.
Hillside, IL 60162-2069

Established around 1995.
Donors: Janice Van Dyke-Zeilstra; Darwill Press.
Grantmaker type: Independent foundation.
Financial data (yr. ended 12/31/10): Assets, $479,075 (M); gifts received, $116,550; expenditures, $130,924; qualifying distributions, $130,668; giving activities include $130,158 for 50 grants (high: $42,200; low: $20).
Fields of interest: Higher education; Human services; International development; Protestant agencies & churches.
Limitations: Applications not accepted. Giving primarily in IL, with some giving in MI. No grants to individuals.
Application information: Contributes only to pre-selected organizations.
Officers and Directors:* Janice K. Van Dyke-Zeilstra,* Pres. and Treas.; Brandon Van Dyke,* V.P. and Secy.; Troy Van Dyke,* V.P.
EIN: 363978469

829
The Weberg Trust
(formerly Weberg Foundation)
P.O. Box 803878
Chicago, IL 60680-8378 (312) 630-6000
E-mail: jwebarg@netcom.com

Established in 1999 in CO; reorganized in 2004. The entity was originally known as Weberg Foundation.
Donors: John P. Weberg; Jacqueline Weberg.
Grantmaker type: Independent foundation.
Financial data (yr. ended 12/31/10): Assets, $22,796,303 (M); expenditures, $8,137,807; qualifying distributions, $7,923,010; giving activities include $7,900,000 for 5 grants (high: $3,400,000; low: $1,000,000).
Purpose and activities: Support for microenterprise development worldwide.
Fields of interest: International economic development.
Limitations: Applications not accepted. Giving in the U.S., with some emphasis on CA and IL. No grants to individuals.
Application information: Contributes only to pre-selected organizations.

Grant Committee: Karen Sue Allen; Linda Lair; Russ Lair; Claudia Weberg; Gary Weberg; Jacqueline Weberg; John P. Weberg.
Trustee: Northern Trust.
EIN: 206382151
Recent grants for international programs:
829-1 Freedom from Hunger, Davis, CA, $1,200,000. For general support. 2009.
829-2 Hope International, Lancaster, PA, $300,000. For general support. 2009.
829-3 Opportunity International, Oak Brook, IL, $2,300,000. For general support. 2009.
829-4 Pro Mujer, New York, NY, $650,000. For general support. 2009.
829-5 World Vision International, Monrovia, CA, $350,000. For general support. 2009.

830
Wein Family Foundation
(formerly Hyman & Susan Wein Foundation)
1550 W. Carroll Ave.
Chicago, IL 60607-1012

Established in IL.
Donors: Irving L. Wein; Zahava Wein; Fantasy Diamond Co.
Grantmaker type: Independent foundation.
Financial data (yr. ended 12/31/10): Assets, $4,708,700 (M); expenditures, $294,344; qualifying distributions, $244,227; giving activities include $237,025 for 55 grants (high: $70,957; low: $25).
Purpose and activities: Giving primarily to Jewish organizations, as well as for education.
Fields of interest: Jewish federated giving programs; Health organizations, association; Education; Human services; Jewish agencies & synagogues.
International interests: Israel.
Type of support: Capital campaigns.
Limitations: Applications not accepted. Giving primarily in Chicago, IL. No grants to individuals.
Application information: Unsolicited requests for funds not accepted.
Officers: Joseph Wein, Pres.; Susan Wein-Bernhardt, Secy.; Zahava Wein, Treas.
EIN: 366065421

831
Marc Weiner Foundation
55 E. Jackson Blvd., Ste. 500
Chicago, IL 60604-4396

Established in 2004 in IL.
Donor: Elliot M. Weiner.
Grantmaker type: Independent foundation.
Financial data (yr. ended 12/31/10): Assets, $4,584 (M); gifts received, $144,500; expenditures, $167,579; qualifying distributions, $167,579; giving activities include $167,500 for 26 grants (high: $55,000; low: $100).
Fields of interest: Health organizations; International affairs, single organization support; Jewish agencies & synagogues.
Limitations: Applications not accepted. No grants to individuals.
Application information: Contributes only to pre-selected organizations.
Officers: Elliot M. Weiner, Pres.; Laurence Weiner, V.P.; Steven Wold, Secy.
EIN: 421653879

832
The Oprah Winfrey Foundation
(formerly For a Better Life Foundation)
110 N. Carpenter St.
Chicago, IL 60607-2104   (312) 633-1000
Contact: Oprah G. Winfrey, Pres.

Established in 1995 in IL.
Donors: Harpo Productions, Inc.; Harpo, Inc.; Oprah G. Winfrey.
Grantmaker type: Independent foundation.
Financial data (yr. ended 12/31/10): Assets, $241,223,048 (M); expenditures, $11,666,860; qualifying distributions, $10,293,238; giving activities include $9,851,212 for 12 grants (high: $1,300,000; low: $2,000), and $43,567 for 1 foundation-administered program.
Purpose and activities: The purpose of the foundation is to focus on education, and empowering women, children, and families.
Fields of interest: Arts; Education; Hospitals (specialty); Health care; Health organizations; Boys & girls clubs; Human services; Children, services; Family services; Community/economic development; Women.
Limitations: Applications not accepted. Giving on a national basis, with emphasis on GA, MD and NY.
Application Information: Contributes only to pre-selected organizations.
Officers and Directors:* Oprah G. Winfrey,* Pres.; Tim Bennett,* V.P.; Letty Tanchum,* V.P.; Julie Hubbard, Treas.; Bob Greene; Gideon Kaufman; Gayle King.
EIN: 363976230
Recent grants for international programs:
832-1 International Education Exchange, Port Chester, NY, $500,000. For general operating support. 2009.
832-2 Kids Haven, Johannesburg, South Africa, $150,000. For general operating support. 2009.
832-3 Malaria No More, New York, NY, $200,000. For general operating support. 2009.

833
The Wristen Family Foundation
7 Turning Shore Dr.
South Barrington, IL 60010-9597

Established in 2005 in IL.
Donors: Edward L. Wristen; Rebecca S. Wristen.
Grantmaker type: Independent foundation.
Financial data (yr. ended 12/31/10): Assets, $951,627 (M); gifts received, $1,287; expenditures, $138,480; qualifying distributions, $136,200; giving activities include $136,200 for 12 grants (high: $76,000; low: $1,000).
Fields of interest: International development; Food services; Christian agencies & churches.
Limitations: Applications not accepted. Giving primarily in CO and IL. No grants to individuals.
Application information: Unsolicited requests for funds not accepted.
Officers and Directors:* Edward L. Wristen,* Pres.; Rebecca S. Wristen,* V.P.; Molly S. Erwin,* Secy.; Sarah E. Brown,* Treas.; Jeffrey T. Brown; Timothy D. Erwin.
EIN: 202271528

INDIANA

834
Benevolent Friends of African Charities, Inc.
8469 Bay Point Dr., Ste. 100
Indianapolis, IN 46240-4313   (317) 848-2013
Contact: Martin J. Moore, Dir.

Established in IN.
Donor: Beverly Richey.
Grantmaker type: Independent foundation.
Financial data (yr. ended 12/31/10): Assets, $1,280,904 (M); gifts received, $10,170; expenditures, $301,561; qualifying distributions, $128,394; giving activities include $128,394 for grants.
Fields of interest: Youth development; Education; Medical care, rehabilitation.
International interests: Kenya.
Type of support: General/operating support.
Limitations: Applications accepted. Giving primarily in IN, with some giving in PA. No grants for seed money, or for educational grants, building or international programs.
Application information: Application form not required.
  Initial approach: Letter or telephone
  Deadline(s): None
  Final notification: Within 60 days
Directors: Martin J. Moore; Susan Joan Moore; Stephen D. Smith.
EIN: 351830834

835
Brotherhood Mutual Foundation, Inc.
6400 Brotherhood Way
Fort Wayne, IN 46825-4235

Established in 2005 in IN.
Donor: Brotherhood Mutual Insurance Co.
Grantmaker type: Company-sponsored foundation.
Financial data (yr. ended 12/31/10): Assets, $95,619 (M); gifts received, $395,960; expenditures, $357,401; qualifying distributions, $357,192; giving activities include $357,192 for 98 grants (high: $35,152; low: $69).
Purpose and activities: The foundation supports health clinics and organizations involved with education, reproductive health, human services, international relief, civic affairs, and Christianity.
Fields of interest: Higher education; Education; Health care, clinics/centers; Reproductive health; Youth, services; Homeless, human services; Human services; International relief; Public affairs, citizen participation; Christian agencies & churches.
Type of support: General/operating support; Annual campaigns; Capital campaigns; Building/renovation; Program development; Sponsorships.
Limitations: Applications not accepted. Giving primarily in IN. No grants to individuals.
Application information: Contributes only to pre-selected organizations.
Officers: James A. Blum, Chair.; Mark A. Robison, Pres.; Hugh W. White, V.P.; Michael J. Allison, Secy.; Matthew G. Hirschy, Treas.
EIN: 203618117

836
Church World Service
(also known as CWS)
28606 Phillips St.
P.O. Box 968
Elkhart, IN 46514-1239   (574) 264-3102
FAX: (574) 262-0966;
E-mail: info@churchworldservice.org; Additional address (New York office): 475 Riverside Dr., Ste. 700, New York, NY 10115-0074; tel.: (212) 870-2061, fax: (212) 879-3523; toll-free tel.: (800) 297-1516; URL: http://www.churchworldservice.org

Established in 1946 in IN.
Grantmaker type: Public charity.
Financial data (yr. ended 06/30/11): Revenue, $82,157,426; assets, $29,848,347 (M); gifts received, $78,732,897; expenditures, $82,029,444; giving activities include $23,894,806 for grants, and $28,280,103 for grants to organizations outside the U.S.
Purpose and activities: The organization partners with indigenous organizations in some eighty countries around the world, supporting sustainable self help development of poor people, meeting emergency needs, and addressing the root causes of poverty and powerlessness.
Fields of interest: International relief; International economic development; International development; Agriculture/food; International agricultural development.
Type of support: In-kind gifts.
Limitations: Applications not accepted. Giving on a national and international basis.
Publications: Annual report.
Application information: Contributes only to pre-selected organizations.
Officers and Directors:* Rt. Rev. Johncy Itty,* Chair.; Rev. John Paterakis,* 1st Vice-Chair.; Rev. Canon Benjamin Musoke-Lubega,* 2nd Vice-Chair.; Rev. John L. McCullough, Exec. Dir. and C.E.O.; Rev. Jennifer Riggs,* Secy.; Rev. Jimmie Hawkins,* Treas.; Bishop Vicken Aykazian; Deborah E. Bass; Rev. Jon T. Chapman; Rev. Peg Chemberlin; Rev. Dr. Kirkpatrick Cohall; Rev. Dr. Margaret Ann Cowden; Bishop Ronald Cunningham; Georgina Dapcevich; Rev. Dr. Kermit DeGraffenreidt; Rev. Dr. David G. Dethmers; and 44 additional directors.
EIN: 134080201

837
The Cummins Foundation
(formerly Cummins Engine Foundation)
500 Jackson St., M.C. 60633
Columbus, IN 47201-6258   (812) 377-3114
Contact: Tracy Souza, Pres. and Secy.
FAX: (812) 377-7897;
E-mail: Cummins.Foundation@cummins.com; Additional tel.: (812) 377-3746; URL: http://www.cummins.com/cmi/navigationAction.do?nodeId=1003&siteId=1&nodeName=Corporate+Responsibility&menuId=1003

Incorporated in 1954 in IN.
Donors: Cummins Engine Co., Inc.; Fleetguard, Inc.; Cummins Inc.
Grantmaker type: Company-sponsored foundation.
Financial data (yr. ended 12/31/10): Assets, $22,316,934 (M); gifts received, $12,280,100; expenditures, $7,289,262; qualifying distributions, $7,258,872; giving activities include $7,258,872 for 198 grants (high: $910,511; low: $16).

Purpose and activities: The foundation supports programs designed to promote education, the environment, and social justice; and programs designed to improve communities in which Cummins does business.

Fields of interest: Disasters, preparedness/ services; Elementary/secondary education; Higher education; Education, services; Education; Environment, climate change/global warming; Environment, natural resources; Environment, energy; Environment; Employment, services; Youth, services; Human services; Civil/human rights; Business/industry; Community/economic development; United Ways and Federated Giving Programs; Mathematics; Science; Economically disadvantaged.

International interests: Brazil; China; India; Mexico; South Africa.

Type of support: General/operating support; Continuing support; Annual campaigns; Building/ renovation; Equipment; Endowments; Emergency funds; Program development; Publication; Curriculum development; Scholarship funds; Technical assistance; Sponsorships; Employee matching gifts; Matching/challenge support.

Limitations: Applications accepted. Giving primarily in areas of company operations, with emphasis on Lake Mills, IA, the Columbus and Seymour, IN, areas, Fridley, MN, Jamestown, NY, Rocky Mount, NC, Findlay, OH, Charleston, SC, Cookeville, Memphis, and Nashville, TN, El Paso, TX, Stoughton, WI and in Brazil, China, India, Mexico, and South Africa; giving also to national organizations. No support for sectarian religious organizations, political candidates, or medical or disease-related organizations. No grants to individuals, or for capital campaigns, business start-up needs or political causes; no loans or product donations.

Publications: Application guidelines; Corporate giving report; IRS Form 990 or 990-PF printed copy available upon request.

Application information: Additional information may be requested at a later date. Organizations receiving support are asked to submit a final report.

Initial approach: Proposal
Copies of proposal: 1
Deadline(s): None
Board meeting date(s): Quarterly
Final notification: Varies by board meeting cycle

Officers and Directors:* Theodore M. Solso,* Chair.; Jean S. Blackwell,* C.E.O.; Tracy H. Souza, Pres. and Secy.; Marsha Allamanno, Treas.; Mark Gerstle; Thomas Linebarger; William I. Miller; Marya M. Rose; Pat Ward.

Number of staff: 2 full-time professional; 1 full-time support.

EIN: 356042373

Recent grants for international programs:

837-1 Asociacion Filantropica Cummins, New York, NY, $16,000. For Hospital. 2010.

837-2 Asociacion Filantropica Cummins, New York, NY, $13,000. For the Steve Knaebel Award to SLP Philanthropy. 2010.

837-3 BOMA Project, Dorset, VT, $25,000. To support BOMA Programs with pastoral nomadic communities of Northern Kenya. 2010.

837-4 Building Tomorrow, Indianapolis, IN, $25,000. For general operating grant to support new staff costs in the U.S. in conjunction with helping to build Cummins' Africa Strategy. 2010.

837-5 Concern Worldwide U.S., New York, NY, $150,000. For Haiti Disaster Relief, for drilling rig for access to clean water on the island of La Gonave. 2010.

837-6 Cummins India Foundation, Pune, India, $50,000. 2010.

837-7 Cummins India Foundation, Pune, India, $25,000. For Street Source Project. 2010.

837-8 Cummins India Foundation, Pune, India, $10,000. For 90th Anniversary Winner, BAIF Foundation, Solve Water Scarcity at Wagholi School Project. 2010.

837-9 Cummins India Foundation, Pune, India, $10,000. For 90th Anniversary Winner, Deep Griha Society, Water Harvesting Project. 2010.

837-10 EARTH University Foundation, Atlanta, GA, $250,000. For Tree Planting Project (tropical reforestration). 2010.

837-11 EARTH University Foundation, Atlanta, GA, $90,000. For Payment for Consulting Services to Earth University. 2010.

837-12 EARTH University Foundation, Atlanta, GA, $32,000. For half of the fee for the VP-Development Search, shared 50/50 with Earth University Foundation. 2010.

837-13 EARTH University Foundation, Atlanta, GA, $15,000. For scholarships. 2010.

837-14 Initiative for Global Development, Seattle, WA, $100,000. 2010.

837-15 Lambi Fund of Haiti, Washington, DC, $50,000. For Haiti Disaster Relief, to assist in rebuilding efforts. 2010.

837-16 Los Ojos De Dios, El Paso, TX, $10,000. For 90th Anniversary Environmental Challenge Winner, raising funds for tree planting campaign. 2010.

837-17 Plan International USA, Warwick, RI, $10,000. For 90th Anniversary Challenge Winner, Increase Public Energy Saving and Reduce Emissions Project. 2010.

837-18 Save the Children Federation, Westport, CT, $150,000. For Haiti Disaster Relief, to rebuild Sainte Agnes de Deslandes School in Leogane. 2010.

837-19 Save the Children Federation, Westport, CT, $50,000. For Pakistan Flood Relief Support. 2010.

837-20 Save the Children Federation, Westport, CT, $25,000. For Cummins China Investment Co., Urumqi Branch Community Involvement Team Partner with Save the Children UK, China Programme, to work with governments at the local level to improve the quality of services they provide to poverty-stricken children in Xinjiang. 2010.

837-21 Save the Children Federation, Westport, CT, $25,000. For Cummins China Investment Co., Xi'an Branch Community Involvement Team Partner with Save the Children UK, China Programme, to work with governments at the local level to improve the quality of services they provide to poverty-stricken children in Xinjiang. 2010.

837-22 Wuxi Library, Wuxi, China, $50,000. For Community Development Grants, WHDB Community Involvement Team and Shanghai Metro Community Involvement Team, to establish children's libraries in elementary schools throughout China. Each library will receive a full range of Chinese language children's books and appropriate furniture. 2010.

837-23 Wuxi Library, Wuxi, China, $22,000. For 2Q Community Development Grant, to create updated computer lab at the Wuxi Migrant Workers Children's School to enable the students to learn basic computer skills in Wuxi, China. 2010.

837-24 Wuxi Library, Wuxi, China, $10,000. For 90th Anniversary Challenge Winner, Cummins woods project. 2010.

838
Cummins Inc. Corporate Giving Program

(formerly Cummins Engine Company, Inc. Corporate Giving Program)
500 Jackson St.
Columbus, IN   47201-6258   (812) 377-5000
URL: http://www.cummins.com/cmi/ sustainabilityDisplayAction.do

Grantmaker type: Corporate giving program.

Purpose and activities: As a complement to its foundation, Cummins also makes charitable contributions to nonprofit organizations directly. Support is given on an international basis in areas of company operations.

Fields of interest: Community/economic development; Civil/human rights, equal rights; Human services; Environment; Education.

International interests: Australia; Africa; Brazil; China; India; Mexico; Russia; United Kingdom.

Type of support: General/operating support; Employee volunteer services; Sponsorships.

Limitations: Giving on an international basis in areas of company operations, including in Africa, Australia, Brazil, China, India, Mexico, and the United Kingdom.

Publications: Grants list.

839
Mark and Anna Ruth Hasten Family Foundation, Inc.

3901 W. 86th St., Ste. 470
Indianapolis, IN   46268-3700   (317) 872-9901
Contact: Mark Hasten, Dir.

Established in 1996 in IN.

Donors: Mark Hasten; Anna Ruth Hasten; Edward Hasten; Michael Hasten.

Grantmaker type: Independent foundation.

Financial data (yr. ended 12/31/10): Assets, $6,598,741 (M); gifts received, $135,400; expenditures, $2,072,637; qualifying distributions, $1,910,528; giving activities include $1,910,528 for 190 grants (high: $1,000,000; low: $25).

Fields of interest: Education; Jewish federated giving programs; Jewish agencies & synagogues.

International interests: Israel.

Limitations: Giving primarily in Indianapolis, IN, New York, NY, and Israel.

Application information:

Initial approach: Letter
Deadline(s): None

Officers and Directors:* Edward Hasten,* Pres.; Judith Hasten,* V.P.; Michael Hasten,* V.P.; Monica Hasten Rosenfeld,* Secy.; Anna Ruth Hasten; Mark Hasten.

EIN: 351998923

840
Eli Lilly and Company Foundation

(also known as Lilly Foundation)
c/o Tax Division
Lilly Corporate Ctr., D.C. 1627
Indianapolis, IN 46285-0001 (317) 428-1130
Contact: Robert Lee Smith, Pres.
URL: http://www.lilly.com/responsibility/
foundation/

Incorporated in 1968 in IN.
Donors: Eli Lilly and Co.; Edmund A Cyrol Trust.
Grantmaker type: Company-sponsored foundation.
Financial data (yr. ended 12/31/09): Assets,
$68,512,626 (M); gifts received, $25,000,000;
expenditures, $30,731,802; qualifying
distributions, $30,345,734; giving activities include
$19,512,712 for 436 grants (high: $2,000,000;
low: $250), and $10,833,022 for 2,668 employee
matching gifts.
Purpose and activities: The foundation supports
organizations involved with arts and culture, K-12
education reform, mental health, disease, youth
development, community development, diversity,
and public policy research. Support is given primarily
in areas of company operations.
Fields of interest: United Ways and Federated Giving
Programs; Arts, cultural/ethnic awareness; Arts;
Education, reform; Elementary/secondary
education; Mental health, depression; Mental
health, schizophrenia; Mental health/crisis
services; Cancer; Heart & circulatory diseases;
Nerve, muscle & bone diseases; Diabetes; Health
organizations; Youth development; Civil rights,
race/intergroup relations; Community/economic
development; Public policy, research; Women.
Type of support: General/operating support;
Continuing support; Annual campaigns; Capital
campaigns; Equipment; Fellowships; Employee
volunteer services; Employee matching gifts;
Donated products; Matching/challenge support.
Limitations: Applications accepted. Giving on a
national and international basis, with emphasis on
areas of company operations, including
Indianapolis, IN. No support for religious or
sectarian organizations not of direct benefit to the
entire community, fraternal, labor, athletic, or
veterans' organizations or bands, or non-accredited
educational organizations. No grants to individuals,
or for scholarships or travel, endowments, debt
reduction, beauty or talent contests, fundraising
activities related to individual sponsorship,
conferences or media production, or memorials; no
loans; no political contributions.
Publications: Application guidelines; Corporate
giving report; Informational brochure (including
application guidelines); Program policy statement.
Application information: Qualifying grant
applications received between January 1 and June
30 are generally reviewed during the third quarter of
the calendar year. Applications selected for a grant
generally receive funding in the fourth quarter of the
same year; applications received between July 1 and
December 31 are generally reviewed in the first
quarter of the following calendar year, with those
selected for grants generally receiving funding in the
second quarter of the following year. Application
form not required.
  Initial approach: Complete online application
  Deadline(s): None
  Board meeting date(s): 1st quarter and 3rd
    quarter
  Final notification: 30 days following board
    meetings

Officer and Directors:* Robert Lee Smith,* Pres.;
Robert A. Armitage; Bryce Carmine; Frank Deane;
John C. Lechleiter, Ph.D.; Susan Mahony; Anthony
T. Murphy; Anne Nobles; Bart Peterson; Steven M.
Paul, M.D.; Derica Rice; Gino Santini.
Number of staff: 1 full-time professional; 3 full-time
support.
EIN: 356202479
Recent grants for international programs:
840-1 American Academy of Family Physicians
Foundation, Leawood, KS, $2,000,000. For
Peers for Progress, global diabetes peer support
program complementing collaborative efforts of
primary care physicians, patients, and diabetes
educators, emphasizing peer-to-peer
interactions, mentoring, and role-modeling
toward sustaining individual behavioral changes
improving long-term diabetes - Cyrol Gift. 2009.
840-2 American Academy of Family Physicians
Foundation, Leawood, KS, $1,359,934. For
Peers for Progress, global diabetes peer support
program complementing collaborative efforts of
primary care physicians, patients, and diabetes
educators, emphasizing peer-to-peer
interactions, mentoring, and role-modeling
toward sustaining individual behavioral changes
improving long-term diabetes - Cyrol Gift. 2009.
840-3 American Academy of Family Physicians
Foundation, Leawood, KS, $179,000. For Peers
for Progress, global diabetes peer support
program complementing collaborative efforts of
primary care physicians, patients, and diabetes
educators, emphasizing peer-to-peer
interactions, mentoring, and role-modeling
toward sustaining individual behavioral changes
improving long-term diabetes - Cyrol Gift. 2009.
840-4 American Red Cross National Headquarters,
Washington, DC, $25,000. For Disaster Relief -
Philippines and Indonesia. 2009.
840-5 Fraser Institute, Vancouver, Canada,
$15,000. For General Operating Support. 2009.
840-6 Heifer Project International, Little Rock, AR,
$100,000. For General Operating Support for
Heifer Project International Programming. 2009.
840-7 Indiana University, Bloomington, IN,
$500,000. For General Operating Support for
AMPATH, Kenya. 2009.
840-8 INSEAD Management Education Foundation,
New York, NY, $33,000. For INSEAD Innovation
MBA Scholarships. 2009.
840-9 International Center of Indianapolis,
Indianapolis, IN, $25,000. For International
Citizen of the Year. 2009.
840-10 Mercy Corps, Portland, OR, $25,000. For
Typhoon Morakot Relief Efforts in Taiwan. 2009.
840-11 Nationalities Council of Indiana,
Indianapolis, IN, $10,000. For World Travelers at
the International Festival. 2009.
840-12 Partners in Health, Boston, MA, $250,000.
For General Operating Support for PIH Rwanda.
2009.
840-13 Project HOPE - The People-to-People Health
Foundation, Millwood, VA, $50,000. For Global
Health and Humanitarian Assistance. 2009.

841
Lilly Cares Foundation, Inc.

c/o Eli Lilly and Co.
Lilly Corp. Ctr.
893 S. Delaware St.
Indianapolis, IN 46285-0001 (800) 545-6962
Application address: P.O. Box 230999, Centerville,
VA 20120; URL: http://www.lilly.com/
responsibility/patients/Pages/programs.aspx

Established as a company-sponsored operating
foundation in 1996 in IN.
Donor: Eli Lilly and Co.
Grantmaker type: Operating foundation.
Financial data (yr. ended 12/31/10): Assets, $0;
gifts received, $308,813,432; expenditures,
$308,813,432; qualifying distributions,
$398,813,432; giving activities include
$308,813,432 for grants to individuals.
Purpose and activities: The foundation distributes
pharmaceuticals to ill, infant, and economically
disadvantaged people who are below the federal
poverty level and who are not eligible for any
third-party medication payment assistance.
Fields of interest: Economically disadvantaged.
International interests: Developing countries.
Type of support: Grants to individuals; Donated
products.
Limitations: Applications accepted. Giving on a
national basis.
Publications: Application guidelines; Informational
brochure.
Application information: Application form required.
  Initial approach: Download application form and
    fax or mail to application address
  Deadline(s): None
  Final notification: 4 weeks
Officers and Directors:* Steven Stapleton,* Chair.
and Pres.; David Garza, V.P.; Bronwen Mantlo,
Secy.; Thomas W. Grein, Treas.; Michael J.
Harrington; Jack Harris; Terrence M. Lyons.
EIN: 352027985

842
NIBCO Inc. Corporate Giving Program

1516 Middlebury St.
Elkhart, IN 46516-4740
URL: http://www.nibco.com/cms.do?id=29

Grantmaker type: Corporate giving program.
Purpose and activities: NIBCO makes charitable
contributions to nonprofit organizations involved
with education, community development, and on a
case by case basis. Support is given primarily in
areas of company operations in Arkansas,
California, Georgia, Indiana, Ohio, Texas, and
Virginia, and in Mexico and Poland.
Fields of interest: United Ways and Federated Giving
Programs; American Red Cross; Recreation;
Recreation, parks/playgrounds; Housing/shelter;
Environment, water resources; Education;
Community/economic development; General
charitable giving.
International interests: Mexico; Poland.
Type of support: General/operating support;
Building/renovation; Employee volunteer services;
Employee-related scholarships; Donated products;
In-kind gifts.
Limitations: Giving primarily in areas of company
operations in AR, CA, GA, IN, OH, TX, and VA, and in
Mexico and Poland; giving also to national
organizations.

843
Overseas Council, Inc.

(also known as Overseas Council for Theological Education and Missions)
P.O. Box 17368
Indianapolis, IN 46217-0368 (317) 788-7250
Contact: Rick Hampton, C.O.O.
FAX: (317) 788-7257; E-mail: info@overseas.org;
Toll-free tel.: (877) 788-7250; URL: http://
www.overseas.org

Established in 1974 in IN.
Grantmaker type: Public charity.
Financial data (yr. ended 09/30/10): Revenue, $6,212,025; assets, $4,427,067 (M); gifts received, $6,086,530; expenditures, $5,351,259; giving activities include $2,381,608 for 51 grants to organizations outside the U.S.
Purpose and activities: The council aims to facilitate excellence in theological education by leveraging people, expertise and resources to advance quality Christian leadership training around the world by providing student scholarships, faculty and staff scholarships, educational resources, and leadership consultation for senior leaders, by facilitating construction of critical educational infrastructure, and by mobilizing individuals, churches and organizations in North America for prayer, financial partnership, understanding and knowledge commitment to the church's leadership training efforts around the world.
Fields of interest: Protestant agencies & churches; Theological school/education; Libraries (special); Scholarships/financial aid; Christian agencies & churches; Religion.
International interests: Middle East; Latin America; Europe; Asia; Africa.
Type of support: Scholarship funds.
Limitations: Applications not accepted. Giving on an international basis, with emphasis on Africa, Asia, Europe, Latin America, and the Middle East.
Publications: Annual report; Newsletter.
Application information: Unsolicited requests for funds not accepted.
   Board meeting date(s): Jan. and June
Officers and Directors:* Norman E. Miller,* Chair.; James C. Blankemeyer,* Vice-Chair.; David A. Baer,* Pres. and C.E.O.; Rick Hampton, C.O.O.; Thomas K. Gabe,* Secy.; Rex E. Bennett, Treas.; Dr. Samuel Barkat; Ann Blaser; Archer D. Bonnema; Dr. David P. Dwight; Richard G. Hagerty; Howard F. Hubler; P. Anthony Lannie; Dr. Robert Petterson; R.T. Rankin; Dr. Ramesh Richard; Lorna Stern-Laniak; Jerry L. Webb.
Number of staff: 17 full-time professional; 17 full-time support.
EIN: 351333030

844
The Melvin and Bren Simon Charitable Foundation Number One

10110 Ditch Rd.
Carmel, IN 46032-9613 (317) 844-9467

Established in 1998 in IN.
Donors: Melvin Simon†; Melvin Simon and Associates, Inc.
Grantmaker type: Independent foundation.
Financial data (yr. ended 12/31/09): Assets, $28,013,162 (M); gifts received, $300,000; expenditures, $2,904,414; qualifying distributions, $2,850,553; giving activities include $2,850,553

for 42 grants (high: $880,000; low: $500; average: $1,000–$100,000).
Purpose and activities: Giving primarily for Jewish organizations, as well as for education and health organizations, particularly for cancer.
Fields of interest: Arts; Higher education; Cancer; Health organizations; Jewish federated giving programs; Jewish agencies & synagogues.
Limitations: Applications not accepted. Giving primarily in Bloomington and Indianapolis, IN. No grants to individuals.
Application information: Contributes only to pre-selected organizations.
Trustee: Bren Simon.
EIN: 352049367
Recent grants for international programs:
844-1 American Friends of the Hebrew University, Chicago, IL, $333,333. For general support. 2008.
844-2 Jewish Federation of Greater Indianapolis, Indianapolis, IN, $100,000. For Israel Emergency Campaign. 2008.
844-3 National Democratic Institute for International Affairs, Washington, DC, $100,000. For general support. 2008.

845
Transformation Trust, Inc.

P. O. Box 80007
Indianapolis, IN 46280-0007 (317) 580-2002

Established in 1997 in IN.
Donors: Edwin H. Klink; Sheila K. Klink.
Grantmaker type: Independent foundation.
Financial data (yr. ended 12/31/10): Assets, $28,962,866 (M); gifts received, $5,027,834; expenditures, $893,368; qualifying distributions, $657,000; giving activities include $657,000 for grants.
Fields of interest: Spirituality; United Ways and Federated Giving Programs; International affairs; Human services; Employment, research; Health care, public policy; Arts; Education.
Limitations: Applications accepted. Giving primarily in CA, IL, IN, VA, and WA.
Application information:
   Initial approach: Letter
   Deadline(s): None
Board Members: Elizabeth Hamilton; Sheila K. Klink.
EIN: 352024586

846
West Foundation, Inc.

c/o JPMorgan Chase Bank, N.A.
111 Monument Cir., Ste. 220
Indianapolis, IN 46204-5168
Application address: c/o Emily West, 4120 N. Illinois St., Indianapolis, IN 46208, tel.: (317) 283-5525

Established in 1954.
Donors: Stephen R. West; Phyllis M. West.
Grantmaker type: Independent foundation.
Financial data (yr. ended 12/31/10): Assets, $6,782,772 (M); expenditures, $482,557; qualifying distributions, $473,297; giving activities include $310,000 for 20 grants (high: $30,000; low: $5,000).
Purpose and activities: Giving primarily for international community development and human service agencies.

Fields of interest: Health care; Human services; International economic development.
International interests: Africa; Europe; South America.
Type of support: General/operating support; Annual campaigns; Capital campaigns; Matching/challenge support.
Limitations: Applications accepted. Giving primarily in the U.S. with some emphasis on CA and NY. No grants to individuals.
Publications: Application guidelines.
Application information: Application form not required.
   Copies of proposal: 1
   Deadline(s): None
   Board meeting date(s): Feb., May, Aug., and Nov.
Officers: Stephen R. West, Pres. and Treas.; Phyllis M. West, V.P.; Emily A. West, Exec. Dir.
EIN: 237416727

IOWA

847
Global Invincibility Foundation

c/o Swartz Co.
200 W. Washington Ave.
Fairfield, IA 52556-3318

Donor: Rafael David.
Grantmaker type: Independent foundation.
Financial data (yr. ended 12/31/10): Assets, $4,420,730 (M); expenditures, $2,127,752; qualifying distributions, $2,127,000; giving activities include $2,127,000 for grants.
Fields of interest: International peace/security.
Limitations: Applications not accepted. Giving primarily in IA.
Application information: Contributes only to pre-selected organizations.
Officers: Rafael David, Pres.; Nancy Diamond, Secy.-Treas.
Director: Steve Brittingham.
EIN: 263418616

848
Holthues Trust

209 Iowa Ave.
Muscatine, IA 52761-3730

Established in 1997 in IA.
Donor: The Stanley Foundation.
Grantmaker type: Independent foundation.
Financial data (yr. ended 12/31/10): Assets, $23,522,234 (M); expenditures, $806,327; qualifying distributions, $756,669; giving activities include $749,000 for 36 grants (high: $100,000; low: $500).
Purpose and activities: Giving primarily for projects that will advance the goals of peace, security, freedom and justice globally, as well as community services locally in Iowa.
Fields of interest: Human services; International human rights; International peace/security; Education; International affairs; Civil/human rights; Community/economic development.

Limitations: Applications not accepted. Giving in the U.S., with emphasis on Washington, DC, IA, MA, MN, and NY. No support for private foundations. No grants to individuals.
Application information: Contributes only to pre-selected organizations.
Officers and Directors:* Richard H. Stanley, Pres.; Joseph H. Stanley,* V.P.; Betty Anders, Secy.; Dana W. Pittman, Treas.; Donna J. Buckles; Elizabeth Shriver; Lincoln Stanley; Lynne E. Stanley.
EIN: 421466786

849
Fred and Charlotte Hubbell Foundation
453 7th St.
Des Moines, IA   50309-4110   (515) 245-2965
Contact: Mindy Nussbaum-Bell

Established in 1997 in IA.
Donors: Charlotte Hubbell; Frederick S. Hubbell.
Grantmaker type: Independent foundation.
Financial data (yr. ended 12/31/10): Assets, $3,849,209 (M); expenditures, $733,630; qualifying distributions, $722,307; giving activities include $711,780 for 84 grants (high: $260,500; low: $100).
Purpose and activities: Giving primarily for education, the environment and the arts; support also for a federated giving program.
Fields of interest: Arts; Foundations (community); Higher education; Environment, association; Human services; International affairs; United Ways and Federated Giving Programs.
Limitations: Applications accepted. Giving primarily in IA, with emphasis on Des Moines.
Application information: Application form not required.
   Initial approach: Letter
   Deadline(s): None
Trustee: Bankers Trust Co.
EIN: 391878112

850
Humanities Iowa
(formerly Iowa Humanities Board)
100 Oakdale Campus, N310 OH
Iowa City, IA   52242-5000   (319) 335-4153
Contact: Christopher R. Rossi, Exec. Dir.; Cheryl Walsh, Grants Dir.
FAX: (319) 335-4154;
E-mail: info@humanitiesiowa.org; Additional email for Cheryl Walsh: cheryl-walsh@uiowa.edu;
URL: http://www.humanitiesiowa.org

Established in 1971 in IA.
Grantmaker type: Public charity.
Financial data (yr. ended 10/31/10): Revenue, $770,385; assets, $542,892 (M); gifts received, $694,468; expenditures, $764,359; giving activities include $350,683 for grants.
Purpose and activities: The organization promotes understanding and appreciation of the people, communities, cultures, and stories of importance to Iowa and to the nation.
Fields of interest: Historical activities, genealogy; Historic preservation/historical societies; Libraries (public); Language/linguistics; Art history; Museums; Museums (history); Media/communications; Media, film/video; Political science; Urban studies; Rural studies; Law/international law; International studies;

Anthropology/sociology; Black studies; Ethnic studies; Adult/continuing education; Arts, cultural/ethnic awareness; Humanities; Arts; Women.
Type of support: Management development/capacity building; Program development; Conferences/seminars; Film/video/radio; Seed money.
Limitations: Applications accepted. Giving primarily in IA. No support for for-profit enterprises, direct social or political action, social services or social training programs, or creative or performing arts. No grants to individuals, or for research (unless integral to a public program), publications outside of a public program, acquisitions, capital projects, equipment, curriculum development, endowment funds, operating support, or international travel.
Publications: Application guidelines; Informational brochure; Newsletter.
Application information: 1 proposal is required for Mini Grants; 21 copies of proposal are required for Major Grants. Application form required.
   Initial approach: Download application guidelines and form; telephone or email with questions
   Deadline(s): May 1 and Oct. 1 for Major Grants; four weeks prior to project start date for Mini Grants
   Board meeting date(s): June and Nov.
   Final notification: Six to seven weeks for Major Grants; two weeks for Mini Grants
Officers and Directors:* Valentina Slater Forminykh,* Pres.; Moudy Nabulsi,* V.P.; Fiona Valentine,* Secy.; Tim Johnson,* Treas.; Christopher R. Rossi, Exec. Dir.; and 16 additional directors.
Number of staff: 3 full-time professional; 1 part-time professional; 1 full-time support.
EIN: 237374180

851
Maharishi Global Development Fund
P.O. Box 1720
Fairfield, IA   52556-0029

Grantmaker type: Public charity.
Financial data (yr. ended 12/31/10): Revenue, $3,579,480; assets, $122,580,646 (M); gifts received, $2,243,751; expenditures, $8,723,632; giving activities include $5,222,269 for grants, and $2,478,266 for grants to organizations outside the U.S.
Purpose and activities: The fund seeks to promote world peace as well as the construction of healthy housing.
Fields of interest: International peace/security; Housing/shelter.
Limitations: Giving on a national and international basis.
Officers and Trustees:* Dr. Benjamin Feldman,* Pres.; Peter Beach, Secy.; Paul Potter,* Treas.; Dr. Christopher Hartnett; Linda Hartnett; Dr. Prakash Srivastava.
EIN: 522052522

852
Ochylski Family Foundation
300 Walnut St., Ste. 295A
Des Moines, IA   50309-2212   (515) 244-6040
Contact: Kathy Hovey

Established in 1996 in IL.
Donors: Edward Ochylski; Mrs. Edward Ochylski.

Grantmaker type: Independent foundation.
Financial data (yr. ended 12/31/10): Assets, $2,378,193 (M); expenditures, $659,412; qualifying distributions, $644,680; giving activities include $644,680 for 25 grants (high: $500,000; low: $500).
Purpose and activities: Giving primarily for Roman Catholic organizations.
Fields of interest: Education; Human services; Children/youth, services; Catholic agencies & churches.
International interests: Vatican City.
Limitations: Applications accepted. Giving primarily in FL, IL, and Warsaw, Poland.
Application information: Application form not required.
   Initial approach: Letter
   Deadline(s): Oct. 1
Officers and Directors:* Edward Ochylski,* Pres.; Kelly Ochylski Butler, V.P.; Gabrielle Klein, V.P.; Daniel Ochylski, V.P.; Edward Ochylski III, V.P.; Juliana Ochylski-Summers, V.P.; Mary C. Ochylski-Wertsch, V.P.; Jessica Stark, V.P.; Eleanor Ochylski,* Secy.-Treas.; Victor Bezman.
EIN: 364110483
Recent grants for international programs:
852-1 Capuchin Poor Clare Nuns, Linares, Mexico, $13,500. 2008.
852-2 Catholic Relief Services, Baltimore, MD, $400,000. 2008.
852-3 Pope John Paul II Foundation, Vatican City, $1,000,000. 2008.
852-4 Smile Train, New York, NY, $25,000. 2008.

853
P.E.O. Foundation
3700 Grand Ave.
Des Moines, IA   50312-2899   (515) 255-3153
Contact: Cathy Brandt, Chair.
FAX: (515) 255-3820; URL: http://www.peointernational.org/peo-foundation

Established in 1961; supporting organization of the P.E.O. Educational Loan Fund, Cottey College, P.E.O. International Peace Scholar Fund, P.E.O. Program Continuing Education, and P.E.O. Scholar Awards.
Grantmaker type: Public charity.
Financial data (yr. ended 06/30/10): Revenue, $6,387,836; assets, $75,160,735 (M); gifts received, $3,326,810; expenditures, $4,585,091; giving activities include $2,911,290 for grants, $500 for grants to organizations outside the U.S., and $1,245,879 for grants to individuals.
Purpose and activities: The foundation provides support for educational opportunities for women.
Fields of interest: Higher education; Education; International exchange, students; Women.
Type of support: Grants to individuals; Scholarships—to individuals; Student loans—to individuals.
Limitations: Applications not accepted. Giving on a national and international basis, primarily in the U.S. and Canada.
Application information: Contributes only to pre-selected organizations.
Officer: Cathy Brandt, Chair.
Trustees: Toots Green; Jayne Pritko.
EIN: 426094564

854
Sehgal Family Foundation
100 Court Ave., Ste. 211
Des Moines, IA 50309-2256 (515) 288-0010
FAX: (515) 288-4501;
E-mail: rclutter@smsfoundation.org; URL: http://www.smsfoundation.org

Established in 1998 in IA.
Donors: Edda G. Sehgal; Surinder M. Sehgal.
Grantmaker type: Independent foundation.
Financial data (yr. ended 12/31/10): Assets, $46,951,920 (M); gifts received, $59,251; expenditures, $4,855,205; qualifying distributions, $1,581,032; giving activities include $1,581,032 for grants.
Purpose and activities: Giving primarily for the environment and natural resource conservation. The foundation also works to address issues in India, such as gender inequality, low literacy, and awareness of reproductive health and family planning. Additionally, the foundation works to facilitate Gurgaon, India villagers in assessing their perceived, met, unmet, hidden health care, and other domestic needs, and it also works to ensure that safe drinking water is available throughout rural Gurgaon, and to promote water literacy. The foundation also works to create village level institutions in India which generate both employment and income, and assist in start up farm production activities.
Fields of interest: International development; Environment, natural resources; Environment; Foundations (community).
International interests: India.
Limitations: Applications not accepted. Giving primarily in India, with some giving in FL and MA, and in Mexico. No grants to individuals.
Application information: Contributes only to pre-selected organizations.
Officers and Directors:* Surinder M. Sehgal,* Pres. and Treas.; Edda G. Sehgal,* V.P. and Secy.; Rajat Sehgal, Exec. Dir.; Ryan Clutter; Bernd U. Sehgal; Kenai K. Sehgal; Oliver S. Sehgal; Vicki D. Sehgal; Maureen Smith.
EIN: 421477858

855
Wallace Research Foundation
c/o RSM McGladrey, Inc.
221 3rd Ave. S.E., Ste. 300
Cedar Rapids, IA 52401-1525
Contact: Joe Gevock

Established in 1996 in IA.
Donors: H.B. Wallace†; Jocelyn M. Wallace; Henry D. Wallace; Linda Wallace-Gray; H.A. Wallace†.
Grantmaker type: Independent foundation.
Financial data (yr. ended 12/31/10): Assets, $76,107,835 (M); expenditures, $3,567,681; qualifying distributions, $3,233,585; giving activities include $3,204,799 for 43 grants (high: $470,000; low: $5,000).
Purpose and activities: Giving primarily for education, the environment, and medical research.
Fields of interest: Medical research; Higher education; Environment, natural resources.
Type of support: Endowments; General/operating support; Research.
Limitations: Applications not accepted. No support for religious or political purposes. No grants to individuals.
Publications: Annual report.

Application information: Contributes only to pre-selected organizations.
Officers and Director:* Henry D. Wallace, Pres.; Linda Wallace-Gray, V.P. and Secy.-Treas.; Alex Gilchrist; Angus Gilchrist.
EIN: 426540579
Recent grants for international programs:
855-1 Arizona State University, Tempe, AZ, $100,000. For research project, NW Mexican Cultures. 2009.
855-2 Lewa Wildlife Conservancy USA, Woodbridge, VA, $90,000. For conservation efforts in various regions. 2009.
855-3 Tostan, Washington, DC, $50,000. For microcredit and training program. 2009.
855-4 Union of Concerned Scientists, Cambridge, MA, $175,000. For climate change impacts assessment. 2009.
855-5 University of Arizona Foundation, Tucson, AZ, $10,800. For survey project at sanctuary of Zeus on Mount Lykaion. 2009.
855-6 University of North Carolina, Chapel Hill, NC, $225,000. For Maya Area Cultural Heritage Initiative. 2009.
855-7 Wildcoast, Inc., Imperial Beach, CA, $50,000. For conservation efforts. 2009.
855-8 Wildlife Alliance, Washington, DC, $95,000. For wildlife tracking to protect against poachers. 2009.
855-9 Wildlife Conservation Society, Bronx, NY, $150,000. To assess and introduce conservation measures in Congo Basin. 2009.

856
John R. Wright and Eloise Mountain Wright Foundation
701 Oaknoll Dr.
Iowa City, IA 52246-5168
Mailing address: c/o Graciela C. Wright, 5218 Redstart St., Houston, TX 77035-3129

Established in 1995 in MO.
Donors: John R. Wright; Eloise M. Wright.
Grantmaker type: Independent foundation.
Financial data (yr. ended 12/31/10): Assets, $3,044,766 (M); gifts received, $4,000; expenditures, $151,751; qualifying distributions, $146,000; giving activities include $146,000 for grants.
Fields of interest: Arts; Education; Christian agencies & churches.
International interests: Central America; Africa; Ireland.
Type of support: Annual campaigns; Building/renovation; Emergency funds; Scholarship funds; Matching/challenge support.
Limitations: Applications not accepted. Giving primarily in IA; some giving also in CA and OR. Funding also in Africa, Central America and Ireland. No grants to individuals.
Application information: Contributes only to pre-selected organizations.
Directors: Charles E. Wright; Graciela C. Wright.
EIN: 431698425

KANSAS

857
Israel Henry Beren Charitable Trust
c/o Robert M. Beren, Tr.
P.O. Box 20380
Wichita, KS 67208-1380

Established in 1995 in OH.
Donor: Israel Henry Beren†.
Grantmaker type: Independent foundation.
Financial data (yr. ended 12/31/10): Assets, $47,920,574 (M); expenditures, $2,145,432; qualifying distributions, $1,943,000; giving activities include $1,943,000 for grants.
Fields of interest: Human services; Education; Jewish agencies & synagogues.
Limitations: Applications not accepted. Giving primarily in NY; some funding also in FL and TX. No grants to individuals.
Application information: Contributes only to pre-selected organizations.
Trustee: Robert M. Beren.
EIN: 486337836
Recent grants for international programs:
857-1 American Friends of Beit Morasha, Rockaway Park, NY, $100,000. For general support. 2009.
857-2 Foundation for Jewish Camping, New York, NY, $100,000. For general support. 2009.
857-3 Hadassah, The Womens Zionist Organization of America, New York, NY, $250,000. For IHB Cardiothoracic Intensive Care Unit. 2009.
857-4 Ohr Torah Stone Colleges and Graduate Programs, New York, NY, $1,000,000. For IHB Academic Center. 2009.

858
Christian Foundation for Children & Aging
1 Elmwood Ave.
Kansas City, KS 66103-3719
Contact: Michael J. Calabria, Dir., Finance
FAX: (913) 384-2211; E-mail: mail@cfcausa.org; Toll-free tel.: (800) 875-6564; URL: http://www.cfcausa.org
Around the World with CFCA: http://blog.cfcausa.org/
Facebook: http://www.facebook.com/sponsorachild
Twitter: http://twitter.com/@cfca
Vimeo: http://vimeo.com/user1580935
YouTube: http://www.youtube.com/user/cfcausa

Established in 1981.
Grantmaker type: Public charity.
Financial data (yr. ended 12/31/10): Revenue, $108,721,821; assets, $38,568,284 (M); gifts received, $107,628,340; expenditures, $107,226,690; giving activities include $93,418,942 for grants to organizations outside the U.S.
Purpose and activities: The foundation connects sponsors in the United States and elsewhere in the world with children, youth, and aging persons in economically-developing countries in Latin America, Asia, Africa, and the Caribbean.
Fields of interest: Human services; Children/youth, services; Family services; International relief.
International interests: Developing countries.

Type of support: Continuing support; Emergency funds.
Limitations: Applications not accepted. Giving to developing countries.
Publications: Occasional report.
Application information: The foundation does not accept individual grant requests.
Officers and Directors:* Scott Wasserman,* Chair.; Robert K. Hentzen,* Pres.; Francis "Paco" Wertin,* C.E.O.; Rev. Allan Weinert,* C.Ss.R., Secy.; Ed Herman,* Treas.; Catherine Crosby; Eileen Greenlay; Louis A. Guillou; Rev. Vince Haselhorst; Carolyn Zimmerman.
Number of staff: 116 full-time professional.
EIN: 431243999

859
Jewish Community Foundation of Greater Kansas City
5801 W. 115th St., Ste. 104
Overland Park, KS   66211-1800   (913) 327-8245
Contact: Lauren Mattleman Hoopes, Exec. Dir.
FAX: (913) 327-8273; E-mail: kevint@jewishkc.org;
URL: http://www.jcfkc.org/

Established in 1959 in KS.
Grantmaker type: Public charity.
Financial data (yr. ended 12/31/09): Revenue, $5,197,981; assets, $108,402,407 (M); gifts received, $3,667,996; expenditures, $6,263,953; giving activities include $5,277,083 for grants.
Purpose and activities: The foundation enhances and promotes the continuity of the Jewish community through a broad range of innovative and charitable programs.
Fields of interest: Jewish agencies & synagogues; Immigrants/refugees.
International interests: Israel.
Type of support: Continuing support; Annual campaigns; Capital campaigns; Building/renovation; Land acquisition; Endowments; Emergency funds; Program development; Conferences/seminars; Publication; Curriculum development; Scholarship funds; Research; Matching/challenge support.
Limitations: Applications accepted. Giving primarily in KS and MO.
Publications: Application guidelines; Annual report.
Application information: Application form required.
Initial approach: Letter
Copies of proposal: 5
Deadline(s): Mar. 15 for Karen and Ed Porter Summer Experience Fund; Apr. 1 and Oct. 15 for Flo Harris Supporting Foundation Grants; July 31 for White Theatre Grantor Fund; Dec. 15 for J-LEAD (Jewish Leadership Education Action and Development); Dec. 31 for Community Legacy Fund
Board meeting date(s): Quarterly
Officers and Trustees:* Michael A. Schultz,* Pres.; Alice Jacks Achtenberg,* V.P.; Jeffrey S. Alpert, V.P.; Ron Goldsmith,* V.P.; Robert Palan,* V.P.; L. Joshua Sosland,* V.P.; Todd L. Stettner,* Secy.; Kevin Taylor, C.P.A., C.F.O.; David Goodman,* Treas.; Lauren Mattleman Hoopes, Exec. Dir.; and 25 additional trustees.
Number of staff: 4 full-time professional; 3 full-time support.
EIN: 436049281

860
Harry J. Lloyd Charitable Trust
(formerly Share Foundation)
7200 W. 132nd St., Ste. 190
Overland Park, KS   66213-1136   (913) 851-2174
Contact: Russell Brown, Pres.
FAX: (913) 851-4892; E-mail: ltrust@ltrust.org;
URL: http://www.hjltrust.org/

Established in 1965 in MO.
Donors: House of Lloyd, Inc.; Harry J. Lloyd†.
Grantmaker type: Independent foundation.
Financial data (yr. ended 12/31/10): Assets, $107,748,033 (M); expenditures, $10,033,216; qualifying distributions, $9,598,201; giving activities include $8,436,639 for 122 grants (high: $368,987; low: $500; average: $25,000–$100,000).
Purpose and activities: The foundation concentrates its support on projects that have a spiritual dimension, with special attention given to evangelical work, especially in the foreign mission field. Interest also in human services and educational organizations that are Christian-based.
Fields of interest: Food services; Education; Health care; Cancer research; Cancer; Christian agencies & churches.
International interests: Africa; China; India; Latin America; Middle East.
Type of support: Scholarship funds; Equipment; Capital campaigns; Program development; Seed money.
Limitations: Applications accepted. Giving worldwide. No support for the arts, organizations that support or prohibit abortion or abortion rights, or for political organizations.
Publications: Application guidelines.
Application information: The foundation's web site is restricted to information on and applications for melanoma research related grants. Not more than one application per institution in each of the three melanoma grant type categories will be funded. See foundation's web site for complete melanoma research grant application policies, guidelines and forms. Application form required.
Initial approach: Proposal
Deadline(s): Feb. 1 for melanoma research grants
Board meeting date(s): Quarterly
Final notification: May for melanoma research grants
Officer and Trustees:* Russell Brown,* Pres.; Janet Ashcroft; Dan Carson; G. Richard Hastings; Jami Kay; Demi Lloyd; Jeanette Lloyd; Timothy J. Oxley.
Number of staff: 6 full-time support.
EIN: 436689416
Recent grants for international programs:
860-1 AMO International, Falls Church, VA, $12,055. For evangelism. 2009.
860-2 Asian Access Life Ministries, San Dimas, CA, $26,000. For evangelism. 2009.
860-3 Asian Partners International, Lubbock, TX, $25,000. For evangelism. 2009.
860-4 Bethlehem Bible College, New Braunfels, TX, $42,501. For evangelism. 2009.
860-5 Biblica, Colorado Springs, CO, $110,000. For evangelism. 2009.
860-6 Blood Water Mission, Nashville, TN, $75,000. For general support. 2009.
860-7 Bombay Teen Challenge, Philadelphia, PA, $97,170. For evangelism. 2009.
860-8 Centro di Riferimento Oncologico, Aviano, Italy, $102,000. For medical research. 2009.
860-9 China Outreach Ministries, Mechanicsburg, PA, $40,000. For evangelism. 2009.
860-10 Christian Community Foundation of France, Marietta, GA, $120,446. For evangelism. 2009.
860-11 Communication Institute, Lisle, IL, $115,300. For evangelism. 2009.
860-12 Create Partners, Tigard, OR, $150,500. For evangelism. 2009.
860-13 Create Partners, Tigard, OR, $10,000. For general support. 2009.
860-14 CURE International, Lemoyne, PA, $76,114. For evangelism. 2009.
860-15 Deaf Opportunity Outreach International, Bunn, NC, $68,000. For evangelism. 2009.
860-16 Development Associates International, Colorado Springs, CO, $201,582. For general support. 2009.
860-17 Development Associates International, Colorado Springs, CO, $157,300. For evangelism. 2009.
860-18 Dynamic Church Planting International, Oceanside, CA, $50,225. For evangelism. 2009.
860-19 Elam Ministries, Alpharetta, GA, $123,250. For general support. 2009.
860-20 English Language Institute in China, Fort Collins, CO, $100,000. For evangelism. 2009.
860-21 Faith Childrens Ministry, Round Hill, VA, $50,820. For evangelism. 2009.
860-22 Foundation for International Research and Education, Colorado Springs, CO, $41,000. For evangelism. 2009.
860-23 Global Partners for Development, Tucker, GA, $75,000. For evangelism. 2009.
860-24 Great Commission Foundation, Hull, GA, $100,000. For general support. 2009.
860-25 Heart to Heart International, Olathe, KS, $30,000. For general support. 2009.
860-26 Hi Kidz International, Suwanee, GA, $90,500. For evangelism. 2009.
860-27 Hope Builders International, Charlottesville, VA, $99,100. For evangelism. 2009.
860-28 Institute for Global Engagement, Arlington, VA, $94,500. For general support. 2009.
860-29 Institute of Cancer Research, London, England, $112,500. For medical research. 2009.
860-30 International Justice Mission, Arlington, VA, $62,500. For general support. 2009.
860-31 International Mission Board of the Southern Baptist Convention, Richmond, VA, $20,000. For evangelism. 2009.
860-32 John Stott Ministries, Menlo Park, CA, $74,567. For evangelism. 2009.
860-33 Lausanne Committee for World Evangelization, South Hamilton, MA, $50,000. For general support. 2009.
860-34 Life in Abundance International, Pasadena, CA, $84,000. For general support. 2009.
860-35 Logosdor, Pompano Beach, FL, $83,168. For evangelism. 2009.
860-36 Mid-India Christian Mission, Greenville, IL, $12,500. For evangelism. 2009.
860-37 Middle East Media, Lynnwood, WA, $59,020. For evangelism. 2009.
860-38 Mission India, Grand Rapids, MI, $250,000. For evangelism work in India. 2009.
860-39 Mission to the World, Lawrenceville, GA, $27,500. For evangelism. 2009.
860-40 Missions International, Franklin, TN, $124,840. For evangelism. 2009.
860-41 Mustard Seed Project, Ambridge, PA, $20,000. For evangelism. 2009.
860-42 Oxford University, Oxford, England, $71,829. For medical research. 2009.
860-43 Partners International, Spokane, WA, $44,500. For evangelism. 2009.

860-44 Reach the Children Foundation, Pompano Beach, FL, $44,000. For evangelism. 2009.

860-45 South Asia Advocates, Kirkland, WA, $148,304. For evangelism. 2009.

860-46 Strategic Global Assistance, Elkhart, IN, $78,450. For general support. 2009.

860-47 Thornston Educational Fund, Glendora, CA, $70,000. For evangelism. 2009.

860-48 Urban Youth Workers Institute, Santa Ana, CA, $50,000. For general support. 2009.

860-49 Viva Network North America, Woodland Park, CO, $25,000. For evangelism. 2009.

860-50 VU University Medical Center, Amsterdam, Netherlands, $112,500. For medical research. 2009.

860-51 Word for the World, USA, Colorado Springs, CO, $102,025. For evangelism. 2009.

860-52 World Sports, Orlando, FL, $88,855. For evangelism. 2009.

860-53 Wycliffe Bible Translators, Orlando, FL, $50,000. For evangelism. 2009.

861
The Shumaker Family Foundation

1948 E. Santa Fe St., Ste. G
Olathe, KS   66062-1894   (913) 764-1772
Contact: Judy Wright, Exec. Dir.
FAX: (913) 764-1772;
E-mail: request@shumakerfamilyfoundation.net;
URL: http://www.shumakerfamilyfoundation.org

Established in 2005 in KS.
Donors: Paul K. Shumaker†; Dianne C. Shumaker.
Grantmaker type: Independent foundation.
Financial data (yr. ended 12/31/10): Assets, $17,054,834 (M); expenditures, $807,291; qualifying distributions, $607,934; giving activities include $607,934 for grants.
Purpose and activities: The foundation exists to promote social justice, environmental justice, spirituality and education.
Fields of interest: Education, early childhood education; Arts, public education; Engineering school/education; Education; Environment; Animal welfare; Animals/wildlife, preservation/protection; Crime/violence prevention, domestic violence; International peace/security; Civil/human rights; Science; Religion, interfaith issues; Spirituality.
Type of support: Capital campaigns; Management development/capacity building; Curriculum development; Program evaluation.
Limitations: Applications accepted. Giving primarily in the greater bi-state Kansas City area; national and international giving for environmental and animal rights. No support for non 501(c)3 organizations, or for churches, or organizations that discriminate or promote violence (including to the environment). In general, no support for schools, except for select organizations. No grants to individuals, or for bricks and mortar, annual campaigns, capital campaigns or for special events.
Publications: Application guidelines; Grants list.
Application information: The foundation will not be awarding any more grants for the 2010 calendar year. Application form available on foundation web site. Application form required for requests of $10,000 or more. For requests under $10,000 a proposal, concise budget and 501(c)(3) confirmation are required. Application form required.
    Initial approach: Letter, telephone or e-mail inquiry
    Copies of proposal: 1

Deadline(s): Mar. 1 for Spirituality and Environmental Justice; July 1 for Social Justice and Education
    Board meeting date(s): Feb., Apr., July and Nov.
    Final notification: Within 6 weeks of decision
Trustees: Dianne C. Shumaker; Eric A. Shumaker; Megan I. Shumaker.
Number of staff: 1 full-time professional.
EIN: 656406193

862
Weskan Charitable Foundation

P.O. Box 4
Lakin, KS   67860-0004

Established in 1996 in KS.
Donors: Don Nightengale; Ralph Reimer; Kearney County Gas Irrigators; Dave R. Unruh; Howard Reimer; Don Toews.
Grantmaker type: Independent foundation.
Financial data (yr. ended 12/31/10): Assets, $261,632 (M); gifts received, $152,323; expenditures, $149,367; qualifying distributions, $149,367; giving activities include $144,228 for 10 grants (high: $49,500; low: $100).
Fields of interest: International development; Education; Christian agencies & churches.
Limitations: Applications not accepted. Giving primarily in KS, with some giving in Jacmel, Haiti. No grants to individuals.
Application information: Contributes only to pre-selected organizations.
Trustees: Don Nightengale; Ralph Reimer.
EIN: 481187938

KENTUCKY

863
The C.E. and S. Foundation, Inc.

101 S. 5th St., Ste. 1650
Louisville, KY   40202-3122   (502) 583-0546
Contact: Bruce A. Maza, Exec. Dir.
FAX: (502) 583-7648;
E-mail: Bruce@cesfoundation.com; URL: http://www.cesfoundation.com

Established in 1984 in FL.
Donors: David A. Jones; and family.
Grantmaker type: Independent foundation.
Financial data (yr. ended 12/31/09): Assets, $59,923,970 (M); gifts received, $802,777; expenditures, $4,022,984; qualifying distributions, $3,934,710; giving activities include $3,645,054 for 163 grants (high: $300,000; low: $70).
Purpose and activities: Giving primarily for higher education, (with a focus on undergraduate liberal arts programs in Louisville, KY), as well as for colleges and universities, and for disaster relief and prevention, international cooperation, Louisville's urban environment, and special projects initiated by the grants committee.
Fields of interest: Safety/disasters; Education; International affairs, goodwill promotion; Urban/community development.
Type of support: General/operating support; Income development; Management development/capacity

building; Capital campaigns; Land acquisition; Endowments; Emergency funds; Program development; Seed money; Internship funds; Scholarship funds; Research; Technical assistance; Consulting services; Program-related investments/loans.
Limitations: Applications accepted. Giving primarily in Louisville, KY. No support for medical research organizations, or for political organizations. No grants to individuals.
Publications: Application guidelines; Annual report; Grants list; Program policy statement.
Application information: Accepts Donors Forum of Kentuckiana Common Application Form. Application form not required.
    Initial approach: Letter, telephone, or web site for guidelines
    Copies of proposal: 1
    Deadline(s): None
    Board meeting date(s): Jan., May, Sept. and Nov.
    Final notification: Up to two months
Officers and Trustee:* David A. Jones,* Pres.; Bruce A. Maza, Exec. Dir.
Number of staff: 2 full-time professional; 1 part-time support.
EIN: 592466943
Recent grants for international programs:
863-1 Asia Institute, Louisville, KY, $25,000. For Sichuan earthquake. 2009.
863-2 Bellarmine University, Louisville, KY, $60,000. For Foreign Study Program. 2009.
863-3 British American Arts Association U.S., Washington, DC, $10,000. For operating support. 2009.
863-4 CARE USA, Atlanta, GA, $35,000. For Typhoon Ketsana relief. 2009.
863-5 CARE USA, Atlanta, GA, $25,000. For Indonesia earthquake. 2009.
863-6 Doctors Without Borders USA, New York, NY, $25,000. For Bangladesh cyclone. 2009.
863-7 Human Rights Watch, New York, NY, $20,000. For Hong Kong Initiative. 2009.
863-8 Yale University, New Haven, CT, $250,000. For International Internships. 2009.

864
Dr. Kirti Jain Family Foundation, Inc.

243 Bellefonte Cir.
Ashland, KY   41101-2195
Contact: Kirti Jain

Established in 2004.
Donors: Kirti Jain; Asha Jain.
Grantmaker type: Independent foundation.
Financial data (yr. ended 12/31/10): Assets, $10,674,020 (M); gifts received, $1,060,000; expenditures, $538,308; qualifying distributions, $538,000; giving activities include $538,000 for 1 grant.
Fields of interest: Education; Human services; International relief.
Application information: Application form not required.
    Initial approach: Letter
Officers: Kirti Jain, Pres.; Asha Jain, Secy.
Director: Anshu Jain.
EIN: 201729881

865
O'Dell Ministries, Inc.
P.O. Box 159
Pine Knot, KY 42635-0159 (606) 354-4422
FAX: (606) 354-4423; E-mail: odellmin@aol.com;
URL: http://www.odellministries.org

Grantmaker type: Public charity.
Financial data (yr. ended 07/31/10): Revenue, $513,507; assets, $16,756 (M); gifts received, $513,415; expenditures, $543,599; giving activities include $4,000 for grants.
Purpose and activities: The organization supports Christian evangelism around the world.
Fields of interest: Christian agencies & churches.
International interests: Honduras; India; Pakistan.
Limitations: Giving primarily in Honduras, India, and Pakistan.
Officers: Jerry R. O'Dell, Pres.; Marilyn O'Dell, V.P.; Monica J. King, Secy.-Treas.
EIN: 731211471

866
Yum! Brands Foundation, Inc.
(formerly Tricon Foundation, Inc.)
P.O. Box 35910
Louisville, KY 40232-5910 (502) 874-8294
Contact: Mary Dossett, Mgr., Community Affairs
Application address: 1441 Gardiner Ln., Louisville, KY 40213-5910

Established in 1998 in KY and TX.
Donors: Tricon Global Restaurants, Inc.; Yum! Brands, Inc.
Grantmaker type: Company-sponsored foundation.
Financial data (yr. ended 12/31/10): Assets, $14,088,021 (M); gifts received, $13,000,000; expenditures, $7,268,714; qualifying distributions, $7,267,870; giving activities include $7,267,870 for 375 grants (high: $2,000,000; low: $25).
Purpose and activities: The foundation supports programs designed to promote hunger relief, youth, and the arts.
Fields of interest: Higher education; Performing arts, theater; Arts; Education; Food services; Food banks; Disasters, preparedness/services; Youth, services; Human services; United Ways and Federated Giving Programs.
Type of support: General/operating support; Continuing support; Annual campaigns; Program development; Employee volunteer services; Employee matching gifts.
Limitations: Applications accepted. Giving primarily in areas of company operations, with some emphasis on Louisville, KY; giving also to national organizations.
Application information: Application form required.
 Initial approach: Contact foundation for
   application form
 Deadline(s): None
Officers and Directors:* David C. Novak,* Chair. and C.E.O.; Jonathan Blum, Pres.; Christian L. Campbell,* V.P. and Secy.; Richard T. Carrucci,* V.P. and Treas.; Donald Phillips, V.P.; W. Lawrence Gathof, C.F.O.; Laura Melilo Barnum, Exec. Dir. and Admin.; Emil Brolick; Anne Byerlein.
EIN: 611327140
Recent grants for international programs:
866-1 Friends of the World Food Program, Washington, DC, $565,786. For unrestricted support. 2009.
866-2 Mali Rising Foundation, Sandy, UT, $10,000. For unrestricted support. 2009.

866-3 One Acre Fund, Falcon Heights, MN, $10,000. For unrestricted support. 2009.
866-4 World Hunger Year, New York, NY, $499,749. For unrestricted support. 2009.

867
Yum! Brands, Inc. Corporate Giving Program
1441 Gardiner Ln.
Louisville, KY 40213-1914 (502) 874-8300
URL: http://www.yum.com/responsibility/default.asp

Grantmaker type: Corporate giving program.
Purpose and activities: As a complement to its foundation, Yum! Brands also makes charitable contributions to nonprofit organizations involved with hunger relief. Support is given on a national and international basis.
Fields of interest: International relief; Food services.
Type of support: General/operating support; Cause-related marketing; Employee volunteer services; Public relations services; Donated products; In-kind gifts.
Limitations: Giving on a national and international basis.
Application information: International donations made via United Nations World Food Program.

LOUISIANA

868
Catholic Charities Archdiocese of New Orleans
1000 Howard Ave., Ste. 1000
New Orleans, LA 70113-1942 (504) 523-3755
FAX: (504) 523-2789;
E-mail: ccano@archdiocese-no.org; Toll-free tel.: (866) 891-2210; URL: http://www.ccano.org

Established in 1938 in LA.
Grantmaker type: Public charity.
Financial data (yr. ended 06/30/10): Revenue, $29,563,670; assets, $27,469,851 (M); gifts received, $26,349,334; expenditures, $32,994,849; giving activities include $870,727 for grants, and $4,223,204 for grants to individuals.
Purpose and activities: The organization collaborates with the wider community to serve those in need by offering life-giving programs, advocating for the voiceless, and empowering the poor and vulnerable to foster a most just society.
Fields of interest: International migration/refugee issues; Housing/shelter, homeless; Nutrition; Family services, domestic violence; Children/youth, services; Human services, emergency aid; Human services; Aging; Economically disadvantaged.
Limitations: Giving limited to New Orleans, LA.
Publications: Annual report.
Officers and Directors :* Paul L. Fine,* Chair.; James R. Kelly, Co-Pres. and C.E.O.; Gordon R. Wadge, Co-Pres. and C.E.O.; Elizabeth E. Adler; David F. Andignac; Sr. Anthony Barczykowski, D.C.; Shawn M. Barney; Dr. Willard L. Dumas, Jr.; John L. Eckholdt; Joseph S. Exnicios; Dr. Ludovico Feoli;

John J. Finan, Jr.; Michael F. Hulefeld; Rev. James J. Jeanfreau; Susan R. Johnson; and 10 additional directors.
EIN: 720408911

869
Park West Children's Fund, Inc.
(also known as Friend Ships Unlimited)
1019 N. 1st Ave.
Lake Charles, LA 70601-1705 (337) 433-5022
FAX: (337) 433-3433; E-mail: info@friendships.org;
URL: http://www.friendships.org/

Established in 1983 in CA.
Grantmaker type: Public charity.
Financial data (yr. ended 02/28/11): Revenue, $5,316,293; assets, $7,790,007 (M); gifts received, $5,312,881; expenditures, $3,060,513; giving activities include $631,895 for grants, and $1,033,726 for 1 grant to an organization outside the U.S.
Purpose and activities: The organization provides large-scale humanitarian and disaster aid and supports ongoing programs that are having an ongoing impact on their communities.
Fields of interest: International relief; Human services, emergency aid.
Type of support: In-kind gifts.
Limitations: Giving on a national and international basis.
Officers: Sandra Tipton, Pres.; Donald Tipton, Secy. and Exec. Dir.; Raymond George, Treas.
EIN: 953917951

870
Irene W. & C. B. Pennington Foundation
2237 S. Acadian Thruway, Ste. 705
Baton Rouge, LA 70808-2380 (225) 928-8346
Contact: To Discuss Current or Proposed Projects: Vonnie L. Hawkins, Prog. Off.
FAX: (225) 928-8375;
E-mail: pff@penningtonfamilyfoundation.org;
URL: http://www.penningtonfamilyfoundation.org

Established in 1982 in LA.
Donors: C.B. Pennington†; Irene W. Pennington†.
Grantmaker type: Independent foundation.
Financial data (yr. ended 12/31/09): Assets, $122,670,711 (M); gifts received, $18,768; expenditures, $10,180,915; qualifying distributions, $6,277,652; giving activities include $6,277,652 for 103 grants (high: $1,000,000; low: $1,000; average: $1,000–$400,000).
Purpose and activities: Giving primarily to provide philanthropic support to promote the overall well-being of families and communities.
Fields of interest: Secondary school/education; Medical specialties research; Youth development, centers/clubs; Human services; Youth, services.
Type of support: General/operating support; Capital campaigns; Building/renovation; Program development.
Limitations: Giving limited to communities within or near Baton Rouge, LA. No grants to individuals.
Publications: Application guidelines.
Application information: Paper proposals which have not been invited will not be accepted, considered or returned. Fax or e-mail proposals, or proposals in spiral or ring binders are not accepted. Unsolicited applications are reviewed once per year in a single step process. Proposal guidelines

available on foundation web site. Application form required.

Initial approach: Online proposal submission
Copies of proposal: 1
Deadline(s): Aug. 15
Final notification: Late Nov.

Officers and Trustees: * William E. Hodgkins,* Chair.; Lori Bertman, C.E.O. and Pres.; Richard Blackstone; Paula P. Delabretonne; Claude B. Pennington III; Daryl B. Pennington, Sr.; Daryl B. Pennington, Jr.; Sharon Palmer Pennington.
Number of staff: 2
EIN: 720938097
Recent grants for international programs:
870-1 Ducks Unlimited, Memphis, TN, $350,000. For general support. 2009.
870-2 Ducks Unlimited, Memphis, TN, $100,000. For general support. 2009.
870-3 Elton John AIDS Foundation, New York, NY, $293,050. For general support. 2009.

871
William B. Wiener, Jr. Foundation
333 Texas St., Ste. 2290
Shreveport, LA   71101-3681

Established in LA.
Donor: William B. Wiener, Jr.
Grantmaker type: Independent foundation.
Financial data (yr. ended 02/28/10): Assets, $19,190,663 (M); expenditures, $1,218,933; qualifying distributions, $825,000; giving activities include $825,000 for grants.
Fields of interest: Environment, reform; Environment, government agencies; Animals/ wildlife; Health organizations; Human services.
International interests: Israel.
Limitations: Applications not accepted. Giving primarily in LA. No grants to individuals.
Application information: Contributes only to pre-selected organizations.
Officers: William B. Wiener, Jr., Pres.; Donald B. Wiener, V.P.; Donald P. Weiss, Secy.
Directors: David Rockefeller, Jr.; Ted Smith.
EIN: 726024398

872
The Woldenberg Foundation
(formerly Dorothy & Malcolm Woldenberg Foundation)
809 Jefferson Hwy.
Jefferson, LA   70121-2522   (504) 849-6078
Contact: Trudi Briede, Dir.
FAX: (504) 849-6515;
E-mail: trudi.briede@RNDC-USA.com; Mailing address: P.O. Box 53333, New Orleans, LA 70153

Incorporated in 1959 in LA as Woldenberg Charitable and Educational Foundation.
Donors: Malcolm Woldenberg‡; Magnolia Liquor Co., Inc.; Sazerac Co., Inc.; Great Southern Liquor Co., Inc.; Duval Spirits, Inc.
Grantmaker type: Independent foundation.
Financial data (yr. ended 12/31/10): Assets, $33,291,635 (M); gifts received, $24,500; expenditures, $2,801,118; qualifying distributions, $2,473,219; giving activities include $2,473,219 for grants.
Purpose and activities: Giving primarily for arts, education, and to Jewish organizations.

Fields of interest: Jewish federated giving programs; Higher education; Museums; Arts; Human services.
International interests: Israel.
Type of support: General/operating support; Continuing support; Capital campaigns; Building/ renovation; Equipment; Emergency funds; Program development; Research.
Limitations: Applications not accepted. Giving primarily in the greater New Orleans, LA, area, with special interest in Miami, FL, the southeastern U.S., and Israel. No support for political organizations. No grants to individuals (except for employee-related scholarships).
Application information: The foundation is not taking on new grantees. Unsolicited requests for funds not accepted.
Board meeting date(s): Varies
Officer and Trustees: * William Goldring,* Pres.; Minette Brown,* V.P.; Mark Halpern,* V.P.; Robert Steeg,* Secy.; Jeffrey Goldring.
Number of staff: 1 part-time professional.
EIN: 726022665
Recent grants for international programs:
872-1 American Friends of Alyn Hospital, New York, NY, $125,000. 2009.
872-2 American Friends of Alyn Hospital, New York, NY, $100,000. 2009.
872-3 American Israel Education Foundation, Washington, DC, $25,000. 2009.
872-4 Israel Education Fund, New York, NY, $300,000. 2009.

873
Zemurray Foundation
228 St. Charles Ave., Ste. 1024
New Orleans, LA   70130-2651
Contact: Kimberley M. Quintana, Treas.

Incorporated in 1951 in LA.
Donor: Sarah W. Zemurray.
Grantmaker type: Independent foundation.
Financial data (yr. ended 12/31/10): Assets, $95,165,250 (M); expenditures, $4,934,749; qualifying distributions, $4,486,543; giving activities include $4,277,307 for 42 grants (high: $1,315,707; low: $500).
Purpose and activities: Grants primarily for education, particularly higher education, cultural programs, civic affairs, hospitals, and medical research.
Fields of interest: Arts; Higher education; Education; Hospitals (general); Medical research, institute; Government/public administration.
Limitations: Applications not accepted. Giving primarily in New Orleans, LA, and Cambridge, MA. No grants to individuals.
Application information: Contributes only to pre-selected organizations.
Board meeting date(s): Usually in Nov.
Officers and Trustees: * Ludovico Feoli,* Co-Chair.; Alison Stone,* Co-Chair.; Stephanie Stone Feoli,* V.P.; Haydee T. Stone,* V.P.; Thomas B. Lemann,* Secy.; Kimberley M. Quintana, Treas.
Number of staff: 1 full-time professional; 2 part-time support.
EIN: 720539603
Recent grants for international programs:
873-1 Alliance Francaise de la Nouvelle Orleans, New Orleans, LA, $10,000. 2009.
873-2 Centro de Investigacion y Adiestramiento Politico Administrativo, Curridabat, Costa Rica, $550,000. 2009.

873-3 Copan Maya Foundation, Pasadena, CA, $20,000. 2009.
873-4 Escuela Agricola Panamericana, Tegucigalpa, Honduras, $300,000. 2009.
873-5 Salvadoran American Humanitarian Foundation, Miami, FL, $175,000. 2009.
873-6 Trinity Episcopal Church, New Orleans, LA, $30,000. For Trinity Medical Mission to remote regions of Nicaragua. 2009.

MAINE

874
Cambodian Arts & Scholarship Foundation
P.O. Box 18186
Portland, ME   04112-8186   (207) 549-7380
E-mail: fredericklipp@roadrunner.com; URL: http:// www.cambodianscholarship.org

Grantmaker type: Public charity.
Financial data (yr. ended 12/31/10): Revenue, $195,024; assets, $442,041 (M); gifts received, $194,423; expenditures, $144,470; program services expenses, $134,572; giving activities include $70,697 for grants.
Purpose and activities: The foundation is committed to improving the lives of children in Cambodia through education, especially poor, at-risk girls who, for a number of reasons, are often denied equal access to schooling.
Fields of interest: International development; International affairs; Education; Children; Girls; Economically disadvantaged.
International interests: Cambodia.
Officers and Directors: * Rev. Frederick Lipp,* Pres.; Hope Hall, Secy.; Tania Hathaway; Shawna Ohm; Jonah Rosenfield; Sam Van Dam.
EIN: 010544749

875
Catalyst for Peace
(formerly The Catalyst Fund)
565 Congress St., Ste. 305
Portland, ME   04101-3308   (207) 775-2616
E-mail: info@catalystforpeace.org; URL: http:// www.catalystforpeace.org/

Established in ME.
Donors: Elisabeth Hoffman; Alan Lukas.
Grantmaker type: Independent foundation.
Financial data (yr. ended 12/31/10): Assets, $13,423,236 (M); gifts received, $47,600; expenditures, $1,295,637; qualifying distributions, $716,285; giving activities include $716,285 for grants.
Purpose and activities: The foundation identifies and supports community based peacebuilding work around the world.
Fields of interest: Higher education; International peace/security; International human rights; Religion, interfaith issues.
International interests: Africa.
Limitations: Applications not accepted. Giving primarily in ME and VA; some funding also in Sierra Leone.

Application information: Unsolicited requests for funds not accepted.
Officers: Elisabeth Hoffman, Pres.; Seth Johnson, Secy.-Treas.
Directors: Alfred Hoffman, Jr.; Cynthia Sampson.
EIN: 352202654
Recent grants for international programs:
875-1 Fambul Tok International, Freetown, Sierra Leone, $548,808. For community reconnection. 2009.
875-2 Forum of Conscience, Freetown, Sierra Leone, $406,230. For community reconnection. 2009.

876
The Dugas Family Foundation
23 Coralburst Ln.
Scarborough, ME   04074-7152
Application Address: c/o Normand Dugas, 12 Sunny Bank Rd., Cape Elizabeth, ME 04107

Established in 1997 in ME.
Donors: Normand Dugas; Agnes Dugas.
Grantmaker type: Independent foundation.
Financial data (yr. ended 05/31/10): Assets, $373,318 (M); gifts received, $8,400; expenditures, $261,678; qualifying distributions, $257,800; giving activities include $257,675 for 11 grants (high: $80,000; low: $2,000).
Purpose and activities: Giving for housing and food services for the poor.
Fields of interest: Health care; Food services; Housing/shelter; Catholic agencies & churches; Economically disadvantaged.
International interests: South America; Africa; Haiti.
Type of support: Continuing support; Seed money.
Limitations: Applications accepted. Giving primarily in ME and NH. No support for arts organizations, or for political groups.
Application information: Application form not required.
   Initial approach: Letter
   Copies of proposal: 2
   Deadline(s): None
   Board meeting date(s): Aug.
   Final notification: Between one and two months
Officers: Normand Dugas, Pres.; Dennis Molleur, V.P.; Agnes Dugas, Treas.
Directors: Felice Colliton; Marc Dugas; Peter Dugas; Michelle McGarrity; Danielle Molleur.
Number of staff: None.
EIN: 010519633

877
The Golden Rule Foundation, Inc.
P.O. Box 658
Camden, ME   04843-0658   (207) 338-1866
E-mail: goldenrule@prexar.com; URL: http://www.goldrule.org

Established in 1981 in DC.
Donor: Jack Evans†.
Grantmaker type: Independent foundation.
Financial data (yr. ended 10/31/10): Assets, $4,110,319 (M); expenditures, $365,613; qualifying distributions, $323,905; giving activities include $280,200 for 47 grants (high: $20,000; low: $500).
Purpose and activities: Giving primarily for the arts, environmental programs, and social services.

Fields of interest: Children, services; Arts; Community/economic development; Education; Environment, alliance/advocacy; Environment, natural resources; Environment, toxics; Human services.
International interests: Mexico.
Type of support: General/operating support; Program development; Seed money.
Limitations: Applications not accepted. Giving primarily in ME. No grants to individuals.
Publications: Informational brochure.
Application information: Unsolicited requests for funds not considered.
   Board meeting date(s): Late Aug.
Officers: Jean Evans, Pres.; Tegan Stephens, Secy.; Salvadore Messina, Treas.
Directors: Gareth Evans; Trevor Evans.
Advisory Board: Sian Evans.
Number of staff: 1 part-time support.
EIN: 599207701

878
The Oak Foundation U.S.A.
511 Congress St., Ste. 800
Portland, ME   04101-3478
E-mail: naep@oakfnd.org; Additional e-mail (Geneva office): info@oakfnd.ch.; URL: http://www.oakfnd.org
Grantee Perception Report: http://www.oakfnd.org/sites/default/files/Oak%20Foundation%20Grantee%20Perception%20Report%202011.pdf
Grants List: http://www.oakfnd.org/about.php

Established in 1986 in DE.
Donors: The Oak Trust; The Forest Trust.
Grantmaker type: Independent foundation.
Financial data (yr. ended 12/31/09): Assets, $195,366,300 (M); gifts received, $840,000; expenditures, $31,653,362; qualifying distributions, $31,059,121; giving activities include $30,212,880 for 191 grants (high: $1,960,149; low: $5,000).
Purpose and activities: The foundation's giving priorities include child abuse, the environment, especially climate change and marine conservation, human rights, issues affecting women, housing and homelessness, learning differences and special interest grants.
Fields of interest: Crime/violence prevention, sexual abuse; Crime/violence prevention, abuse prevention; Crime/violence prevention, domestic violence; Environment, climate change/global warming; Environment, natural resources; Environment, water resources; Environment; Learning disorders; Crime/violence prevention, child abuse; Housing/shelter, homeless; International human rights; Women.
International interests: Africa; Asia; Bulgaria; Burma (Myanmar); East Africa/Horn of Africa; Ethiopia; Europe; India; Latin America; Latvia; Moldova; Russia; South America; Switzerland; Tanzania, Zanzibar and Pemba; Uganda.
Type of support: General/operating support; Continuing support; Management development/capacity building; Building/renovation; Equipment; Program development; Research; Technical assistance; Program evaluation; Matching/challenge support.
Limitations: Applications accepted. Giving on a national basis. No support for religious organizations for religious purposes or for political candidates. No grants to fundraising drives, events

or amounts under $25,000 (except in special circumstances).
Publications: Application guidelines; Annual report (including application guidelines); Grants list; Program policy statement.
Application information: The foundation will respond within two months to inquiries, informing the applicant whether there is sufficient interest to pursue a proposal. If interested, the foundation will request additional information from the organization. Generally grants will not be given for under $25,000. Please see foundation web site for additional information. Application form not required.
   Initial approach: Inquiry via e-mail to the appropriate program or letter addressed to the appropriate office; for initial contact, please do not telephone or visit the offices. See foundation web page for contact information for international offices
   Copies of proposal: 1
   Deadline(s): None
   Final notification: Within two months
Officers and Trustees: * Kristian Parker,* Chair.; Natalie Shipton,* Vice-Chair.; Caroline Turner,* Vice-Chair.; Kathleen Cravero-Kristoffersson, Pres.; Gary Goodman, Secy.; Alan M. Parker; Jette Parker.
Advisory Board Members: William Norris; Julie Sandorf.
Number of staff: 3 full-time professional.
EIN: 133321196

879
The Picker Institute
P.O. Box 777
Camden, ME   04843-0777   (888) 680-7500
FAX: (207) 236-0357;
E-mail: info@pickerinstitute.org; Application e-mail: lhanscom@pickerinstitute.org; contact for application information: Lucile O. Hanscom, tel.: (207) 236-0157; URL: http://pickerinstitute.org
Facebook: http://www.facebook.com/pages/The-Picker-Institute/108428439197671
LinkedIn: http://www.linkedin.com/company/974262
Twitter: http://twitter.com/#!/PickerIns
YouTube: http://www.youtube.com/user/PickerInstitute

Donors: Harvey Picker; Mark Waxman; Samuel Fleming; Steve Schoenbaum; Branta Foundation; The Commonwealth Fund.
Grantmaker type: Independent foundation.
Financial data (yr. ended 12/31/10): Assets, $2,863,292 (M); gifts received, $1,720,000; expenditures, $2,210,141; qualifying distributions, $2,138,330; giving activities include $1,062,539 for 27 grants (high: $461,921; low: $2,200).
Purpose and activities: The institute sponsors education and research in the field of patient-centered care in cooperation with educational institutions and other interested entities and individuals. The institute's goal is to foster a broader understanding of the practical and theoretical implications of patient-centered care by approaching healthcare with a focus on the concerns of patients and other healthcare consumers.
Fields of interest: Medical school/education; Higher education.
Limitations: Giving in the U.S., with some emphasis on CT.
Publications: Annual report.

Application information: Application information available on the institute's web site.

Initial approach: Letter of Inquiry (1-2 pages), submitted via e-mail (text or electronic attachment)

Officers: Mark Waxman, Chair.; Steve Shoenbaum, Vice-Chair.; Samuel Fleming, Secy.-Treas.; Lucile O. Hanscom, Exec. Dir.

Directors: Donald Irvine; David Leach, M.D.; Gail Warden.

EIN: 043238368

Recent grants for international programs:

879-1 Picker Institute Europe, Oxford, England, $461,921. 2010.

880
The Sandy River Charitable Foundation

349 Voter Hill Rd.
Farmington, ME 04938-6030 (207) 779-1682
FAX: (207) 779-1901;
E-mail: info@srcfoundation.org; URL: http://www.srcfoundation.org

Established in 1997 in ME.
Donor: Berry Charitable Trust.
Grantmaker type: Independent foundation.
Financial data (yr. ended 05/31/10): Assets, $32,613,639 (M); expenditures, $761,940; qualifying distributions, $532,405; giving activities include $532,405 for grants.
Purpose and activities: Giving primarily to disaster rehabilitation and hunger relief services; funding also for a community foundation in Ellsworth, Maine, and a mountain alliance in Farmington, Maine. Funding is also made for international and rural development, micro financing, and adoption services.
Fields of interest: Environment; Food services; Disasters, preparedness/services; Children, adoption; Family services; International agricultural development; Rural development; Foundations (community).
Type of support: General/operating support; Continuing support; Income development; Management development/capacity building; Building/renovation; Equipment; Program evaluation; Program-related investments/loans; Matching/challenge support.
Limitations: Applications not accepted. Giving on an international and national basis, (particularly Board/staff areas), with a special emphasis on ME. No grants to individuals.
Application information: Unsolicited proposals not accepted.
Board meeting date(s): June and Dec.
Officers: Archie W. Berry, Jr., Pres.; Nathanael W. Berry, V.P. and Secy.; Jon W. Berry, Treas.
Directors: Marla S. Berry; Nan Berry; Suphaporn V. Berry; Lillian Dox.
Number of staff: 1 full-time professional.
EIN: 522029911

881
Otto and Fran Walter Foundation, Inc.

(formerly Walter & Lorenz Foundation, Inc.)
c/o The Brick House
7 Oak St.
Boothbay Harbor, ME 04538-1972
(207) 633-7300
Contact: Martha H. Peak, V.P. and Grants Dir.

E-mail: grants@walterfoundation.org; URL: http://www.walterfoundation.org/

Established in 1952 in NY.
Donors: Anton Lorenz†; Otto L. Walter†; Fran D. Walter†.
Grantmaker type: Independent foundation.
Financial data (yr. ended 12/31/10): Assets, $12,953,803 (M); expenditures, $1,085,588; qualifying distributions, $838,380; giving activities include $714,880 for 12 grants (high: $312,500; low: $3,380), and $1,600 for foundation-administered programs.
Purpose and activities: Primary areas of interest include education, the arts, the disadvantaged, Holocaust survivorship and international amity.
Fields of interest: Arts; Education; Human services; International affairs, goodwill promotion; Aging; Economically disadvantaged.
Type of support: Seed money; Matching/challenge support.
Limitations: Applications not accepted. Giving on a national and international basis. No support for purely religious or ethnic programs, or for programs with political agendas or programs that discriminate; no support for projects with only local impact. No grants or scholarships to individuals, or for annual or capital campaigns.
Application information: Unsolicited requests for funds not accepted.
Board meeting date(s): As necessary
Officers and Directors:* Frank G. Helman,* Pres.; Martha H. Peak,* V.P.; Carl R. Griffin III,* Secy.; Fritz Weinschenk,* Treas.
Number of staff: 3 part-time professional; 1 part-time support.
EIN: 131625529

MARYLAND

882
ABMRF/The Foundation for Alcohol Research

(formerly Alcoholic Beverage Medical Research Foundation)
1122 Kenilworth Dr., Ste. 407
Baltimore, MD 21204-2147 (410) 821-7066
Contact: Mack C. Mitchell, Jr. M.D., Pres.
FAX: (410) 821-7065; E-mail: info@abmrf.org; Grant Program e-mail: grantinfo@abmrf.org; URL: http://www.abmrf.org/
Facebook: http://www.facebook.com/AlcoholResearch?ref=ts
LinkedIn: http://www.linkedin.com/company/1137768?trk=NUS_CMPE-updater
Twitter: http://twitter.com/AlcoholResearch

Established in 1982 in MD.
Donors: Beer Institute; Brewers Association of Canada; National Beer Wholesalers Association.
Grantmaker type: Independent foundation.
Financial data (yr. ended 12/31/10): Assets, $3,986,753 (M); gifts received, $2,335,882; expenditures, $2,367,642; qualifying distributions, $2,350,464; giving activities include $1,480,631 for 36 grants (high: $50,974; low: $12,500), and $2,367,642 for foundation-administered programs.

Purpose and activities: The mission of the foundation is to achieve a better understanding of the effects of alcohol on the health and behavior of individuals; to provide the scientific basis for prevention and treatment of alcohol misuse and alcoholism; to fund innovative, high-quality research; to support promising new investigations; to communicate effectively with the research community and with other interested parties.
Fields of interest: Medical research; Alcoholism.
International interests: Canada.
Type of support: Research.
Limitations: Applications accepted. Giving primarily in the U.S. and Canada. No grants to individuals, or for education projects, public awareness efforts, treatment or referral services, training of pre- and post-doctoral fellows, undergraduates, graduate students, medical students, interns or residents, or for thesis or dissertation research.
Publications: Annual report; Financial statement; Grants list; Informational brochure.
Application information: See foundation web site for application form and guidelines. Application form required.
Initial approach: Use grant application available on foundation web site
Copies of proposal: 1
Deadline(s): Applications must be postmarked by Feb. 1 or Sept. 1
Board meeting date(s): Apr. and Nov.
Final notification: Within 2 weeks of board meeting
Officers and Trustees:* Bruce Ambler,* M.B.A., Chair.; Raymond Anton, Jr.,* M.D., Vice-Chair.; Mack C. Mitchell, Jr.,* M.D., Pres.; John Hanratty, Cont.; David A. Brenner, M.D.; Thomas A. Collier,* M.D.; Ivan Diamond, M.D., Ph.D.; R. Stuart Dickson; Ian Faris; Steven Hindy; Arthur L. Klatsky; Louis G. Lange, M.D., Ph.D.; Steven W. Leslie, Ph.D.; Ting-Kai Li, M.D.; James G. Martin, Ph.D.; Kim M. Marotta, J.D.; Joseph S. McClain; Craig Purser; John Sleeman; James Villenueve.
Number of staff: 1 full-time professional; 2 part-time professional; 1 part-time support.
EIN: 521234277

883
Adventist Development and Relief Agency International

(also known as A.D.R.A.)
12501 Old Columbia Pike
Silver Spring, MD 20904-6601
Toll-free tel.: (800) 424-2372; URL: http://www.adra.org
Facebook: http://www.facebook.com/joinADRA
Twitter: http://twitter.com/#!/ADRAi

Established in 1956 in DC.
Grantmaker type: Public charity.
Financial data (yr. ended 12/31/10): Revenue, $74,728,346; assets, $41,150,314 (M); gifts received, $72,564,798; expenditures, $69,551,674; program services expenses, $62,814,803; giving activities include $38,009,506 for 81 grants to organizations outside the U.S., and $7,416,306 for foundation-administered programs.
Purpose and activities: The organization works with people in poverty and distress to create positive change and justness through empowering partnerships and responsible action.

Fields of interest: Human services; International development; International relief; Economically disadvantaged.
International interests: Developing countries.
Type of support: In-kind gifts.
Limitations: Giving on a national and international basis, with emphasis on developing countries.
Publications: Annual report; Informational brochure.
Officers and Directors:* Geoffrey Mbwana,* Chair.; Ella Simmons,* Vice-Chair.; Dr. Rudi Maier,* Pres. and Secy.; Ken Flemmer, V.P., Progs.; Robyn Mordeno, V.P., Finance; Mario H. Ochoa, V.P., Network Rels.; Robert Lemon, Treas.; Audrey Andersson; Aho Baliki; Seth Bardu; Renee Battle-Brooks; Guillermo Biaggi; Gilbert Burnham; Zenaida Delica-Willison; Ann Gibson; Sylvana Gittens; A.C. Gulfan; and 23 additional directors.
EIN: 521314847

884
AICE, Inc.
(also known as American-Israeli Cooperative Enterprise)
2810 Blaine Dr.
Chevy Chase, MD 20815-3040 (301) 565-3918
E-mail: aiceresearch@gmail.com; URL: http://www.jewishvirtuallibrary.org/about/index.shtml

Established in 1993.
Grantmaker type: Public charity.
Financial data (yr. ended 12/31/10): Revenue, $1,885,339; assets, $563,051 (M); gifts received, $1,872,754; expenditures, $2,223,888; giving activities include $1,203,000 for grants, and $180,000 for grants to individuals.
Purpose and activities: The organization works to strengthen the U.S.-Israeli relationship by emphasizing the values shared by the two nations.
Fields of interest: International affairs, goodwill promotion; International exchange; International affairs.
International interests: Israel.
Limitations: Applications not accepted. Giving on a national basis.
Application information: Contributes only to pre-selected organizations; unsolicited requests for funds not considered or acknowledged.
Officers: Howard Rosenbloom, Pres. and Treas.; Dr. Arthur Bard, V.P. and Secy.; Mitchell G. Bard, Exec. Dir.
EIN: 521865861

885
American Urological Association Foundation
(formerly American Foundation for Urologic Disease, Inc., also known as AUA Foundation)
1000 Corporate Blvd.
Linthicum, MD 21090-2260 (410) 689-3700
FAX: (410) 689-3800;
E-mail: auafoundation@auafoundation.org; Toll-free tel. (U.S. only): (800) 828-7866; URL: http://www.auafoundation.org
Application information: Rodney Cotten, Research Mgr., tel.: (410) 689-3750, fax: (410) 689-3998, e-mail: grants@auafoundation.org

Founded in 1987 as the American Foundation for Urologic Disease, Inc.; current name adopted in 2005.
Grantmaker type: Public charity.

Financial data (yr. ended 12/31/10): Revenue, $6,869,248; assets, $17,701,115 (M); gifts received, $6,281,226; expenditures, $3,178,091; giving activities include $853,559 for grants, $27,500 for grants to organizations outside the U.S., and $10,250 for grants to individuals.
Purpose and activities: The foundation seeks to prevent and cure urologic disease through the expansion of research, education and public awareness.
Fields of interest: Medical research; Prostate cancer research; Kidney research.
International interests: Canada.
Type of support: Fellowships; Research; Scholarships—to individuals.
Limitations: Applications accepted. Giving in the U.S. and Canada.
Publications: Application guidelines; Newsletter.
Application information: See web site for additional application information. Application form required.
Initial approach: Submit application packet
Deadline(s): Mar. 13 for Bridge Awards; Aug. 10 for Research Scholars Program; Nov. 29 for AUA Foundation/NIDDK/NCI Surgeon-Scientist Award
Officers and Directors:* Datta Wagle,* M.D., Pres.; Sushil S. Lacy,* M.D., Pres.-Elect; Robert C. Flanigan,* M.D., Secy.; Richard A. Memo, M.D., Treas.; Sandra Vassos,* Exec. Dir.; B. Thomas Brown, M.D.; Anton J. Bueschen, M.D.; David F. Green, M.D., F.A.C.S.; John H. Lynch, M.D.; Dennia A. Pessis, M.D., F.A.C.S.; Kevin Pranikoff, M.D.; John C. Prince, M.D.; Pramond C. Sogani, M.D.; J. Brantley Thrasher, M.D.
EIN: 203210212

886
The Kathryn Ames Foundation, Inc.
305 W. Chesapeake Ave., Ste. 308
Towson, MD 21204-4440 (410) 821-3006
Contact: Lu Pierson, Grants Admin.
FAX: (410) 821-3007;
E-mail: info@kathrynames.org; URL: http://www.kathrynames.org/

Established in 1993 in MD.
Donor: Kathryn Ames†.
Grantmaker type: Independent foundation.
Financial data (yr. ended 12/31/10): Assets, $7,627,016 (M); gifts received, $348,714; expenditures, $436,574; qualifying distributions, $335,000; giving activities include $335,000 for grants.
Purpose and activities: Giving primarily to organizations benefiting Israel in social and economic welfare, religious and ethnic pluralism, social justice, and education.
Fields of interest: Religion, interfaith issues; Education; Economic development; Religion.
International interests: Israel.
Type of support: General/operating support; Building/renovation; Equipment; Program development.
Limitations: Applications accepted. Giving primarily in Washington, DC, and New York, NY. No grants to individuals.
Application information: See grantmaker web site for complete application guidelines. Application form required.
Initial approach: Letter of Inquiry (not exceeding 2 pages) by email or mail.
Copies of proposal: 3

Deadline(s): None for Letters of Inquiry.
Board meeting date(s): Quarterly
Officers: W. Michel Pierson, Pres.; Esther E. Saltzman, V.P.; Robert L. Pierson, Secy.-Treas.
EIN: 521828472

887
Asian Relief, Inc.
6411 Ivy Ln., Ste. 204
Greenbelt, MD 20770-1405 (301) 779-4141
FAX: (301) 779-4144;
E-mail: info@worldvillages.org; URL: http://www.worldvillages.org/

Established in 1964.
Grantmaker type: Public charity.
Financial data (yr. ended 12/31/10): Revenue, $9,570,578; assets, $36,096,401 (M); gifts received, $8,336,684; expenditures, $9,796,335; giving activities include $3,422,704 for grants to organizations outside the U.S.
Purpose and activities: The organization works to help poor children around the world break free from a life of poverty, suffering, and despair.
Fields of interest: International relief; Children/youth, services; Children/youth.
Limitations: Giving limited to Brazil, Guatemala, Korea, Mexico, and Philippines.
Officers and Directors:* Sr. Michaela Kim,* Pres.; Joseph F. Vita, V.P.; Dolores Vita, Secy.; Cameron Menzies, C.F.O.; Sr. Elena Belarmino,* Treas.; Sr. Teresita Sumalabe.
EIN: 521440944

888
Association for India's Development, Inc.
5011 Tecumseh St.
College Park, MD 20740-4125
Toll-free tel.: (888) TALK-2-AID; URL: http://aidindia.org

Grantmaker type: Public charity.
Financial data (yr. ended 12/31/09): Revenue, $1,082,470; assets, $3,614,168 (M); gifts received, $958,626; expenditures, $1,028,698; giving activities include $14,215 for grants, $844,944 for grants to organizations outside the U.S., and $18,156 for grants to individuals outside the U.S.
Purpose and activities: The association promotes the sustainable, equitable and just development of India.
Fields of interest: International development.
International interests: India.
Limitations: Giving primarily in India.
Publications: Annual report.
Directors: Satindar Mohan Bhagat; Shrinath Chidambaram; Priya Ranjan; Aniruddha Vaidya; Kirankumar Vissa.
EIN: 043652609

889
Association for International Practical Training, Inc.
10400 Little Patuxent Pkwy., Ste. 250
Columbia, MD 21044-3519 (410) 997-2200
FAX: (410) 993-3924; E-mail: aipt@aipt.org;
URL: http://www.aipt.org

Established in 1948 in MA as the U.S. chapter of the International Association for the Exchange of Students for Technical Experience; incorporated as a separate nonprofit in 1980.

Grantmaker type: Public charity.

Financial data (yr. ended 12/31/09): Revenue, $4,552,298; assets, $4,736,458 (M); gifts received, $12,730; expenditures, $5,606,267; giving activities include $6,250 for grants to individuals.

Purpose and activities: The association works to create the ultimate global training and cultural exchange experience through providing high-quality educational and professional exchange experiences that enhance cultural awareness, develop global competencies, and foster mutual understanding and international cooperation; the association is also a designated J-1 visa sponsor for foreign nationals to gain invaluable career internships and on-the-job training experience.

Fields of interest: International exchange; International conflict resolution; International affairs.

Limitations: Applications accepted. Giving on a national and international basis, with an emphasis on Argentina, Brazil, China, Croatia, and Turkey.

Publications: Application guidelines; Annual report; Newsletter.

Application information: Application form required.
Initial approach: Download application form

Officers and Directors:* Dr. Cheryl A. Matherly,* Chair.; Howard A. Rollins, Jr.,* Chair.-Elect.; Karen Krug,* C.E.O.; Connie Saienga,* Secy.-Treas.; Alpha Conteh; Amb. James Creagan; Sarah E. Cuthill; Amb. David J. Dunford; Robert Gordon; Andrew B. Greenfield; Michael J. Haines; Norman Howard; Noel Kreicker; Aslam Masood; Phyllis Mitchell; Jim Pilarski; Margaret "Peggy" D. Pusch.

EIN: 136199596

890
Herbert Bearman Foundation

101 W. Mount Royal Ave.
Baltimore, MD   21201-5708
Contact: Mark Bearman, C.O.O.
E-mail: mbearman@comcast.net

Established in 2003 in MD.

Grantmaker type: Independent foundation.

Financial data (yr. ended 12/31/10): Assets, $34,809,739 (M); expenditures, $1,743,801; qualifying distributions, $1,349,078; giving activities include $1,349,078 for grants.

Purpose and activities: Giving to improve the quality of life of members of the Baltimore, south Florida, and Israeli communities.

Fields of interest: Higher education; Education; Health care; Mental health, grief/bereavement counseling; Cystic fibrosis; Breast cancer; Autism; Human services; Jewish federated giving programs; Jewish agencies & synagogues; Substance abusers; Physically disabled; Homeless; Economically disadvantaged; Blind/visually impaired; Aging; Disabilities, people with.

International interests: Israel.

Type of support: Research; Management development/capacity building; Annual campaigns; Equipment; Emergency funds; Program development; Conferences/seminars; Seed money; Technical assistance; Program evaluation; Matching/challenge support.

Limitations: Applications accepted. Giving primarily in south FL, Baltimore, MD, and in Israel. No grants

to individuals or for scholarships or capital campaigns.

Application information: Association of Baltimore Area Grantmakers Common Grant Application Format accepted. Application form required.
Initial approach: Letter of inquiry
Copies of proposal: 12
Deadline(s): For letter of inquiry, June 15 and Dec. 15; for full proposal, Feb. 15 and Aug. 15
Board meeting date(s): Apr. and Oct.
Final notification: For letter of inquiry, 2-4 weeks; for full proposal, 1-2 weeks after Apr. and Oct. meetings.

Officers: Sheldon Bearman, Pres. and Treas.; Arlene Bearman, V.P. and Secy.; Mark Bearman, C.O.O.

Number of staff: 1 full-time professional.

EIN: 311602562

891
The Jacob and Hilda Blaustein Foundation, Inc.

10 E. Baltimore St., Ste. 1111
Baltimore, MD   21202-1630   (410) 347-7201
Contact: Betsy F. Ringle, Exec. Dir.
FAX: (410) 347-7210; *E-mail:* info@blaufund.org;
URL: http://www.blaufund.org/foundations/jacobandhilda_f.html

Incorporated in 1957 in MD.

Donors: Jacob Blaustein‡; American Trading and Production Corp.; Barbara B. Hirschhorn; Elizabeth B. Roswell.

Grantmaker type: Independent foundation.

Financial data (yr. ended 12/31/09): Assets, $106,645,728 (M); gifts received, $1,615,601; expenditures, $7,200,891; qualifying distributions, $6,815,741; giving activities include $6,252,500 for 168 grants (high: $1,150,000; low: $50).

Purpose and activities: The foundation promotes social justice and human rights through its five program areas: Jewish life, strengthening Israeli democracy, health and mental health, educational opportunity, and human rights. The foundation supports organizations that promote systematic change; involve constituents in planning and decision making; encourage volunteer and professional development; and engage in ongoing program evaluation.

Fields of interest: Arts education; Arts; Education, reform; Education, public education; Health care; Mental health, treatment; International human rights; Jewish federated giving programs; Jewish agencies & synagogues.

International interests: Israel.

Type of support: General/operating support; Capital campaigns; Building/renovation; Endowments; Program development; Technical assistance; Program evaluation; Program-related investments/loans; Employee matching gifts; Matching/challenge support.

Limitations: Applications accepted. Giving primarily in MD (no local projects outside Baltimore, MD); giving also in Israel. No support for unaffiliated schools or synagogues. No grants to individuals, or for fundraising events, or direct mail solicitations; no loans (except for program-related investments).

Publications: Application guidelines; Grants list.

Application information: The foundation accepts applications that conform to the Association of Baltimore Area Grantmakers Common Grant Application. Application form not required.
Initial approach: Letter

Copies of proposal: 1
Deadline(s): None
Board meeting date(s): Quarterly
Final notification: 4 to 6 months

Officers and Trustees:* Michael J. Hirschhorn,* Pres.; Barbara B. Hirschhorn,* V.P.; Arthur E. Roswell,* V.P.; Elizabeth B. Roswell,* V.P.; Jill R. Robinson, Secy.; Anne Patterson, Treas.; Betsy F. Ringel, Exec. Dir.

Number of staff: 1 part-time professional.

EIN: 526038382

Recent grants for international programs:

891-1 ActionAid USA, Washington, DC, $25,000. For the Right to Education project. 2010.

891-2 ADVA Center, Tel Aviv, Israel, $40,000. For renewed support for programs that analyze government policies and budgets. 2010.

891-3 Agenda-The Israeli Center for Strategic Communication, Tel Aviv, Israel, $50,000. For renewed support to influence Israeli media portrayals of social justice and civil rights issues. 2010.

891-4 AHD: The Association of the Academic Arabs in the Negev, Hura, Israel, $25,000. For the AHD Bedouin High School for Science in Beer-Sheva. 2010.

891-5 AIDS-Free World, New York, NY, $50,000. For general support to integrate human rights perspectives into HIV-AIDS advocacy. 2010.

891-6 Alnuhud: Association to Promote Education for Bedouin Women in the Negev, Beer Sheva, Israel, $25,000. For renewed support for the Mentorship-Community Awareness Project, which provides scholarships to Bedouin women for higher education. 2010.

891-7 American Associates, Ben-Gurion University of the Negev, New York, NY, $25,000. For renewed scholarship support for graduate students from Arab countries at the Blaustein Institutes for Desert Research. 2010.

891-8 American Associates, Ben-Gurion University of the Negev, New York, NY, $25,000. For the BIDR Director. 2010.

891-9 American Friends of the Tel Aviv University, New York, NY, $50,000. For renewed support for the Rights in Education Project. 2010.

891-10 American Jewish Joint Distribution Committee, New York, NY, $50,000. For renewed support for the Inter-Agency Task Force on Israeli-Arab Issues. 2010.

891-11 American Jewish World Service, New York, NY, $200,000. For service learning programs. 2010.

891-12 American Society of the University of Haifa, New York, NY, $25,000. For renewed support for activities to assist Arab master degree candidates in clinical and educational psychology at Haifa University in Israel to complete their degree. 2010.

891-13 Association for Civil Rights in Israel, Tel Aviv, Israel, $15,000. For renewed support of its activities in the Negev. 2010.

891-14 Bimkom - Planners for Planning Rights, Jerusalem, Israel, $150,000. For renewed support for activities in the Negev. 2010.

891-15 Bizchut, The Israel Human Rights Center for People with Disabilities, Jerusalem, Israel, $50,000. For advocacy efforts on behalf of people with mental disabilities. 2010.

891-16 Breakthrough, New York, NY, $50,000. For renewed support for its work to promote women's human rights. 2010.

891-17 Center for Economic and Social Rights, Brooklyn, NY, $20,000. For renewed general support. 2010.

891-18 Center for Health and Gender Equity, Washington, DC, $25,000. For renewed support for activities to promote reproductive health and rights within U.S. international policy. 2010.

891-19 Center for Reproductive Rights, New York, NY, $60,000. For renewed support for the International Legal Program. 2010.

891-20 Center for Womens Justice, Jerusalem, Israel, $20,000. For renewed support for legal aid and advocacy on behalf of women using Israel's rabbinical court system. 2010.

891-21 Community Advocacy, Israel, $25,000. For renewed support for advocacy programs for disadvantaged residents of Beersheva and the Negev. 2010.

891-22 Disability Rights International, Washington, DC, $80,000. For renewed general support to promote the human rights of people with mental disabilities worldwide. 2010.

891-23 Encounter, New York, NY, $80,000. For renewed general support. 2010.

891-24 Fund for Global Human Rights, Washington, DC, $200,000. For renewed general support to make grants to local and regional human rights groups around the world. 2010.

891-25 Global AIDS Alliance, Washington, DC, $30,000. For renewed support for advocacy to link AIDS prevention policy with women's rights and the right to education. 2010.

891-26 Hagar: Bilingual Education for Equality, Beer-Sheva, Israel, $50,000. For general support. 2010.

891-27 Ir Amim, Jerusalem, Israel, $50,000. For renewed support for public education, community work and advocacy to ensure the future of Jerusalem. 2010.

891-28 Israel Association for Child Protection, Tel Aviv, Israel, $50,000. For general support. 2010.

891-29 Israel Association of Community Centers, Jerusalem, Israel, $30,000. For renewed support for the 'Budding Scientists' program for high school students in the Negev. 2010.

891-30 Israel Center for Educational Innovation, Kfar Saba, Israel, $50,000. For renewed support for the Netanya Initiative to raise achievement levels in elementary schools with high concentration of Ethiopian students. 2010.

891-31 Israel Family Planning Association, Tel Aviv, Israel, $55,000. For renewed support for its work in the Negev. 2010.

891-32 Israel Religious Action Center, Jerusalem, Israel, $150,000. For renewed general support for its activities promoting religious pluralism and the rule of law through advocacy, research, public education and litigation. 2010.

891-33 Itach-Maaki, Tel Aviv, Israel, $25,000. For renewed general support for legal aid and litigation for low-income women. 2010.

891-34 Just Vision, Washington, DC, $80,000. For renewed general support. 2010.

891-35 Legal Advocates for Women, Washington, DC, $25,000. For renewed support for the Leadership and Advocacy for Women in Africa Fellowship program. 2010.

891-36 Ma'an: Forum for Arab-Bedouin Womens Organizations of the Negev, Beer Sheva, Israel, $50,000. For renewed general support for activities to empower Bedouin women, including legal aid on matters of family law. 2010.

891-37 Ma'ase, Karmiel, Israel, $25,000. For the Knowledge Center. 2010.

891-38 Middle East Education Through Technology, New York, NY, $50,000. For general support. 2010.

891-39 Negev Institute for Strategies of Peace and Development, Beer Sheva, Israel, $100,000. For general support for activities to promote development in the Bedouin community and positive intergroup relations in the Negev. 2010.

891-40 New Israel Fund, Washington, DC, $200,000. For renewed support for NIF/SHATIL activities in the Negev. 2010.

891-41 Shiluv, Jerusalem, Israel, $22,500. For renewed support for counseling programs. 2010.

891-42 Sikkuy: The Association for the Advancement of Civic Equality in Israel, Jerusalem, Israel, $10,000. For general support. 2010.

891-43 Tebeka: Advocacy for Equality and Justice for Ethiopian Israelis, Netanya, Israel, $20,000. For renewed support for legal aid/representation for Ethiopian Israelis. 2010.

891-44 Tevel b Tzedek: An Israeli Non-Profit for Social and Environmental Justice, Jerusalem, Israel, $10,000. For renewed general support. 2010.

891-45 Tostan, Washington, DC, $35,000. For renewed support for human rights-based work in city of Mbour in the Thies region of Senegal. 2010.

891-46 Witness, Inc., Brooklyn, NY, $50,000. For general support. 2010.

891-47 World Union for Progressive Judaism, New York, NY, $220,000. For renewed support for the young leadership development program in the FSU. 2010.

891-48 Yad L'Isha, Jerusalem, Israel, $20,000. For renewed support for the Legal Aid Center ($10,000) and for ICAR, the International Coalition for Aguna Rights ($10,000). 2010.

891-49 Yedid-Association for Community Empowerment in Israel, Jerusalem, Israel, $100,000. For renewed general support. 2010.

891-50 Yesodot-The Center for the Study of Torah and Democracy, Jerusalem, Israel, $25,000. For renewed support for educational programming. 2010.

892

The Morton K. and Jane Blaustein Foundation, Inc.
10 E. Baltimore St., Ste. 1111
Baltimore, MD 21202-1620 (410) 347-7201
Contact: Mary Jane Blaustein, Pres.
FAX: (410) 347-7210; E-mail: info@bloufund.org;
URL: http://www.blaufund.org/foundations/mortonandjane_f.html

Established in 1988 in MD.
Donors: Morton K. Blaustein†; Mary Jane Blaustein; Lord Baltimore Capital Corp.
Grantmaker type: Independent foundation.
Financial data (yr. ended 12/31/10): Assets, $53,349,504 (M); gifts received, $250,000; expenditures, $2,843,648; qualifying distributions, $2,741,945; giving activities include $2,474,500 for 58 grants (high: $200,000; low: $1,500).
Purpose and activities: The foundation is guided by the principle that people will develop and flourish best through equal opportunities in education, access to quality health care and the freedom to participate in a democratic society. Accordingly, grants are made in the areas of education, health and human rights and social justice.

Fields of interest: Education; Health care; Mental health/crisis services; International human rights.
Type of support: General/operating support; Continuing support; Emergency funds; Program development.
Limitations: Applications accepted. Giving primarily in Washington, DC, Baltimore, MD, and New York, NY. No support for fundraising events, direct mail solicitations, or unsolicited proposals for academic, scientific or medical research. No grants or scholarships to individuals, or for fundraising, capital campaigns, annual campaigns, membership campaigns; no loans.
Application information: See foundation web site for program guidelines. Association of Baltimore Area Grantmakers Common Grant Application Form accepted. Application form not required.
Initial approach: Letter
Copies of proposal: 1
Deadline(s): None
Final notification: 4 to 6 months
Officers and Trustees:* Mary Jane Blaustein,* Pres.; Alan Berlow,* V.P.; Susan B. Blaustein,* V.P.; Jeanne P. Blaustein,* V.P.; Peter Bokor,* V.P.; Jill R. Robinson, Secy.; Anne Patterson, Treas.; Betsy Ringel, Exec. Dir.
Number of staff: 1 full-time professional.
EIN: 521607300
Recent grants for international programs:

892-1 American Jewish World Service, New York, NY, $50,000. For general support for grassroots efforts to promote sustainable development, health, education and human rights in marginalized communities in the developing world. 2010.

892-2 Columbia University, New York, NY, $77,000. For the social sector work of the Millennium Cities Initiative. 2010.

892-3 Committee to Protect Journalists, New York, NY, $90,000. For renewed general support. 2010.

892-4 Disability Rights International, Washington, DC, $30,000. For renewed general support. 2010.

892-5 Nigun HaLev, Nahalal, Israel, $15,000. For the Kol Galgal project for low-income children. 2010.

892-6 Partners in Health, Boston, MA, $50,000. For earthquake relief efforts in Haiti. 2010.

892-7 Physicians for Human Rights, Cambridge, MA, $75,000. For renewed general support. 2010.

892-8 Yotzer Or, Jerusalem, Israel, $25,000. For the Open Horizons program. 2010.

893

BMENA Foundation for the Future
P.O. Box 327
Fulton, MD 20759-0327
Contact: Nabila Hamza, Pres.
E-mail: info@foundationforfuture.org; International address: P.O. Box 18005, Amman 11195 Jordan, Um Uthina - Al Najaf St., Bldg. 7; tel.: +962.6.55.44.906; fax: +962.85.66.44.907; URL: http://www.foundationforfuture.org

Established in 2006 in DC.
Grantmaker type: Public charity.
Financial data (yr. ended 12/31/10): Revenue, $905,524; assets, $16,906,460 (M); expenditures, $5,282,936; giving activities include $3,608,129 for grants to organizations outside the U.S.

Purpose and activities: The foundation works towards promoting democracy and human rights in the broader Middle East and North Africa (BMENA) region.

Fields of interest: Civil/human rights; International affairs.

International interests: Middle East; North Africa.

Limitations: Applications accepted. Giving limited to Afghanistan, Algeria, Bahrain, Egypt, Iran, Iraq, Jordan, Kuwait, Lebanon, Morocco, Oman, Pakistan, Palestine, Qatar, Saudi Arabia, Syria, Tunisia, United Arab Emirates, and Yemen.

Publications: Application guidelines; Annual report; Informational brochure; Newsletter.

Application information: Only those organizations with concept papers of interest to the foundation will be asked to submit full proposals. Application form not required.

   Initial approach: Submit concept paper
   Deadline(s): Apr. 15 (only for existing grantees requests for cost extensions; proposals from Pakistan, Iran, Afghanistan, Algeria, Tunisia, Libya, Syria, and Gulf countries) and Sept. 15
   Final notification: July and Dec.

Officers and Directors:* Rahma Bourqia,* Chair.; Cornelio Sommaruga,* Vice-Chair.; Nabila Hamza,* Pres.; Dr. Kamer Abu Jaber,* Treas.; Dr. Bakhtiar Amin; Amal Basha; Abdul Hassan Buhusian; Sabine Gurtner; Pervez Hassan; Hon. Robert Henry; Zahira Kamal; Andreu Claret Serra.

EIN: 861162123

894
Hershel & Esther Boehm Charity Fund, Inc.
5919 Winner Ave.
Baltimore, MD 21215-3801
Contact: Howard M. Boehm, Pres.

Established in 1997 in MD.

Donors: Howard M. Boehm; Esther Boehm; Hershel Boehm.

Grantmaker type: Independent foundation.

Financial data (yr. ended 12/31/10): Assets, $1,066,922 (M); gifts received, $283,740; expenditures, $315,435; qualifying distributions, $315,435; giving activities include $315,435 for 154 grants (high: $25,360; low: $5).

Purpose and activities: Giving primarily for Jewish agencies and temples.

Fields of interest: Education; Human services; Jewish agencies & synagogues.

International interests: Israel.

Limitations: Applications accepted. Giving primarily in Baltimore, MD and New York, NY; giving also in Israel.

Application information: Application form not required.

   Initial approach: Letter
   Deadline(s): None

Officers: Howard M. Boehm, Pres.; Esther Boehm, V.P.; Ronny S. Retter, Secy.

EIN: 522005744

895
Child Health Foundation
Century Plz.
10630 Little Patuxent Pkwy., Ste. 126
Columbia, MD 21044-3264 (410) 992-5512
Contact: Carol B. Collado, Exec. Dir.

FAX: (410) 992-5641;
E-mail: contact@childhealthfoundation.org;
URL: http://www.childhealthfoundation.org
Facebook: http://www.facebook.com/pages/
Child-Health-Foundation/181380928186
Twitter: http://twitter.com/ChildHealthFnd

Established in 1985 in MD.

Grantmaker type: Public charity.

Financial data (yr. ended 12/31/10): Revenue, $268,644; assets, $171,305 (M); gifts received, $267,791; expenditures, $241,353; giving activities include $156,746 for grants.

Purpose and activities: The foundation seeks to save children's lives through improving the health of infants and young children primarily through the development of biomedical and social technologies, including community mobilization, and the discovery, adaptation and implementation of technologies in local situations.

Fields of interest: Environment, waste management; Environment, water pollution; Environment, water resources; Public health; Children/youth, services; International development; International relief.

International interests: Latin America; Caribbean; Developing countries; Asia.

Type of support: Consulting services; Curriculum development; In-kind gifts; Internship funds; Research; Seed money; Technical assistance.

Limitations: Applications accepted. Giving primarily to developing countries. No grants for international travel, computers, secretarial support, or overhead expenses.

Publications: Application guidelines; Annual report; Financial statement; Informational brochure; Newsletter; Occasional report.

Application information: Proposals should not exceed five pages. Application form required.

   Initial approach: Letter of intent
   Copies of proposal: 1
   Board meeting date(s): Quarterly
   Final notification: Four months after proposal

Officers and Trustees:* Maureen Black,* Chair.; Pamela Johnson,* Ph.D., Vice-Chair.; R. Bradley Sack,* M.D., Pres.; David A. Sack,* M.D., Secy.; Carol B. Collado, Exec. Dir.; Nathaniel F. Pierce,* M.D., Secy.-Treas.; Leonard Andrew; Abdullah H. Baqui, M.P.H., Ph.D.; Rita Colwell, Ph.D., D.Sc.; Jean B. Nachega, M.D., Ph.D.; Tim Shi; Nand Wadhwani.

Number of staff: 2 full-time professional.

EIN: 521429538

896
Naomi and Nehemiah Cohen Foundation
P.O. Box 30100
Bethesda, MD 20824-0639 (301) 652-2230
Contact: Alison McWilliams, Exec. Dir.
FAX: (301) 652-2260; E-mail: info@nncf.net;
URL: http://www.nncf.net

Incorporated in 1959 in DC.

Donors: Emanuel Cohen†; N.M. Cohen†; Naomi Cohen†; Israel Cohen†; Daniel Solomon; Lillian Cohen Solomon†; David Solomon; Stuart Brown; Dr. Diane Solomon Brown.

Grantmaker type: Independent foundation.

Financial data (yr. ended 12/31/10): Assets, $76,815,723 (M); gifts received, $2,208; expenditures, $4,112,701; qualifying distributions, $3,939,995; giving activities include $3,651,336 for 115 grants (high: $350,000; low: $1,000).

Purpose and activities: The focus of the foundation is on human services, reproductive health care, out-of-school time youth development, and civic affairs in Washington, DC, and Jewish-Arab shared society in Israel.

Fields of interest: Human services; International human rights; Civil/human rights; Children/youth; Minorities; Women; Young adults, female; Economically disadvantaged; Homeless.

International interests: Israel.

Type of support: General/operating support; Annual campaigns; Capital campaigns; Building/renovation; Program evaluation.

Limitations: Applications not accepted. Giving primarily in Washington, DC, and Israel. No support for private or parochial schools, universities, or for medical research. No grants to individuals.

Publications: Grants list.

Application information: Unsolicited requests for funds not accepted. Current grantees should refer to application guidelines on foundation web site, and can use the Washington Regional Association of Grantmakers' Common Grant Application Format.

   Board meeting date(s): Quarterly

Officers and Directors:* Dr. Diane Solomon Brown,* Pres.; Daniel Solomon,* V.P.; Jane Solomon,* Secy.; Stuart Brown,* Treas.; Alison McWilliams, Exec. Dir.

Number of staff: 1 full-time professional.

EIN: 201135004

Recent grants for international programs:

896-1 Abraham Fund Initiatives, New York, NY, $50,000. For grant made through Israel Program. 2010.

896-2 Adalah: The Legal Center for Arab Minority Rights in Israel, Shfaram, Israel, $10,000. For grant made through Israel Program. 2010.

896-3 ADVA Center, Tel Aviv, Israel, $10,000. For grant made through Israel Program. 2010.

896-4 American Friends of the Hebrew University, Washington, DC, $10,000. For grant made through Israel Program. 2010.

896-5 American Jewish Joint Distribution Committee, New York, NY, $55,000. For grant made through Israel Program. 2010.

896-6 American Jewish World Service, New York, NY, $35,000. 2010.

896-7 Americans for Peace Now, Washington, DC, $25,000. For grant made through Israel Program. 2010.

896-8 Arava Institute for Environmental Studies, Eilat, Israel, $25,000. For grant made through Israel Program. 2010.

896-9 Association for Civil Rights in Israel, Tel Aviv, Israel, $25,000. For grant made through Israel Program. 2010.

896-10 Bimkom - Planners for Planning Rights, Jerusalem, Israel, $10,000. For grant made through Israel Program. 2010.

896-11 Birthright Israel Foundation, New York, NY, $10,000. 2010.

896-12 Blue White Future, Tel Aviv, Israel, $25,000. For grant made through Israel Program. 2010.

896-13 Bonobo Conservation Initiative, Washington, DC, $230,000. 2010.

896-14 BTselem - Israeli Information Center for Human Rights in the Occupied Territories, Jerusalem, Israel, $25,000. For grant made through Israel Program. 2010.

896-15 Center for Jewish-Arab Economic Development, Herzliya, Israel, $25,000. For grant made through Israel Program. 2010.

896-16 Gilboa Regional Council, Gilboa, Israel, $10,000. For grant made through Israel Program. 2010.

896-17 Givat Haviva Jewish-Arab Center for Peace, Givat Haviva, Israel, $25,000. For grant made through Israel Program. 2010.

896-18 Global Alliance for Incinerator Alternatives, Berkeley, CA, $15,000. 2010.

896-19 GoodWeave USA, Washington, DC, $10,000. 2010.

896-20 Hand in Hand, Jerusalem, Israel, $349,270. For grant made through Israel Program. 2010.

896-21 Inter-Agency Task Force on Israeli Arab Issues, New York, NY, $10,000. For grant made through Israel Program. 2010.

896-22 Ir Amim, Jerusalem, Israel, $10,000. For grant made through Israel Program. 2010.

896-23 Israel Religious Action Center, Jerusalem, Israel, $25,000. For grant made through Israel Program. 2010.

896-24 J Street Education Fund, Washington, DC, $50,000. For grant made through Israel Program. 2010.

896-25 Jewish Federations of North America, Social Venture Fund for Jewish-Arab Equality and Shared Society, New York, NY, $52,566. For grant made through Israel Program. 2010.

896-26 Merchavim: Institute for the Advancement of Shared Citizenship in Israel, Ramla, Israel, $175,000. For grant made through Israel Program. 2010.

896-27 Middle East Education Through Technology, New York, NY, $10,000. For grant made through Israel Program. 2010.

896-28 New Israel Fund, Washington, DC, $100,000. For grant made through Israel Program. 2010.

896-29 Physicians for Human Rights-Israel, Tel Aviv, Israel, $40,000. For grant made through Israel Program. 2010.

896-30 Sikkuy: The Association for the Advancement of Civic Equality in Israel, Jerusalem, Israel, $20,000. For grant made through Israel Program. 2010.

896-31 Sweatfree Communities, Bangor, ME, $40,000. 2010.

896-32 Yedid-Association for Community Empowerment in Israel, Jerusalem, Israel, $40,000. For grant made through Israel Program. 2010.

897
The Haron Dahan Foundation, Inc.
2231 Conowingo Rd.
Bel Air, MD 21015-1436 (410) 879-0200
Contact: Haron Dahan, Pres.

Established in 1986 in MD.
Donors: Haron Dahan; Caddie Homes, Inc.; Dahan Homes, Inc.
Grantmaker type: Independent foundation.
Financial data (yr. ended 12/31/10): Assets, $43,604,034 (M); expenditures, $845,022; qualifying distributions, $769,568; giving activities include $764,886 for 16 grants (high: $390,000; low: $500).
Purpose and activities: Giving primarily for Jewish agencies, temples, and education.
Fields of interest: Higher education; Human services; Jewish federated giving programs; Jewish agencies & synagogues.
International interests: Israel.

Limitations: Giving in the U.S., primarily in Brooklyn and New York, NY, and MD, with emphasis on Baltimore.
Application information:
   Initial approach: Letter
   Deadline(s): None
Officer: Haron Dahan, Pres.
Number of staff: 1 part-time support.
EIN: 521473704

898
Doorstep Ministry Foundation, Inc.
(formerly Criste Family Foundation, Inc.)
c/o Walter F. Galbraith
P.O. Box 710
Riderwood, MD   21139-0710

Established in 1993 in MD.
Donors: Hildebert F. Criste; Mary Ellen Criste.
Grantmaker type: Independent foundation.
Financial data (yr. ended 12/31/10): Assets, $2,079,276 (M); expenditures, $238,717; qualifying distributions, $225,661; giving activities include $219,670 for 33+ grants (high: $49,500).
Purpose and activities: Giving primarily to Christian religious organizations and missions; funding also for human services and education.
Fields of interest: Media, radio; Secondary school/education; Higher education; Human services; Youth, services; Family services; Christian agencies & churches.
International interests: Thailand; South Africa; India; Nepal.
Limitations: Applications accepted. Giving primarily in FL, MD, and VA, as well as in India, Nepal, South Africa, and Thailand.
Application information: Application form not required.
   Initial approach: Letter
   Deadline(s): None
Officers: Mary Ellen Criste, Pres.; Hildebert F. Criste, V.P.; Walter F. Galbraith, Treas.
EIN: 521827165

899
The Dysfunctional Family Foundation, Inc.
308 Montgomery St.
Laurel, MD   20707-4340   (301) 561-2318
Contact: Sharon Hipkins, Dir.

Established in 2001 in MD.
Donor: Lisa M. Losito.
Grantmaker type: Independent foundation.
Financial data (yr. ended 12/31/09): Assets, $1,168,738 (M); expenditures, $464,031; qualifying distributions, $336,386; giving activities include $332,160 for grants (high: $314,040; low: $200).
Fields of interest: Foundations (private operating); Education; Employment; Human services; Children/youth, services; International relief.
Limitations: Applications accepted. Giving primarily in MD. No grants to individuals.
Application information: Application form not required.
   Deadline(s): None
Officers: Douglas E. Humphrey, Pres.; Lisa M. Losito, V.P.
Director: Sharon Hipkins.
EIN: 300002203

900
ELECTRI International
(formerly The Electrical Contracting Foundation, Inc.)
3 Bethesda Metro Ctr., Ste. 1100
Bethesda, MD   20814-5372   (301) 215-4538
Contact: Albert Wendt, Pres.
FAX: (301) 215-4536; E-mail: rja@necanet.org;
URL: http://www.electri21.org

Established in 1989 in MD.
Grantmaker type: Public charity.
Financial data (yr. ended 12/31/10): Revenue, $3,384,410; assets, $18,634,921 (M); gifts received, $3,085,562; expenditures, $1,958,438.
Purpose and activities: The foundation aids in promoting and advancing the ability of electrical contractors to meet the demands of today and the challenges of the future.
Fields of interest: Engineering/technology.
International interests: Canada.
Type of support: Research; Scholarships—to individuals.
Publications: Application guidelines; Annual report; Informational brochure; Newsletter.
Application information: Foundation will invite full proposals after review of summaries. Application form required.
   Initial approach: Letter, telephone, or e-mail
   Copies of proposal: 2
   Deadline(s): Mar. 1
   Board meeting date(s): Oct. 23
   Final notification: Oct.
Officers: E. Milner Irvin III, Chair.; Jerrold H. Nixon, Vice-Chair.; Albert Wendt, Pres.
Trustees: Russell J. Alessi; Richard L. Burns; Larry Cogburn; John R. Colson; Christopher Curtis; Rex A. Ferry; John M. Grau; John M. Guelder; James E. Mackey; John Negro; and 8 additional trustees.
Number of staff: 3 full-time professional; 1 full-time support.
EIN: 521643734

901
The Ellison Medical Foundation
4710 Bethesda Ave., Ste. 204
Bethesda, MD   20814-5226   (301) 657-1830
Contact: Richard L. Sprott Ph.D., Exec. Dir.
FAX: (301) 657-1828;
E-mail: rsprott@ellisonfoundation.org; URL: http://www.ellisonfoundation.org
Lawrence J. Ellison's Giving Pledge: http://givingpledge.org/#enter

Established in 1997 in CA.
Donor: Lawrence J. Ellison.
Grantmaker type: Operating foundation.
Financial data (yr. ended 12/31/10): Assets, $0 (M); gifts received, $9,001,725; expenditures, $40,906,629; qualifying distributions, $40,745,690; giving activities include $7,338,955 for 35 grants (high: $2,093,687; low: $800), $31,625,771 for 192 grants to individuals (high: $291,000; low: $50,000), and $312,124 for 3 foundation-administered programs.
Purpose and activities: The foundation supports basic biomedical research on aging relevant to understanding lifespan development processes and age-related diseases and disabilities. The foundation particularly wishes to stimulate new, creative research that might not be funded by traditional sources or that is often under-funded in the U.S.

Fields of interest: Geriatrics research; Biomedicine; Biomedicine research; Biology/life sciences.

Type of support: Conferences/seminars; Research; Grants to individuals.

Limitations: Applications accepted. Giving limited to U.S. institutions only. No support for commercial or for-profit organizations.

Publications: Informational brochure; Newsletter.

Application information: See foundation web site for additional application information. Senior Scholars letters must be submitted online at: http://www.cybergrants.com/emf/senior_scholar_loi Full applications for Senior Scholars and New Scholars are accepted by invitation only. Application form required.

   Initial approach: Submit Senior Scholar letter of intent via foundation web site

   Copies of proposal: 1

   Deadline(s): Mar. 5th for Senior Scholars letters of intent

   Final notification: Late May for letter of intent decision, Aug. for awardees

Officers and Directors:* Lawrence J. Ellison,* Chair. and Pres.; Andrew L. Dudnick, Corp. Secy.; Philip B. Simon, C.F.O.; Richard L. Sprott, Ph.D., Exec. Dir.; Melanie Craft Ellison.

Scientific Advisory Board: George M. Martin, Chair.; Helen M. Blau, Ph.D.; Eric R. Kandel; Arnold J. Levine; Martin Raff, M.D.; Gerald Weissmann.

Number of staff: 2 full-time professional; 3 full-time support; 1 part-time support.

EIN: 943269827

Recent grants for international programs:

901-1 Baylor College of Medicine, Houston, TX, $10,000. For First International Conference on Molecular Neurodegeneration. 2009.

901-2 Gerontological Society of America, Washington, DC, $10,000. For IAGG (International Association of Gerontology and Geriatrics) World Congress of Gerontology and Geriatrics Symposium. 2009.

901-3 Gordon Research Conferences, West Kingston, RI, $10,000. For Biology of Aging Conference. 2009.

901-4 International Association of Environmental Mutagen Societies, Reston, VA, $10,000. For 10th International Conference on Environmental Mutagens, DNA Damage Repair and Aging Symposium. 2009.

901-5 Tom Lantos Foundation for Human Rights and Justice, Concord, NH, $1,000,000. For endowment fund. 2009.

901-6 University of Texas Medical Branch, Galveston, TX, $10,000. For third US/EU conference on repair of Endogenous Genome Damage. 2009.

902

The Lois & Richard England Family Foundation, Inc.

(formerly The Lois & Richard England Foundation, Inc.)

P.O. Box 341077

Bethesda, MD 20827-1077 (301) 657-7737

Contact: Monica Smith, Prog. Asst.

FAX: (301) 657-7738;

E-mail: englandfamilyfdn@verizon.net; E-mail for Monica Smith: monicasmith.eff@verizon.net;

URL: http://foundationcenter.org/grantmaker/england/

Established in 1990 in MD.

Donors: Richard England; Lois H. England.

Grantmaker type: Independent foundation.

Financial data (yr. ended 12/31/10): Assets, $17,994,510 (M); expenditures, $1,729,540; qualifying distributions, $1,371,285; giving activities include $1,371,285 for grants.

Purpose and activities: The foundation is committed to the improvement of the lives of children living in underserved communities in Washington, DC. Its current focus is out of school time programs that provide academic support and enrichment, athletic activities, and/or arts education to children in grades 3 and above. The foundation also has a strong commitment to strengthening Jewish life in the United States and internationally.

Fields of interest: Arts; Education; Human services; Community development, neighborhood development; Jewish agencies & synagogues.

International interests: Israel.

Type of support: General/operating support; Continuing support; Annual campaigns; Capital campaigns; Building/renovation; Program development; Publication; Seed money; Program evaluation; Program-related investments/loans; Matching/challenge support.

Limitations: Applications not accepted. Giving primarily in the Washington, DC, area, and Israel. No grants to individuals.

Publications: Grants list.

Application information: Unsolicited requests for funds not accepted. The foundation may request letters of inquiry from organizations working in targeted areas of interest.

   Board meeting date(s): May and Nov.

Officers and Board Members:* Catherine S. England,* Chair.; Richard England,* Pres.; Lois H. England,* V.P.; Richard England, Jr.,* Treas.; Larry Akman; Nonie Akman; Diana England.

Number of staff: 1 part-time support.

EIN: 521691418

903

Global Development Network, Inc.

926 Loxford Terr.

Silver Spring, MD 20901-1125 (301) 681-0911

FAX: (301) 592-0442; Toll-free tel.: (866) 580-4364

Grantmaker type: Public charity.

Financial data (yr. ended 06/30/10): Revenue, $29,223,812; assets, $10,122,245 (M); gifts received, $14,611,906; expenditures, $13,249,115; giving activities include $2,395,725 for grants, $5,126,720 for grants to organizations outside the U.S., and $156,275 for grants to individuals.

Purpose and activities: The organization supports the New-Delhi-based Global Development Network in its mission of reducing poverty through better policies driven by more effective research.

Fields of interest: Economically disadvantaged.

International interests: India.

Officer and Directors:* Ernesto Zedillo,* Chair.; Insher Ahluwalia; Mohammed Ariff; Ernest Aryeetey; Abhijit Banerjee; Eliana Cardoso; Alan Gelb; Ravi Kanbur; Olav Korven; Masanori Kondo; Mustapha Nabli; Vijay Naidu; Andres Neumeyer; Jean-Philippe Plateau; Vladimir Popov; and 6 additional directors.

EIN: 542034142

904

Hariri Foundation

7501 Wisconsin Ave., Ste. 715

Bethesda, MD 20814-3602

URL: http://www.haririfoundationusa.org/

Established in 1985 in DC.

Donor: Rafiq Hariri.

Grantmaker type: Independent foundation.

Financial data (yr. ended 12/31/10): Assets, $2,109,196 (M); gifts received, $838,865; expenditures, $1,000,451; qualifying distributions, $989,611; giving activities include $140,000 for 1 grant, and $489,805 for loans to individuals.

Purpose and activities: Giving primarily for international relief, and for student loans and financial assistance to deserving Lebanese and other Middle Eastern students for study at U.S. institutions of higher learning.

Fields of interest: International relief; Higher education; International affairs, goodwill promotion.

Type of support: General/operating support; Student loans—to individuals.

Limitations: Applications not accepted. Giving primarily in the U.S. and in Lebanon.

Application information: Unsolicited requests for funds not accepted.

Officers: Rafic A. Bizri, Pres.; David J. Thompson, Secy.

Directors: Frederick Rizk; Mrs. Bahia B. Al-Hariri; Anthony Essaye.

Number of staff: 4 full-time professional.

EIN: 521386338

905

The David and Barbara B. Hirschhorn Foundation, Inc.

c/o AFS

10 E. Baltimore St., Ste. 1101

Baltimore, MD 21202-1620 (410) 347-7201

Contact: Betsy F. Ringel, Exec. Dir.

E-mail: info@blafund.org

Established in 1986 in MD.

Donors: Barbara B. Hirschhorn; David Hirschhorn†; Daniel B. Hirschhorn; 3510 LLC.

Grantmaker type: Independent foundation.

Financial data (yr. ended 12/31/10): Assets, $40,698,806 (M); gifts received, $503,300; expenditures, $2,956,602; qualifying distributions, $2,651,150; giving activities include $2,651,150 for grants.

Fields of interest: Human services; International relief; Civil rights, race/intergroup relations; Jewish federated giving programs; Jewish agencies & synagogues; Religion, interfaith issues.

Type of support: General/operating support; Annual campaigns; Capital campaigns; Endowments.

Limitations: Applications accepted. Giving primarily in the metropolitan Baltimore, MD, area. No grants to individuals or for fundraisers; no loans.

Application information: Association of Baltimore Area Grantmakers Common Grant Application Form accepted. Application form not required.

   Initial approach: Letter

   Copies of proposal: 1

   Deadline(s): None

   Final notification: 4 to 6 months

Officers and Trustees:* Barbara B. Hirschhorn,* Chair.; Daniel B. Hirschhorn,* Pres.; Michael J. Hirschhorn,* V.P.; Sarah H. Shapiro,* V.P.; Deborah

H. Vogelstein,* V.P.; Jill R. Robinson, Secy.; Betsy F. Ringel, Exec. Dir.
EIN: 521489400
Recent grants for international programs:
905-1 American Jewish World Service, New York, NY, $50,000. For general support. 2010.
905-2 American Jewish World Service, New York, NY, $10,000. For emergency relief efforts in Haiti. 2010.
905-3 AMIT Women, New York, NY, $12,500. For tie-off support for AMIT network of schools in Israel. 2010.
905-4 Breakthrough, New York, NY, $15,000. For general support. 2010.
905-5 Chai Lifeline, New York, NY, $15,000. For general support of US operations ($10,000) and support for Chaiyanu, program in Israel ($5,000). 2010.
905-6 Global Camps Africa, Reston, VA, $15,000. For renewed support for residential camp programs in South Africa for children affected by HIV/AIDS. 2010.
905-7 Just Vision, Washington, DC, $25,000. For general support. 2010.
905-8 New Israel Fund, Washington, DC, $50,000. For general support. 2010.
905-9 Witness, Inc., Brooklyn, NY, $34,000. For general support. 2010.

906
Hoffberger Foundation, Inc.
101 W. Mount Royal Ave.
Baltimore, MD 21201-5781 (410) 369-9336
FAX: (410) 369-9337;
E-mail: info@hoffbergerfoundation.org; URL: http://www.hoffbergerfoundation.org

Incorporated in 1941 in MD.
Donor: The Hoffberger family.
Grantmaker type: Independent foundation.
Financial data (yr. ended 12/31/10): Assets, $20,503,332 (M); expenditures, $650,038, qualifying distributions, $453,094; giving activities include $453,094 for grants.
Purpose and activities: The foundation's mission is to respond with available resources to unmet needs in the greater Baltimore, MD, community, with a significant commitment to the Jewish community.
Fields of interest: Youth development; Theological school/education; Education; Human services; Children/youth, services; Community development, neighborhood development; Economic development; Jewish federated giving programs; Jewish agencies & synagogues.
International interests: Israel.
Type of support: General/operating support; Continuing support; Building/renovation; Endowments; Program development; Seed money; Scholarship funds; Matching/challenge support.
Limitations: Giving primarily in Baltimore, MD. No grants to individuals.
Publications: Grants list; Program policy statement.
Application information: Association of Baltimore Area Grantmakers Common Grant Application Form accepted.
Initial approach: Proposal
Deadline(s): Mar. 1 (no later than 5:00 PM)
Final notification: June 30
Officers and Directors:* LeRoy E. Hoffberger,* Chair.; Sue Gross,* Pres.; Lois Halpert, V.P.; Allison Fass,* Secy.; Bruce Hoffberger,* Treas.; Ann Billingsley, Exec. Dir.; David Hoffberger; Margo Pyes.

Number of staff: 1 part-time professional; 1 part-time support.
EIN: 520794249

907
Howard Hughes Medical Institute
c/o Office of Grants and Special Progs.
4000 Jones Bridge Rd.
Chevy Chase, MD 20815-6789 (301) 215-8500
Contact: For general inquiries: Dr. Peter J. Bruns, V.P., Grants and Special Progs.; Dr. William R. Galey, Prog. Dir., Grad. Prog.; Stephen A. Barkanic, Prog. Dir., Undergrad Prog.; Dr. Jill G. Conley, Prog. Dir., International Prog., Precollege Prog., Research Resources Prog.; Dr. Dennis Liu, Prog. Dir., Educational Products
FAX: (301) 215-8888; E-mail: grantswww@hhmi.org; URL: http://www.hhmi.org
Facebook: http://www.facebook.com/HowardHughesMed
iTunes: http://itunes.apple.com/us/app/hhmi-bulletin/id411540287?mt=8
News Feed: http://www.hhmi.org/news/rss20.xml
Twitter: http://twitter.com/hhminews
Toll-free tel.: (800) 448-4882

Incorporated in 1953 in DE.
Donor: Howard R. Hughes†.
Grantmaker type: Public charity.
Financial data (yr. ended 08/31/11): Assets, $15,739,867,000 (M); expenditures, $870,121,000; giving activities include $80,000,000 for grants, and $825,000,000 for foundation-administered programs.
Purpose and activities: The purpose of the Institute is promotion of human knowledge within the field of basic sciences (chiefly medical research and education) and the effective application thereof to benefit mankind. The Institute is a medical research organization, not a private foundation, under federal tax codes. Through its Medical Research Program, the Institute's scientists conduct fundamental biomedical research throughout the U.S. in the fields of cell biology, computational biology, genetics, immunology, neuroscience, and structural biology. Through its Office of Grants and Special Programs, the Institute awards grants for education in biology and related sciences, funds research at medical schools, and supports fundamental research abroad. The emphasis of the grants program is graduate, undergraduate, and precollege and public science education. Graduate support is primarily awarded under two programs: 1) Research Training Fellowships for Med. Students. Deadline: early Jan.; 2) HHMI-NIH Research Scholars Program. Deadline: Jan. 10. The Undergraduate Science Education Program, awards grants to colleges and universities for 1) student research and expanding access in the sciences; 2) science equipment and lab renovations; 3) faculty and curriculum development; and 4) outreach programs in the sciences and mathematics with elementary and secondary schools, and with junior/community colleges. The HHMI Professors awards, an Undergraduate Program initiative, supports and empowers accomplished research scientists in transmitting the excitement and values of scientific research to undergraduate education. The Institute continues to monitor trends in science education and science, including public and private support. The Precollege Science Education Program addresses concerns about science literacy in the general population by engaging K-12 students, teachers, and families in science education.
Fields of interest: Secondary school/education; Higher education; Medical school/education; Education; Biomedicine; Medical research, institute; Biology/life sciences; Minorities; Asians/Pacific Islanders; African Americans/Blacks; Hispanics/Latinos; Native Americans/American Indians.
International interests: Canada; France; Greece; United Kingdom; Switzerland; Germany; Bulgaria; Czech Republic; Slovakia; Hungary; Poland; Estonia; Lithuania; Russia; Ukraine; Guinea; Uganda; South Africa; Mexico; Argentina; Brazil; Chile; Uruguay; Venezuela; Israel; Bangladesh; India; Taiwan; Australia.
Type of support: Building/renovation; Equipment; Program development; Professorships; Curriculum development; Fellowships; Research; Program evaluation; Grants to individuals.
Limitations: Applications accepted. Giving on a national and international basis. Graduate, undergraduate, and pre-college grants are nationwide; grants to foreign scientists made in selected countries. Some graduate fellowships given outside the U.S. Research grants have gone to scientists in Canada and Mexico (1991), Australia, New Zealand, and the United Kingdom (1992), The Baltics, Cent. Europe, and the former Soviet Union (1995), Argentina, Brazil, Canada, Chile, Mexico, and Venezuela (1997), and Australia, Bangladesh, Bulgaria, Czech Republic, Estonia, France, Germany, Greece, Guinea, Hungary, India, Israel, Lithuania, Mexico, Poland, Russia, Slovakia, South Africa, Switzerland, Taiwan, Uganda, Ukraine, United Kingdom, Uruguay, Venezuela (2000). No support for biomedical research in the U.S., except to scientists employed by the Institute; no grants or fellowships except to individuals or institutions competing under established science education programs. No grants for conferences or publications.
Publications: Application guidelines; Annual report; Informational brochure (including application guidelines); Newsletter; Occasional report; Program policy statement.
Application information: Applicants should consult guidelines in program announcements prior to application. Fellowships and grants are awarded on the basis of national or international competitions. Proposals for the Undergraduate Science Education Program and the Precollege Science Education Program are by invitation only. For the HHMI Professors awards, each invited institution may nominate up to two faculty members. In addition to the science education programs, grants are awarded to biomedical scientists in specified countries under the international program. Awards in all programs are based on peer review. Application form required.
Initial approach: Letter, proposal, or application, depending on program
Deadline(s): Oct. for Gilliam Fellowships
Board meeting date(s): Feb., May, Aug., and Nov.
Final notification: Dec. for Gilliam Fellowships
Officers: Robert Tijan, Pres.; Cheryl Moore, V.P. and C.O.O.; Craig A. Alexander, V.P. and Genl. Counsel; Peter J. Bruns, Ph.D., V.P., Grants and Special Progs.; Sean Carroll, V.P., Science Education; Joseph D. Collins, V.P., Info. Technology; Jack E. Dixon, Ph.D., V.P. and Chief Scientific Off.; Mohamoud Jibrell, V.P. Information Tech; Avice A. Meehan, V.P., Comm. and Pub. Affairs; Edward J. Palmerino, V.P., Fin. and Treas.; Gerald M. Rubin,

Ph.D., V.P. and Exec. Dir., Research Campus Janelia Farm; Landis Zimmerman, V.P. and C.I.O.
Trustees: Kurt L. Schmoke, Chair.; James A. Baker III; Amb. Charlene Barshefsky; Joseph L. Goldstein, M.D.; Garnett L. Keith; Hanna H. Gray, Ph.D.; Fred R. Lummis; Paul Nurse, F.R.S.; Alison F. Richard; Clayton Rose; Anne M. Tatlock.
Number of staff: 2479 full-time professional; 64 part-time professional; 484 full-time support; 105 part-time support.
EIN: 590735717

908
India Development and Relief Fund, Inc.
(also known as IDRF)
5821 Mossrock Dr.
North Bethesda, MD 20852-3238
(301) 704-0032
E-mail: idrfhq@yahoo.com; URL: http://www.idrf.org

Established in 1987 in MD; received tax-exempt status in 1988.
Grantmaker type: Public charity.
Financial data (yr. ended 12/31/10): Revenue, $763,406; assets, $1,418,616 (M); gifts received, $704,974; expenditures, $1,902,609; giving activities include $24,500 for grants, and $1,839,575 for grants to organizations outside the U.S.
Purpose and activities: The fund supports development, relief, and rehabilitation activities in India that are focused on five key areas: education, healthcare, childcare, women, and tribal welfare; relief and rehabilitation support is also funded during natural or man-made disasters.
Fields of interest: International development; International relief; Children/youth; Women; Economically disadvantaged.
International interests: India.
Type of support: General/operating support; Continuing support; Income development; Building/renovation; Endowments; Scholarship funds.
Limitations: Applications not accepted. Giving limited to India. No support for political, religious, sectarian, extremist, or for-profit organizations.
Publications: Annual report; Financial statement; Grants list; Informational brochure; Occasional report.
Application information: Contributes only to pre-selected organizations.
Officer and Directors:* Dr. Vinod Prakash,* Pres. and Treas.; Dr. Ram Gehani; Jatinder Kumar.
EIN: 521555563

909
Interchurch Medical Assistance, Inc.
(also known as IMA World Health)
P.O. Box 429
New Windsor, MD 21776-0429
Contact: Douglas Bright, V.P., Inst. Advance.
FAX: (410) 635-8726;
E-mail: imainfo@imaworldhealth.org; Toll-free tel.: (877) 241-7952; URL: http://imaworldhealth.org/
Charity Navigator: Your Guide to Intelligent Giving: http://www.charitynavigator.org/index.cfm?bay=search.summary&orgid=3877
Facebook: http://www.facebook.com/pages/IMA-World-Health/64232286277?ref=ts
Forbes Magainze: http://www.forbes.com/lists/2009/14/charity-09_IMA-World-Health_CH0297.html

Twitter: http://twitter.com/imaworldhealth
YouTube: http://www.youtube.com/user/IMAWorldHealth

Established in 1960; supporting organization of Adventist Development and Relief Agency, American Baptist Board of International Ministries, Church of the Brethren General Board, Church World Service, Christian Church (Disciples of Christ), Episcopal Church, Lutheran World Relief Inc., Mennonite Central Committee, Presbyterian Church, United Church of Christ, United Methodist Church, and Vellore Christian College Medical Board.
Grantmaker type: Public charity.
Financial data (yr. ended 06/30/10): Revenue, $98,686,426; assets, $9,417,774 (M); gifts received, $98,610,132; expenditures, $129,401,476; giving activities include $6,478,583 for grants, and $114,615,295 for grants to organizations outside the U.S.
Fields of interest: Health care, management/technical assistance; Health care, association; Public health; Health care; AIDS; Parasitic diseases; International relief.
International interests: Africa; Democratic Republic of the Congo; Haiti; Southern Africa; Sudan; Tanzania, Zanzibar and Pemba.
Type of support: General/operating support; Annual campaigns; Emergency funds; In-kind gifts.
Limitations: Applications not accepted. Giving primarily in Haiti and Sub-Saharan Africa.
Publications: Annual report; Financial statement; Informational brochure; Newsletter.
Application information: Contributes only to pre-selected organizations.
  Board meeting date(s): Biannually
Officers and Directors:* Dr. Donald L Parker, Jr.,* Chair.; Timothy McCully,* Vice-Chair.; Roy Winter,* Secy.; Johnny Wray,* Treas.; Paul Derstine, Exec. Dir.; Dr. Sam Dixon; Phyllis Ensor; Bob Ellis; David Martin; Raymond S. Martin; Dr. W. Henry Mosley; Kirsten Laursen Muth; John Scicchitano.
Number of staff: 65 full-time professional.
EIN: 522112460

910
International Eye Foundation
10801 Connecticut Ave.
Kensington, MD 20895-2134 (240) 290-0263
FAX: (240) 290-0269; E-mail: ief@iefusa.org;
URL: http://www.iefusa.org

Established in 1961.
Grantmaker type: Public charity.
Financial data (yr. ended 06/30/10): Revenue, $4,863,374; assets, $2,839,677 (M); gifts received, $4,512,672; expenditures, $4,817,419; giving activities include $3,575,465 for 6 grants to organizations outside the U.S.
Purpose and activities: The foundation is dedicated to helping people see.
Fields of interest: Eye diseases; Eye research.
International interests: Developing countries.
Type of support: In-kind gifts.
Limitations: Giving on a national and international basis. No grants to individuals.
Officers and Directors:* Frank S. Ashburn, Jr.,* M.D., Chair.; Fran Legon,* Vice-Chair.; Victoria M. Sheffield, Pres. and C.E.O.; Barbara Heineback,* Secy.; Roger Jantio,* Treas.; Heather Atkins; Kenneth B. Ball; Allen E. Beach; Robert Best; Rowland R. Bradley; Lawrence S. Clark; Howard P. Cupples, M.D.; James H. Finkelstein, Ph.D.; Mary

Catherine Fischer, M.D.; Susan T. Fritschler; and 11 additional directors.
EIN: 520742301

911
International Orthodox Christian Charities, Inc.
110 West Rd., Ste. 360
Baltimore, MD 21204-2365 (410) 243-9820
FAX: (410) 243-9824; E-mail: relief@iocc.org;
Mailing address: P.O. Box 630225, Baltimore, MD 21263-0225; Toll-free tel.: (877) 803-4622;
URL: http://www.iocc.org

Established in 1992 in DE.
Grantmaker type: Public charity.
Financial data (yr. ended 12/31/10): Revenue, $36,708,530; assets, $7,822,956 (M); gifts received, $36,472,538; expenditures, $40,411,816; giving activities include $10,183,133 for grants, and $19,785,840 for grants to organizations outside the U.S.
Purpose and activities: The organizations works in cooperation with Orthodox churches worldwide as the official humanitarian agency of Orthodox Christians, ministering to those who are suffering and in need of food, shelter, economic self-sufficiency, and hope through the world.
Fields of interest: Housing/shelter; Human services; Orthodox agencies & churches; Catholic agencies & churches.
International interests: Zimbabwe; Thailand; Syria; Greece; Albania; Romania; Armenia; Georgia (Republic of); Russia; Bosnia-Herzegovina; Serbia; Montenegro; Ethiopia; Iraq; Israel; Jordan; Lebanon; Indonesia.
Limitations: Giving on a national and international basis, with emphasis on Albania, Armenia, Bosnia, Ethiopia, Georgia, Greece, Indonesia, Iraq, Israel, Jordan, Lebanon, Montenegro, Romania, Russia, Serbia, Syria, Thailand, and Zimbabwe.
Publications: Annual report; Newsletter.
Officers and Directors:* Michael "Mickey" Homsey,* Chair.; Frank B. Cerra,* M.D., Vice-Chair.; Maria Z. Mossaides,* Secy.; Mark D. Stavropoulos,* Treas.; Jasmina T. Boulanger; Elaine G. Cladis; George Djurasovic; Rev. Michael Ellias; Albert P. Foundos; Jacqueline C. Gigantes; Yousif I. Hamati, M.D.; Charles J. Hinkaty; Elizabeth Oldnow Skouras Huttinger; Rev. Leonid Kishkovsky; Alexander Machaskee; and 11 additional board members.
EIN: 251679348

912
International Youth Foundation
(also known as IYF)
32 South St., Ste. 500
Baltimore, MD 21202-7503 (410) 951-1500
FAX: (410) 347-1188; E-mail: youth@iyfnet.org;
URL: http://www.iyfnet.org
Facebook: http://www.facebook.com/iyfnet
Flickr: http://www.flickr.com/photos/iyfnet/sets/
RSS Feed: http://www.iyfnet.org/rssfeed
YouTube: http://www.youtube.com/user/iyfnet

Established in 1990.
Grantmaker type: Public charity.
Financial data (yr. ended 12/31/10): Revenue, $30,117,234; assets, $36,972,589 (M); gifts received, $29,212,529; expenditures,

$22,493,247; giving activities include $715,773 for grants, $8,789,795 for grants to organizations outside the U.S., and $146,960 for grants to individuals.

Purpose and activities: The organization aims to help young people shape their futures through proven programs that tie education to work, improve employability, and enable and inspire them to play a positive role in their communities.

Fields of interest: International development; Children/youth, services.

International interests: Albania; Argentina; Australia; Bolivia; Bosnia-Herzegovina; Brazil; Bulgaria; Canada; China; Colombia; Croatia; Czech Republic; Dominican Republic; Ecuador; El Salvador; Finland; Germany; Ghana; Greece; Honduras; Hungary; India; Indonesia; Ireland; Israel; Japan; Kenya; Macedonia; Middle East; Mexico; Netherlands; Panama; Paraguay; Peru; Philippines; Poland; Portugal; Romania; Russia; Serbia; South Korea; Slovenia; Slovakia; South Africa; Spain; Taiwan; Tanzania, Zanzibar and Pemba; Thailand; Turkey; Uganda; United Kingdom; Uruguay; Venezuela; Vietnam; Zambia.

Type of support: Seed money.

Limitations: Giving on an international basis.

Publications: Application guidelines; Annual report.

Application information:

Initial approach: Download application for YouthActionNet Global Fellowship Program

Deadline(s): Apr. 9 for YouthActionNet Global Fellowship Program

Officers and Directors:* Douglas L. Becker,* Chair.; William S. Reese,* Pres. and C.E.O.; Richard F. Schubert,* Chair. Emeritus; H.M. Queen Raina Al-Abdullah; Bernise Ang; David Bell; Maria Livanos Cattaui; Bill Conn; Raghda El-Ebrashi; Olivier Fleurot; Henrietta Holsman Fore; Enrique V. Iglesias; Rick R. Little; Helio Mattar; Penina Mlama; Helen Ostrowski; Veli Sundback; Connie Wong.

Number of staff: 80 full-time professional.

EIN: 382935397

913

The Interpreters' Forum

P.O. Box 69150

Mount Washington, MD 21209-9998

Grantmaker type: Public charity.

Financial data (yr. ended 12/31/10): Revenue, $11,147; assets, $16,146 (M); gifts received, $11,147; expenditures, $12,878.

Purpose and activities: The forum is dedicated to peace through education, and to examining, probing, and penetrating the human condition in all its profound differences.

Fields of interest: International peace/security; Education; International affairs, goodwill promotion.

Limitations: Giving primarily in Westminster, MD.

Officers and Directors:* Jack H. Pechter,* Chair.; Sandra Berman, Vice-Chair., Prog. Devel.; Michael L. Combest, Vice-Chair., Devel.; Emanuel Goldman, Ed.D., Pres.; Kathleen Abbot, Secy.; Peter Vinton, Treas.; Arnold Berlin, M.D.; Leo Bretholz; Deborah Davis; Bernard Koman; Michael R. Rosenthal, Ph.D.

EIN: 030533556

914

Janey Foundation

9642 Kanfer Court

Montgomery Village, MD 20886-5065

Grantmaker type: Public charity.

Purpose and activities: The organization supports the operation of Janey Center for the training and rehabilitation of handicapped children in Kerala, India.

Fields of interest: Physically disabled.

International interests: India.

Limitations: Applications not accepted. Giving limited to Kerala, India. No grants to individuals.

Application information: Contributes only to pre-selected organizations.

Officers: Nalini Pillai, Pres.; George Thomas, Secy.; Thomas Kuruvilla, Treas.

Directors: Sathyan Achath; Valsala Pal, M.D.; Mohan Pillai; P.K. Poulose, M.D.; Vasant Telang, M.D.; John C. Thomas; Raju Varghese, M.D.

EIN: 521389615

915

The Jewish Federation of Greater Washington

6101 Montrose Rd.

Rockville, MD 20852-4816 (301) 230-7230

Contact: Erica Pressman, Dir., Fdn. Svcs.

FAX: (301) 230-7273;

E-mail: erica.pressman@shalomdc.org; URL: http://www.shalomdc.org

Established in 1976 in DC.

Grantmaker type: Public charity.

Financial data (yr. ended 06/30/10): Revenue, $26,270,417; assets, $141,227,680 (M); gifts received, $27,758,571; expenditures, $30,991,349; giving activities include $20,384,230 for grants.

Purpose and activities: The fund and its community have created and maintained a permanent philanthropic structure for the enhancement of the Jewish community in Washington, DC, and for others around the world; providing seed money and grants for special and one-time Jewish needs, the fund helps to strengthen and preserve Jewish heritage for future generations.

Fields of interest: Philanthropy/voluntarism; Public affairs; Community/economic development; Civil/human rights; Education; Human services; International affairs; Jewish agencies & synagogues; Religion.

International interests: Israel.

Type of support: General/operating support; Emergency funds; Program development; Seed money; Matching/challenge support.

Limitations: Applications accepted. Giving on a worldwide basis, with emphasis on the greater metropolitan Washington, DC, area; Israel; and the former Soviet Union. No support for political organizations. No grants to individuals, or for endowments, annual campaigns, or capital campaigns.

Publications: Application guidelines; Annual report (including application guidelines); Financial statement; Grants list; Informational brochure; Newsletter.

Application information: Letters of inquiry are required for initial contact; specific application guidelines are available by e-mail after a conversation regarding the nature of the project seeking support. Application form required.

Initial approach: Telephone

Copies of proposal: 1

Deadline(s): Letter of inquiry Feb. 1; formal application May 1

Board meeting date(s): Monthly, except Jan., July, and Aug.

Final notification: June

Directors: Rabbi Bruce D. Aft; Adam August; Ann Bennett; Dr. Brent A. Berger; Miriam Berkowitz; Michele Hymer Blitz; John Bloomfield; Abba Blum; Rabbi Mendel Bluming; Edward B. Bonder; Fay-Ann Brodie; Stuart L. Brown; Gerald Charnoff; Lyn Chasen; Jeffrey Lee Cohen; and 70 additional directors.

Number of staff: 5 full-time professional; 2 full-time support.

EIN: 530212445

916

Lutheran World Relief

700 Light St.

Baltimore, MD 21230-3850 (410) 230-2700

Contact: Rev. John Arthur Nunes, Pres. and C.E.O.

FAX: (410) 230-2882; E-mail: lwr@lwr.org;

URL: http://www.lwr.org

RSS Feed: http://www.lwr.org/xml/LWRnews.asp

Twitter: http://twitter.com/LuthWorldRelief

Established in 1945 in NY.

Grantmaker type: Public charity.

Financial data (yr. ended 09/30/10): Revenue, $41,988,503; assets, $48,870,628 (M); gifts received, $40,852,835; expenditures, $37,106,746; giving activities include $4,184,635 for grants, and $20,292,901 for 167 grants to organizations outside the U.S.

Purpose and activities: The foundation's goals are to alleviate suffering caused by natural disaster, conflict, or poverty; to enable marginalized people to meet basic needs and improve their lives; and to promote a peaceful, just, and sustainable global community.

Fields of interest: Environment; Agriculture; Disasters, preparedness/services; International development; International relief; Civil/human rights, advocacy; Civil liberties, advocacy; Nonprofit management; Community/economic development; AIDS, people with.

International interests: Africa; Asia; Latin America; Middle East.

Type of support: General/operating support; Emergency funds; Program development; Seed money; Technical assistance; Program evaluation; In-kind gifts.

Limitations: Applications accepted. Giving on an international basis, primarily in Africa, Asia, Latin America, and the Middle East. No support for U.S.-based programs. No grants to individuals.

Publications: Application guidelines; Annual report.

Application information: Application form required.

Initial approach: Download application

Deadline(s): Jan. 25 for Scholarships

Board meeting date(s): Jan., June, and Sept.

Officers and Directors:* Rev. Richard A. Nelson,* Chair.; Gloria Edwards,* Vice-Chair.; Rev. John Arthur Nunes,* Pres. and C.E.O.; Lisa Baumgartner Bonds, V.P., Ext. Rels.; Timothy McCully, V.P., Intl. Progs.; Jeffrey S. Whisenant, V.P., Finance and Admin.; Jonathan D. Schultz,* Secy.; Emeried Cole; Rev. Jessica R. Crist; Rev. Dr. Jon T. Diefenthaler; Rev. Matthew C. Harrison; Jayesh Hines-Shah; Rev. Philip D.W. Krey, Ph.D.; Rev. Rafael Malpica-Pedilla; Emma Graeber Porter; Linda K. Reiser; Myrna Sheie.

Number of staff: 32 full-time professional; 1 part-time professional; 7 full-time support; 1 part-time support.

EIN: 132574963

917
Mercy Center Foundation U.S.A., Inc.
P.O. Box 647
Silver Spring, MD 20918-0647 (240) 793-3188
Contact: Laura B. Hunt, Pres.
E-mail: mercyprojectlare@gmail.com; URL: http://www.mercyproject.org/

Grantmaker type: Public charity.
Financial data (yr. ended 07/31/10): Revenue, $57,320; assets, $70,399 (M); gifts received, $34,725; expenditures, $80,944; program services expenses, $84,596; giving activities include $69,028 for grants.
Purpose and activities: The foundation seeks to help combat disease and poverty in Lare, Kenya by providing compassionate and humanitarian assistance toward sustainable and affordable clean water, health care, education, and micro-enterprise initiatives.
Fields of interest: Human services; Economically disadvantaged.
International interests: Kenya.
Type of support: Grants to individuals.
Limitations: Giving limited to Lare, Kenya.
Officers and Directors: John Njoroge,* Chair.; Sr. Esther Wairimu,* Vice-Chair.; David Methu, Secy.; Brian Doherty, M.A.; Dennis Jasinksi, PE, MBA; Geraldine Jasinski, RN, SCM; Paul Muraya; Agnes Mwangi; Lilian Mwangi; Nathalie Sullivan.
EIN: 542124269

918
The Robert Benson Meyer, Jr. Foundation, Inc.
9800 Sotweed Dr.
Potomac, MD 20854-4718 (301) 299-8236
Contact: Maria Teresa De Z. Meyer, Pres.

Established in 1998 in MD.
Donor: Maria Teresa De Z. Meyer.
Grantmaker type: Independent foundation.
Financial data (yr. ended 12/31/10): Assets, $1,109,651 (M); gifts received, $154,565; expenditures, $237,511; qualifying distributions, $230,207; giving activities include $230,207 for 148 grants (high: $25,000; low: $20).
Fields of interest: Animals/wildlife; Education; Human services; International relief; Catholic federated giving programs; Catholic agencies & churches.
Type of support: General/operating support; Grants to individuals.
Limitations: Applications accepted. Giving primarily in Washington, DC, and MD.
Application information: Application form required.
Initial approach: Letter
Deadline(s): None
Officers and Directors:* Maria Teresa De Z. Meyer,* Pres. and Treas.; Carlos Roberto Bensen Meyer,* V.P.; Katharine Maria Meyer,* Secy.
EIN: 522104075

919
The Harvey M. Meyerhoff Fund, Inc.
1 South St., Ste. 1000
Baltimore, MD 21202-7301
E-mail: info@magnajm.com; URL: http://www.meyerhoffcharitablefunds.org/

Established in 1994 in MD.

Grantmaker type: Independent foundation.
Financial data (yr. ended 12/31/10): Assets, $10,514,015 (M); expenditures, $441,036; qualifying distributions, $319,063; giving activities include $319,063 for grants.
Purpose and activities: Giving primarily for the arts, education, and health services; support also for Jewish organizations and agencies.
Fields of interest: Performing arts, orchestras; Libraries/library science; Scholarships/financial aid; Health organizations, association; Jewish agencies & synagogues.
International interests: Israel.
Type of support: General/operating support; Continuing support; Annual campaigns; Capital campaigns; Building/renovation; Equipment; Endowments; Emergency funds; Program development; Conferences/seminars; Professorships; Curriculum development; Scholarship funds; Research; Program evaluation; Matching/challenge support.
Limitations: Applications not accepted. Giving primarily in MD. No grants to individuals.
Application information: Contributes only to pre-selected organizations.
Officers: Harvey M. Meyerhoff, Pres.; Terry M. Rubenstein, Exec. V.P.; Lee M. Hendler, V.P. and Secy.
Trustees: Jill M. Hieronimus; Joseph Meyerhoff II.
EIN: 521904818

920
The Joseph Meyerhoff Fund, Inc.
1 South St., Ste. 1000
Baltimore, MD 21202-7301
E-mail: info@magnajm.com; URL: http://www.meyerhoffcharitablefunds.org/

Incorporated in 1953 in MD.
Donors: Joseph Meyerhoff‡; Mrs. Joseph Meyerhoff‡; Meyerhoff Charitable Income Trust; Katz Charitable Income Trust; Meyerhoff Charitable Income Trust II; Katz Charitable Income Trust II; Rebecca Meyerhoff Memorial Trusts; The Rebecca Meyerhoff Philanthropic Fund.
Grantmaker type: Independent foundation.
Financial data (yr. ended 12/31/10): Assets, $70,373,573 (M); expenditures, $3,641,706; qualifying distributions, $3,080,441; giving activities include $2,783,934 for 72 grants (high: $531,179; low: $119).
Purpose and activities: Giving primarily to support and encourage cultural and higher educational programs and institutions and to facilitate immigration and absorption of new immigrants into Israel.
Fields of interest: Arts; Higher education; Human services; Jewish federated giving programs; Jewish agencies & synagogues; Immigrants/refugees.
International interests: Israel.
Type of support: General/operating support; Continuing support; Annual campaigns; Capital campaigns; Building/renovation; Equipment; Land acquisition; Endowments; Debt reduction; Emergency funds; Program development; Professorships; Publication; Seed money; Fellowships; Scholarship funds; Research; Matching/challenge support.
Limitations: Applications not accepted. Giving primarily in Baltimore, MD, and New York, NY; some funding also to organizations in Israel. No grants to individuals.

Application information: Contributes only to pre-selected organizations.
Board meeting date(s): May and Oct.
Officer: Terry M. Rubinstein, Exec. V.P.
Number of staff: 1 part-time professional; 1 part-time support.
EIN: 526035997

921
Mid Atlantic Arts Foundation
201 N. Charles St., Ste. 401
Baltimore, MD 21201-4199 (410) 539-6656
Contact: Alan W. Cooper, Exec. Dir.
FAX: (410) 837-5517;
E-mail: maaf@midatlanticarts.org; TDD: (410) 539-4241; URL: http://www.midatlanticarts.org

Established in 1979 in DE.
Grantmaker type: Public charity.
Financial data (yr. ended 06/30/10): Revenue, $4,050,717; assets, $6,106,434 (M); gifts received, $3,919,904; expenditures, $4,983,116; program services expenses, $4,208,538; giving activities include $2,519,293 for 147 grants (high: $90,708; low: $5,000), $116,319 for 68 grants to individuals, and $2,635,612 for foundation-administered programs.
Purpose and activities: The foundation provides leadership and support for the arts in the mid-Atlantic region in partnership with state arts councils and commissions, and is dedicated to growth and appreciation of the arts throughout the region, the nation, and the world.
Fields of interest: International exchange; Arts, folk arts; Visual arts; Performing arts; Arts.
Type of support: Program development; Conferences/seminars; Fellowships; Technical assistance; Exchange programs.
Limitations: Applications accepted. Giving on a worldwide basis, with national giving emphasis on Washington, DC; DE; MD; NJ; NY; OH; PA; VA; WV; and VI.
Publications: Application guidelines; Biennial report; Financial statement; Grants list; Informational brochure; Newsletter.
Application information: Application form required.
Initial approach: Letter or telephone
Deadline(s): Varies
Board meeting date(s): Jan., May, and Oct.
Final notification: Varies
Officers and Directors:* Dorothy Pierce McSweeny,* Chair.; Steven D. Spiess,* Vice-Chair.; E. Scott Johnson,* Esq., Secy.; Carol Ann Herbert,* Treas.; Alan W. Cooper, Exec. Dir.; William W. Carter; Theresa Colvin; Elizabeth M. Dubin; Vernon A. Finch; Susan S. Landis; Magda A. Ratajski; Helen M. Stewart; Lavinia Wohlfarth; and 6 additional directors.
Number of staff: 16 full-time professional; 1 part-time professional.
EIN: 521169382

922
The Morningstar Foundation
c/o Gelman, Rosenberg & Freedman
4550 Montgomery Ave., Ste. 650 N.
Bethesda, MD 20814-3250
Contact: Michael C. Gelman, V.P.

Established in 1982 in DC and MD.

Donors: Michael C. Gelman; Susan R. Gelman; Richard Goldman 1997 Charitable Lead Annuity Trust; Susan R. Gelman Charitable Lead Trust; SSR Charitable Lead Annuity Trust 2004.

Grantmaker type: Independent foundation.

Financial data (yr. ended 12/31/09): Assets, $83,669,233 (M); gifts received, $13,153,176; expenditures, $4,644,603; qualifying distributions, $4,292,429; giving activities include $4,187,683 for 108 grants (high: $500,000; low: $300).

Fields of interest: Arts; Education; Environment; Human services; International peace/security; Jewish agencies & synagogues.

International interests: Israel.

Type of support: General/operating support; Annual campaigns; Capital campaigns.

Limitations: Applications not accepted. Giving primarily in the greater Washington, DC, area and in Israel. No grants to individuals.

Application information: Contributes only to pre-selected organizations. Unsolicited requests for funds not accepted.

Board meeting date(s): Quarterly

Officers: Susan R. Gelman, Pres.; Michael C. Gelman, V.P.; George P. Levendis, Esq., Secy.-Treas.

Number of staff: 1 part-time support.

EIN: 521270464

923

Mpala Wildlife Foundation, Inc.

P.O. Box 137
Riderwood, MD 21139-0137 (410) 244-7507
Contact: Jeffrey K. Gonya, Secy.-Treas.
E-mail: jkgonya@venable.com; URL: http://www.mpala.org
E-Newsletter: http://www.mpala.org/Get_our_Newsletter.php

Established in 1989 in MD; funded in 1990.

Donors: George L. Small†; Princeton University; Smithsonian Institute.

Grantmaker type: Operating foundation.

Financial data (yr. ended 12/31/09): Assets, $4,410,667 (M); gifts received, $240,453; expenditures, $426,033; qualifying distributions, $402,427; giving activities include $336,137 for 3 grants (high: $125,000; low: $96,031).

Purpose and activities: Giving primarily to a wildlife sanctuary and preserve, and operation of a scientific research center, as well as for the operation of a mobile clinic.

Fields of interest: Animals/wildlife, preservation/protection.

International interests: Kenya.

Limitations: Applications not accepted. Giving primarily in Nanyuki, Kenya. No grants to individuals.

Application information: Contributes only to pre-selected organizations.

Officers and Trustees:* Donald C. Graham, Chair.; Jeffrey K. Gonya,* Secy.; William S. Eisenhart, Jr., Tr. Emeritus; Giles Davies; Howard Ende; Laurel Harvey; Dennis Keller; Dr. Ira Rubinoff; John Wreford-Smith.

EIN: 521656147

924

National Alliance of Vietnam American Service Agencies

(also known as NAVASA)
1010 Wayne Ave., Ste. 310
Silver Spring, MD 20910-5657 (301) 587-2781
FAX: (301) 587-2783; E-mail: navasa@navasa.org; Additional tel.: (301) 587-2782; URL: http://www.navasa.org

Established in 1995.

Grantmaker type: Public charity.

Financial data (yr. ended 09/30/10): Revenue, $95,342; assets, $800,874 (M); gifts received, $25,000; expenditures, $420,937; giving activities include $835 for grants to individuals.

Purpose and activities: The alliance's mission is to empower the Vietnamese community in the U.S. and facilitate the transition of Vietnamese refugees and immigrants from dependency to self-sufficiency.

Fields of interest: Minorities/immigrants, centers/services; International migration/refugee issues; Immigrants/refugees.

Officers and Directors:* Vee Phan Nelson,* Chair.; Diem Ngo,* Vice-Chair.; Amra Sabanic,* Vice-Chair.; Ducchi Quan,* Secy.; Duy Pham,* Treas.; Diana Bui; Duc Hong Duong; Bob Jones; Dan Krotz; Yen Pham; Tri Duc Ta; Hoang Tran; Dr. Devance Walker.

EIN: 521885019

925

The W. O'Neil Foundation

5454 Wisconsin Ave., Ste. 730
Chevy Chase, MD 20815-6924 (301) 656-5848
Contact: Helene O'Neil Shere, Pres.

Incorporated in 1948 in OH.

Donors: William O'Neil†; Grace O'Neil†; John J. O'Neil†; Grace O'Neil Regan; and others.

Grantmaker type: Independent foundation.

Financial data (yr. ended 12/31/10): Assets, $50,681,692 (M); gifts received, $50; expenditures, $2,717,102; qualifying distributions, $2,555,850; giving activities include $2,555,850 for grants.

Purpose and activities: Grants primarily given to Roman Catholic Church-related organizations for international emergency relief and for programs that bring food, clothing, shelter, basic medical care, and basic education to the poor of the world, preferably through projects that help the poor help themselves toward these goals. International assistance grants are only made to U.S.-based charities.

Fields of interest: Human services; Human services, emergency aid; Homeless, human services; International development; Catholic agencies & churches; Homeless.

Type of support: General/operating support; Equipment; Program development.

Limitations: Applications accepted. Giving primarily in Washington, DC, and New York, NY. No grants to individuals, or for endowment funds, church and school renovations, capital campaigns, administrative overhead, research, conferences, seminars, or matching gifts; no loans.

Publications: Application guidelines.

Application information: If project coincides with the foundation's interests, a proposal will be requested. Application form not required.

Initial approach: Letter of inquiry
Copies of proposal: 1

Deadline(s): None
Board meeting date(s): Feb., Apr., June, and Sept.

Officers and Trustees:* Helene O'Neil Shere,* Chair. and Pres.; Helene Connellan O'Neil,* Vice-Chair. and V.P.; Jane Wieder,* V.P. and Treas.; Grace O'Neil Regan,* V.P.; Ann O'Neil Gradowski,* Secy.; John J. O'Neil, Jr.; Ann Regan; Mary Regan.

EIN: 346516969

926

Howard and Geraldine Polinger Family Foundation

(formerly Howard and Geraldine Polinger Foundation)
5530 Wisconsin Ave., Ste. 1000
Chevy Chase, MD 20815-4330
Contact: Lorre Polinger, Pres.
E-mail: info@polingerfoundation.org; Tel./fax: (617) 964-6199; URL: http://foundationcenter.org/grantmaker/polinger/

Incorporated in 1968 in MD.

Donors: Howard Polinger†; Geraldine Polinger; Geraldine Polinger Family Trust.

Grantmaker type: Independent foundation.

Financial data (yr. ended 06/30/10): Assets, $36,343,028 (M); gifts received, $20,333,391; expenditures, $1,481,102; qualifying distributions, $1,353,275; giving activities include $1,166,050 for 72 grants (high: $150,000; low: $300).

Purpose and activities: The mission of the foundation is to improve the quality of life for families and their communities through support of innovative projects and successful ongoing programs. The trustees are particularly interested in programs that preserve and strengthen Jewish life and the Jewish People, provide access to and appreciation of performing arts, and enhance the well-being of families. Grants in the latter two categories are made primarily in Washington D.C. and Montgomery County, Maryland. For grants serving the Jewish community, support may be provided to local, national, and/or international organizations.

Fields of interest: Jewish federated giving programs; Performing arts; Youth development; Family services; Jewish agencies & synagogues.

International interests: Israel.

Type of support: General/operating support; Continuing support; Program development; Curriculum development; Matching/challenge support.

Limitations: Giving primarily in the Washington, DC, and Montgomery County, MD, area. No grants to individuals. Requests for capital and endowment grants are not normally accepted.

Publications: Application guidelines; Grants list; Newsletter.

Application information: Full proposals accepted by invitation only. If a full proposal is requested, applicants will be required to complete the Polinger Foundation Application Form and related materials. In many cases, board members and/or staff may conduct a site visit after requesting and reviewing a full proposal. Application form required.

Initial approach: 2-page letter of inquiry (email is preferred) with attachments
Copies of proposal: 1
Deadline(s): None
Board meeting date(s): Spring and fall
Final notification: 1 month after board meeting

Officers and Directors:* Lorre Beth Polinger,* Pres.; Arnold Lee Polinger,* V.P., Fin.; Jan Polinger,* V.P., Grants; Margaret Siegel, Secy.; David Marc Polinger,* Treas.; Geraldine H. Polinger.
Number of staff: 3 part-time professional.
EIN: 526078041

927
Quixote Center, Inc.

P.O. Box 5206
Hyattsville, MD 20782-0206 (301) 699-0042
URL: http://www.quixote.org

Established in 1976 in MD.
Grantmaker type: Public charity.
Financial data (yr. ended 06/30/10): Revenue, $1,175,097; assets, $720,142 (M); gifts received, $1,090,061; expenditures, $932,806; program services expenses, $831,275; giving activities include $311,439 for grants to organizations outside the U.S., and $519,836 for foundation-administered programs.
Purpose and activities: The center focuses on religious and educational development and alleviating the plight of the poor in Haiti and Nicaragua.
Fields of interest: Catholic agencies & churches; International human rights; Human services; Economically disadvantaged.
International interests: Nicaragua; Haiti.
Limitations: Giving limited to the U.S., Haiti, and Nicaragua.
Publications: Annual report; Financial statement.
Officers and Directors:* Noelle M. Hanrahan,* Pres.; Frank DeBernardo,* V.P.; William D'Antonio,* Ph.D., Treas.; John F. Bresette, M.D.; Sr. Mary Jeremy Daigler, Ph.D.; Susan Duncan; Martha Turner; Dan Walsh.
EIN: 521055742

928
SAT-7 North America

24 W. Dover St.
Easton, MD 21601-2616 (410) 770-9804
Contact: Ruth S. Thomas, Dir., Finance
FAX: (410) 770-9807; E-mail: usa@sat7.org; Mailing address: P.O. Box 2770, Easton, MD 21601;
URL: http://www.sat7.org

Grantmaker type: Public charity.
Financial data (yr. ended 12/31/10): Revenue, $8,901,131; assets, $1,918,309 (M); gifts received, $8,896,462; expenditures, $8,777,817; giving activities include $6,893,551 for grants to organizations outside the U.S.
Purpose and activities: The organization works to see a growing church in the Middle East and north Africa with an opportunity to witness Christianity through inspirational, informative, and educational television services.
Fields of interest: Christian agencies & churches.
International interests: North Africa; Middle East; Africa.
Limitations: Applications not accepted. Giving primarily to northern Africa and the Middle East.
Publications: Annual report; Financial statement.
Application information: Contributes only to a pre-selected organization.
Board meeting date(s): Apr. and Oct.
Officers and Board Members:* Ray Padron,* Chair.; Habib Badr,* Intl. Chair.; Terence Ascott, C.E.O.;

Debbie Brink, Sr. V.P., Devel.; Peter Schulze,* Secy.; Phyllis Smith, Treas.; James Blankemeyer; Jean Bouchebel; Nancy Stafford.
Number of staff: 6 full-time professional; 4 full-time support; 3 part-time support.
EIN: 232964829

929
The Shared Earth Foundation

113 Hoffman Ln.
Chestertown, MD 21620-1913 (410) 778-6868
Contact: Caroline D. Gabel, C.E.O. and Pres.
FAX: (410) 778-9050;
E-mail: sharedearth@aol.com; URL: http://www.sharedearth.org/

Established in 1999 in MD.
Donor: Caroline D. Gabel.
Grantmaker type: Independent foundation.
Financial data (yr. ended 03/31/11): Assets, $6,342,601 (M); gifts received, $430,000; expenditures, $539,570; qualifying distributions, $475,340; giving activities include $475,340 for grants.
Purpose and activities: Support for the environment, biodiversity, the protection and enhancement of the natural habitat, and the protection of wildlife and endangered species.
Fields of interest: Environment, natural resources; Environment, land resources; Environment; Animals/wildlife, preservation/protection; Animals/ wildlife, endangered species; Indigenous peoples.
International interests: Bolivia; Chile; Guatemala; India; Malaysia; Mexico; Pakistan; Papua New Guinea; Peru.
Type of support: General/operating support; Continuing support; Program development; Research; Technical assistance; Matching/challenge support.
Limitations: Applications not accepted. Giving on a national and international basis. No grants to individuals, or for scholarships, fellowships, or financial aid.
Publications: Annual report; Grants list.
Application information: Unsolicited requests for funds not accepted. Applications are by invitation only. See foundation web site for information.
Board meeting date(s): Quarterly
Officer: Caroline D. Gabel, C.E.O. and Pres.
EIN: 522151843

930
Gordon V. & Helen C. Smith Foundation

8716 Crider Brook Way
Potomac, MD 20854-4547 (301) 469-8597
Contact: Gordon V. Smith, Pres.

Established in 1986 in MD.
Donors: Gordon V. Smith; Helen C. Smith; Douglas I. Smith; Anne U. Smith; Miller and Smith, Inc.
Grantmaker type: Independent foundation.
Financial data (yr. ended 12/31/10): Assets, $13,953,111 (M); gifts received, $88,185; expenditures, $3,746,805; qualifying distributions, $3,286,264; giving activities include $3,207,782 for 45 grants (high: $969,265; low: $100).
Purpose and activities: Support primarily for education; also for Christian and health organizations in which family members are currently involved.

Fields of interest: Christian agencies & churches; Higher education; Theological school/education; Health care; Religion.
Type of support: General/operating support; Building/renovation; Scholarship funds.
Limitations: Applications accepted. Giving primarily in Washington, DC, IL, MD, OH, VA, and WI; funding also in Arusha, Tanzania. No grants to individuals.
Application information: Application form not required.
Deadline(s): None
Officers: Gordon V. Smith, Pres.; Helen C. Smith, V.P.
Directors: Cynthia J. Skarbek; Bruce G. Smith; Douglas I. Smith.
EIN: 521440846
Recent grants for international programs:
930-1 Opportunity International, Oak Brook, IL, $488,628. For general support. 2009.
930-2 School of Saint Jude, Arusha, Tanzania, Zanzibar and Pemba, $743,377. For general support. 2009.
930-3 Synergos Institute, New York, NY, $32,400. For general support. 2009.

931
Strategic Resource Group, Inc.

11 S. Washington St.
Easton, MD 21601-3046
Additional tel. (Columbia/DC): (301) 596-0190;
toll-free tel.: (800) 774-7739

Grantmaker type: Public charity.
Financial data (yr. ended 12/31/10): Revenue, $10,242,475; assets, $9,646,573 (M); gifts received, $10,236,605; expenditures, $7,062,732; giving activities include $2,974,739 for grants, and $2,247,821 for grants to organizations outside the U.S.
Purpose and activities: The organization provides resources to Christian ministries in the Arabian Peninsula, the Middle East, and North Africa.
Fields of interest: Christian agencies & churches; Community/economic development.
International interests: North Africa; Middle East.
Limitations: Giving limited to the Middle East and North Africa.
Directors: Dr. Cliff Daffron; Russell Kerr; Jack Kincaid; Dennis Neal; Bob Roebuck.
EIN: 330780945

932
The Laszlo N. Tauber Family Foundation

6000 Exec. Blvd., Ste. 600
North Bethesda, MD 20852
E-mail: info@tauberfoundation.com; URL: http://www.tauberfoundation.org/page1/about.html
Grants List: http://www.tauberfoundation.org/page3/grants.html

Established in 2004 in MD.
Donor: Laszlo N. Tauber‡.
Grantmaker type: Independent foundation.
Financial data (yr. ended 12/31/09): Assets, $169,104,893 (M); gifts received, $13,661,067; expenditures, $8,278,758; qualifying distributions, $7,318,838; giving activities include $6,986,199 for 63 grants (high: $1,361,875; low: $1,000; average: $1,000–$250,000).

Fields of interest: Medical research; Jewish agencies & synagogues; Elementary/secondary education.
Limitations: Applications not accepted. Giving primarily in Baltimore, MD. No grants to individuals.
Application information: Contributes only to pre-selected organizations.
Officers and Directors: * Ingrid D. Tauber,* Pres.; Alfred I. Tauber,* Secy.-Treas.
Number of staff: 2 full-time professional.
EIN: 300208793
Recent grants for international programs:

932-1 American Friends of Brothers Aid, Monsey, NY, $36,000. For general support. 2008.

932-2 American Friends of Haifa University, New York, NY, $52,300. For Fieldwork Program. 2008.

932-3 American Friends of Meir Panim, Brooklyn, NY, $15,000. To mend rifts in Israeli society. 2008.

932-4 American Friends of Sarah Herzog Hospital, New York, NY, $70,000. For Israel Center for the Treatment of Psychotrauma. 2008.

932-5 American Friends of the Tel Aviv University, New York, NY, $345,000. For Scholarship Fund. 2008.

932-6 American Jewish Joint Distribution Committee, New York, NY, $100,000. For program support. 2008.

932-7 American Society for Technion-Israel Institute of Technology, New York, NY, $25,000. For Jerome and Rose Grossman Scholarship Fund. 2008.

932-8 American Society for Yad Vashem, New York, NY, $25,000. For program support. 2008.

932-9 American Society of the University of Haifa, New York, NY, $246,558. For Fieldwork Program. 2008.

932-10 International Rescue Committee, New York, NY, $10,000. For general support. 2008.

932-11 New Israel Fund, Washington, DC, $1,556,500. For program support. 2008.

932-12 PEF Israel Endowment Funds, New York, NY, $376,668. For general support. 2008.

932-13 Yad Ezra of America Foundation, Brooklyn, NY, $10,000. For program support. 2008.

933
The Taylor Foundation, Inc.
P.O. Box 396
Ellicott City, MD 21041-0396

Established in 1952 in MD.
Donors: Irving J. Taylor, M.D.; Bruce T. Taylor, M.D.; Edith Taylor.
Grantmaker type: Independent foundation.
Financial data (yr. ended 12/31/10): Assets, $3,038,684 (M); expenditures, $184,505; qualifying distributions, $167,110; giving activities include $167,110 for grants.
Purpose and activities: Giving to Jewish agencies.
Fields of interest: Arts; Education; Human services; Jewish federated giving programs; Jewish agencies & synagogues.
International interests: Israel.
Limitations: Applications not accepted. Giving primarily in MD. No grants to individuals.
Application information: Contributes only to pre-selected organizations.
Officers: Irving J. Taylor, M.D., Pres.; Bruce T. Taylor, M.D., Secy.
EIN: 526056357

934
The Harry and Jeanette Weinberg Foundation, Inc.
7 Park Center Ct.
Owings Mills, MD 21117-4200 (410) 654-8500
Contact: Rachel Garbow Monroe, C.O.O.
E-mail: info@theweinbergfoundation.org;
URL: http://www.hjweinbergfoundation.org
Blog: http://hjweinbergfoundation.org/blog/
E-Newsletter: http://hjweinbergfoundation.org/publications/e-newsletters/e-newsletter-sign-up/
Facebook: http://www.facebook.com/pages/The-Harry-and-Jeanette-Weinberg-Foundation-Inc/169299436473114
Grantee Perception Report: http://hjweinbergfoundation.org/publications/what-we-have-learned/
RSS Feed: http://hjweinbergfoundation.org/ficsp/forum/read.php?1,26
Twitter: https://twitter.com/hjweinbergfdn
Weingberg Fellows Program: http://www.hjweinbergfoundation.org/about/fellows_about.php
YouTube: http://www.youtube.com/user/HJWeinbergFoundation

Incorporated in 1959 in MD.
Donors: Harry Weinberg‡; and various companies.
Grantmaker type: Independent foundation.
Financial data (yr. ended 02/28/11): Assets, $2,072,697,349 (M); expenditures, $107,247,858; qualifying distributions, $89,476,093; giving activities include $86,059,465 for 620 grants (high: $3,390,000; low: $250; average: $25,000–$500,000), and $571,717 for 2 foundation-administered programs.
Purpose and activities: Support for programs and direct services (including general operating grants) and capital projects that assist financially disadvantaged individuals primarily located in Maryland, Hawaii, Northeast Pennsylvania, New York, Israel and the Former Soviet Union.
Fields of interest: Education; Health care; Food services; Housing/shelter; Human services; Aging, centers/services; Aging; Disabilities, people with; Economically disadvantaged.
International interests: Israel; Soviet Union (Former).
Type of support: General/operating support; Capital campaigns; Building/renovation; Equipment; Matching/challenge support.
Limitations: Applications accepted. Giving nationally, primarily in MD, HI, northeast PA, NY, and internationally to Israel and the Former Soviet Union. No support for political organizations, colleges, universities, think tanks, or for arts organizations. No grants to individuals, or for deficit financing, annual giving, publications or for scholarships.
Application information: Unsolicited full proposals will not be accepted. The foundation will invite appropriate proposals following submission of letter of inquiry. Guidelines for LOI and invited proposals available on foundation web site. Application form not required.
Initial approach: Complete Letter of Inquiry after reviewing funding guidelines
Copies of proposal: 1
Deadline(s): Rolling basis
Board meeting date(s): Periodically
Final notification: Within 60 days
Officers and Trustees: * Donn Weinberg,* Chair.; Rachel Garbow Monroe, Pres.; John F. Lingenfelter, V.P., Finance; Robin Hutchason, Cont.; Joel Winegarden, Corp. Off.; Barry I. Schloss,*

Secy.-Treas.; Alvin Awaya; Hon. Ellen M. Heller; Robert T. Kelly, Jr.
Number of staff: 22
EIN: 526037034
Recent grants for international programs:

934-1 African Jewish Congress, Johannesburg, South Africa, $36,000. For operation of the only home for older Jewish adults in Zimbabwe. 2010.

934-2 Albert Schweitzer Fellowship, Baltimore, Baltimore, MD, $25,000. For professional and medical students to serve needy individuals. 2010.

934-3 American Committee for Tel Aviv Foundation, New York, NY, $300,000. To support construction of school for students with cerebral palsy. 2010.

934-4 American Committee for Tel Aviv Foundation, New York, NY, $75,000. To support construction of hydrotherapy pool in a school. 2010.

934-5 American Friends of Jordan River Village Foundation, Stamford, CT, $250,000. For construction of Paul Newman, Hole-in-the-Wall camp in Israel. 2010.

934-6 American Friends of Koret Israel Economic Development Fund, San Francisco, CA, $400,000. For Israel Microenterprise Initiative supporting efforts of economically disadvantaged. 2010.

934-7 American Friends of PTACH, Brooklyn, NY, $90,000. For screening and intervention therapies for children with learning disabilities. 2010.

934-8 American Jewish Committee, New York, NY, $300,000. For educational seminars in Israel for civic, ethnic, and religious leaders. 2010.

934-9 American Jewish Joint Distribution Committee, New York, NY, $2,000,000. To provide medicine and welfare for populations in the former Soviet Union. 2010.

934-10 American Jewish Joint Distribution Committee, New York, NY, $2,000,000. To provide medicine and welfare for populations in the former Soviet Union. 2010.

934-11 American Jewish Joint Distribution Committee, New York, NY, $2,000,000. For programs for older adults. 2010.

934-12 American Jewish Joint Distribution Committee, New York, NY, $1,555,000. To provide medicine and welfare for populations in the former Soviet Union. 2010.

934-13 American Jewish Joint Distribution Committee, New York, NY, $1,500,000. For work to ensure a Jewish Future. 2010.

934-14 American Jewish Joint Distribution Committee, New York, NY, $1,500,000. To provide medicine and welfare for populations in the former Soviet Union. 2010.

934-15 American Jewish Joint Distribution Committee, New York, NY, $1,500,000. For the Odessa, Ukraine Jewish Community Center. 2010.

934-16 American Jewish Joint Distribution Committee, New York, NY, $1,500,000. To support JDC's new Employment Initiative in Israel. 2010.

934-17 American Jewish Joint Distribution Committee, New York, NY, $500,000. For Argentina Welfare. 2010.

934-18 American Jewish Joint Distribution Committee, New York, NY, $500,000. For LeDor VaDor Senior Home Argentina. 2010.

934-19 American Jewish Joint Distribution Committee, New York, NY, $500,000. To support groups that help to employ people of Israel's worst areas. 2010.

934-20 American Jewish Joint Distribution Committee, New York, NY, $500,000. To support services for Jews in the Former Soviet Union. 2010.

934-21 American Jewish Joint Distribution Committee, New York, NY, $500,000. To support services for Jews in the Former Soviet Union. 2010.

934-22 American Jewish Joint Distribution Committee, New York, NY, $450,000. For Young Leaders' Institute. 2010.

934-23 American Jewish Joint Distribution Committee, New York, NY, $390,500. For Ensuring a Jewish Future. 2010.

934-24 American Jewish Joint Distribution Committee, New York, NY, $250,000. For ESHEL's Capital projects. 2010.

934-25 American Jewish Joint Distribution Committee, New York, NY, $200,000. For Odessa, Ukraine JCC. 2010.

934-26 American Jewish Joint Distribution Committee, New York, NY, $100,000. For Romanian Older Adults. 2010.

934-27 American Jewish Joint Distribution Committee, New York, NY, $50,000. For general operations of the Grantee. 2010.

934-28 American Jewish Joint Distribution Committee, New York, NY, $50,000. To provide emergency services to Haiti after the earthquake. 2010.

934-29 American Jewish Joint Distribution Committee, New York, NY, $34,000. For Jewish Community Center (JCC) in India. 2010.

934-30 American Jewish Joint Distribution Committee, New York, NY, $20,500. To support the Bayiti Old Age Home in India. 2010.

934-31 American Jewish Joint Distribution Committee, New York, NY, $10,000. For Parents and Children Together Program (PACT) in Israel. 2010.

934-32 American Jewish Joint Distribution Committee, ESHEL, New York, NY, $1,500,000. For capital projects. JDC-ESHEL strives to improve the status of the elderly population in Israel, developing conditions and services to guarantee better quality of life for the elderly, and to improve the image of older people to society as a whole. 2010.

934-33 Beth David Institute, Center for Deaf-Blind Persons, Tel Aviv, Israel, $90,000. For services to assist economically disadvantaged individuals. 2010.

934-34 Boundless Playgrounds, New Haven, CT, $94,488. For promoting and facilitating the development of 5 Boundless playgrounds. 2010.

934-35 David Horowitz Freedom Center, Sherman Oaks, CA, $35,000. To continue support for the Grantee's Defense of Israel Project. 2010.

934-36 David Horowitz Freedom Center, Sherman Oaks, CA, $25,000. To continue support for Grantee's Defense of Israel Project. 2010.

934-37 Defiant Requiem Foundation, Washington, DC, $10,000. For this holocaust related program. 2010.

934-38 ELEM Youth in Distress, New York, NY, $200,000. For funding for drop in and resource center for homeless. 2010.

934-39 Friends of Yad LKashish/Lifeline for the Old, Englewood, NJ, $100,000. For Monthly Stipend Program in which poor older adults work part-time. 2010.

934-40 Friends of Yemin Orde, Rockville, MD, $200,000. For introduction of Yemin Orde's programs into five youth villages in Israel. 2010.

934-41 General Assistance, Southfield, MI, $172,000. For renovation and construction of day center in Haifa. 2010.

934-42 Global FoodBanking Network, Chicago, IL, $500,000. To assist in reaching to food banks in multiple countries. 2010.

934-43 Hawaiian Eye Foundation, Mililani, HI, $75,000. For funds for Pacific Vision Outreach Equipment Project. 2010.

934-44 Hazon Yeshaya, Jerusalem, Israel, $200,000. For food assistance program, free dental clinic, and child day care program. 2010.

934-45 Hillel: The Foundation for Jewish Campus Life, Washington, DC, $37,500. For creation of Tzedek Hillel Centers in the Former Soviet Union. 2010.

934-46 Hillel: The Foundation for Jewish Campus Life, Austin, TX, $50,000. To support Grantee's tzedek service, leadership, and pro-Israel programs. 2010.

934-47 Idan, The Association for Community Services for the Elderly, Jerusalem, Israel, $75,000. For Idan Belt Byer Facility Upgrade project. 2010.

934-48 ImagineNations Group, Pasadena, MD, $250,000. To support start-up expenses of ImagineNations' new and ambitious program. 2010.

934-49 International Rescue Committee, New York, NY, $17,500. For operating support for safe, educational environment for refugee youth. 2010.

934-50 Israel Elwyn, Jerusalem, Israel, $125,000. To expand services to pre-school children with disabilities in Jerusalem. 2010.

934-51 Israel Sports Center for the Disabled, Friends of, Philadelphia, PA, $90,000. For renovation of the Israel Sport Center for the Disabled. 2010.

934-52 Israel Venture Network, Palo Alto, CA, $100,000. For Preparatory for Girls of Ethiopian Origin program. 2010.

934-53 Jerusalem Dental Center for Children, Jerusalem, Israel, $110,000. For Luba Slome Jerusalem Dental Clinic. 2010.

934-54 Jerusalem Foundation, Jerusalem, Israel, $235,998. To assist in purchasing and renovating its current building. 2010.

934-55 Jerusalem Foundation, New York, NY, $10,000. To enable Jerusalem Chamber Music Festival to host older adults. 2010.

934-56 Jewish Agency for Israel, New York, NY, $250,000. For construction of new dormitory at Bat Zion Academy for Girls. 2010.

934-57 Jewish Federations of North America, New York, NY, $400,000. For Operation Promise. 2010.

934-58 Jewish Federations of North America, Overseas Supplemental Giving Israel, New York, NY, $12,000. For volunteer projects by students at the Ruth Z. Korman Pelech School. 2010.

934-59 Konishiki Kids Foundation, Mililani, HI, $10,000. For educational and cultural programs for disadvantaged children. 2010.

934-60 L Man Tishma Foundation, New York, NY, $80,000. To fund vital intervention on behalf of children with autism in Jerusalem. 2010.

934-61 LIGHT Health and Wellness Comprehensive Services, Baltimore, MD, $25,000. For services to women and children involved in prostitution and human trafficking. 2010.

934-62 PEF Israel Endowment Funds, New York, NY, $500,000. For two new buildings at the Jerusalem Hills Children's Home. 2010.

934-63 PEF Israel Endowment Funds, New York, NY, $400,000. For services to Orthodox Jewish women with intellectual disabilities. 2010.

934-64 PEF Israel Endowment Funds, New York, NY, $339,000. For Rehabilitation Day Care Center for toddlers with severe disabilities. 2010.

934-65 PEF Israel Endowment Funds, New York, NY, $300,000. For Home for Life for 28 elderly, mentally impaired residents. 2010.

934-66 PEF Israel Endowment Funds, New York, NY, $300,000. For rehabilitative center for toddlers and children with cerebral palsy. 2010.

934-67 PEF Israel Endowment Funds, New York, NY, $275,000. To improve quality of life of people with special intellectual disabilities. 2010.

934-68 PEF Israel Endowment Funds, New York, NY, $210,000. To assist in building a permanent home for disabled children. 2010.

934-69 PEF Israel Endowment Funds, New York, NY, $200,000. For systemic change in Israel's social and geographic peripheries. 2010.

934-70 PEF Israel Endowment Funds, New York, NY, $200,000. For construction of two buildings for 200 at-risk children. 2010.

934-71 PEF Israel Endowment Funds, New York, NY, $200,000. For food gleaning program. 2010.

934-72 PEF Israel Endowment Funds, New York, NY, $160,000. For dental treatments and oral health care education for low-income persons. 2010.

934-73 PEF Israel Endowment Funds, New York, NY, $140,000. For memory club in Jerusalem for individuals with dementia. 2010.

934-74 PEF Israel Endowment Funds, New York, NY, $140,000. For memory club in Jerusalem for individuals with dementia. 2010.

934-75 PEF Israel Endowment Funds, New York, NY, $125,000. For children with autism home-based treatments. 2010.

934-76 PEF Israel Endowment Funds, New York, NY, $115,000. For The Weekend Retreat Program for children with disabilities. 2010.

934-77 PEF Israel Endowment Funds, New York, NY, $100,000. For providing emotional assistance and psychological support. 2010.

934-78 PEF Israel Endowment Funds, New York, NY, $100,000. For treatments and life skills workshops for mentally ill young people. 2010.

934-79 PEF Israel Endowment Funds, New York, NY, $90,000. To enhance quality of life and level of functioning to mentally ill. 2010.

934-80 PEF Israel Endowment Funds, New York, NY, $80,000. For community clubs that provide psychosocial services to Holocaust survivors. 2010.

934-81 PEF Israel Endowment Funds, New York, NY, $75,000. For program giving to low-income women with the tools to create small business. 2010.

934-82 PEF Israel Endowment Funds, New York, NY, $60,000. For center for people with physical, sensory, and mental disabilities. 2010.

934-83 PEF Israel Endowment Funds, New York, NY, $60,000. For services in the community for poor adults with severe physical disabilities. 2010.

934-84 PEF Israel Endowment Funds, New York, NY, $60,000. For subsidized treatments for over 1,000 children and adults with special needs. 2010.

934-85 PEF Israel Endowment Funds, New York, NY, $60,000. For continued establishment and growth of programs for transitional youth. 2010.

934-86 PEF Israel Endowment Funds, New York, NY, $57,000. For Methadone Day Clinic that will assist care through drug substitutes. 2010.

934-87 PEF Israel Endowment Funds, New York, NY, $50,000. For costs of professional staff, especially caseworkers, for foster care. 2010.

934-88 PEF Israel Endowment Funds, New York, NY, $50,000. For Early Intervention and Rehabilitation Programs for deaf children. 2010.

934-89 PEF Israel Endowment Funds, New York, NY, $50,000. For funding of Tech Careers program that assists poor Ethiopian Jews. 2010.

934-90 PEF Israel Endowment Funds, New York, NY, $50,000. For medical equipment for loan to the needy, adults, sick and individuals with special needs. 2010.

934-91 PEF Israel Endowment Funds, New York, NY, $50,000. For after-school centers for children at risk. 2010.

934-92 PEF Israel Endowment Funds, New York, NY, $50,000. For training of more children, youth, and adults. 2010.

934-93 PEF Israel Endowment Funds, New York, NY, $50,000. To increase of services at Haamakim Community Mental Health Center. 2010.

934-94 PEF Israel Endowment Funds, New York, NY, $50,000. To support outreach to poor and disadvantaged individuals with disabilities. 2010.

934-95 PEF Israel Endowment Funds, New York, NY, $50,000. Toward center for treatment of people with co-occurring illnesses. 2010.

934-96 PEF Israel Endowment Funds, New York, NY, $45,000. For project that will identify 240 children at risk who are learning disabled. 2010.

934-97 PEF Israel Endowment Funds, New York, NY, $45,000. For therapy for children with disabilities in Israel. 2010.

934-98 PEF Israel Endowment Funds, New York, NY, $33,000. To create standardized testing and licensing for Israeli Sign Language. 2010.

934-99 PEF Israel Endowment Funds, New York, NY, $30,000. For Open Door Program for Youth with Physical Disabilities. 2010.

934-100 PEF Israel Endowment Funds, New York, NY, $30,000. For operation of workshop for 65 mentally disabled adults. 2010.

934-101 PEF Israel Endowment Funds, New York, NY, $26,000. For project aimed at increasing awareness and services to Alzheimer's patients. 2010.

934-102 Shekel, Jerusalem, Israel, $50,000. To support establishment of Trauma Center for Children. 2010.

934-103 Tikva Childrens Home, New York, NY, $300,000. To support increasing the capacity to provide homes in Odessa, Ukraine. 2010.

934-104 Yad Sarah, Jerusalem, Israel, $300,000. To support expansion and renovation of headquarters building. 2010.

934-105 Youth Renewal Fund, New York, NY, $100,000. To support program that provides educational help to poor Israeli students. 2010.

935
The Weiss Foundation
c/o Gelman Rosenberg & Freedman
4550 Montgomery Ave., Ste. 650 N.
Bethesda, MD 20814-3250

Established in 1993 in DC.
Donor: Stanley Weiss.
Grantmaker type: Operating foundation.

Financial data (yr. ended 09/30/09): Assets, $429,476 (M); gifts received, $250,000; expenditures, $525,002; qualifying distributions, $517,952; giving activities include $407,250 for 20 grants (high: $208,000; low: $750), and $208,000 for foundation-administered programs.
Purpose and activities: Focus on educating the public on issues concerning national and international security, including matters of defense policy and the promotion of democratic institutions and societies.
Fields of interest: Children/youth, services; International affairs, arms control; International affairs; Public policy, research.
Type of support: Continuing support; Endowments; Program development; Research.
Limitations: Applications not accepted. Giving primarily in the greater metropolitan Washington, DC, area, and New York, NY. No grants to individuals.
Publications: Financial statement.
Application information: Contributes only to pre-selected organizations.
Officers: Stanley Weiss, Pres.; Lisa Weiss, V.P.; Anthony Weiss, Secy.
Director: Lori Christina Lurie.
Number of staff: 1 full-time professional; 1 part-time professional.
EIN: 521848413

936
Windsor Foundation, Inc.
313 Talbot Blvd.
Chestertown, MD 21620-3000
Application address: c/o Joan Farrar, P.O. Box 92, Galena, MD 21635, tel.: (410) 648-5440

Established in 2004 in MD.
Donor: USA Fulfillment, Inc.
Grantmaker type: Independent foundation.
Financial data (yr. ended 12/31/10): Assets, $1,142,678 (M); gifts received, $1,130,090; expenditures, $466,170; qualifying distributions, $459,594; giving activities include $459,594 for grants.
Purpose and activities: Giving primarily for Christian organizations.
Fields of interest: Community/economic development; Christian agencies & churches.
International interests: Romania.
Limitations: Applications accepted. Giving primarily in FL, GA, MD, NC, and PA. No grants to individuals.
Application information: Application form required.
  Initial approach: Letter
  Deadline(s): None
Directors: Glenn Evans; Joan Farrar; Robert R. Farrar; Will Larose.
EIN: 201484900

MASSACHUSETTS

937
Adelson Family Foundation
300 First Ave.
Needham, MA 02494 (781) 972-5950
FAX: (781) 972-5999;
E-mail: proposals@adelsonfoundation.org;
URL: http://www.adelsonfoundation.org/AFF/index.html

Established in 2007.
Donors: Dr. Miriam Adelson; Sheldon G. Adelson.
Grantmaker type: Independent foundation.
Financial data (yr. ended 12/31/09): Assets, $20,827 (M); gifts received, $31,269,849; expenditures, $31,540,340; qualifying distributions, $31,539,517; giving activities include $30,641,159 for 18 grants (high: $21,350,000; low: $10,000).
Purpose and activities: The primary purpose of the foundation is to strengthen the State of Israel and the Jewish people. The foundation focuses on the following categories: Healthcare, Holocaust and Anti-Semitism awareness, Israel Advocacy and defense, Israel studies, Jewish and Zionist identity and education, media and culture, and welfare.
Fields of interest: Human services; Health care; Jewish agencies & synagogues.
International interests: Israel.
Limitations: Applications not accepted. Giving primarily in NY; some giving also in Las Vegas, NV.
Officer: Michael Bohnen, Pres.
Trustees: Sheldon G. Anderson; Dr. Miriam Adelson.
EIN: 047024330
Recent grants for international programs:
937-1 American Society for Yad Vashem, New York, NY, $3,000,000. For general support. 2009.
937-2 Birthright Israel Foundation, New York, NY, $21,350,000. For general support. 2009.
937-3 Girls Town/Or Chadash, Brooklyn, NY, $500,000. For general support. 2009.
937-4 Shalem Foundation, New York, NY, $997,326. For general support. 2009.
937-5 Zionist Organization of America, New York, NY, $250,000. For general support. 2009.

938
Dr. Miriam and Sheldon G. Adelson Medical Research Foundation
300 1st Ave.
Needham, MA 02494-2736 (781) 972-5900
Contact: Marissa White
E-mail: info@adelsonfoundation.org; URL: http://adelsonfoundation.org/AMRF/home.php

Established in 2006 in MA.
Donors: Sheldon G. Adelson; Dr. Miriam Adelson.
Grantmaker type: Independent foundation.
Financial data (yr. ended 12/31/09): Assets, $651,663 (M); gifts received, $10,449,012; expenditures, $10,703,501; qualifying distributions, $10,632,609; giving activities include $8,427,316 for 34 grants (high: $1,736,051; low: $5,000).
Purpose and activities: The foundation is committed to a model of open and highly integrated collaboration among outstanding investigators who participate in goal-directed basic and clinical

research to prevent, reduce or eliminate disabling and life-threatening illness.

Fields of interest: Cancer research; Brain research; Neuroscience research; Medical research.

Limitations: Giving on a national basis.

Application information: Funding for collaborations within program areas only. Application form required.

  Initial approach: Letter

  Deadline(s): None

Officers: Kenneth H. Fasman, Ph.D., V.P. and C.S.O.; Steven Garfinkel, V.P. and General Counsel.

Trustees: Miriam Adelson, M.D.; Sheldon G. Adelson.

EIN: 047023433

Recent grants for international programs:

938-1 Tel Aviv University, Tel Aviv, Israel, $190,000. For medical research. 2009.

938-2 Weizmann Institute of Science, Rehovot, Israel, $598,056. For medical research. 2009.

939
Noubar & Anna Afeyan Foundation

1 Sunset Ridge
Lexington, MA   02421-6031

Established in 1999 in MA.

Donors: Noubar Afeyan; Raffi Festekjian.

Grantmaker type: Independent foundation.

Financial data (yr. ended 12/31/10): Assets, $713,014 (M); gifts received, $773,434; expenditures, $377,249; qualifying distributions, $334,500; giving activities include $334,500 for 20 grants (high: $50,000; low: $500).

Purpose and activities: Giving primarily for Armenian related projects and issues.

Fields of interest: Education; Human services.

International interests: Armenia.

Limitations: Applications not accepted. Giving primarily in Armenia, with some giving in MA. No grants to individuals.

Application information: Contributes only to pre-selected organizations.

Trustees: Noubar Afeyan; Anna Karin M. Gunnarson.

EIN: 043489109

940
The Alchemy Foundation

c/o Kyra L. Montagu
76 Walnut Pl.
Brookline, MA   02445-6750

Established in 2000 in MA.

Donors: Jean I. Montagu; Kyra L. Montagu.

Grantmaker type: Independent foundation.

Financial data (yr. ended 12/31/10): Assets, $3,834,243 (M); gifts received, $2,606; expenditures, $361,967; qualifying distributions, $323,120; giving activities include $323,120 for 200 grants (high: $150,000; low: $25).

Purpose and activities: Giving primarily to international refugee projects in Africa, and health initiatives in Vietnam and internationally.

Fields of interest: International migration/refugee issues; Arts; Education; Human services.

International interests: Africa; Vietnam.

Type of support: Program development.

Limitations: Applications not accepted. Giving on a national basis (with emphasis on MA) and on an international basis (with emphasis on Africa and Vietnam). No grants to individuals, or for capital.

Application information: Contributes only to pre-selected organizations.

  Board meeting date(s): Oct.

Trustees: Jean I. Montagu; Kyra L. Montagu.

EIN: 043541830

941
American Foundation for Bulgaria, Inc.

167 Newbury St.
Boston, MA   02116-2834
E-mail: contact@afbulgaria.org

Grantmaker type: Public charity.

Financial data (yr. ended 12/31/09): Revenue, $3,811,315; assets, $3,230,741 (M); gifts received, $3,766,485; expenditures, $879,470; giving activities include $50,000 for grants, and $478,311 for grants to organizations outside the U.S.

Purpose and activities: The foundation sponsors research, educational, and cultural outreach projects in both Bulgaria and the U.S.

Fields of interest: International affairs; International exchange.

International interests: Bulgaria.

Type of support: Scholarships—to individuals.

Limitations: Giving primarily in Bulgaria.

Officers: Diko Mihov, Pres.; Theodore Vassilev, Exec. Dir.

Director: Alexey Hristov.

EIN: 200361839

942
The American Ireland Fund

211 Congress St.
Boston, MA   02110-2410   (617) 574-0720
FAX: (617) 574-0730; *E-mail:* info@irlfunds.org;
URL: http://www.irlfunds.org/aif/

Established in 1976.

Grantmaker type: Public charity.

Financial data (yr. ended 12/31/10): Revenue, $41,698,499; assets, $11,233,509 (M); gifts received, $43,123,015; expenditures, $44,735,256; giving activities include $1,471,158 for grants, and $39,266,155 for grants to organizations outside the U.S.

Purpose and activities: The fund promotes the peaceful, charitable, and cultural causes in the United States and Ireland for people of both Irish and non-Irish descent.

International interests: Ireland.

Type of support: Scholarships—to individuals.

Limitations: Giving on a national and international basis.

Officers and Directors:* Loretta Brennan Glucksman,* Chair.; Daniel M. Rooney,* Vice-Chair.; A.W.B. Vincent,* Vice-Chair.; Kinglsey Aikins, Pres. and C.E.O.; Sheila O'Malley,* Secy.; Christopher M. Condron,* Treas.; Elizabeth Frawley Bagley; Patrick Broe; Jeremiah M. Callaghan; Thomas Cashman; Gerald Cassidy; Thomas Codd; Christopher Condron; John Connors; Michael Corboy; and 59 additional directors.

EIN: 251306992

943
American Physicians Fellowship for Medicine in Israel

(also known as APF)
2001 Beacon St., Ste. 210
Boston, MA   02135-7787   (617) 232-5382
FAX: (617) 739-2616; *E-mail:* info@apfmed.org;
URL: http://www.apfmed.org

Established in 1952 in MA.

Grantmaker type: Public charity.

Financial data (yr. ended 12/31/10): Revenue, $426,448; assets, $806,332 (M); gifts received, $275,538; expenditures, $567,591; giving activities include $72,400 for grants to organizations outside the U.S., $90,067 for grants to individuals, and $74,260 for grants to individuals outside the U.S.

Purpose and activities: The organization awards fellowships to young Israeli physicians and nurses undertaking specialty training in North America who are committed to returning to Israel. Medical research by young Israeli researchers and grants to educational and health-related Israeli organizations are also supported. It also maintains a number of other educational programs in Israel and North America.

Fields of interest: Health care, formal/general education; Health care; Medical research.

International interests: Israel.

Type of support: Grants to individuals; Conferences/seminars; Fellowships; Research.

Limitations: Applications accepted. Giving limited to Israel.

Publications: Application guidelines; Informational brochure; Newsletter.

Application information: Application form not required.

  Initial approach: Project proposal for research grants; Download application form for fellowships

  Deadline(s): Mar. 15

  Board meeting date(s): Fall and spring

Officers and Directors:* Norton J. Greenberger,* M.D., Pres.; Michael Frogel,* M.D., V.P.; Allen Menkin,* M.D., Secy.; Ivan R. Sabel,* Treas.; Neri M. Cohen, M.D., Ph.D.; Charles M. Kurtzer, DPM, FACFAS; Dan Moskowitz, M.D.; Boaz Tadmor, M.D.; Annekathryn Goodman, M.D.; E. Joseph LeBauer, M.D.; Hiton Mirels, M.D.; Steven J. Tenenbaum, M.D.

Number of staff: 3 full-time professional; 2 part-time professional; 1 full-time support.

EIN: 042207701

944
American Tower Corporation Contributions Program

116 Huntington Ave., 11th Fl.
Boston, MA   02116   (617) 375-7500
URL: http://www.americantower.com/atcweb/AboutUs/SocialResponsibility.htm

Grantmaker type: Corporate giving program.

Purpose and activities: American Tower makes charitable contributions to nonprofit organizations on a case by case basis. Support is given primarily in areas of company operations in Arizona, California, Colorado, Georgia, Illinois, Massachusetts, Nebraska, South Carolina, and Texas, and in Brazil, Chile, Colombia, Ghana, India, Mexico, Peru, South Africa and the United Kingdom.

Fields of interest: General charitable giving.
International interests: United Kingdom; South Africa; Peru; Mexico; India; Ghana; Colombia; Chile; Brazil.
Type of support: General/operating support; Employee volunteer services.
Limitations: Giving primarily in areas of company operations in AZ, CA, CO, GA, IL, MA, NE, SC, and TX, and in Brazil, Chile, Colombia, Ghana, India, Mexico, Peru, South Africa and the United Kingdom.

945
Azadoutioun Foundation
c/o Gravestar, Inc.
160 2nd St.
Cambridge, MA   02142-1515
Contact: Laurie Le Blanc
Application address: 10 Madison Ave., Groveland, MA 01834-1143

Established in 1985 in MA.
Donor: Carolyn G. Mugar.
Grantmaker type: Independent foundation.
Financial data (yr. ended 12/31/10): Assets, $4,724,135 (M); gifts received, $996,799; expenditures, $1,347,884; qualifying distributions, $309,145; giving activities include $309,145 for grants.
Purpose and activities: Giving primarily for education and human services.
Fields of interest: Adult education—literacy, basic skills & GED; Education, reading; Environment; Human services; International economic development.
Type of support: General/operating support; Program development.
Limitations: Applications accepted. Giving on a national basis. No grants to individuals; no loans.
Application information: Application form not required.
  Initial approach: Letter outlining request
  Copies of proposal: 1
  Deadline(s): None
  Board meeting date(s): Annually
Managers: William Allen; Kathleen Dueste.
Trustees: Janet Corpus; Carolyn G. Mugar; Sidney Peck; Sharryn Ross.
Number of staff: 1 part-time professional; 1 part-time support.
EIN: 042876245

946
Beyond the 11th, Inc.
P.O. Box 457
Needham, MA   02494-0004   (781) 465-6464
E-mail: info@beyondthe11th.org; URL: http://www.beyondthe11th.org
Facebook: http://www.facebook.com/pages/Beyond-the-11th/133648413332990
Twitter: http://twitter.com/beyondthe11th

Established in 2003 in MA.
Grantmaker type: Public charity.
Financial data (yr. ended 06/30/11): Revenue, $199,782; assets, $288,270 (M); gifts received, $204,603; expenditures, $50,466; giving activities include $23,746 for grants.
Purpose and activities: The organization is devoted to supporting widows (primarily in Afghanistan) who have been affected by the horrors of war and terrorism, and whose situation and poverty is often compounded by a lack of any support system in their countries to help them survive as widows.
Fields of interest: International affairs; Women.
International interests: Afghanistan.
Limitations: Giving primarily to Atlanta, GA and New York, NY.
Officers and Directors: Susan Retik,* Chair.; Shilpa Phadke,* Secy.; Jennifer Bennet,* Treas.; Deborah Zalesne.
EIN: 562384970

947
The Blossom Fund
c/o Loring Wolcott & Coolidge
230 Congress St.
Boston, MA   02110-2409
Contact: Lindsey W. Parker, Tr.

Established in 1994 in MA.
Grantmaker type: Independent foundation.
Financial data (yr. ended 03/31/11): Assets, $1,025,333 (M); expenditures, $150,149; qualifying distributions, $141,307; giving activities include $140,000 for 10 grants (high: $25,000; low: $5,000).
Purpose and activities: Support for the community and grassroots efforts of women in the Boston, MA area, Central America, and Mexico, and to encourage social and economic development of women and girls; support also for community-based educational and cultural projects in Boston, Brookline and Cambridge, MA, as well as for programs promoting the use of Boston-area outdoor space as described in foundation guidelines.
Fields of interest: Arts; Libraries/library science; Libraries (special); Education; Youth development, centers/clubs; Women, centers/services; International economic development; Women.
International interests: Mexico; Central America.
Type of support: General/operating support; Seed money.
Limitations: Applications not accepted. Giving primarily in MA for local programs; giving nationally for programs benefiting Central America and Mexico. No support for health care or sports. No grants for scholarships, capital campaigns, or construction projects.
Application information: Unsolicited requests for funds not accepted.
  Board meeting date(s): Apr. 20 and Oct. 20
Trustees: Amy L. Domini; Lindsey W. Parker.
EIN: 223297205

948
Boston Jewish Community Women's Fund
c/o Combined Jewish Philanthropies
126 High St.
Boston, MA   02110-2700   (617) 457-8590
Contact: Susan Ebert, Fund Dir.
FAX: (617) 988-6262; E-mail: Susane@cjp.org; URL: http://www.cjp.org/page.aspx?id=101553

Component fund of the Combined Jewish Philanthropies.
Grantmaker type: Public charity.
Financial data (yr. ended 05/31/08): Giving activities include $264,500 for 16 grants.
Purpose and activities: The fund seeks to support innovative, results-oriented programs and projects that benefit Jewish women and girls in the local Jewish community, primarily in Boston, Massachusetts and Israel.
Fields of interest: Jewish agencies & synagogues; Girls; Women.
International interests: Israel.
Limitations: Applications accepted. Giving primarily in the Boston, MA, metropolitan area, and Israel. No grants to individuals, or for scholarships or capital campaigns.
Publications: Application guidelines; Grants list; Informational brochure.
Application information: Application form required.
  Initial approach: Letter of intent (no more than 2 pages) submitted both via e-mail and as hardcopy
  Copies of proposal: 2
  Deadline(s): Oct. 24
  Final notification: Six weeks
Officer: Susan Ebert, Fund Dir.
Number of staff: 1 part-time professional; 1 part-time support.

949
Ella Lyman Cabot Trust, Inc.
c/o Edwards Angell Palmer & Dodge, LLP
P.O. Box 990129
Boston, MA   02199-7618
Contact: P. Brooks Thompson, Clerk
Application address: 86 Rockland St., Holliston, MA 01746-1421

Incorporated in 1939 in MA.
Donor: Richard Cabot‡.
Grantmaker type: Independent foundation.
Financial data (yr. ended 12/31/10): Assets, $3,316,510 (M); expenditures, $170,862; qualifying distributions, $159,984; giving activities include $143,300 for 9 grants (high: $25,000; low: $2,000).
Purpose and activities: Grants primarily to individuals for projects (sometimes involving a departure from one's usual vocation or a creative extension of it) with a promise of good to others. Awards are usually made on a one-year basis and are not renewed.
Fields of interest: Performing arts, music; Humanities; Arts; Child development, education; Education; Environment; Health care; Health organizations, association; Biomedicine; Medical research, institute; Crime/law enforcement; Human services; Youth, services; Child development, services; Women, centers/services; International peace/security; Civil/human rights; Religion; Women.
Type of support: General/operating support; Grants to individuals.
Publications: Application guidelines.
Application information: Application form required.
  Initial approach: Letter
  Deadline(s): Mar. 1 and Oct. 1
Officers and Trustees: * Andrew G. Bodnar,* M.D., Chair.; Mary Jane Gibson,* Exec. Secy.; P. Brooks Thompson, Clerk; Jeffrey Swope,* Treas.; Gene Corbin; Carolyn Darr, Sr.; Helen Glikman; Peter J. Gomes; Ellen T. Harris; Byron Rushing; Constance W. Williams.
Number of staff: 1 part-time professional.
EIN: 042111393

950

Cedar Tree Foundation

(formerly David H. Smith Foundation)
100 Franklin St., Ste. 704
Boston, MA 02110-1401 (617) 695-6767
FAX: (617) 695-1919;
E-mail: info@cedartreefound.org; URL: http://
www.cedartreefound.org
Grants List: http://www.cedartreefound.org/
grants.html

Established in 1994 in DE.
Donors: Dr. David H. Smith†; Andrea L. Smith;
Rachel A. Smith; Jennifer L. Smith; Andrea L. Smith
Charitable Lead Annuity Trust; Jennifer L. Smith
Charitable Lead Annuity Trust; Rachel A. Smith
Charitable Lead Annuity Trust; Jody Leader
Charitable Lead Annuity Trust; Kristen Leader
Charitable Lead Annuity Trust.
Grantmaker type: Independent foundation.
Financial data (yr. ended 12/31/09): Assets,
$92,308,071 (M); gifts received, $2,226,715;
expenditures, $6,279,618; qualifying distributions,
$5,549,379; giving activities include $4,454,619
for 59 grants (high: $1,077,838; low: $2,500).
Purpose and activities: The foundation focuses on
the following areas of concern: sustainable
agriculture, environmental education, and
environmental health. The foundation will give
particular consideration to proposals demonstrating
strong elements of environmental justice, and
conservation.
Fields of interest: Agriculture; Environment, formal/
general education; Environment, legal rights;
Environment.
Type of support: Mission-related investments/
loans.
Limitations: Applications accepted. Giving primarily
in NY; some giving nationally. No grants to
individuals.
Publications: Grants list.
Application information: Application information
available on foundation web site. The foundation will
review letters of inquiry and request additional
information or a proposal if interested. Letters of
inquiry are not accepted via fax or e-mail.
   Initial approach: Letter of inquiry (no more than 3
   pages)
   Deadline(s): None
Officers: Joan M. Smith, Pres.; Andrea L. Smith,
V.P.; Jennifer L. Smith, Clerk; Rachel A. Smith,
Treas.; Martin Teitel, Ph.D., Exec. Dir.
EIN: 133601934
Recent grants for international programs:
950-1 Consultative Group on Biological Diversity,
   San Francisco, CA, $10,000. For Health and
   Environmental Funders Network. 2009.
950-2 Society for Conservation Biology,
   Washington, DC, $1,077,038. For Smith Fellows
   program. 2009.
950-3 World Media Foundation, Living On Earth,
   Somerville, MA, $75,000. For Living On Earth
   radio program. 2009.

951

Center for Balkan Development, Inc.

(formerly Friends of Bosnia, Inc.)
97 Central St., Ste. 403
Lowell, MA 01852-1917 (978) 461-0909
Contact: Glenn Ruga, Pres.

FAX: (978) 461-2552;
E-mail: info@friendsofbosnia.org; URL: http://
www.friendsofbosnia.org/

Grantmaker type: Public charity.
Financial data (yr. ended 06/30/08): Revenue,
$385,896; assets, $3,468 (M); gifts received,
$369,526; expenditures, $396,606; program
services expenses, $366,762; giving activities
include $366,762 for foundation-administered
programs.
Purpose and activities: The organization conducts
benevolent humanitarian activities for the area of
the Balkan states.
Fields of interest: International relief.
International interests: Balkans, The.
Limitations: Giving limited to the Balkan states.
Officers and Directors:* Glenn Ruga,* Pres.; Mary
Ellen Keough,* M.P.H., Secy.; Gina Vanderloop,*
Treas.; Smajl Cengic; Sheri Fink, M.D.; Veton
Kepuska; Stephen Walker; Rob Wilson.
EIN: 043287212

952

China Medical Board, Inc.

(formerly China Medical Board of New York, Inc.)
2 Arrow St.
Cambridge, MA 02138-5102 (617) 979-8000
URL: http://www.chinamedicalboard.org

Incorporated in 1928 in NY.
Donor: The Rockefeller Foundation.
Grantmaker type: Independent foundation.
Financial data (yr. ended 06/30/10): Assets,
$208,555,729 (M); gifts received, $3,285,671;
expenditures, $14,423,970; qualifying
distributions, $11,149,668; giving activities include
$9,309,445 for 49 grants (high: $2,500,000; low:
$15,446), and $590,354 for 4
foundation-administered programs.
Purpose and activities: The foundation works to
catalyze new, evidence-based policies and practices
that will lead to improved health outcomes;
strengthen the development of professional
programs that produce competent graduates to
meet the demands of the health sector; reduce
disparities in access to health services between
rural and urban populations; develop innovative
approaches to major public health challenges, such
as tobacco control; and expand channels that
enable health professionals in China and Asia to
more deeply engage in global health exchange and
development. Southeast Asia remains a focus of the
grantmaker's work and grants to institutions in that
region reflect the same integrated themes of health
policy systems and sciences, medical education,
and rural health.
Fields of interest: Medical school/education;
Libraries/library science; Nursing care; Health care;
Health organizations, association; Medical
research, institute.
International interests: Asia; East Asia; Hong Kong;
Indonesia; Malaysia; Philippines; Southeast Asia;
Singapore; Taiwan; Thailand.
Type of support: Endowments; Program
development; Conferences/seminars; Publication;
Fellowships; Scholarship funds; Research;
Technical assistance.
Limitations: Applications accepted. Giving limited to
East and Southeast Asia, including the People's
Republic of China, Hong Kong, Indonesia, Korea,
Malaysia, the Philippines, Singapore, Taiwan, and
Thailand. No support for professional or scientific

societies, or research institutes not directly under
medical school control. No grants to individuals
(except for scholarships and fellowships), or for
capital projects.
Publications: Annual report.
Application information: Unsolicited requests for
funds not accepted.
   Board meeting date(s): June and Dec.
Officers and Trustees:* Mary Brown Bullock,*
Ph.D., Chair.; Lincoln C. Chen,* Pres.; Laura E.
Butzel, Secy. and Genl. Counsel; Harvey V. Fineberg;
Jane E. Henney, M.D.; Fred Hu; Thomas S. Inui,
M.D.; Tom G. Kessinger, Ph.D.; Jeffrey P. Koplan;
Wendy Harrison O'Neill; Peter J. Robbins; Anthony J.
Saich; Jeffrey R. Williams; William Y. Yun.
Number of staff: 2 full-time professional; 3 full-time
support.
EIN: 131659619
Recent grants for international programs:
952-1 Beijing University, University Health Science
   Center, Beijing, China, $442,000. To establish
   Peking University China Health Development
   Center. 2010.
952-2 Beijing University, University Health Science
   Center, Beijing, China, $95,000. To support
   travel and organization of Chinese scientists to
   First Global Symposium on Health Systems
   research. 2010.
952-3 Beijing University, University Health Science
   Center, Beijing, China, $80,000. For Conference
   of Commission of Education of Health
   Professionals for the 21st Century. 2010.
952-4 Central South University, Changsha, China,
   $200,000. For strategies for mental health
   services in China. 2010.
952-5 Central South University, Changsha, China,
   $165,000. For study of three-in-one model for
   rural doctor training. 2010.
952-6 Central South University, Changsha, China,
   $137,500. To assess student professionalism
   system for medical education. 2010.
952-7 Central South University, Changsha, China,
   $125,000. To develop Regional Medical
   Information Network System. 2010.
952-8 Central South University, Changsha, China,
   $87,500. For Integrated Intervention Model for
   Rural Diabetes Control. 2010.
952-9 Chiang Mai University, Faculty of Nursing,
   Chiang Mai, Thailand, $400,000. To strengthen
   nursing education in four Southeast Asian
   countries. 2010.
952-10 China Medical University, Shenyang, China,
   $197,500. For dissemination and faculty
   development in medical education innovation.
   2010.
952-11 China Medical University, Shenyang, China,
   $165,000. To train rural and urban family
   doctors in regional campuses. 2010.
952-12 China Medical University, Shenyang, China,
   $130,000. To promote patient safety practices
   in China. 2010.
952-13 Fudan University, Shanghai Medical College,
   Shanghai, China, $200,000. To start China
   Center for Health Research. 2010.
952-14 Fudan University, Shanghai Medical College,
   Shanghai, China, $21,971. For nursing policy
   research workshop. 2010.
952-15 Fudan University, Shanghai Medical College,
   Shanghai, China, $15,446. For nursing policy
   research workshop. 2010.
952-16 Guangxi Medical University, Nanning, China,
   $102,650. For innovation management of rural
   healthcare in Guangxi Zhuang Autonomous
   Region. 2010.

952-17 Guryang Medical College, Guiyang, China, $164,950. For medical services training for rural doctors in Guizhou. 2010.

952-18 Hanoi School of Public Health, Hanoi, Vietnam, $104,300. For CHILILAB. 2010.

952-19 Harbin Medical University, Harbin, China, $150,000. For evaluation and capacity building for China's hospital reform pilots. 2010.

952-20 Harbin Medical University, Harbin, China, $100,000. To strengthen rural health workforce in Heilongjiang Province. 2010.

952-21 Inner Mongolia Medical College, Hohhot, China, $179,000. For community-based assessment of regional training of health personnel. 2010.

952-22 Institute of International Education, New York, NY, $2,500,000. For extension of China Medical Board (CMB) Professor, Fellows and Faculty Development awards. 2010.

952-23 Japan Center for International Exchange, New York, NY, $140,000. To organize and host project to produce and publish special series on Japan in The Lancet. 2010.

952-24 Jiujiang Medical College, Jiujiang, China, $200,000. To develop patient referral and transfer system between urban and rural healthcare delivery systems. 2010.

952-25 Jiujiang University Medical Center, Jiujiang, China, $33,064. For planning grant for rural medical education. 2010.

952-26 Mahidol University, Bangkok, Thailand, $30,000. To support travel of Chinese and Asian participants to 4th Asia Pacific Action Alliance on Human Resources for Health (AAAH) annual conference. 2010.

952-27 National University of Laos, Faculty of Medicine, Vientiane, Laos, $76,000. For Laos-Family Medicine. 2010.

952-28 National University of Laos, Faculty of Medicine, Vientiane, Laos, $61,000. For Laos-Family Medicine. 2010.

952-29 Ningxia Medical College, Yinchuan, China, $175,000. For studies on rural health in Western China. 2010.

952-30 Peking Union Medical College, Beijing, China, $410,000. For Young Faculty Development. 2010.

952-31 Peking Union Medical College, Beijing, China, $175,000. To strengthen research and education in health promotion and health risk reduction (health management). 2010.

952-32 Peking Union Medical College, Beijing, China, $173,400. To strengthen management competence of China Medical Board grantee universities. 2010.

952-33 Sichuan University, Chengdu, China, $176,400. To establish evidence-based research center for health in Western China. 2010.

952-34 Sun Yat-Sen University, Guangzhou, China, $125,000. For start-up support for Sun Yat-Sen Center for Migrant Health Policy Studies. 2010.

952-35 Sun Yat-Sen University, Guangzhou, China, $82,500. For China Medical Board President's Council. 2010.

952-36 Sun Yat-Sen University, Guangzhou, China, $43,300. For network research on nursing educational capacity and practice planning new model for Nursing Doctoral Education. 2010.

952-37 Tibet Medical College, Lhasa, China, $157,500. For talent-training in preventive medicine for rural Tibet. 2010.

952-38 Tibet Medical College, Lhasa, China, $100,000. To treat non-communicable diseases among Tibet's high altitude population. 2010.

952-39 Universitas Gadjah Mada, Yogyakarta, Indonesia, $54,402. For author's workshop for Lancet Series on Health in Southeast Asia. 2010.

952-40 University of Medicine, Lanmadow, Burma (Myanmar), $104,000. For capacity building in Human Resources and Information Library. 2010.

952-41 University of Medicine, Mandalay, Burma (Myanmar), $125,000. To strengthen medical education and research. 2010.

952-42 University of Medicine, North Okkalapa, Burma (Myanmar), $100,000. For Faculty and Information Library development. 2010.

952-43 Xian Jiaotong University, Xian, China, $150,000. For study on reform of health care payment system in Shaanxi Province. 2010.

952-44 Xian Jiaotong University, Xian, China, $125,000. To develop model of community health care and general practitioners' training. 2010.

952-45 Xian Jiaotong University, Xian, China, $123,500. For policy study on improving health service equity in west rural areas of China. 2010.

952-46 Xian Jiaotong University, Xian, China, $55,562. For workshop and study tour for rural health. 2010.

952-47 Zhejiang University, Hangzhou, China, $223,500. For Health Policy Development in China's Medical Universities. 2010.

952-48 Zhejiang University, Hangzhou, China, $200,000. To enlarge risk pool to improve sustainability of rural health insurance. 2010.

952-49 Zhejiang University, Hangzhou, China, $127,500. To upgrade public health professional education. 2010.

953
Colombe Foundation

101 University Dr., Ste. A2
Amherst, MA 01002-2385 (413) 256-0349
FAX: (413) 256-0349;
E-mail: grantsmanager@proteusfund.org; Contact for new applicants: Dini Merz, Prog. Dir.: tel.: (203) 439-0076, e-mail: dmerz@proteusfund.org; Contact for current grantees: Beery Adams Jimenez, Grants Mgr., e-mail: bjimenez@proteusfund.org; URL: http://www.proteusfund.org/programs/colombe-foundation

Established in 1996 in DE.
Donor: Edith W. Allen.
Grantmaker type: Independent foundation.
Financial data (yr. ended 06/30/10): Assets, $14,613,647 (M); expenditures, $1,459,707; qualifying distributions, $1,206,500; giving activities include $1,206,500 for 29 grants (high: $150,000; low: $5,000).
Purpose and activities: The foundation supports organizations that are: 1) working for the elimination of weapons of mass destruction; 2) advocating for foreign policy that is balanced with diplomacy and prevention rather than dominated by war and aggression; and 3) supporting a shift from wasteful military spending to investments in programs that create real national security, grounded in environmental protection, alternative energy, education and human services. The foundation's current grantmaking priorities are: 1) changing U.S. policy with regards to nuclear weapons disarmament

and non-proliferation and complex transformation; 2) shifting the priorities of the military budget; and 3) ending the wars in Afghanistan and Iraq.
Fields of interest: Education, public education; Environment, research; International affairs, information services; International peace/security; Social sciences, public policy; Social sciences, government agencies; Social sciences, formal/general education; Political science.
Publications: Application guidelines; Grants list.
Application information:
Initial approach: Telephone or e-mail to Dina Merz to discuss proposal prior to submitting an application; Current grantees should contact Beery Adams Jimenez for current guidelines
Copies of proposal: 2
Deadline(s): See foundation web site for latest deadlines
Final notification: Spring and fall
Officers: Edith W. Allen, Pres.; Frederick Allen, Secy.
EIN: 137103356

954
Conservation, Food and Health Foundation, Inc.

c/o GMA Foundations
77 Summer St., 8th Fl.
Boston, MA 02110-1006 (617) 391-3092
Contact: Prentice Zinn, Admin.
FAX: (617) 426-7087;
E-mail: pzinn@gmafoundations.com; URL: http://cfhfoundation.grantsmanagement08.com/

Established in 1985 in MA.
Grantmaker type: Independent foundation.
Financial data (yr. ended 12/31/10): Assets, $16,024,368 (M); gifts received, $30,000; expenditures, $1,832,534; qualifying distributions, $912,172; giving activities include $912,172 for grants.
Purpose and activities: The purpose of the foundation is to assist in the conservation of natural resources, the production and distribution of food, and the improvement and promotion of health in the developing world. The foundation is especially interested in supporting projects which lead to the transfer of responsibility to the citizens of developing countries for managing and solving their own problems and for developing the capacity of local organizations. Preference will be given to projects, including research projects, in areas that tend to be under-funded.
Fields of interest: Environment, natural resources; Environment; Animals/wildlife, preservation/protection; Health care; Agriculture; Agriculture/food.
International interests: Developing countries.
Type of support: Program development; Seed money; Research; Technical assistance.
Limitations: Giving to benefit developing countries. No support for famine, emergency relief, direct delivery of medical care, or for overhead expenses of large institutions. No grants to individuals (except for research efforts sponsored by organizations and institutions), or for building or land purchase, endowments, fundraising activities, scholarships, tuition, and travel grants or general operating support.
Publications: Application guidelines; Grants list.
Application information: Faxed or e-mailed proposals will not be accepted. In order to try to reduce the number of applicants who are turned down for lack of available funds, and to save time

loss and expense to the applicants, the foundation has adopted a 2-phase application system, comprised of a short concept application, followed by a limited number of full proposals, at the invitation of the foundation. This system is designed to screen out, at the concept application level, projects which appear unlikely to receive final funding. Application guidelines available on foundation web site. Application form required.

Initial approach: Letter of inquiry or concept paper
Copies of proposal: 5
Deadline(s): Jan. 1 and July 1 for concept applications; Mar. 1 and Sept. 1 for requests for proposal; Apr. 1 and Oct. 1 for proposals
Board meeting date(s): May and Nov.
Final notification: June 1 and Dec. 1
Officer: Philip M. Fearnside, Pres.
EIN: 222625024

955
Herman Dana Charitable Trust
1340 Centre St., Ste. 101
Newton, MA   02459-2453
Contact: Myer R. Dana, Tr.

Established in 1969 in MA.
Donor: Herman Dana†.
Grantmaker type: Independent foundation.
Financial data (yr. ended 12/31/10): Assets, $17,428,797 (M); expenditures, $1,992,808; qualifying distributions, $1,027,440; giving activities include $940,200 for 19 grants (high: $153,489; low: $1,000).
Purpose and activities: Grants to participating organizations of the Combined Jewish Philanthropies of greater Boston, MA, for capital purposes or urgent current needs, domestic organizations doing overseas work, and Jewish charitable or educational institutions; support also for organizations and institutions, with the grant to be used for the cost of psychiatric care and counseling of undergraduate students at Harvard University.
Fields of interest: Education; Hospitals (general); Human services; International relief; Jewish federated giving programs; Jewish agencies & synagogues.
Limitations: Applications accepted. Giving primarily in MA; some funding in NY and OK. No grants to individuals.
Application information: Application form not required.
Initial approach: Detailed proposal
Copies of proposal: 2
Deadline(s): None
Final notification: 10-15 days
Trustees: Alan G. Dana; Myer R. Dana.
EIN: 046209497

956
The Daniele Agostino Derossi Foundation, Inc.
(formerly The Daniele Agostino Foundation, Inc.)
40 Wachusett Dr.
Lexington, MA   02421-6936
Contact: Trustees
E-mail: dafound@dafound.org; URL: http://www.dafound.org

Established in 1992 in NY.
Donor: Flavia D. Robinson Derossi.

Grantmaker type: Independent foundation.
Financial data (yr. ended 06/30/10): Assets, $1,795,353 (M); gifts received, $40; expenditures, $277,686; qualifying distributions, $219,527; giving activities include $219,527 for 16 grants (high: $43,330; low: $3,000).
Purpose and activities: The focus of the foundation is helping the indigenous people of Guatemala, especially women and children. There is occasional limited support for unique photography projects and those describing social problems in Latin America.
Fields of interest: Education; Health care; Community/economic development; Indigenous peoples; Children; Women.
International interests: Guatemala.
Type of support: Scholarship funds.
Limitations: Applications accepted. Giving primarily in Guatemala. No support for political organizations. No grants to individuals or building construction.
Publications: Occasional report.
Application information: Application attachments are only required for first-time applicants. E-mail correspondence is preferred. Application guidelines available on foundation web site. Application form not required.
Initial approach: Send e-mail (in English or Spanish)
Deadline(s): None
Board meeting date(s): Annually
Final notification: Within 10 weeks
Officers and Directors:* Daniele Carlo Derossi,* Pres.; Flavia D. Robinson Derossi; Peter De Janosi; David Pollock.
Number of staff: None.
EIN: 133636541

957
Eco-Logic Development Fund
(also known as Eco-Logic)
25 Mt. Auburn St., Ste. 203
Cambridge, MA   02138-6032   (617) 441-6300
Contact: Shaun Paul, Pres. and Exec. Dir.
FAX: (617) 441-6307; *E-mail:* info@ecologic.org; URL: http://www.ecologic.org

Established in 1993 in PA.
Grantmaker type: Public charity.
Financial data (yr. ended 12/31/10): Revenue, $1,997,558; assets, $2,670,985 (M); gifts received, $1,982,449; expenditures, $1,921,144.
Purpose and activities: The fund advances conservation of critical natural resources in rural areas of Latin America by promoting sustainable livelihoods and strengthening community participation in natural resource management.
Fields of interest: Environment; International development; Women; Indigenous peoples; Economically disadvantaged; Children/youth.
International interests: Latin America.
Limitations: Applications not accepted. Giving limited to Latin America.
Publications: Annual report; Financial statement; Newsletter.
Application information: Contributes only to pre-selected organizations; unsolicited requests for funds not considered or acknowledged.
Board meeting date(s): Quarterly
Officers and Directors:* F. William Green,* M.D., Chair.; Nicholas A. Shufro,* Vice-Chair. and Treas.; Shaun Paul,* Pres. and Exec. Dir.; Winstead Rouse,* Secy.; Louise Bowditch; David Bray; David Crocker; Marcela O. de Rovzar; Lisa Leff; Dan Tunstall.

Number of staff: 14 full-time support; 1 part-time support.
EIN: 251704582

958
Families with Children from China - New England
P.O. Box 427
Newton Upper Falls, MA   02464-0002
(617) 876-3042
Contact: Shanti Fry, Pres.
FAX: (617) 441-5449; URL: http://www.fccne.org

Established in 1996 in DC.
Grantmaker type: Public charity.
Financial data (yr. ended 12/31/10): Revenue, $60,332; assets, $355,187 (M); gifts received, $33,018; expenditures, $13,082.
Purpose and activities: The organization provides assistance and support for children living in orphanages in China.
Fields of interest: Children, services; Residential/custodial care.
International interests: China.
Type of support: Continuing support; Equipment.
Limitations: Giving on an international basis, primarily in China.
Application information:
Board meeting date(s): Bimonthly
Officers and Directors:* Shanti Fry,* Pres.; Susan Avery,* Secy.; Bruce Hain,* Treas.; Michael DeLanzo; Janice Litwin; Bonnie Perkel; Martha Volker; Liane Welch.
EIN: 043300403

959
Fidelity Foundation
82 Devonshire St., S2
Boston, MA   02109-3614   (617) 563-6806
Contact: Margaret H. Morton, Sr. V.P., Prog.
E-mail: info@FidelityFoundation.org; URL: http://www.fidelityfoundation.org

Trust established in 1965 in MA.
Donors: FMR Corp.; Fidelity Ventures Ltd.; FMR Capital; The Colt, Inc.
Grantmaker type: Company-sponsored foundation.
Financial data (yr. ended 12/31/09): Assets, $308,280,397 (M); expenditures, $17,680,707; qualifying distributions, $17,237,998; giving activities include $15,992,495 for grants.
Purpose and activities: The foundation supports organizations involved with arts and culture, education, health, human services, and community development. Special emphasis is directed toward programs designed to strengthen long-term effectiveness of nonprofit institutions.
Fields of interest: Arts; Education; Health care; Human services; Community/economic development.
International interests: Canada.
Type of support: Management development/capacity building; Capital campaigns; Building/renovation; Equipment; Program development; Conferences/seminars; Publication; Curriculum development; Technical assistance; Consulting services; Employee matching gifts; Matching/challenge support.
Limitations: Applications accepted. Giving primarily in areas of company operations, including Jacksonville, FL, northern KY, Boston and

Marlborough, MA, Merrimack, NH, Jersey City, NJ, lower Manhattan, NY, Durham and Raleigh, NC, Cincinnati, OH, Smithfield, RI, Dallas, Fort Worth, and northern TX, Salt Lake City, UT, and Toronto, Canada; giving also to regional and national organizations. No support for start-up, sectarian, or civic organizations, public school systems, or disease-specific organizations. No grants to individuals, or for general operating support, sponsorships, scholarships, benefits, corporate memberships, or video or film projects.

Publications: Application guidelines; Informational brochure (including application guidelines).

Application information: Additional information may be requested at a later date. A site visit may be requested. Organizations receiving support are asked submit a six-month progress report and a final report. Application form required.

   Initial approach: Download application form and mail to nearest regional office
   Copies of proposal: 1
   Deadline(s): None
   Final notification: 3 to 6 months

Officers and Trustees:* Anne-Marie Soulliere,* Pres.; Margart H. Morton, Sr. V.P., Prog.; Thomas Ruddy, V.P., Planning and Admin.; Eve K. Nichols, V.P., Science Prog.; Paul Kuenstner, V.P.; Tom Lewis, V.P.; Patricia R. Hurley, Esq., Secy. and Legal Counsel; Charles L. Nickerson, Treas.; Abigail P. Johnson; Edward C. Johnson III; Edward C. Johnson IV; Ross E. Sherbrooke.

Number of staff: 4 full-time professional; 3 full-time support.

EIN: 046131201

Recent grants for international programs:

959-1 Corporation of Massey Hall and Roy Thomson Hall, Toronto, Canada, $50,000. For technology upgrades. 2009.

959-2 Daily Bread Food Bank, Toronto, Canada, $62,500. For technology upgrades. 2009.

959-3 Earthwatch Institute, Boston, MA, $25,000. For consulting services. 2009.

959-4 Edo-Tokyo Museum, Tokyo, Japan, $200,000. For exhibitions. 2009.

959-5 Handel House Foundation of America, New York, NY, $25,000. For technology upgrades. 2009.

959-6 Japan Society, New York, NY, $50,000. For exhibitions. 2009.

959-7 Japan Society of Boston, Boston, MA, $100,000. For consulting services. 2009.

959-8 Right to Play, Toronto, Canada, $38,000. For technology upgrades. 2009.

959-9 Saint Pauls Cathedral Trust in America, New York, NY, $50,000. For program development. 2009.

959-10 Survivor Corps, Washington, DC, $100,000. For technology upgrades. 2009.

960
The Flatley Foundation
35 Braintree Hill Office Park, Ste. 400
Braintree, MA 02184-8754 (781) 849-5100

Established in 1982 in MA.
Donor: Thomas J. Flatley†.
Grantmaker type: Independent foundation.
Financial data (yr. ended 12/31/10): Assets, $560,377,807 (M); expenditures, $17,671,317; qualifying distributions, $16,047,881; giving activities include $14,805,253 for 108 grants (high: $10,000,000; low: $1,000), and $1,135,746 for 1 foundation-administered program.

Purpose and activities: Giving primarily for education, health care, and to Roman Catholic organizations.

Fields of interest: Elementary/secondary education; Higher education; Human services; International affairs; Civil liberties, right to life; Catholic agencies & churches.

Limitations: Applications not accepted. Giving primarily in MA, MD, and Bala Cynwyd, PA. No grants to individuals.

Application information: Contributes only to pre-selected organizations.

Trustees: Mary Margaret Darling; Daniel T. Flatley; John J. Flatley.

EIN: 042763837

Recent grants for international programs:

960-1 American Ireland Fund, Boston, MA, $25,000. For unrestricted support. 2009.

960-2 AmeriCares, Stamford, CT, $500,000. For clinic in El Salvador. 2009.

960-3 Boston College, Newton Centre, MA, $25,000,000. For Irish Famine Institute, initiative to help people in African and Asian countries suffering from famines today. 2009.

960-4 CARE, Cambridge, MA, $100,000. For Mozambique Project. 2009.

960-5 Chernobyl Children Project USA, Dedham, MA, $20,000. For unrestricted support. 2009.

960-6 Concern Worldwide U.S., New York, NY, $1,000,000. For development and relief services. 2009.

960-7 CRUDEM Foundation, Ludlow, MA, $25,000. To renovate Hopital Sacre Coeur. 2009.

960-8 Friends of the Orphans, Chicago, IL, $20,000. For program support. 2009.

960-9 Goal USA Fund, New York, NY, $250,000. For housing programs. 2009.

961
Doug Flutie Jr. Foundation for Autism, Inc.
P.O. Box 767
Framingham, MA 01701-0767 (508) 270-8855
Contact: Lisa Borges, Exec. Dir.
FAX: (508) 270-6868;
E-mail: info@flutiefoundation.org; Toll-free tel.: (866) 3AUTISM; URL: http://www.flutiefoundation.org/
2010 Grants List: http://www.flutiefoundation.org/Grants-2010-Grant-Recipients.asp

Established in 2000 in MA.
Grantmaker type: Public charity.
Financial data (yr. ended 12/31/10): Revenue, $591,613; assets, $2,565,552 (M); gifts received, $459,959; expenditures, $785,760; giving activities include $377,224 for grants, and $20,000 for grants to organizations outside the U.S.

Purpose and activities: The foundation aids financially-disadvantaged families who need assistance in caring for children with autism; funds education and research into the causes and consequences of childhood autism; and serves as a clearinghouse and communications center for new programs and services developed for individuals with autism.

Fields of interest: Autism; Autism research.
International interests: Canada.
Type of support: Research.
Limitations: Applications accepted. Giving on a national basis and select areas of Canada. No grants to individuals.
Publications: Application guidelines.

Application information: Proposals by fax or e-mail not accepted. Application form required.
   Initial approach: Download application
   Copies of proposal: 1
   Deadline(s): Sept. 26 for Grants
   Final notification: Dec. 19

Officers and Directors:* Douglas R. Flutie,* Pres.; Laurie Flutie,* V.P.; David R. Blouin,* Treas.; Lisa Borges, Exec. Dir.; Joseph Bator; Stephen Brackett; Michele Brait; Tom R. Burton III; Tina Cantu; William A. Carlezon, Jr., Ph.D.; Shamez Kanji; Kevin Lane Keller; Donna Lucente; Michael Martini; Michael Shunney.

EIN: 043543134

962
Fowler-Bombardier Family Charitable Trust
195 Hanover St.
Hanover, MA 02339-2205

Established in 2003 in MA.
Donor: Thomas J. Bombardier.
Grantmaker type: Independent foundation.
Financial data (yr. ended 12/31/10): Assets, $2,662 (M); gifts received, $230,000; expenditures, $243,006; qualifying distributions, $240,206; giving activities include $240,206 for grants.

Fields of interest: Christian agencies & churches; Education; Human services; International human rights; LGBTQ.

Limitations: Applications not accepted. No grants to individuals.

Application information: Unsolicited requests for funds not accepted.

Trustees: Thomas J. Bombardier; John Fowler.
EIN: 046987078

963
Friends of Kyrgyzstan, Inc.
28 Old Nourse St.
Westborough, MA 01581-3561
Facebook: http://apps.facebook.com/causes/view_cause/6339?h=plw&recruiter_id=2207700

Established in 2004 in NY.
Grantmaker type: Public charity.
Financial data (yr. ended 12/31/08): Revenue, $1,014; assets, $1,213 (M); gifts received, $1,014; expenditures, $291.

Purpose and activities: The organization is a network of Peace Corps volunteers, other volunteers, and their friends and family who have spent time in Kyrgyzstan and who support the continual learning and development of the culture and people of Kyrgyzstan.

Fields of interest: International development.
International interests: Kyrgyzstan.
Application information:
   Initial approach: Proposal (no more than 5 pages)

Officers and Board Members:* Brian Cowan, Pres.; Linda Lee Blaine,* Secy.; Brandon Boyle,* Treas.; Alice Lee; Kristoffer Rees; Julie Rotherham.
EIN: 562436636

964
Friends of the American Board Schools in Turkey
(also known as FABSIT)
14 Beacon St., Rm. 708
Boston, MA   02108-3733   (617) 523-3433
Contact: Paula Dincer, Exec. Dir.
E-mail: office@fabsit.org; URL: http://www.fabsit.org/

Established in 1987.
Grantmaker type: Public charity.
Financial data (yr. ended 05/31/10): Revenue, $285,979; assets, $868,857 (M); gifts received, $279,064; expenditures, $136,409; program services expenses, $78,266; giving activities include $17,058 for grants.
Purpose and activities: FABSIT is a "friends" organization providing program support and assistance to three secondary schools and a hospital in Turkey, helping to foster excellence in education and health care.
Fields of interest: Elementary/secondary education; Education; Hospitals (general).
International interests: Turkey.
Type of support: Scholarships—to individuals; Scholarship funds; In-kind gifts; Equipment; Building/renovation.
Limitations: Applications not accepted. Giving limited to Turkey.
Publications: Informational brochure; Newsletter.
Application information: Unsolicited requests for funds not considered or acknowledged.
Officers and Directors:* Ismail Ekmekc,* Pres.; Kerem Turunc,* Esq., V.P.; Basar Akyelli,* Secy.; Ismail Ekmekci,* Treas.; Kirkor Balci; Roxanne Scott Barry; Zafer Ecevit; Ismail Ekmekci; Dilhan Kalyon; Dorothy Keller.
EIN: 222789574

965
The Garfield Foundation
89 N. Water St.
New Bedford, MA   02740-6262   (508) 997-3199
Contact: Jennie Curtis, Exec. Dir.
FAX: (508) 997-3122;
E-mail: inquiry@garfieldfoundation.org; URL: http://www.garfieldfoundation.org

Established in 1980.
Grantmaker type: Independent foundation.
Financial data (yr. ended 11/30/10): Assets, $39,159,781 (M); expenditures, $5,140,548; qualifying distributions, $4,683,111; giving activities include $3,569,884 for 79 grants (high: $760,000; low: $27).
Purpose and activities: Giving to stimulate systemic-level solutions to progress towards a more equitable, economically prosperous and environmentally sustainable global society. Grantmaking priorities include sustainable production and consumption, biodiversity conservation, mercury source reduction, and community revitalization. Biodiversity conservation projects are limited to South America, specifically Amazonia and Bolivian Gran Chaco regions.
Fields of interest: Youth development; Environment, climate change/global warming; Environment, toxics; Environment, natural resources; Economic development; Community/economic development.
International interests: South America.

Type of support: General/operating support; Income development; Management development/capacity building; Land acquisition; Program development; Research; Technical assistance; Matching/challenge support.
Limitations: Applications not accepted. Giving primarily in the U.S.; funding also in the Gran Chaco of South America for the Biodiversity Conservation program. No grants to individuals.
Application information: Contributes only to pre-selected organizations.
Officer: Jennie Curtis, Exec. Dir.
Trustees: Michael Baldwin; Ronald Berman; Brian Garfield.
Number of staff: 2 full-time professional; 1 part-time professional.
EIN: 222285358

966
Gerondelis Foundation, Inc.
56 Central Ave., Ste. 201
Lynn, MA   01901-1112   (781) 595-3311
Contact: Gregory C. Demakis, Dir.

Established in 1966 in MA.
Grantmaker type: Independent foundation.
Financial data (yr. ended 12/31/10): Assets, $881,458 (M); expenditures, $564,597; qualifying distributions, $543,597; giving activities include $463,100 for 39 grants (high: $93,000; low: $500).
Purpose and activities: Giving primarily for higher education and for educational scholarships to students who are of at least one-fourth Greek lineage, reside or attend school in Essex County, MA, rank in the upper 15 percent of their class or have achieved a combined verbal math score of at least 1200 on the SAT I test, and officially be admitted to a 4-year college or university.
Fields of interest: Higher education; Education.
International interests: Greece.
Type of support: Scholarship funds; Scholarships—to individuals.
Limitations: Giving primarily in MA.
Application information: Scholarship applicants should contact the foundation or high school guidance counselor for application form.
   Deadline(s): None for grants, July 1 for scholarships
Directors: T. Phillip Comenos; Gregory C. Demakis, Esq.; John N. Demakis; Paul C. Demakis, Esq.; Thomas C. Demakis, Esq.; Thomas L. Demakis; Athas Kourkousis; Nondas Lagonakis; George J. Macropoulous; Christopher Scangas; Russell Smith; Nicholas T. Zervas, M.D.
Number of staff: 1 part-time support.
EIN: 046130871

967
The Goldhirsh Foundation, Inc.
(formerly The Bernard A. and Wendy J. Goldhirsh Foundation, Inc.)
c/o Rinet Co., LLC
101 Federal St., 14th Fl.
Boston, MA   02110-1859
Contact: Tara Ruth McConaghy
Application address: c/o Sally E. McNagny, M.D., M.P.H., Dir., Brain Tumor Research Awards Program, 95 Berkeley St., Ste. 208, Boston, MA 02116; tel.: (617) 279-2254, FAX: (617) 423-4619; E-mail: smcnagny@goldhirshfoundation.org; Tel./FAX For Tara Roth McConaghy: (203) 488-2697,

e-mail: tara@goldhirshfoundation.org; URL: http://www.goldhirshfoundation.org
Grants List: http://www.goldhirshfoundation.org/grant_recipients.htm

Established in 2000 in MA.
Donors: Bernard A. Goldhirsh†; Kendall/Belanger Family; Wasylax Family; Brewster National Crafts; Darrah Feldman; Lisa Tannenbaum; Lloyd Newman; Donna Newman; Todd Yelin; Martin Siroka; Susan Siroka; Victor Suben; Judith Suben; Danile Poswolsky; Brian Martz; Rafael Rosengarten; Ilene S. Cooperman; Jin Kim; Todd Neustat; Philip D. Cutter, M.D.; Marica Yellin; Lawrence Yelin; Laurie Klugman; Geoffrey Gelman; Randi Rothberg; Rinath Benjamin.
Grantmaker type: Independent foundation.
Financial data (yr. ended 12/31/10): Assets, $127,340,495 (M); expenditures, $7,097,238; qualifying distributions, $5,930,591; giving activities include $5,372,716 for 83 grants (high: $2,124,808; low: $1,000).
Purpose and activities: The foundation is interested in providing strategic investment in both pediatric and adult brain tumor research to accelerate progress toward more effective treatment for malignant diffuse glioma tumors. The foundation seeks responses from investigators working in the continuum between basic research and clinical application, integrating and translating knowledge in various disciplines into meaningful progress for patients. Examples of funding areas include, but are not limited to, oncogenomics and proteomics, genetically engineered models, the discovery and testing of small molecule therapies, unusual drug delivery systems, or improved brain imaging techniques. The foundation also encourages submission of research projects at the interface of developmental biology and cancer along the stem cell to glial axis.
Fields of interest: Cancer research.
Limitations: Applications accepted. Giving primarily in MA and NY. No grants to individuals.
Publications: Grants list.
Application information: Proposals are accepted from scientists in research and medical institutions in the United States and Canada for the Brain Tumor Research Awards Program.
Officers and Directors:* Benjamin A. Goldhirsh,* Chair.; Tara Roth McConaghy, Exec. Dir.; Elizabeth A. Goldhirsh; Claire Hoffman; Eric Yellin.
EIN: 043540874
Recent grants for international programs:
967-1 Alliance for Climate Protection, Washington, DC, $50,000. For general operating support. 2009.
967-2 American Friends of the Israel Democracy Institute, Atlanta, GA, $80,000. For Jewish Nation State Project. 2009.
967-3 American Friends of the Reut Institute, Beverly Hills, CA, $50,000. For general operating support. 2009.
967-4 American Israel Education Foundation, Washington, DC, $100,000. For general operating support. 2009.
967-5 American Israel Education Fund, Troy, MI, $100,000. For general operating support. 2009.
967-6 Birthright Israel Foundation, New York, NY, $200,000. For general operating support. 2009.
967-7 Committee for Accuracy in Middle East Reporting in America, Boston, MA, $50,000. For general operating support. 2009.
967-8 Congregation Kehillath Israel, Brookline, MA, $30,000. To send students to Israel. 2009.

967-9 Friends of Ir David, Brooklyn, NY, $250,000. For King Valley Promenade. 2009.

967-10 Friends of Ir David, Brooklyn, NY, $200,000. For general operating support. 2009.

967-11 IKAR, Los Angeles, CA, $30,000. For Israel Programming. 2009.

967-12 Israel Emergency Alliance, StandWithUs, Los Angeles, CA, $50,000. For general operating support. 2009.

967-13 Israel Project, Washington, DC, $50,000. For general operating support. 2009.

967-14 Kiva Microfunds, San Francisco, CA, $150,000. For general operating support. 2009.

967-15 Middle East Media Research Institute, Washington, DC, $50,000. For Palestinian Authority Textbook Project. 2009.

967-16 Milken Institute, Israel Center, Santa Monica, CA, $100,000. For general operating support. 2009.

967-17 Milken Institute, Israel Center, Santa Monica, CA, $50,000. For Medical Records Project. 2009.

967-18 Millennium Promise Alliance, New York, NY, $275,000. For general operating support. 2009.

967-19 Network for Teaching Entrepreneurship, New York, NY, $50,000. For NFTE Israel. 2009.

967-20 PEF Israel Endowment Funds, New York, NY, $25,000. For Wendy Goldhirsh Tel Dor Fellowship. 2009.

967-21 PEF Israel Endowment Funds, New York, NY, $25,000. For Tel-Beth - Shemesh Excavations. 2009.

967-22 Robert I. Lappin 1992 Supporting Foundation, Salem, MA, $50,000. For general operating support. 2009.

967-23 Robert I. Lappin 1992 Supporting Foundation, Salem, MA, $10,000. For general operating support. 2009.

967-24 Robert I. Lappin 1992 Supporting Foundation, Salem, MA, $10,000. For general operating support. 2009.

967-25 Survivor Corps, Washington, DC, $50,000. For general operating support. 2009.

967-26 Survivor Corps, Washington, DC, $50,000. For general operating support. 2009.

967-27 Washington Institute for Near East Policy, Washington, DC, $50,000. For general operating support. 2009.

968
Grand Circle Foundation, Inc.
347 Congress St.
Boston, MA 02210-1280 (617) 346-6602
Contact: Jean Kenney, Mgr.
FAX: (617) 346-6030; E-mail: foundation@gct.com;
E-mail for Jean Kenney: jkenney@gct.com;
URL: http://www.grandcirclefoundation.org/
Facebook: http://www.facebook.com/pages/
Grand-Circle-Foundation/89374752660
Justmeans: http://www.justmeans.com/
companies/grand-circle-foundation/115320.html
Twitter: http://twitter.com/GCFgivesback

Established in 1993 in MA.
Donors: Grand Circle Corp.; Overseas Adventure Travel; Alan E. Lewis; Harriet R. Lewis; Grand Circle Trust; Grand Circle Travel.
Grantmaker type: Company-sponsored foundation.
Financial data (yr. ended 12/31/10): Assets, $904,770 (M); gifts received, $3,092,804; expenditures, $2,993,502; qualifying distributions, $2,129,348; giving activities include $2,071,369 for 220 grants (high: $545,603; low: $25).

Purpose and activities: The foundation supports programs designed to identify and develop gutsy leaders who create social change and economic opportunity; partner with leaders in the villages where Grand Circle travels, live, and work to create jobs, improve school performance, support small business, and promote the health and safety of citizens; and bring together in dialogue and action Grand Circle associates, travelers, travel partners, and leaders around a shared set of values and goals to create change.
Fields of interest: Arts, cultural/ethnic awareness; Education, reading; Education; Health care; Employment; Youth development; Human services; Economic development; Rural development; Social entrepreneurship; Community development, small businesses; Aging.
International interests: Africa; Asia; Europe; Italy; Mexico; South America; Thailand; Turkey.
Type of support: Continuing support; Building/renovation; Equipment; Program development; Curriculum development; Employee volunteer services; Employee matching gifts.
Limitations: Applications accepted. Giving primarily in MA; some giving in Africa, Asia, China, Europe, Italy, Mexico, Peru, South America, Thailand, and Turkey. No support for discriminatory, political, or religious organizations. No grants to individuals, or for general operating support, advertising, or dinner table sponsorship.
Publications: Application guidelines; Program policy statement.
Application information: Proposals should be no longer than 2 pages. Support is limited to 1 contribution per organization during any given year. Organizations receiving support are asked to provide a final report. Application form not required.
　Initial approach: Proposal
　Deadline(s): Mar. 30, July 31, and Nov. 29
　Board meeting date(s): May, Aug., and Dec.
　Final notification: May and Oct.
Officers and Directors:* Alan E. Lewis,* Co-Chair.; Harriet R. Lewis,* Co-Chair.; Martha Prybylo, V.P.
Number of staff: 2 full-time professional.
EIN: 043175434

969
Grantham Foundation for the Protection of the Environment
(formerly Jeremy and Hannelore Grantham Charitable Trust)
40 Rowes Wharf
Boston, MA 02110-3340 (617) 346-7500
Contact: Jeremy Grantham, Tr.
URL: http://www.granthamfoundation.org/

Established in 1997 in MA.
Donors: R. Jeremy Grantham; Eric Oddleifson.
Grantmaker type: Independent foundation.
Financial data (yr. ended 12/31/09): Assets, $354,376,345 (M); gifts received, $66,300,000; expenditures, $14,613,454; qualifying distributions, $12,237,121; giving activities include $12,187,766 for 48 grants (high: $1,527,140; low: $750).
Purpose and activities: To help protect and improve the health of the global environment.
Fields of interest: Environment, legal rights; Education; Environment, natural resources; Environment.

Limitations: Applications not accepted. Giving primarily in MA, VA, and Washington, DC; funding also in London, England. No grants to individuals.
Application information: Contributes only to pre-selected organizations.
Trustees: Isable Grantham; Jeremy Grantham; Oliver Grantham; Rupert Grantham.
EIN: 046856456
Recent grants for international programs:

969-1 Alumni and Friends of the London School of Economics, Arlington, VA, $1,488,490. 2009.

969-2 American Friends of the Royal Society, Wilmington, DE, $50,000. 2009.

969-3 Azuero Earth Project, East Hampton, NY, $25,000. 2009.

969-4 CERES, Boston, MA, $50,000. 2009.

969-5 Imperial College of London, London, England, $1,433,300. 2009.

969-6 Nature Conservancy, Arlington, VA, $1,527,140. 2009.

969-7 Oxfam America, Boston, MA, $150,000. 2009.

969-8 RARE, Arlington, VA, $1,350,000. 2009.

969-9 Smithsonian Institution, Smithsonian Tropical Research Institute, Washington, DC, $31,606. For Smithsonian Tropical Research Institute, which is located in Panama and is dedicated to biodiversity research. 2009.

969-10 Union of Concerned Scientists, Cambridge, MA, $90,000. 2009.

969-11 University of Sheffield in America, Washington, DC, $50,000. 2009.

969-12 WildAid, San Francisco, CA, $25,000. 2009.

969-13 World Wildlife Fund, Washington, DC, $1,232,214. 2009.

970
Grassroots International, Inc.
179 Boylston St., 4th Fl.
Boston, MA 02130 (617) 524-1400
FAX: (617) 524-5525;
E-mail: info@grassrootsonline.org; URL: http://www.grassrootsonline.org
Facebook: http://www.facebook.com/
grassrootsinternational?v=wall&ref=profile
Flickr: http://www.flickr.com/photos/
grassrootsinternational/
Grassroots International, Inc's Philanthropy Promise: http://www.ncrp.org/
philanthropys-promise/who
RSS Feed: http://www.grassrootsonline.org/
rss.xml
Twitter: http://twitter.com/grassrootsintl
YouTube: http://www.youtube.com/GrassrootsIntl

Established in 1983 in MA.
Grantmaker type: Public charity.
Financial data (yr. ended 10/31/10): Revenue, $2,603,253; assets, $2,313,939 (M); gifts received, $2,496,884; expenditures, $2,868,184; giving activities include $142,500 for grants, and $1,581,952 for grants to organizations outside the U.S.
Purpose and activities: The organization works with social movements and progressive organizations to build a global movement for social justice by supporting the initiatives of peasants and family farmers, women, and indigenous groups to protect human rights to land, water, and food.
Fields of interest: Environment; International development; International agricultural development; International relief; International

human rights; International affairs; Indigenous peoples.

Type of support: In-kind gifts.

Limitations: Giving on a national and international basis.

Publications: Annual report; Grants list.

Officers and Board Members: * Devin S. McLachlan,* Chair.; David Holmstrom,* Treas.; Nikhil Aziz,* Exec. Dir.; Rob Baril; Jean Entine; Meg Gage; Ellen Gurzinsky; Catherine Hoffman; Hayat Imam; Soya Jung; Marie Kennedy; Taij Kumarie Moteelall; Anil Naidoo; Tarso Luis Ramos; Robert Warren.

EIN: 042791159

971
The Harold Grinspoon Charitable Foundation

380 Union St.
West Springfield, MA   01089-4132
(413) 736-2552
Contact: Joanna S. Ballantine, Exec. Dir.
FAX: (413) 732-2632; E-mail: info@hgf.org;
URL: http://www.hgcf.org

Established in 1986 in MA.

Donors: Harold Grinspoon; Diane Troderman; Massmutual Financial Group.

Grantmaker type: Independent foundation.

Financial data (yr. ended 08/31/10): Assets, $5,715,233 (M); gifts received, $3,343,645; expenditures, $784,663; qualifying distributions, $756,289; giving activities include $354,304 for 79 grants (high: $100,000; low: $50), and $165,457 for grants to individuals.

Purpose and activities: Giving primarily to: 1) encourage young people to reach their academic and leadership potential; 2) promote literacy and early childhood education; 3) reward excellence in teaching and education; 4) support entrepreneurship among young people; and 5) promote education and health in Cambodia.

Fields of interest: Arts; Education; Cancer research; Youth development; Human services; Jewish agencies & synagogues; Women.

International interests: Cambodia; Israel.

Type of support: General/operating support; Annual campaigns; Endowments; Program development; Scholarship funds; Program-related investments/ loans.

Limitations: Giving primarily in western MA, with emphasis on Springfield. No grants to individuals (except for research projects), or for scholarships or student aid.

Publications: Financial statement; Multi-year report.

Application information:
Initial approach: Letter
Deadline(s): None

Trustees: Harold Grinspoon; Jeremy Pava; Diane Troderman.

Number of staff: 2 full-time professional; 2 part-time support.

EIN: 222738277

972
Hands Together, Inc.

P.O. Box 80985
Springfield, MA   01138-0985   (413) 731-7716
Contact: Doug Campbell, Exec. Dir.

FAX: (413) 731-6405;
E-mail: info@handstogether.org; URL: http://www.handstogether.org

Established in 1986.

Grantmaker type: Public charity.

Financial data (yr. ended 06/30/11): Revenue, $5,425,183; assets, $6,830,298 (M); gifts received, $4,803,553; expenditures, $5,148,988; giving activities include $13,750 for grants, and $4,598,374 for grants to organizations outside the U.S.

Purpose and activities: The organization is devoted to educating, inspiring and encouraging people to understand and respond to the needs of people, especially the poor and disadvantaged. It works to carry out its mission through projects and programs aimed at improving the quality of life for the very poor - primarily in Haiti.

Fields of interest: Human services; Economically disadvantaged.

International interests: Haiti.

Publications: Annual report; Informational brochure.

Officers: Joseph Taylor,* Chair.; Rev. Thomas J. Hagan, O.S.F.S.,* Pres.; Douglas Campbell, Secy. and Exec. Dir.; Tom Gilligan,* Treas.

Directors: Lucille Bongiavanni; John Clarke; Katherine Shafer Coleman; Gary Clayton; Patrick Fiedler; Michael Monteleone; Jann Nohe; Paul Sigmund, Ph.D.

Number of staff: 1 full-time professional; 1 full-time support.

EIN: 232566502

973
Harman Family Foundation

397 South St.
Needham, MA   02492-2761   (781) 449-1911
Contact: Barbara Harman, Treas. and Exec. Dir.
E-mail: bharman@harman-foundation.org;
URL: http://www2.harman-foundation.org
RSS Feed: http://www2.harman-foundation.org/feed/

Established in 1985 in DC.

Donors: Sidney Harman; Hon. Jane Harman.

Grantmaker type: Independent foundation.

Financial data (yr. ended 02/28/09): Assets, $140,659 (M); gifts received, $1,000,337; expenditures, $1,175,629; qualifying distributions, $783,140; giving activities include $772,040 for 101 grants (high: $60,000; low: $500), and $11,100 for 2 employee matching gifts.

Purpose and activities: Giving primarily for the performing arts, international affairs, education, and human services.

Fields of interest: Voluntarism promotion; Performing arts, theater; Performing arts; Performing arts, ballet; Arts; Higher education; Children/youth, services; International affairs; Jewish federated giving programs.

Type of support: General/operating support.

Limitations: Applications not accepted. Giving primarily in Los Angeles, CA, Washington, DC, MD, and New York, NY. No support for religious or political organizations. No grants to individuals.

Application information: The grantmaker is currently not accepting unsolicited letters of inquiry or applications. See foundation web site for current application information.

Officers: Sidney Harman, Pres.; Hon. Jane Harman, V.P.; Barbara Harman, Treas. and Exec. Dir.

Number of staff: 1 full-time professional; 2 part-time professional.

EIN: 521437943

974
Harvard-Yenching Institute

2 Divinity Ave. & Vanserg Hall
25 Francis Ave.
Cambridge, MA   02138-2020   (617) 495-4050
Contact: Peter L. Kelley, Exec. Dir.
FAX: (617) 496-7206;
E-mail: yenching@fas.harvard.edu; Additional address: c/o Harvard Management Co., 600 Atlantic Ave., Boston, MA 02210-2211; Additional tel.: (617) 523-4400; URL: http://www.harvard-yenching.org

Incorporated in 1928 in MA; supporting organization of Harvard University.

Donor: Charles Martin Hall†.

Grantmaker type: Public charity.

Financial data (yr. ended 06/30/10): Revenue, $2,589,449; assets, $171,650,034 (M); expenditures, $7,007,904; giving activities include $2,751,255 for grants, $690,019 for grants to organizations outside the U.S., and $2,681,099 for grants to individuals.

Purpose and activities: The institute seeks to aid the development of higher education in eastern and southern Asia, concentrating on the humanities and social sciences; makes grants to support teaching, research, and study by Asians in these fields; and sponsors fellowships for research at Harvard University, or scholarships for graduate study, by younger faculty members of selected Asian institutions. The institute also helps to support East Asian studies at Harvard through publication of the Harvard Journal of Asiatic Studies, and through the Harvard-Yenching Library, which became an integral part of Harvard University as of July 1, 1976. Grants given only for research or study by faculty members of invited universities in East and Southeast Asia.

Fields of interest: Higher education.

International interests: Asia.

Type of support: Fellowships; Scholarship funds; Research.

Limitations: Applications accepted. Giving primarily in Asia. No grants to individuals except for fellowships or scholarships.

Publications: Application guidelines; Program policy statement.

Application information: Application form required for scholarships; applicants nominated by participating universities. Application form required.
Initial approach: Letter
Copies of proposal: 1
Deadline(s): Dec. 3 for Fellowships for Advanced Research in Chinese Studies
Board meeting date(s): Dec. and Apr.
Final notification: Mar. for Visiting Scholars and Student Exchange Fellowship; May for Doctoral Scholarships

Officers and Trustees: * Peter Geithner,* Chair.; Peter L. Kelley, Exec. Dir.; Weiming Tu, Fdn. Dir.; Charles Booth; Stephen Bosworth; William Kirby; Sarah Reed; Patricia Stranahan; Hue-Ho Tam Tai; Ezra F. Vogel; Ching-Mai Wu.

Number of staff: 6

EIN: 042062394

975
Haymarket People's Fund

42 Seaverns Ave.
Boston, MA 02130-2884 (617) 522-7676
Contact: Karla Nicholson, Exec. Dir.
FAX: (617) 522-9580; URL: http://
www.haymarket.org
Haymarket People's Fund's Philanthropy
Promise: http://www.ncrp.org/
philanthropys-promise/who

Established in 1974 in MA.
Grantmaker type: Public charity.
Financial data (yr. ended 06/30/10): Revenue,
$678,297; assets, $3,995,102 (M); gifts received,
$490,635; expenditures, $1,064,536; giving
activities include $512,858 for grants.
Purpose and activities: The fund is a progressive
organization that makes grants throughout New
England to grassroots groups which organize for
peace, equality, and economic justice.
Fields of interest: Environment; Health care; AIDS;
AIDS research; Employment; International peace/
security; Civil rights, race/intergroup relations; Civil/
human rights; Community development, citizen
coalitions; Community/economic development;
Minorities; Disabilities, people with; Women;
LGBTQ; Immigrants/refugees; Homeless.
International interests: Latin America; Middle East.
Type of support: General/operating support;
Emergency funds; Program development.
Limitations: Applications accepted. Giving limited to
CT, ME, MA, NH, RI, and VT. No support for social
service organizations, government agencies,
alternative businesses, or groups receiving
significant government or corporate funding. No
grants to individuals.
Publications: Application guidelines; Annual report;
Financial statement; Grants list; Newsletter.
Application information: Grant proposals received
by fax or e-mail not accepted. Application form
required.
  Initial approach: Download cover sheet
  Deadline(s): Feb. 1 (CT, ME, NH, RI, and VT) and
  Mar. 30 and Dec. 1 (MA) for Sustaining Grants;
  Oct. 15 for Media Justice Grants; none for
  Bridge and Emergency Grants
  Board meeting date(s): Every two months
  Final notification: Dec. for Media Justice Grants;
  within one month after funding board decisions
  for all others
Officers: Rosemary Candelario, Pres.; Karla Tolbert,
Treas.; Karla Nicholson, Exec. Dir.
EIN: 042586725

976
The Hershey Family Foundation

(formerly Barry J. Hershey Foundation)
c/o Ropes & Gray
1 International Pl.
Boston, MA 02110-2624

Established around 1988 in MA.
Donor: Barry J. Hershey.
Grantmaker type: Independent foundation.
Financial data (yr. ended 12/31/09): Assets,
$63,052,209 (M); gifts received, $71,000;
expenditures, $3,544,183; qualifying distributions,
$3,499,694; giving activities include $3,498,052
for 37 grants (high: $1,330,000; low: $5,000).
Purpose and activities: Giving primarily for the arts,
education, health associations, human services,
Buddhist-related organizations, as well as to a

Montreal, Canada-based organization devoted to
Tibetan culture.
Fields of interest: Performing arts, theater; Arts;
Elementary/secondary education; Libraries (public);
Animals/wildlife; Hospitals (general); Health
organizations, association; Food services; Human
services; International affairs; Public affairs, public
education; Buddhism.
International interests: Canada.
Limitations: Applications not accepted. Giving
primarily in CA and MA, as well as in Montreal,
Canada. Generally, no grants to individuals.
Application information: Contributes only to
pre-selected organizations. Unsolicited requests for
funds not accepted.
Trustees: Barry J. Hershey; Connie Hershey.
EIN: 341574366

977
Homestead Foundation of Washington, D.C.

c/o Russell, Brier & Co. LLP
10 Post Office Sq., 6th Fl.
Boston, MA 02109-4603
Application address: c/o Boston Financial Mgmt.,
Attn.: John S. Goldthwait, 1 Winthrop Sq., Boston,
MA 02110-1257, tel.: (617) 275-0355

Established in 1990 in MA.
Grantmaker type: Independent foundation.
Financial data (yr. ended 12/31/09): Assets,
$2,093,266 (M); expenditures, $271,713;
qualifying distributions, $254,215; giving activities
include $249,000 for 12 grants (high: $54,000;
low: $5,000).
Fields of interest: International studies;
Reproductive health, family planning; Health care;
Children/youth, services; Family services;
Community development, civic centers; Community/
economic development; United Ways and Federated
Giving Programs.
Type of support: Annual campaigns; Building/
renovation; Program development; Program-related
investments/loans.
Limitations: Applications accepted. Giving primarily
in the greater metropolitan Washington, DC, area,
MA and MD. No grants to individuals.
Publications: Application guidelines.
Application information: Application form not
required.
  Initial approach: Letter
  Deadline(s): None
Trustees: Doris D. Blazek-White; John S. Goldthwait.
EIN: 223035067

978
The Lawrence H. Hyde, Jr. Charitable Trust

P.O. Box 854
Harwich Port, MA 02646-0854

Established in 1993 in MA.
Donor: Lawrence H. Hyde, Jr.
Grantmaker type: Independent foundation.
Financial data (yr. ended 12/31/10): Assets,
$2,734,710 (M); gifts received, $96,830;
expenditures, $209,111; qualifying distributions,
$205,800; giving activities include $205,800 for 8
grants (high: $100,000; low: $1,000).
Purpose and activities: Support of Catholic
seminaries in impoverished areas.
Fields of interest: Catholic agencies & churches.

International interests: Africa; South America; Asia.
Type of support: Continuing support.
Limitations: Applications not accepted. Giving
primarily in IL and MD. No grants to individuals.
Application information: Contributes only to
pre-selected organizations.
Officer: Lawrence H. Hyde, Jr., Pres.
EIN: 137024608

979
Indo-American Charities, Inc.

49 Applecrest Rd.
Weston, MA 02493-1101

Established in 2004 in MA as an independent
foundation.
Donors: Lilly J. Fernandez; Joseph D. Fernandez.
Grantmaker type: Independent foundation.
Financial data (yr. ended 12/31/10): Assets,
$12,249 (M); gifts received, $119,992;
expenditures, $208,282; qualifying distributions,
$207,575; giving activities include $207,575 for 1
grant.
Purpose and activities: Giving to implement
programs for the development of the underprivileged
in India and to support programs for the second
generation children in the United States.
Fields of interest: International relief; Economically
disadvantaged; Children/youth.
International interests: India.
Limitations: Applications not accepted. Giving
primarily in India. No grants to individuals.
Application information: Contributes only to
pre-selected organizations.
Officers: Jessy J. Fernandez, Pres.; Premthaj Carlos,
V.P.; Joseph D. Fernandez, Clerk.
Directors: Lilly J. Fernandez; George Nedy; John
Fernz; Jay J. Fernandez.
EIN: 043518827

980
International Fund for Animal Welfare, Inc.

411 Main St.
P.O. Box 193
Yarmouth Port, MA 02675-1843
FAX: (508) 744-2009; E-mail: info@ifaw.org; Toll-free
tel.: (800) 932-4329; URL: http://www.ifaw.org

Established in 1998 in MA, founded in 1969.
Grantmaker type: Public charity.
Financial data (yr. ended 06/30/10): Revenue,
$20,177,095; assets, $51,884,905 (M); gifts
received, $18,916,561; expenditures,
$17,924,874; giving activities include $273,883
for grants, and $1,696,265 for grants to
organizations outside the U.S.
Purpose and activities: The organization seeks to
motivate the public to prevent cruelty to animals and
to promote animal welfare, and conservation
policies that advance the well-being of both animals
and people.
Fields of interest: Animal welfare; Animals/wildlife,
preservation/protection; Animals/wildlife,
endangered species; Animals/wildlife.
International interests: Canada; Russia; Africa;
South Africa; Latin America; China; Australia.
Type of support: General/operating support;
Equipment; Land acquisition; Emergency funds;
Program development; Conferences/seminars;
Publication; Research; Scholarships—to
individuals; In-kind gifts.

Limitations: Applications not accepted. Giving on a national and international basis.
Application information: Contributes only to pre-selected organizations.
Officers and Directors: * Thomas C. Ramey,* Chair.; Frederick O'Regan,* Pres and C.E.O.; Azzedine Downes,* Exec. V.P. and C.O.O.; Barbara Fried,* V.P., Fund Devel.; Melanie B. Powers,* C.F.O.; Angelica Aragon; Keely Shaye Brosnan; Pierce Brosnan; Brian Hutchinson; Margaret A. Kennedy; Sean Rocks; Gary M. Tabor, V.M.D.; and 8 additional directors.
EIN: 311594197

981

International Society for Infectious Diseases, Inc.

(also known as ISID)
9 Babcock Str., 3rd Fl.
Brookline, MA 02446-3202   (617) 277-0551
Contact: Norman Stein, Exec. Dir.
FAX: (617) 278-9113; E-mail: info@isid.org;
URL: http://www.isid.org

Established in 1986 in MA; as a result of the merger of the International Congress on Infectious Diseases (ICID) and the International Federation on Infectious and Parasitic Diseases (IFIPD).
Grantmaker type: Public charity.
Financial data (yr. ended 12/31/10): Revenue, $2,662,902; assets, $4,568,887 (M); gifts received, $2,599,019; expenditures, $2,486,497; giving activities include $96,200 for grants to organizations outside the U.S.
Purpose and activities: The society seeks to improve the care of patients with infectious diseases, the training of clinicians and researchers in infectious diseases and microbiology, and the control of infectious diseases around the world.
Fields of interest: International exchange; Public health, communicable diseases; Medical research.
Type of support: Fellowships; Research; Grants to individuals.
Limitations: Applications accepted. Giving on a national and international basis.
Publications: Application guidelines.
Application information: Application form required.
  Initial approach: Download application form
  Deadline(s): Mar. 1 for Scientific Exchange Fellowship; Apr. 1 for Small Grants Program and SSI/ISID Fellowship
Officers and Directors: * Daniel Lew,* Pres.; Keith Klugman,* Pres.-Elect.; Keryn Christiansen,* Secy.; Jonathan Cohen,* Treas.; Ron Dagan; Raul Isturiz; Adeeba Kamarulzaman; Carlo Odio; Richard Wenzel.
EIN: 222473000

982

Invincibility Foundation

c/o Loring Wolcott Coolidge
230 Congress St.
Boston, MA 02110-2409   (641) 469-5477
Contact: Kenneth Cavanaugh, Pres. and Treas.
Application address: Kenneth Cavanaugh, 2000 N. Court 16-L, Fairfield, IA 52556 tel: (641) 469-5477

Established in 2007 in IA.
Donors: Fay M. Chandler; Howard M. Chandler.
Grantmaker type: Independent foundation.
Financial data (yr. ended 12/31/10): Assets, $182,922 (M); gifts received, $305,000;

expenditures, $194,592; qualifying distributions, $194,018; giving activities include $193,000 for 3 grants (high: $108,000; low: $10,000).
Fields of interest: International peace/security; International development; Hinduism.
International interests: Africa; India.
Limitations: Applications accepted. Giving primarily in IA and NY.
Application information: Application form required.
  Initial approach: Letter
  Deadline(s): None
Officers: Kenneth Cavanaugh, Pres. and Treas.; Gwendolyn Cavanaugh, Secy.
Director: Howard M. Chandler.
EIN: 421745339

983

Izumi Foundation

1 Financial Ctr., 28th Fl.
Boston, MA 02111-2621   (617) 292-2333
FAX: (617) 292-2315; E-mail: info@izumi.org;
URL: http://www.izumi.org

Supporting organization of Shinnyo-En Foundation.
Grantmaker type: Public charity.
Financial data (yr. ended 12/31/10): Revenue, $2,055,951; assets, $59,174,523 (M); expenditures, $1,971,208; giving activities include $1,379,101 for grants, and $194,820 for grants to organizations outside the U.S.
Purpose and activities: The foundation strives to help the earth's poorest people live healthier lives by supporting programs for infectious diseases, particularly neglected infectious diseases, in developing countries.
Fields of interest: International relief.
International interests: Developing countries.
Limitations: Applications accepted. Giving primarily in developing countries.
Publications: Application guidelines.
Application information: The foundation will only consider those organizations that are invited to submit proposals following a letter of inquiry; unsolicited proposals not otherwise considered or acknowledged.
  Initial approach: Letter of inquiry (no more than three pages)
  Deadline(s): None
Officers and Directors: * Shinrei Ito,* Pres.; Yukio Tajiri,* Treas.; Takuji Sano.
EIN: 043439149

984

The Jacobson Family Trust Foundation

14 Highfields Rd.
Wayland, MA 01778-2816

Established in 1997 in MA.
Donor: Jonathon Jacobson.
Grantmaker type: Independent foundation.
Financial data (yr. ended 12/31/09): Assets, $286,669,286 (M); gifts received, $10,000,250; expenditures, $16,071,600; qualifying distributions, $13,139,978; giving activities include $13,127,728 for 70 grants (high: $2,050,000; low: $250).
Fields of interest: Jewish agencies & synagogues; Foundations (private grantmaking); Children/youth, services; Elementary/secondary education; Higher education; Education; Human services; Jewish federated giving programs.

Limitations: Applications not accepted. Giving primarily in MA, with emphasis on the Boston area. No grants to individuals.
Application information: Contributes only to pre-selected organizations.
Trustees: Joanna Jacobson; Jonathon Jacobson.
EIN: 046836735
Recent grants for international programs:
984-1 American Friends of Magen David Adom, New York, NY, $10,000. For general support. 2008.
984-2 American Israel Education Foundation, Washington, DC, $250,000. For general support. 2008.
984-3 Birthright Israel Foundation, New York, NY, $500,000. For general support. 2008.
984-4 David Project, Boston, MA, $100,000. For general support. 2008.
984-5 Middle East Media Research Institute, Washington, DC, $25,000. For general support. 2008.
984-6 My Sisters Keeper, Jamaica Plain, MA, $25,000. For general support. 2008.
984-7 PEF Israel Endowment Funds, Kolot, New York, NY, $35,000. For general support. 2008.
984-8 Project Healthy Children, Newton, MA, $75,000. For general support. 2008.

985

The Jenzabar Foundation

101 Huntington Ave., Ste. 2205
Boston, MA 02199-7603   (617) 492-9099
Contact: John Beahm, Exec. Dir.
FAX: (617) 492-9081;
E-mail: info@thejenzabarfoundation.org; Additional e-mail: foundation@jenzabar.net; URL: http://www.thejenzabarfoundation.org/ics
Facebook: http://www.facebook.com/pages/Student-Leaders-in-Community-Service-SLICS/89407469914
Twitter: http://twitter.com/StudentsCare

Established in 2007.
Donor: Jenzabar, Inc.
Grantmaker type: Public charity.
Financial data (yr. ended 12/31/09): Revenue, $10,164; assets, $468,853 (M); expenditures, $397,978; giving activities include $332,000 for grants.
Purpose and activities: The mission of the foundation is to recognize and support the good works and humanitarian efforts of student leaders serving others across the global community.
Fields of interest: Student services/organizations; Higher education; Human services; International development; Community/economic development; Electronic communications/Internet; Leadership development.
Type of support: Program development; Technical assistance.
Limitations: Applications accepted. Giving in the U.S.
Publications: Application guidelines.
Application information: Applicants must first register online with the foundation before accessing application materials; see foundation web site for application guidelines and requirements, including downloadable application form. Application form required.
  Initial approach: Completed application form may be submitted by e-mail, fax, or postal mail.
  Copies of proposal: 1
  Deadline(s): Mar. 31 for Jenzabar Student Leadership Awards

Officers: Robert A. Maginn, Jr., Chair.; John Beahm, Exec. Dir.
EIN: 261635489

986
The Henry P. Kendall Foundation
176 Federal St.
Boston, MA 02110-2214 (617) 951-2525
Contact: Theodore M. Smith, Exec. Dir.
FAX: (617) 951-2556;
E-mail: request_info@kendall.org; URL: http://www.kendall.org

Trust established in 1957 in MA.
Donors: Henry Kendall†; Henry Way Kendall Trust; and members of the Henry P. Kendall family.
Grantmaker type: Independent foundation.
Financial data (yr. ended 12/31/10): Assets, $79,102,919 (M); expenditures, $1,195,086; qualifying distributions, $225,346; giving activities include $225,346 for grants.
Purpose and activities: Emphasis on strategic environmental policies/ecosystem management.
Fields of interest: Environment, natural resources.
International interests: Canada.
Type of support: Management development/capacity building; Research; General/operating support; Program development; Seed money; Internship funds.
Limitations: Applications not accepted. Giving primarily in western Canada and in New England, the Northeast and the Northwestern United States. No support for waste clean-ups, toxic or air/water pollution prevention or pollution monitoring initiatives, land trusts, or species-specific preservation efforts. No grants to individuals, or for capital or endowment funds, building construction/operation, basic research, scholarships, fellowships, equipment, debt reduction, or conference participation/travel.
Publications: Biennial report.
Application information: Unsolicited proposals and inquiries will not be reviewed.
    Board meeting date(s): Mar., June, and Nov.
Officer: Theodore M. Smith, Exec. Dir.
Trustees: Andrew W. Kendall; John P. Kendall; Phoebe Winder.
Number of staff: 6 full-time professional.
EIN: 046029103

987
Klarman Family Foundation
(formerly The Seth A. & Beth S. Klarman Foundation)
P.O. Box 171627
Boston, MA 02117 (617) 236-7909
Contact: Kim Philbrick McCabe, Exec. Dir.

Established in 1990 in MA.
Donors: Seth A. Klarman; Beth S. Klarman.
Grantmaker type: Independent foundation.
Financial data (yr. ended 12/31/09): Assets, $186,834,234 (M); gifts received, $40,000,000; expenditures, $21,584,774; qualifying distributions, $18,992,839; giving activities include $18,579,700 for 125 grants (high: $2,082,071; low: $235).
Purpose and activities: Giving primarily for the arts, Jewish organizations, education, and healing, including children's hospitals, and human services.

Fields of interest: Education; Hospitals (general); Human services; Children/youth, services; Jewish federated giving programs.
Limitations: Applications not accepted. Giving primarily in MA. No support for political organizations. No grants to individuals, or for endowments.
Trustees: Beth S. Klarman; Seth A. Klarman.
Number of staff: 2 full-time professional; 1 full-time support.
EIN: 043105768
Recent grants for international programs:
987-1 Albert Schweitzer Fellowship, Boston, MA, $25,000. For general operating support. 2009.
987-2 American Friends of LIBI, Brookline, MA, $50,000. For general purposes. 2009.
987-3 American Friends of Yahad in Unum, Chappaqua, NY, $100,000. For general operating support. 2009.
987-4 American Jewish World Service, New York, NY, $34,000. For general operating support. 2009.
987-5 American Society for Yad Vashem, New York, NY, $25,000. For general operating support. 2009.
987-6 Birthright Israel North America, New York, NY, $1,000,000. For general operating support. 2009.
987-7 Center for Security Policy, Washington, DC, $25,000. For general purposes. 2009.
987-8 Central Fund of Israel, New York, NY, $75,000. For general operating support. 2009.
987-9 Committee for Accuracy in Middle East Reporting in America, Boston, MA, $200,000. For general operating support. 2009.
987-10 David Project, Boston, MA, $871,765. For general operating support. 2009.
987-11 Friends of Ir David, Brooklyn, NY, $25,000. For general operating support. 2009.
987-12 Friends of the Israel Defense Forces, Newton, MA, $45,000. For general operating support. 2009.
987-13 HonestReporting.com, Skokie, IL, $20,000. For general operating support. 2009.
987-14 Israel Project, Washington, DC, $800,000. For general operating support. 2009.
987-15 Jewish Institute for National Security Affairs, Washington, DC, $30,000. For general operating support. 2009.
987-16 Middle East Forum, Philadelphia, PA, $50,000. For general operating support. 2009.
987-17 Middle East Media Research Institute, Washington, DC, $75,000. For general operating support. 2009.
987-18 PEF Israel Endowment Funds, New York, NY, $100,000. For general purposes. 2009.
987-19 Shalem Foundation, New York, NY, $250,000. For general operating support. 2009.
987-20 Silk Road Project, Boston, MA, $10,000. For general operating support. 2009.

988
The Peter and Deborah Lamm Foundation
(formerly Peter Lamm Foundation)
c/o Ropes & Gray LLP
1 International Pl.
Boston, MA 02110-2624
Contact: R. Bradford Malt, Tr.

Established in 1997 in MA.
Donor: Peter Lamm.
Grantmaker type: Independent foundation.

Financial data (yr. ended 12/31/10): Assets, $92,869 (M); gifts received, $225,000; expenditures, $219,377; qualifying distributions, $217,426; giving activities include $214,750 for 48 grants (high: $10,000; low: $250).
Purpose and activities: Giving primarily for health organizations, human services, and the arts.
Fields of interest: Jewish agencies & synagogues; International human rights; Arts; Education; Hospitals (general); Health organizations, association; Housing/shelter, search services; Human services; Children.
Limitations: Applications not accepted. Giving primarily in Boston, MA, and New York, NY. No grants to individuals.
Application information: Contributes only to pre-selected organizations.
Trustees: Deborah Lamm; Peter Lamm; R. Bradford Malt.
EIN: 043406251

989
LASPAU: Academic and Professional Program for the Americas, Inc.
25 Mt. Auburn St.
Cambridge, MA 02138-6095 (617) 495-5255
FAX: (617) 495-8990;
E-mail: laspau-webmaster@calists.harvard.edu;
URL: http://www.laspau.harvard.edu/

Established in 1964 in MA.
Grantmaker type: Public charity.
Financial data (yr. ended 12/31/10): Revenue, $17,243,866; assets, $12,344,306 (M); gifts received, $10,862,174; expenditures, $17,098,104; giving activities include $13,013,452 for grants to individuals.
Purpose and activities: The organization, in partnership with Harvard University, works to design, develop, and implement academic and professional programs to benefit the Americas.
Fields of interest: International affairs, public education; International exchange; Higher education.
International interests: Guyana; Haiti; Honduras; Jamaica; Mexico; Nicaragua; Panama; Paraguay; Peru; Saint Kitts-Nevis; Saint Lucia; Saint Vincent & the Grenadines; Suriname; Trinidad & Tobago; Uruguay; Venezuela; Guatemala; Grenada; El Salvador; Ecuador; Dominican Republic; Dominica; Cuba; Costa Rica; Colombia; Chile; Canada; Brazil; Bolivia; Belize; Barbados; Bahamas; Argentina; Antigua & Barbuda; Caribbean; Central America; Italy; South America; Spain.
Limitations: Giving primarily to Central and South America.
Publications: Annual report; Newsletter; Occasional report.
Officers and Trustees:* Gustavo Herrero,* Chair.; Cristian Shea,* Vice-Chair.; Peter Bryant,* Treas.; Ned D. Strong, Exec. Dir.; Alvano Rodriguez Arregui; Brian D. Farrell; William Fulbright Foote; Marilee S. Grindle; Eduardo R. Macagno; Felipe Medina; Lucia Santa Cruz; Jocelyn Sierra; Diana Sorensen; Hilda Catalina Cruz Solis.
EIN: 046151880

990
Lift Up Africa
P.O. Box 3112
Woburn, MA 01888-1912 (503) 408-6838
FAX: (503) 408-5766; E-mail: info@liftupafrica.org;
Toll -free tel. : (888)-854-3887; URL: http://
www.liftupafrica.org

Established in 2004.
Donors: CASE; United Way of King County;
Washington Mutual.
Grantmaker type: Public charity.
Financial data (yr. ended 12/31/10): Revenue,
$348,027; assets, $246,333 (M); gifts received,
$336,813; expenditures, $313,087; giving
activities include $166,066 for grants to
organizations outside the U.S.
Purpose and activities: The organization seeks to
work closely with individual African communities in
developing sustainable mechanisms for combating
the effects of extreme poverty, such as disease,
hunger, and lack of education.
Fields of interest: International development.
International interests: Tanzania, Zanzibar and
Pemba; Kenya.
Type of support: Management development/
capacity building; Land acquisition; Income
development; Building/renovation; Equipment;
Program development; Seed money; Technical
assistance; Program-related investments/loans;
Matching/challenge support.
Limitations: Applications accepted. Giving limited to
Africa. No grants to individuals, or for annual
campaigns, religious purposes, debt reduction,
emergency funds, relief activities, endowments,
exchange programs, fellowships, internships,
professorships, or scholarships.
Publications: Application guidelines; Financial
statement; Grants list; Informational brochure;
Newsletter; Occasional report; Program policy
statement.
Application information: Only organizations whose
letters of inquiry are of interest to the foundation will
be asked to submit an application. Application form
not required.
  Initial approach: Submit letter of inquiry
  Deadline(s): None
  Board meeting date(s): Quarterly
  Final notification: Within one month
Officers and Trustees:* William A. Longbrake,
Chair.; Samuel S. Muinde, V.P.; Richard M. Levy,
C.E.O.; Randy W. Harris.
Number of staff: 1 full-time professional.
EIN: 743116756

991
MacJannet Foundation, Inc.
396 Washington St.
Wellesley Hills, MA 02481-6209
(617) 875-7780
Contact: George R. Halsey, Secy.
FAX: (617) 247-3296;
E-mail: george.halsey@comcast.net; URL: http://
www.macjannet.org

Established in 1968.
Grantmaker type: Public charity.
Financial data (yr. ended 12/31/10): Revenue,
$80,654; assets, $842,600 (M); gifts received,
$34,134; expenditures, $117,606; giving activities
include $100,350 for grants.
Purpose and activities: The foundation seeks to
promote the Prieure in Talloires as a catalyst to

unleash individual potential and inspire
international understanding.
Fields of interest: Education.
International interests: France.
Type of support: Grants to individuals.
Limitations: Applications not accepted.
Application information: Contributes only to
pre-selected organizations.
Officers: Anthony Cook, Pres.; Jean-Marie Herve,
V.P.; George Halsey, Secy.; Douglas Marston, Treas.
Trustees: Willard B. Snyder; Douglas Marston;
Grace Lee Billings; Rocco Carzo.
EIN: 060849139

992
Nicholas C. & Anna F. Marcopolous
Charitable Foundation
c/o D. Ditelberg
4 Longfellow Pl., Ste. 3802
Boston, MA 02114-2835

Established in 1997 in NH.
Donors: Anna F. Marcopoulos; Nicholas C.
Marcopoulos.
Grantmaker type: Independent foundation.
Financial data (yr. ended 12/31/08): Assets,
$1,653 (M); expenditures, $459,291; qualifying
distributions, $435,261; giving activities include
$419,261 for 1 grant.
Fields of interest: Health organizations; Human
services; Orthodox agencies & churches; Aging.
International interests: Greece.
Type of support: General/operating support;
Scholarship funds.
Limitations: Applications not accepted. Giving
primarily in FL; giving also in Sparta, Greece. No
grants to individuals.
Application information: Contributes only to
pre-selected organizations.
Trustees: Dennis L. Ditelberg; John Peter Felopulos;
Kimon Zachos.
EIN: 043358007

993
Maya Educational Foundation
P.O. Box 1483
Wellfleet, MA 02667-1483
Contact: Armando J. Alfonzo, Treas.
E-mail: mef@mayaedufound.org; URL: http://
www.mayaedufound.org

Established in 1993 in VT.
Donor: Christopher Lutz.
Grantmaker type: Public charity.
Financial data (yr. ended 06/30/10): Revenue,
$477,395; assets, $1,313,326 (M); gifts received,
$580,740; expenditures, $574,750; giving
activities include $35,313 for grants, and
$506,671 for grants to organizations outside the
U.S.
Purpose and activities: The foundation provides
scholarships to individuals of Mayan descent in
Central America and Mexico; giving is also allocated
for literacy programs and workshops designed to
empower individuals through skills and knowledge.
Fields of interest: Education.
International interests: Central America;
Guatemala; Mexico.
Type of support: Scholarship funds; Grants to
individuals; Scholarships—to individuals.

Limitations: Applications not accepted. Giving
primarily in Guatemala and southeastern Mexico.
Publications: Annual report; Informational brochure;
Newsletter.
Application information: Unsolicited requests for
funds not accepted.
  Board meeting date(s): Nov.
Officers and Trustees:* Marilyn M. Moors,* Pres.;
Brenda Rosenbaum,* V.P.; Elisabeth S. Nicholson,*
Secy.; Armando J. Alfonzo, Treas.; Pablo Chavjay;
Christine Eber; Susan Feinberg; Robert Greenberg;
Carol Hendrickson; Mimi Laughlin; Robert Laughlin;
Christopher Lutz.
EIN: 030335159

994
Mazar Family Charitable Foundation Trust
c/o The Colony Group
2 Atlantic Ave.
Boston, MA 02110-3918

Established in 1997 in MA.
Donors: Anne Mazar; Brian Mazar.
Grantmaker type: Independent foundation.
Financial data (yr. ended 12/31/10): Assets,
$9,982,417 (M); gifts received, $172,725;
expenditures, $195,685; qualifying distributions,
$188,350; giving activities include $188,350 for 56
grants (high: $55,000; low: $100).
Fields of interest: Environment, natural resources;
Health care; Human services; Children/youth,
services; International development; United Ways
and Federated Giving Programs.
Limitations: Applications not accepted. Giving
primarily in MA. No grants to individuals.
Application information: Unsolicited requests for
funds not accepted.
Trustees: Anne Mazar; Brian Mazar.
EIN: 043344681

995
Memorial Foundation for the Blind, Inc.
(formerly Memorial Homes for the Blind)
799 W. Boylston St.
Worcester, MA 01606-3071 (508) 752-3053
Contact: Jerry Berrier, Pres.
URL: http://www.mfblind.org/

Established in 1951 in MA.
Grantmaker type: Independent foundation.
Financial data (yr. ended 03/31/11): Assets,
$3,717,502 (M); expenditures, $256,551;
qualifying distributions, $225,332; giving activities
include $225,332 for grants.
Purpose and activities: Support primarily for the
care of the visually handicapped.
Fields of interest: Media, radio; Libraries (public);
Eye diseases; Human services.
International interests: Greece.
Type of support: General/operating support.
Limitations: Giving primarily to residents of the
Worcester, MA, area.
Application information:
  Initial approach: Letter or proposal
  Copies of proposal: 1
  Deadline(s): None
Officers: Jerry Berrier, Pres.; T. Ashley Edwards,
V.P.; Jane Wiseman, Clerk; Gary MacConnell, Treas.
Directors: Eleanor Brockway; Helen D. Fifield;
James Gettens; Barbara Higgins; Janice La Breck;

Diane MacConnell; Larry Raymond; Janice Reidy; Joseph Reidy.
EIN: 041611615

996
The John Merck Fund
2 Oliver St., 8th Fl.
Boston, MA 02109 (617) 556-4120
Contact: Ruth G. Hennig, Secy. and Exec. Dir.
FAX: (617) 556-4130; E-mail: info@jmfund.org;
URL: http://www.jmfund.org
Grants List: http://www.jmfund.org/program.list.php

Established in 1970 in NY as a trust.
Donor: Serena S. Merck†.
Grantmaker type: Independent foundation.
Financial data (yr. ended 12/31/09): Assets, $156,239,400 (M); expenditures, $11,769,775; qualifying distributions, $9,604,655; giving activities include $8,348,000 for 133 grants (high: $280,000; low: $5,000; average: $10,000–$100,000).
Purpose and activities: Grants are made in the following areas: for medical research on causes of developmental disabilities in children; to build supply and demand for clear, renewable energy and reduce reliance on coal-fired power plants; to improve the health and vitality of rural communities in Maine, New Hampshire and Vermont by developing a sustainable food systems sector in the region; and to eliminate persistent bio-accumulative toxic chemicals and to encourage comprehensive precaution-based chemicals policy reforms in states to provide both models and upward pressure for eventual reform at the federal level.
Fields of interest: Environment, public policy; Environment, toxics; Environment, climate change/global warming; Environment; Employment, services.
Type of support: Mission-related investments/loans; General/operating support; Program development.
Limitations: Giving on a national basis in the areas of the environment. Generally, no support for large organizations with well-established funding sources. No grants to individuals, or for endowment or capital fund projects, generally no general support grants.
Publications: Grants list; Program policy statement.
Application information: The fund does not encourage the submission of unsolicited applications for grants. The fund prefers to request a grant proposal after receiving preliminary written or verbal information about a project. Application form required.
  Initial approach: Letter of inquiry
  Deadline(s): 1st day of Feb., May, Aug., and Nov.
  Board meeting date(s): Mar., June, Sept., and Dec.
  Final notification: Within 2 months
Officers and Trustees:* George Hatch,* Chair.; Ruth G. Hennig, Secy. and Exec. Dir.; Rick Burnes; Olivia H. Farr; Robert Gardiner; Whitney Hatch; Frederica Perera; Anne Stetson; Serena M. Whitridge.
Number of staff: 3 full-time professional; 1 part-time support.
EIN: 237082558
Recent grants for international programs:
996-1 Alliance for Justice, Washington, DC, $40,000. For Enforcing Human Rights: Torture Accountability. 2009.

996-2 Argentine Association for Civil Rights, Buenos Aires, Argentina, $60,000. For Expanding Equality in Access to Public Education in Argentina. 2009.
996-3 Argentine Forensic Anthropology Team, New York, NY, $55,000. For Scientific Documentation of Human Rights Violations in Argentina and Mexico. 2009.
996-4 Argentine Forensic Anthropology Team, New York, NY, $13,500. For Scientific Documentation of Human Rights Violations in Argentina and Mexico. 2009.
996-5 Asociacion Civil por la Igualdad y la Justicia, Buenos Aires, Argentina, $50,000. For Fundamental Rights: The Struggle to Ensure Equality of Access for the Poor. 2009.
996-6 Asociacion Civil por la Igualdad y la Justicia, Buenos Aires, Argentina, $27,500. For Fundamental Rights: The Struggle to Ensure Equality of Access for Buenos Aires' Poor. 2009.
996-7 Association for the Defense of Human Rights, Lima, Peru, $75,000. For Affirming the Way toward Truth and Justice in Peru. 2009.
996-8 Association for the Defense of Human Rights, Lima, Peru, $22,500. For general support. 2009.
996-9 Center for Justice and International Law, Washington, DC, $75,000. For Human Rights Work in Argentina, Chile, Colombia, Mexico, and Peru. 2009.
996-10 Center for Justice and International Law, Washington, DC, $25,000. For general support. 2009.
996-11 Center for Victims of Torture, Minneapolis, MN, $40,000. For New Strategies and Allies Against Torture. 2009.
996-12 Centro de Derechos Humanos Miguel Agustin Pro Juarez, Mexico City, Mexico, $25,000. For Defending Human Rights in Mexico: Citizen Security and Criminal Justice. 2009.
996-13 Centro de Estudio de Derecho Justicia y Sociedad, Bogota, Colombia, $75,000. For Strategic Plan. 2009.
996-14 Centro de Estudio de Derecho Justicia y Sociedad, Bogota, Colombia, $18,750. For general support. 2009.
996-15 Centro de Estudios Legales y Sociales, Buenos Aires, Argentina, $70,000. For general support. 2009.
996-16 Centro de Estudios Legales y Sociales, Buenos Aires, Argentina, $50,000. For general support. 2009.
996-17 Climate Counts, Manchester, NH, $15,000. For Review of the Merrimac Station Coal-Fired Power Plant. 2009.
996-18 Colombian Commission of Jurists, Bogota, Colombia, $75,000. For general support. 2009.
996-19 Colombian Commission of Jurists, Bogota, Colombia, $18,750. For general support. 2009.
996-20 Coordinadora Nacional de Derechos Humanos, Lima, Peru, $25,000. For Constructing a Human Rights Culture in Peru. 2009.
996-21 Diego Portales University, Santiago, Chile, $40,000. For Annual Report on Human Rights in Chile. 2009.
996-22 Diego Portales University, Santiago, Chile, $20,000. For Centro de Derechos Humanos. 2009.
996-23 Due Process of Law Foundation, Washington, DC, $40,000. For Promoting Access to Justice for Indigenous People in Mexico. 2009.

996-24 Equipo Colombiano de Trabajo Forense y Asistencia Psicosocial, Bogota, Colombia, $25,000. For general support. 2009.
996-25 Human Rights First, New York, NY, $100,000. For Law and Security Program and End Torture Now Campaign. 2009.
996-26 Human Rights First, New York, NY, $25,000. For general support. 2009.
996-27 Human Rights Watch, New York, NY, $25,000. For Emergency Human Rights Defenders Fund (Alison Des Forges Memorial Fund). 2009.
996-28 Human Rights Watch, New York, NY, $25,000. For Terrorism and Counterterrorism Program and Human Rights Defenders. 2009.
996-29 International Center for Transitional Justice, New York, NY, $35,000. For US Accountability Project. 2009.
996-30 International Chemical Secretariat, Gothenburg, Sweden, $48,000. For Promoting Greener Electronics. 2009.
996-31 International Persistent Organic Pollutants Elimination Network, Gothenburg, Sweden, $25,000. For Ensuring Strong Implementation of the Stockholm Convention on Persistent Organic Pollutants. 2009.
996-32 Legal Defense Institute, Lima, Peru, $40,000. For Strategic Litigation in the Context of New Threats to Human Rights, Democracy and the Rule of Law. 2009.
996-33 Legal Defense Institute, Lima, Peru, $20,000. For general support. 2009.
996-34 Mexican Commission for the Defense and Promotion of Human Rights, Mexico City, Mexico, $50,000. For Strategic Litigation in the Field of Human Rights: A Tool for the Strengthening of Mexico's Democratic Institutions. 2009.
996-35 National Religious Campaign Against Torture, Washington, DC, $35,000. For general support. 2009.
996-36 New York University, Law School, Center on Law and Security, New York, NY, $30,000. For Accountability Project. 2009.
996-37 Physicians for Human Rights, Cambridge, MA, $75,000. For Reclaiming Core Values: Health Professionals Unite to Ban Torture. 2009.
996-38 Physicians for Human Rights, Cambridge, MA, $25,000. For general support. 2009.
996-39 Physicians for Social Responsibility, Los Angeles, CA, $40,000. For Women's Environmental Health Organizing Project: Building a Movement for Change. 2009.
996-40 Physicians for Social Responsibility, Seattle, WA, $24,000. For Toxic Free Legacy Campaign. 2009.
996-41 Physicians for Social Responsibility, Greater Boston Chapter, Somerville, MA, $50,000. For Environmental Threats to Healthy Aging. 2009.
996-42 Tlachinollan: Centro de Derechos Humanos de la Montana, Tlapa, Mexico, $45,000. For general support. 2009.
996-43 Tlachinollan: Centro de Derechos Humanos de la Montana, Tlapa, Mexico, $22,500. For general support. 2009.
996-44 Union of Concerned Scientists, Cambridge, MA, $60,000. For Civil Society and Biotechnology Policy: New Opportunities. 2009.
996-45 Union of Concerned Scientists, Cambridge, MA, $25,000. For Civil Society and Biotechnology Policy: New Opportunities. 2009.
996-46 University of Chile, Centro de Derechos Humanos, Santiago, Chile, $90,000. For International Human Rights Fellowship Program. 2009.

996-47 Washington Office on Latin America, Washington, DC, $60,000. For Improving US Policy in Colombia, Mexico, and Peru. 2009.

997
Min Charitable Trust

c/o E. Christopher Palmer
30 Colpitts Rd.
Weston, MA 02493-1534

Established in 1996 in MA.
Donors: Ophelia M. Dahl; Felicity Dahl; Lucy Dahl; Tessa Dahl; Theo M.R. Dahl.
Grantmaker type: Independent foundation.
Financial data (yr. ended 12/31/10): Assets, $43,143 (M); gifts received, $703,506; expenditures, $689,813; qualifying distributions, $686,434; giving activities include $686,434 for grants.
Fields of interest: Museums.
International interests: England.
Type of support: General/operating support.
Limitations: Applications not accepted. Giving primarily in Great Missenden, Buckinghamshire, England. No grants to individuals.
Application information: Contributes only to pre-selected organizations.
Officer: E. Christopher Palmer, Treas.
Trustees: Richard A. Cassell; Ophelia M. Dahl; John Vaughn-Fowler.
EIN: 137070451

998
Alfred L. & Annette S. Morse Foundation

c/o Ropes Gray, LLP
1 International Pl.
Boston, MA 02110-2624

Established in 1962 in MA.
Donors: Alfred L. Morse†; Annette S. Morse.
Grantmaker type: Independent foundation.
Financial data (yr. ended 12/31/10): Assets, $4,098,496 (M); expenditures, $254,543; qualifying distributions, $203,285; giving activities include $201,000 for 4 grants (high: $100,000; low: $32,500).
Purpose and activities: Giving primarily to Jewish organizations and for health care.
Fields of interest: International affairs; Education; Hospitals (general); Health care; Cancer; Human services; Jewish federated giving programs; Jewish agencies & synagogues.
Limitations: Applications not accepted. Giving primarily in Washington, DC, and FL. No grants to individuals.
Application information: Contributes only to pre-selected organizations.
Trustees: Robert N. Shapiro; Harriet M. Zimmerman.
EIN: 046142795

999
New England Biolabs Foundation

240 County Rd.
Ipswich, MA 01938-2723 (978) 998-7990
Contact: Jessica Brown, Exec. Dir.; Susan Foster, Asst. Dir.
FAX: (978) 356-3250; E-mail: fosters@nebf.org;
URL: http://www.nebf.org
Grants List: http://www.nebf.org/previous.html

Established in 1982 in MA.
Donors: New England Biolabs, Inc.; Donald G. Combs; Martine Kellett.
Grantmaker type: Company-sponsored foundation.
Financial data (yr. ended 12/31/10): Assets, $6,900,849 (M); gifts received, $163,739; expenditures, $622,463; qualifying distributions, $395,700; giving activities include $395,700 for grants.
Purpose and activities: The foundation supports programs designed to promote conservation of biological diversity including terrestrial and marine; sustain cultural diversity including linguistic diversity and traditional knowledge systems and practices; maintain ecosystem services with emphasis on water, soil, and carbon sequestration; promote food security and economic vitality of local communities; and sustain healthy reefs and fisheries. The foundation also awards limited grants to individuals for small environmental research projects.
Fields of interest: Animals/wildlife, preservation/protection; Arts; Elementary school/education; Environment, research; Environment, water resources; Environmental education; Animals/wildlife, fisheries; Agriculture, sustainable programs; Food services; Economic development; Biology/life sciences.
International interests: Belize; Bolivia; Cameroon; Central America; Developing countries; Ecuador; El Salvador; Ghana; Guatemala; Honduras; Madagascar; Nicaragua; Papua New Guinea; Peru; South America; Tanzania, Zanzibar and Pemba.
Type of support: Program development; Seed money; Curriculum development; Research; Grants to individuals; Matching/challenge support.
Limitations: Applications accepted. Giving primarily in New England, with emphasis on Boston, MA, area, particularly the North Shore region; giving also in Belize, Bolivia, Cameroon, Central America, Ecuador, El Salvador, Ghana, Guatemala, Honduras, Madagascar, Nicaragua, Papua New Guinea, Peru, South America, and Tanzania. No support for organizations located in Argentina, Belize, Brazil, Chile, Columbia, Costa Rica, French Guiana, Mexico, Panama, the Philippines, Suriname, Uruguay, Venezuela, or Vietnam or private schools. No grants to individuals (except for environmental research), or for non-marine issues in the Caribbean or Madagascar, non-environmental education projects in Guatemala, non-environmental projects in Ghana, educational or community projects of U.S. organizations not located in the Boston, MA, area, art projects located outside the immediate community, capital campaigns, renovations or building funds, conferences, workshops, or travel, production of videos, movies, or books, religious activities, general operating support, scholarships, fellowships, or internships, scientific research eligible for funding by major agencies, services for senior citizens, economically disadvantaged people, or disabled people, or species-specific projects.
Publications: Application guidelines; Grants list; Informational brochure (including application guidelines).
Application information: Letters of inquiry should be no longer than 1 page. A full proposal may be requested at a later date. Grants generally do not exceed $8,000. Priority is given to organizations that have received prior funding. Organizations receiving support are asked to provide a final report. Application form not required.
Initial approach: E-mail or mail letter of inquiry to foundation
Copies of proposal: 1

Deadline(s): None for letter of inquiry; Mar. 1 and Aug. 29 for proposal
Board meeting date(s): May and Dec.
Final notification: 2 months following board meetings
Officer: Jessica Brown, Exec. Dir.
Trustees: David Comb; Heidi Ellard; Henry P. Paulus, Ph.D.
Number of staff: 2 part-time professional.
EIN: 042776213

1000
New England Foundation for the Arts

(also known as NEFA)
145 Tremont St., 7th Fl.
Boston, MA 02111-1214 (617) 951-0010
Contact: Abigail Baisas, Comms. Coord.
FAX: (617) 951-0016; E-mail: info@nefa.org; E-mail for Abigail Baisas: abaisas@nefa.org; URL: http://www.nefa.org
Facebook: http://www.facebook.com/pages/NEFA/343365089783
Foundation blog: http://www.nefa.org/who_we_are/blog

Established in 1976 in MA.
Grantmaker type: Public charity.
Financial data (yr. ended 05/31/11): Revenue, $5,847,612; assets, $17,910,624 (M); gifts received, $5,499,577; expenditures, $5,858,101; giving activities include $3,257,259 for grants, and $192,187 for grants to individuals.
Purpose and activities: The foundation creatively supports the movement of people, ideas, and resources in the arts within New England and beyond; makes vital connections between artists and communities; and builds the strength, knowledge, and leadership of the region's creative sector.
Fields of interest: Performing arts, theater (musical); Performing arts, theater; Performing arts centers; Performing arts; Performing arts, music ensembles/groups; Performing arts, music composition; Performing arts, music (choral); Performing arts, music; Performing arts, dance; Arts, management/technical assistance; Arts, administration/regulation; Arts, fund raising/fund distribution; Arts, cultural/ethnic awareness; Arts councils; Arts.
International interests: Africa; Asia; Australia; Canada; Europe; South America.
Type of support: Program development; Fellowships; Technical assistance; Grants to individuals.
Limitations: Applications accepted. Giving on a national basis, primarily in New England, as well as international.
Publications: Application guidelines; Annual report; Newsletter.
Application information: Grants are awarded to arts organizations with 501(c)(3) status; individual choreographers and artists may apply for grant support if fiscally sponsored by an arts organization with 501(c)(3) status. Application form required.
Deadline(s): Varies
Officers and Directors:* Mary Kelley,* Chair.; Larry Simpson,* Vice-Chair.; Laura Paul, C.F.O.; Byron Champlin,* Secy.; John Plukas,* Treas.; Rebecca Blunk, Exec. Dir.; Jane Preston, Dir., Progs.; Geeta Aiyer; Alex Aldrich; Sandra Burton; Andrew P. Cornell; Lynn Martin Graton; Jane James; Ted Landsmark; Jennifer Lin; Jeremy Liu; Donna McNeil; Christopher "Kip" McMahan; David McWilliams;

Raul Medina; Peter Nessen; Trudie Lamb Richmond; Andrea Rogers; Randy Rosenbaum; An-Ming Truxes; Anita Walker.
Number of staff: 16 full-time professional; 3 part-time professional.
EIN: 042593591

1001
One World Fund
38 Essex St.
Andover, MA   01810-3761
Application address: c/o One World Fund, Attn.: Richard Healy, 64R Prospect St., Cambridge, MA 02139

Established in 1990 in MA.
Donor: Josephine L. Murray.
Grantmaker type: Independent foundation.
Financial data (yr. ended 12/31/10): Assets, $3,641,876 (M); expenditures, $302,269; qualifying distributions, $200,000; giving activities include $200,000 for 15 grants (high: $30,000; low: $5,000).
Fields of interest: Crime/violence prevention; Civil rights, race/intergroup relations; Performing arts, dance; Performing arts, theater; Children, services; International peace/security; United Ways and Federated Giving Programs; Women; Girls.
Limitations: Applications accepted. Giving primarily in CA, MA, MN and NY. No grants to individuals.
Application information:
  Initial approach: Letter
  Deadline(s): None
Trustees: Diana Devegh; Richard Healy; Dr. Josephine Murray.
EIN: 046485766

1002
Oxfam America
226 Causeway St., 5th Fl.
Boston, MA   02114-2155
FAX: (617) 728-2594;
E-mail: info@oxfamamerica.org; Toll-free tel.: (800) 776-9326; Additional tel. (outside the U.S.): (617) 482-1211; URL: http://www.oxfamamerica.org
Blog: http://blogs.oxfamamerica.org/
Facebook: http://www.facebook.com/ oxfamamerica
Flickr: http://www.flickr.com/photos/ oxfamamerica
RSS Feed: http://www.oxfamamerica.org/press/ pressreleases/all-press-releases/RSS
Twitter: http://twitter.com/oxfamamerica
YouTube: http://www.youtube.com/user/ oxfamamerica

Established in 1970 in MA.
Grantmaker type: Public charity.
Financial data (yr. ended 10/31/10): Revenue, $84,865,882; assets, $97,875,378 (M); gifts received, $84,320,475; expenditures, $77,369,224; giving activities include $2,230,737 for grants, and $27,602,836 for 186 grants to organizations outside the U.S.
Purpose and activities: The organization seeks to create lasting solutions to poverty, hunger, and social injustice.
Fields of interest: Disasters, Hurricane Katrina; International development; Civil/human rights, women; Civil/human rights.
International interests: Southern Africa; East Asia.

Type of support: Continuing support; Building/ renovation; Equipment; Emergency funds; Program development; Conferences/seminars; Seed money; Research; Technical assistance; Program evaluation.
Limitations: Applications not accepted. Giving on an international basis, primarily in Central America, Mexico, Caribbean, South America, West Africa, Horn of Africa, Southern Africa, and East Asia.
Publications: Annual report; Informational brochure; Newsletter; Program policy statement.
Application information: Contributes only to pre-selected organizations.
Officers and Directors:* Wendy Sherman, Chair.; Barry Gaberman, Vice. Chair.; Raymond C. Offenheiser,* Pres.; Joe H. Hamilton,* Secy.-Treas.; Elizabeth Becker; Brizio N. Biondi-Morra; Michael Carter; Rosalind Conway; Jonathan Fox; Bennett Freeman; Shigeki Makino; Minh Chau Nguyen; Steven Reiss; Gayle Smith; Janet van Zandt.
Number of staff: 150
EIN: 237069110

1003
The Patagonia Sur Foundation
P. O. Box 1268
Edgartown, MA   02539
Contact: A. Rogovin
E-mail: info@patagoniasurfoundation.org;
URL: http://www.patagoniasurfoundation.org/

Established in 2007.
Donors: Warren Adams; Megan Adams; David Tufaro; Sharon Tufaro; Fred Mouawad; Jim Levitt; Jane Levitt; Brian Hoesterey; Dawn Hoesterey; Elizabeth Daisy Helman; Stephen Reifenberg; Chris Cervenak; Daniel Nowiszewski; Bechler River Partners, LLC; Tufaro Family Ltd. Partnership; Patagonia Resources, LLC; BJP Ventures, LLC; Small Pond Investments, Ltd.; Dasant LTDA; Hvalbukta Ans.
Grantmaker type: Independent foundation.
Financial data (yr. ended 12/31/10): Assets, $233,823 (M); gifts received, $173,333; expenditures, $188,354; qualifying distributions, $171,032; giving activities include $171,032 for grants.
Purpose and activities: Giving primarily to encourage conservation and promote social and economic development in the Patagonia region of Chile.
Fields of interest: International development; Environment.
Limitations: Applications not accepted. Giving primarily in Chile; some funding also in the U.S., with emphasis on Cambridge, MA. No grants to individuals.
Application information: Contributes only to pre-selected organizations.
Board Members: Warren Adams; James Levitt; Brian Milder; Steve Reifenberg; Felipe Valdes.
EIN: 208875388

1004
Pathfinder International
9 Galen St., Ste. 217
Watertown, MA   02472-4521   (617) 924-7200
FAX: (617) 924-3833;
E-mail: information@pathfind.org; URL: http:// www.pathfind.org

Established in 1957.
Grantmaker type: Public charity.
Financial data (yr. ended 06/30/10): Revenue, $99,851,851; assets, $46,581,026 (M); gifts received, $99,826,795; expenditures, $102,298,778; giving activities include $8,967,445 for grants to organizations outside the U.S.
Purpose and activities: Pathfinder International places reproductive health services at the center of all that it does-believing that health care is not only a fundamental human right but is critical for expanding life opportunities for women, families, communities, and nations, while paving the way for transformations in environmental stewardship, decreases in population pressures, and innovations in poverty reduction. Pathfinder provides women, men, and adolescents with a range of quality health services-from contraception and maternal care to HIV prevention and AIDS care and treatment. Pathfinder strives to strengthen access to family planning, ensure availability of safe abortion services, advocate for sound reproductive health policies, and, through all of its work, improve the rights and lives of the people it serves.
Fields of interest: Reproductive health; Reproductive health, family planning; AIDS; Civil liberties, reproductive rights; Youth; Young adults, male; Young adults, female; Young adults; Women; Men; LGBTQ; Girls; Economically disadvantaged; Children/youth; AIDS, people with; Adults, women; Adults, men; Adults.
International interests: Developing countries.
Limitations: Applications not accepted. Giving subgrants only on an international basis.
Publications: Annual report.
Application information: Pathfinder International does not engage in any primary grantmaking activities. Applications will not be accepted or acknowledged.
  Board meeting date(s): May and Nov.
Officers and Directors:* Cynthia A. Fields,* Chair.; Daniel E. Pellegrom,* Pres.; Caroline Crosby, M.D.A., Sr. V.P.; Demet Gural, M.D., M.P.H., V.P., Progs.; Erin S. Majernik, V.P., Resource Devel.; Dr. Manuel Urhina Fuentes,* Secy.; Thomas Downing, C.F.O.; James M. Schwartz,* Treas.; Andrew A. Arkutu; Chaudine Bacher; Richard L. Berkowitz, M.D.; Cornelia L. Cook; Patricia J. Cooper; Andrew L. Frey; Walter J. Gamble; Dr. Susan M. George; Jane L. Havemeyer; Anne H. Johnson; Ben R. Kahrl; Edward M. Kaplan; Rajen A. Kilachand; Elisabeth L. Lyon; Dr. Florence W. Manguyu; Deborah B. Prothrow-Stith, M.D.; Valerie C. Spencer; Kathryn Ketcham Strong; Ronda E. Stryker; John F. Swift; Alfred W. Tate; Ralph S. Tate; June L. Tatelman; Roslyn M. Watson.
Number of staff: 808
EIN: 530235320

1005
Peace Development Fund
44 N. Prospect St
P.O. Box 1280
Amherst, MA   01004-1280   (413) 256-8306
Contact: Kazu Haga, Prog. Coord.
FAX: (413) 256-8871;
E-mail: grants@peacefund.org; URL: http:// www.peacedevelopmentfund.org
Peace Development Fund's Philanthropy Promise: http://www.ncrp.org/ philanthropys-promise/who

Established in 1981 in MA.
Grantmaker type: Public charity.
Financial data (yr. ended 06/30/10): Revenue, $898,842; assets, $1,177,426 (M); gifts received, $849,309; expenditures, $1,113,743; giving activities include $514,624 for grants, and $16,950 for grants to organizations outside the U.S.
Purpose and activities: The fund provides grants to organizations and projects working to achieve peaceful, just, and equitable relationships among people and nations, by focusing on three core areas: relationships between the U.S. and peoples and countries elsewhere in the world; relationships among people and groups within the U.S.; and relationships between institutions, the power that maintains them, and the individuals whom they serve.
Fields of interest: Civil/human rights, equal rights; Environment, legal rights; Crime/law enforcement, equal rights; International peace/security; Civil/human rights, public education; Civil/human rights, LGBTQ; Civil rights, race/intergroup relations; Civil/human rights; Community development, citizen coalitions.
International interests: Haiti; Mexico.
Type of support: General/operating support; Technical assistance.
Limitations: Applications accepted. Giving primarily in the U.S. and its territories, Mexico, and Haiti. No support for academic institutions, audio-visual productions and distribution, organizations with large budgets, or organizations that have access to other sources of funding. No grants to individuals, or for scholarships, research, conferences, or other one-time events.
Publications: Application guidelines; Annual report; Financial statement; Grants list; Newsletter.
Application information: Application form is available on the fund's web site; applications are only accepted via e-mail. Application form required.
   Initial approach: Download application
   Copies of proposal: 1
   Deadline(s): Feb. for Community Organizing Grants; rolling for Fiscal Sponsorship
   Board meeting date(s): June
   Final notification: June/July for Community Organizing Grants; between eight and twelve weeks for Fiscal Sponsorship
Officers and Directors:* Teresa Juarez,* Pres.; Michelle Curry,* Secy.; Lori Goodman,* Treas.; Paul Haible, Exec. Dir.; Kimo Campbell; Ali El-Issa; Vanessa Ramos; Tina Reynolds.
Number of staff: 5 full-time professional.
EIN: 042738794

1006
Peacemaker Circle Foundation, Inc.
177 Ripley Rd.
Montague, MA 01351-9541
Organization Blog: http://peacemakerscircle.blogspot.com/

Grantmaker type: Public charity.
Financial data (yr. ended 06/30/09): Revenue, $50.
Purpose and activities: The foundation works to provide training in peacemaking, social enterprise, and Zen practice.
Fields of interest: International peace/security; Buddhism.
Officers: Bernard Glassman, Pres.; Eve Marko, Secy.
EIN: 800078825

1007
The Pegasus Foundation
c/o Day, Pitney, LLP
One International Pl.
Boston, MA 02110-2602
Contact: Peter A. Bender, Exec. Dir.
E-mail: info@pegasusfoundation.org; Application address for invited organizations only: 27 Merrimack St., Concord, NH 03301, tel.: (603) 225-3918; Fax: (603) 225-4624; e-mail: aostberg@pegasusfoundation.org; URL: http://www.pegasusfoundation.org/

Established in 1996 in MA.
Donor: Barbara U. Birdsey.
Grantmaker type: Independent foundation.
Financial data (yr. ended 12/31/10): Assets, $943,135 (M); gifts received, $352,951; expenditures, $430,738; qualifying distributions, $237,449; giving activities include $220,800 for 25 grants (high: $75,000; low: $200).
Purpose and activities: The Pegasus Foundation was established in 1996 to fund initiatives that benefit animals and the environment. The Foundation's work is concentrated in several regions of the United States: the West and Southwest (Arizona and Montana), Florida, and Cape Cod, Massachusetts. Pegasus also funds animal welfare programs in the Caribbean and Kenya.
Fields of interest: Environment; Education, services; Animal welfare; Animal population control; Animals/wildlife, preservation/protection.
International interests: Kenya; Caribbean.
Type of support: Continuing support; Management development/capacity building; Program development; Conferences/seminars; Program evaluation; Matching/challenge support.
Limitations: Applications not accepted. Giving primarily in FL, MA, select western states, and in the Caribbean and Kenya. No grants to individuals, or for endowments, deficit reduction, or scholarships.
Publications: Annual report; Informational brochure.
Application information: Unsolicited proposals not accepted. Proposals accepted only from current grantees and those who have been invited to apply.
   Board meeting date(s): Quarterly
Officer and Trustees:* Peter A. Bender,* Exec. Dir.; David W. Fitts; George W. Malloy; Stephen Ziobrowski.
Number of staff: 3 full-time professional; 1 part-time professional.
EIN: 223487149

1008
The Perls Foundation
c/o Loring Wolcott & Coolidge
230 Congress St.
Boston, MA 02110-2409

Established in 1998 in MA.
Donors: Klaus G. Perls; Amelia B. Perls.
Grantmaker type: Independent foundation.
Financial data (yr. ended 12/31/10): Assets, $18,949,102 (M); expenditures, $682,183; qualifying distributions, $381,513; giving activities include $381,513 for grants.
Fields of interest: Environment; International human rights; International development; Human services.
Limitations: Applications not accepted. Giving primarily in CA, Washington, DC, MA, and NY. No grants to individuals.

Application information: Contributes only to pre-selected organizations.
Trustees: Lennart C. Braberg; Katherine M. Perls.
EIN: 046864032

1009
Permanent Fund Trust for Harvard Travellers Club
c/o George Bates
P.O. Box 190
Canton, MA 02021-0190
E-mail: jessepage@comcast.net; URL: http://harvardtravellersclub.org

Established in 1937 in MA.
Grantmaker type: Public charity.
Financial data (yr. ended 04/30/11): Revenue, $10,750; assets, $123,578 (M); gifts received, $7,025; expenditures, $2,391; giving activities include $2,000 for grants.
Purpose and activities: The organization supports grants for research activities and exploration throughout the world involving travel.
Fields of interest: International affairs, research.
Type of support: Research; Grants to individuals.
Limitations: Applications accepted. Giving on a national and international basis.
Application information:
   Initial approach: Letter
   Deadline(s): Feb. 28
Officers and Directors: Nils Bonde-Henriksen,* Pres.; Alice Burgess,* V.P.; Marilyn Stempler,* V.P.; Kenneth Bures,* Secy.-Treas.; Madelon Bures; Peter Creighton; Gillian Kellogg; Pam Madigan; Terry Vose.
EIN: 046115589

1010
Planet Aid, Inc.
1 Cross St.
Holliston, MA 01746-2230   (508) 893-0644
FAX: (508) 893-0641; E-mail: info@planetaid.org; Additional tel. for Esther Neltrup: (410) 309-1002; URL: http://www.planetaid.org

Established in 1997 in MA.
Grantmaker type: Public charity.
Financial data (yr. ended 12/31/10): Revenue, $35,915,408; assets, $10,167,545 (M); gifts received, $27,458,861; expenditures, $35,358,402; giving activities include $101,940 for grants, and $11,721,892 for grants to organizations outside the U.S.
Purpose and activities: The organization is dedicated to improving the lives of people in developing countries; objectives include development, protecting the environment, and relief aid.
Fields of interest: Environment; International relief; Human services.
International interests: Developing countries.
Type of support: General/operating support; Program development.
Limitations: Applications not accepted. Giving primarily in developing countries.
Publications: Annual report; Newsletter.
Application information: Unsolicited requests for funds not considered or acknowledged.

Officers and Directors:* Mikael Norling,* Chair.; Ester Neltrup, Pres.; Jytte Martinussen, Treas.; David Hastings; Eva Nielsen; Clifford Reeves.
EIN: 043348171

1011
The Plumsock Fund
c/o JPMorgan Services, Inc.
1 Bridge St., No. 200
Newton, MA 02458-1138

Incorporated in 1959 in IN; supporting organization of the Maya Educational Foundation.
Donors: Evelyn L. Lutz†; Herbert B. Lutz; Sarah L. Lutz.
Grantmaker type: Public charity.
Financial data (yr. ended 06/30/10): Revenue, $29,071; assets, $8,163,868 (M); gifts received, $49,000; expenditures, $264,826; giving activities include $230,000 for grants.
Fields of interest: International development; Education, services; Economically disadvantaged; Indigenous peoples.
International interests: Central America; Mexico.
Limitations: Applications not accepted. Giving limited to South Woodstock, VT. No grants to individuals, for scholarships or fellowships; no loans.
Application information: Contributes only to pre-selected organizations.
Officers and Directors:* Christopher Lutz,* Pres.; Pam Solo,* Secy.-Treas.; Armando Alfonzo; Shelton Davis; Susan Fienberg.
EIN: 356014719

1012
PTC Corporate Giving Program
140 Kendrick St.
Needham, MA 02494-2739 (781) 370-5000
FAX: (781) 370-5647; E-mail: schools@ptc.com;
URL: http://www.ptc.com/company/community-relations.htm
PTC DesignQuest Schools Program: http://www.ptc.com/appserver/mkt/educational/program.jsp?&im_dbkey=52407&icg_dbkey=851

Grantmaker type: Corporate giving program.
Purpose and activities: PTC makes charitable contributions to secondary schools and secondary school teachers and on a case by case basis. Support is given in areas of company operations.
Fields of interest: Cancer; Secondary school/education; Higher education; Education; Voluntarism promotion; Science, formal/general education; Mathematics; Engineering/technology; Science.
International interests: Africa; Asia; China; Europe; Middle East.
Type of support: Conferences/seminars; Curriculum development; Employee volunteer services; Sponsorships; Grants to individuals; Donated equipment; Donated products; In-kind gifts.
Limitations: Applications accepted. Giving in areas of company operations, with emphasis on MA, Africa, Asia, China, Europe, and the Middle East.
Publications: Application guidelines.
Application information: Teachers receiving software donations are expected to attend training classes. The Partners Department handles giving. The company has a staff that only handles contributions. A contributions committee reviews all requests.
  Initial approach: E-mail headquarters for PTC DesignQuest Schools Program
  Deadline(s): None for PTC DesignQuest Schools Program
  Committee meeting date(s): Bimonthly
  Final notification: Following review
Number of staff: 12 full-time professional; 3 part-time professional.

1013
Real Colegio Complutense, Inc.
26 Trowbridge St.
Cambridge, MA 02138-5326 (617) 495-3536
FAX: (617) 496-3401;
E-mail: rcc-info@camail.harvard.edu; URL: http://www.realcolegiocomplutense.harvard.edu/indexEn.htm

Established in 1991 in MA.
Donors: Universidad Complutense; Allen & Overy; Fundacion Ico; Fundacion Rafael Del Pino; J. & A. Garrigues, S.L.; Make a Team Association; CEPSA; Biblioteca Josep LaParte; AFI.
Grantmaker type: Independent foundation.
Financial data (yr. ended 12/31/10): Assets, $0 (M); gifts received, $884,543; expenditures, $1,171,520; qualifying distributions, $1,145,564; giving activities include $298,930 for grants, and $267,410 for 42 grants to individuals (high: $15,500; low: $1,200).
Purpose and activities: Scholarships limited to Spaniards who are graduate students and who are not receiving funds from any other source. Support also for Spanish professors with a priority to those from UCM in Madrid, Spain.
Fields of interest: Education; Adults.
International interests: Spain.
Type of support: Scholarship funds; Grants to individuals; Scholarships—to individuals.
Limitations: Applications accepted. Giving primarily in MA, but limited to Spaniards.
Application information: Application information available on foundation web site. Application form required.
  Deadline(s): Mid-Apr.
  Board meeting date(s): Biannually
Officers: Carlos Berzosa, Pres.; Angel Saenz-Badillos, Clerk; David Kennedy, Treas.
Director: Margot Gill.
Number of staff: 1 full-time professional.
EIN: 043134531

1014
RESIST, Inc.
259 Elm St., No. 201
Somerville, MA 02144-2950 (617) 623-5110
Contact: Robin Carton, Dir., Grantmaking and Fin.
E-mail: grants@resistinc.org; URL: http://www.resistinc.org
Facebook: http://www.facebook.com/calltoresist
Flickr: http://www.flickr.com/photos/calltoresist/
MySpace: http://www.myspace.com/calltoresist
Twitter: http://twitter.com/#!/calltoresist

Established in 1967 in MA.
Grantmaker type: Public charity.
Financial data (yr. ended 12/31/10): Assets, $841,947; gifts received, $1,095,691; expenditures, $829,245; program services expenses, $355,195; giving activities include $321,157 for grants.
Purpose and activities: The organization gives small but timely grants to grassroots groups engaged in activist organizing and educational work within movements for social change. RESIST defines organizing as collective action to challenge the status quo, demand changes in policy and practice, and educate communities about root causes and just solutions. RESIST recognizes that there are a variety of stages and strategies that lead to community organizing. Therefore, RESIST supports strategies that build community, encourage collaborations with other organizations, increase skills and/or access to resources, and produce leadership from the constituency being most directly affected. High priority is given to groups that fall outside of mainstream funding sources because they are considered to be too "radical." To this end, RESIST supports both ongoing and new organizations that address social, racial, gender, economic and/or environmental injustice.
Fields of interest: Media/communications; Media, film/video; AIDS; Offenders/ex-offenders, rehabilitation; Youth development; International peace/security; International affairs, arms control; Civil/human rights, advocacy; Civil/human rights, LGBTQ; Civil rights, race/intergroup relations; Civil/human rights; Native Americans/American Indians; Women; LGBTQ.
Type of support: General/operating support; Emergency funds; Technical assistance.
Limitations: Applications accepted. No support for organizations with an annual budget over $150,000; groups that provide direct services, litigation, or other forms of support for legal organizations (unless directly connected to progressive organizing campaigns); organizations outside the U.S.; development of films or productions; or grant-giving organizations. No grants to individuals, or for research.
Publications: Application guidelines; Financial statement; Grants list; Informational brochure; Newsletter; IRS Form 990 or 990-PF printed copy available upon request.
Application information: RESIST's grant application forms are available on the web site (www.resistinc.org) or by calling in to the office for assistance. Answers to questions 1 - 14 should not exceed ten (10) pages and should use a standard 12 point typeface. One single-sided copy of RESIST's grant package (including cover sheet, application, and attachments) must be submitted in full by the proposal deadline. Do not use staples or binder clips. Common grant application forms are not accepted. Application form required.
  Initial approach: Letter, e-mail or telephone
  Copies of proposal: 1
  Deadline(s): Every eight weeks
  Board meeting date(s): 1st week of Feb., Apr., June, Aug., Oct., and Dec.
  Final notification: One to two weeks following board meeting
Officers and Directors:* Miabi Chatterjee,* Pres.; Becca Howes-Mischel,* Treas.; Cynthia Bargar; Jennifer Bonardi; Melissa Carino; Warren Goldstein-Gelb; Kay Mathew; Marc Miller; Jim O'Brien; Christy Pardew; Greg Pehrson; Nelson Salazar; Carol Schachet; Ragini Shah; Sarah Suong; Camilo Viveiros; Jen Willsea.
Number of staff: 4 full-time professional; 1 part-time professional.
EIN: 042433182

1015
Elizabeth Killam Rodgers Trust
c/o Nutter, McClennen & Fish, LLP
P.O. Box 51400
Boston, MA   02205-8982
Contact: Thomas P. Jalkut, Tr.

Established in 1975 in MA.
Donor: Elizabeth Killam Rodgers†.
Grantmaker type: Independent foundation.
Financial data (yr. ended 04/30/11): Assets,
$8,165,762 (M); expenditures, $227,005;
qualifying distributions, $162,163; giving activities
include $150,000 for 4 grants (high: $125,000;
low: $5,000).
Fields of interest: International exchange, students;
Higher education.
Limitations: Applications not accepted. Giving
primarily in MA and CT; funding also in Nova Scotia,
Canada. No grants to individuals.
Application information: Unsolicited requests for
funds not accepted.
Trustees: Thomas P. Jalkut; John B. Newhall.
EIN: 046385523

1016
The Ruettgers Family Charitable Foundation
c/o Atlantic Trust Co., N.A.
100 Federal St., 37th Fl.
Boston, MA   02110-1802

Established in 1997 in MA.
Donor: Michael Ruettgers.
Grantmaker type: Independent foundation.
Financial data (yr. ended 09/30/09): Assets,
$18,567,414 (M); expenditures, $1,055,272;
qualifying distributions, $917,200; giving activities
include $907,000 for 18 grants (high: $200,000;
low: $5,000).
Fields of interest: Education; Health care; Media/
communications; Libraries (public).
International interests: Rwanda.
Limitations: Applications not accepted. Giving
primarily in MA. No grants to individuals.
Application information: Contributes only to
pre-selected organizations.
Trustees: Abagail Ruettgers; Christopher Ruettgers;
Maureen Ruettgers; Michael Ruettgers; Polly
Ruettgers.
EIN: 043340951

1017
Sabre Foundation, Inc.
872 Massachusetts Ave., Ste. 2-1
Cambridge, MA   02139-3013   (617) 868-3510
FAX: (617) 868-7916; E-mail: inquiries@sabre.org;
URL: http://www.sabre.org

Established in 1969.
Grantmaker type: Public charity.
Financial data (yr. ended 12/31/10): Revenue,
$21,379,206; assets, $254,025 (M); gifts
received, $21,378,698; expenditures,
$21,400,717; giving activities include
$20,691,191 for grants to organizations outside the
U.S.
Purpose and activities: The foundation works to
build free institutions and to examine the ideals that
sustain them. Its largest project makes donated
books available to needy individuals in developing

and transitional societies worldwide through
non-governmental partner organizations, libraries,
universities, schools, research organizations and
other similar institutions.
Fields of interest: International development;
Education.
Type of support: In-kind gifts.
Limitations: Giving primarily on an international
basis.
Officers and Directors:* Kenneth G. Bartels,* Pres.;
Franz F. Colloredo-Mansfield,* V.P.; Charles
Getchell, Secy.; Thomas Conroy,* Treas.; John
Archibald; Jennifer Leaning; Bruce Rabb; Susan
Winthrop; and 7 additional directors.
EIN: 237042881

1018
The Schooner Foundation
(formerly Ryan Family Charitable Foundation)
c/o Schooner Capital LLC
745 Atlantic Ave., 11th Fl.
Boston, MA   02111-2738
Contact: Cynthia Ryan, Tr.
E-mail: cryan@schoonercapital.com

Established in 1996 in MA.
Donor: Vincent J. Ryan.
Grantmaker type: Independent foundation.
Financial data (yr. ended 12/31/08): Assets,
$37,414,716 (M); gifts received, $39,396,466;
expenditures, $5,567,746; qualifying distributions,
$3,753,810; giving activities include $3,666,862
for 96 grants (high: $500,172; low: $250).
Fields of interest: Arts; Higher education;
Education; Environment, natural resources; Health
organizations; Human services; International
peace/security; International affairs; Foundations
(private grantmaking).
Type of support: General/operating support; Income
development; Capital campaigns; Endowments;
Program development; Professorships; Seed
money; Fellowships; Scholarship funds; Consulting
services; Matching/challenge support.
Limitations: Applications not accepted. Giving
primarily in MA; some funding also in TN and
Washington, DC. No grants to individuals.
Application information: Contributes only to
pre-selected organizations.
Officer: Stephen D. Maiocco, Treas.
Trustees: Kimberly R. Dano; Stephanie R.
Ditenhafer; Jennifer R. Flynn; Carla E. Meyer; Cynthia
A. Ryan; Nicholas L. Ryan; Vincent J. Ryan.
Number of staff: 1 full-time professional.
EIN: 043347626

1019
SEVEN Fund
(also known as Social Equity Venture Fund)
1770 Massachusetts Ave., Ste. 247
Cambridge, MA   02140-2808
E-mail: info@sevenfund.org; URL: http://
www.sevenfund.org
Twitter: http://twitter.com/sevenfund

Established in 2007 in MA.
Grantmaker type: Public charity.
Financial data (yr. ended 03/31/10): Revenue,
$6,091,083; assets, $5,830,622 (M); gifts
received, $6,089,686; expenditures, $4,072,545;
giving activities include $248,528 for grants,

$1,253,645 for grants to organizations outside the
U.S., and $63,000 for grants to individuals.
Purpose and activities: The fund works to catalyze,
support, and disseminate research on questions of
economic development, prosperity, and
entrepreneurship, particularly new frontiers related
to enterprise-based solutions to poverty and
innovative ideas unlikely to be supported by
conventional funding sources.
Fields of interest: International affairs; Media, film/
video; Community/economic development,
research; Economic development; Community/
economic development; Economics; Poverty
studies; Economically disadvantaged.
Type of support: Program development; Scholarship
funds; Grants to individuals.
Limitations: Giving on a national and international
basis.
Publications: Application guidelines.
Application information:
  Deadline(s): Feb. 15 for Teaching Fellowship
    Competition; Oct. 15 (request for proposals)
    and Nov. 1 (full proposal) for Enterprise-Based
    Solutions to Poverty RFP; Sept. 15 for Cinema
    Prosperite Film Competition; Oct. 15 for
    SEVEN-CIFA Essay Competition; Dec. 7 for
    Essay Competition; rolling basis for
    Mini-Grants
  Final notification: Feb. 7 for Essay Competition
Officers and Directors:* Andreas Widmer,* Pres.;
Elizabeth Hooper, Exec. Dir.; Michael Brennan;
Regis Dale; Michael Fairbanks; Rev. Peter Gori.
EIN: 208981997

1020
Spero Charitable Foundation
c/o Shirley Spero
79 Florence St., Ste. 200
Chestnut Hill, MA   02467-1957

Established in 1968 in MA.
Donor: Louis Spero†.
Grantmaker type: Operating foundation.
Financial data (yr. ended 12/31/10): Assets,
$2,998,383 (M); expenditures, $293,650;
qualifying distributions, $293,121; giving activities
include $293,121 for 181 grants (high: $20,000;
low: $12).
Fields of interest: Arts; Child development,
education; Higher education; Business school/
education; Hospitals (general); Health care; Health
organizations, association; Cancer; Heart &
circulatory diseases; Cancer research; Heart &
circulatory research; Human services; Children/
youth, services; Child development, services; Aging,
centers/services; Homeless, human services;
Community/economic development; United Ways
and Federated Giving Programs; Catholic federated
giving programs; Jewish federated giving programs;
Government/public administration; Jewish agencies
& synagogues; General charitable giving; Minorities;
Aging; Homeless.
International interests: Israel.
Type of support: General/operating support; Annual
campaigns.
Limitations: Applications not accepted. Giving
primarily in MA. No grants to individuals.
Application information: Contributes only to
pre-selected organizations.
Trustees: Janet Kouroubacalis; Shirley Spero.
EIN: 046183682

1021
State Street Foundation, Inc.
1 Lincoln St
Boston, MA 02111-2900
Contact: Amanda Northrop, V.P., North America and Asia Pacific Grants
E-mail: StateStreetFoundation@statestreet.com; Contact local Community Support Chair. for more information: Los Angeles, CA , Diane Severino; Kansas City, MO, Dorrie Holland; New York, Jessica Hickey; Sacramento, CA, Jeanette Kuhl; Chicago, IL, Adam Browne; Princeton, NJ, Cynthia Pennell; Atlanta, GA, Allison Corbally; Princeton, NJ, Cynthia Pennell; Irvine, CA, Lena Loha;e-mail address for international applicants: statestreet@cafoline.org; URL: http://www.statestreet.com/wps/portal/internet/corporate/home/aboutstatestreet/corporatecitizenship/globalphilanthropy/statestreetfoundation/

Established in 2006 in MA.
Donor: State Street Bank & Trust Co.
Grantmaker type: Company-sponsored foundation.
Financial data (yr. ended 12/31/10): Assets, $36,621,422 (M); gifts received, $19,000,000; expenditures, $18,268,339; qualifying distributions, $18,264,839; giving activities include $15,980,611 for 622 grants (high: $650,267; low: $300); $1,709,642 for 4,316 employee matching gifts and $358,055 for set-asides.
Purpose and activities: The mission of State Street Foundation's strategic grantmaking program is to contribute to the sustainability of communities where State Street operates primarily by investing in education as it relates to employability for disadvantaged populations. Limited funding is also provided, by invitation only, to organizations and programs that deliver critical services to help people along the path to economic self-sufficiency.
Fields of interest: Adult education—literacy, basic skills & GED; Community development, neighborhood development; Community/economic development; Crime/violence prevention, youth; Education; Education, drop-out prevention; Education, services; Employment; Employment, training; Secondary school/education; Vocational education; Vocational education, post-secondary; Youth development; Disabilities, people with; Economically disadvantaged; Immigrants/refugees.
Type of support: Annual campaigns; Building/renovation; Capital campaigns; Continuing support; Emergency funds; Employee matching gifts; Employee volunteer services; General/operating support; In-kind gifts; Program development; Sponsorships.
Limitations: Applications accepted. Giving primarily in areas of company operations in CA, GA, IL, Boston and Quincy, MA, MO, NJ, NY, and NC, and in Australia, Austria, Belgium, Canada, Cayman Islands, Europe, France, Germany, India, Ireland, Italy, Japan, Luxembourg, the Middle East, Netherlands, Poland, Qatar, Singapore, South Africa, South Korea, Switzerland, Taiwan, and the United Kingdom. No support for political candidates or organizations, lobbying organizations, religious organizations not of direct benefit to the entire community, or labor or fraternal organizations. No grants to individuals, or for endowments, political causes or campaigns, sectarian activities for religious organizations, travel, team sponsorships or sporting events, or medical research or disease specific initiatives.
Publications: Application guidelines; Grants list.

Application information: Letters of interest should be no longer than 3 pages. Proposals should be no longer than 6 pages. Organizations receiving support are asked to provide a final report. Visit website for nearest community contact information.
Initial approach: E-mail letter of interest for new applicants to nearest community contact; download grant proposal summary form and e-mail to foundation and mail proposal to nearest company contact for existing applicants; e-mail international contact for organizations located in Canada, the Cayman Islands, Europe, Middle East, and South Africa
Deadline(s): None for letters of interest; Apr. 1, July 1, and Dec. 1 for existing applicants
Final notification: 8 weeks for letters of interest; Mid-March, Mid-July, and Mid-Nov. for existing applicants
Officers and Directors:* George A. Russell, Jr.,* Pres.; Simon Zornoza,* Clerk; James J. Malebra,* Treas.
EIN: 562615567
Recent grants for international programs:
1021-1 Aide a Domicile en Milieu Rural, Chimay, Belgium, $10,157. To provide low back pain prevention training to service providers offering mother's help and home help and care to rural villagers in south of Belgium. 2009.
1021-2 Aktion Sonnenschein, Munich, Germany, $11,000. To integrate children and teenagers with and developing handicaps, in kindergarten and beyond, via assistant. 2009.
1021-3 American Red Cross, Greater Pamlico Area Chapter, Washington, NC, $150,000. Toward relief efforts for series of catastrophic events occurring in Asia Pacific region including Philippines typhoon, Samoa and American Samoa tsunami, and Indonesian earthquakes. 2009.
1021-4 American Red Cross, Greater Pamlico Area Chapter, Washington, NC, $100,000. For Australian wildfires. 2009.
1021-5 American Red Cross, Greater Pamlico Area Chapter, Washington, NC, $100,000. For Italy Earthquake. 2009.
1021-6 Association of People with Disability, Bangalore, India, $10,000. For Mobility Aid program for disabled individuals toward accessing devices, providing assistance in pursuing independent living and careers. 2009.
1021-7 Barnardo's Scotland, Edinburgh, Scotland, $16,155. For Cairn program, providing short-term residential breaks in addition to support at home to children with profound learning disability, and physical and emotional problems. 2009.
1021-8 Belvedere College, Dublin, Ireland, $13,650. For academic support to boys from financially and socially disadvantaged circumstances. 2009.
1021-9 Boundless Adventures Association, Toronto, Canada, $14,505. For Boundless Youth Program blending vocational counseling, alternative education, and outdoor activities toward helping at-risk youth attain high school diplomas, reducing criminality risk. 2009.
1021-10 Bridges, Blacktown, Australia, $13,691. For program support. 2009.
1021-11 C A F Onlus, Milan, Italy, $14,500. To fund support services for children removed from homes due to abuse and neglect. 2009.
1021-12 Caritas Zurich, Zurich, Switzerland, $15,000. For Caritas-Markt Zurich project, toward reduced price groceries and non-food

products to socially disadvantaged people. 2009.
1021-13 Centraide of Greater Montreal, Montreal, Canada, $24,270. For United Way Campaign Contribution. 2009.
1021-14 Chaeli Campaign, Cape Town, South Africa, $10,000. For support services for children with disabilities. 2009.
1021-15 Christie Ossington Neighbourhood Centre, Toronto, Canada, $12,422. For Pedal Pushers Bicycle Share, Cook Nook Nutrition and Cooking Club, and Suspension Help Programs to homeless and marginalized families, children, and youth, improving quality of life. 2009.
1021-16 Christophorus Hospiz Verein, Munich, Germany, $11,000. For task coordinators overseeing volunteers, including accompaniment on assignments, advising, and carrying out general organizational duties and providing training when needed. 2009.
1021-17 Create, London, England, $12,658. 2009.
1021-18 Cultural Industries Development Agency, London, England, $16,203. For Creative Cash program, business development program serving individual entrepreneurs, combination of workshops, panel discussions, and one to one advice sessions. 2009.
1021-19 Die Arche - Das Christliche Kinder- und Jugendwerk e.V., Munich, Germany, $65,000. To create area designated for adolescent population toward development goals, and to fund salary of social worker. 2009.
1021-20 Die Arche - Das Christliche Kinder- und Jugendwerk e.V., Munich, Germany, $25,000. To create area designated for adolescent population toward development goals, and to fund salary of social worker. 2009.
1021-21 Dream A Dream, Bangalore, India, $10,000. To fund Dream Adventure Program for children from vulnerable backgrounds toward life skills. 2009.
1021-22 Dublin City University, Educational Trust, Dublin, Ireland, $40,950. For Access Scholarship program, serving socioeconomically disadvantaged and otherwise underserved students. 2009.
1021-23 Dublin Institute of Technology, Dublin, Ireland, $13,650. For Pathways Through Education Program in secondary schools through Department of Education Social, Personal and Health Education Program toward increasing student confidence. 2009.
1021-24 Dundalk Institute of Technology, Dundalk, Ireland, $13,650. For higher education access for mature students, traditionally underrepresented in third level education. 2009.
1021-25 Early Education, North Sydney, Australia, $12,815. For early intervention programs for young children with disabilities and delays in development. 2009.
1021-26 Education Alive Cape Town, Wynberg, South Africa, $10,000. For training program for educators, improving teaching standard, including discipline, and increasing pass and decreasing dropout rates. 2009.
1021-27 Elizabeth Fry Society of Toronto, Toronto, Canada, $12,900. For Believing in Employment Successes Training program, helping formerly imprisoned women overcome barriers to employment. 2009.
1021-28 Evangelisches Hilfswerk Munchen, Gemeinnuetzige, Munich, Germany, $11,000. For Karla 51 women's shelter, offering short-term lodging and counseling in areas of crisis

intervention and long-term housing to homeless women and children on 24-hour basis. 2009.

1021-29 Evas Initiatives, Toronto, Canada, $21,758. For Life Skills for an Independent Future Program, preparing young clients to live independently in community and work in competitive marketplace by learning variety of skills. 2009.

1021-30 Fairbridge in Scotland, Edinburgh, Scotland, $30,985. To deliver training courses, improving employability prospects of young people through core personal and social skills such as planning, working to deadlines, communication, and teamwork. 2009.

1021-31 Federation Francaise des Banques Alimentaires, Gentilly, France, $10,000. For isothermal bags. 2009.

1021-32 Fondation Caritas Luxembourg, Luxembourg, $21,702. For Employability Alliance Unlimited Potential IT workforce development project. 2009.

1021-33 Fondation Caritas Luxembourg, Luxembourg, $21,702. For Employability Alliance Unlimited Potential IT workforce development project. 2009.

1021-34 Fondation d Auteuil Les Orphelins Apprentis d Auteuil, Paris, France, $25,000. For Mediation Program, structured to provide youth with formal mediation and conflict avoidance training. 2009.

1021-35 Force Femmes, Paris, France, $20,724. For job skills training programs for women over 45. 2009.

1021-36 Franciscan Chapel Center, Tokyo, Japan, $17,184. To distribute rice cakes to homeless people living in and around Shibuya Station and Miyashita Park. 2009.

1021-37 Fred Victor Center, Toronto, Canada, $21,400. For Back to Basics Program, toward high school equivalency for extremely impoverished, and Community Computer Club work on bridging digital divide. 2009.

1021-38 Friends of the Award Edinburgh and the Lothians, Edinburgh, Scotland, $13,086. To help deliver in providing accredited youth work to marginalized young people. 2009.

1021-39 Give2Asia, San Francisco, CA, $100,000. For Taiwan Typhoon Relief Fund at Give2Asia for recovery efforts necessitated by mudslides and rain engulfing southern Taiwan. 2009.

1021-40 Glebe School Childcare Center, Broadway, Australia, $11,720. For Healthy Eating, Healthy Life program, providing nutritious meals to disadvantaged children living in Glebe public housing estate during and after school, as well as during school vacations. 2009.

1021-41 Half the Sky Foundation, Hong Kong, China, $35,000. For Xinyang HTS Centre Infant Nurture, Preschool, and Youth Services Programs for children and youth no longer in birth family care. 2009.

1021-42 HandsOn Tokyo, Tokyo, Japan, $15,000. To fund support services for Wakabaryo Children's Home. 2009.

1021-43 Hangzhou Municipal Charity Federation, Hangzhou, China, $14,706. To train migrant workers in nursing assistant job skills training program serving elderly. 2009.

1021-44 Home-Start Leith and North East Edinburgh, Edinburgh, Scotland, $23,687. For various projects in areas of home visitation, early learning intervention, family crisis, volunteer training and recruitment, and multi-sensory

space, toward strengthening unity between young children and parents. 2009.

1021-45 HOPE Worldwide Hong Kong, Kowloon, China, $25,370. For Volunteers for Senior Days, cleaning and repainting homes of senior citizens in Hong Kong. 2009.

1021-46 HOPE Worldwide Hong Kong, Kowloon, China, $25,000. For Volunteers for Seniors Day program, refurbishing homes of single seniors in Hong Kong and offering seniors fall prevention screenings and assessments by health professionals. 2009.

1021-47 Inner West Neighbour Aid, Croydon Park, Australia, $14,072. For Alive and Kicking project, serving frail, aged, and disabled, experiencing issues caused by social isolation and detachment from local community. 2009.

1021-48 Irish Red Cross, Dublin, Ireland, $25,000. To help people affected by flood disasters. 2009.

1021-49 Isle of Dogs Community Foundation, London, England, $12,088. For Summer Fun Day and Exchange Project, including provision of children's clothing and equipment recycling service of new and nearly new goods for families on low and no income. 2009.

1021-50 Istituto Beata Vergine Addolorata, Milan, Italy, $10,000. For Italian Center for Everybody project, integrating foreign citizens, particularly women, into working, social, and civil life around Milan by offering Italian language classes among other services. 2009.

1021-51 IT Bildungsnetz e V, Berlin, Germany, $35,000. For IT-Fitness initiative toward improving employability of individuals underprivileged on labor market, and otherwise disadvantaged and underserved individuals, by offering basic IT skills training. 2009.

1021-52 IT Bildungsnetz e V, Berlin, Germany, $25,000. For IT-Fitness initiative toward improving employability of individuals underprivileged on labor market, and otherwise disadvantaged and underserved individuals, by offering basic IT skills training opportunities. 2009.

1021-53 Joy Special Educare for Disabled Children, Mitchells Plain, South Africa, $10,000. To deliver community based support services to mothers with disabled children. 2009.

1021-54 Katholische Jugendfursorge der Erzdiozese Munchen und Freising e V, Munich, Germany, $11,000. To continue employability project for young adults in youth welfare system, with social worker hire and special training equipment. 2009.

1021-55 Kildare Youth Services, Naas, Ireland, $13,650. For Stepping Stones Programme, providing support services to young people vulnerable in formal education system toward making successful transition to secondary level education. 2009.

1021-56 Leave Out Violence, Montreal, Canada, $13,423. To continue to support media and arts program for youth ages 13-18 affected by violence. 2009.

1021-57 Lumenvisum, Hong Kong, China, $10,000. To develop visual arts program for disadvantaged students in Sham Shut Po, one of poorest districts. 2009.

1021-58 Mater Dei School, Camden, Australia, $15,000. For pilot project in-around Sydney toward developing self care and independent living skills toward careers for children with intellectual disability. 2009.

1021-59 Mimo Wszystko, Krakow, Poland, $15,000. For rehabilitation sessions for disabled people throughout Poland. 2009.

1021-60 Mitternachtsmission Basel, Basel, Switzerland, $15,000. For Tea on Wheels and Rehab projects targeted to serving marginalized individuals through guidance and field work based on Christian beliefs, toward acquiring perspectives and achieving social integration and related opportunities. 2009.

1021-61 Muenchner Waisenhaus, Munich, Germany, $12,850. To prevent children and young people from sustaining physical, mental, and emotional damage and encourage traumatized to become mentally strong and self-confident. 2009.

1021-62 Muirhouse Youth Development Group, Edinburgh, Scotland, $11,895. For North Edinburgh Arts and MYDG for program of arts activities to engage hard to reach young people. 2009.

1021-63 Munchner Tafel e.V., Munich, Germany, $11,000. To purchase food supplies covering basic needs and finance upkeep of delivery van fleet in effort to feed men, women, and children affected by homelessness and drug addiction among other issues. 2009.

1021-64 National Centre for Childhood Grief, Eastwood, Australia, $11,720. For support activities for bereaved children in form of outdoor activity centers. 2009.

1021-65 National College of Ireland Foundation, Dublin, Ireland, $80,993. For Progressions program. 2009.

1021-66 National College of Ireland Foundation, Dublin, Ireland, $54,600. For Progressions program. 2009.

1021-67 National Council of Social Service, Singapore, Singapore, $27,378. For Spastic Children's Association School, providing special education, rehabilitation services, vocational training, and employment for children and adults with cerebral palsy. 2009.

1021-68 National Council of YMCAs of Japan, Tokyo, Japan, $17,000. For Free School program, offering programming for youth with no history at regular schools to develop social and interpersonal skills and find vocational path. 2009.

1021-69 National Gallery of the Cayman Islands, George Town, Cayman Islands, $15,000. For Art Magnet and Art Haven programs. 2009.

1021-70 Orbis Hong Kong, North Point, China, $30,434. To fund support services for visually impaired individuals and medical training seminars for practitioners. 2009.

1021-71 Oxfam GB, Cowley, England, $129,712. For Oxfam's Anti-Poverty program. 2009.

1021-72 Pathways for Children, Youth, and Families of York Region, Markham, Canada, $17,120. To prepare at-risk youth for employment and life off streets by developing skills in areas of interviewing, resume writing, budgeting, teamwork, and problem solving and offering health workshops. 2009.

1021-73 Pathways to Education Canada, Toronto, Canada, $15,000. For Pathways to Education program to help curb issue of high school dropouts. 2009.

1021-74 Polish Environmental Partnership Foundation, Krakow, Poland, $15,000. For Schools for Sustainable Development, Questing workshops on Greenways, and Tree Day. 2009.

1021-75 Polska Akcja Humanitarna, Krakow, Poland, $20,000. For Humanitarian and Global Education and Repatriates Help, projects raising volunteer qualification level and motivation and assisting repatriates in obtaining skills and confidence. 2009.

1021-76 Rotary Club of Grand Cayman, George Town, Cayman Islands, $12,195. For Cayman Islands Reading Aides Literacy Program, equipping adults and teens with reading, writing, and numeracy literacy. 2009.

1021-77 Saint Felix Centre, Toronto, Canada, $13,055. For Breakfast Plus program, providing hot, nutritious breakfast and packed lunch for school to low-income and inner-city children toward enhanced academic performance. 2009.

1021-78 Saint Josephs Home, Cape Town, South Africa, $10,000. For Creche Program, providing chronically ill children with educational support services to transition from home to grade school successfully. 2009.

1021-79 Saint Pauls Senior National School, Drogheda, Ireland, $10,000. To develop children holistically. 2009.

1021-80 Samu Social de Paris, Paris, France, $30,000. For on the street outreach program providing medical assistance, psychological support, and preventive education for homeless individuals. 2009.

1021-81 Samu Social de Paris, Paris, France, $27,780. For Traces de Pas training program, providing skills training for volunteers and professionals dealing with homeless. 2009.

1021-82 School Home Support, London, England, $22,650. To provide disadvantaged children experiencing educational failure with support services for better outcomes in school. 2009.

1021-83 Science and Mining Traditions Foundation, Krakow, Poland, $12,561. For The Human and Environment, perfect symbiosis project, toward increasing societal awareness of environment protection and spatial development, and fostering durable pro-ecological attitude. 2009.

1021-84 Second Harvest, Toronto, Canada, $21,500. For Harvest Kitchen program, picking up raw food from donors, preparing, and delivering daily to social service agencies. 2009.

1021-85 Serve Canada, Youth Service Organization, Toronto, Canada, $18,857. For Experience This program, focusing on experiential service learning activities in areas of team and leadership development, community engagement, and personal development for youth out of school and work. 2009.

1021-86 Shanghai Cherished Dream Charity Foundation, Shanghai, China, $10,000. For Shanghai Cherished Dream Charity Foundation and Dream Center and Dream Leader Training Programs, promoting learning and developing interactive curriculum. 2009.

1021-87 Smile Foundation, New Delhi, India, $10,000. For access to formal education programs for street children living in shelter. 2009.

1021-88 Sozialwerke Pfarrer Sieber SWS, Zurich, Switzerland, $15,000. For ur-Dorfli, shelter program geared toward treating homeless drug addicted. 2009.

1021-89 Stepping Out Housing Program, Leichhardt, Australia, $12,071. For Fresh Start to Empowered Life project, funding basic household items for women and children transitioning from homelessness to medium term housing. 2009.

1021-90 Stepping Stones for Young Parents, Edinburgh, Scotland, $31,603. To fund groupwork provision for families faced with poverty, difficult housing conditions, substance abuse issues, poor parenting skills, and lack of support, and for Programme Coordinator. 2009.

1021-91 Stichting Computerwijk, Amsterdam, Netherlands, $40,000. For IT skills training to disadvantaged immigrant communities in Geuzenveld-Slotermeer, Slotevaart and Osdorp district on city outskirts. 2009.

1021-92 Stichting Computerwijk, Amsterdam, Netherlands, $30,000. For IT skills training to disadvantaged immigrant communities in Geuzenveld-Slotermeer, Slotevaart and Osdorp district on city outskirts. 2009.

1021-93 Stowarzyszenie WIOSNA, Krakow, Poland, $22,000. For Precious Gift program, toward providing Christmas gifts according to needs of economically disabled social groups via youth volunteers. 2009.

1021-94 Street League, London, England, $41,138. For distinct integrated sports and education program for hard-to-reach men and women ages 16 and up at risk of social exclusion. 2009.

1021-95 Sun Youth Organization, Montreal, Canada, $17,896. For summer and day camp programs for children from less fortunate communities. 2009.

1021-96 Toronto Windfall Clothing, Support Service, Toronto, Canada, $17,833. For youth in shelters, at risk, and homeless. 2009.

1021-97 Touch Community Services, Singapore, $21,614. For TOUCH Home Care, toward enabling frail elderly to live with dignity and have independence and quality of life by providing home medical and nursing services, and housekeeping, personal hygiene, meal, and escort services. 2009.

1021-98 Triangle Wallonie, La Hulpe, Belgium, $29,847. To hire part-time coach toward integrating deaf and hard of hearing children to mainstream classes. 2009.

1021-99 Tung Wah Group of Hospitals, Hong Kong, China, $10,000. For Stride to Serve, Grow and Build Assets program, transforming existing skills of unemployed men and women into employable skills and enhancing self-esteem. 2009.

1021-100 United Way of Greater Toronto, Toronto, Canada, $104,539. For United Way Campaign Contribution. 2009.

1021-101 United Way of Taiwan, Taipei, Taiwan, $14,862. For training program to build foundation for community development, including social welfare. 2009.

1021-102 Verein Strassemagazin Surprise, Basel, Switzerland, $15,000. To fund support services to assist individuals to get back into workforce. 2009.

1021-103 WAC Performing Arts and Media College, InterChange Trust, London, England, $11,325. 2009.

1021-104 Yehudi Menuhin Live Music Now, Munich, Germany, $11,000. To organize music programs for people normally lacking access in greater Munich area. 2009.

1021-105 Young Enterprise London, London, England, $16,428. For Personal Economics financial literacy program serving young students ages 14-16 from disadvantaged backgrounds by providing introduction to personal finance. 2009.

1021-106 Zhejiang Youth Development Foundation, Hangzhou, China, $32,971. For State Street Vocational Fund, helping students from rural, poverty-stricken families receive scholarships to obtain vocational training for job readiness. 2009.

1022
STG International
(formerly Solar Turbine Group, Inc.)
P.O. Box 426152
Cambridge, MA   02142-0021
E-mail: info@stginternational.org; URL: http://www.stginternational.org/

Established in 2006 in MA.
Donors: Massachusetts Institute of Technology; The World Bank.
Grantmaker type: Public charity.
Financial data (yr. ended 09/30/10): Revenue, $9,414; assets, $8,331 (M); gifts received, $9,000; expenditures, $16,692.
International interests: Lesotho.
Limitations: Applications not accepted. No grants to individuals.
Application information: Contributes only to pre-selected organizations.
Officers and Directors:* Matthew Orosz,* Pres.; Elizabeth Wayman,* Clerk; Amy Mueller,* Treas.; Bryan Urban.
EIN: 760834926

1023
Swartz Foundation
c/o Ropes & Gray LLP
800 Boylston St.
Boston, MA   02110-2624   (617) 951-7000
Contact: Janet C. Taylor, Philanthropic Advisor

Established in 1994 in MA.
Donors: Sidney W. Swartz; Judith W. Swartz.
Grantmaker type: Independent foundation.
Financial data (yr. ended 12/31/09): Assets, $139,974,754 (M); expenditures, $8,571,822; qualifying distributions, $8,205,631; giving activities include $8,127,997 for 23 grants (high: $3,192,087; low: $1,000), and $77,634 for foundation-administered programs.
Purpose and activities: Giving primarily to Jewish organizations for medical research, as well as to Jewish temples and federated giving programs; funding also for social services, and education.
Fields of interest: Medical research, institute; Human services; Jewish federated giving programs; Jewish agencies & synagogues; Women.
Type of support: General/operating support; Capital campaigns; Program development.
Limitations: Applications not accepted. Giving primarily in eastern MA, and Palm Beach, FL. No grants to individuals.
Application information: Contributes only to pre-selected organizations.
Trustee: Robert N. Shapiro.
EIN: 043255974
Recent grants for international programs:
1023-1 Friends of Israel Gospel Ministry, Bellmawr, NJ, $100,000. For general support and for The Davidic Covenant Weekly Feature. 2009.
1023-2 Hadassah Medical Relief Association, New York, NY, $1,070,740. For general support. 2009.

1023-3 Jewish National Fund, New York, NY, $21,800. For general support. 2009.

1024
Charles G. Talanian Family Foundation
7 Swan Rd.
Winchester, MA   01890-3719

Established in 2000 in MA.
Donor: Gail O'Reilly.
Grantmaker type: Independent foundation.
Financial data (yr. ended 11/30/10): Assets, $182,313 (M); gifts received, $140,000; expenditures, $272,750; qualifying distributions, $272,750; giving activities include $272,750 for 3 grants (high: $250,000; low: $7,750).
Fields of interest: Recreation, parks/playgrounds; Performing arts; Higher education; International peace/security.
Limitations: Applications not accepted. Giving primarily in Boston, MA. No grants to individuals.
Application information: Contributes only to pre-selected organizations.
Trustee: Gail O'Reilly.
EIN: 046934826

1025
Eliot and June Tatelman Family Foundation
c/o Edwards, Angell, Palmer & Dodge, LLP
111 Huntington Ave.
Boston, MA   02199-7610

Established in 2001 in MA.
Donors: Jordan Furniture Family Foundation; Eliot H. Tatelman.
Grantmaker type: Independent foundation.
Financial data (yr. ended 12/31/10): Assets, $4,690,910 (M); expenditures, $266,264; qualifying distributions, $231,216; giving activities include $220,000 for 7 grants (high: $100,000; low: $5,000).
Fields of interest: Hospitals (general); Reproductive health, family planning; International relief; Jewish federated giving programs.
International interests: South Africa.
Limitations: Applications not accepted. Giving primarily in MA, with some giving in NY. No grants to individuals.
Application information: Contributes only to pre-selected organizations.
Trustees: Lawrence B. Cohen; Laurie J. Hall; Eliot H. Tatelman; June L. Tatelman.
EIN: 456118546

1026
The TJX Foundation, Inc.
(formerly Zayre Foundation, Inc.)
c/o The TJX Cos., Inc.
770 Cochituate Rd., Rte. X3S
Framingham, MA   01701-4666   (508) 390-3199
Contact: Christine A. Strickland, Mgr.
FAX: (508) 390-2091;
E-mail: TJX_Foundation@TJX.com; URL: http://www.tjx.com/corporate_community_foundation.asp

Incorporated in 1966 in MA.
Donors: The TJX Cos., Inc.; Marshalls of MA, Inc.
Grantmaker type: Company-sponsored foundation.
Financial data (yr. ended 01/29/11): Assets, $24,431,377 (M); gifts received, $276,123; expenditures, $7,583,814; qualifying distributions, $7,305,232; giving activities include $6,983,982 for 1,222 grants (high: $270,432; low: $500).
Purpose and activities: The foundation supports programs designed to provide basic-need services to disadvantage women, children, and families. Special emphasis is directed toward programs designed to promote strong families; provide emergency shelter; enhance education and job readiness; and build community ties.
Fields of interest: Alzheimer's disease; Vocational education; Adult education—literacy, basic skills & GED; Education, ESL programs; Education; Health care, infants; Reproductive health, prenatal care; Substance abuse, services; Mental health, counseling/support groups; Genetic diseases and disorders; Medical research; Crime/violence prevention, domestic violence; Food services; Housing/shelter, temporary shelter; Disasters, preparedness/services; Youth development; Children, adoption; Children, services; Family services; Family services, domestic violence; Residential/custodial care; Residential/custodial care, hospices; Developmentally disabled, centers & services; Independent living, disability; Civil/human rights; Children; Disabilities, people with; Women; AIDS, people with; Economically disadvantaged.
Type of support: General/operating support; Continuing support; Program development.
Limitations: Applications accepted. Giving on a national basis in areas of company operations, with emphasis on MA. No support for political, fraternal, or international organizations. No grants to individuals, or for capital campaigns, cash reserves, computer purchases, conferences, seminars, consultant fees, salaries, conventions, education loans, endowments, fellowships, films, photography, renovation, new construction, publications, public policy research, advocacy, seed money, travel, or transportation.
Publications: Application guidelines; Corporate giving report; Program policy statement.
Application information: Additional information may be requested at a later date. Application form required.
   Initial approach: Complete online eligibility quiz and application form
   Copies of proposal: 1
   Deadline(s): Feb. 6, Mar. 19, and July 16
   Board meeting date(s): Week of Apr. 9, June 18, and Oct. 15
   Final notification: 4 weeks following board meeting
Officers and Directors:* Bernard Cammarata, Chair. and Pres.; Scott Goldenberg, V.P.; Paul Kangas, V.P.; Carol M. Meyrowitz, V.P.; Mary B. Reynolds, V.P.; Ann McCauley, Secy.; Jeffrey G. Naylor,* Treas.
Number of staff: 3 full-time professional.
EIN: 042399760
Recent grants for international programs:
1026-1 Save the Children Federation, Westport, CT, $266,976. 2010.
1026-2 UNICEF-New England, Cambridge, MA, $25,000. 2010.

1027
Unitarian Universalist Service Committee, Inc.
689 Massachusetts Ave.
Cambridge, MA   02139-3302   (617) 868-6600
FAX: (617) 868-7102; E-mail: info@uusc.org;
Toll-free tel.: (800) 388-3920; URL: http://www.uusc.org

Established in 1963.
Grantmaker type: Public charity.
Financial data (yr. ended 06/30/11): Revenue, $6,749,374; assets, $22,357,126 (M); gifts received, $5,007,967; expenditures, $6,149,422; giving activities include $495,393 for grants, and $895,923 for grants to organizations outside the U.S.
Purpose and activities: The committee advances human rights and social justice around the world, partnering with those who confront unjust power structures and mobilizing to challenge oppressive policies.
Fields of interest: International human rights; International affairs; Civil liberties, advocacy; Civil/human rights.
Publications: Annual report; Financial statement; Newsletter.
Officers and Trustees:* William F. Schultz,* Chair.; Katherine C. Hall,* Vice-Chair.; Dr. Charlie Clements, Pres. and C.E.O.; David Lysy,* Secy.; Stanley L. Corfman,* Treas.; Mark McPeak, Exec. Dir.; Tom Andrews; John E. Gibbons; Barclay Hudson; Todd Jones; Charlotte Jones-Carroll; Diane Miller; Carolyn Purcell; Lurma Rackley; Susan C. Scrimshaw; Charles Spence; Fasaha M. Traylor.
EIN: 046186012

MICHIGAN

1028
Africa Christian Ministries, Inc.
P.O. Box 461
Keego Harbor, MI   48320-0461   (248) 738-9440
FAX: (248) 738-9441;
E-mail: sgal3333@gmail.com; URL: http://www.africachristian.org

Established in 1993 in MI.
Grantmaker type: Public charity.
Financial data (yr. ended 06/30/11): Revenue, $116,201; assets, $6,423 (M); gifts received, $116,201; expenditures, $162,786; giving activities include $139,523 for grants.
Purpose and activities: The organization supports national and local ministries in South Africa.
Fields of interest: Christian agencies & churches.
International interests: South Africa.
Type of support: Building/renovation; Scholarship funds.
Limitations: Applications not accepted. Giving limited to South Africa. No grants to individuals.
Application information: Contributes only to pre-selected organizations.
Officers and Directors:* Sharon Tice,* Pres.; Deedee Tanana,* V.P.; Sally Galloway,* Secy.; Lisa DaSilva,* Treas.; Cherith Brumfield; Gail Bryan; Rev.

Isaia Mafu; Ndumiso Mafu; Rev. Jerome McAfee; Rev. Vince Messina; Prem Mukherjee.
EIN: 382719112

1029
Amway Corporation Contributions Program

5101 Spaulding Plz. S.E.
Ada, MI   49355-0001
E-mail: contributions@amway.com; URL: http://www.amwayonebyone.com
One by One: http://blogs.amway.com/onebyone/

Grantmaker type: Corporate giving program.
Purpose and activities: Amway makes charitable contributions to nonprofit organizations involved with at-risk children. Support is given primarily in areas of company operations in Buena Park, California, Lakeview, California, Norcross, Georgia, Honolulu, Hawaii, Arlington, Texas, and Kent, Washington, with emphasis on the greater Grand Rapids, Michigan, area, and in Africa, Asia, Australia, Europe, and Latin America.
Fields of interest: Developmentally disabled, centers & services; Children, services; Boys & girls clubs; Disasters, preparedness/services; Nutrition; Health care; Arts; Children.
International interests: Africa; Asia; Australia; Europe; Latin America.
Type of support: General/operating support; Employee volunteer services; In-kind gifts.
Limitations: Applications accepted. Giving primarily in areas of company operations in Buena Park and Lakeview, CA, Norcross, GA, Honolulu, HI, Arlington, TX, and Kent, WA, with emphasis on the greater Grand Rapids, MI, area, and in Africa, Asia, Australia, Europe, and Latin America. No support for fraternal organizations or school athletic teams, bands, or choirs, political, legislative, or lobbying organizations. No grants to individuals, or for travel, scholarships, religious projects, sports or fundraising events, movie, film, or television documentaries, general awareness campaigns, marketing sponsorships, cause-related marketing, or advertising projects; no in-kind gifts for conferences or conventions, personal use, distribution at an expo, fair, or event, family reunions, or sports fundraising events.
Publications: Application guidelines.
Application information: Videos, reports, publications, and other unsolicited materials are not encouraged. In-kind donation values do not exceed $250. Application form required.
   Initial approach: Complete online application form
   Deadline(s): None
   Final notification: 2 months

1030
Arcus Foundation

(formerly Jon L. Stryker Foundation)
402 E. Michigan Ave.
Kalamazoo, MI   49007-3888   (269) 373-4373
Contact: Carol Snapp, Comms. Mgr.
FAX: (269) 373-0277;
E-mail: contact@arcusfoundation.org; New York address: 44 W. 28th St., New York, NY 10011, tel.: (212) 488-3000; URL: http://www.arcusfoundation.org
Arcus Foundation's Philanthropy Promise: http://www.ncrp.org/philanthropys-promise/who

E-Newsletter: http://www.arcusfoundation.org/pages_2/publ.cfm
Grants Database: http://www.arcusfoundation.org/pages_2/funds_n.cfm?

Established in 1997 in MI.
Donor: Jon L. Stryker.
Grantmaker type: Independent foundation.
Financial data (yr. ended 12/31/10): Assets, $179,187,817 (M); gifts received, $30,790,836; expenditures, $36,414,687; qualifying distributions, $36,388,296; giving activities include $29,007,895 for 310 grants (high: $2,130,798; low: $25).
Purpose and activities: The mission of the foundation is to achieve social justice that is inclusive of sexual orientation, gender identity and race, and to ensure conservation and respect of the great apes.
Fields of interest: Animals/wildlife, endangered species; Animals/wildlife, sanctuaries; Animals/wildlife, special services; Civil/human rights, LGBTQ; Civil/human rights; LGBTQ.
Type of support: General/operating support; Management development/capacity building; Capital campaigns; Building/renovation; Endowments; Program development; Conferences/seminars; Publication; Curriculum development; Technical assistance; Consulting services; Program evaluation; Employee matching gifts; Matching/challenge support.
Limitations: Applications accepted. Giving on a national basis, with some emphasis on MI, especially southwest MI. Giving on an international basis, with emphasis on Africa, the Middle East and Southeast Asia. No support for lobby groups or political campaigns. No grants to individuals, or for religious or political activities, scholarships, or for medical research or film production projects.
Publications: Annual report (including application guidelines); Newsletter.
Application information: Application Process: 1) Please confirm that your organization is an eligible tax-exempt organization under Sec. 501(c)(3) of the IRS regulations (or as a non-US organization, can you demonstrate an equivalent status and a non-discrimination or EEO policy compliant); 2) Contact appropriate foundation program officer to discuss interest and ideas for your request; 3) Submit a formal Letter of Inquiry to the foundation; and 4) If invited, submit a full proposal. After reviewing your LOI, the foundation will inform you as to whether a full proposal is being invited. Application form not required.
   Initial approach: Contact a foundation program officer and then submit a formal letter of inquiry
   Copies of proposal: 4
   Deadline(s): Rolling; Once the foundation accepts a Letter of Inquiry and invites a full proposal, a specific deadline for submission of the full proposal will then be provided in the letter of invitation sent by the foundation
   Board meeting date(s): Four board meetings annually
   Final notification: After board meetings; Grant recipients will receive a Grant Award Letter.
Officers and Directors:* Dr. Yvette C. Burton, C.E.O.; Jon L. Stryker,* Pres.; Richard Burns, C.O.O.; Tom Kam, V.P., Social Justice Programming; Bryan E. Simmons, V.P., Global Comms.; Cynthia A. Hallenbeck, V.P., Finance and Opers.; Kristine Stallone, C.F.O.; Stephen Bennett; Cathy J. Cohen; Catherine Pino; Darren Walker.

Number of staff: 21
EIN: 383332791
Recent grants for international programs:

1030-1 African Conservation Foundation, Harden, England, $95,000. To strengthen community support and management of habitat that contributes to conservation of Cross River Gorilla populations in Cameroon. 2010.

1030-2 Akiba Uhaki Foundation, Nairobi, Kenya, $200,000. For support of Small Grants Program, programmatic and convening activities of UHAI - The East African Sexual Health and Rights Initiative, which supports local LGBI and sex worker organizations in Uganda, Kenya, Tanzania, Rwanda, and Burundi. 2010.

1030-3 American Jewish World Service, New York, NY, $200,000. To strengthen and further develop ability of AJWS LGBT program to support most marginalized LGBT groups in Africa and South East Asia through capacity building and small grants. 2010.

1030-4 Arab Foundation for Freedoms And Equality, Beirut, Lebanon, $100,000. To strengthen newly established SOGI Social Justice Fund for Middle East and North Africa (MENA) Region through capacity building support, including facilitating staff exchange and sharing education and training resources with UHAI-the East Africa Sexual Health and Rights Initiative. 2010.

1030-5 Architecture for Humanity, San Francisco, CA, $70,000. For design and construction technical assistance focused on rebuilding housing for low-income communities and educational and civil society facilities in Haiti. 2010.

1030-6 Astraea Lesbian Foundation for Justice, New York, NY, $150,000. For International Fund for Sexual Minorities to continue to support projects and organizations that strategically address needs of LGBT people in the global south and east, as well as to collaborate with these grantees on regional analysis to identify opportunities and resources that can be leveraged for the LGBT groups in the region. 2010.

1030-7 Behind the Mask, Braamfontein, South Africa, $100,000. To employ and train four regional reporters in different parts of sub-Saharan Africa who will actively contribute to an Africa-wide online news publication on LGBTI issues based in South Africa. 2010.

1030-8 Coalition of African Lesbians, Boksburg, South Africa, $100,000. For project support to promote and protect Sexual and Reproductive Health and rights of lesbian, bisexual and trans-diverse people in Africa and to strengthen work and activism of member organizations and partners in regions outside of Southern Africa. 2010.

1030-9 Columbia University, Center for the Study of Human Rights, New York, NY, $62,000. Toward participation of LGBT advocates from Africa, the Middle East and/or Southeast Asia in Human Rights Advocates Program. 2010.

1030-10 Comite IDAHO, Paris, France, $100,000. To support increased recognition and global activities of International Day Against Homophobia campaign, particularly in the global South and East. 2010.

1030-11 Conservation International, Arlington, VA, $99,500. To enhance conservation of priority population of Gibbons in northeastern Cambodia. 2010.

1030-12 Equal Rights Trust, London, England, $100,000. For planning to establish working partnership with Kenyan Human Rights Commission and Gay and Lesbian Coalition of Kenya in order to develop strategies for improving legal protection of LGBI people in Kenya and promoting equality inclusive of sexual orientation and gender identity. 2010.

1030-13 Fahamu Kenya, Nairobi, Kenya, $293,066. For development and implementation of movement building training program for the LGBTI movement in East Africa, in collaboration with East Africa Sexual Rights and Health Initiative (UHAI). 2010.

1030-14 Forest Peoples Programme, Moreton-in-Marsh, England, $172,060. To model and document traditional natural resource management practices and traditional knowledge connected to the forest of the Greater Virunga Area in order to advance conservation of the mountain gorilla and to achieve environmental justice for marginalized communities. 2010.

1030-15 Fund for Global Human Rights, LGBT Program, Washington, DC, $200,000. To increase financial resources, capacity and skills of front-line human rights activists in Africa, the Middle East and Southeast Asia, prioritizing outreach and growth in Southeast Asia where fewer donors and resources are available. 2010.

1030-16 Gender DynamiX, Athlone, South Africa, $100,000. For exchange program for transgender/intersex activists in South Africa and Uganda. 2010.

1030-17 Global Federation of Animal Sanctuaries, Washington, DC, $60,000. For design, development and implementation of accreditation program for great ape sanctuaries in North America, Africa and Asia. 2010.

1030-18 Global Greengrants Fund, Boulder, CO, $150,000. To support community grassroots groups in the Global South working on issues of environmental justice, sustainability and conservation, specifically within and around ape habitats. 2010.

1030-19 Harvard University, Cambridge, MA, $50,000. To support establishment of one-year research and writing fellowship at Law School's Human Rights Program to strengthen international work on human rights framing of sexual orientation and gender identity. 2010.

1030-20 Health in Harmony, Portland, OR, $79,963. For Alam Schat Lestari Program in West Kalimantan, Indonesia to provide conservation-based incentives to local communities that protect key habitat from illegal logging and to reforest ten hectares of critical orangutan habitat that has been deforested. 2010.

1030-21 Heartland Alliance for Human Needs and Human Rights, Chicago, IL, $55,000. For support of Global Equality Network to work with Foundation SEROvie, Haiti's HIV and LGBT resource center, on post-earthquake rebuilding and capacity development. 2010.

1030-22 Highest Common Denominator Fund, Addison, TX, $140,000. For Mideast Youth to create interactive, creative platform tracking anti-LGBT abuses in the Middle East and North Africa, while also providing reliable, safe multimedia platform for LGBT people and their allies to interact. 2010.

1030-23 In Defense of Animals, San Rafael, CA, $35,000. For salaries for Cameroonian caretaker, maintenance and security staff of Sanaga Yong Chimpanzee Rescue Center, a range state sanctuary located in West Africa. 2010.

1030-24 Inclusive and Affirming Ministries, Cape Town, South Africa, $102,761. For Regional Partnerships Africa program to empower African Christian communities by facilitating dialogue between African LGBT communities and mainstream Christian leadership in Africa and providing training and support for local groups. 2010.

1030-25 Inner Circle, Cape Town, South Africa, $100,000. To strengthen outreach to queer Muslims outside of South Africa, including more effective global website and support for Annual International Retreat. 2010.

1030-26 Institute of International Education, New York, NY, $181,073. For International LGBT Learning Initiative to undertake highly participatory process of developing learning frameworks and indicators that will strengthen work of key stakeholders in the international LGBT advocacy sector. 2010.

1030-27 International Gay and Lesbian Human Rights Commission, New York, NY, $125,000. To coordinate initiative with lesbian, bisexual and transgender (LBT) activist organizations from five southeast Asian countries to draw attention to and in the longer term increase services addressing under-reported and misunderstood problem of hate violence on the basis of sexual orientation and gender identity and expression. 2010.

1030-28 International Gay and Lesbian Human Rights Commission, New York, NY, $100,000. To strengthen GATE - Global Action for Trans Equality, global transgender organization working to make knowledge and resources available to activists and working for the rights of trans people at the international level. 2010.

1030-29 International Lesbian and Gay Association, Brussels, Belgium, $70,000. To provide support for four part-time Web managers in four countries in the Global South and East to actively contribute to and regularly update ILGA-World interactive global LGBT map. 2010.

1030-30 International Primate Protection League, Summerville, SC, $230,000. For general operating support to promote well being and provide care for orphaned and captive apes in their native countries. 2010.

1030-31 International Union for Conservation of Nature and Natural Resources, Washington, DC, $212,432. To support activities of Section on Great Apes of the Primate Specialist Group, including efforts to ensure compliance by extractive industries with International Finance Corporation standards, to enable scientists/conservationists in ape range states to attend International Primatological Society Congress and to develop Bonobo Conservation Action Plan. 2010.

1030-32 International Union for Conservation of Nature and Natural Resources, Gland, Switzerland, $297,000. To strengthen global policy work and inform conservation policy and practice in West and Central Africa. 2010.

1030-33 International Union for Conservation of Nature and Natural Resources, Gland, Switzerland, $170,720. For East and Southern Africa Regional Office (ESARO) to strengthen management and conservation of biodiversity in Eastern and Southern Africa through Conservation Areas and Species Development (CASD) program. 2010.

1030-34 Jane Goodall Institute for Wildlife Research, Education and Conservation, Arlington, VA, $192,322. To develop spatially explicit Conservation Action Plan for Maiko-Tanya-Kahuzi-Biega Landscape in eastern Democratic Republic of Congo that identifies highest priority areas for intervention as well as conservation strategies and actions inclusive of specific community development and alternative livelihood interventions. 2010.

1030-35 Lukuru Wildlife Research Foundation, Circleville, OH, $300,000. To enhance awareness and build support for conservation of Tshuapa Lomani Lualaba Landscape in Democratic Republic of Congo and to create blueprint for development of nationally-based conservation organization. 2010.

1030-36 Max Planck Society for the Advancement of Science, Leipzig, Germany, $47,800. To protect great ape populations in Liberia through improved gathering of data on chimpanzee abundance and distribution and through strengthening of national conservation expertise. 2010.

1030-37 MGVP, Inc., Davis, CA, $97,650. To provide delivery of health care to mountain and eastern lowland gorillas at Maryland Zoo in Baltimore and in Democratic Republic of Congo, Rwanda and Uganda, and to build capacity for the development of long-term sustainable health care for gorillas. 2010.

1030-38 Michigan State University College of Law, East Lansing, MI, $42,895. To create Great Apes Information Library within Animal Legal and Historical Web Center. 2010.

1030-39 NAACP, Baltimore, MD, $75,000. For planning to develop UN Charter Membership Program, national and international human rights advocacy program inclusive of racial justice, gender, gender identity, sexual orientation and class. 2010.

1030-40 New Israel Fund, Washington, DC, $150,000. For core program support to further develop New Israel Fund's support to LGBT organizations in Israel. 2010.

1030-41 North American Primate Sanctuary Alliance, Cle Elum, WA, $65,000. For start-up support including infrastructure development which will establish standards of care and best practices for primate sanctuaries. 2010.

1030-42 Ol Pejeta Conservancy, Nanyuki, Kenya, $215,389. To complete construction of new house for orphaned chimpanzees and house for manager of Sweetwaters Chimpanzee Sanctuary. 2010.

1030-43 Ol Pejeta Conservancy, Nanyuki, Kenya, $61,776. For position of Chief Financial Officer in order to provide financial oversight and direction as well as build capacity of financial staff. 2010.

1030-44 Ol Pejeta Conservancy, Nanyuki, Kenya, $60,000. For Veterinary Health Monitoring Program. 2010.

1030-45 Orangutan Appeal UK, Brockenhurst, England, $150,000. To partner with Sepilok Orangutan Rehabilitation Center in Sabah, Borneo, Malaysia for post-release monitoring project to determine effectiveness of rehabilitation program, progress of orangutans after they have been released in the wild and dissemination of findings through published reports. 2010.

1030-46 Pan African Sanctuaries Alliance, Portland, OR, $125,000. For PASA Development Project, capacity building effort focused on board development and growth, financial planning and sustainability and management planning and training to implement newly created strategies. 2010.

1030-47 People, Resources and Conservation Foundation, Amherst, NY, $338,323. To enhance long-term survival of Hoolock Gibbons in Lake Indawgyi Wildlife Sanctuary and build capacity in Myanmar for conservation of globally important primates. 2010.

1030-48 People, Resources and Conservation Foundation, Amherst, NY, $227,160. For critical habitat restoration and expansion as part of work to enhance long-term survival of Hoolock Gibbons in Lake Indawgyi Wildlife Sanctuary and build capacity in Myanmar for conservation of globally important primates. 2010.

1030-49 Political Research Associates, Somerville, MA, $140,000. For Religion and LGBT Equality, research project to expose and confront U.S. religious conservatives who support homophobia in Africa. 2010.

1030-50 Project Primate, Bethesda, MD, $99,990. To support Chimpanzee Conservation Centre in Guinea, West Africa. 2010.

1030-51 Purpose Foundation, New York, NY, $125,000. To establish and develop global online LGBT initiative, including hiring and training an international team of campaigners and building core technology for the site. 2010.

1030-52 Royal Zoological Society of Antwerp, Antwerp, Belgium, $50,000. For Research and Conservation's Projet Grands Singes in collaboration with Ape-assistance to further develop and improve cocoa agro-forestry on the periphery of DJA Biosphere Reserve Centre in Cameroon to reduce hunting pressure on great apes and other protected animals. 2010.

1030-53 Saint James Cathedral, Chicago, IL, $100,000. To support efforts of Chicago Consultation to advance full inclusion of LGBT people within the Episcopal Church and to explore opportunities to promote dialogue and support for LGBT inclusion among leaders of the Anglican Communion in the global South. 2010.

1030-54 Stichting Mama Cash, Amsterdam, Netherlands, $200,000. For general operating support to provide direct grants and accompanying support to lesbian, bisexual and transgender groups in Africa, the Middle East and Southeast Asia that are positioned to take advantage of or to create strategic opportunities to defend and advance LBT human rights. 2010.

1030-55 Transgender Europe, Malmo, Sweden, $100,000. For Transphobia Research Project, collaborative international research project documenting transphobia worldwide and exploring ways in which to promote respect for transgender people. 2010.

1030-56 Two Spirit Society of Denver, Edgewater, CO, $65,111. To organize National Leadership Summit of Two Spirit organizations from the U.S. and Canada. 2010.

1030-57 WCMC 2000, Cambridge, England, $290,225. To support completion (Phase 2) of Apes Mapper, online tool that delivers data and information on great apes in combination with contextual information on location of threats, conservation actions and other issues affecting ape populations. 2010.

1030-58 Wildlife Conservation Society, Bronx, NY, $299,630. To enhance trans-boundary collaboration between Nigeria and Cameroon for conservation of Cross River Gorilla (Gorilla gorilla diehli) and Nigeria-Cameroon chimpanzee (Pan troglodytes ellioti). 2010.

1030-59 Zoological Society of London, London, England, $98,361. For Wildlife Wood Project, effort to ensure responsible wildlife management in areas identified as priority for great ape conservation in Cameroon through improving logging practices and strengthening sustainable natural resource management. 2010.

1030-60 Zoological Society of San Diego, San Diego Zoo, San Diego, CA, $200,091. To strengthen conservation management of Ebo Forest of Northern Cameroon through development of national park and showcase research site. 2010.

1031
Irene M. Auberlin Foundation
11745 Rosa Parks Blvd.
Detroit, MI 48206-1269 (313) 866-5333

Established in 1988 in MI; supporting organization of World Medical Relief, Inc.
Grantmaker type: Public charity.
Financial data (yr. ended 12/31/09): Revenue, $1,741; assets, $995,285 (M); expenditures, $12,414.
Fields of interest: Health care; International relief.
Limitations: Applications not accepted. No grants to individuals.
Application information: Contributes only to a pre-selected organization.
Officers: Dennis T. Torp, Chair.; Dorothea Pomfret, Vice-Chair.; George V. Samson, Pres. and C.E.O.; Rebecca M. Tungol, Secy.; Mike M. Baydoun, Treas.
EIN: 382815534

1032
Mandell L. and Madeleine H. Berman Foundation
(formerly Madeleine and Mandell L. Berman Foundation)
c/o Sarai Brachman Shoup
29100 Northwestern Hwy., Ste. 370
Southfield, MI 48034-1092

Established in 1994 in MI.
Grantmaker type: Independent foundation.
Financial data (yr. ended 12/31/09): Assets, $21,852,765 (M); gifts received, $5,058,140; expenditures, $3,460,412; qualifying distributions, $3,303,366; giving activities include $3,096,995 for 166 grants (high: $338,665; low: $45).
Fields of interest: Jewish agencies & synagogues.
International interests: Israel.
Limitations: Applications not accepted. Giving on a national and international basis, and in the Detroit, MI, area. No grants to individuals.
Application information: Contributes only to pre-selected organizations.
Trustee: Mandell L. Berman.
Number of staff: 2 part-time professional.
EIN: 386644875

1033
BorgWarner Inc. Corporate Giving Program
3850 Hamlin Rd.
Auburn Hills, MI 48326-2872 (248) 754-9200
URL: http://www.borgwarner.com/en/Company/SocialResponsibility/default.aspx

Grantmaker type: Corporate giving program.
Purpose and activities: Borg Warner makes charitable contributions to nonprofit organizations involved with children, education, and the environment. Support is given primarily in areas of company operations in Illinois, Michigan, Mississippi, New York, North Carolina, South Carolina, and Texas, and in Brazil, China, France, Germany, Hungary, India, Ireland, Italy, Japan, Mexico, Monaco, Poland, Portugal, South Korea, Spain, and the United Kingdom.
Fields of interest: General charitable giving; Engineering/technology; Science; Children, services; Disasters, preparedness/services; Health care; Health care, patient services; Environment; Environment, energy; Education; Children.
International interests: Brazil; China; France; Germany; Hungary; India; Ireland; Italy; Japan; Mexico; Monaco; Poland; Portugal; South Korea; Spain; United Kingdom.
Type of support: General/operating support; Employee volunteer services; Employee matching gifts.
Limitations: Giving primarily in areas of company operations in IL, MI, MS, NC, NY, SC, and TX, and in Brazil, China, France, Germany, Hungary, India, Ireland, Italy, Japan, Mexico, Monaco, Poland, Portugal, South Korea, Spain, and the United Kingdom.

1034
The Allen B. Cutting Foundation
c/o Planning Alternatives
36800 Woodward Ave., Ste. 200
Bloomfield Hills, MI 48304

Established in 1996 in MI.
Donors: Joan L. Cutting; Margaret Cutting Manuel; Rebecca Cutting Broderick; Amy E. Cutting.
Grantmaker type: Independent foundation.
Financial data (yr. ended 12/31/10): Assets, $7,549,532 (M); expenditures, $302,365; qualifying distributions, $275,000; giving activities include $275,000 for 9 grants (high: $40,000; low: $15,000).
Fields of interest: Health care, clinics/centers; Arts education; Kidney diseases; International human rights; Elementary/secondary education; Family services, domestic violence; Civil/human rights, minorities; Native Americans/American Indians.
Limitations: Applications not accepted. Giving primarily in FL, Interlochen, MI, Kansas City, MO, Pine Ridge, SD, and Plano, TX. No grants to individuals.
Application information: Contributes only to pre-selected organizations.
Officers: Joan L. Cutting, Pres.; Rebecca Cutting Broderick, V.P. and Secy.; Margaret Cutting Manuel, V.P. and Secy.; Amy E. Cutting, V.P. and Treas.
EIN: 383319000

1035
DENSO North America Foundation
24777 DENSO Dr., MC 4610
Southfield, MI 48086-5047 (248) 372-8225
FAX: (248) 213-2551;
E-mail: densofoundation@denso-diam.com;
Additional tel.: (248) 372-8250; URL: http://
www.densofoundation.org
Grants List: http://www.densofoundation.org/
grants/grants.php

Established in 2001 in MI.
Donor: DENSO International America, Inc.
Grantmaker type: Company-sponsored foundation.
Financial data (yr. ended 12/31/10): Assets,
$9,239,067 (M); expenditures, $545,430;
qualifying distributions, $545,430; giving activities
include $545,430 for grants.
Purpose and activities: The foundation supports
organizations involved with engineering education
and related business areas. Special emphasis is
directed toward programs designed to demonstrate
technological innovation and automotive
engineering.
Fields of interest: Engineering/technology;
Business school/education; Engineering school/
education.
International interests: Canada; Mexico.
Type of support: Capital campaigns; Building/
renovation; Equipment; Program development.
Limitations: Applications accepted. Giving primarily
in CA, MI, MS, OH, and TN, and in Canada and
Mexico. No grants to individuals, or for
administrative costs, stipends, trips, conferences,
or travel expenses.
Publications: Application guidelines; Grants list.
Application information: The foundation considers
proposals on an invitation and request basis. If
applicants are approved, they will be asked to
submit a 1 page concept paper. Application form not
required.
   Initial approach: Telephone foundation to discuss
      possible funding
   Deadline(s): None
   Board meeting date(s): May and Oct.
Officers and Directors: Dennis Dawson,* Pres.;
Robert Townsend, V.P.; Sharon Brosch, Secy.; Kim
Madaj, Treas.; Hugh Cantrell; David Cole; Karen
Cooper-Boyer; Douglas Patton; Richard Shiozaki.
Agent: JPMorgan Chase Bank, N.A.
Number of staff: 1 full-time professional.
EIN: 383547055

1036
Dick & Betsy DeVos Foundation
P.O. Box 230257
Grand Rapids, MI 49523-0257 (616) 643-4700
Contact: Ginny Vander Hart, Exec. Dir.; Sue Volkers,
Fdn. Admin.
FAX (for Ginny Vander Hart): (616) 774-0116; E-mail
(for Ginny Vander Hart): virginiav@rdvcorp.com

Established in 1989 in MI.
Donors: Dick DeVos; Betsy DeVos; Prince
Foundation.
Grantmaker type: Independent foundation.
Financial data (yr. ended 12/31/09): Assets,
$54,829,634 (M); gifts received, $8,000,000;
expenditures, $8,135,254; qualifying distributions,
$9,264,245; giving activities include $7,600,422
for 183 grants (high: $520,000; low: $50), and
$1,300,000 for 1 loan/program-related investment.

Purpose and activities: The foundation seeks to
create a legacy of caring and stewardship through
its support of projects that build a strong
community. To demonstrate this commitment, the
foundation concentrates its funding in support of
various initiatives that promote a healthier
community, with a focus on the arts, health and
children's causes.
Fields of interest: Arts; Education; Children/youth,
services; Family services; Public policy, research;
Christian agencies & churches.
Type of support: Program-related investments/
loans; General/operating support; Continuing
support; Annual campaigns; Capital campaigns.
Limitations: Applications accepted. Giving primarily
in west MI. No grants to individuals.
Publications: Application guidelines.
Application information: Application form not
required.
   Initial approach: Letter
   Copies of proposal: 1
   Deadline(s): 2 weeks prior to review
   Board meeting date(s): Quarterly
   Final notification: 4 to 5 months
Officers and Directors:* Jerry L. Tubergen,* C.O.O.,
V.P. and Secy.; Richard M. DeVos, Jr.,* Pres.;
Elisabeth DeVos,* V.P.; Jeffrey K. Lambert, V.P.;
Robert H. Schierbeek, Treas.; Ginny Vander Hart,
Exec. Dir. and Fdn. Dir.
EIN: 382902412
Recent grants for international programs:
1036-1 Cape Eleuthera Foundation, Lawrenceville,
   NJ, $184,500. For unrestricted grant to general
   fund. 2009.
1036-2 Christian Reformed World Missions, Grand
   Rapids, MI, $15,000. For unrestricted grant to
   general fund. 2009.
1036-3 CURE International, Lemoyne, PA, $46,000.
   For unrestricted grant to general fund. 2009.
1036-4 English Language Institute in China, Fort
   Collins, CO, $10,000. For unrestricted grant to
   general fund. 2009.
1036-5 Global Education Foundation, Pittsburgh,
   PA, $10,000. For unrestricted grant to general
   fund. 2009.
1036-6 Haggai Institute for Advanced Leadership
   Training, Norcross, GA, $500,000. For
   unrestricted grant to general fund. 2009.
1036-7 International Aid, Spring Lake, MI,
   $316,750. For unrestricted grant to general
   fund. 2009.
1036-8 International Justice Mission, Arlington, VA,
   $50,000. For unrestricted grant to general fund.
   2009.
1036-9 Project Rwanda, Salinas, CA, $217,585. For
   unrestricted grant to general fund. 2009.
1036-10 Stephens Children Foundation, Atlanta,
   GA, $100,000. For unrestricted grant to general
   fund. 2009.
1036-11 Thunderbird, The Garvin School of
   International Management, Glendale, AZ,
   $10,000. For unrestricted grant to general fund.
   2009.
1036-12 World Relief, Baltimore, MD, $300,000.
   For unrestricted grant to general fund. 2009.

1037
The Dow Chemical Company Foundation
2030 Dow Ctr.
Midland, MI 48674-0001
Contact: R.N. "Bo" Miller, Pres. and Exec. Dir.

FAX: (989) 636-3518; E-mail: bomiller@dow.com;
URL: http://www.dow.com/about/sponsorship/

Established in 1979 in MI.
Donor: The Dow Chemical Co.
Grantmaker type: Company-sponsored foundation.
Financial data (yr. ended 12/31/10): Assets,
$10,816,562 (M); gifts received, $15,025,000;
expenditures, $24,370,173; qualifying
distributions, $24,370,173; giving activities include
$24,370,173 for 1,274 grants (high: $1,500,000;
low: $75).
Purpose and activities: The foundation supports
organizations involved with K-12 education, the
environment, community development, and
chemical research.
Fields of interest: United Ways and Federated Giving
Programs; Elementary/secondary education;
Environment; Community/economic development;
Chemistry.
Type of support: Equipment; Program development;
Seed money; Employee matching gifts; Donated
products; In-kind gifts.
Limitations: Applications accepted. Giving on a
national and international basis primarily in areas of
company operations. No support for political or
religious organizations. No grants for travel or
administrative costs.
Application information: Application form not
required.
   Initial approach: Letter of inquiry
   Copies of proposal: 1
   Deadline(s): None
   Board meeting date(s): 4 times per year
   Final notification: 2 to 3 months
Officers and Trustees:* Dave E. Kepler, Chair.; R.N.
"Bo" Miller,* Pres. and Exec. Dir.; Nancy Logan,
Secy.; Colleen W. Kay, Treas.; Bill Banholzer;
Gregory M. Freiwald; Geoffery E. Merszei; William H.
Weideman.
Number of staff: 1 full-time professional; 7 part-time
professional.
EIN: 382314603
Recent grants for international programs:
1037-1 American Australian Association, New York,
   NY, $75,000. 2009.
1037-2 American-Australian Education Leadership
   Foundation, Washington, DC, $20,000. 2009.
1037-3 Appeal of Conscience Foundation, New
   York, NY, $10,000. 2009.
1037-4 Bhagwan Mahaveer Viklang Sahayata
   Samiti, Hospital Jaipur, Jaipur, India, $250,000.
   2009.
1037-5 Clinton Global Initiative, New York, NY,
   $38,000. 2009.
1037-6 Dow Center for Youth, Sarnia, Canada,
   $82,372. 2009.
1037-7 Foreign Policy Association, New York, NY,
   $15,000. 2009.
1037-8 Fundacao de Apoio a Universidade de Sao
   Paulo, Sao Paulo, Brazil, $50,000. 2009.
1037-9 Global Water Challenge, Washington, DC,
   $200,000. 2009.
1037-10 Greek Orthodox Archdiocese of North and
   South America, Greek Fire Relief Fund, New York,
   NY, $140,000. 2009.
1037-11 Gulf Coast Bird Observatory, Lake Jackson,
   TX, $25,000. 2009.
1037-12 Junior Achievement China, Beijing, China,
   $200,000. 2009.
1037-13 King Baudouin Foundation United States,
   New York, NY, $540,000. 2009.
1037-14 Kuwait-America Foundation, Washington,
   DC, $250,000. 2009.

1037-15 Resource Foundation, New York, NY, $632,420. 2009.

1037-16 United Nations Environment Programme, Paris, France, $290,000. 2009.

1037-17 Young Arab Leaders, Dubai, United Arab Emirates, $500,000. 2009.

1038
Dow Corning Corporation Contributions Program

P.O. Box 994
Midland, MI 48686-0994 (989) 496-4400
E-mail: community@dowcorning.com; URL: http://www.dowcorning.com/content/about/aboutcomm/?e=About+Dow+Corning

Grantmaker type: Corporate giving program.
Purpose and activities: As a complement to its foundation, Dow Corning also makes charitable contributions to nonprofit organizations directly. Support is given primarily in Seneffe, Belgium, Campinas, Brazil, Songjiang, China, Saint-Laurent-du-Pont, France, Wiesbaden, Germany, Fukui and Yamakita, Japan, Jincheon, South Korea, and Barry, Wales.
Fields of interest: Community/economic development; Mathematics; Science.
International interests: Belgium; Brazil; China; France; Germany; Japan; South Korea; Wales.
Type of support: General/operating support; Employee matching gifts; Donated equipment; Donated products.
Limitations: Applications accepted. Giving primarily in Seneffe, Belgium, Campinas, Brazil, Songjiang, China, Saint-Laurent-du-Pont, France, Wiesbaden, Germany, Fukui and Yamakita, Japan, Jincheon, South Korea, and Barry, Wales. No support for political, veterans', religious, or government-funded organizations. No grants to individuals, or for fundraising, collegiate athletic activities, scholarships, conferences, or travel.
Publications: Application guidelines.
Application information: Organizations receiving support are asked to provide a final report. Application form not required.
Initial approach: E-mail letter of inquiry to headquarters

1039
Earhart Foundation

2200 Green Rd., Ste. H
Ann Arbor, MI 48105-1569 (734) 761-8592
Contact: Ingrid A. Gregg, Pres.

Incorporated in 1929 in MI.
Donor: Harry Boyd Earhart‡.
Grantmaker type: Independent foundation.
Financial data (yr. ended 12/31/09): Assets, $35,723,529 (M); expenditures, $6,154,181; qualifying distributions, $6,003,897; giving activities include $3,273,906 for 123 grants (high: $150,000; low: $1,000), and $1,775,570 for 119 grants to individuals (high: $41,400; low: $1,000).
Purpose and activities: H.B. Earhart Fellowships for graduate study awarded through a special nominating process for which direct applications will not be accepted; research fellowships for individual projects in economics, history, philosophy, international affairs, and political science awarded upon direct application to faculty members; grants

also to educational and research organizations legally qualified for private foundation support.
Fields of interest: History/archaeology; Philosophy/ethics; Graduate/professional education; Economics; Political science; International studies.
Type of support: Conferences/seminars; Publication; Curriculum development; Fellowships; Research; Grants to individuals; Scholarships—to individuals.
Limitations: Applications accepted. Giving on a national basis. No grants for capital, building, or endowment funds, operating budgets, continuing support, annual campaigns, seed money, emergency funds, deficit financing, or matching gifts; no loans.
Publications: Annual report (including application guidelines).
Application information: Direct applications from candidates or uninvited sponsors for H.B. Earhart Fellowships (for graduate study) are not accepted. Application form not required.
Initial approach: Letter
Copies of proposal: 1
Deadline(s): Proposal should be submitted at least 4 months before beginning of project work period
Board meeting date(s): Monthly except in Aug.
Officers and Trustees:* Dennis L. Bark,* Chair.; John H. Moore,* Vice-Chair.; Ingrid A. Gregg,* Pres.; Montgomery B. Brown, Secy. and Dir., Prog(s).; Kathleen B. Mason, Treas.; Peter B. Clark, Tr. Emeritus; Paul W. McCracken, Tr. Emeritus; Richard A. Ware, Tr. Emeritus; Thomas J. Bray; Kimberly O. Dennis; Carl I. Heenan III; Ann K. Irish; David B. Kennedy; Robert L. Queller.
Number of staff: 2 full-time professional; 3 full-time support.
EIN: 386008273
Recent grants for international programs:

1039-1 American Foreign Policy Council, Washington, DC, $15,000. For book, The Closing of the Muslim Mind. 2009.

1039-2 American Islamic Congress, Washington, DC, $11,000. For the Dream Deferred Essay Contest. 2009.

1039-3 Atlas Economic Research Foundation, Washington, DC, $22,500. For Research Program in Foreign Policy of the Centre for Independent Studies. 2009.

1039-4 Atlas Economic Research Foundation, Washington, DC, $16,721. For Graduate Fellowship in Legal Philosophy at Oxford University. 2009.

1039-5 Atlas Economic Research Foundation, Washington, DC, $10,000. For the Institute for Transitional Democracy and International Security. 2009.

1039-6 Cato Institute, Washington, DC, $30,000. For the Agencia Interamericana de Prensa Economica (AIPE). 2009.

1039-7 Educational Initiative for Central and Eastern Europe, Arlington, VA, $15,000. For book, The Black Book of Communism II. 2009.

1039-8 Ethics and Public Policy Center, Washington, DC, $10,000. For the Tertio Millennio Seminar on the Free Society, Krakow, Poland. 2009.

1039-9 George Mason University, Institute for Humane Studies, Fairfax, VA, $14,000. For Graduate Fellowships. 2009.

1039-10 George Mason University, Institute for Humane Studies, Fairfax, VA, $10,000. For Graduate Fellowships. 2009.

1039-11 Haverford College, Department of Economics, Haverford, PA, $26,000. For Study,

National Security and the Soviet Military Sector. 2009.

1039-12 Howard Center for Family, Religion and Society, Rockford, IL, $30,000. For the World Congress of Families V project. 2009.

1039-13 Institute of Economic Affairs, London, England, $22,000. For the Centre for Research Into Post-Communist Economies. 2009.

1039-14 Institute of Economic Affairs, London, England, $17,000. For Graduate Fellowship in Economics at the University of Buckingham. 2009.

1039-15 Institute of Economic Affairs, London, England, $16,500. For Graduate Fellowship at University of Buckingham. 2009.

1039-16 Institute of Economic Affairs, London, England, $10,000. For Conference, Centre for Research Into Post-Communist Economies. 2009.

1039-17 Institute of World Politics, Washington, DC, $118,267. To Support During Academic Year. 2009.

1039-18 Institute of World Politics, Washington, DC, $75,000. For General Operating Support. 2009.

1039-19 Institute of World Politics, Washington, DC, $53,268. To Support During Academic Year. 2009.

1039-20 Institute of World Politics, Washington, DC, $53,268. To Support During Academic Year. 2009.

1039-21 Kansas State University, Department of History, Manhattan, KS, $41,400. For book, Apostles of Liberty French Diplomatic Corps in the Revolution. 2009.

1039-22 Philanthropy Roundtable, Washington, DC, $17,500. For the National Security Breakthrough Group. 2009.

1039-23 University of Bayreuth, Center for American Studies, Bayreuth, Germany, $25,000. For Conference, Market Societies and Their Morality. 2009.

1039-24 University of Bayreuth, Center for American Studies, Bayreuth, Germany, $12,500. For Its Research Programs. 2009.

1039-25 University of Glasgow, Faculty of Law Business and Social Sciences, Glasgow, Scotland, $12,500. For Conference on Adam Smith's the Theory of Moral Sentiments. 2009.

1039-26 University of Notre Dame, Department of Classics, Notre Dame, IN, $30,000. For book, Ephrem the Syrian: an Intellectual and Cultural Biography. 2009.

1039-27 University of Notre Dame, Department of History, Notre Dame, IN, $17,490. For book, Fall of Tsarism. 2009.

1039-28 University of Notre Dame, Department of Political Science, Notre Dame, IN, $10,000. For Study, the Waning Influence of Academics on US National Security Policy. 2009.

1039-29 University of Pennsylvania, Department of East Asian Languages and Civilization, Philadelphia, PA, $21,000. For Graduate Fellowship in History. 2009.

1039-30 University of Pennsylvania, Department of East Asian Languages and Civilization, Philadelphia, PA, $17,666. For Graduate Fellowship in History. 2009.

1039-31 University of Saint Andrews, School of History, Saint Andrews, Scotland, $25,390. For Graduate Fellowship in History. 2009.

1039-32 Victims of Communism Memorial Foundation, Washington, DC, $10,000. For the Global Museum on Communism. 2009.

1039-33 Wheaton College, Department of Politics International Relations, Wheaton, IL, $16,797. For book, Enforcing Property Rights in Common Law Africa. 2009.

1040
Family Christian Stores Foundation
5300 Patterson Ave. S.E.
Grand Rapids, MI 49530-0001

Established in 2003 in MI.
Donors: David M. Browne; Cliff Bartow; Beverly Bartow; Family Christian Stores, Inc.; Thomas Nelson Publishers; Zondervan; Brown Family Agape Foundation.
Grantmaker type: Independent foundation.
Financial data (yr. ended 12/31/09): Assets, $1,991,722 (M); gifts received, $1,197,201; expenditures, $1,069,681; qualifying distributions, $969,692; giving activities include $587,593 for 11 grants (high: $121,803; low: $40), and $277,119 for 4 foundation-administered programs.
Purpose and activities: Giving primarily for the care of orphans, including adoption assistance.
Fields of interest: Children, adoption; International relief, 2004 tsunami; Children/youth, services; Christian agencies & churches.
Limitations: Applications not accepted. Giving primarily in IL, MD, MI and OH. No grants to individuals.
Application information: Contributes only to pre-selected organizations.
Officers: Steve Biondo, Pres.; Amy Anderson, Secy.; Ruth Witte, Treas.
Trustees: Jerry Hal Bailey; Earl C. Bartow; David M. Browne.
EIN: 383673924

1041
Max M. and Marjorie S. Fisher Foundation, Inc.
2 Towne Sq., Ste. 920
Southfield, MI 48075-3761 (248) 415-1444
Contact: Douglas Bitonti Stewart, Exec. Dir.
FAX: (248) 415-1453; E-mail: info@mmfisher.org; Additional e-mail: (for Douglas B. Stewart) dstewart@mmfisher.org; (for Julie M. Howe) jhowe@mmfisher.org; URL: http://www.mmfisher.org

Established in 1955 in MI.
Donors: Max M. Fisher‡; Marjorie M. Fisher; Martinique Hotel, Inc.
Grantmaker type: Independent foundation.
Financial data (yr. ended 12/31/09): Assets, $237,206,127 (M); gifts received, $9,864,725; expenditures, $12,807,544; qualifying distributions, $12,156,208; giving activities include $11,203,928 for 34 grants (high: $2,960,000).
Purpose and activities: The foundation acts from a philosophy grounded in the beliefs of its founders and shared Jewish values that life's purpose is found in service to others, in creating opportunities for those who lack them, empowering individuals in self sufficiency, providing life-saving resources for those without them, and supporting human community in all its forms from families to coalitions, cities to nations.
Fields of interest: Museums; Performing arts; Arts; Elementary/secondary education; Higher education; Education; Health organizations; Human services;

United Ways and Federated Giving Programs; Jewish federated giving programs; Jewish agencies & synagogues; Economically disadvantaged; Youth; Infants/toddlers; Children/youth; AIDS, people with.
International interests: Egypt; Israel; Zambia.
Type of support: General/operating support; Annual campaigns; Capital campaigns; Endowments; Emergency funds; Conferences/seminars; Seed money; Fellowships; Scholarship funds; Matching/challenge support.
Limitations: Applications not accepted. Giving on a national basis, with emphasis on MI, OH, and NY. No grants to individuals.
Application information: Contributes only to pre-selected organizations. At this time the Fisher Foundation is accepting proposals by invitation only.
  Board meeting date(s): Mar. 2, July 28, Sept. 11 and Dec. 16
Officers and Trustees:* Marjorie S. Fisher,* Chair.; Phillip William Fisher,* Secy.; Marjorie M. Fisher,* Treas.; Douglas Bitonti Stewart, Exec. Dir.; Julie Fisher Cummings, Managing Tr.; Mary D. Fisher; Jane F. Sherman.
Number of staff: 3 full-time professional; 1 full-time support.
EIN: 381784340
Recent grants for international programs:
1041-1 Birthright Israel Foundation, New York, NY, $100,000. For Taglit-Birthright Israel trip. 2010.
1041-2 Jewish Funders Network, New York, NY, $10,000. To sponsor International Conference. 2010.
1041-3 Perlman Music Program, New York, NY, $69,000. For residency in Israel. 2010.

1042
Foundation for Theological Education in Southeast Asia
c/o Norman Donkersloot
119 Oak Valley Dr.
Holland, MI 49424-2729
E-mail: ftewilson@gmail.com; URL: http://www.ftesea.org/

Established in 1934 in NY.
Grantmaker type: Independent foundation.
Financial data (yr. ended 12/31/10): Assets, $13,170,763 (M); gifts received, $3,294; expenditures, $695,550; qualifying distributions, $633,066; giving activities include $475,027 for 59 grants (high: $70,000; low: $1,300).
Purpose and activities: Giving primarily for theological education institutions in Southeast Asia, especially China.
Fields of interest: Theological school/education.
International interests: China.
Type of support: Professorships; Curriculum development.
Limitations: Applications not accepted. Giving primarily in Southeast Asia and China. No grants to individuals.
Application information: Contributes only to pre-selected organizations.
  Board meeting date(s): Dec.
Officers and Trustees:* Rev. Benjamin Shun Lai Chan, Chair.; Martha Lund Smalley, Vice-Chair.; Dr. Scott Sunquist,* Secy.; Norman Donkersloot, Treas.; Rev. H.S. Wilson, Exec. Dir.; Gerald Anderson, Tr. Emeritus; Rev. Charles Clark, Tr. Emeritus; Greer Anne Wenh-in Ng, Tr. Emeritus; Rebecca Asedillo; Tammy Jackson; Rev. Dr. Kah-Jin Jeffrey Kuan; Rev. Dr. James Vijayakumar; Dr. Ron

Wallace; Rev. Mienda Uriarte; Rev. Andrew Yutaka Yamamoto.
Number of staff: 1 full-time professional; 1 part-time support.
EIN: 237362344

1043
The Samuel and Jean Frankel Jewish Heritage Foundation
2301 W. Big Beaver Rd., Ste. 900
Troy, MI 48084-3332 (248) 649-2600

Established in 2004 in MI.
Donors: Samuel Frankel‡; Jean Frankel.
Grantmaker type: Independent foundation.
Financial data (yr. ended 12/31/09): Assets, $129,367,963 (M); expenditures, $6,890,536; qualifying distributions, $6,665,991; giving activities include $6,665,991 for 34 grants (high: $2,250,000; low: $1,000).
Fields of interest: Jewish federated giving programs; Theological school/education; Higher education; Education; Jewish agencies & synagogues.
Type of support: Program development; Endowments.
Limitations: Applications not accepted. Giving primarily in MI; giving also in New York, NY. No grants to individuals.
Application information: Contributes only to pre-selected organizations.
Officers and Trustees:* Stanley Frankel,* Pres. and Treas.; Jean Frankel,* V.P.; Judith Frankel,* Secy.
EIN: 300095016
Recent grants for international programs:
1043-1 American Israel Education Fund, Troy, MI, $610,000. 2009.
1043-2 David Project, Boston, MA, $100,000. For general support. 2009.
1043-3 NCSJ: Advocates on Behalf of Jews in Russia, Ukraine, the Baltic States and Eurasia, Washington, DC, $10,000. For general support. 2009.

1044
Global Philanthropy Alliance
P.O. Box 890
St. Joseph, MI 49085-0890 (202) 470-0716
E-mail: info@globalphilanthropyalliance.org; URL: http://www.globalphilanthropyalliance.org Facebook: http://www.facebook.com/pages/Global-philanthropy-Alliance/189999181047663 Twitter: http://twitter.com/#!/AfricaSocEntrep

Established in 2006 in MI.
Grantmaker type: Public charity.
Financial data (yr. ended 09/30/10): Revenue, $13,729; assets, $38,766 (M); gifts received, $13,650; expenditures, $55,903; program services expenses, $52,433; giving activities include $41,256 for grants to organizations outside the U.S., and $11,177 for foundation-administered programs.
Purpose and activities: The organization aims to develop partnerships between people in the United States and Africa, through mutual exchange of ideas and resources to support local organizations, empower youth, promote philanthropy, share knowledge and encourage innovation to achieve sustainable community development.
Fields of interest: Community/economic development; Philanthropy/voluntarism.

International interests: Kenya; Nigeria; South Africa.
Limitations: Applications accepted. Giving primarily in Kenya, Nigeria, and South Africa.
Publications: Application guidelines.
Application information: Grant applications are reviewed twice per year, usually in May and Nov. Application form required.
  Initial approach: Download application
  Deadline(s): Apr. 1 and Oct. 1
Officers and Board Members:* Anne C. Petersen,* Pres.; Robert L. Judd,* V.P. and Secy.; John C. Goff,* Treas.; Erin Brandt, Exec. Dir.; Karen Stone.
EIN: 205715805

1045
Hands of Hope, International
(formerly Hands of Hope, Inc.)
4265 Corporate Exchange Dr.
Hudsonville, MI   49426-1950   (616) 896-4847
FAX: (616) 896-9025;
E-mail: kritz@handsofhopeintl.org; URL: http://www.handsofhopeintl.org

Established in 2000 in MI.
Donors: Donald J. Koop; Al Koop; Robin Koop; Dan Koop; Michelle Koop.
Grantmaker type: Independent foundation.
Financial data (yr. ended 12/31/09): Assets, $32,011 (M); gifts received, $164,823; expenditures, $192,955; qualifying distributions, $183,774; giving activities include $174,882 for 1 grant.
Purpose and activities: Giving for the improvement of the health, education and economic conditions of disabled children and families in Vietnam.
Fields of interest: International relief; Children/youth.
Type of support: General/operating support; Equipment; In-kind gifts; Matching/challenge support.
Limitations: Applications not accepted. Giving primarily in Vietnam. No grants to individuals.
Publications: Annual report; Financial statement; Informational brochure; Occasional report.
Application information: Contributes only to pre-selected organizations.
  Board meeting date(s): Monthly
Officers and Directors:* Donald J. Koop, Chair. and Pres.; Robin Horder-Koop,* Vice-Chair.; Jean Koop,* Secy.; J.P. Koop,* Treas.; Valerie Betten; Al Koop; Dan Koop; Ray Koop; Kim Ritz; Ed Vanessendelft.
Number of staff: 5 full-time professional.
EIN: 383560968

1046
Italian American Delegates, Inc.
15985 Canal Rd., Ste. 5
Clinton Township, MI   48038-5021
(586) 228-5800
Contact: Vito Tocco, Pres.

Established in 1986 in MI.
Grantmaker type: Public charity.
Financial data (yr. ended 10/31/10): Revenue, $30,956; assets, $28,710 (M); gifts received, $10,050; expenditures, $34,551; giving activities include $31,750 for grants.
Purpose and activities: The organization supports cultural and educational programs and provides assistance to the disadvantaged, especially to

those of Italian American heritage, children and senior citizens.
Fields of interest: Arts, cultural/ethnic awareness; Disabilities, people with; Economically disadvantaged.
International interests: Italy.
Type of support: Endowments; Grants to individuals.
Limitations: Giving limited to the Detroit metropolitan area, MI.
Officers: Salvatore Ventimiglia, Pres.; Daniel Patrona, Sr., V.P.; Ted Barrie, Secy.; Frank Coppola, Treas.
EIN: 382840038

1047
Jewish Federation of Metropolitan Detroit
6735 Telegraph Rd.
P.O. Box 2030
Bloomfield Hills, MI   48303-2030
(248) 642-4260
FAX: (248) 642-4941; Toll-free tel.: (888) 902-4673;
URL: http://www.thisisfederation.org

Established in 1926 in MI.
Grantmaker type: Public charity.
Financial data (yr. ended 05/31/11): Revenue, $46,404,915; assets, $36,824,692 (M); gifts received, $43,146,688; expenditures, $68,078,176; giving activities include $56,664,009 for grants, and $156,500 for 2 grants to organizations outside the U.S.
Purpose and activities: The foundation, in partnership with its agencies, plays the leadership role in identifying needs within the metropolitan Detroit Jewish community and in mobilizing human and financial resources, engaging in communal planning, and allocating and advocating to meet those needs.
Fields of interest: Philanthropy/voluntarism; Jewish federated giving programs; Jewish agencies & synagogues.
International interests: Israel.
Type of support: Annual campaigns; Capital campaigns; Program development.
Limitations: Giving on a national and international basis.
Publications: Annual report; Financial statement; Newsletter.
Officers and Directors:* Nancy Grosfeld,* Pres.; Michael P. Horowitz,* Pres.-Elect; Ronald A. Klein,* V.P.; Ronald Krugel,* V.P.; Lawrence S. Lax,* V.P.; Matthew B. Lester,* V.P.; Beverly Liss,* V.P.; Gary Torgow,* V.P.; Marcie Orley,* Secy.; James B. Bellinson,* Treas.; Dr. Lynda Giles; Florine Mark; Marta Rosenthal; Jane Sherman; Paul R. Silverman.
EIN: 381359214

1048
The Jubilee Foundation
(formerly Herman Miller Design Foundation)
c/o Comerica Bank
P.O. Box 75000, M.C. 3462
Detroit, MI   48275-3462

Established in 1994 in MI.
Donor: Herman Miller, Inc.
Grantmaker type: Company-sponsored foundation.
Financial data (yr. ended 05/31/10): Assets, $6,745,347 (M); gifts received, $234,756; expenditures, $2,410,122; qualifying distributions,

$2,410,622; giving activities include $2,410,122 for 217 grants (high: $264,000; low: $250).
Purpose and activities: The foundation supports community foundations and organizations involved with arts and culture, education, the environment, hunger, human services, international affairs, Christianity, neighborhood development, and economically disadvantaged people.
Fields of interest: Arts; Elementary/secondary education; Higher education; Theological school/education; Education; Environment, natural resources; Environment, water resources; Environment; Health care; Food services; Developmentally disabled, centers & services; Human services; International relief; International affairs; Community development, neighborhood development; Foundations (community); Christian agencies & churches; Economically disadvantaged.
Type of support: Scholarship funds; General/operating support.
Limitations: Applications not accepted. Giving primarily in CA, GA, and VA, with emphasis on MI. No grants to individuals.
Application information: Contributes only to pre-selected organizations.
Officers: Michael A. Volkema, Pres.; James E. Christenson, Secy.; Gregory J Bylsma, Treas.
EIN: 383003821

1049
Kellogg Company 25-Year Employees Fund, Inc.
c/o Kellogg Co.
1 Kellogg Sq.
P.O. Box 3599
Battle Creek, MI   49016-3599   (269) 961-2000
Contact: Timothy S. Knowlton, Pres.

Established in 1944 in MI.
Donor: W.K. Kellogg†.
Grantmaker type: Company sponsored foundation.
Financial data (yr. ended 12/31/10): Assets, $62,842,822 (M); expenditures, $3,044,441; qualifying distributions, $3,013,345; giving activities include $1,500,000 for 1 grant, and $1,306,884 for 175 grants to individuals (high: $32,400; low: $324).
Purpose and activities: The fund supports retiree associations and awards grants for living and medical expenses to current and former 25-year employees and the dependents of 25-year employees of Kellogg.
Fields of interest: Zoos/zoological societies; Food banks; Community/economic development; United Ways and Federated Giving Programs; Economically disadvantaged.
International interests: Australia; Canada; Mexico; United Kingdom.
Type of support: Emergency funds; Grants to individuals.
Limitations: Applications not accepted. Giving primarily in areas of company operations, with emphasis on Battle Creek, MI; giving also in Australia, Canada, England, Mexico, and the United Kingdom. No grants to individuals (except for employee-related fund).
Application information: Must be employees or dependents of employees employed by Kellogg or a Kellogg subsidiary for at least 25 years.
  Board meeting date(s): Jan., Apr., July, and Oct.
Officers and Directors:* Timothy S. Knowlton,* Pres.; Joel Vanderkooi, Treas.; Margaret Bath; Celeste A. Clark; Ronald L. Dissinger; Ed Rector.

Number of staff: 1 full-time support.
EIN: 386039770

1050
W. K. Kellogg Foundation

1 Michigan Ave. E.
Battle Creek, MI   49017-4005   (269) 968-1611
URL: http://www.wkkf.org
Grants Database: http://www.wkkf.org/grants/
grants-database.aspx
Knowledge Center: http://www.wkkf.org/
knowledge-center/publications-and-resources.aspx
Multimedia: http://www.wkkf.org/
knowledge-center/multimedia/photos.aspx
RSS Feed: http://www.wkkf.org/news/
newsroom.aspx?rss=true
Twitter: http://www.twitter.com/WK_Kellogg_Fdn
W.K. Kellogg Foundation's Philanthropy
Promise: http://www.ncrp.org/
philanthropys-promise/who
YouTube: http://www.youtube.com/
KelloggFoundation

Incorporated in 1930 in MI.
Donors: W.K. Kellogg‡; W.K. Kellogg Foundation Trust; Carrie Staines Kellogg Trust.
Grantmaker type: Independent foundation.
Financial data (yr. ended 08/31/11): Assets, $7,696,627,040 (M); expenditures, $374,797,004; qualifying distributions, $355,647,496; giving activities include $291,212,363 for grants.
Purpose and activities: The Kellogg Foundation makes grants to organizations that embrace a similar mission of creating communities, systems, and nations in which all children have an equitable and promising future - one in which all children thrive. Grants fund programs and projects that support children, families, and communities as they strengthen and create conditions that propel children to achieve success as individuals and as contributors to the larger community and society.
Fields of interest: Agriculture; Agriculture/food; Community development, neighborhood development; Community/economic development; Education; Education, early childhood education; Elementary school/education; Health care; Health care, reform; Health organizations, association; Leadership development; Minorities/immigrants, centers/services; Rural development; Secondary school/education; Voluntarism promotion; Youth development, services; Youth, services; Youth; Single parents; Native Americans/American Indians; Infants/toddlers; Indigenous peoples; Immigrants/refugees; Hispanics/Latinos; Economically disadvantaged; Children/youth; Asians/Pacific Islanders; African Americans/Blacks; Children; Minorities.
International interests: Brazil; Haiti; Latin America; Mexico.
Type of support: Mission-related investments/loans; Program development; Seed money; Program evaluation; Employee matching gifts; Matching/challenge support.
Limitations: Applications accepted. Giving primarily in the U.S., with emphases on MI, MS, and NM, funding also for programs focused in Southern Mexico, Haiti, and northeast Brazil. No support for religious purposes or for capital facilities. No grants to individuals, or for scholarships, endowment funds, development campaigns, films, equipment, publications, conferences, or radio and television programs unless they are an integral part of a project already being funded; no grants for operating budgets.
Publications: Annual report; Financial statement; Grants list; Occasional report; Program policy statement.
Application information: The foundation requires all proposals to be submitted via an initial process online at www.wkkf.org. Please contact the Proposal Processing office for assistance if you are having difficulty submitting your request online or don't have internet access. Please note only nonprofit organizations are eligible for funding from the foundation and grants are currently limited to programs focused in southern Mexico, Haiti, northeast Brazil, and the United States. While the foundation funds nationally in the United States, it prioritize funding in Michigan, Mississippi, and New Mexico. (While the foundation remains committed to the southern African region, it is not currently accepting proposal submissions.)Should you have additional questions, please contact the Central Proposal Processing office at (269) 969-2329. Application form required.

Initial approach: Online submission is required. Contact the Central Proposal Processing office at (269) 969-2329 for instructions if unable to submit online
Copies of proposal: 1
Deadline(s): None
Board meeting date(s): Monthly
Final notification: 45 days

Officers and Trustees:* Sterling K. Speirn,* C.E.O. and Pres.; La June Montgomery-Tabron, C.O.O. and Treas.; James E. McHale, Chief of Staff; Gail C. Christopher, V.P., Prog. Strategy; Joel R. Wittenberg, V.P. and C.I.O.; Joanne K. Krell, V.P., Comms.; Susan Katz Froning, Corp. Secy. and General Counsel; Celeste A. Clark; Roderick D. Gillum; Dorothy A. Johnson; Fred P. Keller; Hanmin Liu; Cynthia H. Milligan; Wenda Weekes Moore; Bobby Moser; Ramon Murguia; Joseph M. Stewart; Richard M. Tsoumas.
Number of staff: 102 full-time professional; 44 full-time support.
EIN: 381359264
Recent grants for international programs:

1050-1 Academy for Educational Development, Washington, DC, $8,955,462. To promote family and community leadership of Southern African youth as agents of transformation in underserved and/or historically disadvantaged locations in Botswana, Lesotho, Malawi, Mozambique, South Africa, Swaziland and Zimbabwe. 2010.

1050-2 Academy for Educational Development, Washington, DC, $6,306,707. To help capacitate rural leaders from select sites and target areas through grounding in African leadership concepts as well as credentialing through tertiary degree. 2010.

1050-3 Agora Partnerships, Washington, DC, $25,000. To sponsor charitable event to support small and growing businesses throughout Latin America. 2010.

1050-4 Ashoka Mexico y Centroamerica, Mexico City, Mexico, $355,581. To enhance rural development in southeast Mexico by supporting leading social entrepreneurs, developing young social entrepreneurs and promoting hybrid-value chains. 2010.

1050-5 Associacao Frida Kahlo, Sao Paulo, Brazil, $25,000. To promote racial equity and enrich Brazilian diversity by empowering Black youth to stand up for their rights against racism. 2010.

1050-6 Association of Public and Land-grant Universities, Washington, DC, $100,000. To improve the capacity of African higher education institutions to address development problems, including those which have adverse effects on children in their early lives. 2010.

1050-7 Centro de Negocios Sustentables, A.C., Mexico City, Mexico, $50,000. To enhance success of economically, socially, and environmentally sustainable enterprises in central and southern Mexico by studying the feasibility of establishing a venture capital fund. 2010.

1050-8 Chicago Council on Global Affairs, Chicago, IL, $25,000. To explore partnerships with developing nations, international donors, and the private sector to mitigate global hunger and poverty through convening of international conference in Washington, D. C. 2010.

1050-9 Consejo de Organizaciones de la Sociedad Civil de Sinaloa, A.C., Mazatlan, Mexico, $24,998. To promote social development programs in Mazatlan, Sinaloa, Mexico, through the creation of a municipal fund. 2010.

1050-10 Consultative Group on Biological Diversity, San Francisco, CA, $50,000. To enhance the capacity of philanthropy to support environmental health and racial equity work. 2010.

1050-11 Convoy of Hope, Springfield, MO, $377,927. To help meet nutritional and basic needs of children in Haiti who were affected by the recent earthquake. 2010.

1050-12 EARTH University Foundation, Atlanta, GA, $240,000. To enable youth from Mexico, Guatemala, Honduras, and Nicaragua to pursue undergraduate degree in agriculture and natural resource management at EARTH University in Costa Rica by providing scholarships. 2010.

1050-13 EARTH University Foundation, Atlanta, GA, $15,000. To provide educational support for Haitian students. 2010.

1050-14 EARTH University Foundation, Atlanta, GA, $15,000. To provide educational support for Haitian students. 2010.

1050-15 Fundacion del Empresariado en Mexico, Mexico City, Mexico, $145,800. To promote economic development in disadvantaged communities of southeast Mexico by supporting a fund for civil society organizations. 2010.

1050-16 GELEDES Institute of Black Women, Sao Paulo, Brazil, $93,391. To inform and educate public opinion on racial issues in Brazil through the strengthening of the portal GELEDES. 2010.

1050-17 Global Center for Cultural Entrepreneurship, Santa Fe, NM, $249,934. To enhance programs that assist cultural entrepreneurs in New Mexico by strengthening organizational capacity. 2010.

1050-18 Global Food Protection Institute, Battle Creek, MI, $3,801,500. To enhance safety of the global food supply by developing a network which exchanges information, generates new ideas and accelerates applications and processes. 2010.

1050-19 Holt International Childrens Services, Eugene, OR, $75,000. To improve international adoption policies and practices by supporting international forum to explore lessons learned from multiple generations of adoptees. 2010.

1050-20 Iniciativa Ciudadana para la Promocion de la Cultura del Dialogo, A.C., Mexico City, Mexico, $103,479. To assess the state of civil society in Mexico in relation to other countries of the world with a verified methodology developed by

CIVICUS, World Alliance for Citizen Participation. 2010.

1050-21 Instituto de Pesquisas e Estudos Afro-Brasileiros, Rio de Janeiro, Brazil, $75,000. To improve the understanding of Afro-Brazilian history and culture through the organization and preservation of the archives of Abdias Nascimento. 2010.

1050-22 Leon Howard Sullivan Foundation, Washington, DC, $15,000. To support the Global Sullivan Principles of Social Responsibility program. 2010.

1050-23 Links, Renaissance Chapter, Bloomfield Hills, MI, $10,000. To support educational programs in Haiti. 2010.

1050-24 Meharry Medical College, Nashville, TN, $50,000. To improve the lives and survival of children in the developing world and underserved areas of the United States through publications about social determinants of child health. 2010.

1050-25 National Underground Railroad Freedom Center, Cincinnati, OH, $400,000. To increase the awareness of injustice in the global world and inspire participants to become active and engaged members of the community by providing a historical context for issues of racial inequity. 2010.

1050-26 PeaceJam Foundation, Arvada, CO, $10,000. To enable the organization to achieve its mission by providing general operating support. 2010.

1050-27 Royal Family Archives, Museum and Information Center, Maseru, Lesotho, $162,930. To preserve cultural heritage records of the Royal Family found in Matsieng by creating information and resource center. 2010.

1050-28 Salzburg Global Seminar, Washington, DC, $300,000. To enhance civic engagement of emerging leaders by building the Salzburg Global Fellowship network and increase the connectivity of Fellows to the Seminar. 2010.

1050-29 Swazi Indigenous Products, Mpaka, Swaziland, $390,000. To empower rural communities, in particular women's groups, by increasing income through the establishment of innovative, viable rural enterprise using marula and other natural products. 2010.

1050-30 U.S. Human Rights Network, Atlanta, GA, $150,000. To implement a strategy employing human rights education and training activities to increase awareness of the International Convention on the Elimination of all forms of Racial Discrimination and how this ratified treaty can offer structural solutions for addressing racial inequity in Mississippi, Michigan, New Mexico, and Louisiana. 2010.

1050-31 Union de Empresanos para la Tecnologia en la Educacion, Mexico City, Mexico, $350,000. To enable Mexican children and youth in Chiapas, Campeche, and Yucatan to obtain a better education by providing access to the necessary information technology tools. 2010.

1050-32 Womens Funding Network, San Francisco, CA, $3,000,000. To ensure that women and vulnerable children have full access to economic security, education, health care, personal security and human rights by advancing a social justice agenda. 2010.

1050-33 Womens Funding Network, San Francisco, CA, $25,000. To respond to a changing economic and philanthropic landscape by increasing the capacity of its member funds to develop and implement highly relevant and actionable revenue streams and business

models to support social change on behalf of women worldwide. 2010.

1051
Kellogg's Corporate Citizenship Fund
1 Kellogg Sq.
Battle Creek, MI   49016-3599   (269) 961-2867
Contact: Linda Fields
E-mail: linda.fields@kelloggs.com; Additional e-mail: corporateresponsibility@kellogg.com; URL: http://www.kelloggcompany.com/corporateresponsibility.aspx?id=659

Established in 1994 in MI.
Donor: Kellogg Co.
Grantmaker type: Company-sponsored foundation.
Financial data (yr. ended 12/31/10): Assets, $46,895,203 (M); gifts received, $15,000,000; expenditures, $9,504,251; qualifying distributions, $9,458,341; giving activities include $9,035,229 for 479 grants (high: $2,001,781; low: $25).
Purpose and activities: The fund supports food banks and community foundations and organizations involved with arts and culture, education, fitness and health, hunger, nutrition, athletics, and human services.
Fields of interest: Athletics/sports, amateur leagues; Arts; Elementary/secondary education; Higher education; Education; Public health, obesity; Public health, physical fitness; Health care; Food services; Food banks; Nutrition; Athletics/sports, water sports; American Red Cross; YM/YWCAs & YM/YWHAs; Children/youth, services; Human services; Foundations (community); United Ways and Federated Giving Programs.
Type of support: General/operating support; Building/renovation; Program development; Scholarship funds; Research; Technical assistance; Employee volunteer services; Employee matching gifts.
Limitations: Applications accepted. Giving primarily in areas of company operations in CA, Washington, DC, IL, PA, and TX, with emphasis on Battle Creek, MI; some giving also in Australia, Canada, and the United Kingdom.
Application information: Application form not required.
   Initial approach: Letter of inquiry
   Deadline(s): None
Officers and Directors:* Celeste A. Clark,* Pres.; Gary H. Pilnick, V.P.; Janice L. Perkins,* Treas.; Timothy S. Knowlton,* Exec. Dir.; Kris Charles; Paul Norman; Dennis W. Shuler; Mark Wagner.
EIN: 383167772
Recent grants for international programs:
1051-1 ASA, Loughborough, England, $336,000. 2009.
1051-2 Community Foundation for Greater Manchester, Manchester, England, $923,000. 2009.
1051-3 ContinYou, Coventry, England, $141,000. 2009.
1051-4 Global FoodBanking Network, Chicago, IL, $250,000. 2009.
1051-5 Joint Aid Management, Washington, DC, $100,000. 2009.
1051-6 Resource Foundation, New York, NY, $300,000. 2009.
1051-7 Specialty Cereals Ltd., Sydney, Australia, $100,000. 2009.
1051-8 United Way Worldwide, Alexandria, VA, $25,000. 2009.

1052
Latvian Foundation, Inc.
1907 Autumn Crest Ln.
Kalamazoo, MI   49008-4810

Established in 1976.
Grantmaker type: Public charity.
Financial data (yr. ended 04/30/10): Revenue, $63,844; assets, $724,612 (M); gifts received, $18,952; expenditures, $40,894; giving activities include $14,721 for grants.
Purpose and activities: The foundation seeks to preserve Latvian culture.
Fields of interest: Arts; Education.
International interests: Latvia.
Type of support: Grants to individuals.
Limitations: Giving limited to Latvia.
Officers: Valdis Berzins, Pres.; Astrida Levensteins, V.P.; Alfs Berztiss, Secy.; Tua Karklis, Treas.
EIN: 237089477

1053
Edward C. and Linda Dresner Levy Foundation
(formerly Julie & Edward Levy, Jr. Foundation)
9300 Dix Ave.
Dearborn, MI   48120-1528

Established in 1973 in MI.
Donors: Carol Levy; Ellen Levy; Edward C. Levy, Jr.; Edward C. Levy Co.; The Charitable Lead Trust.
Grantmaker type: Independent foundation.
Financial data (yr. ended 09/30/10): Assets, $9,275,419 (M); expenditures, $2,200,022; qualifying distributions, $2,137,725; giving activities include $2,137,725 for 40 grants (high: $1,049,175; low: $250).
Purpose and activities: Giving for primarily health care, particularly to a cancer center, as well as for education, and Jewish organizations.
Fields of interest: Hospitals (specialty); Higher education; Health care; Health organizations, association; Cancer research; International exchange, students; Jewish federated giving programs; Jewish agencies & synagogues.
Limitations: Applications not accepted. Giving primarily in MI, with emphasis on Detroit; some giving also in Washington, DC. No grants to individuals.
Application information: Contributes only to pre-selected organizations.
Officer: Edward C. Levy, Jr., Pres.
Directors: Patrick Duerr; Linda Dresner Levy.
EIN: 386091368

1054
Lot Foundation
13151 Lakeshore Dr.
Grand Haven, MI   49417-9348

Donors: Judith Van Kampen; Grace Foundation.
Grantmaker type: Independent foundation.
Financial data (yr. ended 12/31/10): Assets, $939,560 (M); gifts received, $1,000,000; expenditures, $1,380,135; qualifying distributions, $1,380,135; giving activities include $1,376,800 for 9 grants (high: $650,000; low: $800).
Fields of interest: International relief; Christian agencies & churches; Protestant agencies & churches.

Limitations: Applications not accepted. Giving primarily in MI.
Application information: Contributes only to pre-selected organizations.
Directors: David Wisen; Kristen Wisen.
EIN: 421561347

1055
Manoogian Simone Foundation
(formerly Louise Manoogian Simone Foundation)
21001 Van Born Rd.
Taylor, MI 48180-1340   (313) 274-8799

Established in 1962 in MI.
Donors: Alex Manoogian†; Marie Manoogian; Masco Corp.
Grantmaker type: Independent foundation.
Financial data (yr. ended 12/31/10): Assets, $89,267,244 (M); expenditures, $3,905,904; qualifying distributions, $3,716,551; giving activities include $3,714,500 for 11 grants (high: $1,866,000; low: $1,000).
Purpose and activities: Giving primarily to Armenian organizations, as well as for other human service organizations.
Fields of interest: Human services.
International interests: Armenia.
Limitations: Applications not accepted. Giving primarily in NY; some funding in MA. No grants to individuals.
Application information: Contributes only to pre-selected organizations.
Officers and Directors:* Louise M. Simone,* Pres.; David Simone,* V.P.; Christine M. Simone, Secy.-Treas.; Mark Simone.
EIN: 381799107
Recent grants for international programs:
1055-1 American University of Armenia, Oakland, CA, $820,000. For operating support. 2009.
1055-2 Armenia Fund USA, New York, NY, $10,000. For operating support. 2009.
1055-3 Armenian Eyecare Project, Newport Beach, CA, $25,000. For operating support. 2009.
1055-4 Children of Armenia Fund, New York, NY, $300,000. For operating support. 2009.
1055-5 Doctors Without Borders USA, New York, NY, $50,000. For general support. 2009.
1055-6 Friends of Holy Etchmiadzin, Mahwah, NJ, $600,000. For operating support. 2009.
1055-7 Fund for Armenian Relief, New York, NY, $25,000. For general support. 2009.

1056
Manthei Charitable Trust
3996 Charlevoix Ave.
Petoskey, MI 49770-9722

Established in 1960.
Donors: Theodore W. Manthei; Mary Manthei; Daniel R. Manthei; Tim Manthei; Ben Manthei; Jim Manthei; Mark Manthei; Tom Manthei; Corman Leigh; Dale Northrip; Covenant Development.
Grantmaker type: Independent foundation.
Financial data (yr. ended 12/31/10): Assets, $704,850 (M); gifts received, $144,095; expenditures, $395,153; qualifying distributions, $392,047; giving activities include $392,047 for 8 grants (high: $150,988; low: $1,000).
Fields of interest: Human services; International development; Christian agencies & churches; Asians/Pacific Islanders; Children/youth.

Type of support: General/operating support.
Limitations: Applications not accepted. Giving in the U.S., primarily in CA and WA; giving also in AZ and some funding in Thailand. No grants to individuals.
Application information: Contributes only to pre-selected organizations.
Trustees: Daniel R. Manthei; Mark Manthei; Thomas Manthei.
EIN: 381204856

1057
The Edwin J. May Foundation
615 Abbey St.
Birmingham, MI 48009-5620   (248) 723-9033
Contact: Brian S. May, Tr.

Established in 1994 in FL.
Donors: Daniel May; Dianne L. May.
Grantmaker type: Independent foundation.
Financial data (yr. ended 12/31/10): Assets, $2,344,159 (M); gifts received, $139,726; expenditures, $180,902; qualifying distributions, $172,350; giving activities include $170,000 for 4 grants (high: $50,000; low: $20,000).
Fields of interest: Higher education, college; American Red Cross; International relief; Christian agencies & churches.
International interests: Haiti.
Type of support: General/operating support.
Limitations: Applications accepted. Giving primarily in FL and NC. No grants to individuals.
Application information:
  Initial approach: Letter
  Deadline(s): None
Trustees: Brian S. May; Daniel May; Dianne L. May; Wachovia Bank, N.A.
EIN: 650501566

1058
Charles Stewart Mott Foundation
Mott Foundation Bldg.
503 S. Saginaw St., Ste. 1200
Flint, MI 48502-1851   (810) 238-5651
FAX: (810) 766-1753; E-mail: info@mott.org;
URL: http://www.mott.org/
E-Newsletter: http://www.mott.org/about/thefoundation/newslettersubscribe.aspx
Facebook: http://www.facebook.com/mottfoundation
Flint Area Program's Facebook page: http://www.facebook.com/mottfoundationflint
Grants Database: http://www.mott.org/about/searchgrants.aspx
Program News Feeds: http://feeds.feedburner.com/mott/news/General
RSS Grants Feed: http://feeds.feedburner.com/mott/grant/General
Twitter: http://www.twitter.com/mottfoundation
YouTube: http://www.youtube.com/csmottfoundation

Incorporated in 1926 in MI.
Donors: Charles Stewart Mott†; and members of the Mott family.
Grantmaker type: Independent foundation.
Financial data (yr. ended 12/31/10): Assets, $2,230,528,471 (M); expenditures, $133,800,234; qualifying distributions, $122,672,368; giving activities include $104,656,555 for 492 grants (high: $7,000,000; low: $3,500), $1,319,553 for 727 employee

matching gifts, and $1,440,053 for 17 foundation-administered programs.
Purpose and activities: To support efforts that promote a just, equitable and sustainable society with the primary focus on civil society, the environment, the area of Flint, MI and poverty. The foundation makes grants for a variety of purposes within these program areas including: philanthropy and voluntarism; assisting emerging civil societies in Central/Eastern Europe, Russia and South Africa; conservation of fresh water ecosystems in North America; reform of international finance and trade; improving the outcomes for children, youth and families at risk of persistent poverty; education and neighborhood and economic development. The foundation also makes grants to strengthen the capacity of local institutions in its home community of Flint, MI.
Fields of interest: Employment, services; Education; Environment, pollution control; Environment, natural resources; Human services; Children, services; Child development, services; Family services, parent education; Civil rights, race/intergroup relations; Economic development; Urban/community development; Rural development; Community/economic development; Voluntarism promotion; Leadership development; Children/youth; Young adults; Minorities; Economically disadvantaged.
International interests: Ukraine; Eastern & Central Europe; Latin America; Russia; South Africa.
Type of support: General/operating support; Continuing support; Management development/capacity building; Program development; Conferences/seminars; Seed money; Technical assistance; Program evaluation; Program-related investments/loans; Employee matching gifts; Matching/challenge support.
Limitations: Applications accepted. Giving nationally and to emerging countries in Central and Eastern Europe, Russia, and South Africa. No support for religious activities or programs serving specific religious groups or denominations. Faith based organizations may submit inquiries if the project falls within the foundation's guidelines and serves a broad segment of the population. No grants to individuals or for capital development (with the exception of the Flint area and legacy institutions). Grants for research, project replication or endowments are rarely funded unless these activities grow out of work the foundation already supports. No support for local projects, except in the Flint area, unless they are part of a Mott-planned national demonstration or network of grants. Film and video projects, books, scholarships, and fellowships are rarely funded; no loans.
Publications: Annual report (including application guidelines); Financial statement; Occasional report.
Application information: Applicants strongly encouraged to submit proposals during first quarter of the year. Letter of inquiry form available online. Application form not required.
  Initial approach: Letter of inquiry or proposal
  Copies of proposal: 1
  Deadline(s): None; grants are determined by Aug. 31 of any given year
  Board meeting date(s): Mar., June, Sept., and Dec.
  Final notification: 60 to 90 days
Officers and Trustees:* William S. White,* Chair., C.E.O. and Pres.; Frederick S. Kirkpatrick,* Vice-Chair.; Neal R. Hegarty, Sr. V.P., Progs. and Comms.; Phillip H. Peters, V.P., Admin. Group and Secy.-Treas.; Michael J. Smith, V.P., Investments

and C.I.O.; Gavin T. Clabaugh, V.P., Inf. Svcs.; Carol D. Rugg, V.P., Comms.; Ridgway H. White, V.P., Special Projects and Prog. Off., Flint Area; A. Marshall Acuff, Jr.; Rushworth M. Kidder; Tiffany W. Lovett; Webb F. Martin; Olivia P. Maynard; John Morning; Maryanne Mott; Charlie Nelms; William H. Piper; John W. Porter; Marise M.M. Stewart; Claire M. White; Douglas X. Patino.
Number of staff: 59 full-time professional; 25 full-time support.
EIN: 381211227
Recent grants for international programs:
1058-1 Academy for the Development of Philanthropy in Poland, Warsaw, Poland, $600,000. To strengthen community foundation development in the Czech Republic, Hungary, Poland, and Slovakia (the Visegrad countries) with tailor-made grantmaking and technical assistance programs, networking and learning opportunities. In addition, Grantee will strengthen the Visegrad networks and associations of community foundations. 2010.
1058-2 ActionAid, London, England, $300,000. For Bretton Woods Project continued work in multiple roles as clearinghouse for information and research; advisor to nongovernmental organization networks working on reform of international financial institutions based in the United Kingdom, other European and developing countries; catalyst for strategy development and policy discussions; interlocutor between nongovernmental organizations and British government officials; and as source for information on international financial institutions and policies and practices for the media. 2010.
1058-3 ActionAid, London, England, $85,000. For Bretton Woods Project's leadership role in helping to develop coherent civil society positions in response to the financial crisis, ensuring attention to role of international financial institutions and global economic governance. Grant increase will support efforts to take advantage of opportunities to influence direction of financial reform at the international level. 2010.
1058-4 Afrika Tikkun, Johannesburg, South Africa, $120,000. To strengthen institutional capacity and to partner with community groups, other organizations and government to empower disadvantaged communities. 2010.
1058-5 AGORA Platform: Active Communities for Development Alternatives, Sofia, Bulgaria, $120,000. For general support toward development of local communities and grassroots organizations in Bulgaria. Organizations are called Chitalishtes, community-based, nongovernmental institutions with a history of supporting literacy, education and development in local communities. 2010.
1058-6 Alliance of Religions and Conservation, Manchester, England, $50,000. For collaborative effort between ARC and the United Nations to address issues of environment and climate change. During the grant period, these faith groups will receive assistance on implementing plans and new initiatives and partnerships among religious and secular organizations will be facilitated. 2010.
1058-7 Amazon Watch, San Francisco, CA, $250,000. For work of International Finance and the Amazon Program to strengthen capacity of constituencies in Amazon countries (with focus on Brazil and Peru), particularly environmental and indigenous organizations, to influence and

hold accountable international financial decision makers for environmental and social impacts of energy and infrastructure projects. Grant will support monitoring of emblematic highway, waterway and hydroelectric dam projects in the Amazon region. 2010.
1058-8 American Ireland Fund, Boston, MA, $40,000. To produce a Global Diaspora Strategies Toolkit with practical examples on how to develop diaspora philanthropy programs and encourage growth and effectiveness of diaspora philanthropy globally. Toolkit will be a guide for governments, corporations, foundations and individuals interested in developing programs in this area. Grantee will work with the U.S. State Department to organize a conference which will focus on best practices in diaspora philanthropy and will highlight the work being done in this field throughout the world. 2010.
1058-9 American University, College of Law, Washington, DC, $75,000. For Program on International and Comparative Environmental Law to evaluate current sustainable finance standards, monitor climate change-related policies of financial institutions, strengthen and use existing accountability systems to support affected communities in specific cases, and seek new approaches to increasing accountability of public and private financial institutions as part of Sustainable Finance Project. 2010.
1058-10 ANNA, Moscow, Russia, $150,000. For advocacy in efforts to increase involvement of local communities in prevention of violence against women and girls in Southern Federal District of Russia. 2010.
1058-11 Apartheid Museum, Johannesburg, South Africa, $100,000. For general support of work of the museum and to assist it to introduce new programs including design of new interactive exhibition on South Africa's Truth and Reconciliation Commission which will encourage visitors to add personal stories of human rights violations under apartheid. 2010.
1058-12 Asia Society, New York, NY, $200,000. For research in efforts to raise awareness, build capacity and stimulate new opportunities to integrate global literacy into afterschool initiatives. Overall goals of project are to increase quality and quantity of global learning in afterschool programs and enable collaboration between schools, afterschool programs and community organizations to realize new definition of student success in the 21st century. Specifically, grantee will work closely with leading statewide afterschool networks and experts to further develop tools, materials and training opportunities to add to the afterschool field. In addition, Society's International Studies Schools Network of secondary schools, afterschool experts and national advisors will develop planning process to align school-day curriculum and afterschool experiential learning to help youth achieve global competence. 2010.
1058-13 Asociacion Civil Labor, Moquegua, Peru, $50,000. To coordinate support for national-level civil society coalitions in Peru working to improve environmental and social sustainability of large-scale infrastructure and energy projects in Peru. The Association will carry out strategic analyses, conduct workshops and provide logistical support to inform national dialogues on energy policy. It will provide similar support to coalition of Peruvian organizations concerned

about social and environmental impacts of major highway, hydroelectric dams and other infrastructure being financed as part of Initiative for Integration of Regional Infrastructure for South America. 2010.
1058-14 Association for Civil Society Development-SMART, Rijeka, Croatia, $60,000. For general core support. 2010.
1058-15 Association for Psychosocial Help and Development of Voluntary Work, Centre for Development and Promotion of Voluntary Work, Gracanica, Bosnia-Herzegovina, $60,000. Toward development and promotion of voluntarism and citizen engagement in Bosnia-Herzegovina and South East Europe. 2010.
1058-16 Association Mi, Split, Croatia, $60,000. For general support toward development of civil society and the nonprofit sector in southern Croatia. 2010.
1058-17 Association of Charitable Foundations, London, England, $10,000. For general support. 2010.
1058-18 Association of Community Foundations in Bulgaria, Stara Zagora, Bulgaria, $90,000. For general support. 2010.
1058-19 Balkan Investigative Reporting Network, Sarajevo, Bosnia-Herzegovina, $100,000. For general operating support for work in the area of civil society and public participation. 2010.
1058-20 Bank Information Center, Washington, DC, $25,000. For general support to enable Center to convene two workshops aimed at strengthening policies at the World Bank and International Finance Corporation related to energy and sustainability. 2010.
1058-21 BankTrack, Utrecht, Netherlands, $200,000. For general operating support. 2010.
1058-22 Berne Declaration, Zurich, Switzerland, $200,000. For Sustainable Financial Relations Project, effort to work with partners in the U.S., Europe and developing countries on institutional reform at the World Bank, export credit agencies, and private sector banks including monitoring environmentally and socially harmful projects funded by these institutions and educating Swiss officials and the public about need to ensure that international public and private investments support sustainable development. 2010.
1058-23 Black Sash Trust, Cape Town, South Africa, $200,000. For general operating support for work in South Africa. 2010.
1058-24 BlueLink Foundation, Sofia, Bulgaria, $90,000. For general support toward project to strengthen capacity of nongovernmental organizations in Bulgaria to use Internet communication technology to engage effectively in public policy development and advocacy. BlueLink Foundation maintains an Internet portal through which Bulgarian nongovernmental organizations communicate, network, share and engage in joint activities; provide training and technical assistance to nongovernmental organizations in networking, advocacy and effective use of electronic communication tools and develop specific tools for online communication, campaigning, and advocacy. 2010.
1058-25 Bulgarian Charities Aid Foundation, Sofia, Bulgaria, $75,000. For general support of work to mobilize financial resources and promote philanthropy in Bulgaria. Foundation will promote workplace and payroll giving schemes, administer corporate giving programs and train

nongovernmental organizations on local resource mobilization and financial management. 2010.

1058-26 Bulgarian Donors Forum, Sofia, Bulgaria, $90,000. For general suppor toward consolidating and strengthening the philanthropic community in Bulgaria. 2010.

1058-27 Bulgarian Environmental Partnership Foundation, Sofia, Bulgaria, $200,000. For general support toward strengthening citizen participation at the grassroots level in Bulgaria. During the grant period, the Partnership will provide small grants and technical assistance to nongovernmental organizations and community groups in the fields of environment and community development, raise awareness of the general public about key environmental issues in Bulgaria and increase organizational capacity and financial sustainability. 2010.

1058-28 Bulgarian Environmental Partnership Foundation, Sofia, Bulgaria, $116,070. To strengthen financial stability with fundraising campaign to build endowment. 2010.

1058-29 CARE USA, Atlanta, GA, $160,000. To provide technical assistance in efforts to strengthen youth development and active participation in addressing violence and peace-building challenges in Bosnia-Herzegovina, Croatia, and Serbia. To this end, CARE USA will provide financial and technical assistance to eight nongovernmental organizations across the region to develop and implement programs that promote peace building, address issues of masculinity and violence and engage young people directly in community and civic initiatives Particular focus will be given to working with community-based organizations in eastern Bosnia. 2010.

1058-30 Caring About Rights and Responsibilities Across Society, Ditshwanelo CAR2ASI, Johannesburg, South Africa, $40,000. For general support for work with the Golden Lions Rugby Union to tackle racism in sport and to provide support to the South African Human Rights Commission to address racism and promote reconciliation and community healing in the small town of Skierlik in the Northwest province. Support will also be provided to organizations in Kenya to deal with ethnic conflicts and to promote peace to prevent a repeat of the post-election violence of 2007. 2010.

1058-31 CEE Citizens Network, Banska Bystrica, Slovakia, $130,000. To support networking of nongovernmental organizations working with citizens and local communities. During next two years, network will organize annual Citizen Participation Week simultaneously in 17 countries, conduct study to benchmark levels of citizen participation across the region, promote participation through innovative uses of technology and strengthen cooperation with other networks. 2010.

1058-32 Center for Automotive Research, Ann Arbor, MI, $250,000. To develop Program for Automotive Labor and Education, industry-driven, research-based initiative that will conduct research on size of automotive workforce and timing of any potential new hiring, as well as provide forecast of skill needs and review of best practice programs and curricula. 2010.

1058-33 Center for Civil Initiatives, Zagreb, Croatia, $100,000. For general support for work to stimulate citizen activism and mobilize

community resources to address critical issues facing Croatian communities. 2010.

1058-34 Center for Community Change, Washington, DC, $25,000. To organize training sessions to strengthen capacity of nonprofits and communities in Central and Eastern Europe to use community organizing principles and techniques to engage community residents in addressing issues of common concern. United States-based community organizers will provide training and advice to community leaders and nonprofits in Central and Eastern European countries and consult on development of European network for community organizing. 2010.

1058-35 Center for Humanistic Technologies Ahalar, Chernihiv, Ukraine, $100,000. To strengthen local-level civic participation in decisionmaking and build social capital and cohesion in Ukraine by mobilizing local communities in Ukraine to effectively address and resolve issues of common concern. Specific activities will include organizing trainings, study visits and small pilot projects for community animators, other nonprofits and the media from across Ukraine. The project will emphasize dissemination of results and learning through two national-level conferences and publication of a handbook for practitioners. 2010.

1058-36 Center for Investigative Reporting, Berkeley, CA, $75,000. To focus investigative reporting on development of a global carbon market which will allow for buying and selling of greenhouse gas emission permits-carbon trading. 2010.

1058-37 Center for Research, Documentation and Publication, Pristina, Kosovo, $65,000. To help develop organizational and programmatic capacities to work on justice and reconciliation in Kosovo and the wider region over the long term. 2010.

1058-38 Center for Socio-Environmental Support, Sao Paulo, Brazil, $240,000. To strengthen administrative, operational and resource mobilization capacity. 2010.

1058-39 Centers for Civic Initiatives, Tuzla, Bosnia-Herzegovina, $100,000. For general operating support. 2010.

1058-40 Centre for Promotion of Civil Society, Sarajevo, Bosnia-Herzegovina, $60,000. For general support. 2010.

1058-41 Centre for Public Participation, Local Government Support Programme, Durban, South Africa, $40,000. For conference to strengthen public participation in governance and advance achievement of civil, political and socioeconomic rights and poverty alleviation.Programme helps to build bridges between communities and elected leaders at the local government level in order for people to realize rights and access basic services such as water, electricity and housing. 2010.

1058-42 Charities Aid Foundation-Southern Africa, Johannesburg, South Africa, $70,000. For general support. 2010.

1058-43 Civic Analysis and Independent Research Center, Perm, Russia, $180,000. For Civil Initiatives for Public Benefit Support Service, program to promote capacities for civic awareness and effective civic activism among informal citizen groups in Russia. 2010.

1058-44 Civic Initiatives, Belgrade, Serbia, $100,000. For general support. 2010.

1058-45 Civic Space, Kiev, Ukraine, $100,000. Toward institutional development support to strengthen professional and technological capacity of Ukraine's most prominent Internet portal for civic initiatives and nonprofit organizations. The portal is Internet resource providing a broad spectrum of interactive services to raise the effectiveness of Ukrainian nonprofits including searchable databases, Web page hosting services, discussion forums, analytical and research materials, nonprofit sector news, and other features. 2010.

1058-46 CIVICUS: World Alliance for Citizen Participation, Washington, DC, $120,000. For operating support. 2010.

1058-47 CIVICUS: World Alliance for Citizen Participation, Washington, DC, $80,000. For operating support. 2010.

1058-48 Civil Society Institute, Kiev, Ukraine, $100,000. For general support to conduct detailed monitoring of legislation impacting nonprofit organizations and people's rights and freedoms while educating legislative officials about effective law-making procedures. Institute will work with local and regional partners to promote informed public participation in decision making aimed at improving community development outcomes. It will seek to train a new generation of independent policy professionals capable of carrying on and expanding this work. 2010.

1058-49 Committee of Voters of Ukraine, Kiev, Ukraine, $140,000. For general support toward fostering development of civil society in an open and democratic Ukraine. Committee mobilizes volunteers to monitor elections, promote accountability of elected officials through public information activities, advise citizens on effective means of interacting with local government, educate youth on constitutional and voting rights and advocate for transparent and reliable election procedures in Ukraine. 2010.

1058-50 Common Purpose South Africa, Johannesburg, South Africa, $80,000. For conferences and seminars to train leaders of South African nonprofit organizations. 2010.

1058-51 Community Based Development Programme Trust, Johannesburg, South Africa, $100,000. For general operating support to train, mentor and support community-based organizations in some of the poorest and most marginalized regions of South Africa. Grantee will run Development Management Certificate course in collaboration with University of the Witwatersrand in Johannesburg, which offers specific training to middle- and senior-level leaders of nonprofit organizations. 2010.

1058-52 Community Building Mitrovica, Kosovska Mitrovica, Kosovo, $51,000. To strengthen capacity of this nongovernmental organizational to lead and support economic, social and civic redevelopment in deeply divided city of Mitrovica. 2010.

1058-53 Community Connections, Philippi, South Africa, $80,000. For general support. 2010.

1058-54 Community Development Foundation Western Cape, Cape Town, South Africa, $100,000. For general support toward implementing programs that encourage and enhance local giving within communities and to strengthen community efforts aimed at improving the quality of lives. 2010.

1058-55 Community Foundation Network, London, England, $171,500. For general support toward providing services that will generate new funding, enable more effective work through collaboration and better use of technology and share learning within the United Kingdom and internationally. 2010.

1058-56 Community Foundation Partnership, Togliatti, Russia, $100,000. Toward creating a common identity and purpose and shared base values among Partnership members; 2) supporting learning and professional development opportunities within the membership; and 3) creating a nationally favorable environment supportive of community foundation development in Russia. 2010.

1058-57 Community Foundation Tuzla, Tuzla, Bosnia-Herzegovina, $70,000. For general support. 2010.

1058-58 Community Law and Rural Development Centre, Durban, South Africa, $200,000. For general support toward efforts to strengthen Advice offices through training of paralegals and governing boards and providing hands-on support to ensure that they provide relevant and effective services to communities to deepen democracy. 2010.

1058-59 Community Organisation Resource Centre, Mowbray, South Africa, $80,000. For Learning Through Practice: Building Partnerships Between Organizations of Urban Poor and Local Authorities, initiative to continue work to improve living conditions of people in informal settlements by facilitating various community-driven processes and establishment of network of community-based organizations that represent needs of poor people. 2010.

1058-60 Consultative Group on Biological Diversity, San Francisco, CA, $30,000. For general support. 2010.

1058-61 Consultative Group on Biological Diversity, San Francisco, CA, $10,000. For general support and for consultant who will provide research, networking and administrative support to assist group of funders investigating idea of a national water policy agenda. 2010.

1058-62 Corner House, Sturminster Newton, England, $200,000. For efforts (including research) to reform international financial institutions, in particular the World Bank; export credit agencies; and private banks. In addition, grantee will focus on new trends emerging from the global financial crisis, including monitoring of proposed new regulations for derivatives and other complex financial vehicles and supporting efforts to construct banking and financial systems that reduce systemic risk and promote public interest goals. 2010.

1058-63 Council on Foundations, Arlington, VA, $300,000. For operating support for Global Philanthropy Leadership Initiative, joint project of Council , the European Foundation Centre and Worldwide Initiatives for Grantmaker Support (WINGS). A task force comprising of foundation leaders from around the world will guide work in three areas: 1) improving the legal environment for global philanthropy; 2) developing models/ vehicles for pooling resources together and increasing collaboration; and 3) identifying key political moments and levers to engage with policymakers/multilateral organizations. They will assess and inform current thinking in the three areas and design process through which diverse group of people can explore and jointly shape the agenda and eventual product of the initiative. 2010.

1058-64 Council on Foundations, Arlington, VA, $50,000. To provide technical assistance for Global Philanthropy Program, which aims to promote and help responsible and effective grantmaking among members and to support philanthropy as essential part of a strengthened civil society around the world. 2010.

1058-65 Creating Effective Grassroots Alternatives, Sofia, Bulgaria, $75,000. For general support toward providing capacity building support to local community initiatives working for community change through self-organization and dialogue with local government. Grantee will focus on improving public attitudes toward Roma population and strengthening educational achievements of Roma children. 2010.

1058-66 Czech Association of Community Foundations, Usti nad Labem, Czech Republic, $70,000. For general operating support. 2010.

1058-67 Czech Donors Forum, Prague, Czech Republic, $150,000. For Central and Eastern European Network for Responsible Giving (CEENERGI), Initiative to increase level and effectiveness of corporate giving in Central and Eastern Europe, including work to address critical issues associated with corporate giving at the national and regional levels, including current low levels of corporate contributions to the nonprofit sector and a lack of collaboration between corporate donors and the rest of the philanthropic community. In addition, the grantee will explore ways of encouraging systematic and effective individual giving in the region. 2010.

1058-68 Czech Donors Forum, Prague, Czech Republic, $60,000. For general support for goal to promote philanthropy in the Czech Republic and encourage donor agencies to work together toward using available resources in the most effective way and to coordinate Central and Eastern European Network for Responsible Giving (CEENERGI), initiative to increase level and effectiveness of corporate giving in Central and Eastern Europe. 2010.

1058-69 Dartmouth College, Hanover, NH, $250,000. For emergency relief in Haiti after the 2010 earthquake, Dartmouth College began deploying medical teams to Haiti to assist the relief group, Partners in Health. Teams and medical supplies are assigned as needed by Partners in Health and work in clinics and affiliated hospitals throughout Haiti. 2010.

1058-70 Derecho Ambiente y Recursos Naturales, Lima, Peru, $175,000. For general support. 2010.

1058-71 Diakonia Council of Churches, Durban, South Africa, $50,000. For Social Justice Programme, effort to foster peace, healing, and reconciliation within various communities. It works to increase people's participation in democratic governance, particularly at the local level, to give them a voice in government planning processes. 2010.

1058-72 Duke University, United States-Southern Africa Center for Leadership and Public Values, Durham, NC, $100,000. For Louisiana Effective Leadership Program, created as a training vehicle to address longstanding leadership deficits in Louisiana laid bare by Hurricanes Katrina and Rita. 2010.

1058-73 Eastern Cape NGO Coalition, East London, South Africa, $150,000. For general support toward strengthening networking and mutual learning among members and to continue to train them on topics relevant to work. 2010.

1058-74 Environmental Defence Canada, Toronto, Canada, $75,000. To seek innovative, equitable and cost-effective solutions to Great Lakes water quality problems. Efforts will include engaging in the U.S.-Canada Great Lakes water quality renegotiations, strengthening Ontario's water policies, and increasing public understanding of Great Lakes issues. 2010.

1058-75 Environmental Grantmakers Association, New York, NY, $20,000. For general support for global initiatives. 2010.

1058-76 European Foundation Centre, Brussels, Belgium, $100,000. For general support. 2010.

1058-77 European Foundation Centre, Brussels, Belgium, $30,000. For work to improve effectiveness of grantmaking in Central and Eastern Europe and the former Soviet Union and to encourage new donor activity in the region which includes the following 20 countries Albania, Belarus, Bosnia and Herzegovina, Bulgaria, Croatia, Czech Republic, Estonia, Hungary, Latvia, Lithuania, Macedonia, Moldova, Montenegro, Poland, Romania, Russia, Slovakia, Slovenia, Ukraine and Serbia. Centre will organize annual meeting of Grantmakers East Forum, for interested grantmakers and donors working in this region. Centre will work with Forum's steering committee to further develop format of annual meetings, secure outside speakers, arrange venue and other logistics and disseminate meetings reports. 2010.

1058-78 Five Star Films, Cabin John, MD, $75,000. To film and edit more footage for Breaking the Rules, feature documentary film that tells the story of the whites who fought against apartheid as allies in the struggle for justice in South Africa. Story is told through the voices and memories of five individuals from diverse political and cultural backgrounds who expressed opposition to apartheid in different ways. All five were born into the lives of white privilege, yet each made the choice to dedicate lives to fight racial oppression. The film journeys through five decades of life under apartheid, starting in the 1950s until changes happened in the 1990s. 2010.

1058-79 Forest Peoples Programme, Moreton-in-Marsh, England, $250,000. To assist forest-dependent communities to engage directly in policy debates and ensure that essons learned from projects in the field are fed effectively into advocacy process. 2010.

1058-80 Foundation for Independent Radio Broadcasting, Moscow, Russia, $200,000. To promote processes that strengthen public participation in development of communities through use of participatory radio as means for community development in Russia. Foundation will create replicable model of participatory community radio stations based in universities across Russia and provide training and technical support to forge links between Russian university students, faculty, community stakeholders, and local listeners, with goal of establishing stations that can serve as influential and progressive voices in their communities. 2010.

1058-81 Friends of the Earth, Washington, DC, $50,000. To provide more extensive information on role, effectiveness and regulation of carbon trading scheme as key component of United States and global climate change policy. 2010.

1058-82 Friends of the Earth France, Paris, France, $125,000. For organizational capacity building activities focused on strengthening environmental and social safeguard policies and ensuring that climate policies are in place at European financial institutions, the French export credit agency, French private banks, and the World Bank. 2010.

1058-83 Fund for Active Citizenship, Podgorica, Montenegro, $150,000. For general support for work to strengthen local-level democracy and civil society in Montenegro through development of indigenous grantmaking organization. 2010.

1058-84 Gender Links, Johannesburg, South Africa, $80,000. Toward implementation of action plans for addressing gender-based violence by South African municipalities. Organization will convene first Gender Justice and Local Government Summit, showcasing good practices by local governments in addressing gender-based violence. Summit will bring together local government stakeholders from at least eight countries in southern Africa (including the following 13 countries Angola, Botswana, Lesotho, Malawi, Mauritius, Mozambique, Namibia, Seychelles, South Africa, Swaziland, Tanzania, Zambia, Zimbabwe) and will convene parallel seminars on promoting women's representation and effective participation in local government structures. 2010.

1058-85 Genesee Area Focus Fund, Flint, MI, $75,000. For creation of Energy Council for the City of Flint. Community stakeholders (universities, schools, government and business) will convene regularly in 2010 to develop ideas, identify projects and seek funding to further sustainability agenda of the Flint area including travel to Leksand, Sweden to participate in global conference on green economy. Representatives will visit the city of Linkoping for discussions with government and business officials about economic development and sustainability strategies. 2010.

1058-86 German Marshall Fund of the United States, Black Sea Trust for Regional Cooperation, Washington, DC, $1,000,000. For regranting to support democratic governance and strengthen democratic political institutions in Armenia, Azerbaijan, Bulgaria, Georgia, Moldova, Romania, Turkey, Ukraine and parts of Russia and to advance cross-border cooperation in this region with aim of promoting olitical, social and economic development. 2010.

1058-87 Global Fund for Community Foundations, Belfast, Ireland, $250,000. For regranting work through Small Grants and Capacity Building Program focusing on community foundations and support organizations in developing and transitioning countries around the world. Program activities include making 10 to 15 grants to individual community foundations, providing direct technical assistance support to grantees and documenting grantees' activities and learning. 2010.

1058-88 Global Greengrants Fund, Boulder, CO, $250,000. For regranting efforts which will expand small grants programs for community-based efforts to protect the environment and increase public input into decision making about energy and infrastructure projects in Russia, Eastern Europe and the Central Asian Republics. 2010.

1058-89 Gordon Institute of Business Science, Johannesburg, South Africa, $35,000. To implement Dialogue Circles, core program which works to create opportunities for interaction and exchange across the different sectors of South African society to explore common solutions to the divides of race, poverty, and gender. 2010.

1058-90 Great Lakes Aquatic Habitat Network and Fund, Petoskey, MI, $12,250. For general support, which include providing small grants and technical assistance to local groups working to monitor and address impacts of oil spill in southwestern Michigan and natural gas drilling activities in northern Michigan. 2010.

1058-91 Great Lakes Aquatic Habitat Network and Fund, Freshwater Future, Petoskey, MI, $300,000. For general operating support. 2010.

1058-92 Great Lakes Commission, Ann Arbor, MI, $500,000. To bring together decisionmakers and stakeholders from across the Great Lakes to identify how to restore the natural division between the Mississippi and the Great Lakes as a way to halt Asian Carp movement while providing economic, social, and environmental benefits to the region. Asian Carp is an invasive species poised to enter and disrupt the Great Lakes ecosystem thorugh connections to the Mississippi River. 2010.

1058-93 Great Lakes Indian Fish and Wildlife Commission, Odanah, WI, $65,000. To prepare report examining how tribes can fully participate in the processes for permitting and monitoring sulfide mining operations on land where tribes have hunting and fishing rights. 2010.

1058-94 Great Lakes United, Amherst, NY, $65,000. For general support and to compile report on basin wide mining impacts and implementing public outreach campaign in partnership with American Sail Training Association's Tall Ships Challenge. 2010.

1058-95 Group 484, Belgrade, Serbia, $70,000. To increase participation of young refugees and displaced people in all aspects of decision making and social life in Serbia. To this end, Group 484 will promote the rights of forced migrants and engage young people in communities to work actively with young forced migrants. 2010.

1058-96 Heartefact Fund, Belgrade, Serbia, $70,000. To build organizational and programmatic capacities of the Fund during first years of operation through core operating expenses; training for staff, board and other stakeholders and development of network with beneficiaries and partners. 2010.

1058-97 Helsinki Committee for Human Rights in Republika Srpska, Bijeljina, Bosnia-Herzegovina, $69,800. To build constituency for justice in Bosnia-Herzegovina and work of the War Crimes Chamber of the Bosnian State Court in particular. Committee (in Republika Srpska) will work with local organizations and other stakeholders to raise public awareness about the work of the War Crimes Chamber of the Bosnian State Court and provide assistance to victims and potential witnesses by producing television programs, publishing printed material and providing direct technical assistance and support in the city of Bijeljina and the northeast region of Bosnia. 2010.

1058-98 Hungarian Donors Forum, Budapest, Hungary, $85,000. For general support. 2010.

1058-99 Ikhala Trust, Port Elizabeth, South Africa, $120,000. For general operating support. 2010.

1058-100 Indian Law Resource Center, Helena, MT, $150,000. To increase capacity of indigenous organizations and communities in selected South American countries to protect their environment. Project will combine Washington-based policy work at international financial institutions with capacity building for indigenous people, so that they can more effectively use international rules and safeguard policies to protect their natural resources. In particular project will help communities reduce impact of destructive infrastructure and energy projects in South America where such projects are threatening the environment and local livelihoods. 2010.

1058-101 Institute for Agriculture and Trade Policy, Minneapolis, MN, $75,000. For research as Institute works with national and international nongovernmental organizations as well as researchers and regulators to develop proposals to regulate commodity markets, with particular focus on impacts of potential global carbon market. 2010.

1058-102 Institute for Healing of Memories, Cape Town, South Africa, $120,000. For general support for Healing of Memories Workshops, which provide safe space for dialogue and openness to deal with issues such as reconciliation, forgiveness, dealing with the past, restorative justice, peace building, and conflict resolution and to strengthen partnership and collaboration with various institutions that implement programs related to healing and reconciliation. 2010.

1058-103 Institute for Healing of Memories, Cape Town, South Africa, $80,000. For general support for Healing of Memories Workshops, which provide safe space for dialogue and openness to deal with issues such as reconciliation, forgiveness, dealing with the past, restorative justice, peace building, and conflict resolution and to strengthen partnership and collaboration with various institutions that implement programs related to healing and reconciliation. 2010.

1058-104 Institute for Justice and Reconciliation, Cape Town, South Africa, $120,000. For general operating support for work in South Africa. 2010.

1058-105 Institute for Policy Studies, Washington, DC, $150,000. To support policy research on national and global responses to the economic crisis, with particular focus on role of financial transaction taxes, excess concentration of financial industry and derivatives reform. 2010.

1058-106 Institute for Socioeconomic Studies, Brasilia, Brazil, $100,000. To strengthen capacity of nongovernmental organizations in Brazil, particularly members of the Brazil Network on Multilateral Financial Institutions, to monitor and analyze participation of Brazilian government in financial reform efforts of the Group of 20 nations. Institute will generate informational materials in Portuguese for organizations in Brazil and complement this information with capacity building workshops and coordination with national and international networks promoting meaningful international financial sector reform. 2010.

1058-107 Instituto del Bien Comun, Lima, Peru, $100,000. To develop and promote environmental and social standards for oil and gas and infrastructure investments in Peruvian Amazon and to minimize negative impacts of large-scale energy and infrastructure projects on environment and local communities. Institute will provide local communities in Andean Amazon with maps, policy analysis, and strategic advice on infrastructure and oil and gas investments so they can have more informed voice in shaping these investments to be more sustainable. 2010.

1058-108 Instituto Latinoamericano de Servicios Legales Alternativos, Bogota, Colombia, $110,000. For efforts to strengthen nongovernmental organization and community participation in decisionmaking about investments by the international and regional financial institutions, with a particular focus on the environmental and social effects of infrastructure and energy projects. 2010.

1058-109 Instituto Socioambiental, Sao Paulo, Brazil, $150,000. To produce case studies on two important watersheds in South America, where Brazilian National Development Bank has significant existing and planned investments in infrastructure and energy projects. Information generated will inform strategy for engaging the Bank in developing policies for sustainable investments and increasing transparency and accountability in lending practices. 2010.

1058-110 Inter Press Service, Montevideo, Uruguay, $150,000. To increase quality and quantity of journalistic coverage of infrastructure and energy issues in South America paying particular attention to exploring role that Brazil is playing in large-scale investments in transport and power generation infrastructure across the region. 2010.

1058-111 International Center for Not-for-Profit Law, Washington, DC, $100,000. Toward project, Building an Enabling Legal Environment for Ukraine's Nonprofit Sector which works for development of legal and regulatory environment for Ukraine's nonprofit sector. Grant will enable Center to provide technical assistance in drafting and implementation of legislation affecting nongovernmental organizations and development of philanthropy. Grantee will undertake educational initiatives for lawyers, government officials, parliamentarians and nongovernmental organization leaders on legislation and legal issues affecting the nonprofit sector. Project builds on Grantee's previous efforts, which have resulted in improved opportunity for civic organizations to compete for government-procured goods and services, reduced costs of registering legal entities and coherent government policy for civil society development in Ukraine. 2010.

1058-112 International Rivers Network, Berkeley, CA, $15,000. For general support and toward strategic planning process aimed at strengthening organizational capacity to confront new challenges around climate change and water and energy infrastructure. 2010.

1058-113 Internationales Bildungs und Begegnungswerk, Dortmund, Germany, $100,000. To support civil society development in Belarus by building capacity of Belarusian nongovernmental organizations. 2010.

1058-114 Interreligious Council in Bosnia and Herzegovina, Sarajevo, Bosnia-Herzegovina, $50,000. To promote dialogue and cooperation between Bosnia-Herzegovina's religious communities to build a multiethnic, democratic society. 2010.

1058-115 Isandla Institute, Cape Town, South Africa, $100,000. For advocacy work that focuses on development of effective partnerships between government and the nonprofit sector, especially in terms of poverty alleviation including coordination of Good Governance Learning Network, alliance of 16

South African nonprofit organizations that promotes good local governance. 2010.

1058-116 Isandla Institute, Cape Town, South Africa, $50,000. Toward general support for work to help engagement with local government and urban management using research and knowledge sharing and to develop and promote innovative models for equitable service delivery, leadership and participatory local governance, informed by local and international experiences. 2010.

1058-117 Karoo Centre for Human Rights, Education, Research and Development, Beaufort West, South Africa, $100,000. For general support which will allow grantee to participate in networks and collaborations aimed at improving access to justice and human rights for poor people. 2010.

1058-118 Kosova Womens Network, Prishtina, Kosovo, $50,000. Toward organizational and programmatic development of Network. 2010.

1058-119 Krasnoyarsk Center for Community Partnerships, Krasnoyarsk, Russia, $200,000. For general support toward efforts to foster civic engagement through further development of community schools in Russia. Center works to broaden learning environment for community school practitioners, educational authorities and other stakeholders through training, publications and coaching. Center also works to strengthen network of schools and support centers through regular conferences, mentoring visits and ongoing updating of Web site of the community school movement and focusing on strengthening thier own institutional capacity by raising professional qualifications of staff and through efforts to link into ongoing educational reform activities. 2010.

1058-120 Latvian Rural Forum, Riga, Latvia, $200,000. To strengthen civil society in European Union New Member States and accession countries by promoting dialogue and cooperation between different actors in rural development, helping multinational exchanges and supporting international networking and advocacy for rural development. 2010.

1058-121 Madariaga-College of Europe Foundation, Brussels, Belgium, $150,000. For work to engage citizens and international partners in constructive dialogue on issues that shape Europe's global future. Work will focus on three main issue areas; engaging citizens, empowering Europe and preventing conflicts. 2010.

1058-122 Mani Tese, Milan, Italy, $350,000. To ensure that global financial flows contribute to internationally adopted principles that support and promote sustainable development. To achieve this goal, main areas of focus will be to ensure that public financial institutions support sustainable development; re-regulate the financial sector; hold investors accountable for environmental and social impacts on communities in developing countries and develop new climate finance mechanism. 2010.

1058-123 Mozaik Community Development Foundation, Sarajevo, Bosnia-Herzegovina, $22,000. Toward general operating support and further development of Foundation's two social enterprises. Foundation is based in Sarajevo, works throughout Bosnia-Herzegovina and is networked with other grant making institutions in Eastern Europe. 2010.

1058-124 National Alliance of Latin American and Caribbean Communities, Chicago, IL, $200,000.

For conference as part of capacity-building program for Latin American and Caribbean immigrants, focused on international financial flows and regional integration. 2010.

1058-125 National Council of La Raza, Washington, DC, $225,000. For regranting efforts to provide seed grants and technical assistance to emerging community-based organizations serving low-income neighborhoods in the following Southwest and Western regions of the U.S., Arizona, California, Colorado, New Mexico and Texas and in Puerto Rico as part of Intermediary Support for Organizing Communities program. 2010.

1058-126 Natural Resources and Environment Foundation, Fundacion Ambiente y Recursos Naturales (FARN), Buenos Aires, Argentina, $200,000. To analyze current and proposed energy investments by international financial institutions in Argentina as well as national energy strategies. Project will monitor set of high profile projects including hydroelectric energy, natural gas, biofuels and renewable energy. Information generated on these projects will be disseminated to policymakers, media, and the public, with the goal of improving existing projects and shaping policies for future sustainable energy investments. 2010.

1058-127 Network for the Affirmation of NGO Sector-MANS, Podgorica, Montenegro, $50,000. For general support. 2010.

1058-128 Network of European Foundations for Innovative Cooperation, Brussels, Belgium, $228,000. Toward implementation of Youth Empowerment Partnership Programme in 20 local communities in nine European countries. Network will convene participating foundations, managing grant support from foundations and other donors and building new partnerships to support project's activities. A central project team based in Berlin will assist local sites with intensive monitoring, evaluation and documentation of outcomes; provide specific capacity building and technical support to local practitioners; organize transnational networking and exchanges for young people from local sites and other stakeholders and develop and disseminate information resources throughout the network. 2010.

1058-129 Network of European Foundations for Innovative Cooperation, Brussels, Belgium, $32,000. Toward membership and administrative support. 2010.

1058-130 New Rules for Global Finance Coalition, Washington, DC, $200,000. Toward research and monitoring of reforms at International Monetary Fund and other global financial institutions with goal of making these institutions more accountable and effective at promoting sustainable, equitable growth. 2010.

1058-131 NGO Forum on the Asian Development Bank, Quezon City, Philippines, $17,500. For general support, including participation of civil society organizations in the Asia-Pacific region to attend global meeting on climate finance. 2010.

1058-132 NGO School Foundation, Moscow, Russia, $125,000. To strengthen professional skills of the fundraising community in Russia through series of fundraising and resource mobilization workshops and through ongoing experience sharing within a fundraisers' club. Grantee will seek to use and catalogue successful fundraising strategies employed by pilot project called the Live Foundation, aimed at demonstrating potential impact of innovative fundraising strategies in Russia. 2010.

1058-133 Nizhny Novgorod Volunteer Service, Nizhny Novgorod, Russia, $218,881. To conduct study visits to other countries with successful experience with TimeBank implementation to learn and further adapt different approaches to TimeBank model, expand TimeBank model to two new Russian regions, create strong regional and interregional network, increase number of participants, and establish sustainability and independence of Nizhni Novgorod TimeBank. 2010.

1058-134 Oil Change International, Washington, DC, $100,000. For work of International Program to analyze and present research papers highlighting scope, as well as environmental and social implications, of current global fossil fuel subsidies and organize global nongovernmental organization coalition to build awareness among developed country decision makers. 2010.

1058-135 Organization for Civil Initiatives, Osijek, Croatia, $80,000. For general support for work to promote greater public participation in decision making and to mobilize community resources to address critical issues facing local communities in Croatia. 2010.

1058-136 Partners for Democratic Change, Washington, DC, $75,000. For general support. 2010.

1058-137 Perm Civic Chamber, Perm, Russia, $50,000. For Civic Expeditions-Civil Influence, effort to promote civic awareness and activism in Russia's smaller urban centers and to gather information on successful civil control activities from across Russia. Grantee will conduct civic expeditions to two small cities within the Perm region, conducting workshops on how to adopt these successful strategies. These will be supplemented by further seminars in the city of Perm, which will target government officials, including the regional human rights ombudsman, to generate a greater understanding of civil control methods. 2010.

1058-138 Peruvian Center for Social Studies, Lima, Peru, $140,000. To consolidate new regional network on extractive industries in Latin America. Project provides training and information to local authorities and key opinion leaders and creates spaces for public debate on strategies for shaping infrastructure and energy investments to make them less environmentally damaging and more supportive of local sustainable development. 2010.

1058-139 Philanthropy Bridge Foundation, Dartford, England, $100,000. For general support including tailoring initiatives to engage specific individuals in strategic philanthropy; meetings and conferences for wealthy individuals in Brazil, China, India, Middle East, Russia and South Africa and workshops for public charities to improve understanding of donors in emerging markets. 2010.

1058-140 Pitseng Trust, Braamfontein, South Africa, $40,000. For general support. 2010.

1058-141 PLATFORM, London, England, $150,000. To assist international nongovernmental organizations' efforts to reform global investment in oil and gas development. 2010.

1058-142 Polish Donors Forum, Warsaw, Poland, $90,000. For general support. 2010.

1058-143 Pontis Foundation, Bratislava, Slovakia, $100,000. For Pontis Foundation to work with Belarusian Institute of Strategic Studies to

develop the latter's institutional capacity through a program of training and mentoring. Together they will foster a network of policy fellows and aspiring analysts who will examine specific policy issues and present analyses accessible to the public and government through annual policy conferences and in publications like the Belarus Yearbook. 2010.

1058-144 Populari, Sarajevo, Bosnia-Herzegovina, $60,000. For general support toward carrying out field-based studies and assessments and stimulating discussion of policy issues through seminars, public presentations and bilateral meetings. Center will focus on monitoring and promoting European Union integration and accession; ownership and management of state property and how this complicates Bosnia-Herzegovina's state-building efforts; and working with young people in high schools and colleges to stimulate critical thinking about the country's future. 2010.

1058-145 Regional Foundation for Local Development Zamah, Zagreb, Croatia, $82,000. For general support. 2010.

1058-146 Research Foundation of the City University of New York, New York, NY, $200,000. For International Community Foundation Fellows Program, initiative to enhance development of community philanthropy globally. Program offers emerging leaders and seasoned community foundation practitioners from foreign countries opportunities to learn about community foundations through intensive graduate program of research, seminars, conferences, mentoring, and internships. 2010.

1058-147 Rhodes University, Grahamstown, South Africa, $150,000. To train and mentor Advice Office workers and to provide financial support to Advice Offices as part of support for Rhodes University Legal Aid Clinic: Advice Office Project, established to provide free legal services to indigent people while training law students in practical application of law. 2010.

1058-148 Satyagraha-In Pursuit of Truth, Durban, South Africa, $40,000. For general support toward publication of monthly newspaper in Durban, KwaZulu-Natal, that promotes culture of nonviolence, historic knowledge, civic and community awareness and diversity as well as other activities including high school outreach and youth program, human rights awareness campaigns and development of student research library. 2010.

1058-149 Siberian Civic Initiatives Support Center, Novosibirsk, Russia, $170,000. For program support including seminar with goal to improve quality of life in Russian communities by strengthening partnerships between government and citizens through effective public participation in community development strategies with greater emphasis on economic development strategies, while working to improve citizen input on local budgeting. Work will focus on Irkutsk, Altai and Tyumen regions, with additional efforts made to develop core of civic advocacy specialists in smaller communities throughout the area. 2010.

1058-150 Sluzhenye Association, Nizhny Novgorod, Russia, $125,000. For conference as part of work to introduce new methods of activating communities, increasing local resource mobilization, and promoting social investment in Russia by expanding training program for social animators who will help mobilize and advise civic

groups. Association will increase capacity of local activity centers to act as focal points for community planning and resource mobilization, with particular focus on developing individual giving. Grantee will support further development of Dobriy Nizhny charity festival organized collectively by the Centers. 2010.

1058-151 Social Change Assistance Trust, Cape Town, South Africa, $200,000. For regranting which allow Trust to continue to provide financial resources, training, and hands-on support to between 50 and 60 local, community-based development agencies in rural areas of Eastern, Western and Northern Cape provinces, as well as Northwest and Free State provinces. Interventions will address HIV/AIDS, local economic development, access to justice, gender equity and food security. 2010.

1058-152 South African History Online, Pretoria, South Africa, $80,000. For general operating support. 2010.

1058-153 South African Holocaust Foundation, Cape Town, South Africa, $40,000. For curriculum development which will be used to train senior teachers throughout the country as trainers on Nazi Germany, the Holocaust, and universal lessons on humanity. These teachers will in turn provide ongoing training to grades nine and eleven teachers in respective provinces. 2010.

1058-154 South African Institute for Advancement, Inyathelo, Cape Town, South Africa, $20,000. For general support including hosting a donor conference to promote discussions between grantmakers operating in South Africa on challenges and experiences with grantmaking. Conference is aimed at building effective and impactful philanthropy. 2010.

1058-155 South Centre, Geneva, Switzerland, $100,000. To provide research into key issues of the financial and economic crises to increase capacity of developing countries to better participate in governance of global financial and economic systems. 2010.

1058-156 Step by Step Moldova, Chisinau, Moldova, $150,000. To provide technical assistance toward developing Community School model in Moldova. 2010.

1058-157 Steve Biko Foundation, Johannesburg, South Africa, $100,000. For general support. 2010.

1058-158 Sustainability Institute, Stellenbosch, South Africa, $40,000. To provide technical assistance and curriculum development for Capacity-Building for Development, online training and capacity-building course targeting community-based organizations, with focus on poverty eradication. 2010.

1058-159 Synergos Institute, New York, NY, $150,000. For Senior Fellows Program, which links civil society leaders in a worldwide learning, service and action network. Network strengthens capacities of these leaders and provides them with opportunities to be catalysts in partnerships that address systemic causes of poverty and promote sustainable social change. Senior fellows serve as peer consultants to developing community foundations and other civil society organizations around the world and work produces knowledge on trends and innovative models which Synergos Institute distributes to a wide audience. 2010.

1058-160 Third World Network, Penang, Malaysia, $15,000. For work to inform developing country negotiators about implications of climate finance proposals being put forth for consideration at United Nations climate change negotiations to be held in Mexico. Series of briefing documents and workshops will be prepared for the developing country negotiators, with particular focus on carbon trading as a mechanism for addressing global mitigation and adaptation costs related to climate change. 2010.

1058-161 Tides Canada Foundation, Vancouver, Canada, $50,000. For Halifax Initiative project, coalition of Canadian NGOs that work to promote reforms in international financial institutions with focus on the environment. Initiative will undertake additional work related to the financial transaction tax and organize civil society activities around leaders' summit meetings of the Group of 20 and Group of 8, scheduled to take place in June 2010 in Canada. 2010.

1058-162 Tides Center, Africa Grantmakers' Affinity Group, San Francisco, CA, $75,000. To serve grantmakers working in Africa and strengthen collaboration among them with goal being to improve field of grantmaking in Africa. 2010.

1058-163 Trust for Civil Society in Central and Eastern Europe, Washington, DC, $60,000. For fellowships which will work to strengthen leadership in the nonprofit sector in Central and Eastern Europe. Trust will partner with several European foundations to support fellowships for Central and Eastern European nonprofit leaders with counterparts in Western Europe. Fellowships aim to build capacity of participating organizations through developing professional skills of key staff members while initiating and deepening cooperation between Western and Eastern European organizations. 2010.

1058-164 Trust for Community Outreach and Education, Cape Town, South Africa, $100,000. To continue strengthening voices of the rural poor to engage government and other stakeholders around development needs and interests. Focus areas will continue to be local government, land reform and rural livelihoods, food security, water, and strengthening local organizations and leadership. 2010.

1058-165 U.S.-Mexico Border Philanthropy Partnership, San Diego, CA, $300,000. For general support. 2010.

1058-166 Ukrainian Helsinki Human Rights Union, Kiev, Ukraine, $100,000. For general support. 2010.

1058-167 Ukrainian Step by Step Foundation, Kiev, Ukraine, $180,000. To expand the number of community schools in Ukraine. Work will including promoting adoption of international quality standards; working with education officials and regional teacher training institutes to improve and expand the community school curriculum; advocating for policy changes that will institutionalize best practices of community schools; and assembling, developing and maintaining online database of resources on community school development. 2010.

1058-168 University of KwaZulu-Natal, Centre for Civil Society, Durban, South Africa, $75,000. To conduct research and to critically engage with civil society building on experiences in academic teaching, hosting seminars and publishing and conducting research. Centre will maintain community outreach efforts that include providing opportunities for civil society scholarships and access to information, networking and advocacy. 2010.

1058-169 University of Michigan, International Center, Flint, MI, $405,000. For recruitment of international students through increased funding of international travel for recruiters and scholarship incentives to attract prospective students. Project builds in support after student recruits arrive on campus, through leadership development and student life programming. 2010.

1058-170 University of the Western Cape, School of Government, Bellville, South Africa, $100,000. To offer training and support to community leaders, other interested institutions and individuals focusing on adapting some of Fair Share's training programs and incorporating suggestions and feedback on previous programs. Fair Share is unit of School of Government at the University that focuses on building capacity of ordinary citizens to understand and influence local budgeting processes. It works with municipalities including KwaZulu-Natal and Limpopo, across South Africa sensitizing them to needs of local communities and enhancing ability to involve citizens in planning processes. 2010.

1058-171 Urgewald, Sassenberg, Germany, $250,000. For efforts, including research, education, and advocacy, to establish strong, binding environmental and social standards for international financial institutions and to garner ongoing public support for responsible and accountable financial institutions. 2010.

1058-172 Uruguayan Study Center of Appropriate Technologies, Montevideo, Uruguay, $10,000. For research to explore implications of Brazil's role in South America from sustainable development perspective, including investments in energy and infrastructure across the region. 2010.

1058-173 William J. Clinton Foundation, New York, NY, $20,000. For Clinton Global Initiative, annual meeting (to be held in New York City) with goal to turn ideas into action and help the world move beyond current state of globalization to more integrated global community of shared benefits, responsibilities and values. 2010.

1058-174 World Affairs Council of Northern California, San Francisco, CA, $25,000. For Global Philanthropy Forum, whose mission is to provide best-in-class learning opportunities to donors and foundations committed to making a demonstrable difference on global issues. Featured activity is annual conference. 2010.

1058-175 World Resources Institute, Washington, DC, $340,000. For conference related to International Financial Flows and the Environment project which provides research and data to nongovernmental organizations and key public and private institutions on international financial flows and public policy options.Overarching goal of the project is to improve social and environmental performance of public and private international financial institutions by holding them accountable to investors and to communities in which they invest. Project will continue work to encourage shifts in international financial support for investments that meet high environmental and social standards and that are low-carbon and climate resilient, as well as identify and pursue opportunities to strengthen environmental and social standards of emerging actors in development finance. 2010.

1058-176 World Resources Institute, Washington, DC, $65,000. For conference related to

International Financial Flows and the Environment project. Grant increase will continue work to address financing of response to climate change and related governance issues that have been raised by United Nations negotiations on climate change. It will support partner organizations in developing countries to convene regional strategy meetings on climate finance leading up to next United Nations climate meeting to be held in Mexico. 2010.

1058-177 Youth Communication Center Banja Luka, Banja Luka, Bosnia-Herzegovina, $60,000. For general operating support. 2010.

1058-178 Youth Initiative for Human Rights, Bosnia, Sarajevo, Bosnia-Herzegovina, $70,000. To develop organizational and programmatic capacities to empower and train young people to be more involved in shaping how Bosnian society deals with the legacy of war, addresses ongoing human rights issues, and integrates into the wider Europe. Project goal is to strengthen youth engagement and activism on issues of transitional justice and human rights promotion. Specific activities will include training and mentoring for key staff on financial management and administration, establishing office in Banja Luka and strengthening role of the organization's governing board. 2010.

1058-179 YouthBuild USA, Somerville, MA, $200,000. To increase levels of youth civic participation and initiative for positive social action in the Western Balkans with pilot programs in at least two communities with the goal of demonstrating program's effectiveness and scaling it up to other parts of the region. Young people will receive training, counseling, and mentoring and will directly engage in planning and implementing community improvements, such as building or improving playgrounds and other public spaces and upgrading and weatherizing houses. Young people involved in the project will develop leadership and practical skills by analyzing community development processes, facilitating planning meetings, and interacting with community members. Grantee will develop network of nonprofits and experts that will provide technical assistance to the program over the long term.YouthBuild USA, will implement project through YouthBuild International division and newly established, affiliated nonprofit in Belgrade, Serbia, called YouthBuild Fond Za Balkan. 2010.

1059
Palestine Aid Society of America
c/o Rabia Shafie
3325 Bluett Dr.
Ann Arbor, MI 48105-1556

Grantmaker type: Public charity.
Financial data (yr. ended 12/31/10): Revenue, $85,970; assets, $94,870 (M); gifts received, $72,340; expenditures, $113,286; giving activities include $110,679 for grants, and for 1 grant to an organization outside the U.S.
Purpose and activities: The society provides education and health support to children in need in Palestine.
Fields of interest: Human services; International affairs.
International interests: East Jerusalem; West Bank/Gaza (Palestinian Territories).

Type of support: Grants to individuals.
Limitations: Applications not accepted. Giving primarily in Palestine.
Application information: Unsolicited requests for funds not considered or acknowledged.
Directors: Wadad Abed; Tahani Othman; Huda Karaman Rosen; Karem Sakallah; Silvia Samaan; Rabia Shafie.
EIN: 382381291

1060
Pilgrim Foundation
c/o S. Gunnar Klarr
401 S. Old Woodward Ave., Ste. 465
Birmingham, MI 48009-6622

Established in 1996 in MI.
Donors: Louise S. Klarr; S. Gunnar Klarr; Salwil Foundation.
Grantmaker type: Independent foundation.
Financial data (yr. ended 12/31/10): Assets, $4,833,105 (M); expenditures, $212,859; qualifying distributions, $175,001; giving activities include $175,001 for grants.
Fields of interest: International relief; International development; Human services; Christian agencies & churches; Economically disadvantaged.
Type of support: General/operating support.
Limitations: Applications not accepted. Giving primarily in MI and NC. No grants to individuals.
Application information: Contributes only to pre-selected organizations.
Trustees: Louise S. Klarr; S. Gunnar Klarr.
EIN: 367159136

1061
The Rosenzweig Coopersmith Foundation
c/o Robert Van Dongen
333 Bridge St., N.W., Ste. 1200
Grand Rapids, MI 49504-5367

Established in 1997 in MI.
Donors: Dora Rosenzweig; Leonard Rosenzweig.
Grantmaker type: Independent foundation.
Financial data (yr. ended 12/23/10): Assets, $10,463,534 (M); expenditures, $713,007; qualifying distributions, $636,397; giving activities include $548,500 for 18 grants (high: $130,000; low: $5,000).
Purpose and activities: Support primarily for Jewish organizations; giving also for universities in Israel.
Fields of interest: Higher education; Jewish federated giving programs; Jewish agencies & synagogues.
International interests: Israel.
Limitations: Applications not accepted. Giving primarily in MI, NY, and in Israel. No grants to individuals.
Application information: Contributes only to pre-selected organizations.
Officer: Robert Van Dongen, Financial Off.
Trustees: Monica Armour; Suzanne Fenster; Harry Rosenzweig; Herschel Rosenzweig; Joseph Rosenzweig.
EIN: 383393545

1062
Rotary District 6360 Foundation
316 Beech St.
Charlotte, MI 48813-1006 (517) 543-7929
FAX: (517) 543-3041;
E-mail: district6360@cablespeed.com; URL: http://www.district6360.com/district_foundation/index.htm

Established in 1992 in MI.
Grantmaker type: Public charity.
Financial data (yr. ended 06/30/11): Revenue, $49,522; assets, $163,629 (M); gifts received, $33,714; expenditures, $34,101; giving activities include $32,779 for grants.
Purpose and activities: The foundation supports local area literacy programs and other community service projects, and provides aid for educational and capital improvements in Nicaragua and Mexico.
Fields of interest: Adult education—literacy, basic skills & GED; Education.
International interests: Mexico; Nicaragua.
Type of support: Capital campaigns; Equipment; Program development; Seed money; Matching/challenge support.
Limitations: Applications accepted. Giving on a national and international basis. No grants to District 6360 Rotarians, a Rotary employee or a parent, grandparent, child, grandchild of a Rotarian, or their spouses, or for individual travel expenses, salaries, personnel costs, research consultant fees, operating administrative expenses, or pre-project planning costs.
Publications: Annual report (including application guidelines); Informational brochure; Program policy statement.
Application information: Application form required.
  Initial approach: Download application form
  Copies of proposal: 1
  Deadline(s): None
  Board meeting date(s): Apr. 25, June 10, Aug. 10, Oct. 24, and Dec. 12
  Final notification: Within 30 to 60 days
Officers and Board Members: Terrence J. Allen,* Pres.; Teresa Fitzwater,* Pres.-Elect; Marjorie R. Haas,* Secy.; Nancy L. Thompson Commissaris,* Treas.; Thomas A. Faulkner; James H. Hines; James W. McIntyre; James E. Miyagawa; Carl A. Schoessel; Donald G. Siegel.
Number of staff: 1 part-time support.
EIN: 383002325

1063
Secchia Family Foundation
(formerly Peter F. Secchia Foundation)
c/o Universal Forest Products, Inc.
220 Lyon St. N.W., Ste. 510
Grand Rapids, MI 49503-2210

Established in 1985 in MI.
Donors: Peter F. Secchia; SIBSCO, LLC.
Grantmaker type: Independent foundation.
Financial data (yr. ended 12/31/10): Assets, $13,294,114 (M); gifts received, $100,000; expenditures, $618,685; qualifying distributions, $571,677; giving activities include $528,020 for 78 grants (high: $105,000; low: $40).
Purpose and activities: Giving for education, health associations, youth programs, and religion.
Fields of interest: Higher education; Education; Hospitals (specialty); Health organizations, association; Children/youth, services; Catholic agencies & churches.

International interests: Italy.
Type of support: Building/renovation; Equipment; Scholarship funds.
Limitations: Applications not accepted. Giving primarily in MI. No grants to individuals.
Application information: Contributes only to pre-selected organizations.
Officers: Peter F. Secchia, Pres.; James A. Ens, Secy.; Mark A. Schut, Treas.
EIN: 382641093

1064
Steelcase Foundation
P.O. Box 1967, GH-4E
Grand Rapids, MI 49501-1967
Contact: Susan Broman, Pres.
FAX: (616) 475-2200;
E-mail: sbroman@steelcase.com; Additional Contact: Phyllis Gebben, Coordinator of Donations, E-mail: pgebben@steelcase.com; URL: http://www.steelcase.com/en/company/who/steelcase-foundation/pages/steelcasefoundation.aspx
Grants List: http://www.steelcase.com/en/company/who/steelcase-foundation/pages/updateandreports.aspx

Established in 1951 in MI.
Donor: Steelcase Inc.
Grantmaker type: Company-sponsored foundation.
Financial data (yr. ended 11/30/10): Assets, $84,824,026 (M); expenditures, $3,897,074; qualifying distributions, $3,917,074; giving activities include $3,496,550 for 59 grants (high: $250,000; low: $900), and $400,524 for 929 employee matching gifts.
Purpose and activities: The foundation supports organizations involved with arts and culture, education, the environment, health, human services, and community development. Special emphasis is directed toward programs designed to assist youth, the elderly, disabled people, and economically disadvantaged people.
Fields of interest: Education, early childhood education; Homeless, human services; Arts; Education; Environment; Health care; Human services; Economic development; Community/economic development; Youth; Aging; Disabilities, people with; Economically disadvantaged.
International interests: Canada.
Type of support: General/operating support; Management development/capacity building; Capital campaigns; Building/renovation; Equipment; Land acquisition; Program development; Seed money; Scholarship funds; Employee matching gifts; Employee-related scholarships; Matching/challenge support.
Limitations: Applications accepted. Giving limited to areas of company operations, with emphasis on Athens, AL, City of Industry, CA, Grand Rapids, MI, and Markham, Canada. No support for churches or religious organizations not of direct benefit to the entire community or discriminatory organizations. No grants to individuals (except for employee-related scholarships), or for endowments or conferences or seminars.
Publications: Application guidelines; Annual report; Grants list.
Application information: Letters of inquiry should be submitted using organization letterhead. A full proposal may be requested at a later date. Support is limited to 1 contribution per organization during any given year. Application form required.

Initial approach: Letter of inquiry for application form
Copies of proposal: 1
Deadline(s): Quarterly
Board meeting date(s): Quarterly
Final notification: At least 90 days
Officers and Trustees:* Kate Pew Wolters,* Chair.; Susan K. Broman, Pres.; James P. Hackett; Earl D. Holton; Mary Anne Hunting; Elizabeth Welch Lykins; Mary Goodwillie Nelson; Robert C. Pew III.
Number of staff: 1 full-time professional; 1 full-time support.
EIN: 386050470
Recent grants for international programs:
1064-1 American Red Cross, Greater Grand Rapids, Grand Rapids, MI, $20,000. For Haiti earthquake relief (employee matching gift). 2010.
1064-2 Toronto Windfall Clothing, Toronto, Canada, $13,300. For new fundraising department. 2010.

1065
Ben N. Teitel Charitable Trust
2290 First National Bldg.
Detroit, MI 48226-3506
Contact: Gerald S. Cook, Tr.

Established in 1987 in MI.
Donors: Ben N. Teitel†; Gerald S. Cook.
Grantmaker type: Independent foundation.
Financial data (yr. ended 09/30/10): Assets, $3,590,499 (M); expenditures, $359,707; qualifying distributions, $350,935; giving activities include $350,874 for 48 grants (high: $80,000; low: $100).
Purpose and activities: The trust supports a variety of Jewish community programs for children and the elderly, including camping, teen touring to Israel, and educational programs to train social workers for Jewish agency work.
Fields of interest: Human services; Aging, centers/ services; Jewish federated giving programs; Jewish agencies & synagogues.
International interests: Israel.
Type of support: General/operating support; Continuing support; Annual campaigns; Capital campaigns; Building/renovation; Endowments; Emergency funds; Program development; Seed money; Scholarship funds; Matching/challenge support.
Limitations: Applications not accepted. Giving primarily in southeast MI. No grants to individuals.
Application information: Contributes only to pre-selected organizations.
Trustee: Gerald S. Cook.
EIN: 386512136

1066
Travelers Aid Society of Metropolitan Detroit
30th Fl. Cadillac Twr.
65 Cadillac Square
Detroit, MI 48226-1900   (313) 926-6740
E-mail: info@travelersaiddetroit.org; URL: http:// www.travelersaiddetroit.org

Grantmaker type: Public charity.
Financial data (yr. ended 06/30/10): Revenue, $4,365,752; assets, $945,941 (M); gifts received, $4,364,275; expenditures, $3,921,099; giving

activities include $2,019,366 for grants to individuals.
Purpose and activities: The society provides permanent housing and supportive services to socially-economically challenged individuals and/or disconnected families and travelers by returning them to point of origin, advancing the well-being of the community and empowering them to become self-sufficient contributing members of society.
Fields of interest: Housing/shelter; International migration/refugee issues; Economically disadvantaged.
Type of support: Grants to individuals.
Publications: Annual report.
Officers and Directors:* Eric Foster,* Pres.; Nathaniel Warshay,* V.P.; Alfred J. Gittleman,* Secy.; Wendy L. Smith,* Treas.; Harriet Cosby; Monica Davie; John L. Davis II; Lamar Richardson; and 7 additional directors.
EIN: 381358052

1067
Weingartz Family Foundation
P.O. Box 182008
Shelby Township, MI 48318-2008

Established in 2004 in MI.
Donors: Power Equipment Distributors, Inc.; Weingartz Supply Co.
Grantmaker type: Company-sponsored foundation.
Financial data (yr. ended 12/31/10): Assets, $3,036,024 (M); gifts received, $600,000; expenditures, $475,570; qualifying distributions, $475,570; giving activities include $475,000 for 9 grants (high: $200,000; low: $5,000).
Purpose and activities: The foundation supports organizations involved with hunger, human services, international relief, and religion.
Fields of interest: Food services; Food banks; Homeless, human services; Human services; International relief; Christian agencies & churches; Catholic agencies & churches; Religion.
Type of support: General/operating support.
Limitations: Applications not accepted. Giving primarily in Washington, DC, MI, and NY. No grants to individuals.
Application information: Contributes only to pre-selected organizations.
Officers and Directors:* Raymond Weingartz,* Pres.; Marie Weingartz,* V.P.; Edward Radtke,* Secy.; Daniel Weingartz, Treas.; Beverly Devriendt; Angela Malburg; Donald Malburg; Catherine Radtke; Amy Weingartz; Debbie Weingartz; Kenneth Weingartz; Kris Weingartz; Peggy Weingartz; Ronald Weingartz; Thomas Weingartz.
EIN: 201516609

1068
Whitman Family Foundation
c/o Northpoint Financial
920 E. Lincoln St.
Birmingham, MI 48009-3608

Established in 1994 in MI.
Donors: Marina V.N. Whitman; Robert F. Whitman.
Grantmaker type: Independent foundation.
Financial data (yr. ended 12/31/10): Assets, $1,531,847 (M); expenditures, $190,057; qualifying distributions, $180,517; giving activities include $177,900 for 34 grants (high: $25,000; low: $200).

Fields of interest: Economics; Performing arts; Higher education; Housing/shelter; International relief; Social sciences, interdisciplinary studies; Public policy, research.
Limitations: Applications not accepted. Giving primarily in Washington, DC, Boston, MA, Ann Arbor, MI, Princeton, NJ, and Middlebury, VT. No grants to individuals.
Application information: Contributes only to pre-selected organizations.
Officers and Directors:* Marina V.N. Whitman,* Pres.; Robert F. Whitman,* V.P. and Treas.; Laura Whitman,* Secy.; David Downie; Malcolm Whitman.
EIN: 383191221

1069
Williams Family Foundation
(formerly Koinonia Foundation)
1939 Talamore Ct. S.E.
Grand Rapids, MI 49546-9017

Established in 2004 in MI.
Donors: United Methodist Church; Dale L. Williams, M.D.
Grantmaker type: Operating foundation.
Financial data (yr. ended 12/31/10): Assets, $1,885,988 (M); gifts received, $28,477; expenditures, $250,218; qualifying distributions, $229,639; giving activities include $226,224 for 2 grants (high: $209,824; low: $16,400).
Purpose and activities: Giving primarily for medical and educational supplies for Rwanda.
Fields of interest: Family services; International development; International relief.
International interests: Rwanda.
Type of support: Equipment.
Limitations: Applications not accepted. Giving primarily in MI. No grants to individuals.
Application information: Contributes only to pre-selected organizations.
Officers: Dale L. Williams, Pres.; Christel G. Williams, Secy.; Dale F. Williams, Treas.
Directors: Andrew K. Williams; Peter H. Williams; Susan B. Williams.
EIN: 201025162

1070
World Medical Relief, Inc.
11745 Rosa Parks Blvd.
Detroit, MI 48206-1269   (313) 866-5333
Contact: Rita Montgomery Grezlik, Pres. and C.E.O.
FAX: (313) 866-5588;
E-mail: info@worldmedicalrelief.org; URL: http:// www.worldmedicalrelief.org

Established in 1953.
Grantmaker type: Public charity.
Financial data (yr. ended 12/31/09): Revenue, $20,672,253; assets, $2,361,539 (M); gifts received, $19,928,705; expenditures, $20,000,059; giving activities include $15,445,833 for grants to organizations outside the U.S., and $3,651,925 for grants to individuals.
Purpose and activities: The organization's mission is to help the medically underserved on a local, national, and international basis. It seeks to achieve this mission through the collection of financial donations and goods, including medical, dental, and laboratory items, as well as through the purchase and distribution of such commodities.

Fields of interest: Human services; International relief; Aging; Economically disadvantaged.
International interests: Africa; Middle East; Eastern & Central Europe; Latin America; Oceania; Asia.
Type of support: In-kind gifts.
Limitations: Applications not accepted. Giving on a national and international basis.
Publications: Annual report; Financial statement; Informational brochure; Newsletter; Occasional report; Program policy statement.
Application information: Unsolicited requests for funds not encouraged or acknowledged.
   Board meeting date(s): Jan., Apr., July, and Oct.
Officers and Directors:* John C. Kim,* Chair.; Dennis T. Torp,* Vice-Chair.; Rita Montgomery Grezlik,* Pres. and C.E.O.; Charles L. Myers,* Secy.; Jay K. Ganatra,* Treas.; Wendy R. Acho; Mike M. Baydoun; Bernardo M. Danan, M.D.; Nelson G. Edwards, D.O.; Lola Glass, Esq.; Arthur "Sandy" Hudson; Hanuman Marur; Rebecca M. Tungol.
EIN: 381575570

1071
Worldwide Christian Schools
629 Ionia Ave. S.W.
Grand Rapids, MI   49503-5148   (616) 531-9102
Contact: Scott Vander Kooy, Pres.
FAX: (616) 531-0602; E-mail: info@wwcs.org;
Toll-free tel.: (800) 886-9000; URL: http://www.wwcs.org

Established in 1987 in MI.
Grantmaker type: Public charity.
Financial data (yr. ended 06/30/10): Revenue, $2,132,741; assets, $1,492,601 (M); gifts received, $1,432,086; expenditures, $2,179,365; giving activities include $850,119 for grants to organizations outside the U.S.
Purpose and activities: The organization provides funding to churches and other stable, accountable nonprofits to build schools in developing countries.
Fields of interest: Teacher school/education; Education; Children, services; Christian agencies & churches.
International interests: Developing countries.
Type of support: Building/renovation; Equipment; Program development; Conferences/seminars; Curriculum development; Scholarship funds; Consulting services; Program evaluation.
Limitations: Applications accepted. Giving primarily in developing countries. No support for political organizations.
Publications: Informational brochure (including application guidelines); Newsletter; Occasional report; Program policy statement.
Application information: Application form required.
   Board meeting date(s): 4th Thurs. of every other month
Officers and Directors:* Gloria Stronks,* Ph.D., Chair.; Melvin Busscher,* Vice-Chair.; Scott Vander Kooy,* Pres.; Ken Van Den Bosch,* Treas.; Russell Bloem; Jeni Hoekstra; Robert Jonker.
Number of staff: 8 full-time professional; 1 part-time professional; 1 full-time support.
EIN: 382693388

MINNESOTA

1072
Africa Solutions, Inc.
6066 Shingle Creek Pkwy., No. 314
Minneapolis, MN   55430-2316   (612) 414-5069
E-mail: info@africasolutions.org; URL: http://www.africasolutions.org/index.html

Established in 2001 in MN.
Grantmaker type: Public charity.
Purpose and activities: The organization provides sustainable health and development solutions in African communities.
Fields of interest: Health care.
International interests: Africa.
Officer: Dr. Charles Koudou, Pres.

1073
Andersen Corporate Foundation
(formerly The Bayport Foundation of Andersen Corporation)
White Pine Bldg.
342 5th Ave. N.
Bayport, MN   55003-1201   (651) 275-4450
Contact: Chloette Haley, Prog. Off.
FAX: (651) 439-9480;
E-mail: andersencorpfdn@srinc.biz; Additional tel.: (651) 439-1557; URL: http://www.srinc.biz/bp/index.html

Incorporated in 1941 in MN.
Donor: Andersen Corp.
Grantmaker type: Company-sponsored foundation.
Financial data (yr. ended 11/30/10): Assets, $42,607,257 (M); expenditures, $2,032,151; qualifying distributions, $1,686,250; giving activities include $1,686,250 for grants.
Purpose and activities: The foundation supports programs designed to provide community, social, and support services to better people's lives and strengthen communities. Special emphasis is directed toward programs designed to promote affordable housing; health and safety; education and youth development; human services; and civic support.
Fields of interest: Performing arts, music; Museums; Media/communications; Visual arts; Performing arts; Arts; Elementary/secondary education; Education, services; Education; Environment, natural resources; Hospitals (general); Public health; Health care; Substance abuse, prevention; Mental health/crisis services; Employment, services; Housing/shelter, temporary shelter; Housing/shelter, owner/renter issues; Housing/shelter; Disasters, preparedness/services; Safety/disasters; Recreation; Aging, centers/services; Minorities/immigrants, centers/services; Independent living, disability; Human services; Mathematics; Engineering/technology; Science; Children/youth; Aging; Disabilities, people with; Economically disadvantaged.
International interests: Canada.
Type of support: General/operating support; Annual campaigns; Capital campaigns; Building/renovation; Emergency funds; Program development.
Limitations: Applications accepted. Giving primarily in areas of company operations in Des Moines and

Dubuque, IA, East Metro, MN, North Brunswick, NJ, Luray and Page County, VA, Dunn County, Menomonie, and St. Croix Valley, WI, and to national organizations; some giving also in Huron, London, Middlesex, and Perth, Ontario Province, Canada. No support for national research organizations. No grants to individuals, or for endowments, or the purchase of Andersen products.
Publications: Application guidelines; IRS Form 990 or 990-PF printed copy available upon request.
Application information: Call foundation before sending request. Visit foundation Web site for application address and guidelines. Application form required.
   Initial approach: Download application form and mail proposal and application form to nearest application address
   Copies of proposal: 1
   Deadline(s): Apr. 15, July 15, Oct. 15, and Dec. 15
   Board meeting date(s): Jan., Apr., July, and Nov.
   Final notification: 10 working days
Officers and Directors: Keith D. Olson, Pres.; Maureen E. McDonough, V.P., Grants Admin. and Secy.; Phil Donaldson, Treas.; James E. Humphrey; T. Randall Iles; Jay Lund; Jerry Redmond.
Number of staff: 1 full-time professional; 1 full-time support.
EIN: 416020912

1074
Better Way Foundation, Inc.
(formerly Alpha Omega Foundation, Inc.)
10350 Bren Rd. West
Minnetonka, MN   55343-9014

Established around 1994 in FL.
Donors: North Star Ventures; Arbeit Investment, LP; Arbeit & Co.; Opus Corp.
Grantmaker type: Company-sponsored foundation.
Financial data (yr. ended 12/31/10): Assets, $32,775,603 (M); expenditures, $1,388,076; qualifying distributions, $1,091,731; giving activities include $1,091,731 for grants.
Purpose and activities: The foundation supports organizations involved with higher education, health, human services, international relief, Catholicism, and economically disadvantaged people.
Fields of interest: Higher education; Health care; Children, services; Family services; Human services; International relief; United Ways and Federated Giving Programs; Catholic agencies & churches; Economically disadvantaged.
Type of support: Scholarship funds; General/operating support; Capital campaigns; Program development.
Limitations: Applications not accepted. Giving primarily in MD, and MN; some funding also in NY and Africa. No grants to individuals.
Application information: Contributes only to pre-selected organizations.
Officers and Directors:* Amy R. Goldman,* Pres.; Luz Campa, V.P.; John Crurin, Secy.; Matthew G. Rauenhorst,* Treas.; Anne Mahony; Judith R. Mahoney; Fr. Kevin McDonough; Louise Myers; Gia Rauenhorst; Margaret Rauenhorst.
EIN: 411795984

1075
Dorobo Fund for Tanzania, Inc.
750 S. 2nd St.,
Minneapolis, MN 55401-2363 (612) 313-2030
FAX: (612) 313-2001;
E-mail: SBoren@SpencerStuart.com; URL: http://
www.dorobofund.org/

Established in MN.
Grantmaker type: Public charity.
Financial data (yr. ended 12/31/10): Revenue,
$135,332; assets, $97,040 (M); gifts received,
$135,307; expenditures, $154,178; program
services expenses, $150,616; giving activities
include $150,616 for grants.
Purpose and activities: The fund works at the
community level to develop and carry out both
conservation and education projects that will build
capacity within the local villages of Tanzania, East
Africa.
Fields of interest: Education; Environment, land
resources.
International interests: Tanzania, Zanzibar and
Pemba.
Type of support: General/operating support; In-kind
gifts.
Limitations: Giving primarily in Tanzania.
Trustees: Susan Boren; Jon Cox; Richard Leider;
Daudi Peterson; Mike Peterson; Thad Peterson;
Allan Weber; Shelly Wolfe.
EIN: 411875830

1076
The Dorsey and Whitney Foundation
50 S. 6th St., Ste. 1500
Minneapolis, MN 55402-1498 (612) 343-7900
Contact: Rose Wilson, Comm. Affairs Admin.
FAX: (612) 340-7834;
E-mail: wilson.rose@dorsey.com

Established in 1982 in MN.
Grantmaker type: Public charity.
Financial data (yr. ended 12/31/10): Revenue,
$3,247,043; assets, $364,370 (M); gifts received,
$3,245,429; expenditures, $3,495,977; giving
activities include $3,493,397 for grants, and
$2,000 for grants to individuals.
Purpose and activities: The foundation supports the
communities in which Dorsey & Whitney LLP
operates and provides general support to charitable
organizations and programs which reflect the
diverse interests of its attorneys. Financial support
is provided to established arts, cultural and
community-service organizations.
Fields of interest: Arts; Education; Children/youth,
services.
International interests: Canada.
Type of support: General/operating support.
Limitations: Applications accepted. Giving on a
national and international basis. No support for
religious organizations or their affiliates, or national
fundraising campaigns. No grants to individuals, or
for ticket sales.
Publications: Annual report.
Directors: Brian E. Palmer, Chair.; Jay Swanson,*
Secy.-Treas.; Michael Droke; Kim Severson; Richard
Silberberg.
EIN: 411424522

1077
Duluth Superior Area Community Foundation
Medical Arts Bldg.
324 W. Superior St., Ste. 212
Duluth, MN 55802-1707 (218) 726-0232
Contact: Holly C. Sampson, Pres.
FAX: (218) 726-0257;
E-mail: info@dsacommunityfoundation.com; Grant
application e-mail:
grantsinfo@dsacommunityfoundation.com;
Scholarship application e-mail:
scholarships@dsacommunityfoundation.com;
URL: http://www.dsacommunityfoundation.com
Facebook: http://www.facebook.com/pages/
Duluth-Superior-Area-Community-Foundation/
128701853838939

Established in 1982 in MN.
Grantmaker type: Community foundation.
Financial data (yr. ended 12/31/10): Assets,
$51,800,410 (M); gifts received, $1,913,395;
expenditures, $2,424,560; giving activities include
$1,172,334 for 62+ grants (high: $67,992), and
$287,346 for 150 grants to individuals.
Purpose and activities: The foundation supports a
wide variety of activities in five interest areas: Arts,
Community and Economic Development, Education,
Environment, and Human Services.
Fields of interest: Visual arts; Performing arts;
Performing arts, music; Arts; Child development,
education; Higher education; Education;
Environment; Animal welfare; Crime/violence
prevention; Employment; Food services; Housing/
shelter, development; Human services; Children/
youth, services; Child development, services; Family
services; Homeless, human services; International
affairs, goodwill promotion; International peace/
security; Civil rights, race/intergroup relations;
Economic development; Community/economic
development; Government/public administration;
Disabilities, people with; Minorities; Native
Americans/American Indians; Women; Economically
disadvantaged; Homeless.
Type of support: Film/video/radio; General/
operating support; Emergency funds; Program
development; Publication; Seed money; Curriculum
development; Scholarship funds; Research;
Technical assistance; Consulting services; Program
evaluation; Scholarships—to individuals.
Limitations: Applications accepted. Giving primarily
in Bayfield and Douglas counties, WI, and Atkin,
Carlton, Cook, Itasca, Koochiching, Lake, and St.
Louis counties in northeastern MN. No support for
religious organizations for religious activities. No
grants to individuals (except for designated
scholarship funds), or for capital or annual
campaigns, endowments, debt retirement, medical
research, fundraising, continuing support, deficit
financing, land acquisition, tickets for benefits,
telephone solicitations, or for grants beyond single
funding cycle; no loans.
Publications: Application guidelines; Annual report;
Grants list; Informational brochure (including
application guidelines); Newsletter.
Application information: Based on the outcome of
the online inquiry, an organization may be
encouraged to submit a full proposal. Visit
foundation web site for application forms and
guidelines. Application form required.
  Initial approach: Complete online funding inquiry
    form
  Copies of proposal: 3

Deadline(s): Apr. 1 and Oct. 1 for Community
  Opportunity Fund grants; varies for others
Board meeting date(s): Monthly
Final notification: 60 to 90 days
Officers and Trustees:* Lyle w. Northey,* Chair.;
Jennifer L. Carey,* Vice-Chair.; Holly C. Sampson,
Pres.; Howard T. Klatzky,* Secy.; LeRoy T.
Kolquist,* Treas.; Ryan Boman; Amy Kuronen; David
Nasby; Fariba Pendleton; Philip D. Rolle; Arend J.
Sandbulte; Mia Thibodeau; Donald L. Wallgren;
Claudia Scott Welty.
Number of staff: 8 full-time professional; 1 full-time
support.
EIN: 411429402

1078
Francis H. Fitzgerald Trust
c/o Trust Tax Services
P.O. Box 64713
St. Paul, MN 55164-0713

Established in 1965 in MN.
Grantmaker type: Independent foundation.
Financial data (yr. ended 12/31/10): Assets,
$1,426,795 (M); expenditures, $177,584;
qualifying distributions, $160,000; giving activities
include $160,000 for grants.
Fields of interest: Higher education.
International interests: Scotland.
Type of support: Scholarship funds.
Limitations: Applications not accepted. Giving
primarily to Kirkcaldy District, Scotland.
Application information: Unsolicited requests for
funds not accepted.
Trustee: U.S. Bank, N.A.
EIN: 416053922

1079
Foundation for the Development of Human Potential
30 E. 7th St., Ste. 2000
St. Paul, MN 55101-4930 (651) 228-0935
Contact: Joseph S. Micallef, Pres.

Established in 1974.
Donor: Elizabeth Bentinck-Smith.
Grantmaker type: Independent foundation.
Financial data (yr. ended 12/31/10): Assets,
$56,542 (M); gifts received, $24,461;
expenditures, $159,160; qualifying distributions,
$157,000; giving activities include $157,000 for
grants.
Fields of interest: International peace/security;
Education; Health care; Human services.
Limitations: Applications accepted. Giving primarily
in MA. No grants to individuals.
Application information: Application form not
required.
  Initial approach: Proposal
  Deadline(s): None
Officers and Directors:* Joseph S. Micallef,* Pres.
and Treas; Elizabeth W. Bentinck-Smith,* Clerk;
Charles A. Weyerhaeuser.
EIN: 237368600

1080
H. B. Fuller Company Contributions Program

1200 Willow Lake Blvd.
P.O. Box 64683
St. Paul, MN 55164-0683 (612) 236-5217
Contact: Christine Meyer, Community Affairs Rep.
FAX: (612) 236-5065; URL: http://phx.corporate-ir.net/phoenix.zhtml?c=203756&p=irol-CorporateContributions

Grantmaker type: Corporate giving program.
Financial data (yr. ended 11/30/08): Total giving, $149,625, including $149,625 for grants.
Purpose and activities: As a complement to its foundation, H.B. Fuller also makes charitable contributions to nonprofit organizations directly. Support is given on a national and international basis.
Fields of interest: Arts; Education; Environment; Health care; Human services; Community/economic development.
International interests: Canada; Europe; Latin America.
Type of support: General/operating support; Employee volunteer services; In-kind gifts.
Limitations: Applications accepted. Giving on a national and international basis in areas of company operations, with emphasis on Roseville, CA, Covington and Tucker, GA, Palatine, IL, Paducah, KY, St. Paul, MN, and in Canada, Europe, and Latin America. No support for religious, fraternal, or veterans' organizations not of direct benefit to the entire community, political or lobbying organizations, or disease-specific organizations. No grants to individuals, or for travel, basic or applied research, courtesy or public service advertising, capital campaigns, endowments, or programs which appear to be the responsibility of government which are not community-based efforts directed at improving the delivery of government funded services.
Publications: Corporate giving report (including application guidelines).
Application information: The Community Affairs Department handles giving. The company has a staff that only handles contributions. A contributions committee reviews all requests. Application form required.
Initial approach: Contact headquarters for application form
Copies of proposal: 1
Deadline(s): None
Committee meeting date(s): Monthly
Final notification: Following review
Community Affairs Department: Keralyn Gross, Dir., Community Affairs; Christine Meyer, Community Affairs Rep.
Number of staff: 2 full-time professional.

1081
General Mills Foundation

1 General Mills Blvd.
MS CC-01
Minneapolis, MN 55426-1347
Contact: Ellen Luger, Exec. Dir.
FAX: (763) 764-4114;
E-mail: CommunityActionQA@genmills.com;
URL: http://www.genmills.com/en/Responsibility/Community_Engagement.aspx
Champions for Healthy Kids Recipients: http://www.genmills.com/Home/Responsibility/

Community_Engagement/Grants/Champions_for_healthy_kids/2011_recipients.aspx
Facebook: http://www.facebook.com/GeneralMillsGives
General Mills Foundation's Philanthropy Promise: http://www.ncrp.org/philanthropys-promise/who
Grants Database: http://content.generalmills.com/Responsibility/Community_Engagement/Grants/Grantees.aspx?cat={4020A4F2-C35C-40DD-9CE4-2374486831E7}

Incorporated in 1954 in MN.
Donor: General Mills, Inc.
Grantmaker type: Company-sponsored foundation.
Financial data (yr. ended 05/31/11): Assets, $64,213,355 (M); gifts received, $33,700,000; expenditures, $25,557,668; qualifying distributions, $25,424,899; giving activities include $23,491,183 for 735 grants (high: $4,282,203; low: $700), and $1,909,864 for employee matching gifts.
Purpose and activities: The foundation supports programs designed to support hunger and nutrition wellness; education; family services; and arts and culture.
Fields of interest: Performing arts; Arts; Elementary/secondary education; Education; Public health, physical fitness; Food services; Food banks; Nutrition; Disasters, preparedness/services; Family services; Human services; United Ways and Federated Giving Programs; Economically disadvantaged; Children/youth; Minorities.
Type of support: General/operating support; Capital campaigns; Program development; Scholarship funds; Employee volunteer services; Employee matching gifts; Employee-related scholarships.
Limitations: Applications accepted. Giving primarily in areas of major company operations and headquarters of Twin Cities, MN area; giving also in CA, GA, IA, IL, IN, MA, MD, MI, MO, MT, NJ, NM, NY, OH, TN, WA, and WI for the Community Action Councils Program; limited giving in Malawi and Tanzania. No support for discriminatory organizations, religious, political, social, labor, veterans', alumni, or fraternal organizations, disease-specific organizations, or athletic associations. No grants to individuals, or for endowments, annual appeals, federated campaigns, fund drives, recreational or sporting events, healthcare, research, advertising, political causes, travel, emergency funding, debt reduction or operating deficits, conferences, seminars or workshops, publications, film, or television, sponsorships, special events, or fundraisers; no loans.
Publications: Application guidelines; Corporate report; Corporate giving report; Financial statement; Grants list.
Application information: New applications for Champions for Healthy Kids Program are not accepted for 2012. A full proposal may be requested at a later date for Twin Cities grants. E-mail letter of inquiry to foundation for capital requests. A site visit may be requested for Celebrating Communities of Color. Telephone calls and personal visits are not encouraged. Support is limited to 1 contribution per organization during any given year. Organizations receiving support may be asked to submit an evaluation report. Application form required.
Initial approach: Complete online letter of inquiry for Twin Cities grants; complete online

application for Celebrating Communities of Color
Deadline(s): None for Twin Cities grants; Dec. 15 to Feb. 1 for Celebrating Communities of Color
Board meeting date(s): Ongoing
Final notification: 60 days for Twin Cities grants; Apr. for Celebrating Communities of Color
Officers and Trustees:* Kendall J. Powell,* Chair.; Christina L. Shea,* Pres.; Ellen Goldberg Luger, V.P., Secy., and Exec. Dir.; Marie Pillai, Treas.; Marc Belton; John R. Church; Michael L. Davis; Peter Erickson; Ian R. Friendly; Donal Leo Mulligan*; Kimberly A. Nelson; Shawn O'Grady; Christopher O'Leary; Roderick A. Palmore.
Number of staff: 7 full-time professional; 2 full-time support.
EIN: 416018495
Recent grants for international programs:
1081-1 American Red Cross, Greater Minneapolis Area Chapter, Minneapolis, MN, $25,000. For International Response Fund - Disaster Relief Support for Philippines. 2010.
1081-2 American Red Cross, Greater Minneapolis Area Chapter, Minneapolis, MN, $25,000. For International Response Fund, Samoa-Tonga Tsunami. 2010.
1081-3 American Red Cross, Greater Minneapolis Area Chapter, Minneapolis, MN, $25,000. For International Response Fund-Typhoon Morakot. 2010.
1081-4 American Red Cross National Headquarters, Washington, DC, $100,000. For earthquake relief efforts in Haiti. 2010.
1081-5 American Red Cross National Headquarters, Washington, DC, $50,000. For Chile earthquake relief. 2010.
1081-6 CARE USA, Atlanta, GA, $300,000. For Post-Harvest Loss Reduction and Small-Scale Irrigation Enhancement Project (PHASE). PHASE will contribute to increased food security for 15,000 people in Malawi, focusing on women- and child-headed households, as well as families affected by HIV and AIDS. 2010.
1081-7 CARE USA, Atlanta, GA, $150,000. For long term rebuilding efforts in response to the earthquake in Haiti. 2010.
1081-8 Compatible Technology International, Saint Paul, MN, $15,000. For operating support. 2010.
1081-9 Congressional Hunger Center, Washington, DC, $25,000. For operating support and Emerson-Leland Fellowship Programs Support. 2010.
1081-10 Evangelical Lutheran Church in America, Northwest Synod of Wisconsin, Chetek, WI, $75,000. For Kasungu Integrated Women and Children Hunger Project and Special Feeding Program. 2010.
1081-11 Feed My Starving Children, Coon Rapids, MN, $25,000. For operating support. 2010.
1081-12 Hmong American Mutual Assistance Association, Minneapolis, MN, $10,000. For Center for Hmong Adolescent Development Program. 2010.
1081-13 Save the Children Federation, Westport, CT, $150,000. For Building Partnerships for Sustainable Agriculture Initiatives in Malawi. 2010.
1081-14 TechnoServe, Washington, DC, $75,000. For Tanzania Food Processing Receiver Network. 2010.
1081-15 United Way International, Alexandria, VA, $265,000. For International Donor Advised Giving. 2010.

1081-16 United Way International, Alexandria, VA, $35,000. To support UWI's worldwide charitable activities. 2010.

1081-17 United Way International, Alexandria, VA, $15,000. For Junior Achievement Greece. 2010.

1081-18 University of Minnesota Foundation, Minneapolis, MN, $350,000. For Global Food Safety Systems Initiative. 2010.

1081-19 World Agroforestry Centre, Nairobi, Kenya, $20,000. For Business Alliance Against Chronic Hunger. 2010.

1081-20 Youth Orchestra of the Americas, Arlington, VA, $15,000. For United States - Canada Tour. 2010.

1082
GHR Foundation, Inc.

(formerly Genald and Henrietta Rauenhorst Foundation)
c/o Adler Management, LLC
10350 Bren Road W.
Minnetonka, MN 55343-9002 (952) 656-4850
E-mail: info@ghrfoundaiton.org; URL: http://www.ghrfoundation.org

Established in 2004 in FL.
Donors: Gerald Rauenhorst; Gerald Rauenhorst Family Foundation; National Ore Co.; Omaha Real Estate Investment Partnership; Oire, LLC; Bold, LLC.
Grantmaker type: Independent foundation.
Financial data (yr. ended 12/31/09): Assets, $278,919,779 (M); expenditures, $20,905,270; qualifying distributions, $13,449,113; giving activities include $12,735,485 for 73 grants (high: $1,300,000; low: $1,000).
Fields of interest: Health care; Human services; Higher education.
Limitations: Applications not accepted. Giving primarily in MD, MN, and WI. No grants to individuals.
Application information: Contributes only to pre-selected organizations.
Officers and Directors:* Amy R. Goldman,* Chair. and Exec. Dir.; Luz Campa,* Vice-Chair. and Secy.; Mark Rauenhorst,* Vice-Chair. and Treas.; Peter Karoff; Cardinal Theodore McCarrick; Gerald Rauenhorst; Joseph J. Rauenhorst; Matt Rauenhorst.
EIN: 030547519
Recent grants for international programs:

1082-1 African Sisters Education Collaborative, Scranton, PA, $252,222. For capital and program funding for Bigwa Secondary School. 2009.

1082-2 Carmen Pampa Fund, Saint Paul, MN, $80,000. To extend, deepen and energize donor base to increase general operating funds available to Unidad Academica Campesina-Carmen pampa (UAC-CP) in rural Bolivia. 2009.

1082-3 Catholic Relief Services, Baltimore, MD, $800,000. For Saving Lives, Protecting Livelihoods, and Transforming CRS Emergency Programs. 2009.

1082-4 Catholic Relief Services, Baltimore, MD, $147,975. For faith leaders on Kenyan coast to adopt interfaith approach to eliminate child marriage by raising awareness, promoting children's rights, extending opportunities to girls for microfinance and vocational training. 2009.

1082-5 Catholic Relief Services, Baltimore, MD, $80,000. To build fundraising and advocacy capacity of Caritas Lebanon Migrant Center. 2009.

1082-6 Catholic Relief Services, Baltimore, MD, $56,171. For CRS Vietnam. 2009.

1082-7 Center for Interfaith Action on Global Poverty, Washington, DC, $530,000. For implementation of Nigerian Interfaith Action Association Muslim-Christian faith leader training program in three Nigerian states in support of Nigerian National Malaria Control Programme. 2009.

1082-8 Congressional Coalition on Adoption Institute, Washington, DC, $75,000. For Africa: The Way Forward Policy Summit. 2009.

1082-9 Dominican Sisters of Saint Mary of the Springs, Columbus, OH, $150,000. For project support for the introduction of innovative farming methodologies to improve the lives of the poor in rural Nigeria by providing food and additional income generating activities. 2009.

1082-10 Every Child a Chance Trust, London, England, $244,210. To reduce children in Kyiv Oblast institutions. 2009.

1082-11 Feed My Starving Children, Coon Rapids, MN, $10,000. For general operating support. 2009.

1082-12 Holt International Childrens Services, Eugene, OR, $209,060. To establish new model of child welfare in three communities. 2009.

1082-13 Interfaith Center of New York, New York, NY, $169,000. For Catholic and Muslim social service project to develop ongoing relationships between the two communities through shared social services projects that serve both groups. 2009.

1082-14 Mercy Corps, Portland, OR, $200,000. For providing joint activities to young people in two neighborhoods in Lebanon at the center of sectarian violence to address social and economic needs and build on common interests. 2009.

1082-15 Save the Children Federation, Westport, CT, $125,633. To establish national child welfare model in Nepal. 2009.

1082-16 Sisters of Mercy of the Americas Northeast Community, Cumberland, RI, $57,000. For Counseling Training Program for Sisters at Uganda Martyrs University for academic and programmatic evaluation, scholarships for 10 African religious women to complete the program, and capital funding to construct a building to enhance ministry. 2009.

1082-17 Sisters of Mercy of the Americas Northeast Community, Cumberland, RI, $30,000. For project to assist local African Sisters to plan, develop, present and evaluate a continuing education program for women religious in Sub Saharan Africa. 2009.

1082-18 Sisters of Notre Dame, Ipswich, MA, $200,000. For project and capital funding for African Photovoltaic Project. 2009.

1082-19 United Aid for Azerbaijan, Baku, Azerbaijan, $94,364. To transform national approach to disabled children in Azerbaijan. 2009.

1083
Hegardt Foundation

500 IDS Ctr.
80 S. 8th St.
Minneapolis, MN 55402

Established in 2007 in MN.
Donor: Winifred J. and John M. Harris Charitable Lead Annuity Trust.
Grantmaker type: Independent foundation.

Financial data (yr. ended 12/31/10): Assets, $724,722 (M); gifts received, $401,113; expenditures, $342,088; qualifying distributions, $342,088; giving activities include $335,000 for 11 grants (high: $100,000; low: $5,000).
Fields of interest: Health care, clinics/centers; Foundations (community); Performing arts, dance; Arts; Education; International relief.
Limitations: Applications not accepted. No grants to individuals.
Application information: Unsolicited requests for funds not accepted.
Officers: Carolyn H. Sundquist, Pres.; Marjorie E. Harris, V.P.; Katherine A. Harris, Secy.; W. Gordon Harris, Treas.
EIN: 205814715

1084
India Association of Minnesota, Inc.

(formerly India Club, Inc.)
P.O. Box 130158
St. Paul, MN 55113-0002
Contact: Shalini Thadini, Pres.
E-mail: president@iamn.org; URL: http://www.iamn.org
Facebook: http://www.facebook.com/pages/India-Association-of-Minnesota/89298145823

Grantmaker type: Public charity.
Purpose and activities: The association seeks to educate the public about the culture of India and provide disaster relief.
Fields of interest: Safety/disasters.
International interests: India.
Publications: Newsletter.
Officers: Shalini Thadini, Pres.; Kusum Gosain, V.P.; Anjan Mukherjee, Secy.; Manohar Shintre, Treas.
Board Members: Aarti Koralli; Ameeta Jaiswal-Dale; Dinesh Goel; Hari Pallempati; Hasim Khorakhiwala; Najarjuna Bommareddy; Navnit Narayan; and 10 additional directors.
EIN: 237364647

1085
Kaplan Family Foundation

c/o Harvey Kaplan
6566 France Ave. S., No. 701
Edina, MN 55435-1714
E-mail: aryeh1@aol.com; Winter address: 9405 No. 118th Pl., Scottsdale, AZ 85259

Established in 1994 in MN.
Donors: Harvey Kaplan; Helen Kaplan; Leah Kaplan; Marjorie Kaplan; Rachel Kaplan; Ross Kaplan.
Grantmaker type: Independent foundation.
Financial data (yr. ended 12/31/10): Assets, $3,744,628 (M); gifts received, $57,500; expenditures, $142,909; qualifying distributions, $136,536; giving activities include $135,756 for 40 grants (high: $50,180; low: $85).
Purpose and activities: Giving primarily to Jewish agencies to support Jewish cultural arts, education and camping.
Fields of interest: Jewish federated giving programs; Education; Human services; Family services; Jewish agencies & synagogues.
International interests: Israel.
Type of support: Continuing support; Annual campaigns; Endowments.
Limitations: Applications not accepted. Giving primarily in AZ, IL, MN, NY, PA, the Midwest, and

Israel. No support for political organizations. No grants to individuals.
Application information: Contributes only to pre-selected organizations.
 Board meeting date(s): July-Aug.
Officers and Directors:* Harvey Kaplan,* Pres.; Marjorie Kaplan,* V.P.; Rachel Kaplan,* Secy.; Ross Kaplan,* Treas.; Helen Kaplan; Laura Kaplan; Leah Kaplan; Robert Riesman; Jon Smollen.
Number of staff: None.
EIN: 411794327

1086
Margaret H. and James E. Kelley Foundation, Inc.
408 Saint Peter St., Ste. 425
St. Paul, MN 55102-1187 (651) 222-7463
Contact: Timothy J. Dwyer, Treas.

Established in 1960 in MN.
Grantmaker type: Independent foundation.
Financial data (yr. ended 11/30/10): Assets, $15,324,580 (M); expenditures, $806,037; qualifying distributions, $760,000; giving activities include $760,000 for grants.
Purpose and activities: Giving primarily for human rights, medical disciplines, family planning and social services; support also for higher education and a community fund.
Fields of interest: Arts; Law school/education; Hospitals (specialty); Reproductive health, family planning; Health care; Human services; Children/youth, services; International affairs; Civil liberties, advocacy; United Ways and Federated Giving Programs; Disabilities, people with.
Type of support: General/operating support; Continuing support; Annual campaigns; Capital campaigns; Equipment; Program development; Professorships; Scholarship funds; Program-related investments/loans.
Limitations: Applications accepted. Giving primarily in MN; some funding nationally. No grants to individuals.
Publications: Annual report (including application guidelines); Grants list.
Application information: Application form not required.
 Initial approach: Letter
 Copies of proposal: 1
 Deadline(s): Oct. 1
 Board meeting date(s): Varies
Officers and Directors:* James C. O'Neill,* Pres. and Secy.; Timothy J. Dwyer, Treas.; Hampton K. O'Neill; Mrs. Hampton K. O'Neill; James W. O'Neill; Mrs. James W. O'Neill; Kelley O'Neill; Mrs. Kelley O'Neill.
Number of staff: 2 part-time professional.
EIN: 416017973

1087
Kenya Children's Fund
P.O. Box 4159
Hopkins, MN 55343-0499 (952) 938-2705
Contact: Ginger Palm, Pres. and C.E.O.
FAX: (952) 938-2702;
E-mail: kenyachildrensfd@aol.com; URL: http://www.kenyachildrensfund.org

Established in 1985.
Grantmaker type: Public charity.

Financial data (yr. ended 12/31/10): Revenue, $537,973; assets, $71,651 (M); gifts received, $537,696; expenditures, $615,970; giving activities include $355,418 for grants to organizations outside the U.S.
Purpose and activities: The fund operates a school, nutrition, and health care program in Kinyago-Dandora, a village in Nairobi.
Fields of interest: Children/youth, services.
International interests: Kenya.
Limitations: Applications not accepted. Giving limited to Kenya.
Application information: Contributes only to pre-selected organizations; unsolicited requests for funds not considered or acknowledged.
Officers and Directors:* William B. Parks,* Chair.; Ginger Palm,* Pres. and C.E.O.; Rick McKinley,* Secy.; Robert J. Oehrig,* Treas.; Chad Goehring; Jane Njuguna; Onsando Osiemo.
EIN: 363431216

1088
Lownade Foundation
P.O. Box 3584
Mankato, MN 56002-3584

Established in 2000 in MN.
Donor: David Andreas.
Grantmaker type: Independent foundation.
Financial data (yr. ended 11/30/10): Assets, $12,324 (M); gifts received, $531; expenditures, $392,984; qualifying distributions, $389,000; giving activities include $389,000 for 47 grants (high: $35,000; low: $1,000).
Fields of interest: Elementary/secondary education; Higher education; Children/youth, services; International human rights.
Type of support: General/operating support.
Limitations: Applications not accepted. Giving primarily in Mankato and Minneapolis, MN. No grants to individuals.
Application information: Unsolicited requests for funds not accepted.
Officers: David Andreas, Chair. and C.E.O.; Deb Andreas, C.F.O. and Secy.
EIN: 411989647

1089
Sarah Stevens MacMillan Foundation
P.O. Box 5628
Minneapolis, MN 55440-9300

Established in 1996 in MN.
Donor: Catherine E. Kehoe Trust.
Grantmaker type: Independent foundation.
Financial data (yr. ended 12/31/10): Assets, $6,001,229 (M); expenditures, $340,035; qualifying distributions, $261,500; giving activities include $261,500 for grants.
Fields of interest: Children, day care; Historic preservation/historical societies; Education; Landscaping; Animals/wildlife; Housing/shelter, development; International affairs; Jewish agencies & synagogues.
Limitations: Applications not accepted. Giving primarily in CA, CT, FL, MN, and NY. No grants to individuals.
Application information: Contributes only to pre-selected organizations.
Officers and Directors:* Steven A. Hornig, Secy.; Roger S. Wherry,* Treas.; Alexa M. Daitch;

Katherine W. MacMillan; Sarah MacMillan; Lucy M. Stitzer.
EIN: 411830212

1090
Mano a Mano International Partners
(formerly Mano a Mano Medical Resources)
774 Sibley Memorial Hwy.
Mendota Heights, MN 55118-1707
(651) 457-3141
Contact: Daniel Narr, Exec. Dir.
FAX: (651) 450-9935;
E-mail: dan@manoamano.org; URL: http://www.manoamano.org

Established in 1994.
Grantmaker type: Public charity.
Financial data (yr. ended 12/31/10): Revenue, $1,352,538; assets, $2,631,075 (M); gifts received, $1,336,054; expenditures, $1,287,925; giving activities include $842,879 for grants to organizations outside the U.S.
Purpose and activities: The organization seeks to increase the capability of healthcare providers in Bolivia to serve impoverished patients.
Fields of interest: Health care.
International interests: Bolivia.
Type of support: In-kind gifts.
Limitations: Applications not accepted. Giving limited to Bolivia.
Publications: Annual report; Financial statement; Informational brochure; Newsletter.
Application information: Contributes only to pre-selected organizations.
Officers and Board Members:* Segunda M. Velasquez,* Pres.; John Foxon,* M.D., V.P.; Joan Velasquez,* Ph.D., Secy.-Treas.; Daniel Narr, Exec. Dir.; Terry Crowley; Deborah Kotcher; Christine Verploeg; Nancy White.
Number of staff: 1 full-time professional; 1 full-time support.
EIN: 411796971

1091
Mary's Pence
275 E. 4th St., No. 707
Saint Paul, MN 55101-3375 (651) 788-9869
E-mail: mailbox@maryspence.org; URL: http://www.maryspence.org
Facebook: https://www.facebook.com/pages/Marys-Pence/107261079336288

Established in 1986 in MN.
Grantmaker type: Public charity.
Financial data (yr. ended 06/30/11): Revenue, $279,777; assets, $179,103 (M); gifts received, $269,474; expenditures, $304,559; program services expenses, $265,842; giving activities include $29,450 for grants, $32,500 for grants to organizations outside the U.S., $2,000 for grants to individuals, and $201,892 for foundation-administered programs.
Purpose and activities: The organization collects and distributes funds for the self-empowerment of women. It provides an opportunity for women and men to direct resources to the least powerful members of church and society, and to the Catholic women working in their interests. In addition to giving seed money to emerging or struggling ministries, the organization provides educational and spiritual support for Catholic women seeking to

more fully integrate their faith and work. Programs include monthly spiritual reflection groups nationwide, a biannual newsletter, technical assistance, and networking.

Fields of interest: Civil/human rights, women; Catholic agencies & churches; Women; Disabilities, people with.

International interests: Canada; Caribbean; Central America; Haiti; Mexico; South America.

Type of support: Program development.

Limitations: Applications accepted. Giving primarily in North, South, and Central America, and the Caribbean.

Publications: Application guidelines; Annual report; Financial statement; Grants list; Informational brochure; Newsletter.

Application information: Projects are aimed at empowerment of women and start-up ministries. Organization should have a budget of less than $150,000. Application form required.
  Initial approach: Download application online
  Copies of proposal: 6
  Deadline(s): Feb. 1, June 1, and Oct. 1
  Board meeting date(s): Feb. and July
  Final notification: 15th of the following month after application deadline

Officers and Directors:* Consilia Karli,* SFCC, Pres.; Elise DeGooyer,* Secy.; Judy Diaz Molosky, CSJ; Robbie Pentecost, OSF; Pat Rogucki, SFCC; Ashley Steele.

Number of staff: 1 full-time professional; 1 part-time professional; 1 part-time support.

EIN: 363556481

1092
The McKnight Foundation
710 S. 2nd St., Ste. 400
Minneapolis, MN 55401-2290   (612) 333-4220
Contact: Kate Wolford, Pres.
FAX: (612) 332-3833; E-mail: info@mcknight.org;
URL: http://www.mcknight.org
E-Newsletter: http://visitor.constantcontact.com/manage/optin/ea?v=001mBomMP0GdY8UKXJsN5z3Cw%3D%3D
Facebook: http://www.facebook.com/pages/McKnight-Foundation/131199140270392
Grantee Perception Report: http://www.mcknight.org/files/GPR_10.pdf
Grants Database: http://www.mcknight.org/grantsprograms/findagrantee.aspx
McKnight Foundation's Philanthropy Promise: http://www.ncrp.org/philanthropys-promise/who
RSS Feed: http://www.mcknight.org/rss/rss.aspx
Twitter: http://twitter.com/McKnightFdn

Incorporated in 1953 in MN.

Donors: William L. McKnight‡; Maude L. McKnight‡; Virginia M. Binger‡; James H. Binger‡.

Grantmaker type: Independent foundation.

Financial data (yr. ended 12/31/10): Assets, $2,014,523,000 (M); expenditures, $116,266,000; qualifying distributions, $96,686,000; giving activities include $96,686,000 for grants.

Purpose and activities: The grant maker seeks to improve the quality of life for present and future generations. Through grant making, coalition-building, and encouragement of strategic policy reform, it uses its resources to attend, unite, and empower those it serves.

Fields of interest: Arts; Environment, energy; Environment; Neuroscience; Housing/shelter, development; Youth development; Children/youth, services; Child development, services; Community/economic development; Transportation; Children/youth; Economically disadvantaged.

International interests: Cambodia; Laos; Tanzania, Zanzibar and Pemba; Uganda; Vietnam.

Type of support: General/operating support; Capital campaigns; Building/renovation; Equipment; Program development; Fellowships; Technical assistance; Program evaluation; Employee matching gifts; Matching/challenge support.

Limitations: Applications accepted. Giving limited to organizations in MN, especially the seven-county Twin Cities, MN, area, except for programs in the environment which are made mainly in the 10 states bordering the Mississippi River and in the Twin Cities region, international aid, or research. No support for religious organizations for religious purposes, or for medical health or health-related services, including those for chemical dependency, services for seniors or people with disabilities. No grants to individuals (except for the Virginia McKnight Binger Awards in Human Service and the McKnight Distinguished Artist Award.), or for basic research in academic disciplines (except for defined programs in crop research and neuroscience) endowment funds, scholarships, fellowships, national fundraising campaigns, ticket sales, travel or conferences.

Publications: Application guidelines; Annual report; Financial statement; Grants list; Informational brochure; Newsletter; Occasional report.

Application information: The foundation will e-mail to decline requests or to provide additional instructions for submitting a full proposal online. Application form not required.
  Initial approach: Online grant application
  Deadline(s): Jan. 15, Apr. 15, July 15, and Oct. 15 for arts, and region and communities; Feb. 1, May 1, Aug. 1, Nov. 1 for environment. See foundation web site for additional program deadlines
  Board meeting date(s): Feb., May, Aug., Nov.
  Final notification: 5 months

Officers and Directors:* Robert J. Struyk,* Chair.; Kate Wolford, Pres.; Richard J. Scott, V.P., Finance and Compliance, and Secy.; Ted Staryk,* Treas.; Anne Binger; Erika L. Binger; Patricia S. Binger; Cynthia Binger Boynton; Meghan Binger Brown; Bill Gregg; Richard D. McFarland; John Natoli; Noa Staryk.

Number of staff: 21 full-time professional; 1 part-time professional; 15 full-time support; 1 part-time support.

EIN: 410754835

Recent grants for international programs:

1092-1 3S Rivers Protection Network, Ban Lung, Cambodia, $80,000. For a network of dam-impacted communities in Northeastern Cambodia to protect and improve river-based livelihoods. 2010.

1092-2 Agricultural Research Institute, Uyole, Mbeya, Tanzania, Zanzibar and Pemba, $67,000. For project: Supporting Communities to Increase Bean Productivity Through Enhanced Accessibility to Seed of Preferred Bean Varieties in Malawi, Mozambique, and Tanzania. 2010.

1092-3 Amhara Regional Agricultural Research Institute, Bahir Dar, Ethiopia, $130,000. For project Finger Millet Genetic and Cultivation Improvement, Technology Dissemination, and Seed System Enhancement in the Eastern Horn of Africa Region. 2010.

1092-4 APT Enterprise Development, Moreton-in-Marsh, England, $70,000. To increase incomes of women fruit and vegetable growers by increasing demand for solar-dried produce in Tanzania. 2010.

1092-5 Bioversity International, Rome, Italy, $210,000. For the project Assessing the Success of On-Farm Conservation Projects in Delivering Conservation and Livelihood Outcomes: Identifying Best Practices and Decision Support Tools. 2010.

1092-6 Brigham Young University, Provo, UT, $60,000. For the project development and participative validation of technological innovations that improve the strategies for sustainable management of quinoa and potato in the Bolivian Altiplano. 2010.

1092-7 Cambodia Indigenous Youth Association, Phnom Penh, Cambodia, $50,000. For indigenous communities to promote rights to self-determination and protect lands and natural resources. 2010.

1092-8 Cambodian Volunteers for Community Development, Phnom Penh, Cambodia, $60,000. For general operating support, and for support of Phum Seam Farmers' Cooperative Project. 2010.

1092-9 Center for Forest and Wetland Research and Management, Ho Chi Minh City, Vietnam, $60,000. For project, creating local understanding of impacts of proposed dams on the Mekong Delta. 2010.

1092-10 Center for Marinelife Conservation and Community Development, Hanoi, Vietnam, $120,000. For initiative to empower coastal communities in resources management and sustainable development in area of the Cat Ba Biosphere Reserve, Haiphong, Vietnam. 2010.

1092-11 Centre for Integrated Development, Kampala, Uganda, $75,000. To create opportunities for diversified agricultural income, and enable farmers (primarily women) to apply integrated sustainable farming approaches to increase food production and incomes in Uganda. 2010.

1092-12 Centro de Investigacion de Recursos Naturales y Medio Ambiente, Puno, Peru, $120,000. For the project, Perspectives on the Sustainability of Quinoa Production-Consumption in the Peruvian Altiplano. 2010.

1092-13 ClimateWorks Foundation, San Francisco, CA, $26,000,000. For the overall ClimateWorks Network (Regional Climate Foundations, Best Practice Networks, Global Initiatives, and continuing to build the Network). 2010.

1092-14 Community Capacities for Development, Kampong Chhnang, Cambodia, $70,000. For a community empowerment for sustainable livelihoods development project in Kampong Chnnang Province, Cambodia. 2010.

1092-15 Community Economic Development, Cambodia, $90,000. To carry out awareness raising and capacity building for community biodiversity conservation and resource rights in Kratie and Stung Treng provinces. 2010.

1092-16 Community Volunteer Initiative for Development, Bushenyi, Uganda, $64,000. To strengthen the economic base for sustainable livelihood of women in the fishing communities of Bunyaruguru county, Uganda, through promotion of Village Savings and Loan Associations and training in business skills. 2010.

1092-17 Compatible Technology International, Saint Paul, MN, $30,000. For project Planting and Processing of Small Seeded Crops. 2010.

1092-18 Cord, Leamington Spa, England, $100,000. For capacity development support for NGO's and social networks working with indigenous communities in Cambodia. 2010.

1092-19 Cornell University, Ithaca, NY, $30,000. For project: Integrated Genetic and Cultural Management Approaches for the Improvement of TEFF in Ethiopia. 2010.

1092-20 CUSO-VSO, Ottawa, Canada, $60,000. For the Huamjai Asasamak internship project for young ethnic minority and women volunteers in Laos. 2010.

1092-21 Danish Management Group, Viby, Denmark, $45,000. For the project Innovative Communication Media and Methods for More Effective Aflatoxin Mitigation, Variety Uptake, and Use Interventions in Groundnut in Malawi and Tanzania. 2010.

1092-22 Education Development Foundation, Mwanza, Tanzania, Zanzibar and Pemba, $35,000. To increase the economic potential of existing small businesses and startups through training, counseling, and provision of business-related information and opportunities in urban and rural areas of Mwanza region, Tanzania. 2010.

1092-23 Ekwendeni Hospital, Ekwendeni, Malawi, $48,000. For the project, Best Bets Two: For a Changing World. 2010.

1092-24 EMESCO Development Foundation, Uganda, $75,000. For integrated agriculture development program for women in Uganda. 2010.

1092-25 Ethiopian Institute of Agricultural Research, Addis Ababa, Ethiopia, $298,000. For project: Integrated Genetic and Cultural Management Approaches for the Improvement of TEFF in Ethiopia. 2010.

1092-26 Fauna and Flora International, Washington, DC, $80,000. To continue and expand a project of natural resources management and sustainable livelihoods improvement for ethnic communities living near a gibbon conservation area in far-northern Vietnam. 2010.

1092-27 Foundation for the Promotion and Investigation of Andean Products, Cochabamba, Bolivia, $665,000. For the project, Development and Participative Validation of Technological Innovations that Improve the Strategies for Sustainable Management of Quinoa and Potato in the Bolivian Altiplano. 2010.

1092-28 Friends of Rural Advancement, Rakai, Uganda, $70,000. For a poultry project for women, and to strengthen village savings and loan associations in Uganda. 2010.

1092-29 Global Education Partnership, Tanzania Division, Lushoto, Tanzania, Zanzibar and Pemba, $54,000. For accessible and quality business development and village banking training to young women entrepreneurs in Handeni district of the Tanga Region of Tanzania. 2010.

1092-30 Helen Keller International, New York, NY, $216,000. For project An Be Jigi II: Enhancing Bioavailability of Iron and Zinc in Varieties of Sorghum and Pearl Millet Consumed in Mali. 2010.

1092-31 Highlanders Association, Cambodia, $80,000. For indigenous communities in Ratanakiri province in empowerment to protect lands and natural resources, cultural identity, and right of access to education. 2010.

1092-32 Ilonga Agricultural Research Institute, Morogoro, Tanzania, Zanzibar and Pemba, $224,000. For the project, Development and Promotion of Alectra Resistant Cowpea Cultivars for Smallholder Farmers in Malawi and Tanzania. 2010.

1092-33 Indigenous Community Support Organization, Phnom Penh, Cambodia, $130,000. For land rights and resource management work for indigenous communities in Ratanakiri province, Cambodia. 2010.

1092-34 Initiatives for Development and Equal Access to Services, Karagwe, Tanzania, Zanzibar and Pemba, $86,000. For economic empowerment of rural women in Misenyi district in Tanzania through a program of farmer training and agricultural services. 2010.

1092-35 Institut de lEnvironnement et des Recherches Agricoles, Ouagadougou, Burkina Faso, $330,000. For project Soil (Nutrient and Water) Management to Increase Soil Organic Matter, Sorghum Grain, and Stover Yields. 2010.

1092-36 Institut de lEnvironnement et des Recherches Agricoles, Ouagadougou, Burkina Faso, $149,000. For the project, Technology Introduction, Marketing Strategies, and Farmers' Organizations for Sorghum and Millet in Burkina Faso and Niger. 2010.

1092-37 Institut National de la Recherche Agronomique du Niger, Maradi, Niger, $125,000. For the project, Technology Introduction, Marketing Strategies, and Farmers' Organizations for Sorghum and Millet in Burkina Faso and Niger. 2010.

1092-38 Institute of Rural Economy, Bamako, Mali, $148,000. For project Improvement of Fonio Productivity in Partnership with Farmers in the Sahelian and Northern Guinean Zones of Mali. 2010.

1092-39 Institute of Rural Economy, Bamako, Mali, $80,000. For project An Be Jigi II: Enhancing Bioavailability of Iron and Zinc in Varieties of Sorghum and Pearl Millet Consumed in Mali. 2010.

1092-40 Instituto de Investigacao Agraria de Mocambique, Maputo, Mozambique, $197,000. For the project, Increasing Bean Productivity and Household Food Security in Stressful Environments in Mozambique Through Use of Phosphorus-Efficient Seeds by Farm Households. 2010.

1092-41 Instituto de Investigacao Agraria de Mocambique, Maputo, Mozambique, $67,000. For project Supporting Communities to Increase Bean Productivity Through Enhanced Accessibility to Seed of Preferred Bean Varieties in Malawi, Mozambique, and Tanzania. 2010.

1092-42 Instituto para una Alternativa Agraria, Cusco, Peru, $40,000. For the project, Innovating Concepts and Technology Applied to Achieve Self-Sufficiency, to Improve Livelihoods, and to Ensure Highly Nutritional Diets. 2010.

1092-43 International Center for Tropical Agriculture, Cali, Colombia, $128,000. For project Supporting Communities to Increase Bean Productivity Through Enhanced Accessibility to Seed of Preferred Bean Varieties in Malawi, Mozambique, and Tanzania. 2010.

1092-44 International Centre of Insect Physiology and Ecology, Nairobi, Kenya, $328,000. For project Developing Integrated Management Approach for Napier Stunt Disease in East Africa. 2010.

1092-45 International Centre of Insect Physiology and Ecology, Nairobi, Kenya, $102,000. For project Enhancing Smallholder Farmers' Capacity for Learning and Adoption of Push-Pull Technology Through Video and Computer Communication Tools in East Africa. 2010.

1092-46 International Cooperative Centre for Agricultural Research for Development, Paris, France, $28,000. For Ph.D. program student training. 2010.

1092-47 International Crops Research Institute for the Semi-Arid Tropics, Patancheru, India, $664,000. For the project, Groundnut Varieties Improvement for Yield and Adaptation, Human Health, and Nutrition. 2010.

1092-48 International Crops Research Institute for the Semi-Arid Tropics, Patancheru, India, $567,000. For the project, Sustaining Farmer-Managed Seed Initiatives for Sorghum and Pearl Millet in Mali, Niger, and Burkina Faso. 2010.

1092-49 International Crops Research Institute for the Semi-Arid Tropics, Patancheru, India, $432,000. For the project, Assessing and Refining the Concept of Dynamic Genepool Management and Simultaneous Farmer-Participatory Population Improvement in Pearl Millet and Sorghum. 2010.

1092-50 International Crops Research Institute for the Semi-Arid Tropics, Patancheru, India, $140,000. For project An Be Jigi II: Enhancing Bioavailability of Iron and Zinc in Varieties of Sorghum and Pearl Millet Consumed in Mali. 2010.

1092-51 International Crops Research Institute for the Semi-Arid Tropics, Patancheru, India, $30,000. For project Innovative Communication Media and Methods for More Effective Aflatoxin Mitigation, Variety Uptake, and Use Interventions in Groundnut in Malawi and Tanzania. 2010.

1092-52 International Livestock Research Institute, Nairobi, Kenya, $69,000. For Ph.D. program student training in department of Biology and Biotechnology at Addis Ababa University. 2010.

1092-53 Jalamba Organic Processors and Training Centre, Kampala, Uganda, $70,000. To increase household incomes and food security on the islands of Bussi and Bunjako in Uganda by introducing cash crops of fruit and vegetables along with animal husbandry. 2010.

1092-54 Japan International Volunteer Center, Tokyo, Japan, $80,000. For second phase of community forestry project in south-central Laos. 2010.

1092-55 Kenya Agricultural Research Institute, Nairobi, Kenya, $436,000. For project Multiple Legumes and Management Strategies for Reinvigorating and Maintaining the Health and Productivity of Smallholder Mixed Farming Systems. 2010.

1092-56 Kenya Agricultural Research Institute, Nairobi, Kenya, $256,000. For project Finger Millet Genetic and Cultivation Improvement, Technology Dissemination, and Seed System Enhancement in Eastern Horn of Africa Region. 2010.

1092-57 Kenya Agricultural Research Institute, Nairobi, Kenya, $86,000. For project Improving Food and Livelihood Security in the East and Horn of Africa Using Multiple Stress Tolerant Sorghum Cultivars. 2010.

1092-58 Kulika Charitable Trust Uganda, Kampala, Uganda, $72,000. To promote sustainable agriculture among poor women farmers in Uganda through specialized training, credit, and extension. 2010.

1092-59 Learning Institute, Phnom Penh, Cambodia, $90,000. To coordinate and access Co-Management Learning Network initiative in Cambodia, Laos, and Vietnam. 2010.

1092-60 Makerere University, Kampala, Uganda, $126,000. For project Improving Food and Livelihood Security in the East and Horn of Africa Using Multiple Stress Tolerant Sorghum Cultivars. 2010.

1092-61 Mangrove Action Project, Port Angeles, WA, $80,000. For community capacity building, coastal resources management, and ecological mangrove restoration in Koh Kong province, Cambodia. 2010.

1092-62 Meridian Institute, Dillon, CO, $100,000. For Foundation Working Group on Food and Agriculture Policy. 2010.

1092-63 Messenger Band Association, Phnom Penh, Cambodia, $50,000. For general operating support. 2010.

1092-64 Michigan State University, East Lansing, MI, $130,000. For the Southern Africa Community of Practice project, Best Bets Two: For a Changing World. 2010.

1092-65 Ministry of Agriculture and Irrigation, Lilongwe, Malawi, $67,000. For project Supporting Communities to Increase Bean Productivity Through Enhanced Accessibility to Seed of Preferred Bean Varieties in Malawi, Mozambique, and Tanzania. 2010.

1092-66 Minors in Need of Resettlement, Eagan, MN, $110,000. For a project to improve educational access and increase economic empowerment for ethnic minority girls in northern Vietnam. 2010.

1092-67 Mkombozi Group, Lushoto, Tanzania, Zanzibar and Pemba, $61,000. To build capacities of goat keepers through training on livestock husbandry skills and crossbreeding of local goats with exotic breeds in Tanzania. 2010.

1092-68 Moi University, Eldoret, Kenya, $224,000. For project Improving Food and Livelihood Security in the East and Horn of Africa Using Multiple Stress Tolerant Sorghum Cultivars. 2010.

1092-69 My Village, Phnom Penh, Cambodia, $90,000. For general operating support. 2010.

1092-70 National Agricultural Research Organization, Entebbe, Uganda, $130,000. For project: Finger Millet Genetic and Cultivation Improvement, Technology Dissemination, and Seed System Enhancement in the Eastern Horn of Africa Region. 2010.

1092-71 Organization for Rural Development, Jinja, Uganda, $105,000. To strengthen capacities of rural women to access external credit and assist them to form their own savings and credit associations for increased incomes in Uganda. 2010.

1092-72 Pennsylvania State University, University Park, PA, $270,000. For the project, Increasing Bean Productivity and Household Food Security in Stressful Environments in Mozambique Through Use of Phosphorus-Efficient Seeds by Farm Households. 2010.

1092-73 People, Resources and Conservation Foundation, Amherst, NY, $80,000. To enable the sustainable use of resources and improved

livelihoods for lakeside ethnic minority villagers in Ba Be Lake in northern Vietnam. 2010.

1092-74 Purdue University, West Lafayette, IN, $238,000. For the project Technology Introduction, Marketing Strategies, and Farmers' Organizations for Sorghum and Millet in Burkina Faso and Niger. 2010.

1092-75 Rockefeller Family Fund, New York, NY, $3,025,000. For RE-AMP efforts to promote policies that combat global warming. 2010.

1092-76 Saint Judes Family Projects and Training Centre, Masaka, Uganda, $43,000. To help rural women in Uganda to increase food production, improve nutrition, and earn income from organic fruits, vegetables, and small livestock. 2010.

1092-77 Serengeti Farmers Association, Tanzania, Zanzibar and Pemba, $15,000. For a sustainable agriculture and agro-forestry project for women in Tanzania. 2010.

1092-78 Small Enterprises Foundation, Dar es Salaam, Tanzania, Zanzibar and Pemba, $40,000. For mentorship and business skills training for women entrepreneurs in Temeke and Mkuranga districts in Tanzania. 2010.

1092-79 Social Action for Change, Phnom Penh, Cambodia, $25,000. To strengthen and support a network of women's organizing and empowerment initiatives in Cambodia. 2010.

1092-80 Stichting Centre on Housing Rights and Evictions, Geneva, Switzerland, $120,000. For capacity building and financial support for the 'Housing Rights from Below' project aimed at preventing forced evictions in Cambodia. 2010.

1092-81 Sustainable Laos Education Initiatives, Mississauga, Canada, $50,000. For Sai Nyai Eco-School Project. 2010.

1092-82 Tanzania Forest Conservation Group, Dar es Salaam, Tanzania, Zanzibar and Pemba, $58,000. For a medicinal plant and honey production project for women living near the East Mbara Mountains in Tanzania. 2010.

1092-83 Tanzania Women Volunteers Association, Dar es Salaam, Tanzania, Zanzibar and Pemba, $70,000. For a beekeeping and village community bank project for women in Tanzania. 2010.

1092-84 Tiny Toones Cambodia, Phnom Penh, Cambodia, $35,000. For a youth empowerment and outreach initiative in Phnom Penh, Cambodia. 2010.

1092-85 Uganda Water and Sanitation NGO Network, Kampala, Uganda, $30,000. To help 200 families in Manafwa district get clean water, improve household sanitation, and plant kitchen gardens for better hygiene, nutrition, and income. 2010.

1092-86 University of Greenwich, Chatham, England, $135,000. For Ph.D. student training at Natural Resources Institute at the University of Greenwich. 2010.

1092-87 University of Malawi, Zomba, Malawi, $20,000. For MSc. program student training in Food Science and Human Nutrition at Bunda College of Agriculture, University of Malawi. 2010.

1092-88 University of Malawi, Bunda College of Agriculture, Zomba, Malawi, $254,000. For the project, Best Bets Two: For a Changing World. 2010.

1092-89 University of Malawi, Bunda College of Agriculture, Zomba, Malawi, $154,000. For the project, Development and Promotion of Alectra Resistant Cowpea Cultivars for Smallholder Farmers in Malawi and Tanzania. 2010.

1092-90 University of Nebraska-Lincoln, Lincoln, NE, $106,000. For project: Soil (Nutrient and Water) Management to Increase Soil Organic Matter, Sorghum Grain, and Stover Yields. 2010.

1092-91 University of Virginia, Charlottesville, VA, $54,000. For the project, Development and Promotion of Alectra Resistant Cowpea Cultivars for Smallholder Farmers in Malawi and Tanzania. 2010.

1092-92 Village Focus Cambodia, Phnom Penh, Cambodia, $80,000. For project to improve the capacity of local indigenous leadership in Mondulkiri province, Cambodia. 2010.

1092-93 Village Focus International, New York, NY, $30,000. For the Health, Education, Agriculture, and Leadership community-based development project in Salavan Province of southern Laos. 2010.

1092-94 Wildlife Conservation Society, Bronx, NY, $102,000. For a project to secure the land of indigenous Bunong communities in Mondulkiri Province, Cambodia, to assist them to avoid deepening poverty and to develop the management of lands in line with own priorities. 2010.

1092-95 Woods Hole Oceanographic Institution, Woods Hole, MA, $55,000. To expand shellfish farming activities involving women residents of coastal villages on the island of Unguja in the Zanzibar archipelago. 2010.

1092-96 Worker's Information Center, Phnom Penh, Cambodia, $25,000. For empowerment project for women garment workers to take leadership roles to improve working conditions and lives in Cambodia. 2010.

1092-97 World Education, Boston, MA, $60,000. To develop nonprofit association to improve lives of UXO accident survivors and families in Laos PDR. 2010.

1092-98 World Neighbors, Oklahoma City, OK, $70,000. To improve livelihoods and economic status of vulnerable women in 14 villages in Tanzania. 2010.

1092-99 World Wildlife Fund, Washington, DC, $100,000. To create community networks for fisheries co-management across sub-catchments of the Mekong River basin in Laos. 2010.

1092-100 Yeak Laom Advisory Group, Ban Lung, Cambodia, $10,000. To assist the indigenous Yeak Laom community to maintain and strengthen management rights to Yeak Laom lake in Ratanakiri and to assist in re-building the solidarity, culture, and traditions of the community. 2010.

1093
The Medtronic Foundation
710 Medtronic Pkwy.
Minneapolis, MN 55432-5604 (763) 505-2639
Contact: Deb Anderson, Grants Admin.
FAX: (763) 505-2648;
E-mail: medtronicfoundation@medtronic.com;
Contact for PatientLink and Strengthening Health Systems in Africa, Europe, Middle East, and South America: Luc Girad, Medtronic Fdn., Medtronic Europe, Route du Molliau 31, Case postale, CH—1131 Tolochenaz, Switzerland, e-mail: foundation.emea@medtronic.com; E-mail for Global Heroes: mtcm.globalheroes@medtronic.com; URL: http://www.medtronic.com/foundation Grants List: http://www.medtronic.com/foundation/grants/search-grants.html

HeartRescue Project on Twitter: http://twitter.com/
#!/HeartRescue
Medtronic "What We Care About" Video: http://
www.medtronic.com/foundation/video//
video-what_we_care_about.html
Medtronic "Where We Focus" Video: http://
www.medtronic.com/foundation/video/
video-where_we_focus.html
Medtronic "Who We Are" Video: http://
www.medtronic.com/foundation/video/
video-who_we_are.html
Medtronic Global Heroes on Facebook: http://
www.facebook.com/pages/
Medtronic-Global-Heroes/54011966662

Established in 1979 in MN.
Donor: Medtronic, Inc.
Grantmaker type: Company-sponsored foundation.
Financial data (yr. ended 04/30/11): Assets,
$54,187,794 (M); gifts received, $293,571;
expenditures, $30,589,702; qualifying
distributions, $30,383,841; giving activities include
$25,848,666 for 1,200 grants (high: $2,239,222;
low: $500), and $1,498,281 for employee matching
gifts.
Purpose and activities: The foundation supports
programs designed to promote health, with a focus
on heath systems in developing countries, chronic
disease, patient advocacy and support, and sudden
cardiac arrest; education, including primary and
secondary science, math, and engineering
initiatives and education reform; and community,
through local human services and arts initiatives
and disaster relief efforts providing short- and
long-term help.
Fields of interest: Museums (science/technology);
Arts, cultural/ethnic awareness; Media, radio; Arts;
Education, reform; Elementary/secondary
education; Elementary school/education; Higher
education; Teacher school/education; Education;
Medical care, community health systems; Hospitals
(general); Health care, emergency transport
services; Health care, EMS; Public health; Health
care, patient services; Health care; Cancer; Heart &
circulatory diseases; Lung diseases; Diabetes;
Disasters, preparedness/services; Human
services; United Ways and Federated Giving
Programs; Science, formal/general education;
Mathematics; Engineering/technology; Science;
Public affairs; Youth; Minorities; Women;
Economically disadvantaged.
International interests: Australia; Austria; Belgium;
Brazil; Canada; China; Czech Republic; Denmark;
France; Germany; India; Ireland; Italy; Japan;
Mexico; Netherlands; Poland; Portugal; Russia;
South Africa; Spain; Sweden; Switzerland; United
Kingdom.
Type of support: Continuing support; Management
development/capacity building; Annual campaigns;
Program development; Conferences/seminars;
Publication; Seed money; Curriculum development;
Scholarship funds; Employee volunteer services;
Sponsorships; Employee matching gifts; Donated
products.
Limitations: Applications accepted. Giving primarily
in areas of company operations, with emphasis on
Maricopa County and Tempe, AZ, Santa Clarita, San
Fernando, and Simi Valley regions, western Los
Angeles, and Orange, Santa Barbara, Sonoma,
Sunnyvale, and Ventura counties, CA, Denver metro
area and Louisville, CO, Jacksonville, FL, Kosciusko
County, IN, Beverly, Danvers, Middleton, North
Shore, Peabody, and Salem, MA, Minneapolis, St.
Paul, and Twin Cities-Seven County metro, MN, area,

Humacao, Juncos, and Villalba, PR, Memphis, TN,
Fort Worth and San Antonio, TX, and King and
Snohomish County, WA, and in Africa, Australia,
Austria, Belgium, Brazil, Canada, Czech Republic,
Shanghai, China, Denmark, Europe, France,
Germany, Hungary, India, Ireland, Italy, Japan,
Mexico, Netherlands, Poland, Russia, South Africa,
Spain, Switzerland, and the United Kingdom. No
support for lobbying, political, or fraternal
organizations, fiscal agents, religious groups not of
direct benefit to the entire community, or private
foundations. No grants individuals, or for
scholarships, Continuing Medical Education (CME)
grants, capital campaigns, fundraising events or
activities, social events, goodwill advertising,
general operating support, general support for
educational institutions, long-term counseling or
personal development, endowments, automatic
external defibrillators (AEDs) purchases, or
research.
Publications: Application guidelines; Corporate
giving report; Grants list; Program policy statement.
Application information: Letters of inquiry for
requests outside the U.S.; submissions should be
no longer than 2 to 3 pages. Organizations receiving
support are asked to provide a final report.
Unsolicited applications for HeartRescue,
PatientLink US, and Medtronic Fellows are not
accepted. Application form required.
> *Initial approach:* Letter of inquiry for all requests
> outside the U.S.; complete online application
> form for CommunityLink, Global Heroes, and
> Health in Community Twin Cities
> *Copies of proposal:* 1
> *Deadline(s):* Sept. 1 to Nov. 15 for
> CommunityLink; Apr. 27 for Global Heroes; July
> 15 Health in Community Twin Cities
> *Board meeting date(s):* Quarterly
> *Final notification:* 4 to 5 months for applications
> outside the U.S.; Apr. 15 for CommunityLink;
> Sept. for Health in Community Twin Cities
Officers and Directors:* Gary L. Ellis,* Chair.; H.
James Dallas, Vice-Chair.; Jacob Gayle, V.P.; Kristin
L. Gorsuch; Stephen N. Oesterle, M.D.; Chris J.
O'Connell; Herb F. Riband; Tony B. Semedo; David
M. Steinhaus, M.D.; Caroline Stockdale; Tom M.
Tefft.
Number of staff: 3 full-time professional; 2 part-time
professional; 1 full-time support; 1 part-time
support.
EIN: 411306950
Recent grants for international programs:
1093-1 Ability Online Support Network, Etobicoke,
Canada, $15,000. For Ability Online Vis-Ability
Initiative. 2010.
1093-2 American Austrian Foundation, New York,
NY, $120,000. For Open Medical Institute.
2010.
1093-3 American Austrian Foundation, New York,
NY, $120,000. For Seminars and Internships for
Doctors in Central and Eastern Europe, Asia, and
Russia. 2010.
1093-4 American Refugee Committee, Minneapolis,
MN, $50,000. For Haiti Earthquake Relief. 2010.
1093-5 Americans for Oxford, New York, NY,
$40,000. For Medtronic Scholars and
Lectureships. 2010.
1093-6 Arrhythmia Alliance, Stratford upon Avon,
England, $156,846. For Capacity Building and
Fund Raising Staff. 2010.
1093-7 Arrhythmia Alliance, Stratford upon Avon,
England, $67,191. For World Heart Rhythm Week
Core Campaign and Website Development.
2010.

1093-8 Arrhythmia Alliance, Stratford upon Avon,
England, $48,412. For Arrhythmia Alliance
Spain. 2010.
1093-9 Arrhythmia Alliance, Stratford upon Avon,
England, $18,871. For Restart The Heart - School
Training Programme. 2010.
1093-10 Association des Personnes concernees
par le Tremblement Essentiel, Lyon, France,
$48,020. For A New Communication Strategy.
2010.
1093-11 Association Francaise des Diabetiques,
Paris, France, $42,870. For Cursus Patients
Expert. 2010.
1093-12 Association Francophone pour Vaincre les
Douleurs, Pompaire, France, $34,518. For
Neuropathic Pain Comic Book. 2010.
1093-13 Association Francophone pour Vaincre les
Douleurs, Pompaire, France, $24,438. For
Neuropathic Pain Comic Book. 2010.
1093-14 Association Saint Prex Festival, Saint Prex,
Switzerland, $19,150. 2010.
1093-15 BOSK, Vereniging van Motorisch
Gehandicapten en Hun Ouders, Utrecht,
Netherlands, $22,617. For Interactive
Informative DVD on Cerebral Palsy. 2010.
1093-16 Childrens HeartLink, Minneapolis, MN,
$137,000. For Advancing Pediatric Cardiac Care
in India. 2010.
1093-17 Childrens HeartLink, Minneapolis, MN,
$125,000. For Advancing Pediatric Cardiac Care
in China. 2010.
1093-18 Childrens HeartLink, Minneapolis, MN,
$90,000. To Develop Pediatric Cardiac Surgery
Center in Brazil. 2010.
1093-19 Childrens HeartLink, Minneapolis, MN,
$38,000. For Advancing Pediatric Cardiac Care in
Ukraine. 2010.
1093-20 Childrens HeartLink, Minneapolis, MN,
$25,000. For HeartLink Gala. 2010.
1093-21 Childrens HeartLink, Minneapolis, MN,
$25,000. For Site Development. 2010.
1093-22 Coordination Between Italian Associations
of Youth and Children with Diabetes, Parma, Italy,
$30,818. For Parental Trust Building Workshops.
2010.
1093-23 Danish Continence Foundation,
Copenhagen, Denmark, $30,000. For Special
Ambassador Edition of Continence News. 2010.
1093-24 Diabetes Hope Foundation, Mississauga,
Canada, $15,000. For Diabetes Hope
Scholarship Program. 2010.
1093-25 Diabetes UK, London, England, $33,200.
For national roll-out of Type 1 diabetes Journey of
a Lifetime Starter Pack - Year One. 2010.
1093-26 Dr. Dathu Rao Memorial Charitable Trust,
Chennai, India, $15,000. For program support.
2010.
1093-27 Dystonia Medical Research Foundation
Canada, Toronto, Canada, $30,000. For Twisted
Awareness and Education Screenings. 2010.
1093-28 Ecole Polytechnique Federale de
Lausanne, Lausanne, Switzerland, $31,499. For
Les Science, CA M'Interessel, Raising the
Interest of Young Girls in Scientific and
Engineering Fields. 2010.
1093-29 European Federation of Neurological
Associations, Florence, Italy, $45,075. To hire
Executive Director. 2010.
1093-30 European Multiple Sclerosis Platform,
Brussels, Belgium, $41,271. For Current
Challenges and Opportunities in Europe in the
Work for Young People with Multiple Sclerosis.
2010.

1093-31 European Organization for Rare Diseases, Paris, France, $60,592. For Rare Together. 2010.

1093-32 European Organization for Rare Diseases, Paris, France, $30,290. For Enhancing Outreach with Advanced Electronic Communication for the Rare Disease Community. 2010.

1093-33 European Parkinson's Disease Association, London, England, $41,815. For Annual Member Conference, Translation of Website and Awareness Tool Kit. 2010.

1093-34 European Parkinson's Disease Association, London, England, $22,983. For World Parkinson's Congress. 2010.

1093-35 European Patients Forum, Brussels, Belgium, $38,001. For Young Patients' Advocacy Seminar. 2010.

1093-36 Family House, Tokyo, Japan, $20,031. For National Alliance and Awareness of Family House. 2010.

1093-37 Federacion Espanola Parkinson, Madrid, Spain, $54,252. For Cuentanoslocon arte VIII, Tell Us, with Art. 2010.

1093-38 Fondation Sportsmile, Grand-Saconnex, Switzerland, $19,220. For Communication and Outreach with Obese Children, Adolescents and Their Parents. 2010.

1093-39 Fondation Theodora, Lonay, Switzerland, $44,727. For Hospital Partnership. 2010.

1093-40 Galway Education Center, Galway, Ireland, $82,905. For Medtronic Scientist of the Future. 2010.

1093-41 Galway Education Center, Galway, Ireland, $60,000. For Medtronic Healthy Living. 2010.

1093-42 Grown Up Congenital Heart Patients Association, Ipswich, England, $22,652. For Capacity Building. 2010.

1093-43 Harvard University, Cambridge, MA, $250,000. For School of Public Health in Boston, MA, China Initiative Senior Executive Education Program. 2010.

1093-44 Health Human Resources Development Center of the Ministry of Health, Beijing, China, $200,000. For Hospital Director Training Project on Health System Reform and Public Hospital Development. 2010.

1093-45 Heart to Heart International Childrens Medical Alliance, Oakland, CA, $240,000. For the Into the Heartland Campaign. 2010.

1093-46 Heart to Heart International Childrens Medical Alliance, Oakland, CA, $100,000. To develop Pediatric Cardiac Centers in Russia. 2010.

1093-47 India Diabetes Research Foundation, Chennai, India, $75,000. For strengthening national diabetes care services by enhancing capacity of health care providers. 2010.

1093-48 International Osteoporosis Foundation, Nyon, Switzerland, $37,509. To develop grassroots network and patient support group. 2010.

1093-49 International Society for Pediatric and Adolescent Diabetes, Berlin, Germany, $137,400. To develop common software for benchmarking among EU centers. 2010.

1093-50 Italian Multiple Sclerosis Society, Genoa, Italy, $35,330. For Young People Beyond MS. 2010.

1093-51 Italian Resuscitation Council, Bologna, Italy, $47,000. For Conoscere per salvare. 2010.

1093-52 Japan Association of Cardiac Pacemaker Friends, Tokyo, Japan, $44,586. For Local Pacemaker Users Support. 2010.

1093-53 Japan Chronic Disease Self-Management Association, Tokyo, Japan, $51,161. To expand dissemination of CDSMP workshops to rural areas of Japan. 2010.

1093-54 Japan Chronic Disease Self-Management Association, Tokyo, Japan, $25,017. For Workshops - Tokyo, Nagoya, and Osaka Metropolitan Areas Project. 2010.

1093-55 Japan IDDM Network, Saga, Japan, $39,499. For program support. 2010.

1093-56 Juvenile Diabetes Research Foundation International, London, England, $39,174. For T1 Youth Ambassador programme. 2010.

1093-57 Kardioklub SK, Kosice, Czech Republic, $24,728. For World Heart Day. 2010.

1093-58 Keio University, Tokyo, Japan, $130,000. To develop Japan's Clinical Research Infrastructure. 2010.

1093-59 Kids Against Hunger, New Hope, MN, $20,000. For Haiti Earthquake Relief. 2010.

1093-60 Kontinet, Huddinge, Sweden, $15,054. For website. 2010.

1093-61 Madras Diabetes Research Foundation, Chennai, India, $111,400. For India Diabetes Education Program. 2010.

1093-62 Magyar Cukorbetegek Orszagos Szovetsegenek, Budapest, Hungary, $28,048. For educational program for women with pregestational Diabetes and training for member association leaders. 2010.

1093-63 Minnesota International Center, Minneapolis, MN, $49,000. For International Education Programming. 2010.

1093-64 Minnesota Medical Foundation, Minneapolis, MN, $150,000. For Consortium on Medical Education and Globally Mobile Populations. 2010.

1093-65 Movement Disorders Educational Fund, WE MOVE, New York, NY, $30,000. For Stay Connected, Stay Informed. 2010.

1093-66 National Back Pain Association, Teddington, England, $43,693. For Helpline Development and PR project. 2010.

1093-67 National Tremor Foundation, Disablement Services Center, Harold Wood Hospital, Romford, England, $16,044. For New Web Platform. 2010.

1093-68 Nationales Register fur angeborene Herzfehler, Berlin, Germany, $42,846. For Translation of Corience CHD Website into Spanish and German. 2010.

1093-69 Neurological Alliance of Ireland, Dublin, Ireland, $30,000. To publish The Future for Neurological Conditions in Ireland, A Challenge for Healthcare, opportunity for change. 2010.

1093-70 Osaka Life Support Association, Osaka, Japan, $49,550. For PUSH Project for Schools. 2010.

1093-71 Oxfam America, Boston, MA, $13,250. For match for Trailwalker Japan. 2010.

1093-72 Partners in Health, Boston, MA, $361,977. For match for Haiti earthquake. 2010.

1093-73 Partners in Health, Boston, MA, $150,000. For Human Resources for the Chronic Diseases of the Bottom Billion, A Pathway to Health Systems Strengthening. 2010.

1093-74 Philias Foundation, Carouge, Switzerland, $131,998. For Junior Diabetes Cup. 2010.

1093-75 Prevent Arrhythmic Cardiac Events, Faculty of Health Sciences - Department of Internal Medicine, Tygerberg, South Africa, $81,112. For FIFA Sudden Cardiac Arrest Awareness and Education Campaign. 2010.

1093-76 Prevention Space, La Cote Fondation, Morges, Switzerland, $23,603. For Health Prevention Intervention for Older Citizens. 2010.

1093-77 Project HOPE - The People-to-People Health Foundation, Millwood, VA, $125,000. For Sichuan Province, China Rehabilitation Project. 2010.

1093-78 Public Radio International, Minneapolis, MN, $362,500. To underwrite The World and BBC World Service. 2010.

1093-79 SADS UK, West Horndon, England, $38,270. For Safeguarding the Community. 2010.

1093-80 SAMATVAM Science and Research for Human Welfare Trust, Bangalore, India, $28,000. For Children and Youth with Type 1-Insulin Dependent Diabetes in India Information Technology Enriched Diabetes Care for Both Haves and Have Nots. 2010.

1093-81 Shad Valley International, Waterloo, Canada, $15,000. 2010.

1093-82 SickKids Foundation, Toronto, Canada, $30,000. For Camp Oki. 2010.

1093-83 Svensk dystoniforening, Haninge, Sweden, $15,728. For Reach Out. 2010.

1093-84 Swiss Pain Patients Association, Basel, Switzerland, $34,582. For Leadership Transition. 2010.

1093-85 Syncope Trust and Reflex Anoxic Seizures, Stratford Upon Avon, England, $51,937. For Capacity Building. 2010.

1093-86 Terre des Hommes Foundation, Lausanne, Switzerland, $40,471. For Specialized Healthcare. 2010.

1093-87 Theater de Beausobre, Morges, Switzerland, $28,664. For theater season. 2010.

1093-88 Think First Foundation of Canada, Toronto, Canada, $20,000. For ThinkFirst Brain Day. 2010.

1093-89 United Way of Peel Region, Mississauga, Canada, $42,163. For match of Employee Campaign. 2010.

1093-90 University of the Witwatersrand Fund, New York, NY, $69,589. For Nurse-Facilitated Hypertension Management Program. 2010.

1093-91 World Heart Federation, Geneva, Switzerland, $86,856. To Promote Healthy Lifestyles in Children. 2010.

1093-92 World Heart Federation, Geneva, Switzerland, $84,810. To Promote Healthy Lifestyles in Children. 2010.

1093-93 World Heart Federation, Geneva, Switzerland, $83,150. For Charity Challenge Grant for Rheumatic Heart Disease Prevention Program. 2010.

1093-94 World Internet Resources for Education and Development, Montara, CA, $30,000. To Complete Development of Delivery Tools and Create Medical Content for the International Telemedicine Network. 2010.

1094
The Mortenson Family Foundation
4000 Olson Memorial Hwy.
Minneapolis, MN 55422-5351

Established in 1999 in MN.

Donors: M.A. Mortenson Co.; Alice D. Mortenson; Maurice Mortenson, Jr.

Grantmaker type: Company-sponsored foundation.

Financial data (yr. ended 12/31/10): Assets, $29,591,833 (M); gifts received, $9,636,242;

expenditures, $804,536; qualifying distributions, $550,000; giving activities include $550,000 for grants.
Purpose and activities: The foundation supports organizations involved with education, hunger, youth development, human services, religion, and economically disadvantaged people.
Fields of interest: Higher education; Education; Hospitals (general); Food services; Youth development; Children/youth, services; Human services; United Ways and Federated Giving Programs; Christian agencies & churches; Religion; Economically disadvantaged.
International interests: Guatemala; Honduras; Nicaragua.
Type of support: General/operating support; Program development.
Limitations: Applications not accepted. Giving limited to CA, MN, Guatemala, Honduras, and Nicaragua. No grants to individuals.
Application information: Contributes only to pre-selected organizations.
Officers and Directors:* Alice D. Mortenson,* Chair. and Pres.; Mauritz A. Mortenson, Jr., V.P. and Treas.; Mark A. Mortenson, Secy.; Christopher D. Mortenson; David C. Mortenson; Mathias H. Mortenson.
EIN: 411958621

1095
Kevin J. Mossier Foundation
7201 Ohms Ln., No. 100
Edina, MN 55439-2148

Established in 1998 in MN.
Donor: Kevin J. Mossier.
Grantmaker type: Independent foundation.
Financial data (yr. ended 12/31/10): Assets, $5,019,802 (M); expenditures, $463,705; qualifying distributions, $379,677; giving activities include $379,677 for grants.
Fields of interest: Foundations (public); International human rights; LGBTQ.
Limitations: Applications not accepted. Giving primarily in Washington, DC, MA, MN and New York, NY; some funding nationally. No grants to individuals.
Application information: Contributes only to pre-selected organizations.
Trustees: Steve Brandwein; Larry Bye; Helen Dehner; Donald S. Ofstedal; Charles Rounds.
EIN: 411863691

1096
Oswald Family Foundation
(formerly Oswald Charitable Foundation)
13875 Hwy. 13 S., Ste. 225
Savage, MN 55378-2297   (952) 475-6326
Contact: Susan Cornell Wilkes, Dir.
FAX: (952) 475-6327;
E-mail: scwilkes@adventuresingiving.com

Established in 1986 in MN.
Donor: Charles W. Oswald.
Grantmaker type: Independent foundation.
Financial data (yr. ended 12/31/10): Assets, $17,011,122 (M); expenditures, $804,161; qualifying distributions, $767,412; giving activities include $595,100 for 82 grants (high: $35,000; low: $1,000).

Purpose and activities: Giving primarily for the arts, education, children, youth and social services, international economic and community development, leadership, and social entrepreneurship.
Fields of interest: Arts; Education; Mental health/crisis services; Human services; Children/youth, services; International affairs; Community/economic development.
International interests: Africa; Bolivia; Kenya; Mexico; Peru; Tanzania, Zanzibar and Pemba; Uganda.
Type of support: General/operating support; Continuing support; Management development/capacity building; Program development; Seed money; Program-related investments/loans; Exchange programs; Matching/challenge support.
Limitations: Applications not accepted. Giving primarily in Minneapolis, MN, Troy, OH, Boston, MA, and San Diego, CA. No support for religious organizations. No grants to individuals.
Application information: Contributes only to pre-selected organizations, but will respond to inquiry by letter, telephone or e-mail.
Board meeting date(s): Nov.
Officers and Directors:* Julie Umbarger,* Pres.; David C. Oswald,* Treas.; Charles W. Oswald; Kathleen Oswald; Sara Oswald; Thomas Oswald; Carolyn Workman.
EIN: 363486546

1097
Piper Jaffray Companies Contributions Program
(formerly Piper Jaffray & Co. Contributions Program)
800 Nicollet Mall, Ste. 800
Minneapolis, MN 55402-7020   (612) 303-6000
E-mail: communityrelations@pjc.com.; URL: http://www.piperjaffray.com/2col_largeright.aspx?id=427

Grantmaker type: Corporate giving program.
Purpose and activities: As a complement to its foundation, Piper Jaffray also makes charitable contributions to nonprofit organizations directly. Support is limited to areas of company operations in Arizona, California, Colorado Connecticut, Florida, Iowa, Illinois, Indiana, Kansas, Massachusetts, Minnesota, Missouri, New York, North Carolina, Ohio, Oklahoma, Pennsylvania, Tennessee, Texas, Washington, Wisconsin, and in China, Switzerland, and the United Kingdom.
Fields of interest: Science; Engineering/technology; Mathematics; United Ways and Federated Giving Programs; Community/economic development; Community development, small businesses; Children, services; Economics; Health care; Environment; Education; Arts.
International interests: China; Switzerland; United Kingdom.
Type of support: General/operating support; Program development; Employee volunteer services; Sponsorships; Employee matching gifts.
Limitations: Applications accepted. Giving primarily in Support is limited to areas of company operations in AZ, CA, CO, CT, FL, IA, IL, IN, KS, MA, MN, MO, NC, NY, OH, OK, PA, TN, TX, WA, WI, and in China, Switzerland, and the United Kingdom. No support for lobbying, political, or fraternal organizations, United Way-supported organizations (primary funding), or religious organizations not of direct benefit to the entire community. No grants to individuals (except for employee-related scholarships), or for research, planning, personal needs, or travel, public service or

political campaigns, athletic or pageant scholarships, advertising, publications, or audio or video production.
Publications: Application guidelines.
Application information: Unsolicited requests for capital campaign support are not accepted. Unsolicited requests from health organizations are not accepted. Support for arts and culture organizations are limited to sponsorships. The Community Relations Department handles giving. The company has a staff that only handles contributions. A contributions committee reviews all requests.
Initial approach: Complete online inquiry form
Deadline(s): Jan. 1 to Mar. 15
Final notification: Following review

1098
The Irwin Andrew Porter Foundation
3325 W. 34 1/2 St.
Minneapolis, MN 55416-4652
URL: http://www.iapfoundation.org
Grants List: http://www.iapfoundation.org/?q=about/granthistory

Established in 1996 in MN.
Donor: Amy L. Hubbard.
Grantmaker type: Independent foundation.
Financial data (yr. ended 08/31/10): Assets, $2,900,225 (M); expenditures, $204,041; qualifying distributions, $183,961; giving activities include $183,961 for 24 grants (high: $25,000; low: $800).
Purpose and activities: The mission of the foundation is to fund innovative projects that foster connections between individuals, communities, the environment and the world at large.
Fields of interest: International economic development; YM/YWCAs & YM/YWHAs; Environment, water resources; Museums (art); Arts; Education; Environment; Health care; Human services.
Type of support: Matching/challenge support.
Limitations: Applications accepted. Giving primarily in the U.S., with focus on IA, IL, MI, MN, ND, SD, and WI; also giving on an international basis to projects located outside the U.S. unrestricted by country or region. No support for political organizations or religious programs. No grants to individuals, or for operating expenses, capital campaigns, or endowments.
Application information: Complete application guidelines available on foundation web site.
Copies of proposal: 1
Board meeting date(s): Quarterly
Officer and Directors:* Amy L. Hubbard,* Chair.; Arta Cheney; Scott Elkins; Jay Goldberg; Gloria Perez Jordan; Geoffrey Kehoe; Cari O'Brien.
EIN: 411852392

1099
Reell Precision Manufacturing Corporation Contributions Program
1259 Willow Lake Blvd.
St. Paul, MN 55110-5103   (651) 484-2447
FAX: (651) 484-3867; URL: http://www.reell.com/index.php?page=community-involvement

Grantmaker type: Corporate giving program.
Purpose and activities: Reell makes charitable contributions to nonprofit organizations involved

with arts and culture, education, the environment, wildlife, health, human services, community development, youth, disabled people, and religion. Support is given primarily in areas of company operations in Minnesota, and in China, the Netherlands, and Taiwan.

Fields of interest: Animals/wildlife, preservation/protection; Environment, natural resources; Community/economic development; Health care; Arts; Education; Environment; Human services; Religion; Disabilities, people with; Youth.

International interests: Taiwan; Netherlands; China.

Type of support: General/operating support; Employee volunteer services.

Limitations: Applications accepted. Giving primarily in areas of company operations in MN, and in China, the Netherlands, and Taiwan. No support for political organizations or candidates. No grants to individuals, or for start-up needs or capital campaigns; no loans; no multi-year grants.

Application information:
Initial approach: Contact headquarters for application information
Deadline(s): Sept. 1
Final notification: Oct. 31

1100
Robina Foundation

4900 IDS Ctr.
80 S. 8th St.
Minneapolis, MN 55402-2100
E-mail: info@robinafoundation.org; URL: http://www.robinafoundation.org

Established in 2004.
Donor: James H. Binger‡.
Grantmaker type: Independent foundation.
Financial data (yr. ended 12/31/10): Assets, $35,699,171 (M); expenditures, $8,497,494; qualifying distributions, $8,293,019; giving activities include $8,203,570 for 5 grants (high: $2,373,232; low: $1,000,000).

Purpose and activities: The foundation seeks to positively impact critical social issues by encouraging innovation and financially supporting transformative projects of its four industrial partners. These partners, selected by the foundation's founder, James H. Binger, are: Abbott Northwestern Hospital, Minneapolis, MN; The Council on Foreign Relations, New York, NY; University of Minnesota Law School, Minneapolis, MN; and Yale University, New Haven, CT.

Fields of interest: Animals/wildlife, preservation/protection; Education; Environment, natural resources; Hospitals (general).

Limitations: Applications not accepted. Giving primarily in MN; some giving nationally. No grants to individuals.

Application information: Contributes only to pre-selected organizations.
Board meeting date(s): 4 times per year

Officers and Directors:* Thomas Crosby,* Chair. and Treas.; Steven A. Schroeder,* M.D., Vice-Chair. and Secy.; Gordon M. Aamoth, M.D.; Kathleen Blatz; H. Peter Karoff.

Number of staff: 2 part-time professional.
EIN: 201163610

Recent grants for international programs:
1100-1 Council on Foreign Relations, New York, NY, $2,000,000. For International Institutions and Global Governance. 2010.

1100-2 Yale University, Law School, New Haven, CT, $1,000,000. For Human Rights Project. 2010.

1101
Sit Investment Associates Foundation

3300 IDS Ctr.
80 S. 8th St.
Minneapolis, MN 55402-2100
Contact: Debra Beaudet, Dir.

Established in 1984.
Donor: Sit Investment Associates, Inc.
Grantmaker type: Company-sponsored foundation.
Financial data (yr. ended 12/31/10): Assets, $24,066,231 (M); gifts received, $1,315,278; expenditures, $1,068,655; qualifying distributions, $1,029,350; giving activities include $1,029,350 for 108 grants (high: $100,000; low: $200).

Purpose and activities: The foundation supports organizations involved with arts and culture, education, hunger, housing, human services, international affairs, and military and veterans.

Fields of interest: Education; Arts, cultural/ethnic awareness; Museums; Performing arts, orchestras; Historic preservation/historical societies; Arts; Higher education; Food services; Food banks; Housing/shelter; Boy scouts; Salvation Army; Children/youth, services; Human services; International affairs; United Ways and Federated Giving Programs; Military/veterans' organizations.

Type of support: General/operating support.
Limitations: Applications not accepted. Giving primarily in MN, giving also to national organizations. No grants to individuals.

Application information: Contributes only to pre-selected organizations.
Officer and Director: Paul A. Rasmussen, Secy.; Debra A. Sit.
EIN: 411468021

1102
Sundance Pay It Forward Foundation

3109 W. 50th St.
P.O. Box 129
Minneapolis, MN 55410-2102
Contact: Mary Karen Lynn-Klimenko
E-mail: info@sundancefamilyfoundation.org;
URL: http://www.sundancefamilyfoundation.org/about-pay.html

Established in 2004 in MN.
Donors: Mark Sandercott; Nancy Jacobs.
Grantmaker type: Independent foundation.
Financial data (yr. ended 12/31/10): Assets, $54,978 (M); gifts received, $580,000; expenditures, $580,340; qualifying distributions, $580,339; giving activities include $488,000 for 50 grants (high: $50,000; low: $500).

Purpose and activities: Giving to support and strengthen family stability worldwide.

Fields of interest: Family services; Human services; International affairs.

Limitations: Applications accepted. Giving primarily in the Twin Cities area of MN.

Publications: Application guidelines; Grants list.
Application information: See foundation web site for application information and cover sheet. Application form required.
Initial approach: Proposal
Deadline(s): Refer to web site for current deadline

Officers and Trustees:* Nancy Jacobs,* Pres.; Mark Sandercott,* V.P.; Yvonne Barrett; H. Yvonne Cheek; Mark E. Hamel; John Savereide; Rob Scarlett; Segundo M. Velasquez.
EIN: 300276092

1103
Thomson Reuters Legal Corporate Giving Program

(formerly Thomson West Community Partnership Program)
c/o Community Rels.
610 Opperman Dr.
Eagan, MN 55123-1340 (651) 848-5926
Contact: Martha Field, Mgr., Community Rels.
E-mail: martha.field@thomsonreuters.com;
Additional application address: c/o West Group Community Partnership Prog., 50 E. Broad St., Rochester, NY 14694; URL: http://thomsonreuters.com/products_services/legal/corporate_responsibility/

Established in 1998.
Grantmaker type: Corporate giving program.
Purpose and activities: Thomson Reuters Legal makes charitable contributions to nonprofit organizations involved with educating the future workforce, strengthening youth and families, and advancing legal services. Support is given primarily in areas of company operations in California, Illinois, Maryland, Massachusetts, Minnesota, New Jersey, New Mexico, and New York, and in Argentina, Australia, Belgium, Brazil, Canada, France, Hong Kong, India, Ireland, Japan, Malaysia, the Netherlands, New Zealand, Singapore, Spain, Sweden, and the United Kingdom.

Fields of interest: Education; Community/economic development; Family services; Youth, services; Youth development; Employment, training; Legal services.

International interests: Argentina; Australia; Belgium; Brazil; Canada; France; Hong Kong; India; Ireland; Japan; Malaysia; Netherlands; New Zealand; Singapore; Spain; Sweden; United Kingdom.

Type of support: Program development; General/operating support; Employee volunteer services; Sponsorships; Pro bono services - legal.

Limitations: Applications accepted. Giving primarily in areas of company operations in CA, IL, MA, MD, MN, NJ, NM, and NY, and in Argentina, Australia, Belgium, Brazil, Canada, France, Hong Kong, India, Ireland, Japan, Malaysia, the Netherlands, New Zealand, Singapore, Spain, Sweden, and the United Kingdom.

Publications: Corporate giving report.
Application information: Application form required.
Initial approach: Download application form and mail to headquarters

1104
The Toro Foundation

8111 Lyndale Ave. S.
Bloomington, MN 55420-1196
Contact: Judson McNeil, Pres.
E-mail: community@thetorocompany.com;
URL: http://www.thetorocompany.com/community/foundation.html

Established in 1988 in MN.
Donor: The Toro Co.

Grantmaker type: Company-sponsored foundation.
Financial data (yr. ended 12/31/10): Assets, $3,494,094 (M); gifts received, $927,252; expenditures, $757,157; qualifying distributions, $732,718; giving activities include $730,242 for 214 grants (high: $369,892; low: $25).
Purpose and activities: The foundation supports organizations involved with arts and culture, education, the environment, health, human services, and civic affairs. Special emphasis is directed toward programs designed to promote turf maintenance, water management, and agronomy.
Fields of interest: Public affairs; Agriculture; Environment, land resources; Environment, water resources; Children/youth, services; Media/communications; Arts; Higher education; Education; Environment; Health care; Human services; United Ways and Federated Giving Programs.
International interests: Australia; Mexico.
Type of support: Scholarship funds; General/operating support; Continuing support; Annual campaigns; Program development; Fellowships; Employee volunteer services; Sponsorships; Employee matching gifts; Employee-related scholarships; In-kind gifts; Matching/challenge support.
Limitations: Applications accepted. Giving primarily in areas of company operations in El Cajon and Riverside, CA, Minneapolis and Windom, MN, Beatrice, NE, El Paso, TX, Tomah and western WI, and in Australia and Mexico. No support for political or religious organizations. No grants for capital campaigns.
Publications: Application guidelines; Corporate giving report.
Application information: Requests may be submitted using the Minnesota Common Grant Application Form. Support is limited to 1 contribution per organization during any given year. Multi-year funding is not automatic. Telephone calls during the application process are not encouraged. Application form required.
  Initial approach: Contact foundation via mail for application form
  Board meeting date(s): Quarterly
  Final notification: 3 months
Officers and Directors:* Judson McNeil,* Pres.; Nancy McGrath, Secy.; Blake M. Grams,* Treas.; Timothy P. Dordell; Michael D. Drazen; Michael J. Hoffman; Peter M. Ramstad; Kurt Svendsen; Stephen P. Wolfe.
Number of staff: 1 part-time professional; 1 full-time support; 1 part-time support.
EIN: 363593618

1105
United Jewish Fund and Council

(also known as The United Jewish Fund and Council of St. Paul)
790 Cleveland Ave., Ste. 227
St. Paul, MN 55116-3859 (651) 690-1707
Contact: Eli Skora, Exec. Dir.
FAX: (651) 690-0228; URL: http://www.jewishminnesota.org

Established in MN.
Grantmaker type: Public charity.
Financial data (yr. ended 04/30/10): Revenue, $3,206,238; assets, $12,725,473 (M); gifts received, $3,128,320; expenditures, $3,927,510; giving activities include $2,753,886 for grants, and $24,497 for grants to individuals.

Purpose and activities: The organization's mission is to unite, sustain and enhance the St. Paul area Jewish community and strengthen bonds with Jewish communities in Israel and around the world.
Fields of interest: United Ways and Federated Giving Programs; Education, alliance/advocacy; Higher education, university; Scholarships/financial aid; Youth development, alliance/advocacy; Youth development, religion; Youth development; Human services; Human services; International affairs, alliance/advocacy; International exchange, students; Urban/community development; Economic development, visitors/convention bureau/tourism promotion; Community/economic development; Financial services; Religion, alliance/advocacy; Jewish agencies & synagogues; Religion.
Type of support: General/operating support; Continuing support; Consulting services; Scholarships—to individuals; Exchange programs; Matching/challenge support.
Limitations: Applications accepted. Giving primarily in MN.
Publications: Application guidelines; Annual report; Informational brochure; Newsletter.
Application information: Application form required.
  Initial approach: Download application forms
  Deadline(s): Feb. 11 for The E. David Fischman Scholarship; Apr. 1 for The Jewish Camp Scholarships; Apr. 15 for Higher Education Scholarships, The Milton P. and Irma C. Firestone Fund for Jewish Communal Service, and The Edward Hoffman Scholarship Fund
  Final notification: Apr. 15 for The E. David Fischman Scholarship
Officers and Directors:* Jules Goldstein,* Pres.; Jonathan Parritz,* V.P.; Ed Paster,* V.P.; Karen Gordon,* Secy.; Michael Saxon,* Treas.; Eli Skora, Exec. Dir.; Semyon Axelrod; Steve Baldinger; Wendy Baldinger; Sharon Benmaman; Steve Brand; Charles Fodor; Neal Foman; John Garon; Loren Geller; and 35 additional directors.
EIN: 410693887

1106
WEM Foundation

P.O. Box 5628
Minneapolis, MN 55440-9300
Contact: Robert J. Theiler, Secy.-Treas.

Established in 1988 in MN.
Donors: Whitney MacMillan, Jr.; W. MacMillan 1989 Trust; W. MacMillan, Jr. 2003 Charitable Annuity Trust; W. MacMillan, Jr. 2005 Charitable Annuity Trust; W. MacMillan, Jr. Family '74 Trust; W. MacMillan, Jr. Charitable Annuity Trust.
Grantmaker type: Independent foundation.
Financial data (yr. ended 12/31/09): Assets, $237,575,142 (M); gifts received, $11,264,415; expenditures, $8,834,071; qualifying distributions, $8,690,716; giving activities include $8,690,716 for 115 grants (high: $4,000,000; low: $100).
Purpose and activities: Giving primarily for arts and cultural programs, education, health care and international affairs.
Fields of interest: Museums; Arts; Education; Hospitals (general); Health care; International affairs, public policy.
Limitations: Applications not accepted. Giving primarily in FL and MN. No grants to individuals.
Application information: Contributes only to pre-selected organizations.
Officers and Directors:* Elizabeth S. MacMillan,* Chair.; Whitney MacMillan,* Vice-Chair.; Robert J.

Theiler,* Secy.-Treas.; James Hield; Whitney MacMillan, Jr.; Harriet S. Norgren.
EIN: 411604640
Recent grants for international programs:
1106-1 Diocesan School for Girls, Grahamstown, South Africa, $25,000. For Bruce Probyn Scholarship. 2009.
1106-2 EastWest Institute, New York, NY, $10,000. 2009.
1106-3 International Peace Institute, New York, NY, $15,000. 2009.
1106-4 International Policy Network, London, England, $10,000. 2009.
1106-5 Kingswood College, Grahamstown, South Africa, $25,000. For Bandey Scholarship. 2009.
1106-6 Saint Andrews College, Grahamstown, South Africa, $25,000. For David Wylde Scholarship. 2009.
1106-7 Wallace Collection, London, England, $40,000. 2009.
1106-8 Wild Salmon Center, Portland, OR, $25,000. For Kamchatka Sustainable Fisheries Foundation. 2009.
1106-9 Yale University, Whitney and Betty MacMillan Center for International and Area Studies, New Haven, CT, $4,000,000. 2009.

1107
Weyerhaeuser Family Foundation

(formerly Weyerhaeuser Foundation)
2000 Wells Fargo Pl.
30 E. 7th St.
St. Paul, MN 55101-2201 (651) 215-4408
Contact: Peter Konrad, Prog. Consultant; Gayle Roth, Grants Admin.
E-mail: gmr@fidcouns.com; URL: http://www.wfamilyfoundation.org

Incorporated in 1950 in MN.
Donors: Bette D. Moorman; Stanley R. Day, Jr.; Dana L. Day; George H. Weyerhaeuser; Mrs. George H. Weyerhauser; Lucy R. Jones; Jane Weyerhaeuser-Johnson; Hayley M. Reiter; Kyle W. Reiter; Leilee Weyerhaeuser; Elizabeth Bentinck-Smith; Cody N. Reiter; Carol R. Caruthers; Cherbec Advancement Foundation.
Grantmaker type: Independent foundation.
Financial data (yr. ended 12/31/10): Assets, $21,222,931 (M); gifts received, $210,813; expenditures, $898,777; qualifying distributions, $840,288; giving activities include $657,254 for 27 grants (high: $30,000; low: $9,300).
Purpose and activities: Giving primarily for 1) The Arts: occasional funding to national or international programs in the arts if the project relates to other areas of foundation interest, such as environmental or international areas. Projects that promote cultural exchanges and national and international peace and harmony are of particular interest; 2) Education: multi-site, national or international projects that address needs of at-risk youth; 3) Environment, Conservation and Preservation: multi-site, national or international projects that preserve and protect the environment, promise better utilization of scarce resources and forestry projects. Multi-site, national and international educational projects will also be considered; 4) Health: multi-site, national or international projects dealing with mental health, chemical dependency and population and family planning. Multi-site, national and international educational projects will also be considered; 5) International projects that promote peace and enable people to help themselves through

population planning, agricultural improvements and enterprise development leading to economic self-sufficiency. Educational projects will also be considered; 6) a Children's Initiative to create and promote stability and resiliency for children who have been exposed to domestic violence, and 7) a Sustainable Forest and Communities Initiative that promotes the creation of environmentally and economically sustainable forest communities in the regions in the U.S., where the Weyerhaeuser Family's business interests originated.

Fields of interest: Arts; Environment, natural resources; Environment; Health care; Mental health, treatment; Children, services; International development; International peace/security.

Type of support: Program development; Seed money.

Limitations: Giving for international programs only through U.S.-based organizations. No support for elementary or secondary education, or for books or media projects, unless the project is connected to other areas of foundation interest. No grants to individuals, or for building or endowment funds, annual campaigns, operating budgets, equipment, land acquisitions or trades, research, scholarships, fellowships, travel, or matching gifts; no loans.

Publications: Application guidelines; Annual report (including application guidelines); Grants list.

Application information: Application guidelines for the foundation's General Program, Children's Initiative and Sustainable Forest and Communities Initiative available on web site. Application form required.

Initial approach: Letter of intent (no more than 2 pages) with 1 page budget summary and a coversheet which is to be printed from foundation web site

Copies of proposal: 1

Deadline(s): Submit proposal from Jan. through Apr.; deadline Apr. 1

Board meeting date(s): Program committee meets annually in early summer to review proposals; board usually meets in June and Nov.

Final notification: Notification on Letters of Intent after summer meeting. Notification on proposals in Nov.

Officers and Trustees:* Frederick W. Titcomb,* Pres.; John B. Driscoll,* V.P.; Blaine Gaustad, Secy.; Peter E. Heymann,* Treas.; John L. Davis; Melissa M. Davis; Lucie C. Greer; Anne W. Henderson; Samuel C. Jewett; Amy W. Stried; Daniel L. Titcomb; John W. Titcomb, Jr.; Rohre W.B. Titcomb; W. Drew Weyerhaeuser.

Number of staff: 1 part-time professional.
EIN: 416012062

1108
Winds of Peace Foundation
(formerly Children's Haven, Inc.)
203 S. 6th St.
Kenyon, MN 55946-1036
Contact: Stephen C. Sheppard, C.E.O.
E-mail: peacewinds@peacewinds.org; URL: http://www.peacewinds.org
Blog: http://peacewinds.org/blog

Established in 1978.
Donors: Foldcraft, Inc.; Harold Nielsen; Harlo Investments, Inc.
Grantmaker type: Independent foundation.
Financial data (yr. ended 12/31/10): Assets, $19,259,335 (M); gifts received, $595; expenditures, $870,182; qualifying distributions,

$1,640,914; giving activities include $311,153 for 23 grants (high: $22,910; low: $4,624).

Purpose and activities: The mission of the foundation is to contribute to global peace by promoting economic, social, and environmentally just relations.

Fields of interest: International economic development; International relief; International peace/security; International human rights; Civil/human rights; Economics; Women; Indigenous peoples; Economically disadvantaged.

International interests: Nicaragua.

Type of support: General/operating support; Capital campaigns; Program development; Conferences/seminars; Seed money; Research; Technical assistance; Program evaluation; Program-related investments/loans; Matching/challenge support.

Limitations: Applications not accepted. Giving primarily on an international basis, with an emphasis on Nicaragua. No support for children's organizations, religious organizations, and political groups. No grants to individuals.

Application information: Contributes only to pre-selected organizations.

Board meeting date(s): Mar. and Sept.

Officer and Directors:* Stephen C. Sheppard,* C.E.O.; Annette Bjork; Silvia Conger; Donald J. Fleugel; John T. Kisch; Mark Lester; Harold Nielsen; Louise V. Nielsen.

Number of staff: 1 full-time professional; 1 part-time professional; 1 full-time support.
EIN: 411343012

1109
World-India Diabetes Foundation (USA)
5-194 Joseph, 200 1st St. S.W.
Rochester, MN 55905-0001
E-mail: widfusa@yahoo.com; URL: http://widf.org

Established in 1999.
Grantmaker type: Public charity.
Financial data (yr. ended 12/31/09): Revenue, $818; assets, $18,750 (M); gifts received, $810; expenditures, $5,205.

Purpose and activities: The foundation operates exclusively for charitable, scientific research and educational purposes relating to diabetes mellitus and to educate individuals on the findings with regard to diabetes among people of Indian origin.

Fields of interest: Diabetes research; Diabetes.
International interests: India.
Type of support: Research.
Limitations: Giving on a national and international basis.
Publications: Financial statement.
Officers and Directors:* Sreekumaran Nair,* M.D., Ph.D., Chair.; Prem K. Menon, M.D., Vice-Chair.; Raja Puthoor, M.S., MBA, Secy.; Robert Rizza, M.D., Treas.; Bhishma Agnihota, J.D.; N.R.S. Babu; Reita Powell, M.D.; Madhavan V. Pillai, M.D.; C.S. Pitchumoni, M.D.; Dilip Vellodi; and 8 additional directors.
EIN: 411955380

1110
Youth Hope Foundation
c/o Gray Plant Mooty
500 IDS Ctr.
80 S. 8th St.
Minneapolis, MN 55402-2100

Donors: John Candela; Youth Hope Enterprises, LLC.
Grantmaker type: Independent foundation.
Financial data (yr. ended 12/31/10): Assets, $26,845 (M); gifts received, $692,600; expenditures, $692,305; qualifying distributions, $615,175; giving activities include $615,175 for grants.
Fields of interest: Education; Children, services; International relief; Children; Youth.
Limitations: Applications not accepted. Giving primarily in CO, DC, NY, and WA.
Application information: Contributes only to pre-selected organizations.
Trustees: John Candela; Douglas M. Cravens; Frank Minton; Gary R. Yakes.
EIN: 611509889

MISSISSIPPI

1111
The Lingle Foundation
P.O. Box 1928
Jackson, MS 39215-1928

Established in 2006 in MS.
Donor: Richard M. Lingle.
Grantmaker type: Independent foundation.
Financial data (yr. ended 12/31/10): Assets, $177,926 (M); expenditures, $272,235; qualifying distributions, $264,850; giving activities include $264,850 for 7 grants (high: $250,000; low: $2,475).
Fields of interest: International relief; Protestant agencies & churches.
Limitations: Applications not accepted. Giving primarily in MS. No grants to individuals.
Application information: Contributes only to pre-selected organizations.
Trustees: Richard M. Lingle; Joseph E. Varner III.
EIN: 207159856

1112
Oakwood Foundation Charitable Trust
P.O. Box 4200
Tupelo, MS 38803-4200

Established in 1995 in MS.
Donors: Elizabeth Renee Grisham; John R. Grisham, Jr.; Bennington Press, LLC; Belfry Holdings, Inc.
Grantmaker type: Independent foundation.
Financial data (yr. ended 12/31/10): Assets, $5,388,529 (M); gifts received, $5,100,000; expenditures, $2,541,475; qualifying distributions, $2,536,250; giving activities include $2,536,250 for 65 grants (high: $600,000; low: $500).
Purpose and activities: Giving primarily for Baptist organizations, private foundations and a hospital.
Fields of interest: Hospitals (general); Education; Health care; Housing/shelter, development; Human services; Foundations (private grantmaking); Christian agencies & churches.
Limitations: Applications not accepted. Giving primarily in MS, NJ, and VA.
Application information: Unsolicited requests for funds not accepted.

Officer: Robert E. McDade, Fin. Mgr.
Trustees: Elizabeth Renee Grisham; John R. Grisham.
EIN: 640858879
Recent grants for international programs:
1112-1 Maasai Foundation of East Africa, Santa Barbara, CA, $50,000. 2008.
1112-2 Mission Aviation Fellowship, Nampa, ID, $10,000. 2008.

MISSOURI

1113
A Call to Serve International, Inc.
c/o POC
601 Business Loop 70W
Columbia, MO 65203-2578
URL: http://www.acalltoserve.org

Grantmaker type: Public charity.
Financial data (yr. ended 12/31/10): Revenue, $7,888,812; assets, $28,266 (M); gifts received, $7,888,812; expenditures, $7,921,999; giving activities include $14,450 for grants, and $7,519,788 for grants to organizations outside the U.S.
Purpose and activities: The organization provides donated and purchased medicines, medical supplies, equipment, services, scholarships, and stipends for Georgian medical students to study in the U.S., as well as educational materials, books, and food to Georgia.
Fields of interest: Medical school/education; Scholarships/financial aid; Health care.
International interests: Georgia (Republic of).
Type of support: Scholarships—to individuals.
Limitations: Giving limited to Georgia.
Officers and Directors:* Patricia Blair,* M.D., Pres.; Elizabeth James,* V.P.; Marilyn Sanford,* Secy.; Giorgi Tsilosani,* Treas.; Ted Groshong; Dolores Shearon.
EIN: 954365541

1114
The ASC Foundation
4233 Sulphur Ave.
St. Louis, MO 63109-1517 (314) 351-6294
FAX: (314) 351-6789;
E-mail: ascfoundation@adorers.org; URL: http://www.adorers.org/ascfoundation.html

Established in 2003.
Grantmaker type: Public charity.
Purpose and activities: The foundation provides assistance to promote justice and the principles and practice of social change, striving towards establishing "that beautiful order of things." The foundation is a ministry of the Adorers of the Blood of Christ (ASC), supporting projects within the United States and ASC-affiliated international projects. Grantmaking is focused on four thematic areas: 1) Giving Voice to Those in Need; 2) Reconciliation and Peace; 3) Liberation; and 4) Earth's Resources.
Fields of interest: Environment, natural resources; Human services; International peace/security;

International human rights; Welfare policy/reform; Public affairs; Economically disadvantaged.
International interests: Guatemala; Bolivia.
Type of support: General/operating support; Program development.
Limitations: Applications not accepted. Giving on a worldwide basis, with a special international focus on ASC-affiliated projects in Bolivia, Guatemala, and Korea and other areas of the world where ASCs minister. No support for organizations lacking 501 (c)(3) status, organizations that are the local affiliate of a national disease-specific organization, international projects that are not ASC-affiliated, or hospitals, healthcare systems, or entities sponsored by a healthcare system. No grants to individuals, or for capital expenditures, endowments or development campaigns, conferences, scholarships or tuition, reduction of debt, or operational emergency funds; no loans.
Application information: The organization has currently suspended its grantmaking program. See web site for further information.
Officers and Board Members:* Mary Herman,* Chair.; Mary Louise Degenhart,* Vice-Chair.; Joseph Shaughnessy,* Treas.; Ann Haubrich, Exec. Dir.; Carol Ablah; Barbara Jean Franklin; Kevin Kraft, Sr.; Tarcisia Roths.
EIN: 470931245

1115
BFP International, Inc.
(also known as Bridges for Peace International, Inc.)
1325 W. Sunshine
Springfield, MO 65807-2344
URL: http://www.bridgesforpeace.com/

Established in 2002 in OK.
Grantmaker type: Public charity.
Financial data (yr. ended 12/31/10): Revenue, $6,458,184; assets, $1,465,083 (M); gifts received, $6,442,816; expenditures, $6,364,538; giving activities include $5,249,431 for 1 grant to an organization outside the U.S., and $618,127 for grants to individuals outside the U.S.
Purpose and activities: The organization works to build relationships among people of different faiths through education and practical deeds.
Fields of interest: International affairs; Jewish agencies & synagogues; Christian agencies & churches; Religion.
Limitations: Giving limited to Israel.
Publications: Newsletter.
Officers: Jess Gibson, Chair.; Rebecca Brimmer, Pres. and C.E.O.; James Solberg, Secy.; Peter Robertson, Treas.
EIN: 753077433

1116
Ephraim Block Family Charitable Trust
(formerly Ephraim Block Family Foundation)
P.O. Box 387
St. Louis, MO 63166-0387 (314) 505-8203
Contact: Angela Pearson

Established in 1987 in MO.
Grantmaker type: Independent foundation.
Financial data (yr. ended 06/30/11): Assets, $4,216,588 (M); expenditures, $244,507; qualifying distributions, $175,000; giving activities include $175,000 for grants.

Purpose and activities: Support for organizations providing aid to indigent Jewish people.
Fields of interest: International development; Human services; Jewish federated giving programs.
International interests: Israel.
Application information: Application form required.
Initial approach: Letter
Deadline(s): None
Trustees: Sarah Rosenburg; U.S. Bank, N.A.
EIN: 436331011

1117
The Milford and Lee Bohm Charitable Foundation
11502 New London Dr.
St. Louis, MO 63141-8345
Contact: Leona Lee Bohm, Pres.; Robert Bohm

Established in 1989 in MO.
Donors: Milford Bohm†; Leona Bohm.
Grantmaker type: Independent foundation.
Financial data (yr. ended 12/31/10): Assets, $5,902,304 (M); expenditures, $341,988; qualifying distributions, $323,875; giving activities include $323,875 for 99 grants (high: $50,000; low: $50).
Purpose and activities: Giving primarily to Jewish organizations, including welfare funds; support also for an affiliated fund for the elderly, a community fund, cultural organizations, the United Way, scholarship funds, and art and education funds.
Fields of interest: Performing arts, dance; Performing arts, theater; Performing arts, orchestras; Higher education; Environment; Hospitals (general); Human services; Aging, centers/services; United Ways and Federated Giving Programs; Jewish federated giving programs; Jewish agencies & synagogues; Girls; Disabilities, people with; Children; Youth; Aging; Indigenous peoples; AIDS, people with; Economically disadvantaged.
International interests: Israel.
Type of support: General/operating support; Continuing support; Annual campaigns; Capital campaigns; Building/renovation; Endowments; Emergency funds; Professorships; Fellowships; Internship funds; Scholarship funds; Research; Exchange programs.
Limitations: Applications not accepted. Giving primarily in St. Louis, MO. No support for political or lobbying organizations. No grants to individuals, other than for scholarships.
Publications: Financial statement.
Application information: Unsolicited requests for funds not accepted.
Officer and Trustees:* Leona Lee Bohm,* Pres.; David Bohm; Robert Bohm; Miriam Margulies.
Number of staff: None.
EIN: 436355629

1118
Build-A-Bear Workshop Bear Hugs Foundation
1954 Innerbelt Business Center Dr.
St. Louis, MO 63114-5760 (314) 423-8000
E-mail: giving@buildabear.com; Application address for Bearemy's Kennel Pals Prog.: Pet Prog. Grants, 1954 Innerbelt Business Center Dr., St. Louis, MO 63114-5760; URL: http://www.buildabear.com/shopping/contents/content.jsp?catId=400002&id=700013

Established in 2006 in MO.
Donor: Build-A-Bear Workshop, Inc.
Grantmaker type: Company-sponsored foundation.
Financial data (yr. ended 12/31/10): Assets, $771,256 (M); gifts received, $443,551; expenditures, $584,151; qualifying distributions, $545,858; giving activities include $545,858 for grants.
Purpose and activities: The foundation supports organizations involved with education, animals, children's health and wellness, childhood disease medical research, child safety, and children.
Fields of interest: Animals/wildlife, special services; Education, early childhood education; Education, special; Education, reading; Education; Animals/wildlife, public education; Animal welfare; Animals/wildlife; Health care; Pediatrics research; Medical research; Safety, education; Children, services; Children.
International interests: Canada.
Type of support: General/operating support; Program development; Research; Matching/challenge support.
Limitations: Applications accepted. Giving on a national basis primarily in areas of company operations in CA, CO, KY, MN, MO, NJ, PA, and WI, and in Canada. No support for private foundations, or for religious organizations not of direct benefit to the entire community, or political organizations. No grants for annual campaigns, capital campaigns, construction or "new facility" expense, fundraising or events, or political activities; generally, no grants to individuals.
Publications: Application guidelines; Grants list; IRS Form 990 or 990-PF printed copy available upon request.
Application information: Additional information may be requested at a later date. Support is limited to 1contribution per organization during any given year. Organizations receiving support may be asked to provide a final report. Application form required.
  Initial approach: Complete online application form for Children's Health and Wellness, Domestic Pets, and Literacy and Education Grants
  Copies of proposal: 1
  Deadline(s): Mar.1 to Oct. 28 for Children's Health and Wellness, Domestic Pets, and Literacy and Education Grants
  Final notification: 4 to 6 months
Officers and Director: Dorrie Krueger, Pres.; Jill Saunders, V.P.; Teresa Kroll, Secy.; Jeff Fullmer, Treas.; Maxine Clark, Dir. Emeritus.
EIN: 204961009

1119
Children International
2000 E. Red Bridge Rd.
P.O. Box 219055
Kansas City, MO 64131-3610
E-mail: children@children.org; Toll-free tel.: (800) 888-3089; URL: http://www.children.org
Facebook: http://www.facebook.com/children.international
Twitter: http://twitter.com/Children_Intl

Established in 1936.
Grantmaker type: Public charity.
Financial data (yr. ended 09/30/10): Revenue, $147,801,897; assets, $62,295,256 (M); gifts received, $147,294,643; expenditures, $146,687,857; giving activities include $1,424,415 for grants, and $103,051,993 for grants to organizations outside the U.S.

Purpose and activities: The organization works to help children living in dire poverty.
Fields of interest: International relief; Children; Economically disadvantaged.
Type of support: In-kind gifts.
Limitations: Giving primarily in the U.S., Africa, Asia, Central America, and South America.
Publications: Annual report.
Officers and Directors:* James R. Cook,* Pres. and C.E.O.; David Houchen, Sr. V.P. and C.F.O.; Brian Anderson, V.P., Devel. and Mktg.; Jim Cameron, V.P., Inf. Tech.; Eric McCullough, V.P., Human Resources; Pat McDonnell, V.P., Project Mgmt.; Lisa Thome-Ha, V.P., Sponsorship Svcs.; Andrea Waters, V.P., Creative and Production Svcs.; Vickie Wiedenmann, Secy.; Mark Garrett,* Treas.; Joan Horan; Larry Lee; Charles Maahs.
EIN: 446005794

1120
Clarkson Eyecare Foundation
217 Clarkson Rd.
Ellisville, MO 63011-2219   (636) 227-2600
FAX: (636) 200-4020;
E-mail: tpeel@clarksoneyecare.com; URL: http://www.theclarksoneyecarefoundation.org

Established in 2004 in MO.
Donor: Entergy Arkansas, Inc.
Grantmaker type: Public charity.
Financial data (yr. ended 12/31/10): Revenue, $244,972; assets, $212,437 (M); gifts received, $227,454; expenditures, $227,827; giving activities include $1,500 for grants.
Purpose and activities: The foundation is dedicated to enhancing the quality of life by providing vision improvement and access to a brighter future, including funding Lasik surgery for individuals who are physically challenged and have difficulty wearing eyeglasses and/or contacts.
Fields of interest: Blind/visually impaired.
International interests: Dominican Republic; Vietnam.
Type of support: Annual campaigns; Equipment.
Limitations: Applications accepted. Giving primarily in MO.
Publications: Application guidelines; Occasional report.
Application information: Application form required.
  Initial approach: Letter
  Copies of proposal: 1
  Deadline(s): None
  Board meeting date(s): Quarterly
  Final notification: 1 week
Officers and Directors:* Craig Dorion,* Pres.; Eric Messmer,* Treas.; Dr. Henry Allhoff; Dr. Kathleen Doan; Craig Dorion; Mathew Iovaldi; Dr. Stephen Menzel; Dan Rosen; Dr. James Wachter.
Number of staff: 1 part-time professional.
EIN: 200265693

1121
Enterprise Holdings Foundation
(formerly Enterprise Rent-A-Car Foundation)
600 Corporate Park Dr.
St. Louis, MO 63105-4204   (314) 512-5000
Contact: Jo Ann Taylor Kindle, Pres.
FAX: (314) 512-4754; E-mail: foundation@ehi.com; URL: http://www.enterpriseholdings.com/sustainability/enterprise-holdings-foundation/

Established in 1982 in MO.
Donors: Enterprise Rent-A-Car Co.; Jack C. Taylor.
Grantmaker type: Company-sponsored foundation.
Financial data (yr. ended 07/31/10): Assets, $108,662,616 (M); gifts received, $10,705,426; expenditures, $9,586,513; qualifying distributions, $9,503,731; giving activities include $9,503,731 for 1,877 grants (high: $1,000,000; low: $500).
Purpose and activities: The foundation supports organizations with which employees, family members of employees, and established customers of Enterprise Rent-A-Car are involved and organizations involved with education, reforestation, disaster relief, minorities, and economically disadvantaged people.
Fields of interest: Higher education; Environment, land resources; Environment, forests; Employment, training; Disasters, preparedness/services; General charitable giving; Minorities; Economically disadvantaged.
International interests: Canada; United Kingdom.
Type of support: General/operating support; Capital campaigns; Building/renovation; Equipment; Emergency funds; Program development; Scholarship funds; Research.
Limitations: Applications accepted. Giving on a national basis in areas of company operations, with emphasis on CA, MO, NE, TX, Canada, and the United Kingdom. No support for religious, political, or labor organizations or sports teams. No grants to individuals, or for ongoing operating support, salary costs, debt reduction, sponsorships, tuition, fees, memberships, dues, tickets, subscriptions, telethons, or beauty pageants; no vehicle or rental donations.
Publications: Application guidelines.
Application information: Support is limited to 1 contribution per organization during any given year. Unsolicited requests are accepted from employees and their spouses, and established customers of Enterprise Rent-A-Car on behalf of nonprofit organizations with which there is an established connection. Unsolicited requests on behalf of schools are not accepted. Annual reports, videos, DVD's, CD's and other extraneous materials are not encouraged. Application form not required.
  Initial approach: Complete online application for customers/employees
  Copies of proposal: 1
  Deadline(s): Apr. 1, Aug. 1, and Dec. 1
  Board meeting date(s): Jan.27, May. 12, and Oct. 20
  Final notification: 3 to 4 weeks following board meetings
Officers and Directors:* Jack C. Taylor,* Chair.; Jo Ann Taylor Kindle,* Pres.; Pamela M. Nicholson,* V.P. and Secy.; Rick A. Short,* V.P. and Treas.
EIN: 431262762
Recent grants for international programs:
1121-1 American Red Cross National Headquarters, Washington, DC, $100,000. For Disaster Relief, Haiti Earthquake Relief Fund. 2010.
1121-2 Saint Louis Art Museum, Saint Louis, MO, $25,000. For Five Centuries of Japanese Screens Masterpieces from the Saint Louis Art Museum and the Art Institute of Chicago. 2010.

1122
Fox Family Foundation
7701 Forsyth Blvd., Ste. 600
St. Louis, MO 63105-1875   (314) 889-0890
Contact: Cheri Fox, Exec. Dir.
FAX: (314) 727-7314; E-mail: fff@harbourgroup.com

Established in 1986 in MO.
Donors: Marilyn Fox; Sam Fox.
Grantmaker type: Independent foundation.
Financial data (yr. ended 12/31/10): Assets, $29,101,439 (M); expenditures, $1,926,193; qualifying distributions, $1,687,241; giving activities include $1,556,320 for 252 grants (high: $300,000; low: $100).
Purpose and activities: Giving primarily for projects which meet basic human needs, including food, shelter, basic adult education, job training, early childhood education for the poor, and independence for those dependent on others. In Israel, the foundation supports projects which address the issues of environmental protection, violence in Israeli society, and the full integration of the Ethiopian community.
Fields of interest: Arts; Education, early childhood education; Adult education—literacy, basic skills & GED; Employment, training; Housing/shelter; Human services; Jewish agencies & synagogues; Economically disadvantaged; Homeless.
International interests: Israel.
Type of support: Program development; Seed money; Matching/challenge support.
Limitations: Applications accepted. Giving primarily in St. Louis, MO. No grants to individuals, or for annual campaigns, endowment funds, deficit financing, or operating expenses.
Publications: Application guidelines.
Application information: Application form required.
   Initial approach: Letter requesting application form
   Copies of proposal: 2
   Deadline(s): Contact foundation for annual deadlines
   Board meeting date(s): Biannually
   Final notification: 3 months for preliminary applications; 6 months for formal applications if accepted for review
Officers and Directors: Sam Fox,* Chair.; Marilyn Fox,* Vice-Chair.; Cheri Fox, Exec. Dir.; Gregory Fox; Jeffrey Fox; Steven Fox; Pamela Fox-Claman.
Number of staff: 1 full-time professional; 1 part-time support.
EIN: 431456258

1123
The Ryan Howard Family Foundation
16543 Clayton Rd.
Wildwood, MO   63011-1720

Established in 2007 in MO.
Donors: RJH Enterprises; Casey Close; Boulevard Customs; Palm; Philadelphia Phillies; Subway; PowerAde; Synergy, LLC.
Grantmaker type: Independent foundation.
Financial data (yr. ended 12/31/10): Assets, $277,520 (M); gifts received, $232,555; expenditures, $180,700; qualifying distributions, $145,000; giving activities include $145,000 for 5 grants (high: $50,000; low: $5,000).
Fields of interest: Environment, land resources; Recreation, parks/playgrounds; International development.
Limitations: Applications not accepted. Giving primarily in MO and PA.
Application information: Unsolicited requests for funds not accepted.
Officers: Ron Howard, Chair.; Ryan James Howard, Pres.; Cheryl Howard, Secy.
EIN: 261228464

1124
Lubin-Green Foundation
12 Millstone Campus
St. Louis, MO   63146-5776   (314) 432-0020
Contact: Karole Green, Pres.; Susan Witte, Admin.

Supporting organization of the Jewish Federation of St. Louis.
Grantmaker type: Public charity.
Financial data (yr. ended 12/31/10): Revenue, $347,304; assets, $8,993,503 (M); expenditures, $425,613; giving activities include $354,696 for grants.
Purpose and activities: As a supporting foundation, the overall purpose of the Lubin-Green Foundation is to provide grants that are consistent with the broad mission of the Jewish Federation of St. Louis. The foundation's principal areas of funding are prioritized in the following order: 1) projects and programs of the Jewish Federation of St. Louis and/or its constituent and beneficiary agencies in their service to the Jewish community and the entire St. Louis community; 2) projects and programs of other Jewish agencies and organizations strategically allied with the mission of the Jewish Federation of St. Louis; and 3) projects and programs of any organizations with missions that are consistent with the broad mission of the Jewish Federation of St. Louis to build and serve the Jewish community locally, nationally, and internationally, and to serve the St. Louis community in general.
Fields of interest: Residential/custodial care, senior continuing care; Jewish federated giving programs; Children.
International interests: Israel.
Type of support: Continuing support; Emergency funds; Program development; Seed money; Matching/challenge support.
Limitations: Applications accepted. Giving primarily in St. Louis, MO.
Application information: Application form not required.
   Initial approach: Letter of inquiry
   Board meeting date(s): 3 to 4 times per year
Officers: Karole Green, Pres.; Thomas R. Green, V.P.; Linda Renner, V.P.; Barry Rosenberg, V.P.; Morris Sterneck, V.P.; Michael Newmark, Secy.; Katherine Weber, Treas.
Number of staff: 1 part-time professional.
EIN: 436049332

1125
Maor Foundation
7701 Forsyth Blvd., Ste. 600
Clayton, MO   63105-1875

Established in 2004 in MO.
Donors: Sam Fox; Cheryl Ann Fox.
Grantmaker type: Independent foundation.
Financial data (yr. ended 12/31/10): Assets, $8,118,353 (M); gifts received, $4,875,000; expenditures, $235,648; qualifying distributions, $234,000; giving activities include $234,000 for 11 grants (high: $90,000; low: $500).
Fields of interest: Jewish federated giving programs; Medical school/education; International affairs, public policy; Jewish agencies & synagogues.
International interests: Israel.
Limitations: Applications not accepted. Giving primarily in CA, Washington, DC, IL, and NY. No grants to individuals.
Application information: Contributes only to pre-selected organizations.

Trustees: Cheryl Ann Fox; Hayim Goldgraber.
EIN: 421645906

1126
James S. McDonnell Foundation
(also known as JSMF)
1034 S. Brentwood Blvd., Ste. 1850
St. Louis, MO   63117-1229
Contact: Susan M. Fitzpatrick, V.P.
FAX: (314) 721-7421; E-mail: info@jsmf.org;
URL: http://www.jsmf.org
E-Newsletter: http://www.jsmf.org/about/mailinglist.htm
Grants Database: http://www.jsmf.org/grants/search.php

Established in MO.
Grantmaker type: Independent foundation.
Financial data (yr. ended 12/31/10): Assets, $464,440,606 (M); expenditures, $27,042,224; qualifying distributions, $27,042,224; giving activities include $25,881,175 for 110 grants (high: $2,054,931; low: $50,000).
Purpose and activities: The 21st Century Science Initiative, the foundation's revised program and funding strategy, will award two types of grants in three program areas. The three program areas are Brain Cancer Research, Studying Complex Systems, and Understanding Human Cognition. The long-standing interest of the James S. McDonnell Foundation on human mind/brain is reflected in changes made to the 2008 RFA, including the explicit emphasis on understanding human cognition. The program is intended to help investigators pursue experiments designed to answer well-articulated questions. JSMF Scholar Awards support research studying how neural systems are linked to and support cognitive functions and how cognitive systems are related to an organism's (preferably human) observable behaviors. Studies with model organisms should justify why such models were selected and how data obtained from models advances our understanding of human cognition.
Fields of interest: Science, research; Science; Brain research; Medical research; Cancer research.
Type of support: Research.
Limitations: Applications accepted. Giving on a local, national and international basis. No support for religious, educational or political organizations. No grants to individuals or for ongoing operational support for university-based centers, programs or institutes, no support for tuition, stipends, scholarships, research or travel expenses, underwriting or sponging of charitable functions, or museum exhibitions, expenses tied to projects whose explicit goal is the publication of a work, or expenses tied to the establishment or day-to-day running of a journal or small press.
Publications: Financial statement; Grants list; Program policy statement.
Application information: See foundation's web site for application information, all proposals must be electronically submitted. Institutions sponsoring an application on behalf of a particular principal investigator to JSMF programs (Research Awards, Collaborative Activity Awards) can only submit one application every 3 years on behalf of the named principal investigator. When an investigator submits a proposal for a Research Award the proposal is not funded, the next period of eligibility for that particular investigator and the proposal would begin in CY 2014. This policy is not intended to limit the

number of applications from an institution. The intent of the policy is to encourage investigators and institutions to carefully consider the goodness of fit between a proposal and the goals of JSMF programs prior to submitting. Whether the guideline applies to Co-PI's depends very much on the degree to which they are involved in and contribute to the substance of the application. Letters of intent for Collaborative Activities not accepted until 2013. Application form not required.

> Initial approach: Letter of inquiry for collaborative activity awards
> Copies of proposal: 1
> Deadline(s): Early to mid-Mar. for research awards; no deadline for letters of inquiry for collaborative activity awards
> Board meeting date(s): Varies
> Final notification: Varies depending on submission date

Officers and Directors:* John T. Bruer, Ph.D, Pres.; Susan M. Fitzpatrick, Ph.D., V.P.; James S. McDonnell III,* Secy.; John F. McDonnell,* Treas.; Jeanne M. Champer; Holly M. James; Alicia S. McDonnell; Jeffrey M. McDonnall; Marcella M. Stevens.
Number of staff: 2 full-time professional; 2 full-time support.
EIN: 542074788
Recent grants for international programs:

1126-1 Federal University of Rio de Janeiro, Rio de Janeiro, Brazil, $600,000. For research project: The human brain in numbers: Comparative quantitative studies of the cellular composition of the nervous system of humans and other mammals to investigate the morphological bases of our cognitive advantage. 2010.

1126-2 French National Institute for Health and Medical Research, Paris, France, $600,000. For research project: Spatial awareness: Normality, pathology and rehabilitation. 2010.

1126-3 Hebrew University of Jerusalem, Jerusalem, Israel, $450,000. For research project: The physics of rupture: From the laboratory scale to the scale of our planet. 2010.

1126-4 Hospitaller Order of Saint John of God, Lombardy Veneto Province, Cernusco sul Naviglio, Italy, $50,000. For research project: Noninvasive brain stimulation: new tools, new concepts, and integrated approach to cognitive neurorehabilitation. 2010.

1126-5 Karolinska Institute, Stockholm, Sweden, $600,000. For research project: Multisensory mechanism of body ownership and the projection of ownership onto artificial bodies. 2010.

1126-6 Universitat Rovira i Virgili, Catalan Institution for Research and Advanced Studies (ICREA), Tarragona, Spain, $445,663. For research project: Discovery, decomposition and dynamics of complex networks. 2010.

1126-7 University College London, London, England, $600,000. For research project: Development of human spatial cognition. 2010.

1126-8 University of British Columbia, Vancouver, Canada, $345,664. For research project: Evolution to the edge of chaos: Multilevel selection and life history evolution in metapopulations. 2010.

1126-9 University of Dublin, Trinity College, Dublin, Ireland, $600,000. For research project: How is sensory information encoded in spike trains?. 2010.

1127
Millstone Foundation
7701 Forsyth Blvd., Ste. 925
St. Louis, MO   63105-1842
Contact: I.E. Millstone, Pres; Colleen Millstone, Dir.

Incorporated in 1955 in MO.
Donors: I.E. Millstone; Goldie G. Millstone†.
Grantmaker type: Independent foundation.
Financial data (yr. ended 05/31/11): Assets, $7,659,894 (M); expenditures, $291,520; qualifying distributions, $228,151; giving activities include $228,151 for grants.
Purpose and activities: Giving primarily for higher education and to Jewish organizations. Most giving is in the form of on-going support. Limited new grantmaking.
Fields of interest: Higher education; Education; Human services; Jewish federated giving programs; Jewish agencies & synagogues.
International interests: Israel.
Type of support: General/operating support; Continuing support; Annual campaigns; Emergency funds; Scholarship funds; Research.
Limitations: Giving primarily in St. Louis, MO. No grants to individuals; no loans.
Application information: Funds for new grantmaking are extremely limited. Application form not required.

> Initial approach: Letter
> Copies of proposal: 1
> Deadline(s): None
> Board meeting date(s): Monthly
> Final notification: Within 6-8 weeks

Officer and Directors:* Robert Millstone,* Pres.; Colleen Millstone.
Number of staff: 2 part-time professional.
EIN: 436027373

1128
Monsanto Fund
800 N. Lindbergh Blvd.
St. Louis, MO   63167 7843   (314) 694-4391
Contact: Deborah J. Patterson, Pres.
FAX: (314) 694-7658,
E-mail: monsanto.fund@monsanto.com; Additional tel.: (314) 694-1000, fax: (314) 694-1001; Contact for America's Farmers Grow Communities and America's Farmers Grow Rural Education: Fileen Jensen, 914 Spruce St., St. Louis, MO 63102, tel.: (877) 267-3332; URL: http://www.monsantofund.org/
America's Farmers Grow Communities
Website: http://www.monsanto.com/americasfarmers/Pages/grow-communities.aspx
America's Farmers Grow Rural Education
Website: http://www.monsanto.com/americasfarmers/Pages/grow-rural-education.aspx

Incorporated in 1964 in MO as successor to the Monsanto Charitable Trust.
Donor: Monsanto Co.
Grantmaker type: Company-sponsored foundation.
Financial data (yr. ended 12/31/10): Assets, $5,887,091 (M); gifts received, $7,800,000; expenditures, $19,346,182; qualifying distributions, $19,316,925; giving activities include $15,658,313 for 661 grants (high: $2,500,000; low: $200), and $1,466,778 for 6,808 employee matching gifts.
Purpose and activities: The fund supports programs designed to strengthen farming communities and the communities where Monsanto employees live and work. Special emphasis is directed toward programs designed to improve education in farming communities, including schools, libraries, science centers, farmer training, and academic initiatives that enrich school programming; and meet critical needs in communities through food security, sanitation, access to clean water, public safety, and various other local needs.
Fields of interest: Youth development, agriculture; Disasters, fire prevention/control; Arts education; Visual arts; Performing arts; Literature; Arts; Elementary/secondary education; Libraries (public); Education; Environment, pollution control; Environment, water pollution; Botanical/horticulture/landscape services; Environment; Agriculture/food, research; Agriculture/food, public education; Agriculture; Agriculture, farmlands; Agriculture, farm bureaus/granges; Food services; Nutrition; Safety, education; Safety/disasters; Human services; Science, formal/general education; Mathematics; Science; Public affairs; Children; Youth; Economically disadvantaged.
Type of support: General/operating support; Continuing support; Equipment; Program development; Conferences/seminars; Seed money; Curriculum development; Research; Program evaluation; Employee matching gifts; Matching/challenge support.
Limitations: Applications accepted. Giving on a national and international basis primarily in areas of company operations, with emphasis in the greater St. Louis, MO, area. Giving outside the U.S. in Africa, including Malawi, Burkina Faso, Kenya, South Africa, and Uganda, Asia, including China, India, Indonesia, Philippines, and Thailand, Latin America including Argentina, Brazil, Mexico, and Paraguay, and Canada. No support for start-up organizations, fraternal, labor, or veterans' organizations not of direct benefit to the entire community, religious, politically partisan, or similar organizations, or discriminatory organizations. No grants for debt reduction, benefits, dinners, or advertisements, endowments, marketing, or projects in which Monsanto Company has a financial interest or could derive a financial benefit through cash or rights to intellectual property; no donations of printers, computer software, copiers, scanners, or computers.
Publications: Application guidelines; Grants list; Program policy statement.
Application information: Support is limited to 1 contribution per organization during any given year. Organizations receiving support are asked to submit a mid-year report and a final report. A site visit may be requested for Kids Garden Fresh Program. All applicants in the greater St. Louis, MO area are invited to informational conference calls. Please visit website for conference call dates. Applications from international organizations are by invitation only. International organization should contact a local Monsanto Fund representative.

> Initial approach: Complete online application; complete online nomination form for America's Farmers Grow Communities and America's Farmers Grow Rural Education
> Copies of proposal: 1
> Deadline(s): Jan. 1 to Feb. 28 and July 1 to Aug. 31 for organizations located in the greater St. Louis, MO area; Feb. 1. to May 1 for Kids Garden Fresh Program; Jan. 1 to Feb. 28 for organizations located outside of St. Louis, MO; Aug. 1 to Dec. 31 for America's Farmers Grow Communities; Jan. 1 to Feb. 28 and July 1 to Aug. 31 for international organizations

Board meeting date(s): Twice per year

Final notification: May and Dec. for organizations located in the greater St. Louis, MO area; July for Kids Garden Fresh Program

Officers and Directors:* Brett D. Begemann,* Chair.; Deborah J. Patterson,* Pres.; Sonya Meyers Davis, Secy.; Thomas D. Hartley, Treas.; Janet M. Holloway; Consuelo E. Madere; Kerry J. Preete; Gerald A. Steiner.

Number of staff: 1 full-time professional; 1 part-time professional; 2 full-time support.

EIN: 436044736

Recent grants for international programs:

1128-1 Africare, Washington, DC, $111,860. 2010.

1128-2 Africare, Washington, DC, $88,140. 2010.

1128-3 Akshaya Patra Foundation, Bangalore, India, $22,000. 2010.

1128-4 Akshaya Patra Foundation, Bangalore, India, $21,750. 2010.

1128-5 Akshaya Patra Foundation, Bangalore, India, $20,000. 2010.

1128-6 Australian Foundation for the Peoples of Asia and the Pacific, Saint Leonards, Australia, $64,233. 2010.

1128-7 Australian Foundation for the Peoples of Asia and the Pacific, Saint Leonards, Australia, $38,404. 2010.

1128-8 Australian Foundation for the Peoples of Asia and the Pacific, Saint Leonards, Australia, $17,348. 2010.

1128-9 Bharti Foundation, Gurgaon, India, $24,250. 2010.

1128-10 Biochemical Society, London, England, $83,000. 2010.

1128-11 Biochemical Society, London, England, $41,250. 2010.

1128-12 BioTrek, Winnipeg, Canada, $21,000. 2010.

1128-13 Children International, Kansas City, MO, $24,000. 2010.

1128-14 Children International, Kansas City, MO, $23,590. 2010.

1128-15 China Womens Development Foundation, Beijing, China, $100,000. 2010.

1128-16 Compatible Technology International, Saint Paul, MN, $25,500. 2010.

1128-17 Donald Danforth Plant Science Center, Saint Louis, MO, $2,500,000. 2010.

1128-18 Donald Danforth Plant Science Center, Saint Louis, MO, $791,182. 2010.

1128-19 Donald Danforth Plant Science Center, Saint Louis, MO, $791,182. 2010.

1128-20 Earthwatch Institute, Boston, MA, $70,000. 2010.

1128-21 East African Wildlife Society, Nairobi, Kenya, $26,030. 2010.

1128-22 Entrepreneurs Foundation for Basic Education, Mexico City, Mexico, $35,973. 2010.

1128-23 Escuela Agricola Panamericana, Pan American School of Agriculture, Tegucigalpa, Honduras, $47,500. 2010.

1128-24 Friends of the World Food Program, Washington, DC, $13,677. 2010.

1128-25 Friends of the World Food Program, Washington, DC, $13,090. 2010.

1128-26 Fundacion CasaBasica, Las Condes, Chile, $161,700. 2010.

1128-27 Fundacion Leer, Buenos Aires, Argentina, $11,375. 2010.

1128-28 Fundacion Marzano, Buenos Aires, Argentina, $11,300. 2010.

1128-29 Grand River Conservation Foundation, Cambridge, Canada, $35,000. 2010.

1128-30 Grand River Conservation Foundation, Cambridge, Canada, $35,000. 2010.

1128-31 Habitat for Humanity Indonesia, Jakarta, Indonesia, $40,000. 2010.

1128-32 Helen Keller International, New York, NY, $66,742. 2010.

1128-33 Helen Keller International, New York, NY, $50,000. 2010.

1128-34 Helen Keller International, New York, NY, $50,000. 2010.

1128-35 INICIA Emprender para el Futuro, Buenos Aires, Argentina, $150,000. 2010.

1128-36 INICIA Emprender para el Futuro, Buenos Aires, Argentina, $150,000. 2010.

1128-37 INMED Partnerships for Children, Ashburn, VA, $115,500. 2010.

1128-38 INMED Partnerships for Children, Ashburn, VA, $115,000. 2010.

1128-39 INMED Partnerships for Children, Ashburn, VA, $101,510. For South Africa. 2010.

1128-40 INMED Partnerships for Children, Ashburn, VA, $101,510. For South Africa. 2010.

1128-41 INMED Partnerships for Children, Ashburn, VA, $54,981. 2010.

1128-42 INMED Partnerships for Children, Ashburn, VA, $27,686. 2010.

1128-43 INMED Partnerships for Children, Ashburn, VA, $27,583. 2010.

1128-44 Institute for University Co-operation Onlus, Rome, Italy, $25,000. 2010.

1128-45 Instituto para el Desarrollo de la Mixteca, Huajuapan de Leon, Mexico, $50,000. 2010.

1128-46 Integrated Community Organization for Sustainable Empowerment and Education for Development, Nairobi, Kenya, $65,000. 2010.

1128-47 Integrated Community Organization for Sustainable Empowerment and Education for Development, Nairobi, Kenya, $65,000. 2010.

1128-48 Jaguar Conservation Fund, Brazil, $76,000. 2010.

1128-49 Jaguar Conservation Fund, Brazil, $75,000. 2010.

1128-50 Junior Achievement of Argentina, Buenos Aires, Argentina, $20,000. 2010.

1128-51 Primary Science Program, Braamfontein, South Africa, $41,000. 2010.

1128-52 Research Centre for Non-Formal Education, Hanoi, Vietnam, $46,500. 2010.

1128-53 Rotary Club Laureles, Bogota, Colombia, $25,000. 2010.

1128-54 Rotary Club Laureles, Bogota, Colombia, $25,000. 2010.

1128-55 Saint Leon Interpretive Center, Saint Leon, Canada, $25,000. 2010.

1128-56 Scottish Crop Research Institute, Dundee, Scotland, $59,003. 2010.

1128-57 Scottish Crop Research Institute, Dundee, Scotland, $59,002. 2010.

1128-58 Sikshana Foundation, Bangalore, India, $15,750. 2010.

1128-59 Society for Educational Welfare and Economic Development, New Dehli, India, $51,351. 2010.

1128-60 Society for Educational Welfare and Economic Development, New Dehli, India, $51,350. 2010.

1128-61 SOS Childrens Villages of Pakistan, Lahore, Pakistan, $35,002. 2010.

1128-62 United Nations Foundation, Washington, DC, $15,036. 2010.

1128-63 United Way of Mumbai, Mumbai, India, $42,144. 2010.

1128-64 United Way of Mumbai, Mumbai, India, $42,144. 2010.

1128-65 United Way of Mumbai, Mumbai, India, $38,374. 2010.

1128-66 Voluntary Organization of Rural Development Society, Nandyal, India, $20,000. 2010.

1128-67 Voluntary Organization of Rural Development Society, Nandyal, India, $15,000. 2010.

1128-68 World Initiative for Soy in Human Health, Saint Louis, MO, $25,000. 2010.

1129

People to People International

911 Main St., Ste. 2110
Kansas City, MO 64105-5305 (816) 531-4701
Contact: Mary Eisenhower, Pres. and C.E.O.
FAX: (816) 561-7502; E-mail: ptpi@ptpi.org;
URL: http://www.ptpi.org
Blog: http://blog.ptpi.org/
Facebook: http://www.facebook.com/
PeopletoPeople
LinkedIn: http://www.linkedin.com/groups?
home=&gid=1417967
Twitter: http://twitter.com/ptpi
YouTube: http://www.youtube.com/ptpinetwork

Established in 1961 in MO.

Grantmaker type: Public charity.

Financial data (yr. ended 12/31/10): Revenue, $4,473,670; assets, $5,043,263 (M); gifts received, $509,288; expenditures, $5,110,687; giving activities include $128,633 for grants, $44,106 for 11 grants to organizations outside the U.S., and $60,894 for grants to individuals.

Purpose and activities: The organization enhances international understanding and friendship through educational, cultural, and humanitarian activities involving the exchange of ideas and experiences directly among peoples of different countries and diverse cultures.

Fields of interest: International exchange, students; International affairs, goodwill promotion.

Type of support: Scholarships—to individuals.

Limitations: Applications accepted. Giving on a national and international basis.

Publications: Application guidelines; Newsletter.

Application information: See web site for additional application information and guidelines. Application form required.

Initial approach: Download application form online

Deadline(s): July 5 for Global Youth Forum Scholarship; Oct. 15 for Joyce C. Hall College Scholarship and James & Eunice Doty PTPI/Congressional Award Scholarship; varies for Mary Jean Eisenhower Partner in Peace Scholarship

Officers and Directors:* Mark Stansberry,* Chair.; Rolf Dahlberg,* Vice-Chair.; Mary Eisenhower,* Pres. and C.E.O.; Piya Radia,* Secy.; William Jarvis,* Treas.; Hany Adly; Charlie Cheng; Stephen DiGiacinto; Micah Kubic; Valeria Magistrelli; Anita Manuel; Genci Mucaj; Ruriko Nakajima; Troy Nash; Joseph Patterson; Michael Zanders.

EIN: 440659517

1130
PKD Foundation
(formerly Polycystic Kidney Research Foundation)
8330 Ward Pkwy., Ste. 510
Kansas City, MO 64114-2027 (816) 931-2600
Contact: Teresa Woods, Devel. Asst.
FAX: (816) 931-8655; E-mail: pkdcure@pkdcure.org;
Toll-free tel.: (800) PKD-CURE; URL: http://
www.pkdcure.org
Facebook: https://www.facebook.com/
pkdfoundation

Established in 1982 in MO.
Grantmaker type: Public charity.
Financial data (yr. ended 06/30/11): Revenue,
$7,578,703; assets, $2,390,354 (M); gifts
received, $7,528,329; expenditures, $8,308,496;
program services expenses, $6,568,393; giving
activities include $922,748 for 7 grants (high:
$514,499; low: $39,096), $50,000 for grants to
organizations outside the U.S., $50,000 for 1 grant
to an individual, and $5,545,645 for
foundation-administered programs.
Purpose and activities: The foundation is devoted
to determining the cause, improving clinical
treatment, and discovering a cure for polycystic
kidney disease.
Fields of interest: Kidney diseases; Kidney
research; Terminal illness, people with.
International interests: Canada; England; France;
Italy; Japan; Netherlands; Switzerland.
Type of support: Fellowships; Research; Grants to
individuals.
Limitations: Applications accepted. Giving on a
national and international basis. No support for
pre-doctoral or doctoral awards. No "lifeline" grants
for individuals.
Publications: Annual report; Financial statement;
Informational brochure; Newsletter.
Application information: Application form required.
Initial approach: Download application online
Board meeting date(s): Apr. and Oct.
Officers and Board Members:* Scott Goodman,*
Chair.; Frank C. Condella,* Vice-Chair.; Bill Brazell;
Michael Haggard, Esq.; Walter Hunt, Ph.D.; and 11
additional board members.
Number of staff: 41 full-time professional; 6 full-time
support; 3 part-time support.
EIN: 431266906

1131
Pujols Family Foundation, Inc.
111 Westport Plz., Ste. 255
St. Louis, MO 63146-3013 (314) 878-2105
FAX: (314) 878-2118;
E-mail: info@pujolsfamilyfoundation.org;
URL: http://www.pujolsfamilyfoundation.org/
foundation.htm

Established in 2005 in MO.
Grantmaker type: Public charity.
Financial data (yr. ended 12/31/10): Revenue,
$1,239,116; assets, $2,759,647 (M); gifts
received, $1,016,529; expenditures, $703,955.
Purpose and activities: The foundation aims to
promote awareness, provide hope and meet
tangible needs for families and children with Down
syndrome, and provides extraordinary experiences
for families and children with disabilities and
life-threatening illnesses, especially in the
Dominican Republic.
Fields of interest: Down syndrome.
International interests: Dominican Republic.

Limitations: Applications not accepted. Giving
primarily to the Dominican Republic.
Application information: Contributes only to
pre-selected organizations.
Officers and Directors: Albert Pujols,* Chair.; Deidre
Pujols,* Pres.; Todd Perry, C.E.O. and Exec. Dir.;
Jeanette Bax-Kurtz; Norv Beffa; Daniel Lozano.
EIN: 202272546

1132
Mildred, Herbert and Julian Simon Foundation
P.O. Box 78544
St. Louis, MO 63178-8544 (314) 241-1716
Contact: Charles Baron, Chair., Steering Comm.;
Martin M. Rosen, Exec. Dir.
FAX: (314) 241-1588;
E-mail: mrosen@mersgoodwill.org

Established in 1993 in MO.
Donors: Herbert Simon†; Julian Simon†; Mildred
Simon†.
Grantmaker type: Independent foundation.
Financial data (yr. ended 09/30/10): Assets,
$12,746,665 (M); expenditures, $632,704;
qualifying distributions, $567,825; giving activities
include $445,372 for 33 grants (high: $183,372;
low: $1,000).
Purpose and activities: The foundation is interested
in developing projects which will have a significant
impact on the St. Louis, MO area. It seeks concept
papers concerning programs that will meet unique
specific community needs and seeks the
appropriate organizations to best implement them.
The primary focus includes but is not limited to
programs which enhance the quality of life of senior
citizens and children, with primary consideration
given to the needs of the St. Louis Jewish
community.
Fields of interest: Elementary/secondary
education; Higher education; Employment, services;
Neighborhood centers; Children, services; Jewish
agencies & synagogues; Youth, Disabilities, people
with; Children/youth; Aging.
International interests: Israel; Middle East.
Type of support: Program development; Seed
money; Scholarship funds.
Limitations: Applications accepted. Giving primarily
in St. Louis, MO. No grants to individuals or for
capital campaigns.
Application information: Concepts preferred to
grant applications. Application form not required.
Initial approach: Letter/concept paper
Copies of proposal: 1
Deadline(s): None
Board meeting date(s): Monthly
Final notification: 1-6 months
Officers and Steering Committee:* Charles B.
Baron,* Chair.; Lewis Chartock,* Vice-Chair.; Martin
M. Rosen,* Exec. Dir.; Lucy Lopata; Joan M.
Newman.
Trustee: U.S. Bank, N.A.
Number of staff: 1 part-time professional; 1
part-time support.
EIN: 436498119

1133
Roy W. Slusher Charitable Foundation
c/o U.S. Bank, N.A.
P.O. Box 387
St. Louis, MO 63166-0387

Established in 1988 in MO.
Grantmaker type: Independent foundation.
Financial data (yr. ended 02/28/11): Assets,
$6,501,119 (M); expenditures, $575,479;
qualifying distributions, $324,689; giving activities
include $324,689 for grants.
Purpose and activities: Funding to meet the needs
of disadvantaged youth and their families and to
increase the quality of life for the elderly through the
following broad areas: educational scholarships,
broad national health issues, youth camps and
programs, senior citizens programs, and public radio
and television.
Fields of interest: Boys & girls clubs; Salvation
Army; United Ways and Federated Giving Programs;
Media/communications; Higher education, college;
Education; Medical research, institute; Food
services; Housing/shelter, homeless; Children/
youth, services; Aging, centers/services;
International relief; Christian agencies & churches.
Type of support: General/operating support;
Building/renovation; Seed money; Scholarship
funds; Research.
Limitations: Applications not accepted. Giving
primarily in Taney County, MO. No grants to
individuals or for annual fundraising, endowments,
or routine operating needs.
Publications: Informational brochure.
Application information: Contributes only to
pre-selected organizations.
Board meeting date(s): Mar. and Sept.
Officers: Charles A. Fuller, Jr., Mgr.; Jerry Redfern,
Mgr.
Trustee: U.S. Bank, N.A.
Number of staff: 1 part-time professional.
EIN: 436339151

1134
WaterPartners International
920 Main St., Ste. 1800
Kansas City, MO 64105-2008 (816) 877-8400
URL: http://www.water.org
Twitter: http://twitter.com/Water

Established in 1993 in NC; merged with H2O Africa
in 2009.
Grantmaker type: Public charity.
Financial data (yr. ended 09/30/10): Revenue,
$4,028,659; assets, $3,238,049 (M); gifts
received, $3,994,715; expenditures, $4,999,419;
giving activities include $1,819,632 for 16 grants to
organizations outside the U.S.
Purpose and activities: The organization is
committed to providing safe drinking water and
sanitation to people in developing countries.
Fields of interest: Environment, water resources;
Environment, water pollution.
International interests: Developing countries.
Type of support: Loans—to individuals.
Limitations: Giving primarily on an international
basis, with emphasis on developing countries.
Publications: Annual report; Financial statement;
IRS Form 990 or 990-PF printed copy available upon
request.
Officers and Directors:* Ari Chaney,* Chair.; Tony
Stayner,* Vice-Chair.; Dan Hoskins,* Secy.; Terry
Trayvick,* Treas.; Gary White,* Exec. Dir.; Dawnet
Beverley; Vinod Dasari; Jonathan Greenblatt; Keith
Quinn; Andy Sareyan; Larry Tanz.
EIN: 582060131

MONTANA

1135
Browning-Kimball Foundation
P.O. Box 375
Great Falls, MT   59403-0375   (406) 454-1449
Contact: William S. MacFadden, Admin.

Established in 1981 in UT.
Donors: Barbara K. Browning; Barbara Browning Cowan; Matt S. Browning.
Grantmaker type: Independent foundation.
Financial data (yr. ended 12/31/10): Assets, $17,057,148 (M); expenditures, $658,760; qualifying distributions, $508,000; giving activities include $508,000 for grants.
Purpose and activities: Giving primarily for health care including mental health associations, and for children, youth, and social services.
Fields of interest: Museums; Education; Environment; Animals/wildlife; Mental health, association; Medical research, association; Human services; Children/youth, services; Community/ economic development; Christian agencies & churches; Catholic agencies & churches.
Limitations: Giving primarily in MT and Ogden, UT. No grants to individuals.
Application information: Application form required.
  Initial approach: Request application package
  Deadline(s): None
Officers: Barbara Cowan, Pres.; William S. MacFadden, Admin.
Directors: Lisa Cowan; William Cowan; William B. Cowan.
EIN: 942766079
Recent grants for international programs:
1135-1 Hope Through Health, Medway, MA, $100,000. For unrestricted support. 2009.

1136
O. P. and W. E. Edwards Foundation, Inc.
c/o Jo Ann Eder
P.O. Box 2445
Red Lodge, MT   59068-2445   (406) 446-1077
Contact: Jo Anne Eder, Pres.; Amy Moore, Grants Mgr.
FAX: (406) 446-1363;
E-mail: info@opweedwards.org; E-mail for specific grant questions: amoore@opweedwards.org;
URL: http://opweedwards.org
Grants List: http://opweedwards.org/Grants_List.html

Incorporated in 1962 in NY.
Donors: William E. Edwards†; J.N. Edwards†; Harriet E. Gamper; David E. Gamper†; Jo Ann Eder.
Grantmaker type: Independent foundation.
Financial data (yr. ended 08/31/10): Assets, $28,899,202 (M); gifts received, $1,056,000; expenditures, $4,204,107; qualifying distributions, $4,282,860; giving activities include $3,738,932 for 80 grants (high: $121,355; low: $213), and $110,000 for 2 loans/program-related investments (high: $100,000; low: $10,000).
Purpose and activities: Major interest in programs helping economically disadvantaged young people become able to survive and thrive on their own, with preference to smaller, comprehensive programs

that are integral parts of their communities' networks of services.
Fields of interest: Visual arts; Performing arts; Education; Youth development; Human services; Children/youth, services; Family services; Community/economic development; Astronomy; Infants/toddlers; Children/youth; Youth; Young adults; Native Americans/American Indians; Indigenous peoples; Economically disadvantaged.
International interests: Developing countries.
Type of support: General/operating support; Continuing support; Management development/ capacity building; Debt reduction; Emergency funds; Program development; Seed money; Scholarship funds; Program evaluation; Program-related investments/loans; Matching/challenge support.
Limitations: Giving on a national basis. No grants to individuals.
Publications: Application guidelines; Grants list.
Application information: Unsolicited full proposals not considered. The foundation requests proposals from organizations about which the trustees are personally and directly knowledgeable. See foundation web site for details. Application form required.
  Initial approach: See foundation web site for instructions and guidelines
  Board meeting date(s): As required
Officers and Trustees:* Jo Ann Eder,* Pres. and Treas.; Harriet E. Gamper,* V.P.; Mark D. Eder,* Secy.; Jessica Dunbar; Christopher E. Gamper; Gisela Gamper.
Number of staff: 1 part-time support.
EIN: 136100965
Recent grants for international programs:
1136-1 Media4Good, Manchester, VT, $25,000. For general support for Youth Interactive, and for Montana program and Hub Schools; half the total as a challenge grant. 2010.
1136-2 United Movement to End Child Soldiering, Washington, DC, $30,000. For the Northern Uganda Education Program. 2010.
1136-3 United Movement to End Child Soldiering, Washington, DC, $25,000. For A-Factor Project. 2010.
1136-4 United Movement to End Child Soldiering, Washington, DC, $15,000. For general support. 2010.
1136-5 Vermont Associates for Mexican Opportunity and Support, Weston, VT, $15,000. For annual support to help in funding the classes and training sessions around Cuernavaca, Mexico. 2010.
1136-6 Wycliffe Bible Translators, Orlando, FL, $16,800. For missionary work. 2010.

NEBRASKA

1137
The Susan Thompson Buffett Foundation
(formerly The Buffett Foundation)
222 Kiewit Plz.
Omaha, NE   68131-3302
Contact: Allen Greenberg, Pres.
E-mail: scholarships@stbfoundation.org;
URL: http://www.buffettscholarships.org
Warren Buffett's Giving Pledge: http://givingpledge.org/#enter

Tel. for scholarship information: (402) 943-1383

Incorporated in 1964 in NE. In 2006, Warren Buffett pledged almost $3 billion worth of his Berkshire-Hathaway, Inc. stock to the foundation to be paid out over time. As a result, the Susan Thompson Buffett Foundation's assets and annual giving have risen sharply.
Donors: Warren E. Buffett; Susan T. Buffett†.
Grantmaker type: Independent foundation.
Financial data (yr. ended 12/31/10): Assets, $2,584,393,426 (M); gifts received, $160,478,045; expenditures, $254,824,574; qualifying distributions, $252,575,842; giving activities include $236,866,941 for 278 grants (high: $28,691,307; low: $1,000), and $10,527,654 for grants to individuals.
Purpose and activities: Grants primarily for family planning programs, and scholarships to residents of Nebraska attending Nebraska public colleges or universities.
Fields of interest: Reproductive health, family planning; Civil liberties, reproductive rights.
Type of support: General/operating support; Scholarships—to individuals.
Limitations: Applications accepted. Giving on a national and international basis; scholarships awarded only to residents in NE. No grant to individuals (except for Teacher Awards and scholarships).
Application information: Unsolicited requests for grants not accepted. The foundation accepts scholarship applications. The foundation only responds to questions about scholarships and awards. Please see the foundation's web site for additional details.
  Initial approach: Application form required for scholarship program only
  Deadline(s): Mar. 1 for scholarships
Officers and Directors:* Susan A. Buffett,* Chair. and Treas.; Allen Greenberg, Pres.; Melissa How, Secy.; Peter A. Buffett; Geoffrey Cowan; Carol Loomis; Patti Matson.
Number of staff: 9 full-time professional; 3 full-time support.
EIN: 476032365
Recent grants for international programs:
1137-1 Better World Fund, Washington, DC, $50,000. For project support. 2010.
1137-2 Catolicas por el Derecho de Decidir, Mexico City, Mexico, $1,563,900. For project support. 2010.
1137-3 DKT International, Washington, DC, $12,408,602. For project support. 2010.
1137-4 DKT International, Washington, DC, $931,355. For project support. 2010.
1137-5 EngenderHealth, New York, NY, $1,692,010. For project support. 2010.
1137-6 EngenderHealth, New York, NY, $1,425,642. For project support. 2010.
1137-7 ESAR, Bogota, Colombia, $5,245,556. For project support. 2010.
1137-8 Gender Equity: Citizenship and Work and Family, Mexico City, Mexico, $1,575,000. For project support. 2010.
1137-9 Global Justice Center, New York, NY, $178,109. For project support. 2010.
1137-10 Global Justice Center, New York, NY, $100,000. For project support. 2010.
1137-11 Grupo de Informacion en Reproduccion Elegida, Mexico City, Mexico, $1,361,421. For project support. 2010.
1137-12 Gynuity Health Projects, New York, NY, $2,103,551. For project support. 2010.

1137-13 International Projects Assistance Services, Chapel Hill, NC, $3,012,220. For project support. 2010.

1137-14 International Projects Assistance Services, Chapel Hill, NC, $1,150,695. For project support. 2010.

1137-15 International Projects Assistance Services, Chapel Hill, NC, $601,350. For project support. 2010.

1137-16 International Projects Assistance Services, Chapel Hill, NC, $572,485. For project support. 2010.

1137-17 Marie Stopes International, Washington, DC, $3,140,342. For project support. 2010.

1137-18 Marie Stopes International, Washington, DC, $789,916. For project support. 2010.

1137-19 Marie Stopes International, Washington, DC, $754,930. For project support. 2010.

1137-20 Marie Stopes International, Washington, DC, $749,363. For project support. 2010.

1137-21 Nuclear Threat Initiative, Washington, DC, $7,000,181. For project support. 2010.

1137-22 ONE Campaign, Washington, DC, $1,004,107. For project support. 2010.

1137-23 Options for International Health, Washington, DC, $3,489,039. For project support. 2010.

1137-24 Pathfinder International, Watertown, MA, $23,006. For project support. 2010.

1137-25 Planned Parenthood Federation, International, London, England, $750,128. For project support. 2010.

1137-26 Planned Parenthood Federation, International, London, England, $384,356. For project support. 2010.

1137-27 Planned Parenthood Federation, International, London, England, $359,210. For project support. 2010.

1137-28 Planned Parenthood Federation, International, London, England, $336,258. For project support. 2010.

1137-29 Planned Parenthood Federation, International, London, England, $325,071. For project support. 2010.

1137-30 Planned Parenthood Federation, International, London, England, $315,063. For project support. 2010.

1137-31 Planned Parenthood Federation, International, London, England, $274,097. For project support. 2010.

1137-32 Planned Parenthood Federation, International, London, England, $167,628. For project support. 2010.

1137-33 Planned Parenthood Federation, International, London, England, $166,618. For project support. 2010.

1137-34 Planned Parenthood Federation, International, London, England, $128,650. For project support. 2010.

1137-35 Planned Parenthood Federation, International, London, England, $126,652. For project support. 2010.

1137-36 Planned Parenthood Federation, International, London, England, $79,963. For project support. 2010.

1137-37 Planned Parenthood Federation, International, London, England, $51,152. For project support. 2010.

1137-38 Planned Parenthood Federation, International, New York, NY, $2,346,663. For project support. 2010.

1137-39 Population Council, New York, NY, $1,431,213. For project support. 2010.

1137-40 Population Council, New York, NY, $727,111. For project support. 2010.

1137-41 Population Services International, Washington, DC, $28,691,307. For project support. 2010.

1137-42 Population Services International, Washington, DC, $7,378,682. For project support. 2010.

1137-43 Venture Strategies for Health and Development, Berkeley, CA, $934,787. For project support. 2010.

1137-44 World Health Organization, Geneva, Switzerland, $248,100. For project support. 2010.

1137-45 World Health Partners, New Delhi, India, $1,016,037. For project support. 2010.

1138
Cooper Foundation
870 Wells Fargo Ctr.
1248 O St.
Lincoln, NE 68508-1493 (402) 476-7571
Contact: E. Arthur Thompson, Pres.
FAX: (402) 476-2356;
E-mail: info@cooperfoundation.org; URL: http://www.cooperfoundation.org/

Incorporated in 1934 in NE.
Donor: Joseph H. Cooper†.
Grantmaker type: Independent foundation.
Financial data (yr. ended 12/31/10): Assets, $21,978,666 (M); expenditures, $823,309; qualifying distributions, $784,821; giving activities include $481,628 for grants.
Purpose and activities: The mission of the foundation is to support strong, sustainable organizations, innovative ideas, and ventures of significant promise in Nebraska.
Fields of interest: Humanities; Arts; Education; Environment; Human services.
Type of support: General/operating support; Management development/capacity building; Program development.
Limitations: Giving limited to NE, with emphasis on Lincoln and Lancaster County. No support for religious or health purposes, private foundations, or for businesses. No grants to individuals, or for multi-year grants, memberships, travel, or endowment funds.
Publications: Application guidelines; Financial statement; Grants list.
Application information: Lincoln/Lancaster Grantmakers Common Grant Application Form required only by invitation after having met foundation objectives. See foundation Web site for application guidelines and procedures. Application form required.
  Initial approach: Contact foundation in person, or via telephone, letter, fax, or e-mail to discuss proposal
  Copies of proposal: 1
  Deadline(s): Jan. 15, Apr. 1, Aug. 1, and Oct. 1
  Board meeting date(s): Quarterly
  Final notification: 2 months
Officers and Trustees: * Jack D. Campbell,* Chair.; Jane Renner Hood,* Vice-Chair.; E. Arthur Thompson,* Pres.; Victoria Kovar,* Secy.; Richard J. Vierk,* Treas.; Richard Knudsen, Genl. Counsel; Linda Crump; Brad Korell; Robert Nefsky; Kim Robak.
Number of staff: 2 full-time professional; 1 part-time professional.
EIN: 470401230

Recent grants for international programs:
1138-1 University of Nebraska-Lincoln, E.N. Thompson Forum on World Issues, Lincoln, NE, $400,000. For Campaign for Nebraska. 2010.
1138-2 University of Nebraska-Lincoln, E.N. Thompson Forum on World Issues, Lincoln, NE, $13,921. For Thompson Family Fund. 2010.

1139
Eagle Foundation
1475 Rd. 105
Sidney, NE 69162-4236

Established in 1993 in NE.
Donor: James W. Cabela.
Grantmaker type: Independent foundation.
Financial data (yr. ended 12/31/10): Assets, $76,790,940 (M); expenditures, $3,656,525; qualifying distributions, $3,200,000; giving activities include $3,200,000 for 10 grants (high: $600,000; low: $100,000).
Purpose and activities: Giving primarily to Roman Catholic agencies and churches.
Fields of interest: Health care; Human services; Catholic agencies & churches.
Type of support: General/operating support.
Limitations: Applications not accepted. Giving primarily in MA, NE, and NY. No grants to individuals.
Application information: Contributes only to pre-selected organizations.
Officers and Directors: * James W. Cabela,* Pres. and Treas.; Michael R. McCarthy,* V.P.; Gerald E. Matzke,* Secy.
EIN: 470773892
Recent grants for international programs:
1139-1 Catholic Medical Mission Board, New York, NY, $500,000. 2008.
1139-2 Catholic Near East Welfare Association, New York, NY, $600,000. 2008.
1139-3 Cross International Catholic Outreach, Boca Raton, FL, $500,000. 2008.
1139-4 Doctors Without Borders USA, New York, NY, $200,000. 2008.
1139-5 Food for the Poor, Coconut Creek, FL, $500,000. 2008.
1139-6 Heifer Project International, Little Rock, AR, $100,000. 2008.
1139-7 United States Conference of Catholic Bishops, Washington, DC, $500,000. For subcommittee for church in Africa. 2008.

1140
Himanchal Educational Foundation
5610 Ave. N
Kearney, NE 68847-8545 (308) 234-1243
E-mail: skovl@unk.edu; URL: http://www.himanchal.org

Established in 2000 in NE.
Grantmaker type: Public charity.
Financial data (yr. ended 12/31/10): Revenue, $53,602; assets, $49,133 (M); gifts received, $33,193; expenditures, $51,380; program services expenses, $51,380.
Purpose and activities: The foundation provides direct financial support to Himanchal High School in Nangi, Nepal, as well as scholarship support to its student body.
Fields of interest: Secondary school/education.
International interests: Nepal.

Type of support: General/operating support; Scholarship funds.
Limitations: Applications not accepted. Giving limited to Nangi, Nepal.
Application information: Contributes only to pre-selected organizations.
  Board meeting date(s): Quarterly
Officers and Board Members:* Leonard Skov, Chair.; Jane Sabin-Davis,* Secy.; Bill Ballou,* Treas.; Jiwan Giri; Sandeep Giri; Debra Stoner.
EIN: 470827392

1141
The Kind World Foundation
1125 S. 103rd St., Rm. 200
Omaha, NE 68124-1071 (402) 697-8000
Contact: Patty Killgore

Established in 1991 in SD.
Donor: Norman W. Waitt, Jr.
Grantmaker type: Independent foundation.
Financial data (yr. ended 12/31/09): Assets, $15,819,414 (M); expenditures, $4,424,143; qualifying distributions, $4,305,469; giving activities include $3,990,420 for 53 grants (high: $1,600,000; low: $500).
Purpose and activities: Giving primarily for the arts, particularly a performing arts center, education, and human services.
Fields of interest: International relief; Higher education; Performing arts centers; Arts; Education; Environment, natural resources; Children/youth, services; Family services; Foundations (community).
Type of support: General/operating support; Continuing support; Annual campaigns; Capital campaigns; Building/renovation; Equipment; Land acquisition; Endowments; Program development; Scholarship funds; Research; Consulting services; Matching/challenge support.
Limitations: Giving primarily in Santa Barbara, CA, Sioux City, IA, and nationally for overseas relief programs and projects.
Application information:
  Initial approach: Letter
  Deadline(s): None
Officer: Lee Lysne, Exec. Dir.
Director: Norman W. Waitt, Jr.
Number of staff: 1 full-time professional; 1 part-time professional; 1 part-time support.
EIN: 363776553
Recent grants for international programs:
1141-1 H2O for Life, White Bear Lake, MN, $50,000. 2009.
1141-2 Hesperian Foundation, Berkeley, CA, $37,500. 2009.
1141-3 Potters for Peace, Bisbee, AZ, $12,500. 2009.
1141-4 SEVEN Fund, Cambridge, MA, $75,000. 2009.
1141-5 SEVEN Fund, Cambridge, MA, $35,000. 2009.
1141-6 SEVEN Fund, Cambridge, MA, $20,000. 2009.
1141-7 UNICEF, Washington, DC, $50,000. 2009.
1141-8 Water Advocates, Washington, DC, $50,000. 2009.
1141-9 Waterlines, Santa Fe, NM, $75,000. 2009.
1141-10 World Surgical Foundation, Harrisburg, PA, $50,000. 2009.

1142
The Milton S. and Corinne N. Livingston Foundation, Inc.
11605 Miracle Hills Dr., Ste. 300
Omaha, NE 68154-8005
Contact: Howard N. Epstein, Exec. Dir.

Incorporated in 1948 in NE.
Donor: Milton S. Livingston‡.
Grantmaker type: Independent foundation.
Financial data (yr. ended 12/31/10): Assets, $2,199,357 (M); expenditures, $297,843; qualifying distributions, $272,668; giving activities include $272,668 for grants.
Purpose and activities: Giving for local Jewish welfare funds and temple support, higher education, culture, and health services.
Fields of interest: Arts; Higher education; Health care; Human services; Jewish federated giving programs; Jewish agencies & synagogues; Community/economic development, public education.
International interests: Israel.
Type of support: General/operating support; Continuing support; Emergency funds; Program development; Seed money; Scholarship funds; Matching/challenge support.
Limitations: Applications accepted. Giving primarily in the Omaha, NE, area; funding also in Israel. No grants to individuals, or for capital campaigns or endowments.
Publications: Application guidelines; Financial statement.
Application information: Telephone calls will not be accepted. All applications to be submitted on application form supplied by Exec. Dir. Application form required.
  Initial approach: Letter
  Copies of proposal: 1
  Deadline(s): Nov. 1
  Board meeting date(s): First Tues. after Thanksgiving
  Final notification: Within 1 month of board meeting
Officers and Trustees:* Robert I. Kully,* Pres.; Murray H. Newman,* V.P.; Suzanne Singer,* Secy.; Gerald A. Hoberman,* Treas.; Howard N. Epstein, Exec. Dir.; Robert Belgrade; Patricia Newman, Ph.D.
EIN: 476027670

NEVADA

1143
Dr. Miriam & Sheldon G. Adelson Charitable Trust
3355 Las Vegas Blvd. S.
Las Vegas, NV 89109-8941
Contact: Miriam O. Adelson, Tr.
Mailing address: 901 Trophy Hills Dr., Las Vegas, NV 89134

Established in 1994 in NV.
Donors: Dr. Miriam Adelson; Sheldon G. Adelson.
Grantmaker type: Operating foundation.
Financial data (yr. ended 12/31/09): Assets, $8,738,753 (M); gifts received, $225,000; expenditures, $225,005; qualifying distributions,

$225,000; giving activities include $225,000 for 1 grant.
Purpose and activities: Giving primarily to Jewish organizations, temples, and schools.
Fields of interest: Human services; Aging, centers/services; Arts; Education; Hospitals (general); Jewish federated giving programs; Jewish agencies & synagogues.
International interests: Israel.
Type of support: General/operating support.
Limitations: Applications not accepted. Giving primarily in Washington, DC, MA, Las Vegas, NV, and New York, NY; some funding nationally.
Application information: Unsolicited requests for funds not accepted.
Trustees: Dr. Miriam Adelson; Sheldon G. Adelson.
EIN: 886063073

1144
Boulder City Sunrise Rotary Foundation
P.O. Box 60905
Boulder City, NV 89006-0905 (702) 592-6136

Established in 2005 in NV; supporting organization of the Cabo San Lucas Rotary Club.
Donors: Robert W. Draney; Boulder City Sunrise Rotary.
Grantmaker type: Public charity.
Financial data (yr. ended 06/30/10): Revenue, $33,474; assets, $46,892 (M); gifts received, $10,962; expenditures, $16,225; giving activities include $15,550 for grants.
Fields of interest: Food services; International economic development; Children; Boys.
Type of support: Continuing support; Building/renovation.
Limitations: Applications not accepted. Giving primarily in Mexico.
Application information: Unsolicited requests for funds not accepted.
  Board meeting date(s): Mar.
Trustees: Donna Draney; Eric Estes; Robert Merrell.
EIN: 203507184

1145
A Charitable Foundation Corporation
2657 Windmill Pkwy., Ste. 220
Henderson, NV 89014 (702) 248-8184

Established in 1997 in NV.
Grantmaker type: Independent foundation.
Financial data (yr. ended 12/31/10): Assets, $5,797,872 (M); gifts received, $1,400,100; expenditures, $211,410; qualifying distributions, $165,876; giving activities include $165,030 for 36 grants (high: $36,000; low: $250).
Fields of interest: Education, research; Environment; Food banks; Human services; International development.
Type of support: Annual campaigns; Building/renovation; Emergency funds; Research; Grants to individuals.
Limitations: Giving primarily in California, Hawaii, and New York; some giving also in Brazil.
Application information: Application form not required.
  Initial approach: For scientific research grants, submit brief grant proposal
  Copies of proposal: 2
  Deadline(s): None

Officers and Directors:* David S. Druz,* Pres.;
Colleen A. Haviland,* Secy.-Treas.; Gregg Smith.
EIN: 880375802

1146
Edward Fein Foundation
(formerly Edward Feinstein Foundation)
81 Shoreline Cir.
Incline Village, NV   89451-9504
URL: http://www.foundationcenter.org/
grantmaker/fein/

Established in 1965 in NY.
Donor: Edward Fein.
Grantmaker type: Independent foundation.
Financial data (yr. ended 03/31/11): Assets,
$5,096,191 (M); gifts received, $5,283;
expenditures, $194,062; qualifying distributions,
$187,500; giving activities include $187,500 for
grants.
Fields of interest: Higher education; Education;
Human services; Jewish federated giving programs;
Jewish agencies & synagogues.
International interests: Israel.
Limitations: Applications not accepted. Giving
primarily in CA, MA, and NY. No grants to individuals.
Application information: Contributes only to
pre-selected organizations.
   Board meeting date(s): Jan.
Trustee: Edward Fein.
EIN: 136220451

1147
Fund for the Encouragement of Self Reliance
8021 Golfers Oasis Dr.
Las Vegas, NV   89149-4616
Contact: Thu-Le Doan, Tr.

Established in 1997 in NV.
Donors: Thu-Le Doan; Doan L. Phung; PAI
Corporation; Vietnamese American Scholarship
Fund.
Grantmaker type: Independent foundation.
Financial data (yr. ended 12/31/10): Assets,
$5,218,878 (M); gifts received, $10,590;
expenditures, $249,993; qualifying distributions,
$237,036; giving activities include $237,036 for 6
grants (high: $210,000; low: $816).
Fields of interest: International human rights;
Education; Immigrants/refugees.
Limitations: Applications accepted. Giving in the
U.S. and Vietnam.
Application information: Applicant must document
financial need.
   Initial approach: Letter
   Deadline(s): None
Trustees: Thu-Le Doan; Doan L. Phung.
EIN: 880378074

1148
The Hahn Family Foundation
30 Strada DiVillagio, No. 251
Henderson, NV   89011-2807

Established in 2006 in NV.
Donors: Paul Hahn; David J. Hahn.
Grantmaker type: Independent foundation.
Financial data (yr. ended 12/31/10): Assets,
$9,677,522 (M); expenditures, $2,640,043;

qualifying distributions, $2,600,000; giving
activities include $2,600,000 for grants.
Fields of interest: Christian agencies & churches;
Protestant agencies & churches.
Type of support: General/operating support.
Limitations: Giving primarily in CA; some funding
also in HI and PA. No grants to individuals.
Trustees: Hai Joung Yoon Hahn; Sang Hoon Hahn.
EIN: 207055857
Recent grants for international programs:
1148-1 Africa Inland Mission International, Pearl
   River, NY, $25,000. 2009.
1148-2 Spiritual Awakening Mission, Concord, CA,
   $100,000. 2009.

1149
The M-K LINK Foundation
c/o Stephen Haberkorn
P.O. Box 80270
Las Vegas, NV   89180-0270

Established in 1997 in AZ.
Donor: MK-LINK Investments LP.
Grantmaker type: Independent foundation.
Financial data (yr. ended 05/31/11): Assets,
$10,307,674 (M); expenditures, $4,907,254;
qualifying distributions, $4,889,090; giving
activities include $4,889,090 for grants.
Fields of interest: Community/economic
development; Cancer; Higher education, university;
Medical school/education; Education; Hospitals
(general); Human services; International affairs,
U.N.; Jewish agencies & synagogues.
Limitations: Applications not accepted. Giving
primarily in CA and NV. No grants to individuals.
Application information: Contributes only to
pre-selected organizations.
Officers and Directors:* Stephen Haberkorn,*
Pres.; Matthew Haberkorn, V.P.; Vicki Haberkorn
Abeles,* Secy.
EIN: 860870822

1150
Abraham and Sonia Rochlin Foundation
3690 Grant Dr., Ste. I-2
Reno, NV   89509-5360
Contact: Heidemarie Rochlin, Pres.

Established in 1969 in CA.
Donors: Abraham Rochlin†; Sonia Rochlin;
Heidemarie Rochlin; Heidemarie Rochlin Trust.
Grantmaker type: Independent foundation.
Financial data (yr. ended 12/31/10): Assets,
$45,416,778 (M); expenditures, $1,819,918;
qualifying distributions, $1,626,989; giving
activities include $1,626,989 for grants.
Purpose and activities: Grants primarily for Jewish
organizations, including welfare funds and higher
educational institutions.
Fields of interest: Higher education; Human
services; Jewish federated giving programs; Jewish
agencies & synagogues.
Limitations: Applications not accepted. Giving
primarily in CA, NV, and NY. No grants to individuals.
Publications: Annual report.
Application information: Contributes only to
pre-selected organizations.
Officers: Heidemarie Rochlin, Pres.; Joseph
Schonwald, V.P.
EIN: 941696244
Recent grants for international programs:

1150-1 American Committee for the Weizmann
   Institute of Science, New York, NY, $100,000.
   2009.
1150-2 American Friends of Interdisciplinary Center
   Herzliya, New York, NY, $30,000. 2009.
1150-3 American Jewish Joint Distribution
   Committee, New York, NY, $450,000. 2009.
1150-4 Ben-Gurion University of the Negev, Beer
   Sheva, Israel, $40,000. 2009.
1150-5 Israel Guide Dog Center for the Blind,
   Warrington, PA, $20,000. 2009.
1150-6 Israel Special Kids Fund, New York, NY,
   $10,000. 2009.
1150-7 Livnot ULehibanot, Tzfat, Israel, $25,000.
   2009.
1150-8 Open University of Israel, Friends of the,
   New York, NY, $20,000. 2009.
1150-9 ORT America, New York, NY, $75,000.
   2009.
1150-10 PEF Israel Endowment Funds, New York,
   NY, $690,000. 2009.
1150-11 Schechter Institute of Jewish Studies,
   Jerusalem, Israel, $50,000. 2009.
1150-12 Shalom Hartman Institute of Judaic
   Studies, Jerusalem, Israel, $30,000. 2009.
1150-13 Tevel b Tzedek: An Israeli Non-Profit for
   Social and Environmental Justice, Jerusalem,
   Israel, $25,000. 2009.
1150-14 Tikva Childrens Home, New York, NY,
   $50,000. 2009.

1151
Cyrus Tang Foundation
(formerly Tang Family Foundation)
8960 Spanish Ridge Ave.
Las Vegas, NV   89148-1302   (702) 734-3700
Contact: Stella Liang, Treas.
FAX: (702) 734-6766;
E-mail: tang@tangfoundation.org; URL: http://
www.tangfoundation.org
Photo Galleries: http://www.tangfoundation.org/
index.php?
option=com_content&view=article&id=51&Itemid=
97&site=CTF&sub=7

Established in 1996 in NV.
Donors: Cyrus Tang; Tang Industries, Inc.
Grantmaker type: Independent foundation.
Financial data (yr. ended 12/31/09): Assets,
$116,121,398 (M); gifts received, $16,500;
expenditures, $6,763,623; qualifying distributions,
$6,705,871; giving activities include $6,475,605
for 86 grants (high: $2,198,350; low: $605).
Purpose and activities: Giving primarily to improve
the quality of life in disadvantaged communities of
China, through effective investments in education
and public health, and by fostering community spirit.
Fields of interest: Higher education; Scholarships/
financial aid; Education; Human services.
International interests: China.
Type of support: Building/renovation; Scholarship
funds; Matching/challenge support.
Limitations: Applications not accepted. Giving
primarily in China. No grants to individuals.
Application information: Contributes only to
pre-selected organizations. Applications are by
invitation only, and are also accepted in Chinese
(traditional or simplified).
Officers and Directors:* Cyrus Tang,* Pres.;
Michael Tang,* V.P.; Vytas Ambutas, Secy.; Stella
Liang,* Treas.
Number of staff: 3 full-time professional.
EIN: 880361180

Recent grants for international programs:

1151-1 Anhui University of Technology, Ma'anshan, China, $70,347. For CT scholarship. 2009.

1151-2 Anhui University of Technology, Ma'anshan, China, $11,730. For Reap. Program - Scholarship. 2009.

1151-3 Anhui University of Technology, Ma'anshan, China, $11,725. For CT scholarship. 2009.

1151-4 Beijing Normal University, Beijing, China, $64,485. For CT scholarship. 2009.

1151-5 Chongqing University of Science and Technology, Chongqing, China, $65,071. For CT scholarship. 2009.

1151-6 Fudan University, Shanghai, China, $47,484. For CT scholarship. 2009.

1151-7 Jiangsu Shengze Hospital, Shengze, China, $2,198,350. 2009.

1151-8 Jiangsu Shengze Hospital, Shengze, China, $733,138. 2009.

1151-9 Lailong Middle School, China, $29,326. For Pass the Torch Program. 2009.

1151-10 Nanjing Agricultural University, Nanjing, China, $48,071. For CT scholarship. 2009.

1151-11 Nanjing University, Nanjing, China, $70,933. For CT scholarship. 2009.

1151-12 Nanjing University of Traditional Chinese Medicine, Nanjing, China, $439,670. For research laboratory. 2009.

1151-13 Nanjing University of Traditional Chinese Medicine, Nanjing, China, $78,554. For CT scholarship. 2009.

1151-14 Northwest A&F University, Xian, China, $199,695. For Seed development fund. 2009.

1151-15 Northwest A&F University, Xian, China, $70,347. For CT scholarship. 2009.

1151-16 Northwest A&F University, Xian, China, $29,326. To support Model Village. 2009.

1151-17 Northwest University, Xian, China, $70,347. For CT scholarship. 2009.

1151-18 Northwest University, Xian, China, $11,730. For Reap. Program - Scholarship. 2009.

1151-19 Northwest University, Xian, China, $11,725. For CT scholarship. 2009.

1151-20 Overseas Chinese Affairs Office of Wujiang City, China, $49,267. For CTF Scholarship. 2009.

1151-21 Shanghai Jiao Tong University, Shanghai, China, $46,898. For CT scholarship. 2009.

1151-22 Sichuan University, Chengdu, China, $65,071. For CT scholarship. 2009.

1151-23 Sichuan University, Chengdu, China, $11,730. For Reap. Program - Scholarship. 2009.

1151-24 Sichuan University, Chengdu, China, $11,725. For Zee scholarship. 2009.

1151-25 Soochow University, Suzhou, China, $439,883. For Center for Hem. 2009.

1151-26 Soochow University, Suzhou, China, $72,106. For CT scholarship. 2009.

1151-27 Southeast University, Nanjing, China, $46,898. For CT scholarship. 2009.

1151-28 Suchai Middle School, China, $21,994. For Pass the Torch Program. 2009.

1151-29 Tsinghua University, Beijing, China, $64,485. For CT scholarship. 2009.

1151-30 University of Science and Technology of China, Hefei, China, $82,072. For CT scholarship. 2009.

1151-31 Xian Jiaotong University, Xian, China, $73,202. For Fine Art Garden. 2009.

1151-32 Xian Jiaotong University, Xian, China, $72,106. For CT scholarship. 2009.

1151-33 Xian Jiaotong University, Xian, China, $11,730. For Reap. Program - Scholarship. 2009.

1151-34 Xian Jiaotong University, Xian, China, $11,725. For CT scholarship. 2009.

1151-35 Xian University of Technology, Xian, China, $70,347. For CT scholarship. 2009.

1151-36 Zhou Zi Education Association, China, $73,314. For Pass the Torch Program. 2009.

1151-37 Zhou Zi Education Association, China, $73,202. For Pass the Torch Program. 2009.

1152

The Dale & Edna Walsh Foundation

(also known as D.E.W. Foundation)
6461 Valley Wood Dr.
Reno, NV 89523-1271   (775) 200-3446
Contact: Shai B. Edberg, Dir.
FAX: (775) 787-3069;
E-mail: info@dewfoundation.org; URL: http://www.dewfoundation.org

Established in 1994 in IL.
Donors: Dale Walsh; Edna Walsh; DEW Building.
Grantmaker type: Independent foundation.
Financial data (yr. ended 12/31/10): Assets, $12,841 (M); expenditures, $962,187; qualifying distributions, $885,475; giving activities include $760,457 for 58 grants (high: $110,000; low: $82).
Purpose and activities: The foundation joins hands with effective charitable organizations to meet human need and to promote the common good world-wide, encouraging and empowering the foundation family's personal involvement.
Fields of interest: Arts; Higher education; Environment; Health organizations, association; Human services; Children, services; Family services; International affairs; Foundations (community).
Type of support: General/operating support; Continuing support; Income development; Management development/capacity building; Capital campaigns; Building/renovation; Equipment; Land acquisition; Emergency funds; Program development; Conferences/seminars; Publication; Seed money; Curriculum development; Scholarship funds; Research; Technical assistance; Consulting services; Program evaluation; Employee matching gifts; Matching/challenge support.
Limitations: Applications accepted. Giving limited to U.S.-based organizations only. No support for church operations, or political organizations. No grants to individuals, or for debt retirement or scholarships; no loans.
Application information: Full proposals accepted by invitation only. If proposals are invited, foundation will require additional documentation. Application form required.
  Initial approach: Use online Letter of Inquiry which can be accessed through foundation web site
  Copies of proposal: 1
  Deadline(s): Sept. 1
  Board meeting date(s): Apr. and Nov.
  Final notification: 3 weeks
Officers and Directors:* Dale Walsh,* Chair.; Edna Walsh,* Secy.; Patricia Walsh, Treas.; Jennifer Connell.
Advisory Board: Shai B. Edberg; Joyce Hagberg; Bill Morris; Darin Walsh; Mark Walsh.
Number of staff: 2 full-time professional.
EIN: 363994121

1153

Paul and Pamela Wood Foundation

937 Tahoe Blvd., Ste. 200
Incline Village, NV 89451-7412

Established in 1999 in NV.
Donors: Paul A. Wood; Pamela R. Wood.
Grantmaker type: Independent foundation.
Financial data (yr. ended 12/31/10): Assets, $3,237,712 (M); expenditures, $158,136; qualifying distributions, $149,801; giving activities include $149,801 for 3 grants (high: $70,000; low: $32,300).
Fields of interest: International development; Health organizations; Philosophy/ethics; Higher education; Food services; Children, services; Youth, pregnancy prevention; United Ways and Federated Giving Programs.
International interests: Australia.
Limitations: Applications not accepted. Giving primarily in CA, Washington, DC, NC, NY, and TX; giving internationally in Australia. No grants to individuals.
Application information: Contributes only to pre-selected organizations.
Officers: Pamela R. Wood, Pres.; Paul A. Wood, Secy.
EIN: 880444004

NEW HAMPSHIRE

1154

Brookstone, Inc. Corporate Giving Program

1 Innovation Way
Merrimack, NH 03054-4873   (603) 577-8005
URL: http://www.brookstone.com/brookstone-donate-to-tsunami-relief.html?bkiid=hmpg|hdr|banner|donate

Grantmaker type: Corporate giving program.
Purpose and activities: Brookstone, Inc. makes charitable contributions to nonprofit organizations on a case by case basis.
Fields of interest: International relief; Disasters, floods; Disasters, preparedness/services.
Type of support: General/operating support.

1155

The Butler Foundation

(formerly Neslab Charitable Foundation)
c/o Charter Trust Co.
90 N. Main St.
Concord, NH 03301-4915   (603) 224-1350

Established in 1985 in NH.
Donors: Clara W. Butler Trust; Thomas Butler Trust.
Grantmaker type: Independent foundation.
Financial data (yr. ended 12/31/10): Assets, $9,230,880 (M); expenditures, $705,547; qualifying distributions, $588,005; giving activities include $588,005 for grants.
Purpose and activities: Giving primarily for environmental conservation; scholarship awards to children of employees of NES Labs.

Fields of interest: Arts; Higher education; Environment, natural resources; Animals/wildlife; Community/economic development.
International interests: Ecuador.
Type of support: General/operating support; Program development; Research; Scholarships—to individuals.
Limitations: Applications accepted. Giving primarily in NH and WI.
Application information: Scholarship applicants must submit an essay and high school grades. U.S. applicants are limited to the children of employees of NES Labs.
   Deadline(s): None
Officer and Trustees:* Cynthia Wentworth,* Exec. Dir.; Steven Albrecht; Bonnie B. Bunning; Barbara Butler; Clara W. Butler; Marjorie W. Butler; F. Graham McSwiney, Esq.
EIN: 222701588
Recent grants for international programs:
1155-1 University of Wisconsin, Madison, WI, $33,434. For Archaeological Field School Palmitopamba. 2009.
1155-2 World Land Trust-US, Washington, DC, $23,100. For building of an interpretive center. 2009.

NEW JERSEY

1156
Akhoury Foundation, Inc.
6 Pine Valley Way
Florham Park, NJ   07932-2700

Established in 1995 in NJ.
Donor: Ravindranath Akhoury.
Grantmaker type: Independent foundation.
Financial data (yr. ended 12/31/10): Assets, $668,382 (M); gifts received, $91,930, expenditures, $266,839; qualifying distributions, $266,459; giving activities include $266,459 for 77 grants (high: $25,000; low: $2).
Fields of interest: United Ways and Federated Giving Programs; Elementary/secondary education; Higher education; Libraries (public); Human services; Catholic agencies & churches.
International interests: India.
Limitations: Applications not accepted. Giving primarily in NJ and NY. No grants to individuals.
Application information: Contributes only to pre-selected organizations.
Trustees: Priya Joy Akhoury; Ravindranath Akhoury; Virginia Akhoury.
EIN: 223417520

1157
American Hungarian Foundation
300 Somerset St.
P.O. Box 1084
New Brunswick, NJ   08901-2248
(732) 846-5777
Contact: August J. Molnar, Pres.
FAX: (732) 249-7033;
E-mail: info@ahfoundation.org; URL: http://www.ahfoundation.org

Established in 1954.
Grantmaker type: Public charity.
Financial data (yr. ended 06/30/09): Revenue, $266,426; assets, $2,499,037 (M); gifts received, $296,996; expenditures, $588,994.
Purpose and activities: The foundation is devoted to furthering the understanding and appreciation of Hungarian cultural heritage in the U.S. Through grantmaking activities, the foundation supports student and scholar exchange, publications, academic programs, fellowships, and research at American universities and colleges.
Fields of interest: Arts, cultural/ethnic awareness; Education.
International interests: Hungary.
Type of support: Program development; Publication; Fellowships; Research; Scholarships—to individuals.
Limitations: Giving on a national basis.
Application information: Applicants must submit a letter including applicant's interest in Hungarian studies, program to be pursued, biography, location of proposed study, names and addresses of 3 references, and a list of sources to which applicant applied for assistance. Application form not required.
   Initial approach: Letter
Officers and Directors:* Zsolt Harsanyi,* Ph.D., Chair.; John F. Barna,* Vice-Chair.; Thomas G. Gasper,* Vice-Chair.; Laszlo Papp,* Vice-Chair.; August J. Molnar,* Pres.; Ernest W. Docs,* Secy.; Frank J. Chrinko, Jr.,* Treas.; J. Andrea Alstrup; Alexander Brody; and 16 additional directors.
EIN: 366085105

1158
Aufzien Foundation, Inc.
350 Passaic Ave.
Fairfield, NJ   07004-2025   (973) 575-5132
Contact: Alan Aufzien, Dir.

Established in 1987 in NJ.
Donors: Alan Aufzien; Norma Aufzien; Jonathan Aufzien; Leslie Levine.
Grantmaker type: Independent foundation.
Financial data (yr. ended 12/31/10): Assets, $5,830,638 (M); gifts received, $30,600; expenditures, $548,337; qualifying distributions, $436,500; giving activities include $436,500 for 21 grants (high: $200,000; low: $500).
Purpose and activities: Giving primarily to Jewish organizations and temples.
Fields of interest: International affairs; Arts; Higher education; Health organizations, association; Human services; Jewish federated giving programs; Jewish agencies & synagogues.
Type of support: Annual campaigns; Capital campaigns; Emergency funds; Scholarship funds.
Limitations: Giving primarily in New York, NY; giving also in Washington, DC, NJ, and PA. No grants to individuals.
Application information: Application form not required.
   Initial approach: Letter
   Deadline(s): None
Directors: Alan Aufzien; Jonathan Aufzien; Lisa Aufzien; Norma Aufzien; Meredith Bauer; Leslie Levine.
EIN: 222838652

1159
BD Corporate Giving Program
1 Becton Dr.
Franklin Lakes, NJ   07417-1815
Contact: Jennifer Farrington, Mgr., Community Partnerships
URL: http://www.bd.com/responsibility

Grantmaker type: Corporate giving program.
Financial data (yr. ended 12/31/08): Total giving, $9,718,118, including $6,251,162 for grants, and $3,466,956 for in-kind gifts.
Purpose and activities: BD makes charitable contributions to nonprofit organizations involved with health and human services and community development. Support is given on a national and international basis.
Fields of interest: Public health; Health care; Human services; Community/economic development.
International interests: Africa; Asia; Europe; Latin America; Middle East.
Type of support: General/operating support; Program development; Employee volunteer services; Employee matching gifts; Donated equipment; Donated products; In-kind gifts.
Limitations: Applications not accepted. Giving on a national and international basis, with emphasis on areas of company operations. No grants to individuals, or for fundraising, workshops, sporting events, dinners, or event-driven activities.
Application information: Contributes only to pre-selected organizations. The Community Relations Department handles giving. A contributions committee reviews all requests.
   Committee meeting date(s): Semi-annual
Number of staff: 1 full-time professional; 2 part-time support.

1160
The Russell Berrie Foundation
300 Frank W. Burr Blvd., 7th Fl., Ste. 8
Teaneck, NJ   07666-6704   (201) 928-1880
Contact: Ruth Salzman, C. E. O
E-mail: inquiry@rbfdtn.org; URL: http://www.russellberriefoundation.org
E-Newsletter: http://www.russellberriefoundation.org/getinvolved-enewsletter.php

Established in 1985 in NJ.
Donor: Russell Berrie†.
Grantmaker type: Independent foundation.
Financial data (yr. ended 12/31/10): Assets, $239,173,537 (M); gifts received, $3,000,027; expenditures, $16,639,357; qualifying distributions, $15,722,843; giving activities include $13,788,407 for 99 grants (high: $3,775,000; low: $300), and $100,000 for 11 grants to individuals.
Purpose and activities: The foundation as created to express the values and passions of Russell Berrie through social investments in innovative ideas designed to: 1) Promote the continuity and enrichment of Jewish communal life; 2) Support advances in medicine focusing on diabetes and humanism in medicine; 3) Fostering the spirit of religious understanding and pluralism; 4) Recognizing individuals who have made a significant difference to the lives of others; 5) Elevating the profession of sales; and 6) Raising the awareness of terrorism and promoting its prevention.
Fields of interest: Engineering/technology; Science, research; Health care, clinics/centers; Medical research; Jewish agencies & synagogues; Religion,

interfaith issues; Human services; Hospitals (general); Higher education; Arts.

Type of support: General/operating support; Continuing support; Management development/capacity building; Emergency funds; Program development; Fellowships; Research; Matching/challenge support.

Limitations: Applications not accepted. Giving primarily in northern NJ, New York City, Israel, and Italy.

Application information: Unsolicited requests for funds not accepted.

Officers and Trustees:* Ruth Salzman, C.E.O. and Exec. Dir.; Angelica Berrie,* Pres.; Scott Berrie,* V.P.; Myron Rosner,* Secy.; Adam Hirsch, C.F.O.; Steven Seiden,* Treas.; Ilan Kaufthal; Norman Seiden.

Number of staff: 8 full-time professional.

EIN: 222620908

Recent grants for international programs:

1160-1 American Friends of Beit Morasha, Rockaway Park, NY, $441,500. For Identity and Purpose Program. 2009.

1160-2 American Friends of Beit Morasha, Rockaway Park, NY, $330,000. For Identity and Purpose Program. 2009.

1160-3 American Friends of Interdisciplinary Center Herzliya, New York, NY, $25,000. For conference. 2009.

1160-4 American Friends of NATAL, New York, NY, $50,000. For general operating support. 2009.

1160-5 American Friends of Shalom Hartman Institute, New York, NY, $1,860,000. For Be'eri Initiative. 2009.

1160-6 American Friends of Shalom Hartman Institute, New York, NY, $440,000. For Be'eri Initiative. 2009.

1160-7 American Friends of Shalom Hartman Institute, New York, NY, $217,500. For Melandim Program. 2009.

1160-8 American Friends of Shalom Hartman Institute, New York, NY, $200,000. For general operating support. 2009.

1160-9 American Friends of the Israel Museum, New York, NY, $10,000. For honoring of Judy and Michael Steinhardt. 2009.

1160-10 American Friends of the Reut Institute, Beverly Hills, CA, $50,000. For general operating support. 2009.

1160-11 American Jewish Joint Distribution Committee, New York, NY, $10,000. For general operating support. 2009.

1160-12 American Society for Technion-Israel Institute of Technology, New York, NY, $5,200,000. To establish Russell Berrie Nanotechnology Institute. 2009.

1160-13 American Society for Technion-Israel Institute of Technology, New York, NY, $100,000. For Na'am program. 2009.

1160-14 Boys Town Jerusalem, Jerusalem, Israel, $100,000. For campus renovations. 2009.

1160-15 Counterterrorism and Security Educational Research Foundation, Washington, DC, $36,000. For investigative project capacity building. 2009.

1160-16 FJC, New York, NY, $10,000. For Arts Contemporary Israeli Art Fund. 2009.

1160-17 Friends of Ofanim, Wynnewood, PA, $41,667. To establish northern branch. 2009.

1160-18 Friends of Ofanim, Wynnewood, PA, $10,000. For Israel Discretionary. 2009.

1160-19 Friends of Yemin Orde, Rockville, MD, $20,000. For campaign gift. 2009.

1160-20 Hillel: The Foundation for Jewish Campus Life, Washington, DC, $33,333. For Hillels in Israel. 2009.

1160-21 Institute of International Education, New York, NY, $566,565. For Pope John Paul II Chair. 2009.

1160-22 Investigative Project on Terrorism Foundation, Washington, DC, $100,000. For general operating support. 2009.

1160-23 Israel Documentaries for Education and Scholarship, Tenafly, NJ, $10,000. For Israel discretionary fund. 2009.

1160-24 Jerusalem Foundation, Jerusalem, Israel, $10,000. For Cinematheques' Jewish Film Festival. 2009.

1160-25 KBY Congregations Together, Brooklyn, NY, $10,000. For Beit Tefilah Israel. 2009.

1160-26 Middle East Media Research Institute, Washington, DC, $50,000. For general operating support. 2009.

1160-27 New Israel Fund, Washington, DC, $100,000. For JVP Community Fund the Lab. 2009.

1160-28 New Israel Fund, Washington, DC, $25,000. For Fund Bakehila Leadership. 2009.

1160-29 New Israel Fund, Washington, DC, $20,000. For AHD Agent of Change Grant. 2009.

1160-30 UJA Federation of Northern New Jersey, Paramus, NJ, $25,000. For AJEEC Negev Institute for Strategies of Peace and Development. 2009.

1160-31 UJA Federation of Northern New Jersey, River Edge, NJ, $412,500. For Israel Emergency Aid. 2009.

1160-32 UJA Federation of Northern New Jersey, River Edge, NJ, $10,000. For Israeli Opera. 2009.

1161
Billig Foundation

c/o Gail A. Billig
311 Walnut St.
Englewood, NJ 07631-3105

Established in 1954 in NY.

Donors: Sali Billig; Gail Billig.

Grantmaker type: Independent foundation.

Financial data (yr. ended 10/31/10): Assets, $2,474,940 (M); gifts received, $15,000; expenditures, $158,154; qualifying distributions, $138,510; giving activities include $134,979 for 16 grants (high: $65,000; low: $50).

Purpose and activities: Giving primarily to Jewish organizations and institutes.

Fields of interest: United Ways and Federated Giving Programs; Arts; Theological school/education; Human services; Jewish federated giving programs; Jewish agencies & synagogues.

International interests: Israel.

Limitations: Applications not accepted. Giving primarily in New York, NY; some giving also in NJ. No grants to individuals.

Application information: Unsolicited requests for funds not accepted.

Trustees: Aaron Billig; Gail A. Billig; Evelyn Kenvin; Fred Kenvin.

EIN: 136147322

1162
Borgenicht Foundation, Inc.

392 Fairview Ave.
Long Valley, NJ 07853-3259

Grantmaker type: Independent foundation.

Financial data (yr. ended 03/31/11): Assets, $4,336,676 (M); expenditures, $631,869; qualifying distributions, $602,400; giving activities include $602,400 for grants.

Fields of interest: International affairs, goodwill promotion; Human services; Education; Higher education.

Limitations: Applications not accepted. Giving in the U.S., with some emphasis on DE, NY and PA. No grants to individuals.

Application information: Contributes only to pre-selected organizations.

Trustees: Jan Schwartz Baden; David Bennett; Frances Bordenicht; Yoel Borgenicht; Berta Kerr; James H. Knox.

EIN: 200051444

1163
C.I.S. Development Foundation, Inc.

77 Milltown Rd., Ste. 8C
East Brunswick, NJ 08816-2302
(732) 432-7037
FAX: (732) 432-7034; E-mail: mailto@cisdf.org;
URL: http://www.cisdf.org

Incorporated in 1994 in NJ.

Grantmaker type: Public charity.

Financial data (yr. ended 05/31/10): Revenue, $54,443,006; assets, $5,899,242 (M); gifts received, $54,442,686; expenditures, $55,326,328; giving activities include $54,203,694 for grants to organizations outside the U.S.

Purpose and activities: The foundation, for the mutual benefit of America and Russia, assists in the revival of Russia's (and other republics of the Former Soviet Union - FSU) economy and cultural heritage by sending non-monetary aid.

Fields of interest: International development.

International interests: Russia; Soviet Union (Former).

Type of support: In-kind gifts.

Limitations: Giving primarily in Russia and the republics of the Former Soviet Union.

Officers and Directors:* Alexander Bondarev,* Ph.D., Chair.; Maria Bondarev,* Pres.; Olga Welsh,* Secy.; Elena Iliushecheva; Larisa Poroshina; Igor Troshkin.

EIN: 223304404

1164
Croatian Relief Services, Inc.

225 Anderson Ave.
Fairview, NJ 07022-1401 (201) 945-4891
FAX: (201) 941-1344; E-mail: frgio@aol.com; Toll Free Tel. : (800)-932-4340; URL: http://www.croatianrelief.org

Established in 1991 in NJ.

Grantmaker type: Public charity.

Financial data (yr. ended 09/30/10): Revenue, $751,995; assets, $648,643 (M); gifts received, $741,253; expenditures, $778,726; program services expenses, $660,019; giving activities include $501,750 for grants to organizations outside the U.S.

Fields of interest: International relief.

International interests: Central America; Haiti; Bosnia-Herzegovina; Croatia; Africa.

Type of support: Grants to individuals.

Limitations: Giving on an international basis, with emphasis on Africa, Bosnia-Herzegovina, Central America, Croatia, and Haiti.

Officers: Fr. Giordano Belanich, Pres.; Daria Baricevic, Secy.-Treas.

EIN: 223203653

1165
The Daft Family Foundation
c/o Hamel Assoc., Inc.
615 W. Mt. Pleasant Ave.
Livingston, NJ 07039-1620

Established in 1998 in GA.

Donors: Delphine H. Daft; Douglas N. Daft.

Grantmaker type: Independent foundation.

Financial data (yr. ended 12/31/10): Assets, $3,387,391 (M); expenditures, $357,314; qualifying distributions, $355,000; giving activities include $355,000 for grants.

Fields of interest: Arts; Museums; Performing arts, theater; Elementary/secondary education; Higher education; Hospitals (general); International affairs, goodwill promotion.

International interests: Australia.

Type of support: General/operating support.

Limitations: Applications not accepted. Giving primarily in MA, with emphasis on Williamstown, and New York, NY. No grants to individuals.

Application information: Contributes only to pre-selected organizations.

Distribution Committee: Alexandra Louise Bonner; Delphine H. Daft; Douglas N. Daft; Nicholas Daft.

EIN: 586379765

1166
Danellie Foundation
P.O. Box 375/376
Marlton, NJ 08053-0375 (856) 273-6057
Contact: Nancy L. Dinsmore, Exec. Dir.
FAX: (856) 273-6977.
E-mail: danelliefoundation1@verizon.net

Established in 1988 in NJ.

Donor: Daniel L. Cheney.

Grantmaker type: Independent foundation.

Financial data (yr. ended 12/31/10): Assets, $3,987,388 (M); expenditures, $1,400,315; qualifying distributions, $1,306,830; giving activities include $1,299,220 for 67 grants (high: $140,000; low: $2,500).

Purpose and activities: Primary areas of interest include services for the financially disadvantaged, including housing and social services.

Fields of interest: AIDS; Children/youth, services; Christian agencies & churches; Community/economic development; Education; Employment, training; Homeless, human services; Housing/shelter, development; Human services; International relief; Residential/custodial care, hospices; Adults; Aging; AIDS, people with; Children; Children/youth; Disabilities, people with; Economically disadvantaged; Homeless; Mentally disabled; Offenders/ex-offenders; Single parents; Substance abusers; Young adults; Youth.

International interests: Guatemala; Haiti.

Type of support: General/operating support; Continuing support; Capital campaigns; Building/renovation; Program development; Scholarship funds; Sponsorships.

Limitations: Giving primarily in southern NJ (including Mercer and portions of Monmouth counties), and Baltimore, MD. No support for political organizations or professional sports, libraries or museums. No grants to individuals, or for endowments or radio and television.

Publications: Application guidelines.

Application information: The foundation is not accepting new applicants at this time. Applications are only being accepted from organizations which have received grants from the foundation in the past. Contact foundation for application guidelines. New York/New Jersey Area Common Application Form and New York/New Jersey Common Report Form accepted. Application form required.

Initial approach: Letter of inquiry/telephone
Copies of proposal: 2
Deadline(s): 3 weeks prior to meetings
Board meeting date(s): Varies
Final notification: 2 weeks after board meeting

Officers and Trustees:* Daniel L. Cheney,* Pres.; Eleanora L. Cheney,* Secy.-Treas.; Nancy L. Dinsmore,* Exec. Dir.; Julia Carleton; Richard D. Dinsmore; Keith A. Walter; Patricia E. Walter.

Number of staff: 1 part-time professional.

EIN: 222935245

1167
Mitzi & Warren Eisenberg Family Foundation, Inc.
c/o Rockdale Capital
650 Liberty Ave.
Union, NJ 07083-8130

Established in 1992 in NJ.

Donors: Warren Eisenberg; Bed Bath & Beyond, Inc.

Grantmaker type: Independent foundation.

Financial data (yr. ended 06/30/09): Assets, $73,365,740 (M); expenditures, $4,339,830; qualifying distributions, $4,315,670; giving activities include $4,307,245 for 190 grants (high: $375,207; low: $25).

Purpose and activities: Giving primarily to Jewish organizations and temples; giving also for the arts, medical research, and human services.

Fields of interest: Arts; Environment; Medical research, institute; Human services; Jewish agencies & synagogues.

Limitations: Applications not accepted. Giving primarily in NJ and NY. No grants to individuals.

Application information: Contributes only to pre-selected organizations.

Officers: Warren Eisenberg, Pres.; Maxine Eisenberg, Secy.; Ronald Eisenberg, Treas.

EIN: 521798583

Recent grants for international programs:

1167-1 American Friends of Neve Shalom/Wahat Al-Salam, Sherman Oaks, CA, $57,000. For general support. 2009.

1167-2 American Friends of Neve Shalom/Wahat Al-Salam, School for Peace, Sherman Oaks, CA, $57,000. For general support. 2009.

1167-3 American Friends of Yad Eliezer, Brooklyn, NY, $10,000. For general support. 2009.

1167-4 American Israel Education Foundation, Washington, DC, $75,000. For general support. 2009.

1167-5 American Society for Yad Vashem, New York, NY, $10,000. For general support. 2009.

1167-6 Boys Town Jerusalem Foundation of America, New York, NY, $10,000. For general support. 2009.

1167-7 Friends of the Israel Defense Forces, New York, NY, $300,000. For general support. 2009.

1167-8 Friends of the Israel Defense Forces, New York, NY, $100,000. For general support. 2009.

1167-9 Friends of the Israel Defense Forces, New York, NY, $25,000. For general support. 2009.

1167-10 Hand in Hand, American Friends of the Center for Jewish-Arab Education in Israel, Portland, OR, $25,000. For general support. 2009.

1167-11 Israel Childrens Centers, Deerfield Beach, FL, $10,000. For general support. 2009.

1167-12 Israel Policy Forum, New York, NY, $15,000. For general support. 2009.

1167-13 Israel Project, Washington, DC, $36,000. For general support. 2009.

1167-14 PEF Israel Endowment Funds, New York, NY, $150,000. For general support. 2009.

1168
The Fairbanks Family Foundation
319 Lenox Ave.
Westfield, NJ 07090-2137
Contact: Steven J. Giacona

Established in 2000 in FL.

Donors: Richard M. Fairbanks III; Shannon A. Fairbanks; Fairbanks Charitable Lead Unitrust.

Grantmaker type: Independent foundation.

Financial data (yr. ended 12/31/10): Assets, $5,085,048 (M); expenditures, $794,736; qualifying distributions, $730,150; giving activities include $730,150 for grants.

Fields of interest: Arts; Education; Human services; International affairs, goodwill promotion.

Limitations: Giving primarily in Washington, DC.

Application information:
Initial approach: Letter or proposal (1-2 pages)
Deadline(s): None

Trustees: Jonathan B. Fairbanks; Richard M. Fairbanks III; Shannon A. Fairbanks; Woods A. Fairbanks.

EIN: 582583288

1169
The William and Valerie Gaillard Foundation, Inc.
126 W. Indiana Ave.
Beach Haven, NJ 08008-2807

Established in 2000 in NJ.

Donors: Valerie Gaillard; William Gaillard.

Grantmaker type: Operating foundation.

Financial data (yr. ended 06/30/10): Assets, $770,910 (M); gifts received, $98,930; expenditures, $244,865; qualifying distributions, $187,500; giving activities include $187,500 for 13 grants (high: $68,000; low: $1,000).

Fields of interest: Human services; Children, services; International relief; Christian agencies & churches.

Limitations: Applications not accepted. No grants to individuals.

Application information: Unsolicited requests for funds not accepted.

Officers: William Gaillard, Pres. and Treas.; Larry L. Cook, V.P.; Valerie Gaillard, Secy.
EIN: 223760258

1170
The Jose M. Garcia Foundation, Inc.
851 Franklin Lakes Rd.
Franklin Lakes, NJ 07417-2242
Contact: Donald Quinn, Pres.
E-mail: dhquinn@garciafoundation.org; URL: http://www.garciafoundation.org

Grantmaker type: Independent foundation.
Financial data (yr. ended 10/31/10): Assets, $8,879,312 (M); expenditures, $561,715; qualifying distributions, $390,000; giving activities include $390,000 for grants.
Purpose and activities: Giving primarily to Christian and Lutheran churches and organizations, as well as to other religious organizations; funding also for children, youth and social services.
Fields of interest: Human services; Children/youth, services; Philanthropy/voluntarism; Christian agencies & churches; Religion; Asians/Pacific Islanders; Indigenous peoples; Homeless.
International interests: Latin America; Asia.
Limitations: Applications not accepted. Giving primarily in northern NJ; also giving on an international basis. No grants for administrative costs.
Application information: Unsolicited requests for funds not accepted.
Officer and Trustees:* Donald Quinn,* Pres.; Jorge Corominal; Laura Figueroa; Ella Glover; Gordon Meyer.
EIN: 223369956

1171
Burton G. and Anne C. Greenblatt Foundation, Inc.
111 Coolidge St.
South Plainfield, NJ 07080-3801
Contact: Anne C. Greenblatt, Tr.

Established in 1989 in NJ.
Donors: Anne C. Greenblatt; Burton G. Greenblatt; G & W Laboratories, Inc.
Grantmaker type: Independent foundation.
Financial data (yr. ended 03/31/11): Assets, $1,579,688 (M); gifts received, $2,511; expenditures, $186,261; qualifying distributions, $186,261; giving activities include $184,597 for 67 + grants (high: $40,000).
Purpose and activities: Giving only to cultural, educational, and religious organizations, with emphasis on Jewish organizations.
Fields of interest: Health sciences school/education; Museums (specialized); Arts; Higher education, university; Education; Medical care, in-patient care; Jewish agencies & synagogues.
International interests: Israel.
Limitations: Applications accepted. Giving primarily in NJ. No grants to individuals.
Application information: Application form not required.
  Initial approach: Letter
  Deadline(s): None
Trustees: Anne C. Greenblatt; Burton G. Greenblatt; Ronald Greenblatt.
EIN: 521638050

1172
Harbourton Foundation
47 Hulfish St., Ste. 305
Princeton, NJ 08542-3706
Contact: Amy H. Regan, V.P.

Established in 1982 in NJ.
Donor: James S. Regan.
Grantmaker type: Independent foundation.
Financial data (yr. ended 06/30/11): Assets, $21,888,769 (M); expenditures, $1,165,408; qualifying distributions, $1,146,240; giving activities include $1,083,104 for 38 grants (high: $278,660; low: $695).
Purpose and activities: Giving primarily for educational organizations, an international human rights organization, and children and youth services.
Fields of interest: Homeless, human services; Arts; Education, association; Environment, natural resources; Health organizations; Human services; Children/youth, services; International human rights.
Type of support: General/operating support; Capital campaigns; Program development; Technical assistance.
Limitations: Applications not accepted. Giving primarily in NJ, NY and Washington D.C. No grants to individuals.
Application information: Contributes only to pre-selected organizations.
Officers: James S. Regan, Pres. and Treas.; Amy H. Regan, V.P. and Secy.; Steven Smotrich, V.P.
Directors: Catherine H. Regan Lawliss; James S. Regan III; Patrick H. Regan.
EIN: 222436112

1173
The Harris Foundation for the Living Environment, Inc.
163 Hopewell-Wertsville Rd.
Hopewell, NJ 08525-1106

Established in 1992 in NJ.
Donors: Robert H. Harris; Stephanie G. Harris.
Grantmaker type: Independent foundation.
Financial data (yr. ended 06/30/11): Assets, $2,759,930 (M); expenditures, $157,906; qualifying distributions, $137,880; giving activities include $137,880 for grants.
Fields of interest: International affairs; Education; Environment, natural resources.
Type of support: General/operating support.
Limitations: Applications not accepted. Giving primarily in NJ, with some giving in Washington, DC, and HI. No grants to individuals.
Application information: Contributes only to pre-selected organizations.
Officers: Robert H. Harris, Pres.; Stephanie G. Harris, Treas.
Director: Alexander S. Harris.
EIN: 521743475

1174
Hoffmann-La Roche Inc. Corporate Giving Program
(formerly Roche Laboratories Inc. Corporate Giving Program)
c/o Corp. Donations and Sponsorship
340 Kingsland St.
Nutley, NJ 07110-1150 (973) 235-5000
URL: http://www.rocheusa.com/portal/usa/corporate_responsibility

Grantmaker type: Corporate giving program.
Purpose and activities: As a complement to its foundation, Hoffmann-La Roche also makes charitable contributions to nonprofit organizations directly. Support is given on a national and international basis.
Fields of interest: Science; Science, formal/general education; Science; Community/economic development; International relief; Human services; Disasters, preparedness/services; Health care.
Type of support: Building/renovation; Program development; Seed money; Fellowships; Research; Technical assistance; Sponsorships; In-kind gifts.
Limitations: Applications accepted. Giving primarily in areas of company operations. No support for political or religious organizations. No grants to individuals, or for mass mails, unsigned requests or broadcast requests throughout the corporation, commercial and/or mainstream entertainment events, fundraising events, third-party organizations, or advertising.
Application information: The Corporate Communications Department handles giving. Application form not required.
  Initial approach: Proposal to local General Manager; proposal to local Roche Research organization for scientific grants

1175
Hirair and Anna Hovnanian Foundation, Inc.
4000 Rte. 66, 4th Fl.
Tinton Falls, NJ 07753-7308 (732) 922-6100
Contact: Hirair Hovnanian, Chair.

Established in 1986 in FL.
Donors: Hirair Hovnanian; Anna Hovnanian.
Grantmaker type: Independent foundation.
Financial data (yr. ended 12/31/10): Assets, $52,016,777 (M); gifts received, $4,404,345; expenditures, $2,101,834; qualifying distributions, $1,516,240; giving activities include $1,516,240 for grants.
Purpose and activities: Giving primarily for Armenian culture and education.
Fields of interest: Arts, cultural/ethnic awareness; Higher education; Education; Health organizations; International affairs.
International interests: Armenia.
Limitations: Giving primarily in NJ and Washington, DC. No grants to individuals.
Application information:
  Initial approach: Letter on organization letterhead
  Deadline(s): None
Officers: Hirair Hovnanian, Chair.; Anna Hovnanian, Pres.; Edele Hovnanian, V.P. and Treas.; Armen Hovnanian, V.P.; Leela Hovnanian, V.P.; Siran Sahakian, V.P.; Tanya Hovnanian-Baghdassarian, Secy.
EIN: 592714390

1176
The IDT Charitable Foundation
520 Broad St.
Newark, NJ 07102-3121 (973) 438-1000
Contact: Sidney Mehl

Established as a company-sponsored operating foundation in 2001.
Donor: IDT Corp.
Grantmaker type: Operating foundation.
Financial data (yr. ended 12/31/10): Assets, $7,510,377 (M); expenditures, $1,415,369; qualifying distributions, $1,276,614; giving activities include $1,276,614 for 40 grants (high: $250,000; low: $90).
Purpose and activities: The foundation supports police agencies and organizations involved with education, health, cancer, human services, international relief, and Judaism.
Fields of interest: Crime/law enforcement, police agencies; Breast cancer; Elementary/secondary education; Higher education; Theological school/education; Education; Hospitals (general); Health care; Cancer; Children/youth, services; Human services; International relief; Jewish federated giving programs; Jewish agencies & synagogues.
International interests: Israel.
Type of support: General/operating support; Scholarship funds; Sponsorships; Program-related investments/loans.
Limitations: Applications not accepted. Giving on a national basis in areas of company operations, with emphasis on NJ, NY, and Israel. No grants to individuals.
Application information: Contributes only to pre-selected organizations.
Officers and Directors:* Howard Millendorf,* Pres.; Blake Reiser,* Treas.; Moshe Kaganoff.
EIN: 364450442

1177
The International Foundation
1700 Rte. 23N., Ste. 300
Wayne, NJ 07470-7537 (973) 406-3970
Contact: Edward A. Holmes, Grants Chair.
FAX: (973) 406-3969;
E-mail: info@intlfoundation.org; Additional tel.: (973) 227-6618; URL: http://www.intlfoundation.org

Incorporated in 1948 in DE.
Grantmaker type: Independent foundation.
Financial data (yr. ended 12/31/10): Assets, $0 (M); expenditures, $1,370,548; qualifying distributions, $1,090,263; giving activities include $759,250 for grants.
Purpose and activities: Giving to help people of developing nations in their endeavors to solve some of their problems, to attain a better standard of living, and to obtain a reasonable degree of self-sufficiency. Grants are made in the following general areas: 1) Agriculture: research and production, 2) Health: medical, nutrition, and water, 3) Education: formal at all levels research, 4) Social Development: cultural, economic, community, and entrepreneurial activity, and some aid to refugees, and grants for population planning are given, and 5) Environment.
Fields of interest: Arts; Libraries/library science; Education; Environment, natural resources; Environment; Hospitals (general); Medical care, rehabilitation; Health care; Health organizations, association; AIDS; Biomedicine; Medical research,

institute; AIDS research; Agriculture; Food services; Human services; International economic development; Urban/community development; Rural development; Voluntarism promotion; Marine science; Engineering/technology; Science; Catholic agencies & churches.
International interests: Caribbean; Southern Africa; Latin America; Oceania; Middle East; Philippines.
Type of support: Building/renovation; Equipment; Emergency funds; Program development; Seed money; Matching/challenge support.
Limitations: Applications accepted. Giving primarily to U.S.-based organizations to aid Asia, the Caribbean, Latin America, the Middle East, the Philippines, the South Pacific, and Southern Africa. No grants to individuals, or for endowment funds, operating budgets, scholarships, fellowships, matching gifts, video productions, or conferences; no loans.
Publications: Informational brochure (including application guidelines).
Application information: Unsolicited requests for funds are not accepted. Grant proposals are by invitation only, upon review of initial letter of inquiry. See foundation web site for guidelines. Application form required.
  Initial approach: Use letter of inquiry form on foundation web site
  Board meeting date(s): Jan., Apr., July, and Oct.
Officers and Trustees:* Edward A. Holmes,* Grants Chair.; John D. Carrico,* Pres.; Gary Dicovitsky,* Secy.-Treas.; William McCormack, M.D.; Douglas Walker.
Number of staff: 1 part-time professional; 1 part-time support.
EIN: 131962255

1178
Johnson & Johnson Corporate Giving Program
1 Johnson & Johnson Plz., WH7143
New Brunswick, NJ 08933-0001
FAX: (732) 524-3564; E-mail: smickus@its.jnj.com; Address for Community Health Care Prog.: Sierra Veale, Johnson & Johnson Community Health Care Prog., 615 N. Wolfe St., Ste. E2100, Baltimore, MD 21205, tel.: (443) 287-5138, fax: (410) 510-1974; Additional contacts: Intl. Progs. and Product Donations: Conrad Person, Dir., Intl. Progs./Product Giving, Arts/Culture, K-12 Education, and Employee Volunteer Services: Michael J. Bzdak, Dir., Corp. Contribs., fax: (732) 524-3300; URL: http://www.jnj.com/ourgiving

Grantmaker type: Corporate giving program.
Purpose and activities: As a complement to its foundation, Johnson & Johnson also makes charitable contributions to nonprofit organizations directly. Support is given on a national and international basis.
Fields of interest: Community/economic development; Disasters, preparedness/services; AIDS; Arts; Children, services; Education; Employment, services; Environment; Health care; Health care, cost containment; Human services; International relief; Nursing school/education; Public health; Girls; Women; Disabilities, people with.
International interests: South America; Oceania; South Asia; Southeast Asia; East Asia; Africa.
Type of support: Curriculum development; Donated products; Emergency funds; Employee matching gifts; Fellowships; Internship funds; Management

development/capacity building; Program development; Program evaluation; Research; Scholarship funds; Sponsorships.
Limitations: Applications not accepted. Giving on a national and international basis. No support for religious organizations not of direct benefit to the entire community or political, fraternal, or athletic organizations. No grants to individuals, or for general operating support, scholarships, trips or tours, endowments, or capital campaigns; no loans.
Application information: Unsolicited requests are not accepted. The Corporate Contributions department handles giving. The company has a staff that only handles contributions. A contributions committee reviews all requests.
Corporate Contributions Committee: Brian D. Perkins, Chair.; Sharon D'Agostino, V.P., Worldwide Corp. Contribs. and Community Rels.; Colleen A. Goggins; Raymond C. Jordan; Jose Antonio Justino; Donna Malin; David Norton; Jose V. Sartarelli, Ph.D.; Nicholas J. Valeriani.
Number of staff: 19 full-time professional; 1 part-time professional; 1 part-time support.

1179
Johnson & Johnson Family of Companies Contribution Fund
c/o Michele Lee
1 Johnson & Johnson Plz.
New Brunswick, NJ 08933-0001
URL: http://www.jnj.com/connect/caring/

Incorporated in 1953 in NJ.
Donor: Johnson & Johnson.
Grantmaker type: Company-sponsored foundation.
Financial data (yr. ended 12/31/09): Assets, $8,647,433 (M); gifts received, $52,857,179; expenditures, $49,558,298; qualifying distributions, $49,558,298; giving activities include $38,311,307 for 632 grants, and $11,244,991 for 22,567 employee matching gifts.
Purpose and activities: The foundation supports organizations involved with arts and culture, education, health, HIV/AIDS, hunger, human services, international affairs, philanthropy, and economically disadvantaged people.
Fields of interest: Education, early childhood education; Higher education; Food services; American Red Cross; Children, services; Philanthropy/voluntarism; International development; International affairs, U.N.; International affairs; Arts; Education; Hospitals (general); Health care; AIDS; Human services; United Ways and Federated Giving Programs; Economically disadvantaged.
Type of support: General/operating support; Continuing support; Annual campaigns; Program development; Scholarship funds; Employee matching gifts.
Limitations: Applications not accepted. Giving on a national basis in areas of company operations; giving also to national and international organizations. No support for fraternal, political, religious, or athletic organizations. No grants to individuals, or for debt reduction, trips, tours, capital campaigns or endowments, or publications; no loans.
Publications: Corporate giving report.
Application information: Contributes only to pre-selected organizations.
  Board meeting date(s): Mar., June, Sept., and Dec.

Officers: B.D. Perkins, Pres.; S. Dagostino, V.P.; M.H. Ullmann, Secy.; John A. Papa, Treas.
EIN: 226062811
Recent grants for international programs:

1179-1 African Medical and Research Foundation, New York, NY, $94,000. 2009.

1179-2 African Medical and Research Foundation, New York, NY, $81,508. 2009.

1179-3 African Medical and Research Foundation, New York, NY, $10,000. 2009.

1179-4 Aga Khan Foundation USA, Washington, DC, $24,048. 2009.

1179-5 American Jewish World Service, New York, NY, $50,000. 2009.

1179-6 American Near East Refugee Aid, Washington, DC, $25,000. 2009.

1179-7 Americans for UNFPA, New York, NY, $170,000. 2009.

1179-8 AmeriCares, Stamford, CT, $50,000. 2009.

1179-9 AmeriCares, Stamford, CT, $20,000. 2009.

1179-10 AmeriCares, Stamford, CT, $20,000. 2009.

1179-11 AmeriCares, Stamford, CT, $10,000. 2009.

1179-12 AmericaShare USA, New York, NY, $30,000. 2009.

1179-13 AmericaShare USA, New York, NY, $15,000. 2009.

1179-14 BRAC USA, New York, NY, $10,000. 2009.

1179-15 CARE USA, Atlanta, GA, $250,000. 2009.

1179-16 Catholic Medical Mission Board, New York, NY, $50,000. 2009.

1179-17 Catholic Medical Mission Board, New York, NY, $15,000. 2009.

1179-18 Children of God Relief Fund, Washington, DC, $35,000. 2009.

1179-19 Children of God Relief Fund, Washington, DC, $26,000. 2009.

1179-20 Christian Blind Mission International, Greenville, SC, $90,000. 2009.

1179-21 Direct Relief International, Santa Barbara, CA, $25,000. 2009.

1179-22 Direct Relief International, Santa Barbara, CA, $15,000. 2009.

1179-23 Direct Relief International, Santa Barbara, CA, $15,000. 2009.

1179-24 Encore Service Corps International, Washington, DC, $43,000. 2009.

1179-25 Engineers Without Borders USA, Boulder, CO, $10,000. 2009.

1179-26 FEMAP Foundation, El Paso, TX, $55,000. 2009.

1179-27 Fistula Foundation, Santa Clara, CA, $60,000. 2009.

1179-28 Fonkoze USA, Washington, DC, $15,000. 2009.

1179-29 Freedom from Hunger, Davis, CA, $50,000. 2009.

1179-30 Give2Asia, San Francisco, CA, $150,000. 2009.

1179-31 Give2Asia, San Francisco, CA, $146,403. 2009.

1179-32 Give2Asia, San Francisco, CA, $127,068. 2009.

1179-33 Give2Asia, San Francisco, CA, $122,960. 2009.

1179-34 Give2Asia, San Francisco, CA, $105,000. 2009.

1179-35 Give2Asia, San Francisco, CA, $100,000. 2009.

1179-36 Give2Asia, San Francisco, CA, $96,930. 2009.

1179-37 Give2Asia, San Francisco, CA, $95,000. 2009.

1179-38 Give2Asia, San Francisco, CA, $88,600. 2009.

1179-39 Give2Asia, San Francisco, CA, $88,540. 2009.

1179-40 Give2Asia, San Francisco, CA, $87,200. 2009.

1179-41 Give2Asia, San Francisco, CA, $80,100. 2009.

1179-42 Give2Asia, San Francisco, CA, $80,000. 2009.

1179-43 Give2Asia, San Francisco, CA, $80,000. 2009.

1179-44 Give2Asia, San Francisco, CA, $80,000. 2009.

1179-45 Give2Asia, San Francisco, CA, $75,000. 2009.

1179-46 Give2Asia, San Francisco, CA, $72,500. 2009.

1179-47 Give2Asia, San Francisco, CA, $70,000. 2009.

1179-48 Give2Asia, San Francisco, CA, $58,000. 2009.

1179-49 Give2Asia, San Francisco, CA, $56,177. 2009.

1179-50 Give2Asia, San Francisco, CA, $56,000. 2009.

1179-51 Give2Asia, San Francisco, CA, $55,200. 2009.

1179-52 Give2Asia, San Francisco, CA, $53,253. 2009.

1179-53 Give2Asia, San Francisco, CA, $52,879. 2009.

1179-54 Give2Asia, San Francisco, CA, $51,016. 2009.

1179-55 Give2Asia, San Francisco, CA, $51,000. 2009.

1179-56 Give2Asia, San Francisco, CA, $50,476. 2009.

1179-57 Give2Asia, San Francisco, CA, $50,000. 2009.

1179-58 Give2Asia, San Francisco, CA, $46,000. 2009.

1179-59 Give2Asia, San Francisco, CA, $43,061. 2009.

1179-60 Give2Asia, San Francisco, CA, $42,000. 2009.

1179-61 Give2Asia, San Francisco, CA, $40,919. 2009.

1179-62 Give2Asia, San Francisco, CA, $40,000. 2009.

1179-63 Give2Asia, San Francisco, CA, $37,000. 2009.

1179-64 Give2Asia, San Francisco, CA, $36,716. 2009.

1179-65 Give2Asia, San Francisco, CA, $35,850. 2009.

1179-66 Give2Asia, San Francisco, CA, $35,000. 2009.

1179-67 Give2Asia, San Francisco, CA, $34,400. 2009.

1179-68 Give2Asia, San Francisco, CA, $32,550. 2009.

1179-69 Give2Asia, San Francisco, CA, $31,460. 2009.

1179-70 Give2Asia, San Francisco, CA, $30,000. 2009.

1179-71 Give2Asia, San Francisco, CA, $30,000. 2009.

1179-72 Give2Asia, San Francisco, CA, $29,142. 2009.

1179-73 Give2Asia, San Francisco, CA, $27,368. 2009.

1179-74 Give2Asia, San Francisco, CA, $27,268. 2009.

1179-75 Give2Asia, San Francisco, CA, $25,830. 2009.

1179-76 Give2Asia, San Francisco, CA, $25,000. 2009.

1179-77 Give2Asia, San Francisco, CA, $23,435. 2009.

1179-78 Give2Asia, San Francisco, CA, $22,650. 2009.

1179-79 Give2Asia, San Francisco, CA, $22,500. 2009.

1179-80 Give2Asia, San Francisco, CA, $21,400. 2009.

1179-81 Give2Asia, San Francisco, CA, $20,354. 2009.

1179-82 Give2Asia, San Francisco, CA, $20,000. 2009.

1179-83 Give2Asia, San Francisco, CA, $20,000. 2009.

1179-84 Give2Asia, San Francisco, CA, $19,984. 2009.

1179-85 Give2Asia, San Francisco, CA, $18,947. 2009.

1179-86 Give2Asia, San Francisco, CA, $17,443. 2009.

1179-87 Give2Asia, San Francisco, CA, $16,200. 2009.

1179-88 Give2Asia, San Francisco, CA, $16,000. 2009.

1179-89 Give2Asia, San Francisco, CA, $15,521. 2009.

1179-90 Give2Asia, San Francisco, CA, $15,000. 2009.

1179-91 Give2Asia, San Francisco, CA, $12,267. 2009.

1179-92 Give2Asia, San Francisco, CA, $12,000. 2009.

1179-93 Give2Asia, San Francisco, CA, $11,900. 2009.

1179-94 Give2Asia, San Francisco, CA, $11,775. 2009.

1179-95 Give2Asia, San Francisco, CA, $10,800. 2009.

1179-96 Give2Asia, San Francisco, CA, $10,560. 2009.

1179-97 Give2Asia, San Francisco, CA, $10,000. 2009.

1179-98 Global Fund for Children, Washington, DC, $200,000. 2009.

1179-99 Global Fund for Children, Washington, DC, $138,000. 2009.

1179-100 Global Fund for Women, San Francisco, CA, $129,600. 2009.

1179-101 Global Fund for Women, San Francisco, CA, $60,000. 2009.

1179-102 Harvard University, Cambridge, MA, $50,000. For Center for Health and the Global Environment in Boston. 2009.

1179-103 HealthRight International, New York, NY, $200,000. 2009.

1179-104 HealthRight International, New York, NY, $50,000. 2009.

1179-105 Heart to Heart International, Olathe, KS, $10,000. 2009.

1179-106 Heart to Heart International, Olathe, KS, $10,000. 2009.

1179-107 Heart to Heart International, Olathe, KS, $10,000. 2009.

1179-108 Heart to Heart International, Olathe, KS, $10,000. 2009.

1179-109 Helen Keller International, New York, NY, $100,000. 2009.

1179-110 Helen Keller International, New York, NY, $12,000. 2009.

1179-111 Hopital Albert Schweitzer Haiti, Deschapelles, Haiti, $15,000. 2009.

1179-112 INMED Partnerships for Children, Ashburn, VA, $50,000. 2009.

1179-113 INMED Partnerships for Children, Ashburn, VA, $50,000. 2009.

1179-114 INMED Partnerships for Children, Ashburn, VA, $20,000. 2009.

1179-115 INSEAD Management Education Foundation, New York, NY, $26,060. 2009.

1179-116 Interchurch Medical Assistance, New Windsor, MD, $10,000. 2009.

1179-117 International Aid, Spring Lake, MI, $84,000. 2009.

1179-118 International Aid, Spring Lake, MI, $20,510. 2009.

1179-119 International Aid, Spring Lake, MI, $10,000. 2009.

1179-120 International Rescue Committee, New York, NY, $475,000. 2009.

1179-121 International Rescue Committee, New York, NY, $150,000. 2009.

1179-122 International Rescue Committee, New York, NY, $80,000. 2009.

1179-123 International Rescue Committee, New York, NY, $50,000. 2009.

1179-124 International Youth Foundation, Baltimore, MD, $50,000. 2009.

1179-125 International Youth Foundation, Baltimore, MD, $42,000. 2009.

1179-126 King Baudouin Foundation United States, New York, NY, $200,000. 2009.

1179-127 King Baudouin Foundation United States, New York, NY, $149,000. 2009.

1179-128 King Baudouin Foundation United States, New York, NY, $100,000. 2009.

1179-129 King Baudouin Foundation United States, New York, NY, $66,080. 2009.

1179-130 King Baudouin Foundation United States, New York, NY, $40,000. 2009.

1179-131 King Baudouin Foundation United States, New York, NY, $30,000. 2009.

1179-132 King Baudouin Foundation United States, New York, NY, $20,000. 2009.

1179-133 King Baudouin Foundation United States, New York, NY, $10,000. 2009.

1179-134 King Baudouin Foundation United States, New York, NY, $10,000. 2009.

1179-135 Lions Clubs International Foundation, Oak Brook, IL, $57,500. 2009.

1179-136 Management Sciences for Health, Cambridge, MA, $10,000. 2009.

1179-137 MAP International, Brunswick, GA, $90,000. 2009.

1179-138 MAP International, Brunswick, GA, $75,000. 2009.

1179-139 Medical Teams International, Tigard, OR, $50,000. 2009.

1179-140 Medical Teams International, Tigard, OR, $50,000. 2009.

1179-141 Missionaries of the Poor, Tucker, GA, $30,000. 2009.

1179-142 Mothers2Mothers, Cape Town, South Africa, $667,000. 2009.

1179-143 NBI Foundation, Valhalla, NY, $300,000. 2009.

1179-144 NBI Foundation, Valhalla, NY, $105,000. 2009.

1179-145 NBI Foundation, Valhalla, NY, $90,000. 2009.

1179-146 NBI Foundation, Valhalla, NY, $70,000. 2009.

1179-147 NBI Foundation, Valhalla, NY, $60,000. 2009.

1179-148 NBI Foundation, Valhalla, NY, $60,000. 2009.

1179-149 NBI Foundation, Valhalla, NY, $40,000. 2009.

1179-150 NBI Foundation, Valhalla, NY, $30,000. 2009.

1179-151 NBI Foundation, Valhalla, NY, $30,000. 2009.

1179-152 NBI Foundation, Valhalla, NY, $30,000. 2009.

1179-153 NBI Foundation, Valhalla, NY, $30,000. 2009.

1179-154 NBI Foundation, Valhalla, NY, $11,000. 2009.

1179-155 Operation Smile International, Norfolk, VA, $30,000. 2009.

1179-156 Operation Smile International, Norfolk, VA, $30,000. 2009.

1179-157 Operation Smile International, Norfolk, VA, $20,000. 2009.

1179-158 Partners in Health, Boston, MA, $85,000. 2009.

1179-159 Partnership for Quality Medical Donations, Bernville, PA, $35,000. 2009.

1179-160 Philani Fund USA, Princeton, NJ, $10,000. 2009.

1179-161 Planet Aid, Holliston, MA, $350,000. 2009.

1179-162 Population Services International, Washington, DC, $225,000. 2009.

1179-163 Pratham USA, Houston, TX, $20,305. 2009.

1179-164 Princeton in Africa, Princeton, NJ, $20,000. 2009.

1179-165 Princeton in Africa, Princeton, NJ, $10,000. 2009.

1179-166 Pro Mujer, New York, NY, $50,000. 2009.

1179-167 Project HOPE - The People-to-People Health Foundation, Millwood, VA, $60,000. 2009.

1179-168 Project HOPE - The People-to-People Health Foundation, Millwood, VA, $60,000. 2009.

1179-169 Project HOPE - The People-to-People Health Foundation, Millwood, VA, $30,000. 2009.

1179-170 Project HOPE - The People-to-People Health Foundation, Millwood, VA, $20,000. 2009.

1179-171 Project HOPE - The People-to-People Health Foundation, Millwood, VA, $10,000. 2009.

1179-172 Renascer, Friends of, New York, NY, $60,000. 2009.

1179-173 Resource Foundation, New York, NY, $80,000. 2009.

1179-174 Resource Foundation, New York, NY, $80,000. 2009.

1179-175 Resource Foundation, New York, NY, $70,000. 2009.

1179-176 Resource Foundation, New York, NY, $70,000. 2009.

1179-177 Resource Foundation, New York, NY, $65,000. 2009.

1179-178 Resource Foundation, New York, NY, $65,000. 2009.

1179-179 Resource Foundation, New York, NY, $55,000. 2009.

1179-180 Resource Foundation, New York, NY, $50,000. 2009.

1179-181 Resource Foundation, New York, NY, $50,000. 2009.

1179-182 Resource Foundation, New York, NY, $50,000. 2009.

1179-183 Resource Foundation, New York, NY, $45,000. 2009.

1179-184 Resource Foundation, New York, NY, $40,000. 2009.

1179-185 Resource Foundation, New York, NY, $40,000. 2009.

1179-186 Resource Foundation, New York, NY, $40,000. 2009.

1179-187 Resource Foundation, New York, NY, $35,000. 2009.

1179-188 Resource Foundation, New York, NY, $35,000. 2009.

1179-189 Resource Foundation, New York, NY, $35,000. 2009.

1179-190 Resource Foundation, New York, NY, $32,000. 2009.

1179-191 Resource Foundation, New York, NY, $30,000. 2009.

1179-192 Resource Foundation, New York, NY, $30,000. 2009.

1179-193 Resource Foundation, New York, NY, $30,000. 2009.

1179-194 Resource Foundation, New York, NY, $30,000. 2009.

1179-195 Resource Foundation, New York, NY, $30,000. 2009.

1179-196 Resource Foundation, New York, NY, $30,000. 2009.

1179-197 Resource Foundation, New York, NY, $30,000. 2009.

1179-198 Resource Foundation, New York, NY, $30,000. 2009.

1179-199 Resource Foundation, New York, NY, $30,000. 2009.

1179-200 Resource Foundation, New York, NY, $30,000. 2009.

1179-201 Resource Foundation, New York, NY, $30,000. 2009.

1179-202 Resource Foundation, New York, NY, $30,000. 2009.

1179-203 Resource Foundation, New York, NY, $30,000. 2009.

1179-204 Resource Foundation, New York, NY, $30,000. 2009.

1179-205 Resource Foundation, New York, NY, $30,000. 2009.

1179-206 Resource Foundation, New York, NY, $25,000. 2009.

1179-207 Resource Foundation, New York, NY, $25,000. 2009.

1179-208 Resource Foundation, New York, NY, $24,000. 2009.

1179-209 Resource Foundation, New York, NY, $20,000. 2009.

1179-210 Resource Foundation, New York, NY, $20,000. 2009.

1179-211 Resource Foundation, New York, NY, $20,000. 2009.

1179-212 Resource Foundation, New York, NY, $20,000. 2009.

1179-213 Resource Foundation, New York, NY, $20,000. 2009.

1179-214 Resource Foundation, New York, NY, $20,000. 2009.

1179-215 Resource Foundation, New York, NY, $20,000. 2009.

1179-216 Resource Foundation, New York, NY, $20,000. 2009.

1179-217 Resource Foundation, New York, NY, $20,000. 2009.

1179-218 Resource Foundation, New York, NY, $19,500. 2009.

1179-219 Resource Foundation, New York, NY, $18,000. 2009.

1179-220 Resource Foundation, New York, NY, $18,000. 2009.

1179-221 Resource Foundation, New York, NY, $18,000. 2009.

1179-222 Resource Foundation, New York, NY, $15,000. 2009.

1179-223 Resource Foundation, New York, NY, $15,000. 2009.

1179-224 Resource Foundation, New York, NY, $15,000. 2009.

1179-225 Resource Foundation, New York, NY, $15,000. 2009.

1179-226 Resource Foundation, New York, NY, $15,000. 2009.

1179-227 Resource Foundation, New York, NY, $15,000. 2009.

1179-228 Resource Foundation, New York, NY, $15,000. 2009.

1179-229 Resource Foundation, New York, NY, $15,000. 2009.

1179-230 Resource Foundation, New York, NY, $15,000. 2009.

1179-231 Resource Foundation, New York, NY, $15,000. 2009.

1179-232 Resource Foundation, New York, NY, $15,000. 2009.

1179-233 Resource Foundation, New York, NY, $15,000. 2009.

1179-234 Resource Foundation, New York, NY, $12,000. 2009.

1179-235 Resource Foundation, New York, NY, $11,000. 2009.

1179-236 Resource Foundation, New York, NY, $10,000. 2009.

1179-237 Resource Foundation, New York, NY, $10,000. 2009.

1179-238 Salvatorian Mission Warehouse, New Holstein, WI, $15,000. 2009.

1179-239 Save the Children Federation, Westport, CT, $200,000. 2009.

1179-240 Save the Children Federation, Westport, CT, $70,000. 2009.

1179-241 Save the Children Federation, Westport, CT, $36,000. 2009.

1179-242 Save the Children Federation, Westport, CT, $22,500. 2009.

1179-243 Save the Children Federation, Westport, CT, $12,500. 2009.

1179-244 Shared Interest, New York, NY, $20,000. 2009.

1179-245 Shared Interest, New York, NY, $10,000. 2009.

1179-246 Society of International Humanitarian Surgeons, New York, NY, $40,000. 2009.

1179-247 Solar Electric Light Fund, Washington, DC, $33,000. 2009.

1179-248 Solar Electric Light Fund, Washington, DC, $10,000. 2009.

1179-249 Solidarity and Action Against the HIV Infection in India, New York, NY, $60,000. 2009.

1179-250 Tostan, Washington, DC, $50,000. 2009.

1179-251 United Nations Development Fund for Women, New York, NY, $716,912. 2009.

1179-252 United States Fund for UNICEF, Washington, DC, $400,000. 2009.

1179-253 United States Fund for UNICEF, Washington, DC, $100,000. 2009.

1179-254 United States Fund for UNICEF, Washington, DC, $40,000. 2009.

1179-255 United States Fund for UNICEF, Washington, DC, $40,000. 2009.

1179-256 United States Fund for UNICEF, New York, NY, $200,000. 2009.

1179-257 VisionSpring, New York, NY, $50,000. 2009.

1179-258 Water.org, Kansas City, MO, $55,000. 2009.

1179-259 World Resources Institute, Washington, DC, $50,000. 2009.

1179-260 World Vision, Federal Way, WA, $50,000. 2009.

1179-261 World Wildlife Fund, Washington, DC, $500,000. 2009.

1179-262 World Wildlife Fund, Washington, DC, $58,300. 2009.

1180

Barbara Piasecka Johnson Foundation

c/o Danser Balaam & Frank
5 Independence Way
Princeton, NJ   08540-6627   (609) 688-1030
Contact: Beata P. Piasecka, V.P.

Established in 1976 in DE.
Donors: Barbara Piasecka Johnson; J. Seward Johnson, Sr.‡.
Grantmaker type: Independent foundation.
Financial data (yr. ended 12/31/10): Assets, $1,768,885 (M); gifts received, $261,061; expenditures, $405,222; qualifying distributions, $402,600; giving activities include $368,381 for 6 grants (high: $139,376; low: $15,897), and $7,950 for 3 grants to individuals (high: $5,000; low: $300).
Purpose and activities: Giving to support institutions which promote human rights in Poland, promote institutions of Polish character in the U.S. and abroad, and support artists and scientists, primarily those who are Polish or of Polish extraction, and institutions which support such individuals.
Fields of interest: Media, print publishing; Visual arts; Museums; Performing arts; Language/linguistics; Literature; Arts; Higher education; Medical school/education; Adult/continuing education; Libraries/library science; Education; Environment, natural resources; Environment; Heart & circulatory diseases; Medical research, institute; Heart & circulatory research; International human rights; International affairs; Civil/human rights; Engineering/technology; Biology/life sciences; Science; International studies; Religion; Economically disadvantaged.
International interests: Monaco; Poland.
Limitations: Giving in the U.S. and Poland.
Publications: Application guidelines.
Application information: Contributes generally only to pre-selected organizations. Scholarships and fellowships are for graduate, doctoral and postgraduate education only; no undergraduate programs considered. Application form required.
   Initial approach: Letter or telephone
   Copies of proposal: 1
   Deadline(s): Mar. 30 and Sept. 1; all considered within 3-month basis
   Board meeting date(s): July
Officers and Trustees:* Barbara Piasecka Johnson,* Chair. and Pres.; Beata P. Piasecka,* V.P. and Secy.; Wojciech Piasecki,* V.P.; Christopher Piasecki,* Treas.; Karolina Bandurski; Magdalena Piasecka Ludwin.
Number of staff: 1 part-time professional; 1 part-time support.
EIN: 510201795

1181

J. Seward Johnson, Sr. 1963 Charitable Trust

(formerly J. Seward Johnson, Sr. Charitable Trust)
100 Albany St., Ste. 200
New Brunswick, NJ   08901-2179
Contact: Karen Buyofsky

Established in 1963 in NJ.
Donor: J. Seward Johnson, Sr.‡.
Grantmaker type: Public charity.
Fields of interest: Media/communications; Education; Environment, water resources; Environment; Public health; Health care; Substance abuse, prevention; Crime/law enforcement; International affairs; Marine science.
Type of support: Scholarship funds; Land acquisition; Equipment; Endowments; Capital campaigns; Building/renovation; Program development; Seed money; Research.
Limitations: Applications accepted. Giving primarily in NJ, with emphasis on Princeton and New Brunswick; funding in the area of oceanography is given on a national basis. No grants to individuals, or for long-term support, deficit financing, publications, conferences, symposia, or dinners.
Publications: Informational brochure (including application guidelines).
Application information: Application form not required.
   Initial approach: 1-page letter
   Copies of proposal: 1
   Deadline(s): Rolling
   Board meeting date(s): Mar., June, Sept., and Dec.
Trustees: Robert T. Darretta; Christine A. Poon; William C. Weldon.
Number of staff: None.
EIN: 226054877

1182

Keser Dovid, Inc.

10 Cellar Rd.
Edison, NJ   08817-2903
Contact: Shimon Katz, Tr.

Established in 1991.
Grantmaker type: Public charity.
Financial data (yr. ended 12/31/10): Revenue, $96,180; assets, $11,326 (M); gifts received, $96,178; expenditures, $113,166; giving activities include $89,908 for grants.
Purpose and activities: The organization provides financial support to educational institutions in the U.S. and Israel.
Fields of interest: Education; Jewish agencies & synagogues.
International interests: Israel.
Type of support: Grants to individuals.
Limitations: Giving limited to Boca Raton, FL; Far Rockaway, NY; and Jerusalem, Israel.
Trustees: Eliezer Berger; Jacob Eisner; Shimon Katz.
EIN: 113008841

1183

Fanny and Svante Knistrom Foundation

229 Main St.
Chatham, NJ   07928-2408   (973) 635-5200
Contact: Mr. David Lloyd

Established in 1972 in NJ.

Donors: Svante Knistrom†; Fanny Knistrom†.
Grantmaker type: Independent foundation.
Financial data (yr. ended 05/31/10): Assets, $7,555,476 (M); expenditures, $538,865; qualifying distributions, $469,965; giving activities include $441,000 for grants.
Purpose and activities: Emphasis on health, education, and human rights, especially of marginal groups such as battered women, homeless families, and disabled persons.
Fields of interest: Education; Health care; Crime/ violence prevention, abuse prevention; Children/ youth, services; Youth, pregnancy prevention; International human rights; Minorities; Disabilities, people with.
International interests: Mexico.
Type of support: General/operating support; Capital campaigns; Seed money; Matching/challenge support.
Limitations: Applications accepted. Giving primarily in CA, NH, NJ, and SC. No support for political or religious purposes. No grants to individuals.
Application information: Application form not required.
> *Initial approach:* Letter
> *Deadline(s):* None
> *Board meeting date(s):* Apr. and Oct.
Officers and Trustees:* Virginia Kreuzberger,* Pres.; Gregory P. Buesing,* V.P. and Treas.; Douglas Kreuzberger, Secy.; Donna Barrett; Guy K. Buesing; Jean Buesing; Donald Kreuzberger; Carl A. Frahn; Kurt Kreuzberger; Scott Kreuzberger; Karen Turner.
EIN: 222011417

1184
The MCJ Amelior Foundation
(formerly The MCJ Foundation)
330 South St.
P.O. Box 1975
Morristown, NJ 07962-1975 (973) 540-1946
Contact: Suzanne M. Spero, Exec. Dir.

Established in 1983 in NJ.
Donors: Raymond G. Chambers; Kurt T. Borowsky; Harding Service, LLC.
Grantmaker type: Independent foundation.
Financial data (yr. ended 12/31/09): Assets, $126,148,360 (M); gifts received, $14,570; expenditures, $10,746,894; qualifying distributions, $10,743,590; giving activities include $8,475,997 for 460 grants (high: $500,000; low: $25).
Purpose and activities: Giving primarily for mentoring and youth initiatives.
Fields of interest: Education, early childhood education; Child development, education; Elementary school/education; Education; Health organizations, association; Crime/violence prevention, gun control; Crime/violence prevention, domestic violence; Human services; Children/ youth, services; Youth, pregnancy prevention; Child development, services; Community/economic development; United Ways and Federated Giving Programs; Minorities; Disabilities, people with; Women; AIDS, people with; Economically disadvantaged; Homeless.
Type of support: General/operating support; Seed money; Technical assistance; Matching/challenge support.
Limitations: Applications not accepted. Giving primarily in NJ and NY.
Application information: Contributes only to pre-selected organizations.

Officers and Directors:* Christine Chambers Gilfillan,* Pres.; Suzanne M. Spero,* V.P.; Donald R. Smith, Secy.; Anthony J. Romano, Treas.; Jennifer G. Chambers; Michael J. Chambers; Patricia A. Chambers; Raymond G. Chambers; Tina Brown Chambers; Barbara B. Coleman; Michael Gilfillan; Joseph Walsh.
Number of staff: 2 full-time professional; 1 full-time support.
EIN: 222497895
Recent grants for international programs:
1184-1 Africare, Washington, DC, $10,500. For general operating support. 2009.
1184-2 American Committee for Tel Aviv Foundation, New York, NY, $10,000. For general operating support. 2009.
1184-3 American India Foundation, New York, NY, $10,000. For general operating support. 2009.
1184-4 Better World Fund, Washington, DC, $333,334. For general operating support. 2009.
1184-5 Better World Fund, Washington, DC, $243,334. For general operating support. 2009.
1184-6 Business Executives for National Security, Washington, DC, $10,000. For general operating support. 2009.
1184-7 Business Executives for National Security, Washington, DC, $10,000. For general operating support. 2009.
1184-8 Christian Foundation for the Holy Land, Fort Collins, CO, $50,000. For general operating support. 2009.
1184-9 Dikembe Mutombo Foundation, Atlanta, GA, $10,000. For general operating support. 2009.
1184-10 FACE AIDS, Palo Alto, CA, $10,000. For general operating support. Grant made through Global Health Corps. 2009.
1184-11 Initiative for Global Development, Seattle, WA, $10,000. For general operating support. 2009.
1184-12 Malaria No More, New York, NY, $500,000. For general operating support. 2009.
1184-13 Malaria No More, New York, NY, $420,261. For general operating support. 2009.
1184-14 Malaria No More, New York, NY, $250,000. For general operating support. 2009.
1184-15 Malaria No More, New York, NY, $229,737. For general operating support. 2009.
1184-16 Malaria No More, New York, NY, $147,460. For general operating support. 2009.
1184-17 Malaria No More, New York, NY, $58,966. For general operating support. 2009.
1184-18 Malaria No More, New York, NY, $50,000. For general operating support. 2009.
1184-19 Malaria No More, New York, NY, $40,000. For general operating support. 2009.
1184-20 Malaria No More, New York, NY, $25,000. For general operating support. 2009.
1184-21 Malaria No More, New York, NY, $23,984. For general operating support. 2009.
1184-22 Malaria No More, New York, NY, $23,750. For general operating support. 2009.
1184-23 Malaria No More, New York, NY, $19,369. For general operating support. 2009.
1184-24 Malaria No More, New York, NY, $17,292. For general operating support. 2009.
1184-25 Millennium Promise Alliance, New York, NY, $300,000. For general operating support. 2009.
1184-26 PlayPumps International, Washington, DC, $280,000. For general operating support. 2009.
1184-27 Save the Children Federation, Westport, CT, $50,000. For general operating support. 2009.

1184-28 Shoe4Africa, Inc., New York, NY, $10,000. For general operating support. 2009.
1184-29 Synergos Institute, New York, NY, $25,000. For general operating support. 2009.
1184-30 Synergos Institute, New York, NY, $15,000. For general operating support. 2009.
1184-31 Witness, Inc., Brooklyn, NY, $13,500. For general operating support. 2009.
1184-32 World Health Organization, Geneva, Switzerland, $50,000. For general operating support. 2009.

1185
McMullen Family Foundation
53 Undercliff Rd.
Montclair, NJ 07042-1738
Contact: Linda M. Drasheff, Secy.
FAX: (973) 744-4428;
E-mail: lindamdrasheff@aol.com

Established in 1993 in NY.
Donor: John J. McMullen, Sr.†.
Grantmaker type: Independent foundation.
Financial data (yr. ended 05/31/11): Assets, $27,138,791 (M); expenditures, $738,126; qualifying distributions, $525,011; giving activities include $525,011 for grants.
Purpose and activities: Giving primarily for higher education; funding also for human services.
Fields of interest: Museums (art); Elementary/ secondary education; Higher education; Human services; Foundations (private grantmaking).
International interests: Ireland.
Type of support: General/operating support; Continuing support; Capital campaigns; Endowments; Professorships; Fellowships; Scholarship funds; Exchange programs.
Limitations: Applications not accepted. Giving primarily in NJ, with emphasis on Montclair. No grants to individuals.
Publications: Annual report.
Application information: Contributes only to pre-selected organizations.
Officers: Catherine McMullen, Pres.; John J. McMullen, Jr., V.P.; Linda M. Drasheff, Secy.; Peter McMullen, Treas.; Ilia Scriven, Exec. Dir.
Directors: James Blake; Patrick Gilmartin; Catherine McMullen; Jacqueline McMullen; John J. McMullen, Jr.; Peter McMullen.
Number of staff: 1 part-time professional; 1 part-time support.
EIN: 133721747

1186
The Merck Company Foundation
1 Merck Dr.
P.O. Box 100
Whitehouse Station, NJ 08889-3400
(908) 423-2042
Contact: Ellen Lambert, Exec. V.P.
FAX: (908) 423-1987;
E-mail: OCP_TMCFSupport@Merck.com; Additional tel.: (908) 423-1000; Contact for Neighbor of Choice Program in New Jersey: Doreen Robert, e-mail: doreen_robert@merck.com; URL: http:// www.merckresponsibility.com/giving-at-merck/ home.html
Merck Grants Managment Website: https:// www.mercksupport.com/
RSS Feed: http://www.merck.com/rss/ corporate_responsibility.xml

Incorporated in 1957 in NJ.

Donor: Merck & Co., Inc.

Grantmaker type: Company-sponsored foundation.

Financial data (yr. ended 12/31/10): Assets, $291,071,373 (M); expenditures, $48,631,792; qualifying distributions, $48,113,759; giving activities include $47,673,821 for 122+ grants.

Purpose and activities: The foundation supports programs designed to promote health, education, and community. Special emphasis is directed toward programs designed to improve healthcare quality and capacity; increase access to care for underserved populations; alleviate barriers to good health through strategic collaborations and investments; foster educational opportunity and academic success through initiatives that eliminate achievement gaps among disadvantaged people; expand quality education in science; and programs that include financial support, Merck innovation, and Merck employee expertise to address critical health and social issues in communities where Merck has a presence.

Fields of interest: Pediatrics; Arts; Higher education; Education, services; Education; Environment; Animal welfare; Health care, public policy; Health care, equal rights; Medical care, community health systems; Health care, clinics/centers; Public health; Health care; Asthma; AIDS; Diabetes; Biomedicine; Health organizations; Medical research; Food services; Food banks; Food distribution, meals on wheels; Nutrition; Disasters, preparedness/services; American Red Cross; Children, services; Family services; Aging, centers/services; Human services; Community/economic development; Science, formal/general education; Mathematics; Engineering/technology; Science; African Americans/Blacks; Hispanics/Latinos; Economically disadvantaged.

Type of support: Continuing support; Management development/capacity building; Building/renovation; Program development; Conferences/seminars; Seed money; Curriculum development; Fellowships; Internship funds; Scholarship funds; Research; Employee volunteer services; Employee matching gifts.

Limitations: Applications accepted. Giving on a national and international basis in areas of company operations, with emphasis on CA, Washington, DC, IL, MA, MD, NJ, NY, PA, TN, TX, VA, and WY, and in Africa, China, and Puerto Rico. No support for political organizations, fraternal, labor, or veterans' organizations, religious organizations not of direct benefit to the entire community, or discriminatory organizations. No grants to individuals, or for capital campaigns, endowments, basic or clinical research projects including epidemiological studies, clinical trials, or other pharmaceutical studies, direct medical care including medical screening or testing, or the purchase of medicines, vaccines, or devices, meetings, conferences, symposia or workshops that do not have or are not associated with long-term program objectives, unrestricted general operating support, or fundraising events including concerts, sporting events, annual appeals, membership drives, benefit dinners, or galas unrelated the strategic priorities of the Merck Company Foundation.

Publications: Application guidelines; Corporate giving report; Grants list; Program policy statement.

Application information: Merck typically initiates specific requests for charitable contributions and donations. Support is limited to 1 contribution per organization during any given year. A site visit may be requested for the Neighbor of Choice Program in New Jersey. Organizations receiving support may be asked to submit a final report. Application form not required.

   Initial approach: Complete online application

   Deadline(s): 45 days prior to need; Sept. 1 to 30 for Neighbor of Choice Program in New Jersey

   Board meeting date(s): Semiannually and as required

   Final notification: 4 to 6 weeks; up to 10 weeks for Neighbor of Choice Program in New Jersey

Officers and Trustees:* Richard T. Clark,* Chair.; Geralyn S. Ritter,* Pres.; Ellen Lambert, Exec. V.P.; Leslie M. Hardy, V.P.; Celia A. Colbert, Secy.; Mark E. McDonough, Treas.

EIN: 226028476

Recent grants for international programs:

1186-1 African Comprehensive HIV/AIDS Partnerships, White House Station, NJ, $6,500,000. To improve HIV/AIDS prevention, care, and treatment in Botswana. 2009.

1186-2 American Australian Association, New York, NY, $100,000. 2009.

1186-3 American Australian Association, New York, NY, $25,000. 2009.

1186-4 Brighton and Sussex University Hospitals NHS Trust, Brighton, England, $200,000. 2009.

1186-5 China-Merck Sharp and Dohme HIV-AIDS Partnership, China, $4,515,000. To support partnership with China's Ministry of Health to strengthen HIV/AIDS prevention, patient care, treatment, and support programs. 2009.

1186-6 Freedom House, Washington, DC, $10,000. 2009.

1186-7 Friends of the University of Natal, Rockville, MD, $100,000. 2009.

1186-8 Friends of the University of Natal, Rockville, MD, $100,000. 2009.

1186-9 LSE Foundation, New York, NY, $100,000. 2009.

1186-10 LSE Foundation, New York, NY, $100,000. 2009.

1186-11 Task Force for Global Health, Decatur, GA, $200,000. 2009.

1186-12 Task Force for Global Health, Decatur, GA, $150,000. 2009.

1186-13 Universidad Carlos III de Madrid, Madrid, Spain, $50,000. 2009.

1186-14 Universidad Carlos III de Madrid, Madrid, Spain, $50,000. 2009.

1186-15 Universitat Pompeu Fabra, Barcelona, Spain, $50,000. 2009.

1186-16 Universitat Pompeu Fabra, Barcelona, Spain, $50,000. 2009.

1186-17 Victoria University, Melbourne, Australia, $100,000. 2009.

1186-18 Victoria University, Melbourne, Australia, $100,000. 2009.

1186-19 World Vision, Federal Way, WA, $75,000. 2009.

1187
The Odysseus Foundation

c/o Tina March
14 Yorktown Ct.
Princeton Junction, NJ 08550-1512

Established in 1986 in NY.

Donors: Bernd Diethelm Hoener; Hudson Trust.

Grantmaker type: Independent foundation.

Financial data (yr. ended 12/31/08): Assets, $46,838 (M); expenditures, $353,000; qualifying distributions, $350,000; giving activities include $350,000 for 1 grant (high: $350,000).

Fields of interest: Education; Cancer; Cancer research; United Ways and Federated Giving Programs.

International interests: Germany.

Limitations: Applications not accepted. Giving primarily in NY and Germany. No grants to individuals.

Application information: Contributes only to pre-selected organizations.

Officer: Irene S. March, Pres.

Directors: Michael Hafkisbring; Claudia Wrede.

EIN: 133391991

1188
One Family Fund

300 Frank W. Burr Blvd.
Teaneck, NJ 07666-6704 (201) 227-4660
FAX: (201) 227-4661;
E-mail: ariel@onefamilyfund.org; URL: http://www.onefamilyfund.org

Grantmaker type: Public charity.

Financial data (yr. ended 05/31/10): Revenue, $1,985,442; assets, $968,715 (M); gifts received, $1,973,734; expenditures, $2,553,161; giving activities include $2,090,000 for grants to organizations outside the U.S.

Purpose and activities: The organization provides direct financial, legal, and emotional assistance to victims of terrorism in Israel, and provides a family network for Jewish individuals and families from all over the world to express, cultivate, and actuate friendships that transcend geographic and social boundaries.

Fields of interest: Human services, emergency aid; Jewish agencies & synagogues; International terrorism; International peace/security.

International interests: Israel.

Limitations: Applications not accepted. Giving on an international basis, primarily in Israel.

Application information: Contributes only to pre-selected organizations.

Officers and Directors:* Chantal Belzberg,* Co-Chair.; Marc Belzberg,* Co-Chair.; Julie Franklin,* Vice-Chair.; Martin Franklin; Lisa Belzberg; Rachel Berg; Leonard "Len" Blavatnik; Rabbi Nachum Braverman; Keith Breslauer; Lauren Breslauer; Irwin Cotler; Marion Diner; Martin Donner; Elizabeth Goldhirsh; Michael Gross; and 18 additional directors.

EIN: 113585917

1189
Polish American Enterprise Fund

Harborside Financial Ctr.
2500 Plz. 5
Jersey City, NJ 07311-4026

Established in 1990 in DE.

Grantmaker type: Public charity.

Financial data (yr. ended 09/30/10): Revenue, $605,462; assets, $5,583,991 (M); expenditures, $982,211; giving activities include $500,000 for grants, and $40,000 for 1 grant to an organization outside the U.S.

Purpose and activities: The fund promotes the development of the private sector in Poland, including small business, the agricultural sector, and joint ventures with United States and Polish participants.

Fields of interest: International economic development; International agricultural development; International development.
International interests: Poland.
Limitations: Giving primarily to New York, NY.
Officer and Directors:* John P. Birkelund,* Chair.; Robert G. Faris,* Pres. and C.E.O.; Tadeusz Galkowski, V.P. and C.F.O.; Hon. Zbigniew Brzezinski.
EIN: 133564025

1190
Princeton Brooke Foundation, Inc.
c/o McCabe Heidrich & Wong
4 Gatehall Dr.
Parsippany, NJ 07054-4518

Established in 1998 in NJ.
Donor: James J. Shinn.
Grantmaker type: Independent foundation.
Financial data (yr. ended 12/31/10): Assets, $331,171 (M); expenditures, $144,971; qualifying distributions, $123,070; giving activities include $123,070 for grants.
Fields of interest: Performing arts; Arts; Education; Hospitals (general); International affairs, foreign policy; Museums; Neuroscience; Public affairs.
Limitations: Applications not accepted. Giving primarily in Washington, DC; some giving in NJ. No grants to individuals.
Application information: Contributes only to pre-selected organizations.
Officers and Trustees:* James J. Shinn,* Pres.; Kiyoshi Shinn,* Secy.; Masako Shinn,* Treas.
EIN: 223581925

1191
The Prudential Foundation
Prudential Plz.
751 Broad St., 15th Fl.
Newark, NJ 07102-3777 (973) 802-4791
Contact: Shane Harris, V.P. and Secy.
E-mail: community.resources@prudential.com;
URL: http://www.prudential.com/view/page/public/12182

Incorporated in 1977 in NJ.
Donors: The Prudential Insurance Co. of America; Prudential Equity Group, LLC.
Grantmaker type: Company-sponsored foundation.
Financial data (yr. ended 12/31/10): Assets, $89,063,341 (M); gifts received, $31,009,275; expenditures, $25,351,848; qualifying distributions, $30,521,603; giving activities include $16,753,350 for 982 grants (high: $668,000; low: $250), $7,105,965 for employee matching gifts, and $6,281,242 for loans/program-related investments.
Purpose and activities: The foundation supports organizations involved with education; economic development; and arts and civic infrastructure.
Fields of interest: Military/veterans' organizations; Arts education; Arts; Education, reform; Elementary/secondary education; Education; Employment, training; Food services; Housing/shelter; Recreation, parks/playgrounds; Youth development; Children/youth, services; Homeless, human services; International relief; Economic development; Community/economic development; Leadership development.

International interests: Brazil; Japan; Mexico; North Korea; South Korea; Taiwan.
Type of support: General/operating support; Management development/capacity building; Capital campaigns; Emergency funds; Program development; Seed money; Technical assistance; Program-related investments/loans; Employee matching gifts; Mission-related investments/loans.
Limitations: Applications accepted. Giving primarily in areas of company operations, with emphasis on Phoenix, AZ, Los Angeles, CA, Hartford, CT, Jacksonville, FL, Dubuque, IA, Chicago, IL, New Orleans, LA, Minneapolis, MN, Newark, NJ, New York, NY, Philadelphia and Scranton, PA, Dallas and Houston, TX, Brazil, India, Japan, Korea, Mexico, and Taiwan; giving also to national organizations. No support for discriminatory organizations or veterans', labor, religious, fraternal, or athletic organizations, or single-disease health groups. No grants to individuals or for goodwill advertising.
Publications: Application guidelines; Annual report (including application guidelines).
Application information: Letters of intent should be no longer than 3 pages. The foundation accepts the New York/New Jersey Area Common Application Form and the New York/New Jersey Common Report Form. Additional information may be requested at a later date. Video submissions are not encouraged. Application form not required.
Initial approach: Letter of intent
Deadline(s): None
Board meeting date(s): Feb., June, and Oct.
Final notification: Within 60 days
Officers and Trustees:* Sharon C. Taylor,* Chair.; Gabriella E. Morris, Pres.; Shane Harris, V.P. and Secy.; James W. McCarthy, Treas.; Brian Cloonan, Cont.; Gilbert F. Casellas; Jon F. Hanson; Constance J. Horner; Barbara G. Koster; John R. Strangfeld, Jr.
Number of staff: 5 full-time professional; 4 full-time support.
EIN: 222175290
Recent grants for international programs:
1191-1 Center for Strategic and International Studies, Washington, DC, $16,000. To disseminate study The Graying of the Middle Kingdom Revisited that outlines policy developments on the aging population in China. 2009.
1191-2 United States Fund for UNICEF, New York, NY, $668,000. To create co-branded signature initiative advancing UNICEF's global education goals and to support two in country programs that promote access to quality education to marginalized children in Mexico and Brazil. 2009.
1191-3 Washington Center for Internships and Academic Seminars, Washington, DC, $335,000. To establish Prudential Foundation Global Citizens Program international exchange program providing academic and work experience for college students from India Japan South Korea and Taiwan. 2009.

1192
Ravi and Pratibha Reddy Foundation, Inc.
480 Mundet Pl.
Hillside, NJ 07205-1115

Established in 1997 in DE and NJ.
Grantmaker type: Independent foundation.
Financial data (yr. ended 11/30/10): Assets, $5,114,145 (M); expenditures, $266,742; qualifying distributions, $202,105; giving activities

include $197,600 for 24 grants (high: $100,000; low: $100).
Purpose and activities: Giving primarily for education, human services, and for the relief of poverty.
Fields of interest: Higher education, university; Arts, cultural/ethnic awareness; Education; Health care; Human services; Children/youth, services; International development; Economically disadvantaged.
International interests: India.
Limitations: Applications not accepted. Giving in NJ, NY and RI. No grants to individuals.
Application information: Contributes only to pre-selected organizations.
Trustees: Pratibha B. Reddy; Ravi B. Reddy.
EIN: 223531803

1193
Richer Family Foundation
c/o Merrill Lynch Bank & Trust Co.
P.O. Box 1525, MSC 06-03
Pennington, NJ 08534-1525

Established in 1999 in CA.
Donor: Mark Richer.
Grantmaker type: Independent foundation.
Financial data (yr. ended 07/31/08): Assets, $5,923,203 (M); expenditures, $412,029; qualifying distributions, $366,778; giving activities include $361,392 for 3 grants (high: $330,000; low: $6,000).
Fields of interest: International human rights; Education; Foundations (public).
Limitations: Applications not accepted. Giving primarily in CA, New York, NY and VA. No grants to individuals.
Application information: Contributes only to pre-selected organizations.
Officers: Mark Richer, Pres.; Gwen Owen Richer, Secy.
EIN: 770541926

1194
Salvadore Family Foundation, Inc.
3 Talmadge Dr.
Monroe Township, NJ 08831-2911

Established in 1998 in NJ.
Donor: Richard Salvadore.
Grantmaker type: Independent foundation.
Financial data (yr. ended 09/30/10): Assets, $943,884 (M); expenditures, $256,820; qualifying distributions, $255,320; giving activities include $253,750 for 24 grants (high: $200,000; low: $100).
Fields of interest: Performing arts, ballet; Education; Disasters, Hurricane Katrina; Boys & girls clubs; Human services; Children/youth, services; International relief, 2004 tsunami.
Limitations: Applications not accepted. No grants to individuals.
Application information: Contributes only to pre-selected organizations.
Officers: Richard Salvadore, Pres. and Treas.; Anna Salvadore, V.P. and Secy.; Marcos Rodriquez, V.P.
EIN: 223627335

1195
Segal Family Foundation, Inc.
776 Mountain Blvd., Ste. 202
Watchung, NJ   07069-6269   (908) 279-7881
E-mail: info@segalfamilyfoundation.org;
URL: http://www.segalfamilyfoundation.org
E-Newsletter: http://www.vresp.com/
1092045/203d6165c9/ARCHIVE
Facebook: https://www.facebook.com/pages/
Segal-Family-Foundation/120479467995531

Established in 2004 in NJ.
Donors: Barry Segal; Sydney Siegel; William Siegel;
Martin Segal; Siegel Family Foundation; Retail
Apparel Service Corp.
Grantmaker type: Independent foundation.
Financial data (yr. ended 12/31/10): Assets,
$54,435,179 (M); gifts received, $41,180,702;
expenditures, $3,639,313; qualifying distributions,
$3,050,577; giving activities include $2,592,200
for 86 grants (high: $260,000; low: $1,000).
Purpose and activities: The foundation's mission is
to find its niche where it can help deserving people
and Improve the quality of their lifeperpetually. The
foundation tends to focus on Sub Saharan Africa
where parts of the continent have not benefited from
the modernization that has happened throughout
the world. The foundation would like to find areas
where it can help, whether it be in education, jobs,
economy, health, sports, or most important, family
planning.
Fields of interest: Environment; Medical research,
institute; Human services; Reproductive health,
family planning; Health care; Housing/shelter,
development; Jewish federated giving programs.
International interests: Africa.
Type of support: General/operating support.
Limitations: Giving primarily in NY to organizations
that provide aid in Sub-Saharan Africa, with
emphasis on east Africa; some giving nationally and
in sub-Saharan Africa. No grants to individuals.
Publications: Newsletter.
Application information:
    Initial approach: Letter (2 pages or less)
Officers and Directors:* Barry Segal,* Pres.;
Bradley Segal,* V.P.; Janis Simon,* Secy.; Andy
Bryant, Exec. Dir.; Patti R. Becker; Majora Carter;
Macdella Cooper; Clet Niyikiza; Dolly Segal; Martin
Segal; Richard Segal; Michelle Thompson.
EIN: 562446941

1196
Share and Care Foundation
676 Winters Ave.
Paramus, NJ   07652-3912   (201) 262-7599
Contact: Rajshekhar Parikh, Pres.
FAX: (201) 262-7896;
E-mail: info@shareandcare.org; URL: http://
www.shareandcare.org

Established in 1982 in NJ.
Grantmaker type: Public charity.
Financial data (yr. ended 12/31/10): Revenue,
$914,550; assets, $2,018,138 (M); gifts received,
$934,993; expenditures, $1,028,749; giving
activities include $868,074 for grants to
organizations outside the U.S.
Purpose and activities: The foundation seeks to
enhance the quality of lives of the underprivileged by
supporting programs in the fields of primary
healthcare, education, and the welfare and
development of women and children.

Fields of interest: Youth development; Child
development, services; Women; Economically
disadvantaged.
International interests: India.
Type of support: Program development;
Scholarships—to individuals; In-kind gifts.
Limitations: Applications accepted. Giving on a
national and international basis.
Publications: Application guidelines.
Application information: Application form required.
    Initial approach: Download application form
    Deadline(s): May 1 for Summer Fellowship
    Program
Officers and Trustees:* Arun Bhansali,* Chair.;
Vijay N. Dalal,* Pres.; Dr. Manojkumar Desai, V.P.;
Dr. Mahendra Shah,* Secy.; Dilip Parikh,* Treas.;
Vijay Dalal; Dr. Manojkumar Desai; Rajshekhar
Parikh; Shirish Patrawaala; Bhadra Shah; Jayant
Shroff.
EIN: 222458395

1197
Sweetfeet Foundation, Inc.
c/o Kenneth J. Slutsky
65 Livingston Ave.
Roseland, NJ   07068-1725

Established in 1993 in NJ.
Donors: Andrew J. Shechtel; Stone Holdings LLC.
Grantmaker type: Independent foundation.
Financial data (yr. ended 11/30/10): Assets,
$22,444,384 (M); expenditures, $1,200,000;
qualifying distributions, $1,200,000; giving
activities include $1,200,000 for 1 grant.
Fields of interest: Jewish federated giving programs.
International interests: Middle East; Israel.
Limitations: Applications not accepted. Giving
primarily in New York, NY. No grants to individuals.
Application information: Contributes only to
pre-selected organizations.
Officers: Kenneth J. Slutsky, Pres. and Treas.; Allen
Levithan, V.P. and Secy.; John L. Berger, V.P.
Member: Stone Holdings, LLC.
EIN: 223271692

1198
Sy Syms Foundation
Syms Way
Secaucus, NJ   07094-9421

Established in 1985 in NJ.
Donor: Sy Syms†.
Grantmaker type: Independent foundation.
Financial data (yr. ended 04/30/11): Assets,
$28,065,099 (M); expenditures, $1,866,887;
qualifying distributions, $1,575,350; giving
activities include $1,575,350 for grants.
Purpose and activities: Support for Jewish welfare
and other Jewish organizations, grants also for
higher education and the arts.
Fields of interest: Media, television; Health
organizations, association; Arts; Higher education;
Education; Human services; Jewish federated giving
programs; Jewish agencies & synagogues.
International interests: Israel.
Type of support: General/operating support;
Scholarship funds.
Limitations: Applications not accepted. Giving
primarily in the U.S., with emphasis on NY. No grants
to individuals.

Application information: Contributes only to
pre-selected organizations.
Officers and Trustees:* Marcy Syms Merns,* Pres.;
Mark Freiberg,* Treas.; Robert Syms; Lynn Tamarkin
Syms.
EIN: 222617727

1199
Jane and Tom Tang Foundation for Education, Inc.
c/o Tom Tang
800 Palisades Ave., Ste. 21C
Fort Lee, NJ   07024-4111

Established in 2000 in NJ.
Donor: Tom Y.C. Tang.
Grantmaker type: Operating foundation.
Financial data (yr. ended 12/31/09): Assets,
$315,462 (M); gifts received, $74,721;
expenditures, $316,836; qualifying distributions,
$316,686; giving activities include $266,950 for 6
grants (high: $200,000; low: $1,450), and $35,811
for 2 grants to individuals (high: $34,361; low:
$1,450).
Fields of interest: Higher education.
International interests: China.
Type of support: Scholarships—to individuals;
Program development; Scholarship funds.
Limitations: Applications not accepted. Giving
primarily in China, with some giving in CA and
Canada.
Application information: Unsolicited requests for
funds not accepted.
Trustees: Edwin C. Landis, Jr.; Carl Schwartz; Jane
Y. Tang; Tom Y.C. Tang.
EIN: 223693816

1200
The Henry and Marilyn Taub Foundation
300 Frank W. Burr Blvd., 7th Fl.
Teaneck, NJ   07666-6703

Established in 1967 in DE.
Donors: Henry Taub†; Endowment Foundation of
UJA Federation of Bergen County & North Hudson.
Grantmaker type: Independent foundation.
Financial data (yr. ended 12/31/10): Assets,
$139,106,901 (M); expenditures, $9,954,342;
qualifying distributions, $9,162,421; giving
activities include $8,514,105 for 150 grants (high:
$1,005,000; low: $40; average: $100–$200,000).
Purpose and activities: Grants largely for Jewish
welfare funds; some support for higher and other
education, social service and youth agencies, and
hospitals.
Fields of interest: Higher education; Education;
Hospitals (general); Human services; Children/
youth, services; Jewish federated giving programs;
Jewish agencies & synagogues.
Limitations: Applications not accepted. Giving
primarily in NJ and NY. No grants to individuals.
Application information: Contributes only to
pre-selected organizations.
Officers and Directors:* Fred S. Lafer,* Vice-Chair.;
Steven Taub,* Pres.; Judith Gold,* V.P. and Secy.;
Ira Taub,* V.P. and Treas.; Barbara Lawrence, Exec.
Dir.; Marilyn Taub.
EIN: 226100525
Recent grants for international programs:
1200-1 American Friends of the Hebrew University,
    New York, NY, $50,000. 2010.

1200-2 American Jewish Joint Distribution Committee, New York, NY, $505,000. 2010.

1200-3 American Jewish Joint Distribution Committee, New York, NY, $25,000. For Haiti earthquake relief. 2010.

1200-4 American Society for Technion-Israel Institute of Technology, New York, NY, $1,005,000. 2010.

1200-5 New York University, Taub Center for Israel Studies, New York, NY, $280,000. 2010.

1200-6 Washington Institute for Near East Policy, Washington, DC, $10,000. 2010.

1201
Vollmer Foundation, Inc.
c/o Albert L. Ennist
P.O. Box 704
Butler, NJ   07405-0704

Incorporated in 1965 in NY.
Donor: Alberto F. Vollmer‡.
Grantmaker type: Independent foundation.
Financial data (yr. ended 12/31/10): Assets, $21,970,186 (M); expenditures, $1,368,434; qualifying distributions, $1,316,660; giving activities include $1,204,636 for grants.
Purpose and activities: Giving primarily for health, higher and other education, and social services in Venezuela.
Fields of interest: Higher education; Education; Health care; Youth development; Children/youth, services; Community/economic development; Science, research.
International interests: Venezuela.
Type of support: General/operating support; Continuing support; Research.
Limitations: Applications not accepted. Giving primarily in Venezuela. No grants to individuals, or for building funds or matching gifts; no loans.
Application information: Contributes only to pre-selected organizations. Unsolicited requests for funds not considered.
   Board meeting date(s): As required
Officers and Directors:* Gustavo J. Vollmer,* Pres.; Ana Luisa Wallis, V.P. and Treas.; Carolina V. De Eseverri, Secy.; Gustavo A. Vollmer.
Number of staff: 1 full-time professional; 1 part-time professional.
EIN: 132620718

1202
The Waterview Foundation, Inc.
234 W. Delaware Ave.
Pennington, NJ   08534-1603

Established in 2001 in DE and NJ.
Donors: James L. Mersfelder; Sandra L. Stark.
Grantmaker type: Independent foundation.
Financial data (yr. ended 08/31/10): Assets, $3,741,514 (M); expenditures, $190,025; qualifying distributions, $190,000; giving activities include $190,000 for 4 grants (high: $160,000; low: $5,000).
Fields of interest: Human services; Education; Hospitals (general); International relief.
Limitations: Applications not accepted. Giving primarily in NJ and NY. No grants to individuals.
Application information: Contributes only to pre-selected organizations.

Officers: James L. Mersfelder, Mgr.; Sandra L. Stark, Mgr.
EIN: 223825678

1203
Jack Weisberg Charitable Foundation
c/o SJM & Assocs., Inc.
14 Ridgedale Ave., Ste. 255
Cedar Knolls, NJ   07927-1116
Application address: c/o Jack Weisberg, 173 Franklin St., New York, NY 10013-2805, tel.: (212) 431-7466

Established in 2000 in NY.
Donor: Jack Weisberg.
Grantmaker type: Independent foundation.
Financial data (yr. ended 12/31/10): Assets, $2,952,517 (M); expenditures, $312,016; qualifying distributions, $302,000; giving activities include $302,000 for 1 grant.
Purpose and activities: Giving primarily to an organization which provides performance space and assists artists for presentation of music and art; funding also for international medical relief.
Fields of interest: International affairs; Arts, single organization support.
Limitations: Applications accepted. Giving primarily in New York, NY.
Application information:
   Initial approach: Letter
   Deadline(s): None
Officers: Jack Weisberg, Pres.; Stanley J. Morin, Secy.
EIN: 223771411

1204
The Woodrow Wilson National Fellowship Foundation
5 Vaughn Dr., Ste. 300
Princeton, NJ   08540-6313   (609) 452-7007
Contact: Beverly Sanford, Secy.
FAX: (609) 452-0066;
E-mail: communications@woodrow.org; Application address: P.O. Box 5281, Princeton, NJ 08543-5281; URL: http://www.woodrow.org

Founded in 1945 in NJ.
Grantmaker type: Public charity.
Financial data (yr. ended 06/30/11): Revenue, $17,095,206; assets, $39,594,720 (M); gifts received, $16,838,787; expenditures, $21,555,004; giving activities include $13,624,856 for grants to individuals.
Purpose and activities: The foundation identifies and develops the best minds for the nations' most important challenges, and awards fellowships to enrich human resources, improve public policy, and assist organizations and institutions in enhancing practice in the U.S. and abroad.
Fields of interest: Secondary school/education; Education, reform; Education, public policy; Higher education reform; Education, public education; Education, formal/general education; Education, ethics; Education, administration/regulation; Higher education, college; Education.
Type of support: Program development; Fellowships; Technical assistance; Consulting services; Scholarships—to individuals.
Limitations: Giving on a national basis.
Publications: Annual report; Newsletter.
Application information: Application form required.

Initial approach: Download application or contact participating university
   Deadline(s): Varies
Officers and Trustees:* Nancy Weiss Malkiel,* Chair.; Arthur E. Levine,* Pres.; Raymond Clark,* Sr. V.P. and Treas.; Robert Baird,* V.P., Progs.; Timothy Freeman, V.P., Devel.; Richard Hope, V.P., Progs.; Beverly Sanford,* V.P. and Secy.; George Campbell, Jr.; Jane Phillips Donaldson; Elizabeth Duffy; Frederick Grauer; N. Gerry House; Thomas C. Hudnut; Robert Kasten; Jan Krukowski; and 17 additional trustees.
Number of staff: 37 full-time professional; 12 full-time support; 5 part-time support.
EIN: 210703075

1205
The Alan and Hope Winters Family Foundation
c/o L. Borenstein
P.O. Box 570
Ridgefield, NJ   07657-0570

Established in 1995 in NJ.
Donors: Alan Winters; Hope Winters.
Grantmaker type: Independent foundation.
Financial data (yr. ended 12/31/10): Assets, $5,204,484 (M); gifts received, $335,000; expenditures, $449,803; qualifying distributions, $410,660; giving activities include $410,660 for 72 grants (high: $116,000; low: $40).
Purpose and activities: Giving primarily for higher education and for international aid to children. Funds for seed programs in education to women, children, immigrants, and refugees in areas of tolerance and entrepreneurship.
Fields of interest: Higher education; Education; Health organizations; Human services; International development; Jewish federated giving programs; Jewish agencies & synagogues.
Type of support: Professorships; Seed money; Curriculum development.
Limitations: Applications not accepted. Giving primarily in AZ, Washington, DC, and New York, NY. No grants to individuals.
Application information: Contributes only to pre-selected organizations.
Trustees: Alan Winters; Hope Winters.
Number of staff: 1 part-time professional.
EIN: 526775755

1206
Mel Wolf Foundation
c/o Merrill Lynch Trust Co.
P.O. Box 1501, NJ2-130-03-31
Pennington, NJ   08534-1501

Established in 2005 in NJ.
Donor: Mel Wolf‡.
Grantmaker type: Independent foundation.
Financial data (yr. ended 12/31/10): Assets, $4,182,180 (M); expenditures, $245,678; qualifying distributions, $214,957; giving activities include $146,000 for 8 grants (high: $40,000; low: $5,200).
Fields of interest: YM/YWCAs & YM/YWHAs; International relief; Human services.
Limitations: Applications not accepted. Giving primarily in CO, Washington, DC, and WV. No grants to individuals.

Application information: Contributes only to pre-selected organizations.
Trustees: George Castelle; Susan Giullian; Susan Louise-Brauer.
EIN: 201270730

1207
Worldwide Orphans Foundation
(also known as WWO)
511 Valley St.
Maplewood, NJ 07040-1381   (973) 763-9961
FAX: (973) 763-8640; URL: http://www.wwo.org
YouTube: http://youtube.com/user/WorldWideOrphans

Established in 1997.
Grantmaker type: Public charity.
Financial data (yr. ended 12/31/10): Revenue, $4,635,705; assets, $4,620,650 (M); gifts received, $3,431,847; expenditures, $2,971,783.
Purpose and activities: The foundation works to transform the lives of orphaned children by taking them out of anonymity and helping them to become healthy, independent, and productive members of their communities and the world.
Fields of interest: Children, adoption; Youth development, services; Children/youth, services; Children/youth; Children.
International interests: Vietnam; Serbia; Kenya; Ethiopia; Ecuador; Bulgaria; Azerbaijan.
Limitations: Giving on an international basis, with emphasis on Azerbaijan, Bulgaria, Ecuador, Ethiopia, Kenya, Serbia and Vietnam.
Publications: Annual report; Newsletter; Quarterly report.
Board Members: Dr. Jane Aronson; Anthony Benten; Karen Burnes; Meg Bode D'Ariano; Cynthia Darrison; Mary Knobler; Steve Lerner; Janet Maisel Kagan; Yvette Teofan.
EIN: 133968225

NEW MEXICO

1208
The Angelica Foundation
1688 Cerro Gordo
Santa Fe, NM   87501-6175

Established in 1994 in CA.
Donors: Ruben and Elizabeth Ransing Trust; The Keller Group Investment; Sigrid Rausing Trust; Open Society Institute.
Grantmaker type: Independent foundation.
Financial data (yr. ended 12/31/10): Assets, $4,424,931 (M); gifts received, $250,000; expenditures, $945,550; qualifying distributions, $562,740; giving activities include $562,740 for grants.
Purpose and activities: Giving primarily to support progressive organizations working for democratic change, environmental sustainability, and social justice.
Fields of interest: Foundations (public); Environment; Human services; International human rights.
International interests: Latin America; Mexico.

Type of support: Annual campaigns.
Limitations: Applications not accepted. Giving primarily in San Francisco, CA. No support for public education, political organizations, or programs promoting religious doctrines. No grants to individuals, or for academic scholarships, conferences, or fundraising events.
Publications: Annual report.
Application information: Contributes only to pre-selected organizations.
Officers and Directors:* Suzanne D. Gollin,* Pres.; James D. Gollin,* Secy.-Treas.; Christopher Brown; Nancy Harris Campbell; Nina Royal; Gladys Schmidt.
Number of staff: 1 part-time professional; 2 part-time support.
EIN: 330632647

1209
Atrisco Heritage Foundation
1730 Montano Rd. N.W. Ste. B
Albuquerque, NM 87107   (505) 836-0306
URL: http://www.atriscoheritagefoundation.org

Established in 2007 in NM.
Donor: Suncal Companies.
Grantmaker type: Independent foundation.
Financial data (yr. ended 06/30/10): Assets, $1,574,444 (M); gifts received, $511,200; expenditures, $935,781; qualifying distributions, $761,795; giving activities include $154,655 for 7 grants (high: $60,170; low: $5,000).
Fields of interest: Historic preservation/historical societies.
International interests: Mexico.
Type of support: General/operating support.
Limitations: Applications accepted. Giving primarily in Albuquerque, NM.
Application information: Application form required.
Initial approach: See website for application form
Deadline(s): Nov. 30
Officer: Peter Sanchez, Exec. Dir.
Trustees: Troy Benavidez; Thaddeus Lucero; Ray Mares; Charles Pena; Randolph Sanchez.
EIN: 300392371

1210
Aurora Foundation
c/o Jeffrey Bronfman
551 W. Cordova Rd., PMB 710
Santa Fe, NM 87505-1825   (505) 988-5924

Established in 1993 in TX and NM.
Donor: Jeffrey Bronfman.
Grantmaker type: Operating foundation.
Financial data (yr. ended 09/30/10): Assets, $1,171,634 (M); gifts received, $81,709; expenditures, $210,295; qualifying distributions, $215,987; giving activities include $210,295 for 11 + grants (high: $116,053).
Purpose and activities: Giving for projects that embody strategic efforts for the preservation and protection of planetary ecosystems (i.e. the environment), as well as efforts that secure the perpetuation and practice of indigenous cultures and ancient religious, spiritual and ceremonial traditions (e.g. certain Native American cultures and their religious traditions.).
Fields of interest: Education; Environment.
International interests: Central America; South America.

Limitations: Applications accepted. Giving primarily in NM; some funding also in CA.
Application information:
Deadline(s): None
Officers and Directors:* Jeffrey Bronfman,* Pres. and Treas.; Duncan E. Osborne,* Secy.; Irvin F. Diamond.
EIN: 742660772

1211
Max and Anna Levinson Foundation
P.O. Box 6309
Santa Fe, NM 87502-6309   (505) 995-8802
Contact: Charlotte Talberth, Pres.
FAX: (505) 995-8982;
E-mail: info@levinsonfoundation.org; URL: http://www.levinsonfoundation.org

Incorporated in 1956 in DE.
Donors: Max Levinson†; Carl A. Levinson.
Grantmaker type: Independent foundation.
Financial data (yr. ended 05/31/10): Assets, $13,875,891 (M); expenditures, $535,362; qualifying distributions, $511,955; giving activities include $275,000 for 52 grants (high: $20,000; low: $500).
Purpose and activities: Funding is allocated among three categories: 1) Environment - including preservation of ecosystems and biological diversity, alternative energy and efficiency; toxins, alternative agriculture, environmental restoration, natural resource conservation, and sustainable communities; 2) Social - including urban and rural community economic development, multiculturalism, human rights, youth leadership and empowerment, conflict resolution, and aid to survivors of violence, and health care; and 3) Jewish/Israel - including Jewish culture and spirituality, history and education, eastern and world Jewry, the Israeli peace movement, and social and environmental issues in Israel. Whatever the specific area of interest, the foundation encourages projects which are concerned with promoting community, social justice, a healthy environment and a sustainable economy, either by developing alternatives to the status quo or by responsibly modifying existing systems, institutions, conditions, and attitudes which block promising innovation. Support for large organizations given a lower priority.
Fields of interest: Jewish agencies & synagogues; International human rights; Environment.
International interests: Israel.
Type of support: General/operating support; Equipment; Program development; Conferences/seminars; Publication; Seed money.
Limitations: Applications not accepted. Giving on a national basis. No support for projects of primary local community significance. No grants for capital or endowment funds, building programs, travel, expansion of existing services, matching gifts, scholarships, or fellowships; no loans.
Publications: Grants list.
Application information: Full proposals are accepted by invitation only. However, letter of inquiry may be submitted in format provided on foundation web site.
Board meeting date(s): Varies
Officers: Charlotte Talberth, Pres.; Robin Beck, V.P.; Carol Doroshow, Secy.; Rachel Krich, Treas.
Directors: Peter Gabel; Gordon Levinson; Julian Levinson; Suntara Loba.
Number of staff: 1 full-time professional.
EIN: 236282844

1212
Quail Roost Foundation
P.O. Box 2035
El Prado, NM 87529-2035

Established in 2004 in NM.
Donors: Kerry Heubeck; Jack Dreyfus.
Grantmaker type: Independent foundation.
Financial data (yr. ended 12/31/10): Assets, $4,426,713 (M); gifts received, $1,205,526; expenditures, $211,109; qualifying distributions, $181,932; giving activities include $162,350 for 69 grants (high: $6,000; low: $100).
Fields of interest: Health care; Education; International relief; Religion, interfaith issues.
Limitations: Applications not accepted. No grants to individuals.
Application information: Contributes only to pre-selected organizations.
Officers: Kerry Heubeck, Pres.; Jeff Sanders, V.P.; H'Krih Shelhamer, Secy.
Directors: Bill Rose; Carol White.
EIN: 760754268

1213
Santa Fe Community Foundation
501 Halona
Santa Fe, NM 87505 (505) 988-9715
FAX: (505) 988-1829;
E-mail: foundation@santafecf.org; Mailing address: P.O. Box 1827, Santa Fe, NM, 87504-1827; Workshop registration e-mail: workshops@santafecf.org; URL: http://www.santafecf.org
Facebook: http://www.facebook.com/pages/Santa-Fe-Community-Foundation/108633257617

Incorporated in 1981 in NM.
Grantmaker type: Community foundation.
Financial data (yr. ended 12/31/10): Assets, $33,696,554 (M); gifts received, $3,739,970; expenditures, $4,061,642; giving activities include $3,056,203 for grants.
Purpose and activities: The foundation improves the quality of life for people in Santa Fe and Northern New Mexico, now and for future generations, by: 1) building and managing endowment funds in order to award grants; 2) helping nonprofits operate more effectively; 3) convening area residents to discuss issues of critical importance to the community; and 4) providing leadership for key community initiatives.
Fields of interest: Substance abuse, prevention; Family services, adolescent parents; Family services, domestic violence; Education, drop-out prevention; Adult education—literacy, basic skills & GED; Education, public education; Public affairs, citizen participation; Housing/shelter; Economic development; Arts education; Community development, citizen coalitions; Nonprofit management; Visual arts; Performing arts; Performing arts, music; Humanities; Arts; Child development, education; Elementary school/education; Education; Environment, natural resources; Environment; Animals/wildlife, preservation/protection; Health care; Mental health/crisis services; Health organizations, association; Cancer; AIDS; Alcoholism; Crime/violence prevention, domestic violence; Food services; Children/youth, services; Child development, services; Aging, centers/services; Homeless, human services; Human services; Civil/human rights, immigrants; Civil/human rights, minorities; Civil/human rights, disabled; Civil/human rights, women; Civil/human rights, aging; Civil/human rights, LGBTQ; Civil rights, race/intergroup relations; Community/economic development; Science; Public affairs; Aging; Disabilities, people with; Minorities; Asians/Pacific Islanders; African Americans/Blacks; Hispanics/Latinos; Native Americans/American Indians; Women; AIDS, people with; LGBTQ; Immigrants/refugees; Economically disadvantaged; Homeless.
Type of support: General/operating support; Continuing support; Management development/capacity building; Annual campaigns; Emergency funds; Program development; Publication; Seed money; Scholarship funds; Technical assistance; Matching/challenge support.
Limitations: Applications accepted. Giving limited to northern NM counties, including Los Alamos, Mora, Rio Arriba, San Miguel, Santa Fe and Taos. No support for religious purposes. No grants for capital campaigns, endowments, or technical assistance grants for travel, conferences, start-up costs, or staff salaries or functions.
Publications: Annual report; Informational brochure (including application guidelines); Newsletter.
Application information: Visit foundation web site for online application and guidelines. Free pre-proposal workshops are offered to assist perspective applicants with information on proposal guidelines and the application/grant process for the foundation's grant cycles; telephone or e-mail to register. Faxed proposals are not accepted. Application form required.
Initial approach: Complete online application
Copies of proposal: 1
Deadline(s): May 2, Aug. 31 and Jan. 11
Board meeting date(s): Bimonthly
Final notification: July 6, Nov. 2 and Mar. 14
Officers and Directors:* Jerry G. Jones,* Chair.; Suzanne Ortega Cisneros,* Vice Chair.; Philip S. Cook,* Vice-Chair.; Brian Byrnes, C.E.O. and Pres.; Christa Coggins, V.P., Community Philanthropy; Sarah Sawtell, V.P., Finance and Opers.; Hervey A. Juris,* Secy.; John Vazquez,* Treas.; Darci Burson; Thomas Bustamante; Richard N. Carpenter; Randy Chitto; Patrick Dolan; James Duncan, Jr.; Kelly Egolf; Florian Artie Garcia; Alexis K. Girard; Felice Gonzales; Jill Heppenheimer; Barry Herskowitz; Richard Hertz; Peggy Hubbard; Ruth Ortega; Stephen E. Stork.
Number of staff: 4 full-time professional; 4 part-time professional; 1 full-time support.
EIN: 850303044
Recent grants for international programs:
1213-1 Amnesty International USA, New York, NY, $51,000. For general operating support. 2009.
1213-2 Business Alliance for Local Living Economies, Bellingham, WA, $10,000. For project to create more commercial use of locally grown food. 2009.
1213-3 Creativity for Peace, Santa Fe, NM, $15,183. For general operating support. 2009.
1213-4 Friends of Tibetan Womens Association, Santa Fe, NM, $20,000. For orphanage support. 2009.
1213-5 Interethnic Health Alliance, Salt Lake City, UT, $11,000. For wellness project. 2009.
1213-6 WildAid, San Francisco, CA, $100,000. For general operating support. 2009.

1214
Eugene V. & Clare E. Thaw Charitable Trust
P.O. Box 2422
Santa Fe, NM 87504-2422
Contact: Sherry Thompson, Exec. Dir.
E-mail (for Sherry Thompson): sherryt@thawtrust.org

Established in 1981 in NY as a private operating foundation; status changed to an independent grantmaking foundation in 1994 in NM.
Donors: Eugene Victor Thaw; Clare Eddy Thaw.
Grantmaker type: Independent foundation.
Financial data (yr. ended 12/31/10): Assets, $33,762,685 (M); expenditures, $4,612,739; qualifying distributions, $4,282,320; giving activities include $3,918,188 for 58 grants (high: $325,000; low: $1,300).
Purpose and activities: Support for the arts, ecology and the environment, and animal rights and protection. The trust prefers to make challenge grants that are conditional on recipients matching the funds in an agreed-upon proportion.
Fields of interest: Arts; Environment; Animal welfare.
International interests: United Kingdom; Russia.
Type of support: Program development; Conferences/seminars; Publication; Seed money; Research; Technical assistance; Matching/challenge support.
Limitations: Applications not accepted. Giving on a national basis. No support for political or religious organizations. No grants to individuals or for operating support.
Publications: Biennial report.
Application information: Contributes only to pre-selected organizations.
Board meeting date(s): Fall
Officers and Directors:* Eugene Victor Thaw,* Pres.; Sherry Thompson, Exec. Dir.; William Acquavella; Jeffrey L. Fornaciari; Patricia Tang; Clare Eddy Thaw.
Number of staff: 2 full-time professional.
EIN: 133081491
Recent grants for international programs:
1214-1 British Museum, London, England, $50,000. For conference, Turquoise at the British Museum. 2009.
1214-2 China Institute in America, New York, NY, $20,000. For general support. 2009.
1214-3 Jane Goodall Institute for Wildlife Research, Education and Conservation, Arlington, VA, $10,000. For Roots and Shoots Animal Shelter Youth Leadership Initiative. 2009.
1214-4 Panthera Corporation, New York, NY, $30,000. For Teton Cougar project. 2009.

NEW YORK

1215
The Abraham Fund Initiatives, Inc.
(formerly The Abraham Fund)
9 E. 45th St., 7th Fl.
New York, NY 10017-8458 (212) 661-7770
Contact: Ami Nahshon, Pres. and C.E.O.
FAX: (212) 935-1834;
E-mail: info@abrahamfund.org; Application address:

Grants Dept., G.G. Comms. Ctr., Neve Ilan, Harey Yehuda, 90850, Israel, tel.: 011-972-534-9300; URL: http://www.abrahamfund.org
Facebook: http://www.facebook.com/group.php?gid=2230994522#
Twitter: http://twitter.com/aminahshon
YouTube: http://www.youtube.com/abrahamtafi

Established in 1989 in DE.
Donor: Alan B. Slifka†.
Grantmaker type: Public charity.
Financial data (yr. ended 12/31/09): Revenue, $4,074,292; assets, $3,543,904 (M); gifts received, $4,000,529; expenditures, $3,450,709; program services expenses, $2,710,783; giving activities include $10,000 for 1 grant, $2,353,444 for grants to organizations outside the U.S., and $347,339 for foundation-administered programs.
Purpose and activities: The organization is dedicated to advancing coexistence, equality and cooperation among Israel's Jewish and Arab citizens by promoting its vision of shared citizenship and opportunity for all of Israel's citizens.
Fields of interest: Education, public education; International peace/security; Community/economic development, public education.
International interests: Israel.
Type of support: General/operating support; Program development; Conferences/seminars; Curriculum development; Program evaluation.
Limitations: Applications accepted. Giving on a national and international basis. No support for for-profit organizations or organizations located outside of Israel who do not have Israeli operating affiliates or partners. No grants to individuals, or for projects/activities taking place outside of Israel, endowments, capital projects (including construction, renovation, or building), overseas travel, permanent equipment, retroactive project costs, or projects between Israel and the Palestinian Authority or other countries.
Publications: Application guidelines; Grants list; Informational brochure; Newsletter.
Application information: See web site for current guidelines, deadlines, application procedures and formats. Please direct questions about applications to the Israel office. Application form required.
Deadline(s): Mar. 15
Officers and Directors:* Alan B. Slifka,* Chair.; Orni Petruschka,* Co-Chair., International Board of Dir.; Howard Sohn, Co-Chair., International Board of Dir.; Dov Lautman,* Vice-Chair.; Hon. Abd-El Rahman Zu'bi,* Vice-Chair.; Ami Nahshon,* Pres. and C.E.O.; James R. Cohen,* Secy.; Gary Gladstein,* Treas.; Amnon Be'eri-Sulitzeanu, Exec. Dir.; Dr. Thabet Abu-Ras; Kher Albaz; Faisal Azaiza, Ph.D.; Walter H. Beebe; Michael Bernstein; Mark Blank; and 41 additional directors.
Number of staff: 2 full-time professional; 6 full-time support.
EIN: 133556715

1216

Louis and Anne Abrons Foundation, Inc.
437 Madison Ave.
New York, NY   10022-7001   (212) 756-3376
Contact: Richard Abrons, Pres.

Incorporated in 1950 in NY.
Donors: Anne S. Abrons†; Louis Abrons†.
Grantmaker type: Independent foundation.
Financial data (yr. ended 12/31/10): Assets, $91,010,213 (M); expenditures, $4,507,870;

qualifying distributions, $4,358,919; giving activities include $4,344,750 for 204 grants (high: $300,000; low: $50).
Purpose and activities: Giving primarily to social welfare agencies, Jewish charities, major New York, NY, institutions, civic improvement programs, education, and environmental and cultural projects.
Fields of interest: Museums; Arts; Libraries/library science; Education; Environment; Hospitals (general); Reproductive health, family planning; Legal services; Employment; Human services; Children/youth, services; Family services; Aging, centers/services; Minorities/immigrants, centers/services; Community/economic development; Jewish agencies & synagogues; Aging; Children/youth; Children; Adults; African Americans/Blacks; Offenders/ex-offenders; Economically disadvantaged; Homeless.
International interests: Israel.
Type of support: General/operating support; Continuing support; Annual campaigns; Capital campaigns; Building/renovation; Program development; Scholarship funds; Research; Technical assistance; Consulting services.
Limitations: Applications not accepted. Giving primarily in the metropolitan New York, NY, area. No grants to individuals.
Application information: Contributes only to pre-selected organizations. Telephone calls not accepted. Unsolicited applications not considered or acknowledged.
Board meeting date(s): Feb., June, and Oct.
Officers and Directors:* Richard Abrons,* Pres.; Rita Aranow,* V.P.; Anne S. Abrons,* Secy.-Treas.; Adam Abrons; Alix Abrons; Eleanor Abrons; Henry Abrons; John Abrons; Leslie Abrons; Peter Abrons; Judith Aranow; Stephanie DeChristina; Vicki Feiner; Jennifer Schwartz.
EIN: 136061329

1217

The Abstraction Fund
220 E. 42nd St., Ste. 3105
New York, NY   10017-5815

Established in 2006 in NY.
Grantmaker type: Independent foundation.
Financial data (yr. ended 12/31/10): Assets, $5,896,090 (M); expenditures, $826,488; qualifying distributions, $716,050; giving activities include $716,050 for grants.
Fields of interest: International affairs, public policy; Jewish federated giving programs; Jewish agencies & synagogues; International affairs, foreign policy.
Limitations: Applications not accepted. Giving primarily in Washington, DC, Baltimore, MD, New York, NY, and Philadelphia, PA. No grants to individuals.
Application information: Contributes only to pre-selected organizations.
Officers: David P. Steinmann, Pres. and Treas.; Alexander G. Anagnos, V.P.; Stuart H. Coleman, Secy.
EIN: 205327719

1218

Accenture, Inc. Corporate Giving Program
1345 Avenue of the Americas
New York, NY   10105-0301   (917) 452-4400
FAX: (917) 527-9915; URL: http://www.accenture.com/Global/About_Accenture/

Company_Overview/Corporate_Citizenship/default.htm

Grantmaker type: Corporate giving program.
Purpose and activities: As a complement to its foundation, Accenture also makes charitable contributions to nonprofit organizations directly. Special emphasis is directed towards programs designed to help people build skills that will enable them to find jobs, start businesses, and better their communities. Support is given on a national and international basis in areas of company operations.
Fields of interest: Vocational education; Engineering/technology; Community development, small businesses; International development; Employment.
Type of support: Pro bono services - strategic management; General/operating support; Program development; Employee volunteer services.
Limitations: Giving on a national and international basis in areas of company operations.
Publications: Corporate giving report.

1219

The Achelis Foundation
767 3rd Ave., 4th Fl.
New York, NY   10017-9029   (212) 644-0322
Contact: John B. Krieger, Secy. and Exec. Dir.; Carmel Mazzola, Bookkeeper; Vicki Puluso, Admin. Asst.
FAX: (212) 759-6510;
E-mail: main@achelis-bodman-fnds.org;
URL: http://www.achelis-bodman-fnds.org

Incorporated in 1940 in NY.
Donor: Elisabeth Achelis†.
Grantmaker type: Independent foundation.
Financial data (yr. ended 12/31/10): Assets, $37,602,002 (M); expenditures, $1,761,558; qualifying distributions, $1,540,233; giving activities include $1,400,600 for 48 grants (high: $100,000; low: $400).
Purpose and activities: Giving for some social services includes child welfare and disconnected youth, the disabled, substance abusers, ex-offenders and veterans. Education giving includes a preference for K-12 school reform, school choice, and charter schools rather than nonprofits that provide direct services in public schools. The foundation also makes grants to large arts and cultural institutions in New York City. Other interests include voluntarism, entrepreneurship, employment, strengthening the two-parent family, marriage, fatherhood (and father absence), programs that promote self-help and self-reliance, faith-based programs, and prevention and early intervention. The foundation prefers programs that emphasize measurable participant outcomes and program results, innovations and new cost-saving approaches, consumer choice, and parental involvement.
Fields of interest: Humanities; Education, reform; Medical care, rehabilitation; Health care, cost containment; Substance abuse, prevention; Alcoholism; Medical research, institute; Crime/violence prevention, youth; Offenders/ex-offenders, prison alternatives; Employment; Children/youth, services; Family services; International relief; Public policy, research; Welfare policy/reform; Religion; Children/youth; Youth; Disabilities, people with; Physically disabled; Military/veterans; Offenders/ex-offenders; Substance abusers; Economically disadvantaged.

Type of support: General/operating support; Equipment; Program development; Conferences/seminars; Publication; Seed money; Curriculum development; Scholarship funds; Research; Technical assistance; Program evaluation; Matching/challenge support.

Limitations: Applications accepted. Giving primarily in the New York, NY, area. Generally, no support for political organizations, small art, dance, music, or theater groups, national health or mental health organizations, housing, international projects, government agencies, public schools (except charter schools), or nonprofit programs and services significantly funded or wholly reimbursed by the government. No grants to individuals, or for annual appeals, dinner functions, fundraising events, capital campaigns, deficit financing, or film or travel; no loans.

Publications: Financial statement; Grants list.

Application information: Do not send CDs, DVDs, discs or tapes, or proposals through the internet unless requested; see foundation web site for application guidelines and procedures. New York/New Jersey Area Common Grant Application Form accepted. Application form not required.

   Initial approach: Letter or short proposal
   Copies of proposal: 1
   Deadline(s): None
   Board meeting date(s): Usually in May, Sept., and Dec.
   Final notification: 5 to 6 weeks

Officers and Trustees:* John N. Irwin III,* Chair. and C.E.O.; Russell P. Pennoyer,* Pres.; Peter Frelinghuysen,* V.P.; Mary S. Phipps,* V.P.; John B. Krieger, Secy. and Exec. Dir.; Horace I. Crary, Jr.,* Treas.; Hon. Walter J.P. Curley; Anthony Drexel Duke; Leslie Lenkowsky; Tatiana Pouschine.

Number of staff: 1 full-time professional; 2 part-time support.

EIN: 136022018

Recent grants for international programs:

1219-1 Save the Children Federation, Westport, CT, $15,000. For Haiti Earthquake Children in Emergency Fund. 2010.

1220
Acumen Fund, Inc.
76 9th Ave, Ste. 315
New York, NY 10011-4962 (212) 566-8821
Contact: Jacqueline Novogratz, C.E.O.
FAX: (212) 566-8817; URL: http://www.acumenfund.org/
C.E.O.'s Twitter Feed: http://twitter.com/jnovogratz
Twitter: http://twitter.com/acumenfund

Established in 2001.

Grantmaker type: Public charity.

Financial data (yr. ended 12/31/10): Revenue, $14,253,137; assets, $88,328,834 (M); gifts received, $12,948,757; expenditures, $8,271,911; giving activities include $579,023 for grants to organizations outside the U.S.

Purpose and activities: The fund creates a blueprint for building financially sustainable and scalable organizations that deliver affordable, critical goods and services that elevate the lives of the poor.

Fields of interest: Venture philanthropy; International relief.

Limitations: Giving on a national and international basis.

Officers and Directors:* Margo Alexander,* Chair.; Jacqueline Novogratz,* C.E.O.; Ann MacDougall,* C.A.O. and Genl. Counsel; Brian Trelstad,* C.I.O.;

Angela Glover Blackwell; C. Hunter Boll; Andrea Soros Colombel; Stuart Davidson; William E. Mayer; Catherine S. Muther; Robert H. Niehaus; Michael E. Novogratz; Ali J. Siddiqui; Joseph E. Stiglitz.

EIN: 134166228

1221
Adelson Family Foundation
P.O. Box 820
Katonah, NY 10536-0820

Established in 2000 in NY.

Donors: Andrew Adelson; Nancy Adelson.

Grantmaker type: Independent foundation.

Financial data (yr. ended 12/31/10): Assets, $8,408,990 (M); expenditures, $705,808; qualifying distributions, $699,750; giving activities include $699,500 for 23 grants (high: $333,000; low: $500).

Fields of interest: International migration/refugee issues; Public affairs, ethics; Arts; Higher education; Education; Human services; Jewish federated giving programs; Jewish agencies & synagogues; Women.

Limitations: Applications not accepted. Giving primarily in NJ and NY. No grants to individuals.

Application information: Contributes only to pre-selected organizations.

Trustees: Andrew Adelson; Nancy Adelson.

EIN: 223769645

1222
African Reflection Foundation
87 Chancellor Dr.
Guilderland, NY 12084-9524

Established in 2004 in NY.

Grantmaker type: Public charity.

Financial data (yr. ended 12/31/10): Revenue, $56,121; assets, $750 (M); gifts received, $56,121; expenditures, $64,402; giving activities include $55,385 for grants.

Fields of interest: International development.

International interests: Africa.

Officers and Directors: Sajida Mamdani,* Pres.; Raazaali Mamdani.

EIN: 201621143

1223
African Well Fund, Inc.
P.O. Box 9486
Schenectady, NY 12309-0486 (518) 423-8058
E-mail: info@africanwellfund.org; URL: http://www.africanwellfund.org
Facebook: http://www.facebook.com/AfricanWellFund?ref=ts
Flickr: http://www.flickr.com/photos/africanwellfund/
Fund blog: http://www.africanwellfund.org/blog/
RSS Feed: http://www.africanwellfund.org/atom.xml
Twitter: https://twitter.com/AfricanWellFund
YouTube: http://www.youtube.com/user/AfricanWellFund

Established in 2002.

Grantmaker type: Public charity.

Financial data (yr. ended 12/31/10): Revenue, $27,211; assets, $6,558 (M); gifts received, $24,845; expenditures, $27,086; program services

expenses, $23,772; giving activities include $23,772 for grants.

Purpose and activities: The fund's goal is to raise money for the construction and maintenance of clean water wells throughout sub-Saharan Africa.

Fields of interest: Environment, water resources.

International interests: Sub-Saharan Africa.

Limitations: Applications not accepted. Giving primarily to Angola, Benin, Burkina Faso, Ghana, Liberia, Mali, Malawi, Niger, Rwanda, Sierra Leone, Uganda, Zambia, and Zimbabwe.

Application information: Contributes only to pre-selected organizations.

Officers and Board Members:* Rob Trigalet,* Chair.; Diane Yoder,* Vice-Chair.; Angela Martens,* Secy.; Anne Cimon,* Treas.; Julie Cook; Ayesha Marcel; Devlin Smith; Lara Wineman; Paola Palumbi Yeager.

EIN: 200034483

1224
AFS Intercultural Programs, Inc.
(also known as American Field Service Intercultural Programs, Inc.)
71 W. 23rd St., 6th Fl.
New York, NY 10010 4102 (212) 807-8686
FAX: (212) 807-1001; E-mail: info@afs.org;
URL: http://www.afs.org
Facebook: http://www.facebook.com/AFS.org
YouTube: http://www.youtube.com/afsinterculturalprog

Established in 1946 in NY.

Grantmaker type: Public charity.

Financial data (yr. ended 12/31/10): Revenue, $15,013,837; assets, $10,225,428 (M); gifts received, $328,900; expenditures, $15,245,640; giving activities include $120,940 for grants, and $211,580 for 6 grants to organizations outside the U.S.

Purpose and activities: The organization aims to provide intercultural learning opportunities to help people develop the knowledge, skills, and understanding needed to create a peaceful world.

Fields of interest: International development.

International interests: Argentina; Belgium; Brazil; Canada; Costa Rica; Denmark; Finland; France; Hong Kong; Latvia; South Africa; Thailand; United Kingdom.

Limitations: Applications not accepted. Giving primarily on an international basis, with emphasis on Argentina, Belgium, Brazil, Canada, Costa Rica, Denmark, Finland, France, Hong Kong, Latvia, South Africa, Thailand, and the United Kingdom.

Publications: Annual report.

Application information: Contributes only to pre-selected organizations.

Officers and Directors:* Brian Atwood,* Chair.; Francisco "Tachi" Cazal,* Pres.; Floria Arias; Nils Bauer; Ward Chamberlin, Jr.; Norman Eddy; Maureen Erasmus; Carlo Fusaro; Richardo Garay; Francisco Guerra III; Arthur Howe, Jr.; Richard Hunt; Christian Kurten; Sachiye Kuwamoto; Edwin Masback, Jr.; and 10 additional directors.

EIN: 135596742

1225
AFS-USA, Inc.
(also known as American Field Service - USA, Inc.)
1 Whitehall St., 2nd Fl.
New York, NY   10004-2109   (212) 299-9000
FAX: (212) 299-9090; E-mail: afsinfo@afs.org;
Toll-free tel.: (800) 237-4636; URL: http://
www.afsusa.org/usa_en/home
Facebook: http://www.facebook.com/
StudyAbroadAFSUSA
Flickr: http://www.flickr.com/photos/afsusa
Twitter: http://twitter.com/afsusa
YouTube: http://www.youtube.com/user/AFSTV

Established in 1991 in IL.
Grantmaker type: Public charity.
Financial data (yr. ended 12/31/10): Revenue,
$27,684,792; assets, $21,704,834 (M); gifts
received, $10,478,753; expenditures,
$32,066,430; giving activities include $41,283 for
grants to organizations outside the U.S., and
$1,543,183 for grants to individuals.
Purpose and activities: The organization provides
intercultural learning opportunities to help people
develop the knowledge, skills, and understanding
needed to create a peaceful world.
Fields of interest: International exchange;
International exchange, students.
Type of support: Exchange programs; Scholarships
—to individuals.
Limitations: Applications accepted. Giving on a
worldwide basis.
Application information: Contact organization for
scholarship availability information and additional
deadlines. Application form required.
   Initial approach: E-mail
   Deadline(s): Dec. 15 (nominations) and Jan. 30
   (applications), for Cargill Scholarship; Jan. 13
   (nominations) and Mar. 3 (applications) for
   Ford PAS Scholarship; Mar. 1 for TRUMPF
   Scholarship; Oct. 3, for Scholarships to Japan;
   Dec. 16, for Congress-Bundestag Youth
   Exchange Scholarships; rolling basis
   acceptance for AFS Global Leaders
   Scholarship Program
Officers and Directors:* Mike Sherman,* Chair.;
Judy Weyand,* Vice-Chair.; Jorge Castro, Pres.;
Gerry Bair; Amb. William A. Eaton; William G.
Meserve; Betty McManus; Vincenzo Morlini;
Christopher B. Nelson; Damian Pisanelli; Mary
Porterfield; Tsugiko Scullion; John Schuck; David
Vodila.
EIN: 391711417

1226
AGB Fund, Inc.
c/o CPI Associates, Inc.
32 E. 57th St., 14th Fl.
New York, NY   10022-2513   (212) 421-6600
Contact: Elizabeth B. Nevin, Pres.

Established in 1992 in NY.
Grantmaker type: Independent foundation.
Financial data (yr. ended 12/31/10): Assets,
$3,382,142 (M); expenditures, $253,022;
qualifying distributions, $200,515; giving activities
include $180,000 for 26 grants (high: $24,000;
low: $1,000).
Fields of interest: International relief; Arts;
Education; Environment; Hospitals (general); Food
services; Human services; Children, services;
Science; Public affairs; Religion.

Limitations: Applications accepted. Giving primarily
in NY. No grants to individuals.
Application information: Application form required.
   Initial approach: Letter
   Deadline(s): None
Officers: Elizabeth B. Nevin, Pres.; Stephen C.
Nevin, V.P. and Secy.; Lee R. Robins, Treas.
EIN: 133632843

1227
The Peter C. Alderman Foundation, Inc.
P.O. Box 278
Bedford, NY   10506-0278   (914) 764-1804
E-mail: info@petercaldermanfoundation.org;
Toll-free tel.: (888) 764-1804; URL: http://
www.petercaldermanfoundation.org

Established in 2003 in NY.
Grantmaker type: Public charity.
Financial data (yr. ended 12/31/10): Revenue,
$638,077; assets, $535,765 (M); gifts received,
$521,924; expenditures, $605,034; giving
activities include $147,520 for grants.
Purpose and activities: The foundation's mission is
to alleviate the suffering of victims of terrorism and
mass violence in post-conflict countries by providing
indigenous physicians and other local caregivers
with the tools to treat mental anguish using Western
medical therapies combined with local healing
traditions.
Fields of interest: Health care; International
terrorism.
Officer and Directors:* Alison Pavia,* Exec. Dir.;
Elizabeth R. Alderman; Jeffrey S. Alderman, M.D.;
Stephen James Alderman, M.D.; Anne
Ashmore-Husdon, Ph.D.; Peter Baglieri; Leslie
Corwin, Esq.; Kevin Foley; Brenton Karmen; Stacey
Richman; Daniel Runde; Susan K. Stern.
EIN: 161654102

1228
The Alexander Family Foundation
c/o Margo N. Alexander
15 E. 26th St., Apt. 10A
New York, NY   10010-1424

Established in 2000 in NY.
Donor: Margo N. Alexander.
Grantmaker type: Independent foundation.
Financial data (yr. ended 12/31/10): Assets,
$1,974,764 (M); gifts received, $30,089;
expenditures, $588,809; qualifying distributions,
$546,460; giving activities include $546,460 for
grants.
Fields of interest: International relief; Higher
education; Human services; International affairs,
public policy.
Limitations: Applications not accepted. Giving
primarily in NY. No grants to individuals.
Application information: Contributes only to
pre-selected organizations.
Officer and Trustees:* Margo N. Alexander,* Pres.;
James R. Alexander; Nichol C. Alexander; Robert C.
Alexander.
EIN: 134140292

1229
Allen & Overy LLP Pro Bono Program
1221 Ave. of the Americas
New York, NY   10020-1001   (212) 610-6300
Contact: Chris Marshall
FAX: (212) 610-6399;
E-mail: Chris.Marshall@AllenOvery.com; Additional
tel. for Chris Marshall: +44 20 3088 2949; Contact
for Pro Bono program: Jake Lee, Pro Bono & Comms.
Mgr., tel.: +44 (0)20 3088 4541, e-mail:
jake.lee@allenovery.com; Additional e-mail:
probonoteam@allenovery.com,
community@allenovery.com; URL: http://
www.allenovery.com/AOWEB/Community/
AdditionalPage.aspx?
pageID=21653&prefLangID=410

Grantmaker type: Corporate giving program.
Purpose and activities: Allen & Overy makes
charitable contributions to nonprofit organizations
involved with improving education and employment,
supporting vulnerable people, increasing access to
justice, and helping to eradicate poverty.
Fields of interest: Homeless, human services;
Youth development; Disasters, preparedness/
services; Anti-slavery/human trafficking;
International human rights; International relief;
Children, services; Employment; Education; Arts;
Legal services; Economically disadvantaged.
Type of support: Scholarships—to individuals;
Program development; Continuing support;
Employee volunteer services; General/operating
support; Pro bono services - legal.
Application information: A Pro Bono Committee
manages the Pro Bono Program.
   Initial approach: E-mail letter of inquiry

1230
Alliance for Open Society International, Inc.
400 W. 59th St., 4th Fl.
New York, NY   10019-8023

Grantmaker type: Public charity.
Financial data (yr. ended 12/31/10): Revenue,
$590,556; assets, $547,388 (M); gifts received,
$590,556; expenditures, $350,551.
Purpose and activities: The alliance seeks to
transform closed societies into open societies, and
to protect and expand the values of existing open
societies.
Fields of interest: International affairs, public
education; International democracy & civil society
development; International human rights;
International affairs.
Limitations: Giving on a national and international
basis.
Officers: Robert Kushen,* Chair.; Ricardo Castro,*
Pres.; Stephen Gutmann,* V.P.; Maria Santos
Valentin,* Secy.; Maija Arbolino,* Treas.; Oksana
Korneo, Exec. Dir.
EIN: 810623035

1231
Altman/Kazickas Foundation
c/o Dorian A. Vergos & Co., LLC
352 7th Ave., Ste. 1501
New York, NY   10001-0064

Established in 1996 in NY.
Donors: Robert C. Altman; Roger C. Altman.

Grantmaker type: Independent foundation.
Financial data (yr. ended 04/30/10): Assets, $1,178,244 (M); gifts received, $1,675,312; expenditures, $1,420,512; qualifying distributions, $1,407,668; giving activities include $1,407,568 for 78 grants (high: $100,000; low: $100).
Purpose and activities: Giving primarily for arts and cultural programs, education, social services, and Roman Catholic churches.
Fields of interest: International affairs; Museums (natural history); Arts; Education; Health organizations; Human services; Children/youth, services; Community/economic development; Catholic agencies & churches.
Limitations: Applications not accepted. Giving primarily in NY. No grants to individuals.
Application information: Contributes only to pre-selected organizations.
Trustees: Richard M. Altman; Roger C. Altman; Jurate Kazickas.
EIN: 133944577

1232
The Alvarez Educational Foundation, Inc.
c/o Alvarez & Marsal, Inc.
600 Lexington Ave., 6th Fl.
New York, NY 10022-4834
Application address: c/o Dawn M. Marsal-Wallin, 21677 Sheffield Dr., Farmington Hills, MI 48335-5460, tel.: (212) 759-4433

Established in 1990 in NJ.
Donors: Abigail C. Alvarez; Antonio C. Alvarez.
Grantmaker type: Independent foundation.
Financial data (yr. ended 12/31/10): Assets, $1,200,186 (M); gifts received, $500,000; expenditures, $428,185; qualifying distributions, $427,820; giving activities include $427,820 for grants.
Fields of interest: Business school/education; Cancer; Health organizations; Human services.
International interests: Philippines.
Type of support: Scholarship funds.
Limitations: Applications accepted. Giving primarily in NY.
Application information:
  Initial approach: Letter
  Deadline(s): None
Officers: Antonio C. Alvarez, Pres.; Abigail C. Alvarez, V.P.; Dawn M. Marsal-Wallin, Treas.
EIN: 223479932

1233
America-Israel Cultural Foundation, Inc.
20 E. 46th St., 15th Fl.
New York, NY 10017-5404 (212) 557-1600
FAX: (212) 557-1611; E-mail: admin@aicf.org; URL: http://www.aicf.org

Established in 1939 in NY.
Grantmaker type: Public charity.
Financial data (yr. ended 12/31/10): Revenue, $5,433,509; assets, $6,615,341 (M); gifts received, $5,233,016; expenditures, $2,007,289; giving activities include $1,079,443 for 7 grants to organizations outside the U.S., and $79,870 for grants to individuals.
Purpose and activities: The foundation solicits funds in the United States to promote, nurture, and sustain the cultural life of Israel and Israeli artists exclusively.

Fields of interest: Arts, fund raising/fund distribution.
International interests: Israel.
Limitations: Applications accepted. Giving primarily in Israel.
Publications: Application guidelines; Informational brochure; Newsletter.
Officers and Directors:* William A. Schwartz,* Pres.; Sanford L. Batkin,* V.P.; Linda Schonfeld,* Secy.; Joseph E. Hollander,* Treas.; David Homan, Exec. Dir., USA; Orit Naor, Exec. Dir., Israel; Sanford L. Batkin; Diane Belfer; Ann Bialkin; Renee Cherniak; Lonny Darwin; Debby B. Edelsohn; Stephanie Feldman; Joe Hollander; Jane Stern Lebell; and 18 additional directors.
EIN: 131664048

1234
American Academy in Berlin
14 E. 60th St., Ste. 604
New York, NY 10022-7130 (212) 588-1755
Contact: Dr. Gary Smith, Exec. Dir.
FAX: (212) 588-1758;
E-mail: nyoffice@americanacademy.de; URL: http://www.americanacademy.de

Established in 1991 in DC.
Grantmaker type: Public charity.
Financial data (yr. ended 12/31/10): Revenue, $4,617,380; assets, $32,363,856 (M); gifts received, $4,689,318; expenditures, $2,565,510; giving activities include $1,513,907 for grants to organizations outside the U.S.
Purpose and activities: The academy seeks to strengthen the transatlantic relationship between Germany and the United States by promoting intellectual and cultural exchange by awarding residential fellowships to accomplished Americans in the arts, humanities, social sciences, and public policy, as well as through programming and partnerships with organizations in the United States and Germany.
Fields of interest: International affairs, goodwill promotion; Humanities; Arts; Economics; Public policy, research.
International interests: Germany.
Type of support: Fellowships.
Publications: Application guidelines; Newsletter.
Application information: See web site for additional application information. Application form required.
  Initial approach: Download application form
  Copies of proposal: 5
  Deadline(s): Nov. 3 for music composition fellowship applications; Oct. 13 for general fellowship applications
  Final notification: Early spring
Officers and Trustees:* Henry A. Kissinger,* Co-Chair.; Karl M. von der Heyden,* Co-Chair.; Gahl Hodges Burt,* Vice-Chair.; Norman Pearlstine,* Pres. and C.E.O.; John C. Kornblum, Secy.; Andrew White, Treas.; Dr. Gary Smith, Exec. Dir.; Barbara Balaj; John P. Birkelund; Manfred Bischoff; Stephen Burbank; Caroline Walker Bynum; Mathias Dopfner; Niall Ferguson; Marina Kellen French; Michael E. Geyer; and 27 additional trustees.
EIN: 521726273

1235
American Associates, Ben-Gurion University of the Negev, Inc.
1430 Broadway, 8th Fl.
New York, NY 10018-3308 (212) 687-7721
FAX: (212) 302-6443; E-mail: info@aabgu.org; URL: http://www.aabgu.org

Grantmaker type: Public charity.
Financial data (yr. ended 09/30/10): Revenue, $27,406,664; assets, $176,506,783 (M); gifts received, $20,797,850; expenditures, $22,171,940; giving activities include $15,683,763 for grants to organizations outside the U.S., and $28,500 for grants to individuals.
Purpose and activities: The organization supports Ben-Gurion University and also provides scholarships.
Fields of interest: Higher education, university.
International interests: Israel.
Type of support: Scholarships—to individuals.
Limitations: Giving primarily in the U.S. and Israel.
Officers and Board Members:* Zvi Alon,* Chair.; Lis Gaines, Pres.; Helen R. Katz, C.O.O.; Vivien K. Marion, Exec. V.P.; Martin Blackman, V.P.; Solomon J. Freedman, V.P.; Joseph Friedman, V.P.; Lloyd Goldman, V.P.; Seymour Powers, V.P.; Chaim Reiss, V.P., Finance; Frederick Siegmund, Secy.; Joseph M. Rose, Treas.; and 51 additional board members.
EIN: 237270753

1236
American Australian Association, Inc.
50 Broadway, Ste. 2003
New York, NY 10004-3813 (212) 338-6860
FAX: (212) 338-6864;
E-mail: information@aaanyc.org; URL: http://www.americanaustralian.org
Facebook: http://www.facebook.com/group.php?gid=55116516350&ref=ts
Twitter: http://twitter.com/#!/aaanyc

Established in 1948.
Grantmaker type: Public charity.
Financial data (yr. ended 12/31/09): Revenue, $2,750,532; assets, $8,668,497 (M); gifts received, $2,208,672; expenditures, $2,459,638; giving activities include $221,350 for grants to organizations outside the U.S., and $87,500 for grants to individuals.
Purpose and activities: The association is devoted to building strategic alliances between the U.S., Australia and New Zealand.
Fields of interest: International exchange.
International interests: New Zealand; Australia.
Type of support: Fellowships.
Application information:
  Deadline(s): Apr. 15 for Australia to U.S.A. Fellowships
Officers and Board Members:* Malcolm Binks,* Chair.; Mili Boreham,* Vice-Chair.; Craig E. Chapman,* Vice-Chair.; Frances Cassidy,* Pres.; Anne O. Fulford,* Secy.; Kathryn Holleran,* Treas.; Gavin Anderson; Hugh Killen; Susan Talbot; and 31 additional board members.
EIN: 136151807

1237

American Committee for Shenkar College in Israel, Inc.

307 Seventh Ave., Ste. 1805
New York, NY 10001-6178
Contact: Charlotte Fainblatt, Exec. Dir.

Established in 1971 in NY.
Grantmaker type: Public charity.
Financial data (yr. ended 02/28/10): Revenue, $390,303; assets, $939,339 (M); gifts received, $399,248; expenditures, $612,247; giving activities include $364,467 for grants to organizations outside the U.S.
Purpose and activities: The organization supports Shenkar College of Engineering and Design by providing scholarships, teaching resources, equipment and capital funds for its expansion.
Fields of interest: Higher education, college.
International interests: Israel.
Type of support: Building/renovation; Equipment; Curriculum development; Internship funds; Scholarship funds.
Limitations: Applications not accepted. Giving limited to Israel. No grants to individuals.
Application information: Contributes only to a pre-selected organization.
Officers and Directors:* Bruce Pernick, Pres.; David Blumenthal, V.P.; Leonard Boxer,* V.P.; Elaine Gold,* V.P.; Robert Goldfarb, V.P.; Kenneth S. Grossman, V.P.; Pearlann Marco, V.P.; Sharon Wilkes,* Secy.; Peter Markson,* Treas.; Charlotte Fainblatt, Exec. Dir.; Anne L. Bernstein; Myron Sperber; and 44 additional directors.
Number of staff: 1 full-time professional; 1 part-time support.
EIN: 237090228

1238

American Committee for the David Shapell College of Jewish Studies, Inc.

220 Smith St.
Woodmere, NY 11598

Grantmaker type: Public charity.
Financial data (yr. ended 12/31/09): Revenue, $400,000; assets, $1,008 (M); gifts received, $400,000; expenditures, $401,326; program services expenses, $400,000; giving activities include $400,000 for 1 grant to an organization outside the U.S.
Fields of interest: Education, single organization support; Education; Jewish agencies & synagogues.
International interests: Israel.
Limitations: Applications not accepted. Giving limited to Israel. No grants to individuals.
Application information: Contributes only to pre-selected organizations.
Trustees: Elliott Cahan; Jordan Hirshfeld; David Neiburg; Jack Yellin.
EIN: 237366675

1239

The American Committee for the Tel Aviv Foundation, Inc.

220 5th Ave., Ste. 1301
New York, NY 10001-7708

Grantmaker type: Public charity.
Financial data (yr. ended 12/31/10): Revenue, $3,883,382; assets, $6,067,871 (M); gifts received, $3,880,475; expenditures, $2,519,731; giving activities include $2,149,097 for grants to organizations outside the U.S.
Purpose and activities: The committee is the American fundraising arm for the Tel Aviv Foundation, and supports it in its mission of providing humanitarian, charitable assistance and overall improvement of quality of life to the residents of Tel Aviv-Jaffa, Israel.
Fields of interest: Philanthropy/voluntarism.
International interests: Israel.
Limitations: Applications not accepted. Giving limited to Tel Aviv-Jaffa, Israel. No grants to individuals.
Application information: Contributes only to a pre-selected organization.
Officers: Josh Weston, Chair.; Stephen Greenberg, Secy.-Treas.; Avi Maidenberg, Exec. Dir.
Directors: David C. Albalah; Micky Arison; Gissou Farahi; Jose Galicot; Richard Hirsch; Bernard Kossar; Harvey Kreuger; Walter Lieber; Ira D. Riklis; Shimon Topor; and 5 additional directors.
EIN: 133145161

1240

American Council of Learned Societies

(also known as ACLS)
633 3rd Ave., Ste. 8C
New York, NY 10017-6795 (212) 697-1505
FAX: (212) 949-8058; E-mail: grants@acls.org;
URL: http://www.acls.org

Founded in 1919 in DC.
Grantmaker type: Public charity.
Financial data (yr. ended 06/30/10): Revenue, $25,793,504; assets, $116,036,079 (M); gifts received, $23,491,813; expenditures, $22,097,212; giving activities include $7,339,714 for grants, $2,437,238 for grants to organizations outside the U.S., $4,864,811 for grants to individuals, and $407,416 for grants to individuals outside the U.S.
Purpose and activities: The council's activities are directed toward the advancement of humanistic learning, awarding individual scholarships in all fields of the humanities, and sponsoring projects and works with other organizations who are dedicated to the benefit of scholars in the U.S. and abroad.
Fields of interest: Humanities; Education, services; Social sciences.
Type of support: Fellowships; Research; Grants to individuals.
Limitations: Applications accepted. Giving on a national and international basis.
Publications: Application guidelines; Annual report; Occasional report.
Application information: See web site for application deadlines and additional application guidelines. Application form required.
  Initial approach: Online application
  Deadline(s): Varies
  Final notification: Varies
Officers and Directors:* Kwame Anthony Appiah,* Chair.; Anand A. Yang,* Vice-Chair.; Pauline Yu,* Pres.; James J. O'Donnell,* Secy.; Nancy J. Vickers,* Treas.; Frederick M. Bohen; Nicola Courtright; Jonathan Culler; William E. Davis III; Sarah "Sally" Deutsch; Marjorie Garber; Charlotte V. Kuh; Richard Leppert; Earl Lewis; Teofilo F. Ruiz.
Number of staff: 20 full-time professional; 7 full-time support.
EIN: 131851145

1241

American Express Foundation

World Financial Ctr.
200 Vesey St., 48th Fl.
New York, NY 10285-4804 (212) 640-5661
Contact: Timothy McClimon, Pres.
FAX: (212) 640-5661; Application address for organizations located outside of AZ, FL, NC, and UT: 3 World Financial Center, M.C. 01-48-04, New York, NY 10285-4804; URL: http://home3.americanexpress.com/corp/giving_back.asp
Grants List: http://home3.americanexpress.com/corp/gb/grant.asp

Incorporated in 1954 in NY.
Donor: American Express Co.
Grantmaker type: Company-sponsored foundation.
Financial data (yr. ended 12/31/09): Assets, $8,212,520 (M); gifts received, $7,485,929; expenditures, $7,825,354; qualifying distributions, $7,821,678; giving activities include $7,739,700 for 116 grants (high: $2,000,000; low: $50,000).
Purpose and activities: The foundation supports programs designed to promote community service and engagement; historic preservation and conservation; and leadership.
Fields of interest: Hospitals (general); Education; Employment, services; Foundations (community); Museums; Children/youth, services; Visual arts; Performing arts; Historic preservation/historical societies; Arts; Disasters, preparedness/services; American Red Cross; Human services; Economic development; Nonprofit management; Community/economic development; Leadership development; Public affairs.
International interests: Africa; Asia; Australia; Canada; Caribbean; Europe; Japan; Latin America; Middle East.
Type of support: General/operating support; Management development/capacity building; Annual campaigns; Emergency funds; Program development; Curriculum development.
Limitations: Applications accepted. Giving on a national and international basis primarily in areas of company operations, including in Argentina, Asia, Canada, the Caribbean, Europe, Latin America, and the United Kingdom, with emphasis on AZ, Los Angeles and San Francisco, CA, Washington, DC, southern FL, Atlanta, GA, Chicago, IL, Boston, MA, Greensboro, NC, New York, NY, Philadelphia, PA, Dallas and Houston, TX, and Salt Lake City, UT. No support for discriminatory organizations, religious organizations not of direct benefit to the entire community, or political organizations. No grants to individuals or for fundraising, goodwill advertising, souvenir journals, or dinner programs, travel, books, magazines, or articles in professional journals, endowments or capital campaigns, traveling exhibitions, or sports sponsorships.
Publications: Application guidelines; Grants list; Program policy statement.
Application information: Letters of inquiry should be no longer than 1 to 3 pages. Visit website for e-mail address for letters of inquiry for organizations located in Phoenix, AZ, southern, FL, Greensboro, NC, and Salt Lake City, UT. Organizations receiving support of at least $7,500 are asked to provide a final report. Application form not required.
  Initial approach: Letter of inquiry to application address; e-mail letter of inquiry to organizations located in Phoenix, AZ, southern, FL, Greensboro, NC, and Salt Lake City, UT

Deadline(s): None; Feb. 1 and July 1 for Phoenix, AZ, southern, FL, Greensboro, NC, and Salt Lake City, UT
Board meeting date(s): Biannually
Final notification: 3 to 4 months
Officers and Trustees:* Thomas Schick,* Chair.; Timothy McClimon, Pres.; Judy Tenzer, Secy.; Mary Ellen Craig, Compt.; Kenneth I. Chenault; Edward P. Gilligan; Daniel T. Henry; Stephen J. Squeri.
EIN: 136123529
Recent grants for international programs:
1241-1 Arts and Business, London, England, $210,000. For general support. 2009.
1241-2 Asociacion Civil Responde, Buenos Aires, Argentina, $39,000. For general support. 2009.
1241-3 Asociacion de Amigos de Malba, Buenos Aires, Argentina, $10,000. For general support. 2009.
1241-4 Australian Business and Community Network, Sydney, Australia, $60,000. For general support. 2009.
1241-5 Brighton Dome, Brighton, England, $75,000. For general support. 2009.
1241-6 Corporativa de Fundaciones, Guadalajara, Mexico, $25,000. For general support. 2009.
1241-7 Deutscher Kinderschutzbund Bezirksverband Frankfurt, Frankfurt, Germany, $40,000. For general support. 2009.
1241-8 Entrepreneurial Training for Innovative Community, Tokyo, Japan, $65,000. For general support. 2009.
1241-9 Give2Asia, San Francisco, CA, $75,000. For general support. 2009.
1241-10 International Rescue Committee, New York, NY, $100,000. For general support. 2009.
1241-11 International Rescue Committee, New York, NY, $75,000. For general support. 2009.
1241-12 Japan Philanthropic Association, Tokyo, Japan, $62,000. For general support. 2009.
1241-13 Junior Achievement China, Beijing, China, $50,000. For general support. 2009.
1241-14 King Baudouin Foundation United States, New York, NY, $25,000. For general support. 2009.
1241-15 Money Advice Trust, London, England, $70,000. For general support. 2009.
1241-16 NatureServe, Arlington, VA, $82,500. For general support. 2009.
1241-17 Resource Foundation, New York, NY, $75,000. For general support. 2009.
1241-18 Save the Children Federation, Westport, CT, $83,000. For general support. 2009.
1241-19 Save the Children Federation, Westport, CT, $83,000. For general support. 2009.
1241-20 Sociedad de Amigos del Museo del Palacio de Belles Artes, Mexico, $150,000. For general support. 2009.
1241-21 Springboard Charitable Trust, London, England, $40,000. For general support. 2009.
1241-22 Sussex Community Foundation, Lewes, England, $70,000. For general support. 2009.
1241-23 Tamana Association, New Delhi, India, $45,000. For general support. 2009.
1241-24 World Vision International, Monrovia, CA, $10,000. For general support. 2009.

1242
American Foundation for Charities of Portugal, Inc.
P.O. Box 981
Bethpage, NY   11714-0019   (516) 933-2547
FAX: (516) 933-2598; E-mail: info@afcpinc.org;
URL: http://www.afcpinc.org

Established in 1986.
Grantmaker type: Public charity.
Purpose and activities: The foundation seeks to encourage educational pursuits by Portuguese descendents in America and the raising of their intellectual standards, provide financial assistance in the form of scholarships to deserving students of Portuguese descent, develop fellowship among them, and cultivate in them the spirit of service in the public interest.
Fields of interest: Higher education; Human services.
International interests: Portugal.
Type of support: Scholarships—to individuals.
Publications: Application guidelines.
Application information: Application form required.
Initial approach: Complete online application
Deadline(s): Feb. 28
Officers: Carlos Ferreira, Pres.; Custodio Cerqueira, V.P.; Maria Carvalho Esteves, V.P.; Edgar Joao, V.P.; Avelino Lisboa, V.P.; Maria Augusta Calado, 1st Treas.; Maria do Carmo Correia Secons, Treas.
Directors: Andre Alcobia; Modesta Alcobia; Manuel Correira; Jose Covas; Antonio Dias; Natalia Joao; Americo Magalhaes; Candida Maia; and 15 additional directors.
EIN: 112690312

1243
American Friends of I.D.C.
(formerly The Herzliya Interdisciplinary Center)
116 E. 16th St., 11th Fl.
New York, NY   10003-2112

Established in 1997 in NY.
Donors: Anchorage Charitable Fund; Newton Becker; Chais Family Foundation; Ronald Lauder; McDonald and Company Securities; Samuel Zell; Charles and Lynn Schusterman Family Foundation; Recanati Family Foundation; The American Jewish Joint Distribution Committee, Inc.; Rochelle Becker.
Grantmaker type: Public charity.
Financial data (yr. ended 12/31/09): Revenue, $6,079,604; assets, $13,024,171 (M); gifts received, $6,206,433; expenditures, $8,479,043; giving activities include $7,897,298 for grants to organizations outside the U.S.
Purpose and activities: The organization was established to support educational, charitable, religious, and scientific programs and organizations, including the interdisciplinary center for the study of business, law, and technology in Herzliya, Israel.
Fields of interest: Higher education.
International interests: Israel.
Limitations: Giving limited to Israel. No grants to individuals.
Officers: Samuel Zell, Pres.; Mark Gerson, Secy.; Shimon Topas, Treas.
Board Members: Sheldon Adelson; Gideon Argov; Rebecca Belldegrun, M.D.; Stanley Chais; Barry Cohen; Gerald Cramer; Ellen Davis; Orit Gadiesh; Gary Heiman; Netta Korin; Ronald Lauder; Jonathan

Leitersdorf; David Levy; Eyal Ofer; Michael Recanati; and 9 additional board members.
EIN: 311577589

1244
American Friends of Keshet Eilon, Inc.
P.O. Box 284
Mamaroneck, NY   10543-0284

Established in 1998 in NY.
Donor: Abraham Slivka.
Grantmaker type: Public charity.
Financial data (yr. ended 12/31/09): Revenue, $381,046; assets, $426,044 (M); gifts received, $384,064; expenditures, $321,929; giving activities include $230,000 for grants to organizations outside the U.S.
Purpose and activities: The organization supports Keshet Eilon.
Fields of interest: Education.
International interests: Israel.
Type of support: General/operating support.
Limitations: Applications not accepted. Giving limited to Israel. No grants to individuals.
Application information: Contributes only to a pre-selected organization.
Officers: Abraham Slivka, Pres.; David Oaks, V.P.; Dov Sachter, Secy.-Treas.
EIN: 134015912

1245
American Friends of Kiryat Sanz Laniado Hospital, Inc.
261 W. 35th St., Ste. 803
New York, NY   10001-1900   (212) 944-2690
FAX: (212) 944-7512; E-mail: laniado@verizon.net;
URL: http://www.laniadohospital.org

Established in 1972 in NY.
Grantmaker type: Public charity.
Financial data (yr. ended 06/30/10): Revenue, $2,083,620; assets, $3,339,772 (M); gifts received, $1,437,832; expenditures, $2,279,413; giving activities include $1,809,550 for grants to organizations outside the U.S.
Purpose and activities: The organization provides support for Sanz Medical Center/Laniado Hospital.
Fields of interest: Health care, clinics/centers.
International interests: Israel.
Type of support: Scholarship funds; Research; Program development; Equipment; Continuing support; Building/renovation; Annual campaigns.
Limitations: Applications not accepted. Giving limited to Israel.
Publications: Annual report; Financial statement; Informational brochure.
Application information: Contributes only to a pre-selected organization.
Officers: Stanley Hyman, Chair.; Henry Spitzer, Secy.; Leibis Morgenstern, Treas.
Directors: Norman Dawidowicz; Sigmund Freundlich; Sol Friedman; Leibel Lederman; Olga Lipschitz; Joel Roth.
Number of staff: 3 full-time professional; 1 part-time professional.
EIN: 132724055

1246
American Friends of Mosdos Hakerem, Inc.
4 Treetop Ln.
Monsey, NY 10952-3611 (845) 425-1952
Contact: Jacob Kreitman, Dir.

Established in 1994 in NY.
Donors: Jack Rechnitz; Yisroel Tzvi Jacobs; Sol Marco; Roman Russ; Ida Russ; Harry Jacobs; Genesis Info Security.
Grantmaker type: Operating foundation.
Financial data (yr. ended 08/31/09): Assets, $955,723 (M); gifts received, $83,521; expenditures, $508,185; qualifying distributions, $507,500; giving activities include $507,500 for 1 grant.
Purpose and activities: Giving primarily for yeshivas in Israel.
Fields of interest: Elementary/secondary education; Scholarships/financial aid.
International interests: Israel.
Type of support: Scholarship funds.
Limitations: Applications accepted. Giving limited to Israel.
Application information:
Initial approach: Letter
Deadline(s): None
Directors: Jacob Kreitman; Rivkah Kreitman.
EIN: 133047558

1247
The American Friends of Needy Israeli Sephardic Children
c/o Ventura Corp.
512 7th Ave.
New York, NY 10018-1761 (212) 391-0170

Established in 1983.
Grantmaker type: Public charity.
Financial data (yr. ended 12/31/09): Revenue, $10,094; assets, $127,277 (M); gifts received, $10,000; expenditures, $114,386; program services expenses $113,992; giving activities include $113,992 for grants.
Purpose and activities: The organization seeks to provide financial assistance to poor Israeli Sephardic children.
Fields of interest: Economically disadvantaged.
International interests: Israel.
Type of support: Grants to individuals.
Limitations: Applications accepted. Giving primarily in Israel.
Application information: Applicant must be resident of Israel and be of Sephardic extraction, and the applicant's family must earn no more than $300 per month.
Officers: Ralph Tawil, Pres.; Saul Tawil, Secy.; Moshe Shrem, Asst. Secy.; Sharon Tawil, Asst. Secy.
EIN: 133180929

1248
American Friends of the Children's Nurseries & Children's Town in Israel
c/o Louis J. Septimus & Co.
120 W. 31st St., 7th Fl.
New York, NY 10001-3407

Grantmaker type: Public charity.

Financial data (yr. ended 12/31/10): Revenue, $736,478; assets, $46,315 (M); gifts received, $736,476; expenditures, $712,368; giving activities include $464,802 for grants, and $194,567 for grants to organizations outside the U.S.
Purpose and activities: The organization provides funds for educational institutions and needy families in Israel.
Fields of interest: Education.
International interests: Israel.
Limitations: Giving primarily in Israel. No grants to individuals.
Officers: A.D. Davis, V.P.; Mel Heftler, Secy.; Eli Mendlowitz, Treas.
EIN: 237327778

1249
American Friends of the Israel Museum
500 5th Ave., Ste. 2540
New York, NY 10110-2599 (212) 997-5611
FAX: (212) 997-5536; E-mail: info@afimnyc.org;
URL: http://www.afimnyc.org/

Established in 1972 in NY.
Grantmaker type: Public charity.
Financial data (yr. ended 12/31/10): Revenue, $36,307,108; assets, $184,787,693 (M); gifts received, $33,383,380; expenditures, $23,878,583; giving activities include $21,105,002 for grants to organizations outside the U.S.
Purpose and activities: The organization fosters and encourages the development of liberal arts by obtaining works of art and archaeology for, and obtaining grants for and to, the Israel Museum.
Fields of interest: Museums.
International interests: Israel.
Type of support: In-kind gifts.
Limitations: Applications not accepted. Giving limited to Jerusalem, Israel.
Application information: Contributes only to a pre-selected organization.
Officer: Monique Birenbaum, Exec. Dir.
Directors: Steven Ames; Paul Amir; Eugene Applebaum; Judy Baron; Sanford Batkin; Ruth Baum; Renee Belfer; Robert Beningson; Linda Berley; Irma Braman; David Braver; Melva Bucksbaum; Iris Cantor; Steven Chernys; Maureen Cogan; and 78 additional directors.
EIN: 237182582

1250
The American Friends of the Israel National Museum of Science
390 5th Ave., Ste. 600
New York, NY 10018-8153

Supporting organization of the Israel National Museum of Science.
Donor: H. Merkin.
Grantmaker type: Public charity.
Financial data (yr. ended 12/31/09): Revenue, $4,314,066; assets, $2,422,112 (M); gifts received, $3,734,020; expenditures, $4,650,150; giving activities include $4,325,000 for grants to organizations outside the U.S.
Fields of interest: Museums (science/technology); Science, formal/general education.
International interests: Israel.

Limitations: Applications not accepted. Giving limited to Israel.
Application information: Contributes only to a pre-selected organization; unsolicited requests for funds not considered or acknowledged.
Officer: Eliezer Hemelli, Exec. Dir.
EIN: 133329462

1251
American Friends of the Peres Institute for Peace, Inc.
1270 North Ave.
New Rochelle, NY 10804-2601

Established in 1999 in NY.
Grantmaker type: Public charity.
Financial data (yr. ended 12/31/10): Revenue, $766,187; assets, $125,102 (M); gifts received, $766,158; expenditures, $767,390; giving activities include $665,383 for grants to organizations outside the U.S.
Purpose and activities: The organization supports the Peres Center for Peace in Israel.
Fields of interest: International affairs.
International interests: Israel.
Limitations: Giving limited to Israel.
Officers: Rafael Kravec, Pres.; Steven C. Koppel, V.P.; Rabbi J. Rolando Matalor, Secy.; Saul Kravec, Treas.
Director: Haim Saban.
EIN: 133940178

1252
American Friends of the Yitzhak Rabin Center for the Study of Israel
866 2nd Ave., 10th Fl.
New York, NY 10017-2905 (212) 616-6161
E-mail: info@friendsofrabin.org; URL: http://www.friendsofrabin.org

Grantmaker type: Public charity.
Financial data (yr. ended 12/31/10): Revenue, $1,159,856; assets, $697,701 (M); gifts received, $1,271,465; expenditures, $1,397,636; giving activities include $970,000 for grants to organizations outside the U.S.
Purpose and activities: The organization seeks to educate the general public in the United States, Israel and throughout the world regarding the legacy of Yitzhak Rabin, and to support the educational activities of the Yitzhak Rabin Center for the Study of Israel and other charitable institutions.
Fields of interest: International democracy & civil society development.
International interests: Israel.
Limitations: Applications not accepted. Giving primarily in Israel.
Publications: Informational brochure; Newsletter.
Application information: Contributes only to pre-selected organizations.
Officers: Stuart W. Davidson, Chair.; Toni Verstandig, Pres.; Hon. Ned L. Siegel, V.P.; Jim Gerstein, Secy.; Barbara J. Easterling, Treas.
Board Members: Hon. Madeleine Albright; Etta Brandman; Hon. James A. Baker; Hon. Warren M. Christopher; Lester Crown; Sara Ehrman; Hon. Jay Footlik; Hon. Martin Indyk; Hon. Henry Kissinger; and 9 additional board members.
EIN: 133962392

1253
American Hospital of Paris Foundation
575 Madison Ave., 10th Fl.
New York, NY 10022-8511 (212) 605-0398
Contact: Meg Hammer, Dir. of Development
FAX: (212) 605-0342; E-mail: mhammer@ahpf.org;
URL: http://www.ahpf.org/

Established in 1976 in DC; supporting organization of the American Hospital of Paris.
Grantmaker type: Public charity.
Financial data (yr. ended 12/31/10): Revenue, $870,852; assets, $9,717,798 (M); gifts received, $764,719; expenditures, $706,916; program services expenses, $428,953; giving activities include $40,140 for grants to organizations outside the U.S.
Purpose and activities: The foundation raises funds to provide needed improvements in technology and facilities for the American Hospital of Paris, and to create programs that facilitate a healthy exchange, between the United States and France, of medical ideas, techniques and personnel.
Fields of interest: International exchange; Hospitals (general).
Limitations: Applications not accepted.
Publications: Financial statement; Informational brochure.
Application information: Contributes only to a pre-selected organization.
Officers and Directors:* Donna Pearson Josey,* Chair.; Michel David-Weill,* Vice-Chair.; Hon. Howard H. Leach,* Vice-Chair.; George T. Lowy, V.P.; David G. Hillle,* V.P. and Secy.; Frank Ginsberg,* V.P. and Treas.; Linda F. Barrett; Alex Dongrain; Max Chapman; and 17 additional directors.
Number of staff: 3 full-time professional.
EIN: 541031618

1254
The American India Foundation
216 E. 45th St., 7th Fl.
New York, NY 10017-3304 (646) 530-8977
Contact: Dr. Sanjay Sinho, C.E.O.
FAX: (212) 681-9350; E-mail: info@aif.org;
Additional address: 4800 Great America Pkwy., Ste. 400, Santa Clara, CA 95054-1128, tel.: (408) 916-1976, fax: (408) 982-0784; additional e-mail: luz.pacheco@aif.org; URL: http://www.aif.org
Facebook: http://www.facebook.com/AIFoundation
YouTube: http://www.youtube.com/aifoundation

Established in 2001.
Grantmaker type: Public charity.
Financial data (yr. ended 03/31/10): Revenue, $6,303,089; assets, $7,257,045 (M); gifts received, $6,034,349; expenditures, $8,376,686; program services expenses, $7,057,907; giving activities include $44,742 for 1 grant, $6,183,395 for grants to organizations outside the U.S., and $829,770 for foundation-administered programs.
Purpose and activities: The foundation is devoted to accelerating social and economic change in India; grants are focused on education and livelihood projects, with a particular emphasis on primary education and women's empowerment.
Fields of interest: AIDS; Education; Health care; Safety/disasters; International development; Economic development; Women; Economically disadvantaged.
International interests: India.
Type of support: Fellowships.

Limitations: Applications accepted. Giving limited to India. No support for governmental organizations, religious projects, or other foundations.
Publications: Application guidelines; Annual report; Newsletter.
Application information: Unsolicited proposals for funding not accepted for grants. Application form required.
   Initial approach: Download fellowship application form
   Deadline(s): Feb. 1 for William J. Clinton Fellowship for Service in India
   Final notification: 1st week of Apr. for William J. Clinton Fellowship for Service in India
Officers and Directors:* Rajat K. Gupta,* Co-Chair.; Victor Menezes,* Co-Chair.; Pradeep Kashyap, Vice-Chair.; Lata Krishnan,* Vice-Chair. and Pres.; Dr. Sanjay Sinho,* C.E.O.; Ravi Akhoury; Navneet Chugh; Sridar Iyengar; Diaz Nesamoney; Ravi Reddy; Geoffrey Stewart, Esq.; Chandrika Tandon.
Trustees: Anuradha Aggarwal; Arjun Aggarwal; Ginny Akhoury; Ravi Akhoury; B.N. Bahadur; Rani Bahadur; Balbul Bahuguna; Vimal Bahuguna; William Jefferson Clinton; and 59 additional trustees.
EIN: 134159765

1255
The American Jewish Committee
165 E. 56th St.
New York, NY 10022-2709 (212) 751-4000
FAX: (212) 891-1450; E-mail: pr@ajc.org;
URL: http://www.ajc.org

Established in 1906.
Grantmaker type: Public charity.
Financial data (yr. ended 12/31/10): Revenue, $42,632,422; assets, $131,413,191 (M); gifts received, $38,688,087; expenditures, $40,906,290; giving activities include $194,080 for grants, $347,983 for grants to organizations outside the U.S., and $3,000 for grants to individuals.
Purpose and activities: The mission of the committee is to safeguard the welfare and security of Jews in the United States, in Israel, and throughout the world; to strengthen the basic principles of pluralism around the world, as the best defense against anti-Semitism and other forms of bigotry; and to enhance the quality of American Jewish life by helping to ensure Jewish continuity and deepen ties between American and Israeli Jews.
Fields of interest: International exchange; Jewish agencies & synagogues.
International interests: Israel.
Type of support: Fellowships.
Limitations: Applications accepted. Giving on a national and international basis.
Publications: Annual report; Occasional report.
Application information:
   Initial approach: Submit application
   Deadline(s): Jan. 29 for AJC Goldman Fellowship Program
Officers and Board Members: Mimi Alperin,* Chair.; Richard J. Sideman,* Pres.; Lawrence J. Ramer,* Secy.-Treas.; David A. Harris, Exec. Dir.; Robert Elman; Harris L. Kempner, Jr.; Judah Kraushaar; Karen Levy; John M. Shapiro; Stephen Joel Trachtenberg.
EIN: 135563393

1256
The American Jewish Joint Distribution Committee, Inc.
711 3rd Ave.
New York, NY 10017-4014 (212) 687-6200
E-mail: info@jdc.org; URL: http://www.jdc.org

Established in 1914.
Grantmaker type: Public charity.
Financial data (yr. ended 12/31/10): Revenue, $249,330,587; assets, $445,210,652 (M); gifts received, $244,833,490; expenditures, $247,534,601; giving activities include $99,500 for grants, and $207,516,805 for grants to organizations outside the U.S.
Purpose and activities: The committee's mission is to serve the needs of Jews throughout the world, particularly where their lives as Jews are threatened or made more difficult, and seeks to sponsor programs of relief, rescue, and renewal and help Israel address its most urgent social challenges.
Fields of interest: International relief; Jewish agencies & synagogues.
Type of support: Grants to individuals.
Limitations: Applications accepted. Giving on a national and international basis.
Publications: Application guidelines.
Application information: Application form required.
   Initial approach: E-mail letter of intent for The Ralph I. Goldman Fellowship; download application for Roslyn Z. Wolf Cleveland-JDC Fellowship
   Deadline(s): Dec. 20 (letter of intent) for The Ralph I. Goldman Fellowship
Officers and Directors:* Hon. Ellen M. Heller,* Chair.; Dr. Irving Heller, Pres.; Jane G. Weitzman,* Secy.; Alan S. Jaffe,* Treas.; Steven Schwager, Exec. Dir.; Claude Arnall; Daniel Rader; Nora Lee Barron; Michael Belman; Lisa Belzberg; and 129 additional directors.
EIN: 131656634

1257
American Jewish World Service
45 W. 36th St.
New York, NY 10018-7904 (212) 792-2900
Contact: Josh Berkman, Assoc. Dir., Media and Mktg.
FAX: (212) 792-2930; E-mail: jberkman@ajws.org;
URL: http://www.ajws.org
Facebook: http://www.facebook.com/americanjewishworldservice
RSS Feed: http://feeds.feedburner.com/AjwsNewsFeed
Twitter: http://twitter.com/ajwsdotorg
YouTube: http://www.youtube.com/user/ajwstv

Established in 1985 in MA.
Grantmaker type: Public charity.
Financial data (yr. ended 12/31/10): Revenue, $48,028,998; assets, $31,003,443 (M); gifts received, $48,116,546; expenditures, $43,384,378; giving activities include $3,515,741 for grants, and $20,863,978 for 454 grants to organizations outside the U.S.
Purpose and activities: The organization is dedicated to alleviating poverty, hunger, and disease among the people of the developing world regardless of race, religion, or nationality, through grants to grassroots organizations, volunteer service, advocacy, and education.

Fields of interest: Education, equal rights; Reproductive health; AIDS; Safety/disasters; International development; International relief; International human rights; Civil liberties, reproductive rights; AIDS, people with.
International interests: Africa; Asia; Central America; Developing countries; South America.
Type of support: General/operating support; Continuing support; Capital campaigns; Building/ renovation; Equipment; Land acquisition; Debt reduction; Emergency funds; Program development; Conferences/seminars; Publication; Seed money; Curriculum development; Research; Technical assistance; Program evaluation; In-kind gifts.
Limitations: Applications accepted. Giving on an international basis, primarily in developing countries. No support for organizations not in the developing world. No grants to individuals.
Publications: Application guidelines; Annual report; Financial statement; Grants list; Informational brochure; Newsletter; Occasional report; Program policy statement.
Application information: A report on the progress of the grant must be submitted at the midpoint and end of the project year. Application form required.
  Initial approach: Letter
  Copies of proposal: 1
  Deadline(s): Rolling basis
  Board meeting date(s): Four times annually
  Final notification: Three months
Officers and Trustees:* Barbara Dobkin,* Chair.; Jonathan Cohen, Vice-Chair.; Kathleen Levin,* Vice-Chair.; Ruth Messinger,* Pres.; Robert Bank, Exec. V.P.; Aaron Dorfman, V.P., Progs.; Phyllis Teicher Goldman, V.P., Ext. Affairs; Louis D. Schwartz, V.P., Finance and Admin.; Sara Moore Litt, Secy.; Michael Hirschhorn,* Treas.; Donald Abramson; Marc Baum; Marion J. Bergman, M.D.; Mark Bernstein; James Dubey; Martin Friedman; Sally Gottesman; Rabbi Richard Jacobs; Howard Kleckner; Marion Lev-Cohen; James Meier; and 10 additional trustees.
Number of staff: 48 full-time professional; 4 part-time professional.
EIN: 222584370

1258
American Museum of Natural History
79th St. at Central Park W.
New York, NY 10024-5193 (212) 769-5100
E-mail: grants@amnh.org; URL: http://
www.amnh.org
Facebook: http://www.facebook.com/
naturalhistory
RSS Feed: http://www.amnh.org/news/feeds/
Twitter: http://twitter.com/amnh
YouTube: http://www.youtube.com/user/AMNHorg

Established in 1869 in NY.
Grantmaker type: Public charity.
Financial data (yr. ended 06/30/10): Revenue, $147,774,394; assets, $1,080,940,030 (M); gifts received, $97,085,452; expenditures, $183,122,409; giving activities include $1,021,470 for grants, $131,268 for grants to organizations outside the U.S., and $921,281 for grants to individuals.
Purpose and activities: The museum seeks to discover, interpret, and disseminate - through scientific research and education - knowledge about human cultures, the natural world, and the universe.
Fields of interest: Space/aviation; Astronomy; Physical/earth sciences; Science.

Type of support: Fellowships.
Application information: Applications not accepted by fax or e-mail. Application form required.
  Initial approach: Download application form
  Deadline(s): Feb. 15 for Theodore Roosevelt Memorial Grants; Mar. 15 for Lerner-Gray Grants; Nov. 15 for Research Fellowships and Frank M. Chapman Memorial Grants; Mar. 8, June 15, and Oct. 8 for Annette Kade Graduate Student Fellowship Program
  Final notification: Mar. 15 for Theodore Roosevelt Memorial Grants; Mid-May for Lerner-Gray Grants for Marine research; Mar. for Frank M. Chapman Memorial Grants
Officers and Trustees:* Lewis W. Bernard,* Chair.; Roger C. Altman,* Vice-Chair.; Steven A. Denning,* Vice-Chair.; Fiona Druckenmiller,* Vice-Chair.; Louis V. Gerstner, Jr.,* Vice-Chair.; David S. Gottesman,* Vice-Chair.; Linda R. Macaulay,* Vice-Chair.; Roberto A. Mignone,* Vice-Chair.; Ellen V. Futter,* Pres.; Sibyl R. Golden,* Secy.; Charles H. Mott,* Treas.; Stephanie Bell-Rose; Tom Brokaw; Christopher C. Davis; and 50 additional trustees.
EIN: 136162659

1259
American Patrons of the Tate Gallery Foundation, Inc.
(also known as American Patrons of Tate)
520 W. 27th St., Unit 404
New York, NY 10001-5548 (212) 643-2818
FAX: (212) 643-1001; URL: http://www.aptate.org

Established in 1998 in NY.
Grantmaker type: Public charity.
Financial data (yr. ended 12/31/10): Revenue, $3,007,365; assets, $1,913,119 (M); gifts received, $3,001,947; expenditures, $3,213,559; giving activities include $1,754,764 for grants, and $1,428,828 for 1 grant to an organization outside the U.S.
Purpose and activities: The foundation supports the Tate family of galleries.
Fields of interest: Arts, single organization support; Museums.
International interests: England.
Limitations: Applications not accepted. Giving limited to New York, NY and to the United Kingdom.
Application information: Contributes only to pre-selected organizations.
Officers and Directors:* Lynn Forester de Rothschild,* Chair.; Henry Christensen III,* Pres.; Sandra Morton Niles,* V.P. and Secy.; Richard Hamilton,* Exec. Dir.; Frances Bowes; James Chanos; Jeanne Donovan Fisher; Ella Fontanals-Cinseros; Juan Carlos Verme.
EIN: 133421353

1260
American Society for Yad Vashem, Inc.
500 5th Ave., Ste. 4200
New York, NY 10110-1699 (212) 220-4304
FAX: (212) 220-4308;
E-mail: agoldsmith@yadvashemusa.org;
URL: http://www.yadvashemusa.org

Established in 1981.
Grantmaker type: Public charity.
Financial data (yr. ended 12/31/10): Revenue, $10,249,346; assets, $31,270,504 (M); gifts received, $9,634,538; expenditures,

$10,018,549; giving activities include $7,749,650 for grants to organizations outside the U.S.
Purpose and activities: The society is the development arm of Yad Vashem, Jerusalem, which serves to remember and honor all victims of the Holocaust.
Fields of interest: Jewish agencies & synagogues; Historical activities, genealogy; Historic preservation/historical societies.
International interests: Israel.
Limitations: Giving on an international basis, with emphasis on Israel.
Officers and Directors:* Eli Zborowski,* Chair.; Norman Belfer,* Vice-Chair.; Ira Drukier,* Vice-Chair.; Eugen Gluck,* Vice-Chair.; Mark Palmer,* Vice-Chair.; Sam Skura,* Vice-Chair.; Axel Stawski,* Vice-Chair.; Joseph Wilf,* Vice-Chair.; David Halpern,* Co-Secy.; Ellis Krakowski,* Co-Secy.; Zygmunt Wilf,* Co-Secy.; Ulo Barad,* Co-Treas.; Marvin Zborowski,* Co-Treas.; Elinor Belfer; Jack A. Belz; Sam Halpern; Fanya Gottesfeld Heller; Jack H. Pechter; Marilyn Rubenstein; David Shapell; Sigmund Strochlitz; Fred Weiss; Judith Wilf.
EIN: 133106768

1261
American Society of the French Legion of Honor, Inc.
19 E. 64th St.
New York, NY 10065-7002 (212) 439-0205
Contact: Rhoda Cohen

Established in 1949 in NY.
Donor: Hon. Guy N. Wildenstein.
Grantmaker type: Independent foundation.
Financial data (yr. ended 08/31/10): Assets, $4,566,854 (M); gifts received, $24,028; expenditures, $475,946; qualifying distributions, $397,458; giving activities include $332,610 for 25 grants (high: $35,000; low: $4,500).
Purpose and activities: Grants to promote friendship between France and the U.S. through education and literature. The society also publishes a newsletter and a magazine, and it holds a reception to promote an appreciation of French-American culture.
Fields of interest: Literature; Arts; Higher education; Scholarships/financial aid; Education; International affairs, goodwill promotion; International affairs.
International interests: France.
Limitations: Applications accepted. Giving primarily in New York, NY, and Paris, France.
Application information: Application form not required.
  Initial approach: Submit information outlining activities
  Deadline(s): None
Officers and Board Members:* Hon. Guy N. Wildenstein,* Pres.; Bruno Bich,* V.P.; Hon. Walter J.P. Curley,* V.P.; Edward Finch, Jr.,* V.P.; John Haskell, Jr.,* V.P.; Hon. Joseph Verner Reed,* V.P.; John R. Young,* V.P.; Nicole Hirsh,* Secy.; Ezra K. Zilkha,* Treas.; Serge R.A. Bellanger; Bruce C. Boeglin; Francoise Cestac; Anne Cox Chambers; Roger A. Fessaguet; Steven F. Kovach; Antoine Treuille.
EIN: 130434237

1262
The American Turkish Society, Inc.
3 Dag Hammarskjold Pl., 8th Fl.
New York, NY 10017-2322 (212) 583-7614
FAX: (212) 583-7615;
E-mail: info@americanturkishsociety.org;
URL: http://www.americanturkishsociety.org
Facebook: http://www.facebook.com/
americanturkishsociety
LinkedIn: http://www.linkedin.com/groups?
home=&gid=1821660
Twitter: http://twitter.com/FollowTurkey
Application address: 305 E. 47th St., 8th Fl., New
York, NY 10017-2303

Established in 1949 in NY.
Grantmaker type: Public charity.
Financial data (yr. ended 12/31/09): Revenue,
$627,975; assets, $5,320,326 (M); gifts received,
$8,000; expenditures, $303,056; giving activities
include $54,815 for grants, and $500 for grants to
organizations outside the U.S.
Purpose and activities: The society seeks to
enhance economic, political, and cultural ties
between Turkey and the United States.
Fields of interest: International affairs.
International interests: Turkey.
Publications: Application guidelines; Annual report.
Application information:
Initial approach: Submit two-page project
proposal
Deadline(s): Nov. 1 for Curriculum Development
Grants
Final notification: Dec. 1 for Curriculum
Development Grants
Officers and Directors:* Murat Koprulu,* Chair.;
Lawrence M. Kaye,* Esq., Vice-Chair.; A. Umit
Taftali,* Vice-Chair.; Metin Negrin,* Treas.; Terry
Caloghiris; Haluk Dincer; Ozgen Dogan, M.D.; Nur
Emirgil; Talat S. Halman; Muhtar Kent; Elbrun
Kimmelman; Murad Megalli; Laurence Pettit, Esq.;
Tamer Seckin, M.D.; Shirin Devrim Trainer; Kaya
Tuncer.
EIN: 131978281

1263
American-Italian Cancer Foundation
112 E. 71st St., Ste. 2B
New York, NY 10021-5034 (212) 628-9090
FAX: (212) 517-6089;
E-mail: info@americanitaliancancer.org;
URL: http://www.americanitaliancancer.org

Established in 1980 in NY.
Grantmaker type: Public charity.
Financial data (yr. ended 06/30/10):
$2,035,087; assets, $3,368,361 (M); gifts
received, $1,930,973; expenditures, $2,006,240;
giving activities include $619,000 for grants,
$11,000 for 1 grant to an organization outside the
U.S., and $325,000 for grants to individuals.
Purpose and activities: The foundation supports
research, education, and early detection,
emphasizing the unique resources of Italy and the
United States, recognizing world-class scientific
excellence in medicine, and serving the
economically disadvantaged and medically
underserved in New York City through cancer
screening, outreach, and education.
Fields of interest: Cancer research.
International interests: Europe; Italy.
Type of support: Fellowships; Research.

Limitations: Applications accepted. Giving on a
national and international basis, with a focus on
Europe, particularly Italy.
Publications: Application guidelines; Annual report;
Financial statement; Informational brochure;
Newsletter.
Application information: The completed fellowship
application must be submitted as a digital file on a
CD ROM, along with one full printed original.
Application available at foundation Web site.
Application form required.
Initial approach: Telephone or e-mail
Copies of proposal: 1
Deadline(s): Mar. 1 for Fellowship Program
Board meeting date(s): June
Final notification: June 30
Officers and Directors:* H.E. Amb. Daniele D.
Bodini,* Chair.; Anna Bulgari,* Pres.; George M.
Pavia,* Secy.; Robert F. Agostinelli; Gian Andrea
Botta; Massimo Ferragamo; Mario J. Gabelli; and 13
additional directors.
Number of staff: 4 full-time professional; 1 part-time
support.
EIN: 133035711

1264
The American-Scandinavian Foundation
58 Park Ave.
New York, NY 10016-3007 (212) 779-3587
Contact: Edward P. Gallagher, Pres.
E-mail: info@amscan.org; URL: http://
www.amscan.org

Established in 1910 in NY.
Grantmaker type: Public charity.
Financial data (yr. ended 06/30/10): Revenue,
$4,958,432; assets, $45,551,023 (M); gifts
received, $817,117; expenditures, $4,005,621;
giving activities include $211,740 for grants, and
$769,000 for grants to individuals.
Purpose and activities: The foundation promotes
international understanding through educational
and cultural exchange between the United States
and Denmark, Finland, Iceland, Norway and Sweden.
Fields of interest: International exchange.
International interests: Scandinavia; Denmark;
Finland; Iceland; Norway; Sweden.
Type of support: Scholarships—to individuals;
Grants to individuals; Fellowships; Research.
Limitations: Applications accepted. Giving on a
national and international basis.
Publications: Application guidelines; Annual report;
Newsletter.
Application information: Non-U.S. applicants must
apply through their national cooperating office; see
web site for additional information. Application form
required.
Deadline(s): Nov. 1 for letter of intent and Jan. 30
for full application for Visiting Lectureships
Letter of Intent; Nov. 1 for Awards for Study in
Scandinavia
Final notification: Mar. 15 for Visiting
Lectureships and Awards for Study in
Scandinavia
Officers and Trustees:* Bard Bunaes,* Chair.; Hon.
Robin Chandler Duke,* Vice-Chair., United States; Hon.
Edward E. Elson,* Vice-Chair., Denmark; Bente
Frantz,* Vice-Chair., Norway; Lena Biorck Kaplan,*
Vice-Chair., Sweden; Linda Nordberg,* Vice-Chair.,
Finland; Kristjan T. Ragnarsson,* Vice-Chair.,
Iceland; Edward P. Gallagher,* Pres.; Lynn Carter,*
Exec. V.P. and Secy.; Christian R. Sonne,* Treas.;
Roger E. Anderson; Karl G. Andren; Tor B. Arneberg;

Christina Lang Assael; Hon. Stuart A. Bernstein; and
52 additional trustees.
EIN: 131623897

1265
Amit Women, Inc.
817 Broadway
New York, NY 10003-4709 (212) 477-4720
Contact: Dr. Francine S. Stein, Pres.
FAX: (212) 353-2312; E-mail: info@amitchildren.org;
Toll-free tel.: (800) 989-AMIT; URL: http://
www.amitchildren.org

Established in 1925 in NY.
Grantmaker type: Public charity.
Financial data (yr. ended 12/31/09): Revenue,
$7,532,274; assets, $14,764,191 (M); gifts
received, $7,350,050; expenditures, $7,818,976;
giving activities include $4,002,420 for grants to
organizations outside the U.S.
Purpose and activities: The organization provides
underprivileged children in Israel with
family-centered child care, and operates a network
of quality schools in Israel within a religious, Zionist
framework.
Fields of interest: Children/youth, services; Jewish
agencies & synagogues; Children/youth; Children;
Youth; Young adults; Girls; Young adults, female;
Boys; Young adults, male; Immigrants/refugees;
Economically disadvantaged.
International interests: Israel.
Type of support: Emergency funds; Equipment;
General/operating support; Program development;
Scholarships—to individuals; Curriculum
development; Continuing support; Annual
campaigns; Capital campaigns; Building/
renovation; Endowments; Scholarship funds;
Matching/challenge support.
Limitations: Applications not accepted. Giving
limited to Israel.
Publications: Annual report; Informational brochure;
Newsletter.
Application information: Contributes only to
pre-selected organizations.
Board meeting date(s): Monthly
Officers and Directors:* Mindy Liebman,* Chair.;
Dr. Francine S. Stein,* Pres.; Arnold Gerson,* Exec.
V.P.; Lisa Baratz,* V.P.; Ethylene Brickman,* V.P.;
Vivian Falk,* V.P., Leadership Devel.; Suzanne
Doft,* V.P., Mktg.; Debbi Geller,* V.P.; Ellen
Hellman,* V.P., Israel Amutah; Debbie Herbst,*
V.P.; Brenda Kalter,* V.P., Financial Resource
Devel.; Ellen Koplow,* V.P.; Debbie Moed,* V.P.,
Israel Programming; Sheryle Spar,* V.P.; Ina
Tropper,* V.P., Strategic Planning; Orlee Turitz,*
V.P.; Sharon Merkin,* Secy.; Debbie Isaac,* Treas.;
Laurie S. Bryk; Selma Dyckman; Vivian Falk; Chaiki
Feldman; Dr. Linda D. Garfield; Esther W. Goldman;
Elaine Jacobs; and 10 additional directors.
Number of staff: 42 full-time professional.
EIN: 135631502

1266
Angelina Fund, Inc.
c/o Richard Healy
149 Berkeley Pl.
Brooklyn, NY 11217-3603

Established in 1989 in CT.
Donor: Samuel G. Wiener, Jr.
Grantmaker type: Independent foundation.

Financial data (yr. ended 12/31/10): Assets,
$1,049,421 (M); expenditures, $621,935;
qualifying distributions, $606,100; giving activities
include $606,100 for grants.
Fields of interest: Media/communications;
Environment, land resources; Employment, labor
unions/organizations; International peace/security;
Civil/human rights; Public policy, research.
Limitations: Applications not accepted. Giving
primarily in NY. No grants to individuals.
Application information: Unsolicited requests for
funds not accepted.
Officer and Directors:* Samuel G. Wiener, Jr.,*
Pres.; Ellen Freudenheim; Richard Healy; Sara M.
Wiener.
EIN: 061244000

1267
The Angelson Family Foundation
876 Park Ave.
New York, NY   10075-1843

Established in 2007 in NY.
Donor: Mark Angelson.
Grantmaker type: Independent foundation.
Financial data (yr. ended 12/31/10): Assets,
$8,945,145 (M); gifts received, $2,865,000;
expenditures, $330,563; qualifying distributions,
$297,200; giving activities include $297,200 for 26
grants (high: $125,000; low: $250).
Fields of interest: Education; Arts; International
affairs; Civil/human rights.
Limitations: Applications not accepted. Giving
primarily in IL and NY. No grants to individuals.
Application information: Contributes only to
pre-selected organizations.
Officers and Trustees:* Marilyn Angelson,* Chair.;
Mark Angelson,* Pres. and Treas.; Genevieve
Angelson; Jessica Angelson; Meredith Angelson.
EIN: 566683185

1268
Arkin Family Foundation
857 5th Ave., 16th Fl.
New York, NY   10021-5857

Established in 2002 in NY.
Donor: Stanley S. Arkin.
Grantmaker type: Independent foundation.
Financial data (yr. ended 12/31/10): Assets, $117
(M); gifts received, $239,200; expenditures,
$240,600; qualifying distributions, $240,450;
giving activities include $240,450 for grants.
Fields of interest: Museums (art); Higher education;
Human services; International affairs; Civil/human
rights.
Limitations: Applications not accepted. Giving
primarily in NY. No grants to individuals.
Application information: Contributes only to
pre-selected organizations.
Trustees: Stanley S. Arkin; Suzanne Arkin.
EIN: 137317072

1269
Armenia Fund U.S.A., Inc.
80 Maiden Ln., Ste. 2205
New York, NY   10038-4940   (212) 689-5307
Contact: Irina Lazarian, Exec. Dir.
FAX: (212) 689-5317;
E-mail: info@armeniafundusa.org; Toll-free tel.:

(866)-446-6237; URL: http://
www.armeniafundusa.org

Established in 1992 in DE.
Grantmaker type: Public charity.
Financial data (yr. ended 12/31/10): Revenue,
$1,184,610; assets, $1,410,556 (M); gifts
received, $1,182,460; expenditures, $968,544;
program services expenses, $794,591; giving
activities include $566,355 for grants to
organizations outside the U.S.
Purpose and activities: The fund is dedicated to
supporting large-scale, self-sustaining initiatives in
both Armenia and Nagorno-Karabakh that are in
social and political transition with tremendous
potential for the future; it is primarily focused on
building sustainable infrastructure for the region
through the development of roads, schools, medical
facilities, and utilities.
Fields of interest: Community/economic
development; International development;
International affairs.
International interests: Azerbaijan; Armenia.
Limitations: Applications not accepted. Giving
limited to Armenia and Nagorno-Karabakh.
Publications: Newsletter.
Application information: Contributes only to
pre-selected organizations.
Officers and Directors:* Khoren Bandazian,*
Chair.; Zara Ingilizian,* Secy.; Aram Pehlivanian,
Treas.; Irina Lazarian, Exec. Dir.; Gregory
Amerkanian; Armen Arslanian; Arthur Grigorian;
Jean-Jacques Hajjar; Kharen Musaelian; Tro
Piliguian; Margot Takian; Joshua Tevekelian; Gevorg
Yaghjyan.
Trustees: H.H. Aram, I; Archbishop Khajag
Barsamian; H.E. Abp. Oshagan Choloyan; Hon.
Gagik G. Haroutiunian; Hirair Hovnanian; H.H.
Karekin, II.
EIN: 133696515

1270
Armenian General Benevolent Union
55 E. 59th St.
New York, NY   10022-1112   (212) 319-6383
FAX: (212) 319-6507; E-mail: agbuwb@agbu.org;
URL: http://www.agbu.org

Established in 1906.
Grantmaker type: Public charity.
Financial data (yr. ended 12/31/10): Revenue,
$20,203,542; assets, $194,023,371 (M); gifts
received, $12,304,923; expenditures,
$22,223,330; giving activities include $3,949,311
for grants, $11,989,887 for grants to organizations
outside the U.S., and $23,000 for grants to
individuals.
Purpose and activities: The union seeks to preserve
and promote the Armenian identity and heritage
through educational, cultural and humanitarian
programs.
Fields of interest: Arts, cultural/ethnic awareness.
International interests: Armenia.
Type of support: Scholarships—to individuals.
Publications: Biennial report; Newsletter.
Officers and Directors:* Berge Setrakian,* Pres.;
Arshavir Gundjian,* V.P.; Berge Papazian, Secy.;
Sam Simonian,* Treas.; M. Michael Ansour; Carol
Bagdasarian Aslanian; Aris Atamian; Joseph L.
Basralian; Yervant Demirijian; Nazreth Festekjian;
Vahe Gabrache; Arda Nazerian Haratunian; Sarkis

Jebejian; Levon Kebabdjian; Levon Nazarian; and 4
additional directors.
EIN: 135600421

1271
Armenian Medical Fund
(formerly Armenian-American Medical Philanthropic
Fund, Inc.)
160 Waters Edge
Congers, NY   10920-2622   (845) 268-2069
FAX: (845) 268-1948; URL: http://
www.armenianmedicalfund.org/

Established in 1954 in NY as The Armenian
Association to Aid the Armenian National
Sanatorium of Lebanon, Inc.; changed to current
name in 2004.
Grantmaker type: Public charity.
Financial data (yr. ended 12/31/10): Revenue,
$172,384; assets, $3,866,585 (M); gifts received,
$15,190; expenditures, $165,535; giving activities
include $143,950 for grants to organizations
outside the U.S.
Purpose and activities: The organization works to
help the efforts of all Armenian institutions,
organizations, and individuals that treat, support,
prevent the spread of, research, and educate the
public about tuberculosis and thoracic diseases.
Fields of interest: Lung diseases; Hospitals
(general).
International interests: Armenia; Lebanon.
Limitations: Giving on an international basis,
primarily in Armenia and Lebanon.
Officers: Vahie Balouzian, Pres.; Andrew Torigian,
V.P.; Mesrob Odian, Treas.; Herand M. Markarian,
Ph.D., Exec. Dir.
EIN: 131856369

1272
The Asia Society
725 Park Ave.
New York, NY   10021-5088   (212) 288-6400
FAX: (212) 517-8315; E-mail: info@asiaoc.org;
Toll-free tel.: (888) 275-2742; URL: http://
www.asiasociety.org
YouTube: http://www.youtube.com/user/
asiasociety

Established in 1956 in NY.
Grantmaker type: Public charity.
Financial data (yr. ended 06/30/10): Revenue,
$16,439,022; assets, $104,293,530 (M); gifts
received, $15,006,163; expenditures,
$26,750,978; giving activities include $1,021,064
for grants, and $20,000 for 1 grant to an
organization outside the U.S.
Purpose and activities: The society is one of
America's leading institutions dedicated to fostering
understanding of Asia and communication between
Americans and the people of Asia and the Pacific.
Fields of interest: Education; International
exchange; Asians/Pacific Islanders.
International interests: Asia.
Type of support: Grants to individuals.
Limitations: Giving on a national and international
basis, primarily to Asia.
Publications: Application guidelines.
Application information:

Initial approach: Submit essay
Deadline(s): June 12 for Goldman Sachs Foundation Prizes for Excellence in International Education
Officers and Trustees:* Vishakha N. Desai,* Pres.; Jamie Metzl, Exec. V.P.; Thomas B. Moore, Sr. V.P., Opers.; Todd Michael Galitz, V.P., External Affairs; Deanna Lee, V.P., Comms.; Michael H. Levine, V.P., New Media; Vivien Stewart, V.P., Education; Jon A. Anda; Hushang Ansary; Ajay Banga; Leon D. Black; Ronnie C. Chan; Purnendu Chatterjee; Gina Lin Chu; Betsy Z. Cohen; and 42 additional trustees.
Number of staff: 100
EIN: 133234632

1273
Asian Cultural Council

6 W. 48th St., 12th Fl.
New York, NY 10036-1802 (212) 843-0403
Contact: Dawn Byrnes, Mgr., Comms.
FAX: (212) 843-0343; E-mail: acc@accny.org; Fax for D. Byrnes: (212) 843-0343; URL: http://www.asianculturalcouncil.org
Facebook: http://www.facebook.com/asianculturalcouncil?ref=nf
Grants List: http://www.asianculturalcouncil.org/?page_id=26
Twitter: http://twitter.com/ACCNY

Established in 1980 in NY.
Donors: Asian Oceanic Group; Blanchette H. Rockefeller Fellowship Fund; Blanchette H. Rockefeller‡; The Ford Foundation; The Japan Foundation; The IDR 3rd Fund; The Andrew W. Mellon Foundation; National Endowment for the Humanities; George D. O'Neill; Mrs. George D. O'Neill; Kajitani Textile Fund; Laurance S. Rockefeller‡; Starr Foundation.
Grantmaker type: Public charity.
Financial data (yr. ended 12/31/09): Revenue, $736,928; assets, $32,111,170 (M); gifts received, $1,405,913; expenditures, $4,550,754; program services expenses, $3,631,550; giving activities include $239,100 for 18 grants (high: $22,000; low: $5,100), $353,650 for 1 grant to an organization outside the U.S., $954,710 for 75 grants to individuals, $8,400 for 75 grants to individuals outside the U.S., and $2,075,690 for foundation-administered programs.
Purpose and activities: The ACC's mission is to support international dialogue, understanding and respect through cultural exchange and nurtures the individual talents of artists and scholars in Asia and the United States, while adapting to the ever-changing realities of the world.
Fields of interest: Media, film/video; History/archaeology; Performing arts; Arts, management/technical assistance; Arts, administration/regulation; Arts, multipurpose centers/programs; Arts, cultural/ethnic awareness; Arts councils; Visual arts; Visual arts, architecture; Visual arts, photography; Visual arts, sculpture; Visual arts, drawing; Visual arts, art conservation; Museums (art); Museums (ethnic/folk arts); Art history; Literature; Historic preservation/historical societies; Arts; Graduate/professional education.
International interests: Asia.
Type of support: Conferences/seminars; Professorships; Fellowships; Research; Grants to individuals; Scholarships—to individuals; Exchange programs.
Limitations: Applications accepted. Giving on a national and international basis, primarily in Asia,

with current emphasis on east and southeast Asia. No support for individual exhibitions. No grants for publication costs, performance tours, undergraduate study, or activities conducted by individuals in their home countries, film or video production, lectures, administrative expenses, or capital campaigns.
Publications: Application guidelines; Annual report; Grants list; Informational brochure; Newsletter.
Application information: Applications are accepted by e-mail only. Application form required.
Initial approach: Letter of inquiry
Copies of proposal: 1
Deadline(s): Sept. 1 (letters of inquiry) and Nov. 1 (full applications)
Board meeting date(s): Spring
Final notification: After spring board meeting, typically in June
Officers and Trustees:* Elizabeth J. McCormack,* Chair.; Valerie Rockefeller Wayne,* Vice-Chair.; Richard S. Lanier,* Pres.; Stephen B. Heintz, V.P.; Pauline R. Yu, Secy.; Robert S. Pirie,* Treas.; Jennifer P. Goodale, Exec. Dir.; Hope Aldrich; Jane Debevoise; Jonathan Fanton; John H. Foster; Kenneth H.C. Fung; Curtis Greer; Douglas Tong Hsu; Hans Michael Jebsen; J. Christopher Kojima; and 10 additional trustees.
Number of staff: 8 full-time professional; 7 part-time professional.
EIN: 133018822

1274
Aspen Strategic Initiative Institute

767 Fifth Ave.
New York, NY 10153-0023

Grantmaker type: Public charity.
Financial data (yr. ended 12/31/10): Revenue, $41,935; assets, $128,396 (M); gifts received, $41,935; expenditures, $42,106; giving activities include $41,510 for grants to organizations outside the U.S.
Purpose and activities: The organization supports value-based leadership and trans-Atlantic dialogue.
Fields of interest: International affairs.
Limitations: Giving limited to Germany.
Directors: Bruce Jackson; John O'Sullivan; Allen Roth.
EIN: 300077451

1275
The Assael Foundation

580 5th Ave., 21st Fl.
New York, NY 10036-4701

Established in 1992 in NY.
Donors: Salvador J. Assael; Baruch Assael; Esther Posin.
Grantmaker type: Independent foundation.
Financial data (yr. ended 12/31/10): Assets, $6,548,617 (M); gifts received, $750; expenditures, $248,661; qualifying distributions, $227,665; giving activities include $227,665 for grants.
Purpose and activities: Giving primarily for education and the arts.
Fields of interest: Children, services; Education, special; Elementary/secondary education; Performing arts; Arts, cultural/ethnic awareness; Museums; Arts; Education; International development; Jewish agencies & synagogues.

International interests: Israel.
Limitations: Applications not accepted. Giving primarily in NY, with emphasis on the New York metropolitan area. No grants to individuals.
Application information: Contributes only to pre-selected organizations.
Officers: Salvador J. Assael, Chair. and Pres.; Christina Lang Assael, Vice-Chair.; Bandana Kumar, Secy.-Treas.
Trustees: Rabbi Marc D. Angel; John D. Block; Cyril S. Dwek; Ephraim Propp; Benjamin Zucker.
EIN: 133683069

1276
The Astraea Lesbian Foundation for Justice, Inc.

(formerly ASTRAEA, National Lesbian Action Foundation)
116 E. 16th St., 7th Fl.
New York, NY 10003-2112 (212) 529-8021
Contact: Katherine T. Acey, Exec. Dir.
FAX: (212) 982-3321;
E-mail: info@astraeafoundation.org; URL: http://www.astraeafoundation.org

Established in 1977 in NY; current name adopted in 2003.
Grantmaker type: Public charity.
Financial data (yr. ended 06/30/10): Revenue, $1,886,309; assets, $10,313,330 (M); gifts received, $1,806,698; expenditures, $3,664,608; giving activities include $511,346 for grants, $1,150,563 for grants to organizations outside the U.S., and $20,000 for grants to individuals.
Purpose and activities: The foundation provides support for projects which contribute to the well-being of lesbians and their allies; priorities include organizations directed by or targeted to lesbians of color; multicultural/multiracial lesbian organizations; women's or LGBT that have lesbians in leadership roles, include lesbian issues as an integral part of their work, and are seeking funding for a project that specifically addresses heterocentrism and homophobia; projects focusing on community building and coalition work among lesbian and LGBT organizations and between constituencies for the purpose of promoting a social justice/human rights agenda. The foundation awards grants regionally, nationally, and internationally.
Fields of interest: Civil/human rights, LGBTQ; Disabilities, people with; Women; LGBTQ.
International interests: Africa; Asia; Caribbean; Central America; Eastern & Central Europe; South America; Soviet Union (Former).
Type of support: General/operating support; Continuing support; Conferences/seminars; Seed money; Grants to individuals.
Limitations: Applications accepted. Giving on a national and international basis.
Publications: Application guidelines; Annual report; Grants list; Informational brochure; Newsletter.
Application information: Organizations interested in International Fund for Sexual Minorities Grants who are not current foundation grantees must submit a letter of inquiry to the foundation to be considered to funding; applicants will be notified within twelve weeks of submission as to whether or not they can continue in the application process. Application form required.
Initial approach: Download application form

Copies of proposal: 4

Deadline(s): Feb. 1 and Sept. 5 for International Fund for Sexual Minorities; Feb. 15 for Astraea Visual Arts Fund; June 30 for Lesbian Writers Fund; Dec. 3 for U.S. Fund Panel Grants

Officers and Directors:* Alice Y. Hom,* Chair.; Ileana Jimenez,* Secy.; Rebecca Rolfe,* Treas.; Katherine T. Acey, Exec. Dir.; Marion Banzhaf; Stephanie Blackwood; Louisa Hext; Meg Hickman; Ana Lara; Toni Lester; Kim Mojica; Eleanor Palacios; Miriam Perez; Alejandra Quijada; Robin Rosenbluth.

Number of staff: 2 full-time professional; 4 full-time support.

EIN: 132992977

1277

The Atlantic Foundation of New York

c/o The Atlantic Philanthropies
75 Varick St., 17th Fl.
New York, NY 10017-1950 (212) 916-7300
E-mail: USA@atlanticphilanthropies.org
Charles F. Feeney's Giving Pledge: http://www.givingpledge.org/#enter

Established in 1989 in NY.

Donors: Atlan Management Corp.; Interpacific Holdings, Inc.; General Atlantic Corp.

Grantmaker type: Independent foundation.

Financial data (yr. ended 12/31/10): Assets, $7,496,020 (M); expenditures, $634,221; qualifying distributions, $600,227; giving activities include $600,227 for grants.

Purpose and activities: The purpose of the foundation is to bring about lasting changes that will improve the lives of disadvantaged and vulnerable people.

Fields of interest: Health care; Children, services; Aging, centers/services; International affairs, goodwill promotion; Aging; Economically disadvantaged.

Limitations: Applications not accepted. Giving primarily in Stanford, CA and Washington, DC; some giving also in St. Paul, MN. No grants to individuals.

Publications: Financial statement.

Application information: Contributes only to pre-selected organizations.

Officers and Directors:* Gara LaMarche,* Pres.; Colin McCrea, Sr. V.P., Progs.; Deborah R. Phillips, Sr. V.P., Group Svcs. and Eval.; Cynthia Richards,* V.P.; David Sternlieb, Secy.; Philip Coates, C.I.O.; Harvey Dale; Christine V. Downton; Charles F. Feeney; William Hall; Sara Lawrence-Lightfoot; Elizabeth J. McCormack; Thomas N. Mitchell; Cecilia Munoz; Peter Smitham; Frederick A.O. Schwarz, Jr.; Michael I. Sovern; Cummings V. Zuill.

EIN: 133562971

1278

The AVI CHAI Foundation

(formerly AVI CHAI - A Philanthropic Foundation)
1015 Park Ave.
New York, NY 10028-0904 (212) 396-8850
Contact: Yossi Prager, Exec. Dir., North America
FAX: (212) 396-8833; E-mail: info@avichaina.org;
Additional address (Israel office): 31 Hanevlim, 95103 Jerusalem, tel.: (02) 624-3330, fax: (02) 624-3310, e-mail: office@avichai.org.il;
URL: http://www.avichai.org
Blog: http://www.cmfdn.org/about-us/board-of-directors/

Established in 1984 in NY.

Donor: Zalman C. Bernstein†.

Grantmaker type: Independent foundation.

Financial data (yr. ended 12/31/10): Assets, $614,997,808 (M); gifts received, $29,975; expenditures, $47,175,445; qualifying distributions, $58,594,156; giving activities include $38,851,610 for 75 grants (high: $19,556,301; low: $375), $900,000 for 10 grants to individuals (high: $150,000; low: $75,000), $1,023,857 for foundation-administered programs and $11,805,647 for 16 loans/program-related investments (high: $1,000,000; low: $175,000).

Purpose and activities: The foundation is committed to the perpetuation of the Jewish people, Judaism, and the centrality of the state of Israel to the Jewish people. The objectives of the foundation are to encourage those of the Jewish faith towards greater commitment to Jewish observance and lifestyle by increasing their understanding, appreciation, and practice of Jewish traditions, customs, and laws; and to encourage mutual understanding and sensitivity among Jews of different religious backgrounds and commitments to observance.

Fields of interest: Education; Human services; Youth, services; Jewish federated giving programs.

International interests: Israel.

Type of support: Program development; Conferences/seminars; Curriculum development; Research; Program-related investments/loans.

Limitations: Applications not accepted. Giving primarily in North America and Israel. No grants for building projects or deficits.

Publications: Annual report.

Application information: Unsolicited requests for funds not accepted.

Board meeting date(s): 3 times a year

Officers and Trustees:* Arthur W. Fried,* Chair.; Azriel Novick, C.F.O.; Yossi Prager, Exec. Dir., North America; Eli Silver, Exec. Dir., Israel; Henry Taub, Tr. Emeritus; Mem Dryan Bernstein; Meir Buzaglo; Avital Darmon; Alan R. Feld; Lauren K. Merkin; George Rohr; Lief D. Rosenblatt; David E. Tadmor; Ruth R. Wisse.

Number of staff: 7 full-time professional; 4 full-time support.

EIN: 133252800

Recent grants for international programs:

1278-1 American Friends of Bnei Akiva Yeshivas in Israel, New York, NY, $20,000. To enhance Jewish education and Israel advocacy. 2009.

1278-2 American Friends of Jordan River Village Foundation, Stamford, CT, $10,000. To enhance Jewish summer camps in Israel. 2009.

1278-3 American Pardes Foundation, New York, NY, $1,008,045. For Teacher Training Program. 2009.

1278-4 American-Israeli Cooperative Enterprise, Chevy Chase, MD, $25,000. To enhance Jewish content on the Internet. 2009.

1278-5 Avi Chai, Jerusalem, Israel, $17,000,986. For Jewish Education Projects in Israel. 2009.

1278-6 Bar-Ilan University in Israel, New York, NY, $209,153. To enhance Jewish Day School Education. 2009.

1278-7 Beit Avi Chai, Jerusalem, Israel, $4,477,704. For Jewish Education Projects in Israel. 2009.

1278-8 Birthright Israel Foundation, New York, NY, $1,000,000. For Israel education project. 2009.

1278-9 BlueStar, San Francisco, CA, $294,837. For Israel advocacy project. 2009.

1278-10 Brandeis University, Waltham, MA, $123,831. For project to help Jewish Schools promote Shabbat observance and Judaic commitment and study of effectiveness of Jewish study program in Israel. 2009.

1278-11 Cleveland Jewish News, Beachwood, OH, $144,000. For Israel advocacy project. 2009.

1278-12 Community Foundation for Jewish Education of Metropolitan Chicago, Skokie, IL, $22,220. For Israel advocacy project. 2009.

1278-13 Community Hebrew Academy of Toronto, Toronto, Canada, $23,567. For project to help Jewish schools promote Shabbat observance and Judaic commitment. 2009.

1278-14 Federation Combined Jewish Appeal, Montreal, Canada, $558,402. For Judaic curriculum project. 2009.

1278-15 Federation of Jewish Communities of the CIS and Baltic States, New York, NY, $1,160,555. For Jewish Education Projects in the Former Soviet Union. 2009.

1278-16 Gray Academy of Jewish Education, Winnipeg, Canada, $12,683. To help Jewish Schools to promote Shabbat observance and Judaic commitment. 2009.

1278-17 Hamilton Hebrew Academy, Hamilton, Canada, $43,000. For program to promote cost savings in operation of Jewish Day Schools. 2009.

1278-18 Hebrew University of Jerusalem, Melton Centre for Jewish Education, Jerusalem, Israel, $45,270. For Israel education project. 2009.

1278-19 Hillel: The Foundation for Jewish Campus Life, Washington, DC, $64,550. For Israel advocacy project. 2009.

1278-20 Jewish Agency for Israel, New York, NY, $280,375. To enhance Jewish content in summer camps. 2009.

1278-21 Jewish United Fund of Metropolitan Chicago, Chicago, IL, $50,000. For Israel advocacy project. 2009.

1278-22 Jewish Week, New York, NY, $262,500. For Israel advocacy project. 2009.

1278-23 JOINT Israel, New York, NY, $2,532,916. For Jewish Education Projects in the Former Soviet Union. 2009.

1278-24 JPPS-Bialik, Montreal, Canada, $18,750. For Jewish Schools to promote Shabbat observance and Judaic commitment. 2009.

1278-25 Ohr Avner Foundation, New York, NY, $425,000. For Jewish Education Project in the Former Soviet Union. 2009.

1278-26 TaL AM, Ville Saint Laurent, Canada, $847,650. For Judiac curriculum project. 2009.

1278-27 United Talmud Torahs, Herzliah High School, Canada, $14,900. For Jewish Schools to promote Shabbat observance and Judaic commitment. 2009.

1278-28 World Union for Progressive Judaism, New York, NY, $57,500. For program to enhance Jewish content at summer camp in the Former Soviet Union. 2009.

1279

The AYCO Charitable Foundation

25 British American Blvd.
Latham, NY 12110-1405
Contact: Barry Hamerling, Pres.
URL: http://www.ayco.com/client_services/isg/isg_acf.html

Established in 1995 in NY.

Grantmaker type: Public charity.

Financial data (yr. ended 06/30/10): Revenue, $57,440,200; assets, $232,703,600 (M); gifts received, $57,090,600; expenditures, $67,235,700; giving activities include $64,574,300 for grants.

Purpose and activities: The foundation administers a donor-advised fund by contributing to public charities in the United States in the areas of higher education, human services, the arts, health, the environment, and wildlife preservation.

Fields of interest: Arts, multipurpose centers/programs; Museums; Performing arts; Higher education; Graduate/professional education; Environment, natural resources; Animals/wildlife; Health care; Health organizations; Medical research; Youth development; Human services; International human rights; Community/economic development; United Ways and Federated Giving Programs.

Limitations: Applications not accepted. Giving on a national basis.

Application information: Contributes only to pre-selected organizations.

Officers and Directors:* Barry Hamerling,* Pres.; John Mastriani,* V.P. and C.F.O.; Mae Cavoli,* Secy.; Camille Andrews; Anthony DePaula; David Golub; Peter Heerwagen; William Nutt; Joel Schaller.

EIN: 141782466

1280
B'nai Zion Foundation, Inc.
136 E. 39th St.
New York, NY 10016-0914 (212) 725-1211
Contact: Edna Maayami
FAX: (212) 684-6327;
E-mail: grunspan@bnaizion.org; URL: http://www.bnaizion.org/

Established in 1951 in NY.

Grantmaker type: Public charity.

Financial data (yr. ended 12/31/09): Revenue, $1,206,860; assets, $7,973,191 (M); gifts received, $943,211; expenditures, $2,621,124; program services expenses, $1,867,898; giving activities include $471,366 for grants to organizations outside the U.S., and $1,396,532 for foundation-administered programs.

Purpose and activities: The foundation is dedicated to assisting those in need with humanitarian projects in both Israel and the U.S., supporting the significant and enduring tie between both nations, and advancing the physical, mental, and social well-being of the citizens of Israel.

Fields of interest: Human services; Jewish agencies & synagogues.

International interests: Israel.

Limitations: Giving primarily to Israel.

Officers and Board Members:* George W. Schaeffer,* Pres.; Jack Grunspan,* Exec. V.P. and Secy.; David H. Eisenberg,* V.P.; Rubin Ferziger,* Esq., V.P.; Hon. Benjamin A. Gilman,* V.P.; Harvey Goldfarb,* V.P.; Aaron Ignal,* V.P.; Eleanor Ignal,* V.P.; Roman Kent,* V.P.; Boris Kiderman,* V.P.; Hon. Jerrold Nadler,* V.P.; Eduard Nakhamkin,* V.P.; Arnold Wagner,* V.P.; Sumner Zabriskie,* V.P.; Gabriella Diamond,* Treas.; Sanford L. Batkin; Irwin Blank; Israel Diamond; Rabbi Reuben Katz; Elaine Ordan; and 10 additional board members.

EIN: 132572288

1281
The Banfi Vintners Foundation
(formerly The Villa Banfi Foundation)
1111 Cedar Swamp Rd.
Glen Head, NY 11545-2109 (516) 686-2506
Contact: Frank Savino, Treas.
URL: http://www.banfivintners.com/index.php/about_us/mission

Established in 1982 in NY.

Donor: Banfi Products Corp.

Grantmaker type: Independent foundation.

Financial data (yr. ended 12/31/10): Assets, $12,765,940 (M); expenditures, $658,926; qualifying distributions, $638,863; giving activities include $638,863 for grants.

Fields of interest: Higher education; Hospitals (general); Health organizations, association; International affairs, goodwill promotion.

Limitations: Giving primarily in, but not limited to CA, MA and NY.

Application information:
Deadline(s): None
Board meeting date(s): Nov.

Officers and Directors:* Joan C. Rupp, Secy.; Frank Savino, Treas.; Philip D. Calderone,* Exec. Dir.; Cristina Mariani-May; Harry F. Mariani; James W. Mariani; John Mariani.

EIN: 112622792

1282
The Baobab Fund
200 Madison Ave., 5th Fl.
New York, NY 10016-3912

Established in 2002 in DE.

Donor: Gideon G. Rose.

Grantmaker type: Independent foundation.

Financial data (yr. ended 12/31/10): Assets, $2,305,843 (M); gifts received, $400,000; expenditures, $343,899; qualifying distributions, $343,021; giving activities include $343,021 for grants.

Fields of interest: Higher education, university; Animal welfare; International human rights.

Limitations: Applications not accepted. Giving primarily in CT and NY. No grants to individuals.

Application information: Contributes only to pre-selected organizations.

Officers: Gideon G. Rose, Pres. and Treas.; Sheri Berman, V.P. and Secy.

EIN: 331007796

1283
Bat Hanadiv Foundation No. 3
c/o Carter, Ledyard & Milburn LLP
2 Wall St.
New York, NY 10005-2072
Application address: c/o Yad Hanadiv, 16 Ibn Gvirol St., 92430 Jerusalem, Israel; Application e-mail: website@yadhanadiv.org.il

Established in 1981.

Donors: Bat Hanadiv Foundation; Bat Hanadiv Foundation No. 2.

Grantmaker type: Independent foundation.

Financial data (yr. ended 12/31/10): Assets, $953,358,565 (M); gifts received, $9,714,367; expenditures, $39,267,607; qualifying distributions, $23,331,883; giving activities include $23,331,883 for grants.

Purpose and activities: Grants primarily for higher and other education; support also for conservation, youth and social service agencies, and cultural programs.

Fields of interest: Arts; Environment, natural resources; Human services; Youth, services.

International interests: Israel.

Type of support: General/operating support; Equipment; Program development.

Limitations: Applications accepted. Giving primarily in Israel.

Application information: Grants are administered by Yad Hanadiv. All grantseekers must follow the guidelines on web site http://yadhanadiv.org.il.
Initial approach: See Yad Hanadiv web site for guidelines and eligibility

Trustee: Doder Trust, Ltd.

EIN: 133091620

1284
Batya - Friends of United Hatzalah, Inc.
208 E. 51st St., Ste. 303
New York, NY 10022-6557 (646) 833-7108
FAX: (212) 898-0424;
E-mail: office@israelirescue.org; URL: http://www.unitedhatzalah.org/?categoryid=225

Established in 2000 in NY.

Grantmaker type: Public charity.

Financial data (yr. ended 12/31/10): Revenue, $2,764,069; assets, $664,276 (M); gifts received, $2,763,920; expenditures, $2,200,080, giving activities include $83,170 for grants, and $1,872,250 for grants to organizations outside the U.S.

Purpose and activities: The organization supports United Hatzalah of Israel in its mission of providing emergency medical services and first responders throughout Israel.

Fields of interest: Health care, single organization support; Health care, EMS; Health care, support services.

International interests: Israel.

Limitations: Giving primarily to Israel.

Officers and Trustees:* Eliezer Beer,* Pres.; Moshe Falik,* Secy.; Julius Klein,* Treas.; Aharon Brand; Shlomo Katz; Daniel Katensteim.

EIN: 113533002

1285
The David Berg Foundation, Inc.
16 E. 73rd St., Ste. 1R
New York, NY 10021-4129 (212) 517-8634
Contact: Michele Tocci, Pres.
FAX: (212) 517-8636;
E-mail: mtocci@bergfoundation.org

Established in 1994 in NY.

Donor: David Berg Settlor Trust.

Grantmaker type: Independent foundation.

Financial data (yr. ended 12/31/09): Assets, $1,561,292 (M); gifts received, $3,080,000; expenditures, $2,391,488; qualifying distributions, $1,831,011; giving activities include $1,484,250 for 55+ grants (high: $100,000).

Fields of interest: Legal services; Museums; Law school/education; Jewish agencies & synagogues.

International interests: England; Israel.

Type of support: General/operating support; Continuing support; Annual campaigns; Equipment; Program development; Conferences/seminars;

Professorships; Publication; Curriculum development; Fellowships; Scholarship funds; Research; Exchange programs.
Limitations: Applications accepted. Giving primarily in New York, NY. No grants to individuals.
Publications: Application guidelines; Grants list.
Application information: Application form not required.
   Initial approach: Proposal
   Copies of proposal: 1
   Deadline(s): Dec. 31 for Feb.; Apr. 30 for June; Aug. 30 for Oct.
   Board meeting date(s): June, Oct., and Feb.
Officers: Michele C. Tocci, Pres.; William D. Zabel, V.P.; Jerome Zoffer, Secy.-Treas.
Number of staff: 1 full-time professional; 1 part-time professional; 1 part-time support.
EIN: 133753217

1286
The Judy & Howard Berkowitz Foundation
c/o The Ayco Co., LP
P.O. Box 860
Saratoga Springs, NY   12866-0860
Contact: Joseph N. Vet

Established in 1987 in NY.
Donors: Howard P. Berkowitz; Judith R. Berkowitz.
Grantmaker type: Independent foundation.
Financial data (yr. ended 03/31/11): Assets, $18,331 (M); gifts received, $380,000; expenditures, $871,614; qualifying distributions, $871,302; giving activities include $865,722 for 93 grants (high: $25,000; low: $100).
Purpose and activities: Giving primarily for the arts, particularly the performing arts, as well as for education, health and human services, and Jewish agencies.
Fields of interest: Performing arts; Arts; Higher education, university; Education; Hospitals (general); Health organizations, association; Human services; Children/youth, services; International affairs; Jewish federated giving programs; Jewish agencies & synagogues.
Limitations: Applications not accepted. Giving primarily in New York, NY. No grants to individuals.
Application information: Contributes only to pre-selected organizations.
Trustees: Howard P. Berkowitz; Judith R. Berkowitz; Roger S. Berkowitz; Sandra L. Berkowitz.
EIN: 133371065

1287
The Birkelund Fund
c/o Barry M. Strauss Assoc., Ltd.
307 5th Ave., 8th Fl.
New York, NY   10016-6517

Established in 1989 in DE and NY.
Donor: John P. Birkelund.
Grantmaker type: Independent foundation.
Financial data (yr. ended 04/30/11): Assets, $15,054,553 (M); expenditures, $2,084,441; qualifying distributions, $1,963,079; giving activities include $1,963,079 for grants.
Purpose and activities: Giving primarily for education, including a public library; some giving also for the arts, and health and human services.
Fields of interest: Arts; Museums (art); Higher education; Libraries (public); Education; Health care; Human services; International affairs.

Limitations: Applications not accepted. Giving primarily in CT, NJ, NY, and RI. No grants to individuals.
Application information: Contributes only to pre-selected organizations.
Officer: John P. Birkelund, Pres.
Director: Kenneth W. Orce.
EIN: 133539224

1288
Birthright Israel Foundation
P.O. Box 1784
New York, NY   10156-1784
Contact: Robert Aronson, Pres.
E-mail: foundation@birthrightisrael.org; *URL:* http://www.birthrightisrael.com/site/PageServer?pagename=donate_case
Blog: http://generations.birthrightisrael.com/blog/
Facebook: http://www.facebook.com/TaglitBirthrightIsrael?v=info&ref=ts
Picasa Photo Gallery: https://picasaweb.google.com/birthrightisraelSiteLogs
Twitter: http://twitter.com/TaglitBRI
YouTube: http://www.youtube.com/user/birthrightisrael?blend=2&ob=1&rclk=cti

Established in 1999 in NY.
Grantmaker type: Public charity.
Financial data (yr. ended 12/31/10): Revenue, $51,845,830; assets, $23,347,722 (M); gifts received, $51,823,363; expenditures, $55,033,808; giving activities include $664,467 for grants, and $48,606,219 for grants to organizations outside the U.S.
Purpose and activities: The foundation exists for the sole benefit of Birthright Israel International.
Fields of interest: Jewish agencies & synagogues.
International interests: Israel.
Limitations: Applications not accepted. Giving limited to Los Angeles, CA; Washington, DC; Orlando and Tampa, FL; Atlanta, GA; Chicago, IL; Rockville, MD; Boston, MA; New York City; Philadelphia, PA; Seattle, WA; Montreal, Quebec, Canada; and Jerusalem, Israel.
Publications: Newsletter.
Application information: Contributes only to pre-selected organizations; unsolicited requests for funds not considered or acknowledged.
Officers and Directors:* Daniel S. Och,* Chair.; Charles R. Bronfman,* Vice-Chair.; Joe Gutman,* Vice-Chair.; Sander Levy,* Vice-Chair. and Treas.; Robert Aronson,* Pres.; Marlene Post, Secy.; Madlyn Abramson; Laurie Blitzer; Mark Charendoff; Arlene Kaufman; Michael Steinhardt; Bonnie Tisch; and 15 additional directors.
EIN: 134092050

1289
Laszlo Bito and Olivia Carino Foundation, Inc.
c/o R. Braunschweig
350 5th Ave., Ste. 1000
New York, NY   10118-1099

Established in 2002 in NY.
Donors: Olivia Carino; Laszlo Bito.
Grantmaker type: Independent foundation.
Financial data (yr. ended 12/31/10): Assets, $7,049,732 (M); gifts received, $3,000,000; expenditures, $389,347; qualifying distributions,

$382,500; giving activities include $382,500 for grants.
Fields of interest: International development; Higher education; Human services.
International interests: Hungary.
Limitations: Applications not accepted. Giving primarily in Budapest, Hungary. No grants to individuals.
Application information: Contributes only to pre-selected organizations.
Officer and Directors:* Laszlo Bito,* Pres.; Olivia Carino.
EIN: 223863244

1290
Blacksmith Institute, Inc.
2014 5th Ave.
New York, NY   10035-1803   (646) 742-0200
Contact: Meredith Block
FAX: (212) 779-8044;
E-mail: info@blacksmithinstitute.org; *URL:* http://www.blacksmithinstitute.org

Established in 1999.
Grantmaker type: Public charity.
Financial data (yr. ended 12/31/09): Revenue, $1,748,742; assets, $734,780 (M); gifts received, $1,709,017; expenditures, $2,388,867.
Purpose and activities: The institute supports local champions as they work to solve pollution problems that significantly impact human health.
Fields of interest: Environment; Environment, pollution control; International affairs.
International interests: Developing countries.
Type of support: General/operating support; Research; Technical assistance; Consulting services.
Limitations: Giving on an international basis to less developed countries (LDC's); specifically, developing countries or nations in transition. No support for stand alone research studies, foreign consultants, or budgets that indicate northern wage levels.
Publications: Annual report; Newsletter.
Application information: Non-site specific pollution proposals may apply to Blacksmith Institute directly. Application form not required.
   Copies of proposal: 1
   Deadline(s): None
   Board meeting date(s): Spring and fall
Officer and Directors:* Richard Fuller,* Chair. and Pres.; Joshua Ginsberg; Sheldon Kasowitz; Philip J. Landrigan, M.D., MS.c.; Joshua Mailman; Ronald H. Reede; Siddhartha Sandilya.
EIN: 134075779

1291
Blinken Foundation, Inc.
c/o Allison Blinken
630 Park Ave., Ste. 11B
New York, NY   10065

Established in 1965 in NY.
Donors: Alan J. Blinken; Donald M. Blinken; Milt Blinken†; Robert J. Blinken.
Grantmaker type: Independent foundation.
Financial data (yr. ended 12/31/10): Assets, $1,086,842 (M); expenditures, $197,564; qualifying distributions, $185,600; giving activities include $185,600 for grants.

Fields of interest: Jewish agencies & synagogues; Performing arts; Performing arts, theater; Performing arts, orchestras; Arts; Education; Hospitals (general); Reproductive health, family planning; Biology/life sciences.
International interests: Hungary.
Type of support: General/operating support; Annual campaigns; Fellowships.
Limitations: Applications not accepted. Giving primarily in New York, NY. No grants to individuals.
Application information: Unsolicited requests for funds not accepted.
Officer and Directors:* Donald M. Blinken,* Pres. and Treas.; Alan J. Blinken; Allison Blinken.
EIN: 136190153

1292
The Bloomberg Family Foundation, Inc.
c/o Geller & Co.
909 3rd Ave., 16th Fl.
New York, NY 10022-4797 (212) 205-0100
Michael R. Bloomberg's Giving Pledge: http://givingpledge.org/#enter

Established in 2006 in DE and NY.
Donor: Michael R. Bloomberg.
Grantmaker type: Independent foundation.
Financial data (yr. ended 12/31/10): Assets, $2,734,103,737 (M); gifts received, $361,742,407; expenditures, $123,396,551; qualifying distributions, $108,904,503; giving activities include $107,989,685 for 17 grants (high: $29,590,934; low: $250,000).
Fields of interest: Public health; Mental health, smoking.
International interests: India; Switzerland.
Limitations: Applications not accepted. Giving primarily in NY and on an international basis, with an emphasis in India and Switzerland. No grants to individuals.
Application information: Unsolicited requests for funds not accepted.
Officer and Directors:* Patricia E. Harris,* Chair. and C.E.O.; Tenley Albright; Emma Bloomberg; Georgina Bloomberg; Michael R. Bloomberg; Cory A. Booker; David L. Boren; Jeb Bush; Kenneth I. Chenault; D. Ronald Daniel; Manny Diaz; Fiona Druckenmiller; Walter Isaacson; Maya Lin; John J. Mack; Rev. Joseph McShane; Sam Nunn; Henry M. Paulson, Jr.; Martin Sorrell; Alfred Sommer.
EIN: 205602483
Recent grants for international programs:
1292-1 Association for Safe International Road Travel, Rockville, MD, $200,000. To promote safe international road travel. 2009.
1292-2 EMBARQ, WRI Center for Sustainable Transport, Washington, DC, $4,500,000. To promote safe international road travel. 2009.
1292-3 International Bank for Reconstruction and Development, Washington, DC, $500,000. To promote safe international road travel. 2009.
1292-4 Johns Hopkins University, Bloomberg School of Public Health, Baltimore, MD, $1,000,000. For work of Global Road Safety Program to promote safe international road travel. 2009.
1292-5 Women for Women International, Washington, DC, $3,750,000. To help women in war-torn regions rebuild their lives. 2009.
1292-6 World Health Organization, Geneva, Switzerland, $8,091,828. To promote safe international road travel. 2009.

1292-7 World Lung Foundation, New York, NY, $42,222,917. To end worldwide dependency on tobacco. 2009.
1292-8 World Lung Foundation, New York, NY, $14,186,296. For collaboration with Gates Foundation on work to end dependency on tobacco use. Funds received from Gates Foundation. 2009.

1293
The Bodman Foundation
767 3rd Ave., 4th Fl.
New York, NY 10017-2023 (212) 644-0322
Contact: John B. Krieger, Secy., Exec. Dir. and Asst. Treas.
FAX: (212) 759-6510;
E-mail: main@achelis-bodman-fnds.org;
URL: http://www.achelis-bodman-fnds.org

Incorporated in 1945 in NJ.
Donors: George M. Bodman†; Louise C. Bodman†.
Grantmaker type: Independent foundation.
Financial data (yr. ended 12/31/10): Assets, $58,933,715 (M); expenditures, $3,230,488; qualifying distributions, $3,012,361; giving activities include $2,756,000 for 126 grants (high: $100,000; low: $200).
Purpose and activities: Support largely for poor and disconnected youth; K-12 education, with preference for school reform projects, charter schools, and school choice programs rather than nonprofits that provide direct services in public schools; arts and cultural programs in New York City and northern New Jersey; medical research. Other interests include voluntarism, entrepreneurship, strengthening the two-parent family, fatherhood (and father absence), promoting the institution of marriage, job training and placement, faith-based programs, prevention and early intervention, and measurable participant outcomes and program results, parent involvement, consumer choice, and innovation and cost-saving approaches.
Fields of interest: Arts; Education, reform; Elementary/secondary education; Health care, cost containment; Substance abuse, prevention; Medical research, institute; Employment, services; Children/youth, services; Family services; Family services, adolescent parents; Public policy, research; Children/youth; Youth; Disabilities, people with; Physically disabled; Military/veterans; Offenders/ex-offenders; Substance abusers; Economically disadvantaged.
Type of support: General/operating support; Equipment; Program development; Conferences/seminars; Publication; Seed money; Curriculum development; Scholarship funds; Research; Technical assistance; Program evaluation; Matching/challenge support.
Limitations: Applications accepted. Giving primarily in northern NJ and New York, NY. Generally, no support for political organizations, international projects, government agencies, public schools, (except charter schools), nonprofit programs and services mostly funded or wholly reimbursed by government, small performing arts groups, or national health or mental health organizations. No grants to individuals; generally no grants for travel, endowments, capital campaigns, housing, annual appeals, dinner functions, fundraising events, deficit financing, or films; no loans.
Publications: Application guidelines; Financial statement; Grants list.

Application information: Unless requested, do not send CDs, DVDs, discs, tapes, or proposals through the internet. Application guidelines and procedures are available on foundation web site. Application form not required.
Initial approach: Letter or short proposal
Copies of proposal: 1
Deadline(s): None
Board meeting date(s): Usually May, Sept., and Dec..
Final notification: 5 to 6 weeks
Officers and Trustees:* John N. Irwin III,* Chair. and C.E.O.; Russell P. Pennoyer,* Pres.; Peter Frelinghuysen,* V.P.; Mary S. Phipps,* V.P.; John B. Krieger, Secy. and Exec. Dir.; Horace I. Crary, Jr.,* Treas.; Hon. Walter J.P. Curley; Anthony Drexel Duke; Leslie Lenkowsky; Tatiana Pauschine.
Number of staff: 1 full-time professional; 2 part-time support.
EIN: 136022016
Recent grants for international programs:
1293-1 American Hospital of Paris Foundation, New York, NY, $25,000. For general operating support. 2010.
1293-2 American University in Cairo, Cairo, Egypt, $50,000. For John D. Gerhart Center for Philanthropy and Civic Engagement. 2010.
1293-3 American University of Iraq-Sulaimani, Friends of the, Washington, DC, $35,000. For Provosts Speaker Series on Democracy and Freedom. 2010.
1293-4 Association for the Study of the Middle East and Africa, Washington, DC, $15,000. For Books for the Troops. 2010.
1293-5 Atlas Economic Research Foundation, Washington, DC, $50,000. For Free Markets, Peace and Prosperity in the Muslim World. 2010.
1293-6 Grant Foundation, Pittsburgh, PA, $15,000. For general operating support for Hopital Albert Schweitzer in Haiti. 2010.
1293-7 Hudson Institute, Washington, DC, $25,000. For Center for Global Prosperity. 2010.
1293-8 Middle East Forum, Philadelphia, PA, $50,000. For general operating support. 2010.

1294
Bonide Foundation, Inc.
6301 Sutliff Rd.
Oriskany, NY 13424

Donor: Bonide Products, Inc.
Grantmaker type: Independent foundation.
Financial data (yr. ended 12/31/10): Assets, $793,489 (M); gifts received, $300,000; expenditures, $174,216; qualifying distributions, $174,216; giving activities include $159,850 for 74 grants (high: $35,000; low: $100).
Fields of interest: Children, adoption; Family services; International relief; Christian agencies & churches.
Limitations: Applications not accepted. Giving primarily in NY.
Application information: Unsolicited requests for funds not accepted.
Officers and Directors:* James J. Wurz,* Pres.; Michael Wurz,* Secy.; James H. Wurz,* Treas.; Donald Stevenson; Edward Wurz, Sr.; Gregory Wurz.
EIN: 270951890

1295
Botwinick-Wolfensohn Foundation, Inc.
c/o Bridget Batson
1350 Ave. of the Americas, Ste. 2900
New York, NY 10019-4801 (646) 731-2700

Established in 1952 in NY.
Donors: James D. Wolfensohn; Benjamin
Botwinick†; Edward Botwinick; Bessie Botwinick†.
Grantmaker type: Independent foundation.
Financial data (yr. ended 12/31/10): Assets,
$14,274,605 (M); expenditures, $749,079;
qualifying distributions, $730,000; giving activities
include $730,000 for grants.
Purpose and activities: Emphasis on Israeli and
Jewish interests, music education, medical
research, and social services.
Fields of interest: Performing arts, music;
Education; Medical research, institute; Human
services; Jewish agencies & synagogues.
International interests: Israel.
Type of support: General/operating support;
Continuing support; Annual campaigns; Capital
campaigns; Building/renovation; Program
development; Seed money; Scholarship funds;
Research.
Limitations: Applications not accepted. Giving
primarily in New York, NY. No grants to individuals.
Application information: Unsolicited requests for
funds not accepted.
  Board meeting date(s): Annually in the fall
Officers and Directors: * James D. Wolfensohn,*
Chair.; Edward Botwinick,* Pres.; Adam
Wolfensohn,* V.P.; Elaine R. Wolfensohn,* V.P.;
Sara R. Wolfensohn,* Secy.; Naomi R.
Wolfensohn,* Treas.; Victoria Brown.
Number of staff: 1 part-time professional.
EIN: 136111833

1296
Boys Town Jerusalem Foundation of America, Inc.
1 Penn Plz., Ste. 6250
New York, NY 10119-0002
E-mail: btjnational@boystownjerusalem.org; Toll-free
tel.: (800) 469-2697; toll-free fax: (866) 730-2697;
URL: http://www.boystownjerusalem.org

Established in 1984 in NY.
Grantmaker type: Public charity.
Financial data (yr. ended 12/31/10): Revenue,
$4,421,280; assets, $32,394,522 (M); gifts
received, $3,515,419; expenditures, $5,644,831;
giving activities include $4,305,391 for grants to
organizations outside the U.S.
Purpose and activities: The foundation is the
central support organization for Boys Town
Jerusalem, which serves Jews from all backgrounds
to combine the values of the Jewish heritage and
advanced technology, while inspiring students to
serve the state of Israel as both soldiers and
responsible citizens.
Fields of interest: Jewish agencies & synagogues;
Secondary school/education.
International interests: Israel.
Limitations: Applications not accepted. Giving
limited to Israel.
Publications: Newsletter.
Application information: Contributes only to
pre-selected organizations.
Officers and Directors: * Raphael Benaroya,*
Chair.; Robert Kaswell, Vice-Chair.; Rabbi Moshe

Linchner,* Vice-Chair.; Michael J. Wildes,*
Vice-Chair.; Michael J. Scharf,* Pres.; Rabbi Ronald
Gray,* Exec. V.P.; Lawrence B. Diener,* V.P.; Leo
Goldschmidt, V.P.; Donald L. Soloman,* V.P.;
Marjorie Diener,* Secy.; Dr. Kenneth Garay,*
Treas.; Rabbi Ronald Gray, Exec. Dir.; Albert J. Ades;
Gilbert Aronowitz; Jay Aronowitz; Jack A. Belz; Carl
Cohen; Marc Cooper; Sidney Cooperman; Leslie L.
Dan; and 29 additional directors.
EIN: 115324002

1297
Boys' Town of Italy, Inc.
250 E. 63rd St., Ste. 204
New York, NY 10065-7662 (212) 980-8770
FAX: (212) 644-0766; E-mail: office@briofny.org;
URL: http://boystownofitaly.org/

Established in 1945.
Grantmaker type: Public charity.
Financial data (yr. ended 12/31/10): Revenue,
$1,228,329; assets, $2,413,597 (M); gifts
received, $1,069,491; expenditures, $1,988,068;
giving activities include $1,200,000 for grants to
organizations outside the U.S.
Purpose and activities: The organizations supports
Opera Nazionale per le Citta dei Ragazzi in its
mission of providing programs for youth in Italy.
Fields of interest: Youth development, centers/
clubs; Economically disadvantaged.
International interests: Italy.
Limitations: Applications not accepted. Giving in the
U.S. and Italy.
Publications: Newsletter.
Application information: Contributes only to a
pre-selected organization.
Officers: Mauro C. Romita, Chair.; Lawrence
Auriana, Pres.; Bro. Anthony E. D'Adamo, C.F.C.,
Exec. V.P.
Directors: Dennis Basso; J. Kevin Devlin, C.F.C.;
Florence D'Urso; Robert E. Guglielmo; Grace
Iannuzzi; Laura E. Longodardi, Esq.; Peter Martino;
Edward J. Micone, Jr.; Emilie Puzio; Rev. John
Joseph Serio; Peter Striano.
Number of staff: 4
EIN: 131835632

1298
Brac USA, Inc.
11 E. 44th St., Ste. 1600
New York, NY 10017-0051 (212) 808-5615
Contact: Susan Davis, Pres. and C.E.O.
FAX: (212) 808-0203; E-mail: susan@bracusa.org;
URL: http://www.brac.net/content/about-brac-usa
Facebook: http://www.facebook.com/BRACWorld
LinkedIn: http://www.linkedin.com/groups?
about=&gid=2197400&trk=anet_ug_grppro
Twitter: http://twitter.com/#!/BRACworld
YouTube: http://www.youtube.com/user/bracusa1

Established in 2007 in NY.
Grantmaker type: Public charity.
Financial data (yr. ended 09/30/10): Revenue,
$7,580,890; assets, $12,232,439 (M); gifts
received, $7,060,993; expenditures, $7,812,137;
program services expenses, $7,503,108; giving
activities include $6,443,115 for 8 grants to
organizations outside the U.S., and $1,059,993 for
foundation-administered programs.
Purpose and activities: As the U.S. office of BRAC,
the organization is dedicated to alleviating poverty

by empowering the poor to bring about change in
their own lives.
Fields of interest: International democracy & civil
society development; International human rights;
Community/economic development; Human
services.
Limitations: Giving on an international basis,
primarily to Afghanistan, Bangladesh, Liberia,
Pakistan, Sierra Leone, South Sudan, Sri Lanka,
Tanzania, and Uganda.
Officers and Board Members: * Lincoln C. Chen,*
M.D., Chair.; Raymond C. Offenheiser,* Vice-Chair.;
Susan M. Davis,* Pres. and C.E.O.; Kamal Ahmad,
Secy.; Ronald Grzywinski,* Treas.; Adrienne
Germain; Christina Leijonhufvud; Bridget Liddell;
Cate Muther; Charles Slaughter.
EIN: 208456741

1299
The Brackett Foundation
P.O. Box 8
Hamilton, NY 13346-0008 (315) 824-3435
Contact: Thomas Brackett, Pres.; Elizabeth Brackett,
Treas.
E-mail: lizb@twcny.rr.com; URL: http://
brackett.colgate.edu/

Established in 1997 in NY.
Donors: Ellie Baker; Liz Brackett; Thomas Brackett;
Thomas & Moors Myers; Mark Sommer; Frederick
Watson; David Woods; B.K. Kee Foundation; Virginia
Wellington Cabot Foundation; Dorthea Haus Ross
Foundation; Inavale Foundation.
Grantmaker type: Public charity.
Financial data (yr. ended 12/31/10): Revenue,
$326,433; assets, $584,336 (M); gifts received,
$321,828; expenditures, $269,237; giving
activities include $255,299 for grants to
organizations outside the U.S.
Purpose and activities: The foundation seeks to
provide education for refugees and displaced
persons as near as possible to their country of
origin. Currently the foundation is focused on the
refugees from Burma who are in Thailand and India.
Fields of interest: Education; Immigrants/refugees.
International interests: Thailand; India.
Type of support: Internship funds; Scholarship
funds; Grants to individuals; Scholarships—to
individuals.
Limitations: Applications not accepted. Giving to
refugees from Burma in Thailand, and northeast
India. No support for refugees in the U.S.
Publications: Annual report; Financial statement;
Informational brochure; Newsletter.
Application information: Unsolicited requests for
funds not accepted.
  Board meeting date(s): Apr. and Oct.
Officers and Trustees: * Thomas Brackett,* Pres.;
John A. Novak,* Secy.; Elizabeth Brackett, Treas.;
Cristy R. Ballou; Dianne Becker; J. Phillip Brackett;
T. Theodore Brackett; Hannah Sanger; DeForest
Winfield.
EIN: 161523586

1300
Brazil Foundation
345 7th Ave., No. 1401
New York, NY 10001-5083 (212) 244-3663
Contact: Leona S. Forman, Pres. and C.E.O.
FAX: (212) 244-4334;
E-mail: newyork@brazilfoundation.org; Additional

address: Avenida Calogeras, 15, Cobertura - Centro, Rio de Janeiro, RJ 20030-070, Brazil, tel.: (021) 2532-3029, FAX: (021) 2532-2998, E-mail: info@brazilfoundation.org; URL: http://www.brazilfoundation.org

Established in 2000.
Donors: Arosfa Foundation; Avina Foundation; Ford Foundation; Inter-American Foundation; Kellogg Foundation; HSBC; Tinker Foundation; IBM; Google; TAM Airlines.
Grantmaker type: Public charity.
Financial data (yr. ended 12/31/09): Revenue, $1,996,294; assets, $1,425,033 (M); gifts received, $1,884,546; expenditures, $1,883,230; giving activities include $825,021 for grants to organizations outside the U.S.
Purpose and activities: The organization generates resources for programs that promote social change in Brazil.
Fields of interest: Arts, cultural/ethnic awareness; Education; Health care; Civil/human rights.
International interests: Brazil.
Limitations: Applications accepted. Giving limited to Brazil. No support for shelters, organizations belonging to the S System (SENAI, SESI, SESC, SFRRAE), or religious or political organizations. No grants to individuals, or for travel, conferences, research, publications, construction, restoration/purchase of furniture or vehicles, events, performances, or digital inclusion.
Publications: Application guidelines; Financial statement; Grants list; Multi-year report; Newsletter.
Application information: Application form required.
  Initial approach: Download project application form
  Deadline(s): Varies, usually Dec.
  Final notification: Apr. 28
Officers and Directors:* Leona S. Forman,* Pres. and C.E.O.; Susane Warcman,* V.P.; Roberta Mazzariol,* C.F.O.; Marcello Hallake,* Genl. Counsel; Patricia Cavalcanti Lobaccaro; Marcus Vinicius Ribeiro; Christina Alves Molloy; Flavia Cattan-Naslausky; Cecilia Alves de Freitas; Vanessa S. Pereira; Edineria Pinheiro.
Number of staff: 7 full-time professional; 4 full-time support.
EIN: 134131482

1301
The Breast Cancer Research Foundation, Inc.
60 E. 56th St., 8th Fl.
New York, NY 10022-3343 (646) 497-2600
Contact: Margaret Mastrianni, Deputy Dir.
FAX: (646) 497-0890; E-mail: bcrf@bcrfcure.org; Toll-free tel.: (866) FINDACURE; URL: http://www.bcrfcure.org

Established in 1993 in NY.
Grantmaker type: Public charity.
Financial data (yr. ended 06/30/10): Revenue, $36,214,286; assets, $43,878,604 (M); gifts received, $35,590,918; expenditures, $37,298,691; giving activities include $27,710,238 for grants, and $5,356,734 for grants to organizations outside the U.S.
Purpose and activities: The foundation funds clinical and translational research into the causes and treatment of breast cancer in order to increase the public's awareness and understanding of the disease with an ultimate view towards the reduction, elimination and cure of breast cancer.

Fields of interest: Breast cancer research.
International interests: Middle East; Europe; Latin America; Canada.
Type of support: Research.
Limitations: Applications accepted. Giving on a worldwide basis.
Publications: Financial statement; Grants list; Informational brochure; Newsletter.
Application information: Application by invitation only from the Executive Board and Scientific Advisors.
  Initial approach: Letter or telephone
  Board meeting date(s): July, and as needed throughout the year
Officers and Directors:* Myra Biblowit,* Pres.; Jeanette Wagner,* V.P.; Deborah Krulewitch,* Secy.-Treas.; Carolee Friedlander; Carlyn McCaffrey, Esq.; Josie Robertson; Jackie Zehner.
Number of staff: 12 full-time professional; 1 part-time professional; 3 full-time support.
EIN: 133727250

1302
The Brenner Family Foundation
919 3rd Ave., 24th Fl.
New York, NY 10022-3902

Established in 2005 in NY.
Grantmaker type: Independent foundation.
Financial data (yr. ended 12/31/09): Assets, $4,360,228 (M); expenditures, $283,054; qualifying distributions, $238,300; giving activities include $238,300 for 25 grants (high: $36,800; low: $500).
Fields of interest: International human rights; Arts; Education; Human services.
Limitations: Applications not accepted. No grants to individuals.
Application information: Unsolicited requests for funds not accepted.
Officers: Kim E. Baptiste, Pres. and Secy.; Michele C. Tocci, V.P.; Leslie J. Fishman, Treas.; Pamela Baptiste, Exec. Dir.
EIN: 571217214

1303
The Bristol-Myers Squibb Foundation, Inc.
(formerly The Bristol-Myers Fund, Inc.)
345 Park Ave., 3rd Fl.
New York, NY 10154-0004 (212) 546-4000
Contact: John L. Damonti, Pres.
E-mail for Cancer in Europe - Bridging Cancer Care Initiative: bridgingcancercare@bms.com; E-mail for Together on Diabetes: togetherondiabetes@bms.com; Contact for Mental Health & Well-Being in the U.S.: Catharine Grimes, tel.: (212) 546-4197, e-mail: Catharine.Grimes@bms.com or Christine Newman, Mgr., tel.: (609) 252-4726, e-mail: christine.newman@bms.com; Contact for Secure the Future - Technical Assistance and Skills Transfer Program: Ms. Phangisile Mtshali, Dir., Secure the Future, Bristol-Myers Squibb, P.O. Box 1408, Bedfordview, 2008, South Africa, tel.:+21 11 456 6400, Fax: +27 11 456 6589, E-mail: phangisile.mtshali@bms.com; URL: http://www.bms.com/foundation/Pages/home.aspx
Secure the Future Grant Recipients: http://www.securethefuture.com/our_experience/funding/grant_recipients.shtml

Secure the Future on Facebook: http://www.facebook.com/pages/SECURE-THE-FUTURE/40590021477

Incorporated in 1982 in FL as successor to a foundation established in 1953.
Donor: Bristol-Myers Squibb Co.
Grantmaker type: Company-sponsored foundation.
Financial data (yr. ended 12/31/10): Assets, $145,418,399 (M); gifts received, $2,619,387; expenditures, $37,983,589; qualifying distributions, $35,357,136; giving activities include $30,850,964 for 175 grants (high: $4,500,000; low: $1,250), and $4,506,172 for employee matching gifts.
Purpose and activities: The foundation supports programs designed to reduce health disparities around the world. Special emphasis is directed toward programs designed to improve the health outcomes of populations disproportionately affected by HIV/AIDS in Africa; hepatitis in Asia; type 2 diabetes; mental health and well-being in the United States; and cancer in Europe.
Fields of interest: Higher education; Medical school/education; Education; Health care, public policy; Health care, equal rights; Medical care, community health systems; Hospitals (general); Health care, clinics/centers; Pharmacy/prescriptions; Public health; Public health, STDs; Public health, communicable diseases; Palliative care; Nursing care; Health care; Mental health, treatment; Mental health/crisis services; Cancer; AIDS; Diabetes; Health organizations; Cancer research; AIDS research; American Red Cross; Residential/custodial care, hospices; Human services; African Americans/Blacks; Children; Women; Military/veterans; Economically disadvantaged.
International interests: Africa; China; Europe; India; Japan; Sub-Saharan Africa.
Type of support: General/operating support; Continuing support; Management development/capacity building; Program development; Seed money; Curriculum development; Research; Technical assistance; Employee volunteer services; Program evaluation; Employee matching gifts; Employee-related scholarships; In-kind gifts.
Limitations: Applications accepted. Giving primarily in areas of company operations in Wallingford, CT, Washington, DC, Mount Vernon, IN, Devens, MA, Hopewell, New Brunswick, Plainsboro, Princeton, and West Windsor, NJ, New York and Syracuse, NY, PA, TX, Africa, China, Europe, India, Japan, Sub-Saharan Africa, Taiwan, and Thailand. No support for political, fraternal, social, or veterans' organizations, religious or sectarian organizations not of direct benefit to the entire community, or federated campaign-supported organizations. No grants to individuals (except for employee-related scholarships), or for endowments, capital campaigns, debt reduction, conferences, sponsorships or independent medical research, or specific public broadcasting or films; no loans.
Publications: Application guidelines; Grants list; Informational brochure; Program policy statement.
Application information: Organizations receiving support are asked to submit biannual reports and a final report. Application form required.
  Initial approach: Complete online application; download letter of inquiry form and e-mail for Mental Health & Well-Being in the U.S; download application form and e-mail for Together on Diabetes; complete online

application for Secure the Future - Technical Assistance and Skills Transfer Program

Deadline(s): None; Apr. 13 for Mental Health & Well-Being in the U.S.; Apr. 15 and Aug. 1 for Together on Diabetes; None for Secure the Future - Technical Assistance and Skills Transfer Program

Board meeting date(s): Dec. and as needed

Final notification: 6 to 8 weeks

Officers and Directors:* Lamberto Andreotti, Chair.; John L. Damonti,* Pres.; Sonia Vora,* Secy.; Jeffrey Galik, Treas.; Beatrice Cazala; John E. Celentano; Anthony C. Hooper; Sandra Leung; Elliott Sigal, M.D., Ph.D.

Number of staff: 6 full-time professional; 4 full-time support.

EIN: 133127947

Recent grants for international programs:

1303-1 Accordia Global Health Foundation, Washington, DC, $25,000. 2009.

1303-2 Actions Communautaires contre le SIDA/Avenir Meilleur pour les Orphelins, Kinshasa, Democratic Republic of the Congo, $200,000. For Technical Assistance Program. 2009.

1303-3 Adventist Development and Relief Agency International, Silver Spring, MD, $170,948. For Technical Assistance Program. 2009.

1303-4 American Red Cross National Headquarters, Washington, DC, $25,000. For Italy earthquake. 2009.

1303-5 AmeriCares, Stamford, CT, $33,000. For Disaster Relief. 2009.

1303-6 Asia-Pacific Alliance Against AIDS, Tuberculosis and Malaria of Nuwa, Beijing, China, $168,297. For anti-discrimination and prevention for hepatitis among migrant workers. 2009.

1303-7 Association de Recherche, de Communication et d'Accompagnement a Domicile des Personnes Vivant Avec le VIH/SIDA, Mali, $80,404. For Secure the Future, Technical Assistance Program. 2009.

1303-8 Association de Recherche, de Communication et d'Accompagnement a Domicile des Personnes Vivant Avec le VIH/SIDA, Mali, $64,927. For Secure the Future, Technical Assistance Program - Tech support. 2009.

1303-9 Association Marocaine de Lutte Contre le SIDA, Casablanca, Morocco and the Western Sahara, $44,743. For Technical Assistance Program. 2009.

1303-10 Bambisanani Project, Johannesburg, South Africa, $36,069. For Secure the Future, Technical Assistance Program - Retainer Grant, Phase 2. 2009.

1303-11 Baylor College of Medicine, Baylor Pediatric AIDS Corps, Houston, TX, $4,500,000. For Secure the Future, South Africa. 2009.

1303-12 Baylor College of Medicine, Baylor Pediatric AIDS Corps, Houston, TX, $625,000. For Secure the Future, Technical Assistance Program - Kenya. 2009.

1303-13 Caritas Developpement Congo, Democratic Republic of the Congo, $265,725. For Technical Assistance Program. 2009.

1303-14 CATHCA, Saxsonwold, South Africa, $57,026. For Technical Assistance Program. 2009.

1303-15 Catholic Medical Mission Board, New York, NY, $282,017. For Hepatitis India, Hepatitis Foundation of Tripura, Blood Bank Liver Foundation West Bengal, National Liver Foundation, and Hope Initiative. 2009.

1303-16 Catholic Medical Mission Board, New York, NY, $20,000. 2009.

1303-17 China Foundation for Hepatitis Prevention and Control, China, $110,816. For Rural Medical Workers. 2009.

1303-18 China Foundation for Hepatitis Prevention and Control, China, $76,592. For Rural Medical Workers. 2009.

1303-19 China Foundation for Hepatitis Prevention and Control, China, $68,973. For Hepatitis B education for primary school students in Gansu, Ningxia, and Beijing. 2009.

1303-20 Chizavane Community Development Association, Sao Chizavane, Mozambique, $56,510. For Technical Assistance Program. 2009.

1303-21 Christian HIV/AIDS Network of Liberia, Monrovia, Liberia, $100,000. For Technical Assistance Program. 2009.

1303-22 Christian Medical College Vellore Association, Vellore, India, $119,346. 2009.

1303-23 Community Based Education and Counseling - HIV/AIDS, Liberia, Monrovia, Liberia, $98,368. For Technical Assistance Program. 2009.

1303-24 Direct Relief International, Santa Barbara, CA, $34,000. For Disaster Relief. 2009.

1303-25 Direct Relief International, Santa Barbara, CA, $10,000. 2009.

1303-26 FACE AIDS, Palo Alto, CA, $35,000. For Global Health Corps. 2009.

1303-27 Flanders Interuniversity Institute for Biotechnology, Ghent, Belgium, $100,000. For Neuroscience Research Program. 2009.

1303-28 Foundation for Worldwide Mercy and Sharing, Aspen, CO, $15,000. For Haiti Programs. 2009.

1303-29 Funders Concerned About AIDS, Arlington, VA, $15,000. 2009.

1303-30 Gaia Vaccine Foundation, Providence, RI, $70,570. For Technical Assistance Program - Project Hope. 2009.

1303-31 GBCHealth, New York, NY, $30,000. For Technical Assistance Program grant for Private Sector Delegation to the Board of the Global Fund to Fight AIDS, Tuberculosis and Malaria. 2009.

1303-32 Global Health Council, Washington, DC, $25,000. 2009.

1303-33 Global Medical Relief Program, Evanston, IL, $20,000. 2009.

1303-34 Grandmothers Against Poverty and AIDS, Cape Town, South Africa, $33,093. For Technical Assistance Program - Retainer Grant Phase 2. 2009.

1303-35 GROFORMED, VIH-PAL (Big Idea), Ivory Coast, $125,362. For Secure the Future, West Africa. 2009.

1303-36 Hospice Casa Sperantei Foundation, Brasov, Romania, $71,525. For cancer grant. 2009.

1303-37 Hungarian League Against Cancer, Budapest, Hungary, $93,000. For cancer grant. 2009.

1303-38 Institut Jules Bordet, Brussels, Belgium, $100,000. For Cancer Research Program. 2009.

1303-39 Intelligent Mobility International, Lancaster, CA, $10,000. 2009.

1303-40 International AIDS Society, Geneva, Switzerland, $25,000. For Leading by Example in the Public Health Approach to ART (antiretroviral therapy) - 2nd Global Experts Summit. 2009.

1303-41 International AIDS Society, Geneva, Switzerland, $20,000. For Journal of the International AIDS Society. 2009.

1303-42 International AIDS Vaccine Initiative, New York, NY, $25,000. 2009.

1303-43 Japan Foundation for AIDS Prevention, Tokyo, Japan, $44,643. 2009.

1303-44 Kaohsiung Medical University Hospital, Kaohsiung, Taiwan, $124,384. For Hepatitis C program. 2009.

1303-45 Klinikum der Universitat Munchen, Munchen, Germany, $100,000. For Nutrition Research Grant. 2009.

1303-46 Kyoto University, Kyoto, Japan, $100,000. For Cardiovascular Research Program. 2009.

1303-47 Liberian Womens Empowerment Network, Liberia, $28,175. For Technical Assistance Program. 2009.

1303-48 Light House Association of Liberia, Liberia, $69,812. For Technical Assistance Program. 2009.

1303-49 Liver Disease Prevention and Treatment Research Foundation, Taipei, Taiwan, $63,750. For Hepatitis C Awareness, Prevention and Care Program. 2009.

1303-50 Liver Disease Prevention and Treatment Research Foundation, Taipei, Taiwan, $63,750. For Hepatitis C Awareness, Prevention and Care Program. 2009.

1303-51 Liver Foundation West Bengal, Kolkata, India, $83,431. 2009.

1303-52 Liver Foundation West Bengal, Kolkata, India, $57,842. For Hepatitis C program. 2009.

1303-53 Liver Foundation West Bengal, Kolkata, India, $57,692. For Hepatitis C program. 2009.

1303-54 MAP International, Brunswick, GA, $10,000. For Health Promoters Program Latin America. 2009.

1303-55 Masarykova Univerzita, Brno, Czech Republic, $54,930. For cancer grant. 2009.

1303-56 Melbourne Health, Parkville, Australia, $100,000. For Infectious Diseases Research. Grant made through the VIDRL. 2009.

1303-57 Mieux Vivre Avec le SIDA, Niamey, Niger, $45,810. For Technical Assistance Program. 2009.

1303-58 Mpilonhle Project, Ladysmith, South Africa, $51,897. For Technical Assistance Program - Retainer Grant Phase 2. 2009.

1303-59 National Association of People Living with HIV/AIDS, Newtown, Australia, $56,853. For Technical Assistance Program. 2009.

1303-60 Nedico, Windhoek, Namibia, $95,755. For Technical Assistance Program - Retainer Grant Phase 2. 2009.

1303-61 Positive Living Association of Liberia, Liberia, $99,998. For Technical Assistance Program. 2009.

1303-62 Princeton in Africa, Princeton, NJ, $15,000. 2009.

1303-63 Project HOPE - The People-to-People Health Foundation, Millwood, VA, $33,000. For Disaster Relief. 2009.

1303-64 Project HOPE - The People-to-People Health Foundation, Millwood, VA, $10,000. For Healthcare Worker Training Program - Aceh (Indonesia). 2009.

1303-65 Project HOPE - The People-to-People Health Foundation, Poland, Krakow, Poland, $74,990. For cancer grant. 2009.

1303-66 Regional Charity Community Foundation, Moscow, Russia, $90,000. For cancer grant. 2009.

1303-67 Rutgers, The State University of New Jersey, New Brunswick, NJ, $39,848. For Technical Assistance Program (TAP). 2009.

1303-68 Senkatana, Lesotho, $53,468. For Technical Assistance Program - Retainer Grant Phase 2. 2009.

1303-69 Shanghai Charity Foundation, Shanghai, China, $116,269. For Hepatitis Program. 2009.

1303-70 Shanghai Charity Foundation, Shanghai, China, $60,000. For Migrant Worker's Nursing Assistants Training Project. 2009.

1303-71 Shanghai Charity Foundation, Shanghai, China, $60,000. For Migrant Worker's Nursing Assistants Training Project. 2009.

1303-72 Shanghai Charity Foundation, Shanghai, China, $52,566. To study the Education Model of HCV (hepatitis C virus) Control and Prevention among medical staff, HCV patients, and their family members. 2009.

1303-73 Shanghai Charity Foundation, Shanghai, China, $52,566. To study the Education Model of HCV (hepatitis C virus) Control and Prevention among medical staff, HCV patients, and their family members. 2009.

1303-74 Tanzania Development and AIDS Prevention, Bukoba, Tanzania, Zanzibar and Pemba, $57,936. For Technical Assistance Program. 2009.

1303-75 Technische Universitaet Muenchen, Munich, Germany, $100,000. For Cardiovascular Research Program. 2009.

1303-76 University of Pennsylvania, Philadelphia, PA, $15,000. For Wharton Global Consulting Practicum. 2009.

1303-77 University of Tokyo, Tokyo, Japan, $100,000. For Cancer Research Grant. 2009.

1303-78 World Environment Center, Washington, DC, $12,000. 2009.

1303-79 Worldwide Orphans Foundation, Maplewood, NJ, $10,000. 2009.

1304

The 1994 Sheila Johnson Brutsch Charitable Trust No. 34

630 5th Ave., Ste. 1510
New York, NY   10111-0100

Established in 1994 in NY.
Donor: Betty W. Johnson.
Grantmaker type: Independent foundation.
Financial data (yr. ended 12/31/10): Assets, $4,792,427 (M); expenditures, $216,700; qualifying distributions, $212,750; giving activities include $212,500 for 4 grants (high: $100,000; low: $25,000).
Fields of interest: Media/communications; Higher education; Environment, natural resources; Animals/wildlife, preservation/protection; International relief.
Limitations: Applications not accepted. No grants to individuals.
Application information: Unsolicited requests for funds not accepted.
Trustees: Sheila Johnson Brutsch; Betty W. Johnson.
EIN: 137046312

1305

The Bunson Family Foundation

c/o Goldman Sachs Family Office
Bowling Green Station
P.O. Box 73
New York, NY   10274-0073

Established in 2003 in NY.
Donor: Steven M. Bunson.
Grantmaker type: Independent foundation.
Financial data (yr. ended 12/31/10): Assets, $1,048,784 (M); gifts received, $250,000; expenditures, $341,375; qualifying distributions, $341,000; giving activities include $341,000 for 13 grants (high: $100,000; low: $1,000).
Fields of interest: International development; Higher education; Jewish agencies & synagogues.
Type of support: General/operating support.
Limitations: Applications not accepted. Giving primarily in NY. No grants to individuals.
Application information: Unsolicited requests for funds not accepted.
Trustees: Joy F. Bunson; Steven M. Bunson.
EIN: 450526292

1306

The Burpee Foundation

c/o Windels Marx Lane & Mittendorf, LLP
156 W. 56th St.
New York, NY   10019-3800
Contact: Mel P. Barkan, V.P.

Established in 2002 in NY.
Donor: George C. Ball, Jr.
Grantmaker type: Independent foundation.
Financial data (yr. ended 12/31/10): Assets, $6,858,974 (M); expenditures, $490,948; qualifying distributions, $415,005; giving activities include $365,000 for 12 grants (high: $100,000; low: $5,000).
Fields of interest: Horticulture/garden clubs; Animals/wildlife, bird preserves; Substance abuse, treatment; International relief; Protestant agencies & churches.
Limitations: Applications accepted. Giving on a national basis. No grants to individuals.
Application information: Application form required.
  Initial approach: Completed New York/New Jersey Area Common Application Form
  Copies of proposal: 3
  Deadline(s): None
Officers and Trustees:* George C. Ball, Jr.,* Pres. and Treas.; Mel P. Barkan,* V.P.; David A. Brauner,* Secy.
EIN: 743047509

1307

J. Homer Butler Foundation

30 W. 16th St.
New York, NY   10011-6302
Contact: Dorothy Montalto, Grant Admin.

Incorporated in 1961 in NY.
Donor: Mabel A. Tod†.
Grantmaker type: Independent foundation.
Financial data (yr. ended 12/31/10): Assets, $4,786,860 (M); expenditures, $237,199; qualifying distributions, $204,605; giving activities include $168,500 for 22 grants (high: $40,000; low: $2,000).
Purpose and activities: Grants to Roman Catholic missions and religious orders to help improve the quality of life for the sick, especially those afflicted with leprosy. The foundation does not make direct remittances to foreign countries.
Fields of interest: Health care; Skin disorders; Health organizations, association; Christian agencies & churches; Catholic agencies & churches.

International interests: Africa; Central America; South America; Asia.
Type of support: Equipment; Emergency funds; Seed money.
Limitations: Applications accepted. Giving to domestic organizations for programs in the U.S., Central and South America, Africa, and Asia.
Publications: Informational brochure (including application guidelines).
Application information: Application form required.
  Initial approach: Letter
  Copies of proposal: 1
  Deadline(s): June 30 and Dec. 31
  Board meeting date(s): Sept. and Mar.
  Final notification: 2-4 weeks
Officers and Directors:* Rev. James Yannarell,* Pres.; Rev. James F. Keenan,* V.P.; Nicholas Montalto,* Secy.; Rev. Henry Zenorini,* Treas.; Bro. John J. Campbell; Rev. David Casey; Daniel R. Coleman; John J. Emanuel; Joan MacLean; Dorothy Montalto; Rev. John Replogle; F. Patrick Rogers; Michael Ross; Rev. Raymond Solomon.
Number of staff: 1 part-time professional.
EIN: 136126669

1308

Marilyn and Marshall Butler Foundation

900 3rd Ave., 33rd Fl.
New York, NY   10022-4775
Contact: Marshall D. Butler, Mgr.; Marilyn Butler
FAX: (212) 317-3365; *E-mail:* mdb9695@aol.com

Established in 1990 in NY.
Donors: Marshall D. Butler; The Butler Charitable Lead Annuity Trust 9/30/97; The Butler Charitable Lead Annuity Trust 6/30/99.
Grantmaker type: Independent foundation.
Financial data (yr. ended 12/31/10): Assets, $2,037,638 (M); gifts received, $127,000; expenditures, $165,049; qualifying distributions, $154,683; giving activities include $154,683 for grants.
Purpose and activities: Giving primarily for Jewish organizations.
Fields of interest: Education; Arts; Hospitals (general); Health organizations, association; Human services; Jewish federated giving programs; Jewish agencies & synagogues.
International interests: Israel.
Type of support: Curriculum development; Scholarship funds; Fellowships; Building/ renovation; Capital campaigns; Continuing support; Annual campaigns; General/operating support.
Application information: Application form required.
  Initial approach: Letter
  Copies of proposal: 1
  Deadline(s): None
Trustees: Marilyn Butler; Marshall D. Butler.
EIN: 133591664

1309

Canon U.S.A., Inc. Corporate Giving Program

1 Canon Plz.
Lake Success, NY   11042-1198
Contact: Michael R. Virgintino, Sr. Mgr., Corp. Social Responsibility
URL: http://www.usa.canon.com/templatedata/ AboutCanon/ciwccresp.html

Grantmaker type: Corporate giving program.

Purpose and activities: Canon makes charitable contributions to nonprofit organizations involved with natural resources conservation and protection, youth development, and on a case by case basis. Support is given on a national basis and in Canada, Central America, and South America.

Fields of interest: Environment, natural resources; Youth development; General charitable giving.

International interests: Canada; Central America; South America.

Type of support: General/operating support; Scholarship funds; Employee volunteer services; Scholarships—to individuals; Donated equipment; Donated products.

Limitations: Applications accepted. Giving in areas of company operations in CA, Washington, DC, GA, HI, IL, NJ, NY, TX, and UT; giving also to national organizations. No support for religious, political, or labor organizations. No grants to individuals (except for scholarships).

Publications: Corporate giving report.

Application information: The Corporate Social Responsibility Department handles giving. A contributions committee reviews all requests. Application form not required.

Initial approach: Proposal to headquarters
Copies of proposal: 1
Deadline(s): None
Final notification: 1 to 3 months

Number of staff: 2 full-time professional; 1 part-time professional.

1310
W. P. Carey Foundation
c/o Julianna K. Harris, Exec. Dir.
50 Rockefeller Plz.
New York, NY 10020-1605
Contact: Juliana Harris, Exec. Dir

Established in 1991 in PA.

Donor: William P. Carey.

Grantmaker type: Independent foundation.

Financial data (yr. ended 12/31/10): Assets, $24,930,297 (M); gifts received, $12,000,000; expenditures, $9,297,682; qualifying distributions, $9,199,916; giving activities include $8,524,880 for 60 grants (high: $3,500,000; low: $1,000), $315,927 for 90 employee matching gifts, and $181,126 for foundation-administered programs.

Purpose and activities: Giving primarily for international relief and education.

Fields of interest: Museums; Higher education; Education; International relief; Christian agencies & churches.

Limitations: Applications not accepted. Giving on a national basis. No grants to individuals.

Application information: Contributes only to pre-selected organizations.

Officers and Trustees:* William P. Carey,* Chair.; Francis J. Carey,* Pres.; Juliana K. Harris, Secy. and Exec. Dir.; Jan F. Karst,* C.F.O.; Ricardo A. Vasquez, Treas.; John Miller, C.I.O.; J. Samuel Armstrong IV; Gwendolyn G. Bond; Trevor P. Bond; Francis J. Carey III; Lawrence R. Klein; Edward V. Lapuma; Justin B. Patterson; A. Patterson Pendleton III.

Directors: Timothy W. Burdette; Elizabeth P. Carey; Emily N. Carey; H. Augustus Carey; Christopher E. Franklin; Charles G. Houghton; H. Cabot Lodge III; Marcia Murray; Zachary J. Pack; Douglas S. Parvis; William R. Polk; Anne Coolidge Taylor.

EIN: 133597510

Recent grants for international programs:

1310-1 Johns Hopkins University, School of Advanced International Studies (SAIS), Baltimore, MD, $50,000. For Hopkins - Nanjing Center annual contribution. 2010.

1311
The Carmel Hill Fund
(formerly Ruane Family Fund)
767 5th Ave., Ste. 4701
New York, NY 10153-4798
Contact: Arlene Farrand-Borgerson, Exec. Dir.
E-mail for Arlene Farrand-Borgerson: arlene@ruanecunniff.com; URL: http://www.carmelhill.org/index.htm

Established in 1986 in NY.

Donors: William J. Ruane†; The Riordan Fund; American Institute of Foreign Studies.

Grantmaker type: Independent foundation.

Financial data (yr. ended 12/31/10): Assets, $146,553,957 (M); gifts received, $4,897,075; expenditures, $17,238,797; qualifying distributions, $16,377,392; giving activities include $12,419,816 for 47 grants (high: $3,400,000; low: $500).

Purpose and activities: Giving primarily for education, children and social services, and mental health organizations; some funding also for the arts.

Fields of interest: Arts; Higher education; Education; Mental health/crisis services; Human services; Children/youth, services.

Limitations: Applications not accepted. Giving primarily in NY. No grants to individuals.

Application information: Contributes only to pre-selected organizations.

Officer: Arlene Farrand-Borgerson, Exec. Dir.

Trustees: George J. Gillespie, III; Robert D. Goldfarb.

Number of staff: 22 full-time professional; 5 part-time support.

EIN: 136881103

Recent grants for international programs:

1311-1 Save the Children Federation, Westport, CT, $3,400,000. 2009.

1312
Carnegie Corporation of New York
437 Madison Ave.
New York, NY 10022-7003
Contact: Nicole Howe Buggs, Dir., Grants Management
FAX: (212) 754-4073; E-mail for Nicole Howe Buggs: nb@carnegie.org; URL: http://www.carnegie.org
E-Newsletter: http://carnegie.org/news/enews-sign-up/
Grants Database: http://www.carnegie.org/sub/program/grantsearch.html
iTunes: http://itunes.apple.com/us/podcast/carnegie-corporation-new-york/id275515669?ign-mpt=uo%3D4
RSS Feed: http://carnegie.org/news/rss-subscribe/
Twitter: http://www.twitter.com/carnegiecorp

Incorporated in 1911 in NY.

Donor: Andrew Carnegie†.

Grantmaker type: Independent foundation.

Financial data (yr. ended 09/30/10): Assets, $2,534,623,009 (M); expenditures, $150,087,355; qualifying distributions, $142,711,989; giving activities include $126,171,879 for grants.

Purpose and activities: As a grantmaking foundation, Carnegie Corporation of New York seeks to carry out Andrew Carnegie's vision of philanthropy, which he said should aim 'to do real and permanent good in this world.' Currently the foundation's work is focused in two integrated programs: the National Program, which includes support for education as a pathway to citizenship; and the International Program, which addresses international peace and security issues.

Fields of interest: Civil rights, voter education; Civil/human rights, immigrants; Education, reading; Education, reform; International affairs, arms control; International affairs, national security; International peace/security; Libraries, archives; Teacher school/education; Adults, women.

International interests: Africa; Russia; Sub-Saharan Africa.

Type of support: General/operating support; Continuing support; Program development; Conferences/seminars; Publication; Curriculum development; Research; Technical assistance; Program evaluation; Employee matching gifts.

Limitations: Applications accepted. Giving primarily for U.S. projects, although some grants are made to selected countries in Sub-Saharan Africa. No support for U.S. libraries, cultural institutions, programs or facilities of community-based educational or human services institutions. No grants directly to individuals for scholarships or fellowships (except the Carnegie Scholars Program), travel, capital campaigns, or endowments.

Publications: Annual report; Grants list; Informational brochure (including application guidelines); Occasional report.

Application information: If the project is judged to be within the current program priorities of the corporation, the applicant will be asked to present the narrative and budget in the corporation's format. Before a grant is made, additional materials would be required, including a formal request from the head of the institution involved. Application form required.

Initial approach: Letter
Copies of proposal: 1
Deadline(s): None
Board meeting date(s): Mar., June, and Sept., and Dec.
Final notification: 4-6 months

Officers and Trustees:* Thomas H. Kean,* Chair.; Richard W. Riley,* Vice-Chair.; Vartan Gregorian,* Pres.; Ellen Bloom, V.P., C.A.O. and Corp. Secy.; Robert J. Seman, V.P. and C.F.O.; Deana Arsenian, V.P., Intl. Prog.; Michele Cahill, V.P., Natl. Prog.; Susan King, V.P., External Affairs and Prog. Dir., Journalism Initiative; Meredith Jenkins, Co-C.I.O.; Kim Y. Lew, Co-C.I.O.; Kofi Annan; Pedro Aspe; Richard Beattie; Geoffrey T. Boisi; Richard H. Brodhead; Ralph J. Cicerone; Amb. Edward P. Djerejian; Amy Gutmann; Susan Hockfield; Stephen A. Oxman; Ana Palacio; Norman Pearlstine; Don Michael Randel; Janet L. Robinson; Kurt L. Schmoke; James Wolfensohn.

Number of staff: 41 full-time professional; 1 part-time professional; 30 full-time support; 2 part-time support.

EIN: 131628151

Recent grants for international programs:

1312-1 African Media Initiative, Nairobi, Kenya, $50,000. Toward African Media Leaders Forum, conference to strengthen the continent's media sector. 2010.

1312-2 Alliance for Open Society International, New York, NY, $50,000. Toward research and writing to deepen public understanding of Afghanistan. 2010.

1312-3 American Academy in Berlin, Berlin, Germany, $25,000. Toward series of nuclear nonproliferation roundtables. 2010.

1312-4 American Councils for International Education: ACTR/ACCELS, Washington, DC, $500,000. To open Center for Advanced Study and Education in Belarus. 2010.

1312-5 American Institute of Iranian Studies, New York, NY, $25,000. Toward publication of conference volume on Iranian Studies in America. 2010.

1312-6 American Security Project, Washington, DC, $50,000. For comprehensive strategy for bipartisan nuclear security consensus. 2010.

1312-7 Americas Voice Education Fund, Washington, DC, $10,000. Toward Entre Nos Moms for Family Unity Campaign, to build momentum for comprehensive immigration reform. 2010.

1312-8 Boston College, Center for International Higher Education, Chestnut Hill, MA, $157,500. For publication of International Higher Education. 2010.

1312-9 Brookings Institution, Washington, DC, $600,000. Toward Foreign Policy Program. 2010.

1312-10 Brown University, Providence, RI, $300,000. For project to promote global engagement through new media. 2010.

1312-11 CARE USA, Atlanta, GA, $100,000. For Haiti earthquake relief. 2010.

1312-12 Carnegie Council for Ethics in International Affairs, New York, NY, $500,000. Toward promoting ethics through global education. 2010.

1312-13 Carnegie Endowment for International Peace, Washington, DC, $350,000. Toward developing a new security architecture for the Euro-Atlantic region. 2010.

1312-14 Catholic Relief Services, Baltimore, MD, $200,000. For Haiti earthquake relief. 2010.

1312-15 Center for Policy Studies in Russia, Monterey, CA, $225,000. Toward a program to train and nurture security specialists. 2010.

1312-16 Center for Strategic and International Studies, Washington, DC, $325,000. Toward policy research and outreach on alternatives to centralized state building in states at risk. 2010.

1312-17 Change the Equation, Washington, DC, $600,000. To advance recommendations of Opportunity Equation: Transforming Mathematics and Science Education for Citizenship and the Global Economy. 2010.

1312-18 Columbia University, School of International and Public Affairs, New York, NY, $200,000. Toward Gulf 2000 Project. Created as service to scholars, government officials, business people, journalists and other specialists who have a professional association with the Persian Gulf and Gulf studies, Gulf 2000 Project makes available information on countries of the Persian Gulf region, Bahrain, Iran, Iraq, Kuwait, Oman, Qatar, Saudi Arabia and United Arab Emirates. 2010.

1312-19 Council on Foreign Relations, New York, NY, $25,000. Toward journalism fellowship for covering international affairs. 2010.

1312-20 Doctors Without Borders USA, New York, NY, $200,000. For Haiti earthquake relief. 2010.

1312-21 EastWest Institute, New York, NY, $300,000. Toward U.S.-Russia working group on Afghan narco-trafficking. 2010.

1312-22 eThekwini Municipality, Durban, South Africa, $3,000,000. For one-time grant toward Durban Metropolitan Library System, model city library. 2010.

1312-23 Eurasia Foundation, Washington, DC, $2,000,000. For interdisciplinary research and training centers in the Caucasus. 2010.

1312-24 Fonkoze USA, Washington, DC, $100,000. For Haiti earthquake relief. 2010.

1312-25 Friends of the British Council, USA, Washington, DC, $500,000. Toward American and transnational network and public education campaign on Muslim relations, identity and historical coexistence. 2010.

1312-26 George Washington University, Elliott School of International Affairs, Washington, DC, $751,500. Toward research, dissemination and policy forums on Eurasia, as part of Project on New Approaches to Research and Security in Eurasia, also known as PONARS. 2010.

1312-27 George Washington University, Institute of Middle East Studies at Elliott School of International Affairs, Washington, DC, $475,000. For project building field of political science and international relations of broader Middle East, integrating regional expertise and linking scholarship with policy and outreach. 2010.

1312-28 Harvard University, Cambridge, MA, $885,000. Toward executive training programs for military officers and policymakers. 2010.

1312-29 Harvard University, Cambridge, MA, $50,000. Toward archiving historical record on biological weapons nonproliferation. 2010.

1312-30 Henry L. Stimson Center, Washington, DC, $175,000. Toward project on enhancing public security and the rule of law in post-conflict states at risk. 2010.

1312-31 Henry L. Stimson Center, Washington, DC, $20,000. Toward project on Rule of Law for the Oceans. 2010.

1312-32 Institute for Advanced Study, Princeton, NJ, $500,000. Toward collaborative research and seminars on historical and social developments involving Islam. 2010.

1312-33 Institute for Advanced Study, Regional Initiative in Science and Education (RISE), Princeton, NJ, $200,000. To enhance capacity of selected African science and technology postgraduate training and research networks, which aim to produce and retain in Africa new generation of African scientists, many of whom are expected to remain in the higher education sector as teachers and researchers. Grant will enable networks to engage in activities to strengthen network cohesion, fill skills gaps and foster integration into their host institutions. 2010.

1312-34 Institute for Science and International Security, Washington, DC, $250,000. To expand public education and outreach on Iran's nuclear activities. 2010.

1312-35 Institute for State Effectiveness, Washington, DC, $400,000. For final grant toward creation of handbooks for support of specific functions of states at risk. 2010.

1312-36 Institute of International Education, New York, NY, $100,000. For meeting on developing and retaining the next generation of African academics. 2010.

1312-37 International Crisis Group, New York, NY, $350,000. For final grant toward research, analysis, dialogue and dissemination on preventing state collapse. 2010.

1312-38 International Foundation for Science, Stockholm, Sweden, $1,535,000. For competitive fellowship program for early-career scientists in African universities. 2010.

1312-39 International Institute for Strategic Studies, London, England, $215,200. Toward multilateral dialogue on Iran's nuclear program. 2010.

1312-40 International Peace Institute, New York, NY, $330,000. Toward project to assist development of United Nations Peacebuilding Commission. 2010.

1312-41 International Research and Exchanges Board, Washington, DC, $700,000. For work to improve university administration in Russia, Eurasia and Ghana coordinated through University Administration Support Program (UASP). UASP offers ten-week U.S. visiting fellowships to competitively chosen university administrators and awards pilot project grants to enable them to implement reforms at their home institutions upon their return. Grant will provide exchange opportunities and resources to university administrators from Russia, several Eurasian countries and from Ghana. 2010.

1312-42 Jewish Theological Seminary of America, New York, NY, $30,000. Toward Interfaith Academic Conference as part of Islam Initiative. 2010.

1312-43 Leadership Foundation, Washington, DC, $156,000. Toward higher education fellowship program for African women. 2010.

1312-44 London School of Economics and Political Science, London, England, $25,000. Toward international conference on changes in the news media. 2010.

1312-45 Lutheran World Relief, Baltimore, MD, $50,000. For Haiti earthquake relief. 2010.

1312-46 Makerere University, Kampala, Uganda, $1,900,000. For postgraduate training and research programs to advance scholarship and improve retention of African academics. 2010.

1312-47 Massachusetts Institute of Technology, Cambridge, MA, $600,000. Toward Security Studies Program. 2010.

1312-48 Mercy Corps, Portland, OR, $200,000. For Haiti earthquake relief. 2010.

1312-49 Mercy Corps, Portland, OR, $50,000. Toward Track II dialogue with North Korea. 2010.

1312-50 National Committee on American Foreign Policy, New York, NY, $250,000. Toward multilateral dialogue on North Korea. 2010.

1312-51 National Conference of State Legislatures, Denver, CO, $50,000. For public education for state legislators related to federal policies on immigration. 2010.

1312-52 National Council for Tertiary Education, Accra, Ghana, $845,000. For senior academic leadership training in West Africa. 2010.

1312-53 National Security Archive Fund, Gelman Library, Washington, DC, $600,000. Toward support of Eurasia Initiative to increase transparency and access to historical documents in the Caucasus (Armenia, Azerbaijan, Georgia and Russia) and the former Soviet Union and to strengthen partner networks in these regions. 2010.

1312-54 Near East Foundation, New York, NY, $40,000. Toward program support. 2010.

1312-55 New America Foundation, Washington, DC, $200,000. To produce series of online video dialogues on foreign affairs in collaboration with web site Bloggingheads.tv (BhTV). 2010.

1312-56 New School, New York, NY, $380,000. For final grant for Journal Donation Project, initiative to assist in rebuilding major research and teaching libraries in countries that have fallen victim to political or economic deprivation, and often both, through provision of current subscriptions and back volume sets of English-language scholarly, professional and current events journals. 2010.

1312-57 New York University, New York, NY, $400,000. Toward project on enhancing governmental and intergovernmental capacity to support state-building. 2010.

1312-58 New York University, New York, NY, $50,000. For planning activities for new project concerning nuclear power in developing countries. 2010.

1312-59 New York University, New York, NY, $25,000. For study on health, health behaviors and beliefs and health care needs of the Ghanaian community and other West African immigrants in New York City. Findings will be disseminated through publications and will be used as pilot data for long-term project to develop evaluation and intervention strategies. 2010.

1312-60 Nigeria ICT Forum of Partnership Institutions, Abuja, Nigeria, $400,000. Toward technical training and planning of national research and education network. 2010.

1312-61 Norwegian Institute of International Affairs, Oslo, Norway, $10,000. Toward seminar on peacebuilding. 2010.

1312-62 Nuclear Threat Initiative, Washington, DC, $1,000,000. Toward program support. 2010.

1312-63 Ontario Confederation of University Faculty Associations, Toronto, Canada, $20,000. Toward conference on media coverage of higher education in the 21st century. 2010.

1312-64 Overseas Vote Foundation, Arlington, VA, $50,000. Toward general support. 2010.

1312-65 Oxford Center for Islamic Studies, Oxford, England, $300,000. For challenge grant toward Historical Atlas of the Islamic World, with first volume tracking diffusion of Muslim education, practice, sects and intellectual life through the Indian subcontinent. Corporation's funds will principally support on-staff researchers and visits by specialists to complete the volume. No indirect, overhead or consultancy costs are within range of the grant. 2010.

1312-66 Partners in Health, Boston, MA, $100,000. For Haiti earthquake relief. 2010.

1312-67 Ploughshares Fund, San Francisco, CA, $10,000. For survey and analysis of funding on international peace and security issues. 2010.

1312-68 Princeton University, Princeton, NJ, $295,400. For analysis of post-conflict Afghanistan and future. 2010.

1312-69 Princeton University, Princeton, NJ, $25,000. Toward probabilistic analysis of nuclear terrorism. 2010.

1312-70 Project Medishare for Haiti, Miami, FL, $50,000. For Haiti earthquake relief. 2010.

1312-71 Project on National Security Reform, Arlington, VA, $50,000. For three roundtables and conference on key legal issues of national security reform. 2010.

1312-72 Public Interest Projects, New York, NY, $250,000. Toward supplementing Four Freedoms Funds immigrant integration activities, especially in the area of strategic communications. 2010.

1312-73 Richard Nixon Library and Birthplace Foundation, Yorba Linda, CA, $350,000. Toward research, outreach and international engagement on competing interests of the United States and Asia in the greater Middle East. 2010.

1312-74 Social Science Research Council, Brooklyn, NY, $50,000. To plan program to support early-career social scientists in selected African countries. 2010.

1312-75 Social Science Research Council, Brooklyn, NY, $50,000. Toward conference of scholars from the United States, Eurasia and the Middle East. 2010.

1312-76 Southern Africa Legal Services Foundation, Bethesda, MD, $25,000. Toward transcription of Legal Resource Centers history in South Africa. 2010.

1312-77 Stanford University, Stanford, CA, $750,000. Toward research and training in international security. 2010.

1312-78 Stanford University, Stanford, CA, $25,000. Toward research for book on the rise of new nuclear threats since the end of the Cold War. 2010.

1312-79 Stockholm International Peace Research Institute, Solna, Sweden, $250,000. Toward analysis on Trans-Atlantic dimension of next round of arms reduction negotiations with Russia. 2010.

1312-80 Tides Center, ReThink Media, San Francisco, CA, $220,000. Toward project to strengthen media capacity of select nuclear security grantees. Through this grant, ReThink will work with selected Corporation grantees to help them better articulate and build support for their policy recommendations. In addition to technical support and coaching in media skills, each organization will receive access to state-of-the-art tools that are typically available only to large organizations with a dedicated media shop: a dynamic journalist database and specialized press tracking system. Finally, ReThink will work closely with polling organizations to synthesize latest public opinion research and help Corporation grantees better frame and articulate their message. 2010.

1312-81 Tides Foundation, San Francisco, CA, $400,000. Toward Connect U.S. Funds' efforts to build ties between NGOs. 2010.

1312-82 TrustAfrica, Dakar, Senegal, $590,600. For policy dialog series in higher education transformation in sub-Saharan Africa. 2010.

1312-83 Tufts University, Fletcher School of Law and Diplomacy, Medford, MA, $50,000. Toward Talloires Network's civic global engagement efforts. Network is composed of leaders of institutions of higher education that are committed to civic engagement and strives to accelerate and continue to build civic engagement movement within universities. Network will hold meeting about present state and future goals and strategies of global civic engagement movement. Meeting invitees will include leaders in higher education from Asia, Africa, Europe and North and South America and philanthropy. Results will be disseminated through web-based exchanges and other communications efforts. 2010.

1312-84 U.S. Pugwash, Washington, DC, $320,000. Toward multilateral dialogue on security issues in the Greater Middle East, including organization of workshops and consultations on range of Iran-related security issues bringing Iranians together with Americans, Europeans and others from the region. 2010.

1312-85 University of British Columbia, Vancouver, Canada, $48,500. Toward workshop on transformative evidence-based improvements to teaching and learning in Science, Technology, Engineering and Math (STEM) disciplines in colleges and universities. 2010.

1312-86 University of California, Berkeley, CA, $50,000. To plan Kerr Institute Africa Program, Africa-based higher education institute. 2010.

1312-87 University of California at San Diego, La Jolla, CA, $50,000. For series of nuclear security briefings to government agencies by Institute on Global Conflict and Cooperation. 2010.

1312-88 University of Cape Town, Cape Town, South Africa, $2,500,000. Toward postgraduate training and research programs to advance scholarship and improve the retention of African academics. 2010.

1312-89 University of Georgia, Athens, GA, $299,800. Toward project on strengthening security of nuclear facilities and materials globally. 2010.

1312-90 University of Ghana, Legon, Ghana, $2,000,000. Toward Research Commons at University of Ghana Legon - Balme Library. 2010.

1312-91 University of Ghana, Legon, Ghana, $1,800,000. Toward postgraduate training and research programs to advance scholarship and improve retention of African academics. 2010.

1312-92 University of Pretoria, Pretoria, South Africa, $2,000,000. To establish Masters Program in Information Technology within the School of Information Technology. 2010.

1312-93 University of the Witwatersrand, Johannesburg, South Africa, $2,050,000. Toward postgraduate training and research programs to advance scholarship and improve retention of African academics. 2010.

1312-94 Verification Research, Training and Information Centre, London, England, $48,600. Toward independent assessment of United Kingdom-Norway warhead dismantlement initiative. 2010.

1313
Carnegie Council Fund, Inc.
170 E. 64th St.
New York, NY   10065-7478

Established in NY; supporting organization of the Carnegie Council for Ethics in International Affairs, Inc.

Grantmaker type: Public charity.

Financial data (yr. ended 06/30/10): Revenue, $6; assets, $56,962 (M); expenditures, $17,890.

Fields of interest: International affairs.

Limitations: Applications not accepted. Giving limited to New York, NY.

Application information: Contributes only to a pre-selected organization.

Officers: Alexander Platt, Chair.; Thomas Donaldson, Vice-Chair.; Joel Rosenthal, Pres.; Dr. Charles W. Kegley, Jr., Secy.; Russell Hardin, Treas.

Trustees: Phyllis D. Collins; Barbara Crossette; Philippe Dennery; Imtiaz T. Ladak; E. Scott Mead; Holly Elizabeth Myers; Ann Phillips; Prof. Richard H. Schultz; Prof. Michael J. Smith; Harrison I. Steans; and 6 additional trustees.

EIN: 134185528

1314
Sophia & William Casey Foundation
c/o Steven T. Rosenberg
201 Moreland Rd., Ste. 6
Hauppauge, NY 11788-3922
Application address: c/o Bernadette Casey-Smith,
12 Glenwood Rd., Roslyn Harbor, NY 11576,
tel.: (516) 621-9332

Established in 1974 in NY.
Donors: William J. Casey†; Sophia B. Casey†.
Grantmaker type: Independent foundation.
Financial data (yr. ended 11/30/10): Assets,
$6,789,622 (M); expenditures, $453,944;
qualifying distributions, $393,165; giving activities
include $393,165 for 33 grants (high: $116,500;
low: $125).
Fields of interest: International affairs, national
security; United Ways and Federated Giving
Programs; Higher education; Education; Human
services; International studies; Public affairs;
Catholic agencies & churches.
Limitations: Applications accepted. Giving primarily
in Washington, DC and NY. No grants to individuals.
Application information:
Initial approach: Letter
Deadline(s): None
Officer: Bernadette Casey-Smith, Pres. and Secy.
EIN: 510153218

1315
Lyford Cay Foundation, Inc.
c/o Putney, Twombly, Hall & Hirson
521 5th Ave., 10th Fl.
New York, NY 10175-1099
Contact: Maureen French, Admin.
FAX: (212) 682-9380;
E-mail: lycayfdn@bahamas.net.bs; Additional
address: P.O. Box N7776, Nassau, Bahamas, tel.:
(242) 362-4910, FAX: (242) 362-5449;
URL: http://www.lyfordcayfoundation.com

Established in 1969 in NY.
Grantmaker type: Public charity.
Financial data (yr. ended 12/31/10): Revenue,
$3,140,999; assets, $22,250,874 (M); gifts
received, $1,929,023; expenditures, $4,764,926;
giving activities include $726,707 for grants, and
$3,436,500 for grants to organizations outside the
U.S.
Purpose and activities: The foundation provides
support primarily for educational and charitable
organizations in the Bahamas and organizations
serving Bahamian students.
Fields of interest: Vocational education; Education;
Youth development.
International interests: Bahamas.
Type of support: General/operating support; Annual
campaigns; Capital campaigns; Building/
renovation; Equipment; Endowments; Emergency
funds; Program development; Seed money;
Scholarship funds; Scholarships—to individuals;
Matching/challenge support.
Limitations: Applications accepted. Giving primarily
in the Bahamas. No support for foundations, or
religious or government agencies. No grants for
other endowments or the puchase of vehicles.
Publications: Application guidelines; Informational
brochure (including application guidelines);
Newsletter; Occasional report; Program policy
statement.

Application information: Scholarship applicants
must have Bahamian citizenship. Application form
required.
Initial approach: Letter
Copies of proposal: 1
Deadline(s): Mar. 31 for scholarships; Feb. 1, Apr.
1, and Oct. 1 for grants
Board meeting date(s): Mar., June, and Nov.
Final notification: 2 months
Officers and Directors:* Manuel J. Cutillas, Chair.;
Stuart W. Ray, Pres.; Frank Crothers, V.P.; Alexander
Neave, Secy.; Jeffrey A. Everett, Treas.; Dr. Keva M.
Bethel; Philippe Bonnefoy; LaRita Boren; John T.
Bottomley; Judith L. Chiara; and 23 additional
directors.
Number of staff: 3 full-time professional.
EIN: 237025275

1316
CDS International, Inc.
440 Park Ave. S.
New York, NY 10016-8012 (212) 497-3500
FAX: (212) 497-3535; E-mail: info@cdsintl.org;
URL: http://www.cdsintl.org

Classified as a private operating foundation in
1968; status changed to a public charity in 1991.
Donors: Inwert Capacity Building International,
Germany; Robert Bosch Foundation; German
Marshall Fund; Bayer Foundation; A.G. Bayer; BASF
Corp.
Grantmaker type: Public charity.
Financial data (yr. ended 12/31/10): Revenue,
$4,553,419; assets, $3,792,171 (M); gifts
received, $1,028,189; expenditures, $4,763,577;
giving activities include $24,830 for grants to
individuals.
Purpose and activities: The organization
administers international practical training
programs that stimulate the exchange of knowledge
and technological skills and contribute to the
development of a highly-trained and
interculturally-competent workforce, with the hopes
of strengthening global cooperation and
understanding amongst individuals, businesses,
organizations and communities.
Fields of interest: International exchange;
International affairs.
International interests: Germany.
Type of support: Fellowships; Internship funds;
Grants to individuals; Exchange programs.
Limitations: Applications accepted. Giving on a
national and international basis.
Publications: Annual report; Informational brochure;
Newsletter.
Application information:
Initial approach: Download application form
Deadline(s): Oct. 16 for The Robert Bosch
Foundation Fellowship Program
Officers and Directors:* Karl Geercken,* Chair.;
Linda Boughton,* C.F.O.; Hans W. Decker,* Ph.D.,
Treas.; Robert Fenstermacher,* Exec. Dir.; M.
Blouke Carus; Magda Gohar-Chrobog; Kevin Gully;
H. Friedrich Holzapfel, Ph.D.; Gudrun Johnson-Stein;
Gudrun Kochendoerfer-Lucius, Ph.D.; Fritz E.
Kropatschek; Charles R. Manak; Charles Meier;
Jacqueline Renner; Norbert Schneider, Ph.D.; Jim
Thomas; Andreas Winkler, Ph.D.
Number of staff: 18
EIN: 136275141

1317
CEC ArtsLink, Inc.
435 Hudson St., 8th Fl.
New York, NY 10014-3941 (212) 643-1985
FAX: (212) 643-1996; E-mail: info@cecartslink.org;
URL: http://www.cecartslink.org

Established in 1962.
Grantmaker type: Public charity.
Financial data (yr. ended 12/31/09): Revenue,
$1,634,831; assets, $985,875 (M); gifts received,
$1,613,514; expenditures, $1,580,329; program
services expenses, $1,403,539; giving activities
include $114,050 for grants, $22,400 for grants to
organizations outside the U.S., and $32,500 for 9
grants to individuals.
Purpose and activities: The organization
encourages and supports the exchange of artists
and cultural managers between the United States
and Central Europe, Russia and Eurasia with the
belief that the arts are a society's most deliberate
and complex means of communication, and that
artists and those who work in the arts can help
nations overcome long histories of reciprocal
distrust, insularity and conflict.
Fields of interest: Arts; International exchange, arts;
Adults.
International interests: Asia; Eastern & Central
Europe; Russia.
Type of support: Program development;
Fellowships; Grants to individuals.
Limitations: Applications accepted. Giving on a
national and international basis.
Publications: Application guidelines; Grants list;
Newsletter.
Application information: Application form required.
Initial approach: Download application form
Copies of proposal: 1
Deadline(s): Jan. 15 for ArtsLink Projects; Nov. 9
(visual and media arts) and Nov. 10
(performing arts and literature) for ArtsLink
Residencies
Board meeting date(s): Feb., Mar., and Apr.
Final notification: Apr. for ArtsLink Projects; Mar.
for Independent Project Grants
Officers and Trustees:* Jane K. Lombard,* Chair.;
Amei Wallach,* Secy.; Peter P. Nitze,* Treas.; Fritzie
Brown, Exec. Dir.; Todd Bishop; Hilda Chazanovitz;
Martha Colgney; Ananda Grant; Ellen M. Iseman;
Jane Lombard; Clyde E. Rankin III; Jane Safer; Alexey
F. Surkov; Dimitri Sogoloff.
Number of staff: 3 full-time professional; 3 full-time
support; 4 part-time support.
EIN: 132531695

1318
Center for Global Partnership
c/o The Japan Foundation
152 West 57th St., 17th Fl.
New York, NY 10019-3310 (212) 489-1255
Contact: Melanie Standish, Assoc. Program Officer
FAX: (212) 489-1344; E-mail: info@cgp.org;
URL: http://www.cgp.org
Facebook: http://www.facebook.com/pages/
Japan-Foundation-New-York-and-the-Center-for-Glob
al-Partnership/145339038868893

Established in 1991.
Grantmaker type: Public charity.
Purpose and activities: The organization aims to
promote collaboration between Japan and the U.S.,
with the goal of fulfilling shared global

responsibilities and contributing to improvements in the world's welfare.

Fields of interest: Political science; International studies; International exchange, students; International exchange, arts; International exchange; International economics/trade policy; International economic development; International development; Environment; Education; Economics; Arts, public education; Arts, multipurpose centers/programs; Arts, cultural/ethnic awareness; Anthropology/sociology; International affairs, goodwill promotion; International affairs, foreign policy.

Type of support: Conferences/seminars; Publication; Seed money; Curriculum development; Fellowships; Research; Exchange programs.

Limitations: Giving on a national basis and to Japan. No support for commercial, political or religious activities; activities in support of specific doctrines or claims; language education programs; or tourist-oriented programs. No grants for the creation or support of scholarships or fellowships; medical, technical, or scientific projects that do not focus on policy issues; or goodwill exchanges.

Publications: Application guidelines; Annual report.

Application information: Only projects with successful concept papers will be invited by the center to submit a full proposal. The Intellectual Exchange Program requires ten copies of final proposal; the Grassroots Exchange and Education Programs require one copy of a final proposal.

Initial approach: Submit 2- to 3-page concept paper

Deadline(s): Oct. 1 (concept papers) and Dec. 1 (full proposals) for Intellectual Exchange Program; Oct. 1 for U.S.-Japan Network for the Future; rolling deadline for Grassroots Exchange Program and Education Program

Board meeting date(s): Varies

Final notification: Varies

Officer: Masaru Sakato, Acting Exec. Dir.

1319
Central Fund of Israel

980 Ave. of the Americas
New York, NY   10018-7804

Grantmaker type: Public charity.

Financial data (yr. ended 01/31/11): Revenue, $10,493,530; assets, $3,496,451 (M); gifts received, $10,478,720; expenditures, $10,582,683; giving activities include $10,582,222 for grants to organizations outside the U.S.

Fields of interest: Human services; Economically disadvantaged.

International interests: Israel.

Limitations: Giving primarily in Israel.

Officers: Hadassah K. Marcus, Pres.; Itamar Marcus, V.P.; Jay H. Marcus, V.P.; Morris Stillman, Treas.

Directors: Arthur Marcus; Irwin Peckman.

EIN: 132992985

1320
Chabad of Argentina Relief Appeal, Inc.

675 3rd Ave., Ste. 3210
New York, NY   10017-5707

Established in 2003 in NY.

Grantmaker type: Public charity.

Financial data (yr. ended 12/31/10): Revenue, $1,513,021; assets, $1,420 (M); gifts received, $1,513,021; expenditures, $1,521,977; giving activities include $1,515,924 for grants to organizations outside the U.S.

Purpose and activities: The organization provides grants to assist in humanitarian aid and to assist religious educational institutions affected by the financial crisis in Argentina.

Fields of interest: Religion, formal/general education; International relief; Human services.

International interests: Argentina.

Limitations: Applications not accepted. Giving primarily in Argentina.

Application information: Unsolicited requests for funds not accepted.

Trustees: Chaim Shaul Brook; Joseph Kazarnovki; Mordechai Telsner; David Tessel.

EIN: 270049239

1321
Chamber Music America

305 7th Ave.
New York, NY   10001-6008   (212) 242-2022
FAX: (212) 242-7955;
E-mail: info@chamber-music.org; URL: http://www.chamber-music.org

Established in 1977 in NY.

Grantmaker type: Public charity.

Financial data (yr. ended 06/30/10): Revenue, $1,310,023; assets, $9,971,438 (M); gifts received, $701,988; expenditures, $2,363,013; program services expenses, $2,059,146; giving activities include $425,715 for 32 grants (high: $22,000; low: $5,000), $273,200 for 17 grants to individuals, and $1,360,231 for foundation-administered programs.

Purpose and activities: The organization works to promote artistic excellence and economic stability within the profession and to ensure that chamber music, in its broadest sense, is a vital part of American life.

Fields of interest: International exchange, arts; Performing arts, music; Performing arts, music ensembles/groups; Performing arts, music composition.

Type of support: Grants to individuals; Program development; Conferences/seminars; Technical assistance; Consulting services.

Limitations: Applications accepted. Giving on a national basis.

Publications: Application guidelines; Financial statement; Grants list; Informational brochure; Newsletter.

Application information: Application form required.

Initial approach: Submit application

Deadline(s): Feb. 11 for Residency Partnership Program; Feb. 28 for New Works: Creation and Presentation Program; Apr. 6 for Commissioning Program; Oct. 22 for CMA/FACE French American Jazz Exchange Program; varies for all others

Officers and Trustees:* Louise K. Smith,* Chair.; Margaret M. Lioi,* C.E.O.; Phillip Ying,* Pres.; Daniel R. Gustin, V.P.; Charlotte Schroeder,* Secy.; John R. Kirk,* Treas.; Nadine Asin; Louise Basbas; Billy Childs; James F. Dunham; Derek E. Gordon; Bert Harclerode; Julie Himmelstrup; Laura Kaminsky; Shirley Kirshbaum; and 14 additional trustees.

Number of staff: 12 full-time professional; 1 part-time professional; 2 part-time support.

EIN: 132934575

1322
The Charina Endowment Fund, Inc.

(formerly The HWG Fund, Inc.)
c/o Richard Menschel
375 Park Ave., Ste. 1602
New York, NY   10152-1600

Established in 1992 in NY.

Donor: Horace W. Goldsmith Foundation.

Grantmaker type: Independent foundation.

Financial data (yr. ended 12/31/10): Assets, $221,173,284 (M); expenditures, $9,965,825; qualifying distributions, $9,629,698; giving activities include $9,391,000 for 49 grants (high: $1,000,000; low: $25,000; average: $50,000–$300,000).

Purpose and activities: The fund supports cultural programs, including performing arts and museums. Support also for hospitals and education, with emphasis on higher education.

Fields of interest: Libraries (public); Visual arts; Museums; Performing arts, theater; Arts; Education, research; Higher education; Business school/education; Environment, natural resources; Hospitals (general); Medical care, rehabilitation; Aging, centers/services; Homeless, human services; Children/youth; Children; Economically disadvantaged.

Type of support: General/operating support; Continuing support; Income development; Annual campaigns; Capital campaigns; Building/renovation; Land acquisition; Endowments; Debt reduction; Emergency funds; Professorships; Seed money; Curriculum development; Fellowships; Scholarship funds; Research; Matching/challenge support.

Limitations: Applications not accepted. Giving primarily in New York. No grants to individuals.

Application information: Unsolicited requests for funds not accepted.

Officers and Directors:* Richard L. Menschel,* Pres. and Treas.; Ronay A. Menschel,* Secy.; Robert B. Menschel.

Number of staff: 3 part-time support.

EIN: 133675545

Recent grants for international programs:

1322-1 American Associates, Ben-Gurion University of the Negev, New York, NY, $500,000. For general support. 2009.

1322-2 Human Rights First, New York, NY, $450,000. For general support. 2009.

1322-3 International Institute of Rural Reconstruction, New York, NY, $100,000. For general support. 2009.

1322-4 Rotary Foundation of Rotary International, Evanston, IL, $250,000. For general support. 2009.

1323
Chatterjee Charitable Foundation

888 7th Ave., Ste. 3000
New York, NY   10106-0001

Established in 1995 in NY.

Donors: Purnendu Chatterjee; Sidhartha Maitra; Subir K. Sanyal.

Grantmaker type: Independent foundation.

Financial data (yr. ended 11/30/10): Assets, $10,749,142 (M); expenditures, $713,028; qualifying distributions, $709,814; giving activities include $706,000 for 19 grants (high: $400,000; low: $100).
Purpose and activities: Giving primarily for higher education as well as to Asian and Indian organizations, and to an institute for molecular medicine.
Fields of interest: Higher education; Education; Medical research, institute; Human services.
International interests: India.
Limitations: Applications not accepted. Giving primarily in New York, NY, and England. No grants to individuals.
Application information: Contributes only to pre-selected organizations.
Director: Purnendu Chatterjee.
EIN: 137072667

1324
The Chazen Foundation
c/o Graf Repetti & Co., LLP
1114 Ave. of the Americas, 17th Fl.
New York, NY 10036
Application address: 767 5th Ave., 26th Fl., New York, NY 10153

Established in 1985 in NY.
Donors: Jerome Chazen; Simona Chazen; Jerome Chazen & Graf Repetti & Co., LLP.
Grantmaker type: Independent foundation.
Financial data (yr. ended 12/31/09): Assets, $25,320,800 (M); expenditures, $2,383,972; qualifying distributions, $2,266,804; giving activities include $1,903,738 for grants, and $135,750 for grants to individuals.
Purpose and activities: Giving primarily for Jewish agencies and temples, higher education, the arts, particularly art museums, health associations, and human services.
Fields of interest: Health organizations, association; Performing arts, opera; Museums (art); Arts; Higher education; Human services; Jewish federated giving programs; Jewish agencies & synagogues.
International interests: Israel.
Type of support: General/operating support; Capital campaigns; Building/renovation; Professorships; Scholarship funds; Grants to individuals; Scholarships—to individuals.
Limitations: Giving primarily in the northeastern U.S.; education grants limited to students in the Rockland County, NY, area.
Publications: Application guidelines; Informational brochure.
Application information:
  Initial approach: Letter
  Deadline(s): None
Trustees: Jerome Chazen; Simona Chazen.
Number of staff: 1 part-time professional; 1 part-time support.
EIN: 133229474
Recent grants for international programs:
1324-1 Harvard University, Cambridge, MA, $10,000. For Center for Health and the Global Environment. 2008.

1325
Children's Help Net Foundation
293 Scarborough Rd.
Briarcliff Manor, NY 10510-2027
(914) 923-3774
Contact: Daniel M. Levine Ph.D., Pres.
URL: http://www.childrenshelpnet.org

Grantmaker type: Public charity.
Financial data (yr. ended 12/31/10): Revenue, $23,519; assets, $17,713 (M); gifts received, $23,517; expenditures, $21,234; program services expenses, $20,600; giving activities include $20,600 for grants.
Purpose and activities: The organization supports projects and programs designed to promote child welfare, education, and adoption of children.
Fields of interest: Education; Children/youth, services; Children, adoption.
International interests: Bulgaria; Moldova; Romania.
Type of support: In-kind gifts.
Limitations: Giving on a national and international basis, with emphasis on Bulgaria, Moldova, and Romania.
Officers and Directors:* Daniel M. Levine,* Ph.D., Pres.; Joseph S. Levine, Ph.D., V.P.; Christina Siry, Secy.; James Mahoney, Treas.; Steven A. Caldwell, Ph.D.; Lawrence J. Siry, Esq.; Mary Spaulding.
EIN: 113519076

1326
The Children's Investment Fund Foundation
(formerly Cooper-Hohn Family Foundation)
c/o Perlman & Perlman
41 Madison Ave., Ste. 40T
New York, NY 10010-2202
URL: http://www.ciff.org

Established in 2002 in NY.
Donors: Perry Capital Corp.; The Children's Investment Fund, Ltd.; The Children's Investment Fund, LP; TCIF Fund; TCIFM UK LLP.
Grantmaker type: Independent foundation.
Financial data (yr. ended 12/31/08): Assets, $88,507,120 (M); gifts received, $1,200,000; expenditures, $4,407,290; qualifying distributions, $3,525,793; giving activities include $3,476,774 for 8 grants (high: $2,043,690; low: $25,000).
Purpose and activities: Support for organizations benefiting children in developing countries.
Fields of interest: Education; AIDS; Youth development; International development; International economic development.
International interests: Developing countries.
Limitations: Applications not accepted. Giving on a national and international basis for the benefit of developing countries. No grants to individuals.
Application information: Contributes only to pre-selected organizations.
Trustees: Phyllis Kurlander Constanza; Jamie Cooper-Hohn; Peter McDermott; Joy Phumaphi; William Reeves.
EIN: 043632641

1327
CIT Group Inc. Corporate Giving Program
11 W 42 St.
New York, NY 10036
Contact: Stacy Papas, V.P., Corp. Giving and Community and Employee Affairs
E-mail: stacy.papas@cit.com; *URL:* http://www.cit.com/about-cit/corporate-citizenship/corporate-giving/index.htm

Grantmaker type: Corporate giving program.
Purpose and activities: CIT makes charitable contributions to nonprofit organizations on a case by case basis. Support is given on a national and international basis in areas of company operations.
Fields of interest: General charitable giving.
International interests: Canada.
Type of support: General/operating support; Continuing support; Program development; Employee volunteer services.
Limitations: Giving on a national and international basis in areas of company operations. No support for religious, political, legislative, veteran, fraternal, conference, or sports organizations, or for political candidates. No grants to individuals.
Publications: Application guidelines.
Application information: Grantmaking is currently suspended. The Corporate Giving Department handles giving. Multi-year funding is not automatic. Application form not required.
  Initial approach: Proposal to headquarters
  Deadline(s): None
  Committee meeting date(s): Annually

1328
Citi Foundation
(formerly Citigroup Foundation)
425 Park Ave., 2nd. Fl.
New York, NY 10022-6211
Contact: Sarah Lamothe
E-mail: citifoundation@citi.com; *URL:* http://www.citifoundation.com
Citi Foundation Update: http://www.citifoundation.com/citi/foundation/update vol1_2010.htm
Citi Global Corporate Citizenship: http://a4.g.akamai.net/7/4/22231/v001/citigroupms.download.akamai.com/25801/video/CGCC_2009.wmv
CitiFoundation: http://twitter.com/CitiFoundation
Grant Listing: http://www.citifoundation.com/citi/foundation/grant_search.htm

Established in 1994 in NY.
Donors: Citicorp; Citibank, N.A.; Citigroup Inc.; Citigroup Venture Capital Ltd.; Charles Prince.
Grantmaker type: Company-sponsored foundation.
Financial data (yr. ended 12/31/10): Assets, $63,186,688 (M); gifts received, $66,400,000; expenditures, $63,582,518; qualifying distributions, $63,574,250; giving activities include $63,573,500 for 828 grants (high: $1,500,000; low: $10,000).
Purpose and activities: The foundation supports organizations and programs that enhance economic opportunities for individuals and families, particularly those in need, in areas of company operations. The foundation provides grant support for programs that are aligned with it's economic empowerment mission, promote collaboration and effective use of philanthropic resources, engage it's employees, and demonstrate impact and positive outcomes. Special emphasis is directed toward

programs that promote innovations in microfinance and microenterprise; college and careers; financial capability and asset building; and neighborhood revitalization. The foundation also strives to partner with organizations that demonstrate a commitment to the environment and environmental innovations in each of the core priority areas.

Fields of interest: Business school/education; Business/industry; Community/economic development; Community/economic development, management/technical assistance; Economic development; Education, reading; Elementary/secondary education; Employment; Graduate/professional education; Higher education; Human services, financial counseling; Disabilities, people with; Economically disadvantaged; Minorities; Women; Youth.

Type of support: Continuing support; Curriculum development; Emergency funds; General/operating support; Income development; Management development/capacity building; Program development; Seed money; Technical assistance.

Limitations: Applications not accepted. Giving on a national and international basis in Algeria, Argentina, Australia, Bahamas, Bahrain, Bangladesh, Belgium, Brazil, Brunei, Bulgaria, Cameroon, Canada, China, Colombia, Costa, Rica, Cote d'voire, Czech, Republic, Democratic, Rep, of, Congo, Denmark, Dominican, Republic, Ecuador, Egypt, El, Salvador, Finland, France, Germany, Ghana, Greece, Guam, Guatemala, Honduras, Hong, Kong, Hungary, India, Indonesia, Ireland, Israel, Italy, Jamaica, Japan, Jordan, Kazakhstan, Kenya, Korea, (South), Kuwait, Lebanon, Luxembourg, Malaysia, Morocco, Netherlands, New, Zealand, Nicaragua, Nigeria, Norway, Pakistan, Panama, Paraguay, Peru, Philippines, Poland, Portugal, Qatar, Romania, Russia, Senegal, Singapore, Slovakia, South, Africa, Spain, Sri, Lanka, Sweden, Switzerland, Taiwan, Tanzania, Thailand, Trinidad, &, Tobago, Tunisia, Turkey, Uganda, Ukraine, United, Arab, Emirates, United, Kingdom, Uruguay, Venezuela, Vietnam, and Zambia. No support for political candidates or religious, veterans', or fraternal organizations not of direct benefit to the entire community. No grants to individuals, or for political causes, fundraising events, telethons, marathons, races, or benefits, advertising, sponsorships, dinners or luncheons, or membership fees.

Publications: Corporate giving report; Grants list; Informational brochure.

Application information: The foundation utilizes an invitation only process; unsolicited proposals are not accepted.

Officer and Directors:* Lewis B. Kaden,* Chair.; Bob Annibale; Shirish Apte; Raymond J. McGuire; Paul McKinnon; Manuel Medina-Mora; Francesco Vanni; D'Archirafi Alberto Verme.

Number of staff: 15 full-time professional; 2 full-time support; 3 part-time support.

EIN: 133781879

Recent grants for international programs:

1328-1 ACCION International, Boston, MA, $200,000. For ACCION International: Building Financial Education in Latin America Project. 2010.

1328-2 ACCION International, Boston, MA, $120,000. For ACCION International, LATAM Regional: Citi Microentrepreneurship Awards Support Project. 2010.

1328-3 ACCION International, Boston, MA, $95,000. For Cracking the Capital Markets South Asia Program. 2010.

1328-4 ACCION International, Boston, MA, $50,000. For ACCION International, EMEA Regional: Running with Risk Initiative. 2010.

1328-5 ACCION International, Boston, MA, $25,000. For ACCION International, Peru: PREMIC - Citi Microentrepreneurship Awards Program. 2010.

1328-6 American Friends of the London Business School, London, England, $48,000. For American Friends of the London Business School, EMEA Regional: Citi Foundation Scholarship Program. 2010.

1328-7 American Friends of the New Economic School, University Park, PA, $100,000. For financial literacy in Russian Pedagogical Universities Program. 2010.

1328-8 American Friends of the New Economic School, University Park, PA, $75,000. For Citi Scholarship and Career Exploration Program. 2010.

1328-9 American Ireland Fund, Boston, MA, $50,000. For St. Patrick's College, Ireland: TeachNet Ireland Program. 2010.

1328-10 American Red Cross National Headquarters, Washington, DC, $25,000. For Colombia Floods Disaster Response Initiative. 2010.

1328-11 American University of Beirut, Beirut, Lebanon, $40,000. For American University of Beirut, Lebanon: Citi Scholarship Program. 2010.

1328-12 Americans for Oxford, New York, NY, $78,000. For Oxford University, EMEA Regional: Citi Scholarship Program. 2010.

1328-13 Arc Finance, Glen Ridge, NJ, $200,000. For Arc Finance Partner Performance Measurement System Project. 2010.

1328-14 Aspen Institute, Washington, DC, $175,000. For Aspen Network of Development Entrepreneurs (ANDE) Regional Expansion and Training Project. 2010.

1328-15 Cambridge in America, New York, NY, $78,000. For Cambridge University, EMEA Regional: Citi Bursary Program. 2010.

1328-16 Charities Aid Foundation America, Alexandria, VA, $240,000. For Leopold Kronenberg Foundation, Poland: Junior Achievement Foundation Poland/From Penny to Pound Program. 2010.

1328-17 Charities Aid Foundation America, Alexandria, VA, $240,000. For Leopold Kronenberg Foundation, Poland: Junior Achievement Foundation Poland/My Finances Program. 2010.

1328-18 Charities Aid Foundation America, Alexandria, VA, $240,000. For Leopold Kronenberg Foundation, Poland: Think Foundation/Savings Week Program. 2010.

1328-19 Charities Aid Foundation America, Alexandria, VA, $110,000. For Leopold Kronenberg Foundation, Poland: Debtor's Guide Program. 2010.

1328-20 Charities Aid Foundation America, Alexandria, VA, $90,000. For Leopold Kronenberg Foundation, Poland: Citi Microentrepreneurship Awards Program. 2010.

1328-21 Charities Aid Foundation America, Alexandria, VA, $90,000. For Leopold Kronenberg Foundation, Poland: JA Banks in Action Program. 2010.

1328-22 Children International, Kansas City, MO, $11,000. For Children International, Ecuador: Social and Financial Education (Aflatoun model). 2010.

1328-23 Conservation International, Arlington, VA, $126,000. For Conservation International, Brazil: Promoting Sustainable Businesses in the Atlantic Forest Project. 2010.

1328-24 Conservation International, Arlington, VA, $97,000. For Conservation International Brazil: The Sustainable Piacava Project. 2010.

1328-25 Conservation International, Arlington, VA, $50,000. For Conservation International, South Africa: Building Environmental Enterprises Program. 2010.

1328-26 E and Co, Bloomfield, NJ, $250,000. For Transition and Growth Initiative. 2010.

1328-27 EcoLogic Development Fund, Cambridge, MA, $50,000. For CarbonPlus Program in Honduras. 2010.

1328-28 Endeavor Global, New York, NY, $100,000. For Endeavor Global, EMEA Regional: Search and Selection Program. 2010.

1328-29 Endeavor Global, New York, NY, $10,000. For Endeavor, Uruguay: Entrepreneurs Program. 2010.

1328-30 FINCA International, Washington, DC, $100,000. For FINCA, LATAM Regional: Village Banking in Central America Project. 2010.

1328-31 FINCA International, Washington, DC, $39,000. For FINCA International, Inc, LATAM Regional: FCAT (Client Assessment Tool) and the HOI Correlation Project. 2010.

1328-32 FINCA International, Washington, DC, $10,000. For FINCA International, Inc., Democratic Republic of Congo: Village Banking in DR Congo Project. 2010.

1328-33 FINCA International, Washington, DC, $10,000. For FINCA International, Inc., Zambia: Village Banking in Zambia Project. 2010.

1328-34 FINCA International, Washington, DC, $10,000. For FINCA, Jordan: Village Banking in Jordan Project. 2010.

1328-35 Give to Colombia, Coral Gables, FL, $80,000. For Give to Colombia, Colombia: Analog Forestry in the Atrato River Basin Project. 2010.

1328-36 Global Heritage Fund, Palo Alto, CA, $60,000. For Global Heritage Fund, Colombia: El Mamey-Buritaca Basin Educational Program. 2010.

1328-37 Grameen Foundation USA, Washington, DC, $125,000. For Human Capital Center Program. 2010.

1328-38 Habitat for Humanity International, Americus, GA, $235,000. For Habitat for Humanity International, EMEA Regional: toward Sustainability of Financial Education Program. 2010.

1328-39 Habitat for Humanity International, Americus, GA, $167,000. For Habitat for Humanity Latin America: Center for Innovation in Housing and Finance. 2010.

1328-40 Habitat for Humanity International, Americus, GA, $133,000. For Habitat for Humanity, Latin America and Caribbean: Financial Education Sustainability Program. 2010.

1328-41 Habitat for Humanity International, Americus, GA, $116,000. For Habitat for Humanity, Korea: Citi Family Build Program. 2010.

1328-42 Habitat for Humanity International, Americus, GA, $40,000. For Habitat for Humanity Northern Ireland, United Kingdom: More than Houses at Madrid Street Program. 2010.

1328-43 Habitat for Humanity International, Americus, GA, $30,000. For Habitat for Humanity

Canada, Toronto: 360 Partnership Initiative. 2010.

1328-44 Habitat for Humanity International, Americus, GA, $30,000. For Habitat for Humanity, Canada: Affordable Housing Project. 2010.

1328-45 Habitat for Humanity International, Americus, GA, $25,000. For Habitat for Humanity South Africa, South Africa: Stretford Project. 2010.

1328-46 Habitat for Humanity International, Americus, GA, $20,000. For Habitat for Humanity Cote d'Ivoire: Vulnerable Youths Individual's Permanent Employment Project. 2010.

1328-47 HOPE Worldwide, Johannesburg, South Africa, $170,000. For Hope Worldwide Ltd., Hong Kong: Citi Success Fund. 2010.

1328-48 Idaho Council on Economic Education, Boise, ID, $10,000. For International Economic Summit Program. 2010.

1328-49 INSEAD Management Education Foundation, New York, NY, $40,000. For INSEAD Management Education Foundation, EMEA Regional: MBA Scholarships and Global Leader Series Program. 2010.

1328-50 Integra Ventures, Wheaton, IL, $10,000. For Association Integra-BDS, Bulgaria: Microenterprise Development For Women. 2010.

1328-51 International Institute for Sustainable Development, Winnipeg, Canada, $75,000. For Access to Finance to Sustainable Producers Program. 2010.

1328-52 Junior Achievement Worldwide, Colorado Springs, CO, $500,000. For JA Africa Regional Operating Center and Adapted JA Company Program. 2010.

1328-53 Junior Achievement Worldwide, Colorado Springs, CO, $386,000. For JA Banks in Action Latin America Regional Implementation Initiative. 2010.

1328-54 Junior Achievement Worldwide, Colorado Springs, CO, $230,000. For Junior Achievement Young Enterprise Europe, EMEA Regional: JA Banks in Action EMEA Implementation Initiative. 2010.

1328-55 Junior Achievement Worldwide, Colorado Springs, CO, $140,000. For Young Enterprise London: The Company Program. 2010.

1328-56 Junior Achievement Worldwide, Colorado Springs, CO, $80,000. For Junior Achievement, Spain: Investing in your future. 2010.

1328-57 Junior Achievement Worldwide, Colorado Springs, CO, $75,000. For Junior Achievement, Italy: Financial Education Throughout Italian Youth Program. 2010.

1328-58 Junior Achievement Worldwide, Colorado Springs, CO, $71,000. For Junior Achievement, Turkey: The Company Program. 2010.

1328-59 Junior Achievement Worldwide, Colorado Springs, CO, $60,000. For Junior Achievement, Colombia: The Key That Opens Your Future Program. 2010.

1328-60 Junior Achievement Worldwide, Colorado Springs, CO, $60,000. For Young Enterprise Northern Ireland, United Kingdom: Company Program. 2010.

1328-61 Junior Achievement Worldwide, Colorado Springs, CO, $57,000. For Junior Achievement, EMEA Regional: Real-Time Employability Skills Development Program. 2010.

1328-62 Junior Achievement Worldwide, Colorado Springs, CO, $55,000. For INJAZ Morocco, Morocco: Banks In Action Program. 2010.

1328-63 Junior Achievement Worldwide, Colorado Springs, CO, $55,000. For Young Enterprise East Midlands, United Kingdom: Personal Economics Program. 2010.

1328-64 Junior Achievement Worldwide, Colorado Springs, CO, $50,000. For Junior Achievement Brazil: Learn to Grow Contest Initiative. 2010.

1328-65 Junior Achievement Worldwide, Colorado Springs, CO, $50,000. For Junior Achievement Young Enterprise Ireland, Ireland: Personal Economics Program. 2010.

1328-66 Junior Achievement Worldwide, Colorado Springs, CO, $40,000. For INJAZ United Arab Emirates: Banks in Action Program. 2010.

1328-67 Junior Achievement Worldwide, Colorado Springs, CO, $40,000. For Junior Achievement Nigeria, Nigeria: It's My Biz Program. 2010.

1328-68 Junior Achievement Worldwide, Colorado Springs, CO, $40,000. For Young Enterprise Scotland, United Kingdom: Stairway 2 Success Program. 2010.

1328-69 Junior Achievement Worldwide, Colorado Springs, CO, $34,000. For INJAZ, EMEA Regional: Are They Ready? Evaluation Initiative. 2010.

1328-70 Junior Achievement Worldwide, Colorado Springs, CO, $30,000. For INJAZ, Egypt: It's My Business Program. 2010.

1328-71 Junior Achievement Worldwide, Colorado Springs, CO, $30,000. For Junior Achievement Greece, Greece: Company Program. 2010.

1328-72 Junior Achievement Worldwide, Colorado Springs, CO, $30,000. For Junior Achievement of Central Ontario, Canada: Banks In Action Program. 2010.

1328-73 Junior Achievement Worldwide, Colorado Springs, CO, $30,000. For Junior Achievement, Tanzania: Job Shadow and It's My Business Program. 2010.

1328-74 Junior Achievement Worldwide, Colorado Springs, CO, $30,000. For Young Enterprise Switzerland, Switzerland: Personal Economics Program and Company Program. 2010.

1328-75 Junior Achievement Worldwide, Colorado Springs, CO, $25,000. For INJAZ Al-Arab, Qatar: Personal Economics Program. 2010.

1328-76 Junior Achievement Worldwide, Colorado Springs, CO, $25,000. For INJAZ, Jordan: School Adoption Program. 2010.

1328-77 Junior Achievement Worldwide, Colorado Springs, CO, $25,000. For INJAZ, Lebanon: Banks in Action Program. 2010.

1328-78 Junior Achievement Worldwide, Colorado Springs, CO, $25,000. For Junior Achievement Portugal, Portugal: Company Program. 2010.

1328-79 Junior Achievement Worldwide, Colorado Springs, CO, $25,000. For Junior Achievement, Czech Republic: JA Banks In Action Program. 2010.

1328-80 Junior Achievement Worldwide, Colorado Springs, CO, $23,000. For Junior Achievement El Salvador, El Salvador: Economic for Success Program. 2010.

1328-81 Junior Achievement Worldwide, Colorado Springs, CO, $20,000. For JA-YE Luxembourg, Luxembourg: Fit for Life Program. 2010.

1328-82 Junior Achievement Worldwide, Colorado Springs, CO, $20,000. For Junior Achievement Kazakhstan, Kazakhstan: Banks in Action. 2010.

1328-83 Junior Achievement Worldwide, Colorado Springs, CO, $20,000. For Junior Achievement Kenya: Turning Youth Potential Into Enterprise Program. 2010.

1328-84 Junior Achievement Worldwide, Colorado Springs, CO, $20,000. For Junior Achievement Senegal, Senegal: Company Program, Job Shadow and Our Community Program. 2010.

1328-85 Junior Achievement Worldwide, Colorado Springs, CO, $20,000. For Young Enterprise Trust, New Zealand: Financial Education Course Initiative. 2010.

1328-86 Junior Achievement Worldwide, Colorado Springs, CO, $19,000. For Junior Achievement, Trinidad and Tobago: Economics for Success. 2010.

1328-87 Junior Achievement Worldwide, Colorado Springs, CO, $18,000. For Junior Achievement Young Enterprise Europe, Western Europe Regional: JA Banks in Action European Competition Initiative. 2010.

1328-88 Junior Achievement Worldwide, Colorado Springs, CO, $15,000. For Flemish Young Enterprise, Belgium: Initiative for Ethical Trade Program. 2010.

1328-89 Junior Achievement Worldwide, Colorado Springs, CO, $15,000. For Flemish Young Enterprise, Belgium: Small Business Projects. 2010.

1328-90 Junior Achievement Worldwide, Colorado Springs, CO, $15,000. For Junior Achievement - Young Enterprise Norway/JA-YE Norway, Norway: Pupils Enterprise Program. 2010.

1328-91 Junior Achievement Worldwide, Colorado Springs, CO, $15,000. For Junior Achievement, Finland: Company Program. 2010.

1328-92 Junior Achievement Worldwide, Colorado Springs, CO, $15,000. For Junior Achievement, Japan: MESE National Contest Project. 2010.

1328-93 Junior Achievement Worldwide, Colorado Springs, CO, $15,000. For The Danish Foundation for Entrepreneurship (Young Enterprise), Denmark:(L)earn and Live Program. 2010.

1328-94 Junior Achievement Worldwide, Colorado Springs, CO, $15,000. For Young Enterprise Belgium, Belgium: Young Enterprise Project. 2010.

1328-95 Junior Achievement Worldwide, Colorado Springs, CO, $14,000. For Junior Achievement, Guatemala: Company Program and Job Shadow Day Program. 2010.

1328-96 Junior Achievement Worldwide, Colorado Springs, CO, $10,000. For Junior Achievement Romania, Romania: My Money Business Program. 2010.

1328-97 Junior Achievement Worldwide, Colorado Springs, CO, $10,000. For Junior Achievement Zambia: Company Program. 2010.

1328-98 Junior Achievement Worldwide, Colorado Springs, CO, $10,000. For Junior Achievement, Paraguay: MESE Financial Education Program. 2010.

1328-99 Junior Achievement Worldwide, Colorado Springs, CO, $10,000. For Junior Achievement, Uganda: Company Program. 2010.

1328-100 LSE Foundation, New York, NY, $55,000. For London School of Economics, EMEA Regional: Citi Scholarship Program. 2010.

1328-101 Market Matters, Ithaca, NY, $35,000. For Market Matters, South Africa: Building Management Capacity within Disadvantaged Groups in South Africa's Agribusiness Sector Project. 2010.

1328-102 Mercy Corps, Portland, OR, $100,000. For Mercy Corps, China: Better Finance Better Future Program. 2010.

1328-103 Microfinance Information Exchange, Washington, DC, $250,000. For Enhanced Data Collection and Information Effectiveness Program. 2010.

1328-104 Microfinance Opportunities, Washington, DC, $250,000. For Financial Capabilities for Women Planning Initiative. 2010.

1328-105 Microfinance Opportunities, Washington, DC, $70,000. For MFO-REDCAMIF (Red Centroamericana de Microfinanzas) Alliance For Financial Education Project. 2010.

1328-106 Microfinance Transparency, Lancaster, PA, $50,000. For Transparent Pricing in India Initiative. 2010.

1328-107 Mountain Institute, Washington, DC, $150,000. For The Mountain Institute, China: Guizhou Indigenous Batik Development Program. 2010.

1328-108 New America Foundation, Washington, DC, $100,000. For Savings-Linked Conditional Cash Transfers: A Global Colloquium Initiative. 2010.

1328-109 Nonprofit Enterprise and Self-sustainability Team, San Francisco, CA, $70,000. For Nonprofit Enterprise and Self-sustainability Team, Hungary: NESsT-Citibank Social Business Development Program. 2010.

1328-110 Nonprofit Enterprise and Self-sustainability Team, San Francisco, CA, $14,000. For Nonprofit Enterprise and Self-sustainability Team, Ecuador: Investing in Social Enterprise Program. 2010.

1328-111 One Economy Corporation, Washington, DC, $40,000. For One Economy Corporation, South Africa: Street Vendors Support Initiative. 2010.

1328-112 Operation Hope, Los Angeles, CA, $45,000. For Operation Hope, South Africa: Banking On Our Future Project. 2010.

1328-113 Pan American Development Foundation, Washington, DC, $35,000. For Strengthening Post-Secondary Technical Training in El Salvador Program. 2010.

1328-114 Pan American Development Foundation, Washington, DC, $30,000. For Disaster Management and Response Program. 2010.

1328-115 Pearson Charitable Foundation, New York, NY, $300,000. For Pearson Charitable Foundation, Asia-Pacific Regional: Citi-FT Financial Education Summit Program. 2010.

1328-116 Pearson Charitable Foundation, New York, NY, $50,000. For Pearson Charitable Foundation, Asia-Pac Regional: Citi-FT Financial Education Summit 2010 Program. 2010.

1328-117 Pro Mujer, New York, NY, $50,000. For Pro Mujer, Inc., LATAM Regional: Breaking the Cycle of Poverty: Empowering Women Economically Initiative. 2010.

1328-118 ProLiteracy Worldwide, Syracuse, NY, $75,000. For ProLiteracy Worldwide, EMEA Regional: Learning-based Micro-Finance and Enterprise Program. 2010.

1328-119 ProLiteracy Worldwide, Syracuse, NY, $75,000. For ProLiteracy Worldwide, LATAM Regional: Learning-based Micro-Finance and Enterprise Program. 2010.

1328-120 ProLiteracy Worldwide, Syracuse, NY, $35,000. For ProLiteracy Worldwide, LATAM Regional: ProLiteracy/FINCA El Salvador Village Bank Solidarity Project. 2010.

1328-121 Rainforest Alliance, New York, NY, $150,000. For Rainforest Alliance, LATAM Regional: Supporting Sustainable Forestry and Tourism Enterprises Project. 2010.

1328-122 Rainforest Alliance, New York, NY, $12,000. For Rainforest Alliance, Costa Rica: Rural Costa Rican Sustainable Tourism Training Project. 2010.

1328-123 Resource Foundation, New York, NY, $35,000. For Resource Foundation, Venezuela: Citi Microentrepreneurship Awards Program. 2010.

1328-124 Root Capital, Cambridge, MA, $100,000. For Extending the Impact of Rural Finance Initiative. 2010.

1328-125 Sanabel Microfinance Network of Arab Countries, Giza, Egypt, $55,000. For Citi Microentrepreneurship Awards Program. 2010.

1328-126 Save the Children Federation, Westport, CT, $36,000. For Save the Children Federation, Vietnam: Smart Start for Students Project. 2010.

1328-127 Save the Children Federation, Westport, CT, $30,000. For Save the Children, Guatemala: Financial Literacy for Adolescents in Quiche Project. 2010.

1328-128 Small Enterprise Education and Promotion Network, Washington, DC, $1,150,000. For Advancing Microenterprise Industry's Effectiveness and Practitioner Leadership Initiative. 2010.

1328-129 Small Enterprise Education and Promotion Network, Washington, DC, $10,000. For Small Enterprise Education and Promotion Network, LATAM Regional: Network Annual Conference Program (Foromic). 2010.

1328-130 United Way International, Alexandria, VA, $551,000. For Pratham Mumbai Education Initiative, India: Citi-Pratham Education Project. 2010.

1328-131 United Way International, Alexandria, VA, $500,000. For Indian School of Business: Center for Analytical Finance. 2010.

1328-132 United Way International, Alexandria, VA, $360,000. For National YWCA of Korea: Think Money Program in South Korea. 2010.

1328-133 United Way International, Alexandria, VA, $300,000. For Tsinghua University Center for Financial Research, China: The Tsinghua-Citi Financial Education Hub Project. 2010.

1328-134 United Way International, Alexandria, VA, $281,000. For Learning Society, Hong Kong: Making Sense of Money Program. 2010.

1328-135 United Way International, Alexandria, VA, $280,000. For National Institute of Education, Singapore: Citi-NIE Financial Literacy Hub for Teachers Program. 2010.

1328-136 United Way International, Alexandria, VA, $269,000. For Learning Society Ltd, Hong Kong: Citi Youth Investment Education Program. 2010.

1328-137 United Way International, Alexandria, VA, $264,000. For Institute of Finance, Korea: Citi Finance Sector Talent Development Program. 2010.

1328-138 United Way International, Alexandria, VA, $261,000. For Aflatoun Child Savings International, Netherlands: Child Finance Convening. 2010.

1328-139 United Way International, Alexandria, VA, $260,000. For Korea Small Business Institute: Citi-KOSBI Women's Entrepreneurship Program. 2010.

1328-140 United Way International, Alexandria, VA, $250,000. For International Network for Bamboo and Rattan, China: Sichuan Sustainable Bamboo Enterprise Program. 2010.

1328-141 United Way International, Alexandria, VA, $230,000. For YMCA, Singapore: Youth For Causes Program. 2010.

1328-142 United Way International, Alexandria, VA, $225,000. For Partners in Change, India: Citi Microentrepreneurship Awards Program. 2010.

1328-143 United Way International, Alexandria, VA, $210,000. For Mission Australia: Financial Education, Counseling and Community Hub - Phase II. 2010.

1328-144 United Way International, Alexandria, VA, $185,000. For China Banking Association, China: Citi Microentrepreneurship Awards Program. 2010.

1328-145 United Way International, Alexandria, VA, $185,000. For The Federation for Associations Connected to the International Humana People to People Movement, China: The Wanzhou Rural Small Enterprise Development Program. 2010.

1328-146 United Way International, Alexandria, VA, $172,000. For National YWCA of Korea: Citi-YWCA Success Program. 2010.

1328-147 United Way International, Alexandria, VA, $171,000. For Peking University Center for Economic Research, China: Citi-CCER SME Access to Finance Research Project. 2010.

1328-148 United Way International, Alexandria, VA, $170,000. For National Institute on Consumer Education, Japan: Citi Success Fund. 2010.

1328-149 United Way International, Alexandria, VA, $162,000. For FEBRABAN - Brazilian Banks Federation, LATAM Regional: Financial Education Congress Program. 2010.

1328-150 United Way International, Alexandria, VA, $159,000. For Vision of The Nation Foundation, Indonesia: Your Money TV Program. 2010.

1328-151 United Way International, Alexandria, VA, $154,000. For HOPE Worldwide, Indonesia: Citi Success Fund Program. 2010.

1328-152 United Way International, Alexandria, VA, $150,000. For Citi-Tsao Foundation, Singapore: Financial Education Program. 2010.

1328-153 United Way International, Alexandria, VA, $150,000. For Foundation for Development Cooperation LTD, Asia Pacific Regional: Asia Microfinance Forum. 2010.

1328-154 United Way International, Alexandria, VA, $150,000. For Fudan University School of Management, China: Citi-Fudan SME (small and medium enterprise) Senior Management Training Program. 2010.

1328-155 United Way International, Alexandria, VA, $150,000. For UK Career Academy Foundation: Career Academies Program. 2010.

1328-156 United Way International, Alexandria, VA, $143,000. For Education and Research Association for Consumers, Malaysia: Stretching Your Ringgit. 2010.

1328-157 United Way International, Alexandria, VA, $116,000. For Learning Society, Hong Kong: Smart Kid Financial Education Experiential Program. 2010.

1328-158 United Way International, Alexandria, VA, $115,000. For Partner Toward Self-Reliance Foundation, Indonesia: The Adventures of Agent Penny Program. 2010.

1328-159 United Way International, Alexandria, VA, $105,000. For Association of Center for Women's Resources Development, Indonesia: Financial Education Program. 2010.

1328-160 United Way International, Alexandria, VA, $100,000. For China Friendship Foundation for Peace and Development, China: Sustainable Rural Enterprise TOT Program. 2010.

1328-161 United Way International, Alexandria, VA, $100,000. For Financial Literacy and Education Association, Taiwan: Young Adult Financial Literacy Program. 2010.

1328-162 United Way International, Alexandria, VA, $100,000. For Foundation for the Support of Women's Work, Turkey: Strategic Planning for Capacity Building of Women's Cooperatives Program. 2010.

1328-163 United Way International, Alexandria, VA, $100,000. For Learning Society, Singapore: The Adventures of Agent Penny and Will Power (Book 4) Program. 2010.

1328-164 United Way International, Alexandria, VA, $100,000. For Microcredit Joyful Union, Korea (South): Microfinance Strengthening Program. 2010.

1328-165 United Way International, Alexandria, VA, $100,000. For Russian Microfinance Center, Russia: Support of Small Business Through Assistance to the Unemployed Program. 2010.

1328-166 United Way International, Alexandria, VA, $100,000. For St. Petersburg State University Graduate School of Management, Russia: Project Management for Small and Growing Businesses Program. 2010.

1328-167 United Way International, Alexandria, VA, $100,000. For Taipei Chi Sing Eco-conservation Foundation, Taiwan: Citi Eco-Tourism Capacity Building Program. 2010.

1328-168 United Way International, Alexandria, VA, $100,000. For Teach First, United Kingdom: The Citi English Fellows Program. 2010.

1328-169 United Way International, Alexandria, VA, $100,000. For The Educational Volunteers Foundation, Turkey: Financial Education Project. 2010.

1328-170 United Way International, Alexandria, VA, $100,000. For The Graduate Institute of Network Learning Technology at National Central University, Taiwan: Citi-NCU Online Financial Education Program. 2010.

1328-171 United Way International, Alexandria, VA, $100,000. For Vsemirny Fond Prirody (WWF), Russia: Small Business for Altai Biodiversity Program. 2010.

1328-172 United Way International, Alexandria, VA, $99,000. For Turkish Foundation for Waste Reduction, Turkey: Turkish Grameen Microcredit Program. 2010.

1328-173 United Way International, Alexandria, VA, $95,000. For Arrastao Human Promotion Movement, Brazil: Financial Education Program. 2010.

1328-174 United Way International, Alexandria, VA, $95,000. For China Foundation for Poverty Alleviation, China: CFPA Microfinance Strengthening Program. 2010.

1328-175 United Way International, Alexandria, VA, $95,000. For Civil Association for the Promotion of Popular Development, Venezuela: Finance for Life Educational Program. 2010.

1328-176 United Way International, Alexandria, VA, $95,000. For Youth Off The Streets, Australia: $mart Money (Phase II) Program. 2010.

1328-177 United Way International, Alexandria, VA, $94,000. For Shanghai Technology Entrepreneurship Foundation for Graduates, China: Citi Financial IT Competition. 2010.

1328-178 United Way International, Alexandria, VA, $92,000. For National Agency for Microbusiness Development, Brazil: ANDE - Financial Education Program. 2010.

1328-179 United Way International, Alexandria, VA, $87,000. For Compassion for Migrant Children Limited, China: Life-Vocational Skills Training, Beijing Heiqiao Community Center Program. 2010.

1328-180 United Way International, Alexandria, VA, $85,000. For Microfinance Council of the Philippines, Philippines: Citi Microentrepreneurship Awards Program. 2010.

1328-181 United Way International, Alexandria, VA, $85,000. For Taipei Women's Rescue Foundation, Taiwan: Dollars and $ense Program. 2010.

1328-182 United Way International, Alexandria, VA, $80,000. For Entrepreneurial Training Center Mario Santo Domingo Foundation Accion International, Colombia: Training and Strengthening Small Business Program. 2010.

1328-183 United Way International, Alexandria, VA, $80,000. For Faculty of Economic University of Indonesia, Indonesia: Citi Microentrepreneurship Awards Program. 2010.

1328-184 United Way International, Alexandria, VA, $80,000. For Hong Kong University of Science and Technology School of Business and Management, Hong Kong: International Case Competition 2010 Program. 2010.

1328-185 United Way International, Alexandria, VA, $80,000. For National Association of Citizens Advice Bureaux, United Kingdom: Train the Financial Capability Trainers Project. 2010.

1328-186 United Way International, Alexandria, VA, $80,000. For Teacher Chang Foundation, Taiwan: Debt Counceling and Family Financial Management Program. 2010.

1328-187 United Way International, Alexandria, VA, $80,000. For YouthNet, UK: Budget Challenge and Finance Outreach Program. 2010.

1328-188 United Way International, Alexandria, VA, $79,000. For Paulista Professionalization Institute, Brazil: Pre-employment Program. 2010.

1328-189 United Way International, Alexandria, VA, $75,000. For Association of Microfinance Institutions, Uganda: Citi Microentrepreneurship Awards Program. 2010.

1328-190 United Way International, Alexandria, VA, $75,000. For Goethe University Frankfurt, Germany: Citi Frankfurt Scholars in Economics and Finance Program. 2010.

1328-191 United Way International, Alexandria, VA, $75,000. For Philippine Business for Social Progress, Philippines: Citi Business in Development Challenge Philippines Program. 2010.

1328-192 United Way International, Alexandria, VA, $75,000. For University of New South Wales Foundation, Australia: ASPIRE Project. 2010.

1328-193 United Way International, Alexandria, VA, $70,000. For Bocconi University, Italy: Bocconi Outstanding Students Program. 2010.

1328-194 United Way International, Alexandria, VA, $70,000. For Microfinance and Development Center, Vietnam: Citi Microentrepreneurship Awards Program. 2010.

1328-195 United Way International, Alexandria, VA, $70,000. For Pakistan Poverty Alleviation Fund: Rebuilding Lives- Citi-PPAF Join Hands for a Microfinance Rehabilitation Program for Flood Victims. 2010.

1328-196 United Way International, Alexandria, VA, $70,000. For Russian Microfinance Center, Russia: Citi Microentrepreneurship Awards Program. 2010.

1328-197 United Way International, Alexandria, VA, $70,000. For United Way, Russia: Future Starts Today Program. 2010.

1328-198 United Way International, Alexandria, VA, $65,000. For Learning Society Singapore, Malaysia: Citi Stock Challenge Program. 2010.

1328-199 United Way International, Alexandria, VA, $65,000. For Pakistan Poverty Alleviation Fund, Pakistan: Citi-PPAF Microentrepreneurship Awards Program. 2010.

1328-200 United Way International, Alexandria, VA, $65,000. For PlaNet Finance, Morocco: Citi Microentrepreneurship Awards Program. 2010.

1328-201 United Way International, Alexandria, VA, $65,000. To create Art, United Kingdom: A Wealth of Stages Project. 2010.

1328-202 United Way International, Alexandria, VA, $60,000. For Access Development Services, India: Microfinance India Summit Initiative. 2010.

1328-203 United Way International, Alexandria, VA, $60,000. For CommonWealth Magazine Education Foundation, Taiwan: Future Leaders Development Program. 2010.

1328-204 United Way International, Alexandria, VA, $60,000. For Institute of Management Faculty of Economics University, Indonesia: Financial Education for the Poor Program. 2010.

1328-205 United Way International, Alexandria, VA, $60,000. For IntoUni, United Kingdom: IntoUniversity Secondary FOCUS and Mentoring Program. 2010.

1328-206 United Way International, Alexandria, VA, $60,000. For United Way, Colombia: Finances for Change (Phase VII) Program. 2010.

1328-207 United Way International, Alexandria, VA, $55,000. For City Year, South Africa: School and Community Based Environmental and Educational Service Program. 2010.

1328-208 United Way International, Alexandria, VA, $55,000. For Foundation for the Support of Women's Work, Turkey: Citi Microentrepreneurship Awards Program. 2010.

1328-209 United Way International, Alexandria, VA, $55,000. For Imperial College, EMEA Regional: The Pimlico Connection Program. 2010.

1328-210 United Way International, Alexandria, VA, $55,000. For Jordan River Foundation, Jordan: Citi Microentrepreneurship Awards Program. 2010.

1328-211 United Way International, Alexandria, VA, $55,000. For Young Men's Christian Association of Lebanon: Citi Microentrepreneurship Awards Program. 2010.

1328-212 United Way International, Alexandria, VA, $50,000. For Agency For Inner City Renewal, Jamaica: Building Enterprises through Financial Education Program. 2010.

1328-213 United Way International, Alexandria, VA, $50,000. For Akshara Foundation, India: School Library Program. 2010.

1328-214 United Way International, Alexandria, VA, $50,000. For Association of Alumni and Supporters of the European Business School, Germany: Citi Training Program. 2010.

1328-215 United Way International, Alexandria, VA, $50,000. For Bright Kid Foundation, South Africa: The Zenzele Edutainer Program. 2010.

1328-216 United Way International, Alexandria, VA, $50,000. For Centre for the Study of Financial Innovation, United Kingdom: Microfinance Banana Skins Project. 2010.

1328-217 United Way International, Alexandria, VA, $50,000. For Credit and Development Forum,

Bangladesh: Citi Microentrepreneurship Awards Program. 2010.

1328-218 United Way International, Alexandria, VA, $50,000. For CSR Europe - The Business Network for Corporate Social Responsibility, Western Europe Regional: Financial Capability for Europe's Youth and Retirees Program. 2010.

1328-219 United Way International, Alexandria, VA, $50,000. For FINEX Research and Development Foundation, Philippines: 8th Citi Junior Bankers Congress Program. 2010.

1328-220 United Way International, Alexandria, VA, $50,000. For Frankfurt School of Finance and Management, Germany: New Horizons Program. 2010.

1328-221 United Way International, Alexandria, VA, $50,000. For Global Development of Peaceful Environments, Kenya: Sustainable Cotton Growing Program. 2010.

1328-222 United Way International, Alexandria, VA, $50,000. For Growing Businesses Foundation, Nigeria: Citi Microentrepreneurship Awards Program. 2010.

1328-223 United Way International, Alexandria, VA, $50,000. For Hellenic Children's Museum, Greece: Knowledge with Value Educational Program. 2010.

1328-224 United Way International, Alexandria, VA, $50,000. For Maths Centre, South Africa: Improving Learner Performance in Mathematics and Science Program. 2010.

1328-225 United Way International, Alexandria, VA, $50,000. For Organisation Supporting Youth in Career Guidance, Germany: Finding a Vocation: recognizing and using potential. 2010.

1328-226 United Way International, Alexandria, VA, $50,000. For ProDesarrollo, Finanzas y Microempresa, Mexico: Banamex Microentrepreneurship Awards Program. 2010.

1328-227 United Way International, Alexandria, VA, $50,000. For Prosperity, NGO, Czech Republic: Start Your Own Business Project. 2010.

1328-228 United Way International, Alexandria, VA, $50,000. For Provita, Venezuela: My Business Sustainable Project. 2010.

1328-229 United Way International, Alexandria, VA, $50,000. For The Private Education Development Network, Uganda: Aflatoun, Child Social and Financial Education Program. 2010.

1328-230 United Way International, Alexandria, VA, $50,000. For Tung Wah Group of Hospitals, Hong Kong: Microcredit Feasibility Study Initiative. 2010.

1328-231 United Way International, Alexandria, VA, $48,000. For Marang Financial Services, South Africa: Citi Microentrepreneurship Awards Program. 2010.

1328-232 United Way International, Alexandria, VA, $46,000. For Kenan Foundation, Thailand: Citi Triple Bottom Line Small Business Project. 2010.

1328-233 United Way International, Alexandria, VA, $45,000. For Bahrain Chamber of Commerce and Industry, Bahrain: BCCI Incubation Initiative. 2010.

1328-234 United Way International, Alexandria, VA, $45,000. For Children of Slovakia Foundation, Slovakia: Next Way with the BUS (BUS - Building Understanding and Skills for Independent Life II) Program. 2010.

1328-235 United Way International, Alexandria, VA, $45,000. For Kenan Foundation, Thailand: Phase III Citi At-Risk Women Financial Literacy Program. 2010.

1328-236 United Way International, Alexandria, VA, $45,000. For Kuwait University College of Business Administration, Kuwait: Financial Market Trading Program. 2010.

1328-237 United Way International, Alexandria, VA, $45,000. For National Council on Social Welfare, Thailand: Citi Scholarship and Education and Development Camp Program. 2010.

1328-238 United Way International, Alexandria, VA, $45,000. For Pathways to Education Toronto Programs. 2010.

1328-239 United Way International, Alexandria, VA, $45,000. For PlaNet Finance, South Africa: Client Financial Education Services for Microfinance Institutions in South Africa Program. 2010.

1328-240 United Way International, Alexandria, VA, $44,000. For PlaNet Finance, South Africa: Rural Micro Energy Alliance Program. 2010.

1328-241 United Way International, Alexandria, VA, $43,000. For Grupo ACP, Peru: Mujeres Emprendedoras Program. 2010.

1328-242 United Way International, Alexandria, VA, $40,000. For African and Caribbean Diversity, United Kingdom: Mentoring and Enrichment Program. 2010.

1328-243 United Way International, Alexandria, VA, $40,000. For Asociacion ADRI, Costa Rica: Citi Microentrepreneurship Awards Program. 2010.

1328-244 United Way International, Alexandria, VA, $40,000. For Brussels Capital Region's Debt Mediation Service Support Center, Belgium: Check Your Budget Project. 2010.

1328-245 United Way International, Alexandria, VA, $40,000. For Children's Aid Foundation and Pape Adolescent Resource Centre Financial Literacy and Pre-Employment Program in Canada. 2010.

1328-246 United Way International, Alexandria, VA, $40,000. For Egyptian Association of Comprehensive Development, Egypt: Economic Empowerment of Women Project. 2010.

1328-247 United Way International, Alexandria, VA, $40,000. For IESE, EMEA Regional: Citi Scholarships Program. 2010.

1328-248 United Way International, Alexandria, VA, $40,000. For Microfinance Development Foundation, Argentina: Citi Microentrepreneurship Awards Program. 2010.

1328-249 United Way International, Alexandria, VA, $40,000. For National Competitiveness Center, Panama: PreMic Program. 2010.

1328-250 United Way International, Alexandria, VA, $40,000. For NFTE (Network for Teaching Entrepreneurship) Netherlands: NFTE Aflatoun Young World Entrepreneurs Program. 2010.

1328-251 United Way International, Alexandria, VA, $40,000. For Starehe Girls Centre, Kenya: Education for Young Women Program. 2010.

1328-252 United Way International, Alexandria, VA, $40,000. For Tower Hamlets Education Business Partnership, United Kingdom: Passport to Employability Program. 2010.

1328-253 United Way International, Alexandria, VA, $37,000. For Tel Aviv University, Israel: A Different Economy Financial Education Program. 2010.

1328-254 United Way International, Alexandria, VA, $36,000. For Asociacion Vision Solidaria, Peru: Children and Finance Program. 2010.

1328-255 United Way International, Alexandria, VA, $35,000. For Center in Support of Small Enterprises, Brazil: CEAPE-MA Financial Education Program. 2010.

1328-256 United Way International, Alexandria, VA, $35,000. For Knowledge Channel Foundation, Philippines: Citi Learning Series 4: Entrepreneurship@KnowledgeChannel Project. 2010.

1328-257 United Way International, Alexandria, VA, $35,000. For Network for Training Entrepreneurship, Belgium: Impact Analysis and Entrepreneurship Education Program. 2010.

1328-258 United Way International, Alexandria, VA, $35,000. For Pakistan Microfinance Network, Pakistan: Consumer Protection Initiative. 2010.

1328-259 United Way International, Alexandria, VA, $35,000. For Salvadoran Foundation for Economic and Social Development, El Salvador: Agricultural Modernization Through Indoors Production Program. 2010.

1328-260 United Way International, Alexandria, VA, $35,000. For Social Enterprise Development Centre at Lahore University, Pakistan: Citi-LUMS Youth Initiative. 2010.

1328-261 United Way International, Alexandria, VA, $34,000. For The University of Hong Kong, Hong Kong: Citibank University Banking Course 2010-2011 Program. 2010.

1328-262 United Way International, Alexandria, VA, $33,000. For Ashoka Brazil, Brazil: MFI Acreditar Scale Up Investment Program. 2010.

1328-263 United Way International, Alexandria, VA, $33,000. For China Friendship Foundation for Peace and Development: Central China English Teachers Training Program. 2010.

1328-264 United Way International, Alexandria, VA, $32,000. For Pescar Foundation, Argentina: Pescar Citi Youth Training Center Program. 2010.

1328-265 United Way International, Alexandria, VA, $30,000. For Association for the Right to Economic Initiative, France: Financial Education Program. 2010.

1328-266 United Way International, Alexandria, VA, $30,000. For Books Make You Shine Foundation, Inc., Philippines: The Pasig Citi Reading Program. 2010.

1328-267 United Way International, Alexandria, VA, $30,000. For Budapest University of Economic Sciences Foundation, Hungary: Citi Corvinus University Program. 2010.

1328-268 United Way International, Alexandria, VA, $30,000. For Centre for the Study of Financial Innovation, United Kingdom: Development Fellowship Program. 2010.

1328-269 United Way International, Alexandria, VA, $30,000. For Development Research Network, Bangladesh: Third Citi Financial IT Case Competition Initiative. 2010.

1328-270 United Way International, Alexandria, VA, $30,000. For Grameen Shikkha, Bangladesh: Citi Scholarships for Young Women Program. 2010.

1328-271 United Way International, Alexandria, VA, $30,000. For HOPE Worldwide Nigeria: Rural Micro Enterprise Creation Project. 2010.

1328-272 United Way International, Alexandria, VA, $30,000. For Independent University, Bangladesh: Citi Financial Quiz Competition Initiative. 2010.

1328-273 United Way International, Alexandria, VA, $30,000. For Leadership, Effectiveness, Accountability and Professionalism Africa, Nigeria: Business Leadership Program. 2010.

1328-274 United Way International, Alexandria, VA, $30,000. For Pakistan Microfinance Network: PMN Flood Initiative. 2010.

1328-275 United Way International, Alexandria, VA, $30,000. For Stockholm City Mission, Sweden: Dolly Program. 2010.

1328-276 United Way International, Alexandria, VA, $30,000. For The Association for the Development and Enhancement of Women, Egypt: Know to Grow Program. 2010.

1328-277 United Way International, Alexandria, VA, $30,000. For The Dariu Foundation, Vietnam: Water and Sanitation Improvement Project. 2010.

1328-278 United Way International, Alexandria, VA, $30,000. For Tym Fund Women's Union, Vietnam: Microinsurance Education for the Poor Program. 2010.

1328-279 United Way International, Alexandria, VA, $29,000. For Private Sector for Educational Assistance, Panama: Social Integration and Employability Program. 2010.

1328-280 United Way International, Alexandria, VA, $27,000. For University of Dubai, UAE: Investments in College Degree Program. 2010.

1328-281 United Way International, Alexandria, VA, $26,000. For Fate Foundation, Nigeria: Aspiring Entrepreneurs Program. 2010.

1328-282 United Way International, Alexandria, VA, $25,000. For BRAC, Tanzania: Micro Finance Program. 2010.

1328-283 United Way International, Alexandria, VA, $25,000. For FINEX Research and Development Foundation, Inc., Philippines: FINEX-CITI Rafael B. Buenaventura Outstanding Finance Educator (OFE) Awards Initiative. 2010.

1328-284 United Way International, Alexandria, VA, $25,000. For Fondo Unido de Guatemala, Guatemala: Citi Education Fund For Academic Excellence Program. 2010.

1328-285 United Way International, Alexandria, VA, $25,000. For Fundacion ONCE for Cooperation and Social Inclusion of people with Disabilities, Spain: Learning Personal Finances Project. 2010.

1328-286 United Way International, Alexandria, VA, $25,000. For Gawad Kalinga Community Development Foundation Inc., Philippines: Citi-GK Village Enterprise Initiative. 2010.

1328-287 United Way International, Alexandria, VA, $25,000. For Lebanese American University, Lebanon: Citigroup Scholarship Grants 2010 Program. 2010.

1328-288 United Way International, Alexandria, VA, $25,000. For Salvation Army, Bahamas: After-school Program. 2010.

1328-289 United Way International, Alexandria, VA, $25,000. For Superior School of Economy and Business, El Salvador: Citi Microentrepreneurship Awards Program. 2010.

1328-290 United Way International, Alexandria, VA, $25,000. For Thardeep Rural Development Programme (TRDP), Pakistan: Microfinance based Village Tourism in Tharparkar Program. 2010.

1328-291 United Way International, Alexandria, VA, $25,000. For Tomillo Foundation, Spain: The Adventures of Agent Penny Program. 2010.

1328-292 United Way International, Alexandria, VA, $25,000. For Training and Resources in Early Education, South Africa: An Integrated Early Childhood Development Program. 2010.

1328-293 United Way International, Alexandria, VA, $25,000. For Via Foundation, Czech Republic: Social Enterprise Accelerator Program. 2010.

1328-294 United Way International, Alexandria, VA, $24,000. For Bayan Academy for Social Entrepreneurship and Human Resource Development, Philippines: Citi-Bayan Eskwela Program. 2010.

1328-295 United Way International, Alexandria, VA, $24,000. For Ewha Woman's University, Korea: Citi Ewha Global Finance Academy Program. 2010.

1328-296 United Way International, Alexandria, VA, $24,000. For Student Sponsorship Programme, South Africa: Providing Education to South Africans Program. 2010.

1328-297 United Way International, Alexandria, VA, $23,000. For University of Dubai, UAE: Investments in Entrepreneurship Initiative. 2010.

1328-298 United Way International, Alexandria, VA, $22,000. For Association for the Promotion of Financial Literacy, Japan: National Economics Quiz Tournament Program. 2010.

1328-299 United Way International, Alexandria, VA, $22,000. For Superatec A.C., Venezuela: Finance and Banking for Underprivileged Youth Empowerment Program. 2010.

1328-300 United Way International, Alexandria, VA, $22,000. For Association Nationale Femme et Developpement Rural, Algeria: Creation of Micro-Enterprises for Farmed Rabbit Project. 2010.

1328-301 United Way International, Alexandria, VA, $20,000. For Council of American Development Foundation, Dominican Republic: Citi Microentrepreneurship Awards Program. 2010.

1328-302 United Way International, Alexandria, VA, $20,000. For Dominican Development Foundation, Dominican Republic: Young Entrepreneurs as Economic Change Agents Initiative. 2010.

1328-303 United Way International, Alexandria, VA, $20,000. For Entrepreneurs for Education, Guatemala: Innovation, Creativity, and Entrepreneurship in Our Schools Project. 2010.

1328-304 United Way International, Alexandria, VA, $20,000. For Federation of Thrift and Credit Co-operative Societies LTD, Sri Lanka: Citi-SANASA Young Adults Financial Education Program. 2010.

1328-305 United Way International, Alexandria, VA, $20,000. For King Abdullah Fund for Development, Jordan: Scholarship Program. 2010.

1328-306 United Way International, Alexandria, VA, $20,000. For Network for Teaching Entrepreneurship, Ireland: Entrepreneurship Program. 2010.

1328-307 United Way International, Alexandria, VA, $20,000. For Network Microfinance Institutions of Guatemala, Guatemala: Citi Microentrepreneurship Awards Program. 2010.

1328-308 United Way International, Alexandria, VA, $20,000. For Pathways to Education, Canada: Halifax Program. 2010.

1328-309 United Way International, Alexandria, VA, $20,000. For Pathways to Education, Canada: Winnipeg Program. 2010.

1328-310 United Way International, Alexandria, VA, $20,000. For Plan International, Thailand: Citi Youth School Banks Program. 2010.

1328-311 United Way International, Alexandria, VA, $20,000. For The Hunar Foundation, Pakistan: Expansion of DMS Technical Institute Project. 2010.

1328-312 United Way International, Alexandria, VA, $20,000. For Youth Development Resources, Brunei: Youth Skills Development Program. 2010.

1328-313 United Way International, Alexandria, VA, $20,000. For Youth Initiatives Kenya, Kenya: Youth Entrepreneurial Development Program. 2010.

1328-314 United Way International, Alexandria, VA, $19,000. For Marang Enterprise Development Foundation, South Africa: Product, Branch Management and Assessment Training Program. 2010.

1328-315 United Way International, Alexandria, VA, $18,000. For Fundacion Impulsar, Argentina: Young Entrepreneurs Program. 2010.

1328-316 United Way International, Alexandria, VA, $18,000. For Kids in Need of Direction, Trinidad and Tobago: Sponsor a Child to Learn Program. 2010.

1328-317 United Way International, Alexandria, VA, $18,000. For MIR Foundation (House of Peace), Dominican Republic: MIR Vocational School Program. 2010.

1328-318 United Way International, Alexandria, VA, $18,000. For Youth Business Trinidad and Tobago, Trinidad and Tobago: Mentoring Model For Young Entrepreneurs Project. 2010.

1328-319 United Way International, Alexandria, VA, $17,000. For National Foundation for Honduras Development (FUNADEH), Honduras: Acquiring Basic Computer Skills Program. 2010.

1328-320 United Way International, Alexandria, VA, $15,000. For Al-Aman Fund for the Future of Orphans, Jordan: Scholarship Program. 2010.

1328-321 United Way International, Alexandria, VA, $15,000. For Asociacion Amigos del Aprendizaje (ADA), Costa Rica: Financial Literacy Contest for Children. 2010.

1328-322 United Way International, Alexandria, VA, $15,000. For Economics Education and Research Consortium (EERC), Inc., Ukraine: Master's Degree in Economics Scholarship Program. 2010.

1328-323 United Way International, Alexandria, VA, $15,000. For Esquel Foundation, Ecuador: Taking Care of our Pachamama Program. 2010.

1328-324 United Way International, Alexandria, VA, $15,000. For Fundacion Integral Campesina, Costa Rica: Community Credit Enterprise Program. 2010.

1328-325 United Way International, Alexandria, VA, $15,000. For Private Sector for Educational Assistance, Panama: Entrepreneurship Training for Tourism Development Program. 2010.

1328-326 United Way International, Alexandria, VA, $15,000. For Sarhad Rural Support Programme, Pakistan: School-to-Career Connections Project. 2010.

1328-327 United Way International, Alexandria, VA, $15,000. For The Jordanian Hashemite Fund for Human Development, Jordan: University Scholarship Program. 2010.

1328-328 United Way International, Alexandria, VA, $15,000. For Tunisian Scouts Organization, Tunisia: The Financial Capacities of ACCESS Students. 2010.

1328-329 United Way International, Alexandria, VA, $15,000. For University of Cape Town, South Africa: Academic Development Program (ADP) and Student Scholarship Program. 2010.

1328-330 United Way International, Alexandria, VA, $14,000. For World Literature Center, Bangladesh: Citi Light of the Future Program. 2010.

1328-331 United Way International, Alexandria, VA, $13,000. For Shiur Acher, Israel: Financial Education for School Children Program. 2010.

1328-332 United Way International, Alexandria, VA, $13,000. For University of KwaZulu-Natal Foundation, South Africa: Enriched Management Studies Program. 2010.

1328-333 United Way International, Alexandria, VA, $12,000. For University of Witwatersrand, South Africa: Citigroup Bursaries Program. 2010.

1328-334 United Way International, Alexandria, VA, $11,000. For Rural Financial Network, Ecuador: The RFR Promoting Research and Development of Financial Innovations Project. 2010.

1328-335 United Way International, Alexandria, VA, $10,000. For American University, Bulgaria: Citi Distinguished Scholarship Program. 2010.

1328-336 United Way International, Alexandria, VA, $10,000. For Asociatia Ovidiu Rom, Romania: Citiskool Kindergarten Program. 2010.

1328-337 United Way International, Alexandria, VA, $10,000. For Bernard Eding Fund, Cameroon: Youth Aid Fund for the Creation of Plantations Project. 2010.

1328-338 United Way International, Alexandria, VA, $10,000. For Centre for Adoption and Foster Care, Czech Republic: Money for Living Project. 2010.

1328-339 United Way International, Alexandria, VA, $10,000. For Children With Wings, Uruguay: Secondary Support Looking into Future Program. 2010.

1328-340 United Way International, Alexandria, VA, $10,000. For Exit Foundation, Spain: Financial Education Program. 2010.

1328-341 United Way International, Alexandria, VA, $10,000. For Instituto De Promocion Economico Social Del Uruguay, Uruguay: Women's Microenterprises Program. 2010.

1328-342 United Way International, Alexandria, VA, $10,000. For Maata-N-Tudu Association (MTA), Ghana: the Maata-N-Tudu Microfinance Enhancement Program (MEP). 2010.

1328-343 United Way International, Alexandria, VA, $10,000. For Manzil Centre for Challenged Individuals, UAE: People Receiving Independence and Dignity through Employment (PRIDE) Program. 2010.

1328-344 United Way International, Alexandria, VA, $10,000. For National Trade and Banking High School Trusteeship Association, Bulgaria: Virtual Banks: Increasing Employment Options and Competitiveness Project. 2010.

1328-345 United Way International, Alexandria, VA, $10,000. For Par Foundation, Argentina: Micro-Loans for People With Disabilities Program. 2010.

1328-346 United Way International, Alexandria, VA, $10,000. For Paraguayan Foundation, Paraguay: Women in Development Program. 2010.

1328-347 United Way International, Alexandria, VA, $10,000. For Private Sector Council for Educational Assistance, Panama: Financial Education for Children and Teachers Program: Simon Bolivar Primary School. 2010.

1328-348 United Way International, Alexandria, VA, $10,000. For Superior School of Economy and Business, El Salvador: Effective Management for Microenterprises Program. 2010.

1328-349 United Way International, Alexandria, VA, $10,000. For United Way Romania: To be a Teenage Mother Program. 2010.

1328-350 United Way International, Alexandria, VA, $10,000. For University of the Free State, South Africa: Disadvantaged Students Bursary Initiative. 2010.

1328-351 University of Edinburgh USA Development Trust, New York, NY, $16,000. For The University of Edinburgh, EMEA Regional: Access Bursary Program. 2010.

1328-352 Womens World Banking, New York, NY, $200,000. For Facilitating MFI (Microfinance Institution) Access to Capital Markets Project. 2010.

1328-353 Womens World Banking, New York, NY, $25,000. For Women's World Banking, LATAM Regional: Promoting Visionary Principled Leadership in the Microfinance Sector (Foromic). 2010.

1328-354 World Resources Institute, Washington, DC, $500,000. For New Ventures Program. 2010.

1328-355 World Wildlife Fund, Washington, DC, $75,000. For Increasing Triple Bottom Line: GFTN-Peru (Global Forest and Trade Network) Program. 2010.

1329
Liz Claiborne & Art Ortenberg Foundation
(formerly The Ortenberg Foundation)
650 5th Ave., 15th Fl.
New York, NY 10019-6108 (212) 333-2536
Contact: James Murtaugh, Prog. Dir.
FAX: (212) 956-3531; E-mail: lcaof@lcaof.org;
URL: http://www.lcaof.org/intro.html

Established in 1984 in NY.
Donors: Arthur Ortenberg; Elisabeth Claiborne Ortenberg‡.
Grantmaker type: Independent foundation.
Financial data (yr. ended 12/31/10): Assets, $42,397,722 (M); gifts received, $1,250,000; expenditures, $4,558,795; qualifying distributions, $4,436,701; giving activities include $3,805,578 for 73 grants (high: $650,000; low: $1,000).
Purpose and activities: The board of directors has identified two primary program interests for the foundation: 1) Mitigation of conflict between the land and resource needs of rural communities and conservation of biological diversity; and 2) Implementation of field-based scientific, technical and practical training programs in conservation biology for local people. The foundation typically funds modest, carefully designed field activities—primarily in developing countries and in the northern Rocky Mountains region of the United States—in which local communities have substantial proprietary interest.
Fields of interest: Environment, natural resources; Animals/wildlife, preservation/protection.
International interests: Africa; Central America; South America; Developing countries; Oceania; Asia.
Type of support: Continuing support; Seed money; Matching/challenge support.
Limitations: Applications accepted. Giving primarily in Third World countries in the Tropics and in the Interior West region of the U.S. No grants for general support, or for underwriting of overhead.
Publications: Grants list; Informational brochure (including application guidelines).
Application information: Application information available on foundation web site. Application form not required.
> *Initial approach:* Letter
> *Copies of proposal:* 1
> *Deadline(s):* None

Board meeting date(s): Spring and fall
Final notification: As soon as possible
Directors: William Conway; William deBuys; Robert Dewar; Arthur Ortenberg; Grant Parker; Alison Richard; Dr. David Western.
Number of staff: 3 full-time professional.
EIN: 133200329

1330
Robert Sterling Clark Foundation, Inc.
135 E. 64th St.
New York, NY 10065-7045 (212) 288-8900
Contact: Margaret C. Ayers, C.E.O. and Pres.
FAX: (212) 288-1033; E-mail: rscf@rsclark.org;
URL: http://www.rsclark.org
Grants Database: http://www.rsclark.org/index.php?page=past-grants
Knowledge Center: http://www.rsclark.org/index.php?page=publications
Robert Sterling Clark Foundation's Philanthropy Promise: http://www.ncrp.org/philanthropys-promise/who

Incorporated in 1952 in NY.
Donor: Robert Sterling Clark‡.
Grantmaker type: Independent foundation.
Financial data (yr. ended 10/30/10): Assets, $90,894,758 (M); expenditures, $6,179,675; qualifying distributions, $5,210,522; giving activities include $4,148,600 for 89 grants (high: $150,000; low: $1,000; average: $5,000–$150,000), and $5,370 for 16 employee matching gifts.
Purpose and activities: The foundation supports projects that: 1) promote international cultural engagement and public diplomacy; 2) ensure the effectiveness and accountability of public agencies in New York City and State; and 3) ensure access to comprehensive reproductive health by providing support for litigation and public policy advocacy in New York State and at the federal level.
Fields of interest: Visual arts; Museums; Performing arts; Performing arts, dance; Performing arts, theater; Performing arts, music; Arts; Education; Environment; Reproductive health, family planning; Human services; Family services; Civil liberties, reproductive rights; Urban/community development; Community/economic development; Public policy, research; Government/public administration; Public affairs; Young adults; Children/youth; Aging; Women; Young adults, female; Economically disadvantaged; Homeless.
International interests: Middle East; Latin America; Africa; Global programs.
Type of support: General/operating support; Continuing support; Income development; Management development/capacity building; Program development; Publication; Research; Technical assistance; Employee matching gifts.
Limitations: Applications accepted. Giving primarily in New York State for the Public Institutions Program, giving nationally for reproductive rights; and globally to promote international arts and cultural engagement. No grants to individuals, or for annual campaigns, seed money, emergency funds, deficit financing, capital or endowment funds, general support or scholarships.
Publications: Application guidelines; Annual report (including application guidelines); Grants list; Occasional report; Program policy statement.
Application information: Application form not required.

Initial approach: Proposal (not exceeding 15 pages) and a one-page proposal summary
Copies of proposal: 1
Deadline(s): None
Board meeting date(s): Jan., Apr., July, and Oct.
Final notification: 1 to 6 months
Officers and Directors:* James Allen Smith,* Chair.; Margaret C. Ayers,* C.E.O. and Pres.; Joanna D. Underwood, Secy.; Clara Miller,* Treas.; Paul R. Dolan; Winthrop R. Munyan; John Hoyt Stookey.
Number of staff: 3 full-time professional; 1 full-time support.
EIN: 131957792
Recent grants for international programs:
1330-1 Battery Dance Corporation, New York, NY, $60,000. For hiring of international program coordinator to oversee touring component and development of web-based support materials to enable other companies to plan and execute international exchanges. 2010.
1330-2 Brooklyn Academy of Music, Brooklyn, NY, $60,000. To produce DVD and translation of BAM-sponsored tour of 3 leading dance companies to 9 countries; to translate BAM-curated dance resources into host-country languages; and translate and upload key tour materials to new website. 2010.
1330-3 CEC ArtsLink, New York, NY, $100,000. For arts exchange and services abroad. 2010.
1330-4 Cuban Artists Fund, New York, NY, $10,000. For International Ballet Festival in Cuba. 2010.
1330-5 Independent Curators International, New York, NY, $50,000. To develop online networking platform for international curators; public discussion series with international curators in locations around the U.S.; and training program for independent curators to develop viable exhibition proposals from around the world. 2010.
1330-6 Mid Atlantic Arts Foundation, Baltimore, MD, $200,000. For Global Cultural Connections. 2010.
1330-7 Museum of Arts and Design, New York, NY, $150,000. For Global Africa Project—exhibition, publication and outreach on African art. 2010.
1330-8 National Performance Network, New Orleans, LA, $100,000. For U.S. artists in Latin America and the Caribbean. 2010.
1330-9 New York Foundation for the Arts, Brooklyn, NY, $75,000. For development of full-service fiscal sponsorship website to streamline all aspects of fiscal sponsorship program; marketing of program nationally; and creation of international database of arts opportunities. 2010.
1330-10 New York Live Arts, New York, NY, $75,000. For Suitcase Fund to develop relationships with U.S. and Middle Eastern and African artists and audiences. 2010.
1330-11 New York Theater Workshop, New York, NY, $50,000. For teaching residencies for American artists at theater school on the West Bank; 10-day cultural exchange trip for staff and artists to Israel and West Bank. 2010.
1330-12 Saint Anns Warehouse, Brooklyn, NY, $75,000. For presentation of new productions by Ireland's Druid Theater and the National Theatre of Scotland. 2010.

1331
Cleary Gottlieb Steen & Hamilton LLP Pro Bono Program

1 Liberty Plz.
New York, NY 10006-1404 (212) 225-3136
Contact: Carrie Grimm, Pro Bono Admin.
FAX: (212) 225-3999; E-mail: cgrimm@cgsh.com; Additional tel.: (212) 225-2000; URL: http://www.cgsh.com/about/pro_bono_and_community_service/

Grantmaker type: Corporate giving program.
Purpose and activities: Cleary Gottlieb Steen & Hamilton makes charitable contributions to nonprofit organizations involved with immigration law, affordable housing, family services, and criminal defense.
Fields of interest: Elementary/secondary education; Legal services; Legal services, guardianship; Housing/shelter, homeless; Housing/shelter; Disasters, preparedness/services; Family services, domestic violence; Minorities/immigrants, centers/services; International human rights; Disabilities, people with; Offenders/ex-offenders.
Type of support: General/operating support; Matching/challenge support; Pro bono services - legal.

1332
The Clinton Family Foundation

P.O. Box 937
Chappaqua, NY 10514-0937

Established in 2001 in NY.
Donors: William Jefferson Clinton; Hillary Rodham Clinton.
Grantmaker type: Independent foundation.
Financial data (yr. ended 12/31/10): Assets, $2,682,317 (M); expenditures, $1,411,448; qualifying distributions, $1,404,000; giving activities include $1,404,000 for 65 grants (high: $125,000; low: $1,000).
Purpose and activities: Giving primarily for higher education, health, and social services.
Fields of interest: International democracy & civil society development; Arts; Higher education; Health care; Health organizations, association; Human services; Protestant agencies & churches.
Limitations: Applications not accepted. Giving primarily in AR, NY, and Washington, DC. No grants to individuals.
Application information: Contributes only to pre-selected organizations.
Officers: William Jefferson Clinton, Pres.; Hillary Rodham Clinton, Secy.-Treas.
Director: Chelsea V. Clinton.
EIN: 300048438

1333
Clover Foundation

c/o William Orchard
420 Lexington Ave., Ste. 300
New York, NY 10170-0399

Established in 1986 in NY.
Donors: S.A. Raiser; Francisco Gomez-Franco; Perochena Estate; Ernesto Yamaguchi; Pedro Pasquin; Ralph Coti; Educational Aid Fund; Anatol Financial Assets.
Grantmaker type: Independent foundation.

Financial data (yr. ended 12/31/10): Assets, $97,037,062 (M); gifts received, $59,357; expenditures, $3,458,764; qualifying distributions, $12,566,601; giving activities include $2,859,079 for 8 grants (high: $1,000,000; low: $15,000), and $9,670,000 for 3 loans/program-related investments (high: $6,520,000; low: $1,350,000).
Purpose and activities: Giving primarily for education and human services in the U.S. and Mexico.
Fields of interest: Education; Business school/education; Human services.
International interests: Mexico; Peru.
Type of support: Building/renovation; Program development; Program-related investments/loans.
Limitations: Applications not accepted. Giving primarily in New York, NY, and Mexico City, Mexico.
Application information: Contributes only to pre-selected organizations.
Officers and Directors:* Francisco Gomez-Franco,* Pres.; Begona Laresgoitide Gomez,* V.P.; Alberto Pacheco,* V.P.; Ralph Coti,* Secy.; Federico Riera-Marsa,* Treas.; Pablo Elton; William Kipp.
EIN: 742390003

1334
The Cogitare Foundation

(formerly The Leonard & Charlotte Cooper Foundation)
9 Waccabuc River Ln.
South Salem, NY 10590-1117
FAX: (917) 591-4403;
E-mail: escialo@cogitarefoundation.org; URL: http://cogitarefoundation.org/

Established in 1998 in DE.
Donors: Peter D. Cooper; Elaine Scialo; Joe Scarpinito; S & C Investors, LLC; Weitz & Luxenberg; Sloan Cooper; Mary Cooper.
Grantmaker type: Independent foundation.
Financial data (yr. ended 03/31/11): Assets, $1,945,839 (M); gifts received, $96,902; expenditures, $282,681; qualifying distributions, $232,749; giving activities include $232,749 for grants.
Purpose and activities: Giving primarily for the improvement of people's lives in Africa by funding programs that directly develop African communities, including building houses, providing educational opportunities, improving health care, and any other creative approach to the problems faced by the poor.
Fields of interest: Health care; Higher education; Housing/shelter; Economic development.
International interests: Africa.
Type of support: Continuing support; Building/renovation; Equipment; Internship funds; Scholarship funds; Technical assistance; Consulting services; Grants to individuals.
Limitations: Applications not accepted. Giving primarily in Africa. No support for religious organizations.
Application information: Unsolicited requests for funds not accepted.
Board meeting date(s): Apr. 27, Aug. 21
Officers and Directors:* Randall Cooper,* Chair.; Elaine Scialo,* Pres.; Peter D. Cooper,* V.P.
EIN: 133998983

1335
The Colles-Graves Foundation, Inc.
277 West End Avenue, No. 4C
New York, NY 10023-8714 (212) 686-7544
FAX: (212) 686-8827;
E-mail: info@collesgraves.org; URL: http://
www.collesgraves.org

Grantmaker type: Public charity.
Financial data (yr. ended 12/31/10): Revenue,
$47,781; assets, $176,501 (M); gifts received,
$47,017; expenditures, $53,970; giving activities
include $50,000 for grants.
Purpose and activities: The foundation seeks to
further the advancement of medicine, the natural
sciences, technology and related areas of
educational interest in Ireland. The main beneficiary
of the foundation is the Royal College of Surgeons
in Ireland.
Fields of interest: Science; Health care; Education.
International interests: Ireland.
Limitations: Giving primarily in Ireland.
Officer: Kevin Cahill, Pres.
Trustees: Nid Afdhal, M.D.; David Birnbach, M.D.;
Cathal Kelly; Helen Towers, M.D.
EIN: 237093591

1336
Common Cents New York, Inc.
570 Columbus Ave.
New York, NY 10024-2404 (212) 579-0579
Contact: Teddy Gross, Exec. Dir.
FAX: (212) 579-3488;
E-mail: info@commoncents.org; URL: http://
www.commoncents.org

Established in 1991.
Grantmaker type: Public charity.
Financial data (yr. ended 06/30/10): Revenue,
$1,291,776; assets, $1,080,400 (M); gifts
received, $1,234,052; expenditures, $1,889,755;
giving activities include $441,145 for grants.
Purpose and activities: The organization empowers
young people (K-12) to mobilize resources
(pennies), implement service projects and provides
grants to address community needs, thus creating
a generation of community activists and good
citizens. Each year, approximately one million
students in NYC recycle half a million dollars in
pennies into service projects and grants.
Fields of interest: Education; Environment,
beautification programs; Animal welfare; Health
care; Crime/violence prevention; Food services;
Youth, services; Family services; Homeless, human
services; International affairs; Women;
Economically disadvantaged.
Type of support: Continuing support; Curriculum
development; Emergency funds; General/operating
support; Grants to individuals; Internship funds;
Program development; Publication; Seed money.
Limitations: Applications not accepted. Giving
primarily in CO; FL; the greater metropolitan Albany
and New York, NY, areas; Nashville, TN; and Seattle,
WA.
Publications: Grants list; Informational brochure;
Newsletter.
Application information: Unsolicited requests for
funds not accepted; funding is given only through
participating schools and Student Community Action
Fund (SCAF) councils.
Board meeting date(s): Three times per year
Officers and Directors:* Judith Shapiro,* Chair.;
Erin Shakespeare,* Secy.; Karen Kohler,* Treas.;

Teddy Gross, Exec. Dir.; Susan M. Andersen; Tia
Barancik; Margi Booth; Elizabeth Campbell; Gardner
Dunnan; Joe Goldman; Laird Grant; Nora Gross;
Evelyn Lipper, M.D.; James McGinnis; Jeanne
Mininall; and 4 additional directors.
Number of staff: 15 full-time professional; 1
part-time professional.
EIN: 133613229

1337
The Commonwealth Fund
1 E. 75th St.
New York, NY 10021-2692
Contact: Andrea C. Landes, Dir., Grants Mgmt.
FAX: (212) 606-3500; E-mail: info@cmwf.org; E-mail
for questions from grant applicants:
grants@cmwf.org; URL: http://
www.commonwealthfund.org
Blog: http://www.commonwealthfund.org/
Publications/Blog.aspx
E-Newsletter: http://www.commonwealthfund.org/
Profile/My-Profile.aspx
Facebook: http://www.facebook.com/pages/
The-Commonwealth-Fund/102047517918
Foundation Management and Performance: http://
www.commonwealthfund.org/About-Us/
Foundation-Management-and-Performance.aspx
Grants Database: http://
www.commonwealthfund.org/
Grants-and-Programs/Search-Grants.aspx
Innovations: http://www.commonwealthfund.org/
Innovations.aspx
iTunes: http://phobos.apple.com/WebObjects/
MZStore.woa/wa/viewPodcast?id=284038727
Mobile: http://mobile.commonwealthfund.org/
Multimedia: http://www.commonwealthfund.org/
Multimedia-Center.aspx
Podcasts: http://www.commonwealthfund.org/
podcasts/
RSS Feed: http://feeds.feedburner.com/
TheCommonwealthFund
Twitter: http://twitter.com/commonwealthfnd
YouTube: http://www.youtube.com/
CommonwealthFund

Incorporated in 1918 in NY.
Donors: Mrs. Stephen V. Harkness†; Edward S.
Harkness†; Mrs. Edward S. Harkness†.
Grantmaker type: Independent foundation.
Financial data (yr. ended 06/30/10): Assets,
$604,222,668 (M); expenditures, $48,860,260;
qualifying distributions, $32,509,627; giving
activities include $16,060,432 for 268 grants (high:
$650,000; low: $903); $1,951,838 for grants to
individuals; $467,367 for 178 employee matching
gifts, and $12,559,288 for foundation-administered
programs.
Purpose and activities: The mission of the fund is
to promote a high performing healthcare system that
achieves better access, improved quality, and
greater efficiency, particularly for society's most
vulnerable, including low-income people, the
uninsured, minority Americans, young children, and
elderly adults. The fund carries out this mandate by
supporting independent research on health care
issues and making grants to improve healthcare
practice and policy.
Fields of interest: Health care, financing; Health
care; Minorities; Disabilities, people with; Aging;
Adults.
International interests: Australia; Canada; New
Zealand; United Kingdom.

Type of support: Program development;
Fellowships; Research; Program evaluation;
Employee matching gifts.
Limitations: Applications accepted. Giving on a
national basis. No support for religious
organizations for religious purposes, or basic
biomedical research. No grants to individuals
(except through the Commonwealth Fund's
fellowship programs), or for scholarships, general
planning or ongoing activities, existing deficits,
endowment or capital costs, construction,
renovation, equipment, conferences, symposia,
major media projects, or documentaries (unless
they are an out growth of one of the fund's
programs).
Publications: Annual report; Annual report (including
application guidelines); Financial statement; Grants
list; Informational brochure; Newsletter; Occasional
report; Program policy statement.
Application information: The fund strongly prefers
grant applicants submit letters of inquiry using the
online application form, however, letters submitted
via regular mail or fax will be accepted. The fund
acknowledges letters on receipt; applicants are
typically advised of results of initial staff review
within two months. Application form not required.
Initial approach: Letter of inquiry
Copies of proposal: 1
Board meeting date(s): Apr., July, and Nov.
Final notification: 4-6 weeks
Officers and Directors:* James R. Tallon,* Chair.;
Cristine Russell,* Vice-Chair.; John E. Craig, Jr.,
C.O.O. and Exec. V.P.; Anthony Shih, Exec. V. P.,
Progs.; Cathy Schoen, Sr. V.P., Research and Eval.;
Melinda Abrams, V.P., Patient Centered Coord.
Care; Anne-Marie J. Audet, M.D., M.Sc., V.P., Health
System Quality and Efficiency; Sara Collins, Ph.D.,
V.P., Affordable Health Insurance; Diana Davenport,
V.P., Admin.; Michelle M. Doty, V.P., Survey
Research and Eval.; Stuart Guterman, V.P., Payment
System Reform; Mary Jane Koren, M.D., V.P.,
Quality of Care for Frail Elders; Andrea C. Landes,
V.P., Grants Mgmt.; Robin Osborn, V.P., and Dir.,
International Prog., Health Policy and Innovation;
Barry Scholl, V.P., Comms. and Publishing; Edward
L. Schor, V.P., State Health Policy and Practice;
Jeffry Haber, Cont.; Maureen Bisognano; Benjamin
K. Chu, M.D.; Michael V. Drake, M.D.; Samuel C.
Fleming; Julio Frenk, M.D.; Glen M. Hackbarth; Jane
E. Henney, M.D.; Robert C. Pozen; William Y. Yun.
Number of staff: 28 full-time professional; 21
full-time support.
EIN: 131635260
Recent grants for international programs:
1337-1 Harris Interactive, Rochester, NY,
$407,800. For International Health Policy
Survey. 2010.
1337-2 Johns Hopkins University, Baltimore, MD,
$61,000. For Cross-National Comparisons of
Health Systems Quality Data. 2010.
1337-3 London School of Economics and Political
Science, London, England, $199,650. For
International Lessons On Health Reform:
Learning From the Experiences of European
Nations, Year 2. 2010.
1337-4 London School of Economics and Political
Science, London, England, $49,600. For
Analysis of Prescription Drug Prices in the United
States and Europe. 2010.
1337-5 National Academy of Sciences, Washington,
DC, $40,000. For Commonwealth Fund/Joseph
H. Kanter Family Foundation International
Roundtable on Electronic Medical Records and
Outcomes Research. 2010.

1337-6 RAND Europe Cambridge Limited, Cambridge, England, $17,020. For Updating International Trends in Mortality Amenable. 2010.

1337-7 Scientific Institute for Quality of Healthcare, Nijmegen, Netherlands, $21,102. For Expansion of Commonwealth Fund International Health Policy Survey to Include the Netherlands. 2010.

1337-8 Uniklinik Koln, Cologne, Germany, $50,000. For Patient-Related Outcomes Survey in German Disease Management Programs. 2010.

1337-9 University of British Columbia, Vancouver, Canada, $49,198. For Pharmaceutical Policy: Global Trends, Challenges, and Innovations. 2010.

1337-10 University of California, Oakland, CA, $49,999. For A U.S.-U.K. Comparison of Trends in Quality and Disparities in Diabetes Management. 2010.

1337-11 Urban Institute, Washington, DC, $125,000. For Enhancing the International Program's Communications and Publications Capacity, Year 2. 2010.

1338
Concern Worldwide (U.S.), Inc.
104 E. 40th St., Ste. 903
New York, NY   10016-1809   (212) 557-8000
FAX: (212) 557-8004; URL: http://www.concernusa.org

Grantmaker type: Public charity.
Financial data (yr. ended 12/31/10). Revenue, $32,009,344; assets, $8,339,794 (M); gifts received, $32,261,098; expenditures, $31,344,367; giving activities include $702,722 for grants, and $27,518,796 for grants to organizations outside the U.S.
Purpose and activities: The organization provides emergency relief and long-term assistance throughout Africa, Asia, Central America, and Eastern Europe.
Fields of interest: International relief.
International interests: Eastern & Central Europe; Central America; Asia; Africa.
Limitations: Giving primarily in Africa, Asia, Central America, and Eastern Europe.
Officers and Directors:* Thomas J. Moran,* Chair.; Lynn Tierney,* Secy.; Eugene Keilin,* Treas.; Joan Carroll; Dolores T. Connolly; Lisa D'Urso; Robert M. Fitzgerald; Jack Haire; Kevin Kearney; Alfred F. Kelly, Jr.; Edward J.T. Kenney; Edward McCarrick; Denis O'Brien; Bro. Justin O'Connor; George Pappas; Margaret M. Smyth; Nancy Soderberg.
EIN: 133712030

1339
The Edward T. Cone Foundation
c/o McLaughlin & Stern, LLP
260 Madison Ave., Ste. 1800
New York, NY   10016-2401   (212) 448-1100
Contact: T. Randolph Harris, Tr.

Established in 1991 in NJ.
Donors: Edward T. Cone Charitable Lead Annuity Trust 2; Edward T. Cone Charitable Lead Trust; Edward T. Cone Charitable Lead Annuity Trust 3; Edward T. Cone Charitable Lead Annuity Trust 4; Edward T. Cone Charitable Lead Annuity Trust 6.
Grantmaker type: Independent foundation.

Financial data (yr. ended 12/31/10): Assets, $13,772,744 (M); gifts received, $126,704; expenditures, $2,253,746; qualifying distributions, $2,003,000; giving activities include $2,003,000 for grants.
Fields of interest: Performing arts, music; Arts; Higher education; International affairs.
Limitations: Applications not accepted. Giving primarily in NJ. No grants to individuals.
Application information: Contributes only to pre-selected organizations.
Trustees: T. Randolph Harris; George W. Pitcher.
EIN: 133646357

1340
The Robert M. Conway Foundation
(formerly Robert M. & Lois Conway Foundation)
c/o BCRS Group Associates, LLC
100 Wall St., 11th Fl.
New York, NY   10005-3701

Established in 1982 in NY.
Donors: Robert M. Conway; Ricki Gail Conway.
Grantmaker type: Independent foundation.
Financial data (yr. ended 09/30/10): Assets, $3,692,027 (M); gifts received, $551,076; expenditures, $310,109; qualifying distributions, $301,293; giving activities include $299,293 for 9 grants (high: $94,043; low: $1,000).
Purpose and activities: Giving primarily to U.S.-based organizations for higher education and the arts.
Fields of interest: Performing arts, ballet; Arts; Higher education; Foundations (private grantmaking).
International interests: England.
Limitations: Applications not accepted. Giving primarily in IN and New York, NY; funding also in London, England. No grants to individuals, or for scholarships; no loans.
Application information: Contributes only to pre-selected organizations.
Trustees: Robert M. Conway; Robert J. Hurst.
EIN: 133153721

1341
Bernard and Judy Cornwell Foundation, Inc.
c/o Hogan & Hartson, LLP
875 3rd Ave.
New York, NY   10022-6225

Established in 1999 in MA.
Grantmaker type: Independent foundation.
Financial data (yr. ended 12/31/10): Assets, $1,004,048 (M); gifts received, $294,000; expenditures, $241,368; qualifying distributions, $230,700; giving activities include $230,700 for 18 grants (high: $80,000; low: $500).
Fields of interest: International development; Protestant agencies & churches.
Limitations: Applications not accepted. No grants to individuals.
Application information: Contributes only to pre-selected organizations.
Officers: Bernard Cornwell, Pres.; Kathleen Motz, Clerk; Judith Cornwell, Treas.
Director: Mark Weinsteia.
EIN: 134033628

1342
Berthe M. Cote Foundation, Inc.
c/o Bank of America, N.A.
Bank of America Tower
1 Bryant Park
New York, NY   10036-6728

Grantmaker type: Independent foundation.
Financial data (yr. ended 10/31/10): Assets, $3,046,220 (M); expenditures, $164,176; qualifying distributions, $133,652; giving activities include $133,652 for grants.
Fields of interest: United Ways and Federated Giving Programs; Health care.
International interests: Israel.
Limitations: Applications not accepted. Giving primarily in NY. No grants to individuals.
Application information: Contributes only to pre-selected organizations.
Officers: E. Michael Difabio, Pres.; Linda R. Franciscovich, V.P. and Secy.; Michael D. Difabio, V.P. and Treas.
EIN: 141681452

1343
Council for Canadian American Relations
(formerly American Friends of Canada Committee, Inc.)
670 West End Ave., Ste. 16A
New York, NY   10025-7329   (212) 496-0211
FAX: (212) 496-0213; E-mail: ccar@nyc.rr.com

Established in 1972 in NY.
Grantmaker type: Public charity.
Financial data (yr. ended 12/31/10): Revenue, $320,659; assets, $1,271,932 (M); gifts received, $298,101; expenditures, $983,457; giving activities include $225,555 for grants, and $695,525 for grants to organizations outside the U.S.
Purpose and activities: The council operates a program that enables American art collectors to make tax deductible donations to Canadian museums and galleries. The council also organizes programs and activities in Canada and the United States to stimulate dialogue, disseminate information and facilitate cultural exchange between the two countries.
Fields of interest: International exchange, arts; Arts.
International interests: Canada.
Type of support: In-kind gifts.
Limitations: Applications not accepted. Giving in the U.S. and Canada. No grants to individuals.
Application information: Contributes only to pre-selected organizations.
Directors: Stanley M. Ackert III; John Allison; Maria Beatrice Arco; Sonja Bata; Joel Bell; Michael B. Davies; Gaetana Enders; Daniel Gersen; Ian Griffin; Marife Hernandez; Gregory Kane, Q.C.; James T. Kiernan, Jr.; Ellen Kratzer; Noel Levine; David Manning; David Mirvish; D. Miles Price; W. Brian Rose; Elaine Sargent; Jean-Francois Sauve; Kathy Sloane; Liliane M. Stewart; Kenneth D. Taylor; Emily Anne Tuttle; Harriet "Sis" Bunting Weld; Clark B. Winter, Jr.; and 3 additional directors.
Advisor: James A. Coutts.
Number of staff: 1 part-time professional.
EIN: 237193312

1344
Council on Foreign Relations, Inc.
58 E. 68th St.
New York, NY 10065-5953 (212) 434-9400
FAX: (212) 434-9800; E-mail: fellowships@cfr.org;
Additional address: 1779 Massachusetts Ave.
N.W., Washington, DC 20036-2109, tel.: (202)
518-3400, fax: (202) 986-2984; URL: http://
www.cfr.org
RSS Feed: http://feeds.cfr.org/cfr_main

Established in 1921.
Grantmaker type: Public charity.
Financial data (yr. ended 06/30/10): Revenue,
$42,700,117; assets, $399,766,800 (M); gifts
received, $27,885,600; expenditures,
$50,731,317; giving activities include $14,400 for
grants to organizations outside the U.S., and
$1,446,507 for grants to individuals.
Purpose and activities: The council is an
independent, nonpartisan membership
organization, think tank, and publisher dedicated to
being a resource for its members, government
officials, business executives, journalists,
educators and students, civic and religious leaders,
and other interested citizens in order to help them
better understand the world and the foreign policy
choices facing the U.S. and other countries.
Fields of interest: International affairs.
Type of support: Fellowships.
Publications: Annual report.
Application information:
  Initial approach: Submit fellowship nomination
  Deadline(s): Oct. 31 for International Affairs
    Fellowship in Japan
Officers and Directors:* Carla A. Hills,* Co-Chair.;
Robert E. Rubin,* Co-Chair.; Richard E. Salomon,*
Vice-Chair.; Richard N. Haass,* Pres.; Janice L.
Murray, C.O.O., Sr. V.P., and Treas.; Peter
Ackerman; Fouad Ajami; Madeleine K. Albright;
Charlene Barshefsky; Henry S. Bienen; Alan S.
Blinder; Tom Brokaw; Sylvia Mathews Burwel; Frank
J. Caufield; Hon. Kenneth M. Duberstein; Martin S.
Feldstein; Stephen Friedman; Ann M. Fudge; J.
Tomilson Hill; Shirley Ann Jackson; George E. Rupp;
Colin L. Powell; Christine Todd Whitman; and 16
additional directors.
EIN: 131628168

1345
Cross-Cultural Solutions
2 Clinton Pl.
New Rochelle, NY 10801-7402 (914) 632-0022
FAX: (914) 632-8494;
E-mail: info@crossculturalsolutions.org; Toll-free
tel.: (800) 380-4777; URL: http://
www.crossculturalsolutions.org

Established in 1997.
Grantmaker type: Public charity.
Financial data (yr. ended 12/31/10): Revenue,
$9,226,212; assets, $5,343,568 (M); gifts
received, $9,257,670; expenditures, $9,684,989;
giving activities include $4,276,065 for grants to
organizations outside the U.S., and $4,534,103 for
grants to individuals outside the U.S.
Purpose and activities: The organization operates
volunteer programs around the world in partnership
with sustainable community initiatives, bringing
people together to work side-by-side while sharing
perspectives and fosting cultural understanding.

Fields of interest: Voluntarism promotion;
International affairs; Community/economic
development.
Limitations: Giving on an international basis.
Officer: Steven C. Rosenthal, Exec. Dir.
EIN: 931189960

1346
James H. Cummings Foundation, Inc.
120 W. Tupper Sr., Ste. 201
Buffalo, NY 14201-2170 (716) 874-0040
Contact: William L. Joyce, Secy. and Exec. Dir.
FAX: (716) 854-2659;
E-mail: cummings.foundation@verizon.net; Tel./Fax:
(716) 874-0040; URL: http://
www.jameshcummings.com

Incorporated in 1962 in NY.
Donor: James H. Cummings†.
Grantmaker type: Independent foundation.
Financial data (yr. ended 05/31/11): Assets,
$34,617,981 (M); expenditures, $2,115,170;
qualifying distributions, $1,699,500; giving
activities include $1,699,500 for grants.
Purpose and activities: Giving exclusively for
charitable purposes in advancing medical science,
research, and education in selected cities in the
U.S. and Canada, and for charitable work among
underprivileged boys and girls, and aged and infirm
persons in designated areas. Priority is given to
medical proposals and capital projects, particularly
for equipment needs of various kinds.
Fields of interest: Medical school/education;
Hospitals (general); Biomedicine; Medical research,
institute; Human services; Children/youth, services;
Aging, centers/services; Aging; Economically
disadvantaged.
International interests: Canada.
Type of support: Capital campaigns; Building/
renovation; Equipment; Land acquisition; Seed
money; Research; Matching/challenge support.
Limitations: Applications accepted. Giving limited to
Toronto, Ontario, Canada, and to Hendersonville,
NC, and Buffalo, NY. No support for national health
organizations. No grants to individuals, or for annual
campaigns, program support, endowment funds,
operating budgets, program costs, emergency
funds, deficit financing, scholarships, fellowships,
publications, conferences, contingency reserves, or
continuing support; no loans.
Publications: Annual report (including application
guidelines).
Application information: Application form not
required.
  Initial approach: Preliminary letter (no more than
    2 pages) or telephone inquiry is encouraged
  Copies of proposal: 8
  Deadline(s): 4 weeks prior to board meetings
  Board meeting date(s): Quarterly, usually in Feb.,
    May, Sept. and Dec.
  Final notification: 1 to 4 weeks
Officers and Directors:* Charles F. Kreiner, Jr.,
Pres.; Richard C. Bryan, Jr., V.P.; John P. Naughton,*
M.D., V.P.; William L. Joyce, Secy. and Exec. Dir.;
Robert J.A. Irwin,* Treas.; Theodore I. Putnam, M.D.
Number of staff: 1 part-time professional; 1
part-time support.
EIN: 160864200

1347
The Nathan Cummings Foundation
475 10th Ave., 14th Fl.
New York, NY 10018-9715 (212) 787-7300
Contact: Simon Greer, C.E.O. and Pres.
FAX: (212) 787-7377;
E-mail: contact@nathancummings.org; URL: http://
www.nathancummings.org
E-Newsletter: http://www.nathancummings.net/
news/

Established in 1949 in IL.
Donor: Nathan Cummings†.
Grantmaker type: Independent foundation.
Financial data (yr. ended 12/31/09): Assets,
$415,102,143 (M); expenditures, $26,191,085;
qualifying distributions, $23,915,472; giving
activities include $19,944,000 for 308 grants (high:
$975,000; low: $200), and $297,568 for
foundation-administered programs.
Purpose and activities: The foundation is rooted in
the Jewish tradition and committed to democratic
values and social justice, including fairness,
diversity, and community. It seeks to build a socially
and economically just society that values and
protects the ecological balance for future
generations; promotes humane health care; and
fosters arts and culture that enriches communities.
Fields of interest: Arts; Environment; Health care;
Health organizations, association; Human services;
Jewish agencies & synagogues.
International interests: Israel.
Type of support: Conferences/seminars; General/
operating support; Continuing support; Program
development; Seed money; Research; Program
evaluation.
Limitations: Applications accepted. Giving primarily
in the U.S. No support for specific diseases, general
support for Jewish education, Holocaust-related
projects, foreign-based organizations, or local
synagogues or organizations with local projects. No
grants to individuals, scholarships, sponsorships,
projects with no plans for replication, endowments
or capital campaigns.
Publications: Application guidelines; Annual report;
Financial statement; Grants list.
Application information: Application form required.
  Initial approach: 2- to 3-page letter of inquiry
    required
  Copies of proposal: 1
  Deadline(s): None
  Board meeting date(s): Spring and fall
  Final notification: 30 days
Officers and Trustees:* James K. Cummings,*
Chair.; Ernest Tollerson,* Vice-Chair.; Simon Greer,
C.E.O. and Pres.; Caroline L. Williams, Exec. V.P.;
Stephen P. Durchslag,* Secy.; Adam N.
Cummings,* Treas.; Beatrice Cummings Mayer, Tr.
Emeritus; Adam Blumenthal; Michael A. Cummings;
Ruth Cummings; Sonia Simon Cummings; Danielle
Durchslag; Rachel Durchslag; Andrew Golden; Sara
Horowitz; Robert N. Mayer; Debra Weese-Mayer.
Number of staff: 9 full-time professional; 12 full-time
support; 1 part-time support.
EIN: 237093201
Recent grants for international programs:
1347-1 American Friends of the Reut Institute,
    Beverly Hills, CA, $10,000. For general support
    to strengthen the vision of the state of Israel as
    Jewish, democratic and prosperous. 2010.
1347-2 American Jewish Joint Distribution
    Committee, New York, NY, $150,000. For Israel:
    Portrait of a Work in Progress (IPWP), project that
    aims to explore Israel as both a place and a

metaphor through photography. Grant will support 1) completion of artist residencies and start of additional residencies; 2) selection and shaping of the photographic collection; 3) documentation of the project; 4) creation of a dissemination plan; and 5) strategic planning for a campus engagement project. 2010.

1347-3 American Jewish Joint Distribution Committee, New York, NY, $25,000. For Inter-Agency Task Force on Israeli Arab Issues (Task Force), coalition of North American Jewish organizations, foundations and private philanthropists. Grant will support educating American Jewish community on majority/minority relations in Israel; increasing awareness of economic, educational, and social service weaknesses facing Palestinian-Israeli communities and, in certain cases, leveraging financial resources to provide effective solutions; and working with Israeli organizations to strengthen Palestinian-Israeli leadership. 2010.

1347-4 American Jewish World Service, New York, NY, $150,000. For Pursue: Action for a Just World, joint program of American Jewish World Service and AVODAH: The Jewish Service Corps to inspire, engage and support alumni of volunteer service programs and their peers as lifelong agents for social justice, rooted in and nourished by Jewish values. Pursue will 1) build networks of thousands of young Jewish leaders committed to Tikkun Olam; 2) provide trainings, leadership development and skill building for young Jewish social justice activists; and 3) upgrade its evaluation tools and methodology. 2010.

1347-5 American Jewish World Service, New York, NY, $100,000. For Phase 2 of Jewish Social Justice Coordination Roundtable, which will enable organizations to continue their efforts to deepen relationships, enhance knowledge sharing and coordinate efforts through Jewish Social Justice Roundtable to ultimately strengthen quality and impact of the growing social justice movement. The purpose of Phase 2 is to build on the relationship building and coordination of Phase 1 and to improve collaboration, further expand partnerships, and create intentional space where members both individually and collectively can address issues. There will be two structured and facilitated gatherings attended by the CEO and second senior staff person from each organization. 2010.

1347-6 American Jewish World Service, New York, NY, $99,000. For Phase 3 of Jewish Social Justice Roundtable Table, which will enable organizations to continue their efforts to deepen relationships, enhance knowledge sharing and coordinate efforts to ultimately strengthen the quality and impact of the growing social justice movement. Phase 3 will further deepen relationships, begin action on branded campaigns, support coordinated action among members through clustered organizing, and develop tools for building the sector as a whole. 2010.

1347-7 American Jewish World Service, New York, NY, $21,250. For Immediate emergency aid to Haiti in the wake of the earthquake. 2010.

1347-8 American Pardes Foundation, New York, NY, $30,000. For general support to provide a forum for Jewish men and women of all backgrounds at Pardes Institute of Jewish Studies in Jerusalem. Participants become further acquainted with Jewish traditions, heritage and community life through rigorous textual studies, educational programs and outreach activities within open and free-thinking environment. 2010.

1347-9 American University, Washington, DC, $100,000. For project, Best Practices in Climate Change: Evaluating Resources, Strategies and Communication. Project will evaluate communication challenges facing environmental organizations following the demise of cap and trade legislation, identify false assumptions, failed strategies, and emerging best practices in climate change communication and policy-maker engagement. 2010.

1347-10 Americans for Peace Now, Washington, DC, $100,000. For general support for efforts to educate the American Jewish community and general public through media outreach, policy and government relations, publications, new media, community outreach, grassroots activism, and direct mail about the strategic and economic benefits of peace between Israel and her neighbors. 2010.

1347-11 Ashoka: Innovators for the Public, Youth Venture, Arlington, VA, $15,000. For project to provide young people in the U.S. and internationally with skills to support themselves to become active citizens capable of creating positive social change. 2010.

1347-12 Biomimicry Institute, Missoula, MT, $200,000. For general and program support. 2010.

1347-13 Brandeis University, Waltham, MA, $75,000. To support Acting Together on the World Stage: Performance and the Creative Transformation of Conflict, effort to field test, and disseminate documentary film, discussion guides, policy briefs and anthology that were developed through a partnership with Theatres Without Borders. Acting Together will involve the collaboration of scholars and practitioners working in fifteen conflict regions creating content that will inform practice while building a learning community and strengthening networks. The project will yield rich case studies, useful theoretical frameworks, and recommendations to policymakers about the field of peace-building performance. 2010.

1347-14 Breakthrough, New York, NY, $75,000. For Immigrant Project - Part II, project that uses art and popular culture to explore immigration and migration and promote social change through the ongoing development of innovative interactive multi-player video game. Breakthrough will develop a video game where players will search for clues in various cultural and historical artifacts to solve puzzles that unlock the different levels of a game that address immigration and the larger human rights movement. 2010.

1347-15 Center for American Progress, Washington, DC, $100,000. To support Middle East Progress in their work to advance pragmatic progressive policies to achieve a comprehensive Arab-Israeli peace centered on a two-state resolution to the Israeli-Palestinian conflict. The aim is to: elevate Middle East peace as a core U.S. national security interest; revive cooperation and partnerships among American constituencies strongly supportive of a two-state solution and a comprehensive peace; and offer support for and constructive criticisms of U.S. national security approaches in the Middle East in effort to advance a comprehensive approach to stabilizing the broader region. 2010.

1347-16 CERES, Boston, MA, $50,000. For Investor Strategy on Climate Change, which will work to organize the global warming shareholder campaign and leverage investor pressure to engage with corporate boards and senior management; continue to expand the Investor Network on Climate Risk; enable investors and business leaders to exert their influence in public policy debates around SEC climate disclosure regulations; and implement a strategic communication campaign. 2010.

1347-17 Constitution Project, Washington, DC, $25,000. For the Blue Ribbon Panel on Detainee Treatment, a high-level independent panel of experts who will examine U.S. policies governing the treatment of terrorism suspects in U.S. custody. At the conclusion of its examination, the panel will issue a report that will provide the American people and the Administration with a clear narrative of what is now known about policy missteps and institutional failures that led to detainee mistreatment, identify gaps in the documentary record, highlight the holes in Congressional investigations and explain the importance of filling in missing pieces. The report will fortify the argument that only a full awareness of former policies and their implications can equip this and future Administrations with the necessary tools to keep the nation safe, in keeping with its values and laws. It is not intended to displace government accountability mechanisms, but rather, to recommend steps that only the government can take to pursue a thorough and comprehensive review. 2010.

1347-18 Doctors Without Borders USA, New York, NY, $26,250. For aid to victims of the earthquake in Haiti. 2010.

1347-19 Encounter, New York, NY, $100,000. For general support and program support. 2010.

1347-20 Franklin and Eleanor Roosevelt Institute, New York, NY, $50,000. For Project on Global Finance (PGF), interdisciplinary, multi-platform economic policy initiative to develop and promote frameworks, policies and institutions that can productively and fairly re-align financial markets and incentives for the benefit of society. PGF will address derivative regulation, off balance sheet transactions, too big to fail institutions, regulatory structures, resolution power and related areas. The goal is to provide a sober, coherent set of policy choices to be broadly publicized as a set of approaches for decision makers, the media, and the public. 2010.

1347-21 Global Kids, New York, NY, $75,000. For professional development program called, Playing For Keeps (P4K) Online and for The Virtual Video Project, which teaches students critical human rights and social justice issues and film-making. 2010.

1347-22 Hekima Place, Pittsburgh, PA, $10,000. For general support to provide Kenyan girls, orphaned by AIDS, the opportunity to go to elementary and secondary schools by providing them tuition, books and uniforms. 2010.

1347-23 Interreligious Foundation for Community Organization, New York, NY, $17,495. For Haiti Medical Service Project, which will organize urgent medical mission to Haiti to offer volunteer medical services for a period of one to three months following the earthquake. 2010.

1347-24 J Street Education Fund, Washington, DC, $300,000. For general support for work to promote strong U.S. leadership to resolve the Israeli-Palestinian and Arab-Israeli conflicts peacefully and diplomatically and to broaden discourse on Israel in the American Jewish community. Operations include local field and grassroots organizing, University campus organizing, general programming and education, missions to the Middle East, community and rabbinic outreach, and the national conference. 2010.

1347-25 Just Vision, Washington, DC, $61,000. For general support for work to raise awareness among North American audiences about the range of grassroots Palestinian and Israeli peace building efforts, thereby widening their influence. This grant will support Just Vision to produce and strategically use media to garner attention from press, clergy, community leaders, educators, and students. 2010.

1347-26 LSE Foundation, New York, NY, $50,000. For Hartwell Meeting, conference convened to prepare expanded and updated recommendations on climate policy for government officials, following the failure of the Copenhagen conference to produce a binding treaty on GreenHouse Gas (GHG) emissions. Meeting will produce policy paper authored by recognized international energy experts and strategy to disseminate new policy directions on climate including a Web site and keynote speaking engagements at major conferences in North America and Europe. 2010.

1347-27 Masorti Foundation for Conservative Judaism in Israel, New York, NY, $10,000. For Heart Consciousness, Jewish spiritual meditation retreats, to help participants deepen their Jewish spiritual lives and strengthen their Jewish identity. 2010.

1347-28 Mercy Corps, Action Center to End World Hunger, Washington, DC, $10,000. For interactive space that inspires and empowers visitors to tackle the global challenges hunger and poverty. 2010.

1347-29 New Israel Fund, New York, NY, $950,000. For Women and the Environment: Agents of Change in Israel, initiative to create a more vibrant, just and peaceful Israel through supporting women as agents of change and developing a pro-active environmental movement. Women and the Environment includes three initiatives: 1) The NCF/NIF Women's Initiative to harness the energies of women to create change by advancing the rights and status of disempowered populations to create a more just and vibrant society. The Initiative seeks to cultivate projects in the Orthodox Jewish and Palestinian-Israeli sectors that mobilize women through leadership development, advocacy, networks, and collaborations. 2) The Dafna Fund (DF) to support the work of the NCF/NIF Women's Initiative developing feminist leadership and supporting projects between feminist and mainstream institutions. 3) The Green Environment Fund (GEF) to develop and advance a positive, proactive vision of Israel's future that integrates environmental sustainability and broadly-shared economic prosperity. 2010.

1347-30 New Israel Fund, New York, NY, $100,000. For Responding to Assault on Israeli Democracy, proactive campaign to respond to escalating attacks against fundamental democratic values launched by members of the Israeli media, Knesset, and other public agents. Grant will enable NIF primarily to strengthen public perception of the importance of civil society

organizations through media, communications, and public events. Grant will also provide financial support, as needed, to coordinated efforts among NGOs facing especially harsh attacks and upgrade security for NIF offices and leadership under threat. 2010.

1347-31 New Israel Fund, New York, NY, $50,000. For Green Environment Fund (GEF), project that undertakes strategic design process focused on making Israeli environmentalism more powerful and effective. 2010.

1347-32 New Israel Fund, New York, NY, $15,000. For Sandceil Center Circus Performing Arts School, professional school for modern circus arts and dance in Yakum Israel. The School offers activities for young children and teenagers, and children with disabilities. 2010.

1347-33 New Israel Fund, New York, NY, $10,000. For Sandceil Center Circus Performing Arts School, professional school for modern circus arts and dance in Yakum Israel. The School offers activities for young children and teenagers, and children with disabilities. 2010.

1347-34 Partners in Health, Boston, MA, $51,250. For relief efforts in Haiti in the wake of the earthquake. 2010.

1347-35 Partners in Health, Boston, MA, $10,000. For general support to provide high-quality medical care to the poorest of the poor around the world. 2010.

1347-36 PeaceWorks Foundation, New York, NY, $100,000. For work of OneVoice International Education Program (IEP) to bring moderate, positive discourse around the Middle East conflict and training to American college campuses. Grant will support OneVoice to: 1) bring Israeli and Palestinian OneVoice Youth Leaders to American universities for a series of campus events under the sponsorship of local and diverse student groups and community bodies; 2) provide follow-up training seminars to develop a leadership core; and 3) initiate regional campaigns and networks to sustain student engagement and action. 2010.

1347-37 Religious Action Center of Reform Judaism, Washington, DC, $50,000. To support meetings between National Interreligious Leadership Initiative for Peace in the Middle East (NILI) leaders, senior Administration officials and national leaders and targeted communication to the general public to advance active U.S. leadership toward a two-state solution and comprehensive Israeli-Palestinian peace. 2010.

1347-38 Rockefeller Philanthropy Advisors, Philanthropic Collaborative, New York, NY, $500,000. To support the Breakthrough Institute, which aims to enact paradigm shifts in the way the public, the media, advocates and policymakers think and deal with energy and climate, the economy, and national security. 2010.

1347-39 Rockefeller Philanthropy Advisors, Philanthropic Collaborative, New York, NY, $50,000. For Carbon Disclosure Project (CDP), which uses the power of capital markets - combined with the fiduciary duty of corporations to their shareholders - to pressure corporations to take responsibility for the environmental costs and risks of their activities. 2010.

1347-40 Rockwood Leadership Institute, Berkeley, CA, $100,000. For Leadership Training for Social Change Leaders in Israel to offer its flagship pilot program the Art of Collaborative Leadership and coaching annually to twenty-four leaders of

non-governmental, civil society, and advocacy projects in Israel. 2010.

1347-41 Telos Group, Kairos Project, Washington, DC, $80,000. For general support for work to build a pro-Israel, pro-Palestine, pro-America, pro-peace movement in faith-based mainstream America, and in particular in Christian America. Grant will support expansion and broadening of work through 1) community events and relationship building, 2) conferences on religious leadership, 3) VIP pilgrimages, 4) communication initiatives, and 5) large scale community engagement. 2010.

1348
The John P. & Constance A. Curran Charitable Foundation
101 Park Ave., 23rd Fl.
New York, NY   10178-2399

Established in 1997 in NY.
Grantmaker type: Independent foundation.
Financial data (yr. ended 12/31/10): Assets, $4,615,798 (M); expenditures, $413,172; qualifying distributions, $406,600; giving activities include $406,600 for grants.
Fields of interest: Christian agencies & churches; Education; Health care; Community/economic development.
International interests: Ireland.
Type of support: General/operating support; Continuing support; Annual campaigns; Capital campaigns; Building/renovation; Program development; Curriculum development; Scholarship funds; Research.
Limitations: Applications not accepted. Giving primarily in New York, NY. No grants to individuals, or for the arts, debt reduction, or travel.
Application information: Contributes only to pre-selected organizations.
Trustees: Constance A. Curran; John P. Curran; Meredith Curran; Sean Curran.
EIN: 133923928

1349
The Edmond de Rothschild Foundation
c/o Proskauer Rose LLP
1585 Broadway
New York, NY   10036-8204
Contact: Paul H. Epstein, Pres.

Incorporated in 1963 in NY.
Donor: Edmond de Rothschild‡.
Grantmaker type: Independent foundation.
Financial data (yr. ended 12/31/10): Assets, $59,152,415 (M); expenditures, $4,471,947; qualifying distributions, $2,277,572; giving activities include $2,277,572 for grants.
Purpose and activities: Grants largely for Jewish welfare funds, higher education, and organizations concerned with Israeli affairs in the U.S. and abroad; support also for cultural programs and medical research.
Fields of interest: Higher education; Environment, natural resources; Arts; Medical research, institute.
International interests: France; Israel.
Limitations: Applications not accepted. Giving primarily in New York, NY; giving internationally in France, Switzerland and the UK. No grants to individuals.

Application information: Contributes only to pre-selected organizations.

Board meeting date(s): As required

Officers and Directors:* Benjamin de Rothschild,* Chair.; Ariane de Rothschild,* Pres.; Paul H. Epstein,* V.P.; Stanley Komaroff,* V.P.; Valerie Monchi, V.P.; Francois Morin, V.P.; Philip M. Susswein, Secy.; Firoz Ladak,* Treas.; Nadine de Rothschild.

Number of staff: 1 part-time professional.

EIN: 136119422

1350

The Raymond Debbane Family Foundation

c/o The Invus Group Ltd., Attn.: Raymond Debbane
750 Lexington Ave.
New York, NY 10022-2050

Established in 2001 in NY.

Donor: Raymond Debbane.

Grantmaker type: Independent foundation.

Financial data (yr. ended 02/28/10): Assets, $9,659,007 (M); expenditures, $1,023,494; qualifying distributions, $984,000; giving activities include $984,000 for grants.

Purpose and activities: Giving primarily for the arts, education, international policy programs, and human services.

Fields of interest: International affairs; Human services; Education; Higher education; Museums (history); Economics.

Limitations: Applications not accepted. Giving primarily in England and Lebanon; some funding also in Washington, DC and New York, NY. No grants to individuals.

Application information: Contributes only to pre-selected organizations.

Officers and Directors:* Raymond Debbane,* Pres.; Dr. Randa Hamadeh,* Secy.; Dr. Patrice Hassoun,* Treas.

EIN: 134053653

1351

The Gladys Krieble Delmas Foundation

275 Madison Ave., 33rd Fl.
New York, NY 10016-1101 (212) 687-0011
Contact: Rachel Kimber, Fdn. Admin.
FAX: (212) 687-8877; E-mail: info@delmas.org;
URL: http://www.delmas.org

Established in 1976 in NY.

Donors: Gladys V.K. Delmas†; Jean Paul Delmas†.

Grantmaker type: Independent foundation.

Financial data (yr. ended 12/31/10): Assets, $42,687,787 (M); expenditures, $2,323,053; qualifying distributions, $1,642,406; giving activities include $1,642,406 for grants.

Purpose and activities: The foundation supports the humanities, research libraries, and New York City performing arts organizations, and has a particular interest in encouraging Venetian scholarship.

Fields of interest: Performing arts; Humanities; Libraries/library science.

International interests: Italy.

Type of support: Scholarship funds; General/operating support; Continuing support; Program development; Conferences/seminars; Curriculum development; Fellowships; Research.

Limitations: Applications accepted. Giving on a national basis to organizations, but only in New York, NY, for performing arts grants; giving for individual research projects conducted in Venice or the Veneto, Italy. Research libraries primarily directed toward European and American letters. No grants to individuals (except for advanced research in Venice and the Veneto), or for building campaigns; no loans.

Publications: Application guidelines; Financial statement; Grants list.

Application information: Application form required for grants for independent research on Venetian history and culture. Application form not required.

Initial approach: Letter, not exceeding 2 pages
Copies of proposal: 1
Deadline(s): Dec. 15 for grants for independent research on Venetian history and culture
Board meeting date(s): Varies
Final notification: Apr. 1 for grants for independent research on Venetian history and culture

Trustees: George Labalme, Jr.; Joseph C. Mitchell; David H. Stam.

Number of staff: 1 full-time professional; 1 part-time professional.

EIN: 510193884

1352

Demi and Ashton Foundation

(also known as DNA Foundation)
c/o Altman Greenfield & Selvaggi
200 Park Ave. S., 8th Fl.
New York, NY 10003
E-mail: info@demiandashton.org; URL: http://www.demiandashton.org/
Facebook: http://www.facebook.com/dnafoundation
Twitter: http://twitter.com/dnafoundation

Established in 2010 in CA.

Donors: Ashton Kutcher; Demi Moore.

Grantmaker type: Public charity.

Financial data (yr. ended 12/31/10): Revenue, $689,058; assets, $344,714 (M); gifts received, $689,058; expenditures, $344,344.

Purpose and activities: The foundation aims to eliminate child sex slavery worldwide. Believing that freedom is a fundamental human right, the foundation seeks to help raise awareness about this problem, change cultural stereotypes and rehabilitate the innocent victims.

Fields of interest: Anti-slavery/human trafficking; International human rights.

Officers: Demi Moore, Pres.; Christopher A. Kutcher, V.P.; Stuart Gelwarg, Secy-Treas.

EIN: 270943677

1353

Deutsche Bank Americas Foundation

(formerly BT Foundation)
60 Wall St., NYC60-2112
New York, NY 10005-2858 (212) 250-0539
Contact: Gary S. Hattem, Pres.
FAX: (212) 797-2255; URL: http://www.db.com/us/content/en/1066.html
RSS Feed: http://twitter.com/statuses/user_timeline/64682118.rss
Twitter: http://twitter.com/DBFoundation

Established in 1986 in NY.

Donors: Bankers Trust Co.; BT Capital Corp.; Deutsche Bank Americas Holding Corp.

Grantmaker type: Company-sponsored foundation.

Financial data (yr. ended 12/31/09): Assets, $22,686,138 (M); gifts received, $14,759,991; expenditures, $15,358,193; qualifying distributions, $16,532,600; giving activities include $10,734,213 for grants, $3,085,028 for employee matching gifts, and $1,250,000 for loans/program-related investments.

Purpose and activities: The foundation supports programs designed to promote the arts; education; and community development.

Fields of interest: Arts; Education, services; Education; Employment; Housing/shelter; Human services; Business/industry; Community/economic development; Youth; Boys; Immigrants/refugees; Economically disadvantaged.

International interests: Canada; Latin America.

Type of support: Mission-related investments/loans; General/operating support; Continuing support; Program development; Internship funds; Technical assistance; Employee volunteer services; Sponsorships; Program-related investments/loans; Employee matching gifts.

Limitations: Applications accepted. Giving on a national basis in areas of company operations with emphasis on NY, Canada, and Latin America. No support for political parties or candidates, veterans', military, or fraternal organizations, United Way agencies not providing a fundraising waiver, professional or trade associations, or discriminatory organizations. No grants to individuals, or for endowments, capital campaigns, legal advocacy, or religious purposes.

Publications: Application guidelines; Corporate giving report; Newsletter; Program policy statement.

Application information: Letters of intent should not exceed 3 pages in length. A full proposal may be requested at a later date. The foundation utilizes a Request for Proposal (RFP) process for most programs. Support is limited to 3 years in length. Application form not required.

Initial approach: Letter of intent
Deadline(s): None

Officer and Directors:* Seth Waugh,* Chair.; Gary S. Hattem, Pres.; Alessandra Digiusto, Secy.-Treas. and C.A.O.; Jorge Arce; Gary Beyer; Jacques Brand; Jorge Calderon; Hanns Michael Hoelz; Roelfien Kuijpers; Richard Walker.

Number of staff: 3 full-time professional; 3 full-time support.

EIN: 133321736

Recent grants for international programs:

1353-1 ACCION International, Boston, MA, $50,000. 2009.

1353-2 American Institute for Contemporary German Studies, Washington, DC, $25,000. For Annual Trustee Contribution. 2009.

1353-3 Charities Aid Foundation America, Alexandria, VA, $85,352. For DB Donor Advised Fund. 2009.

1353-4 Charities Aid Foundation America, Alexandria, VA, $60,000. For Donor Advised Fund, Canada. 2009.

1353-5 Council on Foreign Relations, New York, NY, $30,000. For Corporate Program Membership. 2009.

1353-6 European Institute, Washington, DC, $15,000. For Corporate Membership. 2009.

1353-7 Executive Council on Diplomacy, Washington, DC, $10,000. For Program Support. 2009.

1353-8 Global Hunger Project, New York, NY, $10,000. For Women on Wall Street Conference. 2009.

1353-9 HelpArgentina, New York, NY, $15,919. For FONDEA (the Escuela Bicentenario). 2009.

1353-10 Hope International, Lancaster, PA, $30,000. For MF Transparency. 2009.

1353-11 Investing in Education, Washington, DC, $25,000. For Middle School Jazz Academy. 2009.

1353-12 Investing in Education, Washington, DC, $20,000. For 125 Ages Project. 2009.

1353-13 Microfinance Information Exchange, Washington, DC, $75,000. For general operating support. 2009.

1353-14 Out of the Box Foundation for the Arts, New York, NY, $10,000. For MIDE (Museo Interactivo de Economica) Museum. 2009.

1353-15 Resource Foundation, New York, NY, $350,000. For Latin America grants. 2009.

1353-16 Resource Foundation, New York, NY, $100,000. For International Initiative Plus grants. 2009.

1353-17 Resource Foundation, New York, NY, $50,055. For Initiative Plus - Brazil (Instituto Andre Franco). 2009.

1353-18 Resource Foundation, New York, NY, $45,263. For Initiative Plus - Argentina (Fundacion San Martin de Tours). 2009.

1353-19 Resource Foundation, New York, NY, $29,487. For grants in Latin America. 2009.

1353-20 Resource Foundation, New York, NY, $28,223. For Initiative Plus - Brazil. 2009.

1353-21 Resource Foundation, New York, NY, $26,625. For Fideicomiso ProBosque de Chapultepec. 2009.

1353-22 Resource Foundation, New York, NY, $17,841. For Latin America grants. 2009.

1353-23 Resource Foundation, New York, NY, $16,400. For grants in Latin America. 2009.

1353-24 Resource Foundation, New York, NY, $12,340. For MAC - Lima. 2009.

1353-25 Rockefeller Philanthropy Advisors, Philanthropic Collaborative, New York, NY, $20,000. For GIIN (Global Impact Investing Network). 2009.

1353-26 Unitus, Inc., Seattle, WA, $30,000. For Social Performance Management Program. 2009.

1353-27 William J. Clinton Foundation, New York, NY, $100,000. For Clinton Global initiative. 2009.

1353-28 World Education and Development Fund, New York, NY, $15,000. For Instituto de Formacion para la Calidad Educativa. 2009.

1353-29 World Resources Institute, Washington, DC, $10,000. For Paginas Verde. 2009.

1354
Diamonds International Corporate Giving Program
38 W 48th St.
New York, NY 10036-1805
URL: http://www.diamondsinternational.org/

Grantmaker type: Corporate giving program.
Purpose and activities: Diamonds International makes charitable contributions to nonprofit organizations on a case by case basis. Support is given primarily in areas of company operations in Antigua, the Bahamas, Barbados, the Cayman Islands, Cancun and Cozumel, Mexico, and St. Lucia.

Fields of interest: Children/youth, services; Health care; Health organizations, research; Youth development; Human services.
International interests: Antigua & Barbuda; Bahamas; Barbados; Cayman Islands; Mexico; Saint Lucia.
Type of support: In-kind gifts; Sponsorships; Employee volunteer services; Cause-related marketing; Continuing support; General/operating support.
Limitations: Giving primarily in areas of company operations in Antigua, the Bahamas, Barbados, the Cayman Islands, Cancun and Cozumel, Mexico, and St. Lucia; giving also to national and international organizations.

1355
Dobkin Family Foundation
c/o BCRS Assocs., LLC
100 Wall St., 11th Fl.
New York, NY 10005-3701

Established in 1984 in NY.
Donors: Eric S. Dobkin; Barbara Dobkin.
Grantmaker type: Independent foundation.
Financial data (yr. ended 03/31/10): Assets, $46,215,792 (M); expenditures, $5,189,219; qualifying distributions, $3,982,754; giving activities include $3,348,955 for 142 grants (high: $282,000; low: $500).
Purpose and activities: Giving primarily to Jewish organizations and higher education, and for human services.
Fields of interest: Museums; Arts; Higher education; Health organizations, association; Human services; Women, centers/services; Jewish federated giving programs; Jewish agencies & synagogues; Women.
International interests: Israel.
Type of support: General/operating support.
Limitations: Applications not accepted. Giving primarily in New York, NY. No grants to individuals.
Application information: Contributes only to pre-selected organizations.
Trustees: Barbara Dobkin; Eric S. Dobkin; Rachel L. Dobkin.
EIN: 133248042

1356
Doctors Without Borders USA, Inc.
333 7th Ave., 2nd Fl.
New York, NY 10001-5126 (212) 679-6800
FAX: (212) 679-7016; URL: http://www.doctorswithoutborders.org/
Blog: http://msf.ca/blogs/
Facebook: http://www.facebook.com/msf.english
Tumblr: http://doctorswithoutborders.tumblr.com/
Twitter: http://twitter.com/msf_usa
YouTube: http://www.youtube.com/msf

Established in 1971.
Grantmaker type: Public charity.
Financial data (yr. ended 12/31/10): Revenue, $273,934,028; assets, $188,227,319 (M); gifts received, $264,471,272; expenditures, $202,483,543; giving activities include $165,903,069 for grants to organizations outside the U.S.
Purpose and activities: The organization delivers emergency aid to people affected by armed conflict, epidemics, natural or man-made disasters, or

exclusion from health care; the organization also awards grants for emergency and medical relief projects to Medecins Sans Frontieres affiliates for overseas operations.
Fields of interest: International relief; Health care.
Type of support: Emergency funds.
Limitations: Giving on an international basis.
Publications: Annual report.
Officers and Directors:* Matthew Spitzer,* M.D., Pres.; Unni Karunakara,* MB, BS, V.P.; David A. Shevlin,* Esq., Secy.; John E. Plum,* Treas.; Sophie Delaunay, Exec. Dir.; Marie-Pierre Allie, M.D.; Jonathan Fisher, M.D.; Rebecca Golden; Mary Ann Hopkins, M.D.; Deane Marchbein, M.D.; Michael Neuman; Brigg Reilley; Sharmila Shetty, M.D.
EIN: 133433452

1357
Cleveland H. Dodge Foundation, Inc.
420 Lexington Ave., Ste. 2331
New York, NY 10170-2332 (212) 972-2800
Contact: Phyllis M. Criscuoli, Exec. Dir.
FAX: (212) 972-1049;
E-mail: info@chdodgefoundation.org; URL: http://www.chdodgefoundation.org

Incorporated in 1917 in NY.
Donors: Cleveland H. Dodge†; Cleveland H. Dodge, Jr.
Grantmaker type: Independent foundation.
Financial data (yr. ended 12/31/10): Assets, $39,591,625 (M); expenditures, $1,742,825; qualifying distributions, $982,003; giving activities include $982,003 for grants.
Purpose and activities: The purpose of the foundation is to promote the well-being of mankind throughout the world. Grants for a selected list of international organizations in the Near East, including those working toward reversing global overpopulation; grants also to a selected few national agencies in the U.S., the balance directed to organizations located in New York City. Most grants in the U.S. for higher and secondary education, youth agencies and child welfare, and cultural programs.
Fields of interest: Arts; Secondary school/education; Higher education; Children/youth, services; Population studies.
International interests: Middle East.
Type of support: Building/renovation; Equipment; Endowments; Employee matching gifts; Matching/challenge support.
Limitations: Applications accepted. Giving primarily in New York, NY and to national organizations. No support for health care, or schools, colleges, and universities, except those that the foundation has consistently supported. No grants to individuals, including scholarships and fellowships, or for general purposes, medical and other research; no loans.
Publications: Annual report; Grants list; Program policy statement.
Application information: Application guidelines available on foundation web site. Application form not required.
Initial approach: Letter
Copies of proposal: 1
Deadline(s): Submit letter prior to the 15th of Jan., Apr., and Sept.
Board meeting date(s): Mar., June, and Nov.
Final notification: Within 3 months of submitting the proposal

Officers and Directors:* William Dodge Rueckert,* Pres.; Bayard Dodge,* V.P.; Louis E. Black,* Secy.; Phyllis M. Criscuoli, Treas. and Exec. Dir.; Patricia Ares; Simon Dodge; Robert Garrett; Bolling W. Haxall, Jr.; Alfred H. Howell, Jr.; Catherine O. Kerr; Sally Dodge Mole; Bayard D. Rea; William H. Rea III; Ingrid R. Warren.
Number of staff: 1 full-time professional.
EIN: 136015087

1358
Dominican Community Bridge Fund
c/o Rockefeller Philanthropy Advisors
6 W. 48th St., 10th Fl.
New York, NY 10036-1802   (212) 812-4330
FAX: (212) 812-4335; E-mail: info@rockpa.org;
URL: http://dominicanbridgefund.org/

Established in 2004; component fund of Rockefeller Philanthropy Advisors.
Grantmaker type: Public charity.
Financial data (yr. ended 12/31/10): Giving activities include $5,000 for 1 grant.
Purpose and activities: The fund works to generate social investment for education, health, and environmental issues affecting the Dominican Republic and Dominican communities in the U.S.
Fields of interest: Community/economic development; Education; Hispanics/Latinos.
International interests: Dominican Republic.
Limitations: Giving on a national basis, and to the Dominican Republic.
Application information:
Initial approach: Contact Rockefeller Philanthropy Advisors for more information concerning grant applications, including requirements and deadlines

1359
Dominican Foundation, Inc.
74 Secor Lane
Hopewell Junction, NY 12533-5174
URL: http://www.dominicanfoundation.com

Established in 1984; supporting organization of Lebron Barney School and Instituto Dominicano Desarrolo Inegral.
Grantmaker type: Public charity.
Financial data (yr. ended 06/30/10): Revenue, $1,004,383; assets, $123,237 (M); gifts received, $1,004,383; expenditures, $887,672; giving activities include $866,519 for grants to organizations outside the U.S.
Purpose and activities: The organization aims to provide social services in the Dominican Republic.
Fields of interest: Economically disadvantaged; Hispanics/Latinos.
International interests: Dominican Republic.
Limitations: Applications not accepted. Giving limited to the Dominican Republic. No grants to individuals.
Application information: Contributes only to pre-selected organizations.
Officers and Directors:* Tito Coleman,* Ph.D., Pres.; Paul Schenkel,* V.P.; Liv Vesely,* Treas.; Patricia Brunson, Secy.; Jerson Diaz; Juan Manual Diaz Parrondo.
EIN: 650263936

1360
The William H. Donner Foundation
60 E. 42nd St., Ste. 1560
New York, NY 10165-1520   (212) 949-0404
Contact: Deirdre Feeney, Prog. Mgr.
FAX: (212) 949-6022; E-mail: dfeeney@donner.org; Additional tel.: (212) 949-5213; URL: http://www.donner.org

Incorporated in 1961 in DC.
Donor: William H. Donner†.
Grantmaker type: Independent foundation.
Financial data (yr. ended 10/31/10): Assets, $131,177,181 (M); expenditures, $8,182,206; qualifying distributions, $5,125,775; giving activities include $4,566,109 for 153 grants (high: $200,000; low: $1,700).
Purpose and activities: Giving primarily for international development and relief services, education, arts and culture, and public affairs.
Fields of interest: Philanthropy/voluntarism; Human services; Animals/wildlife; Public affairs; Arts; Elementary/secondary education; Education; International relief; International development; International affairs.
Type of support: General/operating support; Program development.
Limitations: Applications not accepted. Giving primarily in CA, CO Washington, DC and NY, with some giving in VA.
Application Information: Only applications invited by the foundation will be considered.
Board meeting date(s): Sept.
Officers and Trustees.* Michael Hunter Spencer,* Pres.; Timothy E. Donner,* V.P.; Cristina Winsor,* Secy.; Joseph W. Donner III,* Treas.; Phaedra Annan; Alexander B. Donner, Esq.; David W. Donner; Deborah Donner; Joseph W. Donner, Jr.; Joseph W. Donner III; Anita Winsor Edwards; Stephanie K. Hanson; Sharon W. Lainhant; Brittany D. Roy; Dillon Roy; Robert D. Spencer; William M. Spencer III; Hon. Curtin Winsor, Jr.; Curtin Winsor III; Monica Winsor; Rebecca Winsor.
Number of staff: 1 full-time professional; 3 part-time professional; 1 full-time support; 1 part-time support.
EIN: 231611346
Recent grants for international programs:
1360-1 African Wildlife Foundation, Washington, DC, $35,000. 2010.
1360-2 Africare, Washington, DC, $30,000. 2010.
1360-3 American Foreign Policy Council, Washington, DC, $47,500. 2010.
1360-4 Amnesty International USA, New York, NY, $20,000. 2010.
1360-5 Association of Former Intelligence Officers, McLean, VA, $10,000. 2010.
1360-6 Center for a Free Cuba, Arlington, VA, $18,000. 2010.
1360-7 Center for Immigration Studies, Washington, DC, $25,000. 2010.
1360-8 Center for Security Policy, Washington, DC, $25,000. 2010.
1360-9 Center for Security Policy, Washington, DC, $24,000. 2010.
1360-10 Center for Security Policy, Washington, DC, $10,000. 2010.
1360-11 Fauna and Flora International, Washington, DC, $30,000. 2010.
1360-12 Fauna and Flora International, Washington, DC, $24,631. 2010.
1360-13 Friends of El Faro Orphanage, Studio City, CA, $10,000. 2010.

1360-14 Fund for Global Human Rights, Washington, DC, $50,000. 2010.
1360-15 Global Water Challenge, Washington, DC, $20,000. 2010.
1360-16 Human Rights Watch, New York, NY, $50,000. 2010.
1360-17 Humanity in Action, New York, NY, $30,000. 2010.
1360-18 Institute of World Politics, Washington, DC, $25,000. 2010.
1360-19 Institute of World Politics, Washington, DC, $25,000. 2010.
1360-20 International Film Seminars, New York, NY, $15,000. 2010.
1360-21 Operation Smile International, Norfolk, VA, $83,253. 2010.
1360-22 Operation USA, Culver City, CA, $20,000. 2010.
1360-23 ORBIS International, New York, NY, $44,967. 2010.
1360-24 Pan American Development Foundation, Washington, DC, $45,000. 2010.
1360-25 Synergos Institute, New York, NY, $25,000. 2010.
1360-26 Video Volunteers, New York, NY, $10,175. 2010.

1361
Doris Duke Charitable Foundation
650 5th Ave., 19th Fl.
New York, NY 10019-6108   (212) 974-7000
FAX: (212) 974-7590; URL: http://www.ddcf.org
CEP Study: http://www.ddcf.org/
Grantmaking-Process/-/
Grantee-Perception-Report/
Grants Database: http://www.ddcf.org/
Grants-Awarded/
Twitter: http://twitter.com/DorisDukeFdn

Established in 1996 in NY.
Donor: Doris Duke†.
Grantmaker type: Independent foundation.
Financial data (yr. ended 12/31/10): Assets, $1,716,471,991 (M); gifts received, $5,802,231; expenditures, $92,544,794; qualifying distributions, $85,744,129; giving activities include $76,569,323 for 222 grants (high: $7,195,686; low: $1,500), and $171,616 for 10 foundation-administered programs.
Purpose and activities: The mission of the foundation is to improve the quality of people's lives through grants supporting the performing arts, environmental conservation, medical research and the prevention of child abuse. In addition to its grantmaking activities, the foundation will support three affiliated operating foundations: Duke Farms Foundation, the Doris Duke Foundation for Islamic Art, and the Newport Restoration Foundation.
Fields of interest: Performing arts; Performing arts, dance; Performing arts, theater; Performing arts, music; Environment, natural resources; Animals/wildlife, preservation/protection; Medical research; Crime/violence prevention, child abuse.
Type of support: Employee matching gifts.
Limitations: Applications accepted. Giving on a national basis. No support for toxic issues, litigation, the visual arts, museums or galleries, or arts programs for rehabilitative or therapeutic purposes. No grants to individuals (except through special foundation programs), or for conferences or publications.
Application information: The foundation staff responds to all letters of inquiry, however, it should

be noted that very few grants result from unsolicited letters of inquiry. Do not send binders, books, CDs, videotapes, or audiotapes.

Initial approach: Online Letter of inquiry (2 pages)
Final notification: 2 months for letter of inquiry

Officers and Trustees:* Nannerl O. Keohane,* Chair.; Anthony S. Fauci, M.D., Vice-Chair.; Edward P. Henry, C.E.O. and Pres.; Peter Simmons, C.F.O. and C.A.O.; Jeffrey Heil, C.I.O.; Eileen Oberlander, Cont. and Dir., Finance; Marion Oates Charles, Emeritus; John J. Mack, Emeritus; Harry B. Demopoulos, M.D.; James F. Gill; Kathy Halbreich; Anne Hawley; Peter A. Nadosy; William H. Schlesinger; Jide Zeitlin; John E. Zuccotti.
EIN: 137043679

Recent grants for international programs:

1361-1 Consortium of Universities for Global Health, San Francisco, CA, $20,000. For annual meeting. 2010.

1361-2 Consultative Group on Biological Diversity, San Francisco, CA, $25,000. For Membership. 2010.

1361-3 Consultative Group on Biological Diversity, San Francisco, CA, $10,000. For Membership in the Energy and Climate workgroup. 2010.

1361-4 Dance/USA, Washington, DC, $20,000. For the U.S. delegation to the 2010 Internationale Tanzmesse. 2010.

1361-5 Environmental Defense, New York, NY, $15,000. To work toward finding a global climate solution, and protecting land and freshwater ecosystems. 2010.

1361-6 Harvard University, Cambridge, MA, $20,400. For a networking session for Doris Duke International Clinical Research Fellows at the 2010 Annual Workshop on Advanced Clinical Care in Durban, South Africa; through Harvard Medical School in Boston, MA. 2010.

1361-7 Imperial College Foundation, Atlanta, GA, $28,000. For two meetings of the Developing Antiretroviral Therapy in Africa (DART) team to enable continued collaboration and development of implementation activities. 2010.

1361-8 International Network for Cancer Treatment and Research USA, Philadelphia, PA, $100,000. For Enhancing Cancer Registration in East Africa. 2010.

1361-9 Mid Atlantic Arts Foundation, Baltimore, MD, $71,725. For The French-American Jazz Exchange. 2010.

1361-10 New York Academy of Medicine, New York, NY, $50,000. For the 9th International Conference on Urban Health. 2010.

1361-11 Oxfam America, Boston, MA, $21,530. For HIV/AIDS projects in Southern Africa. 2010.

1361-12 Peter G. Peterson Institute for International Economics, Washington, DC, $100,000. For analysis of the potential for the G-20 to assume a leadership role in reaching international climate agreement. 2010.

1361-13 Stanford University, Stanford, CA, $100,000. For Web-based interactive course in Ethical Challenges Encountered During Short-Term Overseas Training in Biomedical Research and Practice. 2010.

1361-14 United States Fund for UNICEF, New York, NY, $12,500. For the Unite for Children, Unite Against AIDS campaign. 2010.

1361-15 Universities Allied for Essential Medicines, Berkeley, CA, $10,000. For UAEMs annual training and educational conference. 2010.

1361-16 Wesleyan University, Middletown, CT, $136,585. For the continuation of Feet to the Fire: Exploring Global Climate Change from Science to Art. 2010.

1361-17 Wildlife Conservation Society, Bronx, NY, $4,927,600. For Climate Adaptation Fund. 2010.

1361-18 Women Deliver, New York, NY, $25,000. For a background paper on maternal health and equity for the Women Deliver 2010 Conference. 2010.

1361-19 Yale University, New Haven, CT, $500,000. For Climate Adaptation Mapping Framework. 2010.

1361-20 Yale University, New Haven, CT, $25,000. For Global Health Leadership Institute Conference. 2010.

1362

Dynamic Strategies Research Foundation, Inc.

c/o Landau Arnold Laufer & Company LLP
85 E. Hoffman Ave.
Lindenhurst, NY   11757-5010

Established in 1967 in NY.
Donors: Ethel R. Wells; Marion Rose Wells.
Grantmaker type: Independent foundation.
Financial data (yr. ended 08/31/08): Assets, $188 (M); expenditures, $3,520,313; qualifying distributions, $3,520,256; giving activities include $3,520,256 for 2 grants (high: $2,397,456; low: $1,122,800).
Purpose and activities: Giving primarily for public health and to peace foundations focused on nuclear policy.
Fields of interest: Mental health, smoking; Public health; International peace/security.
Limitations: Applications not accepted. Giving primarily in Santa Barbara, CA, and Washington, DC. No grants to individuals.
Publications: Annual report; Financial statement.
Application information: Contributes only to pre-selected organizations.
Trustee: Marion Rose Wells.
EIN: 116103324

1363

The East West Management Institute

575 Madison Ave., 25th Fl.
New York, NY   10022-8509   (212) 843-7660
FAX: (212) 843-1485; E-mail: info@ewmi.org;
URL: http://www.ewmi.org

Established in 1988 in NY.
Donors: American Association for the Advancement of Sciences; Jewish Coalition for Kosovo Relief Assistance; Soros Foundation; U.S. Agency for International Development; U.S. State Department; Rockefeller Brothers Fund.
Grantmaker type: Public charity.
Financial data (yr. ended 12/31/10): Revenue, $12,573,554; assets, $3,326,406 (M); gifts received, $12,506,089; expenditures, $12,646,367; giving activities include $1,905,587 for grants, and $1,413,206 for grants to organizations outside the U.S.
Purpose and activities: The institute is dedicated to promoting economic and democratic reforms, including financial sector, legal, and accounting reforms as well as NGO development, in the developing and transitional economies of the newly independent states of Central and Eastern Europe and Southeast Asia.
Fields of interest: Leadership development; Financial services; Government/public administration; Urban/community development; Economic development; Civil/human rights, advocacy; International affairs, goodwill promotion; International human rights.
International interests: Eastern & Central Europe; Southeast Asia.
Type of support: General/operating support; Management development/capacity building; Conferences/seminars; Publication; Seed money; Curriculum development; Research; Technical assistance; Consulting services.
Limitations: Applications accepted. Giving primarily in Eastern Europe and Southeast Asia.
Publications: Annual report; Newsletter; Program policy statement.
Application information: Application form not required.
Initial approach: Letter or e-mail
Deadline(s): None
Officers and Directors:* Douglas Rutzen,* Chair.; Adrian B. Hewryk, Pres.; Rachel B. Tritt, Exec. V.P.; Michelle P. Scott, V.P., Secy., and Genl. Counsel; Fron Nazi, V.P., Progs.; Stewart Paperin; Byron Wien.
EIN: 133586432

1364

Lucius & Eva Eastman Fund, Inc.

c/o John Eastman
43-07 42nd St., Apt. 5C
Sunnyside, NY   11104-2853

Established in 1946 in NY.
Grantmaker type: Independent foundation.
Financial data (yr. ended 12/31/10): Assets, $3,319,102 (M); expenditures, $190,804; qualifying distributions, $178,208; giving activities include $144,110 for 31 grants (high: $5,000; low: $2,000).
Fields of interest: Education; Arts; Media/communications; Media, film/video; Performing arts, theater; Aging, centers/services; Women, centers/services; International affairs, arms control; Civil/human rights, advocacy; Community/economic development; Aging; Women.
International interests: Vietnam.
Type of support: Seed money; Matching/challenge support.
Limitations: Giving primarily in NY. No grants to individuals.
Publications: Application guidelines; Grants list.
Application information: Application form not required.
Copies of proposal: 1
Deadline(s): None
Board meeting date(s): Three times per year
Officers: John Eastman, Pres.; Benjamin Eastman, V.P.; Terrell Wilson, Secy.-Treas.
EIN: 131958483

1365

Echoing Green

(formerly Echoing Green Foundation)
494 8th Ave., 2nd Fl.
New York, NY   10001-2519   (212) 689-1165
Contact: Cheryl L. Dorsey, Pres.

FAX: (212) 689-9010;
E-mail: info@echoinggreen.org; URL: http://
www.echoinggreen.org

Established in 1987 in DE.
Donors: Amy Berkower; Peter Bloom; Steve
Denning; Roberta Denning; Bill Ford; Charlotte Ford;
William Grabe; David Hodgson; Laurie Hodgson;
Rene Kern; Marie-France Kern; Michael Loeb; Daniel
Weiss; Michele Snyder; Phil Trahanas; General
Atlantic LLC; Oak Foundation; Advance Magazine
Group; Ford Foundation, The; Morino Institute; Paul,
Weiss, Rifkind, Wharton & Garrison LLP; The Porter
Revocable Trust; The Robert Wood Johnson
Foundation; The Spirit Foundation; Flora Family
Foundation; Friedman French Foundation;
PricewaterhouseCoopers, LLP; Calvert Group; The
Price Family Foundation.
Grantmaker type: Public charity.
Financial data (yr. ended 06/30/10): Revenue,
$5,544,407; assets, $5,844,543 (M); gifts
received, $5,512,455; expenditures, $3,576,391;
giving activities include $489,506 for grants,
$120,669 for grants to organizations outside the
U.S., and $776,033 for grants to individuals.
Purpose and activities: The organization works to
spark social change by identifying, investing, and
supporting the world's most exceptional emerging
leaders and the organizations they launch.
Fields of interest: Social entrepreneurship;
Education; Environment; Health care; Housing/
shelter; Children/youth, services; International
economic development; International relief;
International human rights; Civil/human rights;
Economic development; Community/economic
development; Public affairs.
Type of support: Seed money; Fellowships;
Technical assistance.
Limitations: Applications accepted. Giving on a
national and international basis. No support for
faith-based initiatives, or for the expansion of
existing project or recipients of prior organization
fund recipients. No grants for lobbying or research.
Publications: Application guidelines; Grants list.
Application information: The Fellowship Program
application process has three phases: only those
individuals and partnerships whose applications
successfully pass through the previous round will be
given the materials needed to continue on in the
application process. Application form required.
  Initial approach: Complete online application form
  Copies of proposal: 1
  Deadline(s): Dec. 2 for Fellowship Program
  Final notification: Late May for Fellowship
    Program
Officer and Directors:* David C. Hodgson,* Chair.;
William A. Ackman; Maya Ajmera; Esther Benjamin;
Peter Campbell; Guy de Chazal; Cheryl Dorsey; Betsy
Fader; Marianne Gimon; Andrew Kassoy; Diana
Propper de Callejon; Jerome Vascellaro.
Number of staff: 9 full-time professional; 1 part-time
support.
EIN: 133424419

1366
Edeyo Foundation
P.O. Box 30261
New York, NY 10011-0103 (646) 537-1716
E-mail: info@edeyo.org; URL: http://www.edeyo.org
Facebook: http://www.facebook.com/pages/
New-York-NY/Edeyo-Foundation-Change-in-Haiti/
96059495225
Twitter: http://twitter.com/edeyofoundation

Grantmaker type: Public charity.
Financial data (yr. ended 12/31/10): Revenue,
$453,040; assets, $238,251 (M); gifts received,
$452,734; expenditures, $242,701.
Purpose and activities: The organization improves
the futures of Haitian children by providing them with
access to both education and nutritional support.
Fields of interest: Education; Children.
International interests: Haiti.
Limitations: Giving limited to Haiti.
Publications: Newsletter.
Officers: Patricia Beauvais, Secy.; Mandy Gor,
Treas.; Doris Pradieu, Exec. Dir.
Board Members: Cynthia Bogard; Philip
Charles-Pierre; Simon Doubleday; Dr. Lee Gause;
Nora Gherbi.
EIN: 261478267

1367
The Edouard Foundation, Inc.
c/o Philippe Investment Mgmt., Inc.
2 Penn Plz., Ste. 1920A
New York, NY 10121-1902 (212) 991-6217
E-mail: edouardfoundation@pimf.com

Established in 1987 in NY.
Donor: Christopher E. Finch.
Grantmaker type: Independent foundation.
Financial data (yr. ended 12/31/10): Assets,
$10,321,349 (M); expenditures, $507,945;
qualifying distributions, $405,000; giving activities
include $405,000 for grants.
Purpose and activities: The foundation is
committed to funding programs which improve the
quality of life primarily in the communities in which
the directors reside. The funding is focused in the
areas of human services, education, health care,
art, animal welfare, environmental protection, and
disaster relief.
Fields of interest: Health care; Health
organizations, association; Human services;
Children/youth, services; International relief;
International human rights; United Ways and
Federated Giving Programs; Jewish agencies &
synagogues; Disabilities, people with; Economically
disadvantaged.
Type of support: General/operating support;
Emergency funds; Program development; Research.
Limitations: Applications not accepted. Giving
primarily in CT, NY, TX, and the U.S. Virgin Islands;
some funding nationally. No grants to individuals.
Application information: Contributes only to
pre-selected organizations.
  Board meeting date(s): Oct.
Officers: Sandra Finch-Nguyen, Pres.; Christopher
Finch, V.P.; Ronald Finch, V.P.; Edwin A. Margolius,
Esq., Secy.; Aaron Finch, Treas.
EIN: 133446831

1368
Einhorn Family Charitable Trust
c/o Greenlight Capital, Inc.
140 E. 45th St., 24th Fl.
New York, NY 10017-7142
Contact: David Einhorn, Tr.

Established in 2002 in NY.
Donors: David Einhorn; Cheryl Einhorn.
Grantmaker type: Independent foundation.
Financial data (yr. ended 12/31/09): Assets,
$1,099,825 (M); gifts received, $8,982,776;

expenditures, $9,083,732; qualifying distributions,
$9,079,513; giving activities include $8,714,528
for 47 grants (high: $1,750,000; low: $100).
Fields of interest: Foundations (private
grantmaking); International affairs; Higher
education; Jewish agencies & synagogues.
Limitations: Applications not accepted. Giving
primarily in NY. No grants to individuals.
Application information: Contributes only to
pre-selected organizations.
Officers: Harry Bradler, C.F.O.; Jennifer Hoos
Rothberg, Exec. Dir.
Trustees: Cheryl Einhorn; David Einhorn.
EIN: 226921358

1369
EMpower - The Emerging Markets
Foundation
111 John St., Ste. 1005
New York, NY 10038-3110 (212) 608-4455
E-mail: contactus@empowerweb.org; URL: http://
www.empowerweb.org

Established in 2000.
Grantmaker type: Public charity.
Financial data (yr. ended 06/30/10): Revenue,
$1,048,955; assets, $1,112,612 (M); gifts
received, $825,796; expenditures, $1,784,637;
giving activities include $880,500 for grants to
organizations outside the U.S.
Purpose and activities: The foundation gives grants
to improve opportunities for disadvantaged young
people (defined by the World Health Organization as
ages 10-24) in emerging market countries in three
distinct yet interrelated areas (education, health and
leadership, and livelihoods).
Fields of interest: Education; Reproductive health;
Health care; Employment; International
development; Community/economic development;
Youth; Economically disadvantaged.
International interests: Argentina; Brazil; China;
Colombia; India; Mexico; Nigeria; Peru; Philippines;
South Africa; Thailand; Turkey; Vietnam.
Type of support: Program development.
Limitations: Applications accepted. Giving on an
international basis in Argentina, Brazil, China,
Colombia, India, Mexico, Nigeria, Peru, Philippines,
Russia, South Africa, Thailand, Turkey, and Vietnam.
No support for religious purposes, emergency or
disaster relief, lobbying, or political campaigns. No
grants to individuals, or for scholarships, land
acquisition, construction, major renovation of
facilities, or deficit reduction.
Publications: Annual report; Financial statement.
Application information: Application form required.
  Initial approach: Letter of inquiry (no more than 5
    pages)
  Deadline(s): None
  Final notification: One month
Officers and Directors: Piers Playfair,* Chair.; Marta
Cabrera, Exec. Dir.; Pedro Beroy; Joyce Chang; Peter
Clark; Michael Hirschhorn; Guido Mosca; Sue
Waterbury; and 11 additional directors.
Number of staff: 6 full-time professional; 1 part-time
support.
EIN: 030529005

1370
Endeavor Global, Inc.
(formerly The Endeavor Initiative)
900 Broadway, Ste. 600
New York, NY 10003-1237 (212) 352-3200
FAX: (212) 352-1892; E-mail: info@endeavor.com;
URL: http://www.endeavor.org

Established in 1997.
Grantmaker type: Public charity.
Financial data (yr. ended 12/31/10): Revenue, $8,312,861; assets, $13,144,161 (M); gifts received, $8,329,117; expenditures, $6,613,878; giving activities include $664,050 for grants to organizations outside the U.S., $46,662 for grants to individuals, and $62,929 for grants to individuals outside the U.S.
Purpose and activities: The organization aims to become the leading global supporter of entrepreneurship by breaking down barriers to new venture creation and promoting the next generation of emerging-market business leaders.
Fields of interest: Venture philanthropy; International economic development.
International interests: South Africa; Mexico; Argentina; Brazil; Chile; Uruguay.
Limitations: Giving on an international basis, primarily in Argentina, Brazil, Chile, Mexico, South Africa, and Uruguay.
Publications: Annual report; Informational brochure.
Officers and Directors:* Edgar Bronfman, Jr.,* Chair.; Linda Rottenberg,* C.E.O.; Louise Hulme,* Dir., Finance and Admin.; Emilio Azcarraga-Jean; Nicholas F. Beim; J. Michael Cline; Tim C. Draper; Paul J. Fribourg; Jason Green; Peter Kellner; Michael Klein; Daniel S. Och; Charles B. Seelig; Brian Swette; James D. Wolfensohn.
Number of staff: 7 full-time professional; 3 full-time support.
EIN: 133931449

1371
The Charles Engelhard Foundation
Olympic Twrs.
645 5th Ave., 7th Fl.
New York, NY 10022-5910
Contact: Mary Ogorzaly, Secy.
FAX: (212) 935-2434;
E-mail: mary@engelhardhanovia.com

Incorporated in 1949 in NJ.
Donors: Charles Engelhard†; Jane Engelhard†; Engelhard Hanovia, Inc.; and others.
Grantmaker type: Independent foundation.
Financial data (yr. ended 12/31/09): Assets, $90,889,950 (M); expenditures, $10,915,401; qualifying distributions, $10,427,898; giving activities include $9,974,965 for 214 grants (high: $591,000; low: $500; average: $1,000–$442,301).
Purpose and activities: Emphasis on higher and secondary education, and cultural, medical, religious, wildlife, and conservation organizations.
Fields of interest: Arts; Secondary school/education; Higher education; Environment, natural resources; Animals/wildlife, preservation/protection; Biomedicine; Medical research, institute; Religion; Youth.
Type of support: General/operating support; Continuing support; Annual campaigns; Capital campaigns; Building/renovation; Endowments; Program development; Conferences/seminars; Professorships; Film/video/radio; Publication; Scholarship funds; Research; Matching/challenge support.
Limitations: Applications not accepted. Giving on a national basis. No support for political organizations. No grants to individuals.
Publications: Financial statement.
Application information: Giving only to organizations known to the trustees. Unsolicited requests for funds not considered.
Board meeting date(s): Quarterly
Officers: Mary Ogorzaly, Secy.; Edward G. Beimfohr, Treas.
Trustees: Sophie Engelhard Craighead; Anne E. de la Renta; Charlene B. Engelhard; Susan O'Connor; Sally E. Pingree.
Number of staff: 1 full-time professional; 2 part-time professional.
EIN: 226063032
Recent grants for international programs:
1371-1 Artists for a New South Africa, Los Angeles, CA, $10,000. 2009.
1371-2 Building A Global Community, Minooka, IL, $21,000. 2009.
1371-3 Carter Center, Atlanta, GA, $200,000. 2009.
1371-4 Catholic Relief Services, Baltimore, MD, $35,000. 2009.
1371-5 Compassionate Service Society, City of Industry, CA, $20,000. 2009.
1371-6 Cross Cultural Journeys Foundation, Sausalito, CA, $50,000. 2009.
1371-7 Dilgo Khyentse Fellowship, New York, NY, $25,000. 2009.
1371-8 Doctors Without Borders USA, New York, NY, $100,000. 2009.
1371-9 Friends of the Osa, Washington, DC, $10,000. 2009.
1371-10 Fund for War-Affected Children and Youth in Northern Uganda, New York, NY, $117,000. 2009.
1371-11 Institute for EthnoMedicine, Jackson, WY, $50,000. 2009.
1371-12 International Campaign for Tibet, Washington, DC, $15,000. 2009.
1371-13 International Rescue Committee, New York, NY, $10,000. 2009.
1371-14 Keep a Child Alive, Brooklyn, NY, $60,000. 2009.
1371-15 Missoula Medical Aid, Missoula, MT, $10,000. 2009.
1371-16 Refugees International, Washington, DC, $115,000. 2009.
1371-17 Save the Children Federation, Westport, CT, $210,000. 2009.
1371-18 Shedrub Development Fund, Northampton, MA, $25,000. 2009.
1371-19 Tributary Fund, Bozeman, MT, $35,000. 2009.
1371-20 United States Department of State, Washington, DC, $50,000. 2009.
1371-21 United States Fund for UNICEF, New York, NY, $55,000. 2009.
1371-22 United States Fund for UNICEF, New York, NY, $15,000. 2009.

1372
Engineering Information Foundation
(also known as EiF)
180 W. 80th St., Ste. 207
New York, NY 10024-6301 (212) 579-7596
Contact: Hans Rutimann, Pres.
FAX: (212) 579-7517; E-mail: info@eifgrants.org;
URL: http://www.eifgrants.org

Established in 1934 as a publisher of engineering information with the legal status of a public charity. Restructured in 1994 in NY as a private foundation; approved July 25, 1996, with first round of grants made in Aug. 1997.
Grantmaker type: Independent foundation.
Financial data (yr. ended 12/31/10): Assets, $6,121,850 (M); expenditures, $375,702; qualifying distributions, $291,491; giving activities include $158,283 for grants.
Purpose and activities: Support for educational research programs that advance the availability and use of information related to engineering and applied technologies, programs conducted by engineering educators that encourage women to undertake careers in engineering, and projects to improve access to engineering information for students and faculty of educational institutions in developing countries.
Fields of interest: Women, centers/services; Science, research; Science, information services; Engineering/technology; Women.
International interests: Developing countries.
Type of support: Program development; Research; Matching/challenge support.
Limitations: Applications accepted. Giving on a national and international basis. No grants to individuals, or for general operating expenses, or for equipment, general overhead, capital campaigns, conferences, scholarships, assistantships, doctoral candidates, or fellowships; no loans.
Publications: Application guidelines; Annual report (including application guidelines); Financial statement; Grants list.
Application information: Initial applications are not accepted online. Non-U.S. institutions are required to submit an affidavit of equivalency, and/or name of intermediary organization. Application guidelines available on foundation web site. Application form not required.
Initial approach: Proposal via surface mail
Copies of proposal: 5
Deadline(s): Feb. 28 and Aug. 31
Board meeting date(s): Apr. and Oct.
Final notification: Within 30 days of board meeting
Officers and Directors:* Hans Rutimann,* Pres.; John J. Regazzi,* V.P.; Julie A. Shimer,* Secy.; Ruth A. Miller, Exec. Dir.; Eisen Jo Casaclang.
Number of staff: 1 part-time professional.
EIN: 131679606

1373
Englander Foundation, Inc.
740 Park Ave.
New York, NY 10021-4251 (212) 841-4148

Established in 1991 in NY.
Donors: Israel A. Englander; Englander Capital Corp.
Grantmaker type: Independent foundation.
Financial data (yr. ended 11/30/09): Assets, $5,385,353 (M); gifts received, $8,523,469; expenditures, $12,545,866; qualifying distributions, $11,482,106; giving activities include $11,481,152 for 59 grants (high: $10,651,000; low: $250).
Purpose and activities: Giving primarily for Jewish agencies and temples; some funding for education, health care, and human services.
Fields of interest: Elementary/secondary education; Theological school/education; Hospitals

(general); Human services; Jewish federated giving programs; Jewish agencies & synagogues.
International interests: Israel.
Type of support: General/operating support; Continuing support; Annual campaigns; Capital campaigns; Building/renovation.
Limitations: Applications not accepted. Giving primarily in the metropolitan New York, NY, area. No grants to individuals.
Publications: Financial statement; Grants list.
Application information: Contributes only to pre-selected organizations.
Officers: Israel A. Englander, Pres.; Caryl S. Englander, V.P.; Steven C. Weidman, Secy.-Treas.; Lenard Brafman, V.P.
EIN: 133640833

1374
Epstein Teicher Philanthropies

(formerly Epstein Philanthropies)
c/o Milton S. Teicher
75 Rockefeller Plz., 16th Fl.
New York, NY   10019-6908

Established In 1977 in NY.
Donors: Thomas Epstein†; William A. Epstein†; Florence E. Teicher†.
Grantmaker type: Independent foundation.
Financial data (yr. ended 12/31/10): Assets, $28,339,076 (M); expenditures, $1,572,409; qualifying distributions, $1,283,250; giving activities include $1,283,250 for 57 grants (high: $150,000; low: $750).
Purpose and activities: Giving primarily for the arts, education, and human rights and poverty issues.
Fields of interest: Hospitals (general); Jewish agencies & synagogues; Museums; Arts; Education; Human services; International human rights.
Limitations: Applications not accepted. Giving primarily in New York, NY. No support for religious or political organizations. No grants to individuals.
Application information: Contributes only to pre-selected organizations.
Officers: Seth Teicher, Pres.; Milton S. Teicher, Treas.; Jane E. Heffner, V.P. and Secy.
EIN: 132902852

1375
Estonian Relief Committee, Inc.

243 E. 34th St.
New York, NY   10016-4852   (212) 685-7467
Contact: Endel Reinpoid, Pres.

Established in 1942 in NY.
Grantmaker type: Public charity.
Financial data (yr. ended 12/31/10): Revenue, $64,786; assets, $1,019,174 (M); gifts received, $38,459; expenditures, $133,282; giving activities include $46,997 for grants, $41,940 for grants to organizations outside the U.S., and $21,960 for grants to individuals.
Purpose and activities: The organization supports organizations and individuals involved in relief aid in Estonia.
Fields of interest: Human services.
International interests: Estonia.
Type of support: Grants to individuals.
Limitations: Giving limited to Estonia.
Officers: Endel Reinpoid, Pres.; Merike Grunbaum, V.P.; Paul Samre, V.P.; Virve Vaher, Secy.-Treas.
EIN: 135576607

1376
Eule Charitable Foundation

14 Hampton Rd.
Port Washington, NY   11050-3009

Established in 2003 in NY.
Donors: Daniel Eule; Soros Fund Charitable Foundation.
Grantmaker type: Independent foundation.
Financial data (yr. ended 11/30/10): Assets, $4,056,495 (M); gifts received, $400,000; expenditures, $205,336; qualifying distributions, $203,040; giving activities include $203,040 for 17 grants (high: $35,000; low: $1,000).
Fields of interest: United Ways and Federated Giving Programs; Health organizations, association; Human services; Children/youth, services; International affairs.
Limitations: Applications not accepted. Giving primarily in Maplewood, NJ and NY. No grants to individuals.
Application information: Contributes only to pre-selected organizations.
Trustees: Beth Eule; Daniel Eule.
EIN: 137390001

1377
Ezer M'Zion, Inc.

1281 49th St.
Brooklyn, NY   11219-3055   (718) 853-8400
FAX: (718) 437-4683; E-mail: ezermizion@aol.com

Established in 1979.
Grantmaker type: Public charity.
Financial data (yr. ended 12/31/10): Revenue, $3,453,654; assets, $1,328,994 (M); gifts received, $3,453,541; expenditures, $2,635,299; giving activities include $29,450 for grants, and $1,661,324 for grants to organizations outside the U.S.
Purpose and activities: The organization offers medical and social support services to help Israel's sick, disabled, elderly, and underprivileged populations.
Fields of interest: Health care.
International interests: Israel.
Type of support: Grants to individuals; In-kind gifts.
Limitations: Giving primarily in Israel.
Publications: Newsletter.
Officers and Directors:* Chananya Chollak,* Chair.; Yehoshua Feldstein,* Pres.; Victor Quinn,* V.P.; Sarah L. Mueller,* Treas.; David Breyer; Allan Zucker.
EIN: 133660421

1378
The Howard and Barbara Farkas Foundation

c/o Gasser & Hayes
106-19 Metropolitan Ave.
Forest Hills, NY   11375-6739

Donor: Barbara Farkas†.
Grantmaker type: Independent foundation.
Financial data (yr. ended 12/31/10): Assets, $5,469,710 (M); expenditures, $300,963; qualifying distributions, $292,250; giving activities include $292,250 for grants.
Fields of interest: Homeless, human services; Education; AIDS; Food banks; Human services;

Christian agencies & churches; AIDS, people with; Economically disadvantaged.
International interests: Africa.
Limitations: Applications not accepted. Giving primarily in NY. No grants to individuals.
Application information: Contributes only to pre-selected organizations.
Officers: John C. Crabill, Pres. and Treas.; James A. Beha, V.P.; Macy Ann Beha, Secy.
EIN: 133107852

1379
Fast Retailing USA, Inc.Corporate Giving Program

101 Avenue of the Americas, 11th Fl.
New York, NY   10013   (212) 221-9037
E-mail: marketing@uniqlo-usa.com; URL: http://www.fastretailing.com/eng/csr/

Grantmaker type: Corporate giving program.
Purpose and activities: Fast Retailing USA makes charitable contributions to nonprofit organizations involved with the environment, international refugees, and disaster relief.
Fields of interest: Athletics/sports, Special Olympics; International migration/refugee issues; Disasters, preparedness/services; Environment.
Type of support: General/operating support; Cause-related marketing; Employee volunteer services; Donated products.

1380
Seymour Feldman Foundation, Inc.

277 Broadway, Ste. 601
New York, NY   10007-2029   (212) 233-5688
Contact: Leslie C. Feldman, Pres.

Established in 2005 in NY.
Donor: Seymour Feldman†.
Grantmaker type: Independent foundation.
Financial data (yr. ended 05/31/11): Assets, $4,670,011 (M); expenditures, $244,941; qualifying distributions, $212,332; giving activities include $212,332 for 34 grants (high: $22,100; low: $720).
Fields of interest: Higher education, university; Museums; Medical school/education; Hospitals (general); International affairs, public policy; Jewish agencies & synagogues.
Type of support: General/operating support.
Application information: Application form required.
  Initial approach: Proposal
  Deadline(s): None
Officers: Leslie C. Feldman, Pres. and Treas.; Jeffrey Feldman, V.P. and Secy.
EIN: 203555993

1381
Fellowship of Reconciliation, Inc.

(also known as F.O.R.)
521 N. Broadway
Nyack, NY   10960-1215   (845) 358-4601
Contact: Rachel Pfeffer, Exec. Dir.
FAX: (845) 358-4924; E-mail: for@forusa.org; URL: http://www.forusa.org

Established in 1915 in NY.
Grantmaker type: Public charity.
Financial data (yr. ended 06/30/10): Revenue, $1,498,924; assets, $3,050,195 (M); gifts

received, $1,175,804; expenditures, $1,423,670; giving activities include $97,857 for grants to organizations outside the U.S.

Purpose and activities: The fellowship seeks to replace violence, war, racism, and economic injustice with nonviolence, peace and justice. The fellowship is an interfaith organization committed to active nonviolence as a transforming way of life and as a means of radical change.

Fields of interest: International peace/security.

Application information: See Web site for further application information and guidelines.

   Deadline(s): Apr. 15 for King Awards and Pfeffer Peace Prize

Officers and Directors:* Ed McManus,* Chair.; Dorothy Cotton,* Vice-Chair.; Allie Perry,* V.P.; Rev. Terek El Heneidy,* Treas.; Rachel Pfeffer, Exec. Dir.; Lillian K. Baxter; Michael Brown; Ilise Cohen; Ethan Flad; Susan Glaser; and 11 additional directors.

EIN: 133792144

1382
Fight for Sight, Inc.

381 Park Ave. S., Ste. 809
New York, NY   10016-8806   (212) 679-6060
FAX: (212) 679-4466;
E-mail: info@fightforsight.com; URL: http://www.fightforsight.com

Established in 1946 in NY as National Council to Combat Blindness; current name adopted in 1959.

Grantmaker type: Public charity.

Financial data (yr. ended 03/31/09): Revenue, $673,425; assets, $3,164,860 (M); gifts received, $752,565; expenditures, $686,290; giving activities include $281,000 for grants.

Purpose and activities: The organization finances research in ophthalmology, vision, and related sciences.

Fields of interest: Eye research.

International interests: Canada; Israel.

Type of support: Grants to individuals; General/operating support; Fellowships; Research.

Limitations: Applications accepted. Giving limited to the U.S. and Canada.

Publications: Application guidelines; Annual report; Financial statement; Grants list; Informational brochure; Newsletter.

Application information: Application form required.
   Initial approach: Complete online application
   Copies of proposal: 21
   Deadline(s): Feb. 1 for Summer Student Fellowship; Mar. 1 for Grants-In-Aid and Postdoctoral Fellowships
   Board meeting date(s): Four times per year

Officers and Directors:* Kenneth R. Barasch,* M.D., Pres.; Gaby Kressly,* Secy.; Elaine Hall, Ph.D.; Randy Kardon, M.D., Ph.D.; Tracy S. Keogh; Norman J. Kleiman, Ph.D.; Polly Sheppard; Belinda Walker Terry.

Number of staff: 3 full-time professional; 1 part-time professional.

EIN: 237085732

1383
FIMF, Inc.

c/o Hertz, Herson & Co., LLP
2 Park Ave., Ste. 1500
New York, NY   10016-5701

Established in 1995 in DE and NY.

Grantmaker type: Independent foundation.

Financial data (yr. ended 12/31/10): Assets, $28,816,787 (M); expenditures, $1,368,785; qualifying distributions, $1,250,685; giving activities include $1,250,685 for grants.

Purpose and activities: Giving primarily to Jewish organizations.

Fields of interest: Higher education; Education; Human services; Children/youth, services; Jewish agencies & synagogues.

International interests: Israel.

Limitations: Applications not accepted. Giving primarily in Cambridge, MA, New York, NY, PA, and Israel. No grants to individuals.

Application information: Contributes only to pre-selected organizations.

Officer and Directors:* Susan Wexner,* Pres. and Secy.-Treas.; Dr. Bernard Agus; Dr. Saul G. Agus; Raymond Kanner; Gregg H. Levy, Esq.; Michael S. Oberman, Esq.; Mark Saks, Esq.

EIN: 134072661

1384
Harry and Jane Fischel Foundation

875 Avenue of the Americas, Ste. 1701
New York, NY   10001-3507   (212) 599-2828
FAX: (212) 867-8512;
E-mail: info@fischelfoundation.org; URL: http://fischelfoundation.org/index.htm

Incorporated in 1932 in NY.

Donor: Harry Fischel†.

Grantmaker type: Independent foundation.

Financial data (yr. ended 12/31/10): Assets, $12,504,775 (M); expenditures, $1,039,941; qualifying distributions, $598,968; giving activities include $423,300 for 16+ grants (high: $343,000).

Purpose and activities: Organized to develop Talmudic research to aid Jewish knowledge and to present the Orthodox Jewish contributions to civilization. Funding also to an institute which includes a school for training judges for religious courts, publishes tracts in the field of religious law, and researches and republishes Talmudic commentary in new editions utilizing heretofore unknown manuscripts; some giving also for Jewish education and temples.

Fields of interest: Education; Jewish agencies & synagogues.

International interests: Israel.

Type of support: General/operating support.

Limitations: Applications not accepted. Giving primarily in NY; some giving also in Israel. No grants to individuals.

Application information: Contributes only to pre-selected organizations.

Officers and Directors:* Chief Rabbi S.Y. Cohen,* Chair.; Seth M. Goldstein,* Pres.; Rabbi Hillel Reichel,* V.P.; Rabbi Aaron Reichel,* Secy.; Menachem David,* Treas.; David Locker; Jay Stepelman; Rabbi O. Asher Reichel.

Number of staff: 1 part-time professional; 2 part-time support.

EIN: 135677832

1385
Lawton W. Fitt and James I. McLaren Foundation

c/o Goldman Sachs & Co. - Family Office
Bowling Green Station
P.O. Box 73
New York, NY   10274-0073

Established in 1996 in NY.

Donors: Lawton W. Fitt; James McLaren.

Grantmaker type: Independent foundation.

Financial data (yr. ended 09/30/10): Assets, $7,158,989 (M); expenditures, $359,535; qualifying distributions, $354,750; giving activities include $354,750 for 20 grants (high: $100,000; low: $250).

Purpose and activities: Giving primarily for international relations and education; some giving also for the arts and social services.

Fields of interest: Youth development; Performing arts; Arts; Higher education; Education; Health care; Health organizations, association; Human services; International development; United Ways and Federated Giving Programs.

Limitations: Applications not accepted. Giving primarily in NY and VA. No grants to individuals, or for scholarships; no loans.

Application information: Contributes only to pre-selected organizations.

Trustees: Lawton W. Fitt; James I. McLaren.

EIN: 133919763

1386
The FJJ Foundation, Inc.

c/o Marks Paneth & Shrom, LLP
622 3rd Ave.
New York, NY   10017-6701

Established in 1993 in DE.

Donors: Masham Corp.; Dr. Arturo Constantiner; Leon Constantiner.

Grantmaker type: Independent foundation.

Financial data (yr. ended 12/31/10): Assets, $586,981 (M); expenditures, $303,641; qualifying distributions, $300,000; giving activities include $300,000 for grants.

Purpose and activities: Giving primarily for education and to Jewish organizations; funding also for a nonprofit movie theater.

Fields of interest: Media, film/video; Higher education; Hospitals (general); Jewish federated giving programs; Jewish agencies & synagogues.

International interests: Israel.

Limitations: Applications not accepted. Giving primarily in New York, NY. No grants to individuals.

Application information: Contributes only to pre-selected organizations.

Officer and Directors:* Dr. Arturo Constantiner,* Chair.; Leon Constantiner.

EIN: 133693589

1387
The Fledgling Fund

162 5th Ave., Ste. 901
New York, NY   10010-5967
E-mail: info@thefledglingfund.org; URL: http://www.thefledglingfund.org
Blog: http://www.thefledglingfund.org/blog/
Facebook: http://www.facebook.com/pages/The-Fledgling-Fund/101890706557481
Twitter: http://twitter.com/fledglingfund

Donor: Diana Barrett.
Grantmaker type: Independent foundation.
Financial data (yr. ended 12/31/09): Assets, $18,446,847 (M); expenditures, $2,734,365; qualifying distributions, $2,775,853; giving activities include $2,126,605 for 114 grants (high: $100,000; low: $150).
Purpose and activities: The fund seeks to improve the lives of vulnerable individuals, families and communities by supporting innovative media projects that target entrenched social problems.
Fields of interest: Media, film/video; Environment, beautification programs; Environment; Health care; Substance abuse, prevention; Housing/shelter; Children/youth, services; International affairs; Civil/human rights, advocacy.
Type of support: Film/video/radio.
Limitations: Giving on a national and international basis.
Application information: See foundation web site for application guidelines and procedures. Application form required.
   Initial approach: Complete foundation online letter of inquiry
   Deadline(s): See foundation web site
Officers and Directors:* Diana Barrett,* Pres. and Secy.; Bob Vila,* V.P.; Robert Connor, V.P.; Christopher Vila,* V.P.; Jessica Wolfe, V.P.
Number of staff: 1 full-time professional; 2 part-time professional.
EIN: 202450707

1388
Flowering Tree
225 E. 57th St., Apt. 18D
New York, NY   10022-2861
E-mail: contactus@floweringtreeinc.org;
URL: http://www.floweringtreeinc.org

Established in NY.
Donors: Rajesh Ambasta; Sumita Ambasta; Sansar Capital Foundation.
Grantmaker type: Operating foundation.
Financial data (yr. ended 12/31/10): Assets, $0 (M); expenditures, $262,145; qualifying distributions, $230,000; giving activities include $230,000 for 2 grants (high: $170,000; low: $60,000).
Purpose and activities: The foundation's organization's mission is to support women's development and children's education.
Fields of interest: Education; Women; Children.
International interests: India; Singapore.
Limitations: Applications accepted. Giving primarily in India. No grants to individuals.
Application information: Full proposals accepted by invitation only.
   Initial approach: Letter of inquiry
   Deadline(s): None
Officers: Sumita Ambasta, Pres.
Directors: Lucy Chuah; Christopher McLeod.
EIN: 352278100

1389
The Food Allergy Initiative, Inc.
515 Madison Ave., Ste. 1912
New York, NY   10022-5403   (212) 207-1974
Contact: Robert Pacenza, Exec. Dir.

FAX: (917) 338-5130;
E-mail: info@foodallergyinitiative.org; URL: http://www.foodallergyinitiative.org
Facebook: http://www.facebook.com/FoodAllergyInitiative
Twitter: http://twitter.com/FoodAllergyInit

Established in 1997 in NY.
Grantmaker type: Public charity.
Financial data (yr. ended 12/31/10): Revenue, $5,665,965; assets, $9,382,618 (M); gifts received, $5,564,660; expenditures, $6,361,097; giving activities include $3,360,618 for grants, and $255,000 for grants to individuals.
Purpose and activities: The initiative supports research to find a cure for food allergy and clinical activities to identify and treat those at risk, and to increase public awareness.
Fields of interest: Allergies research; Allergies.
International interests: Asia; Europe.
Type of support: Research.
Limitations: Applications accepted. Giving on a national and international basis. No support for religious or political causes. No grants for capital campaigns.
Publications: Application guidelines; Financial statement; Informational brochure; Occasional report.
Application information: Application form not required.
   Initial approach: Submit concept proposal with coversheet via e-mail or regular mail
   Copies of proposal: 1
   Deadline(s): None
   Final notification: One to two months
Officers and Directors:* Todd J. Slotkin,* Chair. and Pres.; David Bunning,* Vice-Chair.; Sharyn T. Mann,* Vice-Chair.; David R. Jaffe,* Secy.-Treas.; Robert Pacenza, Exec. Dir.; Steven Braverman; Patricia Denner Cayne, Ph.D.; Leslie Cornfeld; John J. Hannan; Robert F. Kennedy, Jr.; Rebecca Lainovic; Amie Rappoport McKenna.
Number of staff: 3 full-time professional
EIN: 133905508

1390
Foot Locker, Inc. Corporate Giving Program
(formerly Venator Group, Inc. Corporate Giving Program)
112 W. 34th St.
New York, NY   10120-0101   (212) 720-3700
URL: http://www.footlocker-inc.com/community.cfm?page=community

Grantmaker type: Corporate giving program.
Purpose and activities: Foot Locker makes charitable contributions to nonprofit organizations involved with education, breast cancer, athletics and sports, children and youth, international affairs, economically disadvantaged people, and other areas. Support is given in areas of company operations.
Fields of interest: General charitable giving; Education; Breast cancer; Athletics/sports, amateur leagues; Children/youth, services; International affairs; Economically disadvantaged.
Type of support: General/operating support; Program development; Employee volunteer services; Sponsorships; Donated equipment; Donated products.
Limitations: Giving primarily in areas of company operations; giving also to national organizations.

1391
Ford Foundation
320 E. 43rd St.
New York, NY   10017-4801   (212) 573-5000
Contact: Secy.
FAX: (212) 351-3677;
E-mail: office-secretary@fordfoundation.org;
URL: http://www.fordfoundation.org
Employment Feed: http://www.fordfoundation.org/feeds/employment
E-Newsletter: http://www.fordfoundation.org/About-Us#sign-up
Flickr: http://www.flickr.com/photos/ford-foundation/
Ford Foundation's Philanthropy Promise: http://www.ncrp.org/philanthropys-promise/who
Foundation News: http://www.fordfoundation.org/newsroom
Grants Database: http://www.fordfoundation.org/grants/search
Issues Center: http://www.fordfoundation.org/issues
Knowledge Center: http://www.fordfoundation.org/impact
Multimedia: http://www.fordfoundation.org/library/search?contenttype=6
News Feed: http://www.fordfoundation.org/feeds/newsroom
Regional Priorities Center: http://www.fordfoundation.org/regions
Vimeo: http://vimeo.com/fordfoundation
YouTube: http://www.youtube.com/fordfoundationTV

Incorporated in 1936 in MI.
Donors: Henry Ford†; Edsel Ford†.
Grantmaker type: Independent foundation.
Financial data (yr. ended 09/30/11): Assets, $10,344,933,000 (M); expenditures, $537,635,000; qualifying distributions, $424,695,000; giving activities include $424,695,000 for grants, $7,897,000 for foundation-administered programs and $16,945,000 for loans/program-related investments.
Purpose and activities: The foundation supports visionary leaders and organizations working on the frontlines of social change worldwide. Its goals for more than half a century have been to strengthen democratic values, reduce poverty and injustice, promote international cooperation, and advance human achievement. The foundation focuses on nine issues: 1) Human Rights; 2) Democratic and Accountable Government; 3) Educational Opportunity and Scholarship; 4) Economic Fairness; 5) Metropolitan Opportunity; 6) Sustainable Development; 7) Freedom of Expression; 8) Sexuality and Reproductive Health and Rights; and 9) Social Justice Philanthropy.
Fields of interest: Agriculture; AIDS; Arts; Civil rights, race/intergroup relations; Civil/human rights; Community/economic development; Crime/violence prevention, abuse prevention; Economic development; Economics; Education; Education, research; Employment; Environment; Environment, natural resources; Government/public administration; Higher education; Housing/shelter, development; Human services; International affairs; International economic development; International human rights; Law/international law; Leadership development; Legal services; Media, film/video; Media/communications; Minorities/immigrants, centers/services; Museums; Performing arts; Performing arts, dance; Performing arts, music;

Performing arts, theater; Philanthropy/voluntarism; Public affairs, citizen participation; Religion, interfaith issues; Reproductive health; Reproductive health, sexuality education; Rural development; Secondary school/education; Social sciences; Urban/community development; Women, centers/services; Youth development, research; Youth; African Americans/Blacks; AIDS, people with; Asians/Pacific Islanders; Economically disadvantaged; Hispanics/Latinos; Immigrants/refugees; Indigenous peoples; LGBTQ; Minorities; Women.

International interests: Africa; Asia; Latin America; Middle East.

Type of support: Continuing support; Employee matching gifts; Endowments; General/operating support; Management development/capacity building; Program development; Program evaluation; Program-related investments/loans.

Limitations: Applications accepted. Giving in the United States, Africa, the Middle East, Asia, Latin America and the Caribbean, and also on a global basis, with a focus on nine core issues. No support for programs for which substantial support from government or other sources is readily available, or for religious sectarian activities. No grants for construction or maintenance of buildings, undergraduate scholarships, or for purely personal or local needs. The vast majority of foundation grants go to organizations. Historically, the foundation has provided a very limited number of fellowship opportunities for individuals, focusing on advanced degrees in areas of interest to the foundation. When available, recipients are selected by universities and other organizations that receive grants from the foundation to support fellowships.

Publications: Annual report; Informational brochure; Occasional report.

Application information: Prospective applicants are advised to carefully review the foundation's initiatives online, and to download and review the Grant Application Guide for additional details about the grant-review process at http://www.fordfoundation.org/pdfs/grants/grant-application-guide.pdf. Application form not required.

Initial approach: After reviewing the Grant Application Guide, submit an inquiry online using the Grant Inquiry Form (http://www.fordfoundation.org/grants/select-country-or-region)

Copies of proposal: 1

Deadline(s): None, grants are made throughout the year

Final notification: Initial indication as to whether proposal falls within program interests within 6 weeks

Officers and Trustees:* Irene Hirano Inouye,* Chairperson; Luis A. Ubinas,* President; John L. Colborn, Vice President for Operations; Eric Doppstadt, Vice President and Chief Investment Officer; Pablo J. Farias, Vice President for Economic Opportunity and Assets; Nancy P. Feller, Vice President, Secretary and General Counsel; Nicholas M. Gabriel, Vice President, Treasurer and Chief Financial Officer; Maya L. Harris, Vice President for Democracy, Rights and Justice; Marta L. Tellado, Vice President for Communications; Darren Walker, Vice President for Education, Creativity, and Free Expression; Kofi Appenteng; Tim Berners-Lee; Afsaneh M. Beschloss; Martin Eakes; Juliet V. Garcia; J. Clifford Hudson; Yolanda Kakabadse; Robert S. Kaplan; Thurgood Marshall, Jr.; N.R. Narayana Murthy; Peter A. Nadosy; Cecile Richards.

Number of staff: 254 full-time professional; 116 full-time support.
EIN: 131684331
Recent grants for international programs:

1391-1 9 to 5 National Association of Working Women, Milwaukee, WI, $250,000. For general support to strengthen women's ability to win economic justice domestically and internationally. 2010.

1391-2 Abhivyakti Media for Development, Nashik, India, $100,000. For final support for training, technical assistance and network building to help grassroots activists and organizations use media to articulate local issues and promote and advance social justice. 2010.

1391-3 ACCESS Development Services, New Delhi, India, $250,000. To launch Livelihoods India Initiative including holding policy retreats and publication of The Yearly State of the Sector Report On Livelihoods In India. 2010.

1391-4 ACCION International, Center for Financial Inclusion, Boston, MA, $175,000. To develop and disseminate toolkit to help microfinance institutions protect their client's rights to transparent, respectful and prudent financial services. 2010.

1391-5 AccountAid India, New Delhi, India, $100,000. To conduct workshops on legal and regulatory frameworks and to strengthen capacities and accountability of Indian NGO sector. 2010.

1391-6 Action Canada for Population and Development, Ottawa, Canada, $500,000. For international collaboration to design and implement strategies for advancing sexual and reproductive rights as human rights at UN human rights council. 2010.

1391-7 Action Health, Lagos, Nigeria, $650,000. To develop strategic plan for training sexuality education teachers, monitor and evaluate delivery of sexuality education and develop pilot economic empowerment program for out-of-school girls. 2010.

1391-8 Action Northeast Trust, Rowmari, India, $199,630. For final support to provide training, technical assistance and working capital for craft and agricultural livelihoods programs in Assam and establish farmers' resource centers. 2010.

1391-9 ActionAid USA, Washington, DC, $250,000. For research, networking and advocacy on unsustainable biofuel production in the Americas and need for regulatory mechanisms to reduce its impacts on food security, land use and climate change. 2010.

1391-10 Active Voice, San Francisco, CA, $125,000. To build makeagentorangehistory.org web site, create social media strategy, produce content and galvanize public support for Agent Orange in Vietnam information initiative. 2010.

1391-11 Advocates Coalition for Development and Environment, Kampala, Uganda, $160,000. To advocate for finalization of national land policy process in Uganda and work with ethnic minorities to claim their rights to land. 2010.

1391-12 Advocates for Youth, Washington, DC, $200,000. To advocate for inclusion of comprehensive, evidence-based HIV prevention programs in U.S. global health initiatives for youth and for integration with reproductive and sexual health services. 2010.

1391-13 Advocates for Youth, Washington, DC, $120,000. To educate policy makers about importance of prioritizing young people's sexual and reproductive health and rights in

implementation of Global Health Initiative and in global HIV/AIDS programs. 2010.

1391-14 Afesis-Corplan, East London, South Africa, $150,000. For research and advocacy to help community participation in local governance in the Eastern Cape. 2010.

1391-15 Afluentes, Mexico City, Mexico, $150,000. To design in- and out-of-school sexual and reproductive health and rights and HIV-prevention model for migrants in collaboration with Ministry of Education's Program for Vulnerable Groups. 2010.

1391-16 Africa 2000 Network-Uganda, Kampala, Uganda, $120,000. To analyze, document and disseminate lessons learned from applying participatory market development methodologies to increase the incomes of poor rural households in Africa. 2010.

1391-17 Africa and Middle East Refugee Assistance, Oxford, England, $121,000. To provide legal assistance and other services to refugees in Egypt. 2010.

1391-18 African Council of AIDS Service Organizations, Dakar, Senegal, $150,000. For final support for developing country NGO delegation to Global Fund To Fight AIDS, Tuberculosis And Malaria to fully participate in governance and work of Fund. 2010.

1391-19 African Film Festival, New York, NY, $50,000. For Artists Support Initiative to provide resources to emerging and established African artists and filmmakers. 2010.

1391-20 African Population and Health Research Center, Nairobi, Kenya, $1,000,000. For Consortium for Advanced Research Training in Africa to award fellowships to doctoral students engaged in sexuality research and strengthen research infrastructure at Carta Universities. 2010.

1391-21 African Population and Health Research Center, Nairobi, Kenya, $200,000. For research on socioeconomic context of masculinities in Nairobi slums, factors that shape practices of manliness and impact of those practices on health, well-being and civic engagement. 2010.

1391-22 African Safari Lodge Foundation, Johannesburg, South Africa, $320,000. To promote conservation-based tourism emphasizing community/private partnerships as means of building and diversifying rural livelihoods and reducing poverty and to expand model to Eastern Africa. 2010.

1391-23 African Woman and Child Feature Service, Nairobi, Kenya, $200,000. For training programs under Media Diversity Centre and for Reject, online publication on social justice and reform issues. 2010.

1391-24 African Womens Millennium Initiative on Poverty and Human Rights, Dakar, Senegal, $100,000. For final support for Young Women Knowledge and Leadership Institute to bring young women together to learn, strategize and network for social change. 2010.

1391-25 AfterImage Public Media, San Francisco, CA, $200,000. To produce Higher Ground, documentary chronicling efforts of Maldives president Mohamed Nasheed to bring democracy to the island and stave off the looming catastrophe of climate change. 2010.

1391-26 Ag Innovations Network, Sebastopol, CA, $198,500. For Sustainable Food Lab to conduct background research for and design an action-research project to determine whether regional and global value chains contribute to pro-poor development. 2010.

1391-27 Aga Khan Foundation - Switzerland, Geneva, Switzerland, $245,000. To assess and scale up a program empowering Egyptian community development associations to increase government transparency and effectiveness at the local level. 2010.

1391-28 Agewell Foundation, New Delhi, India, $30,620. To support network of trained workers to broaden treatment access and secure the well being of low-income elderly people around Delhi. 2010.

1391-29 Agter, Nogent-sur-Marne, France, $100,000. For learning exchanges and training exercises to promote community rights over natural resources. 2010.

1391-30 Ahadi Kenya Trust, Nairobi, Kenya, $30,000. For anti-jigger campaign and to provide treatment and prevention of jigger infestation to curb high rates of school dropouts amongst children in Kiambu District. 2010.

1391-31 AIDS Accountability International, Stockholm, Sweden, $400,000. For final general support to ensure implementation and improve quality of global response to HIV/AIDS pandemic. 2010.

1391-32 AIDS Accountability International, Stockholm, Sweden, $150,000. To develop scorecard for monitoring country reporting on progress toward implementing Maputo Plan of Action on Sexual and Reproductive Health and Rights (Maputo PoA) and to assess reporting process. 2010.

1391-33 AIDS Accountability International, Stockholm, Sweden, $150,000. For HIV/AIDS Forum to provide venue for exchanging knowledge, ideas and experiences on holding governments accountable for not meeting HIV/AIDS commitments and to plan Accountability Conference. 2010.

1391-34 AIDS Law Project, Braamfontein, South Africa, $150,000. For research, advocacy, litigation and training on human rights of people living with HIV/AIDS and for technical assistance to facilitate organizational restructuring. 2010.

1391-35 Airputih Foundation, Baru, Indonesia, $150,000. For research on telecommunications regulatory environment and to develop strategies and applications that assist civil society groups to maximize mobile devices as communications platforms. 2010.

1391-36 Al Kamandjati Association, Ramallah, West Bank/Gaza (Palestinian Territories), $100,000. To build institutional capacity and organize music workshops for young Palestinians. 2010.

1391-37 Al-Kasaba Theater and Cinematheque, Ramallah, West Bank/Gaza (Palestinian Territories), $70,000. For operating support and to undertake in-depth strategic planning process. 2010.

1391-38 Al-Mamal Foundation for Contemporary Art, East Jerusalem, $140,000. For visual arts residency, educational and exhibition program in East Jerusalem. 2010.

1391-39 Aliansi Masyarakat Adat Nusantara, Jakarta, Indonesia, $400,000. For organizational development, training and technical assistance to help indigenous communities resolve land-use conflicts with third parties, with focus on free, prior and informed consent. 2010.

1391-40 All India Artisans and Craftworkers Welfare Association, New Delhi, India, $300,000. To

connect craft producers to mainstream markets in commercially sustainable manner, study feasibility of a bridge loan fund, create an impact assessment system and build institutional capacity. 2010.

1391-41 Alliance Publishing Trust, London, England, $50,000. For final general support for Alliance Magazine to facilitate exchange of information and ideas among philanthropists, social investors and others working for social change worldwide. 2010.

1391-42 Allianz SE, Munich, Germany, $118,872. To pilot and evaluate commercially viable combined savings, life and health insurance product for low-income households in eastern Indonesia. 2010.

1391-43 Alternative Credit Technologies, Washington, DC, $443,248. For Social Performance Task Force to promote transparency about social outcomes achieved by microfinance institutions and increase their effectiveness in improving lives of poor people. 2010.

1391-44 Alternative Information and Development Centre, Cape Town, South Africa, $20,000. For capacity building, training and hosting of series of seminars and dialogues on social justice issues in the context of South African Constitution and Bill Of Rights. 2010.

1391-45 Alzheimers and Related Disorders Society of India, New Delhi, India, $25,000. For final support to create awareness on Alzheimer's and related disorders and provide holistic care and support for affected elderly and their family members. 2010.

1391-46 AMAN, New Delhi, India, $150,000. For final general support to design and implement locally appropriate civic interventions using a human rights framework for addressing and mitigating violent conflict triggered by caste and religious conflicts. 2010.

1391-47 Amazon Institute of People and the Environment, Belem, Brazil, $100,000. To coordinate sustainable Amazon forum and help it develop and promote agenda for sustainable development in the region. 2010.

1391-48 Amazon Institute of People and the Environment, Instituto do Homem e Meio Ambiente da Amazonia (IMAZON), Belem, Brazil, $150,000. To monitor and assess land tenure regularization process in Brazilian Amazon and disseminate findings. 2010.

1391-49 Amazon Working Group, Brasilia, Brazil, $400,000. To establish Reducing Emissions from Deforestation and Degradation (REDD) observatory to monitor public policies related to REDD and build traditional peoples' capacity to influence these policies. 2010.

1391-50 American Bar Association Fund for Justice and Education, Washington, DC, $150,000. To train young male professors in Egyptian public university law faculties in new teaching methods and to develop new curricula. 2010.

1391-51 American Friends of the Ludwig Foundation of Cuba, New York, NY, $50,000. To research, document and publish book for artists and arts professionals on appraising Cuban arts. 2010.

1391-52 American Society for Yad Vashem, New York, NY, $400,000. For Righteous Among the Nations to verify and record acts of courage by non-Jews who risked lives to save Jews during the Holocaust, honor the Righteous and develop online exhibitions. 2010.

1391-53 American University, Washington, DC, $192,500. For Latin American Initiative on

Justice, Gender and Sexuality (ALAS Network) to promote engagement of Latin American academics in advancement of sexual and reproductive rights and gender equity. 2010.

1391-54 American University in Cairo, Social Research Center, Cairo, Egypt, $280,000. To study dynamic relationship among resource rights, marginalization and environmental well-being in rural Egypt and build capacity of young researchers in the field. 2010.

1391-55 American University in Cairo, Social Research Center, Cairo, Egypt, $120,000. To conduct research on equity of access to higher education in Egypt, disseminate findings and mentor junior-level graduate students participating in the project. 2010.

1391-56 American University of Beirut, Beirut, Lebanon, $200,000. For final support for Neighborhood Initiative to strengthen university and community interactions and partnerships. 2010.

1391-57 American University of Beirut, Beirut, Lebanon, $200,000. For capacity building of cadre of educators and practitioners for scaling up sexuality and reproductive health education for youth in Lebanon And Egypt. 2010.

1391-58 Americans for Indian Opportunity, Albuquerque, NM, $300,000. For Ambassadors Program to develop knowledge and skills of emerging indigenous leaders in the U.S. and internationally. 2010.

1391-59 Americas Society, New York, NY, $132,700. To use America's Quarterly as forum for presenting new research and promoting fresh debate on how to address systemic, common problems of social inclusion throughout the Western Hemisphere. 2010.

1391-60 Americas Voice Education Fund, Washington, DC, $400,000. For general support to realize promise of workable and humane comprehensive immigration reform. 2010.

1391-61 Arab Foundation for Freedoms And Equality, Beirut, Lebanon, $140,000. For research and capacity building in documenting discriminatory practices and improving service access by discriminated-against groups. 2010.

1391-62 Arab Fund for Arts and Culture, Geneva, Switzerland, $200,000. To support grant making to stimulate creativity, critical thinking and freedom of expression in the Arab region. 2010.

1391-63 Arab Institute for Human Rights, El Menzah, Tunisia, $278,000. For training and knowledge production to build civil society capacity to promote and advance marginalized groups' access to economic and social rights. 2010.

1391-64 Arab Network of NGOs for Development, Beirut, Lebanon, $270,000. For final support to enhance research-based advocacy aimed at reconciling trade agreements with human development, human rights and democracy. 2010.

1391-65 Argentine Forensic Anthropology Team, Buenos Aires, Argentina, $150,000. To plan creation of and pilot Bi-national Governmental/NGO committee to coordinate identification of remains and search for missing people at U.S.-Mexico border. 2010.

1391-66 Arid Lands Information Network-Eastern Africa, Nairobi, Kenya, $150,000. To help rural communities in Eastern Africa use information and communications technology to increase their access to market opportunities and contribute to policy debates on issues that affect them. 2010.

1391-67 Art Moves Africa, Brussels, Belgium, $150,000. For travel fund to facilitate regional and transregional mobility of artists within Africa and encourage collaboration, learning and exchanges. 2010.

1391-68 Arthur F. Burns Fellowship Program, Washington, DC, $75,000. For travel and research grants to enable program alumni to cover transatlantic issues and to recruit minority fellows , offer intensive foreign language training and hold orientation. 2010.

1391-69 ARTICLE 19, London, England, $230,000. To support Mexico chapter, in partnership with civil society organizations and migration experts, to develop and begin implementation of a joint communications strategy on migration and related policies. 2010.

1391-70 Arts and Business Foundation, Lagos, Nigeria, $2,000,000. To build Federal Government Of Nigeria National Commission And Monument's National Museum Lagos Conservation Centre And Laboratory. 2010.

1391-71 Ashkal Alwan, The Lebanese Association for Plastic Arts, Beirut, Lebanon, $175,000. For Home Works V, regional forum on contemporary art and cultural practices in the Middle East and North Africa region. 2010.

1391-72 Ashoka Trust for Research in Ecology and the Environment, Bangalore, India, $369,031. For endowment support for environment and development activities and to facilitate integration of Centre For Interdisciplinary Studies in Environment and Development Into ATREE. 2010.

1391-73 Asian African Heritage Trust, Nairobi, Kenya, $50,000. For research, dissemination, public education, networking and advocacy to preserve, present and promote recognition of role and experiences of Asian Africans and promote their civic participation. 2010.

1391-74 Asian Centre for Human Rights, New Delhi, India, $200,000. To publish India Human Rights Report Quarterly and take emblematic economic and social rights cases to national and international human rights bodies and constitutional courts. 2010.

1391-75 Asociacion Grupo de Mujeres Mayas Kaqla, Guatemala City, Guatemala, $100,000. To develop institutional strategy for promoting artistic development of Mayan women and create network of Central American indigenous women's organizations to foster Mayan cultural identity. 2010.

1391-76 Asociacion Servicios Educativos Rurales, Lima, Peru, $170,000. For training, technical assistance, dialogue and meetings to promote participation of regional actors in debate and decision making regarding large-scale infrastructure projects in Peru. 2010.

1391-77 Aspen Institute, Washington, DC, $128,150. To manage American side of U.S.-Vietnam Dialogue Group on Agent Orange/ Dioxin and provide technical assistance to and monitor grantees of Agent Orange Vietnam information initiative. 2010.

1391-78 Associacao Brasileira das Emissoras Publicas Educativas e Culturais, Brasilia, Brazil, $149,602. For First International Forum On Digital Content Production For Public TV to discuss Challenges of migrating to digital technology and share best practices in content production & distribution. 2010.

1391-79 Associacao Brasileira de Pesquisadores Negros, Brasilia, Brazil, $200,000. For exchange, research and training among Afro-Brazilian scholars focusing on educational equity. 2010.

1391-80 Associacao Cultural de Mulheres Negras, Porto Alegre, Brazil, $450,000. For Training, monitoring and public education to promote and advocate for Afro-Brazilian women's rights nationally and internationally in partnership with U.S.-based organization, Global Rights. 2010.

1391-81 Associacao de Universidades Amazonicas, Belem, Brazil, $100,000. For social mapping activities in Guyana, Colombia and Bolivia to identify indigenous and traditional peoples. 2010.

1391-82 Associacao dos Magistrados Brasileiros, Brasilia, Brazil, $80,000. To publish the first issue, focused on Afro-Brazilians, of journal on culture and human rights for distribution to all Brazilian judges, educational institutions, journalists and public officials. 2010.

1391-83 Association for Asian Studies, Ann Arbor, MI, $98,808. For series of presentations on topics of public interest by Chinese participants at AAS annual conference and related activities. 2010.

1391-84 Association for Democratic Reforms, Ahmadabad, India, $200,000. To enhance civil society's role in demanding greater transparency and accountability in electoral process and representative institutions in India. 2010.

1391-85 Association for Indonesian Peoples Television, Curug Mekar, Indonesia, $200,000. For network of six regional television stations to develop and exchange programming on cultural and religious minorities and to build technical infrastructure of four regional news agencies. 2010.

1391-86 Association for Nature and Sustainable Development, Cusco, Peru, $150,000. To serve as Secretariat to Indigenous Peoples Climate Change Assessment (IPCCA) to respond to climate change challenges and facilitate community managed assessments. 2010.

1391-87 Association for the Development of the Honduran Mosquitia, Tegucigalpa, Honduras, $105,000. For training and technical assistance to help Miskitu communities demarcate and gain title to their traditional territories and maintain control over their natural resources. 2010.

1391-88 Association for Women's Rights in Development, Toronto, Canada, $350,000. For research, outreach and advocacy to advance women's economic rights at the global level. 2010.

1391-89 Association of African Universities, Accra, Ghana, $150,000. For tie-off support for Research and Education Networking Unit to address issues related to connectivity and access to increased and affordable bandwidth for African universities. 2010.

1391-90 Association of Media Women in Kenya, Nairobi, Kenya, $115,000. To expand community radio and listening group programs promoting interethnic dialogue, reconciliation and respect for human rights, set up production studio and offer microenterprise skills training. 2010.

1391-91 Association of Microfinance Institutions of Uganda, Kampala, Uganda, $100,000. To promote social performance management and reporting on social performance indicators among microfinance institutions in Uganda. 2010.

1391-92 Association of Public Radio Broadcasting Stations of Brazil, Rio de Janeiro, Brazil, $350,015. To strengthen Brazilian public radio stations, foster their integration into unified system and increase membership among public radio stations from the Amazon Region. 2010.

1391-93 Associazione Paolo Sylos Labini, Rome, Italy, $250,000. To complete research on recent financial crises in the European Union and assess potential of proposed new regulatory structures for protecting against similar global crises in the future. 2010.

1391-94 Asuransi Allianz Life Indonesia, Jakarta, Indonesia, $118,872. To pilot and evaluate commercially viable combined savings, life and health insurance product for low-income households in Eastern Indonesia. 2010.

1391-95 Australian National University, Australian Demographic And Social Research Institute, Canberra, Australia, $125,000. For research on impact of demographic youth bulge on gender equality in Indonesia. 2010.

1391-96 Autonomous Group for Environmental Research, Oaxaca, Mexico, $100,000. To study and discuss with communities effect of migration and remittances on natural resource management in Oaxaca and Guerrero and formulate natural resource strategies. 2010.

1391-97 Bainian Vocational School, Beijing, China, $180,000. For organizational development and technical assistance to help school explore ways to replicate and expand model of free education for disadvantaged high school students. 2010.

1391-98 Baitulmaal Muamalat Foundation, Jakarta, Indonesia, $25,000. To develop safe water supply and sanitation facility for poor households in north Jakarta. 2010.

1391-99 Balance, for the Promotion of Youth Development, Mexico City, Mexico, $55,300. For training activities to empower and mobilize women living with HIV/AIDS. 2010.

1391-100 Balance, for the Promotion of Youth Development, Mexico City, Mexico, $50,000. For research, networking and advocacy to promote HIV-positive women's sexual and reproductive rights. 2010.

1391-101 BAMIDELE-Group of Black Women of Paraiba, Joao Pessoa, Brazil, $100,000. For training and technical assistance to local black women's movements, so they can monitor government programs promoting racial equality and conduct public education and outreach and for strategic planning. 2010.

1391-102 Bank Nagari, Padang, Indonesia, $160,630. For microfinance activities targeting low-income people in earthquake-affected regions of West Sumatra, including new products and services, market research, and a study on the feasibility of e-banking. 2010.

1391-103 BAOBAB, Lagos, Nigeria, $400,000. For research, outreach, advocacy and litigation to foster the economic and social rights of women in Nigeria. 2010.

1391-104 Barapani, Bangalore, India, $170,100. For strategic communications support to agriculture and livestock networks advocating for a re-structuring of public investments in India's dry lands. 2010.

1391-105 Bard College, Levy Economics Institute, Annandale on Hudson, NY, $598,000. To conduct research on nature and dynamics of the current global financial crisis and generate a new global regulatory framework to address it. 2010.

1391-106 Beijing China-Dolls Culture Center, Beijing, China, $20,000. To assist rare-disease civil society organizations to publish a newsletter addressing health and social issues affecting people with rare-diseases. 2010.

1391-107 Beijing Mycos Education Consulting Company, Ltd., Beijing, China, $129,821. To introduce new data-based management tool to help university and government improve employment of college students. 2010.

1391-108 Beijing Normal University, Beijing, China, $29,245. To translate Into Chinese and publish book compiling leading articles about the use of empirical research to support criminal justice reform in Western countries. 2010.

1391-109 Beijing Normal University, Institute Of Cognitive Neuroscience And Learning, Beijing, China, $150,000. To work with local educational bureau to promote comprehensive sexual-health education program for migrant school system in Beijing. 2010.

1391-110 Beijing Normal University, Institute of Human Ecology Engineering, Beijing, China, $139,996. To develop case-based learning materials and policy recommendations on protecting herder community resource access in Western China. 2010.

1391-111 Beijing Normal University, School of Social Development and Public Policy, Beijing, China, $100,000. To monitor and advocate for school-based sexuality and reproductive health education. 2010.

1391-112 Beijing Qianqian Law Firm, Beijing, China, $333,897. For legal aid, research and advocacy to protect the rights of women in China. 2010.

1391-113 Beijing University, Beijing, China, $147,007. To review key pastoral policies and provide recommendations for strengthening herder community management over grazing resources in western China. 2010.

1391-114 Beijing University, Center for NPO Law, Beijing, China, $124,743. To conduct research on development of law for nonprofit organizations in China and disseminate findings through conferences and publications. 2010.

1391-115 Beijing University, Center for Public Participation Studies, Beijing, China, $150,350. To expand research, training and monitoring about citizens access to government information and to conduct pilot project in Hunan. 2010.

1391-116 Beijing University, Center For Public Participation Studies and Supports, Beijing, China, $70,000. To organize Open Government Information Week and regular lectures and salons and to maintain a web site. 2010.

1391-117 Better World Fund, Washington, DC, $151,000. For core support for Reproductive Health (RH) Reality Check, project that provides journalism and reporting on reproductive health, rights and justice issues. 2010.

1391-118 Big Fish School of Digital Filmmaking, Johannesburg, South Africa, $200,000. To provide black and female secondary school graduates from throughout South Africa with intermediate-level training in digital filmmaking and prepare them for careers in film and television. 2010.

1391-119 Binational Indigenous Integral Development, Juxtlahuaca, Mexico, $100,000. To help Mixtec small farmers in Oaxaca improve production and marketing practices, develop management and leadership skills and build sustainable livelihoods as an alternative to migration. 2010.

1391-120 Bio oLeos de Maxixe, Inhambane, Mozambique, $200,000. To increase rural income through sustainable forest practices and economic opportunities in Mozambique. 2010.

1391-121 Birzeit University, Edward Said National Conservatory of Music, Ramallah, West Bank/Gaza (Palestinian Territories), $180,000. To develop human and material capacities and resources of Arabic Music Department. 2010.

1391-122 Birzeit University, Women's Studies Institute, Ramallah, West Bank/Gaza (Palestinian Territories), $60,000. To develop new courses and an exhibition on gender representation in the visual arts and the media. 2010.

1391-123 Brazilian Consumer Defense Institute, Sao Paulo, Brazil, $300,000. For public education and advocacy on consumers rights with respect to telecommunications and internet policies, services and use. 2010.

1391-124 Brazilian Forum of Public Safety, Sao Paulo, Brazil, $110,000. For conferences, publications and other activities to promote progressive public security policies and police reform and to establish reserve fund. 2010.

1391-125 Brazilian Institute of Social and Economic Analyses, Rio de Janeiro, Brazil, $200,000. To develop and disseminate materials translating research on international financial reform into plain language for use by civil society organizations and help them use these materials effectively. 2010.

1391-126 Brazilian News Agency for Childrens Rights, Brasilia, Brazil, $150,000. For institutional restructuring and to develop unified media monitoring system, conduct and disseminate research on how media covers itself and develop online database on media policy. 2010.

1391-127 British Council, London, England, $150,000. For Regional Cultural Leadership Development Program. 2010.

1391-128 British Museum, London, England, $300,000. For technical assistance and training to West African museum professionals. 2010.

1391-129 Brookings Institution, John L Thornton China Center, Washington, DC, $100,000. For collaboration with Tsinhua University to implement U.S.-China internship program in research and public policy for young scholars from both countries. 2010.

1391-130 Built Environment Support Group, Deepening Democracy Programme, Pietermaritzburg, South Africa, $200,000. To improve service delivery to and livelihood security of poor communities in Kwazulu-Natal Midlands by building community capacity to engage with government. 2010.

1391-131 Buni Limited, Nairobi, Kenya, $150,000. For XYZ Show, television program using puppeteering for political satire, to encourage public participation in governance debates. 2010.

1391-132 Bureau for International Reporting, New York, NY, $250,000. To produce investigative television reports on foreign affairs for dissemination via multiple media platforms and build institutional capacity to respond to growing demand for foreign news content. 2010.

1391-133 Business and Human Rights Resource Center, New York, NY, $300,000. For general support to advance public awareness of human rights issues relating to business and promote corporate accountability through online legal accountability database and other Web-based programs. 2010.

1391-134 Cabinet Information and Decision Support Center, Cairo, Egypt, $270,000. For comprehensive training program to build staff capacity in areas of public policy analysis, implementation and evaluation. Focus of grant is on educational equity. 2010.

1391-135 Cabinet Information and Decision Support Center, Cairo, Egypt, $180,000. For research on the supply of and demand for Egyptian university graduates in the Egyptian labor market and the miss-match between employers' needs and university training. 2010.

1391-136 Cabinet Information and Decision Support Center, Cairo, Egypt, $180,000. To develop and implement national health sub account analysis of spending on family planning in Egypt. 2010.

1391-137 Cairo Family Planning and Development Association, Cairo, Egypt, $100,000. To develop youth-friendly services, including youth-to-youth and networking activities, on sexuality and reproductive health education. 2010.

1391-138 Cairo University, Cairo, Egypt, $1,500,000. For final support for Pathways Egypt, program to develop language, computer and writing skills of disadvantaged students in public universities. 2010.

1391-139 Cairo University, Cairo, Egypt, $170,000. To improve working facilities and to build academic and professional skills among junior tenured faculty at Faculty of Economics and Political Science. 2010.

1391-140 Cairo University, Center For Research And Social Studies, Cairo, Egypt, $240,000. To develop academic training program for graduate students and younger faculty in five departments of Faculty Of Arts. 2010.

1391-141 Cakrawala Timur Foundation, Surabaya, Indonesia, $245,000. To help participation of poor women in four districts in East Java in decision-making institutions at village and district level to promote gender-responsive budget allocation. 2010.

1391-142 Cape Higher Education Consortium, Cape Town, South Africa, $68,150. To undertake evaluation of all current next generation of academics projects supported by the Foundation in South Africa. 2010.

1391-143 Capital Normal University, Sexual Education Research Center, Beijing, China, $120,000. To strengthen sexual and reproductive health education teaching programs, develop teaching tools and become national resource center for field. 2010.

1391-144 Caribbean Broadcast Media Partnership on HIV/AIDS, Hastings, Barbados, $250,000. For general support to unite broadcasters from across the Caribbean In a coordinated response to the surging pandemic in the region. 2010.

1391-145 Caribbean Broadcast Media Partnership on HIV/AIDS, Hastings, Barbados, $125,000. To develop strategic plan for long-term funding of activities, operations and governance and lay foundation for ongoing financial sustainability and structural soundness. 2010.

1391-146 Caritas Brasileira, Brasllla, Brazil, $200,000. To coordinate National Forum for Agrarian Reform and Justice and help member indigenous and traditional peoples organizations advocate for land-use and ownership policies that protect rights. 2010.

1391-147 Caritas Germany, Freiburg, Germany, $400,000. For expanded efforts to raise awareness about sexuality and reproductive health among young rural women and improve quality of HIV/AIDS care and prevention services in Egypt. 2010.

1391-148 Carlos Chagas Foundation, Sao Paulo, Brazil, $1,200,000. To launch new program to support universities to establish preparatory courses for potential candidates from excluded and disadvantaged groups to ingress in graduation programs. 2010.

1391-149 Catholic University of Mozambique, Beira, Mozambique, $100,000. To strengthen on-going sexual and reproductive health projects in higher education institutions in South Africa, Mozambique and Zimbabwe by integrating piloted sexual rights campaign. 2010.

1391-150 Catolicas por el Derecho de Decidir, Mexico City, Mexico, $200,000. To build public support for sexual and reproductive rights and legal abortion among Catholic constituencies in Mexico and Central America. 2010.

1391-151 CDC Foundation, Atlanta, GA, $32,825. To support international travel for American scientists participating in Vietnam national seminar on birth defects and newborn screening. 2010.

1391-152 Center for Afro Study and Research, Montevideo, Uruguay, $330,000. For training, advocacy, monitoring and dissemination to promote the rights of Afro-descendants in Latin America and strengthen the Afro-descendant movement and Afro-descendant organizations. 2010.

1391-153 Center for American Progress, Washington, DC, $80,000. For research on the economic impact of Arizona immigration policies. 2010.

1391-154 Center for Constitutional Rights, New York, NY, $500,000. For strategic visioning process leading to full integration of international human rights standards in all of programs and for restructuring and staff training to facilitate implementation. 2010.

1391-155 Center for Democracy, Washington, DC, $60,000. For research trips of U.S. delegations to Cuba to help understand real effects of existing embargo. 2010.

1391-156 Center for Economic and Social Rights, Brooklyn, NY, $500,000. For general support to advance economic and social rights worldwide with focus on children. 2010.

1391-157 Center for Health and Gender Equity, Washington, DC, $200,000. For general support for public education, coalition building and advocacy to promote and advance health, rights and gender equity. 2010.

1391-158 Center for Health and Gender Equity, Washington, DC, $135,000. For general support to ensure that U.S. international policies and programs promote women's and girls' sexual and reproductive health within a human rights framework. 2010.

1391-159 Center for Higher Studies of Social Promotion and the Environment, Sao Paulo, Brazil, $150,000. For participatory mapping initiative to guarantee traditional peoples' land rights. 2010.

1391-160 Center for International Forestry Research, Bogor, Indonesia, $100,000. For regional workshop and dissemination activities about rural climate change policies, governance and community rights in Latin America. 2010.

1391-161 Center for International Policy, Washington, DC, $250,000. For research and publications on volume and pattern of cross-border illicit financial flows out of developing and transitional economies and related lost tax revenue. 2010.

1391-162 Center for International Policy, Washington, DC, $100,000. To foster cooperation between Cuba, United States and Mexico in field of natural disasters prevention and explore possibility of re-integrating Cuba in the region. 2010.

1391-163 Center for International Policy, Washington, DC, $80,000. To educate public and policy makers about importance of restoring U.S. academic programs in and people-to-people educational and cultural travel to Cuba. 2010.

1391-164 Center for Investigation and Information, Washington, DC, $50,000. For project support to document difference in speed access and penetration of broadband in other parts of the world. 2010.

1391-165 Center for Justice and Accountability, San Francisco, CA, $300,000. For general support for litigation to combat torture and other severe human rights abuses around the world and advance the rights of survivors to seek truth, justice and redress. 2010.

1391-166 Center for Research and Higher Studies in Social Anthropology, Guadalajara, Mexico, $100,000. To develop and implement joint learning exercise for migrant rights, advocacy and research organizations to identify root causes of migrants rights abuses and efforts to address them. 2010.

1391-167 Center for Studies on Relations and Inequality in the Workplace, Sao Paulo, Brazil, $350,000. For strategic litigation, training and advocacy and to assess public education policies from 2003 through 2010 from a racial equality perspective. 2010.

1391-168 Center of Arab Women for Training and Research, Tunis, Tunisia, $250,000. To produce knowledge and build capacities of civil society organizations developing innovative models that empower marginalized people to access their right to decent housing. 2010.

1391-169 Central American Institute for Social Studies and Development, San Jose, Guatemala, $100,000. For policy-oriented research to facilitate development of comprehensive regional migration policy focused on human security and development. 2010.

1391-170 Central American University, Nitlapan Institute, Managua, Nicaragua, $100,000. To strengthen capacity of Research Center to analyze indigenous tenure, governance and livelihoods issues in Caribbean coast of Nicaragua. 2010.

1391-171 Central American Womens Fund, San Francisco, CA, $100,000. To promote right to safe and legal therapeutic abortion in Nicaragua. 2010.

1391-172 Central Communist Party School, Institute Of International Strategic Studies, Beijing, China, $80,000. To conduct research on impact of domestic developments within China on Sino-U.S. and Sino-U.K. relations. 2010.

1391-173 Centre for Advocacy and Research, New Delhi, India, $150,000. For final support to expand innovative women's forum model using media strategies to develop leadership skills and help innovation among poor women in urban communities. 2010.

1391-174 Centre for Budget and Governance Accountability, New Delhi, India, $350,000. For general support for budget analysis, public education and advocacy to promote transparency, accountable and participatory governance. 2010.

1391-175 Centre for Communication and Development Studies, Pune, India, $280,000. For final support to strengthening innovative communications, dissemination and mobilization programs to strengthen civil society in India. 2010.

1391-176 Centre for Democracy and Social Action, New Delhi, India, $60,000. For action research on public-private partnerships providing basic services in Delhi and to disseminate the findings in meetings with civic groups, publications and online. 2010.

1391-177 Centre for Development and Population Activities, New Delhi, India, $465,000. For partnerships and technical assistance to help three state governments design and test replicable models for empowering adolescent girls with respect to reproductive health, education and livelihoods. 2010.

1391-178 Centre for Higher Education Transformation Trust, Cape Town, South Africa, $200,000. For tie-off support for Higher Education Research and Advocacy Network (HERANA) to help African universities develop information systems and use performance indicators to build institutions. 2010.

1391-179 Centre for Higher Education Transformation Trust, Cape Town, South Africa, $100,000. To develop differentiation methodology to guide Ministry Of Higher Education and Technology in diversifying the higher education system to meet the needs of society, the economy and students. 2010.

1391-180 Centre for Media and Alternative Communication, New Delhi, India, $175,000. For final support to develop new media content and expand public outreach of Women On Record Project in order to promote opportunities for women in media. 2010.

1391-181 Centre for Multiparty Democracy-Kenya, Nairobi, Kenya, $100,000. For series of public reflection forums on leadership and management of public affairs. 2010.

1391-182 Centre for Policy Research, New Delhi, India, $200,000. For core support for accountability initiative to strengthen accountability efforts by government, civil society, research institutes and the media through research, networking and public education. 2010.

1391-183 Centre for Policy Studies, Johannesburg, South Africa, $200,000. To conduct empirical research on politics of service delivery and underlying causes of community protest across South Africa. 2010.

1391-184 Centre for Policy Studies, Johannesburg, South Africa, $100,000. To undertake external, independent organizational review and strategic refocusing process. 2010.

1391-185 Centre for Research, Information, Action for Development in Africa: Southern Africa Development And Consulting, Windhoek, Namibia, $89,436. To partner with International Community of Women Living With HIV and AIDS-Namibia to mentor school dropouts, focusing on HIV and reproductive health issues and provide them with vocational training. 2010.

1391-186 Centre for Rights Education and Awareness, Nairobi, Kenya, $200,000. For research and dialogue to engage education officials with respect to sexual and reproductive health and rights budgets and for litigation to combat gender- and sexuality-based discrimination. 2010.

1391-187 Centre for the Study of Culture and Society, Bangalore, India, $195,000. For research, documentation and an online platform to generate critical public engagement on Unique Identification Number (UID) scheme in India. Project aims to give a unique number to all residents of the country. 2010.

1391-188 Centre International de Developpement et de Recherche, Autreches, France, $123,000. To develop new tools and training manual to assist microfinance organizations improve their ability to serve poor clients. 2010.

1391-189 Centro Agronomico Tropical de Investigacion y Ensenanza, Turrialba, Costa Rica, $125,000. To validate tool for measuring impact of value chains on poverty. 2010.

1391-190 Centro Brasileiro de Analise e Planejamento, Sao Paulo, Brazil, $100,000. To establish new research unit focused on contemporary aspects of racial inequality and to study impact of University for All scholarship program for low-income and black Brazilians. 2010.

1391-191 Centro de Estudios Legales y Sociales, Buenos Aires, Argentina, $445,000. To strengthen regional and universal human rights protection mechanisms, enhance human rights advocacy from the Global South and promote domestic applicability of international human rights law. 2010.

1391-192 Centro de Integridade Publica, Centre For Integrity, Maputo, Mozambique, $200,000. For work on democratic accountability and good governance in Mozambique. 2010.

1391-193 Centro de Investigacion y Docencia Economicas, Mexico City, Mexico, $150,000. To train Mexico-based Central American consular officials to use Mexican law and international treaties to defend and promote the rights of undocumented migrants in Mexico. 2010.

1391-194 Centro de Investigacion y Docencia Economicas, Mexico City, Mexico, $120,000. For Law School to develop and implement course exploring theoretical and normative framework of sexuality and sexual reproductive rights from perspective of fundamental rights. 2010.

1391-195 Centro de Investigacion y Docencia Economicas, Mexico City, Mexico, $100,000. To conduct research on and develop litigation strategy to overcome prevailing culture of impunity in Mexico in cases of feminicide and other crimes against women. 2010.

1391-196 Centro del Obrero Fronterizo, La Mujer Obrera, El Paso, TX, $178,500. To formally establish and administer Red Binacional Niu Matat Napawika, binational fair trade crafts system to help Mexican women and indigenous artisans position their products in the U.S. market. 2010.

1391-197 Centro Mexicano de Derecho Ambiental, Mexico City, Mexico, $100,000. To conduct communications activities that promote community forestry as way to reduce green house gas emissions. 2010.

1391-198 Changsha University of Science and Technology, Changsha, China, $150,000. To expand participatory monitoring and evaluation mechanism for improvement of equity in compulsory education. 2010.

1391-199 Chaoyang Kangzhong Health and Education Service Center of Beijing, Beijing, China, $30,000. To identify opportunities and challenges faced by community-based organizations working in medical and health reform in Beijing and assist in their sustainable development. 2010.

1391-200 Chasing the Flame, LLC, Santa Monica, CA, $75,000. To implement community outreach and engagement program for Sergio, documentary on the life of United Nations diplomat Sergio Vieira de Mello, who was killed in Iraq in 2003. 2010.

1391-201 Chengdu University, Sichuan Research Center of Sexual Sociology and Sex Education, Chengdu, China, $88,276. To develop comprehensive sexual education program for schools in Sichuan Province. 2010.

1391-202 Chiapas Media Project, Promedios, Chiapas, Mexico, $60,000. To organize tour of Cuban films at U.S. universities and cultural institutions. 2010.

1391-203 China Association for NGO Cooperation, Beijing, China, $90,000. To develop manual of good practice for government-civil society partnerships in social service delivery. 2010.

1391-204 China Daily, Beijing, China, $50,000. For Charity China, weekly special insert on charitable activities in China Distributed worldwide with the newspaper and published on the China Daily Web Site and to co-sponsor a charity forum. 2010.

1391-205 China Development Research Foundation, Beijing, China, $199,438. For exploratory research, forums and training and development of multi-channel publishing and feedback system and database related to protection of villagers rights under current laws and policies. 2010.

1391-206 China Development Research Foundation, Beijing, China, $122,500. To conduct field research on and hold workshops to discuss pilot projects in local public service provision, factors conducive to their success and necessary conditions for sustainable replication. 2010.

1391-207 China Education Initiative, New York, NY, $60,000. To scale up innovative approaches to assist local governments to improve quality of instruction for students in rural schools in remote areas. 2010.

1391-208 China Executive Leadership Academy, Pudong, Shanghai, China, $72,650. For research, case study development and publications on innovations in provision of public services, particularly those of most importance to disadvantaged groups, in large municipalities. 2010.

1391-209 China Family Planning Association, Beijing, China, $150,000. To strength, sustain and scale up sexuality and reproductive health peer education program among young migrants and college students. 2010.

1391-210 China Institute of Contemporary International Relations, Beijing, China, $100,000. For research and analysis on current strengths and weaknesses of China-U.S. regional cooperation in third-country sites and prospects for mutual strategic trust in bilateral and multilateral relations. 2010.

1391-211 China National Communication and Education Center for Family Planning, China, $100,000. To strengthen online, television, radio and outreach communication programs for sexual and reproductive health and rights education. 2010.

1391-212 China National Institute for Educational Research, Beijing, China, $187,270. To introduce comprehensive national mechanism to transform safety measures and standards in rural schools in order to improve transitions and success rates among disadvantaged students. 2010.

1391-213 China NPO Network, Beijing, China, $198,886. To establish China Foundation Center program to build capacity of indigenous philanthropy in China. 2010.

1391-214 China Population Welfare Foundation, Beijing, China, $180,000. To strengthen working group of CPWF, Chinese alliance of people living with HIV/AIDS's capacity to advocate for rights of HIV-positive people, including sexual and reproductive rights. 2010.

1391-215 China Prosecutor Society, Beijing, China, $100,000. To train Chinese prosecutors in conduct and use of empirical research methodology to promote criminal justice reform. 2010.

1391-216 China Research Center for Comparative Politics and Economics, Beijing, China, $73,000. For international workshop on dignity in civic, social and international relations. 2010.

1391-217 China Research Center for Comparative Politics and Economics, Beijing, China, $50,000. To analyze and evaluate long-term results of local government innovations and for international conference and publication to disseminate results. 2010.

1391-218 China Sexology Association, Beijing, China, $130,000. To develop and pilot standardized and comprehensive guidelines for sexual and reproductive health education and provide platform for sharing of experience among association's members. 2010.

1391-219 China University of Political Science and Law, Beijing, China, $131,639. For empirical research on juvenile justice reform pilot projects in China and to share best practices and promote systemic reform in juvenile justice. 2010.

1391-220 China University of Political Science and Law, Beijing, China, $62,050. For empirical research on availability, types and effectiveness of legal services in different parts of rural China and for conference and scholarly publications to share the findings. 2010.

1391-221 China University of Political Science and Law, Beijing, China, $30,000. For academic conference to mark tenth anniversary of clinical legal education in China and to bring together clinical professors from China and elsewhere to share experiences and best practices. 2010.

1391-222 China University of Political Science and Law, Constitutionalism Research Institute, Beijing, China, $50,000. To host academic conference to share experiences, lessons learned and best practices on combating employment discrimination in China. 2010.

1391-223 China University of Political Science and Law, Procedural Law Research Institute, Beijing, China, $17,330. To prepare and publish English translations of seminal U.S. Supreme Court cases on search and seizure and hold conference to exchange views about the topic. 2010.

1391-224 Chinese Academy of Social Sciences, Center For Research in Gender and Law, Beijing, China, $25,000. To convene annual conference of law teachers to promote adoption of Gender and Law Course as part of China's Law School curriculum. 2010.

1391-225 Chinese Academy of Social Sciences, Center for Rural Environmental Social Studies, Beijing, China, $72,183. To study impact of climate change in arid grasslands of western China and recommend adaptation policies that protect herder access rights. 2010.

1391-226 Christian Dalit Liberation Movement, Chennai, India, $200,000. For final grant for national federation of Dalit women to deepen and expand leadership training institutes for Dalit women. 2010.

1391-227 Citizen Engagement Laboratory, Berkeley, CA, $300,000. For Presente.org Immigrant Rights Online Organizing and Advocacy Project to respond to the enforcement-only approach to immigration reform and strengthen the immigrants' rights movement. 2010.

1391-228 Citizens Alliance on Prisons and Public Spending, Lansing, MI, $196,625. For general support to promote policies that reduce prison populations and shift resources to public services that prevent crime, rehabilitate offenders and cost-effectively address the needs of all citizens. 2010.

1391-229 Civic: Centre for Indian Visual Culture, New Delhi, India, $200,000. For final support to create digital archive and conduct research, training and dissemination on popular visual culture of the textile industry in western India. 2010.

1391-230 CIVICUS: World Alliance for Citizen Participation, Washington, DC, $200,000. For general support to strengthen citizen action and civil society throughout the world, especially in areas where participatory democracy and citizens freedom of association are threatened. 2010.

1391-231 Clark University, Worcester, MA, $185,000. For research on institutional innovations with the potential for reducing conflicts between extraction and development at sub national levels in the Andean-Amazonian Region and to publish the findings. 2010.

1391-232 Clinton Health Access Initiative, Boston, MA, $250,000. To ensure the continuation of HIV/AIDS treatment and prevention services in Haiti in the aftermath of the devastating earthquake. 2010.

1391-233 Coalition for an Effective African Court, Arusha, Tanzania, Zanzibar and Pemba, $300,000. For advocacy and convenings toward establishment of an effective African Court Of Justice to protect and enforce human rights throughout the continent. 2010.

1391-234 Colombian Commission of Jurists, Bogota, Colombia, $100,000. For general support to promote rule of law and monitor compliance with human rights in Colombia. 2010.

1391-235 Columbia University, Human Rights Institute, New York, NY, $400,000. For core support to provide legal research and assistance to groups working on global human rights. 2010.

1391-236 Columbia University, Initiative for Policy Dialogue, New York, NY, $300,000. For Financial Markets Reform Task Force to conduct research and dialogues on policy options for reforming global financial governance. 2010.

1391-237 Columbia University, School of Law, New York, NY, $75,000. For Human Rights Institute to organize meeting on human rights, gender, sexuality and violence against women in the Americas. 2010.

1391-238 Committee to Protect Journalists, New York, NY, $200,000. For general support to promote press freedom worldwide by defending rights of journalists to report news without fear of reprisal. 2010.

1391-239 Common Cause Education Fund, Washington, DC, $70,000. For outreach activities and public education campaign to educate and engage the public, civic leaders and policy makers about raising profile of The Legacy of War: Addressing Agent Orange In Vietnam. 2010.

1391-240 Communicating for Change, Lagos, Nigeria, $234,000. For strategic use of mass media to promote peaceful, credible and transparent elections at local, state and federal levels in Nigeria. 2010.

1391-241 Communication and Information for Women, Mexico City, Mexico, $100,000. For public information campaign, in print, online and through media workshops, to promote women's sexual and reproductive rights. 2010.

1391-242 Communication University of China, Beijing, China, $89,900. For new media group to determine best communications strategy for promoting sexuality and reproductive health education and help groups working in the field improve their communications strategies. 2010.

1391-243 Communications Consortium Media Center, Washington, DC, $285,000. To develop and implement communications strategies and outreach activities to raise awareness and engagement of key U.S. publics in policy solutions to Agent Orange legacy of the Vietnam war. 2010.

1391-244 Community Forestry Assocation of Guatemala Utz Che, Guatemala, Guatemala, $50,000. For training, technical assistance and dissemination to build capacity of community forestry organizations and encourage local youth to get involved in environmental and forestry activities. 2010.

1391-245 Community Forestry Indigenous-Campesino Coordinating Association, San Jose, Costa Rica, $150,000. To do networking, advocacy, and communications to promote climate change policies that favor forest communities in Central America. 2010.

1391-246 Community Forestry International, Antioch, CA, $200,000. For general support to help rural communities regenerate forests by aiding in development of legal instruments, human resources and negotiation processes and methods to support resident resource managers. 2010.

1391-247 Community Foundation for Northern Ireland, Belfast, Northern Ireland, $250,000. For Working Group on Philanthropy for Social Justice and Peace to develop worldwide community of social justice funders and build capacity of and develop sustainable resources for the field. 2010.

1391-248 Community Friendly Movement, New Delhi, India, $184,796. For final support to design efficient supply-chain and product development interventions for artisans. 2010.

1391-249 Community Life Project, Lagos, Nigeria, $1,290,000. For education, training, organizing and creation of media and cutting-edge information and communications technology platform to promote electoral transparency and democratic accountability in Nigeria. 2010.

1391-250 Community Organisation Resource Centre, Mowbray, South Africa, $150,000. For pilot program on informal settlement upgrading, community participation and accountable government in five South African cities. 2010.

1391-251 Comprehensive Health for Women, Mexico City, Mexico, $100,000. To develop strategies for HIV/AIDS prevention among migrant populations and in their home communities, with special focus on women. 2010.

1391-252 Comunicacion, Cultura y Sociedad, Santiago, Chile, $50,000. To generate and disseminate knowledge and foster debate on communication strategies used by governments of Andean region and Southern Cone in public policies to combat exclusion. 2010.

1391-253 Concern Universal, Hereford, England, $150,000. To strengthen capacity of local communities in Mozambique to participate in government decentralization process and hold their officials accountable to transparent and effective governance. 2010.

1391-254 Conectas Human Rights, Sao Paulo, Brazil, $150,000. To strengthen collaboration among Latin American NGOs and increase presence of Latin American voices in United Nations human rights system, particularly new human rights council. 2010.

1391-255 Consortium of Private Organizations for the Promotion of Small and Micro Enterprise, Lima, Peru, $50,000. To analyze current regulatory framework in Peru, develop strategic agenda and operational plan for promoting inclusive value chains and hold training and policy workshops to advance agenda. 2010.

1391-256 Cooperativa de Profesionales Masangni RL, Puerto Cabezas, Nicaragua, $50,000. For training and technical assistance in community forestry to Miskitu communities in the north Atlantic autonomous region and document and disseminate information on work with these communities. 2010.

1391-257 Coordinating Body for the Indigenous Peoples Organizations of the Amazon Basin, Quito, Ecuador, $200,000. To build capacity and raise public awareness about mining and energy enterprises on indigenous peoples' lands. 2010.

1391-258 Coptic Evangelical Organization for Social Services, Cairo, Egypt, $920,000. For community-based program to promote accountability and economic and social rights. 2010.

1391-259 Corporacion Agencia Afrocolombiana Hileros, Bogota, Colombia, $120,000. For project support to strengthen Afro-descendent organizations throughout Colombia in defense and promotion of their human rights. 2010.

1391-260 Corporation for Innovation in Citizenship, Santiago, Chile, $118,000. For research and learning on public policies to foster sustainable territorial development of indigenous communities. 2010.

1391-261 Council on Foreign Relations, New York, NY, $224,000. For research, publications, meetings and outreach activities to contribute to public debate over U.S.-Cuba relations. 2010.

1391-262 Council on Foreign Relations, New York, NY, $200,000. For final support to maintain Web site's effectiveness as source of nonpartisan information on and analysis of foreign policy issues and for outreach to education, civic and religious leaders. 2010.

1391-263 Council on Foreign Relations, New York, NY, $100,000. For outreach activities to publicize progress made in implementing recommendations of Council's independent task force report on U.S. immigration policy and need for reform. 2010.

1391-264 Counselors Office, Peoples Government of Anhui Province, Hefei, China, $180,000. For action-oriented research to promote vocational education in rural secondary schools. 2010.

1391-265 Creative Time, New York, NY, $100,000. For general support for innovative public art community-based projects. 2010.

1391-266 Credibility Alliance, New Delhi, India, $300,000. For final support to expand membership and develop programmatic norms, accreditation models and code of conduct for civil society. 2010.

1391-267 Culture Resource, Brussels, Belgium, $65,000. For a regional convening of arts and culture donors and the production of learning and resource documents. 2010.

1391-268 Development Action Group, Cape Town, South Africa, $150,000. To build capacity of informal settlements in Cape Town to work with municipality to develop land management policies that facilitate sustainable housing and access to well-located urban land. 2010.

1391-269 Development Alternatives with Women for a New Era, Quezon City, Philippines, $350,000. For general support for feminist research, advocacy and training to promote economic and gender justice and sustainable and democratic development in the Global South. 2010.

1391-270 Development Initiatives Network, Lagos, Nigeria, $540,650. To extend work on access to finance in Nigeria and for support to National Museum in Lagos. 2010.

1391-271 Development Institute for Tradition and Environment, Kunming, China, $194,818. To train national and provincial government rural poverty reduction staff to promote community rights over natural resources through farmer cooperative development. 2010.

1391-272 Development Policy Management Forum, Nairobi, Kenya, $200,000. To develop strategy for using research results to inform advocacy civil society organizations on land ownership issues at coast province of Kenya. 2010.

1391-273 Diego Portales University, Santiago, Chile, $100,000. To analyze Chilean foreign policy over the past 20 years, to generate lessons on the role of Chile as a resource country on key issues of public policy in the region. 2010.

1391-274 Documental Ambulante, Mexico City, Mexico, $135,000. To organize screenings of documentary films on issues relevant to their lives for Central American Indigenous and Afro-descendant women and train them in documentary filmmaking. 2010.

1391-275 Documental Ambulante, Mexico City, Mexico, $60,000. To distribute series of documentaries related to migration and organize video production workshop for women. 2010.

1391-276 Down to Earth, International Campaign for Ecological Justice in Indonesia, London, England, $146,000. To raise awareness of natural resource management practices by indigenous peoples in context of climate change and build capacity for greater participation by communities in decision making. 2010.

1391-277 Due Process of Law Foundation, Washington, DC, $235,000. To strengthen communities affected by the Extractives Sector in Latin America and to help these communities craft legal and advocacy strategies to assert their rights. 2010.

1391-278 Durbar Mahila Samanwaya Committee, Kolkata, India, $150,000. For final support to advocate for economic and social rights of sex workers and for training and technical assistance to reduce violence, improve livelihoods and strengthen their collectives. 2010.

1391-279 EarthRights International, Washington, DC, $150,000. For litigation in U.S. courts to hold corporations accountable for human and environmental rights abuses and to develop accountability mechanisms and enforceable legal standards in other parts of the world. 2010.

1391-280 East Meets West Foundation, Oakland, CA, $195,000. To engage in marketing and fundraising campaign in Vietnam and internationally to further goals of U.S./Vietnam Dialogue Group on Agent Orange/Dioxin Strategic Plan. 2010.

1391-281 East Meets West Foundation, Oakland, CA, $100,000. To launch online network for Vietnamese community worldwide and raise awareness of the Agent Orange legacy to build support for solutions. 2010.

1391-282 Ecociencia Foundation, Quito, Ecuador, $100,000. To develop and publish digital land use atlas of the Ecuadorian Amazon Demarcating Indigenous Peoples' Territories and conservation protected areas and a historical analysis of deforestation in the region. 2010.

1391-283 Ecologists Linked for Organizing Grassroots Initiatives and Action, Whiting, VT, $143,789. To Protect Herder Community Access To Natural Resources Through Sustainable Production And Marketing Of Fair Trade Cashmere And Camel-fiber. 2010.

1391-284 Economic Policy Research Institute, Cape Town, South Africa, $200,000. To expand evaluation of South Africa's Child Support Grant Program to include Program's impact on household assets and opportunities and determine feasibility of a matched savings program. 2010.

1391-285 Economic Research Forum for the Arab Countries, Iran and Turkey, Cairo, Egypt, $250,000. For research, case studies and dissemination on higher education reforms to improve student learning, faculty performance and access by marginalized students to quality higher education. 2010.

1391-286 Economic Research Foundation, New Delhi, India, $330,049. To map evolution of the financial sector in Asia and identify policies that would foster financial stability and development. 2010.

1391-287 EDA Rural Systems Private, Gurgaon, India, $120,000. To develop standard set of social performance reporting metrics for Indian microfinance sector and help microfinance institutions integrate social performance into their management systems. 2010.

1391-288 Egyptian Association for Community Participation Enhancement, Cairo, Egypt, $100,000. To promote social dialogue and community action to achieve economic and social rights. 2010.

1391-289 Egyptian Family Health Society, Cairo, Egypt, $100,000. For training, peer education and coalition building to expand sexuality and reproductive health education for youth in Egypt. 2010.

1391-290 Egyptian NGO Support Center, Giza, Egypt, $600,000. To provide small grants and technical assistance which will help community-based organizations advance youth sexuality and reproductive health education in Egypt. 2010.

1391-291 Egyptian Society for Population Studies and Reproductive Health, Cairo, Egypt, $200,000. For situational analysis to help design rights-based healthcare service models for persons living with HIV/AIDS and to promote dialogue between healthcare and rights stakeholders. 2010.

1391-292 El Colegio de la Frontera Norte, Tijuana, Mexico, $25,000. To build capacity of migrant-serving organizations to monitor performance of Mexican government institutions responsible for protecting migrant rights on both sides of the US-Mexico border. 2010.

1391-293 El Colegio de Mexico, Mexico City, Mexico, $70,000. For Guatemala-Mexico Group on Migration and Development to monitor implementation of migration policy, conduct advocacy on migration- and origin-community development policy and prepare report. 2010.

1391-294 EngageMedia Collective, Collingwood, Australia, $300,000. For an online video-sharing platform and social networking hub focusing on environmental and social justice videos in the Asia Pacific region. 2010.

1391-295 Environmental Protection Agency, Washington, DC, $30,000. To enable EPA scientists to assist in testing new bioremediation technology for cleaning up dioxin contamination at Danang Airport. 2010.

1391-296 Equal Education, Cape Town, South Africa, $350,000. For academic support programme to offer intensive courses to prepare secondary school students in the Western Cape for university matriculation exams and the transition to higher education. 2010.

1391-297 Equal Education, Cape Town, South Africa, $30,000. To prepare proposal for project to form relationships between South Africa's secondary and tertiary education sectors for funding from pathways to higher education initiative. 2010.

1391-298 Eseio Escritura Para Liderar, Santiago, Chile, $230,000. To develop and offer online writing courses in English, Spanish and Portuguese to help Global South scholars working on sexuality and reproductive health and rights produce academic publications. 2010.

1391-299 European Foundation Centre, Brussels, Belgium, $125,000. For general support to create an enabling legal and fiscal environment for foundations, strengthen the structure of the philanthropic sector and promote collaboration to advance the public good. 2010.

1391-300 European Foundation Centre, Brussels, Belgium, $73,780. For contribution to annual membership dues of foundation-supported association of grantmakers. 2010.

1391-301 Fahamu Limited, Oxford, England, $250,000. For Pan-African Fellowship program to develop skills, knowledge and experience of community-based activists and increase effectiveness and professionalism of organizations and movements. 2010.

1391-302 Fair Trade Mexico, Comercio Justo Mexico, Mexico City, Mexico, $100,000. For training, technical assistance and outreach to increase both demand for fair trade products in Mexico and ability of small producers to access this market. 2010.

1391-303 Family Care International, New York, NY, $120,000. For networking, communications and advocacy to promote progressive U.S. leadership on maternal and reproductive health. 2010.

1391-304 Farm Concern International Development Trust, Nairobi, Kenya, $75,000. To build capacity of other organizations in the region on the commercial villages model; test and adapt value chains evaluation tool and to evaluate social impacts. 2010.

1391-305 Federal Fluminense University, Rio de Janeiro, Brazil, $125,000. For anthropological research to delimitate lands traditionally occupied by rural Afro-descendents in state of Para. 2010.

1391-306 Federal University of Para, Belem, Brazil, $300,000. For applied research on reducing emissions resulting from deforestation and forest degradation and agro-biofuels, and on land ownership and carbon in the Amazon. 2010.

1391-307 Federal University of Para, Belem, Brazil, $250,000. For research, dissemination and exchange programs of Latin America Consortium of Postgraduate Programs in Human Rights and to strengthen university's own postgraduate human rights program. 2010.

1391-308 Federal University of Rio de Janeiro, Rio de Janeiro, Brazil, $149,952. For tie-off support for Research Group on Contemporary Forms of Slave Labour to expand and maintain online database on forced labor in Brazil. 2010.

1391-309 Federal University of Sergipe, Aracaju, Brazil, $100,000. For Network on Economic Policies of Information and Communication Technologies to promote civil society engagement in discussions on political economy of communications in Latin America. 2010.

1391-310 Federation of Agencies of Social and Educational Assistance, Rio de Janeiro, Brazil, $250,000. To establish Xingu Indigenous Peoples' Fund to make small grants to community organizations for capacity building, land-use issues and income-generating projects and to monitor and evaluate them. 2010.

1391-311 Feminist Studies and Assistance Center, Brasilia, Brazil, $200,000. For training, monitoring and public education to promote and advocate for women's rights and to conduct strategic review of Center's by-laws, governance systems and communications program. 2010.

1391-312 Final Cut for Real, Copenhagen, Denmark, $201,540. For post-production and outreach in Indonesia for Freemen, documentary film tracing the tumultuous period of political violence in Indonesia during 1965-1966. 2010.

1391-313 Financial Clinic, New York, NY, $30,000. For general support to build financial security of the working poor by addressing their immediate financial challenges and helping them create trajectories for long-term goals and financial mobility. 2010.

1391-314 FIS Social Company, SA, Buenos Aires, Argentina, $100,000. To develop and pilot innovative business model for sustainable distribution of solar panels to poor rural households in Peru and Argentina. 2010.

1391-315 Flint Institute of Arts, Flint, MI, $310,619. For Chiapas Photography Project, initiative to engage indigenous artists and facilitate their use of photography and to digitize and maintain indigenous photographic archive and make it more accessible. 2010.

1391-316 FoodFirst Information and Action Network, Heidelberg, Germany, $150,000. For campaigning and advocacy to deepen knowledge

and support for covenant on economic, social and cultural rights and optional protocol. 2010.

1391-317 Forest Peoples Programme, Moreton-in-Marsh, England, $400,000. For activities to ensure private sector standard-setting processes and codes of conduct related to forest products help secure livelihoods of forest-dependent peoples in Indonesia. 2010.

1391-318 Forest Peoples Programme, Moreton-in-Marsh, England, $150,000. To provide technical and legal assistance to indigenous peoples organizations seeking to promote indigenous rights over natural resources. 2010.

1391-319 Forests and the European Union Resource Network, Moreton-in-Marsh, England, $128,500. To work on European engagement on Reduction in Emissions from Deforestation and Degradation (REDD) in relation to forest governance. 2010.

1391-320 Formacion y Capacitacion, Mexico City, Mexico, $70,000. To mitigate impact of migration on sexual and reproductive health of women from Chiapas and Central America. 2010.

1391-321 Forum Solidaridad Peru, Lima, Peru, $200,000. For International Working Group on Trade-Finance Linkages to promote linked trade and finance policies that serve development based on human rights, gender equality and social and environmental justice. 2010.

1391-322 Forum-Asia, Bangkok, Thailand, $300,000. For final support for advocacy and capacity-building for greater protection of Asian human rights defenders and promotion of human rights in Asia, by national human rights institutions. 2010.

1391-323 Foundation for Contemporary Research, Cape Town, South Africa, $200,000. For general support to build leadership, strengthen structures and expand networks that help development and mobilize marginalized communities to participate in processes that address priority needs. 2010.

1391-324 Foundation for Ecological Security, Anand, India, $25,000. To host series of panels on pastoralism and common pool resources at 13th Biennial Conference of the International Association for the Study of the Commons and to publish proceedings. 2010.

1391-325 Foundation for Education in Multilingual and Pluricultural Contexts, FUNPROEIB ANDES, Cochabamba, Bolivia, $150,000. For action research and regional seminars on role of higher education in sociocultural construction of citizenship in Latin American countries and regions dealing with issues of multinationalism. 2010.

1391-326 Foundation for Salvadoran Program on Environment and Development, San Salvador, El Salvador, $200,000. For case studies, workshops and technical assistance to promote and facilitate greater community access to natural resources both within and outside of protected areas in El Salvador. 2010.

1391-327 Fraternal Black Honduran Organization, Tegucigalpa, Honduras, $90,000. To help the Garifuna communities of coastal Honduras develop a proposal for a multi-community Garifuna territory. 2010.

1391-328 Free State Higher Education ConsortiumTrust, Bloemfontein, South Africa, $450,000. To conduct research on student engagement and use data to inform development

of Skills for a Changing World Programme to prepare youth for study at vocationally oriented schools and colleges. 2010.

1391-329 Freedom Theater, Jenin, West Bank/Gaza (Palestinian Territories), $90,000. For capacity building and core programs for community-based Cultural Center in Jenin. 2010.

1391-330 Fresh Produce Exporters Forum, Cape Town, South Africa, $77,600. To transfer skills, knowledge and experience from South African fruit industry experts to emerging farmers and their communities through Top of the Class Emerging Farmer Training and Mentorship Program. 2010.

1391-331 Friends of the Earth, Washington, DC, $150,000. To protect rights of indigenous peoples and forest-dependent communities in Reduced Emissions from Deforestation and Degradation (REDD) policy development. 2010.

1391-332 Friends of the Earth, Washington, DC, $100,000. For research and advocacy on sustainable governance of new financial markets in carbon and on emergence of new global financiers. 2010.

1391-333 Front Line-International Foundation for the Protection of Human Rights Defenders, Blackrock, Ireland, $335,000. For general support to protect human rights defenders at risk either temporarily or permanently because of work on behalf of others. 2010.

1391-334 Fudan University, Institute for Advanced Study in the Social Sciences, Shanghai, China, $80,102. To conduct research on management of civil society organizations. 2010.

1391-335 Fund for Global Human Rights, Washington, DC, $340,000. For research, advocacy and litigation on youth sexuality and reproductive health, HIV/AIDS human rights and vulnerability, and human rights enforcement in Egypt and North Africa. 2010.

1391-336 Fund for Global Human Rights, Washington, DC, $150,000. For advocacy, legal assistance, policy research and training to develop model promoting access to safe housing in informal areas in Egypt. 2010.

1391-337 Fundacao Viver, Produzir e Preservar, Altamira, Brazil, $200,000. To plan and implement environmentally sound rural settlement project in the Amazon. 2010.

1391-338 Fundacion Ayuda y Esperanza, Santiago, Chile, $600,000. To establish insurance fund and emergency credit fund for microfinance clients whose homes and/or businesses were lost or severely damaged in the earthquake and tsunami. 2010.

1391-339 Fundacion Cerrejon para el Fortalecimiento Institucional de la Guajira, Bogota, Colombia, $140,000. For pilot technical assistance program to promote transparency and accountability in a la Guajira municipality receiving mineral royalties and assist in implementation of its local development plan. 2010.

1391-340 Fundacion DIS, Bogota, Colombia, $100,000. To carry out territorial characterization and institutional mapping of five regions of Colombia and identify opportunities for intersectoral collaboration on core issues of social exclusion. 2010.

1391-341 Fundacion foro Nacional por Colombia, Bogota, Colombia, $134,000. To assess impact of Colombian government's social policies, particularly flagship Families in Action Program, on the country's poorest sectors. 2010.

1391-342 Fundacion las Rosas de Ayuda Fraterna, Santiago, Chile, $25,000. For reconstruction and repair of building destroyed by earthquake. 2010.

1391-343 Fundacion Nacional para el Desarrollo, San Salvador, El Salvador, $702,000. To collaborate with federal and local authorities, NGOs and community associations to build rural economies in San Vicente Directorate and provide incentives for local population not to migrate. 2010.

1391-344 Fundacion para Estudio e Investigacion de la Mujer, Buenos Aires, Argentina, $100,000. For final support to foster collaboration among networks working on sexual and reproductive health and rights, AIDS, women's rights and sexual orientation. 2010.

1391-345 Fundar Center for Research and Analysis, Mexico City, Mexico, $150,000. For research, analysis and information dissemination on migrants and Mexican migration policies and programs and related security policies and for freedom of information litigation. 2010.

1391-346 Funders Concerned About AIDS, Arlington, VA, $125,000. For general support to mobilize and motivate effective funder responses to HIV/AIDS worldwide. 2010.

1391-347 Fuping Vocational School, Henan, China, $238,000. For international workshop to share experiences and look for opportunities for cross-country collaboration to sustain best practices in Population, Health and Environment (PHE) to advance access and success in higher education. 2010.

1391-348 Gandhi Peace Centre, New Delhi, India, $19,380. To establish day care/resource centre in north-West Delhi to ensure meaningful and dignified life for elderly people from four slum clusters. 2010.

1391-349 Gansu Green Camel Bell Environment and Development Center, Lanzhou, China, $60,000. To collaborate with Lanzhou University School of Life Science to promote group-household grazing as mechanism for reducing grassland fragmentation on Qinghai-Tibetan Plateau. 2010.

1391-350 GELEDES Institute of Black Women, Sao Paulo, Brazil, $300,000. For litigation, advocacy and training to address racial and gender discrimination and to implement a strategic management model. 2010.

1391-351 Gender Equity: Citizenship and Work and Family, Mexico City, Mexico, $170,000. For litigation and to strengthen stakeholder groups to expand base of support for reproductive rights. 2010.

1391-352 GESTOS-Soropositivity, Communication and Gender, Recife, Brazil, $400,000. For participation of communities at local and regional level in policy and program activities and to build capacity of affected communities (with focus on teenage girls) to be represented in global HIV agenda. 2010.

1391-353 GESTOS-Soropositivity, Communication and Gender, Recife, Brazil, $250,000. To partner with Foundation grantees and civil society organizations worldwide in campaign to mobilize support for holding governments accountable with respect to their HIV/AIDS funding commitments. 2010.

1391-354 Getulio Vargas Foundation, Rio de Janeiro, Brazil, $80,000. For research on history of media regulation, deregulation and accountability in Brazil. 2010.

1391-355 Getulio Vargas Foundation, Center for Justice and Society, Rio de Janeiro, Brazil, $200,000. To conduct empirical analysis to determine profile of excluded populations seeking access to justice in Rio de Janeiro and disseminate the findings. 2010.

1391-356 Getulio Vargas Foundation, Center Of Development Economics, Rio de Janeiro, Brazil, $257,000. To conduct research on financial instability and exchange rate overvaluation in Latin America and analysis, policy and the case of Brazil. 2010.

1391-357 Global Fund to Fight AIDS, Tuberculosis and Malaria, Geneva, Switzerland, $300,000. To design global system for evaluating performance of its country coordinating mechanism model, with focus on governance, civil society engagement and participation by at-risk populations. 2010.

1391-358 Global Greengrants Fund, Boulder, CO, $110,000. For grant making to strengthen capacity of emerging grassroots environmental groups to expand community rights over natural resources in northwest China. 2010.

1391-359 Global Greengrants Fund, Boulder, CO, $50,000. For small grants program to help indigenous and community organizations in Guatemala, Honduras and Nicaragua participate in policy dialogues and international meetings on forests and climate change. 2010.

1391-360 Global Health Corps, New York, NY, $200,000. To strengthen and expand Fellows Program to provide internships for young leaders in public health organizations with focus on HIV and AIDS. 2010.

1391-361 Global Information Networks, New York, NY, $100,000. To build organizational and journalistic capacity of Saharareporters, news and information web site promoting transparency in African governance. 2010.

1391-362 Global Justice Center, Rio de Janeiro, Brazil, $360,000. For research, documentation and litigation on human rights violations in Brazil. 2010.

1391-363 Global Network of People Living with HIV/AIDS, Amsterdam, Netherlands, $400,000. For general support to advocate for people living with HIV/AIDS and for resource mobilization project to develop and disseminate information on the impact and advocate for continuation of AIDS Financing. 2010.

1391-364 Global Partners and Associates, London, England, $150,000. For research, convening, documentation and dissemination activities to expand role of global civil society in freedom of expression debates. 2010.

1391-365 Global Rights, Washington, DC, $120,000. For training and technical assistance to enable Afro-Peruvian organizations to document human rights abuses and use data for advocacy within inter-American and United Nations human rights systems. 2010.

1391-366 Global Witness, London, England, $250,000. To develop enforceable safeguards and standards for governance in Reduced Emissions From Deforestation and Degradation (REDD) Programs. 2010.

1391-367 Global Workers Justice Alliance, New York, NY, $80,000. To strengthen Defenders Network and increase its capacity to facilitate Mexican and Guatemalan migrants access to legal remedies for labor rights violations. 2010.

1391-368 Go Sheng Services, Nairobi, Kenya, $80,000. To expand digital media platforms, promote content building and develop online organizing strategies. 2010.

1391-369 Gram Abhyudaya Mandali, Nizamabad, India, $200,000. For final support to strengthen financial and management information systems of Women's Dairy Enterprise and train staff to provide extension services. 2010.

1391-370 Grameen Foundation USA, Washington, DC, $290,950. To expand development and use of Progress Out of Poverty Index for measuring poverty levels of clients of microfinance organizations over time and identifying most effective services. 2010.

1391-371 Grantmakers in Health, Washington, DC, $30,000. To integrate reproductive health and rights into program for Forum on Women's Health in partnership with Funders Network on Population, Reproductive Health and Rights. 2010.

1391-372 Grupo de Institutos, Fundacoes e Empresas, Sao Paulo, Brazil, $95,048. For research to strengthen independent and community foundations working on human rights and social justice issues. 2010.

1391-373 Grupo FARO, Quito, Ecuador, $47,000. To convene scholars and practitioners to exchange theoretical analyses and practical experiences on political clientelism, social policy and quality of democracy and disseminate the findings. 2010.

1391-374 Guatemalan Cooperative and NGO Coordinator, Guatemala, $93,000. To establish Agrarian and Rural Observatory to monitor implementation of new law on integrated rural development and analyze impact. 2010.

1391-375 HABI Foundation for Environmental Rights, Cairo, Egypt, $100,000. For research, training and advocacy to promote protection of environmental rights in Egypt. 2010.

1391-376 Handcraft in Transit, Accra, Ghana, $400,000. For tie-off support to complete new office building and provide business development services for craft sectors in Ghana and Nigeria. 2010.

1391-377 Happy Kidney Foundation, Nairobi, Kenya, $25,000. To create awareness on early diagnosis of kidney failure and provide training for underprivileged in Nairobi. 2010.

1391-378 HAQ Centre for Child Rights, New Delhi, India, $200,000. For Budgets for Children, project to develop and use accountability tools, including budget analysis, to promote government responsiveness to children's basic needs and human rights. 2010.

1391-379 Harvard University, Hauser Center For Nonprofit Associations, Cambridge, MA, $70,000. To develop strategic plan for enhancing indigenous support for Chinese NGOs and monitoring, evaluation and learning system for assessing results. 2010.

1391-380 Harvard University, Hauser Center For Nonprofit Organizations, Cambridge, MA, $210,000. To organize and facilitate meeting to help NGOs from countries in conflict strategize about strengthening national and regional justice systems. 2010.

1391-381 Harvard University, John F. Kennedy School of Government, Cambridge, MA, $190,000. To train Chinese scholars in use of empirical research methods to promote criminal justice reform. 2010.

1391-382 Harvard University, Joint Center For Housing Studies, Cambridge, MA, $225,000. For convening activities on urban poverty in developing countries to articulate next generation social and economic policies to help urban poor. 2010.

1391-383 Henry J. Kaiser Family Foundation, Global Media AIDS Initiative, Menlo Park, CA, $1,000,000. For final support for Global Media Partnership Program to enhance efforts to transition leadership of media partnership program to the South. 2010.

1391-384 Hivos, The Hague, Netherlands, $600,000. To establish Ford Foundation-Hivos Fund on Sustainable Rainfed Agriculture for grant making leading to development of new paradigm and policy framework for rainfed agriculture in India. 2010.

1391-385 Hivos, The Hague, Netherlands, $400,000. To establish regional fund addressing sexual and reproductive health and rights of young women and their intersection with HIV/AIDS and gender-based violence in Southern Africa and to begin grant making. 2010.

1391-386 Hivos, The Hague, Netherlands, $300,000. For grant making and other activities of Multi-Agency Grant Initiative, donor collaborative established to help strengthen effectiveness of community-based organizations in South Africa. 2010.

1391-387 Hivos, The Hague, Netherlands, $253,500. For small grants and technical assistance to address sexuality and reproductive health, gender-based violence and HIV/AIDS In rural Zimbabwe and facilitate advocacy on these issues by young women leaders. 2010.

1391-388 HLUVUKU-ADSEMA-Socio-Economic Development Association for the Matutuine and Catembe Districts, Bela Vista, Mozambique, $200,000. For seed capital for coordinated intervention in value chain financing and extension services to help smallholder farmers increase productivity and establish sustainable market linkages in Mozambique. 2010.

1391-389 Hondurans Against AIDS, Bronx, NY, $50,000. For HIV/AIDS Prevention Program aimed at Afro-descendent Honduran communities in the U.S. and Central America. 2010.

1391-390 Horizon Market Research and Policy Analysis, Beijing, China, $147,350. For final phase of work on public assessment of public services, including survey, international symposia and training workshop, local experiments and development of teaching materials. 2010.

1391-391 Hua Dan Limited, Beijing, China, $30,000. To address the psychosocial needs of rural-urban migrant children in Beijing using participatory theatre. 2010.

1391-392 Human Rights First, New York, NY, $850,000. For general support to build respect for human rights and the rule of law to help ensure the dignity to which everyone is entitled and stem intolerance, tyranny and violence and for strategic planning. 2010.

1391-393 Human Rights National Coordinator, Lima, Peru, $30,000. For media campaign on sentencing of Alberto Fujimori in Peru for human rights violations that affirms democratic and human rights culture in Peru. 2010.

1391-394 Human Rights Watch, New York, NY, $400,000. For research and advocacy to encourage international financial institutions to comprehensively integrate human rights into all of their operations and projects. 2010.

1391-395 Human Rights Watch, New York, NY, $150,000. For research, reports and advocacy on human rights in the Andean Region. 2010.

1391-396 HUMANAS Corporation, Regional Center of Human Rights and Gender Justice, Santiago, Chile, $475,000. For research and dissemination on women's rights, regional and global advocacy and expansion of feminist regional articulation to include at least one organization focused on indigenous issues. 2010.

1391-397 Ideosync Media Combine, New Delhi, India, $230,000. For infrastructural and technical support to develop community media content in India. 2010.

1391-398 Independent Television Service, San Francisco, CA, $500,000. For final support for Global Perspectives Project, two-way media exchange using documentaries to transform how Americans see the world and how the world sees the United States. 2010.

1391-399 Indian Institute of Dalit Studies, New Delhi, India, $100,000. For final general support for research, dissemination and other activities related to the nature and consequences of discrimination against and social exclusion of marginalized groups. 2010.

1391-400 Indian Law Resource Center, Helena, MT, $450,000. For general support to strengthen human rights work on behalf of Native Americans and indigenous peoples throughout the world. 2010.

1391-401 Indian Law Resource Center, Helena, MT, $85,500. For education and advocacy to win U.S. endorsement of United Nations Declaration On The Rights Of Indigenous Peoples, increasing potential for achieving climate change agreements that protect those rights. 2010.

1391-402 Indian National Trust for Art and Cultural Heritage, New Delhi, India, $225,000. For final support for training, grant making and a web-based archive to conserve endangered craft traditions and cultural resources in Ladakh. 2010.

1391-403 Indigenous Center for Studies and Research, Manaus, Brazil, $200,000. For Indigenous Rights Observatory to establish regional indigenous rights centers in states of Mato Grosso do Sul, Para and Pernambuco and develop national network of indigenous lawyers. 2010.

1391-404 Indonesia Corruption Watch, Jakarta, Indonesia, $300,000. To establish transparent and accountable Local Information Commissions in six provinces and empower poor to conduct social audits on delivery of public services in six districts/cities. 2010.

1391-405 Indonesia Partnership Committee for Poverty Alleviation, Indonesia, $389,616. To develop resource center for strategic alliance for poverty reduction, integrating many existing poverty reduction data sets and provide technical assistance to local governments and NGOs. 2010.

1391-406 Indonesian Association for Media Development, Jakarta, Indonesia, $239,613. To hold training workshops for mid-career journalists from regional media outlets and develop programming on minority issues for an interactive radio talk show, legal reform and human rights. 2010.

1391-407 Indonesian Association of Community Radio, Bandung, Indonesia, $147,533. To strengthen National Community Radio

Association's provincial branches and conduct training, public outreach and advocacy to safeguard legal provisions for community radio in 10 provinces. 2010.

1391-408 Iniciativa Ciudadana para la Promocion de la Cultura del Dialogo, A.C., Mexico City, Mexico, $60,000. To train Mexican migrant leaders to conduct advocacy in Mexico and United States on key issues that impact their communities on both sides of the border. 2010.

1391-409 Iniciativa Ciudadana y Desarrollo Social, Mexico City, Mexico, $90,000. To assist in design, implementation and monitoring of public policies addressing problems of women migrants on Chiapas-Guatemala border through human rights and gender framework. 2010.

1391-410 Iniciativa Ciudadana y Desarrollo Social, Mexico City, Mexico, $60,000. For final support for Social Policy and Human Rights Observatory to develop tools that help citizen control and oversight of public policies to guarantee rights of all citizens in Mexico. 2010.

1391-411 Innovations for Poverty Action, New Haven, CT, $1,310,762. For Ghana Microfinance Graduation Pilot to test asset transfer, training and support services program to prepare extreme poor for active membership in a microfinance program. 2010.

1391-412 Innovations for Poverty Action, New Haven, CT, $1,014,887. To evaluate pilot programs that provide asset and support services to very poor people in developing countries to help them to increase incomes and gain access to microfinance programs. 2010.

1391-413 Institut Studi Arus Informasi, Jakarta, Indonesia, $270,000. To monitor Information Commission's efforts at national and local level to develop responsible, user-friendly mechanism for providing information on delivery of basic public services. 2010.

1391-414 Institute for Development Education and Learning, Ahmadabad, India, $250,000. For litigation at both the grassroots and constitutional levels, research and monitoring to establish, protect and enforce the socioeconomic rights of vulnerable groups. 2010.

1391-415 Institute for Human Rights and Development in Africa, Banjul, Gambia, $300,000. For research and litigation using national and regional instruments to enforce human rights across Africa and to use litigation before national courts to seed cases for African court of justice. 2010.

1391-416 Institute for Law and Environmental Governance, Nairobi, Kenya, $350,000. To promote implementation of national land policy, equitable access to and ownership of land and land-based natural resources and better reporting on land and natural resource governance. 2010.

1391-417 Institute for Policy and Community Development Studies, Jakarta, Indonesia, $134,239. To assess policy and institutional set up and changes required for nationwide replication of best practices of participation of poor and marginalized groups in public decision making. 2010.

1391-418 Institute for Study and Dissemination on Migration, Mexico City, Mexico, $155,000. To convene working group and conduct advocacy activities to inform Mexican migration policy debate. 2010.

1391-419 Institute for the Development of Journalism, Sao Paulo, Brazil, $295,425. For media observatory to monitor Brazilian media and serve as permanent forum for open discussion on media coverage of issues and to complete and implement plan for achieving financial stability. 2010.

1391-420 Institute of Development Studies, Brighton, England, $140,000. For policy research on social protection in Asia and to nurture regional network of researchers and activists. 2010.

1391-421 Institute of International Education, New York, NY, $1,417,375. For global travel and learning fund for Chinese grantees. 2010.

1391-422 Institute of International Education, Global Travel and Learning Fund, New York, NY, $7,924,400. To administer travel awards to Russia and other program-related learning activities. 2010.

1391-423 Institute of Peruvian Studies, Lima, Peru, $150,000. For comprehensive analysis of data on Peruvian applicants to and participants in international fellowship program to identify Program's Impact on student mobility. 2010.

1391-424 Instituto del Bien Comun, Lima, Peru, $100,000. To map deforestation in the Kakataibo Peoples' Territory in the Peruvian Amazon, publish and disseminate the maps and help Kakataibo Communities monitor and combat deforestation. 2010.

1391-425 Instituto para la Seguridad y la Democracia, INSyDE, Mexico City, Mexico, $183,000. To develop and launch citizen observatory of migrants human rights in southern Mexico. 2010.

1391-426 Instituto Socioambiental, Sao Paulo, Brazil, $155,000. To influence media in relation to World Summit For Sustainable Development (WSSD) - Rio Plus 20. 2010.

1391-427 Instituto Sou da Paz, Sao Paulo, Brazil, $190,000. To develop Local Action Plan for gun control in Sao Paulo, build capacity of Brazilian Disarmament Network and monitor implementation of and attempts to weaken new national disarmament law. 2010.

1391-428 Interaction Institute for Social Change, Cambridge, MA, $145,000. To coordinate International Working Group on Social Justice Philanthropy and Peace and Emerging Global Community of Practice of Thought Leaders in the Field. 2010.

1391-429 Interdisciplinary Group for Appropriate Rural Technology, Patzcuaro, Mexico, $50,000. For research, workshops, media work and advocacy with state officials that help indigenous communities in Michoacan, Mexico to maintain their forests and receive payments for protecting them. 2010.

1391-430 INTERIGHTS: The International Centre for the Legal Protection of Human Rights, London, England, $570,000. For general support to advance human rights worldwide through the use of international and comparative law and mechanisms and project support to advance women's economic and social rights in Africa. 2010.

1391-431 International AIDS Society, Geneva, Switzerland, $500,000. For final general support for work on HIV/AIDS in the global arena and support to strengthen partnerships among HIV/AIDS communities from different sectors, particularly in the Global South. 2010.

1391-432 International AIDS Society, Geneva, Switzerland, $300,000. To strengthen global HIV social science and operational research, generating evidence to promote rights to universal access and quality policy and programmatic response. 2010.

1391-433 International Association for Digital Publications, Sutton, England, $100,000. For E-book And Netlibrary Project. 2010.

1391-434 International Association for Feminist Economics, Lincoln, NE, $250,000. To produce special issue of Feminist Economics on the Intersections Of Gender, Land and Food Security. 2010.

1391-435 International Catholic Migration Commission, Geneva, Switzerland, $228,256. To develop and pilot improved financial service mechanisms for migrant laborers from eastern Indonesia and their families to increase their economic security at home and prevent debt bondage abroad. 2010.

1391-436 International Center, Washington, DC, $140,000. To manage Vietnamese side of U.S.-Vietnam Dialogue Group on Agent Orange/Dioxin and provide technical assistance to and monitor grantees of Agent Orange Vietnam Information Initiative. 2010.

1391-437 International Center for Journalists, Washington, DC, $100,000. For training for minority journalists to become foreign correspondents through World Affairs Journalism Fellowships, in collaboration with Ethics and Excellence in Journalism Foundation. 2010.

1391-438 International Center for Not-for Profit Law, Washington, DC, $200,000. For flexible, targeted technical and legal assistance to safeguard space for civil society and civic participation In politically challenging environments. 2010.

1391-439 International Center for Transitional Justice, New York, NY, $1,500,000. For general support to redress and prevent most severe violations of human rights by confronting legacies of mass abuse. 2010.

1391-440 International Center for Transitional Justice, New York, NY, $1,000,000. For general support to redress and prevent the most severe violations of human rights by confronting legacies of mass abuse. 2010.

1391-441 International Center for Tropical Agriculture, Cali, Colombia, $300,000. To study and disseminate lessons learnt on public policies fostering inclusive value chains in Colombia. 2010.

1391-442 International Coalition of Sites of Conscience, New York, NY, $200,000. For general support to provide technical and financial assistance to and foster collaboration and collective action among regional sites around the world working on social justice issues. 2010.

1391-443 International Community of Women Living with HIV and AIDS, Mbabane, Swaziland, $150,000. For general support to promote human development, gender equality and meaningful and equitable participation of HIV-positive women in all spheres and to advocate for access to quality health care. 2010.

1391-444 International Community of Women Living with HIV and AIDS, Eastern Africa, Kampala, Uganda, $75,000. For general support to advocate for rights of HIV positive women in Uganda, Kenya and Tanzania. 2010.

1391-445 International Community of Women Living with HIV/AIDS, India, $100,000. For advocacy, capacity building and networking among HIV-positive women in Asia. 2010.

1391-446 International Council of AIDS Service Organizations, Toronto, Canada, $200,000. For final general support to mobilize and support diverse HIV and AIDS-affected community organizations to build an effective global response to HIV and AIDS. 2010.

1391-447 International Council on Human Rights Policy, Geneva, Switzerland, $575,000. For general support for applied research, reflection and forward thinking on matters of international human rights policy and to hold meeting on role of human rights in forming macroeconomic policy. 2010.

1391-448 International Development Economics Associates, London, England, $200,000. To develop, sharpen and widely disseminate results emerging from ongoing projects under Reforming Global Finance Initiative, with particular emphasis in Asia. 2010.

1391-449 International Development Law Organization, Rome, Italy, $350,000. To organize regional meetings of AIDS activists and lawyers in Southern Africa, Middle East/North Africa and Latin America and joint meeting prior to the 2010 International AIDS Conference. 2010.

1391-450 International Federation of Human Rights Leagues, Paris, France, $400,000. For advocacy, research and training to advance the accountability of states and private actors for violations of economic and social rights. 2010.

1391-451 International Fellowships Fund, New York, NY, $15,000,000. To carry out activities of International Fellowships Program with focus on women. 2010.

1391-452 International Forum on Globalization, San Francisco, CA, $100,000. To convene indigenous and non-indigenous leaders to protect rights of indigenous peoples and forest communities in decisions at 16th Climate Change Conference of Parties in Mexico. 2010.

1391-453 International Funders for Indigenous Peoples, Akwesasne, NY, $14,500. For annual membership dues. 2010.

1391-454 International Gay and Lesbian Human Rights Commission, New York, NY, $150,000. For general support to advance human rights for everyone, everywhere to end discrimination based on sexual orientation, gender identity or gender expression. 2010.

1391-455 International Institute for Environment and Development, London, England, $48,735. For international platform for research by leading Chinese environmental economists on dilemmas in Chinese environmental sustainability and resource management policy. 2010.

1391-456 International Institute of Rural Reconstruction, New York, NY, $180,000. To develop capacity building program on value chain development. 2010.

1391-457 International Islamic Center for Population Studies and Research, Cairo, Egypt, $90,000. To develop publication and programs on youth reproductive health issues from perspective of Islam. 2010.

1391-458 International Latina Community of Women Living with HIV and AIDS, Buenos Aires, Argentina, $250,000. For transition of headquarters to Global South and to build Latin American women's capacity to participate in policy-making process with respect to HIV/AIDS. 2010.

1391-459 International Latina Community of Women Living with HIV and AIDS, Buenos Aires, Argentina, $200,000. For global human rights advocacy on behalf of women affected by HIV/AIDS. 2010.

1391-460 International Latina Community of Women Living with HIV and AIDS, Buenos Aires, Argentina, $177,000. To complete transition of ICW Global International Support Office from London to Buenos Aires, design communications strategy, strengthen regional networks and develop advocacy strategy. 2010.

1391-461 International Latina Community of Women Living with HIV and AIDS, Buenos Aires, Argentina, $150,000. To strengthen capacity of ICW's Latina chapters to defend rights of women living with HIV with special focus on Central America. 2010.

1391-462 International Latina Community of Women Living with HIV and AIDS, Buenos Aires, Argentina, $50,000. To update donor organizations on recent institutional changes and on ICW Latina's new goals and objectives and for meetings with strategic partners, including donors and UN agencies. 2010.

1391-463 International Livestock Research Institute, Nairobi, Kenya, $61,254. For research to identify livestock products, value chains and markets with greatest potential to benefit poor rural communities and help women transition out of poverty. 2010.

1391-464 International Network of Research Methodologies for Production Systems, RIMISP-Latin American Center for Rural Development, Santiago, Chile, $65,000. To promote innovative policies in rural territorial development and rural advisory services through two international conferences. 2010.

1391-465 International Poverty Reduction Center in China, Beijing, China, $149,970. To document grantee innovations in community-based rural poverty reduction in western China as a reference resource for formulating new national rural poverty reduction policy. 2010.

1391-466 International Poverty Reduction Center in China, Beijing, China, $69,863. To use pastoral areas as test case for incorporating regional and demographic differences into household targeting for new government rural poverty reduction program. 2010.

1391-467 International Projects Assistance Services, Chapel Hill, NC, $260,000. For tie-off core support for IPAS Africa Alliance for Women's Reproductive Health and Rights to advocate for policies that reduce abortion-related death and advance women's reproductive health and rights. 2010.

1391-468 International Projects Assistance Services, Chapel Hill, NC, $200,000. For general support to increase women's ability to exercise sexual and reproductive rights and reduce abortion-related deaths and injuries. 2010.

1391-469 International Projects Assistance Services, Chapel Hill, NC, $175,000. To promote sexual and reproductive rights, including decriminalization of abortion, in Nicaragua and provide technical assistance to a coalition of sexual and reproductive rights advocates in El Salvador. 2010.

1391-470 International Union for Conservation of Nature and Natural Resources, Gland, Switzerland, $120,000. For annual workshop In CIK Countries (China, India, Kenya) on key issues in pastoral rights. 2010.

1391-471 International Union for Conservation of Nature and Natural Resources, Gland, Switzerland, $100,000. For research, training and technical assistance to help indigenous organizations in Mexico and Central America monitor and influence impacts of mining and energy projects in their territories. 2010.

1391-472 International Womens Media Foundation, Washington, DC, $100,000. For grants and training to help women journalists develop and carry out innovative, self-sustaining digital media projects and for Courage In Journalism Awards. 2010.

1391-473 International Womens Rights Action Watch, Kuala Lumpur, Malaysia, $530,000. For tie-off general support to promote women's human rights and the effective implementation of international human rights mechanisms in the Asia Pacific Region. 2010.

1391-474 Internet Sexuality Information Services, Oakland, CA, $62,000. For ISIS (Cal.) Youth and Sexuality Internet Research. 2010.

1391-475 IP Watch Association, Geneva, Switzerland, $200,000. To monitor and disseminate information on issues relating to new developments in intellectual property (IP) rules, agreements and international negotiations and on interconnection between IP and finance. 2010.

1391-476 Isandla Institute, Cape Town, South Africa, $200,000. To coordinate activities of Good Governance Learning Network related to promoting transparent, effective and accountable government. 2010.

1391-477 IT for Change, Bangalore, India, $150,000. For research and advocacy on information and communication technologies and governance reforms in India. 2010.

1391-478 Jawaharlal Nehru University, Centre For Studies In Science Policy, New Delhi, India, $400,000. For new Economic Research Unit to conduct research to advance advocacy initiatives of Revitalizing Rain fed Agriculture and Rain fed Livestock Networks. 2010.

1391-479 Jazz at Lincoln Center, New York, NY, $150,000. For Jazz at Lincoln Center Orchestra to conduct performance and educational residency in Havana, Cuba to explore musical connections among Havana, New Orleans and New York City. 2010.

1391-480 Jumo International, New York, NY, $250,000. To develop online social networking platform for individuals and organizations working toward global economic justice. 2010.

1391-481 K-Republic Development Agency, Nairobi, Kenya, $590,000. To develop, promote and pilot new products and delivery mechanisms for agricultural finance and incubate the Muungano Support Unit, new organization working on urban land tenure and housing finance. 2010.

1391-482 Kampung Halaman Foundation, Jakarta, Indonesia, $300,000. Toward production of multimedia digital content and to conduct online media campaigns and to strengthen youth leadership in local and international forums. Population focus of grant is teenage girls. 2010.

1391-483 Kenya Agricultural Research Institute, Nairobi, Kenya, $200,000. To conduct research and assess different value chains that link rural producers and other marginalized vulnerable markets and to conduct policy analysis research on pro-poor farmer market linkages. 2010.

1391-484 Kenya Land Alliance Trust, Nakuru, Kenya, $300,000. To strengthen capacity of civil society to remain vigilant and to monitor and advocate for inclusive land policy implementation process. 2010.

1391-485 Kenya Women Holding, Nairobi, Kenya, $251,000. To develop new products for agricultural financing that are appropriate and accessible to rural women and to investigate dynamic relationship between women's human rights and economic empowerment. 2010.

1391-486 KHOJ International Artists Association, New Delhi, India, $152,000. To develop and disseminate new media platforms for initiating public outreach and dialogue on urban redevelopment in India. 2010.

1391-487 Kituo Cha Katiba, East African Centre for Constitutional Development, Kampala, Uganda, $200,000. For Education and Resource Centre to conduct training needs assessment and develop programs and curricula and for research, dissemination and workshops on constitution making and good governance. 2010.

1391-488 Koperasi Kerajinan Tenun Ikat Dayak Jasa Menenun Mandiri, Sintang, Indonesia, $124,316. To strengthen financial and livelihood services provided to Dayak women handicraft producers in Sintang District of West Kalimantan. 2010.

1391-489 Labor Project for Working Families, Berkeley, CA, $35,500. For fundraising, relationship building and strategic planning in preparation for launch of the national public policy initiative to increase labor movement engagement on work and family issues. 2010.

1391-490 Labour Awareness Resource Center, Nairobi, Kenya, $50,000. To advocate for women workers' rights on flower farms and in export processing zones, including their sexuality, reproductive health and HIV/AIDS rights. 2010.

1391-491 Land Institute of Para, Belem, Brazil, $250,000. To identify and demarcate rural Afro-descendants' lands on public land in the State of Para. 2010.

1391-492 Land Is Life, Somerville, MA, $200,000. To build capacity of indigenous peoples to protect their rights with respect to climate change policies, adaptation strategies and mitigation projects. 2010.

1391-493 Land of Rights, Curitiba, Brazil, $500,000. For strategic litigation and advocacy on land rights in Brazil. 2010.

1391-494 Lanzhou University, School Of Life Science, Lanzhou, China, $73,332. To help Herder Communities promote group-household grazing as policy alternative to privatized operation and grassland fragmentation on Qinghai-Tibetan Plateau. 2010.

1391-495 Latin American Faculty of Social Sciences, San Jose, Costa Rica, $159,000. To formulate recommendations for modifying Central American regional agreements to protect migrant labor rights. 2010.

1391-496 Latin American Group for Justice and Gender, Buenos Aires, Argentina, $75,000. For tie-off general support to promote gender equality and women's exercise of rights in Latin America. 2010.

1391-497 Law College Association of the University of Arizona, Tucson, AZ, $400,000. For Indigenous People's Law and Policy Program to provide legal advocacy to help indigenous communities and groups promote and secure basic human rights. 2010.

1391-498 Lawyers for Human Rights, Pretoria, South Africa, $200,000. For Strategic Litigation,

Land and Housing and Refugee and Migrant Rights Units to conduct litigation and advocacy on behalf of vulnerable groups about socioeconomic rights. 2010.

1391-499 Le Mouvement Ni Putes Ni Soumises, Paris, France, $100,000. For final support to help women and youth living in French ghettos combat prejudice and promote tolerance and social justice. 2010.

1391-500 Leadership Conference on Civil Rights Education Fund, Washington, DC, $200,000. To undertake public education, advocacy, and outreach on the Convention on the Elimination of All Forms of Discrimination Against Women. 2010.

1391-501 Leadership Institute Simone de Beauvoir, Mexico City, Mexico, $90,000. For training and related activities to build leadership capacity of indigenous women and for new program to improve women's access to justice, focusing on gender-based violence and reproductive rights. 2010.

1391-502 Leadership, Effectiveness, Accountability and Professionalism Africa, LEAP Africa, Vernon Hills, IL, $750,000. To expand Business Leadership Program across Nigeria, organize regional meetings for program's growing alumni network and pilot training of trainers program and for research and publications. 2010.

1391-503 Lebanese Association for Educational Sciences, Beirut, Lebanon, $200,000. To build research program on public/private universities and quality measurement in Mena region. 2010.

1391-504 Legal Defense Institute, Lima, Peru, $350,000. For general support to promote human rights in Peru through national and international efforts with special view to excluded populations including indigenous people. 2010.

1391-505 Legal Resources Trust, Johannesburg, South Africa, $300,000. For litigation, advocacy and public education to protect and promote socioeconomic rights of vulnerable and marginalized groups about land, mineral rights and housing. 2010.

1391-506 Letra S Sida, Cultura y Vida Cotidiana, Mexico City, Mexico, $150,000. To develop and implement media strategy promoting recognition of sexual and reproductive rights of people living with HIV/AIDS and to help clients of Mexico City's HIV/AIDS program defend their rights. 2010.

1391-507 Lexington Institute, Cuba Program, Arlington, VA, $70,000. To bring Cuban academics to the U.S., conduct research on U.S. policy toward Cuban migrants and on state of economic reform in Cuba and disseminate research findings. 2010.

1391-508 LifeLine Pietermaritzburg, Pietermaritzburg, South Africa, $200,000. To expand program addressing problem of teenage pregnancy and sexual and reproductive health and rights of young women to two additional districts in KwaZulu-Natal Province. 2010.

1391-509 Livelihood School, Koti, India, $345,000. To update curriculum on livelihoods training, work with government officials and conduct scoping study for foundation offices in Eastern and Southern Africa regions. 2010.

1391-510 Liverpool VCT and Care Kenya, Nairobi, Kenya, $300,000. For research, capacity building, grant making and expanded sexuality and reproductive health and rights and HIV/AIDS services to at-risk populations and to help them engage in HIV/AIDS policy dialogues. 2010.

1391-511 Living Cities: The National Community Development Initiative, New York, NY, $75,000. For one-year planning grant to support Citiscope, online journalism tool for urban issues globally. 2010.

1391-512 Mahidol University, Southeast Asian Consortium On Gender, Sexuality And Health, Bangkok, Thailand, $100,000. To build capacity of mid-level researchers with project on impact of social and economic change on sexuality and gender. 2010.

1391-513 Mahila Sarvangeen Utkarsh Mandal, Pune, India, $151,000. For final support for building self-advocacy capacities in community-based organizations working with marginalized populations for their basic needs and for strengthening ESR campaigns and networks. 2010.

1391-514 Makerere University, Human Rights and Peace Centre, Kampala, Uganda, $300,000. To conduct research on links between young women's sexual and reproductive health and rights and HIV/AIDS and publish findings. 2010.

1391-515 Management Sciences for Health, Cambridge, MA, $470,000. To conduct management and organizational sustainability assessments of and provide leadership and strategic planning training to global HIV/AIDS initiative grantees. 2010.

1391-516 Maple Womens Psychological Counseling Center, Beijing, China, $100,000. For tie-off support for psychological counseling hotlines for women and single-parent support groups. 2010.

1391-517 Market Theater Foundation, Johannesburg, South Africa, $200,000. For tie-off general support to provide highest level of artistic excellence in performing and visual arts while educating and developing diverse community of artists, audiences and technicians. 2010.

1391-518 Media Development in Africa Limited, Nairobi, Kenya, $300,000. To produce new educational TV series on Kenya's court system and second season of Agenda Uganda; conduct media training program for young Kenyans and build board, staff and institutional capacity. 2010.

1391-519 Media Foundation, New Delhi, India, $80,000. For research and publication activities of The Hoot, media research website, to promote media ethics, accountability and freedom of expression. 2010.

1391-520 Medical Research Council of South Africa, Cape Town, South Africa, $176,000. To test culturally sensitive intervention to improve young women's agency and decisionmaking on sexual and reproductive health and HIV issues in Eastern Cape Province. 2010.

1391-521 Men for the Equality of Men and Women, Nairobi, Kenya, $200,000. For research, networking and training programs on masculinities to strengthen Men For Gender Equality Movement in Kenya. 2010.

1391-522 Men for the Equality of Men and Women, Nairobi, Kenya, $40,000. To produce and distribute edutainment video on progressive masculinities. 2010.

1391-523 Mercy Corps, Portland, OR, $170,282. For China-U.S. International Exchange Program In Philanthropy. 2010.

1391-524 Meridian Institute, Dillon, CO, $200,000. To work with eight foundations to create Initiative on Food and Agriculture that would seek to reform the U.S. Food and Agricultural System to improve the livelihoods of rural poor worldwide. 2010.

1391-525 Mexican Council for Sustainable Forestry, Mexico City, Mexico, $200,000. To conduct research and carry out advocacy and communications activities designed to promote climate change policies that favor community forestry in Mexico. 2010.

1391-526 Microfinance Information Exchange, Washington, DC, $186,266. To create data platform for social indicators reported by microfinance organizations and capacity to analyze the data. 2010.

1391-527 Microfinance Transparency, Lancaster, PA, $284,722. For research on pricing of microfinance loan products in South America and to publish findings online and produce educational materials for investors, regulators, policy makers and the Press. 2010.

1391-528 Ministry of Foreign Affairs, Institute for Diplomatic Studies (IDS), Cairo, Egypt, $200,000. For intensive training program in the U.S. on American foreign policy making and United Nations system for newly appointed Egyptian diplomats. 2010.

1391-529 Mitra Samya Lembaga Studi Partisipasi dan Demokrasi, Mataram, Indonesia, $341,779. To empower poor groups in 60 villages and improve the capacity of village and district officials in Central Lombok to conduct participatory planning and budgeting for fulfillment of basic rights. 2010.

1391-530 Monash University, Clayton, Australia, $100,000. To support post-graduate students studying for Masters and Doctoral degrees. 2010.

1391-531 Moving the Goalposts Kilifi, Kilifi, Kenya, $200,000. To use football (soccer) as starting point for empowering girls and providing reproductive health information and to study Kilifi community's role in addressing sexual and reproductive health and rights and HIV. 2010.

1391-532 Mozambican Association for the Development of Democracy, Maputo, Mozambique, $200,000. To develop training materials on social accountability and provide training and technical assistance to build civil society capacity to promote transparent, effective and accountable government. 2010.

1391-533 Munden Project, Wilmington, DE, $70,000. To design and test model carbon-trading exchange platform focused around rights, needs and livelihood strategies of forest-dependent communities, including rural poor. 2010.

1391-534 Museum for African Art, Long Island City, NY, $250,000. To develop and implement core exhibit for Nelson Mandela Center, a chronicle of the history of apartheid in South Africa, its impact on the rest of the world and Mandela's role in that history. 2010.

1391-535 Muslims for Human Rights, Mombasa, Kenya, $50,000. To build capacity of local communities in Kenya's coast province to secure their land rights and advocate for implementation of national land policy. 2010.

1391-536 Nanjing Community Development Center for Facilitators, Nanjing, China, $260,000. For training and practice programs for social services provision and participatory governance in urban and periurban areas of Nanjing with high concentrations of rural migrants. 2010.

1391-537 Nanjing University, School of Foreign Studies, Nanjing, China, $175,000. To run faculty enhancement program to promote development of American Cultural and Social Studies in China's poorer western regions. 2010.

1391-538 Narada Foundation, Beijing, China, $20,000. For training and services to migrant children kindergartens in Beijing. 2010.

1391-539 National Association for the Rights of Disabled People in Lebanon, Beirut, Lebanon, $170,000. To promote economic and social rights of people with disabilities in Egypt, the Middle East and North Africa. 2010.

1391-540 National Association of Campesino Marketing Organizations, Mexico City, Mexico, $200,000. For policy advocacy and public education on the enabling environment for rural communities in Mexico. 2010.

1391-541 National Association of People Affected by Dams, Sao Paulo, Brazil, $100,000. For activities to protect rights of traditional peoples and rural communities displaced or threatened by construction of large dams in the Amazon. 2010.

1391-542 National Centre for Advocacy Studies, Pune, India, $261,000. For action research and advocacy to identify and address the structural and systemic constraints in the justice delivery mechanism at the grassroots level in India. 2010.

1391-543 National Committee on American Foreign Policy, New York, NY, $70,000. To explore prospects for durable U.S.-China Second Track military-to-military ties. 2010.

1391-544 National Forum on Migration in Guatemala, Guatemala City, Guatemala, $80,000. To strengthen organizational capacities to advocate for migration policy reform, monitor policy implementation and provide legal guidance to migrants. 2010.

1391-545 National Immigration Law Center, Los Angeles, CA, $100,000. To develop bi-national US-Mexico documentation and legal strategies that bolster migrant rights advocacy. 2010.

1391-546 National Immigration Project of the National Lawyers Guild, Boston, MA, $200,000. For general support to defend rights of immigrants facing incarceration and deportation. 2010.

1391-547 National Institute of Public Health, Cuernavaca, Mexico, $250,000. To develop service models for HIV prevention and services for migrants in Mexico and Central America. 2010.

1391-548 National Partnership for Women and Families, Washington, DC, $39,000. To disseminate comparative global research on impact of paid leave policies on competitiveness and unemployment. 2010.

1391-549 National Public Education Support Fund, Education Funder Strategy Group, Washington, DC, $25,000. For research seminar on international strategies for improving teacher and school leader effectiveness. 2010.

1391-550 National Religious Campaign Against Torture, Washington, DC, $200,000. For advocacy work to end the practice of torture and cruel, inhuman and degrading treatment in U.S. prisons and jails and to bring them into compliance with international human rights law. 2010.

1391-551 National Security Archive Fund, Washington, DC, $200,000. To use the right to information to promote accountability and transparency in Mexico and across Latin America, focusing on military, security and

migration issues and providing evidence for human rights cases. 2010.

1391-552 National Security Archive Fund, Washington, DC, $100,000. To catalogue, publish and strategically distribute comprehensive documents collection on untold history of communications and dialogue in U.S.-Cuban relations. 2010.

1391-553 National Social Watch, New Delhi, India, $200,000. For research, advocacy and alliance building to promote accountability of key institutions of governance in India. 2010.

1391-554 National Steering Committee 33, Hanoi, Vietnam, $23,975. To organize seminar on birth defects and newborn screening in collaboration with U.S.-Vietnam Joint Advisory Committee Health Task Force and Centers for Disease Control. 2010.

1391-555 National University of Lanus, Lanus, Argentina, $200,000. For Human Rights Center to survey status of migrant children's rights in Mexico-Guatemala region, design policies that respect those rights and train civil society groups to monitor them. 2010.

1391-556 National University of Singapore, Singapore, Singapore, $164,720. For in-depth research on Chinese higher education sector, analyzing various issues that hamper its development and seeking suggestions for their solutions. 2010.

1391-557 Nelson Mandela Metropolitan University, Port Elizabeth, South Africa, $60,000. To develop systematic links between University and surrounding further education and training colleges. 2010.

1391-558 Netherlands Development Organization, The Hague, Netherlands, $200,000. For research and learning into inclusive business models for scaling up good practices in the Southern Africa region. 2010.

1391-559 Network of European Foundations for Innovative Cooperation, Brussels, Belgium, $100,000. For final core support for European HIV/AIDS Funders Group to mobilize philanthropic leadership and resources to address Global HIV/AIDS pandemic and its social and economic consequences. 2010.

1391-560 New Basket Workshop, Capetown, South Africa, $200,000. To support product development and marketing services to women basket weavers in rural Zimbabwe and Mozambique and implement subsistence agriculture program to provide them with food security. 2010.

1391-561 New Development, Amman, Jordan, $155,000. For dialogue, learning and consensus building to develop and promote rights-driven approach to health, education and governance in Egypt among key stakeholders, thinkers and decision makers. 2010.

1391-562 New Development, Amman, Jordan, $130,000. For a project for research and advocacy on academic freedoms and the right to information in Egyptian universities. 2010.

1391-563 New Israel Fund, Washington, DC, $5,000,000. For final support for Ford Foundation Israel Fund's grant making to promote human rights, social and economic justice and environmental justice. 2010.

1391-564 Nigeria ICT Forum of Partnership Institutions, Abuja, Nigeria, $300,000. For tie-off support to secure and oversee delivery of low-cost bandwidth for research and scholarly

activities to a consortium comprising Association of African Universities and 33 universities. 2010.

1391-565 Non-Profit Incubator, Shanghai, China, $248,000. To establish Social Entrepreneur Institute to provide established practitioners with continuing education directed toward problem solving and for publication of magazine, Social Entrepreneur. 2010.

1391-566 North-South Institute, Ottawa, Canada, $350,000. To develop standards and mechanisms to protect rights of indigenous and Afro-descendent communities affected by large-scale extractive mining in Colombia. 2010.

1391-567 Northeastern University, Boston, MA, $300,000. For core support for Program on Human Rights and the Global Economy to work with scholars, institutions and advocates nationally and internationally to address issues of human rights and economic development. 2010.

1391-568 Northwest University, Xian, China, $229,769. For Northwest Socioeconomic Development Research Center to strengthen partner research and analytical capacity and improve outreach to government, researchers and media. 2010.

1391-569 Northwest University, Northwest Socioeconomic Development Research Center, Xian, China, $281,560. To conduct action research in rural schools on relationship between breakfast consumption and children's health and school performance. 2010.

1391-570 Northwest University of Politics and Law, Xian, China, $148,813. For Criminal Law Scientific Research Center to conduct pilot project providing free criminal defense services to indigent defendants in the city of Xian. 2010.

1391-571 NUPEF Institute-Nucleus for Research, Studies and Formation, Rio de Janeiro, Brazil, $250,000. To coordinate production of knowledge, capacity and public awareness around process of Internet governance and policy making in information and communications technology field. 2010.

1391-572 NUPEF Institute-Nucleus for Research, Studies and Formation, Rio de Janeiro, Brazil, $62,500. To establish Center For Applied Research Studies And Capacity Building On Information And Communications Technologies. 2010.

1391-573 Office of the United Nations High Commissioner for Human Rights, Geneva, Switzerland, $50,000. To train Mexican NGOs in use of indicators from a gender perspective. 2010.

1391-574 Ohio State University Foundation, Kirwan Institute for the Study of Race and Ethnicity, Columbus, OH, $600,000. For core support for Institute's work in partnering with people, communities and institutions worldwide to think about, talk about and engage issues of race and ethnicity and for research on racial justice. 2010.

1391-575 Omi-dudu, Salvador, Brazil, $119,958. To monitor and analyze how Brazil's major print media cover racial disparities and discrimination and movement to combat them. 2010.

1391-576 Open Africa Initiative, Cape Town, South Africa, $200,000. For general support for Pan-African collaborative movement to link splendors of Africa in network of job-creating, conservation-oriented routes from the Cape to Cairo. 2010.

1391-577 Open Democracy Advice Centre, Cape Town, South Africa, $100,000. For Right To

Know, Right To Live Program to help poor communities access information on provision of public housing and use it to make process fairer and more transparent. 2010.

1391-578 Opportunity International Australia, Sydney, Australia, $198,490. To pilot mobile and branchless banking models and new savings products for poor rural households in West Timor. 2010.

1391-579 Organizacion de Estados Iberoamericanos para la Educacion, la Ciencia y la Cultura, Madrid, Spain, $200,000. For activities of Project Of Education Goals 2021, to attend Afro-Colombian populations in the component of higher education. 2010.

1391-580 Overseas Press Club of America, New York, NY, $75,000. For Training And Support For Young Correspondents To Travel And Work Abroad. 2010.

1391-581 Oxfam India, New Delhi, India, $200,000. To help fisher folk in the Bundelkhand region of Madhya Pradesh strengthen their cooperatives; gain access to markets; and develop sustainable, scalable business models for improving their livelihoods. 2010.

1391-582 Oxfam International, Oxford, England, $500,000. To support urgent humanitarian relief efforts for victims of earthquake in Haiti. 2010.

1391-583 Oxfam International, Oxford, England, $300,000. To build capacity of Southern African women's, sexual orientation and gender identity groups to participate effectively in the Global Fund For AIDS, TB and Malaria's funding mechanisms. 2010.

1391-584 Oxfam International, Oxford, England, $200,000. For Pan African project to address impact of punitive laws and policies that criminalize HIV transmission among vulnerable and marginalized groups and strengthen their networks. 2010.

1391-585 Oxfam International, Oxford, England, $75,000. To train indigenous leaders in Honduras in advocacy skills. 2010.

1391-586 Oxfam Novib, The Hague, Netherlands, $200,000. To scale up sustainable palm oil production and build improved models for smallholder production of oil palm to improve the sustainability of key internationally-traded commodities. 2010.

1391-587 Oxford University, Oxford, England, $50,000. For multi-year mentoring for potential Journal Authors and related stakeholders in CIK Countries (China, India, Kenya) on key issues in pastoral rights. 2010.

1391-588 Palestinian Association for Contemporary Art, Ramallah, West Bank/Gaza (Palestinian Territories), $100,000. To build the capacity and sustainability of a four-year degree program in Palestine in contemporary art. 2010.

1391-589 Para Society for the Defense of Human Rights, Belem, Brazil, $100,000. For litigation, communications and seminar on human rights, particularly with respect to land rights and violence against human rights defenders and to monitor enforcement of judicial decisions. 2010.

1391-590 Participatory Ecological Land Use Management, Kampala, Uganda, $60,000. To assess models and policies that help smallholder farmers in eastern Africa access and benefit from markets, develop sub-regional marketing initiative and educate members on national land policy issues. 2010.

1391-591 Participatory Mapping Network Foundation, Bogor, Indonesia, $151,397. To develop management system and capacities in ancestral domain registration for indigenous people and spatial planning. 500,000 hectares are expected to be registered. 2010.

1391-592 Partners for Law in Development, New Delhi, India, $200,000. For general support to advance realization of social justice and women's rights. 2010.

1391-593 Partners in Development for Research, Consulting and Training, Cairo, Egypt, $200,000. For research and training program to promote transparent implementation of social policies. 2010.

1391-594 Partners in Development for Research, Consulting and Training, Cairo, Egypt, $150,000. To host Higher Education Working Group for building knowledge, exchanging experiences and fostering advocacy work on higher education reform. 2010.

1391-595 Partners in Health, Boston, MA, $500,000. To support urgent humanitarian relief efforts for victims of earthquake in Haiti. 2010.

1391-596 Partners in Sexual Health, Parow, South Africa, $155,000. To develop and implement training and mentoring program to prepare young women to become effective leaders and advocates on key sexual and reproductive health and rights issues in Southern Africa. 2010.

1391-597 Pastoral Land Commission, Goiania, Brazil, $450,000. For training and technical assistance to help local civil society organizations in Brazilian Amazon better use legal instruments in defense of identity and land rights. 2010.

1391-598 People Opposing Women Abuse, South Africa, $200,000. For general support for legal advocacy and services to eradicate violence against women. 2010.

1391-599 Performing and Visual Arts Centre, Nairobi, Kenya, $70,000. For Leadership Discussion Forums for inter-generational women from rural Kenya. 2010.

1391-600 Perhimpunan Penggerak Advokasi Kerakyatan untuk Keadilan Sosial, Bandung, Indonesia, $200,232. To transform Secretariat into national resource center offering capacity-building training to grassroots organizations and establish local data and information resource centers in five provinces. 2010.

1391-601 Perkumpulan Pusat Pengembangan Sumberdaya Wanita, Jakarta, Indonesia, $196,286. To strengthen grassroots women's cooperatives and their members' microenterprises and build members' capacity to participate in decisionmaking institutions at local, district and province level. 2010.

1391-602 Peter G. Peterson Institute for International Economics, Washington, DC, $250,000. For research, workshop and conferences on financial institutions that are potentially too big to fail and for policy analysis on how this problem should be tackled. 2010.

1391-603 Physicians for Human Rights, Cambridge, MA, $440,000. For general support to mobilize health professionals to advance health, dignity and justice and promote right to health for all with special focus on women. 2010.

1391-604 Planact, Braamfontein, South Africa, $150,000. For research and advocacy on citizen monitoring of municipal performance and community participation in planning and upgrading of informal settlements. 2010.

1391-605 Planned Parenthood Federation of America, New York, NY, $125,000. For training, technical assistance and other activities to strengthen multidisciplinary group for sexual and reproductive rights in Guatemala and build its capacity to promote safe and legal abortion. 2010.

1391-606 Planned Parenthood Federation, International, Washington, DC, $280,000. To integrate sexual rights framework throughout Federation and its programs, expand services to marginalized groups and promote inclusion of sexual rights language in global agreements. 2010.

1391-607 Plateau Perspectives Canada, Xining, China, $59,045. To explore policy options for sustainable grassland management and poverty reduction in Tibetan Plateau herder communities. 2010.

1391-608 Platform for Citizen Participation And Accountability, Kampala, Uganda, $50,000. To map existing accountability mechanisms for civil society organizations and to design and test new self-assessment tools for civil society organization service delivery. 2010.

1391-609 Points of Encounter for Changes In Daily Life Foundation, Managua, Nicaragua, $150,000. To promote sexual and reproductive rights of young people (with focus on teenage girls) in Central America through media and broadcast. 2010.

1391-610 POLIS - Institute for Research, Training and Advisory Services in Social Policy, Sao Paulo, Brazil, $224,487. For tie-off support to conduct critical analysis of Brazilian experiences of participatory democracy at the national level and develop concrete proposals for improving their effectiveness. 2010.

1391-611 Pontifical Catholic University of Peru, Lima, Peru, $60,000. For Peruvian Social Sciences Network to conduct seminars on such issues as governance, social problems and popular entrepreneurship for social science professors from provincial public universities. 2010.

1391-612 Population Council, New York, NY, $360,000. To map adolescent sexual and reproductive health and rights programs in India, analyze data on parental role in youth transitions to adulthood and to test model for engaging parents in the process. 2010.

1391-613 Population Council, New York, NY, $200,000. For research on barriers to equity of access and success in higher education in Egypt. 2010.

1391-614 Population Council, New York, NY, $100,000. For further analysis of a survey of young people in Egypt. 2010.

1391-615 Practical Action, Bourton on Dunsmore, England, $188,746. To identify principles, approaches and most effective techniques/tools to build capacities of community-based facilitators in pro-poor market development. 2010.

1391-616 Praja Foundation, Mumbai, India, $100,000. To enhance citizen interaction with and oversight of elected representatives in city of Mumbai. 2010.

1391-617 PRAYAS: Initiatives in Health, Energy, Learning and Parenthood, Pune, India, $250,000. To help citizen participation in and oversight of independent regulatory institutions for effective delivery of services in electricity and water sectors in India. 2010.

1391-618 Prayer Movement Trust, Transform Kenya, Nairobi, Kenya, $45,000. To pilot mentoring program to help teenage boys become responsible young men in three high schools in Nairobi. 2010.

1391-619 PROCASUR Corporation, Santiago, Chile, $200,000. For general support to design and provide technical assistance and capacity-building services to improve living conditions of rural poor in Latin America. 2010.

1391-620 Professional Assistance for Development Action, New Delhi, India, $351,160. To train professionals in PRADAN and other NGOs in livelihood promotion and to establish Impact Monitoring Unit. 2010.

1391-621 Professional Assistance for Development Action, New Delhi, India, $300,000. For training, technical assistance, documentation and dissemination to help local governments in West Bengal improve implementation of National Rural Employment Guarantee Act. 2010.

1391-622 Programme on Women's Economic, Social and Cultural Rights, New Delhi, India, $200,000. For general support to promote women's economic, social and cultural rights by bringing gender framework to policy, law and practice at local, national, regional and international levels. 2010.

1391-623 Project Counselling Service for Latin American Refugees, Guatemala, Guatemala, $210,000. To build institutional, rights monitoring and advocacy capacities of southern Mexico and Central American migrant serving organizations, with a specific focus on women. 2010.

1391-624 Project Counselling Service for Latin American Refugees, Guatemala, Guatemala, $99,000. To help Mexican, Colombian and Guatemalan migrants' and human rights organizations develop organizational security plans, including workshop on legal framework for protecting human rights defenders. 2010.

1391-625 Provincial State Museum of East Nusa Tenggara, Kupang, Indonesia, $100,000. For tie-off support for exhibitions, publications and educational outreach programs focusing on minority ethnic groups in East Nusa Tenggara. 2010.

1391-626 Proyectamerica Corporation, Santiago, Chile, $80,000. To assess and monitor government policy toward indigenous peoples, develop recommendations for new institutional framework for indigenous issues and provide technical assistance to indigenous groups. 2010.

1391-627 Public Citizen Foundation, Washington, DC, $200,000. To complete investigation into how investment and financial services policies implemented under the World Trade Organization (WTO) and other trade agreements relate to the global financial crisis. 2010.

1391-628 Public Interest Law Institute, New York, NY, $25,000. Toward staff salaries and associated support for mentoring Chinese Public Interest Fellows and to train Chinese law firms to provide pro bono legal services. 2010.

1391-629 Quiet Pictures, New York, NY, $150,000. For production of documentary, Gardens Of Paradise, that narrates 24-hours in the life of California's Imperial Valley and border cities of Calexico-Mexicali. A series of interconnected stories illuminate challenges facing residents of twin cities Mexicali and Calexico on the U.S.-Mexico border. 2010.

1391-630 Radio Bilingue, Fresno, CA, $325,000. For general and project support for coverage of immigration and census issues and to expand transnational radio programming by and for indigenous communities of the U.S. and Mexico. 2010.

1391-631 Red de Municipalidades Urbanas y Rurales del Peru, Lima, Peru, $140,000. To disseminate mechanism for provision of business development services by rural municipalities in Peru. 2010.

1391-632 Refugees International, Washington, DC, $500,000. For final general support to advocate for lifesaving assistance and protection for refugees and displaced people worldwide and promote solutions to forced migration crises. 2010.

1391-633 Regional Coordinator of Economic and Social Research, Buenos Aires, Argentina, $35,000. To organize Cuban-U.S. academic workshop focused on legacy of distrust between the two countries. 2010.

1391-634 Regional Universities Forum for Capacity Building in Agriculture Limited, Kampala, Uganda, $50,000. To coordinate conceptualization and design of regional masters degree program in agro-enterprise development and for outreach to engage universities in pro-poor activities. 2010.

1391-635 Rehabilitation of Arid Environments Charitable Trust, Nakuru, Kenya, $150,000. To test and develop sustainable and profitable land use and management practices for reclaimed land and natural resources among pastoral communities. 2010.

1391-636 Renmin University of China, Beijing, China, $109,994. To review grassland management rights in herding areas of northern China as a reference for national policy reform. 2010.

1391-637 Renmin University of China, Center for Criminal Procedure and Reform, Beijing, China, $66,745. To study public participation in criminal justice system and practice of using citizen judges alongside professional ones in criminal cases. 2010.

1391-638 Renmin University of China, Center of Research in Comparative Political Economy, Beijing, China, $250,000. To conduct research on financial governance in China and on China's emergence as a global financial player. 2010.

1391-639 Renmin University of China, Institute of Sexuality and Gender, Beijing, China, $200,000. To strengthen China Sexuality Resource Center, build knowledge and conduct research to promote sexuality and reproductive health education in China. 2010.

1391-640 ReServe Elder Service, New York, NY, $30,000. For general support to connect experienced retired professionals with compensated service opportunities that challenge them to use their lifetime skills for public good. 2010.

1391-641 Revenue Watch Institute, New York, NY, $150,000. To strengthen civil society networks monitoring public policies on extractive industries in Latin America. 2010.

1391-642 Rights and Resources Group, Washington, DC, $1,100,000. For general support to reduce poverty, enhance well being and strengthen democratic governance and development in forest communities and to evaluate grants promoting community tenure and resource rights in forests. 2010.

1391-643 Riwaq Centre for Architectural Conservation, Al Bireh, West Bank/Gaza (Palestinian Territories), $250,000. For general support for protection and development of architectural heritage in Palestine. 2010.

1391-644 Rostros y Voces, Faces and Voices Foundation for Social Development, Mexico City, Mexico, $11,500. For emergency food assistance to families who lost their crops in tropical storm Ida and longer term assistance to restore livestock production. 2010.

1391-645 Rutgers, The State University of New Jersey, New Brunswick, NJ, $150,000. For project support for work to promote economic and social rights standards in economic policy making, targeted at national and intergovernmental decision makers. 2010.

1391-646 Rutgers, The State University of New Jersey, Center For Women's Global Leadership, New Brunswick, NJ, $300,000. For core support to develop and facilitate women's leadership for human rights and social justice worldwide. 2010.

1391-647 Sadhna, Udaipur, India, $180,000. For final support to set up small and medium enterprise division and market craft products under its own brand. 2010.

1391-648 SAMA-Resource Group for Women and Health, New Delhi, India, $200,000. For research, knowledge and capacity building, advocacy and monitoring on right to health in India and to strengthen Jan Swasthya Abhiyan, Indian chapter of Global People's Health Movement. 2010.

1391-649 Samaj Pragati Sahayog, Bagli, India, $300,000. To integrate pilot programs in animal husbandry and agriculture with delivery of public services in tribal drylands areas of Madhya Pradesh. 2010.

1391-650 SaveAct, Pietermaritzburg, South Africa, $120,000. For tie-off support to refine and improve effectiveness of group-based savings and lending schemes for asset building and advocacy purposes. 2010.

1391-651 SEMAT for Production and Distribution, Nicosia, Cyprus, $80,000. To train and provide services to young Egyptian filmmakers and to produce and distribute independent films and promote them at film festivals and other cultural venues worldwide. 2010.

1391-652 SEMAT for Production and Distribution, Nicosia, Cyprus, $40,000. To produce and disseminate documentary film that profiles important social change makers in Egypt. 2010.

1391-653 Seven Productions, Nairobi, Kenya, $125,000. To establish a national documentary film fund and leverage private sector and social support for sustainable creation of new content. 2010.

1391-654 Sex Worker Education and Advocacy Taskforce, Cape Town, South Africa, $200,000. For training and technical assistance to build capacity of Sisonke Sex Worker Movement to protect sex workers from human rights abuses and discrimination and address their health and legal needs. 2010.

1391-655 SGS North Amercia, Wilmington, NC, $45,330. For laboratory analysis to determine effectiveness of new bioremediation technology for dioxin at Vietnam's Da Nang Airport. 2010.

1391-656 Shanghai Academy of Educational Sciences, Shanghai, China, $187,654. To assist Ministry Of Education to develop a national monitoring and evaluation system that promotes balanced approach to improve equity in compulsory education. 2010.

1391-657 Shanghai Institute of Planned Parenthood Research, Shanghai, China, $170,000. For research on young people's sexual and reproductive health knowledge, attitudes and behavior and to disseminate the findings to policy makers, educators, practitioners and the general public. 2010.

1391-658 Shashat, Ramallah, West Bank/Gaza (Palestinian Territories), $100,000. For institutional capacity building, strategic planning and core programs using film and video to alter representations of women and girls, including Youth Training Program and Women's Film Festival. 2010.

1391-659 Sisma Mujer, Bogota, Colombia, $110,000. To strengthen women organizations and women's human rights approach in national organizations of people in situations of forced displacement in Colombia. 2010.

1391-660 Social Change Assistance Trust, Cape Town, South Africa, $200,000. For tie-off general support to partner with rural community-based organizations in order to contribute effectively to rights-based endeavors that improve quality of life in their communities. 2010.

1391-661 Social Development Integrated Centre, Port Harcourt, Nigeria, $350,000. For community organizing, advocacy, training and litigation to promote community rights and ensure accountability with respect to natural resource exploitation in Gulf Of Guinea States of West Africa. 2010.

1391-662 Social Science Research Council, Brooklyn, NY, $350,000. For series of meetings in Cuba to explore issues of migration, sexual diversity, HIV/AIDS and disaster prevention strategies with key institutions and individuals. 2010.

1391-663 Social Science Research Council, Brooklyn, NY, $120,000. To develop communications strategy for and launch toward detente in media piracy, foundation-funded analysis of social impact of piracy, including costs and benefits to developing countries. 2010.

1391-664 Social Transformation and Empowerment Projects International Association, Copenhagen, Denmark, $25,000. To host film festival commemorating 20th anniversary of Nelson Mandela's release from prison. 2010.

1391-665 Social Welfare Agency and Training Institute, Kandhamal, India, $75,500. For right to information network in the tribal districts of Orissa to enhance the effectiveness of government policies and programs for tribal communities. 2010.

1391-666 Society for Community Health Awareness, Research and Action, Bangalore, India, $200,000. To strengthen integrated framework of right to basic life needs - food, water, sanitation, health, livelihood - at community level, entrenched by inclusion, equity and state accountability. 2010.

1391-667 Society for Labour and Development, New Delhi, India, $225,000. To develop community-led media platform for poor migrant workers in India's National Capital Region. 2010.

1391-668 Society for Participatory Research in Asia, New Delhi, India, $200,000. To promote and facilitate citizen participation in and oversight of urban reform programs in small and medium towns in India. 2010.

1391-669 Society of Jesus, Near East Province, Beirut, Lebanon, $220,000. To develop coordinated arts and culture projects for young artists (teenagers) at cultural centers in Minia, Cairo and Alexandria in Egypt. 2010.

1391-670 Socio-Economic Rights Institute of South Africa, Braamfontein, South Africa, $300,000. For public interest litigation and research to promote socioeconomic rights and accountable governance. 2010.

1391-671 Socio-Economic Rights Institute of South Africa, Braamfontein, South Africa, $110,000. To organize workshop bringing together key foundation housing rights grantees from Egypt, India, Nigeria, South Africa and the United States to discuss common problems and strategize about solutions. 2010.

1391-672 Soliya, New York, NY, $300,000. For final support for Connect E-Learning program and Soliya Network Students to foster mutual understanding and critical thinking. 2010.

1391-673 SOS Racism-Hands off my Buddy, Paris, France, $100,000. For final support for activities to defend and enforce existing anti-discrimination laws in France and educate citizens about racism and other forms of intolerance. 2010.

1391-674 South African Civil Society Information Service, Johannesburg, South Africa, $60,000. For final general support to produce articles on democracy and governance, human rights and social justice from the perspective of civil society. 2010.

1391-675 South African Institute for Advancement, Inyathelo, Cape Town, South Africa, $109,800, For research, case studies and dissemination on funding and grant-making practices of two state agencies established as conduits for distributing funds to South African nonprofit sector. 2010.

1391-676 South African Institute for Distance Education, Braamfontein, South Africa, $600,000. For final support for grant making and technical assistance to help African universities effectively use information and communications technology to address challenges facing the higher education sector. 2010.

1391-677 South Asia Center for Policy Studies, Kathmandu, Nepal, $153,603. For final support for work to build regional cooperation in South Asia. 2010.

1391-678 South Asia Women's Fund, Colombo, Sri Lanka, $400,000. For final support for institutional and organizational sustainability and for small grants program to advance women's rights in the region. 2010.

1391-679 South Centre, Geneva, Switzerland, $500,000. For capacity building and policy dialogues to help policy makers in developing countries to promote strategic responses to global financial governance in face of the current crisis. 2010.

1391-680 South Centre, Geneva, Switzerland, $200,000. To conduct research and develop recommendations to help developing countries engage productively in global debates on reduction of emissions from deforestation and forest degradation. 2010.

1391-681 Southern Africa HIV and AIDS Information Dissemination Service, Pretoria, South Africa, $150,000. For country-specific interventions to accelerate implementation of Maputo plan of action for achieving universal access to comprehensive sexual and reproductive health services in Africa. 2010.

1391-682 Southern African Development Community Lawyers Association, Gaborone, Botswana, $150,000. For regional project to strengthen role of lawyers in protection of human rights and observance of rule of law in Southern African Development Community. 2010.

1391-683 State Islamic University Syarif Hidayatullah Jakarta, Jakarta, Indonesia, $154,436. For Islamic Credit Co-operatives in South Sulawesi to pilot a health savings product linked to Islamic philanthropic resources. 2010.

1391-684 State University of Amazonas, Manaus, Brazil, $300,000. For series of regional seminars and general meeting of social movements, traditional peoples' organizations and researchers to plan establishment of New Social Cartography Institute. 2010.

1391-685 Stichting Centre on Housing Rights and Evictions, Geneva, Switzerland, $350,000. For general support to ensure full enjoyment of the human right to adequate housing for everyone, everywhere and to prevent forced evictions of persons, families and communities from their homes. 2010.

1391-686 Stichting Global Voices, Amsterdam, Netherlands, $100,000. For Project Lingua To translate English-language news into more than 16 languages, each with its own web site and develop a multilingual newsroom where content is published in its original language. 2010.

1391-687 Stichting Mama Cash, Amsterdam, Netherlands, $200,000. For final general support to mobilize resources from individuals and institutions for grant making to women's and girls human rights organizations and initiatives. 2010.

1391-688 Stichting Panos South Asia, Amsterdam, Netherlands, $238,000. To train media professionals and citizen journalists in Jammu and Kashmir State to cover issues related to urbanization and diversity and build capacity of academic institutions to deliver such training. 2010.

1391-689 Stiftelsen Studio Emad Eddin, Stockholm, Sweden, $200,000. For rehearsal studios and resource services in Cairo for independent performing artists. 2010.

1391-690 Strathmore University, Nairobi, Kenya, $80,000. For research to give meaning, interpretation and expression of community rights over land and natural resources to inform policy making in Kenya. 2010.

1391-691 Studies in Poverty and Inequality Institute, Johannesburg, South Africa, $120,000. To analyze South African Constitutional Court jurisprudence on socioeconomic rights and develop monitoring tool for measuring progressive realization of those rights. 2010.

1391-692 Studies in Poverty and Inequality Institute, Johannesburg, South Africa, $100,000. For conference on chronic and structural poverty in southern Africa. 2010.

1391-693 Sumatera Utara University, Medan, Indonesia, $50,000. For final support to make audiovisual recordings of traditional music from four ethno-linguistic areas of North Sumatra and produce teaching materials to train new generation of traditional musicians. 2010.

1391-694 Sun Culture Foundation, Beijing, China, $170,000. To coordinate and collaborate with other domestic foundations in provision of technical assistance to educational NGOs that provide education to migrant children. 2010.

1391-695 Sun Yat-Sen University, School Of Government, Guangzhou, China, $80,000. For School and partners to conduct research on role of group-differentiated political culture in public policy participation. 2010.

1391-696 Sur-Human Rights University Network, Sao Paulo, Brazil, $400,000. To strengthen human rights infrastructure in the global south and promote access to justice for vulnerable people in Brazil. 2010.

1391-697 Suzhou Industrial Park Institute of Vocational Technology, Suzhou, China, $90,000. For action-oriented research to build partnerships with local enterprises to assist students learning, practice and future employment. 2010.

1391-698 Swisscontact, Zurich, Switzerland, $50,000. For Swisscontact Kenya to develop and introduce microleasing products to help smallholder farmers acquire productive assets, increase productivity and improve livelihoods. 2010.

1391-699 Technical Assistance in Alternative Agriculture, Rio de Janeiro, Brazil, $150,000. To evaluate Lula administration's policies (Luiz Inacio Lula da Silva is the current president of Brazil) to promote agro-ecological development for family farmers in Brazil, with focus on the Western Amazon. 2010.

1391-700 Third World Network, Penang, Malaysia, $400,000. To build capacity of NGOs and policy makers in the global south to manage globalization issues, focusing on finance and finance/trade interface and challenges of the global financial crisis. 2010.

1391-701 Third World Network, Penang, Malaysia, $100,000. For research, analysis, monitoring and communications activities with respect to Reduction In Emissions From Deforestation And Degradation (REDD) Programs and policy making in developing countries. 2010.

1391-702 Tides Center, San Francisco, CA, $250,000. For final core support for International Treatment Preparedness Coalition to advocate for universal access to treatment, prevention and all healthcare services for people living with HIV. 2010.

1391-703 Tides Center, San Francisco, CA, $200,000. For International Treatment Preparedness Coalition to promote access to treatment and prevention for people living with HIV/AIDS in the Middle East and North Africa (especially Egypt) and build regional network. 2010.

1391-704 Tides Center, San Francisco, CA, $200,000. For new policy institute to produce research reports and educate individuals on comprehensive immigration reform. 2010.

1391-705 Tides Center, San Francisco, CA, $200,000. For core support for Detention Watch Network to educate public and policy makers about U.S. detention and deportation system and advocate for humane reform. 2010.

1391-706 Tides Center, International Network on Economic, Social, and Cultural Rights, San Francisco, CA, $250,000. To develop implementation plan for and guide to strategic litigation under Optional Protocol on economic and social rights. 2010.

1391-707 Transparency Brazil, Sao Paulo, Brazil, $225,513. To maintain three very innovative web base tools that promote greater transparency of public budgets and political parties in Brazil. 2010.

1391-708 Treatment Action Campaign, Cape Town, South Africa, $345,000. To build leadership capacity of women and of persons living with AIDS, promote implementation of South Africa's strategic plan on HIV/AIDS and advocate against HIV/AIDS-related stigma and discrimination. 2010.

1391-709 Tribune of Villages and Townships, Beijing, China, $79,418. To establish and staff hotline for villagers seeking information on rights under current laws and policies and to integrate information into broader information platforms. 2010.

1391-710 TrustAfrica, Washington, DC, $3,000,000. For general support to strengthen African initiatives that address the most difficult challenges confronting the continent. 2010.

1391-711 Tsinghua University, Beijing, China, $350,000. To develop, implement and promote clinical legal education programs in key Chinese law schools and for networking, training and curriculum development to strengthen the clinical legal education movement. 2010.

1391-712 Tsinghua University, School Of Public Policy And Management, Beijing, China, $100,000. To conduct research on capacity building of NGOs network participating in prevention and control of HIV/AIDS. 2010.

1391-713 Twaweza Communications, Nairobi, Kenya, $325,000. For media training, monitoring and to explore new distribution strategies for local media content. 2010.

1391-714 Two Tone Productions, HipTruth Productions, New York, NY, $75,000. For documentary that tells the story of immigrants that disappear crossing the harsh desert from Mexico into Arizona in search of better lives for themselves and their families. 2010.

1391-715 U.S. Human Rights Network, Atlanta, GA, $400,000. For general support to promote U.S. accountability to universal human rights standards by building links between organizations and individuals working for human rights in the United States. 2010.

1391-716 Uganda Association of Women Lawyers, Kampala, Uganda, $300,000. For research, litigation, networking and advocacy to promote women's rights in an interdependent and indivisible manner that links constituencies for livelihoods and rights, including sexual rights. 2010.

1391-717 Ujamaa Center, Mombasa, Kenya, $200,000. To create civic spaces for public engagement and build capacity of poor and marginalized groups to negotiate and claim rights to land and natural resources. 2010.

1391-718 Union of Rural Workers of Santarem, Santarem, Brazil, $200,000. For training, technical assistance and monitoring to help rural communities in Para understand rights, retain access to lands and advocate for sustainable use of natural resources. 2010.

1391-719 Union Theological Seminary, New York, NY, $100,000. For core support for Poverty Initiative to raise up generations of religious and community leaders committed to building movement, led by the poor, to end poverty. 2010.

1391-720 United Nations African Institute for Economic Development and Planning, Dakar, Senegal, $500,000. To develop and pilot short courses on trade and mining-contract negotiations for public officials, establish visiting researcher and researcher-in-residence

programs and make library accessible online. 2010.

1391-721 United Nations Development Programme, New York, NY, $200,000. For HIV/AIDS regional program for Arab states to develop strategy for integrating protection of sexual minorities rights into regional and national responses to HIV/AIDS. 2010.

1391-722 United Nations Development Programme, New York, NY, $150,000. To strengthen capacity of civil society organizations to conduct impartial, non-partisan public education around the proposed constitution in Kenya. 2010.

1391-723 United Nations Development Programme, New York, NY, $100,000. For technical assistance to support titling and governance of indigenous territories in Caribbean Coast of Nicaragua. 2010.

1391-724 United Nations Development Programme, New York, NY, $100,000. To help Nicaraguan government develop policies and programs advancing participatory, sustainable management of natural resources by Indigenous and Afro-Descendant communities along the Caribbean coast. 2010.

1391-725 United Nations Educational, Scientific and Cultural Organization, Paris, France, $200,000. For International Institute for Higher Education in Latin America and the Caribbean to coordinate collaborative regional effort to strengthen intercultural higher education institutions and programs. 2010.

1391-726 United Nations Educational, Scientific and Cultural Organization, Paris, France, $100,000. For Inter-Agency Task Team on Education to promote and support good practices in the education sector related to HIV and AIDS. 2010.

1391-727 United Nations Population Fund, New York, NY, $150,000. To foster and strengthen collaboration between state and civil society to eradicate feminicide and other forms of violence against women in Guatemala. 2010.

1391-728 United Nations Programme on HIV/AIDS, Geneva, Switzerland, $1,000,000. For policy and advocacy work to promote human rights, strengthen HIV prevention, expanding universal access to treatment and promote accountability and partnership in the global HIV/AIDS response. 2010.

1391-729 United Nations Programme on HIV/AIDS, Geneva, Switzerland, $200,000. For training, technical assistance and leadership development to build NGO capacity for outreach and service provision to vulnerable men to reduce HIV/AIDS risk in Egypt and for research and advocacy. 2010.

1391-730 United Organisation for Batwa Development in Uganda, Kisoro, Uganda, $300,000. To build capacity of Batwa Forest People and empower them to control and fully participate in efforts to pursue their land rights claims against the government. 2010.

1391-731 Universidad Alberto Hurtado, Santiago, Chile, $60,000. To generate and disseminate knowledge on the right of access to information in Chile. 2010.

1391-732 Universidad Centroamericana Jose Simeon Canas, San Salvador, El Salvador, $52,000. To assess state of migrant labor rights in Central America and develop proposals for Central American regional migration policy. 2010.

1391-733 Universidad Nacional de Rio Negro, Viedma, Argentina, $155,000. To develop southern line of the University, to facilitate access of students of indigenous origin. 2010.

1391-734 Universidad Nacional de San Antonio Abad del Cusco, Cuzco, Peru, $400,000. To consolidate lessons learned from Hatun Nan (Pathways) program and implement intercultural and academic tutoring model throughout the university. 2010.

1391-735 Universidade Federal de Minas Gerais, Public Interest Research Center, Belo Horizonte, Brazil, $200,000. To conduct research on public dimensions of justice in Brazil and to hold seminar, produce CD and publish book to disseminate findings and provoke debate. 2010.

1391-736 Universitas Gadjah Mada, Center for Population and Policy Studies, Yogyakarta, Indonesia, $120,000. To organize Asia Pacific Conference on Reproductive and Sexual Health and Rights. 2010.

1391-737 University of Arizona, Center For Latin American Studies, Tucson, AZ, $115,000. To conduct collaborative research on the relationship between U.S. and Mexican immigration and security policies and violence against undocumented economic migrants. 2010.

1391-738 University of Arizona, School Of Government And Public Policy, Tucson, AZ, $268,943. To conduct annual analyses and rankings of fiscal transparency of China's provincial governments, prepare report and disseminate findings. 2010.

1391-739 University of Brasilia, Brasilia, Brazil, $75,000. To convene national seminar on land and territories in the Amazon in collaboration with Federal University of Amazonas and Federal University of Para. 2010.

1391-740 University of Brasilia, Laboratory Of Communications And Information Policy, Brasilia, Brazil, $350,000. To conduct research and outreach on communications and media policy and establish observatory on public broadcasting in Latin America. 2010.

1391-741 University of British Columbia, Vancouver, Canada, $80,000. For workshops, research and publication on relationship and interplay between participatory and representative approaches to democracy in the Andean region and Southern Cone. 2010.

1391-742 University of California, Berkeley, CA, $50,000. For Institutions and Governance Program to organize annual China Summer Economics Institute at Tsinghua University and underwrite participation of U.S. junior and senior scholars. 2010.

1391-743 University of California, Davis, CA, $265,000. To design index-based insurance scheme for small farmers in Ecuador, determine its likely performance compared to conventional insurance and determine which would best serve for small farm sector. 2010.

1391-744 University of California, Los Angeles, CA, $50,000. For Make Art/Stop AIDS Project to integrate art to promote HIV education and awareness. 2010.

1391-745 University of California, Program in Global Health, Los Angeles, CA, $800,000. For final support for work to develop guidance for foundations on mainstreaming HIV grant making to confront issues of accountability, leadership, equity and partnerships. 2010.

1391-746 University of California, Womens Institute For Leadership Development (WILD) for Human Rights, Berkeley, CA, $85,000. For core support to advance human rights by engaging women in training, research, documentation and advocacy. 2010.

1391-747 University of California at San Diego, La Jolla, CA, $75,000. For coordination and fieldwork travel for Mexican Migration Field Research and training program for students at UCSD and Mexican partner institutions. 2010.

1391-748 University of Cape Town, Cape Town, South Africa, $50,000. For Students' Health and Welfare Centres Organisation's Saturday School Programme to prepare students from disadvantaged communities for grade 12 examination and the transition to University. 2010.

1391-749 University of Cape Town, African Centre for Cities, Cape Town, South Africa, $85,000. To organize international workshop on climate change, asset adaptation and food security in Southern African Cities and edit and publish conference papers. 2010.

1391-750 University of Cape Town, Democratic Governance And Rights Unit, Cape Town, South Africa, $60,000. To coordinate African Network Of Constitutional Lawyers and build its capacity to promote constitutionalism on the African continent. 2010.

1391-751 University of Cape Town, School of Law, Cape Town, South Africa, $145,000. For Academic Scholarship Programme to enable top, particularly Black, graduates to continue their legal studies at the postgraduate level and prepare for careers in teaching and research. 2010.

1391-752 University of Chile, Santiago, Chile, $375,000. For core support for Human Rights Center to promote human rights and strengthening of democracies in Latin America through research, training, publications and networking at local and regional levels. 2010.

1391-753 University of Chile, Santiago, Chile, $100,000. For tie-off support for Chilean Observatory of Education Policies to redefine and strengthen relationship with university and promote networking among universities and research centers. 2010.

1391-754 University of Fort Hare, Alice, South Africa, $350,000. For tie-off support to continue and institutionalize Access Program for poor, rural underprepared students and for research on efficacy of access activities. 2010.

1391-755 University of Indonesia, Center For Global Civil Society Studies, Depok, Indonesia, $15,000. To facilitate dialogues and partnerships for community-level health services. 2010.

1391-756 University of KwaZulu-Natal, Center for Criminal Justice, Durban, South Africa, $220,000. To build capacity of community outreach program to integrate issues of economic empowerment into its work and help Outreach Centers become self-sustaining. 2010.

1391-757 University of KwaZulu-Natal, School of Environmental Sciences, Durban, South Africa, $170,000. To collaborate with Inina Craft Agency and Africa Ignite to strengthen Rural Craft Centers and improve livelihoods of women crafters across Kwazulu-Natal. 2010.

1391-758 University of Manchester, Global Urban Research Centre, Manchester, England, $224,819. To conduct applied research to test assets framework for poverty reduction on the specific challenges of urban poverty and climate change in the Global South. 2010.

1391-759 University of Maryland-College Park, College Park, MD, $198,975. To improve learning skills to augment success rate of disadvantaged students attending non-government universities in less developed regions of China. 2010.

1391-760 University of Massachusetts, Lowell, MA, $199,951. For Center for Industrial Competitiveness in China to conduct comparative research on financial institutions that are central to funding industrial innovation in key high tech sectors of the economy. 2010.

1391-761 University of Pretoria, Pretoria, South Africa, $300,000. For research on Doctoral Studies In South Africa. 2010.

1391-762 University of San Francisco, Center for Law and Global Justice, San Francisco, CA, $300,000. For Marshalling Global Human Rights Project to analyze U.S. criminal punishment and sentencing practices through framework of global human rights-based norms. 2010.

1391-763 University of Stellenbosch, Stellenbosch, South Africa, $200,000. For African doctoral academy to provide prospective doctoral students in the sciences with high-quality research training and scholarships and develop a research program on doctoral studies in Africa. 2010.

1391-764 University of the Andes, Global Justice and Human Rights Program, Bogota, Colombia, $220,000. To use combination of real and virtual networks to promote ideas and practices favorable to social inclusion within the legal field in Latin America. 2010.

1391-765 University of the Andes, Human Rights And Global Justice Program, Bogota, Colombia, $200,000. To sustain research and advocacy activities on affirmative action and minority rights of racial discrimination and Afro-Colombians Rights Watch. 2010.

1391-766 University of the Autonomous Regions of the Caribbean Coast of Nicaragua, Managua, Nicaragua, $125,000. For training and technical assistance to strengthen community forestry in Nicaragua's North Atlantic Coast region. 2010.

1391-767 University of the Autonomous Regions of the Caribbean Coast of Nicaragua, Managua, Nicaragua, $100,000. For training, technical assistance and networking to help Miskitu peoples of Nicaragua and Honduras revitalize Sihkru Tara Ritual commemorating dead ancestors and bring them together as one people. 2010.

1391-768 University of the Frontier, Temuco, Chile, $400,000. For final support to expand Affirmative Action Program for Mapuche students and design new activities to promote pedagogical practices that address cultural diversity. 2010.

1391-769 University of the West Indies, Mona, Jamaica, $350,000. To expand and strengthen Sexual Safety Initiative Program at Mona Campus and surrounding community, providing enabling environment for sexual health and reducing the risk of HIV/AIDS. 2010.

1391-770 University of the Western Cape, Bellville, South Africa, $150,000. For Fairshare to develop course on local economic development to help civil society-based organizations strengthen their ability to engage in an informed way in budget and monitoring processes. 2010.

1391-771 University of the Western Cape, African Centre for Citizenship and Democracy, Bellville, South Africa, $200,000. For core support to examine factors and policy environments that support or inhibit development of more inclusive citizenship in the region. 2010.

1391-772 University World News, Durban, South Africa, $170,000. To produce, disseminate and manage University World News Africa Edition, fortnightly report on African higher education news and issues. 2010.

1391-773 Urgent Action Fund for Women's Human Rights Africa, Nairobi, Kenya, $350,000. For small grants program to promote and protect rights of women and girls and for fundraising, training, technical assistance and networking to build own capacity and that of grantees. 2010.

1391-774 Vale do Rio dos Sinos University, Research Group On Communications, Political Economy And Society, Sao Leopoldo, Brazil, $160,000. To study media digitization and convergence in Brazil and foster debate on their implications for democratization of media. 2010.

1391-775 Vasundhara, Bhubaneswar, India, $165,000. To facilitate improved implementation and policy advocacy on forest rights act in Orissa, Eastern India. 2010.

1391-776 Vietnam Veterans of America National Headquarters, Silver Spring, MD, $50,000. To collaborate with Agent Orange in Vietnam Information Initiative in educating policy makers and the public on urgent need to provide health care to those affected by Agent Orange/Dioxin exposure. 2010.

1391-777 Vikas Samvad Samiti, Bhopal, India, $100,000. To improve standards of investigative research in the mainstream media and enhance media coverage of issues related to migration, displacement and governance in the Indian state of Madhya Pradesh. 2010.

1391-778 Vitae Civilis Institute for Development, Environment and Peace, Sao Lourenco, Brazil, $200,000. For Brazilian civil society engagement on Climate Change And Reduced Emissions From Deforestation And Degradation (REDD). 2010.

1391-779 Volunteer Efforts for Development Concerns, Kampala, Uganda, $120,000. To build capacity of farmers organizations to engage with and benefit from market opportunities and participate in policy debates on issues that affect agricultural production and marketing. 2010.

1391-780 VSO Jitolee, Nairobi, Kenya, $50,000. To test and develop Village Polytechnics Models as hubs for business skills training and develop and evaluate Maasai Women's Beadwork Value Chain and impacts on women's livelihoods. 2010.

1391-781 W E T A-Greater Washington Educational Telecommunications Association, Arlington, VA, $600,000. For core support for expanded international field reporting for Newshour with Jim Lehrer and to send ethnic media fellows on four of television show's international reporting trips. 2010.

1391-782 Walter Sisulu University for Technology and Science, Umtata, South Africa, $250,000. For University and South African Further Education College Staff to undertake graduate study at University of Newcastle, with specialization in technical and vocational education and training. 2010.

1391-783 Well Told Story, Nairobi, Kenya, $100,000. For ShujaazFM, edutainment media project to engage, inform and motivate young Kenyans by providing them with information and inspiration they can use to improve their lives and the world around them. 2010.

1391-784 Wellesley College, Wellesley Centers for Women, Wellesley, MA, $47,347. To continue providing technical assistance to Chinese colleagues concerning regional and global trends and standards in the protection of women's rights. 2010.

1391-785 West Coast Community Foundation, Malmesbury, South Africa, $150,000. For tie-off general support to mobilize, manage and distribute resources to community-based organizations in Western Cape Province of South Africa. 2010.

1391-786 Wildlife SOS, New Delhi, India, $50,000. For final grant for education and training to prepare Kalandar community for sustainable livelihoods to replace their now illegal traditional profession of performing with dancing bears. 2010.

1391-787 Witness, Inc., Brooklyn, NY, $200,000. For general support for video advocacy to open the eyes of the world to human rights violations and empower people to transform personal stories of abuse into powerful tools for justice. 2010.

1391-788 Wits Health Consortium, Johannesburg, South Africa, $151,000. To evaluate impact of integrating work and livelihood skills into on-going youth-friendly reproductive health program in Gauteng Province. 2010.

1391-789 Women Thrive Worldwide, Washington, DC, $350,000. For general support to develop, shape and advocate for international assistance and trade programs and policies that foster economic opportunity for women living in poverty. 2010.

1391-790 Women's Health in Women's Hands, Toronto, Canada, $150,000. For African Black Diaspora Global Network On HIV And AIDS to strengthen response to the epidemic in diaspora communities. 2010.

1391-791 Womens Development Center, Banda Aceh, Indonesia, $243,286. To build capacity of grassroots women's groups in Banda Aceh to participate in bottom-up development planning process for women to promote gender sensitive policies and budget allocations. 2010.

1391-792 Womens Health and Action Research Centre, Benin City, Nigeria, $500,000. For integrated program to strengthen and support adolescent sexuality, reproductive health and rights research, documentation, monitoring and evaluation and advocacy in Nigeria. 2010.

1391-793 Womens Link Worldwide, Northfield, VT, $320,000. For general support to advance women's rights through the use of international human rights law, with a focus on sexual and reproductive rights, gender violence and gender discrimination. 2010.

1391-794 Womens Link Worldwide, Northfield, VT, $280,000. For general support to advance women's rights through the use of international human rights law, with a focus on gender discrimination. 2010.

1391-795 Womens Popular Education Group, Mexico City, Mexico, $100,000. To design educational curriculum and training model on sexuality and reproductive rights for indigenous internal migrants, especially women, and pilot it at a migrants' community center. 2010.

1391-796 Working America Education Fund, Washington, DC, $125,000. For door-to-door outreach among low- to moderate-income households to test messages about and build public support for job quality reforms worldwide. 2010.

1391-797 World AIDS Campaign, Amsterdam, Netherlands, $350,000. For final support to increase capacity to effectively address human rights and HIV and to develop strengthened programs that focus on links between human rights and HIV. 2010.

1391-798 World AIDS Campaign, Amsterdam, Netherlands, $200,000. For public education, monitoring and evaluation to ensure the fulfillment of pledges made by world leaders to aggressively confront HIV. 2010.

1391-799 World Conference of Religions for Peace, New York, NY, $300,000. For final support for Global Women of Faith Network to mobilize and equip women in faith communities worldwide to formulate and pursue agendas for the common good. 2010.

1391-800 World Federalist Movement-Institute for Global Policy, New York, NY, $75,000. For Coalition for International Criminal Court to facilitate civil society preparation for and participation in review conference to evaluate progress of international criminal justice. 2010.

1391-801 World Health Organization, Geneva, Switzerland, $100,000. For final support for Special Programme Of Research, Development And Research Training In Human Reproduction to document and analyze existing human rights standards related to sexuality and sexual health. 2010.

1391-802 World Neighbors, Oklahoma City, OK, $380,000. To promote sustainable natural resource management, secure access to resources and mobilize community resources to improve economic security in Nusa Tenggara. 2010.

1391-803 World Security Institute, Washington, DC, $150,000. To publish China Security and Washington Observer Weekly. 2010.

1391-804 World Security Institute, Washington, DC, $35,000. For high-level delegation of retired U.S. military officers to meet with Cuban officials on issues of regional security. 2010.

1391-805 Yabous Productions, East Jerusalem, $200,000. To renovate abandoned cinema in East Jerusalem and transform it into new multidisciplinary cultural facility. 2010.

1391-806 Yayasan Griya Asih, Jakarta, Indonesia, $25,000. For counseling and educational services to help underprivileged and poor children develop their capabilities, gain living skills and explore life options. 2010.

1391-807 Yayasan Kesehatan Perempuan, Jakarta, Indonesia, $145,000. To help Ministry of Health formulate regulations for implementing Health Law No. 36, which guarantees all Indonesians the right of access to basic health services and programs. 2010.

1391-808 Yayasan Masyarakat Mandiri Film Indonesia, In-Docs, Jakarta, Indonesia, $250,056. For exhibition and education programs to provide training and mentoring to young documentary filmmakers (including teenagers) and for Jakarta International Film Festival to expand script development project. 2010.

1391-809 Yayasan Pendidikan Seni Nusantara, Jakarta, Indonesia, $200,000. For tie-off support to adapt traditional arts curriculum and teaching materials into interactive digital media and online teaching formats. 2010.

1391-810 Yayasan PIRAC, Jakarta, Indonesia, $180,000. To develop and test best practices and accountability standards for managing locally raised funds for humanitarian aid programs in Indonesia. 2010.

1391-811 Yayasan Satu Dunia, Indonesia, $125,688. To develop interactive website as platform for database, information exchanges and impact monitoring for strategic alliance for poverty alleviation program in fifteen districts and cities in Indonesia. 2010.

1391-812 Yayasan Smeru, Jakarta, Indonesia, $150,000. To assess spatial mapping of the urban poor, pro-poor urban planning capacities and asset accumulation strategies for urban poor in the cities of Solo and Makassar, Indonesia. 2010.

1391-813 Young Arab Theater Fund, Brussels, Belgium, $750,000. For grant making, meetings and research to strengthen emerging arts and cultural spaces in the Middle East and North Africa and to build Fund's institutional capacity. 2010.

1391-814 Young Womens Leadership Institute, Nairobi, Kenya, $300,000. For research, internships, networking and other activities to address intersections of sexual and reproductive health and rights, HIV/AIDS and gender inequities. 2010.

1391-815 Youth Agenda, Nairobi, Kenya, $200,000. For Generation of Leaders Initiative to showcase outstanding young Kenyan leaders and to strengthen YA's capacity to empower young people to participate in governance and decision-making processes. 2010.

1391-816 Youth Dreamers of Tomorrow, Cairo, Egypt, $200,000. To develop skill-building program, including information technology and English, for students at four provincial university campuses in Egypt. 2010.

1391-817 Yugantar, Hyderabad, India, $170,842. To build capacity of Muslim women artisans in Hyderabad and their microenterprises to access markets and improve their livelihoods. 2010.

1391-818 Yugantar, Hyderabad, India, $100,000. For final support for Broom Project to produce and disseminate film and catalogue to raise awareness about history of creativity of and discrimination against broom makers in Rajasthan. 2010.

1391-819 Yunnan Normal University, Kunming, China, $120,000. For pilot Comprehensive Learning Center at village level to support life-long learning. 2010.

1391-820 Yunnan Participatory Development Association, Kunming, China, $149,897. To build capacity of regional network to help rural communities maintain control over natural resources. 2010.

1391-821 Zhejiang Academy of Social Sciences, Women And Family Research Center, Hangzhou, China, $90,000. To organize roundtables and public discussions on proper and cultural appropriate sexuality and reproductive health education in China. 2010.

1391-822 Zimbabwe Lawyers for Human Rights, Harare, Zimbabwe, $200,000. For public interest litigation and advocacy to advance socioeconomic rights in Zimbabwe. 2010.

1392
Foundation of Orthopedics and Complex Spine, Inc.

(also known as FOCOS)
Lenox Hill Sta.
P.O. Box 665
New York, NY 10021-0028 (212) 774-2663
FAX: (212) 794-2562; E-mail: orearw@hss.edu;
URL: http://www.orthofocos.org

Grantmaker type: Public charity.
Financial data (yr. ended 12/31/10): Revenue, $1,329,517; assets, $479,324 (M); gifts received, $958,644; expenditures, $3,080,539; giving activities include $69,000 for grants, and $2,702,668 for 1 grant to an organization outside the U.S.
Purpose and activities: The foundation seeks to make optimal surgical and non-surgical care of disabling musculoskeletal problems, including complex spine and pediatric orthopedic disorders, available in developing nations.
Fields of interest: Surgery; Orthopedics; Spine disorders.
International interests: Developing countries.
Type of support: In-kind gifts.
Limitations: Giving primarily to Ghana.
Publications: Newsletter.
Officers and Board Members:* Oheneba Boachie-Adjei,* M.D., Pres.; Sam Owusu-Akyaw,* V.P.; Anna Boutzalis,* Secy.-Treas.; Hank Brown; H.B. Calder, Ph.D.; Jeremiah Callaghan; Rocco Iacoviello; Pamela Lupo, C.O.; Michael Mendelow, M.D.; Joanne Ronson; Bettye Wright, P.A., R.N.
EIN: 134047356

1393
Foundation to Promote Open Society

400 W. 59th St., 4th Fl.
New York, NY 10019-8023

Established in 2008 in DE and NY.
Donors: George Soros; Open Society Institute.
Grantmaker type: Independent foundation.
Financial data (yr. ended 12/31/10): Assets, $2,817,446,416 (M); gifts received, $250,000,000; expenditures, $230,377,590; qualifying distributions, $213,785,765; giving activities include $210,255,130 for 816 grants (high: $29,791,398; low: $610).
Fields of interest: Philanthropy/voluntarism; Human services; Education.
Limitations: Applications not accepted. Giving primarily in Washington, DC and Albany and New York, NY.
Application information: Unsolicited requests for funds not accepted.
Officers and Directors:* George Soros,* Chair.; Jonathan Soros,* Co-Vice-Chair.; Aryeh Neier,* Co-Vice-Chair.; Ricardo A. Castro, Secy.; Daniel R. Eule, Treas.; Susan C. Frunzi; William D. Zabel.
EIN: 263753801
Recent grants for international programs:
1393-1 Abdorrahman Boroumand Foundation, Washington, DC, $20,000. To assist work. 2009.
1393-2 AIDS Project Los Angeles, Los Angeles, CA, $38,236. To plan pre-conference satellite meeting on men having sex with men and HIV at International AIDS Conference in Vienna. 2009.
1393-3 American Bar Association Fund for Justice and Education, Washington, DC, $124,705. To

build capacity of Liberian civil society organizations to provide legal representation to indigent criminal defendants, toward reducing pretrial detention population at Monrovia Central and Harper Prisons. 2009.

1393-4 American Civil Liberties Union Foundation, New York, NY, $127,000. For international network of civil liberties organizations. 2009.

1393-5 American Councils for International Education: ACTR/ACCELS, Washington, DC, $48,045. For Educational Advising Centers in Belarus. 2009.

1393-6 American Friends of the New Economic School, University Park, PA, $25,000. To conduct series of expert-led roundtable discussions to enhance public debate on issues of economic and social policy in Russia. 2009.

1393-7 American Society of International Law, Washington, DC, $225,000. To promote understanding, consideration, and application of international law in U.S. courts by providing trainings, information, and reference materials to judges in partnerships with mainstream judicial institutions and organizations. 2009.

1393-8 American University, Washington, DC, $153,803. To create database of jurisprudence relating to sexual and gender-based crimes from internationalized criminal courts and tribunals. 2009.

1393-9 American University, Washington, DC, $25,000. For Training Course on the Inter-American and International Human Rights Systems. 2009.

1393-10 American University, Washington, DC, $10,000. To edit, publish, and disseminate series of documents on intersection of human rights, human trafficking, sex work, migration, labor, and health, drafted by international experts in human trafficking. 2009.

1393-11 American University in Cairo, Cairo, Egypt, $38,250. For young Egyptian activists training on building and documenting social movements under context of authoritarianism. 2009.

1393-12 Americas Society, New York, NY, $90,000. For Americas Quarterly issues on youth leadership and transnational crime and security. 2009.

1393-13 Americas Voice Education Fund, Washington, DC, $700,000. To shape and drive media and communications work core to Four Pillars Campaign, Reform Immigration for America. 2009.

1393-14 Asia Society, New York, NY, $250,000. For Initiative on U.S.-China Cooperation on Energy and Climate. 2009.

1393-15 Asia Society, New York, NY, $50,000. For Independent Task Force on U.S. Policy Toward Burma. 2009.

1393-16 Aspen Institute, Washington, DC, $125,000. For Justice and Society Program's judicial seminars on international human rights and humanitarian laws. 2009.

1393-17 Bank Information Center, Washington, DC, $85,526. For Strengthening Extractive Industry Revenue and Contract Transparency at the International Financial Institutions - Focus on Europe and Central Asia Region. 2009.

1393-18 Bank Information Center, Washington, DC, $80,000. For project, Promoting Transparency and Accountability in Latin America - Civil Society Advocacy on the World Bank's Information Disclosure Policy. 2009.

1393-19 Bank Information Center, Washington, DC, $56,339. To strengthen capacity of members of

Electricity Governance Initiative coalition in Kyrgyzstan and Tajikistan to achieve better performance of electric power sector by enhancing transparency and accountability in public utilities. 2009.

1393-20 Bank Information Center, Washington, DC, $40,000. For transparency campaign objectives, expanding public access to information on policies and operations of World Bank, reforming World Bank governance and improving accountability through expanded public access to decisionmakers. 2009.

1393-21 Bank Information Center, Washington, DC, $37,000. To form African-led civil society network focused on monitoring and engaging African Development Bank. 2009.

1393-22 Border Network for Human Rights, El Paso, TX, $150,000. To build community, media, networking, and policy capacity through U.S.-Mexico Border and Immigration Task Force and bring ideas and proposals of border communities to national policy discussions. 2009.

1393-23 Brennan Center for Justice, New York, NY, $151,715. For work of Nonprofit Rights Project challenging anti-prostitution pledge requirement contained in Global AIDS Act. 2009.

1393-24 Brookings Institution, Washington, DC, $75,000. For project, Organized Crime and Drug Policy in Latin America. 2009.

1393-25 Brookings Institution, Washington, DC, $23,500. For publication and dissemination of The Obama Administration and the Americas - An Agenda for Change. 2009.

1393-26 Brooklyn Academy of Music, Brooklyn, NY, $10,000. For general support and for Maly Theater from Russia. 2009.

1393-27 Burma Fund, New York, NY, $120,000. For service fees and expenses to obtain advice on diplomatic strategy and technical assistance from Independent Diplomat to improve capacity of advocacy on Burma. 2009.

1393-28 Burma Fund, New York, NY, $75,000. For Burma UN Service Office and Foreign Affairs Coordinating Team. 2009.

1393-29 Business and Human Rights Resource Center, New York, NY, $150,000. For general support. 2009.

1393-30 Case Western Reserve University, School of Law, Cleveland, OH, $10,000. For activities of War Crimes Research Office. 2009.

1393-31 Center for American Progress, Washington, DC, $50,000. To coordinate U.S.-E.U. Dialogue on Counterterrorism and Human Rights Initiative. 2009.

1393-32 Center for Democracy in the Americas, Washington, DC, $50,000. For general support. 2009.

1393-33 Center for Democracy in the Americas, Washington, DC, $25,000. For Honduras Project. 2009.

1393-34 Center for Global Development, Washington, DC, $300,000. For staff of Center for Global Development in Liberian capacity building project. 2009.

1393-35 Center for International Policy, Washington, DC, $127,000. For project, Just the Facts. 2009.

1393-36 Center for Justice and Accountability, San Francisco, CA, $150,000. For general support. 2009.

1393-37 Center for Justice and Accountability, San Francisco, CA, $50,000. For general support. 2009.

1393-38 Center for Justice and International Law, Washington, DC, $150,000. For general support. 2009.

1393-39 Center for Justice and International Law, Washington, DC, $25,000. For project, Monitoring the Human Rights Situation and Strengthening Human Rights Defenders in Honduras. 2009.

1393-40 Center for Strategic and International Studies, Washington, DC, $80,000. For project, Trafficking in the Meso-American Corridor - A Threat to Regional and Human Security. 2009.

1393-41 Center for Strategic and International Studies, Washington, DC, $75,000. For Avoiding False Dichotomies and Crafting New Counterterrorism Policies in the First Year of the Obama Administration Project. 2009.

1393-42 Center for Victims of Torture, Minneapolis, MN, $80,000. For Strengthening Key Validator Voices Against Torture Project. 2009.

1393-43 Church World Service, New York, NY, $150,000. To resource and help mobilize local faith-based initiatives in several states to organize on issues related to immigrant rights and immigration reform. 2009.

1393-44 City of Hope National Medical Center, Duarte, CA, $45,000. For ELNEC's international palliative care nursing projects providing education and training to health care professionals. 2009.

1393-45 Claremont McKenna College, Claremont, CA, $50,000. To translate Chinese book Mubei-Tombstone into English. 2009.

1393-46 Club of Madrid Foundation, Boston, MA, $100,000. For general support. 2009.

1393-47 Columbia University, New York, NY, $115,000. To build capacity of human rights activists through residency. 2009.

1393-48 Columbia University, New York, NY, $10,000. For project on Gaza and the Press, carried out by Columbia Journalism Review. 2009.

1393-49 Columbia University, Graduate School of Journalism, New York, NY, $33,024. For visiting journalists from China. 2009.

1393-50 Coney Island Avenue Project, Brooklyn, NY, $14,021. To enable work of journalist investigating human rights abuses in U.S. and South Asia. 2009.

1393-51 Creating Resources for Empowerment and Action, New York, NY, $11,040. For participation of sex worker rights activists at Human Rights Council in Geneva. 2009.

1393-52 Crimes of War Education Project, Washington, DC, $100,000. For general support. 2009.

1393-53 Crude Accountability, Alexandria, VA, $25,810. To broaden political space for environmental civil society in Turkmenistan. 2009.

1393-54 Cultural Survival, Cambridge, MA, $100,000. For general support. 2009.

1393-55 Democracy Coalition Project, Washington, DC, $116,500. For general support. 2009.

1393-56 Developing Radio Partners, Washington, DC, $68,259. To improve frequency and quality of environmental programming by building network of broadcast journalists with skills necessary to create environmental journalism responding to community needs. 2009.

1393-57 Disability Rights International, Washington, DC, $50,000. For training and advocacy related to implementation of UN Convention on the Rights of Persons with Disabilities in Mexico. 2009.

1393-58 Earth Island Institute, Berkeley, CA, $500,000. For Energy Action Coalition. 2009.

1393-59 EARTH University Foundation, Atlanta, GA, $70,450. For recruitment, selection, travel, and tuition funding for Haitian and African students. 2009.

1393-60 EarthRights International, Washington, DC, $30,000. For Mekong Legal Advocacy Institute. 2009.

1393-61 Economic Policy Institute, Washington, DC, $100,000. For Global Policy Network. 2009.

1393-62 EG Justice, Washington, DC, $21,140. For advocates to attend meetings with lawyers and lawmakers in Spain and Universal Periodic Review of Equatorial Guinea in Geneva. 2009.

1393-63 Eisenhower Project, New York, NY, $160,000. For National Initiative of Foreign and Defense Policy. 2009.

1393-64 Equal Access, San Francisco, CA, $18,000. For Lao Radio Extension Project. 2009.

1393-65 Freedom House, Washington, DC, $54,166. To protect Kazakhstani civil society activists working to improve human rights conditions in run up to and during country chairmanship of Organization for Security and Cooperation in Europe. 2009.

1393-66 French-American Foundation, New York, NY, $25,000. For project Covering Immigration - An International Media Dialogue. 2009.

1393-67 Friends of the Global Fight Against AIDS, Tuberculosis and Malaria, Washington, DC, $91,500. To expand media, communications, and policy capacity toward building support in U.S.. 2009.

1393-68 Fund for the European University at Saint Petersburg, Ann Arbor, MI, $726,921. To establish endowment fund, to support development program and faculty and fund scholarships. 2009.

1393-69 Fund for the European University at Saint Petersburg, Ann Arbor, MI, $201,678. For institutional and program costs for new center for study of rule of law. 2009.

1393-70 GBCHealth, New York, NY, $40,784. To strengthen GBC-Moscow Policy Program capacity to advocate for sustainability of harm reduction services in Russia. 2009.

1393-71 Genocide Intervention Network, Washington, DC, $75,000. For general support. 2009.

1393-72 Global Greengrants Fund, Boulder, CO, $130,000. For Your China Program. 2009.

1393-73 Global Rights, Washington, DC, $150,000. For general support. 2009.

1393-74 Global Rights, Washington, DC, $65,000. To extend access to justice and build capacity of justice sector actors and activists. 2009.

1393-75 Government Accountability Project, Washington, DC, $75,000. To strategically expand Homeland Security Campaign focus on torture, illegal surveillance, excessive secrecy, and politically repressive discrimination. 2009.

1393-76 Graduate Center, City University of New York, New York, NY, $100,000. For Global Centre for the Responsibility to Protect. 2009.

1393-77 Harm Reduction Coalition, New York, NY, $24,475. To sponsor participants from IHRD countries to attend Coalition National Harm Reduction Conference. 2009.

1393-78 Health Global Access Project, New York, NY, $15,000. To promote and advance human rights and access to medical and drug treatment for drug users through mobilization of user groups and medical advocacy, particularly in context of International Harm Reduction Association Conference in Bangkok. 2009.

1393-79 HealthRight International, New York, NY, $100,000. For general support. 2009.

1393-80 HealthRight International, New York, NY, $59,483. To develop case study and collect narratives in Ukraine to examine impact of HIV testing policy implementation on pregnant women's health. 2009.

1393-81 HealthRight International, New York, NY, $35,357. For exchange of civil society organizations, social service providers, local government authorities, and other key stakeholders from Vietnam, Russia, and Ukraine, to share lessons learned, experiences, and tools from partner successes in Russia. 2009.

1393-82 Hudson Institute, Washington, DC, $92,500. For Michael Horowitz work on international and domestic prison policy reform. 2009.

1393-83 Human Rights First, New York, NY, $300,000. For general support. 2009.

1393-84 Human Rights First, New York, NY, $25,000. For Restoring Human Rights to U.S. Detention and Interrogation Policies - How to Evaluate the Obama Administration's First 100 Days Project. 2009.

1393-85 Human Rights First, New York, NY, $25,000. To coordinate media and communications efforts of leading nonprofit organizations toward developing and disseminating streamlined public message. 2009.

1393-86 Human Rights Watch, New York, NY, $1,300,000. For general support. 2009.

1393-87 Human Rights Watch, New York, NY, $154,000. For response to emergency in Gaza. 2009.

1393-88 Human Rights Watch, New York, NY, $128,813. For project, Violence and Intolerance Against Migrants and Roma in Italy. 2009.

1393-89 Human Rights Watch, New York, NY, $110,000. For independent assessment of human rights impact of Cyclone Nargis on Burmese population. 2009.

1393-90 Human Rights Watch, New York, NY, $85,000. For general support of new initiatives. 2009.

1393-91 Human Rights Watch, New York, NY, $75,240. For Terrorism and Counterterrorism Program. 2009.

1393-92 Human Rights Watch, New York, NY, $25,000. For project on Roma in Kosovo - Improving the Rights of a Forgotten Community. 2009.

1393-93 Human Rights Watch, New York, NY, $25,000. For project, Research and Advocacy in Honduras. 2009.

1393-94 Human Rights Watch, New York, NY, $18,000. For general support of new initiatives. 2009.

1393-95 Human Rights Watch, New York, NY, $14,232. To enable Chechnya-based staff member of Memorial, Russian partner organization, to undergo professional development internship toward enhancing Memorial North Caucasus human rights monitoring and advocacy work. 2009.

1393-96 Human Rights Watch, New York, NY, $11,989. To organize roundtable in Geneva on issues of Child Labour in Central Asia. 2009.

1393-97 ImmigrationWorks Foundation, Washington, DC, $150,000. To engage business community in immigration debate and develop policy recommendations on employer-related issues. 2009.

1393-98 Independent Diplomat, New York, NY, $600,000. For general support. 2009.

1393-99 Institute for Policy Studies, Washington, DC, $200,000. For general support. 2009.

1393-100 International Association for Hospice and Palliative Care, Houston, TX, $25,000. To develop and implement strategic plan to improve availability of and access to opioid analgesics in Chile, Peru, and Mexico. 2009.

1393-101 International Association for K-12 Online Learning, Vienna, VA, $30,000. To develop strategic communications plan for Open Educational Resources including higher education institutions. 2009.

1393-102 International Center for Conciliation, Brookline, MA, $50,000. For Justice and History Outreach Project in Cambodia. 2009.

1393-103 International Center for Transitional Justice, New York, NY, $250,000. For general support. 2009.

1393-104 International Center for Transitional Justice, New York, NY, $125,000. For U.S. Accountability Project. 2009.

1393-105 International Center for Transitional Justice, New York, NY, $100,000. For Prosecutions Program. 2009.

1393-106 International Gay and Lesbian Human Rights Commission, New York, NY, $24,000. To promote lesbian, gay, bisexual, and transgender rights through regional mechanisms, public interest litigation, and advocacy. 2009.

1393-107 International Judicial Academy, North American Office, Washington, DC, $69,000. For proposed Sir Richard May Seminar on International Law and International Courts in The Hague, Netherlands. 2009.

1393-108 International Legal Foundation, Brooklyn, NY, $49,691. For interim funding to continue work toward quality legal representation to indigents accused of crime in Nepal. 2009.

1393-109 International Refugee Rights Initiative, New York, NY, $20,000. For seminar to assess range of AU obligations in relation to international justice and existing and incipient mechanisms for pursuing accountability for international crimes. 2009.

1393-110 International Refugee Rights Initiative, New York, NY, $10,000. For funding for activist on Darfur to come to New York to participate in security strategy meetings and write reports assessing security situation, threats, and how NGOs can better collaborate with International Criminal Court related activities. 2009.

1393-111 International Rescue Committee, New York, NY, $50,000. For general support. 2009.

1393-112 International Rivers Network, Berkeley, CA, $25,000. For Protecting the Rights and Resources of Mekong Rivers Communities project. 2009.

1393-113 International Womens Health Coalition, New York, NY, $200,000. For general support. 2009.

1393-114 JSI Research and Training Institute, Boston, MA, $246,000. For fellows to work as special assistants to ministers within Liberian government. 2009.

1393-115 Just Associates, Washington, DC, $10,000. To collect narrative accounts of women's HIV testing experiences during pregnancy through up to a year after in Durban, South Africa, to develop advocacy strategies to promote and protect human rights in provider-initiated HIV testing and counseling. 2009.

1393-116 Justice Policy Institute, Washington, DC, $190,000. For general support, to support network of criminal justice advocates in Maryland to advance policy reforms, and to develop policy report on incarceration rates and social structures in U.S. and other Western democracies. 2009.

1393-117 Latin America Working Group Education Fund, Washington, DC, $100,000. For project, Avoiding Harm, Sharing Responsibility - Human Rights and U.S. Counternarcotics Policy. 2009.

1393-118 Leadership Conference on Civil Rights Education Fund, Washington, DC, $150,000. To organize African American leadership and grassroots in support of immigration reform. 2009.

1393-119 Lebanese American University, New York, NY, $37,008. To promote research and dissemination of updated information regarding condition of women in Arab world through translation of Al-Raida into Arabic. 2009.

1393-120 Lexington Institute, Arlington, VA, $50,000. For Cuba Policy Project. 2009.

1393-121 Link Media, San Francisco, CA, $25,000. For Accountability for Torture Video Resource Project. 2009.

1393-122 Lower East Side Harm Reduction Center, New York, NY, $10,000. For continued technical assistance efforts for international visitors. 2009.

1393-123 Magnum Cultural Foundation, New York, NY, $50,000. For seed funding and to support Emergency Fund for photographers. 2009.

1393-124 Media Development Loan Fund, New York, NY, $2,900,000. For PRI Pool, and Technical Assistance for loanees. 2009.

1393-125 Migration Policy Institute, Washington, DC, $225,000. For work of U.S. Immigration Policy Program to generate analysis, proposals, and policy advocacy for new ideas toward improving national immigration system and treatment of immigrants, both in administrative and legislative arenas. 2009.

1393-126 Millennium Promise Alliance, New York, NY, $190,900. For Scaling Up the Millennium Village approach in Mali. 2009.

1393-127 Moldova Foundation, Washington, DC, $35,000. For general support. 2009.

1393-128 National Iranian American Council, Washington, DC, $25,000. For U.S.-Iran Media Resource Program. 2009.

1393-129 National Religious Campaign Against Torture, Washington, DC, $130,000. For Evangelicals for Human Rights Education Project. 2009.

1393-130 National Religious Campaign Against Torture, Washington, DC, $30,000. For research and plans for possibility of expansion into new areas of work, encouraging U.S. to use influence to end torture by other nations, and ending torture in U.S. prisons. 2009.

1393-131 National Religious Campaign Against Torture, Washington, DC, $25,000. For project, Religious Witness Calling on President Obama to Create a Commission of Inquiry Report. 2009.

1393-132 National Security Initiative, Washington, DC, $100,000. For Creating a Progressive Paradigm Project. 2009.

1393-133 National Whistleblower Center, Washington, DC, $100,000. For Protecting National Security Whistleblowers Campaign to promote human rights and civil liberties through defense of intelligence agency whistleblowers. 2009.

1393-134 New America Foundation, Washington, DC, $200,000. For project, Leaving the Dark Side - Shaping a New Counterterrorism Narrative. 2009.

1393-135 New America Foundation, Washington, DC, $150,000. For Nuclear Strategy and Nonproliferation Initiative. 2009.

1393-136 New School, Parsons School of Design, New York, NY, $87,921. For internship program for Communication Design and Technology graduate students to share expertise in information design and media production with health and human rights advocacy NGOs. 2009.

1393-137 New York University, New York, NY, $150,000. To complete empirical research study on counterterrorism policing in Muslim communities in New York and London, and disseminate findings and recommendations. 2009.

1393-138 New York University, New York, NY, $65,000. For Center for Human Rights and Global Justice's project, Human Rights in Transition - Ensuring Truth and Justice in U.S. National Security. 2009.

1393-139 New York University, New York, NY, $51,000. For International Journal of Constitutional Law - I*CON. 2009.

1393-140 New York University, New York, NY, $25,000. For international conference on ICCPR in Beijing. 2009.

1393-141 Organization of American States, General Secretariat, Washington, DC, $123,000. For project, Technical Assistance on Public Security to Strengthen the Capacity of Latin American Legislatures-Phase I. 2009.

1393-142 Osteopathy Without Borders, New York, NY, $10,000. For general support. 2009.

1393-143 Pacific Environment, San Francisco, CA, $75,000. For project, Strengthening China's Civil Society by Responding to Water Pollution. 2009.

1393-144 Pangaea Global AIDS Foundation, San Francisco, CA, $24,855. To review progress made in implementing substitution treatment since Combating the Twin Epidemics report and to update for use as awareness building tool for policymakers and health providers. 2009.

1393-145 Partners in Health, Boston, MA, $541,955. To work to develop universal guidelines for treatment of MDR/XDR-TB and HIV coinfection. 2009.

1393-146 Partners in Health, Boston, MA, $185,000. To work to develop universal guidelines for treatment of MDR/XDR-TB and HIV coinfection. 2009.

1393-147 Physicians for Human Rights, Cambridge, MA, $200,000. For general support. 2009.

1393-148 Physicians for Human Rights, Cambridge, MA, $25,000. For Afghan Mass Grave Project. 2009.

1393-149 Praxis Institute for Social Justice, Medford, MA, $16,000. For additional support to project, Bringing Justice Home - Alberto Fujimori on Trial for Corruption and Human Rights Violations in Peru. 2009.

1393-150 Public Interest Law Institute, New York, NY, $93,280. For fellows from Nepal in Public Interest Law Fellowship. 2009.

1393-151 Public Interest Law Institute, New York, NY, $36,850. For Russian public interest lawyers to participate in Fellowship program. 2009.

1393-152 Public Interest Law Institute, New York, NY, $35,000. For participation of African fellow as selected by Public Interest Law Institute. 2009.

1393-153 Refugees International, Washington, DC, $350,000. To work on Afghanistan, Iraq and Statelessness. 2009.

1393-154 Refugees International, Washington, DC, $30,000. For general support. 2009.

1393-155 Rehabilitation International, New York, NY, $85,000. For second phase of Global Advocacy Campaign, raising awareness among membership on CRPD, engaging in advocacy at global level, and focusing on legal harmonization in area of legal capacity and access to justice in Latin America. 2009.

1393-156 Res Publica, New York, NY, $300,000. For Avaaz.org work on climate change. 2009.

1393-157 Res Publica, New York, NY, $300,000. For general support to Avaaz.org. 2009.

1393-158 Revenue Watch Institute, New York, NY, $3,000,000. For general support. 2009.

1393-159 Revenue Watch Institute, New York, NY, $47,619. For East Timor research. 2009.

1393-160 Saint Edwards University, Austin, TX, $12,000. For project, Human Rights - Challenges of the Past, Challenges for the Future. 2009.

1393-161 Salzburg Global Seminar, Washington, DC, $100,000. For European Muslim Professionals' Network - Connecting European Dynamic Achievers and Role Models. 2009.

1393-162 San Diego Hospice Foundation, San Diego, CA, $432,808. For Institute for Palliative Medicine development and implementation of International Palliative Care Leadership Development Initiative for one cohort of international fellows. 2009.

1393-163 Save the Children Federation, Westport, CT, $100,000. Toward expanding girls' participation in school and role of young women in basic education through pre-service, in-school teacher training program in Bamyan province of Afghanistan. 2009.

1393-164 Telos Group, Washington, DC, $112,500. To train Israeli and Palestinian civil society leaders and human rights activists on effective engagement with U.S. policymakers and public, and facilitate relationship building between partners and leading U.S. policymakers. 2009.

1393-165 Tides Center, San Francisco, CA, $250,000. For AIDS-Free World. 2009.

1393-166 Tides Center, San Francisco, CA, $200,000. For core support of International Treatment Preparedness Coalition. 2009.

1393-167 Tides Center, San Francisco, CA, $125,000. To strengthen capacity of ITPCru to advocate for access to integrated treatment and care and mobilize affected communities to challenge ineffective HIV, TB, and drug policies and programs in Eastern Europe and Central Asia. 2009.

1393-168 Tides Center, San Francisco, CA, $124,550. For International Treatment Preparedness Coalition. 2009.

1393-169 Tides Foundation, San Francisco, CA, $200,000. For Disability Rights Fund, to expand work in India, Mexico, and Ukraine, and continue existing focus on Bangladesh, Ghana, Uganda, Namibia, Nicaragua, Ecuador, and Peru. 2009.

1393-170 Tides Foundation, San Francisco, CA, $150,000. For China Labour Bulletin. 2009.

1393-171 Trust for the Americas, Washington, DC, $147,000. For project, Proposal to Strengthen the Regional Alliance for Freedom of Expression and Access to Information. 2009.

1393-172 U.S. Office on Colombia, Washington, DC, $25,000. For project, Empowering Colombia's Civil Society to Ensure Their Voices are Heard by U.S. Policymakers. 2009.

1393-173 United States Fund for UNICEF, New York, NY, $55,794. For funding for institutionalizing Step by Step program in Uzbekistan by developing network of trainers throughout country with work feasibly coordinated by regional affiliates. 2009.

1393-174 United States/Middle East Project, New York, NY, $50,000. For general support. 2009.

1393-175 Universities Allied for Essential Medicines, Berkeley, CA, $70,000. For program support. 2009.

1393-176 Universities Allied for Essential Medicines, Berkeley, CA, $20,000. For annual fall conference of coalition of students working to ensure drugs discovered in campus laboratories are accessible to developing countries. 2009.

1393-177 University of Iowa, Iowa City, IA, $15,694. For participation of Burmese writer at International Writing Program. 2009.

1393-178 Urgent Action Fund for Womens Human Rights, Boulder, CO, $200,000. For general support. 2009.

1393-179 W N E T Channel 13 Foundation, WNET.ORG, New York, NY, $300,000. For Wide Angle Series special Women, War and Peace. 2009.

1393-180 Washington Office on Latin America, Washington, DC, $18,000. For project, Toward a New U.S. Policy in Latin America - Strategic Planning for the Washington Office on Latin America. 2009.

1393-181 Washington Office on Latin America, Washington, DC, $15,000. To contribute to bringing justice to cases of women murdered in Ciudad Juarez and Chihuahua City and promote structural changes to combat violence against women in Mexico. 2009.

1393-182 Women for Women International, Washington, DC, $66,473. For program support. 2009.

1393-183 World Professional Association for Transgender Health, Minneapolis, MN, $20,310. To sponsor panel session and policy development process, The Role of Medical and Therapeutic Practitioners in the Development of Law Relating to Transgender and Transsexual Peoples' Rights - Formulating Policy and Practice in Key Areas. 2009.

1394
The William and Eva Fox Foundation
c/o Theatre Communications Group
520 8th Ave., 24th Fl.
New York, NY   10018-4156
URL: http://www.tcg.org/fox/index.htm

Established in 1987 in DE; funded in 1994.
Donor: Belle Fox†.
Grantmaker type: Independent foundation.
Financial data (yr. ended 06/30/10): Assets, $4,633,033 (M); expenditures, $226,767; qualifying distributions, $222,068; giving activities

include $220,000 for 2 grants (high: $200,000; low: $20,000).

Purpose and activities: The foundation's mission is committed to the artistic development of theatre actors as a strategy to strengthen live theatre. The foundation awards fellowships to actors to underwrite periods of advanced training aimed at enhancing their craft and ability to meet the demands of a major role.

Fields of interest: Performing arts; Performing arts, theater.

International interests: United Kingdom.

Type of support: Fellowships.

Limitations: Giving on a national basis and in England.

Publications: Grants list.

Application information: Application guidelines and form available on foundation web site.

Officer and Director:* Robert P. Warren,* Pres. and Treas.

EIN: 133497192

1395
Francqui Foundation
(formerly Foundation Francqui Belgium)
c/o Lutz and Carr
300 E. 42nd St.
New York, NY 10017-5947 (212) 697-2299

Established in Belgium.

Grantmaker type: Independent foundation.

Financial data (yr. ended 12/31/10): Assets, $49,044,301 (M); expenditures, $1,698,614; qualifying distributions, $1,622,651; giving activities include $785,325 for 4 grants (high: $236,562; low: $149,276).

Purpose and activities: Giving primarily for Belgian scholars and education.

Fields of interest: Higher education.

International interests: Belgium.

Limitations: Applications not accepted. Giving limited to Belgium. No grants to individuals.

Application information: Unsolicited requests for funds not accepted.

Officers: Mark Eyskens, Chair.; Herman Balthazar, Vice-Chair.; Viscount Ettiene Davignon, Vice-Chair.; Pierre van Moebeke, Exec. Dir.

Directors: Thierry Boon; Sir Emile L. Boulpaep, M.D.; Baron Jacques Brotchi; Desire Collen; Count Claude d'Aspremont-Lynden; Baron Paul deMeester; Baroness Janine Delruelle; Count Frederic Francqui; Baron Daniel Janssen; Regine Kurgan-Van Hentenryk; Francoise Masai; Baron Niceas Schamp; Alexander Sevrin; Baroness Greta Suetens-Bourgeois; Anton van Rossum; Baron Piet Van Waeyenberge.

EIN: 986001286

1396
Ernst & Elfriede Frank Foundation, Inc
112-01 Queens Blvd., Apt. 11C
Forest Hills, NY 11375-5589

Established around 1962.

Donor: Ernst L. Frank.

Grantmaker type: Independent foundation.

Financial data (yr. ended 08/31/10): Assets, $6,663,449 (M); expenditures, $345,683; qualifying distributions, $333,590; giving activities include $333,590 for grants.

Purpose and activities: Giving primarily for the arts, health, and human services.

Fields of interest: Arts; Education; Health care; Health organizations, association; Human services; Children/youth, services; Religion.

International interests: Canada; South America.

Limitations: Applications not accepted. Giving primarily in MA and NY. No grants to individuals.

Application information: Contributes only to pre-selected organizations.

Officers: Sybil Ann Brennan, V.P.; Jephtha Tausig Edwards, V.P.; Kasara Gage, V.P.; Ernest H. Frank, V.P.; Samantha Starr, V.P.; Eva-Maria Tausig, V.P.

EIN: 136106471

1397
Freeman Foundation
c/o Rockefeller Trust Company, N.A.
10 Rockefeller Plz., 3rd Fl.
New York, NY 10020 (212) 549-5270
Contact: George S. Tsandikos
Application address: 499 Taber Hill Rd., Stowe, VT 05672

Established in 1978 in VT.

Donors: Houghton Freeman; Mansfield Freeman†; members of the Freeman family.

Grantmaker type: Independent foundation.

Financial data (yr. ended 12/31/09): Assets, $270,191,588 (M); expenditures, $31,560,112; qualifying distributions, $30,592,186; giving activities include $29,517,847 for 148 grants (high: $2,100,000; low: $4,000).

Purpose and activities: Support primarily for the promotion of international understanding, farmland preservation projects in the state of VT and special projects in HI.

Fields of interest: Education, public education; Environment, natural resources; International affairs, goodwill promotion; International studies.

International interests: Asia.

Type of support: General/operating support; Land acquisition; Program development; Professorships; Curriculum development; Fellowships; Scholarship funds; Research; Exchange programs; Matching/challenge support.

Limitations: Applications accepted. Giving primarily in VT for conservation and environment grants; Asian studies grants are awarded nationally. No grants to individuals, or for endowments or capital campaigns.

Publications: Annual report.

Application information: Application form not required.

　Initial approach: Letter
　Copies of proposal: 7
　Deadline(s): One month before meetings
　Board meeting date(s): Quarterly

Officer and Trustees:* Graeme Freeman, Pres.; Doreen Freeman; George B. Snell.

Number of staff: 4

EIN: 132965090

Recent grants for international programs:

1397-1 Asian Art Museum of San Francisco, San Francisco, CA, $50,000. For education programs. 2010.

1397-2 California State University, Northridge, CA, $10,000. For the Exploring Deaf Education and Deaf Community Services in Japan project. 2010.

1397-3 Center for Cultural and Technical Interchange Between East and West, East-West

Center, Honolulu, HI, $175,000. For the Jefferson Fellows Program. 2010.

1397-4 Center for Cultural and Technical Interchange Between East and West, East-West Center, Honolulu, HI, $100,000. For Asian Studies Development Program. 2010.

1397-5 Center for Cultural and Technical Interchange Between East and West, East-West Center, Honolulu, HI, $90,000. For the New Generation Seminar. 2010.

1397-6 Chinese American International School, San Francisco, CA, $62,500. For challenge grant for the tuition assistance program. 2010.

1397-7 Columbia University, East Asian Institute, New York, NY, $584,275. For National Consortium for Teaching about Asia. 2010.

1397-8 Cooperating School Districts of the Saint Louis Suburban Area, International Education Consortium, Saint Louis, MO, $138,325. For the China in Missouri program. 2010.

1397-9 Crane House, Louisville, KY, $27,200. For the Teaching in Asia Program. 2010.

1397-10 Doctors Without Borders USA, New York, NY, $50,000. For programs in East Asia. 2010.

1397-11 Five College Center for East Asian Studies, Northampton, MA, $330,000. For National Consortium for Teaching about Asia. 2010.

1397-12 Furman University, Greenville, SC, $30,000. For National Consortium for Teaching about Asia. 2010.

1397-13 Indiana University, East Asian Studies Center, Bloomington, IN, $234,600. For National Consortium for Teaching about Asia. 2010.

1397-14 Institute of International Education, New York, NY, $1,300,000. For Freeman-ASIA (Freeman Awards for Study in Asia) Program. 2010.

1397-15 International Student Conferences, Washington, DC, $25,000. For Japan-America Student Conference. 2010.

1397-16 International Student Conferences, Washington, DC, $25,000. For Korea-America Student Conference. 2010.

1397-17 Iolani School, Honolulu, HI, $40,000. For Freeman Travel Program. 2010.

1397-18 Japan Studies Association, Maryville, MO, $90,000. For Japan Studies Summer Workshop. 2010.

1397-19 Japan-America Society of Hawaii, Honolulu, HI, $50,000. For the Cross-Cultural Education Program Initiative, and for general support. 2010.

1397-20 Japan-America Society of Oregon, Portland, OR, $20,000. For the Japan on the Road program. 2010.

1397-21 Johns Hopkins University, Baltimore, MD, $1,000,000. For R. Kendall Nottingham Fellowship at School of Advanced International Studies in Washington DC. 2010.

1397-22 K C E T Community Television of Southern California, Los Angeles, CA, $200,000. For national distribution of BBC World News. 2010.

1397-23 Korea Society, New York, NY, $96,500. For educational and cultural heritage programs. 2010.

1397-24 Lopez Island School District, Lopez Island, WA, $80,000. For the Japanese Connections project. 2010.

1397-25 National Association of Japan-America Societies, Washington, DC, $665,000. For the U.S. High School Diplomats Program. 2010.

1397-26 National Association of Japan-America Societies, Washington, DC, $35,000. For administration. 2010.

1397-27 National Public Radio, Washington, DC, $25,000. For Asia coverage. 2010.

1397-28 New York University, New York, NY, $135,000. For the Developing Chinese Language Teachers project. 2010.

1397-29 Newton Public Schools, Newton, MA, $300,000. For the China Exchange Initiative. 2010.

1397-30 Northeast Asia Economic Forum, Honolulu, HI, $70,000. For the Young Leaders Program. 2010.

1397-31 Northeast Cultural Coop, Amherst, NH, $15,280. For challenge grant for general support. 2010.

1397-32 Pacific and Asian Affairs Council, Honolulu, HI, $150,000. For PAAC Travel Program. 2010.

1397-33 Peabody Essex Museum, Salem, MA, $150,000. For educational programming related to the exhibition, The Emperor's Private Paradise: Treasures from the Forbidden City, at PEM, The Metropolitan Museum of Art, and The Milwaukee Art Museum. 2010.

1397-34 Peter G. Peterson Institute for International Economics, Washington, DC, $25,000. For dissemination of project on Northeast Asian Economic Relationships. 2010.

1397-35 Primary Source, Watertown, MA, $200,000. For East Asia Programs. 2010.

1397-36 Princeton University, Princeton, NJ, $26,245. For National Consortium for Teaching about Asia. 2010.

1397-37 Public Radio International, Minneapolis, MN, $25,000. For Asia coverage. 2010.

1397-38 Punahou School, Honolulu, HI, $185,000. For Wo International Center initiatives. 2010.

1397-39 Rice University, Houston, TX, $26,675. For National Consortium for Teaching about Asia. 2010.

1397-40 Saint Johnsbury Academy, Saint Johnsbury, VT, $44,000. For the Japan student exchange program. 2010.

1397-41 Stanford University, Stanford Program on International and Cross-Cultural Education (SPICE), Stanford, CA, $98,000. For National Consortium for Teaching about Asia. 2010.

1397-42 Stanford University, Stanford Program on International and Cross-Cultural Education (SPICE), Stanford, CA, $63,900. To develop the curriculum unit, Legacies of the Vietnam War. 2010.

1397-43 Trinity University, San Antonio, TX, $19,700. For National Consortium for Teaching about Asia. 2010.

1397-44 United Board for Christian Higher Education in Asia, New York, NY, $80,000. For the Fellows Program. 2010.

1397-45 United States Indonesia Society, Washington, DC, $45,000. For the Summer Studies program. 2010.

1397-46 University of Arkansas, Little Rock, AR, $108,000. For the Bringing China to Arkansas Program. 2010.

1397-47 University of Arkansas, Little Rock, AR, $33,300. For National Consortium for Teaching about Asia. 2010.

1397-48 University of Colorado, Boulder, CO, $377,500. For National Consortium for Teaching about Asia. 2010.

1397-49 University of Florida, Gainesville, FL, $29,700. For National Consortium for Teaching about Asia. 2010.

1397-50 University of Georgia, Athens, GA, $25,000. For National Consortium for Teaching about Asia. 2010.

1397-51 University of Kansas, Lawrence, KS, $30,000. For National Consortium for Teaching about Asia. 2010.

1397-52 University of Mississippi, University, MS, $19,200. For National Consortium for Teaching about Asia. 2010.

1397-53 University of North Carolina, Chapel Hill, NC, $19,700. For National Consortium for Teaching about Asia. 2010.

1397-54 University of North Texas, Denton, TX, $25,000. For National Consortium for Teaching about Asia. 2010.

1397-55 University of Oklahoma, Tulsa, OK, $14,245. For National Consortium for Teaching about Asia. 2010.

1397-56 University of Pittsburgh, Pittsburgh, PA, $268,300. For National Consortium for Teaching about Asia. 2010.

1397-57 University of Southern California, Los Angeles, CA, $175,000. For the Pacific Rim Internship Program. 2010.

1397-58 University of Southern California, Los Angeles, CA, $158,500. For National Consortium for Teaching about Asia. 2010.

1397-59 University of Tennessee, Chattanooga, TN, $19,500. For National Consortium for Teaching about Asia. 2010.

1397-60 University of Vermont, Asian Studies Program, Burlington, VT, $419,000. For the Asian Studies Outreach Program and the Governor's Institute on Asian Cultures. 2010.

1397-61 University of Washington, Seattle, WA, $317,500. For National Consortium for Teaching about Asia. 2010.

1397-62 University of Washington, Seattle, WA, $75,000. For the East Asia Education Initiative. 2010.

1397-63 Vermont Studio Center, Johnson, VT, $100,000. For the Asian Artists Program. 2010.

1397-64 Volunteers in Asia, Stanford, CA, $17,500. For programs in Indonesia. 2010.

1397-65 W P B T Channel 2, NBR Enterprises, Miami, FL, $12,500. For Asia coverage. 2010.

1397-66 Wesleyan University, Middletown, CT, $2,100,000. For Freeman Asian Scholars Program. 2010.

1397-67 Windham Southeast Supervisory Union, Brattleboro, VT, $340,000. For the Windham County Asian Studies program. 2010.

1398

French American Cultural Exchange

(formerly Society for French American Cultural Services and Educational Aid)
972 5th Ave.
New York, NY   10075-0104   (212) 439-1449
Contact: Elisabeth Hayes
FAX: (212) 439-1455; E-mail: info@facecouncil.org;
URL: http://www.facecouncil.org

Established in 1955 in NY.
Grantmaker type: Public charity.
Financial data (yr. ended 12/31/10): Revenue, $1,998,387; assets, $5,519,129 (M); gifts received, $1,975,698; expenditures, $2,925,572; giving activities include $1,949,093 for grants.
Purpose and activities: The organization is dedicated to nurturing French-American relations through innovative international projects in the arts, education, and cultural exchange.
Fields of interest: International exchange, arts.
International interests: France.
Type of support: Film/video/radio.

Limitations: Applications accepted. Giving on a national and international basis, with emphasis on France.
Publications: Application guidelines.
Application information: Application form required.
  Initial approach: Download application form for French American Fund for Contemporary Music Project Grant; complete online application for Tournees Film Grant
  Deadline(s): Feb. 1 for Etant Donnes: The French-American Fund for the Performing Arts Project Grants; Mar. 1 for French American Fund for Contemporary Music Project Grant and Etant Donnes: The French-American Fund for Contemporary Art Grants; June 30 and Oct. 1 for Tournees Film Grant; Oct. 22 for CMA/FACE French-American Jazz Exchange Program
  Board meeting date(s): Six times per year
Officers and Trustees:* Jacques E. Bouhet,* Chair.; Jean Vallier,* Vice-Chair.; Adrienne Halpern,* Secy.; William A. von Mueffling,* Treas.; Pierre Berge; Grace White Borletti; Alain Coblence; Mary Sharp Cronson; Yves-Andre Istel; Patrick R. Pagni; Richard Pena; Jeanine Parisier Plottel; John S. Reed; Aso Tavitian; Beatrice de Clermont Tonnerre; Jean Vallier; George C. White; Suzi Winson.
Number of staff: 3 full-time professional.
EIN: 136165672

1399

French-American Aid for Children, Inc.

150 E. 58th St., 23rd Fl.
New York, NY   10155-0002   (212) 486-9593
FAX: (212) 486-9594; E-mail: info@faafc.org;
URL: http://www.aidforchildren.org/

Founded in 1939.
Grantmaker type: Public charity.
Financial data (yr. ended 12/31/09): Revenue, $344,049; assets, $394,820 (M); gifts received, $286,290; expenditures, $367,272; giving activities include $310,000 for grants.
Purpose and activities: The organization seeks to give financial assistance to vetted American and French children's charities for programs dealing with health, education and the prevention of abuse.
Fields of interest: Crime/violence prevention, abuse prevention; Health care; Education; Children/youth, services; Children.
International interests: France.
Limitations: Applications not accepted. Giving primarily in the U.S. and France.
Application information: Contributes only to pre-selected organizations.
Officers and Board Members:* Mrs. Charles-Henri Mangin,* Pres.; Mrs. Michel de Schietere Longchampt,* 1st V.P.; Mrs. Walter Jackson,* 2nd V.P.; Jean A. Dricot,* Co-Treas.; Marie-Louise Quere-Messing,* Co-Treas.; Diane L. Ackerman; Susan Andelman; Mrs. Michel Berty; Mrs. Bruno Bich; Mrs. Jonathan Bulkley; Mrs. John Chappell; Mrs. James Cherry; Amrita Douglas; Beatrice DuPont; Mrs. Tilden E. Miller; and 8 additional board members.
EIN: 131616925

1400

French-American Foundation

28 W. 44th St., Ste. 1420
New York, NY   10036-7410   (212) 829-8800
Contact: Nicholas W. F-R. Dungan, Pres.

FAX: (212) 829-8810;
E-mail: info@frenchamerican.org; URL: http://
www.frenchamerican.org

Established in 1976.
Grantmaker type: Public charity.
Financial data (yr. ended 12/31/10): Revenue,
$1,454,417; assets, $3,177,762 (M); gifts
received, $1,374,531; expenditures, $1,737,679.
Purpose and activities: The foundation seeks to
improve relations between France and the U.S. by
professional exchanges, study tours and
conferences.
Fields of interest: International affairs.
International interests: France.
Limitations: Applications not accepted.
Publications: Biennial report; Newsletter;
Occasional report.
Application information: Applications not accepted;
unsolicited requests for funds not considered or
acknowledged.
Officers and Directors: * Michael E. Patterson,*
Chair.; Hon. Walter J.P. Curley,* Honorary Chair.;
Francois Buijon de l'Estang,* Vice Chair.; Elizabeth
Fondaras,* Vice-Chair.; Nicholas W. F-R. Dungan,
Pres.; Felix G. Rohatyn; Anthony A. Smith; and 36
additional directors.
Number of staff: 6 full-time professional; 1 part-time
support.
EIN: 132847092

1401
Friends of Catholic University in Chile
c/o M. Sava Thomas
1150 5th Ave.
New York, NY   10128-0724   (212) 348-8345

Established around 1990; status changed to a
public charity in 2002.
Grantmaker type: Public charity.
Financial data (yr. ended 09/30/10): Revenue,
$513,586; assets, $63,755 (M); gifts received,
$513,081; expenditures, $502,613; giving
activities include $494,207 for grants to
organizations outside the U.S.
Fields of interest: Higher education.
International interests: Chile.
Type of support: Scholarship funds.
Limitations: Applications not accepted. Giving
primarily in Chile. No grants to individuals.
Application information: Contributes only to
pre-selected organizations.
Officers and Directors: * Sava B. Thomas,* Pres.;
Francisco Matte,* Treas.; Juan Carlos Cappello;
Fred Mehlert Fehsenfeld, Jr.; Malcolm Gillis; Arnoldo
C. Hax; William Pounds; and 9 additional directors.
EIN: 521656495

1402
The Friends of Thalamus
200 E. 61st St.
New York, NY   10065-8550

Established in 2004 in NY.
Donor: Scrita Investments, Ltd.
Grantmaker type: Public charity.
Financial data (yr. ended 12/31/10): Revenue,
$441,500; assets, $76,933 (M); gifts received,
$441,500; expenditures, $425,234; giving
activities include $392,000 for grants to
organizations outside the U.S.

Purpose and activities: The organization works to
contribute to Brazil's social development through
the management of socio-economic projects that
serve the poor and foster the development of
ongoing charitable projects in Brazil.
Fields of interest: International development.
International interests: Brazil.
Limitations: Applications not accepted. Giving
limited to Brazil. No grants to individuals.
Application information: Contributes only to
pre-selected organizations.
Officers: Maria Moreira DeSouza-Pierotti, Pres.;
Maris Clara Pierotti-Tassiulas, Secy.-Treas.
EIN: 010748205

1403
Friends of the Israel Defense Forces
350 Fifth Ave., Ste. 2011
New York, NY   10118-2003   (212) 244-3118
E-mail: fidf@israelsoldiers.org; URL: http://
www.israelsoldiers.org

Established in 1983 in NY.
Grantmaker type: Public charity.
Financial data (yr. ended 12/31/10): Revenue,
$58,224,980; assets, $114,476,423 (M); gifts
received, $56,838,499; expenditures,
$49,110,688; giving activities include
$37,687,328 for grants to organizations outside the
U.S.
Purpose and activities: The organization is the
American partner of the Association for the
Wellbeing of Israel's Soldiers, and helps support
social, educational, and recreational programs and
facilities for the young men and women soldiers of
Israel who defend the Jewish homeland.
Fields of interest: Human services, emergency aid;
Military/veterans.
International interests: Israel.
Limitations: Giving limited to Israel.
Officers: Arthur Stark, Chair.; Wily Falic, Pres.;
Maurice Sanderman, V.P.; Adam Tantleff, V.P.;
Joseph Sieber, Secy.; Netta Korin, Treas.; Jonathan
Bernstein, C.F.O.; Yehiel Gozal, Exec. Dir.
Board Members: Caryn Rosen Adelman; Michael
Adler; Daniel Altman; Harvey Axelrod; Moshe Azogui;
Gary Batler; Sammy Bar-Or; Dr. Brian Berman; Craig
Bernfield; Jeffrey Beyda; Scott Black; Dan Brodsky;
Alan Brody; Elliot Broidy; Ruth David; and 48
additional board members.
EIN: 133156445

1404
Friends of Yad Sarah, Inc.
450 Park Ave., Ste. 3201
New York, NY   10022-2633
E-mail: adele@friendsofyadsarah.org; Toll-free tel.:
(888) 923-7272

Established in 1976 in NY.
Grantmaker type: Public charity.
Financial data (yr. ended 06/30/10): Revenue,
$1,938,491; assets, $1,542,809 (M); gifts
received, $1,933,606; expenditures, $2,208,111;
giving activities include $1,488,350 for grants to
organizations outside the U.S.
Purpose and activities: The organization supports
Yad Sarah in Israel.
Fields of interest: Health care; Health
organizations; Jewish agencies & synagogues.
International interests: Israel.

Type of support: Equipment.
Limitations: Applications not accepted. Giving
limited to Israel. No grants to individuals.
Application information: Contributes only to a
pre-selected organization; unsolicited requests for
funds not considered or acknowledged.
Officers: Jay Pomrenze, Pres.; Jack Bendheim,
Secy.; Nathaniel L. Gerber, Treas.; Adele Goldberg,
Exec. Dir.
Number of staff: 2 part-time professional.
EIN: 133106175

1405
Friends of Yeshiva Beer Abraham, Inc.
c/o Meisels
135 Rockaway Tpke., Ste. 111
Lawrence, NY   11559-1023

Grantmaker type: Public charity.
Financial data (yr. ended 12/31/10): Revenue,
$78,760; assets, $311,304 (M); gifts received,
$78,760; expenditures, $47,279; giving activities
include $36,665 for grants, and for 1 grant to an
organization outside the U.S.
Purpose and activities: The organization support
Yeshiva Beer Abraham in Jerusalem.
Fields of interest: Jewish agencies & synagogues.
International interests: Israel.
Limitations: Giving limited to Jerusalem, Israel.
Directors: Rabbi Moshe Chomsky; Rabbi Yehoshua
Karlinsky; Rabbi Chaim Schwartz; Rabbi David
Wacholder; Rabbi Beinyomin Zelingold.
EIN: 112519660

1406
Fund for Armenian Relief, Inc.
630 2nd Ave.
New York, NY   10016-4806   (212) 889-5150
FAX: (212) 889-4849; E-mail: far@farusa.org;
URL: http://www.farusa.org

Established in 1993 in NY.
Grantmaker type: Public charity.
Financial data (yr. ended 12/31/10): Revenue,
$2,916,566; assets, $8,414,955 (M); gifts
received, $2,828,297; expenditures, $3,318,524;
giving activities include $1,173,796 for grants to
organizations outside the U.S.
Purpose and activities: The fund provides
short-term emergency relief and implements
long-term programs for the economic growth and
social development of Armenia.
Fields of interest: International development;
International economic development; International
relief; Children/youth; Children; Adults; Aging;
Young adults; Homeless; Economically
disadvantaged.
International interests: Armenia.
Type of support: Student loans—to individuals;
Scholarships—to individuals; Grants to individuals;
Program evaluation; Technical assistance;
Scholarship funds; Curriculum development;
Professorships; Conferences/seminars; Program
development; Building/renovation; General/
operating support.
Limitations: Giving primarily in Armenia.
Publications: Annual report; Financial statement;
Informational brochure (including application
guidelines); Newsletter; Occasional report.
Officers and Directors: * Randy Sapah-Gulian,*
Chair.; Carl J. Bazarian,* Vice-Chair.; Annette

Choolfaian,* Vice-Chair.; Edgar M. Housepian,* Vice-Chair.; Archbishop Khajag Barsamian,* Pres.; Michael Haratunian,* Secy.; Hagop Kouyoumdjian,* Treas.; Garnik Nanagoulian, Exec. Dir.; Nishan Atinizian; Bishop Vicken Aykazian; Marta Batmasian; Aram V. Chobanian; Dennis R. Tarzian; Oscar Tatosian; Pontish Yeramyan.
Number of staff: 150
EIN: 133706646

1407
Funding Exchange, Inc.
666 Broadway, Ste. 500
New York, NY   10012-2317   (212) 529-5300
Contact: Lucretia John, Prog. Officer
FAX: (212) 982-9272; E-mail: grants@fex.org;
URL: http://www.fex.org
Funding Exchange's Philanthropy Promise: http://www.ncrp.org/philanthropys-promise/who

Established in 1979; supporting organization of Appalachian Community Fund, Bread and Roses Community Fund, Chinook Fund, Crossroads Fund, Fund for Santa Barbara, Fund for Southern Communities, Haymarket People's Fund, Headwaters Foundation for Justice, Liberty Hill Foundation, McKenzie River Gathering Foundation, North Star Fund, The People's Fund, San Diego Foundation for Change, Three Rivers Community Fund, Vanguard Public Foundation, and Wisconsin Community Fund.
Grantmaker type: Public charity.
Financial data (yr. ended 06/30/10): Revenue, $1,773,406; assets, $21,698,462 (M); gifts received, $775,266; expenditures, $3,910,135; giving activities include $2,916,010 for grants, and $42,000 for 7 grants to organizations outside the U.S.
Purpose and activities: The organization is a donor consortium committed to building a permanent institutional and financial base for progressive social change in the U.S. (defined as the process of enabling and encouraging community people to become part of an organization which works against social and economic injustices and educates and challenges the broader community).
Fields of interest: Media/communications; Media, film/video; Environment; Crime/law enforcement; Employment, labor unions/organizations; Safety/disasters; Youth development; International peace/security; Civil/human rights, LGBTQ; Civil rights, race/intergroup relations; Civil liberties, reproductive rights; Economic development; Community/economic development; Minorities; Native Americans/American Indians; Women.
Type of support: General/operating support; Emergency funds; Program development; Seed money; Technical assistance.
Limitations: Giving primarily in the U.S.; there is limited international funding. No support for organizations with access to traditional or mainstream funding sources, community groups with budgets exceeding $500,000, cultural projects or publications not directly connected to organizing campaigns or used as tools for social change organizing, other foundations, or social services that do not have a capacity for organizing recipients around specific issues. No grants to individuals, or for capital campaigns, equipment, endowments, deficit financing, research projects, or fellowships.
Publications: Application guidelines; Annual report; Grants list; Informational brochure (including

application guidelines); Newsletter; Occasional report.
Application information: Due to the current economic crisis, the organization has currently suspended grantmaking operations; see web site for current status of grantmaking programs. Application form required.
  Initial approach: Telephone
  Deadline(s): Varies
  Board meeting date(s): Varies
  Final notification: Varies
Officer and Directors: Casey Cook,* Co-Chair.; Taij Kumarie Moteelall,* Co-Chair.; Jim Sauder,* Secy.-Treas.; Barbara Heisler, Exec. Dir.; Nancy Aleck; Karen Campbell; Gail Heylmum; Jane Kimondo; Demetria Ledbetter; Margo Miller; Nick Palazzetti; Cori Schmanke Parrish; Katie Thiede; Tawnee Walling.
Number of staff: 5 full-time professional; 3 part-time professional; 3 full-time support.
EIN: 133002025

1408
Gabriela Mistral Foundation Inc.
100 Park Ave., Ste. 1600
New York, NY   10017-5516   (212) 984-0632
FAX: (212) 880-6499;
E-mail: info@gabrielamistralfoundation.org;
URL: http://gabrielamistralfoundation.org
Facebook: http://www.facebook.com/pages/gabrielamistralfoundation/286640174382?v=wall&ref=ts

Established in 2007.
Grantmaker type: Public charity.
Purpose and activities: The foundation supports organizations involved with underprivileged children and the aged; support is given primarily in Chile.
Fields of interest: Scholarships/financial aid; Education; Economically disadvantaged; Children; Aging.
International interests: Chile.
Type of support: General/operating support; Scholarships—to individuals.
Limitations: Giving primarily in Chile.
Officers and Directors:* Amb. Heraldo Munoz,* Chair.; Mario J. Paredes,* Vice-Chair.; Felipe Lecaros,* Secy.; Denic Catalan,* Treas.; E. Cecilia Alatriz; Juan Carlos Cappello; Alejandro Cerda; Gloria Garafulich-Grabois; Maria Grasso.
EIN: 743217479

1409
GBRG, Inc.
c/o Hertz, Herson & Company, LLP
2 Park Ave., Ste. 1500
New York, NY   10016-5701

Established in 1995 in DE and NY.
Grantmaker type: Independent foundation.
Financial data (yr. ended 12/31/10): Assets, $28,928,554 (M); expenditures, $1,063,275; qualifying distributions, $945,332; giving activities include $945,332 for grants.
Fields of interest: Elementary/secondary education; Education; Human services; Children/youth, services; International affairs; Jewish federated giving programs; Jewish agencies & synagogues.
International interests: Israel.
Type of support: General/operating support.

Limitations: Applications not accepted. Giving primarily in Washington, DC, Baltimore, MD, and in Jerusalem, Israel. No grants to individuals.
Application information: Contributes only to pre-selected organizations.
Officer and Directors:* Susan Wexner,* Pres. and Secy.-Treas.; Dr. Bernard Agus; Dr. Saul G. Agus; Raymond Kanner; Gregg H. Levy, Esq.; Michael S. Oberman, Esq.; Mark Saks, Esq.
EIN: 134072646

1410
Michael E. Gellert Trust
122 E. 42nd St., 34th Fl.
New York, NY   10168-0001

Established in 1962 in NY.
Donor: Michael E. Gellert.
Grantmaker type: Independent foundation.
Financial data (yr. ended 06/30/10): Assets, $15,622,818 (M); expenditures, $2,009,767; qualifying distributions, $1,950,568; giving activities include $1,950,568 for grants.
Purpose and activities: Giving primarily for education and the arts.
Fields of interest: Performing arts; Arts; Higher education; Education; Human services; International human rights.
Limitations: Applications not accepted. Giving primarily in CT and NY. No grants to individuals.
Application information: Contributes only to pre-selected organizations.
Trustees: David B. Spohn Gellert; Michael E. Gellert; Robert J. Gellert; Hugh McLoughlin.
EIN: 136093842

1411
Genesis Foundation, Inc.
505 Park Ave., 4th Fl.
New York, NY   10022-1106   (212) 763-3703
Contact: Carolina Esquenazi, Pres.
FAX: (917) 591-7858;
E-mail: genesis@genesis-foundation.org;
URL: http://www.genesis-foundation.org
Facebook: http://www.facebook.com/pages/Genesis-Foundation/227677570578716
Twitter: http://twitter.com/#!/GenesisColombia
Vimeo: http://vimeo.com/genesisfoundation

Established in 2001 in FL.
Donors: Genesis Endowment; ReMax of Georgia.
Grantmaker type: Independent foundation.
Financial data (yr. ended 12/31/10): Assets, $1,224,321 (M); gifts received, $1,573,776; expenditures, $2,052,175; qualifying distributions, $1,807,879; giving activities include $1,807,879 for grants.
Purpose and activities: Giving to strengthen and support educational programs for children in Colombia and in Latino communities in the U.S.
Fields of interest: Education, management/technical assistance; Education, reform; Education, equal rights; Education, formal/general education; Education, bilingual programs; Education, ESL programs; Education, community/cooperative; Education; Hispanics/Latinos.
International interests: Colombia.
Type of support: General/operating support; Management development/capacity building; Capital campaigns; Building/renovation;

Equipment; Program development; Curriculum development; Matching/challenge support.
Limitations: Applications accepted. Giving primarily in Colombia, as well as in the metropolitan New York, NY, area, particularly the Corona, Elmhurst, Flushing, Jackson Heights, Sunnyside and Woodside neighborhoods of Queens. No support for religious or political organizations. No grants to individuals.
Publications: Application guidelines; Annual report; Grants list; Informational brochure; Informational brochure (including application guidelines); Newsletter; Occasional report; Occasional report (including application guidelines).
Application information: Application information available on foundation web site. Application form required.
  Initial approach: Use Inquiry Form on foundation web site
  Copies of proposal: 1
  Deadline(s): Mar. 15 and Sept. 15
  Board meeting date(s): May and Nov.
  Final notification: June and Dec.
Officers: Carolina Esquenazi, Pres.; Herbert Selzer, Secy.; Andrea Lawson Gertsacov, Exec. Dir.
Directors: Cristina Gutierrez de Pineres; Susan Mayer.
Number of staff: 4 full-time professional; 1 part-time professional.
EIN: 912120744

1412
The Patrick A. Gerschel Foundation
600 Madison Ave., 16th Fl.
New York, NY 10022-1615

Established in 1986 in NY.
Donor: Patrick A. Gerschel.
Grantmaker type: Independent foundation.
Financial data (yr. ended 12/31/10): Assets, $6,342,319 (M); expenditures, $246,589; qualifying distributions, $186,000; giving activities include $186,000 for grants.
Fields of interest: Museums; Higher education; International affairs, goodwill promotion.
Type of support: Research.
Limitations: Applications not accepted. Giving primarily in New York, NY. No grants to individuals.
Application information: Contributes only to pre-selected organizations.
Officer and Director:* Patrick A. Gerschel,* Pres.
EIN: 133317180

1413
Virginia Gildersleeve International Fund
3 W. 29th St., Rm. 1002
New York, NY 10001-4504 (212) 213-0622
Contact: Fay Kittelson, Exec. Dir.
FAX: (212) 213-0684; E-mail: vgif@vgif.org;
URL: http://www.vgif.org
Facebook: http://www.facebook.com/group.php?gid=6995526839&ref=ts
Grants Database: http://www.thegildersleeve.org/p_projectsfunded.asp
Twitter: http://twitter.com/vgif

Established in 1969 in NY.
Grantmaker type: Public charity.
Financial data (yr. ended 12/31/10): Revenue, $407,447; assets, $13,273,262 (M); gifts received, $161,506; expenditures, $465,720;

giving activities include $120,012 for grants to organizations outside the U.S.
Purpose and activities: The fund provides small grants for grassroots projects that empower women and girls in developing countries. Project areas include community development, health and nutritional support, literacy and leadership training, educational seminars and workshops.
Fields of interest: Education; Health care; International human rights; Leadership development; Women, centers/services; Children; Women.
International interests: Africa; Asia; Caribbean; Central America; Eastern & Central Europe; Oceania; South America.
Type of support: Equipment; Program development; Conferences/seminars; Publication; Seed money.
Limitations: Applications accepted. Giving on an international basis in Africa, Asia, Central and South America, the Caribbean, Eastern Europe, and the Pacific. No support for religious or political organizations, however programs these organizations develop which benefit the greater community of women and girls will be considered. No grants to individuals, or for scholarships, fellowships, staff salaries, building construction, or the purchase of land.
Publications: Application guidelines; Financial statement; Grants list; Informational brochure; Newsletter.
Application information: All applicants must first complete a letter of intent before being invented to complete full application. Application form required.
  Initial approach: Online letter of intent
  Copies of proposal: 1
  Deadline(s): Aug. 31 (letter of intent) Nov. 15 (full application)
  Board meeting date(s): Apr.
  Final notification: Late Apr.
Officers and Directors:* Eileen Menton,* Pres.; Dagmar McGill,* 1st V.P.; Marion Kilson,* 2nd V.P.; Terry Oudraadt,* 3rd V.P.; Karen McKee,* 4th V.P.; Judith Whitelock,* Secy.; Margery Sullivan,* Treas.; Fay Kittelson, Exec. Dir.; and 22 additional directors.
Number of staff: 1 full-time professional; 1 part-time professional.
EIN: 237068080

1414
Gimprich Family Foundation, Inc.
1 W. 4th St.
New York, NY 10012-1105 (212) 824-2208
Contact: Zelda Goldsmith, Exec. Admin.
URL: http://gimprichfamilyfoundation.org/

Established in 1975.
Donor: Marvin Gimprich‡.
Grantmaker type: Independent foundation.
Financial data (yr. ended 05/31/10): Assets, $5,675,909 (M); expenditures, $527,150; qualifying distributions, $527,150; giving activities include $366,100 for grants.
Purpose and activities: Giving primarily for Jewish projects and programs in Israel.
Fields of interest: Human services; Children/youth, services; Civil liberties, advocacy; Jewish agencies & synagogues.
International interests: Israel.
Type of support: Seed money.
Limitations: Applications accepted. Giving in the U.S. and internationally, primarily in Israel. No grants to individuals, or for building.
Application information: Application form required.

Initial approach: Letter
Copies of proposal: 1
Deadline(s): Jan. 1 and July 1
Final notification: Within 4 months
Officers: David M. Fishman, Pres.; Lila Gimprich d'Adolf, V.P.; Rosalie Dolmatch, Recording Secy.; Eric S. Wittstein, Treas.
Directors: Leora Fishman; Jeremy Nussbaum.
Number of staff: 1 part-time professional.
EIN: 510147095

1415
Givat Haviva Educational Foundation, Inc.
114 W. 26th St., Ste. 1001
New York, NY 10001-6812 (212) 989-9272
FAX: (212) 989-9840; E-mail: info@givathaviva.org;
URL: http://www.givathaviva.org

Established in 1949.
Grantmaker type: Public charity.
Financial data (yr. ended 12/31/09): Revenue, $721,506; assets, $2,095,675 (M); gifts received, $680,525; expenditures, $938,086; giving activities include $583,350 for grants to organizations outside the U.S.
Purpose and activities: Givat Haviva Educational Foundation is the American arm representing and supporting the Givat Haviva Institute. The foundation comprises a community of supporters and activist who work to increase awareness of Givat Haviva Institutes role in advancing awareness of Givat Haviva Institutes role in advancing Jewish-Arab relations in Israel.
Fields of interest: Education.
International interests: Israel.
Limitations: Applications not accepted. Giving limited to Israel.
Publications: Newsletter.
Application information: Contributes only to a pre-selected organization; unsolicited requests for funds not considered or acknowledged.
Officers and Board Members:* Michael Ben-Eli,* Chair.; Bruno Aron,* Vice-Chair.; Alex Rosenberg,* Vice-Chair.; Harold Shapiro,* Vice-Chair.; Jo Margolis,* Treas.; Judith Scheuer,* Secy.; Bishara Bahbah; Rachel Oestreicher Bernheim; Joan Bronk; Dan Fleshler; Mort Gerber; Jesse Greenberg; Murray Koppelman; and 15 additional board members.
EIN: 132584337

1416
The GK Foundation
P.O. Box 748120
Rego Park, NY 11374-8120 (718) 897-6500
Contact: David Kuppermann, Tr.

Established in 1987 in NY.
Donors: David Kuppermann; Pola Kuppermann.
Grantmaker type: Independent foundation.
Financial data (yr. ended 11/30/10): Assets, $104,999 (M); expenditures, $502,170; qualifying distributions, $500,000; giving activities include $500,000 for 1 grant.
Fields of interest: Jewish agencies & synagogues; Hospitals (general); Pediatrics.
International interests: Israel.
Limitations: Applications accepted. Giving primarily in New York, NY.
Application information: Application form required.
  Initial approach: Brief resume
  Deadline(s): None

Trustees: Jay Fenster; David Kuppermann; Pola Kuppermann; Salo Mandelbaum; Simeon Zoimen.
EIN: 136892493

1417
The Global Business Coalition on HIV/AIDS, Tuberculosis, and Malaria
110 William St.
New York, NY 10038-3901 (212) 584-1600
FAX: (212) 584-1699; URL: http://www.gbcimpact.org
Facebook: http://www.facebook.com/pages/Global-Business-Coalition-on-HIVAIDS-Tuberculosis-and-Malaria/343501615054
LinkedIn: http://www.linkedin.com/groups?homeNewMember=&gid=844637
Twitter: http://twitter.com/GBCNews
YouTube: http://www.youtube.com/businesshealthaction

Established in 2001 in DE.
Grantmaker type: Public charity.
Financial data (yr. ended 12/31/10): Revenue, $7,088,478; assets, $3,255,932 (M); gifts received, $4,347,569; expenditures, $7,901,848; giving activities include $21,119 for grants.
Purpose and activities: The coalition's mission is to harness the power of the global business community to end the HIV/AIDS, tuberculosis, and malaria epidemics.
Fields of interest: Tropical diseases; Public health, communicable diseases; AIDS; International relief.
Limitations: Giving primarily to DC; New York, NY; and internationally.
Officers and Directors:* Muhtar Kent, Co-Chair.; Sir Mark Moody Stuart, Co-Chair.; John Tedstrom,* Pres. and C.E.O.; Gilles Pelisson; Malva Rabinowitz; Peter Sands.
EIN: 134185520

1418
Global Jewish Assistance and Relief Network
511 Ave. of the Americas, Ste. 18
New York, NY 10011-8436 (212) 868-3636
FAX: (212) 868-7878; E-mail: info@gjarn.org;
Additional address: 1485 Union St., Brooklyn, NY 11213-4447; URL: http://www.globaljewish.org/

Established in 1992 in NY.
Grantmaker type: Public charity.
Financial data (yr. ended 12/31/10): Revenue, $639,747; assets, $221,525 (M); gifts received, $639,747; expenditures, $720,089; giving activities include $342,418 for 5 grants to organizations outside the U.S., and $36,681 for grants to individuals.
Purpose and activities: The network works to provide non-sectarian humanitarian assistance and medical relief throughout the former Soviet Union, with a focus on Russia and Ukraine, as well as in Israel and the U.S.
Fields of interest: Food services; Health care; Human services; Human services, emergency aid.
International interests: Israel; Russia; Soviet Union (Former); Ukraine.
Type of support: In-kind gifts.
Limitations: Giving primarily to the former Soviet Union, particularly to Russia and Ukraine, and to Israel.

Officers: Rabbi Eliezer Avtzon, Pres.; Shneur Z. Baumgarten, Secy.; Eli Tiefrenbrun, Treas.
EIN: 113095240

1419
Global Youth Action Network, Inc.
540 President St. Fl. 3
Brooklyn, NY 11215-1439 (212) 661-6111
FAX: (212) 661-1933; E-mail: gyan@youthlink.org;
URL: http://www.youthlink.org

Established in 1996 in NY.
Grantmaker type: Public charity.
Financial data (yr. ended 11/30/10): Revenue, $503,941; assets, $203,138 (M); gifts received, $503,219; expenditures, $472,445; giving activities include $139,553 for grants to organizations outside the U.S.
Purpose and activities: The network works to facilitate youth participation and intergenerational partnership in global decision-making, support collaboration among diverse youth organizations, and provide tools, resources, and recognition for positive youth action.
Fields of interest: AIDS; Youth development, alliance/advocacy; Youth development, equal rights; Youth development, information services; Youth development; International affairs, goodwill promotion; International affairs.
Limitations: Giving on a national and international basis.
Officer: Franziska Seel, Exec. Dir.
Directors: Carole V. Aciman; Michael Butler; Michael Furdyk; Benjamin Quinto.
EIN: 200479950

1420
Glyndebourne Association America, Inc.
c/o M. Waldstein, McLaughlin & Stern LLP
260 Madison Ave., 19th Fl.
New York, NY 10016-2401

Established in 1971 in NY.
Donors: Robert Montgomery Scott Androssan; Dianne Biennes; Michael Biennes; John Botts; Paul J. Collins; Robert M. Conway; Emily Fletcher; Gordon P. Getty; Mrs. Gordon P. Getty; Carol Colburn Hogel; Paul Saldato; Irmwin Schneiderman; Jayne Wrightsman; Edgar Foster Daniels Foundation; Leonard & Evelyn Lauder Foundation; William C. & Cindy L. Scott Foundation.
Grantmaker type: Independent foundation.
Financial data (yr. ended 12/31/10): Assets, $849,581 (M); gifts received, $666,519; expenditures, $315,343; qualifying distributions, $300,769; giving activities include $281,212 for 1 grant.
Fields of interest: Performing arts, opera; Arts.
International interests: United Kingdom.
Limitations: Applications not accepted. Giving primarily in the United Kingdom. No grants to individuals.
Application information: Contributes only to pre-selected organizations.
Officers: Michael Lynch, Chair.; Mark Waldstein, Treas.
Directors: Henry Astor; John Botts; Robert M. Conway; Mark Flannery; Agustus Christie Glyndebourne Lewes.
EIN: 237174079

1421
The Goldie Anna Charitable Trust
c/o Kenneth L. Stein
5 Woods Witch Ln.
Chappaqua, NY 10514-1223

Established about 1977 in NY.
Grantmaker type: Independent foundation.
Financial data (yr. ended 12/31/10): Assets, $24,726,799 (M); expenditures, $1,280,578; qualifying distributions, $1,086,603; giving activities include $1,086,603 for grants.
Purpose and activities: Emphasis on higher education, including some support in Israel, medical research, hospitals, Jewish giving, cultural organizations, and the elderly and disadvantaged.
Fields of interest: Education; Arts; Higher education; Health organizations; Human services; Jewish agencies & synagogues; Economically disadvantaged.
International interests: Israel.
Limitations: Applications not accepted. Giving primarily in the metropolitan New York, NY, area.
Application information: Contributes only to pre-selected organizations. Unsolicited requests for funds not accepted.
Trustees: Jean Greenfield; Kenneth L. Stein; Nancy C. Stein.
EIN: 132897474

1422
Joyce and Irving Goldman Family Foundation
(formerly Irving Goldman Foundation, Inc.)
417 5th Ave., Ste. 400
New York, NY 10016-2239 (212) 624-4300
Contact: Sarah E. Meyer, Exec. Dir.
E-mail: jigff@jigff.org

Established in 1984 in NY.
Donors: Goldman Children Trust; Goldman Grandchildren Trust.
Grantmaker type: Independent foundation.
Financial data (yr. ended 12/31/09): Assets, $155,514,301 (M); gifts received, $5,135,712; expenditures, $8,678,294; qualifying distributions, $7,889,719; giving activities include $7,754,640 for 140 grants (high: $1,000,000; low: $1,000).
Purpose and activities: Grants are made in the following three issue areas: Jewish life, medical education and community health in Israel's Negev region, and breast cancer cure/eradication.
Fields of interest: Cancer; Medical school/education; Jewish agencies & synagogues.
Type of support: General/operating support; Continuing support; Program development; Conferences/seminars; Seed money; Research; Program evaluation.
Limitations: Applications accepted. Giving primarily in Israel and the U.S., with special emphasis on NY. No grants to individuals, or for capital requests.
Application information: Consideration for support is primarily through invitation to organizations working in the foundation's areas of interest. Unsolicited letters of inquiry are reviewed; unsolicited proposals are discouraged and should not be submitted unless by invitation from foundation staff. Application form not required.
Initial approach: Letter of inquiry
Copies of proposal: 1
Deadline(s): None

Board meeting date(s): Ongoing
Final notification: Acknowledgment of application immediately; decision within 3-9 months
Officers and Director: Dorian Goldman,* Pres.; Lloyd Goldman, Secy.; Katja Goldman, Treas.; Sarah E. Meyer, Exec. Dir.
Number of staff: 1 full-time professional.
EIN: 133216152
Recent grants for international programs:
1422-1 American Associates, Ben-Gurion University of the Negev, New York, NY, $1,000,000. For project support. 2009.
1422-2 American Associates, Ben-Gurion University of the Negev, New York, NY, $36,000. For event support. 2009.
1422-3 American Associates, Ben-Gurion University of the Negev, New York, NY, $25,000. For project support. 2009.
1422-4 American Associates, Ben-Gurion University of the Negev, New York, NY, $10,000. For general operating support. 2009.
1422-5 American Friends of Yahad in Unum, Chappaqua, NY, $22,500. For general operating support. 2009.
1422-6 American Jewish Joint Distribution Committee, New York, NY, $50,000. For general operating support of Agahozo Shalom Youth Village. 2009.
1422-7 American Jewish Joint Distribution Committee, New York, NY, $10,000. For project support of Fredrick Brenner Project. 2009.
1422-8 American Jewish Joint Distribution Committee, New York, NY, $10,000. For project support of Fredrick Brenner Project. 2009.
1422-9 American Jewish World Service, New York, NY, $50,000. For project support. 2009.
1422-10 American Jewish World Service, New York, NY, $10,000. For general operating support. 2009.
1422-11 Ben-Gurion University of the Negev, Beer Sheva, Israel, $350,000. For project support. 2009.
1422-12 Conservation International, Arlington, VA, $25,000. For event support. 2009.
1422-13 Education for Employment Foundation, Washington, DC, $10,000. For general operating support. 2009.
1422-14 Israel Policy Forum, New York, NY, $10,000. For general operating support. 2009.
1422-15 Kivunim, New Directions, New York, NY, $25,000. For general operating support. 2009.
1422-16 Kivunim, New Directions, New York, NY, $25,000. For general operating support. 2009.
1422-17 Miriam Weiner Routes to Roots Foundation, Secaucus, NJ, $10,000. For general operating support. 2009.
1422-18 Nature Conservancy, Arlington, VA, $10,000. For general operating support. 2009.
1422-19 Negev Institute for Strategies of Peace and Development, Beer Sheva, Israel, $10,000. For general operating support. 2009.
1422-20 New Israel Fund, Washington, DC, $15,000. For general operating support. 2009.
1422-21 Synergos Institute, New York, NY, $50,000. For general operating support. 2009.
1422-22 Synergos Institute, New York, NY, $25,000. For general operating support. 2009.

1423
The Goldman Sachs Foundation

(formerly Goldman Sachs Charitable Fund)
200 W. St., 29th FL
New York, NY 10282-2198 (212) 902-3246
Contact: Brenda Lee, Grants Admin.
E-mail: gsfoundation@gs.com; E-mail for 10,000 Small Businesses: 10000SmallBusinesses@gs.com; URL: http://www2.goldmansachs.com/s/esg/HTML1/goldman_sachs-esg_report2010_0022.htm

Established in 1999 in NY.
Donors: Goldman, Sachs & Co.; MTGLQ Investors, L.P.; Goldman Sachs Group, Inc.
Grantmaker type: Company-sponsored foundation.
Financial data (yr. ended 12/31/09): Assets, $523,450,062 (M); gifts received, $318,736,000; expenditures, $39,101,775; qualifying distributions, $36,501,916; giving activities include $24,959,546 for 111 grants (high: $2,750,000; low: $2,280), $441,000 for 72 grants to individuals (high: $10,000; low: $5,000), and $10,629,398 for 9,723 employee matching gifts.
Purpose and activities: The foundation supports strategic programs that include 10,000 Women and 10,000 Small Businesses.
Fields of interest: Community development, small businesses; Community/economic development; Education.
International interests: Africa; Asia; Europe; Middle East; United Kingdom.
Type of support: Continuing support; Program development.
Limitations: Applications not accepted. Giving on a national and international basis primarily in areas of company operations in Asia, Africa, the Middle East, and the United Kingdom. No support for political causes, campaigns, or candidates. No grants for political fundraising events.
Publications: Informational brochure.
Application information: Contributes only to pre-selected organizations and individuals.
Officers and Directors: John F.W. Rogers,* Chair.; Dina H. Powell, Pres.; Peter M. Fahey,* V.P.; Robert J. Katz,* V.P.; Eileen M. Dillion; Lisa D. Hancock; Katherine Jollon; Matthew LoCurto; Noa Meyer; Beverly L. O'Toole; Benjamin J. Radar; Emmett St. John.
EIN: 311678646
Recent grants for international programs:
1423-1 Acumen Fund, New York, NY, $51,077. For Acumen Fund Fellows Programs in partnership with 10,000 Women, which is a five-year initiative to provide a business and management education to underserved female entrepreneurs in developing and emerging markets. The program is designed to drive greater shared economic growth, leading to stronger healthcare, education and greater prosperity in the communities where it operates. 2009.
1423-2 Acumen Fund, New York, NY, $50,000. For Acumen Fund Fellows Programs in partnership with 10,000 Women, which is a five-year initiative to provide a business and management education to underserved female entrepreneurs in developing and emerging markets. The program is designed to drive greater shared economic growth, leading to stronger healthcare, education and greater prosperity in the communities where it operates. 2009.
1423-3 Acumen Fund, New York, NY, $50,000. For Acumen Fund Fellows Programs in partnership with 10,000 Women, which is a five-year initiative

to provide a business and management education to underserved female entrepreneurs in developing and emerging markets. The program is designed to drive greater shared economic growth, leading to stronger healthcare, education and greater prosperity in the communities where it operates. 2009.
1423-4 Africa-America Institute, New York, NY, $329,417. For 10,000 Women initiative in partnership with United States International University in Nairobi Kenya. 10,000 Women is a five-year initiative to provide a business and management education to underserved female entrepreneurs in developing and emerging markets. The program is designed to drive greater shared economic growth, leading to stronger healthcare, education and greater prosperity in the communities where it operates. 2009.
1423-5 Africa-America Institute, New York, NY, $219,611. For 10,000 Women initiative in partnership with United States International University in Nairobi Kenya. 10,000 Women is a five-year initiative to provide a business and management education to underserved female entrepreneurs in developing and emerging markets. The program is designed to drive greater shared economic growth, leading to stronger healthcare, education and greater prosperity in the communities where it operates. 2009.
1423-6 Africa-America Institute, New York, NY, $46,000. For 10,000 Women at the Enterprise Development Services of the Pan African University in Lagos Nigeria. 10,000 Women is a five-year initiative to provide a business and management education to underserved female entrepreneurs in developing and emerging markets. The program is designed to drive greater shared economic growth, leading to stronger healthcare, education and greater prosperity in the communities where it operates. 2009.
1423-7 Africa-America Institute, New York, NY, $19,404. For 10,000 Women initiative in partnership with the University of Dar es Salaam with Women for Women International. 10,000 Women is a five-year initiative to provide a business and management education to underserved female entrepreneurs in developing and emerging markets. The program is designed to drive greater shared economic growth, leading to stronger healthcare, education and greater prosperity in the communities where it operates. 2009.
1423-8 Akanksha Foundation, Mumbai, India, $264,000. To implement Teach for India program. 2009.
1423-9 American University in Cairo, New York, NY, $566,850. For 10,000 Women initiative, five-year project to provide a business and management education to underserved female entrepreneurs in developing and emerging markets. The program is designed to drive greater shared economic growth, leading to stronger healthcare, education and greater prosperity in the communities where it operates. 2009.
1423-10 American University in Cairo, New York, NY, $147,758. For 10,000 Women initiative, five-year project to provide a business and management education to underserved female entrepreneurs in developing and emerging markets. The program is designed to drive

greater shared economic growth, leading to stronger healthcare, education and greater prosperity in the communities where it operates. 2009.

1423-11 Ashoka: Innovators for the Public, Arlington, VA, $300,000. To help launch inaugural program in the United Kingdom and expand newly established program in France and Germany by supporting dynamic social entrepreneurs in the field of education and youth development. 2009.

1423-12 Ashoka: Innovators for the Public, Arlington, VA, $25,000. For partnership with the 10,000 Women initiative, five-year initiative to provide a business and management education to underserved female entrepreneurs in developing and emerging markets. The program is designed to drive greater shared economic growth, leading to stronger healthcare, education and greater prosperity in the communities where it operates. 2009.

1423-13 Ashoka: Innovators for the Public, Arlington, VA, $25,000. For partnership with the 10,000 Women initiative, five-year initiative to provide a business and management education to underserved female entrepreneurs in developing and emerging markets. The program is designed to drive greater shared economic growth, leading to stronger healthcare, education and greater prosperity in the communities where it operates. 2009.

1423-14 Asian University for Women Support Foundation, Cambridge, MA, $650,000. For Access Program which recruits and cultivates high-potential secondary school graduates from disadvantaged backgrounds across Asia. 2009.

1423-15 Association Promotion des Talents, Paris, France, $50,000. To support success of high-potential youth from disadvantaged backgrounds at selective institutions of higher education so they may pursue top careers in France. 2009.

1423-16 Brown University, Providence, RI, $11,610. For 10,000 Women initiative in partnership with the University of Cape Town. 10,000 Women is a five-year initiative to provide a business and management education to underserved female entrepreneurs in developing and emerging markets. The program is designed to drive greater shared economic growth, leading to stronger healthcare, education and greater prosperity in the communities where it operates. 2009.

1423-17 Cambridge in America, New York, NY, $200,000. To support innovative college preparatory program developed at Cambridge University, providing mathematics enrichment for high-potential students from disadvantaged backgrounds. 2009.

1423-18 Camfed USA Foundation, San Francisco, CA, $654,173. For 10,000 Women initiative in Zambia. 10,000 Women is a five-year initiative to provide a business and management education to underserved female entrepreneurs in developing and emerging markets. The program is designed to drive greater shared economic growth, leading to stronger healthcare, education and greater prosperity in the communities where it operates. 2009.

1423-19 Camfed USA Foundation, San Francisco, CA, $519,027. For 10,000 Women initiative in Zambia. 10,000 Women is a five-year initiative to provide a business and management education to underserved female entrepreneurs in

developing and emerging markets. The program is designed to drive greater shared economic growth, leading to stronger healthcare, education and greater prosperity in the communities where it operates. 2009.

1423-20 CHF International, Silver Spring, MD, $180,298. To create and implement 10,000 Women Certificate Program for Women Entrepreneurs in collaboration with Cuttington University in Suakoko, Liberia. 10,000 Women is a five-year initiative to provide a business and management education to underserved female entrepreneurs in developing and emerging markets. The program is designed to drive greater shared economic growth, leading to stronger healthcare, education and greater prosperity in the communities where it operates. 2009.

1423-21 Columbia University, Graduate School of Business, New York, NY, $342,500. For 10,000 Women initiative partnership with United States International University in Nairobi and University of Dar es Salaam in Tanzania. 10,000 Women is a five-year initiative to provide a business and management education to underserved female entrepreneurs in developing and emerging markets. The program is designed to drive greater shared economic growth, leading to stronger healthcare, education and greater prosperity in the communities where it operates. 2009.

1423-22 Ecole des Hautes Etudes Commerciales de Paris, Jouy-en-Josas, France, $150,000. For 10,000 Women initiative in partnership with the Tsinghua School of Management in China. 10,000 Women is a five-year initiative to provide a business and management education to underserved female entrepreneurs in developing and emerging markets. The program is designed to drive greater shared economic growth, leading to stronger healthcare, education and greater prosperity in the communities where it operates. 2009.

1423-23 Ecole des Hautes Etudes Commerciales de Paris, Jouy-en-Josas, France, $150,000. For 10,000 Women initiative in partnership with the Tsinghua School of Management in China. 10,000 Women is a five-year initiative to provide a business and management education to underserved female entrepreneurs in developing and emerging markets. The program is designed to drive greater shared economic growth, leading to stronger healthcare, education and greater prosperity in the communities where it operates. 2009.

1423-24 Financial Services Volunteer Corps, New York, NY, $21,074. For 10,000 Women initiative in partnership with American University in Cairo. 10,000 Women is a five-year initiative to provide a business and management education to underserved female entrepreneurs in developing and emerging markets. The program is designed to drive greater shared economic growth, leading to stronger healthcare, education and greater prosperity in the communities where it operates. 2009.

1423-25 Foreign Policy Association, New York, NY, $15,000. For Great Decision in the Classroom, program which engages secondary teachers and assists them in bringing awareness of foreign policy issues to the classroom. 2009.

1423-26 Friends of Tsinghua School of Economics and Management, Beijing, China, $227,700. For 10,000 Women initiative in China, five-year

initiative to provide a business and management education to underserved female entrepreneurs in developing and emerging markets. The program is designed to drive greater shared economic growth, leading to stronger healthcare, education and greater prosperity in the communities where it operates. 2009.

1423-27 Friends of Tsinghua School of Economics and Management, Beijing, China, $151,800. For 10,000 Women initiative in China. 10,000 Women is a five-year initiative to provide a business and management education to underserved female entrepreneurs in developing and emerging markets. The program is designed to drive greater shared economic growth, leading to stronger healthcare, education and greater prosperity in the communities where it operates. 2009.

1423-28 Gemeinnutzige Hertie-Stiftung, Frankfurt, Germany, $350,000. For START scholarship program for talented immigrant youth in Germany. 2009.

1423-29 Georgetown University, Center for Child and Human Development, Washington, DC, $37,500. For work of U.S. Afghan Women's Council, a 10,000 Women partner. 10,000 Women is a five-year initiative to provide a business and management education to underserved female entrepreneurs in developing and emerging markets. The program is designed to drive greater shared economic growth, leading to stronger healthcare, education and greater prosperity in the communities where it operates. 2009.

1423-30 Hispanic Scholarship Fund, San Francisco, CA, $175,000. For 10,000 Women Business Leadership Award. 10,000 Women is a five-year initiative to provide a business and management education to underserved female entrepreneurs in developing and emerging markets. The program is designed to drive greater shared economic growth, leading to stronger healthcare, education and greater prosperity in the communities where it operates. 2009.

1423-31 Indian School of Business, Hyderabad, India, $483,789. For 10,000 Women initiative in India. 10,000 Women is a five-year initiative to provide a business and management education to underserved female entrepreneurs in developing and emerging markets. The program is designed to drive greater shared economic growth, leading to stronger healthcare, education and greater prosperity in the communities where it operates. 2009.

1423-32 Indian School of Business, Hyderabad, India, $291,000. For 10,000 Women initiative in India. 10,000 Women is a five-year initiative to provide a business and management education to underserved female entrepreneurs in developing and emerging markets. The program is designed to drive greater shared economic growth, leading to stronger healthcare, education and greater prosperity in the communities where it operates. 2009.

1423-33 Institute of International Education, New York, NY, $581,225. For 10,000 Women initiative partnership with IIE who will partner with Fundacao Dom Cabral in Brazil. 10,000 Women is a five-year initiative to provide a business and management education to underserved female entrepreneurs in developing and emerging markets. The program is designed to drive greater shared economic growth, leading to stronger healthcare, education and greater prosperity in the communities where it operates. 2009.

1423-34 Institute of International Education, New York, NY, $66,491. For 10,000 Women initiative in partnership with Keio University in Japan. 10,000 Women is a five-year initiative to provide a business and management education to underserved female entrepreneurs in developing and emerging markets. The program is designed to drive greater shared economic growth, leading to stronger healthcare, education and greater prosperity in the communities where it operates. 2009.

1423-35 Instituto de Empresa Fund, Lawrence, NY, $380,905. For 10,000 Women initiative in Spain in partnership with Fundacao Getulio Vargas (FGV) Escole de Administracao de Empresas de Sao Paulo (EAESP) in Brazil. 10,000 Women is a five-year initiative to provide a business and management education to underserved female entrepreneurs in developing and emerging markets. The program is designed to drive greater shared economic growth, leading to stronger healthcare, education and greater prosperity in the communities where it operates. 2009.

1423-36 International Center for Research on Women, Washington, DC, $48,839. For research in connection with 10,000 Women initiative. 10,000 Women is a five-year initiative to provide a business and management education to underserved female entrepreneurs in developing and emerging markets. The program is designed to drive greater shared economic growth, leading to stronger healthcare, education and greater prosperity in the communities where it operates. 2009.

1423-37 International Center for Research on Women, Washington, DC, $48,839. For research in connection with 10,000 Women initiative. 10,000 Women is a five-year initiative to provide a business and management education to underserved female entrepreneurs in developing and emerging markets. The program is designed to drive greater shared economic growth, leading to stronger healthcare, education and greater prosperity in the communities where it operates. 2009.

1423-38 Keio University, Graduate School of Media Design, Tokyo, Japan, $193,405. For 10,000 Women initiative, five-year initiative to provide a business and management education to underserved female entrepreneurs in developing and emerging markets. The program is designed to drive greater shared economic growth, leading to stronger healthcare, education and greater prosperity in the communities where it operates. 2009.

1423-39 LASPAU: Academic and Professional Programs for the Americas, Cambridge, MA, $326,800. For 10,000 Women initiative at Tecnologico de Monterrey. 10,000 Women is a five-year initiative to provide a business and management education to underserved female entrepreneurs in developing and emerging markets. The program is designed to drive greater shared economic growth, leading to stronger healthcare, education and greater prosperity in the communities where it operates. 2009.

1423-40 LASPAU: Academic and Professional Programs for the Americas, Cambridge, MA, $326,800. For 10,000 Women initiative at Tecnologico de Monterrey. 10,000 Women is a

five-year initiative to provide a business and management education to underserved female entrepreneurs in developing and emerging markets. The program is designed to drive greater shared economic growth, leading to stronger healthcare, education and greater prosperity in the communities where it operates. 2009.

1423-41 LASPAU: Academic and Professional Programs for the Americas, Cambridge, MA, $30,500. For 10,000 Women initiative at Tecnologico de Monterrey. 10,000 Women is a five-year initiative to provide a business and management education to underserved female entrepreneurs in developing and emerging markets. The program is designed to drive greater shared economic growth, leading to stronger healthcare, education and greater prosperity in the communities where it operates. 2009.

1423-42 London School of Economics and Political Science, London, England, $87,500. For CHOICE program which develops academic and leadership skills of talented secondary school students preparing them for admission and success in highly selective colleges and universities. 2009.

1423-43 Management Leadership for Tomorrow, New York, NY, $175,000. For Goldman Sachs Scholars Alumni Program and pilot partnership with 10,000 Women program at Mills College. 10,000 Women is a five-year initiative to provide a business and management education to underserved female entrepreneurs in developing and emerging markets. The program is designed to drive greater shared economic growth, leading to stronger healthcare, education and greater prosperity in the communities where it operates. 2009.

1423-44 Middle East Media Research Institute, Washington, DC, $10,000. For The Reform Project, which monitors advocates of reform in the Arab and Muslim world and the obstacles that they face in advancing their cause. Goal of this project is to provide reformists with a platform from which they can reach out to their societies and to religious, political, and educational leaders while also providing Western policy makers with a solid basis for long-term strategic plans aimed at supporting this effort. 2009.

1423-45 Mills College, Oakland, CA, $300,000. For 10,000 Women Scholarship Program. 10,000 Women is a five-year initiative to provide a business and management education to underserved female entrepreneurs in developing and emerging markets. The program is designed to drive greater shared economic growth, leading to stronger healthcare, education and greater prosperity in the communities where it operates. 2009.

1423-46 Network for Teaching Entrepreneurship, New York, NY, $500,000. To expand and enhance entrepreneurial education initiatives in Germany and China and to support Youth Entrepreneur Expo and Global Young Entrepreneurs Of the Year Awards. 2009.

1423-47 Opportunity International, Oak Brook, IL, $220,194. For 10,000 Women initiative in Kenya. 10,000 Women is a five-year initiative to provide a business and management education to underserved female entrepreneurs in developing and emerging markets. The program is designed to drive greater shared economic growth, leading to stronger healthcare, education

and greater prosperity in the communities where it operates. 2009.

1423-48 Oxford University, Said Business School, Oxford, England, $387,250. For Zhejiang University 10,000 Women Entrepreneurship Certificate Program. 10,000 Women is a five-year initiative to provide a business and management education to underserved female entrepreneurs in developing and emerging markets. The program is designed to drive greater shared economic growth, leading to stronger healthcare, education and greater prosperity in the communities where it operates. 2009.

1423-49 Ozyegin University, Center for Entrepreneurship, Istanbul, Turkey, $354,467. For Goldman Sachs 10,000 Women initiative in Turkey. 10,000 Women is a five-year initiative to provide a business and management education to underserved female entrepreneurs in developing and emerging markets. The program is designed to drive greater shared economic growth, leading to stronger healthcare, education and greater prosperity in the communities where it operates. 2009.

1423-50 Pan-African University, Lagos, Nigeria, $571,935. For 10,000 Women initiative in Nigeria and Liberia. 10,000 Women is a five-year initiative to provide a business and management education to underserved female entrepreneurs in developing and emerging markets. The program is designed to drive greater shared economic growth, leading to stronger healthcare, education and greater prosperity in the communities where it operates. 2009.

1423-51 Pan-African University, Lagos, Nigeria, $245,115. For 10,000 Women initiative in Nigeria and Liberia. 10,000 Women is a five-year initiative to provide a business and management education to underserved female entrepreneurs in developing and emerging markets. The program is designed to drive greater shared economic growth, leading to stronger healthcare, education and greater prosperity in the communities where it operates. 2009.

1423-52 Stanford University, Graduate School of Business, Stanford, CA, $200,000. For 10,000 Women initiative, five-year initiative to provide a business and management education to underserved female entrepreneurs in developing and emerging markets. The program is designed to drive greater shared economic growth, leading to stronger healthcare, education and greater prosperity in the communities where it operates. 2009.

1423-53 TechnoServe, Washington, DC, $52,371. For 10,000 Women initiative, five-year initiative to provide a business and management education to underserved female entrepreneurs in developing and emerging markets. The program is designed to drive greater shared economic growth, leading to stronger healthcare, education and greater prosperity in the communities where it operates. 2009.

1423-54 Thunderbird, The Garvin School of International Management, Glendale, AZ, $309,402. For 10,000 Women initiative in Afghanistan. 10,000 Women is a five-year initiative to provide a business and management education to underserved female entrepreneurs in developing and emerging markets. The program is designed to drive greater shared economic growth, leading to stronger healthcare, education and greater prosperity in the communities where it operates. 2009.

1423-55 Thunderbird, The Garvin School of International Management, Glendale, AZ, $215,389. For 10,000 Women initiative in Afghanistan. 10,000 Women is a five-year initiative to provide a business and management education to underserved female entrepreneurs in developing and emerging markets. The program is designed to drive greater shared economic growth, leading to stronger healthcare, education and greater prosperity in the communities where it operates. 2009.

1423-56 United Negro College Fund, Fairfax, VA, $170,050. To create and implement Goldman Sachs 10,000 Women Business Leadership Award Program. 10,000 Women is a five-year initiative to provide a business and management education to underserved female entrepreneurs in developing and emerging markets. The program is designed to drive greater shared economic growth, leading to stronger healthcare, education and greater prosperity in the communities where it operates. 2009.

1423-57 Universidad de Navarra IESE Business School, Barcelona, Spain, $357,500. For 10,000 Women initiative collaboration with the University of Asia and Pacific Foundation (UAP). 10,000 Women is a five-year initiative to provide a business and management education to underserved female entrepreneurs in developing and emerging markets. The program is designed to drive greater shared economic growth, leading to stronger healthcare, education and greater prosperity in the communities where it operates. 2009.

1423-58 Universidad de Navarra IESE Business School, Barcelona, Spain, $357,500. For 10,000 Women initiative collaboration with the University of Asia and Pacific Foundation (UAP). 10,000 Women is a five-year initiative to provide a business and management education to underserved female entrepreneurs in developing and emerging markets. The program is designed to drive greater shared economic growth, leading to stronger healthcare, education and greater prosperity in the communities where it operates. 2009.

1423-59 University of Cape Town Fund, New York, NY, $141,325. For 10,000 Women initiative at University of Cape Town (UCT). 10,000 Women is a five-year initiative to provide a business and management education to underserved female entrepreneurs in developing and emerging markets. The program is designed to drive greater shared economic growth, leading to stronger healthcare, education and greater prosperity in the communities where it operates. 2009.

1423-60 University of Pennsylvania, Wharton School of Business, Philadelphia, PA, $300,000. For services in connection with creation, development and operation of Program Portal for 10,000 Women Initiative. 10,000 Women is a five-year initiative to provide a business and management education to underserved female entrepreneurs in developing and emerging markets. The program is designed to drive greater shared economic growth, leading to stronger healthcare, education and greater prosperity in the communities where it operates. 2009.

1423-61 University of Pennsylvania, Wharton School of Business, Philadelphia, PA, $250,000. For 10,000 Women initiative in partnership with American University in Cairo. 10,000 Women is

a five-year initiative to provide a business and management education to underserved female entrepreneurs in developing and emerging markets. The program is designed to drive greater shared economic growth, leading to stronger healthcare, education and greater prosperity in the communities where it operates. 2009.

1423-62 University of Pennsylvania, Wharton School of Business, Philadelphia, PA, $100,000. For services in connection with creation, development and operation of Program Portal for 10,000 Women Initiative. 10,000 Women is a five-year initiative to provide a business and management education to underserved female entrepreneurs in developing and emerging markets. The program is designed to drive greater shared economic growth, leading to stronger healthcare, education and greater prosperity in the communities where it operates. 2009.

1423-63 University of Pennsylvania, Wharton School of Business, Philadelphia, PA, $96,000. To develop case study of Brazil involvement of 10,000 Women initiative Case Study Development. 2009.

1423-64 University of Pennsylvania, Wharton School of Business, Philadelphia, PA, $60,000. For services in connection with creation, development and operation of Program Portal for 10,000 Women Initiative. 10,000 Women is a five-year initiative to provide a business and management education to underserved female entrepreneurs in developing and emerging markets. The program is designed to drive greater shared economic growth, leading to stronger healthcare, education and greater prosperity in the communities where it operates. 2009.

1423-65 Vital Voices Global Partnership, Washington, DC, $102,763. For 10,000 Women initiative, five-year initiative to provide a business and management education to underserved female entrepreneurs in developing and emerging markets. The program is designed to drive greater shared economic growth, leading to stronger healthcare, education and greater prosperity in the communities where it operates. 2009.

1423-66 Vital Voices Global Partnership, Washington, DC, $102,763. For 10,000 Women initiative, five-year initiative to provide a business and management education to underserved female entrepreneurs in developing and emerging markets. The program is designed to drive greater shared economic growth, leading to stronger healthcare, education and greater prosperity in the communities where it operates. 2009.

1423-67 William Davidson Institute at the University of Michigan School of Business, Ann Arbor, MI, $385,953. For 10,000 Women initiative in partnership with School of Finance and Banking in Rwanda. 10,000 Women is a five-year initiative to provide a business and management education to underserved female entrepreneurs in developing and emerging markets. The program is designed to drive greater shared economic growth, leading to stronger healthcare, education and greater prosperity in the communities where it operates. 2009.

1423-68 Women for Women International, Washington, DC, $59,173. For 10,000 Women Certificate Program for Women Entrepreneurs in

collaboration with University of Dar es Salaam. 2009.

1423-69 Yale University, School of Public Health, New Haven, CT, $516,612. For Yale-Tsinghua Certificate Program in International Healthcare Management, collaboration with Tsinghua University and part of 10,000 Women, five-year initiative to provide a business and management education to underserved female entrepreneurs in developing and emerging markets. The program is designed to drive greater shared economic growth, leading to stronger healthcare, education and greater prosperity in the communities where it operates. 2009.

1423-70 Yale University, School of Public Health, New Haven, CT, $516,612. For Yale-Tsinghua Certificate Program in International Healthcare Management, collaboration with Tsinghua University and part of 10,000 Women, five-year initiative to provide a business and management education to underserved female entrepreneurs in developing and emerging markets. The program is designed to drive greater shared economic growth, leading to stronger healthcare, education and greater prosperity in the communities where it operates. 2009.

1424
Horace W. Goldsmith Foundation
375 Park Ave., Ste. 1602
New York, NY 10152-1600
Contact: William A. Slaughter, C.E.O.
E-mail for William A Slaughter:
Slaughter@ballardspahr.com

Incorporated in 1955 in NY.
Donor: Horace W. Goldsmith‡.
Grantmaker type: Independent foundation.
Financial data (yr. ended 12/31/10): Assets, $385,953,190 (M); expenditures, $23,218,605; qualifying distributions, $18,014,991; giving activities include $17,460,666 for 219 grants (high: $750,000; low: $5,000).
Purpose and activities: Support for cultural programs, including the performing arts and museums; Jewish and Israeli charitable organizations; hospitals and other health care organizations; and education, especially higher education.
International interests: Israel.
Type of support: Building/renovation; Scholarship funds.
Limitations: Applications not accepted. Giving primarily in NY and PA. No grants to individuals.
Application information: Unsolicited applications are not accepted; foundation grants are internally initiated.
   Board meeting date(s): 4 times a year
Officers and Managing Directors:* William A. Slaughter,* C.E.O.; Charles L. Slaughter,* C.F.O.; Thomas R. Slaughter; R. James Slaughter.
Number of staff: 1 full-time support.
EIN: 136107758
Recent grants for international programs:
1424-1 Albert B. Sabin Vaccine Institute, Washington, DC, $200,000. 2009.
1424-2 American Friends of the Israel Museum, New York, NY, $500,000. 2009.
1424-3 American School of Classical Studies at Athens, Princeton, NJ, $25,000. 2009.
1424-4 Capoeira Foundation, New York, NY, $25,000. 2009.

1424-5 Casey House Foundation, Toronto, Canada, $25,000. 2009.

1424-6 ELEM Youth in Distress, New York, NY, $350,000. 2009.

1424-7 Freedom from Hunger, Davis, CA, $20,000. 2009.

1424-8 Israel Center for Excellence Through Education, Chicago, IL, $25,000. 2009.

1424-9 Jerusalem Foundation, Jerusalem, Israel, $500,000. 2009.

1424-10 Jewish Agency for Israel, North American Council, New York, NY, $187,500. 2009.

1424-11 One Acre Fund, Falcon Heights, MN, $150,000. 2009.

1424-12 Root Capital, Cambridge, MA, $50,000. 2009.

1424-13 Stratford General Hospital Foundation, Stratford, Canada, $20,000. 2009.

1424-14 TechnoServe, Washington, DC, $100,000. 2009.

1424-15 University of California San Francisco Foundation, San Francisco, CA, $120,000. For Global Health. 2009.

1424-16 VisionSpring, New York, NY, $100,000. 2009.

1425

Nathan & Louise Goldsmith Foundation, Inc.

c/o Michael Bernstein
185 E. 85th St., No. 4C
New York, NY 10028-2172

Established in 1986 in NY.
Donor: Nathan Goldsmith‡.
Grantmaker type: Independent foundation.
Financial data (yr. ended 06/30/10): Assets, $2,002,005 (M); expenditures, $156,725; qualifying distributions, $142,100; giving activities include $142,100 for grants.
Purpose and activities: Giving primarily to Jewish-affiliated organizations.
Fields of interest: Elementary/secondary education; Education; Human services; Jewish federated giving programs; Jewish agencies & synagogues; Religion.
International interests: Israel.
Type of support: General/operating support; Building/renovation; Endowments.
Limitations: Applications not accepted. Giving primarily in New York, NY; some giving also in Israel. No grants to individuals.
Application information: Contributes only to pre-selected organizations.
Board meeting date(s): June and Dec.
Officers and Directors: * Rabbi Haskel Lookstein,* Pres.; Michael H. Klein, Secy.; Michael Bernstein, Treas.; Ahuvah Keller; Bernice Reisman; Arthur C. Silverman.
EIN: 133367816

1426

Owen T. Gorman & Alice M. Gorman Testamentary Charitable Trust

447 Kinsley St.
Sherrill, NY 13461-1349 (315) 363-0170
Contact: Amanda Larson, Pres.
FAX: (315) 366-0170;
E-mail: amanda@gormanfoundation.org;
URL: http://www.gormanfoundation.org

Established in 2003 in NY.
Donors: Alice M. Gorman‡; Owen Gorman‡; Catherine Cummings Gorman‡.
Grantmaker type: Independent foundation.
Financial data (yr. ended 12/31/10): Assets, $14,994,195 (M); expenditures, $1,104,445; qualifying distributions, $801,665; giving activities include $801,665 for grants.
Purpose and activities: Giving primarily to organizations that support: 1) faith in action programs, particularly programs and services designed to help people in need gain access to healthcare, education, food, and shelter; 2) the environment, particularly efforts to support sustainable farming programs, and to preserve biodiversity, rehabilitate wildlife, and care for homeless, domestic animals; and 3) community education and enhancement projects, particularly outreach programs that enhance community well being, or preserve historical areas of interest.
Fields of interest: Education; Health care; Human services; Immigrants/refugees; Homeless; Economically disadvantaged; Children.
International interests: Lithuania; Sri Lanka.
Type of support: General/operating support; Continuing support; Building/renovation; Emergency funds; Program development; Scholarship funds; Program-related investments/loans.
Limitations: Applications accepted. Giving primarily in central NY, with emphasis on Madison County. Giving also in Oneida and Onondaga Counties. No grants to individuals, or for debt reduction drives, or lobbying activities as defined by the IRS; no grants to organizations that do not agree with the foundation's policy on non-discrimination.
Publications: Application guidelines; Grants list; Informational brochure; Informational brochure (including application guidelines).
Application information: Hard copy applications are not accepted. Online applications only. Application form required.
Initial approach: Use online application form via foundation web site
Deadline(s): None
Final notification: Approx. 3 months
Officers and Trustees: * Joanne G. Larson,* Chair. and C.I.O.; Amanda Larson,* Pres. and C.O.O.; James F. Sullivan, Sr.,* V.P.
Number of staff: 2 full-time professional; 1 part-time professional; 1 part-time support.
EIN: 226927092

1427

Gould Family Foundation

c/o Baker & McKenzie LLP
1114 Ave. of the Americas
New York, NY 10036-7701
Contact: Edwin S. Matthews, Jr., Tr.; Anthony Gould
E-mail: edwin.s.matthews@beakernet.com; E-mail address for Anthony Gould: magorta@aol.com

Established in 2003 in NY.
Donor: Lois Gould.
Grantmaker type: Independent foundation.
Financial data (yr. ended 12/31/10): Assets, $24,739,958 (M); expenditures, $1,418,914; qualifying distributions, $1,309,951; giving activities include $1,097,500 for 21 grants (high: $250,000; low: $2,500).
Purpose and activities: The foundation funds creative projects for fundamental social change.

Fields of interest: Animals/wildlife; International human rights; Museums; Performing arts; Arts; Higher education; Environment.
International interests: Developing countries.
Limitations: Giving primarily in CT, Washington, DC, New York, NY, and in Kenya, South Africa, and Guatemala.
Application information: Application form not required.
Initial approach: Letter
Copies of proposal: 1
Deadline(s): None
Trustees: Anthony Gould; Edwin S. Matthews, Jr.
EIN: 020595263

1428

The Florence Gould Foundation

c/o Cahill Gordon & Reindel LLP
80 Pine St., Ste. 1548
New York, NY 10005-1702 (212) 701-3400
Contact: John R. Young, Pres.

Incorporated in 1957 in NY.
Donor: Florence J. Gould‡.
Grantmaker type: Independent foundation.
Financial data (yr. ended 12/31/09): Assets, $74,028,098 (M); expenditures, $8,106,217; qualifying distributions, $7,657,363; giving activities include $7,195,073 for 121 grants (high: $347,950; low: $80).
Purpose and activities: Essential aim is to promote French-American amity and understanding.
Fields of interest: Arts.
International interests: France.
Limitations: Applications accepted. Giving primarily in the U.S. and France. No grants to individuals.
Application information: Application form not required.
Initial approach: Letter or telephone inquiry
Copies of proposal: 1
Deadline(s): None
Board meeting date(s): As necessary
Final notification: Varies
Officers and Directors: * John R. Young,* Pres.; Walter C. Cliff,* V.P. and Secy.; Daniel P. Davison,* V.P. and Treas.; Ursula Cliff; Katusha Davison; Mary R. Young.
Number of staff: 1 full-time professional.
EIN: 136176855
Recent grants for international programs:

1428-1 Alliance Francaise de Washington, Washington, DC, $10,000. For outreach French instruction in D.C.. 2009.

1428-2 American Antiquarian Society, Worcester, MA, $25,000. For research on relationship of French and American lithography. 2009.

1428-3 American Foundation for the Paris School of Economics, New York, NY, $55,200. For Florence Gould Fellows. 2009.

1428-4 American Friends of Blerancourt, New York, NY, $30,000. For Anne Morgan exhibition. 2009.

1428-5 American Friends of Coubertin, Chicago, IL, $48,679. For Florence Gould American Fellow. 2009.

1428-6 American Friends of the Franco American Institute, Saranac, MI, $25,000. 2009.

1428-7 American Friends of the Paris Opera and Ballet, New York, NY, $50,000. For exchange with NYC Ballet dancers. 2009.

1428-8 American Philosophical Society, Philadelphia, PA, $50,000. For planning toward Revolutions! The Science and Politics of French Natural History, 1780-1850. 2009.

1428-9 American University of Paris, Paris, France, $100,000. For Arts Arena. 2009.

1428-10 Bibliotheque Americaine de Nancy, Nancy, France, $14,629. 2009.

1428-11 Bibliotheque Anglophone d'Angers, Angers, France, $14,357. 2009.

1428-12 Boston Baroque, Belmont, MA, $18,000. For French Baroque performances. 2009.

1428-13 Boston Early Music Festival, Cambridge, MA, $75,000. For performances in France. 2009.

1428-14 Cambridge University Press, New York, NY, $17,000. For translation of Tocqueville's The Ancient Regime and the Revolution. 2009.

1428-15 Cathedral Church of Saint John the Divine, New York, NY, $45,000. For concerts of French music. 2009.

1428-16 Center for Fiction, New York, NY, $10,000. For French literary programs. 2009.

1428-17 Center for Khmer Studies, New York, NY, $30,000. For Fellows. 2009.

1428-18 Chamber Music Society of Lincoln Center, New York, NY, $20,000. For French programming. 2009.

1428-19 College de France, Paris, France, $100,000. For research by Etienne Baulieu. 2009.

1428-20 Columbia University, New York, NY, $25,000. For French music at Miller Theatre. 2009.

1428-21 CUNY TV Foundation, New York, NY, $25,000. For French programming. 2009.

1428-22 Duke University Press, Durham, NC, $15,000. For translation of Weil's Qu'est-ce Qu'un Francais?. 2009.

1428-23 Educational Broadcasting Corporation, New York, NY, $150,000. For Thirteen documentary about Paris. 2009.

1428-24 European American Musical Alliance, New York, NY, $25,000. For general support. 2009.

1428-25 Foolsfury Theater Company, San Francisco, CA, $18,000. For Contemporary French Plays project. 2009.

1428-26 Foundation for French Museums, New York, NY, $100,000. For FRAME. 2009.

1428-27 French American Cultural Exchange, New York, NY, $165,000. For various projects. 2009.

1428-28 French American Cultural Exchange, New York, NY, $110,000. For various projects. 2009.

1428-29 French American Cultural Exchange, New York, NY, $100,000. For various projects. 2009.

1428-30 French American Cultural Exchange, New York, NY, $80,000. For various projects. 2009.

1428-31 French American Cultural Exchange, New York, NY, $25,000. For various projects. 2009.

1428-32 French Heritage Society, New York, NY, $115,875. For restoration of Abbey of Lagrasse. 2009.

1428-33 French Heritage Society, New York, NY, $76,470. For restoration of Abbey of Savigny. 2009.

1428-34 French Institute Alliance Francaise, New York, NY, $120,000. For performances in Florence Gould Hall. 2009.

1428-35 French Institute Alliance Francaise, New York, NY, $95,000. For performances in Florence Gould Hall. 2009.

1428-36 French-American Aid for Children, New York, NY, $15,000. For support in lieu of attending gala. 2009.

1428-37 French-American Cultural Foundation, Washington, DC, $25,000. For France magazine. 2009.

1428-38 French-American Foundation, New York, NY, $109,424. For Courants program. 2009.

1428-39 French-American Foundation, New York, NY, $66,001. For Translation prize. 2009.

1428-40 Friends of the Institut des Hautes Etudes Scientifiques, New York, NY, $75,000. For Fellowship Program. 2009.

1428-41 Grace Church School, New York, NY, $25,000. For exchange program with France. 2009.

1428-42 International Foundation for Art Research, New York, NY, $15,000. For Web-based catalogue raisonne database of French Art. 2009.

1428-43 Jacobs Pillow Dance Festival, Becket, MA, $12,500. For Grenoble dance company. 2009.

1428-44 Les Amis du Lyrique en Bretagne, Brittany, France, $50,000. For summer festival. 2009.

1428-45 Lincoln Center for the Performing Arts, New York, NY, $100,000. For French programming. 2009.

1428-46 Medici Archive Project, New York, NY, $65,000. For Research Coordinator. 2009.

1428-47 Medici Archive Project, New York, NY, $25,000. For Fellows expenses. 2009.

1428-48 New England Conservatory of Music, Boston, MA, $30,000. For scholarship for French student. 2009.

1428-49 New York City Ballet, New York, NY, $100,000. For French programming. 2009.

1428-50 New York City Ballet, New York, NY, $100,000. For French programming. 2009.

1428-51 New York Public Library, New York, NY, $347,950. For exhibition Between Collaboration and Resistance. 2009.

1428-52 New York Public Library, New York, NY, $200,000. For exhibition Between Collaboration and Resistance. 2009.

1428-53 New York University, New York, NY, $10,000. For conference on French writers and artists in U.S. during WWII. 2009.

1428-54 New York Women in Film and Television, New York, NY, $30,000. For documentary on French farms. 2009.

1428-55 Opera Fuoco, Paris, France, $75,000. 2009.

1428-56 Pasteur Foundation, Paris, France, $240,000. For Paris residencies for American researchers. 2009.

1428-57 Rire Medecin, Paris, France, $50,000. For general support. 2009.

1428-58 School of American Ballet, New York, NY, $13,860. For scholarships for French students. 2009.

1428-59 Tresor Public de La Ville de Paris, Paris, France, $50,000. For Musee d'Art Moderne of City of Paris, American Appropriationist Artists. 2009.

1428-60 University of Chicago, Chicago, IL, $22,800. For Visiting Scholars Program with College de France. 2009.

1428-61 University of Hull, Hull, England, $20,000. For publication of Histoire des Deux Indes. 2009.

1428-62 University of Michigan, Museum of Art, Ann Arbor, MI, $50,000. For exhibition Painting and Photography Along the Normandy Coast. 2009.

1428-63 University of Wisconsin, Madison, WI, $22,600. For symposium A Sea Reshaped. 2009.

1428-64 USA Youth Debates, Venice, FL, $16,414. For debates with French students. 2009.

1428-65 Villa I Tatti, Florence, Italy, $100,000. For library restoration. 2009.

1428-66 World Monuments Fund, New York, NY, $100,000. For Restoration at Royal Palace of Venice. 2009.

1428-67 World Monuments Fund, New York, NY, $90,000. For preservation of Cloister of Saint Trophine. 2009.

1428-68 Z Space Studio, San Francisco, CA, $37,500. For Word for Word performances in France. 2009.

1428-69 Z Space Studio, San Francisco, CA, $37,500. For Word for Word performances in France. 2009.

1429
The Gould-Shenfeld Family Foundation
(formerly The Gould Family Charitable Foundation of New York)
60 Cuttermill Rd.
Great Neck, NY   11021-3152

Established in 1995 in NY.
Donors: Fredric H. Gould; Jeffrey Gould; Matthew Gould; Steven Shenfeld; REIT Management Corp. 401K; REIT Management Corp. Pension.
Grantmaker type: Independent foundation.
Financial data (yr. ended 12/31/10): Assets, $3,461,394 (M); gifts received, $351,254; expenditures, $1,042,734; qualifying distributions, $1,041,069; giving activities include $1,041,069 for grants.
Purpose and activities: Giving primarily for Jewish organizations, as well as for the arts, health, and children, youth and social services.
Fields of interest: Arts; Education; Hospitals (general); Health care; Health organizations, association; Medical research, association; Youth development, services; Human services; Children/youth, services; International conflict resolution; Jewish federated giving programs; Jewish agencies & synagogues.
Limitations: Applications not accepted. Giving primarily in New York, NY. No grants to individuals.
Application information: Contributes only to pre-selected organizations.
Trustees: Fredric H. Gould; Helaine Gould; Jeffrey A. Gould; Matthew J. Gould; Wendy Shenfeld.
EIN: 113262391

1430
Eugene and Emily Grant Family Foundation
277 Park Ave., 47th Fl.
New York, NY   10172-0003   (212) 688-4700
Contact: Eugene M. Grant, Tr.

Established in 1998 in NY.
Donors: Eugene M. Grant; Terry E. Grant; Sol Heligman†.
Grantmaker type: Independent foundation.
Financial data (yr. ended 12/31/10): Assets, $10,527,198 (M); gifts received, $393,000; expenditures, $794,768; qualifying distributions, $777,433; giving activities include $777,433 for grants.
Purpose and activities: Giving primarily to Jewish agencies, the arts and health care; support also to American and Israeli universities, environmental conservation, intermarriage, and holocaust studies.
Fields of interest: Performing arts, music; Performing arts, orchestras; Performing arts, opera; History/archaeology; Arts; Higher education, university; Environment, natural resources; Health

care; Health organizations, association; Jewish federated giving programs; Jewish agencies & synagogues.
International interests: Israel.
Limitations: Giving in the U.S. and Israel.
Application information: Application form not required.
 Initial approach: Letter
 Deadline(s): None
Trustees: Emily Grant; Eugene M. Grant.
EIN: 133997005

1431
Great Charity Chaye Olam
(formerly Great Charity Chaye Olam Institutions of Jerusalem, Inc.)
P.O. Box 786
New York, NY 10101-0787

Established in 1941.
Grantmaker type: Public charity.
Financial data (yr. ended 12/31/10): Revenue, $226,396; assets, $116,920 (M); gifts received, $226,368; expenditures, $224,767; giving activities include $71,300 for grants to organizations outside the U.S.
Purpose and activities: The organization provides educational and human services support to individuals and organizations in Israel.
Fields of interest: Education; Human services.
International interests: Israel.
Limitations: Giving primarily in Israel.
Directors: Sheldon Beren; Isaac Brandwein; Philip Goldberg; Rabbi Chaim Werner.
EIN: 135593820

1432
The William and Mary Greve Foundation, Inc.
c/o Anthony C.M. Kiser
665 Broadway, Ste. 1001
New York, NY 10012-2330

Incorporated in 1964 in NY.
Donor: Mary P. Greve†.
Grantmaker type: Independent foundation.
Financial data (yr. ended 12/31/10): Assets, $28,916,829 (M); expenditures, $3,002,785; qualifying distributions, $2,227,715; giving activities include $1,833,480 for 45+ grants (high: $326,402).
Purpose and activities: Grants largely for education and related fields, U.S.-Eastern Europe relations, the performing arts, and the environment.
Fields of interest: Education; Environment; International affairs, goodwill promotion.
Type of support: General/operating support; Continuing support; Endowments; Matching/challenge support.
Limitations: Applications not accepted. Giving on a national basis, with emphasis on New York, NY. No grants to individuals, or for scholarships or fellowships; no loans.
Application information: Unsolicited requests for funds not accepted.
 Board meeting date(s): Varies
Officers and Directors:* John W. Kiser III,* Chair.; Anthony C.M. Kiser,* Pres.; Victoria Bjorklund, Secy.; Robert E. Cohen; James W. Sykes, Jr.

Number of staff: 1 full-time professional; 1 part-time professional; 1 part-time support.
EIN: 136020724

1433
The William and Sue Gross Family Foundation
c/o The Ayco Co., L.P.
P.O. Box 15014
Albany, NY 12212-5014 (518) 640-5000

Established in 2005 in CA.
Donors: William Gross; Sue Gross.
Grantmaker type: Independent foundation.
Financial data (yr. ended 12/31/10): Assets, $329,912,352 (M); gifts received, $20,000,000; expenditures, $26,404,953; qualifying distributions, $25,806,887; giving activities include $25,806,887 for 6 grants (high: $11,551,887; low: $5,000).
Fields of interest: Higher education, university; Museums; Higher education; Hospitals (general); Human services; Foundations (private grantmaking).
Limitations: Applications not accepted. Giving primarily in CA, NY and Washington, DC.
Application information: Contributes only to pre-selected organizations.
Officers: William Gross, Pres.; Sue Gross, Secy.
EIN: 050563132
Recent grants for international programs:
1433-1 Dikembe Mutombo Foundation, Atlanta, GA, $100,000. For general charitable purposes. 2010.
1433-2 Doctors Without Borders USA, New York, NY, $11,551,887. For general support. 2010.

1434
The Gruss-Lipper Family Foundation
c/o Gruss & Co.
667 Madison Ave.
New York, NY 10065-8029
Contact: Evelyn Gruss Lipper, Tr.; Erika L. Aronson

Established about 1982 in NY.
Donors: Gruss Petroleum Corp.; Evmar Oil Corp.
Grantmaker type: Independent foundation.
Financial data (yr. ended 08/31/10): Assets, $104,388,123 (M); gifts received, $3,000; expenditures, $5,771,657; qualifying distributions, $5,126,143; giving activities include $5,108,402 for 21 grants (high: $1,000,000; low: $250).
Purpose and activities: Giving exclusively for Jewish causes.
Fields of interest: Medical research, institute; Human services; Children/youth, services; Jewish agencies & synagogues.
International interests: Israel.
Type of support: Annual campaigns; Program development; Curriculum development; Research.
Limitations: Applications not accepted. Giving on a national basis and in Israel. No support for non-Jewish charities, organizations or programs.
Application information: Unsolicited requests for funds not accepted.
Trustees: Evelyn Gruss Lipper; Daniella Lipper-Coules; Joanna Lipper.
Number of staff: 1 part-time professional.
EIN: 133188873

1435
The Harry Frank Guggenheim Foundation
25 W. 53rd St., 16th Fl.
New York, NY 10019-5401 (646) 428-0971
Contact: Staff
FAX: (646) 428-0981; E-mail: info@hfg.org;
URL: http://www.hfg.org

Incorporated in 1929 in NY.
Donor: Harry Frank Guggenheim†.
Grantmaker type: Operating foundation.
Financial data (yr. ended 12/31/10): Assets, $80,911,511 (M); expenditures, $3,538,668; qualifying distributions, $2,629,131; giving activities include $228,840 for 13 grants (high: $100,000; low: $1,000), $478,611 for 23 grants to individuals (high: $32,210; low: $9,350), $130,442 for employee matching gifts, and $2,541,194 for foundation-administered programs.
Purpose and activities: Grants for research projects at the postdoctoral level (though not necessarily requiring a Ph.D.) directed toward providing a better understanding of violence, aggression, and dominance in relation to social change; Dissertation Fellowship program to support individuals only during the writing of their Ph.D. dissertation; research grants can be applied for directly. Primary areas of support include anthropology, biological sciences, sociology, history, political science, and psychology.
Fields of interest: History/archaeology; Crime/law enforcement; Child development, services; International peace/security; International affairs, arms control; International affairs, foreign policy; International human rights; International affairs; Civil rights, race/intergroup relations; Biology/life sciences; Science; Social sciences; Anthropology/sociology; Psychology/behavioral science; Political science; Law/international law; International studies; Public policy, research; Government/public administration; Public affairs; Minorities.
Type of support: Fellowships; Research; Employee matching gifts; Grants to individuals.
Limitations: Applications accepted. Giving on a national and international basis. No grants for capital or endowment funds, or for matching funds; no loans. No funds for overhead costs of institutions, travel to professional meetings, publications, conferences (except for those organized by the foundation), subsidiaries, self-education, elaborate fixed equipment, or pre-doctoral support (apart from that indirectly involved in research assistantships and except for a special program of support for dissertation writing).
Publications: Application guidelines; Multi-year report; Occasional report.
Application information: Application guidelines and application forms may be downloaded on foundation Web site. Application form required.
 Initial approach: Letter or telephone
 Copies of proposal: 4
 Deadline(s): Feb. 1 for Ph.D. support; Aug. 1 for research grants
 Board meeting date(s): June and Dec.
 Final notification: Within 3 days of meeting
Officers and Directors:* Peter O. Lawson-Johnston,* Chair.; Josiah Bunting III,* Pres.; Deirdre Hamill, Treas.; William Bardel; Tina Bennett; Dana Draper; Victor Davis Hanson; Donald C. Hood; Patrick Lang; Carol Langstaff; Lewis H. Lapham; Peter Lawson-Johnston II; Lewis Lehrman; Reeve Lindbergh; Gillian Lindt; Tania L.J. McCleery; J.M. Millbank III; Lois Dickson Rice; Andrew Roberts; Patricia Rosenfield; Brogann Sanderson; Kirk Unroh.

Lifetime Directors: James B. Edwards; James Hester; Theodore Lockwood.
Number of staff: 4 full-time professional; 1 part-time professional.
EIN: 136043471

1436
John Simon Guggenheim Memorial Foundation

90 Park Ave.
New York, NY 10016-1302 (212) 687-4470
Contact: Edward Hirsch, Pres.
FAX: (212) 697-3248; E-mail: fellowships@gf.org;
URL: http://www.gf.org
E-Newsletter: http://list-manage.com/subscribe?u=59d983d0914a509b37f82546c&id=5039a73dec

Incorporated in 1925 in NY.
Donors: Simon Guggenheim†; Mrs. Simon Guggenheim†.
Grantmaker type: Independent foundation.
Financial data (yr. ended 12/31/09): Assets, $253,013,678 (M); gifts received, $318,044; expenditures, $14,344,706; qualifying distributions, $12,612,109; giving activities include $8,472,250 for 354 grants to individuals (high: $50,000; low: $5,000).
Purpose and activities: Fellowships offered to further the development of scholars and artists by assisting them to engage in research in any field of knowledge and creation in any of the arts, under the freest possible conditions and irrespective of race, color, or creed. Fellowships are awarded by the trustees upon nomination by a Committee of Selection. Awards are made to citizens and permanent residents of the U.S., Canada, Latin America, and the Caribbean.
Fields of interest: Visual arts; Humanities; Science; Social sciences.
International interests: Canada; Caribbean; Latin America.
Type of support: Fellowships.
Limitations: Applications accepted. Giving to citizens and permanent residents of the U.S., Canada, Latin America, and the Caribbean. No grants for endowments, operating budgets, special projects, or any other expenses of institutions.
Publications: Application guidelines; Annual report; Financial statement; Informational brochure (including application guidelines).
Application information: Grants are awarded to individuals rather than institutions. Application guidelines available on Web site. Application form required.
   Initial approach: Letter
   Copies of proposal: 1
   Deadline(s): Sept. 15 for U.S. and Canada; Dec. 1 for Latin America and the Caribbean
   Board meeting date(s): Apr., June, and as required
   Final notification: Approximately 6 months
Officers and Trustees: * Joseph A. Rice,* Chair.; Edward Hirsch,* Pres.; Andre Bernard, V.P. and Secy.; Coleen P. Higgins-Jacob, V.P., C.F.O., and Treas.; Robert A. Caro; Joel Conarroe; Alphonse Fletcher, Jr.; Michael Hegarty; Joyce Carol Oates; A. Alex Porter; Richard A. Rifkind; Charles Andrew Ryskamp; Charles P. Stevenson, Jr.; Waddell W. Stillman; Patrick J. Waide; Ellen Taaffe Zwilich.
Number of staff: 8 full-time professional; 13 full-time support.
EIN: 135673173

1437
Stella and Charles Guttman Foundation, Inc.

122 E. 42nd St. Ste. 2010
New York, NY 10168-2101
Contact: Elizabeth Olofson, Exec. Dir.
FAX: (212) 371-8936;
E-mail: eolofson@guttmanfoundation.org;
URL: http://www.guttmanfoundation.org/

Incorporated in 1959 in NY.
Donors: Charles Guttman†; Stella Guttman†.
Grantmaker type: Independent foundation.
Financial data (yr. ended 12/31/10): Assets, $52,506,738 (M); expenditures, $3,225,595; qualifying distributions, $2,586,569; giving activities include $1,884,000 for 81 grants (high: $200,000; low: $1,050).
Purpose and activities: The foundation recently completed a strategic review to determine the future direction of its grant program. The Board of Directors has decided to spend half of the foundation's assets, approximately $25 million, over a period of five years beginning in 2012. The board has approved the first program initiative, which will be a significant investment to improve college success for New York City public school students.
Fields of interest: Education.
Type of support: General/operating support; Continuing support; Program development.
Limitations: Applications not accepted. Giving primarily in the metropolitan New York, NY, area; some giving also in Israel. No support for religious organizations for religious purposes, or for public interest litigation or antivivisectionist causes. No grants to individuals, or for foreign travel or foreign study.
Publications: Grants list; Multi-year report.
Application information: Unsolicited requests for funds not accepted. Unsolicited materials will not be acknowledged or returned.
   Board meeting date(s): Quarterly
Officers and Directors: * Ernest Rubenstein,* Pres.; Peter A. Herbert,* V.P.; William S. Rubenstein,* Secy.; Robert S. Gassman,* Treas.; Elizabeth Olofson, Exec. Dir.; Paul R. Gassman; Benjamin Herbert.
Number of staff: 3 full-time professional.
EIN: 136103039
Recent grants for international programs:
1437-1 American Jewish World Service, New York, NY, $51,000. For general support. 2010.
1437-2 American Supporters of YEDID, Teaneck, NJ, $40,000. For general support. 2010.
1437-3 Doctors Without Borders USA, New York, NY, $75,000. For earthquake relief efforts in Haiti. In support of medical and humanitarian relief efforts in Pakistan. 2010.
1437-4 ELEM Youth in Distress, New York, NY, $20,000. For general operations for ELEM's Migdalor Center in Acre. 2010.
1437-5 Haiti Projects, Beverly, MA, $10,000. For general support. 2010.
1437-6 Hand in Hand, American Friends of the Center for Jewish-Arab Education in Israel, Portland, OR, $20,000. For general support. 2010.
1437-7 J. Kirby Simon Foreign Service Trust, New Haven, CT, $27,000. For general support. 2010.
1437-8 New Israel Fund, Washington, DC, $85,000. For 'SHATIL,' which provides technical assistance to Israeli nonprofit organizations. 2010.

1437-9 New Israel Fund, Washington, DC, $40,000. For a grant paid to Trust of Programs for a home-based parenting program for young mothers with children under the age of three that serves Arab populations in Israel. 2010.
1437-10 New Israel Fund, Washington, DC, $10,000. For 'Hillel - The Right to Choose,' a program that provides support services for the newly secular. 2010.
1437-11 PEF Israel Endowment Funds, New York, NY, $20,000. For general support of Neve Michael Children's Village. 2010.
1437-12 Save a Childs Heart Foundation-U.S., Potomac, MD, $20,000. For general support. 2010.

1438
Hadassah Foundation, Inc.

50 W. 58th St.
New York, NY 10019-2505 (212) 451-6245
Contact: Linda Altshuler, Exec. Dir.
FAX: (212) 303-8282;
E-mail: hadassahfoundation@hadassah.org;
URL: http://www.hadassahfoundation.org
Facebook: http://www.facebook.com/Hadassah.org
Twitter: http://twitter.com/HadassahOrg
YouTube: http://www.youtube.com/user/HadassahVideo

Established in 1998 in NY; supporting organization of Hadassah: the Women's Zionist Organization of America, and Hadassah Medical Relief Association, Inc.
Grantmaker type: Public charity.
Financial data (yr. ended 12/31/10): Revenue, $506,695; assets, $11,002,420 (M); gifts received, $118,869; expenditures, $401,484; giving activities include $50,000 for grants, and $118,000 for grants to organizations outside the U.S.
Purpose and activities: The foundation is dedicated to refocusing the priorities of the Jewish community through innovative and creative funding for women and girls in the U.S. and Israel.
Fields of interest: Employment; Jewish agencies & synagogues; Adults, women; Women; Girls.
International interests: Israel.
Type of support: Program development; Seed money; Curriculum development.
Limitations: Applications accepted. Giving in the U.S. and Israel. No support for partisan political activities or direct service. No grants for capital campaigns, endowments, or scholarships.
Publications: Application guidelines; Grants list; Informational brochure.
Application information: See web site for additional application information. Application form required.
   Initial approach: Proposal submitted via e-mail
   Copies of proposal: 1
   Deadline(s): Aug. 9
   Board meeting date(s): Fall/spring
   Final notification: Five months
Officers and Directors: * Rabbi Jacqueline Ellenson,* Chair.; Paula Jarnicki,* Secy.; Rebekah Farber,* Treas.; Linda Altshuler, Exec. Dir.; Froma Benerofe; Georgianne Cutter; Katie Edelstein; Sherri Ades Falchuk; Amy Friedkin; Carol M. Joseph; Rabbi Naamah Kelman; and 8 additional directors; Ellen Landis.
Number of staff: 1 full-time professional; 1 part-time professional.
EIN: 134022483

1439
Lynn Handleman Charitable Foundation
(formerly Joseph & Sally Handleman Charitable
Foundation Trust B)
c/o Bessemer Trust
630 5th Ave., Ste. 3425
New York, NY 10111-0100
Application address: c/o Angela Fitzsimons, P.O. Box
170579, San Francisco, CA 94117

Established in FL.
Grantmaker type: Independent foundation.
Financial data (yr. ended 12/31/10): Assets,
$12,447,725 (M); gifts received, $1,621,574;
expenditures, $602,218; qualifying distributions,
$547,521; giving activities include $547,521 for
grants.
Purpose and activities: Giving primarily for
educational, civic, and healthcare purposes.
Fields of interest: Education; Human services;
International development; Civil/human rights.
International interests: Middle East.
Limitations: Applications accepted. Giving primarily
in CA and Washington DC. No grants to individuals.
Application information: Application form not
required.
　Initial approach: Proposal
　Deadline(s): None
Trustee: Scott Handleman.
Agent: JPMorgan Chase Bank, N.A.
EIN: 656263327

1440
Harbor Lights Foundation
c/o BCRS Assocs., LLC
100 Wall St., 11th Fl.
New York, NY 10005-3701

Established in 1980 in CT.
Donor: J. Fred Weintz, Jr.
Grantmaker type: Independent foundation.
Financial data (yr. ended 04/30/10): Assets,
$13,362,433 (M); expenditures, $679,708;
qualifying distributions, $572,760; giving activities
include $572,760 for grants.
Purpose and activities: Giving primarily for higher
and other education.
Fields of interest: Christian agencies & churches;
International relief; Elementary/secondary
education; Higher education; Business school/
education; Public health school/education; Health
organizations; Human services.
Limitations: Applications not accepted. Giving
primarily in CA, CT, MA, NY, and VT. No grants to
individuals, or for scholarships; no loans.
Application information: Contributes only to
pre-selected organizations.
Trustees: Elizabeth Weintz Cerf; H. Frederick
Krimendahl II; Polly Weintz Sanna; Eric Cortelyou
Weintz; J. Fred Weintz, Jr.; Karl Frederick Weintz.
EIN: 133052490

1441
The Harmon Foundation
c/o Tanton & Co., LLP
37 W. 57th St., 5th Fl.
New York, NY 10019-3411

Established in 1988 in DE.
Donor: James A. Harmon.
Grantmaker type: Independent foundation.

Financial data (yr. ended 08/31/10): Assets,
$4,587,732 (M); expenditures, $189,780;
qualifying distributions, $178,350; giving activities
include $178,350 for grants.
Fields of interest: Performing arts, theater; Arts;
Higher education; Education; International affairs;
Jewish federated giving programs.
Limitations: Applications not accepted. Giving
primarily in FL, NY, and RI. No grants to individuals.
Application information: Contributes only to
pre-selected organizations.
Officers: James Harmon, Pres.; Leonard Leiman,
Secy.; Jane Harmon, Treas.
EIN: 061180560

1442
Mary and Kathleen Harriman Foundation
(formerly W. Averell and Pamela C. Harriman
Foundation)
c/o Brown Brothers Harriman Trust Co., N.A.
140 Broadway, 11th Fl.
New York, NY 10005-1108
Contact: Barbara O'Connell, Asst. Secy.

Established in 1969 in NY.
Donor: W. Averell Harriman†.
Grantmaker type: Independent foundation.
Financial data (yr. ended 12/31/10): Assets,
$4,704,410 (M); expenditures, $307,538;
qualifying distributions, $285,007; giving activities
include $247,250 for 37 grants (high: $30,000;
low: $1,000).
Purpose and activities: Support primarily for the
study of international affairs.
Fields of interest: Animals/wildlife; Education;
Higher education; International affairs.
Type of support: General/operating support; Annual
campaigns; Capital campaigns.
Limitations: Applications not accepted. Giving on a
national basis, with some emphasis on the East
Coast. No grants to individuals.
Application information: Contributes only to
pre-selected organizations.
　Board meeting date(s): May
Officers and Directors:* Kathleen L. Ames,* Pres.;
Robert C. Fisk,* V.P.; Kathleen L. Mortimer,* Secy.;
Averell H. Mortimer,* Treas.; Anna Korniczky;
Barbara O'Connell.
Number of staff: 2 full-time professional.
EIN: 510193921

1443
The John A. Hartford Foundation, Inc.
55 E. 59th St., 16th Fl.
New York, NY 10022-1713
Contact: Corinne H. Rieder, Treas. and Exec. Dir.
FAX: (212) 593-4913; E-mail: mail@jhartfound.org;
URL: http://www.jhartfound.org
CEP Study: http://www.jhartfound.org/files/
CEP_Survey_Ltr.pdf
E-Newsletter: http://www.jhartfound.org/
e_newsletter.htm
Facebook: http://www.facebook.com/jhartfound?
ref=ts
health AGEnda Blog: http://www.jhartfound.org/
blog/
Publications: http://www.jhartfound.org/
publications.htm
Staff Presentations: http://www.jhartfound.org/
staff_presentations.htm

Established in 1929; incorporated in 1942 in NY.
Donors: John A. Hartford†; George L. Hartford†.
Grantmaker type: Independent foundation.
Financial data (yr. ended 12/31/10): Assets,
$484,325,166 (M); expenditures, $35,003,487;
qualifying distributions, $28,164,129; giving
activities include $22,805,443 for 95 grants (high:
$1,912,590; low: $1,700), $903,655 for 255
employee matching gifts, and $475,128 for 2
foundation-administered programs.
Purpose and activities: The foundation addresses
the unique health needs of the elderly, including
long-term care, the use of medication in chronic
health problems, increasing the nation's geriatric
research and training capability, and improving the
integration of financing and care delivery for
comprehensive geriatric services.
Fields of interest: Health care; Geriatrics; Aging,
centers/services; Aging.
Type of support: Conferences/seminars; Continuing
support; Curriculum development; Employee
matching gifts; Fellowships; Management
development/capacity building; Program
development; Program evaluation; Publication;
Research; Scholarship funds.
Limitations: Giving on a national basis. No grants to
individuals (including student loans or
scholarships), or for annual or capital campaigns,
building renovations, equipment, seed money,
emergency or endowment funds, deficit financing,
conferences and seminars, management
development and capacity building, or for
scholarship funds.
Publications: Application guidelines; Annual report;
Newsletter.
Application information: Unsolicited full proposals
or applications not accepted. See foundation's web
site for exact guidelines. Do not send
correspondence by fax or e-mail. Application form
not required.
　Initial approach: Review program areas (see
　　website). May submit a brief letter of inquiry if
　　project falls within this focus
　Copies of proposal: 1
　Board meeting date(s): Mar., June, Sept., and
　　Dec.
　Final notification: 6 weeks
Officers and Trustees:* Norman H. Volk,* Chair.;
Kathryn D. Wriston,* Pres.; William T. Comfort, Jr.,*
Secy.; Corinne H. Rieder, Treas. and Exec. Dir.; Eva
Cheng, Cont. and Dir., Finance; John H. Allen; John
J. Curley; Charles A. Dana; Lile R. Gibbons; John R.
Mach, Jr.; Audrey A. McNiff; Christopher T.H. Pell;
Barbara Paul Robinson; Margaret L. Wolff.
Number of staff: 9 full-time professional; 3 full-time
support; 1 part-time support.
EIN: 131667057
Recent grants for international programs:
1443-1 Association of Directors of Geriatric
Academic Programs, New York, NY, $420,000.
For Geriatric Leadership Development Program,
renewal grant to develop and sustain the
leadership skills of directors of geriatric
academic programs at schools of medicine
across the country. 2010.

1444
The Hauser Foundation, Inc.
c/o Rita E. Hauser
712 5th Ave.
New York, NY 10019-4102 (212) 956-3645
FAX: (212) 956-1413;
E-mail: rhauser@sprintmail.com

Established in 1989 in NY.
Donors: Gustave M. Hauser; Rita E. Hauser.
Grantmaker type: Independent foundation.
Financial data (yr. ended 11/30/10): Assets, $39,551,870 (M); expenditures, $2,515,016; qualifying distributions, $2,215,466; giving activities include $1,831,661 for 31 grants (high: $1,000,000; low: $100).
Purpose and activities: Giving primarily for legal and graduate education, and international affairs; some support for cultural organizations and the arts.
Fields of interest: Media/communications; Visual arts; Performing arts; Performing arts, music; Arts; International peace/security; International affairs, foreign policy; International human rights; Law/international law; Public policy, research; Government/public administration; Women.
International interests: Israel; Middle East.
Type of support: Annual campaigns; Capital campaigns; Endowments; Program development; Conferences/seminars.
Limitations: Applications not accepted. Giving on a national basis. No support for religious organizations. No grants to individuals.
Application information: Unsolicited requests for funds not accepted.
  Board meeting date(s): Fall
Officers and Directors:* Rita E. Hauser,* Pres.; Gustave M. Hauser, V.P. and Secy.-Treas.; Ronald J. Stein.
Number of staff: 1 full-time support.
EIN: 110016142

1445
Hayden Family Foundation
c/o WTAS, Inc.
452 5th Ave., 23rd Fl.
New York, NY 10018-2706
Contact: Marilyn Calister

Established in 1984 in NY.
Donor: Richard M. Hayden.
Grantmaker type: Independent foundation.
Financial data (yr. ended 02/28/10): Assets, $9,741,997 (M); gifts received, $50,000; expenditures, $456,464; qualifying distributions, $383,267; giving activities include $363,534 for grants.
Purpose and activities: Giving primarily for education, arts and culture, health and human services.
Fields of interest: Arts; Higher education; Education; Health care; Health organizations, association; Human services.
International interests: England.
Limitations: Applications not accepted. Giving primarily in the U.S. and London, England. No grants to individuals, or for scholarships, gifts; no loans.
Publications: Financial statement; Grants list.
Application information: Contributes only to pre-selected organizations.
Trustees: Lindsay Hayden; Richard M. Hayden; Susan F. Hayden.
EIN: 133248046

1446
Healthcorps of Florida, Inc.
(formerly Foundation for the Advancement of Cardiac Therapies)
191 7th Ave., 4N
New York, NY 10011-1897
Contact: Mary Lampe, C.E.O. and Exec. Dir.

Established in 2001 in FL and NY; status changed to public charity in 2005.
Grantmaker type: Public charity.
Financial data (yr. ended 06/30/08): Revenue, $4,571,759; assets, $4,024,864 (M); gifts received, $3,173,205; expenditures, $3,067,323; program services expenses, $2,525,064; giving activities include $2,525,064 for foundation-administered programs.
Purpose and activities: The foundation gives to cardiovascular, arterial fibrillation, and cardio-transplant research.
Fields of interest: Medical research, institute; Heart & circulatory research.
International interests: United Kingdom.
Officers and Directors:* Mary Lampe,* C.E.O. and Exec. Dir.; Dr. Mehmet Oz,* Pres.; Dr. Eric Rose,* V.P.; Dr. Morgan Poncy,* M.D., Secy.; Deborah Lysaght,* Esq., Treas.; Dr. Donna Mancini.
EIN: 582586906

1447
Hedge Funds Care, Inc.
(also known as HFC)
70 W. 36th St., Ste. 1404
New York, NY 10018-8014 (212) 991-9600
Contact: Christine Kang, Mgr., Grants and Board Rels.
FAX: (646) 214-1079;
E-mail: ckang@hedgefundscare.org; URL: http://www.hedgefundscare.org
Facebook: https://www.facebook.com/pages/Hedge-Funds-Care-Preventing-and-Treating-Child-Abuse/105032689530589?ref=ts
LinkedIn: http://www.linkedin.com/groups/Hedge-Funds-Care-Preventing-Treating-1878039?home=&gid=1878039&trk=anet_ug_hm
Twitter: http://twitter.com/HedgeFundsCare

Established in 2002 in NY.
Grantmaker type: Public charity.
Financial data (yr. ended 12/31/10): Revenue, $4,026,860; assets, $2,602,643 (M); gifts received, $4,288,050; expenditures, $3,787,643; program services expenses, $2,933,794; giving activities include $2,757,987 for 53 grants (high: $657,100; low: $15,000), and $175,807 for foundation-administered programs.
Purpose and activities: The fund is an international charity, supported largely by the hedge fund industry, whose mission is preventing and treating child abuse.
Fields of interest: Crime/violence prevention, child abuse.
International interests: Canada; Cayman Islands; United Kingdom.
Type of support: Continuing support; Annual campaigns; Program development; Seed money; Research; Program evaluation.
Limitations: Applications accepted. Giving limited to Alameda, Contra Costa, Los Angeles, San Francisco, and San Mateo counties, CA; the greater Denver, CO area; CT; the greater Atlanta, GA area; IL; IN; IA; the greater Boston, MA area; MN; MO; NJ; NY; OH; WI; the greater Toronto, Canada area;

Cayman Islands; and the greater London, United Kingdom area. No support for political organizations.
Publications: Application guidelines; Annual report; Grants list; Informational brochure.
Application information: Application form required.
  Initial approach: Letter of intent (available on web site)
  Copies of proposal: 1
  Deadline(s): Varies by geographical area
  Board meeting date(s): Apr. and Nov.
  Final notification: Two months
Officers and Directors:* John Budzyna,* Chair. and Pres.; Kathryn Conroy, C.E.O. and Exec. Dir.; Dean Backer,* V.P.; Robert Schultz,* V.P.; Melinda Kramer,* Secy.; Donald MacNeal,* Treas.; and 42 additional directors.
Number of staff: 6 full-time professional; 1 part-time professional.
EIN: 431959796

1448
Hess Corporation Contributions Program
(formerly Amerada Hess Corporation Contributions Program)
1185 Ave. of the Americas
New York, NY 10036-2602 (212) 997-8500
URL: http://www.hess.com/sustainability/socialresponsibility/default.aspx

Grantmaker type: Corporate giving program.
Purpose and activities: Hess Corporation makes charitable contributions to nonprofit organizations involved with education, health, and the quality of life in communities where Hess Corporation does business. Support is given on a national and international basis.
Fields of interest: Housing/shelter, development; Education; Environment; Health care; Disasters, preparedness/services; Community/economic development.
International interests: Equatorial Guinea; Azerbaijan; Thailand; United Kingdom; Gabon; Indonesia; Malaysia; Algeria.
Type of support: Building/renovation; Donated equipment; Donated products; Emergency funds; Employee volunteer services; Fellowships; General/operating support; Program development; Scholarship funds; Sponsorships.
Limitations: Giving on a national and international basis primarily in areas of company operations, in Europe, The Americas, Africa, Southeast Asia, and the United Kingdom.

1449
HIAS, Inc.
(also known as The Hebrew Immigrant Aid Society)
333 7th Ave., 16th Fl.
New York, NY 10001-5004 (212) 613-1325
URL: http://www.hias.org
Blog: http://www.hias.org/en/blog/hias-blog/posts

Established in 1889 in NY.
Grantmaker type: Public charity.
Financial data (yr. ended 12/31/10): Revenue, $24,861,010; assets, $62,475,248 (M); gifts received, $20,998,660; expenditures, $26,919,049; giving activities include $5,936,167 for grants, $86,000 for grants to organizations outside the U.S., and $258,000 for grants to individuals.

Purpose and activities: The society works to provide rescue and refuge for persecuted and oppressed Jews around the world, as well as to refugees and immigrants of all backgrounds.

Fields of interest: International migration/refugee issues; Jewish agencies & synagogues; Immigrants/refugees.

Type of support: Grants to individuals; Scholarships —to individuals.

Limitations: Applications accepted. Giving on a national and international basis, primarily to Israel.

Publications: Application guidelines; Annual report; Informational brochure.

Application information: Application form required.
Initial approach: Submit application online
Deadline(s): Feb. 24 for HIAS Scholarship Program

Officers and Directors:* Michael B. Rukin,* Chair.; Marc Silberberg,* 1st Vice-Chair.; Robert D. Aronson,* Vice-Chair.; Suzette Brooks Masters,* Vice-Chair.; Barbara S. Rosenthal,* Vice-Chair.; Dale Schwartz,* Vice-Chair.; Sandra Spinner, Vice-Chair.; Robert S. Whitehill,* Vice-Chair.; Gideon Aronoff, Pres. and C.E.O.; W. Stewart Cahn,* Secy.; Allan J. Rodolitz, Treas.; Elliott Benjamin; Hon. Harold Berger; Eugenia Brin; Alan K. Gidwitz; and 15 additional directors.

EIN: 135633307

1450
HKH Foundation
c/o Anchin Block & Anchin
1375 Broadway
New York, NY 10018-7001
Contact: Harriet Barlow
FAX: (212) 687-8877; E-mail: hkh@hkhfdn.org

Foundation established in 1980 in NY.
Donor: Harold K. Hochschild†.
Grantmaker type: Independent foundation.
Financial data (yr. ended 12/31/10): Assets, $12,992,627 (M); expenditures, $3,424,252; qualifying distributions, $3,158,684; giving activities include $3,158,684 for grants.

Purpose and activities: Funding considered only in the following areas: 1) disarmament and the prevention of war; 2) civil liberties; and 3) environmental protection.

Fields of interest: Environment, natural resources; Environment; International peace/security; International affairs, arms control; Civil liberties, advocacy; Civil/human rights.

Type of support: General/operating support; Program development; Program-related investments/loans.

Limitations: Applications not accepted. Giving on a national basis. No grants to individuals.

Application information: Unsolicited requests for funds not accepted.
Board meeting date(s): Spring and fall (actual dates vary each year)

Trustees: Hermann Hatzfeldt; Adam Hochschild; David Hochschild; Frederick A. Terry, Jr., Esq.; Robert R. Worth.

Number of staff: 2 part-time professional; 1 part-time support.

EIN: 136784950

Recent grants for international programs:
1450-1 Council of Canadians, Ottawa, Canada, $100,000. 2008.
1450-2 Council of Canadians, Ottawa, Canada, $50,000. 2008.

1450-3 ETC Group, Ottawa, Canada, $250,000. 2008.
1450-4 Grassroots International, Boston, MA, $50,000. 2008.
1450-5 National Security Archive Fund, Washington, DC, $200,000. 2008.
1450-6 National Security Initiative, Washington, DC, $130,000. 2008.
1450-7 Peace Action Education Fund, Silver Spring, MD, $50,000. 2008.
1450-8 Tides Foundation, San Francisco, CA, $100,000. For ETC Group/Canada. 2008.

1451
The Howard Hoffman & Sons Foundation, Inc.
1407 Broadway, Ste. 1201
New York, NY 10018-2849
Contact: Jason Hoffman, Treas.

Established in 2003 in NY.
Donors: Howard Hoffman; Jason Hoffman; Nathan Hoffman; 618 Main Clothing Corp.; Madison Brands, Inc.
Grantmaker type: Independent foundation.
Financial data (yr. ended 12/31/10): Assets, $100,675 (M); gifts received, $197,000; expenditures, $423,658; qualifying distributions, $420,456; giving activities include $420,456 for 181 grants (high: $52,851; low: $18).
Fields of interest: Jewish agencies & synagogues; Jewish federated giving programs.
International interests: Israel.
Limitations: Applications accepted. Giving primarily in NJ and NY.
Application information: Application form not required.
Initial approach: Letter
Copies of proposal: 1
Deadline(s): None
Final notification: 1-3 months
Officers: Howard Hoffman, Pres.; Nathan Hoffman, Secy.; Jason Hoffman, Treas.
EIN: 200089283

1452
HOPE Africa Foundation
333 Earle Ovington Blvd., Ste. 903
Mitchell Field, NY 11553-3620   (914) 338-8062
Contact: Onyii Brown, Dir., Development
E-mail: info@hopeafricausa.org; Toll-free fax: (866) 835-9573; URL: http://hopeafricausa.org

Established in NY.
Grantmaker type: Public charity.
Financial data (yr. ended 12/31/10): Revenue, $8,193; assets, $1,698 (M); gifts received, $5,805; expenditures, $6,495; giving activities include $920 for grants.
Purpose and activities: The foundation engages in an international student exchange program that allows American college students to receive experience abroad engaging in African community service and development projects.
Fields of interest: International development; International exchange.
International interests: Africa.
Limitations: Applications not accepted.
Officers: James Ihedigbo, Pres.; Gregory Domond, C.F.O.; Rose Ihedigbo, Exec. Dir.
EIN: 611591538

1453
Howard Family Charitable Foundation
c/o John D. Howard
80 Irving Pl.
New York, NY 10003-2201

Established in 2007 in NY.
Donor: John D. Howard.
Grantmaker type: Independent foundation.
Financial data (yr. ended 12/31/10): Assets, $1,325,826 (M); gifts received, $701,190; expenditures, $567,427; qualifying distributions, $552,950; giving activities include $552,950 for grants.
Fields of interest: International migration/refugee issues; Human services; Housing/shelter, development; Medical school/education; Higher education; Women.
Limitations: Applications not accepted. Giving primarily in NY. No grants to individuals.
Application information: Contributes only to pre-selected organizations.
Officer: John D. Howard, Pres.
EIN: 133549594

1454
Human Rights Watch, Inc.
350 Fifth Ave., 34th Fl.
New York, NY 10118-3299   (212) 290-4700
Contact: Kenneth Roth, Exec. Dir.
FAX: (212) 736-1300; E-mail: hrwnyc@hrw.org; URL: http://www.hrw.org
RSS Feed: http://www.hrw.org/doc/?t=news_rss

Established in 1978.
Grantmaker type: Public charity.
Financial data (yr. ended 06/30/10): Revenue, $42,452,799; assets, $113,930,678 (M); gifts received, $39,220,034; expenditures, $43,033,495; program services expenses, $33,158,554; giving activities include $108,401 for grants to organizations outside the U.S., and $3,000 for grants to individuals.
Purpose and activities: The organization aims to prevent discrimination, to uphold political freedom, to protect people from inhumane conduct in wartime, and to bring offenders to justice.
Fields of interest: International human rights; Civil/human rights.
Type of support: Grants to individuals.
Limitations: Giving on a national and international basis.
Application information: Nominations should try to provide biographical information about the nominee, a list of nominee's published writing, a statement about the political persecution suffered by the writer, and a statement of need. Application form not required.
Initial approach: E-mail nomination materials
Deadline(s): Dec. 17
Board meeting date(s): Jan., Apr., June, and Oct.
Final notification: Spring
Officers and Directors:* James F. Hoge, Jr.,* Chair.; Susan Manilow,* Vice-Chair.; Joel Motley,* Vice-Chair.; John J. Studzinski,* Vice-Chair.; Bruce Rabb, Secy.; Hassan Elmasry, Treas.; Karen Ackman; Jorge Castaneda; Tony Elliott; Michael G. Fisch; and 23 additional directors.
EIN: 132875808

1455
Hungarian Human Rights Foundation
(also known as Magyar Emberi Jogok Alapitvany)
Gracie Sta.
P.O. Box J
New York, NY   10128-0029   (212) 289-5488
FAX: (212) 996-6268; E-mail: hamos@hhrf.org;
Additional address (Budapest office): 1255
Budapest, pf. 66., Magyarorszag, tel.: +36 1 795
5940, fax: +36 1 795 0458; URL: http://
www.hhrf.org/hhrf/index_en.php

Grantmaker type: Public charity.
Financial data (yr. ended 12/31/09): Revenue,
$152,197; assets, $396,579 (M); gifts received,
$86,258; expenditures, $172,731; program
services expenses, $147,906; giving activities
include $4,414 for grants to individuals, and
$143,492 for foundation-administered programs.
Purpose and activities: The foundation provides
humanitarian food and medicine parcels to needy
individuals, material assistance to endangered
minority cultures, and dissident assistance for
individuals suffering repercussions such as
imprisonment, police harassment, torture, job
dismissal, or other forms of reprisal on account of
outspokenness in defense of human rights.
Fields of interest: International human rights.
Type of support: Grants to individuals.
Limitations: Giving primarily in Croatia, Hungary,
Romania, Serbia, Slovakia, and Ukraine.
Officers and Directors:* Laslo Hamos,* Pres.;
Emese Latkoczky,* Secy.
EIN: 133254319

1456
The Hurford Foundation
c/o Davidson, Dawson & Clark, LLP
60 E. 42nd St.
New York, NY   10165-0001

Established in 1986.
Donors: John B. Hurford†; BEA Assocs., Inc.
Grantmaker type: Independent foundation.
Financial data (yr. ended 12/31/10): Assets,
$12,420,446 (M); expenditures, $1,408,286;
qualifying distributions, $1,094,225; giving
activities include $1,038,600 for 16 grants (high:
$217,500; low: $5,000).
Fields of interest: Arts; Higher education; Human
services; Children/youth, services; International
affairs.
Type of support: General/operating support.
Limitations: Applications not accepted. Giving
primarily in NY. Generally no grants to individuals.
Application information: Contributes only to
pre-selected organizations.
   Board meeting date(s): Quarterly
Officers and Directors:* Robert C. Miller,* Pres.
and Treas.; Jayne M. Kurzman,* V.P.; William W.
Priest, Jr.,* Secy.
EIN: 133394688

1457
IBM International Foundation
(formerly IBM South Africa Projects Fund)
c/o Prog. Mgr.
New Orchard Rd.
Armonk, NY   10504-1709   (914) 765-2344
URL: http://www.ibm.com/ibm/ibmgives/
IBM Fellowship Grants Website: http://
www.ibm.com/developerworks/university/
phdfellowship/
KidSmart Early Learning Program Website: http://
www.kidsmartearlylearning.org/
E-mail for IBM Fellowship Grants:
phdfellow@us.ibm.com

Established in 1985 in NY.
Donor: International Business Machines Corp.
Grantmaker type: Company-sponsored foundation.
Financial data (yr. ended 12/31/10): Assets,
$178,699,959 (M); gifts received, $25,404,256;
expenditures, $18,471,060; qualifying
distributions, $19,368,870; giving activities include
$10,422,749 for grants, and $7,141,145 for
employee matching gifts.
Purpose and activities: The foundation supports
organizations involved with arts and culture, K-12
education, the environment, health, employment,
human services, diversity, science, public policy
research, and minorities.
Fields of interest: Engineering; Computer science;
Physics; Mathematics; Arts; Elementary/secondary
education; Education, early childhood education;
Education, continuing education; Education,
reading; Health care; Human services; Civil/human
rights, equal rights; Science, formal/general
education; Engineering/technology; Science; Public
policy, research; Disabilities, people with;
Minorities.
Type of support: General/operating support;
Program development; Publication; Fellowships;
Employee matching gifts; Donated products; In-kind
gifts.
Limitations: Applications accepted. Giving on a
national and international basis, with emphasis on
CA and NY, and in Asia, Victoria, Australia, Canada,
China, Europe, India, Italy, London, England, and
Russia. No support for fraternal, labor, political, or
religious organizations or private or parochial
schools. No grants to individuals (except for
fellowships), or for scholarships, capital campaigns,
fundraising, construction or renovation projects,
chairs, endowments, conferences, symposia, or
sports competitions.
Publications: Application guidelines; Informational
brochure; Program policy statement.
Application information: Proposals should be no
longer than 2 pages. Additional information may be
requested at a later date. Applicants must be
nominated by a faculty member for IBM Fellowship
Grants. Application form not required.
   Initial approach: Proposal; complete online
      nomination form for IBM Fellowship Grants
   Copies of proposal: 1
   Deadline(s): None; Sept. 22 to Nov. 2 for IBM
      Fellowship Grants
   Final notification: 1 month
Officers and Directors:* Samuel J. Palmisano,*
Chair.; John C. Iwata,* Vice-Chair.; Stanley S.
Litow,* Pres.; Andrew Bonzani, Secy.; Robert Del
Bene, Treas.; Nick D'Anniballe, Cont.; Mark
Loughridge; Robin G. Willner.
Number of staff: 1 full-time professional.
EIN: 133267906
Recent grants for international programs:

1457-1 Global Netoptex, San Jose, CA, $60,574.
   For China documentary. 2009.
1457-2 IBM Italy Foundation, Milan, Italy,
   $425,000. For educational and cultural
   initiatives. 2009.
1457-3 IBM United Kingdom Trust, London,
   England, $4,693,000. To deliver educational and
   cultural programs to selected European
   Countries. 2009.
1457-4 United Way of York Region, Markham,
   Canada, $220,497. For IBM Canadian Matching
   Grants Program. 2009.
1457-5 United Way/Centraide Ottawa, Ottawa,
   Canada, $125,000. For local social and
   voluntary initiatives. 2009.

1458
IIMI, Inc.
c/o Hertz, Herson & Company, LLP
477 Madison Ave.
New York, NY   10022-5841

Established in 1997 in DE and NY.
Donor: Susan Wexner Revocable Trust.
Grantmaker type: Independent foundation.
Financial data (yr. ended 06/30/10): Assets,
$21,536,591 (M); expenditures, $1,142,185;
qualifying distributions, $1,089,482; giving
activities include $1,078,423 for 13+ grants (high:
$333,333).
Fields of interest: Education; Human services;
Children/youth, services; International
development; Jewish federated giving programs;
Jewish agencies & synagogues.
International interests: Israel.
Limitations: Applications not accepted. Giving in
Israel and to national organizations for the benefit
of Israel, primarily in CA, Washington, DC, MA, and
New York, NY. No grants to individuals.
Application information: Contributes only to
pre-selected organizations.
Officer and Directors:* Susan Wexner,* Pres. and
Secy.-Treas.; Dr. Bertrand Agus; Dr. Saul G. Agus;
Raymond Kanner; Gregg H. Levy, Esq.; Michael S.
Oberman, Esq.; Mark Saks, Esq.
EIN: 134077817

1459
The Indira Foundation
c/o BCRS Assoc., LLC
100 Wall St., 11th Fl.
New York, NY   10005-3701

Established in 1999 in CT.
Donor: Avi Nash.
Grantmaker type: Independent foundation.
Financial data (yr. ended 08/31/10): Assets,
$6,889,487 (M); gifts received, $150;
expenditures, $189,269; qualifying distributions,
$179,583; giving activities include $175,683 for 17
grants (high: $50,000; low: $332).
Fields of interest: Hinduism; Human services;
Health organizations, association; Higher
education; Elementary/secondary education;
Media/communications; Education.
International interests: India.
Limitations: Applications not accepted. Giving
primarily IL and NY. No grants, gifts, scholarships,
or loans to individuals.
Application information: Contributes only to
pre-selected organizations.

Trustees: Avi Nash; Sandra Nash.
EIN: 134051213

1460
INSEAD Management Education Foundation

(formerly International Management Education Foundation)
FDR Sta.
P.O. Box 7555
New York, NY 10150-7555
Contact: Thomas C. Barry, Pres.

Established in 1990.
Grantmaker type: Public charity.
Financial data (yr. ended 12/31/10): Revenue, $1,725,249; assets, $832,668 (M); gifts received, $1,771,201; expenditures, $1,677,969; giving activities include $21,900 for grants, and $1,618,435 for grants to organizations outside the U.S.
Purpose and activities: The foundation promotes management education in Europe and around the world.
Fields of interest: Business school/education.
International interests: Europe.
Limitations: Giving on a national and international basis.
Officers and Trustees:* Thomas C. Barry,* Pres.; Carol M. Donohue, Secy.; Frank Burgel,* Treas.; Anne C. Holbach; Daniel Lalonde; Margaret E. Osius; Sharyanne J. McSwain; Ilona Nemeth.
EIN: 130209297

1461
Institute of International Education, Inc.

809 United Nations Plz., 9th Fl.
New York, NY 10017-3380 (212) 883-8200
Contact: Allan E. Goodman, Pres. and C.E.O.; Margot Steinberg, Chief Devel. Off.
FAX: (212) 984-5566; E-mail: dkaisth@iie.org; E-mail for Margot Steinberg: msteinberg@iie.org; URL: http://www.iie.org
Facebook: http://www.facebook.com/IIEglobal
Flickr: http://www.flickr.com/photos/iieglobal
Twitter: http://twitter.com/#!/IIEglobal
YouTube: http://www.youtube.com/IIEglobal

Established in 1919 in NY.
Grantmaker type: Public charity.
Financial data (yr. ended 09/30/10): Revenue, $331,251,469; assets, $180,798,884 (M); gifts received, $309,497,032; expenditures, $338,249,112; giving activities include $43,823,838 for grants, $60,595,039 for grants to organizations outside the U.S., and $134,391,685 for grants to individuals.
Purpose and activities: By enabling outstanding men and women to study, conduct research, and receive practical training outside their own countries, the institute fosters mutual understanding, builds global problem-solving capabilities, creates the human resources needed to build democratic and pluralistic societies and market economies, and strengthens the international competence of U.S. citizens; the institute also maintains an emergency loan fund for foreign students and aids in the administration of several government and foundation fellowship and exchange programs.

Fields of interest: International affairs, national security; Higher education; Arts; Education; International exchange.
Type of support: Continuing support; Management development/capacity building; Emergency funds; Conferences/seminars; Curriculum development; Fellowships; Research; Grants to individuals; Scholarships—to individuals; Exchange programs.
Limitations: Applications accepted. Giving on a national and international basis.
Publications: Application guidelines; Annual report; Grants list; Informational brochure.
Application information: Application form required.
    Initial approach: Telephone
    Deadline(s): Jan. 25 for Whitaker International Fellows and Scholars Program; June 25 for Toyota International Teacher Program
    Board meeting date(s): Jan., Apr., and Oct.
Officers and Trustees:* Thomas S. Johnson,* Chair.; Ruth Hinerfeld,* Vice-Chair.; Henry G. Jarecki,* Vice-Chair.; Dr. Allan E. Goodman,* Pres. and C.E.O.; Henrik N. Vanderlip,* Treas.; Mark A. Angelson; Maryam Ansary; Lee Bollinger; Maria Livanos Cattaui; Richard A. Debs; Henry Kaufman; Henry A. Kissinger; John Sexton; Linda Vester; and 33 additional trustees.
EIN: 131624046

1462
Integrative Medicine Foundation, Inc.

P.O. Box 67
New York, NY 10113-0067 (212) 337-3025
FAX: (212) 337-3041;
E-mail: info@integrativemedicinefoundation.org
Facebook: http://www.facebook.com/integrativemedicinefoundation?ref=s
YouTube: http://www.youtube.com/IMFNY

Established in 2007 in NY.
Donor: The Riordan Fund.
Grantmaker type: Operating foundation.
Financial data (yr. ended 06/30/09): Assets, $327,104 (M); gifts received, $679,338; expenditures, $673,914; qualifying distributions, $638,737; giving activities include $160,695 for 1 grant.
Purpose and activities: The mission of the foundation is to build sustainable communities through research and development of traditional medicine to achieve the vision of creating an integrative system of medicine based on best practice research that influences government health policy worldwide.
Fields of interest: Health care, information services; Health care.
International interests: Africa.
Limitations: Applications not accepted. Giving primarily in Kenya and Uganda.
Application information: Unsolicited requests for funds not accepted.
Officers and Directors:* Paige Ruane,* Pres.; Patrick Kearney,* Exec. Dir.; Hadi Ali; Melissa Woodman.
EIN: 651253152

1463
InterExchange, Inc.

161 6th Ave.
New York, NY 10013-1205 (212) 924-0446
FAX: (212) 924-0575;
E-mail: grants@interexchange.org; URL: http://www.interexchange.org

Established in 1988 in NY.
Grantmaker type: Public charity.
Financial data (yr. ended 12/31/10): Revenue, $10,369,280; assets, $32,502,989 (M); expenditures, $9,982,544; giving activities include $66,700 for grants to individuals.
Purpose and activities: The organization seeks to promote cultural awareness through a wide range of work and travel, language, volunteer, professional training, internship, and au pair programs within the U.S. and around the world.
Fields of interest: International affairs, formal/general education; International affairs, public education; International development; International exchange.
Publications: Application guidelines.
Application information: In addition to completed and signed grant application form, applicants must submit two essays, two letters of recommendation from academic instructors or employers, resume, photocopy of U.S. passport or permanent resident card, and $50 application fee (for Christianson Grant applicants only). Telephone interviews may be conducted as part of the selection process. Application form required.
    Initial approach: Download application form from InterExchange web site
    Deadline(s): Mar. 15, July 15, and Oct. 15 for Christianson Grant; eight weeks prior to desired program start date for Working Abroad Grant
    Final notification: Six to eight weeks after deadline
Officers: Uta Christianson, Pres.; Paul Christianson, Secy.; Christine La Monica-Lunn, Exec. Dir.
Board Members: Hope E. Checkley; Janet Johnson; Larry Rothchild.
EIN: 133449415

1464
International Federation of Red Cross and Red Crescent Societies at the United Nations, Inc.

420 Lexington Ave., Ste. 2811
New York, NY 10170

Established in 1992 in NY.
Grantmaker type: Independent foundation.
Financial data (yr. ended 12/31/09): Assets, $0 (M); gifts received, $2,066,006; expenditures, $2,318,028; qualifying distributions, $1,618,194; giving activities include $1,618,194 for 19 grants (high: $200,000).
Fields of interest: International relief; American Red Cross.
International interests: Switzerland; Global programs.
Limitations: Applications accepted. Giving on an international basis, with emphasis on Geneva, Switzerland.
Application information:
    Initial approach: Letter

Officers: Elise Baudot-Queguiner; Bekel Geleta; Andrew Rizk; Matthew Zarghese.
EIN: 133682664

1465
International Fellowships Fund
(also known as IFF)
809 United Nations Plz.
New York, NY 10017-3503 (212) 984-5558
Contact: Joan Dassin, Exec. Dir.
FAX: (212) 984-5594; URL: http://www.fordifp.org

Supporting organization of the Institute of International Education.
Grantmaker type: Public charity.
Financial data (yr. ended 09/30/10): Revenue, $24,735,713; assets, $138,961,386 (M); gifts received, $15,000,000; expenditures, $43,626,362; giving activities include $4,447,609 for grants, $21,667,939 for grants to organizations outside the U.S., and $12,888,379 for grants to individuals.
Purpose and activities: The fund provides opportunities for advanced study to exceptional individuals who will use this education to become leaders in their respective fields.
Fields of interest: Education; International economic development; International human rights; Community/economic development.
International interests: East Jerusalem; Brazil; Chile; China; Egypt; Ghana; Guatemala; India; Indonesia; Kenya; Mexico; Mozambique; Nigeria; Peru; Philippines; Russia; Senegal; South Africa; Tanzania, Zanzibar and Pemba; Thailand; Uganda; Vietnam; West Bank/Gaza (Palestinian Territories).
Type of support: Fellowships; Scholarships—to individuals.
Limitations: Giving limited to Brazil, Chile, China, Egypt, Ghana, Guatemala, India, Indonesia, Kenya, Mexico, Mozambique, Nigeria, Palestinian territories, Peru, Philippines, Russia, Senegal, South Africa, Tanzania, Thailand, Uganda, and Vietnam.
Publications: Informational brochure.
Application information: Applications are currently not being accepted. See website for more information.
Officers and Directors:* Donald McHenry,* Chair.; Joan Dassin, Exec. Dir.; Harriet Elam-Thomas; Pablo J. Farias; Victor J. Goldberg; Dr. Karen A. Holbrook; Barron M. Tenny; Darren C. Walker.
Number of staff: 9 full-time professional; 4 part-time professional.
EIN: 134162722

1466
The International Legal Foundation, Ltd.
55 Washington Str., Ste. 622
Brooklyn, NY 11201-8360 (718) 852-2220
Contact: Natalie Rea, Exec. Dir.
E-mail: info@theilf.org; URL: http://www.theilf.org

Established in 2001in NY.
Donors: The OSI Developement Foundation; Oak Foundation; German Mission to the United States; Canadem; Management Systems International; Daniel & Florence Guggeheim Foundation; Deutshe Gesellschaft Fur Technische; Third Millenium Foundation.
Grantmaker type: Public charity.

Financial data (yr. ended 08/31/10): Revenue, $2,284,129; assets, $1,931,910 (M); gifts received, $2,283,765; expenditures, $2,419,529; program services expenses, $1,839,551.
Purpose and activities: Giving to assist in the establishment of fair criminal justice systems in post-conflict countries.
Fields of interest: International affairs, equal rights.
Limitations: Applications not accepted. No grants to individuals.
Application information: Contributes only to pre-selected organizations.
Officer: Natalie Rea, Exec. Dir.
Directors: Phillip Ackermann; Aileen Donnelly; Henry Gonzalez; Polly Mallinson; Sebastian von Einsiedel.
EIN: 134193728

1467
International Rescue Committee, Inc.
122 E. 42nd St.
New York, NY 10168-1289 (212) 551-3000
Contact: George Rupp, Pres. and C.E.O.
FAX: (212) 551-3179;
E-mail: fundraising@theirc.org; URL: http://www.theirc.org
Facebook: http://www.facebook.com/InternationalRescueCommittee
RSS Feed: http://feeds.feedburner.com/IRCNews
Twitter: http://twitter.com/#!/theirc
Voices from the Field Blog: http://blog.theirc.org
YouTube: http://www.youtube.com/theirc

Founded in 1933 in NY.
Grantmaker type: Public charity.
Financial data (yr. ended 09/30/10): Revenue, $317,301,472; assets, $182,691,961 (M); gifts received, $316,175,409; expenditures, $314,208,514; giving activities include $1,444,533 for grants, $95,099,306 for 190 grants to organizations outside the U.S., and $23,247,232 for grants to individuals.
Purpose and activities: The committee provides relief, rehabilitation, protection, resettlement services, and advocacy for refugees, displaced persons, and victims of oppression and violent conflict.
Fields of interest: Immigrants/refugees.
International interests: Afghanistan; Azerbaijan; Bosnia-Herzegovina; Burundi; Colombia; Croatia; Ethiopia; Georgia (Republic of); Guinea; Indonesia; Iraq; Kenya; Liberia; Macedonia; Pakistan; Rwanda; Sierra Leone; Sudan; Tanzania, Zanzibar and Pemba; Thailand; Uganda; Yugoslavia (Former).
Type of support: Grants to individuals.
Limitations: Applications not accepted. Giving on a national and international basis.
Publications: Annual report; Financial statement; Newsletter.
Application information: Unsolicited requests for funds not accepted.
Officers and Directors:* Sarah O'Hagan,* Co-Chair.; Tom Schick,* Co-Chair.; Liv Ullmann,* Vice-Chair., Intl.; George Rupp,* Pres. and C.E.O.; George Biddle, Sr. V.P.; John Keyes, Sr. V.P., Intl. Progs.; Carrie Ross Welch, Sr. V.P., Ext. Rels.; Edward Bligh, V.P., Comms.; Donna Campbell, V.P., Human Resources; Robert Carey, V.P., Resettlement; Sue Dwyer, V.P., Progs.; Janet Harris, V.P., Devel.; Michael Kocher, V.P., Intl. Progs.; Patricia Long, V.P. and C.F.O.; Ellen O'Connell, V.P., Admin. and Board Rels.; Anne Richard, V.P., Govt. Rels. and Advocacy; Jean Kennedy Smith,* Secy.; Carrie Simon, Genl. Counsel; Tracy Wolstencroft,*

Treas.; Morton I. Abramowitz; Laurent Alpert; Cliff Asness; Christoph Becker; Mary M. Boies; Andrew Brimmer; Glenda Burkhart; Trinh Doan; Kenneth R. French; and 21 additional directors.
EIN: 135660870

1468
Interpeace, Inc.
7001 Brush Hollow Rd.
Westbury, NY 11590-1743

Established in FL and NY.
Donors: Clarence Westbury Foundation; Paul Knight; Jeffrey Lewis; Gile Conway-Gordon; Reverend James Parks Morton; Philip R. Forlenza; Kathleen Forlenza; Robin Johnson; Brownington Foundation; Howard McMorris; Joseph M. Sigelman.
Grantmaker type: Public charity.
Financial data (yr. ended 12/31/09): Revenue, $41,002; assets, $101,960 (M); gifts received, $41,002; expenditures, $8,751.
Purpose and activities: The organization works to promote dialogue between warring parties in conflict-ridden or post-conflict areas throughout the world, in an effort to find peaceful settlements.
Fields of interest: International conflict resolution; International affairs.
Limitations: Giving on an international basis.
Officers: Daniel Hazelton, Pres.; Scott Weber, V.P.; Matthias Stiefel, Secy.-Treas.
EIN: 141877608

1469
The Interpublic Group of Companies, Inc., Corporate Giving Program
1114 Avenue of the Americas
New York, NY 10036 (212) 704-1200
Contact: Tom Cunningham, Corp. Comms.
FAX: (212) 704-1201;
E-mail: tom.cunningham@interpublic.com;
URL: http://www.interpublic.com/corporatecitizenship/communityinvolvement

Grantmaker type: Corporate giving program.
Purpose and activities: The Interpublic Group of Companies, Inc., makes charitable contributions to organizations involved with arts and culture, and education. Support is given primarily in areas of company operations.
Fields of interest: Human services; International relief; Arts; Graduate/professional education; General charitable giving.
Type of support: General/operating support; Employee volunteer services; Pro bono services - marketing/branding; Pro bono services - communications/public relations.
Limitations: Giving primarily in areas of company operations.

1470
Isdell Foundation
136 Madison Ave., 3rd Fl.
New York, NY 10016-6711 (212) 842-8920
Contact: Yodon Thonden, Exec. Dir.
FAX: (212) 842-8936; E-mail: info@isdell.org

Established in 1994 in NY.
Donor: Kevin Toner.
Grantmaker type: Independent foundation.

Financial data (yr. ended 12/31/10): Assets, $12,652,095 (M); gifts received, $5,550,000; expenditures, $726,501; qualifying distributions, $691,666; giving activities include $691,666 for grants.
Purpose and activities: Giving for international affairs and public affairs.
Fields of interest: International affairs; Public affairs.
Type of support: Seed money; Research; Publication; Program evaluation; Program development; Management development/capacity building; General/operating support; Conferences/ seminars.
Limitations: Giving on a national basis.
Publications: Application guidelines.
Application information: Application form not required.
 Initial approach: Letter of inquiry
 Deadline(s): Dec. 31
Officer and Directors:* Yodon Thonden,* Exec. Dir.; Kevin Toner.
EIN: 223341359

1471
Israel Cancer Research Fund, Inc.
295 Madison Ave., Ste. 1030
New York, NY 10104-0095 (212) 969-9800
Contact: Michael Feinman, Exec. Dir.
FAX: (212) 969-9822; E-mail: mail@icrfny.org;
Toll-free tel.: (888) 654-4273; URL: http:// www.icrfonline.org

Established in 1976 in NY.
Grantmaker type: Public charity.
Financial data (yr. ended 12/31/09): Revenue, $3,595,737; assets, $7,862,770 (M); gifts received, $3,652,147; expenditures, $2,807,607; giving activities include $985,382 for grants to organizations outside the U.S.
Purpose and activities: The organization supports cancer research in Israel.
Fields of interest: Cancer research.
International interests: Israel.
Type of support: Research.
Limitations: Applications accepted. Giving on an international basis, primarily in Israel.
Application information: Application form required.
 Initial approach: Download application form
 Deadline(s): Mar. 15 and Sept. 15 for Postdoctoral Fellowships; Dec. 15 for all other grants and awards
Officers and Trustees:* S. Donald Friedman,* Co-Chair.; Yashar Hirshaut,* M.D., Co-Chair.; Michael Rosenfelt,* Co-Chair.; Louis Brause,* Vice-Chair.; Alfred Rosenbaum, M.D., Vice-Chair.; Benjamin Bonavida, Ph.D., Co-Pres.; Harriet Elisofon,* Co-Pres.; Bradley Goldhar, Co-Pres.; Kenneth E. Goodman, 1st V.P.; Louis Brause,* V.P.; Julie S. Mitnick,* M.D., V.P.; Leah Susskind,* M.D., V.P.; Eve Wald,* V.P.; Cynthia Perl,* Secy.; Lawrence D. Loeb,* Treas.; Mitch Orlik, Exec. Dir.; Marc J. Berger, M.D.; Evelyn Bienefeld; Benjamin Bonavida, Ph.D.; Lynda Brafman.
Number of staff: 3 full-time professional; 4 full-time support.
EIN: 510181215

1472
Israel Humanitarian Foundation, Inc.
(formerly Israel Histadrut Foundation, Inc.)
2 W. 46th St., Ste. 1500
New York, NY 10036-4502 (212) 683-5676
Contact: Aaron Hoter-Ishay, Pres.
FAX: (212) 213-9233; E-mail: stanley@ihf.net;
Toll-free tel.: (888) 443-4256; URL: http:// www.ihf.net

Established in 1960.
Grantmaker type: Public charity.
Financial data (yr. ended 09/30/09): Revenue, $1,427,705; assets, $2,453,059 (M); gifts received, $1,426,770; expenditures, $971,657; giving activities include $319,139 for grants.
Purpose and activities: The foundation administers a donor advised fund that supports a wide range of humanitarian causes in the U.S. and Israel.
Fields of interest: Human services.
International interests: Israel.
Type of support: Equipment; Exchange programs; Fellowships; General/operating support; Grants to individuals; Program development; Seed money.
Limitations: Applications not accepted. Giving on a national and international basis, primarily in Israel. No support for political organization.
Application information: Contributes only to pre-selected organizations.
 Board meeting date(s): Quarterly
Officers and Directors:* Aaron Hoter-Ishay, Pres.; Michael Melnicke,* Treas.; Dror Hoter-Ishay; Gatt Hoter-Ishay; Nirit Mola.
Number of staff: 1 full-time professional; 1 part-time professional; 1 full-time support.
EIN: 237088770

1473
Janklow Foundation
445 Park Ave.
New York, NY 10022-2606

Established in 1986 in NY.
Donor: Morton L. Janklow.
Grantmaker type: Independent foundation.
Financial data (yr. ended 06/30/10): Assets, $3,275,937 (M); expenditures, $339,350; qualifying distributions, $307,944; giving activities include $307,502 for 113 grants (high: $35,000; low: $25).
Purpose and activities: Giving primarily for arts and cultural institutions, higher education and human services.
Fields of interest: Arts; Higher education; Education; Hospitals (general); Human services; International affairs.
Limitations: Applications not accepted. Giving primarily in New York, NY. No grants to individuals.
Application information: Contributes only to pre-selected organizations.
Trustees: Angela Janklow Harrington; Linda LeRoy Janklow; Lucas Janklow; Morton L. Janklow.
EIN: 133357111

1474
The Japan Foundation
152 West 57th St., 17th Fl.
New York, NY 10019-3310 (212) 489-0299
FAX: (212) 489-0409; E-mail: info@jfny.org;
Additional address: 333 South Grand Ave., Ste. 2250, Los Angeles, CA 90071, Tel.: (213)

621-2267, Fax: (213) 621-2590, URL: http:// www.jfalc.org, e-mail: jflainfo@jfalc.org;
URL: http://www.jfny.org/

Established in 1972.
Grantmaker type: Public charity.
Purpose and activities: The foundation's objective is to promote international cultural exchange and mutual understanding between Japan and other countries through the exchange of persons, support of Japanese studies, support of Japanese-language instruction, and arts-related exchanges.
Fields of interest: Arts; International affairs, goodwill promotion; International affairs, foreign policy; International studies.
Publications: Informational brochure; Newsletter.
Application information:
 Deadline(s): Varies
Officers: Shin'ichiro Asao, Pres.; Hiroshi Ota, Sr. V.P.; Muneharu Kusaba, Exec. V.P.; Kyoko Nakayama, Exec. V.P.; Masahiko Noro, Dir. General, U.S. Offices.

1475
Jesselson Foundation
445 Park Ave., Ste. 1502
New York, NY 10022-8637 (212) 751-3666
Contact: Michael Jesselson, 1st V.P.

Incorporated in 1955 in NY.
Donors: Ludwig Jesselson†; Erica Jesselson†.
Grantmaker type: Independent foundation.
Financial data (yr. ended 04/30/10): Assets, $7,736,660 (M); expenditures, $1,329,450; qualifying distributions, $1,325,920; giving activities include $1,264,403 for 56 grants (high: $518,000; low: $18).
Purpose and activities: Grants largely for higher and Jewish education, welfare funds, health agencies, and synagogues; some support for cultural programs.
Fields of interest: Museums (ethnic/folk arts); Arts; Secondary school/education; Higher education; Theological school/education; Education; Health organizations, association; Human services; Jewish federated giving programs; Jewish agencies & synagogues.
International interests: Israel.
Limitations: Applications accepted. Giving primarily in New York, NY.
Application information:
 Initial approach: Letter (typed)
 Deadline(s): None
Officers: Michael Jesselson, 1st V.P. and Secy.; Benjamin Jesselson, 2nd V.P. and Treas.
Directors: Steven Chill; Ted Mirvis; Claire Strauss.
EIN: 136075098

1476
Jewelers for Children
52 Vanderbilt Ave., 19th Fl.
New York, NY 10017-3827 (212) 687-2949
FAX: (212) 687-3226;
E-mail: info@jewelersforchildren.org; URL: http:// www.jewelersforchildren.org

Established in 1999 in OH.
Grantmaker type: Public charity.
Financial data (yr. ended 09/30/10): Revenue, $3,782,342; assets, $931,546 (M); gifts received, $3,777,752; expenditures, $3,786,428; program

services expenses, $3,038,170; giving activities include $3,038,170 for 10 grants (high: $600,000; low: $25,000).

Purpose and activities: The organization is supported by members of the jewelry industry to provide funds to charities that support children.

Fields of interest: Children.

International interests: Africa; India.

Type of support: Fellowships; Research.

Limitations: Applications not accepted. Giving on a national and international basis.

Publications: Informational brochure; Newsletter; Program policy statement.

Application information: Unsolicited requests for funding not considered or acknowledged.

Board meeting date(s): Jan. and June

Officers and Directors:* Edward Bridge,* Chair.; Ruth Batson,* V.P., Charity Progs.; Joel Schechter,* V.P., Mktg. and Public Rels.; Peter Engel,* V.P., Fundraising; Terry Chandler,* V.P., Special Progs.; Steven Kaiser,* Secy.; Dennis Ulrich,* Treas.; and 54 additional directors.

Number of staff: 2 full-time professional; 1 full-time support.

EIN: 133716474

1477
Jewish Council for Public Affairs
116 E. 27th St.10 Fl.
New York, NY   10016-8942   (212) 684-6950
E-mail: contactus@thejcpa.org; URL: http://www.jewishpublicaffairs.org

Established in 1944 in NY; as the National Jewish Community Relations Advisory Council; current name adopted in 1997.

Grantmaker type: Public charity.

Financial data (yr. ended 12/31/10): Revenue, $2,511,289; assets, $1,509,991 (M); gifts received, $2,240,224; expenditures, $2,731,707; giving activities include $19,650 for grants.

Purpose and activities: The council works to safeguard the rights of Jews in the U.S., in Israel, and around the world; and, in order to accomplish that, to protect, preserve, and promote a just American society, one that is democratic and pluralistic.

Fields of interest: Public affairs; Human services; International affairs; Jewish federated giving programs; Jewish agencies & synagogues.

Limitations: Giving on a national and international basis.

Officers and Board Members:* Conrad Giles, Chair.; Lawrence M. Gold,* Vice-Chair.; Harold Goldberg,* Vice-Chair.; Bruce Alan Lev,* Vice-Chair.; David Luchins,* Vice-Chair.; Susan Penn,* Vice-Chair.; Midge Perlman Shafton,* Vice-Chair.; Robert H. Siskin,* Vice-Chair.; Marc Stanley, Vice-Chair.; Susan Turnbull, Vice-Chair.; Albert D. Chernin, Exec. Vice-Chair. Emeritus; Rabbi Steve Gutow, Pres.; Stephen Stone,* Secy.; David Bohm,* Treas.; and 70 additional board members.

EIN: 131624104

1478
The Jewish Federations of North America, Inc.
(formerly United Jewish Communities, Inc.)
P. O. Box 157
Wall St. Sta.
New York, NY   10268-0157   (212) 284-6500
E-mail: info@jewishfederations.org; URL: http://www.jewishfederations.org/index.aspx?page=1
RSS Feed: http://www.jewishfederations.org/rss.ashx?Type=2&ComponentID=293194
RSS Feed: http://www.jewishfederations.org/rss.ashx?Type=2&ComponentID=319757
RSS Feed: http://www.jewishfederations.org/rss.ashx?Type=2&ComponentID=332787

Established in 1935 in NY.

Grantmaker type: Public charity.

Financial data (yr. ended 06/30/10): Revenue, $43,059,944; assets, $184,813,491 (M); gifts received, $34,737,311; expenditures, $41,858,650; giving activities include $2,028,923 for grants.

Purpose and activities: The organization seeks to protect and enhance the well-being of Jews in North America, Israel and around the globe.

Fields of interest: Jewish agencies & synagogues.

International interests: Israel.

Limitations: Giving on a national and international basis.

Publications: Annual report; Financial statement.

Officers and Trustees:* Kathy E. Manning,* Chair.; Michael M. Adler,* Vice-Chair.; Marilyn Blumer,* Vice-Chair.; Diane Feinberg,* Vice-Chair.; Harley Gross,* Vice-Chair.; Jerry Silverman,* Pres. and C.E.O.; Harvey J. Barnett,* Secy.; Heschel J. Raskas,* Treas.; Robert Arogeti; Jimmy Berg; Carol Cooper; Betsy Gidwitz; Debbie Horwitz; Bruce Sholk; and 32 additional trustees.

EIN: 131624240

1479
The Jewish Institute for the Blind
353 Lexington Ave., Ste. 1200
New York, NY   10016-0941   (212) 532-4155
Contact: Eric Loeb, Secy.
FAX: (212) 447-7683; E-mail: info@jewishblind.org; URL: http://www.jewishblind.org

Established in 1984.

Grantmaker type: Public charity.

Financial data (yr. ended 06/30/09): Revenue, $64,360; assets, $52,846 (M); gifts received, $63,850; expenditures, $133,162; giving activities include $33,459 for grants.

Purpose and activities: The institute provides a wide range of activities for education, rehabilitation, health and social welfare for the blind and visually impaired.

Fields of interest: Blind/visually impaired.

International interests: Israel.

Limitations: Giving limited to Israel.

Publications: Newsletter; Program policy statement.

Officers: Rabbi David Lapp, Pres.; Eric Loeb, Secy.

EIN: 133193296

1480
Jewish National Fund, Inc.
42 E. 69th St.
New York, NY   10021-5003   (212) 879-9305
FAX: (212) 570-1673;
E-mail: communications@inf.org; Toll-free tel.: (888) 563-0099; URL: http://www.jnf.org
Facebook: http://www.facebook.com/jewishnationalfund
Flickr: http://www.flickr.com/photos/jewishnationalfund
Foursquare URL: http://foursquare.com/venue/1649770
LinkedIn: http://www.linkedin.com/company/20036
Twitter: http://twitter.com/jnfusa
YouTube: http://www.youtube.com/jewishnationalfund

Established in 1901 in NY.

Grantmaker type: Public charity.

Financial data (yr. ended 09/30/10): Revenue, $39,273,484; assets, $105,025,944 (M); gifts received, $37,137,566; expenditures, $36,961,113; giving activities include $3,371,991 for grants, and $11,275,282 for grants to organizations outside the U.S.

Purpose and activities: The fund works to plant trees, build parks, create new communities, construct roads, and build reservoirs throughout Israel.

Fields of interest: Environment; Jewish agencies & synagogues.

International interests: Israel.

Type of support: Scholarship funds.

Limitations: Giving on a national basis, and to Israel.

Publications: Annual report.

Officers: Ronald S. Lauder, Chair. and Co-Pres.; Russell F. Robinson, C.E.O.; Harold Cohen, C.O.O.; Stanley M. Chesley, Co-Pres.; Leonard L. Kleinman, Esq., 1st V.P.; Arthur Silber, Treas.; Mitchel Rosenzweig, C.F.O.

EIN: 131659627

1481
The Jewish Women's Foundation of New York
130 E. 59th St.,
New York, NY   10022-1302   (212) 836-1478
Contact: Joy Sisisky, Exec. Dir.
FAX: (212) 836-1831;
E-mail: trudy@jewishwomenny.org; URL: http://www.jewishwomenny.org

Established in 1995 in NY.

Grantmaker type: Public charity.

Financial data (yr. ended 06/30/10): Revenue, $40,168; assets, $4,554,332 (M); gifts received, $293,706; expenditures, $452,998; giving activities include $50,000 for grants to organizations outside the U.S.

Purpose and activities: The foundation is committed to addressing the unmet needs of Jewish women and girls in the New York area and beyond.

Fields of interest: Jewish agencies & synagogues; Girls; Women.

International interests: Israel.

Type of support: Program development; Conferences/seminars; Publication; Seed money; Curriculum development; Research; Technical assistance; Program evaluation.

Limitations: Applications accepted. Giving primarily in New York City and in Israel. No grants for scholarships, equipment, capital campaigns, or continuing support for existing programs.
Publications: Application guidelines; Grants list; Informational brochure; Newsletter.
Application information: Application form required.
Initial approach: Concept letter (no more than two pages)
Copies of proposal: 10
Deadline(s): Sept. 15
Board meeting date(s): Five meetings each year
Officers and Directors:* Madeleine R. Grant,* Pres.; Miriam Caslow, V.P.; Lauren Wachtle,* Secy.; Peggy Garfunkel,* Treas.; Joy Sisisky, Exec. Dir.; Caryl Ackerman; Madelyn Bucksbaum Adamson; Naomi Altschul; Mady Caslow; and 17 additional directors.
Number of staff: 2 full-time professional; 1 part-time professional; 1 part-time support.
EIN: 133897852

1482
Mata Ji Foundation
P.O. Box 1359
New York, NY 10018-0019 (212) 840-2222
Contact: Anastasios Kopsidas, Secy.

Established in 2001.
Donor: Jai Ma Creation Inc.
Grantmaker type: Company-sponsored foundation.
Financial data (yr. ended 12/31/10): Assets, $164,209 (M); gifts received, $100,000; expenditures, $355,826; qualifying distributions, $354,500; giving activities include $354,500 for grants.
Purpose and activities: The foundation supports organizations involved with education, health, children and youth, and religion.
Fields of interest: Spirituality; Education; Children/youth, services; Health care, patient services; Religion.
International Interests: India.
Type of support: General/operating support.
Limitations: Applications accepted. Giving primarily Phoenix, AR, Little Neck, NY, and in India.
Application information: Application form not required.
Initial approach: Letter of Inquiry
Deadline(s): None
Officers: Shilpi Kopsidas, Pres.; Satmata Kopsidas, V.P.; Anastasios Kopsidas, Secy.
EIN: 113557588

1483
Yibing and Ping Jiang Foundation
c/o Schiff Hardin LLP
666 5th Ave.
New York, NY 10103-0001
Contact: Paul J. Collins

Established in 2006 in NY.
Donors: Ping Jiang; Yibing Guan.
Grantmaker type: Independent foundation.
Financial data (yr. ended 12/31/10): Assets, $10,738,771 (M); gifts received, $150,000; expenditures, $207,799; qualifying distributions, $155,125; giving activities include $155,000 for 3 grants (high: $100,000; low: $5,000).
Fields of interest: Education; Arts.
International interests: China.

Limitations: Applications not accepted. Giving primarily in MN. No grants to individuals.
Application information: Contributes only to pre-selected organizations.
Officers and Director:* Ping Jiang,* Pres. and Treas.; Yibing Guan, V.P. and Secy.
EIN: 205945642

1484
Elton John AIDS Foundation, Inc.
584 Broadway, Ste. 907
New York, NY 10012-3229 (212) 219-0670
E-mail: matt.blinstrubas@ejaf.org; URL: http://www.ejaf.org/
Elton John AIDS Foundation's Philanthropy Promise: http://www.ncrp.org/philanthropys-promise/who

Established in the United States in 1992 and in the United Kingdom (EJAF-UK) in 1993.
Grantmaker type: Public charity.
Financial data (yr. ended 12/31/09): Revenue, $6,255,768; assets, $7,622,184 (M); gifts received, $6,703,357; expenditures, $6,330,158; giving activities include $5,372,703 for grants, and for 1 grant to an organization outside the U.S.
Purpose and activities: The foundation supports innovative HIV prevention programs, efforts to eliminate stigma and discrimination associated with HIV/AIDS, and direct care and support services for people living with HIV/AIDS. EJAF strategically targets its grants to key regions and populations that are poorly served by current prevention efforts and most at risk of infection, including: critically under-served communities of the Southern United States, the Caribbean, and Latin America; highly-marginalized populations (such as injection drug users, men who have sex with men, and incarcerated individuals); and underserved populations (such as African Americans and young people).
Fields of interest: AIDS; Youth; Young adults; Young adults, female; Young adults, male; Women; Minorities; Men; Children; Adults, women; Adults, men; Adults; Children/youth; African Americans/Blacks; Offenders/ex-offenders; Substance abusers; AIDS, people with; LGBTQ.
International interests: Canada; Caribbean; Central America; South America.
Type of support: General/operating support.
Limitations: Applications accepted. Giving to the U.S., Canada, Caribbean, Central and South America. No support for for-profit institutions. No grants to individuals, or for research grants, meetings, conferences, capital, or infrastructure costs.
Publications: Financial statement; Grants list.
Application information: International organizations outside of the foundation's normal geographic boundaries that are interested in funding should contact email@ejaf-uk.org for grant information. Application form required.
Initial approach: Online application
Copies of proposal: 1
Deadline(s): Varies
Officers and Executive Board Members:* Sir Elton John,* CBE, Chair.; Barron Segar,* Secy.; M. Michele Burns,* Treas.; Scott P. Campbell,* Exec. Dir.; Edwina Barbis; David Furnish; Billie Jean King; Ilana Kloss; Sarah McMullen; Frank Presland; John Scott; and 15 additional board members.
Number of staff: 3 full-time professional.
EIN: 582033460

1485
The 1994 Elizabeth R. Johnson Charitable Trust
c/o JH Cohn LLP
1212 Avenue of the Americas
New York, NY 10036-1602

Established in 1994 in NY.
Donor: Elizabeth Ross Johnson.
Grantmaker type: Independent foundation.
Financial data (yr. ended 12/31/10): Assets, $6,807,389 (M); expenditures, $320,000; qualifying distributions, $320,000; giving activities include $320,000 for grants.
Purpose and activities: Giving primarily for children and social services, including U.S.-based organizations which support programs in Cambodia.
Fields of interest: Museums (art); Higher education, college; Education; Human services; Children/youth, services.
International interests: Cambodia.
Limitations: Applications not accepted. Giving primarily in New York, NY. No grants to individuals.
Application information: Contributes only to pre-selected organizations.
Trustees: Betty Wold Johnson; Elizabeth Ross Johnson.
EIN: 137046313

1486
Christian A. Johnson Endeavor Foundation
1060 Park Ave.
New York, NY 10128-1033
Contact: Julie J. Kidd, Pres.

Incorporated in 1952 in NY.
Donors: Christian A. Johnson†; Charlotte Johnson Charitable Lead Trust.
Grantmaker type: Independent foundation.
Financial data (yr. ended 12/31/10): Assets, $204,669,926 (M); expenditures, $10,935,844; qualifying distributions, $10,138,970; giving activities include $7,945,768 for 50 grants (high: $3,180,290; low: $131).
Purpose and activities: Giving concentrated on private institutions of higher learning at the baccalaureate level in the United States and Europe and performing arts organizations in New York City; occasional support for perceived needs in other areas of education and the arts.
Fields of interest: Arts; Higher education; Education.
International interests: Europe.
Type of support: General/operating support; Program development; Seed money; Curriculum development; Matching/challenge support.
Limitations: Applications accepted. Giving primarily in the U.S. and Central and Eastern Europe. No support for government agencies, or for community or neighborhood projects, religious institutions, or for health care. No grants to individuals, or for annual campaigns, emergency funds, deficit financing, land acquisitions, building projects, medical research, demonstration projects, publications, or conferences; no loans (except for program-related investments).
Publications: Application guidelines; Financial statement; Program policy statement.
Application information: Application form not required.
Initial approach: Letter of inquiry
Copies of proposal: 1
Board meeting date(s): Spring

Officers and Trustees:* Julie J. Kidd,* Pres. and Treas.; Christen L. Kidd, Secy.; Donald W. Harward; Ann B. Spence.
Number of staff: 3 full-time professional; 1 full-time support.
EIN: 136147952
Recent grants for international programs:
1486-1 Artes Liberales Institute, Warsaw, Poland, $535,907. For General Operating Support. 2010.
1486-2 Artes Liberales Institute, Warsaw, Poland, $12,508. For General Operating Support. 2010.
1486-3 Bratislava Institute of Humanism, Bratislava, Slovakia, $400,295. For General Operating Support. 2010.
1486-4 European College of Liberal Arts, Berlin, Germany, $3,180,290. For General Operating Support. 2010.
1486-5 European College of Liberal Arts, Berlin, Germany, $969,930. For General Operating Support. Grant made in stock. 2010.
1486-6 European College of Liberal Arts, Berlin, Germany, $334,494. For General Operating Support. 2010.
1486-7 Schoodic International Sculpture Symposium, Steuben, ME, $20,000. For Salaries for Part-Time Director and Project Manager. 2010.
1486-8 University of Chicago, Chicago, IL, $80,000. For Endeavor Chicago Scholars Program. 2010.

1487
Joint Israel
711 3rd Ave.
New York, NY   10017-4014

Grantmaker type: Public charity.
Financial data (yr. ended 12/31/10): Revenue, $56,799,000; assets, $68,899,000 (M); gifts received, $56,618,000; expenditures, $62,889,000; giving activities include $55,714,838 for grants to organizations outside the U.S.
Purpose and activities: The organization seeks to help Israel's most disadvantaged population: children, youth at risk, immigrants, the elderly, and people with disabilities.
Fields of interest: Aging; Disabilities, people with; Immigrants/refugees; Children.
International interests: Israel.
Type of support: Grants to individuals.
Limitations: Giving primarily in Israel.
Directors: Heinz Eppler; Haim Factor; Jack Habib; Sylvia Hassenfeld; Ellen Heller; Jonathan W. Kolker; Arnon Mantvor; Eugene Philips; Eugene Ribakoff; Steven Schwager.
EIN: 134203820

1488
Joukowsky Family Foundation
410 Park Ave., Ste. 1610
New York, NY   10022-4407   (212) 355-3151
Contact: Nina J. Koprulu, Pres. and Dir.
FAX: (212) 355-3147; URL: http://www.joukowsky.org

Established in 1981 in NY as a trust; incorporated in 1983.
Grantmaker type: Independent foundation.
Financial data (yr. ended 10/31/10): Assets, $19,660,084 (M); expenditures, $1,890,452;

qualifying distributions, $1,804,425; giving activities include $531,790 for 50 grants (high: $50,000; low: $250), and $139,017 for foundation-administered programs.
Purpose and activities: Giving primarily for higher and secondary education; support also for a wide range of cultural, social, archaeological and historical activities.
Fields of interest: Education.
Type of support: Scholarship funds; Fellowships; Capital campaigns; General/operating support; Continuing support; Endowments.
Limitations: Applications not accepted. Giving primarily in the northeastern U.S.
Publications: Grants list; IRS Form 990 or 990-PF printed copy available upon request.
Application information: Contributes only to pre-selected organizations.
Officer and Directors:* Nina J. Koprulu,* Pres.; Vivien M. Bailey-Barnum, C.O.O.; Henry Christensen III; Artemis A.W. Joukowsky; Martha S. Joukowsky.
Number of staff: 3 full-time professional; 1 part-time professional.
EIN: 133242753
Recent grants for international programs:
1488-1 American Center of Oriental Research in Amman, Boston, MA, $36,000. For ongoing restoration, Petra Great Temple. 2009.
1488-2 American Community School at Beirut, New York, NY, $10,000. For the Annual Fund. 2009.
1488-3 American Research Institute in Turkey, Philadelphia, PA, $17,050. For Freely Fellowship. 2009.
1488-4 American School of Classical Studies at Athens, Princeton, NJ, $65,000. For the University of Chicago Excavations at Isthmia. 2009.
1488-5 American Turkish Society, New York, NY, $12,750. For institutional promotion. 2009.
1488-6 American University of Beirut, New York, NY, $10,000. For the Annual Fund. 2009.
1488-7 Bogazici University and Robert College International Alumni Association, College Station, TX, $50,000. For renovation of Hamlin Hall. 2009.
1488-8 Bogazici University and Robert College International Alumni Association, College Station, TX, $50,000. For renovation of Hamlin Hall. 2009.
1488-9 Brown University, Providence, RI, $20,506. For Institute for Archaeology for transport of artifacts from Petra. 2009.
1488-10 Council on Foreign Relations, New York, NY, $16,920. For Corporate program. 2009.
1488-11 International Honors Program, Boston, MA, $10,000. For general support. 2009.
1488-12 Robert College of Istanbul, New York, NY, $15,000. For the Annual Fund. 2009.
1488-13 Unitarian Universalist Service Committee, Cambridge, MA, $30,000. For the Martha Sharp Cogan Film Project. 2009.
1488-14 Unitarian Universalist Service Committee, Cambridge, MA, $20,000. For the Martha Sharp Cogan Film Project. 2009.
1488-15 Unitarian Universalist Service Committee, Cambridge, MA, $15,000. For the Martha Sharp Cogan Film Project. 2009.
1488-16 Unitarian Universalist Service Committee, Cambridge, MA, $15,000. For the Martha Sharp Cogan Film Project. 2009.
1488-17 Unitarian Universalist Service Committee, Cambridge, MA, $10,000. For the Martha Sharp Cogan Film Project. 2009.

1488-18 Unitarian Universalist Service Committee, Cambridge, MA, $10,000. For the Martha Sharp Cogan Film Project. 2009.
1488-19 Unitarian Universalist Service Committee, Cambridge, MA, $10,000. For the Martha Sharp Cogan Film Project. 2009.
1488-20 Unitarian Universalist Service Committee, Cambridge, MA, $10,000. For the Martha Sharp Cogan Film Project. 2009.
1488-21 World Monuments Fund, New York, NY, $100,000. For general operating support. 2009.
1488-22 World Monuments Fund, New York, NY, $22,550. For Hadrian Award Luncheon. 2009.

1489
Max Kade Foundation, Inc.
6 E. 87th St., 5th Fl.
New York, NY   10128-0505   (646) 672-4354
Contact: Lya Friedrich Pfeifer, Pres. and Treas.
URL: http://maxkadefoundation.org

Incorporated in 1944 in NY.
Donor: Max Kade†.
Grantmaker type: Independent foundation.
Financial data (yr. ended 12/31/09): Assets, $87,184,576 (M); expenditures, $3,923,503; qualifying distributions, $3,844,480; giving activities include $3,244,575 for 181 grants (high: $250,000; low: $500).
Purpose and activities: Grants primarily to higher educational institutions, with present emphasis on post-doctoral research exchange programs between the United States and Europe in medicine or in the natural and physical sciences. Foreign scholars and scientists are selected by the sponsoring universities upon nomination by the respective Academy of Sciences. Grants also for visiting faculty exchange programs and the training of language teachers.
Fields of interest: Language/linguistics; Literature; Higher education; Biomedicine; Medical research, institute; Physical/earth sciences; Chemistry; Engineering; Biology/life sciences.
International interests: Europe; Germany.
Type of support: Program development; Professorships; Exchange programs.
Limitations: Applications accepted. Giving primarily in the U.S. and Europe. No grants to individuals, or for operating budgets, capital funds, development campaigns, or endowment funds; no loans.
Publications: Occasional report.
Application information:
Initial approach: Letter or proposal
Deadline(s): None
Board meeting date(s): As required
Officers and Directors:* Lya Friedrich Pfeifer,* Pres. and Treas.; Berteline Baier Dale,* Secy.; Reinhard Augustin; Guenter Blobel; Fritz Kade, Jr., M.D.
Number of staff: 4 full-time professional.
EIN: 135658082

1490
The J. M. Kaplan Fund, Inc.
261 Madison Ave., 19th Fl.
New York, NY   10016-2303   (212) 767-0630
Contact: Angela Carabine, Grants Mgr.
FAX: (212) 767-0639; E-mail: info@jmkfund.org; Application address for Furthermore Grants in Publishing program:, c/o Ann Birckmayer, Prog. Assoc., P.O. Box 667, Hudson, NY 12534; tel.: (518) 828-8900; URL: http://www.jmkfund.org

Incorporated in 1948 in NY as Faigel Leah Foundation, Inc.; The J.M. Kaplan Fund, Inc., a DE corporation, merged with it in 1975 and was renamed The J.M. Kaplan Fund, Inc.

Donor: Members of the J.M. Kaplan family.

Grantmaker type: Independent foundation.

Financial data (yr. ended 12/31/09): Assets, $87,279,542 (M); expenditures, $13,990,553; qualifying distributions, $11,522,308; giving activities include $10,102,363 for 439 grants (high: $280,000; low: $75; average: $1,000–$100,000).

Purpose and activities: Giving primarily in three areas: environment, historic preservation, and human migrations. The fund offers program-related investments to encourage ventures of particular interest. The fund also has a trustee-initiated grants program that considers grant requests invited by the trustees.

Fields of interest: Historic preservation/historical societies; Environment, natural resources; Environment; Human services; International migration/refugee issues; Community/economic development.

Type of support: General/operating support; Continuing support; Program development; Publication; Seed money; Research; Technical assistance; Program-related investments/loans.

Limitations: Applications accepted. Giving primarily in New York City; cross-borders of North America; and worldwide. No grants to individuals, including scholarships and fellowships, or for construction or building programs, endowment funds, operating budgets of educational or medical institutions, film or video, or sponsorship of books, dances, plays, or other works of art.

Publications: Annual report (including application guidelines).

Application information: Proposals received by fax will not be considered.

Initial approach: 2- to 3-page letter of inquiry
Copies of proposal: 1
Deadline(s): None; requests received after Oct. 1 will be carried over to next year
Board meeting date(s): Quarterly
Final notification: Applicants will be notified within 30 days of receipt of letter of inquiry if they are to submit a full proposal

Officers and Trustees: * Peter W. Davidson,* Chair.; Conn Nugent, Exec. Dir.; William P. Falahee, Cont.; Joan K. Davidson,* Pres. Emeritus; Betsy Davidson; G. Bradford Davidson; J. Matthew Davidson; Caio Fonseca; Elizabeth K. Fonseca; Isabel Fonseca; Quina Fonseca; Mary E. Kaplan; Richard D. Kaplan.

Number of staff: 4 full-time professional; 1 full-time support.

EIN: 136090286

Recent grants for international programs:

1490-1 Aga Khan Trust for Culture, Geneva, Switzerland, $50,000. For Bi-National Pilot Preservation Project in Pakistan and India. 2009.

1490-2 American Immigration Council, Washington, DC, $100,000. For Rapid Response Project on Immigration Reform by the Immigration Policy Center. 2009.

1490-3 American Immigration Council, Washington, DC, $50,000. For Rapid Response Project on Immigration Reform by the Immigration Policy Center. 2009.

1490-4 American Littoral Society, Highlands, NJ, $25,000. For Regional Marine Conservation Project's Arctic Funders Group Secretariat in 2009 and 2010. 2009.

1490-5 Americas Voice Education Fund, Washington, DC, $150,000. For National Blog Desk and Online Advocacy Project. 2009.

1490-6 Clean Air-Cool Planet, Portsmouth, NH, $30,000. For Avoiding Arctic Tipping Points. 2009.

1490-7 Cotidiano Mujer, Montevideo, Uruguay, $25,000. For Nunca en Domingo (Never on Sunday) Radio Program. 2009.

1490-8 DOCOMOMO International, Paris, France, $25,000. For (1) the attendance of a delegation of 6 members of Docomomo Cuba to the 10th International Conference in September 2008 in Rotterdam; (2) general operating support for Docomomo Cuba. 2009.

1490-9 DOCOMOMO International, Paris, France, $25,000. For the publication of Docomomo Cuba's National Register. 2009.

1490-10 DOCOMOMO International, Paris, France, $10,000. For general operating support for Docomomo Cuba. 2009.

1490-11 Doctors Without Borders USA, New York, NY, $10,000. For general support. 2009.

1490-12 English-Speaking Union of the United States, New York, NY, $10,000. For general support. 2009.

1490-13 Environmental Defense, New York, NY, $37,500. For Protecting Coastal and Ocean Resources in Cuba. 2009.

1490-14 Equal Rights Trust, London, England, $20,000. For Promoting the Principles on Equality Project. 2009.

1490-15 Fundacion Amistad, New York, NY, $50,000. For general operating support. 2009.

1490-16 Fundacion Amistad, New York, NY, $25,000. For the preservation and on-site follow-up for the Calle Cardenas Project. 2009.

1490-17 H. John Heinz III Center for Science, Economics and the Environment, Washington, DC, $30,000. For selected participants to attend the Arctic Governance Project's 2010 Summit in Tromso, Norway. 2009.

1490-18 Harvard University, Cambridge, MA, $35,000. For Conservation of the Lydian Altar and Synagogue Mosaics at Sardis, Turkey. 2009.

1490-19 Human Rights Watch, New York, NY, $25,000. For general support. 2009.

1490-20 Human Rights Watch, New York, NY, $25,000. For general support. 2009.

1490-21 ImmigrationWorks Foundation, Washington, DC, $100,000. For Educating for Comprehensive Reform Project. 2009.

1490-22 International Union for Conservation of Nature and Natural Resources, Washington, DC, $62,500. For High Seas Conservation Initiative. 2009.

1490-23 International Union for Conservation of Nature and Natural Resources, Washington, DC, $25,000. For workshop to develop a strategy and action plan for protecting the Sargasso Sea - The Atlantic Cradle of Life scheduled for February 2010. 2009.

1490-24 Migration Policy Institute, Washington, DC, $50,000. For Labor Market Initiatives. 2009.

1490-25 Migration Policy Institute, Washington, DC, $15,000. For Improving Policy Responses to the Issue of Credentialing. 2009.

1490-26 National Autonomous University of Mexico, Mexico City, Mexico, $100,000. For Understanding Coupled Human-Ecological Systems to Achieve Conservation Goals in Janos Biosphere Reserve. 2009.

1490-27 Natural Resources Defense Council, New York, NY, $75,000. For Integrating Strengthened International Marine Governance into U.S. Arctic Policy. 2009.

1490-28 Natural Resources Defense Council, New York, NY, $37,500. For Improving International Oceans and Arctic Oceans Governance. 2009.

1490-29 New York University, New York, NY, $175,000. For Excavations at Aphrodisias. 2009.

1490-30 Northern Jaguar Project, Tucson, AZ, $10,000. For general operating support. 2009.

1490-31 Pacific Environment, San Francisco, CA, $125,000. For Creating a Circumpolar Civil Society to Protect the Arctic Environment and Promote Sustainable Social Development. 2009.

1490-32 Pacific Environment, San Francisco, CA, $50,000. To build the capacity of the Russian Association of Indigenous Peoples of the North (RAIPON) to conserve the Arctic. 2009.

1490-33 Pew Charitable Trusts, Philadelphia, PA, $50,000. For Oceans North: Protecting Life in the Arctic Campaign. 2009.

1490-34 Progressive States Network, New York, NY, $50,000. For State Immigration Project. 2009.

1490-35 Saskatchewan Heritage Foundation, Regina, Canada, $35,000. For Heritage Conservation Grant Program: Preservation of Saskatchewan's rural churches and heritage sites. 2009.

1490-36 Simon Fraser University, Burnaby, Canada, $25,000. To facilitate the Arctic Governance Project's Tromsu Workshop in January 2010. 2009.

1490-37 Thomas Sill Foundation, Winnipeg, Canada, $35,000. For The Manitoba Prairie Churches/Prairie Icons Project. 2009.

1490-38 Walter and Duncan Gordon Foundation, Toronto, Canada, $100,000. For Gordon-Kaplan Northern Fellowship. 2009.

1490-39 World Monuments Fund, New York, NY, $200,000. For restoration of the Ani Cathedral and restoration of Ani Chruch of the Redeemer. 2009.

1490-40 World Monuments Fund, New York, NY, $100,000. For Stabilization of the Red Church in Cappadoccia. 2009.

1490-41 World Monuments Fund, New York, NY, $55,000. For Preservation of Sites in Islamic Countries: BULLA REGIA, Tunisia MERYEM ANA CHURCH, Turkey. 2009.

1490-42 World Wildlife Fund, Washington, DC, $35,000. For general operating support. 2009.

1490-43 Zoological Society of London, London, England, $150,000. For The First Global State of the Oceans Report: Creation of the International Programme on the State of Oceans and Seas. 2009.

1491
Irfan Kathwari Foundation, Inc.

1875 Palmer Ave.
Larchmont, NY   10538-3053
E-mail: kathwarifoundation@gmail.com

Established in 1992 in NY.

Donors: IFO Enterprises, Ltd.; M. Farooq Kathwari.

Grantmaker type: Independent foundation.

Financial data (yr. ended 06/30/10): Assets, $4,820,682 (M); gifts received, $1,000; expenditures, $251,260; qualifying distributions, $229,875; giving activities include $164,750 for 15 grants (high: $35,000; low: $250), and $24,250 for grants to individuals.

Purpose and activities: The foundation supports organizations involved with education, minority enrollment, humanitarian assistance, and conflict resolution. The foundation grants scholarships to children of employees of Ethan Allen Interiors, Inc. The foundation also supports special projects focused on Kashmir.
Fields of interest: International migration/refugee issues; Education; Women; Girls.
International interests: Southeast Asia; India; Pakistan.
Type of support: General/operating support; Annual campaigns; Equipment; Program development; Employee-related scholarships.
Limitations: Applications accepted. Giving primarily in Washington, DC and NY.
Application information: The foundation generally does not solicit proposals. Application form not required.
  Initial approach: Letter
  Copies of proposal: 1
  Deadline(s): None
Officers: M. Farooq Kathwari, Pres.; Farah Kathwari, V.P.; Farida Kathwari, Secy.; Omar Kathwari, Treas.
EIN: 133681135

1492
Marina P. and Stephen E. Kaufman Foundation
277 Park Ave., 47th Fl.
New York, NY   10172-3699   (212) 826-0820
Contact: Marina P. Kaufman, Tr.; Stephen E. Kaufman, Tr.

Established in 1996 in NY.
Donors: Marina P. Kaufman; Stephen E. Kaufman.
Grantmaker type: Independent foundation.
Financial data (yr. ended 12/31/10): Assets, $307,177 (M); gifts received, $143,818; expenditures, $220,233; qualifying distributions, $203,402; giving activities include $203,402 for 45 grants (high: $30,720; low: $100).
Fields of interest: Museums (ethnic/folk arts); Education; Athletics/sports, amateur leagues; International human rights; Jewish agencies & synagogues.
Application information: Application form required.
  Initial approach: Letter
  Deadline(s): None
Trustees: Marina P. Kaufman; Stephen E. Kaufman.
EIN: 133922035

1493
The Kaye Family Foundation
c/o C. Judge, The Ayco Co., L.P.
321 Broadway
P.O. Box 860
Saratoga Springs, NY   12866-4110

Established in 1999 in NY.
Donors: Charles R. Kaye; Sheryl J. Kaye.
Grantmaker type: Independent foundation.
Financial data (yr. ended 11/30/10): Assets, $935,245 (M); gifts received, $891,380; expenditures, $725,753; qualifying distributions, $725,185; giving activities include $725,185 for 50 grants (high: $400,000; low: $100).
Fields of interest: International economic development; Higher education; Education; Hospitals (general); Health organizations, association; Jewish agencies & synagogues.

Limitations: Applications not accepted. Giving primarily in New York and Westchester counties, NY. No grants to individuals.
Application information: Contributes only to pre-selected organizations.
Trustees: Charles R. Kaye; Sheryl Kaye.
EIN: 134092284

1494
Anna Maria & Stephen Kellen Foundation, Inc.
c/o Joel E. Sammet & Co., LLP
60 Broad St., Ste. 3600
New York, NY   10004-2338   (212) 269-8628

Established in 1984.
Donors: Stephen M. Kellen†; Anna-Maria Kellen.
Grantmaker type: Independent foundation.
Financial data (yr. ended 04/30/09): Assets, $316,585,850 (M); gifts received, $234,400; expenditures, $10,761,887; qualifying distributions, $8,795,139; giving activities include $8,738,050 for 95 grants (high: $2,454,990; low: $250; average: $25,000–$500,000).
Purpose and activities: Giving primarily for cultural programs, including a music school, a school of design, museums, and performing arts groups; support also for higher and secondary education, Protestant churches, and media and communications.
Fields of interest: Media/communications; Museums; Performing arts, music; Arts; Secondary school/education; Higher education; Medical care, outpatient care; Protestant agencies & churches.
Limitations: Applications not accepted. Giving primarily in New York, NY. No grants to individuals.
Application information: Contributes only to pre-selected organizations.
Officers and Directors:* Anna-Maria Kellen,* Pres.; Marina K. French,* V.P.; Michael Kellen,* Secy.-Treas.
EIN: 133173593
Recent grants for international programs:
1494-1 American Academy in Berlin, New York, NY, $2,454,990. 2009.
1494-2 Ashoka: Innovators for the Public, Arlington, VA, $10,000. 2009.
1494-3 Asia Society, New York, NY, $24,600. 2009.
1494-4 Council on Foreign Relations, New York, NY, $300,000. 2009.
1494-5 Elysium Between Two Continents, New York, NY, $20,000. 2009.
1494-6 French Institute Alliance Francaise, New York, NY, $10,000. 2009.
1494-7 Interfaith Center of New York, New York, NY, $98,250. 2009.
1494-8 International House, New York, NY, $48,000. 2009.

1495
Helen Keller International, Inc.
352 Park Ave. S., 12th Fl.
New York, NY   10010-1709   (212) 532-0544
FAX: (212) 532-6014; E-mail: info@hki.org;
URL: http://www.hki.org

Established in 1919.
Grantmaker type: Public charity.
Financial data (yr. ended 06/30/10): Revenue, $94,627,525; assets, $29,308,695 (M); gifts

received, $94,260,165; expenditures, $96,633,370; giving activities include $1,716,846 for grants, and $2,672,307 for grants to organizations outside the U.S.
Purpose and activities: The organization is committed to fighting and treating preventable blindness and malnutrition around the world, including cataracts, trachoma, onchocerciasis (river blindness) and refractive error.
Fields of interest: Health care; Eye diseases; Economically disadvantaged; Blind/visually impaired.
International interests: Africa; Asia.
Limitations: Applications not accepted. Giving limited to the U.S., Africa, and Asia.
Publications: Annual report.
Application information: Contributes only to pre-selected organizations.
Officers and Trustees:* Bradford Perkins,* Chair.; Nancy Smith Lione,* Vice-Chair. and Secy.; Robert M. Thomas, Jr.,* Treas.; Gerald S. Adolph; Mary Lindley Burton; Howard Cohn, M.D.; and 12 additional trustees.
EIN: 135562162

1496
The Kenbe Foundation
c/o Genevieve Lynch
136 Madison Ave., 3rd Fl.
New York, NY   10016-3322

Established in 2001 in NY.
Donors: Robert Lynch; Genevieve Lynch.
Grantmaker type: Independent foundation.
Financial data (yr. ended 12/31/10): Assets, $4,240,201 (M); gifts received, $2,754,000; expenditures, $228,288; qualifying distributions, $225,000; giving activities include $225,000 for 3 grants (high: $100,000; low: $25,000).
Fields of interest: Public affairs; International peace/security.
Limitations: Applications not accepted. Giving primarily in NY and Washington, DC. No grants to individuals.
Application information: Unsolicited requests for funds not accepted.
Officers: Genevieve Lynch, Pres.; Robert Lynch, C.F.O.
Director: Terence Lohman.
EIN: 134200004

1497
The Hagop Kevorkian Fund
1025 Northern Blvd., Ste. 209
Roslyn, NY   11576-1506   (516) 365-5690

Trust established in 1950; incorporated in 1951 in NY.
Donor: Hagop Kevorkian†.
Grantmaker type: Independent foundation.
Financial data (yr. ended 12/31/10): Assets, $4,636,810 (M); expenditures, $423,924; qualifying distributions, $367,625; giving activities include $326,000 for 8 grants (high: $100,000; low: $3,500).
Purpose and activities: Giving to promote interest in Near and Middle Eastern art through exhibitions and fellowships administered by the recipient institutions for research and study in this field.
Fields of interest: Museums (art); Higher education.
International interests: Middle East.

Type of support: Professorships; Curriculum development; Fellowships; Internship funds; Research.
Limitations: Applications not accepted. Giving primarily in NY. No grants to individuals.
Application information: Unsolicited requests for funds not accepted.
  Board meeting date(s): Spring and fall
Officers: Ralph Minasian,* Pres. and Treas.; Martin D. Polevoy,* V.P. and Secy.
Directors: Ralph S. Hattox; Michele C. Tocci.
EIN: 131839686

1498
Kids Can Free The Children
c/o Paul Battaglia-Jackie Fleischman
12 Fountain Plz.
Buffalo, NY 14202-2292
E-mail: info@freethechildren.com; Additional address: 233 Carlton St., Toronto ON, M5A2L2, Canada

Established in 1997 in NY.
Grantmaker type: Public charity.
Financial data (yr. ended 12/31/10): Revenue, $8,126,685; assets, $2,886,807 (M); gifts received, $8,120,986; expenditures, $8,166,992; giving activities include $6,664,896 for grants to organizations outside the U.S.
Purpose and activities: The organization provides international humanitarian relief, including schoolbuilding, medical relief, leadership, and peacebuilding.
Fields of interest: Human services; Human services, emergency aid; Youth development; Health care; Education.
International interests: Sri Lanka; China; Ecuador; Sierra Leone; Kenya.
Type of support: In-kind gifts.
Limitations: Applications not accepted. Giving on an international basis.
Publications: Annual report; Financial statement; Informational brochure; Newsletter.
Application information: Unsolicited requests for funds not accepted.
  Board meeting date(s): Oct.
Officers and Directors:* Eva Haller,* Pres.; Jonathan White,* V.P.; Libby Heimark,* Secy.; Craig Heimark,* Treas.; Marc Kielburger, Exec. Dir.; Virginia Benderly; Josh Cohen; Amy Eldon; Craig Kielburger; Mary Lewis; Jessica Mayberry; Richard Prins; Hal Schwartz; Helaina Roman; Megan Sidhu.
Number of staff: 10 part-time support.
EIN: 161533544

1499
The Helen Kimmel Foundation
445 Park Ave., Ste. 2100
New York, NY   10022-8609   (212) 888-1470

Established in NY.
Donors: Martin Kimmel; Helen Kimmel.
Grantmaker type: Independent foundation.
Financial data (yr. ended 07/31/09): Assets, $34,296,762 (M); expenditures, $6,243,482; qualifying distributions, $6,121,016; giving activities include $6,121,016 for 9 grants (high: $2,000,000; low: $1,000).
Fields of interest: Museums (art); Hospitals (general); Science, single organization support; Science, formal/general education.

Limitations: Applications not accepted.
Application information: Contributes only to pre-selected organizations.
Trustee: Helen Kimmel.
EIN: 136888806
Recent grants for international programs:
1499-1 American Committee for the Weizmann Institute of Science, New York, NY, $1,041,416. For unrestricted support. 2009.
1499-2 American Committee for the Weizmann Institute of Science, New York, NY, $1,000,000. For unrestricted support. 2009.
1499-3 American Committee for the Weizmann Institute of Science, New York, NY, $1,000,000. For unrestricted support. 2009.
1499-4 American Committee for the Weizmann Institute of Science, New York, NY, $993,600. For unrestricted support. 2009.
1499-5 American Friends of Batsheva Dance Company, New York, NY, $25,000. For unrestricted support. 2009.

1500
The Elbrun and Peter Kimmelman Family Foundation, Inc.
800 3rd Ave., Ste. 3100
New York, NY   10022-7604

Established in 1979 in NY.
Donor: Peter Kimmelman.
Grantmaker type: Independent foundation.
Financial data (yr. ended 11/30/10): Assets, $4,337 (M); gifts received, $187,500, expenditures, $191,316; qualifying distributions, $191,197; giving activities include $191,197 for 30 grants (high: $47,566; low: $150).
Purpose and activities: Giving primarily for the arts and education.
Fields of interest: Historic preservation/historical societies; Arts; Education; International affairs.
Type of support: General/operating support; Annual campaigns.
Limitations: Applications not accepted. Giving primarily in Washington, DC and New York, NY. No grants to individuals.
Application information: Contributes only to pre-selected organizations.
Officers: Peter Kimmelman, Pres.; Elbrun Kimmelman, Treas.
Directors: E. Kweilen Kimmelman; P. Damian Kimmelman.
EIN: 132967083

1501
King Baudouin Foundation United States, Inc.
10 Rockefeller Plz., 16th Fl.
New York, NY   10020-1903   (212) 713-7660
Contact: Jean-Paul Warmoes, Exec. Secy.
FAX: (212) 713-7665; *E-mail:* jeanpaul@kbfus.org;
URL: http://www.kbfus.org

Established in 1997 in GA by the King Baudouin Foundation, Belgium.
Grantmaker type: Public charity.
Financial data (yr. ended 12/31/10): Revenue, $9,577,649; assets, $5,180,895 (M); gifts received, $9,443,430; expenditures, $9,263,763; giving activities include $39,107 for grants, and $8,636,936 for grants to organizations outside the U.S.

Purpose and activities: The foundation helps U.S. donors achieve their philanthropic goals in Europe and sub-Saharan Africa. From one-time grants to long-term, structured and effective giving programs, the foundation provides solutions that can be tailored to their needs, interests and priorities. KBFUS helps ensure that their giving remains personalized, efficient, tax deductible and secure.
Fields of interest: Arts, cultural/ethnic awareness; Education; Environment; Health care; Human services; International affairs.
International interests: Europe; Sub-Saharan Africa.
Type of support: General/operating support; Capital campaigns; Building/renovation; Equipment; Conferences/seminars; Publication; Fellowships; Research; Exchange programs.
Limitations: Applications not accepted. Giving on an international basis in Europe and Sub-Saharan Africa.
Publications: Financial statement; Informational brochure; Newsletter.
Application information: Contributes only to pre-selected organizations; unsolicited requests for funds not considered or acknowledged.
  Board meeting date(s): Bi-annually
Officers and Directors:* Georges Jacobs,* Pres.; Alan John Blinken,* V.P.; Gregory A. Dexter,* Secy.; Luc Tayart de Borms,* Treas.; Emile L. Boulpaep, M.D.; Dominique Struye de Swillande; Francois de Visscher; Natalia Kanem; Peter Piot; Shannon E. St. John.
Number of staff: 2 full-time professional.
EIN: 582277856

1502
Kitov Foundation
c/o BCRS Assocs., LLC
100 Wall St., 11th Fl.
New York, NY   10005-3701

Established in 1987 in NY.
Donor: Jacob Z. Schuster.
Grantmaker type: Independent foundation.
Financial data (yr. ended 06/30/11): Assets, $2,632,381 (M); expenditures, $183,268; qualifying distributions, $178,524; giving activities include $178,524 for grants.
Purpose and activities: Giving primarily for Jewish organizations, temples, and yeshivas.
Fields of interest: Elementary/secondary education; Jewish agencies & synagogues.
International interests: Israel.
Limitations: Applications not accepted. Giving primarily in NY; some funding also in Israel. No grants to individuals.
Application information: Contributes only to pre-selected organizations.
Trustees: Diane T. Schuster; Jacob Z. Schuster.
EIN: 133437905

1503
Samuel and Francine Klagsbrun Foundation
c/o Lehman, Newman & Flynn, C.P.A.s
225 W. 34th St., Ste. 2220
New York, NY   10122-2220

Established in 1987 in NY.
Donors: Samuel C. Klagsbrun; Francine Klagsbrun.
Grantmaker type: Independent foundation.

Financial data (yr. ended 12/31/10): Assets, $743,948 (M); expenditures, $211,161; qualifying distributions, $203,303; giving activities include $203,303 for grants.
Purpose and activities: Giving primarily for Jewish agencies and temples.
Fields of interest: Museums (specialized); Arts; Higher education; Theological school/education; Mental health/crisis services; Human services; Residential/custodial care, hospices; Jewish federated giving programs; Jewish agencies & synagogues.
International interests: Israel.
Type of support: General/operating support; Continuing support; Capital campaigns.
Application information: Application form required.
  Initial approach: Letter
  Deadline(s): None
Directors: Francine Klagsbrun; Samuel C. Klagsbrun.
EIN: 133452159

1504
The Reb Ephraim Chaim & Miriam Rochel Klein Charitable Foundation
614 Ave. J
Brooklyn, NY 11230-3504

Established in 1989 in NY.
Donors: Abraham Klein; Sarah Dinah Klein; L. Rubin; Abraham Leizirowitz; Stuart Schlesinger; Barbara Hurwitz; Beach Terrace Care Center; Fairview Nursing Care Center, Inc.; Grandell Rehabilitation; Hyde Park Nursing Home, Inc.; Oceanside Care Center; Park Terrace Care Center; Queens Nassau Nursing Home; Talmide Chidishei Harim.
Grantmaker type: Independent foundation.
Financial data (yr. ended 12/31/10): Assets, $51,337,219 (M); gifts received, $120,000; expenditures, $1,506,118; qualifying distributions, $1,397,611; giving activities include $1,397,611 for grants.
Purpose and activities: Giving primarily to Jewish agencies, temples, and schools.
Fields of interest: Elementary/secondary education; Human services; Jewish federated giving programs; Jewish agencies & synagogues; Religion.
International interests: Israel.
Limitations: Applications not accepted. Giving primarily in Brooklyn, NY; some giving nationally, as well as in Israel. No grants to individuals.
Application information: Contributes only to pre-selected organizations.
Directors: Abraham Klein; Sarah Dinah Klein.
EIN: 223000780

1505
Koha Foundation, Inc.
c/o Mac Corkindale
3960 Merrick Rd.
Seaford, NY 11783-2826

Established in 2005 in CT.
Donor: Craig Nevill-Manning.
Grantmaker type: Independent foundation.
Financial data (yr. ended 12/31/09): Assets, $3,873,903 (M); expenditures, $234,628; qualifying distributions, $231,513; giving activities include $225,130 for 6 grants (high: $200,000; low: $1,000).

Fields of interest: Human services; Philanthropy/voluntarism; International human rights; Education; Health care; Community/economic development.
Limitations: Applications not accepted. No grants to individuals.
Application information: Unsolicited requests for funds not accepted.
Officers: Kirsten Nevill-Manning, Pres.; Craig Nevill-Manning, V.P.
EIN: 202462647

1506
The Kohlberg Foundation, Inc.
111 Radio Cir.
Mount Kisco, NY 10549-2609
Contact: Nancy White McCabe, Exec. V.P. and Exec. Dir.
FAX: (914) 241-1195; E-mail: dehaan@kfound.org; URL: http://www.kohlbergfoundation.org/

Established in 1989 in NY.
Donor: The Kohlberg Foundation.
Grantmaker type: Independent foundation.
Financial data (yr. ended 12/31/09): Assets, $307,143,667 (M); gifts received, $4,502,580; expenditures, $16,475,774; qualifying distributions, $14,629,944; giving activities include $13,443,557 for 159 grants (high: $1,146,750; low: $100).
Purpose and activities: Support for environmental and conservation programs, integrative medicine, community, educational and cultural organizations.
Fields of interest: Environment; Health organizations, association; Medical research, institute; Children/youth, services.
International interests: Mexico.
Type of support: Program-related investments/loans; Annual campaigns; Land acquisition; Program development; Seed money; Program evaluation.
Limitations: Applications not accepted. Giving primarily in the U.S., with emphasis on CA and MA; giving also in Baja CA, Mexico. No grants to individuals.
Publications: Annual report.
Application information: Contributes only to pre-selected organizations.
  Board meeting date(s): Spring and Fall
Officers and Trustees:* Jerome Kohlberg,* Chair. and Pres.; Nancy White McCabe,* Exec. V.P. and Exec. Dir.; Jennifer Magnone,* Secy.; Dave Davis; Karen K. Davis; Leslie G. Fagen; Curt Greer; Andrew Kohlberg; Karen B. Kohlberg; Pamela Kohlberg; Curt Viebranz.
Number of staff: 4 full-time professional; 1 full-time support.
EIN: 133496263
Recent grants for international programs:
1506-1 Bilateral Safety Corridor Coalition, National City, CA, $30,000. For efforts to combat human trafficking and commercial sexual exploitation along the U.S.-Mexico border. 2009.
1506-2 Bilateral Safety Corridor Coalition, National City, CA, $20,000. For Marist Guest House, which provides shelter to victims of human trafficking and helps them transition back into the community. 2009.
1506-3 Climate Lab, Washington, DC, $16,380. For program support for the Climate Lab, located in Washington, D.C. to support interactive wiki (website) designed to provide tools, resources and a discussion platform for climate change related issues. 2009.

1506-4 Human Rights First, New York, NY, $75,000. For general operating support. 2009.
1506-5 Jane Goodall Institute for Wildlife Research, Education and Conservation, Arlington, VA, $250,000. For community-centered ecosystem conservation in Western Tanzania, which is accomplished through a combination of conservation, education, and the promotion of sustainable livelihoods in local African communities. 2009.
1506-6 Waterkeeper Alliance, New York, NY, $10,000. For program support. 2009.
1506-7 World Education, Boston, MA, $10,000. For the Migrating Safely program, developing the knowledge and life skills of young Nepalese girls, enabling them to migrate safely for work and protect themselves against traffickers and HIV/AIDS. 2009.

1507
Kollel Chazon Ish
c/o Max Wasser
132 Nassau St., Ste. 300
New York, NY 10038-2400

Established in 1975; supporting organization of Kollel Chazon Ish, Israel.
Grantmaker type: Public charity.
Financial data (yr. ended 06/30/10): Revenue, $431,029; assets, $3,853 (M); gifts received, $430,980; expenditures, $434,009; giving activities include $434,000 for grants.
Fields of interest: Jewish federated giving programs.
International interests: Israel.
Limitations: Applications not accepted. Giving limited to Israel.
Application information: Contributes only to a pre-selected organization; unsolicited requests for funds not considered or acknowledged.
Trustees: David H. Stefansky; Meir Stefansky.
EIN: 237442270

1508
Kosciuszko Foundation, Inc.
15 E. 65th St.
New York, NY 10065-6501 (212) 734-2130
Contact: Maryla Janiak, V.P., Education
FAX: (212) 628-4552; E-mail: thekf@aol.com; URL: http://www.thekf.org
Address in Poland: ul. Nowy Swiat 4, Rm. 118, 03-921 Warszawa, tel.: (48) (22) 21-7067

Incorporated in 1925 in NY.
Grantmaker type: Public charity.
Financial data (yr. ended 06/30/10): Revenue, $4,680,221; assets, $30,966,337 (M); gifts received, $3,178,752; expenditures, $2,137,138; giving activities include $104,170 for grants to organizations outside the U.S., and $395,842 for grants to individuals.
Purpose and activities: The foundation is dedicated to promoting and strengthening understanding and friendship between the peoples of Poland and the United States through educational, scientific, and cultural exchanges and other related programs and activities.
Fields of interest: Language/linguistics; Higher education.
International interests: Poland.

Type of support: Fellowships; Scholarship funds; Research; Grants to individuals; Scholarships—to individuals; Exchange programs.
Limitations: Applications accepted. Giving primarily in Poland and the U.S.
Publications: Annual report; Informational brochure (including application guidelines); Newsletter.
Application information: See web site for additional application information. Application form required.
  Initial approach: Letter
  Copies of proposal: 1
  Deadline(s): Varies
  Board meeting date(s): Apr. and Nov.
  Final notification: Varies
Officers and Trustees:* Witold S. Sulimirski,* Chair.; Thaddeus V. Gromada,* Ph.D., Vice-Chair.; Christine J. McMullan,* Vice-Chair.; William J. Nareski,* II, Vice-Chair.; Wanda Senko,* Vice-Chair.; Alex Storozynski, Pres. and Exec. Dir.; Maryla Janiak, V.P., Education; Helen Mary M. Tyszka,* Secy.-Treas.; Adam M. Bak; and 9 additional trustees.
Number of staff: 11 full-time professional; 6 part-time professional; 3 full-time support.
EIN: 131628179

1509
Samuel H. Kress Foundation
174 E. 80th St.
New York, NY 10075-0439 (212) 861-4993
Contact: Wyman Meers, Prog. Admin.
FAX: (212) 628-3146;
E-mail: wyman.meers@kressfoundation.org;
URL: http://www.kressfoundation.org

Incorporated in 1929 in NY.
Donors: Samuel H. Kress†; Claude W. Kress†; Rush H. Kress†.
Grantmaker type: Independent foundation.
Financial data (yr. ended 06/30/10): Assets, $79,955,372 (M); expenditures, $6,117,973; qualifying distributions, $5,187,495; giving activities include $1,789,590 for 198 grants (high: $250,000; low: $25), $2,429,250 for 19 grants to individuals (high: $22,500; low: $4,000), $48,381 for 88 employee matching gifts, and $41,526 for foundation-administered programs.
Purpose and activities: Giving through five main programs: 1) fellowships for pre-doctoral research in art history; 2) advanced training and research in conservation of works of art; 3) development of scholarly resources in the fields of art history and conservation; 4) conservation and restoration of monuments in Europe; and 5) occasional related projects.
Fields of interest: Visual arts; Museums; History/archaeology; Arts.
International interests: Europe.
Type of support: Conferences/seminars; Professorships; Publication; Fellowships; Internship funds; Research; Employee matching gifts.
Limitations: Applications accepted. Giving primarily in the U.S. and Europe. No support for art history programs below the pre-doctoral level, or the purchase of works of art. No grants for living artists, or for operating budgets, continuing support, annual campaigns, endowments, deficit financing, capital funds exhibitions, or films; no loans.
Publications: Application guidelines; Annual report (including application guidelines).
Application information: Application forms required for fellowships in art history and art conservation.

Applications sent by fax not considered. Application form not required.
  Initial approach: Proposal
  Copies of proposal: 1
  Deadline(s): Nov. 30 for research fellowships in art history; Mar. 1 for conservation fellowships, Apr. 1 for interpretive fellowships; Quarterly submission deadlines: Jan. 15, Apr. 15 and Oct. 15
  Board meeting date(s): Annually in winter, spring and fall
  Final notification: 3 months
Officers and Trustees:* Frederick W. Beinecke,* Chair.; Max Marmor,* Pres.; David Rumsey, Secy.-Treas.; Carmela Vircillo Franklin; William Higgins; Cheryl Hurley; Barbara A. Shailor; Daniel H. Weiss.
Number of staff: 4 full-time professional; 1 part-time professional.
EIN: 131624176
Recent grants for international programs:
1509-1 American Academy in Rome, New York Office, New York, NY, $80,000. For Institutional Fellowship in the History of Art. 2010.
1509-2 American Academy in Rome, New York Office, New York, NY, $30,000. For Conservation Grant. 2010.
1509-3 American Alumni of Glasgow University, Milford, CT, $11,500. For Digital Resources Grant in the History of Art. 2010.
1509-4 American Associates of the Royal Academy Trust, New York, NY, $23,400. For Digital Resources Grant in the History of Art. 2010.
1509-5 American School of Classical Studies at Athens, Princeton, NJ, $30,000. For Institutional Fellowship in the History of Art. 2010.
1509-6 American School of Classical Studies at Athens, Princeton, NJ, $22,000. For Institutional Fellowship in the History of Art. 2010.
1509-7 American School of Classical Studies at Athens, Princeton, NJ, $18,000. For Digital Resources Grant in the History of Art. 2010.
1509-8 American School of Classical Studies at Athens, Princeton, NJ, $13,000. For Conservation Fellowship. 2010.
1509-9 Burlington Magazine Foundation, London, England, $10,000. For History of Art grant. 2010.
1509-10 Courtauld Institute of Art, London, England, $25,000. For History of Art grant. 2010.
1509-11 Foundation of the American Institute for Conservation of Historic and Artistic Works, Washington, DC, $55,000. For Conservation Fellowship. 2010.
1509-12 Foundation of the American Institute for Conservation of Historic and Artistic Works, Washington, DC, $10,000. For Conservation Grant. 2010.
1509-13 French Regional and American Museums Exchange, Richardson, TX, $25,000. For Digital Resources Grant in the History of Art. 2010.
1509-14 International Center of Medieval Art, New York, NY, $16,000. For Institutional Fellowship in the History of Art. 2010.
1509-15 International Center of Medieval Art, New York, NY, $15,000. For History of Art grant. 2010.
1509-16 Medici Archive Project, New York, NY, $25,000. For Digital Resources Grant in the History of Art. 2010.
1509-17 University of Glasgow, Glasgow, Scotland, $15,000. For Conservation Fellowship. 2010.
1509-18 World Monuments Fund, New York, NY, $250,000. For Conservation Grant. 2010.

1510
The Kurz Family Foundation, Ltd.
c/o Holz, Rubenstein, Reminick LLP
1430 Broadway, 17th Fl.
New York, NY 10018-3308

Established in 1992 in NY.
Donor: Herbert Kurz.
Grantmaker type: Independent foundation.
Financial data (yr. ended 12/31/09): Assets, $51,699,752 (M); expenditures, $7,096,256; qualifying distributions, $7,006,085; giving activities include $6,860,349 for 88 grants (high: $1,674,500; low: $200).
Fields of interest: Higher education; Environment, natural resources; Hospitals (general); Human services; Children/youth, services; International peace/security; Community/economic development; Jewish agencies & synagogues.
Limitations: Applications not accepted. Giving primarily in NY. No grants to individuals.
Application information: Contributes only to pre-selected organizations.
Officers and Directors:* Herbert Kurz,* Chair.; Ellen Kurz,* Secy.; Leonard Kurz,* Treas.
EIN: 133680855

1511
The Lachman Family Foundation, Inc.
138 Rolling Hill Rd.
Manhasset, NY 11030-2517

Established in 2002 in NY.
Donor: Leon Lachman.
Grantmaker type: Independent foundation.
Financial data (yr. ended 12/31/10): Assets, $8,420,306 (M); gifts received, $1,001,807; expenditures, $243,608; qualifying distributions, $192,000; giving activities include $192,000 for grants.
Fields of interest: Scholarships/financial aid; Performing arts, orchestras; Higher education; Health sciences school/education; International relief, 2004 tsunami.
Limitations: Applications not accepted. No grants to individuals.
Application information: Contributes only to pre-selected organizations.
Officers and Directors:* Leon Lachman,* Pres. and Treas.; Joan Lachman,* V.P. and Secy.; Julie Lachman,* V.P.; Lawrence Lachman,* V.P.; David B. Petshaft,* V.P.
EIN: 320033014

1512
Ladenburg Foundation
c/o Anchin Block & Anchin, LLP
1375 Broadway
New York, NY 10018-7001

Established in 2001 in NY.
Donors: Claudia Bussmann; Dr. Martin Bussmann; Margaret Bussmann; Richard Bussmann; Courtney Bussmann.
Grantmaker type: Operating foundation.
Financial data (yr. ended 12/31/10): Assets, $4,603 (M); gifts received, $137,666; expenditures, $137,025; qualifying distributions, $134,625; giving activities include $131,000 for 3 grants (high: $100,000; low: $15,000).

Purpose and activities: Giving primarily for higher education, including journalism scholarships, a German center for American studies, and a student exchange program, as well as for human rights and the Special Olympics.
Fields of interest: Jewish agencies & synagogues; Performing arts, opera; Higher education; Athletics/sports, Special Olympics; International human rights; Disabilities, people with.
International interests: Israel; Germany.
Limitations: Applications not accepted. Giving primarily in NY.; some funding in Heidelberg, Germany and Jerusalem, Israel. No grants to individuals.
Application information: Contributes only to pre-selected organizations.
Officers and Directors:* Claudia Bussmann,* Chair.; Dr. Martin Bussmann,* Pres. and Treas.; Henry Christensen III.
EIN: 134156286

1513
Lane Family Foundation
c/o BCRS Assocs., LLC
100 Wall St., 11th Fl.
New York, NY   10005-3701

Established in 1987 in NY.
Donors: James N. Lane; Susan W. Lane.
Grantmaker type: Independent foundation.
Financial data (yr. ended 06/30/10): Assets, $456,154 (M); expenditures, $135,730; qualifying distributions, $134,225; giving activities include $134,225 for grants.
Fields of interest: Education; Human services; Children/youth, services; International affairs; United Ways and Federated Giving Programs; Christian agencies & churches.
Limitations: Applications not accepted. Giving primarily in CT and NY. No grants to individuals.
Application information: Contributes only to pre-selected organizations.
Trustees: James N. Lane; Susan W. Lane.
EIN: 133437903

1514
LaSalle Adams Fund
c/o Fiduciary Trust Co. International
600 5th Ave.
New York, NY   10020-2326

Established in 1953 in IL; incorporated in 1999 in NY.
Donor: Sydney Stein, Jr.†.
Grantmaker type: Independent foundation.
Financial data (yr. ended 12/31/10): Assets, $26,549,567 (M); expenditures, $1,366,649; qualifying distributions, $1,026,469; giving activities include $1,026,469 for grants.
Purpose and activities: Giving primarily for environmental and wildlife conservation and protection.
Fields of interest: Philanthropy/voluntarism; Environment, natural resources; Animals/wildlife, preservation/protection.
International interests: Canada; Mexico.
Type of support: Land acquisition; Program development; Seed money; Program evaluation; Matching/challenge support.

Limitations: Applications not accepted. Giving primarily in the Rocky Mountain states. No grants to individuals.
Application information: Contributes only to pre-selected organizations.
  Board meeting date(s): 3 times a year
Officers: Edith Carol Stein, Pres. and Treas.; Nancy C. Stein, V.P. and Secy.; Susan S. Stein, Vice-Secy.
EIN: 161562907

1515
Aaron Laub Memorial Foundation, Inc.
30-50 Whitestone Expwy., No. 300
Flushing, NY   11354-1995

Established in 1988 in NY.
Donors: Norman A. Septimies; Perry Chemical Corp.
Grantmaker type: Independent foundation.
Financial data (yr. ended 11/30/10): Assets, $1,133,323 (M); gifts received, $250,000; expenditures, $253,485; qualifying distributions, $251,185; giving activities include $251,185 for 55 + grants.
Fields of interest: Elementary/secondary education; Higher education; Hospitals (general); Jewish agencies & synagogues.
International interests: Israel.
Limitations: Applications not accepted. Giving primarily in NY, especially in Brooklyn and Queens, and NJ; some giving also in Israel. No grants to individuals.
Application information: Contributes only to pre-selected organizations.
Officers: Eva Lamb Kunstler, Pres.; Irving Laub, V.P.; Jack Feigenbaum, Secy.
EIN: 113018695

1516
Lauder Foundation, Inc.
767 5th Ave., 40th Fl.
New York, NY   10153-0003
Contact: Joan Krupskas, Secy.-Treas.

Incorporated in 1962 in NY.
Donors: Estee Lauder†; Joseph H. Lauder†; Leonard A. Lauder; Ronald S. Lauder; Evelyn Lauder; William Lauder; Estee Lauder, Inc.; LWG Family Partners; EL 2002 Trust.
Grantmaker type: Independent foundation.
Financial data (yr. ended 11/30/10): Assets, $2,197,739 (M); expenditures, $2,217,625; qualifying distributions, $2,091,642; giving activities include $2,074,148 for 103 grants (high: $335,714; low: $200).
Purpose and activities: Giving primarily to a university; funding also for the arts.
Fields of interest: Higher education, university; Performing arts centers; Museums (art).
Type of support: General/operating support; Continuing support; Annual campaigns; Capital campaigns.
Limitations: Applications not accepted. Giving primarily in the metropolitan New York, NY, area, and Philadelphia, PA. No grants to individuals.
Application information: Contributes only to pre-selected organizations.
Officers and Directors:* Leonard A. Lauder,* Pres.; Joel Ehrenkranz,* V.P.; George Schiele,* V.P.; Joan Krupskas, Secy.-Treas.
EIN: 136153743
Recent grants for international programs:

1516-1 American Friends of Hala, Cleveland, OH, $100,000. 2009.
1516-2 American Friends of the Israel Museum, New York, NY, $10,000. 2009.
1516-3 Charities Aid Foundation America, Alexandria, VA, $100,000. 2009.
1516-4 Council on Foreign Relations, New York, NY, $200,000. 2009.
1516-5 Foundation for Art and Preservation in Embassies, Washington, DC, $25,000. 2009.

1517
The Ronald S. Lauder Foundation
767 5th Ave., Ste. 4200
New York, NY   10153-0185   (212) 319-6300
Contact: George Ban, C.E.O. and Exec. V.P.
FAX: (212) 319-9411; URL: http://www.rslfoundation.org
RSS Feed: http://feeds.feedburner.com/ronaldlauder
Twitter: http://twitter.com/ronaldlauderfou

Established in 1987 in NY.
Donors: Estee Lauder†; Ronald S. Lauder; Estee Lauder, Inc.; Chaim Z. Roswaski; Aba M. Dunner; Olaf Ossmann; The Estee Lauder 2002 Trust; Jewish Renaissance Foundation; The Taube Foundation for Jewish Life; Jewish Agency for Israel; Chesed Congregation of America; Conference of European Rabbis; Shuvo Yisroel Charity; Javne Fund; Zentgralrat Der Juden; Juedicshe Gemeinde Hamburg.
Grantmaker type: Operating foundation.
Financial data (yr. ended 12/31/09): Assets, $30,766,318 (M); gifts received, $3,700,900; expenditures, $11,698,987; qualifying distributions, $10,833,706; giving activities include $2,119,840 for grants, and $4,366,344 for foundation-administered programs.
Purpose and activities: Support for Central and Eastern European organizations dedicated to revitalization of Jewish life through educational and cultural programs, and the preservation of Jewish monuments and buildings; support also for a nonsectarian international student exchange program at the secondary level.
Fields of interest: Historic preservation/historical societies; Arts; Elementary/secondary education; Education; Jewish agencies & synagogues; Religion.
International interests: Europe; Austria; Germany; Eastern & Central Europe; Bulgaria; Czech Republic; Slovakia; Hungary; Poland; Romania; Belarus; Estonia; Latvia; Lithuania; Moldova; Ukraine.
Type of support: General/operating support; Continuing support; Building/renovation; Program development; Grants to individuals; Exchange programs.
Limitations: Applications not accepted. Giving primarily in Central and Eastern Europe.
Publications: Financial statement; Informational brochure; Newsletter.
Application information: Unsolicited requests for funds are not considered.
  Board meeting date(s): Varies
Officers and Directors:* Ronald S. Lauder,* Chair. and Pres.; Rabbi Joshua Spinner, C.E.O. and Exec. V.P.; Rabbi Jacob I. Biderman, V.P. for Education; Jacob Z. Schuster,* V.P. for Finance; Dr. George Ban; Micki Edelsohn; Rabbi Pinchas Goldschmidt; Malcolm Hoenlein; Jo Carole Lauder; Richard D. Parsons; Steven Schwager.
EIN: 133445910

1518
Lavelle Fund for the Blind, Inc.
307 W. 38th St., Ste. 2010
New York, NY 10018-9507 (212) 668-9801
Contact: Andrew S. Fisher, Exec. Dir.
FAX: (212) 668-9803;
E-mail: afisher@lavellefund.org; URL: http://www.lavellefund.org/
Grants List: http://www.lavellefund.org/grants.html

Established in 1999; Converted to an independent foundation in 2003.
Grantmaker type: Independent foundation.
Financial data (yr. ended 12/31/10): Assets, $94,349,925 (M); expenditures, $4,463,714; qualifying distributions, $3,880,049; giving activities include $3,397,919 for 52 grants (high: $812,888; low: $4,500).
Purpose and activities: The fund is dedicated to supporting programs that promote the spiritual, moral, intellectual, and physical development of blind and low-vision people of all ages, together with programs that help people avoid vision loss. Priority is given to agencies that concentrate on serving the New York City metropolitan area.
Fields of interest: Eye diseases; Disabilities, people with.
Type of support: Program development.
Limitations: Applications accepted. Giving primarily in the New York City metropolitan area. No grants to individuals, or for deficit reduction, emergency funds, medical research programs, conferences or media events (unless an integral part of a broader program of direct service), or advocacy programs; no loans.
Publications: Grants list; Informational brochure (including application guidelines).
Application information: Application guidelines available on foundation web site. New York/New Jersey Area Common Grant Application Form accepted. Application form not required.
   Initial approach: Letter of inquiry on organization's letterhead
   Copies of proposal: 1
   Deadline(s): None
   Board meeting date(s): Quarterly
   Final notification: 1 week
Officers and Trustees:* Daniel M. Callahan,* Pres.; John J. Caffrey,* V.P. and Treas.; Andrew S. Fisher, Exec. Dir.; Nancy L. Brown; Sr. Mary Flood, M.D., Ph.D.; Thomas A. Galvin; Bro. James Kearney, F.M.S.; Michael A. Lemp, M.D.; J. Robert Lunney; Hon. Kevin B. McGrath, Jr.; John J. McNally; Jane B. O'Connell; Paul A. Sidoti, M.D.
Number of staff: 2 full-time professional.
EIN: 131740463
Recent grants for international programs:
1518-1 Indo-American Eye Care Society, L.V. Prasad Eye Institute, Rochester, NY, $550,000. To establish and help operate 30 community-based primary eye care centers (Vision Centers) in three needy districts of south-central India - and to launch a spectacle dispensing unit to help supply these Centers. 2009.
1518-2 International Agency for the Prevention of Blindness, Southampton, NY, $200,000. To strengthen capacity-building organizations in developing world eye care. 2009.
1518-3 International Agency for the Prevention of Blindness, Southampton, NY, $200,000. For the Seva Foundation in strengthening eye care delivery and sustainability among six eye hospitals in India and Bangladesh and for the training competencies of hospitals in Seva's

Centers for Community Ophthalmology (CCO) worldwide network. 2009.
1518-4 Seva Foundation, Berkeley, CA, $360,000. To strengthen and institutionalize 10 primary eye care centers in Nepal and North India and to provide supplemental support for the centers eye care services to a total of 273,275 students and adults. 2009.
1518-5 Task Force for Global Health, Decatur, GA, $244,978. To conduct a comprehensive SAFE program in Ethiopia, including monitoring and evaluation. 2009.
1518-6 VisionSpring, New York, NY, $300,000. For a partnership with the Bangladeshi nonprofit BRAC to sell 360,000 affordable reading glasses to low-income people throughout Bangladesh. 2009.

1519
Bartholomew J. Lawson Foundation for Children
c/o Bank of America, N.A.
114 W. 47th St., 13th Fl.
New York, NY 10036-0001

Established in 2004 in NY.
Donors: Karen Lawson; Careplus; John J.L. Chobor; 1199 SEIU; Moreland Partners.
Grantmaker type: Public charity.
Financial data (yr. ended 12/31/10): Revenue, $177,498; assets, $1,100,048 (M); gifts received, $111,549; expenditures, $417,663; giving activities include $25,000 for grants.
Purpose and activities: The foundation supports children's literacy programs and farm reconstruction training in Grenada.
Fields of interest: Family services, parent education; Child development, services; Hospitals (general).
International interests: Grenada.
Limitations: Applications not accepted. Giving limited to Boston, MA and Bay Shore, NY. No grants to individuals.
Application information: Contributes only to pre-selected organizations.
Officers and Directors:* Karen Lawson,* Pres.; John J.L. Chobor,* Secy.-Treas.; John Erwin.
EIN: 200130110

1520
Legacy Heritage Fund Limited
(formerly KBRK, Inc.)
c/o Hertz, Herson & Co., LLP
477 Madison Ave.
New York, NY 10022-5802 (212) 686-7160

Established in 1997 in NY and DE.
Donors: VHIV, Inc.; IIMI, Inc.; JLRJ, Inc.; MRHM, Inc.; Susan Wexner Revocable Trust; LMCL, Inc.
Grantmaker type: Independent foundation.
Financial data (yr. ended 06/30/10): Assets, $34,136,409 (M); gifts received, $1,324,075; expenditures, $6,604,365; qualifying distributions, $6,294,108; giving activities include $3,993,549 for 412 grants (high: $462,756; low: $375), $907,639 for 38 grants to individuals (high: $44,792; low: $1,714), and $28,929 for 1 foundation-administered program.
Fields of interest: Education; Jewish federated giving programs; Jewish agencies & synagogues.

Limitations: Applications not accepted. Giving primarily in New York, NY; some giving also in MA, and Washington, DC and Israel. No grants to individuals (except for Legacy Heritage fellowships).
Application information: Unsolicited requests for funds not accepted.
Officer and Directors:* Susan Wexner,* Pres. and Secy.-Treas.; Mark Saks, Esq., V.P. and General Counsel; Dr. Bertrand Agus; Dr. Saul G. Argus; Raymond Kanner; Gregg H. Levy, Esq.; Michael S. Oberman, Esq.
EIN: 134077801
Recent grants for international programs:
1520-1 Beit Knesset Ashkenaz, Modiin, Israel, $10,800. For Synagogue Innovation Project. 2010.
1520-2 Beit Knesset Ashkenaz, Modiin, Israel, $10,800. For Synagogue Innovation Project. 2010.
1520-3 Berman Synagogue, Rehovot, Israel, $11,200. For Synagogue Innovation Project. 2010.
1520-4 Berman Synagogue, Rehovot, Israel, $11,200. For Synagogue Innovation Project. 2010.
1520-5 Hadassah Medical Organization, Jerusalem, Israel, $104,870. For stem cell research, purchase research equipment, hire personnel, develop a stem cell society and fund annual conference. 2010.
1520-6 Hebrew University of Jerusalem, Jerusalem, Israel, $100,000. For stem cell research; purchase research equipment, hire personnel, develop a stem cell society and fund annual conference. 2010.
1520-7 Hebrew University of Jerusalem, Jerusalem, Israel, $60,000. For stem cell research; purchase research equipment, hire personnel, develop a stem cell society and fund annual conference. 2010.
1520-8 Kehillah Zichron Yaakov, Zichron Yaakov, Israel, $10,800. For Synagogue Innovation Project. 2010.
1520-9 Kehillah Zichron Yaakov, Zichron Yaakov, Israel, $10,800. For Synagogue Innovation Project. 2010.
1520-10 Kehillat Eshel Avraham, Beer Sheva, Israel, $10,800. For Synagogue Innovation Project. 2010.
1520-11 Kehillat Eshel Avraham, Beer Sheva, Israel, $10,800. For Synagogue Innovation Project. 2010.
1520-12 Marom-Amuta for Education and Advancement of Learning Disabilities, Ramat Hasharon, Israel, $12,000. For a high school that assists special needs students from low socioeconomic backgrounds. 2010.
1520-13 Marom-Amuta for Education and Advancement of Learning Disabilities, Ramat Hasharon, Israel, $11,000. For a high school that assists special needs students from low socioeconomic backgrounds. 2010.
1520-14 Oranienburger Strasse Synagogue, Berlin, Germany, $11,200. For Synagogue Innovation Project. 2010.
1520-15 Oranienburger Strasse Synagogue, Berlin, Germany, $11,200. For Synagogue Innovation Project. 2010.
1520-16 Technion-Israel Institute of Technology, Haifa, Israel, $75,000. For stem cell research; purchase research equipment, hire personnel, develop a stem cell society and fund annual conference. 2010.

1520-17 Tel Aviv University, Tel Aviv, Israel, $462,756. For funding for scholarships and educational programming emphasizing outstanding high school academic performance without regard to standardized admissions criteria. 2010.

1520-18 Tel Aviv University, Tel Aviv, Israel, $100,000. For stem cell research; purchase research equipment, hire personnel, develop a stem cell society and fund annual conference. 2010.

1520-19 Weizmann Institute of Science, Rehovot, Israel, $108,333. For stem cell research, purchase research equipment, hire personnel, develop a stem cell society and fund annual conference. 2010.

1520-20 Weizmann Institute of Science, Rehovot, Israel, $108,333. For stem cell research; purchase research equipment, hire personnel, develop a stem cell society and fund annual conference. 2010.

1521
Edith and Herbert Lehman Foundation, Inc.

c/o Wendy Lehman Lash
151 E. 79th St.
New York, NY 10075-0564
E-mail: wlash@nyc.rr.com

Incorporated in 1952 in NY.
Donors: Edith A. Lehman†; Herbert H. Lehman†.
Grantmaker type: Independent foundation.
Financial data (yr. ended 09/30/10): Assets, $6,743,985 (M); expenditures, $520,923; qualifying distributions, $415,995; giving activities include $412,000 for 45 grants (high: $50,000; low: $500).
Purpose and activities: Giving primarily for the arts and education.
Fields of interest: Arts; Higher education; Education; Animals/wildlife; Health care; Human services; Children, services.
International interests: United Kingdom.
Type of support: Equipment; General/operating support; Continuing support; Annual campaigns; Capital campaigns; Building/renovation; Endowments; Emergency funds; Professorships; Seed money; Curriculum development.
Limitations: Applications not accepted. Giving primarily in NY. No support for political organizations. No grants to individuals.
Publications: Annual report.
Application information: Proposals are accepted by invitation only. Preference is given to organizations which historically have been of interest to the Lehman family and to those in which the family is personally involved.
Board meeting date(s): Quarterly
Officer and Directors:* Wendy Lehman Lash,* Pres.; Robert C. Graham, Jr.;* Abigail S. Lash; Emily Altschul Miller; Catherine J. Wise; Deborah Wise.
EIN: 136094015

1522
Leiden University Fund (U.S.A.), Inc.

c/o Anderson Kill & Olick
1251 Ave. of the Americas, 42nd Fl.
New York, NY 10020-1104
Contact: Hendrik Laverge, Pres. and Treas.

Established in 1998 in NY as a private foundation; supporting organization of Leiden University.
Grantmaker type: Public charity.
Financial data (yr. ended 12/31/09): Revenue, $2,720; assets, $84,528 (M); gifts received, $1,420.
Fields of interest: Higher education, university.
International interests: Netherlands.
Limitations: Applications not accepted. Giving limited to the Netherlands.
Application information: Contributes only to a pre-selected organization.
Officers and Directors:* Hendrik Laverge,* Pres. and Treas.; Isaac E. Druker,* V.P.; Johannes Joosten,* Secy.; Robin Bargmann; Herman Bruggink.
EIN: 133974605

1523
The Leir Foundation, Inc.

570 Lexington Ave., 33rd Fl.
New York, NY 10022-6837

Established in 1996 in CT.
Donors: Henry J. Leir†; Louis Lipton; The Ridgefield Foundation.
Grantmaker type: Operating foundation.
Financial data (yr. ended 12/31/10): Assets, $54,577,696 (M); expenditures, $4,861,330; qualifying distributions, $3,989,800; giving activities include $3,989,800 for 45 grants (high: $1,000,000; low: $1,000).
Fields of interest: Museums (art); Higher education; Human services; Children, services; Jewish federated giving programs; Jewish agencies & synagogues.
International interests: Germany; Luxembourg.
Limitations: Applications not accepted. Giving primarily in CT, with emphasis on Ridgefield, MA, and New York, NY; funding also in Mauth, Germany and Luxembourg. No grants to individuals.
Application information: Contributes only to pre-selected organizations.
Officers and Directors:* Arthur S. Hoffman,* Pres. and Treas.; Margot Gibis,* V.P.; Anthony J. Cernera,* Secy.; Stuart Silver.
EIN: 061466481

1524
The Morris L. Levinson Foundation, Inc.

c/o Weisermazars, LLP
3000 Marcus Ave., Ste. 2W1
Lake Success, NY 11042

Incorporated in 1952 in NY.
Donors: Morris L. Levinson; Barbara Levinson†; Associated Products, Inc.
Grantmaker type: Independent foundation.
Financial data (yr. ended 06/30/10): Assets, $3,169,547 (M); expenditures, $497,111; qualifying distributions, $451,200; giving activities include $450,008 for 2 grants (high: $450,000; low: $8).
Purpose and activities: Giving primarily to Jewish organizations.
Fields of interest: Education; Human services; Jewish federated giving programs; Jewish agencies & synagogues.
International interests: Israel.
Limitations: Applications not accepted. Giving primarily in FL and NY. No grants to individuals.

Application information: Contributes only to pre-selected organizations.
Officers and Directors:* Lawrence Blumberg,* V.P.; Robert Machinist,* V.P.; Judith Oppenheimer, V.P.
EIN: 136132727

1525
The Lewy Family Foundation

c/o Robert Stein
29 W. 38th St., 14th Fl.
New York, NY 10018-5504

Established in 1996 in NY.
Donor: Glen S. Lewy.
Grantmaker type: Independent foundation.
Financial data (yr. ended 12/31/10): Assets, $3,373,067 (M); gifts received, $2,537; expenditures, $311,604; qualifying distributions, $287,700; giving activities include $287,700 for grants.
Fields of interest: United Ways and Federated Giving Programs; Cerebral palsy research; Historic preservation/historical societies; Elementary/secondary education; Higher education; Education, services; International exchange, students; Jewish agencies & synagogues.
Limitations: Applications not accepted. Giving primarily in Washington, DC, New York, NY, and Brattleboro, VT. No grants to individuals.
Application information: Contributes only to pre-selected organizations.
Officer: Glen S. Lewy, Chair.
Directors: Brooke Lewy; Cheryl Winter Lewy; Marshall Lewy; Zachary Jason Lewy.
EIN: 133907886

1526
The Li Foundation, Inc.

57 Glen St., Ste. 1
Glen Cove, NY 11542-2755 (516) 676-1315
Contact: Taie Li, Pres.
FAX: (516) 676-2538; E-mail: info@lifoundation.org;
URL: http://www.lifoundation.org/index.html

Established in 1944 in NY.
Grantmaker type: Independent foundation.
Financial data (yr. ended 12/31/10): Assets, $7,124,697 (M); expenditures, $437,986; qualifying distributions, $335,778; giving activities include $291,000 for 11 grants (high: $52,000; low: $1,000).
Purpose and activities: Scholarship and fellowship awards paid directly to colleges or universities for Chinese students to study in the U.S.
Fields of interest: Higher education.
International interests: China.
Type of support: Fellowships; Scholarship funds.
Application information: Application form required.
Copies of proposal: 2
Deadline(s): Feb. 1
Board meeting date(s): May and Sept.
Officers and Directors:* Taie Li,* Pres.; Marie Chun,* V.P.; Mildred L. Distin,* Secy.; Eric Leong Way,* Treas.; Gail Chun-Deduonni; Minfong Ho Dennis; Carlos Chang Koo; Anna Li; Ling Li; Sebastian Li; Taimim Li; Edward Leong Way.
Number of staff: 3
EIN: 136098783

1527
The Limo Almi Foundation
c/o BSB Assoc., LTD
201 Moreland Rd., Ste. 3
Hauppauge, NY 11788-3922 (631) 543-7700
Contact: Anthony M. Bellissimo, Jr., Mgr.

Established in 1997 in NY.
Grantmaker type: Independent foundation.
Financial data (yr. ended 12/31/10): Assets, $1,909,241 (M); expenditures, $168,673; qualifying distributions, $167,500; giving activities include $167,500 for 18 grants (high: $50,000; low: $1,000).
Fields of interest: Disasters, preparedness/ services; Safety/disasters; International relief.
Limitations: Applications accepted. Giving primarily in NY, with emphasis on Nassau and Suffolk counties.
Application information: Application form required.
Initial approach: Letter
Deadline(s): None
Officer: Anthony M. Bellissimo, Jr., Mgr.
EIN: 116481695

1528
Lisben Charitable Foundation, Inc.
c/o Beno Sternlicht
123 Partridge Run
Schenectady, NY 12309-1321

Established in 1998 in NY.
Donors: Beno Sternlicht; Lisa Sternlicht.
Grantmaker type: Independent foundation.
Financial data (yr. ended 05/31/11): Assets, $8,401 (M); gifts received, $118,793; expenditures, $145,335; qualifying distributions, $143,534; giving activities include $143,534 for 20 grants (high: $105,000; low: $60).
Fields of interest: Higher education, college; Education; Human services; International affairs; Jewish agencies & synagogues.
Type of support: General/operating support.
Limitations: Applications not accepted. Giving primarily in NY. No grants to individuals.
Application information: Unsolicited requests for funds not accepted.
Directors: Hugh Janow; Beno Sternlicht; Lisa Sternlicht.
EIN: 582395697

1529
The Lucius N. Littauer Foundation, Inc.
60 E. 42nd St., Ste. 4600
New York, NY 10165-0009
Contact: William Lee Frost, Pres.

Incorporated in 1929 in NY.
Donor: Lucius N. Littauer‡.
Grantmaker type: Independent foundation.
Financial data (yr. ended 12/31/10): Assets, $40,823,826 (M); expenditures, $2,187,622; qualifying distributions, $2,049,790; giving activities include $1,862,220 for 202 grants (high: $100,000; low: $125).
Purpose and activities: Grants for scholarly research on Jewish studies, for the endowment of Judaica book funds at university libraries, for medical ethics and palliative medical care, and NY public projects.

Fields of interest: Palliative care; Humanities; History/archaeology; Language/linguistics; Literature; Higher education; Environment; Medical care, bioethics; Social sciences; Political science; Jewish agencies & synagogues; Religion.
International interests: Israel.
Type of support: Endowments; Program development; Conferences/seminars; Publication; Seed money; Research; Employee matching gifts; Matching/challenge support.
Limitations: Applications accepted. Giving primarily in NY for medical ethics, and environmental related projects. No support for synagogues. No grants to individuals, or for capital projects or operating funds.
Application information: Application form not required.
Initial approach: Proposal
Copies of proposal: 1
Deadline(s): None
Board meeting date(s): Annually and as required
Final notification: 3 months
Officers and Directors:* Robert D. Frost,* Pres.; Henry A. Lowett,* V.P. and Secy.; Charles Berlin; Berthold Bilski; Mark A. Bilski; Robert D. Frost; George Harris; Noah Perlman; Geula R. Solomon; Peter J. Solomon.
Number of staff: 1 full-time professional; 1 part-time support.
EIN: 131688027

1530
John L. Loeb, Jr. Foundation
c/o Barry M. Strauss Assocs., Ltd.
307 5th Ave., 8th Fl.
New York, NY 10016-6517

Established in 1964.
Donor: John L. Loeb, Jr.
Grantmaker type: Independent foundation.
Financial data (yr. ended 12/31/10): Assets, $7,711,844 (M); expenditures, $2,165,192; qualifying distributions, $2,157,543; giving activities include $2,023,526 for 89 grants (high: $1,690,000; low: $36).
Purpose and activities: Giving primarily for education, Jewish organizations, health organizations and human services.
Fields of interest: Religion, public policy; Arts; Higher education; Education; Environment; Health organizations, association; Human services; International affairs; Foundations (private grantmaking); Jewish agencies & synagogues.
Limitations: Applications not accepted. Giving primarily in NY. No grants to individuals.
Application information: Contributes only to pre-selected organizations.
Officer: John L. Loeb, Jr., Pres. and Treas.
EIN: 136142345

1531
The Henry Luce Foundation, Inc.
51 Madison Ave., 30th Fl.
New York, NY 10010-1603 (212) 489-7700
Contact: Michael Gilligan, Pres.
FAX: (212) 581-9541; E-mail: hlf1@hluce.org;
URL: http://www.hluce.org

Incorporated in 1936 in NY.
Donors: Henry R. Luce‡; Clare Boothe Luce‡.
Grantmaker type: Independent foundation.

Financial data (yr. ended 12/31/10): Assets, $762,603,542 (M); expenditures, $38,808,364; qualifying distributions, $34,970,997; giving activities include $28,555,379 for 263 grants (high: $1,000,000), $539,270 for grants to individuals, and $434,162 for employee matching gifts.
Purpose and activities: Grants for specific projects in the broad areas of Asian affairs, American art, public policy and the environment, theology, advancement of women in science and engineering, and higher education. The Luce Scholars Program gives a select group of young Americans, not Asian specialists, a year's work experience in East and Southeast Asia. Asia grants support the creation of new scholarly and public resources on East and Southeast Asia as well as innovative cultural and intellectual exchange between the Asia-Pacific and the United States. The Henry R. Luce Professorship Program, which supports innovative programs at private colleges and universities, no longer accepts proposals for new grants. The Clare Boothe Luce Program is designed to enhance the careers of women in science and engineering through scholarships, fellowships, and professorships at invited institutions. Funding in the arts focuses on research, scholarship and exhibitions in American art; direct support for specific projects at major museums and service organizations; dissertation support for topics in American art history through the American Council of Learned Societies. Theology grants are made primarily to seminaries and divinity schools for educational purposes. The Henry Luce III Theology Fellows Program is administered through the Association of Theological Schools. Public Policy and the Environment grants are made to support the study of critical issues and environmental training and research.
Fields of interest: Visual arts; Museums; Humanities; Theology; Higher education; Theological school/education; Environment; Engineering/technology; Social sciences; International studies; Public policy, research.
International interests: East Asia; Southeast Asia.
Type of support: Research; General/operating support; Program development; Professorships; Fellowships; Internship funds; Scholarship funds; Employee matching gifts; Grants to individuals; Matching/challenge support.
Limitations: Applications accepted. Giving on a national and international basis; international activities limited to East and Southeast Asia. No support for medical or healthcare projects. No grants to individuals (except for specially designated programs), or for endowments, domestic building campaigns, annual fund drives; no loans.
Publications: Biennial report (including application guidelines); Grants list; Program policy statement.
Application information: Nominees for Luce Scholars Program accepted from invited institutions only; Clare Boothe Luce Program by invitation to institutions only, individual applications cannot be considered; American Art Program requires prior inquiry by Mar.1. Application form not required.
Initial approach: Letter
Copies of proposal: 1
Deadline(s): June 15, for American Art; Nov. 1 for Luce Scholars nominations; all others, no specific deadlines
Board meeting date(s): Mar., June and Nov.
Officers and Directors:* Margaret Boles Fitzgerald,* Chair.; Michael Gilligan,* Pres.; John P. Daley, V.P., Finance and Admin. and Treas.; Toby Volkman, Secy. and Dir., Policy Initiatives; Robert E. Armstrong, Dir., Emeritus; Terrence B. Adamson;

Mary Brown Bullock; John C. Evans; Claire L. Gaudiani; Kenneth T. Jackson; James T. Laney; H. Christopher Luce; Thomas L. Pulling; David V. Ragone.

Number of staff: 11 full-time professional; 2 part-time professional; 8 full-time support; 1 part-time support.

EIN: 136001282

Recent grants for international programs:

1531-1 America Abroad Media, Washington, DC, $350,000. For public radio programming on religion and international affairs. 2010.

1531-2 American Council on Education, Washington, DC, $400,000. To promote effective collaboration between global education and diversity/multicultural initiatives in higher education. 2010.

1531-3 American Studies Association, Washington, DC, $15,000. To support participation of scholars from East and Southeast Asia at ASA's annual meetings. 2010.

1531-4 Americans for Oxford, New York, NY, $13,000. To support international workshop, organized by Refugees Studies Center at University of Oxford, on theme of faith-based humanitarianism, the response of faith communities and faith-based organizations in contexts of forced migration, including climate-induced migration. 2010.

1531-5 Asia Foundation, San Francisco, CA, $2,499,000. For continued administration of Luce Scholars Program, nationally competitive fellowship program launched by the Henry Luce Foundation in 1974 to enhance understanding of Asia among potential leaders in American society. 2010.

1531-6 Asian Cultural Council, New York, NY, $300,000. For program, American Artists and Museum Professionals in Asia. 2010.

1531-7 Aspen Institute, Washington, DC, $30,000. To support travel of members of American delegation to Aspen China Trialogue, Global Governance: Challenges and Expectations, three day conference in Beijing, China. 2010.

1531-8 Association for Asian Studies, Ann Arbor, MI, $135,000. For new program initiatives for Annual Meetings. 2010.

1531-9 Association of American Colleges and Universities, Washington, DC, $400,000. For national project, General Education For a Global Century. 2010.

1531-10 Battery Dance Corporation, New York, NY, $15,000. For project, Dancing to Connect: U.S.-China. 2010.

1531-11 Boston University, Institute on Culture, Religion and World Affairs, Boston, MA, $473,000. For initiative, Religious Pluralism and Civic Peace in Multicultural Societies. 2010.

1531-12 Brookings Institution, Center for Northeast Asia Policy Studies, Washington, DC, $210,000. For fellowships for scholars from Mongolia and Vietnam. 2010.

1531-13 Carnegie Endowment for International Peace, Washington, DC, $200,000. For U.S.-China Policy Dialogue on Advancing Climate Cooperation. 2010.

1531-14 Center for Lao Studies, San Francisco, CA, $30,000. To strengthen organizational and programming capacity. 2010.

1531-15 China Education Initiative, New York, NY, $40,000. For U.S.-China Teaching Fellows Program, to meet need for teachers in China's understaffed low-income rural schools, while fostering constituency of young leaders

positioned to advance cause of educational equity and effect long-term systemic change. 2010.

1531-16 Drew University, Theological School, Madison, NJ, $215,000. To enhance Center for Christianities in Global Contexts. Center's mission is to facilitate, promote and disseminate more accurate understanding of Christianity's place or places within an increasingly complex world.. 2010.

1531-17 Emory University, Candler School of Theology, Atlanta, GA, $325,500. To develop international program of targeted exchanges with seminaries in Africa, Asia and South America. 2010.

1531-18 Freer Gallery of Art and Arthur M. Sackler Gallery, Washington, DC, $133,000. For Southeast Asia Initiatives. 2010.

1531-19 Harvard University, Center for Middle Eastern Studies, Cambridge, MA, $156,000. To support Initiative on Contemporary Islamic Societies, research network on pluralism, coexistence and conflict in Muslim-majority countries. 2010.

1531-20 Hobart and William Smith Colleges, Geneva, NY, $400,000. For Program on Asian Studies and the Environment. 2010.

1531-21 Indiana University, Bloomington, IN, $425,000. For new faculty position and related programming for The Archaeology of Early China in an East Asian Context. 2010.

1531-22 Indiana University, Bloomington, IN, $30,000. For project, The History of Western Medicine in China. 2010.

1531-23 Indiana University, Research Center for Chinese Politics and Business, Bloomington, IN, $250,000. For Initiative on China and Global Governance. 2010.

1531-24 International Crisis Group, Washington, DC, $300,000. To support field research on role of religion in conflict and instability in Yemen, Indonesia, Nigeria and Somalia. 2010.

1531-25 International Student Conferences, Washington, DC, $100,000. For Korea-America Student Conference. 2010.

1531-26 Johns Hopkins University, Baltimore, MD, $390,000. To support new program for specialized Chinese language instruction at Hopkins-Nanjing Center. 2010.

1531-27 Johns Hopkins University, Baltimore, MD, $300,000. For grant to Paul H. Nitze School of Advanced International Studies (SAIS) in Washington, DC which will be used to strengthen coverage of religion and international affairs in the U.S. media. 2010.

1531-28 Lancaster Theological Seminary, Lancaster, PA, $350,000. To support collaborative program on religious pluralism with Institute of Religion, Culture and Peace of Payap University in Thailand. 2010.

1531-29 MUSE Film and Television, New York, NY, $40,000. For documentary project on Chinese artist Ai Weiwei. 2010.

1531-30 National Committee on American Foreign Policy, New York, NY, $250,000. To support policy dialogues on Northeast Asia security issues. 2010.

1531-31 New England Foundation for the Arts, Boston, MA, $48,000. To support Voices from the Shadows, multi-media project on women and religion in Pakistan. 2010.

1531-32 New School, New York, NY, $394,000. For initiative, Everyday Religion and Sustainable Environments in the Himalayas. 2010.

1531-33 New York University, School of Law, New York, NY, $10,000. To support one-day conference of the Center on Law and Security on the subject of the U.S. Constitution and National Security as part of Henry R. Luce Initiative on Religion and International Affairs. 2010.

1531-34 Rice University, Chao Center for Asian Studies, Houston, TX, $273,000. For research project and digital archive. 2010.

1531-35 School for Advanced Research, Santa Fe, NM, $132,000. For residential fellowship on East and Southeast Asia. 2010.

1531-36 Social Science Research Council, Brooklyn, NY, $30,000. To support convening of selected grantees of Henry R. Luce Initiative on Religion and International Affairs for a two-day workshop. 2010.

1531-37 Syracuse University, Syracuse, NY, $25,000. To support travel of delegation of presidents from American research universities to North Korea. 2010.

1531-38 Texas Tech Foundation, Lubbock, TX, $22,000. To support symposium, Vietnam-U.S. Relations: Toward a Brighter Future, co-organized by Vietnam Center and Archive at Texas Tech University and Diplomatic Academy of Vietnam. 2010.

1531-39 Tides Center, San Francisco, CA, $215,000. For Center for Digital TV and The World's journalism training program on coverage of Asia. 2010.

1531-40 University of Illinois at Urbana-Champaign, Urbana, IL, $20,000. For film screenings by Asian Educational Media Service (AEMS) at meeting of Association for Asian Studies. 2010.

1531-41 University of Michigan, Ann Arbor, MI, $30,000. For conference to celebrate 50th anniversary of Center for Southeast Asian Studies. 2010.

1531-42 University of Pennsylvania, Philadelphia, PA, $156,000. For Penn-China Civil Society Initiative. 2010.

1531-43 University of Pennsylvania, Museum of Archaeology and Anthropology, Philadelphia, PA, $28,000. To support symposium, Reconfiguring the Silk Road: New Research on East-West Exchange in Antiquity. 2010.

1531-44 University of Pittsburgh, Pittsburgh, PA, $415,000. For new faculty position of Anthropological Archaeologist specializing in East Asia. 2010.

1531-45 University of Southern California, Los Angeles, CA, $395,000. For Religion on the Move: Crossing Borders, Setting Boundaries, initiative to enhance journalistic and scholarly attention to religion and international relations. 2010.

1532
Georges Lurcy Charitable and Educational Trust

1290 Ave. of the Americas, 29th Fl.
New York, NY 10104-0101
Contact: Seth E. Frank, Tr.

Established in 1985 in NY.
Donor: Georges Lurcy†.
Grantmaker type: Independent foundation.
Financial data (yr. ended 06/30/10): Assets, $24,219,181 (M); expenditures, $1,236,852; qualifying distributions, $1,102,444; giving activities include $953,167 for 73 grants (high: $100,000; low: $1,000).

Purpose and activities: Support primarily for education including fellowships for students of American colleges or universities to study in France, and students of French colleges or universities to study in the U.S.; some support for cultural organizations.

Fields of interest: Arts; Higher education.

International interests: France.

Type of support: Fellowships.

Application information: Fellowship applicants from America must be recommended by their universities; applicants from France must apply to the Franco-American Commission for Educational Exchange. Applicants cannot apply directly to the foundation.

Trustees: Alan S. Bernstein; Daniel L. Bernstein; Georges Lurcy Bernstein; Seth E. Frank.

EIN: 136372044

1533
Lymphoma Research Foundation
115 Broadway, Fl. 13
New York, NY 10006-1901 (212) 349-2910
Contact: Kathleen Brown, Dir., Research
FAX: (212) 349-2886;
E-mail: researchgrants@lymphoma.org; Toll-free tel.: (800) 235-6848; URL: http://www.lymphoma.org
Twitter: http://twitter.com/lymphoma

Established in 1991 in CA.

Donors: Anne Abramson; Fred Abbott; Pam Abbott; William Adams IV; Mrs. William Adams IV; Dr. Richard Adicks; Mrs. Richard Adicks; Nasser A. Ahmad; Larry Akman; Nonie Akman; Jean Aldwell; Robin Armour; Tony Armour; Don B. Baker; Peter Barlin; Anna Becker; Maxa Berid; Mr. and Mrs. Lee M. Blaymore; Donald Blumenthal; Mrs. Donald Blumenthal; Dr. Kenneth Blunt; Mrs. Kenneth Blunt; Allos Therapuetics, Inc.; The Ammon Foundation; John W. Anderson Foundation; Apollo Real Estate Advisors, LP; Argonaut Group, Inc.; Boca Raton Bicycle Club, Inc.; Biogen Idec Foundation; Louis L. Borick Foundation; The Boustead Family Foundation; Centers for Disease Control and Prevention; Cephalon, Inc.; Chattanooga Christian Community Foundation; Condon Family Foundation; Dreams of Life; The Fund for Blood and Cancer Research, Inc.

Grantmaker type: Public charity.

Financial data (yr. ended 06/30/10): Revenue, $7,138,185; assets, $13,070,801 (M); gifts received, $7,004,709; expenditures, $7,600,977; giving activities include $1,732,500 for grants, and $14,192 for grants to individuals.

Purpose and activities: The foundation supports medical research that will result in better, safer treatments and the ultimate cure for lymphoma; and also supports lymphoma patients and their loved ones through education and emotional support services at no charge.

Fields of interest: Cancer research; Medical research.

International interests: Canada.

Type of support: Fellowships; Research.

Limitations: Applications accepted. Giving in Canada, Europe, and the U.S.

Publications: Annual report; Financial statement; Grants list; Informational brochure; Newsletter.

Application information: See web site for current Major Research Grants for Senior Researchers opportunities and application guidelines.

Initial approach: Letter of intent for Major Research Grants for Senior Researchers; online application for all others

Deadline(s): Varies for Major Research Grants for Senior Researchers; Sept. 10 for all others

Board meeting date(s): Quarterly

Final notification: 90 days

Officers and Directors:* Errol M. Cook,* Chair.; Michael Ditzian,* M.D., Exec. V.P.; Tom Condon,* Treas.; John Balan; Joseph R. Bertino, M.D.; Dr. Morton Coleman; Heidi Dieter; Robert E. Fischer; Dr. Richard I. Fisher; Barbara Freundlich; Tom L. Harrison; Marie L. Matthews; Miriam Phalen; Steven J. Prince; Leonard M. Rosen; Michael Werner.

Number of staff: 12 full-time professional; 25 full-time support; 1 part-time support.

EIN: 954335088

1534
The M.A.C. AIDS Fund
(formerly The M.A.C. Global Foundation)
130 Prince St., 4th Fl.
New York, NY 10012-3101 (212) 965-6300
Contact: Bruce Hunter, Exec. Prog. Dir., Canadian Office
FAX: (212) 372-6171;
E-mail: macaidsfund@maccosmetics.com; For applications, address: 360 Adelaide St. W., Ste. 301, Toronto, Ontario, Canada, M5V 1R7, tel.: (866) 244-2356, fax: (416) 599-6311; URL: http://www.macaidsfund.org

Established in 2000 in NY.

Donors: Make-Up Art Cosmetics Inc.; Estee Lauder Companies, Inc.

Grantmaker type: Independent foundation.

Financial data (yr. ended 06/30/10): Assets, $20,015,302 (M); gifts received, $19,803,637; expenditures, $14,219,705; qualifying distributions, $13,664,773; giving activities include $12,713,842 for 185 grants (high: $1,000,000; low: $87).

Purpose and activities: Giving primarily to AIDS research, outreach and resource organizations.

Fields of interest: Food services; AIDS; Human services; International affairs.

Limitations: Applications accepted. Giving on a national basis, with some emphasis on CA and NY; giving on an international basis, with some emphasis on Ontario, Canada. No grants to individuals; general operating expenses. deficit reduction; endowments, capital casts, conferences, summits, briefings, research, or multi-year granting.

Publications: Application guidelines.

Application information: Applicants will receive an acknowledgment letter confirming receipt and advise when request will go forward for Board consideration. If something is missing, applicants will be notified by one of the members of the review committee who makes the funding recommendations. The Board of Dirs. of the fund ultimately makes the final decision. A site visit may be required prior to final review of any grant request and successful grantees can expect to receive payment within the month following. Electronic requests will not be accepted. Please see the fund's Web site for additional information or e-mail the fund with any questions.

Initial approach: Letter

Copies of proposal: 2

Deadline(s): Quarterly

Board meeting date(s): Quarterly, usually Mar., June, Sept. and Dec.

Final notification: Applicants will be notified with the results within a couple of days after board meeting

Officers and Directors:* John D. Demsey,* Chair.; Nancy M. Louden, Secy.; Robert Charles Richards,* Treas.; Nancy Mahon, Exec. Dir.; Bruce Hunter,* Exec. Prog. Dir., Canadian Office; Jennifer Balbier; Karen Buslisi; Frank Doyle; James Gager; Deborah Krulewitch; Ian Ness; Clyde Williams.

EIN: 134144722

Recent grants for international programs:

1534-1 AIDS-Free World, New York, NY, $200,000. 2010.

1534-2 Elton John AIDS Foundation, New York, NY, $100,000. 2010.

1534-3 Elton John AIDS Foundation, New York, NY, $75,000. 2010.

1534-4 Funders Concerned About AIDS, Arlington, VA, $35,000. 2010.

1534-5 FXB USA, New York, NY, $31,065. 2010.

1534-6 Global AIDS Alliance, Washington, DC, $100,000. 2010.

1534-7 Global Fund to Fight AIDS, Tuberculosis and Malaria, Geneva, Switzerland, $500,000. 2010.

1534-8 Grassroot Soccer, Norwich, VT, $85,135. 2010.

1534-9 Helen Keller International, New York, NY, $133,231. 2010.

1534-10 International Center for Research on Women, Washington, DC, $158,217. 2010.

1534-11 Partners in Health, Boston, MA, $175,000. 2010.

1534-12 Partners in Health, Boston, MA, $125,000. 2010.

1534-13 Physicians for Human Rights, Cambridge, MA, $50,000. 2010.

1534-14 Pulitzer Center on Crisis Reporting, Washington, DC, $75,000. 2010.

1534-15 Pulitzer Center on Crisis Reporting, Washington, DC, $50,000. 2010.

1534-16 Tides Center New York, New York, NY, $150,000. For HIV Collaborative Fund. 2010.

1534-17 United States Fund for UNICEF, New York, NY, $195,630. 2010.

1534-18 Weill Medical College of Cornell University, GHESKIO, The Center for Global Health, New York, NY, $125,000. 2010.

1535
MADRE, Inc.
121 W. 27th St., Ste. 301
New York, NY 10001-6207 (212) 627-0444
Contact: Vivian Stromberg, Exec. Dir.
FAX: (212) 675-3704; E-mail: madre@madre.org;
URL: http://madre.org
RSS Feed: http://www.madre.org/rss/news.xml

Established in 1983.

Grantmaker type: Public charity.

Financial data (yr. ended 12/31/09): Revenue, $1,910,770; assets, $2,151,295 (M); gifts received, $1,795,674; expenditures, $1,800,726; giving activities include $20,845 for grants, and $252,004 for grants to organizations outside the U.S.

Purpose and activities: The organization works in partnership with community-based women's organizations worldwide to address issues of health and reproductive rights, economic development, education, and other human rights; also provides resources, training, and support to enable its sister

organizations to meet concrete needs in their communities while working to shift the balance of power to promote long-term development and social justice. Assistance is only provided in the form of fiscal sponsorship; no monetary support is given.
Fields of interest: International peace/security; Education; Reproductive health; Family services; Human services; Women.
Publications: Newsletter.
Officers and Directors:* Anne Hess,* Co-Chair.; Dr. Zala Highsmith-Taylor,* Co-Chair.; Margaret Ratner-Kunstler,* V.P.; Linda Flores Rodriguez,* Secy.; Vivian Stromberg, Exec. Dir.; Hilda Diaz; Laura Flanders; Holly Maguigan; Marie Saint Cyr; Pam Spees.
EIN: 133280194

1536
Maidstone Foundation, Inc.
1225 Broadway, 9th Fl.
New York, NY   10001-4309
Contact: Duncan Whiteside, Pres.
E-mail: maidstoneduncan@aol.com; Tel./fax: (212) 889-5760; additional E-mail: president@maidstonefdn.org; URL: http://maidstonefdn.org/home.html

Established in 1985 in NY.
Grantmaker type: Public charity.
Financial data (yr. ended 06/30/10): Revenue, $774,434; assets, $253,387 (M); gifts received, $351,810; expenditures, $680,001; giving activities include $5,170 for grants to individuals.
Purpose and activities: The foundation's primary interests include unserved people with developmental disabilities (for example, the mentally retarded who have vision problems and mental illness); community services to youth and families (adoption, advocacy for children, training, and policy); and developmental disabilities and community services of a more general nature.
Fields of interest: Arts, association; Genetic diseases and disorders; Brain disorders; Learning disorders; Children/youth, services; Children, adoption; Youth, services; Family services; Developmentally disabled, centers & services; Disabilities, people with.
International interests: Ecuador; Russia.
Type of support: Program development; Seed money; Technical assistance; Consulting services; Grants to individuals.
Limitations: Applications accepted. Giving primarily in NY.
Application information: Application form not required.
    Initial approach: Letter
    Copies of proposal: 1
    Deadline(s): None
    Board meeting date(s): As needed
Officers and Directors:* Duncan Whiteside,* Pres.; Mariette J. Bates,* V.P.; Mohan Badjugar; Nora Chase; Hal Keshner; Daniel B. Rosen, Ph.D.; Nick Whiteside.
Number of staff: 2 full-time professional; 1 full-time support; 19 part-time support.
EIN: 112718381

1537
The Somaly Mam Foundation
360 Park Ave. S.
New York, NY   10010-1710
Contact: Asha Padmanabhan
E-mail: info@somaly.org; URL: http://www.somaly.org
Facebook: http://www.facebook.com/somalymamfoundation
Twitter: http://twitter.com/somalymam
YouTube: http://www.youtube.com/somalymamfoundation

Established in 2007 in CO.
Grantmaker type: Public charity.
Financial data (yr. ended 12/31/10): Revenue, $3,171,726; assets, $2,750,117 (M); gifts received, $3,659,981; expenditures, $3,043,932; giving activities include $73,500 for grants, and $764,059 for 3 grants to organizations outside the U.S.
Purpose and activities: The foundation combats human trafficking by funding organizations that rescue, rehabilitate, and reintegrate victims.
Fields of interest: International human rights; Minorities/immigrants, centers/services; Women, centers/services; Crime/violence prevention, sexual abuse; Women; Crime/abuse victims.
International interests: Cambodia.
Limitations: Applications not accepted. Giving primarily to Cambodia.
Application information: Unsolicited requests for funding neither considered nor acknowledged.
Officers and Directors:* Robert Rigby-Hall,* Chair.; Somaly Mam,* Pres.; Bill Livermore,* C.E.O. and Exec. Dir.; Ed Adams; Kevin Bales; Brandee Barker; Diana Brummer; Bill Fitzgerald; Jennifer Fonstad; Jared Greenberg; Nicholas Lumpp; Rigmor E. Schneider; Norma Jean Roy; Sina Vann; Michael Waldman; Nina You.
EIN: 260392207

1538
The Markle Foundation
(also known as The John and Mary R. Markle Foundation)
10 Rockefeller Plz., 16th Fl.
New York, NY   10020-1903
Contact: Zoe Baird, Pres.
FAX: (212) 765-9690; E-mail: info@markle.org; URL: http://www.markle.org/
E-Newsletter: http://www.markle.org/weekly_digest/
RSS Feed Directory: http://www.markle.org/stay-connected/rss-feeds
Twitter: http://twitter.com/marklefdn

Incorporated in 1927 in NY.
Donors: John Markle†; Mary Markle†.
Grantmaker type: Independent foundation.
Financial data (yr. ended 06/30/10): Assets, $146,884,256 (M); expenditures, $12,080,634; qualifying distributions, $10,785,590; giving activities include $883,795 for grants, and $7,662,689 for foundation-administered programs.
Purpose and activities: The mission of the foundation is to use emerging communication and information technologies to address critical public needs, with emphasis on health and national security.
Fields of interest: Health care; International affairs, national security; Public policy, research.

Limitations: Applications not accepted. Giving primarily in Washington, DC, and New York, NY.
Publications: IRS Form 990 or 990-PF printed copy available upon request.
Application information: The foundation directly supports its work in health and national security.
Officers and Directors:* Lewis B. Kaden,* Chair.; Zoe Baird,* Pres.; Karen Byers, C.F.O. and Secy.-Treas.; John Gage; Suzanne Nora Johnson; Herbert Pardes, M.D.; Edward Rover; Stanley S. Shuman.
Number of staff: 14 full-time professional; 5 full-time support.
EIN: 131770307

1539
The Bob Marley Foundation, Ltd.
60 E. 42nd St., 14th Fl.
New York, NY   10165-0009
E-mail: inquiry@bobmarleyfoundation.org; URL: http://www.bobmarleyfoundation.org/

Established in 2004 in NY.
Grantmaker type: Public charity.
Purpose and activities: The foundation seeks to enable individuals, groups, and/or communities in developing nations, particularly Jamaica and Africa, to create and implement programs that assist in the empowerment of the oppressed and the elimination of generational poverty through sustainable projects.
Fields of interest: Human services.
International interests: Jamaica; Developing countries; Africa.
Publications: Application guidelines.
Application information:
    Initial approach: Submit online proposal form
    Final notification: Six weeks after submission
Officer and Directors:* Rita Marley,* Chair.; Cedella Marley; David "Ziggy" Marley; Eleanor Wint.
EIN: 134146321

1540
The Rita Marley Foundation, Ltd.
c/o Z&L Assocs., C.P.A, P.C.
60 E. 42nd St.
New York, NY   10165-0001
Additional address (Ghana office): P.O. Box 34, Aburi-Akwapim, Ghana; URL: http://ritamarleyfoundation.org

Established in 2000 in NY.
Grantmaker type: Public charity.
Financial data (yr. ended 12/31/08): Revenue, $604,967; assets, $91,969 (M); gifts received, $603,846; expenditures, $645,710; program services expenses, $188,601; giving activities include $133,333 for grants, and $55,268 for foundation-administered programs.
Purpose and activities: The foundation works towards the alleviation of poverty, and funds education for the needy people of developing and less-developed countries.
Fields of interest: Education; Poverty studies.
International interests: Developing countries.
Limitations: Giving on an international basis, with emphasis on developing and less-developed countries.

Officers and Directors:* Rita Marley,* Pres.; Barbara Boahene, Secy.; Marvin Zolt, Treas.; Eleanor Wint.
EIN: 134146177

1541
Marshall Family Foundation
5810 Lake Bluff Rd.
North Rose, NY   14516-9727   (585) 423-1860

Established in 1995 in NY.
Donors: W. Gilman Marshall; Ina Marshall.
Grantmaker type: Independent foundation.
Financial data (yr. ended 10/31/10): Assets, $4,624,212 (M); gifts received, $44,773; expenditures, $241,915; qualifying distributions, $190,000; giving activities include $190,000 for 11 grants (high: $113,500; low: $2,000).
Fields of interest: Historic preservation/historical societies; Hospitals (general); Education; International affairs, U.N.; American Red Cross; AIDS; Health organizations; Youth development, community service clubs; Community/economic development; Foundations (community).
Limitations: Applications accepted. Giving primarily in NY. No grants to individuals.
Application information: Application form not required.
 Initial approach: Letter
 Deadline(s): None
Trustees: Gary Marshall; Gilman Marshall; Ina Marshall; Kent Marshall; Kris T. Marshall.
EIN: 166430502

1542
The Mayday Fund
c/o SPG
127 W. 26th St., Ste. 800
New York, NY   10001-6869   (212) 366-6970
Contact: Christina Spellman, Exec. Dir.
FAX: (212) 366-6979;
E-mail: inquiry@maydayfund.org; URL: http://www.maydayfund.org/

Established in 1992 in NY.
Donors: Shirley S. Katzenbach‡; John C. Beck; Pamela M. Thye; Caroline N. Sidnam; Harold L. Messenger.
Grantmaker type: Independent foundation.
Financial data (yr. ended 12/31/10): Assets, $24,902,424 (M); gifts received, $324,149; expenditures, $1,472,762; qualifying distributions, $1,425,307; giving activities include $1,057,508 for 22 grants (high: $151,000; low: $950).
Purpose and activities: The foundation is dedicated to the reduction of the profound human problems associated with physical pain and its consequences. The fund is particularly interested in projects that result in clinical interventions to reduce the toll of physical pain, pediatric pain, pain in non-verbal populations, and pain in the context of emergency medicine. The fund also promotes networking between veterinary and human medicine.
Fields of interest: Medical research.
International interests: Canada.
Type of support: Research.
Limitations: Giving on a national basis. No grants to individuals, or generally for endowments, capital projects, equipment, general operating expenses, ongoing activities, or annual fundraising drives.

Publications: Annual report; Financial statement; Grants list.
Application information: Mail and phone contacts only after initial e-mail communications. Application form not required.
 Initial approach: E-mail to Exec. Dir.
 Copies of proposal: 1
 Deadline(s): None
 Board meeting date(s): Quarterly
 Final notification: 1-6 weeks
Officer: Christina Spellman, Exec. Dir.
Trustees: John C. Beck; Robert D.C. Meeker, Jr.; Caroline N. Sidnam; Pamela M. Thye.
EIN: 133645438

1543
The McCaddin-McQuirk Foundation, Inc.
60 E. 42nd St.
New York, NY   10165-0006
Application address: c/o Frank J. Hardart, III, P.O. Box 5001, New York, NY 10185; tel.: (646) 258-7172

Incorporated in 1902 in NY.
Donors: Rt. Rev. John McQuirk‡; Ann Eliza McCaddin Walsh‡.
Grantmaker type: Independent foundation.
Financial data (yr. ended 12/31/10): Assets, $4,299,545 (M); expenditures, $481,454; qualifying distributions, $466,800; giving activities include $466,800 for grants.
Purpose and activities: Givint To foster educational opportunities for poorer students to be priests, deacons, catechists, or lay teachers of the Roman Catholic Church in the U.S. or elsewhere.
Fields of interest: Theological school/education; Catholic agencies & churches.
International interests: Africa; Asia; Canada; Europe; India; South America.
Type of support: Scholarship funds.
Limitations: Giving in the U.S. and internationally.
Application information: Applications must be made through a bishop, rector, or head of a seminary. Application form not required.
 Initial approach: Letter
 Deadline(s): Dec. 1
Officers: Frank J. Hardart III, Pres.; John J. Eager, V.P.; Thomas F. Blaney, Secy.; Julien N. Vachon, Treas.
Trustees: John Caffrey; John Cullinane; Tom Galvin; Francis M. Hartman; Robert G. Ix; Patrick Maloney; Rev. Msgr. Thomas A. Modugno; Carrol A. Muccia, Jr.; Martin W. Ronan, Jr., Esq.; Thomas A. Turley; Andy Kalbaugh.
EIN: 136134444

1544
Media Development Loan Fund, Inc.
37 W. 20th St., Ste. 801
New York, NY   10011-3716   (212) 807-1304
FAX: (212) 807-0540;
E-mail: harlan.mandel@mdlf.org; URL: http://www.mdlf.org
RSS Feed: http://www.mdlf.org/en/main/rss_news/

Donor: Media Development Loan Fund.
Grantmaker type: Public charity.
Financial data (yr. ended 12/31/10): Revenue, $6,231,638; assets, $52,961,235 (M); gifts received, $2,402,143; expenditures, $5,573,486;

giving activities include $11,000 for grants, and $663,011 for grants to organizations outside the U.S.
Purpose and activities: The fund supports the growth of independent, indigenous media in developing democracies, primarily by extending low-interest loans and other program-related investments in Central and Eastern Europe, the former Soviet Union, Asia, Africa, and Latin America.
Fields of interest: International development; Media/communications.
International interests: Latin America; Asia; Africa; Soviet Union (Former); Europe; Eastern & Central Europe.
Type of support: Program-related investments/loans.
Limitations: Applications accepted. Giving on an international basis, with emphasis on Africa, Asia, Central and Eastern Europe, Latin America, and the former Soviet Union. No grants to individuals.
Application information: Application form required.
Officers and Directors:* Kenneth Anderson,* Chair.; Sasa Vucinic,* Managing Dir.; Annette Laborey; Gerald Nagler; Aryeh Neier; Alexander Papachristou; Bernard Poulet; John Ryle.
EIN: 134052259

1545
Golda Meir Child Development Fund
505 8th Ave., Ste. 2302
New York, NY   10018-4511   (212) 563-5222
FAX: (212) 563-5710; URL: http://www.naamat.org/

Established in 1984 in NY.
Grantmaker type: Public charity.
Financial data (yr. ended 06/30/10): Revenue, $50,136; assets, $147,741 (M); gifts received, $48,948; expenditures, $37,631.
Purpose and activities: The fund aims to enhance the status of women, children and families in Israel and the U.S.
Fields of interest: Women; Children.
International interests: Israel.
Limitations: Applications not accepted. Giving limited to Israel.
Application information: Contributes only to a pre-selected organization; unsolicited requests for funds not considered or acknowledged.
Officers and Board Members:* Liz Raider, Pres.; Gail Simpson, V.P., Prog. and Edu.; Chellie Goldwater Wilensky, V.P., Membership; Debbie Kohn, Treas.; Lorraine Caris; Jan Gurvitch; Shoshana Riemer; and 11 additional board members.
EIN: 132264004

1546
The Andrew W. Mellon Foundation
140 E. 62nd St.
New York, NY   10065-8124   (212) 838-8400
Contact: Michele S. Warman, Genl. Counsel and Secy.
FAX: (212) 223-2778; E-mail: inquiries@mellon.org; URL: http://www.mellon.org
Knowledge Center: http://www.mellon.org/news_publications/publications
RSS Feed: http://www.mellon.org/search_rss?SearchableText=database

RSS Grants Feed: http://www.mellon.org/news_publications/annual-reports-essays/grants/grants/RSS

Trust established in 1940 in DE as Avalon Foundation; incorporated in 1954 in NY; merged with Old Dominion Foundation and renamed The Andrew W. Mellon Foundation in 1969.

Donors: Ailsa Mellon Bruce†; Paul Mellon†.

Grantmaker type: Independent foundation.

Financial data (yr. ended 12/31/10): Assets, $5,490,877,291 (M); expenditures, $294,396,724; qualifying distributions, $270,123,154; giving activities include $244,723,373 for 644 grants (high: $7,091,000; low: $4,500), $1,076,977 for employee matching gifts, and $644,095 for foundation-administered programs.

Purpose and activities: Grants on a selective basis for higher education; cultural affairs, including the humanities, museums, art conservation, and performing arts; conservation and the environment; and public affairs.

Fields of interest: Museums; Performing arts; Humanities; Arts; Higher education; Environment, natural resources; Environment; Public affairs.

Type of support: Continuing support; Endowments; Program development; Fellowships; Research; Matching/challenge support.

Limitations: Applications accepted. Giving on a national basis with some international giving, primarily focused on South Africa. No support for primarily local organizations. No grants to individuals (including scholarships); no loans.

Publications: Annual report; Grants list.

Application information: Please direct inquiries to appropriate program officers. Contact should be by writing or e-mail. Unsolicited proposals are rarely funded. Application form not required.

Initial approach: Letter
Copies of proposal: 1
Deadline(s): None
Board meeting date(s): Mar., June, Sept., and Dec.
Final notification: After board meetings

Officers and Trustees:* Anne M. Tatlock,* Chair.; Don Michael Randel,* Pres.; John E. Hull, V.P., Finance and C.I.O.; Philip E. Lewis, V.P., Higher Ed. and Scholar; Mariet Westermann, V.P., Higher Ed. and Scholar and Museums and Art Cons.; Michele S. Warman, Genl. Counsel and Secy.; Thomas J. Sanders, Cont. and Dir. of Financial Services; Danielle S. Allen; Lewis W. Bernard; Paul LeClerc; Earl Lewis; Colin Lucas; Eric Mindlich; W. Taylor Reveley III; Lawrence R. Ricciardi.

Number of staff: 57 full-time professional; 3 part-time professional; 9 full-time support; 1 part-time support.

EIN: 131879954

Recent grants for international programs:

1546-1 American Academy in Rome, New York Office, New York, NY, $50,000. For Professional Development and Training Program. 2010.

1546-2 American Political Science Association, Washington, DC, $898,000. For Political Science in Africa. 2010.

1546-3 American University of Paris, Paris, France, $370,000. For Translation, Transnationalism, and Transformation. 2010.

1546-4 American University of Paris, Paris, France, $300,000. For Faculty Career Enhancement. 2010.

1546-5 American University of Paris, Paris, France, $50,000. For Library Renewal. 2010.

1546-6 Appalachian College Association, Berea, KY, $362,000. For Salzburg Global Seminars. 2010.

1546-7 Association Tela Botanica, Montpellier, France, $250,000. For Plants Initiative - JSTOR (with Universite Montpellier II). 2010.

1546-8 Bennett College, Greensboro, NC, $498,000. For Center for Global Studies. 2010.

1546-9 Botanika, Tashkent, Uzbekistan, $32,000. For Plants Initiative - JSTOR. 2010.

1546-10 Botanische Staatssammlung Munchen, Munich, Germany, $143,000. For Plants Initiative (JSTOR). 2010.

1546-11 Botanische Staatssammlung Munchen, Munich, Germany, $30,000. For Plants Initiative - JSTOR. 2010.

1546-12 British Museum, London, England, $675,500. For ResearchSpace. 2010.

1546-13 British Museum, London, England, $100,000. For ResearchSpace. 2010.

1546-14 Cambridge University, Cambridge, England, $2,100,000. For Darwin Correspondence. 2010.

1546-15 Cambridge University, Cambridge, England, $584,000. For CRASSH Postdoctoral Fellowships. 2010.

1546-16 Carleton College, Northfield, MN, $53,286. For The Integration of Global Studies. 2010.

1546-17 Carnegie Institution of Washington, Washington, DC, $550,000. For Research Bridges. 2010.

1546-18 College of Wooster, Wooster, OH, $254,000. For Environmental Studies: Wooster Institute for a Sustainable Global Environment. 2010.

1546-19 Conservatoire et Jardin Botaniques, Geneva, Switzerland, $535,000. For Plants Initiative (JSTOR). 2010.

1546-20 Convergence, Washington, DC, $85,000. For U.S.-Muslim Engagement Initiative (USMEI). 2010.

1546-21 Cornell University, Ithaca, NY, $50,000. For Signale - A Monographic Publication in German Studies. 2010.

1546-22 Courtauld Institute of Art, London, England, $750,000. For Faculty Support. 2010.

1546-23 Courtauld Institute of Art, London, England, $75,000. For Conservation Documentation Pilot Project (Bridge - Pieta). 2010.

1546-24 Dunhuang Academy, Dunhuang, China, $332,000. For Advancing The Dunhuang Academy's Digital Strategy through Professional and Scholarly Exchange. 2010.

1546-25 Foundation of the American Institute for Conservation of Historic and Artistic Works, Washington, DC, $3,460,000. For Photograph Conservation at the State Hermitage Museum. 2010.

1546-26 Free University of Berlin, Berlin, Germany, $196,000. For Plants Initiative - JSTOR. 2010.

1546-27 French American Cultural Exchange, New York, NY, $954,000. For Partner University Fund. 2010.

1546-28 Friedrich-Schiller-Universitat Jena, Jena, Germany, $169,000. For Plants Initiative - JSTOR. 2010.

1546-29 Fundacion Instituto Botanico de Venezuela, Caracas, Venezuela, $24,000. For Plants Initiative - JSTOR. 2010.

1546-30 Georg-August-Universitat Gottingen, Gottingen, Germany, $97,000. For Plants Initiative - JSTOR. 2010.

1546-31 Gettysburg College, Gettysburg, PA, $532,000. For Middle East and Islamic Studies. 2010.

1546-32 Harvard University, Cambridge, MA, $15,000. For Administrative Support for the Program for Latin American Libraries and Archives (PLALA). 2010.

1546-33 IHR Trust, London, England, $730,000. For Graduate Research Fellowships. 2010.

1546-34 Jazz at Lincoln Center, New York, NY, $210,000. For Cuba Residency. 2010.

1546-35 Kenyon College, Gambier, OH, $600,000. For Global Critical Languages and Innovative Pedagogy. 2010.

1546-36 Kings College London, London, England, $50,000. For Prototype Prosopography of Medieval Physicians. 2010.

1546-37 Linnean Society of London, London, England, $104,000. For Plants Initiative - JSTOR. 2010.

1546-38 Linnean Society of London, London, England, $104,000. For Plants Initiative - JSTOR. 2010.

1546-39 Macalester College, Saint Paul, MN, $150,000. For Mid-Career President: Fine Arts and Global Citizenship. 2010.

1546-40 Marie Selby Botanical Gardens, Sarasota, FL, $32,500. For Plants Initiative (JSTOR). 2010.

1546-41 Martin Luther-University Halle-Wittenberg, Halle, Germany, $145,000. For Plants Initiative - JSTOR. 2010.

1546-42 Medici Archive Project, New York, NY, $553,000. For Redesigning the Catalog of the Medici Archives. 2010.

1546-43 Musee National d'Histoire Naturelle, Paris, France, $485,000. For Plants Initiative (JSTOR). 2010.

1546-44 Museo Ecuatoriano de Ciencias Naturales, Quito, Ecuador, $13,000. For Plants Initiative - JSTOR. 2010.

1546-45 National Botanic Garden of Belgium, Meise, Belgium, $206,000. For Plants Initiative - JSTOR. 2010.

1546-46 National Botanic Garden of Belgium, Meise, Belgium, $182,000. For Plants Initiative - JSTOR (Congo). 2010.

1546-47 National Film Preservation Foundation, San Francisco, CA, $22,000. For Repatriating Early American Films at the New Zealand Film Archive. 2010.

1546-48 National Film Preservation Foundation, San Francisco, CA, $21,200. For Repatriating Early American Films at the New Zealand Film Archive. 2010.

1546-49 National Humanities Center, Research Triangle Park, NC, $485,000. For European and American Young Scholars' Summer Institutes (YSSIs). 2010.

1546-50 National Museum Wales, Cardiff, Wales, $15,000. For Plants Initiative - JSTOR. 2010.

1546-51 Natural History Museum, London, England, $446,000. For Plants Initiative - JSTOR. 2010.

1546-52 Natural History Museum, London, England, $91,000. For Plants Initiative (JSTOR). 2010.

1546-53 Natural History Museum, London, England, $72,000. For Plants Initiative - JSTOR. 2010.

1546-54 Natural History Museum, London, England, $60,000. For Plants Initiative - JSTOR (Linnean). 2010.

1546-55 Naturhistorisches Museum Wien, Vienna, Austria, $361,000. For Plants Initiative - JSTOR. 2010.

1546-56 New School, Parsons School of Design, New York, NY, $314,000. For Translation, Transnationalism, and Transformation. 2010.

1546-57 Northwestern University, Evanston, IL, $20,000. For Sawyer Seminar: Theater After Athens. 2010.

1546-58 Organization for Tropical Studies, Durham, NC, $350,000. For Undergraduate Studies in Ecology. 2010.

1546-59 Organization for Tropical Studies, Durham, NC, $300,000. For Environmental Studies. 2010.

1546-60 Oxford Center for Islamic Studies, Oxford, England, $300,000. For Atlas of Muslims in South Asia. 2010.

1546-61 Oxford University, Oxford, England, $517,000. For Digitized Medieval Libraries of Great Britain II. 2010.

1546-62 Oxford University, Oxford, England, $175,000. For Sawyer Seminars: Understanding Human Creativity: Ecologies and Practices of Invention. 2010.

1546-63 Pontifical Institute of Mediaeval Studies, Toronto, Canada, $184,000. For Manuscript Studies. 2010.

1546-64 Pontificia Universidad Catolica del Ecuador, Quito, Ecuador, $52,000. For Plants Initiative - JSTOR. 2010.

1546-65 Queens University, Kingston, Canada, $357,000. For Disraeli Letters. 2010.

1546-66 Real Jardin Botanico de Madrid, Madrid, Spain, $110,000. For Plants Initiative - JSTOR. 2010.

1546-67 Rhodes University, Grahamstown, South Africa, $400,000. For Senior Research Scholars Program. 2010.

1546-68 Rhodes University, Grahamstown, South Africa, $97,000. For Jazz Heritage Studies and Archive Development. 2010.

1546-69 Royal Botanic Garden Edinburgh, Edinburgh, Scotland, $205,000. For Plants Initiative (JSTOR). 2010.

1546-70 Royal Botanic Gardens, Kew, Richmond, England, $620,000. For Plants Initiative - JSTOR. 2010.

1546-71 Royal Botanic Gardens, Kew, Richmond, England, $234,000. For Plants Initiative - JSTOR (Library). 2010.

1546-72 Royal Botanic Gardens, Kew, Richmond, England, $115,000. For Plants Initiative - JSTOR. 2010.

1546-73 Royal Horticultural Society, London, England, $22,000. For Plants Initiative - JSTOR. 2010.

1546-74 Salzburg Global Seminar, Washington, DC, $333,000. For HBCU Fellowship. 2010.

1546-75 Smithsonian Institution, Washington, DC, $420,000. For Plants Initiative (JSTOR). 2010.

1546-76 Sociedad Argentina de Botanica, Corrientes, Argentina, $20,000. For Plants Initiative - JSTOR. 2010.

1546-77 Stanford University, Stanford, CA, $175,000. For Sawyer Seminars: Comparative West: Transnational Perspectives on Rapid Cultural, Economic, and Environmental Transformation in the 19th Century Settler Colonies of Western Australia, Western Canada, the Western United States, and the Pacific Islands. 2010.

1546-78 Stichting tot Exploitatie van het Rijksbureau voor Kunsthistorische Documentatie, The Hague, Netherlands, $1,077,700. For Conservation Documentation Pilot Project (Rembrandt) Phase III. 2010.

1546-79 Stiftung Preussischer Kulturbesitz, Berlin, Germany, $235,000. For Integration of Art Historian and Technical Information. 2010.

1546-80 Swedish Museum of Natural History, Stockholm, Sweden, $270,000. For Plants Initiative - JSTOR. 2010.

1546-81 Swedish Museum of Natural History, Stockholm, Sweden, $187,000. For Plants Initiative - JSTOR. 2010.

1546-82 Tbilisi Botanical Garden and Institute of Botany, Tbilisi, Georgia (Republic of), $23,000. For Plants Initiative - JSTOR. 2010.

1546-83 Theater Communications Group, New York, NY, $300,000. For Services to the Field, Global Connections, and Cultural Exchange. 2010.

1546-84 Tougaloo College, Tougaloo, MS, $100,000. For Global Leadership Curriculum. 2010.

1546-85 Ukraine National Academy of Science, M.G. Kholodny Institute of Botany, Kiev, Ukraine, $64,000. For Plants Initiative - JSTOR. 2010.

1546-86 University College Dublin, Dublin, Ireland, $237,000. For Iberian Books Project, 1601 - 1650. 2010.

1546-87 University of Antioquia, Medellin, Colombia, $10,000. For Plants Initiative (JSTOR). 2010.

1546-88 University of Buenos Aires, Buenos Aires, Argentina, $18,000. For Plants Initiative (JSTOR). 2010.

1546-89 University of California, Berkeley, CA, $90,000. For Research Bridges (Dawson). 2010.

1546-90 University of California, Santa Barbara, CA, $180,000. For Research Bridges (Chadwick). 2010.

1546-91 University of Cape Town, Cape Town, South Africa, $800,000. For MA and PhD Fellowships. 2010.

1546-92 University of Cape Town, Cape Town, South Africa, $800,000. For OpenUCT. 2010.

1546-93 University of Cape Town, Cape Town, South Africa, $750,000. For Senior Research Scholars Program. 2010.

1546-94 University of Cape Town, Cape Town, South Africa, $368,000. For Research Bridges (February). 2010.

1546-95 University of Cape Town, Cape Town, South Africa, $300,000. For Research Bridges (Bond). 2010.

1546-96 University of Cape Town, Cape Town, South Africa, $237,000. For Research Bridges (West). 2010.

1546-97 University of Cape Town, Cape Town, South Africa, $133,000. For Mellon Mays Undergraduate Fellowships (MMUF) South African Regional Leadership. 2010.

1546-98 University of Cape Town, Cape Town, South Africa, $133,000. For Writing Center Internships (MMUF). 2010.

1546-99 University of Cape Town, Cape Town, South Africa, $53,000. For Conservation and Curatorship. 2010.

1546-100 University of Cape Town, Cape Town, South Africa, $17,200. For Higher Education in South Africa (SJS Research). 2010.

1546-101 University of Chicago, Chicago, IL, $600,000. For Islam Initiative. 2010.

1546-102 University of Chicago, Chicago, IL, $175,000. For Sawyer Seminars: Around 1948: Interdisciplinary Approaches to a Global Transformation. 2010.

1546-103 University of Chicago, Chicago, IL, $165,000. For Sawyer Seminars: International Women's Human Rights: Paradigms, Paradoxes, and Possibilities. 2010.

1546-104 University of Florida, Gainesville, FL, $934,800. For Monographs Initiative - Latin American and Caribbean Arts (in collaboration with the University of Oklahoma Press and the University of Texas Press). 2010.

1546-105 University of Graz, Graz, Austria, $76,000. For Plants Initiative - JSTOR. 2010.

1546-106 University of Hamburg, Hamburg, Germany, $145,000. For Plants Initiative (JSTOR). 2010.

1546-107 University of Helsinki, Helsinki, Finland, $114,000. For Plants Initiative - JSTOR. 2010.

1546-108 University of Leeds, Leeds, England, $246,000. For The Cambridge Edition of Ben Jonson Online. 2010.

1546-109 University of Miami, Coral Gables, FL, $172,000. For Rebuilding the Cuban Theater Digital Archive. 2010.

1546-110 University of Minnesota, Minneapolis, MN, $845,000. For Faculty and Graduate Student Exchange Program (in collaboration with the University of the Western Cape). 2010.

1546-111 University of North Carolina, Chapel Hill, NC, $175,000. For Sawyer Seminars: Precarious Work in Asia. 2010.

1546-112 University of Pretoria, Pretoria, South Africa, $150,000. For New Vice-Chancellor Support. 2010.

1546-113 University of Stellenbosch, Stellenbosch, South Africa, $800,000. For Postgraduate Program. 2010.

1546-114 University of Stellenbosch, Stellenbosch, South Africa, $750,000. For Senior Research Scholars Program. 2010.

1546-115 University of the Western Cape, Bellville, South Africa, $200,000. For Visiting Fellows. 2010.

1546-116 University of the Western Cape, Bellville, South Africa, $22,500. For Mellon Mays Undergraduate Fellowship. 2010.

1546-117 University of the Witwatersrand, Johannesburg, South Africa, $800,000. For Centre for Creative Arts of Africa. 2010.

1546-118 University of the Witwatersrand, Johannesburg, South Africa, $350,000. For Postdoctoral Fellowships. 2010.

1546-119 University of the Witwatersrand, Johannesburg, South Africa, $22,500. For Mellon Mays Undergraduate Fellowship. 2010.

1546-120 University of Toronto, Toronto, Canada, $357,000. For New Directions Fellowships (Saleh). 2010.

1546-121 University of Toronto, Toronto, Canada, $305,000. For Making Medieval English Manuscripts: New Knowledge, New Technologies (A group of nine research projects devoted to the advancement of knowledge about the pre- and early modern individuals, institutions, and communities that made and used medieval English books). 2010.

1546-122 University of Toronto, Toronto, Canada, $274,000. For New Directions Fellowships (Everett). 2010.

1546-123 University of Waterloo, Waterloo, Canada, $241,000. For The MARGOT Annotation Tool (MAT) for Interoperable Digital Application. 2010.

1546-124 University of Wisconsin, Madison, WI, $175,000. For Sawyer Seminars: Globalization and the New Politics of Women's Rights. 2010.

1546-125 University of Wyoming, Laramie, WY, $29,000. For Plants Initiative - ALUKA (Aluka is an international, collaborative initiative building an online digital library of scholarly resources from and about Africa). 2010.

1546-126 University of Zurich, Zurich, Switzerland, $499,000. For Developing the Arabic Papyrology Database. 2010.

1546-127 Wabash College, Crawfordsville, IN, $700,000. For Asian Studies (in collaboration with DePauw University). 2010.

1546-128 Wageningen University, Department of Plant Sciences, Wageningen, Netherlands, $607,000. For Plants Initiative - JSTOR. 2010.

1546-129 Washington University, Saint Louis, MO, $175,000. For Sawyer Seminars: Graeco-Arabic Rationalism in Islamic Traditionalism: The Post-Classical Period (ca. 1200-1900 CE). 2010.

1547
The Mendell Family Fund, Inc.

(formerly The Ira L. & Margaret P. Mendell Fund, Inc.)
c/o CBIZ Mahoney & Cohen, CPA
1065 Avenue of the Americas
New York, NY   10018-1878

Established in 1954 in NY.
Donor: Ira L. Mendell.
Grantmaker type: Independent foundation.
Financial data (yr. ended 11/30/10): Assets, $3,060,808 (M); expenditures, $210,181; qualifying distributions, $177,375; giving activities include $175,000 for 18 grants (high: $35,000; low: $1,000).
Fields of interest: International human rights; Youth development; Arts; Higher education; Cancer research; Recreation, centers; Human services.
Type of support: Annual campaigns; Endowments; Scholarship funds.
Limitations: Applications not accepted. Giving primarily in Washington, DC, NY, VA, and VT. No grants to individuals.
Application information: Contributes only to pre-selected organizations.
Officers: Thomas G. Mendell, Pres.; James Mendell, V.P. and Secy.; Alice M. Starr, V.P. and Treas.
EIN: 136159009

1548
Merlin Foundation

c/o Schulte, Roth & Zabel
919 3rd Ave.
New York, NY   10022-3903

Established in 1978 in NY.
Donor: Audrey Sheldon Poon†.
Grantmaker type: Independent foundation.
Financial data (yr. ended 12/31/10): Assets, $626,151 (M); expenditures, $400,477; qualifying distributions, $382,794; giving activities include $372,067 for 52 grants (high: $50,000; low: $500).
Purpose and activities: Emphasis on human rights, higher education, and cultural programs, including music and the arts; some support also for health and hospitals.
Fields of interest: Performing arts, music; Arts; Elementary/secondary education; Higher education; Health care; Health organizations, association; Recreation; International human rights; Catholic agencies & churches; Jewish agencies & synagogues.
Limitations: Applications not accepted. Giving on a national basis. No grants to individuals.

Application information: Contributes only to pre-selected organizations. Unsolicited requests for funds not considered.
Board meeting date(s): Nov.
Officers: William D. Zabel, Esq., Pres. and Treas.; Roger C. Altman, V.P.; Thomas H. Baer, V.P.; John J. McLaughlin, Secy.
EIN: 237418853

1549
The Merow Foundation

c/o John E. Merow, Esq., Sullivan & Cromwell
125 Broad St.
New York, NY   10004-2400

Established in 1997 in NY.
Donors: John E. Merow; Mary Alyce Merow.
Grantmaker type: Independent foundation.
Financial data (yr. ended 12/31/10): Assets, $1,848,263 (M); gifts received, $76,725; expenditures, $128,273; qualifying distributions, $126,090; giving activities include $125,840 for 19 grants (high: $25,000; low: $100).
Purpose and activities: Giving for the arts, education, hospitals, foreign policy, and religious organizations.
Fields of interest: Arts; Higher education; Education; Hospitals (general); International affairs, foreign policy; Religion.
Limitations: Applications not accepted. Giving primarily in NY. No grants to individuals.
Application information: Unsolicited requests for funds not accepted.
Trustees: John E. Merow; Mary Alyce Merow.
EIN: 133913625

1550
The Mesdag Family Foundation

c/o BCRS Assocs., LLC
100 Wall St., 11th Fl.
New York, NY   10005-3701

Established in 1991 in NY.
Donors: T. Willem Mesdag; Goldman Sachs & Co.
Grantmaker type: Independent foundation.
Financial data (yr. ended 03/31/10): Assets, $12,029,473 (M); expenditures, $408,594; qualifying distributions, $299,260; giving activities include $293,937 for 23 grants (high: $65,000; low: $250).
Purpose and activities: Giving primarily for higher education and the arts.
Fields of interest: International affairs; Museums (art); Performing arts, music; Performing arts, opera; Higher education; Medical school/education; Athletics/sports, water sports.
Type of support: General/operating support; Scholarship funds.
Limitations: Applications not accepted. Giving primarily in CA; funding also in CO, Cambridge, MA, and Princeton, NJ. No grants to individuals.
Application information: Contributes only to pre-selected organizations.
Trustees: Lisa Ann Mesdag; T. Willem Mesdag.
EIN: 133651269

1551
The Metropolitan Museum of Art

1000 5th Ave.
New York, NY   10028-0198   (212) 879-5500
FAX: (212) 396-5168;
E-mail: education.grants@metmuseum.org;
URL: http://www.metmuseum.org/en/research/internships-and-fellowships/fellowships

Founded in 1870.
Grantmaker type: Public charity.
Financial data (yr. ended 06/30/10): Revenue, $278,869,051; assets, $2,972,734,449 (M); gifts received, $153,972,180; expenditures, $317,560,714; giving activities include $182,714 for grants to organizations outside the U.S., and $1,279,731 for grants to individuals.
Purpose and activities: The museum encourages and develops the study of the fine arts, and the application of the arts into practical life.
Fields of interest: Museums (art); Arts.
Type of support: Fellowships; Scholarships—to individuals.
Limitations: Applications accepted. Giving on a national and international basis.
Application information: Electronically submitted applications and letters of recommendation will not be accepted; see web site for additional application information. Application form not required.
Copies of proposal: 3
Deadline(s): Jan. 2 for Research Scholarship in Photograph Conservation; Jan. 4 for Conservation Fellowships; Nov. 2 for Art History Fellowships
Officers and Trustees:* David McKinney,* Pres.; Emily K. Rafferty,* Sr. V.P., External Affairs; Deborah Winshel,* Sr. V.P. and C.F.O.; J. Nicholas Cameron, V.P., Construction; Sharon H. Cott,* V.P., Secy., and Genl. Counsel; Harold Holzer, V.P., Comms. and Mktg.; Sally Pearson, V.P. and Genl. Mgr., Merchandise and Retail; Philip Venturino, V.P., Facilities Mgmt.; Suzanne E. Brenner, C.I.O.; Renee E. Belfer; Annette de la Renta; and 36 additional trustees.
EIN: 131624086

1552
Margaret A. Meyer Family Foundation, Inc.

c/o Ocean Road Advisors, Inc.
767 5th Ave., 18th Fl.
New York, NY   10153-0033

Established in 2005 in NY.
Donor: Edward H. Meyer.
Grantmaker type: Independent foundation.
Financial data (yr. ended 12/31/10): Assets, $4,420,490 (M); expenditures, $222,553; qualifying distributions, $201,677; giving activities include $185,000 for 9 grants (high: $30,000; low: $15,000).
Fields of interest: Human services; Education; Environment; International affairs.
Limitations: Applications not accepted. Giving primarily in CA, Washington, DC, MA, and NY. No grants to individuals.
Application information: Contributes only to pre-selected organizations.
Officers and Directors:* Anthony E. Meyer,* Pres.; Margaret A. Meyer,* Secy.; Edward H. Meyer,* Treas.
EIN: 203983138

1553
The Michaels Family Foundation, Inc.
(formerly The Lorne Michaels Foundation, Inc.)
c/o Broadway Video
1619 Broadway, 9th Fl.
New York, NY 10019-7444

Established in 1990 in DE and NY.
Donors: Lorne Michaels; Broadway Video, Inc.
Grantmaker type: Independent foundation.
Financial data (yr. ended 12/31/10): Assets,
$27,600 (M); gifts received, $363,549;
expenditures, $381,298; qualifying distributions,
$375,102; giving activities include $375,102 for
grants.
Fields of interest: Arts, alliance/advocacy;
Education, fund raising/fund distribution; Higher
education, university; Education; Human services;
International relief; Protestant agencies & churches.
Limitations: Applications not accepted. Giving
primarily in NY. No grants to individuals.
Application information: Contributes only to
pre-selected organizations.
Officer: Lorne Michaels, Pres.
EIN: 133584269

1554
The Mihov Foundation
c/o Diko Mihov
111 W. 67th St., Rm. 32E
New York, NY 10023-5959

Established in 2005 in NY.
Grantmaker type: Independent foundation.
Financial data (yr. ended 12/31/09): Assets,
$8,358 (M); expenditures, $292,661; qualifying
distributions, $290,000; giving activities include
$290,000 for 1 grant.
Fields of interest: Arts, cultural/ethnic awareness.
International interests: Bulgaria.
Limitations: Applications not accepted. Giving
primarily in NY.
Application Information: Unsolicited requests for
funds not accepted.
Officers and Directors:* Diko Mihov,* Pres.; Samir
N. Masri,* Treas.; Steven D. Elmert; Theodore
Vassilev.
EIN: 202539551

1555
Mill Reef Fund
190 E. 72nd St.
New York, NY 10021-1108 (212) 954-1971
Contact: Mrs. Hardwick Simmons, Chair.

Established in 1948 in NY.
Grantmaker type: Public charity.
Financial data (yr. ended 12/31/10): Assets,
$284,486 (M); gifts received, $263,426;
expenditures, $327,693; program services
expenses, $318,489; giving activities include
$318,489 for 22 grants to organizations outside the
U.S.
Purpose and activities: The fund renders
educational, medical, and other philanthropic
assistance to the people of Antigua and Barbuda.
Fields of interest: Education; Health care.
International interests: Antigua & Barbuda.
Limitations: Giving on an international basis,
primarily in Antigua and Barbuda.

Officers: Mrs. Hardwick Simmons, Chair.; Barrie M.
Pickering, Treas.
EIN: 136162947

1556
The Millennium Promise Alliance, Inc.
432 Park Ave. S., 13th Fl.
New York, NY 10016-8013 (212) 584-5710
E-mail: info@millenniumpromise.org; URL: http://
www.millenniumpromise.org

Established in 2005 in DE.
Grantmaker type: Public charity.
Financial data (yr. ended 12/31/10): Revenue,
$6,121,624; assets, $27,555,104 (M); gifts
received, $6,159,314; expenditures,
$28,328,099.
Purpose and activities: The organization works to
promote and advocate for its Millennium
Development Goals (MDGs), to be achieved in Africa
by 2015: eradicate extreme hunger and poverty;
achieve universal primary education; promote
gender equality and empower women; reduce child
mortality; improve maternal health; combat HIV/
AIDS, malaria, and other diseases; ensure
environmental sustainability; and develop a global
partnership for development.
Fields of interest: Civil/human rights, women;
Education; Reproductive health; Public health,
communicable diseases; Public health,
environmental health; AIDS; International
development; International relief; International
human rights; International affairs; Economically
disadvantaged.
International interests: Africa.
Limitations: Giving limited to Africa.
Officers and Directors:* Jeffrey C. Walker,* Chair.;
Dr. John W. McArthur, C.E.O.; Dr. Susan Blaustein;
Jimmy Carter; Raymond G. Chambers; Chris Clarke;
Volkert Doeksen; Tracey Durning; Maria Eitel; John
B. Fitzgibbons; Jeffrey S. Flug; Ben Goldhirsh; Rajat
Kumar Gupta; Marjorie Magner; Jeffrey D. Sachs;
and 6 additional directors.
EIN: 203042135

1557
The Miller Family Foundation, Inc.
(formerly The William R. & Irene D. Miller Foundation)
c/o Bessemer Trust Co.
630 5th Ave.
New York, NY 10111-0001
Application address: c/o Judith R. Miller, Pres.,
9462 Brownsboro Rd., No. 131, Louisville, KY
40241, tel.: (502) 243-1252; fax: (502) 243-0951

Established in 1991 in NY; reorganized in 1995 as
The Miller Family Foundation.
Donors: William R. Miller; Irene D. Miller.
Grantmaker type: Independent foundation.
Financial data (yr. ended 12/31/10): Assets,
$308,734 (M); gifts received, $250,000;
expenditures, $337,662; qualifying distributions,
$335,031; giving activities include $210,150 for 23
grants (high: $50,000; low: $200).
Purpose and activities: Giving primarily for
education, including a music school, as well as for
the arts and social services.
Fields of interest: Arts education; Performing arts,
opera; Arts; Education; Hospitals (general); Health
organizations, association; Human services.
International interests: England.

Type of support: Program development.
Limitations: Giving primarily in Louisville, KY, the
metropolitan New York, NY, area, and Portland, OR;
some funding also in England. No grants to
individuals.
Publications: Application guidelines; Program policy
statement.
Application information: Application form required.
Initial approach: Letter requesting update form
Copies of proposal: 1
Deadline(s): Feb. 1 and Aug. 1
Board meeting date(s): Sept. and Mar.
Final notification: Letter
Officers and Directors:* William R. Miller,* Chair.;
Irene D. Miller,* Vice-Chair.; Judith R. Miller,* Pres.
and Exec. Dir.; Jane S. Tierney,* Secy.; Ian W.
Miller,* Treas.
Number of staff: 1 part-time professional.
EIN: 133826612

1558
The Mitrani Family Foundation
c/o Leonard Comerchero
149 Madison Ave., 10th Fl.
New York, NY 10016-6713
Application address: c/o Norman Belmonte, P.O.Box
568, Bloomsburg, PA 17815-0568, tel.: (570)
784-0400

Incorporated in 1959 in NY.
Donors: Members of the Mitrani family; Milco
Industries, Inc.; and others.
Grantmaker type: Independent foundation.
Financial data (yr. ended 12/31/10): Assets,
$1,898,692 (M); expenditures, $220,891;
qualifying distributions, $174,897; giving activities
include $174,897 for grants.
Purpose and activities: Grants largely for
Jewish-sponsored higher and secondary education,
and for vocational and technological training schools
in Israel.
Fields of interest: Higher education; Education;
Human services; United Ways and Federated Giving
Programs; Jewish federated giving programs; Jewish
agencies & synagogues.
International interests: Israel.
Limitations: Applications accepted. Giving primarily
in NY and PA.
Application information:
Initial approach: Contact foundation
Deadline(s): None
Officers: Norman Belmonte, Pres.; Leonard
Comerchero, V.P.
EIN: 246018102

1559
Mitsubishi Corporation Foundation for the Americas
(formerly Mitsubishi International Corporation
Foundation, also known as MC Foundation for the
Americas)
c/o Mitsubishi International Corp.
655 3rd Ave.
New York, NY 10017-5617
Contact: Tracy Austin, Exec. Dir.
FAX: (212) 605-1856;
E-mail: mic.foundation@org.mitsubishicorp.com;
E-mail for Tracy Austin:
tracy.austin@mitsubishicorp.com; Additional
contact: Joseph Reganato, Secy. and Prog. Off,
e-mail: joseph.reganato@mitsubishicorp.com;

URL: http://www.mitsubishicorp.com/us/en/csr/foundation.html

Established in 1992 in NY.
Donors: Mitsubishi Corp.; Mitsubishi International Corp.
Grantmaker type: Company-sponsored foundation.
Financial data (yr. ended 12/31/10): Assets, $4,090,223 (M); expenditures, $684,776; qualifying distributions, $960,737; giving activities include $642,567 for 11 grants (high: $250,000; low: $15,000), and $300,000 for 1 loan/program-related investment.
Purpose and activities: The foundation supports programs designed to promote the physical and social environments in which we live. Special emphasis is directed toward biodiversity conservation; sustainable development; environmental justice; and environmental education.
Fields of interest: Civil/human rights; Environment, natural resources; Environment, water resources; Environment, land resources; Environment, forests; Botanical gardens; Environmental education; Environment.
International interests: Latin America.
Type of support: General/operating support; Continuing support; Land acquisition; Program development; Conferences/seminars; Research; Employee volunteer services; Sponsorships; Program-related investments/loans; Mission-related investments/loans.
Limitations: Applications accepted. Giving primarily in the Americas, with emphasis on areas of company operations; giving also in Latin America. No support for religious, political, or lobbying organizations or discriminatory organizations. No grants to individuals.
Publications: Application guidelines; Grants list.
Application information: Letters of inquiry should be brief. The foundation gives preference to programs where Mitsubishi has a strong presence or where there is an opportunity for employee volunteerism. Application form not required.
Initial approach: Letter of inquiry
Copies of proposal: 1
Deadline(s): None
Board meeting date(s): Fall
Final notification: Summer
Officers and Directors:* Koichi Komatsu,* Chair.; Seiei Ono,* Pres.; Joseph Reganato, Secy. and Prog. Off.; Yuzo Nouchi, Treas.; Tracy L. Austin,* Exec. Dir.; Minoru Akita; Katsuhiro Ito; Seiji Shiraki; Yasuyuki Sugiura; Tetsuro Terada.
Number of staff: 3 part-time professional; 1 part-time support.
EIN: 133676166

1560
The Mitsui U.S.A. Foundation
200 Park Ave.
New York, NY   10166-0001
URL: http://www.mitsui.com/about_mitUSAfound.shtml

Established in 1987 in NY.
Donors: Mitsui & Co. (U.S.A.), Inc.; Intercontinental Terminals Co. LCC.
Grantmaker type: Company-sponsored foundation.
Financial data (yr. ended 03/31/11): Assets, $15,716,925 (M); gifts received, $38,750; expenditures, $688,933; qualifying distributions,

$599,458; giving activities include $599,458 for grants.
Purpose and activities: The foundation supports programs designed to promote education; community welfare and disabled individuals welfare; and arts and culture. Special emphasis is directed toward programs designed to promote international understanding and deepen U.S.-Japan relations.
Fields of interest: Arts education; Arts; Education; Human services; International exchange, students; International affairs; Community/economic development; Disabilities, people with.
Type of support: Conferences/seminars; Fellowships; Employee matching gifts; Employee-related scholarships; Scholarships—to individuals; Exchange programs.
Limitations: Applications not accepted. Giving primarily in Los Angeles, CA, Chicago, IL, and New York, NY. No support for religious, fraternal, veterans', or athletic organizations, or political and lobbying groups. No grants to individuals (except for scholarships), or for endowments, building campaigns, or film or television productions; no in-kind or non-monetary support.
Publications: Informational brochure.
Application information: Contributes only to pre-selected organizations.
Board meeting date(s): Quarterly
Officers and Directors:* Yasunori Yokote,* Chair.; Shinichi Hirabayashi,* C.E.O. and Pres.; Janet E. Garland, Secy.; Anthony Pensabene,* Treas.; Alan Getz; Glenn Clarke; Yoshiyuki Kawashima; Merlin Nelson.
EIN: 133415220

1561
Leo Model Foundation, Inc.
c/o Peter Model
500 E. 63rd St., No. 24K
New York, NY   10065-7946
Additional address: c/o Model Entities, 1500 Walnut St., Ste. 1300, Philadelphia, PA 19103

Established in 1970 in NY.
Donors: Model Charitable Lead Trust; Jane and Leo Model Foundation; Leo Model‡.
Grantmaker type: Independent foundation.
Financial data (yr. ended 12/31/10): Assets, $44,420,866 (M); expenditures, $2,500,960; qualifying distributions, $2,299,235; giving activities include $2,277,700 for 144 grants (high: $420,000; low: $100).
Purpose and activities: Support for museums and the arts, secondary and higher education (including colleges and universities), and public interest organizations.
Fields of interest: Human services; International peace/security; International migration/refugee issues; Environment; Museums; Arts; Higher education; Education; Public affairs.
International interests: Israel.
Limitations: Applications not accepted. Giving primarily in New York, NY, and Philadelphia, PA. No grants to individuals.
Application information: Contributes only to pre-selected organizations.
Board meeting date(s): Mar.
Officers and Directors:* Allen Model,* Chair.; Peter H. Model,* Pres.; Pamela Model,* V.P.; Marjorie Russel,* Secy.-Treas.; Roberta Gausas; Paul Model.
Number of staff: 1 part-time support.
EIN: 237084119

1562
Morgan Stanley Foundation, Inc.
(formerly Morgan Stanley Foundation)
c/o Community Affairs
1633 Broadway, 25th Fl.
New York, NY   10019-6708   (212) 537-1555
FAX: (646) 519-5460;
E-mail: whatadifference@morganstanley.com;
URL: http://www.morganstanley.com/globalcitizen/ms_foundation.html
Contact for Richard B. Scholars Program: Adebola Osakwe, Morgan Stanley, Human Resources, 1221, Avenue of the Americas, 40th FL, New York, NY 10020,
e-mail: adebola.osakwe@morganstanley.com

Trust established in 1961 in NY.
Donors: Morgan Stanley Group Inc.; Morgan Stanley & Co. Inc.; Morgan Stanley, Dean Witter, Discover & Co.; Morgan Stanley Dean Witter & Co.; Morgan Stanley.
Grantmaker type: Company-sponsored foundation.
Financial data (yr. ended 12/31/09): Assets, $53,952,645 (M); gifts received, $5,297,976; expenditures, $14,102,108; qualifying distributions, $14,099,264; giving activities include $14,099,264 for 681 grants.
Purpose and activities: The foundation supports organizations involved with arts and culture, education, children's health, diversity, and underserved populations.
Fields of interest: Civil/human rights, equal rights; Arts; Elementary/secondary education; Secondary school/education; Higher education; Hospitals (general); Health care, clinics/centers; Health care; Pediatrics; Food services; Human services; Children; Disabilities, people with; Minorities; Economically disadvantaged.
Type of support: Fellowships; Internship funds; General/operating support; Program development; Scholarship funds; Employee volunteer services; Scholarships—to individuals.
Limitations: Applications accepted. Giving primarily in areas of company operations, with emphasis on the Phoenix, AZ, Los Angeles and San Francisco, CA, Wilmington, DE, Chicago, IL, MA, New York, NY, Columbus, OH, Philadelphia, PA, Dallas and Houston, TX, Salt Lake City, UT, metropolitan areas, and the United Kingdom; giving also to national organizations. No support for local organizations with which Morgan Stanley employees are not involved, political candidates or lobbying organizations, religious, fraternal, or professional sports organizations, or individual performing arts organizations. No grants to individuals (except for Morgan Stanley Scholarship Initiatives), or for capital campaigns or endowments, dinners, walks or runs, golf events, political causes or campaigns, or documentaries or productions.
Publications: Application guidelines; Corporate giving report.
Application information: Letters of inquiry should be no longer than 1 to 2 pages. Unsolicited requests from local organizations are accepted from Morgan Stanley employees on behalf of nonprofit organizations only. Application form not required.
Initial approach: Letter of inquiry; E-mail letter of inquiry for Richard B. Scholars Program
Deadline(s): None; Jan. 14 for Richard B. Scholars Program
Board meeting date(s): Mar., June, Sept., and Dec.
Officers and Trustees:* Carla Harris,* Chair.; Joan E. Steinberg,* Pres.; Manisha Lalwani, Secy.; Jose

Rivera, Treas.; Marilyn Booker; Charlie Chasin; Gordon Dean; Shelley Hanan; Bill McMahon; Thomas R. Nides; Joanne Pace; William Wright.
EIN: 261226280
Recent grants for international programs:
1562-1 Great Ormond Street Hospital for Children, London, England, $3,500,000. 2009.

1563
The Hilda Mullen Foundation
c/o Milbank Tweed Hadley & McCloy
1 Chase Manhattan Plz.
New York, NY 10005-1413

Established in 1997 in NY.
Donors: Lois Q. Whitman; Martin J. Whitman.
Grantmaker type: Independent foundation.
Financial data (yr. ended 12/31/10): Assets, $12,385,926 (M); expenditures, $1,564,412; qualifying distributions, $1,551,408; giving activities include $1,547,650 for 88 grants (high: $475,000; low: $100).
Purpose and activities: Giving primarily for human rights, education, health services, and Jewish agencies.
Fields of interest: International human rights; Higher education; Education; Environment; Health care; Human services; Civil/human rights; Jewish agencies & synagogues.
Limitations: Applications not accepted. Giving primarily in NY, with emphasis on the metropolitan New York, NY, area; some funding nationally. No grants to individuals.
Application information: Contributes only to pre-selected organizations.
Trustees: Lois Q. Whitman; Martin J. Whitman.
EIN: 137120449

1564
A. J. Muste Memorial Institute, Inc.
339 Lafayette St.
New York, NY 10012-2725 (212) 533-4335
Contact: Murray Rosenblith, Exec. Dir.
FAX: (212) 228-6193; E-mail: info@ajmuste.org;
URL: http://www.ajmuste.org

Established in 1974 in NY.
Grantmaker type: Public charity.
Financial data (yr. ended 06/30/10): Revenue, $1,214,064; assets, $773,254 (M); gifts received, $1,264,814; expenditures, $1,342,094; giving activities include $890,802 for grants, and $242,184 for grants to organizations outside the U.S.
Purpose and activities: The institute makes a limited number of grants to international, national, and local projects, giving priority to those with small budgets and little chance of funding from more traditional sources. Preference is given to new projects or groups over those already in operation for some time. In addition, the institute administers an internship program. The institute has, as one of its programs, the funding and fiscal sponsorship of projects which promote the principles and practice of nonviolent social change. They must be concerned with one or more of the issues to which A.J. Muste dedicated his life: peace and disarmament, social economic justice, racial and sexual equality, and the labor movement.

Fields of interest: International peace/security; International affairs, arms control; International conflict resolution; International human rights.
Type of support: Program development; Publication; Seed money.
Limitations: Applications accepted. Giving on a national and international basis. No support for academic projects, direct social services, organizations with annual budgets exceeding $500,000, projects with budgets exceeding $50,000, or organizations previously funded by the institute within last 2 years. No grants to individuals, or for capital projects, general support of ongoing operations, research, or litigation.
Publications: Application guidelines; Financial statement; Grants list; Informational brochure; Newsletter.
Application information: Accepts National Network of Grantmakers common application form. Application form not required.
  Initial approach: Letter, telephone or e-mail
  Copies of proposal: 2
  Deadline(s): Varies; Feb., Apr., July, and Oct. for General Grants
  Board meeting date(s): Varies
  Final notification: 8 to 10 weeks after deadline
Officers and Directors: * Peter Muste,* Chair.; Martha Thomases,* Vice-Chair.; Bernice Lanning,* Secy.; John Zirinsky,* Treas.; Murray Rosenblith, Exec. Dir.; Karl Bissinger; Susan Kent Cakars; James A. Cole; Christine Halvorson; Melissa Jameson; Carol Kalafatic; David McReynolds; Jill Sternberg; Nina Streich; Robert T. Taylor; Diane Tosh.
Number of staff: 2 full-time professional; 1 part-time professional; 1 part-time support.
EIN: 237379088

1565
Myasthenia Gravis Foundation of America, Inc.
355 Lexington Ave., 15th Fl.
New York, NY 10017-6603
Contact: Janet Golden, Chief Exec.
FAX: (212) 370-9047;
E-mail: mgfa@myasthenia.org; Toll-free tel.: (800) 541-5454; URL: http://www.myasthenia.org

Established in 1952 in NY.
Grantmaker type: Public charity.
Financial data (yr. ended 12/31/09): Revenue, $583,953; assets, $5,245,876 (M); gifts received, $509,692; expenditures, $954,964; program services expenses, $735,239; giving activities include $364,731 for grants, and $370,508 for foundation-administered programs.
Purpose and activities: The foundation seeks to find a cure for myasthenia gravis and related disorders of the neuromuscular function, and to improve the lives of all people affected, through programs of medical research, patient care, patient services, professional education, and public information.
Fields of interest: Myasthenia gravis; Medical research, institute; Myasthenia gravis research.
International interests: Canada.
Type of support: Capital campaigns; Endowments; Fellowships; Research.
Limitations: Giving on a national basis and to Canada.
Publications: Application guidelines; Annual report; Financial statement; Grants list; Informational brochure; Newsletter.

Officers and Directors: * Sam Schulhof,* Chair.; Steve Hawco,* Vice-Chair.; Tor Holtan, Chief Exec.; Janet A. Myder, Secy.; Judy Bodner; Jennifer Faucett; Henry Kaminski, M.D.; Susan Klinger; Wilma Koopman, R.N.; Nancy Law; Marcia Lorimer, R.N., M.S.N; Marie Ronnlof; Robert Ruff, M.D., Ph.D.; Arthur Phillips Sultan; Edward Walsh; and 6 additional directors.
EIN: 135672224

1566
NAON, Inc.
c/o Hertz, Herson & Co., LLP
2 Park Ave., Rm. 1500
New York, NY 10016-5701

Established in 2000 in NY and DE.
Donor: Susan R. Wexner.
Grantmaker type: Independent foundation.
Financial data (yr. ended 12/31/10): Assets, $24,996,719 (M); expenditures, $1,151,938; qualifying distributions, $1,053,453; giving activities include $1,053,453 for grants.
Purpose and activities: Giving primarily for Jewish education, temples, and organizations.
Fields of interest: Human services; Education; Jewish agencies & synagogues.
International interests: Israel.
Limitations: Applications not accepted. Giving primarily in New York, NY, and Israel. No grants to individuals.
Application information: Contributes only to pre-selected organizations.
Officer and Directors: * Susan R. Wexner,* Pres. and Secy.-Treas.; Dr. Bertrand Agus; Dr. Saul G. Agus; Raymond Kanner; Gregg H. Levy, Esq.; Michael S. Oberman, Esq.; Mark Saks, Esq.
EIN: 134099539

1567
Nash Family Foundation
25 W. 45th St., Ste. 1400
New York, NY 10036-4902
Contact: Judith Ginsberg, Exec. Dir.
E-mail: info@nashff.org; Additional e-mail: judith@nashff.org; URL: http://www.nashff.org

Established in 1964 in NY.
Donors: Jack Nash†; Leon Levy†; Helen Nash.
Grantmaker type: Independent foundation.
Financial data (yr. ended 06/30/10): Assets, $71,114,582 (M); expenditures, $11,096,572; qualifying distributions, $10,398,249; giving activities include $9,688,483 for 288 grants (high: $1,000,000; low: $25; average: $10,000–$50,000).
Purpose and activities: Support primarily for underserved Jewish populations, arts and culture, health care organizations.
Fields of interest: Arts; Elementary/secondary education; Theological school/education; Human services; Jewish agencies & synagogues; Economically disadvantaged; Young adults; Mentally disabled; Physically disabled; Disabilities, people with; Aging; Adults.
International interests: Israel.
Type of support: Program development; General/operating support; Management development/capacity building; Building/renovation; Seed money.
Limitations: Applications accepted. Giving primarily in New York, NY and Israel. No support for political

organizations. No grants to individuals or for conferences.

Application information: All doctors, fellows, medical professionals, fiscal sponsors, and other interested parties should please note the discontinuation of the Nash Family Foundation Medical Training Fellowship Program and the Fellowship program. All Nash Family Foundation Medical Training Fellowships awarded must be completed. No further applications will be accepted for this program. Application form not required.

Initial approach: Telephone, letter or e-mail
Copies of proposal: 2
Deadline(s): None
Board meeting date(s): Throughout the year
Final notification: 6 months

Officers and Directors:* Joshua Nash, V.P.; Pamela Rohr, V.P.; Morris H. Rosenthal, Secy.; Helen Nash,* Treas.; Judith Ginsberg, Exec. Dir.; Todd Lang, Tr.

Number of staff: 1 full-time professional; 1 part-time professional; 1 full-time support.

EIN: 136168559

Recent grants for international programs:

1567-1 American Committee for the Weizmann Institute of Science, New York, NY, $10,000. 2010.

1567-2 American Friends of Beit Issie Shapiro, New York, NY, $25,000. 2010.

1567-3 American Friends of Beth Jacob Teachers Institute of Jerusalem, Brooklyn, NY, $20,000. 2010.

1567-4 American Friends of Hazon Yeshaya Institutions, Brooklyn, NY, $25,000. 2010.

1567-5 American Friends of PUAH, Brooklyn, NY, $45,000. 2010.

1567-6 American Friends of the Israel Museum, New York, NY, $33,334. 2010.

1567-7 American Friends of the Israel Museum, New York, NY, $33,333. 2010.

1567-8 American Friends of the Israel Museum, New York, NY, $33,333. 2010.

1567-9 American Friends of the Israel Philharmonic Orchestra, New York, NY, $10,000. 2010.

1567-10 American Friends of the Nancy Caroline Hospice of the Upper Galilee, Providence, RI, $25,000. 2010.

1567-11 American Friends of Yahad in Unum, Chappaqua, NY, $12,500. 2010.

1567-12 American Jewish Joint Distribution Committee, New York, NY, $26,000. 2010.

1567-13 American Society for Yad Vashem, New York, NY, $40,000. 2010.

1567-14 American Supporters of YEDID, Teaneck, NJ, $30,000. 2010.

1567-15 Central Europe Center for Research and Documentation, Atlanta, GA, $10,000. 2010.

1567-16 Central Fund of Israel, New York, NY, $10,000. 2010.

1567-17 Chabads Children of Chernobyl, New York, NY, $25,000. 2010.

1567-18 Ezrat Israel, Brooklyn, NY, $36,000. 2010.

1567-19 Ezrat Israel, Brooklyn, NY, $25,000. 2010.

1567-20 Ezrat Israel, Brooklyn, NY, $20,000. 2010.

1567-21 Friends of the Israel Antiquities, New York, NY, $50,000. 2010.

1567-22 Israel Sports Center for the Disabled, Friends of, Philadelphia, PA, $15,000. 2010.

1567-23 Jerusalem Foundation, New York, NY, $25,000. 2010.

1567-24 Jerusalem Foundation, New York, NY, $20,000. 2010.

1567-25 Jerusalem Foundation, New York, NY, $20,000. 2010.

1567-26 JTA, Inc., New York, NY, $50,000. 2010.

1567-27 One Family Fund, Teaneck, NJ, $10,000. 2010.

1567-28 PEF Israel Endowment Funds, New York, NY, $25,000. 2010.

1567-29 PEF Israel Endowment Funds, New York, NY, $25,000. 2010.

1567-30 PEF Israel Endowment Funds, New York, NY, $24,000. 2010.

1567-31 PEF Israel Endowment Funds, New York, NY, $21,000. 2010.

1567-32 PEF Israel Endowment Funds, New York, NY, $20,000. 2010.

1567-33 PEF Israel Endowment Funds, New York, NY, $10,000. 2010.

1567-34 PEF Israel Endowment Funds, New York, NY, $10,000. 2010.

1567-35 PEF Israel Endowment Funds, New York, NY, $10,000. 2010.

1567-36 Tikva Childrens Home, New York, NY, $27,000. 2010.

1567-37 University College London Friends and Alumni Association, Washington, DC, $20,000. 2010.

1567-38 Untold News, New York, NY, $50,000. 2010.

1568

National Council of Jewish Women - New York Section

820 2nd Ave.
New York, NY   10017-4504   (212) 687-5030
E-mail: info@ncjwny.org; URL: http://www.ncjwny.org

Established in 1894 in NY.
Grantmaker type: Public charity.
Financial data (yr. ended 06/30/11): Revenue, $1,396,618; assets, $4,253,240 (M); gifts received, $746,305; expenditures, $1,944,052; giving activities include $7,338 for grants to individuals.
Purpose and activities: The council provides services which improve the quality of life for all people to foster understanding and action through education and advocacy with an emphasis on aging, children and youth, constitutional rights, Israel, Jewish life and women's issue.
Fields of interest: Children/youth, services; Aging; Women.
International interests: Israel.
Type of support: Scholarship funds.
Limitations: Applications accepted. Giving limited to residents of the New York, NY, metropolitan area.
Publications: Application guidelines; Informational brochure.
Application information: Application form required.
Initial approach: Download application form
Deadline(s): Apr. 18
Officers and Directors:* Shirley Bisgeier,* Co-Chair.; Ruth B. Samuels,* Co-Chair; Beatrice Khan,* Co-Pres.; Beth Mitchel,* Co-Pres.; Susan Sack,* V.P.; Karol Todrys,* V.P.; Joan Shapiro Green,* Exec. Dir.; Lynn Judell,* Secy.; Dayna Langfan,* Treas.; Edward Bartosik.
EIN: 131624132

1569

National Ethnic Albanian American Foundation, Inc.

P.O. Box 70
Ossining, NY   10562-0070
Contact: Shirley A. Cloyes, Pres.

Established in 1991.
Grantmaker type: Public charity.
Financial data (yr. ended 02/28/11): Revenue, $26,800; assets, $9,099 (M); gifts received, $26,800; expenditures, $26,776; giving activities include $5,800 for grants.
Purpose and activities: The foundation educates Americans about Albanian people of the Balkans.
Fields of interest: Human services.
International interests: Albania.
Limitations: Giving on a national basis.
Officers and Directors:* Shirley A. Cloyes,* Pres.; Joseph J. Dioguardi,* Treas.
EIN: 521622672

1570

Nazarian Family Foundation

c/o Marks Paneth & Shron, LLP
88 Froehlich Farm Blvd., Ste. 200
Woodbury, NY   11797-2921

Established in 1987 in NJ.
Donors: Nazar Nazarian; Artemis Nazarian; Seta Albrecht; Levon Nazarian.
Grantmaker type: Independent foundation.
Financial data (yr. ended 11/30/09): Assets, $6,112,295 (M); gifts received, $180,200; expenditures, $210,669; qualifying distributions, $193,109; giving activities include $190,439 for 22 grants (high: $50,000; low: $100).
Purpose and activities: Giving primarily for higher education and to Armenian organizations.
Fields of interest: Higher education; Education; Ethnic studies.
International interests: Armenia.
Limitations: Applications not accepted. Giving primarily in NY. No grants to individuals.
Application information: Unsolicited requests for funds not accepted.
Directors: Seta Albrecht; Artemis Nazarian; Levon Nazarian; Nazar Nazarian.
EIN: 112889824

1571

The NBI Foundation, Inc.

(also known as The Urban Foundation USA, Inc.)
c/o Bencivenga Ward & Co., C.P.A.s
420 Columbus Ave., No. 304
Valhalla, NY   10595-1382
Contact: Lauretta J. Bruno, Pres.

Established in 1985 in NY.
Donors: Johnson & Johnson Corp.; American Express Foundation; Global Initiative Partners.
Grantmaker type: Independent foundation.
Financial data (yr. ended 06/30/10): Assets, $755,950 (M); gifts received, $542,859; expenditures, $570,616; qualifying distributions, $542,859; giving activities include $542,859 for grants.
Purpose and activities: The foundation seeks to improve the quality of life of South African communities, particularly in an urban context, and

to promote peaceful structural change in relation to fundamental aspects of community needs.
Fields of interest: Urban/community development.
International interests: Southern Africa.
Limitations: Giving primarily in South Africa.
Officers and Directors:* Aldrage Cooper, Jr.,* Chair.; Henry R. Slack,* V.P.; Robert Pilkington,* Secy.; Theuns Eloff; Conrad Person; A.M. Rosholt.
EIN: 521402447

1572
The Nduna Foundation
(formerly Amy L. Robbins Foundation)
c/o Perelson Weiner LLP
One Dag Hammarskjold Plz., 42 Fl.
New York, NY 10022 (212) 605-3100

Donors: Amy L. Robbins; Larry Robbins.
Grantmaker type: Independent foundation.
Financial data (yr. ended 12/31/09): Assets, $10,278,388 (M); gifts received, $7,093,282; expenditures, $7,912,925; qualifying distributions, $7,827,324; giving activities include $7,478,146 for 29 grants (high: $1,000,000; low: $10,000).
Purpose and activities: The foundation focuses efforts and investments on improving the lives of children everywhere. In particular, with improved nutrition and food security; supporting those who work diligently to treat and eliminate pediatric HIV/AIDS in developing countries; supporting innovative education programs; on conservation and wildlife restoration efforts in the U.S. and in Africa.
Fields of interest: Environment, natural resources; Elementary/secondary education; Education; Health care; International development; International affairs.
International interests: Africa.
Limitations: Applications not accepted. Giving primarily in NY. No grants to individuals.
Application information: Unsolicited requests for funds not accepted.
Officer and Trustee:* Amy L. Robbins,* Exec. Dir.
EIN: 261641882

1573
Nefesh B'Nefesh Jewish Souls United, Inc.
42 E. 69th St.
New York, NY 10021-5003 (212) 734-2111
FAX: (212) 879-2767; E-mail: nbnusa@nbn.org.il;
URL: http://www.nbn.org.il

Grantmaker type: Public charity.
Financial data (yr. ended 12/31/10): Revenue, $14,766,089; assets, $2,122,801 (M); gifts received, $14,303,041; expenditures, $19,213,352; giving activities include $5,548,270 for grants to organizations outside the U.S.
Purpose and activities: The organization encourages and stimulates the study and promotion of the Jewish religious ideals of the return to Israel, and the centrality of Israel to Jewish religious culture.
Fields of interest: Jewish agencies & synagogues; International migration/refugee issues.
Type of support: Grants to individuals.
Limitations: Applications accepted. Giving on a national and international basis, primarily in Israel.
Publications: Application guidelines; Informational brochure.
Application information: Application form required.

Initial approach: Download application
Deadline(s): Sept. 1 for Aliyah Financial Assistance
Officers: Joshua Fass, Pres.; Tony Gelbart, V.P. and Treas.; Leo Brandstatter, Secy.
EIN: 223804152

1574
The Netherland-America Foundation, Inc.
82 Wall St., Ste. 1101
New York, NY 10005-3613 (212) 825-1221
Contact: Eleanor Prince, Office Mgr.; Angela Molenaar, Exec. Dir.
FAX: (212) 825-9105; E-mail: info@TheNAF.org;
URL: http://www.thenaf.org

Established in 1921.
Grantmaker type: Public charity.
Financial data (yr. ended 12/31/09): Revenue, $826,872; assets, $4,289,471 (M); gifts received, $615,923; expenditures, $852,042; giving activities include $82,239 for grants, $135,386 for grants to organizations outside the U.S., and $169,250 for grants to individuals.
Purpose and activities: The mission of the foundation is to build on the enduring heritage and values shared between the peoples of the Netherlands and the United States. The foundation seeks to further strengthen the bonds between the two countries through exchange in the arts, sciences, education, business and public affairs.
Fields of interest: Education; International exchange, arts.
International interests: Netherlands.
Type of support: Program development; Conferences/seminars; Professorships; Publication; Seed money; Fellowships; Scholarship funds; Research; Program evaluation; Scholarships—to individuals; Student loans—to individuals.
Limitations: Applications accepted. Giving limited to the U.S. and the Netherlands.
Publications: Application guidelines; Annual report; Financial statement; Grants list; Newsletter; Program policy statement.
Application information: Application form not required.

Initial approach: Letter
Copies of proposal: 8
Deadline(s): Feb. 1, May 1, Aug. 1, and Nov. 1 for cultural grants; Mar. 1, May 1, Sept. 1, and Dec. 1 for study loans
Board meeting date(s): Mar., June, Sept., Dec.
Final notification: 1-2 weeks after committee meets
Officers and Directors:* Ennius E. Bergsma,* Chair.; Amb. C. Howard Wilkins, Jr.,* Vice-Chair.; Jan J.H. Joosten,* Secy.; Pauline Verheijen-Dop,* Co-Treas.; Caroline van Scheltinga,* Co-Treas.; Angela Molenaar, Exec. Dir.; John M. Palms; Fred G. Peelen; Theodore Prudon; and 25 additional directors.
Number of staff: 2 full-time professional.
EIN: 132989216

1575
The Neuberger Berman Foundation
(formerly The Lehman Brothers Foundation)
605 Third Ave.
New York, NY 10158-0180
Contact: Melissa Papini, Grants Mgr.

Established in 2000 in NY.
Donors: Lehman Brothers Holdings Inc.; Joseph M. Gregory; LB Foundation; The Action Fund of Lehman Brothers Holdings.
Grantmaker type: Independent foundation.
Financial data (yr. ended 11/30/10): Assets, $14,077,829 (M); expenditures, $4,129,253; qualifying distributions, $3,940,867; giving activities include $3,715,700 for 56 grants (high: $1,000,000; low: $5,000).
Purpose and activities: The foundation supports organizations involved with arts and culture, health, and youth development.
Fields of interest: Arts; Health care; Youth development.
International interests: Africa; Asia; India; Latin America.
Type of support: Building/renovation; Capital campaigns; Continuing support; Emergency funds; General/operating support; Program development; Program evaluation.
Limitations: Applications not accepted. Giving primarily in CA, IL, and NY, and in England, France, Hong Kong, India, Japan and Singapore. No support for religious, political, or fraternal organizations or discriminatory organizations.
Application information: Contributes only to pre-selected organizations.
Officers and Directors: Francine S. Kittredge, Pres.; Elizabeth R. Cribbs, V.P. and Treas.; Kyle Y. Ridaught, Secy.; Ingrid S. Dyott; Theodore P. Janulis; David Pedowitz; Judith M. Vale.
EIN: 311736689
Recent grants for international programs:
1575-1 Camfed USA Foundation, San Francisco, CA, $103,000. For secondary education of girls. 2009.
1575-2 Lehman Brothers Foundation Europe, London, England, $1,112,000. 2009.
1575-3 Magic Bus, Mumbai, India, $24,000. To train youth in the community. 2009.
1575-4 Millennium Promise Alliance, New York, NY, $300,000. For Mbama Tanzania Millennium Village. 2009.
1575-5 SOS Childrens Villages-USA, Washington, DC, $100,000. For construction of medical center in Malawi. 2009.

1576
I. & B. Neuman Foundation, Inc.
122 E. 42nd St.
New York, NY 10168

Established in 1956 in NY.
Donors: Irving Neuman†; Herbert Neuman; Marvin Herbert.
Grantmaker type: Independent foundation.
Financial data (yr. ended 12/31/10): Assets, $1,032,939 (M); expenditures, $220,775; qualifying distributions, $215,125; giving activities include $215,125 for grants.
Purpose and activities: Giving primarily for education and Jewish organizations.
Fields of interest: Education; Human services; Jewish federated giving programs; Jewish agencies & synagogues.
International interests: Israel.
Limitations: Applications not accepted. Giving primarily in NY. No grants to individuals.
Application information: Unsolicited requests for funds not accepted.
Officers: Herbert Neuman, Pres.; Marvin Neuman, Secy.-Treas.

Number of staff: None.
EIN: 136161492

1577
The New World Foundation
666 West End Ave.
New York, NY 10025-7357 (212) 249-1023
Contact: Colin Greer, Pres.
FAX: (212) 472-0508; E-mail: info@newwf.org;
URL: http://www.newwf.org
RSS Feed: http://newwf.org/blog/rss.xml
The New World Foundation's Philanthropy
Promise: http://www.ncrp.org/
philanthropys-promise/who

Incorporated in 1954 in IL and NY.
Donor: Anita McCormick Blaine†.
Grantmaker type: Public charity.
Financial data (yr. ended 09/30/10): Revenue,
$4,260,894; assets, $35,314,197 (M); gifts
received, $3,199,402; expenditures,
$11,825,578; giving activities include $8,757,996
for grants, and $87,830 for grants to organizations
outside the U.S.
Purpose and activities: The foundation places
emphasis on political participation, environmental
justice, economic justice, and media and
democracy.
Fields of interest: Education; Health care; AIDS;
AIDS research; Human services; Children/youth,
services; Minorities/immigrants, centers/services;
International peace/security; International affairs,
arms control; Civil rights, race/intergroup relations;
Civil/human rights; Community/economic
development; Public policy, research; Minorities.
Type of support: Program development;
Conferences/seminars; Seed money; Fellowships;
Technical assistance; Program-related
investments/loans; In-kind gifts; Matching/
challenge support.
Limitations: Applications accepted. Giving on a
national basis. No support for schools, hospitals, or
organizations that discriminate against women or
members of ethnic minority groups, or that do not
have an affirmative action policy and practice. No
grants to individuals (except for fellowships), or for
general operating budgets, community fund drives,
deficit financing, continuing support, capital funding,
building or endowment funds, research that is not
action- or policy-oriented with regard to current
issues and is not of limited scope or duration,
academic research, film and art projects, or
matching gifts. Emergency loans to current grantees
only.
Publications: Biennial report (including application
guidelines); Financial statement.
Application information: Application form not
required.
  Initial approach: Proposal
  Copies of proposal: 1
  Deadline(s): Oct. 30 for Increasing Organizational
    Sustainability: Developing Donor or
    Membership Bases
  Board meeting date(s): Biannually
  Final notification: Six weeks
Officers and Directors:* Nsombi Lambright,*
Chair.; Michael Leon Guerrero,* Vice-Chair.; Colin
Greer,* Pres.; Maria Rodriguez,* Secy.; David
Neubert,* Treas.; Lisa Abbott; Fred Azcarate; Julia
Classen; Maria Echaveste; Jonathan Glionna;
Brenda Hyde; Penn Loh; Charles S. Hey Maestre;
Andrea van der Heever; Vincent Warren.

Number of staff: 3 full-time professional; 3 full-time
support.
EIN: 131919791

1578
The New York Community Trust
909 3rd Ave., 22nd Fl.
New York, NY 10022-4752 (212) 686-0010
FAX: (212) 532-8528; E-mail: aw@nyct-cfi.org;
URL: http://www.nycommunitytrust.org
E-Newsletter: http://www.nycommunitytrust.org/
tabid/251/default.aspx
Facebook: http://www.facebook.com/group.php?
gid=129782847074491
Grants List: http://www.nycommunitytrust.org/
GrantSeekers/RecentGrants/tabid/208/
Default.aspx
Twitter: http://twitter.com/#!/nycommtrust

Established in 1924 in NY by resolution and
declaration of trust.
Grantmaker type: Community foundation.
Financial data (yr. ended 12/31/10): Assets,
$1,877,885,562 (M); gifts received,
$106,535,663; expenditures, $152,355,222;
giving activities include $140,835,396 for grants.
Purpose and activities: Priority given to applications
for projects having particular significance for the
New York City area. Program areas of major interest
are: 1) Children, Youth, and Families - includes
issues of hunger and homelessness, social
services, substance abuse, youth development,
girls and young women; 2) Community Development
and the Environment - includes civic affairs,
community development, conservation,
environment, and technical assistance; 3)
Education, Arts, and the Humanities - includes arts
and culture, education, historic preservation,
immigration, and human justice; and 4) Health and
People With Special Needs - includes health
services and policy, biomedical research, AIDS,
visual handicaps, children and youth with
disabilities, the elderly, and mental health and
retardation. In addition, the trust has established
divisions that reach out to the greater New York
metropolitan area: the Westchester Community
Foundation and the Long Island Community
Foundation.
Fields of interest: Historic preservation/historical
societies; Arts; Education, public education; Child
development, education; Education; Environment;
Health care; Substance abuse, services; Mental
health/crisis services; Health organizations,
association; Cancer; AIDS; Biomedicine research;
Crime/violence prevention, domestic violence;
Legal services; Employment; Food services;
Housing/shelter, development; Youth development;
Children/youth, services; Family services; Aging,
centers/services; Women, centers/services;
Homeless, human services; Human services; Civil/
human rights, immigrants; Civil/human rights,
minorities; Civil/human rights, disabled; Civil/
human rights, women; Civil/human rights, aging;
Civil/human rights, LGBTQ; Civil liberties,
reproductive rights; Community/economic
development; Government/public administration;
Disabilities, people with; Girls; Young adults,
female.
Type of support: Income development; Management
development/capacity building; Program
development; Publication; Seed money;
Fellowships; Scholarship funds; Research;

Technical assistance; Consulting services; Program
evaluation; Employee matching gifts.
Limitations: Applications accepted. Giving limited to
the metropolitan New York, NY, area. No support for
religious purposes. No grants to individuals (except
for scholarships), or for deficit financing, emergency
funds, building campaigns, films, endowment funds,
capital projects or general operating support.
Publications: Application guidelines; Annual report;
Financial statement; Grants list; Informational
brochure (including application guidelines);
Newsletter; Occasional report; Program policy
statement (including application guidelines).
Application information: Visit foundation web site
for application cover sheet and guidelines. Please
submit all written materials before calling the
foundation to discuss ideas. Faxed or e-mailed
proposals are not accepted. The foundation accepts
the New York/ New Jersey Area Common Application
Form. Application form required.
  Initial approach: Submit proposal with cover letter
  Copies of proposal: 1
  Deadline(s): None
  Board meeting date(s): Feb., Apr., June, July, Oct.,
    and Dec.
  Final notification: Within 2 weeks for initial
    response; up to 25 weeks for grant
    determination
Officers and Directors:* Charlynn Goins,* Chair.;
Lorie A. Slutsky,* Pres.; Joyce M. Bove, Sr. V.P.,
Grants and Special Projects; Ani F. Hurwitz, V.P.,
Comms.; Mercedes M. Leon, V.P., Admin.; Gay
Young, V.P., Donor Svcs.; Alan Holzer, C.F.O.; Mary
Z. Greenebaum, C.I.O.; Heidi Hotzler, Cont.; Jane L.
Wilton, Genl. Counsel; Ernest J. Collazo; Jamie
Drake; Roger Juan Maldonado; Anne Moore, M.D.;
Valerie S. Peltier; Samuel S. Polk; Estelle "Nicki"
Newman Tanner; Barron "Buzz" Tenny; Ann
Unterberg; Jason H. Wright.
Trustee Banks: Bank of America, N.A.; Bessemer
Trust Co., N.A.; BNY Mellon, N.A.; Brown Brothers
Harriman Trust Co.; Citigroup; Deutsche Bank
Americas; Fiduciary Trust Co. International; HSBC
Bank USA, N.A.; JPMorgan Chase Bank, N.A.;
Lehman Brothers Trust Co., N.A.; Merrill Lynch Trust
Co.; Rockefeller Trust Co.; Bank of America, N.A.
Number of staff: 23 full-time professional; 1
part-time professional; 18 full-time support; 1
part-time support.
EIN: 133062214
Recent grants for international programs:
1578-1 Action Against Hunger USA, New York, NY,
  $10,000. For general support. 2010.
1578-2 Acumen Fund, New York, NY, $10,000. For
  general support. 2010.
1578-3 Africare, Washington, DC, $15,000. For
  general support. 2010.
1578-4 AFS-USA, New York, NY, $248,000. For
  outreach, support, and scholarships to enable
  40 high school students from New York City to
  participate in summer and academic-year
  international travel programs. 2010.
1578-5 Aish HaTorah New York, New York, NY,
  $12,556. For Aish International Projects. 2010.
1578-6 American Associates of the Royal National
  Theater, New York, NY, $15,000. For general
  support. 2010.
1578-7 American Farm School, New York Office,
  New York, NY, $73,000. For scholarships in
  Velestino, Greece. 2010.
1578-8 American Foundation for the Paris School of
  Economics, New York, NY, $30,000. For general
  support. 2010.

1578-9 American Friends of Rabin Medical Center, New York, NY, $25,000. For general support. 2010.

1578-10 American Friends of the Louvre, New York, NY, $10,000. For the William Kentridge publication. 2010.

1578-11 American Friends of the National Portrait Gallery Foundation, Greenwich, CT, $10,000. For general support. 2010.

1578-12 American Friends of the Tel Aviv Museum, New York, NY, $10,000. For Project India. 2010.

1578-13 American Friends of the Tel Aviv University, New York, NY, $30,000. For general support of Harold Hartog School of Government and Public Policy. 2010.

1578-14 American Friends of the Union of Progressive Jews in Germany, Austria and Switzerland, Pittsburgh, PA, $25,000. For general support of Abraham Geiger Kolleg. 2010.

1578-15 American Friends of the Union of Progressive Jews in Germany, Austria and Switzerland, Pittsburgh, PA, $25,000. For general support. 2010.

1578-16 American Friends Service Committee, Philadelphia, PA, $50,000. For AFSC Haiti Fund. 2010.

1578-17 American Friends Service Committee, Philadelphia, PA, $30,000. For general support. 2010.

1578-18 American Friends Service Committee, Philadelphia, PA, $10,000. For general support. 2010.

1578-19 American Ireland Fund, Boston, MA, $10,000. For general support. 2010.

1578-20 American Jewish Committee, New York, NY, $50,000. For general support of Africa Institute. 2010.

1578-21 American Jewish Joint Distribution Committee, New York, NY, $30,000. For general support of the Better Together Program. 2010.

1578-22 American Patrons of the Tate Gallery Foundation, New York, NY, $25,000. For Transforming Tate Modern. 2010.

1578-23 American Red Cross National Headquarters, Washington, DC, $100,000. For Haiti earthquake - Int'l Response Fund. 2010.

1578-24 American Red Cross National Headquarters, Washington, DC, $10,000. For aid to Haitian Earthquake Victims. 2010.

1578-25 American Red Cross, Westchester County, White Plains, NY, $10,000. For Haitian relief. 2010.

1578-26 American Society for Technion-Israel Institute of Technology, New York, NY, $10,000. 2010.

1578-27 American University in Cairo, New York, NY, $225,000. For general support. 2010.

1578-28 Americans for Oxford, New York, NY, $100,000. For the Endowment of the Alfred Brendel Curator of Music at the Bodleian Library. 2010.

1578-29 Americans for Oxford, New York, NY, $15,000. For general support. 2010.

1578-30 AmeriCares, Stamford, CT, $10,000. For general support. 2010.

1578-31 Appeal of Conscience Foundation, New York, NY, $50,000. For general support. 2010.

1578-32 Asia Society, New York, NY, $25,000. For general support. 2010.

1578-33 Asia Society, New York, NY, $15,000. For Holbrooke Fellowship. 2010.

1578-34 Asia Society, New York, NY, $10,000. For general support. 2010.

1578-35 Atlantic Council of the United States, Washington, DC, $25,000. For general support. 2010.

1578-36 Bahamas Environment Fund, Key Biscayne, FL, $15,000. For general support of the Bahamas National Trust. 2010.

1578-37 Bahamas Environment Fund, Key Biscayne, FL, $10,000. For Bahamas National Trust. 2010.

1578-38 Bahamas Environment Fund, Key Biscayne, FL, $10,000. To support various programs at The Bahamas National Trust. 2010.

1578-39 Bhutan Foundation, Washington, DC, $35,000. For the WWF/Bhutan for roofing in Merak. 2010.

1578-40 Bhutan Foundation, Washington, DC, $25,000. For School of Tourism and Hospitality. 2010.

1578-41 Bishop Museum, Honolulu, HI, $10,000. For Hawaiian Haiti Restoration Fund. 2010.

1578-42 Business Executives for National Security, Washington, DC, $25,000. For general support. 2010.

1578-43 Calvary Episcopal Church, Pittsburgh, PA, $10,000. For capital improvements at Codrington College, Barbados. 2010.

1578-44 CARE, Northeast Region, New York, NY, $15,000. For general support. 2010.

1578-45 Carnegie Council for Ethics in International Affairs, New York, NY, $10,000. For general support. 2010.

1578-46 Catholic Medical Mission Board, New York, NY, $10,000. For Haiti relief. 2010.

1578-47 Catholic Relief Services, Baltimore, MD, $10,000. For Haiti relief. 2010.

1578-48 Catholic Relief Services, Baltimore, MD, $10,000. For survivors of Haitian earthquake. 2010.

1578-49 Catholic Relief Services, Baltimore, MD, $10,000. For general support. 2010.

1578-50 Catholic Relief Services, Baltimore, MD, $10,000. For Pakistan relief. 2010.

1578-51 Center for International Environmental Law, Washington, DC, $75,000. For Rebuilding American Leadership on Chemicals and Health at Home and Abroad. 2010.

1578-52 Center for Strategic and International Studies, Washington, DC, $50,000. For the Global Aging Initiative. 2010.

1578-53 Center for the National Interest, Washington, DC, $25,000. For Distinguished Service Award. 2010.

1578-54 Chicago Council on Global Affairs, Chicago, IL, $10,000. For general support. 2010.

1578-55 Children, Incorporated, Richmond, VA, $12,500. For general support. 2010.

1578-56 City University of New York, New York, NY, $210,000. To enable 128 City University students to participate in summer and academic-year study-abroad programs. 2010.

1578-57 Clean Air Task Force, Boston, MA, $100,000. To reduce black carbon and other short-lived pollutants to protect the Arctic from climate change. 2010.

1578-58 Committee to Protect Journalists, New York, NY, $10,000. For general support. 2010.

1578-59 Committee to Protect Journalists, New York, NY, $10,000. For general support. 2010.

1578-60 Concern Worldwide U.S., New York, NY, $25,000. For general support. 2010.

1578-61 Concern Worldwide U.S., New York, NY, $10,000. For Haiti relief. 2010.

1578-62 Conservation International, Arlington, VA, $10,000. For general support. 2010.

1578-63 Consultative Group on Biological Diversity, San Francisco, CA, $12,000. For operating support for Health and Environmental Funders Network which promotes increased and effective grantmaking at the intersection of health and the environment. 2010.

1578-64 Council on Foreign Relations, New York, NY, $4,000,000. For the Campaign for the Council. 2010.

1578-65 Council on Foreign Relations, New York, NY, $2,300,000. For Campaign for the Council. 2010.

1578-66 Council on Foreign Relations, New York, NY, $50,000. For Annual Fund. 2010.

1578-67 Dalton Schools, New York, NY, $50,000. For Global Initiatives. 2010.

1578-68 Doctors Without Borders USA, New York, NY, $30,000. For general support. 2010.

1578-69 Doctors Without Borders USA, New York, NY, $20,125. For general support. 2010.

1578-70 Doctors Without Borders USA, New York, NY, $10,000. For Haitian relief. 2010.

1578-71 Doctors Without Borders USA, New York, NY, $10,000. For aid to the victims of the flood in Pakistan and for aid to victims of the earthquake in Haiti. 2010.

1578-72 ELEM Youth in Distress, New York, NY, $15,000. For general support. 2010.

1578-73 Endeavor Global, New York, NY, $50,000. For general support. 2010.

1578-74 Fabretto Childrens Foundation, Arlington, VA, $25,000. For general support. 2010.

1578-75 Food for the Poor, Coconut Creek, FL, $30,000. For general support of school in Jamaica. 2010.

1578-76 Food for the Poor, Coconut Creek, FL, $14,000. To build two two-bedroom homes with sanitation in Race Course, Jamaica. 2010.

1578-77 Forest Ethics, San Francisco, CA, $100,000. For campaign to expose false claims of environmental sustainability. 2010.

1578-78 Foundation for Sustainability and Peacemaking in Mesoamerica, Round Rock, TX, $20,000. For general support. 2010.

1578-79 Freer Gallery of Art and Arthur M. Sackler Gallery, Washington, DC, $50,000. For partial funding for a curator of Southeast Asian art. 2010.

1578-80 Freer Gallery of Art and Arthur M. Sackler Gallery, Washington, DC, $10,000. For general support of Cambodian bronze show. 2010.

1578-81 French-American Foundation, New York, NY, $10,000. For general support. 2010.

1578-82 Friends of Dresden, New York, NY, $200,000. For the establishment of acquisitions fund. 2010.

1578-83 Friends of Khmer Culture, Norfolk, CT, $12,120. For NMC - signage and labeling and for general support. 2010.

1578-84 Friends of Khmer Culture, Norfolk, CT, $10,000. For general support. 2010.

1578-85 Friends of the Saint Andrews School Foundation, Nassau, Bahamas, $10,000. For general support. 2010.

1578-86 Friends of the Saint Andrews School Foundation, Nassau, Bahamas, $10,000. For general support. 2010.

1578-87 Friends of the Saint Andrews School Foundation, Nassau, Bahamas, $10,000. For general support. 2010.

1578-88 Global Fund for Children, Washington, DC, $50,000. For general support. 2010.

1578-89 Global Heritage Fund, Palo Alto, CA, $20,000. For general support. 2010.

1578-90 Global Heritage Fund, Palo Alto, CA, $10,000. 2010.

1578-91 Global Heritage Fund, Palo Alto, CA, $10,000. For the Forum on Cultural Heritage in a Developing World. 2010.

1578-92 Global Leadership Foundation, Arlington, VA, $25,000. For general support. 2010.

1578-93 Habitat for Humanity International, Americus, GA, $50,000. For Haiti relief. 2010.

1578-94 Heifer Project International, Little Rock, AR, $150,000. For general support of Tanzania Program. 2010.

1578-95 Heifer Project International, Little Rock, AR, $10,000. For general support. 2010.

1578-96 Human Rights First, New York, NY, $35,000. For general support. 2010.

1578-97 Human Rights Watch, New York, NY, $125,000. For Burma Project for two years. 2010.

1578-98 Human Rights Watch, New York, NY, $26,000. For general support of the SAIS Conference on Burma. 2010.

1578-99 Human Rights Watch, New York, NY, $15,000. For general support. 2010.

1578-100 Institute for Global Ethics, Rockland, ME, $10,000. For general support. 2010.

1578-101 Institute for Shipboard Education, Semester at Sea, Charlottesville, VA, $10,000. For Semester at Sea Annual Fund. 2010.

1578-102 Institute of International Education, New York, NY, $10,000. For support of Haitian students. 2010.

1578-103 International Crisis Group, New York, NY, $25,000. For general support. 2010.

1578-104 International Persistent Organic Pollutants Elimination Network, Berkeley, CA, $50,000. To eliminate use of toxic chemicals through global agreements. 2010.

1578-105 International Rescue Committee, New York, NY, $10,000. For general support. 2010.

1578-106 International Rescue Committee, New York, NY, $10,000. For general support of the Children's Unit. 2010.

1578-107 International Rescue Committee, New York, NY, $10,000. 2010.

1578-108 International Sephardic Education Foundation, New York, NY, $25,000. For general support. 2010.

1578-109 International Womens Health Coalition, New York, NY, $25,000. For general support. 2010.

1578-110 International Womens Health Coalition, New York, NY, $25,000. For general support. 2010.

1578-111 International Womens Health Coalition, New York, NY, $10,000. For general support. 2010.

1578-112 International Womens Health Coalition, New York, NY, $10,000. For general support. 2010.

1578-113 International Youth Leadership Institute, New York, NY, $40,000. To enable nine high school students to participate in a study-abroad program in Tanzania. 2010.

1578-114 J Street Education Fund, Washington, DC, $10,000. For general support. 2010.

1578-115 Jane Addams Peace Association, New York, NY, $10,000. For the Jane Addams Children's Book Award. 2010.

1578-116 Japan Society, New York, NY, $15,000. For general support. 2010.

1578-117 Jesuit Refugee Service, Washington, DC, $30,000. For the Kino Boarder Initiative and for the Fr. Ken Gavin Outreach Fund. 2010.

1578-118 Jordan River Foundation, Washington, DC, $10,000. For general support. 2010.

1578-119 Leo Baeck Education Center Foundation, Houston, TX, $15,000. For the Synagogue Ohel Avraham. 2010.

1578-120 LitWorld International, New York, NY, $10,000. For general support for the Foundation for Literate Youth (FLY). 2010.

1578-121 Long Island University, Brookville, NY, $40,000. To enable ten students attending Long Island University in Brooklyn and community colleges in Brooklyn and Queens to participate in a study program in Costa Rica. 2010.

1578-122 March to the Top Africa, Malibu, CA, $10,000. For general operating support. 2010.

1578-123 Mercy Corps, Action Center to End World Hunger, New York, NY, $40,000. To improve middle and high school global history curricula in City schools. 2010.

1578-124 Metropolitan Museum of Art, New York, NY, $25,000. For the Barbara and William Karatz Fund for Asian Art. 2010.

1578-125 Middlebury College, Middlebury, VT, $40,000. For Russell Leng '60 Professorship of International Politics. 2010.

1578-126 Middlebury College, Middlebury, VT, $40,000. For Russell Leng '60 Professorship of International Politics. 2010.

1578-127 Miracle Corners of the World, New York, NY, $50,000. For general support. 2010.

1578-128 Miracle Corners of the World, New York, NY, $50,000. For general support. 2010.

1578-129 Miracle Corners of the World, New York, NY, $20,000. For the MUHAS Dental Laboratory Project. 2010.

1578-130 Miracle Corners of the World, New York, NY, $10,000. For general support. 2010.

1578-131 Miracle Corners of the World, New York, NY, $10,000. For general support. 2010.

1578-132 Miracle Corners of the World, New York, NY, $10,000. For general support. 2010.

1578-133 Miracle Corners of the World, New York, NY, $10,000. For general support. 2010.

1578-134 Mobility International USA, Eugene, OR, $60,000. To enable seven young people with disabilities from New York City to participate in a homestay and community service program in Spain. 2010.

1578-135 Museum of Fine Arts, Houston, Houston, TX, $210,000. For $100,000 to support exhibition Ife Art in Ancient Nigeria and $110,000 for general support of International Center for Arts of the Americas. 2010.

1578-136 National Committee on United States-China Relations, New York, NY, $10,000. For general support. 2010.

1578-137 Nature Conservancy, Arlington, VA, $50,000. For general support and for the Sakonnet Campaign for the Quicksand Pond Watershed. 2010.

1578-138 Netherland-America Foundation, New York, NY, $17,500. For the Naf-Fulbright Fellowship. 2010.

1578-139 New Energy Foundation, Concord, NH, $10,000. To help underwrite expenses for Energy Conference to take place in India, including early stage planning as well as materials, publicity and documentation. 2010.

1578-140 New York University, New York, NY, $15,000. For Center for French Civilization and Culture. 2010.

1578-141 New York University, New York, NY, $10,000. For the School of Nursing Global Health Scholar Program. 2010.

1578-142 North American Friends of Israel Oceanographic Research, Babylon, NY, $15,000. For the Student and Youth Educational Program. 2010.

1578-143 Ocean Conservancy, Washington, DC, $75,000. To promote federal ocean management policies. 2010.

1578-144 Oceana, Washington, DC, $75,000. To promote offshore wind development and prevent offshore drilling. 2010.

1578-145 Oceana, Washington, DC, $10,000. For general support. 2010.

1578-146 Omprakash Foundation, New Canaan, CT, $50,000. For general support. 2010.

1578-147 One Family Fund, Teaneck, NJ, $12,000. For general support. 2010.

1578-148 Oxfam America, Boston, MA, $100,000. For general support. 2010.

1578-149 Oxfam America, Boston, MA, $100,000. For general support of the Change Program. 2010.

1578-150 Panthera Corporation, New York, NY, $200,000. For the Annual Contribution. 2010.

1578-151 Partners in Health, Boston, MA, $50,000. For POSER (Program on Social and Economic Rights) program in Rwanda. 2010.

1578-152 Partners in Health, Boston, MA, $10,000. For Haiti relief. 2010.

1578-153 Partners in Health, Boston, MA, $10,000. For Haiti relief. 2010.

1578-154 Pathfinder International, Watertown, MA, $30,000. For general support. 2010.

1578-155 Peace Action Education Fund, Princeton, NJ, $50,000. For the Endowment and for general support. 2010.

1578-156 Plan International USA, Warwick, RI, $10,000. For general support. 2010.

1578-157 Ploughshares Fund, San Francisco, CA, $500,000. For general support. 2010.

1578-158 Population Council, New York, NY, $25,000. For general support. 2010.

1578-159 Pro Mujer, New York, NY, $10,000. For general support. 2010.

1578-160 Project Mexico of the Orthodox Church, Chula Vista, CA, $10,000. For general support. 2010.

1578-161 Pure Water for the World, Rutland, VT, $10,000. For benefit of Haiti. 2010.

1578-162 Rainforest Alliance, New York, NY, $10,000. For general support. 2010.

1578-163 Research and Education Project of Long Island, Massapequa, NY, $10,000. For Andolan in support of Indonesian workers rights. 2010.

1578-164 Save the Children Federation, Westport, CT, $25,000. To use in Haiti. 2010.

1578-165 Save the Children Federation, Westport, CT, $10,000. For the Newborn Survival Campaign - Vietnam. 2010.

1578-166 Shared Interest, New York, NY, $25,000. For general support. 2010.

1578-167 Silk Road Project, Boston, MA, $10,000. For general support. 2010.

1578-168 Special Olympics International, Washington, DC, $100,000. For general support. 2010.

1578-169 Student Sponsorship Programme, New York, NY, $10,000. For general support. 2010.

1578-170 Synergos Institute, New York, NY, $25,000. For general support. 2010.

1578-171 Synergos Institute, New York, NY, $10,000. For general support. 2010.

1578-172 TOUCH Foundation, New York, NY, $250,000. For general support. 2010.

1578-173 TOUCH Foundation, New York, NY, $100,000. For general support. 2010.

1578-174 Trickle Up Program, New York, NY, $15,000. For general support. 2010.

1578-175 Union of Concerned Scientists, Cambridge, MA, $10,000. For general support. 2010.

1578-176 United Nations Foundation, Washington, DC, $15,000. For general support. 2010.

1578-177 United States Fund for UNICEF, New York, NY, $10,000. For Haiti relief. 2010.

1578-178 United States Fund for UNICEF, New York, NY, $10,000. For emergency relief in Pakistan. 2010.

1578-179 United States Holocaust Memorial Museum, Washington, DC, $10,000. For education in anti-Semitism and world tolerance. 2010.

1578-180 University of Bath Foundation, Bath, England, $12,000. To support Ph.D. program. 2010.

1578-181 University of the Witwatersrand Fund, New York, NY, $25,000. For general support. 2010.

1578-182 Valentino Achak Deng Foundation, San Francisco, CA, $15,000. For general support of Girl's Dormitory. 2010.

1578-183 Washington Institute for Near East Policy, Washington, DC, $20,000. For general support. 2010.

1578-184 Washington Institute for Near East Policy, Washington, DC, $10,000. For general support. 2010.

1578-185 West Harlem Environmental Action, New York, NY, $75,000. To organize forums on climate change and public health. 2010.

1578-186 William J. Clinton Presidential Foundation, Little Rock, AR, $10,000. For the Clinton Climate Initiative. 2010.

1578-187 Women for Afghan Women, Fresh Meadows, NY, $25,000. Toward salary of part-time person to work on fundraising events, corporate donations, and expanding efforts with private foundations and for the organization's moving costs. 2010.

1578-188 Working World, Hallowell, ME, $20,000. For general support. 2010.

1578-189 World Federation of Hemophilia USA, Albany, NY, $12,000. For the Susan Skinner Memorial Fund. 2010.

1578-190 World Learning, Brattleboro, VT, $248,000. For scholarships to 90 high school students from New York City to participate in international homestay programs. 2010.

1578-191 World Wildlife Fund, Washington, DC, $10,000. For continuing efforts to protect and preserve tigers in their native wild habitats, especially in Sundarban mangrove eco-system. 2010.

1578-192 Wyman Worldwide Health Partners Fund, Lebanon, NH, $25,000. For general support. 2010.

1578-193 YMCA of Greater New York, New York, NY, $130,000. For outreach and scholarships to enable 90 high school students to participate in international, domestic homestay, and work-service programs. 2010.

1579
New York Life Foundation
51 Madison Ave.
New York, NY 10010-1655 (212) 576-7341
Contact: Christine Park, Pres.

E-mail: NYLFoundation@newyorklife.com;
URL: http://www.newyorklife.com/foundation
Grants List: http://www.newyorklife.com/nyl/v/index.jsp?
contentId=18000&vgnextoid=10126f21189d2210a2b3019d221024301cacRCRD
New York Life Foundation Grief Guide: http://www.newyorklife.com/nyl/v/index.jsp?
contentId=17798&vgnextoid=1ec16f21189d2210a2b3019d221024301cacRCRD

Established in 1979 in NY.
Donor: New York Life Insurance Co.
Grantmaker type: Company-sponsored foundation.
Financial data (yr. ended 12/31/10): Assets, $91,521,313 (M); gifts received, $15,753,163; expenditures, $11,288,001; qualifying distributions, $11,257,431; giving activities include $10,270,443 for 608 grants (high: $542,500; low: $400), and $977,858 for 970 employee matching gifts.
Purpose and activities: The foundation supports organizations and programs that benefit young people, particularly in the areas of mentoring, safe places to learn and grow, educational enhancement opportunities and childhood bereavement.
Fields of interest: Boys & girls clubs; Elementary/secondary education; Child development, education; Education, reading; Education; Mental health, grief/bereavement counseling; Youth development, adult & child programs; Youth development, citizenship; Youth development; Children/youth; Children; Economically disadvantaged.
International interests: Mexico.
Type of support: General/operating support; Continuing support; Program development; Curriculum development; Employee volunteer services; Employee matching gifts; Employee-related scholarships.
Limitations: Applications accepted. Giving primarily in New York and Westchester County, NY; giving also to national organizations serving two or more of the following cities and regions: Phoenix, AZ, Los Angeles, Sacramento, San Francisco, and San Ramon, CA, Denver, CO, Washington, DC, Fort Lauderdale, Miami, and Tampa, FL, Atlanta, GA, Chicago, IL, Kansas City, KS, Boston and Westwood, MA, Detroit, MI, Minneapolis, MN, Clinton, Hunterdon, and Morris counties, and Edison and Parsippany, NJ, Cleveland, OH, Philadelphia, PA, Austin, Dallas, and Houston, TX, Salt Lake City, UT, Richmond, VA, Seattle, WA, and Mexico. No support for religious or sectarian organizations not of direct benefit to the entire community, fraternal, social, professional, veterans', or athletic organizations, or discriminatory organizations. No grants to individuals (except for employee-related scholarships) or for seminars, conferences, or trips, endowments, memorials, or capital campaigns, fundraising events, telethons, races, or other benefits, goodwill advertising, or basic or applied research.
Publications: Application guidelines; Annual report; Grants list; Informational brochure (including application guidelines).
Application information: Community Impact Grants must be initiated by a New York Life employee. A full proposal may be requested at a later date. Interviews and site visits may be requested. Organizations receiving support are asked to submit progress reports. Application form required.
   Initial approach: Complete online application form

Deadline(s): None
Board meeting date(s): Apr. and Nov.
Final notification: 2 to 3 months for regular grants
Officers and Directors:* Theodore A. Mathas, Chair.; Christine Park,* Pres.; Steven Rautenberg, Sr. V.P., Corp. Comms.; Lance LaVergne, V.P. and Chief Diversity Off.; Catherine A. Marrion, Secy.; Kenneth Roman, Treas.; Cynthia Bolker; Sheila K. Davidson.
Number of staff: 5 full-time professional; 1 full-time support.
EIN: 132989476
Recent grants for international programs:
1579-1 Fundacion Educa Mexico, Mexico City, Mexico, $100,000. 2010.

1580
The New-Land Foundation, Inc.
1114 Ave. of the Americas, 46th Fl.
New York, NY 10036-7798 (212) 479-6162

Incorporated in 1941 in NY.
Donor: Muriel M. Buttinger‡.
Grantmaker type: Independent foundation.
Financial data (yr. ended 12/31/10): Assets, $26,184,121 (M); expenditures, $1,925,527; qualifying distributions, $1,640,864; giving activities include $1,640,864 for grants.
Purpose and activities: Giving primarily for civil rights, the environment, population control, and peace and arms control.
Fields of interest: Museums (specialized); Environment; Human services; International affairs, arms control; Civil/human rights; Population studies.
International interests: England.
Type of support: General/operating support; Continuing support; Annual campaigns; Program development; Seed money; Research; Matching/challenge support.
Limitations: Giving primarily in CA, CO, Washington, DC, and New York, NY; some funding also in London, England. No support for educational institutions, medicine, religion and general social programs. No grants to individuals or for capital campaigns, publications, films, endowment campaigns, building campaigns, or conferences; no loans.
Publications: Application guidelines.
Application information: Application form required.
   Initial approach: Proposal (no more than 5 pages), or contact foundation for specific application requirements
   Copies of proposal: 1
   Deadline(s): Feb. 1 and Aug. 1
   Board meeting date(s): Spring and fall
   Final notification: Positive responses only; June 1 (spring cycle) and Dec. 31 (fall cycle)
Officers and Directors:* Hal Harvey,* Pres.; Constance Harvey,* V.P.; Renee G. Schwartz,* Secy.-Treas.; Anne Ehrlich; Ann Harvey; Joan Harvey; George Perkovich, Ph.D.
EIN: 136086562

1581
Jerome A. and Estelle R. Newman Assistance Fund, Inc.
43 Appletree Ln.
Carle Place, NY 11514-1320 (516) 279-4900
Contact: Michael Greenberg, Treas.

Incorporated in 1954 in NY.

Donors: Howard A. Newman†; Jerome A. Newman†.
Grantmaker type: Independent foundation.
Financial data (yr. ended 06/30/11): Assets, $8,816,146 (M); expenditures, $464,438; qualifying distributions, $390,000; giving activities include $390,000 for grants.
Purpose and activities: Giving primarily to Jewish education and welfare organizations, including a guild for the blind; support also for higher education.
Fields of interest: Foundations (community); Media/communications; Performing arts, theater; Arts; Higher education; Human services; International relief; Jewish federated giving programs.
Limitations: Applications accepted. Giving primarily in NY. No loans or grants to individuals.
Application information:
  Initial approach: Letter
  Deadline(s): None
  Board meeting date(s): Sept.
  Final notification: Varies
Officers and Directors:* William C. Newman,* Pres.; Robert H. Haines, Secy.; Michael Greenberg,* Treas.; Andrew H. Levy; Jeffrey A. Newman; Victoria Woolner Samuels; William C. Scott*; Catherine N. Woolner.
EIN: 136096241

1582
Nok Charitable Organization, Inc.
(also known as NOK Foundation, Inc.)
c/o Quest Partners LLC
126 E. 56th St., 19th Fl.
New York, NY   10022-3613
E-mail: info@nokfoundation.com; URL: http://www.nokfoundation.com/

Established in 2002 in NY.
Grantmaker type: Independent foundation.
Financial data (yr. ended 12/31/10): Assets, $0 (M); expenditures, $367,210; qualifying distributions, $371,928; giving activities include $249,756 for 34 grants (high: $34,500; low: $675), and $84,850 for 13 grants to individuals (high: $25,800; low: $500).
Purpose and activities: The foundation was created in order to cultivate and promote the study of Eastern philosophy and religion, as well as yoga.
Fields of interest: Hinduism; Buddhism.
International interests: India.
Type of support: General/operating support; Continuing support; Income development; Building/renovation; Endowments; Emergency funds; Program development; Conferences/seminars; Publication; Seed money; Curriculum development; Fellowships; Internship funds; Scholarship funds; Research; Program evaluation; Grants to individuals; In-kind gifts; Student loans—to individuals.
Limitations: Applications accepted. Giving primarily in NY and India.
Publications: Informational brochure.
Application information: The grantmaker is currently focusing on a large scale internal project and will not be accepting applications for scholarships until further notice. Application form required.
  Initial approach: E-mail or letter
  Copies of proposal: 1
  Deadline(s): None
  Final notification: 4 weeks
Officer and Directors:* Nigol Koulajian,* Pres.; Carla Koulajian; Laura Koulajian; Paula Tursi.
EIN: 020654795

1583
North Star Fund, Inc.
520 8th Ave., Ste. 2203
New York, NY   10018-6656   (212) 620-9110
Contact: Hugh Hogan, Exec. Dir.
FAX: (212) 620-8178;
E-mail: info@northstarfund.org; URL: http://www.northstarfund.org
North Star Fund's Philanthropy Promise: http://www.ncrp.org/philanthropys-promise/who
YouTube: http://www.youtube.com/user/NorthStarFund

Established in 1979 in NY.
Grantmaker type: Public charity.
Financial data (yr. ended 06/30/11): Revenue, $1,464,433; assets, $8,765,101 (M); gifts received, $765,968; expenditures, $5,325,927; giving activities include $4,158,235 for grants.
Purpose and activities: The fund fights for equality, economic justice, and peace.
Fields of interest: Media/communications; Media, film/video; Performing arts; Arts; Environment; Health care; Health organizations; Nutrition; Agriculture/food; Housing/shelter, development; Youth, services; International peace/security; Civil/human rights, minorities; Civil/human rights, disabled; Civil/human rights, women; Civil/human rights; Community/economic development; Minorities; Asians/Pacific Islanders; African Americans/Blacks; Hispanics/Latinos; Native Americans/American Indians; Indigenous peoples; Immigrants/refugees; Disabilities, people with; Women; LGBTQ; Economically disadvantaged.
Type of support: Mission-related investments/loans; General/operating support; Emergency funds; Seed money; Technical assistance; Program-related investments/loans.
Limitations: Applications accepted. Giving limited to New York City. No support for private or public schools, colleges, universities, hospitals, clinics, direct service organizations, projects that have large budgets, groups with sufficient access to traditional funding sources, or organizations that lack 501(c)(3) status. No grants to individuals, or for travel expenses for individual speakers or conference participants, fundraising events, feasibility studies, or capital fund drives.
Publications: Application guidelines; Annual report (including application guidelines); Financial statement; Grants list; Informational brochure; Newsletter.
Application information: The foundation accepts the New York/ New Jersey Area Common Application Form. Application form required.
  Initial approach: Telephone
  Copies of proposal: 4
  Deadline(s): Feb. 15 for spring grant cycles; Sept. 15 for fall grant cycles
  Board meeting date(s): Ongoing
  Final notification: Status notification 1 month after deadline; final notification 4 months after deadline
Officers and Directors:* Oona Chatterjee,* Chair.; Kathy Goldman,* Vice-Chair.; Kevin Ryan,* Secy.; Jason Franklin,* Treas.; Hugh Hogan,* Exec. Dir.; Elise Boddie; Lole Demmissie; Sarah Ludwig; Tara Mack; Sheila McDaniel; Jennifer Merschdorf; Julissa Reynoso, Esq.; Maxine Thorne; Jonathan Schorr; Aarti Shahani.
Number of staff: 5 full-time professional; 1 part-time support.
EIN: 132950801

1584
Not On Our Watch, Inc.
162 Fifth Ave., 8th Fl.
New York, NY   10010-1943
E-mail: info@notonourwatchproject.org; URL: http://www.notonourwatchproject.org

Grantmaker type: Public charity.
Financial data (yr. ended 12/31/09): Revenue, $499,069; assets, $2,662,404 (M); gifts received, $318,033; expenditures, $1,673,657; giving activities include $1,063,670 for grants, and $228,740 for grants to organizations outside the U.S.
Purpose and activities: The organization works to focus global attention and resources towards putting an end to mass atrocities around the world by drawing on the powerful voices of artists, activists, and cultural leaders to generate lifesaving humanitarian assistance and protection for the vulnerable, marginalized, and displaced.
Fields of interest: Human services; International relief; International human rights; International affairs.
Limitations: Giving on an international basis.
Officer: Alex Wagner, Exec. Dir.
Board Members: Don Cheadle; George Clooney; Matt Damon; Brad Pitt; David Pressman; Jerry Weintraub.
EIN: 208827879

1585
NoVo Foundation
(formerly The Spirit Foundation)
535 Fifth Ave., 33rd. Fl.
New York, NY   10017-0051
Contact: Kelly Merryman, Opers. Mgr.
E-mail for Kelly Merryman: Kmerryman@novofoundation.org; URL: http://www.novofoundation.org
Warren Buffett's Giving Pledge: http://givingpledge.org/#enter

Established in 1999 in NE; classified as a private operating foundation in 2000; reclassified as an independent foundation in 2001.
Donor: Warren E. Buffett.
Grantmaker type: Independent foundation.
Financial data (yr. ended 12/31/10): Assets, $255,335,455 (M); gifts received, $56,167,099; expenditures, $53,569,207; qualifying distributions, $52,985,952; giving activities include $49,221,448 for 84 grants, and $468,676 for foundation-administered programs.
Purpose and activities: NoVo Foundation seeks to foster a paradigm shift from domination to partnership. Funds are primarily directed toward the empowerment of women and girls, social emotional learning for all, and support for men and boys as their roles transform toward a more balanced society. Strategies include: Education and economic empowerment for young women and girls in the developing world. Ending violence against women and girls. Leadership development for women and men who share our commitment to shifting the paradigm from domination to partnership. Research and advocacy. Advancement of social emotional learning (SEL).
Fields of interest: Civil/human rights, women; Human services, equal rights; Civil/human rights, equal rights; Youth development, equal rights; Child development, services; Women, centers/services; Community/economic development; Women; Girls.

Limitations: Applications not accepted. No grants to individuals.
Publications: Annual report.
Application information: Unsolicited requests for funds not accepted.
  Board meeting date(s): May 5 and Nov. 24
Officer and Directors:* Jennifer Buffett,* Co.-Chair., Pres. and Treas.; Peter Buffett,* Co.-Chair.; Shawn Perrin,* Secy.; Aaron Stern.
Number of staff: 3 full-time professional; 4 full-time support.
EIN: 470824753
Recent grants for international programs:
1585-1 African Medical and Research Foundation, New York, NY, $20,000. For general support. 2010.
1585-2 Alliance for Peacebuilding, Washington, DC, $50,000. For project support for Man Up, international campaign enlisting young people for eradication of violence against women and girls. 2010.
1585-3 Apne Aap Women Worldwide, New Delhi, India, $2,100,000. For general support. 2010.
1585-4 BRAC USA, New York, NY, $200,000. For project support for Pakistan Flood Relief. 2010.
1585-5 Business Alliance for Local Living Economies, Bellingham, WA, $335,000. For general support. 2010.
1585-6 Business Alliance for Local Living Economies, Bellingham, WA, $260,000. For general support. 2010.
1585-7 Close to Home Domestic Violence Prevention Initiative, Dorchester, MA, $32,000. For project support for Resist Exploitation, Embrace Dignity (REED) Campaign, initiative to end trafficking and sexual exploitation. 2010.
1585-8 Coalition Against Trafficking in Women, New York, NY, $200,000. For general support. 2010.
1585-9 Coalition Against Trafficking in Women, New York, NY, $150,000. For project support for Resist Exploitation, Embrace Dignity (REED) Campaign, initiative to end trafficking and sexual exploitation. 2010.
1585-10 Coalition Against Trafficking in Women, New York, NY, $100,000. For project support for Resist Exploitation, Embrace Dignity (REED) Campaign, initiative to end trafficking and sexual exploitation. 2010.
1585-11 Demi and Ashton Foundation, Santa Monica, CA, $500,000. For project support for Real Men Don't Buy Girls Campaign. 2010.
1585-12 Digital Innovations Group, Web Lab, New York, NY, $150,000. For project support for Half the Sky Campaign, which will address two related issues: lack of awareness of issues around gender equality and lack of funding that supports women and girls. They have assembled team of communications, branding, television, film and game production to design and implement four components of campaign: leveraging book publicity, video games/social network, PBS miniseries and Moxie Awards. 2010.
1585-13 Equality Now, New York, NY, $260,000. For project support for strategic planning. 2010.
1585-14 Hastings 1066 Foundation, San Francisco, CA, $150,000. For project support for Center for Gender and Refugee Studies. 2010.
1585-15 Legal Aid Society, New York, NY, $300,000. For project support for Trafficking Victims Legal Defense and Advocacy Project. 2010.
1585-16 Polaris Project, Washington, DC, $100,000. For project support for 20,000 Project. 2010.

1585-17 Population Council, New York, NY, $480,000. For project support to build capacity for girls in Sub-Saharan Africa. 2010.
1585-18 Rebecca Project for Human Rights, Washington, DC, $400,000. For project support for 20,000 Project. 2010.
1585-19 Sanctuary for Families, New York, NY, $25,000. For project support for Sex Trafficking in New York Forum. 2010.
1585-20 Synergos Institute, New York, NY, $10,000. For general support. 2010.
1585-21 William J. Clinton Foundation, Little Rock, AR, $500,000. For Haiti Relief Fund. 2010.
1585-22 Witness, Inc., Brooklyn, NY, $400,000. For project support to produce gender-based violence video. 2010.
1585-23 Women for Women International, Washington, DC, $1,050,000. For general support. 2010.
1585-24 Women Thrive Worldwide, Washington, DC, $375,000. For Campaign to End Violence Against Women. 2010.
1585-25 Women Win Foundation, Northampton, MA, $400,000. For Gender-Based Violence in Conflict-Affected Countries project. 2010.
1585-26 World Affairs Council of Northern California, San Francisco, CA, $25,000. For project support for Global Philanthropy Forum. 2010.

1586
The O'Sullivan Foundation
c/o The Ayco Company, Tax Dept.
P.O. Box 15014
Albany, NY   12212-5014

Established in 1999 in TX.
Donor: Sean M. O'Sullivan.
Grantmaker type: Independent foundation.
Financial data (yr. ended 12/31/10): Assets, $16,172,649 (M); expenditures, $1,024,087; qualifying distributions, $949,600; giving activities include $949,600 for grants.
Fields of interest: International relief; International development; Human services.
Limitations: Applications not accepted. Giving primarily in GA; some funding also in NJ and NY. No grants to individuals.
Application information: Contributes only to pre-selected organizations.
Trustees: Anne S. O'Sullivan; Marie T. O'Sullivan; Sean M. O'Sullivan.
EIN: 066487034

1587
Ralph E. Ogden Foundation, Inc.
Pleasant Hill Rd.
P.O. Box 290
Mountainville, NY   10953-0290

Incorporated in 1947 in DE.
Donors: Ralph E. Ogden†; H. Peter Stern; Margaret H. Ogden†.
Grantmaker type: Independent foundation.
Financial data (yr. ended 12/31/10): Assets, $40,647,824 (M); expenditures, $3,424,386; qualifying distributions, $1,876,485; giving activities include $1,876,485 for grants.
Purpose and activities: Giving primarily for the arts and education.

Fields of interest: Arts; Education; International affairs.
Limitations: Applications not accepted. Giving primarily in Mountainville and New York, NY. No grants to individuals.
Application information: Contributes only to pre-selected organizations.
Officers and Trustees:* H. Peter Stern,* Pres.; Beatrice Stern, V.P.; Elisabeth Ellen Stern, V.P.; Georgene Zlock, Secy.; Eugene L. Cohan,* Treas.; John Peter Stern; Rose Wood; Colleen Zlock.
EIN: 141455902

1588
Ohr Torah Stone Institutions of Israel, Inc.
49 W. 45th St., Ste. 701
New York, NY   10036-4603   (212) 935-8672
Contact: Joel Weiss, Exec. Dir.; Robbie Bensley, Dir., North America
FAX: (212) 935-8683;
E-mail: ots@ohrtorahstone.org.il; URL: http://www.ohrtorahstone.org.il/index.htm

Established in 1983.
Grantmaker type: Public charity.
Financial data (yr. ended 12/31/10): Revenue, $5,390,682; assets, $1,829,862 (M); gifts received, $4,822,132; expenditures, $5,243,768; giving activities include $13,710 for grants, and $4,114,775 for grants to organizations outside the U.S.
Purpose and activities: The organization maintains schools, develops Jewish seminaries, and constructs and maintains facilities.
Fields of interest: Education; Jewish agencies & synagogues.
International interests: United Kingdom; Israel.
Limitations: Giving on an international basis, primarily in Israel and the United Kingdom.
Publications: Informational brochure; Newsletter.
Officers: Fred Ehrman, Pres.; Morton Lamdowne, V.P.; Maurice Spanbock, Secy.; Steve Schlussel, Treas.; Joel Weiss, Exec. Dir.
EIN: 133275531

1589
Olayan Charitable Trust
c/o Olayan America Corp.
505 Park Ave., 11th Fl.
New York, NY   10022-1106

Established in 1993 in NY.
Donors: Hutham S. Olayan; Olayan America Corp.
Grantmaker type: Independent foundation.
Financial data (yr. ended 12/31/10): Assets, $135,938 (M); expenditures, $421,822; qualifying distributions, $417,426; giving activities include $417,426 for 11 grants (high: $235,000; low: $2,426).
Purpose and activities: Giving primarily for education, particularly to a university in Beirut; funding also for a cancer hospital.
Fields of interest: Higher education; Hospitals (specialty); Human services.
International interests: Middle East.
Limitations: Applications not accepted. Giving primarily in NY and in Beirut, Lebanon. No grants to individuals.
Application information: Contributes only to pre-selected organizations.

Trustees: Nazeeh S. Habachy; Hutham S. Olayan.
EIN: 137031747

1590
Vivian and Paul Olum Charitable Foundation

c/o Levene, Gouldin & Thompson, LLP
450 Plaza Dr.
Vestal, NY   13850-3657

Established in 1984 in NY.
Donor: Paul Olum‡.
Grantmaker type: Independent foundation.
Financial data (yr. ended 12/31/10): Assets, $4,003,179 (M); gifts received, $22,232; expenditures, $175,908; qualifying distributions, $156,650; giving activities include $156,650 for grants.
Fields of interest: Health organizations; Human services; Education; Recreation; International peace/security; Civil/human rights.
Limitations: Applications not accepted. Giving primarily in CA, MA and NY. No grants to individuals.
Application information: Contributes only to pre-selected organizations.
Trustees: Joyce Olum Galaski; Kenneth Olum; Michael H. Zuckerman.
EIN: 222559174

1591
Omnicom Group Inc. Corporate Giving Program

437 Madison Ave., 9th Fl.
New York, NY   10022-7000   (212) 415-3600
FAX: (212) 415-3530; URL: http://www.omnicomgroup.com/aboutomnicomgroup/csr

Grantmaker type: Corporate giving program.
Purpose and activities: Omnicom Group Inc. makes charitable contributions to nonprofit organizations involved with education, the environment, human services, international relief, and children. Support is given primarily in areas of company operations.
Fields of interest: Education; Environment; Health organizations; Children/youth, services; Human services; International human rights; International relief.
Type of support: Pro bono services - communications/public relations; Pro bono services - marketing/branding; General/operating support; Employee volunteer services; Sponsorships.
Limitations: Giving primarily in areas of company operations.

1592
One Israel Fund, Ltd.

1175 W. Broadway, Ste. 10
Hewlett, NY   11557   (516) 239-9202
FAX: (516) 239-9203; URL: http://www.oneisraelfund.org

Grantmaker type: Public charity.
Financial data (yr. ended 12/31/09): Revenue, $1,774,726; assets, $885,143 (M); gifts received, $1,748,650; expenditures, $1,805,942; giving activities include $36,000 for grants, and $1,046,940 for grants to organizations outside the U.S.

Purpose and activities: The mission of the fund is to provide essential security, emergency medical and humanitarian aid to the men, women and children living in YESHA (the communities of Judea and Samaria as well as the former residents of the Jewish Communities of Gaza), as well as those communities left vulnerable by the evacuation in the Western Negev Region.
Fields of interest: International relief.
International interests: Israel; West Bank/Gaza (Palestinian Territories).
Publications: Annual report.
Officers and Trustees:* Steven S. Orlow,* Pres.; Scott M. Feldman,* Exec. V.P.; Jay Kestenbaum; Elliott Robinson; Stanley Rosenberg.
Number of staff: 6
EIN: 113195338

1593
Open Society Institute

400 W. 59th St.
New York, NY   10019-1105   (212) 548-0600
Contact: Inquiry Mgr.
FAX: (212) 548-4600; Baltimore, MD office: 201 N. Charles St., Ste. 1300, Baltimore, MD 21201, tel.: (410) 234-1091; Washington, DC office: 1730 Pennsylvania Ave. N.W., 7th fl., Washington, DC 20006, tel.: 202-721-5600; URL: http://www.soros.org
Blog: http://blog.soros.org/
E-Newsletter: http://www.soros.org/resources/newsletters
Facebook: http://www.facebook.com/OpenSocietyInstitute
Multimedia: http://www.soros.org/resources/multimedia
Open Society Institute: United States RSS: http://feeds.feedburner.com/OpenSocietyInstituteUnitedStates
Open Society Institute's Philanthropy Promise: http://www.ncrp.org/philanthropys-promise/who
OSI - Baltimore: http://twitter.com/OSIBaltimore
Podcasts: http://www.soros.org/resources/multimedia/podcasts
RSS Directory: http://www.soros.org/resources/newsfeeds
Twitter: http://www.twitter.com/opensociety
YouTube: http://www.youtube.com/opensocietyinstitute

Established in 1993 in NY.
Donor: George Soros.
Grantmaker type: Operating foundation.
Financial data (yr. ended 12/31/10): Assets, $1,141,004,097 (M); gifts received, $120,510,756; expenditures, $148,864,732; qualifying distributions, $141,437,177; giving activities include $49,608,799 for 280 grants (high: $3,792,489; low: $2,500), $9,547,437 for 791 grants to individuals (high: $132,406; low: $66), $1,514,721 for 547 employee matching gifts, and $5,000,000 for 1 loan/program-related investment.
Purpose and activities: The Open Society Institute (OSI), a private operating and grantmaking foundation, aims to shape public policy to promote democratic governance, human rights, and economic, legal, and social reform. On a local level, OSI implements a range of initiatives to support the rule of law, education, public health, and independent media. At the same time, OSI works to build alliances across borders and continents on issues such as combating corruption and rights

abuses. OSI was created in 1993 by investor and philanthropist George Soros to support his foundations in Central and Eastern Europe and the former Soviet Union. Those foundations were established, starting in 1984, to help countries make the transition from communism. OSI has expanded the activities of the Soros foundations network to other areas of the world where the transition to democracy is of particular concern. The Soros foundations network encompasses foundations, offices, initiatives, and grantees in more than 60 countries and regions including: Asia, Southeast Asia, Central Asia, and Caucasus, Latin America and the Caribbean Central and South Eastern Europe, Africa, the Baltics, and North America.
Fields of interest: Crime/law enforcement; Civil/human rights; Reproductive health; Public health; Palliative care; Media/communications; Law/international law; International human rights; International economic development; Education; Arts; Youth; Terminal illness, people with; Substance abusers; Offenders/ex-offenders; Minorities; Migrant workers; Mentally disabled; LGBTQ; Indigenous peoples; Immigrants/refugees; Hispanics/Latinos; Girls; Economically disadvantaged; Disabilities, people with; Children/youth; Children; Blind/visually impaired; AIDS, people with; African Americans/Blacks.
International interests: Africa; Asia; Caribbean; Central Asia and the Caucasus; Eastern & Central Europe; Global programs; Latin America; Southeast Asia.
Type of support: General/operating support; Continuing support; Program development; Professorships; Publication; Fellowships; Internship funds; Scholarship funds; Research; Technical assistance; Program-related investments/loans; Employee matching gifts; Grants to individuals; Scholarships—to individuals.
Limitations: Applications accepted. Giving on a national and international basis. No support for political parties or organizations connected to political parties.
Publications: Annual report; Informational brochure; Newsletter; Program policy statement.
Application information: For program application guidelines and deadlines see foundation web site. The site includes a wizard to help determine eligibility and submit an inquiry electronically. Application form not required.
Initial approach: Letter of inquiry, only if grantseeker does not have internet access
Officers and Trustees:* George Soros,* Chair.; Aryeh Neier,* C.E.O. and Pres.; Christopher Stone, Pres.-Elect; Stewart J. Paperin, Exec. V.P. and Treas.; Annette Laborey, V.P.; Ricardo A. Castro, Secy. and Genl. Counsel; Maija Arbolino, C.F.O.; Leon Botstein; Jonathan Soros.
EIN: 137029285
Recent grants for international programs:
1593-1 Abdorrahman Boroumand Foundation, Washington, DC, $75,000. For Iran Human Rights Memorial Project. 2009.
1593-2 Aftermath Project, Los Angeles, CA, $20,000. For production support for photographer working on a post-conflict story. 2009.
1593-3 Alliance for Climate Protection, Washington, DC, $5,000,000. For general support. 2009.
1593-4 Alliance for Open Society International, New York, NY, $147,507. For activities in the U.S. and abroad in seeking and implementing U.S. government grants in areas of public health, civil

society development, law reform and education, among others. 2009.

1593-5 America-Mideast Educational and Training Services, Washington, DC, $96,340. To administer Palestinian Rule of Law (PROL) Program in the Palestinian Territories. 2009.

1593-6 American Councils for International Education: ACTR/ACCELS, Washington, DC, $12,251. To support Educational Advising Centers in Belarus. 2009.

1593-7 American Refugee Committee, Minneapolis, MN, $100,000. To build capacity of Foundation for International Dignity (FIND) to reduce violence against women and increase access to justice for violence against women survivors in Lofa County in Liberia. 2009.

1593-8 American University, Washington, DC, $50,824. For Human Rights and Access to Medicines Legal Education and Advocacy Initiative. 2009.

1593-9 American-Iranian Council, Princeton, NJ, $25,000. For U.S.-Iran Relations: Building Constituency, Fostering Engagement project. 2009.

1593-10 Americans for Informed Democracy, Washington, DC, $100,000. For general support. 2009.

1593-11 Amnesty International USA, New York, NY, $500,000. For Counter Terror with Justice Campaign, effort to roll back War on Terror policies and practices disregarding international human rights standards, by mobilizing concerned citizens to apply strategic pressure on key U.S. targets. 2009.

1593-12 Art Works Projects, Chicago, IL, $25,000. For exhibition, BLOOD/STONES Burmese Rubies, consisting of examples of finished (synthetic) ruby jewelry, unset stones, uncut stones and mining implements and materials, along with photos and writing which provide a glimpse into the world of ruby mining and ruby production as a human rights issues. 2009.

1593-13 As You Sow, San Francisco, CA, $45,000. To leverage purchasing power of U.S. and international companies to stop the use of forced child labor in Uzbekistan. 2009.

1593-14 Asia Society, New York, NY, $150,000. For U.S.-Iran Dialogue. 2009.

1593-15 Asian Cultural Council, New York, NY, $25,000. For Mekong Region Fellowship Program. 2009.

1593-16 Baku Educational Information Center Foundation, Baku, Azerbaijan, $61,640. For educational advising services in Central Asia. 2009.

1593-17 Baltic-American Partnership Fund, New York, NY, $83,130. For general support. 2009.

1593-18 Bard College, Annandale on Hudson, NY, $3,000,000. To establish Endowment Fund for benefit of Smolny College in Saint Petersburg, Russia. Smolny College is a liberal arts college and this is a joint undertaking of Bard College and Saint Petersburg State University. 2009.

1593-19 BILIM Educational Advising Center, Almaty, Kazakhstan, $40,882. For educational advising services in Central Asia. 2009.

1593-20 Black Alliance for Just Immigration, Berkeley, CA, $50,000. For efforts to organize national network of African-American and Black immigrant organizations around immigration reform and intra-group relations. 2009.

1593-21 Burma Fund, New York, NY, $32,400. For capacity building, research and outreach for

reform-minded Burmese military officials in exile with links to colleague officials in Burma. 2009.

1593-22 Burma Partnership, Mae Sot, Thailand, $31,000. For project entitled, Strengthening APPPB Burma Regional and International Campaign Activities in Response to the Current Situation in Burma. 2009.

1593-23 Carnegie Endowment for International Peace, Washington, DC, $212,500. For on-going institutional and programmatic work and to allow expansion to new audiences. 2009.

1593-24 Carnegie Endowment for International Peace, Washington, DC, $132,761. For three research directions of Carnegie Moscow Center's two-year civil society initiative. 2009.

1593-25 Carnegie Endowment for International Peace, Washington, DC, $37,850. For conference on security in Shanghai Cooperation Organization (SCO) states, specifically to engage experts from SCO countries on the various dimensions of regional security in Afghanistan's neighborhood. 2009.

1593-26 Carnegie Endowment for International Peace, Washington, DC, $17,540. For initiative, The End of Labor Migration, in discussion of the various dimensions of the end of labor migration in post-Soviet space. 2009.

1593-27 Carter Center, Atlanta, GA, $600,000. To strengthen Rule of law in Liberia. 2009.

1593-28 Cato Institute, Washington, DC, $50,000. For Civil Liberties and Counterterrorism Initiative. 2009.

1593-29 Center for Democracy and Technology, Washington, DC, $300,000. For Freedom, Security and Technology Project and Digital Fourth Amendment Initiative. 2009.

1593-30 Center for International Education, Tbilisi, Georgia (Republic of), $28,141. For educational advising services in Central Asia. 2009.

1593-31 Center for Justice and Accountability, San Francisco, CA, $125,000. For general support. 2009.

1593-32 Center for Strategic and International Studies, Washington, DC, $10,000. To monitor and to produce three web-based reports tracking incidents of violence in the North Caucasus, in order to reach Western policy makers and media. 2009.

1593-33 Center on Budget and Policy Priorities, Washington, DC, $700,000. For International Budget Partnership. 2009.

1593-34 Centrul de Informatii Universitare, Chisinau, Moldova, $30,001. For educational advising services in Central Asia. 2009.

1593-35 Chin Human Rights Organization, Nepean, Canada, $50,000. To provide emergency food relief for Western Burma's Chin State. 2009.

1593-36 CIVIC-Campaign for Innocent Victims in Conflict, Washington, DC, $150,000. For general support. 2009.

1593-37 Climate Policy Initiative, San Francisco, CA, $1,000,000. For startup activities, including early hiring, space acquisition, strategy refinement, communications and preparation for first work products. 2009.

1593-38 Columbia University, Center for the Study of Human Rights, New York, NY, $10,000. For Visiting Scholar. 2009.

1593-39 Committee to Protect Journalists, New York, NY, $10,000. For general support. 2009.

1593-40 Constitution Project, Washington, DC, $50,000. To advance objectives of human rights/liberty and security and criminal justice advocacy communities during transition period by

providing policymakers with collaborative catalogue of policy objectives to promote the rule of law. 2009.

1593-41 Due Process of Law Foundation, Washington, DC, $315,000. For Consolidating the Judicial Accountability and Transparency Program Area. 2009.

1593-42 Earth Island Institute, Berkeley, CA, $500,000. For the Campus Climate Challenge. 2009.

1593-43 EarthRights International, Washington, DC, $100,000. For support related to the Wiwa v. Shell trial. 2009.

1593-44 EarthRights International, Washington, DC, $20,000. For Burma Project/Shwe Gas Project, large-scale natural gas development project in Burma. 2009.

1593-45 East and Horn of Africa Human Rights Defenders Project, Kampala, Uganda, $250,729. For emergency assistance and support for Sudanese human rights defenders at risk exiled in Uganda. 2009.

1593-46 Ethnic Community Development Forum, Chiang Mai, Thailand, $14,193. For capacity building of communities in seven ethnic areas in Burma through community development approach. 2009.

1593-47 Focus Project, Washington, DC, $100,000. For OMB Watch's Charity and Security Network Project, collaboration between humanitarian aid providers, development organizations, charities, civil liberties organizations, civil rights organizations, grantmakers and foundations working to reform counterterrorism measures that place U.S.-based organizations at risk of criminal prosecution and conviction for providing material support to a terrorist organization when they provide humanitarian aid in regions of the world that are under the de facto control of groups designated by the U.S. government as terrorist. 2009.

1593-48 Former Political Prisoners Network, Upper Burma, Monywa, Burma (Myanmar), $22,070. For Internet resource center in Upper Burma. 2009.

1593-49 Forum for Democracy in Burma, Mae Sot, Thailand, $60,000. To support maintaining democracy networks in Burma. 2009.

1593-50 Foundation for Hospices in Sub-Saharan Africa, Alexandria, VA, $25,000. For full-time salary of palliative care leader as Chief Medical Officer at Island Hospice in Zimbabwe. 2009.

1593-51 Foundation for the People of Burma, San Francisco, CA, $30,000. To support Gitameit Music Centre and School, nonprofit community center and music school in downtown Yangon, Burma. 2009.

1593-52 Fund for Global Human Rights, Washington, DC, $50,000. To facilitate technical assistance to grantees seeking to augment their advocacy skills, organizational capacity and effectiveness in Algeria. 2009.

1593-53 Fund for the European University at Saint Petersburg, Ann Arbor, MI, $3,900,000. To establish endowment fund for the benefit of European University of Saint Petersburg, graduate research university located in St. Petersburg, Russia. 2009.

1593-54 GBCHealth, New York, NY, $180,000. To work in Russia and Ukraine. 2009.

1593-55 Generation Wave, Mae Sot, Thailand, $10,000. For public outreach campaigns. 2009.

1593-56 George Mason University, Fairfax, VA, $112,498. For project titled, Efforts to Achieve Accountability for Human Rights Violations in Latin America: A Conference Series on the Trial of Alberto Fujimori in Comparative Perspective. 2009.

1593-57 George Mason University, Fairfax, VA, $15,000. For project titled, Efforts to Achieve Accountability for Human Rights Violations in Latin America: A Conference Series on the Trial of Alberto Fujimori. 2009.

1593-58 Global Action to Prevent War and Armed Conflict, New York, NY, $24,470. To produce publication assessing women's participation in peacemaking, peacekeeping and peace-building through eyes of women participants themselves. 2009.

1593-59 Harm Reduction Coalition, New York, NY, $13,520. For International Harm Reduction Development (IHRD) partner participation at Seventh National Harm Reduction Conference in Miami, FL. 2009.

1593-60 Harvard University, Cambridge, MA, $200,000. Toward Global Disability Law and Policy Project. 2009.

1593-61 Human Rights First, New York, NY, $10,000. For general support. 2009.

1593-62 Human Rights Watch, New York, NY, $381,810. To support activities in Central Asia and the Caucasus. 2009.

1593-63 Human Rights Watch, New York, NY, $126,700. To conduct human rights investigations, publish research reports and engage in regional outreach and advocacy on abuses that result from overreaching drug policies and practices in Thailand, China, Mexico and India. 2009.

1593-64 Human Rights Watch, New York, NY, $93,700. To continue to document human rights violations resulting from Russia-Georgia conflict and to advocate on behalf of civilians in the conflict zone. 2009.

1593-65 Human Rights Watch, New York, NY, $75,000. To support new researcher to work with regional and thematic divisions, as well as external partners, to advance implementation of United Nations Convention on the Rights of Persons with Disabilities. 2009.

1593-66 Human Rights Watch, New York, NY, $75,000. For Aryeh Neier Fellowship. The fellow will work on initiatives to strengthen respect for human rights in the United States. 2009.

1593-67 Hunt Alternatives Fund, Washington, DC, $110,377. To increase capacity and participation of Palestinian women as decision makers in negotiation and reconciliation processes of the Middle East Peace process through development of roster, consultations, trainings and reports. 2009.

1593-68 Indiana University, Bloomington, IN, $2,000,000. To construct dormitory facilities for American University of Central Asia. 2009.

1593-69 Indiana University, Bloomington, IN, $41,541. To contribute to improvement of language education both in Kazakhstan and United States. 2009.

1593-70 Institute for Asian Democracy, Washington, DC, $45,000. To increase awareness of Burma's democracy movement; support non-violent political transition in Burma and coordinate tactical and strategic goals. 2009.

1593-71 Institute for Middle East Understanding, Tustin, CA, $100,000. For general support. 2009.

1593-72 Institute for State Effectiveness, Washington, DC, $30,000. To create effective framework to address reconstruction challenges in Afghanistan. 2009.

1593-73 Institute of International Education, New York, NY, $250,000. For Scholar Rescue Fund, which assists individual scholars who are in imminent danger due to conditions in their home countries. 2009.

1593-74 Inter-American Dialogue, Washington, DC, $150,000. To support Andean Working Group in efforts to identify and generate awareness about pressing issues facing democratic governance in the Andean region, including drug trafficking and demobilization of armed groups in Colombia, centralization and militarization in Venezuela, political tension in Bolivia, institutional conflict in Ecuador, and civil society and international relations in Peru; to draw on expertise of highly informed and experienced policymakers, analysts and academics to propose viable and innovative policies addressing myriad other challenges to democracy confronting the Andes today; and to maximize likelihood that these recommendations are disseminated to a broad audience, debated by relevant and influential actors and ultimately implemented.. 2009.

1593-75 International Accountability Project, San Francisco, CA, $30,000. To support development justice and Video Advocacy Initiative in Southeast Asia. 2009.

1593-76 International Association for Hospice and Palliative Care, Houston, TX, $10,000. For two palliative care leaders from Vietnam to attend the San Diego Hospice and Palliative Care International Palliative Medicine Fellowship Training Program. 2009.

1593-77 International Center for Transitional Justice, New York, NY, $50,000. To develop timely internal memoranda and reports to key partners that discuss international norms, lessons, and experience relevant to U.S. accountability for abuses in its War on Terror. 2009.

1593-78 International Debate Education Association, Salem, OR, $55,000. For general support. 2009.

1593-79 International Gay and Lesbian Human Rights Commission, New York, NY, $70,000. To further the rights of lesbian, gay, bisexual and transgender (LGBT) persons in East, West and Southern Africa. 2009.

1593-80 International Legal Foundation, Brooklyn, NY, $100,000. To increase centralized capacity to support program development and engage in research and advocacy. 2009.

1593-81 International Legal Foundation, Brooklyn, NY, $25,110. To expand presence of legal clinics at Afghan universities. 2009.

1593-82 International Refugee Rights Initiative, New York, NY, $73,000. To support three Congolese activists and to develop domestic outreach and advocacy plan. 2009.

1593-83 International Refugee Rights Initiative, New York, NY, $50,000. For emergency support for eight Sudanese activists. 2009.

1593-84 International Rescue Committee, New York, NY, $10,000. For travel support for two refugees (and one guardian) at Voices of Courage Luncheon hosted by Women's Commission for Refugee Women and Children. 2009.

1593-85 International Senior Lawyers Corporation, New York, NY, $250,000. For $225,000 in general support and $25,000 to support European initiative. 2009.

1593-86 International Womens Health Coalition, New York, NY, $200,000. For general support. 2009.

1593-87 International Womens Tribune Centre, New York, NY, $135,000. To enhance capacity of women working in conflict-affected countries to use legal mechanisms available at international and national level to ensure women's protection, participation and redress and to support their ability to secure their rights. 2009.

1593-88 Justice Africa, London, England, $64,080. To strengthen Sudanese peace and democratic processes through engagement, support and promotion of civil society. 2009.

1593-89 Kachin Development Group, Laiza, Burma (Myanmar), $14,880. For voter education training in Kachin community. 2009.

1593-90 Knowledge Ecology International, Washington, DC, $50,000. For core support for work on Access to Medicines and to develop and promote new paradigms for reconciling the need for both innovation in and access to medical technologies. 2009.

1593-91 Media Development Loan Fund, New York, NY, $1,000,000. For New Media Fund. 2009.

1593-92 Migration Policy Institute, Washington, DC, $100,000. For general support. 2009.

1593-93 Migration Policy Institute, Washington, DC, $50,000. For Mobility and Security Program. 2009.

1593-94 MoeMaKa Radio and Multimedia, San Francisco, CA, $15,000. For general support. 2009.

1593-95 Myanmar AIDS Net, Yangon, Burma (Myanmar), $10,000. For ongoing trainings and support for people in Myanmar/Burma living with HIV/AIDS. 2009.

1593-96 Myanmar Institute of Theology, Yangon, Burma (Myanmar), $25,000. For Cyclone Nargis reconstruction program. 2009.

1593-97 Myanmar Institute of Theology, Yangon, Burma (Myanmar), $20,000. For Bachelor of Arts in Religious Studies (BARS) Scholarship Program. 2009.

1593-98 National Iranian American Council, Washington, DC, $99,010. For Legislative Watch Program to monitor Iran-related legislative activities in Washington. 2009.

1593-99 National Iranian American Council, Washington, DC, $25,000. For U.S.-Iran Media Resource Program. 2009.

1593-100 National Security Archive Fund, Center for National Security Studies, Washington, DC, $400,000. For work to restore civil liberties and human rights in U.S. counter-terrorism policies. 2009.

1593-101 Natural Resources Defense Council, New York, NY, $490,000. For China Public Participation Program. 2009.

1593-102 Nay Kyar Pann, Sunflower, Yangon, Burma (Myanmar), $10,000. For expansion of HIV/AIDS Program. 2009.

1593-103 New Israel Fund, Washington, DC, $67,500. For ongoing support of Israel-U.S. Civil Liberties Law Fellows Program and to mark the 25th anniversary of the program. 2009.

1593-104 New School, New York, NY, $20,000. For Journal Donation Project in Burma, initiative to rebuild major research and teaching libraries in countries that have fallen victim to political or economic deprivation, through provision of current subscriptions and back volume sets of English language scholarly, professional and current events journals. 2009.

1593-105 New School, New York, NY, $10,000. For Journal Donation Project in Cuba, initiative to rebuild major research and teaching libraries in countries that have fallen victim to political or economic deprivation, through provision of current subscriptions and back volume sets of English language scholarly, professional and current events journals. 2009.

1593-106 New York University, Center on International Cooperation, New York, NY, $50,000. For operational support to Afghan Reconstruction Project. 2009.

1593-107 NGO Working Group on Women, Peace and Security, New York, NY, $24,500. To advocate for and monitor participation of women, the prevention of conflict and protection of all civilians so as to ensure full and rapid implementation of Security Council Resolution (SCR) 1325 's promises. 2009.

1593-108 Opening Possibilities Asia, Forest Hills, NY, $20,000. For educational and infrastructural resources for Paung Daw Oo (Phaung Daw Oo) School in Mandalay, Burma. Facility is a monastic high school. 2009.

1593-109 Pan Kachin Development Society, Chiang Mai, Thailand, $15,000. For HIV/AIDS Education Awareness Program. 2009.

1593-110 Physicians for Human Rights, Cambridge, MA, $75,020. To monitor development and implementation of sound U.S. policy that assures universal access to HIV prevention and treatment for injection drug users and their partners, especially in heavily AIDS-burdened countries. 2009.

1593-111 Physicians for Human Rights, Cambridge, MA, $27,267. To assist Colleagues at Risk program. 2009.

1593-112 Planet Care/Global Health Access Program, San Francisco, CA, $46,114. To build capacity of seven local non-governmental and community-based organizations in Burma to develop, implement and manage health and public health programs in manner that is relevant to context and is community-based and scalable. 2009.

1593-113 Planned Parenthood Federation of America, New York, NY, $300,000. For $250,000 in general support and $50,000 to support international programs. 2009.

1593-114 Public Interest Projects, New York, NY, $50,000. For International Human Rights Funders Group. 2009.

1593-115 Public International Law and Policy Group, Washington, DC, $141,345. To provide legal assistance to the Government of South Sudan (GoSS). 2009.

1593-116 Rift Valley Research, Cheltenham, England, $80,000. To organize South Sudan civil society consultation to discuss key themes in rights and governance in South Sudan. 2009.

1593-117 Sabae Phyu White Jasmine, Rangoon, Burma (Myanmar), $10,000. For publication of monthly journal. 2009.

1593-118 Salus World, Denver, CO, $50,000. For training in trauma and mental health issues in Burma and on the Thai-Burma border. 2009.

1593-119 San Diego Hospice Foundation, San Diego, CA, $160,714. For educational intervention and technical assistance in four

countries to help meet the urgent demand for culturally appropriate palliative care. 2009.

1593-120 Soros Foundation-Kyrgyzstan, Bishkek, Kyrgyzstan, $23,614. For educational advising services in Central Asia. 2009.

1593-121 Sudan Center for Justice and Peace, Kampala, Uganda, $45,000. For institutional support to a Sudanese exile organization that aims to promote respect for human rights in Sudan through monitoring and documentation, legal assistance and advocacy. 2009.

1593-122 Sudan Social Development Organization, Khartoum, Sudan, $18,000. To host Open Society Justice Initiative Fellow. 2009.

1593-123 Sudan Tribune, Roubaix, France, $35,820. To enhance capacity of the online news publication. 2009.

1593-124 Synergos Institute, New York, NY, $10,000. For general support. 2009.

1593-125 Synergy Social Re-Engineering Consultancy Firm, Chiang Mai, Thailand, $150,000. For institutional capacity building for Burmese Community-Based Organizations working on Cyclone Nargis reconstruction programs. 2009.

1593-126 Tides Center, San Francisco, CA, $90,000. For Treatment Monitoring and Advocacy Project (part of International Treatment Preparedness Coalition (ITPC) to establish civil society research and advocacy teams in six countries to do independent research on quality and accessibility of HIV services for women and children. 2009.

1593-127 Tides Center, San Francisco, CA, $49,894. To support International Treatment Preparedness Coalition (ITPC) in implementing its new strategic plan and to strengthen ITPC's governance and management capacity. ITPC is comprised of leading treatment advocates and educators from around the world including people living with HIV/AIDS who are directly involved in leadership positions in all aspects of ITPC activities. People involved in and priorities of ITPC reflect a deep understanding of HIV treatment need in every world region, and a commitment to advance HIV treatment while also advancing gender equality and the rights of women, youth, the poor, drug users, sex workers, men who have sex with men, prisoners, migrants, and other vulnerable populations.. 2009.

1593-128 Tides Center, San Francisco, CA, $24,000. For HIV Collaboration Fund in its work on community mobilization to provide education, advocacy and awareness about HIV and TB treatment and prevention in Eastern Europe and Central Asia. 2009.

1593-129 U.S. Campaign for Burma, Washington, DC, $40,000. To increase awareness of Burma's democracy movement and advocacy efforts to press for binding UN Security Council efforts on Burma. 2009.

1593-130 Union of Concerned Scientists, Cambridge, MA, $250,000. To restore integrity of the processes through which scientific knowledge is factored into federal policy decision-making. 2009.

1593-131 University of California, School of Journalism, Berkeley, CA, $24,800. For Burma Visiting Scholar journalist fellowship program. 2009.

1593-132 University of North Carolina, Chapel Hill, NC, $30,000. To conduct case studies in Kenya and South Africa to examine HIV testing programs. 2009.

1593-133 University of Wisconsin, Madison, WI, $239,178. To launch and implement Cohort II of International Pain Policy Fellowship (IPPF) with aim to empower Fellows with knowledge and skills that will help them to improve patient access to opioid analgesics for pain management. 2009.

1593-134 Volunteers for the Vulnerable, Yangon, Burma (Myanmar), $15,000. For Nargis Health Programs. 2009.

1593-135 Washington Office on Latin America, Washington, DC, $250,000. For institutional support. 2009.

1593-136 Women for Women International, Washington, DC, $66,399. To increase women's role as decision-makers and leaders within their own community and to provide forum for collective engagement in civic action and political involvement. 2009.

1593-137 Woodrow Wilson International Center for Scholars, Washington, DC, $200,000. For project, Promoting Citizen Security in Latin America: An Analysis of Public Policy. 2009.

1593-138 World Resources Institute, Washington, DC, $68,112. For Electricity Governance Initiative. 2009.

1593-139 World Resources Institute, Washington, DC, $12,494. To generate dialogue on energy issues in Kyrgyzstan to improve transparency and enhance governance accountability during the privatization and regulation of the energy sector. 2009.

1593-140 Yale University, New Haven, CT, $30,938. To draft report assessing value of information provided by human rights NGOs to Office of the Prosecutor at the International Criminal Court. 2009.

1594
The Overbrook Foundation

122 E. 42nd St., Ste. 2500
New York, NY   10168-2500   (212) 661-8710
Contact: M. Sheila McGoldrick, Grants Mgr.
FAX: (212) 661-8664;
E-mail: contact@overbrookfoundation.org;
URL: http://www.overbrook.org
Blog: http://www.overbrookfoundation.blogspot.com/
E-Newsletter: http://www.overbrook.org/reports/reports.html
Grants Database: http://www.overbrook.org/programs/r_receipents.html#search
The Overbrook Foundation's Philanthropy Promise: http://www.ncrp.org/philanthropys-promise/who

Incorporated in 1948 in NY.
Donors: Frank Altschul†; Helen G. Altschul†; Arthur G. Altschul†; Margaret A. Lang†.
Grantmaker type: Independent foundation.
Financial data (yr. ended 12/31/09): Assets, $127,942,563 (M); expenditures, $10,851,489; qualifying distributions, $8,761,473; giving activities include $7,428,133 for 303 grants (high: $200,000; low: $250).
Purpose and activities: The foundation strives to improve the lives of people by supporting projects that protect human and civil rights, advance the self-sufficiency and well being of individuals and their communities, and conserve the natural environment. The foundation recognizes the importance of a strong community that promotes health, education and opportunity for all of its

members. The foundation values the individual rights of all people and encourages the discussion and analysis of public issues. It is deeply committed to protecting our natural resources.

Fields of interest: Environment, natural resources; AIDS; International human rights; Civil/human rights, advocacy; Civil liberties, advocacy; Civil liberties, reproductive rights; Civil/human rights; LGBTQ; Young adults, female; Women; Girls; Indigenous peoples; Adults; Children; Children/youth.

International interests: Latin America; South Africa.

Type of support: General/operating support; Program development; Fellowships.

Limitations: Applications not accepted. Giving primarily in the U.S. and Latin America, with emphasis on Brazil, Mexico and Ecuador. No grants to individuals.

Publications: Financial statement; Grants list; Newsletter; Program policy statement.

Application information: The foundation no longer accepts unsolicited requests for new projects or operating support from organizations not currently funded by the foundation. Grant requests are now by invitation only for The Emerging Opportunities Fund for advancing human rights and the environment.

Board meeting date(s): 3 times per year, dates vary

Officers and Directors:* Kathryn G. Graham,* Chair.; Serena Altschul,* Vice-Chair. and Secy.; Aaron Labaree,* Vice-Chair. and Treas.; Stephen A. Foster, C.E.O. and Pres.; Arthur G. Altschul, Jr.; Charles Altschul; Emily Altschul-Miller; Robert C. Graham, Jr.; Kathryn C. Graham; Frances Labaree; Helen Lang; Elizabeth Lindemann; Vincent McGee; Isaiah Orozco.

Number of staff: 4 full-time professional; 2 full-time support; 1 part-time support.

EIN: 136088860

Recent grants for international programs:

1594-1 Amazon Watch, San Francisco, CA, $35,000. For Ecuador Rainforest Protection Program. 2010.

1594-2 Borealis Centre for Environment and Trade Research, Vancouver, Canada, $25,000. For work providing environmental organizations with necessary research and strategy to wage successful corporate campaigns as part of Markets-Oriented Research and Investigations Initiative. 2010.

1594-3 Breakthrough, New York, NY, $45,000. For general operating support. 2010.

1594-4 Committee to Protect Journalists, New York, NY, $25,000. For work to defend free media in the Americas. 2010.

1594-5 Conectas Human Rights, Sao Paulo, Brazil, $40,000. To enhance access to justice for vulnerable groups in Brazil through strategic litigation and pro bono advocacy. 2010.

1594-6 Consultative Group on Biological Diversity, San Francisco, CA, $80,000. For ocean acidification message and communications project. 2010.

1594-7 Disability Rights International, Washington, DC, $50,000. For Americas Advocacy Initiative for work in Mexico and the United States. 2010.

1594-8 Ecosystem Sciences Foundation, Boise, ID, $35,000. For Todos por el Agua-Payment for Watershed Services Program in Municipality of San Miguel de Allende, Guanajuato, Mexico. 2010.

1594-9 Environmental Investigation Agency, Washington, DC, $60,000. For continued Work

Leveraging the Lacey Act and Promoting Forest Conservation in Latin America. 2010.

1594-10 Environmental Paper Network, Asheville, NC, $25,000. To support NGO collaboration to accelerate social and environmental transformations in the paper industry. 2010.

1594-11 Forest Ethics, San Francisco, CA, $60,000. For general operating support. 2010.

1594-12 Front Line-International Foundation for the Protection of Human Rights Defenders, Blackrock, Ireland, $40,000. For protection of Latin American human rights defenders. 2010.

1594-13 Fundacion Cordillera Tropical, Cuenca, Ecuador, $80,000. To protect environmental services in Tropical Andes of Ecuador through development of participatory monitoring tools. 2010.

1594-14 Fundacion para el Desarrollo de Alternativas Comunitarias de Conservacion del Tropico, ALTROPICO, Quito, Ecuador, $25,000. To consolidate Cotacachi Cayapas Ecological Reserve and Chachi Territories and extend environmental outreach in Chile's-Mataje Biological Corridor. 2010.

1594-15 Global Fund for Children, Washington, DC, $40,000. To advance the rights of children in Latin America. 2010.

1594-16 Human Rights First, New York, NY, $40,000. To protect human rights defenders in Latin America. 2010.

1594-17 Human Rights Watch, New York, NY, $100,000. For research and advocacy on business and human rights and Mexico's National Human Rights Commission. 2010.

1594-18 IMAFLORA, Piracicaba, Brazil, $35,000. For Phase III of work promoting sustainable cocoa harvesting in Brazil as part of biodiversity conservation in the Brazilian Atlantic Forest. 2010.

1594-19 International Projects Assistance Services, Chapel Hill, NC, $35,000. For advocacy and action on abortion policy in Latin America. 2010.

1594-20 ISEAL Alliance, London, England, $40,000. To bring clarity and order to sustainability standards landscape. 2010.

1594-21 Keystone Center, Keystone, CO, $25,000. For Green Products Roundtable. 2010.

1594-22 Leadership Conference on Civil Rights Education Fund, Washington, DC, $50,000. For Convention on the Elimination of All Forms of Discrimination Against Women (CEDAW) Education Project. 2010.

1594-23 Nature and Culture International, Del Mar, CA, $48,400. For Ecosystem Service Payment Systems for land conservation in Southern Ecuador. 2010.

1594-24 New York Botanical Garden, Bronx, NY, $50,000. To improve timber management and sustainable forestry in Brazilian Amazonia. 2010.

1594-25 New York Civil Liberties Union Foundation, New York, NY, $50,000. To defend civil liberties in a human rights framework. 2010.

1594-26 Peace Brigades International-USA, Washington, DC, $25,000. For Peace Brigades International Mexico, Guatemala, Colombia and USA Protection of Human Rights Defenders. 2010.

1594-27 People and Plants International, Bristol, VT, $60,000. To build local capacity to harvest, market and process bark paper, woodcarvings, honey and other forest products as part of sustainable forest use in Central Mexico. 2010.

1594-28 Planned Parenthood Federation, International, New York, NY, $40,000. For work

to strengthen sexual and reproductive health and rights in Latin America and the Caribbean. 2010.

1594-29 Pronatura Noroeste-Mar de Cortes, Ensenada, Mexico, $50,000. For campaign to halt construction of environmentally destructive Cabo Cortez tourist development as part of effort to protect Cabo Pulmo National Park region in Baja California Sur, Mexico. 2010.

1594-30 Rainforest Action Network, San Francisco, CA, $50,000. For RAN Tropical Forests Program and continued role as watchdog of large corporations. 2010.

1594-31 Rainforest Alliance, New York, NY, $75,000. For Biodiversity Friendly Tourism in the Ecuadorian Amazon and Mexico's Yucatan Peninsula. 2010.

1594-32 Reporters Without Borders, Washington, DC, $30,000. To fight for press freedom in Latin America. 2010.

1594-33 Root Capital, Cambridge, MA, $90,000. For work to provide loans to small businesses that promote conservation in Ecuador and Mexico. 2010.

1594-34 Search for Common Ground, Washington, DC, $25,000. For Search for Common Ground on Issues Affecting LGBT Individuals. 2010.

1594-35 Silicon Valley Toxics Coalition, San Jose, CA, $30,000. Toward a Just and Sustainable Solar Energy Campaign and Stemming the Global Tide of E-Waste. 2010.

1594-36 University of Chile, Human Rights Center, Law School, Santiago, Chile, $50,000. For International Human Rights Fellowship Program. 2010.

1594-37 Urgent Action Fund for Womens Human Rights, Boulder, CO, $40,000. For Women's Rights are Human Rights, program sustaining women human rights defenders and strengthening leadership in peace building and conflict management. 2010.

1594-38 W N E T Channel 13, New York, NY, $35,000. For Wide Angle: Women, War and Peace Online Educational Guide. 2010.

1594-39 Witness, Inc., Brooklyn, NY, $50,000. To promote video advocacy in the Americas. 2010.

1595

P.E.F. Israel Endowment Funds, Inc.

317 Madison Ave., Ste. 607
New York, NY 10017-5301 (212) 599-1260
Contact: Penny Waga, Exec. Dir.
FAX: (212) 599-5981; E-mail: pefisrael@aol.com;
URL: http://www.pefisrael.org

Established in 1922 in NY.

Grantmaker type: Public charity.

Financial data (yr. ended 11/30/10): Revenue, $48,435,468; assets, $112,812,803 (M); gifts received, $45,113,843; expenditures, $60,250,775; program services expenses, $58,918,161; giving activities include $294,906 for 6 grants (high: $253,700; low: $5,000), and $58,623,255 for 538 grants to organizations outside the U.S.

Purpose and activities: The fund supports: primary and secondary education; scientific research; greater tolerance and understanding between religious and secular communities and between Arabs and Jews; the special needs of women, children, and families in distress; special education and education for the gifted; veterans programs; drug abuse; promotion of the arts; and relief for the handicapped.

Fields of interest: Arts; Education; Human services; International relief; Military/veterans; Physically disabled.
International interests: Israel.
Type of support: Research.
Limitations: Giving limited to Israel.
Officers and Trustees:* Harvey Brecher,* Chair.; Dr. Shulamit Bar-Shany,* V.P.; Thmoas J. Fleisch,* V.P.; Sharon Mintz,* V.P.; Mark Bane,* Secy.; Paul J. Isaac,* Treas.; Penny Waga, Exec. Dir., Admin.; Harry S. Allen; Kenneth Abrahami; Ernest Bial; Stephan Brumberg; Joseph Ciechanover; Chaim Edelstein; B. Harrison Frankel; Ernest S. Frefichs; and 12 additional trustees.
EIN: 136104086

1596
Parkinson's Disease Foundation, Inc.
(formerly Parkinson's Disease Research Foundation, Inc.)
1359 Broadway, Ste. 1509
New York, NY 10018-7102 (212) 923-4700
Contact: Robin Elliott, Exec. Dir.
FAX: (212) 923-4778; E-mail: info@pdf.org; Toll-free tel.: (800) 457-6676; URL: http://www.pdf.org

Established in 1957.
Grantmaker type: Public charity.
Financial data (yr. ended 06/30/10): Revenue, $9,133,474; assets, $13,675,022 (M); gifts received, $8,721,024; expenditures, $9,500,399; giving activities include $4,375,840 for grants, $502,500 for 4 grants to organizations outside the U.S., and $44,250 for grants to individuals.
Purpose and activities: The foundation awards grants and fellowships to address the etiology, pathogenesis, and treatment of Parkinson's disease.
Fields of interest: Parkinson's disease; Parkinson's disease research.
International interests: Greece; Israel; United Kingdom.
Type of support: Fellowships; Research.
Limitations: Applications accepted. Giving on a national and international basis.
Publications: Application guidelines; Biennial report; Informational brochure; Newsletter.
Application information: Application form required.
  Deadline(s): Jan. 15 for Clinician Scientist Development Awards; Feb. 1 for International Research Grants Program; Feb. 2 for Postdoctoral Fellowship for Laboratory Research and Postdoctoral Fellowships; July 1 for Summer Student Fellows Program
  Board meeting date(s): Quarterly
  Final notification: Late spring
Officers and Directors:* Page M. Black,* Chair.; Lewis P. Rowland,* M.D., Pres.; Timothy A. Pedley,* M.D., V.P.; Isobel Robins Konecky,* Secy.; Stephen Ackerman,* Treas.; Robin Elliott, Exec. Dir.; Constance Woodruff Atwell, Ph.D.; Karen Elizabeth Burke, M.D., Ph.D.; Margo Castimatidis; Barbara Costikyan; Peter Dorn; George Pennington Egbert III; Stephen B. Flood; Sarah Belk Gambrell; Daniel Gersen, Esq.; Stephanie Goldman-Pittel; Arlene Levine; Marshall Loeb; Howard Dewitt Morgan; Maria D. Schwartz; Domna Stanton, Ph.D.; Sandra Feagan Stern, Ed.D.; Melvin S. Taub; Martin Tuchman.
Number of staff: 5 full-time professional; 4 part-time professional; 3 full-time support; 7 part-time support.
EIN: 131866796

1597
Peierls Foundation
c/o Bank of America, N.A.
114 W. 47th St.
New York, NY 10036-1510
Application address: c/o E. Jeffrey Peierls, Pres., 73 S. Holman Way, Golden, CO 80401

Incorporated in 1956 in NY.
Donors: Brian E. Peierls; Edgar S. Peierls†; Ethel F. Peierls; E. Jeffrey Peierls; Ethel F. Peierls Charitable Lead Trust; and sons.
Grantmaker type: Independent foundation.
Financial data (yr. ended 10/31/10): Assets, $94,001,736 (M); gifts received, $2,035,783; expenditures, $5,112,052; qualifying distributions, $4,803,500; giving activities include $4,803,500 for 56 grants (high: $618,300; low: $7,300).
Purpose and activities: Primary areas of interest include higher education, international relief, and programs benefiting minorities.
Fields of interest: Higher education; Reproductive health, family planning; Health organizations, association; Medical research, institute; Children/youth, services; Minorities/immigrants, centers/services; International relief; Civil rights, race/intergroup relations; Minorities.
Type of support: Annual campaigns; Endowments; Scholarship funds.
Limitations: Applications accepted. Giving primarily in CA, CO, Washington, DC, NJ, NY and TX. No grants to individuals.
Application information: Application form not required.
  Deadline(s): None
  Final notification: Only positive responses will be sent
Officers: E. Jeffrey Peierls, Pres.; Brian Eliot Peierls, V.P.; Malcolm A. Moore, Secy.
EIN: 136082503
Recent grants for international programs:
1597-1 Doctors Without Borders USA, New York, NY, $210,100. 2010.
1597-2 International Rescue Committee, New York, NY, $520,300. 2010.
1597-3 Unitarian Universalist Service Committee, Cambridge, MA, $40,100. 2010.

1598
PEN American Center, Inc.
588 Broadway, Ste. 303
New York, NY 10012-5246 (212) 334-1660
Contact: Linda C. Morgan, Dir., Development; Meghan Kyle-Miller, Devel. Assoc.
FAX: (212) 334-2181; E-mail: info@pen.org; URL: http://www.pen.org
Additional e-mail: awards@pen.org

Established in 1922.
Grantmaker type: Public charity.
Financial data (yr. ended 06/30/10): Revenue, $2,266,865; assets, $2,489,760 (M); gifts received, $2,080,072; expenditures, $2,661,038; giving activities include $65,630 for grants to organizations outside the U.S., and $66,641 for grants to individuals.
Purpose and activities: The center works to advance literature, to defend free expression, and to foster international literary fellowship.
Fields of interest: Media, print publishing; Literature; Arts, artist's services; Civil liberties, first amendment; Minorities.

Type of support: Emergency funds; Grants to individuals.
Limitations: Applications accepted. Giving on a national basis.
Publications: Application guidelines.
Application information: Application form required.
  Initial approach: Letter or telephone
  Deadline(s): Varies
Officers and Directors:* Francine Prose,* Pres.; Billy Collins,* V.P.; Jessica Hagedorn,* V.P.; Lawrence J. Kirshbaum,* V.P.; Benjamin Taylor,* Secy.; A.M. Homes,* Treas.; Michael Roberts, Exec. Dir.; Paul Auster; Maria Campbell; Ron Chernow; Michael Cunningham; Jonathan Safran Foer; Francisco Goldman; Barbara Goldsmith; Beth Gutcheon; and 24 additional directors.
Number of staff: 11 full-time professional; 2 part-time professional.
EIN: 133447888

1599
The Pendill Fund, Inc.
P.O. Box 157
Tarrytown, NY 10591-0157 (914) 332-0238
FAX: (914) 332-0176;
E-mail: gpendill@pendillfund.org; Additional address: 5/7 Rozhdestvensky Blvd., Entrance 2, Apt. 24, Moscow 103045, Russia, tel.: 7 495 208-4493, FAX: 7 495 208-4493; URL: http://www.pendillfund.org

Established in 2005.
Grantmaker type: Public charity.
Financial data (yr. ended 12/31/10): Revenue, $40,453; assets, $453 (M); gifts received, $40,453; expenditures, $107,445; giving activities include $42,141 for grants.
Purpose and activities: The fund seeks to enhance the lives of disadvantaged and at risk children and youth in Russia through support of grassroots programs designed to develop their spirit, mind, and body.
Fields of interest: Children; Economically disadvantaged.
International interests: Russia.
Limitations: Giving primarily in Russia.
Officers and Directors:* Galina S. Pendill,* Pres. and Exec. Dir.; Victor Tchelistcheff,* V.P.; Tamara Geacintov,* Secy.-Treas.; Olga Alexeeva; Jean Berube; Robert Festa; Lyudmila Obolenska; Therese Rafael; Stuart Trager, M.D.
EIN: 203608945

1600
People Allied for Nature, Ltd.
225 W. 34th St., Ste. 1317
New York, NY 10122-1317 (212) 279-7813
E-mail: info@pansite.org; URL: http://www.pansite.org/about%20us.htm

Established in 1994.
Grantmaker type: Public charity.
Purpose and activities: The organization works to help local communities in developing nations safeguard their environment by establishing wildlife and nature reserves, and to encourage conservation by addressing the socioeconomic causes of deforestation at the grassroots level.
Fields of interest: Animals/wildlife; Animals/wildlife, preservation/protection; Environment;

Environment, land resources; Environment, natural resources; Indigenous peoples.
International interests: Ecuador.
Limitations: Giving limited to Loma Alta, Ecuador.
Officers and Directors:* Claude M. Nathan,* Pres.; John M. Walker,* V.P. and Treas.; Myriam A. Lewis,* Secy.; Carmita Bonifaz.
EIN: 133778383

1601
The PepsiCo Foundation, Inc.
700 Anderson Hill Rd.
Purchase, NY 10577-1401 (914) 253-3153
E-mail: pepsico.foundation@pepsi.com;
URL: http://www.pepsico.com/Purpose/
PepsiCo-Foundation.aspx
Grants List: http://www.pepsico.com/Purpose/
PepsiCo-Foundation/Contributions.html

Incorporated in 1962 in NY.
Donor: PepsiCo, Inc.
Grantmaker type: Company-sponsored foundation.
Financial data (yr. ended 12/31/10): Assets, $122,018,651 (M); gifts received, $100,000,000; expenditures, $26,244,577; qualifying distributions, $25,964,268; giving activities include $20,898,478 for 86 grants (high: $3,083,634; low: $66), and $5,065,790 for employee matching gifts.
Purpose and activities: The foundation supports programs designed to promote education, the environment, and health in underserved regions. Special emphasis is directed toward nutrition and safety; safe water and water usage efficiencies; and education and empowerment.
Fields of interest: Food banks; Food services; Higher education; Education; Environment, water pollution; Environment, water resources; Public health; Public health, physical fitness; Public health, clean water supply; Health care; Employment, training; Employment; Nutrition; Agriculture/food; Disasters, preparedness/services; Safety/disasters; Children, services; Civil/human rights, equal rights; Economic development; United Ways and Federated Giving Programs; Minorities; Women; Economically disadvantaged.
International interests: Africa; Asia; Bangladesh; Ghana; India.
Type of support: General/operating support; Continuing support; Management development/capacity building; Program development; Employee volunteer services; Employee matching gifts; Employee-related scholarships; Scholarships—to individuals; In-kind gifts.
Limitations: Applications accepted. Giving on a national and international basis, with emphasis on Washington, DC, FL, IL, MA, NY, TX, and VA, and in Africa, Asia, Bangladesh, Canada, China, Ghana, India, Mexico, and the United Kingdom. No support for private charities or foundations, religious organizations, political candidates or organizations, discriminatory organizations, legislative organizations, playgrounds, or sports fields. No grants to individuals (except for employee-related and Diamond scholarships), or for political causes or campaigns, endowments or capital campaigns, equipment, film, music, TV, video, or media productions, sports sponsorships, performing arts tours, or association memberships.
Publications: Application guidelines; Grants list; Program policy statement.
Application information: A full proposal may be requested at a later date. Grant requests for $100,000 or more are accepted through an

invitation-only Request for Proposal process. Application form not required.
Initial approach: E-mail letter of interest for requests less than $100,000
Deadline(s): None
Board meeting date(s): May and Nov.
Final notification: Several months
Officers and Directors:* Indra K. Nooyi,* Chair.; Larry D. Thompson,* Pres.; Christine Griff, Secy.; Tessa Hilado, Treas.; Zein Abdalla; Saad Abdul-Latif; John C. Compton; Massimo F. d'Amore; Rich Delaney; Richard A. Goodman; Julie Hamp; Hugh F. Johnston; Donald M. Kendall; Mehmood Khan; Cynthia M. Trudell.
Number of staff: 2 full-time professional; 2 full-time support.
EIN: 136163174
Recent grants for international programs:
1601-1 Columbia University, Earth Institute, New York, NY, $2,000,000. Toward a three-year $6 million grant to support an interdisciplinary public-private partnership that leverages market-based solutions and technical knowledge to address water sustenance and the global water supply. In India, the grant supports research and strategies to improve irrigation, focus on contract farming, and encourage private sector partnerships. In China, the grant supports agricultural and irrigation innovation in drought-prone regions, and it encourages partnerships with government ministries for watershed management. In Mali, grant supports innovative pump and water saving technologies in Millennium Village sites. And in Brazil, the grant is directed toward reducing the impact of droughts through water conservation tools, better flow strategies, and financial strategies. 2009.
1601-2 Friends of the World Food Program, Washington, DC, $530,000. 2009.
1601-3 International Union of Nutritional Sciences, Seville, Spain, $100,000. 2009.
1601-4 Oxford Health Alliance, London, England, $1,384,000. 2009.
1601-5 Oxford Health Alliance, London, England, $200,000. 2009.
1601-6 Safe Water Network, Westport, CT, $1,220,000. To support ongoing work in India and Ghana for market-based approaches that provide water and sanitation services for households and communities. In Ghana, the grants supports kiosks, water centers, and new distributed systems, such as trucking to get safe water to people. In India, the focus in on rainwater harvesting and safe water kiosks. In 2010, the grant will support expansion of loan programs for periurban community systems for drinking water supply and sanitation, and hygiene education in Kenya. 2009.
1601-7 Save the Children Federation, Westport, CT, $1,727,189. For a three-year $5 million commitment to create better nutrition for children and mothers who are severely malnourished in India and Bangladesh. The India component of the grant includes a water access, sanitation, and hygiene component that promotes efforts to promote more articulated and integrated health and environmental approaches. 2009.
1601-8 Water.org, Water.org, Kansas City, MO, $1,350,994. Toward a three-year $4.1 million grant to support the WaterCredit Initiative, which seeks to create market-based approaches to water access and sanitation in India. The initiative builds a commercial marketplace in the

financial sector in partnership with micro-finance institutions and WASH NGO's to deliver dedicated loans to individuals and households for water supply and sanitation. 2009.

1602
Perelman Family Foundation
35 E. 62nd St.
New York, NY 10065-8014
Ronald Perelman's Giving Pledge: http://givingpledge.org/#enter

Established in 1999 in NY.
Donors: R G I Group Incorporated; Ronald O. Perelman.
Grantmaker type: Independent foundation.
Financial data (yr. ended 12/31/09): Assets, $4,223,872 (M); gifts received, $12,428,467; expenditures, $13,430,387; qualifying distributions, $13,430,174; giving activities include $13,430,174 for 77 grants (high: $3,125,000; low: $250; average: $1,000–$350,000).
Fields of interest: Arts; Hospitals (general); Health organizations, association; Human services; United Ways and Federated Giving Programs; Jewish agencies & synagogues.
Limitations: Applications not accepted. Giving primarily in NY. No grants to individuals.
Application information: Contributes only to pre-selected organizations.
Officers and Directors:* Ronald O. Perelman,* Chair. and C.E.O.; Barry F. Schwartz, Exec. Vice-Chair. and C.A.O.; Paul Savas, Exec. V.P.; Christine Taylor, Sr. V.P.; Michael C. Borofsky, V.P. and Secy.; Alison Horowitz, V.P., Treas., and Cont.; Joanne DeFreitas, V.P.; Debra G. Perelman, V.P.; Hope G. Perelman, V.P.; Joshua G. Perelman, V.P.; Steven G. Perelman, V.P.; Gary Rozenshteyn, V.P.
EIN: 134008528
Recent grants for international programs:
1602-1 America-Israel Friendship League, New York, NY, $10,000. 2008.
1602-2 American Friends of the Hebrew University, New York, NY, $50,000. 2008.
1602-3 Bryan Adams Foundation, London, England, $15,000. 2008.
1602-4 Machne Israel, Brooklyn, NY, $253,310. 2008.
1602-5 Machne Israel, Brooklyn, NY, $246,620. 2008.
1602-6 Machne Israel, Brooklyn, NY, $198,310. 2008.
1602-7 Machne Israel, Brooklyn, NY, $198,310. 2008.
1602-8 Machne Israel, Brooklyn, NY, $198,310. 2008.
1602-9 Machne Israel, Brooklyn, NY, $125,000. 2008.
1602-10 Machne Israel, Brooklyn, NY, $123,310. 2008.
1602-11 Machne Israel, Brooklyn, NY, $98,310. 2008.
1602-12 Machne Israel, Brooklyn, NY, $73,310. 2008.
1602-13 Machne Israel, Brooklyn, NY, $73,310. 2008.
1602-14 Machne Israel, Brooklyn, NY, $73,310. 2008.
1602-15 Machne Israel, Brooklyn, NY, $50,000. 2008.
1602-16 Machne Israel, Brooklyn, NY, $50,000. 2008.

1602-17 Machne Israel, Brooklyn, NY, $15,000. 2008.

1602-18 Machne Israel, Brooklyn, NY, $13,800. 2008.

1602-19 Ohr Torah Stone Colleges and Graduate Programs, New York, NY, $350,000. 2008.

1603
The Pershing Square Foundation
888 7th Ave., 42nd Fl.
New York, NY 10106-4402

Established in 2007 in NY.

Donors: William Ackman; Karen Ackman; Nicholas Botta; Roy Katzovicz; Lawrence D. Ackman; Pershing Square Capital Mgmt.

Grantmaker type: Independent foundation.

Financial data (yr. ended 09/30/10): Assets, $55,481,569 (M); gifts received, $16,547,500; expenditures, $15,902,382; qualifying distributions, $15,902,382; giving activities include $15,700,102 for 234 grants (high: $1,000,250; low: $50; average: $250–$200,000), and $20,722 for 1 foundation-administered program.

Purpose and activities: Giving primarily for community development, education, the arts, human services, health organizations, and Jewish organizations.

Fields of interest: Human services; Jewish federated giving programs; Leadership development; Foundations (public); Health organizations; Arts, formal/general education; Jewish agencies & synagogues; Arts; Historic preservation/historical societies; Education; Community/economic development.

Limitations: Applications not accepted. Giving primarily in New York, NY; giving also in CA, Washington, DC, and NJ.

Application information: Contributes only to pre-selected organizations.

Trustee: Karen Ackman; William Ackman.

EIN: 208068401

Recent grants for international programs:

1603-1 America Israel Cultural Foundation, New York, NY, $20,000. For general and unrestricted support. 2010.

1603-2 American Friends of the Hebrew University, New York, NY, $100,000. For Science and Math Enrichment. 2010.

1603-3 Center for Jewish History, New York, NY, $75,000. For Genocide Initiative. 2010.

1603-4 Digital Divide Data, New York, NY, $333,333. For general and unrestricted support. 2010.

1603-5 Endeavor Global, New York, NY, $100,250. For general and unrestricted support. 2010.

1603-6 Human Rights Watch, New York, NY, $1,000,250. For general and unrestricted support. 2010.

1603-7 Jerusalem Foundation, New York, NY, $200,000. For Beit Safafa Sports Field Protect. 2010.

1603-8 Jerusalem Foundation, New York, NY, $50,000. For Jerusalem Ambassadors Council Initiative. 2010.

1603-9 Kickstart International, San Francisco, CA, $500,000. For general and unrestricted support. 2010.

1603-10 One Acre Fund, Falcon Heights, MN, $1,000,250. For general and unrestricted support. 2010.

1603-11 Partners in Health, Boston, MA, $1,000,000. For Emergency Relief in Haiti and Documentation of Global Health Delivery in Crisis Situation. 2010.

1603-12 Partners in Health, Boston, MA, $12,825. For Haiti Relief Campaign. 2010.

1603-13 PEF Israel Endowment Funds, New York, NY, $153,598. For Sifting Debris of Temple Mount account at Israel Exploration Society, Jerusalem. 2010.

1603-14 PEF Israel Endowment Funds, New York, NY, $125,000. For MATI-Jerusalem Business Development Center Fund. 2010.

1603-15 PEF Israel Endowment Funds, New York, NY, $100,000. For MAT 1 Business Development Center Fund. 2010.

1603-16 Root Capital, Cambridge, MA, $502,125. For general and unrestricted support. 2010.

1603-17 Salus Foundation, New York, NY, $10,000. For Sulaxmi School for Girls Program. 2010.

1603-18 Seeds of Peace, New York, NY, $10,000. For general and unrestricted support. 2010.

1603-19 Sereolipi Nomadic Education Foundation, New York, NY, $70,000. For Thorn Tree Protect. 2010.

1603-20 Ukrainian National Womens League of America, New York, NY, $15,000. For Rozdil Orphanage Division. 2010.

1604
Peter G. Peterson Foundation
888-C Eighth Ave.
P.O. Box 144
New York, NY 10019 (212) 542-9200
Contact: Rikard Treiber, Dir., Grants Mgmt.
FAX: (212) 542-9250; E-mail: inquiries@pgpf.org;
URL: http://www.pgpf.org/
E-Newsletter: http://www.pgpf.org/
Registration.aspx?ref=/Media/Video/2009/09/
Fiscal-Wake-Up-Tour-Online-Dave-Walker.aspx
Facebook: http://www.facebook.com/pages/
Peter-G-Peterson-Foundation/15503839732
Multimedia: http://www.pgpf.org/Media/Video/
2009/09/
Fiscal-Wake-Up-Tour-Online-Dave-Walker.aspx
Peter G. Peterson's Giving Pledge: http://
givingpledge.org/#enter
RSS Feed: http://www.pgpf.org/rss/Articles.aspx

Established in 2008.

Donors: Peter G. Peterson; David M. Walker; Warren E. Buffett; Georges Marciano.

Grantmaker type: Independent foundation.

Financial data (yr. ended 03/31/10): Assets, $385,027,231 (M); gifts received, $75,000,450; expenditures, $17,396,772; qualifying distributions, $14,663,221; giving activities include $7,981,139 for 20 grants (high: $1,000,000; low: $10,000), $1,785,828 for in-kind gifts, and $4,424,338 for 3 foundation-administered programs.

Purpose and activities: The mission is to increase public awareness of the nature and urgency of key fiscal challenges threatening America's future and to accelerate action on them. To address these challenges successfully, the foundation works to bring Americans together to find and implement sensible, long-term solutions that transcend age, party lines and ideological divides in order to achieve real results.

Fields of interest: Public affairs, citizen participation; International affairs, national security; Health care, financing; Health care, cost containment; Public affairs, finance.

Type of support: Research; Internship funds; Curriculum development; Conferences/seminars.

Limitations: Applications accepted. Giving limited to the U.S. to nonprofits that are regional or national in scope and have the ability to implement programming nationwide. No support for other private grantmaking foundations, foreign organizations, or for political, social or fraternal organizations. No grants to individuals, or for general operating support, unrestricted purposes, indirect expenses, ongoing funding, capital campaigns, annual appeals, ongoing sponsorships, fundraising events, or to underwrite chairs, endowments or scholarships sponsored by academic or nonprofit institutions.

Publications: Financial statement; Informational brochure; Newsletter; Occasional report.

Application information: The foundation gives only in pre-selected program areas. Application form required.

Initial approach: Submit initial inquiry via inquiries@pgpf.org. If invited, a proposal will be requested
Copies of proposal: 1
Deadline(s): Initial inquiries are accepted throughout the year
Final notification: Varies

Officers and Directors: * Peter G. Peterson,* Chair.; Michael Peterson,* Vice-Chair.; Susan Tanaka, V.P., Policy and Research; Loretta Ucelli, V.P., Comms. and Public Affairs; Paul Newman, C.F.O.; Joan Ganz Cooney.

Number of staff: 16 full-time professional; 4 part-time professional.

EIN: 260316905

Recent grants for international programs:

1604-1 Nuclear Threat Initiative, World Institute for Nuclear Security, Washington, DC, $2,000,000. To implement more effective and efficient security programs for nuclear materials and foster appropriate exchange of best practices and lessons learned by operators. 2009.

1604-2 Peter G. Peterson Institute for International Economics, Washington, DC, $100,000. For research and White Paper examining dependence on foreign capital and America's growing position as world's largest debtor country. 2009.

1604-3 Peter G. Peterson Institute for International Economics, Washington, DC, $50,000. To support a writer to bring key messages of the Peterson Institute to the broader public. 2009.

1604-4 Transatlantic Futures, The Globalist, Washington, DC, $40,000. For analysis of fiscal issues, including demographics and pensions, health care, trade and budget deficits, energy policies, education and youth engagements. 2009.

1605
Petra Foundation Charitable Trust
315 Duke Ellington Blvd., 16C
New York, NY 10025-3449 (212) 665-6673
FAX: (212) 864-4924;
E-mail: info@petrafoundation.org; URL: http://
www.petrafoundation.org/index.html
Application address: c/o Muriel Morisey Spence, Chair., Award Comm., P.O. Box 11579, Washington, DC 20008-0779, tel.: (202) 364-8964

Established in 1988 in MA.

Donors: Eli Segal; Mark Munger; John Shattuck; Richard T. Balzer; Margret Rey; Arnold Hiatt; Mrs. Arnold Hiatt; Eileen Hsu.
Grantmaker type: Public charity.
Financial data (yr. ended 03/31/10): Revenue, $138,011; assets, $195,882 (M); gifts received, $138,266; expenditures, $214,134; program services expenses, $166,226; giving activities include $30,000 for grants to individuals, and $136,226 for foundation-administered programs.
Purpose and activities: The trust works to enable recipients to carry on research, teaching, and education in the areas of civil and human rights and social justice.
Fields of interest: Crime/law enforcement; International human rights; Civil/human rights.
Type of support: Grants to individuals.
Officers and Trustees: * Richard Balzer,* Chair.; Preble Jacques, Treas.; Meg Fidler, Exec. Dir.; Ann Beaudry; Robert Borosage; Katherine Bourne; Drew S. Days III; Michael Hurwitz; Kay Kohl; Cantwell Muckenfuss III; John Shattuck; Gina B. Womack.
EIN: 046603552

1606
The Pfizer Foundation, Inc.
235 E. 42nd St.
New York, NY 10017-5703
URL: http://www.pfizer.com/pfizer/subsites/philanthropy/index.jsp

Incorporated in 1953 in Brooklyn, NY.
Donor: Pfizer Inc.
Grantmaker type: Company-sponsored foundation.
Financial data (yr. ended 12/31/10): Assets, $209,307,790 (M); gifts received, $825,000; expenditures, $22,150,833; qualifying distributions, $21,575,195; giving activities include $8,790,715 for grants, and $10,336,140 for employee matching gifts.
Purpose and activities: The foundation supports programs designed to promote access to quality health care; nurture innovation; and support the community involvement of Pfizer colleagues. Special emphasis is directed toward four strategies to improve health care for people in need: Treat, including helping health organizations reach people in need with quality care; Teach, including providing health education and prevention messages to individuals and health care workers; Build, including increasing the capacity of health organizations to provide care to people in need; and Serve, including partnering with experts and organizations to measure impact and share best practices with others.
Fields of interest: Science; Mathematics; Cancer; Elementary/secondary education; Education, services; Education; Health care; AIDS; United Ways and Federated Giving Programs; Science, formal/general education.
Type of support: General/operating support; Management development/capacity building; Building/renovation; Program development; Curriculum development; Technical assistance; Employee volunteer services; Sponsorships; Program evaluation; Employee matching gifts.
Limitations: Applications not accepted. Giving on a national and international basis. No support for political organizations. No grants to individuals, or for capital campaigns or scholarships; no loans to individuals.

Publications: Corporate giving report; Financial statement; Grants list; Informational brochure; Program policy statement.
Application information: Contributes only to pre-selected organizations.
  Board meeting date(s): As required
Officers and Directors: * William C. Steere, Jr.,* Chair.; Caroline Roan, Pres.; Dezarie Mayers, Secy; Richard Passov, Treas.; Anneka Norgren, Exec. Dir.; C. L. Clemente*; Frank D'Amelio; Jean-Michel Halfon; Kirsten Lund-Jurgensen; Gary Nicholson; Sally Susman.
EIN: 136083839
Recent grants for international programs:
1606-1 Give2Asia, San Francisco, CA, $1,063,000. 2009.
1606-2 Heart and Stroke Foundation of Canada, Ottawa, Canada, $231,000. 2009.
1606-3 King Baudouin Foundation United States, New York, NY, $2,875,700. 2009.
1606-4 Resource Foundation, New York, NY, $327,000. 2009.

1607
Pfizer Inc. Corporate Giving Program
235 E. 42nd St.
New York, NY 10017
URL: http://www.pfizer.com/pfizer/subsites/philanthropy/index.jsp

Grantmaker type: Corporate giving program.
Purpose and activities: As a complement to its foundation, Pfizer also makes charitable contributions to nonprofit organizations directly. Support is given on a national and international basis.
Fields of interest: AIDS; Arts; Education; Health care, equal rights; Public health; Health care; Health organizations; Human services; International relief; Community/economic development; Biology/life sciences; Minorities; Economically disadvantaged.
International interests: Eastern & Central Europe; Africa; Asia.
Type of support: Fellowships; General/operating support; Continuing support; Program development; Curriculum development; Technical assistance; Consulting services; Program evaluation; Donated products.
Limitations: Applications not accepted. Giving on a national and international basis in areas of company operations, with emphasis on La Jolla, CA, Groton, CT, Terre Haute, IN, Cambridge, MA, Ann Arbor and Kalamazoo, MI, Lee's Summit and St. Louis, MO, Lincoln, NE, Parsippany, NJ, New York, NY, Exton, PA, Barceloneta, PR, and in Africa, Asia, and Eastern Europe; giving also to national organizations.
Publications: Informational brochure.
Application information: Contributes only to pre-selected organizations. The Corporate Affairs and Corporate Philanthropy Department handles giving. The company has a staff that only handles contributions.

1608
Philippe Foundation, Inc.
c/o Philippe Investment Mgmt., Inc.
2 Penn Plz., Ste. 1920A
New York, NY 10121-0101
Contact: Beatrice Philippe, V.P.; Alain Philippe, Pres.

Incorporated in 1953 in NY.

Donors: Pierre Philippe; Alain Philippe; Anne-Marie Philippe; Beatrice Philippe; European-American Economic Corp.
Grantmaker type: Independent foundation.
Financial data (yr. ended 12/31/10): Assets, $6,275,775 (M); gifts received, $27,469; expenditures, $517,968; qualifying distributions, $502,566; giving activities include $99,399 for 3 grants (high: $65,880; low: $13,519), and $380,490 for 60 grants to individuals (high: $15,000; low: $2,500).
Purpose and activities: Support primarily for the exchange of physicians and scientists between the U.S. and France for advanced study and scientific research, emphasizing cancer research.
Fields of interest: Cancer research; Science.
International interests: France.
Type of support: Conferences/seminars; Fellowships; Internship funds; Research; Grants to individuals; Exchange programs.
Limitations: Applications accepted. Giving on a national basis; funding also in France.
Publications: Application guidelines.
Application information: Application form not required.
  Initial approach: Letter
  Copies of proposal: 3
  Board meeting date(s): Mar., June, Sept., and Dec.
  Final notification: 3 months
Officers and Directors: * Alain Philippe,* Pres.; Beatrice Philippe,* V.P.; Lenore Thornton, V.P.; Zoltan Hankovszky, Secy.; Patricia Reischour, Treas.; Helene P. Grenier; Marie-Josette Larrieu; Irving London; Dominique Meyer; Anne Philippe-Vaysse; Benjamin Grenier.
EIN: 136087157

1609
Polish Scholarship Fund, Inc.
P.O. Box 2025
Syracuse, NY 13220-2025 (315) 687-1076
E-mail: info@polishscholarship.com; *URL:* http://www.polishscholarship.com

Grantmaker type: Public charity.
Financial data (yr. ended 10/31/10): Revenue, $47,662; assets, $67,976 (M); gifts received, $9,251; expenditures, $44,498.
Purpose and activities: The fund helps talented students of Polish descent achieve their academic goals by providing them with financial assistance.
International interests: Poland.
Type of support: Scholarships—to individuals.
Limitations: Applications accepted. Giving limited to residents of Cayuga, Cortland, Madison, Oneida, Onondaga, and Oswego counties, NY.
Publications: Application guidelines.
Application information: Application form required.
  Initial approach: Download application form
  Deadline(s): Mar. 15 for Scholarships
Officers and Directors: * Kasia Prus,* Pres.; Tad Szyszka,* V.P.; Lucian Konarski,* Secy.; Andre Siok,* Treas.; John Bielak; Andre Bugajski; Marian Bysiak; Nancy Cummings; Allen Czelusniak; and 17 additional directors.
EIN: 160959507

1610
Polish-American Freedom Foundation
410 Park Ave., 15th Fl.
New York, NY 10022-4407 (212) 551-3544
URL: http://www.pafw.pl/strona.php?
setlanguage=2

Grantmaker type: Public charity.
Financial data (yr. ended 12/31/10): Revenue,
$7,194,247; assets, $297,978,780 (M);
expenditures, $9,767,885; giving activities include
$7,268,662 for grants to organizations outside the
U.S.
Purpose and activities: The foundation seeks to
advance democracy, civil society, economic
development and equal opportunity in Poland and,
ultimately, in other Central and Eastern European
countries.
Fields of interest: International democracy & civil
society development; International economic
development; International development.
International interests: Eastern & Central Europe;
Poland.
Limitations: Giving primarily in Poland.
Publications: Annual report; Informational brochure.
Officers and Directors:* John P. Birkelund,* Chair.;
Jerzy Kozminski,* Pres. and C.E.O.; C. Douglas
Ades, Secy.; Marek Belka; Joseph C. Bell; Frederick
M. Bohen; Hon. Zbigniew Brzezinski; Robert G. Faris;
Anna Fornalczyk; Aleksander Koj; Krzysztof
Pawlowski; Nicholas A. Rey.
EIN: 522193529

1611
The Population Council, Inc.
1 Dag Hammarskjold Plz.
New York, NY 10017-2203 (212) 339-0500
FAX: (212) 756-6052;
E-mail: pubinfo@popcouncil.org; URL: http://
www.popcouncil.org

Established in 1952 in NY.
Grantmaker type: Public charity.
Financial data (yr. ended 12/31/10): Revenue,
$56,113,356; assets, $157,996,594 (M); gifts
received, $42,845,550; expenditures,
$90,277,162; giving activities include $4,518,773
for grants, $10,593,204 for grants to organizations
outside the U.S., and $746,409 for grants to
individuals.
Purpose and activities: The council, an
international, nonprofit, nongovernmental
organization, seeks to improve the well-being and
reproductive health of current and future
generations around the world and to help achieve a
humane, equitable, and sustainable balance
between people and resources.
Fields of interest: Population studies; Reproductive
health.
International interests: Middle East; Latin America;
Asia; Africa.
Type of support: Fellowships.
Limitations: Applications not accepted. Giving on a
national and international basis.
Publications: Annual report; Newsletter.
Application information: Unsolicited requests for
funds not accepted.
Board meeting date(s): June and Dec.
Officers and Trustees:* Mark A. Walker,* Chair.;
Peter J. Donaldson,* Pres.; Darcy Bradbury; Howard
Cox; Wafaa El-Sadr; Lynn A. Foster; Anna Glasier;
Victor Halberstadt; Werner Holzer; Henry L. King;
Charles D. Klein; Anna Mastroianni; Cheikh Mbacke;

Robert B. Millard; Jotham Musinguzi; Anne R.
Pebley.
Number of staff: 600
EIN: 131687001

1612
Porat Yosef Foundation
1879 E. 2nd St.
Brooklyn, NY 11223-2822 (718) 336-9570

Established in 1966.
Grantmaker type: Public charity.
Financial data (yr. ended 12/31/10): Revenue,
$852,726; assets, $17,065 (M); gifts received,
$852,726; expenditures, $853,705.
Purpose and activities: The foundation aids
Orthodox Jewish parochial schools.
Fields of interest: Elementary/secondary
education; Jewish agencies & synagogues.
International interests: Israel.
Limitations: Giving primarily in Jerusalem, Israel;
some giving also in NY.
Officers and Trustees:* Isaac Hidary,* Pres.; Sonny
Laniado,* Secy.; Elie Marcus.
EIN: 116077810

1613
The PRASAD Project, Inc.
(also known as Philanthropic Relief, Altruistic
Service, and Development)
465 Brickman Rd.
Hurleyville, NY 12747-6002 (845) 454-0376
FAX: (854) 434-0377; E-mail: prasad@prasad.org;
URL: http://www.prasad.org
Facebook: http://www.facebook.com/
PRASADProject

Established in 1992.
Grantmaker type: Public charity.
Financial data (yr. ended 12/31/09): Revenue,
$881,708; assets, $1,670,130 (M); gifts received,
$733,403; expenditures, $752,707; giving
activities include $133,621 for grants, and
$132,277 for grants to organizations outside the
U.S.
Purpose and activities: The organization is
committed to improving the quality of life of
economically-disadvantaged people around the
world, and to help people become self-reliant and
live a life of dignity.
Fields of interest: Education; Dental care;
Optometry/vision screening; Public health; Health
care; Human services; International affairs;
Community/economic development; Economically
disadvantaged; AIDS, people with.
Limitations: Giving on a national and international
basis.
Officers and Trustees:* Frederic Dacqmine,*
Chair.; Peri Lynne Johnson,* Secy.; Steve Lane,*
Treas.; Dr. Gary Barth; Jyotika Patel.
EIN: 141751086

1614
The Preservation Fund
c/o Julius Paige, PC
501 E. 79th St., Ste. 10G
New York, NY 10075-0715

Established in 1992 in NY.
Grantmaker type: Independent foundation.

Financial data (yr. ended 10/31/10): Assets,
$4,556,880 (M); expenditures, $338,987;
qualifying distributions, $335,581; giving activities
include $250,000 for 54 grants (high: $10,000;
low: $1,000).
Fields of interest: Human services; Arts; Higher
education; Children/youth, services; International
affairs, foreign policy; Christian agencies &
churches.
Limitations: Applications not accepted. Giving
primarily in NY. No grants to individuals.
Application information: Contributes only to
pre-selected organizations.
Officers: Ponchitto Pierce, Pres.; Jay Julien, V.P.;
Tapio Vaskio, V.P.; Rev. Andrew Young, Secy.; Julius
Paige, Treas.
EIN: 133690790

1615
PricewaterhouseCoopers LLP Corporate Giving Program
300 Madison Ave., 24th Fl.
New York, NY 10017-6232 (312) 298-6669
Contact: Shannon Schuyler, U.S. Managing Dir.,
Corp. Responsibility
FAX: (813) 286-6000; Contacts for Impact Program:
Charlotte Coker Gibson, Prog. Dir. tel.: (703)
918-3286, e-mail:
charlotee.coker.gibson@us.pwc.com; Heather Tilis,
Sr. Assoc., tel. (877) 934-6722, fax: (813)
281-6238, e-mail: heather.tilis@us.pwc.com;
Additional e-mail: impact@us.pwc.com; Application
address for Impact Program: Attn: Heather Tilis,
Pricewaterhouse Coopers LLC, 1900 St. Antoine St.,
Detroit, MI, 48226; URL: http://www.pwc.com/
extweb/aboutus.nsf/docid/
84ED407A7C7CA1BE8525744E0055C716

Grantmaker type: Corporate giving program.
Purpose and activities: As a complement to its
foundation, PricewaterhouseCoopers also makes
charitable contributions to nonprofit organizations
directly. Support is given primarily in areas of
company operations, with emphasis on Washington,
DC, Atlanta, Georgia, Boston, Massachusetts, New
York, New York, Charlotte, North Carolina, and
Philadelphia, Pennsylvania.
Fields of interest: International affairs, U.N.;
Secondary school/education; Higher education;
Education; Disasters, preparedness/services;
Youth development, business; Youth, services;
United Ways and Federated Giving Programs;
General charitable giving; African Americans/
Blacks.
Type of support: General/operating support;
Program development; Conferences/seminars;
Employee volunteer services; Employee matching
gifts.
Limitations: Applications accepted. Giving primarily
in areas of company operations, with emphasis on
Washington, DC, Atlanta, GA, Boston, MA, Charlotte,
NC, New York, NY, and Philadelphia, PA.
Publications: Application guidelines.
Application information: An interview may be
requested for Impact Program. Application form
required.
Initial approach: Download application form and
mail to application address for Impact Program
Deadline(s): Dec. 1 for Impact Program

1616
Project ORBIS International, Inc.

(also known as ORBIS)
520 8th Ave., 11th Fl.
New York, NY   10018-6507   (646) 674-5500
Contact: Stephanie Huggins, Devel. Asst.
FAX: (646) 674-5599; E-mail: info@orbis.org;
Toll-free tel.: (800) ORBIS.US; URL: http://www.orbis.org

Established in 1973.
Grantmaker type: Public charity.
Financial data (yr. ended 12/31/10): Revenue, $80,836,868; assets, $45,588,797 (M); gifts received, $78,443,310; expenditures, $78,236,450; program services expenses, $67,612,063; giving activities include $5,789,682 for grants to organizations outside the U.S.
Purpose and activities: The organization works to preserve and restore sight by strengthening the capacity of local partners to prevent and treat blindness.
Fields of interest: Hospitals (general); Health care; Eye diseases; Children; Economically disadvantaged; Blind/visually impaired.
International interests: Africa; Asia; Bangladesh; Caribbean; China; Developing countries; Ethiopia; India; Latin America; Middle East; Vietnam.
Limitations: Applications not accepted. Giving primarily in developing countries.
Publications: Annual report.
Application information: Unsolicited requests for funds not accepted.
   Board meeting date(s): Quarterly
Officers and Directors:* Robert F. Walters, Chair.; James R. Parker,* Vice-Chair.; Jack McHale, Pres. and C.E.O.; Mohan Jacob Thazhathu, C.O.O.; Peter P. Mullen,* Secy.; Peter Hickson, Treas.; Geoffrey Holland, Exec. Dir.; Desmond G. Fitzgerald; Thomas S. Knight, Jr.; Francis A. L'Esperance, Jr.; Brian C. Leonard; Richard T. Lewis; Dina Merrill-Hartly; Dato' Kulasegaran Sabaratnam; John S. Slattery; Frederick W. Telling; Albert L. Ueltschi*; Bruce N. Whitman.
EIN: 237297651

1617
ProLiteracy Worldwide

1320 Jamesville Ave.
Syracuse, NY   13210-4224   (315) 422-9121
Contact: David C. Harvey, Pres. and C.E.O.
FAX: (315) 422-6369; E-mail: info@proliteracy.org;
Toll-free tel.: (888) 528-2224; URL: http://www.proliteracy.org

Established in 2002 in NY as a result of the merger of Literacy Volunteers of America and Laubach Literacy International.
Grantmaker type: Public charity.
Financial data (yr. ended 06/30/10): Revenue, $10,062,001; assets, $10,631,969 (M); gifts received, $3,581,802; expenditures, $10,083,346; program services expenses, $8,215,002; giving activities include $228,172 for 3 grants (high: $9,000; low: $6,000), and $282,020 for grants to organizations outside the U.S.
Purpose and activities: ProLiteracy Worldwide provides small direct grants in support of grassroots nongovernmental organizations in Africa, Asia, Latin America, and the Middle East that incorporate adult literacy into a broader process of community change.

Fields of interest: Adult education—literacy, basic skills & GED; Education, ESL programs.
International interests: Middle East; Latin America; Africa; Asia.
Type of support: Technical assistance; Internship funds.
Limitations: Applications accepted. Giving on a national and international basis. No grants to individuals.
Publications: Application guidelines; Annual report.
Application information:
   Initial approach: Letter with resume for internships; Application form for National Book Scholarship Fund
   Deadline(s): Apr. 14 for National Book Scholarship Fund
Officers and Directors:* Kevin Morgan,* Chair.; John Ward,* Vice-Chair.; David C. Harvey, Pres. and C.E.O.; Anne DuPrey,* Secy.; Thomas Fiscoe,* Treas.; Ruth Colvin; Dr. Robert Laubach; Tosca Bruno-van Vijfeijken; Sherrie Claiborne; Shari Daw; and 8 additional directors.
EIN: 166076384

1618
The Prospect Hill Foundation, Inc.

99 Park Ave., Ste. 2220
New York, NY   10016-1601   (212) 370-1165
FAX: (212) 599-6282;
E-mail: grants@prospect-hill.org; URL: http://www.prospect-hill.org/

Incorporated in 1960 in NY; absorbed The Frederick W. Beinecke Fund in 1983.
Donor: William S. Beinecke.
Grantmaker type: Independent foundation.
Financial data (yr. ended 06/30/09): Assets, $52,985,454 (M); gifts received, $146,243; expenditures, $3,906,959; qualifying distributions, $3,597,351; giving activities include $2,859,500 for 99 grants, and $310,427 for 233 employee matching gifts.
Purpose and activities: The foundation's mission is to advance the human experience while ensuring the well being of the earth. The foundation pursues this mission by making grants in four main program areas: 1) environmental conservation - to support conservation strategies that protect natural systems and to improve air quality for the benefit of human and ecological health; 2) nuclear nonproliferation - to limit the spread of nuclear weapons by providing reliable information to U.S. policy makers, the media, and the public; 3) reproductive health and rights - to support the right of women and men to be informed of and have access to safe, effective, affordable and acceptable methods of fertility regulation of their choice; and 4) criminal justice - to promote a fair and humane criminal justice system. In addition, the foundation makes a number of core grants that support the general philanthropic interests and goals of the foundation's directors and their family.
Fields of interest: Courts/judicial administration; Arts; Education; Environment, natural resources; Reproductive health, family planning; International affairs, arms control.
Type of support: Mission-related investments/loans; General/operating support; Capital campaigns; Land acquisition; Employee matching gifts; Matching/challenge support.
Limitations: Applications accepted. Giving primarily on a national basis with emphasis on MA, NJ, NY, and RI. No support for sectarian religious activities,

political organizations or non-tax exempted organizations. No grants to individuals, or for basic scientific research.
Publications: Grants list; Informational brochure.
Application information: Unsolicited proposals are not normally considered. Invited applicants should see the foundation Web site for specific guidelines. The foundation accepts the New York/ New Jersey Area Common Application Form and the New York/ New Jersey Common Report Form.
   Board meeting date(s): 3 times annually
Officers and Directors:* William S. Beinecke,* Chair.; John B. Beinecke,* Pres.; Frederick W. Beinecke, V.P. and Secy.; Robert J. Barletta, Treas.; Penny Fujiko Willgerodt, Exec. Dir.; Frances Beinecke Elston; Sarah Beinecke Richardson.
Number of staff: 1 full-time professional; 1 part-time support.
EIN: 136075567
Recent grants for international programs:
1618-1 Arms Control Association, Washington, DC, $50,000. For general support. 2010.
1618-2 Arms Control Association, Washington, DC, $50,000. To launch the New Voices Nonproliferation Fellowship. 2010.
1618-3 Asociacion Pro Bienestar de la Familia de Guatemala, Guatemala City, Guatemala, $35,000. For the San Benito Youth Clinic in Peten, Guatemala. 2010.
1618-4 Bulletin of the Atomic Scientists, Chicago, IL, $20,000. For general support. 2010.
1618-5 Carnegie Endowment for International Peace, Washington, DC, $50,000. For the Nuclear Nonproliferation Project. 2010.
1618-6 Centro de Accion Legal Ambiental y Social de Guatemala, Guatemala City, Guatemala, $25,000. For general support. 2010.
1618-7 EcoLogic Development Fund, Cambridge, MA, $35,000. For programs in Guatemala. 2010.
1618-8 Henry L. Stimson Center, Washington, DC, $35,000. For the Security for a New Century Program. 2010.
1618-9 Institute for Science and International Security, Washington, DC, $32,000. For general support. 2010.
1618-10 Marie Stopes International, London, England, $35,000. For programs in Chiapas, Mexico. 2010.
1618-11 National Security Archive Fund, Washington, DC, $35,000. For the Nuclear Weapons Documentation Project. 2010.
1618-12 Natural Resources Defense Council, New York, NY, $50,000. For the Nuclear Program. 2010.
1618-13 Planned Parenthood of South Florida and the Treasure Coast, West Palm Beach, FL, $20,000. For youth sexuality programs in Tan Ux'il, Peten, Guatemala. 2010.
1618-14 Pro Mujer, New York, NY, $35,000. For network coordination of reproductive health services. 2010.
1618-15 Search for Common Ground, Washington, DC, $25,000. For Iran program. 2010.
1618-16 Wildlife Conservation Society, Bronx, NY, $50,000. For environmental programs in Peten, Guatemala. 2010.
1618-17 World Neighbors, Oklahoma City, OK, $35,000. For reproductive health and natural resources management activities in Guatemala. 2010.
1618-18 World Resources Institute, Washington, DC, $25,000. For the Climate and Energy Program. 2010.

1619
QIBQ Foundation
(also known as Susan Wexner Charitable
Foundation)
c/o Hertz, Herson & Co., LLP
477 Madison Ave.
New York, NY   10022-5802

Established in 1986 in NY.
Donor: Susan R. Wexner.
Grantmaker type: Independent foundation.
Financial data (yr. ended 12/31/10): Assets,
$5,286,237 (M); expenditures, $139,346;
qualifying distributions, $139,096; giving activities
include $139,096 for 1 grant.
Fields of interest: International affairs; Jewish
federated giving programs.
Limitations: Applications not accepted. Giving in
New Haven, CT. No grants to individuals.
Application information: Contributes only to
pre-selected organizations.
Trustees: Michael S. Oberman; Mark Saks; Susan
R. Wexner.
EIN: 133424462

1620
Sanam Vaziri Quraishi Foundation
305 E. 63rd St., PH-A
New York, NY   10065-7772
URL: http://www.svqf.org
Facebook: https://www.facebook.com/TheSVQF

Established in NY.
Grantmaker type: Independent foundation.
Financial data (yr. ended 12/31/10): Assets,
$39,677 (M); gifts received, $383,161;
expenditures, $346,509; qualifying distributions,
$186,864; giving activities include $186,864 for
grants.
Purpose and activities: The foundation seeks to
alleviate extreme poverty and inequality through
tangible philanthropy.
Fields of interest: International development;
Human services; Children.
Limitations: Applications not accepted. Giving
primarily in NY, TN and TX.
Application information: Contributes only to
pre-selected organizations.
Officers and Directors:* Sanam Vaziri Quraishi,*
Chair.; Corinne A. Richardson,* Secy.; Shahid H.
Quraishi,* Treas.
EIN: 205243999

1621
Rainforest Alliance, Inc.
665 Broadway, Ste. 500
New York, NY   10012-2420   (212) 677-1900
Contact: Tensie Whelan, Exec. Dir.; Deanna Newsom
FAX: (212) 677-2187; E-mail: kleinhans@ra.org;
Toll-free tel.: (888) MY-EARTH; URL: http://
www.rainforest-alliance.org

Established in 1987 in NY.
Grantmaker type: Public charity.
Financial data (yr. ended 06/30/10): Revenue,
$34,346,469; assets, $13,697,054 (M); gifts
received, $20,824,703; expenditures,
$33,951,722; giving activities include $534,553
for grants, $1,694,258 for 12 grants to
organizations outside the U.S., $5,000 for grants to

individuals, and $15,000 for grant to an individual
outside the U.S.
Purpose and activities: The mission of the alliance
is to protect ecosystems and the people and wildlife
that live within them by implementing better
business practices for biodiversity conservation and
sustainability companies, cooperatives, and
landowners that participate in the alliance's
programs meet strict standards for protecting the
environment, wildlife, workers, and local
communities.
Fields of interest: Environment, research;
Environment, public education; Environment, natural
resources; Environment, forests; Environment.
International interests: Latin America.
Type of support: General/operating support; Land
acquisition; Emergency funds; Program
development; Seed money; Fellowships;
Program-related investments/loans.
Limitations: Applications accepted. Giving limited to
Latin America. No grants for unnecessary or
unreasonable equipment.
Publications: Application guidelines.
Application information: See web site for additional
application information. Application form required.
Deadline(s): Dec. 31 for Kleinhans Fellowship
Officers and Directors:* Daniel R. Katz,* Chair.;
Wendy Gordon,* Vice-Chair.; Tensie Whelan, Exec.
Dir.; Labeeb M. Abboud; John D. Adams; Adam
Albright; Dr. Noel Brown; Daniel Cohen; Henry P.
Davison II; Marilu Hernandez de Bosoms; Roger
Deromedi; Karl Fossum; Sudhakar Kesavan; Mary
Stuart Masterson; Brendan May; and 4 additional
directors.
EIN: 133377893

1622
Rainforest Foundation, Inc.
180 Varick St., Ste. 528
New York, NY   10014-5431   (212) 431-9098
Contact: Christine Halvorson, Exec. Dir.
FAX: (212) 431-9197; E-mail: christinch@rffny.org;
URL: http://www.rainforestfoundation.org
Facebook: http://www.facebook.com/pages/
Rainforest-Foundation-US/36085812354
MySpace: http://profile.myspace.com/index.cfm?
fuseaction=user.viewProfile&friendID=125355212
Twitter: http://twitter.com/RainforestUS
YouTube: http://www.youtube.com/user/
rainforestfoundation

Established in 1989 in CA and NY.
Donors: Glenda Bailey; Joenia Carvalho; S. Todd
Crider; Cuca Fresca; Gilbert B. Friesen; Dustin
Hoffman; Lynn Maas; Carlos Miele; Carol Sue
Sandler; Kathy Schenker; Jessica Serafin; Linda
Stein†; Laurie & Paul Sturz; Trudie Styler; Gordon
"Sting" Sumner; Donald S. Sussman; Jill Swinton;
Gary Martin Wexler; Amnesty International of the
U.S.A., Inc.; Aravis Ltd.; Durst Organization L.P.;
Entertainment Industry Foundation; The Frank and
Fred Friedman Family Foundation; Richard and
Rhoda Goldman Fund; Grubman, Indursky P.C.;
HSBC Bank USA, N.A.; Latin America Fund; Moss
Foundation; Newman's Own Foundation;
Philosophy; Rainforest Foundation Fund; Rainforest
Foundation U.K.; Sony Corporation of America; The
Charles H. Stout Foundation; The Tomorrow
Foundation; Travel Dynamics.
Grantmaker type: Public charity.
Financial data (yr. ended 12/31/10): Revenue,
$1,005,217; assets, $318,748 (M); gifts received,
$996,388; expenditures, $1,146,425; giving

activities include $409,126 for grants to
organizations outside the U.S.
Purpose and activities: The foundation supports
indigenous people and traditional populations of the
rainforest in their efforts to protect their
environment and fulfill their rights.
Fields of interest: Environment, forests; Indigenous
peoples.
International interests: South America; Central
America.
Type of support: Continuing support; Management
development/capacity building; Program
development; Conferences/seminars; Scholarship
funds; Consulting services; Program evaluation;
Scholarships—to individuals.
Limitations: Applications not accepted. Giving
primarily on an international basis.
Publications: Annual report; Financial statement;
Informational brochure; Newsletter.
Application information: Unsolicited requests for
funds not accepted.
Board meeting date(s): Three times per year
Officers and Board Members:* S. Todd Crider,*
Chair.; Suzanne Pelletier, Exec. Dir.; John Copeland;
Ivan Gallegos-Rivas; Heloisa Griggs; Jean La Rose;
Veronique Pittman; Jessica Serafin.
Number of staff: 2 full-time professional; 1 part-time
professional.
EIN: 951622945

1623
Rainforest Foundation Fund, Inc.
180 Varick St., Ste. 528
New York, NY   10014-5431   (212) 431-9098
Contact: Athos Gontijo, Dir., Finance; Franca Sciuto,
Chair.
FAX: (212) 431-9197; E-mail: agontijo@rffny.org;
URL: http://www.rainforestfoundationfund.org

Established in 1989 in NY as Rainforest Foundation
International; name changed in 1999 to Rainforest
Foundation Fund.
Grantmaker type: Public charity.
Financial data (yr. ended 12/31/10): Revenue,
$2,874,409; assets, $10,312,655 (M); gifts
received, $2,683,037; expenditures, $2,294,454;
giving activities include $1,017,942 for 16 grants to
organizations outside the U.S.
Purpose and activities: The mission of the
foundation is to support indigenous and traditional
people of the world's rainforests in their efforts to
protect their environment and fulfill their rights by
assisting them in: securing and controlling the
natural resources necessary for their long-term
well-being and managing these resources in ways
which do not harm their environment, violate their
culture, or compromise their future; and developing
the means to protect their individual and collective
rights and to obtain, shape, and control basic
services from the state.
Fields of interest: Environment, natural resources;
Environment, forests; Indigenous peoples.
International interests: Africa; South America;
Southeast Asia.
Type of support: Management development/
capacity building; Capital campaigns; Emergency
funds; Scholarship funds; Program evaluation;
Scholarships—to individuals.
Limitations: Applications not accepted. Giving
primarily in Africa, Brazil, Ecuador, Guyana,
Indonesia, Peru, and Suriname.
Publications: Annual report; Biennial report;
Financial statement.

Application information: Unsolicited requests for funds not accepted.

Board meeting date(s): Dec.

Officers: Franca Sciuto, Chair.; Trudie Styler, Vice-Chair.; Li Lu, Treas.

Number of staff: 1 full-time professional.

EIN: 133710434

1624

V. Kann Rasmussen Foundation

475 Riverside Dr., Ste. 900
New York, NY 10115-0066 (212) 812-4268
Contact: Irene Krarup, Assoc. Dir.
FAX: (212) 812-4299; E-mail: vkrfinfo@vkrf.org;
E-mail for Irene Krarug: ikrarup@vkrf.org;
URL: http://www.vkrf.org/

Established in 1991 in MA.

Donor: The Velux Trust.

Grantmaker type: Independent foundation.

Financial data (yr. ended 06/30/10): Assets, $76,482,246 (M); expenditures, $3,473,697; qualifying distributions, $3,076,177; giving activities include $2,213,664 for 31 grants (high: $250,000; low: $450), and $167,500 for foundation-administered programs.

Purpose and activities: Giving primarily for the environment.

Fields of interest: Environment; Higher education; Environment, natural resources; Medical research, institute.

Type of support: Mission-related investments/loans; General/operating support; Program development.

Limitations: Applications accepted. Giving to national and international programs, with a special interest in SC. No grants to individuals.

Publications: Informational brochure; Occasional report.

Application information: Full proposals are by invitation only. Application form not required.

Initial approach: Letter of inquiry, 2 pages, e-mail only

Copies of proposal: 1

Deadline(s): See foundation web site for current deadlines

Board meeting date(s): Mar./Apr. and Oct./Nov.

Final notification: 30 days or see foundation web site

Officer and Trustees:* Hans Kann Rasmussen,* Chair.; Lois E. H. Smith,* Ph.D., M.D., Managing Dir.; Irene Krarup, Assoc. Dir.; Anne-Margrete Ogstrup-Pedersen; Astrid Kann Rasmussen; Kristian Kann Rasmussen; Julie Wilson.

EIN: 223101266

Recent grants for international programs:

1624-1 Avaaz Foundation, New York, NY, $11,723. For grant expenses at COP15. 2009.

1624-2 Better World Fund, Washington, DC, $50,000. For Energy Future Coalition. 2009.

1624-3 Center for Climate Strategies, Washington, DC, $11,162. For grant expenses at COP15. 2009.

1624-4 Center for International Environmental Law, Washington, DC, $200,000. For Climate Change Program. 2009.

1624-5 Center for Media and Democracy, Madison, WI, $200,000. For SourceWatch coverage of COP15. 2009.

1624-6 CERES, Boston, MA, $125,000. For investor strategy on climate change. 2009.

1624-7 CERES, Boston, MA, $16,949. For grant expenses at COP15. 2009.

1624-8 EARTH University Foundation, Atlanta, GA, $175,000. For the Community Development Program of EARTH University in Costa Rica. 2009.

1624-9 EcoHealth Alliance, New York, NY, $975,000. For Consortium for Conservation Medicine and Wildlife Trust alliance. 2009.

1624-10 Energy and Resources Institute, North America, Washington, DC, $68,750. For the Yale-TERI collaborative. 2009.

1624-11 Environmental Defense, New York, NY, $100,000. For the program, A Path to a Low Carbon Future in Mexico. 2009.

1624-12 Friends of the Earth, Washington, DC, $100,000. For campaign to engage United States in effective and equitable climate policy. 2009.

1624-13 Grist Magazine, Seattle, WA, $11,723. For grant expenses at COP15. 2009.

1624-14 International Action Center, New York, NY, $20,000. For campaign for clean water in Haiti. 2009.

1624-15 Internews Network, Washington, DC, $150,000. For Earth Journalism Network's climate change media coverage in the developing world. 2009.

1624-16 New York Botanical Garden, Bronx, NY, $125,000. For Biodiversity and Human Health in Micronesia Project. 2009.

1624-17 Pew Charitable Trusts, Philadelphia, PA, $500,000. For the Pew Environmental Group's global public campaign on climate change. 2009.

1624-18 Rainforest Action Network, San Francisco, CA, $100,000. For efforts to challenge financing of carbon-intensive projects. 2009.

1624-19 Root Capital, Cambridge, MA, $75,000. For micro-finance projects for sustainable agriculture in Latin America. 2009.

1624-20 Sustainability Institute, Hartland, VT, $26,224. For grant expenses at COP15. 2009.

1624-21 Sustainable Markets Foundation, New York, NY, $50,000. For Project 350 and its global grassroots movement to address climate change. 2009.

1624-22 Sustainable Markets Foundation, New York, NY, $20,000. For Project 350.org efforts in connection with COP15. 2009.

1624-23 Sustainable Sciences Institute, San Francisco, CA, $100,000. For program, Knowledge-Based Approach to Infectious Disease Control in the Developing World. 2009.

1624-24 U.S. Climate Action Network, Washington, DC, $500,000. For CAN International and NGO's participation in climate negotiations at COP15. 2009.

1624-25 U.S. Climate Action Network, Washington, DC, $150,000. For climate policy program. 2009.

1624-26 U.S. Climate Action Network, Washington, DC, $125,000. For strategic media initiative and communications needs of NGO community for COP15. 2009.

1624-27 U.S. Climate Action Network, Washington, DC, $65,000. For CAN International for staff support in connection with COP15. 2009.

1624-28 U.S. Climate Action Network, Washington, DC, $50,676. For grant expenses at COP15. 2009.

1624-29 U.S. Climate Action Network, Washington, DC, $50,000. For CAN International media efforts for COP14 and 15. 2009.

1624-30 Union of Concerned Scientists, Cambridge, MA, $170,000. For climate campaign undertaken at COP15. 2009.

1624-31 Union of Concerned Scientists, Cambridge, MA, $42,452. For Non-Profit Organization center in Copenhagen for COP15. 2009.

1624-32 Union of Concerned Scientists, Cambridge, MA, $26,056. For grant expenses at COP15. 2009.

1624-33 Yale University, New Haven, CT, $68,750. Support for the Yale-TERI collaborative. 2009.

1624-34 Yellowstone to Yukon Conservation Initiative, Canmore, Canada, $125,000. For the Center for Large Landscape Conservation and Science. 2009.

1625

Rattner Family Foundation, Inc.

(formerly Steven L. Rattner and P. Maureen White Foundation, Inc.)
c/o Quadrangle Group LLC
998 5th Ave., 9th Fl.
New York, NY 10028-0102

Established in 1989 in NY.

Donors: Steven L. Rattner; The Steven Rattner 2000 LT Trust; 2000 LTT Asset Corp.

Grantmaker type: Independent foundation.

Financial data (yr. ended 12/31/10): Assets, $1,985,348 (M); expenditures, $763,503; qualifying distributions, $699,905; giving activities include $699,905 for grants.

Purpose and activities: Giving primarily for higher education; support also for cultural institutions, and human services.

Fields of interest: Human services; International relief; Museums; Arts; Higher education; Education.

Limitations: Applications not accepted. Giving primarily in New York, NY. No grants to individuals.

Application information: Contributes only to pre-selected organizations.

Officers and Directors:* Steven L. Rattner, Pres.; P. Maureen White,* V.P. and C.F.O.; Michael Minars, Secy.-Treas.

EIN: 133519099

1626

Recanati Foundation

590 5th Ave., 19th Fl.
New York, NY 10036-4702

Incorporated in 1956 in NY.

Donors: Guardian Industries Corp.; OSG Foundation.

Grantmaker type: Independent foundation.

Financial data (yr. ended 06/30/11): Assets, $1,733,319 (M); expenditures, $335,141; qualifying distributions, $329,656; giving activities include $329,656 for grants.

Purpose and activities: Giving primarily to medical and Jewish organizations, including welfare funds.

Fields of interest: Medical research, institute; Museums (science/technology); Education; Human services; Jewish agencies & synagogues.

International interests: Israel.

Type of support: Research.

Limitations: Applications not accepted. Giving primarily in NY. No grants to individuals, or for building funds.

Application information: Contributes only to pre-selected organizations.

Officers: Diane Recanati, Chair.; Leon Recanati, Vice-Chair.; Oudi Recanati, Vice-Chair.; Michael A. Recanati, V.P.; Yudith Recanati, V.P.
Directors: Daniel Pearson; Ariel Recanati.
EIN: 136113080

1627
The Reed Foundation, Inc.
500 5th Ave., Ste. 2222
New York, NY 10110-0004
E-mail: lathamdc@thereedfoundation.org;
URL: http://www.thereedfoundation.org

Incorporated in 1949 in NY.
Donor: Samuel Rubin†.
Grantmaker type: Independent foundation.
Financial data (yr. ended 12/31/10): Assets, $17,169,304 (M); expenditures, $4,998,236; qualifying distributions, $4,990,155; giving activities include $3,769,703 for 61 grants (high: $2,500,000; low: $200), and $332,045 for 14 grants to individuals (high: $60,000; low: $7,500).
Purpose and activities: The foundation's focus is on the support of programs in the arts, related libraries, social services, and both domestic and international civil rights. The arts and literature of the Caribbean Basin, through programs at a university and a research institute, are of major interest at present.
Fields of interest: Visual arts; Museums (art); Performing arts; Performing arts, opera; Arts; Higher education; Libraries/library science; Education; Human services; Civil/human rights.
International interests: Caribbean.
Type of support: General/operating support; Continuing support; Endowments; Program development; Fellowships; Scholarship funds; Research; Exchange programs; Matching/challenge support.
Limitations: Applications not accepted. Giving primarily in the metropolitan New York, NY, area; some limited funding also in the Caribbean Basin. No grants to individuals.
Publications: Program policy statement.
Application Information: Unsolicited requests for funds not accepted.
Board meeting date(s): Varies
Officers and Directors: Reed Rubin, Pres.; Jane Gregory Rubin, Secy.; Maia A. Rubin, Treas.; Lara R. Rubin; Peter L. Rubin.
Number of staff: 3 full-time professional.
EIN: 131990017

1628
The Susie Reizod Foundation
P.O. Box 816
New Paltz, NY 12561-0816 (845) 255-9708
Contact: Cynthia E. Dozier, Pres.
FAX: (845) 255-0608;
E-mail: info@thesusiereizodfoundation.org;
Additional e-mail: cdreizod@aol.com; URL: http://www.thesusiereizodfoundation.org

Established in 2001 in NY.
Grantmaker type: Public charity.
Financial data (yr. ended 12/31/10): Revenue, $121,943; assets, $34,574 (M); gifts received, $60,438; expenditures, $145,948.
Purpose and activities: The organization provides new shoes to children in need in poor urban and rural areas of the United States and developing countries.

Fields of interest: Children/youth, services; Infants/toddlers; Children; Children/youth; Youth; Girls; Boys; Disabilities, people with; AIDS, people with; Economically disadvantaged.
International interests: Africa; Asia; Caribbean; Developing countries; Latin America.
Type of support: In-kind gifts.
Limitations: Applications not accepted. Giving primarily in the U.S., Africa, Asia, the Caribbean, and Latin America.
Publications: Annual report.
Application information: Contributes only to pre-selected organizations.
Board meeting date(s): Quarterly
Officers and Directors: Cynthia E. Dozier, Pres.; Derrick E. Dozier, V.P.; Racquel Dozier, Secy.; Steven A. Yergan, Treas.; and 11 additional directors.
Number of staff: 2
EIN: 141836352

1629
Religious Zionists of America, Inc.
500 7th Ave., 2nd Fl.
New York, NY 10018-4502 (212) 465-9234
Contact: Rabbi Yosef Blau, Pres.
FAX: (212) 465-9246; E-mail: mizrachi@rza.org;
URL: http://www.rza.org

Established in 1916 in NY.
Grantmaker type: Public charity.
Financial data (yr. ended 08/31/11): Revenue, $360,633; assets, $414,088 (M); gifts received, $153,116; expenditures, $382,339; giving activities include $92,335 for grants to organizations outside the U.S.
Purpose and activities: The organization aims to instill in the American Jewish community a commitment to religious Zionism.
Fields of interest: Jewish agencies & synagogues.
International interests: Israel.
Limitations: Giving in the U.S. and Israel.
Officers: Martin Oliner, Chair.; Rabbi Yosef Blau, Pres.; Ernest Agatstein, Ph.D., V.P.; Isaac Blachor, V.P.; Martin Cohen, V.P.; Chanania Gang, Ph.D., V.P.; Rabbi William Kanter, V.P.; Rabbi Ariel Konstantyn, V.P.; Rabbi Solomon Rybak, V.P.; Mark S. Cohen, Secy.; Asher Brukner, Ph.D., Treas.
EIN: 135611746

1630
The Resource Foundation, Inc.
237 W. 35th St., Ste. 1203
New York, NY 10001-6216 (212) 675-6170
Contact: Loren Finnell, Pres. and C.E.O.
FAX: (212) 268-5325; E-mail: info@resourcefnd.org;
URL: http://www.resourcefnd.org

Established in 1987.
Grantmaker type: Public charity.
Financial data (yr. ended 12/31/10): Revenue, $7,277,765; assets, $2,498,119 (M); gifts received, $7,285,970; expenditures, $7,675,953; giving activities include $6,743,964 for 164 grants to organizations outside the U.S.
Purpose and activities: The foundation administers donor-advised funds and provides representation, networking, training, technical assistance, and fundraising to Latin American private development organizations (PDOs) that implement self-help projects in the areas of microenterprise,

environmental conservation, sustainable agriculture, basic education, low-cost housing, and primary healthcare.
Fields of interest: Education; Environment, natural resources; Health care; Agriculture; Housing/shelter; International development; International agricultural development; International economic development; Community development, small businesses; Hispanics/Latinos; Girls; Economically disadvantaged; Children/youth; Children; Adults, women; Adults, men; Adults.
International interests: Latin America.
Type of support: Technical assistance.
Limitations: Applications not accepted. Giving limited to Latin America and the Caribbean.
Publications: Financial statement; Newsletter.
Application information: Unsolicited requests for funds not encouraged or acknowledged.
Board meeting date(s): Six times a year
Officers and Directors: Loren Finnell, Pres. and C.E.O.; Marcela Lopez-Macedonio, Esq., Exec. Dir.; Manochere Alamgir; Michael Archer; Alejandro Bernal; Jovita Castillo; Alain Concher; Antonio Costa, Jr.; Jose M. De Lasa; William Hockman; Darryl Hunt; Rudolf Laager; Colleen May; Carla V. Porter; Kenneth Ricci; and 7 additional directors.
Number of staff: 4 full-time professional; 4 part-time professional.
EIN: 133421446

1631
Charles H. Revson Foundation, Inc.
55 E. 59th St., 23rd Fl.
New York, NY 10022-1112 (212) 935-3340
Contact: Julie A. Sandorf, Pres.
FAX: (212) 688-0633;
E-mail: info@revsonfoundation.org; Contact inf. for A. Akst, e-mail: aakst@revsonfoundation.org, tel.: (212) 935-3340, ext. 13; URL: http://www.revsonfoundation.org
Grants List: http://www.revsonfoundation.org/programs.html

Incorporated in 1956 in NY.
Donor: Charles H. Revson†.
Grantmaker type: Independent foundation.
Financial data (yr. ended 12/31/09): Assets, $150,891,126 (M); expenditures, $7,399,834; qualifying distributions, $6,931,913; giving activities include $5,625,130 for 58 grants (high: $937,500; low: $3,000).
Purpose and activities: Grants for urban affairs and public policy, with a special emphasis on New York, NY, problems, as well as national policy issues; education, including higher education; biomedical research policy; and Jewish philanthropy and education.
Fields of interest: Biology/life sciences; Community/economic development, public education; Education; Government/public administration; Higher education; Media/communications; Public affairs; Public policy, research.
International interests: Israel.
Type of support: Program-related investments/loans; Continuing support; Program development; Fellowships; Internship funds; Research.
Limitations: Applications accepted. Giving primarily in New York, NY and Israel. No support for local or national health appeals. No grants to individuals generally, or for film projects, endowments, capital or building campaigns or fundraising dinner events.

Application information: See foundation web site for application information. Application form not required.

Initial approach: Letter
Copies of proposal: 1
Deadline(s): None
Board meeting date(s): 3 times per year
Final notification: 6 months

Officers and Directors:* Reynold Levy,* Chair.; Julie A. Sandorf,* Pres.; Azade Ardali, C.F.O. and C.A.O.; Cheryl Cohen Effron, Secy.; Gerald Rosenfeld,* Treas.; Stacy S. Dick; Suzanne Gluck; Jeffrey Goldberg; Jerome Groopman; Steven Hyman; Martha Minow; Charles H. Revson, Jr.; Clifford Tabin.

Number of staff: 3 full-time professional; 5 full-time support; 1 part-time support.

EIN: 136126105

Recent grants for international programs:

1631-1 Center for Independent Documentary, Sharon, MA, $15,000. For production of feature-length documentary Nuclear Underground. 2010.

1631-2 Jewish Federations of North America, New York, NY, $50,000. For Social Venture Fund for Jewish-Arab Equality and Shared Society, which uses collective resources of contributors, each donating $50,000, to help promote a positive shared future in Israel of social and political equality, equal opportunity, and fair access to resources for all its citizens. 2010.

1631-3 Khiraquna, Beer Sheva, Israel, $25,000. For consortium of Arab-Israeli NGOs involved in voluntarism in development of a conceptual framework and proposal for government funding in order to expand the participation of Arab youth. 2010.

1631-4 Ma'ase, Karmiel, Israel, $200,000. For NGOs of the Civic Service Forum in their enrichment programming for 70 newly created civic service slots designated for disadvantaged Israeli youth: Arab Israelis, at-risk youth, and the physically and mentally disabled. 2010.

1631-5 Ma'ase, Karmiel, Israel, $180,000. For establishment of Civic Service Forum of Israeli NGOs working to improve the quantity and quality of volunteer year-of-service opportunities for disadvantaged Israeli youth. 2010.

1631-6 Toldot Yisrael, Jerusalem, Israel, $30,000. For cost of recording video testimonies of 50 men and women of Israel's founding generation. 2010.

1632
The Christopher Reynolds Foundation, Inc.

267 5th Ave., Ste. 1001
New York, NY 10016-7504 (212) 532-1606
Contact: Andrea Panaritis, Exec. Dir.
FAX: (212) 532-1403; E-mail: Panaritis@aol.com;
URL: http://www.creynolds.org

Incorporated in 1952 in NY.

Donors: Libby Holman Reynolds†; Atlantic Philanthropies.

Grantmaker type: Independent foundation.

Financial data (yr. ended 12/31/09): Assets, $24,319,916 (M); gifts received, $953,000; expenditures, $2,899,403; qualifying distributions, $2,552,129; giving activities include $2,037,986 for 75 grants (high: $268,667; low: $200).

Purpose and activities: In the foundation's first 12 years, it was principally supportive of innovative work toward international peace and disarmament,

civil rights, and against racism. Since 1995, the foundation has been steadily increasing its support of work that focuses on: U.S. relations with Cuba, and more recently, it has provided assistance to a limited number of initiatives examining U.S. policy and the U.S. presence in Iraq and possible policy options.

Fields of interest: International studies; Human services; International affairs.

International interests: Cuba; Iraq.

Type of support: Mission-related investments/ loans; General/operating support; Continuing support; Conferences/seminars; Technical assistance; Exchange programs.

Limitations: Giving primarily in the U.S., with emphasis on national organizations in Washington, DC, New York, NY, and Arlington, VA. No grants to individuals, or for capital or endowment funds, annual campaigns, emergency funds, deficit financing, scholarships, or matching gifts; no loans.

Publications: Financial statement; Grants list; Multi-year report (including application guidelines).

Application information: Application form available on foundation web site. The foundation does not accept full-length proposals that have not been requested by our staff and approved for receipt by the Executive Director. Application form required.

Initial approach: Telephone, or fax or e-mail letter of inquiry, no more than 3 typewritten pages.
Copies of proposal: 6
Deadline(s): Submit proposal preferably 30 days prior to board meeting
Board meeting date(s): Quarterly
Final notification: 1 week

Officers and Directors:* John R. Boettiger,* Ph.D., Pres. and Treas.; Suzanne Derrer,* V.P.; Andrea Panaritis,* Secy. and Exec. Dir.; Michael Kahn; Virginia Kahn.

Number of staff: 1 full-time professional; 1 part-time professional; 1 full-time support.

EIN: 136129401

1633
Richie-Madden Children's Foundation

c/o Inspired Philanthropy Group
70A Greenwich Ave., Ste. 268
New York, NY 10011-8300
URL: http://richiemaddenfoundation.com/
Facebook: http://www.facebook.com/group.php?gid=6259064403
MySpace: http://www.myspace.com/richiemadden

Established in 2007; donor-advised fund of the Tides Foundation.

Grantmaker type: Public charity.

Purpose and activities: The foundation provides general and program grants to nonprofit organizations in the U.S. and abroad, primarily in the areas of healthcare, education, and human rights.

Fields of interest: International human rights; Human services; Health care; Youth development; Children, services; Economically disadvantaged; Children.

Limitations: Giving on a national and international basis.

Directors: Pam Hicks; Benji Madden; Joel Madden; Brenda Richie; Lionel Richie; Nicole Richie.

1634
The William L. Richter Family Foundation

(formerly Richter Family Foundation)
c/o Richter Investment Corp.
299 Park Ave., 22nd Fl.
New York, NY 10171-0001 (212) 891-2109
Contact: William L. Richter, Tr.

Established in 2005 in NY.

Donors: William Richter; Richter Investment Corp.

Grantmaker type: Independent foundation.

Financial data (yr. ended 12/31/10): Assets, $4,312,643 (M); expenditures, $187,409; qualifying distributions, $153,951; giving activities include $112,995 for 37 grants (high: $60,000; low: $25), and $37,628 for 3 grants to individuals (high: $27,628; low: $5,000).

Fields of interest: International economic development; Arts; Higher education; Human services; Jewish agencies & synagogues.

Limitations: Applications accepted. Giving primarily in CT and NY.

Application information:

Deadline(s): None

Trustees: Ari Richter; William L. Richter.

EIN: 203467361

1635
The Ridgefield Foundation

c/o Arthur S. Hoffman
570 Lexington Ave., 33rd Fl.
New York, NY 10022-6837

Incorporated in 1956 in NY.

Donors: Henry J. Leir†; Erna D. Leir†; Continental Ore Corp.; International Ore and Fertilizer Corp.; Joan Corley.

Grantmaker type: Independent foundation.

Financial data (yr. ended 12/31/10): Assets, $80,830,313 (M); gifts received, $2,717; expenditures, $5,699,264; qualifying distributions, $4,757,483; giving activities include $4,182,000 for 76 grants (high: $430,000; low: $500).

Purpose and activities: Support for education in the U.S. and Israel, Jewish welfare funds, social service agencies, and cultural programs; most support is for past donees or for organizations recommended by board members.

Fields of interest: Arts; Education; Human services; Jewish federated giving programs; Jewish agencies & synagogues.

International interests: Israel.

Limitations: Applications not accepted. Giving primarily in NY for local services; giving in the U.S. and Israel for education. No grants to individuals, or for scholarships, fellowships, or matching gifts; no loans.

Application information: Contributes only to pre-selected organizations.

Board meeting date(s): Oct.

Officers and Directors:* Arthur S. Hoffman,* Pres. and Treas.; Margot Gibis,* V.P.; Anthony J. Cernera,* Secy.; Stuart Silver.

Number of staff: 1 part-time professional.

EIN: 136093563

Recent grants for international programs:

1635-1 American Friends of the Alliance Israelite Universelle, New York, NY, $150,000. For libraries. 2010.

1635-2 American Friends of the Hebrew University, New York, NY, $50,000. 2010.

1635-3 American Friends of the Israel Museum, New York, NY, $260,000. 2010.

1635-4 Bar-Ilan University in Israel, New York, NY, $50,000. 2010.

1635-5 Boys Town Jerusalem Foundation of America, New York, NY, $75,000. 2010.

1635-6 Charities Aid Foundation UK, West Malling, England, $20,000. For Georgian Foundation (Children of the Caucasus). 2010.

1635-7 Childrens Help Net Foundation, Briarcliff Manor, NY, $10,000. For children's' programs. 2010.

1635-8 Doctors Without Borders USA, New York, NY, $25,000. 2010.

1635-9 Friends of Yad Sarah, U.S. Office, New York, NY, $100,000. For relief of the disadvantaged. 2010.

1635-10 Jaffa Institute for Social Advancement, Flushing, NY, $20,000. For education. 2010.

1635-11 Jerusalem Foundation, New York, NY, $250,000. For relief of disadvantages. 2010.

1636
Rivendell Foundation
c/o The Philanthropic Group
630 5th Ave., 20th Fl.
New York, NY   10111-0100   (212) 501-7785
Contact: Barbara R. Greenberg, Fdn. Advisor
E-mail: BGreenberg@philanthropicgroup.com;
URL: http://foundationcenter.org/grantmaker/
rivendell/

Established in 1987 in NJ.
Donor: Kenneth I. Goldman.
Grantmaker type: Independent foundation.
Financial data (yr. ended 12/31/09): Assets, $0 (M); gifts received, $331,082; expenditures, $495,419; qualifying distributions, $440,750; giving activities include $440,750 for 20+ grants (high: $50,000; low: $1,000).
Purpose and activities: Giving primarily for out-of-school time programming for Newark, NJ, children and youth, and international human rights.
Fields of interest: International human rights; Neighborhood centers; Children/youth.
Type of support: Program development.
Limitations: Applications not accepted. Giving primarily in NJ. No grants to individuals.
Publications: Grants list.
Application information: Applications by invitation only.
   Board meeting date(s): 3 times per year
Trustee: Kenneth J. Goldman.
Advisor: Barbara R. Greenberg.
EIN: 222876727

1637
Roche Foundation, Inc.
c/o Robert G. Wilmers
350 Park Ave., 6th Fl.
New York, NY   10022-6081   (212) 350-2497

Established in 1997 in NY.
Donor: Robert G. Wilmers.
Grantmaker type: Independent foundation.
Financial data (yr. ended 11/30/10): Assets, $6,482,529 (M); expenditures, $223,408; qualifying distributions, $208,750; giving activities include $208,750 for 7 grants (high: $100,000; low: $1,000).
Fields of interest: Botanical gardens; Museums (art); Language (foreign); International exchange, arts.

Limitations: Applications not accepted. Giving primarily in MA and NY. No grants to individuals.
Application information: Contributes only to pre-selected organizations.
Officers: Robert G. Wilmers, Pres.; Elisabeth Roche Wilmers, Treas.
EIN: 161543635

1638
Rockefeller Brothers Fund, Inc.
475 Riverside Dr., Ste. 900
New York, NY   10115   (212) 812-4200
Contact: Hope Lyons, Dir., Grants Mgmt.
FAX: (212) 812-4299; E-mail: grantsmgmt@rbf.org;
URL: http://www.rbf.org
Blog: http://www.rbf.org/newsroom/all/all/
The-RBF-Journal%3A-The-Official-Blog
CEP Study: http://www.rbf.org/resource/
2010-grantee-and-applicant-perception-reports
David Rockefeller's Giving Pledge: http://
givingpledge.org/#enter
E-Newsletter: http://rbf.us1.list-manage.com/
subscribe/post?
u=8ced17726d46f75e118db9da7&id=2a6d5fa7b
5
Facebook: http://www.facebook.com/pages/
Rockefeller-Brothers-Fund/181125435234193
Grants Database: http://www.rbf.org/content/
grants-search
Knowledge Center: http://www.rbf.org/resources
Multimedia: http://www.rbf.org/resources/
browse?tid[]=3
RSS Feed: http://www.rbf.org/content/rss-feeds
Twitter: http://twitter.com/rockbrosfund
YouTube: http://www.youtube.com/user/
RBFCommunications

Incorporated in 1940 in NY.
Donors: John D. Rockefeller, Jr.†; Martha Baird Rockefeller†; Abby Rockefeller Mauze†; David Rockefeller; John D. Rockefeller III†; Laurance S. Rockefeller†; Nelson A. Rockefeller‖; Winthrop Rockefeller‡.
Grantmaker type: Independent foundation.
Financial data (yr. ended 12/31/10): Assets, $789,378,035 (M); expenditures, $71,768,485; qualifying distributions, $28,004,330; giving activities include $28,004,330 for grants, and $5,752,223 for foundation-administered programs.
Purpose and activities: The Rockefeller Brothers Fund promotes social change that contributes to a more just, sustainable, and peaceful world. Through its grantmaking, the Fund supports efforts to expand knowledge, clarify values and critical choices, nurture creative expression, and shape public policy. The Fund's programs are intended to develop leaders, strengthen institutions, engage citizens, build community, and foster partnerships that include government, business, and civil society. Respect for cultural diversity and ecological integrity pervades the Fund's activities.
Fields of interest: Arts, cultural/ethnic awareness; Arts; Environment, climate change/global warming; Environment, natural resources; Environment; International peace/security.
International interests: China; Montenegro; Serbia.
Type of support: Mission-related investments/ loans; General/operating support; Program development; Conferences/seminars; Seed money; Technical assistance; Consulting services; Employee matching gifts; Matching/challenge support.

Limitations: Applications accepted. Giving primarily in the United States and internationally, with an emphasis on three pivotal places: New York City, Southern China and the Western Balkans. No grants to individuals, or for land acquisitions or building funds.
Publications: Annual report; Grants list; Occasional report; IRS Form 990 or 990-PF printed copy available upon request.
Application information: Application guidelines available on foundation web site.
   Initial approach: Online letter of inquiry and preliminary grant compatibility quiz. For Pivotal Place: New York City Arts and Culture Grants use online application
   Deadline(s): See foundation web site
   Board meeting date(s): Mar., June, and Nov.
   Final notification: 3 months
Officers and Trustees:* Richard G. Rockefeller,* Chair.; Valerie Rockefeller Wayne,* Vice-Chair.; Stephen B. Heintz,* Pres.; Elizabeth C. Campbell, V.P., Progs.; Geraldine F. Watson, V.P., Opers. and Finance; Nancy L. Muirhead, Corp. Secy.; Jonathan F. Fanton, Advisory Tr.; William H. Luers, Advisory Tr.; Robert B. Oxnam, Advisory Tr.; David Rockefeller, Advisory Tr.; Anne Bartley; Nicholas Burns; Wendy Gordon; Miranda M. Kaiser; James E. Moltz; Vali Nasr; Timothy O'Neill; Wendy O'Neill; Joseph A. Pierson; Kavita Ramdas; Justin Rockefeller; Steven C. Rockefeller; Arlene Shuler; Marsha Simms; James Gustave Speth.
Number of staff: 19 full-time professional; 28 full-time support.
EIN: 131760106
Recent grants for international programs:

1638-1 35mm, Podgorica, Montenegro, $120,000. For work monitoring public services and its investigative reporting program.

1638-2 Abraham Path Initiative, Boulder, CO, $100,000. For general support. 2010.

1638-3 ActionAid USA, Washington, DC, $80,000. For Haiti relief efforts. 2010.

1638-4 Alliance for Climate Protection, Washington, DC, $250,000. For general support. 2010.

1638-5 American Councils for International Education: ACTR/ACCELS, Washington, DC, $50,000. For Kosovo American Education Fund. 2010.

1638-6 American University in Kosovo Foundation, Whitefield, ME, $65,000. For Center for Energy and Natural Resource Development and summer school program on European integration and peace-building, post-conflict reconstruction, and development. 2010.

1638-7 American University of Beirut, New York, NY, $50,000. For the Issam Fares Institute for Public Policy and International Affairs. 2010.

1638-8 Architecture for Humanity, San Francisco, CA, $45,000. For Haiti Schools Initiative. 2010.

1638-9 Asia Society, New York, NY, $75,000. For U.S.-Iran dialogue. 2010.

1638-10 Asian Cultural Council, New York, NY, $200,000. For general support. 2010.

1638-11 Aspen Global Change Institute, Basalt, CO, $100,000. For Climate Science Outreach Project. 2010.

1638-12 Aspen Institute, Washington, DC, $75,000. For Partners for a New Beginning. 2010.

1638-13 Association of Womens Business Centers, Camden, ME, $10,000. For Global Student Leadership program activities in the Western Balkans and to increase the capacity and sustainability of the program. 2010.

1638-14 Balkan Community Initiatives Fund-Serbia and Montenegro, Belgrade, Serbia, $70,000. For project, Together toward Sustainable Development. 2010.

1638-15 Balkan Investigative Reporting Network Kosovo, Prishtina, Kosovo, $65,000. For parliamentary election debates project. 2010.

1638-16 Bank Information Center, Washington, DC, $250,000. For general support. 2010.

1638-17 Bank Information Center, Washington, DC, $30,000. For a conference on international finance and coal. 2010.

1638-18 Belgrade Fund for Political Excellence, Belgrade, Serbia, $25,000. For general support. 2010.

1638-19 Bibliotheca Alexandrina, Alexandria, Egypt, $50,000. For New Beginning: U.S.-Muslim Relations Conference. 2010.

1638-20 Business for Social Responsibility, San Francisco, CA, $100,000. For the project, Sustainable Supply Chains in South China: Building Efficiency and Transparency of Green Factories and Ports. 2010.

1638-21 Carnegie Council for Ethics in International Affairs, New York, NY, $125,000. For program on U.S. Global Engagement. 2010.

1638-22 Carnegie Endowment for International Peace, Washington, DC, $200,000. For post-Copenhagen dialogue between the U.S. and China on climate and energy issues. 2010.

1638-23 Centar Za Nove Medije_kuda.org, Novi Sad, Serbia, $30,000. For general support. 2010.

1638-24 Center for Arms Control and Non-Proliferation, Washington, DC, $50,000. For project, Advocacy 2.0: From Information to Influence. 2010.

1638-25 Center for Clean Air Policy, Washington, DC, $50,000. For From Fast Start to Successful Finish initiative. 2010.

1638-26 Center for Climate Strategies, Washington, DC, $350,000. For general support. 2010.

1638-27 Center for Climate Strategies, Washington, DC, $90,000. For the project, United States-China Partnership on Climate Action Planning and Policy Development. 2010.

1638-28 Center for Research, Documentation and Publication, Pristina, Kosovo, $58,000. For general support. 2010.

1638-29 Center for U.S. Global Engagement, Washington, DC, $75,000. For Brasstops Initiative. 2010.

1638-30 Century Foundation, New York, NY, $100,000. For Khyber connection project. 2010.

1638-31 CERES, Boston, MA, $200,000. For We Can Lead campaign. 2010.

1638-32 China Dialogue, London, England, $120,000. For Web-based work focusing on energy and climate, and environment and health. 2010.

1638-33 China Primary Health Care Foundation, Beijing, China, $20,000. For Soil Pollution and Environmental Health Forum. 2010.

1638-34 China Youth Climate Action Network, Beijing, China, $35,000. For U.S.-China Youth Dialogue project. 2010.

1638-35 Chinese Academy of Sciences, Beijing, China, $300,000. For project, Forum on Health, Environment and Development. 2010.

1638-36 Chinese University of Hong Kong, Hong Kong, China, $200,000. For Civil Society Visiting Fellows Program. 2010.

1638-37 Christian Aid, London, England, $200,000. For continued support of its global Southern Advocacy and Outreach program. 2010.

1638-38 Civic Exchange, Hong Kong, China, $200,000. For project, Health Impacts of Marine Emissions in the Pearl River Delta. 2010.

1638-39 Civic Initiatives, Belgrade, Serbia, $30,000. For general support. 2010.

1638-40 Civil Society Institute, Newton, MA, $100,000. For the Global Warming Legal Action Project. 2010.

1638-41 Climate Central, Princeton, NJ, $25,000. For Communications Campaign on Sea Level Rise. 2010.

1638-42 Climate Change Organisation, Climate Group, London, England, $100,000. For China Carbon Treasure Program. 2010.

1638-43 Climate Registry, Los Angeles, CA, $80,000. For technical support to the Innovation Center for Energy and Transportation's project, The China Energy and Climate Registry. 2010.

1638-44 Columbia University, New York, NY, $100,000. For program, the Initiative for Policy Dialogue, for research, convening, and communications on the economics of equity in global climate policies. 2010.

1638-45 Community Partners, Los Angeles, CA, $35,000. For project, the Funders Network on Transforming the Global Economy. 2010.

1638-46 Connexus Communications, Arcata, CA, $75,000. For project, Better Together: U.S.-China Cooperation in Environmental Innovation. 2010.

1638-47 Consensus Building Institute, Cambridge, MA, $100,000. For U.S.-Muslim Engagement Initiative. 2010.

1638-48 Cornell University, Ithaca, NY, $125,000. For Global Labor Institute's Labor Leaders Climate Forum and Global Trade Union Task Force for Development Alternatives. 2010.

1638-49 Corporate Ethics International, Suisun City, CA, $300,000. For Tar Sands Campaign. 2010.

1638-50 Council of Canadians, Ottawa, Canada, $25,000. For work coordinating dissemination, outreach, and networking on Earth jurisprudence. 2010.

1638-51 Council of Canadians, Ottawa, Canada, $20,000. For publication of materials on Earth jurisprudence. 2010.

1638-52 Cuban Artists Fund, New York, NY, $100,000. For capacity building. 2010.

1638-53 Demos: A Network for Ideas and Action, New York, NY, $100,000. For U.S. in the World initiative. 2010.

1638-54 Dialogo 2000, Buenos Aires, Argentina, $15,000. For project, Jubilee South, for its South-South Summit on Climate Justice and Finance. 2010.

1638-55 DokuFest, Prizren, Kosovo, $35,000. For documentary and short film festival. 2010.

1638-56 EastWest Institute, New York, NY, $25,000. For mission to Ankara, Erbil, and Tel Aviv. 2010.

1638-57 ecoAmerica, Washington, DC, $15,000. For America the Best Climate Solutions Conference. 2010.

1638-58 ENCOMPASS, Centre for Social and Psychological Studies and Services, Prishtina, Kosovo, $50,000. For project, ATOMI. 2010.

1638-59 European Foundation Centre, Brussels, Belgium, $40,000. For foundation law project. 2010.

1638-60 European Foundation Centre, Brussels, Belgium, $10,000. For Grantmakers East Forum. 2010.

1638-61 Forum for Civic Initiatives, Prishtina, Kosovo, $52,740. For project, Go to Vote-Shape Your Future. 2010.

1638-62 Forum for Civic Initiatives, Prishtina, Kosovo, $50,000. For civil society training program on the processes and frameworks of international financial institutions and multinational corporations. 2010.

1638-63 Forum on Democracy and Trade, Washington, DC, $200,000. For general support. 2010.

1638-64 Foundation for a Civil Society, New York, NY, $25,000. For Iran project. 2010.

1638-65 Fresh Energy, Saint Paul, MN, $100,000. For Global Warming Solutions program. 2010.

1638-66 Friends of the Earth International, London, England, $100,000. For the development of a network of advocates for justice and equity in global climate change policy processes. 2010.

1638-67 Fund for Active Citizenship, Podgorica, Montenegro, $120,000. For small grants program. 2010.

1638-68 Georgetown University, Washington, DC, $400,000. For the Georgetown Climate Center. 2010.

1638-69 Global Environmental Institute, Beijing, China, $400,000. For project, China-U.S. Cooperation: Low Carbon Planning and Energy Efficiency. 2010.

1638-70 Global Exchange, San Francisco, CA, $35,000. For innovative communications platforms to link climate advocates. 2010.

1638-71 Global Fund for Community Foundations, Belfast, Ireland, $50,000. For program support for its institutional, operational, and program development. 2010.

1638-72 Global Justice Ecology Project, Hinesburg, VT, $15,000. For climate justice media and communications work around COP 16 in Cancun, Mexico. 2010.

1638-73 Guangdong Energy Conservation Center, Guangzhou, China, $100,000. For project, Improving Energy Efficiency in Small Medium-sized Enterprises (SMEs) in Guangdong. 2010.

1638-74 Harvard University, Cambridge, MA, $50,000. For Western Balkan Civil Society Leadership Development Program. 2010.

1638-75 Henry L. Stimson Center, Washington, DC, $50,000. For project, the Global Systems Initiative. 2010.

1638-76 Henry L. Stimson Center, Washington, DC, $50,000. For Security for a New Century program. 2010.

1638-77 Horizon Research Consultancy Group, Beijing, China, $160,000. For Black Apple Youth Project: Promoting University Students' Social Entrepreneurship and Social Engagement. 2010.

1638-78 Indiana University, Bloomington, IN, $200,000. To work with Zhongshan University to establish a Center on Philanthropy in southern China. 2010.

1638-79 Inicijativa Mladih za Ljudska Prava-Crna Gora, Podgorica, Montenegro, $25,000. For School of Democratic Leadership. 2010.

1638-80 Initiative for Kosova Community, Shtime, Kosovo, $30,000. For project to replace environmentally damaging economic activities with sustainable development activities. 2010.

1638-81 Innovation Center for Energy and Transportation, South Pasadena, CA, $200,000.

For project, The China Energy and Climate Registry. 2010.

1638-82 Institute for Agriculture and Trade Policy, Minneapolis, MN, $100,000. For work on climate change, trade, and agriculture. 2010.

1638-83 Institute for State Effectiveness, Washington, DC, $100,000. For the Kabul Conference. 2010.

1638-84 Institute of Public and Environmental Affairs, Beijing, China, $300,000. For general support. 2010.

1638-85 Investor Watch, Richmond, England, $90,000. For Investor Disclosure Project's analytic work on energy-related initial public offerings. 2010.

1638-86 Islands First, Brooklyn, NY, $40,000. For general support. 2010.

1638-87 J Street Education Fund, Washington, DC, $25,000. For National Conference. 2010.

1638-88 Johns Hopkins University, Baltimore, MD, $125,000. For International Reporting Project. 2010.

1638-89 Kosovar Institute for Policy Research and Development, Prishtina, Kosovo, $74,000. For work to strengthen the rule of law in Kosovo. 2010.

1638-90 Kosovo Law Institute, Prishtina, Kosovo, $30,000. For project to strengthen judicial sector accountability in Kosovo. 2010.

1638-91 LiNet, Belgrade, Serbia, $50,000. For government monitoring and investigative journalism project, Truth-o-meter. 2010.

1638-92 Mary Robinson Foundation, Dublin, Ireland, $100,000. For general support. 2010.

1638-93 Meedan, Inc., San Francisco, CA, $100,000. To build capacity in the Middle East. 2010.

1638-94 Natural Capitalism Solutions, Longmont, CO, $100,000. For Presidential Climate Action Project. 2010.

1638-95 Natural Resources Defense Council, New York, NY, $200,000. For continuing work on heavy metal pollution. 2010.

1638-96 Network for the Affirmation of NGO Sector-MANS, Podgorica, Montenegro, $70,000. For general support. 2010.

1638-97 New Venture Fund, Washington, DC, $75,000. For Turnwell/Climate Interactive project to support the development of the C-ROADS Climate simulation. 2010.

1638-98 New York Immigration Coalition, New York, NY, $20,000. For mobilization of New York City community groups to Washington, D.C., for the March 21st March for America. 2010.

1638-99 New York University, New York, NY, $100,000. For project, The Center for Dialogues: Islamic World-U.S.-The West; of which $20,000 is for a development consultant. 2010.

1638-100 Oceana, Washington, DC, $200,000. For general support. 2010.

1638-101 Partneret-Shqiperi, Qendra per Ndryshim dhe Manaxhim Konflikti, Tirana, Albania, $70,000. For efforts to develop philanthropy in Albania. 2010.

1638-102 Partnership for a Secure America, Washington, DC, $50,000. For Congressional Fellows program. 2010.

1638-103 PeaceWorks Foundation, New York, NY, $50,000. For OneVoice Movement project. 2010.

1638-104 Polaris Institute USA, Essex, NY, $100,000. For project, Our World is Not For Sale network. 2010.

1638-105 Political Security Domain, Ramat HaSharon, Israel, $50,000. For general support. 2010.

1638-106 Princeton University, Princeton, NJ, $25,600. For the Program on Science and Global Security at the Woodrow Wilson School of Public and International Affairs. 2010.

1638-107 Project on Middle East Democracy, Washington, DC, $100,000. For general support. 2010.

1638-108 Public Citizen Foundation, Washington, DC, $200,000. For Global Trade Watch program. 2010.

1638-109 Quebec-Labrador Foundation/Atlantic Center for the Environment, Ipswich, MA, $20,000. For general support. 2010.

1638-110 Ramon Magsaysay Award Foundation, Manila, Philippines, $150,000. For the Ramon Magsaysay Awards. 2010.

1638-111 Rekonstrukcija Zenski Fond, Belgrade, Serbia, $30,000. For Special Focus Program. 2010.

1638-112 Resource Media, San Francisco, CA, $250,000. For Climate Science Initiative. 2010.

1638-113 Resource Media, San Francisco, CA, $75,000. For project, Defending Climate Science: Communications Support for the Intergovernmental Panel on Climate Change. 2010.

1638-114 Save the Children Federation, Westport, CT, $80,000. For Haiti relief efforts. 2010.

1638-115 Search for Common Ground, Washington, DC, $75,000. For Iran project. 2010.

1638-116 Smart Kolektiv, Belgrade, Serbia, $30,000. For project, Business Contributions to Tackle Climate Change. 2010.

1638-117 Social Science Research Council, Brooklyn, NY, $500,000. For China Environment and Health Initiative. 2010.

1638-118 Society for Harmonious Development, Ting Kau, China, $35,000. For a youth engagement project in Guangzhou. 2010.

1638-119 Soliya, New York, NY, $75,000. For Connect Program. 2010.

1638-120 South Centre, Geneva, Switzerland, $200,000. For general support. 2010.

1638-121 Sustainable Markets Foundation, New York, NY, $25,000. For Eco-Accountability project. 2010.

1638-122 TechSoup Global, San Francisco, CA, $80,000. For work to strengthen the technology infrastructure of civil society organizations in the Western Balkans. 2010.

1638-123 TechSoup Global, San Francisco, CA, $75,000. For the launch, operation, and growth of its project, NGOsource, the NGO Repository of Equivalency Determination Information. 2010.

1638-124 Third World Network, Accra, Ghana, $150,000. For regional work on trade. 2010.

1638-125 Third World Network, Penang, Malaysia, $40,000. For analysis and strategy-setting meeting of international climate policy nongovernmental organizations and their networks. 2010.

1638-126 Truman National Security Project Educational Institute, Washington, DC, $100,000. For work on climate change. 2010.

1638-127 Tsinghua University, Beijing, China, $100,000. For Institute of Energy, Environment and Economy for the project, Creating a Common Platform Simulator to Support the Disaggregation of National Carbon Emissions Reduction Target. 2010.

1638-128 U.S. Climate Action Network, Washington, DC, $100,000. For Facing the Climate Security Threat project. 2010.

1638-129 U.S. Climate Action Network, Washington, DC, $50,000. For China Strategy project. 2010.

1638-130 U.S. Climate Action Network, Washington, DC, $20,000. To help bridge a budget gap. 2010.

1638-131 United Nations, New York, NY, $35,000. For program, the United Nations Conference on Trade and Development, for its mapping study of multilateral negotiating processes. 2010.

1638-132 United Nations, New York, NY, $20,000. To its program, the United Nations Non-Governmental Liaison Service, for its work on climate finance. 2010.

1638-133 W E T A-Greater Washington Educational Telecommunications Association, Arlington, VA, $130,000. For the International Reporting Unit of the PBS NewsHour, a project of the Greater Washington Educational Telecommunications Association, Inc. 2010.

1638-134 Washington State University, Pullman, WA, $51,300. For Muslim World Media Survey in Pakistan. 2010.

1638-135 Welfare Association, East Jerusalem, $50,000. For the Arab Foundations Forum. 2010.

1638-136 What Is Missing? Foundation, New York, NY, $25,000. For the development of core media content. 2010.

1638-137 WildAid, San Francisco, CA, $200,000. For 5 TO DO TODAY campaign in China for energy conservation to combat climate change. 2010.

1638-138 Wilderness Foundation, Port Elizabeth, South Africa, $40,000. For project, The Development of a Universal Declaration of the Rights of Mother Earth. 2010.

1638-139 Woodrow Wilson International Center for Scholars, Washington, DC, $25,000. For public diplomacy initiative working group. 2010.

1638-140 World Resources Institute, Washington, DC, $100,000. For U.S.-China Climate and Energy Information Network: Advancing Climate Protection through Better Information. 2010.

1638-141 World Resources Institute, Washington, DC, $70,000. For the International Financial Flows and Environment Project of its Institutions and Governance Program, for its work on emerging financial actors and social and environmental safeguards. 2010.

1638-142 Yunnan Health and Development Research Association, Kunming, China, $150,000. For general support for work on environment and health. 2010.

1639
The Rockefeller Foundation
420 5th Ave.
New York, NY 10018-2702 (212) 869-8500
URL: http://www.rockefellerfoundation.org/
E-Newsletter: http://www.rockefellerfoundation.org/sign-up
Facebook: http://www.facebook.com/rockefellerfoundation
Grants Database: http://www.rockefellerfoundation.org/grants/search
Multimedia: http://www.rockefellerfoundation.org/news/multimedia
RSS Feed: http://www.rockefellerfoundation.org/rockfound.xml

Incorporated in 1913 in NY.
Donor: John D. Rockefeller, Sr.†.
Grantmaker type: Independent foundation.
Financial data (yr. ended 12/31/10): Assets, $3,593,289,629 (M); expenditures, $190,391,999; qualifying distributions, $176,058,849; giving activities include $133,475,179 for 596 grants (high: $6,000,000; low: $340), $244,600 for 7 grants to individuals, $1,734,190 for 285 employee matching gifts, $3,954,257 for 1 foundation-administered program and $1,132,991 for loans/program-related investments.
Purpose and activities: Operating both within the United States and around the world, the Rockefeller Foundation supports work that expands opportunity and strengthens resilience to social, economic, health and environmental challenges-affirming its pioneering philanthropic mission since 1913 to "promote the well-being" of humanity.
Fields of interest: International economic development; Health care; Environment, climate change/global warming; Community/economic development.
International interests: Global programs.
Type of support: General/operating support; Continuing support; Program development; Conferences/seminars; Publication; Seed money; Curriculum development; Fellowships; Research; Technical assistance; Program-related investments/loans; Employee matching gifts; Scholarships—to individuals.
Limitations: Applications accepted. Giving primarily in New York City, Africa, North America, and Southeast Asia. No grants to individuals for personal aid, or, except in rare cases, for endowment funds or building or operating funds.
Publications: Annual report (including application guidelines); Financial statement; Grants list.
Application information: Organizations submitting inquiries that foundation staff thinks might contribute to a defined area of work will be asked to submit a full proposal. Please do not send a proposal by mail or e-mail unless invited to do so. See foundation web site for the Ballagio Center application information. Application form not required.
   Initial approach: Online funding inquiry form
   Copies of proposal: 1
   Board meeting date(s): Apr., Aug., and Dec.
   Final notification: 6 to 8 weeks
Officers and Trustees:* David Rockefeller, Jr.,* Chair.; Dr. Judith Rodin,* Pres.; Peter Madonia, C.O.O.; Heather Grady, V.P., Fdn. Initiatives; Zia Khan, V.P., Strategy and Eval.; Shari L. Patrick, Genl. Counsel and Corp. Secy.; Ellen Taus, C.F.O. and Treas.; Donna Dean, C.I.O.; Ann M. Fudge; Helene D. Gayle; Thomas J. Healey; Alice S. Huang; Strive Masiyiwa; Diana Natalicio; Sandra Day O'Connor; Dr. Ngozi Okonjo-Iweala; Richard D. Parsons; Surin Pitsuwan; John W. Rowe.
Number of staff: 171 full-time professional; 2 part-time professional.
EIN: 131659629
Recent grants for international programs:
1639-1 Access Health International, Washington, DC, $153,100. For project, as member organization of Center for Health Market Innovations, to identify, map, track and analyze innovative private sector health organizations and programs in Brazil and Bangladesh, foster links among key stakeholders and cultivate future support for this sector. 2010.

1639-2 African Center for Economic Transformation, Washington, DC, $85,000. For project to conduct trend monitoring and horizon scanning on issues relevant to poverty and human development, focused on West Africa. 2010.

1639-3 African Center for Economic Transformation, Washington, DC, $30,500. For study to map efforts related to strengthening health systems in Ghana and more broadly in sub-Saharan Africa and to identify research needed for knowledge base capable of serving as resource for informed national policy choices that will improve access to universal health coverage for poor and vulnerable people. 2010.

1639-4 African Centre for Global Health and Social Transformation, Kampala, Uganda, $613,800. Toward Secretariat to coordinate African Network for Health Systems Governance, regional effort to improve health and health systems performance by supporting capacity, expertise and leadership development within Ministries of Health in Africa. 2010.

1639-5 African Health Economics and Policy Association, Croydon, England, $69,500. To engage Accenture Development Partnerships to develop plan to promote and strengthen capacity to conduct health economics and policy analysis in order to improve health outcomes in African countries. 2010.

1639-6 African Technology Policy Studies Network, Nairobi, Kenya, $75,952. For workshop, Strengthening Linkages between Policy Research and Policymaking for African Development, to be held in Mombasa, Kenya. 2010.

1639-7 Agora Partnerships, Washington, DC, $200,000. Toward Accelerator initiative, which seeks to leverage impact investing to support small and growing businesses that, through their operations, generate social, environmental and economic impact for poor and vulnerable populations in El Salvador, Honduras and Nicaragua and to encourage adoption of Global Impact Investment Rating System (GIIRS) in Central America and Mexico. 2010.

1639-8 Alliance for a Green Revolution in Africa, Nairobi, Kenya, $8,000,000. Toward Market Access Program to direct investments and resources to improve market infrastructure for core food staples of selected countries in Africa, leading to increased incomes for smallholder farmers. 2010.

1639-9 American Planning Association, Washington, DC, $25,000. For travel scholarships for delegates from Latin America to attend conference launching Ashoka Changemakers' Sustainable and Inclusive Housing and Livable Cities Challenge, to be held in Sao Paulo, Brazil. 2010.

1639-10 Arsom Silp Institute of the Arts, Bangkok, Thailand, $85,000. To develop preservation and restoration activities and guidelines in two historic Thai neighborhoods - one in Bangkok and one in the province of Chanthaburi - by making use of multi-stakeholder participatory process. 2010.

1639-11 Ashoka: Innovators for the Public, Arlington, VA, $510,000. For Changemakers Initiative, in collaboration with member governments of Group of 20, in support of the design and launch of inclusive global competition to identify innovative ideas for investing in small- and medium-scale businesses whose growth can promote pro-poor development either through job- and income-generation or the provision of services at affordable prices. 2010.

1639-12 Ashoka: Innovators for the Public, Arlington, VA, $499,000. For Changemakers Initiative in support of Sustainable and Inclusive Housing and Livable Cities Challenge, collaborative competition for innovations in sustainable housing design for Latin America and the Caribbean and Sustainable Housing Solutions Guide for innovators, entrepreneurs, investors and consumers addressing urban housing issues. 2010.

1639-13 Asia Foundation, San Francisco, CA, $164,750. For project, as member organization within Center for Health Market Innovations, to identify, map, track and analyze innovative private sector health organizations and programs in Pakistan, to foster links among key stakeholders and to cultivate additional future support for this sector. 2010.

1639-14 Asia Society, New York, NY, $100,000. Toward Nine Lives: In Search of the Sacred in Modern India, readings and performances based on William Dalrymple's book, which examines the way social changes have affected great Indian traditions of mysticism, monasticism, music and dance. 2010.

1639-15 Asian Disaster Preparedness Center, Bangkok, Thailand, $96,440. To develop and implement training course on climate and disaster risk management and provide technical assistance to Asian Cities Climate Change Resilience Network (ACCCRN) partners. 2010.

1639-16 Aspen Institute, Congressional Program, Washington, DC, $250,000. Toward nonpartisan project to educate members of the U.S. Congress on confluence of forces, including transportation, that impact energy security and climate change. 2010.

1639-17 Aspen Institute, Philanthropy and Social Innovation Program, Washington, DC, $500,000. Toward designing and implementing new initiative on social enterprise and the impact economy to create a more robust enabling environment for market-based models and private sector mechanisms that address social challenges and advance social goals. 2010.

1639-18 Bangabandhu Sheikh Mujib Medical University, Dhaka, Bangladesh, $400,420. For project to launch new Department of Public Health and Informatics in Bangladesh. 2010.

1639-19 Bangladesh Enterprise Institute, Dhaka, Bangladesh, $204,000. To develop scenario planning workshop for future of eHealth in Bangladesh, organizing mHealth (mobile health) innovators student competition and drafting of national strategy for eHealth in Bangladesh. 2010.

1639-20 Bloodlink Foundation, Nairobi, Kenya, $76,100. To launch and implement FrontlineSMS mobile-phone-based feedback and reminder system to track and manage blood donors in Kenya, increasing regular donation rate needed for a safe, steady supply of blood in its healthcare system. FrontlineSMS is free, open source software that turns a laptop and a mobile phone into a central communications hub. 2010.

1639-21 BRAC, Dhaka, Bangladesh, $200,000. For use by Manoshi Maternal and Neonatal Care Service Delivery Program, in collaboration with ClickDiagnostics Inc., toward scaling up mHealth (mobile health) application for community health workers. 2010.

1639-22 BRAC University, BRAC Development Institute, Dhaka, Bangladesh, $29,850. Toward conference, Transcending Binaries: The Politics of Islam in South Asia to be held in Dhaka, Bangladesh. 2010.

1639-23 Bridges Ventures Limited, London, England, $10,000. Toward disseminating collection of case studies of impact investments across asset classes that will inform impact investing community about opportunities to increase flow of capital to address pressing social challenges faced by poor and vulnerable people. 2010.

1639-24 Brookings Institution, African Growth Initiative, Washington, DC, $307,300. To raise visibility among African policymakers and international researchers of Africa-based researchers doing policy relevant work on African growth and structural transformation by convening its inaugural annual growth forum, to be held in Washington, DC. 2010.

1639-25 Calvert Social Investment Foundation, Bethesda, MD, $268,200. For research with actionable insights on current and potential impact investment vehicles that could be offered to non-accredited investors, in order to inform efforts to increase significantly the flow of capital to benefit poor and vulnerable communities globally. 2010.

1639-26 Calvert Social Investment Foundation, Enterprise Innovation Fund, Bethesda, MD, $124,500. Toward symposium to enlist support, feedback and expertise from key leaders from multiple sectors in establishing public-private partnership that will strengthen and catalyze impact investing in social enterprises that seek to solve social and environmental problems that address needs of poor and vulnerable people. 2010.

1639-27 CARE USA, Poverty, Environment and Climate Change Network, Atlanta, GA, $494,000. To develop and implement sustainable agriculture and land management carbon project in western Kenya. 2010.

1639-28 Carleton University, Centre for Trade Policy and Law, Ottawa, Canada, $218,950. Toward project to strengthen emerging Global Health Diplomacy Network by creating and maintaining website for collecting and disseminating key information about current global health diplomacy negotiations and other issues. 2010.

1639-29 Carleton University, Centre for Trade Policy and Law, Ottawa, Canada, $160,500. Toward Interim Secretariat to support activities of Global Health Diplomacy Network. 2010.

1639-30 Carnegie Endowment for International Peace, Washington, DC, $150,000. To organize four conferences and meetings to advance vision of pioneering global think tank committed to collaborative international research, analysis and policy work, to be held at Rockefeller Foundation Bellagio Center. 2010.

1639-31 Cedar Associates, LLC, Menlo Park, CA, $169,100. For study to document and verify scope of benefits available within national health coverage programs in low- and middle-income countries, including identification of factors that influenced those coverage decisions and publishing results in order to provide evidence-based resource for developing strategies to strengthen health systems and increase access to care. 2010.

1639-32 Center for Creative Initiatives in Health and Population, Hanoi, Vietnam, $160,160. For project, as member organization within Center for Health Market Innovations, to identify, map, track and analyze innovative private sector health organizations and programs in Vietnam and Cambodia, to foster links among key stakeholders and to cultivate additional future support for this sector. 2010.

1639-33 Center for National Policy, Washington, DC, $499,241. For Global Summit on Resilience, to mark 10th anniversary of the September 11 terrorist attacks, showcase ongoing, new and planned resilience efforts including initiatives on climate adaptation and global economic development and offer templates for successful resilience building activities that can be pursued on a national and international scale. 2010.

1639-34 Center for the Advancement of Women, New York, NY, $50,000. For general support to promote and protect women's rights and opportunities, worldwide, by conducting national opinion research among women to measure experiences in their daily lives in order to present a profile of women that is used to educate opinion leaders, policymakers and the general public. 2010.

1639-35 Centre for Democracy and Development, Nigeria, Abuja, Nigeria, $85,900. For project to conduct trend monitoring and horizon scanning on issues relevant to poverty and human development, focused on West Africa. 2010.

1639-36 Centre for Health and Social Services, Accra, Ghana, $69,445. Toward engaging Accenture Development Partnerships to develop strategic plan Centre and outline growth strategy to promote and strengthen capacity to conduct research, develop evidence and provide policy analysis that supports strengthening of health systems in Africa. 2010.

1639-37 CEOs for Cities, Chicago, IL, $59,900. To address urban poverty and sustainability and resilience of cities by convening international urban and governance experts to develop parameters of roles and responsibilities of cities and city-wide actors and to identify individuals or institutions that can further define these roles. 2010.

1639-38 CERES, Boston, MA, $400,000. Toward improving stewardship of water resources by large companies operating in water-stressed regions throughout the world and encouraging best practices by companies on a broad range of sustainability issues worldwide. 2010.

1639-39 Cherie Blair Foundation for Women, London, England, $120,000. Toward hiring program manager for Women Entrepreneurs and Mobile Technology Program, which seeks to provide women with improved access to mobile phones as a way to develop and improve their entrepreneurial ventures in the Middle East, South Asia and sub-Saharan Africa. 2010.

1639-40 Chiang Mai University, Faculty of Veterinary Medicine, Chiang Mai, Thailand, $45,130. Toward convening international training course on One Health Leadership to be held in Chiang Mai, Thailand. 2010.

1639-41 Childline Kenya, Nairobi, Kenya, $403,800. To professionalize and increase efficiency of toll-free child abuse hotline to ensure better response and support to vulnerable children in Kenya. 2010.

1639-42 Chulalongkorn University, Department of Urban and Regional Planning, Bangkok, Thailand, $45,360. Toward support of lecture series on inequality and injustice in access to resources and basic services in Thailand. 2010.

1639-43 Chulalongkorn University, Department of Urban and Regional Planning, Bangkok, Thailand, $43,890. To explore approaches for arts to serve as tool for community revitalization in two Bangkok neighborhoods and to share lessons learned to inform policymaking. 2010.

1639-44 City Parks Alliance, Washington, DC, $100,000. Toward International Urban Parks Conference: Leveraging the Power of Parks, to address role parks can play in solving challenges faced by cities, to be held in New York City. 2010.

1639-45 Claremont Graduate University, School of Behavioral and Organizational Sciences, Claremont, CA, $350,000. To provide grantees and partners, particularly those in Africa and Asia, with better tools to design strategies and evaluation practices around the kind of complex outcomes that are common to the Foundation's Initiatives. 2010.

1639-46 Clinton Health Access Initiative, Boston, MA, $311,300. Toward collaboration with Kenya's Ministries of Medical Services and Public Health and Sanitation to develop and launch open standard automated system for annual operational planning activities facilitating faster, informed-response capacity by health system at local and national levels. 2010.

1639-47 Columbia University, Earth Institute's Tropical Agriculture and Rural Environment Program, New York, NY, $250,000. Toward Meeting the Challenge of 2050: Intelligent Agriculture and Food Systems to Feed the Global Population, program to continue development of sustainable food and agriculture systems and to launch university-wide Center for Agriculture and Food Systems. 2010.

1639-48 Columbia University, Mailman School of Public Health, New York, NY, $500,000. For support of three projects designed to strengthen health systems and related activities: 1) conference on scaling up HIV/AIDS services in sub-Saharan Africa to be held at Rockefeller Foundation Bellagio Center, Italy; 2) effort to identify new funders of health systems and universal health coverage; and 3) conference on the Changing Landscape of Global Public Health, to be held in New York City. 2010.

1639-49 Crown Agents for Oversea Governments and Administrations, Legal Division, Sutton, England, $500,000. Toward launching Secretariat to coordinate Harnessing Non-State Actors for Better Health for the Poor (HANSHEP) project, partnership to enable pooled donor funds and expertise to support innovative private sector health programs and approaches globally. 2010.

1639-50 Dalberg Consulting CC, Johannesburg, South Africa, $122,350. For scoping study in West Africa to identify current impact investing activities, key players, successes, failures, lessons learned, policy issues, and steps required to grow the sector for the benefit of poor and vulnerable populations in the region. 2010.

1639-51 Diabetic Association of Bangladesh, Dhaka, Bangladesh, $450,000. Toward work of Bangladesh Institute of Sciences to establish Department of Health Informatics to launch Masters of Science curriculum on health informatics. 2010.

1639-52 Digital Divide Data, New York, NY, $895,000. To establish program in Kenya to operate local impact outsourcing centers employing disadvantaged youth, host management training institute to build capacity of impact outsourcing managers and conduct market research to understand the emerging sector. 2010.

1639-53 Duke University, Center for the Advancement of Social Entrepreneurship, Fuqua School of Business, Durham, NC, $84,500. To support planning potential multi-year effort to research trends and lessons for field of impact investing from data gathered by two impact rating systems, B Lab's B Corporations and the Global Impact Investing Ratings System. 2010.

1639-54 E and Co, Bloomfield, NJ, $300,000. Toward transitioning to new organizational model that will promote aggregation of capital to scale new clean energy enterprises serving poor, environmentally vulnerable people in Africa, Asia and Latin America. 2010.

1639-55 East Africa Association of Grantmakers, Nairobi, Kenya, $125,000. For research to study state and nature of philanthropy in East Africa in effort to develop evidence-based programs for informing and promoting philanthropy in the region. 2010.

1639-56 East, Central and Southern African Health Community, Arusha, Tanzania, Zanzibar and Pemba, $238,120. For initiative to strengthen leadership and increase capacity and strategic information resources at Ministries of Health in East, Central and Southern African countries in order to maximize benefits from future negotiations related to global health diplomacy. 2010.

1639-57 EcoHealth Alliance, New York, NY, $216,200. To develop feasibility plan for launching new disease surveillance network, One Health Alliance of South Asia (OHASA), in conjunction with stakeholders in Bangladesh, India and Pakistan. 2010.

1639-58 Egerton University, Egerton, Kenya, $483,900. For initiative to help farmers and pastoralists in Kenya to adequately adapt to climate change as part of effort to lead a regional climate change adaptation movement. 2010.

1639-59 Egerton University, Tegemeo Institute of Agricultural Policy and Development, Egerton, Kenya, $297,500. To support building institutional capacity in climate change research and analysis by conducting socio-economic study on effects of climate change on rural communities in Kenya and identifying adaptation responses. 2010.

1639-60 Energy and Resources Institute, New Delhi, India, $100,000. Toward 2010 Delhi Sustainable Development Summit, international forum for analysis and debate on climate change mitigation and adaptation, to be held in New Delhi, India. 2010.

1639-61 Ethiopian Institute of Agricultural Research, Addis Ababa, Ethiopia, $420,000. For mainstreaming of climate change adaptation into food security and sustainable development in Ethiopia. 2010.

1639-62 Farm Concern International, Nairobi, Kenya, $75,000. For project to design, test and implement pilot projects in order to develop business model for expanding youth participation in agricultural systems in Kenya as means to address anticipated future youth unemployment and low agricultural productivity. 2010.

1639-63 Financial Sector Deepening Trust Tanzania, Dar es Salaam, Tanzania, Zanzibar and Pemba, $250,000. Toward study of agriculture finance in Tanzania that aims to encourage increased lending and investment in the agricultural sector to improve the livelihoods and incomes of local smallholder farmers. 2010.

1639-64 Financial Times Limited, London, England, $69,600. For use by This is Africa publication in support of baseline research, publication and supplemental articles about impact investing in Africa that will enhance profile of the industry and deepen the understanding of how impact investment in Africa can benefit the poor and vulnerable. 2010.

1639-65 Forest Trends Association, Washington, DC, $600,000. To launch African Agriculture Climate Finance Facility (AACFF) in two countries in effort to innovate, test and document new set of transaction models that can be used to access carbon and climate finance sources for smallholder farmer-driven agricultural climate mitigation and adaptation projects. 2010.

1639-66 FORO Nacional Internacional, Lima, Peru, $159,400. For project to conduct trend monitoring and horizon scanning research on issues relevant to poverty and human development, focused on South America. 2010.

1639-67 Forum for African Women Educationalists, Nairobi, Kenya, $100,000. For general support of mission to promote gender equity and equality in education in Africa by fostering positive policies, practices and attitudes toward girls' education. 2010.

1639-68 Foundation Center, New York, NY, $100,000. Toward building global data platform for philanthropy that will enhance accessibility of information on philanthropic activity around the world. 2010.

1639-69 Freedom from Hunger, Davis, CA, $248,600. For project, as member organization of Center for Health Market Innovations, to identify, map, track and analyze innovative private sector health organizations and programs in the Andes region of Latin America and foster links among key stakeholders to cultivate additional future support for this sector. 2010.

1639-70 Global Healthcare Information Network, Charlbury, England, $50,000. For project to develop monitoring and evaluation framework and process for Health Information for All by 2015 (HIFA2015) online network, which is committed to promoting access to reliable healthcare information for healthcare providers in developing countries. 2010.

1639-71 GlobalGiving Foundation, Washington, DC, $150,000. For Phase II of project that will make use of stories and short narratives to develop evaluation tool to improve monitoring and evaluation capability, increase accountability to donors, recognize social change and impact that have resulted from projects in Africa supported through its marketplace, improve organizational performance, and share methodology and lessons learned with the broader not-for-profit community. 2010.

1639-72 Goldmark Productions, Richmond Hill, Canada, $70,354. For radio and online segments covering important trends in impact investing to be aired as part of American Public Media's Marketplace programming, in order to educate the public about the opportunities for social benefit and financial return from impact investing. 2010.

1639-73 Gorakhpur Environmental Action Group, Gorakhpur, India, $479,150. To develop model for ward-level climate change resilience planning that can be integrated into the overall development planning process in Gorakhpur, India, as part of Asian Cities Climate Change Resilience Network. 2010.

1639-74 Graduate Institute of International and Development Studies, Geneva, Switzerland, $205,000. For conference for authors contributing to a textbook on Global Health Diplomacy and for training of trainer's workshop - both to be held at the Rockefeller Foundation Bellagio Center, Italy. 2010.

1639-75 Grameen Foundation USA, Washington, DC, $252,486. For demonstration project, in collaboration with BASIX in India, to test sustainable business model for providing financial and livelihood development services to the poorest populations in a way that benefits the poor and the institution providing the services. 2010.

1639-76 Growth Philanthropy Network, New York, NY, $300,000. Toward Social Impact Exchange initiative to develop practices for studying, implementing and funding large-scale expansions of top-performing social purpose organizations that seek to solve social and environmental problems that affect poor and vulnerable people. 2010.

1639-77 GSMA Foundation, Atlanta, GA, $50,000. For use by GSMA Development Fund, toward book that chronicles innovative development of mobile-phone based money transfer platform mPesa, and its transformative impact on poor and vulnerable people in Kenya. 2010.

1639-78 GuideStar International, London, England, $77,000. For continuing development of Guidestar India, searchable online database that provides philanthropic sector in India with better access to information on credible non-government organizations. 2010.

1639-79 Habitat for Humanity International, Atlanta, GA, $165,000. To facilitate and administer activities at World Urban Forum, conference to address rapid urbanization and its impact on communities, cities, economies, climate change and policies, to be held in Rio de Janeiro, Brazil. 2010.

1639-80 Hanoi Medical University, Hanoi, Vietnam, $301,640. Toward establishing Center for Health System Research to promote implementation of evidence-based health policies in Vietnam. 2010.

1639-81 Hanoi School of Public Health, Hanoi, Vietnam, $500,000. For project to develop and implement Bachelor's degree program in public health informatics in Vietnam. 2010.

1639-82 Hanoi School of Public Health, Hanoi, Vietnam, $285,000. To build capacity to foster Universal Health Coverage with emphasis on health economics and health financing through staff training and curriculum development. 2010.

1639-83 Harvard University, School of Public Health, Cambridge, MA, $250,000. Toward support of planning process to determine need for and design of new initiative to translate global health research evidence into policy recommendations for country-level health systems strengthening implementation efforts. 2010.

1639-84 Heartfile, Inc., Islamabad, Pakistan, $25,000. For two-day meeting to conduct peer reviews of four papers for possible publication in the Lancet focused on health systems in Pakistan. 2010.

1639-85 ICLEI Australia/New Zealand, Melbourne, Australia, $180,000. Toward developing and testing set of calibrated tools, materials and processes for engaging new cities in India in understanding challenges and opportunities for addressing urban climate change resilience, in order to disseminate the lessons from and begin to replicate the successes of the Asian Cities Climate Change Resilience Network. 2010.

1639-86 Indian School of Business, Center for Emerging Market Solutions, Hyderabad, India, $250,000. Toward research, analysis and convenings focused on urbanization and affordable housing in India. 2010.

1639-87 Institute for Social and Environmental Transition, Boulder, CO, $1,582,240. To establish city climate change coordination offices in three Vietnamese cities (Can Tho, Da Nang and Quy Nhon) that will enable local government planning, decision making and policy implementation for climate change resilience and adaptation that is consistent with requirements of Vietnam National Target Program for Climate Change, as part of Asian Cities Climate Change Resilience Network (ACCCRN). 2010.

1639-88 Institute for Social and Environmental Transition, Boulder, CO, $1,300,000. To collect and analyze evidence documenting effectiveness of Asian Cities Climate Change Resilience Network (ACCCRN) methodologies and interventions for replication, and including dissemination of lessons and tools for adoption by other local, national and international actors through variety of peer-reviewed products and publications. 2010.

1639-89 Institute for Social and Environmental Transition, Boulder, CO, $781,790. To assist three cities in Vietnam - Can Tho, Da Nang and Quy Nhon - to plan and implement climate resilience projects, provide project management and financial oversight for resilience projects, map key climate change policies and networks and identify new sources of funding, as part of Asian Cities Climate Change Resilience Network (ACCCRN). 2010.

1639-90 Institute for Social and Environmental Transition, Boulder, CO, $367,160. For project, in collaboration with Da Nang University and city agencies in Da Nang, Vietnam, to build, test and share data from two hydrological models to understand impacts of urban development and climate change in the city, partial participant in Asian Cities Climate Change Resilience Network (ACCCRN). 2010.

1639-91 Institute for Social and Environmental Transition, Boulder, CO, $337,800. For impact assessment of flooding and inundation scenarios on planned urban development in Nhon Binh Ward in the city of Quy Nhon, Vietnam, in context of potential climate change impact and recent extreme storm events, in connection with Asian Cities Climate Change Resilience Network (ACCCRN). 2010.

1639-92 Institute for Social and Environmental Transition, Boulder, CO, $69,920. For feasibility study of ways to provide livelihood skills, technologies and storm-resistant building techniques to poor female-headed households in Da Nang City, Vietnam. 2010.

1639-93 Institute for the Future, Palo Alto, CA, $298,500. For project to synthesize and visualize trend and horizon scanning information on issues relevant to poverty and human development through signals database, web-based map and interactive game platform. 2010.

1639-94 Institute for the Future, Palo Alto, CA, $94,200. For project to conduct research and create forecast map on cities, information systems and citizen engagement that focuses on emerging technologies and poor and vulnerable in the developed and the developing world. 2010.

1639-95 Institute of Health Policy, Management and Research, Nairobi, Kenya, $196,160. For project, as member organization of Center for Health Market Innovations, to identify, map, track and analyze innovative private sector health organizations and programs in east Africa, foster links among key stakeholders and cultivate future support for this sector. 2010.

1639-96 Institute of International Education, New York, NY, $1,217,000. Toward administering several activities related to Rockefeller Foundation Bellagio Center, Italy including semi-annual competitions for creative arts and scholarly residencies, Bellagio Travel and Learning Fund and support for outreach activities. 2010.

1639-97 Institute of International Education, New York, NY, $91,900. Toward administering selection process for 2011 Bellagio Creative Arts Fellows program and producing brochure of the work created by 2009 fellowship recipients while in residency at Rockefeller Foundation Bellagio Center. 2010.

1639-98 Intellecap, Palo Alto, CA, $500,000. Toward organizing Sankalp Social Enterprise and Investment Forum, to bring together stakeholders in Asia to share information on how market-based mechanisms can provide efficient and innovative solutions that address needs of poor and vulnerable people. 2010.

1639-99 Intellecap, Palo Alto, CA, $345,800. Toward project to conduct trend monitoring and horizon scanning research on issues relevant to poverty and human development, focused on India, Bangladesh and Pakistan, and meeting of Searchlight grantees to be held in Mumbai, India. 2010.

1639-100 InterAction: American Council for Voluntary International Action, Evaluation and Program Effectiveness Working Group, Washington, DC, $171,200. To improve capacity of non-governmental organizations globally to conduct impact evaluations, through production of guidance notes and webinar series. 2010.

1639-101 International Bank for Reconstruction and Development, Independent Evaluation Group, Washington, DC, $500,000. Toward Centers for Learning on Evaluation and Results, to support development and implementation of four Centers - in Africa, East Asia, and South Asia - to strengthen monitoring and evaluation and results based management capacity of public and private development institutions working in the Global South. 2010.

1639-102 International Centre for Diarrheal Disease Research, Bangladesh, Dhaka, Bangladesh, $2,283,000. To launch, in collaboration with BRAC University, Centre of Excellence on Universal Health Coverage at James P. Grant School of Public Health in Bangladesh. 2010.

1639-103 International Centre for Diarrheal Disease Research, Bangladesh, Dhaka, Bangladesh, $307,270. For project to develop and implement pilot health insurance scheme in Bangladesh. 2010.

1639-104 International Centre for Diarrheal Disease Research, Bangladesh, Dhaka, Bangladesh, $95,000. Toward publication and dissemination of special issue of The Lancet focusing on various aspects of health in Bangladesh. 2010.

1639-105 International Centre for Diarrheal Disease Research, Bangladesh, Dhaka, Bangladesh, $70,000. For site visits to India and Thailand to study their respective national health insurance schemes and post-visit workshop to integrate lessons learned for achieving universal health coverage. 2010.

1639-106 International Health Policy Program Thailand, Nonthaburi, Thailand, $25,000. For attendance of 12-15 Asian participants at Fifth Asia-Pacific Action Alliance on Human Resources for Health conference to be held in Bali, Indonesia. 2010.

1639-107 International Housing Coalition, Washington, DC, $152,600. To develop educational activities and resources, including issue-oriented advocacy campaigns, topical seminars and web-based platform, to disseminate research on importance and impact of housing and urban issues to policy makers, development practitioners and leaders in developing countries. 2010.

1639-108 International Institute for Environment and Development, London, England, $175,000. For research on urban adaptation to climate change for incorporation into Fifth Assessment of the Intergovernmental Panel on Climate Change. 2010.

1639-109 Jazz at Lincoln Center, New York, NY, $50,000. Toward Orchestra's week-long residency in Cuba and related programs exploring the musical connections among Havana, New Orleans and New York City. 2010.

1639-110 Kenya Community Development Foundation, Nairobi, Kenya, $103,000. For use by African Grantmakers Network toward inaugural Pan African Assembly, which aims to strengthen network of African grantmaking organizations and create common strategy for advocacy of philanthropy within Africa, to be held in Nairobi, Kenya. 2010.

1639-111 Keystone Accountability, London, England, $50,000. Toward developing and implementing impact investing survey that will enable social enterprises to increase performance measurement and effectiveness. 2010.

1639-112 Lions Head Global Partners LLP, London, England, $450,000. To develop and syndicate guiding principles and framework for impact investing in African agriculture as means to ensure that socially- and environmentally-oriented capital is deployed to improve African food security and increase incomes for the poor and vulnerable. 2010.

1639-113 London School of Hygiene and Tropical Medicine, London, England, $253,170. For project to strengthen evidence base related to global health diplomacy and to plan for further research that supports the goals of the Global Health Diplomacy Network. 2010.

1639-114 Mahidol University, Institute for Population and Social Research, Nakhon Pathom, Thailand, $175,000. To strengthen emerging Global Health Diplomacy Network by supporting expansion of work into Southeast

Asia and organize meeting to enhance local capacity to be held at Rockefeller Foundation Bellagio Center. 2010.

1639-115 Maker Faire Africa Foundation, Amsterdam, Netherlands, $150,000. Toward Maker Faire 2011 and 2012, annual event that convenes innovators from around Africa and links them with mentors who can help bring their innovations to scale, to help spur entrepreneurship and manufacturing as a poverty reduction vehicle for the African continent. 2010.

1639-116 Makerere University, School of Public Health, Kampala, Uganda, $150,000. For use by Leadership Initiative for Public Health in East Africa in support of Health Emergency Management Program's efforts to build disease outbreak response and emergency management capacity in district health teams in Eastern Africa. 2010.

1639-117 Mary Robinson Foundation, Dublin, Ireland, $149,500. For work to build women's leadership in the area of climate justice and in particular, including gender and climate perspective in negotiations at 16th United Nations Framework Convention on Climate Change. 2010.

1639-118 Massachusetts Institute of Technology, Department of Urban Studies and Planning, Cambridge, MA, $65,000. For use by SENSEable City Lab in support of conference to begin mapping plan to establish new international research network or center focused on cultivating vision of the future city and, in particular, the impacts of technology on cities. 2010.

1639-119 McGill University, McGill World Platform for Health and Economic Convergence, Montreal, Canada, $161,000. To convene meeting on intersections of the business sector and the global health diplomacy field, to be held at Rockefeller Foundation Bellagio Center, Italy. 2010.

1639-120 McKinsey and Company, New York, NY, $100,000. For landscape analysis of current and nascent technologies that cities and their residents in the U.S. and globally can use to collect and analyze city-level information and of key drivers, trends and leverage points related to application of such technologies to cities. 2010.

1639-121 Mercy Corps, Portland, OR, $785,780. To assist two cities in Indonesia (Semerang and Bandar Lampung) to plan and implement climate resilience projects, map key climate change policies and networks and identify new sources of funding, as part of Asian Cities Climate Change Resilience Network. 2010.

1639-122 Mercy Corps, Portland, OR, $249,180. For project, as member organization within Center for Health Market Innovations, to identify, map, track and analyze innovative private sector health organizations and programs in Indonesia, to foster links among key stakeholders and to cultivate additional future support for this sector. 2010.

1639-123 Mercy Corps, Portland, OR, $233,530. To incorporate climate change and urban growth considerations into development of Integrated Solid Waste Management master plan, as well as assessment of solid waste management technology, in Bandar Lampung City, Indonesia, as part of Asian Cities Climate Change Resilience Network. 2010.

1639-124 Mercy Corps, Portland, OR, $189,520. For pre-feasibility study of potential for rainwater harvest to be available and effective alternative source of (domestic and drinking) water in Semarang City, Indonesia, as part of Asian Cities Climate Change Resilience Network. 2010.

1639-125 Meridian Institute, Dillon, CO, $193,600. Toward Global Dialogue on Agriculture and Climate Change, initiative that seeks to include agriculture as major mitigation and adaptation strategy in international climate negotiations, including convening of key stakeholders at the Rockefeller Foundation Bellagio Center, Italy. 2010.

1639-126 Meridian Institute, Dillon, CO, $150,000. For series of convenings to engage systems experts in effort to explore role of systems thinking in solving complex global problems. 2010.

1639-127 Meridian Institute, Dillon, CO, $100,000. Toward launching Initiative on Food and Agriculture Policy (IFAP), effort to develop donor coalition to examine opportunities where U.S. farm, food and climate change policy reforms could help break cycles of hunger in developing countries. 2010.

1639-128 Microfinance Information Exchange, Washington, DC, $187,600. To collaborate with Global Impact Investing Network to develop data-sharing platform that will enable exchange of performance data on microfinance and the broader field of impact investing to lead to better outcomes for poor and vulnerable populations. 2010.

1639-129 Millennium Project Corporation, Washington, DC, $124,700. For project to assist in improving capacity of developing countries to conduct futures research by providing targeted travel support for participants from developing countries to attend Millennium Project Planning Committee Meeting, to be held in Boston and to create long-term financial sustainability and feasibility plan for the organization. 2010.

1639-130 Ministry of Health of Ghana, Private Sector Unit, Accra, Ghana, $257,900. To incubate Private Health Sector Alliance of Ghana and support further development of appropriate private sector policy to coordinate and leverage public and private sectors' collective capacities to improve national health care services and accessibility. 2010.

1639-131 Monitor Group, Cambridge, MA, $585,000. For research project exploring the potential of outsourcing employment opportunities for providing jobs and economic growth to very poor populations in emerging economies in India and Kenya. 2010.

1639-132 Monitor Group, Cambridge, MA, $354,000. To monitor and evaluate unintended consequences of low-income housing projects for urban poor in India, and develop approaches to address negative consequences of them and propagate strategies for improving them. 2010.

1639-133 Monitor Group, Cambridge, MA, $300,000. Toward research to identify and document new business models and market-based solutions for development and poverty alleviation for poor and vulnerable populations in Africa. 2010.

1639-134 Museum of Arts and Design, New York, NY, $75,000. Toward organization and presentation of Global Africa Project, exhibition focusing on aspects of contemporary design, craft and art by individuals working in Africa, Asia, the Caribbean, Europe and the United States whose work exemplifies the creativity coming out of or inspired by Africa. 2010.

1639-135 Museum of Contemporary African Diasporian Arts, Brooklyn, NY, $175,000. Toward Soul of Brooklyn, consortium of 22 African Diaspora Arts Organizations working to brand Brooklyn as the destination for unique and authentic African diasporan cultural experience. Grant made as part of New York City Cultural Innovation Fund Award Program. 2010.

1639-136 National Bureau of Asian Research, Seattle, WA, $50,000. For workshop on current efforts to implement universal health coverage through lens of maternal and newborn health at 2010 Pacific Health Summit to be held in London. 2010.

1639-137 National Institute of Development Administration, Centre for Philanthropy and Civil Society, Bangkok, Thailand, $19,000. Toward travel support for representatives from Thai NGOs to attend International Anti-Corruption Conference, to be held in Bangkok. 2010.

1639-138 National Museums of Kenya, Nairobi, Kenya, $50,000. To construct canopy for open-air amphitheatre that will optimize use of the space for visitors to the museum including audiences attending educational and cultural events. 2010.

1639-139 National Religious Partnership for the Environment, Amherst, MA, $80,100. For Conference on International Adaptation to highlight need for greater policy support and financing for international climate change adaptation efforts, to be held in Washington, D.C. 2010.

1639-140 National University of Rwanda, School of Public Health, Butare, Rwanda, $964,340. To support launch Centre of Excellence in Health Systems Strengthening to benefit health professionals and practitioners in East and Central Africa. 2010.

1639-141 National Womens Law Center, Washington, DC, $100,000. Toward collaboration with American Civil Liberties Union, Citizens for Global Solutions, Communications Consortium Media Center, Leadership Conference on Civil Rights Education Fund and YWCA-USA to educate thought leaders, media, policymakers and the public on benefits of the United Nations Convention on the Elimination of All Forms of Discrimination Against Women. 2010.

1639-142 NetHope, Fairfax, VA, $430,000. For collaboration with Accenture Development Partnerships to develop plan to build and launch Innovation for Development (I4D) Office, which will seek to incubate, partner and scale most recent successful information and communications strategies, to improve operational capacity of global international development organizations. 2010.

1639-143 New School, Milano New School for Management and Urban Policy, New York, NY, $50,000. To support research for comparative case study examining role and impact of arts and culture in New York City and Toronto. 2010.

1639-144 New York Academy of Medicine, International Society for Urban Health, New York, NY, $120,000. Toward travel and other associated support for participants from developing countries to attend 9th International Conference on Urban Health, to be held in New York City. 2010.

1639-145 New York Foundation for the Arts, Brooklyn, NY, $175,000. Toward first multi-disciplinary festival of Cambodian arts to be produced in the United States and first of its scale to take place outside Cambodia. Grant made as part of New York City Cultural Innovation Fund Award Program. 2010.

1639-146 New York University, Institute for International Law and Justice, New York, NY, $51,500. Toward study to analyze usefulness of indicators in designing interventions tackling complex problems that affect poor and vulnerable populations. 2010.

1639-147 Nuclear Threat Initiative, Global Health and Security Initiative, Washington, DC, $275,000. Toward Connecting Health Organizations for Regional Disease Surveillance (CHORDS), project to promote global collaboration in disease surveillance across existing and emerging regional disease surveillance networks by building capacity and improving communication and collaboration. 2010.

1639-148 Operation USA, Culver City, CA, $21,200. For workshop bringing together international experts on refugee housing, including practitioners, academics and advocates, to address issues around design and functionality of refugee camps, many of which eventually become permanent settlements. 2010.

1639-149 Ove Arup and Partners International, London, England, $1,649,960. To provide strategic planning, program management support and technical assistance to ensure program credibility, knowledge management support and knowledge dissemination and replication support to Asian Cities Climate Change Resilience Network program and its partners. 2010.

1639-150 Oxfam International, Oxford, England, $50,000. Toward project to promote climate change justice and sustainable resolution of land ownership conflicts in Thailand through deployment of appropriate strategies that take into consideration community rights of local indigenous populations and to promote sustainable livelihood and natural resources management. 2010.

1639-151 Pacific Community Ventures, San Francisco, CA, $139,700. For use by InSight Program, in collaboration with Initiative for Responsible Investment in support of in-depth study of global impact investing policy landscape to inform global audience about how to better use advantageous policies to advance the field and its impact on poor and vulnerable people. 2010.

1639-152 Pact Institute, Southeast Asia Change Project (SEA Change), Washington, DC, $400,000. To establish Southeast Asia Community of Practice of monitoring and evaluation of adaptive responses to climate change, to facilitate learning and to capture and disseminate promising monitoring and evaluation practices. 2010.

1639-153 Palli Karma-Sahayak Foundation, Dhaka, Bangladesh, $105,000. To conduct study tours of national health insurance schemes of India, the Philippines, and Thailand in order to inform implementation of micro-health insurance in Bangladesh. 2010.

1639-154 Pamoja Media East Africa, Nairobi, Kenya, $89,950. To develop online and mobile social networking platform to build agricultural capacity among new generation of farmers in Kenya. 2010.

1639-155 Pamoja Media East Africa, Nairobi, Kenya, $81,200. To develop online knowledge sharing and management system for research and development work on climate change resilience for African agriculture. 2010.

1639-156 Partners in Health, Boston, MA, $296,900. For collaboration with Inshuti Mu Buzima and Ministry of Health in Rwanda to expand core OpenMRS electronic medical record platform to include primary health care, as part of national effort to deliver more effective care to populations living in rural areas. 2010.

1639-157 PATH, Seattle, WA, $1,000,000. For project to begin development of global health enterprise architecture for national health insurance information systems with the aim of strengthening health systems in the Global South through improved access to and use of health information. 2010.

1639-158 Pathfinder International, Watertown, MA, $120,000. For project to develop mHealth (mobile health) information-education-communication system by using mobile phones to disseminate culturally and linguistically relevant healthcare information to underserved populations in Central Highlands and Northern Mountains of Vietnam. 2010.

1639-159 PharmAccess Foundation, Amsterdam, Netherlands, $190,000. For use by Ghana office in support of project to develop Ghana Health Certification and Accreditation Board and launch Capacity Building and Quality Improvement Program that will improve quality and increase access to health services in Ghana. 2010.

1639-160 Philippine Institute for Development Studies, Makati, Philippines, $249,890. For project, as member organization within the Center for Health Market Innovations, to identify, map, track and analyze innovative private sector health organizations and programs in the Philippines, to foster links among key stakeholders and to cultivate additional future support for this sector. 2010.

1639-161 Population and Community Development Association, Bangkok, Thailand, $50,990. For piloting philanthropy workshop for young Thai business executives and high net worth individuals to raise awareness of philanthropy and encourage further philanthropic activities. 2010.

1639-162 Public Health Foundation of India, New Delhi, India, $354,450. To establish technical and administrative Secretariat for assisting government of India to develop framework for universal healthcare in India. 2010.

1639-163 PUKAR-Partners for Urban Knowledge Action and Research, Mumbai, India, $431,107. For multifaceted research study, in collaboration with Harvard University's School of Public Health and New York University, on physical and social determinants of health in disadvantaged urban settings in Mumbai, India in effort to identify replicable solutions for improving health among urban populations. 2010.

1639-164 Regional Universities Forum for Capacity Building in Agriculture Limited, Kampala, Uganda, $99,000. For event to build capacity for African tertiary institutions to use foresight methods and techniques to plan for training Africa's agriculture sector in near- and long-term, to be held at Ministerial Conference on Higher Education in Africa, Uganda. 2010.

1639-165 Regional Universities Forum for Capacity Building in Agriculture Limited, Kampala, Uganda, $84,600. For work to strengthen resilience of African agriculture to climate change by helping 25 East, Southern and Central African universities in its consortium to access climate change adaptation funds and training opportunities. 2010.

1639-166 Results for Development Institute, Washington, DC, $3,508,000. For efforts to create more awareness and analytical understanding of possibilities for, and direct facilitation of, country-level efforts to expand and deepen, universal health coverage, including through creation of Joint Learning Network among implementing countries. 2010.

1639-167 Root Capital, Cambridge, MA, $500,000. Toward transitioning to multiple loan fund model that will expand and accelerate positive impact on small and growing businesses operating in poor, environmentally vulnerable regions of Africa and Latin America. 2010.

1639-168 Royal Melbourne Institute of Technology, School of Global Studies, Social Science and Planning, Melbourne, Australia, $223,350. Toward Phase II of project BetterEvaluation, international Web 2.0 evaluation resource aimed at assisting the Foundation, its grantees and partners to better choose tools and use them to articulate, measure and report on their results and strategies in order to achieve impact. 2010.

1639-169 Rwanda Agriculture Research Institute, Kigali, Rwanda, $440,000. To strengthen climate change adaptation research to create demand-driven, market-responsive practices that improve food security for smallholder farmers in Rwanda. 2010.

1639-170 Samasource, San Francisco, CA, $799,200. To further refine and execute business model, which uses innovative technology platforms to train, manage and outsource distributed digital work to small impact outsourcing providers in urban and rural Kenya, Rwanda and Uganda and create jobs for very poor populations. 2010.

1639-171 Santa Fe Institute, Santa Fe, NM, $231,400. For research project to develop theory and application for understanding structure, dynamics and organization of cities and for related meeting to be held at Rockefeller Foundation Bellagio Center, Italy. 2010.

1639-172 Shack/Slum Dwellers International, Cape Town, South Africa, $4,000,002. Toward developing more inclusive shelter strategies for cities in the developing world by increasing engagement and building partnerships between urban poor and local governments. 2010.

1639-173 Shared Interest, New York, NY, $120,000. To engage Nonprofit Finance Fund's Sustainable Enhancement Grant model to refine capital raising and business plan for using partial loan guarantees to encourage commercial banks to lend to businesses in low-income townships and rural communities in South Africa. 2010.

1639-174 Small Enterprise Education and Promotion Network, Washington, DC, $75,000. Toward Social Performance Working Group for Microfinance Associations, global platform for enhancing peer learning among microfinance organizations and encouraging development and use of social metrics in effort to ensure that impact investments succeed in producing better outcomes for poor and vulnerable populations. 2010.

1639-175 Sokoine University of Agriculture, Department of Agricultural Engineering and Land Planning, Morogoro, Tanzania, Zanzibar and Pemba, $359,600. To support capacity building on climate change adaptation in the agricultural sector in Tanzania. 2010.

1639-176 South African Health Informatics Association, Durban, South Africa, $120,000. Toward supporting 13th World Congress on Medical and Health Informatics: Partnerships for Effective eHealth Solutions to be held in Cape Town, South Africa, including support for participation of health informatics researchers and practitioners from developing countries and coordination of the eHealth Innovators Awards. 2010.

1639-177 South African Node of the Millennium Project, Johannesburg, South Africa, $150,900. Toward building and maintaining Internet-based information repository and networking platform for pro-poor foresight - forward looking analysis that focuses on poor and vulnerable people by way of anticipating long-term trends through the use of various research methodologies. 2010.

1639-178 Strategic Foresight Group, Mumbai, India, $302,400. Toward project to conduct trend monitoring and horizon scanning research on issues relevant to poverty and human development, focused on India, Bangladesh, Indonesia, Thailand, Vietnam and Middle East countries. 2010.

1639-179 Swiss Tropical and Public Health Institute, Basel, Switzerland, $234,440. To evaluate Foundation's Disease Surveillance Networks initiative work in Africa, in collaboration with Africa Population and Health Research Center, to capture and share lessons learned about ability of complex networks to achieve improved disease surveillance and response and to foster learning, accountability and performance improvements in the Foundation and among its grantees. 2010.

1639-180 Synergos Institute, New York, NY, $50,000. For general support of mission to mobilize resources and bridge social and economic divides to reduce poverty and increase equity around the world. 2010.

1639-181 Taru Leading Edge Private Limited, Gurgaon, India, $825,420. To assist three cities in India (Surat, Indore, and Gorakhpur) to plan and implement climate resilience projects, by building capacity of city partners and other actors in those cities to undertake urban climate resilience work, partner with national, state and local governments to initiate reforms that support urban climate resilience in India and document methodologies and lessons learned as part of Asian Cities Climate Change Resilience Network. 2010.

1639-182 Taru Leading Edge Private Limited, Gurgaon, India, $509,900. To model end-to-end early warning system that will help improve management of reservoir releases and reduce intensity of floods and resultant damage in city of Surat, India, as part of Asian Cities Climate Change Resilience Network. 2010.

1639-183 Taru Leading Edge Private Limited, Gurgaon, India, $239,850. To develop and demonstrate range of models for cost effective, reliable, decentralized urban water management that are driven by differentiated end-use demands in Indore, India, as part of Asian Cities Climate Change Resilience Network. 2010.

1639-184 Thai Breastfeeding Center Foundation, Bangkok, Thailand, $25,000. Toward disseminating publication, Thai Breastfeeding Atlas in Thailand, and developing plan for possible replication in Vietnam. 2010.

1639-185 Thai Fund Foundation, Bangkok, Thailand, $35,240. To develop accredited program to train fundraisers at nonprofit organizations in Thailand in order to strengthen their capacity to mobilize resources and ensure sustainability. 2010.

1639-186 United Nations Economic Commission for Africa, Addis Ababa, Ethiopia, $250,900. In support of funding participants and speakers to strengthen sessions on climate change mitigation and adaptation at Seventh African Development Forum, high-level bi-annual event focused on key African development issues, under 2010 theme of Acting on Climate Change for Sustainable Development in Africa, to be held in Addis Ababa, Ethiopia. 2010.

1639-187 Universidad del Desarrollo, Center for Epidemiology and Public Health Policy, Santiago, Chile, $171,800. Toward study to assess equity of health coverage for pre-natal care and hypertension in Chile and to develop methodological tools for evaluating health coverage that will be effective under a variety of conditions and in different countries. 2010.

1639-188 University of California, Department of City and Regional Planning, Institute of Urban and Regional Development, Berkeley, CA, $250,326. To support collaborative project to ensure that recently launched infrastructure development programs in Kenya are scalable and responsive to local community needs. 2010.

1639-189 University of California, Global Health Group, San Francisco, CA, $104,000. To support establishment of Secretariat to organize symposium to be held in Toronto, Canada, as part of continuing effort to map what is known about the role of the private sector in health care and to identify related research priorities to further strengthen health systems in developing countries. 2010.

1639-190 University of Dar es Salaam, Institute of Resource Assessment, Dar es Salaam, Tanzania, Zanzibar and Pemba, $340,600. To support design and delivery of training on climate change adaptation to researchers at Tanzania's seven autonomous zonal agriculture research centers and to staff seven other East African research and development institutions. 2010.

1639-191 University of Ghana, School of Public Health, Legon, Ghana, $167,700. To enhance health informatics curriculum and establish Health Informatics Society that will promote development of health informatics capacities that leverage eHealth to improved access to health services in Ghana. 2010.

1639-192 University of KwaZulu-Natal, Faculty of Science and Agriculture, Westville, South Africa, $600,000. Toward establishing Health Enterprise Architecture Laboratory (HEAL), research laboratory focused on application of enterprise architecture and health informatics to low-resource settings. 2010.

1639-193 University of Liberia, College of Agriculture and Forestry, Monrovia, Liberia, $364,000. To revitalize capacity and initiate research and begin multiplication and distribution of improved rice varieties to enhance Liberia's national food security. 2010.

1639-194 University of Manchester, Institute of Innovation Research, Manchester, England, $39,740. To support project to synthesize and visualize trend and horizon scanning information on issues relevant to poverty and human

development including publication of a special issue of journal, Foresight. 2010.

1639-195 University of Minnesota, Minneapolis, MN, $265,870. For activities related to assessing state of global One Health movement and related high-level meeting at the Rockefeller Foundation Bellagio Center. One Health Initiative is a movement to forge co-equal, all inclusive collaborations between physicians, osteopaths, veterinarians, dentists, nurses and other scientific-health and environmentally related disciplines. 2010.

1639-196 University of Nairobi, Department of Urban and Regional Planning, Nairobi, Kenya, $245,150. To support collaborative project in Kenya to ensure that recently launched infrastructure development programs are scalable and responsive to local community needs. 2010.

1639-197 University of Pennsylvania, Institute for Strategic Threat Analysis and Response, Philadelphia, PA, $27,100. To support welcome reception for International Study of Radicalization and Political Violence Peace and Security Summit to be held in New York City, which will provide leading international policymakers, experts and other stakeholders opportunities to engage in outcome driven discussions about potential threats to peace and security. 2010.

1639-198 University of Pretoria, Gordon Institute for Business Science, China-Africa Network, Pretoria, South Africa, $366,300. To support educating Chinese stakeholders about opportunities for socially and environmentally responsible investing in Africa. 2010.

1639-199 University of Reading, Walker Institute for Climate System Research, Reading, England, $599,400. Toward collaboration with Statistical Services Centre, in support of providing capacity building assistance to climate change units of seven agriculture research and development institutions in East and Central Africa. 2010.

1639-200 University of Sussex, Science and Technology Policy Research Department, Brighton, England, $63,100. Toward support of collaboration with Social, Technological and Environmental Pathways to Sustainability (STEPS) Centre to conduct research on application of new models for technology assessment in the Global South and their potential to foster development in health, climate change and agriculture. 2010.

1639-201 University of the Free State, Directorate for Research Development, Bloemfontein, South Africa, $400,000. Toward collaboration with EvalNet, to engage development evaluation leaders to provide practical assistance to Rockefeller Foundation Initiative teams, key grantees and partners, to better articulate, monitor, evaluate and report on their results and strategies in order to achieve impact. 2010.

1639-202 Wildlife Conservation Society, Bronx, NY, $360,030. For use by Animal and Human Health for the Environment and Development (AHEAD) project to engage program officer who will support One Health activities that link human, animal, wildlife activities in the Southern African region. One Health Initiative is a movement to forge co-equal, all inclusive collaborations between physicians, osteopaths, veterinarians, dentists, nurses and other scientific-health and environmentally related disciplines. 2010.

1639-203 William J. Clinton Foundation, Little Rock, AR, $350,000. Toward Clinton Global Initiative, designed to catalyze a community of global leaders to devise and implement innovative solutions to global challenges such as energy and climate change, poverty alleviation, global health, and education. 2010.

1639-204 William J. Clinton Foundation, Clinton Climate Initiative's Carbon and Poverty Reduction Program, Little Rock, AR, $3,000,000. To support efforts to develop, deploy and demonstrate carbon measurement and accounting systems that enable poor people in rural areas of developing countries to participate in and benefit from global climate markets. 2010.

1639-205 Wilton Park, Steyning, England, $100,000. Toward Africa 2010: The Key Challenges, conference to review achievements made toward Africa's development at mid-point between completion of Africa Commission Report in 2005 and 2015 target date for achievement of the Millennium Development Goals. 2010.

1639-206 Womens Campaign International, Bala Cynwyd, PA, $100,000. Toward First Ladies' Legacy Project, to provide training on strategic planning and capacity building to group of African First Ladies to enable them to create and sustain their respective legacy plans to work toward social improvement and development, to be held during the African Union summit in Ethiopia. 2010.

1639-207 World Affairs Council of Northern California, San Francisco, CA, $75,000. Toward Global Philanthropy Forum, which brings together foundation leaders, individual donors, social investors, and agents of change to learn more about opportunities for international philanthropy. 2010.

1639-208 World Federation of Public Health Associations, Geneva, Switzerland, $28,868. To support presenters and developing country practitioners at 12th World Congress of Public Health Associations, held in Istanbul, Turkey. 2010.

1639-209 World Food Programme, Climate and Disaster Risk Solutions (CDRS) Unit, Rome, Italy, $1,000,000. To support partnering with African Union Commission to establish African Risk Capacity project, optimized global risk management system for providing natural disaster assistance to African countries. 2010.

1639-210 World Health Organization, Global Observatory for eHealth, Geneva, Switzerland, $120,000. Toward analyzing results of recent survey of eHealth activities in 115 countries and development of series of monographs for publication, which will inform decisions of countries planning to incorporate information technology into their healthcare systems. 2010.

1639-211 World Vision, Federal Way, WA, $600,000. Toward designing and implementing field-based shared service center in Nairobi, Kenya to enhance delivery of information and communication technology services and support field operations across Africa; and conducting design study and pilot implementation of business process outsourcing centers in rural and semi-rural Tanzania and Ghana to generate income and economic empowerment for poor and vulnerable people in those communities. 2010.

1639-212 World Wide Web Foundation, Cambridge, MA, $396,000. To conduct study of users' experiences accessing the Internet in the developing world and a pilot experiment on the use of Interactive Voice Response (IVR) systems by poor and vulnerable communities. 2010.

1639-213 Young Foundation, London, England, $212,000. For research to assess need and demand for Innovation Academy and Social Innovation eXchange, global community of social entrepreneurs, businesses, governments and charities committed to building a broader knowledge base about how to apply innovation to social problems. 2010.

1640
Rosenblatt Family Foundation, Inc.
155 Riverside Dr.
New York, NY 10024-2207

Incorporated in 1956 in NY.
Donors: Marcus Retter; Betty Retter†; C. Rosenblatt.
Grantmaker type: Independent foundation.
Financial data (yr. ended 12/31/10): Assets, $4,788,327 (M); expenditures, $1,333,529; qualifying distributions, $710,592; giving activities include $710,592 for grants.
Purpose and activities: Giving primarily to Jewish temples and yeshivas.
Fields of interest: Education; Human services; Jewish agencies & synagogues.
International interests: Israel.
Limitations: Applications not accepted. Giving primarily in NY.
Application information: Contributes only to pre-selected organizations.
Officers: Mary Schreiber, Pres.; Daniel Retter, V.P.; Leah Eisenberg, Treas.; Margot Pollak, Secy.
EIN: 136145385

1641
Alfred & Jane Ross Foundation, Inc.
c/o Hecht & Co.
622 3rd Ave., 8th Fl.
New York, NY 10017-6720

Established in 1992 in DE.
Donors: Arthur Ross†; Jane Ross.
Grantmaker type: Independent foundation.
Financial data (yr. ended 12/31/10): Assets, $17,117,536 (M); expenditures, $801,642; qualifying distributions, $744,516; giving activities include $726,800 for 67 grants (high: $235,000; low: $300).
Purpose and activities: Giving primarily for art, with some emphasis on music, and cultural institutes, education, and youth services.
Fields of interest: Performing arts, opera; Arts; Higher education; Education; Youth, services; International exchange, arts; International affairs, foreign policy.
Limitations: Applications not accepted. Giving primarily in New York, NY. No grants to individuals.
Application information: Contributes only to pre-selected organizations.
Officers: Alfred F. Ross, Pres.; Jane Ross, V.P. and Secy.; Michael Hecht, Treas.
EIN: 133680380

1642
Royal Oak Foundation
35 W. 35th St., Ste. 1200
New York, NY 10001-2205 (212) 480-2889
FAX: (212) 785-7234;
E-mail: general@royal-oak.org; Toll-free tel.: (800) 913-6565; URL: http://www.royal-oak.org

Established in 1973 in NY.
Grantmaker type: Public charity.
Financial data (yr. ended 12/31/09): Revenue, $2,489,741; assets, $4,243,961 (M); gifts received, $1,832,211; expenditures, $1,685,171; giving activities include $20,000 for grants, and $248,035 for grants to organizations outside the U.S.
Purpose and activities: The foundation raises funds for the conservation of areas of historic properties, including houses and gardens in Britain and elsewhere. It sponsors educational programs which address issues in conservation and preservation.
Fields of interest: Visual arts, architecture; Historic preservation/historical societies; Arts; Environment; Animals/wildlife.
International interests: United Kingdom.
Type of support: General/operating support; Continuing support; Annual campaigns; Program development; Publication; Scholarship funds; Employee-related scholarships; Scholarships—to individuals; In-kind gifts.
Limitations: Applications accepted. Giving limited to the U.S., England, Wales, Scotland, and Northern Ireland.
Publications: Application guidelines; Financial statement; Grants list; Informational brochure; Newsletter.
Application information: A non-refundable fee of $25 must accompany each application. Application form not required.
  Initial approach: Download application form
  Deadline(s): Apr. 25 for fellowships
  Board meeting date(s): Mar., June, Sept., and Dec.
  Final notification: May 17 for fellowships
Officers: Patrick S. Gallagher, Chair.; Herbert L. Camp, Vice-Chair.; Ian Hooper, Secy.; David O. Brownwood, Treas.; John J. Oddy, Exec. Dir.; Henry J. Heinz II, Hon. Chair.
Directors: Charlotte P. Armstrong; Carrie Rebora Barratt; David Beal; Friederike K. Biggs; Mary Rose Bolton; J. Scott Burns; James F. Caughman; Tracey W. Dart; Ronald Lee Fleming; Suzy Grote; Josephine W. Patton; J. Rodney Pleasants; J. Thomas Savage, Jr.; Suzanne C. Schutz; P. Allen Smith; and 12 additional directors.
Number of staff: 8 full-time professional; 2 part-time support.
EIN: 237349380

1643
Samuel Rubin Foundation, Inc.
777 United Nations Plz.
New York, NY 10017-3521 (212) 697-8945
Contact: Lauranne Jones, Grants Admin.
FAX: (212) 682-0886; E-mail: laurannc@igc.org;
URL: http://www.samuelrubinfoundation.org

Established in 1958 in NY.
Donors: Samuel Rubin†; Samuel Rubin Foundation, Inc.
Grantmaker type: Independent foundation.
Financial data (yr. ended 06/30/11): Assets, $11,947,419 (M); expenditures, $810,005;

qualifying distributions, $548,361; giving activities include $548,361 for grants.
Purpose and activities: Grants for the pursuit of peace and justice; for an equitable reallocation of the world's resources; and to promote social, economic, political, civil, and cultural rights.
Fields of interest: Higher education; International peace/security; International affairs, arms control; International affairs, foreign policy; International human rights; Civil/human rights; Women.
Type of support: Film/video/radio; General/operating support; Seed money.
Limitations: Applications accepted. Giving on a national and international basis. No grants to individuals, or for endowments, scholarships, or building funds.
Publications: Grants list; Program policy statement.
Application information: Applications sent by e-mail or fax will not be accepted, nor will telephone solicitations. Application form not required.
  Initial approach: Proposal (not to exceed 5 pages)
  Copies of proposal: 1
  Deadline(s): First Fri. in Jan., May, and Sept.
  Board meeting date(s): 3 times per year; generally at the end of Feb., June, and Oct.
  Final notification: 2 weeks following board meetings
Officers: Cora Weiss, Pres.; Daniel Weiss, V.P.; Judy Weiss, V.P.; Tamara Weiss, V.P.; Peter Weiss, Treas.
Director: Alison R. Bernstein.
Number of staff: 2 full-time professional.
EIN: 136164671

1644
Russian Children's Welfare Society, Inc.
200 Park Ave. S., Ste. 1617
New York, NY   10003-1503   (212) 473-6263
FAX: (212) 473-6301; E-mail: main@rcws.org;
Toll-free tel.: (888) 732-7297; URL: http://www.rcws.org

Established in 1926 in NY.
Grantmaker type: Public charity.
Financial data (yr. ended 12/31/10): Revenue, $1,310,119; assets, $4,305,098 (M); gifts received, $776,813; expenditures, $1,272,951; giving activities include $901,555 for grants to organizations outside the U.S.
Purpose and activities: The society assists disadvantaged children in Russia to improve their lives and enhance their health, education and social welfare.
Fields of interest: Children/youth, services.
International interests: Russia.
Type of support: Grants to individuals.
Limitations: Giving limited to Russia.
Publications: Grants list.
Officers and Directors:* Igor P. Holodry,* M.D., Chair.; Vladimir P. Fekula,* Pres. and C.E.O.; Georges Nahitchevansky,* V.P.; Serge M. Ossorguine,* V.P. and Secy.; John L. Pouschine,* Treas.; Peter A. Basilevsky; Beatrice Fekula; Cyril E. Geacintov, M.D.; Samuel Harding; Michael A. Jordan; Nadia Lipsky; Thomas McPartland; Georges Nahitchevansky; Serge M. Ossorguine; Douglas L. Paul; and 2 additional directors.
EIN: 135562332

1645
The Richard Salomon Family Foundation, Inc.
(formerly Richard & Edna Salomon Foundation, Inc.)
c/o Richard E. Salomon
610 5th Ave., Ste. 506
New York, NY   10020-2403

Established in 1964 in NY.
Donors: Richard B. Salomon†; Richard E. Salomon; Edna Salomon†.
Grantmaker type: Independent foundation.
Financial data (yr. ended 12/31/10): Assets, $17,094,368 (M); expenditures, $831,500; qualifying distributions, $477,509; giving activities include $477,509 for grants.
Purpose and activities: Giving for education, cancer research, and human services.
Fields of interest: Human services; Museums (art); Elementary/secondary education; Higher education; Education; Cancer research; International affairs, foreign policy.
Type of support: General/operating support.
Limitations: Applications not accepted. Giving primarily in New York, NY and Providence, RI. No grants to individuals.
Application information: Contributes only to pre-selected organizations.
Officers: David Salomon, Chair.; Jennifer Salomon, Exec. Dir.
Directors: Evanne S. Gargiulo; Laura A. Landro; Frederick Lubcher; Christina Salomon; Richard E. Salomon.
EIN: 136163521

1646
The Sapling Foundation
c/o Ted Conf.
250 Hudson St., No. 1002
New York, NY   10013

Established in 1995 in CA.
Grantmaker type: Independent foundation.
Financial data (yr. ended 12/31/09): Assets, $22,775,384 (M); gifts received, $9,972,122; expenditures, $23,777,249; qualifying distributions, $2,827,292; giving activities include $485,600 for 3 grants (high: $235,600; low: $50,000).
Purpose and activities: Giving primarily to the environment, and to U.S.-based organizations that support global health and poverty issues.
Fields of interest: International affairs.
Limitations: Applications not accepted. Giving primarily in CA and NY. No grants to individuals.
Application information: Contributes only to pre-selected organizations.
Officers: Christopher Anderson, Pres.; Katherine McCartney, Secy.
EIN: 943235545

1647
The Schaffner Family Foundation
252 7th Ave., Ste. 17M
New York, NY   10001-7351
Contact: Valentine Schaffner, Tr.
E-mail: val@nabigallery.com

Established in 2002 in NY.
Grantmaker type: Independent foundation.

Financial data (yr. ended 12/31/09): Assets, $6,040,507 (M); expenditures, $955,709; qualifying distributions, $885,400; giving activities include $885,400 for grants.
Fields of interest: International affairs; Human services; Arts; Environment.
International interests: Africa; Asia.
Type of support: General/operating support; Continuing support; Annual campaigns; Capital campaigns; Building/renovation; Land acquisition; Emergency funds; Program development; Conferences/seminars; Film/video/radio; Publication; Seed money; Scholarship funds; Research; Matching/challenge support.
Limitations: Applications accepted. Giving primarily in NY. No grants to individuals.
Application information: Application form not required.
  Initial approach: Letter
  Copies of proposal: 1
  Deadline(s): None
Trustees: Valentine Schaffner, Mgr.; Elizabeth B. Schaffner; Timothy Schaffner.
EIN: 383652881

1648
Priscilla & Richard J. Schmeelk Foundation, Inc.
c/o J. Anderson
1003 Park Blvd.
Massapequa Park, NY   11762-2741

Established in 1983 in NY.
Donor: Richard J. Schmeelk.
Grantmaker type: Independent foundation.
Financial data (yr. ended 12/31/10): Assets, $1,627,910 (M); gifts received, $7,050; expenditures, $294,882; qualifying distributions, $282,099; giving activities include $282,099 for 68 grants (high: $60,000; low: $50).
Fields of interest: Education; Hospitals (general); Health care; Children/youth, services; Catholic agencies & churches; Jewish agencies & synagogues; Children; Youth.
International interests: Canada.
Type of support: Continuing support; Annual campaigns; Endowments; Scholarship funds.
Limitations: Applications not accepted. Giving primarily in New York, NY. No grants to individuals.
Publications: Annual report.
Application information: Contributes only to pre-selected organizations.
Officers and Directors:* Richard J. Schmeelk,* Pres. and Treas.; Priscilla M. Schmeelk,* V.P. and Secy.
EIN: 133126387

1649
SDialogue, LLC Corporate Giving Program
314 Wall St., 1st Fl.
Kingston, NY   12401-3820   (866) 210-1183
URL: http://sdialogue.com/about-us/

Grantmaker type: Corporate giving program.
Purpose and activities: SDialogue donates a percentage of profits to nonprofit organizations involved with human rights and the environment.
Fields of interest: International human rights; Environment.
Type of support: General/operating support.

1650
Select Equity Group Foundation
380 Lafayette St., Ste. 6
New York, NY   10003-6933
Contact: Robert Wilson, Dir., Corp. Giving
E-mail: rwilson@selectequity.com; URL: https://
www.selectequity.com/foundation.aspx

Established in 2000 in NY.
Donors: Select Equity Group, Inc.; Lyster Watson.
Grantmaker type: Company-sponsored foundation.
Financial data (yr. ended 12/31/09): Assets,
$4,188,688 (M); expenditures, $1,615,134;
qualifying distributions, $1,273,002; giving
activities include $1,273,002 for 246 grants (high:
$75,000; low: $60).
Purpose and activities: The foundation supports
organizations involved with arts and culture,
education, the environment, health, cancer, kidney
disease, human services, youth development,
international economic development, and civil and
human rights.
Fields of interest: Arts; Secondary school/
education; Education; Environment, water
resources; Environment; Health care; Cancer;
Kidney diseases; Youth development; Children,
services; Human services; International economic
development; Civil/human rights.
Type of support: General/operating support;
Program development; Scholarship funds; Employee
matching gifts.
Limitations: Applications not accepted. Giving
primarily in AL, MA, MD, NJ, NY, OH, TX, and VA, with
emphasis on NY. No grants to individuals.
Application information: Contributes only to
pre-selected organizations. Preference is given to
organizations endorsed by Select Equity employees.
Trustees: Christopher Arndt; John Britton; George S.
Loening; Darren Seirer; Amor Towles.
EIN: 134148796

1651
Shalem Foundation
845 3rd Ave., 6th Fl.
New York, NY   10022-6601

Established in 1997 in NY.
Grantmaker type: Public charity.
Financial data (yr. ended 12/31/09): Revenue,
$7,313,967; assets, $2,185,686 (M); gifts
received, $7,311,878; expenditures, $6,487,775;
giving activities include $6,037,565 for grants to
organizations outside the U.S.
Purpose and activities: The foundation works to
promote and foster the creation of an intellectual
infrastructure for the state of Israel, the
development of a Jewish national culture, and the
promotion of intellectual and economic liberty.
Fields of interest: Education; Jewish agencies &
synagogues.
International interests: Israel.
Limitations: Applications not accepted. Giving
limited to Israel.
Application information: Unsolicited requests for
funds not considered or acknowledged.
Officers and Directors:* Ronald S. Lauder,* Chair.;
Roger Hertog,* Vice-Chair.; Daniel Polisar,* Pres.;
Ahavia Scheindlin, V.P., Devel.; David Messer,
Treas.; Yitz Applbaum; Jed Arkin; Yoram R. Haznoy;
Howard Jonas; Leon Kass; Barry Klein; William
Kristol; Izhak Lax; Allen Roth; Yair Shamir; Natan
Sharansky; Aliza Sharon.
EIN: 133941865

1652
J. D. Shatford Memorial Trust
c/o JPMorgan Chase Bank, N.A.
270 Park Ave., 16th Fl.
New York, NY   10017-2014
E-mail: connie.a.brandeis@JPMorgan.com;
Application address: c/o Advisory Committee, P.O.
Box 192, Hubbards, Nova Scotia B0J 1T0; e-mail:
info@jdshatfordmemorialtrust.org; URL: http://
foundationcenter.org/grantmaker/shatford/

Trust established in 1955 in NY.
Grantmaker type: Independent foundation.
Financial data (yr. ended 12/31/09): Assets,
$6,471,774 (M); expenditures, $380,014;
qualifying distributions, $342,675; giving activities
include $24,000 for 1 grant, and $305,865 for 46
grants to individuals (high: $36,500; low: $600).
Purpose and activities: Emphasis on scholarship
aid, secondary and higher education, and charities
limited to Hubbards, Nova Scotia, Canada,
organizations and residents.
Fields of interest: Secondary school/education;
Protestant agencies & churches.
International interests: Canada.
Type of support: General/operating support;
Scholarships—to individuals.
Limitations: Applications accepted. Giving limited to
Hubbards, Nova Scotia, Canada.
Publications: Grants list; Informational brochure.
Application information: Complete application
guidelines available on Trust web site. Application
form required.
  Deadline(s): None
Trustee: JPMorgan Chase Bank, N.A.
EIN: 136029993

1653
Shaw Family Foundation
c/o Resource Holdings Assoc.
520 Madison Ave., 33rd Fl.
New York, NY   10022-4213

Established in 1998 in CT.
Donors: John C. Shaw; Jay Shaw.
Grantmaker type: Independent foundation.
Financial data (yr. ended 04/30/10): Assets,
$319,291 (M); gifts received, $235,000;
expenditures, $837,276; qualifying distributions,
$835,825; giving activities include $835,825 for 31
grants (high: $500,000; low: $25).
Fields of interest: Health organizations,
association; Foundations (private operating);
Military/veterans' organizations; Higher education;
Human services; Children/youth, services.
International interests: China.
Limitations: Applications not accepted. Giving
primarily in CT. No grants to individuals.
Application information: Contributes only to
pre-selected organizations.
Officer: John C. Shaw, Mgr.
EIN: 061486109

1654
Murray & Beatrice Sherman Foundation
115 Central Park West, Ste. 29F
New York, NY   10023-4198

Established in 1999 in NY.
Grantmaker type: Independent foundation.

Financial data (yr. ended 12/31/10): Assets,
$5,254,075 (M); expenditures, $335,356;
qualifying distributions, $301,852; giving activities
include $268,728 for 20 grants (high: $50,000;
low: $1,000).
Fields of interest: Arts; Libraries (public); Education;
Hospitals (general); Human services; Youth,
services; International relief; International
migration/refugee issues; Community/economic
development; United Ways and Federated Giving
Programs.
Limitations: Applications not accepted. Giving
primarily in New York, NY. No grants to individuals.
Application information: Contributes only to
pre-selected organizations.
Trustees: Mary Sherman Mittleman; William S.
Sherman.
Agent: Citibank, N.A.
EIN: 311623371

1655
The Nick Simons Foundation
160 5th Ave., 7th Fl.
New York, NY   10010-7003
James and Marilyn Simons's Giving Pledge: http://
givingpledge.org/#enter

Established in 2006 in NY.
Donors: James Simons; Nick Simons†.
Grantmaker type: Independent foundation.
Financial data (yr. ended 06/30/10): Assets,
$13,081,815 (M); gifts received, $16,800,000;
expenditures, $3,924,982; qualifying distributions,
$3,924,982; giving activities include $3,215,830
for 14 grants (high: $2,414,000; low: $1,000).
Purpose and activities: Giving primarily for health
care.
Fields of interest: Hospitals (general); Health care;
Foundations (private grantmaking).
International interests: Nepal.
Limitations: Applications not accepted. Giving
primarily in CA, CO, and in Nepal.
Application information: Contributes only to
pre-selected organizations.
Officers: James Simons, Pres.; Marilyn Simons,
Secy.-Treas.
Trustees: Caitlin Heising; Mark Heising; Audrey
Simons; Laura Baxter Simons; Liz Simons; Nat
Simons.
EIN: 203101239

1656
The Simons Foundation
160 5th Ave., 7th Fl.
New York, NY   10010-7037   (646) 654-0066
Contact: Marilyn Simons, Pres.
E-mail: admin@simonsfoundation.org; URL: http://
www.simonsfoundation.org
James and Marilyn Simons's Giving Pledge: http://
givingpledge.org/#enter
Knowledge Center: https://sfari.org/
news-and-opinion
On SFARI Blog: https://sfari.org/news-and-opinion/
blog/going-on-sfari
Vimeo: http://vimeo.com/simonsfoundation

Established in 1994 in NY.
Grantmaker type: Independent foundation.
Financial data (yr. ended 12/31/10): Assets,
$1,862,188,781 (M); gifts received,
$270,395,620; expenditures, $169,138,764;

qualifying distributions, $132,374,789; giving activities include $132,374,789 for grants, and $17,056,217 for foundation-administered programs.

Purpose and activities: The primary mission of the foundation is to advance the frontiers of research in the basic sciences and mathematics.

Fields of interest: Autism research; Science, research; Mathematics.

Type of support: General/operating support; Capital campaigns; Endowments; Professorships; Research.

Publications: Annual report; Financial statement.

Application information: The foundation does not accept proposals outside its established programs. In almost all cases grants are made in response to announced requests for proposals and funding decisions are made through a peer-reviewed proposal process. See foundation web site for requests for applications.

Board meeting date(s): Throughout the year

Officers and Trustees:* Marilyn Simons,* Pres.; Maria Adler, V.P., Finance; David Eisenbud, V.P., Mathematics and Physical Sciences; Marion Greenup, V.P., Admin.; James Simons,* Ph.D., Secy.-Treas.; Mark Silber.

Number of staff: 2 part-time professional; 1 full-time support.

EIN: 133794889

Recent grants for international programs:

1656-1 American University of Beirut, Beirut, Lebanon, $500,000. For chair in mathematics. 2009.

1656-2 Chern Medal Foundation, Houston, TX, $2,000,000. 2009.

1656-3 Friends of the Institut des Hautes Etudes Scientifiques, New York, NY, $4,666,244. 2009.

1656-4 Friends of the Institut des Hautes Etudes Scientifiques, New York, NY, $4,294,359. 2009.

1656-5 Friends of the Institut des Hautes Etudes Scientifiques, New York, NY, $100,000. For benefit. 2009.

1656-6 Friends of the Institut des Hautes Etudes Scientifiques, New York, NY, $21,879. 2009.

1656-7 Friends of the Institut des Hautes Etudes Scientifiques, New York, NY, $10,400. 2009.

1656-8 Friends of the Institut des Hautes Etudes Scientifiques, New York, NY, $10,000. 2009.

1656-9 Geohazards International, Palo Alto, CA, $10,000. 2009.

1656-10 International Society for Autism Research, West Hartford, CT, $50,000. For IMFAR meeting. 2009.

1656-11 McGill University, Montreal, Canada, $224,434. For SFARI Simplex Collection (SSC), core project and resource of Simons Foundation Autism Research Initiative (SFARI), using family genetic samples. 2009.

1656-12 McGill University, Montreal, Canada, $16,070. For SFARI Simplex Collection (SSC), core project and resource of Simons Foundation Autism Research Initiative (SFARI), using family genetic samples. 2009.

1656-13 Oxford University, Oxford, England, $204,810. 2009.

1656-14 Oxford University, Oxford, England, $204,810. 2009.

1656-15 Science Festival Foundation, New York, NY, $500,000. For World Science Festival. 2009.

1656-16 Science Festival Foundation, New York, NY, $500,000. For World Science Festival. 2009.

1657
Singh Foundation, Inc.
c/o Rajasekhar Ramakrishnan
50 W. 97th St., Apt. 15T
New York, NY   10025-0681   (212) 866-1616
FAX: (212) 305-5834; E-mail: rr6@columbia.edu;
URL: http://www.singhfoundation.org/

Established in 1993 in NY.

Grantmaker type: Public charity.

Financial data (yr. ended 12/31/10): Revenue, $83,858; assets, $273,514 (M); gifts received, $70,520; expenditures, $117,871; program services expenses, $117,683; giving activities include $94,200 for grants.

Fields of interest: International relief; Media, film/video; Community/economic development.

International interests: South Asia.

Type of support: Grants to individuals.

Limitations: Applications not accepted. Giving primarily in India and Dhaka, Bangladesh, with some giving in NY.

Application information: Unsolicited requests for funds not accepted.

Officers: Deepak Kapur, Pres.; Abha Sur, V.P.; R. Ramakrishnan, Secy.-Treas.

EIN: 133719319

1658
The Skadden Fellowship Foundation, Inc.
(formerly Skadden, Arps, Slate, Meagher & Flom Fellowship Foundation)
360 Hamilton Ave.
White Plains, NY   10601-1811   (212) 735-2956
Contact: Susan Butler Plum, Dir.
FAX: (917) 777-2956; Application address: 4 Times Sq., Rm. 29-218, New York, NY 10036; URL: http://www.skaddenfellowships.org/

Grants List: http://www.skaddenfellowships.org/sitecontent.cfm?page=recentFellows

Established in 1988 in NY.

Donor: Skadden, Arps, Slate, Meagher & Flom.

Grantmaker type: Company-sponsored foundation.

Financial data (yr. ended 12/31/09): Assets, $8,453,072 (M); gifts received, $6,637,406; expenditures, $4,247,332; qualifying distributions, $4,200,126; giving activities include $3,770,101 for grants to individuals.

Purpose and activities: The foundation awards fellowships to graduating law students and outgoing judicial clerks who create projects at public interest organizations designed to provide legal services to the poor, the elderly, the disabled, and those deprived of their civil rights or human rights.

Fields of interest: Leadership development; Civil/human rights, advocacy; Law school/education; Aging; Disabilities, people with; Economically disadvantaged.

Type of support: Fellowships.

Limitations: Applications accepted. Giving on a national basis, with emphasis on Berkeley, Los Angeles, Oakland, San Diego, and San Francisco, CA, Washington, DC, Chicago, IL, MA, and Bronx, Brooklyn, and New York, NY. No grants to individuals who do not secure a potential position with a sponsoring public interest organization.

Publications: Application guidelines; Informational brochure; Multi-year report.

Application information: Application form required.

Initial approach: Download application form and mail application form and supporting materials to foundation

Copies of proposal: 1
Deadline(s): Oct. 3
Board meeting date(s): Dec. 3
Final notification: Dec. 2

Trustees: Jacqeuline Anchondo; Eric J. Friedman; Barry H. Garfinkel; Judith S. Kaye; Jose Lozano; Suzanne Mckechnie Klahr; Mathew Minow; Peter P. Mullen; Michael H. Schill; Kurt Schmoke; Robert C. Sheehan; Solomon Watson IV; Peter P. Mullen.

Advisory Committee: Lauren E. Aguiar; Jose R. Allen; Thomas J. Allingham II; Margaret A. Brown; C. Benjamin Crisman, Jr.; Eric J. Gorman; Alan C. Myers; Harriet S. Posner; Peter Simshauser; Stephanie C. Robinson; Ronald J. Tabak; Vaughn C. Williams.

Number of staff: 1 full-time professional; 1 part-time support.

EIN: 133455231

1659
Skirball Foundation
31 W. 52nd St., 21st Fl.
New York, NY   10019-6396   (212) 832-8500
Contact: Martin Blackman, Pres.

Established in 1950 in OH.

Donors: Members of the Skirball family; Skirball Investment Co.

Grantmaker type: Independent foundation.

Financial data (yr. ended 12/31/10): Assets, $82,105,676 (M); expenditures, $32,652,194; qualifying distributions, $30,612,382; giving activities include $29,024,789 for 148 grants (high: $11,420,454; low: $2).

Purpose and activities: Giving primarily for Jewish welfare and temple support; support also for education, the arts, and medicine.

Fields of interest: Media/communications; Arts; Education; Human services; Jewish federated giving programs; Jewish agencies & synagogues.

Limitations: Applications accepted. Giving primarily in CA. No grants to individuals.

Application information: Contributes primarily to pre-selected organizations and accepts limited applications for funds.

Officers and Trustees:* Martin Blackman,* C.E.O. and Pres.; Marvin Goldstein, V.P., Secy. and C.F.O.; Robert D. Goldfarb,* Treas.; Nympha H. Cody, Cont.; Uri D. Herscher.

EIN: 346517957

Recent grants for international programs:

1659-1 African Wildlife Foundation, Washington, DC, $25,000. For operating support. 2009.

1659-2 American Associates, Ben-Gurion University of the Negev, New York, NY, $320,000. For operating support. 2009.

1659-3 American Committee for the Weizmann Institute of Science, Los Angeles, CA, $182,120. For operating support. Grant given in form of securities. 2009.

1659-4 American Committee for the Weizmann Institute of Science, New York, NY, $17,880. For operating support. 2009.

1659-5 American Friends of Hazon Yeshaya Institutions, Brooklyn, NY, $50,000. For operating support. 2009.

1659-6 American Friends of Shalom Hartman Institute, New York, NY, $50,000. For endowed chair. 2009.

1659-7 American Friends of the Hebrew University, New York, NY, $250,000. For endowed chair. 2009.

1659-8 American Friends of the Israel Museum, New York, NY, $270,818. For operating support. Grant given in form of securities. 2009.

1659-9 American Friends of the Israel Museum, New York, NY, $29,183. For operating support. 2009.

1659-10 American Friends of the Tel Aviv University, New York, NY, $17,480. For operating support. 2009.

1659-11 American Jewish Joint Distribution Committee, New York, NY, $91,595. For operating support. Grant given in form of securities. 2009.

1659-12 American Jewish Joint Distribution Committee, New York, NY, $83,787. For operating support. Grant given in form of securities. 2009.

1659-13 American Jewish Joint Distribution Committee, New York, NY, $81,972. For operating support. Grant given in form of securities. 2009.

1659-14 American Jewish Joint Distribution Committee, New York, NY, $58,499. For operating support. Grant given in form of securities. 2009.

1659-15 American Jewish Joint Distribution Committee, New York, NY, $45,742. For operating support. 2009.

1659-16 American Society for Technion-Israel Institute of Technology, New York, NY, $46,312. For operating support. Grant given in form of securities. 2009.

1659-17 Auschwitz Jewish Center Foundation, New York, NY, $25,000. For operating support. 2009.

1659-18 Ben-Gurion University of the Negev, Beer Sheva, Israel, $100,000. For operating support and for the emergency fund. 2009.

1659-19 Ben-Gurion University of the Negev, Faculty of Health Sciences, Beer Sheva, Israel, $40,000. For general support of the Center for Emerging Diseases, Tropical Diseases and AIDS (CEMTA). 2009.

1659-20 Daniel Pearl Foundation, Encino, CA, $25,000. For operating support. 2009.

1659-21 Friends of Beit Daniel Synagogue and Community Center, Chevy Chase, MD, $50,000. For operating support. 2009.

1659-22 Friends of Yemin Orde, Rockville, MD, $25,000. For operating support. 2009.

1659-23 Helen Keller International, New York, NY, $40,000. For operating support. 2009.

1659-24 Human Rights Watch, Los Angeles, CA, $10,000. For operating support. 2009.

1659-25 Israel at Heart, New York, NY, $50,000. For operating support. 2009.

1659-26 Israel Center for Excellence Through Education, Chicago, IL, $250,000. For operating support. 2009.

1659-27 Israel Emergency Alliance, StandWithUs (SWU), Los Angeles, CA, $50,000. For operating support. 2009.

1659-28 Israeli Education Fund, Los Angeles, CA, $45,000. For operating support. 2009.

1659-29 Jerusalem Foundation, New York, NY, $25,000. For operating support. 2009.

1659-30 Jewish World Watch, Encino, CA, $25,000. For operating support. 2009.

1659-31 Museum Computer Network, Ottawa, Canada, $15,000. For operating support. 2009.

1659-32 North American Conference on Ethiopian Jewry, New York, NY, $25,000. For operating support. 2009.

1659-33 Operation Smile International, Norfolk, VA, $50,000. For operating support. 2009.

1659-34 Oxford Centre for Hebrew and Jewish Studies, Oxford, England, $92,611. For operating support. Grant given in form of securities. 2009.

1659-35 Pontifical Gregorian University, Institute for the Study of Religions and Cultures, Rome, Italy, $20,000. For operating support. 2009.

1659-36 Seacology, Berkeley, CA, $10,000. For operating support. 2009.

1659-37 W. F. Albright Institute of Archaeological Research, Philadelphia, PA, $100,077. For operating support. Grant given in form of securities. 2009.

1660
Alan B. Slifka Foundation, Inc.

477 Madison Ave., 8th Fl.
New York, NY   10022-5802   (212) 303-9470
Contact: Sarah Silver, Exec. Dir.
E-mail: programofficer@halcyonllc.com

Established in 1963 in NY.
Donors: Alan B. Slifka†; Sylvia Slifka†.
Grantmaker type: Independent foundation.
Financial data (yr. ended 11/30/09): Assets, $30,556,989 (M); gifts received, $4,357,938; expenditures, $6,688,276; qualifying distributions, $6,592,929; giving activities include $6,092,308 for 429 grants (high: $600,000; low: $50).
Purpose and activities: Support primarily for Jewish interest projects and cultural activities and for endeavors that promote coexistence and a world safe for difference.
Fields of interest: Jewish agencies & synagogues; International peace/security; International affairs; Religion, interfaith issues; Religion.
International interests: Israel; Middle East.
Type of support: Research; General/operating support; Continuing support; Program development; Seed money; Curriculum development; Program evaluation; Matching/challenge support.
Limitations: Applications accepted. No support for political organizations, environmental, medical, or health-related fields. No grants to individuals, or for endowments, for-profit organizations or acquisitions of land. Generally no grants for major equipment purchases, individual research or media projects.
Application information: Telephone or e-mail the foundation for a copy of the current guidelines which has all the necessary information for applying.
  Initial approach: Letter
  Copies of proposal: 1
  Board meeting date(s): Varies
Officers and Board Members:* Shira Levin,* Secy.; Sarah Silver, Exec. Dir.; Gary Gladstein; Rachelle Markowitz; Riva Ritro Slitka.
Number of staff: 3 full-time professional; 1 full-time support.
EIN: 136192257
Recent grants for international programs:

1660-1 Abraham Fund Initiatives, New York, NY, $600,000. For unrestricted support. 2009.

1660-2 Abraham Fund Initiatives, New York, NY, $600,000. For unrestricted support. 2009.

1660-3 Abraham Fund Initiatives, New York, NY, $40,000. For unrestricted support. 2009.

1660-4 Abraham Fund Initiatives, New York, NY, $25,000. For unrestricted support. 2009.

1660-5 Abraham Fund Initiatives, New York, NY, $25,000. For unrestricted support. 2009.

1660-6 Abraham Fund Initiatives, New York, NY, $25,000. For unrestricted support. 2009.

1660-7 Abraham Joshua Heschel Center for Environmental Learning and Leadership, Tel Aviv, Israel, $10,000. For unrestricted support. 2009.

1660-8 Abraham Path Initiative, Boulder, CO, $10,000. For unrestricted support. 2009.

1660-9 Abrahams Vision, Redwood City, CA, $25,000. For unrestricted support. 2009.

1660-10 American Friends of Shalom Hartman Institute, New York, NY, $35,000. For unrestricted support. 2009.

1660-11 American Friends of Shalom Hartman Institute, New York, NY, $25,000. For unrestricted support. 2009.

1660-12 American Friends of the College of Management, New York, NY, $12,000. For unrestricted support. 2009.

1660-13 American Friends of the Israel Museum, New York, NY, $200,000. For unrestricted support. 2009.

1660-14 American Friends of the Yaacov Herzog Center for Jewish Studies, Chicago, IL, $15,000. For unrestricted support. 2009.

1660-15 American Jewish Joint Distribution Committee, New York, NY, $10,000. For unrestricted support. 2009.

1660-16 American Pardes Foundation, New York, NY, $20,000. For unrestricted support. 2009.

1660-17 American Society of the University of Haifa, New York, NY, $45,000. For unrestricted support. 2009.

1660-18 American Society of the University of Haifa, New York, NY, $15,000. For unrestricted support. 2009.

1660-19 American Supporters of YEDID, Teaneck, NJ, $10,000. For unrestricted support. 2009.

1660-20 Central Fund of Israel, New York, NY, $10,000. For unrestricted support. 2009.

1660-21 Club of Madrid Foundation, Boston, MA, $425,000. For unrestricted support. 2009.

1660-22 Earthville Network, Evergreen, CO, $25,000. For unrestricted support. 2009.

1660-23 Gesher Foundation, New York, NY, $20,000. For unrestricted support. 2009.

1660-24 Hand in Hand, Jerusalem, Israel, $10,000. For unrestricted support. 2009.

1660-25 Human Dignity and Humiliation Studies, Lake Oswego, OR, $10,000. For unrestricted support. 2009.

1660-26 International Society for Autism Research, West Hartford, CT, $25,000. For unrestricted support. 2009.

1660-27 Israel Guide Dog Center for the Blind, Warrington, PA, $11,500. For unrestricted support. 2009.

1660-28 Israel Venture Network, Israel Office, Kadima, Israel, $10,000. For unrestricted support. 2009.

1660-29 Jewish Agency for Israel, New York, NY, $10,000. For unrestricted support. 2009.

1660-30 Judaism and Democracy Action Alliance of North America, New York, NY, $30,000. For unrestricted support. 2009.

1660-31 Judaism and Democracy Action Alliance of North America, New York, NY, $25,000. For unrestricted support. 2009.

1660-32 Judaism and Democracy Action Alliance of North America, New York, NY, $25,000. For unrestricted support. 2009.

1660-33 Judaism and Democracy Action Alliance of North America, New York, NY, $25,000. For unrestricted support. 2009.

1660-34 Judaism and Democracy Action Alliance of North America, New York, NY, $20,000. For unrestricted support. 2009.

1660-35 Judaism and Democracy Action Alliance of North America, New York, NY, $15,000. For unrestricted support. 2009.

1660-36 Kivunim, New York, NY, $30,000. For unrestricted support. 2009.

1660-37 Meretz USA, New York, NY, $20,000. For unrestricted support. 2009.

1660-38 New Israel Fund, Washington, DC, $30,000. For unrestricted support. 2009.

1660-39 New Israel Fund, Washington, DC, $22,000. For unrestricted support. 2009.

1660-40 New Israel Fund, Washington, DC, $15,000. For unrestricted support. 2009.

1660-41 New Israel Fund, Washington, DC, $15,000. For unrestricted support. 2009.

1660-42 New Israel Fund, Washington, DC, $15,000. For unrestricted support. 2009.

1660-43 New Israel Fund, Washington, DC, $14,000. For unrestricted support. 2009.

1660-44 New Israel Fund, Washington, DC, $12,500. For unrestricted support. 2009.

1660-45 New Israel Fund, Washington, DC, $10,000. For unrestricted support. 2009.

1660-46 New Israel Fund, Washington, DC, $10,000. For unrestricted support. 2009.

1660-47 New Israel Fund, Washington, DC, $10,000. For unrestricted support. 2009.

1660-48 North American Friends of Oranim, Milwaukee, WI, $15,000. For unrestricted support. 2009.

1660-49 Ohr Torah Stone Colleges and Graduate Programs, New York, NY, $25,000. For unrestricted support. 2009.

1660-50 Ohr Torah Stone Colleges and Graduate Programs, New York, NY, $25,000. For unrestricted support. 2009.

1660-51 PEF Israel Endowment Funds, New York, NY, $25,000. For unrestricted support. 2009.

1660-52 PEF Israel Endowment Funds, New York, NY, $25,000. For unrestricted support. 2009.

1660-53 PEF Israel Endowment Funds, New York, NY, $15,000. For unrestricted support. 2009.

1660-54 PEF Israel Endowment Funds, New York, NY, $15,000. For unrestricted support. 2009.

1660-55 PEF Israel Endowment Funds, New York, NY, $11,000. For unrestricted support. 2009.

1660-56 PEF Israel Endowment Funds, New York, NY, $10,000. For unrestricted support. 2009.

1660-57 PEF Israel Endowment Funds, New York, NY, $10,000. For unrestricted support. 2009.

1660-58 PEF Israel Endowment Funds, New York, NY, $10,000. For unrestricted support. 2009.

1660-59 PEF Israel Endowment Funds, New York, NY, $10,000. For unrestricted support. 2009.

1660-60 PEF Israel Endowment Funds, New York, NY, $10,000. For unrestricted support. 2009.

1660-61 PEF Israel Endowment Funds, New York, NY, $10,000. For unrestricted support. 2009.

1660-62 PEF Israel Endowment Funds, New York, NY, $10,000. For unrestricted support. 2009.

1660-63 PEF Israel Endowment Funds, New York, NY, $10,000. For unrestricted support. 2009.

1660-64 Washington Institute, Alexandria, VA, $10,000. For unrestricted support. 2009.

1660-65 Washington Institute for Near East Policy, Washington, DC, $10,000. For unrestricted support. 2009.

1660-66 Zionism 2000, Beit Yehoshea, Israel, $10,000. For unrestricted support. 2009.

1661
Smile Train, Inc.

41 Madison Ave., Fl. 28
New York, NY 10010-2351 (212) 689-9199
Contact: Priscilla Ma, V.P., Mktg.; Shari Mason, Mktg. Coord.
FAX: (212) 689-9299; E-mail: info@smiletrain.org; Additional e-mail: pma@smiletrain.org; URL: http://www.smiletrain.org

Established in 1998 in NY.
Grantmaker type: Public charity.
Financial data (yr. ended 06/30/10): Revenue, $105,677,409; assets, $145,352,003 (M); gifts received, $102,277,208; expenditures, $86,267,187; giving activities include $257,500 for grants, and $35,128,006 for grants to organizations outside the U.S.
Purpose and activities: The organization is dedicated to helping the millions of children in the world who suffer from cleft lip and palate through free surgery for children, free training for doctors, and research to find a cure.
Fields of interest: Genetic diseases and disorders; Health care.
International interests: Afghanistan; Argentina; Armenia; Bangladesh; Bhutan; Bolivia; Bosnia-Herzegovina; Brazil; Bulgaria; Cambodia; Chile; China; Colombia; Ecuador; Egypt; El Salvador; Ethiopia; East Timor; Georgia (Republic of); Ghana; Guatemala; Guyana; Haiti; Honduras; Hungary; India; Indonesia; Iran; Iraq; Kenya; Laos; Malaysia; Mexico; Moldova; Mongolia; Nepal; Nicaragua; Nigeria; Pakistan; Peru; Philippines; Poland; Romania; Russia; Rwanda; Senegal; South Africa; Sri Lanka; Taiwan; Tanzania; Zanzibar and Pemba; Thailand; Turkey; Uganda; Ukraine; Uzbekistan; Venezuela; Vietnam; Yemen; Zambia.
Type of support: General/operating support; Continuing support; Equipment; Program development; Consulting services; Program evaluation; In-kind gifts.
Limitations: Applications accepted. Giving in the U.S. and to Afghanistan, Argentina, Armenia, Bangladesh, Bhutan, Bolivia, Bosnia and Herzegovina, Brazil, Bulgaria, Cambodia, Chile, China, Colombia, East Timor, Ecuador, Egypt, El Salvador, Ethiopia, Georgia, Ghana, Guatemala, Guyana, Haiti, Honduras, Hungary, India, Indonesia, Iran, Iraq, Israel, Kenya, Laos, Malaysia, Mexico, Moldova, Mongolia, Nepal, Nicaragua, Nigeria, Pakistan, Peru, Philippines, Poland, Romania, Russia, Rwanda, Senegal, South Africa, Sri Lanka, Taiwan, Tanzania, Thailand, Turkey, Uganda, Ukraine, Uzbekistan, Venezuela, Vietnam, Yemen, and Zambia.
Publications: Application guidelines; Annual report; Financial statement; Informational brochure; Newsletter; Program policy statement.
Application information: Application form required.
   Initial approach: Download application form
   Deadline(s): Rolling basis
   Final notification: Within six weeks of application submission
Officers and Board Members:* Charles B. Wang,* Chair.; Brian F. Mullaney,* Pres.; DeLois Greenwood, V.P.; Mark E. Atkinson; Robert T. Bell; Donald B. Murphy; Susannah Schaefer; Robert K. Smits, Esq.; Tamsen Ann Ziff.
Number of staff: 38
EIN: 133661416

1662
George D. Smith Fund, Inc.

c/o L.W. Milas & W.B. Norden
620 8th Ave.
New York, NY 10018-1415 (212) 218-5500
Contact: Lawrence W. Milas, V.P.

Incorporated in 1956 in DE.
Donor: George D. Smith, Sr.‡.
Grantmaker type: Independent foundation.
Financial data (yr. ended 12/31/10): Assets, $136,275,295 (M); expenditures, $5,300,258; qualifying distributions, $5,202,859; giving activities include $5,200,000 for 10 grants (high: $1,200,000; low: $100).
Fields of interest: Media, television; Higher education; Biomedicine; Medical research, institute.
Type of support: Research.
Limitations: Applications not accepted. Giving primarily in CA.
Application information: Unsolicited requests for funds not considered.
Officers: George D. Smith, Jr., Pres. and Secy.-Treas.; Lawrence W. Milas, V.P.; Camilla M. Smith, V.P.
Director: Sarah A. Smith.
EIN: 136138728
Recent grants for international programs:
1662-1 Carter Center, Atlanta, GA, $600,000. 2010.

1663
Social Science Research Council

(also known as SSRC)
1 Pierrepoint Plz., 15th Fl.
Brooklyn, NY 11201-2776 (212) 377-2700
Contact: Gail Kovach, Dir., Admin. Svcs.
FAX: (212) 377-2727; E-mail: info@ssrc.org; URL: http://www.ssrc.org
Facebook: http://www.facebook.com/SSRC.org
RSS Feed: http://www.ssrc.org/feed/
Twitter: http://twitter.com/#!/SSRC_org

Established in 1923 in IL.
Grantmaker type: Public charity.
Financial data (yr. ended 06/30/10): Revenue, $18,826,627; assets, $31,314,933 (M); gifts received, $18,153,252; expenditures, $20,333,708; giving activities include $1,605,805 for grants, $502,618 for grants to organizations outside the U.S., and $3,336,290 for grants to individuals.
Purpose and activities: The council is devoted to the advancement of interdisciplinary research in the social sciences by means of a wide variety of interdisciplinary workshops and conferences, fellowships and grants, summer training institutes, scholarly exchanges, and publications; the council also offers support for dissertation fellowships, grants for advanced research, and grants to institutions.
Fields of interest: Telecommunications; Media/communications; Social sciences.
Type of support: Program development; Fellowships; Research.
Limitations: Applications accepted. Giving on a national and international basis.
Publications: Application guidelines; Informational brochure; Newsletter.
Application information: Applications are particularly encouraged from women and members of minority groups. Application form required.
   Initial approach: Complete online application

Deadline(s): Apr. 16 for Social Science Fellowship Program; Apr. 22 for Collaborative Grants; Sept. 1 for Abe Fellowship Program; Oct. 3 for Dissertation Proposal Development Fellowships; Nov. 1 for Mellon Mays Graduate Initiatives Program; Nov. 6 for International Dissertation Research Fellowship; Nov. 13 for Eurasia Fellowship Program; varies for all others

Board meeting date(s): Mar. and Nov.

Final notification: Varies

Officers and Directors:* Michael J. Watts,* Chair.; Craig Calhoun,* Pres.; Ira Katznelson,* Secy.; Michael D. Kennedy, Treas.; Mary Byrne McDonnell, Exec. Dir.; Jonathan Aronson; John Seely Brown; Lincoln C. Chen; David Coulter; Dame Sandra Dawson; Edward Glaeser; Alfred Gusenbauer; Caroline Humphrey; William H. Janeway; Margaret Levi; and 5 additional directors.

Number of staff: 30 full-time professional; 2 part-time professional; 21 full-time support; 2 part-time support.

EIN: 131325070

1664

Sony USA Foundation Inc.

c/o Communicatons and Public Affairs Dept.
550 Madison Ave., 33rd Fl.
New York, NY 10022-3211
Contact: Karen E. Kelso, V.P.

Established in 1972 in NY.

Donors: Sony Corp. of America; Sony Electronics, Inc.

Grantmaker type: Company-sponsored foundation.

Financial data (yr. ended 12/31/10): Assets, $675,370 (M); expenditures, $191,392; qualifying distributions, $190,867; giving activities include $190,867 for 3 grants (high: $106,535; low: $56,832).

Purpose and activities: The foundation supports organizations involved with education, youth development, and international exchange.

Fields of interest: Education; Youth development; International exchange, students.

Type of support: General/operating support; Continuing support; Program development; Curriculum development; Scholarship funds.

Limitations: Applications accepted. Giving primarily in MD and NY; giving also to national and international organizations. No grants to individuals, or for special projects, research, publications, or conferences; no loans.

Application information: Application form not required.

Initial approach: Letter of inquiry

Deadline(s): None

Officers and Directors:* Naofumi Hara,* Chair.; Mark Khalil, Pres.; Karen E. Kelso,* V.P. and Secy.; Edward Wallace, V.P.; H. Paul Burak,* V.P.; Ann L. Morfogen; Kenneth L. Nees.

EIN: 237181637

1665

Soros Fund Charitable Foundation

(formerly SGM Scholarship Foundation)
888 7th Ave., 33rd Fl.
New York, NY 10106-0011

Established in 1986 in NY.

Donors: George Soros; Soros Charitable Foundation; Soros Foundation-Hungary; Centennial Foundation.

Grantmaker type: Independent foundation.

Financial data (yr. ended 12/31/10): Assets, $194,530,861 (M); expenditures, $15,008,360; qualifying distributions, $14,845,950; giving activities include $14,845,950 for 281 grants (high: $10,000,000; low: $75).

Purpose and activities: Awards scholarships to students who have demonstrated an ability for contributing to the scientific, cultural, or economic development of China, and fellowships to individuals involved in the fields of culture, economics, and science. The scholarships and fellowships may be used for trips to the U.S. and other countries by Chinese nationals and trips to China by non-Chinese nationals. Support also for international organizations and U.S. philanthropic organizations supporting international issues.

Fields of interest: Education; Health care; Health organizations, association; Human services; Children/youth, services; International affairs, goodwill promotion; Civil rights, race/intergroup relations; Christian agencies & churches; Jewish agencies & synagogues.

International Interests: East Asia.

Type of support: General/operating support; Fellowships; Scholarship funds.

Limitations: Applications not accepted. Giving primarily in CT, NJ, and NY. No grants to individuals.

Application information: Contributes only to pre-selected organizations.

Officers and Directors:* Gary Gladstein,* Pres.; Daniel R. Eule,* V.P. and Secy.; Maryann Canfield, Treas.; Armando Belly; George Soros; Jonathan Allan Soros; William D. Zabel.

EIN: 133388177

Recent grants for international programs:

1665-1 Acumen Fund, New York, NY, $75,000. For general support. 2010.

1665-2 Alliance for Open Society International, New York, NY, $90,000. For general support. 2010.

1665-3 American Near East Refugee Aid, Washington, DC, $30,000. For general support. 2010.

1665-4 Birthright Israel Foundation, New York, NY, $75,000. For general support. 2010.

1665-5 CARE USA, Atlanta, GA, $15,750. For general support. 2010.

1665-6 DASRA, Sugar Land, TX, $150,000. For general support. 2010.

1665-7 Hoops for Hope, East Hampton, NY, $15,000. For general support. 2010.

1665-8 Human Rights Watch, New York, NY, $45,000. For general support. 2010.

1665-9 Institute for Middle East Understanding, Tustin, CA, $132,600. For general support. 2010.

1665-10 Israel-America Academic Exchange, Beverly Hills, CA, $13,500. For general support. 2010.

1665-11 King Baudouin Foundation United States, New York, NY, $82,500. For general support. 2010.

1665-12 Middle East Institute, Washington, DC, $37,500. For general support. 2010.

1665-13 Pratham USA, Houston, TX, $16,500. For general support. 2010.

1665-14 Shoe4Africa, Inc., New York, NY, $32,325. For general support. 2010.

1665-15 United States Fund for UNICEF, New York, NY, $15,000. For general support. 2010.

1666

Sotheby's Holdings, Inc. Corporate Giving Program

1334 York Ave.
New York, NY 10021-4806
FAX: (212) 606-7027;
E-mail: courtney.king@sothebys.com

Grantmaker type: Corporate giving program.

Purpose and activities: Sotheby's makes charitable contributions to nonprofit organizations involved with arts and culture. Support is given primarily in North America.

Fields of interest: Arts.

International interests: Canada; Mexico.

Type of support: General/operating support; Cause-related marketing; Sponsorships; In-kind gifts.

1667

Sparkplug Foundation

Park West Finance Station
P.O. Box 20956
New York, NY 10025 (877) 866-8285
Contact: Dorothy Zellner, Admin.
FAX: (877) 866-8285;
E-mail: info@sparkplugfoundation.org; URL: http://www.sparkplugfoundation.org/

Established in 2003 in NY.

Donors: Felice Gelman; Yoram Gelman; Emmaia Gelman.

Grantmaker type: Independent foundation.

Financial data (yr. ended 12/31/10): Assets, $6,642,799 (M); expenditures, $478,831; qualifying distributions, $351,418; giving activities include $351,418 for grants.

Purpose and activities: Giving is focused on providing seed money for new organizations, projects or ideas. The foundation makes one-time grants for activities which create sustainable organizing and communities, while recognizing the importance of developing individual cultures by favoring projects that promote diversity. The main areas of focus are music, education, and grassroots organizations, as well as exploring funding projects in the area of alternative and sustainable energies.

Fields of interest: Environment; Science; Performing arts, music ensembles/groups; International migration/refugee issues; International human rights; International affairs; Education; Community/economic development; Young adults; Adults, women; Native Americans/American Indians; Minorities; Indigenous peoples; Hispanics/Latinos; Asians/Pacific Islanders; AIDS, people with; African Americans/Blacks; LGBTQ; Immigrants/refugees.

International interests: East Jerusalem; Israel; West Bank/Gaza (Palestinian Territories).

Type of support: Management development/capacity building; Program development; Conferences/seminars; Publication; Seed money; Curriculum development; Research; Technical assistance; Program evaluation; Grants to individuals.

Limitations: Giving to every state in the USA. Some giving in Israel for projects that involve Palestinian communities. No support for university-based projects, or for non-secular activities. No grants to non-501(c)(3) organizations unless they have a fiscal sponsor. No grants for performances, tickets or tuitions, equipment, computers or for operating support.

Application information: Application process begins following initial phone call. Applications may be downloaded after determination from the foundation. Application form required.

Initial approach: Initial phone inquiry is required before an application can be considered and/or accepted

Copies of proposal: 1

Deadline(s): Spring and fall. See foundation web site for application deadline dates

Board meeting date(s): Within 4 weeks of deadline dates

Final notification: Usually within 1 month

Trustees: Felice Gelman; Yoram Gelman.

Number of staff: 1 part-time professional.

EIN: 331033952

1668

The Speyer Family Foundation, Inc.

(formerly Tishman Speyer Properties Foundation, Inc.)

45 Rockefeller Plz., 7th Fl.

New York, NY   10111-0100

Established in NY.

Donors: Katherine G. Farley; Jerry I. Speyer; Robert Speyer.

Grantmaker type: Independent foundation.

Financial data (yr. ended 09/30/09): Assets, $23,907 (M); gifts received, $1,802,559; expenditures, $3,376,530; qualifying distributions, $3,282,927; giving activities include $3,282,927 for 44 grants (high: $948,343; low: $500).

Purpose and activities: Giving primarily for museums, education, health care, and the arts.

Fields of interest: Museums (art); Museums (natural history); Performing arts; Arts; Higher education; Education; Hospitals (general); Health organizations; Human services; International human rights; Civil/human rights, immigrants; Jewish agencies & synagogues.

Limitations: Applications not accepted. Giving primarily in New York, NY. No grants to individuals.

Application information: Contributes only to pre-selected organizations.

Officers: Jerry I. Speyer, Pres.; Katherine G. Farley, V.P.; Linda Szoldatits, Secy.; Richard Welch, Treas.

Directors: Holly Lipton; Valerie Peltier; Robert Speyer.

EIN: 136158848

Recent grants for international programs:

1668-1 American Friends of the Israel Museum, New York, NY, $25,000. For education support. 2008.

1668-2 American Friends of the Israel Philharmonic Orchestra, New York, NY, $50,000. For production support. 2008.

1668-3 Americans for UNFPA, New York, NY, $15,000. For new projects support. 2008.

1668-4 International Rescue Committee, New York, NY, $76,750. For humanitarian services. 2008.

1668-5 University of Manitoba, Winnipeg, Canada, $25,000. For medicine scholarship program. 2008.

1669

Sam Spiegel Foundation, Inc.

(formerly Sam Spiegel Foundation)

c/o David N. Bottoms Jr.

30 Wall St., Ste. 1203

New York, NY   10005-2201   (212) 269-6720

Contact: David N. Bottoms, Jr., Dir.

Established in 1958 in NY.

Donors: Sam Spiegel; Albatros Enterprises Trust.

Grantmaker type: Independent foundation.

Financial data (yr. ended 12/31/10): Assets, $11,126,840 (M); expenditures, $319,716; qualifying distributions, $255,500; giving activities include $255,500 for grants.

Fields of interest: Hospitals (general); Arts; Education; Human services; Children/youth, services; Jewish federated giving programs; Jewish agencies & synagogues.

International interests: England.

Limitations: Applications accepted. Giving primarily in NY. No grants to individuals.

Application information:

Initial approach: Letter

Deadline(s): None

Directors: David N. Bottoms, Jr.; Raya Dreben; Alisa S. Freedman; Adam Spiegel; Michael Freedman.

EIN: 136163123

1670

St. George's Society of New York

216 E. 45th St., Ste. 901

New York, NY   10017-3304   (212) 682-6110

Contact: John Shannon, Exec. Dir.

FAX: (212) 682-3465;

E-mail: info@stgeorgessociety.org; URL: http://www.stgeorgessociety.org

Facebook: https://www.facebook.com/pages/St-Georges-Society-of-New-York/16723030430738

Established in 1770 in NY.

Donors: Charlotte M. F. Bentley†; British Embassy; DeCoizart Charitable Trust; Andrew MacKenzie Hay†; Florence Davis; Francis Finlay; Richard Grasso; Sir Deryck C. Maughan; Sir Edwin Manton†; William R. Miller; Martin Sullivan; Aetna; Citigroup UK; D'Amato & Lynch; HSBC Bank USA, N.A.; McGraw Hill Companies; Sherman & Sterling; Skaden Arps; JPMorgan Chase Bank, N.A.; Starr Foundation; Revolution Studios; CSFB; Bloomberg; Sony Corp.; AIG; WWP/Young & Rubicam; Hearst Corp.; Sir Howard Stringer; R. Brandon Fradd; Mark C. Pigott; PACCAR, Inc.; Ford Motor Co.

Grantmaker type: Operating foundation.

Financial data (yr. ended 12/31/10): Assets, $11,294,474 (M); gifts received, $932,688; expenditures, $1,308,099; qualifying distributions, $1,143,232; giving activities include $68,787 for 1 grant, $458,823 for 85 grants to individuals, and $766,598 for foundation-administered programs.

Purpose and activities: A private operating foundation dedicated to helping men and women from the United Kingdom and the British Commonwealth and their children who find themselves in need, trouble, sickness or other adversity in the New York, NY, area. Current programs include stipends, emergency grants, and burial funds.

Fields of interest: Health care; Disabilities, people with; Aging; Economically disadvantaged.

International interests: United Kingdom.

Type of support: Emergency funds; Grants to individuals.

Limitations: Giving limited to the metropolitan New York, NY, area.

Publications: Application guidelines; Annual report; Informational brochure; Newsletter.

Application information: Applicant must be a native of the United Kingdom or the British Commonwealth, residing in the New York, NY, metropolitan region, with a legal status. Personal interviews and visits from the Society's social worker. Application form not required.

Initial approach: Letter or telephone

Copies of proposal: 1

Deadline(s): None

Board meeting date(s): Quarterly

Final notification: 4-6 weeks

Officers: John C. Harvey, Pres.; Robert J.K. Titley, 1st V.P.; Richard Sexton, 2nd V.P.; Keith Simpson, Secy.; Stephen J. Storen, Treas.

Directors: Lewis Stetson Allen; Maria Allen; Ceasar N. Anquillare; Margot W. Astrachan; JoAnne Davidson; Vicki Downey; Hilda Frost; John Oden; Richard Powell; Nicholas C. Walsh; Philip Warner, OBE; John D. Wiltshire.

Number of staff: 2 full-time professional; 1 part-time professional; 2 full-time support.

EIN: 237426425

1671

The Stainman Family Foundation, Inc.

c/o Arthur J. Stainman

320 E. 72nd St.

New York, NY   10021-4769

Donors: Arthur J. Stainman; Lois Stainman.

Grantmaker type: Independent foundation.

Financial data (yr. ended 12/31/10): Assets, $13,351,436 (M); gifts received, $261,206; expenditures, $556,308; qualifying distributions, $534,090; giving activities include $534,090 for grants.

Fields of interest: Civil liberties, reproductive rights; Reproductive health, family planning; Arts; Human services; International affairs; Higher education, university; Animals/wildlife, preservation/protection; Food services.

Limitations: Applications not accepted. Giving primarily in NY; some giving also in Washington, DC. No grants to individuals.

Application information: Contributes only to pre-selected organizations.

Officers: Arthur J. Stainman, Pres.; Lois Stainman, V.P.; Evan Stainman, Secy.

EIN: 133980213

1672

The Starr Foundation

399 Park Ave., 17th Fl.

New York, NY   10022-4614   (212) 909-3600

Contact: Suzanne Eden, Prog. Off.

FAX: (212) 750-3536;

E-mail: suzanne.eden@starrfoundation.org;

URL: http://www.starrfoundation.org/

Incorporated in 1955 in NY.

Donor: Cornelius V. Starr†.

Grantmaker type: Independent foundation.

Financial data (yr. ended 12/31/10): Assets, $1,342,712,927 (M); expenditures, $124,194,477; qualifying distributions, $108,203,104; giving activities include $104,010,034 for 272 grants (high: $20,000,000;

low: $25), $925,850 for 112 grants to individuals (high: $19,040; low: $1,830), and $9,110 for 44 employee matching gifts.

Purpose and activities: The foundation makes grants in a number of areas, including education, medicine and health care, human needs, public policy, culture and the environment.

Fields of interest: Arts; Higher education; Education; Environment; Health care; Health organizations, association; Medical research; Human services; Social sciences; Aging; Youth; Military/veterans; Immigrants/refugees; Economically disadvantaged; Disabilities, people with; Deaf/hearing impaired; Children; Blind/visually impaired; AIDS, people with; Adults.

International interests: Asia.

Type of support: Building/renovation; Capital campaigns; Continuing support; Emergency funds; Employee matching gifts; Employee-related scholarships; Endowments; Exchange programs; Fellowships; General/operating support; Management development/capacity building; Matching/challenge support; Professorships; Program development; Research; Scholarship funds.

Limitations: Applications not accepted. Giving on a national and international basis, with emphasis on New York, NY and Asia. No support for religious institutions (except for non-denominational human services). No grants to individuals (except for children of C.V. Starr & Co. and Starr International Co. employees, pursuant to a qualified scholarship program).

Publications: IRS Form 990 or 990-PF printed copy available upon request.

Application information: The foundation does not accept unsolicited applications. Unsolicited applications will be declined summarily and will not be saved by the foundation.

Board meeting date(s): Six times per year

Officers and Directors:* Maurice R. "Hank" Greenberg,* Chair.; Florence A. Davis,* Pres.; Paula S. Lawrence, V.P.; Courtney O'Malley, V.P.; Joan Katz, Corp. Secy. of the Board; Howard I. Smith,* Treas.; T.C. Hsu; Edward E. Matthews; John J. Roberts.

Number of staff: 8 full-time professional; 1 part-time professional; 4 full-time support.

EIN: 136151545

Recent grants for international programs:

1672-1 America-Israel Friendship League, New York, NY, $10,000. For general operating support. 2010.

1672-2 American Public Media Group, Saint Paul, MN, $25,000. For Asia economic coverage on Marketplace. 2010.

1672-3 Business Council for International Understanding, New York, NY, $10,000. For general operating support. 2010.

1672-4 Business Executives for National Security, Washington, DC, $225,000. For general operating support. 2010.

1672-5 Business Executives for National Security, Washington, DC, $25,000. For general operating support. 2010.

1672-6 Business Executives for National Security, Washington, DC, $25,000. For table at Eisenhower Award Dinner. 2010.

1672-7 Center for Strategic and International Studies, Washington, DC, $10,000,000. For new conference center. 2010.

1672-8 Center for Strategic and International Studies, Washington, DC, $150,000. For Greenberg-Cohen Commission (also known as U.S.-ASEAN Strategy Commission), which will bring together thought leaders including top executives from American companies, former government officials, and civil society leaders. The initiative will include an extensive review of American interests in Southeast Asia ranging from security and political to trade and investment to social cultural and people to people ties and then present a set of recommendations representing key elements of a long-term US strategy for Southeast Asia to the President and the Congress. 2010.

1672-9 Center for Strategic and International Studies, Washington, DC, $100,000. For Sanya Initiative, Track Two military dialogue between retired service chiefs from China and the U.S. 2010.

1672-10 Center for the National Interest, Washington, DC, $75,000. For American National Security in the 21st Century program. 2010.

1672-11 Center for the National Interest, Washington, DC, $50,000. For general operating support. 2010.

1672-12 China Development Research Foundation, Beijing, China, $209,000. For China Development Forum. 2010.

1672-13 China Institute in America, New York, NY, $40,000. For table at China Institute Gala. 2010.

1672-14 Columbia University, School of International and Public Affairs, New York, NY, $10,000. To augment C.V. Starr Scholarship Fund. 2010.

1672-15 Council on Foreign Relations, New York, NY, $35,000. For Annual Fund. 2010.

1672-16 Eisenhower Exchange Fellowships, Philadelphia, PA, $50,000. For exchange programs. 2010.

1672-17 ELEM Youth in Distress, New York, NY, $12,000. For general operating support. 2010.

1672-18 Financial Services Volunteer Corps, New York, NY, $15,000. For general operating support. 2010.

1672-19 Foreign Policy Association, New York, NY, $25,000. For general operating support. 2010.

1672-20 Foreign Policy Association, New York, NY, $15,000. For general operating support. 2010.

1672-21 French-American Foundation, New York, NY, $15,000. For general operating support. 2010.

1672-22 Friends of Tsinghua SEM, San Jose, CA, $50,000. To augment support to Zhu Rongji Scholarship Fund. 2010.

1672-23 Institute of International Education, New York, NY, $50,000. For general operating support. 2010.

1672-24 Institute of International Education, New York, NY, $15,000. For general operating support. 2010.

1672-25 Institute of World Politics, Washington, DC, $10,000. For general operating support. 2010.

1672-26 International Rescue Committee, New York, NY, $100,000. For table at Freedom Award Dinner. 2010.

1672-27 Japan Society, New York, NY, $15,000. For general operating support. 2010.

1672-28 Kings Academy, Madaba-Manja, Jordan, $50,000. To augment C.V. Starr Scholarship Fund. 2010.

1672-29 Kings Academy, Madaba-Manja, Jordan, $50,000. To augment C.V. Starr Scholarship Fund. 2010.

1672-30 National Chamber Foundation, Washington, DC, $100,000. For China Corporate Social Responsibility (CSR) and corporate governance issues. 2010.

1672-31 National Committee on American Foreign Policy, New York, NY, $10,000. For general operating support. 2010.

1672-32 National Committee on United States-China Relations, New York, NY, $50,000. For table at Gala Dinner. 2010.

1672-33 National Committee on United States-China Relations, New York, NY, $25,000. For table at reception and dinner in honor of China's Premier. 2010.

1672-34 New York City Police Foundation, New York, NY, $250,000. For International Liaison Program. 2010.

1672-35 Project HOPE - The People-to-People Health Foundation, Millwood, VA, $15,000. For general operating support. 2010.

1672-36 Rice University, James A. Baker III Institute for Public Policy, Houston, TX, $2,500,000. For Transnational China Fellowship. 2010.

1672-37 U.S.-China Policy Foundation, Washington, DC, $50,000. For general operating support. 2010.

1672-38 U.S.-China Policy Foundation, Washington, DC, $10,000. For general operating support. 2010.

1672-39 Woodrow Wilson International Center for Scholars, Washington, DC, $150,000. For Kissinger Institute on China and the United States. 2010.

1672-40 Yale University, New Haven, CT, $15,000,000. For World Fellows Program. 2010.

1673
The Robert K. Steel Family Foundation
c/o BCRS Assocs.
100 Wall St., 11th Fl.
New York, NY 10005

Established in 1989 in NY.

Donors: Robert K. Steel; Robert K. Steel Family; Goldman, Sachs, & Co.

Grantmaker type: Independent foundation.

Financial data (yr. ended 04/30/10): Assets, $12,082,562 (M); gifts received, $4,852,179; expenditures, $5,575,563; qualifying distributions, $5,330,626; giving activities include $5,330,626 for grants.

Purpose and activities: Giving primarily for higher education, and to health associations and hospitals.

Fields of interest: Arts; Higher education; Health care; Health organizations, association; International studies; Protestant agencies & churches.

Type of support: General/operating support; Annual campaigns; Capital campaigns; Endowments.

Limitations: Applications not accepted. Giving primarily in NC and NY. No grants to individuals.

Application information: Contributes only to pre-selected organizations.

Trustees: Gillian V. Steel; Robert K. Steel.

EIN: 133531990

Recent grants for international programs:

1673-1 Akanksha Fund, New York, NY, $100,000. 2010.

1673-2 Global Fund for Children, Washington, DC, $100,000. 2010.

1673-3 Global Fund for Children, Washington, DC, $100,000. 2010.

1673-4 Humanity in Action, New York, NY, $100,000. 2010.

1673-5 Right to Play USA, New York, NY, $100,000. 2010.

1674
Allen A. Stein Family Foundation, Inc.

c/o Davidson, Dawson & Clark LLP
60 E. 42nd St., 38th Fl.
New York, NY   10165-0006
Contact: Christine A. Kehoe, Admin. Dir.
E-mail: cakehoe@davidsondavidson.com

Established in 2002 in NY.
Donor: Allen A. Stein†.
Grantmaker type: Independent foundation.
Financial data (yr. ended 12/31/10): Assets, $8,974,704 (M); expenditures, $483,607; qualifying distributions, $366,995; giving activities include $366,745 for 115 grants (high: $25,000; low: $180).
Purpose and activities: Giving primarily for Jewish education, organizations and temples.
Fields of interest: Theological school/education; Jewish federated giving programs; Jewish agencies & synagogues.
International interests: Israel.
Type of support: General/operating support; Continuing support; Annual campaigns; Capital campaigns; Building/renovation; Equipment; Program development; Research.
Limitations: Applications not accepted.
Application information: Unsolicited requests for funds not accepted.
   Board meeting date(s): Quarterly
Officers and Directors:* Elaine Stein Roberts,* Pres.; Bernard Roberts,* V.P. and Treas.; Eric Stein,* V.P.; Sharon Stein,* V.P.; Margot Stein,* Secy.
Number of staff: 1 part-time professional.
EIN: 134153383

1675
The Judy and Michael Steinhardt Foundation

650 Madison Ave., 17th Fl
New York, NY   10022-1029   (212) 371-7300
Contact: Michael H. Steinhardt, Tr.

Established in 1986 in NY.
Donor: Michael H. Steinhardt.
Grantmaker type: Independent foundation.
Financial data (yr. ended 09/30/10): Assets, $647,020 (M); gifts received, $1,515,125; expenditures, $1,515,532; qualifying distributions, $1,515,225; giving activities include $1,515,000 for 3 grants (high: $515,000; low: $500,000).
Purpose and activities: Support for Jewish giving and Jewish welfare, including organizations supporting Israel; support also for higher and other education and a botanical garden.
Fields of interest: Higher education; Education; Environment, natural resources; Human services; Jewish federated giving programs; Jewish agencies & synagogues.
International interests: Israel.
Limitations: Applications not accepted. Giving primarily in NY. No grants to individuals.
Application information: Contributes only to pre-selected organizations.
Trustees: Judith Steinhardt; Michael H. Steinhardt.
EIN: 133357500
Recent grants for international programs:

1675-1 American Friends of Shavei Israel, New York, NY, $10,000. For unrestricted support. 2009.
1675-2 American Friends of the Israel Museum, New York, NY, $1,000,000. For unrestricted support. 2009.
1675-3 American Friends of the Israel Museum, New York, NY, $100,000. For unrestricted support. 2009.
1675-4 American Pardes Foundation, New York, NY, $10,000. For unrestricted support. 2009.
1675-5 Birthright Israel Foundation, New York, NY, $1,850,000. For unrestricted support. 2009.
1675-6 Birthright Israel Foundation, New York, NY, $1,000,000. For unrestricted support. 2009.
1675-7 Birthright Israel Foundation, New York, NY, $10,000. For unrestricted support. 2009.
1675-8 Council on Foreign Relations, New York, NY, $25,000. For unrestricted support. 2009.
1675-9 Ezrat Israel, Brooklyn, NY, $10,000. For unrestricted support. 2009.
1675-10 Israel Youth Village, Brooklyn, NY, $10,000. For unrestricted support. 2009.
1675-11 Middle East Media Research Institute, Washington, DC, $10,000. For unrestricted support. 2009.

1676
Ernest E. Stempel Foundation

c/o Eisenberg
150 Broadway, Ste. 1102
New York, NY   10038-4367

Established in 1994 in DE.
Donor: Ernest E. Stempel†.
Grantmaker type: Independent foundation.
Financial data (yr. ended 12/31/10): Assets, $29,363,934 (M); gifts received, $1,556,269; expenditures, $1,697,781; qualifying distributions, $1,335,104; giving activities include $1,335,104 for grants.
Fields of interest: Museums (marine/maritime); Higher education; Law school/education; Education; Zoos/zoological societies; Hospitals (general); Human services.
International interests: Bermuda.
Limitations: Applications not accepted. Giving primarily in FL and NY, as well as in Bermuda. No grants to individuals.
Application information: Contributes only to pre-selected organizations.
Trustees: Diana S. Bergquist; Calvin P. Stempel; Neil F. Stempel.
EIN: 510363381

1677
Ernest E. and Brendalyn Stempel Foundation

c/o Eisenberg & Blau
150 Broadway, Ste. 1102
New York, NY   10038-4367

Established in 2002 in DE.
Donor: Ernest E. Stempel Foundation.
Grantmaker type: Independent foundation.
Financial data (yr. ended 12/31/10): Assets, $4,917,870 (M); expenditures, $291,101; qualifying distributions, $250,000; giving activities include $250,000 for grants.
Purpose and activities: Giving primarily for an art school, as well as for higher and other education,

hospitals, children's reconstructive surgery, human services, and federated giving programs.
Fields of interest: International development; Arts education; Higher education; Education; Hospitals (general); Surgery; Human services; Children, services; United Ways and Federated Giving Programs.
Limitations: Applications not accepted. Giving primarily in NY. No grants to individuals.
Application information: Contributes only to pre-selected organizations.
Trustees: Richard Eisenberg; Brendalyn Stempel.
EIN: 306015902

1678
Walter P. & Elizabeth M. Stern Foundation, Inc.

450 Fort Hill Rd.
Scarsdale, NY   10583-2413
Contact: Walter P. Stern, Pres.
FAX: (212) 649-1533; E-mail: wps@capgroup.com

Established in 1963 in NY.
Donors: Elizabeth M. Stern; Walter P. Stern.
Grantmaker type: Independent foundation.
Financial data (yr. ended 12/31/10): Assets, $4,765,746 (M); gifts received, $80,557; expenditures, $255,616; qualifying distributions, $243,406; giving activities include $243,406 for grants.
Fields of interest: Higher education; International affairs, national security; International affairs; United Ways and Federated Giving Programs; Jewish federated giving programs; Public policy, research; Jewish agencies & synagogues.
International interests: Israel.
Type of support: General/operating support; Continuing support; Endowments; Scholarship funds.
Limitations: Applications not accepted. Giving primarily in Washington, DC, and New York and Westchester counties, NY. No grants to individuals.
Application information: Unsolicited requests for funds not accepted.
   Board meeting date(s): Varies annually
Officers and Directors:* Walter P. Stern,* Pres.; Elizabeth M. Stern,* Secy.; David M.C. Stern; Sarah M. Stern; William M. Stern.
Number of staff: None.
EIN: 136111129

1679
The Strauss Foundation, Inc.

c/o Sacks Press & Lacher
600 3rd Ave.
New York, NY   10016-1901

Established in 2005 in NY.
Donors: Strauss Family Trust; Noemi Strauss; Noemi Strauss Trust; Roberto Strauss Trust; Renato Strauss Trust; Sylvie Strauss Trust.
Grantmaker type: Independent foundation.
Financial data (yr. ended 12/31/10): Assets, $1,036,166 (M); gifts received, $150,000; expenditures, $136,308; qualifying distributions, $134,966; giving activities include $134,966 for 10 grants (high: $100,000; low: $500).
Fields of interest: Higher education; Jewish agencies & synagogues.
International interests: Israel.

Limitations: Applications not accepted. No grants to individuals.
Application information: Unsolicited requests for funds not accepted.
Directors: Warren Gleicher; Ernst Strauss; Renato Strauss.
EIN: 202357393

1680
The Synergos Institute, Inc.
51 Madison Ave., 21st Fl.
New York, NY 10010-1603 (212) 447-8111
FAX: (212) 447-8119;
E-mail: synergos@synergos.org; URL: http://www.synergos.org

Established in 1987.
Grantmaker type: Public charity.
Financial data (yr. ended 12/31/10): Revenue, $6,256,411; assets, $18,181,859 (M); gifts received, $5,460,135; expenditures, $7,691,153; giving activities include $637,703 for grants to organizations outside the U.S.
Purpose and activities: The institute works to reduce poverty and increase equality around the world in innovative ways that lead to meaningful, long-term change.
Fields of interest: International human rights; International relief; International development; International affairs, equal rights; Economically disadvantaged.
Type of support: Fellowships.
Limitations: Applications not accepted. Giving on a national and international basis, with emphasis on Brazil, Ecuador, India, Indonesia, Mexico, Mozambique, Namibia, the Philippines, southern Africa, South Africa, Thailand, and Zimbabwe.
Publications: Annual report; Newsletter.
Application information: Contributes only to pre-selected organizations.
Officers and Directors:* Peggy Dulany,* Chair.; Robert H. Dunn,* Pres. and C.E.O.; Wanda Engel Aduan; Sabina Alkire; Hylton Appelbaum; Edward Bergman; William Bohnett; Alan Detheridge; Youssef Dib; Nili Gilbert; and 14 additional directors.
Number of staff: 45 full-time professional; 3 part-time professional; 1 part-time support.
EIN: 133392006

1681
Tanaka Memorial Foundation, Inc.
711 5th Ave., 16th Fl.
New York, NY 10022-3111
Contact: Kenji Tanaka, Chair.

Established in 1991 in NY.
Donor: Tanaka Ikubikai Educational Corp.
Grantmaker type: Independent foundation.
Financial data (yr. ended 06/30/11): Assets, $19,699,136 (M); expenditures, $900,508; qualifying distributions, $900,508; giving activities include $558,000 for 22 grants (high: $100,000; low: $3,000).
Purpose and activities: Giving primarily for higher education, including support for Asian studies through programs and scholarship funds, arts, and human services.
Fields of interest: Performing arts centers; Higher education; Education.
International interests: United Kingdom.

Type of support: General/operating support; Capital campaigns; Endowments; Scholarship funds.
Limitations: Applications not accepted. Giving on a national and international basis, with emphasis on New York, NY, Washington, DC, and England. No grants to individuals.
Application information: Unsolicited requests for funds not accepted.
Officers and Directors:* Kenji Tanaka,* Chair.; Taeko Tanaka,* Vice-Chair.; Makiko Tanaka,* Pres.; Kimiko Tanaka,* V.P.; Takeshi Hashimoto, Secy.; Tokiwa Morimoto, Treas.; Kiyoshi Okada; Yoshihiro Tajima; Takeshi Ueshima.
EIN: 110235010

1682
Tandon Family Foundation, Inc.
c/o M. Baharestani, CPA
148 Madison Ave.
New York, NY 10016-6700

Established in NY.
Donor: Chandrika Tandon.
Grantmaker type: Independent foundation.
Financial data (yr. ended 12/31/10): Assets, $11,898,067 (M); gifts received, $4,941,068; expenditures, $2,388,800; qualifying distributions, $2,074,747; giving activities include $2,074,747 for 22 grants (high: $1,500,000; low: $100), and $72,658 for foundation-administered programs).
Purpose and activities: Giving primarily for U.S.-based organizations and programs concerning India.
Fields of interest: Arts; Education; Hinduism.
International interests: India.
Limitations: Applications not accepted. Giving primarily in New Haven, CT, and New York, NY. No grants to individuals.
Application information: Contributes only to pre-selected organizations.
Directors: Martin Baharestani; Chandrika Tandon; Ranjan Tandon.
EIN: 043744965

1683
The Tang Fund
c/o Gwenn Winkhaus
P.O. Box 31259
New York, NY 06831-0959 (212) 830-5305

Established in 1984 in NY.
Donors: Oscar L. Tang; Reich & Tang; Robert F. Hoerle; and members of the Tang family.
Grantmaker type: Independent foundation.
Financial data (yr. ended 11/30/10): Assets, $54,248,744 (M); expenditures, $1,584,719; qualifying distributions, $1,270,857; giving activities include $1,270,857 for 40 grants (high: $400,000; low: $250).
Purpose and activities: Giving primarily for higher and secondary education; support also for cultural programs and community development.
Fields of interest: Arts; Secondary school/education; Higher education; International affairs, goodwill promotion; Community/economic development.
International interests: China.
Limitations: Applications not accepted. Giving primarily in NY. No grants to individuals.
Application information: Contributes only to pre-selected organizations.

Officers and Directors:* Oscar L. Tang,* Pres. and Treas.; Gwenn S. Winkhaus, Secy.; Tracy L. Tang.
EIN: 133256295

1684
The Tanzania Wildlife Fund, Inc.
560 Broadway, Ste. 202
New York, NY 10012-3945 (212) 431-5508
Contact: Kate McLetchie, Exec. Dir.
E-mail: info@africarainforest.org; URL: http://www.africarainforest.org

Grantmaker type: Public charity.
Financial data (yr. ended 12/31/10): Revenue, $227,481; assets, $38,390 (M); gifts received, $227,458; expenditures, $308,857; giving activities include $155,000 for grants to organizations outside the U.S.
Purpose and activities: The fund promotes wildlife conservation throughout Africa, primarily in Tanzania.
Fields of interest: Animals/wildlife, preservation/protection.
International interests: Tanzania, Zanzibar and Pemba; Africa.
Limitations: Giving limited to Africa, primarily in Tanzania.
Officers and Directors:* Carter Coleman,* Pres.; Beth O'Donnell,* Secy.; David Yamner,* Treas.; Kate McLetchie, Exec. Dir.; Michelle Clark; P. Jay Cone, II; George Grayson; Lindy Reilly; Sheila Rooney; Peter Wirth; Joe Zammit-Lucia.
EIN: 133582323

1685
Theatre Communications Group
520 Eighth Ave., 24th Fl.
New York, NY 10018-4156 (212) 609-5900
Contact: Teresa Eyring, Exec. Dir.
FAX: (212) 609-5901; E-mail: grants@tcg.org;
URL: http://www.tcg.org
Facebook: http://www.facebook.com/tcg.org
Twitter: http://twitter.com/#!/tcg

Established in 1961 in NY.
Grantmaker type: Public charity.
Financial data (yr. ended 06/30/10): Revenue, $6,445,994; assets, $12,243,818 (M); gifts received, $2,373,952; expenditures, $9,219,741; giving activities include $1,697,061 for grants, and $374,582 for grants to individuals.
Purpose and activities: The group aims to strengthen, mature, and promote the professional nonprofit American theatre.
Fields of interest: Arts, research; Performing arts, theater; Performing arts, theater (playwriting); Arts.
International interests: Eastern & Central Europe.
Type of support: Program development; Grants to individuals.
Limitations: Applications accepted. Giving on a national basis.
Publications: Application guidelines; Annual report.
Application information: Application form required.
 Initial approach: Submit application
 Deadline(s): Varies
 Final notification: Varies
Officers and Directors:* Martha Lavey,* Pres.; James Bundy,* V.P.; Dawn Chiang,* V.P.; Olga Sanchez,* Secy.; Andrew Hamingson,* Treas.; Teresa Eyring,* Exec. Dir.; Peter C. Brosius; Douglas R. Brown; Ralph Bryan; Mark Cuddy; Lydia Diamond;

Philip Himberg; Robert Hupp; Paul Nicholson; Jeffrey Woodward; and 20 additional directors.
EIN: 136160130

1686
The Tibet Fund
241 E. 32nd St.
New York, NY 10016-6305 (212) 213-5011
FAX: (212) 213-1219; E-mail: info@tibetfund.org;
URL: http://www.tibetfund.org

Established in 1987 in NY.
Grantmaker type: Public charity.
Financial data (yr. ended 12/31/10): Revenue, $5,388,103; assets, $8,091,646 (M); gifts received, $4,957,796; expenditures, $8,041,890; giving activities include $3,069,010 for grants, $3,559,403 for grants to organizations outside the U.S., and $755,729 for grants to individuals.
Purpose and activities: The fund works to address the health, educational, cultural, economic, and community development needs of the Tibetan refugee community.
Fields of interest: Civil/human rights; International affairs; International migration/refugee issues.
Limitations: Giving limited to Tibet.
Publications: Annual report.
Officers and Directors:* Mickey Lemle,* Chair.; Rinchen Dharlo, Pres.; Geoffrey Menin, V.P.; Jessica Brackman,* Secy.; Susan M. Holgate,* Treas.; Pema Chhinjor; Shep Gordon; Dr. Gail Gross; Dr. Thupten Jinpa; Elizabeth Lindsey; Ven. Gehlek Rinpoche; T.C. Tethong; Yodon Thonden.
EIN: 133115145

1687
Tikva Corporation
40 W. 23rd St., 3rd Fl.
New York, NY 10010-5263

Grantmaker type: Public charity.
Financial data (yr. ended 12/31/09): Revenue, $8,264,973; assets, $7,960,084 (M); gifts received, $8,264,973; expenditures, $9,317,188; giving activities include $7,082,907 for grants to organizations outside the U.S.
Purpose and activities: The corporation supports a Ukrainian orphange that serves underprivileged children.
Fields of interest: Children, adoption; Children/youth, services; Children/youth.
International interests: Ukraine.
Limitations: Applications not accepted. Giving limited to Odessa, Ukraine.
Application information: Contributes only to pre-selected organizations.
Officers: Edward Frankel, Chair.; Seth M. Gerzberg, Pres.; Rabbi Shlomo Baksht, V.P.; Andrew J. Stamelman, Secy.; Richard Thrush, Treas.
Trustees: Marc Ecko; Sydney Faber; Leah Frankel; Rose Gerszberg; Morey Goldberg; Carla Harman; Ethan Keiser; Lenny Krayzelburg; Refael Kruskal; Martin Paisner; Lenny Piontak; Sandra Piontak; Steven Poznak; Warren Steiglitz; Effy Zinkin; and 8 additional trustees.
EIN: 223779212

1688
The Tikvah Fund
745 5th Ave., Ste. 1400
New York, NY 10151-1402 (212) 796-1672
Contact: Roger Hertog, Chair.
FAX: (646) 794-0172; E-mail: info@tikvahfund.org;
URL: http://tikvahfund.org/

Established in 1992 in NY.
Donor: Zalman C. Bernstein†.
Grantmaker type: Independent foundation.
Financial data (yr. ended 12/31/09): Assets, $164,527,991 (M); gifts received, $5,000,000; expenditures, $8,743,683; qualifying distributions, $8,441,616; giving activities include $5,289,492 for 18 grants (high: $3,187,500; low: $1,000).
Purpose and activities: Giving primarily for Jewish affairs. Makes grants and program-related investments to companies located in areas of high unemployment or development in Israel, and to companies that are owned by or employ new immigrants or veteran soldiers.
Fields of interest: Religion, public policy; Jewish agencies & synagogues.
International interests: Israel.
Limitations: Applications not accepted. Giving primarily in NY and NJ; some giving in Israel.
Application information: Contributes only to pre-selected organizations.
Officers and Directors:* Roger Hertog,* Chair.; Arthur W. Fried,* C.F.O.; Eric Cohen, Exec. Dir.; Mem Dryan Bernstein; William Kristol; Jay Lefkowitz; David Stone.
EIN: 133676152
Recent grants for international programs:
1688-1 Herzog College, Gush Etzion, Israel, $27,368. For specific program. 2009.
1688-2 Mezaref, Kfar Sava, Israel, $10,000. For specific program. 2009.
1688-3 PEF Israel Endowment Funds, New York, NY, $202,000. For specific programs. 2009.
1688-4 Shalem Foundation, New York, NY, $3,187,500. For general support. 2009.
1688-5 University of Toronto, Toronto, Canada, $272,213. For specific program. 2009.

1689
The Tinker Foundation Inc.
55 E. 59th St., 21st Fl.
New York, NY 10022-1112 (212) 421-6858
Contact: Renate Rennie, Chair. and Pres.
FAX: (212) 223-3326; E-mail: tinker@tinker.org;
URL: http://foundationcenter.org/grantmaker/tinker

Trust established in 1959 in NY; incorporated in 1975 in NY.
Donor: Edward Larocque Tinker†.
Grantmaker type: Independent foundation.
Financial data (yr. ended 12/31/10): Assets, $81,909,717 (M); expenditures, $4,924,597; qualifying distributions, $3,008,050; giving activities include $3,008,050 for grants.
Purpose and activities: The mission of the foundation is to promote the development of an equitable, sustainable, and productive society in Latin America and to enhance the understanding in the U.S. of Latin America and of how U.S. policies may impact the region. Grants are awarded primarily in the areas of democratic governance, education, and sustainable resource management. More limited support is given for projects addressing U.S. policy toward Latin America and Antarctica.

Fields of interest: International affairs, goodwill promotion; Education; Environment, natural resources; Environment; International affairs, foreign policy; International affairs; Marine science; Economics; Political science; Public policy, research; Government/public administration.
International interests: Antarctica; Latin America; Mexico.
Type of support: Program development; Conferences/seminars; Seed money; Research.
Limitations: Applications accepted. Giving limited to projects related to Latin America and Antarctica. No support for projects concerned with health or medical issues or the arts and humanities. No grants to individuals, or for building or endowment funds, equipment, annual campaigns, operating budgets, annual appeals or production costs for film, television, and radio projects.
Publications: Application guidelines; Annual report.
Application information: Application form for Institutional grants available on foundation web site. Use application guidelines and proposal cover sheet found on the web site or in paper copy, available upon request. Application form required.
Initial approach: Request application procedures on the foundation web site, by telephone or in writing
Copies of proposal: 2
Deadline(s): Mar. 1 for June meeting and Sept. 15 for Dec. meeting
Board meeting date(s): June and Dec.
Final notification: 2 weeks after board meetings
Officers and Directors:* Renate Rennie,* Chair. and Pres.; Richard de J. Osborne,* Secy.; Kathleen Waldron,* Treas.; John H. Coatsworth; Sally Grooms Cowal; Arturo C. Porzecanski; Susan L. Segal; Luis Rubio; Alan Stoga.
Number of staff: 4 full-time professional; 1 part-time professional; 1 full-time support.
EIN: 510175449

1690
Tisch Foundation, Inc.
655 Madison Ave., 19th Fl.
New York, NY 10065-8043 (212) 521-2930
Contact: Mark J. Krinsky, V.P.

Incorporated in 1957 in FL.
Donors: Hotel Americana; Tisch Hotels, Inc.; members of the Tisch family; and closely held corporations.
Grantmaker type: Independent foundation.
Financial data (yr. ended 12/31/10): Assets, $42,504,145 (M); expenditures, $14,379,964; qualifying distributions, $14,328,314; giving activities include $14,320,076 for 115 grants (high: $6,000,300; low: $20; average: $1,000–$1,000,000).
Purpose and activities: Emphasis on higher education, including institutions in Israel, and research-related programs; support also for Jewish organizations and welfare funds, museums, and secondary education.
Fields of interest: Museums; Secondary school/education; Higher education; AIDS; Medical research, institute; Human services; Jewish federated giving programs; Jewish agencies & synagogues.
International interests: Israel.
Type of support: Continuing support; Building/renovation; Equipment; Research.
Limitations: Applications not accepted. Giving primarily in NY. No grants to individuals, or for

endowment funds, scholarships, fellowships, or matching gifts; no loans.

Application information: Contributes only to pre-selected organizations.

   Board meeting date(s): Mar., June, Sept., Dec., and as required

Officers and Directors:* Wilma S. Tisch,* Co-Pres.; Joan H. Tisch,* Co-Pres.; Mark J. Krinsky, V.P.; Thomas M. Steinberg, V.P.; Andrew H. Tisch, V.P.; Daniel R. Tisch, V.P.; James S. Tisch, V.P.; Jonathan M. Tisch, V.P.; Laurie M. Tisch, V.P.; Steven E. Tisch, V.P.; Thomas J. Tisch,* V.P.; Barry L. Bloom,* Secy.-Treas.

EIN: 591002844

Recent grants for international programs:

1690-1 American Friends of the Israel Museum, New York, NY, $102,500. 2010.

1690-2 Haitian Education and Leadership Program, New York, NY, $10,000. 2010.

1690-3 Health and Humanitarian Aid Foundation, Garnerville, NY, $160,000. 2010.

1691
Touch Foundation, Inc.

P.O. Box 1420
New York, NY   10028-0011
E-mail: touch_foundation@mckinsey.com; Additional address: P.O. Box 1464, Mwanza, Tanzania; URL: http://www.touchfoundation.org
Facebook Causes URL: http://www.causes.com/causes/61469?recruiter_id=11003477
RSS Feed: http://www.touchfoundation.org/rss/news.rss
Twitter: http://twitter.com/touchfoundation
YouTube: http://www.youtube.com/user/TheTouchFoundation

Established in 2004 in CT.
Grantmaker type: Public charity.
Financial data (yr. ended 06/30/10): Revenue, $2,343,070; assets, $1,444,718 (M); gifts received, $2,334,204; expenditures, $3,088,125; giving activities include $2,414 for grants, and $1,293,646 for grants to organizations outside the U.S.
Purpose and activities: The foundation works to provide funding and management resources to developing countries for local programs that create human resources for health (HRH); build awareness around problems in health care delivery in developing countries; and create, collect, store, and provide access to the leading information about global health, and share the knowledge gained from programs it supports.
Fields of interest: Health care.
International interests: Developing countries.
Limitations: Applications not accepted. Giving primarily in developing countries.
Publications: Annual report.
Application information: Contributes only to pre-selected organizations.
Officers and Directors:* Lowell L. Bryan,* Chair. and Pres.; David W. Lowden,* Secy.; Richard M. Cashin; Kevin J. Curnin; Celia A. Felsher; Jane Fraser; Mbago Kaniki; Frederick Kigadye, M.D.; Vikram Malhotra; Robert H. Niehaus.
EIN: 201469976

1692
Toyota USA Foundation

c/o Fdn. Admin.
601 Lexington Ave., 49th Fl.
New York, NY   10022-4611   (212) 715-7486
Tel. for problems with online applications: (212) 715-7490; URL: http://www.toyota.com/foundation

Established in 1987 in CA.
Donors: Toyota Motor Sales, U.S.A., Inc.; Toyota Motor Manufacturing North America, Inc.
Grantmaker type: Company-sponsored foundation.
Financial data (yr. ended 06/30/10): Assets, $94,843,911 (M); expenditures, $5,336,614; qualifying distributions, $4,700,040; giving activities include $4,700,040 for 24 grants (high: $800,000; low: $50,000).
Purpose and activities: The foundation supports organizations involved with K-12 education. Special emphasis is directed toward math, science, and environmental science.
Fields of interest: Environment, natural resources; Environment; Science; Elementary/secondary education; Higher education; Science, formal/general education; Mathematics.
Type of support: Equipment; Program development; Curriculum development; Program evaluation.
Limitations: Giving primarily in areas of major company operations in AZ, CA, Washington, DC, IL, MD, NM, NY, and TX; giving also to national organizations. No support for discriminatory organizations, government agencies, private or public K-12 schools, religious, fraternal, or lobbying organizations, or political parties or candidates. No grants to individuals, or for general operating support, annual campaigns, or debt reduction, endowments, capital campaigns, fundraising events, or construction or equipment, conferences, meals, or travel, or publication subsidies, advertising, or mass mailings.
Publications: Application guidelines; Grants list.
Application information: Grants range from $50,000 to $500,000. A site visit may be requested. Additional information may be requested at a later date.

   Initial approach: Complete online application
   Deadline(s): None
   Board meeting date(s): Twice per year
   Final notification: Up to 6 months

Officers and Directors:* Yoshimi Inaba,* Pres.; Dian Ogilvie,* Secy.; Katsuyuki Kusakawa,* Treas.; Tetsuo Agata; Chuck Brown; Barbra Cooper; Robert C. Daly; Jim Lentz; Patricia Salas Pineda; Steve St. Angelo; James Weisman.
Number of staff: 2 full-time professional; 1 full-time support.
EIN: 953255038
Recent grants for international programs:

1692-1 Earthecho International, Washington, DC, $552,000. To help youth restore and protect the water on the planet by providing both science-based environmental education materials and service-learning tools and resources to improve the health of the environment. 2010.

1692-2 Nature Conservancy, Arlington, VA, $800,000. To establish the first nationwide network for environmental high schools and provide students from these schools with real world, paid summer internships in the conservation field, ultimately servicing over 17,000 students. 2010.

1693
Trace Foundation

132 Perry St., Ste. 2B
New York, NY   10014-2703   (212) 367-7380
FAX: (212) 367-7383; E-mail: info@trace.org;
URL: http://www.trace.org
Facebook: http://www.facebook.com/TraceFoundation
Flickr: http://www.flickr.com/photos/tracefoundation
Twitter: http://twitter.com/tracefoundation
YouTube: http://www.youtube.com/user/tracefoundation

Established in 1993 in NY.
Donors: Andrea Soros; George Soros.
Grantmaker type: Operating foundation.
Financial data (yr. ended 12/31/09): Assets, $36,368,410 (M); expenditures, $6,631,009; qualifying distributions, $5,802,393; giving activities include $3,367,309 for grants, and $3,412,223 for foundation-administered programs.
Purpose and activities: The foundation supports the continuity of Tibetan culture and language, and strengthens the ability of Tibetan communities within China to meet their own needs. The foundation implements and funds projects, and offers support to individuals through scholarships that integrate culture and development goals and respect environmental principles. Projects fall within four sectors: Education, Healthcare, Rural Development and Culture.
Fields of interest: Arts, cultural/ethnic awareness; Education; International development; Philanthropy/voluntarism.
International interests: China.
Type of support: Scholarship funds.
Limitations: Applications not accepted. Giving primarily in China.
Publications: Annual report.
Application information: Unsolicited requests for funds not considered. See foundation web site for scholarship and fellowship information.
Officers: Enrico Dell' Angelo, Exec. Dir.; Jeremy Burke, Cont.
Trustees: Eric Colombel; Andrea Soros.
Number of staff: 1 full-time professional; 2 full-time support.
EIN: 137008868

1694
Trickle Up Program, Inc.

104 W. 27th St., 12th Fl.
New York, NY   10001-6210
Contact: Daynelle Williams, Office Mgr.
FAX: (212) 255-9974;
E-mail: daynellew@trickleup.org; Toll-free tel.: (866) 246-9980; URL: http://www.trickleup.org

Established in 1979.
Grantmaker type: Public charity.
Financial data (yr. ended 08/31/10): Revenue, $3,997,360; assets, $2,644,864 (M); gifts received, $3,938,895; expenditures, $4,115,992; giving activities include $927,472 for grants to organizations outside the U.S.
Purpose and activities: The organization seeks to help the lowest income people worldwide take the first step up out of poverty, by providing conditional seed capital and business training essential to the launch of a microenterprise.

Fields of interest: Venture philanthropy; International economic development; Economic development; Economically disadvantaged.
Type of support: Seed money; Grants to individuals.
Limitations: Giving on a national and international basis.
Publications: Annual report; Newsletter.
Officers and Directors: * Wendy Gordon Rockefeller,* Chair.; William M. Abrams, Pres.; Peter Baird; Thomas C. Barry; Robert J. Berg; Lynette Cameron; Margaret Cantarella; Marcia Cantarella; Alexander W. Casdin; Joyce Chang; Mildred Robbins Leet; and 13 additional directors.
EIN: 061043042

1695
Trinity Wall Street
(formerly Trinity Church)
74 Trinity Pl., 21st Fl.
New York, NY   10006-2002   (212) 602-0710
FAX: (212) 602-0717; Tel. for Jamila Jabulani: (212) 602-0713; URL: http://www.trinitywallstreet.org

Established in 1846.
Grantmaker type: Public charity.
Purpose and activities: The church's mission is to spread the Gospel and participate in God's salvation according to the divine intention, using the tools of philanthropy to strengthen the church's witness both locally and globally.
Fields of interest: Protestant agencies & churches.
International interests: Africa.
Type of support: Program-related investments/ loans; Program development; Matching/challenge support.
Limitations: Applications accepted. Giving on a national and international basis, with emphasis on the Global South and the metropolitan New York, NY area. No support for secular programs that have no participation by churches, feeding programs, disaster response, programs that do not have the active involvement of an Anglican/Episcopal church jurisdiction, operation of neighborhood service facilities (such as pre-schools, day-care centers, community centers, orphanages, shelters), or arts and cultural programs. No grants for land purchases, construction, renovation, establishment of endowments funds, general operating expenses of established organizations, deficit financing, or emergency relief.
Publications: Annual report; Grants list.
Application information: Application form not required.
  Initial approach: Letter
  Copies of proposal: 1
  Deadline(s): Feb., May, and Nov.
  Board meeting date(s): Feb., May, and Nov.
Officer and Board Members: * Susan V. Berresford,* Chair.; Rev. James H. Cooper; J. Christopher Daly; Evan A. Davis; Stefan Ford; Cynthia Pardy; Maribel Ruiz; Dr. Westina Matthews Shateen; Mary H. White, M.D.
Number of staff: 4 full-time professional; 1 part-time professional; 2 full-time support.

1696
Trust for Mutual Understanding
6 W. 48th St., 12th Fl.
New York, NY   10036-1802   (212) 843-0404
Contact: Jennifer P. Goodale, Exec. Dir.; Barbara Lanciers, Assoc. Dir.

FAX: (212) 843-0344; E-mail: tmu@tmuny.org; URL: http://www.tmuny.org
Blog: http://www.tmuny.org/connect/blog
E-Newsletter: http://www.tmuny.org/connect/ tmuniverse
Facebook: http://www.facebook.com/pages/ Trust-for-Mutual-Understanding/112446932323
Grants Database: http://www.tmuny.org/grantees

Established in 1984 in NY.
Grantmaker type: Independent foundation.
Financial data (yr. ended 12/31/09): Assets, $39,587,275 (M); expenditures, $4,977,556; qualifying distributions, $4,876,968; giving activities include $3,477,627 for 157 grants (high: $150,000; low: $1,000).
Purpose and activities: Support to American nonprofit organizations for professional exchanges in the arts and environmental fields between the United States, Russia, and Eastern and Central Europe. Support is provided for travel and related expenses for exchange projects that involve direct, in-depth professional interaction, with the potential for sustained collaboration; that show evidence of professional accomplishment and innovation; and/ or that respond to social contexts and engage local communities.
Fields of interest: Visual arts; Museums; Performing arts; Performing arts, dance; Performing arts, theater; Performing arts, music; Historic preservation/historical societies; Arts; Environment, natural resources; Environment; Animals/wildlife, preservation/protection; International exchange.
International interests: Albania; Armenia; Azerbaijan; Belarus; Bosnia-Herzegovina; Bulgaria; Croatia; Czech Republic; Estonia; Georgia (Republic of); Hungary; Kazakhstan; Kosovo; Kyrgyzstan; Latvia; Lithuania; Macedonia; Montenegro; Moldova; Mongolia; Poland; Romania; Russia; Serbia; Slovenia; Slovakia; Tajikistan; Turkmenistan; Ukraine; Uzbekistan.
Type of support: Exchange programs.
Limitations: Applications accepted. Giving for exchanges between the U.S. and Russia, Central and Eastern Europe, Central Asia, the Caucasus, and Mongolia. No support for one-person exhibitions of work by living artists, solo performance tours or youth programs. No grants to individuals, or for fellowships for individual research or academic study, operating expenses, capital campaigns, construction costs, salaries, honoraria or fees, student exchanges, performing or visual arts competitions, literature or publication projects, library acquisitions or equipment purchases, film production, media training, mass communication programs, activities pertaining to arms control or security issues, economic development, medicine, public health, agriculture, activities in which only a single participant is involved, multi-year commitments, retroactive funding, or, except in special circumstances, interregional travel or travel by project participants in their home countries.
Publications: Application guidelines; Annual report; Grants list; Newsletter.
Application information: Grants are made only to tax-exempt organizations in the United States for exchange projects involving Russia, Central Asia, Mongolia and the Caucasus, and Eastern and Central Europe. Grant funds may only be used for international travel costs. Application form required.
  Initial approach: Letter of Inquiry (refer to form on foundation web site); initial contact should be

established at least 3 months prior to the application deadline
  Copies of proposal: 1
  Deadline(s): Feb. 1 and Aug. 1
  Board meeting date(s): Spring and fall
  Final notification: 3-4 months after proposal submission
Director and Trustees: * Jennifer P. Goodale,* Exec. Dir.; Richard S. Lanier; Elizabeth J. McCormack; Donal C. O'Brien, Jr.
Board of Advisors: Laura Chasin; Wade Greene; William H. Luers; Joseph Polisi; Blair Ruble; Isaac Shapiro; Arlene Shuler.
Number of staff: 3 full-time professional; 1 part-time professional; 1 part-time support.
EIN: 133212724

1697
Tsadra Foundation
P.O. Box 20192
New York, NY   10014-0710
URL: http://www.tsadra.org

Established in 2000 in NY.
Donors: Eric Colombel; Andrea Soros; Leon Sauke; Trace Foundation.
Grantmaker type: Independent foundation.
Financial data (yr. ended 12/31/10): Assets, $503,350 (M); gifts received, $2,162,000; expenditures, $2,219,945; qualifying distributions, $1,404,608; giving activities include $1,404,608 for grants.
Fields of interest: Education; International development; Buddhism.
Type of support: General/operating support; Program development; Fellowships.
Limitations: Applications not accepted. Giving in the U.S., with emphasis on CA, as well as in Canada, France, India and Nepal.
Application information: Unsolicited requests for funds not accepted.
Trustee: Eric Colombel.
EIN: 137224970

1698
Turkish Philanthropy Funds
216 E. 45th St., 7th Fl.
New York, NY   10017-3304   (646) 530-8988
Contact: Senay Ataselim
E-mail: info@tpfund.org; URL: http://www.tpfund.org
Blog: http://tpfund.blogspot.com/
Facebook: http://www.facebook.com/pages/ Turkish-Philanthropic-Fund/82036262510
LinkedIn: http://www.linkedin.com/groups? home=&gid=1850909
Twitter: http://twitter.com/tphilanthropy
YouTube: http://www.youtube.com/user/ TurkishPhilanthropy

Established in 2007 in DE.
Grantmaker type: Public charity.
Financial data (yr. ended 06/30/11): Revenue, $1,129,127; assets, $4,229,988 (M); gifts received, $839,065; expenditures, $8,897,963; giving activities include $8,631,539 for grants, and $71,925 for grants to organizations outside the U.S.
Purpose and activities: The fund helps donors realize their philanthropic goals to meet community needs in the U.S. and Turkey, and works to increase philanthropy among the Turkish-American community in general.

Fields of interest: Arts; Public health; Human services; Environment; Education; International economic development; Philanthropy/voluntarism.

Limitations: Applications accepted. Giving primarily to Turkey. No support for religious or political organizations. No grants to individuals.

Publications: Application guidelines; Annual report; Newsletter.

Application information: Application form required.
 Initial approach: Submit grant eligibility Form
 Copies of proposal: 1
 Deadline(s): None
 Board meeting date(s): Every other month
 Final notification: One to three months

Officers and Directors:* Haldun Tashman,* Chair.; Enrich R. Ozada, Vice-Chair.; Ozlenen Eser Kalav,* Pres. and C.E.O.; Gamze Ates, Secy.; Mustafa Kemal Abadan,* Treas.; Murat Agirnasli; Mehmet Lutfi Kirdar; Aydin Koc; Nicholas C. Pocaro.

EIN: 208392006

1699
The Desmond Tutu Peace Foundation

205 E. 64th St., Ste. 503
New York, NY 10065-6635 (212) 750 5504
Contact: Donna Blackwell Ph.D., C.E.O.
FAX: (212) 371-2776;
E-mail: info@tutufoundation-usa.org; URL: http://www.tutufoundation-usa.org

Established in 2000.

Grantmaker type: Public charity.

Financial data (yr. ended 12/31/10): Revenue, $314,726; assets, $344,589 (M); gifts received, $314,620; expenditures, $124,600; giving activities include $10,000 for grants to organizations outside the U.S.

Purpose and activities: The mission of the foundation is to support and promote the creation of a culture of peace throughout the world, through helping to build, equip, and support programs at the new Desmond Tutu Peace Centre in Cape Town, South Africa.

Fields of interest: Youth development, ethics; International peace/security; International conflict resolution; Women; Youth; Children/youth.

Type of support: Capital campaigns; Program development.

Limitations: Applications not accepted. Giving limited to Cape Town, South Africa.

Application information: Contributes only to a pre-selected organization.
 Board meeting date(s): Quarterly

Officers and Directors:* Patricia A. McLagan,* Pres.; David Pierce,* Ph.D., Secy.; Barry Smith, M.D., Ph.D., Treas.; Very Rev. Dr. Michael Jesse Battle; Alicia Bythewood; Gloria Hartley; Craig Hatkoff; Rabbi Irwin Kula; Judith A. Mayotte, Ph.D.; Trevor Neilson; Very Rev. Robert Taylor; Robert White.

Number of staff: 2 full-time professional.

EIN: 134092458

1700
Maoz Tzur Foundation, Inc.

1860 Flatbush Ave.
Brooklyn, NY 11210-4831 (718) 377-8700
Contact: Charles Neiss, Pres.

Donors: Charles Neiss; Fay Neiss; Martin Rappaport; Yeshaya Elefant; Manny Weiss; Joseph Tabak; Chana Tabak; Abraham Wolfson; Berger Boiler Corp.; Diamond Services; Green Hill Industrial Supply.

Grantmaker type: Operating foundation.

Financial data (yr. ended 12/31/09): Assets, $64,703 (M); gifts received, $788,573; expenditures, $715,194; qualifying distributions, $714,901; giving activities include $272,249 for 31 grants (high: $84,419; low: $100), and $442,652 for 100 grants to individuals (high: $94,000; low: $100).

Fields of interest: Jewish agencies & synagogues.

International interests: Israel.

Application information: Any applicable brochures concerning the foundation may be submitted with letter.
 Initial approach: Letter
 Deadline(s): None

Officers: Charles Neiss, Pres.; Jacob Neiss, V.P.

EIN: 113423569

1701
UJA - Federation of New York

130 E. 59th St.
New York, NY 10022-1302 (212) 980-1000
E-mail: contact@ujafedny.org; URL: http://www.ujafedny.org
Facebook: http://www.facebook.com/ujafedny
Twitter: http://twitter.com/UJAfedNY
YouTube: http://www.youtube.com/user/ujafedny

Established in 1917.

Grantmaker type: Public charity.

Financial data (yr. ended 06/30/10): Revenue, $260,755,000; assets, $1,110,867,000 (M); gifts received, $173,778,000; expenditures, $218,276,000; giving activities include $150,447,000 for grants, $306,000 for grants to organizations outside the U.S., and $2,709,000 for grants to individuals.

Purpose and activities: The federation conducts fundraising activities to support cultural, social, health-related, educational, and other services to millions of people each year in Israel, New York, and throughout the world.

Fields of interest: Jewish federated giving programs; Jewish agencies & synagogues.

International interests: Israel.

Limitations: Giving on a worldwide basis, with emphasis on NY and Israel.

Officers and Trustees:* Susan K. Stern,* Chair.; John S. Ruskay,* C.E.O. and Exec. V.P.; Morris W. Offit,* Pres.; Jane F. Karlin, Sr. V.P., Financial Resource Devel.; William D. Samers, V.P., Gift Devel. and Compliance; Esther Treitel,* Secy.; David Silvers,* Treas.; Robert H. Arnow; Lawrence B. Buttenwieser; William Kahn; Irving Schneider; and 14 additional trustees.

EIN: 510172429

1702
Unbound Philanthropy

120 Wooster St., Ste. 3N
New York, NY 10012-5203 (212) 219-1009
FAX: (212) 219-1129;
E-mail: mail@unboundphilanthropy.org; URL: http://www.unboundphilanthropy.org
Grants List: http://www.unboundphilanthropy.org/grantees.php

Established in 2004 in HI.

Donors: William Reeves; Deborah K. Berger.

Grantmaker type: Independent foundation.

Financial data (yr. ended 12/31/08): Assets, $97,035,932 (M); gifts received, $2,619,583; expenditures, $2,989,042; qualifying distributions, $2,734,097; giving activities include $2,200,460 for grants.

Purpose and activities: The grantmaker is dedicated to securing justice and opportunity for migrants and refugees.

Fields of interest: Education; Human services; Philanthropy/voluntarism; Immigrants/refugees; Women; Children/youth.

International interests: United Kingdom; Africa.

Limitations: Applications not accepted. Giving on a national basis and in Africa and the U.K. No grants to individuals.

Publications: Grants list.

Application information: Contributes only to pre-selected organizations.

Officers: Deborah K. Berger, Chair.; Taryn Higashi, Exec. Dir.

Directors: Richard Graham; Bill Reeves; Kikilia Fordham Schaefer; Hilary Weinstein.

Number of staff: 3 full-time professional.

EIN: 830411606

Recent grants for international programs:

1702-1 Asylum Aid, London, England, $180,000. For Refugee Women's Resource Project, which aims to enable women seeking asylum in the United Kingdom to obtain protection and security, to maintain their dignity and to be treated with respect during the asylum process.. 2010.

1702-2 Childrens Legal Centre, Colchester, England, $160,000. For Migrant Children's Project. 2010.

1702-3 Childrens Legal Centre, Colchester, England, $102,942. For communications project. 2010.

1702-4 Citizens UK, London, England, $159,864. To organize key immigrant communities in the United Kingdom and continue building stakeholder relationships. 2010.

1702-5 Global Fund for Children, Washington, DC, $100,000. For Supporting the Grassroots in East Africa. 2010.

1702-6 Immigration Law Practitioners Association, London, England, $199,603. For On-Line Communications Capacity-Building Project. 2010.

1702-7 Institute for Public Policy Research, London, England, $47,746. For Communicating Migration, conference about immigration to the United Kingdom (31,000 GBP). 2010.

1702-8 Jesuit Refugee Service, Washington, DC, $100,000. For Eastern Africa Project on Education in Emergencies. 2010.

1702-9 Migrants' Rights Network, London, England, $211,000. For Communications Strategy Project (CSP). 2010.

1702-10 Oxford University, Centre on Migration, Policy and Society, Oxford, England, $525,000. To establish Migration Observatory, formerly known as MIDAS, website for data on migration issues. 2010.

1702-11 Population Council, New York, NY, $80,000. For Migratory Girls East Africa. 2010.

1702-12 Refugee and Migrant Justice, London, England, $110,134. For advocacy work. 2010.

1702-13 Tides Foundation, San Francisco, CA, $500,000. For Immigration Reform Collaboration Fund (IRCF). 2010.

1702-14 Urgent Action Fund for Womens Human Rights, Boulder, CO, $100,000. For Urgent Action Fund Africa. 2010.

1703
UncommonGoods Corporate Giving Program

140 58th St.
Bldg. B, Ste. 5A
Brooklyn, NY 11220-2523 (888) 365-0056
URL: http://www.uncommongoods.com/about/better.jsp

Grantmaker type: Corporate giving program.
Purpose and activities: UncommonGoods is a certified B Corporation that donates a percentage of profits to nonprofit organizations.
Fields of interest: Anti-slavery/human trafficking; Environment, forests; Health care; Mental health/crisis services, rape victim services; Food services; Children/youth, services.
Type of support: Continuing support.
Limitations: Applications not accepted.
Application information: Contributes only to pre-selected organizations.

1704
United Board for Christian Higher Education in Asia

475 Riverside Dr., Ste. 1221
New York, NY 10115-0047 (212) 870-2600
Contact: Jonathan Wolff, Dir., Grants Mgmt.
FAX: (212) 870-2322;
E-mail: staff@unitedboard.org; Application address: 1/F, Chung Chi College, Administration Building, The Chinese University of Hong Kong, Shatin, N.T., HK; Prog. Dir.: Dr. Avron Boretz; e-mail: aboretz@unitedboard.org; fax: 852-3163-4219; Dir. of Fellowship and Scholarship Prog.: Anne Ofstedal; e-mail: aofstedal@unitedboard.org; fax: 212-870-2322; URL: http://www.unitedboard.org

Established in 1922 in NY.
Grantmaker type: Public charity.
Financial data (yr. ended 06/30/10): Revenue, $4,564,214; assets, $95,904,638 (M); gifts received, $1,900,905; expenditures, $5,686,038; program services expenses, $3,680,146; giving activities include $2,149,926 for grants to organizations outside the U.S., $162,563 for 20 grants to individuals, and $1,367,657 for foundation-administered programs.
Purpose and activities: The board works to support a Christian presence in academic communities in Asia by working with higher education institutions in Asia to develop leadership, collaboration, and such values as justice, care for the environment, reconciliation and harmony among ethnic and religious communities, and civil societies.
Fields of interest: Environmental education; Higher education; Education; Environment, research; Religion, interfaith issues.
International interests: Asia.
Type of support: Building/renovation; Equipment; Program development; Conferences/seminars; Seed money; Curriculum development; Fellowships; Scholarship funds; Research; Technical assistance; Consulting services.
Limitations: Applications accepted. Giving primarily in Asia. No support for non-Asian institutions not in collaboration with the board's Asian partners. No grants to individuals, or for church or relief work or community outreach that has no relation to higher education, student scholarships (except for designated grants), requests for funding to turn theses/dissertations into research publications, requests for attending or sponsoring conferences, buildings and building materials (except for designated grants), salaries or salary supplements (except for designated grants), or equipment or furniture (except for designated grants).
Publications: Application guidelines; Annual report; Financial statement; Grants list.
Application information:
  Initial approach: Proposal submitted to Hong Kong office
  Copies of proposal: 1
  Deadline(s): Oct. 31
  Board meeting date(s): Apr. and Nov.
  Final notification: June
Officers and Trustees:* Dr. Ching-Mai Wu,* Chair.; Dr. Michael Gilligan,* Vice-Chair.; Patricia Stranahan, Pres.; Betty Cernol-McCann, V.P., Progs.; Candy Eng, V.P., Finance and Admin.; Rita Pullium, Ph.D., V.P. and Dir., United Board Fellows Prog. and Regional Scholars Prog.; Ruth Hayhoe,* Ph.D., Secy.; Anthony Ruger,* Treas.; Dr. Paul P. Appasamy; Judith A. Berling, Ph.D.; Dr. Charles Booth; Dr. Nancy Chapman; Dr. Shin Chiba; Dr. I. John Hesselink; Janet E. Hunt, Esq.
Number of staff: 14 full-time professional; 2 part-time professional; 2 part-time support.
EIN: 135562367

1705
The United Fund for the Education of Russian Immigrant Children in Israel

5417 18th Ave.
Brooklyn, NY 11204-1928

Grantmaker type: Public charity.
Financial data (yr. ended 12/31/10): Revenue, $5,236,545; assets, $11,837,127 (M); gifts received, $5,367,219; expenditures, $4,328,056; giving activities include $12,500 for grants, and $3,066,475 for grants to organizations outside the U.S.
Purpose and activities: The fund supports institutions in New York City and Israel, which cater to the needs of Russian immigrant children.
Fields of interest: Elementary/secondary education; Jewish agencies & synagogues; Children.
International interests: Israel.
Limitations: Giving limited to the New York, NY, area, NJ, and Israel.
Officer: Abraham Biederman, Pres.
Directors: Baruch Greisman; Max Knopf.
EIN: 113064893

1706
United States Fund for UNICEF

125 Maiden Ln.
New York, NY 10038-4912 (212) 686-5522
FAX: (212) 779-1670; Toll-free tel: (800) 486-4233; URL: http://www.unicefusa.org
Blog: http://fieldnotes.unicefusa.org/
RSS Feed: http://www.unicefusa.org/system/rss/channel.jsp?subsiteID=36107&feed=feed-678514&feedFormat=rss2

Established in 1949.
Donor: GE Foundation.
Grantmaker type: Public charity.
Financial data (yr. ended 06/30/11): Revenue, $252,625,352; assets, $138,970,269 (M); gifts received, $248,654,701; expenditures, $244,547,822; giving activities include $8,302,418 for grants, and $184,933,740 for grants to organizations outside the U.S.
Purpose and activities: The fund supports child survival, protection, and development worldwide through education, advocacy, and fundraising.
Fields of interest: Children/youth, services; International affairs; Children.
Type of support: General/operating support; In-kind gifts.
Limitations: Giving on a national and international basis.
Officers and Directors:* Caryl M. Stern,* Pres. and C.E.O.; Edward G. Lloyd, Exec. V.P., Opers., and C.F.O.; Cynthia McCaffrey, Sr. V.P., Progs.; Robert Thompson, Sr. V.P., Devel.; Jay Aldous, V.P., Mktg., Comms., and Corp. Partnerships; Roslyn Carnage, V.P., Human Resources; Richard Esserman, V.P., Finance and Budget; Susan Kotcher, V.P., Devel.; Martin Rendon, V.P., Public Policy and Advocacy; Lisa Szarkowski, V.P., Public Rels.; Susan V. Berresford; James A. Block; Dan Brutto; Nelson Chai; Gary M. Cohen; Mary Callahan Erdoes; Pamela Fiori; Dolores Rice Gahan, D.O.; and 10 additional directors.
Number of staff: 122 full-time professional; 8 part-time professional.
EIN: 131760110

1707
United States Fund for UNICEF In-Kind Assistance Corporation

c/o Edward G Lloyd
125 Maiden Lane
New York, NY 10038-4912 (212) 686-5522

Supporting organization of United States Fund for UNICEF.
Grantmaker type: Public charity.
Financial data (yr. ended 06/30/11): Revenue, $202,547,353; assets, $106,041 (M); gifts received, $202,547,353; expenditures, $202,547,353; giving activities include $202,377,253 for grants to organizations outside the U.S.
Fields of interest: Human services; International affairs.
Limitations: Giving limited to New York, NY and Toronto, Canada.
Officers and Directors:* Antony Pantaleoni,* Chair.; Caryl Stern,* Pres. and C.E.O.; Edward G. Lloyd, Treas.; James Block; Albert Kaneb; Anthony Lake; Susan Rice; Amy Robbins.
EIN: 203287404

1708
United States-Japan Foundation

145 E. 32nd St., 12th Fl.
New York, NY 10016-6055 (212) 481-8753
FAX: (212) 481-8762; E-mail: info@us-jf.org; Tokyo office address: Reinanzaka Bldg. 1F, 1-14-2 Akasaka, Minato-ku, Tokyo 107-0052, Japan, tel.: (03) 3586-0541; fax: (03) 3586-1128; e-mail: infotokyo-usjf@nifty.com; URL: http://www.us-jf.org
Sign up for current newsletter: http://www.us-jf.org/

Foundation incorporated in 1980 in NY.
Donor: The Nippon Foundation.
Grantmaker type: Independent foundation.
Financial data (yr. ended 12/31/09): Assets, $81,040,832 (M); gifts received, $13,898; expenditures, $4,073,432; qualifying distributions, $3,292,991; giving activities include $949,393 for 35 grants (high: $538,199; low: $3,000).
Purpose and activities: The United States-Japan Foundation is committed to promoting stronger ties between Americans and Japanese by supporting projects that foster mutual knowledge and education, deepen understanding, create effective channels of communication, and address common concerns in an increasingly interdependent world. The current focus of grantmaking activities is in the areas of communication/public opinion, precollege education and policy studies.
Fields of interest: Elementary school/education; Secondary school/education; Education; Environment, energy; Environment; International economic development; International affairs, foreign policy; International affairs; Economics; Public policy, research; Government/public administration; Youth; Adults.
International interests: Asia; Japan.
Type of support: Program development; Publication; Curriculum development; Research; Matching/challenge support.
Limitations: Applications accepted. Giving primarily in the U.S. and Japan. No support for projects in the arts involving performances, exhibitions, or productions, or for sports exchanges or student exchanges. No grants to individuals, or for building or endowment funds, capital campaigns, deficit operations.
Publications: Application guidelines; Financial statement; Grants list.
Application information: The foundation only accepts unsolicited letters of inquiry, not proposals. Application form not required.
  Initial approach: Letter (no longer than 4 pages)
  Copies of proposal: 2
  Deadline(s): July 15 and Dec. 15
  Board meeting date(s): Apr. and Oct.
  Final notification: 1 to 3 months
Officers and Trustees:* Thomas S. Johnson, Chair.; Shinji Fukukawa,* Vice-Chair.; George R. Packard,* Pres.; Takeo Takuma,* V.P. and Dir., Tokyo office; Yusuke Saraya,* Board Secy.; Christine Manapat-Sims, Treas.; Gerald L. Curtis; Hon. Robin Chandler Duke; Jane M. Gould; Yoriko Kawaguchi; Shiichi Kitaoka; Yotaro Kobayashi; Akira Kojima; Taro Kono; James W. Lintott; Alexandra Munroe; T. Timothy Ryan, Jr.; Yohei Sasakawa; Thomas W. Strauss.
Number of staff: 8 full-time professional; 1 full-time support.
EIN: 133054425

1709
University of Cape Town Fund, Inc.
51 W. 52nd St.
New York, NY   10019-6119   (212) 403-1333

Grantmaker type: Public charity.
Financial data (yr. ended 12/31/10): Revenue, $1,951,211; assets, $339,058 (M); gifts received, $1,943,560; expenditures, $1,997,582; giving activities include $1,837,545 for grants to organizations outside the U.S.
Purpose and activities: The organization makes grants to programs and organizations in South Africa

which support Black advancement in the academic world and to organizations which are committed to non-racism and to non-racial future for South Africa.
Fields of interest: African Americans/Blacks.
International interests: South Africa.
Limitations: Giving primarily in South Africa.
Officer and Directors:* Trevor Norwitz,* Chair.; Kofi Appenteng, Esq.; Michelle M. Le Roux; Vincent Mai; David J.P. Meachin.
EIN: 133202349

1710
Uphill Foundation
31 W. 27th St., 4th Fl.
New York, NY   10001-6914
Contact: Jean Crawford, U.S. Trust

Established in 2000 in PA.
Donor: Frances A. Velay†.
Grantmaker type: Independent foundation.
Financial data (yr. ended 12/31/10): Assets, $23,499,024 (M); gifts received, $639,552; expenditures, $978,327; qualifying distributions, $650,000; giving activities include $650,000 for grants.
Purpose and activities: Giving primarily for human services.
Fields of interest: Arts; Education; Environment; Human services; Children/youth, services; International relief; Economically disadvantaged.
Limitations: Applications not accepted. Giving primarily in AR, NY, and VA. No grants to individuals.
Application information: Contributes only to pre-selected organizations.
Trustees: Dan McCarthy; Barbara Paul Robinson; Christophe Velay.
EIN: 137196672

1711
Usha Foundation
226 Idlewood Rd.
Rochester, NY   14618-3948   (585) 244-3632
Contact: Brijen Gupta, Exec. Dir.

Established in 1998 in IA.
Grantmaker type: Independent foundation.
Financial data (yr. ended 12/31/09): Assets, $13,621 (M); gifts received, $500; expenditures, $135,350; qualifying distributions, $135,350; giving activities include $135,350 for 4 grants (high: $135,000; low: $50).
Purpose and activities: Giving primarily to educational institutions and healthcare facilities in the U.S. and India.
Fields of interest: Education; Hospitals (general).
International interests: India.
Limitations: Giving on a national basis and in India. No grants to individuals.
Application information:
  Initial approach: Proposal
  Deadline(s): None
Officers: Nalini Mullapudi, Pres.; Ratnam V. Mullapudi, Secy.; Brijen Gupta, Exec. Dir.
Trustees: Sudhir Koneru; G.N. Rao.
EIN: 391900020

1712
The Vanderbilt Family Foundation
(formerly The William H. & Helen C. Vanderbilt Foundation)
c/o Fiduciary Trust International
600 Fifth Ave.
New York, NY   10020-2326

Established in MA.
Donor: William H. Vanderbilt Charitable Trust.
Grantmaker type: Independent foundation.
Financial data (yr. ended 02/28/11): Assets, $5,319,269 (M); expenditures, $264,461; qualifying distributions, $230,000; giving activities include $230,000 for grants.
Purpose and activities: Giving primarily for education, employment services, parks, and international development.
Fields of interest: Arts; Elementary/secondary education; Environmental education; Environment; Health care; Employment, training; Housing/shelter, development; Recreation, parks/playgrounds; Human services; International economic development; International relief; Science.
Limitations: Applications not accepted. Giving primarily in Washington, DC, New York, NY, Boston, MA and VT; giving also on an international basis, primarily in the Caribbean and Honduras. No grants to individuals.
Application information: Contributes only to pre-selected organizations.
Trustees: Ellen F. Vanderbilt Aidnoff; Anne C. Vanderbilt Hartwell; William Henry Vanderbilt, Jr.; Emily Vanderbilt Wade.
EIN: 042743143

1713
The G. Unger Vetlesen Foundation
c/o Fulton, Rowe, & Hart
1 Rockefeller Plz., Ste. 301
New York, NY   10020-2002   (212) 586-0700
Contact: George Rowe, Jr., Pres.
FAX: (212) 245-1863;
E mail: info@monellvetlesen.org; URL: http://www.monellvetlesen.org/

Incorporated in 1955 in NY.
Donor: George Unger Vetlesen†.
Grantmaker type: Independent foundation.
Financial data (yr. ended 12/31/10): Assets, $119,039,383 (M); expenditures, $4,895,249; qualifying distributions, $4,644,874; giving activities include $4,406,500 for 35 grants (high: $600,000; low: $10,000).
Purpose and activities: Established a biennial international science award for discoveries in the earth sciences; grants for biological, geophysical, and environmental research, including scholarships, and cultural organizations, including those emphasizing Norwegian-American relations and maritime interests. Support also for public policy research and libraries.
Fields of interest: Arts; Libraries/library science; Environment; Marine science; Physical/earth sciences; Engineering/technology; Biology/life sciences; Science; Public policy, research.
Type of support: General/operating support; Continuing support; Annual campaigns; Capital campaigns; Building/renovation; Equipment; Endowments; Program development; Professorships; Scholarship funds; Research.

Limitations: Applications accepted. Giving primarily in NY; some giving in other areas. No grants to individuals.
Publications: Application guidelines; Annual report; Financial statement; Grants list.
Application information: Full proposals are accepted by invitation only following positive response to letter of inquiry. Unsolicited full proposals will not be reviewed. Application form not required.
Initial approach: Letter of inquiry (not exceeding 3 pages)
Copies of proposal: 1
Deadline(s): None for letters of inquiry
Board meeting date(s): June and Dec.
Final notification: Positive responses are sent within 4-6 weeks
Officers and Directors:* George Rowe, Jr.,* Pres. and Treas.; Eugene P. Grisanti,* V.P.; Ambrose K. Monell, V.P.; Maurizio J. Morello, Secy.; Gary K. Beauchamp.
EIN: 131982695
Recent grants for international programs:
1713-1 American-Scandinavian Foundation, New York, NY, $10,000. For general operating support. 2009.
1713-2 Bermuda Institute of Ocean Sciences, Saint Georges, Bermuda, $100,000. For general operating support. 2009.
1713-3 Cape Eleuthera Island School, Eleuthera, Bahamas, $50,000. For general operating support. 2009.
1713-4 Oceana, Washington, DC, $25,000. For Dirty Fishing campaign. 2009.
1713-5 Organization for Tropical Studies, Durham, NC, $75,000. For general operating support. 2009.
1713-6 University of Rhode Island, Graduate School of Oceanography, Kingston, RI, $300,000. For general operating support ($200,000) and for the URI Honors Colloquium on Global Environmental Change ($100,000). 2009.
1713-7 University of Texas, Institute for Geophysics, Austin, TX, $200,000. For Antarctic aerogeophysical research project. 2009.
1713-8 University of the South Pacific, Suva, Fiji, $93,500. For research on how global change affects Oceanic Islands. 2009.
1713-9 University of Washington, Center of Excellence at the College of Ocean and Fishery Sciences, Seattle, WA, $225,000. For general operating support ($200,000) and for work on whales in Greenland. 2009.
1713-10 Wildlife Conservation Society, Bronx, NY, $650,000. For the Global Health Program ($50,000), the Marine Conservation Program ($50,000), for general operating support ($50,000), and for predevelopment costs of the renovations to the New York Aquarium ($500,000). 2009.
1713-11 Yale University, Department of Astronomy, New Haven, CT, $200,000. For research on solar variability and global temperature. 2009.

1714
VHIV, Inc.

(formerly The Bella Wexner Charitable Foundation)
c/o Hertz, Herson, & Co., LLP
2 Park Ave., Ste. 1500
New York, NY 10016-5701

Established in 1990 in OH.

Donors: Bella Wexner; Susan R. Wexner Revocable Trust.
Grantmaker type: Independent foundation.
Financial data (yr. ended 12/31/10): Assets, $38,271,558 (M); expenditures, $1,304,458; qualifying distributions, $1,098,166; giving activities include $1,098,166 for grants.
Fields of interest: Youth development; Jewish federated giving programs; Jewish agencies & synagogues.
International interests: Israel.
Limitations: Applications not accepted. Giving primarily in New York, NY. No grants to individuals.
Application information: Contributes only to a pre-selected organization.
Officer and Directors:* Susan R. Wexner,* Pres. and Secy.-Treas.; Dr. Bertrand Agus; Dr. Saul G. Agus; Raymond Kanner; Gregg H. Levy, Esq.; Michael S. Oberman, Esq.; Mark Saks, Esq.
EIN: 311324522

1715
Vietnam Relief Effort

845 United Nations Plz., 90A
New York, NY 10017-3539 (917) 668-2600

Established in 1999 in NY.
Grantmaker type: Public charity.
Financial data (yr. ended 12/31/10): Revenue, $3,388; assets, $167,938 (M); gifts received, $2,092; expenditures, $62,503; giving activities include $35,453 for grants.
Purpose and activities: The organization seeks to bring aid, through education, medical, and relief projects, to impoverished regions of Vietnam.
Fields of interest: Education; Health care; International relief; Economically disadvantaged.
International interests: Vietnam.
Type of support: Grants to individuals.
Limitations: Giving primarily to Vietnam.
Board Members: John Altorelli; Amy Braunschweiger; Chinh Chu; Kathy Chu; Thien Le; Steven Nguyen; Truc To; Jonathan Wall; Mindy Williams.
EIN: 134095507

1716
The Vine Group USA, Inc.

4634 White Plains Rd.
Bronx, NY 10470-1610
URL: http://tvgint.org/index.html

Established in 2000.
Grantmaker type: Public charity.
Financial data (yr. ended 12/31/09): Revenue, $153,602; assets, $50,704 (M); gifts received, $153,602; expenditures, $153,080.
Purpose and activities: The organization works to provide educational resources and scholarship opportunities to tertiary instutitions in Sub-Saharan Africa, in order to alleviate poverty and help in building a workforce necessary for a sustainable economic development.
Fields of interest: Scholarships/financial aid; Education; Economically disadvantaged.
International interests: Sub-Saharan Africa.
Type of support: Scholarships—to individuals.
Limitations: Giving limited to Sub-Saharan African.
Officers: Mekhi Phifer, Chair.; Gale Stevens-Hayes, Vice-Chair.; Henry Akintunde, Pres.; Tammy Musiowksy, C.F.O.

Board Members: Corine Petty; Rosemary Santana-Ramirez.
EIN: 113593033

1717
The Virtue Foundation

1040 1st Ave., Ste. 116
New York, NY 10022-2991 (212) 355-2227
FAX: (212) 583-1150;
E-mail: info@virtuefoundation.org; URL: http://www.virtuefoundation.org

Established in 2002 in NY.
Donor: John Haskell, Jr.
Grantmaker type: Public charity.
Financial data (yr. ended 12/31/10): Revenue, $301,769; assets, $953,003 (M); gifts received, $295,899; expenditures, $68,779; program services expenses, $58,640; giving activities include $58,640 for grants.
Purpose and activities: The foundation's mission is to increase awareness of prevalent global issues, to inspire people to action, and to render humanitarian assistance through healthcare, education, and empowerment initiatives.
Fields of interest: Education; Health care; International affairs; International human rights; International relief.
Type of support: General/operating support; Equipment; Program development; Conferences/seminars; Curriculum development; Technical assistance; Consulting services; Program evaluation.
Limitations: Applications accepted. Giving primarily in the U.S., Africa, and Southeast Asia. No support for religious organizations, governmental organizations, or political groups. No grants to individuals.
Publications: Annual report; Financial statement; Informational brochure.
Application information: Application form not required.
Initial approach: Letter
Copies of proposal: 4
Deadline(s): Nov. 15
Board meeting date(s): 2nd week of Feb., May, Sept., and Dec.
Final notification: Four weeks
Officers and Directors: Joseph Salim,* M.D., Pres.; John Larovere,* M.D., V.P.; Richard Rass,* Secy.; Shane Nazeri,* M.D., Treas.; George C. Biddle; John A. Bradley; Ebby M.D. Elahi; Jim Fowler; Roy M. Goodman; Richard W. Murphy.
EIN: 562289262

1718
Vital Projects Fund, Inc.

c/o Robert B. Menschel
375 Park Ave., Ste. 1602
New York, NY 10152-1600

Established in 1992 in NY, funded in 2006.
Donor: Horace W. Goldsmith†.
Grantmaker type: Independent foundation.
Financial data (yr. ended 12/31/10): Assets, $220,575,402 (M); expenditures, $10,013,653; qualifying distributions, $9,599,455; giving activities include $9,222,500 for 136 grants (high: $500,000; low: $7,500; average: $25,000–$100,000).

Purpose and activities: The fund primarily supports cultural programs, including performing arts and museums, support also for hospitals, and higher education.
Fields of interest: International relief; Homeless, human services; Human services; Crime/law enforcement; Medical research, institute; Medical research; AIDS research; Cancer research; Medical care, rehabilitation; Health care; Hospitals (general); Environment, natural resources; Education; Libraries/library science; Higher education; Education, research; Arts; Performing arts, music; Visual arts; Performing arts, theater; Performing arts, dance; Museums; Disabilities, people with.
Type of support: General/operating support; Continuing support; Income development; Annual campaigns; Capital campaigns; Building/renovation; Land acquisition; Endowments; Debt reduction; Emergency funds; Professorships; Curriculum development; Fellowships; Scholarship funds; Research; Matching/challenge support.
Limitations: Applications not accepted. Giving on a national basis. No grants to individuals, or for scholarships or loans to individuals.
Application information: Unsolicited requests for funds not accepted.
Officers and Directors:* Robert B. Menschel,* Pres. and Treas.; David F. Menschel,* Secy.; Lauren E. Menschel; Richard B. Menschel; Ronay Menschel.
Number of staff: 1 part-time professional; 3 part-time support.
EIN: 133711340
Recent grants for international programs:
1718-1 American Academy in Rome, New York, NY, $25,000. For general purpose fund. 2010.
1718-2 Architecture for Humanity, San Francisco, CA, $25,000. For general purpose fund. 2010.
1718-3 Ashoka: Innovators for the Public, Arlington, VA, $25,000. For general purpose fund. 2010.
1718-4 Council on Foreign Relations, New York, NY, $25,000. For general purpose fund. 2010.
1718-5 Doctors Without Borders USA, New York, NY, $100,000. For general purpose fund. 2010.
1718-6 Human Rights Watch, New York, NY, $100,000. For general purpose fund. 2010.
1718-7 International Rescue Committee, New York, NY, $100,000. For general purpose fund. 2010.
1718-8 Just Vision, Washington, DC, $20,000. For general purpose fund. 2010.
1718-9 Seeds of Peace, New York, NY, $300,000. For general purpose fund. 2010.
1718-10 Ubuntu Education Fund, New York, NY, $25,000. For general purpose fund. 2010.

1719
The Volcker Family Foundation, Inc.
c/o Hill Rivkins & Hayden, LLP
45 Broadway, Ste. 1500
New York, NY   10006-3007

Established in 1996 in DE.
Donor: Paul A. Volcker.
Grantmaker type: Independent foundation.
Financial data (yr. ended 12/31/10): Assets, $6,405,903 (M); gifts received, $300,000; expenditures, $257,085; qualifying distributions, $250,000; giving activities include $250,000 for grants.
Purpose and activities: Giving primarily for a health organization and education.

Fields of interest: Higher education; Education; Cerebral palsy; International affairs.
Limitations: Applications not accepted. Giving primarily in Washington, DC, and New York, NY.
Application information: Unsolicited requests for funds not accepted.
Officers and Directors:* Paul A. Volcker,* Pres.; Ernesto V. Luzzatto, Secy.-Treas.; James P. Volcker; Janis Volcker Zima.
EIN: 133917327

1720
The Walker Family Foundation
c/o BCRS Assocs., Inc.
77 Water St., 9th Fl.
New York, NY   10005-4414   (212) 440-0800

Established in 1999 in CT.
Donor: Jeffrey Walker.
Grantmaker type: Independent foundation.
Financial data (yr. ended 03/31/11): Assets, $1,619,646 (M); expenditures, $1,809,830; qualifying distributions, $1,808,730; giving activities include $1,779,130 for 54 grants (high: $300,000; low: $500).
Purpose and activities: Giving primarily for higher education, human services, and the arts.
Fields of interest: Human services; International development; Business school/education; Arts education; Arts; Higher education; Libraries (public); Education; Children, services; Family services.
Limitations: Applications not accepted. Giving primarily in New York, NY, and the greater Boston, MA, area. No grants to individuals, or for scholarships; no loans.
Application information: Contributes only to pre-selected organizations.
Trustees: Jeffrey C. Walker; Suzanne Walker.
EIN: 061543752

1721
Miriam G. and Ira D. Wallach Foundation
3 Manhattanville Rd.
Purchase, NY   10577-2110

Incorporated in 1956 in NY.
Grantmaker type: Independent foundation.
Financial data (yr. ended 10/31/09): Assets, $130,662,000 (M); expenditures, $9,099,437; qualifying distributions, $8,210,669; giving activities include $8,014,117 for 50 grants (high: $6,500,000; low: $100; average: $2,500–$250,000).
Purpose and activities: Support primarily for higher education, international relations, social services, Jewish organizations, and cultural programs, including a public television station.
Fields of interest: Media, television; Museums; Performing arts; Historical activities; Higher education; Environment; Human services; International affairs; Jewish federated giving programs; Jewish agencies & synagogues.
Limitations: Applications not accepted. Giving primarily in NY. No grants to individuals.
Application information: Contributes only to pre-selected organizations.
Officers and Directors:* Miriam G. Wallach,* Chair.; Kenneth L. Wallach,* Pres.; Edgar Wachenheim III,* V.P.; Peter C. Siegfried, Secy.; Steven M. Eigen, Treas. and C.F.O.; Kate W. Cassidy; Martin W.

Cassidy; Sue W. Wachenheim; Mary K. Wallach; Susan S. Wallach.
EIN: 136101702
Recent grants for international programs:
1721-1 Asia Society, New York, NY, $10,000. For general support. 2009.
1721-2 e-Parliament, Wye, England, $25,000. For general support. 2009.
1721-3 Human Rights First, New York, NY, $25,000. For general support. 2009.
1721-4 Human Rights Watch, New York, NY, $10,000. For general support. 2009.
1721-5 Lawyers Committee on Nuclear Policy, New York, NY, $75,000. For general support. 2009.
1721-6 United Nations Association of the United States of America, New York, NY, $100,000. For general support. 2009.

1722
The Walters Family Foundation, Inc.
c/o Eisner & Lubin, LLP
444 Madison Ave., 11th Fl.
New York, NY   10022
Application address: c/o Kathryn S. Walters, 742B Cienequitas Rd., Santa Barbara, CA 93110

Established in 1960 in NY.
Grantmaker type: Independent foundation.
Financial data (yr. ended 12/31/10): Assets, $3,342,431 (M); expenditures, $169,456; qualifying distributions, $150,000; giving activities include $150,000 for grants.
Fields of interest: International relief; Health care; Heart & circulatory research; Alzheimer's disease research; Housing/shelter; Human services.
Type of support: General/operating support; Emergency funds; Research; Matching/challenge support.
Limitations: Applications accepted. Giving primarily in NY. No grants to individuals.
Application information:
   Initial approach: Letter
   Deadline(s): None
Officers and Directors:* Sarah Walters,* Pres. and Secy.; Kathryn S. Walters,* V.P.; Mary E. Rust,* Treas.
EIN: 136107423

1723
Weeden Foundation
747 3rd Ave., 34th Fl.
New York, NY   10017-2803
Contact: Donald A. Weeden, Exec. Dir.; Gillian Beach, Research Asst.
FAX: (212) 888-1354;
E-mail: weedenfdn@weedenfdn.org; URL: http://www.weedenfdn.org

Established 1963 in CA.
Donors: Frank Weeden†; Alan N. Weeden; Donald E. Weeden; John D. Weeden; William F. Weeden, M.D.; Frank Weeden Fund; Holloman-Price Fdn.
Grantmaker type: Independent foundation.
Financial data (yr. ended 06/30/11): Assets, $29,160,269 (M); gifts received, $60,000; expenditures, $2,407,654; qualifying distributions, $1,816,269; giving activities include $1,478,322 for grants.
Purpose and activities: Giving primarily to environmental organizations working to preserve biological diversity. Program interests also include

organizations working to stabilize human population and organizations working to address the over consumption of the earth's resources.

Fields of interest: Environment, natural resources; Environment; Population studies.

International interests: Chile; Russia.

Type of support: General/operating support; Continuing support; Land acquisition; Emergency funds; Program development; Seed money; Program-related investments/loans.

Limitations: Applications accepted. Giving on a national and international basis, primarily in northern CA, the Pacific Northwest, Latin America (Chile), Central Siberia and the Altai Republic in Russia. No grants to individuals, or for multi-year requests; generally no funding for films, conferences, or scientific research.

Publications: Application guidelines; Annual report; Financial statement; Grants list; Program policy statement.

Application information: The foundation strongly encourages potential applicants to submit a letter of inquiry before presenting a complete proposal. Proposal guidelines available on foundation web site. Application form not required.

> *Initial approach:* Letter of inquiry via e-mail or U.S. mail only
> *Copies of proposal:* 2
> *Deadline(s):* 6 weeks prior to each board meeting; check web site for dates
> *Board meeting date(s):* 3 times a year
> *Final notification:* 8-10 weeks

Officers and Directors: * Norman Weeden, * Ph.D., Pres.; Tina Roux, V.P.; H. Leslie Weeden, * Secy.; Bob Weeden, Treas.; Donald A. Weeden, Exec. Dir.; Barbara Daugherty; David Davies; Alan N. Weeden; Donald E. Weeden; Jack D. Weeden; John D. Weeden; William Weeden, M.D.

Number of staff: 2 full-time professional.

EIN: 946109313

1724
Weil, Gotshal & Manges Foundation

c/o Weil, Gotshal & Manges LLP
767 5th Ave.
New York, NY 10153-0001 (212) 310-6813
Contact: Dennis Foley, Treas.

Established in 1983 in NY.

Donors: Weil, Gotshal & Manges LLP; Robert Todd Lang; Ira M. Millstein; Harvey R. Miller.

Grantmaker type: Company-sponsored foundation.

Financial data (yr. ended 12/31/10): Assets, $6,210,328 (M); gifts received, $1,500,000; expenditures, $1,856,830; qualifying distributions, $1,856,430; giving activities include $1,856,305 for 112 grants (high: $345,000; low: $100).

Purpose and activities: The foundation supports museums and organizations involved with education, legal services, disaster relief, children and youth, international relief, civil and human rights, business, and Judaism.

Fields of interest: Museums; Elementary school/education; Higher education; Law school/education; Education; Legal services; Disasters, 9/11/01; American Red Cross; Children/youth, services; International relief; Civil/human rights; Business/industry; United Ways and Federated Giving Programs; Jewish federated giving programs; Jewish agencies & synagogues.

Type of support: General/operating support; Scholarship funds.

Limitations: Applications accepted. Giving primarily in NJ and NY. No grants to individuals.

Application information: Application form not required.

> *Initial approach:* Proposal
> *Copies of proposal:* 1
> *Deadline(s):* Nov. 1

Officer and Directors: * Dennis Foley, * Treas.; Stephen Dannhauser; Richard Davis; Thomas Roberts.

EIN: 133158325

1725
Weingarten Family Foundation

1661 53rd St.
Brooklyn, NY 11204-1421

Established in 1992 in NY.

Donor: Otto I. Weingarten.

Grantmaker type: Independent foundation.

Financial data (yr. ended 12/31/10): Assets, $6,044,096 (M); gifts received, $451,966; expenditures, $244,557; qualifying distributions, $218,370; giving activities include $216,620 for 9 grants (high: $53,000; low: $360).

Purpose and activities: Giving primarily for Jewish organizations and yeshivas.

Fields of interest: Human services; Elementary/secondary education; Jewish agencies & synagogues.

International interests: Israel.

Limitations: Applications not accepted. Giving primarily in NJ and Brooklyn, NY. No grants to individuals.

Application information: Contributes only to pre-selected organizations.

Officers: Otto I. Weingarten, Pres.; Rosemarie Weingarten, V.P.; Simone Krause, Secy.; Hershie Weingarten, Treas.

EIN: 113133160

1726
Jeffrey and Susan Weingarten Foundation

c/o BCRS Assocs., LLC
100 Wall St., 11th Fl.
New York, NY 10005-3701

Established in 1991 in NY.

Donors: Jeffrey M. Weingarten; Susan Weingarten.

Grantmaker type: Independent foundation.

Financial data (yr. ended 06/30/11): Assets, $611,141 (M); expenditures, $153,345; qualifying distributions, $153,120; giving activities include $153,120 for grants.

Purpose and activities: Giving primarily to education; support also for Jewish agencies, the performing arts, and health and medicine.

Fields of interest: Elementary/secondary education; Performing arts; Higher education; Education; Jewish agencies & synagogues.

International interests: England.

Limitations: Applications not accepted. Giving primarily in London, England; some funding also in Philadelphia, PA. No grants to individuals.

Application information: Contributes only to pre-selected organizations.

Trustees: Michael R. Armellino; Jeffrey M. Weingarten; Amanda Weingarten.

EIN: 133639274

1727
J. Weinstein Foundation, Inc.

Rockridge Farm, 961 Rte. 52
Carmel, NY 10512 (845) 225-7647
Contact: Salvatore Cappuzzo, Secy.-Treas.

Incorporated in 1948 in NY.

Donors: Joe Weinstein†; J.W. Mays, Inc.

Grantmaker type: Independent foundation.

Financial data (yr. ended 12/31/10): Assets, $5,410,521 (M); gifts received, $507,193; expenditures, $214,066; qualifying distributions, $213,000; giving activities include $213,000 for grants.

Purpose and activities: Support for higher education in the U.S. and Israel, temple support, hospitals, and Jewish welfare funds.

Fields of interest: Museums; Higher education; Hospitals (general); Human services; Jewish federated giving programs; Jewish agencies & synagogues.

International interests: Israel.

Type of support: General/operating support; Continuing support; Endowments; Research.

Limitations: Applications accepted. Giving primarily in NY.

Application information:

> *Initial approach:* Letter
> *Deadline(s):* None

Officers and Directors: * Lloyd J. Shulman, * Pres.; Sylvia W. Shulman, * V.P.; Salvatore Cappuzzo, * Secy.-Treas.

EIN: 116003595

1728
The Margaret L. Wendt Foundation

40 Fountain Plz., Ste. 277
Buffalo, NY 14202-2220 (716) 855-2146
Contact: Robert J. Kresse, Tr.

Trust established in 1956 in NY.

Donor: Margaret L. Wendt†.

Grantmaker type: Independent foundation.

Financial data (yr. ended 01/31/10): Assets, $93,552,774 (M); expenditures, $4,715,993; qualifying distributions, $8,894,158; giving activities include $3,501,553 for 153 grants (high: $262,018; low: $93), and $5,138,235 for loans/program-related investments.

Purpose and activities: Emphasis on education, the arts, and social services; support also for churches and religious organizations, health associations, public interest organizations, and youth agencies.

Fields of interest: Visual arts; Museums; Performing arts; Performing arts, theater; History/archaeology; Historic preservation/historical societies; Arts; Education, fund raising/fund distribution; Education; Education, early childhood education; Higher education; Libraries/library science; Education; Environment, natural resources; Hospitals (general); Substance abuse, services; Mental health/crisis services; Health organizations, association; Cancer; AIDS; Alcoholism; Biomedicine; Medical research, institute; Cancer research; AIDS research; Legal services; Crime/law enforcement; Human services; Children/youth, services; Residential/custodial care, hospices; Aging, centers/services; Minorities/immigrants, centers/services; International human rights; Community/economic development; United Ways and Federated Giving Programs; Political science; Government/public administration; Public affairs; Religion; Minorities; Disabilities, people with; Aging; Economically disadvantaged.

Limitations: Applications accepted. Giving primarily in Buffalo and western NY. No grants to individuals, or for scholarships.
Publications: Application guidelines.
Application information: Application form not required.
  Initial approach: Letter or application form
  Copies of proposal: 4
  Deadline(s): 1 month prior to board meeting
  Board meeting date(s): Quarterly; no fixed dates
  Final notification: Usually 4 to 6 months
Trustees: Janet L. Day; Robert J. Kresse; Thomas D. Lunt.
Number of staff: 1 part-time support.
EIN: 166030037

1729
Western Wall Heritage Foundation, Inc.
587 5th Ave., 7th Fl.
New York, NY 10017-6202 (212) 725-0598
URL: http://english.thekotel.org

Established in 1988.
Grantmaker type: Public charity.
Financial data (yr. ended 12/31/10): Revenue, $3,855,329; assets, $11,636,614 (M); gifts received, $3,509,407; expenditures, $3,719,144; giving activities include $2,889,000 for grants to organizations outside the U.S.
Purpose and activities: The foundation seeks to convey to all segments of the Jewish people the values inherent in the heritage of the Western Wall in Jerusalem, Israel.
Fields of interest: Jewish agencies & synagogues; Historical activities; Historic preservation/historical societies.
International interests: Israel.
Limitations: Applications not accepted. Giving limited to Israel.
Publications: Newsletter.
Application information: Contributes only to a pre-selected organization; unsolicited requests for funds not considered or acknowledged.
Officers: Joseph Loshinsky,* Pres.; Issac Applebaum, V.P. and Treas.; Jay Marcus, Secy.
Board Member: Benjamin Sambul.
EIN: 133468352

1730
Whalesback Foundation
1 Pierrepont St.
Brooklyn, NY 11201-3302

Established in 1996 in PA.
Donors: Theodore Roosevelt III; Theodore Roosevelt IV.
Grantmaker type: Independent foundation.
Financial data (yr. ended 12/31/10): Assets, $4,217,955 (M); expenditures, $215,752; qualifying distributions, $195,500; giving activities include $195,500 for grants.
Fields of interest: Museums (art); Business school/education; Animals/wildlife; International affairs.
Limitations: Applications not accepted. Giving primarily in NY. No grants to individuals.
Application information: Contributes only to pre-selected organizations.
Officer and Trustees: Theodore Roosevelt IV,* Pres. and Secy.-Treas.; Constance Roosevelt.
EIN: 311478498

1731
Whispering Bells Foundation
c/o RSM McGladrey, Inc.
1185 Ave. of the Americas
New York, NY 10036-2601

Established in 1990 in NY.
Donors: Peter Workman; Carolan Workman; Workman Publishing Co.
Grantmaker type: Independent foundation.
Financial data (yr. ended 12/31/10): Assets, $875,806 (M); gifts received, $575,000; expenditures, $642,501; qualifying distributions, $639,457; giving activities include $639,357 for 121 grants (high: $177,500; low: $100).
Fields of interest: Education; Human services; Neighborhood centers; International human rights; Jewish federated giving programs; Economically disadvantaged.
Limitations: Applications not accepted. Giving primarily in NY. No grants to individuals.
Application information: Contributes only to pre-selected organizations.
Officer and Trustees: Peter Workman,* Pres.; Edward Klagsbrun; Carolan Workman.
EIN: 136962126

1732
White Flowers Foundation
c/o J.C. Flowers & Co., LLC
717 5th Ave., 26th Fl.
New York, NY 10022-8100

Established in 1989 in NY.
Donors: J. Christopher Flowers; E. Neville Isdell; Church of Our Savior.
Grantmaker type: Independent foundation.
Financial data (yr. ended 05/31/10): Assets, $5 (M); gifts received, $153,370; expenditures, $193,765; qualifying distributions, $237,188; giving activities include $204,578 for 10 grants (high: $100,000; low: $1,000).
Purpose and activities: Giving primarily for healthcare, the arts, higher education and to Christian churches.
Fields of interest: Health care; Hospitals (specialty); Performing arts, orchestras; Higher education; Education; Human services; International relief; Christian agencies & churches.
Type of support: General/operating support; Continuing support; Annual campaigns; Capital campaigns; Endowments; Emergency funds; Research.
Limitations: Applications not accepted. Giving primarily in Boston, MA and the metropolitan New York, NY, area, including Long Island and Westchester. No grants to individuals, or for scholarships; no loans.
Application information: Contributes only to pre-selected organizations.
Trustees: J. Christopher Flowers; Mary H. White.
EIN: 133532030

1733
Malcolm Hewitt Wiener Foundation, Inc.
c/o The Millburn Corporation
1270 Ave. of the Americas
New York, NY 10020-1700
Contact: Christina Padgett

Incorporated in 1984 in NY.

Donor: Malcolm H. Wiener.
Grantmaker type: Independent foundation.
Financial data (yr. ended 12/31/10): Assets, $50,777,134 (M); expenditures, $4,314,543; qualifying distributions, $3,866,113; giving activities include $3,532,829 for 119 grants (high: $540,000; low: $4).
Purpose and activities: Giving primarily for international affairs, arts and cultural programs, and higher education. Support also for public affairs.
Fields of interest: Museums (art); Humanities; Higher education; International affairs, goodwill promotion; International peace/security; International affairs, foreign policy.
Limitations: Applications not accepted. Giving primarily in CT, NJ, NY and PA. No grants to individuals.
Application information: Contributes only to pre-selected organizations.
Officers and Directors: Malcolm H. Wiener,* Pres. and Treas.; Harvey Beker,* V.P.; George E. Crapple,* V.P.; Martin J. Whitman; Carolyn S. Wiener.
EIN: 133250321

1734
The Elie Wiesel Foundation for Humanity
555 Madison Ave., 20th Fl.
New York, NY 10022-3301 (212) 490-7788
Contact: Alex Heit, Exec. Asst.
FAX: (212) 490-6006; *URL:* http://www.eliewieselfoundation.org
Facebook: http://www.facebook.com/EWFDN
Twitter: http://twitter.com/#!/eliewieselfdn

Established in 1986 in NY.
Grantmaker type: Public charity.
Financial data (yr. ended 12/31/10): Revenue, $1,328,105; assets, $5,429,771 (M); gifts received, $1,252,743; expenditures, $1,152,008; giving activities include $484,338 for 1 grant to an organization outside the U.S., and $10,333 for grants to individuals.
Purpose and activities: The foundation advances the causes of human rights throughout the world by creating forums for the discussion of urgent ethical and moral issues confronting humankind; it also awards prizes to winners of a college essay contest.
Fields of interest: Humanities; International affairs; Young adults; Minorities; Children/youth; Children.
Type of support: Program development; Conferences/seminars; Scholarship funds; Grants to individuals; Scholarships—to individuals.
Limitations: Applications accepted. Giving primarily in the U.S. and Israel.
Publications: Application guidelines; Annual report; Informational brochure; Newsletter.
Application information: Applications must be mailed. Application form required.
  Initial approach: Download application
  Copies of proposal: 3
  Deadline(s): Dec. 19
Officers and Directors: Elie Wiesel,* Pres.; Marion Wiesel,* V.P.; Mark Winkelman,* Secy.-Treas.; Roger Barnett; Joseph Ciechanover; David Pincus; Mark Podwal; Sheila Robbins; William H. Webb; Elisha Wiesel; Stephen I. Willis.
Number of staff: 3 full-time professional; 1 part-time support.
EIN: 133398151

1735
Barrie A. & Dee Dee Wigmore Foundation
c/o BCRS Assocs., LLC
77 Water St., 9th Fl.
New York, NY   10005-4414

Established in 1978 in NY.
Donor: Barrie A. Wigmore.
Grantmaker type: Independent foundation.
Financial data (yr. ended 03/31/11): Assets, $10,451,252 (M); expenditures, $803,849; qualifying distributions, $706,958; giving activities include $704,273 for 47 grants (high: $99,518; low: $665).
Purpose and activities: Giving primarily for arts and culture, particularly art museums; support also for human services and education.
Fields of interest: Museums (art); Performing arts; Higher education; Human services; United Ways and Federated Giving Programs.
International interests: Canada; England.
Limitations: Applications not accepted. Giving primarily in the U.S., with emphasis on New York and Saranac Lake, NY; some funding also in Saskatchewan Province, Canada, and Oxford, England. No grants to individuals; no loans.
Application information: Contributes only to pre-selected organizations.
Trustees: Donald Lenz; Barrie A. Wigmore; DeeDee Wigmore.
EIN: 132967487

1736
Raybin Q. Wong Foundation
5 Roland Dr.
White Plains, NY   10605-5406

Established in 2000 in NY.
Donors: Raybin Q. Wong†; Raybin Q. Wong Trust.
Grantmaker type: Independent foundation.
Financial data (yr. ended 12/31/10): Assets, $5,390,037 (M); gifts received, $1,200; expenditures, $236,229; qualifying distributions, $153,823; giving activities include $153,823 for grants.
Purpose and activities: Giving primarily to benefit educational programs in China.
Fields of interest: Libraries (school); Education.
International interests: China.
Type of support: Scholarship funds.
Limitations: Applications not accepted. Giving primarily in VA. No grants to individuals.
Application information: Unsolicited requests for funds not accepted.
Officers: Martin Young, Pres.; Peizhen Shao, V.P.
Trustees: Abraham Chen; Yaupui Wong; Yanan Xia.
Number of staff: 2 full-time professional.
EIN: 113472626

1737
The Woods Foundation
(formerly The Ward W. Woods Foundation)
c/o Bessemer Trust Co., N.A.
630 5th Ave., 34th Fl.
New York, NY   10111-0001

Established in 1985 in NY.
Donors: Ward W. Woods, Jr.; Priscilla B. Woods; Katherine Weld Bacon; Nebris Corporation; North Hailey Corporation.
Grantmaker type: Independent foundation.

Financial data (yr. ended 09/30/10): Assets, $942 (M); gifts received, $2,679,758; expenditures, $2,708,298; qualifying distributions, $2,708,280; giving activities include $2,704,000 for 40 grants (high: $1,500,000; low: $100).
Purpose and activities: Giving primarily for wildlife conservation and the environment; funding also for the arts, education, recreation, and international affairs.
Fields of interest: Higher education; Animals/wildlife, preservation/protection; Arts; Athletics/sports, amateur leagues; Environment, natural resources; International affairs, U.N..
Limitations: Applications accepted. Giving primarily in CA, New York, NY and Washington, DC. No grants to individuals.
Application information:
  Initial approach: Letter
  Deadline(s): None
Officers and Directors:* Ward W. Woods, Jr.,* Pres.; Priscilla B. Woods,* V.P.; Robert Roriston, Secy.-Treas.; Katherine Woods Emerick; Alexandra Woods.
EIN: 133314966

1738
World Federation of Hemophilia - USA
(formerly World Hemophilia Alliance)
911 Central Ave.
PMB 142
Albany, NY   12206-1350
E-mail: wfh@wfh.org; URL: http://www.wfh.org

Grantmaker type: Public charity.
Financial data (yr. ended 12/31/09): Revenue, $15,650,953; assets, $230,101 (M); gifts received, $15,650,647; expenditures, $15,637,261; giving activities include $15,566,847 for grants to organizations outside the U.S., and $1,500 for grants to individuals.
Purpose and activities: The federation distributes hemophilia treatment products to developing countries for treatment of persons with hemophilia and related bleeding disorders.
Fields of interest: Hemophilia.
International interests: Developing countries.
Type of support: In-kind gifts.
Limitations: Applications not accepted. Giving primarily in developing countries.
Application information: Unsolicited requests for funds not accepted.
Officers: Mark W. Skinner, Pres.; Craig M. Kessler, M.D., V.P.; Miklos Fulop, Treas.
Board Members: Trish Dominic; Sally Owen, M.D.
EIN: 161513923

1739
World Hunger Year, Inc.
(also known as WHY)
505 8th Ave., Ste. 2100
New York, NY   10018-6582   (212) 629-8850
Contact: William Ayres, Exec. Dir.
FAX: (212) 465-9274;
E-mail: why@worldhungeryear.org; Toll-free tel: (800) 548-6479; URL: http://www.worldhungeryear.org
Facebook: http://www.facebook.com/WHYhunger
Twitter: http://twitter.com/hungerthon

Established in 1975.
Grantmaker type: Public charity.

Financial data (yr. ended 03/31/11): Revenue, $3,049,058; assets, $1,656,334 (M); gifts received, $2,228,912; expenditures, $2,665,922; giving activities include $97,848 for grants, $230,000 for 6 grants to organizations outside the U.S., and $12,999 for grants to individuals.
Purpose and activities: The organization attacks the root causes of hunger and poverty by promoting effective and innovative community based solutions that create self-reliance, economic justice, and food security.
Fields of interest: Agriculture; Food services; Human services; International agricultural development; Community/economic development.
Type of support: General/operating support; Program development; Conferences/seminars; Program evaluation.
Limitations: Applications accepted. Giving on a national basis.
Publications: Application guidelines; Annual report; Financial statement; Grants list; Informational brochure (including application guidelines); Newsletter.
Application information: Application form required.
  Initial approach: Download application form
  Copies of proposal: 2
  Deadline(s): Feb. 2 for Media Awards; June 16 for Self-Reliance Awards
  Board meeting date(s): Quarterly
  Final notification: June for Media Awards
Officers and Directors:* Charles Sanders,* Pres.; Brian McMorrow, V.P.; Jennifer Chapin,* Secy.; Stephen Beninati,* Treas.; William Ayres, Exec. Dir.; Stephen Apkon; Edward Barron; Tom Chapin; Cliff Chenfeld; Betsy Friedlander; Alan C. Handell; Michael Keats; Paul C. Kurland; Carl Austin Lukens; David Miller; Anne Johns Ruckert; and 7 additional directors.
Number of staff: 12 full-time professional; 1 part-time professional; 1 full-time support; 1 part-time support.
EIN: 132805575

1740
Yele Haiti Foundation
(formerly Wyclef Jean Foundation, Inc.)
P.O. Box 5057
New York, NY   10185-5057
Contact: Suzie Sylvain
E-mail: info@yele.org; URL: http://www.yele.org

Grantmaker type: Public charity.
Financial data (yr. ended 12/31/10): Revenue, $15,941,122; assets, $6,888,870 (M); gifts received, $15,941,122; expenditures, $9,157,065; giving activities include $4,189,874 for grants to organizations outside the U.S.
Purpose and activities: The foundation's mission is to use the potent combination of music and development to create small-scale, manageable, and replicable projects to contribute to Haiti's long-term progress.
Fields of interest: Performing arts, music; International development.
International interests: Haiti.
Type of support: Scholarship funds.
Limitations: Giving primarily in Haiti.
Officer: Hugh Locke, Exec. Dir.
Directors: Jerry Duplessis; Wyclef Jean; Seth Kanegis.
Advisory Board Members: Tyra Banks; Vikram Chatwal; Jonathan Demme; Angelina Jolie; Norah

Jones; Maryse Kedar; Gepsie Metellus; Susan Sarandon; Mona Scott; Russell Simmons.
EIN: 650823881

1741
The Yoreinu Foundation
443 N. Franklin St., Ste. 210
Syracuse, NY   13204-5426
Contact: David Roth, Exec. Dir.
E-mail: dtroth@gmail.com; Mailing and application address: c/o David Roth, Exec. Dir., 24 Derech Beit Lechem, Apt. 25, Jerusalem, 93109 Israel, tel.: 011-972-50-538-2353, fax: 011-972-2-671-3830

Established in 1991 in NY.
Donors: Laurence Roth†; Marsha Roth.
Grantmaker type: Independent foundation.
Financial data (yr. ended 12/31/10): Assets, $3,938,534 (M); gifts received, $40,000; expenditures, $273,309; qualifying distributions, $212,000; giving activities include $212,000 for 21 grants (high: $15,000; low: $5,000).
Purpose and activities: The Yoreinu Foundation is an American private philanthropic foundation that seeks to strengthen Israel's development as a Jewish, democratic, and just society by funding programs in Israel that strengthen religious Zionist periphery populations; promote a modern Orthodox worldview among Israel's religious Zionist sector; and engage and empower secular Israelis' Jewish and Zionist identity. Priority will be given to organizations that have a Modern Orthodox and Zionist outlook; that have a social justice component; and that work to bridge rifts between religious and secular communities in Israel.
Fields of interest: Jewish agencies & synagogues; Youth; Young adults.
International interests: Israel.
Type of support: General/operating support; Program development; Seed money; Technical assistance.
Limitations: Applications accepted. Giving limited to Israel. No grants to individuals or for capital projects; no loans.
Application Information: The foundation is not accepting new inquiries for funding at the present time. Application form required.
 Initial approach: Letter of inquiry via e-mail
 Board meeting date(s): Twice a year, or when necessary
Officer: David Roth, Exec. Dir.
Trustees: Alexander S. Pasquale; Marsha Roth.
EIN: 161404154

1742
Youth Renewal Fund
250 W. 57th St., Ste. 632
New York, NY   10107-0609   (212) 207-3195
Contact: Karen Berman, Exec. Dir.
FAX: (212) 207-8379;
E-mail: karen@youthrenewalfund.org; URL: http://www.youthrenewalfund.org
Facebook: http://www.facebook.com/YouthRenewalFund
Twitter: http://twitter.com/#!/youthrenewalfnd
YouTube: http://www.youtube.com/user/YouthRenewalFund

Established in 1989.
Grantmaker type: Public charity.

Financial data (yr. ended 06/30/10): Revenue, $2,163,365; assets, $3,771,634 (M); gifts received, $898,961; expenditures, $2,505,910; giving activities include $1,995,000 for grants to organizations outside the U.S.
Purpose and activities: The fund provides supplemental education to underprivileged Israeli youth.
Fields of interest: Education.
International interests: Israel.
Limitations: Applications not accepted. Giving primarily in Israel.
Publications: Annual report; Newsletter.
Application information: Contributes only to pre-selected organizations.
Officer: Karen Berman, Exec. Dir.
Directors: Stuart Angowitz; Harlan Cherniak; David Feldman; Susan Zelnick Flaxman; David Fox; Jeffrey Freed; Michael Gross; Karen Herron; Sam Katz; Doug Korn; and 11 additional directors.
EIN: 133641489

1743
Zenkel Foundation
15 W. 53rd St.
New York, NY   10019-5410

Established in 1987 in NY.
Donor: Lois Zenkel.
Grantmaker type: Independent foundation.
Financial data (yr. ended 12/31/10): Assets, $1,743,891 (M); expenditures, $246,294; qualifying distributions, $222,501; giving activities include $216,025 for 21 grants (high: $90,000; low: $350).
Purpose and activities: Giving primarily for Jewish welfare, the arts, higher education, the environment, and human rights.
Fields of interest: Visual arts, photography; Museums (art); Arts; Higher education; Environment; Hospitals (general); Health organizations, association; Medical research, institute; Human services; International human rights; Civil rights, race/intergroup relations; Community/economic development; Jewish federated giving programs; Jewish agencies & synagogues.
Type of support: General/operating support; Annual campaigns; Capital campaigns; Building/renovation; Professorships; Scholarship funds.
Limitations: Applications not accepted. No grants to individuals.
Application information: Unsolicited requests for funds not accepted.
 Board meeting date(s): Apr.
Officers and Directors:* Lois S. Zenkel,* Pres.; Daniel R. Zenkel,* Secy.-Treas.; Bruce Zenkel; Gary B. Zenkel; Lisa Z. Zenkel.
EIN: 133380631

1744
The Zilkha Foundation, Inc.
450 Park Ave., Ste. 2102
New York, NY   10022-2675
Contact: Ezra K. Zilkha, Pres. and Treas.

Incorporated in 1948 in NY.
Donors: Zilkha & Sons, Inc.; Ezra K. Zilkha; Cecile E. Zilkha.
Grantmaker type: Company-sponsored foundation.

Financial data (yr. ended 08/31/11): Assets, $1,938,992 (M); expenditures, $825,515; qualifying distributions, $818,140; giving activities include $818,140 for grants.
Purpose and activities: The foundation supports hospitals and organizations involved with opera, K-12 and higher education, human services, international affairs, public policy research, and Judaism.
Fields of interest: Performing arts, opera; Elementary/secondary education; Higher education; Hospitals (general); Human services; International affairs, foreign policy; Jewish federated giving programs; Public policy, research; Jewish agencies & synagogues.
Type of support: General/operating support.
Limitations: Applications not accepted. Giving primarily in Washington, DC and New York, NY. No grants to individuals.
Application information: Contributions only to pre-selected organizations.
 Board meeting date(s): Dec.
Officers: Ezra K. Zilkha, Pres. and Treas.; Cecile E. Zilkha, V.P. and Secy.
EIN: 136090739

1745
Ziv Israel Association
c/o Kamerman
708 Third Ave, No. 1610
New York, NY   10017

Established in 1989 in NY.
Donors: Emanuel Toporowitz; Sport/Ellie Inc.; Marc L. Geraldine Schottenstein; Mark Blisko; Imra Reich Foundation; Suzan Z. Glenn Prisc; Louis Altman; David Altman; Olga Kuchevsky; Vaad Mishmeres ML; Steven Weiss; Naomi Weiss.
Grantmaker type: Independent foundation.
Financial data (yr. ended 12/31/09): Assets, $173,542 (M); gifts received, $263,741; expenditures, $244,913; qualifying distributions, $243,981; giving activities include $243,981 for 3 grants (high: $179,175; low: $13,806).
Purpose and activities: Giving for rabbinical education.
Fields of interest: Theological school/education; Jewish agencies & synagogues.
International interests: Israel.
Limitations: Applications not accepted. Giving limited to Haifa, Israel. No grants to individuals.
Application information: Unsolicited requests for funds not accepted.
Trustees: Aric Bodenstein; Emanuel Toporowitz.
EIN: 237321981

1746
The Zyman Foundation, Inc.
c/o The Ayco Co., L.P.
321 Broadway
P.O. Box 860
Saratoga Springs, NY   12866-4110

Established in 2005 in FL.
Donors: Sergio Zyman; Sylvia Zyman.
Grantmaker type: Independent foundation.
Financial data (yr. ended 06/30/10): Assets, $2,975,645 (M); expenditures, $181,908; qualifying distributions, $166,774; giving activities include $166,774 for 9 grants (high: $60,000; low: $260).

Fields of interest: International development; Christian agencies & churches.
Limitations: Applications not accepted. No grants to individuals.
Application information: Unsolicited requests for funds not accepted.
Officers and Director:* Sergio Zyman,* Chair.; Sylvia Zyman, Pres. and Secy.; Jennifer Zyman, V.P.; Jessica Zyman, V.P.
EIN: 203624795

NORTH CAROLINA

1747
African Medical Mission of WNC, Inc.
P.O. Box 2756
Hendersonville, NC 28793-2756
(828) 696-9930
Contact: Carla Schell, Pres.
FAX: (828) 696-8799; E-mail: info@ammsa.org; URL: http://ammsa.org/?page_id=350&id=11

Grantmaker type: Public charity.
Financial data (yr. ended 12/31/10): Revenue, $186,072; assets, $45,781 (M); gifts received, $146,876; expenditures, $177,536; giving activities include $137,294 for grants.
Purpose and activities: The organization supports medical care and educational training in the rural area of Transkei, South Africa.
Fields of interest: Health care, support services; Health care.
International interests: South Africa.
Type of support: Annual campaigns; In-kind gifts.
Limitations: Applications not accepted. Giving limited to Transkei, South Africa.
Application information: Unsolicited requests for funds not accepted.
Board meeting date(s): 2nd Wed. of each month
Officers: Carla Schell, Pres.; Joe Poole, V.P.; Siobhan Gore, Secy.; Alex Kealy, Treas.
Directors: Susan Bullard; Lee Burdett; Frank Byrd; Demme Foresman; Andy Gilboy; Randy Hunter; Maureen Linneman.
Number of staff: 1 part-time professional.
EIN: 561308802

1748
AlphaMed Cancer Foundation
3920 Dover Rd.
Durham, NC 27707-5157

Established in 2002 in NC.
Donors: AlphaMed Press, Inc.; Martin J. Murphy; Ann A. Murphy.
Grantmaker type: Independent foundation.
Financial data (yr. ended 12/31/10): Assets, $1,201,308 (M); gifts received, $400,000; expenditures, $198,254; qualifying distributions, $190,000; giving activities include $190,000 for grants (high: $75,000; low: $500).
Fields of interest: Health organizations, formal/general education; International affairs, formal/general education; Cancer.
Limitations: Applications not accepted. No grants to individuals.

Application information: Unsolicited requests for funds not accepted.
Officers: Martin J. Murphy, Jr., Pres.; Ann A. Murphy, V.P.; Sean P. Murphy, Secy.; Brendan A. Murphy, Treas.
EIN: 421564194

1749
American Kennel Club Canine Health Foundation, Inc.
c/o The American Kennel Club
8051 Arco Corporate Dr., Ste. 300
Raleigh, NC 27617-3901
E-mail: info@akcchf.org; Toll-free tel.: (888) 682-9696; application address: P.O. Box 900061, Raleigh, NC 27690-3526; URL: http://www.akcchf.org
Facebook: http://www.facebook.com/pages/American-Kennel-Club-Canine-Health-Foundation/75007816144
Twitter: http://twitter.com/CanineHealthFnd

Founded in 1995 in NC.
Grantmaker type: Public charity.
Financial data (yr. ended 12/31/10): Revenue, $3,640,223; assets, $10,605,119 (M); gifts received, $3,543,390; expenditures, $2,575,084; giving activities include $1,415,949 for grants, and $111,400 for grants to organizations outside the U.S.
Purpose and activities: The foundation raises funds to support non-invasive canine health research worldwide.
Fields of interest: Spine disorders research; Science, research; Pathology research; Pathology; Parasitic diseases research; Parasitic diseases; Orthopedics research; Organ research; Organ diseases; Neuroscience; Medical specialties research; Adult/continuing education; Allergies; Allergies research; Anatomy (animal); Anesthesiology; Anesthesiology research; Animal welfare; Animals/wildlife; Animals/wildlife, formal/general education; Animals/wildlife, public education; Animals/wildlife, research; Animals/wildlife, special services; Arthritis; Arthritis research; Biology/life sciences; Biomedicine; Biomedicine research; Brain disorders; Brain research; Cancer; Cancer research; Diabetes; Diabetes research; Digestive diseases; Digestive disorders research; Disasters, search/rescue; Ear, nose & throat diseases; Ear, nose & throat research; Epilepsy; Epilepsy research; Eye diseases; Eye research; Genetic diseases and disorders research; Heart & circulatory diseases; Heart & circulatory research; Hemophilia; Hemophilia research; Internal medicine; Internal medicine research; Kidney diseases; Kidney research; Lung diseases; Lung research; Medical care, bioethics; Medical research; Neuroscience research; Orthopedics; Skin disorders; Spine disorders; Veterinary medicine; Veterinary medicine, hospital.
International interests: Canada; Europe; France; United Kingdom.
Type of support: Conferences/seminars; Research; Seed money.
Limitations: Applications accepted. Giving on a national basis. No support for the purchase of animals for research purposes, support of animal research colonies, disease induction or injury models, or euthanasia of healthy animals. No grants to non-disposable equipment or repair, software development, salaries of tenure-track or

professional, salaried investigators, tuition or registration fees, travel expenses, or transportation of animals.
Publications: Application guidelines; Annual report; Grants list; Informational brochure (including application guidelines); Newsletter.
Application information: Application form not required.
Initial approach: Telephone or e-mail
Copies of proposal: 1
Deadline(s): Mar. 1 for Research Grants; at least six months in advance for Education Grants; none for ACORN Research Grants: Small Grants for Quick Results
Board meeting date(s): Sept.
Final notification: Sept. for Research Grants
Officers and Trustees:* Cindy Vogels,* Chair.; Lee Arnold,* Vice-Chair.; Connie Field,* Secy.; Dr. J. Charles Gravin,* Treas.; Deborah A. DiLalla, M.B.A., Exec. Dir.; A. Duane Butherus, Ph.D.; Howard Falberg; Susan LaCroix Hamil; J. David Haworth; D.V.M., Ph.D.; Mary Edwards Hayes; Hon. Iris Cornelia Love; Andrew Mills; Steve T. Rernspecher; Dr. Howard Spey; James Stevens; William C. Truesdale.
Number of staff: 5 full-time professional; 2 full-time support; 1 part-time support.
EIN: 133813813

1750
ANAI, Inc.
1120 Meadows Rd.
Franklin, NC 28734-4369 (828) 524-8369

Established in 1980.
Grantmaker type: Public charity.
Financial data (yr. ended 04/30/10): Revenue, $219,155; assets, $67,011 (M); gifts received, $219,127; expenditures, $187,384; program services expenses, $156,710; giving activities include $123,353 for grants to organizations outside the U.S.
Purpose and activities: The organization is dedicated to advancing the work of Asociacion ANAI, and its mission of supporting the indigenous population of Talamanca region, Costa Rica, through promoting self-sufficiency and locally-based production.
Fields of interest: International development; International affairs; Agriculture; Indigenous peoples.
International interests: Costa Rica.
Limitations: Giving limited to the Talamanca region, Costa Rica.
Officers and Directors:* Billy Campbell,* M.D., Pres.; Stanley Polanski,* V.P.; Susan Ervin, Secy.; Dr. William O. McLarney,* Treas.; James J. Kennedy; Paul Carlson.
EIN: 581618989

1751
Burroughs Wellcome Fund
21 T. W. Alexander Dr.
P.O. Box 13901
Research Triangle Park, NC 27709-3901
(919) 991-5100
Contact: Russell Campbell III, Comms. Off.
FAX: (919) 991-5160; E-mail: info@bwfund.org; Contact info. for Russ Campbell III tel.: (919) 991-5119; fax: (919) 991-5179, e-mail:

rcampbell@bwfund.org; URL: http://www.bwfund.org

Incorporated in 1955 in NY.

Donors: Burroughs Wellcome Co.; The Wellcome Trust.

Grantmaker type: Independent foundation.

Financial data (yr. ended 08/31/10): Assets, $633,871,299 (M); expenditures, $28,143,014; qualifying distributions, $23,777,011; giving activities include $19,946,661 for 717 grants (high: $275,087; low: $400).

Purpose and activities: The fund is an independent private foundation dedicated to advancing the medical sciences by supporting research and other scientific and educational activities. Major program areas include: basic biomedical sciences, infectious diseases, interfaces between physical and biological sciences, translational research, and science education.

Fields of interest: Medical research, institute; Biology/life sciences.

International interests: Canada.

Type of support: Program development; Research.

Limitations: Applications accepted. Giving limited to the U.S. and Canada. No grants to individuals, or for building or endowment funds, equipment, operating budgets, continuing support, annual campaigns, deficit financing, publications, conferences, or matching gifts; no loans.

Publications: Annual report (including application guidelines); Informational brochure (including application guidelines); Newsletter; Occasional report.

Application information: See fund web site for application information. Application form required.

  Initial approach: All applications for Career Awards must be submitted electronically or they will not be reviewed

  Deadline(s): Varies depending on the program. See fund web site for information

  Board meeting date(s): Feb., May, July, and Oct.

  Final notification: Varies

Officers and Directors:* Carlos J. Bustamante, Ph.D., Chair.; Jerome F. Strauss III, M.D., Ph.D., Vice-Chair.; John E. Burris,* Pres.; Steven D. Corman, Hon. Dir.; Philip R. Tracy, J.D., Hon. Dir.; Bruce Alberts; Nancy Andrews; J. Michael Bishop, M.D.; Geoff Gerber, Ph.D.; Phil Gold; George Langford, Ph.D.; Carla Shatz; Judith L. Swain, M.D.; Chris Viehbacher; Dyann Wirth, Ph.D.

Number of staff: 17 full-time professional; 4 full-time support; 2 part-time support.

EIN: 237225395

Recent grants for international programs:

1751-1 Fundacio Clinic per a la Recerca Biomedica, Barcelona, Spain, $15,000. For Malaria Eradication Research Agenda (malERA) initiative. 2010.

1751-2 Gordon Research Conferences, West Kingston, RI, $20,000. For Gordon Research Conference titled Sensory Coding in the Natural Environment held at Bates College, Maine. 2010.

1751-3 Gordon Research Conferences, West Kingston, RI, $10,000. For new Gordon Research Conference titled Immunology of fungal infections, in Galveston, Texas. 2010.

1751-4 Gordon Research Conferences, West Kingston, RI, $10,000. For 2010 Host-Parasite Interactions Gordon Research Conference, Salve Regina University, Newport, Rhode Island. 2010.

1751-5 Hospital for Sick Children, Toronto, Canada, $10,000. For Third Annual Canadian Human Genetics Conference, Saint Sauveur, Quebec. 2010.

1751-6 North Carolina Museum of Natural Sciences, Raleigh, NC, $20,000. For general support of 2010 North Carolina International Science Challenge. 2010.

1751-7 North Carolina School of Science and Mathematics Foundation, Durham, NC, $16,000. For participation in Singapore International Mathematics Challenge. 2010.

1751-8 University of California, San Francisco, CA, $30,000. For collaboration over next two years by funding travel and living expenses for students or postdocs who will serve as bridges between laboratories worldwide. 2010.

1751-9 University of Edinburgh, Edinburgh, Scotland, $25,000. For Helminth Parasite meeting in Hydra, Greece. 2010.

1751-10 University of Western Ontario, London, Canada, $10,000. For 2010 Clinician Investigator Trainee Association of Canada's general meeting and international workshop held in Ottawa, Canada. 2010.

1751-11 Walter and Eliza Hall Institute of Medical Research, Parkville, Australia, $10,000. For protozoan databases workshop at International Congress on Parasitology (ICOPA XII), Melbourne, Australia. 2010.

1751-12 Wellcome Trust, London, England, $15,000. For Genomic Epidemiology of Malaria Conference held in Hinxton, Cambridge, United Kingdom. 2010.

1752
Carlson Family Foundation, Inc.

206 Brookgreen Dr.
Chapel Hill, NC 27516-4462 (201) 760-2170
Contact: Mary N. Owen, Dir.

Established in 2000 in NJ.

Grantmaker type: Independent foundation.

Financial data (yr. ended 12/31/10): Assets, $18,987,491 (M); expenditures, $1,006,135; qualifying distributions, $888,063; giving activities include $736,109 for 122 grants (high: $26,000; low: $50).

Fields of interest: Health organizations; Education; Environment, natural resources; Cancer research; Human services; Children/youth, services; Foundations (private grantmaking); Foundations (community).

International interests: Spain.

Type of support: General/operating support; Capital campaigns; Matching/challenge support.

Limitations: Giving primarily in the U.S., with emphasis on KY and NC; some funding also in CT, MD, NY, and Spain.

Application information:

  Initial approach: Letter

  Deadline(s): None

Officers: Paul S. Norton, Pres.; Lenore "Trilby" Norton, V.P.; Michael A. Norton, Secy.; John A. Norton, Treas.

Directors: Elaine Boylen; James M. Norton; Mary N. Owen.

EIN: 311678303

1753
Evrytanian Association Velouchi, Inc.

(formerly Evrytanian Association of America)
121 Greenwich Rd.
Charlotte, NC 28211-2313 (704) 366-6571
FAX: (704) 366-6571;
E-mail: velouchi@bellsouth.net; Toll-free tel.: (800) 307-4795; URL: http://www.velouchiusa.org

Established in 1947.

Grantmaker type: Public charity.

Financial data (yr. ended 05/31/11): Revenue, $119,291; assets, $743,090 (M); gifts received, $39,367; expenditures, $118,764; giving activities include $36,959 for grants to organizations outside the U.S., and $28,750 for grants to individuals.

Purpose and activities: The association awards scholarships and provides aid to people of Evrytanian origin.

Fields of interest: Secondary school/education; Higher education, college.

International interests: Greece.

Type of support: Grants to individuals; Scholarships—to individuals.

Application information:

  Initial approach: Download application

  Deadline(s): Mar. 1

Officers: Sam Nikopoulos, Pres.; Tom Skenteris, 1st V.P.; Dr. Steve Hodges, 2nd V.P.; Spiro Pappas, 1st Secy.; John Pappas, 2nd Secy.; James Kastriches,* 1st Treas.; Jim N. Kontos, 2nd Treas.

EIN: 566061036

1754
Harry Kramer Memorial Fund

c/o Wachovia Bank, N.A.
1525 W. WT Harris Blvd.
Charlotte, NC 28262-8522

Established in 1982 in FL.

Grantmaker type: Independent foundation.

Financial data (yr. ended 12/31/09): Assets, $5,510,470 (M); gifts received, $1,198; expenditures, $376,377; qualifying distributions, $259,800; giving activities include $256,600 for grants.

Fields of interest: Arts; Higher education; Disasters, 9/11/01; Human services; Aging, centers/services; International terrorism; Jewish federated giving programs; Disabilities, people with.

International interests: Israel.

Type of support: Capital campaigns; Building/renovation; Program development; Seed money; Scholarship funds.

Limitations: Applications not accepted. Giving primarily in FL. No grants to individuals or for operating budgets or continuing support.

Application information: Contributes only to pre-selected organizations.

Trustees: Leslie J. August; Wachovia Bank, N.A.

EIN: 596644290

1755
The Lookout Foundation

300 N. Greene St., Ste. 1750
Greensboro, NC 27401-2270

Established in 1999 in NC.

Donors: Stephen C. Hassenfelt; Pamela H. Hassenfelt.

Grantmaker type: Independent foundation.

Financial data (yr. ended 06/30/10): Assets, $93,762 (M); expenditures, $142,455; qualifying distributions, $142,455; giving activities include $142,455 for 65 grants (high: $40,000; low: $100).
Fields of interest: International conflict resolution; Medical school/education; Human services; Protestant agencies & churches.
Limitations: Applications not accepted. No grants to individuals.
Application information: Unsolicited requests for funds not accepted.
Officers: Stephen C. Hassenfelt, Pres. and Treas.; Pamela H. Hassenfelt, V.P. and Secy.
EIN: 562173641

1756
Mafraq Sanatorium Association
P.O. Box 2001
Boone, NC 28607-2001
Contact: Aileen Coleman, Pres.

Established in 1977.
Grantmaker type: Public charity.
Financial data (yr. ended 12/31/10): Revenue, $662,486; assets, $203,410 (M); gifts received, $662,150; expenditures, $787,963; giving activities include $340,112 for grants to organizations outside the U.S.
Purpose and activities: The association provides services to Annoor Sanatorium for treatment of chest diseases in Mafraq, Jordan.
Fields of interest: Health care.
International interests: Jordan.
Limitations: Giving primarily in Mafraq, Jordan.
Officers and Directors:* Sean P. Campbell,* Chair.; Aileen Coleman,* Pres.; Dr. Wesley Ulrich, V.P.; Dr. Richard Furman, Secy.; Phyllis T. Payne,* Treas.; David Allen; David C. Shultz; and 5 additional directors.
EIN: 591761378

1757
Microelectronics Advanced Research Corporation
P.O. Box 12053
Research Triangle Park, NC 27709-2053
(919) 941-9400

Grantmaker type: Public charity.
Financial data (yr. ended 12/31/10): Revenue, $39,989,421; assets, $25,273,677 (M); gifts received, $39,870,627; expenditures, $39,367,660; giving activities include $36,813,817 for grants.
Purpose and activities: The corporation acts as subsidiary of the Semiconductor Research Corporation, and works to maintain a program of university-based research centers focused on long-range research that would benefit both private industry and U.S. defense capabilities.
Fields of interest: International peace/security; Public affairs; Higher education, university.
Type of support: Research.
Limitations: Applications accepted. Giving on a national basis.
Publications: Application guidelines.
Application information: Application form required.
Initial approach: Download proposal guide
Deadline(s): May 29

Officers and Directors:* Larry W. Sumney,* Pres. and C.E.O.; Dr. Elizabeth Weitzman,* Exec. Dir.; Dr. Steven Hillenius; Dr. Dinesh Mehta.
EIN: 562038762

1758
New Directions International, Inc.
2806 Eric Ln.
Burlington, NC 27215-5491 (326) 227-1273
Mailing address: P.O. Box 2347, Burlington NC 27216-2347; URL: http://www.newdirections.org

Established in 1971 in NC.
Grantmaker type: Public charity.
Financial data (yr. ended 12/31/10): Revenue, $573,367; assets, $787,203 (M); gifts received, $1,761,322; expenditures, $2,238,276; giving activities include $1,447,553 for 24 grants to organizations outside the U.S.
Purpose and activities: The organization serves missions projects globally, through church planting, agricultural and medical projects, child and pastor sponsorships, training, teaching, and evangelism.
Fields of interest: Health care; International agricultural development; International relief; Religion; Education.
Limitations: Giving on a national and international basis.
Officers and Board Members: Jack Frank,* Chair.; Vee Chandler,* Vice-Chair.; J.L. Williams, C.E.O.; Tony Holt,* Secy.; Ed Wooten,* Treas.; Tom L. Coble; Keith Kiser; Donald Lyons; Mark Thompson.
EIN: 560953324

1759
Nickel Producers Environmental Research Association, Inc.
(also known as NiPERA)
2525 Meridian Pkwy., Ste. 240
Durham, NC 27713-5244 (919) 544-7722
Contact: Hudson K. Bates, Exec. Dir.
FAX: (919) 544-7724; E-mail: nipera@nipera.org

Established in 1980 in NY.
Donors: Anglo Platinum; Billiton; Empress Nickel Refinery, Ltd.; Eramet; Inco, Ltd.; International Cobalt; Nippon Yakin; Noranda; Sumitomo; Pharma; Unicore; Nickel Institute.
Grantmaker type: Independent foundation.
Financial data (yr. ended 12/31/10): Assets, $617,483 (M); gifts received, $2,860,822; expenditures, $1,828,825; qualifying distributions, $1,828,825; giving activities include $1,093,018 for grants.
Purpose and activities: Giving primarily for research investigations, studies, and surveys relating to occupational health and safety aspects of the nickel producing industries and related environmental matters.
Fields of interest: Higher education; Environment; Health care; Health organizations, association; Safety/disasters; Engineering/technology; Science.
International interests: Canada; Europe; Japan.
Type of support: Fellowships; Research.
Limitations: Giving primarily in the U.S., Europe, Canada, and Japan.
Application information:
Initial approach: Proposal
Deadline(s): Varies
Board meeting date(s): Sept.

Officers: Steve Barnett, Co-Chair.; Kevin Bradley, Co-Chair.; David Butler, Secy.; Victor Kerchenko, Treas.; Hudson K. Bates, Exec. Dir.
Board Members: Michael Chalkley; Gordon Hall; Tetsuya Kubota; L.J.G. Nacken; Jacques-Antoine Rondeau; Catherine Tissot-Colle.
EIN: 133070077

1760
North Carolina Center for International Understanding Council, Inc.
100 E. Six Forks Rd., Ste. 300
Raleigh, NC 27609-7752 (919) 420-1360
Contact: Cindy DeFoor, Interim Exec. Dir.
FAX: (919) 420-1371;
E-mail: ciu_info@ciu.northcarolina.edu; Cindy DeFoor Ph. No.:919-420-1360 ext. 203Cindy DeFoor Email: cdefoor@northcarolina.edu;
URL: http://ciu.northcarolina.edu/

Established in 1979 in NC.
Grantmaker type: Public charity.
Financial data (yr. ended 06/30/11): Revenue, $248,136; assets, $338,813 (M); gifts received, $142,445; expenditures, $201,792; giving activities include $43,100 for grants.
Purpose and activities: The center is committed to helping North Carolinians live and work effectively with people of all cultures.
Fields of interest: International exchange; International affairs.
Type of support: Grants to individuals.
Publications: Annual report; Informational brochure; Newsletter.
Officers and Directors:* Tom McGuire,* Chair.; Pell Tanner,* Vice-Chair.; Leslie Boney; Anita Brown Graham; Tony Caravano; Swadesh Chatterjee; Phillip R. Dixon; Dianne English; Ann B. Goodnight; and 13 additional directors.
EIN: 561751280

1761
Project Health for Leon
P.O. Box 30953
Raleigh, NC 27622-0953 (919) 787-7292
Contact: John A. Paar M.D., Pres.
E-mail: jpaar@bellsouth.net; URL: http://projecthealthforleon.org

Established in 1995 in NC.
Grantmaker type: Public charity.
Financial data (yr. ended 11/30/10): Revenue, $60,582; assets, $38,527 (M); gifts received, $60,447; expenditures, $58,858; program services expenses, $46,708; giving activities include $46,707 for grants.
Purpose and activities: The organization provides for the transportation and housing of Nicaraguan health professionals training in the United States.
Fields of interest: Health care, formal/general education.
International interests: Nicaragua.
Type of support: In-kind gifts.
Limitations: Applications not accepted. Giving limited to Leon, Nicaragua. No support for political organizations.
Publications: Annual report; Financial statement; Newsletter.
Application information: Unsolicited requests for funds not accepted.
Board meeting date(s): Biannually

Officers and Directors:* John A. Paar,* M.D., Pres.; Manuel Suarez, Treas.; Harry Adams; Laurence Dahners, M.D.; Charles Helton, M.D.; Luanne Lapio, R.N.; Gregory Murphy, M.D.; John Rose, M.D.; William Sullivan, M.D.; Osi Udekwu; Ross Vaughan, M.D.
EIN: 561917546

1762
The Mary Lynn Richardson Fund
c/o Piedmont Financial Co.
P.O. Box 20124
Greensboro, NC 27420-0124 (336) 274-5471
FAX: (336) 272-8921; E-mail: sgreen@piedfin.com

Trust established in 1940 in NC.
Donor: Mary Lynn Richardson†.
Grantmaker type: Independent foundation.
Financial data (yr. ended 12/31/10): Assets, $6,441,900 (M); expenditures, $303,201; qualifying distributions, $259,770; giving activities include $259,770 for grants.
Purpose and activities: Though the foundation is not a bricks and mortar fund, the foundation does make grants for basic needs funding (health, education and shelter). The foundation also dispenses half its monies to foreign missions.
Fields of interest: Higher education; Health care; volunteer services; Human services; YM/YWCAs & YM/YWHAs; Children/youth, services; Aging, centers/services; International affairs; Christian agencies & churches; Aging; Economically disadvantaged.
Type of support: General/operating support; Seed money; Research.
Limitations: Applications accepted. Giving primarily in NC, with an emphasis on Guilford County; giving internationally also to 501(c)(3) foreign organizations. No grants for building funds.
Publications: Application guidelines.
Application information: Application form required.
  Initial approach: Proposal
  Copies of proposal: 1
  Deadline(s): Aug. 31
  Board meeting date(s): Nov.
  Final notification: Dec. 31
Trustees: Patricia S. Agnew; Eric R. Calhoun; Betsy Boney Mead; Rachel P. Mermey; Britt A. Preyer.
Advisory Committee: Martin M. Boney; Samuel W. Tripp.
EIN: 066025946

1763
Oscar C. Rixson Foundation, Inc.
P.O. Box 19255
Asheville, NC 28815-1255
Contact: Alan L. Mojonnier, Pres.
E-mail: mojo@asheville.com

Incorporated in 1925 in NY.
Donors: Oscar C. Rixson†; Mary Rixson†; Eleanor Rixon Cannon†; Ulrika Rixon Booth†.
Grantmaker type: Independent foundation.
Financial data (yr. ended 12/31/10): Assets, $2,737,191 (M); gifts received, $83,990; expenditures, $265,649; qualifying distributions, $217,600; giving activities include $154,800 for 100 grants (high: $58,500; low: $500), and $62,800 for 113 grants to individuals (high: $2,000; low: $400).

Purpose and activities: Grants only to evangelical churches, missions, and organizations in support of missionaries. Grant requests for non-Protestant, non-evangelical purposes will not be considered. Since grants originate within the Rixson Board, requests for grants are neither solicited nor desired.
Fields of interest: Protestant agencies & churches.
International interests: Canada; Europe; Africa; South America.
Type of support: General/operating support; Continuing support; Grants to individuals.
Limitations: Applications not accepted. Giving throughout the U.S., Canada, Africa, Europe, South America, and the Far East. No support for welfare programs, or for non-Protestant evangelical programs.
Application information: General applications for grants are not solicited.
  Board meeting date(s): Last Sat. of Apr.
Officers and Directors:* Alan L. Mojonnier,* Pres.; James M. Gilbert,* V.P.; Richard Yeskoo,* Secy.; Timothy VanWyck,* Treas.; Donald Dunkerton; Thomas J. Elliott, Sr.; RADM. Thomas J. Elliot, Jr.; William R. Kusche; Sajan Joseph; Raul Sanchez.
Number of staff: 2 part-time support.
EIN: 136129767

1764
The Rolander Family Foundation
203 Cedar Berry Ln.
Chapel Hill, NC 27517-7204
E-mail: RoloSBR@aol.com; Application address: c/o Stephen B. Rolander, 7413 Spyglass Way, Raleigh, NC 27615

Established in 2000 in PA.
Grantmaker type: Independent foundation.
Financial data (yr. ended 12/31/10): Assets, $5,966,735 (M); expenditures, $304,223; qualifying distributions, $303,340; giving activities include $281,300 for 42 grants (high: $35,000; low: $500).
Purpose and activities: Giving primarily for the arts, public broadcasting, medical research, programs and facilities for children with special needs, religion, and housing development.
Fields of interest: Media/communications; Museums; Performing arts, orchestras; Historic preservation/historical societies; Medical research, institute; Housing/shelter, development; Human services; Children, services; Religion.
International interests: South America; Central America; Haiti; Africa.
Type of support: General/operating support; Annual campaigns; Capital campaigns; Building/renovation; Equipment; Program development; Research.
Limitations: Applications accepted. Giving on a national basis, particularly to areas where members of the board or family reside.
Publications: Application guidelines.
Application information: Application form not required.
  Initial approach: Letter
  Copies of proposal: 1
  Deadline(s): None
  Board meeting date(s): Twice yearly
  Final notification: 1 month from receipt
Officers and Directors:* C. Arthur Rolander, Jr.,* Pres.; Stephen B. Rolander,* V.P.; Stephen C. Leroy,* Secy.; Nancy R. Leroy; William B. Leroy; C. Arthur Rolander III; Mildred D. Rolander.

Number of staff: 2 part-time professional.
EIN: 912080946

1765
Samaritan's Purse
P.O. Box 3000
Boone, NC 28607-3000 (828) 262-1980
FAX: (828) 266-1053; E-mail: info@samaritan.org;
URL: http://www.samaritanspurse.org/
Facebook: http://www.facebook.com/
SamaritansPurse
RSS Feed: http://feeds.feedburner.com/
SamaritansPurseNewsFeed
Social Wire: http://www.samaritanspurse.org/
socialwire/
Twitter: http://twitter.com/SamaritansPurse
Vimeo: http://vimeo.com/channels/
samaritanspurse
YouTube: http://www.youtube.com/user/
SamaritansPurseVideo

Established in 1970 in CA.
Grantmaker type: Public charity.
Financial data (yr. ended 12/31/10): Revenue, $373,235,481; assets, $244,100,086 (M); gifts received, $369,514,498; expenditures, $335,882,005; giving activities include $1,712,395 for grants, $155,971,411 for grants to organizations outside the U.S., and $260,283 for grants to individuals.
Purpose and activities: The organization provides spiritual and physical aid to victims of war, poverty, natural disasters, disease, and famine.
Fields of interest: AIDS; Theological school/education; Health care; Disasters, preparedness/services; International relief; Religion; Economically disadvantaged; Children; Immigrants/refugees; Homeless; AIDS, people with.
International interests: Africa; Asia; Central America; Europe; India; South America.
Type of support: General/operating support; Continuing support; Equipment; Emergency funds; Technical assistance.
Limitations: Applications not accepted. Giving on a national and international basis.
Publications: Annual report; Informational brochure; Newsletter.
Application information: Unsolicited requests for funds not accepted.
  Board meeting date(s): 2-3 times yearly
Officers and Board Members:* W. Franklin Graham III,* Chair. and C.E.O.; Phyllis T. Payne,* V.P., Corp. Affairs, and Secy.; Sterling Carroll,* Treas.; Felix Martin Del Campo; James Furman; and 14 additional board members.
Number of staff: 409 full-time professional; 255 full-time support; 7 part-time support.
EIN: 581437002

1766
Stop Hunger Now
615 Hillsborough St., Ste. 200
Raleigh, NC 27603-1771 (919) 839-0689
FAX: (919) 839-8971;
E-mail: info@stophungernow.org; Toll-free tel.: (888) 501-8440; URL: http://www.stophungernow.org
Stop Hunger Now Blog: http://
thefaceofhunger.stophungernow.org

Established in 1998 in VA.
Grantmaker type: Public charity.

Financial data (yr. ended 12/31/10): Revenue, $6,804,737; assets, $1,931,625 (M); gifts received, $6,780,892; expenditures, $5,716,756; giving activities include $2,274,659 for 7 grants to organizations outside the U.S.
Purpose and activities: The organization coordinates the distribution of food and other life-saving aid around the world, seeks to end world hunger by providing food and life-saving aid to the world's most vulnerable, and strives to create a global commitment to mobilize necessary resources.
Fields of interest: International relief; Food services.
Type of support: In-kind gifts.
Limitations: Applications accepted. Giving on a national and international basis.
Application information: Unsolicited application for meals are currently accepted. Application form required.
　Initial approach: E-mail
　Final notification: Three to six months from application
Officers and Board Members:* Rev. Ray A. Buchanan,* Pres.; Rod Brooks,* C.E.O.; Rev. JoElaine Harris,* Secy.; Tom Proctor,* Treas.; Jacob S. Blass; Michael Constantino; Rev. Steve Hickle; David Johnston; Rev. Dr. Reggie Ponder; Dr. Adam Saffer; Dr. A. Hope Williams; Rosemary Wyche.
EIN: 161541024

1767
Strauss Foundation
c/o Wells Fargo
1525 W. WT Harris Blvd.
Charlotte, NC   28288-5709
Contact: Reginald Middleton, V.P., Wells Fargo

Trust established in 1951 in PA.
Donor: Maurice L. Strauss.
Grantmaker type: Independent foundation.
Financial data (yr. ended 12/31/10): Assets, $37,817,603 (M); expenditures, $2,079,221; qualifying distributions, $1,831,940; giving activities include $1,831,940 for grants.
Purpose and activities: Emphasis on Jewish welfare funds in the U.S. and Israel, child welfare and youth agencies, education, hospitals, and cultural programs.
Fields of interest: Arts; Higher education; Education; Hospitals (general); Human services; Children/youth, services; Jewish federated giving programs.
International interests: Israel.
Limitations: Applications not accepted. Giving primarily in PA. No grants to individuals.
Application information: Contributes only to pre-selected organizations. Unsolicited applications are not encouraged.
Trustees: Henry A. Gladstone; Scott Rosen Isdaner; Sandra S. Krause; Benjamin Strauss; Robert Perry Strauss.
Corporate Trustee: Wells Fargo.
EIN: 236219939

1768
Triangle Community Foundation
324 Blackwell St., Ste. 1220
Durham, NC   27701-3690   (919) 474-8370
Contact: For grants: Robyn Ferhman, Community Prog. Off.; For Scholarships: Libby Long, Scholarship, Special Proj. Coord.
FAX: (919) 941-9208; E-mail: info@trianglecf.org;
Grant application e-mail: robyn@trianglecf.org;
URL: http://www.trianglecf.org
Blog: http://www.philanthrospeak.com/
E-Newsletter: http://www.trianglecf.org/contact_us/email_newsletters
Facebook: http://www.facebook.com/pages/Triangle-Community-Foundation/113419701016
Twitter: http://twitter.com/TriComFdn
YouTube: http://www.youtube.com/user/TriangleCF
E-mail for scholarship: libby@trianglecf.org

Incorporated in 1983 in NC.
Grantmaker type: Community foundation.
Financial data (yr. ended 06/30/10): Assets, $122,492,712 (M); gifts received, $14,130,752; expenditures, $14,069,670; giving activities include $11,738,053 for 1,500+ grants.
Purpose and activities: The foundation seeks to connect philanthropic resources with community needs, create opportunity for enlightened change, and encourage philanthropy as a way of life.
Fields of interest: Visual arts; Museums; Performing arts; Performing arts, dance; Performing arts, theater; Performing arts, music; Humanities; Historic preservation/historical societies; Arts; Education, early childhood education; Child development, education; Elementary school/education; Vocational education; Higher education; Adult/continuing education; Adult education—literacy, basic skills & GED; Libraries/library science; Education, reading; Education; Environment, natural resources; Environment, energy; Environment; Animal welfare; Animals/wildlife, preservation/protection; Reproductive health, family planning; Medical care, rehabilitation; Health care; Substance abuse, services; Mental health/crisis services; Health organizations, association; AIDS; Alcoholism; Crime/violence prevention, youth; Legal services; Crime/law enforcement; Food services; Housing/shelter, development; Recreation; Youth development, services; Human services; Children/youth, services; Child development, services; Family services; Residential/custodial care, hospices; Aging, centers/services; Women, centers/services; Minorities/immigrants, centers/services; Homeless, human services; International peace/security; Civil rights, race/intergroup relations; Urban/community development; Rural development; Community/economic development; Voluntarism promotion; Government/public administration; Leadership development; Public affairs; Aging; Disabilities, people with; Minorities; Native Americans/American Indians; Women; LGBTQ; Economically disadvantaged; Homeless.
Type of support: Continuing support; Management development/capacity building; Annual campaigns; Capital campaigns; Emergency funds; Program development; Seed money; Scholarship funds; Research; Technical assistance; Program-related investments/loans; Employee matching gifts; Employee-related scholarships; Scholarships—to individuals; In-kind gifts; Matching/challenge support.

Limitations: Applications accepted. Giving limited to Chatham, Durham, Orange, and Wake counties, NC. No grants for budget deficits.
Publications: Annual report; Newsletter.
Application information: Visit foundation web site for application form and guidelines. Application form required.
　Initial approach: E-mail application form and attachments
　Deadline(s): Feb. 15 and Aug. 15 for Community Grantmaking program
　Board meeting date(s): Feb., May, Aug., and Nov.
　Final notification: June 30 and Nov. 30 for Community Grantmaking program
Officers and Directors:* Rick Guirlinger,* Chair.; Cecile Noel,* Secy. and Chair., Philanthropic Svcs.; Willy Stewart,* Treas. and Chair., Finance Comm.; Ken Troshinsky,* C.F.O.; MaryAnn Black,* Chair., Nominating and Governance Comm.; Donovan Moxey,* Chair., Devel. Comm.; Peter J. Meehan,* Chair., Leadership Council; Joel M. Sheer, Chair., Mktg. and Comms. Comm.; Mary Braxton-Joseph; Jack O. Clayton; C. Perry Colwell; Diane Evia-Lanevi; John H. Idler; James A. Joseph; Anu Kumar; Pat Nathan; Steven Nelson; Frank Phoenix; Lacy M. Presnell III; Thomas R. Staab II; Dr. Phail Wynn, Jr.
Number of staff: 13 full-time professional; 2 part-time professional.
EIN: 561380796
Recent grants for international programs:
1768-1 Accordia Global Health Foundation, Washington, DC, $50,000. For work of foundation. 2010.
1768-2 American Friends Service Committee, Philadelphia, PA, $10,000. For Nuclear Disarmament Initiative. 2010.
1768-3 American Red Cross, Central Iowa Chapter, Des Moines, IA, $41,843. For disaster relief in Haiti. 2010.
1768-4 American Red Cross, Central Iowa Chapter, Des Moines, IA, $19,735. For Haiti relief work. 2010.
1768-5 Doctors Without Borders USA, New York, NY, $10,000. For Haiti relief efforts. 2010.
1768-6 Duke University, Global Health Institute, Durham, NC, $57,076. 2010.
1768-7 Family Health Ministries, Chapel Hill, NC, $10,000. For Haiti relief. 2010.
1768-8 Friends of Canadian Education, West Orange, NJ, $100,000. 2010.
1768-9 International Affairs Council, Raleigh, NC, $10,000. For planning for the Teachers and Technology - Linking NC and the Middle East program. 2010.
1768-10 International Hospital for Children, Richmond, VA, $10,000. 2010.
1768-11 International Hospital for Children, Richmond, VA, $10,000. 2010.
1768-12 Medical Missionaries, Manassas, VA, $10,000. 2010.
1768-13 Non-Profit Incubator, Shanghai, China, $21,000. 2010.
1768-14 North Carolina Center for International Understanding Council, Raleigh, NC, $60,000. For International School Partnerships with Mexico. 2010.
1768-15 Partners in Health, Boston, MA, $52,441. For Haiti relief efforts. 2010.
1768-16 Provo Childrens Home, Providenciales, Turks & Caicos Islands, $10,000. 2010.
1768-17 University of Ottawa, Law School, Ottawa, Canada, $30,000. 2010.
1768-18 University of Toronto, Toronto, Canada, $25,000. For Dictionary of Old English. 2010.

1768-19 Willka Tika Childrens Fund, Portland, OR, $10,000. 2010.

1768-20 Womens Forum Initiative Partnership, Paris, France, $20,000. 2010.

1769
With Love From Jesus Ministries, Inc.
P.O. Box 37713
Raleigh, NC   27627-7713
Contact: Linda Williams, Exec. Dir.
Mailing address: P.O. Box 37713, Raleigh, NC 27627-7713

Established in 2001 in NC.
Grantmaker type: Public charity.
Financial data (yr. ended 12/31/10): Revenue, $1,399,360; assets, $43,201 (M); gifts received, $1,399,360; expenditures, $1,426,733; giving activities include $20,684 for grants to organizations outside the U.S., and $1,112,707 for grants to individuals.
Purpose and activities: The organization distributes needed resources, such as food, clothing, appliances, furniture, computers, etc., to high need populations.
Fields of interest: Economically disadvantaged.
International interests: India.
Type of support: In-kind gifts.
Limitations: Applications not accepted. Giving limited to Wake County, NC.
Application information: Unsolicited requests for funds not considered or acknowledged.
Board meeting date(s): Third Thurs. of each month
Officers and Directors: Keith Strandtman,* Pres.; Jerry Boyd,* V.P.; Terri Smith,* Treas.; Linda Williams,* Exec. Dir.; Becky Armistead; Jack Brinson; Vince DiMondi; Scott Gottfried; Sonny Wilson; Tina Wilson.
EIN: 562271441

NORTH DAKOTA

1770
Noel & Judith Fedje Foundation
2429 E. Country Club Dr.
Fargo, ND   58103-5730

Established in 1990.
Donors: Noel I. Fedje; Judith A. Fedje.
Grantmaker type: Independent foundation.
Financial data (yr. ended 12/31/10): Assets, $3,424,528 (M); expenditures, $167,085; qualifying distributions, $165,105; giving activities include $165,105 for 69 grants (high: $25,500; low: $50).
Fields of interest: Arts; Education; Hospitals (general); Health organizations, association; Human services; YM/YWCAs & YM/YWHAs; Children, services; United Ways and Federated Giving Programs; Religious federated giving programs; Protestant agencies & churches.
Limitations: Applications not accepted.
Application information: Unsolicited requests for funds not accepted.

Officers and Trustees:* Noel I. Fedje,* Pres.; Judith A. Fedje,* V.P.; Jill Fedje Johnson; Julie Fedje Johnston; Lori Fedje Paulson; Kari Fedje Rasmus.
EIN: 450418868
Recent grants for international programs:
1770-1 World Relief, Baltimore, MD, $15,000. 2010.

1771
Ekberg Johnson Family Foundation
P.O. Box 4067
Bismarck, ND   58502-4067

Established in 2007 in ND.
Donors: Judith E. Johnson; Bruce D. Johnson; DN, LLLP; TBP, LLLP; RSB, LLLP.
Grantmaker type: Independent foundation.
Financial data (yr. ended 06/30/11): Assets, $3,223,486 (M); expenditures, $237,496; qualifying distributions, $225,250; giving activities include $225,250 for grants.
Fields of interest: Human services; Christian agencies & churches.
Limitations: Applications not accepted. Giving primarily in FL, NY and OK. No grants to individuals.
Application information: Contributes only to pre-selected organizations.
Officers: Aaron D. Johnson, Pres.; Judith E. Johnson, V.P. and Secy.-Treas.; Amelia C. Beatty, V.P.; Bruce D. Johnson, V.P.; Victoria M. Johnson, V.P.
EIN: 260856315
Recent grants for international programs:
1771-1 World Compassion Foundation, Tulsa, OK, $127,000. For humanitarian relief and education. 2009.

1772
Los Amigos de Padre Juan
P.O. Box 717
West Fargo, ND   58078-6506   (701) 540-7242
Contact: Susan Trnka, Exec. Dir.
E-mail: strnka@losamigos-chimbote.org;
URL: http://www.losamigos-chimbote.org/

Established in 1998 in ND; received 501(c)(3) status in 2002.
Grantmaker type: Public charity.
Financial data (yr. ended 12/31/10): Revenue, $2,138,085; assets, $452,152 (M); gifts received, $2,135,493; expenditures, $2,129,112; giving activities include $1,964,461 for grants to organizations outside the U.S.
Purpose and activities: The organization is dedicated to supporting programs that improve and transform the lives of the poor of Chimbote, Peru.
Fields of interest: Health care; Community/economic development; Human services; Christian agencies & churches.
International interests: Peru.
Type of support: In-kind gifts.
Limitations: Giving limited to West Fargo, ND and Chimbote, Peru.
Publications: Newsletter.
Officers and Directors:* Susan Trnka,* Pres. and Exec. Dir.; Dr. Mark Christenson, V.P.; Tim Killeen,* V.P.; Ron Stensgard,* V.P.; Gary Zespy,* V.P.; Earl Milbrath,* Secy.; Nancy Evans,* Treas.; Fr. Al Bitz; Hector Bosse; Sr. Peggy Byrne; Marlene

Christenson; Fr. Jack Davis; Dr. Lucho Espejo; Sue Leahy; Mark Pominville; and 4 additional directors.
EIN: 450453441

1773
John L. McCormick Memorial Trust
902 3rd Ave. S.
Fargo, ND   58103-1707
Application address: c/o Maurice McCormick, 218 N. P Ave., Fargo, ND 58102, tel.: (701) 237-6983

Established in 2005 in ND.
Donor: John L. McCormick, Jr.†.
Grantmaker type: Independent foundation.
Financial data (yr. ended 12/31/10): Assets, $3,402,966 (M); expenditures, $159,486; qualifying distributions, $159,486; giving activities include $158,500 for 16 grants (high: $20,000; low: $1,000).
Fields of interest: Education; Higher education; Human services; Christian agencies & churches.
Type of support: General/operating support.
Application information: Application form required.
Initial approach: Letter
Deadline(s): None
Trustees: Maurice McCormick; Steve McCormick; Tom McCormick.
EIN: 206285678
Recent grants for international programs:
1773-1 Los Amigos del Padre Juan Foundation, West Fargo, ND, $15,000. 2010.

1774
The R. B. Nordick Foundation
675 12th Ave. N.E.
West Fargo, ND   58078-3500

Established in 1995 in ND.
Donor: Ralph B. Nordick.
Grantmaker type: Independent foundation.
Financial data (yr. ended 12/31/10): Assets, $43,887,261 (M); expenditures, $2,053,840; qualifying distributions, $2,000,000; giving activities include $2,000,000 for grants.
Fields of interest: Christian agencies & churches.
Limitations: Applications not accepted. Giving in the U.S., with emphasis on CA, GA and MN. No grants to individuals.
Application information: Contributes only to pre-selected organizations.
Officers: Ralph B. Nordick, Pres.; Brett A. Nordick, V.P.; Douglas R. Geeslin, Secy.-Treas.
EIN: 450442920
Recent grants for international programs:
1774-1 China Harvest, Wichita, KS, $71,000. 2009.
1774-2 Cornerstone Ministries International, Tustin, CA, $169,500. 2009.
1774-3 Development Associates International, Colorado Springs, CO, $150,000. 2009.
1774-4 Disciple the Nations, Trenton, KY, $38,100. 2009.
1774-5 Elam Ministries, Alpharetta, GA, $220,000. 2009.
1774-6 Emmanuel Ministries International, Waite Park, MN, $10,000. 2009.
1774-7 Foundation for International Research and Education, Colorado Springs, CO, $35,000. 2009.
1774-8 New India Evangelistic Association, Harbor Springs, MI, $25,000. 2009.

1774-9 Operation Mobilization USA, Tyrone, GA, $412,000. 2009.

1774-10 Seeds of Life Ministries, Makanda, IL, $10,000. 2009.

1774-11 South Asia Advocates, Kirkland, WA, $130,000. 2009.

1774-12 Strategic Global Assistance, Elkhart, IN, $255,000. 2009.

1774-13 Systematic Asian Leadership Training, Charlotte, NC, $30,000. 2009.

1774-14 Trans World Radio, Cary, NC, $45,000. 2009.

OHIO

1775
AK Steel Foundation
9227 Centre Pointe Dr.
West Chester, OH   45069-4822   (513) 425-5038
URL: http://www.aksteel.com/company/
corporate-citizenship/
Application address for scholarships: c/o Middletown Community Foundation, 36 Donham Plaza, Middletown, OH 45042, tel.: (513) 424-7369; URL: http://www.mcfoundation.org

Established in 1989 in OH.
Donors: AK Steel Corp.; Kawasaki Steel Investments, Inc.
Grantmaker type: Company-sponsored foundation.
Financial data (yr. ended 12/31/10): Assets, $13,639,139 (M); expenditures, $1,630,475; qualifying distributions, $1,621,764; giving activities include $1,052,845 for 65 grants (high: $100,000; low: $200), $406,000 for grants to individuals, and $120,884 for 375 employee matching gifts.
Purpose and activities: The foundation supports museums and community foundations and organizations involved with health, Down syndrome, cancer, heart disease, diabetes, human services, and international relief and awards college scholarships to the children of employees of AK Steel and to African-American high school seniors attending high schools in Butler and Warren counties, Ohio.
Fields of interest: Museums; Health care, volunteer services; Hospitals (general); Health care, clinics/centers; Health care; Down syndrome; Cancer; Cancer, leukemia; Heart & circulatory diseases; Diabetes; Cancer research; Boy scouts; American Red Cross; YM/YWCAs & YM/YWHAs; Children/youth, services; Aging, centers/services; Developmentally disabled, centers & services; Human services; International relief; Foundations (community); United Ways and Federated Giving Programs; African Americans/Blacks.
Type of support: General/operating support; Continuing support; Annual campaigns; Employee matching gifts; Employee-related scholarships; Scholarships—to individuals.
Limitations: Applications accepted. Giving primarily in areas of company operations, with emphasis on OH.
Application information: The Louis F. Cox Memorial AK Steel African-American Scholarships are administered by the Middletown Community Foundation.

Initial approach: Contact application address for application form for Louis F. Cox Memorial AK Steel African-American Scholarships
Deadline(s): Dec. 31 for Louis F. Cox Memorial AK Steel African-American Scholarships
Officers and Trustees:* James L. Wainscott,* Chair.; Sarah Cunningham, Secy. and Exec. Dir.; Doug Mitterholzer, Treas.; Alan H. McCoy; Albert E. Ferrara, Jr.; David C. Horn; John F. Kaloski.
Number of staff: 1 part-time professional.
EIN: 311284344

1776
Arab Student Aid International Corp.
P.O. Box 3546
Dublin, OH   43016-0271   (614) 889-9420
FAX: (614) 889-9430;
E-mail: president@arabstudentaid.org; URL: http://www.arabstudentaid.org

Established in 1998 in NJ.
Donor: HRH Prince Turkin bin Abdul Aziz.
Grantmaker type: Public charity.
Financial data (yr. ended 06/30/10): Revenue, $622,577; assets, $4,123,950 (M); gifts received, $132,528; expenditures, $557,141; giving activities include $413,686 for grants to organizations outside the U.S.
Purpose and activities: Support primarily for interest-free loans to full-time students of Arab descent who will be studying in the U.S. and Europe on a student visa, are pursuing a Ph.D., and who plan to return to the Arab world after graduation. Funding also for scholarship grants for training programs for NGO's in Arab states.
Fields of interest: Graduate/professional education; Scholarships/financial aid; Economically disadvantaged; Adults, women; Adults, men.
International interests: Middle East.
Type of support: Management development/capacity building; Equipment; Emergency funds; Scholarship funds; In-kind gifts; Student loans—to individuals; Loans—to individuals.
Limitations: Applications accepted. Giving primarily in the U.S. and the Middle East. No support for the study of languages before enrolling at a university, or for more than one student per family; no support for religious or political organizations. No grants for trips or travel expenses.
Publications: Application guidelines; Informational brochure; Multi-year report; Newsletter; Program policy statement.
Application information: Application form required.
Initial approach: E-mail or fax
Copies of proposal: 1
Deadline(s): Sept. 1 for fall semester, Jan. 1 for spring semester
Final notification: One week
Officers: Ishaq Y. Al-Qutub, Pres.; Mustafa D. Shamy, V.P. and Treas.; Robert W. Thabit, Secy.
Number of staff: 1 full-time professional; 1 part-time professional; 3 part-time support.
EIN: 208113798

1777
The Evenor Armington Fund
P.O. Box 1558, Dept. EA4E86
Columbus, OH   43216-1558

Established in 1954 in OH.

Donors: Everett Armington; and members of the Armington family.
Grantmaker type: Independent foundation.
Financial data (yr. ended 06/30/11): Assets, $2,220,612 (M); expenditures, $308,880; qualifying distributions, $288,000; giving activities include $288,000 for grants.
Purpose and activities: Grants primarily for special projects, usually short-term, in education, child welfare, medical research, health, the arts, the environment, and public policy organizations, including human rights, peace and justice, and the struggle against poverty.
Fields of interest: Arts; Education; Environment, natural resources; Environment; Health care; Medical research, institute; Human services; Children/youth, services; International peace/security; International human rights; Civil/human rights; Public policy, research.
Type of support: General/operating support; Continuing support; Annual campaigns; Emergency funds; Program development; Publication; Research; Consulting services.
Limitations: Applications not accepted. Giving primarily in CA and NY. No grants to individuals.
Application information: Contributes only to pre-selected organizations.
Board meeting date(s): Summer
Trustee: The Huntington National Bank.
EIN: 346525508

1778
Becker Family Foundation
c/o Fifth Third Bank
P.O. Box 630858
Cincinnati, OH   45263-0858
Application address: c/o Fifth Third Bank, 401 S. 4th Ave., Louisville, KY 40202-3426, tel.: (502) 562-5254

Established in 2001 in KY.
Donors: Gary Becker; Mary Becker; Gary E. Becker Unitrust.
Grantmaker type: Independent foundation.
Financial data (yr. ended 12/31/10): Assets, $2,648,053 (M); expenditures, $254,334; qualifying distributions, $233,400; giving activities include $233,400 for grants.
Fields of interest: International development; Education; Human services; Foundations (public); Christian agencies & churches.
Limitations: Applications accepted. Giving primarily in Louisville, KY and NY.
Application information: Application form not required.
Initial approach: Letter with prior 2 years financial statements
Deadline(s): None
Trustee: Fifth Third Bank.
EIN: 306006912

1779
The Brush Foundation
25350 Rockside Rd., 3rd Fl.
Bedford Heights, OH   44146   (216) 334-2209
Contact: Judy Wright, Prog. Off.
FAX: (216) 334-2211;
E-mail: brushfoundation@hotmail.com; URL: http://foundationcenter.org/grantmaker/brush/

Established in 1928 in OH.

Donors: Charles F. Brush†; Maurice Perkins†; Rufus S. Day, Jr. Trust.
Grantmaker type: Independent foundation.
Financial data (yr. ended 12/31/10): Assets, $6,746,780 (M); expenditures, $339,468; qualifying distributions, $323,587; giving activities include $297,500 for 18 grants (high: $25,000; low: $2,500).
Purpose and activities: To ensure that family planning worldwide becomes acceptable, available, accessible, affordable, effective and safe. Funding is focused, nationally and internationally, on those organizations with innovative projects which will: 1) Protect and enhance people's ability to manage their reproductive health; 2) Carry out public policy analysis and/or public education in areas related to reproductive behavior and its social implications; and 3) Advance the knowledge and purposeful behavior of young people regarding sexuality within both a social and health context. The current major interests of the foundation are adolescent sexuality and the control of adolescent pregnancy, preservation of the freedom of choice of women to plan the spacing and number of children, how laws and regulations may control population growth, and pilot family planning programs in Third World countries. Grants range from $5,000 to $25,000.
Fields of interest: Reproductive health, family planning; Civil liberties, reproductive rights; Youth; Young adults, male; Young adults, female; Young adults; Women; Girls; Adults, women; Adults.
International interests: Developing countries.
Type of support: Scholarships—to individuals; General/operating support; Program development.
Limitations: Giving in the U.S., with some emphasis on northeast OH; giving also on an international basis. No grants for capital endowment funds, operating support, or fellowships; no loans.
Publications: Application guidelines.
Application information: Core grants and scholarships are provided on an invitation-only basis. Uninvited requests for core support or scholarship support will not be funded. Check foundation web site for updated information. Application form required.
   Deadline(s): Twice annually. Contact foundation for specific deadlines or refer to foundation web site
   Board meeting date(s): Spring and fall
   Final notification: Notice of awards will be made within 4 months
Officers: Jacqueline Darroch, Pres.; Gita P. Gidwani, V.P.; Elizabeth Stites, Secy.; Ellen Rome, M.D., Treas.
Board of Managers: Barbara Brush-Wright; Daphne Byers; Cindie Carroll-Pankhurst; Stacey Easterling; Abigail English; Dan Pellegrom; Gordon Weir, M.D.
Trustee Bank: KeyBank N.A.
Number of staff: 1 part-time professional.
EIN: 346000445

1780
Catholic Mission Aid
17826 Brian Ave.
Cleveland, OH   44119-2933   (216) 481-3155

Grantmaker type: Public charity.
Financial data (yr. ended 12/31/10): Revenue, $109,303; assets, $111,470 (M); gifts received, $78,841; expenditures, $205,944; giving activities include $202,180 for grants.

Purpose and activities: The organization supports Catholic missionaries and Catholic missionary organizations.
Fields of interest: International relief; Human services; Catholic agencies & churches.
Type of support: Grants to individuals.
Limitations: Giving on a national and international basis.
Officers and Trustees: * Marisa Lavrisha,* Pres.; Mary Zupancic,* Treas.; Mary Celestina*; Helena Gorshe*; Rudy Knez; Antonia Lamovec; Mary Miklavcic; Anne Nemec; Lawrence Rozman; Ivanka Tominec; Victor Tominec; Antonia Urankar.
EIN: 237299558

1781
Christian Aid Ministries, Inc.
P.O. Box 360
Berlin, OH   44610-0360   (330) 893-2428
FAX: (330) 893-2305; Additional address: R.R. 3, Wallenstein, Ontario N0B2S0 Canada, tel.: (519) 664-2440

Established in 1981 in OH.
Grantmaker type: Public charity.
Financial data (yr. ended 12/31/10): Revenue, $155,208,072; assets, $47,214,064 (M); gifts received, $154,977,118; expenditures, $150,445,823; giving activities include $7,763,599 for grants, $127,146,860 for grants to organizations outside the U.S., and $7,823 for grants to individuals.
Purpose and activities: The ministries provide spiritual and material assistance ,such as food, clothing, medicine, and Christian literature, to needy people in various countries.
Fields of interest: Medical care, bioethics; Food services; International relief; Christian agencies & churches; Religion.
Type of support: Emergency funds; Grants to individuals; In-kind gifts.
Limitations: Giving on an international basis.
Publications: Informational brochure; Newsletter.
Application information:
   Board meeting date(s): Quarterly
Officers and Directors: * Nolan Dyler,* Chair.; Laverne Miller,* Secy.-Treas.; Roman B. Mullet, C.F.O.; David Troyer, Exec. Dir.; Amsey Drubacher; James Miller; James Mullet; Stephen Stoltzfus; Paul Weaver; Allen Yoder.
EIN: 341344364

1782
Cintas Cares
(formerly Cintas Corporation Contributions Program)
6800 Cintas Blvd.
P.O. Box 625737
Cincinnati, OH   45262-5737
URL: http://www.cintas.com/company/

Grantmaker type: Corporate giving program.
Purpose and activities: Cintas makes charitable contributions to nonprofit organizations involved with the military, human services, international relief, and on a case by case basis. Support is given primarily in areas of company operations.
Fields of interest: Disasters, preparedness/services; Human services; International relief; General charitable giving; Military/veterans.

Type of support: General/operating support; Employee volunteer services; Donated products; In-kind gifts.
Limitations: Giving primarily in areas of company operations; giving also to national and international organizations.

1783
The Convergys Foundation, Inc.
201 E. 4th St., Ste. 102-1400
Cincinnati, OH   45202-4122

Established in 1999 in OH.
Donor: Convergys Corp.
Grantmaker type: Company-sponsored foundation.
Financial data (yr. ended 12/31/10): Assets, $2,589 (M); gifts received, $759,000; expenditures, $756,665; qualifying distributions, $755,665; giving activities include $755,665 for grants.
Purpose and activities: The foundation supports organizations involved with arts and culture, education, youth development, and human services.
Fields of interest: Museums; Performing arts; Arts; Higher education; Education; Youth development; Human services; Children/youth, services; United Ways and Federated Giving Programs.
International interests: India; Asia; Oceania; Latin America; Europe; Canada.
Type of support: Capital campaigns; Building/renovation; Endowments; Seed money; Internship funds; Research; Sponsorships; Employee matching gifts.
Limitations: Applications accepted. Giving primarily in Jacksonville and Orlando, FL, Cincinnati, OH, TX, Salt Lake City, UT, and on an international basis in Asia, Canada, Europe, India, Latin America, and Oceania. No support for political or religious organizations. No grants to individuals.
Publications: Application guidelines.
Application Information: Regional Association of Grantmakers form is accepted. Application form not required.
   Initial approach: Written proposal
   Copies of proposal: 1
   Deadline(s): Feb. 29 for Spring consideration
   Board meeting date(s): Spring and fall
   Final notification: Varies
Trustees: Karen R. Bowman; David F. Dougherty; Clark D. Handy; Sajud Malhorta; Earl C. Shanks.
EIN: 311619871

1784
Danaher Foundation
6095 Parkland Blvd., Ste. 310
Mayfield Heights, OH   44124-6140

Established in 1952 in IL.
Donors: Joslyn Corp.; Steven M. Rales.
Grantmaker type: Company-sponsored foundation.
Financial data (yr. ended 12/31/10): Assets, $93,586 (M); gifts received, $125; expenditures, $307,177; qualifying distributions, $300,144; giving activities include $300,144 for grants.
Purpose and activities: The foundation supports organizations involved with arts and culture, higher education, health, cancer, kidney disease, international relief, philanthropy, and women.
Fields of interest: Arts; Media, print publishing; Cancer, leukemia; Philanthropy/voluntarism;

International relief; Visual arts; Higher education; Health care; Cancer; Kidney diseases; Women.
Type of support: General/operating support.
Limitations: Applications not accepted. Giving primarily in areas of company operations, with emphasis on Washington, DC, MD, PA, and VA. No grants to individuals.
Application information: Contributes only to pre-selected organizations.
Officers and Directors:* Robert S. Lutz,* Pres.; James F. O'Reilly, V.P. and Treas.; Laurence S. Smith, V.P.
EIN: 366042871

1785
William Dauch Foundation
(formerly Believers Foundation)
1570 Dutch Hollow Rd.
Elida, OH   45807-1803   (419) 339-4441
Contact: Thomas E. Brown, Pres.

Established in 1986 in OH.
Donors: Gladys Dauch; Thomas E. Brown; Marilyn Brown; Brown Supply Co.; Debra Grant; Bible Believers of Lima.
Grantmaker type: Independent foundation.
Financial data (yr. ended 12/31/10): Assets, $5,129,017 (M); gifts received, $88,848; expenditures, $552,683; qualifying distributions, $160,950; giving activities include $160,950 for grants.
Purpose and activities: Support to organizations that promote Christian knowledge and dissemination of the Gospel.
Fields of interest: Christian agencies & churches.
International interests: Canada; South Africa; India; Philippines.
Limitations: Applications accepted. Giving primarily in OH and WA; giving internationally in South Africa. No grants to individuals.
Application information:
  Initial approach: Letter
  Deadline(s): None
Officers and Trustees:* Thomas E. Brown,* Pres.; Marilyn Brown,* Secy.; Debra Grant,* Treas.; Tamara Brown LeRoux.
EIN: 341516486

1786
Eaton Corporation Contributions Program
1111 Superior Ave., N.E.
Eaton Ctr.
Cleveland, OH   44114-2584   (216) 523-4944
Contact: William B. Doggett, Sr. V.P., Public and Community Affairs
FAX: (216) 479-7013;
E-mail: barrydoggett@eaton.com

Grantmaker type: Corporate giving program.
Financial data (yr. ended 12/31/09): Total giving, $1,058,214, including $1,048,723 for grants, and $9,491 for 7 employee matching gifts.
Purpose and activities: As a complement to its foundation, Eaton also makes charitable contributions to nonprofit organizations directly. Support is given on a national and international basis.
Fields of interest: Arts; Elementary/secondary education; Vocational education; Higher education; Engineering school/education; Education, drop-out prevention; Education; Health care; Disasters,

preparedness/services; Family services; Human services; Urban/community development; Community/economic development; Public affairs.
International interests: Argentina; Australia; Belgium; Brazil; Canada; Chile; China; Colombia; Czech Republic; Denmark; Dominican Republic; Finland; France; Germany; Hungary; India; Indonesia; Ireland; Kenya; Mexico; Netherlands; Norway; Peru; Poland; Russia; Singapore; South Africa; Sweden; Taiwan; United Kingdom.
Type of support: Capital campaigns; Employee volunteer services; Program-related investments/loans; Donated products; In-kind gifts; Matching/challenge support.
Limitations: Applications accepted. Giving on a national and international basis in areas of company operations. No support for religious, fraternal, political, or labor organizations. No grants to individuals, or for endowments, debt reduction, or general operating support.
Publications: Application guidelines; Corporate giving report.
Application information: The Public and Community Affairs Department handles giving. A contributions committee reviews all requests. Application form not required.
  Initial approach: Proposal to nearest company facility
  Copies of proposal: 1
  Deadline(s): None
  Committee meeting date(s): Bimonthly
  Final notification: Following review
Corporate Contributions Committee: Alexander M. Cutler, Chair., Pres., and C.E.O.; Craig Arnold, Vice-Chair. and C.O.O.; Susan J. Cook, Exec. V.P., Human Resources; William W. Blausey, Jr., Sr. V.P. and C.I.O.; Ken D. Semelsberger, Sr. V.P., Finance and Planning; William B. Doggett, V.P., Public and Community Affairs; James E. Sweetnam.
Number of staff: 2 part-time professional; 1 part-time support.

1787
The Cyrus Eaton Foundation
The Heights Rockefeller Bldg.
2475 Lee Blvd., Ste. 2B
Cleveland Heights, OH   44118-1214
(216) 320-2285
FAX: (216) 320-2287;
E-mail: cyrus.eaton.foundation@deepcove.org;
URL: http://www.deepcove.org

Established in 1955 in DE.
Grantmaker type: Independent foundation.
Financial data (yr. ended 12/31/10): Assets, $3,134,702 (M); expenditures, $181,535; qualifying distributions, $132,850; giving activities include $132,850 for grants.
Purpose and activities: Giving primarily to support non-profit organizations in Cleveland and northeast Ohio whose programs enhance the quality of life in the area, and whose aims are in accord with Cyrus Eaton, the founder of the foundation.
Fields of interest: Arts; Education; Environment, natural resources; Environment; Human services; International peace/security; Community/economic development; Public affairs.
International interests: Canada.
Type of support: General/operating support; Endowments; Program development; Seed money.
Limitations: Giving primarily in OH, with emphasis on Cleveland. No support for municipalities or

organizations lacking 501(c)(3) status. No grants to individuals, or for tickets or tables for events.
Application information: See foundation web site for complete guidelines. Application form required.
  Initial approach: Cover letter (no more than 2 pages)
  Copies of proposal: 1
  Deadline(s): May 1 and Oct. 1
  Board meeting date(s): Oct.
  Final notification: Following board meeting
Officers and Trustees:* Raymond Szabo,* Pres.; Catherine I. Eaton,* V.P.; Alice J. Gulick,* Secy.; Henry W. Gulick,* Treas.; Ralph P. Higgins; Pamela Niedes.
Number of staff: 1 part-time support.
EIN: 237440277

1788
Ethicon Endo-Surgery, Inc. Corporate Giving Program
4545 Creek Rd.
Cincinnati, OH   45242-2803   (513) 337-7000
E-mail: fundingrequests@eesus.jnj.com;
URL: http://www.ethiconendosurgery.com/Corporate/ourconnections/funding

Grantmaker type: Corporate giving program.
Purpose and activities: Ethicon Endo-Surgery makes charitable contributions to nonprofit organizations involved with helping disease prevention through early detection and prevention of childhood obesity, colorectal cancer, breast cancer, and diabetes. Support is given primarily in areas of company operations, with emphasis on the greater Cincinnati, Ohio, area, and in Brazil, China, Germany, India, Japan, and Russia.
Fields of interest: Surgery; Diabetes; Pediatrics; Cancer; Breast cancer; Health care; Public health, obesity.
International interests: Brazil; China; Germany; India; Japan; Russia.
Type of support: General/operating support; Program development; Conferences/seminars; Faculty/staff development; Research; Employee volunteer services; Sponsorships; Donated products.
Limitations: Applications accepted. Giving primarily in areas of company operations, with emphasis on the greater Cincinnati, OH, area, and in Brazil, China, Germany, India, Japan, and Russia; giving also to national and international organizations. No support for religious or political organizations. No grants for for "bricks-and-mortar" projects.
Application information: Application form required.
  Initial approach: Complete online application form
  Deadline(s): None

1789
Ethnic Voice of America
5360 Brookpark Rd.
Cleveland, OH   44134-4640   (440) 845-0922

Established in 1995 in OH.
Grantmaker type: Public charity.
Financial data (yr. ended 10/31/10): Revenue, $90,597; assets, $1,150,095 (M); expenditures, $220,530; giving activities include $37,527 for grants to organizations outside the U.S.
Purpose and activities: Support for children and families, including specific assistance to children requiring medical treatment.

Fields of interest: Health care; Children/youth, services.
International interests: Eastern & Central Europe.
Type of support: Grants to individuals.
Limitations: Giving primarily for the benefit of Eastern Europe.
Officers: Irene Smirnov, Pres.; Mario Kavic, V.P.; George Smirnov, Treas.
EIN: 341649643

1790

John F. and Mary A. Geisse Foundation

(formerly The Geisse Foundation)
38050 Jackson Rd.
Chagrin Falls, OH   44022-2025   (440) 893-9458
Contact: Tim Geisse, Managing Tr.
FAX: (440) 247-8903; E-mail: timegeisse@aol.com

Established in 1969 in MO.
Donors: John F. Geisse†; Mary A. Geisse†.
Grantmaker type: Independent foundation.
Financial data (yr. ended 12/31/10): Assets, $10,382,845 (M); expenditures, $1,097,903; qualifying distributions, $1,176,025; giving activities include $988,448 for 64 grants (high: $200,420; low: $25), and $137,000 for 1 foundation-administered program.
Purpose and activities: Giving for economic development in the developing world, rural development, and water development.
Fields of interest: International development; Economically disadvantaged.
International interests: Central America; Developing countries.
Type of support: General/operating support; Continuing support; Annual campaigns; Equipment; Program-related investments/loans; Matching/challenge support.
Limitations: Giving to U.S. organizations that work internationally, in the developing world. No support for purely religious or environmental protection purposes, or for arts and culture. No grants or scholarships to individuals.
Publications: Informational brochure; Informational brochure (including application guidelines).
Application information: Unsolicited requests for funds generally not accepted. Application form not required.
  Initial approach: 1-2-page letter
  Copies of proposal: 1
  Deadline(s): None
  Board meeting date(s): As needed
  Final notification: Varies
Trustees: Lawrence J. Geisse, M.D.; Timothy F. Geisse, J.D.
Number of staff: 1 full-time professional.
EIN: 237049780
Recent grants for international programs:
1790-1 American Nicaraguan Foundation, Miami, FL, $50,000. For general support. 2009.
1790-2 Amigos de Honduras, Seattle, WA, $50,000. For rural development work in Honduras. 2009.
1790-3 Association for a More Just Society-US, Grand Rapids, MI, $65,100. For land titling work. 2009.
1790-4 Cooperative for Education, Cincinnati, OH, $20,000. For education programs in Guatemala. 2009.
1790-5 El Porvenir, Denver, CO, $20,000. For general support. 2009.
1790-6 EndPoverty.org, Bethesda, MD, $30,000. For general support. 2009.

1790-7 Fabretto Childrens Foundation, Arlington, VA, $100,000. For general support. 2009.
1790-8 Foundation for Management Education in Central America, Glen Echo, MD, $48,750. For general support. 2009.
1790-9 Goodwill Association of America, Penfield, NY, $10,000. For general support. 2009.
1790-10 Lifewater International, San Luis Obispo, CA, $90,000. For water, sanitation, and hygiene in rural northern Uganda. 2009.
1790-11 Rainbow Network, Springfield, MO, $300,300. For general support. 2009.
1790-12 Strategies for International Development, Arlington, VA, $140,000. For general support. 2009.
1790-13 Village Enterprise Fund, San Carlos, CA, $20,000. For general support. 2009.

1791

Give the Gift of Sight Foundation

(formerly LensCrafters Foundation)
4000 Luxottica Pl.
Mason, OH   45040-8114   (513) 765-6248
Contact: Susan Knobler, V.P.
FAX: (513) 492-6248;
E-mail: gos_info@luxotticaretail.com; E-mail for Susan Knobler: sknobler@luxotticaretail.com; additional tel.: (513) 765-6000; URL: http://www.givethegiftofsight.org

Established in 1988.
Donor: LensCrafters, Inc.
Grantmaker type: Public charity.
Financial data (yr. ended 12/31/09): Revenue, $8,129,565; assets, $11,365,232 (M); gifts received, $7,987,480; expenditures, $7,180,284.
Purpose and activities: The foundation sponsors missions in developing countries, where LensCrafters associates and doctors deliver eye exams and recycled glasses to the needy. The foundation also sponsors two vision vans that traverse across North America, delivering eye exams and new glasses to children.
Fields of interest: Optometry/vision screening; Eye diseases.
International interests: Developing countries.
Type of support: In-kind gifts.
Limitations: Giving on a national and international basis. No cash grants.
Application information:
  Board meeting date(s): Quarterly
Officers and Trustees:* Frank Baynham,* Chair.; Susan Knobler,* V.P.; Jeanine McHugh,* Secy.; Brian Haigis,* Treas.; Joseph R. DeZenzo,* Exec. Dir.; Mark Durkan; Emma Horn; Mark Jacquot; Wallace W. Lovejoy; Robin Wilson.
EIN: 311385607

1792

The Goatie Foundation

c/o KeyBank N.A.
4900 Tiedman Rd.
OH-01-49-0150
Brooklyn, OH   44144-2338
Application address: c/o Michael Simmons, 127 Public Sq., Cleveland, OH 44113; tel.: (216) 689-5834

Established in 2001 in OH.
Donors: Louise Gund; Women's Project Foundation.
Grantmaker type: Independent foundation.

Financial data (yr. ended 12/31/10): Assets, $1,856,359 (M); gifts received, $4,156,510; expenditures, $5,431,414; qualifying distributions, $5,428,000; giving activities include $5,428,000 for 50 grants (high: $600,000; low: $2,000).
Purpose and activities: Giving primarily for educational purposes including, but not limited to, the welfare of children, women, and families, the expansion of opportunities for women, and the elimination of prejudice and discrimination against women.
Fields of interest: Environment; Animals/wildlife; Human services; Women.
Limitations: Applications accepted. Giving primarily in CA, NJ and NY, with some giving in MD.
Application information: Application form not required.
  Deadline(s): None
Trustee: KeyBank N.A.
EIN: 347158309
Recent grants for international programs:
1792-1 Dian Fossey Gorilla Fund International, Atlanta, GA, $90,000. For Karisoke research center program. 2010.
1792-2 Dian Fossey Gorilla Fund International, Atlanta, GA, $80,000. For Freedom Fence at Grace. 2010.
1792-3 Earth Island Institute, Berkeley, CA, $50,000. For dolphin projects. 2010.
1792-4 Ecojustice Canada, Vancouver, Canada, $100,000. For general support. 2010.
1792-5 Ploughshares Fund, San Francisco, CA, $80,000. For general support. 2010.
1792-6 World Society for the Protection of Animals, Boston, MA, $150,000. For orangutan reintroduction project. 2010.

1793

Haskell Fund

c/o Advisory Svcs., Inc.
1010 Hanna Bldg.
1422 Euclid Ave.
Cleveland, OH   44115-2001
Contact: James C. Sekerak, Treas.

Incorporated in 1955 in OH.
Donors: Melville H. Haskell†; Coburn Haskell; Melville H. Haskell, Jr.†; Mark Haskell.
Grantmaker type: Independent foundation.
Financial data (yr. ended 12/31/10): Assets, $4,374,337 (M); expenditures, $255,275; qualifying distributions, $216,342; giving activities include $203,000 for 85 grants (high: $12,000; low: $500).
Purpose and activities: Giving locally for community services; national support for education, including building funds, hospitals and health agencies, community funds and social services, and the environment.
Fields of interest: History/archaeology; Education, fund raising/fund distribution; Education; Environment, natural resources; Environment; Animal welfare; Animals/wildlife, preservation/protection; Hospitals (general); Health care; AIDS; AIDS research; Human services; International human rights; United Ways and Federated Giving Programs; Marine science.
Type of support: Research; Scholarship funds; Program development; General/operating support; Endowments; Continuing support; Building/renovation; Annual campaigns.

Limitations: Applications accepted. Giving on a national basis, with emphasis on AZ, CA, and Cleveland, OH. No grants to individuals.
Application information: Application form not required.
  Initial approach: 1-2 page letter
  Copies of proposal: 1
  Deadline(s): None
  Board meeting date(s): Early fall
  Final notification: Late Fall
Officers and Trustees:* Coburn Haskell,* Chair.; Eric T. Haskell,* Co-Pres.; Coburn T. Haskell,* Co-Pres.; Schuyler A. Haskell,* V.P.; Mark Haskell,* V.P.; Paulette Kitko, Secy.; James C. Sekerak, Treas.; Sally Bell; Sarah Haskell Greene; Mary E. Haskell.
Number of staff: None.
EIN: 346513797

1794
Hazelbaker Foundation
1661 Old Henderson Rd.
Columbus, OH 43220-3644

Established in 1985 in OH.
Donors: Ralph E. Hazelbaker; Billie E. Hazelbaker.
Grantmaker type: Independent foundation.
Financial data (yr. ended 02/28/10): Assets, $1,896,130 (M); expenditures, $161,853; qualifying distributions, $154,246; giving activities include $154,246 for 40 grants (high: $36,913; low: $68).
Fields of interest: Youth, services; Performing arts, theater; Arts; Higher education; Health care; Health organizations, association; Athletics/sports, Special Olympics; Homeless, human services; International development.
Limitations: Applications not accepted. Giving primarily in Columbus, OH.
Application information: Unsolicited requests for funds not accepted.
  Board meeting date(s): Quarterly
Officers: Ralph E. Hazelbaker, Pres.; Billie E. Hazelbaker, Secy.; R. Brian Hazelbaker, Treas.
EIN: 311131197

1795
International Partners in Mission
3091 Mayfield Rd., Ste. 320
Cleveland Heights, OH 44118-1732
(216) 932-4082
Contact: Joseph F. Cistone, C.E.O. and Exec. Dir.
FAX: (216) 932-4084;
E-mail: office@ipmconnect.org; Toll Free Tel. : (866)-932-4082; URL: http://www.ipmconnect.org

Established in 1974 in MO.
Grantmaker type: Public charity.
Financial data (yr. ended 12/31/10): Revenue, $1,204,680; assets, $639,835 (M); gifts received, $796,450; expenditures, $1,189,459; program services expenses, $1,083,708; giving activities include $64,604 for grants, and $250,405 for grants to organizations outside the U.S.
Purpose and activities: The organization works across borders of faith and culture on behalf of children, women, and youth to create partnerships that build justice, peace, and hope.
Fields of interest: Environment; Health care; Children/youth, services; Community/economic development; Native Americans/American Indians; Women.
International interests: Asia; Canada; Central America; Europe; Middle East; North Africa; South America; Sub-Saharan Africa.
Type of support: Income development; Emergency funds; Program development; Seed money; Technical assistance.
Limitations: Applications accepted. Giving internationally to Sub Saharan and North Africa, Asia, Europe, the Middle East, and North, Central and South America. Giving in the U.S. is limited to Cleveland, OH, St. Louis, MO, and Native American communities.
Publications: Application guidelines; Annual report; Financial statement; Informational brochure; Newsletter.
Application information: Application form required.
  Initial approach: Letter or e-mail
Officers and Directors:* Elizabeth T. Reichard-Sims,* Chair.; Antonina Aura,* Vice-Chair.; Christine E. Henry,* Vice-Chair.; Joseph F. Cistone,* C.E.O. and Exec. Dir.; Caroline Mills,* Secy.; Michael S. Mayor,* Treas.; Beth Damsgaard-Rodriguez; Tony Dowell; Mark Falbo; Nadine Hopwood Feighan; Ana Grieg; Stephanie Hiedemann; Douglas Horner; Jim Kamphoefner; Mark Schulte; and 8 additional trustees.
Number of staff: 4 full-time professional; 2 part-time professional.
EIN: 431487311

1796
Carl Jacobs Foundation
38 Fountain Square Plz., MD 1090CA
Cincinnati, OH 45263
Contact: Heidi B. Jark, Mgr., Fifth Third Bank

Established in 1997 in DE.
Donor: Carl Jacobs.
Grantmaker type: Independent foundation.
Financial data (yr. ended 12/31/09): Assets, $14,859,740 (M); gifts received, $10,000,000; expenditures, $306,928; qualifying distributions, $245,024; giving activities include $238,950 for 41 grants (high: $25,000; low: $500).
Purpose and activities: Giving primarily to the arts; funding also for human services.
Fields of interest: Museums (art); Performing arts; Performing arts, ballet; Performing arts, theater; Performing arts, opera; Arts; Higher education; Libraries (public); Animals/wildlife; Health care; Human services; International affairs.
Limitations: Giving primarily in New York, NY; some funding nationally.
Application information:
  Initial approach: Letter
  Deadline(s): None
Trustee: Carl M. Jacobs III.
EIN: 133933000

1797
Jewish Community Federation of Cleveland
25701 Science Park Dr.
Cleveland, OH 44122-7302 (216) 593-2900
Contact: Hedy P. Milgrom, Asst. V.P., Endowments and Fdns.
E-mail: info@jcfcleve.org; Toll-free tel.: (888) 467-1125; URL: http://www.jewishcleveland.org
Blog: http://jewishcleveland.wordpress.com/
Facebook: http://www.facebook.com/JewishCleveland
Twitter: http://twitter.com/jewishcleveland
YouTube: http://www.youtube.com/user/JewishCleveland

Founded in 1903 in OH.
Grantmaker type: Public charity.
Financial data (yr. ended 06/30/10): Revenue, $57,028,958; assets, $378,467,985 (M); gifts received, $44,635,447; expenditures, $59,994,102; giving activities include $47,592,554 for grants, and $25,000 for grants to organizations outside the U.S.
Purpose and activities: The federation acts to produce the resources, ideas, and commitment necessary to preserve and strengthen Jewish life in Cleveland; to identify needs and provide funding to agencies that can help address those needs; to empower individual Jews or Jewish families to live quality Jewish lives; and to contribute to the creative survival of Jews in the U.S., in Israel, and throughout the world.
Fields of interest: Jewish agencies & synagogues.
International interests: Israel.
Limitations: Applications accepted. Giving on a national and international basis, primarily in Cleveland, OH and Israel. No grants to individuals.
Publications: Application guidelines; Annual report.
Application information: Application form required.
  Initial approach: Contact federation prior to preparing application
  Copies of proposal: 2
Officers and Trustees:* Michael D. Siegal,* Chair.; Renee Chelm,* Vice-Chair.; Jeffrey M. Kahn,* Vice-Chair.; Keith Libman,* Vice-Chair.; Betty Rosskamm,* Vice-Chair.; Judy Klein Willensky,* Vice-Chair.; Stephen H. Hoffman,* Pres.; Harvey A. Freiman, Secy.; J. David Heller,* Treas.; David Adler; Trish Adler; Vlad Agranovich; Cindy J. Attias; Eric E. Bell; Susan R. Borison; Rabbi Naphtali Burnstein; and 89 additional trustees.
EIN: 340714445

1798
The Jewish Foundation of Cincinnati
4555 Lake Forest Dr., Ste. 645
Cincinnati, OH 45242-3785
Contact: Connie M. Hinitz, Admin.
FAX: (513) 792-2716; E-mail: jfdncin@supern.com

Established in 1995 in OH; created when the Jewish Hospital of Cincinnati's entry into the Health Alliance of Cincinnati produced assets in excess of what was required by each participating entity.
Donor: Orla Miezinert†.
Grantmaker type: Independent foundation.
Financial data (yr. ended 10/31/10): Assets, $74,696,726 (M); gifts received, $33,157; expenditures, $5,971,207; qualifying distributions, $4,246,780; giving activities include $4,119,231 for 14 grants (high: $1,505,000; low: $750).
Purpose and activities: Giving limited to health care initiatives of the Jewish Hospital of Cincinnati, trauma medicine in Israel during times of exigent circumstances, Jewish capital needs in the greater Cincinnati area and Israel Experience Grants for Jewish young people ages 16-26 whose permanent residence is in the Greater Cincinnati Area.
Fields of interest: Hospitals (general); Jewish agencies & synagogues.
International interests: Israel.

Type of support: Capital campaigns; Building/renovation; Equipment; Emergency funds; Matching/challenge support.
Limitations: Applications not accepted. Giving primarily in Cincinnati, OH, and to health organizations benefiting Israel. No grants to individuals, or for general operating support, or for debt reduction or for endowments.
Application information: Unsolicited requests for funds not accepted.
Board meeting date(s): Varies
Officers and Trustees:* Phyllis S. Sewell,* Chair.; Gary Heiman,* Pres.; Warren C. Falberg,* Secy.; Philip T. Cohen,* Treas.; Bernard L. Dave; Benjamin Gettler; Gloria S. Haffer; Robert Kanter; Michael Oestreicher; J. David Rosenberg; Jeffrey Zipkin, M.D.
Number of staff: 1 part-time professional.
EIN: 311451489

1799
The Lerner Foundation
26500 Curtiss Wright Pkwy.
Highland Heights, OH 44143-1438
(440) 891-5000
Contact: Douglas Jacobs

Established in 1993 in OH.
Donors: Alfred Lerner†; Norma Lerner.
Grantmaker type: Independent foundation.
Financial data (yr. ended 12/31/10): Assets, $18,100,398 (M); gifts received, $220,936; expenditures, $18,983,396; qualifying distributions, $18,608,960; giving activities include $18,602,510 for 61 grants (high: $3,325,100; low: $5).
Purpose and activities: Support primarily for medical care, Jewish agencies and temples and Jewish federated giving programs.
Fields of interest: Museums (art); Higher education; Health care, single organization support; Hospitals (general); Jewish federated giving programs; Jewish agencies & synagogues.
Limitations: Applications accepted. Giving primarily in NY, OH and VA. No grants to individuals.
Application information:
Initial approach: Letter
Deadline(s): None
Officers and Trustees:* Norma Lerner,* Pres. and Treas.; Nancy Fisher,* V.P.; Randolph Lerner,* V.P.; James H. Berick,* Secy.
EIN: 341744726
Recent grants for international programs:
1799-1 Foundation for Art and Preservation in Embassies, Washington, DC, $20,000. For general operating support. 2009.
1799-2 Jewish Foundation for the Righteous, New York, NY, $10,000. For general operating support. 2009.
1799-3 National Portrait Gallery, London, England, $3,325,200. For general operating support. 2009.

1800
Limited Brands, Inc. Corporate Giving Program
(formerly The Limited, Inc. Corporate Giving Program)
3 Limited Pkwy.
Columbus, OH 43230-1467   (614) 415-6400
FAX: (614) 415-7786;
E-mail: MakeADifference@LimitedBrands.com;

URL: http://www.limitedbrands.com/responsibility/community/community_overview.aspx

Grantmaker type: Corporate giving program.
Purpose and activities: As a complement to its foundation, Limited Brands also makes charitable contributions to nonprofit organizations directly. Special emphasis is directed towards programs designed to address women and children's health, welfare, and education. Support is given primarily in areas of company operations in Rio Rancho, New Mexico, New York, New York, Columbus and Kettering, Ohio, and Montreal, Canada.
Fields of interest: Cancer research; United Ways and Federated Giving Programs; Women, centers/services; Children, services; Health care; Education; Arts.
International interests: Canada.
Type of support: General/operating support; Program development; Employee volunteer services; Donated products; In-kind gifts.
Limitations: Applications accepted. Giving primarily in areas of company operations in Rio Rancho, NM, New York, NY, Columbus and Kettering, OH, and Montreal, Canada; giving also to national organizations. No support for fraternal, labor, social, or veterans' organizations, religious organizations not of direct benefit to the entire community, discriminatory organizations, individual K-12 schools (unless the Limited Brand has a business partnership with the school), organizations with overhead and fundraising expenses exceeding 20 percent of the total operating budget, or public service agencies. No grants to individuals, or for non-academic educational activities, staff positions for governmental agencies, fundraising events, athletes, teams, sporting events, or tournaments, fashion shows, beauty pageants, or contestants, publications, audio or video productions (although exceptions may be made if they serve as supporting materials to a project within Limited Brand's focus), or travel.
Publications: Application guidelines; Grants list.
Application information: Telephone calls during the application process are not encouraged. Support is limited to 1 contribution per organization during any given year. Application form required.
Initial approach: Complete online application form
Deadline(s): Nov. 1, Mar. 1, and July 1 for grant requests; 1 month prior to need for product donations
Committee meeting date(s): Dec. 30, Apr. 30, and Aug. 30 for grant requests
Final notification: 30 days for grant requests

1801
Lowe Family Foundation, Inc.
c/o Ignite Philanthropy Advisors
1776 Mentor Ave., Ste. 310
Cincinnati, OH 45212   (513) 351-1945
Contact: Lyn Martin

Established in 2000 in OH.
Donors: Kenneth W. Lowe; Mary E. Lowe.
Grantmaker type: Independent foundation.
Financial data (yr. ended 12/31/10): Assets, $4,356,242 (M); expenditures, $197,113; qualifying distributions, $136,000; giving activities include $136,000 for grants.
Purpose and activities: Giving primarily for international development, with a focus on the empowerment of women.

Fields of interest: International development; Women.
Type of support: General/operating support; Program development.
Limitations: Applications not accepted. No grants to individuals.
Application information: Contributes only to pre-selected organizations.
Officers and Trustees:* Kenneth W. Lowe,* Pres. and Treas.; Mary E. Lowe,* V.P. and Secy.
EIN: 311739056

1802
Lowe-Marshall Trust
c/o C. Marshall Lowe
5301 C. Huffman Ln.
Chesterhill, OH 43728-9021
E-mail: mblowe@morganco.net

Established in 1968.
Donors: James T. Lowe†; Constance M. Lowe†.
Grantmaker type: Independent foundation.
Financial data (yr. ended 12/31/10): Assets, $6,108,136 (M); expenditures, $255,000; qualifying distributions, $255,000; giving activities include $255,000 for 3 grants (high: $145,000; low: $5,000).
Purpose and activities: Primary areas of interest include peacemaking and conflict resolution projects, and sustainable development in Appalachia and other economically depressed rural areas. Funding also for environmental quality, protection and beautification, and community improvement and capacity building.
Fields of interest: Environment, natural resources; Environment; International development; Community/economic development.
International interests: Central America.
Type of support: General/operating support; Continuing support; Annual campaigns; Program development; Seed money; Program-related investments/loans.
Limitations: Applications not accepted. Giving primarily in OH. No grants to individuals.
Publications: Program policy statement.
Application information: Contributes only to pre-selected organizations.
Officer and Trustees:* C. Marshall Lowe,* Chair.; Betty M. Lowe; Peter A. Lowe.
EIN: 316084154

1803
The Milton and Tamar Maltz Family Foundation
1600 W. 2nd St.
800 Skylight Office Tower
Cleveland, OH 44113-1461
Contact: Kittie D. Warshawsky Esq., Exec. V.P.
FAX: (216) 781-3611;
E-mail: kwarshawsky@maltzfamilyfoundation.org;
URL: http://maltzfoundation.org/

Established in 1989 in FL.
Donors: Milton S. Maltz; Tamar Maltz; Daniel Maltz; David Maltz; Julie E. Konigsberg.
Grantmaker type: Independent foundation.
Financial data (yr. ended 12/31/10): Assets, $67,318,781 (M); gifts received, $4,085,299; expenditures, $2,932,333; qualifying distributions, $2,482,825; giving activities include $2,482,825 for grants.

Purpose and activities: The foundation supports programs in the areas of the arts, health and human services, medical research, education, the environment and Jewish federated giving.

Fields of interest: Arts; Education; Environment, natural resources; Health care; Medical research; Human services; Aging, centers/services; Jewish federated giving programs; Military/veterans' organizations.

International interests: Israel.

Type of support: General/operating support; Management development/capacity building; Annual campaigns; Capital campaigns; Building/renovation; Land acquisition; Endowments; Professorships; Scholarship funds; Research; Matching/challenge support.

Limitations: Applications not accepted. Giving on a national basis, with emphasis on AZ, FL, and Cleveland, OH. No support for lobbying. No grants to individuals.

Application information: Contributes only to pre-selected organizations.

Officers: Milton S. Maltz, Pres.; Julie E. Konigsberg, V.P.; Daniel Maltz, V.P.; Tamar Maltz, Secy.; David Maltz, Treas.

Number of staff: 1 full-time professional.

EIN: 650164300

1804

The Morton and Barbara Mandel Family Foundation

(formerly Morton and Barbara Mandel Foundation)
2829 Euclid Ave.
Cleveland, OH 44115-2413   (216) 875-6500
Contact: Morton L. Mandel, Tr.
E-mail for JoAnn White, Prog. Off.:
JWhite@mandel-Foundation.org; URL: http://www.mandelfoundation.org

Established in 1963 in OH.

Donors: Morton L. Mandel; Barbara A. Mandel.

Grantmaker type: Independent foundation.

Financial data (yr. ended 12/31/09): Assets, $108,348,876 (M); gifts received, $679,421; expenditures, $9,223,755; qualifying distributions, $6,225,865; giving activities include $6,006,145 for 165 grants (high: $4,616,956).

Purpose and activities: Support primarily for leadership, management of nonprofits, higher education, Jewish education and continuity, and for urban neighborhood renewal.

Fields of interest: Leadership development; Nonprofit management; Urban/community development; Higher education; Education; Community/economic development; United Ways and Federated Giving Programs; Jewish federated giving programs; Jewish agencies & synagogues.

International interests: Israel.

Type of support: General/operating support.

Limitations: Applications not accepted. Giving primarily in Cleveland, OH; and the U.S. & Israel. No grants to individuals.

Application information: Contributes only to pre-selected organizations.

Officers and Trustees:* Morton L. Mandel,* Pres.; Barbara A. Mandel,* V.P.; Karen A. Vereb, Secy.; Anthony J. Pishkula, Treas.; Amy C. Mandel; Stacy L. Mandel; Thomas A. Mandel; Bradley S. Smith.

Number of staff: 1 full-time professional; 1 part-time professional; 2 full-time support.

EIN: 346546420

Recent grants for international programs:

1804-1 American Friends of the Hebrew University, New York, NY, $100,000. For general support. 2009.

1804-2 American Friends of the Israel Philharmonic Orchestra, New York, NY, $25,000. For general support. 2009.

1804-3 American Friends of the Israel Philharmonic Orchestra, New York, NY, $25,000. For general support. 2009.

1804-4 American Friends of the Israel Philharmonic Orchestra, New York, NY, $25,000. For general support. 2009.

1804-5 American Israel Environmental Council, New York, NY, $13,333. For general support. 2009.

1804-6 American Jewish World Service, New York, NY, $50,000. For general support. 2009.

1804-7 American Jewish World Service, New York, NY, $20,000. For general support. 2009.

1804-8 New Israel Fund, Washington, DC, $30,000. For general support. 2009.

1804-9 New Israel Fund, Washington, DC, $25,000. For general support. 2009.

1804-10 New Israel Fund, Washington, DC, $25,000. For general support. 2009.

1805

Mandel Supporting Foundations-Jack N. and Lilyan Mandel Fund

c/o Jewish Community Federation of Cleveland
1750 Euclid Ave.
Cleveland, OH 44115-2106
Contact: Marianne Lax, Grants Coord., Jewish Comm. Fed. of Cleveland

Established in 1982; supporting organization of the Jewish Community Federation of Cleveland.

Grantmaker type: Public charity.

Financial data (yr. ended 06/30/10): Revenue, $2,188,903; assets, $487,563,244 (M); gifts received, $12,917,263; expenditures, $11,669,587; giving activities include $10,224,350 for grants, and $2,218,814 for grants to organizations outside the U.S.

Purpose and activities: As a supporting foundation of the Jewish Community Federation of Cleveland, the fund makes grants to organizations supported by the Federation and to other organizations that further the charitable purposes of the fund.

Fields of interest: Jewish agencies & synagogues; Nonprofit management; Philanthropy/voluntarism; United Ways and Federated Giving Programs; Jewish federated giving programs.

International interests: Israel.

Type of support: General/operating support; Program development.

Limitations: Applications accepted. Giving in the U.S. and Israel. No support for organizations lacking 501(c)(3) status. No grants to individuals.

Application information: All grant proposals must be submitted on a Supporting Foundation of the Jewish Community Federation Grant Application form (form and guidelines are available to be downloaded from Federation Web site). Application form required.

Officers and Trustees:* Henry J. Goodman,* V.P. and Treas.; Joseph C. Mandel,* V.P.; Morton L. Mandel,* V.P.; David Fleshler, Secy.; Robert Goldberg; Stephen H. Hoffman; Barbara Mandel; Charles Ratner; Sally H. Wertheim.

EIN: 341350566

1806

Mandel Supporting Foundations-Joseph C. and Florence Mandel Fund

c/o Jewish Comm. Fed. of Cleveland
1750 Euclid Ave.
Cleveland, OH 44115-2106
Contact: Marianne Lax, Grants Coord., Jewish Comm. Fed. of Cleveland

Established in 1982; supporting organization of the Jewish Community Federation of Cleveland.

Grantmaker type: Public charity.

Financial data (yr. ended 06/30/10): Assets, $299,769,408 (M); gifts received, $3,586,011; expenditures, $12,213,674; giving activities include $10,224,348 for grants, and $2,218,814 for grants to organizations outside the U.S.

Purpose and activities: As a supporting foundation of the Jewish Community Federation of Cleveland, the fund makes grants to organizations supported by the Federation and to other organizations that further the charitable purposes of the fund.

Fields of interest: Philanthropy/voluntarism; Nonprofit management; Jewish agencies & synagogues; United Ways and Federated Giving Programs; Jewish federated giving programs.

International interests: Israel.

Type of support: General/operating support; Program development.

Limitations: Applications accepted. Giving in the U.S. and Israel.

Application information: All grant proposals must be submitted on a Supporting Foundation of the Jewish Community Federation Grant Application form (form and guidelines are available to be downloaded from Federation Web site). Application form required.

Officers and Trustees:* Joseph C. Mandel,* Pres.; Henry J. Goodman,* V.P. and Treas.; Morton L. Mandel,* V.P.; David Fleshler,* Secy.; Robert Goldberg; Stephen H. Hoffman; Barbara Mandel; Charles Ratner; Sally H. Wertheim.

EIN: 341350568

1807

Marion Community Foundation, Inc.

(formerly Ohio MedCenter Foundation, Inc.)
504 S. State St.
Marion, OH 43302-5036   (740) 387-9704
Contact: Bradley C. Bebout, C.E.O.
FAX: (740) 375-0665;
E-mail: marionlegacy@frontier.com; URL: http://www.marioncommunityfoundation.org

Established in 1998 in OH; converted from the sale of MedCenter Hospital.

Grantmaker type: Community foundation.

Financial data (yr. ended 06/30/10): Assets, $30,967,257 (M); gifts received, $17,671,813; expenditures, $870,609; giving activities include $478,109 for 10 grants (high: $134,982).

Purpose and activities: The foundation is dedicated to enhancing the quality of life for the greater Marion area through fostering philanthropy consistent with community values by providing a vehicle for planned giving through acceptance management and distribution of endowed funds in accordance with the wishes of their donors.

Fields of interest: Food banks; Youth development; Health care.

International interests: Dominican Republic.

Type of support: General/operating support; Annual campaigns; Capital campaigns; Building/

renovation; Equipment; Endowments; Program development; Conferences/seminars; Publication; Seed money; Curriculum development; Scholarship funds; Research; Technical assistance; Program evaluation; Scholarships—to individuals.

Limitations: Applications accepted. Giving limited to the greater Marion County, OH, area.

Publications: Application guidelines; Annual report; Financial statement; Grants list; Informational brochure; Newsletter.

Application information: Visit foundation web site for application form and guidelines. Application form required.

  Initial approach: Submit application form and attachments
  Copies of proposal: 1
  Deadline(s): Aug. 1
  Board meeting date(s): Monthly

Officers and Trustees:* Rex Parrott,* Chair.; Bradley C. Bebout,* C.E.O. and Pres.; Larry Geissler,* Secy.; Sue Jacob,* Treas.; Dr. James Barney; Nicolle Brooks; Susie Brown; Ronald D. Cramer; Anne J. Davy, R.N.; Pastor Doug Ford; Dr. Charles Garvin; Ted Graham; Hon. Thomas K. Jenkins; Tom Johnston; Nicole Workman; Dr. Scott Yancey.

Number of staff: 1 full-time professional; 1 part-time professional; 1 full-time support.

EIN: 314446189

1808
The Raymond E. Mason Foundation

c/o The Columbus Foundation
1234 E. Broad St.
Columbus, OH 43205-1453
URL: http://columbusfoundation.org/giving/foundations/mason/

Established in 1987 in OH; a supporting organization of the Columbus Foundation.

Grantmaker type: Public charity.

Financial data (yr. ended 12/31/10): Assets, $504,289 (M); gifts received, $6,194; expenditures, $111,581; giving activities include $73,500 for grants.

Purpose and activities: The grantmaking activities of the foundation support higher education, including the areas of transportation and logistics; American military history; art museums; historical societies; liberal arts; international refugee problems; assistance to disadvantaged families and individuals; and expanding the facilities and colleges serving the Appalachian area.

Fields of interest: Museums (art); International migration/refugee issues; Historic preservation/historical societies; History/archaeology; Transportation; Higher education; Military/veterans.

Limitations: Applications not accepted. Giving primarily in the Columbus, OH area; giving also in Sarasota, FL, and KY.

Application information: Currently only accepting requests from organizations that have previously received funding from the foundation; requests for funds from other organizations are not considered or acknowledged.

Trustees: John B. Gerlach, Jr.; Raymond E. Mason III; John R. Pine.

EIN: 311220052

1809
Middletown Community Foundation

300 N. Main St., Ste. 300
Middletown, OH 45042 (513) 424-7369
Contact: T. Duane Gordon, Exec. Dir.
FAX: (513) 424-7555;
E-mail: info@mcfoundation.org; URL: http://www.mcfoundation.org/

Incorporated in 1976 in OH.

Grantmaker type: Community foundation.

Financial data (yr. ended 12/31/10): Assets, $24,699,273 (M); gifts received, $2,098,053; expenditures, $2,354,574; giving activities include $1,047,141 for 50 grants (high: $74,158), and $804,270 for 378 grants to individuals.

Purpose and activities: The mission of the foundation is to: 1) serve as a leader, catalyst and resource for philanthropy; 2) serve as a permanent and growing endowment for the community's changing needs and opportunities; 3) strive for excellence through strategic grantmaking in the areas of the arts, education, health, social services, recreation and community development; 4) provide a flexible and cost-effective way for donors to improve their community.

Fields of interest: Recreation; Performing arts; Arts; Elementary/secondary education; Education, early childhood education; Elementary school/education; Higher education; Libraries/library science; Education; Health care; Youth development, services; Youth development, citizenship; Human services; Youth, services; Family services; Community/economic development; Public affairs, citizen participation; Leadership development; Aging.

Type of support: Capital campaigns; Building/renovation; Equipment; Emergency funds; Program development; Seed money; Curriculum development; Scholarship funds; Employee matching gifts; Scholarships—to individuals; Matching/challenge support.

Limitations: Applications accepted. Giving limited to the greater Middletown, OH area. No support for religious organizations other than religious schools, medical or other research organizations, or national or regional organizations (unless program addresses local needs). No grants to individuals (except for scholarships), or for endowments or general operating budgets of established organizations.

Publications: Application guidelines; Annual report; Financial statement; Informational brochure (including application guidelines); Newsletter.

Application information: Visit foundation web site for application guidelines. Common Grant Application may be submitted for grant requests. Application form not required.

  Initial approach: Submit application form and attachments
  Copies of proposal: 1
  Deadline(s): Mar. 1 and Sept. 1 for Recreation, Arts, Festivals, and Community Devel. grants and June 1 and Dec. 1 for Education and Human Needs grants; varies for scholarships
  Board meeting date(s): Quarterly
  Final notification: 60 to 90 days

Officers and Trustees:* Bob Flagel,* Pres.; Cathie Mulligan,* V.P.; Jim Burke,* Secy.; John Venturella,* Treas.; T. Duane Gordon, Exec. Dir.; Ron Ely, Tr. Emeritus; Doug Bean; Tim Carlson; Edwina Blackwell Clark; Roger Conner; Kee Edwards; Hon. Rhonda Freeze; Patricia Miller Gage; Richard Isroff; Hon. Larry Mulligan; Hon. Noah

Powers; G. Michael Pratt; Hon. Kathleen Dobrozki Romans; Michael J. Sanders; Carole Schul; Tom Scott; John Singleton; Verlena Stewart; Bill Triick; Mike Wallner; Tom Wiley; Mary Dees Wortley.

Number of staff: 1 full-time professional; 1 full-time support.

EIN: 310898380

Recent grants for international programs:

1809-1 Caring Partners International, Franklin, OH, $318,005. 2008.

1809-2 Caring Partners International, Franklin, OH, $10,000. 2008.

1809-3 Caring Partners International, Franklin, OH, $10,000. 2008.

1810
David & Inez Myers Foundation

c/o Jewish Federation of Cleveland
25701 Science Park Dr.
Cleveland, OH 44122-7302

Supporting organization of the Jewish Community Federation of Cleveland.

Donors: David N. Myers†; Inez P. Myers†.

Grantmaker type: Public charity.

Financial data (yr. ended 12/31/09): Assets, $172,766,506 (M); expenditures, $2,257,653; program services expenses, $1,930,086; giving activities include $8,253,502 for 39 grants (high: $2,476,000; low: $10,000).

Fields of interest: Performing arts; Museums; Higher education; Elementary/secondary education; United Ways and Federated Giving Programs; Jewish agencies & synagogues; Jewish federated giving programs.

International interests: Israel.

Limitations: Applications accepted. Giving primarily in Cleveland, OH and Israel.

Application information:

  Initial approach: Letter
  Deadline(s): May 15 and Nov. 15
  Board meeting date(s): June and Dec.
  Final notification: 60 days

Officers and Trustees:* S. Lee Kohrman,* Pres.; Henry J. Goodman,* V.P.; Stephen H. Hoffman,* Secy.; Barry M. Reis,* Treas.; Leslie Dunn; Morton G. Epstein; Robert Goldberg; Marc Krantz; Dieter Myers, D.D.S.; Charles A. Ratner.

EIN: 346560945

1811
Donald and Alice Noble Foundation, Inc.

(formerly Donald E. and Alice M. Noble Charitable Foundation, Inc.)
2000 Noble Dr.
Wooster, OH 44691-5353
Contact: David D. Noble, Pres.
FAX: (330) 264-8083;
E-mail: noblefound@tgstech.com

Established in 1990 in OH.

Donors: Donald E. Noble†; Alice M. Noble.

Grantmaker type: Independent foundation.

Financial data (yr. ended 12/31/08): Assets, $14,120,697 (M); expenditures, $5,012,891; qualifying distributions, $3,244,423; giving activities include $3,244,423 for 76 grants (high: $600,500; low: $100).

Purpose and activities: Giving for education and human services.

Fields of interest: Education, public education; Secondary school/education; Human services; Foundations (community); Youth; Economically disadvantaged; Children/youth.
International interests: Ghana; Honduras; Kenya; Namibia; Nicaragua; South Africa.
Type of support: General/operating support; Capital campaigns; Program development.
Limitations: Giving primarily in Wooster, OH and in Ghana and Honduras. No grants to individuals.
Application information:
  Initial approach: Letter
  Copies of proposal: 1
  Deadline(s): None
  Board meeting date(s): Spring and fall
  Final notification: 2 weeks
Officer: David D. Noble, Pres.
Trustees: Nancy L. Holland; Steve Matthew; Donald Noble II; Matthew Noble; Chris Schmid.
Number of staff: 1 full-time professional; 1 full-time support.
EIN: 341665641

1812
Oberlin Shansi Memorial Association
103 Peters Hall
50 North Prof. Str.
Oberlin, OH 44074 (440) 775-8605
FAX: (440) 775-8116; URL: http://www.oberlin.edu/cgi-bin/cgiwrap/shansi/shansi06.php?section=home

Supporting organization of Oberlin College.
Grantmaker type: Public charity.
Financial data (yr. ended 06/30/10): Revenue, $273,229; assets, $12,231,306 (M); gifts received, $230,293; expenditures, $713,487; program services expenses, $569,366; giving activities include $44,126 for grants to organizations outside the U.S., and $39,084 for grants to individuals.
Purpose and activities: The association promotes understanding and communication between Asians and Americans.
Fields of interest: International exchange; Higher education; Asians/Pacific Islanders.
Type of support: Exchange programs; Fellowships.
Application information: Application forms are available on the association's web site. Application form required.
Directors: Harry Pfeifer,* Chair.; Eric Estes,* Secy.; Phillip Braun,* Treas.; Midge Wood Brittingham; Michael Beebe; Timothy Henrich; Ziyad Hopkins; Carol Lasser; Tim Liang; Anya Desai; Qiusha Ma; Henry McCann; and 4 additional Directors.
EIN: 340768350

1813
OMNOVA Solutions Foundation Inc.
175 Ghent Rd.
Fairlawn, OH 44333-3300 (330) 869-4289
Contact: Theresa Carter, Pres.
FAX: (330) 869-4272;
E-mail: theresa.carter@omnova.com; URL: http://www.omnova.com/about/community/community.aspx

Established in 1999 in OH.
Donor: GenCorp Foundation Inc.
Grantmaker type: Company-sponsored foundation.

Financial data (yr. ended 11/30/10): Assets, $24,035,627 (M); expenditures, $1,917,265; qualifying distributions, $1,841,615; giving activities include $1,528,667 for 474 grants (high: $118,000; low: $25), and $155,833 for 93 grants to individuals (high: $3,000; low: $1,000).
Purpose and activities: The foundation supports organizations involved with arts and culture, education, health, drug prevention, crime prevention, disaster relief, safety, human services, urban renewal, and civic affairs. Special emphasis is directed toward programs designed to help motivate our future leaders and workers to gain the desire, knowledge, and work readiness skills required for companies to succeed and maintain a competitive edge.
Fields of interest: Arts, public education; Arts; Elementary/secondary education; Adult education—literacy, basic skills & GED; Education, reading; Education; Medical care, in-patient care; Health care; Substance abuse, prevention; Crime/violence prevention; Disasters, preparedness/services; Safety, education; Human services; Urban/community development; Science, formal/general education; Mathematics; Public affairs, public education; Public affairs.
International interests: Canada; Finland; France; India; Italy.
Type of support: General/operating support; Continuing support; Annual campaigns; Capital campaigns; Building/renovation; Endowments; Program development; Scholarship funds; Employee volunteer services; Employee matching gifts; Employee-related scholarships; In-kind gifts.
Limitations: Applications accepted. Giving primarily in areas of company operations in GA, MA, MS, NC, OH, PA, SC, WI, and in Canada, China, Finland, France, India, and Italy; giving also to national organizations. No support for private foundations, fraternal, social, labor, or veterans' organizations, discriminatory organizations, organizations not of direct benefit to the entire community, political parties or candidates, organizations posing a conflict of interest with OMNOVA, or churches or religious organizations. No grants to individuals (except for employee-related scholarships), or for lobbying activities, local athletic or sports programs or sports equipment, travel, advertising, benefits, raffles, or similar fundraising events, or research or conferences.
Publications: Application guidelines; Annual report; Corporate report.
Application information: Organizations receiving support are asked to provide periodic progress reports. Multi-year funding is not automatic. Proposals should be brief. Application form not required.
  Initial approach: Mail proposal to foundation
  Copies of proposal: 1
  Deadline(s): None
  Board meeting date(s): As required
  Final notification: 4 to 6 weeks
Officers and Trustees:* Michael E. Hicks,* Chair.; Theresa Carter, Pres.; Kristine C. Syrvalin,* Secy.; Frank P. Robers,* Treas.; Robin McCain; Nick Triantafillopoulos.
Number of staff: 1 full-time professional; 1 part-time support.
EIN: 341909350

1814
The Partridge Foundation
925 Euclid Ave, Ste. 2000
Cleveland, OH 44115-1407

Established in 1992 in NY.
Donors: Polly Guth; P.W. Guth Charitable Lead Unitrust.
Grantmaker type: Independent foundation.
Financial data (yr. ended 11/30/09): Assets, $39,306,599 (M); gifts received, $2,775,387; expenditures, $10,302,348; qualifying distributions, $8,870,157; giving activities include $8,870,157 for 22 grants (high: $2,500,000; low: $157; average: $250,000–$1,000,000).
Fields of interest: Performing arts, opera; Arts, cultural/ethnic awareness; Performing arts; Environment, land resources; Reproductive health, family planning; Cancer research; International affairs, goodwill promotion; International affairs; Public affairs; Women.
Limitations: Applications not accepted. Giving primarily in NY, with some giving in MA and ME. No grants to individuals.
Application information: Unsolicited requests for funds not accepted.
Trustees: Virginia Montgomery; Richard T. Watson.
EIN: 341742512
Recent grants for international programs:
1814-1 Acumen Fund, New York, NY, $250,000. For general support. 2009.
1814-2 Asia Society, New York, NY, $50,000. For general support. 2009.
1814-3 Community and Family Services International, Manila, Philippines, $160,000. To provide social services. 2009.
1814-4 Doctors Without Borders USA, New York, NY, $125,000. For general support. 2009.
1814-5 Population Council, New York, NY, $60,000. For general support. 2009.

1815
The Procter & Gamble Fund
2 Procter & Gamble Plz.
Cincinnati, OH 45202-3315 (513) 983-2139
Contact: Tawnia True
FAX: (513) 983-2147; E-mail: pgfund.im@pg.com; Additional contact: Paula Long, V.P. and Secy., tel.: (512) 983-2143; URL: http://www.pg.com/company/our_commitment/community.jhtml

Incorporated in 1952 in OH.
Donor: The Procter & Gamble Co.
Grantmaker type: Public charity.
Financial data (yr. ended 06/30/08): Assets, $21,013 (M); gifts received, $10,000,000; expenditures, $23,044,862; giving activities include $15,193,570 for 164 grants (high: $4,965,491; low: $450).
Purpose and activities: The fund supports food banks and organizations involved with arts and culture, education, clean water, animals, health, disaster relief, human services, international relief, community development, civic affairs, and economically disadvantaged people. Special emphasis is directed toward children in need.
Fields of interest: Animals/wildlife; Arts; Higher education; Education; Environment, water pollution; Health care; Food banks; Disasters, preparedness/services; Homeless, human services; Human services; International relief; Community/economic development; United Ways and Federated Giving

Programs; Public affairs; Children; Economically disadvantaged.

Type of support: General/operating support; Program development; Curriculum development; Employee volunteer services; Employee matching gifts; Employee-related scholarships.

Limitations: Applications accepted. Giving on a national and international basis primarily in areas of company operations, with emphasis on Washington, DC, NY, and OH, and in China, Costa Rica, Mexico, and Zimbabwe. No support for religious organizations, political, legislative, or fraternal organizations, or athletic, social, or veterans' organizations. No grants to individuals (except for employee-related scholarships) or for endowments; generally, no fundraisers.

Publications: Application guidelines.

Application information: Application form required.

Initial approach: Complete online application

Deadline(s): July 1 to Sept. 30; Dec. 1 to Feb. 29

Officers and Trustees:* C.R. Otto,* Pres.; Paula S. Long, V.P. and Secy.; R.L. Antoine,* V.P.; C.C. Dailey, Jr.,* V.P.; John P. Goodwin, Treas.

EIN: 316019594

1816

The Jay and Jean Schottenstein Foundation

(formerly Jay L. Schottenstein Foundation)

c/o Charles Spicer Inc.

4300 E. Fifth Ave.

Columbus, OH 43219-1816 (614) 449-4253

Established in OH.

Donors: Jay Schottenstein; Jeffrey Schottenstein; Jonathan Schottenstein; Joseph Schottenstein.

Grantmaker type: Independent foundation.

Financial data (yr. ended 12/31/09): Assets, $12,872,279 (M); gifts received, $2,152,900; expenditures, $5,628,654; qualifying distributions, $5,597,291; giving activities include $5,597,291 for 56 grants (high: $1,100,000; low: $54; average: $50,000–$150,000).

Purpose and activities: Support only for Jewish agencies, temples, and schools.

Fields of interest: Elementary/secondary education; Theological school/education; Jewish federated giving programs; Jewish agencies & synagogues.

Type of support: General/operating support.

Limitations: Applications not accepted. Giving limited to NY and OH. No grants to individuals.

Application information: Contributes only to pre-selected organizations.

Officers: Jay Schottenstein, Pres.; Geraldine Schottenstein Hoffman, V.P.

EIN: 311111955

Recent grants for international programs:

1816-1 American Friends of Ateret Cohanim - Jerusalem Reclamation Project, New York, NY, $10,000. 2008.

1816-2 American Friends of Bet El Yeshiva Center, Hempstead, NY, $15,000. 2008.

1816-3 American Friends of Brothers Aid, Monsey, NY, $36,000. 2008.

1816-4 American Friends of Nishmat, New York, NY, $400,000. 2008.

1816-5 American Friends of Old City Charities, Staten Island, NY, $30,000. 2008.

1816-6 Ariel American Friends of Midrasha and United Israel Institutions, New York, NY, $18,000. 2008.

1816-7 Chabads Children of Chernobyl, New York, NY, $27,000. 2008.

1816-8 Friends of the Israel Antiquities, New York, NY, $1,000,000. 2008.

1816-9 Jewish National Fund, New York, NY, $150,000. 2008.

1816-10 Western Wall Heritage Foundation, New York, NY, $133,334. 2008.

1817

Dale & Alyce Sheely Family Foundation

c/o The Huntington National Bank

23 Federal Plz.

Youngstown, OH 44503-1411

Contact: David Sabine, Sr. V.P., The Huntington National Bank

Established in 1994 in OH.

Donor: Dale R. Sheely, Sr.

Grantmaker type: Independent foundation.

Financial data (yr. ended 12/31/10): Assets, $1,105,965 (M); gifts received, $200,000; expenditures, $199,294; qualifying distributions, $194,428; giving activities include $189,000 for 383 grants.

Purpose and activities: Support for churches, religious groups, education, and a relief program in Columbiana, Mahoning, and Trumbull counties, Ohio.

Fields of interest: Human services; Religion; Elementary/secondary education; Protestant agencies & churches.

International interests: Scotland.

Type of support: Emergency funds.

Limitations: Applications not accepted. Giving limited to Mahoning Valley, OH.

Application information: Contributes only to pre-selected organizations.

Officer: Dale R. Sheely, Sr., Chair.

Directors: Albert Ortenzio; David Sabine; Alyce Sheely; Linda Cappelli Sladick.

Trustee: The Huntington National Bank.

EIN: 347012061

1818

The Taj Foundation

3136 Campbell Dr.

Springfield, OH 45503

Application address: c/o Tajuddin Ahmed, 1174 East Home Rd., Springfield, OH 45503, tel.: (937) 398-0054

Established in 1987 in OH.

Donors: Tajuddin Ahmed; Shahana Ahmed; Satiad H. Siddiqi; Edith Siddiqi.

Grantmaker type: Independent foundation.

Financial data (yr. ended 12/31/10): Assets, $3,695,128 (M); gifts received, $80,755; expenditures, $226,738; qualifying distributions, $209,024; giving activities include $209,024 for grants.

Purpose and activities: Giving primarily for education and Islamic associations.

Fields of interest: Education; Arts, multipurpose centers/programs; Health care; Human services; International affairs; Islam.

Type of support: General/operating support; Scholarship funds.

Application information: Application form required.

Initial approach: Letter

Deadline(s): None

Officers: Tajuddin Ahmed, Pres.; Shahana Ahmed, V.P.; Afshan Ahmed, Secy.-Treas.

EIN: 311191104

1819

Thanksgiving Fund

c/o American Endowment Foundation

1521 Georgetown Rd.

P.O. Box 911

Hudson, OH 44236-4066

E-mail: info@thanksgivingfund.org; URL: http://www.thanksgivingfund.org/index.html

Donor-advised fund of the American Endowment Foundation.

Grantmaker type: Public charity.

Purpose and activities: The fund seeks to empower people and organizations to act with integrity to achieve sustainable and creative changes impacting the quality of our shared lives. The fund makes grants that address the root causes of social and environmental issues, and enables individuals and communities to express and celebrate their full creative potential. The fund focuses its giving on the following areas: social and economic justice, environmental protection and restoration, the arts, hunger and affordable housing, International health and development, and gender equality.

Fields of interest: Social sciences, equal rights; International development; Social sciences; Arts; Housing/shelter; Human services.

Application information: Applicants are encouraged to submit all materials in all stages of the application process electronically. Phone calls will not be accepted.

Initial approach: Letter of inquiry (no more than 3 pages)

Deadline(s): None

1820

Dave Thomas Foundation for Adoption

545 Metro Place N., Ste. 200

Dublin, OH 43017-5014

Contact: Rita L. Soronen, Exec. Dir.

FAX: (614) 766-3871;

E-mail: info@davethomasfoundation.org; Toll-free tel.: (800) 275-3832; URL: http://www.davethomasfoundationforadoption.org

Facebook: http://www.facebook.com/pages/Dublin-OH/Dave-Thomas-Foundation-for-Adoption/88485759616

LinkedIn: http://www.linkedin.com/groups?gid=1910609

Twitter: http://twitter.com/DTFA

YouTube: http://youtube.com/user/dtfa

Established in 1992 in OH.

Grantmaker type: Public charity.

Financial data (yr. ended 06/30/11): Revenue, $11,018,479; assets, $13,231,141 (M); gifts received, $10,614,923; expenditures, $11,437,374; giving activities include $8,194,791 for grants, and $66,900 for grants to individuals.

Purpose and activities: The foundation seeks to raise public awareness about children awaiting adoption in the U.S., to educate prospective parents about the adoption process, and to form public and private partnerships to make the process easier and more affordable.

Fields of interest: Children, foster care; Children, adoption.

International interests: Canada.

Type of support: Program development; Publication; Seed money; Curriculum development; Technical assistance; Consulting services; Matching/challenge support.

Limitations: Giving in the U.S. and Canada. No support for religious purposes, adoption searches, or special events. No grants to individuals for adoption expenses, or for operational budgets, budget deficits, endowments, or capital projects.

Publications: Grants list; Informational brochure; Newsletter.

Application information:

Board meeting date(s): Biannually

Officers and Trustees:* Denny L. Lynch,* Pres.; Joyce Eufemi,* V.P.; Mary A. Schell,* Secy.; Ed Austin,* Treas.; Rita L. Soronen, Exec. Dir.; John D. Barker; Jeffrey J. Coghlan; Brad Conner; Michael J. Givens; J. David Karam; Wendy Morse; Doug Nichols; Deborah Pryce; Roland C. Smith; Lorraine Thomas; Joseph Turner, Jr.; Debra S. Waller.

Number of staff: 8 full-time professional; 1 full-time support.

EIN: 311356151

1821

The Timken Company Charitable and Educational Fund, Inc.

(formerly The Timken Company Educational Fund, Inc.)

1835 Dueber Ave. S.W.
Canton, OH 44706-2728
URL: http://www.timken.com/EN-US/ABOUT/CITIZENSHIP/SCHOLARSHIP/Pages/Scholarship.aspx

Established in 1957.

Donor: The Timken Co.

Grantmaker type: Company-sponsored foundation.

Financial data (yr. ended 12/31/10): Assets, $3,570,944 (M); gifts received, $2,000,000; expenditures, $1,022,486; qualifying distributions, $1,021,436; giving activities include $680,000 for grants, and $196,239 for grants to individuals.

Purpose and activities: The foundation awards college scholarships to children of associates and retirees of the Timken Company, its subsidiaries, and joint ventures.

Fields of interest: Higher education.

International interests: Asia; Brazil; China; Eastern & Central Europe; India; Latin America; Poland; Romania; South Africa.

Type of support: Employee-related scholarships.

Limitations: Applications not accepted. Giving primarily in areas of company operations, with emphasis on Brazil, China, Poland, and Romania.

Application information: Contributes only through employee-related scholarships.

Board meeting date(s): Quarterly

Officers and Trustees:* G. A. Eisenberg,* Exec. V.P.; Donald L. Walker,* Sr. V.P.; K. L. Groh,* V.P., Comms.

EIN: 346520257

1822

Timken Foundation of Canton

200 Market Ave. N., Ste. 210
Canton, OH 44702-1437 (330) 452-1144
Contact: Nancy Knudsen, Secy.-Treas.

Incorporated in 1934 in OH.

Donor: Members of the Timken family.

Grantmaker type: Independent foundation.

Financial data (yr. ended 09/30/10): Assets, $257,081,371 (M); expenditures, $8,061,177; qualifying distributions, $7,781,527; giving activities include $7,430,178 for 88 grants (high: $357,488; low: $500).

Purpose and activities: To promote broad civic betterment by capital fund grants; support largely for colleges, schools, hospitals, cultural centers, social services and recreation, and other charitable institutions.

Fields of interest: Historic preservation/historical societies; Arts; Education, early childhood education; Child development, education; Elementary school/education; Secondary school/education; Higher education; Adult education—literacy, basic skills & GED; Libraries/library science; Education, reading; Education; Hospitals (general); Health care; Health organizations, association; Crime/violence prevention, abuse prevention; Recreation; Youth development, services; Child development, services; Community/economic development; Computer science; Leadership development; Economically disadvantaged.

International interests: Brazil; Canada; China; Czech Republic; France; Germany; India; Italy; Poland; Romania; South Africa; United Kingdom.

Type of support: Capital campaigns; Building/renovation; Equipment; Land acquisition; Matching/challenge support.

Limitations: Applications not accepted. Giving primarily in local areas of Timken Co. domestic operations in Manchester, CT; Bucyrus, Canton, Eaton, New Philadelphia, OH; Ashboro, Columbus, and Lincolnton, NC; Keene, and Lebanon, NH; Honea Path, Union, and Gaffney, SC; Altavista, VA; and Mascot and Pulaski, TN. Giving also in local areas in Canada, China, France, Great Britain, India, Italy, Poland, Romania, and South Africa where Timken Co. has manufacturing facilities. No support for projects for religious or political purposes. No grants to individuals. Generally, no grants for operating budgets, endowments, or program development.

Application information: Unsolicited requests for funds not accepted.

Board meeting date(s): As required

Officers and Trustees:* Ward J. Timken,* Pres.; W.J. Timken, Jr.,* V.P.; Nancy Knudsen,* Secy.-Treas.; Joy A. Timken; W. R. Timken, Jr.

Number of staff: 1 full-time professional; 1 part-time professional; 1 full-time support.

EIN: 346520254

Recent grants for international programs:

1822-1 CAP Foundation, Hyderabad, India, $50,000. To construct a community college. 2010.

1822-2 Habitat for Humanity India, Mumbai, India, $50,667. To fund half the cost of building 38 homes for female supported families. 2010.

1822-3 Italian Red Cross, Rome, Italy, $42,000. To purchase a new medical car (changed to allow the grant to be used for their disaster fund) for Red Cross in Brescia. 2010.

1822-4 Jean Monnet National College Ploiesti, Ploiesti, Romania, $63,000. To renovate and equip the kitchen and dining areas. 2010.

1822-5 Medical and Social Welfare Center, Ploiesti, Romania, $95,700. To purchase testing and rehabilitation equipment and a platform wheelchair lift. 2010.

1822-6 North America Railway Hall of Fame, Saint Thomas, Canada, $111,500. To restore the waiting room and second floor hallway. 2010.

1822-7 Rabindranath Tagore International Institute of Cardiac Sciences, Kolkata, India, $185,900. To purchase equipment for early detection of cancer and congenital heart disease. 2010.

1822-8 Round Table India, Chennai, India, $48,500. To rebuild four classrooms and two toilet blocks, replace two roofs and purchase furniture. 2010.

1822-9 Schongauer Society, Colmar, France, $333,000. To expand the Unterlinden Museum by renovating the old public baths and adding some new construction. 2010.

1822-10 School of Arts and Crafts Toma Caragiu Ploiesti, Ploiesti, Romania, $60,150. To construct and furnish a physics lab and a carpentry workshop for the second chance program. 2010.

1822-11 Sosnowiec, Town of, Sosnowiec, Poland, $357,488. To provide funding for a sports and recreation hall. 2010.

1822-12 Special Education School of Wuhou District, Chengdu, China, $48,337. To purchase equipment to treat developmentally disabled and autistic children. 2010.

1822-13 Wuxi Charity Hospital, China, $112,060. To purchase equipment for a new rehabilitation centre. 2010.

1822-14 Wuxi Dongjiang Experimental School, Wuxi, China, $86,100. To construct eight indoor badminton courts at Taihu Gym Centre. 2010.

1822-15 Xiangtan Welfare Center, China, $37,300. To purchase physical therapy and fitness equipment for use by disabled and abandoned children. 2010.

1822-16 Yantai Library, Yantai, China, $116,600. To purchase furnishings and equipment to preserve ancient works. 2010.

1822-17 YWCA-England and Wales, Oxford, England, $54,800. To remove a metal extension to the building and construct a brick addition. 2010.

1823

Tri-State International Education Fund, Inc.

300 Carew Twr.
441 Vine St.
Cincinnati, OH 45201 (513) 579-3150
Contact: Barry Scott Myers

Established in 1991.

Grantmaker type: Public charity.

Financial data (yr. ended 03/31/10): Revenue, $108,739; assets, $103,674 (M); gifts received, $89,750; expenditures, $116,883; giving activities include $100,500 for grants.

Purpose and activities: The fund seeks to collect and disperse funds to promote international issues in elementary and secondary schools in the greater Cincinnati metropolitan area.

Fields of interest: Elementary/secondary education; International studies.

Limitations: Applications not accepted. Giving primarily in the greater Cincinnati, OH, area.

Application information: Contributes only to pre-selected organizations.

Officers and Trustees:* Junichiro Morita,* Chair.; Kazuhiro Fukuda,* Treas.; Katsuhiro Harada; Seiichi Matsui; Kazunari Matsunami; Takahiro Morooka; Takashi Narushima; Kiyoshi Shima; Toshiyuki

Sotojima; Nobuyuki Suguyama; Keizo Takeuchi; Hiroyuki Uoi.
EIN: 311328977

1824
The Veale Foundation
(formerly V and V Foundation)
30195 Chagrin Blvd., Ste. 310-N
Pepper Pike, OH 44124-5703

Established in 1965 in OH.
Donors: Tinkham Veale II; Harriet Ernst Veale†.
Grantmaker type: Independent foundation.
Financial data (yr. ended 12/31/10): Assets, $39,782,287 (M); expenditures, $2,001,703; qualifying distributions, $1,842,700; giving activities include $1,842,700 for 44 grants (high: $625,000; low: $2,500).
Fields of interest: Human services; Elementary/secondary education; Higher education; Education; Health care; International affairs, foreign policy; United Ways and Federated Giving Programs; Christian agencies & churches.
Type of support: General/operating support.
Limitations: Applications not accepted. Giving primarily in OH, with emphasis on Cleveland. No grants to individuals.
Application information: Contributes only to pre-selected organizations.
  Board meeting date(s): Sept. and Dec.
Trustees: Daniel P. Harrington; John Kennedy; Jane Kober; Tinkham Veale II.
Number of staff: 1 part-time professional.
EIN: 346565830

OKLAHOMA

1825
Blessings International
5881 S. Garnett Rd.
Tulsa, OK 74146-6848 (918) 250-8101
FAX: (918) 250-1281; E-mail: info@blessing.org;
URL: http://www.blessing.org

Established in 1981.
Grantmaker type: Public charity.
Financial data (yr. ended 08/31/10): Revenue, $39,023,841; assets, $20,551,595 (M); gifts received, $35,821,999; expenditures, $41,333,019; giving activities include $545,603 for grants, and $38,392,074 for grants to organizations outside the U.S.
Purpose and activities: The organization serves as a source of pharmaceuticals, vitamins, and medical supplies for clinics and hospitals in developing nations that serve indigent populations, and short-term medical teams that travel to such sites to provide donated medical services.
Fields of interest: Health care.
International interests: Developing countries.
Type of support: Grants to individuals.
Limitations: Giving on an international basis, primarily in developing nations.
Publications: Annual report.
Officers and Directors:* Harold C. Harder,* Ph.D., Pres.; Chisoo Choi,* M.D., V.P.; Linda J. Harder,*

Secy.; Sharon C. Blaho,* Treas.; William Mast, M.D.; Paul McClendon, Ph.D.; John E. Merriman, M.D.; Leslie Pierce; Roger Youmans, M.D.
EIN: 731130590

1826
Broken Arrow Medical Center Foundation
P.O. Box 470372
Tulsa, OK 74147-0372
Contact: W.R. Lissau, Pres.

Established in 1998 in OK.
Grantmaker type: Independent foundation.
Financial data (yr. ended 12/31/10): Assets, $5,115,114 (M); expenditures, $240,957; qualifying distributions, $237,000; giving activities include $237,000 for 6 grants (high: $162,000; low: $5,000).
Purpose and activities: Giving primarily to local Catholic healthcare facilities; funding also for community services.
Fields of interest: Catholic agencies & churches; Performing arts, theater; Hospitals (general); Reproductive health, prenatal care; Health organizations, association; Alzheimer's disease research; Youth, services; International affairs, goodwill promotion; Community/economic development.
Limitations: Giving primarily in Broken Arrow and Tulsa, OK. No grants to individuals.
Application information: Application form not required.
  Initial approach: Lottor
  Copies of proposal: 1
  Deadline(s): None
Officers and Directors:* W.R. Lissau,* Pres.; J. Henry, Jr.,* V.P.; D.B. Whitehill,* Secy.; M.A. Buntz,* Treas.; J.H. Beavers; R.L. Carr; S.I. Graham; J. Neely.
EIN: 731532494

1827
Crio Ministries Evangelistic Association, Inc.
c/o Ronald N. Hesser
5905 Witteville Dr.
Poteau, OK 74953-1947
URL: http://www.crioministries.org

Established in OK.
Donors: Ronald N. Hesser; George Ollie; Bob Kanak; Linda Kanak.
Grantmaker type: Operating foundation.
Financial data (yr. ended 12/31/10): Assets, $10,678 (M); gifts received, $266,390; expenditures, $268,989; qualifying distributions, $268,388; giving activities include $220,979 for 2 + grants.
Purpose and activities: Giving to support member evangelists, assist in planting churches (buying property, buildings, and sound equipment), provide leadership training and developmental resources, and provide social services to orphans, widows and the poor.
Fields of interest: Christian agencies & churches; Elementary/secondary education.
International interests: Africa.
Type of support: Building/renovation; Land acquisition; Scholarship funds.
Limitations: Applications not accepted. No grants to individuals.

Application information: Contributes only to pre-selected organizations.
Officers: Ronald N. Hesser, Pres.; Curtis B. Hesser, V.P.; Hillary Grantham, Secy.-Treas.
Board Members: Reggie Goodin; Glenn Quirk; Leanne Robertson.
EIN: 731579626

1828
Devon Energy Corporation Contributions Program
c/o Community Rels.
20 N. Broadway
Oklahoma City, OK 73102-8260
(405) 235-3611
Contact: Christina Rehkop
FAX: (405) 552-4550;
E-mail: christina.rehkop@dvn.com; For organizations located in Canada: Paula King, e-mail: paula.king@dvn.com; URL: http://www.dvn.com/CommunityRelations/Pages/Overview.aspx

Grantmaker type: Corporate giving program.
Purpose and activities: Devon Energy makes charitable contributions to nonprofit organizations involved with arts and culture, education, health, the environment, youth development, emergency response, human services, community development, and civic affairs. Support is given primarily in areas of significant company operations in Louisiana, Montana, New Mexico, Oklahoma, Texas, Utah, and Wyoming, and in Canada.
Fields of interest: Public affairs; Science, formal/general education; Human services; Youth development; Community/economic development; Disasters, preparedness/services; Health care; Environment; Education; Arts.
International interests: Canada.
Type of support: Program development; Curriculum development; Employee volunteer services; Sponsorships; In-kind gifts.
Limitations: Applications accepted. Giving primarily in areas of significant company operations in LA, MT, NM, OK, TX, UT, and WY, and in Canada. No support for religious or political organizations, fraternal or partisan organizations, or disease-specific organizations. No grants to individuals, or for team sports, or sporting events.
Application information: Application form required.
  Initial approach: Complete online application form

1829
Love Without Boundaries Foundation
306 S. Bryant, Ste. C-145
PMB 145
Edmond, OK 73034-5620 (405) 216-5837
FAX: (405) 445-7485; E-mail: info@lwbmail.com;
URL: http://www.lovewithoutboundaries.com
Flickr: http://www.flickr.com/photos/43781165@N07/
Organization blog: http://www.lwbstories.com/
Twitter: http://twitter.com/lovewb
YouTube: http://youtube.com/federov9

Established in 2003 in OK.
Grantmaker type: Public charity.
Financial data (yr. ended 12/31/10): Revenue, $1,539,401; assets, $813,221 (M); gifts received, $1,471,975; expenditures, $1,407,836.

Purpose and activities: The foundation's mission is to brighten the lives of orphaned and impoverished children in China.
Fields of interest: Health care; Children, foster care; Nutrition; International relief; Children, services.
International interests: China.
Type of support: In-kind gifts.
Publications: Annual report; Newsletter.
Officers and Board Members:* Paul Duggan,* Chair.; Joe Hampton,* Secy.; Chris Ingoldsby,* Treas.; Amy Eldridge, Exec. Dir.; Ben Glass; Don White.
EIN: 061710161

1830
Charles and Lynn Schusterman Family Foundation

Two W. 2nd St., 20th Fl.
Tulsa, OK   74103-3123   (918) 591-1090
Contact: Sanford "Sandy" R. Cardin, Pres.
FAX: (918) 591-1758; Additional address: Washington, DC Office: 800 8th St. N.W., Washington, DC 2000; URL: http://www.schusterman.org
Blog: http://www.schusterman.org/category/blog
Facebook: http://www.facebook.com/schustermanfamilyfoundation?ref=sgm
Flickr: http://www.flickr.com/photos/schustermanfoundation/
Knowledge Center: http://www.schusterman.org/resources
LinkedIn: http://www.linkedin.com/company/charles-and-lynn-schusterman-family-foundation?goback=.cps_1286207986738_1
Lynn Schusterman's Giving Pledge: http://givingpledge.org/#enter
Multimedia: http://www.schusterman.org/resources/videos-gallery
RSS Feed: http://www.schusterman.org/feed
Twitter-DC: http://www.twitter.com/schustermanfoun
Twitter-Tulsa: http://twitter.com/clsff
YouTube: http://www.youtube.com/user/SchustermanFoun

Established in 1987 in OK.
Donors: Charles Schusterman†; Lynn Schusterman; LJS Revocable Trust.
Grantmaker type: Independent foundation.
Financial data (yr. ended 12/31/09): Assets, $66,063,572 (M); gifts received, $1,050,000; expenditures, $28,623,098; qualifying distributions $28,384,151; giving activities include $27,695,685 for 204 grants (high: $2,689,619; low: $40).
Purpose and activities: The foundation is dedicated to helping the Jewish people flourish by supporting programs throughout the world that spread Jewish living, giving and learning. The foundation also provides assistance to non-sectarian charitable organizations dedicated to enhancing the quality of life in Tulsa, Oklahoma, especially in the areas of education, child development, and community service.
Fields of interest: Arts; Higher education; Education; Health organizations, association; Crime/violence prevention, child abuse; Human services; Children/youth, services; Community/economic development; Jewish federated giving programs; Jewish agencies & synagogues.
International interests: Israel; Ukraine.

Type of support: General/operating support; Continuing support; Annual campaigns; Capital campaigns; Building/renovation; Emergency funds; Program development; Conferences/seminars; Professorships; Publication; Seed money; Curriculum development; Fellowships; Internship funds; Scholarship funds; Research; Technical assistance; Consulting services; In-kind gifts; Matching/challenge support.
Limitations: Applications not accepted. Giving primarily to nonsectarian organizations in OK; giving on a local, national, and international basis for Jewish organizations. No grants to individuals, or for endowment funds, deficit funds, media based projects, or programs that require expenditure responsibility.
Publications: Grants list.
Application information: Unsolicited requests for funds not accepted.
Officers and Directors:* Lynn Schusterman,* Chair.; Sanford "Sandy" R. Cardin, Pres.; Stacy H. Schusterman,* V.P.; Jerome R. Schusterman, Secy.
Number of staff: 5 full-time professional.
EIN: 731312965
Recent grants for international programs:
1830-1 American Friends of the Israel Museum, New York, NY, $1,500,000. For matching grant for campus renewal project. 2009.
1830-2 American Friends of the Israel Museum, New York, NY, $100,000. For Director's Circle. 2009.
1830-3 American Friends of the Israel Museum, New York, NY, $26,830. For Ulman Project. 2009.
1830-4 American Friends of the Israel Museum, New York, NY, $25,000. For youth program. 2009.
1830-5 American Friends of the Israel Philharmonic Orchestra, New York, NY, $85,000. For keynote program. 2009.
1830-6 American Friends of the Reut Institute, Beverly Hills, CA, $75,000. For strategy and leadership training program of Israel's future policy designers. 2009.
1830-7 American Friends of the Tel Aviv University, New York, NY, $20,000. For the graduate program for teacher training in Jewish Studies. 2009.
1830-8 American Friends of the United Jewish Israel Appeal, Philadelphia, PA, $70,000. For operating support. 2009.
1830-9 American Israel Education Foundation, Washington, DC, $484,600. For PLDP program. 2009.
1830-10 American Jewish Joint Distribution Committee, New York, NY, $81,500. For elderly jews in the FSU. 2009.
1830-11 American Jewish Joint Distribution Committee, New York, NY, $51,500. For Beit Lynn National Coordinator. 2009.
1830-12 American Jewish Joint Distribution Committee, New York, NY, $25,000. For Tevel b'Tzedek. 2009.
1830-13 American Jewish Joint Distribution Committee, New York, NY, $20,620. For increasing capacity of volunteer programs. 2009.
1830-14 American Jewish World Service, New York, NY, $161,000. For alumni service center. 2009.
1830-15 American Jewish World Service, New York, NY, $88,000. For expansion of alternative break program. 2009.
1830-16 American Jewish World Service, New York, NY, $22,000. For expanison of altrenative break program. 2009.

1830-17 American Society for the Protection of Nature in Israel, Great Neck, NY, $65,000. For A Beautiful Israel. 2009.
1830-18 American Society for the Protection of Nature in Israel, Great Neck, NY, $23,000. For Israel Clean-Up Project. 2009.
1830-19 American Zionist Movement, New York, NY, $72,500. For PresenTense Group. 2009.
1830-20 American-Israeli Cooperative Enterprise, Chevy Chase, MD, $1,156,173. For Israel Scholar Development Fund. 2009.
1830-21 American-Israeli Cooperative Enterprise, Chevy Chase, MD, $210,000. For Schusterman Israel Scholar Awards. 2009.
1830-22 American-Israeli Cooperative Enterprise, Chevy Chase, MD, $10,000. For Yarden Fanta-Vagenshtein at Harvard. 2009.
1830-23 Birthright Israel Foundation, New York, NY, $1,250,000. For Birthright NEXT, alumni peer-based Jewish communities in the United States. 2009.
1830-24 Birthright Israel Foundation, New York, NY, $1,000,000. For 2010 support. 2009.
1830-25 Birthright Israel Foundation, New York, NY, $1,000,000. For For Taglit-Birthright subsidies for participants. 2009.
1830-26 Birthright Israel Foundation, New York, NY, $250,000. For Adelson Challenge. 2009.
1830-27 Brandeis University, Waltham, MA, $2,700,000. For Schusterman Center for Israel Studies. 2009.
1830-28 Brandeis University, Waltham, MA, $1,000,000. For Schusterman Center for Israel Studies. 2009.
1830-29 Brandeis University, Waltham, MA, $25,000. For long term evaluation of Birthright Israel applicants. 2009.
1830-30 Central Fund of Israel, New York, NY, $30,000. For Hatch a Match. 2009.
1830-31 FJC, New York, NY, $75,000. For Israeli Art and Culture. 2009.
1830-32 Hillel: The Foundation for Jewish Campus Life, Washington, DC, $32,500. For Israel Amplified. 2009.
1830-33 Israel Center for Excellence Through Education, Chicago, IL, $125,000. For renovation and upgrade. 2009.
1830-34 Israel Center for Excellence Through Education, Chicago, IL, $100,000. For general support. 2009.
1830-35 Israel Center for Excellence Through Education, Chicago, IL, $25,000. To Get the Ball Rolling. 2009.
1830-36 Jewish National Fund, New York, NY, $40,000. For alternative spring break. 2009.
1830-37 Judaism and Democracy Action Alliance of North America, New York, NY, $300,000. For pluralistic educational system. 2009.
1830-38 Judaism and Democracy Action Alliance of North America, New York, NY, $60,000. 2009.
1830-39 Middle East Media Research Institute, Washington, DC, $15,000. For general support. 2009.
1830-40 Moishe House, Oakland, CA, $175,000. 2009.
1830-41 PEF Israel Endowment Funds, New York, NY, $339,068. For New Beginnings Early Childhood Initiative. 2009.
1830-42 PEF Israel Endowment Funds, New York, NY, $65,000. For prevention of shaken baby syndrome campaign. 2009.
1830-43 PEF Israel Endowment Funds, New York, NY, $60,000. For Hatch a Match. 2009.

1830-44 PEF Israel Endowment Funds, New York, NY, $25,000. For children at risk mentoring and tutorial project. 2009.

1830-45 PEF Israel Endowment Funds, New York, NY, $20,000. For Compassion Worshop National Expansion. 2009.

1830-46 PEF Israel Endowment Funds, New York, NY, $20,000. For operating support. 2009.

1830-47 PEF Israel Endowment Funds, New York, NY, $20,000. For training for early childhood teachers for screen for children at risk of abuse. 2009.

1830-48 PEF Israel Endowment Funds, New York, NY, $12,500. For compassion workshop. 2009.

1830-49 Schusterman Foundation - Israel, Jerusalem, Israel, $2,689,619. For grants. 2009.

1830-50 Schusterman Foundation - Israel, Jerusalem, Israel, $687,840. For administrative support. 2009.

1830-51 University of California, Oakland, CA, $20,000. For study abroad in Israel. 2009.

1830-52 Washington Institute for Near East Policy, Washington, DC, $53,600. For Schusterman Research Assistant and Internship Program. 2009.

1830-53 World Union for Progressive Judaism, Jerusalem, Israel, $51,975. For roof repairs. 2009.

1831
The Maxine and Jack Zarrow Family Foundation

(formerly The Maxine and Jack Zarrow Foundation)
c/o Zarrow Family Office, LLC
401 S. Boston Ave., Ste. 900
Tulsa, OK 74103-4012   (918) 295-8004
Contact: Bill Major, Exec. Dir.
FAX: (918) 295-8049; *E-mail:* jgillert@zarrow.com;
URL: http://www.zarrow.com/mjz.htm

Established in 1988 in OK.
Donor: Jack C. Zarrow†.
Grantmaker type: Independent foundation.
Financial data (yr. ended 12/31/10): Assets, $44,088,484 (M); expenditures, $2,111,806; qualifying distributions, $1,886,317; giving activities include $1,886,317 for 190 grants (high: $500,000; low: $75).
Purpose and activities: The foundation is committed to helping support education, social services, Jewish causes, health programs, medical research and mental health programs. The foundation is also very interested in helping to provide food, clothing, and shelter for the challenged, disadvantaged and homeless, with a geographical preference for the Tulsa, OK, area.
Fields of interest: Foundations (community); Museums; Higher education; Health care; Mental health/crisis services; Health organizations, association; Human services; Jewish agencies & synagogues.
Type of support: General/operating support; Program development.
Limitations: Applications accepted. Giving primarily in the Tulsa, OK, area.
Application information: See foundation web site for application requirements. Proposals received after due date will be held until next quarter's meeting. Application form required.
Initial approach: Use online grant application

Deadline(s): Jan. 15, Apr. 15, Aug. 15, and Oct. 15
Board meeting date(s): Quarterly in Feb., May, Sept., and Nov.
Officers and Trustees:* Eric Richards,* Pres.; Gail Richards,* V.P. and Secy.; Scott F. Zarrow,* V.P. and Treas.; Rebecca Richards,* V.P.; Maxine Zarrow,* V.P.; Bill Major, Exec. Dir.
Number of staff: 1 full-time professional.
EIN: 316640903
Recent grants for international programs:

1831-1 American Jewish Joint Distribution Committee, New York, NY, $100,000. For The Plight of Jews in Belarus: Providing Critical Welfare Support to Impoverished Elderly Jews and Children at Risk. 2010.

1831-2 PEF Israel Endowment Funds, New York, NY, $40,000. For providing a menu of Therapeutic and Rehabilitative Assistance to the severely mentally challenged residents at the Gan-Or Daycare Center near the coastal city of Haifa. 2010.

1831-3 PEF Israel Endowment Funds, New York, NY, $20,000. For Enosh Family Counseling Centers — Providing Supportive Intervention Programs for Families of Mentally Ill Individuals. 2010.

1831-4 PEF Israel Endowment Funds, New York, NY, $10,000. For LOTEM: Mother Nature: A Program for Battered Women and Children. 2010.

1831-5 PEF Israel Endowment Funds, New York, NY, $10,000. For Na Lagaat Organization - New Theater Production The Ball, Performed by Deaf-blind, Deaf and Blind Actors. 2010.

1832
The Anne and Henry Zarrow Foundation

401 S. Boston Ave., Ste. 900
Tulsa, OK 74103-4012   (918) 295-8004
Contact: Bill Major, Exec. Dir.
FAX: (918) 295-8049; *E-mail:* Bmajor@zarrow.com;
URL: http://www.zarrow.com/ahz.htm

Established in 1986 in OK.
Donor: Henry H. Zarrow.
Grantmaker type: Independent foundation.
Financial data (yr. ended 12/31/10): Assets, $94,522,168 (M); gifts received, $5,002,350; expenditures, $7,822,526; qualifying distributions, $7,396,616; giving activities include $7,396,616 for 481 grants (high: $1,000,000; low: $150).
Purpose and activities: Giving primarily for education, social services, Jewish causes, health programs, medical research and mental health programs. The foundation is also very interested in helping to provide food, clothing, and shelter for the challenged, disadvantaged and homeless. The foundation also funds scholarships at selected universities in OK.
Fields of interest: Arts; Education; Health care; Human services; Aging, centers/services; United Ways and Federated Giving Programs; Disabilities, people with.
Type of support: General/operating support; Annual campaigns; Scholarship funds.
Limitations: Applications accepted. Giving primarily in the Tulsa, OK, area. No grants to individuals.
Publications: Application guidelines.
Application information: See foundation's web site for detailed application information and guidelines.The foundation will no longer take scholarship applications from students who are not already receiving scholarship assistance from the foundation. Application form not required.

Initial approach: Letter
Copies of proposal: 1
Deadline(s): Jan. 15, Apr. 15, Aug. 15, and Oct. 15 for grants.
Board meeting date(s): Feb., Apr., Sept., and Nov.
Officers and Directors:* Judith Z. Kishner,* Pres.; Stuart A. Zarrow,* V.P.; Henry H. Zarrow, Secy.; Bill Major, Exec. Dir.; Julie W. Cohen; Jay Wohlgemuth; Dr. Edward Zarrow.
Number of staff: 1 full-time professional; 2 part-time professional.
EIN: 731286874
Recent grants for international programs:

1832-1 American Jewish Joint Distribution Committee, New York, NY, $100,000. For The Plight of Jews in Belarus: Providing Critical Welfare Support to Impoverished Elderly Jews and Children at Risk. 2010.

1832-2 American Jewish World Service, New York, NY, $15,000. For Haiti. 2010.

1832-3 Dillon International, Tulsa, OK, $25,000. For Heritage Camps for Internationally Adopted Children and Parenting Education Workshops for Adoptive Parents. 2010.

1832-4 Doctors Without Borders USA, New York, NY, $15,000. For Aid for Haiti. 2010.

1832-5 Habitat for Humanity, Dallas Area, Dallas, TX, $500,000. For the disaster that struck Haiti on January 12th, Habitat is initiating plans to build new homes, as well as Habitat Resource Centers. 2010.

1832-6 PEF Israel Endowment Funds, New York, NY, $30,000. For Galila - the Northern Galilee Development Foundation for the Holocaust Survivors program of the Association of Concentration Camp and Ghetto Survivors in Israel. 2010.

1832-7 PEF Israel Endowment Funds, New York, NY, $25,000. For Amutat Misgav Hagalil for the Nitzanim - Special Needs Children's Center. 2010.

1832-8 PEF Israel Endowment Funds, New York, NY, $25,000. For Matan - Your Way to Give for Tesafchin - the Association for the Integration of Ethiopian Youth - Ethiopian Toddlers and Tutors Program. 2010.

1832-9 PEF Israel Endowment Funds, New York, NY, $25,000. For The Summit Institute program for Recruitment and Training Foster Parents Project for the placement of children at high risk. 2010.

OREGON

1833
Alima Cosmetics, Inc. Corporate Giving Program

18342 SE River Rd.
Portland, OR 97267-6026   (503) 786-8224
URL: http://www.alimapure.com
B Corporation Profile: http://www.bcorporation.net/alimapure

Grantmaker type: Corporate giving program.
Purpose and activities: Alima Cosmetics is a certified B Corporation that donates a percentage of net profits to nonprofit organizations. Special emphasis is directed toward organizations involved with the environment. Support is given on a national

and international basis, with some emphasis on Portland, Oregon.

Fields of interest: International human rights; Environment, toxics; Environment; Women.

Type of support: Continuing support.

Limitations: Giving on a national and international basis, with some emphasis on Portland, OR.

1834
Franklin Conklin Foundation
6015 N.W. Rosewood Dr.
Corvallis, OR 97330-9567

Established in 1997 in OR.

Grantmaker type: Independent foundation.

Financial data (yr. ended 12/31/10): Assets, $4,681,082 (M); expenditures, $274,087; qualifying distributions, $258,025; giving activities include $257,000 for 40 grants (high: $27,500; low: $500).

Fields of interest: Civil/human rights, advocacy; International affairs; Public affairs; Education; Human services.

Limitations: Applications not accepted. Giving on a national basis, with some emphasis on Washington, DC, MA, NY, and OR. No grants to individuals.

Application information: Unsolicited requests for funds not accepted.

Officers: Harold H. Demarest, Jr., Pres.; David P. Demarest, V.P.; Frank C. Demarest, Secy.; Anne Demarest Taft, Treas.

EIN: 911844877

1835
Evergreen Humanitarian & Relief Services, Inc.
3850 Three Mile Ln.
McMinnville, OR 97128-9402 (503) 472-9361
Contact: A. Blythe Berselli, Pres.
FAX: (503) 472-1048; E-mail: info@ehrsi.org;
URL: http://www.ehrsi.org

Grantmaker type: Public charity.

Financial data (yr. ended 12/31/10): Revenue, $577; assets, $9,747 (M); gifts received, $577; expenditures, $427.

Purpose and activities: The organization supports local and international humanitarian and relief projects.

Fields of interest: International relief; Medical research.

Type of support: Research.

Limitations: Giving on a national and international basis.

Officers: Delford M. Smith, Chair.; A. Blythe Berselli, Pres.; Gwenna R. Wootress, Secy.; John A. Irwin, Treas.

EIN: 400001619

1836
Fohs Foundation
P.O. Box 1001
Roseburg, OR 97470-0232
Contact: Howard Sohn, Exec. Dir.; Jami Seal, Secy.-Treas.

Established in 1937 in NY.

Donors: F. Julius Fohs†; Cora B. Fohs†; Fred & Frances Sohn Charitable Lead Trust.

Grantmaker type: Independent foundation.

Financial data (yr. ended 12/31/10): Assets, $15,746,110 (M); gifts received, $303,544; expenditures, $896,332; qualifying distributions, $641,739; giving activities include $545,000 for 18 grants (high: $75,000; low: $5,000).

Purpose and activities: Giving to ensure the viability of a Jewish homeland in Israel by improving relations between the Jewish majority and Arab minority within the state.

Fields of interest: Education; Civil/human rights; Community/economic development; Social sciences, research; Public affairs; Jewish agencies & synagogues; Minorities; Economically disadvantaged.

International interests: Israel.

Type of support: General/operating support; Income development; Management development/capacity building; Program development; Seed money; Curriculum development; Research.

Limitations: Giving primarily in the U.S. and Israel. No support for programs that do not address majority-minority issues in Israel.

Application information: Generally does not accept unsolicited requests for funds. Application form not required.

> *Initial approach:* Letter
> *Copies of proposal:* 1
> *Deadline(s):* Mar. 31
> *Board meeting date(s):* Apr. or May
> *Final notification:* Varies

Officers: Frances F. Sohn, Chair.; Howard F. Sohn, Vice-Chair.; Jami Seal, Secy.-Treas.

Trustees: Frances Sohn; Fred Sohn; Ruth Sohn; Barbara Tint.

Number of staff: 1 part-time support.

EIN: 746003165

1837
Foreign Mission Foundation
10875 S.W. 89th St.
Tigard, OR 97223-8323
Contact: Gene Davis

Established around 1982 in OR.

Donors: Eugene L. Davis; Miriam Larson; Harold Kent; JoAnn Kent; Joanne Kendall; John Cooner; Harry Lloyd Charitable Trust; GTI Services, Inc.; Living Water Foundation; NW Christian Community Foundation; Synergy Resource Group; Synergy Resource Group; WF Foundation.

Grantmaker type: Independent foundation.

Financial data (yr. ended 02/28/11): Assets, $6,678,773 (M); gifts received, $141,079; expenditures, $805,892; qualifying distributions, $391,637; giving activities include $391,637 for grants.

Purpose and activities: Giving primarily for missionary programs in the U.S. and India.

Fields of interest: Elementary/secondary education; Christian agencies & churches; Religion.

International interests: India.

Limitations: Applications not accepted. Giving primarily in India; some funding in the U.S. No grants to individuals.

Application information: Contributes only to pre-selected organizations.

Officers and Directors:* Eugene L. Davis,* Pres.; Vivian Davis,* Secy.; Don Chapman; George Hughes; Robert Waymire.

Number of staff: 1 full-time professional; 1 part-time professional.

EIN: 930763215

1838
The Grass Foundation
P.O. Box 3101
Eugene, OR 97403-0101 (541) 346-3540
Contact: Sylvie Spengler
FAX: (541) 346-4548;
E-mail: info@grassfoundation.org; URL: http://www.grassfoundation.org

Incorporated in 1957 in MA.

Donors: Albert M. Grass†; Ellen R. Grass†; Grass Instrument Co.; Cannon Manufacturing Co.; The Ellen R. Grass Trust.

Grantmaker type: Independent foundation.

Financial data (yr. ended 12/31/10): Assets, $20,090,928 (M); gifts received, $500; expenditures, $911,178; qualifying distributions, $759,825; giving activities include $332,753 for 10 grants (high: $100,000; low: $100), and $287,937 for foundation-administered programs.

Purpose and activities: Giving to encourage research in neurophysiology and the neurosciences; grants primarily for fellowships for summer study at a marine biological laboratory, lectureships, and for higher education.

Fields of interest: Marine science; Biology/life sciences; Biomedicine; Medical research; Neuroscience.

International interests: Africa; Latin America.

Type of support: Fellowships; Research.

Limitations: Applications accepted. Giving primarily in the U.S., with emphasis on Woods Hole, MA; some funding internationally.

Publications: Application guidelines; Informational brochure (including application guidelines); Program policy statement.

Application information: Application formats and deadlines depend upon type of grant; specific information will be sent upon request. Application guidelines and form are available on foundation web site. Application form required.

> *Initial approach:* Refer to foundation web site
> *Board meeting date(s):* Jan. and July

Officers and Trustees:* Janis C. Weeks,* Ph.D., Pres.; Bernice Grafstein,* Ph.D., V.P.; Henry J. Grass,* M.D., Clerk; Richard Larkin,* C.P.A., Treas.; Shelley Adamo, Ph.D.; Catherine E. Carr, Ph.D.; Graeme W. Davis, Ph.D; Henry J. Grass, M.D.; Ronald R. Hoy, Ph.D.; Darcy B. Kelley, Ph.D; Kamran Khodakhah, Ph.D.; Jeffrey Noebels, M.D., Ph.D.; Amy R. Segal, Esq.; Steven J. Zottoli, Ph.D.

Number of staff: 2 part-time support.

EIN: 046049529

1839
Intel Foundation
2111 NE 25th Ave., JF3-165
Hillsboro, OR 97124-6497
Contact: Wendy Ramage Hawkins, Exec. Dir.
FAX: (503) 254-3913;
E-mail: intel.foundation@intel.com; Additional E-mail for Wendy Ramage Hawkins: wendy.hawkins@intel.com; E-mail for Intel Schools of Distinction: schoolsofdistinction@ce.uoregon.edu; URL: http://www.intel.com/intel/foundation/; CSR@Intel: http://blogs.intel.com/csr/; Intel International Science and Engineering Fair Winners: http://www.intel.com/about/corporateresponsibility/education/isef/winners.htm

Intel Schools of Distinction Winners: http://www.intel.com/about/corporateresponsibility/education/soda/winners.htm
Intel Science Talent Search Winners: http://www.intel.com/about/corporateresponsibility/education/sts/winners.htm

Established in 1988 in OR.
Donors: Intel Corp.; Intel Capital Corp.
Grantmaker type: Company-sponsored foundation.
Financial data (yr. ended 12/31/10): Assets, $56,991,245 (M); gifts received, $31,000,000; expenditures, $48,726,165; qualifying distributions, $48,242,053; giving activities include $46,539,084 for grants, and $1,569,390 for employee matching gifts.
Purpose and activities: The foundation supports organizations that help to advance education and improve communities worldwide. Special emphasis is directed toward programs that promote innovation in classrooms; empower women and underserved youth; enable Intel employees to serve the needs of their communities; and increase interest in math, science, and engineering education.
Fields of interest: Disasters, preparedness/services; Elementary/secondary education; Elementary/secondary school reform; Higher education; Higher education, college; Engineering school/education; Education; Science, formal/general education; Mathematics; Science; Youth; Minorities; African Americans/Blacks; Hispanics/Latinos; Native Americans/American Indians; Women.
Type of support: General/operating support; Program development; Curriculum development; Fellowships; Scholarship funds; Employee volunteer services; Sponsorships; Employee matching gifts; Matching/challenge support.
Limitations: Applications accepted. Giving primarily in Phoenix, AZ, Folsom and Santa Clara, CA, Hudson, MA, Albuquerque, NM, Portland, OR, and DuPont, WA; Sao Paulo, Brazil, San Jose, Costa Rica, Israel, Taiwan, and Istanbul, Turkey; limited giving to select national organizations. No support for religious, sectarian, fraternal, or political organizations, arts or health care organizations, environmental organizations, private schools, or sports teams. No grants to individuals (except for fellowships and scholarships), or for endowments, capital campaigns, general fund drives, annual campaigns, fundraising events, sporting events, television or radio production costs, creation of personal/organization websites, travel or tours, or equipment.
Publications: Application guidelines; Corporate giving report.
Application information: Unsolicited applications for general grants are not accepted. Applications are only accepted from K-12 schools for Intel Schools of Distinction. Application form required.
   Initial approach: Complete online application for Intel Schools of Distinction
   Deadline(s): Sept. 15 to Feb. 17 for Intel Schools of Distinction
   Board meeting date(s): Semiannually
   Final notification: Apr. for Intel Schools of Distinction
Officers and Directors:* Richard Taylor, Chair.; Shelly Esque, Pres.; Suzan A. Miller, Secy.; Ravi Jacob, Treas.; Wendy Ramage Hawkins,* Exec. Dir.; Deborah Conrad; Justin Rattner.
Number of staff: 2 part-time professional; 1 full-time support.
EIN: 943092928

Recent grants for international programs:
1839-1 Alona Memorial Elementary School, General Trias, Philippines, $18,990. 2009.
1839-2 American Red Cross National Headquarters, Washington, DC, $45,500. For Typhoon Ketsana relief matching program. 2009.
1839-3 American Red Cross National Headquarters, Washington, DC, $45,500. For Typhoon Ketsana relief matching program. 2009.
1839-4 APM, Fundacao Liberato, Novo Hamburgo, Brazil, $20,000. For Brazil science fair. 2009.
1839-5 APM, Fundacao Liberato, Novo Hamburgo, Brazil, $20,000. For Brazil science fair. 2009.
1839-6 Arab Science and Technology Foundation, Sharjah, United Arab Emirates, $80,000. For Arab Technology Business Plan Competition. 2009.
1839-7 Arab Science and Technology Foundation, Sharjah, United Arab Emirates, $80,000. For Arab Technology Business Plan Competition. 2009.
1839-8 Argentina Ministry of Education, Buenos Aires, Argentina, $20,000. For Argentina National Science Fair Program. 2009.
1839-9 Argentina Ministry of Education, Buenos Aires, Argentina, $20,000. For Argentina National Science Fair Program. 2009.
1839-10 Asociacion de Voluntarios pare el Servicio en las Areas Protegidas, San Jose, Costa Rica, $10,736. 2009.
1839-11 Asociacion Empresarial para el Desarrollo, San Jose, Costa Rica, $15,770. For Costa Rica earthquake relief. 2009.
1839-12 Asociacion Empresarial para el Desarrollo, San Jose, Costa Rica, $15,770. For Costa Rica earthquake relief. 2009.
1839-13 Associacao do Laboratorio de Sistemas Integraveis Tecnologica, Sao Paulo, Brazil, $20,000. For Science Fair. 2009.
1839-14 Associacao do Laboratorio de Sistemas Integraveis Tecnologico, Sao Paulo, Brazil, $20,000. For Science Fair. 2009.
1839-15 Association for Indias Development, Beaverton, OR, $10,000. 2009.
1839-16 Autonomous Organization IT Training Centre, Novosibirsk, Russia, $55,000. For Intel Learn, program to help youth ages 8-16 develop 21st century skills, with focus on digital literacy, critical thinking, problem solving and collaboration. 2009.
1839-17 Autonomous Organization IT Training Centre, Novosibirsk, Russia, $55,000. For Intel Learn, program to help youth ages 8-16 develop 21st century skills, with focus on digital literacy, critical thinking, problem solving and collaboration. 2009.
1839-18 Bangalore Medical Services Trust, Bangalore, India, $13,796. 2009.
1839-19 Beijing University, Department of Education Technology, Graduate School of Education, Beijing, China, $10,000. For TE Web Curriculum. 2009.
1839-20 Bilge Adam, Istanbul, Turkey, $60,000. For Intel Learn, program to help youth ages 8-16 develop 21st century skills, with focus on digital literacy, critical thinking, problem solving and collaboration. 2009.
1839-21 Bilge Adam, Istanbul, Turkey, $60,000. For Intel Learn, program to help youth ages 8-16 develop 21st century skills, with focus on digital literacy, critical thinking, problem solving and collaboration. 2009.
1839-22 Bilge Adam, Istanbul, Turkey, $30,000. For Intel Learn, program to help youth ages 8-16

develop 21st century skills, with focus on digital literacy, critical thinking, problem solving and collaboration. 2009.
1839-23 Bilge Adam, Istanbul, Turkey, $30,000. For Intel Learn, program to help youth ages 8-16 develop 21st century skills, with focus on digital literacy, critical thinking, problem solving and collaboration. 2009.
1839-24 Bradesco Foundation, Brazil, $20,000. For Intel Learn, program to help youth ages 8-16 develop 21st century skills, with focus on digital literacy, critical thinking, problem solving and collaboration. 2009.
1839-25 Bradesco Foundation, Brazil, $20,000. For Intel Learn, program to help youth ages 8-16 develop 21st century skills, with focus on digital literacy, critical thinking, problem solving and collaboration. 2009.
1839-26 Buenavista Elementary School, General Trias, Philippines, $14,062. 2009.
1839-27 Bulgarian Institute for Management and Technology, Sofia, Bulgaria, $80,000. For NOVATech Competition. 2009.
1839-28 Bulgarian Institute for Management and Technology, Sofia, Bulgaria, $80,000. For NOVATech Competition. 2009.
1839-29 Bureau of Jail Management and Penology, General Trias, Philippines, $15,008. 2009.
1839-30 Cats Aid, Dublin, Ireland, $10,000. 2009.
1839-31 Childrens Hospital Costa Rica Foundation, San Jose, Costa Rica, $16,808. 2009.
1839-32 China Association for Science and Technology, Beijing, China, $233,000. For Intel Learn program. 2009.
1839-33 China Association for Science and Technology, Beijing, China, $75,000. For School of Distinction Award (SODA) Program In China. 2009.
1839-34 China Association for Science and Technology, Children and Youth Science Center, Beijing, China, $202,000. For Intel Learn, program to help youth ages 8-16 develop 21st century skills, with focus on digital literacy, critical thinking, problem solving and collaboration. 2009.
1839-35 China Association for Science and Technology, Children and Youth Science Center, Beijing, China, $202,000. For Intel Learn, program to help youth ages 8-16 develop 21st century skills, with focus on digital literacy, critical thinking, problem solving and collaboration. 2009.
1839-36 China Association for Science and Technology, Children and Youth Science Center, Beijing, China, $90,000. For CAST-C. 2009.
1839-37 Ciencia Joven, Puebla, Mexico, $30,000. For National Science Fair. 2009.
1839-38 Clane Gaelic Athletic Association, Clane, Ireland, $10,470. 2009.
1839-39 Clane Rugby Club, Clane, Ireland, $13,240. 2009.
1839-40 Clane United Football Club, Clane, Ireland, $11,720. 2009.
1839-41 Corporacion Encuentro, Chile, $69,985. For Intel Learn, program to help youth ages 8-16 develop 21st century skills, with focus on digital literacy, critical thinking, problem solving and collaboration. 2009.
1839-42 Cumann Luthchleas Gael Na Fianna, Dublin, Ireland, $10,000. 2009.
1839-43 Direccion de Innovacion, Ciencia y Tecnologia para el Desarrollo, Montevideo, Uruguay, $10,000. For National Science Fair Sponsorship. 2009.

1839-44 Eco-Watch, Bangalore, India, $25,000. 2009.

1839-45 Fundacion CRUSA, San Jose, Costa Rica, $50,000. For Strengthening the ISEF (International Science and Engineering Fair) path. 2009.

1839-46 Fundacion Evolucion, Buenos Aires, Argentina, $30,000. For Intel Learn, program to help youth ages 8-16 develop 21st century skills, with focus on digital literacy, critical thinking, problem solving and collaboration. 2009.

1839-47 Fundacion Feria Nacional de Ciencia y Tecnologia de Colombia, Bogota, Colombia, $10,000. For First National Science Faire - FENCYT Intel Awards. 2009.

1839-48 Fundacion Paniamor, San Jose, Costa Rica, $13,000. For SW Refresh Intel Computer Clubhouse - Costa Rica. 2009.

1839-49 Fundacion para la Sostenibilidad y la Equidad, San Jose, Costa Rica, $10,748. 2009.

1839-50 General Trias Municipal Social Welfare and Development Office, Training and Productivity Center, General Trias, Philippines, $13,596. 2009.

1839-51 Getulio Vargas Foundation, Rio de Janeiro, Brazil, $60,000. For 4th GV Intel Challenge. 2009.

1839-52 GlobalGiving Foundation, Washington, DC, $10,300. For Italy earthquake relief. 2009.

1839-53 Good Friend Mission, Taipei, Taiwan, $10,000. For SW Refresh - Taiwan. 2009.

1839-54 Governor Ferrer Memorial National High School, Biclatan Annex, General Trias, Philippines, $17,168. 2009.

1839-55 Help Them Grow, VIBHA, Sunnyvale, CA, $10,000. 2009.

1839-56 Inquiry Facilitators, Bernalillo, NM, $30,000. For RoboRave International Program. 2009.

1839-57 IT-Blocks, Cairo, Egypt, $75,000. For Intel Learn program. 2009.

1839-58 IT-Blocks, Cairo, Egypt, $75,000. For Intel Learn program. 2009.

1839-59 Jordanian Hashemite Fund for Human Development, Amman, Jordan, $12,000. For SW Refresh - Jordan. 2009.

1839-60 Kinderzukunft, Grundau-Lieblos, Germany, $15,590. 2009.

1839-61 Kochav David, Kiryat Gat, Israel, $13,580. 2009.

1839-62 Korea Environmental Education Association, Seoul, South Korea, $80,000. For K-12 Green Initiative. 2009.

1839-63 Kreisjugendring Muenchen-Stadt, Munich, Germany, $10,600. 2009.

1839-64 Learning Links Foundation, New Delhi, India, $130,000. For Intel Learn program. 2009.

1839-65 Learning Links Foundation, New Delhi, India, $120,000. For Intel Learn program. 2009.

1839-66 Magen David Adom, Jerusalem, Israel, $25,000. For IIMGP - Magen David Adom Blood Services (Tel Aviv Branch). 2009.

1839-67 Make-A-Wish Foundation Ireland, Dublin, Ireland, $10,600. 2009.

1839-68 Malaysian Red Crescent Society, Kuala Lumpur, Malaysia, $70,000. For Intel Malaysia Gives Back. 2009.

1839-69 Museum of Science, Boston, MA, $50,000. For Teen Summit Global Community impact. 2009.

1839-70 Nan-shan Elementary School of Yilan, Nan-shan Village, Taiwan, $13,120. 2009.

1839-71 National Council for Volunteering in Israel, Tel Aviv, Israel, $25,000. 2009.

1839-72 Neve Yosef Community Center, Haifa, Israel, $15,915. 2009.

1839-73 Nizhny Novgorod Regional Scientific and Technological Small Business Venture Investments Assistance Foundation, Nizhny Novgorod, Russia, $95,000. For IBTEC (Intel + UC Berkeley Technology Entrepreneurship Challenge for youth) - Russia. 2009.

1839-74 Non-Profit Incubator, Shanghai, China, $75,000. For Intel China CSR Award for non-profit capacity. 2009.

1839-75 Northern Star Twirlers, Dublin, Ireland, $16,170. 2009.

1839-76 Parostok Charitable Foundation, Kiev, Ukraine, $15,000. For Ukraine Intel ISEF affiliated fair. 2009.

1839-77 Pasong Camachile Elementary School, General Trias, Philippines, $13,732. 2009.

1839-78 Philippine National Red Cross, Manila, Philippines, $13,334. 2009.

1839-79 Rathdangan Community Council, Rathdangan, Ireland, $20,240. 2009.

1839-80 Russian Federation for Vocational Education, Moscow, Russia, $73,000. For Science Fair. 2009.

1839-81 Saint John of God Kildare Services, Celbridge, Ireland, $22,130. 2009.

1839-82 Salesian Scouts, 19th Kildare, Celbridge, Ireland, $11,710. 2009.

1839-83 Sekolah Jenis Kebangsaan (China) Kelang Lama, Kulim, Malaysia, $16,086. 2009.

1839-84 Sekolah Jenis Kebangsaan (China) Yang Cheng, Bayan Lepas, Malaysia, $37,764. 2009.

1839-85 Sekolah Jenis Kebangsaan (Tamil) Ladang Henrietta, Kulim, Malaysia, $14,130. 2009.

1839-86 Sekolah Jenis Kebangsaan (Tamil) Subramaniya Barathee, Gelugor, Malaysia, $45,656. 2009.

1839-87 Sekolah Kebangsaan Minden Height, Georgetown, Malaysia, $35,280. 2009.

1839-88 Sekolah Kebangsaan Sungai Ular, Kulim, Malaysia, $18,228. 2009.

1839-89 Sekolah Menegah Kebangsaan Lunas, Kulim, Malaysia, $47,162. 2009.

1839-90 Sekolah Menengah Jenis Kebangsaan Chung Hwa Confucian High School, Georgetown, Malaysia, $11,416. 2009.

1839-91 Sekolah Menengah Kebangsaan Bukit Gambir, Bukit Gambir, Malaysia, $30,140. 2009.

1839-92 Sekolah Menengah Kebangsaan Chio Min, Kulim, Malaysia, $58,088. 2009.

1839-93 Sekolah Menengah Kebangsaan Junjong, Kulim, Malaysia, $17,258. 2009.

1839-94 Sekolah Menengah Kebangsaan Raja Tun Uda, Bayan Lepas, Malaysia, $12,198. 2009.

1839-95 Sekolah Menengah Kebangsaan Sungai Kob, Kulim, Malaysia, $13,704. 2009.

1839-96 Sekolah Menengah Kebangsaan Sungai Nibong, Sungai Nibong, Malaysia, $18,698. 2009.

1839-97 Seneschalstown Gaelic Athletic Association Club, Navan, Ireland, $10,440. 2009.

1839-98 Society of Saint Vincent de Paul, Dublin, Ireland, $11,500. 2009.

1839-99 Taiwan Buddhist Tzu Chi Foundation USA, San Dimas, CA, $137,479. For Taiwan Typhoon matching program. 2009.

1839-100 Tapuah-The Israel Society for the Advancement of the Information Age, Tel Aviv, Israel, $200,000. For Intel Learn, program to help youth ages 8-16 develop 21st century skills, with focus on digital literacy, critical thinking, problem solving and collaboration. 2009.

1839-101 Tapuah-The Israel Society for the Advancement of the Information Age, Tel Aviv, Israel, $118,000. For Intel Learn, program to help youth ages 8-16 develop 21st century skills, with focus on digital literacy, critical thinking, problem solving and collaboration. 2009.

1839-102 Tapuah-The Israel Society for the Advancement of the Information Age, Tel Aviv, Israel, $105,000. For Intel Learn, program to help youth ages 8-16 develop 21st century skills, with focus on digital literacy, critical thinking, problem solving and collaboration. 2009.

1839-103 Tapuah-The Israel Society for the Advancement of the Information Age, Tel Aviv, Israel, $104,000. For Intel Learn, program to help youth ages 8-16 develop 21st century skills, with focus on digital literacy, critical thinking, problem solving and collaboration. 2009.

1839-104 Technische Universitaet Muenchen, UnternehmerTUM (Center for Innovation and Business Creation at TUM), Munich, Germany, $42,000. For Business Plan-Seminars. 2009.

1839-105 Tsinghua University, Beijing, China, $65,000. For Tsinghua University Entrepreneurship program. 2009.

1839-106 United Nations Educational, Scientific and Cultural Organization, Brasilia, Brazil, $30,000. For Intel Learn, program to help youth ages 8-16 develop 21st century skills, with focus on digital literacy, critical thinking, problem solving and collaboration. 2009.

1839-107 Universitat des Saarlandes, Competence Center of Computer Science, Saarbrucken, Germany, $106,000. For Intel Visual Computing Conference. 2009.

1839-108 University of Electronic Science and Technology of China, Zhongshan Institute, Chengdu, China, $25,000. 2009.

1839-109 World Vision Taiwan, Taipei, Taiwan, $18,000. 2009.

1839-110 WWF-Malaysia, Petaling Jaya, Malaysia, $10,638. 2009.

1839-111 YouNoodle, San Francisco, CA, $64,192. For LAR Competition. 2009.

1839-112 Zabota, Nizhny Novgorod, Russia, $14,000. For SW Refresh - Russia. 2009.

1840
Kalakendra Society for the Performing Arts of India

16401 S.W. Timberland Dr.
Beaverton, OR 97007-7807
Contact: Satya Narayanan, Pres.
FAX: (503) 645-3915; E-mail: info@kalakendra.org;
URL: http://www.kalakendra.org

Established in 1987 in OR.

Grantmaker type: Public charity.

Financial data (yr. ended 06/30/10): Revenue, $43,181; assets, $34,519 (M); gifts received, $21,488; expenditures, $36,003.

Purpose and activities: The foundation introduces, promotes and enhances awareness of the various performing arts of the Indian subcontinent through presenting concerts, classical dances, recitals and lecture demonstrations.

Fields of interest: Performing arts.

International interests: India.

Type of support: Annual campaigns; Scholarships—to individuals; In-kind gifts.

Limitations: Applications not accepted. Giving primarily in OR.
Application information: Unsolicited requests for funds not considered or acknowledged.
Board meeting date(s): 1st Sun. of each month
Officers and Directors:* Satya Narayanan,* Ph.D., Pres.; Sunanda Sen,* V.P., Membership; Nagendra Tirumali,* V.P., Concerts; Rose Okada,* Secy.; Durgam G. Chakrapani,* Co-Treas.; Mahendra Shah,* Co-Treas.; Steve Amdahl; Mitch Haas; Sathya Narayanan; and 7 additional directors.
EIN: 943044192

1841
KEEN, Inc. Contributions Program
926 N.W. 13th Ave., Ste. 210
Portland, OR 97209-3083

Grantmaker type: Corporate giving program.
Purpose and activities: KEEN partners with environmental, conservation and social organizations, particularly those interested in connecting people with the outdoors.
Fields of interest: International relief; Environmental education; Environment.
Limitations: Giving on an international basis.

1842
The Larson Legacy
14404 S.E. Krause Ln.
Happy Valley, OR 97086-6534 (503) 593-5674
Contact: Leland E.G. Larson, Pres.

Established in 1997 in OR.
Donors: Leland E.G. Larson; Kathleen C. Larson.
Grantmaker type: Independent foundation.
Financial data (yr. ended 12/31/10): Assets, $3,034,259 (M); gifts received, $100,000; expenditures, $240,116; qualifying distributions, $208,866; giving activities include $161,424 for 35 + grants (high: $25,000; low: $180).
Purpose and activities: Giving for the environment, human rights, and civil liberties, thereby creating a more compassionate, kinder world.
Fields of interest: Education; Environment; Human services; International human rights; Civil liberties, advocacy.
Type of support: Annual campaigns.
Limitations: Applications not accepted. Giving primarily on an international basis, with some emphasis on India, as well as in the northwestern U.S., with a focus on CA, OR, and WA. No support for religious organizations.
Publications: Multi-year report.
Application information: Unsolicited requests for funds not accepted.
Board meeting date(s): Annually
Officers: Leland E.G. Larson, Pres.; Kathleen Larson, V.P.; David Larson, Secy.-Treas.
Number of staff: None.
EIN: 911859861

1843
The Lemelson Foundation
45 S.W. Ankeny St., Ste. 200
Portland, OR 97204 (503) 827-8910
E-mail: webmaster@lemelson.org; URL: http://www.lemelson.org/
E-Newsletter: http://lemelson.us1.list-manage.com/subscribe?u=de855f63e59f43c6bce8afdd2&id=eb6afc211b
Facebook: http://www.facebook.com/TheLemelsonFoundation?ref=ts
RSS Feed: http://www.lemelson.org/news/rss.xml
Twitter: http://twitter.com/LemelsonFdn
YouTube: http://www.youtube.com/lemelsonfoundation

Established in 1994 in NV.
Donors: Dorothy Lemelson; Eric Lemelson; Jerome Lemelson†; Robert B. Lemelson.
Grantmaker type: Independent foundation.
Financial data (yr. ended 12/31/09): Assets, $320,780,264 (M); expenditures, $22,263,329; qualifying distributions, $21,796,861; giving activities include $14,486,574 for 89 grants (high: $2,948,825; low: $1,000; average: $10,000–$1,791,221), $118,274 for 4 foundation-administered programs and $525,000 for 3 loans/program-related investments (high: $200,000; low: $125,000).
Purpose and activities: The foundation celebrates and supports inventors and entrepreneurs in order to strengthen social and economic life in the United States and developing countries. The foundation is a private philanthropy established by U.S. inventor Jerome Lemelson, and his family. It uses its resources to inspire, encourage and recognize inventors, innovators and entrepreneurs, with a growing emphasis on those who harness invention for sustainable development where the needs are the greatest.
Fields of interest: Higher education; Economic development; Business/industry; Engineering/technology.
International interests: Developing countries.
Type of support: Program-related investments/loans.
Limitations: Applications not accepted. Giving primarily in the United States and internationally in Africa, Asia and Latin America. No grants to individuals.
Application information: Contributes only to pre-selected organizations.
Officers and Directors:* Dorothy Lemelson,* Chair and Pres.; Robert Lemelson,* Ph.D., V.P. and Secy.; Eric Lemelson,* V.P. and Treas.; Philip Varnum, C.F.O. and C.A.O.; Carol Dahl, Exec. Dir.; Denis J. Prager; Jennifer Bruml Lemelson; Susan Morse.
EIN: 880391959
Recent grants for international programs:
1843-1 Ashoka: Innovators for the Public, Arlington, VA, $95,000. For public relations, online activities and additional travel for Ashoka's global celebration event in India. 2009.
1843-2 Ashoka: Innovators for the Public, Arlington, VA, $30,000. Toward documentary that will air on MTV internationally to spread stories of invention ventures launched through Invent Your World program and inspire more young people to develop invention-based ventures. 2009.
1843-3 Bogor Agricultural University, Bogor, Indonesia, $594,168. To improve Institut Pertanian Bogor's existing university-level technopreneurship curricula, to develop new courses focused on inventions for social

applications and to develop new pre-mentoring program for students. 2009.
1843-4 International Development Enterprises - India, New Delhi, India, $827,744. For creation of Center for Innovation to Impact. 2009.
1843-5 Mahila Housing SEWA Trust, Ahmadabad, India, $450,000. For creation of Innovation Center for the Poor. 2009.
1843-6 Massachusetts Institute of Technology, Cambridge, MA, $30,500. To publish special edition of quarterly journal, Innovations, for Tech4Society's event in Hyderabad, India as part of participation in Ashoka-Lemelson celebration of current fellows. Partnership supports fellows whose work focuses on invention and social entrepreneurship for social good, especially in the developing world. 2009.
1843-7 Mercy Corps, Portland, OR, $10,000. To co-host grand opening of new building. 2009.
1843-8 Sambotha, San Diego, CA, $350,000. To further develop technology and markets for Sambotha's three product lines (Isolyak, Yak Dream and Norlha). 2009.
1843-9 SELCO Solar Light Company, Bangalore, India, $58,128. For pilot project of low-cost solar lighting systems for poor households. 2009.
1843-10 SolarAid, London, England, $265,000. To design, develop prototypes for and test solar LED retrofit kit for kerosene lanterns and low-cost gravity-powered LED light. 2009.
1843-11 Sustainable Harvest, Portland, OR, $600,000. For farmer training, technology dissemination and market link development program in Tanzania. 2009.
1843-12 Villgro, Chennai, India, $2,365,262. To coordinate and lead India Recognition and Mentoring Program (RAMP) in partnership with Indian Institute of Technology, Madras. 2009.
1843-13 Villgro, Chennai, India, $702,000. To coordinate and lead India Recognition and Mentoring Program (RAMP) in partnership with Indian Institute of Technology, Madras. 2009.

1844
McKenzie River Gathering Foundation
(also known as MRG)
2705 E. Burnside, Ste. 210
Portland, OR 97214-1768 (503) 289-1517
Contact: Marjory Hamann, Exec. Dir.
FAX: (503) 232-1731; Toll-free tel.: (800) 489-6743;
URL: http://www.mrgfoundation.org
Facebook: http://www.facebook.com/pages/MRG-Foundation/113047983234
McKenzie River Gathering Foundation's Philanthropy Promise: http://www.ncrp.org/philanthropys-promise/who

Established in 1976 in OR.
Grantmaker type: Public charity.
Financial data (yr. ended 06/30/10): Revenue, $946,794; assets, $6,693,242 (M); gifts received, $794,204; expenditures, $1,534,270; giving activities include $841,011 for grants.
Purpose and activities: The foundation funds Oregon-based organizations that organize people to work for progressive social change. It aims to champion groups that challenge the vast social, economic, and political inequities that exist in society, with the goal of creating a peaceful, just, and environmentally sound world. The foundation's grantmaking focuses on efforts within communities that bring people together to address issues in the following areas: human and civil rights, racial

justice, economic justice, environmental protection, peace, and international solidarity.

Fields of interest: Environment, natural resources; Environment; International peace/security; International affairs; Civil/human rights.

Type of support: General/operating support; Equipment; Program development; Publication; Seed money; Technical assistance.

Limitations: Applications accepted. Giving limited to OR. No support for schools, co-ops, or social services. No grants to individuals.

Publications: Application guidelines; Annual report; Grants list; Informational brochure; Newsletter.

Application information: The foundation requires all new applicants to speak with the foundation staff before submitting an application. Application form not required.

> *Initial approach:* Telephone
> *Copies of proposal:* 17
> *Deadline(s):* Feb. 19 and Sept. 5 for General Funding Cycle Grants; Mar. 21 for Peace Fund; Oct. 12 for Lilla Jewel Award; none for Critical Response or Travel Grants
> *Board meeting date(s):* Bimonthly
> *Final notification:* June 15 and Dec. 15 for General Funding Cycle Grants; June 7 for Peace Fund

Officers and Directors:* Kayse Jama,* Chair.; Chris Winter,* Vice-Chair.; Marcy Middleton,* Secy.; Marjory Hamann, Exec. Dir.; Gil Avery; Ibrahim Hamide; Arbrella Luvert; Suk Rhee; Rich Rohde; Chris Winter; Carole Zoom.

Number of staff: 4 full-time professional; 2 full-time support.

EIN: 930691187

1845
Medical Teams International

(formerly Northwest Medical Teams International)
14150 S.W. Milton Ct.
Tigard, OR 97224-8024   (503) 624-1000
FAX: (503) 624-1001;
E-mail: info@medicalteams.org; Mailing address: P.O. Box 10, Portland, OR 97207-0010;
URL: http://www.medicalteams.org
Facebook: http://www.facebook.com/pages/ Medical-Teams-International/91223411833
RSS Feed: http://www.medicalteams.org/sf/ rss.aspx
Twitter: http://twitter.com/medteams
YouTube: http://www.youtube.com/medicalteams

Grantmaker type: Public charity.

Financial data (yr. ended 06/30/11): Revenue, $142,601,466; assets, $28,814,233 (M); gifts received, $140,993,004; expenditures, $142,552,080; giving activities include $59,559,093 for grants, and $60,681,188 for grants to organizations outside the U.S.

Purpose and activities: The organization's mission is to demonstrate the love of Christ to people affected by disaster, conflict, and poverty.

Fields of interest: International relief; Safety/ disasters; Economically disadvantaged.

Type of support: In-kind gifts.

Limitations: Giving on a national and international basis.

Publications: Annual report; Financial statement.

Officers and Directors:* Bert Waugh,* Chair.; Ron King,* Vice-Chair.; Bas Vanderzalm, Pres.; Pamela Blikstad, V.P., Finance; Bill Essig, V.P., Intl. Progs.; David van Vuuren, V.P., Admin.; Joan Wallace,* Secy.; Don Petersen,* Treas.; Mark Dodson; Gary T. Duim; Paul Hathaway; Ann Klein; Phil Lane; Nate

Miles; Jin Park; Jeff Pinneo; Jeff Rideout; Todd Ulmer; Nancy Wilgenbusch.

EIN: 930878944

1846
Mercy Corps

45 S.W. Ankeny St.
Portland, OR 97204-3504   (503) 896-5000
Contact: Neal Keny-Guyer, C.E.O.
E-mail: info@mercycorps.org; Toll-free tel.: (800) 292-3355; URL: http://www.mercycorps.org
Facebook: http://www.facebook.com/mercycorps
Flickr: http://www.flickr.com/photos/mercycorps
The Mercy Corps Blog: http://www.mercycorps.org/ blog
Twitter: http://twitter.com/mercycorps
YouTube: http://www.youtube.com/mercycorps

Established in 1981 in WA.

Grantmaker type: Public charity.

Financial data (yr. ended 06/30/10): Revenue, $244,942,281; assets, $130,684,971 (M); gifts received, $237,872,770; expenditures, $242,559,032; giving activities include $368,556 for grants, and $72,943,782 for grants to organizations outside the U.S.

Purpose and activities: The organization provides international humanitarian aid and seeks to alleviate suffering, poverty, and oppression by helping people build secure, productive, and just communities.

Fields of interest: AIDS; Health care; Food services; Education; Economic development; International conflict resolution; International affairs; Community/economic development; Agriculture; Safety/disasters; International relief; Migrant workers; Indigenous peoples; Minorities; Economically disadvantaged; Children/youth.

Type of support: Loans—to individuals; Grants to individuals; In-kind gifts.

Limitations: Giving on a worldwide basis.

Publications: Annual report; Financial statement; Informational brochure.

Application information:

> *Board meeting date(s):* Three times each year

Officers and Directors:* Linda A. Mason,* Chair.; Robert D. Newell,* J.D., Vice-Chair. and Treas.; Neal Keny-Guyer,* C.E.O.; Nancy Lindborg, Pres.; George Devendorf, V.P., Global Engagement; Johanna Thoeresz, V.P., Devel.; Shyama Venkateswar, Exec. Dir.; Dr. Jay A. Barber, Jr.; Anita Beckenstein; Scott Brown; Gun Denhart; Phyllis Dobyns; Jock Encombe; Mark Gordon; Allen Grossman; and 8 additional directors.

EIN: 911148123

1847
NIKE Foundation

(formerly NIKE P.L.A.Y. Foundation)
1 Bowerman Dr.
Beaverton, OR 97005-6453   (888) 448-6453
E-mail: nike.foundation@nike.com; URL: http:// nikeinc.com/pages/the-nike-foundation
The Girl Effect on Facebook: http:// www.facebook.com/girleffect
The Girl Effect on Twitter: http://twitter.com/ girleffect
The Girl Effect on YouTube: http:// www.youtube.com/girleffect

Established in 1994 in OR.

Donors: NIKE, Inc.; Michael Jordan; NoVo Foundation.

Grantmaker type: Company-sponsored foundation.

Financial data (yr. ended 05/31/11): Assets, $39,761,379 (M); gifts received, $27,164,207; expenditures, $23,513,239; qualifying distributions, $23,512,332; giving activities include $17,108,276 for 83 grants (high: $1,003,312; low: $5,000).

Purpose and activities: The foundation supports programs designed to empower adolescent girls in the developing world. Special emphasis is directed toward ending early marriage and delaying first birth; ensuring health and safety; secondary school completion and transitions to employment; and expanding direct access to economic assets.

Fields of interest: Microfinance/microlending; Secondary school/education; Education; Health care; Employment; Safety/disasters; Youth development, adult & child programs; Human services, financial counseling; Economic development; Social entrepreneurship; Girls; Economically disadvantaged.

International interests: Africa; Brazil; Developing countries; India.

Type of support: General/operating support; Management development/capacity building; Program development.

Limitations: Applications not accepted. Giving primarily in CA, Washington, DC, NY; giving on an international basis in Africa, Bangladesh, Brazil, India, Kenya, Nigeria, Paraguay, Tanzania, Uganda, and Zambia. No support for discriminatory organizations. No grants to individuals, or for general operating support for established programs, research or travel, films, television, or radio programs not an integral part of a project, religious programs, endowments or fundraising campaigns, lobbying or political activities, or depreciation or debt reduction.

Application information: Contributes only to pre-selected organizations. The foundation utilizes an invitation only Request for Proposal (RFP) process.

Officers and Directors:* Maria S. Eitel,* C.E.O. and Pres.; Howard Taylor, V.P. and Managing Dir.; Donald W. Blair; Jennifer Buffet; Peter Buffet; Charlie D. Denson; Gary DeStefano; Trevor Edwards; Hannah Jones; Hilary Krane*; Mark Parker.

EIN: 931159948

Recent grants for international programs:

1847-1 Academia para o Desenvolvimento da Educacao-Brasil, Recife, Brazil, $586,342. To develop and test urban, scalable, multi-component, project-based learning employability model for girls in Northeast Brazil. 2010.

1847-2 Academia para o Desenvolvimento da Educacao-Brasil, Recife, Brazil, $93,795. To develop and test urban, scalable, multi-component, project-based learning employability model for girls in Northeast Brazil. 2010.

1847-3 Academy for Educational Development, Washington, DC, $88,899. To develop and test urban, scalable, multi-component, project-based learning employability model for girls in Northeast Brazil. 2010.

1847-4 American Jewish World Service, New York, NY, $700,000. To make grants to grassroots organizations for appropriate programming and advocacy for adolescent girls ages 10-19; strengthen mechanisms and systems for reaching girls through grassroots organizations;

build capacity of grassroots organizations to deliver quality programs for girls; and contribute to creating knowledge and evidence about these programs in collaboration with Grassroots Girls Initiative. 2010.

1847-5 American Jewish World Service, New York, NY, $17,050. To make grants to grassroots organizations for appropriate programming and advocacy for adolescent girls ages 10-19; strengthen mechanisms and systems for reaching girls through grassroots organizations; build capacity of grassroots organizations to deliver quality programs for girls; and contribute to creating knowledge and evidence about these programs in collaboration with Grassroots Girls Initiative. 2010.

1847-6 Ashoka: Innovators for the Public, Arlington, VA, $13,000. To coordinate prize distribution management by Changemakers on behalf of Nike Foundation for winners of Gamechangers Change the Game for Women in Sport Competition. 2010.

1847-7 Cardno Emerging Markets USA, Ltd., Arlington, VA, $474,103. To develop, test and document replicable and sustainable model for economically empowering girls by increasing their participation in vegetable and poultry value chains in region of Lake Victoria, Kenya. 2010.

1847-8 CARE USA, Atlanta, GA, $730,873. To adapt self-managed Savings and Loan program (VSL) for girls outside the reach of microfinance institutions. 2010.

1847-9 CARE USA, Atlanta, GA, $661,847. To improve economic, sexual and reproductive health of girls that have been married, divorced and/or widowed (ever-married) in Ethiopia. Project also seeks to provide an evidence base that will address key gaps in knowledge in field of adolescent girl programming, by understanding to what extent combined economic empowerment and sexual reproductive health intervention drives better sexual reproductive health and economic outcomes for ever-married, adolescent girls compared to programs that offer each component in isolation. 2010.

1847-10 CARE USA, Atlanta, GA, $64,066. To develop and design project with focus on Reproductive Health and Economic Empowerment. 2010.

1847-11 Carolina for Kibera, Chapel Hill, NC, $32,553. To sustain and expand viral network of girls' groups and pilot evolution of program model to address girls' economic vulnerability. 2010.

1847-12 Center for Global Development, Washington, DC, $100,000. To expand focus on Millennium Development Goals and global poverty solutions, with particular focus on role of adolescent girls in household, community and national welfare, both today and in future generations and to explore how donor agencies and corporations can more effectively create opportunities for young girls to reach their potential. 2010.

1847-13 Center for Global Development, Washington, DC, $50,000. To expand focus on Millennium Development Goals and global poverty solutions, with particular focus on role of adolescent girls in household, community and national welfare, both today and in future generations and to explore how donor agencies and corporations can more effectively create opportunities for young girls to reach their potential. 2010.

1847-14 Center for Interfaith Action on Global Poverty, Washington, DC, $133,051. To identify dynamic faith and traditional leaders whose efforts championing cause of girls in their communities will inspire others. 2010.

1847-15 Chicago Council on Global Affairs, Chicago, IL, $200,000. To research, write, design, produce and disseminate report focusing on adolescent girls in rural economies in the developing world. 2010.

1847-16 Columbia University, New York, NY, $50,000. To empower girls aged 10-14 in the Kilmanjaro region of Tanzania with knowledge of how their bodies change during puberty and to contribute to building a culture of reading by enabling Grantee to finalize, publish and distribute culturally appropriate book based on Tanzanian girls' menstrual stories and their recommendations for younger girls. 2010.

1847-17 Columbia University, New York, NY, $31,000. To empower girls aged 10-14 in the Kilmanjaro region of Tanzania with knowledge of how their bodies change during puberty and to contribute to building a culture of reading by enabling Grantee to finalize, publish and distribute culturally appropriate book based on Tanzanian girls' menstrual stories and their recommendations for younger girls. 2010.

1847-18 DASRA, Sugar Land, TX, $300,000. To design and launch creative multi-media curriculum in India to cultivate entrepreneurship among low-income youth ages 9 to 14. 2010.

1847-19 EMpower, The Emerging Markets Foundation, New York, NY, $405,000. To make grants to grassroots organizations for appropriate programming and advocacy for adolescent girls aged 10-19 years old; to strengthen mechanisms and systems for reaching girls through grassroots orgnizations; to build capacity of grassroots organizations to deliver quality programs for girls; and to contribute to creating knowledge and evidence about such programs in collaboration with Grassroots Girls Initiative. 2010.

1847-20 EMpower, The Emerging Markets Foundation, New York, NY, $39,385. To bring practitioners, business experts, and adolescent girls together to create package of knowledge (toolkit/guidelines) about how to expand girls' income-generating opportunities in the informal sector. 2010.

1847-21 EMpower, The Emerging Markets Foundation, New York, NY, $25,000. To bring practitioners, business experts, and adolescent girls together to create package of knowledge (toolkit/guidelines) about how to expand girls' income-generating opportunities in the informal sector. 2010.

1847-22 EngenderHealth, New York, NY, $183,487. To transform informal network of young indigenous Guatemalan female leaders into permanent indigenous Guatemalan girl-led organization and to support lateral viral expansion of local, sustainable, indigenous girl-led network. 2010.

1847-23 Equality Now, New York, NY, $100,000. To support landmark cases that exemplify severe, consequential, and widespread violation of girls' rights and to create awareness around these cases. 2010.

1847-24 Equality Now, New York, NY, $65,000. To provide strategic response to girls in need of legal support around the world through capacity provided by Adolescent Girls Legal Defense Fund Program Officer. 2010.

1847-25 Equality Now, New York, NY, $50,000. To establish Rapid Response Fund for quick and effective response to major violations of girls' rights as they arise. 2010.

1847-26 European Parliamentary Forum on Population and Development, Brussels, Belgium, $10,000. To research options to maximize European aid flows to adolescent girls in the developing world to improve adolescent girl programming. 2010.

1847-27 Four-H Council, National, Chevy Chase, MD, $107,985. To support co-facilitator for 4-H African Conference to give training on best practices on girl programming; identify what optimal 4-H model is for girls under 19 years old in a pilot country in Africa, which will include utilizing girls' input directly as well as Nike Foundation's input on the pilot model; develop 4-H Knowledge Center on Africa-specific content; and develop and implement an M+E system, including qualitative data gathered on characteristics of programs that more effectively engage girls. 2010.

1847-28 Friends of WWB/USA, New York, NY, $603,389. To enable Grantee to support two WWB members (Asia and Latin America) to design, market and deliver savings products and financial education to girls ages 7 to 24. Grant enables Grantee to test microfinance institution-led sustainable business model for girls' savings products on 2 continents and, if successful, paves the way for uptake among greater number of WWB network members and other microfinance institutions. 2010.

1847-29 Fundacion Paraguaya de Cooperacion y Desarrollo, Asuncion, Paraguay, $548,100. To design and test an all-girls, financially self-sufficient farm school model adapted from successful co-ed model. 2010.

1847-30 Futures Without Violence, San Francisco, CA, $533,805. To adapt and test Coaching Boys Into Men program within context of the sport of cricket in India. 2010.

1847-31 Global Fund for Children, Washington, DC, $550,000. To make grants to grassroots organizations for appropriate programming and advocacy for adolescent girls ages 10-19; strengthen mechanisms and systems for reaching girls through grassroots organizations; build capacity of grassroots organizations to deliver quality programs for girls; and contribute to creating knowledge and evidence about these programs in collaboration with Grassroots Girls Initiative. 2010.

1847-32 Global Fund for Children, Washington, DC, $16,725. To make grants to grassroots organizations for appropriate programming and advocacy for adolescent girls ages 10-19; strengthen mechanisms and systems for reaching girls through grassroots organizations; build capacity of grassroots organizations to deliver quality programs for girls; and contribute to creating knowledge and evidence about these programs in collaboration with Grassroots Girls Initiative. 2010.

1847-33 Global Fund for Women, San Francisco, CA, $400,000. To make grants to grassroots organizations for appropriate programming and advocacy for adolescent girls ages 10-19; strengthen mechanisms and systems for reaching girls through grassroots organizations; build capacity of grassroots organizations to deliver quality programs for girls; and contribute to creating knowledge and evidence about these programs in collaboration with Grassroots Girls Initiative. 2010.

1847-34 GlobalGirl Media, Culver City, CA, $135,400. To train South African girls to report on 2010 FIFA World Cup and to be broadcast voice for South African girls. 2010.

1847-35 GlobalGirl Media, Culver City, CA, $10,000. To train South African girls to report on 2010 FIFA World Cup and to be broadcast voice for South African girls. 2010.

1847-36 Grameen Foundation USA, Washington, DC, $44,793. To provide resources to allow Grameen to acquire an expert in monitoring evaluation and impact assessment, with specific experience in gender in development. 2010.

1847-37 Grameen Healthcare Trust, Dhaka, Bangladesh, $540,000. To qualify young women in delivering primary healthcare. Key strategic objectives are to address shortage of nurses with innovative teaching techniques and recruitment of rural young women, create first of its kind curriculum focused on health needs of adolescent girls, deliver sustainable social business model with nurses as central actors of the healthcare economy. 2010.

1847-38 Instituto Companheiros das Americas, Rio de Janeiro, Brazil, $869,465. To develop and test sport-based, comprehensive economic empowerment model for girls in Brazil. 2010.

1847-39 International Bank for Reconstruction and Development, Washington, DC, $1,000,000. For Gender Action Plan: Gender Equality as Smart Economics, to promote economic empowerment of adolescent girls. 2010.

1847-40 International Center for Research on Women, Washington, DC, $514,771. To provide capacity-building support for Nike Foundation grantees so they can more effectively carry out grant missions and to assist grantees with monitoring and evaluation. 2010.

1847-41 International Womens Health Coalition, New York, NY, $20,000. For general operating support to run effective programs for adolescent girls. 2010.

1847-42 JSI Research and Training Institute, Boston, MA, $150,868. For fellowships as part of Liberia Fellows Program in which fellows serve as assistants to Minister of Gender and Development and Minister of Youth and Sports and work on policies focusing on economic empowerment of adolescent girls. 2010.

1847-43 Kakenya Center for Excellence, Washington, DC, $25,000. For general operating support. 2010.

1847-44 Landesa, Seattle, WA, $290,055. To provide programs to improve adolescent girls' social and economic situation by securing land rights for them and their families through leveraging Government of West Bengal's land redistribution program, improving community awareness of girls' issues and assets and assisting Government of West Bengal to scale program throughout the state. 2010.

1847-45 Landesa, Seattle, WA, $57,029. To explore feasibility of programming options and build relationships with key stakeholders to eventually grant girls and their families secure rights to land in West Bengal and Orissa (Odisha). 2010.

1847-46 Maplecroft, Bath, England, $102,098. To support Fellow who will be seated with the Foundation during the term. Grant will support

Fellow's salary, benefits, communicaitons and agreed-upon travel expenses during the grant term. 2010.

1847-47 Maplecroft, Bath, England, $35,780. To support Fellow who will be seated with the Foundation during the term. Grant will support Fellow's salary, benefits, communicaitons and agreed-upon travel expenses during the grant term. 2010.

1847-48 Maplecroft, Bath, England, $33,095. For maintenance and updates of Girls Discovered website, user-friendly database focusing on adolescent girls with regard to general and reproductive health, security, education, economic opportunities and policy environments. 2010.

1847-49 Massachusetts Institute of Technology, Cambridge, MA, $11,860. To prepare two research reports that will support Nike Foundation's development of an evidence base for girls' programming. 2010.

1847-50 Massachusetts Institute of Technology, Cambridge, MA, $11,860. To prepare two research reports that will support Nike Foundation's development of an evidence base for girls' programming. 2010.

1847-51 McGill University, Montreal, Canada, $22,963. For research and publication around female-headed households in Sub-Saharan Africa. 2010.

1847-52 Mercy Corps, Portland, OR, $129,324. For NIKE Foundation-Mercy Corps fellowship program. Fellow will oversee set of Nike Foundation grantees, provide strategic input into Foundation's strategic planning process, and deliver body of work defining how international NGOs can better address needs of AGs to both Nike Foundation and Mercy Corps. Fellow will be a senior staff member from Mercy Corps who will be seconded to Nike Foundation. 2010.

1847-53 Mercy Corps, Portland, OR, $78,411. To support Fellow under Nike Foundation-Mercy Corps Fellowship program. Grant will be used for Fellow's salary, benefits, communcations and agreed-upon travel expenses during grant term. Fellowship is designed to integrate private sector and adolescent girl expertise to Mercy Corps through targeted projects and deliverables. 2010.

1847-54 Mercy Corps, Portland, OR, $30,000. To support Communications Fellow through Nike Foundation-Mercy Corps Fellowship program. Fellowship is designed to channel communcations/branding expertise to Mercy Corps through targeted projects and deliverables. 2010.

1847-55 Mercy Corps, Portland, OR, $19,000. To support Fellow under Nike Foundation-Mercy Corps Fellowship program. Grant will be used for Fellow's salary, benefits, communcations and agreed-upon travel expenses during grant term. Fellowship is designed to integrate private sector and adolescent girl expertise to Mercy Corps through targeted projects and deliverables. 2010.

1847-56 Microfinance Opportunities, Washington, DC, $158,722. To work in partnership with three Savings grantees (CARE, Population Council Kenya, and Women's World Banking) to develop financial education products adapted to each cultural context and to help identify and develop appropriate delivery systems for financial education. 2010.

1847-57 Millennium Promise Alliance, New York, NY, $300,000. To support a Millennium Village in Africa, providing Village with scientific and other interventions in areas such as health, food production, education, access to clean water and essential infrastructures allowing Villagers the opportunity and tools to escape extreme poverty. 2010.

1847-58 Pacific Institute for Womens Health, Los Angeles, CA, $500,000. To develop, pilot and document effective strategies for empowering girls, initiate development of active network of girls in Northeast Brazil, and increase donor support for girls' empowerment programs. 2010.

1847-59 PACT, Washington, DC, $86,485. To test and refine package of interventions supporting adolescent girls' success in secondary school and transitions from secondary school to economic activity when school is no longer an option. 2010.

1847-60 PATH, Seattle, WA, $341,917. To provide resources for adolescent Yi girls (Yi are an ethnic minority group in China) to develop and build skills to implement appropriate health curriculum to increase health knowledge, improve attitudes and build skills for healthy behaviors. 2010.

1847-61 Population Council, New York, NY, $498,348. To build on Grantee's and MicroSave's market research work to develop, pilot and scale up savings products for girls in urban Kenya and Uganda. Work will combine market research and product development expertise of MicroSave, implementation expertise of local financial institutions (FIs) and girl and research expertise of Grantee to form powerful combination for girls' economic empowerment. 2010.

1847-62 Population Council, New York, NY, $235,851. To provide expertise in continuing to nurture capacity to do targeted and focused investments and work with adolescent girls in poverty. 2010.

1847-63 Population Council, New York, NY, $151,460. To lead Brain Trust of Practitioners in Ethiopia to inform, expand and leverage programming for rural girls. 2010.

1847-64 Population Council, New York, NY, $36,641. To conduct qualitative research that evaluates what facilitates and/or hinders translation of knowledge into behavior change for adolescent girls and why social asset building programs, such as Binti Pamoja Center, prepare adolescent girls for economic activity. 2010.

1847-65 Reach Global, Berkeley, CA, $150,000. To support Reach India's training infrastructure and increase capacity to serve more women and children. 2010.

1847-66 Reach Global, Berkeley, CA, $150,000. To support Reach India's training infrastructure and increase capacity to serve more women and children. 2010.

1847-67 Reach Global, Berkeley, CA, $150,000. To support Reach India's training infrastructure and increase capacity to serve more women and children. 2010.

1847-68 Save the Children Federation, Westport, CT, $83,909. To improve health and physical security, educational and economic security and social opportunity and voice of adolescent girls in Bangladesh and Malawi by expanding integrated food security programs in both countries. 2010.

1847-69 Synergos Institute, New York, NY, $100,000. To develop and pilot low-cost and replicable girls' component within larger, comprehensive child malnutrition program (herein called Integration Model). Girls' component will test whether investing in girls empowerment, knowledge of and access to government programs/services and nutrition/ health education before girls have children can affect health of their children, rates of girls' anemia, age at the time of first pregnancy, age of marriage and retention rates of girls in school. 2010.

1847-70 Tostan, Washington, DC, $378,331. To adapt Community Empowerment Program in Senegal. Program will sharpen girl lens and more broadly measure its impact on girls' empowerment. Program will empower girl and boy leaders to drive adoption of more equitable gender attitudes and behaviors in their own neighboring communities. 2010.

1847-71 Tostan, Washington, DC, $140,000. For general operating support to expand Community Empowerment Program to seven new villages in The Gambia. 2010.

1847-72 Tostan, Washington, DC, $41,089. To adapt Community Empowerment Program in Senegal. Program will sharpen girl lens and more broadly measure its impact on girls' empowerment. Program will empower girl and boy leaders to drive adoption of more equitable gender attitudes and behaviors in their own neighboring communities. 2010.

1848
Sustainable Harvest Coffee Importers Corporate Giving Program

Natural Capital Ctr.
721 N.W. 9th Ave., Ste. 235
Portland, OR 97209-3451 (503) 235-1119
E-mail: info@sustainableharvest.com; URL: http://www.sustainableharvest.com
B Corporation Profile: http://www.bcorporation.net/sustainableharvest

Grantmaker type: Corporate giving program.
Purpose and activities: Sustainable Harvest Coffee Importers is a certified B Corporation that donates a percentage of profits to charitable organizations. Support is given primarily in Oaxaca, Mexico, Lima, Peru, and Moshi, Tanzania.
Fields of interest: Agriculture/food, formal/general education; Agriculture, sustainable programs.
International interests: Mexico; Peru; Tanzania, Zanzibar and Pemba.
Limitations: Giving primarily in Oaxaca, Mexico, Lima, Peru, and Moshi, Tanzania.

1849
Tazo Corporate Giving Program

c/o Donations
P.O. Box 66
Portland, OR 97207-0066
URL: http://www.tazo.com/tazo.asp?init=

Grantmaker type: Corporate giving program.
Purpose and activities: Tazo makes charitable contributions to nonprofit organizations involved with arts and culture, education, the environment, HIV/AIDS, diversity, and children. Support is given on a national and international basis, with emphasis on Portland, Oregon, and India.

Fields of interest: Children, services; Civil/human rights, equal rights; Environment; Literature; Arts; Education; AIDS.
International interests: India.
Type of support: General/operating support; Donated products.
Limitations: Applications accepted. Giving on a national and international basis, with emphasis on Portland, OR, and India.
Application information: Unsolicited requests for monetary contributions are not accepted. Application form required.
   Initial approach: Download application form and mail to headquarters
   Deadline(s): 1 month prior to need

1850
Weatherspoon Charitable Foundation

2325 N.E. Flanders St., No. 16
Portland, OR 97232-3184
Contact: Kristen MacDonald

Established in 1988 in IA.
Donor: Margaret Weatherspoon.
Grantmaker type: Independent foundation.
Financial data (yr. ended 12/31/10): Assets, $3,227,623 (M); expenditures, $184,945; qualifying distributions, $178,000; giving activities include $178,000 for grants.
Purpose and activities: Giving for childhood development and education, Christian services, food services to the needy, aid to the homeless, and environmental conservation.
Fields of interest: Higher education; Education; Environment, land resources; Environment; Food services; American Red Cross; YM/YWCAs & YM/YWHAs; Children/youth, services; International relief; Christian agencies & churches; Homeless.
Limitations: Applications not accepted. Giving on a national basis, with some emphasis on IA and OR.
Application information: Unsolicited requests for funds not accepted.
   Board meeting date(s): Annually
Officer: Martha Stevenson, Pres.
Board Members: James Bowden; Mary Bowden; Sara Christie; Andrew McDonald; Jacqueline Reineke; Jennifer Reynoldson; Joann Weatherspoon; Margaret Weatherspoon.
Number of staff: None.
EIN: 421324028

1851
The Wyss Foundation

620 S.W. 5th Ave., Ste. 1010
Portland, OR 97204-1424
Contact: Loren L. Wyss, Pres.
E-mail: lwyss@aol.com

Established in 1989 in OR.
Donors: Judith Wyss; Loren L. Wyss.
Grantmaker type: Independent foundation.
Financial data (yr. ended 04/30/11): Assets, $5,167,487 (M); expenditures, $274,248; qualifying distributions, $274,248; giving activities include $216,575 for 80 grants (high: $10,000; low: $75).
Purpose and activities: Giving primarily for the arts, education, religion, and community and social services.
Fields of interest: Arts; Education; Environment; Animals/wildlife, association; Human services.

International interests: United Kingdom.
Type of support: General/operating support; Program development.
Limitations: Applications accepted. Giving primarily in the Portland, OR, area. No support for political causes, medical research or for lobbying groups. No grants to individuals.
Publications: Grants list; Informational brochure.
Application information: Until further notice, new applications are confined to the fine and performing arts. Previous recipients are still invited to apply for existing or new programs. The foundation attempts to inform applicants who supply an e-mail address what the status of their request is. Application form not required.
   Initial approach: Letter
   Copies of proposal: 2
   Deadline(s): Nov. 1 and Mar. 1
   Board meeting date(s): Apr. and Dec.
   Final notification: Usually Jan. 31 and Apr. 30
Officers and Directors:* Loren L. Wyss,* Pres. and Treas.; Judith Wyss,* Secy.
Trustees: Edmund Wyss; Emily A. Wyss; Isabel J. Wyss; Jennifer Wyss-Jones.
Number of staff: None.
EIN: 931010019

1852
Zwaanstra Foundation

452 N.E. Lincoln St.
Hillsboro, OR 97124-3148

Established in OR.
Grantmaker type: Independent foundation.
Financial data (yr. ended 12/31/10): Assets, $743,150 (M); expenditures, $1,001,256; qualifying distributions, $1,000,000; giving activities include $1,000,000 for grants.
Fields of interest: International exchange; Higher education; Education, reading.
Limitations: Applications not accepted. Giving primarily in MA. No grants to individuals.
Application information: Contributes only to pre-selected organizations.
Trustees: James E. Zwaanstra; John Zwaanstra III; John Zwaanstra IV; Shizuka Zwaanstra; Todd D. Zwaanstra.
EIN: 911751312

PENNSYLVANIA

1853
Alcoa Foundation

Alcoa Corporate Ctr.
201 Isabella St.
Pittsburgh, PA 15212-5858 (412) 553-2348
E-mail: alcoafoundation@alcoa.com; URL: http://www.alcoa.com/global/en/community/foundation.asp
Alcoa Foundation's Conservation and Sustainability Program E-Newsletter: http://www.alcoa.com/global/en/community/csf_releases/releases_overview.asp
Grants Database: http://www.alcoa.com/global/en/community/foundation/grants.asp

Trust established in 1952 in PA; incorporated in 1964.

Donors: Aluminum Co. of America; Alcoa Inc.

Grantmaker type: Company-sponsored foundation.

Financial data (yr. ended 12/31/09): Assets, $435,170,273 (M); gifts received, $500,000; expenditures, $20,870,580; qualifying distributions, $17,724,699; giving activities include $16,222,038 for 1,057 grants (high: $778,404; low: $100).

Purpose and activities: The foundation supports programs designed to promote environmental stewardship; prepare tomorrow's leaders; and enable economic and social sustainability. Special emphasis is directed toward programs designed to address the environment; empowerment; education; and sustainable design.

Fields of interest: Transportation; Higher education; Teacher school/education; Adult/continuing education; Education; Environment, public policy; Environment, pollution control; Environment, waste management; Environment, recycling; Environment, climate change/global warming; Environment, natural resources; Environment, water resources; Environment, land resources; Environment, energy; Environment, forests; Environment; Employment, training; Employment; Disasters, preparedness/services; Safety/disasters; Youth development; American Red Cross; Children/youth, services; Mathematics; Engineering/technology; Science; Leadership development; Women; Girls.

International interests: Africa; Asia; Australia; Caribbean; Central America; Europe; Mexico; South America.

Type of support: Continuing support; Management development/capacity building; Annual campaigns; Building/renovation; Equipment; Emergency funds; Program development; Conferences/seminars; Curriculum development; Scholarship funds; Research; Employee volunteer services; Sponsorships; Employee matching gifts; Employee-related scholarships; Scholarships—to individuals; Matching/challenge support.

Limitations: Applications accepted. Giving on a national and international basis in areas of company operations, with emphasis on New York, NY, Pittsburgh, PA, Africa, Asia, Australia, Canada, Caribbean, Central America, Europe, Mexico, and South America; giving also to national and international organizations. No support for political or lobbying organizations, sectarian or religious organizations not of direct benefit to the entire community, private foundations, or trust funds. No grants to individuals (except for scholarships), or for endowments, capital campaigns, debt reduction, or general operating support, fundraising events or sponsorships, trips, conferences, seminars, festivals, one-day events, documentaries, videos, or research projects/programs, or indirect or overhead costs.

Publications: Application guidelines; Corporate giving report; Grants list; Informational brochure (including application guidelines); Program policy statement.

Application information: Organizations receiving support are asked to submit interim reports and a final report.

  Initial approach: Proposal to nearest company facility; complete online application for Alcoa Global Service Leaders Scholarship

  Copies of proposal: 1

  Deadline(s): Contact nearest company facility; Apr. 22 for Alcoa Global Service Leaders Scholarship

Board meeting date(s): Monthly

Final notification: May 2 for Alcoa Global Service Leaders Scholarship

Officers and Directors:* Paula Davis,* Pres.; Velma Monteiro-Tribble, Secy.; Dean Will, Cont. and Business Mgr.; Nicholas J. Ashooh; John D. Bergen; Alan Cransberg; Franklin L. Feder; Vanessa Lau; Lysane Martel; Charles D. McLane, Jr.; Raymond B. Mitchell; Tim D. Myers; William J. O'Rourke; Shannon Parks; Marcos Ramos; Helmut O. Wieser.

Corporate Trustee: The Bank of New York Mellon, N.A.

Number of staff: 6 full-time professional; 1 full-time support.

EIN: 251128857

Recent grants for international programs:

1853-1 Academy for Educational Development, Washington, DC, $75,000. For Phase II of program, Improving Girls Education in Guinea. 2010.

1853-2 American Australian Association, New York, NY, $125,000. For Alcoa Foundation Fellowship supporting Australian researchers conducting post-graduate research in conservation, sustainability or materials technology. 2010.

1853-3 American Enterprise Institute for Public Policy Research, Washington, DC, $30,000. For Russian Studies Program. 2010.

1853-4 American Forests, Washington, DC, $600,000. For multi-year tree planting program. 2010.

1853-5 American Institute for Contemporary German Studies, Washington, DC, $15,000. For Project Support Initiative. 2010.

1853-6 American Institute for Contemporary German Studies, Washington, DC, $15,000. For Global Leadership Award Dinner. 2010.

1853-7 American Red Cross National Headquarters, Washington, DC, $100,000. For earthquake relief efforts in Haiti. 2010.

1853-8 American Red Cross National Headquarters, Washington, DC, $50,000. For disaster relief for victims of the recent earthquake in Chile. 2010.

1853-9 Appeal of Conscience Foundation, New York, NY, $20,000. For Annual Awards Dinner. 2010.

1853-10 Aranyeso Alapitvany, Szekesfehervar, Hungary, $20,000. For Fultorna Dyslexia Prevention Program. 2010.

1853-11 Arc-en-ciel, Donnacona, Canada, $15,000. To provide breakfasts and social-professional reintegration program. 2010.

1853-12 Aspen Institute, New York, NY, $50,000. For forum, scholarship and operating support for Aspen Network of Development Entrepreneurs (ANDE), global network of organizations that invest money and expertise to propel entrepreneurship in emerging markets in Brazil, China, Jamaica, Russia and Suriname. 2010.

1853-13 Association Le Relais, Blagnac, France, $20,000. For skills assessment for clients and to establish vocational training activities. 2010.

1853-14 Association of Regional Extended Families, Szekesfehervar, Hungary, $21,000. For Healthy Families program. 2010.

1853-15 Banco Internacional de Alimentos, Ciudad Acuna, Mexico, $15,000. For disaster relief for victims of the flood. 2010.

1853-16 Banco Internacional de Alimentos, Ciudad Acuna, Mexico, $10,000. For disaster relief for victims of flooding in Acuna. 2010.

1853-17 Beijing Environmental Protection Foundation, Beijing, China, $53,468. For aluminum pot disposal project. 2010.

1853-18 Birmingham City Council, Birmingham, England, $20,000. For Kingfisher Country Park Cole Valley Environmental Improvement project. 2010.

1853-19 Borgunarsveitin Arsol-Arsol Rescue Squad, Reydarfjordur, Iceland, $10,000. For general programs. 2010.

1853-20 Breiddalssetur, Breiddalsvik, Iceland, $40,000. For Capacity Building and Community Involvement Program. 2010.

1853-21 Brothers Brother Foundation, Pittsburgh, PA, $20,000. For disaster recovery and medical supplies for hospitals and clinics damaged by the Hait earthquake. 2010.

1853-22 Caribbean Institute, Paramaribo, Suriname, $49,964. For program to transition to organic agriculture for food safety and income security. 2010.

1853-23 Carrefour-Rue, Geneva, Switzerland, $10,000. For general programs. 2010.

1853-24 Centacare Catholic Family Services, East Melbourne, Australia, $120,000. For Advancing Diversity and Women in Australia program. 2010.

1853-25 Central South University, Changsha, China, $49,000. For Alcoa Excellent Female Scholarship in Science, Technology, Engineering and Mathematics (STEM) education. 2010.

1853-26 Centre for European Policy Studies, Brussels, Belgium, $15,000. For program to boost European Union competitiveness in a global economy and the carbon market. 2010.

1853-27 Chambre de Commerce de Portneuf, Secteur Ouest, Saint-Marc-des-Carrieres, Canada, $15,000. To hire development agent to assure revitalization of the community. 2010.

1853-28 Chambre de Commerce et d Industrie de Becancour, Becancour, Canada, $50,000. For Defi, on recyle (Recycling Challenge) program, initiative to develop waste management plan with view to achieving ICI ON RECYCLE! designation from Recyc-Quebec. 2010.

1853-29 Charities Aid Foundation Australia, North Sydney, Australia, $100,000. For project to enhance and maintain quality of Timehelp volunteer demonstration models and to facilitate strategy to deliver Australia's first national program of retiree volunteers. 2010.

1853-30 China Center for International Economic Exchanges, Alcoa Advancing Sustainability Initiative, Beijing, China, $220,000. To research and leverage actionable solutions for project, Chinese Public Policy of Promoting Low-Carbon Economy. 2010.

1853-31 China Center for International Economic Exchanges, Alcoa Advancing Sustainability Initiative, Beijing, China, $180,000. To research and leverage actionable solutions for Voluntary Emissions Reduction (VER) and NGO Participation in China. 2010.

1853-32 China Forum of Environmental Journalists, Beijing, China, $40,000. For Alcoa Environmental Base. 2010.

1853-33 CLD de la MRC de Becancour, Becancour, Canada, $15,000. For Innovative Expertise Development Project with small and medium-size businesses and social economy enterprises. 2010.

1853-34 Clontarf Foundation, Burswood, Australia, $85,400. For Gilmore College-Clontarf Academy Leadership Works Program. 2010.

1853-35 Coaldale Baseball Association, Coaldale, Canada, $15,000. For upgrades to the Quad. 2010.

1853-36 Colegio de Educacion Infantil y Primaria El Palmeral, Alicante, Spain, $44,000. To modernize educational offer. 2010.

1853-37 Colegio Oficial de Quimicos de Galicia, Vigo, Spain, $53,430. For III Secondary School Galician Chemical Olympiad. 2010.

1853-38 Comite de la Reserve Mondiale de la Biosphere Manicouagan Uapishka, Baie-Comeau, Canada, $80,000. To support Reference Center of sustainable development and commitment chart. 2010.

1853-39 Comite ZIP de la Rive Nord de l'Estuaire, Baie-Comeau, Canada, $15,000. For school awareness development tour about coastal habitats on the north shore of the estuary. 2010.

1853-40 Comune di Dolo, Dolo, Italy, $10,000. For general operating support. 2010.

1853-41 Comune di Tratalias, Tratalias, Italy, $73,000. To create craft laboratories for youth in the village of Tratalias. 2010.

1853-42 Conalep Plantel Ciudad Acuna, Ciudad Acuna, Mexico, $15,000. For comprehensive service for students in graphic design training. 2010.

1853-43 Conservation International, Arlington, VA, $10,000. For sponsorship of Conservation International dinner in New York City. 2010.

1853-44 COOP de Solidarite Sante JP Despins, Saint Leonard D Aston, Canada, $15,000. For medical equipment upgrade. 2010.

1853-45 Cooperative de Solidarite du Marche Godefroy, Becancour, Canada, $20,000. For activities targeting sustainable development and life quality of the community. 2010.

1853-46 Cooperative de Solidarite la Residence Portneuvienne, Portneuf, Canada, $20,000. For construction of housing units for elderly people age 75 and older. 2010.

1853-47 Cooperative de Solidarite Sante de Sainte-Gertrude, Becancour, Canada, $15,000. For acquisition of X-ray machine. 2010.

1853-48 Corporation Veloroute des Baleines, Baie-Comeau, Canada, $20,000. For welcoming and information pavilion project fo Cycle Path of the Whales. 2010.

1853-49 Council on Foreign Relations, New York, NY, $100,000. For Global Brazil program. 2010.

1853-50 Devon Wildlife Trust, Exeter, England, $44,985. For Exeter Wild City - Swifts Project. 2010.

1853-51 Earthwatch Institute, Boston, MA, $519,355. For Alcoa Employee Sustainability Fellowships in Brazil and China. 2010.

1853-52 Ecole Polytechnique, Alcoa Advancing Sustainability Initiative, Montreal, Canada, $350,000. To research and leverage actionable solutions toward sustainable landscapes for project, ImpactWorld+ : An Improved Environmental Footprint Methodology for Life Cycle Assessment (LCA) at Interuniversity Research Centre for the Life Cycle of Products, Processes and Services (CIRAIG). 2010.

1853-53 Economics for Energy, Vigo, Spain, $20,000. For workshops and reports on energy economic issues. 2010.

1853-54 Egry Street Kindergarten, Veszprem, Hungary, $15,000. For Developing Sustainable Communities Through Children program. 2010.

1853-55 Eichendorffschule Kelkheim, Kelkheim, Germany, $30,000. For tuition program. 2010.

1853-56 Emaus Fundacion Social, Donostia San Sebastian, Spain, $29,500. For Aviles Collects Oil: Oil Recycling in Schools program. 2010.

1853-57 Ente Parco Naturale Regionale del Fiume Sile, Treviso, Italy, $30,000. For Firemen City (Pompieropoli). 2010.

1853-58 Farsund Undervannsklubb, Farsund, Norway, $30,000. For Backes Bu Restoration Project. 2010.

1853-59 Fjardabyggd Cultural Center, Eskifjordur, Iceland, $15,000. For Singing for Life program, organized professional vocal training for choir members in East Iceland. 2010.

1853-60 Fondation au Coeur des Grottes, Geneva, Switzerland, $15,000. For program to provide food and shelter to disadvantaged women and their children. 2010.

1853-61 Fondation de lEcole Saint-Gabriel Archange, Trois Rivieres, Canada, $50,000. For Program Environmental Education and Citizenship (PEEC). 2010.

1853-62 Foundation Center, New York, NY, $15,000. For specific research to identify nonprofits focused on environment, empowerment, education, design and disaster relief in specific regions of the world. 2010.

1853-63 Fund Aid for Community Sustainable Development, Moscow, Russia, $205,000. For Youth Votes for Health program. 2010.

1853-64 Fund Aid for Community Sustainable Development, Alcoa Advancing Sustainability Initiative, Moscow, Russia, $250,000. To research and leverage actionable solutions for project, Responsible Water Resources Management for Sustainable Development. 2010.

1853-65 Fundacion La Laboral -Centro de Arte y Creacion Industrial, Gijon, Spain, $80,000. For Platform 0 - Production Center. 2010.

1853-66 Fundacion Privada Trinijove, Barcelona, Spain, $37,000. For Recicla@luminio, environmental program. 2010.

1853-67 Fundacion Publica de Deportes, Amorebieta, Spain, $49,500. For Active Ageing Program. 2010.

1853-68 Gaja Kornyezetvedo Egyesulet, Szekesfehervar, Hungary, $22,000. To protect healthy living areas and to support protection of climate program. 2010.

1853-69 Gaja Kornyezetvedo Egyesulet, Szekesfehervar, Hungary, $10,000. For facility expansion of Green cottage at Sosto Natural Protected Area. 2010.

1853-70 Gemeente Zeewolde, Zeewolde, Netherlands, $30,000. For Energyweek program. 2010.

1853-71 Global Links, Pittsburgh, PA, $20,000. To provide dialysis unit and general material support for Mandeville Hospital in Jamaica. 2010.

1853-72 Global Rivers Environmental Education Network Belgium, Brussels, Belgium, $15,000. For educational program on climate change and sustainable mobility through climate action and through schools transport plans. 2010.

1853-73 Greening Australia, Deakin, Australia, $500,000. For Make an Impact, program to help Alcoa employees and their families reduce their household water and energy use and become part of the solution to climate change. 2010.

1853-74 Greening Australia, Deakin, Australia, $120,000. For Putting It Back, national revegetation project. 2010.

1853-75 Greening Australia, Alcoa Advancing Sustainability Initiative, Deakin, Australia, $355,000. To research and leverage actionable solutions toward sustainable landscapes for

project, Harnessing Bioenergy Markets to Build Resilient Landscapes. 2010.

1853-76 Greening Australia, Alcoa Advancing Sustainability Initiative, Deakin, Australia, $355,000. To research and leverage actionable solutions toward sustainable landscapes for project, Phosphorus Management to protect RAMSAR Wetlands. 2010.

1853-77 Groupe Essec, Cergy Pontoise, France, $30,000. For Higher Education Equal Opportunities programs. 2010.

1853-78 H. John Heinz III Center for Science, Economics and the Environment, Washington, DC, $50,000. For project to finance sustainable land use in Brazil. 2010.

1853-79 Halton Borough Council, Widnes, England, $30,000. For Castlefield Regeneration Partnership's project, Wild About Town Park Lake. 2010.

1853-80 Halton District School Board, Burlington, Canada, $15,000. For Georgetown Field of Dreams, initiative to replace natural outdoor track and field at Georgetown District High School with artificial turf sports field and all-weather rubberized track. Field will be avaiable for use by the School and the community. 2010.

1853-81 Heart of Eden Project, Birmingham, England, $25,000. For participation in Green Community Programme supported by The Energy Saving Trust project. 2010.

1853-82 Heart to Heart International Childrens Medical Alliance, Oakland, CA, $50,000. For Into the Heartland Campaign, Rostov-on-Don, initiative to expand services and programs to eastern and rural Russia. 2010.

1853-83 Hildesheim, City of, Hildesheim, Germany, $30,000. For Ecological Brainfood, program to provide comprehensive environmental education for 6 to 16-year olds. Program aims to sensitize young people on environmental issues through mobile media delivery in form of media boxes, combined with environmental workshops and provision of specific media in context of environmental issues series. 2010.

1853-84 Historical and Archaeological Society of Montreal, Pointe-a-Calliere, Montreal, Canada, $26,188. For lighting upgrade for Pointe-a-Callieres. 2010.

1853-85 Hungarian Red Cross Fejer County Organization, Szekesfehervar, Hungary, $20,000. For disaster relief to victims of recent Bakonycsernye flood, protection against future flooding and repair of damages in Bakonycsernye. 2010.

1853-86 Icelandic Church Aid, Reykjavik, Iceland, $50,000. For Family Assistance Program. 2010.

1853-87 IGS Muehlenberg, Europagesamtschule, Hannover, Germany, $30,000. For Success By Professionalism program. 2010.

1853-88 Institute for Sustainable Communities, Montpelier, VT, $300,000. For Environment, Health and Safety Academy in Jiangsu, China. 2010.

1853-89 Institute of International Education, New York, NY, $1,737,766. To act as Managing Partner for Advancing Sustainability Academic Partnership. 2010.

1853-90 Institute of International Education, New York, NY, $222,500. For Alcoa Foundation Technical Support Program in Russia for Science, Technology, Engineering and Mathematics (STEM) education. 2010.

1853-91 International Foundation for Education and Self-Help, Scottsdale, AZ, $29,987. For program,

Teacher Education and Training in Guinea (STEG). 2010.

1853-92 Jane Goodall Institute for Wildlife Research, Education and Conservation, Arlington, VA, $50,000. For Chimpanzee Conservation and Sensitization Program in Guinea, West Africa. 2010.

1853-93 Jour de la Terre Quebec, Montreal, Canada, $15,000. For La Ville en Vert (The City in Green). 2010.

1853-94 Jugendhilfe Selbecke gGmbH, Hagen, Germany, $30,000. For Theatre Pedagogical Concept. 2010.

1853-95 Junior Achievement of Spain, Madrid, Spain, $70,000. For RetoAlcoa, Simulador de Direccion Estrategica de Empresas. 2010.

1853-96 Junior Achievement Young Enterprise Italy, Milan, Italy, $18,000. For entrepreneurship education program, Impresa in Azione: Students Mini-Companies in Vocational Schools. 2010.

1853-97 Kunshan Charity Federation, Kunshan, China, $15,000. For environmental protection Aisle made of recycled materials in Huaqiao Cao An kindergarten. 2010.

1853-98 La Canal Public School, Luanco, Spain, $15,000. For program to make exercise through new technologies. 2010.

1853-99 La Maison des Enfants le Dauphin, Laval, Canada, $30,000. For renovation project. 2010.

1853-100 Le Boulot Vers, Montreal, Canada, $15,000. For Healthy Lifestyle Habits training program for interns. 2010.

1853-101 Les Appartements Sainte-Jeanne, Pont-Rouge, Canada, $50,000. For Social Housing Program. 2010.

1853-102 Les Restaurants du Coeur de LAriege, Varilhes, France, $18,000. To purchase IT equipment for social assistance and education of the needy population of Ariege. 2010.

1853-103 Lethbridge Public Library, Lethbridge, Canada, $15,000. For West Lethbridge Library Branch Collection. 2010.

1853-104 Lycee Immaculee Conception, Laval, France, $25,000. For English Intensive preparation project. 2010.

1853-105 Lycee Polyvalent Theodore Deck, Guebwiller is a commune in the Haut-Rhin department in Alsace in northeastern France, Guebwiller, France, $15,000. For Deck High School (Lycee Polyvalent Theodore Deck) Communication Center. 2010.

1853-106 Mercy Corps, Portland, OR, $80,000. For disaster recovery assistance for victims of the earthquake which struck Haiti. 2010.

1853-107 Multiple Sclerosis Society of Canada, Quebec Division, Montreal, Canada, $15,000. For MS Kids Camp Program. 2010.

1853-108 Musee de la Civilisation, Quebec City, Canada, $185,000. For Aqua exhibition, bicycle rack stations and outdoor urban design furniture projects. 2010.

1853-109 Musee de la Civilisation, Quebec City, Canada, $15,000. For program to offer educational kits in Quebec primary schools. 2010.

1853-110 Nature Conservancy, Arlington, VA, $200,000. For Plant a Billion Trees Campaign, part of Reforestation Program in Brazil. 2010.

1853-111 Organisme de Bassins Versants Manicouagan, Baie-Comeau, Canada, $20,000. For Resort Lake Characterization Project. 2010.

1853-112 Polgardi Kolyokkucko Kozhasznu Alapitvany, Budapest, Hungary, $25,000. To support day care centre for the Szekesfehervar community. 2010.

1853-113 Quad Counties Council on Alcohol and Drug Abuse, Del Rio, TX, $15,000. For Binational Youth Substance Abuse Prevention Conference. 2010.

1853-114 Quebec Society for Disabled Children, Montreal, Canada, $10,000. To purchase safety equipment for clientele. 2010.

1853-115 Red Cross of France, Paris, France, $20,000. For disaster relief to flood victims in southern France. 2010.

1853-116 Red Cross of France, Paris, France, $20,000. For disaster relief to victims of Xynthia storm. Xynthia was a violent European windstorm which crossed Western Europe between 27 February and 1 March 2010. 2010.

1853-117 Red Cross Society of China, Beijing, China, $20,000. For disaster relief to victims of Yushu earthquake. 2010.

1853-118 Redningsselskapet Distrikt Agder, Hovik, Norway, $30,000. For Safety On and By the Sea Program. 2010.

1853-119 Regional Ministry of Education and University Organization of the Regional Governement of Galicia, Santiago De Compostela, Spain, $54,800. For program to prevent occupational hazards in technical colleges in La Coruna. 2010.

1853-120 Regroupement National des Conseils Regionaux de Lenvironnement du Quebec, Montreal, Canada, $15,000. For Defi Climat - Chaque Geste Compte (Climate Challenge - Every Bit Counts). 2010.

1853-121 Restaurants du Coeur du Haut-Rhin, Colmar, France, $20,000. To implement educational kitchen. 2010.

1853-122 Reykjavik University, Reykjavik, Iceland, $150,000. For Alcoa Visir 2 - A Developmental Project on the Advancement of a Knowledge Community in Fjardabyggd, Iceland. 2010.

1853-123 Saint George Hospital of Fejer County, Szekesfehervar, Hungary, $47,000. For programs to improve services at Fejer County Hospital. 2010.

1853-124 Samara Regional Fund for Social Development Time to Live, Samara, Russia, $15,000. For Healthy Youth Is a Healthy Future for Russia program. 2010.

1853-125 Samara Regional Fund for Social Development Time to Live, Samara, Russia, $10,000. For general operating support. 2010.

1853-126 School-to-School International, Pacifica, CA, $49,266. For capacity building for Alcoa School Health and Education Program in Guinea. 2010.

1853-127 Secretaria Especial da Casa Militar, Governo do Estado de Pernambuco, Recife, Brazil, $20,000. For disaster relief to flooding victims in Pernambuco, Brazil. 2010.

1853-128 Shanghai Expo 2010, Pasadena, CA, $170,120. For USA National Pavilion at Shanghai World Expo. 2010.

1853-129 SIPEP de Merxheim Gundolsheim, Gundolsheim, France, $15,000. For program to raise awareness of need to rehabilitate water resources. 2010.

1853-130 Sistema Para el Desarrollo Integral de la Familia, Monterrey, Mexico, $10,000. For disaster relief for victims of Hurricane Alex which struck Nuevo Leon. 2010.

1853-131 Sociedad Deportiva Amorebieta, Amorebieta, Spain, $15,000. For Proyecto Gimnasio SDA (SDA Gym Project). 2010.

1853-132 Strategies for the Global Environment, Arlington, VA, $323,500. For Make an Impact, program to help Alcoa employees and their families reduce their household water and energy use and become part of the solution to climate change in the United States, Canada and Brazil. 2010.

1853-133 Sustainable Pittsburgh, Pittsburgh, PA, $35,000. For Water Matters Global Water Conference. 2010.

1853-134 Szekesfehervar Megyei Jogu Varos Onkormanyzata Kriziskezelo Kozpont, Szekesfehervar, Hungary, $20,000. For housing programmed for individuals, married couples and families, both those with housing and those who have become homeless. 2010.

1853-135 United Way of Jamaica, Kingston, Jamaica, $90,943. For Centers of Excellence Project. 2010.

1853-136 United Way of Jamaica, Kingston, Jamaica, $55,000. For Jamalco Career Enhancement Programme. 2010.

1853-137 Universidad de Navarra IESE Business School, IESE Business School, Barcelona, Spain, $166,931. For research on effects of European Union (EU) sustainable development policies on construction and aluminum. 2010.

1853-138 Universidad de Vigo, Alcoa Advancing Sustainability Initiative, Vigo, Spain, $350,000. To research and leverage actionable solutions for advanced research in energy and environmental economics. 2010.

1853-139 Universita Ca Foscari Venezia, Department of Environmental Sciences (Dipartimento di Scienze Ambientali), Venice, Italy, $30,000. For project about ecosustainability of metallurgical industrial circles. 2010.

1853-140 University of Arkansas Foundation, Applied Sustainability Center, Fayetteville, AR, $80,000. For Sustainability Consortium. 2010.

1853-141 Vefsn Kommune, Mosjoen, Norway, $60,000. For Mosjoen Torg - meeting point and playground. 2010.

1853-142 Victoria Road Primary School, Runcorn, England, $15,000. To create outdoor learning environment and engage local community in the process. 2010.

1853-143 Villa Zapakara Kindermuseum, Paramaribo, Suriname, $78,250. For Star in the City, educational interactive exhibition on Mumbai, India. 2010.

1853-144 Ville de Baie-Comeau, Baie-Comeau, Canada, $28,000. For community development activities throughout World Cup of Para-Cycling of Baie-Comeau with focus on community health. 2010.

1853-145 Voluntarios en Equipo Trabajando por la Superacion con Amor, Monterrey, Mexico, $15,000. For Escobedo Community Activation program. 2010.

1853-146 Windmill Primary School and Childrens Centre, Telford, England, $45,000. For Sustainable Living in Brookside program. 2010.

1853-147 World Resources Institute, Washington, DC, $600,000. For New Ventures: Supporting Environmental Entrepreneurship in Emerging Markets. 2010.

1853-148 World Resources Institute, Washington, DC, $250,000. For Greenhouse Gas (GHG) Protocol Product and Supply Chain Initiative. 2010.

1853-149 World Resources Institute, Washington, DC, $50,000. For programs providing innovative financing to improve industrial energy efficiency in Shanghai. 2010.

1853-150 World Wildlife Fund, Washington, DC, $250,000. For Building on Success: Community Stakeholder Workshops in Kunshan and Shanghai China. 2010.

1853-151 World Wildlife Fund, Washington, DC, $200,000. For Advancing Sustainable Hydropower Project in Mekong, China. 2010.

1853-152 World Wildlife Fund, Washington, DC, $50,000. For Promoting Water Stewardship through Industry Dialogues in China. 2010.

1853-153 Zapovedniks Center, Moscow, Russia, $42,571. For Samara and Belaya Kalitva Young Friends of Protected Areas Program. 2010.

1854
American Foundation for Children with Aids, Inc.

6221 Blue Grass Ave.
Harrisburg, PA   17112-2331   (717) 489-0206
FAX: (717) 489-0214; E-mail: info@afcaids.org;
Toll-free tel.: (888) 683-8323; URL: http://www.helpchildrenwithaids.org/
Facebook: http://www.facebook.com/AFCAids
Twitter: http://twitter.com/#!/AFCA1

Established in 2004 in PA.
Grantmaker type: Public charity.
Financial data (yr. ended 12/31/10): Revenue, $6,266,392; assets, $1,049,316 (M); gifts received, $6,318,154; expenditures, $6,167,582; program services expenses, $5,152,956; giving activities include $302,546 for foundation-administered programs.
Purpose and activities: The organization works to help HIV-positive children, their guardians, and HIV-positive pregnant women in sub-Saharan Africa who have no other access to aid.
Fields of interest: AIDS; Health care; AIDS, people with.
International interests: Sub-Saharan Africa.
Type of support: In-kind gifts.
Limitations: Giving limited to Sub-Saharan Africa.
Publications: Annual report; Financial statement.
Officers and Directors:* Nick Cassino,* Pres.; Robert Maynard,* V.P.; Bill Garbarino,* Treas.; Tanya Weaver, Exec. Dir.; Mary Engelking; Michael Kracht; Al Manji; Lindsey Walker.
EIN: 300247823

1855
AmerisourceBergen Corporation Contributions Program

(formerly AmeriSource Health Corporation Contributions Program)
1300 Morris Dr.
Chesterbrook, PA   19087-5559   (610) 727-7000
URL: http://www.amerisourcebergen.com/abc/Charitable_Giving/index.jsp

Grantmaker type: Corporate giving program.
Purpose and activities: AmerisourceBergen makes charitable contributions to nonprofit organizations involved with improving the mental, social, and physical well-being of the elderly. Support is given primarily in North Carolina, Pennsylvania, Texas, and in Canada.
Fields of interest: Public health; Health care; United Ways and Federated Giving Programs; Aging.
International interests: Canada.

Type of support: General/operating support; Employee volunteer services.
Limitations: Applications not accepted. Giving primarily in areas of company operations in NC, PA, and TX, and in Canada.
Application information: Unsolicited requests are currently not accepted.

1856
AMETEK Foundation, Inc.

1100 Cassatt Rd.
Berwyn, PA   19312-1177
Contact: Kathryn E. Sena, Secy.-Treas.

Incorporated in 1960 in NY.
Donor: AMETEK, Inc.
Grantmaker type: Company-sponsored foundation.
Financial data (yr. ended 12/31/10): Assets, $4,779,024 (M); gifts received, $1,000,000; expenditures, $1,165,550; qualifying distributions, $1,165,550; giving activities include $1,148,870 for 79 grants (high: $108,444; low: $1,000).
Purpose and activities: The foundation supports hospitals and organizations involved with arts and culture, education, the environment, cancer, diabetes, human services, international affairs, and community economic development.
Fields of interest: Museums; Arts; Elementary school/education; Higher education; Scholarships/financial aid; Education; Environment, natural resources; Environment; Hospitals (general); Cancer; Diabetes; American Red Cross; Youth, services; Human services; International affairs; Business/industry; Community/economic development; United Ways and Federated Giving Programs.
Type of support: Program development; General/operating support; Annual campaigns; Building/renovation; Equipment; Endowments; Scholarship funds; Research; Technical assistance; Exchange programs; Matching/challenge support.
Limitations: Applications accepted. Giving primarily in areas of company operations, with emphasis on PA. No support for organizations lacking significant employee interest or involvement. No grants to individuals; no loans.
Application information: Application form not required.
  Initial approach: Proposal
  Copies of proposal: 1
  Deadline(s): None
  Board meeting date(s): Apr. and Oct.
Officers and Directors:* Frank S. Hermance,* Chair. and Pres.; Elizabeth R. Varet,* V.P.; Kathryn E. Sena, Secy.-Treas.; Dennis K. Williams.
EIN: 136095939

1857
The Argus Fund

2200 Hillendale Dr.
Doylestown, PA   18901
Contact: Mark Dibner, Trustee
E-mail: mark@theargusfund.org

Established in 2006 in PA.
Donors: Mark Dibner; Rachel Zax Dibner; The Dibner Fund, Inc.
Grantmaker type: Independent foundation.
Financial data (yr. ended 12/31/10): Assets, $22,362,225 (M); expenditures, $994,377;

qualifying distributions, $713,234; giving activities include $713,234 for grants.
Purpose and activities: The fund will be dedicated, within its financial ability, to provide leadership and supportive funding to organizations, programs and institutions that provide individuals and families with opportunities to help themselves improve the quality of their lives. The fund will also serve to initiate and assist a broad range of activities and projects which tend to improve the human condition, bringing better health, education, self-sufficiency, and cross-cultural understanding to individuals and groups worldwide. To this end, initially, the fund will make local, national, and international grants related but not restricted to: 1) The Arts and Humanities; 2) Humanitarian Aid; 3) Environmental Protection & Conservation; 4) Peaceful Coexistence; 5) Social Reform & Progressive problem solving; 6) Educational Access; 7) Health Care Advocacy; 8) Technological Accessibility & Empowerment; 9) Historical Preservation; and 10) Multi-Cultural Awareness Legacy Giving.
Fields of interest: Arts, cultural/ethnic awareness; Historic preservation/historical societies; Health care; Education; Civil/human rights; International democracy & civil society development; International peace/security; Environment; International relief; Humanities; Arts.
Limitations: Giving primarily in NY and PA.
Application information: Application form not required.
  Initial approach: Letter
  Deadline(s): None
Trustees: Mark Dibner; Rachel Zax Dibner.
EIN: 205045447

1858
The Arronson Foundation

c/o Joseph C. Kohn, Esq.
2400 One Reading Ctr., Ste. 2100
Philadelphia, PA   19107-3304
Application address: c/o Joseph C. Kohn, Esq., One S. Broad St., Philadelphia, PA 19107

Established in 1957 in DE.
Donor: Gertrude Arronson†.
Grantmaker type: Independent foundation.
Financial data (yr. ended 10/31/10): Assets, $4,404,715 (M); expenditures, $152,100; qualifying distributions, $130,475; giving activities include $130,475 for grants.
Purpose and activities: Emphasis on Jewish organizations and education, particularly higher education; support also for the performing arts and other cultural programs, hospitals and hospices, nursing and medical research, women's issues, and family planning.
Fields of interest: Jewish federated giving programs; Performing arts; Performing arts, theater; Performing arts, music; Arts; Higher education; Education; Hospitals (general); Reproductive health, family planning; Nursing care; Medical research, institute; Residential/custodial care, hospices; Women, centers/services; Jewish agencies & synagogues; Women.
International interests: Israel.
Type of support: Annual campaigns; Capital campaigns; Building/renovation; Endowments; Seed money; Scholarship funds.
Limitations: Applications accepted. Giving primarily in Philadelphia, PA.
Application information: Application form required.
  Initial approach: Letter

Copies of proposal: 1
Deadline(s): None
Board meeting date(s): Mar., June, Sept., and Dec.
Final notification: Generally within two weeks
Officers: Joseph C. Kohn, Esq., Pres. and Treas.; Edith Kohn, V.P. and Secy.; Amy D. Goldberg, V.P.; Ellen Kohn, V.P.
EIN: 236259604

1859
Association of Theological Schools in the U.S. & Canada
10 Summit Park Dr.
Pittsburgh, PA   15275-1103   (412) 788-6505
Contact: Daniel O. Aleshire, Exec. Dir.
FAX: (412) 788-6510; E-mail: ats@ats.edu; Tel. for Daniel O. Aleshire : (412)-788-6505 Ext. 227; URL: http://www.ats.edu

Established in 2004 in PA; supporting organization of the Commission on Accreditation of the Association of Theological Schools.
Grantmaker type: Public charity.
Financial data (yr. ended 06/30/10): Revenue, $3,059,904; assets, $18,900,316 (M); gifts received, $1,320,633; expenditures, $4,510,248; program services expenses, $3,678,352; giving activities include $54,430 for grants to organizations outside the U.S., and $706,332 for 22 grants to individuals (high: $75,000; low: $3,665).
Purpose and activities: The association promotes the improvement and enhancement of theological schools for the benefit of communities of faith and the broader public.
Fields of interest: Theology; Theological school/education; Religion.
International interests: Canada.
Type of support: Fellowships; Grants to individuals.
Limitations: Applications accepted. Giving in the U.S. and Canada.
Publications: Application guidelines; Grants list; Informational brochure (including application guidelines); Newsletter.
Application information: Applications accepted only from full time faculty of ATS accredited and Candidate for Accreditation member schools; inappropriate requests for funds not considered or acknowledged. Application form required.
Initial approach: Application
Copies of proposal: 1
Deadline(s): Jan. for Lilly Grants; Dec. for Luce Grants
Officers and Directors:* Donald Senior,* Pres.; John W. Kinney,* V.P.; Leland V. Elliason,* Secy.; Thomas R. Johnson,* Esq., Treas.; Daniel O. Aleshire, Exec. Dir.; Linda Cannell; Ward B. Ewing; Dorcas Gordon; James W. Holsinger, Jr., M.D.; James Hudnut-Beumler; Florence Johnson; Robert E. Manning; Myron F. McCoy; William T. McGrattan; William McKinney; Mary E. McNamara; David Neff; Mark R. Ramseth; Brian C. Stiller; Edward L. Wheeler; G. Craig Williford.
Number of staff: 10 full-time professional; 10 full-time support.
EIN: 562476876

1860
Azavea Inc. Contributions Program
340 N. 12th St., Ste. 402
Philadelphia, PA   19107   (215) 925-2600
E-mail: info@azavea.com; URL: http://www.azavea.com
B Corporation Profile: http://www.bcorporation.net/azavea

Grantmaker type: Corporate giving program.
Purpose and activities: Azavea is a certified B Corporation that donates a percentage of profits to charitable organizations. Support is given primarily in Philadelphia, Pennsylvania.
Fields of interest: Environment; Community/economic development; Computer science; International development; Human services; Arts.
Type of support: Pro bono services - interactive/website technology.
Limitations: Giving primarily in Philadelphia, PA; giving also to national and international organizations.

1861
The Barrack Foundation
930 Rock Creek Rd.
Bryn Mawr, PA   19010-1923

Established in 1978.
Donor: Leonard Barrack.
Grantmaker type: Independent foundation.
Financial data (yr. ended 11/30/10): Assets, $2,735,245 (M); gifts received, $1,000,000; expenditures, $1,146,189; qualifying distributions, $1,146,102; giving activities include $1,146,102 for 29 grants (high: $820,050; low: $50).
Purpose and activities: Giving primarily for Jewish organizations, including Jewish federated giving programs; some giving also to international relief organizations and federated giving programs.
Fields of interest: Children/youth, services; Animals/wildlife, preservation/protection; International relief; Health organizations, association; Human services; Jewish federated giving programs; Jewish agencies & synagogues.
Limitations: Giving primarily in PA. No grants to individuals.
Officer: Leonard Barrack, Mgr.
EIN: 232084461

1862
The Beach Foundation
300 Barr Harbor Dr., Ste. 220
West Conshohocken, PA   19428-3902
Contact: Thomas E. Beach, Pres.

Established in 1997 in PA.
Donor: Thomas E. Beach.
Grantmaker type: Independent foundation.
Financial data (yr. ended 12/31/10): Assets, $6,029,611 (M); gifts received, $2,907,950; expenditures, $295,631; qualifying distributions, $280,000; giving activities include $280,000 for 42 grants (high: $120,000; low: $50).
Fields of interest: Disasters, Hurricane Katrina; Human services; Education; Environment, natural resources; International affairs, public policy; United Ways and Federated Giving Programs; Public affairs.
Limitations: Applications accepted. Giving primarily in CA, NH and PA. No grants to individuals.
Application information:

Initial approach: Letter
Deadline(s): None
Officers and Directors:* Thomas E. Beach,* Pres.; Walter T. Beach,* V.P.; Jonathan T. Beach,* Secy.; Theodore T. Beach,* Treas.
EIN: 232897351

1863
The Benter Foundation
c/o William Benter
4 Smithfield St., 9th Fl.
Pittsburgh, PA   15222-2226

Established in 2007 in PA.
Donor: William F. Benter.
Grantmaker type: Independent foundation.
Financial data (yr. ended 12/31/10): Assets, $54,785 (M); gifts received, $1,150,000; expenditures, $1,280,773; qualifying distributions, $1,280,577; giving activities include $1,109,350 for 25 grants (high: $103,600; low: $10,000).
Purpose and activities: Giving primarily for higher education, as well as for international and cultural affairs.
Fields of interest: Arts, cultural/ethnic awareness; Performing arts, ballet; Higher education; Education; Boy scouts; International affairs; Foundations (public).
Limitations: Applications not accepted. Giving primarily in PA, with emphasis on Pittsburgh. No grants to individuals.
Application information: Contributes only to pre-selected organizations.
Officers and Directors:* William F. Benter,* Pres.; Bruce Benter,* Secy.; Bruce Pyle,* Treas.
EIN: 208807953

1864
The Edwin J. and Barbara R. Berkowitz Family Foundation
506 Oak Terr.
Merion Station, PA   19066-1341
(610) 664-8335
Contact: Edwin J. Berkowitz, Tr.

Established in 1998.
Donor: Edwin J. Berkowitz.
Grantmaker type: Independent foundation.
Financial data (yr. ended 12/31/10): Assets, $39,243 (M); gifts received, $199,975; expenditures, $169,850; qualifying distributions, $169,600; giving activities include $169,600 for grants.
Purpose and activities: Giving primarily for education and to Jewish organizations.
Fields of interest: Higher education, university; Education; Jewish federated giving programs; Jewish agencies & synagogues.
International interests: Israel.
Limitations: Applications accepted. Giving primarily in PA and NJ; some giving also in Israel.
Application information:
Initial approach: Letter
Deadline(s): None
Trustees: Alan Berkowitz; Arthur M. Berkowitz; Barbara R. Berkowitz; Daniel M. Berkowitz; Edwin J. Berkowitz; Pnina B. Siegler.
EIN: 237978506

1865
The Raymond and Elizabeth Bloch Foundation

603 Frick Bldg.
Pittsburgh, PA 15219
Contact: Bernard L. Bloch, C.E.O. and Pres.

Established in 1989 in PA.
Donor: Raymond Bloch†.
Grantmaker type: Independent foundation.
Financial data (yr. ended 12/31/10): Assets, $3,165,980 (M); expenditures, $234,949; qualifying distributions, $161,500; giving activities include $161,500 for grants.
Purpose and activities: Giving primarily for self-help projects for children in impoverished parts of the world and to organizations concerned with issues of world peace through international law and arms control; some support also for medical research to relieve pain caused primarily by headaches.
Fields of interest: Children/youth, services; Medical research, institute; International peace/security; International affairs, arms control; Law/international law.
Limitations: Applications accepted. Giving primarily in PA. No grants to individuals.
Application information: Application form not required.
Deadline(s): None
Officer: Bernard L. Bloch, C.E.O. and Pres.
EIN: 251561204

1866
Bread and Roses Community Fund

(formerly The People's Fund)
1500 Walnut St., Ste. 1305
Philadelphia, PA 19102-3514   (215) 731-1107
Contact: Christie Balka, Exec. Dir.
FAX: (215) 731-0453;
E-mail: info@breadrosesfund.org; URL: http://www.breadrosesfund.org/

Established in 1971 in PA.
Grantmaker type: Public charity.
Financial data (yr. ended 06/30/10): Revenue, $553,711; assets, $1,348,888 (M); gifts received, $537,435; expenditures, $523,328; giving activities include $63,750 for grants, and $22,000 for grants to individuals.
Purpose and activities: The fund is a unique partnership of donors and activists committed to supporting social change in the Delaware Valley, primarily in the areas of greater access to health care, economic justice, procuring a clean and safe environment, civil and human rights, peace, and other issues.
Fields of interest: Environment; Health care; International peace/security; Civil/human rights, advocacy; Civil liberties, advocacy; Civil/human rights.
Type of support: General/operating support; Continuing support; Program development; Conferences/seminars; Seed money; Technical assistance; Scholarships—to individuals.
Limitations: Applications accepted. Giving limited to Philadelphia, Bucks, Chester, Delaware, and Montgomery counties, PA, and Camden County, NJ. No support for direct service organizations (unless involved in social change) or generally for organizations with budgets exceeding $150,000. No grants to individuals (except for scholarships), or for capital campaigns or building projects.

Publications: Application guidelines; Grants list; Informational brochure; Newsletter.
Application information: Organizations must be located in the Delaware Valley (Bucks, Chester, Delaware, Montgomery, and Philadelphia counties, PA; and Camden County, NJ), and must have an organizational and/or distinct project budget that is less than $150,000. Application form required.
Initial approach: Download application
Deadline(s): 1st day of each month for The Opportunity Fund; Jan. 15 for Lax Scholarship Fund; Mar. 1 for The Media Justice Fund; July 6 for The Future Fund and The Racial and Economic Justice Fund; Dec. 1 for Phoebus Criminal Justice Initiative;
Board meeting date(s): Jan., Mar., May, June, Sept., Oct., and Nov.
Final notification: May for LAX Scholarships; within 3 to 4 weeks for Discretionary/Emergency Grants; 2 months for Phoebus
Officers and Directors: Denise Brown,* Co-Chair.; Tom Sugure,* Co-Chair.; Christie Balka, Exec. Dir.; Richard Baron; Gloria Casarez; Andy Lamas; Arun Prabhakaran; Chris Rabb; Aissia Richardson; Ellen Somekawa; Joel Steiker.
Number of staff: 6 full-time professional.
EIN: 232047297

1867
The Brother's Brother Foundation

1200 Galveston Ave.
Pittsburgh, PA 15233-1604   (412) 321-3160
FAX: (412) 321-3325,
E-mail: mail@brothersbrother.org; URL: http://www.brothersbrother.org
Facebook: http://www.facebook.com/pages/Brothers-Brother-Foundation/141763585250

Established in 1958.
Grantmaker type: Public charity.
Financial data (yr. ended 12/31/10): Revenue, $273,450,919; assets, $18,804,595 (M); gifts received, $272,736,024; expenditures, $274,423,849; giving activities include $63,883,610 for grants, and $208,372,703 for 2 grants to organizations outside the U.S.
Purpose and activities: The foundation promotes international health and education for those in need overseas through the efficient and effective distribution and provision of donated medical, educational, agricultural, and other resources, including pharmaceuticals, medical supplies, medical equipment, text books, and educational and humanitarian supplies.
Fields of interest: Education; Health care; Nutrition; International affairs.
Type of support: In-kind gifts.
Limitations: Applications not accepted. Giving on an international basis.
Publications: Annual report; Newsletter.
Application information: Unsolicited requests for funds not accepted.
Officers and Trustees:* Richard Milner,* Chair.; Roy G. Dorrance,* Vice-Chair.; Luke L. Hingson, Pres.; Daniel Simpson,* Secy.; Joseph T. Senko,* Treas.; Rachel Lorey Allen; Elena A. Baylis; Seth Bekoe, M.D.; Michael R. Doherty; Carolyn D. Ellis, M.D.; Paul Euwer; Michael R. Foster; Walter B. Fowler; Mariann Geyer; and 12 additional trustees.
Number of staff: 5 full-time professional; 2 part-time professional; 5 full-time support; 2 part-time support.
EIN: 346562544

1868
Carnegie Hero Fund Commission

436 7th Ave., Ste. 1101
Pittsburgh, PA 15219-1841
Contact: Jeffrey A. Dooley, Investigations Mgr.
FAX: (412) 281-5751;
E-mail: carnegiehero@carnegiehero.org; Toll free tel.: (800) 447-8900; URL: http://www.carnegiehero.org/

Established in 1904 in PA.
Donor: Andrew Carnegie†.
Grantmaker type: Operating foundation.
Financial data (yr. ended 12/31/09): Assets, $38,115,097 (M); gifts received, $9,392; expenditures, $1,738,879; qualifying distributions, $1,618,233; giving activities include $862,104 for grants to individuals.
Purpose and activities: A private operating foundation established to recognize, with the award of medals and sums of money, heroism voluntarily performed by civilians within the U.S. and Canada in saving or attempting to save the lives of others; and to grant monetary assistance, including scholarship aid, to awardees and to the dependents of those who have lost their lives or who have been disabled in such heroic manner.
Fields of interest: Human services; Voluntarism promotion.
International interests: Canada.
Type of support: Continuing support; Grants to individuals; Scholarships—to individuals.
Limitations: Applications accepted. Giving primarily in the U.S.; some giving also in Canada.
Publications: Annual report; Informational brochure; Newsletter.
Application information: Awards by nomination only. Refer to the commission web site for complete nominating guidelines and form. Application form required.
Initial approach: Letter
Copies of proposal: 1
Deadline(s): Within 2 years of the act for nominations
Board meeting date(s): Mar., June, Sept., and Dec.
Final notification: Following board meetings
Officers and Trustees:* Mark Laskow,* Pres.; Priscilla J. McCrady,* V.P.; Walter F. Rutkowski, Secy. and Exec. Dir.; James M. Walton,* Treas.; Albert H. Burchfield III; Elizabeth H. Genter; Thomas J. Hilliard, Jr.; David McL. Hillman; Linda T. Hills; Peter J. Lambrou; Christopher R. McCrady; Ann M. McGuinn; Nancy L. Rackoff; Frank Brooks Robinson; Dan D. Sandman; William P. Snyder III; Sybil P. Veeder; Thomas L. Wentling, Jr.; Alfred W. Wishart, Jr.; Carol A. Word.
Number of staff: 5 full-time professional; 2 part-time professional; 2 full-time support; 1 part-time support.
EIN: 251062730

1869
The Carthage Foundation

1 Oxford Ctr.
301 Grant St., Ste. 3900
Pittsburgh, PA 15219-6401   (412) 392-2900
Contact: Michael W. Gleba, Treas.
URL: http://www.scaife.com/carthage.html

Incorporated in 1964 in PA.
Donor: Richard M. Scaife.
Grantmaker type: Independent foundation.

Financial data (yr. ended 12/31/10): Assets, $26,390,356 (M); expenditures, $1,277,438; qualifying distributions, $1,164,566; giving activities include $602,500 for 6 grants (high: $200,000; low: $37,500).

Purpose and activities: Grants primarily for public policy research, particularly in the areas of government and international affairs and only to U.S. 501(c)(3) organizations.

Fields of interest: Crime/law enforcement, counterterrorism; International affairs; Political science; Public policy, research; Government/public administration.

Type of support: General/operating support; Conferences/seminars.

Limitations: Applications accepted. Giving on a national basis, with emphasis on the Washington, DC, metro area. No support for nationally-organized fundraising groups. No grants to individuals. Generally, no grants for event sponsorships, endowments, capital campaigns, renovations or government agencies.

Publications: Annual report.

Application information: The foundation does not issue a separate program policy statement or grant application guidelines. The foundation acknowledges receipt of proposals. Application form not required.

    Initial approach: Letter
    Copies of proposal: 1
    Deadline(s): None
    Board meeting date(s): Quarterly
    Final notification: 1 to 3 weeks

Officers and Trustees:* Richard M. Scaife,* Chair.; R. Daniel McMichael,* Secy.; Michael W. Gleba,* Treas.; Alexis J. Konkol; W. McCook Miller, Jr.; Roger W. Robinson, Jr.

Number of staff: 2 part-time professional; 2 part-time support.

EIN: 256067979

1870
Cephalon, Inc. Corporate Giving Program

c/o Mgr., Corp. Contribs.
41 Moores Rd.
P.O. Box 4011
Frazer, PA 19355-1113
URL: http://www.cephalon.com/our-responsibility/commitment-to-community.shtml

Grantmaker type: Corporate giving program.

Purpose and activities: As a complement to its foundation, Cephalon also makes charitable contributions to nonprofit organizations directly. Support is given primarily in Minneapolis, Minnesota, the greater Philadelphia, Pennsylvania area, and Salt Lake City, Utah, and in Australia, France, Germany, and Switzerland.

Fields of interest: General charitable giving; Residential/custodial care, hospices; Disasters, preparedness/services; Cancer, leukemia; Disabilities, people with.

International interests: Australia; France; Germany; Switzerland.

Type of support: General/operating support; Employee volunteer services.

Limitations: Applications not accepted. Giving primarily in Minneapolis, MN, the greater Philadelphia, PA area, and Salt Lake City, UT, and in Australia, France, Germany, and Switzerland.

Application information: Unsolicited requests for funds are not accepted.

1871
Children's Medical Foundation of Central and Eastern Europe

c/o Scott P. Bartlett
10 Penn Tower, 3400 Spruce St.
Philadelphia, PA 19104-4206
Contact: Anne Van Gilson, Secy.-Trees.; Scott Bartlett M.D., Pres.
E-mail: cmfcee@gmail.com; E-mail for Dr. Scott Bartlett: scott.bartlett@uphs.upenn.edu; URL: http://www.cmfcee.org

Established in 2005 in PA.

Grantmaker type: Public charity.

Financial data (yr. ended 12/31/10): Revenue, $32,962; assets, $257,382 (M); gifts received, $31,637; expenditures, $44,210; program services expenses, $36,414; giving activities include $6,982 for grants.

Purpose and activities: The foundation is dedicated to improving the lives of children in Central and Eastern Europe by providing desperately needed funding to well-managed yet under-funded hospitals of the region.

Fields of interest: Pediatrics; Medical care, outpatient care; Medical care, in-patient care; International development; International affairs, fund raising/fund distribution; International affairs; Health care, association; Hospitals (general).

International interests: Ukraine; Poland; Romania; Lithuania; Georgia (Republic of); Bulgaria; Eastern & Central Europe; Europe.

Type of support: Equipment; Seed money; Scholarship funds.

Limitations: Applications accepted. Giving on an international basis in Central and Eastern Europe. No grants to individuals.

Publications: Newsletter.

Application information: Applications must be either electronic or hardcopy. Application form required.

    Initial approach: E-mail to request application form
    Copies of proposal: 1
    Deadline(s): None
    Final notification: 1-2 months

Officers: Scott P. Bartlett, M.D., Pres.; Anne Van Gilson, Secy.-Treas.

EIN: 251915857

1872
The Clayman Family Foundation

One Presidential Blvd., Ste. 200
Bala Cynwyd, PA 19004-1007

Established in 1997 in PA.

Grantmaker type: Independent foundation.

Financial data (yr. ended 12/31/10): Assets, $9,050,600 (M); expenditures, $461,392; qualifying distributions, $448,560; giving activities include $336,980 for 87 grants (high: $110,000; low: $10).

Fields of interest: Higher education; Education; Health organizations, association; Crime/law enforcement, police agencies; Human services; Children, services; International affairs; Jewish federated giving programs; Christian agencies & churches; Catholic agencies & churches; Jewish agencies & synagogues.

Limitations: Applications not accepted. Giving primarily in NJ and PA. No grants to individuals.

Application information: Contributes only to pre-selected organizations.

Directors: Bradford Clayman; Deborah Clayman; Roberta Clayman; Stephen A. Cohen.

EIN: 232893816

1873
Colcom Foundation

2 Gateway Ctr., Ste. 1800
Pittsburgh, PA 15222-1442
Contact: John F. Rohe, V.P., Philanthropy
E-mail: contact@colcomfdn.org; URL: http://www.colcomfdn.org/

Established in 1996 in PA.

Donor: Cordelia S. May†.

Grantmaker type: Independent foundation.

Financial data (yr. ended 06/30/10): Assets, $387,247,859 (M); gifts received, $1,329,763; expenditures, $23,343,785; qualifying distributions, $19,972,241; giving activities include $19,158,060 for 108 grants (high: $1,500,000; low: $400).

Purpose and activities: The primary mission of the foundation is to foster a sustainable environment to ensure quality of life for all Americans by addressing major causes and consequences of overpopulation and its adverse effects on natural resources. Regionally, the foundation supports conservation and environmental projects and cultural assets.

Fields of interest: Environment, beautification programs; Recreation; Human services; Environment, administration/regulation; Environment; Community/economic development; Population studies.

Type of support: Technical assistance; Seed money; Publication; Program evaluation; Internship funds; Film/video/radio; Equipment; Endowments; Continuing support; Capital campaigns; Annual campaigns; General/operating support; Land acquisition; Management development/capacity building; Matching/challenge support; Program development; Research.

Limitations: Giving nationally in the areas of population and immigration, regionally (southwestern PA) for the environment and conservation, and locally (Pittsburgh, PA) for community and economic development. No grants to individuals, or for scholarships; no loans.

Publications: Application guidelines; Annual report; Financial statement; Grants list; Informational brochure.

Application information: Grant applications are not accepted unless in response to an invitation following a letter of inquiry. See web site for additional application information. Grantmakers of Western Pennsylvania's Common Grant Application Format accepted. Application form required.

    Initial approach: Letter of inquiry not exceeding 2 pages
    Copies of proposal: 1
    Deadline(s): Varies
    Board meeting date(s): Feb., May, Aug. and Nov.
    Final notification: Up to 4 months

Officers and Directors:* Timothy M. Inglis,* Pres. and Treas.; John F. Rohe, V.P., Philanthropy and Secy.; John S. Barsotti,* V.P., Investments; Donna M. Panazzi; Michael M. Strueber.

Number of staff: 2 full-time professional; 1 full-time support.

EIN: 311479839

Recent grants for international programs:

1873-1 American Immigration Control Foundation, Monterey, VA, $50,000. For public education on a balanced immigration policy. 2009.

1873-2 American Immigration Control Foundation, Monterey, VA, $40,000. For public awareness program. 2009.

1873-3 Center for Immigration Studies, Washington, DC, $225,000. For research and public education on the effects of immigration. 2009.

1873-4 Center for Immigration Studies, Washington, DC, $200,000. For journalism articles on immigration. 2009.

1873-5 Center for Immigration Studies, Washington, DC, $100,000. For public awareness programs. 2009.

1873-6 Center for Immigration Studies, Washington, DC, $100,000. For research on security issues. 2009.

1873-7 Center for Immigration Studies, Washington, DC, $75,000. For public education of immigration impact on a group. 2009.

1873-8 Center for Immigration Studies, Washington, DC, $55,000. For communications work related to immigration. 2009.

1873-9 International Services Assistance Fund, Research Triangle Park, NC, $50,000. For research on safe, affordable, and accessible contraception. 2009.

1873-10 NumbersUSA Education and Research Foundation, Arlington, VA, $900,000. For research and public education on impact of immigration levels. 2009.

1873-11 NumbersUSA Education and Research Foundation, Arlington, VA, $500,000. For public education on sustainable immigration levels. 2009.

1873-12 NumbersUSA Education and Research Foundation, Arlington, VA, $465,000. For public awareness program. 2009.

1873-13 NumbersUSA Education and Research Foundation, Arlington, VA, $300,000. To expand media's understanding of immigration issues. 2009.

1873-14 NumbersUSA Education and Research Foundation, Arlington, VA, $45,000. To advance understanding of immigration consequences by the media. 2009.

1873-15 NumbersUSA Education and Research Foundation, Arlington, VA, $40,000. For internships. 2009.

1873-16 US, Petoskey, MI, $1,000,000. For public education on effects of immigration on natural resources, wages, schools, infrastructure, and taxes. 2009.

1873-17 US, Petoskey, MI, $465,000. For public awareness programs. 2009.

1873-18 US, Petoskey, MI, $160,000. For public education on advantages of official English and on personal value of familiarity with other languages. 2009.

1874
Copernicus Society of America
1 Reiffs Mill Rd.
Ambler, PA 19002-4280

Established in 1972 in PA.
Donors: Edward J. Piszek, Sr.†; James A. Michener†.
Grantmaker type: Independent foundation.
Financial data (yr. ended 06/30/11): Assets, $3,351,272 (M); gifts received, $9,960;

expenditures, $322,851; qualifying distributions, $170,263; giving activities include $170,263 for grants.
Purpose and activities: Giving primarily for the support and advancement of the Polish culture and heritage. Giving also for education and Roman Catholic organizations.
Fields of interest: Higher education, university; Education; Catholic agencies & churches.
International interests: Poland.
Type of support: Continuing support; Endowments; Conferences/seminars; Publication.
Limitations: Applications not accepted. Giving primarily in PA. No grants to individuals, or for special projects, operating budgets, annual campaigns, seed money, emergency funds, deficit financing, building funds, equipment and materials, land acquisition, matching gifts, scholarships, fellowships, or research; no loans.
Application information: Unsolicited requests for funds not accepted.
   Board meeting date(s): Monthly
Officers: Helen P. Nelson, Pres.; Francis Keenan, V.P.; Edward J. Piszek, Jr., V.P.; George W. Piszek, V.P.; William P. Piszek, V.P.; P. Erik Nelson, Exec. Dir.
Number of staff: 1 full-time professional; 3 part-time support.
EIN: 237184731

1875
The Cotswold Foundation
234 Broughton Ave.
Villanova, PA 19085-1914

Established in 1994 in PA.
Donors: I. Wistar Morris III; Martha Morris; Melissa H. Morris; Lydia P. Morris; Eleanor W. Morris; Eleventh Generation, LP.
Grantmaker type: Independent foundation.
Financial data (yr. ended 12/31/10): Assets, $36,050,793 (M); gifts received, $343,075; expenditures, $1,557,722; qualifying distributions, $1,556,367; giving activities include $1,556,367 for grants.
Fields of interest: Medical research; Museums (art); Higher education; Human services; International affairs, foreign policy; Biology/life sciences.
Type of support: General/operating support.
Limitations: Applications not accepted. Giving in the U.S., particularly in PA, with emphasis on Philadelphia. No grants to individuals.
Application information: Contributes only to pre-selected organizations.
Trustees: I. Wistar Morris III; Martha H. Morris.
EIN: 237767257

1876
The Francis J. Dixon Foundation
P.O. Box 333
Lebanon, PA 17042-0333 (717) 389-0995
Contact: Stephan Vegoe, Exec. Dir.
E-mail: svegoe@fjdixonfoundation.org

Established in 1989 in PA.
Donors: Francis J. Dixon; Brandywine Recyclers, Inc.
Grantmaker type: Independent foundation.
Financial data (yr. ended 12/31/10): Assets, $10,599,323 (M); gifts received, $3,000,000; expenditures, $794,686; qualifying distributions,

$364,700; giving activities include $364,700 for grants.
Purpose and activities: Support for education, medical and community organizations, scholarships, and disaster relief.
Fields of interest: Health care; Education, fund raising/fund distribution; Higher education, college (community/junior); Safety/disasters; International relief; United Ways and Federated Giving Programs.
Type of support: Equipment; Emergency funds; Program development; Scholarship funds; Technical assistance.
Limitations: Applications accepted. Giving primarily in Lebanon County, PA. No support for businesses, private foundations, large community based or national charities, or religious organizations. No grants to individuals, or for endowments, capital expenditures, general operating expenses, or debt reduction.
Publications: Annual report; Financial statement; Grants list.
Application information: Application form required.
   Initial approach: 1-2 page cover letter outlining grant request
   Copies of proposal: 1
   Deadline(s): None
   Board meeting date(s): 2nd Wed. of Mar., July, & Nov.
   Final notification: 2-3 weeks
Officers: Frank Dixon, Chair.; Daniel Dixon, Vice-Chair.; Christine Dixon, Pres.; JoAnn D. White, Treas.; Stephan Vegoe, Exec. Dir.
Directors: David Dixon; Thomas Dixon; Timothy J. Huber; Robert J. Phillips; Richard P. Scott; Thomas I. Siegel.
Number of staff: 1 full-time professional.
EIN: 251600852

1877
The Samuel Epstein Foundation Trust
248 Seneca St.
Oil City, PA 16301-1371

Established in 1988 in PA.
Donor: Samuel Epstein†.
Grantmaker type: Independent foundation.
Financial data (yr. ended 12/31/10): Assets, $4,634,296 (M); expenditures, $220,974; qualifying distributions, $200,956; giving activities include $180,000 for 11 grants (high: $72,000; low: $10,800).
Purpose and activities: Giving primarily for human services, and Jewish organizations; scholarships are limited to Sheffield High School, Warren County, Pennsylvania.
Fields of interest: Education; Human services; Jewish federated giving programs; Jewish agencies & synagogues.
International interests: Israel.
Type of support: General/operating support; Scholarships—to individuals.
Limitations: Applications not accepted. Giving primarily in Warren, PA.
Application information: Unsolicited requests for grants not accepted.
Trustee: National City Bank.
EIN: 256311365

1878
Gene & Marlene Epstein Humanitarian Fund

1238 Wrightstown Rd.
Newtown, PA   18940-9602   (215) 968-2200
Contact: Gene Epstein

Established in 2007 in PA.
Donors: Gene Epstein; Marlene Epstien.
Grantmaker type: Operating foundation.
Financial data (yr. ended 12/31/09): Assets, $0 (M); gifts received, $75,252; expenditures, $150,799; qualifying distributions, $146,964; giving activities include $146,964 for 24+ grants (high: $50,000).
Fields of interest: Jewish agencies & synagogues; International development.
International interests: Israel.
Type of support: General/operating support.
Application information:
  Initial approach: Letter or phone call
  Deadline(s): None
Directors: Gene Epstein; Marlene Epstein.
EIN: 061813910

1879
Federated Investors Foundation, Inc.

1001 Liberty Avenue, 21st Fl
Pittsburgh, PA   15222-3779

Established in 1997.
Donor: Federated Investors, Inc.
Grantmaker type: Company-sponsored foundation.
Financial data (yr. ended 04/30/11): Assets, $1,266,514 (M); gifts received, $1,251,300; expenditures, $646,152; qualifying distributions, $646,000; giving activities include $646,000 for grants.
Purpose and activities: The foundation supports organizations involved with arts and culture, education, human services, international affairs, civil liberties, and public policy.
Fields of interest: Media/communications; Arts; Secondary school/education; Higher education; Education; Children, services; Human services; International affairs; Civil liberties, advocacy; Civil liberties, right to life; United Ways and Federated Giving Programs; Public policy, research.
Type of support: General/operating support; Annual campaigns; Capital campaigns; Building/renovation; Program development; Scholarship funds.
Limitations: Applications not accepted. Giving primarily in Pittsburgh, PA. No grants to individuals.
Application information: Contributes only to pre-selected organizations.
Officers and Directors:* J. Christopher Donahue,* Pres.; John W. McGonigle, Secy.; Thomas R. Donahue, Treas.; John F. Donahue; Thomas J. Donnelly.
EIN: 232913182

1880
Foundation for a Christian Civilization, Inc.

P.O. Box 341
Hanover, PA   17331-0341   (717) 225-7147
FAX: (717) 225-7382; E-mail: tfp@tfp.org; Toll-free tel.: (866) 661-0272; URL: http://www.tfp.org/

Established in 1973 in NY.
Grantmaker type: Public charity.

Financial data (yr. ended 06/30/10): Revenue, $7,318,696; assets, $5,744,309 (M); gifts received, $7,026,371; expenditures, $7,052,062; giving activities include $150,902 for grants, $188,500 for grants to organizations outside the U.S., and $1,838 for grants to individuals.
Purpose and activities: The foundation is a civic organization of Catholic inspiration that seeks to defend in a legal and peaceful way, the basic values of Christian civilization, namely tradition, family, and property.
Fields of interest: Christian agencies & churches; Catholic agencies & churches.
Type of support: Scholarships—to individuals; In-kind gifts.
Limitations: Giving on a national and international basis.
Publications: Informational brochure.
Officers and Directors:* Raymond E. Drake,* Pres.; John W. Horvat II,* V.P.; Benjamin A. Hiegert,* Secy.-Treas.; Luiz A. Fragelli; Gary J. Isbell; Charles P. Noell III; Robert E. Ritchie.
EIN: 237325778

1881
Friends of Via

P.O. Box 82556
Pittsburgh, PA   15218-0556   (412) 855-6581
Contact: Carol Hochman, Pres.
E-mail: carolh1541@aol.com; URL: http://viafoundation.org/friends-of-via/

Established in 2005 in PA as a United States-based partner to support the charitable activities of the Via Foundation in Prague, Czech Republic.
Grantmaker type: Public charity.
Financial data (yr. ended 06/30/10): Revenue, $76,284; assets, $17,793 (M); gifts received, $76,284; expenditures, $92,303; giving activities include $8,000 for grants, and $81,692 for grants to individuals.
Purpose and activities: The organization aims to increase awareness of the Czech Republic and of the Via Foundation's charitable work in the areas of Czech Cultural Heritage, community development, youth, and the environment. Through these areas of interest, Friends of Via works to empower citizens and nonprofit organizations, promoting philanthropy, community activism, and respect for the environment through support and proliferation of successful models, in order to cultivate a strong civil society in the Czech Republic.
International interests: Czech Republic.
Officer and Directors:* Carol Hochman,* Pres.; William Lafe; Kevin Kearns; Vera Krofcheck; Robin Zoufalik.
EIN: 820546000

1882
Friendship Fund, Inc.

c/o BNY Mellon, N.A.
P.O. Box 185
Pittsburgh, PA   15230-0185
Application address: c/o Eleanor Millan, 1 Boston Pl., Boston, MA 02108, tel.: (617) 722-7772

Incorporated in 1918 in NY.
Donor: Charles R. Crane†.
Grantmaker type: Independent foundation.
Financial data (yr. ended 06/30/11): Assets, $4,398,473 (M); expenditures, $300,009;

qualifying distributions, $245,000; giving activities include $245,000 for grants.
Purpose and activities: Giving for the advancement of the humanities and the sciences and for the welfare of humanity. Emphasis on local giving for environmental protection, social services, and international affairs. Funds largely committed in advance.
Fields of interest: Science; Education; Environment; Human services; International affairs.
Type of support: Capital campaigns; Building/renovation; Equipment; Land acquisition; Program development; Publication; Seed money.
Limitations: Applications accepted. Giving primarily in CA, CO, CT, MA, NY and VA. No grants to individuals.
Application information: Application form not required.
  Initial approach: Letter
  Deadline(s): Apr. 1
  Board meeting date(s): Aug.
Officers and Trustees:* Ellen D.B.F. Tully,* Pres.; Thomas S. Crane,* Treas.; Darby Bradley; Charles M. Crane; Diane Crane; Sylvia E. Crane; Josephine DeGive; Elizabeth McLane-Bradley.
EIN: 136089220

1883
Global Links

4809 Penn Ave., No. 2
Pittsburgh, PA   15224-1301   (412) 361-3424
FAX: (412) 361-4950; E-mail: info@globallinks.org; URL: http://www.globallinks.org

Established in 1989.
Grantmaker type: Public charity.
Financial data (yr. ended 12/31/10): Revenue, $5,051,684; assets, $4,511,310 (M); gifts received, $5,003,945; expenditures, $5,034,048; giving activities include $9,658 for grants, and $3,745,084 for grants to organizations outside the U.S.
Purpose and activities: The organization recovers unused medical supplies, equipment, and furnishings from U.S. hospitals for distribution to hospitals and clinics that serve the poorest segments of the population in developing countries.
Fields of interest: Health care; Economically disadvantaged.
International interests: Developing countries.
Type of support: In-kind gifts.
Limitations: Applications not accepted. Giving primarily in developing countries.
Publications: Financial statement.
Application information: Unsolicited applications not accepted or acknowledged.
Officers and Directors:* Margaret Larkins-Pettigrew,* M.D., Chair.; Jeffrey Ford,* C.P.A., Vice-Chair.; Rev. Eugene F. Lauer,* S.T.D., Secy.; Charles Vargo,* Treas.; Kathleen G. Hower,* Exec. Dir.; Mimi Falbo, R.N., M.S.N.; Daniel Kovalik; Miguel Marquez, M.D.; Patricia Rambasek, C.F.R.E.; Robin Sheldon; Barry L. Silverman; Mahmood Mike Usman, M.D.; Daniel T. Wagner, R.Ph., MBA.
EIN: 521629060

1884
Global Security Institute
GSB Bldg., Ste. 400
1 Belmont Ave.
Bala Cynwyd, PA   19004-1607   (610) 668-5488
FAX: (610) 668-5489;
E-mail: general@gsinstitute.org; URL: http://
www.gsinstitute.org

Established in 1999.
Grantmaker type: Public charity.
Financial data (yr. ended 12/31/10): Revenue,
$911,486; assets, $56,684 (M); gifts received,
$863,549; expenditures, $931,847.
Purpose and activities: The institute is dedicated to
strengthening international cooperation and security
based on the rule of law, with a particular focus on
nuclear arms control, non-proliferation, and
disarmament.
Fields of interest: International affairs, arms
control; International peace/security; International
conflict resolution; International affairs.
Limitations: Giving on a worldwide basis.
Publications: Newsletter; Occasional report.
Officers and Directors:* Kim Cranston,* Chair.;
C.E. "Pat" Patterson,* Pres.; Zachary Allen,*
Secy.-Treas.; Christie Brinkley; Amb. Thomas
Graham, Jr.; Jonathan Granoff; Robert Klein II; Fred
Matser; Berniece Patterson; Kim Polese; Christina
Sidoti; Tyler Wigg Stevenson; Lynne Twist; Dolf
Zantinge.
EIN: 943347331

1885
Grass Family Foundation
1000 N. Front St., Ste. 503
Wormleysburg, PA   17043-1043

Established in 1972 in PA.
Donor: Alex Grass.
Grantmaker type: Independent foundation.
Financial data (yr. ended 11/30/10): Assets,
$9,043,569 (M); expenditures, $1,256,549;
qualifying distributions, $1,193,429; giving
activities include $1,184,374 for 49 grants (high:
$381,720; low: $100).
Purpose and activities: Giving primarily for Jewish
welfare funds; some support also for education, and
arts and culture.
Fields of interest: Arts; Education; Human services;
Jewish federated giving programs.
International interests: Israel.
Limitations: Applications not accepted. Giving
primarily in FL; Baltimore, MD; New York, NY; and
Harrisburg, PA. No grants to individuals.
Application information: Contributes only to
pre-selected organizations.
Officers and Directors:* Linda Shapiro Chemtob,*
Secy.; Elizabeth Grass Weese.
EIN: 237218002

1886
Guanacaste Dry Forest Conservation Fund
University of Penn., Biology Dept.
Philadelphia, PA   19104-4274   (215) 898-5636
Contact: Daniel Janzen, Pres.

Grantmaker type: Public charity.
Financial data (yr. ended 12/31/10): Revenue,
$1,743,523; assets, $16,761,701 (M); gifts
received, $1,604,619; expenditures, $933,533;

giving activities include $30,000 for grants to
organizations outside the U.S.
Purpose and activities: The fund supports
organizations that work for wildlife conservation and
preservation of the Rincon rainforest in Costa Rica.
Fields of interest: Environment, forests; Animals/
wildlife, preservation/protection; Animals/wildlife.
International interests: Costa Rica.
Type of support: Land acquisition.
Limitations: Giving on an international basis,
primarily in Costa Rica.
Officers and Directors:* Daniel Janzen,* Pres.;
Winnie Hallwachs,* Secy. and C.F.O.; George
Gorman.
EIN: 943280315

1887
H. J. Heinz Company Contributions Program
1 PPG Place
Pittsburgh, PA   15222-5400   (412) 237-5100
FAX: (412) 237-3881; URL: http://www.heinz.com/
sustainability.aspx

Grantmaker type: Corporate giving program.
Purpose and activities: As a complement to its
foundation, Heinz also makes charitable
contributions to nonprofit organizations directly.
Support is given on a national and international
basis in areas of company operations.
Fields of interest: Disasters, preparedness/
services; Food banks; Elementary/secondary
education; Health care; Nutrition; Children, services;
Human services; International affairs; Civil/human
rights, equal rights.
International interests: China; India; Indonesia.
Type of support: General/operating support;
Program development; Employee volunteer
services; Donated products; In-kind gifts.
Limitations: Giving on a national and international
basis in areas of company operations, with
emphasis on China, India, and Indonesia.

1888
The Hellendall Family Foundation
8119 Heacock Ln.
Wyncote, PA   19095-1818

Established in 1994 in PA.
Donors: Walter Hellendall; Gretel Hellendall.
Grantmaker type: Independent foundation.
Financial data (yr. ended 12/31/10): Assets,
$331,192 (M); gifts received, $49,664;
expenditures, $153,135; qualifying distributions,
$151,000; giving activities include $151,000 for 11
grants (high: $30,000; low: $1,000).
Fields of interest: Human services; International
affairs; Hospitals (general); Higher education,
university; Higher education; Performing arts,
orchestras; Performing arts, opera; Performing arts,
music; Education.
Limitations: Applications not accepted. Giving
primarily in PA. No grants to individuals.
Application information: Unsolicited requests for
funds not accepted.
Trustees: Gretel Hellendall; Kenneth C. Hellendall;
Ronald D. Hellendall.
EIN: 232798144

1889
The Hershey Company Contributions Program
(formerly Hershey Foods Corporation Contributions
Program)
100 Crystal A Dr., P.O. Box 810
Hershey, PA   17033-0810   (800) 468-1714
URL: http://www.thehersheycompany.com/
social-responsibility/community.aspx

Grantmaker type: Corporate giving program.
Purpose and activities: The Hershey Company
makes charitable contributions to organizations
involved with arts and culture, education, the
environment, health and human services, and civic
and community initiatives. Special emphasis is
directed towards programs designed to help at-risk
children. Support is limited to areas of company
operations in Hawaii, Illinois, Pennsylvania,
Tennessee, and Virginia, and in Brazil, China, India,
and Mexico.
Fields of interest: Children/youth, services; Arts;
Education; Environment; Health care; Human
services; Community/economic development;
Public affairs.
International interests: Brazil; China; India; Mexico.
Type of support: General/operating support;
Continuing support; Program development;
Employee volunteer services; Donated products.
Limitations: Applications accepted. Giving limited to
areas of company operations in HI, IL, PA, TN, and
VA, and in Brazil, China, India, and Mexico. No
support for political or lobbying organizations,
churches or religious organizations, fraternal
organizations, or labor organizations. No grants to
individuals, political campaigns, or for general
operating support for Cultural Enrichment Fund- or
United Way-supported organizations; no student
loans.
Publications: Application guidelines.
Application information: Proposals should be
submitted using organization letterhead. Video and
other unsolicited submissions are not encouraged.
Application form not required.
   Initial approach: Proposal to nearest company
      facility
   Copies of proposal: 1
   Deadline(s): 3 months prior to need for product
      donations
Administrators: Jennifer M. Goss, Corp. Contribs.
and Community Rels. Rep.; John C. Long, V.P., Corp.
Affairs.
Number of staff: 2 full-time professional; 1 part-time
support.

1890
HJW Foundation
(formerly Hansjoerg Wyss Foundation)
c/o Joseph M. Fisher
1302 Wrights Ln. E.
West Chester, PA   19380-3417

Established in 1999 in PA.
Donor: Hansjoerg Wyss.
Grantmaker type: Independent foundation.
Financial data (yr. ended 12/31/09): Assets,
$98,884,259 (M); expenditures, $10,717,000;
qualifying distributions, $9,931,507; giving
activities include $9,888,344 for 24 grants (high:
$1,394,100; low: $5,000).
Purpose and activities: Giving primarily for
education, the environment, health and human
services.

Fields of interest: Reproductive health, family planning; Human services; Environment, land resources; Environment, natural resources; Foundations (private grantmaking); Higher education; Education; Hospitals (general); Medical research, institute; Biomedicine research.
International interests: Germany; Switzerland.
Limitations: Applications not accepted. Giving on a national and international basis, with emphasis on Switzerland and Germany. No grants to individuals.
Application information: Contributes only to pre-selected organizations.
Officers: Hansjoerg Wyss, Chair.; Molly Mcusic, Pres.; Joseph M. Fisher, Treas.
EIN: 233012622
Recent grants for international programs:
1890-1 AOSpine International, Duebendorf, Switzerland, $248,886. 2009.
1890-2 Childrens Medical Foundation of Central and Eastern Europe, Philadelphia, PA, $100,000. 2009.
1890-3 Ecole Cantonal DArt du Valais, Sierre, Switzerland, $94,483. 2009.
1890-4 Fondation Beyeler, Basel, Switzerland, $1,394,100. 2009.
1890-5 Kunstmuseum Bern, Bern, Switzerland, $1,266,394. 2009.
1890-6 Stiftung PROGR, Berne, Switzerland, $919,400. 2009.

1891
Hope Worldwide, Ltd.
353 W. Lancaster Ave., Ste. 200
Wayne, PA 19087-3907 (610) 254-8800
FAX: (610) 254-8989;
E-mail: hope_worldwide@hopeww.org

Established in 1991.
Grantmaker type: Public charity.
Financial data (yr. ended 12/31/09): Revenue, $20,731,598; assets, $5,364,458 (M); gifts received, $19,793,626; expenditures, $20,202,749; giving activities include $10,500 for grants, $13,983,181 for grants to organizations outside the U.S., and $13,522 for grants to individuals.
Purpose and activities: The organization seeks to deliver sustainable, high-impact, community-based services to the poor and needy.
Fields of interest: Education; Employment; Health care; Human services; International relief; Economically disadvantaged.
Type of support: Grants to individuals; In-kind gifts.
Limitations: Applications not accepted. Giving on a national and international basis.
Publications: Annual report; Financial statement; Newsletter.
Application information: Contributes only to pre-selected organizations.
Officers and Directors:* Frank Kim,* Chair.; Randolph Jordan, C.E.O.; Andy Blocker; Dinesh George; Gregg Marutzky; Albert May; Jenny Nash; Wendy Richard; Charlie Stolper; Jenny Tate.
EIN: 043129839

1892
The Huston Foundation
900 W. Valley Rd., Ste. 204
Wayne, PA 19087-1849 (610) 832-4955
Contact: Susan B. Heilman, Exec. Asst.

FAX: (610) 832-4960; E-mail: hustonfndn@aol.com;
URL: http://www.hustonfoundation.org

Incorporated in 1957 in PA.
Donors: Charles L. Huston, Jr.†; Ruth Huston†.
Grantmaker type: Independent foundation.
Financial data (yr. ended 12/31/10): Assets, $23,612,406 (M); expenditures, $1,558,915; qualifying distributions, $813,950; giving activities include $813,950 for grants.
Purpose and activities: Giving primarily to Protestant evangelical ministries, health organizations, and human service organizations. Also some support for education and the arts.
Fields of interest: Arts; Education; Health care; Human services; Public policy, research; Christian agencies & churches; Protestant agencies & churches.
International interests: Italy; Africa.
Type of support: General/operating support; Annual campaigns; Equipment; Emergency funds; Program development; Seed money; Research; Technical assistance; Matching/challenge support.
Limitations: Giving primarily in southeastern PA; some funding nationally. No grants to individuals, or for research programs, endowments, fellowships, capital campaigns or salaries; no loans.
Publications: Application guidelines; Annual report.
Application information: Application form required.
Initial approach: Letter of request or telephone call
Copies of proposal: 1
Deadline(s): Mar. 15 and Sept. 15
Board meeting date(s): May and Nov.
Officers and Directors:* Elinor Huston Lashley,* C.E.O. and Pres., Education and Cultural Rels.; Nancy Huston Hansen,* V.P., Evangelical Rels.; Charles L. Huston III,* V.P., Community Rels. and C.O.O.; Rebecca H. Mathews,* Secy.; Charles L. Huston IV,* Treas.; Charles B. Chadwick; Nancy C. DeWind; Scott G. Huston.
Number of staff: 4 full-time professional; 1 part-time professional.
EIN: 236284125

1893
The Institute for Aegean Prehistory
2133 Arch St., Ste. 300
Philadelphia, PA 19103 (215) 496-9914
Contact: Karen B. Vellucci, Dir., Grants
FAX: (215) 496-9925; E-mail: instap@hotmail.com;
Application e-mail: instapplications@gmail.com;
URL: http://www.aegeanprehistory.net

Established in 1983 in NY.
Donor: Malcolm H. Wiener.
Grantmaker type: Operating foundation.
Financial data (yr. ended 06/30/10): Assets, $10,732,230 (M); gifts received, $6,112,019; expenditures, $7,205,334; qualifying distributions, $6,644,139.
Purpose and activities: The Institute for Aegean Prehistory (INSTAP) is a private operating foundation; opportunities to participate in the organization's activities are given only for the purpose of allowing and encouraging persons to study Aegean prehistory with expectation of research publication under the direct supervision of the institute. The goal of the Institute's grant program is to promote knowledge of the Aegean region, and to support archaeological fieldwork and research in that area in the chronological span of the

Paleolithic period through to the First Olympiad in 776 BC.
Fields of interest: History/archaeology.
International interests: Greece.
Type of support: Internship funds; Research; Grants to individuals.
Limitations: Applications accepted. Giving on a national and international basis, with emphasis on Greece. No grants for students obtaining degrees, travel or maintenance of children or spouses, research expenses incurred before the date of a grant, salaries for researchers, purchase of expensive individual items of equipment such as computers, cameras and video recorders, or general activities of other institutions, or entities including "overhead expenses".
Application information: Application forms are available on the institute's web site. The institute prefers applications and final reports submitted by e-mail. Faxed applications not accepted. Application form required.
Initial approach: Letter
Deadline(s): New Research Grants and Renewal Grants applications due Nov. 1
Final notification: 60 days
Officers and Directors:* Malcolm H. Wiener, Pres. and Treas.; Phillip Betancourt, V.P. and Secy.; Harvey Beker,* V.P.; George E. Crapple,* V.P.; Martin J. Whitman; Carolyn S. Wiener.
EIN: 133137391

1894
Jewish Community Foundation of Central Pennsylvania
3301 N. Front St.
Harrisburg, PA 17110-1436 (717) 236-9555
Contact: Nachman Rosenberg, Fdn. Dir.; Michele Wickwire, Fdn. Admin.
FAX: (717) 236-0965;
E-mail: foundation@jewishfedhbg.org; URL: http://jewishharrisburg.org/section.html?id=1121

Established in PA.
Grantmaker type: Public charity.
Financial data (yr. ended 08/31/10): Revenue, $3,235,138; assets, $16,013,712 (M); gifts received, $2,965,992; expenditures, $1,644,124; giving activities include $1,398,987 for grants.
Purpose and activities: The foundation seeks to promote philanthropy through meaningful relationships with donors and community organizations to carry out charitable purposes, and to increase current and future support for the Jewish community in central Pennsylvania, Israel, and the world.
Fields of interest: Jewish agencies & synagogues.
International interests: Israel.
Limitations: Applications not accepted. Giving primarily in central PA. No support for organizations lacking 501(c)(3) status.
Publications: Annual report; Informational brochure.
Application information: Unsolicited requests for funds not considered or acknowledged.
Officers: Ted Bernstein, Chair.; Dorothea Aronson, Vice-Chair.
Trustees: Leonard Berman; Sanford Cohen; Dr. Donald Freedman; Herman Gordon; Gerald Gorelick; Peggy Grove; David Kornblatt; Morris Schwab; Susan Symons; David Weisberg.
Number of staff: 1 full-time professional; 1 full-time support.
EIN: 231352587

1895
Key Foundation
345 Quarry Rd.
Wellsville, PA   17365-9798

Established in 1997 in PA.
Donors: Joelle Margolis; Martin Margolis.
Grantmaker type: Independent foundation.
Financial data (yr. ended 12/31/10): Assets, $2,285,091 (M); gifts received, $200,000; expenditures, $150,533; qualifying distributions, $148,750; giving activities include $148,750 for 49 grants (high: $25,000; low: $50).
Fields of interest: Arts; Education; Health organizations, association; Medical research, institute; International human rights; Jewish agencies & synagogues.
Limitations: Giving primarily in NY and PA. No grants to individuals.
Application information: Application form not required.
   Deadline(s): None
Officers: Martin Margolis, Pres.; Joelle Margolis, Secy.
EIN: 232894154

1896
KL Felicitas Foundation
(formerly Kleissner Family Foundation)
c/o Febert & Assocs., LLC
707 Grant St., Ste. 1140
Pittsburgh, PA   15219-1909
Contact: Lisa Kleissner, Pres.
E-mail: lisa@kleissner.com; URL: http://www.klfelicitasfoundation.org/

Established in 2000 in CA.
Donors: Karl Kleissner; Lisa Kleissner; KD Primus Trust.
Grantmaker type: Independent foundation.
Financial data (yr. ended 12/31/10): Assets, $10,513,963 (M); gifts received, $45,000; expenditures, $490,618; qualifying distributions, $186,474; giving activities include $186,474 for grants.
Purpose and activities: Giving to enable social entrepreneurs worldwide to develop and grow economically sustainable, scalable enterprises with high measurable social impact and to empower rural communities and families through sustainable economic and social change.
Fields of interest: Environment; Community/economic development.
International interests: Brazil; India; Sri Lanka.
Type of support: Mission-related investments/loans; General/operating support; Income development; Management development/capacity building; Annual campaigns; Capital campaigns; Building/renovation; Endowments; Program development; Seed money; Curriculum development; Research; Technical assistance; Consulting services; Program-related investments/loans; Matching/challenge support.
Limitations: Applications not accepted. Giving in the U.S., as well as in Brazil, India, and Sri Lanka. No support for religious organizations. No grants to individuals.
Application information: Contributes only to pre-selected organizations.
   Board meeting date(s): Jan. 2, June 12-13, and Oct. 30-31

Officers: Lisa Kleissner, Pres.; Alex Kleissner, V.P.; Karl Kleissner, Secy.; Andrea Kleissner, Treas.
EIN: 770539366

1897
Macha Malaria Research Institute, Inc.
P.O. Box 388
Dillsburg, PA   17019-0388
Contact: Phil Thuma, Exec. Dir.
E-mail: pthuma@mmri.net; Tel./Fax: (717) 432-1775; URL: http://www.mmri.net

Grantmaker type: Public charity.
Financial data (yr. ended 12/31/10): Revenue, $465,711; assets, $190,140 (M); gifts received, $465,323; expenditures, $479,832.
Purpose and activities: The institute exists to foster, support and undertake activities that will improve the understanding and increase the scientific knowledge of malaria.
Fields of interest: Tropical diseases research; Parasitic diseases research; Tropical diseases; Parasitic diseases.
International interests: Zambia; Africa.
Type of support: Research; Grants to individuals.
Limitations: Giving to Southern Africa, primarily Zambia.
Publications: Newsletter.
Officers and Directors:* Mary Holland,* Chair.; David Millary,* Vice-Chair.; Gary Lebo,* Secy.-Treas.; Phil Thuma,* Exec. Dir.; David Byer; Dorothy Gish; Rufus Good; Kenneth O. Hoke; Cynthia Holac; Elliot Munsanje; Linda Worman.
EIN: 232913099

1898
Mama Project, Inc.
2781A Gerryville Pike
Pennsburg, PA   18073-2306
E-mail: mamaproject@enter.net; Tel./fax: (215) 679-4338; URL: http://www.mamaproject.org
YouTube: http://www.youtube.com/user/mamaproject

Established in 1987 in PA.
Grantmaker type: Public charity.
Financial data (yr. ended 12/31/09): Revenue, $1,691,494; assets, $139,703 (M); gifts received, $1,684,646; expenditures, $1,671,076; giving activities include $1,396,289 for grants to organizations outside the U.S.
Purpose and activities: The organization works to provide health and wholeness services, focused on nutrition, wellness, hygiene, and education, in Honduras, Haiti, and Nigeria.
Fields of interest: Human services; Community/economic development; Nutrition; Health care.
International interests: Niger; Haiti; Honduras.
Type of support: In-kind gifts.
Limitations: Giving limited to Haiti, Honduras, and Nigeria.
Officers and Directors:* Priscilla J. Brenner,* M.D., Pres.; Ruth Cole,* V.P.; Barbara Schieck,* Secy.; Barbara Rice,* Treas.; Marlene Frankenfield; Steven Hackman; Judy Jones; Richard A. Moyer; Chidi Ukazim; Timothy Weaver; Jan Weikel.
EIN: 232993647

1899
Mine Safety Appliances Company Charitable Foundation
P.O. Box 426
Pittsburgh, PA   15230-0426   (412) 967-3000
Contact: Dennis L. Zeitler, V.P.
URL: http://www.msanorthamerica.com/communityrelations.html

Established in 1991 in PA as successor to the Mine Safety Appliances Company Charitable Trust.
Donor: Mine Safety Appliances Co.
Grantmaker type: Company-sponsored foundation.
Financial data (yr. ended 12/31/10): Assets, $67,062 (M); gifts received, $503,273; expenditures, $673,742; qualifying distributions, $673,679; giving activities include $673,679 for grants.
Purpose and activities: The foundation supports botanical gardens and organizations involved with performing arts, education, health, lung diseases, children, foreign policy, and community development.
Fields of interest: Performing arts; Higher education; Libraries (public); Education; Botanical gardens; Hospitals (general); Health care; Lung diseases; YM/YWCAs & YM/YWHAs; Children, services; International affairs, foreign policy; Community/economic development; United Ways and Federated Giving Programs.
Type of support: Conferences/seminars; General/operating support; Continuing support; Annual campaigns; Capital campaigns; Building/renovation; Emergency funds; Employee volunteer services.
Limitations: Applications accepted. Giving primarily in Pittsburgh, PA. No grants to individuals.
Application information: Application form not required.
   Initial approach: Letter of inquiry
   Deadline(s): None
Officers and Directors:* John T. Ryan III, Pres.; Dennis L. Zeitler, V.P. and Secy.-Treas.; William Lambert, V.P.; Douglas K. McClaine; Paul R. Uhler.
EIN: 256023104

1900
The Nararo Foundation
P.O. Box 4937
Philadelphia, PA   19119-0037

Established in 2002 in PA.
Donors: Thomas I. Whitman; Mira Rabin; Martin J. Whitman.
Grantmaker type: Independent foundation.
Financial data (yr. ended 12/31/10): Assets, $13,733,852 (M); gifts received, $2,503,814; expenditures, $645,340; qualifying distributions, $637,500; giving activities include $637,500 for 63 grants (high: $50,000; low: $1,000).
Fields of interest: International human rights; Human services.
Limitations: Applications not accepted. Giving primarily in NY and PA, some giving also in MA. No grants to individuals.
Application information: Contributes only to pre-selected organizations.
Trustees: Mira Rabin; Thomas I. Whitman.
EIN: 020229861

1901
National Philanthropic Trust
165 Township Line Rd., Ste. 150
Jenkintown, PA   19046-3533   (215) 277-3010
Contact: Andrew W. Hastings, V.P.
FAX: (215) 277-3029; E-mail: npt@nptrust.org;
Toll-free tel.: (888) 878-7900; URL: http://
www.nptrust.org

Established in 1996 in PA.
Grantmaker type: Public charity.
Financial data (yr. ended 06/30/10): Revenue,
$272,093,046; assets, $670,680,521 (M); gifts
received, $283,194,785; expenditures,
$224,612,863; giving activities include
$197,127,860 for grants, and $3,682,978 for
grants to organizations outside the U.S.
Purpose and activities: The trust is dedicated to
creating tailored philanthropic solutions for each of
its donors that best serves their specific goals and
interests, while expanding their knowledge in their
field of philanthropy. It helps individuals meet their
philanthropic goals by establishing donor-advised
funds, supporting organizations, bequests, and
other gift arrangements.
Fields of interest: Social sciences; Science;
Philanthropy/voluntarism; Civil/human rights;
International affairs; Human services; Community/
economic development; Youth development;
Recreation; Safety/disasters; Housing/shelter;
Agriculture/food; Mental health/crisis services;
Medical research; Employment; Environment;
Religion; Arts; Education; Animal welfare; Health
care.
International interests: Middle East; South
America; Asia; Europe.
Type of support: Annual campaigns; Building/
renovation; Capital campaigns; Conferences/
seminars; Consulting services; Continuing support;
Curriculum development; Debt reduction;
Emergency funds; Employee matching gifts;
Endowments; Equipment; Exchange programs;
Fellowships; Film/video/radio; General/operating
support; Internship funds; Land acquisition;
Management development/capacity building;
Matching/challenge support; Professorships;
Program development; Program evaluation;
Publication; Research; Scholarship funds; Seed
money; Technical assistance.
Limitations: Applications not accepted. Giving on a
national and international basis. No support for
private, non-operating foundations, political
campaigns, or lobbying activities. No grants for
membership fees, tuition, goods from charitable
auction, acquisition of a benefit, good, or service for
any specific individual, or fullfillment of existing
pledge.
Publications: Annual report; Financial statement;
Grants list; Informational brochure; Newsletter.
Application information: Contributes only to
pre-selected organizations.
   Board meeting date(s): Feb., May and Sept.
Officers and Trustees:* Howard Brownstein,*
Chair.; Eileen R. Heisman, Pres. and C.E.O.; Tom
Grace, C.O.O.; Margaret A. Bandera,* V.P. and
Treas.; Andrew W. Hastings, V.P., Ext. Affairs;
Amanda High, V.P., Philanthropic Svcs.; Patricia
Renzulli, V.P., NPT Breast Cancer 3-Day; Jeffrey R.
Lauterbach,* Secy.; Gennaro J. Fulvio; Cecilia
Mendez Hodes; Dirk Junge, C.F.A.; Joseph Kluger;
Rosalyn McPherson; Sharon Mueller; June Noronha;
Clark D. Pitcairn; Wayne R. Walker.
Number of staff: 25 full-time professional.
EIN: 237825575

1902
The Nazareth Project, Inc.
237 N. Prince St., Ste. 203
Lancaster, PA   17603-3527   (717) 290-1800
Contact: Midge Crystle, Exec. Dir.
FAX: (717) 290-1827;
E-mail: npi@nazarethproject.org; URL: http://
www.nazarethproject.org

Established in 1991.
Donors: Roberto Abello; Carl Beck; Mark Lacy, M.D.;
J. Paul Lehman.
Grantmaker type: Public charity.
Financial data (yr. ended 06/30/10): Revenue,
$172,016; assets, $39,363 (M); gifts received,
$171,247; expenditures, $166,047; giving
activities include $115,580 for grants.
Purpose and activities: The organization supports
and promotes a Christian ministry of healing, peace,
and reconciliation in the Middle East through health
care services.
Fields of interest: Civil rights, race/intergroup
relations; Crime/violence prevention; Crime/
violence prevention, domestic violence; Child
development, education; Adult/continuing
education; Nursing school/education; Hospitals
(general); Health care, patient services; Health care.
International interests: East Jerusalem; Israel;
Middle East; West Bank/Gaza (Palestinian
Territories).
Type of support: General/operating support;
Continuing support; Equipment; Program
development; Seed money; Scholarship funds;
Grants to individuals.
Limitations: Giving limited to Nazareth, Israel; and
Nablus, the West Bank. No grants for undergraduate
scholarships.
Publications: Annual report; Informational brochure;
Newsletter.
Application information: Unsolicited applications
not accepted.
   Board meeting date(s): May 22 and Oct. 22
Officers and Directors:* Robert Martin,* M.D.,
Chair.; Nelson R. Lehman,* M.D., Vice-Chair.; Roy
E. Wert,* M.D., Secy.-Treas.; Midge Crystle, Exec.
Dir.; Rev. Christine J. Day, M.S.; Rev. S. George
Dirghalli; Rev. W. Richard Foster, Jr.; Rev. Ronald B.
Fritts, Ph.D.; Roger K. Glick; David Hiebert; J. Welby
Leaman; Ponnuswamy Swamidoss, Ph.D.
Number of staff: 2 part-time professional.
EIN: 232619395

1903
One Village Coffee Corporate Giving
   Program
18 Cassel Rd.
Souderton, PA   18964-2603   (215) 721-4818
URL: http://www.onevillagecoffee.com
B Corporation Profile: http://www.bcorporation.net/
onevillagecoffee

Grantmaker type: Corporate giving program.
Purpose and activities: One Village Coffee is a
certified B Corporation that donates a percentage of
revenues of designated products to nonprofit
organizations. Special emphasis is directed toward
international organizations and programs that help
to alleviate poverty.
Fields of interest: Community/economic
development; Education; Environment, water
resources; International economic development.
Type of support: General/operating support.

Limitations: Giving in Egypt, Honduras, Indonesia,
and Kenya.

1904
The Pacem in Terris Institute
9000 Babcock Blvd.
Pittsburgh, PA   15237-5808

Supporting organization of La Roche College.
Grantmaker type: Public charity.
Financial data (yr. ended 06/30/10): Assets,
$103,943 (M); expenditures, $3,982; giving
activities include $3,982 for grants to individuals.
Fields of interest: International affairs;
Scholarships/financial aid.
Limitations: Giving limited to Pittsburgh, PA.
Officers: Sr. Candace Introcaso, Pres.; Janet
Dennis, V.P., Devel.; Dr. Howard Ishiyama, V.P.,
Academic Affairs; Colleen Ruefle, V.P., Student Life;
Kenneth P. Service, V.P., Institutional Rels.; Robert
Vogel, V.P., Finance and C.F.O.; George Zaffuto,
V.P., Admin. Svcs.
Trustees: Kathy Kozdemba; Joseph Dimario; J.
Douglas Austin; Sr. Mary Jane Beatty; Don L.
Canterna; Sr. Mary Joan Coultas; James A.
Delligatti; Sr. Sandra Denardis; Gennaro Dibello;
Richard B. Fisher; Sr. Mary Francis Fletcher; Robert
Fragasso; Ralph W. Gilbert, Jr.; V. James Gregory;
Howard W. Hanna III; and 14 additional trustees.
EIN: 251733322

1905
Pan-Icarian Foundation
P.O. Box 79037
Pittsburgh, PA   15216-0037   (412) 563-0547
URL: http://www.pan-icarian.com/foundation
Application address: Steve Stratakos, Chair., c/o
Pan-Icarian Scholarship Comm., 9305 S. 85th Ct.,
Hickory Hills, IL 60457; E-mail for additional
inquires: generalequity@comcast.net

Established in 1961 in PA.
Grantmaker type: Public charity.
Financial data (yr. ended 06/30/11): Revenue,
$131,601; assets, $4,119,206 (M); gifts received,
$30,334; expenditures, $136,921; giving activities
include $81,500 for grants to individuals.
Purpose and activities: The foundation provides
support for medical aid, scholarships, disaster
relief, and other causes in North America and
Greece. It is the charitable arm of the Pan-Icarian
Brotherhood of America, an organization focused on
Hellenic culture.
Fields of interest: International relief; Safety/
disasters.
International interests: Greece.
Type of support: Scholarships—to individuals.
Limitations: Giving limited to North America and
Greece.
Officers and Directors:* C.D. Yiakas,* Chair.; John
A. Lygizos,* Vice-Chair.; Nikolaos J. Pasamihalis,
Pres.; George Koklanaris, V.P.; E. Terry Platis,*
Secy.; George Paralemos, Treas.; Chris Aivaliotis;
Steve Stratakos; Dr. Nikitas Tripodes.
EIN: 256085664

1906
The Pew Charitable Trusts

1 Commerce Sq.
2005 Market St., Ste. 1700
Philadelphia, PA 19103-7077 (215) 575-9050
Contact: Rebecca W. Rimel, C.E.O. and Pres.
FAX: (215) 575-4939; E-mail: info@pewtrusts.org;
Additional address: 901 E St., NW, Washington, DC
20004-2037; tel.: (202) 552-2000, fax: (202)
552-2299; URL: http://www.pewtrusts.org
E-Newsletter: http://www.pewtrusts.org/
news_room_alerts.aspx
Grants and Program Investments Database: http://
www.pewtrusts.org/
program_investments_database.aspx
News Feed: http://www.pewtrusts.org/
rss_feed.aspx?category=news
YouTube: http://www.youtube.com/pew

Established in 1948; the trusts reorganized into a
public charity in 2004.
Donors: Mary Ethel Pew†; Mabel Pew Myrin†; J.
Howard Pew†; Joseph N. Pew, Jr.†.
Grantmaker type: Public charity.
Financial data (yr. ended 06/30/10): Revenue,
$303,511,412; assets, $752,424,802 (M); gifts
received, $285,992,854; expenditures,
$258,909,146; program services expenses,
$239,231,130; giving activities include
$110,954,646 for grants.
Purpose and activities: The Pew Charitable Trusts
support nonprofit activities in the areas of culture,
education, the environment, health and human
services, public policy and religion. Based in
Philadelphia, the trusts make strategic investments
to help organizations and citizens develop practical
solutions to difficult problems.
Fields of interest: Media, print publishing; Visual
arts; Museums; Performing arts; Performing arts,
dance; Performing arts, theater; Performing arts,
music; Humanities; Historic preservation/historical
societies; Arts; Education, research; Child
development, education; Education; Environment,
natural resources; Environment, energy;
Environment; Animals/wildlife, preservation/
protection; Public health; Health care; Biomedicine;
Employment; Housing/shelter, development; Youth
development, services; Youth development,
citizenship; Human services; Children/youth,
services; Child development, services; Family
services; Aging, centers/services; Minorities/
immigrants, centers/services; Homeless, human
services; Voluntarism promotion; Biology/life
sciences; Science; Social sciences; Government/
public administration; Public affairs, election
regulation; Public affairs, citizen participation;
Leadership development; Public affairs; Religion,
research; Religion, public policy; Physically
disabled; Offenders/ex-offenders; Mentally
disabled; Homeless; Economically disadvantaged;
Children/youth; Aging; Adults.
International interests: Australia; Canada; Europe.
Type of support: Continuing support; Program
development; Research; Technical assistance;
Program-related investments/loans; Employee
matching gifts.
Limitations: Applications accepted. Giving on an
international basis, with a special commitment to
the Philadelphia, PA, region. No grants to
individuals, or for endowment funds, capital
campaigns, construction, equipment, deficit
financing, scholarships, or fellowships (except
those identified or initiated by the trusts).

Publications: Application guidelines; Grants list;
Occasional report.
Application information: Contact Pew for specific
guidelines and limitations or visit the trusts' web
site; applicants should not send full proposals
unless requested by trustee representatives.
Examples of past work, articles, reports, videos or
other material should not be submitted with the
letter of inquiry. Application form required.
  Initial approach: Letter of inquiry (2 to 3 pages)
  Copies of proposal: 1
  Deadline(s): See foundation web site for current
    deadlines
  Board meeting date(s): Mar., June, Sept., and
    Dec.
  Final notification: Approximately 4 to 6 weeks
Officer and Board Members:* Rebecca W. Rimel,*
C.E.O. and Pres.; Robert H. Campbell; Susan W.
Catherwood; Gloria Twine Chisum; Aristides W.
Georgantas; J. Howard Pew II; J.N. Pew IV, M.D.;
Mary Catherine Pew, M.D.; R. Anderson Pew; Sandy
Pew; Robert G. Williams; Ethel Benson Wister.
Trustee: The Glenmede Trust Co.
Number of staff: 398 full-time professional; 17
part-time professional; 128 full-time support; 6
part-time support.
EIN: 562307147

1907
The Pilgrim Foundation

107 E. Chestnut St.
West Chester, PA 19380-2631
E-mail: info@thepilgrimfoundation.org; URL: http://
www.thepilgrimfoundation.org
Blog: http://thepilgrimfoundation.org/blog/

Established in 1998 in PA.
Donor: Gary L. Pilgrim.
Grantmaker type: Independent foundation.
Financial data (yr. ended 06/30/10): Assets,
$13,708,446 (M); gifts received, $1,250,000;
expenditures, $507,441; qualifying distributions,
$482,125; giving activities include $433,715 for 30
grants (high: $50,000; low: $2,500).
Purpose and activities: Giving primarily to Christian
organizations and churches, and to Evangelical
Christian organizations benefiting women and
children, primarily in Chester County, PA.
Fields of interest: Christian agencies & churches;
Education; Family services; Reproductive health;
Women, centers/services; Boys; Children;
Children/youth; Economically disadvantaged; Girls;
Infants/toddlers; Infants/toddlers, female; Infants/
toddlers, male; Minorities; Single parents; Women;
Youth.
International interests: India; Zimbabwe.
Type of support: General/operating support;
Scholarship funds.
Limitations: Applications accepted. Giving primarily
in Chester County, PA. No grants to individuals.
Application information: Application guidelines
available on foundation web site. Application form
not required.
  Initial approach: Half-page of inquiry by letter or
    e-mail
  Copies of proposal: 1
  Deadline(s): None
  Board meeting date(s): No set dates
  Final notification: 6 weeks
Officer: Gary L. Pilgrim, Pres.
Director: Suzanne T. Daniel.
Number of staff: 1 part-time support.
EIN: 232955610

1908
Pine Tree Foundation

120 Righters Mill Rd.
Gladwyne, PA 19035-1531 (610) 649-4601
Contact: A. Morris Williams, Jr., Chair.; Ruth W.
Williams, Pres.

Established in 1986 in PA.
Donors: A. Morris Williams, Jr.; Ruth W. Williams.
Grantmaker type: Independent foundation.
Financial data (yr. ended 07/31/10): Assets,
$26,542,296 (M); expenditures, $2,179,843;
qualifying distributions, $2,118,628; giving
activities include $2,118,628 for grants.
Purpose and activities: Giving primarily for
education and human services.
Fields of interest: International relief; Performing
arts; Higher education; Education; Housing/shelter,
development; Human services; Salvation Army.
Type of support: General/operating support.
Limitations: Applications accepted. Giving primarily
in CO, GA, NC, OH, and PA. No grants to individuals.
Application information:
  Initial approach: Letter
  Deadline(s): None
Officers and Directors:* A. Morris Williams, Jr.,*
Chair. and Treas.; Ruth W. Williams,* Pres. and
Secy.; Susan W. Beltz; Joanne W. Markman.
EIN: 222751187

1909
Progressive Business Publications
Charitable Trust

c/o Edward M. Satell
376 Technology Dr.
Malvern, PA 19355-1315

Established in 1996 in PA.
Donors: American Future Systems, Inc.; Edward M.
Satell.
Grantmaker type: Company-sponsored foundation.
Financial data (yr. ended 12/31/10): Assets,
$784,491 (M); gifts received, $200,000;
expenditures, $235,606; qualifying distributions,
$141,216; giving activities include $141,216 for
grants.
Purpose and activities: The foundation supports
organizations involved with arts and culture, food
services, business youth development, and
international affairs.
Fields of interest: Museums (history); Performing
arts, theater; Arts; Food services; Youth
development, business; International affairs; United
Ways and Federated Giving Programs.
Type of support: General/operating support.
Limitations: Applications not accepted. Giving
primarily in Philadelphia, PA. No grants to
individuals.
Application information: Contributes only to
pre-selected organizations.
Trustee: Edward M. Satell.
EIN: 237835073

1910
The Rosenstiel Foundation

c/o John R. Latourette
1500 Market St., Ste. 3500E
Philadelphia, PA 19102-2101

Incorporated in 1950 in OH.
Donor: Lewis S. Rosenstiel†.

Grantmaker type: Independent foundation.
Financial data (yr. ended 12/31/10): Assets, $18,939,942 (M); expenditures, $793,406; qualifying distributions, $620,750; giving activities include $620,750 for grants.
Purpose and activities: Grants largely for Polish cultural programs, the arts, health organizations, and higher education.
Fields of interest: Arts; Higher education; Education; Health organizations, association; Medical research, institute; Human services.
International interests: Poland.
Type of support: General/operating support; Continuing support; Seed money.
Limitations: Applications not accepted. Giving primarily in FL and NY. No grants to individuals.
Application information: Contributes only to pre-selected organizations.
Officers and Trustees: * Blanka A. Rosenstiel,* Pres.; Elizabeth R. Kabler,* V.P.; Robert I. Fisher,* V.P.
EIN: 066034536

1911
Sarah Scaife Foundation, Inc.
1 Oxford Ctr.
301 Grant St., Ste. 3900
Pittsburgh, PA 15219-6401 (412) 392-2900
Contact: Michael W. Gleba, Exec. V.P.
URL: http://www.scaife.com/sarah.html

Trust established in 1941; incorporated in 1959 in PA; present name adopted in 1974.
Donor: Sarah Mellon Scaife†.
Grantmaker type: Independent foundation.
Financial data (yr. ended 12/31/10): Assets, $255,540,386 (M); expenditures, $16,527,275; qualifying distributions, $14,174,000; giving activities include $14,174,000 for 89 grants (high: $760,000; low: $7,500).
Purpose and activities: Grants primarily directed toward public policy programs that address major international and domestic issues.
Fields of interest: Higher education; Education; International affairs; Economics; Political science; Law/international law; International studies; Public policy, research.
Type of support: General/operating support; Continuing support; Program development; Conferences/seminars; Publication; Seed money; Curriculum development; Fellowships; Research.
Limitations: Applications accepted. Giving primarily in Washington, DC and VA. No support for nationally organized fundraising groups or generally for government agencies. No grants to individuals, or generally for event sponsorships, endowments, capital campaigns, or renovations; no loans.
Publications: Annual report (including application guidelines).
Application information: Application form not required.
  Initial approach: Letter signed by the organization's President, or authorized representative and have the approval of the board
  Copies of proposal: 1
  Deadline(s): None
  Board meeting date(s): Feb., May, Sept., and Nov.
  Final notification: 2 - 4 weeks
Officers and Trustees: * Richard M. Scaife,* Chair.; Michael W. Gleba,* Pres.; Barbara L. Slaney, V.P. and Treas.; R. Daniel McMichael,* Secy.; T. Kenneth Cribb, Jr.; Edwin J. Feulner, Jr.; Allan H.

Meltzer, Ph.D.; E. Van R. Milbury; Roger W. Robinsin, Jr.; James C. Roddey; James M. Walton; Arthur P. Ziegler, Jr.
Number of staff: 1 full-time professional; 2 part-time professional; 2 full-time support; 4 part-time support.
EIN: 251113452
Recent grants for international programs:
1911-1 American Bar Association Fund for Justice and Education, Standing Committee on Law and National Security, Chicago, IL, $115,000. 2009.
1911-2 American Foreign Policy Council, Washington, DC, $125,000. For general support. 2009.
1911-3 Americas Survival, Owings, MD, $150,000. For program support. 2009.
1911-4 Center for Immigration Studies, Washington, DC, $125,000. For general operating support. 2009.
1911-5 Center for Security Policy, Washington, DC, $175,000. For general operating support. 2009.
1911-6 Center for Strategic and International Studies, Washington, DC, $325,000. For position of Senior Advisor and project support. 2009.
1911-7 Defense Forum Foundation, Falls Church, VA, $50,000. For program support. 2009.
1911-8 Foundation for the Defense of Democracies, Washington, DC, $150,000. For project support. 2009.
1911-9 George C. Marshall Institute, Arlington, VA, $230,000. For general operating support. 2009.
1911-10 High Frontier, Alexandria, VA, $100,000. For program support. 2009.
1911-11 Hudson Institute, Washington, DC, $100,000. For Project for Civil Justice Reform and International Religious Liberty. 2009.
1911-12 Human Rights Foundation, New York, NY, $75,000. For general operating support. 2009.
1911-13 Institute for Foreign Policy Analysis, Cambridge, MA, $550,000. For general operating support and project support. 2009.
1911-14 Institute for Foreign Policy Analysis, Cambridge, MA, $160,000. For Economic Security Program. 2009.
1911-15 Institute for International Studies, Washington, DC, $45,000. For project support. 2009.
1911-16 International Policy Network, Washington, DC, $50,000. For general operating support. 2009.
1911-17 Jamestown Foundation, Washington, DC, $125,000. For general operating support. 2009.
1911-18 Johns Hopkins University, Baltimore, MD, $120,000. For grant to Paul H. Nitze School of Advanced International Studies in Washington, DC. 2009.
1911-19 Maldon Institute, Baltimore, MD, $200,000. For general operating support. 2009.
1911-20 Missouri State University Foundation, Springfield, MO, $140,000. For Department of Defense and Strategic Studies. 2009.
1911-21 NumbersUSA Education and Research Foundation, Arlington, VA, $37,500. For project support. 2009.
1911-22 Tufts University, Fletcher School of Law and Diplomacy, Medford, MA, $280,000. 2009.
1911-23 University of Virginia Law School Foundation, Charlottesville, VA, $325,000. For Center for National Security Law. 2009.
1911-24 World Affairs Council of Pittsburgh, Pittsburgh, PA, $70,000. For Teacher-Student Educational Projects. 2009.

1912
The Scranton Area Foundation, Inc.
321 Spruce St., Ste. 608
Scranton, PA 18503-1409 (570) 347-6203
Contact: Jeanne A. Bovard, C.E.O.
FAX: (570) 347-7587; E-mail: safinfo@safdn.org; Additional E-mail: jab@safdn.org; URL: http://www.safdn.org

Established in 1954 in PA by resolution and declaration of trust; reorganized in 1998.
Grantmaker type: Community foundation.
Financial data (yr. ended 12/31/10): Assets, $25,571,974 (M); gifts received, $675,051; expenditures, $1,502,316; giving activities include $600,632 for 150+ grants (high: $100,000), and $286,538 for 65 grants to individuals.
Purpose and activities: The foundation encourages and helps to build community endowment through grants for new projects and services to address unmet needs. The foundation primarily supports organizations involved with health, education, arts, environment, human services, and civic affairs.
Fields of interest: Historic preservation/historical societies; Arts; Child development, education; Vocational education; Higher education; Libraries/library science; Education; Environment, natural resources; Environment; Animal welfare; Health care; Mental health/crisis services; Health organizations, association; Housing/shelter; Youth development, services; Human services; Children/youth, services; Child development, services; International human rights; Community/economic development; Voluntarism promotion; Leadership development; Public affairs; Religion; Aging.
Type of support: General/operating support; Continuing support; Program development; Conferences/seminars; Publication; Seed money; Curriculum development; Scholarship funds; Research; Technical assistance; Consulting services; Matching/challenge support.
Limitations: Applications accepted. Giving limited to Lackawanna County and Scranton, PA, area. No grants for building funds, annual campaigns, deficit financing, or emergency funds.
Publications: Application guidelines; Annual report; Annual report (including application guidelines); Grants list; Informational brochure; Informational brochure (including application guidelines); Newsletter; Occasional report.
Application information: Visit foundation web site for application guidelines. The foundation strongly recommends submission of letter of intent; immediate response as to the potential for the project will be provided. Application forms may be requested by calling the foundation. Application form required.
  Initial approach: Submit letter of intent (1-2 pages maximum)
  Copies of proposal: 1
  Deadline(s): None
  Board meeting date(s): Feb., May, Sept., and Dec.
  Final notification: Applications are reviewed quarterly
Officers and Governors: * Karen Clifford, Chair.; Thomas G. Speicher,* Vice-Chair.; Jeanne A. Bovard, C.E.O.; William J. Calpin, Secy.; Kathleen Graff,* Treas.; James B. Baker; Rosemary Broderick; Dante A. Cancelli; Joanne P. Corbett; Cathy Ann Hardaway; Matthew E. Haggerty; David Hawk; Alan F. Hughes; John P. Kearney; Jane Oppenheim; Ann Lavelle Powell; James A. Ross; Cynthia Yevich.

Investment Managers: Penn Security; Smith Barney; Wachovia Securities.
Number of staff: 1 full-time professional; 3 full-time support.
EIN: 232890364

1913
Abantika Piyush Shah Foundation
c/o Piyush A. Shah
P.O. Box 462
Quakertown, PA 18951-0462

Established in 2004 in PA.
Donors: Piyush A. Shah; Abantika A. Shah.
Grantmaker type: Independent foundation.
Financial data (yr. ended 12/31/10): Assets, $524,703 (M); gifts received, $100,000; expenditures, $280,100; qualifying distributions, $280,000; giving activities include $280,000 for grants.
Fields of interest: Safety/disasters; International relief; Education.
Limitations: Applications not accepted. No grants to individuals.
Application information: Contributes only to pre-selected organizations.
Officers: Piyush A. Shah, Pres.; Abantika A. Shah, Secy. and Treas.
EIN: 201320572

1914
The Shiloh Foundation
c/o David C. Paul
123 Anderson Farm Rd.
Phoenixville, PA 19460-5769

Established in 2007 in PA.
Donors: David Paul; Sonali Paul.
Grantmaker type: Independent foundation.
Financial data (yr. ended 12/31/10): Assets, $2,824,277 (M); expenditures, $250,045; qualifying distributions, $250,000; giving activities include $250,000 for 1 grant.
Fields of interest: Christian agencies & churches.
International interests: India.
Limitations: Applications not accepted. Giving primarily in India and PA. No grants to individuals.
Application information: Contributes only to pre-selected organizations.
Trustees: David C. Paul; Sonali Paul.
EIN: 256915616

1915
The Sidewater Family Foundation, Inc.
(formerly The Morris & Evelyn Sidewater Foundation, Inc.)
c/o Morris Sidewater
1 Wynnewood Rd.
Wynnewood, PA 19096-1918

Established in 1989 in PA.
Donor: Morris Sidewater.
Grantmaker type: Independent foundation.
Financial data (yr. ended 12/31/10): Assets, $4,645,031 (M); expenditures, $242,865; qualifying distributions, $208,678; giving activities include $205,234 for 32 grants (high: $60,000; low: $65).
Fields of interest: Arts; Medical research; Alzheimer's disease research; Education; Human

services; International affairs; Jewish federated giving programs; Jewish agencies & synagogues.
Limitations: Applications not accepted. No grants to individuals.
Application information: Unsolicited requests for funds not accepted.
Officers: Morris Sidewater, Pres.; Steven Sidewater, V.P. and Secy.; Samuel Sidewater, V.P. and Treas.
EIN: 232573603

1916
John Templeton Foundation
300 Conshohocken State Rd., Ste. 500
West Conshohocken, PA 19428-3801
(610) 941-2828
Contact: Grant Admin.
FAX: (610) 825-1730; E-mail: info@templeton.org; URL: http://www.templeton.org/
Facebook: http://www.facebook.com/TempletonFoundation
Twitter: http://twitter.com/templeton_fdn
YouTube: http://www.youtube.com/user/TempletonFoundation

Established in 1988 in TN.
Donors: Sir. John Marks Templeton†; Templeton Religious Trust; Templeton World Charity Foundation.
Grantmaker type: Independent foundation.
Financial data (yr. ended 12/31/09): Assets, $1,689,804,911 (M); gifts received, $599,917,290; expenditures, $81,500,582; qualifying distributions, $69,768,437; giving activities include $58,197,202 for 438 grants (high: $3,382,161; low: $50), $1,607,593 for 13 grants to individuals (high: $1,405,900; low: $1,720), and $2,573,741 for 4 foundation-administered programs.
Purpose and activities: The John Templeton Foundation serves as a philanthropic catalyst for discoveries relating to the Big Questions of human purpose and ultimate reality. It supports research on subjects ranging from complexity, evolution, and infinity to creativity, forgiveness, love, and free will. It encourages civil, informed dialogue among scientists, philosophers, and theologians and between such experts and the public at large, for the purposes of definitional clarity and new insights. Its vision is derived from the late Sir John Templeton's optimism about the possibility of acquiring "new spiritual information" and from his commitment to rigorous scientific research and related scholarship. The foundation's motto, "How little we know, how eager to learn," exemplifies its support for open-minded inquiry and its hope for advancing human progress through breakthrough discoveries.
Fields of interest: Health care; Youth development; Economic development; Science; Leadership development; Religion.
Type of support: Program development; Conferences/seminars; Publication; Curriculum development; Fellowships; Research; Grants to individuals; Matching/challenge support.
Limitations: Applications accepted. Giving on a national and international basis. No support for the development of new business ventures or the creation of for-profit companies. No grants for academic scholarships for individuals or groups, endowment funds, building funds, real estate holdings, capital campaigns, or artistic productions; no grants for the purchase of equipment, unless deemed a vital and necessary component of a larger research project falling within the foundation's

funding purposes; and no grants for general operating support to universities, institutions, or organizations.
Publications: Annual report; Financial statement; Informational brochure; Newsletter.
Application information: The foundation has established a new online grantmaking process for its Core Funding and Funding Priorities areas. Grants to individuals are a tiny portion of its grant-making because the foundation focuses on making grants in its area of interest. The foundation will award a grant to an applicant, whether an individual or an organization, if the applicant establishes an ability to make a contribution in one of the foundation's areas of interest. Generally, individual applicants must be associated with a 501 (c) (3) organization and the grant will be made to the organization. Full proposals will be accepted by invitation only. Application form required.
  Initial approach: Submit online funding inquiry form
  Deadline(s): Deadlines for inquiries: Feb. 1 - Apr. 16 and Aug.1 - Oct. 15
  Board meeting date(s): Varies
  Final notification: May 23
Officers and Trustees:* John Marks Templeton, Jr.,* M.D., Chair. and Pres.; Douglas W. Scott, Exec. V.P. and C.A.O.; Dawn Bryant, Exec. V.P. and General Counsel; Michael J. Murray, Exec. V.P., Progs.; Barnaby Marsh, Sr. V.P., Management and Strategic Initiatives; Mauro De Lorenzo, V.P., Freedom and Free Enterprise; Kent Hill, V.P. Character Devel.; Judith Marchand, V.P., Special Projects; Kimon Howland Sargeant, Ph.D., V.P., Human Sciences; Pamela Thompson, V.P., Comms.; Harvey M. Templeton III,* Secy.; Valerie K. Martin, C.F.O.; Anne Templeton Cameron, Treas.; Denis R. Alexander; John D. Barrow; Heather Templeton Dill; David G. Myers; Stephen G. Post; Jeffrey P. Schloss; John W. Schott, M.D.; Jane M. Siebels, Ph.D.; Josephine "Pina" Templeton; Gail Zimmerman, Ph.D.
Number of staff: 12 full-time professional; 6 full-time support.
EIN: 621322826
Recent grants for international programs:
1916-1 Acton Institute for the Study of Religion and Liberty, Grand Rapids, MI, $295,004. For Educating Future and Present Catholic Leadership on Free Enterprise Solutions to Poverty in Developing/Transitioning Countries. 2009.
1916-2 America Abroad Media, Washington, DC, $238,204. For Television Programming in the Muslim world on Religion, Liberty, and Constitutionalism in the 21st Century. 2009.
1916-3 America Abroad Media, Washington, DC, $75,267. For filming of the Istanbul Darwin conference public event. 2009.
1916-4 American Fund of the National Maritime Museum and Royal Observatory, Wilmington, DE, $12,283. For The Paradox between Religion and Cosmology. 2009.
1916-5 Anti-Slavery International, Free the Slaves, Washington, DC, $600,000. For The Freedom Prizes: Furthering Human Purpose through Ending Slavery. 2009.
1916-6 Association for the Dialogue between Science and Theology, Romania, Bucharest, Romania, $197,190. For Science and Orthodoxy: Research and Education. 2009.
1916-7 Australian Catholic University, North Sydney, Australia, $92,000. For Exploring Economics and Theology. 2009.

1916-8 Baylor University, Waco, TX, $25,000. For The Empirical Study of Religions in China. 2009.

1916-9 Bildung Und Begabung, Bonn, Germany, $128,369. For The 50th International Mathematics Olympiad Highlighting Young Mathematical Genius. 2009.

1916-10 Calvin College, Grand Rapids, MI, $657,630. For Advancing Scholarship on Science and Religion in Chinese Philosophy and Religious Studies. 2009.

1916-11 Calvin College, Grand Rapids, MI, $56,984. For Chinese Cognitive Science of Religion. 2009.

1916-12 Cambridge in America, New York, NY, $25,225. For Creativity in Action: A Comparative Historical Study of Highly Gifted Individuals, Geniuses, and Polymaths. 2009.

1916-13 Cambridge University, Cambridge, England, $278,424. For Templeton-Cambridge Journalism Fellowships and Seminars in Science and Religion. 2009.

1916-14 Cambridge University, Cambridge, England, $206,135. For Cambridge Programme for Research in Spiritual Realities. 2009.

1916-15 Cambridge University, Cambridge, England, $177,559. For interactive online education programme for young people with exceptional mathematical ability. 2009.

1916-16 Cambridge University, Cambridge, England, $29,869. For Further Development of PLUS, and Internet Mathematics Magazine. 2009.

1916-17 Cambridge University, Saint Edmunds College, Cambridge, England, $245,203. For Promoting the Public Understanding of Science and Christianity in the International Church Community. 2009.

1916-18 Cambridge University, Saint Edmunds College, Cambridge, England, $224,438. For Darwin Anniversary Conference, Istanbul. 2009.

1916-19 Cambridge University, Saint Edmunds College, Cambridge, England, $82,143. For The Faraday Institute Project on the Interactions between Science and Religious Belief in the Secondary School Context in England. 2009.

1916-20 Cambridge University, Saint Edmunds College, Cambridge, England, $37,120. For Faraday Projects. 2009.

1916-21 Cambridge University, Saint Edmunds College, Cambridge, England, $29,484. For Newton, Science and Religion: A Dramatisation for the Cambridge University 800th Founding Anniversary. 2009.

1916-22 Canterbury Christ Church University, Canterbury, England, $983,625. For Learning for Life: Strengthening Character in United Kingdom Civil Society. 2009.

1916-23 Centre de Recerca Matematica, Barcelona, Spain, $111,375. For The Myriad Aspects of Infinity. 2009.

1916-24 Centre for Development and Enterprise, Johannesburg, South Africa, $267,735. For Un Tercemundismo del Centro: A New Paradigm for Development Policy. 2009.

1916-25 Centre for Development and Enterprise, Johannesburg, South Africa, $75,000. For The Role of Private Entrepreneurs and Competition in Educating the Poor in South Africa. 2009.

1916-26 Charles University, Prague, Czech Republic, $27,000. For Proof Complexity and Infinite Structures. 2009.

1916-27 Christian Education Movement, Birmingham, England, $18,872. For Tackling Tough Questions, DVD Project. 2009.

1916-28 Christian Educational Center, Minsk, Belarus, $12,000. For Formation of a Competent Dialogue between the Religious and the Scientific Elites of Belarus and Promotion in the Media Pilot Phase. 2009.

1916-29 Columbia University, New York, NY, $300,000. For Program on Indian Economic Policies: Free Trade, Democracy, and Entrepreneurial Development. 2009.

1916-30 Concerned Nigerian Youth Action, Aba, Nigeria, $21,240. For Laws of Life Essay Contest. 2009.

1916-31 Conversations Essentielles, Paris, France, $17,967. For Fund Raising Department, Geographical Extension and DVD. 2009.

1916-32 Cornell University, Ithaca, NY, $56,870. For Research: China's Free Enterprise Economy. 2009.

1916-33 Dalberg Consulting-U.S., LLC, San Francisco, CA, $176,048. For Franchising in Frontier Markets: Can A Commercial Model For Replication Be Applied In The Fight Against Poverty To Create Financial And Social Return?. 2009.

1916-34 Ethics and Public Policy Center, Washington, DC, $55,000. For The Tertio Millennio Seminar on the Free Society. 2009.

1916-35 Euresis, Milan, Italy, $95,550. For Science and Ultimate Reality: A San Marino Symposium. 2009.

1916-36 Excelsis Center, Orlando, FL, $135,000. For Exploring Life's Biggest Questions in London and the University Cities of Oxford and Edinburgh. 2009.

1916-37 Freedom Lights Our World, Austin, TX, $22,500. For Be the Solution: How Entrepreneurs and Conscious Capitalists Can Solve All the World's Problems. 2009.

1916-38 Harvard University, Cambridge, MA, $225,180. For Transatlantic Comparison of Religion's Role in Society. 2009.

1916-39 Harvard University, Cambridge, MA, $19,000. For Uganda Symposium. 2009.

1916-40 Historical Society, Boston, MA, $19,518. For British Abolitionism and Noble Purpose: A Planning Grant to Organize a Conference on the Role of Progress in History. 2009.

1916-41 Hudson Institute, Washington, DC, $162,500. For The Index of Global Philanthropy and Report on Remittances: A Guide to the Sources and Magnitude of Global Giving to the Developing World. 2009.

1916-42 Human Rights Foundation, New York, NY, $28,600. For The Nobility of the Human Spirit and the Power of Freedom: Testimonies to Human Dignity and Character. 2009.

1916-43 Ian Ramsey Centre for Science and Religion, Oxford, England, $19,369. For Religious Freedom. 2009.

1916-44 Image Bearer Pictures, Washington, DC, $236,415. For the As We Forgive International Outreach Campaign. 2009.

1916-45 Intercollegiate Studies Institute, Wilmington, DE, $510,030. For Project to Foster the Culture of Enterprise in Age of Globalization. 2009.

1916-46 Intercollegiate Studies Institute, Wilmington, DE, $126,000. For Lecture Series to Foster the Culture of Enterprise in Age of Globalization. 2009.

1916-47 International Society for Science and Religion, Cambridge, England, $172,974. For The Science and Religion Library Initiative. 2009.

1916-48 International Society for Science and Religion, Cambridge, England, $39,134. For Cambridge Office. 2009.

1916-49 Istituto Niels Stensen, Florence, Italy, $54,569. For International Congress, the Galileo Affair: A Historical, Philosophical and Theological Re-Examination. 2009.

1916-50 Jnana-Deepa Vidyapeeth, Pune, India, $40,760. For University/College Project for Science-Religion Interfacing, Networking and Research (UPSR). 2009.

1916-51 Jnana-Deepa Vidyapeeth, Pune, India, $30,000. For seminar on Science and Religion in India. 2009.

1916-52 Junior Achievement China, Beijing, China, $427,680. For Laws of Life in China Three Year Program. 2009.

1916-53 Junior Achievement China, Beijing, China, $21,700. For Investing in China Next Generation - Laws of Life Essay Contest. 2009.

1916-54 Kalligram Foundation, Bratislava, Slovakia, $20,000. For Translation and Publication of New Books in Slovakia and in Hungary. 2009.

1916-55 Kings College London, London, England, $391,436. For The Genetics of High Cognitive Abilities. 2009.

1916-56 Kurt Godel Society, Vienna, Austria, $142,250. For Kurt Godel Research Prize Fellowships Program. 2009.

1916-57 Kurt Godel Society, Vienna, Austria, $20,000. For Godel Centenary Research Prize Fellowship. 2009.

1916-58 Landesa, Seattle, WA, $132,500. Toward a Global Homestead Program: Exploring the Potential of Homestead Plot Ownership for Improving the Livelihoods of the Poor. 2009.

1916-59 London School of Economics and Political Science, London, England, $272,666. For God's Order, Man's Order and the Order of Nature. 2009.

1916-60 Metanexus Institute on Religion and Science, Bryn Mawr, PA, $316,000. For Metanexus Global Network Initiative. 2009.

1916-61 National Opinion Research Center, Chicago, IL, $75,000. For The Changing Role of Religion and Spirituality around the World. 2009.

1916-62 New Vision Partners, Pasadena, CA, $60,000. For Healing, Forgiveness, and Reconciliation in Post-Genocide Rwanda. 2009.

1916-63 Open University, Milton Keynes, England, $34,859. For Boundaries of the Knowable: A Web-Based Video Presentation. 2009.

1916-64 Oxford University, Oxford, England, $581,437. For Empirical Expansion in Cognitive Science and Religion. 2009.

1916-65 Oxford University, Oxford, England, $162,001. For God, Philosophy and Science: Science and Religion Program Support for the Ian Ramsey Centre. 2009.

1916-66 Oxford University, Oxford, England, $65,643. For Philosophy of Cosmology: Characterising Science and Beyond. 2009.

1916-67 Oxford University, Oxford, England, $56,994. For Modern Cosmology and Philosophy: A Detailed Examination of Fine-Tuning and Implications. 2009.

1916-68 Oxford University, Oxford, England, $13,627. For Seeking Wisdom? Engaging the Academic Disciplines from the Standpoint of Faith (Annual Conference). 2009.

1916-69 Philantrust, Paris, France, $27,021. For Frontiers of Science Funding Initiative: Asian perspectives on the cognitive and neurosciences. 2009.

1916-70 Pointy Shoe Productions, Alexandria, VA, $22,500. For Let My People Go: Documentary and Education Project. 2009.

1916-71 Pontifical Council for Culture, Vatican City, Vatican City, $662,652. For Science, Theology and Ontological Quest IV Project. 2009.

1916-72 Pontifical Council for Culture, Vatican City, Vatican City, $127,770. For Science, Theology and Ontological Quest II Project Continuation and Science, Theology and Ontological Quest III New Activities. 2009.

1916-73 Pontifical Gregorian University, Rome, Italy, $56,493. For Biological Evolution Facts and Theories: A Critical Appraisal 150 Years after the Origin of Species. 2009.

1916-74 Purdue University, West Lafayette, IN, $400,000. For Beijing summit on Chinese Spirituality and Society. 2009.

1916-75 Purdue University, West Lafayette, IN, $100,000. For Chinese Spirituality and Society Program: A Research and Training Initiative. 2009.

1916-76 Quality Education for Minorities Network, Washington, DC, $17,666. For The Pan-African Mathematics Olympiad Committee of Visitors (PAMOCOV). 2009.

1916-77 Regent College, Vancouver, Canada, $105,000. For Pastoral Science: Reading, Teaching, and Delighting in God's Two Books. 2009.

1916-78 Royal Institution of Great Britain, London, England, $24,730. For Events Series Partnership for the Big Questions on Humanity and the Universe. 2009.

1916-79 Ruprecht-Karls-Universitat, Heidelberg, Germany, $277,000. For John Templeton Award for Theological Promise. 2009.

1916-80 Ruprecht-Karls-Universitat, Heidelberg, Germany, $154,600. For John Templeton Award for Theological Promise. 2009.

1916-81 Rutgers, The State University of New Jersey, New Brunswick, NJ, $56,000. For Laws of Life: Mishma'ut V' Mishma'at in Israel. 2009.

1916-82 Saint Andrews Biblical Theological College, Moscow, Russia, $85,004. For Science for Young Scholars from Russia and the Former Soviet Union. 2009.

1916-83 Search Institute, Minneapolis, MN, $157,299. For Discovering Common and Unique Patterns in Adolescent Spiritual Development across Global Cultures and Traditions. 2009.

1916-84 SEVEN Fund, Cambridge, MA, $1,474,331. For The Enterprise-Based Solutions to Poverty. 2009.

1916-85 SEVEN Fund, Cambridge, MA, $448,600. For Pioneers at Prosperity (POP) Grants and Awards Program for Innovation and Entrepreneurship in the Caribbean and Central America. 2009.

1916-86 SEVEN Fund, Cambridge, MA, $200,000. For Building Linkages between Prosperity and Progressive Human Values for Citizens of Developing Nations. 2009.

1916-87 SEVEN Fund, Cambridge, MA, $57,750. For Success Stories of Africa Grant and Award Program. 2009.

1916-88 Society for Interaction of Religion, Science, and Technology, Mansehra, Pakistan, $44,000. For Introduction, Expansion and Institutionalization of Science-Religion Discourse in Pakistan. 2009.

1916-89 Society of Christian Philosophers, Grand Rapids, MI, $10,000. For Science and Human Nature: Russian and Western Perspectives. 2009.

1916-90 Sparks Rising, Goshen, NH, $618,768. For Sparks, Rising Stories from Rwanda - A feature film intended for theatrical release. 2009.

1916-91 Stanford University, Stanford, CA, $768,664. For Religion as the Basis for Power and Property in the First Civilizations: The Analysis and Publication of Catalhoyuk, Turkey. 2009.

1916-92 Theos, the Public Theology Think Tank, London, England, $135,242. For Rescuing Darwin: Research, Report, Debate and Launch on the Need to Save Darwinism from Invalid and Damaging religious and atheist Interpretations. 2009.

1916-93 Trinity College, Bristol, England, $34,826. For Origins - A DVD Project for UK Schools and Churches. 2009.

1916-94 Universidad de Navarra, Pamplona, Spain, $12,756. For The Human Singularity: The Origin, Nature and Destiny of the Human Being. 2009.

1916-95 Universidad Pontificia Comillas, Pamploma, Spain, $51,064. For Sophia-Iberia in Europe. 2009.

1916-96 Universitas Gadjah Mada, Center for Religious and Cross-Cultural Studies, Yogyakarta, Indonesia, $125,000. For Understanding and Healing after Natural Disaster: Scientific and Inter-Religious Reflections. 2009.

1916-97 Universite Interdisciplinaire de Paris, Paris, France, $123,064. For Bridge Grant for Science and Religion in Islam Project. 2009.

1916-98 Universite Interdisciplinaire de Paris, Paris, France, $46,669. For Strengthening the Field of Science and Religion in France through the Promotion of the Ideas of Six Top Scholars in the Field. 2009.

1916-99 Universite Interdisciplinaire de Paris, Paris, France, $20,000. For Global Perspective on Science and Spirituality, The Major Awards Program. 2009.

1916-100 Universiteit Gent, Ghent, Belgium, $41,175. For Phase Transitions in Logic and Combinatorics (PTLC). 2009.

1916-101 Universitetet i Oslo, Center for the Study of Mind in Nature, Oslo, Norway, $85,000. Toward a Defensible Platonism: Outline of Epistemology for Non-Material Objects. 2009.

1916-102 University of Birmingham, Birmingham, England, $25,273. For Toward a Nonphysicalist Monist Solution to the Mystery of Consciousness. 2009.

1916-103 University of Bristol, Bristol, England, $45,000. For The Study of Unprovability. 2009.

1916-104 University of British Columbia, Vancouver, Canada, $17,410. For Beyond Myths and Christians: Expanding and Correcting the Historical Record. 2009.

1916-105 University of Edinburgh, Edinburgh, Scotland, $450,000. For The Adaptive Logic of Religious Belief and Behavior. 2009.

1916-106 University of Erfurt, Max Weber Center for Advanced Cultural and Social Studies, Erfurt, Germany, $47,307. For The Axial Age and Consequences for Subsequent History and the Present. 2009.

1916-107 University of Iowa Foundation, Iowa City, IA, $99,311. For Making a Global Impact on

Gifted Education: A proposal to translate A Nation Deceived into seven languages. 2009.

1916-108 University of Manchester, Manchester, England, $16,206. For A Dialogue on Infinity. 2009.

1916-109 University of Puerto Rico, Mayaguez, PR, $64,155. For The 12th Central American and Caribbean Mathematical Olympiad Supporting Young Mathematical Genius. 2009.

1916-110 University of Saint Andrews, Saint Andrews, Scotland, $42,327. For James Gregory Lectures on Science and Religion. 2009.

1916-111 University of South Carolina Research Foundation, Columbia, SC, $14,653. For Science and the Orthodox Church in North America. 2009.

1916-112 University of Southern California, Los Angeles, CA, $850,000. For Spirit in the World: A Global Pentecostal Research Initiative. 2009.

1916-113 University of Southern California, Los Angeles, CA, $50,516. For Heart and Virtue: The Revival of Confucian Education In Contemporary China. 2009.

1916-114 Zhejiang University, Hangzhou, China, $120,000. For Mathematics Competition for Chinese High School Students. 2009.

1917
Charles K. Williams II Trust

c/o BNY Mellon, N.A.
P.O. Box 185
Pittsburgh, PA   15230-0185
Application address: c/o BNY Mellon, N.A., 1735 Market St., Philadelphia, PA 19101, tel.: (215) 553-3344

Established in 1985 in PA.
Donor: Charles K. Williams.
Grantmaker type: Independent foundation.
Financial data (yr. ended 11/30/10): Assets, $6,305 (M); gifts received, $200,000; expenditures, $199,369; qualifying distributions, $199,356; giving activities include $199,348 for 10 grants (high: $80,000; low: $1,700).
Purpose and activities: Scholarship awards for postgraduate studies limited to the field of scientific archaeology; also providing awards and fellowships for individuals and/or projects in specific archaeology endeavors.
Fields of interest: History/archaeology.
International interests: Greece.
Type of support: Fellowships; Scholarship funds; Research.
Limitations: Applications accepted. Giving primarily in DE and Italy.
Application information: Application form not required.
    Initial approach: Proposal
    Deadline(s): None
Trustee: BNY Mellon, N.A.
EIN: 236758319

1918
Wollowick Family Foundation
(formerly Rubin and Gladys Wollowick Foundation, Inc.)

c/o BNY Mellon, N.A.
P.O. Box 185
Pittsburgh, PA   15230-0185
c/o Joseph Fernandez, 1111 Brickell Ave., 30th Fl., Miami, FL 33131-3155; tel.: (305) 810-2936

Established in 1984 in FL.
Donor: Gladys Wollowick‡.
Grantmaker type: Independent foundation.
Financial data (yr. ended 01/31/09): Assets, $3,784,781 (M); expenditures, $721,885; qualifying distributions, $613,222; giving activities include $595,000 for 35 grants (high: $150,000; low: $1,000).
Purpose and activities: Giving primarily for education, hospitals and health organizations, social services, and Jewish organizations.
Fields of interest: Higher education; Hospitals (general); Health organizations, association; Medical research, institute; Human services; American Red Cross; Jewish federated giving programs; Jewish agencies & synagogues.
International interests: Israel.
Type of support: General/operating support; Annual campaigns; Equipment; Emergency funds; Research; Matching/challenge support.
Limitations: Giving primarily in Miami, FL. No grants to individuals.
Application information: Application form not required.
  Initial approach: Letter
  Deadline(s): None
  Board meeting date(s): Varies
Directors: Richard Lowe; Sandra Lois Lowe; Rhoda Stein; Dr. Robert Tesher; Al Wollowick; Janet Amy Wollowick.
Trustee: BNY Mellon, N.A.
EIN: 592469452

1919
Zeldin Family Foundation
c/o Claudia Zeldin, Martex Fiber Corp.
325-341 Chestnut St.
Constitution Pl., Ste. 1320
Philadelphia, PA   19106-2614
E-mail: claudiazeldin@yahoo.com; Additional address: 921 President St., Brooklyn, NY 11215

Established in 1986 in PA.
Donor: Martin Zeldin.
Grantmaker type: Independent foundation.
Financial data (yr. ended 11/30/10): Assets, $2,473,472 (M); gifts received, $199,536; expenditures, $166,714; qualifying distributions, $166,061; giving activities include $165,849 for 78 grants (high: $20,000; low: $250).
Purpose and activities: Giving primarily for education, youth and children's services, and for women's interests.
Fields of interest: Arts; Higher education; Education; Health organizations, association; Children/youth, services; Women, centers/ services; International relief.
Type of support: General/operating support; Annual campaigns; Capital campaigns; Emergency funds; Program development; Scholarship funds; Matching/challenge support.
Limitations: Applications not accepted. Giving on a national basis. No support for religious or political organizations. No grants to individuals.
Application information: Unsolicited requests for funds will not be accepted.
  Board meeting date(s): Nov.
Trustees: Claudia Zeldin; Jessica Zeldin; Martin Zeldin; Stefanie Zeldin; Sybille Zeldin.
Number of staff: None.
EIN: 236861835

PUERTO RICO

1920
FNZ Foundation, Inc.
Box 3425
Carolina, PR   00984-3425
Contact: James D. Klau, Pres.
FAX: (787) 768-9850; E-mail: jdklau@cs.com

Established in 1996 in DE.
Grantmaker type: Independent foundation.
Financial data (yr. ended 12/31/10): Assets, $6,819,863 (M); expenditures, $411,560; qualifying distributions, $394,717; giving activities include $394,717 for grants.
Purpose and activities: Giving primarily for Jewish organizations and temples, youth, health care, animals, education and social action.
Fields of interest: Arts; Education; Animals/wildlife; Health care; Urban League; Youth, services; Jewish agencies & synagogues.
International interests: Soviet Union (Former); Israel.
Limitations: Giving on a national basis.
Officers: James D. Klau, Pres.; Susan L. Klau, V.P.
EIN: 660535017

RHODE ISLAND

1921
Collette Foundation
162 Middle St.
Pawtucket, RI   02860-1013   (401) 642-4576
Contact: Allison Villasenor, Prog. Mgr.
E-mail: info@collettefoundation.org; URL: http://www.collettefoundation.org/
RSS Feed: http://collettefoundation-org.securec8.ezhostingserver.com/blog/?feed=rss2

Established in 2007 in RI.
Donors: Jack Carley; Collette Travel Service, Inc.
Grantmaker type: Company-sponsored foundation.
Financial data (yr. ended 12/31/10): Assets, $882,673 (M); gifts received, $41,428; expenditures, $363,564; qualifying distributions, $352,900; giving activities include $352,900 for 33 grants (high: $50,000; low: $100).
Purpose and activities: The foundation supports programs designed to improve and extend the quality of life of children in worldwide destinations with which Collette explores.
Fields of interest: Education; Human services; International relief; Economically disadvantaged; Children.
Type of support: General/operating support; Continuing support; Annual campaigns; Building/ renovation; Equipment; Program development; Employee volunteer services; Sponsorships; Matching/challenge support.
Limitations: Applications not accepted. Giving primarily in areas of company operations in Brazil, Cambodia, China, Costa Rica, Kenya, Mexico, Peru, and South Africa. No grants to individuals.

Application information: Contributes only to pre-selected organizations.
Directors: John Galvin; Michael Horan.
Trustee: Daniel J. Sullivan, Jr.
EIN: 208256603

1922
CVS Caremark Charitable Trust, Inc.
(formerly CVS/pharmacy Charitable Trust, Inc.)
1 CVS Dr.
Woonsocket, RI   02895-6146   (401) 770-4561
Contact: Eileen Howard Boone, V.P.
Additional contact: Jennifer Veilleux,
e-mail: jhveilleux@cvs.com; URL: http://www.cvscaremark.com/community/our-impact/charitable-trust
All Kids Can CREATE Call for Art Website: http://www.vsarts.org/prebuilt/showcase/gallery/exhibits/calls/allkidscan/index.html
Charitable Trust Featured Recipients: http://info.cvscaremark.com/community/ways-we-give/charitable-trust/featured-recipients
CVS Caremark All Kids Can on Facebook: http://www.facebook.com/CVSCaremarkAllKidsCan
RSS Feed: http://info.cvscaremark.com/newsroom/press-releases/community/feed

Established in 1992 in DE and MA.
Donors: Melville Corp.; CVS Corp.; CVS Pharmacy, Inc.
Grantmaker type: Company-sponsored foundation.
Financial data (yr. ended 12/31/09): Assets, $65,501,659 (M); expenditures, $7,286,914; qualifying distributions, $7,276,849; giving activities include $6,675,001 for 656 grants (high: $500,000; low: $7), and $428,000 for 178 grants to individuals (high: $5,000; low: $1,000).
Purpose and activities: The trust supports programs designed to serve children with disabilities; and uninsured or underserved people with healthcare needs.
Fields of interest: Disasters, preparedness/ services; Visual arts; Medical school/education; Health care, equal rights; Medicine/medical care, public education; Health care, infants; Medical care, rehabilitation; Public health, obesity; Public health, physical fitness; Health care, insurance; Health care, patient services; Health care; Autism; Family services, parent education; Independent living, disability; Assistive technology; Children; Youth; Aging; Disabilities, people with; Physically disabled; Blind/visually impaired; Deaf/hearing impaired; Mentally disabled.
Type of support: General/operating support; Capital campaigns; Building/renovation; Program development; Scholarship funds; Employee volunteer services; Employee-related scholarships.
Limitations: Applications accepted. Giving on a national basis in areas of company operations including Puerto Rico.
Publications: Application guidelines; Program policy statement.
Application information: Additional information may be requested at a later date. Support is limited to 1 contribution per organization during any given year. E-mail messages and telephone calls during the application process are not encouraged. Organizations receiving support are asked to submit a final report. Application form required.
  Initial approach: Complete online application form; submit artwork online for Call for Art
  Deadline(s): May 1 to June 15 for applications targeting children with disabilities; July 1 to

Aug. 15 for applications targeting healthcare services for underserved populations; Feb. 4 for Call for Art

Final notification: Nov. 1 for applications targeting children with disabilities; Dec. 1 for applications targeting healthcare services for underserved populations

Officers and Directors: * Zenon P. Lankowsky,* Pres; David M. Denton, V.P. and Co-Treas.; Eileen Howard Boone,* V.P.; V. Michael Ferdinandi, V.P.; Michael K. Golub, V.P.; David B. Rickard,* V.P.; Carole A. DeNale, Co-Treas.

EIN: 223206973

Recent grants for international programs:

1922-1 Boundless Playgrounds, New Haven, CT, $233,406. For program funding. 2009.

1922-2 Boundless Playgrounds, New Haven, CT, $135,000. For program funding. 2009.

1922-3 Boundless Playgrounds, New Haven, CT, $127,699. For program funding. 2009.

1922-4 Boundless Playgrounds, New Haven, CT, $101,250. For program funding. 2009.

1922-5 Boundless Playgrounds, New Haven, CT, $90,000. For program funding. 2009.

1922-6 Boundless Playgrounds, New Haven, CT, $55,000. For program funding. 2009.

1922-7 Boundless Playgrounds, New Haven, CT, $50,000. For program funding. 2009.

1922-8 Boundless Playgrounds, New Haven, CT, $30,000. For program funding. 2009.

1922-9 Boundless Playgrounds, New Haven, CT, $25,000. For program funding. 2009.

1922-10 Boundless Playgrounds, New Haven, CT, $15,000. For program funding. 2009.

1923
Dorot Foundation

401 Elmgrove Ave.
Providence, RI 02906-3451 (401) 351-8866
Contact: Michael Hill, Exec. V.P.
FAX: (401) 351-4975; E-mail: Info@dorot.org;
URL: http://www.dorot.org

Incorporated in 1958 in NY as Joy and Samuel Ungerleider Foundation.

Donors: Joy G. Ungerleider-Mayerson†; D.S. and R.H. Gottesman Foundation; Yesod Fund.

Grantmaker type: Independent foundation.

Financial data (yr. ended 03/31/10): Assets, $62,663,734 (M); gifts received, $2,683,030; expenditures, $4,198,704; qualifying distributions, $3,653,634; giving activities include $2,464,573 for 40 grants (high: $297,073; low: $2,500), and $223,000 for 12 grants to individuals (high: $21,500; low: $4,000).

Purpose and activities: Grants primarily for informal education, the Dorot Fellowship in Israel, cultural organizations with which the foundation has an existing relationship, and organizations supporting adult education for democratic participation in Israel.

Fields of interest: International affairs; Arts, cultural/ethnic awareness; Education; Public affairs, citizen participation.

International interests: Israel.

Type of support: General/operating support; Continuing support; Program development; Publication; Seed money; Fellowships; Internship funds; Technical assistance; Program evaluation; Matching/challenge support.

Limitations: Applications accepted. Giving primarily in Washington, DC, MA, NY, and Israel. No support for acquisitions for museums or excavation phase

of archaeological work. No grants for endowments, capital campaigns, equipment, debt reduction, consultants or technical assistance, or events.

Publications: Application guidelines; Financial statement; Grants list.

Application information: See foundation's web site for application information. Application form not required.

Initial approach: Letter of inquiry (2-3 pages)
Copies of proposal: 1
Deadline(s): 60 days prior to board meetings
Board meeting date(s): Apr./May and Oct./Nov.
Final notification: 4-6 weeks

Officers and Director: * Ernest S. Frerichs,* Pres.; Michael Hill, Exec. V.P.; Steven M. Jackson, V.P. Strategy.

Number of staff: 3 full-time professional; 1 part-time professional.

EIN: 136116927

Recent grants for international programs:

1923-1 Alma Hebrew College, Tel Aviv, Israel, $20,000. For Education of Jewish Heritage. 2009.

1923-2 American Friends of the Israel Museum, New York, NY, $15,000. For Director's Fund and Shrine of the Book Information. 2009.

1923-3 American Jewish World Service, New York, NY, $40,000. For Jewish College Corps and Tsunami Relief. 2009.

1923-4 Elil Communication, Tel Aviv, Israel, $30,000. For Trude Dothan Film. 2009.

1923-5 Encounter, New York, NY, $20,000. For Jewish Leaders' Exposure to Palestinian Life. 2009.

1923-6 Friends of Kol Haneshama, New York, NY, $75,000. For fellowships. 2009.

1923-7 Habitus: A Diaspora Journal, Brooklyn, NY, $20,000. For Jewish Newspaper. 2009.

1923-8 Israel Exploration Society, Jerusalem, Israel, $40,000. For IES journal, encyclopedia, and translations. 2009.

1923-9 Just Vision, New York, Washington, DC, $50,000. For salaries. 2009.

1923-10 New Israel Fund, Washington, DC, $250,000. For social change in Israel. 2009.

1923-11 New Israel Fund, Shatil, New York, NY, $25,000. For fellowship/internship and college volunteer. 2009.

1923-12 Projects for Global Harmony, Concord, NH, $20,000. For program support. 2009.

1923-13 Schechter Institute of Jewish Studies, Center for Women in Jewish Law, Jerusalem, Israel, $35,000. 2009.

1923-14 Shomrey Mishpat Rabbis for Human Rights North America, West Tisbury, MA, $20,000. For general operating support. 2009.

1923-15 Survivor Corps, Washington, DC, $25,000. For general operating support. 2009.

1923-16 Van Leer Foundation/Jerusalem Cinematheque, Jerusalem, Israel, $20,000. For Jewish Film Festival. 2009.

1923-17 W. F. Albright Institute of Archaeological Research, Jerusalem, Israel, $130,000. For fellowships and Director's Fund. 2009.

1924
The Feinstein Foundation, Inc.

37 Alhambra Cir.
Cranston, RI 02905-3416 (401) 467-5155
Contact: Alan Shawn Feinstein, Pres.

FAX: (401) 941-0988;
E-mail: asf@feinsteinfoundation.org; URL: http://www.feinsteinfoundation.org
Facebook: http://www.facebook.com/pages/The-Feinstein-Foundation/310441040233?ref=search

Established in 1991 in RI.

Donors: Alan Shawn Feinstein; Leila Feinstein; Ari Feinstein; Fidelity Charitable Gift Fund; The Rhode Island Foundation.

Grantmaker type: Independent foundation.

Financial data (yr. ended 12/31/09): Assets, $39,220,248 (M); gifts received, $1,510; expenditures, $1,672,053; qualifying distributions, $1,436,250; giving activities include $1,436,250 for 884 grants (high: $320,679; low: $8).

Purpose and activities: Giving primarily for public service and fighting hunger.

Fields of interest: Elementary/secondary education; Higher education; Education; Food services; Food banks; Human services.

Limitations: Applications not accepted. Giving on a national basis.

Application information: Unsolicited requests for funds not accepted.

Board meeting date(s): Varies

Officers and Directors: * Alan Shawn Feinstein, Pres.; Edward Valenti, V.P.; Michael Finer,* Secy.; Ari Feinstein; Leila Feinstein; Richard Feinstein; Kevin Hanlon; Ofir Katz; Reza Khoyi; Edward Walton.

Number of staff: 1 full-time professional; 1 part-time professional.

EIN: 223142312

Recent grants for international programs:

1924-1 American Jewish World Service, New York, NY, $24,272. 2009.

1924-2 Feed My Hungry People, Scottsdale, AZ, $19,607. 2009.

1924-3 Flying Kites, Brooklyn, NY, $18,885. 2009.

1924-4 Flying Kites, Brooklyn, NY, $17,200. 2009.

1924-5 Hasdei Naomi, Bnei Brak, Israel, $20,814. 2009.

1924-6 Hasdei Naomi, Bnei Brak, Israel, $10,000. 2009.

1924-7 Operation Blessing International Relief and Development Corporation, Virginia Beach, VA, $10,919. 2009.

1924-8 PEF Israel Endowment Funds, New York, NY, $11,900. 2009.

1925
FM Global Foundation

(formerly Allendale Insurance Foundation)
270 Central Ave.
P.O. Box 7500
Johnston, RI 02919-4923
URL: http://www.fmglobal.com/page.aspx?id=01060100

Established in 1986 in RI.

Donors: Allendale Mutual Insurance Co.; Factory Mutual Insurance Co.

Grantmaker type: Company-sponsored foundation.

Financial data (yr. ended 12/31/10): Assets, $13,041,916 (M); gifts received, $42,000; expenditures, $4,097,624; qualifying distributions, $3,996,717; giving activities include $3,996,717 for grants.

Purpose and activities: The foundation supports museums and organizations involved with education, human services, community development, and public policy research.

Fields of interest: Public policy, research; Museums; Elementary/secondary education; Scholarships/financial aid; Education; Human services; Economic development, visitors/ convention bureau/tourism promotion; Community/ economic development; United Ways and Federated Giving Programs.
International interests: Canada.
Type of support: General/operating support; Scholarship funds; Employee volunteer services; Employee matching gifts.
Limitations: Applications not accepted. Giving primarily in NJ, RI, WA and in Canada. No grants to individuals.
Application information: Contributes only to pre-selected organizations.
Officers and Directors: Shivan S. Subramaniam,* Chair., C.E.O., and Pres.; Paul E. LaFleche, Sr. V.P., Investments; Nelson G. Wester, V.P. and Secy.; William A. Mekrut,* V.P. and Treas.; John N. Lemieux, V.P.
Trustee: JPMorgan Chase Bank, N.A.
Number of staff: 1
EIN: 222773230
Recent grants for international programs:
1925-1 American Red Cross National Headquarters, Washington, DC, $25,000. For Haiti programs. 2010.
1925-2 Centraide of Greater Montreal, Montreal, Canada, $43,911. 2010.
1925-3 Dalhousie University, Halifax, Canada, $10,000. 2010.
1925-4 Pakistan Red Crescent Society, Lahore, Pakistan, $25,000. 2010.
1925-5 United Way of York Region, Markham, Canada, $45,010. 2010.

1926
Hasbro Children's Fund, Inc.
(formerly Hasbro Charitable Trust, Inc.)
c/o Hasbro, Inc.
1027 Newport Ave.
Pawtucket, RI 02861-2539 (401) 727-5429
Contact: Karen Davis, V.P., Community Rels.
E-mail: kdavis@hasbro.com; URL: http:// www.hasbro.org

Established in 1984 in RI.
Donor: Hasbro, Inc.
Grantmaker type: Company-sponsored foundation.
Financial data (yr. ended 12/26/10): Assets, $14,713,306 (M); gifts received, $5,964; expenditures, $7,850,686; qualifying distributions, $7,850,104; giving activities include $7,774,485 for 159 grants (high: $1,350,000; low: $125), and $54,300 for employee matching gifts.
Purpose and activities: The fund supports programs designed to assist children in triumphing over critical life obstacles; and bring the joy of play into their lives. Special emphasis is directed toward programs designed to provide hope to children who need it most; play for children who otherwise would not be able to experience that joy; and empowerment of youth through service.
Fields of interest: Food banks; Mental health/crisis services; Disasters, preparedness/services; Recreation, parks/playgrounds; Elementary/ secondary education; Zoos/zoological societies; Hospitals (general); Health care; Food services; Housing/shelter; Recreation; Philanthropy/ voluntarism; Economically disadvantaged; Children.
Type of support: General/operating support; Continuing support; Capital campaigns; Building/

renovation; Program development; Employee volunteer services; Employee matching gifts.
Limitations: Applications accepted. Giving primarily in Los Angeles, CA, Springfield, MA, RI, and Renton, WA; giving also to regional, national, and U.S.-based international organizations through strategic partnership program. No support for religious organizations, political organizations, or schools. No grants to individuals, or for research, scholarships, travel, endowments, advertising, sponsorship of recreational activities, fundraisers, or auctions; no loans; no cash free grants.
Publications: Application guidelines; Corporate giving report.
Application information: The fund awards grants through an RFP process. Visit website for updated guidelines. Unsolicited requests from regional, national, and U.S.-based international organizations are not accepted. Application form required.
Initial approach: Complete online letter of inquiry
Deadline(s): Varies
Board meeting date(s): Oct./Nov.
Officers: David D.R. Hargreaves, C.O.O.; Brian Goldner, Pres.; Barbara Finigan, Sr. V.P. and Secy.; Deborah Thomas, Sr. V.P. and C.F.O.; Martin Trueb, Sr. V.P. and Treas.; Jeff Barkan, Sr. V.P and Cont.
Number of staff: 3 full-time professional; 1 full-time support; 1 part-time support.
EIN: 222538470
Recent grants for international programs:
1926-1 Angel Flight New England, North Andover, MA, $50,000. For Hasbro Helping Wings Program. 2009.
1926-2 Boundless Playgrounds, New Haven, CT, $125,000. For project for military installations, giving military children of all ages and abilities a place to play with others. 2009.
1926-3 Operation Smile International, Norfolk, VA, $150,000. For Brazil Smile Mission, which provides educational opportunities to in-country healthcare professionals. Operation Smile plush Mr. Potato Head toys were again distributed as a source of comfort to children seeking surgery. 2009.
1926-4 Operation Smile International, Norfolk, VA, $19,355. For Operation Smile China Mission. 2009.
1926-5 SOS Childrens Villages-USA, Washington, DC, $125,000. To support SOS Villages in Brazil, China, Mexico, Poland and Russia. 2009.
1926-6 United States Fund for UNICEF, Boston, MA, $10,000. For Project Zambi for AIDS orphans in Rwanda. Project Zambi is a global initiative to raise awareness of the estimated 15 million children who have been orphaned as a result of the AIDS epidemic in Africa and to support programs that serve them. 2009.
1926-7 University of Rhode Island Foundation, Kingston, RI, $100,000. For Chinese International Engineering Program (IEP) and Chinese International Business Program (IBP) and Hasbro Scholars Fund, which provides support for undergraduates who study in China and take part in internships in that country. 2009.
1926-8 World Vision, Federal Way, WA, $125,000. For RAPIDS HIV/AIDS partnership in Zambia. 2009.
1926-9 World Vision, Federal Way, WA, $14,595. For World Vision Care Giver Kits. 2009.
1926-10 Youth Venture, Arlington, VA, $15,000. For Youth Venture Summit U.S. Ambassador Program for Youth Empowerment. YVS is the annual gathering of Youth Venture. The

conference brings together Youth Venturers and young leaders interested in creating change, as well as the adult allies and professionals who support young changemakers. 2009.

1927
Hassenfeld Foundation
101 Dyer St., Ste. 401
Providence, RI 02903-3908

Established in 1944 in RI.
Donors: Sylvia Hassenfeld; Hasbro, Inc.; Stephen Hassenfeld Charitable Lead Trust; Sylvia K. Hassenfeld Revocable Trust; and members of the Hassenfeld family.
Grantmaker type: Independent foundation.
Financial data (yr. ended 12/31/10): Assets, $25,303,737 (M); gifts received, $1,065,000; expenditures, $5,113,451; qualifying distributions, $5,059,451; giving activities include $4,929,875 for 94 grants (high: $717,689; low: $500).
Purpose and activities: Giving primarily for higher education and Jewish federated giving programs.
Fields of interest: Higher education; Hospitals (general); Jewish federated giving programs.
Limitations: Applications not accepted. Giving primarily in MA, NY, PA, RI. No grants to individuals.
Application information: Contributes only to pre-selected organizations.
Officers and Director:* Sylvia K. Hassenfeld,* Pres.; Alan G. Hassenfeld, V.P. and Treas.; Ellen Block, Secy.
EIN: 056015373
Recent grants for international programs:
1927-1 American Friends of the Israel Museum, New York, NY, $220,096. For unrestricted support. 2009.
1927-2 American Jewish Joint Distribution Committee, New York, NY, $37,650. For unrestricted support. 2009.
1927-3 Institute for International Sport, Kingston, RI, $62,928. For unrestricted support. 2009.
1927-4 Relief International, Los Angeles, CA, $42,615. For unrestricted support. 2009.
1927-5 Transfair USA, Oakland, CA, $25,000. For unrestricted support. 2009.

1928
Hoag Family Charitable Foundation
P.O. Box 1802
Providence, RI 02901-1802

Established in 2005 in NY.
Donors: Bruce Hoag; Barbara Hoag.
Grantmaker type: Independent foundation.
Financial data (yr. ended 12/31/10): Assets, $3,631,225 (M); expenditures, $228,450; qualifying distributions, $207,380; giving activities include $194,500 for grants.
Fields of interest: Education; Human services; International relief.
Limitations: Applications not accepted. No grants to individuals.
Application information: Unsolicited requests for funds not accepted.
Trustee: Bank of America, N.A.
EIN: 204058314

1929
Cornelius L. King Foundation
c/o Bank of America, N.A.
P.O. Box 1802
Providence, RI 02901-1802
Application address: c/o Bank of America,
Attn.: Christine O'Donnell, 1 Bryant Park, New York,
NY 10036, tel.: (646) 855-1011

Established in 2003 in NY.
Donor: Cornelius L. King Charitable Trust.
Grantmaker type: Independent foundation.
Financial data (yr. ended 09/30/10): Assets,
$443,034 (M); gifts received, $2,000;
expenditures, $231,879; qualifying distributions,
$224,598; giving activities include $222,250 for 38
grants (high: $25,000; low: $500).
Fields of interest: Environment; Education; Health
organizations; International relief; Jewish federated
giving programs; Jewish agencies & synagogues.
International interests: Israel.
Limitations: Applications accepted. Giving primarily
in NY; some giving in CT, NJ, and VT. No grants to
individuals.
Application information:
  Initial approach: 3-page letter of inquiry
  Deadline(s): None
Trustees: Bruce Alter; Bank of America, N.A.
EIN: 137425372

1930
Koonce Family Foundation
c/o Bank of America, N.A.
P.O. Box 1802
Providence, RI 02901-1802

Established in 2005 in TX.
Donors: K. Terry Koonce; Beverly Koonce.
Grantmaker type: Independent foundation.
Financial data (yr. ended 12/31/10): Assets,
$8,318,694 (M); gifts received, $984,408;
expenditures, $318,967; qualifying distributions,
$295,412; giving activities include $278,500 for 20
grants (high: $50,000; low: $3,000).
Fields of interest: Human services; International
development; Christian agencies & churches.
Limitations: Applications not accepted. Giving
primarily in TX. No grants to individuals.
Application information: Contributes only to
pre-selected organizations.
Trustees: Charlene C. Koonce; K. Terry Koonce;
Kelly M. Koonce; Kenneth T. Koonce; Kimberly
Koonce; Diana Koonce Walla; Richard E. Walla.
EIN: 766211703

1931
Luke Charitable Foundation
333 Roosevelt Ave.
Pawtucket, RI 02860-2123

Established in 2005.
Donor: Chinese Christian Church.
Grantmaker type: Independent foundation.
Financial data (yr. ended 12/31/10): Assets,
$4,550,082 (M); expenditures, $234,640;
qualifying distributions, $171,910; giving activities
include $171,910 for grants.
Purpose and activities: Giving primarily to Chinese
organizations.

Fields of interest: Arts, cultural/ethnic awareness;
Higher education; Minorities/immigrants, centers/
services; International relief.
Limitations: Applications not accepted. Giving
primarily in RI. No grants to individuals.
Application information: Unsolicited requests for
funds not accepted.
Trustees: Robert Billington; Tze Ping Ng; Nai Che
Tsai; Shirley Wu; Chiu Yip.
EIN: 202597824

1932
F. Mason Perkins Trust
c/o Bank of America, N.A.
P.O. Box 1802
Providence, RI 02901-1802

Established in 1955.
Donor: F. Mason Perkins†.
Grantmaker type: Independent foundation.
Financial data (yr. ended 12/31/10): Assets,
$4,175,170 (M); expenditures, $207,955;
qualifying distributions, $170,000; giving activities
include $170,000 for grants.
Purpose and activities: Giving exclusively to
charities in Italy for aid to the poor and less
fortunate, particularly children and the aged, and for
the protection of animals; first consideration for
grants is given to organizations providing for the
poor, orphans, children and Sisters of Charity.
Fields of interest: Animal welfare; Nursing care;
Human services; Children/youth, services; Aging,
centers/services; Disabilities, people with; Aging;
Economically disadvantaged.
International interests: Italy.
Type of support: Continuing support; Endowments;
Emergency funds; Program development;
Curriculum development; Fellowships; Scholarship
funds; Research.
Limitations: Applications accepted. Giving limited to
Italy. No grants to individuals.
Publications: Application guidelines.
Application information: Application form required.
  Initial approach: Grant request on requesting
  organization's letterhead
  Copies of proposal: 3
  Deadline(s): May 1 and Nov. 1
  Final notification: June 30 and Dec. 31
Trustee: Bank of America, N.A.
EIN: 226040411

1933
Plan International, Inc.
155 Plan Way
P.O. Box 7670
Warwick, RI 02886-1011
URL: http://www.planusa.org
Facebook: http://www.facebook.com/planusa
Twitter: http://twitter.com/planusa
YouTube: http://www.youtube.com/planusavideos

Supporting organization of Foster Parents Plan of
Canada, Foster Parents Plan Japan, Plan
International Australia, Plan International Belgium,
Plan International Denmark, Plan International
Deutschland, Plan International Finland, Plan
International France, Plan International Korea, Plan
International Norway, Plan International Spain, Plan
International Sweden, Plan International (UK), Plan
International USA, and Stichting Foster Parents Plan
Nederland.

Grantmaker type: Public charity.
Financial data (yr. ended 06/30/10): Revenue,
$531,763,649; assets, $267,552,541 (M); gifts
received, $531,292,446; expenditures,
$438,216,171; giving activities include
$211,521,560 for grants to organizations outside
the U.S.
Fields of interest: Children/youth, services;
Economically disadvantaged; Children.
International interests: Developing countries.
Limitations: Applications not accepted. Giving on a
worldwide basis.
Application information: Contributes only to
pre-selected organizations.
Officers: Paul Arlman, Chair.; Wendy McCarthy,
Vice-Chair.; Peter Gross, Treas.
Directors: Stan Bartholomeeussen; Srilatha
Batliwala; John Bonnycastle; Miguel Canalejo; Anne
Grant; Viveka Hirdman-Ryrberg; Ezra Mbogori.
EIN: 510169168

1934
Jacob F. & Wilma S. Schoellkopf Foundation
c/o Bank of America, N.A.
P.O. Box 1802
Providence, RI 02901-1802

Established in MA.
Grantmaker type: Independent foundation.
Financial data (yr. ended 09/30/10): Assets,
$19,123,324 (M); expenditures, $213,275;
qualifying distributions, $180,933; giving activities
include $177,158 for grants.
Fields of interest: Foundations (private operating);
Philanthropy/voluntarism.
International interests: Germany.
Limitations: Applications not accepted. Giving in NY
and Germany. No grants to individuals.
Application information: Contributes only to
pre-selected organizations.
Trustee: Bank of America, N.A.
EIN: 046008242

1935
Edwin S. Soforenko Foundation
870 Westminster St.
Providence, RI 02903-4024 (401) 282-4743
Application address: c/o RBS Citizens, N.A.,
Attn.: Palmira Azevedo, 1 Citizens Plz., Providence,
RI 02903, tel.: (401) 282-4743

Established in 1967 in RI.
Donors: Edwin S. Soforenko†; Lawrence Soforenko.
Grantmaker type: Independent foundation.
Financial data (yr. ended 12/31/10): Assets,
$3,033,300 (M); gifts received, $2,965;
expenditures, $210,750; qualifying distributions,
$202,599; giving activities include $192,100 for 52
grants (high: $47,500; low: $1,000).
Purpose and activities: Giving primarily to Jewish
organizations; some support also for education,
health and human services and international relief
for victims of earthquakes.
Fields of interest: Education; Hospitals (general);
Human services; International relief; United Ways
and Federated Giving Programs; Jewish federated
giving programs; Jewish agencies & synagogues.
Type of support: Continuing support; Annual
campaigns; Capital campaigns; Building/
renovation; Endowments; Emergency funds;

Program development; Professorships; Fellowships; Scholarship funds; Research.
Limitations: Applications accepted. Giving primarily in Providence, RI. No grants to individuals.
Application information: Application form required.
  Initial approach: Proposal
  Deadline(s): None
  Final notification: Within 1 month
Trustees: Max Kohlenberg; Lawrence Soforenko; RBS Citizens, N.A.
EIN: 056019803

SOUTH CAROLINA

1936
American Leprosy Missions, Inc.
1 ALM Way
Greenville, SC   29601-3060   (864) 271-7040
Contact: Christopher Doyle, Pres.; Jennifer Englert-Copeland, Public Affairs and Comms.
FAX: (864) 271-7062; E-mail: amlep@leprosy.org; Toll-free tel.: (800) 543-3135; URL: http://www.leprosy.org

Established in 1906.
Grantmaker type: Public charity.
Financial data (yr. ended 12/31/10): Revenue, $6,681,699; assets, $14,351,751 (M); gifts received, $6,415,839; expenditures, $6,424,631; giving activities include $450,000 for grants, and $2,224,917 for grants to organizations outside the U.S.
Purpose and activities: The organization strives to support persons affected by leprosy and related conditions, helping them to be healed in body and spirit and restored to lives of dignity and hope.
Fields of interest: Skin disorders; Diseases (rare).
International interests: Angola; Brazil; Burma (Myanmar); China; Congo; Ethiopia; Ghana; India; Ivory Coast; Thailand.
Limitations: Applications not accepted. Giving primarily on an international basis, primarily in Angola, Brazil, China, Congo, Cote d'Ivoire, Ethiopia, Ghana, India, Myanmar, Nepal, Philippines, and Thailand.
Publications: Annual report; Financial statement.
Application information: Unsolicited requests for funds not accepted.
  Board meeting date(s): May, June, and Nov.
Officers and Directors:* Neal Joseph,* Chair.; Thomas M. Young,* Vice-Chair.; Christopher Doyle, Pres.; Ron Doucette, Secy.; Chris Pott, C.F.O.; Mary Phillips, Treas.; James Oehrig, Chief Progs. Off.; and 7 additional directors.
Number of staff: 11 full-time professional; 8 full-time support; 3 part-time support.
EIN: 135562163

1937
AVX/Kyocera Foundation
801 17th Ave. S.
P.O. Box 867
Myrtle Beach, SC   29577-4245

Established in 1996 in SC.
Donor: AVX Corp.

Grantmaker type: Company-sponsored foundation.
Financial data (yr. ended 03/31/11): Assets, $9,998,883 (M); expenditures, $512,664; qualifying distributions, $429,317; giving activities include $429,317 for grants.
Purpose and activities: Giving primarily for education and human services.
Fields of interest: Education; Human services; International relief.
International interests: China; El Salvador; Israel.
Type of support: General/operating support; Scholarships—to individuals.
Limitations: Applications not accepted. Giving primarily in the U.S., with emphasis on SC; some international giving also, including but not limited to China, El Salvador, and Israel.
Application information: Unsolicited requests for funds not accepted.
Officers: John S. Gilbertson, Pres.; C. Marshall Jackson, V.P.; Larry Edwards, Treas.
EIN: 571057142

1938
Calabar Foundation
3 Castlebridge Ct.
Hilton Head Island, SC   29928-3362
(843) 341-5675
Contact: Andrew Summers, Secy.-Treas.

Established in 2007 in SC.
Donor: Andrew Summers.
Grantmaker type: Independent foundation.
Financial data (yr. ended 06/30/11): Assets, $1,251,747 (M); gifts received, $247,096; expenditures, $528,767; qualifying distributions, $513,917; giving activities include $225,291 for 5 grants (high: $59,971; low: $13,821).
Fields of interest: Human services; Education.
International interests: South Africa.
Limitations: Applications accepted. Giving primarily in South Africa.
Application information: Application form required.
  Initial approach: Letter
  Deadline(s): None
Officers and Directors:* Darisse Summers,* Pres.; Andrew Summers,* Secy.-Treas.; Walt Howell.
EIN: 020787615

1939
Michelin North America, Inc. Corporate Giving Program
c/o Community Rels.
P.O. Box 19001
Greenville, SC   29602-9001
URL: http://www.michelin-us.com/communityrelations/index.html

Grantmaker type: Corporate giving program.
Purpose and activities: Michelin makes charitable contributions to nonprofit organizations involved with STEM (science, technology, engineering, and math) education, the environment, and automotive safety. Support is given on a national basis in areas of company operations in Alabama, Indiana, Kentucky, North Carolina, Oklahoma, and South Carolina, and in Canada.
Fields of interest: Engineering/technology; Mathematics; Science; Human services; Safety, automotive safety; Health care; Environment; Education; Arts.
International interests: Canada.

Type of support: Program development; Employee volunteer services; Sponsorships; In-kind gifts.
Limitations: Applications accepted. Giving primarily in areas of company operations in AL, IN, KY, NC, OK, SC, and in Canada. No support for religious organizations not of direct benefit to the entire community, political candidates or lobbying organizations, fraternal, labor, veterans', or similar organizations with a limited constituency, or anti-business organizations. No grants to individuals, or for travel, national conferences, sports events, or other one-time, short-term events, advertising, or team sponsorships or athletic scholarships.
Application information: Application form required.
  Initial approach: Download application form and upload completed application form to web site
  Deadline(s): None

1940
TSC Foundation, Inc.
104 E. Springs St.
Lancaster, SC   29720-2159   (803) 286-2172

Established in 2001 in SC.
Donors: Derick S. Close; Crandall C. Bowles; Leroy S. Close; Springs Industries, Inc.; Patricia Close Charitable Lead Trust No. 2; Springs Window Fashions, Inc.; 09 PGC Charitable Lead Annuity Trust.
Grantmaker type: Independent foundation.
Financial data (yr. ended 12/31/10): Assets, $751,028 (M); gifts received, $1,878,288; expenditures, $2,224,816; qualifying distributions, $2,224,616; giving activities include $2,224,616 for grants.
Purpose and activities: Giving primarily to public and community foundations, health associations and medical research, particularly for Lou Gehrig's disease and juvenile diabetes, social services, farmworker legal services, Episcopal churches, and a women's shelter; funding also for children's services, education, and the arts.
Fields of interest: Arts; Elementary school/education; Higher education; Animals/wildlife; Health organizations, association; Medical research, institute; Nerve, muscle & bone research; Diabetes research; Legal services; Food banks; Boy scouts; Human services; American Red Cross; Children, services; Residential/custodial care, hospices; Women, centers/services; Foundations (public); Foundations (community); Protestant agencies & churches.
Limitations: Applications not accepted. Giving primarily in NC and SC. No grants to individuals.
Application information: Contributes only to pre-selected organizations.
Officers: William Taylor, Pres.; Harry Emerson, V.P. and Secy.; Peyton Worley, V.P. and Treas.
EIN: 571124837
Recent grants for international programs:
1940-1 1000 Jobs Haiti, Little Compton, RI, $20,000. 2010.
1940-2 1000 Jobs Haiti, Little Compton, RI, $20,000. 2010.
1940-3 1000 Jobs Haiti, Little Compton, RI, $20,000. 2010.
1940-4 1000 Jobs Haiti, Little Compton, RI, $15,000. 2010.
1940-5 1000 Jobs Haiti, Little Compton, RI, $13,500. 2010.
1940-6 1000 Jobs Haiti, Little Compton, RI, $10,000. 2010.

1940-7 1000 Jobs Haiti, Little Compton, RI, $10,000. 2010.

1940-8 1000 Jobs Haiti, Little Compton, RI, $10,000. 2010.

1940-9 1000 Jobs Haiti, Little Compton, RI, $10,000. 2010.

1940-10 1000 Jobs Haiti, Little Compton, RI, $10,000. 2010.

1940-11 1000 Jobs Haiti, Little Compton, RI, $10,000. 2010.

1940-12 1000 Jobs Haiti, Little Compton, RI, $10,000. 2010.

1940-13 Fonkoze USA, Washington, DC, $10,000. 2010.

1940-14 Friends of the Earth, Washington, DC, $25,000. 2010.

1940-15 Friends of the Earth, Washington, DC, $25,000. 2010.

1940-16 Grant Foundation, Pittsburgh, PA, $125,000. For Hopital Albert Schweitzer in Haiti. 2010.

1940-17 Grant Foundation, Pittsburgh, PA, $25,000. For Hopital Albert Schweitzer in Haiti. 2010.

1940-18 Partners in Health, Boston, MA, $30,000. 2010.

1940-19 Partners in Health, Boston, MA, $10,000. 2010.

1941
Youths' Friends Association, Inc.
P.O. Box 5387
Hilton Head Island, SC 29938-5387
(843) 671-5060
Contact: Walter J. Graver, Secy.-Treas.

Incorporated in 1950 in NY.
Donors: Johan J. Smit†; Mrs. Johan J. Smit†.
Grantmaker type: Independent foundation.
Financial data (yr. ended 12/31/09): Assets, $9,195,717 (M); expenditures, $528,966; qualifying distributions, $506,300; giving activities include $438,300 for 121 grants (high: $13,000; low: $500).
Purpose and activities: Grants largely for international relief, and higher and secondary education, through scholarship support earmarked for high school students; support also for social services, youth, health, and cultural programs.
Fields of interest: Children, adoption; Arts; Secondary school/education; Higher education; Health care; Health organizations, association; Human services; Children/youth, services; International relief; Youth; Children.
Type of support: General/operating support; Seed money; Scholarship funds.
Limitations: Applications accepted. Giving on a national basis. No grants to individuals.
Publications: Financial statement.
Application information: Application form not required.
> *Initial approach:* Letter
> *Copies of proposal:* 1
> *Deadline(s):* None
> *Board meeting date(s):* Semiannually
Officers and Directors:* Sheila Smit,* Pres.; Stephen C. Smit,* V.P.; Walter J. Graver,* Secy.-Treas.; Evan Kirchen; Helen Kirchen; Robert Kirchen; Judith Rist; Peta Smit Santos; Lisa Smit; Barbara Weiler.
Number of staff: 1 part-time support.
EIN: 136097828

1942
The Zvejnieks Foundation
4 Ashfield Ln.
Blythewood, SC 29016-9091 (803) 754-8184
Contact: Peter Zvejnieks, Tr.

Established in 1990 in GA.
Donor: Andrejs Zvejnieks†.
Grantmaker type: Independent foundation.
Financial data (yr. ended 12/31/08): Assets, $0 (M); expenditures, $286,828; qualifying distributions, $265,500; giving activities include $265,500 for 14 grants (high: $120,000; low: $1,000).
Purpose and activities: Giving primarily for financial support to students from any of the Baltic states and the United States for travel and study in other foreign countries, particularly students with a special interest and competency in Latvian language and culture.
Fields of interest: Children/youth, services; Education; Christian agencies & churches; Human services.
International interests: Latvia.
Limitations: Applications accepted. Giving limited to students from any of the Baltic states and the U.S. No grants to individuals.
Application information: Application form not required.
> *Initial approach:* Letter
> *Deadline(s):* None
Trustee: Peter Zvejnieks.
EIN: 581912848

SOUTH DAKOTA

1943
Branches Foundation
c/o Dorsey & Whitney Trust
401 E. 8th St., Ste. 319
Sioux Falls, SD 57103-7031

Established in 1999 in MN.
Donors: David O. Christianson; Branches Charitable Annuity Trust; Gustafson 2003 Charitable Lead Annuity Trust; Branches 1999 Charitable Lead Annuity Trust.
Grantmaker type: Independent foundation.
Financial data (yr. ended 12/31/10): Assets, $25,083,296 (M); gifts received, $2,819,900; expenditures, $1,214,914; qualifying distributions, $1,029,025; giving activities include $1,029,000 for 20 grants (high: $260,000; low: $5,000).
Fields of interest: Protestant agencies & churches; Human services; Christian agencies & churches.
Limitations: Applications not accepted. Giving primarily in CO and MN. No grants to individuals.
Application information: Contributes only to pre-selected organizations.
Trustees: Todd J. Christianson; Trudy A. Christianson.
EIN: 416463939
Recent grants for international programs:
1943-1 Compassion International, Colorado Springs, CO, $260,000. For general operating support. 2010.

1943-2 English Language Institute in China, Fort Collins, CO, $68,000. For general operating support. 2010.

1943-3 Josiah Venture, Wheaton, IL, $25,000. For general operating support. 2010.

1943-4 Samaritans Purse, Boone, NC, $100,000. For general operating support. 2010.

1944
Opus Prize Foundation
(formerly Alpha & Omega Family Foundation)
c/o Adler Mgmt., LLC
401 E. 8th St., Ste. 250A
Sioux Falls, SD 57103-7034

Established in 1994 in SD.
Grantmaker type: Independent foundation.
Financial data (yr. ended 12/31/10): Assets, $27,996,898 (M); expenditures, $1,461,154; qualifying distributions, $1,215,936; giving activities include $1,215,936 for grants.
Purpose and activities: Giving primarily for human services.
Fields of interest: Catholic federated giving programs; Education; Human services; Economically disadvantaged.
International interests: Brazil; Colombia; Jamaica; Mexico; Morocco and the Western Sahara.
Type of support: General/operating support; Capital campaigns; Program development.
Limitations: Applications not accepted. Giving primarily on a national and international basis. No grants to individuals.
Application information: Contributes only to pre-selected organizations.
Officers and Directors:* Michael Rauenhorst,* Pres.; Luz Campa, V.P.; Loretta Rauenhorst,* Secy.; Kristine Rauenhorst,* Treas.; Amy Sunderland, Exec. Dir.; Janine Geske; Katherine Marshall; Susan R. Turner.
EIN: 460434399
Recent grants for international programs:
1944-1 Asociacion Hogares Luz y Vida, Bogota, Colombia, $100,000. For charitable mission and activities. 2009.

1944-2 Association Solidarite Feminine, Morocco and the Western Sahara, $1,000,000. For charitable mission and activities. 2009.

1944-3 Obra Social Nossa Senhora da Gloria Fazenda da Esperanca, Brazil, $100,000. For Fazenda da Esperanca's charitable mission and activities. 2009.

TENNESSEE

1945
African Christian Schools Foundation, Inc.
P.O. Box 41120
Nashville, TN 37204-1120
E-mail: info@africanchristianschools.org;
URL: http://africanchristianschools.org/
RSS Feed: http://africanchristianschools.org/rss

Established in 1960 in TN.
Grantmaker type: Public charity.

Financial data (yr. ended 12/31/10): Revenue, $329,953; assets, $496,803 (M); gifts received, $328,892; expenditures, $363,546; giving activities include $133,999 for grants to organizations outside the U.S.
Purpose and activities: The foundation works to provide, through African partnership, centers of educational excellence that equip students for leadership, evangelism, and ministry in Africa.
Fields of interest: Religion, public education; Christian agencies & churches.
International interests: Africa.
Limitations: Applications not accepted. Giving limited to Africa.
Application information: Contributes only to pre-selected organizations.
Officers: Bruce Church, Chair.; Mike Cochrane, Vice-Chair.; Don Harrison, Secy.; Carlton "Butch" Stinson, Treas.
Board Members: John Amey; William Bagents; Dr. Ron Butterfield; Janice Crowder; Euel Fountain; E. Henry Huffard, Jr.; Alan Hutchison; Ron Laughery; Larry D. Mathis; Edward L. Palmer; Dr. Jill Parker; Brandon Potter; Dr. Elizabeth Saunders; Jack Thorn.
EIN: 620701124

1946
African Leadership, Inc.
233 Wilson Pike Cir., Bldg. 2A
Brentwood, TN 37027-5263 (615) 595-8238
E-mail: info@africanleadershipinc.org; *URL:* http://www.africanleadershipinc.org

Established in 2000 in TN.
Grantmaker type: Public charity.
Financial data (yr. ended 12/31/10): Revenue, $3,812,846; assets, $1,459,406 (M); gifts received, $3,772,435; expenditures, $3,823,510; giving activities include $255,000 for grants, $1,334,664 for 7 grants to organizations outside the U.S., and $295,931 for grants to individuals outside the U.S.
Purpose and activities: The organization trains pastors and church leaders, funds relief and development projects in Africa, and assists refugees in central Tennessee.
Fields of interest: International migration/refugee issues; Community/economic development; Christian agencies & churches.
Limitations: Giving limited to AL and VA, and to Africa.
Officer: Jerry Heffel, Chair.; Larry Warren, Pres.; Eddy Messick, V.P. and Secy.; Rick DeSoto, Treas.
Directors: Mike Gay; Dick Wright.
EIN: 311736706

1947
Bala Cares Foundation
c/o Ganapathy Lakshmanan, M.D.
211-B E. Court Ave.
Selmer, TN 38375
E-mail: balacenter@balacares.com; India address: c/o R. Ariyadoss, Managing Dir., 11/49 Woodville Rd., Kodaikanal, Tamilnadu, India - 624101, tel.: 91-4542-243070, or 243071, or 241214: FAX: 91-4542-241252; E-mail: hotelbala@balacares.com; *URL:* http://www.balacares.com

Established in 1999 in TN.
Donor: Ganapathy Lakshmanan, M.D.

Grantmaker type: Independent foundation.
Financial data (yr. ended 12/31/10): Assets, $32,377 (M); gifts received, $199,325; expenditures, $167,278; qualifying distributions, $166,595; giving activities include $166,595 for 4 grants (high: $100,000; low: $25).
Purpose and activities: Giving to help and assist distressed people from disease and poverty, irrespective of color, religion, or country of origin.
Fields of interest: Education; Hospitals (general).
International interests: India.
Limitations: Applications not accepted. Giving primarily in India. No grants to individuals.
Application information: Contributes only to pre-selected organizations.
Officers: Ganapathy Lakshmanan, M.D., Chair. and Pres.; Gail Shultz, Secy.
Director: Charlene Hawkins.
EIN: 621763812

1948
Belz Foundation
100 Peabody Pl., Ste. 1400
Memphis, TN 38103-3648

Incorporated in 1952 in TN.
Donors: Philip Belz†; Martin S. Belz; Ronald A. Belz; Jack A. Belz; Andrew Groveman; Jan B. Groveman; Philip Bell Charitable Lead Annuity II; The 1992 Belz Charitable Trust.
Grantmaker type: Independent foundation.
Financial data (yr. ended 12/31/10): Assets, $24,612,047 (M); gifts received, $1,060,239; expenditures, $1,980,457; qualifying distributions, $1,513,103; giving activities include $1,513,103 for grants.
Purpose and activities: Emphasis on Jewish welfare funds, temple support, Israel, education, including higher education and yeshivas, cultural organizations, and health and welfare organizations.
Fields of interest: Arts; Elementary/secondary education; Higher education; Theological school/education; Education; Health care; Health organizations, association; Medical research, institute; Human services; Jewish federated giving programs; Jewish agencies & synagogues.
International interests: Israel.
Limitations: Applications not accepted. Giving primarily in Memphis, TN. No grants to individuals.
Application information: Contributes only to pre-selected organizations.
Officers and Directors:* Jack A. Belz,* Pres.; Martin S. Belz,* V.P.; Jimmie D. Williams,* Secy.-Treas.; Ronald A. Belz; Andrew Groveman; Jan B. Groveman; Raymond Shainberg.
EIN: 626046715

1949
Cloud Forest School Foundation
P.O. Box 3223
Sewanee, TN 37375-3223
E-mail: foundation@cloudforestschool.org; *URL:* http://cloudforestschool.org/?page_id=68

Established in 1991.
Donors: C. Nelle Alexander; Dr. Henry Arnold; Mrs. Henry Arnold; Garnett Ashby; Mrs. Garnett Ashby; Blake Audsley; Robert A. Ayres; Mrs. Robert A. Ayres; Daniel Backlund; Mrs. Daniel Backlund.
Grantmaker type: Public charity.

Financial data (yr. ended 06/30/11): Revenue, $86,567; assets, $281,300 (M); gifts received, $68,028; expenditures, $66,119; giving activities include $52,273 for grants.
Purpose and activities: The organization supports Centro de Educacion Creativa, a bilingual school located in Monteverde, Costa Rica.
Fields of interest: Elementary/secondary education; Environment.
International interests: Costa Rica.
Type of support: Annual campaigns; Capital campaigns; Building/renovation; Equipment; Endowments; Program development; Professorships; Scholarship funds; In-kind gifts.
Limitations: Applications not accepted. Giving limited to Costa Rica.
Publications: Newsletter.
Application information: Contributes only to a pre-selected organization.
 Board meeting date(s): Mar. and Oct.
Officers and Trustees:* Christopher R. Tompkins,* Chair.; Scott Shannon,* Vice-Chair.; Elizabeth M. Lowell,* Secy.; Douglas A. Caves,* Treas.; Mary Bruce Alford; Douglas Cameron; Jason Hamilton; Thomas McPartland; Stephen Watters.
Number of staff: None.
EIN: 621532788

1950
The Community Foundation of Greater Chattanooga, Inc.
1270 Market St.
Chattanooga, TN 37402-2713 (423) 265-0586
Contact: Peter T. Cooper, Pres.; For grants: Robin Posey, Prog. Off.
FAX: (423) 265-0587; *E-mail:* info2@cfgc.org; Additional e-mail: pcooper@cfgc.org; Grant application e-mail: rposey@cfgc.org; *URL:* http://www.cfgc.org
Facebook: http://www.facebook.com/pages/Community-Foundation-of-Greater-Chattanooga/90899078728
RSS Feed: http://www.cfgc.org/index.php?format=feed&type=rss
Twitter: http://www.twitter.com/WEAREGREATER
Scholarship e-mail: rsmith@cfgc.org

Incorporated in 1963 in TN.
Grantmaker type: Community foundation.
Financial data (yr. ended 12/31/09): Assets, $74,507,958 (M); gifts received, $10,299,813; expenditures, $14,560,244; giving activities include $12,488,375 for 3,848 grants (high: $800,000), and $1,024,119 for 484 grants to individuals.
Purpose and activities: The foundation seeks to promote and enhance the well-being of the inhabitants of the greater Chattanooga, TN area.
Fields of interest: Community development, neighborhood development; Human services; Child development, education; Immigrants/refugees.
International interests: Japan.
Type of support: Management development/capacity building; Capital campaigns; Building/renovation; Equipment; Land acquisition; Program development; Seed money; Scholarship funds; Scholarships—to individuals.
Limitations: Applications accepted. Giving limited to the Hamilton County, TN, area. No support for private schools, religious causes, or veterans' or fraternal organizations, public agencies, state, national or regional organizations. No grants to

individuals (except for scholarship programs), endowment campaigns, operating support for existing programs, conferences, advertising, telephone solicitations, fundraising expenses, or federated fund drives; no loans.

Publications: Application guidelines; Annual report; Biennial report (including application guidelines); Grants list; Informational brochure; Informational brochure (including application guidelines).

Application information: Visit foundation web site for online application form and guidelines. Applicants are required to submit a Letter of Intent form and receive written approval from the foundation to continue the application process. Application form required.

  Initial approach: Submit Letter of Intent form
  Copies of proposal: 1
  Deadline(s): Jan. 14, May 20, and Sept. 9 for letter of intent; Jan. 28, June 3, and Sept. 23 for full application
  Board meeting date(s): Quarterly; Prog. Comm. meets 3 times per year
  Final notification: Apr., Aug., and Dec.

Officers and Directors:* Paul Campbell,* Chair.; Patsy Hazlewood,* Vice-Chair.; Peter T. Cooper, Pres.; Marty Robinson, V.P., Donor Rels.; Rebecca Underwood, V.P., Finance and Admin.; Ansley Moses,* Secy.; Linda Mosley,* Treas.; Mike Berry; Charlie Brock; Jeff Cannon; Lakweshia Ewing; Tom Glenn; Helen Johnson; Alison Lebovitz; Hugh Moore; Ward Nelson; Michelle Ruest; Rachel Schulson; Chris Smith; Niti Tejani; Carolyn Thompson; Edna Varner.

Number of staff: 8 full-time professional; 2 full-time support.

EIN: 626045999

1951
Peter Hawkins Dobberpuhl Foundation
12 Cadillac Dr., Ste. 280
Brentwood, TN 37027-5360

Established in 2007 in TN.
Donor: Joel F. Dobberpuhl.
Grantmaker type: Independent foundation.
Financial data (yr. ended 12/31/10): Assets, $45,625,938 (M); gifts received, $4,000,000; expenditures, $15,539,271; qualifying distributions, $15,516,014; giving activities include $15,492,654 for 15 grants (high: $12,010,000; low: $10,000).
Fields of interest: Christian agencies & churches; Education; Children/youth, services.
Limitations: Applications not accepted. Giving primarily in TN. No grants to individuals.
Application information: Contributes only to pre-selected organizations.
Officers and Directors:* Joel E. Dobberpuhl,* Pres.; Holly S. Dobberpuhl,* Secy.; Mark Ezell.
EIN: 261454348
Recent grants for international programs:
1951-1 Agros International, Seattle, WA, $1,567,649. For family support. 2010.
1951-2 Pura Vida Partners, Seattle, WA, $100,000. For family support. 2010.

1952
The Drake Foundation
482 Halle Park Dr., Ste. 101
Collierville, TN 38017-7089
Contact: Pansy L. Drake, Pres.

Established in 1997 in TN.
Donors: Hendrick Manufacturing Co.; Drake Industries, LLC.
Grantmaker type: Company-sponsored foundation.
Financial data (yr. ended 12/31/10): Assets, $255,771 (M); gifts received, $176,292; expenditures, $305,800; qualifying distributions, $305,800; giving activities include $305,800 for grants.
Purpose and activities: The foundation supports organizations involved with cancer, domestic violence, international relief, leadership development, and Christianity.
Fields of interest: Cancer; YM/YWCAs & YM/YWHAs; Family services, domestic violence; International relief; Leadership development; Christian agencies & churches.
Type of support: General/operating support.
Limitations: Applications accepted. Giving primarily in KY, MO, TN, and TX. No grants to individuals.
Application information: Application form not required.
  Initial approach: Letter of inquiry
  Deadline(s): None
Officers and Directors:* Pansy L. Drake,* Pres.; Darin Drake,* Secy.
EIN: 621684643

1953
Ezell Foundation, Inc.
P.O. Box 100957
Nashville, TN 37224-0957
Contact: F. Miles Ezell, Jr., Pres.

Established in 1964.
Donors: F. Miles Ezell, Sr.†; and members of the Ezell family.
Grantmaker type: Independent foundation.
Financial data (yr. ended 12/31/10): Assets, $14,933,452 (M); gifts received, $14,500; expenditures, $873,215; qualifying distributions, $657,450; giving activities include $657,450 for 72 grants (high: $125,000; low: $150).
Purpose and activities: Giving primarily to the Church of Christ and related educational programs.
Fields of interest: Education; Christian agencies & churches; Religion.
International interests: Guatemala; Honduras; Nigeria.
Type of support: General/operating support; Continuing support; Capital campaigns; Equipment.
Limitations: Giving primarily in TN.
Application information:
  Initial approach: Letter
  Deadline(s): None
  Board meeting date(s): Annually
Officers: F. Miles Ezell, Jr., Pres.; Roy C. Ezell, 1st V.P.; David Thomas, 2nd V.P.; Stanley M. Ezell, Secy.; John W. Ezell, Treas.
EIN: 626046865

1954
FedEx Corporation Contributions Program
(formerly FDX Corporation Contributions Program)
c/o Global Citizenship
3610 Hacks Cross Rd.
Bldg. A
Memphis, TN 38125-8800
E-mail: communityrelations@fedex.com;
URL: http://about.van.fedex.com/corporate_responsibility
FedEx Blog | Community Involvement: http://blog.fedex.designcdt.com/fedexblog/community_involvement
FedEx Cares: http://twitter.com/#!/FedExCares

Grantmaker type: Corporate giving program.
Purpose and activities: FedEx makes charitable contributions to nonprofit organizations involved with disaster relief, child pedestrian safety, and environmental sustainability. Support is on a national and international basis.
Fields of interest: Environment; Safety/disasters, public education; Disasters, preparedness/services; Safety, automotive safety; Safety/disasters; American Red Cross; Salvation Army; International relief; Children.
Type of support: General/operating support; Continuing support; Program development; Employee volunteer services; In-kind gifts.
Limitations: Applications accepted. Giving on a national and international basis. Generally, no support for athletic organizations, exclusively tax-supported educational institutions, labor or political organizations, public or private elementary or secondary schools or colleges, sectarian or religious organizations, or discriminatory organizations. Generally, no grants to individuals, or for athletic activities, beauty contests, endowments or memorials, scholarships, membership dues, general operating support for United Way-associated organizations, or travel; no shipping donations for items sold through fundraisers; no FedEx promotional merchandise donations.
Publications: Application guidelines.
Application information: Application form required.
  Initial approach: Complete online eligibility quiz and application form

1955
Fugitive Foundation
(formerly Wills Foundation)
c/o W. Ridley Wills, II
2156 Golf Club Ln.
Nashville, TN 37215-1224

Established in 1992 in TN.
Donors: W. Ridley Wills II; Irene J. Wills; Morgan J. Wills; Thomas W. Wills; W. Ridley Wills III.
Grantmaker type: Independent foundation.
Financial data (yr. ended 12/31/10): Assets, $5,097,768 (M); expenditures, $273,589; qualifying distributions, $240,000; giving activities include $240,000 for 26 grants (high: $58,000; low: $500).
Fields of interest: Historical activities; Arts; Education; Health care; Human services; Christian agencies & churches; Youth; Young adults, male; Young adults, female; Young adults; Women; Single parents; Physically disabled; Minorities; Migrant workers; Men; Infants/toddlers, female; Infants/toddlers; Infants/toddlers, male; Homeless; Hispanics/Latinos; Economically disadvantaged;

Children/youth; Children; Boys; African Americans/ Blacks; Adults, women; Adults, men; Adults.
International interests: Ghana.
Type of support: General/operating support; Annual campaigns; Capital campaigns; Building/ renovation; Endowments; Scholarship funds.
Limitations: Applications not accepted. Giving primarily in Nashville, TN.
Application information: Unsolicited requests for funds not accepted.
  Board meeting date(s): late Dec.
Trustees: Irene J. Wills; Morgan J. Wills; Thomas W. Wills; W. Ridley Wills II; W. Ridley Wills III.
Number of staff: None.
EIN: 626245453

1956
Global Ministries Foundation

P.O. Box 1150
Cordova, TN 38088-1150 (901) 684-5556
FAX: (901) 684-5558; E-mail: info@gmfonline.org; URL: http://gmfonline.org

Established in 2003.
Grantmaker type: Public charity.
Financial data (yr. ended 12/31/10): Revenue, $2,442,659; assets, $2,456,684 (M); gifts received, $2,265,567; expenditures, $2,858,487; giving activities include $84,670 for grants, $1,111,713 for grants to organizations outside the U.S., and $653,941 for grants to individuals.
Fields of interest: International relief; Housing/ shelter, services; Housing/shelter; Disasters, preparedness/services; Safety/disasters; Christian agencies & churches.
Limitations: Applications not accepted. Giving on an international basis, with emphasis on Africa, Australia, Eastern Europe, India, Indonesia, Korea, Latin America, the Middle East, the Philippines, and Western Europe.
Application information: Unsolicited requests for funds not considered or acknowledged.
Officers: Richard L. Hamlet, Pres.; Ginger S. Hamlet, Secy.
Directors: Eric Busby; Dr. Thomas Stovall; Alan Swafford.
EIN: 562378045

1957
Grandview Foundation, Inc.

601 Grandview Ave.
Lookout Mountain, TN 37350-1225

Established in 1991 in GA.
Donors: Carter N. Paden, Jr.; Janet C. Paden.
Grantmaker type: Independent foundation.
Financial data (yr. ended 11/30/10): Assets, $1,237,449 (M); gifts received, $320,360; expenditures, $208,236; qualifying distributions, $197,789; giving activities include $175,203 for 41 grants (high: $22,500; low: $100).
Purpose and activities: Giving primarily for Christian evangelism and education.
Fields of interest: Youth development; Higher education; Human services; Christian agencies & churches; Protestant agencies & churches.
International interests: Soviet Union (Former).
Type of support: Capital campaigns.
Limitations: Applications not accepted. Giving primarily in TN. No grants to individuals.

Application information: Contributes only to pre-selected organizations.
  Board meeting date(s): May and Dec.
Officers: Carter N. Paden, Jr.,* Pres. and Treas.; Carter N. Paden III, Secy.
Directors: Curtis L. Knorr; Dean P. North; Robert M. Paden; Janet C. Paden; Thomas C. Paden.
Number of staff: None.
EIN: 582004351

1958
Improved Health Systems for Iraq, Inc.

108 Cape Breton Ct.
Franklin, TN 37067-1325
FAX: (619) 444-2941;
E-mail: bekhtyarg@hotmail.com
Facebook: http://www.facebook.com/group.php? gid=20769221159

Grantmaker type: Public charity.
Purpose and activities: The organization aims to improve the health of the poor and most vulnerable populations through reducing inequalities and promoting sustainable development.
Fields of interest: Reproductive health; Health care; International development; International affairs.
Type of support: In-kind gifts; Management development/capacity building.
Limitations: Giving limited to Iraq. No support for INo support for.
Publications: Newsletter.
Officers: Dr. Goran Bekhtyar,* Pres.; Sozan Bekhtyar,* Secy.; Karwan Mahmood-Salih, Treas. and C.F.O.; Dr. Jamal Abdul-Hameed; Galavej Barwari; Barzan Barzani; Hunar Bekhtyar.
EIN: 203193924

1959
International Board of Jewish Missions, Inc.

P.O. Box 1386
Hixson, TN 37343-4909 (423) 876-8150
FAX: (423) 876-8156; URL: http://www.ibjm.org/

Established in 1949 in TN.
Grantmaker type: Public charity.
Financial data (yr. ended 12/31/10): Revenue, $3,063,664; assets, $3,545,067 (M); gifts received, $2,651,237; expenditures, $3,452,224; giving activities include $70,490 for grants to organizations outside the U.S., and $1,722,330 for grants to individuals.
Purpose and activities: The organization works to support Jewish causes in Israel and throughout the world.
Fields of interest: Community/economic development; Jewish agencies & synagogues.
International interests: Israel.
Limitations: Giving primarily to Israel.
Publications: Occasional report.
Officers and Board Members:* Dr. Orman L. Norwood,* Pres.; Terry Bolden,* Secy.-Treas.; Rev. Edward Frampton; Frances Hardy; Dr. Mike Patterson; Rev. Dan Rodgers; Dr. James H. Sims; Miriam Stanly; Rev. Fred Stanly.
EIN: 580669998

1960
International Paper Company Foundation

6400 Poplar Ave.
Memphis, TN 38197-0100 (800) 236-1996
Contact: Kimberly Wirth, Exec. Dir.
E-mail: ipfoundationfeedback@ipaper.com; E-mail for Coins 4 Kids Program: coins4kids@ipaper.com; URL: http://www.internationalpaper.com/US/EN/ Company/IPGiving/IPFoundation.html

Incorporated in 1952 in NY.
Donor: International Paper Co.
Grantmaker type: Company-sponsored foundation.
Financial data (yr. ended 12/31/10): Assets, $54,359,066 (M); gifts received, $15,000,000; expenditures, $2,845,949; qualifying distributions, $2,579,859; giving activities include $2,579,859 for grants.
Purpose and activities: The foundation supports organizations involved with literacy, environmental education, and critical community needs.
Fields of interest: Environment, recycling; Education, ESL programs; Education, reading; Education; Environment, air pollution; Environment, water pollution; Environment, forests; Environmental education; Food services; Human services; Children; Youth.
International interests: Africa.
Type of support: Equipment; Employee matching gifts; Continuing support; Program development; Seed money; Curriculum development; Employee volunteer services; In-kind gifts.
Limitations: Applications accepted. Giving on a national basis in areas of company operations, with some emphasis on Memphis, TN; giving also in Africa through the World Food Program. No support for veterans' or labor groups, religious or political groups, lobbying organizations, or discriminatory organizations. No grants to individuals, or for scholarships, endowments, capital campaigns, sponsorships, advertising, travel, national conferences, sporting events, or other one-time events; no loans.
Publications: Application guidelines; Corporate giving report; Program policy statement.
Application information: All applications are routed to a local IP facility. Please contact the facility for local submission deadlines. Multi-year funding is not automatic. Application form required.
  Initial approach: Complete online eligibility quiz and application
  Copies of proposal: 1
  Deadline(s): Varies
  Board meeting date(s): Sept.
Officers and Directors:* Patricia Neuhoff, Pres.; Joe Saab, Secy.; Carol Tusch, Treas.; Kimberly Wirth, Exec. Dir.; Bob Grillet; Terri Herrington; Jean-Michel Ribieras; Carol Roberts; Mark Sutton; Greg Wanta.
Number of staff: 3 full-time professional; 1 part-time support.
EIN: 136155080
Recent grants for international programs:
1960-1 Friends of the World Food Program, Washington, DC, $375,000. For Coins 4 Kids program. 2009.
1960-2 Friends of the World Food Program, Washington, DC, $375,000. For Coins 4 Kids. 2009.
1960-3 Responsible Environmentalism Foundation, Temperate Forest Foundation, Beaverton, OR, $25,000. For teacher education projects. 2009.

1961
The Lazarus Foundation, Inc.
340 Martin Luther King Blvd., Rm. 200
Bristol, TN 37620-2313
Contact: Mary Ann Blessing, Treas.

Established in 1992 in VA.
Donors: John M. Gregory; Joan P. Gregory.
Grantmaker type: Operating foundation.
Financial data (yr. ended 12/31/10): Assets, $619,609 (M); gifts received, $3,250,000; expenditures, $3,523,290; qualifying distributions, $3,320,577; giving activities include $3,316,077 for 19 grants (high: $990,300; low: $650), and $4,500 for 1 grant to an individual.
Purpose and activities: Giving primarily to Christian organizations for family financial distress.
Fields of interest: Food services; Human services; International development; Christian agencies & churches; Economically disadvantaged.
International interests: Developing countries.
Type of support: Grants to individuals.
Limitations: Applications not accepted. Giving primarily in Bristol, TN, and surrounding communities.
Application information: Unsolicited requests for funds not accepted.
Officers: John M. Gregory, Pres.; Joan P. Gregory, V.P. and Secy.; Mary Ann Blessing, Treas.
Board Member: James Gregory.
Number of staff: 1 part-time professional.
EIN: 541654943
Recent grants for international programs:
1961-1 Children of the World, Fairhope, AL, $10,000. For ministry and orphanage. 2010.
1961-2 Children of the World Ministries, Bristol, TN, $825,822. For ministry and orphanage. 2010.
1961-3 Church of God, Cleveland, TN, $150,000. For Youth World Evangelism Action (YWEA) Project. 2010.
1961-4 Church of God World Missions, Cleveland, TN, $990,300. For ministry and orphanage. 2010.
1961-5 People for Care and Learning, Cleveland, TN, $150,000. 2010.

1962
The Maclellan Foundation, Inc.
820 Broad St., Ste. 300
Chattanooga, TN 37402-2604 (423) 755-1366
Contact: Hugh O. Maclellan, Jr., Pres.
FAX: (423) 755-1640; E-mail: info@maclellan.net;
URL: http://www.maclellan.net/family-foundations/maclellan

Incorporated in 1945 in DE; reincorporated in TN in 1992.
Donors: Robert J. Maclellan†; and members of the Maclellan family.
Grantmaker type: Independent foundation.
Financial data (yr. ended 12/31/09): Assets, $354,589,110 (M); expenditures, $27,492,766; qualifying distributions, $20,331,106; giving activities include $16,807,484 for 6+ grants (high: $16,285,000), and $2,400 for employee matching gifts.
Purpose and activities: Grants largely for Protestant missions support and religious organizations.
Fields of interest: Religion, association; Protestant agencies & churches; Christian agencies & churches.
International interests: Eastern & Central Europe; Africa; Latin America; Asia; Middle East.

Type of support: General/operating support; Equipment; Program development; Seed money; Consulting services; Program evaluation.
Limitations: Applications accepted. Giving nationally, with emphasis on the Chattanooga, TN, area; giving internationally in Eastern Europe, Asia, Africa, Latin America, and the Middle East. No grants to individuals, or for emergency funds, deficit financing, land acquisition, endowment funds, health services, medical research, publications scholarships, or for renovations.
Application information: See foundation's web site for eligibility quiz and online application. Inquires via fax are not considered. Only online applications will be considered. No unsolicited requests for educational institutions. Application form not required.
Initial approach: Application online required
Copies of proposal: 1
Deadline(s): 6-8 weeks prior to board meetings
Board meeting date(s): 3-4 times per year
Final notification: 1 month after meeting
Officers and Trustees:* Hugh O. Maclellan, Jr.,* Pres.; David Denmark, Exec. Dir.; Sandy Barber, Compt.; Mrs. R.L. Maclellan, Tr. Emeritus; Tom Lowe, C.F.O.; Ronald W. Blue; Frank A. Brock; Mrs. Catherine Maclellan Heald; G. Richard Hostetter; Christopher Maclellan; Daniel Maclellan; Robert H. Maclellan; Pat MacMillan; Niel Nielson; Laurence Powell; W. Miller Welborn.
Number of staff: 12 full-time professional; 6 full-time support.
EIN: 626041468

1963
Nissan North America, Inc. Corporate Giving Program
c/o Nissan Neighbors
1 Nissan Way
Franklin, TN 37067-6367 (615) 725-1000
URL: http://www.nissanusa.com/about/corporate-info/community-relations.html

Grantmaker type: Corporate giving program.
Purpose and activities: As a complement to its foundation, Nissan also makes charitable contributions to nonprofit organizations directly. Support is given primarily in areas of company operations in southern California, metropolitan Detroit, Michigan, south central Mississippi, middle Tennessee, and Dallas and Fort Worth, Texas.
Fields of interest: International relief; Human services; Education; Environment.
Type of support: General/operating support; Scholarships—to individuals; In-kind gifts.
Limitations: Applications accepted. Giving primarily in southern CA, metropolitan Detroit, MI, south central MS, middle TN, and Dallas and Fort Worth, TX.
Application information:
Initial approach: Complete online application form
Deadline(s): None

1964
Operation Compassion, Inc.
114 Stuart Rd., N.E., Ste. 370
Cleveland, TN 37312-4803 (423) 728-3932
URL: http://www.operationcompassion.org

Established in 1999 in TN.
Grantmaker type: Public charity.

Financial data (yr. ended 12/31/10): Revenue, $262,681,170; assets, $92,102,377 (M); gifts received, $262,678,210; expenditures, $204,441,347; giving activities include $76,722,083 for grants, $124,069,592 for grants to organizations outside the U.S., and $15,000 for grants to individuals.
Purpose and activities: The organization focuses on three priorities: responding to natural disasters nationally and around the world; providing inspiration, information, training, and resources to help mobilize churches, individuals, and community groups to provide food and basic necessities to the poor and needy; and concentrating on international distribution to widows, single mothers, and children.
Fields of interest: Christian agencies & churches; Human services, victim aid; Human services; International relief.
Type of support: Emergency funds; In-kind gifts.
Limitations: Giving on a national and international basis.
Publications: Newsletter; IRS Form 990 or 990-PF printed copy available upon request.
Officer: David Lorency, Pres.
Directors: Kevin Brooks; Randy Johnson; Daniel Moore; Steven L. Lowery; Donnie W. Smith; Tom Sterbens; Ronnie W. Stewart; Jackie T. Walker.
EIN: 621697490

1965
Outpost Centers International
5340 Layton Ln.
Apison, TN 37302-9556 (423) 236-5600
FAX: (423) 236-5650;
E-mail: info@outpostcenters.org; URL: http://www.outpostcenters.org

Established in 1984 in TN.
Grantmaker type: Public charity.
Financial data (yr. ended 12/31/10): Revenue, $2,156,101; assets, $5,603,345 (M); gifts received, $2,019,326; expenditures, $2,659,626; giving activities include $28,205 for grants, $2,036,844 for grants to organizations outside the U.S., and $26,019 for grants to individuals.
Purpose and activities: The organization networks and nurtures Adventist supporting ministries around the world by providing counseling, training, encouragement, and coordination.
Fields of interest: International development; Christian agencies & churches; International affairs; Religion.
Limitations: Giving on a national basis, and to Australia, Austria, Bulgaria, Canada, Chile, Colombia, Czech Republic, Democratic Republic of the Congo, Dominican Republic, France, Germany, India, Japan, Madagascar, Mexico, Moldova, Nicaragua, Norway, Peru, Poland, Portugal, Romania, Serbia, South Korea, Spain, Sweden, Switzerland, Tanzania, Ukraine, Uruguay, Venezuela, and Zambia.
Publications: Newsletter.
Officers and Directors:* Frank Fournier,* Chair.; Markus Jaudas,* Pres.; Steven Grabiner,* V.P.; Naomi Pirraglia,* Secy.; Wilbur Atwood; Bernard Beranger; Kim Busi; Gayle Clark; Charles Cleveland; Nick Dan; Viriato Ferreira; Ronald Jaudas; Oscar Newball; Scott Richards; Sidney Sweet; and 6 additional directors.
EIN: 581570279

1966
Redbird Foundation
4624 Chambliss Ave.
Knoxville, TN 37919-5118

Established in 1995 in TN.
Donors: B. Ray Thompson Charitable Trust; Juanne Thompson Charitable Trust.
Grantmaker type: Independent foundation.
Financial data (yr. ended 12/31/10): Assets, $7,860,156 (M); expenditures, $390,448; qualifying distributions, $325,000; giving activities include $325,000 for 1 grant.
Purpose and activities: Giving primarily to Christian humanitarian organizations.
Fields of interest: International relief; Christian agencies & churches.
Limitations: Applications not accepted. Giving on a national basis. No grants for endowments or funds to support operating deficits.
Publications: Annual report.
Application information: Contributes only to pre-selected organizations.
Officers and Directors:* B. Ray Thompson, Jr.,* Pres.; Adella Sands Thompson,* V.P.; Juanne J. Thompson,* Secy.; Rebekah Thompson Palmer; Sarah Thompson Tarver; B. Ray Thompson III; Catherine Vance Thompson.
EIN: 621591527

1967
UnumProvident Corporation Contributions Program
(formerly Provident Companies, Inc. Corporate Giving Program)
1 Fountain Sq.
Chattanooga, TN 37402-1306 (423) 755-1011
Contact: Cathy Barrett, Community Rels. Mgr.
FAX: (423) 755-3194;
E-mail: CommunityRelations@unum.com; Application addresses: Portland, ME: Susan Austin, 2211 Congress St., B118, Portland, ME 04122; and Worcester, MA: Meghan Maceiko, 18 Chestnut St., Worcester, MA 01608; Tel. for Cathy Barrett: (423) 294-7579, FAX: (423) 755-3194, E-mail: cbarrett@unum.com; URL: http://www.unum.com/aboutus/Responsibility/CommunityGiving.aspx

Grantmaker type: Corporate giving program.
Financial data (yr. ended 12/31/08): Total giving, $6,200,000, including $5,000,000 for grants, and $1,200,000 for employee matching gifts.
Purpose and activities: UnumProvident makes charitable contributions to nonprofit organizations involved with arts and culture; public education; health and wellness; and disability services. Support is given in areas of company operations.
Fields of interest: Food services; Hospitals (general); Arts; Elementary/secondary education; Education; Health care; Boys & girls clubs; Children, services; Independent living, disability; Human services; United Ways and Federated Giving Programs; Disabilities, people with.
International interests: Canada; United Kingdom.
Type of support: General/operating support; Program development; Employee volunteer services; Sponsorships; Employee matching gifts; Employee-related scholarships; Scholarships—to individuals.
Limitations: Applications accepted. Giving in areas of company operations, with emphasis on Worcester, MA, Portland, ME, SC, Chattanooga, TN, and in Canada and the United Kingdom. No support

for political organizations or political candidates, or religious organizations not of direct benefit to the entire community. No grants for general operating support for higher education.
Publications: Application guidelines; Corporate giving report.
Application information: Proposal should be submitted using organization letterhead. Support is limited to 1 contribution per organization during any given year.
  Initial approach: Proposal to local community relations representative; download application form and mail for headquarters for Unum Strong Schools Grants Program
  Deadline(s): None; Jan. 9 for Unum Strong Schools Grants Program
  Final notification: Feb. for Unum Strong Schools Grants Program

1968
Vine International, Inc.
P.O. Box 52086
Knoxville, TN 37950-2086 (865) 690-6857
FAX: (865) 531-8477;
E-mail: woody@vineinternational.org; Additional address (Guatemala office): Km. 25.5 Carratera Mataquescuintla, Bodega 6 - Cypress Business Ctr. 2, Hacienda Nueva, San Jose Pinula, Guatemala; URL: http://www.vineinternational.org
Bodega Update: News from Vine International's U.S. Collection Center Manager: http://bodegaupdate.blogspot.com/
End of the Pipeline: http://dennis51.wordpress.com/
Facebook: http://www.facebook.com/pages/Vine-International/107345333118
LinkedIn: http://www.linkedin.com/pub/vine-international/14/895/506
RSS Feed: http://vineinternational.org/?feed=rss2
Twitter: http://twitter.com/Vine_Friends

Established in 1993 in TN.
Grantmaker type: Public charity.
Financial data (yr. ended 12/31/09): Revenue, $11,767,016; assets, $26,945 (M); gifts received, $11,767,016; expenditures, $11,770,984; giving activities include $11,440,430 for grants to organizations outside the U.S.
Purpose and activities: The organization provides medical supplies primarily to remote areas in Guatemala.
Fields of interest: International relief.
International interests: Guatemala.
Type of support: In-kind gifts.
Limitations: Applications not accepted. Giving primarily in Guatemala.
Application information: Contributes only to pre-selected organizations.
Officers and Board Members:* T. Warren Woodson,* Pres.; Chris Hughes,* Secy.; Mike Turner,* Treas.; Bruce Allsop; Norris Hill; Mike Turner.
EIN: 621533189

1969
Westwood Endowment, Inc.
P.O. Box 4268
Chattanooga, TN 37405-0268 (423) 755-3964
Contact: Thomas H. McCallie III, Pres.
FAX: (423) 755-1640;
E-mail: mccallie60@hotmail.com

Established in 1986 in IN.
Donors: Richard A. West; Florence G. West; Marie G. Byers†; West Baking Co.; Single Family Residential Property.
Grantmaker type: Independent foundation.
Financial data (yr. ended 11/30/10): Assets, $10,259,165 (M); gifts received, $8,950; expenditures, $525,048; qualifying distributions, $400,000; giving activities include $400,000 for grants.
Purpose and activities: Support for various needs of the Third World through organizations with tax-exempt status.
International interests: Africa; Asia; India.
Type of support: General/operating support.
Limitations: Applications not accepted. Giving primarily to U.S.-based organizations for benefit of third world countries.
Application information: The foundation initiates funding for service opportunities in its target fields. Unsolicited requests for funds not considered or acknowledged.
  Board meeting date(s): As necessary
Officers and Directors:* Richard A. West,* Chair.; Thomas H. McCallie III,* Pres.; Craig Hammon,* Secy.
Number of staff: 2 part-time support.
EIN: 311197125

TEXAS

1970
A Glimmer of Hope Foundation
3600 N. Capital of TX Hwy, Bldg. B, Ste. 330
Austin, TX 78746-3209 (512) 328-9944
Contact: Michael O'Keefe, Comms. Dir.
FAX: (512) 328-8872;
E-mail: inquiries@aglimmerofhope.org; URL: http://www.aglimmerofhope.org
Facebook: http://www.facebook.com/pages/A-Glimmer-of-Hope-Foundation/102487557749
Founder's Blog: http://aglimmerofhopefoundation.blogspot.com/
Multimedia: http://www.aglimmerofhope.org/success-stories
Twitter: http://twitter.com/aglimmerofhope
Vimeo: http://www.vimeo.com/aglimmerofhope
YouTube: http://www.youtube.com/aglimmerofhopeorg

Established in 2000 in TX.
Donors: Donna Berber; Philip Berber; Eric Schmidhauser; Lucie Schmidhauser; Leslie Moore; Kathy Moore; Neil Webber; Ronnie Morgan; Bill Parrish; Margaret Parrish; Neil Webber; Ernst & Young; Tim Brosnan; Tony Gannon; Berberfam, Ltd.; Operation Days Work; Berberfam, Ltd.; Austin Ethiopian Women Assn.; Lee Portnoi; Mark Stryker; Oregon Ethiopian Community Organization; Robert Epstein; Preston Ctr.; The Andrew S. Roddick Foundation.
Grantmaker type: Independent foundation.
Financial data (yr. ended 12/31/09): Assets, $47,270,846 (M); gifts received, $5,361,165; expenditures, $8,167,566; qualifying distributions, $8,148,531; giving activities include $6,467,723 for 6 grants (high: $5,629,570; low: $750).

Purpose and activities: The foundation serves to ease some of the pain and suffering on the planet. It currently operates a national aid program in Ethiopia as well as programs for excluded youth in the U.S. and the U.K.
Fields of interest: Business school/education; Human services; Children/youth, services; International relief; International affairs; Economically disadvantaged.
International interests: Ireland; England; Ethiopia.
Limitations: Applications not accepted. Giving primarily in Austin, TX, London, England, and Ethiopia.
Application information: Contributes only to pre-selected organizations.
Officers: Donna Berber, Co-Chair.; Philip Berber, Co-Chair.; Brian Cooper, C.E.O.; David Porter III, Exec. Dir.; Carla Power, Cont.
EIN: 311758218
Recent grants for international programs:
1970-1 A Glimmer of Hope-Ethiopia, Addis Ababa, Ethiopia, $5,629,570. For Ethiopia projects. 2009.
1970-2 A Glimmer of Hope-UK, London, England, $14,437. For operating support. 2009.

1971
The ADR Foundation, Inc.
P.O. Box 118953
Carrollton, TX   75011-8953

Established in 1999 in TX.
Donors: Danny L. Dansby; Linda L. Dansby.
Grantmaker type: Independent foundation.
Financial data (yr. ended 12/31/10): Assets, $3,355,594 (M); expenditures, $160,412; qualifying distributions, $158,199; giving activities include $150,000 for 9 grants (high: $30,000; low: $10,000).
Fields of interest: Family services; Children/youth, services; Residential/custodial care; International development; Christian agencies & churches.
Limitations: Applications not accepted. Giving primarily in TX. No grants to individuals.
Application information: Unsolicited requests for funds not accepted.
Officer: Danny L. Dansby, Pres.
Directors: John Lawrence; David Meyer.
EIN: 752849058

1972
Africa Leadership and Reconciliation Ministries of Texas
13154 Coit Rd., Ste. 102
Dallas, TX   75240-5787   (972) 671-8522
FAX: (972) 437-1350; URL: http://alarm-inc.org/

Established in 1994.
Grantmaker type: Public charity.
Financial data (yr. ended 12/31/10): Revenue, $3,091,840; assets, $245,812 (M); gifts received, $3,091,840; expenditures, $3,166,476; giving activities include $2,428,164 for 1 grant to an organization outside the U.S.
Purpose and activities: The organization works to empower the African church to impact the African continent by developing and equipping leaders with skills and tools to nurture and deepen the Christian faith, for the transformation and reconciliation of the African communities.

Fields of interest: International conflict resolution; Community/economic development; Christian agencies & churches.
International interests: Sub-Saharan Africa.
Limitations: Giving limited to sub-Saharan Africa.
Publications: Financial statement; IRS Form 990 or 990-PF printed copy available upon request.
Officers and Board Members:* Greg Gilkerson,* Chair.; Celestin Musekura,* Pres.; Ruth Calver; Joe Hanson; Steve Rose; Karen Smith; Joseph D. Storey.
EIN: 311660877

1973
Africa Renewal Ministries, Inc.
P.O. Box 13733
San Antonio, TX   78213-0733   (210) 979-7441
E-mail: armusa@africarenewal.org; URL: http://www.africarenewal.org
Facebook Causes URL: http://www.causes.com/causes/146493-africa-renewal-ministries-arm

Established in 2003 in TX.
Grantmaker type: Public charity.
Financial data (yr. ended 12/31/10): Revenue, $4,091,186; assets, $832,183 (M); gifts received, $4,089,688; expenditures, $3,973,491; giving activities include $3,614,622 for grants to organizations outside the U.S., and $2,570,304 for grants to individuals outside the U.S.
Purpose and activities: The organization seeks to reach the lost and to renew the people of Africa through salvation and education.
Fields of interest: Human services; Christian agencies & churches.
International interests: Africa.
Limitations: Giving primarily in Africa.
Publications: Financial statement.
Officers and Directors:* Karl J. Zeile, Chair.; Rev. Peter Kasirivu, Pres.; Donald M. Jones, Secy.; Thomas Brown,* Treas.; Craig DuBois, Co-Exec. Dir.; Johnny Karls, Co-Exec. Dir.; Larry Thrasher; Thomas Gore.
EIN: 432004779

1974
The Alcon Foundation, Inc.
6201 S. Freeway
Fort Worth, TX   76134-2099
Contact: Sara Woodward, Pres.
FAX: (817) 615-3811; Additional tel.: (817) 293-0450; URL: http://www.alcon.com/en/corporate-responsibility/alcon-foundation.asp

Established in 1962 in TX.
Donor: Alcon Laboratories, Inc.
Grantmaker type: Company-sponsored foundation.
Financial data (yr. ended 12/31/10): Assets, $30,000 (M); gifts received, $7,574,599; expenditures, $7,604,526; qualifying distributions, $7,574,599; giving activities include $7,574,599 for 129 grants (high: $685,195; low: $250).
Purpose and activities: The foundation supports programs designed to advance eye health education, research, and awareness; improve the quality of eye health care and patient access to care; and enhance and create sound communities where Alcon has a facility. Special emphasis is directed toward programs designed to advance the education and skill levels of eye care professionals.

Fields of interest: Arts; Higher education; Medical school/education; Education; Hospitals (general); Hospitals (specialty); Optometry/vision screening; Health care; Eye diseases; Medical research, institute; Eye research; American Red Cross; Human services; Community/economic development; United Ways and Federated Giving Programs; Public affairs; Blind/visually impaired.
Type of support: General/operating support; Capital campaigns; Building/renovation; Endowments; Program development; Scholarship funds; Research.
Limitations: Applications accepted. Giving primarily in areas of company operations in Irvine, CA, Orlando, FL, Sinking Spring, PA, Fort Worth and Houston, TX, and Huntington, WV. No support for fraternal, labor, political, or veterans' organizations, discriminatory organizations, or private K-12 schools. No grants to individuals, or for family requests for scholarships, fellowships, religious activities, endowments, capital, or building campaigns outside of Community-Aligned Grants; matching gifts, university administrative, management, or indirect fees, golf tournaments, athletic events, league or team sponsorships, school-affiliated orchestras, bands, choirs, students trips, or tours, unrestricted grants, books, research papers, or articles in professional journals, travel, or fundraising activities or advertising sponsorships.
Publications: Application guidelines; Corporate giving report.
Application information: Application form required.
   Initial approach: Complete online application form
   Deadline(s): None; Feb. 1 to July 31 for requests of $50,000 and above
   Board meeting date(s): Mar., July, and Nov.
   Final notification: 45 days
Officers and Directors:* Kevin J. Buehler, Chair.; Sara Woodward, Pres.; Tamara Dean, V.P. and Treas.; David Bass, Secy.; Kay A. Cox; Tom Hohman; Kuritis Klein; Scott Manning; John Via; Terry Wiernas; Steven Wilson.
EIN: 200166600
Recent grants for international programs:
1974-1 Friends of Aravind, Manchester, MI, $367,614. 2009.
1974-2 Friends of Aravind, Manchester, MI, $125,000. 2009.
1974-3 Helen Keller International, New York, NY, $50,000. 2009.
1974-4 International Rescue Committee, New York, NY, $36,066. 2009.
1974-5 International Sister Cities Association of Fort Worth, Fort Worth, TX, $25,000. 2009.
1974-6 Mercy Ships, Garden Valley, TX, $50,000. 2009.
1974-7 ORBIS International, New York, NY, $600,000. 2009.
1974-8 Project HOPE - The People-to-People Health Foundation, Millwood, VA, $65,200. 2009.
1974-9 Van Cliburn Foundation, Fort Worth, TX, $50,000. 2009.

1975
Alliance for Multicultural Community Services
6440 Hillcroft, Ste. 411
Houston, TX   77081-3104   (713) 776-4700
FAX: (713) 776-4730;
E-mail: info@allianceontheweb.org; URL: http://www.allianceontheweb.org

Established in 1986 in TX.
Grantmaker type: Public charity.
Financial data (yr. ended 09/30/10): Revenue, $6,071,296; assets, $3,679,666 (M); gifts received, $4,243,691; expenditures, $6,236,169; giving activities include $2,269,537 for grants to individuals.
Purpose and activities: The alliance provides a comprehensive mix of social and community development services to allow refugees, immigrants, and low-income residents of Harris County to become self-sufficient and improve their quality of life.
Fields of interest: Family services; Children/youth, services; International migration/refugee issues.
Limitations: Giving primarily to Harris County, TX.
Officers and Directors:* Sue Davis,* Chair.; Abdullah S. Jafari, C.I.O.; Astatkie Zikarge,* M.D., M.P.H., Secy.; Stacey-Ann Williams,* Treas.; Cuong M. Le; Gin Ru Lee; Dr. Patrick Leung; Kheang Ven.
EIN: 760171217

1976
Amazon Christian Missions
2200 High Point Dr.
Carrollton, TX   75007-1701

Established in 2005.
Donors: Ron Crosby; Gary & Diane Heavin Fund; Kinnie Gibson; Sheri Gibson.
Grantmaker type: Public charity.
Financial data (yr. ended 12/31/10): Revenue, $215,084; assets, $243,329 (M); gifts received, $212,230; expenditures, $231,194; giving activities include for 2 grants to organizations outside the U.S.
Purpose and activities: The organization supports mission services in the Amazon region of Brazil.
Fields of interest: Christian agencies & churches.
International interests: Brazil.
Limitations: Applications not accepted. Giving limited to Brazil. No grants to individuals.
Application information: Contributes only to pre-selected organizations.
Directors: Kinnie Gibson; Sheri Gibson; Elmer B. Lessa; Mark L. Pharo.
EIN: 201936712

1977
AMD Foundation, Inc.
7171 Southwest Pkwy., MS 100.3
Austin, TX   78735-8953
E-mail: amd.foundation@amd.com; URL: http://www.amd.com/foundation

Established in TX.
Donor: Advanced Micro Devices, Inc.
Grantmaker type: Company-sponsored foundation.
Financial data (yr. ended 12/31/10): Assets, $398,901 (M); gifts received, $1,884,000; expenditures, $1,726,728; qualifying distributions, $1,726,728; giving activities include $1,726,728 for grants.
Purpose and activities: The foundation supports schools and nonprofits involved with education. Special emphasis is directed toward programs that target disadvantaged youth. Support is given in areas of company operations.
Fields of interest: Education; Recreation; information services; Science; Youth development; Economically disadvantaged.

International interests: Canada; China; India; Malaysia; Singapore; Taiwan.
Type of support: Employee matching gifts; General/operating support.
Limitations: Applications accepted. Giving primarily in areas of company operations in Sunnyvale (Silicon Valley), CA, Ft. Collins, CO, Orlando, FL, Boston, MA, Austin, TX, and Bellevue, WA, and in Canada, China, India, Malaysia, Singapore, and Taiwan.
Application information: Application form required.
Officers and Directors:* Alex Brown, Chair.; J. Michael Woollems, Vice-Chair.; Allyson W. Peerman, Pres.; Devinder Kumar, Treas.; Ben Bar-Haim; Robert Feldstein; Annie Flaig; Roger Pineiro; Thomas Seifert; Leslie Sobon; Kathleen Woodhouse.
EIN: 711036553

1978
American Research Center in Egypt, Inc.
8700 Crownhill Blvd., Ste. 507
San Antonio, TX   78209-1130   (210) 821-7000
Contact: Rachel Mauldin; Dina Saad
FAX: (210) 821-7007; E-mail: info@arce.org; URL: http://www.arce.org

Established in 1948.
Grantmaker type: Public charity.
Financial data (yr. ended 06/30/10): Revenue, $7,738,287; assets, $59,469,594 (M); gifts received, $5,920,755; expenditures, $6,136,614; giving activities include $423,736 for grants, $735,875 for grants to organizations outside the U.S., $434,748 for grants to individuals, and $718,885 for grants to individuals outside the U.S.
Purpose and activities: The center is a nonprofit consortium of individuals and North American research institutions dedicated to an understanding of all aspects of Egyptian history and culture up to the present. To these ends, the center promotes scholarly research and the dissemination of its results; encourages cultural and academic ties among its members and their Egyptian counterparts; and fosters broader knowledge and appreciation of Egypt and its culture among the general public.
Fields of interest: History/archaeology.
International interests: Egypt.
Type of support: Fellowships.
Publications: Application guidelines.
Application information: Application form required.
  Initial approach: Download application form
  Deadline(s): Jan. 5 for fellowships
Officers and Governors:* Carol Redmount,* Pres.; Richard C. Martin, V.P.; Brienne Lofits, Treas.; Jonathan Berkey; Leonard Binder; Peter Dorman; Marjorie M. Fisher; Ogden Goelet; William Granara; and 25 additional governors.
Number of staff: 40 full-time professional; 20 full-time support.
EIN: 042319500

1979
Apache Corporation Contributions Program
2000 Post Oak Blvd., Ste. 100
Houston, TX   77056-4400   (713) 296-6000
Contact: Obie O'Brien
URL: http://www.apachecorp.com/Resources/Upload/Sustainability/community/index.html

Grantmaker type: Corporate giving program.

Purpose and activities: As a complement to its foundation, Apache also makes charitable contributions to nonprofit organizations directly. Support is given on a national and international basis.
Fields of interest: Human services; Environment; Environment, natural resources; Arts; Education.
International interests: Australia; Canada; Egypt.
Type of support: Donated products; General/operating support; Annual campaigns; Employee volunteer services; Sponsorships; Employee matching gifts; In-kind gifts.
Limitations: Applications accepted. Giving on a national and international basis in areas of company operations, with emphasis on LA, NM, OK, and Houston, TX, and in Australia, Argentina, Egypt, the United Kingdom, and Canada, in Saskatchewan, Alberta, British Columbia, and the Northwest Territories. No grants to individuals, or for annual tithes, building campaigns, or religious activities.
Publications: Application guidelines; Corporate giving report (including application guidelines).
Application information: The Investor Relations Department handles giving. Application form not required.
  Initial approach: Proposal to headquarters
  Copies of proposal: 1
  Deadline(s): Jan. 1 to Dec. 1
  Final notification: 45 days
Number of staff: 1 full-time professional.

1980
Austin Community Foundation for the Capital Area, Inc.
(formerly Austin Community Foundation)
P.O. Box 5159
Austin, TX   78763-5159   (512) 472-4483
Contact: MariBen Ramsey, V.P.
FAX: (512) 472-4486;
E-mail: info@austincommunityfoundation.org;
Additional e-mail: mbramsey@austincommunityfoundation.org;
URL: http://www.austincommunityfoundation.org
E-Newsletter: http://www.austincommunityfoundation.org/?nd=email
Facebook: http://www.facebook.com/pages/Austin-Community-Foundation/250561989784?ref=ts
LinkedIn: http://www.linkedin.com/groups?about=&gid=2640460&trk=anet_ug_grppro
Twitter: http://twitter.com/#!/AustinCommFound
YouTube: http://www.youtube.com/user/AustinCommunityFound

Established in 1977 in TX.
Grantmaker type: Community foundation.
Financial data (yr. ended 12/31/10): Assets, $116,382,049 (M); gifts received, $25,959,630; expenditures, $26,714,089; giving activities include $16,208,515 for grants.
Purpose and activities: The foundation promotes philanthropy in Central Texas to improve the quality of life now and in the future. The foundation provides support for arts and culture, education and training, community development and community services, the environment, health, human services, recreation, and animal-related services.
Fields of interest: Animal welfare; Disasters, Hurricane Katrina; Environment; History/archaeology; Arts; Child development, education; Education; Medical care, rehabilitation; Health care;

Recreation; Child development, services; Human services; Community/economic development.
Type of support: Continuing support; Annual campaigns; Capital campaigns; Building/renovation; Equipment; Land acquisition; Program development; Conferences/seminars; Professorships; Publication; Seed money; Research; Technical assistance; Consulting services; Matching/challenge support.
Limitations: Applications accepted. Giving limited to Travis County, TX, for discretionary grants. No support for religious organizations for religious purposes. No grants to individuals (except for scholarships), or for deficit financing, emergency funds, endowments, unrestricted general operating expenses, fundraising activities or events, or fellowships; no loans.
Publications: Application guidelines; Annual report; Informational brochure; Newsletter; Program policy statement.
Application information: Visit foundation web site for Agency Information Sheet and application guidelines. Faxed proposals are not accepted. Application form required.
Initial approach: Submit online Agency Information Sheet and attachments
Copies of proposal: 1
Deadline(s): None
Board meeting date(s): At least 9 times per year
Final notification: 4 to 6 months
Officers and Board of Governors:* JoLynn Free,* Chair.; Max Sherman,* Vice-Chair.; Jeff Garvey, C.E.O. and Pres.; MariBen Ramsey,* V.P. and C.O.O.; Donna Stockton Hicks,* Secy.; William Volk,* Treas.; Steve Shook,* Chair.-Elect; Sylvia Acevedo; Aimee Boone; Gigi Bryant; Graciela Cigarroa; Carolyn Gallagher; Sandy Gottesman; Chris Harte; Dan Herd; Lew Little, Jr.; Cliff Mountain; Hal Peterson; Rob Repass; Rick Salwen; Mark Seriff; Tejas Vakil.
Number of staff: 3 full-time professional; 1 part-time professional; 1 full-time support.
EIN: 741934031
Recent grants for international programs:
1980-1 Afghan Hands, New York, NY, $20,000. For Unrestricted Support. 2008.
1980-2 Airline Ambassadors International, Moss Beach, CA, $10,000. For Unrestricted Support. 2008.
1980-3 Association of Junior Leagues International, New York, NY, $17,984. 2008.
1980-4 Audubon Society, National, New York, NY, $25,000. For International Program. 2008.
1980-5 Austin Independent School District, Austin, TX, $142,000. For Global Studies Academy. 2008.
1980-6 Evangel Fellowship International, Conway, SC, $12,000. For New Life Nicaragua Orphanage. 2008.
1980-7 Fabretto Childrens Foundation, Arlington, VA, $18,000. For Feeding Program. 2008.
1980-8 Heifer Project International, Little Rock, AR, $10,000. For South Africa Country Endowment. 2008.
1980-9 Hope Nicaragua, Fairfax, VA, $36,840. For Unrestricted Support. 2008.
1980-10 Makarios, Austin, TX, $18,500. For Missionary Support. 2008.
1980-11 Manna Project International, Nashville, TN, $24,000. For Unrestricted Support. 2008.
1980-12 Manna Project International, Nashville, TN, $24,000. For Casa Base de Salud. 2008.

1980-13 Medical, Eye and Dental International Care Organization, Georgetown, TX, $16,300. For Unrestricted Support. 2008.
1980-14 Miracle Foundation, Austin, TX, $10,200. For Unrestricted Support. 2008.
1980-15 Peace Corps of the United States, Washington, DC, $15,000. For Unrestricted Support. 2008.
1980-16 Project HOPE - The People-to-People Health Foundation, Millwood, VA, $50,000. For Unrestricted Support. 2008.
1980-17 Students Partnership Worldwide USA, Washington, DC, $15,000. For Unrestricted Support. 2008.
1980-18 SWCM, Inc., Austin, TX, $10,000. For Unrestricted Support. 2008.
1980-19 Tribal Outreach Medical Assistance Foundation, Northridge, CA, $13,500. For unrestricted support. 2008.
1980-20 University of Texas, Austin, TX, $2,000,000. For Institute of Latin American Studies. 2008.

1981
Leo Baeck Education Center Foundation
3555 Timmons Ln., Ste. 1440
Houston, TX 77027-6435

Established in 1987.
Grantmaker type: Public charity.
Financial data (yr. ended 08/31/10): Revenue, $1,438,079; assets, $41,372 (M); gifts received, $1,433,845; expenditures, $1,289,093; giving activities include $4,130 for grants, and $859,965 for grants to organizations outside the U.S.
Fields of interest: Education.
International interests: Israel.
Limitations: Applications not accepted. Giving limited to Haifa, Israel.
Application information: Contributes only to a pre-selected organization; unsolicited requests for funds not considered or acknowledged.
Directors: Herschel M. Rich; J. Victor Samuels.
EIN: 760205816

1982
The Baldridge Foundation
4925 Greenville, No. 1050
Dallas, TX 75206-4084

Established in 2004 in TX.
Grantmaker type: Independent foundation.
Financial data (yr. ended 12/31/10): Assets, $1,149,232 (M); expenditures, $355,365; qualifying distributions, $354,143; giving activities include $352,365 for 18 grants (high: $100,000; low: $1,000).
Fields of interest: Human services; Museums; Humanities; Education, reading; International affairs, public policy; International development; Public policy, research.
Type of support: General/operating support.
Limitations: Applications not accepted. Giving primarily in New York, NY, and Dallas, TX.
Application information: Contributes only to pre-selected organizations.
Officers and Directors:* Jerald T. Baldridge,* Pres. and Treas.; Emily Z. Baldridge,* V.P. and Secy.; Jeffrey Turner Baldridge; Kimberly Baldridge Solomon.
EIN: 201806185

1983
The Anne Hendricks Bass Foundation
1801 Deepdale Dr.
Fort Worth, TX 76107-3517 (817) 735-1840
Contact: Anne H. Bass, Tr.

Established in 1997 in TX.
Donor: Anne H. Bass.
Grantmaker type: Independent foundation.
Financial data (yr. ended 12/31/09): Assets, $4,136,419 (M); expenditures, $265,947; qualifying distributions, $256,981; giving activities include $256,981 for 14 grants (high: $25,000; low: $1,000).
Fields of interest: Museums; Performing arts; History/archaeology; Libraries (public); Education; Environment, natural resources; International studies.
Limitations: Giving primarily in NY, with emphasis on New York City. No grants to individuals.
Application information:
Initial approach: Letter
Deadline(s): None
Trustees: Anne H. Bass; Hyatt A. Bass; Samantha S. Bass.
EIN: 137117629

1984
The Dan and Martha Lou Beaird Foundation
c/o Dan L. Beaird
5121 McKinney Ave.
Dallas, TX 75205-3321

Established in 2001 in TX.
Donors: Dan L. Beaird; Martha Lou Beaird.
Grantmaker type: Independent foundation.
Financial data (yr. ended 12/31/10): Assets, $4,657 (M); gifts received, $145,000; expenditures, $145,575; qualifying distributions, $144,798; giving activities include $144,798 for 66 grants (high: $18,200; low: $100).
Fields of interest: International development; Athletics/sports, amateur competition; Children, services; Christian agencies & churches.
Limitations: Applications not accepted. Giving primarily in TX. No grants to individuals.
Application information: Unsolicited requests for funds not accepted.
Officers and Directors:* Dan L. Beaird,* Pres.; Martha Lou Beaird,* Secy.; Benjamin H. Beaird; Gayden B. Breckwoldt; John R. Hudson.
EIN: 752943958

1985
Henry & Eileen Beyer Foundation
P.O. Box 1104
Sugar Land, TX 77487-1104

Donors: Henry T. Beyer III; Juliette E. Beyer.
Grantmaker type: Independent foundation.
Financial data (yr. ended 12/31/10): Assets, $4,405,180 (M); gifts received, $2,500,000; expenditures, $2,326,685; qualifying distributions, $2,325,785; giving activities include $2,325,785 for grants.
Fields of interest: International relief; Christian agencies & churches.
Limitations: Applications not accepted. Giving primarily in TX.

Application information: Contributes only to pre-selected organizations.
Directors: Darren R. Beyer; Henry T. Beyer III; Juliette E. Beyer.
EIN: 203905824

1986
Bhutada Family Foundation
4018 Westhollow Pkwy.
Houston, TX 77082-4604

Established in 2005 in TX.
Donors: Ramesh Bhutada; Rishi Bhutada.
Grantmaker type: Independent foundation.
Financial data (yr. ended 12/31/10): Assets, $2,327,230 (M); expenditures, $174,425; qualifying distributions, $168,653; giving activities include $168,653 for grants.
Fields of interest: Education; Hinduism.
International interests: India.
Limitations: Applications not accepted. Giving in the U.S., with emphasis on TX. No grants to individuals.
Application information: Unsolicited requests for funds not accepted.
Officers: Ramesh Bhutada, Pres.; Kiran Bhutada, V.P.; Rishi Bhutada, Secy.
EIN: 202051596

1987
BMC Software, Inc. Corporate Giving Program
2101 CityWest Blvd.
Houston, TX 77042-2828 (713) 918-8800
Contact: Dan D'Armond, Dir., Community and Govt. Rels.
E-mail: dan_darmond@bmc.com; URL: http://www.bmc.com/corporate/corporate-commitment

Grantmaker type: Corporate giving program.
Purpose and activities: BMC Software makes charitable contributions to nonprofit organizations involved with social services, and health and wellness. Support is given primarily in areas of company operations, with emphasis on San Jose, California, Boston, Massachusetts, and Houston and Austin, Texas, and in India, Israel, the Netherlands, and Singapore.
Fields of interest: Human services; Public health.
International interests: India; Israel; Netherlands; Singapore.
Type of support: General/operating support; Program development; Employee volunteer services.
Limitations: Giving on a national and international basis in areas of company operations, with emphasis on San Jose, CA, Boston, MA, Houston and Austin, TX, and in India, Israel, the Netherlands, and Singapore.
Application information:
Initial approach: E-mail headquarters for application information
Administrator: Dan D'Armond, Dir., Comms. and Govt. Rels.

1988
Simon Bolivar Foundation, Inc.
1293 Eldridge Pkwy., N5033
Houston, TX 77077-1670
Contact: Brenda Estrada-Torres

E-mail: sbf@citgo.com; URL: http://www.simonbolivarfoundation.org/

Established in 2007 in TX.
Donor: CITGO Petroleum Corporation.
Grantmaker type: Company-sponsored foundation.
Financial data (yr. ended 12/31/09): Assets, $9,752,009 (M); gifts received, $8,407,400; expenditures, $7,136,375; qualifying distributions, $9,542,310; giving activities include $562,424 for 2 grants (high: $390,992; low: $171,432), and $8,979,886 for foundation-administered programs.
Purpose and activities: The foundation supports programs designed to expand access to healthcare to underprivileged individuals who are affected by critical illness and poverty.
Fields of interest: Environment; Human services; Hospitals (general); Health care, clinics/centers; Speech/hearing centers; Health care, support services; Health care, organ/tissue banks; Health care, patient services; Health care; Economically disadvantaged.
International interests: Venezuela.
Type of support: Building/renovation; Equipment; Program development.
Limitations: Applications accepted. Giving primarily in Washington, DC, New York, NY, Argentina, Italy, and Venezuela.
Publications: Application guidelines; Program policy statement.
Application information: Application form required.
Initial approach: Complete online application for medical assistance and Bronx Social Programs
Deadline(s): None for medical assistance; varies for Bronx Social Programs
Officers and Directors:* Maritza Rojas de Villanueva,* Chair.; Gustavo Cardenas, Pres.; Patricia Milano, V.P.; Arnaldo Arcay, Secy.; Daniel Beuses, Treas.; Daniel Cortez; Rosana Delgado de Granado; Brian O'Kelly.
EIN: 205787382

1989
BP Foundation, Inc.
(formerly BP Amoco Foundation, Inc.)
501 Westlake Park Blvd., 25th FL
Houston, TX 77079-2604
URL: http://www.bp.com/sectiongenericarticle800.do?categoryId=9036288&contentId=7067020

Incorporated in 1952 in IN.
Donors: Amoco Corp.; BP Amoco Corp.; BP Corp. North America Inc.; BP America Inc.; Amoco Production Co.; Atlantic Richfield Co.; BP Products North America, Inc.
Grantmaker type: Company-sponsored foundation.
Financial data (yr. ended 12/31/10): Assets, $83,951,643 (M); expenditures, $32,436,570; qualifying distributions, $32,158,399; giving activities include $31,248,005 for 92 grants (high: $6,597,980; low: $4,200).
Purpose and activities: The foundation supports organizations involved with arts and culture, education, the environment, animals and wildlife, disaster relief, human services, community development, minorities, and economically disadvantaged people.
Fields of interest: Animals/wildlife; Libraries (public); Environment, natural resources; Museums (art); Aquariums; Media/communications; Museums; Performing arts, orchestras; Arts; Higher education; Scholarships/financial aid; Education;

Environment, air pollution; Environment, climate change/global warming; Environment, energy; Environment; Disasters, preparedness/services; American Red Cross; Children/youth, services; Human services; Community/economic development; Minorities; Economically disadvantaged.
Type of support: General/operating support; Emergency funds; Scholarship funds; Research; Employee volunteer services; Sponsorships; Employee matching gifts.
Limitations: Applications not accepted. Giving primarily in AK, CA, Washington, DC, Chicago, IL, IN, LA, TX, China, Germany, Indonesia, and the United Kingdom. No support for religious, fraternal, political, social, or athletic organizations; generally no support for organizations already receiving general operating support through the United Way. No grants to individuals, or for endowments, medical research, publications, or conferences.
Publications: Financial statement.
Application information: Contributes only to pre-selected organizations.
Board meeting date(s): Apr., July, and Nov.
Officers and Directors:* Andy P. Hopwood,* Chair.; Steven L. Bray, Secy.; Don Eldred,* C.F.O.; Mark E. Thompson, Treas.; Ben E. Cannon, Exec. Dir.; Sherry Strasner, Assoc. Dir.; Claire Bebbington; Iris M. Cross; Ray C. Dempsey.
Number of staff: 4 full-time professional; 1 full-time support.
EIN: 366046879
Recent grants for international programs:
1989-1 Agency for International Development, Washington, DC, $500,000. For unrestricted support. 2009.
1989-2 Alaska World Affairs Council, Anchorage, AK, $15,840. For unrestricted support. 2009.
1989-3 Australian Red Cross, Carlton, Australia, $250,394. For unrestricted support. 2009.
1989-4 Australian Red Cross, Carlton, Australia, $56,934. For unrestricted support. 2009.
1989-5 BirdLife International, Cambridge, England, $744,132. For unrestricted support. 2009.
1989-6 Cambridge in America, New York, NY, $238,301. For unrestricted support. 2009.
1989-7 Charities Aid Foundation UK, West Malling, England, $1,656,055. For unrestricted support. 2009.
1989-8 Conservation International, Arlington, VA, $320,103. For unrestricted support. 2009.
1989-9 Deutscher Verein fur offentliche und private Fursorge e. V., Berlin, Germany, $144,161. For unrestricted support. 2009.
1989-10 Deutscher Verein fur offentliche und private Fursorge e. V., Berlin, Germany, $130,342. For unrestricted support. 2009.
1989-11 Deutscher Verein fur offentliche und private Fursorge e. V., Berlin, Germany, $130,082. For unrestricted support. 2009.
1989-12 Fauna and Flora International, Cambridge, England, $268,930. For unrestricted support. 2009.
1989-13 Fauna and Flora International, Cambridge, England, $266,973. For unrestricted support. 2009.
1989-14 Gawad Kalinga USA, Del Mar, CA, $70,000. For unrestricted support. 2009.
1989-15 Gawad Kalinga USA, Del Mar, CA, $20,000. For unrestricted support. 2009.
1989-16 Gawad Kalinga USA, Del Mar, CA, $12,326. For unrestricted support. 2009.

1989-17 Indonesian Red Cross Society, Jakarta, Indonesia, $75,000. For unrestricted support. 2009.

1989-18 John Smith Memorial Trust, London, England, $123,458. For unrestricted support. 2009.

1989-19 Maecenata Management, Munich, Germany, $1,038,236. For unrestricted support. 2009.

1989-20 Pacific Council on International Policy, Los Angeles, CA, $140,000. For unrestricted support. 2009.

1989-21 Stifting Deutsch-Russischer Jugendaustausch, Hamburg, Germany, $90,583. For unrestricted support. 2009.

1989-22 Tsinghua University, Beijing, China, $600,000. For unrestricted support. 2009.

1989-23 World Resources Institute, Washington, DC, $200,000. For unrestricted support. 2009.

1989-24 World Vision UK, Milton Keynes, England, $153,535. For unrestricted support in Angola. 2009.

1989-25 Yayasan Dompet Dhuafa Republika, Tangerang, Indonesia, $100,000. For unrestricted support. 2009.

1990
Bridgeway Charitable Foundation
20 Greenway Plz. ste. 450
Houston, TX   77046-2009   (832) 204-8170
FAX: (713) 807-8071;
E-mail: info@bridgewayfoundation.org.; *URL:* http://www.bridgewayfoundation.org/

Established in 2000 in TX.
Donor: Bridgeway Capital Management, Inc.
Grantmaker type: Company-sponsored foundation.
Financial data (yr. ended 12/31/10): Assets, $366,137 (M); expenditures, $1,078,061; qualifying distributions, $1,066,627; giving activities include $782,198 for 10 grants (high: $333,333; low: $15,000).
Purpose and activities: The foundation supports programs designed to eliminate genocide; promote peace and reconciliation; and promote human rights.
Fields of interest: Health care; Education; International conflict resolution; Higher education; Disasters, preparedness/services; Children/youth, services; Human services; International relief; International peace/security; Civil/human rights; Christian agencies & churches; Economically disadvantaged.
Type of support: General/operating support; Capital campaigns; Emergency funds; Program development; Scholarship funds; Matching/challenge support.
Limitations: Applications not accepted. Giving primarily in TX and the United Kingdom. No grants to individuals, or for scholarships, fellowships, sponsorship of golf tournaments, galas, award dinners, or other fundraising events, debt reduction, endowments, or religious activities not of direct benefit to the entire community.
Application information: Unsolicited applications are currently not accepted.
  Board meeting date(s): Quarterly
Officers and Directors:* John Montgomery,* Pres.; Ann M. Montgomery,* V.P.; Bill Baumeyer,* V.P.; Ashley Rodriguez,* Secy.; Von Celestine, Treas.
Partners: Shannon Sedgwick Davis; Rebecca Hove.
EIN: 760666069

1991
H. E. Butt Grocery Company Contributions Program
646 S. Main Ave.
San Antonio, TX   78204-1210   (210) 938-8592
Contact: Dya Campos, Dir., Public Affairs
E-mail: campos.dya@heb.com; Additional application addresses: Austin and central TX: Leslie Sweet, Dir., Public Affairs, 6929 Airport, Ste. 176, Austin, TX 78752, tel.: (512) 421-1017; Houston, TX: Cyndy Garza-Roberts, Dir., Public Affairs, 4301 Windfern, Houston, TX 77041, tel.: (713) 329-3920; Gulf Coast, TX, area: Shelley Parks, Dir., Public Affairs, 4428 Kostoryz, Corpus Christi, TX 78415, tel.: (361) 857-1708; Border Region: Virginia Perez, Public Affairs Specialist, 2502 Cornerstone Blvd., Edinburg, TX 78752, tel.: (956) 225-3659; *URL:* http://www.heb.com/sectionpage/about-us/community/community-involvement/sd80002 Excellence in Education Award Winners: http://www.heb.com/sectionpage/about-us/community/excellence-in-education/2011-award-winners/sd30410039
Excellence in Education Awards: Jill Reynolds, 6929 Airport Blvd., Ste. 176, Austin, TX 78752, e-mail: reynolds.jill@heb.com

Grantmaker type: Corporate giving program.
Purpose and activities: H.E. Butt makes charitable contributions to nonprofit organizations involved with arts and culture, education, hunger, recreation, economic development, and to food banks and awards grants to K-12 teachers. Support is given primarily in areas of company operations.
Fields of interest: Health care; Nutrition; Arts; Elementary/secondary education; Education; Food services; Food banks; Recreation; Economic development.
International interests: Mexico.
Type of support: General/operating support; Program development; Research; Consulting services; Loaned talent; Grants to individuals; Donated equipment; Donated products.
Limitations: Applications accepted. Giving primarily in areas of company operations in TX and in Mexico; giving also to national organizations.
Publications: Application guidelines; Grants list.
Application information: Proposals should be submitted using organization letterhead. Organizations located in the Dallas, TX, area should use headquarters application address. Application form required.
  Initial approach: Download application form and mail proposal and application form to nearest application address; complete online application for Excellence in Education Awards and Healthy Campus Grant
  Deadline(s): 60 days prior to need; Jan. 6 for Excellence in Education Awards; Nov. 11 for Healthy Campus Grant
  Final notification: 30 days

1992
C.I.O.S.
P.O. Box 20815
Waco, TX   76702-0815   (254) 752-5551

Incorporated about 1952 in TN; corporation liquidated into a charitable trust in 1987.
Donors: Paul P. Piper, Sr.; Mrs. Paul P. Piper; Paul P. Piper, Jr.; Piper Industries, Inc.

Grantmaker type: Independent foundation.
Financial data (yr. ended 06/30/10): Assets, $116,406,373 (M); gifts received, $35,000; expenditures, $8,302,085; qualifying distributions, $7,688,106; giving activities include $7,180,664 for 31 grants (high: $3,999,500; low: $3,420; average: $25,000–$120,000), and $90,000 for 1 loan/program-related investment.
Purpose and activities: Grants for Protestant church support and religious programs, including Christian education, evangelism, welfare, and support for foreign missions.
Fields of interest: Theological school/education; Human services; Christian agencies & churches; Protestant agencies & churches.
Type of support: Program-related investments/loans.
Limitations: Applications not accepted. Giving primarily in TX. No grants to individuals.
Application information: Contributes only to pre-selected organizations.
  Board meeting date(s): Monthly
Trustees: Mary J. Piper; Paul Piper, Jr.; Shirley Piper; Polly Piper Rickard.
EIN: 742472778
Recent grants for international programs:
1992-1 Baptist Child and Family Services, San Antonio, TX, $100,000. For work in Haiti. 2010.
1992-2 Cooperative Baptist Fellowship, Atlanta, GA, $110,373. For UBLA. 2010.
1992-3 Global Women, Pelham, AL, $75,000. For development. 2010.
1992-4 Gloria al Padre, Temple, TX, $25,000. 2010.
1992-5 Haggai Institute for Advanced Leadership Training, Norcross, GA, $3,999,500. 2010.

1993
Casa Sonrisa, Inc.
3300 FM 1431
Round Rock, TX   78681-1075   (512) 797-2353
Contact: Maurice Kemper, Dir., Opers.
E-mail: info@casasonrisa.org; Additional tel.: (512) 388-9999; additional e-mail: gkemper@joimail.com; *URL:* http://www.casasonrisa.org/

Established in 1993 in Mexico.
Grantmaker type: Public charity.
Financial data (yr. ended 12/31/10): Revenue, $125,191; assets, $209,067 (M); gifts received, $124,400; expenditures, $123,496; giving activities include $120,279 for grants, and for 1 grant to an organization outside the U.S.
Purpose and activities: The organization promotes the physical, emotional, and spiritual well being of homeless and needy children in Mexico.
Fields of interest: Economically disadvantaged; Homeless.
International interests: Mexico.
Limitations: Applications not accepted. Giving primarily in Mexico. No support for political organizations.
Publications: Annual report; Financial statement; Newsletter; Occasional report.
Application information: Contributes only to pre-selected organizations; unsolicited requests for funds not considered or acknowledged.
  Board meeting date(s): Six to seven times per year
Trustees: Bob Bledsoe; Kit B'Smith; Bill Goff; Lee Jackson; Floyd Odom.
EIN: 742656238

1994
Chrest Foundation, Inc.

(formerly J. Jensen Family Foundation, Inc.)
130 E. John Carpenter Freeway
Irving, TX 75062-2708 (972) 999-4514
Contact: Lou Anne King Jensen, Pres.
FAX: (972) 999-4502;
E-mail: administrator@chrestfoundation.org;
URL: http://www.chrestfoundation.org

Established in 1999 in TX.
Donors: Jeffrey J. Jensen; Gladys Margaret Jensen.
Grantmaker type: Independent foundation.
Financial data (yr. ended 12/31/10): Assets,
$8,864,517 (M); gifts received, $140,480;
expenditures, $470,627; qualifying distributions,
$347,653; giving activities include $347,653 for 13
grants.
Purpose and activities: The foundation believes
that social action and civic participation contribute
to the creation of a more equitable and tolerant
society. The foundation concentrates its resources
on civil society organizations in Turkey that focus on
increasing gender equality and fostering
communication and dialogue through arts and
culture.
Fields of interest: Children; Youth; Women; Adults,
women.
International interests: Turkey.
Type of support: Emergency funds; Film/video/
radio; Management development/capacity building;
Matching/challenge support; Program development;
Program evaluation; Program-related investments/
loans; Research; Technical assistance.
Limitations: Applications accepted. Giving primarily
in Turkey, with occasional support to Cyprus and the
Caucasus. No grants to individuals.
Publications: Application guidelines; Grants list;
Program policy statement; Program policy statement
(including application guidelines).
Application information: Application guidelines
available on foundation web site. Application form
required.
  Initial approach: E-mail, telephone, or grant
    inquiry form on foundation web site
  Copies of proposal: 1
  Deadline(s): None
  Board meeting date(s): Two times per year
  Final notification: Ranges from days to eight
    weeks
Officers: Lou Anne King Jensen, Pres.; Jeffrey J.
Jensen, V.P.; Haley Barb, Secy.; Julie J. Jensen,
Treas.
Number of staff: 1 full-time professional; 1 part-time
support.
EIN: 752840026

1995
The Coneway Family Foundation

(formerly Lynn & Peter Coneway Foundation)
2247 Troon Rd.
Houston, TX 77019-1417

Established in 1983 in TX.
Donors: Lynn M. Coneway; Peter R. Coneway; Peter
R. Coneway Charitable Lead Trust; Natalie Coneway
Page.
Grantmaker type: Independent foundation.
Financial data (yr. ended 04/30/11): Assets,
$10,745,048 (M); expenditures, $492,525;
qualifying distributions, $224,767; giving activities
include $224,767 for grants.
Purpose and activities: Giving primarily for the arts,
higher education, health care, and human services.
Fields of interest: Cancer; Museums (art); Arts;
Higher education; Education; Health care; Human
services; Foundations (community).
International interests: Switzerland.
Type of support: Continuing support; Endowments;
Fellowships.
Limitations: Applications not accepted. Giving
primarily in TX, with emphasis on Austin and
Houston. No grants, scholarships, or loans to
individuals.
Application information: Contributes only to
pre-selected organizations.
Trustees: Cecile L. Coneway; Lynn M. Coneway;
Natalie Coneway; Peter R. Coneway.
Number of staff: 1 full-time professional.
EIN: 133188841

1996
Cooper Industries, Inc. Corporate Giving
Program

P.O. Box 4446
Houston, TX 77210-4446 (713) 209-8800
FAX: (713) 209-8982;
E-mail: info@cooperindustries.com; URL: http://
www.cooperindustries.com/content/public/en/
company/corporate_giving.html

Grantmaker type: Corporate giving program.
Purpose and activities: As a complement to its
foundation, Cooper Industries also makes
charitable contributions to nonprofit organizations
directly. Support is given in areas of company
operations.
Fields of interest: Recreation, parks/playgrounds;
Recreation, fairs/festivals; Arts; Vocational
education; Higher education; Education;
Environment; Health care; Human services;
Community/economic development.
International interests: China; Mexico; United
Kingdom.
Type of support: General/operating support;
Employee volunteer services; Loaned talent;
Sponsorships; Employee-related scholarships;
Donated equipment; Donated products; In-kind gifts.
Limitations: Giving on a national and international
basis in areas of company operations, with
emphasis on Peachtree, GA, Highland, IL, St. Louis,
MO, Syracuse, NY, Houston, TX, and Waukesha, WI
and China, Mexico, and the United Kingdom. No
support for discriminatory organizations or religious,
veterans', or political organizations. No grants to
individuals (except for employee-related
scholarships).
Application information:
  Initial approach: Contact nearest facility for
    application information
Administrator: Victoria B. Guennewig, V.P., Public
Affairs.
Number of staff: 1 full-time professional; 1 full-time
support.

1997
Opal G. Cox Charitable Trust

c/o Bank of America, N.A.
P.O. Box 831041
Dallas, TX 75283-1041
Scholarship application addresses: Office of
Academic Scholarships and Financial Aid, Baylor
University, 1 Bear Pl., No. 97028, Waco, TX
76798-7028, tel.: (254) 710-2611; Office of
Financial Aid, Southwestern Baptist Theological
Seminary, P.O. Box 22510, Fort Worth, TX 76122,
tel.: (817) 923-1921

Established in 1982 in TX.
Donor: Opal G. Cox‡.
Grantmaker type: Independent foundation.
Financial data (yr. ended 08/31/10): Assets,
$4,722,514 (M); expenditures, $221,396;
qualifying distributions, $165,683; giving activities
include $152,574 for 2 grants (high: $76,287; low:
$76,287).
Purpose and activities: Provides educational funds
available to students attending or wishing to attend
Baylor University or Southwestern Baptist
Theological Seminary. Preference is given to
students studying to become missionaries or
medical missionaries.
Fields of interest: Higher education, university;
Theological school/education.
Type of support: Scholarship funds.
Limitations: Applications accepted. Giving primarily
in TX. No grants to individuals directly.
Application information: Applications are available
at financial aid office. Application form required.
  Deadline(s): May 15 for Baylor University; for
    Southwestern Baptist Theological Seminary
    call for deadline
Trustee: Bank of America, N.A.
EIN: 746307500

1998
The Bill and Helen Crowder Foundation

P.O. Box 1421
La Porte, TX 77572-1421 (281) 470-1001
Contact: Linda Windham, Admin.
FAX: (281) 471-4376; Application address: 1001
West H St., La Porte, TX 77571

Established in 1999 in TX.
Grantmaker type: Independent foundation.
Financial data (yr. ended 12/31/10): Assets,
$4,382,658 (M); expenditures, $244,060;
qualifying distributions, $218,288; giving activities
include $208,000 for 53 grants (high: $20,000;
low: $500).
Purpose and activities: Giving primarily for
hospitals, health associations, and human services;
funding also for children and youth services and an
Episcopal church.
Fields of interest: Hospitals (general); Health
organizations; Human services; Salvation Army;
Children/youth, services; United Ways and
Federated Giving Programs; Protestant agencies &
churches.
International interests: Asia; Africa.
Type of support: General/operating support; Annual
campaigns; Capital campaigns; Emergency funds;
Program development; Scholarship funds;
Research.
Limitations: Applications accepted. Giving primarily
in TX. No support for political organizations. No
grants to individuals.
Application information: Application form not
required.
  Initial approach: Letter
  Copies of proposal: 1
  Deadline(s): None
  Board meeting date(s): Quarterly
Officers: Helen S. Crowder, Pres.; James R. Keeney,
Jr., V.P.

Directors: Stephen Arthur; R.N. Domec; Marilyn Sims.
Number of staff: 1 part-time professional; 1 part-time support.
EIN: 760555573

1999
The Cultural Heritage Preservation Fund
800 Gessner Rd., Ste. 1260
Houston, TX 77024-4273

Established in 2004 in TX.
Donor: Laurans Trust.
Grantmaker type: Independent foundation.
Financial data (yr. ended 12/31/10): Assets, $1,721,294 (M); expenditures, $1,085,897; qualifying distributions, $1,075,000; giving activities include $1,075,000 for 5 grants (high: $1,000,000; low: $12,500).
Fields of interest: Media, film/video; Arts.
International interests: France.
Limitations: Applications not accepted. Giving primarily in Paris, France; some giving also in the U.S., primarily in New York, NY. No grants to individuals.
Application information: Contributes only to pre-selected organizations.
Officers: Francois Letaconnoux, Pres.; Jacques Le Blevennec, V.P.; Marvin A. Wurzer, Secy.-Treas.
EIN: 201442065

2000
The Michael and Susan Dell Foundation
P.O. Box 163867
Austin, TX 78716-3867
E-mail: info@msdf.org; URL: http://www.msdf.org/
Facebook: http://www.facebook.com/dellfamilyfoundation?v=info
Grants Database: http://www.msdf.org/Grants/Master_Grant_List.aspx
Twitter: http://twitter.com/msdf_foundation

Established in 1999 in TX.
Donors: Michael Dell; Susan Dell.
Grantmaker type: Independent foundation.
Financial data (yr. ended 12/31/10): Assets, $934,701,114 (M); expenditures, $114,061,461; qualifying distributions, $112,936,978; giving activities include $93,673,023 for 329 grants (high: $9,500,000; low: $261), $4,268,048 for 2 foundation-administered programs and $1,839,404 for 3 loans/program-related investments.
Purpose and activities: The foundation's mission is to fund initiatives that seek to foster active minds, healthy bodies and a safe environment where children can thrive. It proactively seeks out opportunities to support or develop programs that address five essential focus areas: children's health, education, safety, youth development and early childhood care.
Fields of interest: Elementary/secondary school reform; Elementary/secondary education; Education; Health care, HMOs; Health care, clinics/centers; Health care, infants; Health care; Health care, patient services; Crime/violence prevention, abuse prevention; Crime/violence prevention, child abuse; Youth development; Children/youth, services; Children, day care; Community/economic development.
Limitations: Applications accepted. Giving on a local (central TX), regional, national and international

basis (international emphasis is on India). No support for medical research. No grants to individuals except for scholarship program, or for fundraisers, sponsorships, or endowments.
Publications: Grants list.
Application information: See foundation Web site for guidelines and requirements. Unsolicited full proposals are not accepted. If the foundation finds that the preliminary grant request fulfills its mission, grant seekers will be notified and provided a password to access official grant application forms through its Web site.
Initial approach: Submit preliminary grant request online
Officers and Directors:* Michael Dell,* Pres.; Susan Dell,* 1st V.P.; Alexander Dell,* 2nd V.P.; Marc Lisker, Secy.; Tricia Teegardin, Treas.; Janet Mountain, Exec. Dir.
Number of staff: 35
EIN: 364336415
Recent grants for international programs:
2000-1 African Leadership Foundation, African Leadership Academy, Michael and Susan Dell Science and Technology Center, New York, NY, $75,000. 2009.
2000-2 Akanksha Foundation, Mumbai, India, $84,612. For Akanksha Schools. 2009.
2000-3 Akanksha Foundation, Mumbai, India, $82,148. For Akanksha Schools. 2009.
2000-4 Akshara Foundation, Bangalore, India, $106,165. For School-Based Libraries in Bangalore. 2009.
2000-5 Alternative for India Development, Chennai, India, $110,000. For Equivalency Determination Eureka Quality Improvement Programme - EQUIP. 2009.
2000-6 Alternative for India Development, Chennai, India, $96,492. For Equivalency Determination Eureka Quality Improvement Programme, EQUIP. 2009.
2000-7 Andhra Pradesh Mahila Abhivruddhi Society, Hyderabad, India, $138,156. For Integrated Access to Clean Water and Sanitation in Urban Slums Through the Microfinance Delivery Channel. 2009.
2000-8 Andhra Pradesh Mahila Abhivruddhi Society, Hyderabad, India, $138,156. For Integrated Access to Clean Water and Sanitation in Urban Slums Through the Microfinance Delivery Channel. 2009.
2000-9 Bandhan-Konnagar, Kolkata, India, $313,125. For transforming poor, excluded women in Kolkata into viable micro-entrepreneurs. 2009.
2000-10 Bandhan-Konnagar, Kolkata, India, $87,777. For transforming poor, excluded women in Kolkata into viable micro-entrepreneurs. 2009.
2000-11 Bharat Integrated Social Welfare Agency, Sambalpur, India, $53,000. For microfinance-enabled access to water and sanitation services. 2009.
2000-12 Bodh Shiksha Samiti, Jaipur, India, $97,463. For Janbodh Karyakram. 2009.
2000-13 Bodh Shiksha Samiti, Jaipur, India, $91,085. For Janbodh Karyakram. 2009.
2000-14 Bodh Shiksha Samiti, Jaipur, India, $77,412. For Janbodh Karyakram. 2009.
2000-15 Bodh Shiksha Samiti, Jaipur, India, $18,037. For Janbodh Karyakram. 2009.
2000-16 CAP Foundation, Hyderabad, India, $167,233. For Teen Channel Ek Mouka Community Learning Initiative. 2009.

2000-17 Consultative Group to Assist the Poor, Washington, DC, $200,000. For Microfinance Donor Consortium. 2009.
2000-18 Doctor Reddys Foundation, Hyderabad, India, $1,052,634. For A Generation of Urban Livelihoods Across India. 2009.
2000-19 Doctor Reddys Foundation, Hyderabad, India, $801,183. For A Generation of Urban Livelihoods Across India. 2009.
2000-20 Education Support Organisation, Ahmadabad, India, $402,996. For Gyan Shala - Quality Education for Slum Children in Ahmadabad. 2009.
2000-21 Endeavor Global, New York, NY, $300,000. For economic development through supporting entrepreneurs. 2009.
2000-22 Friends of WWB, India, Ahmadabad, India, $53,821. To develop sustainable model to enable urban poor in India to access water and sanitation services. 2009.
2000-23 Friends of WWB, India, Ahmadabad, India, $41,750. To develop sustainable model to enable urban poor in India to access water and sanitation services. 2009.
2000-24 Good360, Alexandria, VA, $59,256. For Printer Technology Program. 2009.
2000-25 Good360, Alexandria, VA, $28,800. For Printer Technology Program. 2009.
2000-26 Good360, Alexandria, VA, $13,233. For Printer Technology Program. 2009.
2000-27 Grameen Foundation USA, Washington, DC, $255,000. For standards in measurement of microfinance's social impact, and to catalyze growth of poverty focused microfinance institutions. 2009.
2000-28 Grameen Foundation USA, Washington, DC, $236,131. To provide sustainable, impact-focused financial support to enable microfinance institutions to reach poor families globally. 2009.
2000-29 Grameen Foundation USA, Washington, DC, $217,228. To provide sustainable, impact-focused financial support to enable microfinance institutions to reach poor families globally. 2009.
2000-30 Grameen Foundation USA, Washington, DC, $181,235. To provide sustainable, impact-focused financial support to enable microfinance institutions to reach poor families globally. 2009.
2000-31 Helen Keller International, New York, NY, $600,000. For Fortification of Staple Foods in Cameroon in Central Africa. 2009.
2000-32 Helen Keller International, New York, NY, $600,000. For Fortification of Staple Foods in Cameroon in Central Africa. 2009.
2000-33 Helen Keller International, New York, NY, $500,000. For Wheat Flour Fortification in West Africa. 2009.
2000-34 KATHA, New Delhi, India, $53,250. For Mapping the Future - Katha Lab School. 2009.
2000-35 Keep a Child Alive, Brooklyn, NY, $45,000. For Nutritional Support to Aid AIDS Orphans in Soweto in Continuing Their Education. 2009.
2000-36 LEAP Science and Maths School, Pinelands, South Africa, $208,405. For supporting university-preparatory high school for young people from South Africa's townships. 2009.
2000-37 Mahila Housing SEWA Trust, Ahmadabad, India, $177,271. For Renewal of Inclusive Cities - Provision of Water and Sanitation for Urban Poor. 2009.

2000-38 Mahila Housing SEWA Trust, Ahmadabad, India, $174,708. For Renewal of Inclusive Cities - Provision of Water and Sanitation for Urban Poor. 2009.

2000-39 Mahila Housing SEWA Trust, Ahmadabad, India, $162,691. For Renewal of Inclusive Cities - Provision of Water and Sanitation for Urban Poor. 2009.

2000-40 Microfinance Information Exchange, Washington, DC, $154,500. For promoting public reporting and transparency of social performance indicators in microfinance. 2009.

2000-41 Microfinance Information Exchange, Washington, DC, $130,500. For promoting public reporting and transparency of social performance indicators in microfinance. 2009.

2000-42 Microfinance Information Exchange, Washington, DC, $19,320. For Social Performance Reporting Awards for Microfinance Institutions. 2009.

2000-43 Monitor Group, Market Based Solutions to Create Social Change Initiative, Cambridge, MA, $150,000. For microfinance-enabled low-income housing for India's urban poor. 2009.

2000-44 Naandi Foundation, Hyderabad, India, $1,310,164. For Integrated Proposal for School Programs in Hyderabad and Mumbai. 2009.

2000-45 Naandi Foundation, Hyderabad, India, $258,926. For Ensuring Children Learn, Mumbai. 2009.

2000-46 Naandi Foundation, Hyderabad, India, $199,169. For interim grant, Ensuring Children Learn, Hyderabad. 2009.

2000-47 Naandi Foundation, Hyderabad, India, $183,600. For interim grant, Ensuring Children Learn, Hyderabad. 2009.

2000-48 Naandi Foundation, Hyderabad, India, $145,905. For Ensuring Children Learn, Mumbai. 2009.

2000-49 Navjyoti India Foundation, Delhi, India, $120,000. For Improving Re-Settled Slum Children's Learning and Growth. 2009.

2000-50 Navjyoti India Foundation, Delhi, India, $115,848. For Improving Re-Settled Slum Children's Learning and Growth. 2009.

2000-51 NetHope, Fairfax, VA, $150,000. For addressing the humanitarian productivity gap in the non-profit sector. 2009.

2000-52 NIIT Institute of Information Technology, New Delhi, India, $224,409. For Community Learning Centres. 2009.

2000-53 NIIT Institute of Information Technology, New Delhi, India, $64,208. For playground learning centers in Jaipur. 2009.

2000-54 Parikrma Humanity Foundation, Bangalore, India, $110,419. For Parikrma Circle of Life Program. 2009.

2000-55 Parikrma Humanity Foundation, Bangalore, India, $57,718. For Parikrma Circle of Life Program. 2009.

2000-56 PATH, Seattle, WA, $1,300,000. For Eliminating the Meningitis Epidemic in Africa. 2009.

2000-57 PATH, Seattle, WA, $500,000. For Saving Children's Lives Through Immunization. 2009.

2000-58 PlayPumps International, Washington, DC, $50,000. For installation of PlayPumps Systems which bring play opportunities and improved access to safe water to communities and schools in Africa. 2009.

2000-59 Pratham-Mumbai Education Initiative, Mumbai, India, $506,726. For Large Scale Improvement in Children's Learning Levels. 2009.

2000-60 Pratham-Mumbai Education Initiative, Mumbai, India, $322,697. For Large Scale Improvement in Children's Learning Levels. 2009.

2000-61 Pratham-Mumbai Education Initiative, Mumbai, India, $277,813. For Large Scale Improvement in Children's Learning Levels. 2009.

2000-62 Ruchika Social Service Organization, Bhubaneswar, India, $33,327. For Alternative Schooling with Remedial Support for Slum Children. 2009.

2000-63 Save the Children India, Mumbai, India, $144,359. For Saksham - Education Project. 2009.

2000-64 Save the Children India, Mumbai, India, $123,272. For Saksham - Education Project. 2009.

2000-65 Sesame Workshop, New York, NY, $258,960. For Galli Galli Sim Sim Outreach, Hindi language adaptation of Sesame Street for India. 2009.

2000-66 Sesame Workshop, New York, NY, $180,000. For Galli Galli Sim Sim Outreach, Hindi language adaptation of Sesame Street for India. 2009.

2000-67 Svasti Financial Services Pvt. Ltd., Mumbai, India, $365,000. For Svasti project - funding support to provide microfinance services in slums. 2009.

2000-68 Swadhaar FinAccess, Mumbai, India, $100,000. For Start-Up Capital for Microfinance Institution in Mumbai Slums. 2009.

2000-69 Swadhaar FinAccess, Mumbai, India, $100,000. For start-up support for microfinance institution in Mumbai slums. 2009.

2000-70 Swami Vivekananda Youth Movement of North America, Fullerton, CA, $281,025. For Prema Vidya Center. 2009.

2000-71 Swami Vivekananda Youth Movement of North America, Fullerton, CA, $260,719. For Prema Vidya Center. 2009.

2000-72 Swami Vivekananda Youth Movement of North America, Fullerton, CA, $159,791. For Prema Vidya Center. 2009.

2000-73 Teach for America, New York, NY, $53,300. For Building Teach For India with Teach For All Support. 2009.

2000-74 Teach for America, New York, NY, $20,306. For Building Teach For India with Teach For All Support. 2009.

2000-75 Teacher Foundation, Bangalore, India, $86,114. For Turning Schools Around. 2009.

2000-76 Teacher Foundation, Bangalore, India, $84,800. For Turning Schools Around. 2009.

2000-77 Ubuntu Education Fund, New York, NY, $163,038. For Ubuntu Scholars Initiative. 2009.

2000-78 Unitus, Inc., Seattle, WA, $189,775. For Enhancing Adoption of Social Performance Reporting Tools and Indicators by Microfinance Institutions. 2009.

2000-79 Unitus, Inc., Seattle, WA, $155,185. For Enhancing Adoption of Social Performance Reporting Tools and Indicators by Microfinance Institutions. 2009.

2000-80 Urban Health Resource Center, New Delhi, India, $101,500. For Urban Health Program for Maternal and Child Health. 2009.

2000-81 Vidya Bhawan Society, Udaipur, India, $139,992. For QUEST- Qualitative Universalization of Education and School Transformation. 2009.

2000-82 Vidya Bhawan Society, Udaipur, India, $139,635. For QUEST- Qualitative

Universalization of Education and School Transformation. 2009.

2000-83 Vidya Bhawan Society, Udaipur, India, $136,048. For QUEST- Qualitative Universalization of Education and School Transformation. 2009.

2000-84 Vikramshila Education Resource Society, Kolkata, India, $79,478. For Education to Employability - E2E. 2009.

2000-85 Vikramshila Education Resource Society, Kolkata, India, $24,404. For Education to Employability - E2E. 2009.

2000-86 Vikramshila Education Resource Society, Kolkata, India, $22,193. For Education to Employability - E2E. 2009.

2001

Dudley T. Dougherty Foundation, Inc.

P.O. Box 4310
Beeville, TX   78104-4310   (361) 358-1464
Contact: Patricia Dougherty, Pres.
FAX: (361) 358-1244;
E-mail: contact@dudleytdoughertyfoundation.org;
URL: http://www.dudleytdoughertyfoundation.org/

Established in 2002 in TX.
Donor: The James R. Dougherty, Jr. Foundation.
Grantmaker type: Independent foundation.
Financial data (yr. ended 12/31/10): Assets, $3,044,647 (M); expenditures, $203,146; qualifying distributions, $145,595; giving activities include $145,595 for grants.
Fields of interest: Human services; Education; Environment, natural resources; International human rights.
International interests: Netherlands.
Limitations: Applications accepted. Giving primarily in TX. No grants to individuals.
Application information: Guidelines and application available on foundation web site.
   Deadline(s): Nov. 30
   Board meeting date(s): Fall
Officers and Trustees:* Patricia Dougherty,* Pres.; Erin Marcotte Marmor,* V.P. and Secy.; Kevin Dougherty,* V.P.; Tim Fitch, Treas.
EIN: 943418539

2002

El Paso Community Foundation

123 West Mills, Ste. 520
P.O. Box 272
El Paso, TX   79901   (915) 533-4020
Contact: Virginia S. Martinez, Pres.
FAX: (915) 532-0716; E-mail: info@epcf.org;
URL: http://www.epcf.org
Grants List: http://www.epcf.org/recent_grants

Incorporated in 1977 in TX.
Grantmaker type: Community foundation.
Financial data (yr. ended 12/31/09): Assets, $89,586,983 (M); gifts received, $9,464,601; expenditures, $7,777,453; giving activities include $3,389,187 for grants.
Purpose and activities: The foundation seeks to: 1) establish permanent charitable endowments; 2) provide a vehicle for donors' varied interests; 3) promote local philanthropy; and 4) provide leadership and resources in addressing local challenges and opportunities. Primary areas of interest include education, human services, health and disabilities, arts and humanities, the

environment and animals, and community development.

Fields of interest: Animal welfare; Humanities; Arts; Education; Environment; Health care; Human services; Community/economic development.

International interests: Mexico.

Type of support: Management development/capacity building; Equipment; General/operating support; Program development; Seed money; Scholarship funds; Technical assistance; Matching/challenge support.

Limitations: Applications accepted. Giving limited to the El Paso, TX region: far west Texas, southern NM, and northern Chihuahua, Mexico. No support for medical or academic research, or religious purposes. No grants to individuals (except for scholarships), or for deficit financing, annual campaigns, travel, capital campaigns, fundraising events, endowments, or ongoing support.

Publications: Application guidelines; Annual report; Financial statement; Grants list; Informational brochure; Newsletter; Occasional report.

Application information: Visit foundation web site for application form and guidelines. Application form required.

  Initial approach: Submit application
  Copies of proposal: 1
  Deadline(s): Feb. 1 and Aug. 1
  Board meeting date(s): May and Nov.
  Final notification: Following board consideration

Officers and Directors: Sharon Smith Kidd,* Chair.; Virginia Martinez, Pres.; Eric Pearson, Exec. V.P.; Carmen M. Vargas, V.P., Finance; Cathy Hill, V.P., Donor Rels.; Richard Harlan "Rickie" Feuille,* Chair. Emeritus; Leigh V. Bloss,* Secy.-Treas.; Joe Alcantar, Jr.; Frances R. Axelson; Patricia Saucedo Burdick; Lillian Crouch; Charles de Wetter; Steve Hoy; John S. McKee, Jr.; Roger Ortiz, D.D.S.; Lupe Rivera; Jonathan Rogers, Jr.; Felipa Solis.

Number of staff: 8 full-time professional; 4 full-time support; 1 part-time support.

EIN: 741839536

2003
The Roger and Rosemary Enrico Foundation

3831 Turtle Creek Blvd., No. 23B
Dallas, TX 75219-4480

Established in 2000 in TX.

Donor: Roger A. Enrico.

Grantmaker type: Independent foundation.

Financial data (yr. ended 12/31/09): Assets, $19,468,055 (M); gifts received, $1,000,000; expenditures, $5,639,820; qualifying distributions, $5,039,135; giving activities include $5,039,135 for 21 grants (high: $1,570,000; low: $1).

Fields of interest: Higher education; Arts, cultural/ethnic awareness; Media, film/video; Elementary/secondary education; Health care; Human services; International relief; Catholic federated giving programs; Social sciences; Catholic agencies & churches.

Type of support: General/operating support.

Limitations: Applications not accepted. Giving primarily in Washington, DC, and Dallas, TX; giving also in CA, FL, MT, and NY. No grants to individuals.

Application information: Contributes only to pre-selected organizations.

Officer: Terence C. Sullivan, Treas.

Directors: Aaron J. Enrico; Roger A. Enrico; Rosemary Enrico.

EIN: 752871636

2004
ExxonMobil Foundation

(formerly ExxonMobil Education Foundation)
5959 Las Colinas Blvd.
Irving, TX 75039-2298
Contact: Gerald W. McElvy, Pres.
URL: http://www.exxonmobil.com/Corporate/community_foundation.aspx

Incorporated in 1955 in NJ as Esso Education Foundation; name changed to Exxon Education Foundation in 1972; name changed to ExxonMobil Foundation in 1999.

Donors: Exxon Corp.; Exxon Mobil Corp.

Grantmaker type: Company-sponsored foundation.

Financial data (yr. ended 12/31/10): Assets, $67,519,747 (M); gifts received, $111,908,579; expenditures, $72,363,241; qualifying distributions, $72,363,241; giving activities include $42,669,655 for grants, and $29,484,908 for employee matching gifts.

Purpose and activities: The foundation supports organizations involved with education, the environment, endangered species and habitats, health, medical research, human services, community development, civic affairs, and women. Special emphasis is directed toward programs designed to provide mathematics, engineering, science, and technology education. Support is given primarily in areas of company operations; giving also to national and international organizations.

Fields of interest: Higher education; Engineering school/education; Education, reading; Education; Environment, natural resources; Environment; Animals/wildlife, endangered species; Health care; Parasitic diseases; Medical research; Human services; Economic development; Business/industry; Community/economic development; Science, formal/general education; Mathematics; Public policy, research; Public affairs; Women.

International interests: Africa; Developing countries.

Type of support: General/operating support; Program development; Employee volunteer services; Employee matching gifts.

Limitations: Applications not accepted. Giving on national and international basis, primarily in areas of company operations in Baldwin and Mobile counties, AL, Anchorage, Fairbanks, and North Slope, AK, Santa Barbara County and Torrance, CA, Cortez and Rio Blanco County, CO, Washington, DC, LaGrange, GA, Joliet, IL, Kingman and Stevens County, KS, Baton Rouge, Chalmette, and Grand Isle, LA, Billings, MT, Clinton and Paulsboro, NJ, Rochester, NY, Akron, OH, Shawnee and Texas County, OK, Baytown, Beaumont, Dallas, Fort Worth, Houston, Midland, Odessa, and Tyler, TX, San Juan County, UT, Fairfax County and northern VA, and Lincoln, Sublette, and Sweetwater counties, WY; giving also to national and international organizations. No support for political or religious organizations or youth sports organizations. No grants to individuals, or for institutional scholarship or fellowship programs, capital campaigns, land acquisition, equipment, renovation projects, endowments, athletics, or scholarships; no loans.

Publications: Annual report; Corporate giving report; Grants list.

Application information: Contributes only to pre-selected organizations.

Officers and Trustees: K. P. Cohen,* Chair.; Suzanne M. McCarron, Pres.; N. H. Jenkins, Secy.; L. M. Rubin, Treas.; B. A. Babock, Cont.; F. W. Bass;

N. A. Chapman; B. G. Macklin; J. M. Spellings; S. K. Stuewer.

Number of staff: 5 part-time professional; 3 part-time support.

EIN: 136082357

Recent grants for international programs:

2004-1 Accordia Global Health Foundation, Washington, DC, $550,000. For Malaria Training Program - Infectious Disease Institute, Makerere University, Uganda. 2010.

2004-2 Africare, Washington, DC, $325,000. For Malaria Prevention in Nigeria Program. 2010.

2004-3 Africare, Washington, DC, $300,000. For CORE - Angola Community Malaria Program. 2010.

2004-4 Africare, Washington, DC, $250,000. For Coconda Community-Based Malaria Program in Angola. 2010.

2004-5 Agency for International Development, Washington, DC, $500,000. For President's Malaria Initiative. 2010.

2004-6 Ajuda de Desenvolvimento de Povo para Povo, Luanda, Angola, $260,000. For Malaria and HIV-AIDS Prevention. 2010.

2004-7 Ajuda de Desenvolvimento de Povo para Povo, Luanda, Angola, $100,000. For Benguela Malaria Consortium. 2010.

2004-8 American Red Cross National Headquarters, International Response Fund, Washington, DC, $100,000. For flood relief and recovery efforts in Pakistan. 2010.

2004-9 Americans for Oxford, New York, NY, $680,000. For ExxonMobil Scholars in Global Health Science. 2010.

2004-10 Bermuda Institute of Ocean Sciences, Saint Georges, Bermuda, $125,000. For Fellowships-Marine Carbon Cycle. 2010.

2004-11 Centre for Development and Population Activities, Washington, DC, $1,855,000. For institutional capacity building, training and communications support for Global Women in Management Program. 2010.

2004-12 Centre for Development and Population Activities, Washington, DC, $200,000. For WEOI - Capacity Building. 2010.

2004-13 Eisenhower Exchange Fellowships, Philadelphia, PA, $150,000. For WEOI - General Support. 2010.

2004-14 Episcopal Relief and Development, New York, NY, $333,000. For Nets for Life Program. 2010.

2004-15 Friends of WWB/USA, New York, NY, $250,000. For WWB in a Box Toolkit - Microfinance Training, Mexico. 2010.

2004-16 Giant Sable Fund, Boston, MA, $50,000. For general support. 2010.

2004-17 JHPIEGO, Baltimore, MD, $1,000,000. For Malaria in Pregnancy Intervention Programs in Angola and Nigeria. 2010.

2004-18 Kopernik Solutions, New York, NY, $100,000. For WEOI, Empowering Women Through Solar Technology in Indonesia. 2010.

2004-19 Leuser International Foundation, Jakarta, Indonesia, $100,000. For Ecosystem Preservation. 2010.

2004-20 Massachusetts Institute of Technology, Global Change Program, Cambridge, MA, $200,000. For Joint Program on the Science and Policy of Global Change. 2010.

2004-21 Medicines for Malaria Venture, Geneva, Switzerland, $500,000. For anti-malarial drug Pyramax, PNG Plan. 2010.

2004-22 MediSend International, Dallas, TX, $800,000. For Biomedical Training. 2010.

2004-23 MediSend International, Dallas, TX, $380,000. For Container Shipment. 2010.

2004-24 National Fish and Wildlife Foundation, Washington, DC, $1,000,000. For Save the Tiger Fund Council Expenses. 2010.

2004-25 Nature Conservancy, Arlington, VA, $25,000. For Leadership Council. 2010.

2004-26 PATH Vaccine Solutions, Malaria Vaccine Initiative, Seattle, WA, $500,000. For Malaria Vaccine Projects. 2010.

2004-27 Population Services International, Washington, DC, $300,000. For Lasting Insecticide Treated Nets Distribution in Angola. 2010.

2004-28 Saint Francis Xavier University, Friends of, Antigonish, Canada, $1,500,000. For Indigenous Women in Community Leadership, Developing the Next Generation. 2010.

2004-29 United Nations Foundation, Washington, DC, $500,000. For Nothing But Nets. 2010.

2004-30 Vital Voices Global Partnership, Washington, DC, $1,450,000. For WEOI - African Women as Economic Force. 2010.

2004-31 Vital Voices Global Partnership, Washington, DC, $250,000. For Women's Supplier Diversity Program. 2010.

2004-32 Vital Voices Global Partnership, Washington, DC, $200,000. For Measuring and Evaluation for BWNs in MENA and Latin America. 2010.

2004-33 World Health Organization, Geneva, Switzerland, $500,000. For Research and Training in Tropical Diseases. 2010.

2005
The Feldman Family Foundation
1431 Greenway Dr., No. 360
Irving, TX   75038-2442
Contact: Robert L. Feldman, V.P.

Established in 2005 in TX as successor foundation to The Feldman Foundation.
Donor: The Feldman Foundation.
Grantmaker type: Independent foundation.
Financial data (yr. ended 12/31/10): Assets, $38,459,425 (M); expenditures, $2,384,255; qualifying distributions, $2,143,758; giving activities include $1,774,500 for 34 grants (high: $275,000; low: $500).
Fields of interest: Education; Human services; Jewish federated giving programs; Jewish agencies & synagogues.
International interests: Israel.
Limitations: Applications accepted. Giving primarily in CA and TX.
Application information: Application form not required.
   Initial approach: Letter
   Copies of proposal: 1
   Deadline(s): None
   Board meeting date(s): Late summer/early fall
Officers and Directors:* Daniel E. Feldman,* Pres.; Robert L. Feldman,* V.P.
Number of staff: 1 part-time support.
EIN: 202098529

2006
Fluor Corporation Contributions Program
6700 Las Colinas Blvd.
Irving, TX   75039-2902
Contact: Suzanne Huffmon Esber, Dir., Community Rels.
URL: http://www.fluor.com/sustainability/community/fluor_giving/Pages/default.aspx

Grantmaker type: Corporate giving program.
Purpose and activities: As a complement to its foundation, Fluor also makes charitable contributions to nonprofit organizations directly. Support is given on a national and international basis.
Fields of interest: Arts; Education; Health care; Human services; Public affairs.
International interests: Canada; Netherlands; United Kingdom; Spain; Poland; South Africa; Chile; India; Philippines; China; Australia.
Type of support: General/operating support; Annual campaigns; Building/renovation; Program development; Employee volunteer services; Loaned talent; Use of facilities.
Limitations: Giving on a national and international basis in areas of company operations, with emphasis on Orange County, CA, Fernald, OH, Greenville, SC, Fort Bend County, TX, Richland, WA, and in Australia, Canada, Chile, China, India, the Netherlands, the Philippines, Poland, South Africa, Spain, and the United Kingdom. No support for religious or political organizations.
Publications: Application guidelines.
Application information: The Community Relations Department handles giving. The company has a staff that only handles contributions. Application form not required.
   Initial approach: Letter of inquiry to nearest company facility
   Copies of proposal: 1
   Deadline(s): None
   Final notification: 2 to 3 months
Number of staff: 7 full-time professional; 2 full-time support.

2007
Flynn Family Foundation
203 Bluffcove
San Antonio, TX   78216-1920

Established in 1994 in TX.
Donors: Patricia A. Flynn; Robert W. Flynn.
Grantmaker type: Independent foundation.
Financial data (yr. ended 12/31/10): Assets, $770,044 (M); expenditures, $180,650; qualifying distributions, $180,000; giving activities include $180,000 for grants.
Fields of interest: International human rights; Food services; Reproductive health, family planning; Higher education; Crime/violence prevention, gun control; Courts/judicial administration.
Limitations: Applications not accepted. No grants to individuals.
Application information: Unsolicited requests for funds not accepted.
Trustees: Patricia A. Flynn; Robert W. Flynn.
EIN: 746423178

2008
The Fondren Foundation
c/o JPMorgan Chase Trust Dept.
P.O. Box 2558
Houston, TX   77252-8037
Contact: Martie Herrick

Established in 1948 in TX.
Donor: Mrs. W.W. Fondren, Sr.‡.
Grantmaker type: Independent foundation.
Financial data (yr. ended 10/31/09): Assets, $177,864,747 (M); expenditures, $9,091,548; qualifying distributions, $8,021,290; giving activities include $7,710,500 for 76 grants (high: $350,000; low: $12,500; average: $25,000–$150,000).
Purpose and activities: Emphasis on higher and secondary education, social service and youth agencies, cultural organizations, and health.
Fields of interest: Arts; Secondary school/education; Higher education; Health care; Human services; Youth, services.
Type of support: Continuing support; Capital campaigns; Building/renovation; Program development.
Limitations: Applications accepted. Giving primarily in TX, with emphasis on Houston. No grants to individuals, or for annual or operating fund drives.
Publications: Application guidelines.
Application information: Application form not required.
   Initial approach: Letter
   Copies of proposal: 1
   Deadline(s): Feb. 1, May 1, Aug. 1, Nov. 1
   Board meeting date(s): Mar., June, Sept., and Dec.
   Final notification: 3 to 6 months
Officers and Trustees:* Robert E. Fondren,* Chair.; Michael E. Hanson, Jr.,* Vice-Chair.; Laura Trammell Baird,* Secy.-Treas.; Doris Fondren Allday; R. Edwin Allday; Ellanor Allday Camberg; Celia Whitfield Crank; Bentley B. Fondren; Frances Fondren; Leland T. Fondren; Walter W. Fondren III; Walter W. Fondren IV; Marie Fondren Hall; Burton M. Hunson; Catherine Underwood Murray; Michael W. Springer; Carrie Trammell Sturges; Ann Gordon Trammell; Harper B. Trammell; David M. Underwood; David M. Underwood, Jr.; Duncan K. Underwood; Lynda Knapp Underwood; Sue Trammell Whitfield; W. Trammell Whitfield; William F. Whitfield, Jr.
EIN: 746042565
Recent grants for international programs:
2008-1 Amigos de las Americas, Houston, TX, $250,000. For challenge grant. 2009.

2009
The Regina Bauer Frankenberg Foundation
c/o JPMorgan Private Bank, Philanthropic Svcs.
P.O. Box 227237 TX1-2963
Dallas, TX   75222-7237
Contact: Casey Castaneda, Prog. Off.
FAX: (212) 464-2305;
E-mail: casey.b.castaneda@jpmchase.com;
URL: http://foundationcenter.org/grantmaker/frankenberg/

Established in 1994 in NY.
Donor: Regina Bauer Frankenberg‡.
Grantmaker type: Independent foundation.
Financial data (yr. ended 12/31/10): Assets, $21,086,466 (M); expenditures, $1,084,185;

qualifying distributions, $920,052; giving activities include $900,000 for 14 grants (high: $125,000; low: $40,000).

Purpose and activities: Giving exclusively for animal welfare, particularly for the protection of endangered wild animals or threatened species by supporting conservation and research, and for strengthening the capacity of organizations working to reduce the homelessness, mistreatment and euthanasia of companion animals through adoption, training, spaying/neutering, and other programs.

Fields of interest: Animal welfare; Animals/wildlife, preservation/protection.

Type of support: Capital campaigns; Management development/capacity building; Program development.

Limitations: Applications accepted. Giving for companion animals limited to New York, NY; giving for wildlife on a national and international scope. No support for private foundations, or for organizations that will engage in or supply animals for vivisection. No grants to individuals, or for matching gifts; no loans.

Publications: Application guidelines; Grants list.

Application information: Application form not required.

  Initial approach: Proposal
  Copies of proposal: 1
  Deadline(s): July 1
  Board meeting date(s): Nov.
  Final notification: Dec. 31

Trustee: JPMorgan Chase Bank, N.A.

Number of staff: None.

EIN: 133741659

Recent grants for international programs:

2009-1 African People and Wildlife Fund, Bernardsville, NJ, $40,000. For first installment of $80,000 grant for efforts to protect African lion population in Tanzania. 2009.

2009-2 American Bird Conservancy, The Plains, VA, $75,000. For second installment of $150,000 grant for Alliance for Zero Extinction. 2009.

2009-3 Finding Species, Takoma Park, MD, $45,000. For work to save Andean Tapir in Ecuador. 2009.

2010
Freedom Ministries, Inc.

P.O. Box 838
Raymondville, TX   78580-0838   (956) 347-3802
FAX: (956) 347-3430; URL: http://www.freedom-ministries.us

Established in 1981.

Grantmaker type: Public charity.

Financial data (yr. ended 12/31/10): Revenue, $1,077,352; assets, $986,919 (M); gifts received, $1,073,924; expenditures, $1,144,818; program services expenses, $1,116,486; giving activities include $4,000 for grants, $167,250 for grants to organizations outside the U.S., and $2,398 for grants to individuals.

Purpose and activities: The organization conducts missionary work in Mexico and Central America.

Fields of interest: Christian agencies & churches; Religion.

International interests: Mexico; Central America.

Limitations: Applications not accepted. Giving limited to Central America and Mexico.

Application information: Contributes only to pre-selected organizations.

Officers: David Hogan, Pres.; Deborah A. Hogan, V.P.; Joseph Hogan, Secy.; Shawn Williamson, Treas.

EIN: 720991267

2011
Freescale Semiconductor, Inc. Corporate Giving Program

6501 William Cannon Dr. W.
Austin, TX   78735-8523
Contact: Tamika Hickstubbs
E-mail: tamika.hickstubbs@freescale.com; For Asia Pacific and Japan: gloria.shiu@freescale.com; For Europe, the Middle East, and Africa: michel.abitteboul@freescale.com; URL: http://www.freescale.com/webapp/sps/site/homepage.jsp?nodeId=06PfBm

Grantmaker type: Corporate giving program.

Purpose and activities: Freescale makes charitable contributions to nonprofit organizations involved with education, the environment, health, and human services. Support is given primarily in areas of company operations in Arizona and Texas, and in Brazil, Canada, the Czech Republic, Denmark, Finland, France, Germany, Hong Kong, India, Israel, Italy, Japan, Korea, Malaysia, Mexico, the Netherlands, Romania, Russia, Singapore, South Korea, Spain, Sweden, Switzerland, Taiwan, and the United Kingdom.

Fields of interest: Engineering/technology; Mathematics; Science; Elementary/secondary education; Environment; Health care; Human services.

International interests: Brazil; Canada; Czech Republic; Denmark; Finland; France; Germany; Hong Kong; India; Israel; Italy; Japan; Malaysia; Mexico; Netherlands; Romania; Russia; Scotland; Singapore; Spain; Sweden; Switzerland; Taiwan; United Kingdom.

Type of support: General/operating support; Program development; Employee volunteer services; Sponsorships.

Limitations: Applications accepted. Giving primarily in areas of company operations in AZ and TX, and in Brazil, Canada, the Czech Republic, Denmark, Finland, France, Germany, Hong Kong, India, Israel, Italy, Japan, Malaysia, Mexico, the Netherlands, Romania, Russia, Singapore, South Korea, Spain, Sweden, Switzerland, Taiwan, and the United Kingdom.

Application information: Application form required.

  Initial approach: Download online application form and e-mail with required attachments to Community Contact
  Deadline(s): June 1 and Dec. 1

2012
Friedkin Conservation Fund

1375 Enclave Pkwy.
Houston, TX   77077-2026
Contact: Charles L. Williams, Pres.

Grantmaker type: Public charity.

Financial data (yr. ended 12/31/09): Revenue, $310,805; assets, $12,100 (M); gifts received, $310,805; expenditures, $310,805; giving activities include $309,725 for grants.

Purpose and activities: The fund concentrates on the conservation of wildlife, and village assistance such as food, clothing, shelter, and education in Tanzania.

Fields of interest: Environment, natural resources; Economically disadvantaged.

International interests: Tanzania, Zanzibar and Pemba.

Limitations: Giving on an international basis, primarily in Tanzania.

Officers and Directors:* Charles L. Williams,* Pres.; L. Michael Phelps,* Secy.-Treas. and Cont.; Frank X. Gruen; Jerry H. Pyle.

EIN: 760438974

2013
GAIN International

(also known as Global Aid Network)
P.O. Box 139020
Dallas, TX   75313-9020   (972) 234-0800
E-mail: info@gainusa.org; URL: hhttp://www.gainusa.org/
Facebook: http://www.facebook.com/GlobalAidNetwork
Twitter: http://twitter.com/#!/GAINUSA
YouTube: http://www.youtube.com/user/GlobalAidNetwork

Established in 1991.

Grantmaker type: Public charity.

Financial data (yr. ended 08/31/10): Revenue, $33,416,338; assets, $9,700,139 (M); gifts received, $31,775,326; expenditures, $32,140,659; giving activities include $2,788,125 for grants, and $24,262,496 for grants to organizations outside the U.S.

Purpose and activities: The organization is a multi-national network of ministries serving to demonstrate the love of God, through word and deed, to hurting and needy people around the world through relief and development projects.

Fields of interest: Christian agencies & churches; International relief.

Type of support: In-kind gifts.

Limitations: Applications not accepted. Giving on a national and international basis.

Publications: Informational brochure.

Application information: Contributes only to pre-selected organizations.

Officers: Steve Sellers, Chair.; Dr. Marvin Kehler, Pres.; Duane Zook, Pres. and C.E.O.; Rick Ragan, C.O.O. and V.P.; Sally Hauer, Secy.; Roger Craft, Treas.

Directors: Dr. Stephen B. Douglass; Tom Manthei; Dr. Josh McDowell; Tim Starling; Anne Wallace.

EIN: 954578963

2014
General Motors Financial Company, Inc. Contributions Program

(formerly AmeriCredit Corp. Contributions Program)
801 Cherry St., Ste. 3500
Fort Worth, TX   76102-6854
URL: http://www.americredit.com/Customers/About/community_involvement.asp

Grantmaker type: Corporate giving program.

Purpose and activities: AmeriCredit makes charitable contributions to nonprofit organizations involved with health, human services, and on a case by case basis. Support is given primarily in areas of company operations in Chandler, Arizona, Charlotte, North Carolina, and Arlington and Fortworth, Texas, and in Ontario, Canada; giving also to national organizations.

Fields of interest: United Ways and Federated Giving Programs; Salvation Army; Health organizations; Genetic diseases and disorders; General charitable giving.

International interests: Canada.

Type of support: General/operating support; Employee volunteer services.

Limitations: Giving primarily in areas of company operations in Chandler, AZ, Charlotte, NC, and Fortworth, TX, and in Canada; giving also to national organizations.

Application information: National organizations are chosen for Signature Events based on employee interest, number of people and communities served, and availability of volunteer opportunities for AmeriCredit employees.

2015
Vijay and Marie Goradia Charitable Foundation

16800 Imperial Valley Dr., Ste. 499
Houston, TX 77060-3134

Established in 2006 in TX.

Donors: Vijay P. Goradia; Marie G. Goradia.

Grantmaker type: Independent foundation.

Financial data (yr. ended 12/31/10): Assets, $11,047,112 (M); gifts received, $9,414,208; expenditures, $330,473; qualifying distributions, $318,336; giving activities include $317,000 for 14 grants (high: $125,000; low: $1,000).

Fields of interest: Minorities/immigrants, centers/services; United Ways and Federated Giving Programs; International development.

Limitations: Applications not accepted. Giving primarily in NY and TX. No grants to individuals.

Application information: Contributes only to pre-selected organizations.

Officers: Sapphira Goradia, Pres. and Treas.; Vijay P. Goradia, V.P.; Marie G. Goradia, Secy.

EIN: 205835715

2016
Antonio Haghenbeck y de La Lama Foundation, Inc.

1319 Edwards Dr.
San Leon, TX 77539-9647

Established in 1986 in TX.

Donor: Antonio Haghenbeck y de La Lama†.

Grantmaker type: Independent foundation.

Financial data (yr. ended 11/30/10): Assets, $4,145,331 (M); expenditures, $1,061,330; qualifying distributions, $142,715; giving activities include $142,715 for grants.

Purpose and activities: Giving for prevention of cruelty to animals.

Fields of interest: Animal welfare.

International interests: Mexico.

Limitations: Applications accepted. Giving primarily in Mexico. No grants to individuals.

Application information:
Initial approach: Letter
Deadline(s): None

Officers and Directors:* Carmela Rivero Jimenez,* Pres.; Mary Jo Gutierrez,* V.P. and Treas.; Roy Diaz Gonzalez,* Secy.

EIN: 760227001

2017
James and Gayle Halperin Foundation
(formerly James Halperin Foundation)
3500 Maple Ave., Ste. 1700
Dallas, TX 75219-3941

Established in 1989 in TX.

Donor: James L. Halperin.

Grantmaker type: Independent foundation.

Financial data (yr. ended 12/31/10): Assets, $4,754,762 (M); gifts received, $590,000; expenditures, $182,704; qualifying distributions, $164,954; giving activities include $164,954 for grants.

Purpose and activities: Giving primarily for the arts, education, health, and international relief.

Fields of interest: Performing arts; Performing arts, dance; Education; Health care; Health organizations; Genetic diseases and disorders research; Youth, services; International relief.

Limitations: Applications not accepted. No grants to individuals.

Application information: Unsolicited requests for funds not accepted.

Officers: James L. Halperin, Pres.; Abigail Halperin, V.P.; Marjorie Halperin, V.P.

EIN: 752294319

2018
Hines Interests L.P. Corporate Giving Program

2800 Post Oak Blvd.
Houston, TX 77056-6100 (713) 621-8000
FAX: (713) 966-2636; URL: http://www.hines.com/careers/community.aspx

Grantmaker type: Corporate giving program.

Purpose and activities: Hines makes charitable contributions to nonprofit organizations involved with arts and culture, the environment, youth development, community development, and on a case by case basis. Support is given primarily in areas of company operations in San Francisco, California, Atlanta, Georgia, Chicago, Illinois, New York, New York, and Houston, Texas, and in Brazil, Canada, China, France, Germany, India, Ireland, Italy, Luxembourg, Mexico, Panama, Poland, Russia, Spain, Turkey, the United Arab Emirates and the United Kingdom.

Fields of interest: Community/economic development; Youth development; Environment; Elementary/secondary education; Arts; General charitable giving.

International interests: Brazil; Canada; China; France; Germany; India; Ireland; Italy; Luxembourg; Mexico; Panama; Poland; Russia; Spain; Turkey; United Arab Emirates; United Kingdom.

Type of support: General/operating support; Employee volunteer services.

Limitations: Giving primarily in areas of company operations in San Francisco, CA, Atlanta, GA, Chicago, IL, New York, NY, and Houston, TX, and in Brazil, Canada, China, France, Germany, India, Ireland, Italy, Luxembourg, Mexico, Panama, Poland, Russia, Spain, Turkey, the United Arab Emirates and the United Kingdom.

2019
His Broadcasting, Inc.

P.O. Box 247
Comfort, TX 78013-0247

Established in TX.

Grantmaker type: Public charity.

Financial data (yr. ended 12/31/10): Revenue, $21,985; assets, $103,915 (M); gifts received, $21,985; expenditures, $23,789; giving activities include $20,339 for grants.

Fields of interest: Education; Christian agencies & churches.

International interests: Uganda.

Type of support: Scholarships—to individuals.

Limitations: Applications not accepted. Giving primarily in TX, NJ, FL, and CA.

Application information: Unsolicited requests for funds not accepted.

Officers: M. Diane White, Pres.; Ted Lyons, Secy.-Treas.

Directors: Winston Martin; Kay Pergrem.

EIN: 237212872

2020
Huntsman Corporation Contributions Program

10003 Woodloch Forest Dr., Ste. 260
The Woodlands, TX 77380-1955
URL: http://www.huntsman.com/eng/Sustainability/Social_responsibility/Social_responsibility/index.cfm?PageID=8646

Grantmaker type: Corporate giving program.

Purpose and activities: Huntsman makes charitable contributions to nonprofit organizations involved with education, cancer, international relief, and homeless people. Support is given primarily in areas of company operations, with emphasis on Utah, and in Armenia.

Fields of interest: International relief; Education; Cancer; International development; Economic development; Business/industry; Community/economic development; Economically disadvantaged; Homeless.

International interests: Armenia.

Type of support: General/operating support; Scholarship funds; Employee volunteer services; Grants to individuals.

Limitations: Giving primarily in areas of company operations, with emphasis on UT, and in Armenia.

2021
Interdenominational Christian Missions, Inc.

30260 Saratoga Ln.
Fair Oaks Ranch, TX 78015-4232
URL: http://www.icmweb.org
Blog: http://www.icmweb.org/category/blog/
Video: http://www.icmweb.org/category/video/

Established in 1997 in TX.

Donors: Ralph E. Fair, Jr.; Michael Clark; Carole Clark; William Greendyke; Craig Spalding; Darlene Spalding; M.L. Stanley; First Baptist Church Boerne; The Covenant Foundation; Community Bible Church; Woodbridge Baptist Church; Tim Hill Evangelical Ministry.

Grantmaker type: Operating foundation.

Financial data (yr. ended 12/31/10): Assets, $97,205 (M); gifts received, $546,736; expenditures, $672,179; qualifying distributions, $667,786; giving activities include $509,133 for 8 grants (high: $390,056; low: $2,642).

Purpose and activities: Giving to Christian organizations performing evangelistic and human services, and for operating orphanages.
Fields of interest: Human services; Christian agencies & churches.
International interests: Central America; Costa Rica; Honduras; Peru; South America.
Limitations: Applications not accepted. Giving primarily in Peru, with some giving in Costa Rica and Honduras.
Application information: Unsolicited requests for funds not accepted.
Officers and Directors:* Ralph E. Fair, Jr.,* Pres.; Dennis Smith,* V.P.; Michael Gauntt, Secy.; Greg Harper,* Treas.; Fred Jones; John Kelly; John Davis Martinez; Tim Stromstad; Robert Trolese; Robert Wilmarth.
EIN: 742798861

2022
Interfaith Ministries for Greater Houston
3217 Montrose Blvd.
Houston, TX   77006-3929   (713) 533-4900
URL: http://www.imgh.org

Established in 1992 in TX.
Grantmaker type: Public charity.
Financial data (yr. ended 12/31/10): Revenue, $11,868,520; assets, $5,685,240 (M); gifts received, $11,548,099; expenditures, $11,276,062; giving activities include $4,692,132 for grants to individuals.
Purpose and activities: The organization brings together people of all faiths from the greater Houston area to advocate for the needs and rights of at-risk and special needs children, enhance the independence and dignity of low-income seniors, and improve the quality of life for refugees. Financial assistance, including rental and food assistance, is provided.
Fields of interest: Food distribution, meals on wheels; Children/youth, services; Children, services; Family services; Aging, centers/services; International migration/refugee issues; Religion, interfaith issues; Aging.
Type of support: Grants to individuals.
Limitations: Giving limited to the greater metropolitan Houston, TX, area.
Officers and Directors:* Rev. Dr. L. James Bankston,* Chair.; Charles Erickson,* 1st Vice-Chair.; Elliot Gershenson,* Pres. and C.E.O.; Jay Thomas,* Secy.; Pat Brown, Treas.; James Calaway; Brian Cooper; Dr. Jaime de la Sala; Deacon Sam Dunning; Hon. Robert Eckels; Charles Foster; Ajit Giani; Aziz Jamaluddin; Judy Jeng; Hon. William E. King; Dr. Fatima Mawji; Albert Myres; Bobbie Osadchey; Zuhaira Razzack; Dick Steele; Chris Wilmot.
EIN: 741488102

2023
International Medical Outreach, Inc.
915 Gessner Rd., Ste. 620
Houston, TX   77024-2551   (713) 935-9057
Contact: Todd Price, Pres.
URL: http://www.imoutreach.com

Established in 1997 in TX.
Donors: Todd Price, M.D.; William Lee; Donna Greer; Ingrid Sharon, M.D.; Leticia J. Dizov; Lakewood Church; Christian Alliance for

Humanitarian Aid; Medical Bridges, Inc.; Feed the Children.
Grantmaker type: Operating foundation.
Financial data (yr. ended 12/31/10): Assets, $1,255,092 (M); gifts received, $166,615,340; expenditures, $170,171,278; qualifying distributions, $170,001,005; giving activities include $170,001,005 for 29 grants (high: $47,350,000; low: $250).
Purpose and activities: The grantmaker provides health care for those in need on a worldwide basis. It concentrates on efforts towards the relief of infectious diseases, including malaria, HIV/AIDS, tuberculosis, pneumonia, and diarrhea in addition to other diseases. It also establishes and assists existing medical clinics, orphanages, feeding centers, drug rehabilitation projects and teaching centers among other humanitarian efforts.
Fields of interest: Diseases (rare); Food services; Children, services; Children, adoption; AIDS; Substance abuse, treatment; Health care; Health care, clinics/centers; Public health; Health care, support services; International relief.
Type of support: General/operating support.
Limitations: Giving primarily on an international basis.
Application information: Applicants must also include the need for medical supplies and equipment, as well as the Christian-related organization with which they are affiliated.
  Initial approach: Letter
  Deadline(s): None
Officers: Todd Price, M.D., Pres.; Susan Price, V.P.; Robert Liken, Secy.; Justin Osteen, Treas.
EIN: 760392915

2024
International Technical Assistance Group
P.O. Box 861482
Plano, TX   75086-1482   (206) 781-5138
E-mail: info@itagonline.org; URL: http://www.itagonline.org/

Established in 1983.
Grantmaker type: Public charity.
Financial data (yr. ended 09/30/10): Revenue, $4,990,963; assets, $38,461 (M); gifts received, $4,990,907; expenditures, $4,990,963; giving activities include $1,969,003 for grants to organizations outside the U.S., and $144,693 for grants to individuals.
Purpose and activities: The organization works to promote holistic development in Asia and Eastern Europe by helping people become more productive members of society through helping the ppor so that they can leave lives of poverty through various community and business development projects, assisting nationals with education and services (such as teaching English), and facilitating ex-patriate Western workers to adapt and live cross-culturally.
Fields of interest: Human services; International development; International affairs.
Limitations: Giving on a national and international basis.
Officers: Laron Olson, Chair.; Ken Smith, Treas.; Annetta Whiteley, Secy.
Board Members: Jerry Carlisle; Peter Henley; Gib Martin; Laron Olson; Kent Parks; Gwen Reese; Kyle Usrey; Rick Watkins.
EIN: 911216866

2025
Jiv Daya Foundation
12222 Merit Dr., Ste. 820
Dallas, TX   75251-3207   (214) 360-7473
Contact: Sarah Hunt Oswald, Grants Coord.
FAX: (214) 360-7471;
E-mail: info@jivdayafound.org; Tel. for Sarah Hunt Oswald: (214) 360-7484; e-mail: shoswald@jivdayafound.org. Additional fax: (214) 593-1902; URL: http://www.jivdayafound.org

Established in 2002 in TX.
Donors: Vinay K. Jain; Kanika Virmani Jain.
Grantmaker type: Independent foundation.
Financial data (yr. ended 12/31/09): Assets, $76,570,783 (M); gifts received, $6,500,000; expenditures, $3,562,785; qualifying distributions, $3,501,222; giving activities include $3,405,448 for 17 grants (high: $2,750,000; low: $912).
Purpose and activities: Giving to support education and health care internationally.
Fields of interest: Education; Medical research, institute; Philanthropy/voluntarism.
International interests: India.
Limitations: Giving primarily in MA and India.
Application information: Application guidelines and information available on foundation web site.
  Initial approach: Letter via e-mail or U.S. mail
Officers and Directors:* Vinay K. Jain,* Pres. and Treas.; Kanika Virmani Jain,* V.P. and Secy.; Yash Paul Virmani.
EIN: 320045123

2026
Jubilee Centre, Inc.
c/o Dr. Bryan Boatwright, M.D.
2704 Hartlee Ct.
Denton, TX   76208-3544
E-mail: mail@jubileecentre.org; URL: http://jubileecentre.org
Facebook: https://www.facebook.com/pages/Jubilee-Centre-Zambia/121811704557647
RSS Feed: http://www.jubileecentre.org/feed/

Established in 2000.
Grantmaker type: Public charity.
Financial data (yr. ended 12/31/10): Revenue, $112,539; assets, $30,550 (M); gifts received, $112,385; expenditures, $129,098; program services expenses, $127,275; giving activities include $127,275 for 3 grants (high: $97,000; low: $13,000).
Purpose and activities: The organization supports missionary work in Zambia.
Fields of interest: Religion.
International interests: Zambia.
Limitations: Applications not accepted. Giving limited to AR and Zambia. No grants to individuals.
Application information: Contributes only to pre-selected organizations.
Officers: Prisca Kambole, Chair.; Rev. Joe Simfukwe, Vice-Chair.; Dr. Neal Smith, Secy.; Rev. Lawrence Temfwe, Exec. Dir.
EIN: 860845171

2027
The Karakin Foundation
P.O. Box 2079
Abilene, TX   79604-2079

Established in 1997 in TX.

Donors: Joseph B. Matthews; Julia Jones Matthews.
Grantmaker type: Independent foundation.
Financial data (yr. ended 12/31/10): Assets, $52,662,650 (M); gifts received, $150,807; expenditures, $2,705,348; qualifying distributions, $1,801,964; giving activities include $1,801,964 for grants.
Fields of interest: International affairs, equal rights; Children/youth, services.
Limitations: Applications not accepted. Giving primarily in NJ. No grants to individuals.
Application information: Contributes only to pre-selected organizations.
Officers and Directors:* Joseph B. Matthews,* Pres.; Leroy Bolt,* V.P. and Treas.; David L. Buhrmann,* Secy.
EIN: 752692023

2028
Kimberly-Clark Corporation Contributions Program
351 Phelps Dr.
Irving, TX 75038-6507
URL: http://www.kimberly-clark.com/sustainability/people/communities.aspx

Grantmaker type: Corporate giving program.
Purpose and activities: As a complement to its foundation, Kimberly-Clark also makes charitable contributions to nonprofit organizations directly. Support is given on a national and international basis in areas of company operations.
Fields of interest: YM/YWCAs & YM/YWHAs; United Ways and Federated Giving Programs; Youth development, business; Hospitals (general); Education; Environment, natural resources; Environment, forests; Health care; Breast cancer; Boys & girls clubs; American Red Cross; Children, services; Family services; International relief; General charitable giving.
Type of support: General/operating support; Continuing support; Scholarship funds; Cause-related marketing; Employee volunteer services; Sponsorships; Donated products; In-kind gifts.
Limitations: Giving on a national and international basis in areas of company operations.

2029
Kimberly-Clark Foundation, Inc.
351 Phelps Dr.
Irving, TX 75038-6507 (972) 281-1200
Application address: P.O. Box 619100, Dallas, TX 75261-9100; URL: http://www.kimberly-clark.com/ourcompany/community/kc_foundation.aspx

Incorporated in 1952 in WI.
Donors: Kimberly-Clark Corp.; P.D. and Tracy Parsons Trust.
Grantmaker type: Company-sponsored foundation.
Financial data (yr. ended 12/31/10): Assets, $21,511 (M); gifts received, $4,498,414; expenditures, $4,371,346; qualifying distributions, $4,366,470; giving activities include $1,476,104 for grants, $1,472,500 for grants to individuals, and $1,325,001 for employee matching gifts.
Purpose and activities: The foundation supports organizations involved with arts and culture, education, the environment, health, and human services.

Fields of interest: Arts; Higher education; Education; Environment, natural resources; Environment; Hospitals (general); Health care; Salvation Army; Children/youth, services; Family services; Human services; United Ways and Federated Giving Programs.
Type of support: Capital campaigns; General/operating support; Continuing support; Program development; Curriculum development; Employee volunteer services; Sponsorships; Employee matching gifts; Employee-related scholarships.
Limitations: Applications accepted. Giving primarily in areas of company operations, with emphasis on CA and TX; giving also to national organizations. No support for religious or political organizations. No grants to individuals (except for employee-related scholarships), or for sports or athletic activities; no loans.
Publications: Corporate giving report; Financial statement.
Application information: Unsolicited requests from national or international organizations are not accepted. Application form not required.
   Initial approach: Proposal to nearest K-C site manager
   Deadline(s): None
Officers and Directors: Anthony J. Palmer, Pres.; Mark A. Buthman, V.P.; Jennifer L. Lewis, V.P.; Timothy C. Everett, Secy.; Steven E. Voskuil, Treas.; Thomas J. Falk.
Number of staff: 1 full-time professional; 1 full-time support.
EIN: 396044304
Recent grants for international programs:
2029-1 CARE USA, Atlanta, GA, $50,000. For general operating support. 2009.
2029-2 Conservation International, Arlington, VA, $250,000. For general operating support. 2009.
2029-3 Nanjing Charity Foundation, Nanjing, China, $100,000. For general operating support. 2009.
2029-4 Salvation Army Australia, Southern Territory, Blackburn, Australia, $50,000. For general operating support. 2009.
2029-5 World Resources Institute, Washington, DC, $50,000. For general operating support. 2009.
2029-6 World Vision Taiwan, Taipei, Taiwan, $50,000. For general operating support. 2009.

2030
Kingdom Foundation
109 Enterprise Pkwy., Ste. 202
Boerne, TX 78006

Established in 2005 in NM.
Grantmaker type: Independent foundation.
Financial data (yr. ended 12/31/10): Assets, $359,039 (M); gifts received, $300,785; expenditures, $237,921; qualifying distributions, $230,000; giving activities include $230,000 for 1 grant.
Purpose and activities: Giving primarily to further the charitable and religious mission of a Christian organization in Japan.
Fields of interest: Pregnancy centers; Christian agencies & churches.
International interests: Japan.
Limitations: Applications not accepted. Giving primarily in Japan; some giving also in TX.
Application information: Contributes only to pre-selected organizations.
Officers and Directors:* Charles J. Gyurko,* Pres. and Exec. Dir.; Sadie D. Gyurko,* V.P.; William H.

Arthur, Secy.-Treas. and C.F.O.; James A. Arthur; Paul C. Arthur; Claire Arthur Honsalek.
EIN: 203816832

2031
Kowitz Family Foundation
1901 N. Akard St.
Dallas, TX 75201-2305

Established in 1997 in TX.
Donors: Sarah Kowitz; David Kowitz.
Grantmaker type: Independent foundation.
Financial data (yr. ended 12/31/09): Assets, $1,268,957 (M); expenditures, $305,921; qualifying distributions, $302,800; giving activities include $301,800 for 11 grants (high: $100,000; low: $300), and $1,000 for 1 grant to an individual.
Fields of interest: Museums; Visual arts; Education; Environment; Human services; International development; Children/youth.
Type of support: General/operating support; Scholarships—to individuals.
Limitations: Applications not accepted. Giving primarily in NY, with emphasis on Garrison and New York; giving also in Washington, DC, and London, England.
Application information: Unsolicited requests for funds not accepted.
Officers and Trustees:* David Kowitz,* Pres. and Treas.; Sarah Kowitz,* V.P. and Secy.; Julie Miller.
EIN: 752707561

2032
Limiar U.S.A., Inc.
111 Broken Bough
San Antonio, TX 78231-1203 (210) 479-0300
FAX: (210) 479-3835; E-mail: limiar@limiar.org; URL: http://www.limiar.org

Established in 1987.
Grantmaker type: Public charity.
Financial data (yr. ended 12/31/10): Revenue, $118,503; assets, $12,930 (M); gifts received, $99,516; expenditures, $131,139.
Purpose and activities: The organization provides assistance in adoptions and sponsorships that benefit Brazilian children.
Fields of interest: Children, adoption.
International interests: Brazil.
Type of support: Grants to individuals.
Limitations: Giving primarily in Brazil.
Officers: Stuart Cameron, Pres.; Lane Cameron, V.P. and Secy.; Thomas Cameron, V.P. and Treas.
EIN: 341461670

2033
The Link Foundation
c/o H. David Hughes
111 Congress Ave., Ste. 1400
Austin, TX 78701-4093 (512) 472-5456
Contact: Joe W. Bratcher III, Pres.

Established in 1985 in TX.
Donor: Joe W. Bratcher III.
Grantmaker type: Independent foundation.
Financial data (yr. ended 12/31/10): Assets, $1,283,027 (M); gifts received, $153,350; expenditures, $388,255; qualifying distributions, $381,666; giving activities include $381,666 for grants.

Purpose and activities: Giving primarily for human services, health care, and relief organizations.
Fields of interest: Hospitals (general); Arts; Health organizations, association; Food banks; Human services; Children/youth, services; Family services, domestic violence; International relief; International human rights; United Ways and Federated Giving Programs.
Limitations: Giving primarily in Austin, TX. No grants to individuals.
Application information:
Initial approach: Letter
Deadline(s): Sept. 30
Officers: Joe W. Bratcher III, Pres. and Treas.; Brigid Anne Cockrum, V.P. and Secy.
Director: Elizbieta Szoka.
EIN: 742387802

2034
Living Water International
P.O. Box 35496
Houston, TX 77235-5496 (281) 207-7800
Contact: Gary L. Evans, Exec. Dir.
FAX: (281) 207-7845; E-mail: info@water.cc; Additional address (Great Lakes office): 100 S. Pine St., Ste. 388, Zeeland, MI 49464-2612; toll-free tel.: (877) 594-4426; e-mail for Gary L. Evans: gary@water.cc; URL: http://www.water.cc/
Facebook: http://www.facebook.com/livingwaterinternational
Flickr: http://www.flickr.com/photos/lwi/
RSS Feed: http://feeds2.feedburner.com/lwinews
YouTube: http://www.youtube.com/results?search_query=living+water+international

Established in 1990 in TX.
Grantmaker type: Public charity.
Financial data (yr. ended 12/31/10): Revenue, $17,271,070; assets, $7,987,109 (M); gifts received, $17,281,951; expenditures, $16,211,788; giving activities include $96,447 for grants, and $13,000 for grants to individuals.
Purpose and activities: The organization provides desperately needed clean water and medical attention.
Fields of interest: Health care; Environment, waste management; Environment, water resources; Christian agencies & churches; Religion.
International interests: Africa; Asia; Central America; South America.
Limitations: Applications not accepted. Giving on an international basis, with emphasis on Africa, Central and South America, Europe, India, and Mexico.
Publications: Annual report; Financial statement; Informational brochure; Newsletter.
Application information: Unsolicited requests for funds not accepted or acknowledged.
Board meeting date(s): Jan. 18, Apr. 19, July 19, and Oct. 18
Officers: Gary W. Loveless,* Chair.; Jerry Wiles, Pres.; Malcolm Morris, Exec. V.P.; Lewis "Lew" Hough, V.P.; Tim Mulville, V.P.; Bruce Whitmire, V.P.; Jay Brown,* Treas.; Gary L. Evans, Exec. Dir.
Directors: Mollie J. Allen; Richard Bischoff; Bob D. Boozer; Hollis Bullard; Keith D. Hatch; Becky Morris; Robert J. Pettigrew; Dr. Roy Rhodes; Jeffrey R. Singer; Mark D. Stouse.
Number of staff: 25 full-time professional; 5 part-time professional; 36 full-time support; 5 part-time support.
EIN: 760324875

2035
Manna Energy Foundation
957 NASA Pkwy., Ste. 560
Houston, TX 77058-3039
URL: http://www.mannaenergy.org
Facebook: http://www.facebook.com/MannaEnergy

Established in TX.
Grantmaker type: Public charity.
Financial data (yr. ended 12/31/10): Revenue, $336,285; assets, $337,880 (M); gifts received, $336,263; expenditures, $40,835; giving activities include $8,220 for grants to individuals.
Purpose and activities: Giving to systematically eradicate poverty, in the long term, in the developing world through the application of sustainable economies that are enabled through technology development and the provision of sustainable systems to provide clean energy and clean water.
Fields of interest: International development; Environment, water resources; Environment, energy; Community/economic development, management/technical assistance.
Limitations: Applications not accepted. Giving primarily in CO. No grants to individuals.
Application information: Contributes only to pre-selected organizations.
Officers: Christopher Stott, Chair.; Michael Potter, Vice-Chair.; John Garan, Treas.; Ron Garan, Founder.
EIN: 202915348

2036
The Carolyn and Mike Maples Foundation
2208 Windsor Rd.
Austin, TX 78703-3115
Contact: Michael J. Maples, Ir.

Established in 2000 in TX.
Donors: Jane Carolyn Maples; Michael J. Maples.
Grantmaker type: Independent foundation.
Financial data (yr. ended 04/30/10): Assets, $236,433 (M); gifts received, $50,000; expenditures, $144,596; qualifying distributions, $141,500; giving activities include $141,500 for 12 grants (high: $100,000; low: $500).
Fields of interest: International affairs; Museums (children's); Museums (history); Education; Hospitals (general); Human services; United Ways and Federated Giving Programs.
Limitations: Applications accepted. Giving primarily in TX.
Application information:
Initial approach: Letter
Deadline(s): None
Trustees: Jane Carolyn Maples; Michael J. Maples.
EIN: 916500136

2037
Tom and Charlene Marsh Family Foundation
P.O. Box 460
Dallas, TX 75221-0460

Established in 2007 in TX.
Donors: Marsh Foundation, Inc.; Estelle Fariss Marsh†.
Grantmaker type: Independent foundation.
Financial data (yr. ended 12/31/10): Assets, $8,138,828 (M); gifts received, $18,357;

expenditures, $369,202; qualifying distributions, $345,250; giving activities include $345,250 for 40 grants (high: $35,000; low: $100).
Fields of interest: Christian agencies & churches; Museums (art); Performing arts, orchestras; International affairs, foreign policy; Performing arts; Elementary/secondary education; Higher education; Hospitals (general); Human services; International affairs; Protestant agencies & churches.
Type of support: General/operating support; Endowments; Program development.
Limitations: Applications not accepted. Giving primarily in NJ, New York, NY, and Dallas and San Antonio, TX. No grants to individuals.
Application information: Contributes only to pre-selected organizations.
Officers: Tom F. Marsh, Chair.; Charlene Marsh, Pres.; Joe Coffman, V.P. and Secy.; William E. Allen, Treas.
Directors: Tennessee E. Kellogg; Charlene C. Marsh; Charles A. Marsh.
EIN: 260177017

2038
The Mattsson McHale Foundation
3300 Bee Cave Rd., Ste. 650, No. 1311
Austin, TX 78746-6663
Contact: Christine Mattsson, Dir.

Established in 1995 in TX.
Donors: John McHale; Christine Mattsson.
Grantmaker type: Independent foundation.
Financial data (yr. ended 12/31/10): Assets, $2,468,658 (M); expenditures, $731,276; qualifying distributions, $727,011; giving activities include $727,011 for grants.
Fields of interest: International affairs, national security; Museums (art); Elementary/secondary education.
Limitations: Applications accepted. Giving primarily in TX; some giving also in Washington, DC. No grants to individuals.
Publications: Annual report.
Application information: Application form not required.
Initial approach: Letter
Deadline(s): None
Directors: Christine Mattsson; Sharon Mattsson; John McHale.
EIN: 752623152

2039
The Eugene McDermott Foundation
3808 Euclid Ave.
Dallas, TX 75205-3102
Contact: Mary McDermott Cook, Pres.

Incorporated in 1972 in TX; absorbed The McDermott Foundation in 1977.
Donors: Eugene McDermott†; Mrs. Eugene McDermott.
Grantmaker type: Independent foundation.
Financial data (yr. ended 08/31/10): Assets, $91,691,115 (M); expenditures, $6,645,640; qualifying distributions, $6,317,263; giving activities include $6,228,740 for 108 grants (high: $1,000,000; low: $1,000; average: $5,000–$100,000).
Purpose and activities: Support primarily for cultural programs, higher and secondary education, health, and general community interests.

Fields of interest: Arts; Children/youth, services; Community/economic development; Education; Education, early childhood education; Elementary school/education; United Ways and Federated Giving Programs; Government/public administration; Health care; Health organizations, association; Higher education; Historic preservation/historical societies; Hospitals (general); International human rights; Medical research, institute; Museums; Secondary school/education; Homeless; Economically disadvantaged; Terminal illness, people with; Substance abusers; Single parents; Crime/abuse victims; AIDS, people with; Young adults, male; Boys; Men; Young adults, female; Girls; Women; Disabilities, people with; Native Americans/American Indians; Indigenous peoples; Hispanics/Latinos; African Americans/Blacks; Physically disabled; Mentally disabled; Deaf/hearing impaired; Blind/visually impaired; Young adults; Children/youth; Children; Youth; Aging; Adults; Minorities.
Type of support: General/operating support; Continuing support; Annual campaigns; Capital campaigns; Building/renovation; Equipment; Land acquisition; Endowments; Program development; Professorships; Seed money; Curriculum development; Scholarship funds; Research; Matching/challenge support.
Limitations: Applications accepted. Giving primarily in Dallas, TX. No grants to individuals.
Application information: No printed material available. Application form not required.
  Initial approach: Letter
  Copies of proposal: 1
  Deadline(s): None
  Board meeting date(s): Quarterly
  Final notification: Prior to Aug. 31
Officers and Trustees:* Mary McDermott Cook,* Pres.; Patricia Brown, Secy.; J.H. Cullum Clark; Dr. Liza Lee; Mrs. Eugene McDermott; Sam Self; C.J. Thomsen.
Agent: Bank of America, N.A.
Number of staff: 2 part-time professional.
EIN: 237237919
Recent grants for international programs:
2039-1 Angel Wings International, Fort Lauderdale, FL, $10,000. For Hope and Health in Haiti. 2010.

2040
Menil Foundation, Inc.
1519 Branard St.
Houston, TX   77006-4721

Incorporated in 1953 in TX. Classified as a private operating foundation in 1972.
Donors: Dominique de Menil‡; John de Menil‡.
Grantmaker type: Public charity.
Financial data (yr. ended 06/30/10): Revenue, $49,629,246; assets, $567,939,489 (M); gifts received, $40,359,679; expenditures, $14,474,717; giving activities include $95,470 for grants.
Purpose and activities: A private operating foundation primarily exhibiting its art collection at Rice University in Houston, and museums throughout the world; currently building a museum in Houston, to permanently house and exhibit its collection; supports art centers at Rice University.
Fields of interest: Visual arts; Performing arts; Arts.
International interests: Italy.
Limitations: Applications not accepted. Giving primarily in Houston, TX. No grants to individuals.

Application information: Contributes only to pre-selected organizations.
Officers and Directors:* Louisa Sarofim,* Pres.; Miles Glaser,* V.P. and C.F.O.; James A. Elkins, V.P.; L. Henry Gissel, Jr., Secy.; Adelaide Carpenter; Mrs. Christopher DeMenil; Francois DeMenil; Walter Hopps; Susan O'Connor; Francesco Pellizzi; George Stark; Paul Winkler; and 2 additional directors.
EIN: 746045327

2041
Mercy Ships
P.O. Box 2020
Lindale, TX   75771-2020   (903) 939-7000
FAX: (903) 882-0336; E-mail: info@mercyships.org; URL: http://www.mercyships.org

Established in 1978.
Grantmaker type: Public charity.
Financial data (yr. ended 12/31/08): Revenue, $23,584,963; assets, $7,403,216 (M); gifts received, $21,583,441; expenditures, $29,587,411; giving activities include $330,540 for grants, $4,247,886 for grants to organizations outside the U.S., and $40,808 for grants to individuals.
Purpose and activities: Mercy Ships seeks to bring hope and healing to the poor by mobilizing people and resources worldwide.
Fields of interest: International relief; Human services; Voluntarism promotion.
Type of support: In-kind gifts.
Limitations: Applications not accepted. Giving on a national and international basis.
Publications: Annual report.
Application information: Unsolicited requests for funds not accepted.
  Board meeting date(s): Quarterly
Officers and Directors:* Myron E. Ullman III,* Chair.; William S. Kanaga,* Vice-Chair.; Prof. Lord McColl, Vice-Chair.; Donald K. Stephens,* Pres.; Sam Smith,* C.E.O.; Ronald L. Goode,* Secy.; Peter B. Schulze,* Treas.; Gary Brown; Michael Cowan; and 12 additional directors.
EIN: 953793975

2042
Mission to Unreached Peoples
P.O. Box 860548
Plano, TX   75086-0548   (469) 814-8222
Contact: Tim Swaugar, U.S. Dir.
FAX: (469) 375-1794; E-mail: mupinfo@mup.org; Toll-free tel.: (888) 847-6950; URL: http://www.mup.org

Established in 1981.
Grantmaker type: Public charity.
Financial data (yr. ended 09/30/10): Revenue, $5,775,536; assets, $1,915,357 (M); gifts received, $5,729,403; expenditures, $6,034,469; giving activities include $4,901,631 for grants.
Purpose and activities: The organization works to champion the potential of lay people and create a channel for ministry by recruiting, training, placing, facilitating, and caring for them, and to gain access to unreached people groups by responding to both physical and spiritual needs; services include Bible schools and training centers, children's ministries, church planting/evangelism, ESL teaching, health care, relief and development, and youth ministry.

Fields of interest: Religion, association; Christian agencies & churches.
International interests: Europe; Asia.
Type of support: Technical assistance; Management development/capacity building; In-kind gifts; General/operating support; Endowments; Employee matching gifts; Continuing support; Capital campaigns.
Limitations: Applications not accepted. Giving on an international basis.
Publications: Annual report; Financial statement; Informational brochure; Newsletter.
Application information: Unsolicited requests for funds not accepted.
  Board meeting date(s): Jan., Apr., July, and Oct.
Officers and Directors:* Dan Edds,* Chair.; Annetta Whiteley,* Secy.; Gib Martin; Todd Smith; Ron Wayman.
Number of staff: 6 full-time support; 6 part-time support.
EIN: 911171837

2043
New Media Centers
6101 W. Courtyard, Bldg. 1, Ste. 100
Austin, TX   78730-5115   (512) 425-4200
FAX: (512) 445-4205; URL: http://www.nmc.org

Established in 1994 in CA.
Grantmaker type: Public charity.
Financial data (yr. ended 12/31/08): Revenue, $2,085,169; assets, $1,133,524 (M); gifts received, $545,031; expenditures, $2,066,379; program services expenses, $1,772,729.
Purpose and activities: The organization is an international consortium of learning-focused organization dedicated to the exploration and use of new media and new technologies.
Fields of interest: Higher education; Education, association; Education; Public affairs.
International interests: Vietnam; Venezuela; United Arab Emirates; Turkey; Thailand; Taiwan; Switzerland; Sweden; Spain; South Africa; Slovakia; Singapore; Russia; Romania; Portugal; Poland; Philippines; Peru; Norway; New Zealand; Netherlands; Mexico; Malaysia; Luxembourg; South Korea; Kenya; Japan; Italy; Israel; Ireland; Indonesia; India; Hungary; Hong Kong; United Kingdom; Greece; Germany; France; Finland; Egypt; Ecuador; Denmark; Czech Republic; Costa Rica; Colombia; China; Chile; Canada; Brazil; Belgium; Australia; Austria; Argentina.
Limitations: Giving on a national and international basis.
Publications: Annual report; Informational brochure.
Officers and Directors:* Don Henderson,* Chair.; Holly Willis,* Vice-Chair.; Larry Johnson,* C.E.O.; Matt Woolsey,* Treas.; Danah Boyd; Gardner Campbell; Peter Isaacson; Clifford Lynch; Peter Samis; Marco Torres.

2044
The Marilyn and Sonny Oates Foundation
6300 Cedar Springs
Dallas, TX   75235-5809

Established in 2006 in TX.
Donors: B. Marilyn Oates; William D. Oates.
Grantmaker type: Independent foundation.
Financial data (yr. ended 12/31/10): Assets, $6,293,434 (M); expenditures, $185,776;

qualifying distributions, $152,500; giving activities include $152,500 for 8 grants (high: $50,000; low: $2,500).

Fields of interest: Recreation, camps; Animal welfare; International development; Community/economic development; Public affairs; Protestant agencies & churches; Children/youth.

Type of support: General/operating support.

Limitations: Applications not accepted. Giving primarily in TX, with emphasis on Dallas County. No grants to individuals.

Application information: Contributes only to pre-selected organizations.

Officers: William D. Oates, Pres. and Treas.; B. Marilyn Oates, V.P. and Secy.; W. Hunter Oates, V.P.

EIN: 208084868

2045
The Jesse H. & Susan R. Oppenheimer Foundation

711 Navarro St., Ste. 620
San Antonio, TX 78205-1893
Contact: Jesse H. Oppenheimer, Tr.; J. David Oppenheimer, Tr.

Established in 1964 in TX.

Donors: Jesse H. Oppenheimer; Susan R. Oppenheimer; J. David Oppenhelmer.

Grantmaker type: Independent foundation.

Financial data (yr. ended 12/31/10): Assets, $5,443,221 (M); expenditures, $258,619; qualifying distributions, $242,693; giving activities include $242,693 for 81 grants (high: $60,000; low: $75).

Purpose and activities: Giving for conservation, education, and medical purposes.

Fields of interest: Arts; Education; Environment; Reproductive health, family planning; Health organizations, association; Medical research, institute; International peace/security; Jewish federated giving programs; Disabilities, people with; Deaf/hearing Impaired; Mentally disabled.

Type of support: Endowments; Scholarship funds; Research.

Limitations: Applications not accepted. Giving primarily in Bexar County, TX.

Application information: Unsolicited requests for funds not accepted; all donations are trustee generated.

Board meeting date(s): Varies

Trustees: J. David Oppenheimer; Jesse H. Oppenheimer; Susan R. Oppenheimer.

Number of staff: None.

EIN: 746032845

2046
Paso del Norte Health Foundation

221 N. Kansas St., Ste. 1900
El Paso, TX 79901-1428   (915) 544-7636
Contact: Myrna Deckert, C.E.O. and Pres.
FAX: (915) 544-7713; E-mail: health@pdnhf.org;
Additional E-mail: mdeckert@pdnhf.org; URL: http://www.pdnhf.org
Blog: http://www.pdnhf.org/Blog.asp
Grants Database: http://www.pdnhf.org/searchgrantdb.asp

Established in 1995 in TX; converted from sale of the assets of Providence Memorial Hospital.

Grantmaker type: Independent foundation.

Financial data (yr. ended 12/31/09): Assets, $177,598,518 (M); gifts received, $859,960; expenditures, $6,361,645; qualifying distributions, $8,086,092; giving activities include $6,361,645 for 63 grants (high: $1,500,000; low: $1,500).

Purpose and activities: The foundation's mission is to promote health and prevent disease in the region through leadership in health education, research, and advocacy.

Fields of interest: Education, public education; Health care, support services; Health care; Mental health/crisis services; Nutrition; Youth development; Human services; Hispanics/Latinos; Youth; Children.

International interests: Mexico.

Type of support: Program development.

Limitations: Applications not accepted. Giving limited to west TX, southern NM, and northern Mexico. No support for political organizations. No grants to individuals, or for building/renovation, capital campaigns, or research.

Publications: Annual report.

Application information: Unsolicited applications not accepted.

Board meeting date(s): Jan., Mar., May, July, Sept., and Nov.

Officers and Directors:* Susana Navarro, Chair.; Sandra Sanchez Almanzan, Vice-Chair.; Myrna Deckert, C.E.O. and Pres.; Marcela Garcia, C.F.O.; Robert Ash; Jack Cardwell; George Drake; Allan Goldfarb; Rene Hurtado; Cindy Lyons; Carolyn Mora; Eduardo Sanchez; Eduardo Sanchez, M.D.

Number of staff: 10 full-time professional; 2 full-time support.

EIN: 741143071

Recent grants for international programs:

2046-1 FEMAP Foundation, El Paso, TX, $108,578. For Youth Culture and Sexuality program which will provide 11,000 youth of Ciudad Juarez with educational workshops, including puppet shows, art exhibit for promotion of sexual health and teen group discussions. 2010.

2046-2 FEMAP Foundation, El Paso, TX, $15,000. For FEMAP/SADEC in Juarez to develop modified form of KIDS EXCEL program to be called 'Valor Arte.' The program will target approximately 210 4th grade children from Moises Soteno and Amado Nervo schools in Ciudad Juarez. The program concept ' Education through Art' launched by New York National Dance Institute has been implemented in El Paso area by KIDS EXCEL El Paso with significant local support. 2010.

2047
The PHM Foundation

P.O. Box 1333
Coppell, TX 75019-1333
URL: http://phmfoundation.org/

Established in 2006 in TX.

Donors: Care Now; Dura Medical Inc.; Primary Health Management, Ltd.; Primary Health, Inc.

Grantmaker type: Operating foundation.

Financial data (yr. ended 12/31/10): Assets, $2,582,103 (M); gifts received, $5,000,000; expenditures, $7,167,941; qualifying distributions, $7,158,845; giving activities include $7,153,304 for 14 grants (high: $5,770,000; low: $824), and $5,541 for 1 foundation-administered program.

Purpose and activities: The foundation supports religious ministries and organizations involved with print publishing, reproductive health, and youth. The

foundation also operates an economic development program to promote entrepreneurship and development in developing countries.

Fields of interest: Media, print publishing; Reproductive health; Youth, services; International economic development; Social entrepreneurship; Christian agencies & churches; Jewish agencies & synagogues; Religion, interfaith issues; Religion.

International interests: Developing countries.

Type of support: General/operating support; Program-related investments/loans.

Limitations: Applications not accepted. Giving primarily in CA, Washington, DC, FL, MO, NM, NV, and TX; giving also to developing countries through program-related investments. No grants to individuals.

Application information: Unsolicited applications are not accepted. The foundation utilizes an invitation only process for giving.

Officers and Directors:* David Walter,* Pres.; Jennifer L. Walter,* Secy.; Daniel E. Walter,* Exec. Dir.

EIN: 204948182

2048
Pizza Hut, Inc. Corporate Giving Program

c/o Community Rels.
14841 Dallas Pkwy.
Dallas, TX 75254-7685
For the BOOK IT! Program: P.O. Box 2999, Wichita, KS, 67201; For the BOOK IT! Program in Canada: Zerina Pai, YUM! Restaurants International (Canada) LP, 101 Exchange Ave., Vaughan, Ontario L4K 5R6, tel.: (416) 664-5316, fax: (416) 739-6158, e-mail: Zerina.Pai@yum.com; For the BOOK IT! Program in Puerto Rico: Veronica Sanchez, Encanto Restaurants, Inc., Amelia Industrial Park, Diana St., Guaynabo, PR 00968, tel.: (787) 277-7765, fax: (787) 277-7783, e-mail: veronica.sanchez@encantopr.com; URL: http://www.pizzahut.com/ContactUs/CorporateContributionGuidelines.aspx
Additional URL: http://www.bookitprogram.com

Grantmaker type: Corporate giving program.

Purpose and activities: Pizza Hut makes charitable contributions to nonprofit organizations involved the arts, reading, and food services. Special emphasis is directed towards programs designed to encourage at-risk youths to express themselves through the arts. Support is given on a national basis, with emphasis on Dallas, Texas, and in Canada and Puerto Rico.

Fields of interest: Youth development; Food services; Education; Arts; Elementary/secondary education; Education, early childhood education; Education, reading; Economically disadvantaged.

International interests: Canada.

Type of support: General/operating support; Program development; In-kind gifts.

Limitations: Applications accepted. Giving on a national basis, with emphasis on Dallas, TX, and in Canada and Puerto Rico. No support for religious or political organizations. No grants to individuals, or for athletic groups, activities, or fundraisers, endowments, capital campaigns, or memorials, religious organizations or programs, travel expenses for school groups or individuals, or medical care.

Application information:

Initial approach: Contact nearest restaurant for application information; mail proposal to headquarters for funding requests for arts programs in the Dallas-Fort Worth, TX area;

complete online application form for BOOK IT!
Program
Deadline(s): June for BOOK IT! Program

2049
Plitt Southern Theatres, Inc. Employees Fund
1000 N. Central Expwy., Ste. 400
Dallas, TX 75231

Established in 1945 in TX.
Donors: Plitt Southern Theatres, Inc.; Sedge Plitt Charitable Trust III.
Grantmaker type: Company-sponsored foundation.
Financial data (yr. ended 12/31/10): Assets, $486,968 (M); expenditures, $358,858; qualifying distributions, $334,518; giving activities include $334,518 for grants.
Purpose and activities: The foundation supports hospitals and organizations involved with arts and culture, higher education, mental health, medical research, children and youth, and Israeli defense.
Fields of interest: International affairs; Arts; Higher education; Hospitals (general); Mental health/crisis services; Medical research; Children/youth, services.
International interests: Israel.
Type of support: General/operating support; Program-related investments/loans; Grants to individuals.
Limitations: Applications not accepted. Giving primarily in TX; giving also in Israel.
Application information: Contributes only to pre-selected organizations.
Officers and Trustees:* Joe S. Jackson,* Pres.; W.R. Curtis,* V.P. and Secy.; Roy H. Aaron; Raymond C. Fox; Henry G. Plitt.
EIN: 756037855

2050
Pratham U.S.A.
9703 Richmond Ave., Ste. 102
Houston, TX 77036-2612 (713) 774-9599
FAX: (713) 583-6779; E-mail: info@prathamusa.org;
URL: http://www.prathamusa.org

Established in 1999 in TX.
Donors: G.E. Foundation; Johnson & Johnson; Douglas Foundation; Wells Fargo.
Grantmaker type: Public charity.
Financial data (yr. ended 12/31/10): Revenue, $8,632,046; assets, $7,266,596 (M); gifts received, $6,757,309; expenditures, $8,421,968; giving activities include $7,830,409 for 3 grants to organizations outside the U.S.
Purpose and activities: The organization seeks to be the unifying movement which connects the Indian community in the U.S. to the cause of a literate India.
Fields of interest: International exchange; Education, reading; Education; Children.
International interests: India.
Limitations: Giving primarily to India.
Publications: Annual report; Financial statement; Newsletter.
Officer and Directors:* Vijay Goradia,* Chair.; Avinash Ahuja; Sudesh Arora; Jaideep Khanna; Sanjay Motwani; Paul Pandian; Arvind Sanger.
EIN: 760620808

2051
The Jay Pritzker Foundation
c/o Eric Brandfonbrener
3555 Timmons Ln., Ste. 800
Houston, TX 77027-6498

Established in 2002 in IL.
Donor: Daniel Pritzker.
Grantmaker type: Independent foundation.
Financial data (yr. ended 12/31/10): Assets, $8,256,454 (M); gifts received, $100; expenditures, $6,516,241; qualifying distributions, $6,447,177; giving activities include $6,440,000 for 10 grants (high: $2,500,000; low: $5,000).
Fields of interest: Elementary school/education; Higher education; Higher education, university; Education.
Limitations: Applications not accepted. Giving primarily in CA and MA; some funding also in Chicago, IL. No grants to individuals.
Application information: Contributes only to pre-selected organizations.
Officers and Directors:* Daniel F. Pritzker,* Pres.; Karen M. Pritzker,* Secy.; Diana E. Conway,* Treas.
EIN: 020550210
Recent grants for international programs:
2051-1 American Friends of the Hebrew University, New York, NY, $500,000. For general operating support. 2009.

2052
The Reilly Family Foundation
c/o The Ballpark
1017 S. FM Road 5
Aledo, TX 76008-4558 (817) 265-2364
Contact: Michael A. Reilly, Chair.; Beverly Reilly, V.P.

Established in 1996 in TX.
Donors: John C. Franklin; Stars for Children; Peter Baldwin; Reilly Parkway; Beverly Reilly; Michael Reilly.
Grantmaker type: Independent foundation.
Financial data (yr. ended 12/31/10): Assets, $2,064,871 (M); gifts received, $98,300; expenditures, $539,760; qualifying distributions, $411,975; giving activities include $345,167 for 63 grants (high: $42,000; low: $100), and $66,808 for grants to individuals.
Purpose and activities: Giving primarily for education, including scholarships to high school graduates pursuing higher education.
Fields of interest: Christian agencies & churches; International development; Health care; Higher education; Education; Human services.
Type of support: General/operating support; Scholarship funds; Scholarships—to individuals.
Limitations: Applications accepted. Giving in the U.S., primarily in the Dallas-Fort Worth, TX, area.
Application information: Contact foundation for application form and guidelines. Application form required.
   Initial approach: Telephone or letter requesting application form
Officers and Directors:* Michael A. Reilly,* Chair.; Richard D. Trubitt,* V.P. and Secy.-Treas.; Beverly A. Reilly,* V.P.; Robert Barnes; Anson Reilly; Asher Reilly; Atlee Reilly; Austin Reilly.
EIN: 752366809

2053
The Charles and Betti Saunders Foundation
19 Willowron Dr.
Houston, TX 77024-7618

Established in 1993 in TX.
Donors: Charles A. Saunders; Betti F. Saunders.
Grantmaker type: Independent foundation.
Financial data (yr. ended 06/30/10): Assets, $4,432,103 (M); expenditures, $199,750; qualifying distributions, $199,200; giving activities include $197,800 for 39 grants (high: $15,000; low: $1,500).
Fields of interest: YM/YWCAs & YM/YWHAs; Performing arts centers; Education; Human services; Religion.
International interests: Russia.
Limitations: Applications not accepted. Giving primarily in TX. No grants to individuals.
Application information: Unsolicited requests for funds not accepted.
Trustees: Cynthia S. Buggs; Shelly S. Eatherly; Melanie S. Mahoney; Betti F. Saunders; Charles A. Saunders; C. Stephen Saunders.
EIN: 760410069

2054
Scaler Foundation, Inc.
800 Gessner Rd., Ste. 1260
Houston, TX 77024-4276

Incorporated in 1954 in TX.
Donor: Eric Boissonnas.
Grantmaker type: Independent foundation.
Financial data (yr. ended 12/31/10): Assets, $22,252,462 (M); expenditures, $929,363; qualifying distributions, $686,821; giving activities include $686,821 for 10 grants (high: $177,252; low: $21,000).
Purpose and activities: Giving primarily for arts and culture, social services, and to French Protestant federated giving programs.
Fields of interest: Performing arts, music; Visual arts; Human services; United Ways and Federated Giving Programs; Protestant federated giving programs.
International interests: France.
Type of support: General/operating support; Continuing support; Income development; Building/renovation; Program development; Seed money.
Limitations: Applications not accepted. Giving primarily in Paris, France; some giving in the U.S., primarily in Brooklyn, NY. No grants to individuals, or for building or endowment funds, research, scholarships, fellowships, or matching gifts; no loans.
Application information: Contributes only to pre-selected organizations.
Officers and Directors:* Jacques C. Boissonnas,* Pres.; Nicolas N. Boissonnas,* V.P.; Marvin A. Wurzer, Secy.-Treas.; Catherine B. Coste.
EIN: 746036684

2055
The Search Foundation
(formerly The Sophia Foundation)
800 Gessner, Ste. 1260
Houston, TX 77024-4273

Established in 1996 in TX.

Donors: Catherine B. Coste; Fondation Ventose.
Grantmaker type: Independent foundation.
Financial data (yr. ended 12/31/10): Assets, $11,768,353 (M); expenditures, $515,213; qualifying distributions, $425,125; giving activities include $425,125 for 9 grants (high: $175,607; low: $10,000).
Fields of interest: History/archaeology; Libraries (special); Medical research; International development; Philanthropy/voluntarism; Science.
Type of support: General/operating support; Program development; Research.
Limitations: Applications not accepted. Giving primarily in Paris, France, as well as Melbourne, Australia; Athens, Greece; and Kiev, Ukraine; some giving also in the U.S. No grants to individuals.
Application information: Contributes only to pre-selected organizations.
Officers and Directors:* Roger Coste,* Chair.; Catherine B. Coste,* Pres.; Bertrand Coste,* Sr. V.P.; Mathilde Coste,* V.P.; Stephane Coste,* V.P.; Marvin A. Wurzer, Secy.-Treas.
EIN: 760520202

2056
Seegers Foundation
12720 Hillcrest Rd., Ste. 530
Dallas, TX   75230 2000

Established in 1984 in TX.
Donors: Paul Ray Seegers; Phyllis Ann Seegers; Steven P. Seegers; Scott R. Seegers.
Grantmaker type: Independent foundation.
Financial data (yr. ended 12/31/10): Assets, $5,095,211 (M); expenditures, $317,572; qualifying distributions, $299,021; giving activities include $292,571 for 31 grants (high: $125,000; low: $500).
Fields of interest: Theological school/education; Higher education; Health organizations, association; Human services; Children/youth, services; Christian agencies & churches.
International interests: Mexico.
Type of support: General/operating support.
Limitations: Applications not accepted. Giving primarily in TX. No grants to individuals.
Application information: Unsolicited requests for funds not accepted.
Officers: Phyllis Ann Seegers, Pres. and Treas.; Paul Ray Seegers, V.P.; Scott R. Seegers, V.P.; Pamela Seegers Gaulding, Secy.
Directors: David G. Glickman; Jacob P. Seegers.
EIN: 752001868

2057
Shepherds for the Savior
19380 Hwy. 105 W., Ste. 516
Montgomery, TX   77356-1984
Contact: Tracey Magee

Established in 2004 in TX.
Donor: Christ Church of Conroe.
Grantmaker type: Independent foundation.
Financial data (yr. ended 12/31/10): Assets, $6,170,685 (M); gifts received, $3,755; expenditures, $465,451; qualifying distributions, $298,817; giving activities include $298,817 for 7 grants (high: $195,314; low: $3,000).
Fields of interest: Christian agencies & churches; Human services; Children/youth, services; International relief, 2004 tsunami.

Limitations: Giving primarily in TX.
Publications: Informational brochure; Informational brochure (including application guidelines); Newsletter.
Application information:
   Initial approach: Letter
   Deadline(s): None
Officers: Mike Landes, Pres.; Becky Thompson, V.P.; Rhonda Saldivar, Secy.; David Johnson, Treas.
Directors: Scott Barr; Ed Bishop; Bill Hamlin.
EIN: 200554658

2058
The Six Four Foundation
(formerly The Sixty Four Foundation)
2850 Lake Vista Dr., Ste. 150
Lewisville, TX   75067-4189

Donor: Crum & Forster Holdings Corporation.
Grantmaker type: Independent foundation.
Financial data (yr. ended 12/31/10): Assets, $15,003,248 (M); gifts received, $4,282,000; expenditures, $7,029,027; qualifying distributions, $6,982,333; giving activities include $6,982,333 for grants.
Fields of interest: Higher education; Education; Health care; Cancer; International development; International relief; Children/youth.
Type of support: General/operating support; Scholarship funds; Research.
Limitations: Applications not accepted. Giving primarily in CA and NY. No grants to individuals.
Application information: Contributes only to pre-selected organizations.
Officers and Directors:* V. Prem Wasta,* Pres.; Ronald Schokking, V.P. and Treas.; Anthony F. Griffiths; Eric Salsberg.
EIN: 980364976

2059
The Sooch Foundation
c/o Navdeep Sooch
600 W. 7th St.
Austin, TX   78701-2710   (512) 472-5754
FAX: (512) 472-5748;
E-mail: info@soochfoundation.org; URL: http://www.soochfoundation.org

Established in 2003 in TX.
Donors: Janet Harman; Navdeep S. Sooch.
Grantmaker type: Independent foundation.
Financial data (yr. ended 12/31/10): Assets, $14,816,322 (M); gifts received, $500; expenditures, $1,037,872; qualifying distributions, $681,050; giving activities include $681,050 for grants.
Purpose and activities: The foundation seeks to make a positive and permanent change in the lives of economically disadvantaged people in Austin, Texas and in India. In Austin, the foundation will support educational activities and social services that facilitate educational activities. In India, the foundation will support programs that lift people out of poverty.
Fields of interest: Human services; Education; Economically disadvantaged.
International interests: India.
Limitations: Applications accepted. Giving primarily in the Austin, TX area and in India. No support for for-profit organizations, or for on-going fund drives or organizations not classified as public charities by

the IRS. No grants to individuals, or for endowments, capital campaigns, gala, dinner or raffle tickets, operating expenses or deficits.
Publications: Annual report.
Application information: Use Central Texas Education Funders Common Grant Application which can be downloaded from foundation web site. At this time, the foundation is not soliciting proposals for international projects.
   Initial approach: Check foundation web site to determine suitability, then follow up with a 1-2 page summary via e-mail
   Deadline(s): None
   Board meeting date(s): Quarterly
Officers and Trustees:* Navdeep S. Sooch, Pres. and Treas.; David R. Welland, V.P.; Isabel Welland,* Secy.; Mary Ellen Pietruszynski, Exec. Dir.; John McGovern.
Number of staff: 2 full-time professional; 1 part-time professional.
EIN: 200399480

2060
Spark Energy, L.P., Corporate Giving Program
2501 Citywest Blvd., Ste. # 100
Houston, TX   77042 3019   (713) 977-5634
URL: https://www.sparkenergy.com/Community-Involvement

Grantmaker type: Corporate giving program.
Purpose and activities: Spark Energy, L.P. makes charitable contributions to nonprofits involved with children, military personnel, the mentally disabled, and homeless families. Support is given primarily in areas of company operations in Arizona, California, Colorado, Connecticut, Florida, Illinois, Indiana, Maryland, Massachusetts, Michigan, Nevada, New Mexico, New York, Ohio, Pennsylvania, and Texas; giving also to national organizations.
Fields of interest: International relief, Children, services; Children's rights; Family services; Homeless, human services; Children; Homeless; Mentally disabled; Military/veterans.
Type of support: General/operating support.
Limitations: Giving primarily in areas of company operations in AZ, CA, CO, CT, FL, IL, IN, MA, MD,MI, NM, NV, NY, OH, PA, and TX.
Officer: Frode Helgerud, C.E.O.

2061
The Sparrow Charitable Foundation
211 N. Record St., Ste. 222
Dallas, TX   75202-3347

Established in 2003 in TX.
Donors: Marydel Harris; Raymond Harris.
Grantmaker type: Independent foundation.
Financial data (yr. ended 12/31/09): Assets, $1,664,270 (M); gifts received, $5,150,000; expenditures, $6,315,424; qualifying distributions, $6,314,055; giving activities include $6,313,100 for 65 grants (high: $3,886,700; low: $100).
Fields of interest: Health organizations, association; Human services; Christian agencies & churches; Protestant agencies & churches.
Limitations: Applications not accepted. Giving primarily in TX. No grants to individuals.
Application information: Contributes only to pre-selected organizations.

Directors: Elizabeth A. Harris; Marydel Harris; Raymond Harris; Stephen R. Harris.
EIN: 200488561
Recent grants for international programs:
2061-1 Apostrophe Mission Foundation, Richardson, TX, $50,000. For general fund. 2009.
2061-2 Bridge2Rwanda, Little Rock, AR, $100,000. For Rwanda School Project. 2009.
2061-3 Buckner Baptist Benevolences, Dallas, TX, $250,000. For Community Centers in Ethiopia. 2009.
2061-4 Buckner Baptist Benevolences, Dallas, TX, $150,000. For Africa Initiative. 2009.
2061-5 Campus Crusade for Christ International, Orlando, FL, $50,000. For Global Campus Forum - Thailand. 2009.
2061-6 Crown Financial Ministries, Gainesville, GA, $150,000. For India Sustainability. 2009.
2061-7 Enright Flight Ministries, Daytona Beach, FL, $175,000. For Kafakumba Training Center. 2009.
2061-8 Enright Flight Ministries, Daytona Beach, FL, $150,000. For Kafakumba Training Center. 2009.
2061-9 Faith Comes By Hearing International Foundation, Albuquerque, NM, $1,000,000. For Africa Initiative. 2009.
2061-10 Faith Comes By Hearing International Foundation, Albuquerque, NM, $100,000. For general fund. 2009.
2061-11 Faith Comes By Hearing International Foundation, Albuquerque, NM, $10,000. For general fund. 2009.
2061-12 Family Legacy Missions International, Irving, TX, $100,000. For Tree of Life Village. 2009.
2061-13 Frontiers, Phoenix, AZ, $10,000. For general fund. 2009.
2061-14 Greater Europe Mission, Monument, CO, $15,000. 2009.
2061-15 Heres Life Mission to Africa, Decatur, TX, $50,000. For General Fund - Tanzania project. 2009.
2061-16 International Students, Colorado Springs, CO, $20,000. 2009.
2061-17 Land and Water Resources International, Lynnwood, WA, $100,000. For Honduras Project. 2009.
2061-18 Medical Ambassadors International, Salida, CA, $100,000. For general fund. 2009.
2061-19 Navigators, The, Colorado Springs, CO, $150,000. For Africa Initiative. 2009.
2061-20 Operation Mobilization USA, Tyrone, GA, $10,000. For general fund. 2009.
2061-21 Overseas Missionary Fellowship International, Littleton, CO, $50,000. For Chiang Mai Seminary. 2009.
2061-22 Overseas Missionary Fellowship International, Littleton, CO, $10,000. 2009.
2061-23 Overseas Missionary Fellowship International, Littleton, CO, $10,000. 2009.
2061-24 Precept Ministries International, Chattanooga, TN, $10,000. For general fund. 2009.
2061-25 United States Center for World Missions, Pasadena, CA, $50,000. For general fund. 2009.
2061-26 United States Center for World Missions, Pasadena, CA, $20,000. 2009.

2062
Spectra Energy Foundation
c/o Community Rels.
5400 Westheimer Ct.
Houston, TX 77056 (713) 627-5036
Contact: Regan Kasman, Mgr., Community Rels.

Grantmaker type: Corporate giving program.
Purpose and activities: Spectra Energy makes charitable contributions to nonprofit organizations primarily in areas of company operations.
Fields of interest: General charitable giving.
International interests: Canada.
Type of support: General/operating support; Employee volunteer services; Employee matching gifts; Employee-related scholarships.
Limitations: Applications not accepted. Giving primarily in areas of company operations.
Application information: Contributes only to pre-selected organizations.

2063
The Marlene and J. O. Stewart, Jr. Foundation
124 W. Castellano, Ste. 100
El Paso, TX 79912-6139
Contact: Ron F. Acton, Pres.

Established in 2000 in TX.
Donors: Marlene Stewart; James O. Stewart, Jr.
Grantmaker type: Independent foundation.
Financial data (yr. ended 12/31/10): Assets, $1,706,406 (M); expenditures, $310,662; qualifying distributions, $241,815; giving activities include $241,815 for 23 grants (high: $60,000; low: $200).
Purpose and activities: Giving primarily for Christian agencies and churches.
Fields of interest: International affairs; Higher education; Arts; Health organizations, association; Human services; Christian agencies & churches.
Limitations: Applications accepted. Giving primarily in TX. No grants to individuals.
Application information: Application form not required.
  Initial approach: Letter
  Copies of proposal: 1
  Deadline(s): None
  Board meeting date(s): Annually, in Jan, and thereafter as needed
Officers and Directors:* Ron F. Acton,* Pres.; Myron Brown,* V.P.; James O. Stewart, Jr.,* V.P.; James O. Stewart III,* V.P.; Marlene Stewart,* V.P.
EIN: 742958268

2064
The Summerlee Foundation
5556 Caruth Haven Ln.
Dallas, TX 75225-8146 (214) 363-9000
Contact: John W. Crain, Pres.
FAX: (214) 363-1941; E-mail: info@summerlee.org; Animal Protection Program Address: c/o Melanie A. Lambert, Prog. Dir., 716 N. Tejon, Ste. 9, Colorado Springs, CO, 80903; tel.: (800) 256-7515, fax: (719) 266-5459; URL: http://www.summerlee.org/

Established in 1988 in TX.
Donor: Annie Lee Roberts‡.
Grantmaker type: Independent foundation.
Financial data (yr. ended 06/30/10): Assets, $57,027,928 (M); expenditures, $2,362,667;

qualifying distributions, $2,204,468; giving activities include $1,066,001 for 45 grants (high: $250,000; low: $550), and $399,368 for foundation-administered programs.
Purpose and activities: Giving limited to 1) the alleviation of pain and suffering and the prevention of cruelty to animals; and 2) for the study, promotion, preservation, and documentation of all facets of TX history.
Fields of interest: History/archaeology; Historic preservation/historical societies; Animal welfare; Animals/wildlife, preservation/protection.
International interests: Canada; Mexico.
Type of support: Capital campaigns; Building/renovation; Equipment; Land acquisition; Program development; Conferences/seminars; Professorships; Film/video/radio; Publication; Seed money; Curriculum development; Fellowships; Internship funds; Research; Technical assistance; Matching/challenge support.
Limitations: Applications accepted. Giving primarily in TX for history programs; National and international giving for animal welfare program. No support for religious purposes. No grants to individuals.
Publications: Application guidelines; Grants list.
Application information: See foundation web site for programs, and application guidelines including deadlines and procedures. Faxed, e-mailed or incomplete applications will not be accepted. Application form not required.
  Initial approach: Telephone, letter, e-mail
  Copies of proposal: 1
  Deadline(s): Deadlines vary every year. See foundation web site.
  Board meeting date(s): Quarterly
  Final notification: 3 months
Officers and Directors:* John W. Crain,* Pres. and Prog. Dir., TX history; Melanie A. Lambert,* V.P. and Prog. Dir., Animal Protection; Hon. Nikki DeShazo,* Secy.; Hon. David D. Jackson,* V.P.; Martha Benson, Treas.; Michael H. Collins; Ron Tyler, Ph.D.
Number of staff: 2 full-time professional; 1 full-time support.
EIN: 752252355

2065
Teen Mania Ministries, Inc.
P.O. Box 2000
Lindale, TX 75771-2000 (903) 324-8000
Contact: Ronald Luce, Pres.

Established in 1987 in OK.
Grantmaker type: Public charity.
Financial data (yr. ended 08/31/10): Revenue, $17,119,135; assets, $10,234,420 (M); gifts received, $10,458,327; expenditures, $16,830,148; program services expenses, $14,995,408; giving activities include $2,493 for grants.
Purpose and activities: The organization promotes worldwide evangelism through the granting of fellowships to individuals for short-term missionary trips to Latin America, Europe, Africa, and Asia.
Fields of interest: Religion.
International interests: Europe; Africa; Latin America; Asia.
Type of support: Fellowships.
Officers and Board Members:* Dr. Daniel Williams,* Chair.; Ronald Luce,* Pres.; David Hasz,* V.P.; Kathryn Luce,* Secy.; Jonathan Hasz,* C.F.O.; Dr. George Babbes; Dr. Myles Munroe; Tom Mucio; Paul Nelson; Lisa Robertson.
EIN: 731284606

2066
Thirst No More Ministries
P.O. Box 2290
Cedar Park, TX 78630-2290 (512) 382-4318
FAX: (512) 259-7186;
E-mail: office@thirstnomore.org; URL: http://
www.thirstnomore.org
Facebook Causes URL: http://www.causes.com/
causes/6784?recruiter_id=2242675
Organization Blog: http://
thirstnomoreassociation.wordpress.com/

Established in 1995 in TX.
Grantmaker type: Public charity.
Financial data (yr. ended 12/31/10): Revenue,
$851,476; assets, $109,852 (M); gifts received,
$841,961; expenditures, $738,920; giving
activities include $391,836 for grants to
organizations outside the U.S.
Purpose and activities: The organization seeks to
relieve human suffering through compassion
projects.
Fields of interest: International relief; Human
services.
Type of support: Grants to individuals.
Limitations: Giving primarily in Springdale, AR and
Richmond, VA.
Officer and Board Members:* Steven Craig Miller,*
Pres.; Charles Damron; Stan Bedford; Greg Maphet.
EIN: 710774001

2067
The Trull Foundation
404 4th St.
Palacios, TX 77465-4812 (361) 972-5241
Contact: E. Gail Purvis, Exec. Dir.
FAX: (361) 972-1109;
E-mail: gpurvis@trullfoundation.org; URL: http://
www.trullfoundation.org

Established in 1967 in TX. Originally established in
1948 as The B.W. Trull Foundation.
Donors: R.B. Trull†; Florence M. Trull†; Gladys T.
Brooking; Jean T. Herlin†; Laura Shiflett.
Grantmaker type: Independent foundation.
Financial data (yr. ended 12/31/10): Assets,
$24,166,506 (M); expenditures, $1,949,341;
qualifying distributions, $1,712,091; giving
activities include $1,590,670 for 240 grants (high:
$50,000; low: $150).
Purpose and activities: The foundation's grant
focus areas include: concern for needs of the
Palacios and Matagorda County, where the
foundation has its roots; concern for children and
families, channeling lives away from abuse, neglect,
hunger, and poverty; concern for those persons and
families devastated by the effects of substance
abuse; concern for the coastal Texas environment,
recognizing and including farming, ranching,
aquaculture, and birds.
Fields of interest: Museums; Elementary/
secondary education; Child development,
education; Elementary school/education;
Secondary school/education; Higher education;
Theological school/education; Adult education—
literacy, basic skills & GED; Libraries/library
science; Education; Environment; Substance abuse,
services; Food services; Human services; Children/
youth, services; Child development, services; Family
services; Minorities/immigrants, centers/services;
Homeless, human services; International relief;
International peace/security; Community/economic
development; Protestant agencies & churches;

Religion; Infants/toddlers; Children/youth; Youth;
Minorities; Hispanics/Latinos; Women; Adults,
women; Adults, men; Substance abusers;
Immigrants/refugees; Economically disadvantaged;
Homeless.
Type of support: General/operating support;
Continuing support; Management development/
capacity building; Annual campaigns; Building/
renovation; Equipment; Program development;
Conferences/seminars; Publication; Seed money;
Curriculum development; Scholarship funds;
Technical assistance; Matching/challenge support.
Limitations: Applications accepted. Giving primarily
in TX, with emphasis on the rural TX, south TX, and
the Palacios and Matagorda County areas. No
grants to individuals directly, or for capital building
campaigns, endowment funds; no loans.
Publications: Application guidelines; Biennial report
(including application guidelines); Grants list; IRS
Form 990 or 990-PF printed copy available upon
request.
Application information: Applications must include
an application letter and The Trull Foundation's
proposal fact sheet. Proposals submitted by fax or
e-mail not considered. Telephone inquiries about
proposals and grants will be answered Mon.-Fri.,
from 8:00am-12:00pm. Application guidelines and
proposal fact sheet available on foundation Web
site. Please do not send 990s, audits, CDs, videos,
information concerning staff, Board of Dirs., plaques
or certificates of appreciation. Application form
required.
  Initial approach: Proposal
  Copies of proposal: 2
  Deadline(s): See foundation web site for
    application deadlines
  Board meeting date(s): Usually twice a year;
    contributions committee meets monthly and
    as required
  Final notification: 2 months
Officers and Trustees:* Colleen Claybourn,* Chair.;
Cara P. Herlin,* Vice-Chair.; R. Scott Trull,*
Secy.-Treas.; E. Gail Purvis, Exec. Dir.; Craig A.
Hallis, Advisory Tr.; Susan Herlin, Advisory Tr.; Mike
McAllister, Advisory Tr.; Sarah H. Olfers.
Number of staff: 1 full-time professional; 1 full-time
support.
EIN: 237423943
Recent grants for international programs:
2067-1 Church World Service, Elkhart, IN, $10,000.
  For Haiti Relief. 2010.
2067-2 Church World Service, Elkhart, IN, $10,000.
  For Pakistan Flooding. 2010.
2067-3 Environmental Defense, Austin, TX,
  $15,000. To safeguard Gulf of Mexico fisheries
  and marine ecosystems through Recreational
  Fishing Catch Share Management Program.
  2010.
2067-4 Freedom from Hunger, Davis, CA, $10,000.
  For Haiti Relief. 2010.
2067-5 International Rescue Committee, New York,
  NY, $10,000. For Haiti Relief. 2010.
2067-6 Medical Benevolence Foundation, Houston,
  TX, $10,000. For Haiti Medical Recovery Needs.
  2010.
2067-7 World Neighbors, Oklahoma City, OK,
  $20,000. For emergency funding for Bolivia and
  Peru. 2010.

2068
Vietnamese Culture & Science Association
4615 Belle Pk. Dr.
Houston, TX 77072-1819 (281) 933-8118
FAX: (281) 933-8187;
E-mail: vcsa-scholarships@vcsa.org; URL: http://
www.vcsa.org
RSS Feed: http://vcsa.org/rss.xml

Established in 1991 in TX.
Grantmaker type: Public charity.
Financial data (yr. ended 12/31/10): Revenue,
$329,841; assets, $165,512 (M); gifts received,
$166,252; expenditures, $347,185; giving
activities include $1,263 for grants, $71,028 for
grants to organizations outside the U.S., and
$14,688 for grants to individuals.
Purpose and activities: The organization seeks to
promote excellence in education, leadership and
skills development through culture and science. Our
organization encourages multi-generational and
cross-cultural collaborations.
Fields of interest: International exchange.
International interests: Vietnam.
Limitations: Applications accepted. Giving on an
international basis.
Publications: Application guidelines; Newsletter.
Application information: Resume and essay are
required with application. Application form required.
  Initial approach: Submit application form online
  Deadline(s): April
Officers and Directors:* Anhlan Nguyen,* Chair.;
Mr. Hung Le,* Pres.; Ms. Bao Ngan Nguyen, V.P.,
Internal Affairs; Mr. Kim Yen Vu, V.P., Internal
Affairs; Mr. Duy Anh Truong, Secy.; Mr. Peter Hop
Pham,* Treas.; Michael Dao, C.P.A.; Dr. Nguyen
Minh "Mark" Duy; Ms. Tieu Muoi "Sophia" Huynh;
Mr. Doan D. Khoa; Tuong Vu Nguyen; Tinh Tien Trinh.
EIN: 760360557

2069
Rob and Bessie Welder Wildlife Foundation
P.O. Box 1400
Sinton, TX 78387-1400 (361) 364-2643
Contact: Dr. Selma Glasscock, Asst. Dir.
FAX: (361) 364-2650;
E-mail: welderfoundation@welderwildlife.org;
URL: http://www.welderwildlife.org

Trust established in 1954 in TX.
Donors: R.H. Welder†; Mrs. R.H. Welder†; Edward
H. & Winnie H. Smith Fellowship Trust Fund.
Grantmaker type: Operating foundation.
Financial data (yr. ended 12/31/09): Assets,
$22,760,126 (M); gifts received, $62,208;
expenditures, $1,107,072; qualifying distributions,
$992,670; giving activities include $118,461 for 1
grant, and $131,694 for 8 grants to individuals
(high: $20,200; low: $5,800).
Purpose and activities: Established to further
research and education in wildlife conservation, to
support graduate-level research (M.Sc., Ph.D.) at
bona fide universities into wildlife problems, and to
develop scientific methods for increasing wildlife
populations; operates a wildlife refuge.
Fields of interest: Animals/wildlife; Environment,
natural resources; Environment.
International interests: Canada.
Type of support: Fellowships; Internship funds.

Limitations: Applications accepted. Giving primarily in the Coastal Bend and South Plains areas of TX. No grants for building or endowment funds, work/study programs, or operating budgets.
Publications: Application guidelines; Biennial report; Informational brochure (including application guidelines); Multi-year report; Newsletter.
Application information: Application guidelines available on web site. Application form required.
  Initial approach: Letter, preferably submitted as e-mail
  Copies of proposal: 1
  Deadline(s): Submit application preferably in fall; deadline Oct. 1
  Board meeting date(s): Usually in Nov. and June
  Final notification: Prior to Dec. 15
Director: Dr. Terry Blankenship.
Trustees: Hughes C. Thomas; H.C. Weil; John J. Welder V.
Number of staff: 2 full-time professional; 5 full-time support; 2 part-time support.
EIN: 741381321

2070
The Clarence Westbury Foundation
(formerly The Scaler Westbury Foundation)
800 Gessner Rd., Ste. 1260
Houston, TX 77024-4273

Established in 1996 in TX.
Donors: Jacques C. Boissonnas; Jaguar Trust; Jasper Trust.
Grantmaker type: Independent foundation.
Financial data (yr. ended 12/31/10): Assets, $7,005,687 (M); gifts received, $2,000,000; expenditures, $2,255,349; qualifying distributions, $2,153,621; giving activities include $2,153,621 for 10 grants (high: $1,270,300; low: $4,600).
Fields of interest: Human services; Museums; Health organizations, association.
International interests: France.
Limitations: Applications not accepted. Giving primarily in Paris, France; giving also in the U.S. with emphasis on TX. No grants to individuals.
Application information: Contributes only to pre-selected organizations.
Officers and Directors:* Jacques C. Boissonnas,* Pres.; Nicolas N. Boissonnas,* Sr. V.P.; Catherine B. Coste,* V.P.; Marvin A. Wurzer, Secy.-Treas.
EIN: 760507294

2071
Whole Planet Foundation
550 Bowie St.
Austin, TX 78703-4677   (512) 542-3834
FAX: (512) 482-7000;
E-mail: general_info@wholeplanetfoundation.org;
URL: http://www.wholeplanetfoundation.org
E-Newsletter: http://www.wholeplanetfoundation.org/newsroom/newsletters/
Facebook: http://www.facebook.com/group.php?gid=9953259175&ref=ts
Twitter: http://twitter.com/wholeplanet
Whole Planet Foundation Videos: http://www.wholeplanetfoundation.org/newsroom/videos/
Whole Story: The Official Whole Foods Market Blog: http://www.wholeplanetfoundation.org/newsroom/blog/

Established in 2005 in DE and TX.
Donors: Whole Foods Market Services, Inc.; Pepsico; Seventh Generation; ITO EN.
Grantmaker type: Company-sponsored foundation.
Financial data (yr. ended 12/31/10): Assets, $5,375,235 (M); gifts received, $5,743,567; expenditures, $4,739,572; qualifying distributions, $4,728,364; giving activities include $3,727,805 for 19 grants (high: $343,608; low: $47,304), and $4,728,364 for foundation-administered programs.
Purpose and activities: The foundation creates and supports economic partnerships with the poor in developing-world communities that supply Whole Foods stores with product. Special emphasis is directed toward microfinance institutions in Latin America, Africa and Asia who in turn develop and offer microenterprise loan programs, training and other financial services to the self-employed poor.
Fields of interest: Community development, small businesses; Microfinance/microlending; International development; International economic development; Economic development; Community development, business promotion; Social entrepreneurship; Economically disadvantaged.
International interests: Africa; Asia; Latin America.
Type of support: General/operating support; Capital campaigns.
Limitations: Applications not accepted. Giving primarily in NY and in developing communities in Africa, Argentina, Asia, Bangladesh, Costa Rica, Ethiopia, Guatemala, Haiti, Honduras, India, Indonesia, Kenya, Latin America, Nepal, Nicaragua, Peru, and Thailand. No grants to individuals.
Publications: Annual report; Financial statement; Newsletter; IRS Form 990 or 990-PF printed copy available upon request.
Application information: Contributes only to pre-selected organizations.
Officers and Directors:* John P. Mackey,* Co-Chair.; Lee Valkenaar,* Co-Chair.; Philip Sansone,* Pres. and Exec. Dir.; Roberta Lang,* V.P. and Treas.; Scott Allshouse; Michael Besancon; Glenda F. Flanagan; Ken Meyer; Will Paradise; Walter E. Robb IV; Jeff Teter.
Number of staff: 6 full-time professional.
EIN: 202376273

2072
The Windmill Foundation
P.O. Box 941401
Plano, TX 75094-1401

Established in 2007 in TX.
Donors: Radu Achiriloaie; Raluca Moucha.
Grantmaker type: Independent foundation.
Financial data (yr. ended 12/31/10): Assets, $3,281,305 (M); gifts received, $100,000; expenditures, $176,859; qualifying distributions, $176,859; giving activities include $175,000 for 16 grants (high: $30,000; low: $1,000).
Fields of interest: Human services; Environment, natural resources; Food banks; International development.
Limitations: Applications not accepted. Giving primarily to national organizations in CA, IL, NY, and VA. No grants to individuals.
Application information: Contributes only to pre-selected organizations.
Officers and Directors:* Radu Achiriloaie,* Chair. and Secy.; Raluca Moucha,* Pres. and Treas.; Robert G. Hamm.
EIN: 331195770

UTAH

2073
The Force for Good Foundation
c/o Nu Skin Enterprises, Inc.
75 W. Center St.
Provo, UT 84601-4432   (801) 345-2187
Contact: Jordan Karpowitz
E-mail: forceforgood@nuskin.com; Additional contact: Kara Schneck, tel.: (801) 345-2116, e-mail: kschneck@nuskin.com; E-mail for Jordan Karpowitz: jkarpowi@nuskin.com; URL: http://www.forceforgood.org

Established in 1998 in UT.
Donors: Diamond Technology Partners Inc.; Nu Skin Enterprises, Inc.
Grantmaker type: Company-sponsored foundation.
Financial data (yr. ended 12/31/10): Assets, $407,655 (M); gifts received, $906,344; expenditures, $1,135,846; qualifying distributions, $1,096,076; giving activities include $1,096,076 for grants.
Purpose and activities: The foundation supports programs designed to improve the lives of children by offering hope for a life free for disease, illiteracy, and poverty.
Fields of interest: Disasters, preparedness/services; Economic development; Elementary/secondary education; Heart & circulatory diseases; Medical research; Education, reading; Education; Health care; Skin disorders research; Children, services; Human services; Economically disadvantaged.
Type of support: General/operating support; Continuing support; Building/renovation; Equipment; Research.
Limitations: Applications not accepted. Giving primarily in CA, UT, China, Ethiopia, Kenya, Malawi, and Uganda; giving also to national and international organizations. No support for fraternal organizations, religious organizations, or political lobbyists. No grants to individuals, or for administrative costs, capital campaigns, seed money, advertising, or travel.
Application information: Contributes only to pre-selected organizations.
Officers and Trustees:* Blake M. Roney,* Chair. and Pres.; Gary Garrett, V.P.; M. Truman Hunt,* V.P.; Brooke Roney, V.P.; Sandra N. Tillotson,* V.P.; Steven J. Lund,* Secy.; B.G. Hunt, Cont.
EIN: 870577244
Recent grants for international programs:
2073-1 American Chamber Foundation Philippines, Hilton Head Island, SC, $15,000. 2009.
2073-2 Angel Guardian Foundation, Malibu, CA, $10,000. 2009.
2073-3 China Foundation for Poverty Alleviation, Beijing, China, $554,194. 2009.
2073-4 China Youth Development Foundation, China Hope Project, Beijing, China, $13,250. For Nu Hope Schools in China. 2009.
2073-5 Fundanica, Valencia, Venezuela, $15,000. 2009.
2073-6 PKPU, Jakarta, Indonesia, $10,000. 2009.
2073-7 Shanghai Charity Foundation, Shanghai, China, $20,000. 2009.
2073-8 Support Africa Empowerment Foundation International, Aurora, CO, $245,450. 2009.

2074
The Miner Foundation
(formerly The Miner Family Foundation)
c/o T. Monson
1173 S. 250 W., Ste. 204
St. George, UT 84770-6742 (435) 628-3930
Contact: Allen P. Miner, Pres.

Established in 2004 in DE.
Donor: Allen P. Miner.
Grantmaker type: Independent foundation.
Financial data (yr. ended 12/31/10): Assets,
$3,012,540 (M); gifts received, $50,000;
expenditures, $269,406; qualifying distributions,
$239,479; giving activities include $239,479 for 6
grants (high: $172,524; low: $1,455).
Fields of interest: Education; International
economics/trade policy.
Type of support: General/operating support.
Limitations: Applications accepted. Giving primarily
in Japan.
Application information:
Initial approach: Letter
Deadline(s): None
Officers and Directors:* Allen P. Miner,* Pres.,
Secy. and Exec. Dir.; Thomas S. Monson,* Treas.;
Michiko Minor.
EIN: 980441716

2075
Semnani Foundation
630 E. South Temple
Salt Lake City, UT 84102-1102 (801) 321-7725
Contact: Khosrow B. Semnani, Dir.

Established in 1991 in UT.
Donor: Khosrow B. Semnani.
Grantmaker type: Independent foundation.
Financial data (yr. ended 12/31/10): Assets,
$54,723,224 (M); expenditures, $2,200,759;
qualifying distributions, $2,006,621; giving
activities include $2,006,621 for grants.
Purpose and activities: Giving primarily for social
services, with emphasis on Islamic charity services.
Fields of interest: Foundations (private
grantmaking); Foundations (public); Arts, cultural/
ethnic awareness; Higher education; Education;
Health care, clinics/centers; Health organizations,
association; Medical research, institute; Human
services; International relief; Islam.
International interests: Iran.
Limitations: Giving primarily in UT, with emphasis on
Salt Lake City; some funding also in PA. No grants
to individuals.
Application information: Application form not
required.
Initial approach: Letter
Deadline(s): None
Officer: John Pingree, Exec. Dir.
Directors: Nolan Karras; Shirin Kia; Ghazelah
Semnani; Khosrow Semnani.
EIN: 742639794
Recent grants for international programs:
2075-1 Deseret International Foundation, Provo,
UT, $35,000. For general contribution. 2009.
2075-2 Hope Arising, Gilbert, AZ, $10,000. For
general contribution. 2009.
2075-3 Rising Star Outreach, Provo, UT, $14,200.
For general contribution. 2009.

2076
William E. Slaughter, Jr. Foundation, Inc.
375 S. Main St., No. 144
Moab, UT 84532-2557

Incorporated in 1959 in MI.
Donor: William E. Slaughter, Jr.†
Grantmaker type: Independent foundation.
Financial data (yr. ended 12/31/10): Assets, $0;
expenditures, $181,689; qualifying distributions,
$160,000; giving activities include $160,000 for 33
grants.
Purpose and activities: Giving primarily for wildlife
and animal preservation, world improvement, and
the environment.
Fields of interest: Environment, natural resources;
Environment; Animal welfare; International peace/
security.
Type of support: General/operating support;
Continuing support; Annual campaigns; Seed
money.
Limitations: Applications not accepted. Giving
primarily in AZ, HI, and UT. No grants to individuals
or for scholarships.
Application information: Contributes only to
pre-selected organizations.
Officers and Directors:* Kent C. Slaughter,* Pres.
and Secy.; Gloria Slaughter,* V.P.; William E.
Stillwater,* V.P.; William A. Corbett, C.F.O.
Number of staff: None.
EIN: 386065616

2077
SmartGo Foundation
3021 Chaucer Pl.
Salt Lake City, UT 84108-2503

Established in 2006 in UT.
Grantmaker type: Independent foundation.
Financial data (yr. ended 12/31/10): Assets,
$5,214,728 (M); expenditures, $353,624;
qualifying distributions, $176,500; giving activities
include $176,500 for grants.
Fields of interest: Human services; Education;
Horticulture/garden clubs; International relief.
Limitations: Applications not accepted. Giving
primarily in UT, with some giving in CA, GA, and NY.
No grants to individuals.
Application information: Contributes only to
pre-selected organizations.
Directors: Anders Kierulf; Bjorn Kierulf; Sara A. Rich.
EIN: 205290408

2078
The Sorenson Legacy Foundation
2511 S. West Temple St.
Salt Lake City, UT 84115-3060
Contact: Lisa Meiling, Exec. Dir.
E-mail for Lisa Meiling:
lisa@sorensonlegacyfoundation.org; URL: http://
www.sorensonlegacyfoundation.org

Established in 2001 in UT.
Donors: James LeVoy Sorenson†; Sorenson Devel.,
Inc.
Grantmaker type: Independent foundation.
Financial data (yr. ended 12/31/10): Assets,
$540,414,148 (M); gifts received, $10,179,000;
expenditures, $24,455,571; qualifying
distributions, $23,478,113; giving activities include

$21,827,533 for 89 grants (high: $9,350,813; low:
$4,000).
Purpose and activities: The Sorenson Legacy
Foundation is a non-profit corporation established by
the James LeVoy Sorenson family for the exclusive
purpose of promoting charitable, religious,
educational, literary and scientific endeavors.
Fields of interest: Elementary school/education;
Health organizations, association; Human services;
Children/youth, services; Foundations (private
grantmaking).
Type of support: General/operating support;
Continuing support; Building/renovation; Program
development; Matching/challenge support.
Limitations: Applications accepted. Giving primarily
in Salt Lake City, UT. No support for political
organizations.
Application information: Submissions sponsored by
Sorenson Legacy Foundation member have a better
chance for funding. Application form required.
Initial approach: Letter
Copies of proposal: 2
Deadline(s): 1 month prior to meeting
Board meeting date(s): First 2 weeks of April, July,
Oct. and Jan.
Final notification: 2 weeks following meeting
Trustees: Jim Sorenson, Jr.; Shauna Johnson.
EIN: 870669065
Recent grants for international programs:
2078-1 Africa Help Line Society, West Jordan, UT,
$18,000. For general support. 2009.
2078-2 Cause for Hope, South Jordan, UT,
$60,000. For general support. 2009.
2078-3 Church of Jesus Christ of Latter Day Saints,
Salt Lake City, UT, $1,475,000. For Missionary
Fund. 2009.
2078-4 Patel Foundation for Global Understanding,
Tampa, FL, $13,000. For general support. 2009.
2078-5 Save a Child Foundation, Salt Lake City, UT,
$15,000. For general support. 2009.
2078-6 Unitus, Inc., Seattle, WA, $206,000. For
general support. 2009.
2078-7 Utah State University, Logan, UT,
$1,521,000. For Uganda Project, initiative where
Engineers Without Borders travel to Uganda, to
implement engineering projects designed to
provide clean drinking water for an orphanage.
2009.

2079
Dr. W. C. Swanson Family Foundation, Inc.
2520 N. 1500 W.
Ogden, UT 84404-2823 (801) 392-0360
Contact: Bridgett Tasker, Grants Admin.
FAX: (801) 392-0429; E-mail: SFF@swanfound.org;
Additional tel.: (801) 540-8783; e-mail (for Bridgett
Tasker): bridgett@swanfound.org

Established in 1977; incorporated in 1999.
Donor: W.C. Swanson†.
Grantmaker type: Independent foundation.
Financial data (yr. ended 12/31/09): Assets,
$27,063,926 (M); gifts received, $126,294;
expenditures, $2,498,869; qualifying distributions,
$1,012,836; giving activities include $443,695 for
grants, and $437,352 for foundation-administered
programs.
Purpose and activities: Giving primarily for
education, arts and culture, human services, and
the prevention of cruelty to children and animals.
Fields of interest: Crime/law enforcement; Arts;
Education; Animal welfare; Children/youth,
services; Homeless, human services.

International interests: Mongolia.
Type of support: General/operating support; Continuing support; Equipment; Emergency funds; Program development; Conferences/seminars; Scholarship funds; Research; In-kind gifts; Matching/challenge support.
Limitations: Applications accepted. Giving primarily in UT, with emphasis on Weber County and Ogden City. No grants to individuals, or for salaries and benefits, "bricks and mortar," or capital campaigns.
Publications: Application guidelines.
Application information: Must complete application and provide all requested information. Application form required.
Initial approach: Letter
Copies of proposal: 1
Deadline(s): End of the quarter/prior to the quarter when grant request will be considered. Contact Grants Admin. for specific deadline dates, they may vary year to year
Board meeting date(s): Quarterly
Advisory Board and Directors:* W. Charles Swanson,* Chair. and C.E.O.; Cindy Purcell, Pres.; Annabel Hofer,* Exec. V.P.; Kim Dohrer; Michael Fosmark; Jon Greiner; Marcy Korgenski; Tami Swanson.
Number of staff: 35
EIN: 870578540
Recent grants for international programs:
2079-1 International Volunteers in Urology, Salt Lake City, UT, $15,000. For Mongolian trip. 2008.
2079-2 International Volunteers in Urology, Salt Lake City, UT, $15,000. For in-kind support for Mongolian trip. 2008.

2080
Tanner Charitable Trust
1930 S. State St.
Salt Lake City, UT 84115-2311

Incorporated in 1965 in UT.
Donors: Obert C. Tanner; O.C. Tanner Co.
Grantmaker type: Independent foundation.
Financial data (yr. ended 12/31/10): Assets, $2,626,002 (M); expenditures, $3,008,409; qualifying distributions, $2,993,257; giving activities include $2,993,257 for 38 grants (high: $500,000; low: $300).
Fields of interest: Performing arts; Arts; Higher education; Human services.
Limitations: Applications not accepted. Giving primarily in Salt Lake City, UT. No grants to individuals.
Application information: Contributes only to pre-selected organizations.
Officer and Trustees:* Carolyn T. Irish,* Chair.; David A. Petersen.
EIN: 876125059
Recent grants for international programs:
2080-1 Americans for Oxford, New York, NY, $500,000. 2010.

2081
The Taylor Family Foundation
1822 E. Sawgrass Cir.
Draper, UT 84020-8302

Established in 2002 in UT.
Donors: J. Steven Taylor; Kelly A. Taylor.
Grantmaker type: Independent foundation.

Financial data (yr. ended 12/31/10): Assets, $1,062,174 (M); expenditures, $214,667; qualifying distributions, $201,014; giving activities include $201,014 for grants.
Fields of interest: International relief; Human services; Education.
International interests: Latin America.
Limitations: Applications not accepted. Giving primarily in UT; some giving in Honduras. No grants to individuals.
Application information: Contributes only to pre-selected organizations.
Trustees: J. Steven Taylor; Kelly A. Taylor.
EIN: 743067797

2082
Trivani Foundation
198 S. Main St.
Springville, UT 84663-1849

Established in 2007 in UT.
Grantmaker type: Independent foundation.
Financial data (yr. ended 12/31/10): Assets, $1,341 (M); gifts received, $407,980; expenditures, $412,947; qualifying distributions, $341,110; giving activities include $341,110 for grants.
Fields of interest: Health care, clinics/centers; International relief; Children.
International interests: Kenya; Philippines.
Limitations: Applications not accepted. Giving primarily in UT. No grants to individuals.
Application information: Contributes only to pre-selected organizations.
Officers: Robert I. Steed, Pres.; Megan McMillan, Secy.
Manager: Chad A. Spiers.
Trustee: Allen K. Davis.
EIN: 260446110

2083
C. Scott and Dorothy E. Watkins Charitable Foundation
1935 E. Vine St., Ste. 260
Salt Lake City, UT 84121-6559

Established in 1992.
Donor: C. Scott Watkins‡.
Grantmaker type: Operating foundation.
Financial data (yr. ended 12/31/10): Assets, $41,979,452 (M); expenditures, $2,079,142; qualifying distributions, $2,000,000; giving activities include $2,000,000 for 59 grants (high: $160,000; low: $2,000).
Purpose and activities: Giving primarily for higher education, medical research, and health care.
Fields of interest: Higher education; Nursing school/education; Hospitals (general); Health care; Health organizations, association; Food banks; Youth development; Human services; Children/youth, services.
Limitations: Applications not accepted. Giving primarily in UT. No grants to individuals.
Application information: Contributes only to pre-selected organizations.
Trustees: Jay Rasmussen; Carol Watkins; Gary Watkins.
EIN: 876218993
Recent grants for international programs:
2083-1 Latter-Day Saints Humanitarian Center, Salt Lake City, UT, $90,000. 2009.

2083-2 Latter-Day Saints Humanitarian Center, Salt Lake City, UT, $75,000. For Perpetual Education Fund. 2009.
2083-3 Operation Smile International, Utah Chapter, Salt Lake City, UT, $28,000. 2009.

VERMONT

2084
Jan & David Blittersdorf Foundation, Inc.
P.O. Box 549
Hinesburg, VT 05461-0549
E-mail: info@blittersdorffamilyfoundation.org

Established in 2005 in VT.
Donors: David C. Blittersdorf; Jan L. Blittersdorf.
Grantmaker type: Independent foundation.
Financial data (yr. ended 12/31/10): Assets, $1,556,635 (M); expenditures, $1,720,971; qualifying distributions, $1,716,382; giving activities include $1,716,382 for grants.
Purpose and activities: The foundation is committed to promoting the development of renewable energy sources, building a sustainable world infrastructure, and celebrating arts and culture in order to help society make better long term choices while lessening the impact on world energy and natural resources.
Fields of interest: Reproductive health; Humanities; Education; Arts; Environment, energy; Environment.
Type of support: General/operating support; Program development; Seed money; Scholarship funds.
Limitations: Giving primarily in Vermont, with some support to national nonprofits connected to renewable energy and the environment. No grants to individuals.
Application information: Unsolicited full proposals not accepted. However, grantseekers may contact the foundation by e-mail to discuss funding priorities and opportunities to submit a proposal.
Deadline(s): None
Officers: Alyssa L. Blittersdorf, V.P.; Evan D. Blittersdorf, Secy.; David C. Blittersdorf, Treas.
EIN: 061764244
Recent grants for international programs:
2084-1 Bulletin of the Atomic Scientists, Chicago, IL, $10,000. 2009.
2084-2 Ecologists Linked for Organizing Grassroots Initiatives and Action, Whiting, VT, $10,000. 2009.
2084-3 Union of Concerned Scientists, Cambridge, MA, $50,000. 2009.

2085
Harris & Frances Block Foundation, Inc.
491 Ennis Hill Rd.
Marshfield, VT 05658-8250 (802) 426-3806
Contact: Betsy Chodorkoff, Treas.
E-mail: info@blockfound.org; URL: http://www.blockfound.org

Established in 2001 in VT.
Donor: Carol Maurer‡.
Grantmaker type: Independent foundation.

Financial data (yr. ended 12/31/10): Assets, $5,948,500 (M); gifts received, $520,730; expenditures, $320,855; qualifying distributions, $281,254; giving activities include $248,535 for 30 grants (high: $16,000; low: $3,000).
Purpose and activities: Giving primarily in the areas of economic justice, environmental protection, arms control, community development, and historic preservation.
Fields of interest: Historic preservation/historical societies; Environment, natural resources; International affairs, arms control; Civil/human rights; Economic development.
Limitations: Applications accepted. Giving in the U.S., primarily in VT; giving also in CT, MA, NC, and VA.
Application information:
Initial approach: Typed-written letter
Deadline(s): None
Officers: Nancy M. Sluys, V.P.; Diane Maurer Schatz, Secy.; Betsy M. Chodorkoff, Treas. and Exec. Dir.
EIN: 311784246

2086
The Evslin Family Foundation, Inc.
c/o Mary Evslin
2398 Stowe Hollow Rd.
Stowe, VT 05672-4430
E-mail: mary@evslin.com

Established in 2000 in NJ.
Donors: Mary Evslin; Tom Evslin.
Grantmaker type: Independent foundation.
Financial data (yr. ended 12/31/10): Assets, $1,308,774 (M); expenditures, $393,249; qualifying distributions, $389,807; giving activities include $388,617 for 35 grants (high: $166,667; low: $250).
Fields of interest: Medical school/education; Arts; Education; Medical research; Disasters, preparedness/services; International economic development; Economic development; Economically disadvantaged.
International interests: Developing countries.
Type of support: General/operating support; Emergency funds; Research; Technical assistance; Program-related investments/loans; Matching/challenge support.
Limitations: Applications not accepted. No support for religious or political organizations. No grants to individuals.
Publications: Grants list.
Application information: Contributes only to pre-selected organizations.
Board meeting date(s): Jan.
Officers: Mary A. Evslin,* Pres.; Tom I. Evslin, V.P. and Secy.
Directors: Kate Morris; Kelly Evans; Jarah Evslin.
Number of staff: None.
EIN: 223778394

2087
Himalayan Cataract Project, Inc.
P.O. Box 55
Waterbury, VT 05676-0055 (802) 522-9976
Contact: Emily Newick, C.O.O.; Job C. Heintz J.D., M.S.C., C.E.O.
FAX: (802) 649-1041;
E-mail: info@cureblindness.org; E-mail for Emily Newick: enewick@cureblindness.org; email for Job

C. Heintz: jheintz@cureblindness.org; URL: http://www.cureblindness.org

Established in 1995 in VT.
Grantmaker type: Public charity.
Financial data (yr. ended 12/31/10): Revenue, $4,309,220; assets, $7,930,510 (M); gifts received, $4,018,200; expenditures, $3,241,837; giving activities include $2,479,365 for grants to organizations outside the U.S., and $91,489 for grants to individuals.
Purpose and activities: The organization strives to eradicate preventable and curable blindness through high-quality ophthalmic care, education, and the establishment of a sustainable eye care infrastructure.
Fields of interest: Education; Health care; Optometry/vision screening; Eye diseases.
International interests: Asia; Bhutan; China; Ghana; India; Nepal.
Limitations: Applications not accepted. Giving on an international basis, primarily in the Himalayan region.
Publications: Annual report; Financial statement; Newsletter.
Application information: Unsolicited requests for funds not accepted.
Board meeting date(s): Oct.
Officer: Job Heintz, J.D., M.S.C., C.E.O.; Emily Newick, C.O.O.
Directors: Richard Litwin, M.D.; Matt Oliva, M.D.; Randall Olson, M.D.; Sanduk Ruit, M.D.; Geoffrey C. Tabin, M.D.; Hugh Taylor, M.D.
Number of staff: 2 full-time professional.
EIN: 030362926

2088
Institute for Sustainable Communities
535 Stone Cutters Way
Montpelier, VT 05602-3795 (802) 229-2900
FAX: (802) 229-2919; E-mail: isc@iscvt.org;
URL: http://www.iscvt.org
Facebook: http://www.facebook.com/SustainableComm
Twitter: http://twitter.com/SustainableComm

Established in 1991 in VT.
Grantmaker type: Public charity.
Financial data (yr. ended 09/30/10): Revenue, $14,030,981; assets, $4,730,016 (M); gifts received, $13,787,270; expenditures, $13,505,877; giving activities include $674,445 for grants, and $4,685,950 for 54 grants to organizations outside the U.S.
Purpose and activities: The institute's mission is to promote environmental protection and economic and social well-being through integrated strategies at the local level.
Fields of interest: Economic development; Environment; International development; Community/economic development.
Limitations: Giving on a national and international basis, with emphasis on Bulgaria, China, Hungary, Japan, Macedonia, Poland, Romania, Russia, Serbia, and Ukraine.
Officers and Directors:* Stephen D. Ramsey,* Esq., Chair.; John A. Dooley,* Vice-Chair.; Jan Blittersdorf, Pres. and C.E.O.; Harry Barnes, Jr.,* Secy.; Jerry Greenfield,* Treas.; Laura Colless; Perez Ehrich; George Hamilton; Elizabeth Knup; Madeleine M. Kunin; Ramsey A. Luhr; Richard D.

Paisner; James Gustave "Gus" Speth; Sandy Stash; Anne van Dusen.
EIN: 223098727

2089
C. Kaufman Family Foundation
c/o Stacey Gerrish
P.O. Box 120
Newport, VT 05855-0120

Established in 2004 in VT.
Donors: Barbara Kaufman; Kaufman Revocable Trust "B".
Grantmaker type: Independent foundation.
Financial data (yr. ended 12/31/10): Assets, $5,221,606 (M); expenditures, $242,670; qualifying distributions, $228,916; giving activities include $223,139 for 21 grants (high: $30,000; low: $650).
Fields of interest: Animals/wildlife, preservation/protection; Education; Health organizations; International economic development; Civil/human rights.
Type of support: General/operating support.
Limitations: Applications not accepted. No grants to individuals.
Application information: Unsolicited requests for funds not accepted.
Trustee: Community Financial Services Group.
EIN: 036111428

2090
Russian Arts Foundation
P.O. Box 248
Montpelier, VT 05602-0248 (802) 223-4955
FAX: (802) 223-6105;
E-mail: membership@russianarts.org; URL: http://www.russianarts.org

Established in 1992.
Grantmaker type: Public charity.
Financial data (yr. ended 12/31/10): Revenue, $1,968,288; assets, $4,426,786 (M); gifts received, $1,718,295; expenditures, $1,798,403; giving activities include $23,500 for grants, and $962,958 for grants to organizations outside the U.S.
Purpose and activities: The organization is dedicated to promoting international understanding through the arts, especially between Russia and the rest of the world.
Fields of interest: Arts, alliance/advocacy; Performing arts; Arts, cultural/ethnic awareness; Arts.
International interests: Russia.
Limitations: Giving primarily to Russia.
Publications: Newsletter.
Officers and Directors:* Thomas Ferguson,* Chair.; Richard P. Walker, Pres.; Kelly Kaplan,* Secy.; David L. Taub,* C.F.O.; Gordon Getty; Mikhail Gorbachev; Diana P. Kern; Michael J. Polenske; Barbara F. Roach; Helmut Schmidt; Shand S. Stephens; Marianne Wyman.
EIN: 943165716

2091
Underdog Foundation

23 Rte. 105, E. Brighton Rd.
P.O. Box 443
Island Pond, VT   05846-0443   (802) 723-9909
FAX: (802) 723-9933;
E-mail: info@underdogventures.com; URL: http://www2.underdogventures.com/underdog-foundation/

Established in 2001 in VT; supporting organization of Tides Foundation.
Grantmaker type: Public charity.
Financial data (yr. ended 12/31/10): Assets, $4,697,481 (M); expenditures, $37,707; giving activities include $34,500 for grants.
Fields of interest: International economic development; Animals/wildlife, preservation/protection; Environment; International development; Community/economic development; Women.
Type of support: Technical assistance.
Limitations: Applications not accepted. Giving on a national basis.
Application information: Contributes only to pre-selected organizations.
Officer and Directors:* David Berge,* Pres.; Alisa Gravitz; Drummond Pike; Joel Solomon.
EIN: 030368814

VIRGINIA

2092
Algerian-American Foundation for Culture, Education, Science and Technology

2001 Jefferson Davis Hwy., Ste. 208
Arlington, VA   22202-3604
E-mail: info@algerianamericanfoundation.org;
URL: http://algerianamericanfoundation.org/

Established in 2010.
Grantmaker type: Public charity.
Purpose and activities: The mission of the foundation is to: 1) Develop and foster strategic relations of cooperation between Algeria and the USA; 2) To promote progress of science and health between the two countries; 3) Advance the national interest in education in both countries; encourage innovative ideas whenever they arise; 4) Explore and identify opportunities and resources to promote training and community relations; and 5) to promote Algerian and American cultural exchange activities.
Fields of interest: International exchange; International exchange, arts; Science; Arts, cultural/ethnic awareness.
International interests: Algeria.
Limitations: Giving primarily in the United States and Algeria.
Officers and Directors:* Dr. Elias Zerhouni,* Chair.; Farid Amirouche,* Pres.; Zenagui Brahim, V.P.; James H. Bailey,* Secy.; Yacine Rahmoun, V.P.; Dr. Ismael Chikhoune, Treas.

2093
America's Development Foundation

101 N. Union St., Ste. 200
Alexandria, VA   22314-3231   (703) 836-2717
Contact: Michael D. Miller, Pres.
FAX: (703) 836-3379; E-Mail for Michael D. Miller : mmiller@adfusa.org; URL: http://www.adfusa.org

Established in 1980 in DC.
Grantmaker type: Public charity.
Financial data (yr. ended 12/31/10): Revenue, $1,485,092; assets, $519,968 (M); gifts received, $1,476,404; expenditures, $2,153,019; program services expenses, $1,584,950; giving activities include $590,926 for grants to organizations outside the U.S.
Purpose and activities: The foundation is dedicated to the international development of democracy and the belief that a strong civil society, comprising a diversity of autonomous economic, political, social, and cultural institutions, provides the indispensable foundation of a sustainable democracy.
Fields of interest: International democracy & civil society development.
International interests: Zimbabwe; Congo; Mozambique; Mali; Ethiopia; Ivory Coast; Burkina Faso; Benin; Angola; Panama; Nicaragua; Guatemala; El Salvador; Haiti; Iraq; West Bank/Gaza (Palestinian Territories); Morocco and the Western Sahara; Jordan; Egypt; Ukraine; Russia; Romania; Croatia; Bosnia-Herzegovina; Serbia; Uzbekistan; Kazakhstan; Afghanistan.
Limitations: Giving on an international basis with emphasis on Afghanistan, Angola, Benin, Bosnia-Herzegovina, Burkina Faso, Congo, Croatia, Egypt, El Salvador, Ethiopia, Guatemala, Iraq, Ivory Coast, Jordan, Kazakhstan, Mali, Morocco, Mozambique, Nicaragua, Panama, Romania, Russia, Serbia, Ukraine, Uzbekistan, West Bank/Gaza, and Zimbabwe.
Publications: Occasional report.
Officers and Directors:* Joseph Coblentz,* Chair.; Michael D. Miller,* Pres.; Nina Bention,* Secy.; Peter Goldmark; Heather Paul; Nader Tadros; Ross Worthington.
EIN: 521197547

2094
American Society for Industrial Security Foundation

(also known as ASIS Foundation)
1625 Prince St.
Alexandria, VA   22314-2882   (703) 519-6200
Contact: Robert Rowe, Dir., Devel.
FAX: (703) 519-6299;
E-mail: foundation@asisonline.org; URL: http://www.asisonline.org/foundation/noframe/about.html

Established in 1967; supporting organization of ASIS International, Inc.
Grantmaker type: Public charity.
Financial data (yr. ended 12/31/09): Revenue, $149,289; assets, $713,583 (M); gifts received, $140,829; expenditures, $236,403; program services expenses, $148,406; giving activities include $84,792 for 104 grants to individuals, and $63,614 for foundation-administered programs.
Purpose and activities: The foundation provides funding at the national and local levels to individuals seeking educational opportunities and to researchers in the security industry.

Fields of interest: Education; Safety, education.
International interests: South America; Central America.
Type of support: Matching/challenge support; Grants to individuals; Curriculum development; Conferences/seminars; Research; Scholarships—to individuals.
Limitations: Applications accepted. Giving on a national basis.
Publications: Application guidelines; Informational brochure; Newsletter.
Application information: Application form required.
   Deadline(s): Jan. 1 for Allan J. Cross Award; Feb. 6 for Timothy J. Walsh APC I Award; Mar. 1 for Roy Bordes Award for Physical Security;
   Board meeting date(s): Jan., June, and Sept.
Officers and Trustees:* David Davis,* C.P.P., Pres.; John A. Petruzzi, jr.,* C.P.P., V.P.; Brian J. Allen,* C.P.P., Secy.; Edward G. Hallen,* C.P.P., Treas.; Linda Florence, Ph.D., C.P.P.; Peter J. Mazzaroni, C.P.P.; Kaj Moller.
Number of staff: 1 full-time professional.
EIN: 520848090

2095
Ashoka: Innovators for the Public

1700 N. Moore St., Ste. 2000
Arlington, VA   22209-1939   (703) 527-8300
Contact: William Drayton, Chair. and C.E.O.
FAX: (703) 527-8383; E-mail: info@ashoka.org;
E-mail for individuals working in the U.S.: usprogram@ashoka.org; URL: http://www.ashoka.org
Facebook: http://www.facebook.com/pages/Ashoka/66279444793
Flickr: http://www.flickr.com/photos/ashokaphotos/
LinkedIn: http://www.linkedin.com/groups?gid=65728
RSS Feed: http://www.ashoka.org/rss/clippings
Scribd URL: http://www.scribd.com/AshokaDocs
Twitter: http://twitter.com/ashoka
YouTube: http://www.youtube.com/ashokavideos

Established in 1980.
Grantmaker type: Public charity.
Financial data (yr. ended 08/31/10): Revenue, $25,152,575; assets, $68,712,967 (M); gifts received, $24,813,865; expenditures, $30,268,073; giving activities include $630,000 for grants, $4,127,493 for grants to organizations outside the U.S., and $198,348 for grants to individuals.
Purpose and activities: The organization gives fellowships internationally to individuals who possess the innovation and drive to realize social change in education and youth development, health care, environment, human rights, access to technology, and economic development.
Fields of interest: Youth development, services; Youth development, ethics; Youth development, citizenship; Youth development, business; Youth development, association; Education; Environment; Animals/wildlife, preservation/protection; Animals/wildlife; Health care; AIDS; Employment; Nutrition; Agriculture/food; Housing/shelter; Youth development; International development; International agricultural development; International economic development; Civil/human rights; Urban/community development; Business/industry; Community/economic development; Venture philanthropy; Engineering/technology; Social sciences; Welfare policy/reform.

Type of support: In-kind gifts; Program development; Fellowships.

Limitations: Applications accepted. Giving on a national and international basis. No support for political or religious organizations.

Publications: Application guidelines; Informational brochure; Newsletter.

Application information: Visit http://www.changemakers.com for more information about the organization's Changemakers initiatives, including application guidelines and deadlines. Application form not required.

Initial approach: E-mail
Deadline(s): Rolling basis for Ashoka Fellowships; varies for Changemakers initiatives
Board meeting date(s): Monthly
Final notification: Acknowledgement within one month for Ashoka Fellowships

Officers and Directors:* William Drayton,* Chair. and C.E.O.; C. William Carter,* Secy.-Treas.; Gloria de Souza; Mary Gordon; Roger Harrison; Fred Hehuwat; William Kelly, Jr.; Kyle Zimmer.

Number of staff: 134 full-time professional; 11 part-time professional.

EIN: 510255908

2096
Associates of the American Foreign Service Worldwide

4001 9th St. N. No. 214
Arlington, VA 22203-1900
FAX: (703) 820-5421; E-mail: office@aafsw.org;
URL: http://www.aafsw.org

Established in 1960 in DC.

Grantmaker type: Public charity.

Financial data (yr. ended 06/30/10): Revenue, $127,945; assets, $290,985 (M); gifts received, $95,558; expenditures, $125,475; giving activities include $24,690 for grants.

Purpose and activities: The organization acts as an independent advocate for Foreign Service spouses, employees and retirees, attempting to give members a stronger voice when working on common concerns and a chance to enjoy shared interests.

Fields of interest: Scholarships/financial aid; International affairs, government agencies.

Type of support: Grants to individuals; Scholarship funds.

Application information:

Initial approach: Download application or contact the organization
Deadline(s): Mar. 1 for The J. Kirby Simon Foreign Service Trust; Apr. for Cox Professional Fellowship for Foreign Service Spouses
Board meeting date(s): 2nd Tuesday of each month

Officers and Directors:* Faye Barnes,* Pres.; Elaine Neumann,* 1st V.P.; Katherine Koch,* 2nd V.P.; Barbara Ratigan,* Secy.; Lucy Whitley,* Treas.; Mette Beecroft; Lesley Dorman; Judy Felt; Barbara Gordon; Katarina Hamilton; Terri Williams.

Number of staff: 1 part-time professional; 1 part-time support.

EIN: 526041153

2097
Bangs-Russell Foundation

c/o The Trust Company of Virginia
4097 Ironbound Rd., Ste. B
Williamsburg, VA 23188-2676

Established in 2004 in VA.

Donors: Archie E. Russell†; Marion B. Russell.

Grantmaker type: Independent foundation.

Financial data (yr. ended 12/31/10): Assets, $5,762,454 (M); expenditures, $491,768; qualifying distributions, $443,520; giving activities include $443,520 for grants.

Fields of interest: Christian agencies & churches; Salvation Army; American Red Cross; Higher education; Business school/education; Housing/shelter, development; Human services; International development; Catholic agencies & churches.

Type of support: General/operating support.

Limitations: Applications not accepted. Giving primarily in Washington, DC, GA, MO, NC and VA. No grants to individuals.

Application information: Contributes only to pre-selected organizations.

Officers: Marion B. Russell, Pres.; Elizabeth R. Ogburn, Secy.

Directors: William F. Russell; Barbara R. Valenti.

EIN: 201840390

2098
Aimee & Frank Batten, Jr. Foundation

150 Granby St.
Norfolk, VA 23510-1604

Established in 1998 in VA.

Donor: Frank Batten, Jr.

Grantmaker type: Independent foundation.

Financial data (yr. ended 12/31/09): Assets, $59,534,481 (M); expenditures, $4,547,982; qualifying distributions, $4,330,800; giving activities include $4,330,800 for 50 grants (high: $1,000,000; low: $2,500).

Purpose and activities: Giving primarily for Christian causes.

Fields of interest: Foundations (private grantmaking); Arts; Human services; Christian agencies & churches.

Limitations: Applications not accepted. Giving primarily in VA. No grants to individuals.

Application information: Contributes only to pre-selected organizations.

Officer and Director:* Frank Batten, Jr.,* Pres. and Secy. Treas.

EIN: 541879266

Recent grants for international programs:

2098-1 Elam Ministries, Alpharetta, GA, $50,000. 2009.

2098-2 Evangelical Alliance Mission, Carol Stream, IL, $120,000. 2009.

2098-3 Gods Story Project, Hemet, CA, $50,000. 2009.

2098-4 Gods Story Project, Hemet, CA, $50,000. 2009.

2098-5 Harvest Foundation, Phoenix, AZ, $75,000. 2009.

2098-6 Harvest Foundation, Phoenix, AZ, $25,000. 2009.

2098-7 Kanakuk Ministries, Branson, MO, $25,000. 2009.

2098-8 Medical Ambassadors International, Salida, CA, $250,000. 2009.

2098-9 Medical Ambassadors International, Salida, CA, $100,000. 2009.

2098-10 Opportunity International, Oak Brook, IL, $25,000. 2009.

2098-11 Physicians for Peace Foundation, Norfolk, VA, $25,000. 2009.

2098-12 Rafiki Foundation, Eustis, FL, $1,000,000. 2009.

2098-13 SAT-7 North American, Easton, MD, $25,000. 2009.

2098-14 World Mission Prayer League, Minneapolis, MN, $50,000. 2009.

2098-15 Wycliffe Bible Translators, Orlando, FL, $789,000. 2009.

2099
Blue Moon Fund, Inc.

(formerly W. Alton Jones Foundation, Inc.)
222 W. South St.
Charlottesville, VA 22902 (434) 295-5160
FAX: (434) 295-6894;
E-mail: info@bluemoonfund.org; URL: http://www.bluemoonfund.org
Grants Database: http://www.bluemoonfund.org/grantmaking/search/

Incorporated in 1944 in NY as W. Alton Jones Foundation.

Donor: W. Alton Jones†.

Grantmaker type: Independent foundation.

Financial data (yr. ended 12/31/10): Assets, $178,887,119 (L); expenditures, $17,224,193; qualifying distributions, $13,377,552; giving activities include $12,575,793 for 95 grants (high: $2,500,000; low: $25; average: $50,000–$200,000), and $85,082 for foundation-administered programs.

Purpose and activities: The fund supports initiatives that work to build human and natural resilience to a changing and warming world. It uses natural, social, and financial capital to implement new models in high-diversity regions around the world.

Fields of interest: Economic development; Environment, climate change/global warming; Environment, natural resources; Environment, energy.

Type of support: General/operating support; Program development; Program-related investments/loans; Matching/challenge support; Mission-related investments/loans.

Limitations: Applications accepted. Giving in Asia, primarily in China, the Greater Mekong region, and the Himalayas, in North America primarily in the Chesapeake, Appalachian and Gulf Coast regions, and in the Tropical Americas, primarily in the Andes-Amazon, the Eastern Amazon, and the Mesoamerica regions. No grants for lobbying, advertising, dissertations, thesis and other academic work.

Application information: The fund is an initiative-based organization and generally does not take unsolicited proposals. Staff selects organizations to fund that have the skills to further the projects developed by the staff. Organizations may also submit letters of inquiry through the foundation's web site. LOI's are reviewed periodically by staff who may invite full proposals.

Initial approach: Eligibility quiz on foundation web site
Board meeting date(s): Typically, five times annually

Officers and Trustees:* Diane Edgerton Miller,* C.E.O. and Pres.; Adrian Forsyth, Ph.D., V.P., Progs.; Ji-Qiang Zhang, V.P., Progs.; Diane Schmidt, C.F.O.; Beverly Lamb, Compt.

EIN: 136034219

Recent grants for international programs:

2099-1 Amazon Alliance for Indigenous and Traditional Peoples of the Amazon Basin,

Washington, DC, $80,000. For key program operations and coordination of indigenous groups in the Amazon Basin with a focus on creating a unified and positive stance on reduced emissions from degradation and deforestation (REDD) policy in the build-up to Copenhagen. 2009.

2099-2 Amazon Institute of People and the Environment, Belem, Brazil, $100,000. For the reduction of illegal logging and deforestation in the protected areas of the Brazilian Amazon by strengthening environmental law enforcement. 2009.

2099-3 Amazon Watch, San Francisco, CA, $56,000. For protection of the rainforests of the northern Peruvian Amazon by supporting indigenous organizations, challenging the oil and gas industry's expansion into pristine areas, and holding specific companies responsible for past ecological and social damage. 2009.

2099-4 Amazonicos por la Amazonia, Moyobamba, Peru, $145,500. For biodiversity conservation by supporting the operation and sustainable management of the Alto Huayabamba Conservation Concession in collaboration with local communities. 2009.

2099-5 American Museum of Natural History, New York, NY, $138,000. For the development of training materials for National Protected Area (NPA) managers aimed at the effective conservation of biodiversity and to provide training at the National University of Laos. 2009.

2099-6 Ashoka Trust for Research in Ecology and the Environment, Belmont, MA, $200,000. For building a model of natural resource management in India to enhance livelihoods, sustain ecological services and create institutions capable of scaling up and supporting this model. 2009.

2099-7 Asia Network for Sustainable Agriculture and Bioresources, Kathmandu, Nepal, $89,500. For biodiversity conservation through the creation of the Center of Excellence which will provide management solutions to others that balances social, economic and environmental concerns associated with effective rural development in Nepal and surrounding areas. 2009.

2099-8 Asociacion Centroamericana para la Economia, la Salud y el Ambiente, San Jose, Costa Rica, $49,500. For the identification of wetlands contamination in the Osa region in collaboration with local stakeholders, institutions and community organizations; for a demonstration prototype bio-garden; to promote environmental education and awareness about the importance of mangroves as natural resources. 2009.

2099-9 Asociacion Peruana para la Conservacion de la Naturaleza, Lima, Peru, $110,000. For the implementation of the regional protected area system of Amazonas department and to develop programs to manage solid waste and water contamination in region's rivers. 2009.

2099-10 Asociacion Peruana para la Conservacion de la Naturaleza, Lima, Peru, $26,500. For the incorporation of a Regional Protected Area System in the biodiverse frontier region of the Andean-Amazon mountain forests of Peru. 2009.

2099-11 Association for Children and their Environment, Lima, Peru, $35,000. For community dialogue in the southwestern Amazon region of Peru concerning the environmental impacts and other changes that will result from paving the interoceanic highway from Brazil to ports in the Pacific Ocean. 2009.

2099-12 Carnegie Endowment for International Peace, Washington, DC, $50,000. For substantive US-China energy and environmental collaboration by providing technical analysis, building high-level support for energy efficiency action and promoting innovative solutions to reduce the barriers to collaboration. 2009.

2099-13 Center for Climate Strategies, Washington, DC, $75,000. For training and technical assistance to bring CCS economic modeling tools to China as a resource for climate change planning and policy evaluation. 2009.

2099-14 Center for Responsible Travel, Washington, DC, $25,000. For completion of the first comprehensive analysis of coastal tourism development in Costa Rica and dissemination of the report to policymakers and the general public. 2009.

2099-15 Centre for the Development of the Amazonian Indigenous People, Lima, Peru, $84,250. For the design and implementation a sustainable development strategy for 11 million acres of tilled Malses indigenous territory and create a state-designated reserve to protect the Wises watershed. 2009.

2099-16 CERES, Boston, MA, $125,000. For public education regarding the importance of a global climate agreement. 2009.

2099-17 Children, Incorporated, Richmond, VA, $20,000. For the development of a community market space for people living on the indigenous reservation in Santa Luisa, Costa Rica to create sustainable economic growth. 2009.

2099-18 Conservation International, Arlington, VA, $266,000. For conservation of forests and biodiversity by engaging Peruvian NGOs in developing and managing three pilot high-quality forest carbon projects and to establish best practices for forest carbon management in the Amazonian Peru. 2009.

2099-19 Conservation International, Arlington, VA, $74,500. For proposed policies and practices regarding the management of land and water resources in the Sierpe-Terraba wetland system and associated ecosystems in Costa Rica's Osa Peninsula. 2009.

2099-20 Conservation International, Arlington, VA, $46,000. For a feasibility study to assess the potential for creating carbon offsets for a pilot Reduced Emissions from Deforestation and Forest Degradation (REDD) project in Prey Long, Cambodia. 2009.

2099-21 ECOA - Ecology and Action, Campo Grande, Brazil, $60,500. For conservation in the Amolar region of the Pantanal in Brazil through promotion of sustainable livelihoods focused on the tourism fishing industry, and activities supporting creation of a new federal protected area of at least 10,000 hectares. 2009.

2099-22 Environmental Defense, New York, NY, $52,000. For technical and social design of a collaborative Reduced Emissions from Deforestation and Degradation (REDD) project with indigenous peoples in the Xingu protected area. 2009.

2099-23 Falls Brook Centre, Knowlesville, Canada, $70,000. For restoration and rehabilitation of native mangrove forests and provide access to a diversity of food sources and value-added livelihood opportunities using the Analog Forestry system in the Cuero y Salado wetlands of Honduras. 2009.

2099-24 Field Museum of Natural History, Chicago, IL, $100,000. For conservation efforts in the Cerros Campanquiz in northern Peru by conducting a rapid biological and social inventory, to be used as a catalyst for creation of a large binational protected area on the Peru-Ecuador border. 2009.

2099-25 Freeland Foundation, Bangkok, Thailand, $102,500. For ex-poaching communities living near national parks in Cambodia to develop income alternatives to poaching, and to build the capacity of the ASEAN Wildlife Enforcement Network (ASEAN-WEN) and Laotian and Cambodian forest rangers to stop illegal poaching and wildlife trafficking. 2009.

2099-26 Friends of the Earth Brazil, Sao Paulo, Brazil, $80,000. For establishment of independent agricultural certification system in Brazil that will allow consumers to make informed decisions about their purchasing, reduce the socioenvironmental impacts of agricultural enterprises, and increase market access for certified producers. 2009.

2099-27 Fundacao Vitoria Amazonica, Manaus, Brazil, $43,000. For conservation of Protected Areas of the Lower Rio Negro Basin by providing technical assistance to distressed rural communities to bring their sustainably harvested non-timber forest products and handicrafts to market. 2009.

2099-28 Fundacion Cordillera Tropical, Cuenca, Ecuador, $20,000. For landowner outreach, technical studies and national Payments for Environmental Services (PES) program. 2009.

2099-29 Global Fund for Children, Washington, DC, $100,000. For general support. 2009.

2099-30 Global Fund for Children, Washington, DC, $25,000. For general support. 2009.

2099-31 GreenWood, South Berwick, ME, $75,000. For consolidation and expansion of lumber research, artisan training and wood product marketing program in the Palcazu Valley of the Peruvian Amazon in partnership with local NGOs and businesses. 2009.

2099-32 Guanacaste Dry Forest Conservation Fund, Philadelphia, PA, $20,000. For general support. 2009.

2099-33 Helvetas, Zurich, Switzerland, $80,000. For improved livelihoods of residents of upland regions by bringing clean, affordable and reliable energy to remote communities in Laos and by supporting productive uses of electricity consistent with conservation. 2009.

2099-34 Instituto Socioambiental, Sao Paulo, Brazil, $50,000. For the coordination Xingu Campaign aimed at conserving and restoring areas of the Rio Xingu basin and increasing forest governance, to consolidate the Xingu Seed Gatherers Network for facilitation of reforestation projects and to initiate place-based reforestation efforts in the Tanguro and Corgao sub-basins. 2009.

2099-35 International Network for Bamboo and Rattan, Beijing, China, $112,000. For the commercialization of pre-fabricated bamboo modular housing through strategic private public partnerships. 2009.

2099-36 International Network for Bamboo and Rattan, Beijing, China, $30,500. For bamboo as a viable option for disaster relief housing and to promote policies that favor bamboo's use in the housing sector in Peru. 2009.

2099-37 International Rivers Network, Berkeley, CA, $134,671. For education on the greenhouse gas emissions from dam reservoirs, the impact of climate change on the performance and safety of dams, and the need to help communities adapt to the impacts of climate change. 2009.

2099-38 International Rivers Network, Berkeley, CA, $120,000. For environmental reforms at the most important Chinese hydropower institutions to strengthen the environmental standards of China Exim Bank, and to mediate the development of Chinese dams based on compliance with international best practices. 2009.

2099-39 International Rivers Network, Berkeley, CA, $100,000. For public education regarding the planned dam construction on the rivers of the Amazon Basin including monitoring licensing and compliance and analyzing energy alternatives. 2009.

2099-40 International Snow Leopard Trust, Seattle, WA, $13,000. For the protection of the highly-endangered snow leopards in the rural communities in the North West Frontier Province and the Northern Areas of Pakistan through a participatory vaccination program. 2009.

2099-41 International Union for Conservation of Nature and Natural Resources, Washington, DC, $67,000. For educational efforts to help countries understand the governance and institutional arrangements required under REDD and build capacity on best practice guidance and principals. 2009.

2099-42 La Fundacion para la Sobrevivencia del Pueblo Cofan, Quito, Ecuador, $37,500. For key operations of the Cofan Ranger Program which provides effective control and management for Cotes territories containing over one million acres of highly biodiverse and pristine rain forests. 2009.

2099-43 McGill University, Montreal, Canada, $69,000. For the implementation of a Reducing Emissions from Deforestation and Degradation (REDD) project with indigenous communities in the Darien Peninsula. 2009.

2099-44 Nectandra Institute, Alameda, CA, $75,000. For conservation and restoration of water resources and forest ecosystems by engaging local communities in managing and valuing ecosystem services. 2009.

2099-45 New Global Citizens, Phoenix, AZ, $10,000. For general support. 2009.

2099-46 Organization for Tropical Studies, Durham, NC, $119,000. For the technical capacity of Guyana and Suriname in applied conservation and biodiversity science. 2009.

2099-47 RARE, Arlington, VA, $71,500. For pride campaigns for conservation in the Eastern Andes-Amazon Region of Peru. 2009.

2099-48 Shangri-la Alpine Botanical Garden, Diqing, China, $100,000. For a demonstration project for bare land vegetation restoration in Northwest Yunnan with native species and to establish the related climate change monitoring systems. 2009.

2099-49 Small-Scale Sustainable Infrastructure Development Fund, Cambridge, MA, $115,000. For further development and expansion of the S3IDF Social Merchant Bank's (SMB) portfolio of explicitly pro-poor small-scale investments in South India and to disseminate the SMB model. 2009.

2099-50 Sociedad Peruana de Derecho Ambiental, Lima, Peru, $113,000. For the dissemination and implementation of the initiative for private and community-based conservation in San

Marlin, Loreto and Amazonas in order to consolidate and increase the areas under formal instruments for conservation and to provide legal and technical support to regional governments. 2009.

2099-51 Stroud Water Research Center, Avondale, PA, $30,000. For assessment of water and habitat quality of streams and rivers in the Sierpe watershed. 2009.

2099-52 United Nations Foundation, Washington, DC, $100,000. For momentum for a strong international climate agreement by providing high-level convening, policy and technical support to the UNFCCC process. 2009.

2099-53 Wake Forest University, Winston-Salem, NC, $249,500. For collection of basic scientific data and development of carbon projects in highly threatened Andean forest ecosystems. 2009.

2099-54 Wake Forest University, Winston-Salem, NC, $178,000. For innovative remote sensing technique to estimate carbon stocks in high conservation priority areas of southeastern Peru to provide critical data for valuation of ecosystem services projects. 2009.

2099-55 Wildlife Conservation Nepal, Kathmandu, Nepal, $80,000. For the reduction in wildlife crime by creating a curriculum and training program on wildlife conservation and trafficking for the Nepal Police Academy. 2009.

2099-56 Wildlife Conservation Society, Bronx, NY, $383,000. For development and establishment of sustainable financing for a protected area in South Sudan encompassing East Africa's largest intact wild grassland and site of one of the world's largest mammalian migrations. 2009.

2099-57 Wildlife Conservation Society, Bronx, NY, $150,000. To continue support of the China Border Wildlife Guardian Award to promote cross-border wildlife conservation and law enforcement by providing training to top border guards and recognizing commitment and excellence in wildlife enforcement. 2009.

2099-58 Wildlife Conservation Society, Bronx, NY, $100,000. For the Takana Indigenous Council (CIPTA) in the Madidi region of Bolivia to develop updated sustainable management strategy for the Takana Indigenous Territory, to develop a proposal for the international carbon credit market using the avoided deforestation mechanism (REDD), and structure a community-based trust fund for CIPTA and the Takana to hold the proceeds of the avoided deforestation. 2009.

2099-59 Wildlife Conservation Society, Bronx, NY, $65,000. For a biodiversity friendly rotational grazing system for cattle ranching in deforested regions of the Brazilian Pantanal which will mitigate harmful effects of cattle ranching in these areas and allow the region to sustain stable populations of key wildlife species. 2009.

2099-60 Wildlife Conservation Society, Bronx, NY, $30,000. For a feasibility assessment for payment of ecosystem services (PES) project in Laos that will bundle watershed and forest carbon values. 2009.

2099-61 Woodrow Wilson International Center for Scholars, Washington, DC, $100,000. For US-China dialogue on energy and environmental collaboration by providing educational opportunities aimed at promoting dialogue and debate on China's efforts to lower carbon emissions and highlighting cooperative

opportunities to make a global transition to lower carbon economies. 2009.

2099-62 World Wildlife Fund, Washington, DC, $156,000. For the continued monitoring and documentation of the movement of keystone species in the lowlands being bisected by the Interoceanic Highway and the potential impact of the proposed Inambari hydroelectric project. 2009.

2100
Bread and Water for Africa, Inc.
2550 Huntington Ave., Ste. 200
Alexandria, VA   22303-1400   (703) 317-9440
FAX: (703) 317-9690; URL: http://africanrelief.org/
Flickr: http://www.flickr.com/photos/
bread_and_water_for_africa/
YouTube: http://www.youtube.com/AfricanRelief

Established in 1986.
Grantmaker type: Public charity.
Financial data (yr. ended 06/30/10): Revenue, $6,813,429; assets, $145,282 (M); gifts received, $6,813,429; expenditures, $6,808,149; giving activities include $6,721,936 for grants to organizations outside the U.S.
Purpose and activities: The organization aims to support and strengthen grassroots intiatives for community self-sufficiency, health and education in Africa.
International interests: Africa.
Limitations: Giving primarily in Africa.
Officers and Directors: * James J. O'Brien,* Esq., Chair.; Eugene L. Krizek,* Pres.; Bryan L. Krizek,* C.E.O.; Clyde B. Richardson,* Treas.; Bethelhem Tessema, Exec. Dir.; Myriam Jones, M.D.; Marshall A. Mackler; and 4 additional directors.
EIN: 541884520

2101
Cedars Foundation, Inc.
40123 Bond St.
P.O. Box 55
Waterford, VA   20197

Established in 1999 in DE and VA.
Donor: W. Bowman Cutter.
Grantmaker type: Independent foundation.
Financial data (yr. ended 12/31/10): Assets, $1,015,638 (M); gifts received, $144,367; expenditures, $235,226; qualifying distributions, $197,750; giving activities include $197,750 for 36 grants (high: $75,000; low: $100).
Purpose and activities: Giving primarily for environmental conservation and international relief efforts.
Fields of interest: International relief; Public policy, research; Environment, natural resources; Higher education; Human services.
Limitations: Applications not accepted. No grants to individuals.
Application information: Unsolicited requests for funds not accepted.
Officer: W. Bowman Cutter III, Managing Dir.
EIN: 223651734

2102
Center for the Support of Native Lands
3503 13th St. N.
Arlington, VA   22201-4907   (703) 243-1526

Grantmaker type: Public charity.
Purpose and activities: The center works to protect biological and cultural diversity throughout the world, with a strong focus on Latin America.
Fields of interest: Arts; Environment; Indigenous peoples.
International interests: Latin America.
Board Members: Jack Vanderryn; Wilbur Wright; Sally Yudelman.
EIN: 541861490

2103
Kamlesh & Luci Chainani Foundation
c/o Argy
8405 Greensboro Dr., Ste. 700
McLean, VA 22102-5108

Established in 2001 in VA.
Donors: Kamlesh Chainani; FC Business Systems; Luci Chainani.
Grantmaker type: Independent foundation.
Financial data (yr. ended 12/31/10): Assets, $4,100,464 (M); expenditures, $207,815; qualifying distributions, $181,871; giving activities include $176,096 for 1 grant.
Fields of interest: Hospitals (specialty); Food services; Children/youth, services; Health care; Human services; International relief.
Limitations: Applications not accepted.
Application information: Unsolicited requests for funds not accepted.
Officers: Kamlesh Chainani, Pres.; Angela Gilbert, V.P. and Secy.
EIN: 542061344

2104
Charities Aid Foundation America
(also known as CAFAmerica)
King St. Sta.
1800 Diagonal Rd., Ste. 150
Alexandria, VA 22314-2840 (703) 549-8931
Contact: Susan K.E. Saxon-Harrold, C.E.O.
FAX: (703) 549-8934; E-mail: info@cafamerica.org;
URL: http://www.cafamerica.org

Founded in 1992.
Grantmaker type: Public charity.
Financial data (yr. ended 04/30/11): Revenue, $46,886,137; assets, $55,116,367 (M); gifts received, $45,406,767; expenditures, $39,666,406; giving activities include $6,678,745 for grants, and $31,087,137 for grants to organizations outside the U.S.
Purpose and activities: The foundation administers donor-advised funds that encourage cross-border philanthropy by providing grantmaking and advice about international philanthropic issues to donors who want to support charitable organizations throughout the world.
Fields of interest: International affairs, fund raising/fund distribution.
Limitations: Applications not accepted. Giving on an international basis. No support for political organizations or organizations in countries sanctioned by the U.S. government. No grants to individuals.
Publications: Annual report; Financial statement; Informational brochure; Newsletter.
Application information: Contributes only to pre-selected organizations.
    Board meeting date(s): Feb., June, and Oct.

Officers and Directors:* Janet Boyd,* Pres.; Susan K.E. Saxon-Harrold,* Ph.D., C.E.O.; Sarah Allan; Mara-Michelle Batlin; Anthony C. Rogers, F.C.A.; Russell Prior.
Number of staff: 3 full-time professional; 1 part-time support.
EIN: 431634280

2105
ChildFund International
(formerly Christian Children's Fund)
2821 Emerywood Pkwy.
Richmond, VA 23294-3725 (804) 756-2700
E-mail: questions@childfund.org; Toll-free tel.: (800) 776-6767; URL: http://www.childfund.org
Blog: http://childfundinternational.wordpress.com/
Facebook: http://www.facebook.com/ChildFundInternational
LinkedIn: http://www.linkedin.com/companies/childfund-international
Twitter: http://twitter.com/ChildFund
YouTube: http://www.youtube.com/user/childfundtube

Established in 1951.
Grantmaker type: Public charity.
Financial data (yr. ended 06/30/10): Revenue, $215,772,220; assets, $83,079,438 (M); gifts received, $212,431,296; expenditures, $212,581,677; giving activities include $2,082,249 for grants, and $136,861,146 for grants to organizations outside the U.S.
Purpose and activities: The fund provides long-term sustainable assistance to impoverished children around the world through its educational opportunities, nutritional assistance, health benefits, and access to safe water and waste disposal programs.
Fields of interest: Children, services; International relief.
Type of support: In-kind gifts; Emergency funds; Scholarships—to individuals; Matching/challenge support.
Limitations: Giving on a national and international basis.
Publications: Annual report; Informational brochure; Newsletter.
Officers and Directors:* Ann C. Crouter,* Ph.D., Chair.; William E. Leahey, Jr.,* 1st Vice-Chair. and Pres.; Steven A. Markel,* 2nd Vice-Chair.; Charles M. Caravati, Jr.,* M.D., Secy.; Lewis T. Booker,* Treas.; Jesus M. Amadeo; A. Scott Andrews; Jenny Taylor Bond, Ph.D.; Austin Brockenbrough III; Lisa D. Collis; Glenn Davidson; Maureen J. Denlea; Roger L. Gregory; Karen Hein, M.D.; Stephen F. Keller; and 8 additional directors.
EIN: 540536100

2106
Christian Relief Services, Inc.
2550 Huntington Ave., Ste. 200
Alexandria, VA 22303-1400 (703) 317-9086
Contact: Paul Krizek, V.P.
E-mail: info@christianrelief.org; Toll-free tel.: (800) 33-RELIEF; URL: http://www.christianrelief.org

Established in 1985 in VA.
Grantmaker type: Public charity.
Financial data (yr. ended 06/30/10): Revenue, $18,558,744; assets, $1,048,817 (M); gifts received, $18,284,869; expenditures,

$18,150,057; giving activities include $10,274,955 for grants, and $520,272 for grants to organizations outside the U.S.
Purpose and activities: The organization assists in the alleviation of human suffering, misery, pain, and disability in the world by advancing and improving the welfare of all persons and the international community while preserving native cultures, heritage, customs, and beliefs.
Fields of interest: Agriculture; Housing/shelter; Human services, emergency aid; Human services; International development.
Type of support: In-kind gifts.
Limitations: Applications not accepted. Giving on a national and international basis. No support for organizations lacking 501 (c)(3) status. No grants to individuals.
Publications: Annual report; Financial statement; Newsletter.
Application information: Contributes only to pre-selected organizations.
    Board meeting date(s): Quarterly
Officers and Directors:* James J. O'Brien,* Chair.; Eugene L. Krizek,* Pres.; Bryan Krizek,* V.P. and C.F.O.; Paul Krizek,* V.P.; Miriam Jones,* M.D., Secy.; Clyde B. Richardson,* Treas.; Emil Her Many Horses; Robert J. Hisel; Rev. Charles T. Holliday; Tracy Kelso; Marshall A. Mackler; Frank Stitely, C.P.A.
Number of staff: 140 full-time professional; 12 part-time professional.
EIN: 541884868

2107
Christian Training Foundation
8800 Arlington Blvd.
Fairfax, VA 22031-2706

Established in 2006 in VA.
Donors: Claudia Moore; Vernon Lewis; Mamie Burton; Jane Snyder; Ellen K. Blackwell; Robert S. Burt; Leni A. Christian; Frederick A. Merana; Way of Faith Assembly of God.
Grantmaker type: Public charity.
Financial data (yr. ended 12/31/10): Revenue, $946,627; assets, $14,902 (M); gifts received, $946,593; expenditures, $1,136,910; giving activities include $24,381 for grants, and $1,099,313 for grants to organizations outside the U.S.
Purpose and activities: Giving primarily to a Christian fellowship house in Israel.
Fields of interest: Christian agencies & churches.
International interests: Israel.
Limitations: Applications not accepted. Giving primarily in Israel. No grants to individuals.
Application information: Contributes only to pre-selected organizations.
Officers: Ellen K. Blackwell, Pres.; Robert S. Burt, V.P.; Eugene Pearson, Secy.; Kathryn N. Thomas, Treas.
EIN: 202699636

2108
City of Joy Aid, Inc.
c/o Marie B. Allizon
9501 4th Pl.
Lorton, VA 22079-2700 (703) 847-6147
FAX: (703) 734-6956; E-mail: marie@4dshift.com;
URL: http://www.cityofjoyaid.org/

Established in 1981.
Grantmaker type: Public charity.
Financial data (yr. ended 12/31/10): Revenue, $95,868; assets, $17,357 (M); gifts received, $95,868; expenditures, $80,737; giving activities include $80,200 for grants.
Purpose and activities: The organization is dedicated to helping the underprivileged and impoverished in Kolkata and Bengal in India, and the Dominican Republic.
Fields of interest: Human services; Economically disadvantaged; Children; Children/youth; Mentally disabled; Minorities.
International interests: India.
Limitations: Giving primarily in Kolkata and Bengal, India, and the Dominican Republic.
Director: Marie Allizon.
EIN: 541566941

2109
Cooperative Development Foundation
(also known as CDF)
2011 Crystal Dr., Ste. 800
Arlington, VA   22202-3734   (703) 302-8094
E-mail: info@cdf.coop; URL: http://www.cdf.coop
Facebook: http://www.facebook.com/group.php?gid=17109752406
Flickr: http://www.flickr.com/photos/50062413@N07/
Twitter: http://twitter.com/CoopFoundation
YouTube: http://www.youtube.com/user/CoopHall

Established in 1944 in IL.
Grantmaker type: Public charity.
Financial data (yr. ended 12/31/10): Revenue, $569,608; assets, $4,121,856 (M); gifts received, $307,766; expenditures, $559,966; giving activities include $211,835 for grants.
Purpose and activities: The foundation promotes community, economic, and social development through cooperative enterprise.
Fields of interest: Aging, centers/services; Agriculture; Agriculture, farm cooperatives; Housing/shelter; International economic development; Leadership development.
Limitations: Applications accepted. Giving on a national and international basis.
Publications: Application guidelines; Annual report; Financial statement.
Application information: Application form not required.
 Initial approach: Letter, e-mail, or telephone
 Copies of proposal: 1
 Deadline(s): Varies
 Board meeting date(s): Jan., Apr., July, and Oct.
Officers and Directors:* Gasper Kovach, Jr.,* Chair.; James Johnson,* Secy.; Rebecca Dunn, Jr.,* Treas.; Douglas Graham; Paul Hazen; Terry Lewis, Esq.; Mary McLaury; Ralph Paige; Ira Schwartz.
Number of staff: 3 full-time professional.
EIN: 237044533

2110
Corporations to End World Hunger Foundation
1350 Beverly Rd., Ste. 617
McLean, VA   22101-0856   (703) 917-9500
Contact: Gilbert A. Robinson, Chair.

Established in 1999 as a private foundation; became a public charity in 2002.

Grantmaker type: Public charity.
Purpose and activities: The foundation provides aid for economically-disadvantaged families and orphans residing in Russia.
Fields of interest: Human services; Residential/custodial care; Economically disadvantaged.
International interests: Russia.
Limitations: Giving primarily in Russia.
Officers: Gilbert A. Robinson, Chair.; Kenneth T. Hoeck, Treas.
EIN: 521458696

2111
Crosslink International, Ltd.
427 N. Maple Ave.
Falls Church, VA   22046-3428   (703) 534-5465
Contact: Malcolm Cook, Chair.; Dan Henneberg, Exec. Dir.
FAX: (703) 536-8349;
E-mail: dan@crosslinkinternational.net; URL: http://www.crosslinkinternational.net

Incorporated in 1996.
Grantmaker type: Public charity.
Financial data (yr. ended 09/30/09): Revenue, $5,325,467; assets, $789,759 (M); gifts received, $5,171,886; expenditures, $5,530,040; giving activities include $4,902,886 for grants.
Purpose and activities: The organization supplies medical mission teams, humanitarian aid organizations, free clinics and hospitals with medicines and supplies to reduce suffering among the world's most needy.
Fields of interest: Health care; International relief.
Type of support: In-kind gifts.
Limitations: Giving on a national and international basis.
Publications: Annual report; Newsletter.
Officers and Directors:* Daryl Jackson,* Chair.; Carl Biggs,* Vice-Chair.; Mary Ellen Gannon,* Secy.; Will Soza,* Treas.; Amy Hammer; Glenn Letham; James L. Oakes; Pete Sparber; and 4 additional directors.
Number of staff: 4 full-time professional; 8 part-time professional.
EIN: 541827160

2112
Dayspring International, Inc.
P.O. Box 3309
Virginia Beach, VA   23454-9409   (757) 428-1092
URL: http://www.dayspringinternational.org

Established in 1979 in VA.
Grantmaker type: Public charity.
Financial data (yr. ended 12/31/10): Revenue, $5,580,994; assets, $1,265,171 (M); gifts received, $5,572,058; expenditures, $5,476,541; giving activities include $3,499,352 for grants to organizations outside the U.S.
Purpose and activities: The organization works to transform villages all across India by engaging each person with powerful, culturally-relevant media, establishing local churches as community centers, and elevating the individual through education, training, and relief.
Fields of interest: Christian agencies & churches; Community/economic development; Economically disadvantaged.
International interests: India.
Type of support: In-kind gifts.

Limitations: Giving primarily to India.
Publications: Financial statement; Newsletter.
Officers and Directors:* Rev. George Ivey III,* Chair.; Deborah B. Darnell, Secy.; Scott Mitchell,* Treas.; Dr. Dale Berkey; John Gilman, Jr.; Timothy Persons.
EIN: 510237239

2113
The Charles Delmar Foundation
5205 Leesburg Pike, Ste. 209
Falls Church, VA   22041-3858

Established in 1957 in DC.
Donors: Charles Delmar†; Roland H. Delmar†; Elizabeth A. Delmar†; Mareen D. Hughes.
Grantmaker type: Independent foundation.
Financial data (yr. ended 12/31/10): Assets, $7,045,330 (M); expenditures, $316,453; qualifying distributions, $291,942; giving activities include $291,942 for 122 grants (high: $10,000; low: $32).
Purpose and activities: Special interests include inter-American studies, higher, secondary, elementary, and other education, underprivileged youth, the disadvantaged, the aged, the homeless and housing issues, general welfare organizations, and fine and performing arts.
Fields of interest: Reproductive health, family planning; Performing arts; Higher education; Environment, natural resources; Hospitals (general); Health organizations; Human services; Children/youth, services; Protestant agencies & churches; Catholic agencies & churches; Youth; Substance abusers; Mentally disabled; Deaf/hearing impaired; Infants/toddlers; Children/youth; Children; Adults; Aging; Disabilities, people with; Physically disabled; Blind/visually impaired; Minorities; African Americans/Blacks; Hispanics/Latinos; Native Americans/American Indians; Indigenous peoples; Women; Girls; Adults, women; Men; Boys; Adults, men; Military/veterans; AIDS, people with; Economically disadvantaged; Homeless; Migrant workers.
International interests: Europe; Latin America.
Type of support: General/operating support; Continuing support; Annual campaigns; Capital campaigns; Building/renovation; Endowments; Conferences/seminars; Seed money; Internship funds; Scholarship funds.
Limitations: Applications accepted. Giving primarily in the Washington, DC area in the U.S., and in Europe and South America. No support for religious or political organizations. No grants to individuals, or for building or endowment funds, or matching gifts; no loans.
Publications: Financial statement.
Application information: Application form not required.
 Initial approach: Letter
 Copies of proposal: 1
 Deadline(s): None
 Board meeting date(s): As required
Officers and Trustees:* Mareen D. Hughes,* Pres.; R. Bruce Hughes,* Secy.-Treas.
EIN: 526035345

2114
Diema's Dream Foundation
9103 Dellwood Dr.
Vienna, VA 22180-6120
Contact: Debra Cockrell, C.F.O. and Exec. Dir.
FAX: (703) 319-0011;
E-mail: debra@diemasdream.com; URL: http://www.diemasdream.com

Established in 1998.
Grantmaker type: Public charity.
Financial data (yr. ended 12/31/09): Revenue, $371,189; assets, $474,608 (M); gifts received, $187,485; expenditures, $577,176; giving activities include $505,605 for grants.
Purpose and activities: The foundation provides financial, medical and educational support to mentally and/or physically disabled Eastern European children.
Fields of interest: Children, services; Disabilities, people with.
International interests: Eastern & Central Europe; Russia.
Type of support: General/operating support; Continuing support; Building/renovation; Equipment; Conferences/seminars; Exchange programs.
Limitations: Applications not accepted. Giving primarily in Russia. No support for political organizations.
Publications: Financial statement; Informational brochure; Newsletter; Program policy statement.
Application information: Contributes only to pre-selected organizations.
Officers and Director:* Mary Dudley,* Pres. and Founder; Debra Cockrell,* C.F.O. and Exec. Dir.
Number of staff: 3 part-time support.
EIN: 364254630

2115
Donors Capital Fund, Inc.
P.O. Box 1305
Alexandria, VA 22313-1305

Supporting organization of American Enterprise Institute, Americans for Limited Government, Cato Institute, Center for Islamic Pluralism, Center of the American Experiment, Commonwealth Foundation for Public Policy, Evergreen Freedom Foundation, Federalist Society, George Mason University Foundation Inc., Goldwater Institute, Heartland Institute, Hudson Institute, Independence Institute, Institute for Justice, James Madison Institute, LEAD Foundation, Palmer R. Chester Fund, Reason Foundation, South Carolina Center for Grassroots and Community Alternatives, South Carolina Political Council Education Foundation, Texas Public Policy Foundation, U.S. Term Limits Foundation, Yankee Institute for Public Policy Studies, and 59 other organizations.
Grantmaker type: Public charity.
Financial data (yr. ended 12/31/09): Revenue, $57,298,374; assets, $55,638,563 (M); gifts received, $56,570,167; expenditures, $60,457,404; giving activities include $59,781,233 for grants.
Fields of interest: Philanthropy/voluntarism; Arts; Education; Environment; Health care; Human services; International affairs; Public affairs.
Limitations: Applications not accepted. Giving on a national basis.

Application information: Contributes only to pre-selected organizations.
Board meeting date(s): Annually
Officers: Bruce H. Jacobs, Pres.; Adam Meyerson, V.P.; Whitney L. Ball, Secy.; Steven Hayward, Treas.
Board Members: Melissa M. Cliett; Christopher DeMuth; Kris Alan Mauren; William H. Mellor; Stephen Moore; John Von Kannon.
EIN: 541934032

2116
The Dorothy-Ann Foundation
c/o Vernon Geddy III
1177 Jamestown Rd.
Williamsburg, VA 23185-3315

Established in 1999 in VA.
Donors: Darwin O'Ryan Curtis; Darwin O'Ryan Curtis Charitable Lead Annuity Trust.
Grantmaker type: Independent foundation.
Financial data (yr. ended 12/31/10): Assets, $483,368 (M); gifts received, $179,789; expenditures, $278,763; qualifying distributions, $272,873; giving activities include $222,237 for 9 grants (high: $64,242; low: $495).
Purpose and activities: Giving primarily for international health and environmental conservation.
Fields of interest: Environment, natural resources; Health care.
International interests: Latin America; Africa.
Type of support: General/operating support; Program development; Seed money; Matching/challenge support.
Limitations: Applications not accepted. Giving on an international basis. No grants to individuals.
Publications: Occasional report.
Application information: Contributes only to pre-selected organizations.
Board meeting date(s): Fall
Officer: Vernon M. Geddy III, Secy.-Treas.
Number of staff: None.
EIN: 541965966

2117
Earthrights International, Inc.
4306 Evergreen Ln., Ste. 202
Annandale, VA 22003-3217
E-mail: infousa@earthrights.org; URL: http://www.earthrights.org
causes: http://www.causes.com/causes/8766-earthrights-international
Facebook: http://www.facebook.com/EarthRightsIntl
RSS Feed: http://feeds.feedburner.com/EarthRightsInternational
Twitter: http://twitter.com/#!/earthrightsintl

Grantmaker type: Public charity.
Financial data (yr. ended 01/31/10): Revenue, $2,141,615; assets, $3,786,663 (M); gifts received, $1,590,071; expenditures, $1,845,402; giving activities include $43,861 for grants to organizations outside the U.S.
Purpose and activities: The organization works to combine the power of law and the power of people in defense of human rights and the environment, with the goals of ending earth rights abuses, providing real solutions for real people, and promoting and protecting human rights and the environment in all communities.

Fields of interest: Civil/human rights; Civil/human rights, advocacy; International affairs; Environment, pollution control; Environment.
Type of support: Grants to individuals.
Limitations: Giving on an international basis, primarily in Thailand.
Publications: Annual report; Informational brochure.
Officers and Directors:* Dr. Charlie Clements,* Co-Chair. and Secy.; Marianne Manilov,* Co-Chair.; David Hunter,* Esq., Treas.; Ka Hsaw Wa, Exec. Dir.; Toshiyuki Doi; Kumi Naidoo; Neil Popovic; Rebecca Rockefeller; Kate Tillery.
EIN: 043265555

2118
EduCare Education Inc. Contributions Program
12809 Glendale Ct
Fredericksburg, VA 22407-2060
(866) 338-7217
E-mail: info@educatencare.com; URL: http://www.educateNcare.com
B Corporation Profile: http://www.bcorporation.net/educare

Grantmaker type: Corporate giving program.
Purpose and activities: EduCare is a certified B Corporation that donates a percentage of net profits to charitable organizations. Support is given primarily in Africa and Asia.
Fields of interest: Elementary/secondary education; Economically disadvantaged.
International interests: Africa; Asia.
Type of support: General/operating support.
Limitations: Giving primarily in Africa and Asia.

2119
Feris Foundation of America, Inc.
120 Vincennes Rd.
Charlottesville, VA 22911-8538
(434) 977-1868
Contact: Allen Lynch, V.P.

Established in 1972.
Donors: Carter Gallatin Fund; Eberly Family Trust; Bank Switzerland Alumni Assn.; Shelby Cullom Davis & Co.
Grantmaker type: Independent foundation.
Financial data (yr. ended 12/31/10): Assets, $358,585 (M); gifts received, $258,650; expenditures, $296,277; qualifying distributions, $296,159; giving activities include $292,703 for 2 grants (high: $290,000; low: $2,703).
Fields of interest: Higher education; International studies.
International interests: Global programs.
Type of support: Fellowships; Scholarships—to individuals.
Limitations: Applications accepted. Giving on an international basis.
Publications: Newsletter.
Application information: Application form required.
Initial approach: Letter
Deadline(s): None
Officers: Alexander Swoboda, Pres.; Allen Lynch, E.V.P.; David Carmack, Secy.; Paul Mathieu, Treas.
Directors: Alain Dick; Bates Gill; Ernesto Hernandez-Cata.
EIN: 132748862

2120
The Foster Family Foundation
14501 George Carter Way
Chantilly, VA 20151-1770

Established in 1998 in VA.
Donors: Betty Flanders Foster; Wesley Foster, Jr.
Grantmaker type: Independent foundation.
Financial data (yr. ended 12/31/10): Assets, $3,025,951 (M); expenditures, $163,544; qualifying distributions, $140,000; giving activities include $140,000 for grants.
Purpose and activities: Giving primarily for international relief and local environmental concerns.
Fields of interest: Education; Environment; International relief.
International interests: Honduras.
Type of support: Emergency funds; Program development.
Limitations: Applications not accepted. Giving primarily in the Washington, DC, area.
Application information: Contributes only to pre-selected organizations.
Officers and Directors:* Betty Flanders Foster,* Pres.; Julia Heather Hanks,* V.P. and Secy.; Philip Rodney Lawrence, Jr.,* V.P. and Treas.; P. Wesley Foster, Jr.,* V.P.; Paul Wesley Foster III,* V.P.; Amanda Foster Spahr,* V.P.; George W. Spahr,* V.P.
EIN: 541902260

2121
Galapagos Conservancy
(formerly Charles Darwin Foundation, Inc.)
11150 Fairfax Blvd., Ste. 408
Fairfax, VA 22030-5066 (703) 383-0077
E-mail: comments@galapagos.org; URL: http://www.galapagos.org

Founded in 1986; supporting organization of Charles Darwin Foundation for the Galapagos Isles.
Grantmaker type: Public charity.
Financial data (yr. ended 03/31/11): Revenue, $413,273; assets, $5,074,527 (M); gifts received, $389,300; expenditures, $437,287; giving activities include $112,679 for grants to organizations outside the U.S., and $1,260 for grants to individuals.
Fields of interest: Animal welfare; Environment; Environment, natural resources; Environment, public education.
International interests: Ecuador.
Limitations: Giving on a national and international basis, with emphasis on Ecuador.
Officers and Directors:* Richard Wood,* Chair.; Johannah E. Barry,* Pres.; Elizabeth Nassikas,* Secy.; Jon Stufflebeem,* Treas.; Ian Bowers; Veronique Chopin de la Bruyere; Maria Markham; Ray Rifenburg.
EIN: 133281486

2122
Gannett Foundation, Inc.
7950 Jones Branch Dr.
McLean, VA 22107-0001 (703) 854-6000
Contact: Pat Lyle, Mgr.

FAX: (703) 854-2167;
E-mail: foundation@gannett.com; URL: http://www.gannettfoundation.org
Media Grants: http://www.gannettfoundation.org/media.htm

Established in 1991 in VA.
Donor: Gannett Co., Inc.
Grantmaker type: Company-sponsored foundation.
Financial data (yr. ended 12/31/09): Assets, $15,547,586 (M); expenditures, $4,240,103; qualifying distributions, $4,193,623; giving activities include $2,725,750 for 69 grants (high: $1,500,000; low: $250), and $1,394,196 for 4,118 employee matching gifts.
Purpose and activities: The foundation supports organizations involved with arts and culture, media and journalism, education, conservation, health, youth development, human services, diversity, community development, minorities, women, and economically disadvantaged people.
Fields of interest: Arts; Arts, cultural/ethnic awareness; Civil liberties, first amendment; Civil/human rights, equal rights; Community development, neighborhood development; Community/economic development; Economic development; Education; Environment, natural resources; Health care; Human services; Journalism school/education; Media, print publishing; Media/communications; Youth development; Economically disadvantaged; Minorities; Women.
International interests: United Kingdom.
Type of support: Capital campaigns; Conferences/seminars; Employee matching gifts; Equipment; Program development; Scholarship funds.
Limitations: Applications accepted. Giving on a national and international basis in areas of company operations, with emphasis on AZ, Washington DC, FL, IN, MI, NY, OH, VA and the United Kingdom. No support for private foundations, regional or national organizations not addressing local needs, elementary or secondary schools (except for special initiatives not provided by regular school budgets), political action or legislative advocacy groups, medical or research organizations, fraternal groups, athletic teams, bands, veterans' organizations, or volunteer firefighters. No grants to individuals (except for employee-related scholarships), or for religious programs or initiatives, endowments, or multi-year pledge campaigns.
Publications: Application guidelines; Annual report; Informational brochure; IRS Form 990 or 990-PF printed copy available upon request; Program policy statement.
Application information: Proposals should be no longer than 5 pages. Telephone calls during the application process are not encouraged. Visit website to confirm application deadline for specific areas. Application form required.
Initial approach: Download application form and mail proposal and application form to nearest company daily newspaper or broadcast station
Copies of proposal: 1
Deadline(s): Feb. 16 and Aug. 17; Mar. 15, July 15, and Nov. 15 for Media Grants; Autumn for Newsquest Grants
Board meeting date(s): 3 times per year from Feb. to Oct.
Final notification: 90 to 120 days
Officers and Director:* Craig A. Dubow,* Chair. and Pres.; Daniel S. Ehrman, V.P.; Gracia C. Martore,* V.P.; Todd A. Mayman, Secy.; Michael A. Hart, Treas.; Robin Pence, Exec. Dir.

Number of staff: 1 full-time professional; 1 full-time support.
EIN: 541568843
Recent grants for international programs:
2122-1 Quartet Community Foundation, Bristol, England, $640,000. 2010.

2123
Global Impact
66 Canal Ctr. Plz., Ste. 310
Alexandria, VA 22314-1568 (703) 717-5200
FAX: (703) 717-5215; E-mail: mail@charity.org;
Toll-free tel.: (800) 836-4620; URL: http://www.charity.org
Facebook: http://www.facebook.com/globalimpact.charity
Twitter: http://twitter.com/@charitydotorg
YouTube: http://www.youtube.com/user/charitydotorg

Established in 1956; supporting organization of ACCION International, Accumen Fund, Africa-America Institute, African Medical and Research Foundation, Africare, American Ireland Fund, American Jewish World Service, American Leprosy Foundation, American Near East Refugee Aid, American Refugee Committee, AmeriCares, Boy Scouts of America - Aloha Council, Boy Scouts of America - Far East Council, Boy Scouts of America - Transatlantic Council, CARE, Catholic Relief Services - USCCB, Plan USA, Children International, Children Inc., Christian Children's Fund, Christian Reformed World Relief Committee, Church World Service/CROP, Doctors Without Borders USA, ECHO Inc., FINCA International, Freedom from Hunger, Girl Scouts of the USA - Overseas, Goodwill Global Inc., Health Volunteers Overseas, Heifer Project International, Helen Keller Worldwide, International Eye Foundation, International Orthodox Christian Charities, International Relief Teams, and International Rescue Committee.
Grantmaker type: Public charity.
Financial data (yr. ended 06/30/10): Revenue, $105,437,964; assets, $22,681,065 (M); gifts received, $104,868,838; expenditures, $105,085,822; giving activities include $92,029,941 for grants, and $700,467 for grants to organizations outside the U.S.
Purpose and activities: The organization is dedicated to helping the poorest people on earth.
Fields of interest: Human services; International relief; Economically disadvantaged.
International interests: Developing countries.
Limitations: Giving on a national and international basis.
Publications: Annual report; Newsletter.
Officers and Directors:* Peter Grant,* Chair.; Joseph A. Crupi,* Vice-Chair.; Renee S. Acosta, Pres.; H. Kenneth Fleishman,* Secy.-Treas.; Kenneth I. Schaner, Esq., Genl. Counsel; Timothy Bloechl; Lawrence J. Cavaiola; Julius E. Coles; Lt. Genl. Robert R. Dierker; Mamadu M. Djalo; Stan M. Harrell; Scott Jackson; Karen R. Johnson; Genl. George A. Joulwan; James B. Kanuch, C.P.A.; Nancy A. Kelly; Maryon Davies Lewis; Darius Mans, Ph.D.; Steve Polo; Rabih T. Torbay; Mauricio Vivero.
EIN: 521273585

2124
Good360

(formerly Gifts In Kind International)
333 N. Fairfax St.
Alexandria, VA 22314-2632 (703) 836-2121
Contact: Judy Mercadal Ewing, V.P., Charity Svcs.
E-mail: jmercadal@giftsinkind.org; Toll-free tel.:
(877) 798-3192; URL: http://www.giftsinkind.org

Founded in 1983 in VA.
Grantmaker type: Public charity.
Financial data (yr. ended 12/31/10): Revenue,
$289,609,075; assets, $34,829,005 (M); gifts
received, $286,426,533; expenditures,
$280,849,523; giving activities include
$273,485,852 for grants, $671,565 for grants to
organizations outside the U.S., and $11,990 for
grants to individuals.
Purpose and activities: The organization assists
companies to effectively and efficiently donate
top-quality products and services to nonprofit
organizations worldwide.
Fields of interest: Education; Health care;
Employment, retraining; Youth development; Human
services; Community/economic development;
Philanthropy/voluntarism; Engineering/technology.
International interests: Asia; Canada; Europe; Latin
America; Mexico; Southern Africa.
Type of support: Building/renovation; Equipment;
In-kind gifts.
Limitations: Applications accepted. Giving
worldwide, specifically in the U.S., Asia, Canada,
Europe, Latin America, Mexico, the Pacific, and
South Africa. No support for for-profit organizations.
No grants to individuals.
Publications: Application guidelines; Annual report;
Financial statement; Informational brochure
(including application guidelines).
Application information: Eligible charities pay a
nominal membership fee, after which they can
select needed products through weekly notices,
monthly updates, and quarterly catalogs.
Application form required.
  Initial approach: Letter (including SASE), fax, or
    e-mail
  Deadline(s): None
  Board meeting date(s): May and Nov.
Officers and Directors:* Gail Aldrich,* Chair.;
Elisabeth Barna, Vice-Chair.; Barry R. Anderson,
Interim Pres. and C.E.O.; Judy Mercadal Ewing, V.P.,
Charity Svcs.; Alan R. Andreasen; Alan Benjamin;
John Connolly; and 10 additional directors.
Number of staff: 28 full-time professional.
EIN: 541282616

2125
The Robert and Mary Haft Foundation, Inc.

3216 Spring Rain Ct.
Oak Hill, VA 20171-1931
Contact: Robert M. Haft, Pres.

Established in 1997 in MD.
Donors: Mary Z. Haft; Robert M. Haft.
Grantmaker type: Independent foundation.
Financial data (yr. ended 12/31/09): Assets,
$187,196 (M); expenditures, $152,652; qualifying
distributions, $140,152; giving activities include
$140,152 for grants.
Purpose and activities: Giving primarily to
education, health care, children and youth services,
philanthropy and voluntarism groups, and religious
organizations.

Fields of interest: Performing arts, ballet; Libraries
(public); Education, reading; Hospitals (specialty);
Health organizations, association; Children/youth,
services; International relief; Foundations (private
operating); Philanthropy/voluntarism; Catholic
agencies & churches.
Limitations: Applications not accepted. No grants to
individuals.
Application information: Unsolicited requests for
funds not accepted.
Officers: Robert M. Haft, Pres.; Mary Z. Haft, V.P.
EIN: 522034198

2126
Hansen Family Foundation

2241 Hatton St.
Virginia Beach, VA 23451-1703

Established in 2006.
Donors: Richard C. Hansen; Cherrie L. Hansen.
Grantmaker type: Independent foundation.
Financial data (yr. ended 12/31/10): Assets,
$2,519,061 (M); expenditures, $242,947;
qualifying distributions, $218,854; giving activities
include $170,000 for 10 grants (high: $50,000;
low: $5,000).
Fields of interest: International relief; Education;
Hospitals (specialty); Children, services; Catholic
agencies & churches.
Limitations: Applications not accepted. Giving
primarily in VA. No grants to individuals.
Application information: Contributes only to
pre-selected organizations.
Officers and Directors:* Richard D. Hansen,* Pres.;
Cherrie L. Hansen,* Secy.; Larry Biddle; Keith Carl;
Caitlin Hansen; Caleb Hansen; Rebecca Hansen.
EIN: 208102394

2127
The Hitt Foundation, Inc.

2900 Fairview Park Dr.
Falls Church, VA 22042-4513

Established in 1999 in VA.
Donor: Myrtle Lee Hitt.
Grantmaker type: Independent foundation.
Financial data (yr. ended 12/31/10): Assets,
$5,076,307 (M); expenditures, $306,264;
qualifying distributions, $279,000; giving activities
include $279,000 for grants.
Fields of interest: Military/veterans' organizations;
Secondary school/education; Historic preservation/
historical societies; Higher education; Cancer
research; Residential/custodial care, hospices;
International studies.
Type of support: General/operating support.
Limitations: Applications not accepted. Giving
primarily in Washington, DC, and VA. No grants to
individuals.
Application information: Contributes only to
pre-selected organizations.
Officers: Russell A. Hitt, Pres.; Brett R. Hitt, V.P.;
James Millar, Secy.
EIN: 541963708

2128
India National Inland Mission

P.O. Box 2603
Forest, VA 24551-6603

Grantmaker type: Public charity.
Financial data (yr. ended 05/31/11): Revenue,
$2,858,740; assets, $223,246 (M); gifts received,
$2,857,744; expenditures, $2,783,156; giving
activities include $2,607,000 for grants to
organizations outside the U.S.
Purpose and activities: The mission exists to
support a orphanage, bible college and missionaries
in India.
Fields of interest: Higher education, college;
Christian agencies & churches; Children, adoption.
International interests: India.
Limitations: Giving limited to India.
Officers: Dr. H. Ronald Vandermey,* Chair.; Larry
Vonada, Vice-Chair.; Ajay Pillai, V.P.; Semon Vincent,
Treas.
Directors: Paul C. Nelson; Denise Vandermey; Dr.
Vance Vandermey; Dixana Vincent; Kathleen
Vonada.
EIN: 956116077

2129
Ivy Inter-American Foundation

P.O. Box 248
Ivy, VA 22945-0248 (434) 295-4698
Contact: Anabella Jordan, Pres.
E-mail: ivyinteram@aol.com; URL: http://
www.ivyinteramericanfoundation.org

Established in 1987.
Grantmaker type: Public charity.
Financial data (yr. ended 12/31/10): Revenue,
$109,049; assets, $224,469 (M); gifts received,
$92,670; expenditures, $103,193; giving activities
include $97,200 for grants.
Purpose and activities: The foundation provides
direct aid to projects to assist, educate, and
empower children and impoverished people
throughout the Americas.
Fields of interest: International relief; Hispanics/
Latinos; Economically disadvantaged; Children/
youth.
International interests: Peru; Argentina; Nicaragua;
Latin America.
Limitations: Giving primarily in Latin America.
Officers and Directors:* Maria Bonnemaison,*
Chair.; Anabella Jordan,* Pres.; David C. Jordan,*
V.P.; Joachim Funck,* Secy.; John Wood Bolton,*
Treas.; Carol Einaudi; Susan Quainton.
EIN: 541428167

2130
Jubilee Campaign USA, Inc.

9689-C Main St.
Fairfax, VA 22031-3764 (703) 503-0791
FAX: (703) 503-0792; Toll-free tel.: (877) 654-4331;
URL: http://www.jubileecampaign.org
causes: http://www.causes.com/causes/
93553-jubilee-campaign?recruiter_id=19609873

Established in 1990 in VA.
Grantmaker type: Public charity.
Financial data (yr. ended 12/31/10): Revenue,
$187,334; assets, $47,886 (M); gifts received,
$187,226; expenditures, $216,905; program
services expenses, $201,004; giving activities
include $79,079 for grants.
Purpose and activities: The organization works to
protect the human rights and religious liberty of
ethnic and religious minorities in countries which
imprison, terrorize, or otherwise oppress them by

advocating the release of prisoners of conscience and the change of laws as necessary to achieve these purposes, and by advocating against the exploitation of children.

Fields of interest: International conflict resolution; International affairs; Children's rights; Civil liberties; freedom of religion; Civil/human rights; Christian agencies & churches; Minorities.

Type of support: Program development.

Limitations: Giving on an international basis.

Officers and Directors: Danny Smith, Pres.; Ann Buwalda, V.P.; Polly Coen, Secy.; Patricia Tanaka, Treas.; Brian Coen, Asst. Secy.; Faith McDonnell; Paul Miller; Mary Miller; Marlene Rice; Joan Smith.

EIN: 521645262

2131
King Hussein Foundation International

(formerly Jordan Society, Inc.)
P.O. Box 1195
McLean, VA 22101-1195 (202) 833-4999
Contact: Nicole Carey, Exec. Dir.
FAX: (202) 833-5666;
E-mail: khfi@peacebuilders.org

Established in 1999 in NY.

Grantmaker type: Public charity.

Financial data (yr. ended 12/31/09): Revenue, $262,201; assets, $3,088,493 (M); gifts received, $182,500; expenditures, $440,271; giving activities include $95,669 for grants to organizations outside the U.S., and $50,000 for grants to individuals.

Purpose and activities: As the U.S. affiliate of the King Hussein Foundation, the foundation supports programs for community development in education, leadership, health, democracy, peace and the environment.

Fields of interest: International economics/trade policy; International human rights; Education; Environment; Health care; International peace/security; Community/economic development, public education; Community/economic development.

International interests: Jordan.

Limitations: Giving on an international basis, primarily in Amman, Jordan.

Publications: Informational brochure.

Officers and Trustees: * HM Queen Noor, Chair.; Alexa Halaby,* Secy.; Rebecca Walldorf, Exec. Dir.; Tala Abu-Ghalzeh; Zoe Baird; HRH Prince Firas bin Ra'ad; Camille Douglas; Samia Farouki; Dr. Rima Khalaf Hunaidi; Artemis Joukowsky; Nemir Kirdar; Story Clark Resor; Sen. Leila Sharaf.

EIN: 133064429

2132
Minnie & Bernard Lane Foundation

c/o Mrs. Bernard Lane
414 Washington St.
Altavista, VA 24517-1952
Contact: Cindy Jester, Admin. Asst.
Mailing address: P.O. Box 359, Altavista, VA 24517

Established in 1957 in VA.

Donors: Bernard B. Lane†; Minnie B. Lane.

Grantmaker type: Independent foundation.

Financial data (yr. ended 03/31/11): Assets, $5,032,023 (M); gifts received, $273,747; expenditures, $646,390; qualifying distributions, $603,986; giving activities include $603,986 for 62 grants (high: $145,000; low: $125).

Purpose and activities: Giving primarily for a food distribution program; support also for Methodist churches and other Christian organizations, social and human services, and international giving, including relief and missionary programs. Support is for U.S.-based organizations only, and primarily for projects in Campbell County, VA.

Fields of interest: Food services; Human services; International relief; Christian agencies & churches; Protestant agencies & churches.

Type of support: Seed money; Matching/challenge support.

Limitations: Applications not accepted. Giving primarily in Campbell County, VA, for new projects. No support for foreign organizations. No grants to individuals; no loans.

Application information: Unsolicited requests for funds not accepted; funds fully committed.

Trustees: Bernard B. Lane, Jr.; Douglas B. Lane; Minnie B. Lane.

Number of staff: 1 part-time professional.

EIN: 546052404

2133
The Living Waters Trust

c/o Keel Point
8065 Leesburg Pike, Ste. 300
Vienna, VA 22182-2738

Established in 1993 in MA.

Donors: Peter B. Schulze; Karen Schulze; The Procter & Gamble Co.; Greenwich Financial.

Grantmaker type: Independent foundation.

Financial data (yr. ended 12/31/10): Assets, $1,977,831 (M); gifts received, $176,368; expenditures, $571,408; qualifying distributions, $567,832; giving activities include $565,700 for 15 grants (high: $104,000; low: $1,000).

Fields of interest: Health care; Human services; International relief; Religion; Economically disadvantaged.

Limitations: Applications not accepted. Giving in the U.S., with some emphasis on CA, MD, OH and PA. No grants to individuals.

Application information: Contributes only to pre-selected organizations.

Trustees: Karen Gottlieb Schulze; Peter B. Schulze.

EIN: 046746134

2134
The Loyola Foundation, Inc.

10335 Democracy Ln., No. 202
Fairfax, VA 22030-2527 (571) 435-9401
Contact: Albert G. McCarthy III; Christine M. Rice
FAX: (571) 435-9402;
E-mail: info@loyolafoundation.org; URL: http://www.loyolafoundation.org/

Incorporated in 1957 in DC.

Donor: Members of the Albert Gregory McCarthy, Jr. family.

Grantmaker type: Independent foundation.

Financial data (yr. ended 10/31/10): Assets, $37,838,709 (M); expenditures, $1,663,908; qualifying distributions, $867,490; giving activities include $867,490 for grants.

Purpose and activities: Grants primarily for basic overseas Roman Catholic missionary work and other Catholic activities of special interest to the trustees. Primary interest in nonrecurring requests for capital improvements in the missionary area, which are self-sustaining after completion; special consideration given to requests where there are matching contributions from the missionary area, itself.

Fields of interest: Catholic agencies & churches.

International interests: Africa; Developing countries; Latin America; Asia.

Type of support: Building/renovation; Equipment; Matching/challenge support.

Limitations: Applications accepted. Giving primarily in Third World developing nations. Grants made in the U.S. only to institutions or organizations of special interest to the trustees. No support for minor seminaries. No grants to individuals, or for annual budgets, endowment funds, research, continuing support, operating expenses, emergency funds, deficit financing, publications, conferences, scholarships, fellowships, travel and meetings, or for used or reconditioned vehicles; no loans.

Publications: Application guidelines; Multi-year report.

Application information: All requests must be in English. If the initial request meets the foundation guidelines, an application form will be sent. For requests for projects whose cost is in excess of $50,000, applications cannot be accepted until at least 75 percent of the total funds needed for the project have been secured from other sources. Application form required.

> *Initial approach:* Letter
> *Copies of proposal:* 1
> *Deadline(s):* Apr. 30 and Oct. 31
> *Board meeting date(s):* June and Dec.
> *Final notification:* Jan. and July

Officers and Trustees: * Andrea M. Hattler-Bramson, Pres.; John N. Malyska,* V.P.; Denise M. Hattler,* Treas.; A. Gregory McCarthy IV,* Exec. Dir.; Daniel J. Altobello; Rev. William J. Byron, S.J.; Kathleen D.H. Carr; Paul R. Dean; Ann M. Farrell; William J. Fiore; Hillary A. Hattler; Cardinal Theodore E. McCarrick; Albert G. McCarthy III; Diana Hattler McDonough; Raymond W. Merritt; Rev. Allen P. Novotny, S.J.; Amy Hattler Page.

Number of staff: 2 full-time professional; 1 part-time professional.

EIN: 520781255

2135
Mercatus Center at George Mason University, Inc.

3351 N. Fairfax Dr., 4th Fl.
Arlington, VA 22201-4426 (703) 993-4930
FAX: (703) 993-4935; E-mail: mercatus@gmu.edu;
Toll-free tel.: (800) 815-5711; URL: http://www.mercatus.org
Facebook: http://www.facebook.com/mercatuscenter
RSS Feed: http://feeds.feedburner.com/MercatusHome
Twitter: http://twitter.com/Mercatus
YouTube: http://www.youtube.com/user/MercatusCenter

Established in 1994 in VA.

Grantmaker type: Public charity.

Financial data (yr. ended 08/31/10): Revenue, $8,075,737; assets, $4,691,315 (M); gifts received, $8,042,253; expenditures, $7,723,974; giving activities include $1,047,675 for grants.

Purpose and activities: The center works to apply scholarly research to the problems facing policy makers by bringing together a network of scholars

and experts from around the globe to provide them with the economic tools necessary to make sense of today's most pressing issues.
Fields of interest: International economics/trade policy; Higher education, university; Education; International affairs; Economics.
Limitations: Giving primarily to Fairfax, VA.
Publications: Occasional report.
Directors: Frank Atkinson; Tyler Cowen; Richard Fink; Manuel Johnson; Charles Koch; Edwin Meese; Menlo Smith; Vernon Smith.
EIN: 541436224

2136
The Mousetrap Foundation
c/o Sterling Foundation Mgmt., LLC
2325 Dulles Corner Blvd., Ste. 670
Herndon, VA 20171-4683 (703) 437-9720

Established in 2002 in VA.
Donor: Judith Randal Hines.
Grantmaker type: Independent foundation.
Financial data (yr. ended 12/31/10): Assets, $12,009,901 (M); expenditures, $470,185; qualifying distributions, $363,751; giving activities include $300,000 for 5 grants (high: $110,000; low: $40,000).
Fields of interest: Environment, natural resources; Health care, clinics/centers; Legal services; International development.
Limitations: Applications accepted. Giving primarily in VA. No grants to individuals.
Application information: Application form not required.
Initial approach: Letter
Deadline(s): None
Officers: Judith Randal Hines, Pres.; Georgia H. Herbert, V.P. and Secy.
Directors: Rudy Abramson; Rosina Bierbaum; Sue Scheer.
EIN: 522285383

2137
Mustard Seed Foundation, Inc.
7115 Leesburg Pike, Ste. 304
Falls Church, VA 22043 (703) 524-5620
Contact: Brian Bakke, Regional Dir., North America
FAX: (703) 533-7340; E-mail: info@msfdn.org;
URL: http://www.msfdn.org

Established in 1983 in SC.
Donors: Eileen Harvey Bakke; Dennis W. Bakke; Warren Harvey; and members of the Bakke and Harvey families.
Grantmaker type: Independent foundation.
Financial data (yr. ended 12/31/10): Assets, $5,760,874 (M); gifts received, $9,942,500; expenditures, $5,549,919; qualifying distributions, $4,613,666; giving activities include $4,613,666 for grants.
Purpose and activities: To advance the Kingdom of God through granting and scholarships. Provides grants to churches and Christian organizations worldwide engaged in ministries such as outreach, discipleship, and empowerment. Provides scholarships to Christians pursuing advanced education in non-western theological studies or under-represented fields.
Fields of interest: Theological school/education; Christian agencies & churches.

International interests: Africa; Asia; Europe; Latin America; Middle East; South America.
Type of support: Fellowships; Scholarship funds; Scholarships—to individuals; Matching/challenge support.
Limitations: Applications accepted. Giving on a national basis in Los Angeles, CA, Washington, DC, Miami, FL, Chicago, IL, New York City, and Houston, TX, and internationally in large urban centers. No support for parachurch organizations, only local churches can apply. No support for U.S. elementary or secondary education. No grants for general purposes, or for television or radio projects, or for buildings, land purchases, small towns or rural projects, administrative costs or for ongoing operations, projects without local church financial support, or scholarships to undergraduate programs, or multi-year grants.
Publications: Application guidelines; Annual report.
Application information: Check foundation web site for more information. Please submit one copy of application for grants. Application form required.
Initial approach: Letter, e-mail or telephone. Online application for Harvey Fellows
Copies of proposal: 1
Deadline(s): Grants - revolving; Harvey Fellows - Nov. 1
Board meeting date(s): Every 7 or 8 weeks
Final notification: Up to 3 months from submission date
Officers and Directors:* Dennis W. Bakke, Co-Chair.; Eileen Harvey Bakke,* Co-Chair.; Eric Hornberger, Co-Exec. Dir.; Lonni Jackson, Co-Exec. Dir.; Elizabeth Bakke; Lowell Bakke; Raymond J. Bakke; Margaret Bakke; Helen C. Harvey; W. Brantley Harvey, Jr.; Warren Harvey; Helen Laffitte; Jill Nauta; Margaret Thompson; Carolyn Thompson.
Number of staff: 11 full-time professional.
EIN: 570748914

2138
National Rural Electric Cooperative International Foundation
(also known as NRECA International Foundation)
4301 Wilson Blvd., IPD7-202
Arlington, VA 22203-1860 (703) 907-5645
Contact: Dan Waddle, Sr. V.P.
FAX: (703) 907-5532;
E-mail: internationalprograms@nreca.coop; E-Mail for Dan Waddle : dan.waddle@nreca.coop;
URL: http://www.nrecainternational.org

Established in 1985 in DC.
Grantmaker type: Public charity.
Financial data (yr. ended 12/31/09): Revenue, $1,174,024; assets, $624,839 (M); gifts received, $1,143,922; expenditures, $1,171,954; program services expenses, $960,381; giving activities include $450,382 for grants to organizations outside the U.S.
Purpose and activities: The foundation strives to help rural populations around the world get electricity and provide opportunities for these people to enjoy the social, economic, and improved health benefits that come with electricity.
Fields of interest: International development.
International interests: Philippines; Haiti; Guatemala; Costa Rica.
Type of support: Program development; Technical assistance.

Limitations: Applications not accepted. Giving on a national and international basis. No support for organizations lacking 501(c)(3) IRS status.
Publications: Annual report.
Application information: Contributes only to pre-selected organizations.
Officers and Directors:* Charles L. Dawsey,* Chair.; Glen English,* Pres.; Vivek Talvadkar, Sr. V.P.; Veneicia Lockhart,* V.P.; Daniel B. Waddle, V.P., Opers.; Norma Hiller,* Secy.-Treas.; Dave Predmore, Asst. Secy.; Joe Bongiovanni; Dennis M. Esaki; and 7 additional directors.
EIN: 521409279

2139
North American Regional Committee for St. Georges College, Inc.
(also known as NARC)
3737 Seminary Rd.
Alexandria, VA 22304-5202 (703) 461-1754

Grantmaker type: Public charity.
Financial data (yr. ended 12/31/10): Revenue, $82,850; assets, $153,454 (M); gifts received, $82,036; expenditures, $153,702; giving activities include $102,593 for grants.
Purpose and activities: The organization supports St. George's College.
Fields of interest: Higher education, college.
International interests: Israel.
Type of support: General/operating support; Scholarship funds.
Limitations: Applications not accepted. Giving limited to Jerusalem, Israel.
Application information: Contributes only to a pre-selected organization.
Officers: Rev. Allen L. Bartlett, Jr., Pres.; Rev. William B. Lane, V.P.; Rev. Keith Owen, Exec. Secy.; Judith T. Milone, Secy.; Rev. J. Barney Hawkins IV, Treas.
EIN: 621343994

2140
Operation Blessing International Relief and Development Corp.
977 Centerville Tpke.
Virginia Beach, VA 23463-1001
FAX: (757) 226-3657; URL: http://www.ob.org
Facebook: http://www.facebook.com/operationblessingintl?ref=ts
Twitter: http://twitter.com/operationbless
YouTube: http://www.youtube.com/user/operationblessing

Established in 1978.
Grantmaker type: Public charity.
Financial data (yr. ended 03/31/10): Revenue, $473,062,348; assets, $17,879,439 (M); gifts received, $473,093,551; expenditures, $472,252,932; giving activities include $649,946 for grants, $346,351,056 for grants to organizations outside the U.S., and $108,028,234 for grants to individuals.
Purpose and activities: The organization's mission is to demonstrate God's love by alleviating human need and suffering in the United States and around the world.
Fields of interest: International relief; Human services.
Type of support: Grants to individuals.

Limitations: Giving on a national and international basis.
Publications: Annual report.
Officers and Directors:* Dr. M.G. "Pat" Robertson,* Chair.; Michael D. Little,* Vice-Chair.; Bill Horan, Pres. and C.O.O.; James R. Barr, Jr., V.P. and C.F.O.; Pam Erickson, V.P., Procurement and Corp. Rels.; A.E. "Dede" Robertson,* V.P.; Randy J. Morell,* Secy.; Thomas W. Daugherty, M.D.; William Dooner; Max C. Karrer, M.D.; David Melilli; Gordon P. Robertson.
EIN: 541382657

2141
Practical Small Projects, Inc.
4801 Courthouse St., Ste. 300
Williamsburg, VA 23188-2678
E-mail: info@practicalsmallprojects.com;
URL: http://www.practicalsmallprojects.com
causes: http://www.causes.com/causes/
38945-practical-small-projects
Facebook: http://www.facebook.com/pages/
Practical-Small-Projects-PSP/232882116747215?
sk=info
vimeo: http://vimeo.com/5415144

Established in 2006 in VA.
Donors: Melissa Thompson; David Graham.
Grantmaker type: Public charity.
Financial data (yr. ended 12/31/10): Revenue, $123,344; assets, $19,799 (M); gifts received, $123,320; expenditures, $112,731; giving activities include $94,430 for grants.
Purpose and activities: The foundation's mission is to facilitate the implementation of practical, small, self-sustaining projects that benefit the developing world.
Fields of interest: International development.
International interests: Mali.
Officers: Mary K. Graham, Pres.; Kriston Johnson, Secy.; David B. Graham, Treas.
Directors: Carolina Barreto Casina; Daniel Dembele.
EIN: 203793469

2142
Project HOPE - The People-to-People Health Foundation, Inc.
255 Carter Hall Ln.
Millwood, VA 22646-0255 (540) 837-2100
FAX: (540) 837-1813;
E-mail: hope@projecthope.org; Toll-free tel.: (800) 544-4673; URL: http://www.projecthope.org

Grantmaker type: Public charity.
Financial data (yr. ended 06/30/11): Revenue, $203,901,912; assets, $64,025,519 (M); gifts received, $199,606,684; expenditures, $202,363,497; giving activities include $195,562 for grants to organizations outside the U.S.
Purpose and activities: The organization's mission is to achieve sustainable advances in health care around the world by implementing health education programs and providing humanitarian assistance in areas of need.
Fields of interest: International relief; Health care.
Type of support: Fellowships.
Limitations: Giving on a national and international basis.
Publications: Annual report.

Officers: Charles A. Sanders, M.D., Chair.; John P. Howe III, M.D., Pres. and C.E.O.; Stuart L. Myers, Sr. V.P.; Anthony Buchard, V.P., Devel. and Comms.; Susan Dentzer, V.P., Health Policy; Abul Hashem, V.P., New Business Devel.; Deborah R. Iwig, V.P. and C.F.O.; M. Miriam Wardak, V.P., Human Resources and Admin.; Dayton Ogden, Secy.; William F. Brandt, Jr., Treas.
Directors: George B. Abercrombie; Richard T. Clark; Mrs. Edward N. Cole; John D. Fowler; John W. Galiardo; Jack M. Gill, Ph.D.; Robert A. Ingram; Gerhard N. Mayr; J. Michael McQuade, Ph.D.; Viren Mehta, Pharm.D.; Walter G. Montgomery; Phebe Novakovic; Steven B. Pfeiffer, Esq.; Stephen H. Rusckowski; Curt M. Selquist; and 6 additional board members.
EIN: 530242962

2143
Rare
(formerly Rare Center for Tropical Conservation)
1840 Wilson Blvd., Ste. 204
Arlington, VA 22201-3000 (703) 522-5070
Contact: Brett S. Jenks, Pres. and C.E.O.
FAX: (703) 522-5027;
E-mail: rare@rareconservation.org; URL: http://www.rareconservation.org

Established in 1973.
Grantmaker type: Public charity.
Financial data (yr. ended 09/30/10): Revenue, $7,094,477; assets, $26,341,836 (M); gifts received, $6,511,551; expenditures, $10,806,827; giving activities include $1,179,844 for grants to organizations outside the U.S.
Purpose and activities: The organization protects wildlands of globally significant biological diversity by empowering local people to benefit from their preservation. Current areas of focus include the Caribbean, Latin America, the Pacific, and South Africa.
Fields of interest: Environment, natural resources.
International interests: Oceania; Caribbean; Latin America; South Africa.
Limitations: Giving on an international basis.
Publications: Annual report.
Officers and Trustees:* Wendy J. Paulson,* Chair.; Angus Parker,* Vice-Chair.; Brett S. Jenks,* Pres. and C.E.O.; Dale Galvin, C.O.O.; Joseph H. Ellis,* Secy.; Edward Soule,* Treas.; Melissa Shackleton Dann; Mark DiMassimo; Barbara R. Hernandez; Dexter C. Mead; and 8 additional trustees.
EIN: 237380563

2144
The Salvation Army World Service Office
615 Slaters Ln.
P.O. Box 269
Alexandria, VA 22314-1112 (703) 684-5528
FAX: (703) 684-5536;
E-mail: saws@ousn.salvationarmy.org; URL: http://www.sawso.org

Established in 1977; supporting organization of The Salvation Army.
Grantmaker type: Public charity.
Financial data (yr. ended 12/31/10): Revenue, $51,933,064; assets, $44,988,577 (M); gifts received, $50,973,913; expenditures, $32,515,814; giving activities include

$17,002,429 for grants to organizations outside the U.S.
Purpose and activities: The organization seeks to support and strengthen The Salvation Army's efforts to work hand in hand with communities to improve the health, education, living, economic and spiritual conditions of the poor throughout the world.
Fields of interest: Salvation Army; Human services.
International interests: Trinidad & Tobago; South Africa; Spain; Liberia; Tanzania, Zanzibar and Pemba; Uganda; Zambia; Zimbabwe; Sri Lanka; Singapore; Taiwan.
Limitations: Giving on a worldwide basis.
Publications: Financial statement.
Officers: Israel L. Gaither, Pres.; Barry C. Swanson, V.P.; Patricia Kiddoo, Secy.; John Falin, Treas.; Harden White, Exec. Dir.
Trustees: Kenneth Baillie; Maxwell Feener; Lawrence R. Moretz; Philip Swyers.
EIN: 132923701

2145
Samberg Family Foundation
3101 Wilson Blvd., Suite 220
Arlington, VA 22201-4445 (703) 351-9405
Contact: Laura J. Samberg, Co-Dir.
URL: http://www.sambergfdn.org

Established in 1996.
Donor: Arthur Samberg.
Grantmaker type: Independent foundation.
Financial data (yr. ended 11/30/09): Assets, $74,068,236 (M); expenditures, $6,412,017; qualifying distributions, $6,068,427; giving activities include $5,464,369 for 25 grants (high: $1,000,000; low: $8,365).
Purpose and activities: Giving primarily for children, youth and families; health; and Jewish issues.
Fields of interest: Youth development, services; Museums; Education; Health care; Children/youth, services; Family services; Jewish federated giving programs.
International interests: Israel.
Type of support: General/operating support; Continuing support; Management development/capacity building; Program development; Seed money; Curriculum development; Research; Technical assistance; Program evaluation; Matching/challenge support.
Limitations: Applications not accepted. Giving primarily in NY. No grants to individuals.
Publications: Grants list.
Application information: Unsolicited requests for funds not accepted.
Director: Laura J. Samberg.
Trustees: Arthur Samberg; Jeffrey Samberg; Joseph Samberg; Laura Samberg; Rebecca Samberg.
Number of staff: 3 full-time professional.
EIN: 066439895
Recent grants for international programs:
2145-1 Birthright Israel Foundation, New York, NY, $750,000. 2009.
2145-2 Center for Leadership Initiatives, Jerusalem, Israel, $32,500. 2009.

2146
Robert H. Smith Family Foundation
2345 Crystal Dr.
Arlington, VA 22202-4801 (703) 769-1023

Established in 1987 in VA.

Donors: Robert H. Smith†; Clarice R. Smith; CES Mgmt., Inc.; RCS II, LLC; Charles E. Smith Family Foundation.
Grantmaker type: Independent foundation.
Financial data (yr. ended 11/30/10): Assets, $8,362,108 (M); gifts received, $9,900,000; expenditures, $16,881,449; qualifying distributions, $16,770,308; giving activities include $16,667,520 for 55 grants (high: $5,600,000; low: $898).
Purpose and activities: Giving primarily for the arts and education.
Fields of interest: Historic preservation/historical societies; Performing arts, opera; Museums; Arts; Higher education; Education; Environment; Hospitals (general); Jewish agencies & synagogues.
Limitations: Applications not accepted. Giving primarily in Washington, DC. No grants to individuals.
Application information: Contributes only to pre-selected organizations.
Officer and Directors:* Michelle Smith,* Pres.; Clarice R. Smith,* V.P. and Secy.; David B. Smith, Treas.
EIN: 521502273
Recent grants for international programs:
2146-1 American Academy in Rome, New York, NY, $50,000. 2010.
2146-2 American Friends of Shalom Hartman Institute, New York, NY, $25,000. 2010.
2146-3 American Friends of the Hebrew University, Washington, DC, $5,600,000. 2010.
2146-4 American Friends of the Israel Museum, New York, NY, $25,000. 2010.
2146-5 Foundation for Art and Preservation in Embassies, Washington, DC, $72,500. 2010.
2146-6 Friends of Benjamin Franklin House, London, England, $150,000. 2010.

2147
Somali Family Care Network

2724 Dorr Ave., Ste. 102
Fairfax, VA   22031-4903   (703) 560-0005
FAX: (703) 560-9523; URL: http://www.somalifamily.org

Grantmaker type: Public charity.
Financial data (yr. ended 09/30/10): Revenue, $107,288; assets, $52,015 (M); gifts received, $99,158; expenditures, $135,984.
Purpose and activities: The network's mission is to serve as a national resource center and referral network for the Somali immigrant community in the U.S., as well as for the U.S. refugee and mainstream service providers who interface with the Somali communities in the U.S.
Fields of interest: International migration/refugee issues; Immigrants/refugees.
International interests: Somalia, Somaliland and Puntland.
Officer: Raqiya Abdalla, Pres.
EIN: 541993544

2148
Three Swallows Foundation

12608 Wyclow Dr.
Clifton, VA   20124-1616

Established in 1981 in VA.
Grantmaker type: Independent foundation.

Financial data (yr. ended 10/31/10): Assets, $1,530,255 (M); expenditures, $1,418,877; qualifying distributions, $603,931; giving activities include $603,931 for grants.
Fields of interest: Education; Health organizations, association; Neuroscience research; Human services; International development; United Ways and Federated Giving Programs; Christian agencies & churches.
Type of support: Research.
Limitations: Applications not accepted. Giving primarily in CA, CO and Washington, DC. No grants to individuals; no program-related investments.
Application information: Contributes only to pre-selected organizations.
Officers and Directors:* Paul N. Temple, Pres.; Steven Greenberg,* Treas.; D. Barry Abell; Pamela T. Abell; Lise Temple Greenberg; G. Michael Moore; Diane E. Temple; Nancy L. Temple; Robin R. Temple.
EIN: 521234546

2149
Trehan Foundation

(formerly Trehan Family Foundation, Inc.)
1308 Ballantrae Farm Dr.
McLean, VA   22101-3028

Established in 2003 in VA.
Donor: Ranvir Trehan.
Grantmaker type: Independent foundation.
Financial data (yr. ended 12/31/10): Assets, $13,338,152 (M); expenditures, $645,591; qualifying distributions, $613,699; giving activities include $610,000 for 10 grants (high: $450,000; low: $2,000).
Purpose and activities: Giving primarily for international development, particularly an organization focused on global poverty, as well as a performing arts center and human services.
Fields of interest: International development; Performing arts centers; Human services; Children, services; Public policy, research; Children.
International interests: India.
Limitations: Applications not accepted. Giving primarily in Washington, DC. No grants to individuals.
Application information: Contributes only to pre-selected organizations.
Officer: Ranvir Trehan, Pres. and Secy.
EIN: 270073510

2150
The U.S. Civilian Research and Development Foundation

(also known as CRDF Global)
1530 Wilson Blvd., 3rd Fl.
Arlington, VA   22209-2459   (703) 526-9720
Contact: David Lindeman, Devel. Dir.
FAX: (703) 526-9721; E-mail: information@crdf.org;
URL: http://www.crdf.org
Facebook: http://www.facebook.com/pages/CRDF-Global/113271435392699
LinkedIn: http://www.linkedin.com/companies/crdf-global
Twitter: http://twitter.com/crdfglobal

Established in 1995 in VA.
Grantmaker type: Public charity.
Financial data (yr. ended 12/31/10): Revenue, $14,999,467; assets, $31,034,730 (M); gifts received, $13,621,179; expenditures,

$21,509,358; giving activities include $2,588,765 for grants, $4,143,803 for grants to organizations outside the U.S., and $721,704 for grants to individuals.
Purpose and activities: The foundation promotes scientific and technological collaboration between the U.S. and other countries, and assists researchers of the former Soviet Union to transfer their skills and experience to civilian science.
Fields of interest: Business/industry; Environmental education; Health care; Medical research; International exchange; Science, research; Engineering/technology; Science.
International interests: Jordan; Iraq; Middle East; Libya; Serbia; Albania; Eastern & Central Europe; Soviet Union (Former); Armenia; Azerbaijan; Estonia; Georgia (Republic of); Kazakhstan; Kyrgyzstan; Latvia; Lithuania; Moldova; Russia; Tajikistan; Turkmenistan; Ukraine; Uzbekistan.
Type of support: Equipment; Conferences/seminars; Fellowships; Research; Program evaluation; Grants to individuals.
Limitations: Applications accepted. Giving in the U.S. and the countries of the former Soviet Union, Baltic States, Central and Eastern Europe, Middle East, and North Africa. No grants for commercial manufacturing or weapons development.
Publications: Application guidelines; Annual report; Informational brochure; Newsletter; Occasional report.
Application information: See web site for current RFPs and application guidelines and deadlines. Application form required.
Initial approach: Nomination form for George Brown Awards; download application form for all others
Deadline(s): Apr. 25 for Biomedical Research Competition; May 4 for George Brown Awards; varies for all others
Board meeting date(s): Quarterly
Officers and Directors:* Dr. William Wulf,* Chair.; Dona L. Crawford,* Vice-Chair.; Dr. Rodney Nichols,* Secy.; Paul Longsworth,* Treas.; Dr. Jaleh Daie; Dr. Farouk El-Baz; Dr. Howard Frank; Irma Gigli, M.D.; Dr. Malcolm Gillis; David Kay, Ph.D.; John H. Moore, Ph.D.; Dr. Gilbert S. Omenn; Elizabeth Rindskopf Parker; Dr. Anne C. Petersen; Victor Rabinowitch, Ph.D.
Number of staff: 68 full-time professional.
EIN: 541773406

2151
United Negro College Fund Special Programs Corporation

6402 Arlington Blvd., Ste. 600
Falls Church, VA   22042-2343   (703) 677-3400
Contact: Melissa C. Green Ph.D., Dir.
FAX: (703) 205-7645; E-mail: portal@uncfsp.org;
URL: http://www.uncfsp.org
IIPP: http://www.facebook.com/pages/Falls-Church-VA/Institute-for-International-Public-Policy-IIPP/53552591814
UMCFSPIIPP: http://twitter.com/uncfspiipp

Established in 2000 in VA.
Grantmaker type: Public charity.
Financial data (yr. ended 12/31/09): Revenue, $9,070,444; assets, $2,589,387 (M); gifts received, $9,067,384; expenditures, $9,325,884; giving activities include $1,410,720 for grants, and $2,186,329 for grants to individuals.

Purpose and activities: The corporation's mission is to organize and deliver educational support services such as capacity building, technical assistance, and workforce development programs to minority serving institutions of higher learning.
Fields of interest: Science; Science, research; International affairs, formal/general education; International affairs, alliance/advocacy; International development; Historic preservation/historical societies; Education, management/technical assistance; Higher education, university; Graduate/professional education; Scholarships/financial aid; Youth development, management/technical assistance; Youth development; Minorities/immigrants, centers/services; Minorities.
Type of support: General/operating support; Continuing support; Internship funds; Technical assistance; Scholarships—to individuals.
Limitations: Applications accepted. Giving on a national basis.
Publications: Annual report; Newsletter.
Application information: Application form required.
  Initial approach: Telephone or e-mail
  Copies of proposal: 4
  Deadline(s): June 15 for the Curriculum Improvement Partnership Award for Integration of Research
  Final notification: Aug. 1 for the Curriculum Improvement Partnership Award for Integration of Research
Officers and Directors:* Michael L. Lomax,* Ph.D., Chair.; Aaron R. Andrews,* Pres. and C.E.O.; Michael J. Hester, C.O.O. and V.P.; Veronica Biggins; Rev. Floyd H. Flake; Dr. Norman C. Francis; Lloyd Howell, Jr.; Dr. Sebetha Jenkins; Lynn Martin; Dr. Henry N. Tisdale; Dr. Dorothy C. Yancy.
EIN: 541980487

2152
United States Geospatial Intelligence Foundation
2325 Dulles Corner Blvd., Ste. 450
Herndon, VA 20171-4676 (703) 793-0109
URL: http://www.usgif.org
Email for the Scholarship Subcommittee:
scholarships@usgif.org

Established in 2004.
Grantmaker type: Public charity.
Financial data (yr. ended 12/31/10): Revenue, $4,890,367; assets, $3,917,020 (M); gifts received, $932,966; expenditures, $4,850,534; program services expenses, $4,310,859; giving activities include $69,000 for grants to individuals.
Purpose and activities: The foundation seeks to improve the nation's national and homeland security. It hopes to bring together the many disciplines involved in the geospatial intelligence sector to exchange ideas, share best practices, and promote the education and importance of a national geospatial intelligence agenda.
Fields of interest: International affairs, national security.
Type of support: Scholarships—to individuals.
Limitations: Giving on a national basis.
Officers and Directors:* K. Stuart Shea,* Chair. and CEO; Aimee Correnti,* V.P., Opers.; Dr. William L. Ballhaus; Dr. Jack Dangermond; Hon. Joan Avalyn Dempsey; Dr. Michael F. Goodchild; Mr. Arthur V Grant; Mr. Paul L. Graziani; Dr. Leo A. Hazlewood; Michael G. Lee.
EIN: 200668409

2153
Universal Cultural Foundation, Inc.
P.O. Box 8603
Reston, VA 20195-2503

Established in DC.
Donors: Unification Church International; Korean Cultural Foundation; Universal Ballet Foundation.
Grantmaker type: Operating foundation.
Financial data (yr. ended 12/31/10): Assets, $6,166,284 (M); gifts received, $4,423,342; expenditures, $1,227,583; qualifying distributions, $1,163,369; giving activities include $123,970 for 6 grants (high: $39,800; low: $4,170), and $1,039,399 for foundation-administered programs.
Fields of interest: Performing arts; Performing arts, ballet; Human services.
International interests: Colombia; South Korea.
Limitations: Applications not accepted. Giving primarily in Washington, DC, NJ, and NY; some funding also in Bogota, Columbia, and Seoul, South Korea.
Application information: Contributes only to pre-selected organizations.
Officers: Julia H. Moon, Chair.; Antonio Betancourt, Vice-Chair.; Jonathan Park, Pres.; Bill Selig, Secy.-Treas.
Director: Jenny Kim.
EIN: 203755855

2154
WestWind Foundation
232 E. High St.
Charlottesville, VA 22902-5178
Contact: Guinevere Higgins, Prog. Asst.
FAX: (434) 977-3176;
E-mail: info@westwindfoundation.org; Additional e-mail for Guinevere Higgins:higgins@westwindfoundaiton.org;
URL: http://www.westwindfoundation.org

Established in 1987 in DC.
Donors: Edward M. Miller; WWF, Ltd.
Grantmaker type: Independent foundation.
Financial data (yr. ended 12/31/10): Assets, $54,043,325 (M); expenditures, $3,689,419; qualifying distributions, $3,499,007; giving activities include $3,499,007 for 123 grants (high: $313,500; low: $100).
Purpose and activities: The foundation is dedicated to protecting the integrity of natural ecosystems and the health of human communities through its grantmaking programs. WestWind tends to provide more general support grants, but the foundation will also provide grants for project or program specific requests.
Fields of interest: Education; Environment, land resources; Environment, forests; Environment; Reproductive health, family planning; Youth development; Human services; Youth; Young adults.
International interests: Caribbean; Latin America.
Type of support: General/operating support; Continuing support; Land acquisition; Program development; Conferences/seminars; Matching/challenge support.
Limitations: Giving on a national level, with emphasis on the Southeast, for environment program. Giving is primarily targeted toward benefiting Latin America and the Caribbean for Reproductive Health and Rights program, although domestic support is available. No support for religious organizations. No grants to individuals, or

for capital campaigns, endowments or brick and mortar projects.
Publications: Application guidelines; Grants list.
Application information: Organizations that have never received a grant from the foundation before, must first submit an online letter of inquiry 60 days before program deadline. Proposal submission is by invitation only. See foundation web site for application guidelines and procedures. Currently, letters of inquiry are not being accepted for either the Environmental Program or the Reproductive Health and Rights Program. The foundation tends to provide more general support grants, but the foundation will also provide grants for project or program specific requests. Application form required.
  Initial approach: See foundation web site for current guidelines
  Copies of proposal: 1
  Deadline(s): Reproductive Health and Rights grants deadline is Apr.; Forests deadline is Aug.; Climate deadline is Oct.
  Board meeting date(s): May, Sept., and Nov.
  Final notification: Late June for Reproductive Health and Rights Program; Oct. for Forests; Dec. for Climate
Trustees: Janet H. Miller; Edward M. Miller.
Number of staff: 1 full-time support.
EIN: 526358830

2155
Woodbury Fund, Inc.
(formerly Do'Ikyte Foundation)
21570 Schoolhouse Ct.
Ashburn, VA 20148-5018

Established in 1993 in DC.
Donors: Daniel Solomon; Lillian Cohen Solomon Trust.
Grantmaker type: Independent foundation.
Financial data (yr. ended 12/31/09): Assets, $9,679,289 (M); expenditures, $773,017; qualifying distributions, $544,800; giving activities include $544,800 for grants.
Fields of interest: Education; Human services; International human rights; Jewish federated giving programs; Jewish agencies & synagogues.
Limitations: Applications not accepted. Giving primarily in Washington, DC. No grants to individuals.
Application information: Contributes only to pre-selected organizations.
Officers and Directors:* Daniel Solomon,* Pres.; Jane Solomon,* V.P.; Thomas R. Asher,* Secy.; Liza Albright, Treas.
EIN: 043198227

2156
World Hope International, Inc.
625 Slaters Ln., Ste. 200
Alexandria, VA 22314-1169 (703) 923-9414
FAX: (703) 923-1169; E-mail: whi@worldhope.net;
Toll-free tel.: (888) 466-4673; URL: http://www.worldhope.org
Facebook: http://www.facebook.com/worldhopeorg?v=wall&ref=ts
Twitter: http://twitter.com/worldhopeorg

Established in 1996.
Grantmaker type: Public charity.

Financial data (yr. ended 12/31/10): Revenue, $11,659,913; assets, $8,352,046 (M); gifts received, $11,209,155; expenditures, $13,518,634; giving activities include $58,001 for grants, and $1,524,848 for grants to organizations outside the U.S.
Purpose and activities: The organization works to alleviate suffering and injustice through education, enterprise, and community health.
Fields of interest: Health care; International relief; Economically disadvantaged.
Limitations: Giving on a national and international basis.
Publications: Annual report; Financial statement; Newsletter.
Application information:
 Board meeting date(s): Aug. and Mar.
Officers and Directors: Jo Anne Lyon,* Chair.; Gary St. John, C.F.O.; Karl D. Eastlack,* C.E.O.; Dr. David Blanchard; Steve Brown; Kevin Batman; Dr. Ewy Hay Campbell; Dr. Dan Chamberlain; Mike Chambers; Robert Clyde; Dr. Clint Curle; Norwood Davis; John Lyon; Dr. Jerry Pence; Dr. Thomas E. Phillippe, Sr.; Jeri Sape, J.D.; Bobby Strand; H.C. Wilson.
EIN: 351985485

2157
Youth Venture
1700 N. Moore St., Ste. 2000
Arlington, VA   22209-1921   (703) 527-4126
FAX: (703) 527-8383;
E-mail: info@youthventure.org; URL: http://www.genv.net/
YouTube: http://www.youtube.com/user/youthventure

Established in 1997 in VA.
Donors: Allianz Foundation; Corporation for National and Community Service; Cricket Island Foundation; Bill and Melinda Gates Foundation; The Robert Wood Johnson Foundation; New Hampshire Charitable Foundation; William McGowan Charitable Fund; Public Welfare Foundation; Starbucks Foundation.
Grantmaker type: Public charity.
Financial data (yr. ended 12/31/10): Revenue, $1,434,003; assets, $1,000,316 (M); gifts received, $1,361,882; expenditures, $1,676,811; giving activities include $164,391 for grants.
Purpose and activities: The organization seeks to inspire and invest in teams of young people to design and launch their own lasting social ventures, enabling them to have the transformative experience of leading positive social change.
Fields of interest: Youth development; Leadership development; Children/youth.
International interests: Argentina; Belgium; Brazil; Canada; Chile; France; Germany; India; Ireland; Mexico; South Africa; Spain; Thailand.
Type of support: Management development/capacity building; Conferences/seminars; Seed money; Curriculum development; Technical assistance; Consulting services.
Limitations: Applications accepted. Giving on a national and international basis. No support for religious or political organizations. No grants for operating losses.
Publications: Application guidelines; Financial statement; Informational brochure; Newsletter.
Application information: Applicants must be teams of youth predominately between the ages of 12 and 20; applicants for Dream It, Do It Grants may be submitted in English, Spanish, Portuguese, or French. Application form required.
 Initial approach: Complete application online
 Copies of proposal: 1
 Deadline(s): Rolling basis for Basic Grants; May 31 for The Dr. Seuss Lorax Grants; Dec. 31 for Dream It, Do It Grants
 Final notification: 1 to 2 weeks for Basic Grants
Officers and Directors: * Bill Drayton,* Chair.; Roy Gamse, Acting Pres.; Gretchen Zucker, Exec. Dir.; Howard Gardner, Ph.D.; Lou Harris; Joe Onek; Kyle Zimmer.
Number of staff: 21 full-time professional.
EIN: 541744720

WASHINGTON

2158
444S Foundation
(also known as 444 Sierra Foundation)
P.O. Box 1128
Bellevue, WA   98009-1128
Contact: Peggy Ford, Fdn. Admin.
E-mail: 444s@kamutlake.net

Established in 1998 in WA.
Donor: G. James Roush.
Grantmaker type: Independent foundation.
Financial data (yr. ended 12/31/10): Assets, $35,877,844 (M); expenditures, $1,935,637; qualifying distributions, $1,670,966; giving activities include $1,433,000 for 45 grants (high: $137,000; low: $5,000).
Purpose and activities: Giving to support environmental, wild lands and wildlife protection efforts. This includes northern wild lands and forests.
Fields of interest: Environment, natural resources; Animals/wildlife, preservation/protection.
International interests: Canada.
Type of support: General/operating support; Program development; Matching/challenge support.
Limitations: Applications not accepted. Giving primarily for the benefit of the Pacific Northwest, including western Canada, AK, and the Arctic. No grants to individuals or for media projects.
Application information: Contributes only to pre-selected organizations. Foundation will solicit proposals. Unsolicited requests for funds not accepted.
 Board meeting date(s): Varies
Trustees: Del Langbauer; G. James Roush; William Morgan Roush; James Sheldon; Cynthia Wayburn.
Number of staff: 1 full-time professional; 1 part-time support.
EIN: 916468421

2159
Bainbridge-Ometepe Sister Islands Association
P.O. Box 4484
Rollingbay, WA   98061-0484   (206) 842-8148
FAX: (206) 842-6907; E-mail: info@bosia.org;
URL: http://www.bosia.org

Established in 1986 in WA.
Grantmaker type: Public charity.
Financial data (yr. ended 12/31/10): Revenue, $159,675; assets, $271,332 (M); gifts received, $119,777; expenditures, $180,055; program services expenses, $171,506; giving activities include $110,101 for grants to organizations outside the U.S.
Purpose and activities: The association provides grants to enable Bainbridge Island residents to join delegations to Ometepe Island on Lake Nicaragua, and to enable their residents to visit Bainbridge. It promotes friendship and mutual understanding between the residents of the islands through peaceful exchanges of all sorts. It aims to support educational, technical, and cultural exchange; and promote understanding of the special problems faced by the people of Nicaragua.
Fields of interest: Humanities; Arts; Education; Public health.
International interests: Nicaragua.
Type of support: Building/renovation; Program development; Grants to individuals; Scholarships—to individuals; Exchange programs.
Limitations: Giving limited to residents of Bainbridge Island, WA, and Ometepe Island, Nicaragua.
Publications: Annual report; Newsletter.
Officers and Directors: * Betsy Carroll,* Pres.; Don Duprey,* V.P.; Jeanne Huber, Past Pres.; Barb Pettit,* Secy.; Dana Quitslund,* Treas.; Carol Cassell; Monica Jones; Kari Lagerloef; Cestjon McFarland; George Schneider; Tim Sell; Linda Shadwell; Susan Shaffer; James Templeton; Dallas Young.
Number of staff: 1 part-time professional; 1 part-time support.
EIN: 911433369

2160
Bezos Family Foundation
7683 S.E. 27th St., No. 224
Mercer Island, WA   98040-2804

Established in 2000 in WA.
Donors: Miguel A. Bezos; Jacklyn G. Bezos.
Grantmaker type: Independent foundation.
Financial data (yr. ended 12/31/10): Assets, $45,669,948 (M); expenditures, $3,981,690; qualifying distributions, $3,981,477; giving activities include $3,490,413 for 71 grants (high: $497,139; low: $349).
Fields of interest: Education; Children/youth, services; International exchange; Children/youth.
Limitations: Applications not accepted. Giving in the U.S., with emphasis on NY and WA. No grants to individuals.
Application information: Contributes only to pre-selected organizations.
Directors: Jacklyn G. Bezos; Jeffrey P. Bezos; Lisa Bezos; Mackenzie T. Bezos; Mark S. Bezos; Miguel A. Bezos; Christina Bezos Poore; Stephen S. Poore.
EIN: 912073258

2161
The Bullitt Foundation
1212 Minor Ave.
Seattle, WA   98101-2825   (206) 343-0807
Contact: Denis Hayes, Pres.

FAX: (206) 343-0822; E-mail: info@bullitt.org;
URL: http://www.bullitt.org
Grants Database: http://www.bullitt.org/
grant-history
RSS Feed: http://www.bullitt.org/resources/
resources/RSS

Incorporated in 1952 in WA.
Donors: Dorothy S. Bullitt†; Members of the Bullitt family.
Grantmaker type: Independent foundation.
Financial data (yr. ended 12/31/09): Assets, $100,160,268 (M); gifts received, $200; expenditures, $8,073,484; qualifying distributions, $6,801,198; giving activities include $6,618,467 for grants, and $100,000 for 1 grant to an individual.
Purpose and activities: Support primarily to safeguard the natural environment by promoting responsible human activities and sustainable communities in the Pacific Northwest.
Fields of interest: Transportation; Public affairs, citizen participation; Environment, water resources; Environment, water pollution; Environment, toxics; Environment, pollution control; Environment, radiation control; Environment, land resources; Environment, climate change/global warming; Environment, energy; Employment, public policy; Animals/wildlife; Agriculture/food, public policy; Agriculture/food.
International interests: Canada.
Type of support: General/operating support; Continuing support; Income development; Management development/capacity building; Equipment; Emergency funds; Program development; Seed money; Fellowships; Technical assistance; Program-related investments/loans; Employee matching gifts; Matching/challenge support.
Limitations: Applications accepted. Giving in the Pacific Northwest including AK, OR, WA, and British Columbia; giving also in ID and MT. No support for political organizations. No grants to individuals (except for fellowships), or for capital campaigns, equipment, building construction, or land acquisition.
Publications: Application guidelines; Grants list.
Application information: Once invited, the full application is available on the foundation web site. Full applications are by invitation only. The foundation is in the process of revising its grantmaking priorities and procedures. Please follow the online inquiry process even if you have applied for or received a Bullitt Foundation grant in the past. Application form required.
   Initial approach: Inquiry form to determine eligibility found on foundation web site. (Full applications are only accepted upon invitation, following letter of inquiry)
   Copies of proposal: 1
   Deadline(s): May 1 and Nov. 1 for full applications
   Board meeting date(s): Apr. and Oct.
   Final notification: 5 months by letter for full applications
Officers and Trustees:* Maggie Walker,* Chair.; Harriet Bullitt,* Vice-Chair.; Denis Hayes,* C.E.O. and Pres.; Anne Fennessy,* Secy.; Phyllis Wise,* Treas.; Jabe Blumenthal; Maud Daudon; Estella Leopold; Michael Parham; Doug Raff.
Number of staff: 6 full-time professional.
EIN: 916027795
Recent grants for international programs:
2161-1 Bonneville Environmental Foundation, Portland, OR, $50,000. For Green Sports

Alliance. To support the organization's efforts to advance professional sports teams', players', owners', and venue managers' adoption of best practices in water and energy conservation, waste minimization, purchasing policies, and transportation. 2010.
2161-2 British Columbia Spaces for Nature, Gibsons, Canada, $15,000. For Howe Sound UN Biosphere Reserve. To assess the feasibility of a campaign to designate the Howe Sound and associated uplands near Vancouver as a major new protected area in British Columbia. 2010.
2161-3 Canadian Center for Policy Alternatives, Vancouver, Canada, $22,000. For Climate Justice Project - Paths to Equitable and Sustainable BC Economy. To lead a collaborative outreach initiative to generate climate change mitigation and adaptation policies that integrate social justice objectives. 2010.
2161-4 Canadian Parks and Wilderness Society, Ottawa, Canada, $40,000. For Working toward protecting 50 percent of British Columbia in light of climate change. The award is for year five of a five-year grant. 2010.
2161-5 Carpe Diem West, Sausalito, CA, $25,000. For Carpe Diem - Western Water and Climate Change Project. To advance policy reforms necessary to protect the headwater source areas for western watersheds, and to illuminate the linkages among water management, energy development, and climate change. 2010.
2161-6 Cascadia Region Green Building Council, Seattle, WA, $75,000. For general support. 2010.
2161-7 Community Energy Association, Vancouver, Canada, $40,000. For Green Landlords Project - Phase 2. To support a pilot project that advances energy efficiency in the rental-housing sector in British Columbia. 2010.
2161-8 EarthCorps, Seattle, WA, $10,000. For EarthCorps-Friends of the Hylebos Merger Evaluation and Integration. For expenses associated with the proposed merger of EarthCorps and Friends of the Hylebos (FOH), two organizations dedicated to restoring urban parks and open space. 2010.
2161-9 Ecojustice Canada, Vancouver, Canada, $50,000. For Ensuring Wise Water Governance in BC: A Legal and Scientific Approach to Protecting In-Stream Flows and Habitat. The award is for year four of a five-year grant. 2010.
2161-10 Ecotrust Canada, Vancouver, Canada, $40,000. For FSC Market Development in British Columbia. The award is for year three of a three-year grant. 2010.
2161-11 Forest Ethics, San Francisco, CA, $30,000. For Conservation-Based Solutions to Climate Change: Protecting Temperate Wildlands So They Can Protect Us. For work in British Columbia to ensure that high level climate change policies properly incorporate and accurately account for land-based carbon dioxide emissions, sequestration, and storage. 2010.
2161-12 Fraser Riverkeeper, Vancouver, Canada, $30,000. For Fraser Riverkeeper Program. For general support. 2010.
2161-13 Friends of the Earth, San Francisco, CA, $30,000. For Cleaner Ship-Healthier Ports: Improving community health and our marine environment. To reduce pollution from Northwest coastal short-sea shipping in Seattle, Vancouver, and Victoria. 2010.
2161-14 Georgia Strait Alliance, Nanaimo, Canada, $35,000. For Sustaining the Strait: Increasing

Sustainability Within Georgia Strait Alliance. For general support. 2010.
2161-15 Groundwire, Seattle, WA, $15,000. For a comprehensive redesign of Groundwire's current business model with assistance from expert legal, financial, and fundraising firms. 2010.
2161-16 ICLEI - Local Governments for Sustainability USA, Oakland, CA, $50,000. For STAR Community Index - A national sustainability framework for local governments. For the development of the STAR Community Index, a rating system for cities to advance sustainable policies and practices modeled after the LEED standard for green buildings. Funding will support completion of the STAR framework and pilot training in Pacific Northwest cities. 2010.
2161-17 Land Trust Alliance of British Columbia, Victoria, Canada, $35,000. For Protecting Ecosystem Services for Sustainable Communities. To provide training resources and technical assistance to improve the effectiveness and impact of member organizations. 2010.
2161-18 Pembina Foundation for Environmental Research and Education, Drayton Valley, Canada, $45,000. For Power My Ride - Sparking Sustainable Transportation in the Lower Mainland. For initiative that accelerates deployment of electric vehicles in British Columbia. 2010.
2161-19 Pembina Foundation for Environmental Research and Education, Drayton Valley, Canada, $30,000. For Strengthening the Western Climate Initiative by Ensuring the Active Participation of British Columbia. For activities to encourage British Columbia to implement the Western Climate Initiative protocol on January 1, 2012. 2010.
2161-20 Sightline Institute, Seattle, WA, $90,000. For research and communications programs that provide regional advocates and policy makers with tools to advance solutions to environmental, economic, and social problems. 2010.
2161-21 Tides Foundation, San Francisco, CA, $55,000. For Greening Markets to Conserve Forests of the Pacific Northwest and Their Ecosystem Services. To advance Forest Stewardship Council standards for timber production and practices and expand usage of recycled content for books and other printed materials. 2010.
2161-22 Tides Foundation, San Francisco, CA, $50,000. For Vancouver Greenest City Fund. For expenses associated with the establishment of a fund to enable Vancouver, BC to realize its vision of becoming the greenest city in the world. 2010.
2161-23 Tides Foundation, San Francisco, CA, $30,000. For Organizing for Change. To advance progressive environmental policies and achieve greater influence and effectiveness with citizens and decisionmakers in British Columbia. 2010.
2161-24 University of Victoria, Victoria, Canada, $50,000. For The Future of Water Law, Policy and Governance in the Pacific Northwest: Building capacity and action for sustainability in the 21st century. For efforts to advance reforms to British Columbia's water management policies and governance mechanisms. 2010.
2161-25 University of Washington, Seattle, WA, $35,000. For Enhancements to OneBusAway, Transit Traveler Information Systems. For enhancements to OneBusAway, a set of transit

tools that provide real-time arrival information by various media. 2010.

2161-26 Urban Greenspaces Institute, Portland, OR, $25,000. For Regional Biodiversity Conservation. To support continuing efforts to create a comprehensive, integrated network of open space in the Portland-Vancouver metropolitan region with a specific focus on biodiversity conservation, green infrastructure, and climate adaptation. 2010.

2161-27 Watershed Watch Salmon Society, Port Coquitlam, Canada, $25,000. Toward Water Reform in British Columbia: Implementation of the Living Water Smart program. For support of efforts to advance improved water management policies in British Columbia. 2010.

2162
Campion Foundation

1904 3rd Ave., Ste. 405
Seattle, WA 98101-1150   (206) 686-5310
Contact: Melanie Mathews, Opers. Dir.
FAX: (206) 260-0106;
E-mail: info@campionfoundation.org; URL: http://www.campionfoundation.org

Established in 2005 in WA.
Donors: Thomas D. Campion; Sonya Campion.
Grantmaker type: Independent foundation.
Financial data (yr. ended 12/31/10): Assets, $30,131,130 (M); expenditures, $6,236,562; qualifying distributions, $5,988,845; giving activities include $5,151,280 for 53 grants (high: $1,615,000; low: $480).
Purpose and activities: The foundation focuses on three program areas: Protecting Wilderness, Ending Homelessness, and Strengthening Nonprofits.
Fields of interest: Environment; Housing/shelter; Community/economic development; Homeless.
Type of support: Matching/challenge support; General/operating support; Management development/capacity building; Program development; Program evaluation.
Limitations: Applications not accepted. Giving primarily in WA, ID, MT, AK and Western Canada (British Columbia, the North Western Territories and the Yukon) for wilderness protection. No support for salmon protection programs, or for water quality programs, environmental education programs or for energy, transportation or air-quality programs. No grants to individuals, or for land acquisition, capital construction projects.
Application information: Unsolicited requests for funds not accepted. Proposals accepted by invitation only.
Trustees: Sonya Campion; Thomas D. Campion.
Number of staff: 4 full-time professional.
EIN: 203421717
Recent grants for international programs:
2162-1 Alaska Wilderness League, Washington, DC, $1,615,000. 2010.
2162-2 Canadian Parks and Wilderness Society, Ottawa, Canada, $50,000. 2010.
2162-3 Forest Ethics, San Francisco, CA, $150,000. 2010.
2162-4 Northern Alaska Environmental Center, Fairbanks, AK, $25,000. 2010.
2162-5 Ocean Conservancy, Washington, DC, $50,000. 2010.
2162-6 Oceana, Washington, DC, $100,000. 2010.
2162-7 Yukon Conservation Society, Whitehorse, Canada, $15,000. 2010.

2163
Channel Foundation

603 Stewart St., Ste. 415
Seattle, WA 98101-1247
E-mail: info@channelfoundation.org; URL: http://www.channelfoundation.org

Established in 1998 in WA.
Donor: Elaine M. Nonneman.
Grantmaker type: Independent foundation.
Financial data (yr. ended 12/31/10): Assets, $8,010,577 (M); gifts received, $1,002,575; expenditures, $494,906; qualifying distributions, $311,000; giving activities include $311,000 for grants.
Purpose and activities: The foundation promotes leadership in women's human rights around the globe by supporting organizations engaged in combating gender inequality. Through grantmaking, advocacy, and collaboration with an international network of women's rights organizations and funders, the foundation seeks to create opportunities in order to ensure that women's rights are respected, protected, and fulfilled.
Fields of interest: Housing/shelter, services; Higher education; Women, centers/services; International affairs, equal rights; International human rights; Civil/human rights, women; Women.
Type of support: General/operating support; Scholarship funds; Scholarships—to individuals.
Limitations: Applications not accepted. Giving on a worldwide basis, with some emphasis on global organizations in CA, Washington, DC, and MA. No grants to individuals (except for the Women's Leadership Scholarship Program), or for service delivery projects, capital campaigns or electoral campaigns.
Application information: Unsolicited requests for funds not accepted.
Officer: Katrin Wilde, Exec. Dir.
Trustee: Elaine M. Nonneman.
EIN: 916478055

2164
Colson Family Foundation

9310 N.E. Vancouver Mall Dr.
Vancouver, WA 98662-8210

Established in 2003 in OR.
Donors: Hugh Colson; Hugh Colson Living Trust.
Grantmaker type: Independent foundation.
Financial data (yr. ended 12/31/10): Assets, $26,168,256 (M); gifts received, $7,845,719; expenditures, $4,228,723; qualifying distributions, $4,152,347; giving activities include $4,150,162 for 29 grants (high: $1,250,000; low: $2,500).
Fields of interest: Higher education; Human services; Christian agencies & churches.
International interests: Africa.
Limitations: Applications not accepted. Giving primarily in OR and WA. No grants to individuals.
Application information: Contributes only to pre-selected organizations.
Officers: Barton G. Colson, Pres.; Norman L. Brenden, V.P.; Bradley A. Colson, V.P.; Patrick Kennedy, V.P.; Bruce D. Thorn, Secy.; Susan Haider, Treas.
Director: Bonnie Colson.
EIN: 931326316

2165
Common Ground Foundation

c/o King & Oliason
514 2nd Ave. W
Seattle, WA 98119-3928
Application address: c/o Charles C. Perkins, 1325 N. Allen Pl., Apt. 420, Seattle, WA 98103, tel.: (206) 632-2375

Established in 1997 in KS.
Donors: Charles C. Perkins; Nancy P. Perkins.
Grantmaker type: Independent foundation.
Financial data (yr. ended 12/31/10): Assets, $5,499,375 (M); gifts received, $3,646,647; expenditures, $202,974; qualifying distributions, $189,118; giving activities include $185,733 for 16 grants (high: $118,527; low: $200).
Purpose and activities: Giving primarily for family planning, human rights, and public policy research.
Fields of interest: Higher education, university; Reproductive health, family planning; International human rights; Public policy, research.
Type of support: General/operating support.
Limitations: Applications accepted. Giving primarily in CA, MA, and NY. No grants to individuals.
Application information:
Initial approach: Letter
Deadline(s): None
Officers: Charles C. Perkins, Pres.; Nancy P. Perkins, Secy.-Treas.
Director: Mary L. Perkins.
EIN: 742831671

2166
Community Building Foundation

(formerly The Quiet Group Foundation)
c/o Jim Sheehan
35 W. Main, Ste. 300
Spokane, WA 99201-1405

Established in 2003 in WA.
Donor: James L. Sheehan.
Grantmaker type: Independent foundation.
Financial data (yr. ended 12/31/10): Assets, $3,839,173 (M); gifts received, $127,587; expenditures, $917,015; qualifying distributions, $171,121; giving activities include $171,121 for grants.
Fields of interest: Community development, civic centers; International human rights.
Limitations: Applications not accepted. Giving primarily in WA. No grants to individuals.
Application information: Contributes only to pre-selected organizations.
Officers: James L. Sheehan, Pres.; Kathryn C. Sheehan, Secy.
Director: Joseph M. Sheehan.
EIN: 371465273

2167
Crystal Springs Foundation

c/o Filament, LLC
701 Pike St., Ste. 2225
Seattle, WA 98101-2370

Established in 1999 in WA.
Donors: Michael R. Murray; Joyce B. Murray.
Grantmaker type: Independent foundation.
Financial data (yr. ended 12/31/10): Assets, $43,338,053 (M); expenditures, $1,780,386;

qualifying distributions, $1,139,949; giving activities include $1,139,949 for grants.
Purpose and activities: Giving primarily for international economic development, education, as well as for social services.
Fields of interest: International economic development; Higher education; Health organizations, association; Human services; Children/youth, services; Foundations (private grantmaking).
Limitations: Applications not accepted. Giving primarily in UT, with emphasis on Salt Lake City, and Seattle, WA. No grants to individuals.
Application information: Contributes only to pre-selected organizations.
Officers and Directors:* Michael R. Murray,* Pres. and Treas.; Joyce B. Murray,* V.P. and Secy.
Number of staff: 1 full-time support.
EIN: 912008832

2168
Duim Family Foundation
8518 146th Pl. S.E.
Newcastle, WA 98059-9267

Established in 1997 in WA.
Donors: Gary T. Duim; Linda K. Duim; Duim Charitable Lead Trust.
Grantmaker type: Independent foundation.
Financial data (yr. ended 12/31/10): Assets, $2,007,942 (M); gifts received, $75,549; expenditures, $203,989; qualifying distributions, $191,000; giving activities include $191,000 for 9 grants (high: $100,000; low: $1,000).
Fields of interest: International affairs; Human services; Christian agencies & churches.
Limitations: Applications not accepted. No grants to individuals.
Application information: Unsolicited requests for funds not accepted.
Officers: Gary T. Duim, Pres.; Linda K. Duim, V.P.; Douglas A. Duim, Secy.-Treas.
Directors: Deanna K. Duim; Duane M. Duim; Rae Ann Duim.
EIN: 911872763

2169
Friends of Woodstock School, Inc.
724 2nd St., Ste. A
Mukilteo, WA 98275-1577   (425) 353-8422
FAX: (425) 438-8951;
E-mail: mail@fwsfoundation.org; URL: http://www.fwsfoundation.org

Grantmaker type: Public charity.
Financial data (yr. ended 06/30/10): Revenue, $1,305,435; assets, $3,565,671 (M); gifts received, $941,519; expenditures, $1,335,839; giving activities include $973,548 for grants to organizations outside the U.S.
Purpose and activities: The organization supports the educational mission and purposes of Woodstock School in India.
Fields of interest: Scholarships/financial aid; Education, single organization support.
International interests: India.
Type of support: Scholarships—to individuals.
Limitations: Applications not accepted. Giving on a national and international basis.
Publications: Financial statement.

Application information: Unsolicited requests for funds not considered or acknowledged.
Officers and Directors:* Glenn Conrad,* Pres.; Marlin Schoonmaker,* Secy.; Bruce Davis,* Treas.; Stephen Alter; Rick Downs; Anne Lind; David Laurenson.
EIN: 591588857

2170
Bill & Melinda Gates Foundation
(formerly William H. Gates Foundation)
P.O. Box 23350
Seattle, WA 98102-0650   (206) 709-3100
Contact: Inquiry Admin.
FAX: (206) 709-3180;
E-mail: info@gatesfoundation.org; Tel. for grant inquiries: (206) 709-3140; East Coast Office address: P.O. Box 6176, Benjamin Franklin Station, Washington, DC 20044; URL: http://www.gatesfoundation.org
Bill and Melinda Gates and Warren Buffett's Giving Pledge: http://givingpledge.org/#enter
Blog: http://www.impatientoptimists.org/
E-Newsletter: http://www.gatesfoundation.org/Pages/subscribe-email-rss.aspx
Facebook: http://www.facebook.com/billmelindagatesfoundation?v=info
Flickr: http://www.flickr.com/photos/gatesfoundation/
Foundation News: http://www.gatesfoundation.org/FileReturn.aspx?returntype=rss&feed=PressRelease
Grantee Perception Report: http://www.gatesfoundation.org/learning/Pages/grantee-perception-report.aspx
Grants Database: http://www.gatesfoundation.org/grants/Pages/search.aspx
Knowledge Center: http://www.gatesfoundation.org/learning/Pages/overview.aspx
Twitter: http://www.twitter.com/gatesfoundation
YouTube: http://www.youtube.com/GatesFoundation

Established in 1994 in WA as the William H. Gates Foundation; The Gates Library Foundation was created in 1997 and its name changed to the Gates Learning Foundation in Aug. 1999; The Gates Learning Foundation merged into the foundation Jan. 1, 2000 and was renamed the Bill & Melinda Gates Foundation; In May 2006 the foundation reorganized its grantmaking programs.
Donors: William H. "Bill" Gates III; Melinda French Gates; Warren E. Buffett.
Grantmaker type: Independent foundation.
Financial data (yr. ended 12/31/10): Assets, $37,430,150,458 (M); gifts received, $3,163,183,326; expenditures, $2,947,705,793; qualifying distributions, $3,196,164,408; giving activities include $2,482,720,907 for 1,786 grants (high: $155,184,851; low: $360), $3,621,302 for 1,282 employee matching gifts, $100,051,599 for foundation-administered programs and $7,175,528 for loans/program-related investments.
Purpose and activities: Guided by the belief that every life has equal value, the Bill & Melinda Gates Foundation works to reduce inequities and improve lives around the world. Grantmaking is focused among 3 major initiatives: 1) Global Development, which has such priorities as poverty, agricultural development, emergency relief, access to technology and libraries, and water and sanitation; 2) Global Health, which includes major initiatives

towards controlling or eliminating AIDS and Malaria, as well as nutrition, tobacco issues, polio, tuberculosis and other diseases, and 3) United States, which focuses on community grants, libraries and learning.
Fields of interest: Public health, clean water supply; Rural development; Reproductive health, family planning; Public health, sanitation; Public health; Philanthropy/voluntarism, alliance/advocacy; Parasitic diseases research; Nutrition; Libraries/library science; International development; Human services; Higher education, college (community/junior); Health care; Environment, water resources; Electronic communications/Internet; Education; Economic development; Community/economic development; Civil/human rights; AIDS; Agriculture.
International interests: Africa; Asia; Australia; Developing countries; Europe.
Type of support: General/operating support; Continuing support; Annual campaigns; Capital campaigns; Building/renovation; Program development; Publication; Scholarship funds; Research; Technical assistance; Program-related investments/loans; Employee matching gifts; Scholarships—to individuals; Matching/challenge support.
Limitations: Applications accepted. Giving on a national and international basis to support initiatives in health, learning, poverty alleviation and development. United States giving has an emphasis on the Pacific Northwest, international giving emphasis is on South America, Africa, Europe, Asia and Australia. No support for religious purposes. No grants to individuals directly.
Publications: Application guidelines; Annual report; Financial statement; Grants list; Informational brochure; Newsletter; Occasional report; Program policy statement.
Application information: Review funding guidelines and eligibility overview on foundation's web site before initial contact with foundation; proposals should not be submitted without prior invitation by the foundation. No mail-in applications are accepted. Application form required.
> *Initial approach:* Letter of inquiry (not exceeding 4 pages and only accepted in Global Health and Pacific Northwest giving areas); submit formal funding proposal upon invitation from foundation
> *Deadline(s):* Generally none
> *Final notification:* 10-12 weeks

Officers and Trustees:* Melinda French Gates,* Co-Chair.; William H. "Bill" Gates III,* Co-Chair.; William H. Gates, Sr., Co-Chair.; Jeff Raikes, C.E.O.; Christopher Elias, Pres., Global Devel. Prog.; Allan C. Golston, Pres., U.S. Prog.; Trevor Mundel, Pres.-Elect, Global Health Prog.; Connie Collingsworth, Secy. and Genl. Counsel; Richard Henriques, C.F.O.; Martha Choe, C.A.O.; Kate James, C.C.O.; Geoff Lamb, Managing Dir., Public Policy, Fdn. Opers.; Warren E. Buffett.
Global Development Advisory Board: Joaquim Alberto Chissano; Amina J. Ibrahim; Kavita N. Ramdas; Lawrence H. Summers; Ernesto Zedillo; Philip Zelikow.
U.S. Program Advisory Board: Ann Fudge, Chair.; Henry Cisneros; Christopher Edley; Edward Glaeser; Walter Massey.
Global Health Advisory Board: Harold Varmus, Chair.; John Bell; Cheryl Scott; Jay Naidoo; Joy Phumaphi; Sujatha Rao; Daniel Vasella.
Number of staff: 980
EIN: 562618866
Recent grants for international programs:

2170-1 Aarhus, City of, Aarhus, Denmark, $85,000. For Aarhus Next Library conference and to provide scholarships for select attendees. 2010.

2170-2 Aeras Global TB Vaccine Foundation, Rockville, MD, $20,000. For premiere international TB Vaccine Conference, which will incorporate the current goals of the STOP TB working group on TB Vaccines and other national and international TB initiatives, and will emphasize coordination with TB diagnostics. 2010.

2170-3 African Agricultural Technology Foundation, Nairobi, Kenya, $200,000. For Open Forum on Agricultural Biotechnology in Africa (OFAB) conferences that enhance knowledge-sharing and awareness on biotechnology and contribute to building enabling environment for decision making. 2010.

2170-4 African Leaders Malaria Alliance, Francistown, Botswana, $450,858. For African Leaders Malaria Alliance (ALMA) secretariat. 2010.

2170-5 African Malaria Network Trust, Dar es Salaam, Tanzania, Zanzibar and Pemba, $223,830. To strengthen institutional capacities in Health Research Ethics (HRE) in Africa, foster and promote discussion, debate, research and publications in HRE, highlighting African perspectives. 2010.

2170-6 African Monitor, Cape Town, South Africa, $1,517,491. To monitor the impact of development programs on poor communities in Africa, elevate the voices of African citizens in development decisions, and build support in Africa for pro-poor policies. 2010.

2170-7 Albert B. Sabin Vaccine Institute, Washington, DC, $3,322,780. To serve as effective secretariat for the Coalition against Typhoid (CaT) so that Sabin and CaT are able to expedite and sustain evidence-informed decisions at the global, regional, and country levels regarding the use of typhoid vaccination to prevent childhood enteric fever in areas of high risk. 2010.

2170-8 Albert B. Sabin Vaccine Institute, Washington, DC, $199,898. To commemorate the 30th anniversary of the declaration that smallpox was eradicated and bring together persons involved to determine lessons that might be applied to future global collaborative efforts. 2010.

2170-9 Albert Einstein College of Medicine of Yeshiva University, Bronx, NY, $100,000. To create a low cost diagnostic test for the detection and quantification of amastigotes, the parasites that cause clinical manifestations in Leishmaniasis, using a simple and inexpensive microfluidics device. 2010.

2170-10 AllAfrica Foundation, Washington, DC, $2,311,529. For The Development Challenge: Reporting Africa's Promise and Possibilities, which will provide coverage of the challenges, opportunities and advances of sustainable development efforts to reduce poverty. 2010.

2170-11 Alliance for a Green Revolution in Africa, Nairobi, Kenya, $28,000,000. To increase the livelihoods of smallholder farmers in African countries through meaningful improvements to their farm business operations and the market infrastructure of core food staples. 2010.

2170-12 Alliance for a Green Revolution in Africa, Nairobi, Kenya, $5,474,390. To improve the livelihoods of smallholder farmers in sub-Saharan Africa by strengthening Farm

Organization Support Centre for Africa (FOSCA), member-based farmer organizations, to deliver demand-driven, income-enhancing services to their members; by 2020, FOSCA envisions significant contributions to tripling the membership of farmer organizations in sub-Saharan Africa (SSA) and to AGRA's objective to double the incomes of 20 million smallholder farmers through robust and relevant institutions. 2010.

2170-13 American Cancer Society, Atlanta, GA, $451,720. To support Tobacco Conference where participants will share experiences and key findings from case studies with others in the field and to identify tobacco control policy and research priorities for the short-, medium- and longer-term at the national and regional level. 2010.

2170-14 American Society of Tropical Medicine and Hygiene, Deerfield, IL, $352,027. For conference support for annual meetings of the American Society of Tropical Medicine and Hygiene. 2010.

2170-15 AMT, Cherry Hill, NJ, $100,000. To develop and test a prototype, battery run photovoltaic driven blue LED portable blanket phototherapy system to provide light therapy for the treatment of jaundiced newborn infants in developing countries at risk for acute bilirubin encephalopathy. 2010.

2170-16 Applied Research and Technical Services LLC, Washington, DC, $14,698,635. To create Haiti Mobile Money Initiative (HMMI), incentive fund to enable financial services by mobile phone in Haiti that will support economic recovery and development. 2010.

2170-17 Arizona State University, Tempe, AZ, $100,000. For Round 4, Phase I of Grand Challenges Explorations-Noroviral Replicon: VLP for Gut Mucosal Immunity, project to develop and test a vaccine delivery system that uses Norovirus virus-like particles (VLPs) to deliver desired antigens directly to the gut mucosa. The self-replicating RNA in the VLP will not only encode those antigens, it will also act as an adjuvant by activating several signaling pathways for an enhanced and sustained immune response. 2010.

2170-18 Arizona State University, Tempe, AZ, $100,000. To develop and test malaria prevention novel skin-binding insect repellents that slowly release the repellent over a period of weeks. 2010.

2170-19 Ashoka: Innovators for the Public, Arlington, VA, $10,000. For general operating support. 2010.

2170-20 Asian Forum of Parliamentarians on Population and Development, Bangkok, Thailand, $25,000. For general operating support. 2010.

2170-21 Asian Vegetable Research and Development Center, Tainan, Taiwan, $250,000. For general support for AVRDC-The World Vegetable Center to increase vegetable production, marketing, and consumption in order to reduce poverty and increase the livelihood of vulnerable groups; in particular woman and children in Sub-Saharan Africa. 2010.

2170-22 Asociacion Benefica PRISMA, Lima, Peru, $100,000. To develop a rapid method of evaluating treatment response to tuberculosis and multidrug-resistant TB by measuring exhaled nitric oxide. 2010.

2170-23 Aspen Institute, Washington, DC, $450,248. To support global development as a strategic interest by strengthening links between

the development, diplomacy, and defense communities within the U.S. government. 2010.

2170-24 Association of Charitable Foundations, London, England, $25,000. For general operating support. 2010.

2170-25 Athabasca University, Athabasca, Canada, $10,000. For International Conference on Learning Analytics and Knowledge (LAK 11). Learning analytics is the measurement, collection, analysis and reporting of data about learners and their contexts, for purposes of understanding and optimizing learning and the environments in which it occurs. 2010.

2170-26 Australian National University, Canberra, Australia, $100,000. To test a new vaccine technology that modulates a host cytokine response to HIV vaccines. If successful, this cytokine trap technology may enhance T-cell mediated immunity to other vaccine antigens, such as tuberculosis. 2010.

2170-27 AVAC: Global Advocacy for HIV Prevention, New York, NY, $121,597. To create a favorable social environment for accelerated ethical research and global delivery of HIV/AIDS vaccines. 2010.

2170-28 Bansefi, Mexico City, Mexico, $2,989,493. To build innovative national correspondent banking network for low-income families in Mexico. 2010.

2170-29 Bar-Ilan University, Ramat Gan, Israel, $100,000. To design and test molecules that will inactivate specific genes within sperm that are essential to the fertilization process for potential use in a reversible oral male contraceptive. 2010.

2170-30 BBC World Service Trust, London, England, $19,998,393. To shape demand and social norms and improve family health practices in Bihar, through integrated and sustainable multi-channel communication strategy, empowering those who currently lack the information and agency to make informed decisions about their health. 2010.

2170-31 BBC World Service Trust, London, England, $623,045. To support improved media coverage of development issues in Africa through a facility to coordinate and streamline media development investments, research, and activities across the continent. 2010.

2170-32 Beijing University, Beijing, China, $1,104,400. To develop new in vitro culture systems for blood-stage and liver-stage Plasmodium vivax to facilitate anti-malaria drug screening. 2010.

2170-33 Better World Fund, Washington, DC, $25,000. For general operating support. 2010.

2170-34 Biomedical Primate Research Centre, Rijswijk, Netherlands, $1,414,793. To address present limitations in long-term cultivation of P. vivax (Pv) that seriously hamper research into the biology of this malaria parasite and vaccine/drug development. 2010.

2170-35 Biotechnology and Biological Sciences Research Council, Swindon, England, $8,000,000. For high quality research on sustainable crop production in sub-Saharan Africa and South Asia. 2010.

2170-36 Bond, London, England, $258,304. To catalyze United Kingdom and European Union leadership for Millennium Development Goals achievement through network building, policy engagement and increased awareness of the goals. 2010.

2170-37 Boston University, Boston, MA, $100,000. To develop and test low-cost maternal and infant mechanical ventilators for developing countries. 2010.

2170-38 Boston University, School of Medicine, Office of Continuing Medical Education, Boston, MA, $899,114. To improve accuracy and reporting of procurement transaction data and establish single global price and reporting database for HIV, tuberculosis, and malaria medicines and consumables for the purposes of identifying sub-optimal procurement spending and targeting interventions. 2010.

2170-39 Bread for the World Institute, Washington, DC, $1,784,791. To strengthen U.S. constituency for global maternal and child nutrition and promote a stronger U.S. response to under-nutrition in developing countries. 2010.

2170-40 Brigham and Womens Hospital, Boston, MA, $10,000. For conference support for the U.S.-Japan Tuberculosis and Leprosy Research Conference. 2010.

2170-41 Broad Institute, Cambridge, MA, $5,174,653. For P. falciparum genetic diversity: drug, vaccine, and disease severity applications. 2010.

2170-42 Broad Institute, Cambridge, MA, $1,535,508. To aid drug discovery and vaccine development toward the eradication of malaria. 2010.

2170-43 Brookings Institution, Washington, DC, $6,270,792. To conduct high-quality policy research focused on sustainable economic development in Africa, while amplifying the voice of African researchers in policymaking in the United States and Africa Ghana, Kenya, Nigeria, Senegal, South Africa, Uganda. 2010.

2170-44 Brookings Institution, Washington, DC, $280,438. To design innovative fund which will provide growth capital to successful, scalable development projects focused on agriculture, financial access and health. 2010.

2170-45 Brookings Institution, Washington, DC, $149,150. For Africa Growth Initiative Conference to identify coordinated or joint initiatives in three areas: research on growth, partnering with African research organizations, and new ideas to create an African voice. 2010.

2170-46 CAB International, Wallingford, England, $4,529,792. To distribute up-to-date knowledge on integrated soil fertility management to drive increased productivity on smallholder farms in sub-Saharan Africa. 2010.

2170-47 California Institute of Technology, Pasadena, CA, $471,918. To engineer immunity against HIV and other dangerous pathogens. 2010.

2170-48 California Institute of Technology, Pasadena, CA, $100,000. For Round 4, Phase I of Grand Challenges Explorations-Stable Protein Capture Agents with Antibody-like Properties, project to build stable, low-cost protein capture agents to target proteins. If successful, these agents could replace expensive and unstable monoclonal antibodies that are currently needed for diagnostic tests. 2010.

2170-49 Cardiff University, Cardiff, Wales, $848,000. To evaluate the capacity of a new intradermal vaccine using polypropylene sulfide nanoparticles to induce immunity against HIV, Tuberculosis, and Cytomegalovirus infections. 2010.

2170-50 CARE USA, Atlanta, GA, $30,000,000. To develop and adopt Family Health Initiative in Bihar, promoting effective approaches to scaling up coverage of essential family health interventions within the National Rural Health Mission in India. 2010.

2170-51 CARE USA, Atlanta, GA, $1,000,000. For emergency response for flood-affected communities in Benin. 2010.

2170-52 CARE USA, Atlanta, GA, $56,873. To implement a joint emergency capacity building initiative with 6 of the world's leading humanitarian aid organizations to improve their speed, quality and effectiveness in saving lives and improving the welfare of people affected by emergencies. 2010.

2170-53 Carter Center, Atlanta, GA, $196,868. To integrate malaria and lymphatic filariasis (LF) programs in seven southeastern states of Nigeria to demonstrate proof of concept that insecticide impregnated (bed)nets (ITNs) alone can eliminate lymphatic filariasis transmission. 2010.

2170-54 Catholic Relief Services, Baltimore, MD, $1,000,000. For emergency response to the earthquake in Haiti. 2010.

2170-55 Catholic Relief Services, Baltimore, MD, $400,000. For emergency response following the eruption of Mount Merapi volcano in Indonesia. 2010.

2170-56 Catholic University of America, Washington, DC, $100,000. To develop and test Phage DNA vaccine for HIV. 2010.

2170-57 CDC Foundation, Atlanta, GA, $345,000. To complete a systematic review of the evidence on how to improve health worker performance in low- and middle-income countries, and to disseminate findings and recommendations to policy makers and practitioners. 2010.

2170-58 Centers for Disease Control and Prevention, Atlanta, GA, $2,989,588. To measure the public health benefits of integrated Neglected Tropical Diseases (NTD) programs and to correlate expanded disease-specific indicators with other health outcomes. 2010.

2170-59 Centers for Disease Control and Prevention, Atlanta, GA, $2,388,869. To develop the strategy for onchocerciasis elimination in Africa building on the roll out of Neglected Tropical Disease (NTD) mass drug administration programs. 2010.

2170-60 Centre Hospitalier Universitaire Vaudois, Lausanne, Switzerland, $5,498,371. For work of Poxvirus T-Cell Vaccine Discovery Consortium (PTVDC) to develop one potential vaccine strategy that may contribute to the global effort of stopping the HIV pandemic. 2010.

2170-61 Charities Aid Foundation UK, West Malling, England, $250,000. To act as intermediary for co-grant to support small-scale strategic initiatives for Global Health and Global Development in the United Kingdom. 2010.

2170-62 Cheikh Anta Diop University, Dakar, Senegal, $513,036. To reduce mortality and morbidity from malaria in Senegalese children by the administration of anti-malarial drugs to children under the age of five years on three occasions during the high transmission season. 2010.

2170-63 Chicago Council on Global Affairs, Chicago, IL, $2,249,999. For design, adoption, implementation and accountability of Global Agricultural Development Initiative (GADI) which details U.S. policy for international agricultural development with focus on Sub-Saharan African and Southern Asia. 2010.

2170-64 Chicago Council on Global Affairs, Girls in Rural Economies Initiative, Chicago, IL, $250,000. To develop recommendations to better support the growth and development of adolescent girls working in the agriculture and food sectors in rural parts of Africa, Asia, Latin America, and the Caribbean. 2010.

2170-65 Child Health Research Foundation, Dhaka, Bangladesh, $3,413,171. For etiology (bacterial and viral agents) of neonatal sepsis in Asia and Africa, specifically Bangladesh, India and Pakistan. 2010.

2170-66 Childrens Hospital Corporation, Boston, MA, $3,179,639. To test novel technologies for developing more effective neonatal vaccines, which can be applied across a broad range of vaccinal antigens, to improve infant health and survival, particularly in low-income countries and the world's poorest communities, where neonatal and infant infections are endemic. 2010.

2170-67 Childrens Hospital Corporation, Boston, MA, $100,000. To develop XoutTB: A Mobile Phone Enabled Diagnostic Platform, drug compliance platform that uses mobile phones to administer, read and submit a simple diagnostic test, resulting in economic incentives for the user, such as additional cell phone minutes. 2010.

2170-68 Childrens Hospital Corporation, Boston, MA, $100,000. To develop and test a nanoparticle contraceptive that releases sperm tail inhibitors in response to vaginal pH changes or exposure to prostatic fluid. 2010.

2170-69 Childrens Hospital Los Angeles, Los Angeles, CA, $100,000. For Round 4, Phase I of Grand Challenges Explorations-Nonlinear Approaches to Rational Control of HIV-1 Infection. 2010.

2170-70 Childrens Hospital Medical Center, Cincinnati, OH, $100,000. To test the hypothesis that the protein mTor, which regulates cell growth and survival, plays a critical role in premature uterine aging that lead to preterm birth, difficult labor and fetal death. 2010.

2170-71 Childrens Hospital Medical Center, Cincinnati, OH, $79,925. To evaluate the effect of pneumococcal conjugate vaccine given in the routine infant schedule. 2010.

2170-72 China NPO Network, Beijing, China, $50,000. To develop public database of knowledge on China's private foundations. 2010.

2170-73 China University of Petroleum (East China), Qingdao, China, $100,000. For Round 4, Phase I of Grand Challenges Explorations-Simple Early Breath Diagnosis of Pneumococcal Pneumonia. 2010.

2170-74 Clemson University, Clemson, SC, $100,000. To develop low-cost diagnostic tools for priority global health conditions using highly-sensitive and specific and direct-molecule interfacing biosensors that are cheap to produce, easy to operate, and rugged to deploy and handle. 2010.

2170-75 Clinton Health Access Initiative, Boston, MA, $4,164,598. To improve the efficiency of commodity spending in public health programs across the developing world by pursuing targeted interventions that significantly reduce per-patient commodity costs for HIV/AIDS and, to a lesser degree, malaria and tuberculosis. 2010.

2170-76 Clinton Health Access Initiative, Boston, MA, $999,074. To secure sustained financing for malaria control in target countries to enable them to reduce malaria infections on their path to malaria elimination. 2010.

2170-77 Collaborative Drug Discovery, Burlingame, CA, $899,999. To develop, populate and operate a novel database to spark collaborative efforts to discover more effective drugs against TB. 2010.

2170-78 Colorado State University, Fort Collins, CO, $100,000. To develop new rice varieties (specifically Rice Bran) that can non-specifically increase mucosal intestinal immunity to enteric infections. 2010.

2170-79 Colorado State University, Fort Collins, CO, $100,000. To develop non-invasive phage particle based sensors for active tuberculosis. 2010.

2170-80 Columbia University, New York, NY, $1,433,058. To determine causes of pediatric pneumonia in The Gambia using molecular tools for viral and bacterial surveillance and discovery to inform prioritization of microbial targets for vaccine development. 2010.

2170-81 Columbia University, New York, NY, $1,000,000. To research how optical irradiation might be used to physically disrupt mosquitoes' sensory systems to mitigate the transmission of malaria. 2010.

2170-82 Columbia University, New York, NY, $467,110. To learn from BRAC's Urban slum health delivery model in Bangladesh. 2010.

2170-83 Columbia University, New York, NY, $100,000. For Round 4, Phase I of Grand Challenges Explorations-Defeating Insect-Borne Diseases Using Atomic-Level Structure, project to perform crystallization experiments on a key olfactory receptor used by mosquitoes to detect humans. The aim of these studies is to determine at an atomic level the common regions on the olfactory receptor in order to develop drug therapies to block these receptors. 2010.

2170-84 Columbia University, New York, NY, $50,000. For Earth Institute's 5th International Nitrogen Conference. 2010.

2170-85 Columbia University, Earth Institute, Center on Globalization and Sustainable Development, New York, NY, $599,623. To promote effective, evidence-based public health policies in India implemented by International Advisory Panel to the National Rural Health Mission (NRHM) with the goal of improving the wellbeing of rural populations. 2010.

2170-86 Community Organisation Resource Centre, Mowbray, South Africa, $3,000,000. To align communities with local and national governments to improve the shelter and livelihoods of the poor living in urban South Africa. 2010.

2170-87 Conservation International, Arlington, VA, $338,741. To develop operational strategy for measuring natural resource indicators through Metrics for Ecosystem Services. 2010.

2170-88 Convergent Engineering, Newberry, FL, $100,000. To develop and test handheld, easy to use, maternal/fetal early warning system that uses reusable capacitive sensors and smart phones that provide early diagnosis for preeclampsia, labor dystocia, and the presence of preterm labor. 2010.

2170-89 Cornell University, Ithaca, NY, $1,968,450. To promote development of faster-acting drugs for tuberculosis through academic-industrial collaborations under global access provisions by developing high-throughput screens for compounds that kill Mycobacterium tuberculosis both when it is replicating and during exposure to physiological stresses that prevent it from replicating. 2010.

2170-90 Cornell University, Ithaca, NY, $1,459,311. To identify Mycobacterium tuberculosis proteins that are best suited as targets for the development of new and improved drugs against Tuberculosis. 2010.

2170-91 Cornell University, Ithaca, NY, $739,859. To furnish a metabolomic toolset that will accelerate Tuberculosis drug development. 2010.

2170-92 Cornell University, Ithaca, NY, $496,100. To understand political economy determinants of food policy decisions. 2010.

2170-93 Cornell University, Ithaca, NY, $100,000. To define/identify in Mycobacterium tuberculosis (Mtb) exiting latency the identity and distribution of irreversibly oxidized proteins; the relative growth rates of senescent and rejuvenant lineages; and the genes controlling the asymmetric distribution. 2010.

2170-94 Cornell University, Ithaca, NY, $100,000. To test the hypothesis that ability of Mycobacterium tuberculosis (Mtb) to enter into, dwell in, and exit from, latency (as modeled by non-replicating physiology) is mediated by the reversible assembly and disassembly of specific, physically compartmentalized, metabolic structures (metabolosomes). 2010.

2170-95 CSS Institute of International Health, Immunology and Microbiology, Copenhagen, Denmark, $100,000. To develop and test a vaccine combining a novel placental malaria vaccine candidate with the cervical cancer vaccine, with the potential of inducing a strong protective response against both diseases simultaneously. 2010.

2170-96 D-Tree, Inc., Weston, MA, $100,000. To develop and test a mobile phone-based tool that rapidly identifies women at risk during labor and delivery and facilitate emergency transfer to a hospital. The tool is a combination of phone decision support, data storage, on-line banking and communications on a single device at the point of care. 2010.

2170-97 Daystar University, Nairobi, Kenya, $100,000. For Round 4, Phase I of Grand Challenges Explorations-Biological Control for Sandflies Using Free-Living Fungi Found in the Local Soil in Kenya. These entomopathogenic fungi, which attach like parasites onto adult insects and larvae and kill them, will be harvested and cultured to isolate virulent strains that can eradicate sandflies, which are responsible for the spread of visceral leishmaniasis. 2010.

2170-98 Deutsche Gesellschaft fur Internationale Zusammenarbeit, Eschborn, Germany, $4,996,172. To develop Integrated Community-Based Solid Waste Management Project in Qalyubeya - Greater Cairo, solid waste management system that promotes waste as a resource and integrates the urban poor in the management of municipal waste services. 2010.

2170-99 Development Workshop Angola, Luanda, Angola, $5,000,000. For work of Voices of Citizens for Urban Change in promoting more inclusive public planning processes that will help improve basic services for Luanda residents. 2010.

2170-100 Diagnostics for All, Cambridge, MA, $100,000. To develop a disposable paper-based diagnostic device embedded with ultrathin, photosensitive electronics to provide HIV viral loads via light transmittance detection. 2010.

2170-101 Diconsa, Mexico City, Mexico, $961,264. To improve access to affordable financial services in Mexico's poorest, most isolated communities. 2010.

2170-102 Direccion de Bibliotecas, Archivos y Museos, Santiago, Chile, $430,000. For DIBAM's Bibliored program as it develops digital and virtual library services. 2010.

2170-103 DNA Medicine Institute, Cambridge, MA, $100,000. For Round 4, Phase I of Grand Challenges Explorations-Optomagnetic Finger Scanner for Malaria, project o develop a battery-powered non-invasive finger scanner to detect and measure hemozoin, a byproduct formed by malaria parasites, through the finger's capillaries. If successful, mass manufacturing of the scanner should be possible due to basic components. 2010.

2170-104 Donald Danforth Plant Science Center, Saint Louis, MO, $8,257,560. To develop high iron, protein and proVitamin A cassava for Nigeria and Kenya. 2010.

2170-105 Drugs for Neglected Diseases Initiative, Geneva, Switzerland, $1,500,000. To develop new drug candidates for human African trypanosomiasis (HAT) and visceral leishmaniasis (VL) through the pre-clinical stage and ready for Investigational New Drug (IND) filing, and the completion of Phase I clinical studies with one drug candidate for each disease. 2010.

2170-106 Duke University, Durham, NC, $2,267,252. To establish a global laboratory support network that will benefit AIDS vaccine development as it relates to vaccine-elicited antibody responses. 2010.

2170-107 Duke University, Durham, NC, $426,990. To plan for evaluation of Bihar Evaluation of Social Franchising and Telemedicine (BEST), project designed to engage private health providers to improve management of infectious diseases in Bihar, India. 2010.

2170-108 Duke University, Durham, NC, $42,634. To co-sponsor a scientific workshop to discuss immune correlates of protection on HIV vaccines. 2010.

2170-109 Ecoagriculture International, Washington, DC, $275,000. For general operating support. 2010.

2170-110 Ecole de Technologie Superieure, Montreal, Canada, $100,000. To design and test a diagnostic tool using computer acoustical analysis of newborn cries to complement conventional diagnostic techniques in detecting medical conditions such as asphyxia, hypoglycemia, and infections. 2010.

2170-111 Ecole Polytechnique Federale de Lausanne, Lausanne, Switzerland, $2,930,889. For platform technology for immunogenic, thermostable, needle-free, dose-sparing, and low-cost protective vaccines via intradermal administration. 2010.

2170-112 Eidgenoessische Technische Hochschule, Institute of Microbiology, Zurich, Switzerland, $100,000. To study the swimming behavior of diarrhea-causing pathogens, which move using tiny tails called flagella, to develop micro-structures that can trap the pathogen before it infects tissues. 2010.

2170-113 Emory University, Atlanta, GA, $2,499,890. To develop cost-effective tools for assessing exposure to fecal contamination in urban areas of low-income countries with focus on Ghana. 2010.

2170-114 Emory University, Atlanta, GA, $373,151. To conduct analyses of the COHORTS database to address critical questions concerning the determinants and consequences of healthy child growth, which will inform policy surrounding early child development, complementary feeding, nutritional rehabilitation, and supplemental food assistance programs. 2010.

2170-115 Engineering Conferences Foundation, New York, NY, $95,795. For Vaccine Technology III conference (taking place in Mexico) that addresses process engineering technology aspects of vaccine production and how the vaccine development cycle integrates with regulatory issues, clinical development, and public policy. 2010.

2170-116 Equilibres and Populations, Paris, France, $357,696. To share evidence-based data on family planning to meet the Millennium Development Goals (MDGs) and follow up action/disseminations plans in selected Francophone countries of Benin, Burkina Faso, Cote d'Ivoire, Mali, Niger, Senegal and Togo. 2010.

2170-117 European Foundation Centre, Brussels, Belgium, $95,000. For general operating support. 2010.

2170-118 European Molecular Biology Laboratory, European Bioinformatics Institute, Hinxton, England, $478,458. To develop strategies to protect cereals against rust pathogens and diagnostic tools for rust research. 2010.

2170-119 European Parliamentary Forum on Population and Development, Brussels, Belgium, $118,519. To ensure environment of increased resources that allows the advancement of the basic human right for individuals to make free and informed choices in their reproductive lives and to have access to high quality information, education, and health services. 2010.

2170-120 Family Care International, New York, NY, $977,326. To revitalize the global emergency contraception agenda and increase access in Sub-Saharan Africa and South Asia. 2010.

2170-121 Family Health International, Research Triangle Park, NC, $1,500,000. For Sino-implant (II) Initiative's continued quality assurance and introduction in the following countries and regions Burundi, Ethiopia, Ghana, Kenya, Madagascar, Malawi, Nigeria, Rwanda, Uganda, United Republic of Tanzania, Zambia, Zimbabwe, Dominican Republic and Colombia. 2010.

2170-122 Farm Concern International, Nairobi, Kenya, $5,596,772. To increase the profitability of horticulture production by creating efficient marketing mechanisms to serve domestic markets in four countries in Sub-Saharan Africa. 2010.

2170-123 FARM-Africa, London, England, $5,188,438. To develop Animal Health Services Franchising Business for the delivery of vaccines and pharmaceuticals to smallholder farmers in Kenya. 2010.

2170-124 Fiorello H. LaGuardia Foundation, New York, NY, $138,833. To support conference in Brazil to design a Program of Projects to transfer successful smallholder conservation agricultural strategies from Latin America to Africa including Ghana, Mali, Mozambique and Tanzania. 2010.

2170-125 Food and Agriculture Organization of the United Nations, Rome, Italy, $860,737. To construct a statistical framework and apply information technology solution for countries and regions, to consolidate food and agricultural statistics into integrated solution to support policy decisions and their monitoring. 2010.

2170-126 Food and Agriculture Organization of the United Nations, Rome, Italy, $350,285. For 5th International Conference on Agricultural Statistics. 2010.

2170-127 Foundation for the National Institutes of Health, Bethesda, MD, $6,781,984. To produce high-quality chemical hit series with defined, tractable targets as drug leads for tuberculosis. 2010.

2170-128 Foundation for the National Institutes of Health, Bethesda, MD, $1,756,879. To initiate a more comprehensive follow-up grant program to discover novel vector-based approaches to prevent disease transmission and encourage their translation through initial proof of principle. 2010.

2170-129 Foundation for the National Institutes of Health, Bethesda, MD, $843,121. For work of Grand Challenges in Global Health to develop a funding mechanism that will accelerate scientific progress in addressing the diseases of the most impoverished. 2010.

2170-130 Four-H Council, National, Chevy Chase, MD, $129,076. For African-based program that will help youth participate productively in the agricultural sector. 2010.

2170-131 Friends of the Global Fight Against AIDS, Tuberculosis and Malaria, Washington, DC, $850,000. For general operating support. 2010.

2170-132 Fundacao Ataulpho de Paiva, Rio de Janeiro, Brazil, $3,138,113. To ensure the successful delivery and integration of innovative tools for Tuberculosis control into the Brazilian public health system, effectively reducing infection rates and improving treatment outcomes while generating data and creating partnerships that promote Tuberculosis innovation in other countries. 2010.

2170-133 Gairdner Foundation, Toronto, Canada, $30,000. For conference, Eradicating Malaria: Prospects and Perils. 2010.

2170-134 GBCHealth, New York, NY, $500,000. To catalyze the international business community and mobilize its resources, reach and expertise in the global fight against HIV/AIDS, TB, and malaria. 2010.

2170-135 George Washington University, Washington, DC, $400,929. To convene a meeting to discuss findings on the status of medical education in Sub-Saharan Africa, policy development implication, and how to move forward. 2010.

2170-136 Georgia Tech Research Corporation, Atlanta, GA, $100,000. To develop complement-based antibiotic microbeads to create new ways to protect against infectious disease. 2010.

2170-137 Global Action for Children, Washington, DC, $500,000. To raise awareness about the biggest causes of child mortality worldwide and the need for the expansion of childhood immunization programs to scale up the delivery of existing, underused and new vaccines in developing countries. 2010.

2170-138 Global Alliance for Improved Nutrition, Geneva, Switzerland, $3,251,905. To reduce malnutrition by supporting food fortification and sustainable nutrition strategies. 2010.

2170-139 Global Alliance for Improved Nutrition, Geneva, Switzerland, $1,199,275. To contribute to improved nutrition for mothers and children by increasing access to and utilization of fortified foods in the following countries Egypt, Morocco, Cote d'Ivoire, Ghana, Mali, Nigeria, Uganda, Dominican Republic, Bolivia, China, Vietnam, Bangladesh, Georgia, Kazakhstan, Pakistan and Uzbekistan. 2010.

2170-140 Global Alliance for TB Drug Development, New York, NY, $164,910,038. To accelerate development of anti-tuberculosis treatments by filling the drug development pipeline with novel candidates, developing single drug candidates, and working as a part of the Critical Path to TB drug Regimens to develop a completely novel anti-tuberculosis drug regimen. 2010.

2170-141 Global Business School Network, Washington, DC, $182,205. To support consortium of African business schools in developing a plan to increase their course offerings and programs aimed at the agriculture and health sectors. 2010.

2170-142 Global HIV Vaccine Enterprise, New York, NY, $400,000. For conference support related to work on the AIDS vaccine. 2010.

2170-143 Global Solutions for Infectious Diseases, South San Francisco, CA, $637,174. To acquire and disseminate information that will further the development of a safe and effective HIV vaccine. 2010.

2170-144 Global Washington, Seattle, WA, $20,000. For general operating support. 2010.

2170-145 Gordon Research Conferences, West Kingston, RI, $46,120. To convene the Gordon Research Conference of Acute Lower Respiratory Infection Researchers, with the strategic approach of accelerating discovery by scientists working to create health tools such as vaccines, drugs, and diagnostics. 2010.

2170-146 Gordon Research Conferences, West Kingston, RI, $33,750. For Gordon Research Conference on the Biology of Host-Parasite Interactions. 2010.

2170-147 Grameen Foundation USA, Washington, DC, $100,000. To develop a prototype of content authoring and management software for the delivery of health information and tools to low-end mobile phones that can often only display 160-character SMS messages on small screens. 2010.

2170-148 Harvard University, Cambridge, MA, $1,500,000. For work at School of Public Health in Boston to develop a robust in vitro culture system for the human malaria parasite, Plasmodium vivax, that will facilitate biological studies and support the design of health interventions. 2010.

2170-149 Harvard University, Cambridge, MA, $500,000. For NGO Leaders Forum to promote strategic dialogue among large U.S. development and humanitarian organizations on issues of concern in the area of development assistance. 2010.

2170-150 Harvard University, Cambridge, MA, $100,000. For Round 4, Phase I of Grand Challenges Explorations-Separation of Malaria-Infected Erythrocytes From Whole Blood. 2010.

2170-151 Health Protection Agency, London, England, $3,382,414. To improve incidence measurement with improved biological assays and analytical methods, reducing the cost and time necessary to achieve accurate incidence measurements of HIV. 2010.

2170-152 Helmholtz Center for Infection Research, Braunschweig, Germany, $211,604. To create novel mouse models for testing HIV and Hepatitis C Virus (HCV) vaccines. 2010.

2170-153 Helmholtz Center for Infection Research, Braunschweig, Germany, $100,000. To develop a versatile pollen mimetic transcutaneous vaccination platform with built-in adjuvant properties for needle-free transdermal delivery of vaccine antigens via hair follicles. 2010.

2170-154 Hervana, Ltd., Beit Shemesh, Israel, $100,000. For Round 4, Phase I of Grand Challenges Explorations-Biologic Contraceptive, project to develop and test a vaginal formulation that secretes an agent which inhibits sperm motility thus interfering with fertilization. It is hoped that this non-hormonal contraceptive will need only infrequent administration to maintain its effectiveness. 2010.

2170-155 HLL Lifecare, Ltd., Thiruvananthapuram, India, $100,000. To attempt to eliminate side effects associated with copper T intrauterine devices by coating the copper with biodegradable polymers, leading to increased acceptance of this contraceptive device. 2010.

2170-156 IDEO, Palo Alto, CA, $499,979. For effort to improve livelihoods in rural communities by freely distributing the Human Centered Design (HCD) toolkit to the non-profit public and creating a peer-based hub of ongoing support for social innovation at the local level. 2010.

2170-157 Immunocore, Abingdon, England, $100,000. To test whether a novel biologic therapy, engineered from immune cells, can clear virus from latently-infected HIV cells. 2010.

2170-158 Imperial College of London, London, England, $2,692,835. To enable the UK, French, and European Commission governments to provide more effective agricultural development support for smallholder farmers in sub-Saharan Africa. 2010.

2170-159 Imperial College of London, London, England, $2,035,793. To improve scientific support for decision making by co-coordinating a wide range of research activities in mathematical modeling of the HIV epidemic. 2010.

2170-160 Imperial College of London, London, England, $1,500,000. To identify the molecular signatures of latent TB in human tissues, and target them with novel drugs. 2010.

2170-161 Imperial College of London, London, England, $1,499,341. To widen the scope of existing Neglected Tropical Disease chemotherapeutic control programmes to include taeniosis/cysticercosis, a zoonotic diseases that causes significant morbidity and economic hardship in many countries in sub Saharan Africa, which will evaluate whether praziquantal used in existing Mass Drug Administration (MDA) programs will safely and effectively treat cysticercosis and plan a pilot of interventions needed for effective control/elimination program. 2010.

2170-162 Indian Institute of Technology Kharagpur, Kharagpur, India, $100,000. To test a new transcervical contraceptive made from a polymer compound for its ability to incapacitate both sperm and egg. 2010.

2170-163 Infectious Disease Research Institute, Seattle, WA, $3,733,444. To identify chemical genomics for new leads and new drug targets for

tuberculosis suitable for further drug development with the ultimate goal of producing new drugs to treat tuberculosis. 2010.

2170-164 Information Training and Outreach Centre for Africa, Johannesburg, South Africa, $39,956. To provide access to comprehensive, up-to-date information on agricultural tertiary education and extension in Africa. 2010.

2170-165 Innolytics, LLC, Rancho Santa Fe, CA, $100,000. For Round 4, Phase I of Grand Challenges Explorations-Contraception Based on Inhibition of the Sperm Receptor. 2010.

2170-166 Innovations for Poverty Action, New Haven, CT, $3,300,000. For project that will refine technology, business models and evidence around chlorine dispensers to take the approach from a small-scale pilot to one that has been proven at medium-scale and is primed for widespread replication. 2010.

2170-167 Innovations for Poverty Action, New Haven, CT, $1,618,047. For series of randomized interventions in Bangladesh to promote improved sanitation behavior and products that account for different forms of social interactions in communities - learning through social networks, reacting to social pressures and a sense of shame. 2010.

2170-168 Institute for Financial Management and Research, Chennai, India, $1,179,717. To conduct research to identify ways to increase the availability of safe savings services for the poor through improving regulated chit funds, a particular type of rotating savings and credit association (ROSCA), in India. 2010.

2170-169 Institute for OneWorld Health, San Francisco, CA, $4,499,050. To keep and build upon organizational capacity to further the work of the organization, especially in the Diarrhea/ Enteric Diseases strategic area. 2010.

2170-170 Institute of Medicine, Washington, DC, $100,000. To conduct expert consensus process to offer conclusions and recommendations on a long term strategy for responding to the global HIV/AIDS burden as it is projected to be manifest 10 to 15 years in the future. 2010.

2170-171 Instituto de Estudios de la Inmunidad Humoral, National Council of Scientific and Technical Research (CONICET), Buenos Aires, Argentina, $100,000. For work with National Council of Scientific and Technical Research (CONICET) to research whether a bacterial protein can function as both a protease inhibitor to protect antigens delivered in oral vaccine from degradation and as adjuvant to stimulate enhanced mucosal immune response. 2010.

2170-172 Instituto de Medicina Molecular, Lisbon, Portugal, $100,000. To test the theory that modified live rodent malaria parasites (P. berghei) can be used in a vaccine to elicit a strong immune response in humans without being able to infect human red blood cells and cause illness. 2010.

2170-173 Instituto Gulbenkian de Ciencia, Oeiras, Portugal, $100,000. To test the theory that antibodies directed against a specific carbohydrate produced by gut pathogens play a role in immunity against severe forms of malaria. 2010.

2170-174 InterAction: American Council for Voluntary International Action, Washington, DC, $76,945. To build awareness and support for the benefits of foreign assistance in aiding the world's poorest and most vulnerable populations

through educational and capacity-building activities. 2010.

2170-175 International AIDS Society, Geneva, Switzerland, $1,472,345. To promote efficiencies and accountability for prevention through global advocacy. 2010.

2170-176 International Association for K-12 Online Learning, Vienna, VA, $64,628. To assist with the design of the digital learning initiative, marketing it to the field, recruiting applicants and advisors, and processing applications. 2010.

2170-177 International Bank for Reconstruction and Development, Washington, DC, $30,000,000. To improve the income and food security of poor people in developing countries through improved public and private sector investment in the agriculture and rural sectors. 2010.

2170-178 International Bank for Reconstruction and Development, Washington, DC, $11,366,492. To incorporate financial questions into existing global Gallup poll to measure and track financial inclusion levels across 150 countries every three years. 2010.

2170-179 International Bank for Reconstruction and Development, Washington, DC, $10,566,855. To support activities that advance World Bank Water and Sanitation Program (WSP) strategy to scaling up rural sanitation for poor people through the provision of technical assistance, capacity building and knowledge. 2010.

2170-180 International Bank for Reconstruction and Development, Washington, DC, $6,000,000. For Phase II of the Consultative Group to Assist the Poor (CGAP) Technology Program, initiative to promote branchless banking models to increase the number of poor people who have access to a range of safe, convenient, and affordable financial services, particularly savings. 2010.

2170-181 International Center for Journalists, Washington, DC, $2,038,716. To develop high-impact fellowships in Ethiopia, Kenya, Mozambique, Nigeria, South Africa, Uganda and Zambia focusing on health issues. 2010.

2170-182 International Center for Not-for-Profit Law, Washington, DC, $400,000. For comprehensive, accessible online legal resource center. 2010.

2170-183 International Center for Not-for-Profit Law, Washington, DC, $200,000. For general operating support. 2010.

2170-184 International Center for Research on Women, Washington, DC, $67,229. To apply research methodologies and participatory approaches to implement a national assessment focused on understanding the current situation of the HIV and AIDS response with respect to gender in Cambodia and Rwanda. 2010.

2170-185 International Center for Research on Women, Washington, DC, $10,000. For general operating support. 2010.

2170-186 International Center for Tropical Agriculture, Cali, Colombia, $1,390,571. For efforts to accelerate breeding of cassava in Sub-Saharan Africa for greater productivity, disease resistance and other traits that will benefit smallholder farmers in the developing world. 2010.

2170-187 International Center for Tropical Agriculture, Cali, Colombia, $140,000. For strategic planning workshop entitled, Repositioning PRGA in Times of Change, to help reform the Consultative Group on International

Agricultural Research's Participatory Research and Gender Analysis Program (PRGA), which supports gender-sensitive participatory research on agricultural issues focused on the needs and preferences of resource-limited women and men farmers. 2010.

2170-188 International Centre for Diarrheal Disease Research, Bangladesh, Dhaka, Bangladesh, $100,000. To develop and test inexpensive, biodegradable absorbent mat that can be placed under mothers who have just delivered babies to assess immediate postpartum blood loss. 2010.

2170-189 International Centre for Diarrheal Disease Research, Bangladesh, Dhaka, Bangladesh, $100,000. To improve mucosal immune responses to oral typhoid vaccine. 2010.

2170-190 International Centre for Genetic Engineering and Biotechnology, New Delhi, India, $51,500. To organize Tuberculosis Diagnostics: Challenges, Innovations and Applications, international symposium on tuberculosis. 2010.

2170-191 International Clinical Epidemiology Network, Philadelphia, PA, $1,274,157. To evaluate the impact of topical application of emollient(s) for prevention of neonatal infections, and mortality in Asia, Africa and India. 2010.

2170-192 International Federation of Red Cross and Red Crescent Societies, Geneva, Switzerland, $309,788. For efforts to eradicate polio by increasing polio vaccination coverage to reduce number of missed children and non-compliance through intensified social mobilization/communications activities conducted by Red Cross National Societies in Africa. 2010.

2170-193 International Finance Corporation, Washington, DC, $330,997. To analyze payments in selected health programs in Bihar State to identify systemic solutions to improve efficiency, transparency, and accountability. 2010.

2170-194 International Food Policy Research Institute, Washington, DC, $8,522,236. To develop a model that will assist in making agricultural technology development and adoption investment choices. 2010.

2170-195 International Food Policy Research Institute, Washington, DC, $5,006,540. To determine the knowledge and capacity needs of evidence and outcome based agricultural policy planning and implementation among African countries. 2010.

2170-196 International Food Policy Research Institute, Washington, DC, $2,999,197. To assess how well current donor and grant programs address gender inequalities in developing countries in order to improve women's control and ownership of productive assets. 2010.

2170-197 International Food Policy Research Institute, Washington, DC, $300,000. For conference Accelerating Agricultural Growth: Synergies with Nutrition and Health. 2010.

2170-198 International Food Policy Research Institute, Washington, DC, $150,000. For internationally available database in agricultural research investments in developing countries. 2010.

2170-199 International Institute for Environment and Development, London, England, $4,000,000. To catalyze and strengthen the community development process in twenty countries across Asia. 2010.

2170-200 International Institute for Environment and Development, London, England, $1,512,100. To develop innovative tools to secure land rights in West Africa. 2010.

2170-201 International Livestock Research Institute, Nairobi, Kenya, $75,000. To develop business plan for Biosciences Eastern and Central Africa Initiative (BECA-ILRI) Hub. 2010.

2170-202 International Maize and Wheat Improvement Center, Mexico City, Mexico, $8,468,135. To contribute to the development of improved legume varieties in sub-Saharan Africa (Burkina Faso, Cameroon, Ethiopia, Kenya, Malawi, Nigeria, Zambia, Niger, Nigeria, Senegal, Tanzania, Zimbabwe) and South Asia (India) by advancing molecular breeding for traits of importance in both regions. 2010.

2170-203 International Medical Corps, Santa Monica, CA, $700,000. To respond to the cholera outbreak in Cameroon. 2010.

2170-204 International Rescue Committee, New York, NY, $2,479,514. To support multidisciplinary emergency responders with training and technical support for the practical application of models that improve the safety and security of women and children. 2010.

2170-205 International Rescue Committee, New York, NY, $700,000. For emergency relief for flood affected communities in Pakistan. 2010.

2170-206 International Rice Research Institute, Manila, Philippines, $10,287,784. To address the problem of Vitamin A deficiency among millions of people in the Philippines and Bangladesh through introduction of Golden Rice, high beta-carotene rice varieties. 2010.

2170-207 International Rice Research Institute, Manila, Philippines, $480,000. To monitor the diffusion of improved crop varieties in rain-fed areas of South Asia including Bangladesh, Bhutan, India, Nepal and Sri Lanka. 2010.

2170-208 International Society for Influenza and other Respiratory Virus Diseases, Atlanta, GA, $100,942. For general operating support for conference, Options for the Control of Influenza VII. 2010.

2170-209 International Vaccine Institute, Seoul, South Korea, $6,987,482. To accelerate the introduction of safe and broadly protective dengue vaccines into public sector programs, especially for children, as well as by supporting the continued development of promising dengue vaccine candidates. 2010.

2170-210 International Vaccine Institute, Seoul, South Korea, $4,664,890. To reduce the burden of cholera in India through the deployment of the killed whole cell oral cholera vaccine in endemic and epidemic settings. 2010.

2170-211 International Vaccine Institute, Seoul, South Korea, $1,342,461. For a project, which is part of World Health Organization's (WHO) pre-emptive use of a cholera vaccine in vulnerable populations at risk which will determine whether cholera vaccines can be utilized as a public health response to protect high-risk populations from cholera in Zanzibar. 2010.

2170-212 International Vaccine Institute, Seoul, South Korea, $100,000. For Round 4, Phase I of Grand Challenges Explorations-A Novel Test to Measure Mucosal Immunity to Vaccines in Whole Blood Samples from Children. 2010.

2170-213 International Vaccine Institute, Seoul, South Korea, $35,415. To bring together a panel of global experts to review what is currently known and identify opportunities for action toward reduction of Hepatitis A and E burden in developing country populations. 2010.

2170-214 International Water Management Institute, Battaramulla, Sri Lanka, $1,526,702. To create and disseminate a portfolio of promising technologies/interventions that can be deployed in support of agrarian poverty reduction for smallholders in Burkina Faso, Ethiopia, Ghana, Tanzania, Zambia and India. 2010.

2170-215 International Womens Health Coalition, New York, NY, $25,000. For general operating support. 2010.

2170-216 Iowa State University, Ames, IA, $1,459,460. To implement policy changes aimed at increasing supply and access to seed of improved varieties across selected countries in sub-Saharan Africa to enhance productivity on small farms. 2010.

2170-217 Japan Center for International Exchange, New York, NY, $3,000,000. For general operating support. 2010.

2170-218 Jenner Institute, Oxford, England, $100,000. To test three components from the mosquito's innate signaling pathways for possible use in a malaria vaccine. 2010.

2170-219 JHPIEGO, Baltimore, MD, $1,999,527. To provide technical assistance to the Ministry of Health and Family Welfare India for integrating postpartum Intra Uterine Contraceptive Device (IUCD) services into family planning programs and monitor the progress of this component of the national program. 2010.

2170-220 Johns Hopkins University, Baltimore, MD, $5,865,167. To develop comprehensive approach to the disease burden of pneumonia and diarrhea in children in under age 5 in India. 2010.

2170-221 Johns Hopkins University, Baltimore, MD, $4,134,423. To conduct a study that informs and improves child health and nutrition programs globally and results in reduced stunting and anemia in the first years of life. Focus of study is Zimbabwe. 2010.

2170-222 Johns Hopkins University, Baltimore, MD, $665,685. To conduct evidence-based, rigorous, and transparent process for collecting, analyzing and interpreting the evidence for pneumococcal serotype replacement conjugate vaccine. 2010.

2170-223 Johns Hopkins University, Baltimore, MD, $498,333. To evaluate the accuracy of diagnosis of Acute Lower Respiratory Infection (ALRI) in children and severe ALRI when standardized measurement and interpretation of chest auscultation is included as a diagnostic technology. 2010.

2170-224 Johns Hopkins University, Baltimore, MD, $367,941. For a reporting fellowship at School of Advanced International Studies (SAIS) in Washington, DC for influential journalists in the U.S. media to cover global health stories in different countries around the world. 2010.

2170-225 Johns Hopkins University, Baltimore, MD, $100,000. For Round 4, Phase I of Grand Challenges Explorations-An "Evolution-Proof" Bio-Pesticide to Control Malaria. 2010.

2170-226 Johns Hopkins University, Bloomberg School of Public Health, Center for Communication Programs, Baltimore, MD, $636,801. For work of Voices for a Malaria Free Future II to increase access to and use of prevention and treatment by expanding resources for malaria control in Africa in order to reduce malaria morbidity and mortality. 2010.

2170-227 Justus Liebig University, Giessen, Germany, $100,000. To test the effectiveness of the cancer drug Imatinib (also known as Gleevec) to impair and kill parasitic worms which carry Schistosomiasis. 2010.

2170-228 K and S Consulting, Dodewaard, Netherlands, $100,000. To develop and test a surface coating that slowly releases mosquito attractants and a pesticide that female mosquitoes take back to breeding sites to kill emerging larvae which would transmit dengue fever. 2010.

2170-229 Karolinska Institute, Stockholm, Sweden, $100,000. To develop a computational model to identify new DNA sequences in the Tuberculosis bacterium that can be used as biomarkers, and then employ zinc-finger tags to detect the identified DNA sequence in a diagnostic test. 2010.

2170-230 Keystone Symposia on Molecular and Cellular Biology, Silverthorne, CO, $116,951. For conference support for the Global Health Conference Series. 2010.

2170-231 Khyber Pakhtunkhwa, Government of, Peshawar, Pakistan, $600,000. For emergency response to the floods in Pakistan. 2010.

2170-232 Kickstart International, San Francisco, CA, $2,259,380. For KickStart in Tanzania, initiative to develop improved small-scale pump technologies, expand nationally the market distribution network for pumps, and monitor the impact on smallholder farmers in Tanzania. 2010.

2170-233 Kings College London, London, England, $100,000. To field test a new blood pressure monitor which uses solar power and requires little training for its ability to increase detection rates and improve outcomes of women with pre-eclampsia in rural Africa as part of COBRA Project. 2010.

2170-234 Landesa, Seattle, WA, $15,000. For general operating support. 2010.

2170-235 Landesa, Seattle, WA, $10,000. For general operating support. 2010.

2170-236 Lavax, Inc., Palatine, IL, $100,000. To develop and test female-controlled antiviral contraceptive, vaginal suppository that uses a strain of commensal bacteria which has the ability to immobilize sperm and capture viruses. If successful, the bacteria could be used as a reversible contraceptive that affords protection against viruses such as HIV and herpes. 2010.

2170-237 League for Innovation in the Community College, Phoenix, AZ, $50,000. For STEMtech Conference. 2010.

2170-238 League for Innovation in the Community College, Phoenix, AZ, $50,000. For Virtual Conference Collaboration. 2010.

2170-239 Lilongwe City Assembly, Lilongwe, Malawi, $2,572,188. For project, Sustainable Improvement of Livelihood of the Lilongwe Slum Dwellers: an Integrated Approach to Urban Planning, initiative to improve the general livelihood of Lilongwe's informal settlements through a detailed survey of the needs of their residents and a range of interventions aimed at upgraded service delivery. 2010.

2170-240 Lincoln Square Productions, LLC, New York, NY, $1,500,000. For production of Be the Change: Save a Life - An ABC News Initiative, news story working to bring greater public awareness to critical, underreported health issues plaguing the poorest of the poor around the globe, and to inspire and motivate viewers to take action. 2010.

2170-241 Link Media, San Francisco, CA, $376,629. To develop digital media hub that highlights progress in reducing hunger, poverty and disease in developing nations. 2010.

2170-242 Lions Clubs International Foundation, Oak Brook, IL, $400,000. To reduce measles mortality and morbidity by strengthening delivery and access to quality immunizations during supplementary immunization activities and routine immunization. 2010.

2170-243 Liverpool School of Tropical Medicine, Liverpool, England, $50,000,000. For Product Development Partnership with Innovative Vector Control Consortium (IVCC) to eliminate transmission of mosquito-borne pathogens through improved insect vector control with innovative products. 2010.

2170-244 London School of Hygiene and Tropical Medicine, London, England, $14,790,459. To learn, improve on, scale and sustain impact through harmonized, synthesized, and applied results measurement, while providing the needed evidence to influence and leverage global action and optimize our critical path in Maternal, Newborn and Child Health (MNCH) work. 2010.

2170-245 London School of Hygiene and Tropical Medicine, London, England, $1,545,508. For cluster-randomized, controlled field trial in Orissa, India, to assess the effectiveness of basic sanitation to reduce diarrhoeal disease and lower the prevalence and intensity of worm infection among a rural population practicing open defecation. Project will generate information on how the intervention actually impacts exposure to human excreta along principal transmission pathways, and explore the extent to which different levels of acquisition and use of on-site sanitation among households impact disease throughout the community. Project will also report on cost and cost-effectiveness of intervention and its impact of lost days at school and work and expenditures on drugs and medical treatment. 2010.

2170-246 London School of Hygiene and Tropical Medicine, London, England, $999,570. To build public confidence in immunization through a global information surveillance system that identifies and tracks rumors/inaccuracies about vaccines and information, and assist national programs in overcoming this misinformation. 2010.

2170-247 London School of Hygiene and Tropical Medicine, London, England, $995,826. To evaluate the impact of a new serogroup A meningococcal conjugate vaccine on pharyngeal carriage and transmission of serogroup A meningococcal infection in countries of the African meningitis belt. 2010.

2170-248 London School of Hygiene and Tropical Medicine, London, England, $172,155. To advocate the value of diagnostics for improving global health and to build future leadership in critical decision making in diagnostics in both developed and developing countries. 2010.

2170-249 London School of Hygiene and Tropical Medicine, London, England, $89,000. To convene international symposium to review the potential contribution of new vaccines to improving global health. 2010.

2170-250 London School of Hygiene and Tropical Medicine, London, England, $35,650. To organize and convene international meeting on diagnostics for enteric typhoid fever. 2010.

2170-251 Lowy Institute for International Policy, Sydney, Australia, $768,246. To create Friends of the Global Fund Pacific, advocacy organization dedicated to building strong political and financial support for the work of the Fund and the fight against HIV, TB and Malaria in the Pacific region. 2010.

2170-252 Loyola University of Chicago, Chicago, IL, $1,100,544. For Master's Program in Rule of Law for Development. 2010.

2170-253 Lutheran World Relief, Baltimore, MD, $949,959. For emergency assistance to protect and increase food and animal production in Adouna, Niger. 2010.

2170-254 Lutheran World Relief, Baltimore, MD, $68,342. To mitigate the impact of rising food prices on rural communities through optimum rice and wheat production in Mali and Niger. 2010.

2170-255 Makerere University, Kampala, Uganda, $100,000. For Round 4, Phase I of Grand Challenges Explorations-A Novel Way of Controlling Malaria Transmitting Mosquitoes. 2010.

2170-256 Malaria Consortium, London, England, $100,000. For Round 4, Phase I of Grand Challenges Explorations-Insecticide-Treated Traditional Scarves Among Migrants, project to treat the traditional scarves worn by migrant workers along the Thai-Cambodia border with insecticides to reduce the overall malaria disease burden. Sintasath will then monitor subsequent infection rates reported by area health facilities, and survey participants to learn more about their knowledge, attitude and use of the treated scarves. 2010.

2170-257 Malaria No More, New York, NY, $944,350. To advance high-impact international efforts to achieve universal access to malaria interventions in Africa and eliminate preventable deaths from malaria through a broad range of partnerships. 2010.

2170-258 Manobi Development Foundation, Pasadena, CA, $100,000. To launch free-range freshwater prawn farming in rivers and canals to reduce the incidence of schistosomiasis among children and provide income-generating activity for village women who can harvest and sell the prawns. 2010.

2170-259 Massachusetts General Hospital, Boston, MA, $100,000. For Round 4, Phase I of Grand Challenges Explorations-G-Protein Coupled Receptors to Detection Infectious Agents, project to reverse engineer in vitro G-protein coupled receptors (GPCRs), which usually are used by the human body to sense light, odors, tastes and hormones, to detect selected parasite biomarkers. If successful, these engineered receptors could be used to develop a diagnostic sensor for infectious agents. 2010.

2170-260 Mater Medical Research Institute, South Brisbane, Australia, $204,922. To produce a series of papers for The Lancet entitled, Lancet Stillbirth Series, placing stillbirths as a priority within the context of maternal and child survival, bringing together epidemiology, evidence for interventions, costing estimates, and policy analysis to promote action and guide priority-setting for programs and research. 2010.

2170-261 Medicines for Malaria Venture, Geneva, Switzerland, $9,328,358. To further develop and accelerate antimalarial discovery and development projects. 2010.

2170-262 Mercy Corps, Portland, OR, $700,000. For emergency response to the humanitarian crisis in Kyrgyzstan. 2010.

2170-263 Mercy Corps, Portland, OR, $649,995. To provide emotional and psychological support to children affected by the earthquake in Haiti. 2010.

2170-264 Mercy Corps, Portland, OR, $400,000. For emergency response to the earthquake and tsunami in Indonesia. 2010.

2170-265 Mercy Corps, Global Food Crisis Response, Portland, OR, $495,458. To meet immediate humanitarian needs within targeted food insecure communities while increasing resiliency to weather future emergencies. 2010.

2170-266 Meridian Institute, Dillon, CO, $72,429. For a study of innovations for agricultural value chains using science and technology. 2010.

2170-267 Miami University, Oxford, OH, $100,000. To use high-end nanotechnology to enable very low-cost, low-end nature-provided spectroscopy technology to produce a diagnostic system focused on color change in body fluids. 2010.

2170-268 Middlesex University, London, England, $357,624. To research the role of floodplain community-based organizations in coping with risk in Bangladesh, Bhutan, India, Nepal, Pakistan and Sri Lanka. Good practices and innovations identified with the community-based organization will be piloted by CBOs to improve risk coping mechanisms and ultimately the livelihoods of poor fishers and farmers. Lessons will be drawn and disseminated to practitioners and policy makers who have scope to scale up the findings to potentially benefit a large part of the rural poor population facing natural and climatic hazards. 2010.

2170-269 Milken Institute, Santa Monica, CA, $435,950. To bring together leaders in health and medical research to identify innovative approaches for accelerating progress to finding cures for neglected diseases. 2010.

2170-270 Milken Institute, Santa Monica, CA, $25,000. To explore catalytic capital market solutions to leverage aid and stimulate investment in developing countries with focus on African, Asia and South America. 2010.

2170-271 Millennium Health Microscope Foundation, Bedford, England, $100,000. To develop portable fluorescence microscopy by designing a variant of the Millennium Health Microscope (MHM) to enable better diagnosis of priority global health conditions in resource-poor settings. 2010.

2170-272 Monash University, Clayton, Australia, $100,000. To develop and test the stability and efficacy of a dry powder formulation of the drug oxytocin, which is used to treat post-partum bleeding, in inexpensive inhalant format that would be a needle-free, non-refrigerated option suitable for use in remote areas with limited training. 2010.

2170-273 Monash University, Clayton, Australia, $100,000. To engineer a live virus with a self-destruct sequence for use in a vaccine. 2010.

2170-274 Monash University, Institute of Medical Research, Clayton, Australia, $100,000. To test the antioxidant melatonin as a simple and inexpensive intervention to reduce and prevent birth asphyxial brain injury. 2010.

2170-275 Monrovia City Corporation, Monrovia, Liberia, $5,000,000. To work with community groups and city officials to create a sustainable municipal solid waste management and recycling system. 2010.

2170-276 Murdoch University, Perth, Australia, $100,000. To develop and test Inject and Forget Contraceptive Drug Delivery, implantable subcutaneous device made from same calcium mineral that bones are made of to release contraceptive drugs in a sustained and controlled way for a period of months. 2010.

2170-277 Nankai University, School of Medicine, Tianjin, China, $100,000. To develop HIV interference (HIVi), which is interfering virus against HIV via stable intracellular siRNA expression and competitive replication with HIV. 2010.

2170-278 NanoBio Corporation, Ann Arbor, MI, $5,930,094. To develop effective, stable intranasal nanoemulsion adjuvanted Respiratory Syncytial Virus (RSV) vaccine for the developing world without the hyper-reactivity observed with prior RSV vaccines in clinical trials. 2010.

2170-279 Nanyang Technological University, Singapore, $100,000. To develop rapid malaria diagnosis using magnetic nanoparticles. 2010.

2170-280 National Academy of Sciences, Washington, DC, $436,967. For Agriculture-Nutrition Linkages Workshops/Conferences in Uganda and Nigeria. 2010.

2170-281 National Academy of Sciences, Washington, DC, $150,000. To convene experts from the public and private sector in agricultural development to help establish the dimensions of the food security challenge and explore how to sustainably meet growing food demands during the coming decades. 2010.

2170-282 National Bureau of Asian Research, Seattle, WA, $700,000. For Pacific Health Summit Conference. 2010.

2170-283 National Institute for the Control of Pharmaceutical and Biological Products, Beijing, China, $100,000. To assess the effectiveness of a new inexpensive skin test that can differentiate between true Tuberculosis infection and the markers of the BCG vaccination. 2010.

2170-284 National Institute of Child Health and Human Development, Biomarkers of Nutrition for Development (BOND), Bethesda, MD, $397,435. To establish a forum for the discovery, validation, and utilization of biomarkers relevant across the range of uses and interests represented in the global food and nutrition community. 2010.

2170-285 National Public Radio, Washington, DC, $1,800,005. For balanced, in-depth coverage of global health and development in the developing world. 2010.

2170-286 NEPAD e-Africa Commission, NEPAD Planning and Coordinating Agency, Pretoria, South Africa, $1,078,107. To build capacity for drug regulatory harmonization in Africa. 2010.

2170-287 NetHope, Fairfax, VA, $155,000. For planning and business development for Weather Information for Development (WIND), initiative to increase reliable weather and climate information for farmers throughout Africa with focus on Kenya. 2010.

2170-288 New Mexico State University, Las Cruces, NM, $100,000. To develop a low-cost, rapid, and sensitive malaria diagnostic tool. 2010.

2170-289 New Venture Fund, Washington, DC, $2,718,750. For Global Health Advocacy Small Grants Initiative making small and timely grants to domestic and international projects that are focused on global health issues. 2010.

2170-290 New Venture Fund, Global Health CEO Roundtable, Washington, DC, $961,559. To increase the level of attention and investment devoted to global health issues by the research-based biopharmaceutical industry, and to coordinate their activities to achieve the greatest amount of impact and efficiency with respect to neglected tropical and other diseases that have a disproportionate impact upon developing world countries. 2010.

2170-291 New Venture Fund, Global Health CEO Roundtable, Washington, DC, $823,879. To increase the level of attention and investment devoted to global health issues by the research-based biopharmaceutical industry, and to coordinate their activities to achieve the greatest amount of impact and efficiency with respect to neglected tropical and other diseases that have a disproportionate impact upon developing world countries. 2010.

2170-292 New York University, New York, NY, $2,087,034. To communicate research results that will provide the foundations for policy and product innovation aimed at expanding access to financial services for low-income individuals in developing countries. 2010.

2170-293 New York University, New York, NY, $100,000. For Round 4, Phase I of Grand Challenges Explorations-Enhancing Innate Vaginal Defenses to Reduce the Risk of HIV, project to test the hypothesis that eliminating intra-vaginal practices such as douching will allow the return of healthy vaginal flora conditions which includes ideal pH and an intact vaginal mucosa. By restoring and maintaining this healthy environment, researcher proposes that incidences of pelvic inflammatory disease and HIV infection can be reduced. 2010.

2170-294 Northwestern University, Evanston, IL, $492,506. To complete development of infant HIV rapid test and transfer design to a global diagnostic company for regulatory approvals and market introduction in high prevalence countries. 2010.

2170-295 Norwegian Institute of Public Health, Oslo, Norway, $100,000. To develop a simple and rapid saliva-based screening test for the detection of tuberculosis (TB) disease in the developing world. 2010.

2170-296 Ohio State University, Columbus, OH, $100,000. To develop engineered strain of bacteria used to ferment beans in traditional Asian and African diets, to display antigen from the Tuberculosis bacterium. The engineered bacillus will then be used to make the traditional Asian dish natto, which can serve as a kind of oral vaccine to elicit a strong immune response. 2010.

2170-297 ONE Campaign, Washington, DC, $7,010,364. To promote health, agriculture, and development. 2010.

2170-298 OneWorld Now, Seattle, WA, $250,000. For additional support to event in Seattle to increase understanding between the United States and the Muslim world, including cultural exchanges for young people. 2010.

2170-299 OneWorld Now, Seattle, WA, $150,000. For additional support to event in Seattle to increase understanding between the United States and the Muslim world, including cultural exchanges for young people. 2010.

2170-300 Oregon Health and Science University, Portland, OR, $100,000. To test the feasibility of using the varicose vein treatment polidocanol in a foam format to permanently close fallopian tubes. If validated, the method could offer a low-cost, nonsurgical sterilization method for administration by minimally trained healthcare workers in the developing world. 2010.

2170-301 Osaka University, School of Dentistry, Osaka, Japan, $100,000. To construct and test synthetic immunoglobulin derived from the human immune system for their ability to provide protection against a broad range of bacteria, including multiple-antibiotic resistant pathogens. 2010.

2170-302 Ottawa Health Research Institute, Ottawa, Canada, $100,000. To research whether the antimicrobial peptide LL-37 can be used simultaneously as a contraceptive and anti-HIV treatment. 2010.

2170-303 Overseas Development Institute, London, England, $487,899. For Progress in Development: A Library of Stories and Outreach, project to identify untold stories of sustained, macro-level development progress. 2010.

2170-304 Overseas Development Institute, London, England, $119,782. For Progress in Development: A Library of Stories and Outreach, project to identify untold stories of sustained, macro-level development progress. 2010.

2170-305 Overseas Development Institute, London, England, $23,125. For Progress in Development: A Library of Stories and Outreach, project to identify untold stories of sustained, macro-level development progress. 2010.

2170-306 Oxfam America, Boston, MA, $4,297,750. To implement a series of innovations in Ethiopia's extension system, one of the largest in the world, to improve the system's overall performance at a national-scale and generate productivity improvements for smallholders. 2010.

2170-307 Oxfam America, Boston, MA, $500,000. For emergency response to flash floods in Senegal and The Gambia. 2010.

2170-308 Oxfam America, Boston, MA, $500,000. For emergency response to the flooding and mudslides in Guatemala. 2010.

2170-309 Oxfam America, Boston, MA, $467,556. To advance understanding of the relationship between community-based coping mechanisms, external interventions, and the pressures of climate change in sub-Saharan Africa, specifically Ethiopia and Mali. 2010.

2170-310 Oxfam America, Boston, MA, $57,793. To assist in alleviating hunger, malnutrition, and the deterioration of health of vulnerable families caused by the food crisis and drought in the Oromia and Tigray regions of Ethiopia. 2010.

2170-311 Oxfam France - Agir Ici, Paris, France, $37,047. To raise the profile of and support for global health issues in France through public outreach, advocacy, media engagement, and partnership building. 2010.

2170-312 Oxford University, Oxford, England, $11,807,540. For work of International Fetal and Newborn Growth Consortium for the 21st Century (INTERGROWTH-21st) to develop international Fetal and Newborn Growth Standards and to relate these to neonatal health risk. 2010.

2170-313 Oxford University, Oxford, England, $48,814. To promote policy-relevant research and targeted media and communications work of Oxford University's Centre for the Study of African Economies (CSAE). 2010.

2170-314 Oxford University, Oxford, England, $25,000. To sponsor the attendance of scientists and clinicians from malaria-endemic countries at international conference on Genomic Epidemiology of Malaria being held at the Wellcome Trust Conference Center. 2010.

2170-315 Palo Alto Institute for Research and Education, Palo Alto, CA, $100,000. For Round 4, Phase I of Grand Challenges Explorations-Plasmablast-Based Assays for Mucosal Antibody Response, project to develop a new assay that evaluates the function and phenotype of plasmablasts in peripheral blood after infection or vaccination. By determining how many of these cells have mucosal-homing receptors, this new test could provide an accurate measurement of mucosal immune response. 2010.

2170-316 Panos Institute, Dakar, Senegal, $1,818,421. To improve the radio quality and quantity of key development topics by building a pilot Pan-African radio platform to inform and amplify marginalized and citizens voices with content and resource-sharing networks in sub-Saharan Africa. 2010.

2170-317 Partners in Health, Boston, MA, $500,000. For emergency response to the earthquake in Haiti. 2010.

2170-318 PATH, Seattle, WA, $35,540,719. To consolidate work of Malaria Control and Evaluation Partnership in Africa (MACEPA) and scale up coverage of effective interventions and by disseminating operational guidance to inform the policies and practices of donors, implementing partners, and national governments. 2010.

2170-319 PATH, Seattle, WA, $17,232,724. For Meningitis Vaccine Project (MVP), initiative to eliminate epidemic of meningitis in Sub-Saharan Africa. 2010.

2170-320 PATH, Seattle, WA, $10,971,107. To consolidate work of Malaria Control and Evaluation Partnership in Africa (MACEPA) and scale up coverage of effective interventions and by disseminating operational guidance to inform the policies and practices of donors, implementing partners, and national governments. 2010.

2170-321 PATH, Seattle, WA, $4,999,724. To develop evidence for improving the performance of live, attenuated, orally delivered rotavirus vaccines in infants in the developing world. 2010.

2170-322 PATH, Seattle, WA, $3,056,772. To make available a rapid, affordable, and field-friendly Ov-16 antigen-based antibody test (Ov-16 rapid test) for use in onchocerciasis programs for disease control and eventual elimination in Africa. 2010.

2170-323 PATH, Seattle, WA, $1,448,532. To use market research and a willingness-to-pay study in India and East Africa to identify one or more target product profiles for improved Oral Rehydration Salts and Zinc (ORS-Zn) and to begin to align stakeholders toward ultimate goal of sustained public health impact. 2010.

2170-324 PATH, Seattle, WA, $1,370,050. For limited introduction of contraceptive, Depot MedroxyProgesterone Acetate (DMPA-SC) in the Uniject device in Kenya, Malawi, Pakistan, Rwanda and Senegal. 2010.

2170-325 PATH, Seattle, WA, $1,198,870. To understand the intensity of transmission as malaria control increases and the impact on clinical trials for new tools. 2010.

2170-326 PATH, Seattle, WA, $1,000,000. For general operating support. 2010.

2170-327 PATH, Seattle, WA, $887,850. To establish a home for this cross-Product Development Partnership (PDP) regulatory support, and provide evidence that this model both strengthens regulatory capacities for PDP products and is more efficient than establishing these resources at individual PDPs. 2010.

2170-328 PATH, Seattle, WA, $600,000. For Reproductive Health Supplies Coalition (RHSC). 2010.

2170-329 PATH, Seattle, WA, $66,700. To ensure broad participation by African researchers at the International Rotavirus Symposium in Johannesburg and the related African Rotavirus Symposium through PATH-directed support to conference hosts. 2010.

2170-330 PATH, Seattle, WA, $50,000. For a cooperative initiative aimed at catalyzing the discovery, development, and delivery of global health solutions. 2010.

2170-331 PATH Vaccine Solutions, Seattle, WA, $29,999,216. To advance clinical development of late-stage rotavirus vaccine candidate by a developing-country manufacturer, ultimately increasing affordability and access to sustainable rotavirus vaccine introduction in low-resource settings. 2010.

2170-332 PATH Vaccine Solutions, Seattle, WA, $989,356. For planning and preparations for bioprocess, formulation, and early clinical development of non-replicating rotavirus vaccines. 2010.

2170-333 Pennsylvania State University, University Park, PA, $100,000. For Round 4, Phase I of Grand Challenges Explorations-Scent of Disease: Diagnostic for Malaria Infection in Humans, project to test the theory that malaria infection induces characteristic odor cues, even in asymptomatic individuals. By identifying these chemical cues with gas chromatography and mass spectrometry it will be determined if there are biomarkers for diagnosis of infection. 2010.

2170-334 Planned Parenthood Federation, International, Brussels, Belgium, $7,298,377. To protect and increase European donor commitment to universal access to reproductive health and family planning with focus on Africa and Asia. 2010.

2170-335 Policlinico S.Orsola-Malpighi, Bologna, Italy, $100,000. To attempt to produce engineered HIV integrase, enzyme produced by the virus to integrate itself into host chromosomes, and test its ability to instead cut the virus' DNA at its integration sites in the human genome. 2010.

2170-336 Population Action International, Washington, DC, $2,991,037. To expand upon the successful model established via the Mobilizing for Reproductive Health/HIV Integration Initiative to unleash resources for, generate demand for, increase capacity around, and bolster political will for the financing and implementation of integrated Reproductive Health/HIV services. 2010.

2170-337 Population Reference Bureau, Washington, DC, $759,500. For RENEW Project (Reenergizing Nutrition Worldwide), initiative to increase commitment and resources in addressing undernutrition globally, using data visualization tools for advocacy. 2010.

2170-338 Population Services International, Washington, DC, $1,499,978. For market/supply chain research and policy recommendations for antimalarial drugs. 2010.

2170-339 Population Services International, Washington, DC, $31,960. For market/supply chain research and policy recommendations for antimalarial drugs. 2010.

2170-340 Prince Henrys Institute of Medical Research, Clayton, Australia, $100,000. To develop a new assay to measure a protein that is produced by the placenta during its development, and will test the theory that monitoring this protein can reflect placental abnormalities that indicate a high risk for preeclampsia very early in pregnancy. 2010.

2170-341 Prince Henrys Institute of Medical Research, Clayton, Australia, $100,000. To test whether a peptide inhibitor that has been shown to inhibit protein processing critical to HIV transmission can be used as a non-hormonal contraceptive which protects against HIV. 2010.

2170-342 ProCredit Holding, Frankfurt, Germany, $2,600,000. To increase the access of micro entrepreneurs, small businesses and low-income groups to responsible banking services in Africa, especially savings accounts. 2010.

2170-343 Project HOPE - The People-to-People Health Foundation, Millwood, VA, $1,411,815. To publish papers on global health issues in the U.S. and abroad. 2010.

2170-344 Public Health Institute, Oakland, CA, $198,750. To convene a conference on the impact of tobacco tax adjustment on tobacco control in China and recommend further reform. 2010.

2170-345 Purdue University, West Lafayette, IN, $100,000. For Round 4, Phase I of Grand Challenges Explorations-Blocking the P. falciparum Transporter PfCRT, research project to develop novel dimeric drugs designed to block a key protein in the malaria parasite that limits the accumulation of anti-malarials in the parasite's digestive system. By inhibiting this protein, this new therapy could eliminate drug resistance in malaria parasites. 2010.

2170-346 Queen Mary University of London, London, England, $100,000. For Round 4, Phase I of Grand Challenges Explorations-Inducing Mucosal Immunity using Retinoids and Oral Vaccines, project to test the theory that a measured dose of vitamin A (retinoic acid) given with an oral vaccine will enhance immunoglobulin secretions in the gut, thus boosting the mucosal immune response. If successful, vitamin A could be used as an effective adjuvant for oral vaccines that target diarrhea, a leading cause of death among children worldwide. 2010.

2170-347 Research America, Alexandria, VA, $1,711,296. To help increase investment in research focused on diseases and health conditions that have the greatest burden in the developing world. 2010.

2170-348 Results for Development Institute, Washington, DC, $196,089. To communicate to key audiences the findings of AIDS 2031 Costs and Financing Project, in order to engage high-level decision makers at the global, regional, and national levels (in selected countries) in policy discussions that will shape efficient and sustainable long-term strategies and actions for financing the growing gaps in the HIV/AIDS response. 2010.

2170-349 Rhodes University, Grahamstown, South Africa, $193,774. For activities to improve the quality of coverage on development topics in the African media in order to better inform public opinion and policy decisions. 2010.

2170-350 Richards Rwanda, Seattle, WA, $10,000. For general operating support. 2010.

2170-351 Rockefeller University, New York, NY, $100,000. To identify single gene mutations that are critical to immunity against bacterial infections to provide insight into a genetic basis for the susceptibility of some children to Tuberculosis and inform a recombinant IFN-y drug therapy. 2010.

2170-352 Royal Melbourne Institute of Technology, Melbourne, Australia, $100,000. To develop a nanochip patch that utilizes a surface enhanced raman scattering platform to detect infectious diseases along with Malaria. 2010.

2170-353 Royal Society of Tropical Medicine and Hygiene, London, England, $45,457. For international three-day meeting in Liverpool, UK to explore and debate ideas and advances relating to a range of communicable and non-communicable diseases and related global health issues. 2010.

2170-354 Rush University Medical Center, Chicago, IL, $100,000. For Round 4, Phase I of Grand Challenges Explorations-Detecting Pathogenic Microbes by a "Microbial Litmus Strip", project to develop nanoparticles which react to the presence of pathogenic microbes by releasing encapsulated substances that quickly amplify the binding signals. These nanoparticles can be placed on the tip of a litmus strip as a colorimetric assay to indicate the presence and concentration of pathogens. 2010.

2170-355 Rutgers, The State University of New Jersey, New Brunswick, NJ, $100,000. To evaluate the effectiveness of the natural antimicrobial protein subtilosin to not only treat vaginal infections but act as a spermicidal agent. 2010.

2170-356 Saint Georges University of London, London, England, $280,236. To develop a novel delivery strategy for HIV vaccine antigens. 2010.

2170-357 Saint Georges University of London, London, England, $35,975. For Parasite to Prevention Conference. 2010.

2170-358 SANGONet Information Association, Braamfontein, South Africa, $2,957,196. To develop mobile phone applications that will help agricultural support organizations boost incomes of small-scale farmers and increase the effectiveness of selected agricultural development programs. 2010.

2170-359 Sasakawa Africa Association, Tokyo, Japan, $5,730,825. To promote the scaling up of modern agricultural technologies that can increase the productivity and incomes of resource-poor smallholder farmers in Ethiopia. 2010.

2170-360 Save the Children Federation, Westport, CT, $7,478,197. To test and evaluate a critical set of newborn health care tools, technologies and approaches to improve newborn health and survival. 2010.

2170-361 Save the Children Federation, Westport, CT, $600,000. For emergency response to Cyclone Giri in Myanmar. 2010.

2170-362 Save the Children Federation, Westport, CT, $300,000. For emergency relief to communities in Guatemala affected by Tropical Storm Agatha. 2010.

2170-363 Seattle Biomedical Research Institute, Seattle, WA, $3,559,859. To develop the knowledge which is needed to develop vaccines and drugs for global infectious diseases including malaria, tuberculosis, HIV/AIDS, and emerging and neglected diseases. 2010.

2170-364 Seattle Childrens Hospital Foundation, Seattle, WA, $100,000. To develop a low cost pulmonary surfactant that can be administered by minimally educated health care workers to premature infants as they are being born as a means to avoid infant intubation as well as injury to premature lungs. 2010.

2170-365 Seattle International Foundation, Seattle, WA, $250,000. For Global Giving Campaign, ongoing efforts to expand and increase philanthropic giving from individuals and corporations. 2010.

2170-366 Self Employed Women's Association, Ahmadabad, India, $1,361,315. For work of A Space of My Own: Integrating the Urban Poor in City Development, initiative to organize workers to achieve their goals of full employment and self reliance. 2010.

2170-367 Seoul National University, Seoul, South Korea, $100,000. For Round 4, Phase I of Grand Challenges Explorations-Use of Fusobacterium Nucleatum as a Vaccine Vector, project to test whether Fusobacterium nucleatum, a common bacteria often found in human mouths, can be used to deliver antigens to the oral mucosa. This bacteria has the ability to invade epithelial tissues, and researchers hope to engineer a strain to express a vaccine antigen when given under the tongue to induce both antibody production and a strong cell-mediated immune response. 2010.

2170-368 Shack/Slum Dwellers International, SDI International, Mowbray, South Africa, $7,029,460. For work of Building Inclusive Cities from the Bottom Up to enable organized communities of the urban poor to engage key stakeholders, especially local governments, in upgrading informal settlements and the overall planning of cities. 2010.

2170-369 Shanghai Institute of Biological Sciences, Shanghai, China, $481,388. For research that will guide the C4 rice project, initiative to use cutting edge science to discover the genes that will supercharge photosynthesis, boost food production and improve the lives of billions of poor people in the developing world. 2010.

2170-370 ShoreBank International, Washington, DC, $10,000,000. To work with BRAC Bank Limited to build bKash, a scalable mobile money platform that will allow poor Bangladeshis to store, transfer, and receive money safely via mobile phone. 2010.

2170-371 ShoreBank International, Washington, DC, $6,948,436. To scale up United Banking Limited's branchless banking platform in Pakistan in a way that encourages account uptake and usage among the poor and unbanked. 2010.

2170-372 Sickle Cell Cure Foundation, Oklahoma City, OK, $100,000. To test whether a peptide inhibitor that has been shown to inhibit protein processing critical to HIV transmission can be used to prevent embryo implantation in the uterus. 2010.

2170-373 Simon Fraser University, Burnaby, Canada, $100,000. To develop novel antibiotics by combining regions of insect antibacterial peptides in abnormal conformations that will increase the types of organisms they will control and reduce the drug concentration required to kill existing and drug resistant bacteria. 2010.

2170-374 Sister Cities International, Washington, DC, $306,903. For sustainable and collaborative cross-sector solution models to address pressing causes of urban poverty with focus on the following 13 African countries Egypt, Ethiopia, Ghana, Kenya, Liberia, Malawi, Mali, Morocco, Nigeria, Senegal, South Africa, Swaziland, United Republic of Tanzania. 2010.

2170-375 Small Enterprise Finance Trust, Hyderabad, India, $431,253. To identify ways to improve informal saving and credit associations practices that can increase access to financial services to the rural poor. 2010.

2170-376 Social Transformation and Empowerment Projects International Association, Copenhagen, Denmark, $1,595,097. For Why Poverty?, global documentary series on the causes of and innovative solutions to persistent global poverty. 2010.

2170-377 Society for Vector Ecology, Corona, CA, $26,000. For conference support. 2010.

2170-378 South Africa Development Fund, Boston, MA, $3,230,123. For targeted policy and advocacy that builds government accountability for health financing (specifically HIV treatment and prevention) and strengthens the community engagement capacity of the government in South Africa. 2010.

2170-379 Southern Africa Trust, Midrand, South Africa, $3,000,000. To link research, advocacy and media groups for more coordinated and effective delivery of pro-poor policies in Africa. 2010.

2170-380 Southern African Confederation of Agricultural Unions, City of Tshwane, South Africa, $3,232,942. To increase the incomes of smallholder farmers in Southern Africa by strengthening Farmers' Organizations and increasing their smallholder membership. 2010.

2170-381 SRI International, Menlo Park, CA, $100,000. To develop Vitamin A-secreting probiotics to activate mucosal immunity. 2010.

2170-382 Stanford University, Stanford, CA, $1,000,000. To establish proof concept for the application of mass spectrometry-based flow cytometry and microfluidic-based single cell RT-PCR technologies as applied to priority diseases, and to undertake a large-scale characterization, and subsequent phenotyping, of antigen-specific T-cell responses to rotavirus and influenza virus infection and vaccination in humans. 2010.

2170-383 Stanford University, Stanford, CA, $995,844. To develop open access lecture series, twelve integrated lectures on food policy, food security and the environment in effort to help build a global education network. 2010.

2170-384 Stanford University, Stanford, CA, $100,000. For Round 4, Phase I of Grand Challenges Explorations-Hand-Held Proteomic NanoLab for Infectious Diseases, project to refine a prototype diagnostic platform which uses GMR sensors, commonly used in hard disk drives, to detect proteins labeled with magnetic nanoparticles. By employing GMR sensors on disposable "NanoLab" sticks, Wang and his team hope to produce an easy to use, ultraportable diagnostic device for rapid

point-of-care HIV screening in the developing world. 2010.

2170-385 Stanford University, Stanford, CA, $100,000. To create a cell phone application that collects information on an individual's menstrual cycle, processes the information with a calendar algorithm, and sends free text messages as a reminder to a woman of her menstrual status. 2010.

2170-386 Stanford University, Stanford, CA, $100,000. To develop mass-producible microscopes for low-cost diagnosis of tuberculosis. 2010.

2170-387 Stichting eIFL.net, Rome, Italy, $1,700,000. To accelerate development of replicable, innovative library services that meet user needs. 2010.

2170-388 Stichting Global Voices, Amsterdam, Netherlands, $20,000. For conference support for Global Voices annual summit, to be held at Santiago Public Library in Chile. 2010.

2170-389 Swiss Agency for Development and Cooperation, Bern, Switzerland, $475,000. To research scalable, sustainable sanitation service chains in low-income urban areas in Sub-Saharan Africa. Grant made as part of SPLASH-the European Union Water Initiative Research Area Network. 2010.

2170-390 Swiss Federal Institute of Aquatic Science and Technology, Dubendorf, Switzerland, $2,999,920. To recover nutrients from urine in small decentralized reactors, in an effort to develop a dry sanitation system, which is affordable for the poor, produces a valuable fertilizer, promotes entrepreneurship and reduces pollution of water resources. 2010.

2170-391 Symbiora, Grantham, NH, $100,000. To evaluate the safety and effectiveness of a low-cost oral solution derived from beneficial strains of human gut bacteria to prevent and treat acute diarrheal illness in infants. 2010.

2170-392 Task Force for Global Health, Decatur, GA, $6,793,782. For Polio Antivirals Initiative. 2010.

2170-393 Technische Universitat Darmstadt, Darmstadt, Germany, $100,000. To research whether early-stage pneumonia infection produces specific biomarkers that can be detected in a breath analysis. 2010.

2170-394 TechnoServe, Washington, DC, $8,000,000. To link small-scale soy producers to industrial feed processors in Zambia and Mozambique. 2010.

2170-395 Texas A & M Research Foundation, College Station, TX, $1,053,395. To identify new protein targets that will lead to the discovery of new drugs that will dramatically shorten chemotherapy for treatment of tuberculosis. 2010.

2170-396 Thomson Foundation, Cardiff, Wales, $860,628. To promote in-depth and accurate information about policy-relevant economic research in regional markets in Africa. 2010.

2170-397 Treatment Action Group, New York, NY, $2,834,582. To strengthen domestic and international HIV community responses to TB/HIV by creating and implementing a research, policy, education, and mobilization agenda with community groups from around the world. 2010.

2170-398 Tsinghua University, Beijing, China, $100,000. To design and test a portable, non-invasive device (Local Skin Hyperthermia) for its ability to kill the worm larvae that causes the

chronic parasitic disease Schistosomiasis. 2010.

2170-399 Tufts University, Fletcher School, Medford, MA, $568,679. To support leadership education program for banking policymakers from developing countries and accelerate their leadership on financial inclusion. 2010.

2170-400 Tulane Educational Fund, New Orleans, LA, $762,198. To evaluate and assess the humanitarian responses to the earthquake in Haiti. 2010.

2170-401 Tulane Educational Fund, New Orleans, LA, $124,644. To develop a strategy to build a Global Disaster Resilience Network through partnerships with local universities. 2010.

2170-402 Tulane University, School of Public Health and Tropical Medicine, New Orleans, LA, $786,576. To expand evidence base for integrated urban family planning in Francophone countries of Burkina Faso, Democratic Republic of the Congo and Mali. 2010.

2170-403 UNICEF, New York, NY, $87,000,001. For polio eradication through enhanced communication, vaccine supply, and operational support. 2010.

2170-404 UNICEF, New York, NY, $22,122,396. For polio eradication through enhanced communication, vaccine supply, and operational support. 2010.

2170-405 UNICEF, New York, NY, $3,500,000. For polio eradication through enhanced communication, vaccine supply, and operational support. 2010.

2170-406 United Nations Capital Development Fund, New York, NY, $718,967. For the United Nations Special Advocate for Inclusive Finance for Development to promote sound policies to increase poor people's access to financial services, especially savings and in rural areas of developing countries. 2010.

2170-407 United Nations Department of Economic and Social Affairs, Advisory Board on Water and Sanitation, New York, NY, $1,023,441. To support a group of water and sanitation champions, created by the UN Secretary-General to galvanize the international community and generate political will for improved access to drinking water and sanitation. 2010.

2170-408 United Nations Development Programme, New York, NY, $485,000. For African Human Development Report on Food Security for Human Development. 2010.

2170-409 United Nations Foundation, Washington, DC, $29,999,683. To raise awareness of and mobilize resources in support of Millennium Development Goals 4, 5 and 6, which are to reduce child mortality, improve maternal health and combat HIV/AIDS, malaria and other diseases. 2010.

2170-410 United Nations Foundation, Washington, DC, $1,499,408. To develop a strategic approach increasing U.S. support for global (with focus on Africa and Asia) family planning and reproductive health. 2010.

2170-411 United Nations Foundation, Washington, DC, $494,500. To support organizations that aid the Global Fund to Fight AIDS, Tuberculosis and Malaria in Africa from constituencies based in Africa, Australia, Europe, Japan, and USA. 2010.

2170-412 United Nations Foundation, Washington, DC, $200,100. To support policymaker roundtable on Millennium Development Goals and the United Nations Summit. 2010.

2170-413 United States Department of State, Washington, DC, $4,500,000. To establish Women's Leadership Fund as part of Women's Health Innovation Program. 2010.

2170-414 United States Fund for UNICEF, New York, NY, $12,637,231. For Diarrhea Alleviation through Zinc and ORS Therapy (DAZT), integrated strategy to provide zinc Oral Rehydration Salts (ORS) in Gujarat and Uttar Pradesh regions in India. 2010.

2170-415 United States Fund for UNICEF, New York, NY, $5,000,000. For general operating support. 2010.

2170-416 United States Fund for UNICEF, New York, NY, $1,000,000. For emergency response to the measles outbreak in southern Africa, specifically Central African Republic, Lesotho and Madagascar. 2010.

2170-417 United States Fund for UNICEF, New York, NY, $1,000,000. For emergency response to polio outbreak in the Congo. 2010.

2170-418 United States Fund for UNICEF, New York, NY, $1,000,000. To respond to flooding and a cholera outbreak in Chad. 2010.

2170-419 Universidad Peruana Cayetano Heredia, Lima, Peru, $2,779,521. For the results of the proof of concept of the Cysticercosis (common parasitic infestation of the central nervous system) and Taeniasis (tapeworm (cestode) infection acquired by the ingestion of raw or undercooked meat of infected animals) elimination grant to the Universidad Peruana Cayetano, which will look at the sustainability of the elimination after the program stopped interventions and expands the sites with a simplified regimen for scale up outside a research setting. 2010.

2170-420 Universidad Peruana Cayetano Heredia, Lima, Peru, $100,000. To develop a harmless probiotic bacterium capable of binding and neutralizing enterotoxins of Enterotoxigenic Escherichia coli to prevent diarrheal disease. 2010.

2170-421 University College London, Institute of Child Health, London, England, $1,053,162. For exploratory study to guide the design of emollient field trial in Africa. 2010.

2170-422 University of Adelaide, Adelaide, Australia, $100,000. To develop a harmless probiotic bacterium capable of binding and neutralizing Enterotoxigenic Escherichia Coli (ETEC), which produces two distinct enterotoxins that attack intestinal cells, by mimicking their respective receptors, thereby preventing disease. 2010.

2170-423 University of Alabama, Birmingham, AL, $100,000. To develop a novel, cheap, simple, and rapid method for detecting and tracking fecal coliform contamination in drinking water. 2010.

2170-424 University of Bonn, Center for Development Research, Bonn, Germany, $450,300. To design strategies for livelihood improvement in marginal environments through Marginality Reduction for Enhanced Investments for and with the Poorest. (MARGIP) program, with focus on Bangladesh and Ethiopia. 2010.

2170-425 University of British Columbia, Vancouver, Canada, $6,999,991. To bring together a suite of interventions to test new strategies for monitoring, prevention, and treatment of pre-eclampsia in various low resource settings. 2010.

2170-426 University of California, Berkeley, CA, $100,000. For Round 4, Phase I of Grand Challenges Explorations-Discovery of Chemosensory Molecules as Novel Contraceptives, project to identify chemical compounds in the female reproductive system that guide sperm cells to the egg. By characterizing these "odorants," synthetic versions can be produced and administered to disrupt this navigation system thus inhibiting fertilization. 2010.

2170-427 University of California, Berkeley, CA, $100,000. To develop newly discovered RNA restriction enzymes into low-cost diagnostics for viral and bacterial infections. 2010.

2170-428 University of California, Berkeley, CA, $89,433. To determine whether and why individual or combined water, sanitation and hygiene interventions are more or less effective at realizing health, social and/or economic impacts, and to provide data that will influence water, sanitation and hygiene policy and practice. 2010.

2170-429 University of California, Davis, CA, $100,000. For Round 4, Phase I of Grand Challenges Explorations-Prevention of Infection by Bovine Milk Oligosaccharides, project to determine whether oligosaccharides found in cow's milk can be used to enrich nutritional strategies of children who have been weaned. While human milk contains oligosaccharides that have been shown protect breast-feeding infants, the older children could benefit from enrichment of intestinal microbiota to prevent intestinal diseases. 2010.

2170-430 University of California, Irvine, CA, $363,849. To support Institute that will research money and technology for those who live on less than $1 per day. 2010.

2170-431 University of California, Irvine, CA, $100,000. To develop and field test Long-Lasting Biological Larvicide for Malaria Vector Control in Africa, which will provide new formulations of biological larvicides which utilize plaster matrix materials for the slow release of the insecticide in aquatic environment, as well as chemical lures that attract and stimulate feeding by the mosquito larvae. 2010.

2170-432 University of California, Los Angeles, CA, $100,000. For Round 4, Phase I of Grand Challenges Explorations-Cost-Effective Testing of Blood Samples using Cell phones, project to test the feasibility of a lens-free cell phone microscope for rapid, automated and accurate diagnosis of malaria in field settings. This on-chip cell phone microscope is based on digital holography and does not require any lenses, lasers or other bulky components making it extremely cost-effective and compact. 2010.

2170-433 University of California, Los Angeles, CA, $100,000. To develop a disposable malaria biosensor based on a SIM card platform, which will allow malaria detection to be performed using a cell phone, making diagnostic testing more widely available. 2010.

2170-434 University of California, Riverside, CA, $100,000. To develop low-cost hardware that can automatically count mosquitoes as they fly past a sensor. Accurate counts of the sex/species of mosquitoes are critical for planning intervention and control strategies to reduce malaria disease transmission. 2010.

2170-435 University of California, San Francisco, CA, $4,430,611. To gather, analyze, and disseminate evidence on malaria elimination and to synthesize new evidence into practical guidance for strategic planning and decision making at global, regional, and country levels. 2010.

2170-436 University of California, San Francisco, CA, $3,609,195. To allow broad evaluation of available compounds that can be used in mass drug administration programs to kill adult filarial worms (a macrofilaricide) that cause Onchocerciasis and Lymphatic Filariasis. 2010.

2170-437 University of California, San Francisco, CA, $1,499,993. To establish Consortium of Universities for Global Health (CUGH) as a self-sustaining organization representing North American university-based global health programs. 2010.

2170-438 University of California, San Francisco, CA, $100,000. For Round 4, Phase I of Grand Challenges Explorations-Identification of a Viral Pathogen in Nematodes. 2010.

2170-439 University of California, San Francisco, CA, $100,000. To develop a new drug delivery technology that exploits the high ferrous iron concentrations in malaria parasites. 2010.

2170-440 University of California, San Francisco, CA, $100,000. To engineer a virus that expresses a killer gene when a mosquito is old enough to reproduce, but not old enough to transmit the malaria parasite. By allowing the mosquito to reproduce, the virus not only will be transmitted vertically to the next generation, but will significantly slow the evolution of resistance to the gene. 2010.

2170-441 University of California, Santa Barbara, CA, $100,000. To develop inexpensive, hand-held electronic device that will allow healthcare workers in the developing world to rapidly and conveniently quantify antibodies indicative of vaccination status or inherent mucosal immunity. 2010.

2170-442 University of California at San Diego, La Jolla, CA, $100,000. To develop a novel delivery system for non-toxic, anti-roundworm proteins. 2010.

2170-443 University of Cape Town, Cape Town, South Africa, $5,352,811. To identify predictive gene expression signatures of risk of tuberculosis (TB) disease, following natural infection with Mycobacterium tuberculosis (Mtb); these signatures will facilitate rapid screening of new, better TB vaccine candidates, and will allow targeted isoniazid therapy to prevent disease after Mtb infection. 2010.

2170-444 University of Cape Town, Cape Town, South Africa, $23,000. For conference support. 2010.

2170-445 University of Cincinnati, Cincinnati, OH, $100,000. To develop and test a tampon-like, biodegradable foam device made from polymers that contain a safe spermicide and a microbicide. 2010.

2170-446 University of Colorado, Boulder, CO, $828,817. To study the use of nanocrystal therapeutics for the treatment of multi-drug resistant pathogens. 2010.

2170-447 University of Colorado, Denver, CO, $117,658. To identify the most sensitive and specific method for detecting viruses causing acute lower respiratory infections in Philippine children by testing different multiplex PCR methods to complement global epidemiological studies. 2010.

2170-448 University of Florida, Gainesville, FL, $100,000. To develop a dry powder pulmonary surfactant formulation for the treatment of respiratory distress syndrome in newborns. 2010.

2170-449 University of Georgia Research Foundation, Athens, GA, $150,000. For research that will reduce the spread of disease in poultry. 2010.

2170-450 University of Illinois at Chicago, Chicago, IL, $100,000. To investigate the use of a copper-based compound as a microbicide to prevent HIV infection through sexual transmission. 2010.

2170-451 University of Kansas Center for Research, Lawrence, KS, $100,000. To develop point-of-care diagnostic platforms using microfluidic structures fabricated onto compact disc (CD) media for detection in conventional computer compact disk drives. 2010.

2170-452 University of Liverpool, Liverpool, England, $1,499,862. To enable and drive development of improved and appropriate vaccines against invasive pneumococcal disease for use in high burden low-income countries with focus on sub-Saharan Africa. 2010.

2170-453 University of Manchester, Manchester, England, $100,000. To test affordable, sustained drug delivery formulation made of microparticle doughnuts combined with recently identified non-hormonal substances that immobilize sperm for possible use in a vaginal contraceptive device. 2010.

2170-454 University of Manitoba, Winnipeg, Canada, $2,000,000. To reduce the risk of transmission of HIV and STIs among sex workers in the Learning Sites of Mysore and Mandya. 2010.

2170-455 University of Maryland-Baltimore, Baltimore, MD, $4,708,596. To improve understanding of the causes of severe diarrhea among children in high mortality areas. 2010.

2170-456 University of Maryland-Baltimore, Baltimore, MD, $100,000. To develop a diagnostic platform based on seed germination by integrating DNA amplification with the expression of reporter proteins in plant seeds to aid in the detection of infectious diseases, specifically Filariasis. 2010.

2170-457 University of Maryland-Baltimore, Baltimore, MD, $100,000. To genetically integrate heat shock proteins from thermopilic organisms, which thrive at relatively high temperatures, into attenuated bacterial vaccines to try to enhance the viability and immunogenicity of these vaccines during the freeze-drying process. 2010.

2170-458 University of Maryland-Baltimore, School of Medicine, Baltimore, MD, $100,000. To test the ability of AT1002, innovative 6-mer peptide regulator of mucosalbarrier function, to elicit protective local and systemic immune responses by increasing antigens delivery through the airway mucosa. 2010.

2170-459 University of Maryland-College Park, College Park, MD, $100,000. To construct and test a vaccine platform that utilizes low-cost, stable surfactant vesicles to deliver antigens for a sustained mucosal immune response. 2010.

2170-460 University of Miami, Institute of Renal Medicine, School of Medicine, Miami, FL, $100,000. To develop low-cost, rapid, multiplexed detection of Tuberculosis. 2010.

2170-461 University of Michigan, Ann Arbor, MI, $100,000. For Round 4, Phase I of Grand Challenges Explorations-Circumcision Tool for Traditional Ceremonies in Africa, project to

develop prototype circumcision tool for use in traditional ceremonies in Africa and demonstrate the functionality, cultural suitability, and potential for low-cost mass production of the device. Such a tool could increase the circumcision rates leading to lower rates of HIV transmission in the region. 2010.

2170-462 University of Nairobi, Nairobi, Kenya, $100,000. For Round 4, Phase I of Grand Challenges Explorations-A Zeolite Hydrogel 'Nano-Mop' for Contraception. 2010.

2170-463 University of Nebraska Foundation, Lincoln, NE, $50,000. To assemble a diverse group of representatives from government, research institutions, and the private sector to focus on issues of water for agricultural production. 2010.

2170-464 University of New England, Armidale, Australia, $2,895,698. To improve the livelihoods of small-holder dairy farmers in East Africa by supplying the genotypes that best suit the production level and system of individual farmers. 2010.

2170-465 University of Newcastle, Callaghan, Australia, $100,000. To study mechanisms by which organic compounds called quinones may provide simultaneous protection against pregnancy and sexually transmitted disease. 2010.

2170-466 University of North Carolina, Chapel Hill, NC, $500,000. To publish special issue of Lancet on population and family planning in relation to achieving Millennium Development Goals. 2010.

2170-467 University of North Carolina, Chapel Hill, NC, $100,000. For Round 4, Phase I of Grand Challenges Explorations-Ultrasound as a Long-Term, Reversible Male Contraceptive, project to study the ability of therapeutic ultrasound to deplete testicular sperm counts. Characterizing the most beneficial timing and dosage could lead to the development of a low-cost, non-hormonal and reversible method of contraception for men. 2010.

2170-468 University of North Carolina, Chapel Hill, NC, $100,000. To create simple, sensitive, fast and affordable instrument-free detection platforms for nucleic-acid disease-markers that integrate the rapid expression of reporter proteins in plant-seeds with DNA amplification at room temperature. 2010.

2170-469 University of North Carolina, Chapel Hill, NC, $100,000. To develop synthetic lymph node, bio-compatible, biodegradable polymer device that can be placed under the skin to introduce vaccines and antigens to the immune system. 2010.

2170-470 University of North Carolina, Chapel Hill, NC, $100,000. To test whether antibodies within mucus interact with viruses to create adhesive traps that prevents them from reaching target cells, for potential use in the development of a new vaccine platform that could target many infectious diseases at their point of entry. 2010.

2170-471 University of Notre Dame, Notre Dame, IN, $999,999. To support consortium for improved methods to design and evaluate malaria control programs. 2010.

2170-472 University of Notre Dame, Notre Dame, IN, $163,125. To provide essential treatment for Lymphatic Filariasis (LF) and intestinal helminths with the goal of eliminating LF from Haiti. 2010.

2170-473 University of Oklahoma Health Sciences Center, Oklahoma City, OK, $100,000. To

develop low-cost delivery of controlled short and low-voltage Square-Wave Electrical Pulses (SWEP) in the vicinity of lymphoid tissues (through skin surface; non-invasive) which can induce the long-lived, functional, robust immunity by enhancing the immune-functions of dendritic cells. 2010.

2170-474 University of Pennsylvania, Philadelphia, PA, $100,000. For Round 4, Phase I of Grand Challenges Explorations-Unleashing Protein Disaggregases to Prevent HIV Infection. 2010.

2170-475 University of Pennsylvania, Philadelphia, PA, $100,000. For Round 4, Phase I of Grand Challenges Explorations-Sentinel Commensals for in situ Temporal Protection against Bacterial Diarrheas. 2010.

2170-476 University of Pittsburgh, Pittsburgh, PA, $2,990,342. To develop a whole body imaging technology as a means to shorten the duration of chemotherapy in patients suffering from tuberculosis. 2010.

2170-477 University of Quebec, Center Hospitalier, Montreal, Canada, $100,000. To hold the biennial meeting of International Society for Sexually Transmitted Diseases Research (ISSTDR), the largest international research conference in the field of sexually transmitted diseases (STDs), including presentation of the most recent advances in the field, information sharing between scientists, and capacity building activities. 2010.

2170-478 University of Queensland, Brisbane, Australia, $100,000. To develop a new diagnostic test using a low-cost magnetic reader to detect biomarkers in saliva that are present during infection. 2010.

2170-479 University of Rochester, Rochester, NY, $100,000. For Round 4, Phase I of Grand Challenges Explorations-Symbiont-Mediated Control of River Blindness, project to test the hypothesis that infecting blackflies with the bacteria Spiroplasma could impair the ability to transmit the parasite responsible for River Blindness, and also increase fertility of female flies that can pass along this beneficial bacteria to its offspring. 2010.

2170-480 University of Saskatchewan, Saskatoon, Canada, $100,000. For Round 4, Phase I of Grand Challenges Explorations-Bacteriophage Lambda Mucosal Vaccine Delivery System, proposal that bacteriophage lambda, a virus that invades bacterial cells and uses the host's genome to replicate, can be used as a vector to deliver DNA vaccines into targeted cells. Results will test this lambda delivery platform in its ability to induce long-term systemic and mucosal immune responses. 2010.

2170-481 University of Science and Technology of China, Hefei, China, $305,813. To promote evidence-based decision making in policies, investments and foundings on health research and development-related projects in China. 2010.

2170-482 University of South Florida, Orlando, FL, $2,142,862. For xenomonitoring fly trap needed to guide treatment areas of Onchocerciasis and monitor for recurrence after elimination. 2010.

2170-483 University of South Florida, Tampa, FL, $4,056,644. For effective therapeutics to prevent and cure malaria by developing long-term continuous culture system for Plasmodium vivax blood-stages. 2010.

2170-484 University of South Florida, Tampa, FL, $1,387,061. To develop a new malaria liver stage model that will support the normal development of EE stages, enhance infection rates, allow the visualization of the complete development of human malaria EE stages, and provide a platform to accelerate drug discovery. 2010.

2170-485 University of Southern Mississippi, Hattiesburg, MS, $30,459. To convene experts to discuss new information about Vibrios in the Environment particularly in relation to diarrhea/enteric diseases, diagnostics, and vaccines. 2010.

2170-486 University of Strathclyde, Glasgow, Scotland, $100,000. To develop innovative, optics-based seek-and-destroy' system to combat Leishmania infection in vivo, to provide unconventional mechanism of inducing long-lived protective immunity. 2010.

2170-487 University of Texas, Austin, TX, $100,000. To develop BTI-engineered green-algal food source for mosquito larvae into a biological control agent by engineering their chloroplasts to produce larvacidal proteins. 2010.

2170-488 University of Texas Health Science Center, San Antonio, TX, $100,000. For Round 4, Phase I of Grand Challenges Explorations-Triggered Release Microcapsules for Barrier Contraception, project to test the feasibility of developing a vaginal tablet containing adhesive microcapsules that would adhere to the vaginal wall and release spermicidal agents upon contact with semen as a method for contraception. 2010.

2170-489 University of the Witwatersrand, Johannesburg, South Africa, $9,999,558. For a field study in Africa on maternal influenza immunization. 2010.

2170-490 University of Toledo, Health Science Campus, Toledo, OH, $100,000. For Round 4, Phase I of Grand Challenges Explorations-Transgenic Cow Milk Containing Human Antimicrobial Protein, project to test the hypothesis that adding an antimicrobial peptide to powdered milk products can confer protection against enteric diseases. Research will focus on testing the peptide for its ability to kill pathogens in stomach conditions, and on its ability to maintain integrity through the milk pasteurization and drying processes. 2010.

2170-491 University of Virginia, Charlottesville, VA, $14,711,019. To identify why oral poliovirus and rotavirus vaccines are less effective in the developing world, in order to develop new approaches to protect children from enteric diseases. 2010.

2170-492 University of Virginia, Charlottesville, VA, $3,958,587. To improve the ability for field sites to detect enteropathogens by facilitating high quality multiplexed molecular diagnostics through manageable protocols, specifically on direct fecal specimens instead of the existing cumbersome array of culture, microscopy, and ELISA. 2010.

2170-493 University of Washington, Seattle, WA, $1,000,000. To deliver HIV-specific homing endonucleases to latently infected cells, inducing deletions within integrated HIV DNA and rendering the virus harmless. 2010.

2170-494 University of Washington, Seattle, WA, $611,554. To develop Population Health Metrics Research Consortium Project (IHME) providing valid population health metrics for managing interventions. 2010.

2170-495 University of Washington, Seattle, WA, $100,000. To develop and test a streamlined, inexpensive mobile ultrasound device for midwives with limited functionality, a simplified user interface, and a contextual help system. 2010.

2170-496 Vanderbilt University, Nashville, TN, $1,462,929. For study of Respiratory Syncytial Virus (RSV) burden of disease. RSV is a respiratory virus that infects the lungs and breathing passages. Most otherwise healthy people recover from RSV infection in 1 to 2 weeks. However, infection can be severe in some people, such as certain infants, young children, and older adults. 2010.

2170-497 VaxTrac, Chicago, IL, $100,000. To field test a mobile phone-based vaccination registry that uses fingerprint scans to track those who have received immunizations in hopes of reducing redundant doses and boosting coverage levels in developing countries. 2010.

2170-498 Vellore Christian Medical College Board, New York, NY, $92,123. To organize the first advanced course in Vaccinology in India, on the ADVAC model of Vaccinology courses, while aiming to provide a comprehensive overview of Vaccinology, and strengthen the capacity within India in this field. 2010.

2170-499 Veria Central Public Library, Veria, Greece, $1,000,000. For Access to Learning Award (ATLA), which recognizes the innovative efforts of public libraries or similar organizations outside the United States to connect people to information through free access to computers and the Internet. 2010.

2170-500 Vindico NanoBioTechnology, Lexington, KY, $100,000. For Round 4, Phase I of Grand Challenges Explorations-Polymersome-Based Novel Spermicide/Therapeutic Delivery, project to develop a vaginal gel that uses nano-sacs called polymersomes, which can control the delivery of spermicides as a contraceptive and other sexually transmitted agents. 2010.

2170-501 Vital Voices Global Partnership, Washington, DC, $15,000. For general operating support. 2010.

2170-502 Vodacom Tanzania Limited, Dar es Salaam, Tanzania, Zanzibar and Pemba, $4,774,530. To increase awareness and usage of M-PESA ((M for mobile, Pesa is Swahili for money) in Tanzania and reach at least 2 million people in 18 months. M-PESA is a mobile-phone based money transfer service for Safaricom, which is a Vodafone affiliate. 2010.

2170-503 Walter and Eliza Hall Institute of Medical Research, Parkville, Australia, $52,890. To convene international conference and forum for the dissemination and discussion of new research findings into parasites. 2010.

2170-504 Wamax, Bellevue, WA, $100,000. To develop a tooth filler which can be applied by hand into cavities to provide long-lasting anti-viral and anti-bacterial functions. 2010.

2170-505 Washington State University, Pullman, WA, $100,000. For Round 4, Phase I of Grand Challenges Explorations-Long Lasting Male Contraceptive Pill Development. 2010.

2170-506 Washington State University, Pullman, WA, $100,000. To study whether commensal bacteria in human milk is related to maternal consumption of probiotic foods, and whether these microorganisms in breast milk can help prevent infectious diarrhea in infants. 2010.

2170-507 Washington University, Saint Louis, MO, $100,000. To formulate a vaginal gel that contains nanoparticles which serve as decoys to attract both sperm and HIV. 2010.

2170-508 Water for People, Denver, CO, $5,659,264. To catalyze sanitation business models supported by local finance and to demonstrate a sustainable, scalable approach to increasing sustainable sanitation service delivery in three target countries of India, Malawi and Uganda. 2010.

2170-509 White Ribbon Alliance for Safe Motherhood, Washington, DC, $503,365. To improve maternal health worldwide and to contribute to the achievement of MDG5, while mobilizing high-level global and country leadership for greater investments and better policies for maternal, newborn, and child health programs. 2010.

2170-510 William J. Clinton Foundation, Boston, MA, $500,000. For Clinton Global Initiative, annual meeting with goal to turn ideas into action and help the world move beyond current state of globalization to more integrated global community of shared benefits, responsibilities and values. 2010.

2170-511 William J. Clinton Foundation, Boston, MA, $313,145. To convene a conference of scientific experts to review and prioritize opportunities for technical interventions that will lead to reductions in commodity spending for the treatment of HIV/AIDS in emerging markets. 2010.

2170-512 Women in Informal Employment: Globalizing and Organizing, WIEGO, Manchester, England, $3,998,857. To improve the status of the working poor, especially women, in the informal economies of developing world countries. 2010.

2170-513 World Affairs Council, Seattle, WA, $10,000. For general operating support. 2010.

2170-514 World Affairs Council of Northern California, San Francisco, CA, $3,246,774. To build the capacity of the Global Philanthropy Forum to promote, enable and inform funding and co-funding partnerships among high net worth individuals - and between high net worth individuals and institutional donors— in global health and related fields. 2010.

2170-515 World Faiths Development Dialogue International, Washington, DC, $85,120. To enhance the understanding of non-traditional actors, such as faith-inspired organizations, in agricultural development. 2010.

2170-516 World Health Organization, Geneva, Switzerland, $197,957,720. To intensify the Global Polio Eradication Initiative. 2010.

2170-517 World Health Organization, Geneva, Switzerland, $79,827,856. To intensify the Global Polio Eradication Initiative. 2010.

2170-518 World Health Organization, Geneva, Switzerland, $27,042,282. To intensify the Global Polio Eradication Initiative. 2010.

2170-519 World Health Organization, Geneva, Switzerland, $23,500,002. To intensify the Global Polio Eradication Initiative. 2010.

2170-520 World Health Organization, Geneva, Switzerland, $8,100,983. To improve and sustain engagement of Nigeria's most influential traditional and religious leaders in the country's polio eradication and routine immunization efforts, in order to stop transmission of wild polio virus in Nigeria and improve child health indicators. 2010.

2170-521 World Health Organization, Geneva, Switzerland, $4,641,083. To help develop and update guidance in priority nutrition areas, which will identify good practices for delivery. 2010.

2170-522 World Health Organization, Geneva, Switzerland, $3,810,475. To promote evidence-based decision-making to accelerate scale-up of priority Maternal, Newborn, and Child Health (MNCH) interventions and to increase visibility and funding for Maternal, Newborn, and Child Health, which will contribute to the goals of achieving significant reductions in Maternal, Newborn, and Child mortality and morbidity in low-income countries. 2010.

2170-523 World Health Organization, Geneva, Switzerland, $3,499,530. To improve policymaking process at WHO's Malaria Programme. 2010.

2170-524 World Health Organization, Geneva, Switzerland, $3,001,914. For leadership, support, coordination, and oversight for the implementation of the Global Plan for Artemisinin Resistance Containment (GPARC). Document is a companion to the Global report on antimalarial drug efficacy and drug resistance, which provides the extensive evidence on which the GPARC was based. The GPARC sets out a high-level plan of attack to protect Artemisinin-Combination Therapies (ACTs) as an effective treatment for Plasmodium falciparum malaria. 2010.

2170-525 World Health Organization, Geneva, Switzerland, $1,568,578. To help countries take advantage of the increased attention to child health arising out of the Millennium Development Goals and programs such as the USG Global Health Initiative to improve implementation of interventions against pneumonia and diarrhea. 2010.

2170-526 World Health Organization, Geneva, Switzerland, $1,063,641. For conference support for meeting and retreat for New and Under Utilized Vaccine Implementation (NUVI). 2010.

2170-527 World Health Organization, Geneva, Switzerland, $614,901. To strengthen the capacity of WHO to serve endemic countries and malaria control partners with evidence-based norms, standards, policies and guidelines, capacity building of countries and partners, documented success stories and best practices, and malaria-free certification procedures for all countries that are aiming to achieve malaria elimination. 2010.

2170-528 World Health Organization, Geneva, Switzerland, $406,214. For World Health Day, which will aim to raise awareness of the drivers of antimicrobial resistance and to build commitment to common solutions across diseases, through fostering urgent implementation of effective policies and practices. 2010.

2170-529 World Health Organization, Geneva, Switzerland, $347,576. To contribute to a reduction in under five mortality by promoting research and development, access and use of essential medicines for children, particularly for diarrhea and malaria in priority countries in Africa (Ghana and Tanzania) and India. 2010.

2170-530 World Health Organization, Geneva, Switzerland, $344,388. For core support for Roll Back Malaria (RBM) Secretariat in support of work for the Roll Back Malaria Global Partnership. 2010.

2170-531 World Health Organization, Geneva, Switzerland, $280,806. For efficient and effective allocation of resources for tuberculosis (TB) control. 2010.

2170-532 World Health Organization, Geneva, Switzerland, $272,352. For conference on mass administration of antimalarial drugs in the context of containment of artemisinin resistant malaria in South East Asia. 2010.

2170-533 World Health Organization, Geneva, Switzerland, $202,878. To promote and evaluate pilot models of effective, affordable, cost-effective, and financially-sustainable diagnosis through treatment of multidrug-resistant tuberculosis in China. 2010.

2170-534 World Health Organization, Geneva, Switzerland, $197,246. To assess the feasibility of onchocerciasis elimination by ivermectin treatment in Africa, specifically Guinea-Bissau, Mali and Senegal. 2010.

2170-535 World Health Organization, Geneva, Switzerland, $187,525. To advocate for HIV vaccines research and development and facilitate the African AIDS Vaccine Programme's (AAVP) transition to a fully independent operational African programme outside of WHO, led by Africans and effectively connected with the international HIV vaccine community. 2010.

2170-536 World Health Organization, Geneva, Switzerland, $150,000. For conference support for international forum on vaccine research and development issues with leading scientists and representatives of vaccine industry from developed and developing countries. 2010.

2170-537 World Health Organization, Geneva, Switzerland, $120,000. For conference support for meetings regarding the evaluation of pandemic influenza vaccines in clinical trials. 2010.

2170-538 World Health Organization, Geneva, Switzerland, $113,014. To improve policymaking process at WHO's Malaria Programme. 2010.

2170-539 World Health Organization, Geneva, Switzerland, $100,886. To bring together key stakeholders in Myanmar and representatives from neighboring countries with the ultimate aim to adopt a strategic framework to contain Artemisinin resistant parasites in Myanmar in articulation with similar activities implemented on its borders with China (Yunnan province) and Thailand. 2010.

2170-540 World Health Organization, Geneva, Switzerland, $80,569. Toward survey of Neglected Tropical Disease (NTD) community, at the global and country level, to obtain information on the flow of NTD medicines throughout the supply chain, identify problems and hurdles, and identify useful elements for developing strategies that will improve the effectiveness of the NTD medicines supply chain. 2010.

2170-541 World Health Organization, Geneva, Switzerland, $75,000. For TechNet consultations and meetings of the Technologies and Logistics Advisory Panel. 2010.

2170-542 World Health Partners, New Delhi, India, $23,350,000. To establish a state-wide network of private health providers in Bihar, India to improve management of infectious diseases, including diarrhea, pneumonia, tuberculosis and Visceral Leishmaniasis. 2010.

2170-543 World Resources Institute, Washington, DC, $100,000. For joint initiative of World Resources Institute and Rural Development Institute to conduct interactive mapping to strengthen property rights in Ghana, Kenya, Mali, Mozambique, Uganda and Tanzania by providing policymakers in government, donor and development agencies with the information and ideas needed to make well-informed decisions and to take appropriate actions. 2010.

2170-544 World Savings Banks Institute, Brussels, Belgium, $600,000. To double the number of savings accounts held by poor people by identifying viable projects for future funding at major member savings banks. 2010.

2170-545 World University Service of Canada, Ottawa, Canada, $3,995,720. For Farm Radio International in the African Farm Radio Research Initiative to scale-up the adoption of proven technologies to reach smallholder farmers, and ensure the sustainability of radio for agriculture. 2010.

2170-546 World Vision, Federal Way, WA, $8,999,542. To support The CORE Group in their global polio eradication efforts by bridging implementation gaps, improving performance monitoring/management and building capacity. 2010.

2170-547 World Vision, Federal Way, WA, $600,000. For emergency relief response to Typhoon Megi in the Philippines. 2010.

2170-548 World Vision, Federal Way, WA, $100,000. To field test in central Mozambique two mobile phone modules that prompt community health workers caring for pregnant women and newborns to assess, to take action, and to refer care in cases of complications and emergencies as part of Maternal, Neonatal and Child Health (MNCH) care. 2010.

2170-549 Yale University, New Haven, CT, $7,299,052. To expand Microsavings and Payments Innovation Initiative (MPII), developing country research network and conduct more than 20 studies to identify the best financial products for the poor and their economic benefits. 2010.

2170-550 Yale University, New Haven, CT, $2,983,165. To develop humanized mouse models for testing anti-malarial intervention strategies. 2010.

2170-551 Yale University, New Haven, CT, $436,592. To create novel mouse models for testing live attenuated vaccines. 2010.

2170-552 Yale University, New Haven, CT, $100,000. For Round 4, Phase I of Grand Challenges Explorations-Microchips to Assess Multifunctionality of Single T Cells. 2010.

2170-553 Yale University, New Haven, CT, $100,000. To optimize a simple diagnostic urine test that uses the synthetic dye Congo Red to stain misfolded proteins that have been recently found to be excreted in the urine of women either suffering from or at high risk for preeclampsia, to increase treatment and lower rates of maternal deaths. 2010.

2171
Gateway Medical Alliance

10611 Canyon Rd., E PMB 172
Puyallup, WA 98373-4256
URL: http://www.gatewayma.org/

Established in 1997 in WA.
Grantmaker type: Public charity.
Financial data (yr. ended 12/31/10): Revenue, $1,199,578; assets, $226,038 (M); gifts received, $1,198,403; expenditures, $1,192,937; giving

activities include $1,108,517 for 7 grants to organizations outside the U.S.

Purpose and activities: The alliance provides humanitarian medical aid and community development to underprivileged people in Morocco.

Fields of interest: International relief; Community/economic development; Health care; Economically disadvantaged.

International interests: Morocco and the Western Sahara.

Type of support: In-kind gifts.

Limitations: Giving primarily to Morocco.

Officers and Directors: * Michael Spiger,* Pres.; Derald Baskin,* V.P.; David Knight,* Secy.-Treas.; Ray Fricks; Jerry Kind; Scott Kronlund; Steve MacLurg; David Martz; J. Anne Spiger*.

EIN: 911851462

2172
Glaser Progress Foundation
(formerly The Glaser Foundation)
1601 2nd Ave., Ste. 1080
Seattle, WA 98101-3526
Contact: Melessa Rogers, Operations Mgr.
FAX: (206) 728-1123;
E-mail: grants@glaserprogress.org; E-mail for application questions: melessa@glaserprogress.org; URL: http://www.glaserprogress.org

Established in 1993 in WA.

Donor: Robert D. Glaser.

Grantmaker type: Independent foundation.

Financial data (yr. ended 12/31/10). Assets, $13,688,276 (M); expenditures, $2,211,267; qualifying distributions, $1,709,900; giving activities include $1,709,900 for grants.

Purpose and activities: The foundation focuses on four program areas: 1) Measuring Progress: build a more equitable and sustainable world by improving our understanding and measurement of human progress, 2) Animal Advocacy: make animal treatment a crucial consideration in business, policy and personal decision-making, 3) Independent Media: strengthen democracy by making independent voices heard (the foundation has also launched a Progress Education Project which will influence all grant awards in this area), and 4) Global HIV/AIDS: to identify and implement programs that provide support for and fulfillment of the goals of the Global Fund to Fight AIDS, tuberculosis, and malaria.

Fields of interest: Media/communications; Animal welfare; International economic development.

Type of support: General/operating support; Program development; Conferences/seminars; Technical assistance.

Limitations: Applications accepted. Giving on a national basis. No support for political organizations. No grants to individuals.

Publications: Application guidelines; Grants list.

Application information: Guidelines available on foundation web site. Application form not required.
  Initial approach: Letter or e-mail
  Copies of proposal: 1
  Deadline(s): None
  Board meeting date(s): Approx. 6 months after receipt of application letter to staff and board review

Officer: Martin Collier, Exec. Dir.

Trustee: Robert D. Glaser.

Number of staff: 3 full-time professional.

EIN: 911626010

2173
Global Partnerships Foundation
1932 First Ave., Ste. 400
Seattle, WA 98101-2442 (206) 652-8773
FAX: (206) 264-3009;
E-mail: info@globalpartnerships.org; URL: http://www.globalpartnerships.org

Established in 1993 in WA; status changed to a public charity in 2003.

Grantmaker type: Public charity.

Financial data (yr. ended 06/30/10): Revenue, $3,894,039; assets, $5,950,396 (M); gifts received, $1,710,671; expenditures, $12,940,597; giving activities include $9,000,000 for grants to organizations outside the U.S.

Purpose and activities: The foundation supports programs in Latin America that help people overcome poverty, primarily through microfinance funding.

Fields of interest: International development; Community development, business promotion; Economically disadvantaged.

International interests: Latin America.

Type of support: Technical assistance; Program-related investments/loans.

Limitations: Applications not accepted. Giving limited to Latin America. No grants to individuals.

Publications: Annual report; Newsletter.

Application information: Unsolicited requests for funds not accepted or acknowledged.

Officers and Directors: * Bill Clapp, Chair.; Richard J. "Dick" Robbins,* Vice-Chair.; Rick Beckett, Pres. and C.E.O.; Paula Clapp,* Secy.; Tom Waldron,* Treas.; Dean C. Allen; Christopher Alston; Sherilyn Anderson; Sandra O. Archibald; Doug Boyden; Steve Davis; Walter Euyang; Jack Faris; William Foege, M.D.; Mike T. Galgon; Bert Green; Margaret Larson; Virginia Meisenbach; Jose Pinero; Eddie Poplawski; Bob Wright.

EIN: 820574491

2174
Harnish Foundation
17035 W. Valley Hwy.
Tukwila, WA 98188-5519

Established in 2005 in WA.

Donor: Harnish Group, Inc.

Grantmaker type: Company-sponsored foundation.

Financial data (yr. ended 12/31/10): Assets, $10,853,221 (M); gifts received, $5,535,675; expenditures, $729,949; qualifying distributions, $715,000; giving activities include $715,000 for grants.

Fields of interest: Family resources and services, disability; Food services; Housing/shelter, temporary shelter; International economic development.

Limitations: Applications not accepted. No grants to individuals.

Application information: Contributes only to pre-selected organizations.

Officers: John J. Harnish, Pres. and Treas.; Richard C. Bellin, V.P.; Katherine A. Harnish, V.P.; Jennifer C. Harnish, Secy.

EIN: 383730146

2175
Helping and Loving Orphans
2416 2nd Ave. N.
Seattle, WA 98109-2007 (206) 282-7337
E-mail: bettytisdale@aol.com; URL: http://www.bettytisdale.com
Facebook: http://www.facebook.com/pages/HALO-Helping-and-Loving-Orphans-Betty-Tisdale/336965935274

Established in 2000 in WA.

Grantmaker type: Public charity.

Financial data (yr. ended 12/31/10): Revenue, $102,287; assets, $110,587 (M); gifts received, $101,923; expenditures, $88,758; giving activities include $88,500 for grants.

Purpose and activities: The organization is dedicated to bettering the lives of orphans and at-risk children around the world, especially in developing countries, by providing them with the best possible healthcare, education, and training available.

Fields of interest: Children, services; Children/youth, services; Youth development; Children/youth.

International interests: Developing countries.

Type of support: In-kind gifts.

Limitations: Giving primarily in Afghanistan, Colombia, Mexico, Vietnam, and developing countries.

Officers: Cindy McCain, Chair.; Betty Tisdale, Pres.; Thu van DeBellis, V.P.; Trang Hanh, Secy.; Geoff Shelton, Treas.

EIN: 912056117

2176
The Hyder Family Foundation
105 Windsor Dr. S.E.
Sammamish, WA 98074-3420

Established in 2001 in WA.

Donors: Ifrah Hyder; Jameel Hyder.

Grantmaker type: Independent foundation.

Financial data (yr. ended 12/31/10): Assets, $1,184,068 (M); gifts received, $275,000; expenditures, $375,135; qualifying distributions, $373,350; giving activities include $373,350 for 13 grants (high: $170,000; low: $350).

Purpose and activities: Giving primarily for Islamic education and communities.

Fields of interest: Education; International relief; Islam.

International interests: England; India.

Limitations: Applications not accepted. Giving primarily in Seattle, WA; giving also in London, England, and Hyderabad, India.

Application information: Contributes only to pre-selected organizations.

Directors: Ifrah Hyder; Jameel Hyder; Rizwan Hyder.

EIN: 912159711

2177
International Children's Care, Inc.
2711 N.E. 134th Way
Vancouver, WA 98686-2796 (360) 573-0429
FAX: (360) 573-0491; E-mail: info@forhiskids.org; Mailing address: P.O. Box 820610, Vancouver, WA 98682-0013; toll-free tel.: (800) 422-7729; URL: http://www.forhiskids.org

Established in 1977 in WA.

Grantmaker type: Public charity.
Financial data (yr. ended 12/31/10): Revenue, $3,963,469; assets, $924,029 (M); gifts received, $3,970,118; expenditures, $4,015,586; giving activities include $2,622,662 for 7 grants to organizations outside the U.S.
Purpose and activities: The organization works to enhance life-preparation for orphaned and vulnerable children in developing countries.
Fields of interest: Children/youth, services.
International interests: Developing countries.
Limitations: Applications not accepted. Giving primarily on an international basis, with emphasis on Asia, Asia Pacific, Europe, and Latin America.
Publications: Informational brochure; Newsletter.
Application information: Unsolicited requests for funds not accepted.
Officers and Board Members:* Paul Edgren,* Chair.; Richard G. Fleck, Pres. and C.E.O.; Marilyn Patchin,* Secy.-Treas.; Lutz Binus; Janet Edgren; Cody Erwin; Renee Erwin; Don Folkenberg; Robert Folkenberg; Magda Triantos; Leon Wellington; Norm Woods.
EIN: 930717332

2178
Islands Fund
c/o John Munn
6523 California Ave., S.W., Ste. 137
Seattle, WA 98136-1833
Contact: Sarah R. Werner, Dir.

Established in 1995.
Grantmaker type: Independent foundation.
Financial data (yr. ended 12/31/10): Assets, $106,268,066 (M); gifts received, $8,000,000; expenditures, $4,577,263; qualifying distributions, $4,215,572; giving activities include $4,200,000 for 64 grants (high: $490,000; low: $5,000; average: $25,000–$100,000).
Purpose and activities: Giving primarily for conservation and the environment.
Fields of interest: Education; Environment, natural resources; Children/youth, services.
Limitations: Applications not accepted. Giving primarily in VA, WA, WV and Canada. No grants to individuals.
Application information: Contributes only to pre-selected organizations.
Directors: James Flaggert; E. Leeds Gulick; George G. Gulick; Rick S. Werner; Sarah R. Werner.
EIN: 911663838
Recent grants for international programs:
2178-1 Conservation International, Arlington, VA, $60,000. 2010.
2178-2 Ecotrust Canada, Vancouver, Canada, $54,500. 2010.
2178-3 Future Generations, Franklin, WV, $490,000. 2010.
2178-4 New Summit Academy, Atenas, Costa Rica, $25,000. 2010.

2179
The Henry M. Jackson Foundation
1501 4th Ave., Ste. 1580
Seattle, WA 98101-1653 (206) 682-8565
Contact: Lara Iglitzin, Exec. Dir.
FAX: (206) 682-8961;
E-mail: foundation@hmjackson.org; URL: http://www.hmjackson.org

Established in 1983 in DC.
Grantmaker type: Public charity.
Financial data (yr. ended 09/30/10): Revenue, $162,493; assets, $3,003,527 (M); gifts received, $21,050; expenditures, $408,274; giving activities include $31,685 for grants.
Purpose and activities: Through its grantmaking and strategic initiatives, the foundation seeks to make a lasting impact in the areas of international affairs education, human rights, environment and natural resources management, and public service, and to perpetuate the legacy of Senator Henry M. Jackson for the benefit of future generations.
Fields of interest: Civil/human rights, advocacy; Environment, natural resources; Environment; International affairs, research.
Type of support: Program development; Conferences/seminars; Professorships; Publication; Fellowships; Internship funds; Scholarship funds; Research; Matching/challenge support.
Limitations: Applications accepted. Giving primarily in WA. No support for political campaigns or efforts to influence legislation other than making available results of nonpartisan analysis and research. No grants to individuals, or for unrestricted operating expenses, operating deficits, or capital expenditures, except in rare circumstances.
Publications: Application guidelines; Annual report; Financial statement; Grants list; Informational brochure; Newsletter.
Application information: Application form not required.
    Initial approach: Submit application
    Copies of proposal: 1
    Deadline(s): Nov. 9 for Sterling and Gene Munro Public Service Fellowship; Dec. 4 for Sterling Munro Public Service Teaching Award
    Board meeting date(s): Annually
Officers and Governors:* Helen Hardin Jackson,* Chair.; William J. Van Ness, Jr.,* Pres.; John W. Hempelmann,* V.P.; Anna Marie Laurence, Secy.; Keith D. Grinstein,* Treas.; Lara Iglitzin, Exec. Dir.; Joel C. Merkel, Genl. Counsel; Julia P. Cancio; Thomas C. Dickson; Manny Weiss; and 19 additional governors.
Number of staff: 5
EIN: 521313011

2180
The Jernigan Foundation
343 Westhampton Ln. S.W.
Olympia, WA 98512-9475 (360) 455-0077
Contact: Tanya S. Jernigan, V.P.

Established in 2006 in WA.
Donors: Theodore E. Jernigan; Tanya S. Jernigan.
Grantmaker type: Independent foundation.
Financial data (yr. ended 06/30/10): Assets, $173,429 (M); gifts received, $150,750; expenditures, $170,009; qualifying distributions, $146,263; giving activities include $146,263 for 10 grants (high: $115,000; low: $500).
Fields of interest: Performing arts, orchestras; Pregnancy centers; Youth development; Boys & girls clubs; International human rights; United Ways and Federated Giving Programs; Christian agencies & churches.
Type of support: General/operating support; Scholarship funds.
Limitations: Applications accepted. Giving primarily in WA. No grants to individuals.

Application information: Application form not required.
    Initial approach: Proposal
    Deadline(s): None
Officers: Theodore E. Jernigan, Pres.; Tanya S. Jernigan, V.P. and Secy.-Treas.
EIN: 208111798

2181
The Kaphan Foundation
c/o King & Oliason, P.S.
514 2nd Ave. W.
Seattle, WA 98119-3928

Established in 2003 in WA.
Donor: Sheldon J. Kaphan.
Grantmaker type: Independent foundation.
Financial data (yr. ended 12/31/10): Assets, $32,440,629 (M); gifts received, $2,090,823; expenditures, $1,085,548; qualifying distributions, $842,500; giving activities include $842,500 for grants.
Fields of interest: Foundations (private grantmaking); Arts; Medical research; Human services; Children/youth, services; International development; Civil/human rights.
Limitations: Applications not accepted. Giving in the U.S., with some emphasis in AZ, CA, Washington DC, MA, MO, NY and WA. No grants to individuals.
Application information: Contributes only to pre-selected organizations.
Officers: Sheldon J. Kaphan, Pres., V.P. and Treas.; Matthew B. McCutchen, Secy.
EIN: 651211107

2182
Khaki Foundation
901 197th Ave. S.E.
Sammamish, WA 98075-8610

Established in 2003 in WA.
Donors: Kanize Fatima Khaki; Mohamed Jawad Khaki.
Grantmaker type: Independent foundation.
Financial data (yr. ended 12/31/10): Assets, $5,752,207 (M); gifts received, $207,505; expenditures, $454,480; qualifying distributions, $376,401; giving activities include $376,401 for grants.
Fields of interest: Education; Housing/shelter; Children/youth, services; International relief; Community/economic development; Islam; Economically disadvantaged.
Limitations: Applications not accepted. Giving primarily on an international basis; some giving in MN. No grants to individuals.
Application information: Contributes only to pre-selected organizations.
Officers and Directors:* Mohamed Jawad Khaki,* Pres. and Treas.; Kanize Fatima Khaki,* V.P. and Secy.; Ali Raza Khaki; Asiya Khaki; Ateqah Khaki.
EIN: 200461805

2183
Kongsgaard-Goldman Foundation
1932 1st Ave., Ste. 602
Seattle, WA 98101-2447 (206) 448-1874
Contact: Martha Kongsgaard, Pres.

FAX: (206) 448-1973;
E-mail: kgf@kongsgaard-goldman.org; URL: http://www.kongsgaard-goldman.org

Established in 1988 in WA.
Donors: Peter Goldman; Martha Kongsgaard; Ross Goldman.
Grantmaker type: Independent foundation.
Financial data (yr. ended 12/31/10): Assets, $263,408 (M); gifts received, $920,017; expenditures, $678,215; qualifying distributions, $674,816; giving activities include $631,293 for 50 grants (high: $60,000; low: $1,000).
Purpose and activities: Giving primarily for Puget Sound restoration and protection, including public policy, citizen involvement, education, restoration, sustainable land use and environmental justice. Grants in this area are awarded for both general operating expenses and special projects. Funding also is for forest protection in WA and OR, including conservation, policy, sustainable land use; and for climate change initiatives aimed at addressing climate change challenges in Washington State.
Fields of interest: Environment, land resources; Education; Environment.
International interests: Canada.
Type of support: General/operating support; Continuing support; Annual campaigns; Equipment; Land acquisition; Emergency funds; Program development; Conferences/seminars; Seed money; Technical assistance; Matching/challenge support.
Limitations: Giving limited to AK, ID, MT, OR, and WA, with emphasis on Seattle; giving also in British Columbia, Canada. No support for institutions of higher learning, medical institutions, or for wildlife rehabilitation programs. No grants to individuals, or for scholarships, fellowships, medical research or general animal welfare; no direct services in the human services sector, or for land acquisition.
Publications: Grants list; Informational brochure (including application guidelines).
Application information: Accepts Philanthropy Northwest Common Grant Application Form; eligible organizations will be invited to send a full proposal; foundation does not accept faxed letters of intent or full proposals; discourages the use of folders, plastic binders and videos, but encourages the use of recycled paper, double sided paper and re-used envelopes. Refer to foundation web site for application guidelines. Application form not required.
  Initial approach: Letter of intent
  Copies of proposal: 1
  Deadline(s): Letter of intent due Mar. 16 and Sept. 16; full proposal Apr. 30 and Oct. 31
  Board meeting date(s): Contributions made in Feb. and Aug.
  Final notification: Feb. and Aug.
Officers and Directors:* Martha Kongsgaard,* Pres.; Peter Goldman,* V.P. and Secy.-Treas.
Number of staff: 1 full-time professional.
EIN: 943088217

2184
Luke 12:48 Foundation
c/o Heather Tuininga, Exec. Dir.
333 108th Ave., N.E., Ste. 2010
Bellevue, WA 98004-5777 (425) 974-3755
E-mail: heather@luke1248.org; URL: http://www.luke1248.org

Established in 2007 in WA.
Grantmaker type: Independent foundation.

Financial data (yr. ended 12/31/10): Assets, $1,573,222 (M); gifts received, $500,000; expenditures, $2,082,611; qualifying distributions, $1,759,223; giving activities include $1,759,223 for grants.
Purpose and activities: The vision of the foundation is to serve as witness to the realness of Jesus and His relentless, transforming love by supporting organizations that: 1) make fishers of men, 2) transform communities, 3) promote justice and 4) care for the least of these.
Fields of interest: Community/economic development; Human services; Children/youth, services; Christian agencies & churches.
International interests: Uganda.
Limitations: Applications not accepted. Giving primarily in the Pacific Northwest and Uganda, Africa.
Publications: Grants list.
Application information: Contributes only to pre-selected organizations.
  Board meeting date(s): Quarterly
Officers: Marybeth Johnston, Pres. and Treas.; J. Michael Johnston, V.P. and Secy.; Heather Tuininga, Exec. Dir.
Number of staff: 2 full-time professional.
EIN: 261110518

2185
McKinstry Company Charitable Foundation
P.O. Box 24567
Seattle, WA 98124-0567
Contact: J. William Teplicky, Tr.
URL: http://www.mckinstry.com/about/giving

Established in 1998 in WA.
Donors: McKinstry Co.; Dean Allen; Earl Davie; Anita Davie; George Allen.
Grantmaker type: Company-sponsored foundation.
Financial data (yr. ended 09/30/10): Assets, $11,825 (M); gifts received, $747,500; expenditures, $763,570; qualifying distributions, $763,570; giving activities include $760,350 for 425 grants (high: $100,250; low: $250).
Purpose and activities: The foundation supports arts museums and organizations involved with education, global health, medical research, human services, international development, and microfinance.
Fields of interest: Museums (art); Higher education; Education; Hospitals (general); Health care, clinics/centers; Health care; Diabetes research; Biomedicine research; Medical research; Boys & girls clubs; Boy scouts; YM/YWCAs & YM/YWHAs; Children/youth, services; Developmentally disabled, centers & services; Human services; International development; Microfinance/microlending; Economically disadvantaged.
Type of support: General/operating support; Annual campaigns; Program development; Scholarship funds.
Limitations: Applications not accepted. Giving primarily in Seattle, WA. No grants to individuals.
Application information: Contributes only to pre-selected organizations.
Trustees: Dean C. Allen; Vicki Allen; J. William Teplicky, Jr.
EIN: 911942024

2186
Mona Foundation
218 Main St., Ste. 404
Kirkland, WA 98033-6108 (425) 743-4550
Contact: Mahnaz A. Javid Ed.D., Pres.
E-mail: monafoundation@monafoundation.org;
URL: http://www.monafoundation.org
Grants List: http://www.monafoundation.org/grants-scholarships.htm

Established in 1999 in WA; status changed to a public charity in 2002.
Donors: Mahnaz Javid; Patrece Banks.
Grantmaker type: Public charity.
Financial data (yr. ended 12/31/10): Revenue, $1,193,568; assets, $755,593 (M); gifts received, $1,200,237; expenditures, $1,031,105; giving activities include $30,500 for grants, and $744,710 for grants to organizations outside the U.S.
Purpose and activities: The foundation is dedicated to supporting grassroots educational initiatives, and raising the status of women and girls in the U.S. and abroad.
Fields of interest: Education; Girls; Women.
International interests: Honduras; Panama.
Type of support: Technical assistance; Scholarship funds; Program development; General/operating support.
Limitations: Giving on a national and international basis. No grants to individuals.
Publications: Annual report; Newsletter.
Application information:
  Board meeting date(s): Jan. and June
Officers and Directors:* Mahnaz Aflatooni Javid,* Ed.D., Pres.; Sima Mobini,* Secy.; Rita Azizi Egrari,* Ph.D., Treas.; Duy-Loan Le; Diane Marie Samandi; Stephen Waite, Ed.D.
Number of staff: 2 full-time professional; 1 part-time professional.
EIN: 911968512

2187
Neukom Family Foundation
99 Union St., Ste. 1703
Seattle, WA 98101-5004

Established in 1998 in WA.
Donor: William H. Neukom.
Grantmaker type: Independent foundation.
Financial data (yr. ended 03/31/10): Assets, $53,560,784 (M); expenditures, $4,419,385; qualifying distributions, $3,005,374; giving activities include $3,005,374 for 12+ grants (high: $500,000).
Fields of interest: Civil/human rights, women; United Ways and Federated Giving Programs; Higher education; Education; Environment; Human services; Family services; International development.
Limitations: Applications not accepted. Giving primarily in NY and WA. No grants to individuals.
Application information: Contributes only to pre-selected organizations.
Directors: Gillian Neukom; John McMakin Neukom; Josselyn Neukom; Samantha Neukom; William H. Neukom.
EIN: 911737888

2188
Northwest Danish Foundation
(also known as Northwest Danish Association)
1833 N. 105th St., Ste. 101
Seattle, WA 98133-8973   (206) 523-3263
FAX: (206) 729-6997;
E-mail: seattle@nwdanish.org; Toll-free tel. (Seattle office): (800) 564-7736; additional address (Portland office): 4330 N.E. 37th Ave., Portland, OR 97211-8208; URL: http://www.northwestdanishfoundation.org

Established in 1923 in WA.
Grantmaker type: Public charity.
Financial data (yr. ended 06/30/11): Revenue, $99,233; assets, $1,683,562 (M); gifts received, $54,396; expenditures, $140,331; giving activities include $500 for grants to individuals.
Purpose and activities: The association works to enrich community life experience through cultural exchange and social outreach in the areas of contemporary issues, arts, education, families, and seniors.
Fields of interest: Arts, cultural/ethnic awareness; Education; Human services.
International interests: Denmark.
Type of support: Grants to individuals; Scholarships—to individuals.
Limitations: Applications accepted. Giving limited to residents of OR and WA.
Publications: Application guidelines; Annual report; Newsletter.
Application information: Application form required.
  Initial approach: Letter, telephone, or e-mail
  Deadline(s): Mar. 31 for The Kaj Christiansen Scholarship for Vocational Training and scan/design Foundation by Inger and Jens Bruun Scholarship
  Board meeting date(s): Apr.
  Final notification: Early May
Officers and Board Members: Edith E. Christensen,* EdD, Pres.; Erik Laursen,* V.P.; Sonja Kroman,* Secy.; Kenneth Kroman,* Treas.; Ole Brahe-Pedersen*; Jette Bunch; Britt Pfaff Dunton; Gary Korsgaard; Sonja Kroman; Jens Laundrup; Joseph Matsen; Bodil Muller; Betty Ravenholt; Carla Parks Schultz; Larry West*.
Number of staff: 1 full-time professional; 2 part-time professional; 2 part-time support.
EIN: 910565541

2189
Pangea: Giving for Global Change
(formerly World Venture Partners)
P.O. Box 46653
Seattle, WA 98146-0653
E-mail: info1@pangeagiving.org; URL: http://www.pangeagiving.org

Established in 2003 in WA.
Grantmaker type: Public charity.
Financial data (yr. ended 12/31/10): Revenue, $138,286; assets, $136,266 (M); gifts received, $129,707; expenditures, $24,797; giving activities include $11,324 for grants.
Purpose and activities: The giving circle is dedicated to increasing the philanthropic resources flowing to international projects that help people in economically disadvantaged countries lead healthy, productive lives, and to inform its members and others about global problems and about the process of effective grant making through travel opportunities.
Fields of interest: International economic development; International affairs; Economically disadvantaged.
Limitations: Giving on an international basis, with emphasis on Latin America and sub-Saharan Africa.
Officers and Board Members: Allan Paulson, Pres.; Sydney Munger, V.P.; Linda Mason, Secy.; Duane Edwards, Treas.; Walt Adams; Christine Doerr; Dee Endelman.
EIN: 342060541

2190
Pura Vida Partners
3517 Stone Way N.
Seattle, WA 98103-8923
E-mail: info@puravidacoffee.org
Facebook: http://www.facebook.com/puravidacreategood
Twitter: http://twitter.com/#!/pvcreategood
YouTube: http://www.youtube.com/user/puravidacoffee

Established in 1998 in WA.
Donor: Stewardship Foundation.
Grantmaker type: Public charity.
Financial data (yr. ended 12/31/10): Revenue, $256,668; assets, $178,767 (M); gifts received, $256,668; expenditures, $237,817; giving activities include $142,416 for grants to organizations outside the U.S.
Purpose and activities: The organization is committed to creating good in the lives of poor people who live and work in coffee-growing communities around the world.
Fields of interest: Health care; Community/economic development; Children/youth, services; International development.
Limitations: Applications not accepted. Giving primarily to Costa Rica, Ethiopia, Guatemala, Nicaragua, and Peru. No grants to individuals.
Application information: Contributes only to pre-selected organizations.
Officers: John Sage, Chair.; Ken Kierstead, Secy.; Jeff Hussey, Treas.; Samuel Snyder, Exec. Dir.
EIN: 912032119

2191
RealNetworks Foundation
c/o RealNetworks, Inc.
2601 Elliot Ave.
Seattle, WA 98121-1399   (866) 545-9205
E-mail: RealGrants@easymatch.com; URL: http://www.realnetworks.com/realnetworks-foundation/

Established in 2000 in WA.
Donor: RealNetworks, Inc.
Grantmaker type: Company-sponsored foundation.
Financial data (yr. ended 12/31/10): Assets, $18,276,688 (M); expenditures, $1,820,952; qualifying distributions, $1,816,236; giving activities include $1,140,745 for 110 grants (high: $50,000; low: $500), and $450,257 for employee matching gifts.
Purpose and activities: The foundation supports programs designed to enhance the quality of life in areas of company operations; and enable alternative voices or foster the right of free speech throughout the world.
Fields of interest: Arts; Civil liberties, first amendment; Community/economic development; Electronic communications/Internet; Family services; Health care; Human services; Economically disadvantaged.
International interests: Czech Republic; France; United Kingdom.
Type of support: Employee matching gifts.
Limitations: Applications not accepted. Giving primarily in areas of company operations for Community Enhance Grants, with emphasis on San Jose, CA (San Francisco Bay Area), New York, NY, Reston, VA (Metro D.C.), and Seattle, WA (Puget Sound Region); also national and international giving for Freedom of Expression & Independent Media Grants. No support for religious or membership-based organizations unless the program is open to the public without regard to affiliation, discriminatory organizations, organizations designated under Section 509 of the U.S. Internal Revenue Service code, individual, K-12 schools, youth groups, clubs, teams, choirs, bands, or PTSA. No grants to individuals. or for capital campaigns, general operating funds, endowments, or event or conference sponsorships.
Publications: Grants list.
Application information: Contributes only to pre-selected organizations.
Officers: Robert Glaser, Pres.; Sid Ferrales, V.P.
EIN: 912033075

2192
Red Lion Hotels Corporation Contributions Program
(formerly WestCoast Hospitality Corporation Contributions Program)
201 W. North River Dr., Ste. 100
Spokane, WA 99201-2262   (509) 459-6100
FAX: (509) 325-7324;
E-mail: teamred@redlion.com; URL: http://redlion.rdln.com/Corporate/AboutTeamRed.aspx

Grantmaker type: Corporate giving program.
Purpose and activities: Red Lion makes charitable contributions to organizations involved with animal welfare. Support is given primarily in areas of company operations in Alaska, California, Colorado, Idaho, Montana, Nevada, Oregon, and Utah, with emphasis on Spokane, Washington, and in Canada.
Fields of interest: Animal welfare.
International interests: Canada.
Type of support: General/operating support; Employee volunteer services.
Limitations: Giving primarily in areas of company operations in AK, CA, CO, ID, MT, NV, OR, and UT, with emphasis on Spokane, WA, and in Canada; giving also to national organizations.

2193
RHEMA Ministry
P.O. Box 31651
Seattle, WA 98103-1651   (206) 525-9252

Status changed to a public charity in 2002.
Grantmaker type: Public charity.
Financial data (yr. ended 12/31/10): Revenue, $977,923; assets, $2,719,683 (M); gifts received, $968,999; expenditures, $1,336,201; giving activities include $465,030 for grants to organizations outside the U.S.
Purpose and activities: The organization supports religious books, booklets, and magazines distribution in the former USSR.
Fields of interest: Christian agencies & churches.

International interests: Soviet Union (Former).
Limitations: Giving primarily in Seattle, WA.
Officers: Joel W. Kennon, Pres.; John Brooks, V.P.;
Richard C.T. Li, Secy.; Phil Neher, Treas.
Director: Tim Graver.
EIN: 911183911

2194
RISA Charitable Trust
(formerly Kearsarge Institute)
9120 173rd Ave. S.E.
Snohomish, WA   98290-4105   (774) 276-0202
Contact: Elena Pullen-Venema, Exec. Dir.

Grantmaker type: Public charity.
Financial data (yr. ended 06/30/08): Revenue,
$46,827; assets, $31,143 (M); gifts received,
$35,869; expenditures, $16,432; program services
expenses, $11,368; giving activities include
$4,940 for grants, and $6,428 for
foundation-administered programs.
Purpose and activities: The trust provides capacity
building grants to small businesses that are creating
jobs and economic empowerment in South Africa's
poorest communities.
International interests: South Africa.
Type of support: Management development/
capacity building.
Limitations: Giving in the U.S. and South Africa. No
grants to individuals.
Officer: Elena Pullen-Venema, Exec. Dir.
EIN: 232699699

2195
The Russell Family Foundation
P.O. Box 2567
Gig Harbor, WA   98335-4567   (253) 858-5050
Contact: Linsey Sauer, Grants Mgr.
FAX: (253) 851-0460; E-mail: info@trff.org; Toll Free
tel.: (888) 252-4331; URL: http://trff.org/
default.aspx
Grants Database: http://www.trff.org/
grants_search.aspx

Established in 1994 in WA.
Donors: George F. Russell, Jr.; Jane T. Russell†.
Grantmaker type: Independent foundation.
Financial data (yr. ended 12/31/09): Assets,
$130,939,740 (M); expenditures, $8,787,225;
qualifying distributions, $7,621,808; giving
activities include $5,635,162 for 109 grants (high:
$1,000,000; low: $500; average: $5,000–
$100,000), $255,135 for 10 grants to individuals
(high: $11,500; low: $10,000), $9,550 for 20
employee matching gifts, and $250,000 for 1 loan/
program-related investment.
Purpose and activities: The foundation invests in
resources and relationships in grassroots leaders,
environmental sustainability and global peace.
Fields of interest: Environment.
Type of support: Mission-related investments/
loans; General/operating support; Program
development; Fellowships; Program-related
investments/loans; Employee matching gifts;
Grants to individuals.
Limitations: Applications accepted. Giving primarily
in the Puget Sound region of WA. No support for
lobbying, city or county government programs, work
on water quantity or water rights, watershed
planning, or corporate development of new products
or services, energy-related programs or for land use

planning. No grants for capital construction or
purchases of land.
Publications: Application guidelines; Financial
statement; Newsletter.
Application information: Full proposals are
accepted by invitation only. Application form
required.
  Initial approach: Online letter of inquiry
  Copies of proposal: 1
  Deadline(s): See foundation website for current
  deadlines
  Board meeting date(s): Quarterly; grants awarded
  in May and Nov/Dec.
  Final notification: Following board meeting
Officers: Richard Woo, C.E.O.; Phyllis Gill, Pres.;
Dion Rurik, Secy.; Tim Cavanaugh, Treas.
Directors: Sarah Cavanaugh; Hubert Locke; George
F. Russell, Jr.; Jileen Russell; Richard Russell.
Number of staff: 5 full-time professional; 1 part-time
professional.
EIN: 911663336
Recent grants for international programs:
2195-1 Coast Watch Society, Whale Trail,
  Bellingham, WA, $50,000. For project support.
  2010.
2195-2 Discovery Institute, Seattle, WA, $50,000.
  For Real Russia Project. 2010.
2195-3 EastWest Institute, New York, NY,
  $2,150,000. For general operating support.
  2010.
2195-4 EastWest Institute, New York, NY,
  $200,000. For general operating support. 2010.
2195-5 National Bureau of Asian Research, Seattle,
  WA, $1,000,000. For general operating support.
  2010.
2195-6 National Bureau of Asian Research, Seattle,
  WA, $100,000. For John M. Shalikashvili Chair in
  National Security Studies. 2010.
2195-7 National Bureau of Asian Research, Seattle,
  WA, $100,000. For Kenneth B. Pyle Center for
  Northeast Asia Studies. 2010.

2196
Samis Foundation
208 James St., Ste. C
Seattle, WA   98104-2220   (206) 622-3363
Contact: Eddie I. Hasson, Co-Chair.
FAX: (206) 622-4918; E-mail: samis@samis.com;
URL: http://www.samis.com/foundation/
index.html

Established in 1979.
Donor: Samuel Israel.
Grantmaker type: Independent foundation.
Financial data (yr. ended 12/31/10): Assets,
$118,747,565 (M); expenditures, $9,338,507;
qualifying distributions, $4,657,200; giving
activities include $4,202,594 for 20 grants (high:
$948,371; low: $1,000).
Purpose and activities: Giving primarily for Jewish
day schools, Jewish overnight camps and Israel
experiences for students in WA, with a focus on
grades K-12.
Fields of interest: Education; Jewish agencies &
synagogues; Religion.
International interests: Israel.
Type of support: General/operating support;
Continuing support; Building/renovation; Emergency
funds; Program development; Publication; Seed
money; Scholarship funds; Research; Technical
assistance; Exchange programs; Matching/
challenge support.

Limitations: Applications not accepted. Giving
limited to WA and Israel. No grants to individuals.
Publications: Grants list.
Application information: Contributes only to
pre-selected organizations.
  Board meeting date(s): Quarterly
Officers and Directors:* Eddie I. Hasson,* Co-Chair.
and Pres.; Albert S. Maimon,* Co-Chair. and V.P.;
Irwin L. Treiger,* Secy.; Morris Piha, Tr. Emeritus;
Victor D. Alhadeff; Eli J. Almo; David Azose; Jerome
O. Cohen; Barry D. Ernstoff; David Friedenberg; Eli
Genauer; Rabbi William Greenberg; Mike Israel; Lucy
Pruzan; Martin Selig; Ernest Sherman; Alex Sytman.
Number of staff: 2 full-time professional; 1 part-time
professional; 1 full-time support.
EIN: 911641746

2197
Scan Design By Inge & Jens Bruun
Foundation
800 5th Ave., Ste. 4000
Seattle, WA   98104-3180
E-mail: Mary.DeLorme@scandesignfoundation.org;
Additional U.S. e-mail:
admin.us@scandesignfoundation.org;Danish
contact: Kurt Andersson, Grants and Opers. Mgr.,
Kornmodvaenget 29, DK 5210 Odense Nv; e-mails:
kurt.andersson@scandesignfoundation.org or
admin.dk@scandesignfoundation.org; URL: http://
www.scandesignfoundation.org

Established in 2003 in WA.
Donor: Jens C. Bruun†.
Grantmaker type: Independent foundation.
Financial data (yr. ended 12/31/10): Assets,
$42,365,848 (M); expenditures, $2,720,572;
qualifying distributions, $1,707,033; giving
activities include $1,707,033 for grants.
Purpose and activities: Giving primarily to promote
Danish-American relations; giving also for medical
research, particularly pain research, as well as for
education; including the funding of student
exchange programs between U.S. and Danish
Universities, as well as programs which send U.S.
students and professors to Denmark to engage in a
specialized study curriculum at a Danish University.
Fields of interest: Higher education; Medical
research; International affairs, goodwill promotion;
International affairs.
Limitations: Applications not accepted. Giving
primarily in Seattle, WA. No grants to individuals.
Publications: Grants list.
Application information: Contributes only to
pre-selected organizations.
Officers and Directors:* Mark T. Schleck,* Pres.;
Robert Thompson,* Secy.-Treas.; Rob Harris; Tage
Kristensen.
EIN: 680537904

2198
Schuler Family Foundation
(formerly Force Schuler Family Foundation)
P.O. Box 2438
Seattle, WA   98111-2438

Established in 2002 in WA.
Donor: Jean A. Schuler.
Grantmaker type: Independent foundation.
Financial data (yr. ended 12/31/10): Assets,
$5,386,953 (M); expenditures, $269,185;

qualifying distributions, $254,175; giving activities include $254,175 for grants.

Fields of interest: International development; Higher education; Hospitals (general); Housing/shelter, development; Human services; Child development, services; Family services; Family services, domestic violence; Women, centers/services.

Limitations: Applications not accepted. Giving primarily in AR, CA and WA. No grants to individuals.

Application information: Contributes only to pre-selected organizations.

Trustees: Jean A. Schuler; Keith R. Vernon.

EIN: 916557029

2199

The Seattle Foundation

1200 5th Ave., Ste. 1300
Seattle, WA 98101-3151 (206) 622-2294
Contact: Ceil Erickson, Dir., Grantmaking
FAX: (206) 622-7673;
E-mail: info@seattlefoundation.org; Grant application e-mail: grantmaking@seattlefoundation.org; URL: http://www.seattlefoundation.org
Facebook: http://www.facebook.com/TheSeattleFoundation
Giving Center: http://www.seattlefoundation.org/givingcenter/Pages/default.aspx
Grants List: http://www.seattlefoundation.org/nonprofits/grantmaking/Pages/RecentGrants.aspx
Twitter: http://twitter.com/TheSeattleFdn/

Incorporated in 1946 in WA.

Grantmaker type: Community foundation.

Financial data (yr. ended 12/31/10): Assets, $663,201,900 (M); gifts received, $64,883,181; expenditures, $62,314,757; giving activities include $52,117,881 for grants.

Purpose and activities: The foundation is creating a healthy community through engaged philanthropy, community knowledge, and leadership.

Fields of interest: Media, radio; Media, film/video; Recreation, parks/playgrounds; Medical research; Education, reading; Agriculture/food; Visual arts; Performing arts, dance; Performing arts, music; Humanities; Literature; Historic preservation/historical societies; Arts; Education, early childhood education; Adult/continuing education; Education, ESL programs; Libraries (public); Education, Environment, public education; Environment, air pollution; Environment, water pollution; Environment; Animals/wildlife; Health care; Mental health/crisis services; Health organizations, association; Housing/shelter; Recreation; Youth development; Children/youth, services; Homeless, human services; Human services; Economic development; Community development, small businesses; Community/economic development; Public affairs.

Type of support: Mission-related investments/loans; General/operating support; Capital campaigns; Building/renovation; Equipment.

Limitations: Applications accepted. Giving limited to King County, WA. No support for religious purposes. No grants for endowment funds, debt reduction, fundraising events, fundraising feasibility projects, conferences or seminars, film or video production, publications, first year organizations, or operating expenses for public or private elementary and secondary schools, colleges, and universities.

Publications: Application guidelines; Annual report; Financial statement; Grants list; Informational brochure; Newsletter; Program policy statement.

Application information: Visit foundation web site for application form and guidelines. Application form required.

  Initial approach: Telephone or e-mail
  Copies of proposal: 1
  Deadline(s): Varies
  Board meeting date(s): Mar., June, Sept., and Dec.
  Final notification: Approx. 8 months

Officers and Trustees:* Margaret Walker,* Chair.; Martha Choe,* 1st Vice-Chair.; Bradford L. Smith,* 2nd Vice-Chair.; Norman Rice,* C.E.O. and Pres.; Jared Watson, Sr. V.P., Grantmaking and Community Leadership; Michael Brown, V.P., Community Leadership; Bill Sperling, V.P, Foundation Affairs; Susan G. Duffy,* Secy.; Jeffrey Rudd, C.F.O.; Pete Shimer,* Treas.; Kareen Holmquist, Cont. and Dir., Finance; Libby Armintrout; Nathaniel T. "Buster" Brown; Kevin Daniels; Steve Davis; Jean Enersen; Joe Gaffney; Mark Gibson; Linda Park, Ph.D.; Mary Pugh; John Stanton; Kevin Washington; Robert A. Watt; Jan Whitsitt; James Williams; Tay Yoshitani; Grace T. Yuan.

Number of staff: 17 full-time professional; 1 part-time professional; 8 full-time support; 1 part-time support.

EIN: 916013536

Recent grants for international programs:

2199-1 Action International Ministries, Mountlake Terrace, WA, $50,000. To work in Cuba, Mexico and to provide general support. 2010.

2199-2 Action International Ministries, Mountlake Terrace, WA, $20,000. For general support. 2010.

2199-3 ActionAid USA, Washington, DC, $25,000. For emergency relief and humanitarian assistance to families living in shelters and/or displaced in Guatemala due to Storm Agatha. 2010.

2199-4 ActionAid USA, Washington, DC, $25,000. For emergency relief and humanitarian assistance to families living in shelters and/or displaced in Guatemala due to Storm Agatha. 2010.

2199-5 Agros International, Seattle, WA, $12,500. For expansion of coffee and vegetable programs to include communities adjacent to Agros villages Cotzal and Nebaj, Guatemala and partner in income-generating projects and women's community banking program. 2010.

2199-6 Alaska Wilderness League, Washington, DC, $75,000. For December Arctic event. 2010.

2199-7 Alliance for Tompotika Conservation, Vashon, WA, $12,000. For general support. 2010.

2199-8 American Friends of the University of Calgary, Houston, TX, $500,000. For climate change research. 2010.

2199-9 American Friends of the University of Calgary, Houston, TX, $250,000. For climate change research. 2010.

2199-10 American Red Cross National Headquarters, Washington, DC, $10,000. For Aid to Haiti. 2010.

2199-11 American Red Cross National Headquarters, International Response Relief Fund, Washington, DC, $10,000. For Pakistan flood relief. 2010.

2199-12 American Trust for Oxford University, Tuscaloosa, AL, $25,000. For general support. 2010.

2199-13 Amigos de Santa Cruz Foundation, Lopez Island, WA, $15,000. To implement vocational training courses in CECAP center. 2010.

2199-14 Amnesty International USA, New York, NY, $15,000. For website development and building netroots capacity. 2010.

2199-15 Ashoka: Innovators for the Public, Arlington, VA, $50,000. To expand Avacemos pilot program to six more cities in El Salvador and support formation of 290 youth collectives over next two years, involving between 1,500 and 2,000 youth directly. 2010.

2199-16 Ashoka: Innovators for the Public, Arlington, VA, $25,000. For general support. 2010.

2199-17 Ayni Education International, Seattle, WA, $12,500. For salary for Deputy Director managing Afghan and US programs. 2010.

2199-18 Bahia Street, Seattle, WA, $12,500. To fund comprehensive education program and provide social development support for 60 impoverished girls in Bahia, Brazil. 2010.

2199-19 Burkitts Lymphoma Kenya Fund, Seattle, WA, $60,000. For general support. 2010.

2199-20 Burkitts Lymphoma Kenya Fund, Seattle, WA, $50,000. For general support. 2010.

2199-21 CARE, Seattle, WA, $40,000. For scholarships in Cambodia. 2010.

2199-22 CARE, Seattle, WA, $15,000. For Northwest Community for CARE. 2010.

2199-23 CARE, Northwest Office, Seattle, WA, $25,214. For Republic of Mali School Stores Project. 2010.

2199-24 Catholic Relief Services, Baltimore, MD, $20,000. For relief in Haiti. 2010.

2199-25 Center for Global Development, Washington, DC, $75,000. For research and publication of special report and other materials related to poverty and development in Central America. 2010.

2199-26 Center for Global Development, Washington, DC, $25,000. For general support. 2010.

2199-27 Central Asia Institute, Bozeman, MT, $15,000. For general support. 2010.

2199-28 Central Asia Institute, Bozeman, MT, $10,000. For general operating support. 2010.

2199-29 Cheetah Conservation Fund USA, Alexandria, VA, $10,000. For general support. 2010.

2199-30 Conservation International, Arlington, VA, $15,000. For YUS Ecosystem Research Project in Papua, New Guinea. 2010.

2199-31 Conservation International, Seattle, WA, $10,000. For Annual Fund. 2010.

2199-32 CRUDEM Foundation, Ludlow, MA, $10,000. For Haiti Relief at Hospital Sacre Coeur. 2010.

2199-33 Doctors Without Borders USA, New York, NY, $25,000. For relief in Haiti. 2010.

2199-34 Doctors Without Borders USA, New York, NY, $10,000. For Haiti emergency relief efforts. 2010.

2199-35 Due Process of Law Foundation, Washington, DC, $65,000. To establish network and provide technical assistance to NGOs working on judicial transparency and independence issues in Central America. 2010.

2199-36 EarthCorps, Seattle, WA, $25,000. For general operating support. 2010.

2199-37 EarthCorps, Seattle, WA, $12,500. For six training positions to environmental leaders from Latin America. 2010.

2199-38 Environmental Law Alliance Worldwide, Eugene, OR, $58,000. For regional conference of ELAW fellows from Central America and other related meetings in San Jose, CA. 2010.

2199-39 Environmental Law Alliance Worldwide, Eugene, OR, $10,000. For regional conference of ELAW fellows from Central America. 2010.

2199-40 Esperanza International Foundation, Bellevue, WA, $10,000. For Haiti Rehabilitation Program with focus on three key areas: Education and vocational training, water access and nutrition, and income generation through microfinance. 2010.

2199-41 Fondo Centroamericano de Mujeres, Managua, Nicaragua, $32,000. For 7-10 women's groups in Ola Joven program. 2010.

2199-42 Foundation for Management Education in Central America, Glen Echo, MD, $50,000. For general operating support to Central America Leadership Initiative. 2010.

2199-43 Friends of the Orphans Northwest, Bellevue, WA, $10,000. For Haiti Earthquake Relief Fund. 2010.

2199-44 Fundacion del Camino, Puerto Barrios, Guatemala, $14,000. For youth leadership and computer education programs. 2010.

2199-45 Fundacion Nacional para el Desarrollo, San Salvador, El Salvador, $17,000. For ongoing research on poverty in Central America and support SIF's Central America Network. 2010.

2199-46 Global Fund for Women, San Francisco, CA, $15,000. For general support. 2010.

2199-47 Global Fund for Women, San Francisco, CA, $12,500. To work with local women's groups in Central America through grants and technical assistance. 2010.

2199-48 Global Hunger Project, New York, NY, $50,000. For fund raising match. 2010.

2199-49 Global Partnerships, Seattle, WA, $500,000. To expand programs. 2010.

2199-50 Global Partnerships, Seattle, WA, $300,000. For operations and expansion of programs. 2010.

2199-51 Global Partnerships, Seattle, WA, $35,000. For general support. 2010.

2199-52 Global Partnerships, Seattle, WA, $32,000. For Legacy Fund. 2010.

2199-53 Global Partnerships, Seattle, WA, $20,000. For Business of Hope. 2010.

2199-54 Global Partnerships, Seattle, WA, $10,000. For Microfinance Health Initiative. 2010.

2199-55 Global Visionaries, Seattle, WA, $12,500. For general operating support to educate and empower 87 Guatemalan and 140 Seattle youth to become active, global leaders. 2010.

2199-56 Global Visionaries, Seattle, WA, $11,000. For mentoring program. 2010.

2199-57 Global Washington, Seattle, WA, $125,000. For general support. 2010.

2199-58 Global Washington, Seattle, WA, $125,000. For general operating support. 2010.

2199-59 Global Washington, Seattle, WA, $80,000. For general support. 2010.

2199-60 Global Washington, Seattle, WA, $35,000. For communication and messaging efforts. 2010.

2199-61 Global Washington, Seattle, WA, $15,000. For NPR radio advertising program. 2010.

2199-62 Global Washington, Seattle, WA, $15,000. For 10 additional spots for NPR radio program. 2010.

2199-63 Grassroots International, Boston, MA, $10,000. For sustainable agriculture projects and advocacy for agriculture reform. 2010.

2199-64 Grassroots International, Boston, MA, $10,000. For general support. 2010.

2199-65 Greater Essex County School Board, Windsor, Canada, $10,000. For Begley School for school year. 2010.

2199-66 HEAL Africa, Monroe, WA, $15,000. For general operating support. 2010.

2199-67 Healing the Children Oregon/Western Washington, Everett, WA, $15,000. For construction of community clinic and educational center in Monterrico, Guatemala. 2010.

2199-68 iLEAP: The Center for Critical Service, Seattle, WA, $49,000. For Central America Women's Leadership Program. 2010.

2199-69 Indiana University Foundation, Bloomington, IN, $10,000. For general support for AMPATH-IU (Academic Model for the Prevention and Treatment of HIV/AIDS) Kenya Program. 2010.

2199-70 Initiative for Global Development, Seattle, WA, $50,000. For general operating support. 2010.

2199-71 International Snow Leopard Trust, Seattle, WA, $10,000. For general support. 2010.

2199-72 Jolkona Foundation, Kirkland, WA, $15,000. For Global Project Expansion. 2010.

2199-73 Jumpstart Network, Novato, CA, $15,000. For church's mission work in India and elsewhere. 2010.

2199-74 Just Associates, Washington, DC, $10,000. For leadership training event in Guatemala for indigenous, female leaders from Central America. 2010.

2199-75 Lambi Fund of Haiti, Washington, DC, $10,000. For building of latrines in rural Haiti. 2010.

2199-76 Landesa, Seattle, WA, $20,000. For general support. 2010.

2199-77 Natural Resources Defense Council, New York, NY, $30,000. For China Program. 2010.

2199-78 New Tribes Mission, Sanford, FL, $10,000. For emergency relief project. 2010.

2199-79 New Tribes Mission, Sanford, FL, $10,000. For ministry. 2010.

2199-80 New Venture Fund, Washington, DC, $25,000. For general support to Easter Congo Initiative. 2010.

2199-81 One By One, Seattle, WA, $10,000. To fund building of GynoCare Fistula Prevention, Treatment, and Reintegration Center in Eldoret, Kenya. 2010.

2199-82 Orphanage Outreach, Glendale, AZ, $10,000. For general operating support. 2010.

2199-83 Oxfam America, Boston, MA, $10,000. For general support. 2010.

2199-84 Pangea: Giving for Global Change, Seattle, WA, $10,000. For general support. 2010.

2199-85 Pangea: Giving for Global Change, Seattle, WA, $10,000. For Pangea grant pool. 2010.

2199-86 Partners in Health, Boston, MA, $25,000. For Haiti relief. 2010.

2199-87 Partners in Health, Boston, MA, $10,000. For Haiti emergency relief efforts. 2010.

2199-88 PeaceTrees Vietnam, Seattle, WA, $15,000. For general operating support. 2010.

2199-89 Prosthetics Outreach Foundation, Seattle, WA, $12,500. For general support. 2010.

2199-90 Rafiki Foundation, Eustis, FL, $10,000. To Koop No. 164, Tanzania. 2010.

2199-91 Rwanda Girls Initiative, Medina, WA, $45,000. For general support. 2010.

2199-92 Rwanda Girls Initiative, Medina, WA, $15,000. For hiring of Rwandan teachers For Gashora Girls Academy, Rwanda. 2010.

2199-93 Save the Children Federation, Westport, CT, $50,000. For Malawi initiatives. 2010.

2199-94 Save the Children Federation, Westport, CT, $10,000. To assist in emergency relief in Haiti. 2010.

2199-95 Save the Children Federation, Westport, CT, $10,000. For general support. 2010.

2199-96 Seattle Rotary Service Foundation, Seattle, WA, $12,500. To fund assessment of training midwives in limited obstetric ultrasound and to finalize curriculum and training method in preparation for clinical trial in Uganda. 2010.

2199-97 Seattle University, Seattle, WA, $35,000. For research on effectiveness of International Development Internship Program. 2010.

2199-98 Seattle University, Seattle, WA, $15,000. For International Development Internship, providing 10-12 Seattle University students with opportunities to work with impoverished communities in developing countries. 2010.

2199-99 Student Sponsorship Programme, New York, NY, $18,000. To 3 students in program. 2010.

2199-100 U.S. Foundation for the United World College of the Atlantic, New York, NY, $18,000. For general support. 2010.

2199-101 United States Fund for UNICEF, New York, NY, $10,000. For general support. 2010.

2199-102 Unitus, Inc., Seattle, WA, $25,000. For general support. 2010.

2199-103 University of Washington, Seattle, WA, $12,500. For roofs-and-stoves project in Piriquina, Bolivia. 2010.

2199-104 University of Washington, Seattle, WA, $10,000. For UW Department of Radiology: To assess effectiveness of training of midwives in limited obstetric ultrasound and to finalize curriculum and training method in preparation for clinical trial in Uganda. 2010.

2199-105 University of Washington Foundation, Seattle, WA, $30,000. For Gondar and Peru projects. 2010.

2199-106 VillageReach, Seattle, WA, $15,000. For vaccination program to reach about over 39,000 children in remote areas of Mozambique. 2010.

2199-107 Water First International, Seattle, WA, $10,000. For distribution system for clean water for community members in Kelecho Gerbi, Ethiopia. 2010.

2199-108 Wild Salmon Center, Portland, OR, $20,000. For general support. 2010.

2199-109 Woodland Park Zoological Society, Woodland Park Zoo, Seattle, WA, $10,000. For restoration of seven waterholes with goal of increasing eco-tourism, benefiting Merrueshi community in Kenya. 2010.

2199-110 World Impact Network, Bellevue, WA, $10,000. For general operating support. 2010.

2199-111 World Neighbors, Oklahoma City, OK, $15,000. For general support. 2010.

2199-112 World Vision, Federal Way, WA, $10,000. For Haiti earthquake relief. 2010.

2199-113 World Vision, Federal Way, WA, $10,000. For program support for efforts in Bangladesh. 2010.

2200
Seattle Mariners Corporate Giving Program

c/o Charitable Donations
P.O. Box 4100
Seattle, WA 98194-0100 (206) 346-4000
URL: http://seattle.mariners.mlb.com/sea/
community/mariners_care_donations.jsp

Grantmaker type: Corporate giving program.
Purpose and activities: As a complement to its foundation, the Seattle Mariners also make charitable contributions of memorabilia and game tickets to nonprofit organizations directly. Support is limited to Alaska, Hawaii, Idaho, Montana, Oregon, Washington, and British Columbia.
Fields of interest: General charitable giving.
International interests: Canada.
Type of support: Donated products; In-kind gifts.
Limitations: Giving limited to AK, HI, ID, MT, OR, WA, and British Columbia. No grants to individuals.
Publications: Application guidelines.
Application information: Proposals should be submitted using organization letterhead. Faxed or e-mailed proposals are not accepted. Personal items or fan merchandise to be autographed are not accepted. Support is limited to 1 contribution per organization during any given year. The Community Relations Department handles giving.
  Initial approach: Mail proposal to headquarters
  Deadline(s): 6 weeks prior to event

2201
Charles See Foundation

1215 120th Ave. N.E., Rm. 202
Bellevue, WA 98005
Contact: Anne R. See, Pres.

Incorporated in 1960 in CA.
Donors: Charles B. See; Anne R. See.
Grantmaker type: Independent foundation.
Financial data (yr. ended 12/31/10): Assets, $1,687,472 (M); expenditures, $151,854; qualifying distributions, $129,531; giving activities include $125,000 for 29 grants (high: $10,000; low: $500).
Purpose and activities: Emphasis on education and hospitals; giving also for mental health, church support, conservation, cultural programs, and international affairs.
Fields of interest: Cancer research; Arts; Education; Environment, natural resources; Animal welfare; Hospitals (general); Mental health/crisis services; Human services; International affairs; Religion.
Limitations: Applications accepted. Giving primarily in CA and WA. No grants to individuals.
Application information: Application form not required.
  Initial approach: Letter
  Copies of proposal: 1
  Deadline(s): Nov. 1
  Board meeting date(s): Nov. 15
Officers: Anne R. See, Pres. and Treas.; Harry A. See, V.P. and Secy.; Richard W. See, V.P.
Directors: Bruce M. Pym; Maureen See; Stephen D. Varon.
EIN: 956038358

2202
The Starbucks Foundation

c/o Starbucks Corp.
2401 Utah Ave. S.
Seattle, WA 98134-1436
Contact: Joelle Skaga Nausin
E-mail: foundationgrants@starbucks.com;
URL: http://www.starbucks.com/responsibility/
community
Ethos Water Fund: http://www.ethoswater.com/
Shared Planet Youth Action Grants
Database: http://www.starbucksfoundation.com/
organizations/index.cfm
Shared Planet Youth Action Grants Web site: http://
www.starbucksfoundation.com/index.cfm?
objectid=525D51E7-1D09-317F-BBF9A860BE884
D22

Established in 1997 in WA.
Donors: Starbucks Corp.; Starbucks Coffee Co.; Pepsico; Schultz Family Foundation.
Grantmaker type: Company-sponsored foundation.
Financial data (yr. ended 09/30/10): Assets, $13,252,553 (M); gifts received, $1,664,450; expenditures, $5,398,699; qualifying distributions, $5,394,503; giving activities include $4,318,001 for 1,438 grants.
Purpose and activities: The foundation supports programs designed to support young people creating change in local communities; water projects through the Ethos Water Fund; and social investments in countries where Starbuck buys coffee, tea, and cocoa.
Fields of interest: Arts, cultural/ethnic awareness; Media/communications; Arts; Education, reading; Environment, water resources; Environmental education; Environment; Disasters, preparedness/services; Disasters, Hurricane Katrina; Youth development; International economic development; Social entrepreneurship; Community/economic development; Children/youth.
International interests: Middle East; Africa; Asia; Canada; China; Ecuador; Europe; Latin America; South Africa; Thailand; United Kingdom.
Type of support: Continuing support; Emergency funds; Employee matching gifts; Program development.
Limitations: Applications accepted. Giving on a national and international basis in areas of company operations and in countries where the company buys coffee, tea, and cocoa. No support for private foundations, political, labor, or fraternal organizations, religious organizations not of direct benefit to the entire community, hospitals or medical research institutions, universities or academic research institutions, individual schools or parent teacher associations, or sporting teams. No grants to individuals, or for neighborhood clean-ups or tree plantings, wildlife conservation projects, capital campaigns, capital expenditures or land acquisition, school bands or orchestras or non-literacy art programs, fundraising events, one-time events or programs, event sponsorships, trips or travel, league sports programs, scholarships or fellowships, expeditions, political campaigns, the production of marketing material promoting Starbucks, the production of products to sell in Starbucks stores, endowments, conferences or symposia, contests, festivals, or parades, advertising, tickets to events, or supply drives.
Publications: Application guidelines; Grants list.
Application information: A full proposal may be requested at a later date for Starbucks Shared Planet Youth Action Grants. Unsolicited requests are

currently not accepted for the Ethos Water Fund and Social Investments in Coffee, Tea, & Cocoa Communities.
  Initial approach: Complete online letter of inquiry for Starbucks Shared Planet Youth Action Grants
  Deadline(s): Oct. 1 to Jan. 31 for Starbucks Shared Planet Youth Action Grants
Officers and Directors:* Orin Smith,* Pres.; Paula E. Boggs,* Secy.; Donna Brooks, Treas.; Rodney Hines, Exec. Dir.; Martin Coles.
Number of staff: 3 part-time professional; 1 part-time support.
EIN: 911795425
Recent grants for international programs:
2202-1 Bridges to Understanding, Seattle, WA, $15,000. 2010.
2202-2 Foundation Rwanda, New York, NY, $29,905. 2010.
2202-3 Give2Asia, San Francisco, CA, $297,000. 2010.
2202-4 Heifer Project International, Little Rock, AR, $10,000. 2010.
2202-5 OneWorld Now, Seattle, WA, $10,000. 2010.
2202-6 Resource Foundation, New York, NY, $110,000. 2010.
2202-7 Save the Children Federation, Westport, CT, $25,000. 2010.
2202-8 Save the Children Federation, Westport, CT, $25,000. 2010.
2202-9 Vancouver Foundation, Vancouver, Canada, $75,000. 2010.
2202-10 Vancouver Foundation, Vancouver, Canada, $12,025. 2010.
2202-11 Vancouver Foundation, Vancouver, Canada, $10,500. 2010.
2202-12 Vancouver Foundation, Vancouver, Canada, $10,472. 2010.

2203
The Stewardship Foundation

P.O. Box 1278
Tacoma, WA 98401-1278
Contact: Cary Paine, Exec. Dir.
E-mail: info@stewardshipfdn.org; URL: http://
www.stewardshipfdn.org

Trust established in 1962 in WA.
Donor: C. Davis Weyerhaeuser Irrevocable Trust.
Grantmaker type: Independent foundation.
Financial data (yr. ended 12/31/09): Assets, $116,562,116 (M); expenditures, $7,766,798; qualifying distributions, $7,058,613; giving activities include $6,381,310 for 155 grants (high: $250,000; low: $733).
Purpose and activities: The foundation provides resources to Christ centered organizations which have their primary goal to bring people into a relationship with God through faith in Jesus Christ. The foundation will consider making grants to organizations that promote: 1) Leadership: Preparation and training of servant leaders for the church and marketplace; favors mentoring and discipleship of indigenous leadership in the least evangelized world. 2) Poverty: community development (i.e. health, agriculture, water, education); economic development primarily in the developing world. 3) Reconciliation and Justice: advocacy and intervention on behalf of people suffering injustice, oppression and persecution; protection for refugees and displaced people around the world, and efforts which seek to end the

conditions that create displacement; promotion of reconciliation and healing among current and historic enemies; and advocacy and promotion of religious liberty. 4) Relational Evangelism and Discipleship: building relationships and friendships with people for the purpose of introducing them to Jesus Christ. 5) Children at Risk: outreach and support of vulnerable children, protecting then from abuse and unfair treatment; solutions and best practices which enable children to develop into the people God created them to be.

Fields of interest: Public health, clean water supply; Youth development, services; Youth development, religion; Youth, services; International economic development; International peace/security; Community/economic development; Leadership development; Christian agencies & churches.

Type of support: General/operating support; Continuing support; Program development; Matching/challenge support.

Limitations: Applications accepted. Giving internationally, nationally and in western WA, especially in Tacoma and King, Snohomish counties. No support for churches (except for religious support to Christian parachurch organizations and Christian-Evangelical purposes). No grants to individuals, or for seed money, endowment funds, deficit financing, research, videos, media time or program production.

Publications: Application guidelines.

Application information: Application limited to once a year. Applicants should not submit full proposals unless requested to do so by the foundation or have received a grant payment from the foundation within the past three years. Application form not required.

Initial approach: Letter of inquiry (1-2 pages)
Copies of proposal: 1
Deadline(s): None for letter of inquiry
Board meeting date(s): Mar., June, Sept., and Dec.
Final notification: 30 days for letter of inquiry

Officers and Directors:* William T. Weyerhaeuser,* Chair.; Gail T. Weyerhaeuser,* Vice-Chair. and Treas.; Cary A. Paine, Exec. Dir.; Wesley J. Anderson; Kerry L. Dearborn; Susan S. Hutchison; Chi-Dooh "Skip" Li; Todd D. Silver; Annette B. Weyerhaeuser.

Number of staff: 1 full-time professional.

EIN: 916020515

Recent grants for international programs:

2203-1 Agros International, Seattle, WA, $50,000. For general operations. 2009.

2203-2 American Bible Society, New York, NY, $34,982. For Scripture for Rape Survivors. 2009.

2203-3 Awana Clubs International, Streamwood, IL, $15,000. For Expanding the Leader-Based Strategy Program in India. 2009.

2203-4 Bible League, Chicago, IL, $26,950. For Sabah Borneo Evangelism Impact Zone in Malaysia. 2009.

2203-5 Care for Children, Northfield, IL, $75,000. For National Foster Care Project in China. 2009.

2203-6 Christian Veterinary Mission, Seattle, WA, $16,000. For VetRed in Latin America. 2009.

2203-7 Christian Veterinary Mission, Seattle, WA, $12,000. For Project Living Hope: Reaching the Gumuz People for Christ. 2009.

2203-8 CURE International, Lemoyne, PA, $100,000. For Ethiopia Children's Hospital. 2009.

2203-9 Development Associates International, Colorado Springs, CO, $50,000. For general operations. 2009.

2203-10 Entrust, Colorado Springs, CO, $50,000. For general operations. 2009.

2203-11 Entrust, Colorado Springs, CO, $18,000. For Women to Women Leadership Training - Russia. 2009.

2203-12 Fellowship Foundation, International Foundation, Bethesda, MD, $20,000. For National Prayer Breakfast. 2009.

2203-13 GANSU, Warner Robins, GA, $10,000. For general operations. 2009.

2203-14 Hagar USA, Eau Claire, WI, $50,000. For Aftercare in Cambodia. 2009.

2203-15 Headington Institute, Pasadena, CA, $105,000. For Efficacy-Outcomes Programmatic Research. 2009.

2203-16 Headington Institute, Pasadena, CA, $50,000. For general operations. 2009.

2203-17 Hope Haven, Rock Valley, IA, $42,680. For Gospel Outreach in Vietnam. 2009.

2203-18 India Gospel Outreach, Rancho Cucamonga, CA, $25,000. For general operations. 2009.

2203-19 Institute for Global Engagement, Arlington, VA, $50,000. For general operations. 2009.

2203-20 Institute for Sustainable Peace, Houston, TX, $10,000. For ROM - Renewing Our Minds. 2009.

2203-21 Institute of Chinese Studies, Orange, CA, $15,000. For CEO Initiative. 2009.

2203-22 International Center for Religion and Diplomacy, Washington, DC, $60,000. For general operations. 2009.

2203-23 International Center for Religion and Diplomacy, Washington, DC, $60,000. For general operations. 2009.

2203-24 International Center for Religion and Diplomacy, Washington, DC, $25,000. For general operations. 2009.

2203-25 International Justice Mission, Arlington, VA, $100,000. For general operations. 2009.

2203-26 International Justice Mission, Arlington, VA, $75,000. For Global Affiliate Expansion. 2009.

2203-27 InterVarsity Christian Fellowship/USA, Platteville, WI, $50,000. For IFES - Middle East and North Africa Region. 2009.

2203-28 John Stott Ministries, Menlo Park, CA, $100,000. For Scholars' Program. 2009.

2203-29 Joni and Friends International Disability Center, Agoura Hills, CA, $90,000. For Wheels for the World. 2009.

2203-30 Landesa, Seattle, WA, $150,000. For general operations. 2009.

2203-31 Lausanne Committee for World Evangelization, South Hamilton, MA, $150,000. For Cape Town. 2009.

2203-32 Loma Linda University, Loma Linda, CA, $180,000. For Service Opportunities in the Muslim World - Niger and Mauritania. 2009.

2203-33 Medical Teams International, Tigard, OR, $100,000. For general operations. 2009.

2203-34 Mercy Ships Foundation, Lindale, TX, $35,000. For Fistula Prevalence Reduction and National Health Training in Benin, West Africa. 2009.

2203-35 Middle East Fellowship, Brea, CA, $71,000. For Empowering Citizen Peacebuilders in Palestine and Israel. 2009.

2203-36 Mission Aviation Fellowship, Nampa, ID, $50,000. For Plane Maintenance Fund. 2009.

2203-37 Mission India, Grand Rapids, MI, $67,551. For adult literacy classes. 2009.

2203-38 Navigators, The, Colorado Springs, CO, $50,000. For Capacity Building. 2009.

2203-39 Open Doors with Brother Andrew, Santa Ana, CA, $85,000. For IBADAT Literacy Training in Pakistan. 2009.

2203-40 Opportunity International, Oak Brook, IL, $150,000. For Chief Transformation Officers' Strategy. 2009.

2203-41 Partners International, Spokane, WA, $40,000. For Reaching Mekong Southeast Asia for Christ. 2009.

2203-42 Peter Deyneka Russian Ministries, Wheaton, IL, $60,000. For general operations. 2009.

2203-43 Reconciliation Ministries, Medina, WA, $45,000. For Musalaha's general operations. 2009.

2203-44 Refugees International, Washington, DC, $150,000. For general operations. 2009.

2203-45 Rwanda Partners, Bellevue, WA, $20,000. For general operations. 2009.

2203-46 Shelter for Life International, Minnetonka, MN, $111,377. For sustainable livelihood development in returning communities, Eastern Equatoria, Sudan. 2009.

2203-47 Systematic Asian Leadership Training, Charlotte, NC, $25,000. For general operations. 2009.

2203-48 Willow Creek Association, South Barrington, IL, $25,000. For Global Leadership Summit, South Africa. 2009.

2203-49 Word for the World, USA, Colorado Springs, CO, $25,000. For general operations. 2009.

2203-50 World Bicycle Relief, Chicago, IL, $75,000. For Bicycles for Educational Empowerment Program. 2009.

2203-51 World Concern, Seattle, WA, $75,000. For World Concern's General Operations. 2009.

2203-52 World Concern, Seattle, WA, $25,000. For World Concern's Community HIV/AIDS Mainstreaming Project, Kachin, Myanmar. 2009.

2203-53 World Concern, Seattle, WA, $25,000. For World Concern's Hope for Children Affected by HIV/AIDS in Kenya. 2009.

2203-54 World Hope International, Alexandria, VA, $35,000. For Community Orphan Trust. 2009.

2203-55 World Relief, Baltimore, MD, $75,000. For Choose Peace. 2009.

2203-56 World Relief, Baltimore, MD, $10,000. For Refugee Needs Fund. 2009.

2204
Tulalip Tribes Charitable Fund

8802 27th Ave. N.E.
Tulalip, WA 98271-8063 (360) 716-5000
Contact: Marilyn Sheldon, Charitable Contribs.
FAX: (360) 716-0126;
E-mail: msheldon@tulaliptribes-nsn.gov;
URL: http://www.quilcedavillage.org/ charitable_fund/index.asp

Established by the Tulalip Tribes.

Grantmaker type: Corporate giving program.

Financial data (yr. ended 12/31/09): Total giving, $2,832,066, including $2,832,066 for 225 grants.

Purpose and activities: The fund supports organizations involved with arts and culture, pre-K and K-12 education, youth athletics, environment, and wildlife conservation.

Fields of interest: Animals/wildlife; Arts; Education, early childhood education; Elementary/secondary education; Environment; Health care; Human services; International affairs; Performing arts, music; Public affairs; Recreation; Religion; Youth.

Type of support: Capital campaigns; Conferences/seminars; Consulting services; Curriculum development; General/operating support; Matching/challenge support; Program development; Scholarship funds.
Limitations: Applications accepted. Giving limited to WA, with emphasis on King, Skagit, and Snohomish counties. No support for political candidates or organizations. No grants to individuals, or for memorials or endowments, travel expenses, or legal fees.
Publications: Application guidelines; Grants list.
Application information: The Charitable Contributions Department handles giving. The company has a staff that only handles contributions. A contributions committee reviews all requests. Application form required.
   Initial approach: Download application form and mail proposal and application form to foundation
   Copies of proposal: 1
   Deadline(s): Mar. 1, June 1, Sept. 1, and Dec. 1
   Committee meeting date(s): Quarterly
   Final notification: 60 days following deadline if approved
Number of staff: 1 full-time professional.

2205
Vista Hermosa
1111 Fishhook Park Rd.
Prescott, WA 99348-9618 (509) 749-2217
Contact: Suzanne Broetje, Exec. Dir.
FAX: (509) 749-2354;
E-mail: SuzanneB@firstfruits.com; URL: http://www.broetjeorchards.com/index.cfm?pageId=17775C08-D0B3-A2C5-0AF1EB652A2D8C6A

Established in 1990 in WA.
Donors: Cheryl Broetje; Ralph Broetje; Broetje Orchards.
Grantmaker type: Independent foundation.
Financial data (yr. ended 12/31/10): Assets, $28,338,141 (M); gifts received, $2,504,072; expenditures, $5,191,270; qualifying distributions, $4,961,451; giving activities include $3,059,895 for 38 grants (high: $482,000; $71,183 for 27 grants to individuals (high: $10,000; low: $89), $7,375 for 4 employee matching gifts, and $958,119 for 4 foundation-administered programs.
Purpose and activities: The foundation was established for the purpose of using proceeds from Broetje Orchards to serve children and underserved communities, both at home and around the world. The foundation also provides FirstFruits Scholarships for children of Broetje Orchards' employees, and graduates of Jubilee Christian Academy.
Fields of interest: Education; Agriculture/food; Housing/shelter, development; Youth development, services; International relief; Community/economic development; Children/youth; Hispanics/Latinos; Women; Girls; Economically disadvantaged.
International interests: Central America; Dominican Republic; East Africa/Horn of Africa; Haiti; India; Mexico.
Type of support: Income development; Program development; Employee-related scholarships; Matching/challenge support.
Limitations: Applications not accepted. Giving primarily in WA; giving also in Mexico, Central America, Haiti, Dominican Republic, India, Kenya and Uganda. No support for universities or

university-led programs. No grants to individuals (except for scholarships), or endowments, professorships; no student loans, or loans to individuals.
Application information: Unsolicited queries or proposals not accepted. See foundation web site for additional information.
   Board meeting date(s): Monthly
Officers: Ralph Broetje, Pres.; Suzanne Broetje, Exec. Dir.; Cheryl Broetje, V.P.
Directors: Sandra Gamble; Theresa Morton.
Number of staff: 1 full-time professional.
EIN: 911491438

2206
Weyerhaeuser Company Foundation
P.O. Box 9777
CH 3E22
Federal Way, WA 98063-9777 (253) 924-3159
Contact: Bruce Amundson, Pres.
FAX: (253) 924-3658;
E-mail: bruce.amundson@weyerhaeuser.com;
Additional contacts: Karen Veitenhans, Exec. Dir., e-mail: karen.veitenhans@weyerhaeyser.com; Anne Leyva, Secy., e-mail: anne.leyva@weyerhaeuser.com; URL: http://www.weyerhaeuser.com/Sustainability/People/Communities
MakingWaves on Facebook: http://www.facebook.com/WYMakingWAVES

Incorporated in 1948 in WA.
Donors: Weyerhaeuser Co.; Gareth Curtiss.
Grantmaker type: Company-sponsored foundation.
Financial data (yr. ended 12/31/10): Assets, $14,168,286 (M); gifts received, $3,000,000; expenditures, $4,566,931; qualifying distributions, $3,983,182; giving activities include $3,983,182 for grants.
Purpose and activities: The foundation supports organizations involved with the education, the environment, affordable housing and shelter, and the forest products industry. Support is given primarily in areas of company operations.
Fields of interest: Higher education; Food banks; United Ways and Federated Giving Programs; Youth development; Education; Environment, research; Environment, public policy; Environment, natural resources; Environment, forests; Environmental education; Housing/shelter, temporary shelter; Housing/shelter; Human services; Business/industry; Children.
Type of support: General/operating support; Capital campaigns; Building/renovation; Equipment; Emergency funds; Program development; Conferences/seminars; Curriculum development; Research; Employee volunteer services; Employee matching gifts; Employee-related scholarships.
Limitations: Applications accepted. Giving on a national and international basis primarily in areas of company operations, with emphasis on Washington, DC, GA, MN, OR, WA, Canada, and China. No support for religious organizations not of direct benefit to the entire community; generally, no support for disease-specific organizations. No grants to individuals (except for employee-related scholarships), or for political campaigns, lobbying activities, general operating support for organizations indirectly receiving Weyerhaeuser Foundation support through a federated organization or combined campaign, tickets or tables, or activities providing benefits to Weyerhaeuser or employees of Weyerhaeuser;

generally, no grants for services the public sector should be reasonably expected to provide, endowments or memorials, research or conferences unrelated to the forest products industry, hospital capital campaigns resulting in higher costs to health care users, or debt reduction.
Application information:
   Initial approach: Letter of inquiry or contact foundation for application form
   Deadline(s): Varies
   Board meeting date(s): Feb. and mid-year
   Final notification: 60 to 120 days
Officers and Trustees:* Ernesta Ballard,* Chair.; Bruce Amundson, Pres.; Karen L. Veitenhans, V.P. and Exec. Dir.; Anne Leyva, Secy.; Jeffrey W. Nitta, Treas.; Jeanne M. Hillman, Cont.; Patricia M. Bedient; Mike Branson; Lawrence Burrows; Miles Drake; Daniel S. Fulton; Thomas F. Gideon; Sandy D. McDade.
Number of staff: 4 full-time professional; 2 full-time support.
EIN: 916024225
Recent grants for international programs:
2206-1 Environmental Law Institute, Washington, DC, $10,000. For New Vision and Future Challenges Fund. 2010.
2206-2 Japan-America Society of the State of Washington, Seattle, WA, $10,000. For Japan in the Schools program. 2010.
2206-3 North Carolina Agricultural Foundation, Raleigh, NC, $296,500. For ongoing water footprint and sustainability platform underlying the range of biomass production and use for food, fiber and fuels in Uruguay. 2010.
2206-4 World Resources Institute, Washington, DC, $35,000. To work to address global issues relative to climate protection, sustainable forestry and water management. 2010.

2207
The Wilburforce Foundation
3601 Fremont Ave. N., Ste. 304
Seattle, WA 98103-8753
Contact: Timothy Greyhavens, Secy. and Exec. Dir.
FAX: (206) 632-2326;
E-mail: grants@wilburforce.org; Additional address (Montana office): P.O. Box 296, Bozeman, MT 59771-0296, tel.: (406) 586-9796, fax: (406) 586-3076, e-mail: jennifer@wilburforce.org; Additional tel.: (800) 201-0148 (Seattle office), (800) 317-8180 (Montana office); URL: http://www.wilburforce.org
Grants Database: http://www.wilburforce.org/grantees/grantees_search.cfm

Established in 1990 in WA.
Donors: James Letwin; Rosanna W. Letwin.
Grantmaker type: Independent foundation.
Financial data (yr. ended 12/31/10): Assets, $7,856,921 (M); gifts received, $13,139,395; expenditures, $12,163,075; qualifying distributions, $12,066,421; giving activities include $9,884,000 for 217 grants (high: $900,000; low: $500; average: $25,000–$100,000), and $30,000 for 3 grants to individuals (high: $10,000; low: $10,000).
Purpose and activities: The foundation is dedicated to protecting nature's richness and diversity through funding programs that help to preserve our remaining wild places. The foundation focuses on increasing the amount of protected critical wildlife habitat, assuring the quality and extent of key connective land between core habitat areas,

lessening immediate threats to critical wildlife habitat, improving management programs that preserve the ecological integrity of existing or proposed protected areas, increasing knowledge of wildlife populations and/or improving managements plans that ensure the viability of local species in a region and building the capacity of organizations working to protect priority areas.

Fields of interest: Environment, natural resources; Environment.

International interests: Canada.

Type of support: General/operating support; Continuing support; Management development/capacity building; Capital campaigns; Equipment; Program development; Seed money; Research; Technical assistance; Consulting services; Program evaluation; Matching/challenge support.

Limitations: Applications accepted. Giving primarily in the western U.S. and western Canada, particularly AK, AZ, MT, NM, OR, UT, WA, British Columbia, and the Yellowstone to Yukon region of U.S.-Canada. No support for schools or universities, governmental agencies, agricultural issues, air quality or other clean air programs, energy-related programs; environmental education, environmental justice programs, habitat restoration, marine or other water-only programs, pollution prevention on other pollution-related projects, salmon recovery programs, sustainable development or other economically based programs, sprawl or other growth management programs, transportation-related programs, wildlife rehabilitation programs or youth education programs. No grants to individuals (except for Leadership Awards), or for fellowships or scholarships, endowment funds, operating budgets, deficit financing or indirect costs, annual meetings, conferences or symposia, or land acquisition and/or stewardship; no loans.

Publications: Application guidelines; Grants list.

Application information: Applicants who are interested in submitting a grant proposal must contact the appropriate staff member prior to developing a proposal. Please do not submit a full proposal without first contacting a program officer. When contacting a program officer regarding the possibility of a grant, be sure to specify the dollar level of your request. Grant Application Form will be sent to an organization only after it has received approval to submit a full proposal. Application form required.

Initial approach: Telephone
Copies of proposal: 1
Deadline(s): See web site for details
Board meeting date(s): Feb., Mar., July and Nov.
Final notification: Grants of more than $25,000: Quarterly; Six to eight weeks for grants of $25,000 or less

Officers and Directors:* Rosanna W. Letwin,* Chair. and Treas.; Stephanie Nichols-Young,* Pres.; Timothy Greyhavens, Secy. and Exec. Dir.

Number of staff: 11 full-time professional.

EIN: 943137894

Recent grants for international programs:

2207-1 Alaska Wilderness League, Washington, DC, $30,000. For General Support. 2009.

2207-2 Alberta Wilderness Association, Calgary, Canada, $20,000. For Conservation in the Castle and Southwest Alberta. 2009.

2207-3 American Littoral Society, Highlands, NJ, $12,000. For Arctic Funders Group Secretariat. 2009.

2207-4 British Columbia Spaces for Nature, Gibsons, Canada, $50,000. For a Biodiversity Survival Strategy for a Changing Climate. 2009.

2207-5 Canadian Parks and Wilderness Society, Ottawa, Canada, $120,000. For Protecting Habitat and Corridors in Northern Y2Y. 2009.

2207-6 Canadian Parks and Wilderness Society, Ottawa, Canada, $85,000. For British Columbia and Southern Alberta Chapters: Protecting Habitat and Corridors in the Northern Crown of the Continent. 2009.

2207-7 Canadian Parks and Wilderness Society, Ottawa, Canada, $50,000. For Completing a Visionary Atlin-Taku Land Use Plan that plans for the impacts of climate change. 2009.

2207-8 Canadian Parks and Wilderness Society, Ottawa, Canada, $25,000. For CPAWS BC: Creating and Presenting the ENGO Conservation Vision for the Atlin-Taku Land Use Plan Area. 2009.

2207-9 Canadian Parks and Wilderness Society, Ottawa, Canada, $10,000. For Integration Feasibility Study. 2009.

2207-10 Castle-Crown Wilderness Coalition, Pincher Creek, Canada, $15,000. For General Support. 2009.

2207-11 Chinook Institute for Community Stewardship, Carmore, Canada, $20,000. For Southwestern Alberta Stewardship: Castle Special Place Working Group. 2009.

2207-12 Council of Yukon First Nations, Whitehorse, Canada, $25,000. For Arctic Athabaskan Council: Caribou, community adaptation, and short-lived climate change forcers: perspectives from northern Canada and Alaska. 2009.

2207-13 David Suzuki Foundation, Vancouver, Canada, $100,000. For British Columbia Species at Risk Working Group. 2009.

2207-14 Defenders of Wildlife, Washington, DC, $10,000. For Naturalia: Mexican Wolves in Mexico. 2009.

2207-15 Driftwood Foundation, Smithers, Canada, $45,000. For Skeena Watershed Conservation Coalition Organizational Capacity. 2009.

2207-16 Ecotrust Canada, Vancouver, Canada, $50,000. For Scaling up EBM in Heiltsuk Territory and the Great Bear Rainforest. 2009.

2207-17 Forest Ethics, San Francisco, CA, $125,000. For New Frontiers in Conservation: Protecting the Great Bear Rainforest and Beyond. 2009.

2207-18 Greenpeace Fund, Washington, DC, $60,000. For Greenpeace Canada: Beyond Promises to a Reality on the Ground in the GBR. 2009.

2207-19 Headwaters Montana, Whitefish, MT, $10,000. For Transboundary Project. 2009.

2207-20 Idaho Conservation League, Boise, ID, $60,000. For Yellowstone to Yukon. 2009.

2207-21 Miistakis Institute for the Rockies, Calgary, Canada, $25,000. For General Support and Road Watch in the Pass. 2009.

2207-22 Montana State University Foundation, Bozeman, MT, $10,000. For Western Transportation Institute Cascades Carnivore Connectivity Project. 2009.

2207-23 Nature Conservancy, Arlington, VA, $13,000. For TNC Alaska: Climate Change and Development by Design in Arctic Alaska. 2009.

2207-24 Nature Conservancy of Canada, Toronto, Canada, $80,000. For Chilcotin Coast Grizzly Bear Project. 2009.

2207-25 Northern Alaska Environmental Center, Fairbanks, AK, $12,000. For Alaskan's for Protecting America's Arctic. 2009.

2207-26 Ocean Conservancy, Washington, DC, $13,000. For Taking Ocean-Climate Action in the Arctic. 2009.

2207-27 Oceana, Washington, DC, $13,000. For United States Arctic Large Marine Ecosystem Protection. 2009.

2207-28 Pembina Foundation for Environmental Research and Education, Drayton Valley, Canada, $70,000. For Pembina Institute: Advancing New Decision Making Frameworks and Planning for the MacKenzie Gas Pipeline Decision. 2009.

2207-29 Raincoast Conservation Foundation, Sidney, Canada, $80,000. For Carnivore and Wilderness Protection in the Great Bear Rainforest: Science and Informed Advocacy. 2009.

2207-30 Round River Conservation Studies, Salt Lake City, UT, $100,000. For Taku River Wildlife Conservation Project. 2009.

2207-31 Sierra Club Canada Foundation, Ottawa, Canada, $20,000. For Action Grizzly Bear, campaign initiated by local and international conservation voices focused on advocating the recovery of Alberta's grizzly bear. It is a grassroots campaign designed to network people concerned about the imperiled grizzly and mobilizes them with the knowledge and tools to take action. 2009.

2207-32 Sierra Club Canada Foundation, Ottawa, Canada, $20,000. For Alberta WILD. 2009.

2207-33 Sierra Club Foundation, San Francisco, CA, $40,000. To protect America's Arctic Campaign. 2009.

2207-34 Sierra Club of British Columbia Foundation, Victoria, Canada, $60,000. For Sierra Club of Canada, BC Chapter: Conserving BC's Great Bear Rainforest Now and into the Future. 2009.

2207-35 Sierra Club of British Columbia Foundation, Victoria, Canada, $45,000. For Inspiring British Columbians to Protect the Flathead River Valley. 2009.

2207-36 Sky Island Alliance, Tucson, AZ, $75,000. For General Support. 2009.

2207-37 Sky Island Alliance, Tucson, AZ, $20,000. For Coalition for Sonoran Desert Protection. Sonoran Desert is located in North America and covers the southwestern parts of the state of Arizona, southeastern parts of the state of California in the United States and the state of Sonora in Mexico. 2009.

2207-38 Tides Canada Foundation, Initiatives Society, Vancouver, Canada, $25,000. For Headwaters Initiative Project. 2009.

2207-39 Tides Center, San Francisco, CA, $80,000. For Rivers Without Borders: Transboundary Watershed Conservation Campaign. 2009.

2207-40 Tides Foundation, San Francisco, CA, $90,000. For Canopy: Mobilizing Markets for Great Bear Rainforest Conservation. 2009.

2207-41 Tides Foundation, San Francisco, CA, $25,000. For Dogwood Initiative: Expanding the Reach - Coastal Oil Tanker Campaign. 2009.

2207-42 Trustees for Alaska, Anchorage, AK, $19,000. For Protecting America's Unique Arctic Ecosystems. 2009.

2207-43 University of Alaska Fairbanks, Fairbanks, AK, $60,000. For SNAP: Climate Adaptation Scenario Planning for Wilburforce Arctic and Tongass Grantees. 2009.

2207-44 University of Calgary, Calgary, Canada, $10,000. For Wolf Publications. 2009.

2207-45 University of California, Santa Barbara, CA, $45,000. For Integrating Conservation Science for the Coastal Temperate Rainforests (Tongass and Great Bear). 2009.

2207-46 University of Montana, Missoula, MT, $25,000. For Projecting the Impacts to Grizzly Bears, Wolverine and River Otters of the Proposed Lodgepole Coal Mine and Coal Bed Methane Development in the Upper Flathead River Drainage in British Columbia. 2009.

2207-47 Walter and Duncan Gordon Foundation, Toronto, Canada, $25,000. For Indigenous Approaches to Arctic Governance. 2009.

2207-48 West Coast Environmental Law Research Foundation, Vancouver, Canada, $25,000. For Protecting the Great Bear Rainforest from Oil Supertankers: Legal Strategies. 2009.

2207-49 WILD Foundation, Boulder, CO, $50,000. For Flathead Campaign. 2009.

2207-50 Wilderness Society, Washington, DC, $20,000. For Unified Arctic Campaign. 2009.

2207-51 Wildsight, Kimberley, Canada, $68,500. For Flathead Wild Campaign. 2009.

2207-52 Yellowstone to Yukon Conservation Initiative, Bozeman, MT, $275,000. For Organizational Capacity Support and Project Implementation. 2009.

2207-53 Yellowstone to Yukon Conservation Initiative, Bozeman, MT, $10,000. For Yellowstone to Yukon Climate Adaptation Report. 2009.

2207-54 Yukon Conservation Society, Whitehorse, Canada, $20,000. For Partnering in the Peel. 2009.

2208
World Concern Development Organization
(also known as WCDO)
19303 Fremont Ave. N.
Seattle, WA 98133-3800 (206) 546-7201
FAX: (206) 546-7269;
E-mail: info@worldconcern.org; Toll-free tel.: (800) 755-5022; URL: http://www.worldconcern.org
E-Newsletter: http://www.worldconcern.org/newsletter/
Facebook: http://www.facebook.com/worldconcern
Flickr: http://www.flickr.com/people/worldconcern
FriendFeed URL: http://friendfeed.com/worldconcern
Twitter: http://twitter.com/worldconcern
Vimeo: http://www.vimeo.com/worldconcern
YouTube: http://www.youtube.com/user/WorldConcernVideos

Established in 1981 in WA.
Grantmaker type: Public charity.
Financial data (yr. ended 06/30/11): Revenue, $9,083,551; assets, $1,126,445 (M); gifts received, $9,083,475; expenditures, $9,092,677; giving activities include $885,203 for grants to organizations outside the U.S.
Purpose and activities: The organization provides community development and disaster response to the world's poor in Africa, Asia, and the Americas.
Fields of interest: Human services, emergency aid; Disasters, preparedness/services; Human services; Community/economic development; Christian agencies & churches; Economically disadvantaged.
International interests: Nicaragua; Cambodia; Nepal; Zimbabwe; Zambia; Burkina Faso; Sierra Leone; Rwanda; Niger; Ethiopia; Haiti; Bolivia; Vietnam; China; Thailand; Sri Lanka; Burma (Myanmar); Laos; Bangladesh; Uganda; Sudan; Somalia, Somaliland and Puntland; Kenya; Chad; Africa; Asia; Caribbean; Central America; South America.
Type of support: Loans—to individuals.
Limitations: Giving primarily to Bangladesh, Bolivia, Burkina Faso, Cambodia, Chad, Ethiopia, Haiti, Kenya, Laos, Myanmar, Nepal, Nicaragua, Niger, Rwanda, Sierra Leone, Somalia, Sri Lanka, Sudan, Thailand, Tibet, Uganda, Vietnam, Zambia, and Zimbabwe.
Publications: Financial statement; Newsletter; Occasional report.
Officers and Directors:* Fred Stabbert,* Chair.; Deborah Limb,* Vice-Chair.; David Eller,* Pres.; Stephen Grey,* Secy.; Michael Eggers,* Treas.; Dr. Margaret Brand; Reg Branston; Joe Bundrant; Dale Cowles; Brad Decker; David Ederer; Jim Funfar; Kevin Gabelein; E. Kent Halvorsen; Dr. Daniel Hayden; and 7 additional directors.
EIN: 911155150

WEST VIRGINIA

2209
One Foundation
125 Whitestick Rd.
Beckley, WV 25801-3625 (304) 256-6427
Contact: Tom R. Attar, Tr.

Established in 1999 in WV.
Donors: Faramarz Attar; Rama N. "Tom" Attar; Mohan "Scott" Attar; Kalindi Attar.
Grantmaker type: Independent foundation.
Financial data (yr. ended 12/31/10): Assets, $15,388,279 (M); expenditures, $539,530; qualifying distributions, $401,303; giving activities include $373,314 for 38 grants (high: $50,000; low: $75).
Fields of interest: Environment; Human services; Community/economic development; United Ways and Federated Giving Programs.
Limitations: Applications accepted. Giving primarily in CA, NY, PA, and WV. No grants to individuals.
Application information:
  Initial approach: Letter
  Deadline(s): None
Directors: Reinhard Bouman; David B. McClure.
Trustees: Marz Attar; Tom R. Attar.
EIN: 316622764
Recent grants for international programs:
2209-1 Acumen Fund, New York, NY, $50,000. For working capital operations. 2010.
2209-2 Care for Vrindavan, Saratoga Springs, NY, $10,000. For working capital operations. 2010.
2209-3 Just Vision, Washington, DC, $25,000. For working capital operations. 2010.
2209-4 Mapendo International, Cambridge, MA, $10,000. For working capital operations. 2010.
2209-5 Shadduli Center, San Anselmo, CA, $20,000. For working capital operations. 2010.
2209-6 Turkish Philanthropy Funds, New York, NY, $20,000. For working capital operations. 2010.

WISCONSIN

2210
The Argosy Foundation
(formerly The Abele Family Charitable Trust)
555 E. Wells St., Ste. 1650
Milwaukee, WI 53202-3819
Contact: Jeneye Abele, C.E.O.
E-mail address for inquiries in Spanish: ayuda@argosyfnd.org; URL: http://www.argosyfnd.org/
E-Newsletter: http://www.argosyfnd.org/enews/

Established in 1997 in MA. Over the next few years, the Abele family plans to more than double the foundation's endowment, which would make it one of the larger foundations in the nation with assets eventually approaching $2 billion.
Donor: John E. Abele.
Grantmaker type: Independent foundation.
Financial data (yr. ended 12/31/10): Assets, $25,826,690 (M); expenditures, $3,082,538; qualifying distributions, $2,994,644; giving activities include $1,700,500 for 84 grants (high: $125,000; low: $400).
Purpose and activities: The mission of the foundation is to support people and programs that make our society a better place to live. The foundation seeks to employ creative and entrepreneurial approaches that help people to help themselves, and become self-sustaining whenever possible. The intention is to solve systemic problems, build teams and communities, create replicable solutions, and inspire others to contribute in their own ways.
Fields of interest: Public affairs; Arts; Education; Environment; Health care; Human services; International affairs.
Type of support: Annual campaigns; Emergency funds; Program development; Conferences/seminars; Scholarship funds; Research; Matching/challenge support.
Limitations: Applications not accepted. Giving primarily to CO, MA, VT and WI. No grants to individuals.
Publications: Annual report.
Application information: Unsolicited requests for funds not accepted.
Officers and Trustees:* John E. Abele,* Chair.; Jeneye Abele, C.E.O. and Pres.
EIN: 046752868
Recent grants for international programs:
2210-1 Clean Air Task Force, Boston, MA, $48,000. To work on climate change. 2008.
2210-2 Engineers Without Borders USA, Boulder, CO, $22,500. For a construction project. 2008.
2210-3 Global Greengrants Fund, Boulder, CO, $50,000. For strategic planning. 2008.
2210-4 Greater Milwaukee Committee for Community Development, Milwaukee, WI, $12,500. For knowledge and cultural understanding of China. 2008.
2210-5 Philharmonic Orchestra of the Americas, New York, NY, $10,000. For the commission, performance and recording of contemporary music. 2008.
2210-6 Public Citizen, Texas, Austin, TX, $40,000. To work to abate global warming. 2008.
2210-7 Rockefeller Family Fund, New York, NY, $50,000. To work to reverse global warming. 2008.

2210-8 Royal Shakespeare Company America, New York, NY, $170,000. For the commissioning of contemporary music. 2008.

2210-9 Royal Shakespeare Company America, New York, NY, $27,000. For education and outreach. 2008.

2211

Helen Bader Foundation, Inc.

233 N. Water St., 4th Fl.
Milwaukee, WI 53202-5729 (414) 224-6464
Contact: Daniel J. Bader, Pres.
FAX: (414) 224-1441; E-mail: info@hbf.org;
URL: http://www.hbf.org
Grants Database: http://www.hbf.org/search_grants.aspx

Established in 1991 in WI.
Donors: Daniel Bader Charitable Trust; David Bader Charitable Trust.
Grantmaker type: Independent foundation.
Financial data (yr. ended 08/31/10): Assets, $5,866,947 (M); gifts received, $10,700,000; expenditures, $12,394,768; qualifying distributions, $12,482,152; giving activities include $9,968,114 for 257 grants (high: $1,578,600; low: $500; average: $25,000–$250,000), $33,114 for 3 foundation-administered programs and $135,000 for 2 loans/program related investments (high: $125,000; low: $10,000).
Purpose and activities: The Helen Bader Foundation, Inc. strives to be a philanthropic leader in improving the quality of life of the diverse communities in which it works. The foundation makes grants, convenes partners, and shares knowledge to affect emerging issues in key areas: Alzheimer's and Aging, Economic Development, and Community Partnerships for Youth.
Fields of interest: Youth development; Alzheimer's disease; Medical research, institute; Human services; Children/youth, services; Economic development; Community/economic development; Jewish federated giving programs; Jewish agencies & synagogues; Religion.
International interests: Israel.
Type of support: General/operating support; Annual campaigns; Capital campaigns; Building/renovation; Debt reduction; Program development; Conferences/seminars; Seed money; Scholarship funds; Research; Technical assistance; Program-related investments/loans.
Limitations: Applications accepted. Giving primarily in the greater Milwaukee, WI, area for education and economic development; giving locally and nationally for Alzheimer's disease and dementia; giving in Israel for early childhood development. PRI emphasis is Milwaukee. No grants to individuals, including individual scholarships.
Publications: Application guidelines; Annual report (including application guidelines); Grants list.
Application information: The grants process has now moved online. After receipt of the preliminary application form, the foundation will send an e-mail regarding the status of the application. If a full proposal is requested, an on-site visit will also be required. Full proposals may not be submitted via fax or E-mail. Application form required.
Initial approach: Preliminary application form
Copies of proposal: 1
Deadline(s): Preliminary application: Dec. 9; Full proposal: Jan.15
Board meeting date(s): May and Nov.
Final notification: Within 2 weeks

Officers and Directors:* Jere D. McGaffey,* Chair. and Treas.; Daniel J. Bader,* Pres.; David M. Bader,* V.P.; Lisa G. Hiller, V.P., Admin.; Robin B. Mayrl, V.P., Prog. Devel.; Deirdre H. Britt,* Secy.; Linda C. Bader; Michelle Berrong; Frances Klitsner Wolff.
Number of staff: 10 full-time professional; 2 part-time professional; 3 full-time support; 1 part-time support.
EIN: 391710914
Recent grants for international programs:

2211-1 Alzheimers Association of Israel, Ramat Gan, Israel, $64,000. For Capacity Building and Creativity and Dementia Education and Training Initiative. 2010.

2211-2 Alzheimers Disease International, London, England, $20,000. For Alzheimer University Training Program. 2010.

2211-3 American Jewish Joint Distribution Committee, New York, NY, $150,000. For Day Care Center for Elderly with Dementia in Ramat Gan. 2010.

2211-4 American Jewish Joint Distribution Committee, New York, NY, $10,000. For JDC Programs in Tunisia and Turkey. 2010.

2211-5 Doctors Without Borders USA, New York, NY, $10,000. For Emergency Relief Programs in Haiti. 2010.

2211-6 International Centre for Democratic Transition, Budapest, Hungary, $25,000. For General Operations. 2010.

2211-7 Israel Association of Community Centers, Jerusalem, Israel, $38,000. For Gonenim Multicultural Music Center. 2010.

2211-8 MELABEV-Community Clubs for Eldercare, Jerusalem, Israel, $70,000. For English Speakers Center. 2010.

2211-9 Mi Refugio, Rockville, MD, $10,000. For Purchase of a New 75 Passenger International School Bus. 2010.

2211-10 Prevent Alzheimers Disease 2020, Rockville, MD, $56,000. For Proposal for the Establishment of Israeli Successful Replication of WRAP. 2010.

2211-11 University of Wisconsin Foundation, Wisconsin Alzheimers Institute, Madison, WI, $118,000. For Alzheimer's Prevention, Education, and Research Initiative in Israel: Feasibility and Planning Meeting. 2010.

2212

The Lynde and Harry Bradley Foundation, Inc.

1241 N. Franklin Pl.
Milwaukee, WI 53202-2901 (414) 291-9915
Contact: Daniel P. Schmidt, V.P., Progs.
FAX: (414) 291-9991; URL: http://www.bradleyfdn.org
Grants Database: http://www.bradleyfdn.org/2008_grantees.asp

Incorporated in 1942 in WI as the Allen-Bradley Foundation, Inc.; adopted present name in 1985.
Donors: Harry L. Bradley‡; Caroline D. Bradley‡; Margaret B. Bradley‡; Margaret Loock Trust; Allen-Bradley Co.; Michael Keiser; Mrs. Michael Keiser.
Grantmaker type: Independent foundation.
Financial data (yr. ended 12/31/10): Assets, $561,556,697 (M); gifts received, $1,266,000; expenditures, $51,842,750; qualifying distributions, $47,639,126; giving activities include

$42,346,950 for 716 grants (high: $3,000,000; low: $500).
Purpose and activities: Support for projects that cultivate a renewed, healthier, and more vigorous sense of citizenship, at home and abroad. Projects will reflect the assumption that free men and women are genuinely self-governing, personally responsible citizens, able to run their daily affairs without the intrusive therapies of the bureaucratic, social service state. Consequently, they will seek to reinvigorate and revive the authority of the traditional institutions of civil society - families, schools, churches, neighborhoods, and entrepreneurial enterprises - that cultivate and provide room for the exercise of citizenship, individual responsibility, and strong moral character. Projects reflecting this view of citizenship and civil society may be demonstrations with national significance; public policy research in economics, politics, culture, or foreign affairs; or media and public education undertakings. Local support is directed toward cultural programs, education, social services, medical and health programs, and public policy research.
Fields of interest: Humanities; History/archaeology; Arts; Education, research; Higher education; Education; Youth development, citizenship; International affairs, foreign policy; International affairs; Economics; Political science; Public policy, research; Public affairs, citizen participation; Public affairs.
Type of support: General/operating support; Continuing support; Annual campaigns; Building/renovation; Equipment; Program development; Conferences/seminars; Professorships; Publication; Curriculum development; Fellowships; Internship funds; Scholarship funds; Research; Program-related investments/loans; Matching/challenge support.
Limitations: Applications accepted. Giving primarily in Milwaukee, WI; giving also on a national and international basis. No support for strictly denominational projects. No grants to individuals (except for Bradley Prizes), or for endowment funds.
Publications: Application guidelines; Annual report; Grants list; Occasional report (including application guidelines).
Application information: Application form not required.
Initial approach: Letter of inquiry
Copies of proposal: 1
Deadline(s): Feb. 1, May 1, Aug. 1 and Nov. 1
Board meeting date(s): Feb., May or June, Aug., and Nov.
Final notification: 3 to 5 months
Officers and Directors:* Terry Considine,* Chair.; David V. Uihlein, Jr.,* Vice-Chair.; Michael W. Grebe,* C.E.O. and Pres.; Cynthia K. Friauf, V.P., Finance and Treas.; Terri L. Farmer, V.P., Admin.; R. Michael Lempke, V.P., Investments; Robert E. Norton II, V.P., Donor Relations; Daniel P. Schmidt, V.P., Progs.; Thomas L. Smallwood,* Secy.; Mandy L. Hess, Cont.; Robert P. George; Dennis J. Kuester; San W. Orr, Jr.; Br. Bob Smith; George F. Will.
Number of staff: 9 full-time professional; 8 full-time support; 3 part-time support.
EIN: 396037928
Recent grants for international programs:

2212-1 Abdorrahman Boroumand Foundation, Washington, DC, $30,000. For The Foundation's program activities. 2010.

2212-2 American Foreign Policy Council, Washington, DC, $110,000. For general operations. 2010.

2212-3 American Foreign Policy Council, Washington, DC, $50,000. For accounting-system upgrade. 2010.

2212-4 AmeriCares, Stamford, CT, $50,000. For general operations. 2010.

2212-5 Association for the Study of the Middle East and Africa, Washington, DC, $50,000. For the annual conference. 2010.

2212-6 CARE USA, Atlanta, GA, $100,000. For general operations. 2010.

2212-7 Catholic Committee for Cultural Collaboration, Rome, Italy, $80,000. For the Committee's work with the Eastern Orthodox and the organization of the meeting of the Joint Commission for Theological Dialogue. 2010.

2212-8 Cato Institute, Washington, DC, $100,000. For a senior fellowship at the Center for Global Liberty and Prosperity. 2010.

2212-9 Center for a Free Cuba, Arlington, VA, $25,000. For general programming. 2010.

2212-10 Center for European Policy Analysis, Washington, DC, $45,000. For the Keeping New Allies project. 2010.

2212-11 Center for Immigration Studies, Washington, DC, $25,000. For work on national security as it relates to population and immigration. 2010.

2212-12 Center for Security Policy, Washington, DC, $75,000. For general operations. 2010.

2212-13 Center for Strategic and Budgetary Assessments, Washington, DC, $80,000. For research and education activities. 2010.

2212-14 Centre for Development and Enterprise, Johannesburg, South Africa, $200,000. For the development of a consortium of think tanks focusing on growth and development issues in Brazil, India, and South Africa. 2010.

2212-15 Centre for Social Justice, London, England, $50,000. For general operations. 2010.

2212-16 Consilium Conferentiarum Episcoporum Europae, Saint Gallen, Switzerland, $100,000. For program activities. 2010.

2212-17 Council on Foreign Relations, New York, NY, $25,000. For the Middle Eastern Studies program. 2010.

2212-18 Doctors Without Borders USA, New York, NY, $25,000. For general operations. 2010.

2212-19 Duke University, Durham, NC, $21,000. For the New Faces conference of the Triangle Institute for Security Studies. 2010.

2212-20 East-West Church and Ministry Report, Wilmore, KY, $25,000. For general operations. 2010.

2212-21 Foreign Policy Research Institute, Philadelphia, PA, $75,000. For the Center for the Study of America and the West. 2010.

2212-22 Foundation for the Defense of Democracies, Washington, DC, $125,000. For the Center for Law and Counterterrorism and the Investigative Reporting Project. 2010.

2212-23 Foundation for the Defense of Democracies, Washington, DC, $72,150. For a conference on US-Israel relations, sponsored jointly with the Hudson Institute. 2010.

2212-24 Freedom House, Washington, DC, $100,000. For a project on how technology impacts on the development of democratic institutions. 2010.

2212-25 George Washington University, Elliott School of International Affairs, Washington, DC, $25,000. For the Bradley Graduate and Post Graduate Fellowship Program. 2010.

2212-26 German Marshall Fund of the United States, Washington, DC, $375,000. For the Transatlantic Academy and the Funds Black Sea programming. 2010.

2212-27 German Marshall Fund of the United States, Washington, DC, $300,000. For the survey Transatlantic Trends: Immigration project. 2010.

2212-28 Heartland Institute, Chicago, IL, $75,000. For the International Conference on Climate Change. 2010.

2212-29 Heartland Institute, Chicago, IL, $50,000. For distribution of climate-change research in India. 2010.

2212-30 Hoover Institution on War, Revolution and Peace, Stanford, CA, $50,000. For the Working Group on Islamism and International Order. 2010.

2212-31 Hudson Institute, Washington, DC, $200,000. For the Center on Islam, Democracy and the Future of the Muslim World. 2010.

2212-32 Human Rights Foundation, New York, NY, $30,000. For general operations. 2010.

2212-33 Human Rights Foundation, New York, NY, $10,000. For general operations. 2010.

2212-34 Institute for Foreign Policy Analysis, Cambridge, MA, $100,000. For the Democracy in Latin America research and seminar project. 2010.

2212-35 Institute for Global Engagement, Arlington, VA, $150,000. For general operations. 2010.

2212-36 Institute for International Studies, Washington, DC, $200,000. For Culture of Lawfulness education in the Americas. 2010.

2212-37 Institute for the Study of War, Washington, DC, $30,000. For general operations. 2010.

2212-38 International Association for K-12 Online Learning, Vienna, VA, $16,000. For messaging project on on-line learning. 2010.

2212-39 International Theological Institute for Studies on Marriage and the Family, Trumau, Austria, $25,000. For a conference program for legislators. 2010.

2212-40 Johns Hopkins University, Baltimore, MD, $75,000. For Foreign Policy Institute at School of Advanced International Studies in Washington, DC. 2010.

2212-41 Johns Hopkins University, Baltimore, MD, $25,000. For the Bradley Graduate and Post Graduate Fellowship Program at School of Advanced International Studies in Washington, DC. 2010.

2212-42 Johns Hopkins University, Baltimore, MD, $25,000. For the Bradley Graduate and Post Graduate Fellowship Program in Middle East Studies at School of Advanced International Studies in Washington, DC. 2010.

2212-43 Johns Hopkins University, Baltimore, MD, $25,000. For the Strategic Studies program at School of Advanced International Studies in Washington, DC. 2010.

2212-44 Johns Hopkins University, Baltimore, MD, $20,000. For a seminar series on U.S. foreign policy at the School of Advanced International Studies in Washington, DC. 2010.

2212-45 Lay Centre at Foyer Unitas, Rome, Italy, $20,000. For general operations. 2010.

2212-46 Loyola University of Chicago, Chicago, IL, $25,000. For Loyola's Cuba Program. 2010.

2212-47 Mercy Ships, Garden Valley, TX, $10,000. For general operations. 2010.

2212-48 Middle East Forum, Philadelphia, PA, $25,000. For Campus Watch, Islamist Watch, and the Legal Project. 2010.

2212-49 Middle East Media Research Institute, Washington, DC, $35,000. For general operations. 2010.

2212-50 Mississippi State University, Mississippi State, MS, $25,000. For a project on maritime security at the Center for International Security and Strategic Studies. 2010.

2212-51 National Bureau of Asian Research, Seattle, WA, $190,000. For Strategic Asia and the Pyle Center for Northeast Asian Studies. 2010.

2212-52 National Bureau of Asian Research, Seattle, WA, $50,000. For the PLA Resource project. 2010.

2212-53 National Endowment for Democracy, Washington, DC, $75,000. For the Journal of Democracy. 2010.

2212-54 National Endowment for Democracy, Washington, DC, $25,000. For the NED Democracy Award program. 2010.

2212-55 National Strategy Information Center, Washington, DC, $375,000. For general operations. 2010.

2212-56 Pacific Academy for Advanced Studies, Aliso Viejo, CA, $40,000. For the Alamos Alliance. 2010.

2212-57 Project on Transitional Democracies, Washington, DC, $75,000. For the Formalizing the Eastern Policy of the West project. 2010.

2212-58 Russian-American Christian University, Wheaton, MD, $40,000. For a lectureship series. 2010.

2212-59 Saint Gregory the Theologian Charity Foundation, Moscow, Russia, $300,000. For a series of educational and cultural initiatives. 2010.

2212-60 SAT-7 North American, Easton, MD, $20,000. For program activities. 2010.

2212-61 Southeastern Legal Foundation, Marietta, GA, $25,000. For the Global Warming Litigation Project. 2010.

2212-62 Stanford University, Stanford Institute for Economic Policy Research, Stanford, CA, $100,000. For the Center on Democracy, Development, and the Rule of Laws Program on Liberation Technology. 2010.

2212-63 Tufts University, Fletcher School of Law and Diplomacy, Medford, MA, $25,000. For the Bradley Graduate and Post Graduate Fellowship Program. 2010.

2212-64 Tufts University, Fletcher School of Law and Diplomacy, Medford, MA, $25,000. For the Bradley Graduate and Post Graduate Fellowship Program. 2010.

2212-65 Tufts University, Fletcher School of Law and Diplomacy, Medford, MA, $25,000. For the Bradley Graduate and Post Graduate Fellowship Program. 2010.

2212-66 Ukrainian Catholic Education Foundation, Chicago, IL, $100,000. For general program activities. 2010.

2212-67 We Remember Foundation, Washington, DC, $25,000. For publication projects promoting democracy principles and values. 2010.

2212-68 Witherspoon Institute, Princeton, NJ, $75,000. For a research project on national security. 2010.

2213
Central Asian Development Agency
656 Stourbridge Pl.
Wales, WI   53183-9766   (262) 490-8589

Established in 1995 in GA.
Grantmaker type: Public charity.
Financial data (yr. ended 12/31/09): Assets, $297 (M); expenditures, $1,209.
Purpose and activities: The agency supports the building of a national training center in Nepal.
Fields of interest: Community/economic development.
International interests: Nepal.
Limitations: Giving limited to Nepal.
Officers: Henry Couser, Chair.; Will Longenecker,* Vice-Chair.; Dave Lovett, Pres. and Treas.; Patrick Railey, Secy.
Board Members: David Nelson.
EIN: 391746442

2214
The Cops Foundation of Kimberly, Inc.
(formerly Cops Foundation, Inc.)
P.O. Box 12800
Green Bay, WI 54307-2800

Established in 1988 in WI.
Donors: Henry P. Cops†; James G. Cops†; Joyce Cops; Thomas P. Cops†.
Grantmaker type: Independent foundation.
Financial data (yr. ended 12/31/10): Assets, $2,309,977 (M); gifts received, $21,215; expenditures, $169,396; qualifying distributions, $149,687; giving activities include $149,687 for grants.
Purpose and activities: Giving primarily to religious organizations.
Fields of interest: Religion; Christian agencies & churches.
International interests: Africa; Central America; South America; Asia.
Type of support: General/operating support.
Limitations: Applications accepted. Giving primarily on an international basis. No grants to individuals.
Application information:
    Initial approach: Letter
    Deadline(s): None
Officers: James G. Cops, Pres.; Thomas Cops, V.P.; Henry Cops, Secy.-Treas.
EIN: 391633247

2215
Patrick and Anna M. Cudahy Fund
P.O. Box 11978
Milwaukee, WI 53211-0978 (414) 271-6020
E-mail: secretary@cudahyfund.org; IL address: 1609 Sherman Ave., Ste. 207, Evanston, IL, 60201-3753; IL tel.: (847) 866-0760; fax: (847) 475-0679; URL: http://www.cudahyfund.org

Incorporated in 1949 in WI.
Donor: Michael F. Cudahy†.
Grantmaker type: Independent foundation.
Financial data (yr. ended 12/31/10): Assets, $12,945,169 (M); expenditures, $1,268,937; qualifying distributions, $1,228,828; giving activities include $1,066,382 for 167 grants (high: $48,132; low: $750).
Purpose and activities: Primary areas of interest include the arts, education, youth, international relief, and social services. Support for the homeless, family services, and international development programs; support also for national programs concerned with environmental and public interest issues, and cultural and civic affairs programs.
Fields of interest: Arts; Adult/continuing education; Adult education—literacy, basic skills & GED; Education, reading; Education; Environment; Food services; Housing/shelter, development; Human services; Youth, services; Family services; Homeless, human services; International economic development; International relief; International human rights; Rural development; Public affairs; Catholic agencies & churches; Children/youth; Aging; Disabilities, people with; Women; Immigrants/refugees; Economically disadvantaged; Homeless.
International interests: Africa.
Type of support: General/operating support; Continuing support; Annual campaigns; Building/ renovation; Equipment; Program development; Seed money; Technical assistance; Matching/challenge support.
Limitations: Applications not accepted. Giving limited to Chicago, IL, and WI for local programs and for international (U.S.-based) programs. No grants to individuals, or for endowments; no loans.
Publications: Grants list.
Application information: Unsolicited requests for funds not accepted or considered.
    Board meeting date(s): Usually in Mar., June, Sept., and Dec.
Officers and Directors:* Hon. Richard D. Cudahy,* Chair.; Janet S. Cudahy,* M.D., Pres.; Richard D. Cudahy, Jr., Secy.-Treas.; James Bailey; Kit Cudahy; Molly Cudahy; Patrick G. Cudahy; Barbara Holtz; Kristi Leswing; Annette Stoddard-Freeman.
Number of staff: 1 part-time professional; 1 part-time support.
EIN: 390991972

2216
Nelson B. Delavan Foundation
c/o JPMorgan Chase Bank, N.A.
P.O. Box 3038
Milwaukee, WI 53201-1308
Application address: c/o JPMorgan Chase Bank, N.A., Attn.: Paul Hurley, One Chase Square, Rochester, NY 14643, tel.: (585) 797-2618

Established in 1983 in NY.
Grantmaker type: Independent foundation.
Financial data (yr. ended 12/31/10): Assets, $5,763,631 (M); expenditures, $296,580; qualifying distributions, $262,395; giving activities include $262,395 for grants.
Purpose and activities: Giving primarily to organizations that support performances of fine arts.
Fields of interest: Performing arts; Arts; Medical school/education; Animal welfare; Health care; Health organizations, association; Human services; Children/youth, services; Women, centers/ services; International affairs; Women.
Type of support: General/operating support.
Limitations: Applications accepted. Giving primarily in the Finger Lakes area and Monroe County, NY. No grants to individuals.
Application information: Application form not required.
    Initial approach: Letter
    Copies of proposal: 2
    Deadline(s): Most applications reviewed between Feb. 1 and Mar. 15, and between Sept. 1 and Oct. 15

Trustee: JPMorgan Chase Bank, N.A.
EIN: 166260274

2217
Eastman Kodak Charitable Trust
c/o JPMorgan Chase Bank, N.A.
P.O. Box 3038
Milwaukee, WI 53201-1308
Application address: Essie Calhoun, Dir., Corp. Contribs., 343 State St., Rochester, NY 14650, tel.: (585) 724-2434

Trust established in 1952 in NY.
Donor: Eastman Kodak Co.
Grantmaker type: Company-sponsored foundation.
Financial data (yr. ended 12/31/10): Assets, $1,281,710 (M); expenditures, $446,667; qualifying distributions, $440,500; giving activities include $440,500 for grants.
Purpose and activities: The trust supports organizations involved with education, health, asthma, human services, international relief, and community development.
Fields of interest: Higher education; Education; Hospitals (general); Health care; Asthma; Children/ youth, services; Family services; Human services; International relief; Community/economic development.
Type of support: Conferences/seminars; Equipment; General/operating support; Continuing support; Program development; Scholarship funds.
Limitations: Applications accepted. Giving primarily in areas of company operations in Canada, China, Japan, Mexico, and the United Kingdom. No grants to individuals; low priority for building or endowments; no loans; no matching gifts.
Publications: Corporate giving report.
Application information: Application form not required.
    Initial approach: Proposal
    Deadline(s): None
    Board meeting date(s): Monthly
Trustee: JPMorgan Chase Bank, N.A.
EIN: 166015274

2218
Global Christian Interaction, Inc.
9667 S. 20th St.
Oak Creek, WI 53154-4931

Established in 1990 in WI.
Donor: Michael H. Polaski.
Grantmaker type: Operating foundation.
Financial data (yr. ended 12/31/09): Assets, $7,248,292 (M); expenditures, $527,402; qualifying distributions, $412,486; giving activities include $412,486 for grants.
Fields of interest: Human services; Christian agencies & churches.
International interests: Bulgaria; Kenya; Global programs.
Limitations: Applications not accepted. Giving primarily in TX and WI, and in Sofia, Bulgaria, and Meru, Kenya. No grants to individuals.
Application information: Contributes only to pre-selected organizations.
Officers and Directors:* Michael H. Polaski,* Pres. and Treas.; Michael J. Polaski,* Secy.; Catherine J. Polaski.
EIN: 391695712

2219
Joseph & Sally Handleman Charitable Foundation Trust A
c/o JPMorgan Chase Bank, N.A.
P.O. Box 3038
Milwaukee, WI 53201-3038
Application address: c/o JPMorgan Chase Bank, N.A., 3399 PGA Blvd., Ste. 100, Palm Beach Gardens, FL 33410, tel.: (561) 799-1132

Donor: Joan Sadoff.
Grantmaker type: Independent foundation.
Financial data (yr. ended 12/31/10): Assets, $6,335,060 (M); expenditures, $711,403; qualifying distributions, $663,782; giving activities include $654,000 for 13 grants (high: $600,000; low: $500).
Purpose and activities: Giving primarily to Jewish organizations and for higher education.
Fields of interest: Health sciences school/education; Arts; Higher education; Business school/education; Education; Legal services; Housing/shelter, development; Human services; American Red Cross; Residential/custodial care, hospices; Aging, centers/services; Jewish agencies & synagogues; Women.
International interests: Israel.
Limitations: Applications accepted. Giving primarily in FL, MI, NY, and PA.
Application information: Application form not required.
   Initial approach: Proposal
   Deadline(s): None
Trustee: Joan Ara Sadoff.
Agent: JPMorgan Chase Bank, N.A.
EIN: 656263326

2220
International Children's Fund, Inc.
(formerly Son Light Ministries, Inc.)
P.O. Box 583
Neenah, WI 54957-0583
Contact: David J. Bruenning, Pres. and C.E.O.

Grantmaker type: Public charity.
Financial data (yr. ended 09/30/10): Revenue, $38,273,722; assets, $504,063 (M); gifts received, $38,272,615; expenditures, $38,196,737; giving activities include $37,264,604 for grants to organizations outside the U.S.
Purpose and activities: The fund distributes supplies to relief organization in the U.S. and Africa that help needy children.
Fields of interest: Children, services; Human services; International relief.
International interests: Africa.
Type of support: In-kind gifts.
Limitations: Giving limited to the U.S. and Africa.
Officers and Directors:* David J. Bruenning,* Pres. and C.E.O.; Larry Oettel,* V.P.; Jean Hoppe,* Secy.; Carol Grady,* Treas.; Mary Bruenning.
EIN: 391303430

2221
C. Paul Johnson Family Charitable Foundation
10000 Innovation Dr., No. 250
Milwaukee, WI 53226-4837

Established in 1988 in IL.

Donor: C. Paul Johnson.
Grantmaker type: Independent foundation.
Financial data (yr. ended 12/31/10): Assets, $42,594 (M); gifts received, $233,361; expenditures, $354,221; qualifying distributions, $352,007; giving activities include $352,007 for grants.
Fields of interest: Higher education; Education; Environment, natural resources; Human services; Science.
International interests: Africa; Israel.
Type of support: Endowments; Capital campaigns; General/operating support; Scholarship funds; Research.
Limitations: Applications not accepted. Giving on a national basis. No grants to individuals.
Application information: Contributes only to pre-selected organizations.
Trustees: Adrienne Johnson; C. Paul Johnson; Debra Johnson; Julianne Johnson; Vince Mancuso; Rebecca Milne; Deborah Reguera.
EIN: 366891454

2222
Kikkoman Foods Foundation, Inc.
P.O. Box 69
Walworth, WI 53184-0069   (262) 275-6181
Contact: Robert V. Conover, Dir.

Established in 1993 in WI.
Donor: Kikkoman Foods, Inc.
Grantmaker type: Company-sponsored foundation.
Financial data (yr. ended 12/31/10): Assets, $9,879,003 (M); gifts received, $500,000; expenditures, $452,536; qualifying distributions, $449,420; giving activities include $449,410 for 80 grants (high: $100,000; low: $250).
Purpose and activities: The foundation supports organizations involved with arts and culture, education, human services, and international exchange and economics.
Fields of interest: Performing arts; Arts; Secondary school/education; Higher education; Education; Disasters, preparedness/services; Youth, services; Developmentally disabled, centers & services; Human services; International exchange, students; International economics/trade policy.
Type of support: General/operating support; Annual campaigns; Scholarship funds; Sponsorships.
Limitations: Applications accepted. Giving primarily in WI. No support for private organizations, political organizations, religious or sectarian organizations, or discriminatory organizations. No grants to individuals, or for raffle tickets or product purchases, non-food-related scientific or development research, travel or lodging, or promotional events.
Publications: Application guidelines.
Application information: Application form not required.
   Initial approach: Proposal
   Deadline(s): None
   Board meeting date(s): Monthly
Directors: Robert V. Conover; Noriaki Horikiri; Satoshi Kawamata; Karl N. Keane; Daniel P. Miller; Yuzaburo Mogi; Milton E. Neshek; Takashi Ozawa; Kazuo Shimizu; Mitsuo Someya; Ryohei Tsuji, Ph.D.
EIN: 391763633

2223
John M. Kohler Foundation, Inc.
c/o US Bank, N.A.
P.O. Box 2043
Milwaukee, WI 53201-9668
Application address: c/o US Bank, N.A., Attn.: Brian Versey, 605 N. 8th St., Ste. 2, Sheboygan, WI, 53081-4520; tel.: (920) 459-6942

Established in 2003 in WI.
Donor: W.M. Collins Kohler.
Grantmaker type: Independent foundation.
Financial data (yr. ended 12/31/10): Assets, $2,591 (M); gifts received, $207,620; expenditures, $228,084; qualifying distributions, $227,296; giving activities include $227,296 for grants.
Fields of interest: Environment, water resources; Arts, multipurpose centers/programs; Higher education; Human services; International affairs.
Limitations: Applications accepted. Giving primarily in WI, with some giving in GA.
Application information: Application form not required.
   Deadline(s): None
Directors: Julilly W. Kohler; Robert T. Melzer; Cindy Miller.
EIN: 200497413

2224
John N. & Kathleen S. MacDonough Foundation, Inc.
6208 Brumder Dr.
Hartland, WI 53029-9709

Established in 1998 in WI.
Donors: John N. MacDonough; Kathleen S. MacDonough.
Grantmaker type: Independent foundation.
Financial data (yr. ended 12/31/10): Assets, $2,065,182 (M); expenditures, $148,445; qualifying distributions, $144,805; giving activities include $144,805 for 25 grants (high: $75,000; low: $500).
Fields of interest: Higher education, university; Education; Health organizations; Human services; International relief; Christian agencies & churches.
Limitations: Applications not accepted. Giving primarily in NC and WI. No grants to individuals.
Application information: Contributes only to pre-selected organizations.
Trustees: Michael W. Grebe; John N. MacDonough; Kathleen S. MacDonough; Stephen J. MacDonough.
EIN: 391924028

2225
Madison Rotary Foundation
22 N. Carroll St., Ste. 202
Madison, WI 53703-3377
E-mail: office@rotarymadison.org; URL: http://rotarymadison.org/

Established in 1942.
Grantmaker type: Public charity.
Financial data (yr. ended 06/30/10): Revenue, $207,201; assets, $7,114,886 (M); gifts received, $256,190; expenditures, $562,928; giving activities include $224,723 for grants, $9,700 for grants to organizations outside the U.S., and $216,825 for grants to individuals.

Purpose and activities: The foundation awards scholarships to students, and grants to community charitable organizations.
Fields of interest: International development; Education; Community/economic development.
Type of support: Scholarships—to individuals.
Limitations: Applications accepted. Giving primarily in Madison, WI.
Publications: Application guidelines; Newsletter.
Application information: Application form required.
  Initial approach: Download application form
  Deadline(s): Nov. 30 for International and
    Community Grants
Officers and Trustees: Kathryne M. McGowan,* Pres.; Eleanor M. Schatz, V.P.; Patricia L. Jenkins, Secy.; Bruce D. Westervelt, Treas.; Terry C. Anderson; Nathan F. Brand; Laura M. Davis; Dale J. Henricks; Stanley L. Inhorn; Mary Carr Lee; and 7 additional trustees.
EIN: 930757050

2226
Meehan Family Foundation, Inc.
(formerly Daniel E. Meehan Foundation, Inc.)
1473 E. Goodrich Ln.
Fox Point, WI 53217-2950
Contact: Daniel E. Meehan, Chair.

Established in 1983 in WI.
Donors: Daniel E. Meehan; Eileen Meehan.
Grantmaker type: Independent foundation.
Financial data (yr. ended 12/31/10): Assets, $2,765,202 (M); gifts received, $4,853; expenditures, $893,529; qualifying distributions, $890,323; giving activities include $886,283 for 32 grants (high: $157,500; low: $250).
Purpose and activities: Support for higher and secondary education, and social services. Also awards scholarships to children of employees of Meehan Seaway Service.
Fields of interest: Jewish agencies & synagogues; Catholic agencies & churches; Secondary school/education; Higher education; Hospitals (specialty); Human services; International relief.
Type of support: Scholarship funds; Employee-related scholarships.
Publications: Application guidelines.
Application information: Individual scholarships are awarded only to children or grandchildren of employees of Meehan Seaway Service. Foundation is currently accepting applications from organizations. Application form required.
  Initial approach: Letter or inter-company mail
  Deadline(s): May 15
  Board meeting date(s): June and Nov.
Officers: Daniel E. Meehan, Chair.; Laurie Lukaszewicz, Pres.; Eileen Meehan, V.P.; Theresa R Meehan-Felknor, Treas.
Director: Henry Loos.
EIN: 391445333

2227
Milwaukee Jewish Federation, Inc.
1360 N. Prospect Ave.
Milwaukee, WI 53202-3016 (414) 390-5700
FAX: (414) 390-5782;
E-mail: info@milwaukeejewish.org; URL: http://www.milwaukeejewish.org

Grantmaker type: Public charity.

Financial data (yr. ended 06/30/10): Revenue, $19,270,188; assets, $168,802,473 (M); gifts received, $15,213,836; expenditures, $27,824,189; giving activities include $8,498,918 for 40 grants (high: $584,985; low: $5,000), and $539,636 for 3 grants to individuals (high: $50,000; low: $15,856).
Purpose and activities: The federation's mission is to ensure the continuity of the Jewish people, to enhance the quality of Jewish life and to build a strong unified Jewish community in Milwaukee, in Israel and throughout the world.
Fields of interest: Community/economic development; Human services; Jewish agencies & synagogues.
International interests: Israel.
Directors: Jerry Benjamin, Pres.; Frederick R. Croen, Vice Pres.; Moshe Katz, Vice Pres.; Marlene Lauwasser, Vice Pres.; Marci Taxman, Vice Pres.; Andrea Schneider, Secy.; Richard H. Meyer, Exec. Vice Pres.; and 51 additional directors.
EIN: 390806312

2228
Sand County Foundation, Inc.
c/o David Allen
16 N. Carroll St., Ste 450
Madison, WI 53703-2784 (608) 663-4605
FAX: (608) 663-4617; E-mail: info@sandcounty.net;
URL: http://www.sandcounty.net
E-Newsletter: http://sandcounty.net/newsletter/subscriber/signup.aspx
Facebook: http://www.facebook.com/pages/Monona-WI/Sand-County-Foundation/50784653564
Twitter: http://twitter.com/sandcountyfdn/
YouTube: http://www.youtube.com/SandCountyFdn

Classified as a private operating foundation in 1987.
Donors: Nash Williams†; Wisconsin Dept. of Natural Resources; Norman Basset Foundation; U.S. Fish and Wildlife Service; Ed Warner; Wisconsin Dept. of Transportation; Lynde & Harry Bradley Foundation.
Grantmaker type: Operating foundation.
Financial data (yr. ended 12/31/10): Assets, $8,589,795 (M); gifts received, $2,713,179; expenditures, $2,192,753; qualifying distributions, $2,158,318; giving activities include $412,718 for 19 grants (high: $170,309; low: $1,062), $55,071 for 19 grants to individuals (high: $10,000; low: $150), and $1,588,792 for foundation-administered programs.
Purpose and activities: Giving to advance the use of ethical and scientifically sound land management practices and partnerships for the benefit of people and the ecological landscape.
Fields of interest: Environment, water resources; Environment, land resources; Education.
International interests: Southern Africa.
Type of support: General/operating support; Program development; Conferences/seminars; Research.
Limitations: Applications not accepted. No grants to individuals.
Publications: Annual report; Newsletter.
Application information: Contributes only to pre-selected organizations.
  Board meeting date(s): Feb., June, Sept., and Dec.

Officers and Directors: Reed Coleman,* Chair.; David J. Hanson,* Vice-Chair. and Secy.; Brent M. Haglund,* Pres.; Dr. Ingrid "Indy" Burke; George Kennedy; Scott Klug; Terry Mulcahy; Dr. Stanley A. Temple; Charles H. Thompson; John N. Umlauf; Ed Warner.
Number of staff: 6 full-time professional; 1 full-time support.
EIN: 396089450

2229
Sarvodaya U.S.A.
122 State St., Ste. 5101
Madison, WI 53703-2500 (608) 442-5945
FAX: (608) 310-5865;
E-mail: info@sarvodayausa.org; URL: http://www.sarvodayausa.org

Grantmaker type: Public charity.
Financial data (yr. ended 12/31/10): Revenue, $216,873; assets, $106,652 (M); gifts received, $206,802; expenditures, $217,912; giving activities include $105,012 for grants to organizations outside the U.S.
Purpose and activities: The mission of the organization is to learn from and support the work of the Sarvodaya Shramadana Movement of Sri Lanka and worldwide, and to facilitate the application of the Movement's holistic community development vision and philosophy in the U.S.
Fields of interest: International relief; International development; Community/economic development.
Limitations: Giving limited to Sri Lanka and Nepal
Officers and Board Members: Richard Brooks,* Chair.; Mary Woodward,* Treas.; Shisir Khanal, Exec. Dir.; Dr. Vinya Ariyaratne; George Bond, Ph.D.; Karen Faster; Richard Flyer; Dr. Harsha P. Jayatilake; Patricia Masters, Ph.D.; Michael Trainer.
EIN: 133358148

2230
Jack DeLoss Taylor Charitable Trust
c/o Buttonwood Partners, Inc.
701 Deming Way, No. 100
Madison, WI 53717-2916 (608) 827-6400
Contact: Christopher Bugg, Tr.

Established in 1989 in WI.
Grantmaker type: Independent foundation.
Financial data (yr. ended 06/30/11): Assets, $7,434,651 (M); expenditures, $560,114; qualifying distributions, $526,323; giving activities include $496,000 for 61 grants (high: $102,000; low: $500).
Purpose and activities: Giving primarily to organizations which provide financial assistance to needy people throughout the world, with preference given to children of underdeveloped countries whose needs are the most fundamental, such as food and medical care.
Fields of interest: Food services; Nutrition; Housing/shelter, development; Human services; Children/youth, services; Child development, services; United Ways and Federated Giving Programs; Christian agencies & churches.
International interests: Developing countries.
Type of support: Building/renovation; Equipment; Emergency funds; Program development; Matching/challenge support.

Limitations: Applications accepted. Giving in the U.S., with some emphasis on WI. No grants to individuals.
Application information: Application form not required.
Initial approach: Letter
Copies of proposal: 1
Deadline(s): Jan. 31
Board meeting date(s): Early May
Final notification: June 30
Trustees: Christopher Bugg; Lyle Larson; Dr. Catherine H. Taylor.
EIN: 396510710

2231
The Wagner Foundation, Ltd.
(formerly R. H. Wagner Foundation, Ltd.)
P.O. Box 307
Lyons, WI 53148-0307

Established in 1981 in WI.
Donors: Richard H. Wagner; Roberta L. Wagner; Ken Essman; Marcy Essman; Bob O'Neil; Julie O'Neil; S. Heekin; Molly Carl; Roger Ringelman; Burlington Rotary Club; Robert W. Baird Foundation; The Word at Work Foundation; Rotary Club of Elmbrook; Kikkoman Foods Foundation.
Grantmaker type: Independent foundation.
Financial data (yr. ended 06/30/11): Assets, $9,715,782 (M); gifts received, $62,000; expenditures, $464,989; qualifying distributions, $458,665; giving activities include $411,026 for 26 grants (high: $65,750; low: $50).
Purpose and activities: Giving primarily for humanitarian aid in Central America and Africa; support also for education, including Roman Catholic schools, and human services.
Fields of interest: Education; Human services; Children/youth, services; International relief; Catholic agencies & churches.
International interests: Bermuda; Central America; Belize; Philippines.

Type of support: Grants to individuals; Equipment; Scholarship funds.
Limitations: Applications not accepted. Giving in the U.S. and in Africa, Central America and South America.
Application information: Unsolicited requests for funds not accepted.
Officers: Richard H. Wagner, Pres.; Roberta L. Wagner, V.P.
Directors: Melissa Doyle; Adam Essman; Emily Essman; Ken Essman; Marcy Essman; Emily Labadie; Bob O'Neill; Julie O'Neill; Marci O'Neill; Meghan O'Neill; Molly O'Neill.
EIN: 391311452

2232
Wisconsin Community Fund
1202 Williamson St., Ste. 109
Madison, WI 53703-4830 (608) 251-6834
Contact: Bruce Moffat, Exec. Dir.
FAX: (815) 361-9183; E-mail: info@wcfund.org;
Additional address: 1442 N. Farwell Ave., Ste. 100, Milwaukee, WI 53202-2913, tel.: (414) 225-9965, fax: (414) 225-9964; URL: http://www.wcfund.org
Wisconsin Community Fund's Philanthropy Promise: http://www.ncrp.org/philanthropys-promise/who

Established in 1982 in WI.
Grantmaker type: Public charity.
Financial data (yr. ended 06/30/10): Revenue, $279,680; assets, $391,452 (M); gifts received, $260,694; expenditures, $196,621; program services expenses, $135,797; giving activities include $85,999 for grants.
Purpose and activities: The fund provides assistance to grassroots organizations in Wisconsin working for social justice.
Fields of interest: Environment, legal rights; Health care; Employment, labor unions/organizations; International peace/security; International human

rights; Civil/human rights, LGBTQ; Civil rights, race/intergroup relations; Civil/human rights; Minorities; Native Americans/American Indians; Women.
International interests: Central America; South America.
Type of support: General/operating support; Income development; Management development/capacity building; Equipment; Emergency funds; Program development; Conferences/seminars; Publication; Seed money; Scholarship funds; Technical assistance; Consulting services; Program evaluation; In-kind gifts; Matching/challenge support.
Limitations: Applications accepted. Giving primarily in WI. No support for social service, research organizations, or groups with budgets over $200,000. No grants for academic, cultural, or religious projects; annual fund drives; endowments; or capital campaigns.
Publications: Application guidelines; Annual report (including application guidelines); Grants list; Informational brochure; Multi-year report; Newsletter; Program policy statement.
Application information: General Fund Grants are limited to WI and are only granted to social change organizations. Application form required.
Initial approach: Letter or telephone
Copies of proposal: 16
Deadline(s): Varies annually; contact fund for updates
Board meeting date(s): Eight times per year
Final notification: Mar.
Officers and Directors:* Karen Campbell,* Pres.; Timeka Rumph,* V.P.; Cathy Miller,* Secy.; Mik Engleson,* Treas.; Bruce Moffat, Exec. Dir.; Dennis M. Grzezinski; Rob Meiksins; Hanif NuMan; Kathy Ronco.
Number of staff: 2 full-time professional; 2 part-time professional; 1 part-time support.
EIN: 391398124

INDEX TO DONORS, OFFICERS, TRUSTEES

Capital Research & Management Co., 91
Capital Source Finance LLC, 509
Capital Trust Co. of Delaware, The, 402
Caplan, Barry, 293
Capozzi, Lou, 582
Cappello, Alexander, 554
Cappello, Juan Carlos, 1401, 1408
Cappuzzo, Salvatore, 1727
Caravano, Tony, 1760
Caravati, Charles M., Jr., 2105
Cardenas, David, 618
Cardenas, Gustavo, 1988
Cardenas, Mar, 125
Cardin, Sanford "Sandy" R., 1830
Cardoso, Eliana, 903
Cardoso, Fernando Henrique, 501
Cardwell, Jack, 2046
Care Bags Foundation, 47
Care Now, 2047
Careplus, 1519
Carey, Andy, 350
Carey, Elizabeth P., 1310
Carey, Emily N., 1310
Carey, Francis J., 1310
Carey, Francis J., III, 1310
Carey, H. Augustus, 1310
Carey, Jennifer L., 1077
Carey, Robert, 1467
Carey, William P., 1310
Cargo Express International, 402
Carino, Melissa, 1014
Carino, Olivia, 1289
Caris, Lorraine, 1545
Carl, Keith, 2126
Carl, Molly, 2231
Carleton, Julia, 1166
Carlezon, William A., Jr., 961
Carliner, David, 535
Carlisle, Jerry, 2024
Carlos, Maria H., 820
Carlos, Premthaj, 979
Carlson, Mary, 290, 374
Carlson, Paul, 1750
Carlson, Richard E., 286
Carlson, Tim, 1809
Carlston, Doug, 280
Carmack, David, 2119
Carmichael, Barie, 508
Carmine, Bryce, 840
Carnage, Roslyn, 1706
Carnegie Corporation of New York, 574
Carnegie, Andrew, 1312, 1868
Carnival Cruise Lines, Inc., 616
Caro, Elias, 629
Caro, Robert A., 1436
Carol Oates, Joyce, 1436
Carol, Dan, 345
Carpendale, Roesemary, 66
Carpenter, Adelaide, 2040
Carpenter, Richard N., 1213
Carpenter, Russell H., Jr., 535
Carr, Archie F., III, 625
Carr, Catherine E., 1838
Carr, Gregory C., 536
Carr, Kathleen D.H., 2134
Carr, R.L., 1826
Carrey Family Trust, 80
Carrey, James, 80
Carrick, Elizabeth, 820
Carrico, John D., 1177
Carrillo, Jenny Cooney, 67
Carroll, Betsy, 2159
Carroll, Catherine, 190
Carroll, Constance M., 307
Carroll, Joan, 1338
Carroll, Karen M., 525
Carroll, Nina, 222
Carroll, Sean, 907
Carroll, Sterling, 1765
Carroll-Pankhurst, Cindie, 1779
Carrucci, Richard T., 866
Carrus, Gerald, 746
Carrus, Janet, 746
Carsey, Eben, 386

Carson, Dan, 860
Carson, Emmett D., 323
Carter Gallatin Fund, 2119
Carter, C. William, 2095
Carter, David, 501
Carter, David H., 597
Carter, James E., 690
Carter, Jason, 690
Carter, Jimmy, 1556
Carter, Larry R., 100
Carter, Lynn, 1264
Carter, Majora, 1195
Carter, Michael, 1002
Carter, Quincy, 568
Carter, Rosalynn, 690
Carter, Theresa, 1813
Carter, William W., 921
Cartmill, Molly, 315
Cartner, Holly, 531
Carus, M. Blouke, 1316
Caruthers, Carol R., 1107
Carvalho, Joenia, 1622
Carvalho, Ricardo, 696
Carver, Doris, 402
Carzo, Rocco, 991
Casaclang, Eisen Jo, 1372
Casarez, Gloria, 1866
Casasbuenas, Julian, 517
Casdin, Alexander W., 1694
CASE, 990
Case, Jean, 584
Case, Jean N., 503
Case, Stephen M., 503
Casellas, Gilbert F., 1191
Casey Close, 1123
Casey, David, Rev., 1307
Casey, Sophia B., 1314
Casey, William J., 1314
Casey-Smith, Bernadette, 1314
Cashdin, Jeffrey, 541
Cashin, Richard M., 1691
Cashman, Thomas, 942
Casina, Carolina Barreto, 2141
Caslow, Mady, 1481
Caslow, Miriam, 1481
Cason, Roxanne Mankin, 440
Casper, Gerhard, 824
Cassell, Carol, 2159
Cassell, Richard A., 997
Cassidy, Frances, 1236
Cassidy, Gerald, 942
Cassidy, Kate W., 1721
Cassidy, Martin W., 1721
Cassino, Nick, 1854
Castaneda, Jorge, 1454
Castelle, George, 1206
Casten, Judith A., 747
Casten, Thomas R., 747
Castillo, Jovita, 1630
Castimatidis, Margo, 1596
Castonguay, Lyne, 699
Castro, Jorge, 1225
Castro, Ricardo, 1230
Castro, Ricardo A., 1393, 1593
Catalan, Denic, 1408
Catellus Land & Development
    Corporation and Subsidiaries, 404
Caterpillar Inc., 748
Cathay Pacific Airlines, 47
Catherwood, Susan W., 1906
Catholic Relief Services, 47
Cattan-Naslausky, Flavia, 1300
Cattaui, Maria Livanos, 912, 1461
Catto, Henry E., 497
Caufield, Frank J., 92, 1344
Caufield, Frank R., 92
Caufield, Kirsten N., 92
Caufield, Marilyn, 424
Caughman, James F., 1642
Cavaiola, Lawrence J., 2123
Cavanaugh, Gwendolyn, 982
Cavanaugh, Kenneth, 982
Cavanaugh, Peggy M., 625
Cavanaugh, Sarah, 2195

Cavanaugh, Tim, 2195
Caves, Douglas A., 1949
Cavoli, Mae, 1279
Cayce, Eugenia Topple, 696
Cayne, Patricia Denner, 1389
Cayton, Andrea Goldrich, 160
Cayton, Barry, 160
Cazal, Francisco "Tachi", 1224
Cazala, Beatrice, 1303
Celentano, John E., 1303
Celestina, Mary, 1780
Celestine, Von, 1990
Cengic, Smajl, 951
Centennial Foundation, 1665
Centers for Disease Control and
    Prevention, 1533
Central Pacific Bank, 719
Cephalon, Inc., 1533
CEPSA, 1013
Cerda, Alejandro, 1408
Ceremsak, Robert J., 146
Ceres Foundation, 231
Cerf, Elizabeth Weintz, 1440
Cernera, Anthony J., 1523, 1635
Cernol-McCann, Betty, 1704
Cerqueira, Custodio, 1242
Cerra, Frank B., 911
Cerrell, Joe, 577
Cervenak, Chris, 1003
CES Mgmt., Inc., 2146
Cestac, Francoise, 1261
Chabraja, Eleanor, 750
Chabraja, Nicholas, 750
Chadwick, Charles B., 1892
Chai, Nelson, 1706
Chainani, Kamlesh, 2103
Chainani, Luci, 2103
Chais Family Foundation, 1243
Chais, Stanley, 1243
Chakrapani, Durgam G., 1840
Chalkley, Michael, 1759
Cham, Mbye, Dr., 513
Chamberlain, Dan, Dr., 2156
Chamberlin, Ward, Jr., 1224
Chambers, Anne Cox, 1261
Chambers, Jennifer G., 1184
Chambers, John T., 100
Chambers, Michael J., 1184
Chambers, Mike, 2156
Chambers, Patricia A., 1184
Chambers, Raymond G., 1184, 1556
Chambers, Tina Brown, 1184
Chameli, Kathy Wahlert, 679
Champer, Jeanne M., 1126
Champion, Don, 680
Champlin, Byron, 1000
Chan, Benjamin Shun Lai, Rev., 1042
Chan, Chi-Chao, 432
Chan, Kenyon, 432
Chan, Ronnie C., 1272
Chan, Ted, 307
Chandler, Fay M., 982
Chandler, Howard M., 982
Chandler, Kay, 307
Chandler, Terry, 1476
Chandler, Vee, 1758
Chaney, Ari, 1134
Chang, Frederic C., 432
Chang, Joyce, 1369, 1694
Chang, Robert, 342
Chang, William H.C., 64
Chanin, Anthony, 203
Chanos, James, 1259
Chao Family Trust, 93
Chao, Amy, 93
Chao, Mark, 95
Chao, Ping, 93
Chao, Shiu-Kai, 93
Chapin, Jennifer, 1739
Chapin, Tom, 1739
Chapman, Craig E., 1236
Chapman, Debbie, 270
Chapman, Don, 1837
Chapman, Jon T., Rev., 836

Chapman, Max, 1253
Chapman, N. A., 2004
Chapman, Nancy, Dr., 1704
Chapman, Tom, 720
Chappell, John, Mrs., 1399
Charendoff, Mark, 1288
Charitable Lead Trust, The, 1053
Charities Aid Foundation, 106
Charles, Kris, 1051
Charles, Marion Oates, 1361
Charles-Pierre, Philip, 1366
Charnoff, Gerald, 915
Chartock, Lewis, 1132
Chase, Gregory C., 739
Chase, Nora, 1536
Chasen, Lyn, 915
Chasin, Charlie, 1562
Chasin, Laura, 1696
Chastang, Lawrence J., 568
Chatlos, Janet, 626
Chatlos, William F., 626
Chatlos, William J., 626
Chatlos, William J., III, 626
Chattanooga Christian Community
    Foundation, 1533
Chatterjee, Miabi, 1014
Chatterjee, Oona, 1583
Chatterjee, Purnendu, 1272, 1323
Chatterjee, Swadesh, 1760
Chaturvedi, Vinayak, 738
Chatwal, Vikram, 1740
Chaudhary, Tariq Mahmood, 130
Chaudhary, Uzma, 130
Chavarria-Lara, Clarissa, 797
Chavjay, Pablo, 993
Chazanovitz, Hilda, 1317
Chazen & Graf Repetti & Co., Jerome,
    LLP, 1324
Chazen, Jerome, 1324
Chazen, Simona, 1324
Cheadle, Don, 1584
Checkley, Hope E., 1463
Cheek, H. Yvonne, 1102
Chelm, Renee, 1797
Chemberlin, Peg, Rev., 836
Chemerinsky, Erwin, 241
Chemtob, Linda Shapiro, 1885
Chen, Abraham, 1736
Chen, Chang-Hua, 342
Chen, Ho-Yuan, 342
Chen, Jackson, 339
Chen, Lincoln C., 952, 1298, 1663
Chen, Stanley, 373
Chenal West Development, Inc., 34
Chenault, Kenneth I., 1241, 1292
Cheney, Arta, 1098
Cheney, Daniel L., 1166
Cheney, Eleanora L., 1166
Cheney, Richard B., Hon., 488
Chenfeld, Cliff, 1739
Cheng, Charlie, 1129
Cheng, Eva, 1443
Cheng, Paul M.F., 716
Cherbec Advancement Foundation, 1107
Cherng, Andrew, 275
Cherniak, Harlan, 1742
Cherniak, Renee, 1233
Chernin, Albert D., 1477
Chernow, Ron, 1598
Chernys, Steven, 1249
Cherry, James, Mrs., 1399
Cherry, Stanton, 673
Cherukuri, Peter, 572
Chesed Congregation of America, 1517
Chesley, Stanley M., 1480
Chesnoff, Adam, 302
Cheves, Bettye A., 685
Cheves, Cecil M., 685
Chevez, Cecil, 685
Chhinjor, Pema, 1686
Chiang, Anne, 373
Chiang, Dawn, 1685
Chiar, Paul, 373
Chiara, Judith L., 1315

Ford Motor Co., 1670
Ford, Bill, 1365
Ford, Charlotte, 1365
Ford, Doug, Pastor, 1807
Ford, Edsel, 1391
Ford, Gary M., 244
Ford, Henry, 1391
Ford, Jeffrey, 1883
Ford, Stefan, 1695
Fore, Henrietta Holsman, 912
Foresman, Demme, 1747
Forest Trust, The, 878
Forlenza, Kathleen, 1468
Forlenza, Philip R., 1468
Forman, Leona S., 1300
Forman, Lori A., 714
Forminykh, Valentina Slater, 850
Fornaciari, Jeffrey L., 1214
Fornalczyk, Anna, 1610
Forneris, Stephen, 47
Forrester, Robert, 435
Forsyth, Adrian, 485, 2099
Forsyth, Doug, 286
Fortier, Alison B., 549
Fosmark, Michael, 2079
Fossum, Karl, 1621
Foster, Angela, 280
Foster, Badi, 582
Foster, Betty Flanders, 2120
Foster, Charles, 2022
Foster, David, 57
Foster, Eric, 1066
Foster, Geoff, 132
Foster, John H., 1273
Foster, Lynn A., 1611
Foster, Michael R., 1867
Foster, P. Wesley, Jr., 2120
Foster, Paul, 413
Foctor, Paul Wesley, III, 2120
Foster, Stephen A., 1594
Foster, W. Richard, Jr., Rev., 1902
Foster, Wesley, Jr., 2120
Foulke, Mellisa, 805
Foundation, Ostara, 523
Foundos, Albert P., 911
Fountain, Euel, 1945
Fournier, Frank, 1965
Fowler, Jerry, 589
Fowler, Jim, 1717
Fowler, John, 962
Fowler, John D., 2142
Fowler, Stephen, 270
Fowler, Walter B., 1867
Fowler, Wyche, Amb., 159
Fox, Belle, 1394
Fox, Cheri, 1122
Fox, Cheryl Ann, 1125
Fox, Craig, 121
Fox, David, 682, 1742
Fox, Gregory, 1122
Fox, Jeffrey, 1122
Fox, Jonathan, 1002
Fox, Marilyn, 1122
Fox, Raymond C., 2049
Fox, Sam, 1122, 1125
Fox, Steven, 1122
Fox-Claman, Pamela, 1122
Foxley, Zoe L., 392
Foxon, John, 1090
Fracyon, Noelle M., 467
Fradd, R. Brandon, 1670
Frade, Leopold, Rev., 635
Fragasso, Robert, 1904
Fragelli, Luiz A., 1880
Frahn, Carl A., 1183
Frampton, Edward, Rev., 1959
Francis, Helen Lovely, 454
Francis, Norman C., Dr., 2151
Francis, Philip L., 26
Franciscovich, Linda R., 1342
Franck, Gail, 503
Francqui, Frederic, Count, 1395
Frank, Adrienne, 653
Frank, Elizabeth E., 763

Frank, Elizabeth Furst, 534
Frank, Ernest H., 1396
Frank, Ernst L., 1396
Frank, Howard, Dr., 2150
Frank, Jack, 1758
Frank, Lois, 241
Frank, Michele, 157
Frank, Norman, 268
Frank, Seth E., 1532
Frank, Sidney E., 142
Frankel, B. Harrison, 1595
Frankel, Edward, 1687
Frankel, Jean, 1043
Frankel, Judith, 1043
Frankel, Leah, 1687
Frankel, Samuel, 1043
Frankel, Stanley, 1043
Frankenberg, Regina Bauer, 2009
Frankenfield, Marlene, 1898
Franklin, Barbara Jean, 1114
Franklin, Carmela Vircillo, 1509
Franklin, Christopher E., 1310
Franklin, Jason, 1583
Franklin, Jeff, 266
Franklin, John C., 2052
Franklin, Julie, 1188
Franklin, Martin, 1188
Frantz, Bente, 1264
Fraser, E. W., 428
Fraser, Jane, 1691
Frederick, Nan, 513
Free, Francl, 286
Free, JoLynn, 1980
Freed, Jeffrey, 1742
Freedman, Alisa S., 1669
Freedman, Donald, Dr., 1894
Freedman, Michael, 1669
Freedman, Roger, Dr., 826
Freedman, Solomon J., 1235
Freeman, Bennett, 1002
Freeman, Deena, 651
Freeman, Doreen, 1397
Freeman, Douglas K., 211
Freeman, Graeme, 1397
Freeman, Houghton, 1397
Freeman, Mansfield, 1397
Freeman, Timothy, 1204
Freeze, Rhonda, Hon., 1809
Frefichs, Ernest S., 1595
Frehling, Robert, 622
Frelberg, Mark, 1198
Freidus, Bernice, 412
Freiman, Harvey A., 1797
Freiwald, Gregory M., 1037
Frelinghuysen, Peter, 1219, 1293
Fremont Sequoia Holding, L.P., 143
French, John, 774
French, John P., 774
French, Kenneth R., 1467
French, Marina K., 1494
French, Marina Kellen, 1234
Frenk, Julio, 534, 1337
Frenzel, William, 522
Frerichs, Ernest S., 1923
Fresca, Cuca, 1622
Freston, Tom, 577
Freudenheim, Ellen, 1266
Freund, William, 671
Freundlich, Barbara, 1533
Freundlich, Sigmund, 1245
Frey, Andrew L., 1004
Frey, Marcia, 620
Friauf, Cynthia K., 2212
Friberg, Susan, 423
Fribourg, Paul J., 1370
Frichner, Tonya Gonnella, 317
Fricks, Ray, 2171
Fried, Arthur W., 1278, 1688
Fried, Barbara, 980
Friedenberg, David, 2196
Friedkin, Amy, 1438
Friedlander, Betsy, 1739
Friedlander, Carolee, 1301

Friedman Family Foundation, Frank and Fred, The, 1622
Friedman French Foundation, 1365
Friedman, Anita, 204, 216
Friedman, Bernie, 653
Friedman, David, 309
Friedman, Ellen, 105, 255, 345, 346
Friedman, Eric J., 1658
Friedman, Gary, 45
Friedman, Howard E., 491
Friedman, Joseph, 1235
Friedman, Judy, 302
Friedman, Leslie, 241
Friedman, Martin, 1257
Friedman, Michael, 538
Friedman, Phil, 514
Friedman, S. Donald, 1471
Friedman, Sol, 1245
Friedman, Stephen, 1344
Friedman, Tully M., 488
Friedmann, Theodore, Dr., 45
Friedrichs, Jay, 357
Friel, Thomas J., 323
Friend, Don, 204
Friend, Patricia S., 570
Friend, Robert, 216
Friendly, Alfred, 528
Friendly, Ian R., 1081
Friendly, Jonathan, 528
Friendly, Nicholas, 528
Friendly, Victoria, 528
Friendship Fund, Inc., 542
Friesen, Gilbert B., 1622
Friesen, Robert, 17
Friess, Robert M., 58
Frist, William H., 505
Frist, William Harrison, 440
Fritschler, Susan T., 910
Fritts, Ronald B., Rev., 1902
Frogel, Michael, 943
Frohlich, Susan, 309
Fromm Charitable Lead Annuity Trust, Alfred and Hanna, 145
Fromm, Alfred, 145
Fromm, Barbara, 145
Fromm, David George, 145
Fromm, Hanna, 145
Froning, Susan Katz, 1050
Frost, Carolyn Barry, 739
Frost, Hilda, 1670
Frost, Robert D., 1529
Frunzi, Susan C., 1393
Fry, Shanti, 958
Frye, Nancy P., 545
Fudge, Ann, 2170
Fudge, Ann M., 1344, 1639
Fuente, Carlos, Jr., 627
Fuente, Carlos, Sr., 627
Fuentes, Manuel Urbina, Dr., 1004
Fujimoto, Isao, 157
Fukuda, Kazuhiro, 1823
Fukukawa, Shinji, 1708
Fukuyama, Francis, Dr., 570
Fulbright, Harriet Mayor, 487
Fulford, Anne O., 1236
Fuller, Charles A., Jr., 1133
Fuller, Jack, 788
Fuller, Kathryn S., 592
Fuller, Richard, 1290
Fuller, Richard H., 64
Fuller, Sandra, 637
Fuller, Stephen M., 637
Fuller, Victor, 637
Fuller, William, 372
Fuller, William P., 155
Fullerton, Scott, 284
Fullmer, James L., 147
Fullmer, Jeff, 1118
Fulop, Miklos, 1738
Fulton, Daniel S., 2206
Fulvio, Gennaro J., 1901
Funaro, Charles, 243
Funck, Joachim, 2129

Fund for Blood and Cancer Research, Inc., The, 1533
Fund for Santa Barbara, Inc., 317
Fund for the Poor Inc., 402
Fund for the Poor, Inc., 402
Fund, John, 526
Fundacao Ciocle AE Tecnologia, 536
Fundacion Ico, 1013
Fundacion Rafael Del Pino, 1013
Funfar, Jim, 2208
Fung, Clair, 813
Fung, Daniel, 714
Fung, David, 813
Fung, Kenneth H.C., 1273
Fuqua, J.B., 574
Furdyk, Michael, 1419
Furman, James, 1765
Furman, Richard, Dr., 1756
Furness, Deborra-Lee, 459
Furnish, David, 1484
Furth, Frederick P., 548
Fusaro, Carlo, 1224
Fussel, Stephen R., 735
Fustero, Steven, 514
Futter, Ellen V., 1258

G & W Laboratories, Inc., 1171
G.E. Foundation, 2050
Gabe, Thomas K., 843
Gabel, Caroline D., 929
Gabel, Peter, 1211
Gabelein, Kevin, 2208
Gabelli, Mario J., 1263
Gaberman, Barry, 1002
Gabrache, Vahe, 1270
Gabriel, Nicholas M., 1391
Gadala-Maria, Jacobo, 671
Gadbois, Richard A., III, 284
Gadiel, Andy, 293
Gadiesh, Orit, 1243
Gaffney, Joe, 2199
Gage, John, 1538
Gage, Kasara, 1396
Gage, Meg, 970
Gage, Patricia Miller, 1809
Gager, James, 1534
Gaguine, Alexander, 57
Gaguine, Benito, 57
Gaguine, John, 9, 57
Gahan, Dolores Rice, 1706
Gall, Max, Jr., 330
Gaillard, Valerie, 1169
Gaillard, William, 1169
Gaines, Barbara, 803
Gaines, Billie Davis, 487
Gaines, Lis, 1235
Gainsley, Gloria, 719
Gainsley, Gloria J., 719
Gainsley, Stephen E., 719
Gaither, Israel L., 2144
Gaither, James C., 251
Galaski, Joyce Olum, 1590
Galbraith, James R., 178
Galbraith, Walter F., 898
Gale, Fred, 334
Galen, Michele, 534
Galgon, Mike T., 2173
Galiardo, John W., 2142
Galicot, Jose, 1239
Galik, Jeffrey, 1303
Galil, Uzia, 601
Galinson, Murray, 226
Galitz, Todd Michael, 1272
Galkowski, Tadeusz, 1189
Gallagher, Carolyn, 1980
Gallagher, Edward P., 1264
Gallagher, James, 492
Gallagher, Patricia A., 457
Gallagher, Patrick S., 1642
Gallegos, Herman, 180
Gallegos-Rivas, Ivan, 1622
Gallo, Gregory M., 323
Galloway, Sally, 1028

Smith, Gare, 544
Smith, Gary, Dr., 1234
Smith, Gayle, 1002
Smith, George D., Jr., 1662
Smith, George D., Sr., 1662
Smith, Gordon V., 930
Smith, Gregg, 1145
Smith, Helen C., 930
Smith, Howard I., 1672
Smith, James, 386
Smith, James Allen, 1330
Smith, Jean Kennedy, 1467
Smith, Jean Kennedy, Amb., 556
Smith, Jennifer L., 950
Smith, Joan, 2130
Smith, Joan M., 950
Smith, Jolene, 495
Smith, Judith C., 328
Smith, Juel Shannon, Dr., 665
Smith, Karen, 1972
Smith, Katherine M., 231
Smith, Ken, 2024
Smith, Larry, 701, 813
Smith, Laurence S., 1784
Smith, Lois E. H., 1624
Smith, Louise K., 1321
Smith, Maureen, 854
Smith, May, 327
Smith, Menlo, 2135
Smith, Michael, 503
Smith, Michael J., 1058
Smith, Michael J., Prof., 1313
Smith, Michelle, 2146
Smith, Neal, Dr., 2026
Smith, Orin, 2202
Smith, P. Allen, 1642
Smith, Paul J., 821
Smith, Paul R., 603
Smith, Peter C., 328
Smith, Phyllis, 928
Smith, Rachel A., 950
Smith, Randall, 528
Smith, Robert H., 2146
Smith, Robert Lee, 840
Smith, Roland C., 1820
Smith, Russell, 966
Smith, Sam, 2041
Smith, Sarah A., 1662
Smith, Scott C., 792
Smith, Stephen D., 834
Smith, Stephen E., Jr., 556
Smith, Stephen W., 328
Smith, Stephen W., Jr., 328
Smith, Steve, 307
Smith, Ted, 871
Smith, Terri, 1769
Smith, Theodore M., 986
Smith, Todd, 2042
Smith, Tricia, 707
Smith, Vernon, 2135
Smith, Wendy L., 1066
Smith, William, 582
Smitham, Peter, 1277
Smithsonian Institute, 923
Smits, Robert K., 1661
Smollen, Jon, 1085
Smollett, Jurnee, 63
Smotrich, Steven, 1172
Smyth, Margaret M., 1338
Smyth, Maureen, 594
Smythe, James J., 329
Smythe, Linda, 329
Smythe, Michael D., 329
Smythe, William D., 329
Smythe, William D., Jr., 329
Snell, George B., 1397
Snider, Jody, 502
Snidow, Robin, 392
Snowe, Parker, 472
Snowmass Chapel, 402
Snyder, Don, 386
Snyder, Jane, 2107
Snyder, Michele, 1365
Snyder, Samuel, 2190

Snyder, Tanya, 604
Snyder, Willard B., 991
Snyder, William P., III, 1868
Sobon, Leslie, 1977
Sobrato, John M., 323
Soderberg, Nancy, 511, 1338
Sofaer, Abraham D., 216
Soforenko, Edwin S., 1935
Soforenko, Lawrence, 1935
Sogani, Pramond C., 885
Sogoloff, Dimitri, 1317
Sohcot, Sandy, 293
Sohn Charitable Lead Trust, Fred &
    Frances, 1836
Sohn, Frances, 1836
Sohn, Frances F., 1836
Sohn, Fred, 1836
Sohn, Howard, 1215
Sohn, Howard F., 1836
Sohn, Ruth, 1836
Sohnchen, Randy, 680
Solberg, James, 1115
Soleman, Mumtaz, 41
Solheim, Allan, 28
Solheim, Allan, Jr., 28
Solheim, Andrew, 28
Solheim, David, 28
Solheim, Joy, 28
Solheim, Karsten, 28
Solheim, Karsten Louis, 28
Solheim, Louise, 28
Solheim, Louise C., 28
Solis, Felipa, 2002
Solis, Francisco, 350
Solis, Hilda Catalina Cruz, 989
Solo, Pam, 1011
Soloman, Donald L., 1296
Solomon Trust, Lillian Cohen, 2155
Solomon, Andrew, 788
Solomon, Daniel, 896, 2155
Solomon, David, 896
Solomon, Geula R., 1529
Solomon, Jacob, 669
Solomon, Jane, 896, 2155
Solomon, Joel, 346, 2091
Solomon, Kimberly Baldridge, 1982
Solomon, Lillian Cohen, 896
Solomon, Peter J., 1529
Solomon, Raymond, Rev., 1307
Solomon, Richard H., 520
Solomon, Ron, 83
Solomon, Steven, 353
Solso, Theodore M., 837
Soltani, Atossa, 97, 330
Somekawa, Ellen, 1866
Someya, Mitsuo, 2222
Sommaruga, Cornelio, 893
Sommer, Alfred, 1292
Sommer, Mark, 1299
Sonabend, Roberto, 682
Sonn, Tamara, 507
Sonne, Christian R., 1264
Sony Corp., 1670
Sony Corp. of America, 1664
Sony Corporation of America, 1622
Sony Electronics, Inc., 1664
Sooch, Navdeep S., 2059
Sorbo, Gunnar M., 547
Sordoni, Stephen, 287
Sorensen, Diana, 989
Sorenson Devel., Inc., 2078
Sorenson, James LeVoy, 2078
Sorenson, Jim, Jr., 2078
Soronen, Rita L., 1820
Soros Charitable Foundation, 1665
Soros Foundation, 1363
Soros Foundation-Hungary, 1665
Soros Fund Charitable Foundation, 1376
Soros, Andrea, 1693, 1697
Soros, George, 1393, 1593, 1665,
    1693
Soros, Jonathan, 1393, 1593
Soros, Jonathan Allan, 1665
Sorrell, Martin, 1292

Sosland, L. Joshua, 859
Sotojima, Toshiyuki, 1823
Sotos, Marybeth M., 560
Soule, Edward, 2143
Soulliere, Anne-Marie, 959
Soulon, Deena, 202
Sousa, Jan, 536
Southard, Dawn, 715
Southby, Janet, 611
Souza, Tracy H., 837
Sovern, Michael I., 1277
Sovey, Mara L., 757
Sowards, Michael, Ms., 267
Sowards, Stacey, 267
Sowards, Wayne, 267
Soza, Will, 2111
Spacinsky, Charlotte L., 660
Spahr, Amanda Foster, 2120
Spahr, George W., 2120
Spalding, Craig, 2021
Spalding, Darlene, 2021
Spalding, Mark J., 575
Spanbock, Maurice, 1588
Spar, Sheryle, 1265
Sparber, Pete, 2111
Spaulding, Mary, 1325
Spector, Deborah, 45
Spector, Nancy, 307
Spees, Pam, 1535
Speicher, Thomas G., 1912
Speirn, Sterling K., 1050
Spellings, J. M., 2004
Spellman, Christina, 1542
Spence, Ann B., 1486
Spence, Charles, 1027
Spence, David, 334
Spence, Imagene, 260
Spencer, John, 542
Spencer, John, Prof., 513
Spencer, Lyle M., 820
Spencer, Martin, 316
Spencer, Michael Hunter, 1360
Spencer, Robert D., 1360
Spencer, Roderick, 63
Spencer, Valerie C., 1004
Spencer, William M., III, 1360
Sperber, Myron, 1237
Sperling, Bill, 2199
Spero, Louis, 1020
Spero, Shirley, 1020
Spero, Suzanne M., 1184
Speth, James Gustave, 585, 1638
Speth, James Gustave "Gus", 2088
Spey, Howard, Dr., 1749
Speyer, Jerry I., 1668
Speyer, Robert, 1668
Spezzaferro, Patrisia, 283
Spiccia, Joseph, 42
Spickler, Julie, 125
Spiegel, Adam, 1669
Spiegel, Sam, 1669
Spiers, Chad A., 2082
Spiess, Steven D., 921
Spiger, J. Anne, 2171
Spiger, Michael, 2171
Spillman, Rita, 523
Spinelli, Francesca, 26
Spinner, Joshua, Rabbi, 1517
Spinner, Sandra, 1449
Spire-Joaquin, Zem, 159
Spirit Foundation, The, 1365
Spitzer, Henry, 1245
Spitzer, Matthew, 1356
Spivey, Paul, 180
Splinter, Michael R., 58
Spoelman, Roger, 265
Spogli, Ronald P., 153
Sport/Ellie Inc., 1745
Spradlin, Greg, 33
Spring, Grace, 544
Springer, Michael W., 2008
Springs Industries, Inc., 1940
Springs Window Fashions, Inc., 1940
Sprott, Richard L., 901

Spruce 2007 Charitable Trust, 161
Squeri, Stephen J., 1241
Sreedhar, Kathy, 495
Srinivasan, M., Dr., 316
Srivastava, Prakash, Dr., 851
SSR Charitable Lead Annuity Trust 2004,
    922
St. Amour, Denis, 375
St. Angelo, Steve, 1692
St. Cyr, Marie Marthe, 558
St. John, Emmett, 1423
St. John, Gary, 20, 2156
St. John, Shannon E., 1501
Staab, Thomas R., II, 1768
Stabbert, Fred, 2208
Stacy Charitable Trust, Helen, 675
Stacy, Festus, 675
Staff, Marilyn, 382
Staffieri, Michael, 314
Stafford, Nancy, 928
Stafford, Tim, 334
Stainman, Arthur J., 1671
Stainman, Evan, 1671
Stainman, Lois, 1671
Stallone, Kristine, 1030
Stam, David H., 1351
Stamelman, Andrew J., 1687
Stanley Foundation, The, 848
Stanley, Joseph H., 848
Stanley, Lincoln, 848
Stanley, Lynne E., 848
Stanley, M.L., 2021
Stanley, Marc, 1477
Stanley, Richard H., 848
Stanly, Fred, Rev., 1959
Stanly, Miriam, 1959
Stansberry, Mark, 1129
Stansberry, Mark A., 530
Stantic, Lita, 110
Stanton, Carrie M., 758
Stanton, Domna, 1596
Stanton, John, 2199
Stapleton, Craig R., 390
Stapleton, John F., 603
Stapleton, Katharine H., 390
Stapleton, Steven, 841
Star, Sara Crown, 756
Starbucks Coffee Co., 2202
Starbucks Corp., 2202
Starbucks Foundation, 2157
Starer, Brian, 648
Stark, Arthur, 1403
Stark, George, 2040
Stark, Jessica, 852
Stark, Sandra L., 1202
Starling, Tim, 2013
Starr Foundation, 1273, 1670
Starr, Alice M., 1547
Starr, Cornelius V., 1672
Starr, Maria, 372
Starr, Samantha, 1396
Stars for Children, 2052
Staryk, Noa, 1092
Staryk, Ted, 1092
Stasch, Julia M., 788
Stash, Sandy, 2088
Stash, Sharon, 571
State Farm Mutual Automobile Insurance
    Co., 821
State Street Bank & Trust Co., 1021
Statt, Darren, 297
Stavropoulos, Mark D., 911
Stawski, Axel, 1260
Stayner, Tony, 1134
Steans, Harrison I., 1313
Steckler Charitable Lead Trust, Lois R.,
    425
Steckler, Alan R., 425
Steckler, Deborah S., 425
Steed, Robert I., 2082
Steeg, Robert, 872
Steel Family, Robert K., 1673
Steel, Gillian V., 1673
Steel, John, 412

GEOGRAPHIC INDEX

Grantmakers in boldface type make grants on a national, regional, or international basis; the others generally limit giving to the city or state in which they are located. For local funders with a history of giving in another state, consult the "see also" references at the end of each state section.

COLORADO

CONNECTICUT

DELAWARE

DISTRICT OF COLUMBIA

FLORIDA

Jupiter: Abramson 613
Key West: Around 617
Longwood: **Chatlos 626**
Lutz: **Watoto 680**
Miami: **Alfalit 614, American 615,** Assurant 619, Blank 622, Coulter 629, Greenburg 645, **Peterson 666,** Russell 669, **Salvadoran 671**
Miami Springs: **Transitions 677**
Naples: Cafesjian 623, Gorin 642, **Hope 649,** Second 674
New Smyrna Beach: Atlantic 620
Orange City: **Global 640**
Orlando: Murphy 663
Oviedo: Duda 632
Palm Beach: Engelberg 634, Hertog 646, **Working 681**
Palm Beach Gardens: Himmel 647
Pembroke Pines: Assn. of Amer. Schools SA 618, De La Pena 631
Plantation: Kerzner 658
Sebastian: Green 644
St. Petersburg: Jabil 652, Pruitt 668
Tampa: Basham 621, **Cigar 627, Holland 648,** Patel 664, Patel 665
Tarpon Springs: Cantonis 624
West Palm Beach: Clark 628, **Israel 651**

see also 2, 3, 89, 175, 249, 261, 313, 402, 407, 413, 416, 433, 435, 539, 704, 705, 706, 708, 743, 749, 767, 789, 798, 819, 852, 854, 857, 872, 890, 898, 936, 959, 992, 998, 1007, 1023, 1034, 1057, 1089, 1093, 1097, 1106, 1182, 1191, 1241, 1288, 1336, 1441, 1524, 1579, 1601, 1676, 1754, 1771, 1783, 1803, 1808, 1885, 1910, 1918, 1974, 2003, 2019, 2047, 2060, 2122, 2219

GEORGIA

Atlanta: American 682, Atlanta 686, Bancker 687, **Carter 690,** Chesed 691, **Coca 692,** Coca 693, Delta 694, Gray 696, **Halle 697, Home 699,** Livingston 700, Marous 701, Rosenberg 703, South 705, **Turner 708, UPS 709, Wardlaw 710**
Buford: **Amigos 683**
Carrollton: Southwire 706
Columbus: Amos 684, Amos-Cheves 685
Lawrenceville: Scientific 704
Peachtree City: Global 695
Savannah: **Belize 688, Cambodia 689,** Masroor 702
St. Marys: St. 707
Woodstock: **His 698**

see also 5, 7, 127, 137, 298, 428, 471, 477, 619, 629, 657, 663, 743, 744, 757, 798, 832, 842, 936, 944, 946, 1021, 1029, 1048, 1080, 1081, 1128, 1241, 1288, 1309, 1447, 1579, 1586, 1615, 1774, 1813, 1822, 1908, 1996, 2004, 2018, 2077, 2097, 2206, 2223

GUAM

see 596

HAWAII

Honolulu: Akihito 711, Alexander 712, **Center 714, Community 715,** East-West 716, Hau'Oli 717, Honda 718, Kosasa 719, Pacific 720, People's 721, Scott 723, **Shaw 724,** Shiraki 725, Watumull 726, Yoshimoto 727
Kailua Kona: Burke 713
Kula: Sangham 722

see also 142, 238, 458, 743, 934, 1029, 1145, 1148, 1173, 1309, 1889, 2076, 2200

IDAHO

Boise: Boise 728, Micron 730, Micron 731, Rebholtz 732, Thomas 734
Ketchum: **Schultz 733**
Sun Valley: Good 729

see also 536, 722, 1128, 2161, 2162, 2183, 2192, 2200, 2207

ILLINOIS

Abbott Park: Abbott 735
Arlington Heights: Magnus 791
Bloomington: **State 821**
Buffalo Grove: **New 800,** Simonsen 819
Burbank: **United 827**
Burr Ridge: King 777
Carol Stream: **Messengers 796**
Champaign: Eades 763
Chicago: Abelson 736, Alphawood 737, **American 738,** Aon 739, Bobolink 742, Boeing 743, Build 745, Carrus 746, Communitas 752, Conduit 753, Crown 756, **Demos 758,** Driehaus 761, Edgerly 764, Hebrew 768, Heritage 769, IDP 770, Illinois 772, **International 774,** Jocarno 775, Joy 776, Landau 780, Legion 781, Libra 782, Logos 785, Lohengrin 786, Lurie 787, **MacArthur 788,** MacDonald 789, Madigan 790, McCormick 792, **Mission 797,** Novak 801, Penrose 803, Pritzker 804, Rosenthal 805, Rossman 806, Rothman 808, Rubin 809, Rumsfeld 810, Sarkisian 811, Schneider 812, Shapiro 816, Shifting 817, **Spencer 820,** Stern 822, **Terra 824,** Weberg 829, Wein 830, Weiner 831, Winfrey 832
Decatur: Archer 740, Buffett 744
Deerfield: Baxter 741, CF 749
Evanston: **New 799, Rotary 807, Sigma 818, Two 826**
Glenview: Lindon 783, Mead 794
Hillside: Van Dyke 828
Hinsdale: Casten 747
Lake Forest: Chabraja 750, **Scholar 813,** Stuart 823
Lemont: **Lithuanian 784**
Lincolnwood: Mermelstein 795
Mokena: Divac 760
Moline: Deere 757
Naperville: **India 773**
Northbrook: Dunard 762, **Scholl 814**
Northfield: **Kraft 778**
Oak Brook: Cooper 754, **Opportunity 802**
Park Ridge: **IFSA 771**
Peoria: Caterpillar 748
Rockford: **Circle 751**
Rosemont: McShane 793
Schaumburg: Motorola 798
Skokie: Goodman 767
South Barrington: Wristen 833
Western Springs: **Foods 765**
Wheaton: Crane 755, **Deyneka 759**
Wilmette: Krehbiel 779, Shamrock 815
Winnetka: Gochnauer 766, Tinberg 825

see also 7, 137, 150, 173, 187, 197, 262, 298, 304, 378, 402, 406, 410, 413, 429, 435, 454, 458, 502, 579, 704, 706, 712, 845, 852, 930, 944, 978, 1021, 1033, 1040, 1051, 1080, 1081, 1085, 1097, 1098, 1103, 1125, 1186, 1191, 1241, 1267, 1288, 1309, 1447, 1459, 1560, 1562, 1575, 1579, 1601, 1658, 1692, 1889, 1989, 1996, 2004, 2018, 2051, 2060, 2072, 2215

INDIANA

Carmel: Simon 844
Columbus: Cummins 837, Cummins 838
Elkhart: **Church 836,** NIBCO 842
Fort Wayne: Brotherhood 835

Indianapolis: Benevolent 834, Hasten 839, Lilly 840, **Lilly 841, Overseas 843,** Transformation 845, West 846

see also 706, 735, 737, 741, 763, 1081, 1093, 1097, 1303, 1340, 1447, 1607, 1939, 1989, 2060, 2122

IOWA

Cedar Rapids: Wallace 855
Des Moines: Hubbell 849, Ochylski 852, **P.E.O. 853,** Sehgal 854
Fairfield: Global 847, **Maharishi 851**
Iowa City: Humanities 850, Wright 856
Muscatine: Holthues 848

see also 166, 277, 462, 679, 749, 757, 837, 982, 1073, 1081, 1097, 1098, 1128, 1141, 1191, 1447, 1850

KANSAS

Kansas City: **Christian 858**
Lakin: Weskan 862
Olathe: **Shumaker 861**
Overland Park: Jewish 859, **Lloyd 860**
Wichita: Beren 857

see also 7, 410, 743, 757, 1097, 1579, 2004

KENTUCKY

Ashland: Jain 864
Louisville: C.E. 863, Yum! 866, Yum! 867
Pine Knot: **O'Dell 865**

see also 54, 428, 652, 705, 706, 801, 959, 1080, 1118, 1557, 1752, 1778, 1808, 1939, 1952

LOUISIANA

Baton Rouge: Pennington 870
Jefferson: Woldenberg 872
Lake Charles: **Park 869**
New Orleans: Catholic 868, Zemurray 873
Shreveport: Wiener 871

see also 266, 428, 463, 705, 757, 1128, 1191, 1828, 1979, 1989, 2004

MAINE

Boothbay Harbor: **Walter 881**
Camden: Golden 877, Picker 879
Farmington: **Sandy 880**
Portland: Cambodian 874, Catalyst 875, **Oak 878**
Scarborough: Dugas 876

see also 975, 999, 1000, 1814, 1967

MARYLAND

Baltimore: **ABMRF/The 882,** Bearman 890, **Blaustein 891,** Blaustein 892, Boehm 894, Hirschhorn 905, Hoffberger 906, **International 911, International 912, Lutheran 916,** Meyerhoff 919, Meyerhoff 920, **Mid 921**
Bel Air: Dahan 897
Bethesda: Cohen 896, ELECTRI 900, **Ellison 901,** England 902, **Hariri 904,** Morningstar 922, Weiss 935
Chestertown: **Shared 929,** Windsor 936
Chevy Chase: **AICE 884, Hughes 907,** O'Neil 925, Polinger 926

1729, Whispering 1731, White 1732, Wiener 1733, **Wiesel 1734**, Wigmore 1735, Woods 1737, **World 1739**, **Yele 1740**, **Youth 1742**, Zenkel 1743, Zilkha 1744, **Ziv 1745**
North Rose: Marshall 1541
Nyack: Fellowship 1381
Oriskany: Bonide 1294
Ossining: **National 1569**
Port Washington: Eule 1376
Purchase: **PepsiCo 1601**, Wallach 1721
Rego Park: GK 1416
Rochester: **Usha 1711**
Roslyn: Kevorkian 1497
Saratoga Springs: Berkowitz 1286, Kaye 1493, Zyman 1746
Scarsdale: Stern 1678
Schenectady: **African 1223**, Lisben 1528
Seaford: Koha 1505
Sherrill: Gorman 1426
South Salem: **Cogitare 1334**
Sunnyside: Eastman 1364
Syracuse: Polish 1609, **ProLiteracy 1617**, **Yoreinu 1741**
Tarrytown: **Pendill 1599**
Valhalla: **NBI 1571**
Vestal: Olum 1590
Westbury: **Interpeace 1468**
White Plains: **Skadden 1658**, Wong 1736
Woodbury: Nazarian 1570
Woodmere: **American 1238**

see also 10, 18, 40, 60, 75, 86, 87, 88, 89, 90, 91, 93, 99, 112, 127, 137, 142, 150, 160, 166, 168, 175, 181, 187, 214, 220, 224, 228, 229, 240, 262, 288, 298, 313, 318, 319, 320, 322, 335, 343, 358, 362, 367, 368, 378, 381, 383, 389, 396, 402, 413, 416, 418, 428, 429, 433, 434, 435, 438, 442, 443, 444, 445, 446, 447, 453, 454, 457, 458, 460, 463, 464, 471, 476, 478, 502, 537, 538, 541, 555, 616, 617, 623, 624, 628, 629, 633, 634, 645, 646, 652, 655, 657, 658, 659, 667, 670, 672, 682, 693, 702, 703, 735, 742, 746, 750, 753, 756, 762, 779, 789, 795, 798, 804, 809, 816, 817, 822, 832, 837, 839, 846, 848, 857, 886, 892, 894, 897, 920, 921, 925, 934, 935, 937, 946, 950, 955, 959, 967, 973, 982, 988, 1001, 1008, 1021, 1025, 1033, 1041, 1043, 1055, 1061, 1067, 1074, 1081, 1085, 1089, 1095, 1097, 1103, 1110, 1125, 1139, 1143, 1145, 1146, 1150, 1153, 1156, 1158, 1160, 1161, 1162, 1165, 1167, 1172, 1176, 1182, 1184, 1186, 1187, 1189, 1191, 1192, 1193, 1195, 1197, 1198, 1200, 1202, 1203, 1205, 1752, 1771, 1777, 1778, 1792, 1796, 1799, 1800, 1814, 1815, 1816, 1834, 1847, 1853, 1857, 1882, 1885, 1895, 1900, 1910, 1923, 1927, 1929, 1934, 1982, 1983, 1988, 1996, 1999, 2003, 2004, 2009, 2015, 2018, 2031, 2037, 2054, 2058, 2060, 2071, 2072, 2077, 2122, 2145, 2153, 2160, 2165, 2181, 2187, 2191, 2209, 2216, 2219

NORTH CAROLINA
Asheville: **Rixson 1763**
Boone: **Mafraq 1756**, **Samaritan's 1765**
Burlington: **New 1758**
Chapel Hill: Carlson 1752, **Rolander 1764**
Charlotte: Evrytanian 1753, Kramer 1754, Strauss 1767
Durham: AlphaMed 1748, **Nickel 1759**, Triangle 1768
Franklin: **ANAI 1750**
Greensboro: Lookout 1755, Richardson 1762
Hendersonville: **African 1747**
Raleigh: **American 1749**, North 1760, **Project 1761**, **Stop 1766**, With 1769
Research Triangle Park: Burroughs 1751, **Microelectronics 1757**

see also 7, 89, 99, 175, 261, 367, 469, 579, 705, 757, 837, 936, 959, 1021, 1033, 1057, 1060, 1097, 1153, 1241, 1346, 1615, 1673, 1822, 1855, 1908, 1939, 1940, 2014, 2085, 2097, 2224

NORTH DAKOTA
Bismarck: Johnson 1771
Fargo: Fedje 1770, McCormick 1773
West Fargo: **Los 1772**, Nordick 1774

see also 757, 1098

OHIO
Bedford Heights: **Brush 1779**
Berlin: **Christian 1781**
Brooklyn: Goatie 1792
Canton: Timken 1821, **Timken 1822**
Chagrin Falls: **Geisse 1790**
Chesterhill: Lowe 1802
Cincinnati: Becker 1778, Cintas 1782, Convergys 1783, Ethicon 1788, Jacobs 1796, Jewish 1798, Lowe 1801, Procter 1815, Tri-state 1823
Cleveland: **Catholic 1780**, Eaton 1786, **Ethnic 1789**, Haskell 1793, **Jewish 1797**, Maltz 1803, **Mandel 1804**, **Mandel 1805**, **Mandel 1806**, **Myers 1810**, Partridge 1814
Cleveland Heights: Eaton 1787, **International 1795**
Columbus: Armington 1777, Hazelbaker 1794, Limited 1800, Mason 1808, Schottenstein 1816
Dublin: **Arab 1776**, **Thomas 1820**
Elida: Dauch 1785
Fairlawn: OMNOVA 1813
Highland Heights: Lerner 1799
Hudson: Thanksgiving 1819
Marion: Marion 1807
Mason: **Give 1791**
Mayfield Heights: Danaher 1784
Middletown: Middletown 1809
Oberlin: Oberlin 1812
Pepper Pike: Veale 1824
Springfield: Taj 1818
West Chester: AK Steel 1775
Wooster: Noble 1811
Youngstown: Sheely 1817

see also 7, 15, 428, 435, 735, 743, 837, 842, 921, 930, 959, 1035, 1040, 1041, 1081, 1096, 1097, 1447, 1562, 1579, 1650, 1908, 2004, 2006, 2060, 2122, 2133

OKLAHOMA
Edmond: Love 1829
Oklahoma City: Devon 1828
Poteau: Crio 1827
Tulsa: **Blessings 1825**, Broken 1826, **Schusterman 1830**, Zarrow 1831, Zarrow 1832

see also 619, 743, 749, 955, 1097, 1771, 1939, 1979, 2004

OREGON
Beaverton: Kalakendra 1840, NIKE 1847
Corvallis: **Conklin 1834**
Eugene: Grass 1838
Happy Valley: Larson 1842
Hillsboro: Intel 1839, Zwaanstra 1852
McMinnville: **Evergreen 1835**

Portland: **Alima 1833**, **KEEN 1841**, **Lemelson 1843**, McKenzie 1844, **Mercy 1846**, **Sustainable 1848**, **Tazo 1849**, **Weatherspoon 1850**, Wyss 1851
Roseburg: **Fohs 1836**
Tigard: **Foreign 1837**, **Medical 1845**

see also 89, 94, 261, 377, 381, 722, 735, 743, 856, 1557, 2161, 2164, 2183, 2188, 2192, 2200, 2206, 2207

PENNSYLVANIA
Ambler: Copernicus 1874
Bala Cynwyd: Clayman 1872, **Global 1884**
Berwyn: AMETEK 1856
Bryn Mawr: Barrack 1861
Chesterbrook: AmerisourceBergen 1855
Dillsburg: **Macha 1897**
Doylestown: Argus 1857
Frazer: Cephalon 1870
Gladwyne: Pine 1908
Hanover: **Foundation 1880**
Harrisburg: **American 1854**, Jewish 1894
Hershey: Hershey 1889
Jenkintown: **National 1901**
Lancaster: **Nazareth 1902**
Lebanon: Dixon 1876
Malvern: Progressive 1909
Merion Station: Berkowitz 1864
Newtown: Epstein 1878
Oil City: Epstein 1877
Pennsburg: **Mama 1898**
Philadelphia: Arronson 1858, Azavea 1860, Bread 1866, **Children's 1871**, **Guanacaste 1886**, **Institute 1893**, Nararo 1900, Pew 1906, Rosenstiel 1910, **Zeldin 1919**
Phoenixville: Shiloh 1914
Pittsburgh: Alcoa 1853, **Association 1859**, Benter 1863, Bloch 1865, **Brother's 1867**, **Carnegie 1868**, **Carthage 1869**, **Colcom 1873**, Federated 1879, Friends 1881, Friendship 1882, **Global 1883**, Heinz 1887, **KL 1896**, Mine 1899, Pacem 1904, **Pan 1905**, Scaife 1911, Williams 1917, Wollowick 1918
Quakertown: Shah 1913
Scranton: Scranton 1912
Souderton: **One 1903**
Villanova: Cotswold 1875
Wayne: **Hope 1891**, Huston 1892
Wellsville: Key 1895
West Chester: **HJW 1890**, Pilgrim 1907
West Conshohocken: Beach 1862, **Templeton 1916**
Wormleysburg: Grass 1885
Wyncote: Hellendall 1888
Wynnewood: Sidewater 1915

see also 79, 89, 137, 187, 428, 458, 461, 468, 470, 472, 502, 613, 706, 743, 762, 789, 834, 921, 934, 936, 960, 1051, 1085, 1097, 1118, 1123, 1148, 1158, 1162, 1186, 1191, 1217, 1241, 1288, 1303, 1383, 1424, 1516, 1558, 1561, 1562, 1579, 1607, 1615, 1726, 1733, 1767, 1784, 1813, 1927, 1974, 2060, 2075, 2133, 2209, 2219

PUERTO RICO
Carolina: **FNZ 1920**

see also 54, 596, 619, 731, 735, 1093, 1186, 1607, 2048

RHODE ISLAND
Cranston: **Feinstein 1924**
Johnston: FM 1925

Pawtucket: Collette 1921, Hasbro 1926, Luke 1931
Providence: Dorot 1923, Hassenfeld 1927, Hoag 1928, King 1929, Koonce 1930, **Perkins 1932**, Schoellkopf 1934, Soforenko 1935
Warwick: **Plan 1933**
Woonsocket: CVS 1922

see also 18, 54, 959, 975, 999, 1000, 1192, 1287, 1441, 1645

SOUTH CAROLINA

Blythewood: **Zvejnieks 1942**
Greenville: **American 1936**, Michelin 1939
Hilton Head Island: **Calabar 1938**, **Youths' 1941**
Lancaster: TSC 1940
Myrtle Beach: AVX 1937

see also 197, 428, 637, 685, 705, 708, 743, 837, 944, 1033, 1183, 1813, 1822, 1967, 2006

SOUTH DAKOTA

Sioux Falls: Branches 1943, **Opus 1944**

see also 1034, 1098

TENNESSEE

Apison: **Outpost 1965**
Brentwood: **African 1946**, Dobberpuhl 1951
Bristol: Lazarus 1961
Chattanooga: Community 1950, **Maclellan 1962**, UnumProvident 1967, **Westwood 1969**
Cleveland: **Operation 1964**
Collierville: Drake 1952
Cordova: **Global 1956**
Franklin: **Improved 1958**, Nissan 1963
Hixson: **International 1959**
Knoxville: **Redbird 1966**, **Vine 1968**
Lookout Mountain: Grandview 1957
Memphis: Belz 1948, **FedEx 1954**, International 1960
Nashville: **African 1945**, Ezell 1953, Fugitive 1955
Selmer: **Bala 1947**
Sewanee: **Cloud 1949**

see also 7, 31, 187, 240, 416, 652, 685, 687, 705, 757, 837, 1018, 1035, 1081, 1093, 1097, 1186, 1336, 1620, 1822, 1889

TEXAS

Abilene: Karakin 2027
Aledo: Reilly 2052
Austin: A Glimmer 1970, AMD 1977, Austin 1980, **Dell 2000**, Freescale 2011, Link 2033, Maples 2036, Mattsson 2038, **New Media 2043**, Sooch 2059, Whole 2071
Beeville: Dougherty 2001
Boerne: Kingdom 2030
Carrollton: ADR 1971, **Amazon 1976**
Cedar Park: Thirst 2066
Comfort: His 2019
Coppell: PHM 2047
Dallas: **Africa 1972**, Baldridge 1982, Beaird 1984, Cox 1997, Enrico 2003, **Frankenberg 2009**, **GAIN 2013**, Halperin 2017, Jiv 2025, Kowitz 2031, Marsh 2037, McDermott 2039, Oates 2044, **Pizza 2048**, Plitt 2049, Seegers 2056, Sparrow 2061, Summerlee 2064
Denton: Jubilee 2026
El Paso: El Paso 2002, Paso 2046, Stewart 2063
Fair Oaks Ranch: **Interdenominational 2021**
Fort Worth: Alcon 1974, Bass 1983, General 2014

Houston: Alliance 1975, Apache 1979, **Baeck 1981**, Bhutada 1986, BMC 1987, Bolivar 1988, BP 1989, Bridgeway 1990, Coneway 1995, Cooper 1996, Cultural 1999, Fondren 2008, **Friedkin 2012**, Goradia 2015, Hines 2018, Interfaith 2022, **International 2023**, **Living 2034**, Manna 2035, Menil 2040, **Pratham 2050**, Pritzker 2051, Saunders 2053, Scaler 2054, Search 2055, Spark 2060, Spectra 2062, **Vietnamese 2068**, Westbury 2070
Irving: **Chrest 1994**, ExxonMobil 2004, Feldman 2005, Fluor 2006, Kimberly 2028, Kimberly 2029
La Porte: Crowder 1998
Lewisville: Six 2058
Lindale: **Mercy 2041**, Teen 2065
Montgomery: Shepherds 2057
Palacios: Trull 2067
Plano: **International 2024**, **Mission 2042**, Windmill 2072
Raymondville: **Freedom 2010**
Round Rock: **Casa 1993**
San Antonio: **Africa 1973**, American 1978, Butt 1991, Flynn 2007, **Limiar 2032**, Oppenheimer 2045
San Leon: **Haghenbeck 2016**
Sinton: Welder 2069
Sugar Land: Beyer 1985
The Woodlands: Huntsman 2020
Waco: C.I.O.S. 1992

see also 28, 59, 89, 96, 137, 187, 193, 197, 261, 350, 437, 455, 637, 652, 706, 731, 735, 743, 798, 815, 837, 842, 857, 944, 959, 1029, 1033, 1034, 1051, 1093, 1097, 1104, 1121, 1153, 1186, 1191, 1241, 1303, 1309, 1367, 1562, 1579, 1597, 1601, 1620, 1650, 1692, 1783, 1828, 1855, 1930, 1952, 1963, 2218

UTAH

Draper: Taylor 2081
Moab: Slaughter 2076
Ogden: Swanson 2079
Provo: Force 2073
Salt Lake City: Semnani 2075, SmartGo 2077, Sorenson 2078, Tanner 2080, Watkins 2083
Springville: Trivani 2082
St. George: **Miner 2074**

see also 59, 89, 261, 706, 731, 743, 959, 1135, 1241, 1309, 1562, 1579, 1783, 1828, 1870, 2004, 2020, 2167, 2192, 2207

VERMONT

Hinesburg: Blittersdorf 2084
Island Pond: **Underdog 2091**
Marshfield: Block 2085
Montpelier: **Institute 2088**, **Russian 2090**
Newport: Kaufman 2089
Stowe: Evslin 2086
Waterbury: **Himalayan 2087**

see also 800, 975, 999, 1000, 1011, 1068, 1397, 1440, 1525, 1547, 1712, 1929, 2210

VIRGIN ISLANDS

see 596, 921, 1367

VIRGINIA

Alexandria: **America's 2093**, **American 2094**, **Bread 2100**, **Charities 2104**, **Christian 2106**, **Donors 2115**, **Global 2123**, **Good360 2124**, **North 2139**, **Salvation 2144**, **World 2156**

Altavista: Lane 2132
Annandale: **Earthrights 2117**
Arlington: **Algerian-American 2092**, **Ashoka: 2095**, Associates 2096, Center 2102, **Cooperative 2109**, Mercatus 2135, **National 2138**, **Rare 2143**, Samberg 2145, Smith 2146, **U.S. 2150**, **Youth 2157**
Ashburn: Woodbury 2155
Chantilly: Foster 2120
Charlottesville: **Blue 2099**, **Feris 2119**, **WestWind 2154**
Clifton: Three 2148
Fairfax: **Christian 2107**, **Galapagos 2121**, **Jubilee 2130**, **Loyola 2134**, Somali 2147
Falls Church: **Crosslink 2111**, Delmar 2113, Hitt 2127, **Mustard 2137**, **United 2151**
Forest: **India 2128**
Fredericksburg: **EduCare 2118**
Herndon: Mousetrap 2136, **United 2152**
Ivy: **Ivy 2129**
Lorton: **City 2108**
McLean: Chainani 2103, **Corporations 2110**, Gannett 2122, **King 2131**, Trehan 2149
Millwood: **Project 2142**
Norfolk: Batten 2098
Oak Hill: Haft 2125
Reston: Universal 2153
Richmond: **ChildFund 2105**
Vienna: **Diema's 2114**, Living 2133
Virginia Beach: **Dayspring 2112**, Hansen 2126, **Operation 2140**
Waterford: Cedars 2101
Williamsburg: Bangs-Russell 2097, **Dorothy 2116**, Practical 2141

see also 7, 86, 114, 193, 197, 240, 261, 428, 464, 469, 477, 515, 518, 555, 562, 579, 636, 603, 694, 730, 731, 735, 742, 750, 842, 845, 875, 898, 921, 930, 969, 1073, 1112, 1186, 1193, 1360, 1385, 1547, 1579, 1601, 1632, 1650, 1710, 1784, 1799, 1822, 1882, 1889, 1911, 1946, 2004, 2066, 2072, 2085, 2178, 2191

WASHINGTON

Bellevue: 444S 2158, Luke 2184, See 2201
Federal Way: Weyerhaeuser 2206
Gig Harbor: Russell 2195
Kirkland: **Mona 2186**
Mercer Island: Bezos 2160
Mukilteo: **Friends 2169**
Newcastle: Duim 2168
Olympia: Jernigan 2180
Prescott: Vista 2205
Puyallup: **Gateway 2171**
Rollingbay: **Bainbridge 2159**
Sammamish: Hyder 2176, Khaki 2182
Seattle: Bullitt 2161, Campion 2162, **Channel 2163**, Common 2165, Crystal 2167, **Gates 2170**, **Glaser 2172**, **Global 2173**, **Helping 2175**, **Islands 2178**, Jackson 2179, Kaphan 2181, Kongsgaard 2183, McKinstry 2185, Neukom 2187, Northwest 2188, **Pangea: 2189**, **Pura 2190**, RealNetworks 2191, RHEMA 2193, Samis 2196, Scan 2197, Schuler 2198, Seattle 2199, Seattle 2200, Starbucks 2202, Wilburforce 2207, **World 2208**
Snohomish: **RISA 2194**
Spokane: Community 2166, Red 2192
Tacoma: **Stewardship 2203**
Tukwila: Harnish 2174
Tulalip: Tulalip 2204
Vancouver: Colson 2164, **International 2177**

see also 39, 54, 89, 137, 261, 355, 410, 435, 437, 476, 693, 734, 743, 845, 1029, 1056, 1081, 1093, 1097, 1110, 1288, 1336, 1579, 1785, 1839, 1842, 1925, 1926, 2006

TYPE OF SUPPORT INDEX

Grantmakers in boldface type make grants on a national, regional, or international basis; the others generally limit giving to the city or state in which they are located.

Advocacy: cash grants for services related to advocacy, including advocating for better assistance in various program areas (for example school reform, full access to health care, legal reform, environmental clean-up work, etc.) and providing assistance in planning advocacy campaigns.

Annual campaigns: any organized effort by a nonprofit to secure gifts on an annual basis; also called annual appeals.

Building/renovation: money raised for construction, renovation, remodeling, or rehabilitation of buildings; may be part of an organization's capital campaign.

Camperships: funding to organizations to provide partial or full tuition subsidies to enable participants who would not otherwise be financially able to participate in fee-based camping programs.

Capital campaigns: a campaign, usually extending over a period of years, to raise substantial funds for enduring purposes, such as building or endowment funds.

Cause-related marketing: linking gifts to charity with marketing promotions. This may involve donating products which will then be auctioned or given away in a drawing with the proceeds benefiting a charity. The advertising campaign for the product will be combined with the promotion for the charity. In other cases it will be advertised that when a customer buys the product a certain amount of the proceeds will be donated to charity. Often gifts made to charities stemming from cause-related marketing are not called charitable donations and may be assigned as expenses to the department in charge of the program. Public affairs and marketing are the departments usually involved.

Computer technology: grants to acquire, upgrade or develop computer technology. Includes hardware, software, peripherals, systems, networking components and mobile devices.

Conferences/seminars: a grant to cover the expenses of holding a conference or seminar.

Consulting services: professional staff support provided by the foundation to a nonprofit to consult on a project of mutual interest or to evaluate services (not a cash grant).

Continuing support: a grant that is renewed on a regular basis.

Curriculum development: grants to schools, colleges, universities, and educational support organizations to develop general or discipline-specific curricula.

Debt reduction: also known as deficit financing. A grant to reduce the recipient organization's indebtedness; frequently refers to mortgage payments.

Donated equipment: surplus furniture, office machines, paper, appliances, laboratory apparatus, or other items that may be given to charities, schools, or hospitals.

Donated land: land or developed property Institutions of higher education often receive gifts of real estate; land has also been given to community groups for housing development or for parks or recreational facilities.

Donated products: companies giving away what they make or produce. Product donations can include periodic clothing donations to a shelter for the homeless or regular donations of pharmaceuticals to a health clinic resulting in a reliable supply.

Emergency funds: a one-time grant to cover immediate short-term funding needs on an emergency basis.

Employee matching gifts: a contribution to a charitable organization by a corporate employee which is matched by a similar contribution from the employer. Many corporations support employee matching gift programs in higher education to stimulate their employees to give to the college or university of their choice. In addition, many foundations support matching gift programs for their officers and directors.

Employee volunteer services: an ongoing coordinated effort through which the company promotes involvement with nonprofits on the part of employees. The involvement may be during work time or after hours. (Employees may also volunteer on their own initiative; however, that is not described as corporate volunteerism). Many companies honor their employees with awards for outstanding volunteer efforts. In making cash donations, many favor the organizations with which their employees have worked as volunteers. Employee volunteerism runs the gamut from school tutoring programs to sales on work premises of employee-made crafts or baked goods to benefit nonprofits. Management of the programs can range from fully-staffed offices of corporate volunteerism to a part-time coordinating responsibility on the part of one employee.

Employee-related scholarships: a scholarship program funded by a company-sponsored foundation usually for children of employees; programs are frequently administered by the National Merit Scholarship Corporation which is responsible for selection of scholars.

Endowments: a bequest or gift intended to be kept permanently and invested to provide income for continued support of an organization.

Equipment: a grant to purchase equipment, furnishings, or other materials.

Exchange programs: usually refers to funds for educational exchange programs for foreign students.

Faculty/staff development: grants to institutions or organizations to train or further educate staff or faculty members

Fellowships: usually indicates funds awarded to educational institutions to support fellowship programs. A few foundations award fellowships directly to individuals.

Film/video/radio: grants to fund a specific film, video, or radio production.

General/operating support: a grant made to further the general purpose or work of an organization, rather than for a specific purpose or project; also called unrestricted grants.

Grants to individuals: awards made directly by the foundation to individuals rather than to nonprofit organizations; includes aid to the needy. (See also "Fellowships," "Scholarships—to individuals," and "Student loans—to individuals.")

In-kind gifts: a contribution of equipment, supplies, or other property as distinct from a monetary grant. Some organizations may also donate space or staff time as an in-kind contribution.

Income development: grants for fundraising, marketing, and to expand audience base.

Internship funds: usually indicates funds awarded to an institution or organization to support an internship program rather than a grant to an individual.

Land acquisition: a grant to purchase real estate property.

Lectureships: see "Curriculum development."

Loaned talent: an aspect of employee volunteerism. It differs from the usual definition of such in that it usually involves loaned professionals and executive staff who are helping a nonprofit in an area involving their particular skills. Loaned talents can assist a nonprofit in strategic planning, dispute resolution or negotiation services, office administration, real estate technical assistance, personnel policies, lobbying, consulting, fundraising, and legal and tax advice.

Loans: see "Program-related investments/loans" and "Student loans—to individuals."

Loans—to individuals: assistance distributed directly to individuals in the form of loans.

Management development/capacity building: grants for salaries, staff support, staff training, strategic and long-term planning, capacity building, budgeting and accounting.

Matching/challenge support: a grant which is made to match funds provided by another donor. (See also "Employee matching gifts.")

Mission-related investments/loans: Market-rate loans or other investments (as distinguished from grants) to organizations to finance projects related to the foundation's stated charitable purpose and interests. Organizations invested in may be for-profit entities.

Operating budgets: see "General/operating support."

Pro bono services: pro bono services rendered by a company, professional services firm, intermediary,association or individual professional leveraging the core competencies and expertise of the professional(s) engaged to meet the client's need.

Pro bono services-advocacy: pro bono consulting assistance related to advocacy, including advocating for better services in various program areas (for example school reform, full access to health care, legal reform, environmental clean-up work, etc.) and providing assistance in planning advocacy campaigns that will follow current legal guidelines preventing certain kinds of advocacy by nonprofits

Pro bono services-board: pro bono consulting assistance in board effectiveness assessment, board recruitment process design, board reporting, meeting facilitation, executive coaching, and performance review.

Pro bono services-communications/public relations: pro bono consulting assistance in external communications and public relations, including but not limited to assistance with the development of an annual report, brochure, newsletter design, and/or public service announcement.

Pro bono services-financial management: pro bono consulting assistance in financial management, including but not limited to program cost analysis, financial audit, financial controls assessment and design, budgeting process design, pricing strategy, and purchase and supply chain audit.

Pro bono services-fundraising: Pro bono consulting assistance in programs or projects directly relating to fundraising. These may include event planning and production, executive fundraising coaching, donor segmentation, in-kind opportunity assessment, capital campaign design and management, and the development of capital campaign materials.

Pro bono services-human resources: pro bono consulting assistance in the area of human resources, including a strategic assessment and recommendations for a human resources plan, organizational diversity plan, performance management system, back office systems implementation, staff compensation and incentive plan, staff training and development plan, and an internal communications plan.

Pro bono services-interactive/website technology: pro bono consulting assistance in website technology, including the design and development of a basic website, interactive website, intranet, and extranet.

Pro bono services-legal: pro bono consulting assistance in the area of legal support, including donation of legal services in court situations, review of various legal documents, including those related to incorporation and other law, justice, and counsel issues.

Pro bono services-marketing/branding: pro bono consulting assistance in marketing and branding. Programs or projects may cover issues such as a program marketing, organizational positioning and key messages, visual identity or re-naming.

Pro bono services-medical: pro bono consulting assistance in the medical area, including donation of medical services and equipment.

Pro bono services-strategic management: pro bono consulting assistance in the area of strategic management, including the development of a strategic plan, refined mission, environmental and sustainability policy and plan, internal capacity assessment, strengths, weaknesses, opportunities, and threats analysis, competitive analysis, earned income business plan, geographic expansion plan, and logic model design

Pro bono services-technology infrastructure: pro bono consulting assistance in technology infrastructure such as donor database implementation, the development of an organizational IT plan, installation of office networking, remote IT access set up, and program database implementation.

Professorships: a grant to an educational institution to endow a professorship or chair.

Program development: grants to support specific projects or programs as opposed to general purpose grants.

Program evaluation: grants to evaluate a specific project or program; includes awards both to agencies to pay for evaluation costs and to research institutes and other program evaluators.

Program-related investments/loans: a loan is any temporary award of funds that must be repaid. A program-related investment is a loan or other investment (as distinguished from a grant) made by a foundation to another organization for a project related to the foundation's stated charitable purpose and interests.

Public relations services: may include printing and duplicating, audio-visual and graphic arts services, helping to plan special events such as festivals, piggyback advertising (advertisements that mention a company while also promoting a nonprofit), and public service advertising.

Publication: a grant to fund reports or other publications issued by a nonprofit resulting from research or projects of interest to the foundation.

Renovation projects: see "Building/renovation."

Research: usually indicates funds awarded to institutions to cover costs of investigations and clinical trials. Research grants for individuals are usually referred to as fellowships.

Scholarship funds: a grant to an educational institution or organization to support a scholarship program, mainly for students at the undergraduate level. (See also "Employee-related scholarships.")

Scholarships—to individuals: assistance awarded directly to individuals in the form of educational grants or scholarships. (See also "Employee-related scholarships.")

Seed money: a grant or contribution used to start a new project or organization. Seed grants may cover salaries and other operating expenses of a new project. Also known as "start-up funds."

Special projects: see "Program development."

Sponsorships: endorsements of charities by corporations; or corporate contributions to all or part of a charitable event.

Student aid: see "Fellowships," "Scholarships—to individuals," and "Student loans—to individuals."

Student loans—to individuals: assistance awarded directly to individuals in the form of educational loans.

Technical assistance: operational or management assistance given to nonprofit organizations; may include fundraising assistance, budgeting and financial planning, program planning, legal advice, marketing, and other aids to management. Assistance may be offered directly by a foundation staff member or in the form of a grant to pay for the services of an outside consultant.

Travel awards: funding to organizations to provide awards to individuals to cover transportation and/or out-of-town living expenses while attending a conference or completing a period of studt or special project. Enrollment in a college or university is not a requirement.

Use of facilities: this may include rent free office space for temporary periods, dining and meeting facilities, telecommunications services, mailing services, transportation services, or computer services.

Annual campaigns

Arizona: Duffy 18, Freeport-McMoRan 21

California: Autodesk 68, Eisenberg 123, Flora 135, Fremont 143, Goldsmith 161, Ingram 187, Jacobs 197, Koret 216, Leichtag 226, Philibosian 278, Saban 302, Sempra 315, **Seventh 317**, Strome 336, Teichman 343, **Tides 346**

Colorado: **Global 393**

Connecticut: Oristano 436

Delaware: Colgate 453, Jewish 461

District of Columbia: Bernstein 500, **Centre 508**, Poretsky 586, **Sons 591**, Zients 609

Florida: Cafesjian 623, Engelberg 634, Greenburg 645, **Katz 656**, Kaufman 657, Russell 669, **Uncle 678**, Wahlert 679

Georgia: Global 695, Livingston 700, Scientific 704

Hawaii: Alexander 712

Illinois: Caterpillar 748, Crane 755, Crown 756, Deere 757, Dunard 762, Jocarno 775, King 777, Lindon 783, Logos 785, **New 799**, **Rotary 807**, Stuart 823

Indiana: Brotherhood 835, Cummins 837, Lilly 840, West 846

Iowa: Wright 856

Kansas: Jewish 859

Kentucky: Yum! 866

Maryland: Bearman 890, Cohen 896, England 902, Hirschhorn 905, **Interchurch 909**, Meyerhoff 919, Meyerhoff 920, Morningstar 922

Massachusetts: Grinspoon 971, Homestead 977, Spero 1020, State 1021

Michigan: DeVos 1036, Fisher 1041, **Jewish 1047**, Teitel 1065

Minnesota: Andersen 1073, Kaplan 1085, Kelley 1086, Medtronic 1093, Toro 1104

Missouri: Bohm 1117, Clarkson 1120, Millstone 1127

Nebraska: Kind 1141

Nevada: Charitable 1145

New Jersey: Aufzien 1158, Johnson 1179

New Mexico: Angelica 1208, Santa Fe 1213

New York: Abrons 1216, American 1241, **American 1245, Amit 1265**, Berg 1285, Blinken 1291, Botwinick 1295, Butler 1308, **Cay 1315**, Charina 1322, Curran 1348, **Engelhard 1371**, Englander 1373, **Gruss 1434, Harriman 1442, Hauser 1444**, Hedge 1447, Kathwari 1491, Kimmelman 1500, **Kohlberg 1506**, Lauder 1516, Lehman 1521, Mendell 1547, New 1580, Peierls 1597, **Royal 1642**, Schaffner 1647, Schmeelk 1648, Steel 1673, Stein 1674, Vetlesen 1713, **Vital 1718**, White 1732, Zenkel 1743

North Carolina: **African 1747, Rolander 1764**, Triangle 1768

Ohio: AK Steel 1775, Armington 1777, **Geisse 1790**, Haskell 1793, Lowe 1802, Maltz 1803, Marion 1807, OMNOVA 1813

Oklahoma: **Schusterman 1830**, Zarrow 1832

Oregon: Kalakendra 1840, Larson 1842

Pennsylvania: Alcoa 1853, AMETEK 1856, Arronson 1858, **Colcom 1873**, Federated 1879, Huston 1892, **KL 1896**, Mine 1899, **National 1901**, Wollowick 1918, **Zeldin 1919**

Rhode Island: Collette 1921, Soforenko 1935

Tennessee: **Cloud 1949**, Fugitive 1955

Texas: Apache 1979, Austin 1980, Crowder 1998, Fluor 2006, McDermott 2039, Trull 2067

Utah: Slaughter 2076

Virginia: Delmar 2113

Washington: **Gates 2170**, Kongsgaard 2183, McKinstry 2185

Wisconsin: Argosy 2210, Bader 2211, **Bradley 2212**, Cudahy 2215, Kikkoman 2222

Building/renovation

Arkansas: **Tech 36**

California: Agilent 44, Autodesk 68, **AWESNA 69**, Chevron 94, Columbia 104, Firedoll 131, **Firelight 132**, Flora 135, **Global 158**, Goldsmith 161, **Hilton 178**, Jewish 203, Kvamme 219, Leichtag 226, McConnell 242, **Milarepa 247**, Rancho 286, Reve 292, Saban 302, **Seacology 314, Seventh 317**, Teichman 343, World 374

Colorado: **AfricAid 380**, Bohemian 384, **Global 393**, Mercy 402, **Queen 405, Someone 409, Western 413, World 415**

Connecticut: **Lingnan 432**, Oristano 436

Delaware: **Glencoe 456**, Jewish 461, **Raskob 467**, Shoemaker 472

District of Columbia: Gottesman 537, Gudelsky 538, **Ocean 575**

Florida: **Davis 630**, Engelberg 634, Freewill 636, Kerzner 658, Russell 669, **Uncle 678**, Wahlert 679

Georgia: Amos 684, Amos-Cheves 685, Delta 694, Livingston 700, Scientific 704

Hawaii: Alexander 712, Watumull 726

Idaho: **Schultz 733**

Illinois: Abbott 735, Aon 739, Boeing 743, Caterpillar 748, Crown 756, Deere 757, King 777, McCormick 792

Indiana: Brotherhood 835, Cummins 837, NIBCO 842

Iowa: Wright 856

Kansas: Jewish 859

Louisiana: Pennington 870, Woldenberg 872

Maine: **Oak 878, Sandy 880**

Maryland: **Ames 886, Blaustein 891**, Cohen 896, England 902, Hoffberger 906, **Hughes 907, India 908**, Meyerhoff 919, Meyerhoff 920, Smith 930, **Weinberg 934**

Massachusetts: Fidelity 959, **Friends 964**, Grand 968, Homestead 977, **Lift 990, Oxfam 1002**, State 1021

Michigan: **Africa 1028, Arcus 1030**, DENSO 1035, Kellogg's 1051, Secchia 1063, Steelcase 1064, Teitel 1065, **Worldwide 1071**

Minnesota: Andersen 1073, McKnight 1092

Missouri: Bohm 1117, Enterprise 1121, Slusher 1133

Nebraska: Kind 1141

Nevada: **Boulder 1144**, Charitable 1145, **Tang 1151, Walsh 1152**

New Jersey: Danellie 1166, Hoffmann-La 1174, **International 1177**, Johnson 1181, Merck 1186

New York: Abrons 1216, **American 1237, American 1245, American 1257, Amit 1265**, Botwinick 1295, Butler 1308, **Cay 1315**, Charina 1322, Chazen 1324, **Clover 1333, Cogitare 1334**, Cummings 1346, Curran 1348, Dodge 1357,

Engelhard 1371, Englander 1373, **Fund 1406**, Genesis 1411, Goldsmith 1424, Goldsmith 1425, Gorman 1426, Hess 1448, **King 1501, Lauder 1517**, Lehman 1521, **Nash 1567**, Neuberger 1575, Nok 1582, **Pfizer 1606**, Schaffner 1647, **Starr 1672**, Stein 1674, Tisch 1690, **United 1704**, Vetlesen 1713, **Vital 1718**, Zenkel 1743

North Carolina: Kramer 1754, **Rolander 1764**

Ohio: Convergys 1783, Haskell 1793, Jewish 1798, Maltz 1803, Marion 1807, Middletown 1809, OMNOVA 1813, **Timken 1822**

Oklahoma: Crio 1827, **Schusterman 1830**

Pennsylvania: Alcoa 1853, AMETEK 1856, Arronson 1858, Federated 1879, Friendship 1882, **KL 1896**, Mine 1899, **National 1901**

Rhode Island: Collette 1921, CVS 1922, Hasbro 1926, Soforenko 1935

Tennessee: **Cloud 1949**, Community 1950, Fugitive 1955

Texas: Alcon 1974, Austin 1980, Bolivar 1988, Fluor 2006, Fondren 2008, McDermott 2039, Scaler 2054, Summerlee 2064, Trull 2067

Utah: Force 2073, Sorenson 2078

Virginia: Delmar 2113, **Diema's 2114, Good360 2124, Loyola 2134**

Washington: **Bainbridge 2159, Gates 2170**, Samis 2196, Seattle 2199, Weyerhaeuser 2206

Wisconsin: Bader 2211, **Bradley 2212**, Cudahy 2215, Taylor 2230

Capital campaigns

Alabama: Ard 1

Arizona: Lodestar 25

California: Amgen 54, Autodesk 68, Firedoll 131, Flora 135, Goldsmith 161, **Hilton 178**, Leichtag 226, McConnell 242, Strauss 335

Colorado: Bohemian 384

Connecticut: Oristano 436, United 444

Delaware: Jewish 461, Shoemaker 472

District of Columbia: Bernstein 500, El-Hibri 519, Gottesman 537, Gudelsky 538

Florida: Atlantic 620, Cafesjian 623, **Davis 630**, EIS 633, Engelberg 634, **Katz 656**, Russell 669, **Uncle 678**, Wahlert 679

Georgia: Livingston 700, Scientific 704

Hawaii: Alexander 712, Sangham 722, Watumull 726

Illinois: Boeing 743, Caterpillar 748, Crown 756, Driehaus 761, Gochnauer 766, King 777, Lindon 783, **New 799**, Shifting 817, Stuart 823, Wein 830

Indiana: Brotherhood 835, Lilly 840, West 846

Kansas: Jewish 859, **Lloyd 860, Shumaker 861**

Kentucky: C.E. 863

Louisiana: Pennington 870, Woldenberg 872

Maryland: **Blaustein 891**, Cohen 896, England 902, Hirschhorn 905, Meyerhoff 919, Meyerhoff 920, Morningstar 922, **Weinberg 934**

Massachusetts: Fidelity 959, Schooner 1018, State 1021, Swartz 1023

Michigan: **Arcus 1030**, DENSO 1035, DeVos 1036, Fisher 1041, **Jewish 1047, Rotary 1062**, Steelcase 1064, Teitel 1065

Cause-related marketing

Conferences/seminars

Consulting services

Continuing support

1488, Kaplan 1490, Klagsbrun 1503, Lauder 1516, **Lauder 1517**, Lehman 1521, **Mellon 1546**, Mitsubishi 1559, Neuberger 1575, New York 1579, New 1580, Nok 1582, **Open 1593, PepsiCo 1601**, Pfizer 1607, **Rainforest 1622**, Reed 1627, Revson 1631, Reynolds 1632, **Rockefeller 1639, Royal 1642**, Schaffner 1647, Schmeelk 1648, Slifka 1660, **Smile 1661**, Sony 1664, **Starr 1672**, Stein 1674, Stern 1678, Tisch 1690, UncommonGoods 1703, Vetlesen 1713, **Vital 1718, Weeden 1723**, Weinstein 1727, White 1732

North Carolina: **Rixson 1763, Samaritan's 1765**, Triangle 1768

Ohio: AK Steel 1775, Armington 1777, **Geisse 1790**, Haskell 1793, Lowe 1802, OMNOVA 1813

Oklahoma: **Schusterman 1830**

Oregon: **Alima 1833**

Pennsylvania: Alcoa 1853, Bread 1866, **Carnegie 1868, Colcom 1873**, Copernicus 1874, Hershey 1889, Mine 1899, **National 1901, Nazareth 1902**, Pew 1906, Rosenstiel 1910, Scaife 1911, Scranton 1912

Rhode Island: Collette 1921, Dorot 1923, Hasbro 1926, **Perkins 1932**, Soforenko 1935

Tennessee: Ezell 1953, **FedEx 1954**, International 1960

Texas: Austin 1980, Coneway 1995, Fondren 2008, Kimberly 2028, Kimberly 2029, McDermott 2039, **Mission 2042**, Scaler 2054, Trull 2067

Utah: Force 2073, Slaughter 2076, Sorenson 2078, Swanson 2079

Virginia: Delmar 2113, **Diema's 2114**, Samberg 2145, **United 2151, WestWind 2154**

Washington: Bullitt 2161, **Gates 2170**, Kongsgaard 2183, Samis 2196, Starbucks 2202, **Stewardship 2203**, Wilburforce 2207

Wisconsin: **Bradley 2212**, Cudahy 2215, Eastman 2217

Curriculum development

Arizona: Duffy 18, Freeport McMoRan 21

Arkansas: Walton 37

California: Agilent 44, Applied 59, **Asia 64**, Autodesk 68, Bickerstaff 81, Cisco 100, Columbia 104, Flora 135, **Global 158, Hilton 178**, Rancho 286, Reinhard 289, **Rivendell 295**, Saban 302, Telchman 343

Colorado: **AfricAid 380, Oreg 403**

Connecticut: **GE 428, Lingnan 432**, United 444

Delaware: Jackman 459, **Raskob 467**, Shoemaker 472

District of Columbia: **Endowment 520, Eurasia 522, Institute 543, Ocean 575**

Florida: **Chatlos 626, Davis 630**, Engelberg 634, Freewill 636, **Koch 660**, Pruitt 668, **Uncle 678**

Georgia: Livingston 700, Scientific 704

Hawaii: People's 721

Idaho: Micron 730

Illinois: Abbott 735, Caterpillar 748, King 777, Logos 785, McCormick 792, Mead 794, Motorola 798

Indiana: Cummins 837

Kansas: Jewish 859, **Shumaker 861**

Maryland: **Child 895, Hughes 907**, Meyerhoff 919, Polinger 926

Massachusetts: Fidelity 959, Grand 968, New England 999, PTC 1012

Michigan: **Arcus 1030, Earhart 1039, Foundation 1042, Worldwide 1071**

Minnesota: Duluth 1077, Medtronic 1093

Missouri: Monsanto 1128

Nevada: **Walsh 1152**

New Jersey: **Johnson 1178**, Merck 1186, Winters 1205

New York: **Abraham 1215**, Achelis 1219, **American 1237**, American 1241, **American 1257, Amit 1265, AVI 1278**, Berg 1285, Bodman 1293, Bristol 1303, Butler 1308, **Carnegie 1312, Center 1318**, Charina 1322, Citi 1328, **Common 1336**, Curran 1348, **Delmas 1351, East 1363**, Freeman 1397, **Fund 1406**, Genesis 1411, **Gruss 1434, Hadassah**

1438, Hartford 1443, Institute 1461, Jewish 1481, **Johnson 1486**, Kevorkian 1497, Lehman 1521, New York 1579, Nok 1582, **Peterson 1604**, Pfizer 1606, Pfizer 1607, **Rockefeller 1639**, Slifka 1660, Sony 1664, **Sparkplug 1667**, Toyota 1692, **United 1704, United 1708, Virtue 1717, Vital 1718**

Ohio: Marion 1807, Middletown 1809, Procter 1815, **Thomas 1820**

Oklahoma: Devon 1828, **Schusterman 1830**

Oregon: **Fohs 1836**, Intel 1839

Pennsylvania: Alcoa 1853, **KL 1896, National 1901**, Scaife 1911, Scranton 1912, **Templeton 1916**

Rhode Island: **Perkins 1932**

Tennessee: International 1960

Texas: Kimberly 2029, McDermott 2039, Summerlee 2064, Trull 2067

Virginia: **American 2094**, Samberg 2145, **Youth 2157**

Washington: Tulalip 2204, Weyerhaeuser 2206

Wisconsin: **Bradley 2212**

Debt reduction

California: Flora 135

Florida: **Chatlos 626**

Maryland: Meyerhoff 920

Montana: **Edwards 1136**

New York: **American 1257**, Charina 1322, **Vital 1718**

Pennsylvania: **National 1901**

Wisconsin: Bader 2211

Donated equipment

California: Cadence 89, Gap 150, Spansion 331

Georgia: Delta 694

Illinois: Boeing 743

Massachusetts: PTC 1012

Michigan: Dow 1038

New Jersey: **BD 1159**

New York: Canon 1309, Foot 1390, Hess 1448

Texas: Butt 1991, Cooper 1996

Donated products

Arizona: U-Haul 29

California: **Adobe 39**, Autodesk 68, Gap 150, Google.org 163, Ingram 187, Palm 274, Quiksilver 284, San Diego 308, Symantec 337

Connecticut: United 444

Georgia: Delta 694

Illinois: Mead 794

Indiana: Lilly 840, **Lilly 841**, NIBCO 842

Kentucky: Yum! 867

Massachusetts: PTC 1012

Michigan: Dow 1037, Dow 1038

Minnesota: Medtronic 1093

New Jersey: **BD 1159, Johnson 1178**

New York: Canon 1309, Fast 1379, Foot 1390, Hess 1448, **IBM 1457**, Pfizer 1607

Ohio: Cintas 1782, Eaton 1786, Ethicon 1788, Limited 1800

Oregon: **Tazo 1849**

Pennsylvania: Heinz 1887, Hershey 1889

Texas: Apache 1979, Butt 1991, Cooper 1996, Kimberly 2028

Washington: Seattle 2200

Emergency funds

Alabama: Ard 1

Arizona: Duffy 18, **PetSmart 26**

California: **ANGELCARE 56, Armenian 61**, Autodesk 68, Firedoll 131, Flora 135, Fund 149, **Give2Asia 155, Global 158, Hilton 178**, Kee 212, Lutz 235, **Milarepa 247, Omega 263, Orangutan 267**,

Ploughshares 280, Rancho 286, **Seventh 317, Taiwan 339**, Teichman 343, World 374

Colorado: **General 392, Global 393, Urgent 411**

Connecticut: **AmeriCares 421**, International 431

Delaware: **Glencoe 456, Raskob 467**

District of Columbia: **American 492, Eritrean 521, Franciscan 525**, Gottesman 537, Gudelsky 538, **Jerusalem 552, Moriah 562, Ocean 575, Sons 591, United 599, United 600**

Florida: EIS 633, Engelberg 634, Freewill 636, Greenburg 645, **Peterson 666**, Wahlert 679

Georgia: Coca 693, Global 695

Hawaii: People's 721

Idaho: Boise 728

Illinois: Boeing 743, **Circle 751**, Deere 757, Driehaus 761, Jocarno 775, King 777, Landau 780, Lindon 783, **Rotary 807**, Stern 822

Indiana: Cummins 837

Iowa: Wright 856

Kansas: **Christian 858**, Jewish 859

Kentucky: C.E. 863

Louisiana: Woldenberg 872

Maryland: Bearman 890, Blaustein 892, **Interchurch 909, Jewish 915, Lutheran 916**, Meyerhoff 919, Meyerhoff 920

Massachusetts: Haymarket 975, **International 980, Oxfam 1002**, RESIST 1014, State 1021

Michigan: Fisher 1041, Kellogg 1049, Teitel 1065

Minnesota: Andersen 1073, Duluth 1077

Missouri: Bohm 1117, Enterprise 1121, Lubin 1124, Millstone 1127

Montana: **Edwards 1136**

Nebraska: Livingston 1142

Nevada: Charitable 1145, **Walsh 1152**

New Jersey: Aufzien 1158, Berrie 1160, **International 1177, Johnson 1178**, Prudential 1191

New Mexico: Santa Fe 1213

New York: American 1241, **American 1257, Amit 1265, Butler 1307, Cay 1315**, Charina 1322, Citi 1328, **Common 1336, Doctors 1356**, Edouard 1367, **Funding 1407**, Gorman 1426, Hess 1448, **Institute 1461**, Lehman 1521, Neuberger 1575, Nok 1582, North 1583, **PEN 1598, Rainforest 1621, Rainforest 1623**, Schaffner 1647, St. George's 1670, **Starr 1672, Vital 1718**, Walters 1722, **Weeden 1723**, White 1732

North Carolina: **Samaritan's 1765**, Triangle 1768

Ohio: **Arab 1776**, Armington 1777, **Christian 1781, International 1795**, Jewish 1798, Middletown 1809, Sheely 1817

Oklahoma: **Schusterman 1830**

Pennsylvania: Alcoa 1853, Dixon 1876, Huston 1892, Mine 1899, **National 1901**, Wollowick 1918, **Zeldin 1919**

Rhode Island: **Perkins 1932**, Soforenko 1935

Tennessee: **Operation 1964**

Texas: BP 1989, Bridgeway 1990, **Chrest 1994**, Crowder 1998

Utah: Swanson 2079

Vermont: Evslin 2086

Virginia: **ChildFund 2105**, Foster 2120

Washington: Bullitt 2161, Kongsgaard 2183, Samis 2196, Starbucks 2202, Weyerhaeuser 2206

Wisconsin: Argosy 2210, Taylor 2230, Wisconsin 2232

Employee matching gifts

Arizona: Freeport-McMoRan 21

California: **Adobe 39**, Agilent 44, Amgen 54, Applied 58, Autodesk 68, Cadence 89, **Capital 91**, Cisco 100, Flora 135, Fremont 143, Gap 150, **Getty 153, Give2Asia 155**, Google.org 163, Hewlett 172, **Hilton 178**, Ingram 187, Intuit 193, McConnell 242, NVIDIA 261, **Omidyar 264, Packard 271**, Palm 274, **salesforce.com 305**, San Diego 307, San Francisco 309, Sempra 315, Strauss 335, Symantec 337

Colorado: First 389, ProLogis 404, **Western 413**
Connecticut: **GE 428**, United 444
Florida: Assurant 619, Atlantic 620, **Davis 630**
Georgia: Coca 693, Gray 696, Scientific 704, **UPS 709**
Hawaii: Alexander 712
Idaho: Micron 730
Illinois: Abbott 735, Aon 739, Archer 740, Baxter 741, Boeing 743, Caterpillar 748, Crane 755, Crown 756, Deere 757, **MacArthur 788**, McCormick 792, **Spencer 820, State 821**
Indiana: Cummins 837, Lilly 840
Kentucky: Yum! 866
Maryland: **Blaustein 891**
Massachusetts: Fidelity 959, Grand 968, State 1021
Michigan: **Arcus 1030**, BorgWarner 1033, Dow 1037, Dow 1038, **Kellogg 1050**, Kellogg's 1051, **Mott 1058**, Steelcase 1064
Minnesota: General 1081, McKnight 1092, Medtronic 1093, Piper 1097, Toro 1104
Missouri: Monsanto 1128
Nevada: **Walsh 1152**
New Jersey: **BD 1159, Johnson 1178**, Johnson 1179, Merck 1186, Prudential 1191
New York: Bristol 1303, **Carnegie 1312**, Clark 1330, **Commonwealth 1337**, Deutsche 1353, Dodge 1357, **Duke 1361, Ford 1391, Guggenheim 1435, Hartford 1443, IBM 1457, Kress 1509**, Littauer 1529, **Luce 1531**, Mitsui 1560, New York 1578, New York 1579, **Open 1593, PepsiCo 1601, Pfizer 1606**, PricewaterhouseCoopers 1615, **Prospect 1618, Rockefeller 1638, Rockefeller 1639**, Select 1650, **Starr 1672**
North Carolina: Triangle 1768
Ohio: AK Steel 1775, Convergys 1783, Middletown 1809, OMNOVA 1813, Procter 1815
Oregon: Intel 1839
Pennsylvania: Alcoa 1853, **National 1901**, Pew 1906
Rhode Island: FM 1925, Hasbro 1926
Tennessee: International 1960, UnumProvident 1967
Texas: AMD 1977, Apache 1979, BP 1989, ExxonMobil 2004, Kimberly 2029, **Mission 2042**, Spectra 2062
Virginia: Gannett 2122
Washington: Bullitt 2161, **Gates 2170**, RealNetworks 2191, Russell 2195, Starbucks 2202, Weyerhaeuser 2206

Employee volunteer services

Alabama: Protective 7
Arizona: Freeport-McMoRan 21
California: **Adobe 39**, Advent 40, Agilent 44, Amgen 54, Applied 58, Autodesk 68, Cadence 89, Cisco 100, Fremont 143, Gap 150, Google.org 163, Ingram 187, Intuit 193, NVIDIA 261, Palm 274, Sempra 315, Spansion 331, Strauss 335, Symantec 337, Xilinx, 377
Colorado: First 389, **Western 413**
Connecticut: United 444
Delaware: ING 458
Florida: Assurant 619, Jabil 652
Georgia: **Coca 692**, Delta 694, Global 695, Southwire 706, **UPS 709**
Hawaii: Alexander 712
Idaho: Micron 730, Micron 731
Illinois: Archer 740, Baxter 741, Boeing 743, Caterpillar 748, Mead 794, Motorola 798, **State 821**
Indiana: Cummins 838, Lilly 840, NIBCO 842
Kentucky: Yum! 866, Yum! 867
Massachusetts: American 944, Grand 968, PTC 1012, State 1021
Michigan: Amway 1029, BorgWarner 1033, Kellogg's 1051
Minnesota: Fuller 1080, General 1081, Medtronic 1093, Piper 1097, Reell 1099, Thomson 1103, Toro 1104
New Jersey: **BD 1159**, Merck 1186

New York: Accenture 1218, Allen 1229, Bristol 1303, Canon 1309, **CIT 1327**, Deutsche 1353, Diamonds 1354, Fast 1379, Foot 1390, Hess 1448, Interpublic 1469, Mitsubishi 1559, Morgan 1562, New York 1579, Omnicom 1591, **PepsiCo 1601, Pfizer 1606**, PricewaterhouseCoopers 1615
Ohio: Cintas 1782, Eaton 1786, Ethicon 1788, Limited 1800, OMNOVA 1813, Procter 1815
Oklahoma: Devon 1828
Oregon: Intel 1839
Pennsylvania: Alcoa 1853, AmerisourceBergen 1855, Cephalon 1870, Heinz 1887, Hershey 1889, Mine 1899
Rhode Island: Collette 1921, CVS 1922, FM 1925, Hasbro 1926
South Carolina: Michelin 1939
Tennessee: **FedEx 1954**, International 1960, UnumProvident 1967
Texas: Apache 1979, BMC 1987, BP 1989, Cooper 1996, ExxonMobil 2004, Fluor 2006, Freescale 2011, General 2014, Hines 2018, Huntsman 2020, Kimberly 2028, Kimberly 2029, Spectra 2062
Washington: Red 2192, Weyerhaeuser 2206

Employee-related scholarships

Arizona: Freeport-McMoRan 21
Arkansas: Walton 37
California: Sempra 315
Connecticut: **GE 428**
District of Columbia: **Ocean 575**
Georgia: Scientific 704
Hawaii: Alexander 712
Illinois: Baxter 741, **State 821**
Indiana: NIBCO 842
Michigan: Steelcase 1064
Minnesota: General 1081, Toro 1104
New York: Bristol 1303, Kathwari 1491, Mitsui 1560, New York 1579, **PepsiCo 1601, Royal 1642, Starr 1672**
North Carolina: Triangle 1768
Ohio: AK Steel 1775, OMNOVA 1813, Procter 1815, Timken 1821
Pennsylvania: Alcoa 1853
Rhode Island: CVS 1922
Tennessee: UnumProvident 1967
Texas: Cooper 1996, Kimberly 2029, Spectra 2062
Washington: Vista 2205, Weyerhaeuser 2206
Wisconsin: Meehan 2226

Endowments

Arizona: Lodestar 25
Arkansas: Darragh 32
California: Amgen 54, Berman 79, Bickerstaff 81, Flora 135, Goldsmith 161, **Hilton 178**, Lutz 235, McConnell 242, Philibosian 278
Delaware: Colgate 453, Shoemaker 472
District of Columbia: Gudelsky 538, **Moriah 562**
Florida: Atlantic 620, Cafesjian 623, **Davis 630**, Greenburg 645, **Uncle 678**
Georgia: Livingston 700
Hawaii: Honda 718, Watumull 726
Illinois: Aon 739, Crown 756, Dunard 762, King 777, Lurie 787, **New 799**
Indiana: Cummins 837
Iowa: Wallace 855
Kansas: Jewish 859
Kentucky: C.E. 863
Maryland: **Blaustein 891**, Hirschhorn 905, Hoffberger 906, **India 908**, Meyerhoff 919, Meyerhoff 920, Weiss 935
Massachusetts: **China 952**, Grinspoon 971, Schooner 1018
Michigan: **Arcus 1030**, Fisher 1041, Frankel 1043, Italian 1046, Teitel 1065

Minnesota: Kaplan 1085
Missouri: Bohm 1117
Nebraska: Kind 1141
New Jersey: Johnson 1181, McMullen 1185
New York: **Amit 1265, Cay 1315**, Charina 1322, Dodge 1357, **Engelhard 1371, Ford 1391**, Goldsmith 1425, Greve 1432, **Hauser 1444**, Joukowsky 1488, Lehman 1521, Littauer 1529, **Mellon 1546**, Mendell 1547, **Myasthenia 1565**, Nok 1582, Peierls 1597, Reed 1627, Schmeelk 1648, Simons 1656, **Starr 1672**, Steel 1673, Stern 1678, Tanaka 1681, Vetlesen 1713, **Vital 1718**, Weinstein 1727, White 1732
Ohio: Convergys 1783, Eaton 1787, Haskell 1793, Maltz 1803, Marion 1807, OMNOVA 1813
Pennsylvania: AMETEK 1856, Arronson 1858, **Colcom 1873**, Copernicus 1874, **KL 1896, National 1901**
Rhode Island: **Perkins 1932**, Soforenko 1935
Tennessee: **Cloud 1949**, Fugitive 1955
Texas: Alcon 1974, Coneway 1995, Marsh 2037, McDermott 2039, **Mission 2042**, Oppenheimer 2045
Virginia: Delmar 2113
Wisconsin: **Johnson 2221**

Equipment

Alaska: Alaska 8
Arizona: **PetSmart 26**
Arkansas: Walton 37
California: Amgen 54, **ANGELCARE 56, Asia 64**, Autodesk 68, **Christensen 97**, Firedoll 131, Flora 135, **Global 156, Global 158, Hilton 178, Karisma 210**, Kvamme 219, Leichtag 226, McConnell 242, Rancho 286, **Rock 297**, S.G. 300, **salesforce.com 305**, San Diego 307, **Seacology 314, Seventh 317, Smith 327**, Strauss 335, World 374
Colorado: **AfricAid 380**, Bohemian 384, **Western 413**
Connecticut: **Aid 417**
Delaware: **Glencoe 456, Raskob 467**
District of Columbia: **Eurasia 522, Ocean 575**
Florida: **Chatlos 626, Davis 630**, Freewill 636, **Koch 660, Peterson 666, Uncle 678**, Wahlert 679
Georgia: Amos-Cheves 685
Hawaii: Alexander 712, People's 721
Idaho: Boise 728, **Schultz 733**
Illinois: Boeing 743, Caterpillar 748, Crown 756, Motorola 798, **Rotary 807, Scholl 814**, Stern 822
Indiana: Cummins 837, Lilly 840
Kansas: **Lloyd 860**
Louisiana: Woldenberg 872
Maine: **Oak 878, Sandy 880**
Maryland: **Ames 886**, Bearman 890, **Hughes 907**, Meyerhoff 919, Meyerhoff 920, O'Neil 925, **Weinberg 934**
Massachusetts: **Families 958**, Fidelity 959, **Friends 964**, Grand 968, **International 980, Lift 990, Oxfam 1002**
Michigan: DENSO 1035, Dow 1037, **Hands 1045, Rotary 1062**, Secchia 1063, Steelcase 1064, Williams 1069, **Worldwide 1071**
Minnesota: Kelley 1086, McKnight 1092
Missouri: Clarkson 1120, Enterprise 1121, Monsanto 1128
Nebraska: Kind 1141
Nevada: **Walsh 1152**
New Jersey: **International 1177**, Johnson 1181
New Mexico: **Levinson 1211**
New York: Achelis 1219, **American 1237, American 1245, American 1257, Amit 1265, Bat 1283**, Berg 1285, Bodman 1293, **Butler 1307, Cay 1315, Cogitare 1334**, Cummings 1346, Dodge 1357, **Friends 1404**, Genesis 1411, **Gildersleeve 1413, Israel 1472, King 1501**, Lehman 1521, **Smile 1661**, Stein 1674, Tisch 1690, Toyota 1692, **United 1704**, Vetlesen 1713, **Virtue 1717**
North Carolina: **Rolander 1764, Samaritan's 1765**

1010, RESIST 1014, Schooner 1018, Spero 1020, State 1021, Swartz 1023, TJX 1026

Michigan: Amway 1029, **Arcus 1030**, BorgWarner 1033, DeVos 1036, Dow 1038, Fisher 1041, **Hands 1045**, Jubilee 1048, Kellogg's 1051, Manthei 1056, May 1057, **Mott 1058**, Pilgrim 1060, Steelcase 1064, Teitel 1065, Weingartz 1067

Minnesota: Andersen 1073, Better 1074, **Dorobo 1075, Dorsey 1076**, Duluth 1077, Fuller 1080, General 1081, Kelley 1086, Lownade 1088, McKnight 1092, Mortenson 1094, Oswald 1096, Piper 1097, Reell 1099, Sit 1101, Thomson 1103, Toro 1104, United 1105, **Winds 1108**

Missouri: **ASC 1114**, Bohm 1117, Build 1118, Enterprise 1121, Millstone 1127, Monsanto 1128, Slusher 1133

Montana: **Edwards 1136**

Nebraska: **Buffett 1137**, Cooper 1138, Eagle 1139, **Himanchal 1140**, Kind 1141, Livingston 1142

Nevada: Adelson 1143, Hahn 1148, **Walsh 1152**

New Hampshire: Brookstone, 1154, Butler 1155

New Jersey: **BD 1159**, Berrie 1160, Daft 1165, Danellie 1166, Harbourton 1172, Harris 1173, IDT 1176, Johnson 1179, Knistrom 1183, MCJ 1184, McMullen 1185, Prudential 1191, Segal 1195, Syms 1198, **Vollmer 1201**

New Mexico: Atrisco 1209, **Levinson 1211**, Santa Fe 1213

New York: **Abraham 1215**, Abrons 1216, Accenture 1218, Achelis 1219, Allen 1229, American 1241, **American 1244, American 1257, Amit 1265, Astraea 1276, Bat 1283**, Berg 1285, **Blacksmith 1290**, Blinken 1291, Bodman 1293, Botwinick 1295, Bristol 1303, Bunson 1305, Butler 1308, Canon 1309, **Carnegie 1312, Cay 1315**, Charina 1322, Chazen 1324, **CIT 1327**, Citi 1328, Clark 1330, Cleary 1331, **Common 1336, Cummings 1347**, Curran 1348, **Delmas 1351**, Deutsche 1353, Diamonds 1354, Dobkin 1355, Donner 1360, **East 1363**, Edouard 1367, **Engelhard 1371**, Englander 1373, Fast 1379, Feldman 1380, **Fight 1382**, Fischel 1384, Foot 1390, **Ford 1391**, Freeman 1397, **Fund 1406, Funding 1407, Gabriela 1408**, GBRG 1409, Genesis 1411, **Goldman 1422**, Goldsmith 1425, Gorman 1426, Greve 1432, Guttman 1437, **Harriman 1442**, Hess 1448, **HKH 1450**, Hurford 1456, **IBM 1457**, Interpublic 1469, **Isdell 1470, Israel 1472**, Mata 1482, **John 1484, Johnson 1486**, Joukowsky 1488, Kaplan 1490, Kathwari 1491, Kimmelman 1500, **King 1501**, Klagsbrun 1503, Lauder 1516, **Lauder 1517**, Lehman 1521, Lisben 1528, **Luce 1531**, Mesdag 1550, Mitsubishi 1559, Morgan 1562, **Nash 1567**, Neuberger 1575, New York 1579, New 1580, Nok 1582, North 1583, Omnicom 1591, **Open 1593, Overbrook 1594, PepsiCo 1601, Pfizer 1606**, Pfizer 1607, PricewaterhouseCoopers 1615, **Prospect 1618, Rainforest 1621, Rasmussen 1624**, Reed 1627, Reynolds 1632, **Rockefeller 1638, Rockefeller 1639, Royal 1642, Rubin 1643**, Salomon 1645, Schaffner 1647, SDialogue, 1649, Select 1650, **Shatford 1652**, Simons 1656, Slifka 1660, **Smile 1661**, Sony 1664, Soros 1665, Sotheby's 1666, **Starr 1672**, Steel 1673, Stein 1674, Stern 1678, Tanaka 1681, Tsadra 1697, **United 1706**, Vetlesen 1713, **Virtue 1717, Vital 1718**, Walters 1722, **Weeden 1723**, Weil 1724, Weinstein 1727, White 1732, **World 1739**, Yoreinu 1741, Zenkel 1743, Zilkha 1744

North Carolina: Carlson 1752, Richardson 1762, **Rixson 1763, Rolander 1764, Samaritan's 1765**

North Dakota: McCormick 1773

Ohio: AK Steel 1775, Armington 1777, **Brush 1779**, Cintas 1782, Danaher 1784, Eaton 1787, Ethicon 1788, **Geisse 1790**, Haskell 1793, Limited 1800, Lowe 1801, Lowe 1802, Maltz 1803, **Mandel 1804, Mandel 1805, Mandel 1806**, Marion 1807, Noble 1811, OMNOVA 1813, Procter 1815, Schottenstein 1816, Taj 1818, Veale 1824

Oklahoma: **Schusterman 1830**, Zarrow 1831, Zarrow 1832

Oregon: **Fohs 1836**, Intel 1839, McKenzie 1844, NIKE 1847, **Tazo 1849**, Wyss 1851

Pennsylvania: AmerisourceBergen 1855, AMETEK 1856, Bread 1866, **Carthage 1869**, Cephalon 1870, **Colcom 1873**, Cotswold 1875, Epstein 1877, Epstein 1878, Federated 1879, Heinz 1887, Hershey 1889, Huston 1892, **KL 1896**, Mine 1899, **National 1901, Nazareth 1902, One 1903**, Pilgrim 1907, Pine 1908, Progressive 1909, Rosenstiel 1910, Scaife 1911, Scranton 1912, Wollowick 1918, **Zeldin 1919**

Rhode Island: Collette 1921, CVS 1922, Dorot 1923, FM 1925, Hasbro 1926

South Carolina: AVX 1937, **Youths' 1941**

South Dakota: **Opus 1944**

Tennessee: Drake 1952, Ezell 1953, **FedEx 1954**, Fugitive 1955, **Maclellan 1962**, Nissan 1963, UnumProvident 1967, **Westwood 1969**

Texas: Alcon 1974, AMD 1977, Apache 1979, Baldridge 1982, BMC 1987, BP 1989, Bridgeway 1990, Butt 1991, Cooper 1996, Crowder 1998, El Paso 2002, Enrico 2003, ExxonMobil 2004, Fluor 2006, Freescale 2011, General 2014, Hines 2018, Huntsman 2020, **International 2023**, Kimberly 2028, Kimberly 2029, Kowitz 2031, Marsh 2037, McDermott 2039, **Mission 2042**, Oates 2044, PHM 2047, **Pizza 2048**, Plitt 2049, Reilly 2052, Scaler 2054, Search 2055, Seegers 2056, Six 2058, Spark 2060, Spectra 2062, Trull 2067, Whole 2071

Utah: Force 2073, **Miner 2074**, Slaughter 2076, Sorenson 2078, Swanson 2079

Vermont: Blittersdorf 2084, Evslin 2086, Kaufman 2089

Virginia: Bangs-Russell 2097, **Blue 2099**, Delmar 2113, **Diema's 2114, Dorothy 2116, EduCare 2118**, Hitt 2127, **North 2139**, Samberg 2145, **United 2151, WestWind 2154**

Washington: 444S 2158, Bullitt 2161, Campion 2162, **Channel 2163**, Common 2165, **Gates 2170, Glaser 2172**, Jernigan 2180, Kongsgaard 2183, McKinstry 2185, **Mona 2186**, Red 2192, Russell 2195, Samis 2196, Seattle 2199, **Stewardship 2203**, Tulalip 2204, Weyerhaeuser 2206, Wilburforce 2207

Wisconsin: Bader 2211, **Bradley 2212, Cops 2214**, Cudahy 2215, Delavan 2216, Eastman 2217, **Johnson 2221**, Kikkoman 2222, Sand 2228, Wisconsin 2232

Grants to individuals

Alaska: Sealaska 12

Arizona: Jewish 22, U-Haul 29

California: **AIDS 46, Airline 47**, Alalusi 50, Amgen 54, Bickerstaff 81, **Children's 95, CW 110**, Foundation 138, **Foundation 141, Getty 153**, Humanitarian 183, Jewish 204, **Koulaieff 217, PADI 273, Ploughshares 280**, Rancho 286, **Seacology 314**

Colorado: Colorado 385, **Grassroots 394**, Society 408

Connecticut: **AmeriCares 421, Belgian 423**, International 431, **Save 440**

District of Columbia: **Accordia 479, Atlas 498**, Center 505, **Friendly 528, Global 534, Institute 543, International 544, International 546, International 551**, National 571, National 572, **Ocean 575, Teamster 593, Women 607**

Florida: **Food 635, Global 640**, Holland 648

Georgia: American 682, Amos-Cheves 685, Rosenberg 703

Idaho: Boise 728, Rebholtz 732

Illinois: **American 738**, CF 749, **Circle 751**, Divac 760, Driehaus 761

Indiana: **Lilly 841**

Iowa: **P.E.O. 853**

Maryland: **Ellison 901, Hughes 907, Mercy 917**, Meyer 918

Massachusetts: **American 943**, Cabot 949, **International 981**, MacJannet 991, **Maya 993**, New England 999, **New 1000, Permanent 1009**, PTC 1012, Real 1013, **SEVEN 1019**

Michigan: **Earhart 1039**, Italian 1046, Kellogg 1049, **Latvian 1052, Palestine 1059**, Travelers 1066

Missouri: **PKD 1130**

Nevada: Charitable 1145

New Jersey: **Croatian 1164**, Keser 1182

New York: **American 1240, American 1247, American 1256, American 1264, Asia 1272, Asian 1273, Astraea 1276, Brackett 1299, CDS 1316, CEC 1317, Chamber 1321**, Chazen 1324, **Cogitare 1334, Common 1336**, Estonian 1375, **Ezer 1377, Fight 1382, Fund 1406, Guggenheim 1435, HIAS 1449, Human 1454, Hungarian 1455, Institute 1461, International 1467, Israel 1472, Joint 1487, Kosciuszko 1508, Lauder 1517, Luce 1531**, Maidstone 1536, **Nefesh 1573**, Nok 1582, **Open 1593, PEN 1598**, Petra 1605, **Russian 1644**, Singh 1657, **Sparkplug 1667**, St. George's 1670, **Theatre 1685, Trickle 1694, Vietnam 1715, Wiesel 1734**

North Carolina: Evrytanian 1753, North 1760, **Rixson 1763**

Ohio: **Catholic 1780, Christian 1781, Ethnic 1789**

Oklahoma: **Blessings 1825**

Oregon: **Mercy 1846**

Pennsylvania: **Association 1859, Carnegie 1868, Hope 1891, Institute 1893, Macha 1897, Nazareth 1902, Templeton 1916**

Tennessee: Lazarus 1961

Texas: Butt 1991, Huntsman 2020, Interfaith 2022, **Limiar 2032**, Plitt 2049, **Thirst 2066**

Virginia: **American 2094**, Associates 2096, **Earthrights 2117, Operation 2140, U.S. 2150**

Washington: **Bainbridge 2159**, Northwest 2188, Russell 2195

Wisconsin: **Wagner 2231**

In-kind gifts

Arizona: Children's 16, **Food 20**

California: **African 42, ANGELCARE 56, Armenian 61, Asia 64**, Autodesk 68, **Bangladesh 70**, Cadence 89, **Fistula 134**, ForceBrain.com 137, Gap 150, **Global 158**, Google.org 163, **Hidaya 174**, Ingram 187, McConnell 242, **Medical 243, Middle 245, Nora 258**, Quiksilver 284, **Rescue 290, Rock 297**, San Diego 308, Spansion 331, **Taiwan 339**, Tides 345, **United 352, World 373**, World 374, **World 375**, Xilinx, 377

Colorado: **Global 393, H.E.L.P. 395**

Connecticut: **AmeriCares 421, Save 440**, United 444

District of Columbia: **ACDI 480, American 492, Eritrean 521, Moriah 562, Most 564, Pan 580, Teamster 593, United 600, Vishnevskaya-Rostropovich 603**

Florida: **Alfalit 614, American 615**, Atlantic 620, **Hope 649**, Jabil 652, **Stacy 675**

Georgia: **Amigos 683, Coca 692**, Delta 694, Scientific 704, **UPS 709**

Hawaii: **Center 714**

Illinois: Boeing 743, **Circle 751**, Mead 794, **Messengers 796**

Indiana: **Church 836**, NIBCO 842

Kentucky: Yum! 867

Louisiana: **Park 869**

Maryland: **Adventist 883, Child 895, Interchurch 909, International 910, Lutheran 916**

Massachusetts: **Friends 964, Grassroots 970, International 980**, PTC 1012, **Sabre 1017**, State 1021

Michigan: Amway 1029, Dow 1037, **Hands 1045, World 1070**

Minnesota: **Dorobo 1075**, Fuller 1080, **Mano 1090**, Toro 1104

Missouri: **Children 1119**

New Jersey: **BD 1159, C.I.S. 1163**, Hoffmann-La 1174, **Share 1196**

New York: **American 1249, American 1257**, Bristol 1303, **Children's 1325, Council 1343**, Diamonds 1354, **Ezer 1377, Foundation 1392, Global 1418, IBM 1457, Kids 1498, New 1577**, Nok 1582, **PepsiCo 1601, Reizod 1628, Royal 1642, Smile 1661**, Sotheby's 1666, **United 1706, World 1738**

North Carolina: **African 1747, Project 1761, Stop 1766**, Triangle 1768, With 1769

North Dakota: **Los 1772**

Ohio: **Arab 1776, Christian 1781**, Cintas 1782, Eaton 1786, **Give 1791**, Limited 1800, OMNOVA 1813

Oklahoma: Devon 1828, Love 1829, **Schusterman 1830**

Oregon: Kalakendra 1840, **Medical 1845, Mercy 1846**

Pennsylvania: **American 1854, Brother's 1867, Foundation 1880, Global 1883**, Heinz 1887, **Hope 1891, Mama 1898**

South Carolina: Michelin 1939

Tennessee: **Cloud 1949, FedEx 1954, Improved 1958**, International 1960, Nissan 1963, **Operation 1964, Vine 1968**

Texas: Apache 1979, Cooper 1996, **GAIN 2013**, Kimberly 2028, **Mercy 2041, Mission 2042, Pizza 2048**

Utah: Swanson 2079

Virginia: **Ashoka: 2095, ChildFund 2105, Christian 2106, Crosslink 2111, Dayspring 2112, Good360 2124**

Washington: **Gateway 2171, Helping 2175**, Seattle 2200

Wisconsin: **International 2220**, Wisconsin 2232

Income development

California: **Asia 64**, Atkinson 65, Flora 135, **Global 158, Nonprofit 257**, San Diego 308, **Seacology 314**

Delaware: Jackman 459

District of Columbia: **Agora 483, Moriah 562**

Florida: Freewill 636

Hawaii: Sangham 722

Idaho: **Schultz 733**

Kentucky: C.E. 863

Maine: **Sandy 880**

Maryland: **India 908**

Massachusetts: **Garfield 965, Lift 990**, Schooner 1018

Nevada: **Walsh 1152**

New York: Charina 1322, Citi 1328, Clark 1330, New York 1578, Nok 1582, **Vital 1718**

Ohio: **International 1795**

Oregon: **Fohs 1836**

Pennsylvania: **KL 1896**

Texas: Scaler 2054

Washington: Bullitt 2161, Vista 2205

Wisconsin: Wisconsin 2232

Internship funds

Alabama: Corman 3

Arizona: Duffy 18, Freeport-McMoRan 21

California: **Asia 64**, Flora 135, **Getty 153**

Connecticut: **Lingnan 432**

District of Columbia: **Ocean 575, Sons 591, Wilson 606**

Florida: **Davis 630**, Greenburg 645, **Uncle 678**

Hawaii: People's 721

Illinois: **IFSA 771**, King 777, **Scholl 814**

Kentucky: C.E. 863

Maryland: **Child 895**

Massachusetts: Kendall 986

Missouri: Bohm 1117

New Jersey: **Johnson 1178**, Merck 1186

New York: **American 1237, Brackett 1299, CDS 1316, Cogitare 1334, Common 1336**, Deutsche 1353, Kevorkian 1497, **Kress 1509, Luce 1531,**

Morgan 1562, Nok 1582, **Open 1593, Peterson 1604, Philippe 1608, ProLiteracy 1617**, Revson 1631

Ohio: Convergys 1783

Oklahoma: **Schusterman 1830**

Pennsylvania: **Colcom 1873, Institute 1893, National 1901**

Rhode Island: Dorot 1923

Texas: Summerlee 2064, Welder 2069

Virginia: Delmar 2113, **United 2151**

Washington: Jackson 2179

Wisconsin: **Bradley 2212**

Land acquisition

Arizona: Duffy 18

California: **Compton 105**, Firedoll 131, Flora 135, Foundation 138, **Moore 251, Packard 271**, Rancho 286, San Diego 307, **Tides 346**

Colorado: Warner 412

Delaware: **Raskob 467**

District of Columbia: **Wallace 605**

Florida: Freewill 636, **Peterson 666, Uncle 678**

Illinois: Jocarno 775

Kansas: Jewish 859

Kentucky: C.E. 863

Maryland: Meyerhoff 920

Massachusetts: **Garfield 965, International 980, Lift 990**

Michigan: Steelcase 1064

Nebraska: Kind 1141

Nevada: **Walsh 1152**

New Jersey: Johnson 1181

New York: **American 1257**, Charina 1322, Cummings 1346, Freeman 1397, **Kohlberg 1506**, LaSalle 1514, Mitsubichi 1559, **Prospect 1618, Rainforest 1621**, Schaffner 1647, **Vital 1718, Weeden 1723**

Ohio: Maltz 1803, **Timken 1822**

Oklahoma: Crio 1827

Pennsylvania: **Colcom 1873**, Friendship 1882, **Guanacaste 1886, National 1901**

Tennessee: Community 1950

Texas: Austin 1980, McDermott 2039, Summerlee 2064

Virginia: **WestWind 2154**

Washington: Kongsgaard 2183

Loaned talent

Delaware: ING 458

Illinois: Boeing 743

Texas: Butt 1991, Cooper 1996, Fluor 2006

Loans—to individuals

District of Columbia: **American 492, FINCA 523, Women 607**

Illinois: **Opportunity 802**

Missouri: **WaterPartners 1134**

Ohio: **Arab 1776**

Oregon: **Mercy 1846**

Washington: **World 2208**

Management development/capacity building

Arizona: Duffy 18, Freeport-McMoRan 21, Lodestar 25

Arkansas: Walton 37

California: Atkinson 65, Columbia 104, **Draper 119, Firelight 132**, Flora 135, **Fund 148**, Gap 150, **Give2Asia 155, Global 158, Hilton 178**, Kee 212, Koret 216, **Nonprofit 257, Pacific 270, Packard 271**, Rancho 286, **Rivendell 295**, Silicon 323, **Smith 327**, Strauss 335

Connecticut: **GE 428, Lingnan 432, Newman's 435**

Delaware: Jewish 461, **Raskob 467**

District of Columbia: **African 481, Arca 496, Centre 508**, El-Hibri 519, **Moriah 562, Ocean 575, United 600**

Florida: Kerzner 658, **Peterson 666, Uncle 678**

Georgia: South 705, **UPS 709**

Hawaii: People's 721, Sangham 722

Idaho: **Schultz 733**

Illinois: Abbott 735, King 777

Iowa: Humanities 850

Kansas: **Shumaker 861**

Kentucky: C.E. 863

Maine: **Oak 878, Sandy 880**

Maryland: Bearman 890

Massachusetts: Fidelity 959, **Garfield 965**, Kendall 986, **Lift 990**, Pegasus 1007

Michigan: **Arcus 1030, Mott 1058**, Steelcase 1064

Minnesota: Medtronic 1093, Oswald 1096

Montana: **Edwards 1136**

Nebraska: Cooper 1138

Nevada: **Walsh 1152**

New Jersey: Berrie 1160, **Johnson 1178**, Merck 1186, Prudential 1191

New Mexico: Santa Fe 1213

New York: American 1241, Bristol 1303, Citi 1328, Clark 1330, **East 1363, Ford 1391**, Genesis 1411, **Hartford 1443, Institute 1461, Isdell 1470, Nash 1567**, New York 1578, **PepsiCo 1601**, Pfizer 1606, **Rainforest 1622, Rainforest 1623, Sparkplug 1667, Starr 1672**

North Carolina: Triangle 1768

Ohio: **Arab 1776**, Maltz 1803

Oregon: **Fohs 1836**, NIKE 1847

Pennsylvania: Alcoa 1853, **Colcom 1873, KL 1896, National 1901**

Tennessee: Community 1950, **Improved 1958**

Texas: **Chrest 1994**, El Paso 2002, **Frankenberg 2009, Mission 2042**, Trull 2067

Virginia: Samberg 2145, **Youth 2157**

Washington: Bullitt 2161, Campion 2162, **RISA 2194**, Wilburforce 2207

Wisconsin: Wisconsin 2232

Matching/challenge support

Alabama: Ard 1, Corman 3

Alaska: Alaska 8

Arizona: Community 17, Freeport-McMoRan 21

Arkansas: Walton 37

California: Amgen 54, Applied 58, Autodesk 68, **Christensen 97, Compton 105**, Firedoll 131, Flora 135, **Getty 153**, Goldsmith 161, Hewlett 172, **Hilton 178**, Ingram 187, Jacobs 197, Koret 216, Kvamme 219, Marra 239, **MAZON 241**, McConnell 242, **Milarepa 247, Packard 271, Rivendell 295**, Roth 299, S.G. 300, Saban 302, San Diego 307, **Spencer 332, Tides 346**, World 374

Colorado: Bohemian 384, JFM 398, **Living 400, Oreg 403, Western 413**

Connecticut: **Aid 417, Newman's 435**

Delaware: Jewish 461, **Raskob 467**

District of Columbia: **Arca 496, Banyan 499, Centre 508, Council 513, Eurasia 522**, Foundation 524, Henry 539, **Institute 543**, Kimsey 557, **Moriah 562, Ocean 575**, Palmer 579, **Summit 592, Wallace 605**

Florida: Cafesjian 623, **Chatlos 626, Davis 630**, Freewill 636, **Koch 660**, Russell 669, **Stacy 675, Uncle 678**

Georgia: Gray 696, Livingston 700, Scientific 704, South 705, **Turner 708**

Hawaii: People's 721, Sangham 722

Idaho: **Schultz 733**

Illinois: Boeing 743, Caterpillar 748, Crown 756, Driehaus 761, **IFSA 771**, King 777, **MacArthur 788**, McCormick 792, **Rotary 807**

Indiana: Cummins 837, Lilly 840, West 846

Iowa: Wright 856

Kansas: Jewish 859
Maine: **Oak 878, Sandy 880, Walter 881**
Maryland: Bearman 890, **Blaustein 891**, England 902, Hoffberger 906, **Jewish 915**, Meyerhoff 919, Meyerhoff 920, Polinger 926, **Shared 929, Weinberg 934**
Massachusetts: Fidelity 959, **Garfield 965, Lift 990**, New England 999, Pegasus 1007, Schooner 1018
Michigan: **Arcus 1030**, Fisher 1041, **Hands 1045, Kellogg 1050, Mott 1058, Rotary 1062**, Steelcase 1064, Teitel 1065
Minnesota: McKnight 1092, Oswald 1096, Porter 1098, Toro 1104, United 1105, **Winds 1108**
Missouri: Build 1118, Fox 1122, Lubin 1124, Monsanto 1128
Montana: **Edwards 1136**
Nebraska: Kind 1141, Livingston 1142
Nevada: **Tang 1151, Walsh 1152**
New Jersey: Berrie 1160, **International 1177**, Knistrom 1183, MCJ 1184
New Mexico: Santa Fe 1213, **Thaw 1214**
New York: Achelis 1219, **Amit 1265**, Bodman 1293, **Cay 1315**, Charina 1322, Claiborne 1329, Cleary 1331, Cummings 1346, Dodge 1357, Eastman 1364, **Engelhard 1371, Engineering 1372**, Freeman 1397, Genesis 1411, Greve 1432, **Johnson 1486**, LaSalle 1514, Littauer 1529, **Luce 1531, Mellon 1546, New 1577**, New 1580, **Prospect 1618**, Reed 1627, **Rockefeller 1638**, Schaffner 1647, Slifka 1660, **Starr 1672**, Trinity 1695, **United 1708, Vital 1718**, Walters 1722
North Carolina: Carlson 1752, Triangle 1768
Ohio: Eaton 1786, **Geisse 1790**, Jewish 1798, Maltz 1803, Middletown 1809, **Thomas 1820, Timken 1822**
Oklahoma: **Schusterman 1830**
Oregon: Intel 1839
Pennsylvania: Alcoa 1853, AMETEK 1856, **Colcom 1873**, Huston 1892, **KL 1896, National 1901**, Scranton 1912, **Templeton 1916**, Wollowick 1918, **Zeldin 1919**
Rhode Island: Collette 1921, Dorot 1923
Texas: Austin 1980, Bridgeway 1990, **Chrest 1994**, El Paso 2002, McDermott 2039, Summerlee 2064, Trull 2067
Utah: Sorenson 2078, Swanson 2079
Vermont: Evslin 2086
Virginia: **American 2094, Blue 2099, ChildFund 2105, Dorothy 2116**, Lane 2132, **Loyola 2134, Mustard 2137**, Samberg 2145, **WestWind 2154**
Washington: 444S 2158, Bullitt 2161, Campion 2162, **Gates 2170**, Jackson 2179, Kongsgaard 2183, Samis 2196, **Stewardship 2203**, Tulalip 2204, Vista 2205, Wilburforce 2207
Wisconsin: Argosy 2210, **Bradley 2212**, Cudahy 2215, Taylor 2230, Wisconsin 2232

Mission-related investments/loans

California: Cienega 99, **Compton 105**, Flora 135, Silicon 323, Skoll 325
Colorado: **General 392**
Massachusetts: Cedar 950, **Merck 996**
Michigan: **Kellogg 1050**
New Jersey: Prudential 1191
New York: Deutsche 1353, Mitsubishi 1559, North 1583, **Prospect 1618, Rasmussen 1624**, Reynolds 1632, **Rockefeller 1638**
Pennsylvania: **KL 1896**
Virginia: **Blue 2099**
Washington: Russell 2195, Seattle 2199

Pro bono services - communications/public relations

New York: Interpublic 1469, Omnicom 1591

Pro bono services - interactive/website technology

Pennsylvania: Azavea 1860

Pro bono services - legal

Minnesota: Thomson 1103
New York: Allen 1229, Cleary 1331

Pro bono services - marketing/branding

New York: Interpublic 1469, Omnicom 1591

Pro bono services - strategic management

New York: Accenture 1218

Professorships

California: Flora 135, Goldsmith 161, **Kavli 211**
Connecticut: **Lingnan 432**
District of Columbia: Gudelsky 538
Florida: **Davis 630**, Engelberg 634, **Peterson 666**, Pruitt 668
Idaho: Micron 730
Illinois: Boeing 743, Crown 756
Maryland: **Hughes 907**, Meyerhoff 919, Meyerhoff 920
Massachusetts: Schooner 1018
Michigan: **Foundation 1042**
Minnesota: Kelley 1086
Missouri: Bohm 1117
New Jersey: McMullen 1185, Winters 1205
New York: **Asian 1273**, Berg 1285, Charina 1322, Chazen 1324, **Engelhard 1371**, Freeman 1397, **Fund 1406, Kade 1489**, Kevorkian 1497, **Kress 1509**, Lehman 1521, **Luce 1531, Netherland-America 1574, Open 1593**, Simons 1656, **Starr 1672**, Vetlesen 1713, **Vital 1718**, Zenkel 1743
Ohio: Maltz 1803
Oklahoma: **Schusterman 1830**
Pennsylvania: **National 1901**
Rhode Island: Soforenko 1935
Tennessee: **Cloud 1949**
Texas: Austin 1980, McDermott 2039, Summerlee 2064
Washington: Jackson 2179
Wisconsin: **Bradley 2212**

Program development

Alabama: Corman 3
Alaska: Alaska 8
American Samoa: Amerika 13
Arizona: Community 17, Lodestar 25, **PetSmart 26**
Arkansas: Darragh 32, Walton 37
California: **Adobe 39**, Agilent 44, Amgen 54, **ANGELCARE 56**, Applied 58, Applied 59, Arntz 62, **Asia 64**, Atkinson 65, Autodesk 68, Berman 79, Chevron 94, **Christensen 97**, Cisco 100, **Clarity 102**, Columbia 104, **Compton 105, Draper 119, Dzambuling 120, Energy 124**, Firedoll 131, **Firelight 132**, Flora 135, Foundation 138, **Foundation 141**, Fremont 143, **Fund 148**, Gap 150, **Getty 153, Give2Asia 155, Global 156, Global 157, Global 158**, Handlery 170, Hewlett 172, **Hilton 178**, Ingram 187, Intuit 193, Koret 216, **Lift 231**, Lutz 235, **Marisla 238**, Marra 239, **Milarepa 247, Moore 251, Pacific 270, Packard 271, Ploughshares 280**, Quiksilver 284, Rancho 286, Reinhard 289, Resnick 291, **Rivendell 295, Rock 297**, Roth 299, S.G. 300, Saban 302, **salesforce.com 305**, San Diego 307, San Francisco 309, Sempra 315, **Seventh 317**, Silicon 323, **Smith 327**, Social 330, Spansion 331, **Spencer 332**, Strauss 335, Strome 336, Symantec 337, Tides 345, **Tides 346**, Xilinx, 377

Colorado: **AfricAid 380**, Bohemian 384, First 389, **General 392**, JFM 398, Mercy 402, **Oreg 403**, ProLogis 404, Warner 412, **Western 413**
Connecticut: **Aid 417, GE 428, Lingnan 432, Newman's 435**, United 444, Valentine 445
Delaware: Jackman 459, Jewish 461, **Raskob 467**, Shoemaker 472
District of Columbia: **American 491, Americans 493, Arca 496, Atlas 498, Banyan 499**, Bernstein 500, Butler 502, **Centre 508, CityBridge 509, DeMoss 516, Eurasia 522, Fund 531**, Gottesman 537, Gudelsky 538, Henry 539, **Institute 543, International 546, International 550, Jerusalem 552**, Kaye 555, **Kennedy 556**, Kimsey 557, **Moriah 562, NAFSA 567, National 570, Ocean 575**, Palmer 579, **Phelps 582**, Poretsky 586, **Sons 591, Summit 592, United 597, United 600, Wallace 605**, Zients 609
Florida: Assurant 619, **Chatlos 626, Davis 630**, Engelberg 634, Gainesville 638, Greenburg 645, Jabil 652, **Katz 656**, Kerzner 658, **Koch 660**, Patel 664, **Peterson 666**, Russell 669, Wahlert 679
Georgia: Amos-Cheves 685, Bancker 687, **Coca 692**, Coca 693, Gray 696, Scientific 704, South 705, **Turner 708, UPS 709**
Hawaii: Alexander 712, People's 721, Sangham 722, Watumull 726, Yoshimoto 727
Idaho: Boise 728, Micron 730, **Schultz 733**
Illinois: Abbott 735, Aon 739, Archer 740, Baxter 741, Boeing 743, Caterpillar 748, CF 749, Crown 756, Deere 757, Driehaus 761, Dunard 762, Heritage 769, **IFSA 771**, King 777, Landau 780, Lindon 783, Logos 785, **MacArthur 789**, MacDonald 789, McCormick 792, Motorola 798, **Rotary 807, Scholl 814**, Shifting 817, Stern 822, **Terra 824**
Indiana: Brotherhood 835, Cummins 837
Iowa: Humanities 850
Kansas: Jewish 859, **Lloyd 860**
Kentucky: C.E. 863, Yum! 866
Louisiana: Pennington 870, Woldenberg 872
Maine: Golden 877, **Oak 878**
Maryland: **Ames 886**, Bearman 890, **Blaustein 891**, Blaustein 892, England 902, Hoffberger 906, **Hughes 907, Jewish 915, Lutheran 916**, Meyerhoff 919, Meyerhoff 920, **Mid 921**, O'Neil 925, Polinger 926, **Shared 929**, Weiss 935
Massachusetts: **Alchemy 940, Azadoutioun 945, China 952, Conservation 954**, Fidelity 959, **Garfield 965**, Grand 968, Grinspoon 971, Haymarket 975, Homestead 977, **International 980, Jenzabar 985**, Kendall 986, **Lift 990, Merck 996**, New England 999, **New 1000, Oxfam 1002**, Pegasus 1007, **Planet 1010**, Schooner 1018, **SEVEN 1019**, State 1021, Swartz 1023, TJX 1026
Michigan: **Arcus 1030**, DENSO 1035, Dow 1037, Frankel 1043, **Jewish 1047, Kellogg 1050**, Kellogg's 1051, **Mott 1058, Rotary 1062**, Steelcase 1064, Teitel 1065, **Worldwide 1071**
Minnesota: Andersen 1073, Better 1074, Duluth 1077, General 1081, Kelley 1086, **Mary's 1091**, McKnight 1092, Medtronic 1093, Mortenson 1094, Oswald 1096, Piper 1097, Thomson 1103, Toro 1104, **Weyerhaeuser 1107, Winds 1108**
Missouri: **ASC 1114**, Build 1118, Enterprise 1121, Fox 1122, Lubin 1124, Monsanto 1128, Simon 1132
Montana: **Edwards 1136**
Nebraska: Cooper 1138, Kind 1141, Livingston 1142
Nevada: **Walsh 1152**
New Hampshire: Butler 1155
New Jersey: **American 1157, BD 1159**, Berrie 1160, Danellie 1166, Harbourton 1172, Hoffmann-La 1174, **International 1177, Johnson 1178**, Johnson 1179, Johnson 1181, Merck 1186, Prudential 1191, **Share 1196**, Tang 1199, **Wilson 1204**
New Mexico: **Levinson 1211**, Santa Fe 1213, **Thaw 1214**
New York: **Abraham 1215**, Abrons 1216, Accenture 1218, Achelis 1219, Allen 1229, American 1241, **American 1245, American 1257, Amit 1265**, AVI

California: Agilent 44, **AIDS 46**, Amgen 54, **Asia 64**, Berman 79, Bickerstaff 81, Chevron 94, **Christensen 97**, Columbia 104, **Compton 105**, Eisenberg 123, **Fistula 134**, Flora 135, **Getty 153, Give2Asia 155, Global 158**, Goldsmith 161, Handlery 170, **Hilton 178, Hirshberg 179, Hispanics 180**, Jagadeesh 198, **Kapnek 209, Kavli 211**, Koret 216, Kvamme 219, **Leakey 222**, Milarepa 247, **Moore 251, Neilsen 253, Orangutan 267, Packard 271, PADI 273**, Preuss 281, Quiksilver 284, Rifkind 294, Saban 302, San Diego 307, Strauss 335, Strome 336, Teichman 343, **Tides 346**

Colorado: Bohemian 384, **Ecumenical 388, Living 400**

Connecticut: **Belgian 423, GE 428, Lingnan 432, Newman's 435, Rett 437, Richardson 439**

District of Columbia: **Amazon 485, American 487, American 489**, Anti-Slavery 495, **Arca 496, Aspen 497, CityBridge 509**, Counterterrorism 514, **Endowment 520**, Foundation 524, **German 532, Heritage 540, Institute 543, Jerusalem 552, Ocean 575**, Phelps 582, **PVA 587, Sons 591**, U.S. 595, **Wallace 605, Wilson 606**

Florida: Caribbean 625, Coulter 629, **Davis 630**, Duda 632, Freewill 636, Greenburg 645, **Israel 651**, Kerzner 658, Pruitt 668

Georgia: Delta 694, Gray 696, **Turner 708, UPS 709**

Hawaii: East-West 716, People's 721

Idaho: Micron 730

Illinois: Abbott 735, **American 738**, Boeing 743, Deere 757, **IFSA 771, MacArthur 788**, McCormick 792, **New 799, Scholl 814, Spencer 820, Two 826**

Iowa: Wallace 855

Kansas: Jewish 859

Kentucky: C.E. 863

Louisiana: Woldenberg 872

Maine: **Oak 878**

Maryland: **ABMRF/The 882, American 885**, Bearman 890, **Child 895**, ELECTRI 900, **Ellison 901, Hughes 907**, Meyerhoff 919, Meyerhoff 920, **Shared 929**, Weiss 935

Massachusetts: **American 943, China 952, Conservation 954, Flutie 961, Garfield 965, Harvard 974, International 980, International 981**, Kendall 986, New England 999, **Oxfam 1002, Permanent 1009**

Michigan: **Earhart 1039**, Kellogg's 1051

Minnesota: Duluth 1077, **Winds 1108, World-India 1109**

Missouri: Bohm 1117, Build 1118, Enterprise 1121, **McDonnell 1126**, Millstone 1127, Monsanto 1128, **PKD 1130**, Slusher 1133

Nebraska: Kind 1141

Nevada: Charitable 1145, **Walsh 1152**

New Hampshire: Butler 1155

New Jersey: **American 1157**, Berrie 1160, Hoffmann-La 1174, **Johnson 1178**, Johnson 1181, Merck 1186, **Vollmer 1201**

New Mexico: **Thaw 1214**

New York: Abrons 1216, Achelis 1219, **American 1240, American 1245, American 1257, American 1263, American 1264, Asian 1273, AVI 1278**, Berg 1285, **Blacksmith 1290**, Bodman 1293, Botwinick 1295, **Breast 1301**, Bristol 1303, **Carnegie 1312, Center 1318**, Charina 1322, Clark 1330, **Commonwealth 1337, Cummings 1347**, Curran 1348, **Delmas 1351, East 1363**, Edouard 1367, **Engelhard 1371, Engineering 1372, Fight 1382, Food 1389**, Freeman 1397, Gerschel 1412, **Goldman 1422, Gruss 1434, Guggenheim 1435, Hartford 1443**, Hedge 1447, **Institute 1461, Isdell 1470, Israel 1471, Jewelers 1476**, Jewish 1481, Kaplan 1490, Kevorkian 1497, **King 1501, Kosciuszko 1508, Kress 1509**, Littauer 1529, **Luce 1531, Lymphoma 1533, Mayday 1542, Mellon 1546**, Mitsubishi 1559, **Myasthenia 1565, Netherland-America 1574**, New York 1578, New 1580, Nok 1582, **Open 1593, P.E.F. 1595, Parkinson's 1596**, Peterson 1604, **Philippe 1608**, Recanati 1626, Reed 1627,

Revson 1631, **Rockefeller 1639**, Schaffner 1647, Simons 1656, Slifka 1660, Smith 1662, **Social 1663, Sparkplug 1667, Starr 1672**, Stein 1674, **Tinker 1689**, Tisch 1690, **United 1704, United 1708**, Vetlesen 1713, **Vital 1718**, Walters 1722, Weinstein 1727, White 1732

North Carolina: **American 1749, Burroughs 1751, Microelectronics 1757, Nickel 1759**, Richardson 1762, **Rolander 1764**, Triangle 1768

Ohio: Armington 1777, Convergys 1783, Ethicon 1788, Haskell 1793, Maltz 1803, Marion 1807

Oklahoma: **Schusterman 1830**

Oregon: **Evergreen 1835, Fohs 1836**, Grass 1838

Pennsylvania: Alcoa 1853, AMETEK 1856, **Colcom 1873**, Huston 1892, **Institute 1893, KL 1896, Macha 1897, National 1901**, Pew 1906, Scaife 1911, Scranton 1912, **Templeton 1916**, Williams 1917, Wollowick 1918

Rhode Island: **Perkins 1932**, Soforenko 1935

Texas: Alcon 1974, Austin 1980, BP 1989, Butt 1991, **Chrest 1994**, Crowder 1998, McDermott 2039, Oppenheimer 2045, Search 2055, Six 2058, Summerlee 2064

Utah: Force 2073, Swanson 2079

Vermont: Evslin 2086

Virginia: **American 2094**, Samberg 2145, Three 2148, **U.S. 2150**

Washington: **Gates 2170**, Jackson 2179, Samis 2196, Weyerhaeuser 2206, Wilburforce 2207

Wisconsin: Argosy 2210, Bader 2211, **Bradley 2212, Johnson 2221**, Sand 2228

Scholarship funds

Alaska: Alaska 8

Arizona: Community 17, Duffy 18, Freeport-McMoRan 21, Rosztoczy 27

Arkansas: Darragh 32

California: **Adobe 39**, Applied 58, **Asia 64**, Atkinson 65, Autodesk 68, Farahnik 128, Flora 135, Fremont 143, Gap 150, **Give2Asia 155, Hilton 178**, Jacobs 197, Kee 212, Koret 216, **Lebanese 223**, McConnell 242, Philibosian 278, Preuss 281, Quiksilver 284, Rancho 286, **Rivendell 295**, Saban 302, Silicon 323, **Smith 327**, Smith 328, Strauss 335, Teichman 343

Colorado: Fishback 390, ProLogis 404, **Western 413**

Connecticut: **GE 428, Lingnan 432, Newman's 435**

Delaware: Shoemaker 472

District of Columbia: **Endowment 520**, Gottesman 537, Gudelsky 538, **Institute 543, Ocean 575**, Poretsky 586, **Sons 591, Union 596**

Florida: Assurant 619, **Chatlos 626, Davis 630**, EIS 633, Freewill 636, Gainesville 638, Greenburg 645, **Peterson 666**, Russell 669, **Scholarship 673, Uncle 678**, Wahlert 679

Georgia: Amos-Cheves 685, Bancker 687, **Belize 688**, Coca 693, Delta 694, Scientific 704, **UPS 709**

Hawaii: Honda 718, Shiraki 725, Watumull 726

Idaho: Micron 730

Illinois: Abbott 735, Aon 739, Boeing 743, Caterpillar 748, Crane 755, Crown 756, Deere 757, **Demos 758**, Dunard 762, Eades 763, **IFSA 771**, King 777, **Lithuanian 784**, Logos 785, MacDonald 789, **New 799, Rotary 807, Scholl 814, State 821, United 827**

Indiana: Cummins 837, **Overseas 843**

Iowa: Wright 856

Kansas: Jewish 859, **Lloyd 860**

Kentucky: C.E. 863

Maryland: Hoffberger 906, **India 908**, Meyerhoff 919, Meyerhoff 920, Smith 930

Massachusetts: **China 952, Derossi 956, Friends 964**, Gerondelis 966, Grinspoon 971, **Harvard 974**, Marcopolous 992, **Maya 993**, Real 1013, Schooner 1018, **SEVEN 1019**

Michigan: **Africa 1028**, Fisher 1041, Jubilee 1048, Kellogg's 1051, Secchia 1063, Steelcase 1064, Teitel 1065, **Worldwide 1071**

Minnesota: Better 1074, Duluth 1077, **Fitzgerald 1078**, General 1081, Kelley 1086, Medtronic 1093, Toro 1104

Missouri: Bohm 1117, Enterprise 1121, Millstone 1127, Simon 1132, Slusher 1133

Montana: **Edwards 1136**

Nebraska: **Himanchal 1140**, Kind 1141, Livingston 1142

Nevada: **Tang 1151, Walsh 1152**

New Jersey: Aufzien 1158, Danellie 1166, IDT 1176, **Johnson 1178**, Johnson 1179, Johnson 1181, McMullen 1185, Merck 1186, Syms 1198, Tang 1199

New Mexico: Santa Fe 1213

New York: Abrons 1216, Achelis 1219, Alvarez 1232, **American 1237, American 1245, American 1246, Amit 1265**, Berg 1285, Bodman 1293, Botwinick 1295, **Brackett 1299**, Butler 1308, Canon 1309, **Cay 1315**, Charina 1322, Chazen 1324, **Cogitare 1334**, Curran 1348, **Delmas 1351, Engelhard 1371**, Freeman 1397, **Friends 1401, Fund 1406**, Goldsmith 1424, Gorman 1426, **Hartford 1443**, Hess 1448, **Jewish 1480**, Joukowsky 1488, **Kosciuszko 1508**, Li 1526, **Luce 1531, McCaddin 1543**, Mendell 1547, Mesdag 1550, Morgan 1562, National 1568, **Netherland-America 1574**, New York 1578, Nok 1582, **Open 1593**, Peierls 1597, **Rainforest 1622, Rainforest 1623**, Reed 1627, **Royal 1642**, Schaffner 1647, Schmeelk 1648, Select 1650, Sony 1664, Soros 1665, **Starr 1672**, Stern 1678, Tanaka 1681, **Trace 1693, United 1704**, Vetlesen 1713, **Vital 1718**, Weil 1724, **Wiesel 1734**, Wong 1736, **Yele 1740**, Zenkel 1743

North Carolina: Kramer 1754, Triangle 1768

Ohio: **Arab 1776**, Haskell 1793, Maltz 1803, Marion 1807, Middletown 1809, OMNOVA 1813, Taj 1818

Oklahoma: Crio 1827, **Schusterman 1830**, Zarrow 1832

Oregon: Intel 1839

Pennsylvania: Alcoa 1853, AMETEK 1856, Arronson 1858, **Children's 1871**, Dixon 1876, Federated 1879, **National 1901, Nazareth 1902**, Pilgrim 1907, Scranton 1912, Williams 1917, **Zeldin 1919**

Rhode Island: CVS 1922, FM 1925, **Perkins 1932**, Soforenko 1935

South Carolina: **Youths' 1941**

Tennessee: **Cloud 1949**, Community 1950, Fugitive 1955

Texas: Alcon 1974, BP 1989, Bridgeway 1990, Cox 1997, Crowder 1998, El Paso 2002, Huntsman 2020, Kimberly 2028, McDermott 2039, Oppenheimer 2045, Reilly 2052, Six 2058, Trull 2067

Utah: Swanson 2079

Vermont: Blittersdorf 2084

Virginia: Associates 2096, Delmar 2113, Gannett 2122, **Mustard 2137, North 2139**

Washington: **Channel 2163, Gates 2170**, Jackson 2179, Jernigan 2180, McKinstry 2185, **Mona 2186**, Samis 2196, Tulalip 2204

Wisconsin: Argosy 2210, Bader 2211, **Bradley 2212**, Eastman 2217, **Johnson 2221**, Kikkoman 2222, Meehan 2226, **Wagner 2231**, Wisconsin 2232

Scholarships—to individuals

Alaska: Sealaska 12

Arizona: Community 17, Freeport-McMoRan 21, Rosztoczy 27

California: **Adobe 39, Australians 67**, Bickerstaff 81, **Foundation 139, Invisible 194**, Jewish 204, **Koulaieff 217, Middle 245**, San Diego 307, San Francisco 309, Silicon 323, **Stott 334, Taiwan 339**, Tawa 342, World 372

Colorado: **AfricAid 380, Western 413**

Seed money

Sponsorships

Student loans—to individuals

Technical assistance

New York: Abrons 1216, Achelis 1219, **American 1257, Blacksmith 1290**, Bodman 1293, Bristol 1303, **Carnegie 1312, Chamber 1321**, Citi 1328, Clark 1330, **Cogitare 1334**, Deutsche 1353, **East 1363, Echoing 1365, Fund 1406, Funding 1407**, Jewish 1481, Kaplan 1490, Maidstone 1536, **New 1577**, New York 1578, North 1583, **Open 1593, Pfizer 1606**, Pfizer 1607, **ProLiteracy 1617, Resource 1630**, Reynolds 1632, **Rockefeller 1638, Rockefeller 1639, Sparkplug 1667, United 1704, Virtue 1717, Yoreinu 1741**

North Carolina: **Samaritan's 1765**, Triangle 1768

Ohio: **International 1795**, Marion 1807, **Thomas 1820**

Oklahoma: **Schusterman 1830**

Oregon: McKenzie 1844

Pennsylvania: AMETEK 1856, Bread 1866, **Colcom 1873**, Dixon 1876, Huston 1892, **KL 1896, National 1901**, Pew 1906, Scranton 1912

Rhode Island: Dorot 1923

Texas: Austin 1980, **Chrest 1994**, El Paso 2002, **Mission 2042**, Summerlee 2064, Trull 2067

Vermont: Evslin 2086, **Underdog 2091**

Virginia: **National 2138**, Samberg 2145, **United 2151, Youth 2157**

Washington: Bullitt 2161, **Gates 2170, Glaser 2172, Global 2173**, Kongsgaard 2183, **Mona 2186**, Samis 2196, Wilburforce 2207

Wisconsin: Bader 2211, Cudahy 2215, Wisconsin 2232

Use of facilities

California: **Adobe 39**, Autodesk 68, Social 330

Delaware: Jewish 461

Florida: Atlantic 620

Hawaii: **Center 714**

Illinois: Boeing 743

Texas: Fluor 2006

SUBJECT INDEX

Terms used in this index conform to the Foundation Center's Grants Classification System's comprehensive subject area coding scheme. In the index itself, grantmakers are arranged under each term by state location, abbreviated name, and sequence number. Grantmakers in boldface type make grants on a national, regional, or international basis. The others generally limit their giving to the state or city in which they are located. For a subject index to the individual grants in this volume, see the Index to Grants by Subject.

Afghanistan

California: **Afghanistan 41**
District of Columbia: **Aga 482, Women 607**
Georgia: Global 695
Idaho: **Schultz 733**
Illinois: **Messengers 796**
Massachusetts: Beyond 946
New York: **International 1467, Smile 1661**
Virginia: **America's 2093**

Africa

Alabama: Ard 1
Arizona: Duffy 18, **Esperanca 19**, Lodestar 25
California: **African 42, African 43, AIDS 46, America 52, ANGELCARE 56**, Battle 71, Egg 122, Flynt 136, **Hilton 178, Leakey 222**, Lee 224, Marra 239, **New 255, Open 265**, Otto 269, **Ploughshares 280**, Roth 299, Strauss 335, Strome 336, **Wildlife 366**, World 374
Colorado: **AfricAid 380**
Connecticut: **GE 428**
District of Columbia: **African 481, Aga 482, Banyan 499, Eritrean 521, Free 526, International 551, Joint 553, MAG 559, Ocean 575, One 577, Phelps 582, PlayPumps 584, Wilson 606**
Florida: **Alfalit 614**, Patel 665, **Stacy 675, Working 681**
Georgia: Bancker 687, Coca 693, St. 707
Hawaii: Sangham 722
Illinois: Deere 757, IDP 770, Illinois 772, King 777, **Opportunity 802, Scholar 813**
Indiana: Cummins 838, **Overseas 843**, West 846
Iowa: Wright 856
Kansas: **Lloyd 860**
Maine: Catalyst 875, Dugas 876, **Oak 878**
Maryland: **Interchurch 909, Lutheran 916, SAT-7 928**
Massachusetts: **Alchemy 940**, Grand 968, Hyde 978, **International 980**, Invincibility 982, **New 1000**, PTC 1012
Michigan: Amway 1029, **World 1070**
Minnesota: Africa 1072, Oswald 1096
New Jersey: **BD 1159, Croatian 1164, Johnson 1178**, Segal 1195
New York: African 1222, American 1241, **American 1257, Astraea 1276**, Bristol 1303, **Butler 1307,**
Carnegie 1312, Claiborne 1329, Clark 1330, **Cogitare 1334, Concern 1338**, Farkas 1378, **Ford 1391, Gildersleeve 1413**, Goldman 1423, HOPE 1452, **Integrative 1462, Jewelers 1476, Keller 1495**, Marley 1539, **McCaddin 1543, Media 1544, Millennium 1556**, Nduna 1572, Neuberger 1575, **Open 1593, PepsiCo 1601**, Pfizer 1607, **Population 1611, Project 1616, ProLiteracy 1617, Rainforest 1623, Reizod 1628**, Schaffner 1647, **Tanzania 1684**, Trinity 1695, **Unbound 1702**
North Carolina: **Rixson 1763, Rolander 1764, Samaritan's 1765**
Oklahoma: Crio 1827
Oregon: Grass 1838, NIKE 1847
Pennsylvania: Alcoa 1853, Huston 1892, **Macha 1897**
Tennessee: **African 1945**, International 1960, **Maclellan 1962, Westwood 1969**
Texas: **Africa 1973**, Crowder 1998, ExxonMobil 2004, **Living 2034**, Teen 2065, Whole 2071
Virginia: **Bread 2100, Dorothy 2116, EduCare 2118**, Loyola 2134, **Mustard 2137**
Washington: Colson 2164, **Gates 2170**, Starbucks 2202, **World 2208**
Wisconsin: **Cops 2214**, Cudahy 2215, **International 2220**, Johnson 2221

Albania

Illinois: **Messengers 796**
Maryland: **International 911, International 912**
New York: **National 1569, Trust 1696**
Virginia: **U.S. 2150**

Algeria

District of Columbia: **Fund 531**
New York: Hess 1448
Virginia: **Algerian-American 2092**

Angola

South Carolina: **American 1936**
Virginia: **America's 2093**

Antarctica

New York: **Tinker 1689**

Antigua & Barbuda

Massachusetts: **LASPAU: 989**
New York: Diamonds 1354, **Mill 1555**

Argentina

California: Conservation 106, ForceBrain.com 137, Foundation 138
Colorado: First 389, Rio 406
Florida: Assurant 619
Georgia: Rosenberg 703
Illinois: **Messengers 796**
Maryland: **Hughes 907, International 912**
Massachusetts: **LASPAU: 989**
Minnesota: Thomson 1103
New York: **AFS 1224, Chabad 1320, EMpower 1369, Endeavor 1370, Smile 1661**
Ohio: Eaton 1786
Texas: **New Media 2043**
Virginia: **Ivy 2129, Youth 2157**

Armenia

California: Akian 48, **Armenian 61**, Hampar 169, **Karisma 210, United 352**
District of Columbia: **Eurasia 522**
Florida: Cafesjian 623
Illinois: Sarkisian 811
Maryland: **International 911**
Massachusetts: Afeyan 939
Michigan: Manoogian 1055
New Jersey: Hovnanian 1175
New York: **Armenia 1269**, Armenian 1270, **Armenian 1271, Fund 1406**, Nazarian 1570, **Smile 1661, Trust 1696**
Texas: Huntsman 2020
Virginia: **U.S. 2150**

Arms control

California: **Global 159**, **Nuclear 260**, **Ploughshares 280**, **Working 371**
Colorado: Warner 412
Connecticut: Oristano 436
Delaware: James 460
District of Columbia: Connect 511, **MAG 559**, **Mott 565**, **Nuclear 574**, **Physicians 583**
Illinois: MacDonald 789
Maryland: Weiss 935
Massachusetts: RESIST 1014
New York: **Carnegie 1312**, Eastman 1364, **Guggenheim 1435**, **HKH 1450**, **Muste 1564**, **New 1577**, New 1580, **Prospect 1618**, **Rubin 1643**
Pennsylvania: Bloch 1865, **Global 1884**
Vermont: Block 2085

Asia

Arizona: Kearny 23, Lodestar 25
California: Agilent 44, **AIDS 46**, **Asia 64**, Autodesk 68, **Dzambuling 120**, **Gere 152**, **Give2Asia 155**, Gupta 168, **Hilton 178**, Ingram 187, **International 189**, **Leakey 222**, **Open 265**, Otto 269, **PADI 273**, **Ploughshares 280**, Quiksilver 284, **Rescue 290**, **salesforce.com 305**, Social 330, **Spencer 332**, Strauss 335, Strome 336, Symantec 337, World 374
Colorado: **Asia 382**, **Grassroots 394**
Connecticut: **Richardson 439**
District of Columbia: **Aga 482**, **American 487**, Dingwall 518, **Ocean 575**, **Wilson 606**
Florida: Kerzner 658, **Stacy 675**
Hawaii: **Center 714**
Illinois: Baxter 741, Illinois 772, Mead 794, **Opportunity 802**, **Scholar 813**, **Terra 824**
Indiana: **Overseas 843**
Maine: **Oak 878**
Maryland: **Child 895**, **Lutheran 916**
Massachusetts: **China 952**, Grand 968, **Harvard 974**, Hyde 978, **New 1000**, PTC 1012
Michigan: Amway 1029, **World 1070**
New Jersey: **BD 1159**, Garcia 1170
New York: American 1241, **American 1257**, Asia 1272, **Asian 1273**, **Astraea 1276**, Butler 1307, **CEC 1317**, Claiborne 1329, **Concern 1338**, Food 1389, **Ford 1391**, Freeman 1397, **Gildersleeve 1413**, Goldman 1423, **Keller 1495**, **McCaddin 1543**, **Media 1544**, Neuberger 1575, **Open 1593**, **PepsiCo 1601**, Pfizer 1607, **Population 1611**, **Project 1616**, **ProLiteracy 1617**, **Reizod 1628**, Schaffner 1647, **Starr 1672**, **United 1704**, **United 1708**
North Carolina: **Samaritan's 1765**
Ohio: Convergys 1783, **International 1795**, Timken 1821
Pennsylvania: Alcoa 1853, **National 1901**
Tennessee: **Maclellan 1962**, **Westwood 1969**
Texas: Crowder 1998, **Living 2034**, **Mission 2042**, Teen 2065, Whole 2071
Vermont: **Himalayan 2087**
Virginia: **EduCare 2118**, **Good360 2124**, **Loyola 2134**, **Mustard 2137**
Washington: **Gates 2170**, Starbucks 2202, **World 2208**
Wisconsin: **Cops 2214**

Australia

California: **Adobe 39**, **Australians 67**, **Christensen 97**, Google.org 163, **PADI 273**, Quiksilver 284, **Smith 327**
Colorado: First 389
Connecticut: Tudor 443
Delaware: ING 458
Illinois: Boeing 743, Illinois 772, **Two 826**
Indiana: Cummins 838
Maryland: **Hughes 907**, **International 912**
Massachusetts: **International 980**, **New 1000**
Michigan: Amway 1029, Kellogg 1049
Minnesota: Medtronic 1093, Thomson 1103, Toro 1104
Nevada: Wood 1153

New Jersey: Daft 1165
New York: American 1236, American 1241, **Commonwealth 1337**
Ohio: Eaton 1786
Pennsylvania: Alcoa 1853, Cephalon 1870, Pew 1906
Texas: Apache 1979, Fluor 2006, **New Media 2043**
Washington: **Gates 2170**

Austria

Colorado: Avenir 383
Delaware: ING 458
Florida: Jabil 652
Minnesota: Medtronic 1093
New York: **Lauder 1517**
Texas: **New Media 2043**

Azerbaijan

District of Columbia: **Eurasia 522**
New Jersey: **Worldwide 1207**
New York: **Armenia 1269**, Hess 1448, **International 1467**, **Trust 1696**
Virginia: **U.S. 2150**

Bahamas

California: Bercaw 76, **Smith 327**
Colorado: YPI 416
District of Columbia: Merriman 560
Massachusetts: LASPAU: 989
New York: **Cay 1315**, Diamonds 1354

Balkans, The

Massachusetts: **Center 951**

Bangladesh

California: **Bangladesh 70**
District of Columbia: **Aga 482**
Florida: Freewill 636
Illinois: **Messengers 796**
Maryland: **Hughes 907**
New York: **PepsiCo 1601**, **Project 1616**, **Smile 1661**
Washington: **World 2208**

Barbados

Massachusetts: **LASPAU: 989**
New York: Diamonds 1354

Belarus

District of Columbia: **Eurasia 522**
Illinois: **Deyneka 759**
New York: **Lauder 1517**, **Trust 1696**

Belgium

Colorado: Rio 406
Connecticut: **Belgian 423**
Florida: Jabil 652
Georgia: **Coca 692**
Michigan: Dow 1038
Minnesota: Medtronic 1093, Thomson 1103
New York: **AFS 1224**, **Francqui 1395**
Ohio: Eaton 1786
Texas: **New Media 2043**
Virginia: **Youth 2157**

Belize

District of Columbia: **Summit 592**, U.S. 595
Georgia: **Belize 688**
Massachusetts: **LASPAU: 989**, New England 999
Wisconsin: **Wagner 2231**

Benin

Florida: Freewill 636
Virginia: **America's 2093**

Bermuda

New York: Stempel 1676
Wisconsin: **Wagner 2231**

Bhutan

New York: **Smile 1661**
Vermont: **Himalayan 2087**

Bolivia

District of Columbia: **Amazon 485**
Maryland: **International 912**, Shared 929
Massachusetts: **LASPAU: 989**, New England 999
Minnesota: **Mano 1090**, Oswald 1096
Missouri: **ASC 1114**
New York: **Smile 1661**
Washington: **World 2208**

Bosnia-Herzegovina

California: **Whalen 364**
District of Columbia: **Women 607**
Maryland: **International 911**, **International 912**
New Jersey: **Croatian 1164**
New York: **International 1467**, **Smile 1661**, **Trust 1696**
Virginia: **America's 2093**

Brazil

California: Google.org 163, **PADI 273**, Palm 274
Colorado: Rio 406, **Western 413**
District of Columbia: **Amazon 485**
Florida: Assurant 619, Jabil 652
Georgia: **UPS 709**
Illinois: **Messengers 796**
Indiana: Cummins 837, Cummins 838
Maryland: **Hughes 907**, **International 912**
Massachusetts: American 944, **LASPAU: 989**
Michigan: BorgWarner 1033, Dow 1038, **Kellogg 1050**
Minnesota: Medtronic 1093, Thomson 1103
New Jersey: Prudential 1191
New York: **AFS 1224**, **Brazil 1300**, **EMpower 1369**, **Endeavor 1370**, **Friends 1402**, **International 1465**, **Smile 1661**
Ohio: Eaton 1786, Ethicon 1788, Timken 1821, **Timken 1822**
Oregon: NIKE 1847
Pennsylvania: Hershey 1889, **KL 1896**
South Carolina: **American 1936**
South Dakota: **Opus 1944**
Texas: **Amazon 1976**, Freescale 2011, Hines 2018, **Limiar 2032**, New Media 2043
Virginia: **Youth 2157**

Bulgaria

District of Columbia: **Trust 594**
Illinois: **Messengers 796**
Maine: **Oak 878**
Maryland: **Hughes 907**, **International 912**
Massachusetts: **American 941**
New Jersey: **Worldwide 1207**
New York: **Children's 1325**, **Lauder 1517**, Mihov 1554, **Smile 1661**, **Trust 1696**
Pennsylvania: **Children's 1871**
Wisconsin: Global 2218

Burkina Faso

California: **New 255**
Virginia: **America's 2093**
Washington: **World 2208**

Fiji

California: **Omega 263**, Resnick 291, **Seacology 314**

Finland

California: NVIDIA 261
Maryland: **International 912**
New York: **AFS 1224, American 1264**
Ohio: Eaton 1786, OMNOVA 1813
Texas: Freescale 2011, **New Media 2043**

Foreign policy

California: Caipirinha 90, Smythe 329
Connecticut: **Belgian 423, Richardson 439**
Delaware: James 460
District of Columbia: **Arca 496**, Cox 515, **German 532, Mott 565**, Open 578
Illinois: Cooper 754, Edgerly 764, Heritage 769, Madigan 790, Rubin 809
New Jersey: Princeton 1190
New York: Abstraction 1217, **Center 1318, Guggenheim 1435, Hauser 1444**, Japan 1474, Merow 1549, Preservation 1614, Ross 1641, **Rubin 1643**, Salomon 1645, **Tinker 1689, United 1708**, Wiener 1733, Zilkha 1744
Ohio: Veale 1824
Pennsylvania: Cotswold 1875, Mine 1899
Texas: Marsh 2037
Wisconsin: **Bradley 2212**

France

California: **Adobe 39**, Applied 59, Google.org 163, NVIDIA 261, Palm 274
Colorado: Fishback 390, Rio 406
Delaware: Colgate 453, Cornwell 454, ING 458
Florida: Jabil 652
Georgia: **Coca 692**
Maryland: **Hughes 907**
Massachusetts: MacJannet 991
Michigan: BorgWarner 1033, Dow 1038
Minnesota: Medtronic 1093, Thomson 1103
Missouri: **PKD 1130**
New York: **AFS 1224**, American 1261, de Rothschild 1349, **French 1398, French 1399**, French 1400, **Gould 1428**, Lurcy 1532, **Philippe 1608**
North Carolina: **American 1749**
Ohio: Eaton 1786, OMNOVA 1813, **Timken 1822**
Pennsylvania: Cephalon 1870
Texas: Cultural 1999, Freescale 2011, Hines 2018, **New Media 2043**, Scaler 2054, Westbury 2070
Virginia: **Youth 2157**
Washington: RealNetworks 2191

Gabon

New York: Hess 1448

Gambia, The

Illinois: **Messengers 796**

Georgia (Republic of)

District of Columbia: **Eurasia 522**
Maryland: **International 911**
Missouri: **A Call 1113**
New York: **International 1467, Smile 1661, Trust 1696**
Pennsylvania: **Children's 1871**
Virginia: **U.S. 2150**

Germany

California: **Adobe 39**, Applied 59, Google.org 163, **Hirshberg 179**, NVIDIA 261, Preuss 281
Colorado: First 389, Rio 406
Delaware: Hofmann 457, ING 458
Florida: Assurant 619, Jabil 652
Georgia: **Halle 697**

Illinois: **Two 826**
Maryland: **Hughes 907, International 912**
Michigan: BorgWarner 1033, Dow 1038
Minnesota: Medtronic 1093
New Jersey: Odysseus 1187
New York: American 1234, **CDS 1316, Kade 1489**, Ladenburg 1512, **Lauder 1517**, Leir 1523
Ohio: Eaton 1786, Ethicon 1788, **Timken 1822**
Pennsylvania: Cephalon 1870, **HJW 1890**
Rhode Island: Schoellkopf 1934
Texas: Freescale 2011, Hines 2018, **New Media 2043**
Virginia: **Youth 2157**

Ghana

Connecticut: **GE 428**
Georgia: Gray 696
Maryland: **International 912**
Massachusetts: American 944, New England 999
New York: **International 1465, PepsiCo 1601, Smile 1661**
Ohio: Noble 1811
South Carolina: **American 1936**
Tennessee: Fugitive 1955
Vermont: **Himalayan 2087**

Global programs

California: Chevron 94, **Hilton 178, Packard 271**
Colorado: Society 408, **Western 413**
Delaware: Jackman 459, **Raskob 467**
District of Columbia: **Case 503, Global 533**
Florida: **Working 681**
Illinois: Deere 757
New York: Clark 1330, **International 1464, Open 1593, Rockefeller 1639**
Virginia: **Feris 2119**
Wisconsin: Global 2218

Greece

Colorado: First 389
District of Columbia: American 490, **Fund 530**
Florida: Cantonis 624
Illinois: **Demos 758**
Maryland: **Hughes 907, International 911, International 912**
Massachusetts: Gerondelis 966, Marcopolous 992, Memorial 995
New York: **Parkinson's 1596**
North Carolina: Evrytanian 1753
Pennsylvania: **Institute 1893, Pan 1905**, Williams 1917
Texas: **New Media 2043**

Grenada

Massachusetts: **LASPAU: 989**
New York: Lawson 1519

Guatemala

California: **Leadership 221, Network 254, Rock 297**
Connecticut: Richardson 438
District of Columbia: **Fund 531, Moriah 562**, Palmer 579, **Summit 592**
Florida: **Transitions 677**
Illinois: **Circle 751, Messengers 796**
Maryland: **Shared 929**
Massachusetts: **Derossi 956, LASPAU: 989, Maya 993**, New England 999
Minnesota: Mortenson 1094
Missouri: **ASC 1114**
New Jersey: Danellie 1166
New York: **International 1465, Smile 1661**
Tennessee: Ezell 1953, **Vine 1968**
Virginia: **America's 2093, National 2138**

Guinea

California: **New 255**

District of Columbia: **Fund 531**
Maryland: **Hughes 907**
New York: **International 1467**

Guyana

Massachusetts: **LASPAU: 989**
New York: **Smile 1661**

Haiti

California: S.G. 300, Strauss 335
Colorado: **Colorado 386**, Mercy 402
Florida: **Hope 649**
Maine: Dugas 876
Maryland: **Interchurch 909, Quixote 927**
Massachusetts: Hands 972, **LASPAU: 989, Peace 1005**
Michigan: **Kellogg 1050**, May 1057
Minnesota: **Mary's 1091**
New Jersey: **Croatian 1164**, Danellie 1166
New York: **Edeyo 1366, Smile 1661, Yele 1740**
North Carolina: **Rolander 1764**
Pennsylvania: **Mama 1898**
Virginia: **America's 2093, National 2138**
Washington: Vista 2205, **World 2208**

Honduras

District of Columbia: **Summit 592**
Florida: Wahlert 679
Illinois: **Messengers 796, Mission 797**
Kentucky: **O'Dell 865**
Maryland: **International 912**
Massachusetts: **LASPAU: 989**, New England 999
Minnesota: Mortenson 1094
New York: **Smile 1661**
Ohio: Noble 1811
Pennsylvania: **Mama 1898**
Tennessee: Ezell 1953
Texas: **Interdenominational 2021**
Virginia: Foster 2120
Washington: **Mona 2186**

Hong Kong

California: **Adobe 39**, NVIDIA 261, **Smith 327**
Connecticut: **Lingnan 432**
District of Columbia: **Fund 530**
Massachusetts: **China 952**
Minnesota: Thomson 1103
New York: **AFS 1224**
Texas: Freescale 2011, **New Media 2043**

Hungary

Arizona: Rosztoczy 27
District of Columbia: **Trust 594**
Florida: Jabil 652
Maryland: **Hughes 907, International 912**
Michigan: BorgWarner 1033
New Jersey: **American 1157**
New York: **Bito 1289**, Blinken 1291, **Lauder 1517, Smile 1661, Trust 1696**
Ohio: Eaton 1786
Texas: **New Media 2043**

Iceland

New York: **American 1264**

India

Alabama: Corman 3
California: **Adobe 39**, Advent 40, Amar 51, **Amritraj 55**, Applied 59, **Auroville 66**, Benaka 72, Cadence 89, ForceBrain.com 137, **Foundation 139, Foundation 141**, Gap 150, Google.org 163, Gupta 168, Huneeus 185, India 186, Jagadeesh 198, **Kulkarni 218**, Marra 239, Patel 277, Reve 292, **Sai**

303, **Sathya 310**, **Seacology 314**, Sikand 321, **Sri 333**, Tarsadia 341, Wadhwani 360, Xilinx, 377
Colorado: **Living 400**, **Western 413**
Connecticut: **Avatar 422**, United 444
District of Columbia: **Aga 482**, **Centre 508**, **Fund 531**
Florida: Freewill 636, Jabil 652, Patel 664, Patel 665
Georgia: Delta 694, Gray 696
Hawaii: Sangham 722, Watumull 726
Idaho: Micron 731
Illinois: **American 738**, Deere 757, **India 773**, **MacArthur 788**, **Messengers 796**
Indiana: Cummins 837, Cummins 838
Iowa: Sehgal 854
Kansas: **Lloyd 860**
Kentucky: **O'Dell 865**
Maine: **Oak 878**
Maryland: **Association 888**, Doorstep 898, Global 903, **Hughes 907**, **India 908**, **International 912**, **Janey 914**, **Shared 929**
Massachusetts: American 944, **Indo-American 979**, Invincibility 982
Michigan: BorgWarner 1033
Minnesota: India 1084, Medtronic 1093, Thomson 1103, **World-India 1109**
New Jersey: Akhoury 1156, Reddy 1192, **Share 1196**
New York: **American 1254**, Bloomberg 1292, **Brackett 1299**, Bristol 1303, Chatterjee 1323, **EMpower 1369**, **Flowering 1388**, Indira 1459, **International 1465**, **Jewelers 1476**, Mata 1482, Kathwari 1491, **McCaddin 1543**, Neuberger 1575, Nok 1582, **PepsiCo 1601**, **Project 1616**, **Smile 1661**, Tandon 1682, **Usha 1711**
North Carolina: **Samaritan's 1765**, With 1769
Ohio: Convergys 1783, Dauch 1785, Eaton 1786, Ethicon 1788, OMNOVA 1813, Timken 1821, **Timken 1822**
Oregon: **Foreign 1837**, Kalakendra 1840, NIKE 1847, **Tazo 1849**
Pennsylvania: Heinz 1887, Hershey 1889, **KL 1896**, Pilgrim 1907, Shiloh 1914
South Carolina: **American 1936**
Tennessee: **Bala 1947**, **Westwood 1969**
Texas: AMD 1977, Bhutada 1986, BMC 1987, Fluor 2006, Freescale 2011, Hines 2018, Jiv 2025, **New Media 2043**, **Pratham 2050**, Sooch 2059
Vermont: **Himalayan 2087**
Virginia: **City 2108**, **Dayspring 2112**, **India 2128**, Trehan 2149, **Youth 2157**
Washington: **Friends 2169**, Hyder 2176, Vista 2205

Indonesia

California: **Orangutan 267**, **Seacology 314**
Illinois: **Messengers 796**
Maryland: **International 911**, **International 912**
Massachusetts: **China 952**
New York: Hess 1448, **International 1465**, **International 1467**, **Smile 1661**
Ohio: Eaton 1786
Pennsylvania: Heinz 1887
Texas: **New Media 2043**

International affairs

Arizona: Barrett 14, World 30
California: Amar 51, **American 53**, **Appleton 57**, **Asia 64**, **Bergstrom 78**, Caufield 92, Consortium 107, **Cuore 109**, **CW 110**, Deng 114, Do 116, Draper 118, Esperanto 125, Foundation 138, **Foundation 141**, Fremont 143, Gap 150, **Give2Asia 155**, Hitz 181, Hoppe 182, **Humanity 184**, Huneeus 185, International 190, Jacobs 197, Jewish 204, **Jewish 205**, Lee 224, Lemelson 227, **Middle 245**, **Network 254**, **New 255**, **Pacific 270**, **Raising 285**, RM 296, Saban 302, Saje 304, Tides 345, **Tides 346**, Tosa 347, U.S.-Mexico 350, Unique 351, Uplands 354, Venture 356, Von der Ahe 358, Wadhwani 360, Wong 370, World 372, **X Prize 376**
Colorado: **Asia 382**, **Ecumenical 388**, Japan 397
Connecticut: Allison 418, **GE 428**, **Newman's 435**, **Richardson 439**, Shenandoah 441

Delaware: Adobe 447, Colgate 453, JNT 462, Sager 468
District of Columbia: **Aga 482**, Alliance 484, American 488, American 490, **American 491**, **Americans 493**, **Atlas 498**, **Better 501**, Center 504, Center 505, **Center 506**, Coleman 510, Connect 511, **Council 513**, Counterterrorism 514, **Eritrean 521**, **Free 526**, **Global 534**, **Global 535**, **Institute 542**, **International 544**, **International 546**, **International 547**, **International 548**, **International 549**, **Lambi 558**, **MAG 559**, **Migration 561**, **National 568**, Open 578, **Population 585**, **Sons 591**, **United 600**, **Wilson 606**
Florida: **American 615**, Assn. of Amer. Schools SA 618, Cafesjian 623, De La Pena 631, **Give 639**, **Global 640**, Patel 665, **Salvadoran 671**, Schecter 672
Georgia: American 682, **Carter 690**, **Halle 697**
Hawaii: Burke 713, **Center 714**, **Community 715**, Honda 718, Pacific 720, Scott 723
Illinois: Abelson 736, Build 745, Communitas 752, Divac 760, Joy 776, Krehbiel 779, Penrose 803, Pritzker 804, Rosenthal 805, Shifting 817
Indiana: Transformation 845
Iowa: Holthues 848, Hubbell 849
Maine: Cambodian 874
Maryland: **AICE 884**, **Association 889**, **BMENA 893**, **Jewish 915**, Weiss 935
Massachusetts: **American 941**, Beyond 946, Flatley 960, **Grassroots 970**, Harman 973, Hershey 976, Morse 998, Schooner 1018, **SEVEN 1019**, Unitarian 1027
Michigan: Jubilee 1048, **Palestine 1059**
Minnesota: Kelley 1086, MacMillan 1089, Oswald 1096, Sit 1101, Sundance 1102
Missouri: **BFP 1115**
Nevada: **Walsh 1152**
New Jersey: Aufzien 1158, Harris 1173, Hovnanian 1175, Johnson 1179, **Johnson 1180**, Johnson 1181, Weisberg 1203
New York: **Alliance 1230**, Altman 1231, **American 1251**, American 1261, American 1262, Angelson 1267, Arkin 1268, **Armenia 1269**, **Aspen 1274**, Berkowitz 1286, Birkelund 1287, **Blacksmith 1290**, Carnegie 1313, **CDS 1316**, **Common 1336**, Cone 1339, Council 1344, **Cross-Cultural 1345**, Debbane 1350, Donner 1360, Einhorn 1368, Eule 1376, **Fledgling 1387**, Foot 1390, **Ford 1391**, French 1400, GBRG 1409, **Global 1419**, **Guggenheim 1435**, Harmon 1441, **Harriman 1442**, Hurford 1456, **Interpeace 1468**, **Isdell 1470**, Janklow 1473, **Jewish 1477**, Kimmelman 1500, **King 1501**, Lane 1513, Lisben 1528, Loeb 1530, **M.A.C. 1534**, Mesdag 1550, Meyer 1552, **Millennium 1556**, Mitsui 1560, Nduna 1572, **Not 1584**, Ogden 1587, **PRASAD 1613**, QIBQ 1619, Reynolds 1632, Sapling 1646, Schaffner 1647, Slifka 1660, **Sparkplug 1667**, Stalnman 1671, Stern 1678, **Tibet 1686**, **Tinker 1689**, **United 1706**, United 1707, **United 1708**, **Virtue 1717**, Volcker 1719, Wallach 1721, Whalesback 1730, **Wiesel 1734**
North Carolina: **ANAI 1750**, North 1760, Richardson 1762
Ohio: Jacobs 1796, Partridge 1814, Taj 1818
Oregon: **Conklin 1834**, McKenzie 1844, **Mercy 1846**
Pennsylvania: AMETEK 1856, Benter 1863, **Brother's 1867**, **Carthage 1869**, **Children's 1871**, Clayman 1872, Federated 1879, Friendship 1882, **Global 1884**, Heinz 1887, Hellendall 1888, **National 1901**, Pacem 1904, Progressive 1909, Scaife 1911, Sidewater 1915
Rhode Island: Dorot 1923
Tennessee: **Improved 1958**, **Outpost 1965**
Texas: A Glimmer 1970, **International 2026**, Maples 2036, Marsh 2037, Plitt 2049, Stewart 2063
Virginia: **Donors 2115**, **Earthrights 2117**, **Jubilee 2130**, Mercatus 2135
Washington: Duim 2168, **Pangea: 2189**, Scan 2197, See 2201, Tulalip 2204
Wisconsin: Argosy 2210, **Bradley 2212**, Delavan 2216, Kohler 2223

International affairs, alliance/advocacy

California: **Network 254**, **United 353**
District of Columbia: **United 599**
Florida: **Jewish 653**
Minnesota: United 1105
Virginia: **United 2151**

International affairs, equal rights

California: **Draper 119**, **Global 158**
District of Columbia: **International 548**
New York: International 1466, **Synergos 1680**
Texas: Karakin 2027
Washington: **Channel 2163**

International affairs, formal/general education

Florida: Assn. of Amer. Schools SA 618
Illinois: Casten 747
New York: InterExchange 1463
North Carolina: AlphaMed 1748
Virginia: **United 2151**

International affairs, fund raising/fund distribution

California: Kadima 206
Pennsylvania: **Children's 1871**
Virginia: **Charities 2104**

International affairs, goodwill promotion

Alaska: Sealaska 12
California: Chao 93, Cienega 99, **Foundation 140**, Hidden 175, Van Konynenburg 355
Colorado: Japan 397
District of Columbia: Kaye 555, **National 570**
Florida: Hsu 650
Georgia: **Wardlaw 710**
Hawaii: East-West 716, Honda 718
Illinois: Stuart 823
Kentucky: C.E. 863
Maine: **Walter 881**
Maryland: **AICE 884**, **Hariri 904**, Interpreters' 913
Minnesota: Duluth 1077
Missouri: **People 1129**
New Jersey: Borgenicht 1162, Daft 1165, Fairbanks 1168
New York: American 1234, American 1261, Atlantic 1277, Banti 1281, **Center 1318**, **East 1363**, Freeman 1397, Gerschel 1412, **Global 1419**, Greve 1432, Japan 1474, Soros 1665, Tang 1683, **Tinker 1689**, Wiener 1733
Ohio: Partridge 1814
Oklahoma: Broken 1826
Washington: Scan 2197

International affairs, government agencies

District of Columbia: **Eurasia 522**
Virginia: Associates 2096

International affairs, information services

District of Columbia: **International 546**, Open 578
Massachusetts: Colombe 953

International affairs, management/technical assistance

District of Columbia: **Eurasia 522**

International affairs, national security

California: Caipirinha 90
District of Columbia: **Arca 496**
New York: **Carnegie 1312**, Casey 1314, **Institute 1461**, Markle 1538, **Peterson 1604**, Stern 1678
Texas: Mattsson 2038

Texas: **Pratham 2050**, **Vietnamese 2068**
Virginia: **Algerian-American 2092**, **U.S. 2150**
Washington: Bezos 2160

International exchange, arts

Connecticut: Creative 425
District of Columbia: **American 489**, Mosaic 563, **San Giacomo 588**
New York: **CEC 1317**, **Center 1318**, **Chamber 1321**, **Council 1343**, **French 1398**, **Netherland-America 1574**, Roche 1637, Ross 1641
Virginia: **Algerian-American 2092**

International exchange, students

California: **Wang 361**
Illinois: **IFSA 771**, **Rotary 807**
Iowa: **P.E.O. 853**
Massachusetts: Rodgers 1015
Michigan: Levy 1053
Minnesota: United 1105
Missouri: **People 1129**
New York: **AFS-USA 1225**, **Center 1318**, Lewy 1525, Mitsui 1560, Sony 1664
Wisconsin: Kikkoman 2222

International human rights

California: Alalusi 50, Benjamin 75, Better 80, **Brilliant 85**, Caipirinha 90, Coalition 103, Falling 126, **Fund 148**, Fund 149, Genocide 151, **Gere 152**, **Global 157**, **Global 158**, Humanitarian 183, Jennings 200, **Jewish 205**, Keller 213, Leibowitz 225, Levy 228, **Lift 231**, Lutz 235, **Milarepa 247**, **Network 254**, Otto 269, PTSRK 283, San Francisco 309, Von der Ahe 358, **Working 371**, Yen 378
Colorado: Econscious 387, **Ecumenical 388**, Free 391, **General 392**, **Urgent 411**, Warner 412
Connecticut: Mahadeva 434, Tierney 442, Valentine 445
Delaware: James 460, Jolie-Pitt 463
District of Columbia: Anti-Slavery 495, **Arca 496**, Connect 511, El-Hibri 519, Freedom 527, **Fund 531**, **Global 535**, Gorongosa 536, **International 544**, **International 546**, International 549, Kimsey 557, **MAG 559**, **Moriah 562**, **Mott 565**, Open 578, **Pan 580**, **Save 589**, **Summit 592**, **United 597**, **Women 608**
Florida: Around 617, Patel 664
Georgia: **Wardlaw 710**
Illinois: **MacArthur 788**, Magnus 791, **New 799**, Rothman 808
Iowa: Holthues 848
Maine: Catalyst 875, **Oak 878**
Maryland: **Blaustein 891**, Blaustein 892, Cohen 896, **Quixote 927**
Massachusetts: Fowler 962, **Grassroots 970**, Lamm 988, Perls 1008, Unitarian 1027
Michigan: Cutting 1034
Minnesota: Lownade 1088, Mossier 1095, **Winds 1108**
Missouri: **ASC 1114**
Nevada: **Fund 1147**
New Jersey: Harbourton 1172, **Johnson 1180**, Knistrom 1183, Richer 1193
New Mexico: Angelica 1208, **Levinson 1211**
New York: Allen 1229, **Alliance 1230**, **American 1257**, **AYCO 1279**, Baobab 1282, **Brac 1298**, Brenner 1302, Cleary 1331, Demi 1352, **East 1363**, **Echoing 1365**, Edouard 1367, Epstein 1374, **Ford 1391**, Gellert 1410, **Gildersleeve 1413**, Gould 1427, **Guggenheim 1435**, **Hauser 1444**, **Human 1454**, **Hungarian 1455**, **International 1465**, Kaufman 1492, Koha 1505, Ladenburg 1512, **Mam 1537**, Mendell 1547, **Merlin 1548**, **Millennium 1556**, Mullen 1563, **Muste 1564**, **Not 1584**, Omnicom 1591, **Open 1593**, **Overbrook 1594**, Petra 1605, **Richie-Madden 1633**, Rivendell 1636, **Rubin 1643**, SDialogue, 1649, **Sparkplug 1667**, Speyer 1668, **Synergos 1680**, **Virtue 1717**, Wendt 1728, Whispering 1731, Zenkel 1743

Ohio: Armington 1777, Haskell 1793
Oregon: **Alima 1833**, Larson 1842
Pennsylvania: Key 1895, Nararo 1900, Scranton 1912
Texas: Dougherty 2001, Flynn 2007, Link 2033, McDermott 2039
Virginia: **King 2131**, Woodbury 2155
Washington: **Channel 2163**, Common 2165, Community 2166, Jernigan 2180
Wisconsin: Cudahy 2215, Wisconsin 2232

International migration/refugee issues

California: Deng 114, **Humanity 184**, **Jewish 205**, Otto 269, World 374
Colorado: Colorado 385
Connecticut: International 431
District of Columbia: **Migration 561**, **Save 589**
Illinois: Hebrew 768
Louisiana: Catholic 868
Maryland: National 924
Massachusetts: **Alchemy 940**
Michigan: Travelers 1066
New York: Adelson 1221, Fast 1379, **HIAS 1449**, Howard 1453, Kaplan 1490, Kathwari 1491, Model 1561, **Nefesh 1573**, Sherman 1654, **Sparkplug 1667**, Tibet 1686
Ohio: Mason 1808
Tennessee: **African 1946**
Texas: Alliance 1975, Interfaith 2022
Virginia: Somali 2147

International peace/security

Arkansas: Darragh 32
California: **American 53**, Firedoll 131, Fund 149, **Invisible 194**, Lainer 220, **Milarepa 247**, **Nuclear 260**, **Ploughshares 280**, **Sloss 326**, **Taiwan 339**
Colorado: Arsenault 381, **Ecumenical 388**, **General 392**, Huntor 396, Warner 412
Delaware: Shoemaker 472, Winky 478
District of Columbia: **Better 501**, Center 504, Connect 511, El-Hibri 519, **Endowment 520**, Foundation 524, **International 546**, **International 549**, **Mott 565**, National 571, **Nuclear 574**
Florida: Schecter 672
Georgia: **Wardlaw 710**
Hawaii: Burke 713, People's 721, Scott 723
Illinois: Communitas 752, Jocarno 775, **MacArthur 788**, **New 799**, **New 800**
Iowa: Global 847, Holthues 848, **Maharishi 851**
Kansas: **Shumaker 861**
Maine: Catalyst 875
Maryland: Interpreters' 913, Morningstar 922
Massachusetts: Cabot 949, Colombe 953, **Haymarket 975**, Invincibility 982, One 1001, **Peace 1005**, Peacemaker 1006, RESIST 1014, Schooner 1018, Talanian 1024
Minnesota: Duluth 1077, Foundation 1079, **Weyerhaeuser 1107**, **Winds 1108**
Missouri: **ASC 1114**
New Jersey: **One 1188**
New York: **Abraham 1215**, Angelina 1266, **Carnegie 1312**, Dynamic 1362, Fellowship 1381, **Funding 1407**, **Guggenheim 1435**, **Hauser 1444**, **HKH 1450**, Kenbe 1496, Kurz 1510, MADRE, 1535, Model 1561, **Muste 1564**, **New 1577**, North 1583, Olum 1590, **Rockefeller 1638**, **Rubin 1643**, Slifka 1660, **Tutu 1699**, Wiener 1733
North Carolina: **Microelectronics 1757**, Triangle 1768
Ohio: Armington 1777, Eaton 1787
Oregon: McKenzie 1844
Pennsylvania: Argus 1857, Bloch 1865, Bread 1866, **Global 1884**
Texas: Bridgeway 1990, Oppenheimer 2045, Trull 2067
Utah: Slaughter 2076
Virginia: **King 2131**
Washington: **Stewardship 2203**
Wisconsin: Wisconsin 2232

International relief

Alaska: Gaguine 9
Arizona: **Food 20**, Solheim 28
California: **Afghanistan 41**, **Airline 47**, Alalusi 50, **America 52**, **Amritraj 55**, Applied 58, Arlene 60, **Bangladesh 70**, Benham 73, Caipirinha 90, Chintu 96, Do 116, East 121, Egg 122, Fanuk 127, **Grameen 164**, Grove 167, Hexberg 173, **Hidaya 174**, Higgins 176, **Humanity 184**, **International 191**, Jennings 200, **Jewish 205**, Kaiser 208, Kerby 214, **Medical 243**, Neeley 252, **Nora 258**, Novellus 259, Oak 262, Operation 266, Otto 269, **Rawat 287**, Ray 288, Sabadia 301, Saje 311, **Seva 316**, Simms 324, **Sloss 326**, **Sri 333**, **Tibetan 344**, Tres 348, **World 373**, World 374, **World 375**, Ying 379
Colorado: **Colorado 386**, **H.E.L.P. 395**, ProLogis 404, **Someone 409**
Connecticut: **AmeriCares 421**, Crew 426, Macauley 433, Vranos 446
Delaware: **Birch 452**, Jackman 459, Jolie-Pitt 463, Kuehner 465, **Raskob 467**, Schejola 471, Three 474, Weissman 476, Williams 477
District of Columbia: **CityBridge 509**, El-Hibri 519, Kaye 555, Mosaic 563, Omega 576, **Pan 580**, **United 600**, **Voices 604**, Zonta 611
Florida: Abraham 612, **American 615**, Green 644, **Holland 648**, Patel 664, **Working 681**
Georgia: Amos-Cheves 685, Masroor 702
Idaho: **Schultz 733**
Illinois: Carrus 746, Lohengrin 786, McShane 793, **Messengers 796**, Rothman 808, Shifting 817, **United 827**
Indiana: Brotherhood 835, **Church 836**
Kansas: **Christian 858**
Kentucky: Jain 864, Yum! 867
Louisiana: **Park 869**
Maryland: **Adventist 883**, **Asian 887**, **Child 895**, Dysfunctional 899, **Hariri 904**, Hirschhorn 905, **India 908**, **Interchurch 909**, **Lutheran 916**, Meyer 918
Massachusetts: **Center 951**, Dana 955, **Grassroots 970**, **Indo-American 979**, **Izumi 983**, **Planet 1010**, Tatelman 1025
Michigan: Auberlin 1031, **Hands 1045**, Jubilee 1048, Lot 1054, May 1057, Pilgrim 1060, Weingartz 1067, Whitman 1068, Williams 1069, **World 1070**
Minnesota: Better 1074, Hegardt 1083, **Winds 1108**, Youth 1110
Mississippi: Lingle 1111
Missouri: **Children 1119**, Slusher 1133
Nebraska: Kind 1141
New Hampshire: Brookstone, 1154
New Jersey: **Croatian 1164**, Danellie 1166, Gaillard 1169, Hoffmann-La 1174, IDT 1176, **Johnson 1178**, Prudential 1191, Waterview 1202, Wolf 1206
New Mexico: Quail 1212
New York: Achelis 1219, **Acumen 1220**, AGB 1226, Alexander 1228, Allen 1229, **American 1256**, **American 1257**, Bonide 1294, Brutsch 1304, **Burpee 1306**, **Carey 1310**, **Chabad 1320**, **Concern 1338**, **Doctors 1356**, Donner 1360, **Echoing 1365**, Edouard 1367, **Fund 1406**, **Global 1417**, Harbor 1440, **International 1464**, Interpublic 1469, Limo 1527, Michaels 1553, **Millennium 1556**, Newman 1581, **Not 1584**, O'Sullivan 1586, Omnicom 1591, One 1592, **P.E.F. 1595**, Peierls 1597, Pfizer 1607, Rattner 1625, Sherman 1654, Singh 1657, **Synergos 1680**, Uphill 1710, Vanderbilt 1712, **Vietnam 1715**, **Virtue 1717**, **Vital 1718**, Walters 1722, Weil 1724, White 1732
North Carolina: **New 1758**, **Samaritan's 1765**, **Stop 1766**
Ohio: AK Steel 1775, **Catholic 1780**, **Christian 1781**, Cintas 1782, Danaher 1784, Procter 1815
Oklahoma: Love 1829
Oregon: **Evergreen 1835**, **KEEN 1841**, **Medical 1845**, Mercy 1846, Weatherspoon 1850
Pennsylvania: Argus 1857, Barrack 1861, Dixon 1876, **Hope 1891**, **Pan 1905**, Pine 1908, Shah 1913, **Zeldin 1919**

2043, Paso 2046, Seegers 2056, Summerlee 2064
Virginia: **Good360 2124**, **Youth 2157**
Washington: Vista 2205

Middle East

California: Firedoll 131, **Middle 246**, **Open 265**, Philibosian 278, **Ploughshares 280**, **salesforce.com 305**, Unique 351
Colorado: **Living 400**
Connecticut: **Richardson 439**
District of Columbia: **American 492**, **Americans 494**, El-Hibri 519, Foundation 524, **Franciscan 525**, **Jerusalem 552**, **MAG 559**, **Most 564**, **Ocean 575**, **Wilson 606**
Florida: Kerzner 658
Illinois: Landau 780
Indiana: **Overseas 843**
Kansas: **Lloyd 860**
Maryland: **BMENA 893**, **International 912**, **Lutheran 916**, **SAT-7 928**, **Strategic 931**
Massachusetts: Haymarket 975, PTC 1012
Michigan: **World 1070**
Missouri: Simon 1132
New Jersey: **BD 1159**, **International 1177**, Sweetfeet 1197
New York: American 1241, **Breast 1301**, Clark 1330, Dodge 1357, **Ford 1391**, Goldman 1423, Handleman 1439, **Hauser 1444**, Kevorkian 1497, Olayan 1589, **Population 1611**, **Project 1616**, **ProLiteracy 1617**, Slifka 1660
Ohio: **Arab 1776**, **International 1795**
Pennsylvania: **National 1901**, **Nazareth 1902**
Tennessee: **Maclellan 1962**
Virginia: **Mustard 2137**, **U.S. 2150**
Washington: Starbucks 2202

Moldova

District of Columbia: **Eurasia 522**
Illinois: **Deyneka 759**
Maine: **Oak 878**
New York: **Children's 1325**, **Lauder 1517**, **Smile 1661**, **Trust 1696**
Virginia: **U.S. 2150**

Monaco

Georgia: **Coca 692**
Michigan: BorgWarner 1033
New Jersey: **Johnson 1180**

Mongolia

Illinois: **Messengers 796**
New York: **Smile 1661**, **Trust 1696**
Utah: Swanson 2079

Montenegro

Maryland: **International 911**
New York: **Rockefeller 1638**, **Trust 1696**

Morocco and the Western Sahara

District of Columbia: **Fund 531**
South Dakota: **Opus 1944**
Virginia: **America's 2093**
Washington: **Gateway 2171**

Mozambique

District of Columbia: **Aga 482**
Georgia: St. 707
New York: **International 1465**
Virginia: **America's 2093**

Namibia

Ohio: Noble 1811

Nepal

California: McConnell 242
Colorado: Free 391
Delaware: Sager 468
District of Columbia: **Centre 508**
Illinois: **Messengers 796**
Maryland: Doorstep 898
Nebraska: **Himanchal 1140**
New York: Simons 1655, **Smile 1661**
Vermont: **Himalayan 2087**
Washington: **World 2208**
Wisconsin: **Central 2213**

Netherlands

California: Advent 40, Google.org 163
Colorado: Rio 406
Florida: Jabil 652
Georgia: **Coca 692**, South 705
Maryland: **International 912**
Minnesota: Medtronic 1093, Reell 1099, Thomson 1103
Missouri: **PKD 1130**
New York: **Leiden 1522**, **Netherland-America 1574**
Ohio: Eaton 1786
Texas: BMC 1987, Dougherty 2001, Fluor 2006, Freescale 2011, **New Media 2043**

New Zealand

Illinois: **Messengers 796**
Minnesota: Thomson 1103
New York: American 1236, **Commonwealth 1337**
Texas: **New Media 2043**

Nicaragua

District of Columbia: **Kennedy 556**
Florida: **American 615**, Himmel 647
Georgia: **Amigos 683**
Illinois: **Messengers 796**
Maryland: **Quixote 927**
Massachusetts: **LASPAU: 989**, New England 999
Michigan: **Rotary 1062**
Minnesota: Mortenson 1094, **Winds 1108**
New York: **Smile 1661**
North Carolina: **Project 1761**
Ohio: Noble 1811
Virginia: **America's 2093**, **Ivy 2129**
Washington: **Bainbridge 2159**, **World 2208**

Niger

California: **New 255**
Pennsylvania: **Mama 1898**
Washington: **World 2208**

Nigeria

District of Columbia: **Centre 508**, **Women 607**
Florida: Freewill 636
Illinois: **MacArthur 788**, **Messengers 796**
Michigan: **Global 1044**
New York: **EMpower 1369**, **International 1465**, **Smile 1661**
Tennessee: Ezell 1953

North Africa

Maryland: **BMENA 893**, **SAT-7 928**, **Strategic 931**
Ohio: **International 1795**

North Korea

California: **Ploughshares 280**

Illinois: **Messengers 796**
New Jersey: Prudential 1191

Norway

California: Advent 40
New York: **American 1264**
Ohio: Eaton 1786
Texas: **New Media 2043**

Oceania

California: Ingram 187, **Packard 271**, **Seacology 314**, Symantec 337
Colorado: **Living 400**
Hawaii: Alexander 712, **Center 714**
Michigan: **World 1070**
New Jersey: **International 1177**, **Johnson 1178**
New York: Claiborne 1329, **Gildersleeve 1413**
Ohio: Convergys 1783
Virginia: **Rare 2143**

Pakistan

California: Al-Ameen 49, Fatima 130
District of Columbia: **Aga 482**, **Fund 531**
Georgia: Masroor 702
Illinois: Eades 763, **Messengers 796**
Kentucky: **O'Dell 865**
Maryland: **Shared 929**
New York: **International 1467**, Kathwari 1491, **Smile 1661**

Palau

California: **Seacology 314**

Panama

Maryland: **International 912**
Massachusetts: **LASPAU: 989**
Texas: Hines 2018
Virginia: **America's 2093**
Washington: **Mona 2186**

Papua New Guinea

California: **Christensen 97**, **Seacology 314**
Maryland: **Shared 929**
Massachusetts: New England 999

Paraguay

Florida: Freewill 636
Illinois: **Messengers 796**
Maryland: **International 912**
Massachusetts: **LASPAU: 989**

Peru

Connecticut: **Hampshire 430**
District of Columbia: **Amazon 485**
Illinois: **Messengers 796**
Maryland: **International 912**, **Shared 929**
Massachusetts: American 944, **LASPAU: 989**, New England 999
Minnesota: Oswald 1096
New York: **Clover 1333**, **EMpower 1369**, **International 1465**, **Smile 1661**
North Dakota: **Los 1772**
Ohio: Eaton 1786
Oregon: **Sustainable 1848**
Texas: **Interdenominational 2021**, **New Media 2043**
Virginia: **Ivy 2129**

Philippines

Arizona: Children's 16

New York: **American 1257, Astraea 1276, Butler 1307,** Canon 1309, Claiborne 1329, Frank 1396, **Gildersleeve 1413, John 1484, McCaddin 1543, Rainforest 1622, Rainforest 1623**
North Carolina: **Rixson 1763, Rolander 1764, Samaritan's 1765**
Ohio: **International 1795**
Pennsylvania: Alcoa 1853, **National 1901**
Texas: **Interdenominational 2021, Living 2034**
Virginia: **American 2094, Mustard 2137**
Washington: **World 2208**
Wisconsin: **Cops 2214,** Wisconsin 2232

South Asia

California: **Packard 271**
District of Columbia: **MAG 559**
New Jersey: **Johnson 1178**
New York: Singh 1657

South Korea

California: Applied 59, Spansion 331
District of Columbia: Dingwall 518
Idaho: Micron 731
Maryland: **International 912**
Michigan: BorgWarner 1033, Dow 1038
New Jersey: Prudential 1191
Texas: **New Media 2043**
Virginia: Universal 2153

Southeast Asia

California: **ANGELCARE 56,** East 121, **Open 265, Ploughshares 280, Seacology 314**
District of Columbia: **Banyan 499**
Hawaii: Shiraki 725
Massachusetts: **China 952**
New Jersey: **Johnson 1178**
New York: **East 1363,** Kathwari 1491, **Luce 1531, Open 1593, Rainforest 1623**

Southern Africa

Georgia: St. 707
Illinois: **Circle 751**
Maryland: **Interchurch 909**
Massachusetts: **Oxfam 1002**
New Jersey: **International 1177**
New York: **NBI 1571**
Virginia: **Good360 2124**
Wisconsin: Sand 2228

Soviet Union (Former)

Alabama: Corman 3
Colorado: **Queen 405**
Connecticut: **Richardson 439**
District of Columbia: **American 487, Eurasia 522, Vishnevskaya-Rostropovich 603, Wallace 605**
Georgia: Rosenberg 703
Maryland: **Weinberg 934**
New Jersey: **C.I.S. 1163**
New York: **Astraea 1276, Global 1418, Media 1544**
Puerto Rico: **FNZ 1920**
Tennessee: Grandview 1957
Virginia: **U.S. 2150**
Washington: RHEMA 2193

Spain

California: Google.org 163
Colorado: Rio 406
Delaware: ING 458
Florida: **Alfalit 614,** Assurant 619
Maryland: **International 912**
Massachusetts: **LASPAU: 989,** Real 1013
Michigan: BorgWarner 1033
Minnesota: Medtronic 1093, Thomson 1103
North Carolina: Carlson 1752

Texas: Fluor 2006, Freescale 2011, Hines 2018, **New Media 2043**
Virginia: **Salvation 2144, Youth 2157**

Sri Lanka

California: **Seacology 314**
Illinois: **Circle 751**
New York: Gorman 1426, **Kids 1498, Smile 1661**
Pennsylvania: **KL 1896**
Virginia: **Salvation 2144**
Washington: **World 2208**

Sub-Saharan Africa

California: **Compton 105, Firelight 132,** Hewlett 172, **Packard 271**
Delaware: Sager 468
District of Columbia: **Accordia 479, Joint 553**
New York: **African 1223,** Bristol 1303, **Carnegie 1312, King 1501, Vine 1716**
Ohio: **International 1795**
Pennsylvania: **American 1854**
Texas: **Africa 1972**

Sudan

California: **African 42,** Deng 114
Colorado: Colorado 385
District of Columbia: **Save 589, Women 607**
Florida: Freewill 636
Illinois: **Circle 751**
Maryland: **Interchurch 909**
New York: **International 1467**
Washington: **World 2208**

Suriname

Massachusetts: **LASPAU: 989**

Sweden

California: **Adobe 39,** Advent 40, Agouron 45, Google.org 163
Minnesota: Medtronic 1093, Thomson 1103
New York: **American 1264**
Ohio: Eaton 1786
Texas: Freescale 2011, **New Media 2043**

Switzerland

California: Advent 40, Applied 59, Google.org 163, NVIDIA 261
Connecticut: **American 419**
District of Columbia: **Aga 482**
Idaho: Micron 731
Maine: **Oak 878**
Maryland: Hughes 907
Minnesota: Medtronic 1093, Piper 1097
Missouri: **PKD 1130**
New York: Bloomberg 1292, **International 1464**
Pennsylvania: Cephalon 1870, **HJW 1890**
Texas: Coneway 1995, Freescale 2011, **New Media 2043**

Syria

California: **Middle 246**
District of Columbia: **Aga 482**
Maryland: **International 911**

Taiwan

California: **Adobe 39,** Applied 59, **Lyu 236,** NVIDIA 261, Spansion 331
Colorado: Rio 406
Florida: Jabil 652
Idaho: Micron 731
Illinois: Eades 763
Maryland: Hughes 907, **International 912**

Massachusetts: **China 952**
Minnesota: Reell 1099
New Jersey: Prudential 1191
New York: **Smile 1661**
Ohio: Eaton 1786
Texas: AMD 1977, Freescale 2011, **New Media 2043**
Virginia: **Salvation 2144**

Tajikistan

California: **Christensen 97**
District of Columbia: **Aga 482, Eurasia 522**
Illinois: **Messengers 796**
New York: **Trust 1696**
Virginia: **U.S. 2150**

Tanzania, Zanzibar and Pemba

California: **Firelight 132, Seacology 314,** Smith 328, Wade 359
Colorado: **AfricAid 380**
District of Columbia: **Aga 482, DeMoss 516**
Georgia: St. 707
Illinois: **Messengers 796**
Maine: **Oak 878**
Maryland: **Interchurch 909, International 912**
Massachusetts: **Lift 990,** New England 999
Minnesota: **Dorobo 1075,** McKnight 1092, Oswald 1096
New York: **International 1465, International 1467, Smile 1661, Tanzania 1684**
Oregon: **Sustainable 1848**
Texas: **Friedkin 2012**
Virginia: **Salvation 2144**

Thailand

California: **Foundation 141,** Otto 269, Spansion 331
District of Columbia: **Fund 531**
Illinois: **Circle 751, Messengers 796**
Maryland: Doorstep 898, **International 911, International 912**
Massachusetts: **China 952,** Grand 968
New York: **AFS 1224, Brackett 1299, EMpower 1369,** Hess 1448, **International 1465, International 1467, Smile 1661**
South Carolina: **American 1936**
Texas: **New Media 2043**
Virginia: **Youth 2157**
Washington: Starbucks 2202, **World 2208**

Trinidad & Tobago

Massachusetts: **LASPAU: 989**
Virginia: **Salvation 2144**

Tunisia

District of Columbia: **Fund 531**

Turkey

California: **Turkish 349**
District of Columbia: **Institute 543**
Illinois: **Messengers 796**
Maryland: **International 912**
Massachusetts: **Friends 964,** Grand 968
New York: American 1262, **EMpower 1369, Smile 1661**
Texas: **Chrest 1994,** Hines 2018, **New Media 2043**

Turkmenistan

District of Columbia: **Eurasia 522**
Illinois: **Messengers 796**
New York: **Trust 1696**
Virginia: **U.S. 2150**

Uganda

California: **African 42**, **Invisible 194**
Connecticut: **GE 428**
District of Columbia: **Aga 482**, **DeMoss 516**, **Fund 531**
Florida: **Watoto 680**
Georgia: **His 698**, St. 707
Illinois: **Messengers 796**
Maine: **Oak 878**
Maryland: **Hughes 907**, **International 912**
Minnesota: McKnight 1092, Oswald 1096
New York: **International 1465**, **International 1467**, **Smile 1661**
Texas: His 2019
Virginia: **Salvation 2144**
Washington: Luke 2184, **World 2208**

Ukraine

California: **International 192**
District of Columbia: **Eurasia 522**
Florida: Jabil 652
Illinois: **Deyneka 759**, Heritage 769
Maryland: **Hughes 907**
Michigan: **Mott 1058**
New York: **Global 1418**, **Lauder 1517**, **Smile 1661**, **Tikva 1687**, **Trust 1696**
Oklahoma: **Schusterman 1830**
Pennsylvania: **Children's 1871**
Virginia: **America's 2093**, **U.S. 2150**

United Arab Emirates

Texas: Hines 2018, **New Media 2043**

United Kingdom

California: **Adobe 39**, Advent 40, Agouron 45, Cadence 89, Gap 150, **Global 156**, Google.org 103, NVIDIA 261, Palm 274, **Smith 327**
Colorado: First 389
Delaware: **American 449**, ING 458
District of Columbia: **Aga 482**, Butler 502
Florida: Assurant 619, Taylor 676
Idaho: Micron 731
Indiana: Cummins 838
Maryland: **Hughes 907**, **International 912**
Massachusetts: American 944
Michigan: BorgWarner 1033, Kellogg 1049
Minnesota: Medtronic 1093, Piper 1097, Thomson 1103
Missouri: Enterprise 1121
New Mexico: **Thaw 1214**
New York: **AFS 1224**, **Commonwealth 1337**, **Fox 1394**, **Glyndebourne 1420**, Goldman 1423, Healthcorps 1446, Hedge 1447, Hess 1448,

Lehman 1521, **Ohr 1588**, **Parkinson's 1596**, **Royal 1642**, St. George's 1670, Tanaka 1681, **Unbound 1702**
North Carolina: **American 1749**
Ohio: Eaton 1786, **Timken 1822**
Oregon: Wyss 1851
Tennessee: UnumProvident 1967
Texas: Cooper 1996, Fluor 2006, Freescale 2011, Hines 2018, **New Media 2043**
Virginia: Gannett 2122
Washington: RealNetworks 2191, Starbucks 2202

Uruguay

Maryland: **Hughes 907**, **International 912**
Massachusetts: **LASPAU: 989**
New York: **Endeavor 1370**

Uzbekistan

District of Columbia: **Eurasia 522**
Illinois: **Messengers 796**
New York: **Smile 1661**, **Trust 1696**
Virginia: **America's 2093**, **U.S. 2150**

Vanuatu

California: **Christensen 97**, **Seacology 314**

Vatican City

Iowa: Ochylski 852

Venezuela

Maryland: **Hughes 907**, **International 912**
Massachusetts: **LASPAU: 989**
New Jersey: **Vollmer 1201**
New York: **Smile 1661**
Texas: Bolivar 1988, **New Media 2043**

Vietnam

California: Cienega 99, East 121, **Milkcare 248**, **Seacology 314**
Florida: Freewill 636, Jabil 652
Idaho: **Schultz 733**
Maryland: **International 912**
Massachusetts: **Alchemy 940**
Minnesota: McKnight 1092
Missouri: Clarkson 1120
New Jersey: **Worldwide 1207**

New York: Eastman 1364, **EMpower 1369**, **International 1465**, **Project 1616**, **Smile 1661**, **Vietnam 1715**
Texas: **New Media 2043**, **Vietnamese 2068**
Washington: **World 2208**

Wales

Georgia: **Coca 692**
Michigan: Dow 1038

West Bank/Gaza (Palestinian Territories)

District of Columbia: **American 492**, **Franciscan 525**, **Jerusalem 552**, **United 598**
Idaho: **Schultz 733**
Illinois: **United 827**
Michigan: **Palestine 1059**
New York: **International 1465**, One 1592, **Sparkplug 1667**
Pennsylvania: **Nazareth 1902**
Virginia: **America's 2093**

Western Africa

Alabama: Corman 3

Yemen

New York: **Smile 1661**

Yugoslavia (Former)

New York: **International 1467**

Zambia

California: **African 42**, **Firelight 132**
Georgia: St. 707
Maryland: **International 912**
Michigan: Fisher 1041
New York: **Smile 1661**
Pennsylvania: **Macha 1897**
Texas: Jubilee 2026
Virginia: **Salvation 2144**
Washington: **World 2208**

Zimbabwe

California: **Firelight 132**, **Kapnek 209**, **Rock 297**
Delaware: Jackman 459
Maryland: **International 911**
Pennsylvania: Pilgrim 1907
Virginia: **America's 2093**, **Salvation 2144**
Washington: **World 2208**

INDEX TO GRANTS BY SUBJECT

For each subject term, grants are listed first by grantmaker entry number, then by grant number within the grantmaker entry. When known, type of support is also included. For a general subject index to the international activities of the grantmakers in this volume, see the Index to Grantmakers by Subject.

Abortion clinics/services, economically disadvantaged, 172-60, 172-106, 271-77, 271-78, 271-79, 271-123, 271-164, 271-165, 782-20, 788-93, 788-108, 1391-467, 1391-469, 1391-605, 1594-19
Abortion clinics/services, girls, 1391-469
Abortion clinics/services, indigenous peoples, 1391-605
Abortion clinics/services, program evaluation, 271-78
Abortion clinics/services, research, 271-123, 1391-605
Abortion clinics/services, technical assistance, 271-77, 1391-469, 1391-605
Abortion clinics/services, women, 172-60, 172-106, 271-77, 271-78, 271-79, 271-123, 271-130, 271-164, 271-165, 782-14, 782-20, 788-93, 788-108, 1391-150, 1391-171, 1391-467, 1391-469, 1391-605, 1594-19
Abortion clinics/services, youth, 271-123
Abuse prevention, AIDS, people with, 1391-385, 1391-387
Abuse prevention, awards/prizes/competitions, 1916-5
Abuse prevention, boys, 709-103
Abuse prevention, children/youth, 271-134, 1585-16, 1585-22
Abuse prevention, conferences/seminars, 1391-237
Abuse prevention, economically disadvantaged, 708-11, 1030-27, 1391-385, 1391-387, 1391-501, 1391-727, 1585-24, 1916-5
Abuse prevention, film/video/radio, 1393-121, 1585-22
Abuse prevention, girls, 708-11, 709-103, 1391-385, 1391-387, 1585-2
Abuse prevention, immigrants/refugees, 1585-16
Abuse prevention, indigenous peoples, 1391-501
Abuse prevention, LGBTQ, 1030-27
Abuse prevention, management development/capacity building, 271-134, 1030-27
Abuse prevention, migrant workers, 1391-195
Abuse prevention, military/veterans, 1393-30
Abuse prevention, minorities, 1585-16
Abuse prevention, offenders/ex-offenders, 1393-130
Abuse prevention, research, 788-137, 1391-195, 1391-387, 1393-30, 1393-130
Abuse prevention, technical assistance, 1391-387
Abuse prevention, women, 271-134, 708-11, 709-103, 1030-27, 1058-84, 1391-195, 1391-237, 1391-387, 1391-501, 1391-598, 1391-727, 1393-181, 1585-2, 1585-16, 1585-22, 1585-24
Abuse prevention, youth, 1391-237
Accessibility/universal design, 934-34, 1922-1, 1922-2, 1922-3, 1922-4, 1922-5, 1922-6, 1922-7, 1922-8, 1922-9, 1922-10, 1926-2
Accessibility/universal design, children/youth, 934-34, 1922-1, 1922-2, 1922-3, 1922-4, 1922-5, 1922-6, 1922-7, 1922-8, 1922-9, 1922-10, 1926-2
Accessibility/universal design, disabilities, people with, 934-34, 1922-1, 1922-2, 1922-3, 1922-4, 1922-5, 1922-6, 1922-7, 1922-8, 1922-9, 1922-10, 1926-2
Accessibility/universal design, military/veterans, 1926-2

Adoption, conferences/seminars, 1050-19, 1082-8
Adoption, economically disadvantaged, 132-15, 1050-19, 1082-8, 1082-12, 1832-3, 1961-1, 2078-5
Adoption, homeless, 1832-3
Adoption, research, 1050-19
Adoption, seed money, 1082-12
Adult education—literacy, basic skills & GED, 172-68, 271-7, 323-113, 499-4, 499-15, 499-34, 660-123, 709-89, 1021-37, 1021-76, 1128-52, 2203-37
Adult education—literacy, children, 499-15
Adult education—literacy, children/youth, 499-4
Adult education—literacy, curriculum development, 271-7
Adult education—literacy, economically disadvantaged, 172-68, 499-15, 499-34, 1021-37
Adult education—literacy, homeless, 323-113
Adult education—literacy, men, 660-123
Adult education—literacy, program evaluation, 172-68
Adult education—literacy, women, 271-7, 499-34
Adult education—literacy, youth, 1021-76
Adult/continuing education, 132-11, 172-16, 1082-17, 1328-118, 1328-119, 1391-565
Adult/continuing education, economically disadvantaged, 172-16, 1328-119
Adult/continuing education, emergency funds, 172-16
Adult/continuing education, indigenous peoples, 172-16
Adult/continuing education, publication, 1391-565
Adult/continuing education, seed money, 1391-565
Adult/continuing education, women, 1082-17
Adult/continuing education, youth, 172-16
Afghanistan, arts/culture/humanities, 97-8, 135-15, 271-155, 439-1, 439-49, 735-6
Afghanistan, civil rights, 323-90, 323-91, 1578-187
Afghanistan, community improvement/development, 1423-29, 1423-54, 1423-55, 1980-1
Afghanistan, crime/courts/legal services, 1393-148, 1593-81
Afghanistan, education, 323-90, 323-91, 1393-163, 1423-29, 1423-54, 1423-55, 1593-81, 2199-17
Afghanistan, environment, 1531-32
Afghanistan, health—general, 309-4, 1393-148, 2170-403, 2170-404, 2170-405, 2170-516, 2170-517, 2170-518, 2170-519
Afghanistan, health—specific diseases, 2170-403, 2170-404, 2170-405
Afghanistan, human services—multipurpose, 309-4
Afghanistan, international affairs/development, 135-15, 148-12, 172-69, 271-155, 323-91, 325-8, 413-75, 439-1, 439-6, 439-19, 439-24, 439-43, 439-46, 439-49, 463-9, 463-10, 646-18, 735-6, 1312-2, 1312-21, 1312-68, 1393-148, 1393-153, 1393-163, 1423-29, 1423-54, 1423-55, 1531-32, 1578-187, 1593-25, 1593-72, 1593-81, 1593-106, 1638-30, 1638-83, 1980-1, 2170-403, 2170-404, 2170-405, 2170-516, 2170-517, 2170-518, 2170-519, 2199-17
Afghanistan, medical research, 2170-516, 2170-517, 2170-518, 2170-519
Afghanistan, public affairs/government, 148-12, 439-1, 646-18
Afghanistan, religion, 97-8, 439-1, 1531-32

Afghanistan, social sciences, 439-6, 439-49, 1312-2, 1312-21, 1312-68, 1593-25, 1593-81
Africa, animals/wildlife, 742-1, 744-16, 744-35, 1030-17, 1214-4, 1360-1, 1578-150, 1659-1, 2199-29
Africa, arts/culture/humanities, 97-41, 172-95, 172-125, 251-52, 309-60, 744-47, 787-5, 1030-25, 1312-1, 1330-7, 1330-10, 1391-19, 1391-23, 1391-67, 1391-133, 1391-361, 1531-17, 1546-117, 1546-125, 1639-134, 1639-135, 2061-9, 2170-31, 2170-349, 2170-396
Africa, civil rights, 271-119, 271-161, 271-166, 562-4, 788-114, 891-35, 1030-3, 1030-8, 1030-9, 1030-15, 1030-24, 1030-25, 1030-49, 1030-53, 1030-54, 1058-84, 1361-18, 1391-20, 1391-23, 1391-24, 1391-430, 1391-467, 1391-773, 1639-206, 1702-14, 2170-119
Africa, community improvement/development, 74-4, 142-20, 172-91, 309-57, 309-69, 323-220, 323-261, 323-378, 323-379, 323-380, 347-12, 466-1, 709-2, 709-3, 735-11, 744-2, 855-3, 1030-49, 1050-2, 1128-1, 1128-2, 1179-4, 1184-1, 1328-4, 1328-28, 1328-118, 1360-2, 1391-16, 1391-188, 1391-463, 1391-576, 1391-720, 1391-780, 1578-3, 1603-9, 1639-54, 1639-64, 1639-112, 1639-115, 1639-133, 1639-155, 1639-167, 1639-198, 1639-211, 1790-13, 1916-87, 2170-64, 2170-166, 2170-179, 2170-287, 2170-342, 2170-374, 2199-48
Africa, crime/courts/legal services, 562-4, 788-8, 788-115, 788-136, 1058-84, 1391-233, 1391-415, 1391-750, 1393-152
Africa, education, 21-12, 135-1, 166-1, 172-95, 172-125, 172-134, 172-139, 178-36, 323-5, 323-12, 323-62, 347-1, 435-31, 499-5, 499-7, 499-12, 499-13, 626-23, 660-268, 744-56, 788-8, 820-10, 891-35, 1050-2, 1050-6, 1058-168, 1082-1, 1312-33, 1312-36, 1312-38, 1312-43, 1312-46, 1312-74, 1312-83, 1312-86, 1312-88, 1312-91, 1328-118, 1391-89, 1391-178, 1391-564, 1391-634, 1391-676, 1391-720, 1391-763, 1393-59, 1531-17, 1546-125, 1575-1, 1639-67, 1639-164, 1639-201, 1847-57, 2000-1, 2170-164
Africa, employment, 788-9, 1328-61, 1353-8, 1639-133, 1639-211
Africa, environment, 97-41, 172-2, 172-3, 251-38, 323-35, 1058-79, 1082-18, 1328-13, 1391-576, 1393-21, 1546-125, 1639-6, 1639-54, 1639-65, 1639-155, 1639-167, 1639-186, 1639-198, 1639-209, 2170-124, 2170-166, 2170-179
Africa, food/nutrition/agriculture, 172-86, 744-30, 744-50, 1092-47, 1391-463, 1391-634, 1639-6, 1639-8, 1639-65, 1639-112, 1639-155, 1639-164, 1847-57, 2170-11, 2170-64, 2170-124, 2170-130, 2170-139, 2170-164, 2170-194, 2170-287
Africa, health—general, 172-4, 172-100, 172-102, 178-36, 271-119, 271-130, 271-161, 271-166, 302-7, 323-121, 323-123, 323-124, 323-332, 435-4, 503-4, 503-6, 503-7, 735-14, 744-51,

Arts/culture/humanities, Kenya, 97-63, 153-31, 787-5, 1312-1, 1391-23, 1391-66, 1391-90, 1391-131, 1391-368, 1391-518, 1391-522, 1391-599, 1391-653, 1391-713, 1391-783, 1639-138, 2170-181

Arts/culture/humanities, Kosovo, 1638-55

Arts/culture/humanities, Kyrgyzstan, 97-4, 97-13, 97-20, 97-21, 97-22, 97-64, 97-85, 97-97, 97-98, 97-104, 97-109

Arts/culture/humanities, Laos, 1393-64

Arts/culture/humanities, Latin America, 153-1, 153-5, 153-6, 153-7, 238-59, 309-64, 467-95, 1039-6, 1330-8, 1353-11, 1391-164, 1391-309, 1391-325, 1391-740, 1393-12, 1546-75, 1546-104, 1594-4, 1594-32, 1594-39, 2210-5

Arts/culture/humanities, Lebanon, 153-9, 660-129, 1391-71, 1391-669, 1393-119

Arts/culture/humanities, Lesotho, 1050-27

Arts/culture/humanities, Libya, 153-18

Arts/culture/humanities, Madagascar, 660-191

Arts/culture/humanities, Malawi, 2170-545

Arts/culture/humanities, Maldives, 1391-25

Arts/culture/humanities, Mali, 2170-545

Arts/culture/humanities, Mexico, 97-24, 97-39, 97-53, 97-83, 153-23, 172-119, 413-7, 413-31, 855-1, 855-6, 1241-20, 1353-14, 1353-29, 1391-196, 1391-202, 1391-241, 1391-274, 1391-275, 1391-315, 1391-629, 1391-714, 1393-22, 1638-72, 1853-42, 2046-1, 2046-2, 2210-5

Arts/culture/humanities, Middle East, 216-19, 439-2, 626-14, 626-20, 701-21, 814-15, 860-37, 967-7, 967-15, 984-5, 987-9, 987-13, 987-17, 1030-22, 1039-26, 1160-26, 1330-10, 1347-25, 1391-62, 1391-71, 1391-813, 1393-119, 1546-101, 1546-126, 1546-129, 1638-2, 1660-8, 1675-11, 1830-39, 2098-13, 2212-49, 2212-60

Arts/culture/humanities, Montenegro, 1638-1

Arts/culture/humanities, Morocco and the Western Sahara, 153-32

Arts/culture/humanities, Mozambique, 1391-560, 2170-181

Arts/culture/humanities, Netherlands, 153-24, 153-25, 739-11, 788-182, 788-183, 1093-15, 1391-686, 1490-8, 1546-78, 2170-388

Arts/culture/humanities, New Zealand, 97-49, 660-275, 1546-47, 1546-48

Arts/culture/humanities, Nicaragua, 1391-609, 1391-767

Arts/culture/humanities, Nigeria, 153-31, 1391-70, 1391-240, 1391-249, 1391-270, 1578-135, 2170-181

Arts/culture/humanities, North Africa, 626-14, 626-20, 814-15, 1030-22, 1391-71, 1391-813, 1393-119, 1546-101, 1546-126, 1546-129, 2098-13, 2212-60

Arts/culture/humanities, North Korea, 1397-23

Arts/culture/humanities, Norway, 1916-101

Arts/culture/humanities, Oceania, 105-43, 1391-294, 1397-3, 1546-77

Arts/culture/humanities, Pakistan, 439-1, 439-49, 1490-1, 1531-31, 1638-134

Arts/culture/humanities, Panama, 630-3

Arts/culture/humanities, Papua New Guinea, 97-7, 97-91, 97-101, 97-106

Arts/culture/humanities, Paraguay, 153-8

Arts/culture/humanities, Peru, 153-26, 562-17, 626-8, 824-9, 1391-393

Arts/culture/humanities, Philippines, 335-1

Arts/culture/humanities, Poland, 216-21, 216-30, 216-32, 709-56, 1624-29, 1659-17

Arts/culture/humanities, Portugal, 153-10, 1546-86, 1916-95

Arts/culture/humanities, Romania, 272-11, 1822-10

Arts/culture/humanities, Russia, 97-99, 105-5, 335-6, 693-47, 693-55, 788-62, 788-67, 788-103, 788-221, 1039-27, 1058-80, 1330-3, 1393-26, 1546-25, 1916-89

Arts/culture/humanities, Rwanda, 105-3, 323-73, 1916-44, 1916-90

Arts/culture/humanities, Scotland, 323-369, 1021-62, 1039-25, 1039-31, 1330-12, 1509-3, 1509-17, 1916-36, 1916-105, 1916-110

Arts/culture/humanities, Senegal, 172-14, 2170-316

Arts/culture/humanities, Serbia, 1638-14, 1638-23, 1638-91

Arts/culture/humanities, Sierra Leone, 105-2, 105-20

Arts/culture/humanities, Slovakia, 1486-3, 1916-54

Arts/culture/humanities, Solomon Islands, 97-106

Arts/culture/humanities, South Africa, 153-11, 153-31, 172-125, 1030-7, 1030-25, 1058-11, 1058-78, 1058-152, 1391-118, 1391-517, 1391-534, 1391-560, 1391-664, 1391-757, 1546-68, 1546-98, 1546-99, 1546-117, 1847-34, 1847-35, 2170-181, 2170-349

Arts/culture/humanities, South America, 97-41, 1058-110, 1391-92, 1391-252, 1531-17

Arts/culture/humanities, South Asia, 1312-65, 1393-50

Arts/culture/humanities, South Korea, 1397-23

Arts/culture/humanities, Southeast Asia, 2-2, 1036-4, 1531-18, 1531-35, 1578-79, 1593-15, 1593-75, 1943-2

Arts/culture/humanities, Southern Africa, 153-11

Arts/culture/humanities, Spain, 153-22, 1039-6, 1546-86, 1853-65, 1916-95

Arts/culture/humanities, Sub-Saharan Africa, 1030-7, 2170-316, 2170-396

Arts/culture/humanities, Sudan, 272-9, 272-14, 1593-123

Arts/culture/humanities, Suriname, 1853-143

Arts/culture/humanities, Sweden, 1391-689, 1546-80, 1546-81

Arts/culture/humanities, Switzerland, 788-190, 824-11, 1093-14, 1093-39, 1093-87, 1391-62, 1490-1, 1546-126, 1890-3, 1890-4, 1890-5, 1890-6

Arts/culture/humanities, Taiwan, 737-2

Arts/culture/humanities, Tajikistan, 97-4, 97-8, 97-22, 97-31, 97-38, 97-81, 97-89, 97-100, 97-109

Arts/culture/humanities, Tanzania, Zanzibar and Pemba, 499-9, 2170-545

Arts/culture/humanities, Thailand, 1531-28, 1639-10, 1639-43

Arts/culture/humanities, Tunisia, 1490-41

Arts/culture/humanities, Turkey, 97-45, 323-371, 439-1, 1488-3, 1490-18, 1490-29, 1490-39, 1490-40, 1490-41, 1916-3, 1916-91

Arts/culture/humanities, Uganda, 105-11, 323-211, 323-212, 2170-181, 2170-545

Arts/culture/humanities, Ukraine, 272-15, 660-29, 987-3, 1422-5, 1567-11

Arts/culture/humanities, United Kingdom, 142-15, 1328-201, 1702-9, 1916-40

Arts/culture/humanities, Uruguay, 1058-110, 1490-7

Arts/culture/humanities, Vanuatu, 97-35, 97-106

Arts/culture/humanities, Vatican City, 1916-71, 1916-72

Arts/culture/humanities, Vietnam, 172-143, 1391-10, 1391-281, 1397-42

Arts/culture/humanities, Wales, 1546-50, 2170-396

Arts/culture/humanities, West Bank/Gaza (Palestinian Territories), 1330-11, 1347-25, 1391-36, 1391-37, 1391-121, 1391-122, 1391-329, 1391-588, 1391-643, 1391-658, 1393-48

Arts/culture/humanities, Western Africa, 1391-128, 2170-316

Arts/culture/humanities, Yugoslavia (Former), 1330-3

Arts/culture/humanities, Zambia, 153-31, 2170-181

Arts/culture/humanities, Zimbabwe, 1391-560

Asia, animals/wildlife, 135-43, 271-156, 693-42, 1030-17, 1214-4, 1578-150, 2199-71

Asia, arts/culture/humanities, 97-41, 323-41, 323-42, 439-2, 626-25, 987-20, 1391-294, 1397-1, 1397-3, 1397-9, 1397-27, 1397-31, 1397-37, 1397-63, 1397-65, 1494-3, 1531-6, 1531-17, 1531-39, 1531-40, 1531-43, 1578-32, 1578-33, 1578-34, 1578-124, 1578-167, 1638-10, 1639-134, 1672-2, 1721-1, 1814-2

Asia, civil rights, 271-161, 987-3, 1030-6, 1030-10, 1391-473, 1391-736, 1393-96, 2170-119

Asia, community improvement/development, 142-20, 309-57, 323-378, 323-379, 323-380, 347-12, 413-25, 1179-4, 1328-153, 1391-780, 1639-54, 1639-73, 1639-85, 1639-88, 1639-98, 1790-13, 1847-28, 2170-64, 2170-166, 2199-48

Asia, crime/courts/legal services, 562-4, 1391-74, 1393-60

Asia, education, 17-3, 100-9, 626-23, 1058-12, 1093-3, 1312-41, 1312-83, 1328-115, 1328-116, 1397-1, 1397-4, 1397-7, 1397-9, 1397-11, 1397-12, 1397-21, 1397-32, 1397-36, 1397-38, 1397-39, 1397-41, 1397-43, 1397-44, 1397-47, 1397-48, 1397-49, 1397-50, 1397-51, 1397-52, 1397-53, 1397-54, 1397-55, 1397-56, 1397-57, 1397-58, 1397-59, 1397-60, 1397-61, 1397-66, 1397-67, 1423-14, 1531-3, 1531-17, 1531-34, 1923-3

Asia, employment, 1353-8

Asia, environment, 97-41, 172-87, 271-56, 271-135, 322-3, 323-35, 693-42, 1058-79, 1058-131, 1328-13, 1391-294, 1393-60, 1531-20, 1531-32, 1639-15, 1639-54, 1639-73, 1639-85, 1639-88, 1639-149, 2170-166, 2170-199, 2199-71

Asia, food/nutrition/agriculture, 2170-64, 2170-138, 2170-139

Asia, health—general, 271-117, 271-130, 271-161, 323-332, 335-26, 737-3, 1093-3, 1148-2, 1303-6, 1391-445, 1391-736, 1639-106, 1639-136, 2170-20, 2170-41, 2170-119, 2170-138, 2170-139, 2170-166, 2170-191, 2170-261, 2170-282, 2170-334, 2170-397, 2170-409, 2170-410, 2170-509

Asia, health—specific diseases, 335-8, 335-9, 335-10, 335-26, 737-3, 1303-6, 1391-445

Asia, human services—multipurpose, 17-3, 335-9, 335-10, 1328-115, 1328-116

Asia, international affairs/development, 17-3, 37-9, 100-9, 119-2, 142-20, 172-33, 172-55, 172-87, 242-1, 271-56, 286-1, 309-57, 323-40, 323-41, 323-42, 323-149, 323-150, 323-151, 323-152, 323-153, 323-154, 323-378, 323-379, 323-380, 335-8, 335-9, 335-10, 335-62, 347-12, 413-25, 439-2, 439-18, 447-11, 562-4, 709-1, 709-71, 734-9, 737-3, 748-11, 748-12, 748-13, 748-14, 748-15, 748-16, 748-17, 748-18, 748-19, 748-20, 748-21, 748-22, 748-23, 748-24, 748-25, 748-26, 748-27, 748-28, 748-29, 748-30, 788-102, 860-2, 860-27, 960-3, 987-20, 1030-6, 1030-10, 1058-12, 1058-43, 1058-79, 1058-131, 1093-3, 1128-6, 1128-7, 1128-8, 1128-13, 1128-14, 1148-2, 1179-4, 1179-30, 1179-31, 1179-32, 1179-33, 1179-34, 1179-35, 1179-36, 1179-37, 1179-38, 1179-39, 1179-40, 1179-41, 1179-42, 1179-43, 1179-44, 1179-45, 1179-46, 1179-47, 1179-48, 1179-49, 1179-50, 1179-51, 1179-52, 1179-53, 1179-54, 1179-55, 1179-56, 1179-57, 1179-58, 1179-59, 1179-60, 1179-61, 1179-62, 1179-63, 1179-64, 1179-65, 1179-66, 1179-67, 1179-68, 1179-69, 1179-70, 1179-71, 1179-72, 1179-73, 1179-74, 1179-75, 1179-76, 1179-77, 1179-78, 1179-79, 1179-80, 1179-81, 1179-82, 1179-83, 1179-84, 1179-85, 1179-86, 1179-87, 1179-88, 1179-89, 1179-90, 1179-91, 1179-92, 1179-93, 1179-94, 1179-95, 1179-96, 1179-97, 1241-9, 1312-26, 1312-41, 1312-73, 1312-75, 1312-83, 1328-13, 1328-153, 1391-74, 1391-254, 1391-286, 1391-294, 1391-322, 1391-420, 1391-445, 1391-448, 1391-473, 1391-780, 1393-60, 1397-1, 1397-3, 1397-4, 1397-5, 1397-9, 1397-21, 1397-27, 1397-30, 1397-31, 1397-32, 1397-37, 1397-38, 1397-44, 1397-57, 1397-60, 1397-63, 1397-65, 1397-66, 1397-67, 1423-14, 1494-3, 1531-5, 1531-6, 1531-7, 1531-17, 1531-30, 1531-32, 1546-111, 1578-32, 1578-33, 1578-34, 1578-167, 1593-25, 1606-1, 1638-10, 1639-15, 1639-54, 1639-73, 1639-85, 1639-88, 1639-98, 1639-106, 1639-134, 1639-136, 1639-149, 1721-1, 1790-13, 1814-2, 1847-28, 1923-3, 1980-17, 2170-20, 2170-41, 2170-64, 2170-119, 2170-138, 2170-139, 2170-166, 2170-191, 2170-199, 2170-252, 2170-261, 2170-270, 2170-282, 2170-334, 2170-397, 2170-409, 2170-410, 2170-509, 2195-5, 2195-6, 2195-7, 2199-48, 2202-3, 2212-51, 2212-52

Asia, medical research, 1916-69, 2170-41, 2170-191, 2170-261, 2170-397, 2170-409

Asia, mental health/substance abuse, 737-3

Asia, philanthropy/voluntarism, 37-9, 323-149, 323-150, 323-151, 447-11, 748-11, 748-12, 748-13, 748-14, 748-15, 748-16, 748-17, 748-18,

748-19, 748-20, 748-21, 748-22, 748-23, 748-24, 748-25, 748-26, 748-27, 748-28, 748-29, 748-30, 1179-30, 1179-31, 1179-32, 1179-33, 1179-34, 1179-35, 1179-36, 1179-37, 1179-38, 1179-39, 1179-40, 1179-41, 1179-42, 1179-43, 1179-44, 1179-45, 1179-46, 1179-47, 1179-48, 1179-49, 1179-50, 1179-51, 1179-52, 1179-53, 1179-54, 1179-55, 1179-56, 1179-57, 1179-58, 1179-59, 1179-60, 1179-61, 1179-62, 1179-63, 1179-64, 1179-65, 1179-66, 1179-67, 1179-68, 1179-69, 1179-70, 1179-71, 1179-72, 1179-73, 1179-74, 1179-75, 1179-76, 1179-77, 1179-78, 1179-79, 1179-80, 1179-81, 1179-82, 1179-83, 1179-84, 1179-85, 1179-86, 1179-87, 1179-88, 1179-89, 1179-90, 1179-91, 1179-92, 1179-93, 1179-94, 1179-95, 1179-96, 1179-97, 1241-9, 1606-1, 1639-45, 1916-69, 1923-3, 2202-3

Asia, public affairs/government, 335-62, 562-4, 788-102, 1058-43, 1058-79, 1058-131, 1312-83, 1328-115, 1328-116, 1328-153, 1391-448, 1397-5, 1397-30, 1531-5, 1531-34, 1531-39, 1638-110, 1847-28

Asia, religion, 265-1, 286-1, 516-3, 626-25, 734-9, 860-2, 860-27, 860-47, 1312-75, 1531-32, 1774-13, 2061-22, 2061-23

Asia, safety/disaster relief, 863-4, 1639-15

Asia, science, 1916-69

Asia, social sciences, 439-18, 709-71, 1312-26, 1312-73, 1312-75, 1391-74, 1391-83, 1391-286, 1391-448, 1391-736, 1397-1, 1397-3, 1397-4, 1397-5, 1397-7, 1397-11, 1397-12, 1397-21, 1397-32, 1397-36, 1397-38, 1397-39, 1397-41, 1397-43, 1397-47, 1397-48, 1397-49, 1397-50, 1397-51, 1397-52, 1397-53, 1397-54, 1397-55, 1397-56, 1397-57, 1397-58, 1397-59, 1397-60, 1397-61, 1397-66, 1397-67, 1531-3, 1531-5, 1531-7, 1531-8, 1531-20, 1531-34, 1531-39, 1531-40, 1531-43, 1546-111, 1546-127, 1593-25, 1639-45, 1672-2, 1916-69, 2170-252, 2170-270, 2195-5, 2195-6, 2195-7, 2212-51, 2212-52

Asia, youth development, 119-2, 172-55, 323-152, 323-153, 323-154, 1058-12, 2170-64

Asians/Pacific Islanders, arts/culture/humanities, 309-26, 709-72, 934-59, 1391-10, 1391-200, 1391-281, 1391-437, 1391-580, 1391-781, 1393-50, 1397-1, 1397-9, 1578-80, 1593-94

Asians/Pacific Islanders, civil rights, 1391-580, 1393-50

Asians/Pacific Islanders, community improvement/development, 1393-50

Asians/Pacific Islanders, crime/courts/legal services, 1081-12

Asians/Pacific Islanders, education, 286-10, 1397-1, 1397-6, 1397-9

Asians/Pacific Islanders, employment, 1081-12, 1578-163

Asians/Pacific Islanders, environment, 1391-10, 1391-243, 1391-280, 1391-281, 1391-554

Asians/Pacific Islanders, food/nutrition/agriculture, 135-40

Asians/Pacific Islanders, health—general, 1391-10, 1391-243, 1391-280, 1391-281, 1391-554

Asians/Pacific Islanders, health—specific diseases, 1391-554

Asians/Pacific Islanders, human services—multipurpose, 309-15, 323-61, 1081-12, 1213-4

Asians/Pacific Islanders, international affairs/development, 135-40, 286-10, 309-15, 323-61, 863-1, 934-59, 1391-10, 1391-73, 1391-200, 1391-243, 1391-280, 1391-281, 1391-437, 1391-554, 1391-781, 1393-50, 1397-1, 1397-9

Asians/Pacific Islanders, public affairs/government, 1391-781

Asians/Pacific Islanders, safety/disaster relief, 863-1

Asians/Pacific Islanders, social sciences, 1391-243, 1397-1, 1397-6, 1531-14

Asians/Pacific Islanders, youth development, 1081-12

Assistive technology, 443-13, 814-27, 1021-6, 1021-14, 1303-39, 2203-29

Assistive technology, children/youth, 443-13, 814-27, 1021-14

Assistive technology, disabilities, people with, 443-13, 814-27, 1021-6, 1021-14, 1303-39

Assistive technology, economically disadvantaged, 1303-39

Assistive technology, equipment, 814-27, 1021-6

Assistive technology, physically disabled, 2203-29

Astronomy, 211-2, 338-1, 1916-4, 1916-66, 1916-67

Astronomy, research, 338-1, 1916-66, 1916-67

Athletics/sports, AIDS, people with, 735-2

Athletics/sports, amateur competition, 154-36, 860-52

Athletics/sports, amateur leagues, 734-4, 892-5, 1093-71, 1839-38, 1839-39, 1839-42, 1839-97, 1847-6, 1847-38, 1847-42, 1853-48, 1853-80

Athletics/sports, awards/prizes/competitions, 1847-6

Athletics/sports, baseball, 1853-35

Athletics/sports, basketball, 1665-7

Athletics/sports, boys, 1847-30, 1853-34

Athletics/sports, building/renovation, 1822-14, 1853-35, 1853-58, 1853-131

Athletics/sports, children/youth, 154-9, 616-11, 693-9, 734-4, 735-2, 756-23, 892-5, 1093-74, 1167-11, 1534-8, 1665-7, 1822-14, 1853-35, 1853-80, 1853-98

Athletics/sports, disabilities, people with, 616-11, 709-18, 814-24

Athletics/sports, economically disadvantaged, 21-4, 756-23, 892-5, 1021-94, 1093-71, 1167-11, 1391-531, 1665-7, 1847-6, 1847-34, 1847-35, 1847-38, 1847-42, 1853-34

Athletics/sports, electronic media/online services, 1847-34, 1847-35

Athletics/sports, equestrianism, 616-11, 709-18, 814-24

Athletics/sports, fellowships, 1847-42

Athletics/sports, fishing/hunting, 238-27, 1058-93

Athletics/sports, football, 323-144

Athletics/sports, girls, 154-33, 154-34, 1391-531, 1839-75, 1847-34, 1847-35, 1847-38, 1847-42

Athletics/sports, income development, 1093-71

Athletics/sports, indigenous peoples, 1853-34

Athletics/sports, minorities, 756-23, 1167-11

Athletics/sports, Native Americans/American Indians, 1058-93

Athletics/sports, physically disabled, 435-39

Athletics/sports, professional leagues, 2161-1

Athletics/sports, publication, 1058-93, 1058-94

Athletics/sports, racquet sports, 154-9, 154-33, 154-34, 756-23, 1167-11, 1847-30

Athletics/sports, research, 1058-93, 1058-94, 1847-30, 1847-38

Athletics/sports, school programs, 1822-14, 1839-75, 1853-80, 1853-98

Athletics/sports, seed money, 1847-38

Athletics/sports, soccer, 21-4, 735-2, 1021-94, 1093-74, 1391-531, 1534-8, 1839-40, 1847-34, 1847-35, 1853-34, 1853-131

Athletics/sports, Special Olympics, 616-40, 693-53, 693-54, 1578-168

Athletics/sports, training, 435-39, 693-9, 1603-7, 1927-3

Athletics/sports, water sports, 323-146, 1051-1, 1058-94, 1853-58

Athletics/sports, women, 1847-6

Athletics/sports, youth, 1021-94

Australia, animals/wildlife, 271-168, 435-33, 628-1

Australia, arts/culture/humanities, 97-1, 97-19, 97-61, 97-75, 97-116, 272-16, 307-28, 1391-294, 1546-77, 1916-7

Australia, civil rights, 97-77, 335-49

Australia, community improvement/development, 97-47, 271-90, 1051-7, 1241-4, 1328-143, 1391-578, 1639-85, 1853-74, 1853-75, 1853-76

Australia, crime/courts/legal services, 335-49, 788-73

Australia, education, 45-3, 97-59, 323-45, 323-51, 788-198, 1021-25, 1186-17, 1186-18, 1328-192, 1391-530, 1853-2, 1853-34, 1916-7

Australia, employment, 709-31, 1021-58

Australia, environment, 97-6, 97-10, 97-115, 251-51, 271-90, 271-168, 435-33, 628-1, 693-40, 709-23, 788-73, 788-198, 1391-294, 1546-58, 1546-59, 1639-85, 1713-5, 1853-2, 1853-73, 1853-74, 1853-75, 1853-76

Australia, food/nutrition/agriculture, 788-199, 1021-40, 1051-7, 2170-194, 2170-464

Australia, health—general, 335-49, 735-23, 1303-56, 1303-59, 2170-26, 2170-251, 2170-260, 2170-272, 2170-273, 2170-274, 2170-276, 2170-340, 2170-341, 2170-352, 2170-411, 2170-465, 2170-478, 2170-503

Australia, health—specific diseases, 335-49, 443-2, 1303-59, 2170-251, 2170-411

Australia, human services—multipurpose, 97-61, 323-338, 443-2, 709-12, 709-31, 709-113, 1021-10, 1021-25, 1021-47, 1021-58, 1021-89, 1328-143, 1328-176, 1853-24, 1989-3, 1989-4, 2029-4

Australia, international affairs/development, 97-1, 97-6, 413-26, 413-27, 788-199, 1021-4, 1037-1, 1037-2, 1128-6, 1128-7, 1128-8, 1186-2, 1186-3, 1328-143, 1328-176, 1328-192, 1391-294, 1639-85, 1853-2, 2170-26, 2170-194, 2170-251, 2170-260, 2170-272, 2170-273, 2170-274, 2170-276, 2170-341, 2170-352, 2170-411, 2170-422, 2170-464, 2170-465, 2170-478, 2170-503

Australia, medical research, 443-3, 1303-56, 1751-11, 2170-26, 2170-272, 2170-273, 2170-274, 2170-276, 2170-340, 2170-341, 2170-352, 2170-422, 2170-465, 2170-478, 2170-503

Australia, mental health/substance abuse, 323-51, 443-1, 1021-10, 1021-64

Australia, philanthropy/voluntarism, 97-47, 693-15, 693-16, 693-17, 693-18, 1853-29

Australia, public affairs/government, 97-77, 323-110, 323-338, 1037-2, 1328-143, 1328-176, 1391-578, 1639-168

Australia, recreation/sports/athletics, 1021-64, 1853-34

Australia, religion, 467-71

Australia, safety/disaster relief, 709-12, 1021-4, 1989-3, 1989-4

Australia, science, 45-3, 323-346, 1186-17, 1186-18, 1546-58, 1546-59, 1546-77, 1713-5, 1853-2, 2170-352, 2170-464

Australia, social sciences, 788-199, 1391-95, 1546-77, 1639-168, 1916-7

Australia, youth development, 1328-176, 1391-95, 1853-34

Austria, animals/wildlife, 271-168

Austria, arts/culture/humanities, 97-1, 97-90, 153-16, 824-13, 1546-55, 1916-56, 1916-57

Austria, civil rights, 413-38

Austria, education, 660-125, 660-192, 1093-2, 1546-6, 1578-14, 2212-39

Austria, environment, 271-168, 1546-55, 1546-105

Austria, health—general, 1093-2

Austria, health—specific diseases, 1393-2

Austria, human services—multipurpose, 413-15, 1393-2

Austria, international affairs/development, 97-1, 97-90, 413-15, 413-38, 1093-2, 1486-8

Austria, public affairs/government, 2212-39

Austria, religion, 1578-15

Austria, science, 1546-55, 1546-105, 1916-56, 1916-57

Austria, social sciences, 660-125, 2212-39

Austria, youth development, 413-38

Autism, 135-37, 443-2, 709-13, 709-109, 934-75, 1822-12

Autism research, 1656-10, 1656-11, 1656-12, 1660-26

Autism research, conferences/seminars, 1656-10

Autism research, mentally disabled, 1656-10, 1656-11, 1656-12, 1660-26

Autism, children, 135-37

Autism, children/youth, 934-75, 1822-12

Autism, equipment, 1822-12

Autism, mentally disabled, 135-37, 443-2, 709-13, 709-109, 934-75, 1822-12

Azerbaijan, civil rights, 1312-53

Azerbaijan, community improvement/development, 1312-23

Azerbaijan, education, 1312-53, 1593-16

Azerbaijan, human services—multipurpose, 1082-19

Azerbaijan, international affairs/development, 439-28, 1058-86, 1082-19, 1312-23, 1312-53

Azerbaijan, public affairs/government, 1058-86

Bahamas, animals/wildlife, 1578-36, 1578-37, 1578-38

860-51, 860-52, 860-53, 1036-2, 1036-6, 1036-8,
1036-10, 1039-12, 1039-26, 1112-2, 1136-6,
1148-1, 1179-260, 1186-19, 1241-24, 1393-43,
1531-16, 1771-1, 1774-1, 1774-2, 1774-3,
1774-4, 1774-5, 1774-6, 1774-7, 1774-8, 1774-9,
1774-10, 1774-11, 1774-12, 1774-13, 1774-14,
1809-1, 1809-2, 1809-3, 1839-109, 1916-6,
1916-17, 1916-27, 1916-93, 1926-9, 1943-4,
1961-1, 1961-3, 1961-4, 1980-9, 1980-18,
1989-24, 1992-4, 1992-5, 2029-6, 2061-1,
2061-5, 2061-6, 2061-8, 2061-9, 2061-10,
2061-11, 2061-13, 2061-14, 2061-15, 2061-16,
2061-18, 2061-19, 2061-20, 2061-24, 2061-25,
2061-26, 2067-1, 2098-1, 2098-2, 2098-5,
2098-6, 2098-7, 2098-8, 2098-9, 2098-12,
2098-13, 2098-15, 2199-1, 2199-2, 2199-79,
2199-90, 2199-110, 2199-112, 2199-113,
2203-2, 2203-3, 2203-4, 2203-6, 2203-7, 2203-9,
2203-12, 2203-17, 2203-18, 2203-19, 2203-25,
2203-26, 2203-27, 2203-28, 2203-31, 2203-35,
2203-36, 2203-38, 2203-41, 2203-42, 2203-43,
2203-45, 2203-47, 2203-48, 2203-49, 2212-20,
2212-35, 2212-60
Christian agencies & churches, AIDS, people with,
860-7
Christian agencies & churches, building/renovation,
323-134, 626-12, 2203-36
Christian agencies & churches, children/youth, 286-11,
323-399, 626-7, 798-68, 860-7, 860-14, 860-21,
860-26, 860-35, 860-44, 860-49, 1036-10,
1179-260, 1186-19, 1916-93, 1926-9, 1961-1,
2098-7, 2098-12, 2199-90, 2199-112, 2199-113,
2203-3
Christian agencies & churches, computer technology,
626-6
Christian agencies & churches, conferences/seminars,
626-13, 1039-12, 2061-5, 2203-12, 2203-48
Christian agencies & churches, crime/abuse victims,
91-25, 455-1, 860-7, 860-30, 1036-8, 2203-2,
2203-25, 2203-26
Christian agencies & churches, curriculum
development, 626-20, 1916-93
Christian agencies & churches, deaf/hearing impaired,
860-15
Christian agencies & churches, disabilities, people with,
860-14, 2203-17
Christian agencies & churches, economically
disadvantaged, 135-20, 286-11, 307-5, 323-399,
413-72, 413-73, 413-74, 516-8, 626-6, 709-129,
734-7, 734-9, 798-68, 829-5, 860-7, 860-12,
860-13, 860-14, 860-21, 860-22, 860-23, 860-41,
860-44, 860-45, 860-47, 860-48, 860-49,
1036-10, 1179-260, 1186-19, 1241-24, 1393-43,
1771-1, 1774-1, 1774-7, 1774-8, 1774-11,
1839-109, 1926-9, 1943-4, 1961-1, 1980-9,
1989-24, 2029-6, 2061-8, 2061-18, 2067-1,
2098-8, 2098-9, 2098-12, 2199-90, 2199-110,
2199-112, 2199-113, 2203-17
Christian agencies & churches, equipment, 626-4,
1926-9
Christian agencies & churches, faculty/staff
development, 626-2, 626-4, 626-13, 626-19
Christian agencies & churches, film/video/radio,
626-3, 626-4, 626-14, 626-20, 626-22, 1916-27,
1916-93
Christian agencies & churches, immigrants/refugees,
1393-43, 2067-1
Christian agencies & churches, indigenous peoples,
860-22, 1774-7
Christian agencies & churches, management
development/capacity building, 2203-38
Christian agencies & churches, minorities, 860-48,
1393-43, 2203-7
Christian agencies & churches, publication, 626-7,
1039-26
Christian agencies & churches, research, 1916-6
Christian agencies & churches, seed money, 626-8
Christian agencies & churches, student aid/financial
aid, 2203-28
Christian agencies & churches, substance abusers,
860-7
Christian agencies & churches, women, 2098-12,
2199-90, 2203-2
Christian agencies & churches, youth, 860-48, 1961-3

Circus arts, children/youth, 1093-39, 1347-32,
1347-33, 1428-57
Circus arts, disabilities, people with, 1347-32, 1347-33
Circus arts, youth, 271-28
Civil liberties, advocacy, 172-119, 216-20, 562-18,
562-23, 562-26, 562-33, 562-38, 562-39, 562-58,
562-60, 782-2, 782-9, 782-15, 788-40, 788-104,
788-40, 788-104, 891-9, 891-21, 934-35, 934-36,
1039-2, 1347-5, 1347-6, 1347-11, 1391-62,
1391-154, 1393-4, 1393-11, 1393-75, 1393-91,
1393-133, 1393-134, 1393-138, 1393-140,
1593-28, 1593-29, 1593-40, 1593-100,
1593-103, 1594-25, 1916-2
Civil liberties, African Americans/Blacks, 1391-580
Civil liberties, Asians/Pacific Islanders, 1391-580
Civil liberties, awards/prizes/competitions, 1039-2,
1853-9
Civil liberties, children/youth, 562-23, 782-2, 1039-2,
1347-11
Civil liberties, conferences/seminars, 1347-5, 1347-6,
1391-116, 1391-223, 1393-62, 1393-140
Civil liberties, crime/abuse victims, 562-23, 782-2,
782-15, 1393-48, 1393-62, 1393-75
Civil liberties, disabilities, people with, 782-25
Civil liberties, due process, 788-68, 1347-17,
1391-277, 1391-705, 1393-62, 1593-41,
2199-35
Civil liberties, economically disadvantaged, 172-10,
172-23, 172-119, 562-18, 782-9, 782-15, 782-21,
891-21, 1347-5, 1347-6, 1347-11, 1391-62,
1391-562, 1391-665, 1391-705, 1393-62,
1393-171
Civil liberties, electronic media/online services,
1391-116, 1391-519, 1593-29
Civil liberties, film/video/radio, 788-123, 1916-2
Civil liberties, first amendment, 172-10, 309-64,
499-32, 537-6, 562-61, 788-123, 892-3,
1391-238, 1391-519, 1391-580, 1393-48,
1393-171, 1578-58, 1578-59, 1593-39, 1594-4,
1594-32
Civil liberties, freedom of information, 172-10, 172-23,
788-127, 1312-53, 1391-116, 1391-551,
1391-562, 1391-665, 1391-731, 1393-171
Civil liberties, freedom of religion, 860-28, 891-32,
896-23, 1037-3, 1578-31, 1853-9, 1911-11,
1916-43, 2203-19, 2212-35
Civil liberties, Hispanics/Latinos, 1391-580
Civil liberties, homeless, 782-15
Civil liberties, immigrants/refugees, 562-18, 562-23,
562-60, 782-15, 1037-3, 1391-551, 1391-705,
1578-31, 1853-9
Civil liberties, income development, 1853-9
Civil liberties, indigenous peoples, 788-68
Civil liberties, management development/capacity
building, 1391-154
Civil liberties, men, 782-9, 1391-62
Civil liberties, mentally disabled, 782-15
Civil liberties, migrant workers, 562-60, 1391-551
Civil liberties, minorities, 562-18, 562-33, 562-39,
562-58, 782-2, 782-21, 1037-3, 1039-2, 1391-62,
1391-562, 1391-665, 1391-705, 1393-48,
1393-75, 1578-31, 1853-9
Civil liberties, Native Americans/American Indians,
1391-580
Civil liberties, offenders/ex-offenders, 788-68
Civil liberties, publication, 1347-17, 1391-223,
1391-519, 1393-48
Civil liberties, reproductive rights, 105-6, 105-17,
172-63, 172-106, 172-153, 271-46, 271-80,
271-119, 271-161, 271-163, 271-166, 562-5,
562-6, 562-7, 562-16, 562-27, 562-72, 782-14,
782-20, 782-23, 782-28, 788-43, 788-44, 788-70,
788-91, 788-141, 891-18, 891-19, 1137-2,
1137-7, 1137-11, 1391-6, 1391-13, 1391-15,
1391-20, 1391-32, 1391-53, 1391-99, 1391-100,
1391-117, 1391-147, 1391-149, 1391-150,
1391-157, 1391-158, 1391-171, 1391-186,
1391-194, 1391-211, 1391-237, 1391-241,
1391-298, 1391-320, 1391-344, 1391-351,
1391-371, 1391-385, 1391-467, 1391-468,
1391-469, 1391-506, 1391-508, 1391-512,
1391-514, 1391-573, 1391-596, 1391-605,
1391-606, 1391-609, 1391-612, 1391-727,
1391-736, 1391-755, 1391-792, 1391-795,

1391-801, 1391-814, 1391-821, 1594-19,
1594-28, 2170-119
Civil liberties, research, 891-32, 1347-17, 1391-154,
1391-223, 1391-277, 1391-519, 1391-551,
1391-562, 1593-29, 1593-40, 1916-43
Civil liberties, right to privacy, 1391-223
Civil liberties, women, 562-23, 782-2, 782-9,
1391-562, 1391-665
Civil rights, Afghanistan, 323-90, 323-91, 1578-187
Civil rights, Africa, 271-119, 271-161, 271-166, 562-4,
788-114, 891-35, 1030-3, 1030-8, 1030-9,
1030-15, 1030-24, 1030-25, 1030-49, 1030-53,
1030-54, 1058-84, 1361-18, 1391-20, 1391-23,
1391-24, 1391-32, 1391-430, 1391-467,
1391-773, 1639-206, 1702-14, 2170-119
Civil rights, Arctic Region, 2207-12
Civil rights, Argentina, 335-27, 996-5, 996-6,
1391-344, 1391-459, 1391-461, 1391-462,
1391-496, 1391-555, 1638-54
Civil rights, Armenia, 1312-53
Civil rights, Asia, 271-161, 562-4, 1030-6, 1030-10,
1391-473, 1391-736, 1393-96, 2170-119
Civil rights, Australia, 97-77, 335-49
Civil rights, Austria, 413-38
Civil rights, Azerbaijan, 1312-53
Civil rights, Balkans, The, 1638-61, 2203-20
Civil rights, Bangladesh, 135-23, 1393-169
Civil rights, Belgium, 1030-29, 1093-35, 1847-26,
2170-119
Civil rights, Bolivia, 1137-7
Civil rights, Botswana, 105-14
Civil rights, Brazil, 148-14, 335-25, 335-31, 335-32,
413-17, 1050-5, 1050-16, 1050-21, 1391-79,
1391-80, 1391-101, 1391-124, 1391-126,
1391-146, 1391-167, 1391-190, 1391-305,
1391-308, 1391-311, 1391-350, 1391-352,
1391-353, 1391-362, 1391-403, 1391-491,
1391-493, 1391-575, 1391-589, 1391-597,
1391-718, 1391-735, 1594-5
Civil rights, Bulgaria, 1058-65
Civil rights, Burma (Myanmar), 1593-89
Civil rights, Burundi, 1030-2
Civil rights, Cambodia, 323-71, 693-6, 1092-7,
1092-33, 1092-63, 1092-79, 1092-80, 1393-102,
2170-184, 2203-14
Civil rights, Canada, 105-14, 335-12, 335-17, 335-18,
447-6, 447-7, 782-17, 1030-56, 1391-6, 1391-88,
1391-237, 1594-4, 1638-50, 1638-51, 1847-51,
2004-28, 2161-3, 2207-12
Civil rights, Caribbean, 782-23, 1393-171, 1594-28
Civil rights, Central America, 105-6, 562-11, 562-25,
782-17, 1391-75, 1391-150, 1391-274,
1391-320, 1391-461, 1391-609, 1391-623,
1391-662, 1391-732, 2199-35
Civil rights, Chile, 148-3, 996-21, 996-22, 1391-298,
1391-396, 1391-731, 1391-752, 1391-768
Civil rights, China, 335-2, 439-33, 788-123, 1128-15,
1391-112, 1391-116, 1391-205, 1391-211,
1391-214, 1391-219, 1391-220, 1391-221,
1391-223, 1391-224, 1391-570, 1391-637,
1391-709, 1391-711, 1391-784, 1391-821,
1393-140, 1853-152
Civil rights, Colombia, 148-4, 148-7, 148-16, 148-17,
1137-7, 1391-259, 1391-340, 1391-624,
1391-659
Civil rights, Cuba, 782-18, 1391-662
Civil rights, Cyprus, 1391-652
Civil rights, Denmark, 820-4
Civil rights, Developing countries, 172-106, 172-146,
172-153, 271-54, 271-162, 562-21, 782-6, 782-9,
782-20, 891-1, 891-25, 1030-6, 1030-10,
1030-29, 1030-53, 1030-54, 1093-86, 1292-5,
1391-32, 1391-269, 1391-298, 1391-316,
1391-353, 1391-500, 1391-606, 1391-687,
1585-24, 1593-87, 1593-110, 1638-54, 1638-66,
1639-117, 1847-10, 1847-23, 1847-24, 1847-25,
1847-26, 2004-28, 2170-196, 2170-413
Civil rights, East Africa/Horn of Africa, 1030-2,
1030-13, 1593-79, 1702-11
Civil rights, East Jerusalem, 323-118, 562-61, 562-65,
891-23, 891-27, 891-38, 896-14, 896-22, 896-27,
1213-3, 1347-19, 1660-9, 1923-5, 1923-14
Civil rights, Ecuador, 148-4, 1137-7, 1393-169

Civil rights, Egypt, 1391-147, 1391-258, 1391-288, 1391-291, 1391-375, 1391-539, 1391-562, 1391-652, 1393-11

Civil rights, El Salvador, 1391-343, 1391-469, 1391-732

Civil rights, England, 172-10, 335-55, 499-32, 788-161, 820-4, 1030-12, 1391-430, 1638-66, 1702-1, 1702-2, 1702-3, 1702-4, 1702-6, 1702-7, 1702-9, 1702-12, 1916-43, 2212-15

Civil rights, Equatorial Guinea, 1393-62

Civil rights, Ethiopia, 97-95, 788-143, 1639-206, 1847-9

Civil rights, Europe, 172-153, 335-55, 1030-10, 1093-29, 1093-35, 1391-672, 1847-26, 2170-119, 2203-20

Civil rights, France, 1030-10, 1391-450, 1391-499, 1391-673

Civil rights, Georgia (Republic of), 1312-53

Civil rights, Germany, 820-4, 1241-7, 1391-147, 1391-316

Civil rights, Ghana, 1393-169

Civil rights, Global programs, 105-14, 148-14, 148-19, 166-8, 172-10, 172-56, 172-63, 172-106, 172-146, 226-5, 238-26, 271-162, 271-163, 309-54, 309-56, 323-130, 323-131, 323-133, 323-162, 323-376, 323-377, 325-12, 325-13, 325-14, 325-43, 325-44, 335-4, 335-12, 335-39, 413-16, 413-38, 413-39, 435-28, 447-8, 447-15, 447-21, 499-17, 499-32, 537-6, 562-5, 562-7, 562-12, 562-18, 562-19, 562-20, 562-22, 562-23, 562-27, 562-69, 562-70, 562 72, 562-73, 655-7, 708-11, 782-2, 782-3, 782-4, 782-11, 782-12, 782-14, 782-16, 782-19, 782-20, 782-21, 782-25, 782-26, 782-27, 782-28, 788-40, 788-43, 788-44, 788-91, 788-127, 788-161, 860-28, 891-16, 891-17, 891-18, 891-19, 891-22, 891-25, 891-48, 892-3, 892-4, 996-35, 1030-6, 1030-10, 1030-19, 1030-25, 1030-26, 1030-28, 1030-29, 1030-39, 1030-51, 1030-55, 1037-3, 1050-10, 1050-22, 1050-25, 1050-26, 1050-30, 1050-32, 1050-33, 1058-153, 1093-48, 1093-86, 1137-9, 1137-10, 1179-100, 1179-101, 1292-5, 1312-64, 1312-72, 1347-5, 1347-6, 1347-11, 1347-14, 1347-17, 1347-21, 1391-1, 1391-6, 1391-13, 1391 32, 1391-61, 1391-75, 1391-80, 1391-88, 1391-117, 1391-154, 1391-156, 1391-157, 1391-158, 1391-165, 1391-221, 1391-223, 1391-227, 1391-238, 1391-247, 1391-263, 1391-316, 1391-321, 1391-352, 1391-353, 1391-371, 1391-393, 1391-400, 1391-428, 1391-430, 1391-434, 1391-442, 1391 450, 1391-454, 1391-459, 1391-461, 1391-462, 1391-468, 1391-500, 1391-504, 1391-546, 1391-550, 1391-555, 1391-574, 1391-580, 1391-589, 1391-606, 1391-622, 1391-646, 1391-672, 1391-705, 1391-746, 1391-755, 1391-793, 1391-794, 1391-799, 1391-801, 1393-4, 1393-10, 1393-23, 1393-36, 1393-37, 1393-42, 1393-51, 1393-54, 1393-75, 1393-91, 1393-106, 1393-125, 1393-129, 1393-131, 1393-133, 1393-134, 1393-138, 1393-140, 1393-155, 1393-178, 1393-183, 1531-11, 1546-103, 1546-124, 1578-31, 1578-58, 1578-59, 1578-179, 1585-2, 1585-12, 1585-13, 1585-14, 1585-15, 1585-24, 1585-25, 1593-13, 1593-28, 1593-29, 1593-31, 1593-38, 1593-39, 1593-40, 1593-41, 1593-58, 1593-60, 1593-65, 1593-66, 1593-87, 1593-100, 1593-107, 1593-110, 1593-127, 1593-136, 1594-3, 1594-22, 1594-25, 1594-34, 1594-37, 1638-50, 1638-51, 1638-66, 1638-72, 1638-99, 1638-138, 1639-34, 1639-76, 1639-117, 1639-141, 1659-20, 1659-30, 1702-2, 1702-3, 1702-13, 1847-6, 1847-10, 1847-14, 1847-23, 1847-24, 1847-25, 1853-9, 1853-133, 1911-11, 1916-2, 2004-28, 2170-196, 2170-298, 2170-299, 2170-413, 2203-19, 2212-35

Civil rights, Guatemala, 562-6, 562-8, 562-15, 562-28, 744-25, 744-32, 1137-7, 1391-75, 1391-293, 1391-409, 1391-555, 1391-605, 1391-623, 1391-624, 1391-727, 1618-6, 1847-22

Civil rights, Haiti, 1030-21, 1093-4

Civil rights, Honduras, 1391-87, 1391-327

Civil rights, India, 97-105, 172-82, 172-88, 271-46, 905-4, 1128-66, 1128-67, 1391-84, 1391-173,

1391-175, 1391-226, 1391-348, 1391-378, 1391-399, 1391-513, 1391-519, 1391-542, 1391-592, 1391-612, 1391-622, 1391-665, 1391-667, 1391-775, 1391-818, 1393-169, 1847-44, 1847-45

Civil rights, Indonesia, 335-46, 788-228, 1391-39, 1391-141, 1391-406, 1391-407, 1391-529, 1391-600, 1391-601, 1391-736, 1391-755, 1391-791

Civil rights, Ireland, 1639-117

Civil rights, Israel, 154-23, 154-24, 167-3, 216-20, 226-8, 323-118, 413-16, 562-31, 562-33, 562-35, 562-38, 562-39, 562-41, 562-42, 562-45, 562-47, 562-48, 562-49, 562-51, 562-55, 562-56, 562-58, 562-59, 562-60, 562-61, 613-5, 616-18, 655-7, 798-22, 891-3, 891-9, 891-10, 891-13, 891-14, 891-15, 891-20, 891-21, 891-23, 891-26, 891-27, 891-32, 891-33, 891-36, 891-37, 891-38, 891-39, 891-42, 891-43, 891-48, 891-49, 896-1, 896-2, 896-3, 896-9, 896-10, 896-14, 896-15, 896-17, 896-20, 896-22, 896-23, 896-25, 896-26, 896-27, 896-30, 896-32, 934-31, 934-35, 934-36, 1030-40, 1167-1, 1167-2, 1167-10, 1213-3, 1347-10, 1347-19, 1437-2, 1437-6, 1567-14, 1593-103, 1603-18, 1631-2, 1631-4, 1631-5, 1660-1, 1660-2, 1660-3, 1660-4, 1660-5, 1660-6, 1660-9, 1660-19, 1660-24, 1660-30, 1660-31, 1660-32, 1660-33, 1660-34, 1660-35, 1718-9, 1830-37, 1830-38, 1923-5, 1923-14, 2211-7

Civil rights, Italy, 1093-29, 1393-88

Civil rights, Jordan, 1391-562

Civil rights, Kenya, 105-23, 271-119, 1030-2, 1030-12, 1030-13, 1058-30, 1082-4, 1391-20, 1391-21, 1391-23, 1391-90, 1391-186, 1391-444, 1391-481, 1391-485, 1391-490, 1391-521, 1391-522, 1391-535, 1391-722, 1391-773, 1391-814

Civil rights, Kosovo, 1058-37, 1058-118, 1393-92, 1638-15, 1638-28, 1638-61

Civil rights, Latin America, 105 17, 271 161, 309 64, 562-4, 562-26, 782-23, 1391-53, 1391-237, 1391-277, 1391-496, 1391-551, 1391-752, 1393-155, 1393-171, 1594-4, 1594-15, 1594-19, 1594-28, 1594-32

Civil rights, Lebanon, 1030-4, 1391-61, 1391-539, 1393-119

Civil rights, Lesotho, 335-7

Civil rights, Liberia, 1303-47, 1593-7

Civil rights, Malaysia, 1391-473

Civil rights, Mexico, 97-24, 97-94, 148-5, 172-10, 172-23, 172 119, 271-149, 335-20, 335-22, 335-57, 562-16, 562-25, 782-17, 788-68, 788-70, 788-91, 788-104, 788-141, 788-160, 788-164, 788-176, 788-179, 996-12, 996-23, 996-34, 996-42, 996-43, 1137-2, 1137 7, 1137 8, 1137-11, 1391-15, 1391-99, 1391-100, 1391-150, 1391 166, 1391-194, 1391-195, 1391-241, 1391-274, 1391-275, 1391-292, 1391-293, 1391-320, 1391-345, 1391-351, 1391-409, 1391-410, 1391-425, 1391-501, 1391-506, 1391-545, 1391-551, 1391-555, 1391-573, 1391-623, 1391-624, 1391-629, 1391-630, 1391-662, 1391-714, 1391-737, 1391-795, 1393-22, 1393-57, 1393-169, 1393-181, 1594-7, 1594-17, 1638-72

Civil rights, Middle East, 613-5, 756-12, 1030-4, 1030-9, 1030-15, 1030-22, 1030-54, 1039-2, 1347-10, 1391-62, 1391-539, 1391-672, 1391-721, 1393-119, 1603-18, 1660-9, 1718-9

Civil rights, Montenegro, 1058-37

Civil rights, Morocco and the Western Sahara, 1944-2

Civil rights, Mozambique, 1391-149, 1391-192

Civil rights, Namibia, 1393-169

Civil rights, Nepal, 242-5, 323-117, 499 6, 499-28, 499-29, 709-103

Civil rights, Netherlands, 172-153, 820-4, 1030-54, 1391-385, 1391-387, 1391-687

Civil rights, Nicaragua, 562-11, 1391-171, 1391-469, 1391-609, 1393-169, 2199-41

Civil rights, Nigeria, 788-114, 788-177, 788-186, 788-206, 788-215, 1391-103, 1391-240, 1391-249, 1391-792

Civil rights, North Africa, 1030-4, 1030-22, 1391-539, 1393-119

Civil rights, Northern Ireland, 1391-247

Civil rights, Oceania, 1391-473, 1391-736

Civil rights, Pakistan, 271-88, 271-137, 1531-31

Civil rights, Papua New Guinea, 271-23

Civil rights, Paraguay, 1137-7

Civil rights, Peru, 148-2, 251-39, 996-7, 996-8, 996-20, 996-32, 996-33, 1137-7, 1391-321, 1391-393, 1391-424, 1391-504, 1391-611, 1393-169

Civil rights, Philippines, 1391-269

Civil rights, Poland, 709-112

Civil rights, race/intergroup relations, 167-3, 226-5, 226-8, 323-118, 413-38, 613-5, 616-18, 655-7, 756-12, 820-4, 891-10, 891-23, 891-26, 891-27, 891-37, 891-38, 891-39, 891-49, 896-1, 896-14, 896-15, 896-17, 896-20, 896-22, 896-25, 896-26, 896-27, 896-32, 1039-2, 1050-5, 1050-25, 1050-26, 1058-30, 1058-37, 1058-65, 1058-71, 1058-78, 1058-153, 1167-1, 1167-2, 1167-10, 1213-3, 1347-10, 1347-19, 1391-90, 1391-672, 1391-673, 1393-88, 1393-102, 1437-2, 1437-6, 1531-11, 1567-14, 1578-179, 1603-18, 1631-2, 1631-4, 1631-5, 1638-99, 1639-42, 1659-20, 1660-1, 1660-2, 1660-3, 1660-4, 1660-5, 1660-6, 1660-9, 1660-19, 1660-24, 1660-30, 1660-31, 1660-32, 1660-33, 1660-34, 1660-35, 1718-9, 1830-37, 1830-38, 1923-5, 2170-298, 2170-299, 2203-20, 2211-7

Civil rights, Russia, 335-6, 788-13, 788-62, 788-98, 788-214, 1058-137, 1312-53, 1853-64

Civil rights, Rwanda, 132-7, 132-8, 132-9, 132-20, 132 51, 1030-2, 2170-184

Civil rights, Senegal, 1391-24, 1847-70, 1847-72

Civil rights, Serbia, 1058-37, 1058-118, 1638-111

Civil rights, Sierra Leone, 105-26

Civil rights, South Africa, 105-14, 132-16, 132 17, 309-12, 335-3, 1030-7, 1030-8, 1030-16, 1030-24, 1030-25, 1058-11, 1058-23, 1058-30, 1058-71, 1058-78, 1058-84, 1058-89, 1058-102, 1058-103, 1058-140, 1058-151, 1058-153, 1371-1, 1391-34, 1391-44, 1391-149, 1391-498, 1391-505, 1391-508, 1391-596, 1391-598, 1391-654, 1391-660, 1391 670, 1391-674, 1391-692, 1638-138

Civil rights, South America, 782-17

Civil rights, South Asia, 97-105, 896-19, 1391-622, 1391-678, 1393-50

Civil rights, Southeast Asia, 271-80, 788-228, 1030-3, 1030-9, 1030-15, 1030-27, 1030-54, 1391-512

Civil rights, Southern Africa, 1030-8, 1391-385, 1391-443, 1391-596, 1391-654, 1391-692, 1593-79

Civil rights, Soviet Union (Former), 1593-26

Civil rights, Spain, 782-28, 1393-62, 1578-134

Civil rights, Sri Lanka, 1391-678

Civil rights, Sub-Saharan Africa, 271-80, 1030-7, 1585-17, 1847-51

Civil rights, Sudan, 1593-122

Civil rights, Swaziland, 1391-443

Civil rights, Sweden, 1030-55, 1391-32

Civil rights, Switzerland, 271-166, 1092-80, 1093-48, 1093-86, 1391-62, 1391-573, 1391-801, 1393-51, 1393-62, 1393-96

Civil rights, Tanzania, Zanzibar and Pemba, 132-63, 1030-2, 1391-444

Civil rights, Thailand, 335-58, 1391-512, 1639-42

Civil rights, Uganda, 1030-2, 1030-16, 1391-11, 1391-444, 1391-514, 1391-716, 1391-730, 1393-169

Civil rights, Ukraine, 413-39, 1058-49, 1393-169

Civil rights, United Kingdom, 1702-1, 1702-2, 1702-3, 1702-4, 1702-7, 1702-9

Civil rights, Uruguay, 1328-341, 1490-7

Civil rights, Uzbekistan, 1593-13

Civil rights, Venezuela, 148-4

Civil rights, Vietnam, 413-70

Civil rights, voter education, 172-82, 788-114, 788-186, 788-206, 1058-49, 1312-64, 1391-84, 1391-240, 1391-249, 1391-722, 1593-89, 1638-15, 1638-61

Civil rights, West Bank/Gaza (Palestinian Territories), 167-3, 323-118, 562-50, 562-65, 613-5, 891-13, 891-23, 891-38, 896-9, 896-14, 896-17, 896-25, 896-27, 1213-3, 1347-19, 1391-122, 1391-658,

1423-43, 1423-45, 1423-52, 1423-53, 1423-56,
1423-60, 1423-62, 1423-64, 1423-65, 1423-66,
1424-14, 1424-16, 1450-3, 1578-174, 1638-125,
1639-11, 1639-38, 1639-79, 1639-128,
1639-142, 1639-144, 1639-172, 1639-174,
1639-203, 1639-204, 1790-12, 1843-1, 1843-6,
1847-15, 1847-20, 1847-21, 1847-36, 1847-56,
1916-58, 1916-84, 1916-86, 2000-17, 2000-27,
2000-28, 2000-29, 2000-30, 2000-40, 2000-41,
2000-42, 2000-78, 2000-79, 2078-6, 2098-10,
2099-45, 2170-126, 2170-156, 2170-177,
2170-196, 2170-234, 2170-235, 2170-258,
2170-292, 2170-406, 2170-549, 2199-70,
2199-76, 2199-102, 2199-111, 2203-30,
2203-40
Community improvement/development, Dominican
Republic, 37-5, 335-11, 1328-301
Community improvement/development, East Africa/
Horn of Africa, 323-256, 325-31, 866-3, 1391-22,
1391-66, 1391-509, 1391-590, 1603-10,
2170-125
Community improvement/development, East
Jerusalem, 891-27
Community improvement/development, Eastern &
Central Europe, 1058-34, 1058-67, 1058-68,
1058-88, 1058-120, 1638-116
Community improvement/development, Ecuador,
251-45, 1092-5, 1328-110, 1391-257, 1594-14,
1594-23, 1594-31, 1594-33
Community improvement/development, Egypt,
1328-125, 1328-276, 1391-27, 1391-54,
1391-258, 1391-288, 1391-561, 1423-9,
1423-10, 1423-24, 1423-61, 2170-98
Community improvement/development, El Salvador,
467-99, 1328-120, 1328-289, 1328-348,
1391-326, 1391-343, 1639-7
Community improvement/development, England,
97-37, 97-79, 172-1, 251-36, 271-83, 416-4,
428-24, 443-23, 499-16, 709-90, 788-25,
788-189, 1021-18, 1092-4, 1092-18, 1092-86,
1391-41, 1391-615, 1423-48, 1638-85, 1639-23,
1639-39, 1639-64, 1639-108, 1639-111,
1639-112, 1639-150, 1639-213, 1702-4,
1853-79, 1853-81, 1853-146, 2170-123,
2170-245, 2170-268, 2211-2
Community improvement/development, Ethiopia, 97-3,
97-9, 97-25, 97-32, 97-62, 97-67, 97-76, 97-79,
132-33, 271-60, 788-143, 1639-61, 1847-63,
1970-1, 2199-107
Community improvement/development, Europe,
335-23, 335-36, 1058-34, 1328-4, 1328-28,
1328-118, 1328-218, 1393-17, 1393-161,
2170-389
Community improvement/development, Federated
States of Micronesia, 271-95, 271-151
Community improvement/development, Fiji, 97-112,
788-83
Community improvement/development, France, 97-4,
97-5, 335-23, 709-8, 1391-188, 1423-11,
1423-22, 1423-23
Community improvement/development, Georgia
(Republic of), 1312-23
Community improvement/development, Germany,
335-43, 1058-113, 1391-42, 1423-11, 1839-104,
1989-19, 2170-98, 2170-342
Community improvement/development, Ghana,
435-18, 435-35, 435-36, 1328-342, 1391-376,
1391-411, 1601-6, 1639-211, 2170-342
Community improvement/development, Global
programs, 21-9, 86-1, 97-49, 105-46, 105-48,
119-4, 135-3, 172-151, 238-1, 238-18, 251-36,
264-5, 264-6, 264-14, 271-83, 271-133, 271-145,
302-2, 309-53, 309-89, 312-3, 313-1, 323-37,
323-38, 323-39, 323-55, 323-127, 323-376,
323-377, 325-2, 325-3, 325-9, 325-10, 325-11,
325-43, 325-44, 335-16, 335-56, 384-3, 384-4,
413-5, 428-24, 428-33, 435-1, 447-5, 460-1,
464-21, 605-11, 709-58, 744-22, 782-1, 782-3,
782-4, 782-5, 782-8, 782-21, 782-29, 788-25,
788-55, 788-189, 798-5, 798-45, 814-6, 837-14,
840-9, 967-14, 969-4, 1050-17, 1050-22,
1092-86, 1179-14, 1179-135, 1184-11, 1303-31,
1303-76, 1322-4, 1328-14, 1328-104, 1328-352,
1330-9, 1347-11, 1347-16, 1347-39, 1353-1,

1391-4, 1391-41, 1391-43, 1391-86, 1391-133,
1391-246, 1391-302, 1391-313, 1391-401,
1391-464, 1391-511, 1391-524, 1391-533,
1391-548, 1391-586, 1391-615, 1391-640,
1393-29, 1423-1, 1423-2, 1423-3, 1423-12,
1423-13, 1423-30, 1423-36, 1423-37, 1423-43,
1423-45, 1423-52, 1423-53, 1423-56, 1423-60,
1423-62, 1423-64, 1423-65, 1423-66, 1450-3,
1494-2, 1578-17, 1578-18, 1578-73, 1578-127,
1578-128, 1578-130, 1578-131, 1578-132,
1578-133, 1578-188, 1594-10, 1603-5, 1638-31,
1638-104, 1638-121, 1638-125, 1639-9,
1639-11, 1639-17, 1639-23, 1639-25, 1639-26,
1639-27, 1639-37, 1639-38, 1639-44, 1639-53,
1639-64, 1639-76, 1639-79, 1639-100,
1639-108, 1639-111, 1639-118, 1639-119,
1639-120, 1639-142, 1639-144, 1639-151,
1639-172, 1639-174, 1639-203, 1639-213,
1672-3, 1718-3, 1768-2, 1790-6, 1839-111,
1843-1, 1843-2, 1847-20, 1847-21, 1847-56,
1916-37, 2000-21, 2099-45, 2170-19, 2170-126,
2170-156, 2170-177, 2170-196, 2170-258,
2170-366, 2170-389, 2170-406, 2170-549,
2199-16, 2199-70, 2211-2
Community improvement/development, Guatemala,
467-70, 562-8, 562-15, 562-28, 605-1, 1328-303,
1328-307, 1391-244, 1391-374, 2199-5
Community improvement/development, Haiti, 21-2,
21-3, 37-5, 97-65, 323-126, 323-223, 467-44,
788-146, 837-15, 1030-5, 1578-16, 1940-1,
1940-2, 1940-3, 1940-4, 1940-5, 1940-6, 1940-7,
1940-8, 1940-9, 1940-10, 1940-11, 1940-12,
2199-40, 2199-75
Community improvement/development, Honduras,
1328-27, 1391-87, 1391-327, 1639-7, 1790-2,
1790-3, 2099-23
Community improvement/development, Hong Kong,
1328-230
Community improvement/development, Hungary,
335-13, 1058-67, 1328-109, 1853-54
Community improvement/development, Iceland,
1853-122
Community improvement/development, India, 264-11,
271-6, 271-22, 271-129, 307-27, 323-173,
323-174, 325-22, 325-23, 413-45, 428-58,
435-35, 435-36, 467-4, 467-6, 467-30, 467-35,
467-37, 467-39, 467-63, 467-66, 467-67, 467-81,
467-90, 499-8, 709-39, 709-106, 735-27, 735-33,
788-174, 860-22, 1128-59, 1128-60, 1128-66,
1128-67, 1328-106, 1328-142, 1328-202,
1391-2, 1391-3, 1391-5, 1391-8, 1391-40,
1391-72, 1391-104, 1391-173, 1391-176,
1391-177, 1391-248, 1391-287, 1391-369,
1391-397, 1391-478, 1391-486, 1391-509,
1391-513, 1391-581, 1391-620, 1391-621,
1391-647, 1391-649, 1391-688, 1391-775,
1391-786, 1391-817, 1423-31, 1423-32, 1601-6,
1601-8, 1639-73, 1639-75, 1639-86, 1639-132,
1639-153, 1639-163, 1639-181, 1665-6, 1774-7,
1790-9, 1822-8, 1839-15, 1839-44, 1843-1,
1843-4, 1843-5, 1843-6, 1843-8, 1843-9,
1843-12, 1843-13, 1847-18, 1847-44, 1847-45,
1847-65, 1847-66, 1847-67, 1916-29, 2000-7,
2000-8, 2000-9, 2000-10, 2000-11, 2000-38,
2000-39, 2000-43, 2000-67, 2000-68, 2000-69,
2170-50, 2170-85, 2170-168, 2170-245,
2170-268, 2170-366, 2170-368, 2170-375,
2170-508
Community improvement/development, Indonesia,
271-67, 271-90, 693-50, 788-100, 1328-183,
1328-204, 1391-42, 1391-94, 1391-98,
1391-102, 1391-141, 1391-160, 1391-405,
1391-488, 1391-578, 1391-601, 1391-683,
1391-791, 1391-802, 1391-811, 1391-812,
1843-3, 2004-18
Community improvement/development, Ireland,
1021-65, 1021-66, 1839-79
Community improvement/development, Israel, 154-1,
154-23, 154-24, 154-35, 154-37, 154-38, 154-39,
154-40, 154-42, 154-43, 154-44, 154-45, 167-3,
562-41, 562-44, 562-48, 562-54, 562-58, 616-36,
701-4, 891-14, 891-21, 891-27, 891-39, 891-49,
896-10, 896-15, 896-25, 896-32, 934-6, 934-81,

967-11, 1347-40, 1437-2, 1567-14, 1603-14,
1603-15, 1638-2, 1660-7, 1660-8, 1660-19
Community improvement/development, Italy, 435-12,
1092-5, 1639-119, 1853-96, 1853-139,
2170-125, 2170-126
Community improvement/development, Jamaica,
788-146, 1328-212, 1853-12
Community improvement/development, Japan, 238-23,
1241-8, 1423-34, 1423-38
Community improvement/development, Jordan,
1328-34, 1328-210, 1391-561, 1839-59
Community improvement/development, Kenya, 97-62,
97-63, 97-72, 132-24, 166-13, 166-14, 323-252,
323-253, 435-35, 435-36, 467-87, 734-2, 837-3,
1082-4, 1128-46, 1128-47, 1303-60, 1328-221,
1328-313, 1391-30, 1391-66, 1391-90,
1391-304, 1391-463, 1391-481, 1391-483,
1391-484, 1391-485, 1391-490, 1391-535,
1391-599, 1391-635, 1391-690, 1391-698,
1391-717, 1391-780, 1391-814, 1423-4, 1423-5,
1423-21, 1423-47, 1601-6, 1639-58, 1639-59,
1639-154, 1639-155, 1639-170, 1639-188,
1639-196, 1639-211, 1847-56, 2073-8,
2170-123, 2170-166, 2170-287, 2170-368,
2199-109
Community improvement/development, Kosovo,
1638-13, 1638-62, 1638-80
Community improvement/development, Kyrgyzstan,
97-4, 97-13, 97-70, 97-71, 97-88, 97-97, 97-98
Community improvement/development, Laos,
1092-59, 1092-93, 1092-99
Community improvement/development, Latin America,
251-8, 309-57, 323-295, 323-350, 413-55, 829-4,
1050-3, 1179-166, 1328-2, 1328-31, 1328-117,
1328-119, 1328-121, 1328-129, 1328-353,
1391-160, 1391-302, 1391-619, 1391-641,
1578-159, 1624-19, 1639-9, 1639-12, 1639-54,
1639-167, 1847-28, 2008-1, 2170-64, 2199-48,
2199-49, 2199-50, 2199-51, 2199-52, 2199-53,
2199-54, 2203-1
Community improvement/development, Latvia,
1058-120
Community improvement/development, Lebanon,
1328-211, 1391-56
Community improvement/development, Lesotho,
1303-60, 1371-2
Community improvement/development, Liberia, 264-2,
1423-20, 1423-50, 1423-51, 2170-275
Community improvement/development, Macedonia,
1638-13, 1638-122
Community improvement/development, Madagascar,
323-86, 788-80, 788-82, 788-118, 788-151
Community improvement/development, Malawi,
132-31, 307-26, 1092-88, 1092-89, 1092-91,
1847-68, 2170-216, 2170-239, 2170-508
Community improvement/development, Malaysia,
1638-125
Community improvement/development, Mali, 172-93,
1092-38, 1092-39, 2170-254, 2170-402
Community improvement/development, Mexico, 17-1,
37-5, 37-12, 97-24, 97-74, 97-94, 172-28, 172-29,
172-44, 172-65, 172-73, 238-32, 271-2, 271-18,
271-25, 271-27, 271-33, 271-57, 271-74,
271-105, 271-141, 271-154, 323-299, 413-30,
788-180, 1050-4, 1050-7, 1050-15, 1128-45,
1179-26, 1328-226, 1353-29, 1391-96,
1391-119, 1391-196, 1391-197, 1391-302,
1391-429, 1391-525, 1391-540, 1393-22,
1423-39, 1423-40, 1423-41, 1594-17, 1594-21,
1594-27, 1594-29, 1594-31, 1594-33, 1639-7,
1853-145, 1951-1, 1980-3, 2004-15, 2170-28,
2170-101, 2199-5
Community improvement/development, Middle East,
154-42, 154-43, 154-44, 154-45, 435-12, 1328-4,
1328-28, 1328-118, 1638-2, 1639-39, 1660-8,
1839-6, 1839-7
Community improvement/development, Montenegro,
1058-127, 1638-13, 1638-96, 1638-122
Community improvement/development, Morocco and
the Western Sahara, 1328-200
Community improvement/development, Mozambique,
172-1, 1092-40, 1391-120, 1391-388, 1391-560,
2170-342, 2170-394

829-2, 829-3, 829-4, 837-3, 837-14, 837-15,
855-3, 860-22, 866-3, 891-14, 891-21, 892-2,
896-10, 896-15, 930-1, 934-6, 934-81, 967-14,
1021-65, 1021-66, 1030-5, 1050-2, 1050-3,
1050-4, 1050-15, 1050-22, 1050-29, 1058-4,
1058-13, 1058-29, 1058-32, 1058-34, 1058-51,
1058-53, 1058-54, 1058-58, 1058-59, 1058-99,
1058-107, 1058-116, 1058-120, 1058-125,
1058-140, 1058-151, 1058-158, 1058-164,
1058-167, 1058-179, 1081-14, 1082-4, 1092-4,
1092-11, 1092-12, 1092-14, 1092-16, 1092-22,
1092-24, 1092-28, 1092-29, 1092-31, 1092-34,
1092-38, 1092-39, 1092-40, 1092-42, 1092-58,
1092-59, 1092-66, 1092-67, 1092-71, 1092-76,
1092-77, 1092-78, 1092-83, 1092-85, 1092-92,
1092-93, 1092-94, 1092-98, 1128-1, 1128-2,
1128-28, 1128-45, 1128-46, 1128-47, 1128-59,
1128-60, 1128-66, 1128-67, 1137-43, 1141-4,
1141-5, 1141-6, 1179-4, 1179-14, 1179-26,
1179-166, 1179-244, 1179-245, 1179-257,
1184-1, 1184-11, 1213-2, 1303-60, 1322-3,
1328-2, 1328-3, 1328-4, 1328-5, 1328-26,
1328-27, 1328-30, 1328-31, 1328-32, 1328-33,
1328-34, 1328-37, 1328-50, 1328-103,
1328-104, 1328-105, 1328-106, 1328-111,
1328-117, 1328-119, 1328-123, 1328-125,
1328-128, 1328-129, 1328-195, 1328-202,
1328-258, 1328-276, 1347-11, 1353-1, 1353-10,
1353-13, 1353-26, 1360-2, 1371-2, 1391-2,
1391-3, 1391-4, 1391-7, 1391-8, 1391-11,
1391-16, 1391-22, 1391-27, 1391-30, 1391-40,
1391-42, 1391-43, 1391-66, 1391-72, 1391-76,
1391-86, 1391-87, 1391-90, 1391-91, 1391-94,
1391-96, 1391-98, 1391-102, 1391-103,
1391-104, 1391-113, 1391-119, 1391-120,
1391-130, 1391-141, 1391-146, 1391-153,
1391-159, 1391-170, 1391-173, 1391-177,
1391-188, 1391-189, 1391-196, 1391-199,
1391-203, 1391-208, 1391-212, 1391-220,
1391-225, 1391-231, 1391-244, 1391-245,
1391-246, 1391-248, 1391-250, 1391-255,
1391-256, 1391-257, 1391-258, 1391-264,
1391-268, 1391-269, 1391-270, 1391-271,
1391-284, 1391-287, 1391-288, 1391-302,
1391-304, 1391-305, 1391-310, 1391-313,
1391-314, 1391-326, 1391-327, 1391-330,
1391-338, 1391-339, 1391-340, 1391-343,
1391-349, 1391-369, 1391-370, 1391-374,
1391-376, 1391-386, 1391-388, 1391-401,
1391-405, 1391-411, 1391-412, 1391-424,
1391-429, 1391-441, 1391-456, 1391-463,
1391-465, 1391-466, 1391-478, 1391-481,
1391-483, 1391-485, 1391-488, 1391-490,
1391-491, 1391-494, 1391-509, 1391-511,
1391-513, 1391-524, 1391-525, 1391-526,
1391-527, 1391-533, 1391-535, 1391-536,
1391-540, 1391-541, 1391-558, 1391-560,
1391-569, 1391-578, 1391-581, 1391-586,
1391-590, 1391-601, 1391-604, 1391-607,
1391-615, 1391-619, 1391-620, 1391-621,
1391-635, 1391-636, 1391-641, 1391-647,
1391-649, 1391-650, 1391-660, 1391-684,
1391-688, 1391-690, 1391-698, 1391-699,
1391-717, 1391-718, 1391-730, 1391-754,
1391-756, 1391-757, 1391-759, 1391-766,
1391-775, 1391-779, 1391-780, 1391-786,
1391-791, 1391-802, 1391-811, 1391-812,
1391-814, 1391-817, 1391-820, 1393-22,
1393-50, 1393-97, 1423-1, 1423-2, 1423-3,
1423-4, 1423-5, 1423-6, 1423-7, 1423-9,
1423-10, 1423-11, 1423-12, 1423-13, 1423-16,
1423-18, 1423-19, 1423-20, 1423-21, 1423-22,
1423-23, 1423-24, 1423-26, 1423-27, 1423-29,
1423-30, 1423-31, 1423-32, 1423-33, 1423-34,
1423-35, 1423-36, 1423-37, 1423-38, 1423-39,
1423-40, 1423-41, 1423-43, 1423-45, 1423-47,
1423-48, 1423-49, 1423-50, 1423-51, 1423-52,
1423-53, 1423-54, 1423-55, 1423-56, 1423-57,
1423-58, 1423-59, 1423-60, 1423-61, 1423-62,
1423-63, 1423-64, 1423-65, 1423-66, 1423-67,
1423-68, 1424-14, 1424-16, 1450-3, 1494-2,
1506-5, 1518-6, 1578-3, 1578-40, 1578-127,
1578-128, 1578-130, 1578-131, 1578-132,
1578-133, 1578-159, 1578-166, 1578-174,

1578-188, 1585-5, 1585-6, 1593-46, 1594-33,
1601-6, 1601-8, 1603-9, 1603-10, 1624-8,
1624-19, 1639-7, 1639-11, 1639-12, 1639-23,
1639-25, 1639-26, 1639-27, 1639-37, 1639-39,
1639-50, 1639-54, 1639-58, 1639-59, 1639-61,
1639-63, 1639-64, 1639-73, 1639-75, 1639-76,
1639-79, 1639-86, 1639-87, 1639-88, 1639-89,
1639-90, 1639-91, 1639-92, 1639-98, 1639-100,
1639-112, 1639-115, 1639-119, 1639-128,
1639-132, 1639-133, 1639-142, 1639-144,
1639-150, 1639-151, 1639-153, 1639-156,
1639-161, 1639-163, 1639-167, 1639-169,
1639-170, 1639-172, 1639-173, 1639-174,
1639-181, 1639-188, 1639-196, 1639-203,
1639-204, 1639-211, 1639-213, 1702-4, 1718-3,
1774-7, 1790-2, 1790-3, 1790-6, 1790-9,
1790-10, 1790-12, 1790-13, 1822-8, 1839-15,
1843-1, 1843-3, 1843-4, 1843-5, 1843-6, 1843-9,
1843-11, 1843-12, 1843-13, 1847-15, 1847-18,
1847-20, 1847-21, 1847-28, 1847-29, 1847-36,
1847-37, 1847-38, 1847-44, 1847-45, 1847-56,
1847-63, 1847-65, 1847-66, 1847-67, 1847-68,
1853-12, 1853-22, 1853-66, 1853-145,
1853-147, 1916-25, 1916-58, 1916-84, 1916-85,
1916-86, 1916-87, 1940-1, 1940-2, 1940-3,
1940-4, 1940-5, 1940-6, 1940-7, 1940-8, 1940-9,
1940-10, 1940-11, 1940-12, 1951-1, 1970-1,
1980-1, 2000-7, 2000-8, 2000-9, 2000-10,
2000-11, 2000-17, 2000-27, 2000-28, 2000-29,
2000-30, 2000-38, 2000-39, 2000-40, 2000-41,
2000-42, 2000-43, 2000-67, 2000-68, 2000-69,
2000-78, 2000-79, 2004-3, 2004-4, 2004-18,
2008-1, 2009-1, 2067-7, 2073-8, 2078-2, 2078-6,
2098-10, 2099-15, 2099-27, 2161-20, 2170-19,
2170-28, 2170-50, 2170-64, 2170-82, 2170-85,
2170-86, 2170-98, 2170-99, 2170-101,
2170-123, 2170-125, 2170-126, 2170-156,
2170-166, 2170-168, 2170-177, 2170-179,
2170-196, 2170-216, 2170-232, 2170-234,
2170-236, 2170-239, 2170-245, 2170-254,
2170-258, 2170-268, 2170-275, 2170-287,
2170-292, 2170-342, 2170-366, 2170-368,
2170-374, 2170-375, 2170-389, 2170-390,
2170-394, 2170-402, 2170-406, 2170-502,
2170-508, 2170-549, 2199-5, 2199-16, 2199-27,
2199-28, 2199-40, 2199-48, 2199-49, 2199-50,
2199-51, 2199-52, 2199-53, 2199-54, 2199-70,
2199-75, 2199-76, 2199-102, 2199-111, 2203-1,
2203-30, 2203-40, 2203-50

Economically disadvantaged, crime/courts/legal
services, 97-95, 172-10, 172-30, 172-32,
172-142, 242-3, 323-339, 335-20, 335-44,
335-45, 335-46, 413-17, 467-73, 467-78, 562-4,
562-18, 708-11, 782-6, 782-16, 788-15, 788-115,
788-160, 788-176, 788-177, 891-33, 891-36,
891-43, 891-48, 934-61, 996-26, 1021-60,
1030-27, 1058-23, 1058-58, 1058-100,
1058-147, 1312-76, 1322-2, 1391-17, 1391-34,
1391-39, 1391-65, 1391-87, 1391-103,
1391-167, 1391-220, 1391-228, 1391-233,
1391-260, 1391-279, 1391-336, 1391-385,
1391-387, 1391-392, 1391-403, 1391-406,
1391-415, 1391-449, 1391-493, 1391-497,
1391-498, 1391-501, 1391-505, 1391-542,
1391-545, 1391-546, 1391-550, 1391-570,
1391-597, 1391-623, 1391-624, 1391-670,
1391-690, 1391-691, 1391-696, 1391-705,
1391-716, 1391-727, 1393-3, 1393-43, 1393-60,
1393-62, 1393-83, 1393-84, 1393-85, 1393-97,
1506-4, 1578-96, 1585-11, 1585-15, 1585-19,
1585-24, 1593-7, 1593-8, 1593-13, 1593-43,
1593-61, 1593-87, 1594-5, 1594-16, 1639-41,
1702-1, 1702-2, 1702-6, 1702-12, 1721-3,
1790-3, 1847-23, 1847-24, 1847-25, 1916-5

Economically disadvantaged, education, 37-17, 58-4,
91-9, 91-10, 91-22, 97-39, 100-8, 100-9, 105-3,
132-35, 132-59, 132-60, 135-2, 135-16, 142-3,
142-4, 142-5, 142-6, 142-10, 142-15, 154-27,
154-47, 166-12, 172-14, 172-15, 172-16, 172-37,
172-42, 172-50, 172-61, 172-68, 172-75, 172-80,
172-81, 172-88, 172-93, 172-95, 172-96, 172-97,
172-113, 172-115, 172-125, 172-134, 172-139,
172-141, 172-143, 178-38, 216-17, 216-22,
271-1, 271-3, 271-50, 286-3, 307-10, 309-7,

309-17, 309-18, 309-19, 309-20, 309-21, 309-22,
309-23, 309-76, 309-109, 309-110, 312-7, 323-6,
323-45, 323-62, 323-70, 323-75, 323-76, 323-90,
323-91, 323-111, 323-112, 323-116, 323-128,
323-132, 323-137, 323-140, 323-141, 323-157,
323-158, 323-159, 323-160, 323-161, 323-185,
323-191, 323-240, 323-298, 323-307, 323-308,
323-309, 323-310, 323-311, 323-333, 323-334,
323-345, 323-383, 323-384, 325-18, 325-19,
347-2, 347-11, 384-10, 384-16, 413-10, 413-11,
413-22, 413-28, 413-52, 413-54, 413-63, 413-76,
428-58, 435-6, 435-31, 443-21, 447-2, 447-3,
447-6, 447-7, 447-8, 447-12, 447-14, 447-16,
447-19, 447-20, 447-21, 447-23, 447-24, 463-3,
463-13, 464-18, 467-1, 467-18, 467-19, 467-24,
467-41, 467-43, 467-50, 467-58, 467-59, 467-65,
467-73, 467-78, 467-79, 467-80, 467-87, 467-96,
467-98, 499-1, 499-2, 499-3, 499-6, 499-7,
499-8, 499-11, 499-12, 499-13, 499-15, 499-16,
499-18, 499-19, 499-20, 499-21, 499-22, 499-23,
499-24, 499-28, 499-29, 499-30, 499-33, 499-34,
562-51, 562-54, 562-64, 562-68, 616-7, 616-25,
616-32, 616-35, 616-45, 626-23, 660-16, 660-18,
660-19, 660-23, 660-50, 660-105, 660-138,
693-10, 693-11, 693-24, 693-29, 701-14, 701-15,
709-104, 709-117, 709-118, 719-1, 729-5, 744-3,
744-26, 744-65, 748-58, 756-18, 788-57,
788-142, 798-14, 798-16, 798-19, 798-43,
798-44, 820-4, 820-10, 837-4, 837-8, 837-18,
866-2, 891-1, 891-6, 891-25, 905-3, 930-2,
934-40, 934-89, 934-105, 952-31, 1021-8,
1021-15, 1021-21, 1021-22, 1021-37, 1021-65,
1021-66, 1021-73, 1021-77, 1021-78, 1021-82,
1021-86, 1021-93, 1021-106, 1050-1, 1050-2,
1050-6, 1050-12, 1050-13, 1050-14, 1050-23,
1050-31, 1058-32, 1058-65, 1058-147,
1058-167, 1082-1, 1082-10, 1082-16, 1092-31,
1092-66, 1092-93, 1128-3, 1128-4, 1128-5,
1128-9, 1128-22, 1128-58, 1141-4, 1160-17,
1160-18, 1160-19, 1179-98, 1179-99, 1191-2,
1241-21, 1303-64, 1312-17, 1328-11, 1328-47,
1328-115, 1328-116, 1328-119, 1328-126,
1328-237, 1328-238, 1328-288, 1328-308,
1328-309, 1328-316, 1328-336, 1328-350,
1347-22, 1353-11, 1353-12, 1353-17, 1353-18,
1353-28, 1391-30, 1391-97, 1391-118,
1391-135, 1391-138, 1391-148, 1391-167,
1391-177, 1391-185, 1391-186, 1391-190,
1391-207, 1391-212, 1391-222, 1391-264,
1391-285, 1391-296, 1391-297, 1391-315,
1391-325, 1391-328, 1391-340, 1391-369,
1391-507, 1391-509, 1391-562, 1391-567,
1391-569, 1391-579, 1391-613, 1391-618,
1391-634, 1391-656, 1391-688, 1391-726,
1391-733, 1391-734, 1391-748, 1391-751,
1391-754, 1391-759, 1391-768, 1391-806,
1391-816, 1391-819, 1393-163, 1393-176,
1423-1, 1423-2, 1423-3, 1423-4, 1423-5, 1423-6,
1423-7, 1423-8, 1423-9, 1423-10, 1423-11,
1423-12, 1423-13, 1423-14, 1423-15, 1423-16,
1423-17, 1423-18, 1423-19, 1423-20, 1423-21,
1423-22, 1423-23, 1423-24, 1423-26, 1423-27,
1423-28, 1423-29, 1423-30, 1423-31, 1423-32,
1423-33, 1423-34, 1423-35, 1423-36, 1423-37,
1423-38, 1423-39, 1423-40, 1423-41, 1423-42,
1423-43, 1423-45, 1423-47, 1423-48, 1423-49,
1423-50, 1423-51, 1423-52, 1423-53, 1423-54,
1423-55, 1423-56, 1423-57, 1423-58, 1423-59,
1423-60, 1423-61, 1423-62, 1423-63, 1423-64,
1423-65, 1423-66, 1423-67, 1423-68, 1423-69,
1423-70, 1520-12, 1520-13, 1531-15, 1575-1,
1578-40, 1578-88, 1578-108, 1578-120,
1578-123, 1578-169, 1593-108, 1603-4,
1603-17, 1603-19, 1624-8, 1635-10, 1639-52,
1639-203, 1659-22, 1673-1, 1673-2, 1673-3,
1690-2, 1702-5, 1702-8, 1768-19, 1790-4,
1822-1, 1822-8, 1839-24, 1839-25, 1839-41,
1847-1, 1847-2, 1847-3, 1847-16, 1847-17,
1847-18, 1847-29, 1847-37, 1847-43, 1847-48,
1847-57, 1847-59, 1847-68, 1847-69, 1853-1,
1853-10, 1853-13, 1853-34, 1853-91, 1853-112,
1853-126, 1923-3, 1960-1, 1960-2, 1980-10,
2000-2, 2000-3, 2000-5, 2000-6, 2000-16,
2000-18, 2000-19, 2000-20, 2000-35, 2000-36,

1594-38, 1624-5, 1638-32, 1638-34, 1638-91, 1639-72, 1702-6, 1702-9, 1702-10, 1847-34, 1847-35, 1847-48, 1853-83, 1853-143, 1916-16, 2161-25, 2170-388

Electronic media/online services, civil rights, 788-206, 1030-22, 1030-25, 1030-29, 1030-51, 1050-16, 1347-14, 1347-21, 1391-23, 1391-116, 1391-126, 1391-205, 1391-211, 1391-227, 1391-241, 1391-249, 1391-298, 1391-308, 1391-519, 1391-654, 1391-672, 1490-5, 1593-29, 1702-6, 1702-9

Electronic media/online services, community improvement/development, 97-2, 100-12, 1058-80, 1058-158, 1330-9, 1391-102, 1391-133, 1391-176, 1391-511, 1391-526, 1391-527, 1391-720, 1391-811, 1423-60, 1423-62, 1423-64, 1639-39, 1639-72, 1639-100, 1639-128, 1639-154, 1639-155, 1639-156, 1639-170, 1639-211, 1843-1, 2004-18, 2170-502

Electronic media/online services, crime/courts/legal services, 788-170, 1393-8, 1593-29, 1702-6

Electronic media/online services, education, 54-17, 100-5, 142-2, 142-17, 142-19, 172-37, 172-50, 172-94, 172-96, 172-125, 172-141, 172-143, 323-228, 616-13, 788-183, 820-1, 952-40, 952-42, 1021-86, 1312-83, 1361-13, 1391-89, 1391-107, 1391-178, 1391-298, 1391-315, 1391-402, 1391-433, 1391-564, 1391-672, 1391-676, 1391-720, 1391-772, 1391-809, 1391-816, 1393-101, 1423-60, 1423-62, 1423-64, 1457-3, 1531-34, 1546-42, 1546-47, 1546-48, 1546-61, 1546-86, 1546-109, 1546-121, 1546-123, 1546-125, 1594-38, 1618-11, 1768-9, 1847-48, 1853-143, 1916-15, 2170-102, 2170-164, 2170-176, 2170-238, 2170-387, 2170-499, 2212-38

Electronic media/online services, employment, 1391-107, 1639-170, 1639-211

Electronic media/online services, environment, 97-2, 97-18, 105-5, 105-43, 251-3, 251-6, 251-24, 271-91, 312-8, 788-28, 1347-26, 1391-10, 1391-281, 1391-282, 1391-294, 1393-156, 1506-3, 1546-9, 1546-125, 1624-5, 1638-32, 1638-34, 1638-97, 1639-155, 1853-83, 2004-18

Electronic media/online services, food/nutrition/ agriculture, 1347-26, 1639-154, 1639-155, 2170-114, 2170-164, 2170-198

Electronic media/online services, health—general, 54-17, 100-13, 172-4, 172-64, 271-24, 323-347, 952-7, 1093-7, 1093-60, 1093-67, 1093-68, 1093-80, 1093-94, 1361-13, 1391-10, 1391-211, 1391-241, 1391-281, 1391-298, 1391-474, 1391-654, 1638-32, 1639-18, 1639-19, 1639-20, 1639-21, 1639-28, 1639-29, 1639-70, 1639-156, 1639-158, 1639-176, 1639-191, 1847-48, 2170-67, 2170-77, 2170-114, 2170-147, 2170-246, 2170-385, 2170-433, 2170-451

Electronic media/online services, health—specific diseases, 323-347, 1093-7, 1093-32, 1093-33, 1093-60, 1093-65, 1093-67, 1093-68, 1093-80, 2170-114

Electronic media/online services, human services— multipurpose, 1093-1, 1093-67, 1391-176

Electronic media/online services, international affairs/ development, 97-52, 100-3, 105-43, 172-4, 172-96, 251-6, 439-28, 439-55, 439-57, 439-60, 439-65, 788-170, 788-183, 788-190, 788-206, 788-221, 1030-25, 1093-94, 1312-55, 1312-83, 1330-1, 1330-2, 1330-5, 1330-9, 1347-21, 1347-26, 1347-28, 1391-10, 1391-23, 1391-133, 1391-227, 1391-262, 1391-281, 1391-282, 1391-294, 1391-298, 1391-308, 1391-480, 1391-526, 1391-654, 1391-672, 1391-720, 1391-764, 1393-8, 1393-64, 1393-156, 1393-179, 1423-60, 1423-62, 1423-64, 1457-3, 1546-47, 1546-48, 1546-109, 1546-125, 1593-29, 1593-32, 1594-38, 1618-11, 1638-97, 1639-39, 1639-78, 1639-93, 1639-100, 1639-128, 1639-155, 1639-158, 1639-170, 1639-177, 1639-211, 1639-212, 1702-9, 1702-10, 1768-9, 1843-1, 1847-48, 2004-18, 2170-16, 2170-67, 2170-77, 2170-114, 2170-147, 2170-180, 2170-182, 2170-198,

2170-246, 2170-370, 2170-433, 2170-451, 2170-502, 2199-14

Electronic media/online services, medical research, 1361-13, 2170-67, 2170-77, 2170-433, 2170-451

Electronic media/online services, philanthropy/ voluntarism, 251-24, 1058-158, 1391-204, 1639-68, 1639-72, 1639-78, 2170-72, 2170-182

Electronic media/online services, public affairs/ government, 97-2, 97-52, 100-3, 100-5, 100-12, 105-5, 142-16, 172-4, 172-64, 172-141, 271-24, 312-8, 323-228, 323-347, 439-60, 616-13, 788-170, 788-183, 788-190, 788-206, 788-221, 820-1, 824-6, 952-7, 952-40, 1030-22, 1030-25, 1030-29, 1030-38, 1030-51, 1030-57, 1050-16, 1058-24, 1058-80, 1058-158, 1093-32, 1093-65, 1093-67, 1093-80, 1093-94, 1278-4, 1312-55, 1312-83, 1330-1, 1330-5, 1347-14, 1347-26, 1347-28, 1391-23, 1391-78, 1391-89, 1391-102, 1391-107, 1391-116, 1391-176, 1391-178, 1391-204, 1391-205, 1391-249, 1391-308, 1391-315, 1391-361, 1391-368, 1391-474, 1391-480, 1391-519, 1391-526, 1391-527, 1391-564, 1391-672, 1391-676, 1391-686, 1391-707, 1391-720, 1391-764, 1391-772, 1391-811, 1391-816, 1393-64, 1393-101, 1393-156, 1423-60, 1423-62, 1423-64, 1490-5, 1531-34, 1546-9, 1546-123, 1593-29, 1593-32, 1593-48, 1594-38, 1618-11, 1638-91, 1639-19, 1639-20, 1639-28, 1639-29, 1639-39, 1639-68, 1639-70, 1639-72, 1639-78, 1639-93, 1639-100, 1639-128, 1639-154, 1639-155, 1639-156, 1639-158, 1639-168, 1639-176, 1639-177, 1639-191, 1639-211, 1639-212, 1702-10, 1847-34, 1847-35, 1853-83, 1916-16, 2004-18, 2161-25, 2170-16, 2170-67, 2170-72, 2170-102, 2170-147, 2170-164, 2170-176, 2170-180, 2170-182, 2170-198, 2170-238, 2170-246, 2170-370, 2170-385, 2170-387, 2170-388, 2170-433, 2170-499, 2170-502, 2212-38

Electronic media/online services, recreation/sports/ athletics, 1847-34, 1847-35

Electronic media/online services, religion, 660-275, 1278-4

Electronic media/online services, safety/disaster relief, 1391-102, 2170-16

Electronic media/online services, science, 97-18, 142-16, 788-190, 1457-3, 1546-9, 1546-125, 1546-126, 1638-97, 1639-20, 1843-1, 1916-15, 1916-16, 1916-63, 2004-18, 2170-385, 2170-451

Electronic media/online services, social sciences, 172-4, 172-64, 251-6, 439-60, 788-190, 1030-29, 1030-38, 1312-55, 1391-227, 1391-308, 1391-511, 1391-764, 1393-8, 1393-179, 1531-34, 1546-21, 1546-126, 1593-32, 1639-93, 1639-168, 1639-177, 2170-182

Electronic media/online services, youth development, 660-275, 1347-21, 1391-482, 1638-34, 1847-34, 1847-35, 1847-48, 1853-83

Elementary school/education, 91-36, 100-5, 172-81, 172-113, 172-114, 172-126, 323-185, 323-226, 323-264, 323-314, 323-315, 428-42, 467-49, 467-76, 562-30, 562-36, 616-38, 660-14, 660-46, 660-86, 660-217, 660-240, 660-243, 660-262, 660-271, 709-32, 798-67, 837-22, 891-30, 930-2, 1021-79, 1082-10, 1093-88, 1179-163, 1278-26, 1303-19, 1328-347, 1397-20, 1665-13, 1839-1, 1839-26, 1839-70, 1839-77, 1839-83, 1839-84, 1839-85, 1839-86, 1839-88, 1847-43, 1853-109, 2000-4, 2000-59, 2000-60, 2000-61, 2046-2, 2073-4, 2199-65

Elementary school/education, building/renovation, 323-226, 323-264, 467-49, 467-76, 660-14, 660-46, 660-86, 660-217, 660-240, 660-243, 2073-4

Elementary school/education, children, 100-5, 172-81, 172-113, 467-49, 616-38, 660-14, 660-46, 660-86, 660-217, 660-240, 660-243, 660-271, 798-67, 837-22, 891-30, 1082-10, 1093-88, 1278-26, 1303-19, 1397-20, 1853-109, 2000-4, 2046-2

Elementary school/education, children/youth, 323-185, 323-226, 562-30, 562-36, 660-262, 1328-347, 2073-4

Elementary school/education, computer technology, 323-314, 323-315

Elementary school/education, crime/abuse victims, 616-38

Elementary school/education, curriculum development, 100-5, 1278-26, 1303-19

Elementary school/education, economically disadvantaged, 172-81, 172-113, 323-185, 930-2, 1082-10, 1847-43, 2046-2, 2073-4

Elementary school/education, electronic media/online services, 100-5

Elementary school/education, equipment, 467-49, 837-22, 1853-109

Elementary school/education, girls, 467-76, 1847-43

Elementary school/education, immigrants/refugees, 562-30, 562-36, 616-38

Elementary school/education, indigenous peoples, 1847-43

Elementary school/education, infants/toddlers, 798-67

Elementary school/education, minorities, 891-30

Elementary/secondary education, 37-7, 54-8, 58-4, 91-3, 91-4, 91-9, 91-10, 97-51, 105-3, 132-59, 132-60, 135-2, 142-15, 154-3, 154-5, 154-27, 154-47, 166-12, 172-93, 172-95, 172-97, 172-125, 178-39, 216-22, 226-8, 271-3, 271-50, 307-10, 309-7, 309-76, 309-109, 309-110, 323-6, 323-12, 323-45, 323-62, 323-70, 323-75, 323-112, 323-116, 323-128, 323-188, 323-191, 323-240, 323-289, 323-308, 323-330, 323-333, 323-335, 347-2, 347-11, 384-10, 384-16, 413-11, 413-28, 413-52, 413-54, 413-59, 413-63, 416-7, 428-39, 435-5, 435-13, 435-16, 443-21, 447-17, 447-18, 447-23, 447-24, 463-3, 463-11, 463-13, 464-18, 467-1, 467-9, 467-11, 467-18, 467-24, 467-27, 467-41, 467-65, 467-73, 467-78, 467-84, 499-4, 499-5, 499-6, 499-8, 499-9, 499-10, 499-11, 499-14, 499-18, 499-19, 499-20, 499-21, 499-22, 499-23, 499-24, 499-27, 499-28, 499-29, 516-9, 562-62, 562-64, 616-4, 616-7, 616-10, 616-24, 616-27, 616-32, 660-18, 660-19, 660-27, 660-28, 660-50, 660-57, 660-66, 660-105, 660-113, 660-138, 660-148, 660-151, 660-155, 660-163, 660-173, 660-202, 660-206, 660-208, 660-215, 660-236, 660-256, 660-284, 693-10, 693-11, 701-9, 701-14, 701-15, 709-21, 709-104, 744-3, 744-65, 748-58, 756-7, 788-71, 788-142, 788-165, 788-188, 798-14, 798-19, 798-43, 798-44, 820-11, 832-1, 837-8, 837-18, 866-2, 891-50, 892-8, 896-19, 896-20, 905-3, 934-40, 934-52, 934-56, 934-58, 934-105, 1021-74, 1021-77, 1021-82, 1021-87, 1050-31, 1093-9, 1093-40, 1093-41, 1093-70, 1128-3, 1128-4, 1128-5, 1141-1, 1160-14, 1160-17, 1160-18, 1160-19, 1167-6, 1167-10, 1191-2, 1278-1, 1278-3, 1278-6, 1278-10, 1278-13, 1278-16, 1278-17, 1278-24, 1278-27, 1312-17, 1328-9, 1328-47, 1328-76, 1328-126, 1328-168, 1328-205, 1328-207, 1328-209, 1328-215, 1328-224, 1328-270, 1328-316, 1328-331, 1328-339, 1347-22, 1391-109, 1391-111, 1391-201, 1391-423, 1391-549, 1391-656, 1391-694, 1391-809, 1393-101, 1393-163, 1397-1, 1397-6, 1397-7, 1397-8, 1397-11, 1397-12, 1397-13, 1397-17, 1397-24, 1397-29, 1397-32, 1397-35, 1397-36, 1397-38, 1397-39, 1397-41, 1397-42, 1397-43, 1397-46, 1397-47, 1397-48, 1397-49, 1397-50, 1397-51, 1397-52, 1397-53, 1397-54, 1397-55, 1397-56, 1397-58, 1397-59, 1397-61, 1397-67, 1437-6, 1488-2, 1488-12, 1531-15, 1578-67, 1578-85, 1578-86, 1578-87, 1578-123, 1603-17, 1603-19, 1635-5, 1638-8, 1659-22, 1660-23, 1660-24, 1702-8, 1768-9, 1768-14, 1768-19, 1790-4, 1816-2, 1822-14, 1839-8, 1839-9, 1839-13, 1839-14, 1839-33, 1839-47, 1839-62, 1839-76, 1839-87, 1853-1, 1853-34, 1853-37, 1853-39, 1853-55, 1853-56, 1853-72, 1853-98, 1853-126, 1853-146, 1911-24, 1916-93, 1916-113, 1960-1, 1960-2, 1960-3, 2000-2, 2000-3, 2000-12, 2000-13, 2000-14, 2000-15, 2000-34, 2000-44, 2000-45, 2000-46, 2000-47, 2000-48, 2000-54,

271-41, 271-46, 271-54, 271-64, 271-76, 271-86, 271-88, 271-115, 271-116, 271-117, 271-118, 271-119, 271-120, 271-121, 271-122, 271-125, 309-105, 1030-8, 1137-3, 1137-4, 1137-17, 1137-18, 1137-19, 1137-20, 1137-24, 1391-12, 1391-32, 1391-303, 1391-508, 1391-531, 1391-606, 1578-154, 1594-28, 1618-10, 1873-9, 2170-29, 2170-68, 2170-116, 2170-120, 2170-121, 2170-154, 2170-155, 2170-162, 2170-165, 2170-219, 2170-236, 2170-276, 2170-300, 2170-302, 2170-324, 2170-334, 2170-336, 2170-341, 2170-402, 2170-410, 2170-445, 2170-453, 2170-462, 2170-465, 2170-466, 2170-488, 2170-500, 2170-507

Family planning, electronic media/online services, 271-24

Family planning, girls, 271-20, 271-24, 1391-12, 1391-13, 1391-289, 1391-508, 1391-531, 1391-788, 1618-3, 1618-13

Family planning, immigrants/refugees, 1391-209

Family planning, income development, 271-122

Family planning, indigenous peoples, 788-120

Family planning, LGBTQ, 1030-8

Family planning, management development/capacity building, 172-107, 172-110, 271-116

Family planning, men, 2170-29, 2170-68, 2170-165, 2170-445, 2170-467, 2170-488, 2170-500, 2170-505

Family planning, migrant workers, 1391-209

Family planning, minorities, 1391-209, 1391-606

Family planning, program evaluation, 1391-32, 1391-788

Family planning, publication, 2170-466

Family planning, research, 271-54, 788-157, 1391-32, 1391-143, 1391-639, 1873-9, 2170-29, 2170-68, 2170-116, 2170-120, 2170-121, 2170-154, 2170-155, 2170-162, 2170-165, 2170-236, 2170-276, 2170-300, 2170-302, 2170-336, 2170-341, 2170-402, 2170-410, 2170-426, 2170-445, 2170-453, 2170-462, 2170-465, 2170-467, 2170-488, 2170-500, 2170-505, 2170-507

Family planning, technical assistance, 271-86

Family planning, women, 105-24, 105-38, 135-29, 172-41, 172-100, 172-104, 172-105, 172-107, 172-110, 271-20, 271-21, 271-41, 271-45, 271-46, 271-54, 271-64, 271-76, 271-86, 271-88, 271-115, 271-116, 271-117, 271-118, 271-119, 271-120, 271-121, 271-122, 271-125, 309-105, 782-23, 788-154, 788-157, 891-31, 1030-8, 1137-3, 1137-4, 1137-17, 1137-18, 1137-19, 1137-20, 1137-24, 1137-25, 1137-26, 1137-27, 1137-28, 1137-29, 1137-30, 1137-31, 1137-32, 1137-33, 1137-34, 1137-35, 1137-36, 1137-37, 1137-38, 1391-32, 1391-136, 1391-143, 1391-149, 1391-209, 1391-303, 1391-508, 1391-606, 1391-639, 1578-154, 1593-113, 1594-28, 1618-10, 1873-9, 2170-29, 2170-68, 2170-116, 2170-120, 2170-121, 2170-154, 2170-155, 2170-162, 2170-165, 2170-219, 2170-236, 2170-276, 2170-300, 2170-302, 2170-324, 2170-334, 2170-336, 2170-341, 2170-402, 2170-410, 2170-426, 2170-445, 2170-453, 2170-462, 2170-465, 2170-466, 2170-488, 2170-500, 2170-507

Family planning, youth, 271-28, 788-120, 1391-32, 1391-137, 1391-290, 1391-606

Family resources and services, aging, 2211-1

Family resources and services, children/youth, 443-6, 1021-7, 1021-53, 1853-114

Family resources and services, crime/abuse victims, 1021-7

Family resources and services, disabilities, people with, 443-6, 1021-25, 1021-53, 1853-114

Family resources and services, disability, 443-6, 1021-7, 1021-25, 1021-53, 1831-3, 1853-114, 2211-1

Family resources and services, equipment, 1853-114

Family resources and services, infants/toddlers, 1021-25

Family resources and services, management development/capacity building, 2211-1

Family resources and services, mentally disabled, 1021-7, 1831-3, 2211-1

Family resources and services, women, 1021-53

Family services, 132-5, 132-32, 132-36, 132-54, 132-58, 142-14, 154-16, 323-44, 323-338, 413-4, 413-62, 435-9, 447-23, 467-90, 616-43, 660-42, 693-27, 701-17, 701-18, 701-19, 709-27, 798-43, 798-44, 934-61, 1021-44, 1021-49, 1021-50, 1021-89, 1021-90, 1093-36, 1303-34, 1328-173, 1391-341, 1391-489, 1391-612, 1639-184, 1853-14, 1853-24, 1853-86, 1951-1, 1951-2, 2000-54, 2000-55, 2170-28, 2170-50, 2199-3

Family services, adolescent parents, 1328-349

Family services, aging, 1021-1, 1021-47, 1021-97, 1391-45, 2211-8

Family services, AIDS, people with, 132-32, 132-36, 132-54, 132-58, 1303-34

Family services, Asians/Pacific Islanders, 1081-12

Family services, building/renovation, 467-90

Family services, children/youth, 132-32, 132-42, 132-43, 132-54, 154-16, 323-44, 323-338, 413-4, 443-17, 447-23, 616-43, 709-27, 709-97, 798-34, 798-43, 798-44, 934-61, 1021-44, 1021-50, 1021-89, 1093-22, 1093-36, 1832-3, 1951-2, 2000-54, 2000-55

Family services, conferences/seminars, 1039-12, 1093-22

Family services, counseling, 891-41, 1021-10, 1021-44, 1021-90

Family services, crime/abuse victims, 709-27, 798-34, 934-61, 1021-89, 1081-12

Family services, disabilities, people with, 467-90, 1021-1, 1021-47

Family services, domestic violence, 309-49, 309-50, 443-10, 1021-28, 1058-10, 1831-4, 1853-60

Family services, economically disadvantaged, 132-5, 132-36, 132-58, 323-44, 323-338, 413-62, 435-9, 447-23, 467-90, 798-43, 798-44, 934-61, 1021-49, 1021-90, 1021-97, 1303-34, 1391-341, 1391-612, 1639-184, 1853-2, 1853-14, 1853-24, 1853-86, 1951-1, 1951-2, 2000-54, 2000-55, 2170-28, 2170-50, 2199-3

Family services, equipment, 1021-49

Family services, faculty/staff development, 1021-90

Family services, home/homemaker aid, 443-17, 709-97, 1021-1, 1021-47, 1021-97, 1391-45, 2211-8

Family services, homeless, 1832-3

Family services, immigrants/refugees, 413-4, 1021-50, 1081-12

Family services, income development, 1391-489

Family services, infants/toddlers, 1021-44, 1437-9, 1639-184

Family services, management development/capacity building, 1391-489

Family services, mentally disabled, 1391-45, 2211-8

Family services, military/veterans, 413-62, 1081-12

Family services, minorities, 1437-9, 1853-24

Family services, parent education, 132-42, 132-43, 798-34, 1021-90, 1039-12, 1081-12, 1093-22, 1437-9, 1832-3

Family services, program evaluation, 1391-341

Family services, publication, 1639-184

Family services, research, 1391-341, 1391-612, 2170-50

Family services, sex workers, 934-61

Family services, single parents, 1391-516

Family services, substance abusers, 467-90, 1021-10, 1021-90

Family services, technical assistance, 1303-34

Family services, women, 413-4, 934-61, 1021-50, 1021-89, 1303-34, 1437-9, 1639-184, 1853-24

Family services, youth, 1081-12, 1391-612

Federated States of Micronesia, animals/wildlife, 271-151

Federated States of Micronesia, community improvement/development, 271-95, 271-151

Federated States of Micronesia, environment, 238-40, 271-34, 271-95, 271-151

Federated States of Micronesia, food/nutrition/agriculture, 271-151

Federated States of Micronesia, health—general, 1624-16

Federated States of Micronesia, science, 238-40, 1624-16

Fellowships, animals/wildlife, 97-96

Fellowships, arts/culture/humanities, 216-30, 323-371, 439-2, 814-1, 824-4, 1039-4, 1039-29, 1039-30, 1039-31, 1312-19, 1330-11, 1347-2, 1391-38, 1391-437, 1391-781, 1397-3, 1428-5, 1428-17, 1428-47, 1488-3, 1509-1, 1509-5, 1509-6, 1509-8, 1509-11, 1509-14, 1509-17, 1531-35, 1546-33, 1546-74, 1578-33, 1593-15, 1593-131, 1639-96, 1639-97, 1916-13, 1916-56, 1916-57, 1923-17, 2170-181, 2170-224

Fellowships, civil rights, 891-35, 1030-19, 1391-20, 1391-79, 1593-38, 1593-66, 1593-122

Fellowships, community improvement/development, 105-46, 105-48, 119-1, 119-4, 1391-720, 1423-1, 1423-2, 1423-3, 1638-36

Fellowships, crime/courts/legal services, 1391-628, 1393-150, 1393-151, 1393-152, 1593-140

Fellowships, education, 21-11, 97-96, 97-107, 178-38, 320-4, 323-187, 820-3, 820-5, 820-11, 891-35, 952-22, 1039-4, 1039-9, 1039-10, 1039-14, 1039-15, 1039-29, 1039-30, 1039-31, 1058-146, 1312-38, 1312-41, 1312-43, 1328-168, 1391-79, 1391-423, 1391-451, 1391-628, 1391-720, 1397-21, 1397-44, 1423-1, 1423-2, 1423-3, 1428-3, 1428-47, 1509-1, 1509-5, 1509-6, 1509-14, 1531-15, 1546-15, 1546-20, 1546-33, 1546-74, 1546-91, 1546-115, 1546-116, 1546-118, 1546-119, 1546-120, 1546-122, 1593-131, 1594-36, 1638-5, 1639-96, 1672-36, 1672-40, 1853-2, 2212-25, 2212-41, 2212-42, 2212-63, 2212-64, 2212-65

Fellowships, environment, 97-96, 105-10, 105-33, 105-46, 105-48, 251-75, 950-2, 1853-2, 1853-51

Fellowships, food/nutrition/agriculture, 119-5, 1081-9

Fellowships, health—general, 119-3, 119-7, 178-38, 952-22, 1361-6, 1391-20, 1393-114, 1393-162, 1593-76, 1593-133, 2170-181, 2170-224

Fellowships, health—specific diseases, 119-8, 1593-133

Fellowships, human services—multipurpose, 1393-162, 1593-76

Fellowships, international affairs/development, 97-107, 105-10, 105-33, 105-46, 105-48, 119-1, 119-2, 119-4, 119-5, 119-6, 119-8, 178-38, 439-2, 820-3, 820-5, 891-35, 967-20, 996-46, 1030-19, 1039-9, 1039-10, 1050-28, 1058-146, 1058-159, 1058-163, 1312-19, 1312-41, 1312-43, 1328-268, 1347-2, 1391-301, 1391-437, 1391-720, 1391-781, 1393-114, 1393-150, 1393-151, 1393-152, 1393-162, 1397-3, 1397-21, 1397-44, 1423-1, 1423-2, 1423-3, 1531-12, 1531-15, 1546-20, 1546-74, 1578-33, 1578-138, 1593-15, 1593-24, 1593-38, 1593-66, 1593-122, 1593-140, 1594-36, 1618-2, 1638-5, 1638-36, 1638-102, 1639-96, 1672-36, 1847-42, 1847-46, 1847-47, 1847-52, 1847-53, 1847-54, 1847-55, 1853-2, 1853-51, 1923-17, 2170-181, 2212-8, 2212-25, 2212-41, 2212-42

Fellowships, medical research, 1361-6

Fellowships, mental health/substance abuse, 1593-133

Fellowships, philanthropy/voluntarism, 1058-146, 1058-159, 1490-38

Fellowships, public affairs/government, 891-35, 1058-72, 1058-146, 1058-159, 1058-163, 1328-268, 1391-720, 1391-781, 1393-114, 1546-97, 1638-36, 1638-102, 2212-8, 2212-63, 2212-64, 2212-65

Fellowships, recreation/sports/athletics, 1847-42

Fellowships, religion, 323-187, 1347-2, 1923-6

Fellowships, science, 950-2, 1312-38, 1428-40, 1853-2, 1916-13, 1916-56, 1916-57, 2004-10

Fellowships, social sciences, 21-11, 105-10, 105-39, 216-35, 820-3, 820-5, 820-11, 1030-19, 1039-9, 1039-10, 1039-14, 1039-29, 1039-30, 1328-268, 1391-20, 1391-628, 1393-150, 1393-151, 1393-152, 1397-3, 1397-21, 1428-3, 1428-17, 1531-12, 1531-35, 1546-74, 1546-97, 1593-38, 1593-140, 1594-36, 1672-36, 1672-40, 1923-17, 2170-224, 2212-8, 2212-25, 2212-41, 2212-42, 2212-63, 2212-64, 2212-65

Fellowships, youth development, 97-107, 119-2, 1847-42, 1847-53, 1847-55

Fiji, animals/wildlife, 271-159, 271-169, 788-60

Fiji, arts/culture/humanities, 97-106

2170-481, 2170-489, 2170-509, 2170-522, 2170-523, 2170-527, 2170-538, 2170-542, 2170-548

Health care, rural areas, 132-34, 178-11, 309-34, 467-41, 735-1, 787-1, 788-120, 788-180, 952-5, 952-8, 952-11, 952-16, 952-17, 952-20, 952-24, 952-25, 952-29, 952-34, 952-37, 952-38, 952-45, 952-46, 952-48, 1093-53, 1137-45, 1303-17, 1303-18, 1578-192, 1639-156, 1639-158, 2170-85, 2170-542

Health care, seed money, 271-43, 934-102, 952-34, 1639-18

Health care, single organization support, 709-14, 709-64, 872-1, 872-2, 1293-1, 1424-13, 1578-9, 1635-9, 1839-31, 1940-16, 1940-17

Health care, single parents, 467-36

Health care, substance abusers, 335-6, 1393-78, 1393-167, 1593-110

Health care, support services, 10-1, 91-12, 226-2, 309-33, 629-5, 709-59, 709-69, 735-13, 735-24, 934-90, 984-1, 1037-4, 1093-80, 1093-94, 1179-21, 1179-22, 1179-23, 1179-116, 1179-159, 1303-24, 1303-25, 2004-22, 2004-23, 2199-89

Health care, technical assistance, 271-77, 467-53, 1303-14, 1303-23, 1303-68, 1639-162

Health care, terminal illness, people with, 1393-162

Health care, volunteer services, 17-2, 91-13, 166-4, 238-15, 309-35, 309-36, 309-37, 309-38, 309-39, 309-40, 309-41, 309-42, 309-43, 309-44, 309-45, 323-100, 323-101, 323-102, 323-103, 323-104, 323-105, 323-106, 323-107, 323-108, 428-12, 435-11, 562-9, 562-10, 605-8, 660-30, 717-1, 735-17, 934-104, 1055-5, 1139-4, 1141-10, 1371-8, 1397-10, 1433-2, 1437-3, 1490-11, 1578-68, 1578-69, 1578-70, 1578-71, 1597-1, 1635-8, 1718-5, 1768-5, 1814-4, 1832-4, 2039-1, 2079-1, 2079-2, 2098-11, 2199-33, 2199-34, 2211-5, 2212-18

Health care, women, 105-38, 172-6, 172-48, 172-60, 172-103, 271-20, 271-21, 271-46, 271-59, 271-61, 271-70, 271-76, 271-77, 271-78, 271-86, 271-87, 271-88, 271-89, 271-117, 271-123, 271-128, 271-130, 271-136, 271-162, 271-166, 335-44, 467-16, 467-17, 467-36, 562-5, 562-6, 562-16, 562-68, 660-263, 729-7, 735-3, 782-9, 782-14, 788-3, 788-4, 788-53, 788-59, 788-72, 788-93, 788-94, 788-119, 788-148, 788-154, 788-157, 788-180, 1093-48, 1137-5, 1137-6, 1137-12, 1137-17, 1137-18, 1137-19, 1137-20, 1179-27, 1391-42, 1391-94, 1391-136, 1391-443, 1391-458, 1391-807, 1393-80, 1393-115, 1593-126, 1618-10, 1639-32, 1639-36, 1639-69, 1639-136, 1639-157, 1639-158, 1639-184, 1639-187, 2000-80, 2004-17, 2170-66, 2170-70, 2170-188, 2170-244, 2170-260, 2170-274, 2170-312, 2170-318, 2170-320, 2170-326, 2170-327, 2170-338, 2170-339, 2170-409, 2170-489, 2170-509, 2170-522, 2170-548, 2199-96, 2199-104

Health care, youth, 271-123, 562-16, 788-120

Health organizations, 735-19, 1093-73, 1393-70, 1593-54, 1639-46, 2170-107, 2170-363, 2203-34

Health organizations, AIDS, people with, 735-19, 1093-73, 1393-70, 1593-54, 1639-46, 2170-363

Health organizations, children/youth, 2199-19, 2199-20

Health organizations, economically disadvantaged, 1093-73, 1639-46, 2170-107, 2170-363, 2199-19, 2199-20, 2203-34

Health organizations, fund raising/fund distribution, 1578-189, 2199-19, 2199-20

Health organizations, men, 1578-189

Health organizations, program evaluation, 2170-107

Health organizations, technical assistance, 1639-46

Health sciences school/education, 178-36, 309-121, 735-36, 952-1, 952-2, 952-3, 1303-64, 1303-70, 1303-71, 1424-15, 1578-172, 1578-173, 1639-51, 1659-19, 2004-9, 2170-437, 2170-498

Health sciences school/education, conferences/ seminars, 952-2, 952-3

Health sciences school/education, curriculum development, 1639-51

Health sciences school/education, economically disadvantaged, 1303-64, 2170-437, 2170-498

Health sciences school/education, faculty/staff development, 309-121, 1303-64, 1303-70, 1303-71

Health sciences school/education, migrant workers, 1303-70, 1303-71

Health sciences school/education, minorities, 2170-498

Health sciences school/education, research, 2170-498

Health sciences school/education, seed money, 2170-437

Health—general, Afghanistan, 309-4, 1393-148, 2170-403, 2170-404, 2170-405, 2170-516, 2170-517, 2170-518, 2170-519

Health—general, Africa, 172-4, 172-100, 172-102, 178-36, 271-119, 271-130, 271-161, 271-166, 302-7, 323-121, 323-123, 323-124, 323-332, 435-4, 503-4, 503-6, 503-7, 735-14, 744-51, 744-52, 832-3, 934-2, 987-1, 1030-8, 1092-47, 1137-22, 1179-1, 1179-2, 1179-3, 1184-10, 1184-12, 1184-13, 1184-14, 1184-15, 1184-16, 1184-17, 1184-18, 1184-19, 1184-20, 1184-21, 1184-22, 1184-23, 1184-24, 1184-26, 1184-28, 1303-26, 1361-10, 1361-18, 1361-20, 1391-18, 1391-20, 1391-24, 1391-32, 1391-467, 1391-584, 1391-681, 1391-790, 1585-1, 1639-4, 1639-5, 1639-36, 1639-179, 1665-14, 1847-57, 2000-56, 2000-58, 2004-5, 2004-26, 2170-4, 2170-5, 2170-13, 2170-41, 2170-59, 2170-105, 2170-119, 2170-139, 2170-166, 2170-179, 2170-191, 2170-226, 2170-233, 2170-247, 2170-257, 2170-261, 2170-286, 2170-318, 2170-320, 2170-329, 2170-334, 2170-338, 2170-339, 2170-397, 2170-409, 2170-410, 2170-411, 2170-421, 2170-431, 2170-461, 2170-471, 2170-489, 2170-509, 2170-535

Health—general, Angola, 2004-17, 2004-27, 2170-403, 2170-404, 2170-405, 2170-546

Health—general, Argentina, 335-27, 335-35, 467-85, 1391-344, 1391-458, 1391-459, 1391-460, 1391-461, 1391-462, 2170-171

Health—general, Armenia, 1055-3

Health—general, Asia, 271-117, 271-130, 271-161, 323-332, 335-26, 737-3, 1093-3, 1148-2, 1303-6, 1391-445, 1391-736, 1639-106, 1639-136, 2170-20, 2170-41, 2170-119, 2170-138, 2170-139, 2170-166, 2170-191, 2170-261, 2170-282, 2170-334, 2170-397, 2170-409, 2170-410, 2170-509

Health—general, Australia, 335-49, 735-23, 1303-56, 1303-59, 2170-26, 2170-251, 2170-260, 2170-272, 2170-273, 2170-274, 2170-276, 2170-340, 2170-341, 2170-352, 2170-411, 2170-465, 2170-478, 2170-503

Health—general, Austria, 1093-2

Health—general, Bahrain, 857-3

Health—general, Bangladesh, 100-13, 135-27, 238-15, 264-3, 264-4, 709-15, 1179-258, 1518-6, 1601-7, 1639-1, 1639-18, 1639-19, 1639-21, 1639-51, 1639-57, 1639-102, 1639-103, 1639-104, 1639-105, 1639-153, 1847-37, 2170-65, 2170-82, 2170-167, 2170-188, 2170-189, 2170-197, 2170-206, 2170-428

Health—general, Barbados, 1391-144

Health—general, Belgium, 693-26, 1021-1, 1093-35, 1391-559, 1853-72, 2170-119, 2170-334

Health—general, Benin, 814-18, 2170-116, 2203-34

Health—general, Bhutan, 2170-197

Health—general, Bolivia, 748-44, 1137-7, 2170-138, 2170-139, 2199-103

Health—general, Botswana, 323-347, 1186-1, 1303-14, 2170-4

Health—general, Brazil, 172-71, 335-25, 335-31, 428-23, 798-6, 1093-18, 1093-20, 1128-37, 1128-38, 1128-41, 1128-42, 1128-43, 1179-112, 1179-113, 1179-114, 1179-172, 1391-352, 1391-353, 1601-1, 1639-1, 1847-58, 1926-3, 2170-132

Health—general, Burkina Faso, 2170-116, 2170-192, 2170-402

Health—general, Burma (Myanmar), 135-30, 1593-44, 1593-95, 1593-102, 1593-112, 1593-134, 2170-539, 2203-52

Health—general, Burundi, 1030-2

Health—general, Cambodia, 91-19, 91-42, 323-137, 335-19, 443-12, 463-5, 1639-32, 2170-184, 2170-256

Health—general, Cameroon, 178-24, 2000-31, 2000-32, 2170-203

Health—general, Canada, 605-4, 709-109, 1021-15, 1021-72, 1058-74, 1093-24, 1093-88, 1337-9, 1391-6, 1391-790, 1424-13, 1639-28, 1639-29, 1639-119, 1639-189, 1853-44, 1853-48, 1853-100, 1853-114, 1853-144, 1926-1, 2161-1, 2161-13, 2170-110, 2170-133, 2170-302, 2170-373, 2170-425, 2170-437, 2170-454, 2170-477, 2170-480

Health—general, Caribbean, 428-23, 467-5, 782-23, 870-3, 1128-37, 1128-38, 1128-41, 1128-42, 1128-43, 1137-38, 1179-112, 1179-113, 1179-114, 1391-144, 1534-2, 1534-3, 1594-28

Health—general, Cayman Islands, 1021-69

Health—general, Central Africa, 1639-140, 2170-121

Health—general, Central Africa Republic, 2170-416

Health—general, Central America, 100-13, 105-6, 135-20, 178-18, 178-19, 744-7, 1179-258, 1391-150, 1391-320, 1391-389, 1391-461, 1391-547, 1391-609, 1980-13, 2170-179

Health—general, Central Asia and the Caucasus, 1393-167, 1593-128

Health—general, Chad, 2170-192, 2170-403, 2170-404, 2170-405, 2170-418

Health—general, Chile, 1391-298, 1391-342, 1393-100, 1639-187

Health—general, China, 100-7, 312-5, 335-2, 335-40, 335-59, 428-40, 693-9, 693-12, 709-85, 729-7, 952-1, 952-2, 952-5, 952-7, 952-8, 952-11, 952-12, 952-13, 952-14, 952-15, 952-16, 952-17, 952-19, 952-20, 952-21, 952-24, 952-25, 952-29, 952-31, 952-33, 952-34, 952-35, 952-36, 952-37, 952-38, 952-43, 952-44, 952-45, 952-46, 952-47, 952-48, 952-49, 1021-43, 1021-46, 1021-99, 1093-17, 1093-43, 1093-44, 1151-7, 1151-8, 1151-12, 1151-13, 1186-5, 1303-6, 1303-17, 1303-18, 1303-19, 1303-69, 1303-70, 1303-71, 1303-72, 1303-73, 1391-106, 1391-109, 1391-111, 1391-143, 1391-199, 1391-201, 1391-209, 1391-211, 1391-214, 1391-218, 1391-242, 1391-347, 1391-569, 1391-639, 1391-657, 1391-712, 1391-821, 1423-69, 1423-70, 1531-22, 1601-1, 1638-32, 1638-33, 1638-35, 1638-38, 1638-117, 1638-142, 1822-13, 1822-15, 1847-60, 1853-88, 1853-152, 1926-4, 2170-277, 2170-283, 2170-344, 2170-398, 2170-481, 2170-533, 2170-539

Health—general, Colombia, 1137-7, 2170-121

Health—general, Congo, 798-18, 2170-516, 2170-517, 2170-518, 2170-519

Health—general, Costa Rica, 1839-31

Health—general, Czech Republic, 54-1, 709-108, 1093-57

Health—general, Democratic Republic of the Congo, 21-4, 21-5, 21-6, 798-18, 1184-9, 1303-13, 1433-1, 2170-242, 2170-402, 2170-403, 2170-404, 2170-405, 2170-516, 2170-517, 2170-518, 2170-519, 2199-66

Health—general, Denmark, 1093-23, 2170-95

Health—general, Developing countries, 91-14, 91-15, 91-30, 91-43, 100-2, 105-38, 119-3, 119-7, 135-17, 135-18, 142-11, 166-9, 166-11, 166-16, 166-17, 172-40, 172-41, 172-48, 172-54, 172-64, 172-103, 172-104, 172-105, 172-106, 172-107, 172-111, 172-146, 172-151, 172-152, 172-153, 178-9, 271-21, 271-32, 271-40, 271-43, 271-54, 271-61, 271-116, 271-120, 271-122, 271-136, 271-162, 271-165, 271-167, 307-25, 309-105, 309-117, 309-118, 309-123, 323-53, 323-196, 323-197, 323-207, 323-208, 323-209, 323-210, 323-237, 323-276, 323-279, 323-336, 323-337, 323-382, 325-34, 325-35, 347-9, 428-12, 435-25, 435-37, 460-7, 503-9, 562-68, 605-4, 605-5, 605-6, 605-12, 605-13, 605-16, 605-17, 605-18, 605-23, 605-25, 605-26, 605-27, 605-28, 626-17, 629-5, 693-45, 709-59, 709-69, 735-15, 735-21,

735-24, 735-30, 735-32, 735-36, 756-28, 782-9,
782-20, 782-24, 787-4, 788-72, 788-93, 788-109,
788-111, 788-154, 840-13, 852-4, 891-25, 984-8,
1036-3, 1037-9, 1050-24, 1093-73, 1093-86,
1093-91, 1093-92, 1093-93, 1137-3, 1137-4,
1137-5, 1137-6, 1137-12, 1137-13, 1137-14,
1137-15, 1137-16, 1137-17, 1137-18, 1137-19,
1137-20, 1137-22, 1137-24, 1137-25, 1137-26,
1137-27, 1137-28, 1137-29, 1137-30, 1137-31,
1137-32, 1137-33, 1137-34, 1137-35, 1137-36,
1137-37, 1137-39, 1137-40, 1137-43, 1137-45,
1141-1, 1141-2, 1141-8, 1141-9, 1141-10,
1179-7, 1179-116, 1179-137, 1179-138,
1179-155, 1179-156, 1179-157, 1179-158,
1179-167, 1179-168, 1179-169, 1179-170,
1179-171, 1179-246, 1179-257, 1186-11,
1186-12, 1292-3, 1303-30, 1303-33, 1303-63,
1347-35, 1360-15, 1360-21, 1361-14, 1361-15,
1391-18, 1391-32, 1391-33, 1391-177,
1391-298, 1391-303, 1391-346, 1391-353,
1391-360, 1391-383, 1391-431, 1391-432,
1391-449, 1391-458, 1391-515, 1391-559,
1391-606, 1391-726, 1391-728, 1391-744,
1391-790, 1391-798, 1393-113, 1393-142,
1393-144, 1393-145, 1393-146, 1393-175,
1393-176, 1424-16, 1534-6, 1534-11, 1534-12,
1578-109, 1578-110, 1578-111, 1578-112,
1578-154, 1578-158, 1578-172, 1578-173,
1593-86, 1593-90, 1593-110, 1601-4, 1601-5,
1603-11, 1624-23, 1639-31, 1639-38, 1639-40,
1639-49, 1639-70, 1639-83, 1639-144,
1639-147, 1639-157, 1639-166, 1639-176,
1639-189, 1639-195, 1639-200, 1639-203,
1639-208, 1639-210, 1659-33, 1668-3, 1672-35,
1768-10, 1768-11, 1814-5, 1847-10, 1847-41,
1847-48, 1847-69, 1853-129, 1873-9, 1940-18,
1940-19, 1974-6, 1974-8, 1980-16, 2000-57,
2004-11, 2004-12, 2004-21, 2004-22, 2004-23,
2061-18, 2075-1, 2083-3, 2098-8, 2098-9,
2098-11, 2170-2, 2170-7, 2170-8, 2170-9,
2170-13, 2170-14, 2170-15, 2170-18, 2170-22,
2170-26, 2170-27, 2170-29, 2170-34, 2170-37,
2170-38, 2170-39, 2170-40, 2170-42, 2170-47,
2170-56, 2170-57, 2170-58, 2170-60, 2170-61,
2170-66, 2170-67, 2170-68, 2170-70, 2170-71,
2170-74, 2170-75, 2170-76, 2170-77, 2170-78,
2170-79, 2170-81, 2170-83, 2170-88, 2170-89,
2170-90, 2170-91, 2170-93, 2170-94, 2170-95,
2170-96, 2170-100, 2170-106, 2170-108,
2170-110, 2170-111, 2170-112, 2170-114,
2170-115, 2170-127, 2170-128, 2170-129,
2170-132, 2170-133, 2170-134, 2170-136,
2170-137, 2170-140, 2170-142, 2170-143,
2170-145, 2170-147, 2170-148, 2170-151,
2170-152, 2170-153, 2170-154, 2170-155,
2170-157, 2170-159, 2170-160, 2170-162,
2170-163, 2170-165, 2170-169, 2170-170,
2170-171, 2170-172, 2170-173, 2170-175,
2170-188, 2170-189, 2170-190, 2170-208,
2170-209, 2170-212, 2170-213, 2170-215,
2170-218, 2170-222, 2170-223, 2170-224,
2170-227, 2170-228, 2170-229, 2170-230,
2170-236, 2170-240, 2170-241, 2170-243,
2170-246, 2170-248, 2170-249, 2170-250,
2170-258, 2170-259, 2170-260, 2170-267,
2170-269, 2170-271, 2170-272, 2170-273,
2170-274, 2170-276, 2170-277, 2170-278,
2170-279, 2170-283, 2170-284, 2170-285,
2170-288, 2170-289, 2170-290, 2170-291,
2170-293, 2170-294, 2170-295, 2170-296,
2170-300, 2170-301, 2170-302, 2170-311,
2170-312, 2170-314, 2170-321, 2170-322,
2170-325, 2170-326, 2170-327, 2170-328,
2170-330, 2170-331, 2170-332, 2170-337,
2170-338, 2170-339, 2170-340, 2170-341,
2170-343, 2170-346, 2170-347, 2170-348,
2170-351, 2170-352, 2170-353, 2170-354,
2170-355, 2170-356, 2170-357, 2170-363,
2170-364, 2170-367, 2170-372, 2170-373,
2170-377, 2170-381, 2170-382, 2170-384,
2170-385, 2170-386, 2170-392, 2170-393,
2170-395, 2170-397, 2170-398, 2170-407,
2170-409, 2170-413, 2170-423, 2170-425,
2170-427, 2170-433, 2170-434, 2170-435,

2170-436, 2170-437, 2170-438, 2170-439,
2170-440, 2170-441, 2170-442, 2170-443,
2170-445, 2170-446, 2170-448, 2170-449,
2170-450, 2170-451, 2170-453, 2170-455,
2170-457, 2170-458, 2170-459, 2170-460,
2170-462, 2170-465, 2170-466, 2170-468,
2170-469, 2170-470, 2170-473, 2170-476,
2170-477, 2170-478, 2170-480, 2170-483,
2170-484, 2170-485, 2170-486, 2170-487,
2170-488, 2170-491, 2170-492, 2170-493,
2170-494, 2170-495, 2170-496, 2170-497,
2170-500, 2170-503, 2170-504, 2170-506,
2170-507, 2170-509, 2170-511, 2170-514,
2170-516, 2170-517, 2170-518, 2170-519,
2170-521, 2170-522, 2170-523, 2170-524,
2170-526, 2170-527, 2170-528, 2170-530,
2170-531, 2170-532, 2170-535, 2170-536,
2170-537, 2170-538, 2170-540, 2170-541,
2170-550, 2170-551, 2170-553, 2199-89,
2212-47
Health—general, Dominican Republic, 1768-12,
    2170-121, 2170-138, 2170-139
Health—general, East Africa/Horn of Africa, 1030-2,
    1030-13, 1361-8, 1639-95, 1639-116, 1639-140,
    2170-121, 2170-323
Health—general, East Asia, 1397-10
Health—general, Eastern & Central Europe, 1093-3,
    1303-65, 1593-128, 1890-2, 2170-139
Health—general, Ecuador, 660-263, 1137-7
Health—general, Egypt, 172-6, 1391-57, 1391-136,
    1391-137, 1391-147, 1391-289, 1391-290,
    1391-291, 1391-335, 1391-457, 1391-561,
    1391-614, 1391-703, 2170-44, 2170-98,
    2170-138
Health—general, El Salvador, 467-99, 960-2,
    1391-343, 1391-469
Health—general, England, 172-116, 335-40, 443-7,
    503-6, 709-28, 709-61, 788-30, 788-94, 788-154,
    788-163, 814-5, 814-24, 879-1, 1093-6, 1093-7,
    1093-8, 1093-9, 1093-25, 1093-56, 1093-66,
    1093-67, 1093-79, 1137-25, 1137-26, 1137-27,
    1137-28, 1137-29, 1137-30, 1137-31, 1137-32,
    1137-33, 1137-34, 1137-35, 1137-36, 1137-37,
    1186-4, 1337-3, 1337-4, 1337-6, 1391-460,
    1391-584, 1562-1, 1601-4, 1601-5, 1618-10,
    1638-32, 1639-5, 1639-49, 1639-70, 1639-113,
    1639-136, 1639-200, 1847-48, 2170-30,
    2170-61, 2170-151, 2170-157, 2170-159,
    2170-160, 2170-161, 2170-218, 2170-233,
    2170-243, 2170-244, 2170-245, 2170-246,
    2170-247, 2170-248, 2170-249, 2170-250,
    2170-256, 2170-271, 2170-312, 2170-314,
    2170-346, 2170-353, 2170-356, 2170-357,
    2170-421, 2170-452, 2170-453
Health—general, Ethiopia, 100-13, 178-23, 271-3,
    271-7, 271-28, 271-39, 271-45, 271-50, 271-60,
    271-109, 744-4, 788-143, 1179-27, 1179-258,
    1518-5, 1847-9, 2170-181, 2170-242, 2170-244,
    2170-310, 2170-336, 2170-360, 2170-421,
    2170-546, 2199-107, 2203-8
Health—general, Europe, 105-27, 172-153, 693-26,
    1093-3, 1093-29, 1093-35, 1093-49, 1337-3,
    1337-4, 1391-559, 1393-167, 2170-119,
    2170-297, 2170-334, 2170-389, 2170-411
Health—general, Federated States of Micronesia,
    1624-16
Health—general, Finland, 709-64
Health—general, France, 54-17, 709-7, 1021-80,
    1093-11, 1093-12, 1093-13, 1293-1, 1391-726,
    1428-57, 1853-102, 1853-121, 1853-129,
    2170-116, 2170-311
Health—general, Gambia, The, 2170-80
Health—general, Germany, 172-40, 271-39, 271-40,
    428-12, 709-30, 1093-49, 1093-68, 1303-45,
    1337-8, 1391-42, 1391-147, 2170-98, 2170-152,
    2170-153, 2170-227, 2170-393
Health—general, Ghana, 100-13, 172-64, 435-35,
    435-36, 660-171, 660-198, 660-204, 660-213,
    660-232, 1179-258, 1312-59, 1601-6, 1639-3,
    1639-36, 1639-130, 1639-159, 1639-191,
    2170-113, 2170-529
Health—general, Global programs, 54-17, 91-12,
    91-13, 105-8, 105-27, 105-36, 105-38, 105-42,
    105-47, 119-3, 166-4, 172-4, 172-12, 172-40,

172-54, 172-62, 172-63, 172-64, 172-100,
172-105, 172-106, 172-107, 172-110, 172-116,
172-146, 172-151, 178-9, 178-38, 238-5, 238-20,
238-21, 238-22, 238-24, 238-35, 238-49, 238-51,
271-4, 271-30, 271-61, 271-87, 271-120,
271-122, 271-138, 271-145, 271-162, 271-163,
271-165, 286-5, 307-11, 307-12, 307-19, 307-25,
309-33, 309-35, 309-39, 309-43, 309-53, 309-63,
309-105, 309-121, 323-102, 323-103, 323-104,
323-106, 323-107, 323-108, 323-123, 323-124,
323-341, 325-39, 335-33, 335-34, 435-11,
439-69, 455-2, 464-3, 464-9, 464-21, 562-5,
562-7, 562-9, 562-10, 605-8, 605-11, 605-12,
605-13, 605-18, 605-19, 605-27, 660-30, 684-3,
717-1, 735-7, 735-9, 735-12, 735-13, 735-14,
735-15, 735-17, 735-19, 735-21, 735-32, 744-10,
748-31, 782-14, 782-20, 782-22, 787-4, 788-21,
788-36, 788-43, 788-57, 788-85, 788-91, 788-93,
788-148, 788-154, 788-163, 829-1, 840-1, 840-2,
840-3, 840-13, 879-1, 891-18, 891-25, 892-7,
896-18, 934-61, 950-1, 952-2, 952-22, 996-31,
996-37, 996-38, 996-39, 996-40, 996-41, 1023-2,
1037-9, 1050-10, 1050-18, 1055-5, 1058-61,
1058-112, 1081-18, 1093-2, 1093-7, 1093-21,
1093-48, 1093-57, 1093-64, 1093-86, 1093-91,
1093-92, 1093-93, 1093-94, 1137-12, 1137-13,
1137-14, 1137-15, 1137-16, 1137-17, 1137-18,
1137-19, 1137-20, 1137-23, 1137-25, 1137-26,
1137-27, 1137-28, 1137-29, 1137-30, 1137-31,
1137-32, 1137-33, 1137-34, 1137-35, 1137-36,
1137-37, 1137-41, 1137-42, 1137-44, 1139-1,
1139-4, 1179-16, 1179-17, 1179-21, 1179-22,
1179-23, 1179-29, 1179-102, 1179-103,
1179-104, 1179-136, 1179-139, 1179-140,
1179-159, 1179-162, 1179-167, 1179-168,
1179-169, 1179-170, 1179-171, 1184-10,
1184-32, 1292-1, 1292-2, 1292-3, 1292-4,
1292-6, 1292-7, 1292-8, 1303-16, 1303-24,
1303-25, 1303-26, 1303-31, 1303-32, 1303-33,
1303-40, 1303-41, 1303-42, 1303-63, 1324-1,
1337-1, 1337-2, 1337-5, 1337-6, 1337-7, 1337-9,
1337-11, 1347-38, 1360-15, 1361-1, 1361-6,
1361-10, 1361-13, 1361-20, 1371-8, 1371-11,
1391-6, 1391-12, 1391-13, 1391-31, 1391-32,
1391-33, 1391-106, 1391-117, 1391-151,
1391-157, 1391-158, 1391-303, 1391-346,
1391-347, 1391-352, 1391-353, 1391-357,
1391-360, 1391-363, 1391-371, 1391-383,
1391-431, 1391-432, 1391-449, 1391-458,
1391-459, 1391-460, 1391-461, 1391-462,
1391-468, 1391-474, 1391-515, 1391-559,
1391-603, 1391-606, 1391-666, 1391-702,
1391-726, 1391-728, 1391-744, 1391-745,
1391-755, 1391-790, 1391-797, 1391-798,
1391-801, 1393-10, 1393-44, 1393-51, 1393-67,
1393-77, 1393-78, 1393-79, 1393-122,
1393-136, 1393-144, 1393-147, 1393-155,
1393-162, 1393-165, 1393-166, 1393-168,
1393-183, 1424-1, 1424-7, 1424-15, 1433-2,
1437-3, 1490-11, 1506-7, 1534-6, 1534-7,
1534-13, 1534-18, 1578-51, 1578-63, 1578-68,
1578-69, 1578-104, 1578-129, 1578-185,
1593-4, 1593-8, 1593-59, 1593-76, 1593-90,
1593-110, 1593-111, 1593-113, 1593-119,
1593-126, 1593-133, 1597-1, 1601-4, 1601-5,
1635-8, 1638-32, 1639-28, 1639-29, 1639-31,
1639-38, 1639-40, 1639-48, 1639-49, 1639-74,
1639-83, 1639-106, 1639-113, 1639-119,
1639-144, 1639-147, 1639-166, 1639-176,
1639-189, 1639-195, 1639-203, 1639-208,
1639-210, 1672-35, 1718-5, 1768-6, 1768-12,
1814-4, 1847-10, 1847-48, 1853-133, 1873-9,
1890-1, 1974-8, 1980-16, 2004-33, 2170-2,
2170-4, 2170-7, 2170-8, 2170-9, 2170-13,
2170-14, 2170-15, 2170-18, 2170-22, 2170-26,
2170-27, 2170-29, 2170-34, 2170-37, 2170-38,
2170-39, 2170-40, 2170-42, 2170-47, 2170-56,
2170-57, 2170-58, 2170-60, 2170-61, 2170-66,
2170-67, 2170-68, 2170-70, 2170-71, 2170-74,
2170-75, 2170-76, 2170-77, 2170-78, 2170-79,
2170-81, 2170-83, 2170-84, 2170-88, 2170-89,
2170-90, 2170-91, 2170-93, 2170-94, 2170-95,
2170-96, 2170-100, 2170-106, 2170-108,
2170-110, 2170-111, 2170-112, 2170-114,

International affairs/development, Rwanda, 105-3, 166-7, 323-73, 1030-2, 1036-9, 1423-67, 1578-151, 1578-192, 1639-170, 1916-44, 1916-62, 1916-90, 1926-6, 2061-2, 2170-184, 2170-324, 2170-350, 2199-91, 2199-92, 2203-45

International affairs/development, Samoa, 1021-3, 1081-2

International affairs/development, Saudi Arabia, 439-10, 439-23, 439-24, 1312-18

International affairs/development, Scandinavia, 1713-1

International affairs/development, Scotland, 335-37, 1330-12, 2170-486

International affairs/development, Senegal, 172-134, 499-34, 744-28, 891-45, 1391-18, 1391-24, 1391-720, 1847-70, 1847-72, 2170-43, 2170-62, 2170-116, 2170-192, 2170-307, 2170-316, 2170-324, 2170-534

International affairs/development, Serbia, 1058-19, 1058-29, 1058-95, 1058-96, 1058-179, 1638-13, 1638-74, 1638-122

International affairs/development, Sierra Leone, 105-20, 105-26, 264-1, 264-4, 323-186, 735-10, 744-65, 875-2, 2170-192, 2170-342

International affairs/development, Singapore, 323-146, 323-150, 820-8, 1328-135, 1328-141, 1328-152, 1328-198, 2170-279

International affairs/development, Slovakia, 1058-31, 1058-143, 1328-234

International affairs/development, Slovenia, 1058-31

International affairs/development, Solomon Islands, 97-6, 788-83

International affairs/development, Somalia, Somaliland and Puntland, 744-68, 1531-24, 2170-265

International affairs/development, South Africa, 91-44, 105-14, 172-91, 226-7, 309-12, 428-23, 467-20, 735-26, 934-1, 1030-25, 1050-1, 1058-30, 1058-78, 1058-84, 1058-104, 1058-117, 1058-139, 1050-153, 1050-157, 1120-37, 1128-38, 1128-39, 1128-40, 1128-41, 1128-42, 1128-43, 1179-112, 1179-113, 1179-114, 1179-143, 1179-144, 1179-145, 1179-146, 1179-147, 1179-148, 1179-149, 1179-150, 1179-151, 1179-152, 1179-153, 1179-154, 1179-244, 1179-245, 1312-76, 1328-45, 1328-47, 1328-101, 1328-111, 1328-215, 1328-231, 1328-239, 1328-240, 1328-296, 1328-314, 1328-333, 1371-1, 1391-386, 1391-498, 1391-534, 1391-560, 1391-576, 1391-596, 1391-654, 1391-664, 1391-670, 1391-671, 1391-691, 1391-749, 1391-750, 1391-751, 1391-756, 1393-115, 1423-16, 1423-59, 1546-17, 1546-89, 1546-90, 1546-94, 1546-96, 1546-110, 1578-166, 1593-132, 1639-50, 1639-172, 1639-173, 1639-177, 1639-198, 1718-10, 1916-25, 1980-8, 2000-77, 2170-6, 2170-43, 2170-181, 2170-286, 2170-349, 2170-358, 2170-360, 2170-368, 2170-378, 2170-379, 2170-380, 2170-390, 2170-443, 2170-444, 2170-512, 2212-14

International affairs/development, South America, 251-86, 251-87, 322-1, 1058-79, 1058-100, 1058-106, 1058-109, 1058-110, 1058-126, 1058-172, 1312-83, 1391-47, 1391-49, 1391-231, 1391-252, 1391-273, 1391-282, 1391-306, 1391-307, 1391-337, 1391-395, 1391-541, 1391-739, 1391-741, 1531-17, 1593-74, 1639-66, 1639-69, 1980-19, 2099-1, 2099-39, 2170-41, 2170-166, 2170-179, 2170-187, 2170-252, 2170-261, 2170-270, 2212-36

International affairs/development, South Asia, 97-105, 323-8, 323-9, 439-34, 788-22, 788-95, 788-106, 1328-3, 1391-46, 1391-287, 1391-622, 1391-677, 1393-50, 1639-39, 1639-57, 1639-101, 1639-114, 1774-11, 2170-35, 2170-63, 2170-120, 2170-179, 2170-199, 2170-358

International affairs/development, South Korea, 172-26, 788-112, 1191-3, 1328-132, 1328-137, 1328-139, 1328-164, 1328-295, 1397-16, 1397-23, 1531-25, 1774-1, 2170-199, 2170-209,

2170-210, 2170-211, 2170-212, 2170-213, 2170-367

International affairs/development, Southeast Asia, 271-70, 271-80, 709-125, 788-125, 788-199, 788-228, 1030-3, 1030-9, 1030-15, 1030-27, 1030-54, 1391-287, 1397-14, 1593-15, 1593-75, 1639-152, 1672-8, 2170-179, 2170-199, 2170-512, 2170-532, 2203-41

International affairs/development, Southern Africa, 172-11, 172-21, 172-22, 172-39, 1058-117, 1092-64, 1371-2, 1391-385, 1391-443, 1391-509, 1391-558, 1391-583, 1391-596, 1391-654, 1391-671, 1391-682, 1391-749, 1593-79, 1639-165, 1639-202, 2170-121, 2170-380, 2170-383

International affairs/development, Soviet Union (Former), 216-31, 413-25, 439-34, 655-6, 655-9, 934-9, 934-10, 934-12, 934-14, 934-20, 934-21, 1039-11, 1039-13, 1043-3, 1058-149, 1106-2, 1278-25, 1278-28, 1593-26, 1989-18, 2212-57

International affairs/development, Spain, 782-28, 1039-6, 1328-340, 1391-579, 1393-62, 1423-35, 1423-57, 1423-58, 1578-134, 1601-3, 1853-137, 1853-138

International affairs/development, Sri Lanka, 1328-304, 2170-197, 2170-198, 2170-207, 2170-214, 2170-265, 2170-268, 2170-281, 2170-383

International affairs/development, Sub-Saharan Africa, 119-8, 172-38, 271-59, 271-70, 271-80, 309-1, 323-176, 323-271, 837-4, 892-2, 1303-1, 1391-272, 1391-304, 1585-17, 1639-3, 1639-39, 1639-48, 1768-1, 1847-51, 2170-3, 2170-6, 2170-10, 2170-35, 2170-46, 2170-63, 2170-84, 2170-120, 2170-122, 2170-125, 2170-138, 2170-141, 2170-158, 2170-161, 2170-174, 2170-186, 2170-187, 2170-195, 2170-198, 2170-202, 2170-257, 2170-266, 2170-281, 2170-297, 2170-316, 2170-319, 2170-358, 2170-370, 2170-380, 2170-396, 2170-408, 2170-452

International affairs/development, Sudan, 463-12, 467-15, 782-10, 1393-71, 1393-110, 1593-45, 1593-83, 1593-88, 1593-116, 1593-121, 1593-122, 2203-7, 2203-46

International affairs/development, Suriname, 1853-12

International affairs/development, Swaziland, 748-3, 1050-1, 1371-2, 1391-443

International affairs/development, Sweden, 1030-55, 1058-85, 1312-79, 1328-275, 1391-31, 1391-33, 2170-229

International affairs/development, Switzerland, 172-7, 172-39, 335-14, 335-38, 335-41, 335-42, 335-61, 413-12, 443-4, 788-190, 1021-12, 1021-60, 1058-22, 1058-155, 1093-86, 1137-44, 1184-32, 1292-6, 1391-27, 1391-62, 1391-357, 1391-431, 1391-432, 1391-435, 1391-447, 1391-470, 1391-471, 1391-475, 1391-573, 1391-679, 1391-680, 1391-685, 1391-698, 1391-728, 1391-729, 1391-801, 1393-51, 1393-62, 1490-1, 1638-120, 1639-74, 1639-179, 1639-210, 2004-33, 2099-33, 2170-60, 2170-105, 2170-111, 2170-112, 2170-138, 2170-139, 2170-175, 2170-192, 2170-261, 2170-389, 2170-390, 2170-516, 2170-517, 2170-518, 2170-519, 2170-520, 2170-521, 2170-522, 2170-523, 2170-524, 2170-525, 2170-526, 2170-527, 2170-528, 2170-529, 2170-530, 2170-531, 2170-532, 2170-533, 2170-534, 2170-535, 2170-536, 2170-537, 2170-538, 2170-539, 2170-540, 2170-541

International affairs/development, Syria, 693-38, 693-39, 814-7

International affairs/development, Taiwan, 17-3, 840-10, 1021-39, 1081-3, 1191-3, 1328-161, 1328-167, 1328-181, 1328-186, 1328-203, 1839-99, 1839-109, 2029-6, 2170-21

International affairs/development, Tajikistan, 97-4, 97-5

International affairs/development, Tanzania, Zanzibar and Pemba, 309-7, 309-76, 323-229, 660-136, 660-139, 660-140, 660-141, 660-144, 660-145, 660-146, 788-8, 1030-2, 1081-14, 1092-2, 1092-4, 1092-21, 1092-43, 1092-51, 1092-65,

1092-91, 1092-95, 1092-98, 1328-282, 1391-233, 1423-7, 1423-21, 1423-68, 1575-4, 1578-94, 1578-113, 1639-190, 1639-211, 1843-11, 2009-1, 2170-5, 2170-12, 2170-21, 2170-124, 2170-211, 2170-214, 2170-232, 2170-336, 2170-360, 2170-368, 2170-421, 2170-502, 2170-529, 2170-543, 2170-545, 2199-90

International affairs/development, Thailand, 91-24, 335-9, 335-10, 788-96, 1328-232, 1328-235, 1328-237, 1328-310, 1391-322, 1393-78, 1393-112, 1593-22, 1593-46, 1593-49, 1593-55, 1593-63, 1593-118, 1593-125, 1639-15, 1639-40, 1639-106, 1639-114, 1639-137, 1639-150, 1639-178, 2170-20, 2170-256, 2170-539

International affairs/development, Togo, 2170-116

International affairs/development, Tonga, 1081-2

International affairs/development, Trinidad & Tobago, 1328-318

International affairs/development, Tunisia, 1328-328, 1391-63, 1391-168, 2211-4

International affairs/development, Turkey, 135-44, 172-43, 439-1, 1058-86, 1058-120, 1328-162, 1328-172, 1328-208, 1393-53, 1423-49, 1488-5, 1638-56, 2211-4, 2212-57

International affairs/development, Uganda, 105-11, 105-45, 132-34, 172-102, 309-14, 323-211, 323-212, 384-7, 1030-2, 1092-60, 1092-70, 1136-2, 1328-189, 1371-10, 1391-16, 1391-634, 1393-169, 1593-45, 1593-121, 1639-4, 1639-116, 1639-164, 1639-165, 1639-170, 184/-61, 1916-39, 2078-7, 2170-43, 2170-181, 2170-242, 2170-255, 2170-280, 2170-360, 2170-508, 2170-543, 2170-545

International affairs/development, Ukraine, 413-39, 439-46, 709-94, 934-103, 960-5, 1058-111, 1058-166, 1150-14, 1393-80, 1393-81, 1393-169, 1567-17, 1567-36, 1816-7

International affairs/development, United Arab Emirates, 439-24, 439-32, 1312-18, 1328-66, 1328-297, 1839-6, 1839-7

International affairs/development, United Kingdom, 1058-55, 1312-94, 1328-185, 1328-201, 1328-216, 1328-242, 1328-252, 1328-268, 1391-172, 1393-137, 1423-11, 1702-1, 1702-2, 1702-7, 1702-9, 2170-36, 2170-52, 2170-61

International affairs/development, Uruguay, 1058-110, 1058-172, 1328-29, 1328-339, 1328-341, 1391-152, 2206-3

International affairs/development, Uzbekistan, 1393-173, 1593-13

International affairs/development, Vanuatu, 788-83

International affairs/development, Venezuela, 148-4, 788-144, 1328-123, 1328-175, 1328-228, 1328-299

International affairs/development, Vietnam, 309-47, 335-42, 439-22, 788-96, 1082-6, 1092-26, 1092-66, 1092-73, 1328-126, 1328-194, 1328-277, 1328-278, 1391-10, 1391-77, 1391-239, 1391-243, 1391-280, 1391-281, 1391-295, 1391-436, 1391-554, 1391-655, 1393-81, 1393-112, 1397-42, 1531-12, 1531-38, 1639-32, 1639-87, 1639-89, 1639-90, 1639-91, 1639-92, 1639-158, 1639-178, 2199-88

International affairs/development, Wales, 2170-49, 2170-396

International affairs/development, West Bank/Gaza (Palestinian Territories), 135-5, 322-5, 323-118, 467-17, 499-12, 499-13, 562-46, 562-50, 562-65, 613-5, 891-13, 891-23, 891-34, 891-38, 896-9, 896-12, 896-14, 896-17, 896-24, 896-27, 905-7, 1179-6, 1347-3, 1347-19, 1347-24, 1347-25, 1347-36, 1347-37, 1347-41, 1393-48, 1393-87, 1393-164, 1546-102, 1578-114, 1593-5, 1593-67, 1603-18, 1638-87, 1638-103, 1660-9, 1660-37, 1665-3, 1718-8, 1718-9, 1923-5, 1923-9, 1923-14, 2203-35, 2203-43, 2209-3

International affairs/development, Western Africa, 323-301, 788-206, 1092-49, 1092-90, 1391-661, 1593-79, 1639-2, 1639-35, 1639-50, 2170-125, 2170-316, 2170-383, 2170-516, 2170-517, 2170-518, 2170-519

International affairs/development, Yemen, 1531-24

413-67, 413-68, 413-71, 413-72, 413-73, 413-74,
413-75, 416-8, 428-4, 428-5, 428-6, 428-8,
428-18, 428-23, 428-33, 428-34, 428-45, 428-46,
428-48, 428-49, 428-50, 435-2, 435-3, 435-4,
435-9, 435-10, 435-18, 435-29, 435-30, 435-34,
439-54, 443-4, 443-18, 447-1, 447-11, 447-22,
460-8, 463-9, 463-12, 463-13, 464-11, 467-15,
467-17, 467-19, 467-44, 467-59, 499-7, 499-34,
503-1, 503-3, 503-4, 503-5, 503-6, 503-7, 503-8,
537-2, 537-3, 537-9, 537-10, 562-17, 562-42,
562-67, 605-1, 605-7, 605-9, 605-28, 616-33,
626-1, 626-2, 626-6, 626-16, 626-17, 629-1,
629-2, 629-3, 629-4, 629-5, 655-1, 655-3, 655-6,
655-9, 655-11, 655-13, 657-2, 660-136, 660-139,
660-140, 660-141, 660-143, 660-144, 660-145,
660-146, 660-153, 684-1, 693-1, 709-2, 709-3,
709-4, 709-59, 709-84, 709-91, 709-122,
709-128, 709-129, 717-2, 728-1, 729-6, 729-9,
734-2, 734-3, 734-7, 734-8, 734-10, 735-10,
735-21, 735-24, 735-29, 735-32, 737-3, 737-7,
744-3, 744-24, 744-26, 744-27, 744-48, 744-52,
748-3, 748-5, 748-9, 748-11, 748-12, 748-13,
748-14, 748-15, 748-16, 748-17, 748-18, 748-19,
748-20, 748-21, 748-22, 748-23, 748-24, 748-25,
748-26, 748-27, 748-28, 748-29, 748-30, 748-32,
748-33, 748-34, 748-35, 748-36, 748-37, 748-38,
748-39, 748-40, 748-41, 748-42, 748-43, 748-44,
748-48, 748-49, 748-51, 748-52, 748-53, 748-54,
748-55, 748-56, 748-57, 753-2, 756-1, 756-9,
756-18, 756-27, 782-19, 788-21, 788-25, 788-29,
788-30, 788-46, 788-63, 788-65, 788-78, 788-79,
788-83, 788-94, 788-96, 788-100, 788-106,
788-109, 788-121, 788-124, 788-130, 788-144,
788-148, 788-154, 788-166, 788-172, 788-187,
788-188, 788-208, 788-209, 788-226, 798-3,
798-4, 798-12, 798-13, 798-15, 798-18, 798-24,
798-35, 798-55, 798-62, 798-68, 798-69, 814-9,
814-26, 816-3, 820-10, 829-1, 829-5, 837-2,
837-4, 837-14, 837-17, 837-18, 837-20, 837-21,
840-1, 840-2, 840-3, 840-13, 852-4, 855-3,
860-2, 860-12, 860-13, 860-22, 860-23, 860-27,
860-38, 891-1, 891-11, 892-1, 892-2, 896-5,
896-6, 896-8, 905-1, 930-3, 932-3, 932-6, 932-12,
934-1, 934-2, 934-9, 934-10, 934-12, 934-13,
934-14, 934-17, 934-20, 934-21, 934-23, 934-26,
934-27, 934-42, 934-48, 934-68, 934-69, 934-71,
934-91, 934-92, 937-4, 959-8, 960-6, 960-7,
967-18, 967-20, 967-21, 969-7, 984-6, 984-7,
987-1, 987-4, 987-18, 987-19, 1021-12, 1021-71,
1023-3, 1026-1, 1026-2, 1030-18, 1030-20,
1030-31, 1036-2, 1036-3, 1036-7, 1036-10,
1037-5, 1037-13, 1037-15, 1050-1, 1050-6,
1050-8, 1050-24, 1050-33, 1051-4, 1051-5,
1051-6, 1058-9, 1058-21, 1058-81, 1058-88,
1058-105, 1058-106, 1058-124, 1058-126,
1058-138, 1058-139, 1058-165, 1081-10,
1081-13, 1081-15, 1081-16, 1081-17, 1082-7,
1082-14, 1082-15, 1082-18, 1082-19, 1092-4,
1092-13, 1092-18, 1092-20, 1092-54, 1092-66,
1092-81, 1092-94, 1092-98, 1093-18, 1093-46,
1093-71, 1093-77, 1093-86, 1093-94, 1112-2,
1128-1, 1128-2, 1128-6, 1128-7, 1128-8,
1128-13, 1128-14, 1128-37, 1128-38, 1128-39,
1128-40, 1128-41, 1128-42, 1128-43, 1128-44,
1128-62, 1136-1, 1136-5, 1137-3, 1137-4,
1137-22, 1137-23, 1137-24, 1137-25, 1137-26,
1137-27, 1137-28, 1137-29, 1137-30, 1137-31,
1137-32, 1137-33, 1137-34, 1137-35, 1137-36,
1137-37, 1137-38, 1137-44, 1137-45, 1139-2,
1139-5, 1141-2, 1141-3, 1141-7, 1141-9, 1148-1,
1150-3, 1150-10, 1160-11, 1160-30, 1167-14,
1179-1, 1179-2, 1179-3, 1179-4, 1179-5, 1179-6,
1179-7, 1179-12, 1179-13, 1179-20, 1179-24,
1179-25, 1179-29, 1179-30, 1179-31, 1179-32,
1179-33, 1179-34, 1179-35, 1179-36, 1179-37,
1179-38, 1179-39, 1179-40, 1179-41, 1179-42,
1179-43, 1179-44, 1179-45, 1179-46, 1179-47,
1179-48, 1179-49, 1179-50, 1179-51, 1179-52,
1179-53, 1179-54, 1179-55, 1179-56, 1179-57,
1179-58, 1179-59, 1179-60, 1179-61, 1179-62,
1179-63, 1179-64, 1179-65, 1179-66, 1179-67,
1179-68, 1179-69, 1179-70, 1179-71, 1179-72,
1179-73, 1179-74, 1179-75, 1179-76, 1179-77,
1179-78, 1179-79, 1179-80, 1179-81, 1179-82,

1179-83, 1179-84, 1179-85, 1179-86, 1179-87,
1179-88, 1179-89, 1179-90, 1179-91, 1179-92,
1179-93, 1179-94, 1179-95, 1179-96, 1179-97,
1179-98, 1179-99, 1179-100, 1179-101,
1179-112, 1179-113, 1179-114, 1179-116,
1179-117, 1179-118, 1179-119, 1179-124,
1179-125, 1179-126, 1179-127, 1179-128,
1179-129, 1179-130, 1179-131, 1179-132,
1179-133, 1179-134, 1179-137, 1179-138,
1179-143, 1179-144, 1179-145, 1179-146,
1179-147, 1179-148, 1179-149, 1179-150,
1179-151, 1179-152, 1179-153, 1179-154,
1179-159, 1179-161, 1179-164, 1179-165,
1179-167, 1179-168, 1179-169, 1179-170,
1179-171, 1179-173, 1179-174, 1179-175,
1179-176, 1179-177, 1179-178, 1179-179,
1179-180, 1179-181, 1179-182, 1179-183,
1179-184, 1179-185, 1179-186, 1179-187,
1179-188, 1179-189, 1179-190, 1179-191,
1179-192, 1179-193, 1179-194, 1179-195,
1179-196, 1179-197, 1179-198, 1179-199,
1179-200, 1179-201, 1179-202, 1179-203,
1179-204, 1179-205, 1179-206, 1179-207,
1179-208, 1179-209, 1179-210, 1179-211,
1179-212, 1179-213, 1179-214, 1179-215,
1179-216, 1179-217, 1179-218, 1179-219,
1179-220, 1179-221, 1179-222, 1179-223,
1179-224, 1179-225, 1179-226, 1179-227,
1179-228, 1179-229, 1179-230, 1179-231,
1179-232, 1179-233, 1179-234, 1179-235,
1179-236, 1179-237, 1179-239, 1179-240,
1179-241, 1179-242, 1179-243, 1179-250,
1179-251, 1179-252, 1179-253, 1179-254,
1179-255, 1179-256, 1179-260, 1184-1, 1184-3,
1184-9, 1184-11, 1184-25, 1184-26, 1184-27,
1184-28, 1184-29, 1184-30, 1184-32, 1186-11,
1186-12, 1186-19, 1191-2, 1200-2, 1241-9,
1241-14, 1241-17, 1241-18, 1241-19, 1241-24,
1278-28, 1292-1, 1292-2, 1292-3, 1292-4,
1292-6, 1303-1, 1303-3, 1303-32, 1303-33,
1303-54, 1303-62, 1303-64, 1303-67, 1303-79,
1311-1, 1312-31, 1312-33, 1312-54, 1322-3,
1322-4, 1328-14, 1328-22, 1328-45, 1328-47,
1328-126, 1328-130, 1328-135, 1328-140,
1328-141, 1328-148, 1328-192, 1328-197,
1328-201, 1328-203, 1328-215, 1328-234,
1328-237, 1328-242, 1328-263, 1328-270,
1328-275, 1328-277, 1328-284, 1328-287,
1328-295, 1328-305, 1328-323, 1328-326,
1328-330, 1328-333, 1328-335, 1328-337,
1328-339, 1328-349, 1328-352, 1347-2,
1347-11, 1347-16, 1347-22, 1347-26, 1347-28,
1347-35, 1347-39, 1353-9, 1353-12, 1353-15,
1353-17, 1353-18, 1353-19, 1353-20, 1353-22,
1353-23, 1353-24, 1353-27, 1360-2, 1360-6,
1360-23, 1360-24, 1360-25, 1360-26, 1361-7,
1371-2, 1371-5, 1371-10, 1371-15, 1371-17,
1371-19, 1371-21, 1371-22, 1391-9, 1391-13,
1391-16, 1391-18, 1391-23, 1391-27, 1391-29,
1391-31, 1391-33, 1391-41, 1391-43, 1391-66,
1391-75, 1391-81, 1391-86, 1391-88, 1391-93,
1391-168, 1391-177, 1391-207, 1391-231,
1391-236, 1391-246, 1391-252, 1391-282,
1391-283, 1391-286, 1391-295, 1391-303,
1391-304, 1391-306, 1391-321, 1391-324,
1391-332, 1391-337, 1391-346, 1391-347,
1391-352, 1391-359, 1391-360, 1391-363,
1391-366, 1391-382, 1391-383, 1391-386,
1391-394, 1391-401, 1391-408, 1391-426,
1391-431, 1391-432, 1391-436, 1391-445,
1391-446, 1391-452, 1391-453, 1391-456,
1391-458, 1391-464, 1391-467, 1391-469,
1391-471, 1391-475, 1391-480, 1391-509,
1391-515, 1391-547, 1391-548, 1391-549,
1391-554, 1391-558, 1391-559, 1391-576,
1391-581, 1391-583, 1391-587, 1391-596,
1391-605, 1391-615, 1391-642, 1391-655,
1391-680, 1391-688, 1391-700, 1391-701,
1391-702, 1391-706, 1391-710, 1391-719,
1391-723, 1391-724, 1391-739, 1391-744,
1391-749, 1391-758, 1391-759, 1391-790,
1391-796, 1391-798, 1391-799, 1393-34,
1393-56, 1393-64, 1393-113, 1393-126,
1393-163, 1393-171, 1393-173, 1393-176,

1422-6, 1422-7, 1422-8, 1422-9, 1422-10,
1422-13, 1422-19, 1422-21, 1422-22, 1423-8,
1423-11, 1423-14, 1424-7, 1424-15, 1433-1,
1437-1, 1437-5, 1437-11, 1437-12, 1450-4,
1457-3, 1490-1, 1494-2, 1516-1, 1518-1, 1518-4,
1518-5, 1531-32, 1534-5, 1534-17, 1534-18,
1567-12, 1567-18, 1567-19, 1567-20, 1567-28,
1567-29, 1567-30, 1567-31, 1567-32, 1567-33,
1567-34, 1567-35, 1575-4, 1575-5, 1578-1,
1578-2, 1578-3, 1578-21, 1578-39, 1578-55,
1578-60, 1578-75, 1578-76, 1578-78, 1578-88,
1578-92, 1578-109, 1578-110, 1578-111,
1578-112, 1578-118, 1578-120, 1578-122,
1578-148, 1578-149, 1578-154, 1578-156,
1578-164, 1578-170, 1578-171, 1578-176,
1578-192, 1585-1, 1585-20, 1585-26, 1593-30,
1593-44, 1593-46, 1593-75, 1593-86, 1593-90,
1593-101, 1593-112, 1593-124, 1593-126,
1593-128, 1593-132, 1593-138, 1593-139,
1594-6, 1594-8, 1594-9, 1594-24, 1594-27,
1594-30, 1594-31, 1597-3, 1601-3, 1601-7,
1602-3, 1603-14, 1603-15, 1606-1, 1606-3,
1606-4, 1618-17, 1638-6, 1638-42, 1638-60,
1638-78, 1638-83, 1638-86, 1638-117,
1638-120, 1639-1, 1639-3, 1639-4, 1639-5,
1639-11, 1639-13, 1639-24, 1639-32, 1639-37,
1639-38, 1639-40, 1639-46, 1639-48, 1639-50,
1639-52, 1639-57, 1639-60, 1639-64, 1639-69,
1639-73, 1639-74, 1639-77, 1639-79, 1639-83,
1639-85, 1639-87, 1639-88, 1639-89, 1639-90,
1639-91, 1639-92, 1639-93, 1639-95, 1639-98,
1639-100, 1639-106, 1639-107, 1639-108,
1639-112, 1639-113, 1639-114, 1639-116,
1639-119, 1639-121, 1639-122, 1639-123,
1639-125, 1639-126, 1639-128, 1639-129,
1639-132, 1639-133, 1639-136, 1639-137,
1639-139, 1639-142, 1639-144, 1639-146,
1639-147, 1639-149, 1639-150, 1639-151,
1639-152, 1639-157, 1639-158, 1639-159,
1639-160, 1639-166, 1639-172, 1639-177,
1639-179, 1639-180, 1639-186, 1639-188,
1639-189, 1639-190, 1639-195, 1639-198,
1639-199, 1639-200, 1639-202, 1639-204,
1639-205, 1639-207, 1639-210, 1639-211,
1639-212, 1639-213, 1656-9, 1659-11, 1659-12,
1659-13, 1659-14, 1659-15, 1659-32, 1660-15,
1660-22, 1660-51, 1660-52, 1660-53, 1660-54,
1660-55, 1660-56, 1660-57, 1660-58, 1660-59,
1660-60, 1660-61, 1660-62, 1660-63, 1665-1,
1665-3, 1665-11, 1665-14, 1665-15, 1668-3,
1672-17, 1672-30, 1672-35, 1673-2, 1673-3,
1673-5, 1675-9, 1688-3, 1688-4, 1702-5, 1718-2,
1718-3, 1718-10, 1768-1, 1768-6, 1768-12,
1771-1, 1773-1, 1774-1, 1774-7, 1774-8,
1774-10, 1774-11, 1790-1, 1790-2, 1790-3,
1790-6, 1790-9, 1790-11, 1790-12, 1804-5,
1804-6, 1804-7, 1814-1, 1816-1, 1816-5, 1816-9,
1830-10, 1830-11, 1830-12, 1830-13, 1830-14,
1830-15, 1830-16, 1830-36, 1830-41, 1830-43,
1830-45, 1830-46, 1830-48, 1832-2, 1832-6,
1839-15, 1839-55, 1839-109, 1843-7, 1847-12,
1847-13, 1847-14, 1847-18, 1847-22, 1847-26,
1847-28, 1847-41, 1847-42, 1847-44, 1847-45,
1847-46, 1847-47, 1847-49, 1847-50, 1847-52,
1847-53, 1847-54, 1847-55, 1847-57, 1847-58,
1847-59, 1847-60, 1847-62, 1847-63, 1847-64,
1847-69, 1847-70, 1847-71, 1847-72, 1853-2,
1853-4, 1853-12, 1853-26, 1853-30, 1853-31,
1853-51, 1853-52, 1853-82, 1853-88, 1853-89,
1853-110, 1853-133, 1853-137, 1853-138,
1853-140, 1853-147, 1853-148, 1853-150,
1853-151, 1916-25, 1916-37, 1916-41, 1916-58,
1916-85, 1916-86, 1916-107, 1924-1, 1924-7,
1924-8, 1926-6, 1926-8, 1926-9, 1927-2, 1943-1,
1951-2, 1961-3, 1970-2, 1974-7, 1974-8, 1980-9,
1980-10, 1980-11, 1980-12, 1980-14, 1980-15,
1980-16, 1980-17, 1980-19, 1989-1, 1989-14,
1989-15, 1989-16, 1989-24, 1992-4, 2000-22,
2000-23, 2000-51, 2000-58, 2000-70, 2000-71,
2000-72, 2000-73, 2000-74, 2000-77, 2004-2,
2004-4, 2004-5, 2004-11, 2004-12, 2004-15,
2004-18, 2004-26, 2004-27, 2004-29, 2004-30,
2004-33, 2008-1, 2009-1, 2029-6, 2061-2,
2061-7, 2061-8, 2061-12, 2061-13, 2067-4,

International migration/refugee issues, sex workers, 1393-10

International migration/refugee issues, technical assistance, 1391-623

International migration/refugee issues, women, 562-4, 562-23, 562-69, 1391-275, 1391-623, 1593-84, 2170-204

International peace/security, 105-9, 105-15, 105-18, 105-25, 105-28, 105-29, 105-34, 105-41, 135-34, 135-38, 148-12, 148-18, 148-20, 172-19, 172-24, 172-128, 309-55, 323-49, 323-200, 323-342, 435-21, 439-3, 439-6, 439-7, 439-9, 439-15, 439-17, 439-18, 439-20, 439-25, 439-28, 439-34, 439-42, 439-43, 439-44, 439-48, 439-50, 439-55, 439-57, 439-62, 439-63, 439-66, 460-5, 460-6, 562-3, 605-14, 646-16, 657-2, 756-24, 788-39, 788-40, 788-41, 788-49, 788-58, 788-71, 788-97, 788-102, 788-125, 788-178, 788-199, 891-10, 896-7, 896-21, 896-22, 987-15, 1039-5, 1039-9, 1039-10, 1050-26, 1058-29, 1106-2, 1106-3, 1167-12, 1312-10, 1312-13, 1312-15, 1312-18, 1312-21, 1312-26, 1312-28, 1312-47, 1312-55, 1312-56, 1312-61, 1312-73, 1312-81, 1312-84, 1347-41, 1391-200, 1391-239, 1391-543, 1391-677, 1391-799, 1393-40, 1393-69, 1393-76, 1393-140, 1393-164, 1393-179, 1422-14, 1578-16, 1578-17, 1578-18, 1593-14, 1593-23, 1593-25, 1593-27, 1593-58, 1593-74, 1593-88, 1593-121, 1593-137, 1594-38, 1618-8, 1618-9, 1638-6, 1638-7, 1638-12, 1638-19, 1638-21, 1638-22, 1638-30, 1638-47, 1638-53, 1638-56, 1638-64, 1638-75, 1638-83, 1638-88, 1638-99, 1638-105, 1638-134, 1638-139, 1639-30, 1639-197, 1660-37, 1916-37, 2195-3, 2195-4, 2203-55, 2212-19, 2212-50

International peace/security, African Americans/ Blacks, 1391-200

International peace/security, aging, 323-49

International peace/security, Asians/Pacific Islanders, 1391-200

International peace/security, children/youth, 788-71, 1050-26

International peace/security, collections management/ preservation, 1312-56

International peace/security, conferences/seminars, 105-34, 135-34, 435-21, 439-28, 439-48, 1312-26, 1312-61, 1312-84, 1393-140, 1593-25, 1638-19, 1638-83, 1639-30, 1639-197, 2212-19

International peace/security, crime/abuse victims, 1393-40, 1393-76, 1593-121

International peace/security, curriculum development, 439-48, 788-71

International peace/security, disabilities, people with, 1391-239

International peace/security, economically disadvantaged, 105-25, 105-41, 172-24, 323-200, 1058-29, 1391-799, 1593-121, 2203-55

International peace/security, electronic media/online services, 439-28, 439-55, 439-57, 1312-55, 1393-179, 1594-38

International peace/security, faculty/staff development, 1638-99

International peace/security, fellowships, 1039-9, 1039-10

International peace/security, film/video/radio, 1312-55, 1391-200, 1393-179

International peace/security, Hispanics/Latinos, 1391-200

International peace/security, immigrants/refugees, 105-41, 2203-55

International peace/security, management development/capacity building, 1593-23, 1593-121

International peace/security, military/veterans, 148-12, 439-48, 1312-28, 1391-239, 1393-76

International peace/security, minorities, 105-41, 1050-26, 1058-29, 1347-41, 1393-164, 1593-121, 1638-47

International peace/security, Native Americans/ American Indians, 1391-200

International peace/security, offenders/ex-offenders, 1393-40

International peace/security, publication, 105-15, 439-6, 439-9, 439-15, 439-17, 439-18, 439-20,

439-25, 439-34, 439-42, 439-43, 439-44, 439-50, 439-62, 439-63, 439-66, 460-6, 788-41, 788-49, 1312-26, 1593-58, 1916-37

International peace/security, research, 105-9, 105-15, 105-29, 105-34, 105-41, 439-3, 439-6, 439-7, 439-9, 439-15, 439-17, 439-18, 439-20, 439-25, 439-28, 439-34, 439-42, 439-43, 439-44, 439-50, 439-62, 439-63, 439-66, 788-44, 788-178, 788-199, 1312-26, 1312-47, 1312-56, 1312-73, 1312-84, 1391-543, 1393-40, 1593-74, 1593-137, 1639-30

International peace/security, technical assistance, 1058-29

International peace/security, women, 105-41, 309-55, 1391-799, 1393-40, 1393-179, 1593-58, 1594-38

International peace/security, youth, 435-21, 1058-29

International relief, 9-1, 10-1, 17-2, 17-4, 21-2, 21-3, 21-13, 54-4, 54-5, 54-9, 54-15, 54-16, 84-2, 86-2, 86-4, 86-5, 91-5, 91-12, 91-13, 91-23, 91-24, 91-29, 91-44, 97-44, 97-65, 100-1, 100-6, 100-7, 100-8, 105-35, 119-6, 135-2, 135-5, 135-6, 135-22, 135-36, 166-2, 166-4, 167-4, 167-5, 172-108, 178-2, 178-4, 178-8, 178-10, 178-14, 178-15, 178-21, 178-27, 178-28, 178-29, 178-30, 178-31, 178-35, 178-40, 216-8, 226-2, 238-7, 238-15, 271-16, 286-9, 307-4, 307-5, 307-8, 307-9, 309-9, 309-10, 309-11, 309-15, 309-16, 309-24, 309-27, 309-33, 309-34, 309-35, 309-36, 309-37, 309-38, 309-39, 309-40, 309-41, 309-42, 309-43, 309-44, 309-45, 309-66, 309-67, 309-77, 309-78, 309-79, 309-80, 309-81, 309-82, 309-83, 309-84, 309-85, 309-87, 309-88, 309-90, 309-91, 309-92, 309-93, 309-94, 309-95, 309-96, 309-97, 309-98, 309-99, 309-100, 309-101, 309-102, 309-113, 309-115, 309-120, 320-1, 320-2, 323-14, 323-16, 323-17, 323-18, 323-19, 323-20, 323-21, 323-22, 323-23, 323-24, 323-25, 323-26, 323-27, 323-28, 323-29, 323-30, 323-31, 323-32, 323-33, 323-36, 323-54, 323-61, 323-63, 323-67, 323-68, 323-69, 323-70, 323-92, 323-93, 323-99, 323-100, 323-101, 323-102, 323-103, 323-104, 323-105, 323-106, 323-107, 323-108, 323-109, 323-126, 323-175, 323-181, 323-186, 323-202, 323-204, 323-214, 323-236, 323-237, 323-239, 323-266, 323-268, 323-272, 323-273, 323-274, 323-275, 323-277, 323-278, 323-280, 323-282, 323-283, 323-304, 323-322, 323-324, 323-325, 323-329, 323-344, 323-356, 323-357, 323-358, 323-360, 323-361, 323-362, 323-398, 325-36, 335-30, 335-50, 335-51, 335-52, 335-53, 335-61, 347-5, 347-6, 347-7, 384-8, 384-11, 384-12, 384-13, 384-14, 413-13, 413-14, 413-40, 413-41, 413-42, 428-1, 428-9, 428-12, 428-17, 428-37, 428-38, 435-8, 435-11, 435-22, 435-23, 435-24, 443-23, 447-9, 447-10, 460-1, 463-3, 463-8, 463-10, 464-18, 467-16, 467-20, 469-1, 499-28, 499-29, 516-8, 562-2, 562-9, 562-10, 562-24, 562-66, 605-8, 616-46, 626-10, 655-5, 660-17, 660-22, 660-30, 693-7, 709-4, 709-16, 709-17, 709-62, 709-69, 709-125, 717-1, 729-1, 730-7, 732-1, 734-9, 735-1, 735-4, 735-8, 735-9, 735-13, 735-18, 735-26, 744-6, 744-8, 744-9, 744-10, 744-11, 744-12, 744-14, 744-63, 744-64, 744-65, 744-66, 744-67, 744-68, 744-69, 748-6, 748-7, 748-10, 756-22, 787-1, 788-24, 788-110, 788-146, 788-149, 788-155, 788-191, 788-192, 798-8, 798-9, 798-10, 801-1, 801-2, 814-13, 814-18, 814-23, 837-5, 837-19, 840-10, 852-2, 860-6, 860-25, 863-1, 863-6, 866-1, 866-4, 873-5, 892-6, 905-2, 932-10, 934-28, 934-103, 960-2, 960-3, 960-4, 960-5, 960-9, 984-1, 1021-3, 1021-4, 1021-5, 1021-39, 1021-75, 1023-1, 1023-2, 1030-5, 1030-21, 1036-12, 1037-10, 1050-11, 1050-19, 1051-5, 1055-2, 1055-4, 1055-5, 1055-7, 1058-69, 1064-1, 1081-1, 1081-2, 1081-3, 1081-4, 1081-5, 1081-6, 1081-7, 1081-11, 1082-3, 1082-4, 1082-6, 1082-11, 1082-12, 1092-30, 1092-97, 1093-4, 1093-59, 1093-72, 1128-24, 1128-25, 1128-32, 1128-33, 1128-34, 1128-68, 1139-1, 1139-3, 1139-4, 1148-2, 1150-14, 1160-31, 1179-8, 1179-9, 1179-10, 1179-11, 1179-15, 1179-16, 1179-17, 1179-18, 1179-19, 1179-21, 1179-22,

1179-23, 1179-105, 1179-106, 1179-107, 1179-108, 1179-109, 1179-110, 1179-120, 1179-121, 1179-122, 1179-123, 1179-139, 1179-140, 1200-3, 1219-1, 1241-10, 1241-11, 1293-6, 1303-4, 1303-5, 1303-15, 1303-16, 1303-24, 1303-25, 1303-28, 1303-63, 1312-11, 1312-14, 1312-20, 1312-24, 1312-45, 1312-48, 1312-66, 1312-70, 1328-10, 1328-114, 1328-195, 1328-274, 1347-7, 1347-18, 1347-23, 1347-30, 1347-34, 1360-22, 1371-4, 1371-8, 1371-13, 1371-14, 1371-16, 1391-162, 1391-232, 1391-582, 1391-595, 1391-632, 1391-644, 1391-662, 1393-78, 1393-111, 1393-153, 1393-154, 1397-10, 1428-36, 1433-2, 1437-3, 1490-11, 1518-2, 1518-3, 1534-9, 1567-17, 1567-36, 1578-23, 1578-24, 1578-25, 1578-30, 1578-44, 1578-46, 1578-47, 1578-48, 1578-49, 1578-50, 1578-61, 1578-68, 1578-69, 1578-70, 1578-71, 1578-93, 1578-105, 1578-106, 1578-107, 1578-151, 1578-152, 1578-153, 1578-160, 1578-161, 1578-177, 1578-178, 1585-4, 1585-21, 1593-35, 1593-47, 1593-84, 1593-106, 1593-118, 1593-125, 1597-1, 1597-2, 1601-2, 1603-11, 1603-12, 1635-8, 1638-3, 1638-8, 1638-114, 1639-15, 1639-148, 1639-209, 1659-23, 1665-5, 1668-4, 1672-26, 1690-3, 1702-8, 1718-5, 1718-7, 1768-3, 1768-4, 1768-5, 1768-7, 1768-15, 1770-1, 1814-4, 1816-7, 1831-1, 1832-1, 1832-4, 1832-5, 1839-2, 1839-3, 1839-11, 1839-12, 1839-52, 1839-99, 1853-7, 1853-8, 1853-21, 1853-62, 1853-86, 1853-106, 1916-39, 1924-3, 1924-4, 1925-1, 1927-4, 1943-4, 1960-1, 1960-2, 1961-5, 1974-3, 1974-4, 1974-6, 1980-2, 1980-13, 1992-1, 2004-3, 2004-8, 2004-14, 2004-17, 2004-22, 2004-23, 2029-1, 2039-1, 2067-1, 2067-2, 2067-5, 2067-6, 2078-5, 2170-16, 2170-51, 2170-52, 2170-54, 2170-55, 2170-204, 2170-205, 2170-231, 2170-253, 2170-254, 2170-262, 2170-263, 2170-264, 2170-265, 2170-307, 2170-308, 2170-317, 2170-361, 2170-362, 2170-400, 2170-401, 2170-418, 2170-547, 2199-3, 2199-4, 2199-10, 2199-11, 2199-21, 2199-22, 2199-23, 2199-24, 2199-32, 2199-33, 2199-34, 2199-78, 2199-86, 2199-87, 2199-94, 2203-33, 2203-44, 2203-55, 2203-56, 2209-2, 2209-4, 2211-5, 2212-4, 2212-6, 2212-18, 2212-47

International relief, 2004 tsunami, 1923-3

International relief, aging, 1831-1, 1832-1

International relief, AIDS, people with, 91-44, 178-8, 178-29, 178-30, 178-31, 309-90, 309-91, 309-92, 309-93, 309-94, 309-95, 309-96, 309-97, 309-98, 309-99, 309-100, 309-101, 309-102, 323-273, 323-274, 323-275, 323-277, 323-278, 323-280, 323-282, 323-283, 335-53, 384-14, 709-4, 735-26, 788-149, 860-6, 892-6, 1030-21, 1081-6, 1093-72, 1312-66, 1347-34, 1371-14, 1391-232, 1391-595, 1391-662, 1393-78, 1578-151, 1578-152, 1578-153, 1603-11, 1768-15, 1916-39, 2170-317, 2199-86, 2199-87

International relief, Asians/Pacific Islanders, 309-15, 323-61, 863-1

International relief, awards/prizes/competitions, 435-24

International relief, blind/visually impaired, 1092-30, 1128-32, 1128-33, 1128-34, 1179-109, 1179-110, 1518-2, 1518-3, 1534-9, 1659-23, 1974-3

International relief, building/renovation, 135-2, 323-70, 463-3, 660-17, 788-149, 1030-5, 1593-106, 1638-8, 1832-5

International relief, children/youth, 54-15, 54-16, 86-2, 86-4, 86-5, 91-24, 91-29, 91-44, 100-8, 135-2, 135-36, 178-2, 178-8, 178-29, 309-15, 309-27, 309-113, 309-115, 309-120, 320-1, 320-2, 323-54, 323-61, 323-186, 323-272, 323-322, 323-324, 323-325, 323-329, 323-360, 323-361, 323-362, 323-398, 435-8, 464-18, 709-4, 709-62, 735-26, 744-65, 814-13, 814-23, 837-19, 934-103, 960-5, 1050-11, 1050-19, 1055-4, 1081-6, 1081-11, 1082-4, 1082-11, 1082-12, 1093-59, 1128-68, 1150-14, 1179-18, 1179-19, 1219-1, 1303-28, 1371-14, 1428-36, 1567-17,

Lebanon, human services—multipurpose, 467-27, 1082-14, 1328-211
Lebanon, international affairs/development, 435-34, 1030-4, 1082-5, 1082-14, 1179-6, 1328-287, 1391-64, 1391-71, 1393-119, 1638-7, 1665-3
Lebanon, public affairs/government, 1328-77, 1391-56, 1391-61, 1638-7
Lebanon, recreation/sports/athletics, 435-34
Lebanon, religion, 660-8, 660-129
Lebanon, science, 1656-1
Lebanon, social sciences, 1393-119
Lebanon, youth development, 1328-77, 1391-57, 1391-669
Legal services, 97-95, 148-7, 238-50, 271-23, 335-17, 335-20, 335-27, 335-31, 335-32, 335-38, 335-44, 335-45, 335-46, 413-17, 562-4, 562-8, 562-31, 562-45, 562-50, 562-61, 709-26, 782-6, 788-51, 788-134, 788-176, 891-20, 891-32, 891-36, 891-43, 891-48, 896-2, 896-23, 1058-23, 1058-58, 1058-147, 1391-17, 1391-39, 1391-50, 1391-87, 1391-103, 1391-112, 1391-167, 1391-215, 1391-220, 1391-235, 1391-279, 1391-318, 1391-336, 1391-350, 1391-351, 1391-362, 1391-403, 1391-438, 1391-449, 1391-493, 1391-497, 1391-498, 1391-542, 1391-544, 1391-546, 1391-570, 1391-592, 1391-597, 1391-623, 1391-624, 1391-637, 1391-673, 1391-682, 1391-690, 1391-696, 1391-716, 1391-750, 1393-3, 1490-2, 1490-3, 1585-15, 1593-8, 1593-81, 1593-85, 1593-87, 1593-100, 1593-115, 1594-5, 1702-1, 1702-2, 1702-3, 1702-12, 1790-3, 1847-23, 1847-24, 1847-25, 2099-25, 2099-57, 2212-48
Legal services, African Americans/Blacks, 1058-23, 1312-76, 1391-350, 1391-505
Legal services, AIDS, people with, 335-17, 335-27, 335-31, 335-32, 335-38, 335-45, 335-46, 335-49, 1391-34, 1391-449
Legal services, awards/prizes/competitions, 335-38
Legal services, building/renovation, 788-177
Legal services, children/youth, 1506-2, 1585-15, 1702-2, 1702-3
Legal services, conferences/seminars, 335-45, 788-139, 1391-220, 1391-449, 1393-183, 2199-38, 2199-39
Legal services, crime/abuse victims, 335-17, 562-4, 562-73, 782-16, 788-15, 788-139, 891-33, 1393-181, 1506-2, 1585-15
Legal services, curriculum development, 1391-50
Legal services, disabilities, people with, 1393-155
Legal services, economically disadvantaged, 97-95, 172-10, 172-30, 172-32, 335-20, 335-44, 335-45, 335-46, 413-17, 562-4, 562-18, 782-6, 782-16, 788-15, 788-115, 788-176, 788-177, 891-33, 891-36, 891-43, 891-48, 996-26, 1058-23, 1058-58, 1058-100, 1058-147, 1312-76, 1322-2, 1391-17, 1391-34, 1391-39, 1391-87, 1391-103, 1391-167, 1391-220, 1391-260, 1391-279, 1391-336, 1391-392, 1391-403, 1391-449, 1391-493, 1391-497, 1391-498, 1391-505, 1391-542, 1391-545, 1391-546, 1391-570, 1391-597, 1391-623, 1391-624, 1391-670, 1391-690, 1391-696, 1391-716, 1393-3, 1393-60, 1393-83, 1393-84, 1393-85, 1506-4, 1578-96, 1585-15, 1593-8, 1593-61, 1593-87, 1594-5, 1594-16, 1702-1, 1702-2, 1702-6, 1702-12, 1721-3, 1790-3, 1847-23, 1847-24, 1847-25
Legal services, electronic media/online services, 1702-6
Legal services, equipment, 788-177
Legal services, faculty/staff development, 271-38, 1058-147, 1391-50, 1391-215, 1391-628
Legal services, fellowships, 1391-628, 1393-150, 1393-151, 1393-152
Legal services, girls, 1847-23, 1847-24, 1847-25
Legal services, Hispanics/Latinos, 1391-545, 1506-2
Legal services, homeless, 562-4
Legal services, immigrants/refugees, 335-20, 413-17, 562-4, 562-18, 562-45, 782-16, 788-176, 891-36, 891-43, 996-26, 1322-2, 1391-17, 1391-392, 1391-498, 1391-544, 1391-545, 1391-546, 1391-597, 1391-623, 1391-624, 1393-83, 1393-84, 1393-85, 1393-125, 1490-2, 1490-3,

1506-2, 1506-4, 1578-96, 1593-61, 1594-16, 1702-1, 1702-2, 1702-6, 1702-12, 1721-3
Legal services, indigenous peoples, 97-16, 97-17, 562-8, 782-6, 782-17, 788-176, 891-36, 1058-100, 1391-39, 1391-87, 1391-167, 1391-260, 1391-279, 1391-318, 1391-403, 1391-493, 1391-497, 1391-597, 1391-690, 1393-60, 1594-5, 1790-3, 2099-22
Legal services, LGBTQ, 1393-106, 1393-183
Legal services, management development/capacity building, 271-23, 996-13, 1058-100, 1391-34, 1391-39, 1391-544, 1391-623, 1391-624, 1593-80, 1702-6, 1847-24
Legal services, men, 1391-50
Legal services, migrant workers, 788-176
Legal services, minorities, 562-18, 562-50, 782-16, 891-33, 891-43, 896-2, 996-26, 1322-2, 1391-17, 1391-392, 1391-498, 1391-542, 1391-546, 1391-623, 1391-624, 1391-673, 1393-83, 1393-84, 1393-85, 1490-2, 1490-3, 1506-4, 1578-96, 1593-61, 1594-16, 1702-1, 1702-2, 1721-3
Legal services, Native Americans/American Indians, 782-17, 1391-497
Legal services, offenders/ex-offenders, 788-139, 1391-637, 1393-3
Legal services, program evaluation, 1393-84
Legal services, public interest law, 97-16, 97-17, 172-10, 172-30, 172-32, 238-24, 271-26, 271-38, 335-49, 562-18, 562-73, 782-14, 782-16, 782-17, 788-15, 788-44, 788-73, 788-74, 788-75, 788-98, 788-115, 788-139, 788-156, 788-177, 891-33, 996-13, 996-14, 996-26, 996-32, 996-33, 1058-100, 1312-76, 1322-2, 1391-34, 1391-260, 1391-392, 1391-505, 1391-545, 1391-628, 1391-670, 1391-822, 1393-60, 1393-83, 1393-84, 1393-85, 1393-106, 1393-108, 1393-125, 1393-150, 1393-151, 1393-152, 1393-155, 1393-181, 1393-183, 1490-13, 1506-2, 1506-4, 1578-96, 1593-61, 1593-80, 1594-16, 1638-40, 1702-6, 1721-3, 1792-4, 2099-22, 2099-50, 2161-9, 2161-24, 2199-38, 2199-39, 2207-48, 2212-61
Legal services, publication, 1312-76, 1391-220, 1391-362
Legal services, research, 891-32, 1058-100, 1391-34, 1391-103, 1391-112, 1391-167, 1391-215, 1391-220, 1391-235, 1391-260, 1391-336, 1391-350, 1391-362, 1391-438, 1391-542, 1391-544, 1391-570, 1391-624, 1391-637, 1391-670, 1391-690, 1391-716, 1393-84, 1393-125, 1393-183, 1593-80
Legal services, single parents, 891-33
Legal services, technical assistance, 1391-34, 1391-39, 1391-87, 1391-318, 1391-438, 1391-623, 2099-50
Legal services, women, 335-44, 335-45, 562-4, 562-73, 782-14, 788-15, 788-44, 891-20, 891-33, 891-36, 891-48, 1391-103, 1391-112, 1391-350, 1391-351, 1391-542, 1391-592, 1391-623, 1391-716, 1393-181, 1506-2, 1585-15, 1593-87, 1702-1
Lesotho, arts/culture/humanities, 1050-27
Lesotho, civil rights, 335-7
Lesotho, community improvement/development, 1303-60, 1371-2
Lesotho, crime/courts/legal services, 335-7
Lesotho, education, 1050-1, 1050-27
Lesotho, employment, 335-41, 1050-1
Lesotho, food/nutrition/agriculture, 660-158
Lesotho, health—general, 335-7, 1303-68, 1639-56, 2170-416
Lesotho, health—specific diseases, 132-57, 335-7, 1303-60, 1303-68, 2170-416
Lesotho, human services—multipurpose, 132-55, 335-41
Lesotho, international affairs/development, 335-41, 1050-1, 1371-2, 2170-416
Lesotho, public affairs/government, 1639-56
Lesotho, religion, 660-158
Lesotho, youth development, 1050-1
LGBTQ, arts/culture/humanities, 1030-7, 1030-22, 1030-25, 1030-29, 1030-51

LGBTQ, civil rights, 335-4, 335-22, 335-39, 1030-2, 1030-3, 1030-4, 1030-6, 1030-7, 1030-8, 1030-9, 1030-10, 1030-12, 1030-13, 1030-15, 1030-16, 1030-19, 1030-21, 1030-22, 1030-24, 1030-25, 1030-26, 1030-27, 1030-28, 1030-29, 1030-39, 1030-40, 1030-49, 1030-51, 1030-53, 1030-54, 1030-55, 1030-56, 1391-61, 1391-344, 1391-353, 1391-454, 1391-662, 1391-721, 1391-784, 1393-106, 1393-183, 1593-79, 1594-34
LGBTQ, community improvement/development, 1030-49
LGBTQ, crime/courts/legal services, 335-22, 1030-27, 1391-278, 1393-106, 1393-183, 1594-34
LGBTQ, education, 1030-26
LGBTQ, employment, 1391-278
LGBTQ, health—general, 335-22, 335-26, 1030-2, 1030-8, 1030-13, 1030-21, 1391-344, 1391-353, 1391-721, 1393-183, 1639-32
LGBTQ, health—specific diseases, 335-4, 335-22, 335-26, 1030-21, 1391-344, 1391-353, 1391-583, 1391-662, 1391-721
LGBTQ, international affairs/development, 335-4, 335-39, 1030-2, 1030-3, 1030-4, 1030-6, 1030-9, 1030-10, 1030-12, 1030-13, 1030-15, 1030-19, 1030-21, 1030-25, 1030-27, 1030-28, 1030-39, 1030-40, 1030-49, 1030-53, 1030-54, 1030-55, 1391-278, 1391-454, 1391-583, 1391-662, 1391-721, 1391-729, 1391-784, 1393-106, 1393-183, 1593-79, 1594-34, 1639-32
LGBTQ, medical research, 1391-729
LGBTQ, public affairs/government, 1030-22, 1030-25, 1030-29, 1030-51, 1030-56, 1391-61, 1391-353, 1391-729
LGBTQ, religion, 1030-24, 1030-53
LGBTQ, social sciences, 1030-19, 1030-29, 1391-662, 1391-784, 1639-32
Liberia, animals/wildlife, 1030-36
Liberia, civil rights, 1303-47, 1593-7
Liberia, community improvement/development, 264-2, 1423-20, 1423-50, 1423-51, 2170-275
Liberia, crime/courts/legal services, 1393-3, 1593-7
Liberia, education, 1423-20, 1423-50, 1423-51
Liberia, environment, 1639-193, 2170-275
Liberia, food/nutrition/agriculture, 264-3, 1639-193
Liberia, health—general, 105-31, 264-3, 1303-23, 1303-48, 1393-114, 2170-192
Liberia, health—specific diseases, 1303-21, 1303-23, 1303-47, 1303-48, 1303-61, 2170-192
Liberia, human services—multipurpose, 105-31
Liberia, international affairs/development, 8-12, 105-31, 264-2, 264-3, 1393-3, 1393-114, 1423-20, 1423-50, 1423-51, 1593-7, 1593-27, 1847-42, 2170-192
Liberia, mental health/substance abuse, 1303-61
Liberia, public affairs/government, 1393-114
Liberia, recreation/sports/athletics, 1847-42
Liberia, social sciences, 1593-7, 1593-27
Liberia, youth development, 1847-42
Libraries (academic/research), 605-21, 1312-56, 1312-90, 1391-720, 1428-65, 1546-5, 1546-32, 1546-61, 1578-28, 1593-104, 1593-105
Libraries (academic/research), building/renovation, 1428-65
Libraries (academic/research), capital campaigns, 1312-90
Libraries (academic/research), collections management/preservation, 1312-56, 1546-61
Libraries (academic/research), conferences/seminars, 605-21
Libraries (academic/research), electronic media/online services, 1391-720, 1546-61
Libraries (academic/research), endowments, 1578-28
Libraries (academic/research), faculty/staff development, 1578-28
Libraries (academic/research), fellowships, 1391-720
Libraries (academic/research), publication, 1593-104, 1593-105
Libraries (academic/research), research, 1312-56, 1391-720, 1593-104, 1593-105
Libraries (medical), 952-40, 952-42
Libraries (medical), electronic media/online services, 952-40, 952-42
Libraries (medical), faculty/staff development, 952-42

Nerve, children/youth, 2170-192, 2170-392, 2170-403, 2170-404, 2170-405, 2170-417, 2170-491, 2170-516, 2170-517, 2170-518, 2170-519, 2170-520, 2170-546

Nerve, disabilities, people with, 814-18, 2170-192, 2170-392, 2170-403, 2170-404, 2170-405, 2170-491, 2170-516, 2170-517, 2170-518, 2170-519, 2170-520, 2170-546

Nerve, economically disadvantaged, 814-18, 2170-192, 2170-392, 2170-403, 2170-404, 2170-405, 2170-417, 2170-491, 2170-516, 2170-517, 2170-518, 2170-519, 2170-520, 2170-546

Nerve, electronic media/online services, 1093-65

Nerve, muscle & bone diseases, 814-18, 1093-48, 1093-65, 1093-83, 2170-192, 2170-392, 2170-403, 2170-404, 2170-405, 2170-417, 2170-546

Nerve, muscle & bone research, 1093-27, 2170-491, 2170-516, 2170-517, 2170-518, 2170-519, 2170-520

Nerve, physically disabled, 1093-65, 2170-417

Nerve, women, 1093-48

Netherlands, arts/culture/humanities, 153-24, 153-25, 739-11, 788-182, 788-183, 1093-15, 1391-686, 1490-8, 1546-78, 2170-388

Netherlands, civil rights, 172-153, 820-4, 1030-54, 1391-385, 1391-387, 1391-687

Netherlands, community improvement/development, 1391-386, 1391-558, 1391-586, 1391-688, 1639-115

Netherlands, crime/courts/legal services, 428-36, 1391-385, 1391-387, 1393-107

Netherlands, education, 626-23, 788-183, 820-4, 820-8, 1391-688

Netherlands, employment, 788-9, 1021-91, 1021-92

Netherlands, environment, 172-49, 271-153, 313-3, 428-19, 1058-21, 1546-128, 1853-70

Netherlands, food/nutrition/agriculture, 1391-384, 1391-586, 1546-128

Netherlands, health—general, 172-100, 172-152, 172-153, 271-167, 1337-7, 1391-363, 1391-385, 1391-387, 1391-797, 1391-798, 1639-159, 2170-34, 2170-228

Netherlands, health—specific diseases, 1093-15, 1391-363, 1391-385, 1391-387, 1391-797, 1391-798, 2170-34

Netherlands, human services—multipurpose, 820-4, 1391-363

Netherlands, international affairs/development, 172-152, 172-153, 271-167, 413-61, 428-19, 428-36, 788-9, 788-183, 798-55, 820-8, 1030-54, 1058-21, 1328-250, 1391-363, 1391-384, 1391-385, 1391-386, 1391-387, 1391-558, 1391-586, 1391-687, 1391-688, 1391-797, 1391-798, 1578-138, 1639-115, 1639-159, 2170-34, 2170-228

Netherlands, medical research, 629-7, 860-50, 2170-34, 2170-228

Netherlands, philanthropy/voluntarism, 1391-384, 1391-386, 1391-687

Netherlands, public affairs/government, 788-182, 788-183, 798-55, 1021-91, 1021-92, 1058-21, 1391-686, 2170-388

Netherlands, religion, 265-2, 265-3, 265-5, 265-8, 748-64

Netherlands, science, 211-4, 629-7, 1021-91, 1021-92, 1546-128

Netherlands, social sciences, 820-4, 1337-7, 1391-688, 1393-107

Netherlands, youth development, 820-4, 1328-138, 1328-250

Neuroscience, 443-19, 1093-12, 1093-13, 1093-65, 1093-69, 1593-133

Neuroscience research, 211-5, 901-1, 1126-4, 1126-9, 1303-27, 1916-69

Neuroscience research, conferences/seminars, 901-1

Neuroscience, disabilities, people with, 443-19

Neuroscience, electronic media/online services, 1093-65

Neuroscience, fellowships, 1593-133

Neuroscience, physically disabled, 1093-65

Neuroscience, publication, 1093-12, 1093-13, 1093-69

New Zealand, animals/wildlife, 271-168

New Zealand, arts/culture/humanities, 97-49, 660-275, 1546-47, 1546-48

New Zealand, community improvement/development, 97-49, 709-79

New Zealand, education, 820-5, 1546-47, 1546-48

New Zealand, environment, 97-49, 271-168, 709-79

New Zealand, food/nutrition/agriculture, 2170-194

New Zealand, health—general, 735-23, 2170-251

New Zealand, health—specific diseases, 2170-251

New Zealand, human services—multipurpose, 1328-85

New Zealand, international affairs/development, 820-5, 1546-47, 1546-48, 2170-194, 2170-251

New Zealand, public affairs/government, 660-276

New Zealand, religion, 660-275, 660-276

New Zealand, social sciences, 820-5

New Zealand, youth development, 660-275, 1328-85

Nicaragua, animals/wildlife, 238-48

Nicaragua, arts/culture/humanities, 1391-609, 1391-767

Nicaragua, civil rights, 562-11, 1391-171, 1391-469, 1391-609, 1393-169, 2199-41

Nicaragua, community improvement/development, 1391-170, 1391-256, 1391-766, 1639-7

Nicaragua, education, 467-43, 629-2, 1050-12

Nicaragua, employment, 1391-170

Nicaragua, environment, 1050-12, 1391-170, 1391-256, 1391-359, 1391-723, 1391-724, 1391-766, 1639-7

Nicaragua, food/nutrition/agriculture, 467-43, 1050-12, 1980-7

Nicaragua, health—general, 873-6, 1391-171, 1391 469, 1391-609, 1790-5

Nicaragua, human services—multipurpose, 467-43, 1578-74, 1790-7, 1980-6

Nicaragua, international affairs/development, 629-2, 629-3, 744-12, 1391-171, 1391-359, 1391-469, 1391-723, 1391-724, 1391-766, 1639-7, 1790-1, 1790-5, 1790-11, 1980-9, 1980-11, 1980-12

Nicaragua, philanthropy/voluntarism, 562-11, 1790-11, 2199-41

Nicaragua, religion, 873-6, 1980-9

Nicaragua, social sciences, 1391-469, 1391-767

Nicaragua, youth development, 1980-11, 1980-12

Niger, community improvement/development, 1092-74

Niger, education, 660-194

Niger, environment, 744-28, 1092-36, 1092-37

Niger, food/nutrition/agriculture, 467-12, 1092-36, 1092-37, 1092-48, 1092-74, 2170-253

Niger, health—general, 323-302, 2004-17

Niger, health—specific diseases, 1303-57, 2004-17

Niger, human services—multipurpose, 413-34, 1303-57

Niger, international affairs/development, 323-302, 323-356, 323-357, 744-28, 1092-48, 1092-74, 2004-17, 2170-253, 2203-32

Niger, religion, 660-194

Nigeria, animals/wildlife, 788-11, 1030-46, 1030-58

Nigeria, arts/culture/humanities, 153-31, 1391-70, 1391-240, 1391-249, 1391-270, 1578-135, 2170-181

Nigeria, civil rights, 788-114, 788-177, 788-186, 788-206, 788-215, 1391-103, 1391-240, 1391-249, 1391-792

Nigeria, community improvement/development, 271-115, 467-49, 1328-222, 1328-271, 1328-273, 1328-281, 1391-7, 1391-103, 1391-270, 1391-502, 1423-6, 1423-50, 1423-51, 2170-216, 2170-254

Nigeria, crime/courts/legal services, 788-51, 788-115, 788-134, 788-136, 788-156, 788-177, 788-215, 1391-103, 1593-43

Nigeria, education, 271-1, 467-49, 660-43, 708-8, 788-11, 788-121, 788-128, 788-134, 788-193, 788-195, 798-1, 798-21, 1312-60, 1391-564, 1423-6, 1423-50, 1423-51

Nigeria, environment, 788-193, 788-197, 1391-661, 1593-43, 2170-43

Nigeria, food/nutrition/agriculture, 788-23, 2170-104, 2170-216, 2170-254, 2170-265, 2170-280

Nigeria, health—general, 271-1, 271-5, 271-20, 271-115, 271-118, 271-128, 271-148, 271-164, 467-49, 788-2, 788-5, 788-11, 788-12, 788-59, 788-87, 788-94, 788-121, 788-153, 788-194,

788-229, 1082-7, 1391-7, 1391-792, 2004-2, 2170-53, 2170-104, 2170-116, 2170-181, 2170-242, 2170-244, 2170-280, 2170-336, 2170-403, 2170-404, 2170-405, 2170-421, 2170-520

Nigeria, health—specific diseases, 788-2, 788-5, 788-229, 1082-7, 2004-2, 2170-242, 2170-336, 2170-403, 2170-404, 2170-405, 2170-421

Nigeria, housing/shelter, 1391-671

Nigeria, human services—multipurpose, 271-148, 709-22, 788-2, 788-5, 788-229, 798-21

Nigeria, international affairs/development, 788-49, 788-51, 788-58, 788-94, 788-114, 788-115, 788-121, 788-136, 788-150, 788-186, 788-206, 1082-7, 1082-9, 1328-222, 1328-271, 1328-273, 1328-281, 1391-103, 1391-502, 1391-661, 1391-671, 1423-6, 1423-50, 1423-51, 1531-24, 1593-43, 1639-35, 2004-2, 2170-43, 2170-52, 2170-53, 2170-104, 2170-116, 2170-181, 2170-216, 2170-242, 2170-244, 2170-254, 2170-265, 2170-280, 2170-336, 2170-403, 2170-404, 2170-405, 2170-421, 2170-520

Nigeria, medical research, 2170-53, 2170-520

Nigeria, public affairs/government, 788-10, 788-58, 788-150, 788-156, 788-186, 788-206, 1312-60, 1328-222, 1328-271, 1391-240, 1391-249, 1391-502, 1391-564

Nigeria, religion, 660-43, 660-52, 660-53, 660-90, 660-111, 660-186, 660-211, 660-259, 660-260, 1082-7, 1531-24

Nigeria, science, 788-197, 2170-104

Nigeria, social sciences, 153-31, 788-10, 788-51, 788-115, 788-121, 788-186, 788-193, 788-194, 788-195, 788-197, 788-215, 1391-671, 1593-43, 1639-35, 2170-116

Nigeria, youth development, 1328-67, 1916-30

Nonprofit management, 172-93, 271-6, 271-133, 309-75, 693-49, 709-29, 782-8, 782-21, 782-29, 1058-35, 1058-45, 1058-48, 1058-50, 1058-51, 1058 111, 1058 127, 1058 143, 1058 154, 1058-158, 1092-18, 1328-109, 1328-110, 1330-9, 1347-40, 1391-5, 1391-114, 1391-340, 1391-379, 1391-675, 1638-36, 1638-96, 1638-122, 1638-125, 1639-64, 1639-142, 1639-185, 1665-6, 1768-13, 1839-74, 1989-19, 2199-80, 2211-2

Nonprofit management, aging, 2211-2

Nonprofit management, awards/prizes/competitions, 1839-74

Nonprofit management, conferences/seminars, 271-6, 1058-35, 1058-50, 1058-154, 1391-5, 1391-114, 1638-125

Nonprofit management, curriculum development, 1058-158

Nonprofit management, economically disadvantaged, 172-93, 782-21, 1058-51, 1058-158, 1391-340, 1639-64, 1639-142

Nonprofit management, electronic media/online services, 1058-158, 1330-9

Nonprofit management, faculty/staff development, 1058-35, 1639-185

Nonprofit management, fellowships, 1638-36

Nonprofit management, income development, 1330-9, 1639-185

Nonprofit management, indigenous peoples, 1092-18

Nonprofit management, management development/capacity building, 1058-45, 1058-158, 1639-185

Nonprofit management, mentally disabled, 2211-2

Nonprofit management, minorities, 782-21

Nonprofit management, program evaluation, 1391-379

Nonprofit management, publication, 1058-35, 1391-114, 1391-675, 1639-64

Nonprofit management, research, 172-93, 1058-35, 1058 143, 1347 40, 1391 114, 1391-340, 1391-379, 1391-675, 1639-64, 1639-142

Nonprofit management, technical assistance, 1058-111, 1058-158

North Africa, arts/culture/humanities, 626-14, 626-20, 814-15, 1030-22, 1391-71, 1391-813, 1393-119, 1546-101, 1546-126, 1546-129, 2098-13, 2212-60

North Africa, civil rights, 1030-4, 1030-22, 1391-539, 1393-119

North Africa, community improvement/development, 1839-6, 1839-7
North Africa, education, 1546-20
North Africa, employment, 1422-13
North Africa, health—general, 1391-335, 1391-703
North Africa, health—specific diseases, 1391-335, 1391-703
North Africa, international affairs/development, 216-29, 286-2, 323-192, 323-215, 1030-4, 1139-2, 1391-63, 1391-71, 1391-335, 1391-703, 1393-119, 1422-13, 1546-20, 1639-2, 1665-12, 1839-6, 1839-7, 2004-32
North Africa, public affairs/government, 1030-22, 2004-32
North Africa, religion, 626-14, 626-20, 1546-101, 1546-129, 2098-13, 2203-27, 2212-60
North Africa, science, 428-3, 1546-126, 1839-6, 1839-7
North Africa, social sciences, 814-15, 1393-119, 1546-101, 1546-126, 1546-129, 1639-2, 1665-12
North Korea, arts/culture/humanities, 1397-23
North Korea, education, 1531-37
North Korea, international affairs/development, 439-13, 788-178, 1312-49, 1312-50, 1397-23
North Korea, social sciences, 216-35, 439-13, 788-178, 1312-50, 1531-37
Northern Ireland, civil rights, 1391-247
Northern Ireland, education, 748-50
Northern Ireland, international affairs/development, 1391-247, 2170-52
Northern Ireland, philanthropy/voluntarism, 1391-247
Norway, arts/culture/humanities, 1916-101
Norway, community improvement/development, 97-76
Norway, education, 1490-36
Norway, environment, 1490-17
Norway, health—general, 2170-295
Norway, human services—multipurpose, 709-80
Norway, international affairs/development, 97-76, 1312-61, 1312-94, 2170-295
Norway, medical research, 211-5, 2170-295
Norway, recreation/sports/athletics, 1853-58, 1853-141
Norway, religion, 660-166
Norway, safety/disaster relief, 709-80, 1853-118
Norway, social sciences, 1312-94, 1490-17
Norway, youth development, 1328-90
Nursing care, 709-30, 709-108, 788-85, 952-9, 952-14, 952-15, 952-36, 1021-43, 1093-90, 1303-70, 1303-71, 1393-44, 1847-37
Nursing care, aging, 709-108, 1021-43
Nursing care, children/youth, 709-30
Nursing care, conferences/seminars, 952-14, 952-15
Nursing care, curriculum development, 1847-37
Nursing care, economically disadvantaged, 1847-37
Nursing care, faculty/staff development, 1303-70, 1303-71
Nursing care, girls, 1847-37
Nursing care, migrant workers, 1021-43, 1303-70, 1303-71
Nursing care, research, 952-14, 952-15, 952-36, 1847-37
Nursing care, women, 1847-37
Nursing home/convalescent facility, 467-85, 660-277, 709-67, 934-30, 934-65, 1391-342
Nursing home/convalescent facility, aging, 467-85, 660-277, 709-67, 934-30, 934-65, 1391-342
Nursing home/convalescent facility, building/renovation, 467-85, 660-277, 1391-342
Nursing home/convalescent facility, disabilities, people with, 660-277, 709-67
Nursing home/convalescent facility, economically disadvantaged, 467-85, 709-67
Nursing home/convalescent facility, mentally disabled, 934-65
Nursing school/education, 952-9, 952-14, 952-15, 952-36, 1578-141, 1847-37
Nursing school/education, conferences/seminars, 952-14, 952-15
Nursing school/education, curriculum development, 1847-37
Nursing school/education, economically disadvantaged, 1847-37
Nursing school/education, girls, 1847-37

Nursing school/education, research, 952-14, 952-15, 952-36, 1847-37
Nursing school/education, scholarship funds, 1578-141
Nursing school/education, women, 1847-37
Nutrition, 166-17, 467-34, 467-43, 467-87, 693-5, 735-3, 744-10, 788-199, 984-8, 1021-15, 1050-11, 1051-7, 1081-18, 1081-19, 1092-30, 1092-39, 1092-42, 1092-47, 1092-50, 1092-72, 1092-76, 1092-85, 1128-68, 1179-160, 1303-45, 1391-569, 1601-3, 1601-7, 1639-184, 1847-69, 1853-102, 1853-121, 2000-31, 2000-32, 2000-33, 2000-35, 2170-39, 2170-104, 2170-114, 2170-138, 2170-139, 2170-197, 2170-206, 2170-221, 2170-280, 2170-284, 2170-296, 2170-337, 2170-429, 2170-521, 2199-40
Nutrition, AIDS, people with, 2000-35
Nutrition, blind/visually impaired, 1092-30, 2000-31, 2000-32, 2000-33
Nutrition, building/renovation, 467-34, 1853-121
Nutrition, children/youth, 166-17, 467-87, 984-8, 1021-15, 1050-11, 1128-68, 1391-569, 1601-7, 2000-35, 2170-39, 2170-114, 2170-139, 2170-284, 2170-429
Nutrition, computer technology, 1853-102
Nutrition, conferences/seminars, 2170-197, 2170-280, 2170-284
Nutrition, economically disadvantaged, 166-17, 467-43, 467-87, 735-3, 744-10, 984-8, 1021-15, 1050-11, 1081-19, 1092-30, 1092-39, 1092-42, 1092-47, 1092-50, 1092-76, 1092-85, 1128-68, 1179-160, 1391-569, 1601-7, 1639-184, 1847-69, 1853-102, 1853-121, 2000-31, 2000-32, 2000-33, 2000-35, 2170-39, 2170-104, 2170-114, 2170-138, 2170-139, 2170-197, 2170-206, 2170-221, 2170-280, 2170-284, 2170-296, 2170-337, 2170-429, 2170-521, 2199-40
Nutrition, electronic media/online services, 2170-114
Nutrition, equipment, 1853-102
Nutrition, girls, 467-34, 1847-69
Nutrition, homeless, 1021-15
Nutrition, immigrants/refugees, 744-10
Nutrition, infants/toddlers, 467-43, 735-3, 1179-160, 1639-184, 2170-221
Nutrition, program evaluation, 467-43
Nutrition, publication, 1639-184
Nutrition, research, 788-199, 1092-30, 1092-39, 1092-50, 1303-45, 1391-569, 1847-69, 2170-39, 2170-104, 2170-114, 2170-138, 2170-206, 2170-221, 2170-284, 2170-296, 2170-337, 2170-429, 2170-521
Nutrition, women, 166-17, 735-3, 984-8, 1092-76, 1179-160, 1601-7, 1639-184, 2170-39, 2170-139
Obstetrics/gynecology, 309-123, 2199-81
Obstetrics/gynecology, economically disadvantaged, 309-123, 2199-81
Obstetrics/gynecology, women, 309-123, 2199-81
Oceania, animals/wildlife, 271-168
Oceania, arts/culture/humanities, 105-43, 1391-294, 1397-3, 1546-77
Oceania, civil rights, 1391-473, 1391-736
Oceania, community improvement/development, 309-89
Oceania, crime/courts/legal services, 788-73
Oceania, education, 1397-4, 1397-32, 1713-8
Oceania, environment, 105-43, 238-57, 271-56, 271-168, 309-89, 788-28, 788-73, 788-201, 1058-131, 1391-294, 1639-15, 1713-8
Oceania, food/nutrition/agriculture, 788-199
Oceania, health—general, 271-117, 335-26, 1391-445, 1391-736, 1639-106, 2170-251
Oceania, health—specific diseases, 335-9, 335-10, 335-26, 335-43, 1391-445, 2170-251
Oceania, human services—multipurpose, 335-9, 335-10
Oceania, international affairs/development, 105-43, 271-56, 335-9, 335-10, 788-199, 1058-131, 1128-6, 1128-7, 1128-8, 1391-294, 1391-445, 1391-473, 1397-3, 1397-4, 1397-5, 1397-32, 1639-15, 1639-106, 2170-251
Oceania, public affairs/government, 1058-131, 1397-5

Oceania, safety/disaster relief, 1639-15
Oceania, science, 238-63, 788-201, 1546-77, 1713-8
Oceania, social sciences, 788-199, 1391-736, 1397-3, 1397-4, 1397-5, 1397-32, 1546-77
Offenders/ex-offenders, arts/culture/humanities, 788-67
Offenders/ex-offenders, civil rights, 148-4, 562-12, 782-4, 788-13, 788-68, 996-35, 1391-219, 1391-550, 1391-637, 1393-23, 1393-129, 1393-131
Offenders/ex-offenders, community improvement/development, 782-4
Offenders/ex-offenders, crime/courts/legal services, 616-34, 782-4, 788-13, 788-67, 788-139, 1021-27, 1021-60, 1391-219, 1391-228, 1391-550, 1391-637, 1391-762, 1393-3, 1393-23, 1393-40, 1393-82, 1393-110, 1393-116, 1393-130, 1839-29
Offenders/ex-offenders, economically disadvantaged, 1391-228
Offenders/ex-offenders, education, 616-34, 788-139
Offenders/ex-offenders, employment, 1021-27
Offenders/ex-offenders, health—general, 1021-60
Offenders/ex-offenders, human services—multipurpose, 646-4, 788-13, 934-38, 1021-60, 1391-219, 1424-6, 1437-4, 1578-72, 1672-17
Offenders/ex-offenders, international affairs/development, 148-4, 562-12, 782-4, 788-13, 788-68, 788-139, 1021-60, 1391-228, 1391-550, 1391-762, 1393-3, 1393-23, 1393-40, 1393-110, 1393-130, 1585-18, 1672-17
Offenders/ex-offenders, mental health/substance abuse, 616-14, 1021-60
Offenders/ex-offenders, prison alternatives, 1391-228, 1393-82
Offenders/ex-offenders, public affairs/government, 782-4, 1391-219
Offenders/ex-offenders, publication, 788-67
Offenders/ex-offenders, rehabilitation, 1021-27
Offenders/ex-offenders, religion, 996-35, 1393-129, 1393-131
Offenders/ex-offenders, services, 616-34, 788-67, 1393-82
Offenders/ex-offenders, social sciences, 1391-637, 1391-762, 1393-40, 1393-110, 1393-116
Offenders/ex-offenders, women, 616-34, 1021-27
Oman, international affairs/development, 1312-18
Oman, social sciences, 1312-18
Opera, performance/productions, 1428-44
Optometry/vision screening, 323-332, 323-382, 1055-3, 1179-257, 1424-16, 1518-1, 1518-4, 1518-6
Optometry/vision screening, blind/visually impaired, 1055-3
Optometry/vision screening, economically disadvantaged, 323-332, 323-382, 1179-257, 1424-16, 1518-1, 1518-4, 1518-6
Optometry/vision screening, women, 323-382, 1179-257, 1424-16, 1518-6
Orchestras, commissioning new works, 2210-5
Orchestras, equipment, 97-104
Orchestras, management development/capacity building, 97-104
Orchestras, performance/productions, 216-21, 1668-2, 2210-5
Orchestras, youth, 216-21
Organ diseases, 1093-23, 2079-1, 2079-2
Organ diseases, publication, 1093-23
Orthodox agencies & churches, 467-93, 1055-6, 1916-28, 1916-111
Orthodox agencies & churches, management development/capacity building, 467-93
Orthodox agencies & churches, research, 1916-111
Other, Slovakia, 798-52
Painting, collections management/preservation, 153-3, 153-22, 153-24, 153-25, 153-27
Painting, conferences/seminars, 153-25
Painting, electronic media/online services, 153-24
Painting, exhibitions, 97-36, 153-19, 824-7, 824-8, 824-10, 824-11, 824-12
Painting, film/video/radio, 153-25
Painting, publication, 824-8, 824-10, 824-11, 824-12
Painting, research, 153-3, 153-19, 153-22, 153-24, 153-25, 153-27, 1546-78

Pakistan, animals/wildlife, 2099-40, 2170-268
Pakistan, arts/culture/humanities, 439-1, 439-49, 1490-1, 1531-31, 1638-134
Pakistan, civil rights, 271-88, 271-137, 1531-31
Pakistan, community improvement/development, 271-89, 271-96, 271-99, 323-195, 323-216, 323-217, 323-218, 325-24, 325-25, 325-26, 325-27, 325-28, 413-1, 735-34, 1328-195, 1328-199, 1328-258, 1328-260, 1328-274, 1328-290, 2170-268
Pakistan, crime/courts/legal services, 271-134
Pakistan, education, 91-10, 439-40, 467-19, 814-12, 1328-311, 1328-326, 2170-383, 2203-39
Pakistan, employment, 335-15, 693-43
Pakistan, environment, 1531-32, 2099-40, 2170-383
Pakistan, food/nutrition/agriculture, 178-27, 2170-197, 2170-198, 2170-268, 2170-281, 2170-383
Pakistan, health—general, 172-122, 178-2, 178-14, 178-21, 178-27, 178-28, 271-64, 271-88, 271-89, 271-96, 271-139, 335-15, 562-24, 709-15, 788-192, 1393-142, 1578-71, 1639-13, 1639-57, 1639-84, 2170-65, 2170-197, 2170-324, 2170-360, 2170-403, 2170-404, 2170-405, 2170-516, 2170-517, 2170-518, 2170-519
Pakistan, health—specific diseases, 178-21, 709-15, 2170-324, 2170-403, 2170-404, 2170-405
Pakistan, human services—multipurpose, 97-44, 271-65, 271-98, 271-137, 693-43, 1128-61, 1925-4
Pakistan, international affairs/development, 54-9, 54-15, 91-10, 97-44, 178-2, 178-14, 178-21, 178-27, 178-28, 307-8, 323-23, 323-31, 323-54, 323-109, 323-358, 323-359, 325-38, 335-61, 435-10, 439-1, 439-5, 439-19, 439-24, 439-35, 439-49, 439-57, 439-67, 447-10, 463-8, 467-19, 562-2, 562-24, 788-192, 837-19, 1328-195, 1328-199, 1328-260, 1328-274, 1328-290, 1328-326, 1490-1, 1531-32, 1578-71, 1578-178, 1585-4, 1638-30, 1638-134, 1639-13, 1639-57, 1639-99, 2004-8, 2067-2, 2170-65, 2170-197, 2170-198, 2170-205, 2170-231, 2170-268, 2170-281, 2170-324, 2170-360, 2170-371, 2170-383, 2170-403, 2170-404, 2170-405, 2170-516, 2170-517, 2170-518, 2170-519, 2199-11
Pakistan, medical research, 2170-65, 2170-360, 2170-516, 2170-517, 2170-518, 2170-519
Pakistan, mental health/substance abuse, 271-134
Pakistan, public affairs/government, 439-1, 1328-199, 1328-258, 1328-198, 2170-371
Pakistan, religion, 439-1, 439-35, 439-40, 1531-31, 1531-32, 1638-134, 1916-88
Pakistan, safety/disaster relief, 97-44, 178-2, 178-14, 178-21, 178-27, 178-28, 271-65, 271-98, 271-139, 307-8, 323-23, 323-31, 323-54, 323-109, 323-145, 323-323, 323-358, 323-364, 447-10, 562-2, 562-24, 788-192, 837-19, 1578-71, 1578-178, 1585-4, 1925-4, 2067-2, 2170-205, 2170-231, 2170-268, 2199-11
Pakistan, science, 1916-88
Pakistan, social sciences, 172-122, 439-5, 439-35, 439-49, 439-67, 1639-13, 1639-99
Pakistan, youth development, 1328-260
Palau, community improvement/development, 271-63, 271-111
Palau, environment, 271-62, 271-63, 271-111, 271-112
Palliative care, 1093-12, 1093-13, 1393-44, 1393-100, 1393-162, 1593-50, 1593-76, 1593-119, 1593-133
Palliative care, AIDS, people with, 1593-50
Palliative care, economically disadvantaged, 1593-119
Palliative care, faculty/staff development, 1593-50
Palliative care, fellowships, 1393-162, 1593-76, 1593-133
Palliative care, immigrants/refugees, 1593-119
Palliative care, minorities, 1593-119
Palliative care, publication, 1093-12, 1093-13
Palliative care, technical assistance, 1593-119
Palliative care, terminal illness, people with, 1393-100, 1393-162, 1593-50, 1593-76, 1593-119
Panama, animals/wildlife, 969-3, 969-9
Panama, arts/culture/humanities, 630-3

Panama, community improvement/development, 1328-249, 1328-325
Panama, education, 1328-347
Panama, employment, 1328-279
Panama, environment, 969-3, 969-9, 2099-43
Panama, human services—multipurpose, 1328-347
Panama, international affairs/development, 1328-249, 1328-325, 1328-347
Panama, public affairs/government, 1328-249
Panama, youth development, 1328-279
Papua New Guinea, arts/culture/humanities, 97-7, 97-91, 97-101, 97-106
Papua New Guinea, civil rights, 271-23
Papua New Guinea, community improvement/development, 97-2, 97-16, 97-17, 97-68, 97-73, 97-84, 97-112, 271-90, 271-113, 788-100, 788-147
Papua New Guinea, crime/courts/legal services, 97-16, 97-17, 271-23
Papua New Guinea, environment, 97-2, 97-6, 97-7, 97-12, 97-16, 97-17, 97-18, 97-68, 97-73, 97-80, 97-84, 97-86, 97-103, 97-106, 271-90, 271-113, 788-100, 788-147, 2199-30
Papua New Guinea, food/nutrition/agriculture, 97-12, 97-16, 97-17, 97-84, 97-91
Papua New Guinea, international affairs/development, 97-6, 788-100
Papua New Guinea, public affairs/government, 97-2
Papua New Guinea, recreation/sports/athletics, 97-101
Papua New Guinea, religion, 467-71, 660-134
Papua New Guinea, safety/disaster relief, 97-103
Papua New Guinea, science, 97-18, 97-80
Papua New Guinea, social sciences, 97-12, 97-106, 97-112
Paraguay, arts/culture/humanities, 153-8
Paraguay, civil rights, 1137-7
Paraguay, community improvement/development, 323-2, 1328-346, 1847-29
Paraguay, education, 1847-29
Paraguay, environment, 323-392
Paraguay, food/nutrition/agriculture, 1847-29
Paraguay, health—general, 11-1, 1137-7
Paraguay, human services—multipurpose, 1328-98, 1328-346
Paraguay, international affairs/development, 1328-346
Paraguay, youth development, 1328-98, 1847-29
Parasitic diseases, 178-3, 2170-34, 2170-357, 2170-419, 2170-472, 2170-482
Parasitic diseases research, 1659-19, 1751-4, 1751-9, 1751-11, 2170-9, 2170-41, 2170-53, 2170-97, 2170-103, 2170-105, 2170-112, 2170-148, 2170-172, 2170-210, 2170-211, 2170-227, 2170-258, 2170-259, 2170-322, 2170-331, 2170-332, 2170-354, 2170-398, 2170-420, 2170-422, 2170-436, 2170-442, 2170-456, 2170-479, 2170-486, 2170-487, 2170-503, 2170-534, 2170-539
Parasitic diseases research, blind/visually impaired, 2170-479, 2170-534
Parasitic diseases research, children/youth, 2170-258, 2170-322, 2170-332
Parasitic diseases research, conferences/seminars, 1751-4, 1751-9, 1751-11, 2170-503, 2170-539
Parasitic diseases research, disabilities, people with, 2170-322
Parasitic diseases research, economically disadvantaged, 2170-9, 2170-41, 2170-53, 2170-97, 2170-103, 2170-105, 2170-112, 2170-148, 2170-172, 2170-210, 2170-211, 2170-227, 2170-258, 2170-259, 2170-322, 2170-331, 2170-332, 2170-354, 2170-398, 2170-420, 2170-422, 2170-436, 2170-442, 2170-456, 2170-479, 2170-486, 2170-487, 2170-503, 2170-534, 2170-539
Parasitic diseases research, program evaluation, 2170-436
Parasitic diseases research, women, 2170-258, 2170-322, 2170-486
Parasitic diseases, blind/visually impaired, 2170-482
Parasitic diseases, children/youth, 2170-472
Parasitic diseases, conferences/seminars, 2170-357

Parasitic diseases, economically disadvantaged, 2170-34, 2170-357, 2170-419, 2170-472, 2170-482
Parkinson's disease, 1093-33, 1093-34, 1093-37
Parkinson's disease, conferences/seminars, 1093-33, 1093-34
Parkinson's disease, electronic media/online services, 1093-33
Parkinson's disease, equipment, 1093-33
Parkinson's disease, physically disabled, 1093-33, 1093-34, 1093-37
Parks/playgrounds, building/renovation, 142-7, 2000-53
Parks/playgrounds, children/youth, 416-8, 934-34, 1021-64, 1021-74, 1853-79, 1853-141, 1922-1, 1922-2, 1922-3, 1922-4, 1922-5, 1922-6, 1922-7, 1922-8, 1922-9, 1922-10, 1926-2, 2000-53
Parks/playgrounds, conferences/seminars, 1639-44
Parks/playgrounds, disabilities, people with, 934-34, 1922-1, 1922-2, 1922-3, 1922-4, 1922-5, 1922-6, 1922-7, 1922-8, 1922-9, 1922-10, 1926-2
Parks/playgrounds, economically disadvantaged, 416-8, 788-65, 1353-21
Parks/playgrounds, equipment, 2000-53
Parks/playgrounds, military/veterans, 1926-2
Parks/playgrounds, research, 1030-60
Patients' rights, 335-58, 1093-29, 1093-35, 1093-48, 1391-214, 1391-291, 1391-352, 1391-353, 1593-110
Patients' rights, AIDS, people with, 335-58, 1391-214, 1391-291, 1391-352, 1391-353, 1593-110
Patients' rights, children/youth, 1093-35, 1391-214
Patients' rights, conferences/seminars, 1093-35
Patients' rights, disabilities, people with, 1093-29
Patients' rights, economically disadvantaged, 1391-214, 1391-291, 1391-352, 1391-353, 1593-110
Patients' rights, girls, 1391-352
Patients' rights, LGBTQ, 1391-353
Patients' rights, management development/capacity building, 1093-29
Patients' rights, research, 1391-291, 1593-110
Patients' rights, substance abusers, 1391-353, 1593-110
Patients' rights, women, 1093-48, 1391-214, 1391-291, 1391-353
Pediatrics, 1050-24, 1093-18, 1093-46, 1303-11, 1768-10, 1768-11, 2170-110, 2170-114, 2170-220, 2170-221, 2170-222, 2170-421, 2170-529
Pediatrics research, 1303-11, 2170-65, 2170-66, 2170-70, 2170-71, 2170-80, 2170-191, 2170-360, 2170-364, 2170-391, 2170-429
Pediatrics research, AIDS, people with, 1303-11
Pediatrics research, children/youth, 1303-11, 2170-80, 2170-429
Pediatrics research, economically disadvantaged, 2170-65, 2170-66, 2170-70, 2170-71, 2170-80, 2170-191, 2170-360, 2170-364, 2170-391, 2170-429
Pediatrics research, infants/toddlers, 2170-65, 2170-66, 2170-70, 2170-71, 2170-191, 2170-360, 2170-364, 2170-391
Pediatrics research, program evaluation, 2170-71, 2170-191, 2170-391
Pediatrics research, women, 2170-66, 2170-70, 2170-191
Pediatrics, AIDS, people with, 1303-11
Pediatrics, children/youth, 1050-24, 1093-18, 1093-46, 1303-11, 1768-10, 1768-11, 2170-114, 2170-421
Pediatrics, economically disadvantaged, 1050-24, 1093-18, 1768-10, 1768-11, 2170-110, 2170-114, 2170-220, 2170-221, 2170-222, 2170-421, 2170-529
Pediatrics, electronic media/online services, 2170-114
Pediatrics, infants/toddlers, 2170-110, 2170-220, 2170-221, 2170-222, 2170-529
Pediatrics, minorities, 1050-24
Pensions, 684-2
Pensions, aging, 684-2
Pensions, economically disadvantaged, 684-2

735-15, 735-17, 735-20, 735-21, 735-27, 735-35, 737-3, 744-1, 744-4, 744-7, 744-10, 744-51, 744-52, 756-28, 787-4, 788-57, 788-59, 798-18, 814-9, 829-1, 837-5, 837-8, 837-9, 873-6, 891-25, 934-61, 952-31, 984-8, 1021-15, 1021-46, 1021-60, 1030-13, 1030-21, 1037-9, 1050-10, 1050-24, 1081-6, 1082-7, 1092-39, 1092-47, 1092-50, 1092-85, 1092-93, 1128-37, 1128-38, 1128-39, 1128-40, 1128-41, 1128-42, 1128-43, 1137-13, 1137-14, 1137-15, 1137-16, 1137-22, 1137-41, 1137-42, 1137-43, 1141-1, 1141-2, 1141-8, 1141-9, 1179-1, 1179-2, 1179-3, 1179-26, 1179-29, 1179-112, 1179-113, 1179-114, 1179-136, 1179-160, 1179-162, 1179-172, 1179-249, 1179-258, 1184-9, 1184-26, 1184-28, 1186-1, 1186-11, 1186-12, 1213-5, 1292-3, 1303-1, 1303-9, 1303-13, 1303-15, 1303-33, 1303-40, 1303-41, 1303-48, 1303-54, 1312-59, 1360-15, 1361-14, 1371-15, 1391-7, 1391-12, 1391-18, 1391-21, 1391-30, 1391-31, 1391-33, 1391-34, 1391-98, 1391-99, 1391-100, 1391-144, 1391-147, 1391-199, 1391-232, 1391-280, 1391-281, 1391-346, 1391-352, 1391-353, 1391-357, 1391-360, 1391-363, 1391-377, 1391-383, 1391-389, 1391-431, 1391-432, 1391-443, 1391-444, 1391-445, 1391-449, 1391-458, 1391-459, 1391-460, 1391-461, 1391-462, 1391-506, 1391-510, 1391-514, 1391-515, 1391-520, 1391-547, 1391-559, 1391-569, 1391-584, 1391-648, 1391-666, 1391-681, 1391-702, 1391-703, 1391-708, 1391-712, 1391-726, 1391-728, 1391-744, 1391-745, 1391-790, 1391-797, 1391-798, 1393-67, 1393-122, 1393-144, 1423-69, 1423-70, 1424-7, 1433-1, 1506-7, 1518-4, 1518-5, 1534-6, 1534-7, 1578-161, 1578-185, 1585-1, 1593-44, 1593-95, 1593-102, 1593-109, 1593-110, 1593-112, 1593-126, 1593-128, 1593-132, 1593-134, 1601-4, 1601-5, 1601-6, 1601-7, 1601-8, 1639-5, 1639-21, 1639-28, 1639-29, 1639-36, 1639-46, 1639-48, 1639-49, 1639-56, 1639-57, 1639-80, 1639-83, 1639-104, 1639-106, 1639-113, 1639-119, 1639-124, 1639-130, 1639-144, 1639-147, 1639-163, 1639-179, 1639-183, 1639-187, 1639-189, 1639-191, 1639-192, 1639-195, 1639-200, 1639-202, 1639-203, 1639-208, 1639-210, 1665-14, 1768-1, 1790-5, 1790-10, 1847-57, 1847-58, 1847-60, 1847-69, 1853-14, 1853-100, 1853-102, 1853-121, 1853-124, 1853-126, 1926-6, 1926-8, 2000-7, 2000-8, 2000-11, 2000-22, 2000-23, 2000-31, 2000-32, 2000-33, 2000-35, 2000-37, 2000-38, 2000-39, 2000-56, 2000-57, 2000-58, 2004-2, 2004-26, 2004-27, 2046-1, 2046-2, 2067-4, 2078-7, 2170-2, 2170-5, 2170-7, 2170-8, 2170-9, 2170-13, 2170-14, 2170-18, 2170-22, 2170-26, 2170-30, 2170-34, 2170-38, 2170-39, 2170-40, 2170-41, 2170-42, 2170-44, 2170-47, 2170-49, 2170-50, 2170-53, 2170-56, 2170-57, 2170-58, 2170-59, 2170-60, 2170-61, 2170-62, 2170-65, 2170-66, 2170-67, 2170-71, 2170-74, 2170-75, 2170-76, 2170-77, 2170-78, 2170-79, 2170-80, 2170-81, 2170-82, 2170-83, 2170-84, 2170-85, 2170-89, 2170-90, 2170-91, 2170-93, 2170-94, 2170-95, 2170-98, 2170-100, 2170-104, 2170-105, 2170-106, 2170-108, 2170-110, 2170-111, 2170-112, 2170-113, 2170-114, 2170-115, 2170-116, 2170-119, 2170-121, 2170-127, 2170-128, 2170-129, 2170-131, 2170-132, 2170-133, 2170-134, 2170-136, 2170-137, 2170-138, 2170-139, 2170-140, 2170-141, 2170-142, 2170-143, 2170-145, 2170-147, 2170-148, 2170-151, 2170-152, 2170-153, 2170-157, 2170-159, 2170-160, 2170-161, 2170-163, 2170-166, 2170-167, 2170-169, 2170-170, 2170-171, 2170-172, 2170-173, 2170-175, 2170-179, 2170-181, 2170-184, 2170-189, 2170-190, 2170-191, 2170-192, 2170-193, 2170-197, 2170-203, 2170-206, 2170-209, 2170-210, 2170-211, 2170-212, 2170-213, 2170-218, 2170-221, 2170-222, 2170-223, 2170-224, 2170-226, 2170-227, 2170-228, 2170-229, 2170-230,

2170-236, 2170-240, 2170-241, 2170-242, 2170-243, 2170-245, 2170-247, 2170-248, 2170-249, 2170-250, 2170-251, 2170-257, 2170-258, 2170-259, 2170-260, 2170-261, 2170-267, 2170-269, 2170-271, 2170-272, 2170-273, 2170-277, 2170-278, 2170-279, 2170-280, 2170-282, 2170-283, 2170-284, 2170-288, 2170-289, 2170-290, 2170-291, 2170-294, 2170-295, 2170-296, 2170-297, 2170-301, 2170-302, 2170-310, 2170-311, 2170-312, 2170-314, 2170-318, 2170-319, 2170-320, 2170-321, 2170-322, 2170-323, 2170-325, 2170-326, 2170-327, 2170-328, 2170-329, 2170-330, 2170-331, 2170-332, 2170-336, 2170-337, 2170-338, 2170-339, 2170-341, 2170-343, 2170-344, 2170-346, 2170-347, 2170-348, 2170-351, 2170-352, 2170-353, 2170-354, 2170-355, 2170-356, 2170-357, 2170-363, 2170-367, 2170-372, 2170-373, 2170-377, 2170-378, 2170-381, 2170-382, 2170-384, 2170-386, 2170-389, 2170-390, 2170-392, 2170-393, 2170-395, 2170-397, 2170-398, 2170-402, 2170-403, 2170-404, 2170-405, 2170-407, 2170-409, 2170-410, 2170-411, 2170-414, 2170-416, 2170-418, 2170-419, 2170-421, 2170-423, 2170-425, 2170-427, 2170-428, 2170-431, 2170-433, 2170-434, 2170-435, 2170-436, 2170-437, 2170-438, 2170-439, 2170-440, 2170-441, 2170-442, 2170-443, 2170-444, 2170-446, 2170-447, 2170-449, 2170-450, 2170-451, 2170-452, 2170-454, 2170-455, 2170-457, 2170-458, 2170-459, 2170-460, 2170-461, 2170-462, 2170-465, 2170-466, 2170-468, 2170-469, 2170-470, 2170-473, 2170-476, 2170-477, 2170-478, 2170-480, 2170-481, 2170-483, 2170-484, 2170-485, 2170-486, 2170-487, 2170-489, 2170-491, 2170-492, 2170-493, 2170-494, 2170-497, 2170-498, 2170-500, 2170-503, 2170-504, 2170-506, 2170-508, 2170-509, 2170-511, 2170-515, 2170-517, 2170-518, 2170-519, 2170-520, 2170-521, 2170-523, 2170-524, 2170-525, 2170-526, 2170-527, 2170-528, 2170-529, 2170-530, 2170-531, 2170-532, 2170-533, 2170-534, 2170-535, 2170-536, 2170-537, 2170-538, 2170-539, 2170-541, 2170-546, 2170-548, 2170-550, 2170-551, 2199-40, 2199-54, 2199-67, 2199-106, 2203-34, 2203-52, 2203-53

Public health, electronic media/online services, 100-13, 172-4, 172-64, 323-347, 1093-7, 1093-60, 1093-68, 1391-10, 1391-281, 1391-474, 1391-654, 1638-32, 1639-18, 1639-19, 1639-21, 1639-28, 1639-29, 1639-176, 1639-191, 2170-67, 2170-77, 2170-114, 2170-147, 2170-246, 2170-433, 2170-451

Public health, endowments, 178-38, 323-341, 744-52

Public health, environmental health, 105-36, 172-62, 172-71, 238-5, 238-20, 238-21, 238-22, 238-24, 238-35, 238-49, 238-50, 238-51, 309-53, 312-5, 464-9, 464-21, 605-11, 605-19, 693-57, 788-112, 896-18, 950-1, 996-31, 996-39, 996-40, 996-41, 1050-10, 1058-74, 1179-102, 1324-1, 1391-10, 1391-77, 1391-239, 1391-243, 1391-280, 1391-281, 1391-295, 1391-436, 1391-655, 1391-776, 1578-51, 1578-104, 1593-44, 1638-32, 1638-33, 1638-35, 1638-38, 1638-117, 1638-142, 2078-7, 2161-13, 2199-103

Public health, epidemiology, 693-57, 788-11, 788-59, 1371-11, 2170-191, 2170-260, 2170-447, 2170-492

Public health, equipment, 302-7, 467-5, 467-7, 467-10, 467-15, 467-49, 467-92, 467-99, 660-216, 1853-102, 2004-27, 2170-328, 2170-461

Public health, faculty/staff development, 467-7, 952-22, 1303-17, 1303-18, 1639-202

Public health, fellowships, 119-7, 178-38, 952-22, 1393-114, 2170-181, 2170-224

Public health, film/video/radio, 97-24, 1391-10, 2170-240, 2170-285

Public health, girls, 309-20, 467-76, 1391-7, 1391-12, 1391-13, 1391-352, 1391-461, 1506-7, 1847-58, 1847-60, 1847-69

Public health, Hispanics/Latinos, 172-124, 1391-458, 1391-459, 1391-460, 1391-461, 1391-462

Public health, homeless, 1021-15, 1021-80, 1030-21

Public health, hygiene, 562-24, 605-6, 605-27, 1601-6, 1601-7, 1790-10, 2000-22, 2000-23, 2170-113, 2170-167, 2170-428, 2170-508, 2199-107

Public health, immigrants/refugees, 178-4, 467-20, 467-50, 562-24, 562-63, 744-1, 744-10, 1303-6, 1312-59, 1391-506, 1393-10

Public health, income development, 100-2, 1093-6, 1093-66, 1391-280, 1393-67, 1847-58, 2170-76, 2170-129, 2170-251

Public health, indigenous peoples, 97-24, 178-35, 323-229, 323-344, 562-17, 1092-93, 1371-11, 1391-15, 1391-251, 1391-547, 1391-648, 1593-44, 1593-112, 1639-187

Public health, infants/toddlers, 91-14, 91-15, 271-43, 1093-25, 1179-160, 1639-187, 2170-62, 2170-65, 2170-66, 2170-71, 2170-110, 2170-191, 2170-221, 2170-222, 2170-260, 2170-294, 2170-312, 2170-321, 2170-372, 2170-409, 2170-489, 2170-496, 2170-506, 2170-509, 2170-529, 2170-548

Public health, infants/toddlers, male, 2170-461

Public health, internship funds, 323-341, 1391-360, 1853-100

Public health, LGBTQ, 335-22, 335-26, 1030-13, 1030-21, 1391-353, 1391-721

Public health, management development/capacity building, 100-7, 172-54, 335-2, 335-21, 1030-13, 1058-112, 1093-6, 1391-34, 1391-280, 1391-445, 1391-460, 1391-510, 1391-515, 1391-797, 1639-5, 1639-130, 1853-126, 2170-179, 2170-251, 2170-527

Public health, men, 1391-654, 2170-500

Public health, mentally disabled, 934-101, 1021-60

Public health, migrant workers, 335-2, 335-21, 1303-6, 1391-15, 1391-251, 1391-506, 1506-7, 2170-256

Public health, military/veterans, 1391-239, 1391-436, 1391-776

Public health, minorities, 323-301, 323-302, 735-12, 756-28, 1030-21, 1050-10, 1050-24, 1303-6, 1391-474, 1391-584, 1391-790, 1393-51, 1578-185, 1847-60, 1853-100, 2170-498

Public health, Native Americans/American Indians, 97-74

Public health, obesity, 1093-38

Public health, occupational health, 178-5, 335-45, 428-40, 1021-1, 1303-6, 1853-119

Public health, offenders/ex-offenders, 1021-60

Public health, physical fitness, 693-9, 693-23, 1093-38, 1853-48, 1853-98, 1853-131, 1853-144

Public health, physically disabled, 86-4, 323-137, 1093-66, 2170-247

Public health, professorships, 952-22

Public health, program evaluation, 178-23, 1391-515, 1639-179, 1639-187, 1847-58, 2170-49, 2170-71, 2170-191, 2170-223, 2170-247, 2170-355, 2170-436, 2170-533, 2170-537

Public health, publication, 1093-23, 1303-41, 1312-59, 1391-514, 1393-10, 1639-104, 1639-210, 2170-5, 2170-343, 2170-466

Public health, research, 105-8, 105-36, 312-5, 323-341, 605-16, 693-57, 788-59, 788-112, 788-194, 952-13, 952-31, 952-33, 952-46, 1058-112, 1092-39, 1092-50, 1093-61, 1303-56, 1312-59, 1391-7, 1391-21, 1391-33, 1391-34, 1391-99, 1391-100, 1391-199, 1391-243, 1391-251, 1391-295, 1391-357, 1391-432, 1391-445, 1391-460, 1391-474, 1391-510, 1391-514, 1391-515, 1391-520, 1391-547, 1391-569, 1391-648, 1391-655, 1391-712, 1393-67, 1593-110, 1593-126, 1593-132, 1601-1, 1624-16, 1638-35, 1638-38, 1638-117, 1639-5, 1639-19, 1639-21, 1639-36, 1639-40, 1639-48, 1639-57, 1639-80, 1639-83, 1639-113, 1639-114, 1639-116, 1639-124, 1639-163, 1639-176, 1639-179, 1639-183, 1639-187,

323-189, 323-350, 443-15, 463-2, 467-13,
467-14, 467-36, 467-88, 660-251, 701-14,
701-15, 709-22, 709-34, 709-55, 709-92,
709-101, 709-102, 709-113, 709-126, 709-137,
709-139, 735-29, 788-13, 798-11, 837-16,
934-40, 934-62, 934-68, 934-70, 934-103, 960-8,
1021-42, 1150-14, 1160-19, 1213-4, 1360-13,
1391-806, 1437-11, 1567-36, 1578-182,
1603-20, 1659-22, 1675-10, 1768-16, 1839-60,
1839-81, 1944-1, 1961-1, 1961-2, 1961-4,
1980-6, 1980-14, 2199-43
Residential/custodial care, aging, 616-28, 709-92,
709-102, 709-137, 1391-348, 2211-3
Residential/custodial care, AIDS, people with, 467-14,
709-34
Residential/custodial care, Asians/Pacific Islanders,
1213-4
Residential/custodial care, boys, 178-22, 309-13
Residential/custodial care, building/renovation,
467-13, 467-26, 467-47, 934-62, 934-70
Residential/custodial care, children/youth, 8-2, 8-3,
8-4, 8-5, 8-6, 8-7, 8-8, 8-9, 8-10, 8-11, 8-13, 91-35,
132-15, 132-44, 307-7, 309-115, 320-1, 323-189,
323-350, 463-2, 467-13, 467-14, 467-26, 467-36,
467-47, 660-251, 701-14, 701-15, 709-20,
709-22, 709-34, 709-92, 709-101, 709-102,
709-110, 709-126, 709-137, 709-139, 735-29,
788-13, 798-11, 837-16, 934-40, 934-62, 934-68,
934-70, 934-103, 960-8, 1021-42, 1128-61,
1150-14, 1160-19, 1360-13, 1391-806, 1437-11,
1567-36, 1603-20, 1659-22, 1675-10, 1768-16,
1839-60, 1926-5, 1944-1, 1961-1, 1961-2,
1980-6, 1980-14, 2199-43
Residential/custodial care, crime/abuse victims,
309-13, 709-110, 788-13, 934-103, 1021-42,
1128-61, 1150-14, 1567-36, 1675-10, 1839-60,
1926-5
Residential/custodial care, disabilities, people with,
91-35, 307-7, 616-28, 709-92, 709-101, 709-126,
709-139, 837-16, 934-68, 1944-1
Residential/custodial care, economically
disadvantaged, 8-2, 8-3, 8-4, 8-5, 8-6, 8-7, 8-8,
8-9, 8-10, 8-11, 8-13, 91-35, 132-15, 132-44,
178-22, 307-7, 309-13, 309-70, 309-115, 320-1,
323-350, 463-2, 467-13, 467-47, 616-28,
660-251, 701-14, 701-15, 709-92, 709-101,
709-102, 709-110, 709-137, 735-29, 798-11,
934-40, 934-103, 960-8, 1021-42, 1128-61,
1150-14, 1160-19, 1360-13, 1391-348,
1391-806, 1567-36, 1603-20, 1659-22, 1675-10,
1768-16, 1839-60, 1926-5, 1961-1, 1961-2,
1980-14, 2199-43
Residential/custodial care, equipment, 467-14,
467-26, 467-36, 616-28
Residential/custodial care, girls, 309-13, 309-70,
1578-182
Residential/custodial care, group home, 467-26,
467-47, 709-20, 709-110, 1128-61, 1926-5,
2211-3
Residential/custodial care, homeless, 467-13, 709-92,
709-113, 709-137, 798-11, 837-16, 934-103,
1150-14, 1391-806, 1567-36, 1675-10
Residential/custodial care, hospices, 443-22, 709-61,
709-120, 814-11, 1021-16, 1393-100, 1393-162,
1424-5, 1567-10, 1593-50, 1593-76
Residential/custodial care, immigrants/refugees,
701-14, 701-15, 934-40, 1160-19, 1213-4,
1578-182, 1659-22
Residential/custodial care, income development,
837-16
Residential/custodial care, infants/toddlers, 443-15,
709-55
Residential/custodial care, mentally disabled, 467-26,
467-36, 467-88, 1839-81, 2211-3
Residential/custodial care, offenders/ex-offenders,
788-13
Residential/custodial care, physically disabled,
443-15, 467-26, 467-88
Residential/custodial care, research, 788-13
Residential/custodial care, senior continuing care,
660-265, 709-108, 934-1, 934-18, 1853-46
Residential/custodial care, single parents, 467-36
Residential/custodial care, special day care, 616-28,
1391-348

Residential/custodial care, student aid/financial aid,
8-6, 8-8, 8-10, 8-11
Residential/custodial care, women, 467-36
Residential/custodial care, youth, 709-113
Romania, arts/culture/humanities, 272-11, 1822-10
Romania, education, 1328-336, 1822-4, 1822-10
Romania, health—general, 1822-5
Romania, health—specific diseases, 1303-36
Romania, human services—multipurpose, 709-110,
1328-96, 1328-349, 1822-5
Romania, international affairs/development, 934-26,
1058-19, 1058-31, 1058-86, 1328-349
Romania, public affairs/government, 1058-31,
1058-86
Romania, religion, 1916-6
Romania, science, 1822-10, 1916-6
Romania, youth development, 1328-96
Rural development, 37-5, 74-3, 91-20, 91-27, 91-28,
97-4, 97-5, 97-9, 97-13, 97-16, 97-17, 97-24,
97-25, 97-31, 97-32, 97-37, 97-42, 97-63, 97-70,
97-71, 97-72, 97-79, 97-88, 97-97, 97-98, 100-10,
105-48, 132-12, 132-26, 132-31, 135-35, 148-2,
166-13, 166-14, 172-44, 172-65, 172-151, 251-4,
251-7, 251-8, 251-33, 251-34, 251-39, 264-12,
271-33, 271-60, 271-99, 271-115, 271-129,
271-154, 309-57, 309-58, 323-74, 323-86,
323-94, 323-95, 323-96, 323-97, 323-117,
323-173, 323-174, 323-188, 323-229, 323-252,
323-253, 323-256, 323-394, 325-22, 325-23,
325-31, 384-2, 413-33, 413-52, 416-4, 435-18,
443-23, 467-4, 467-6, 467-37, 467-39, 467-63,
467-66, 467-81, 499-8, 499-16, 562-15, 709-39,
709-79, 709-117, 709-118, 729-6, 735-10,
735-33, 735-34, 744-22, 744-55, 788-83,
788-180, 837-3, 860-22, 866-3, 1050-2, 1050-4,
1050-29, 1058-58, 1058-90, 1058-120,
1058-135, 1058-140, 1058-145, 1058-151,
1058-164, 1092-11, 1092-5, 1092-6, 1092-11,
1092-12, 1092-14, 1092-16, 1092-24, 1092-27,
1092-28, 1092-34, 1092-38, 1092-39, 1092-40,
1092-42, 1092-53, 1092-58, 1092-59, 1092-69,
1092-71, 1092-74, 1092-76, 1092-77, 1092-78,
1092-82, 1092-83, 1092-88, 1092-89, 1092-91,
1092-92, 1092-93, 1092-94, 1092-95, 1092-98,
1092-99, 1092-100, 1128-28, 1128-45, 1128-46,
1128-47, 1128-59, 1128-60, 1128-66, 1128-67,
1151-9, 1151-28, 1151-36, 1151-37, 1322-3,
1328-37, 1391-2, 1391-8, 1391-11, 1391-16,
1391-22, 1391-48, 1391-66, 1391-76, 1391-86,
1391-87, 1391-96, 1391-104, 1391-110,
1391-113, 1391-119, 1391-120, 1391-141,
1391-146, 1391-159, 1391-160, 1391-197,
1391-212, 1391-220, 1391-225, 1391-231,
1391-244, 1391-245, 1391-246, 1391-256,
1391-257, 1391-264, 1391-270, 1391-271,
1391-302, 1391-305, 1391-306, 1391-314,
1391-330, 1391-337, 1391-343, 1391-349,
1391-369, 1391-370, 1391-374, 1391-388,
1391-401, 1391-424, 1391-429, 1391-456,
1391-463, 1391-464, 1391-465, 1391-466,
1391-478, 1391-483, 1391-484, 1391-491,
1391-494, 1391-513, 1391-524, 1391-525,
1391-533, 1391-535, 1391-536, 1391-540,
1391-541, 1391-569, 1391-578, 1391-590,
1391-599, 1391-607, 1391-615, 1391-619,
1391-620, 1391-621, 1391-631, 1391-635,
1391-636, 1391-649, 1391-660, 1391-698,
1391-699, 1391-718, 1391-730, 1391-754,
1391-759, 1391-766, 1391-775, 1391-779,
1391-802, 1391-820, 1423-53, 1424-14, 1450-3,
1450-8, 1594-14, 1594-18, 1594-23, 1594-27,
1603-10, 1624-8, 1638-80, 1638-109, 1639-27,
1639-58, 1639-59, 1639-61, 1639-73, 1639-75,
1639-150, 1639-154, 1639-155, 1639-156,
1639-169, 1639-173, 1639-204, 1639-211,
1774-7, 1790-2, 1790-9, 1790-10, 1790-12,
1843-4, 1843-9, 1843-12, 1843-13, 1847-15,
1847-29, 1847-36, 1847-37, 1847-44, 1847-45,
1847-63, 1853-22, 1853-45, 1916-58, 1951-1,
1970-1, 2000-27, 2000-28, 2000-29, 2000-30,
2008-1, 2009-1, 2067-7, 2073-8, 2099-4, 2099-7,
2099-15, 2099-23, 2099-27, 2170-50, 2170-64,
2170-85, 2170-101, 2170-125, 2170-126,
2170-156, 2170-177, 2170-179, 2170-216,

2170-234, 2170-235, 2170-245, 2170-254,
2170-287, 2170-406, 2199-5, 2199-27, 2199-28,
2199-48, 2199-76, 2199-107, 2199-111, 2203-1,
2203-30, 2203-50
Rural development, African Americans/Blacks,
1391-491
Rural development, AIDS, people with, 132-26,
1058-151, 1639-156
Rural development, building/renovation, 467-81
Rural development, capital campaigns, 323-394
Rural development, children/youth, 132-26, 148-2,
309-57, 323-74, 323-188, 384-2, 413-52, 435-18,
499-8, 499-16, 735-33, 837-3, 1092-83, 1128-66,
1128-67, 1391-212, 1391-569, 1639-211,
2199-27, 2199-28, 2199-48, 2203-50
Rural development, computer technology, 271-99
Rural development, conferences/seminars, 97-13,
251-8, 1391-76, 1391-160, 1391-220, 1391-429,
1391-464, 1391-599, 2170-126
Rural development, curriculum development, 1050-2,
1847-37
Rural development, disabilities, people with, 1391-369
Rural development, economically disadvantaged, 37-5,
74-3, 91-20, 91-27, 91-28, 97-4, 97-5, 97-9,
97-31, 97-32, 97-37, 97-42, 100-10, 132-12,
132-26, 132-31, 135-35, 148-2, 166-13, 166-14,
172-44, 172-65, 172-151, 251-33, 264-12,
271-60, 271-99, 271-115, 271-129, 309-57,
309-58, 323-74, 323-86, 323-94, 323-95, 323-96,
323-97, 323-117, 323-173, 323-174, 323-229,
323-252, 323-253, 323-256, 323-394, 325-22,
325-23, 325-31, 384-2, 413-33, 413-52, 435-18,
443-23, 467-6, 467-37, 467-39, 467-63, 467-66,
467-81, 499-8, 499-16, 709-39, 709-117,
709-118, 735-10, 735-33, 735-34, 744-22,
744-55, 837-3, 860-22, 866-3, 1050-2, 1050-4,
1050-29, 1058-58, 1058-120, 1058-140,
1058-151, 1058-164, 1092-11, 1092-12,
1092-14, 1092-16, 1092-24, 1092-28, 1092-34,
1092-38, 1092-39, 1092-40, 1092-42, 1092-58,
1092-59, 1092-71, 1092-76, 1092-77, 1092-78,
1092-83, 1092-92, 1092-93, 1092-94, 1092-98,
1128-28, 1128-45, 1128-46, 1128-47, 1128-59,
1128-60, 1128-66, 1128-67, 1322-3, 1328-37,
1391-2, 1391-8, 1391-11, 1391-16, 1391-22,
1391-66, 1391-76, 1391-86, 1391-87, 1391-96,
1391-104, 1391-113, 1391-119, 1391-120,
1391-141, 1391-146, 1391-159, 1391-212,
1391-220, 1391-225, 1391-231, 1391-244,
1391-245, 1391-246, 1391-256, 1391-257,
1391-264, 1391-270, 1391-271, 1391-302,
1391-305, 1391-314, 1391-330, 1391-343,
1391-349, 1391-369, 1391-370, 1391-374,
1391-388, 1391-401, 1391-424, 1391-429,
1391-456, 1391-463, 1391-465, 1391-466,
1391-478, 1391-483, 1391-491, 1391-494,
1391-513, 1391-524, 1391-525, 1391-533,
1391-535, 1391-536, 1391-540, 1391-541,
1391-569, 1391-578, 1391-590, 1391-607,
1391-615, 1391-619, 1391-620, 1391-621,
1391-635, 1391-636, 1391-649, 1391-660,
1391-698, 1391-699, 1391-718, 1391-730,
1391-754, 1391-759, 1391-766, 1391-775,
1391-779, 1391-802, 1391-820, 1423-53,
1424-14, 1450-3, 1603-10, 1624-8, 1639-27,
1639-58, 1639-59, 1639-61, 1639-73, 1639-75,
1639-150, 1639-156, 1639-169, 1639-173,
1639-204, 1639-211, 1774-7, 1790-2, 1790-9,
1790-10, 1790-12, 1843-4, 1843-9, 1843-12,
1843-13, 1847-15, 1847-29, 1847-36, 1847-37,
1847-44, 1847-45, 1847-63, 1853-22, 1916-58,
1951-1, 1970-1, 2000-27, 2000-28, 2000-29,
2000-30, 2008-1, 2009-1, 2067-7, 2073-8,
2099-15, 2099-27, 2170-50, 2170-64, 2170-85,
2170-101, 2170-125, 2170-126, 2170-156,
2170-177, 2170-179, 2170-216, 2170-234,
2170-235, 2170-245, 2170-254, 2170-287,
2170-406, 2199-5, 2199-27, 2199-28, 2199-48,
2199-76, 2199-111, 2203-1, 2203-30, 2203-50
Rural development, electronic media/online services,
1639-154, 1639-155, 1639-156, 1639-211
Rural development, equipment, 467-63
Rural development, faculty/staff development, 467-39,
1391-76, 1391-620, 1391-621, 1847-36

GRANTMAKER NAME INDEX

Foot Locker, Inc. Corporate Giving Program, NY, 1390
For a Better Life Foundation, IL, see 832
Force for Good Foundation, The, UT, 2073
ForceBrain.com Contributions Program, CA, 137
Ford Foundation, NY, 1391
Foreign Mission Foundation, OR, 1837
Foster Family Foundation, The, VA, 2120
Foundation for a Christian Civilization, Inc., PA, 1880
Foundation for Deep Ecology, CA, 138
Foundation for Excellence, Inc., CA, 139
Foundation for Global Community, CA, 140
Foundation for Middle East Peace, DC, 524
Foundation for Partnerships Trust, IL, see 764
Foundation for the Advancement of Cardiac Therapies, NY, see 1446
Foundation for the Development of Human Potential, MN, 1079
Foundation for the People of Burma, CA, 141
Foundation for Theological Education in Southeast Asia, MI, 1042
Foundation for Worldwide Mercy & Sharing, CO, see 402
Foundation Francqui Belgium, NY, see 1395
Foundation of Orthopedics and Complex Spine, Inc., NY, 1392
Foundation to Promote Open Society, NY, 1393
Fowler-Bombardier Family Charitable Trust, MA, 962
Fox Family Foundation, MO, 1122
Fox Foundation, William and Eva, The, NY, 1394
Franciscan Foundation for the Holy Land, DC, 525
Francqui Foundation, NY, 1395
Frank Foundation, Inc, Ernst & Elfriede, NY, 1396
Frank Foundation, Sidney E., CA, 142
Frankel Jewish Heritage Foundation, Samuel and Jean, The, MI, 1043
Frankenberg Foundation, Regina Bauer, The, TX, 2009
Free A Child, CO, 391
Free Africa Foundation, Inc., The, DC, 526
Free the Slaves, DC, see 495
Freedom House, Inc., DC, 527
Freedom Ministries, Inc., TX, 2010
Freeman Foundation, NY, 1397
Freeport-McMoRan Copper & Gold Foundation, AZ, 21
Freescale Semiconductor, Inc. Corporate Giving Program, TX, 2011
Freewill Charitable Trust, FL, 636
Fremont Group Foundation, The, CA, 143
French American Cultural Exchange, NY, 1398
French-American Aid for Children, Inc., NY, 1399
French-American Foundation, NY, 1400
Friedkin Conservation Fund, TX, 2012
Friend Ships Unlimited, LA, see 869
Friendly Foundation, Alfred, The, DC, 528
Friends of Bosnia, Inc., MA, see 951
Friends of Catholic University in Chile, NY, 1401
Friends of Kyrgyzstan, Inc., MA, 963
Friends of Sheba Medical Center, Inc., CA, 144
Friends of Thalamus, The, NY, 1402
Friends of the American Board Schools in Turkey, MA, 964
Friends of the Israel Defense Forces, NY, 1403
Friends of the World Food Program, Inc., DC, 529
Friends of Via, PA, 1881
Friends of Woodstock School, Inc., WA, 2169
Friends of Yad Sarah, Inc., NY, 1404
Friends of Yeshiva Beer Abraham, Inc., NY, 1405
Friendship Fund, Inc., PA, 1882
Fromm Fund, Alfred & Hanna, The, CA, 145
Fugitive Foundation, TN, 1955
Fuller Company Contributions Program, H. B., MN, 1080
Fuller Family Foundation, Inc., Victor & Sandra, FL, 637
Fuller Foundation, The, CA, 146
Fullmer Charitable Fund, J. L., CA, see 147
Fullmer Memorial Fund, Jamie Lynn, The, CA, 147
Fund for American Studies, The, DC, 530
Fund for Armenian Relief, Inc., NY, 1406
Fund For Global Human Rights, Inc., DC, 531
Fund for Nonviolence, CA, 148
Fund for Santa Barbara, Inc., CA, 149
Fund for the Encouragement of Self Reliance, NV, 1147
Funding Exchange, Inc., NY, 1407

Gabriela Mistral Foundation Inc., NY, 1408
Gaguine Foundation, Benieo & Frances C., AK, 9

Gaillard Foundation, Inc., William and Valerie, The, NJ, 1169
GAIN International, TX, 2013
Gainesville Community Foundation, Inc., FL, 638
Galapagos Conservancy, VA, 2121
Gannett Foundation, Inc., VA, 2122
Gap Foundation, The, CA, 150
Garcia Foundation, Inc., Jose M., The, NJ, 1170
Garfield Foundation, The, MA, 965
Gates Foundation, Bill & Melinda, WA, 2170
Gates Foundation, William H., WA, see 2170
Gateway Medical Alliance, WA, 2171
GBRG, Inc., NY, 1409
GE Foundation, CT, 428
GE Fund, CT, see 428
Geisse Foundation, John F. and Mary A., OH, 1790
Geisse Foundation, The, OH, see 1790
Gellert Trust, Michael E., NY, 1410
General Mills Foundation, MN, 1081
General Motors Financial Company, Inc. Contributions Program, TX, 2014
General Service Foundation, CO, 392
Genesis Foundation, Inc., NY, 1411
Genocide Education Project, The, CA, 151
Gere Foundation, The, CA, 152
German Marshall Fund of the United States, The, DC, 532
Gerondelis Foundation, Inc., MA, 966
Gerschel Foundation, Patrick A., The, NY, 1412
Getty Trust, J. Paul, CA, 153
GHR Foundation, Inc., MN, 1082
Gifts In Kind International, VA, see 2124
Gilbert Foundation, Rosalinde and Arthur, The, CA, 154
Gildersleeve International Fund, Virginia, NY, 1413
Gimprich Family Foundation, Inc., NY, 1414
Givat Haviva Educational Foundation, Inc., NY, 1415
Give the Gift of Sight Foundation, OH, 1791
Give to Colombia, Inc., FL, 639
Give2Asia, CA, 155
GK Foundation, The, NY, 1416
Glaser Foundation, The, WA, see 2172
Glaser Progress Foundation, WA, 2172
Glencoe Foundation, Inc., DE, 456
Global Aero Logistics Corporate Giving Program, Inc., GA, see 695
Global Aid Network, TX, see 2013
Global Aviation Holdings Inc. Corporate Giving Program, GA, 695
Global Business Coalition on HIV/AIDS, Tuberculosis, and Malaria, The, NY, 1417
Global Catalyst Foundation, CA, 156
Global Christian Interaction, Inc., WI, 2218
Global Development Network, Inc., MD, 903
Global Exchange, CA, 157
Global Film Initiative, The, CA, see 110
Global Fund for Children, DC, 533
Global Fund for Women, CA, 158
Global Green USA, CA, 159
Global Health Council, DC, 534
Global Impact, VA, 2123
Global Invincibility Foundation, IA, 847
Global Jewish Assistance and Relief Network, NY, 1418
Global Links, PA, 1883
Global Ministries Foundation, TN, 1956
Global Partnerships Foundation, WA, 2173
Global Philanthropy Alliance, MI, 1044
Global Rights, DC, 535
Global Security Institute, PA, 1884
Global Servants, Inc., FL, 640
Global Volunteer Network Foundation, The, CO, 393
Global Youth Action Network, Inc., NY, 1419
Glyndebourne Association America, Inc., NY, 1420
Goatie Foundation, The, OH, 1792
Gochnauer Family Foundation, IL, 766
Golden Rule Foundation, Inc., The, ME, 877
Goldhirsh Foundation, Inc., Bernard A. and Wendy J., The, MA, see 967
Goldhirsh Foundation, Inc., The, MA, 967
Goldie Anna Charitable Trust, The, NY, 1421
Goldman Family Foundation, Joyce and Irving, NY, 1422
Goldman Foundation, Inc., Irving, NY, see 1422
Goldman Sachs Charitable Fund, NY, see 1423
Goldman Sachs Foundation, The, NY, 1423

Goldrich Family Foundation, The, CA, 160
Goldsmith Family Foundation, CA, 161
Goldsmith Foundation, Horace W., NY, 1424
Goldsmith Foundation, Inc., Nathan & Louise, NY, 1425
Gondobay Manga Foundation, The, CA, 162
Good Works Institute, Inc., The, ID, 729
Good360, VA, 2124
Goodman Foundations, Lillian and Larry, IL, 767
Google.org, CA, 163
Goradia Charitable Foundation, Vijay and Marie, TX, 2015
Gordon Foundation, Gail and Mark, FL, see 641
Gordon Foundation, Mark J., FL, 641
Gorin Foundation, Nehemias, FL, 642
Gorman Foundation, The, NY, see 1426
Gorman Testamentary Charitable Trust, Owen T. Gorman & Alice M., NY, 1426
Gorongosa Restoration Project, Inc., DC, 536
Gottesman Fund, The, DC, 537
Gottstein Family Foundation, AK, 10
Gould Family Charitable Foundation of New York, The, NY, see 1429
Gould Family Foundation, NY, 1427
Gould Foundation, Florence, The, NY, 1428
Gould-Shenfeld Family Foundation, The, NY, 1429
Grameen de la Frontera Norte, CA, 164
Grand Circle Foundation, Inc., MA, 968
Grandview Foundation, Inc., TN, 1957
Grant Family Foundation, Eugene and Emily, NY, 1430
Grantham Charitable Trust, Jeremy and Hannelore, MA, see 969
Grantham Foundation for the Protection of the Environment, MA, 969
Grass Family Foundation, PA, 1885
Grass Foundation, The, OR, 1838
Grassroots Asia, CO, 394
Grassroots International, Inc., MA, 970
Gray Matters Charitable Foundation, Inc., GA, 696
Great Charity Chaye Olam Institutions of Jerusalem, Inc., NY, see 1431
Great Charity Chaye Olam, NY, 1431
Green Family Foundation, Inc., FL, 643
Green Park Foundation, FL, 644
Greenblatt Foundation, Inc., Burton G. and Anne C., NJ, 1171
Greenburg-May Foundation, Inc., The, FL, 645
Greenlight Apparel Corporate Giving Program, CA, 165
Greve Foundation, Inc., William and Mary, The, NY, 1432
Grinspoon Charitable Foundation, Harold, The, MA, 971
Gross Family Foundation, William and Sue, The, NY, 1433
Grossman Charitable Trust, Sanford J., CT, 429
Group Seven Children's Foundation Corporation, IL, see 760
Grousbeck Family Foundation, CA, 166
Grove Foundation, The, CA, 167
Gruss-Lipper Family Foundation, The, NY, 1434
Guanacaste Dry Forest Conservation Fund, PA, 1886
Gudelsky Family Foundation, Inc., Isadore and Bertha, The, DC, 538
Guggenheim Foundation, Harry Frank, The, NY, 1435
Guggenheim Memorial Foundation, John Simon, NY, 1436
Gupta Foundation, Naren & Vinita, The, CA, 168
Guttman Foundation, Inc., Stella and Charles, NY, 1437

H.E.L.P. International, CO, 395
Hadassah Foundation, Inc., NY, 1438
Haft Foundation, Inc., Robert and Mary, The, VA, 2125
Haghenbeck y de La Lama Foundation, Inc., Antonio, TX, 2016
Hahn Family Foundation, The, NV, 1148
Halle Foundation, The, GA, 697
Halperin Foundation, James and Gayle, TX, 2017
Halperin Foundation, James, TX, see 2017
Hampar Family Foundation, Armen and Gloria, The, CA, 169
Hampshire Foundation, The, CT, 430
Handleman Charitable Foundation Trust A, Joseph & Sally, WI, 2219
Handleman Charitable Foundation Trust B, Joseph & Sally, NY, see 1439

Handleman Charitable Foundation, Lynn, NY, 1439
Handlery Foundation, The, CA, 170
Hands of Hope, Inc., MI, see 1045
Hands of Hope, International, MI, 1045
Hands Together, Inc., MA, 972
Hansen Family Foundation, VA, 2126
Harbor Lights Foundation, NY, 1440
Harbourton Foundation, NJ, 1172
Hariri Foundation, MD, 904
Harkham Foundation, CA, 171
Harman Family Foundation, MA, 973
Harmon Foundation, The, NY, 1441
Harnish Foundation, WA, 2174
Harriman Foundation, Mary and Kathleen, NY, 1442
Harriman Foundation, W. Averell and Pamela C., NY, see 1442
Harris Foundation for the Living Environment, Inc., The, NJ, 1173
Hartford Foundation, Inc., John A., The, NY, 1443
Harvard-Yenching Institute, MA, 974
Hasbro Charitable Trust, Inc., RI, see 1926
Hasbro Children's Fund, Inc., RI, 1926
Haskell Fund, OH, 1793
Hassenfeld Foundation, RI, 1927
Hasten Family Foundation, Inc., Mark and Anna Ruth, IN, 839
Hau'Oli Mau Loa Foundation, The, HI, 717
Hauser Foundation, Inc., The, NY, 1444
Hawaii People's Fund, HI, see 721
Hayden Family Foundation, NY, 1445
Haymarket People's Fund, MA, 975
Hazelbaker Foundation, OH, 1794
Healthcorps of Florida, Inc., NY, 1446
Hebrew Immigrant Aid Society of Chicago, IL, 768
Hebrew Immigrant Aid Society, The, NY, see 1449
Hedge Funds Care, Inc., NY, 1447
Hegardt Foundation, MN, 1083
Heifer International Foundation, AR, 33
Heinz Company Contributions Program, H. J., PA, 1887
Hellendall Family Foundation, The, PA, 1888
Helping and Loving Orphans, WA, 2175
Henry Foundation, Inc., The, DC, 539
Heritage Foundation of First Security Federal Savings Bank, Inc., The, IL, 769
Heritage Foundation, The, DC, 540
Hershey Company Contributions Program, The, PA, 1889
Hershey Family Foundation, The, MA, 976
Hershey Foods Corporation Contributions Program, PA, see 1889
Hershey Foundation, Barry J., MA, see 976
Hertog Foundation, Inc., FL, 646
Herzliya Interdisciplinary Center, The, NY, see 1243
Hess Corporation Contributions Program, NY, 1448
Hewlett Foundation, William and Flora, The, CA, 172
Hexberg Family Foundation, The, CA, 173
HFC, NY, see 1447
HIAS, Inc., NY, 1449
Hidaya Foundation, CA, 174
Hidden Leaf Foundation, CA, 175
Higgins-Trapnell Family Foundation, The, CA, 176
Hills Fund, Edward E., The, CA, 177
Hilton Foundation, Conrad N., CA, 178
Himalayan Cataract Project, Inc., VT, 2087
Himanchal Educational Foundation, NE, 1140
Himmel Anton Foundation, Inc., The, FL, 647
Hines Interests L.P. Corporate Giving Program, TX, 2018
Hirschhorn Foundation, Inc., David and Barbara B., The, MD, 905
Hirshberg Foundation for Pancreatic Cancer Research, The, CA, 179
Hirshberg Memorial Foundation, Ronald S., The, CA, see 179
His Broadcasting, Inc., TX, 2019
His Hands Foundation, Inc., GA, 698
His Trust Foundation, Inc., GA, see 685
Hispanics in Philanthropy, CA, 180
Hitt Foundation, Inc., The, VA, 2127
Hitz Foundation, The, CA, 181
HJW Foundation, PA, 1890
HKH Foundation, NY, 1450
Hoag Family Charitable Foundation, RI, 1928
Hoffberger Foundation, Inc., MD, 906

Hoffman & Sons Foundation, Inc., Howard, The, NY, 1451
Hoffmann-La Roche Inc. Corporate Giving Program, NJ, 1174
Hofmann Article 5 Charitable Trust, DE, see 457
Hofmann Trust, Renate, Hans & Maria, DE, 457
Holland & Knight Charitable Foundation, Inc., FL, 648
Holthues Trust, IA, 848
Holy Land Trust, CA, see 246
Home Depot Foundation, Inc., GA, 699
Homestead Foundation of Washington, D.C., MA, 977
Honda Foundation, The, HI, 718
HOPE Africa Foundation, NY, 1452
Hope for Haiti, Inc., FL, 649
Hope Worldwide, Ltd., PA, 1891
Hoppe Foundation, The, CA, 182
Hovde Foundation, Eric D. & Steven D., The, DC, 541
Hovnanian Foundation, Inc., Hirair and Anna, NJ, 1175
Howard Family Charitable Foundation, NY, 1453
Howard Family Foundation, Ryan, The, MO, 1123
Hsu Family Foundation, Inc., FL, 650
Hubbell Foundation, Fred and Charlotte, IA, 849
Hughes Medical Institute, Howard, MD, 907
Human Rights Watch, Inc., NY, 1454
Humanitarian Media Foundation, The, CA, 183
Humanitarian Organization Divac Corporation, IL, see 760
Humanities Iowa, IA, 850
Humanity United, CA, 184
Huneeus Foundation, The, CA, 185
Hungarian Human Rights Foundation, NY, 1455
Hunter-White Foundation, CO, 396
Huntsman Corporation Contributions Program, TX, 2020
Hurford Foundation, The, NY, 1456
Huston Foundation, The, PA, 1892
HWG Fund, Inc., The, NY, see 1322
Hyde, Jr. Charitable Trust, Lawrence H., The, MA, 978
Hyder Family Foundation, The, WA, 2176

IBM International Foundation, NY, 1457
IBM South Africa Projects Fund, NY, see 1457
IDP Foundation, Inc., IL, 770
IDRF, MD, see 908
IDT Charitable Foundation, The, NJ, 1176
IFES, Inc., DC, see 548
IFF, NY, see 1465
IFPRI, DC, see 547
IFSA Foundation, Inc., IL, 771
IHCenter, CA, see 190
IIMI, Inc., NY, 1458
Illinois Arts Council Foundation, IL, 772
IMA World Health, MD, see 909
Improved Health Systems for Iraq, Inc., TN, 1958
India Association of Minnesota, Inc., MN, 1084
India Club, Inc., MN, see 1084
India Development and Relief Fund, Inc., MD, 908
India Development Service, IL, 773
India Literacy Project-USA, CA, 186
India National Inland Mission, VA, 2128
Indira Foundation, The, NY, 1459
Indo-American Charities, Inc., MA, 979
ING DIRECT Corporate Giving Program, DE, 458
Ingram Micro Inc. Corporate Giving Program, CA, 187
INSEAD Management Education Foundation, NY, 1460
Institute for Aegean Prehistory, The, PA, 1893
Institute for OneWorld Health, CA, 188
Institute for Sustainable Communities, VT, 2088
Institute of Current World Affairs, Inc., DC, 542
Institute of International Education, Inc., NY, 1461
Institute of Turkish Studies, DC, 543
Integrative Medicine Foundation, Inc., NY, 1462
Intel Foundation, OR, 1839
Interchurch Medical Assistance, Inc., MD, 909
Interdenominational Christian Missions, Inc., TX, 2021
InterExchange, Inc., NY, 1463
Interfaith Ministries for Greater Houston, TX, 2022
International Board of Jewish Missions, Inc., TN, 1959
International Campaign for Tibet, DC, 544
International Center for Journalists, Inc., The, DC, 545
International Children's Care, Inc., WA, 2177
International Children's Fund, Inc., WI, 2220
International Community Foundation, CA, 189
International Crisis Group, DC, 546

International Eye Foundation, MD, 910
International Federation of Red Cross and Red Crescent Societies at the United Nations, Inc., NY, 1464
International Fellowship of Christians and Jews, Inc., IL, 774
International Fellowships Fund, NY, 1465
International Food Policy Research Institute, DC, 547
International Foundation for Electoral Systems, DC, 548
International Foundation, The, NJ, 1177
International Fund for Animal Welfare, Inc., MA, 980
International Humanities Center, CA, 190
International Institute of Connecticut, Inc., CT, 431
International Legal Foundation, Ltd., The, NY, 1466
International Management Education Foundation, NY, see 1460
International Medical Corps, CA, 191
International Medical Outreach, Inc., TX, 2023
International Orthodox Christian Charities, Inc., MD, 911
International Paper Company Foundation, TN, 1960
International Partners in Mission, OH, 1795
International Project Advisory Board, CA, 192
International Republican Institute, DC, 549
International Rescue Committee, Inc., NY, 1467
International Society for Infectious Diseases, Inc., MA, 981
International Technical Assistance Group, TX, 2024
International Utility Efficiency Partnerships, Inc., DC, 550
International Women's Media Foundation, DC, 551
International Youth Foundation, MD, 912
Interpeace, Inc., NY, 1468
Interpreters' Forum, The, MD, 913
Interpublic Group of Companies, Inc., Corporate Giving Program, The, NY, 1469
Intuit Foundation, The, CA, 193
Invincibility Foundation, MA, 982
Invisible Children, Inc., CA, 194
Iowa Humanities Board, IA, see 850
Isdell Foundation, NY, 1470
Ishiyama Foundation, The, CA, 195
ISID, MA, see 981
Islands Fund, WA, 2178
Israel Cancer Association USA, FL, 651
Israel Cancer Research Fund, Inc., NY, 1471
Israel Histadrut Foundation, Inc., NY, see 1472
Israel Humanitarian Foundation, Inc., NY, 1472
Israel Venture Network, CA, 196
Italian American Delegates, Inc., MI, 1046
Ivy Inter-American Foundation, VA, 2129
IYF, MD, see 912
Izumi Foundation, MA, 983

Jabil Circuit, Inc. Contributions Program, FL, 652
Jackman Family Foundation, The, DE, 459
Jackson Foundation, Henry M., The, WA, 2179
Jacobs Engineering Foundation, CA, 197
Jacobs Foundation, Carl, OH, 1796
Jacobson Family Trust Foundation, The, MA, 984
Jagadeesh Family Foundation, CA, 198
Jain Family Foundation, Inc., Dr. Kirti, KY, 864
James Foundation, Robert & Ardis, DE, 460
Janey Foundation, MD, 914
Janklow Foundation, NY, 1473
Jao Foundation, The, CA, 199
Japan America Society of Colorado, CO, 397
Japan Foundation, The, NY, 1474
Jennings Foundation, Alan K. and Cledith M., The, CA, 200
Jensen Family Foundation, Inc., J., TX, see 1994
Jenzabar Foundation, The, MA, 985
Jernigan Foundation, The, WA, 2180
Jerome Foundation, CA, 201
Jerusalem Fund for Education and Community Development, The, DC, 552
Jerusalem Fund, The, DC, see 552
Jesselson Foundation, NY, 1475
Jewelers for Children, NY, 1476
Jewish Community Federation of Cleveland, OH, 1797
Jewish Community Federation of San Francisco, the Peninsula, Marin and Sonoma Counties, CA, 202
Jewish Community Foundation of Central Pennsylvania, PA, 1894

Sidewater Family Foundation, Inc., The, PA, 1915
Sidewater Foundation, Inc., Morris & Evelyn, The, PA, see 1915
Siebel Foundation, Thomas and Stacey, The, CA, 320
Sigma Chi Foundation, IL, 818
Sikand Foundation, Inc., The, CA, 321
Silberstein Foundation, Stephen M., The, CA, 322
Silicon Valley Community Foundation, CA, 323
Simms Family Foundation, CA, 324
Simon Charitable Foundation Number One, Melvin and Bren, The, IN, 844
Simon Foundation, Mildred, Herbert and Julian, MO, 1132
Simone Foundation, Louise Manoogian, MI, see 1055
Simons Foundation, Nick, The, NY, 1655
Simons Foundation, The, NY, 1656
Simonsen Foundation, Arnold J., IL, 819
Singgod Foundation, CA, see 341
Singh Foundation, Inc., NY, 1657
Sister Cities International, Inc., DC, 590
Sit Investment Associates Foundation, MN, 1101
Six Four Foundation, The, TX, 2058
Sixty Four Foundation, The, TX, see 2058
Skadden Fellowship Foundation, Inc., The, NY, 1658
Skadden, Arps, Slate, Meagher & Flom Fellowship Foundation, NY, see 1658
Skirball Foundation, NY, 1659
Skoll Foundation, The, CA, 325
Slaughter, Jr. Foundation, Inc., William E., UT, 2076
Slifka Foundation, Inc., Alan B., NY, 1660
Sloss Foundation, Margaret K., CA, 326
Slusher Charitable Foundation, Roy W., MO, 1133
SmartGo Foundation, UT, 2077
Smile Train, Inc., NY, 1661
Smith Charitable Trust, May and Stanley, CA, 327
Smith Family Foundation, Robert H., VA, 2146
Smith Foundation, Crawford, The, CA, 328
Smith Foundation, David H., MA, see 950
Smith Foundation, Gordon V. & Helen C., MD, 930
Smith Fund, Inc., George D., NY, 1662
Smythe Family Foundation, William D., CA, 329
Social and Environmental Entrepreneurs, CA, 330
Social Equity Venture Fund, MA, see 1019
Social Science Research Council, NY, 1663
Society for French American Cultural Services and Educational Aid, NY, see 1398
Society of Economic Geologists Foundation, Inc., CO, 408
Soforenko Foundation, Edwin S., RI, 1935
Solar Turbine Group, Inc., MA, see 1022
Solheim Foundation, AZ, 28
Somali Family Care Network, VA, 2147
Someone Cares Charitable Trust, CO, 409
Son Light Ministries, Inc., WI, see 2220
Sons of Italy Foundation, DC, 591
Sony USA Foundation Inc., NY, 1664
Sooch Foundation, The, TX, 2059
Sophia Foundation, The, TX, see 2055
Sorenson Legacy Foundation, The, UT, 2078
Soros Fund Charitable Foundation, NY, 1665
Sotheby's Holdings, Inc. Corporate Giving Program, NY, 1666
South Arts, GA, 705
Southern Arts Federation, GA, see 705
Southwire Company Contributions Program, GA, 706
Spansion Inc. Corporate Giving Program, CA, 331
Spark Energy, L.P., Corporate Giving Program, TX, 2060
Sparkplug Foundation, NY, 1667
Sparrow Charitable Foundation, The, TX, 2061
Spectra Energy Foundation, TX, 2062
Spencer Foundation, The, IL, 820
Spencer Foundation, W. L. S., The, CA, 332
Spero Charitable Foundation, MA, 1020
Speyer Family Foundation, Inc., The, NY, 1668
Spiegel Foundation, Inc., Sam, NY, 1669
Spiegel Foundation, Sam, NY, see 1669
Spirit Foundation, The, NY, see 1585
Sri Sathya Sai World Foundation, CA, 333
SSRC, NY, see 1663
St. George's Society of New York, NY, 1670
St. Marys United Methodist Church Foundation, Inc., GA, 707
Stacy Foundation, Inc., Festus and Helen, FL, 675

Stainman Family Foundation, Inc., The, NY, 1671
Starbucks Foundation, The, WA, 2202
Starr Foundation, The, NY, 1672
State Farm Companies Foundation, IL, 821
State Street Foundation, Inc., MA, 1021
Steel Family Foundation, Robert K., The, NY, 1673
Steelcase Foundation, MI, 1064
Steffens Foundation, CO, 410
Stein Family Foundation, Inc., Allen A., NY, 1674
Steinhardt Foundation, Judy and Michael, The, NY, 1675
Stempel Foundation, Ernest E. and Brendalyn, NY, 1677
Stempel Foundation, Ernest E., NY, 1676
Stern Foundation, Inc., Walter P. & Elizabeth M., NY, 1678
Stern Foundation, Irvin, IL, 822
Stewardship Foundation, The, WA, 2203
Stewart, Jr. Foundation, Marlene and J. O., The, TX, 2063
STG International, MA, 1022
Stone Family Foundation, Inc., Michael and Karen, The, DE, 473
Stop Hunger Now, NC, 1766
Stott Ministries, John, CA, 334
Strategic Resource Group, Inc., MD, 931
Strauss Foundation, Inc., The, NY, 1679
Strauss Foundation, Levi, CA, 335
Strauss Foundation, NC, 1767
Strome Family Foundation, CA, 336
Stryker Foundation, Jon L., MI, see 1030
Stryker-Short Foundation, The, CO, see 384
Stuart Family Foundation, IL, 823
Stuart Foundation, Barbara and Robert, The, IL, see 823
Summerlee Foundation, The, TX, 2064
Summit Charitable Foundation, Inc., The, DC, see 592
Summit Foundation, The, DC, 592
Sundance Pay It Forward Foundation, MN, 1102
Sustainable Harvest Coffee Importers Corporate Giving Program, OR, 1848
Swanson Family Foundation, Inc., Dr. W. C., UT, 2079
Swartz Foundation, MA, 1023
Sweetfeet Foundation, Inc., NJ, 1197
Symantec Corporation Contributions Program, CA, 337
Syms Foundation, Sy, NJ, 1198
Synergos Institute, Inc., The, NY, 1680

Tabasco Foundation, The, CA, 338
Taiwan Buddhist Tzu Chi Foundation, U.S.A., CA, 339
Taj Foundation, The, OH, 1818
Takahashi Charitable Foundation, Henri & Tomoye, CA, 340
Talanian Family Foundation, Charles G., MA, 1024
Tanaka Memorial Foundation, Inc., NY, 1681
Tandon Family Foundation, Inc., NY, 1682
Tang Family Foundation, NV, see 1151
Tang Foundation for Education, Inc., Jane and Tom, NJ, 1199
Tang Foundation, Cyrus, NV, 1151
Tang Fund, The, NY, 1683
Tanner Charitable Trust, UT, 2080
Tanzania Wildlife Fund, Inc., The, NY, 1684
Tarsadia Foundation, CA, 341
Tatelman Family Foundation, Eliot and June, MA, 1025
Taub Foundation, Henry and Marilyn, The, NJ, 1200
Tauber Family Foundation, Laszlo N., The, MD, 932
Tawa Charitable Foundation, CA, 342
Taylor Charitable Trust, Jack DeLoss, WI, 2230
Taylor Family Foundation, Inc., FL, 676
Taylor Family Foundation, The, UT, 2081
Taylor Foundation, Inc., The, MD, 933
Tazo Corporate Giving Program, OR, 1849
Teamster Disaster Relief Fund, DC, 593
Tech Serve International, Inc., AR, 36
Teen Mania Ministries, Inc., TX, 2065
Teichman Family Charitable Foundation, The, CA, 343
Teitel Charitable Trust, Ben N., MI, 1065
Tekchand Foundation, CA, see 360
Templeton Foundation, John, PA, 1916
Terra Foundation for American Art, IL, 824
Thanksgiving Fund, OH, 1819
Thaw Charitable Trust, Eugene V. & Clare E., NM, 1214
Theatre Communications Group, NY, 1685
Thirst No More Ministries, TX, 2066

Thomas Foundation for Adoption, Dave, OH, 1820
Thomas Foundation, Harold E. & Phyllis S., ID, 734
Thomson Reuters Legal Corporate Giving Program, MN, 1103
Thomson West Community Partnership Program, MN, see 1103
Three Sisters Foundation, The, DE, 474
Three Swallows Foundation, VA, 2148
Tibet Fund, The, NY, 1686
Tibetan Nyingma Relief Foundation, CA, 344
Tides Center, CA, 345
Tides Foundation, CA, 346
Tierney Family Foundation, Inc., The, CT, 442
Tikva Corporation, NY, 1687
Tikvah Fund, The, NY, 1688
Timken Company Charitable and Educational Fund, Inc., The, OH, 1821
Timken Company Educational Fund, Inc., The, OH, see 1821
Timken Foundation of Canton, OH, 1822
Tinberg Foundation, The, IL, 825
Tinker Foundation Inc., The, NY, 1689
Tisch Foundation, Inc., NY, 1690
Tishman Speyer Properties Foundation, Inc., NY, see 1668
TJX Foundation, Inc., The, MA, 1026
Toro Foundation, The, MN, 1104
Tosa Foundation, CA, 347
Touch Foundation, Inc., NY, 1691
Town Affiliation Association of the U.S., Inc., Sister Cities International, DC, see 590
Toyota USA Foundation, NY, 1692
Trace Foundation, NY, 1693
Transformation Trust, Inc., IN, 845
Transitions Foundation of Guatemala, Inc., FL, 677
Travelers Aid Society of Metropolitan Detroit, MI, 1066
Trehan Family Foundation, Inc., VA, see 2149
Trehan Foundation, VA, 2149
Tres Chicas Foundation, The, CA, 348
Tri-State International Education Fund, Inc., OH, 1823
Triangle Community Foundation, NC, 1768
Trickle Up Program, Inc., NY, 1694
Tricon Foundation, Inc., KY, see 866
Trinity Church, NY, see 1695
Trinity Wall Street, NY, 1695
Trivani Foundation, UT, 2082
Trull Foundation, The, TX, 2067
Trust for Civil Society in Central and Eastern Europe, DC, 594
Trust for Mutual Understanding, NY, 1696
Trust in Diversity, DE, 475
Tsadra Foundation, NY, 1697
TSC Foundation, Inc., SC, 1940
Tudor Foundation, Inc., The, CT, 443
Tulalip Tribes Charitable Fund, WA, 2204
Turkish Educational Foundation, CA, 349
Turkish Philanthropy Funds, NY, 1698
Turner Foundation, Inc., GA, 708
Tutu Peace Foundation, Desmond, The, NY, 1699
Two Blades Foundation, IL, 826
Tzu Chi Foundation, CA, see 339
Tzur Foundation, Inc., Maoz, NY, 1700

U-Haul International, Inc. Corporate Giving Program, AZ, 29
U.S. Civilian Research and Development Foundation, The, VA, 2150
U.S. for Belize Foundation for Research & Environmental Education, Inc., DC, 595
U.S.-Mexico Border Philanthropy Partnership, CA, 350
UJA - Federation of New York, NY, 1701
Unbound Philanthropy, NY, 1702
Uncle Larry's Fund, FL, 678
UncommonGoods Corporate Giving Program, NY, 1703
Underdog Foundation, VT, 2091
UNDP-USA, DC, see 600
Union Plus Education Foundation, DC, 596
Unique Zan Foundation, CA, 351
Unitarian Universalist Service Committee, Inc., MA, 1027
United Armenian Fund, The, CA, 352
United Board for Christian Higher Education in Asia, NY, 1704